中国统计年鉴

CHINA STATISTICAL YEARBOOK

2004

(总第23期 No.23)

中华人民共和国国家统计局　编

Compiled by

National Bureau of Statistics of China

（京）新登字041号

©中国统计出版社。
版权所有。未经许可，本书的任何部分不准以任何方式在世界任何地区以任何文字翻印、拷贝、仿制或转载。

Copyright © China Statistics Press.
All rights reserved. No part of the publication may be reproduced or transmitted in any form or by any means, electronic or mechanical, including photocopying, recording, or any information storage and retrieval system, without written permission from the publisher.

图书在版编目(CIP)数据

中国统计年鉴.2004/国家统计局 编
-北京：中国统计出版社，2004.9
ISBN 7-5037-4352-2

I.中 …

II.国 …

III.社会经济统计-统计资料-中国-2004-年鉴

IV.C832-54

中国版本图书馆CIP数据核字(2004)第034153号

中国统计年鉴-2004

作　　者／中华人民共和国国家统计局
责任编辑／叶礼奇　王立群　刘金成
E-mail: yearbook@stats.gov.cn
Address: No.75 Yuetan Nanjie, Sanlihe, Beijing 100826, China Statistics Press
封面设计／艺编广告
出版发行／中国统计出版社
通信地址／北京市西城区三里河月坛南街75号　　邮政编码／100826
办公地址／北京市丰台区西三环南路甲6号
电　　话／(010)63459084、63266600-22500（发行部）、63321207（编辑部）
印　　刷／北京中科印刷有限公司
经　　销／新华书店
开　　本／890 × 1240 毫米　　1/16
字　　数／210万字
印　　张／66
版　　别／2004年9月第1版
版　　次／2004年9月第1次印刷
书　　号／ISBN 7-5037-4352-2/F · 1817
定　　价／298.00元　　Price: 298.00 yuan (RMB)

本书附同版本CD-ROM一张，光盘内容以书面文字为准。
中国统计版图书，如有印装错误，本社发行部负责调换。

《中国统计年鉴—2004》

编委会和编辑出版人员

一、编委会

主　　任：李德水

副 主 任：邱晓华　林贤郁　朱向东　张为民　徐一帆　章国荣
郑京平

编　　委：（以姓氏笔画为序）
万东华　马京奎　冯乃林　任才方　刘　科　朱维盛
汲凤翔　许宪春　严建辉　李　强　李晓超　周小知
金兆丰　姚景源　徐铁夫　黄朗辉　谢鸿光　翟志宏
鲜祖德　魏贵祥

二、编辑工作人员

总 编 辑：郑京平

副总编辑：金兆丰　朱维盛

编辑部主任：郝胜龙　李小维　叶礼奇

编辑部副主任：黄　培　卞丽华

编辑人员：（以姓氏笔画为序）
王　强　王立群　王贵銮　龙　玲　刘金成　孙梅君
张　昕　张　琪　李万茂　李仁元　李花菊　李金宽
李俊波　李锁强　肖　云　肖　丽　陈晓杰　周学文
孟合合　郑学工　金　红　胡晓微　唐　平　徐　岚
铁　兵　梁尔卫　董礼华　董雅秀　阙小青　翟善清
鞠传玲

英文校订：冯乃林　朱维盛　叶礼奇

英文翻译：冯乃林　杜卫群　叶礼奇　宋少英　郝胜龙

责任编辑：叶礼奇　王立群　刘金成

光盘设计：王立群　张　旭　刘金成

三、出版发行工作人员

出版部主任：卢宝臻

发行部主任：宋安辉

China Statistical Yearbook - 2004

EDITORIAL BOARD AND STAFF

I. Editorial Board

Chairman: Li Deshui

Vice-chairmen: Qiu Xiaohua Lin Xianyu Zhu Xiangdong Zhang Weimin Xu Yifan Zhang Guorong Zheng Jingping

Editorial Board: (in order of strokes of Chinese surname)

Wan Donghua Ma Jingkui Feng Nailin Ren Caifang Liu Ke Zhu Weisheng Ji Fengxiang Xu Xianchun Yan Jianhui Li Qiang Li Xiaochao Zhou Xiaozhi Jin Zhaofeng Yao Jingyuan Xu Tiefu Huang Langhui Xie Hongguang Zhai Zhihong Xian Zude Wei Guixiang

II. Editorial Staff

Editor-in-chief: Zheng Jingping

Associate Editors-in-chief: Jin Zhaofeng Zhu Weisheng

Directors of Editorial Department: Hao Shenglong Li Xiaowei Ye Liqi

Deputy Directors of Editorial Department: Huang Pei Bian Lihua

Editorial Staff : (in order of strokes of Chinese surname)

Wang Qiang Wang Liqun Wang Guiluan Long Ling Liu Jincheng Sun Meijun Zhang Xin Zhang Qi Li Wanmao Li Renyuan Li Huaju Li Jinkuan Li Junbo Li Suoqiang Xiao Yun Xiao Li Chen Xiaojie Zhou Xuewen Meng Hehe Zheng Xuegong Jin Hong Hu Xiaowei Tang Ping Xu Lan Tie Bing Liang Erwei Dong Lihua Dong Yaxiu Que Xiaoqing Zhai Shanqing Ju Chuanling

English Proofreaders: Feng Nailin Zhu Weisheng Ye Liqi

English Translators: Feng Nailin Du Weiqun Ye Liqi Song Shaoying Hao Shenglong

Coordinators: Ye Liqi Wang Liqun Liu Jincheng

CD-ROM Designer: Wang Liqun Zhang Xu Liu Jincheng

III. Other Related Staff

Director of Publishing Department: Lu Baozhen

Directors of Distribution Department: Song Anhui

编 者 说 明

一、《中国统计年鉴－2004》系统收录了全国和各省、自治区、直辖市2003年经济、社会各方面的统计数据，以及历史重要年份和近二十年的全国主要统计数据，是一部全面反映中华人民共和国经济和社会发展情况的资料性年刊。

二、本年鉴正文内容分为25个篇章，即：1.行政区划和自然资源；2.综合；3.国民经济核算；4.人口；5.就业人员和职工工资；6.固定资产投资；7.能源；8.财政；9.价格指数；10.人民生活；11.城市概况；12.环境保护；13.农业；14.工业；15.建筑业；16.运输和邮电；17.国内贸易；18.对外经济贸易；19.旅游；20.金融业；21.教育和科技；22.文化、体育和卫生；23.其他社会活动；24.香港特别行政区主要社会经济指标；25.澳门特别行政区主要社会经济指标。同时附录两个篇章：台湾省主要社会经济指标和我国经济、社会统计指标同世界主要国家比较。为方便读者使用，各篇章前设有《简要说明》，对本篇章的主要内容、资料来源、统计范围、统计方法以及历史变动情况予以简要概述，篇末附有《主要统计指标解释》。

三、本年鉴所涉及的全国性统计数据，除行政区划、国土面积和森林资源外，均未包括香港、澳门特别行政区和台湾省数据。

四、香港特别行政区和澳门特别行政区的统计是构成国家统计总体的一部分。但根据中华人民共和国“香港特别行政区基本法”和“澳门特别行政区基本法”的有关原则，香港、澳门与内地是相对独立的统计区域，根据各自不同的统计制度和法律规定，独立进行统计工作。本年鉴中香港和澳门特别行政区统计资料分别由香港特别行政区政府统计处、澳门特别行政区政府统计暨普查局提供，国家统计局进行编辑。

五、资料中所使用的度量衡单位均采用国际统一标准计量单位。

六、本年鉴部分数据合计数或相对数由于单位取舍不同而产生的计算误差均未作机械调整。

七、本年鉴各表中，有关对全表的注解均在该表上方，对表中部分指标的注解则在该表下方。凡带续表的资料，对部分指标的注解一律放在最后一张续表的下方。

八、本年鉴表中的符号使用说明：“…”表示数据不足本表最小单位数；“空格”表示该项统计指标数据不详或无该项数据；“＃”表示其中的主要项；“＊”或“①”表示本表下有注解。

PREFACE

I. *China Statistical Yearbook 2004* is an annual statistics publication, which covers very comprehensive data in 2003 and some selected data series in historically important years and the most recent twenty years at national level and local levels of province, autonomous region, and municipality directly under the central government and therefore, reflects various aspects of China's social and economic development.

II. The yearbook contains the following twenty-five chapters, 1. Division of Administrative Areas and Natural Resources; 2. General Survey; 3. National Accounts; 4. Population; 5. Employment and Wages; 6. Investment in Fixed Assets; 7. Energy; 8. Government Finance; 9. Price Indices; 10. People's Livelihood; 11. General Survey of Cities; 12. Environment Protection; 13. Agriculture; 14. Industry; 15. Construction; 16. Transport, Post and Telecommunication Services; 17. Domestic Trade; 18. Foreign Trade and Economic Cooperation; 19. Tourism; 20. Financial Intermediation; 21. Education, Science and Technology; 22. Culture, Sports and Public Health; 23. Other Social Activities ; 24. Main Social and Economic Indicators of Hong Kong Special Administrative Region (SAR); 25. Main Social and Economic Indicators of Macao Special Administrative Region (SAR). Two chapters listed as the appendices are Main Social and Economic Indicators of Taiwan Province and A Comparison of Economic and Social Indicators among the People's Republic of China and Other Countries. In brief introduction at the beginning of each chapter, mainly coverage of this chapter, data sources, statistical coverage, statistical methods and historical changes are concerned. In addition, Explanatory Notes on Main Statistical Indicators are provided at the end of each chapter.

III. The national data in this book do not include that of Hong Kong Special Administrative Region, Macao Special Administrative Region and Taiwan Province except for divisions of administrative areas, territory and forest resources.

IV. Statistics of Hong Kong Special Administrative Region and Macao Special Administrative Region constitute an integral part of the national statistics of China. According to the principles set forth in *the Basic Law of Hong Kong Special Administrative Region*, and *the Basic Law of Macao Special Administrative Region* statistically Hong Kong, Macao and the mainland of China are three mutually independent regions, and follow their own and different statistical systems in carrying out independent statistical operation. Statistics on Hong Kong Special Administrative Region and Macao Special Administrative Region as included in this yearbook are provided by the Department of Census and Statistics of the Government of Hong Kong Special Administrative Region, the Department of Census and Statistics of the Government of Macao Special Administrative Region, and edited by National Bureau of Statistics. Users are alerted to the difference in the concepts, definitions and coverage of statistics when using and comparing data of the mainland of China, Hong Kong and Macao.

V. The units of measurement used in this yearbook are internationally standard measurement units.

VI. Statistical discrepancies due to rounding are not adjusted in this yearbook.

VII. The notes concerning the whole table are placed at the upper part of the table, while the notes concerning individual indicators are placed at the lower part. If the table is a continued one, the footnotes are placed in the last page.

VIII. Notations used in this yearbook:

" ..." indicates that the figure is not large enough to be measured with the smallest unit in the table;

"(blank) " indicates that the data not available;

" # " indicates the major items of the total;

" * " or " ① " indicated "see footnotes below ".

目　录

CONTENTS

一、行政区划和自然资源

Divisions of Administrative Areas and Natural Resources

二、综合
General Survey

三、国民经济核算
National Accounts

四、人口
Population

五、就业人员和职工工资
Employment and Wages

六、固定资产投资
Investment in Fixed Assets

七、能源
Energy

八、财政
Government Finance

九、价格指数
Price Indices

十、人民生活
People's Livelihood

十一、城市概况
General Survey of Cities

十二、环境保护
Enviornment Protection

十三、农业
Agriculture

十四、工业
Industry

十五、建筑业
Construction

十六、运输和邮电
Transport, Post and Telecommunication Services

十七、国内贸易
Domestic Trade

十八、对外经济贸易
Foreign Trade and Economic Cooperation

十九、旅游
Tourism

二十、金融业
Financial Intermediation

二十一、教育和科技
Education , Science and Technology

二十二、文化、体育和卫生
Culture, Sports and Public Health

二十三、其他社会活动
Other Social Activities

二十四、香港特别行政区主要社会经济指标
Main Social and Economic Indicators of Hong Kong Special Administrative Region

二十五、澳门特别行政区主要社会经济指标
Main Social and Economic Indicators of Macao Special Adminstrative Region

附录一、台湾省主要社会经济指标
APPENDIX I. Main Social and Economic Indicators of Taiwan Province

附录二、我国经济、社会统计指标同世界主要国家比较

APPENDIX II. A Comparison of Indicators of Economy and Society Among the People's Republic of China and Other Countries

一、行政区划和自然资源

Divisions of Administrative Areas and Natural Resources

简要说明

本篇内容主要包括我国行政区划、自然状况、自然资源及开发和利用等资料。

1．“全国行政区划”资料，由民政部根据国务院批准的，截止到上一年末全国行政区划变更情况汇总整理并提供。

2.自然状况包括国土、山脉、河流、海洋、气候等数据资料，由国家统计局综合司根据有关历史资料进行整理和编辑。

3.自然资源包括土地、林木、水、海洋、矿产、气象等资料。其中，耕地面积来自国家统计局1996年农业普查数据；荒地面积和草原面积来自农业部调查数据；林业用地面积和林木资源数据来自国家林业局1994-1998年清查数据；水资源数据由水利部提供；海洋资源数据由国家海洋局提供；矿产资源数据由国土资源部提供；气象资料由中国气象局提供。

Brief Introduction

This chapter mainly covers data on China's divisions of administrative areas, natural conditions and the exploitation and utilization of the natural resources.

1) Data on divisions of administrative areas in China are prepared and provided by the Ministry of Civil Affairs on the basis of the changes in the divisions of administrative areas approved by the State Council by the end of the previous year.

2) Data on natural conditions cover land area, mountain ranges, rivers, ocean and meteorological phenomena. Statistics are compiled by the Department of Integrated Statistics of the National Bureau of Statistics using relevant historical data.

3) Data on natural resources cover land, forest, water, ocean and mineral resources. Data on cultivated land are from the 1996 agriculture census conducted by the National Bureau of Statistics. Data on idle land and grassland are collected from surveys conducted by the Ministry of Agriculture. Data on land occupied by forest industry and on forest resources are prepared according to checks conducted by the National Bureau of Forestry in 1994-1998. Data on water resources are provided by the Ministry of Water Conservancy. Data on oceanic resources are provided by the State Oceanic Administration. Data on mineral resources are provided by the Ministry of Land and Resources. Meteorological data are provided by the China Meteorological Bureau.

1-1 全国行政区划(2003年底)

Divisions of Administrative Areas in China (End of 2003)

单位: 个 (unit)

省级区划名称 Provinces, Autonomous Regions and Municipalities		地级区划数 Number of Regions at Prefecture Level	#地级市 Cities at Prefecture Level	县级区划数 Number of Regions at County Level	#县级市 Cities at County Level	#市辖区 Districts under the Jurisdiction of Cities	乡镇级区划数 Number of Regions at Townships Level	#街道办事处 Street Communities	#镇 Towns
全国	**National Total**	**333**	**282**	**2861**	**374**	**845**	**44067**	**5751**	**20226**
北京市	Beijing			18		16	318	131	142
天津市	Tianjin			18		15	241	101	120
河北省	Hebei	11	11	172	22	36	2207	235	937
山西省	Shanxi	11	11	119	11	23	1386	188	564
内蒙古自治区	Inner Mongolia	12	9	101	11	21	1431	195	527
辽宁省	Liaoning	14	14	100	17	56	1532	539	614
吉林省	Jilin	9	8	60	20	19	1011	240	456
黑龙江省	Heilongjiang	13	12	130	19	64	1314	381	475
上海市	Shanghai			19		18	221	100	118
江苏省	Jiangsu	13	13	106	27	53	1518	275	1117
浙江省	Zhejiang	11	11	90	22	32	1598	275	783
安徽省	Anhui	17	17	105	5	44	1936	220	997
福建省	Fujian	9	9	85	14	26	1111	151	608
江西省	Jiangxi	11	11	99	10	19	1548	120	770
山东省	Shandong	17	17	139	31	48	1928	395	1237
河南省	Henan	17	17	158	21	48	2440	328	866
湖北省	Hubei	13	12	102	24	38	1234	273	737
湖南省	Hunan	14	13	122	16	34	2587	225	1098
广东省	Guangdong	21	21	122	23	54	1710	380	1318
广西壮族自治区	Guangxi	14	14	109	7	33	1396	72	748
海南省	Hainan	2	2	20	6	4	218	17	181
重庆市	Chongqing			40	4	15	1259	106	648
四川省	Sichuan	21	18	181	14	43	5144	202	1934
贵州省	Guizhou	9	4	88	9	10	1539	86	693
云南省	Yunnan	16	8	129	9	12	1574	57	580
西藏自治区	Tibet	7	1	73	1	1	692	9	140
陕西省	Shaanxi	10	10	107	3	24	1744	142	919
甘肃省	Gansu	14	11	86	4	16	1569	101	463
青海省	Qinghai	8	1	43	2	4	429	31	115
宁夏回族自治区	Ningxia	5	5	21	2	8	227	39	92
新疆维吾尔自治区	Xinjiang	14	2	99	20	11	1005	137	229
香港特别行政区	Hong Kong Special Administrative Region								
澳门特别行政区	Macao Special Administrative Region								
台湾省	Taiwan								

注：本表资料由民政部提供。

a) The data in the table are provided by the Ministry of Civil Affairs.

1-2 自　然　状　况

Natural Conditions

项　目		Item		2003
国土		**Territory**		
国土面积	(万平方公里)	Area of Territory	(10 000 sq.km)	960
海域面积	(万平方公里)	Area of Sea	(10 000 sq.km)	473
海洋平均深度	(米)	Average Depth of Sea	(m)	961
海洋最大深度	(米)	Maximum Depth of Sea	(m)	5377
岸线总长度	(公里)	Length of Coastline	(km)	32000
大陆岸线长度	(公里)	Mainland Shore	(km)	18000
岛屿岸线长度	(公里)	Island Shore	(km)	14000
岛屿个数	(个)	Number of Islands		5400
岛屿面积	(万平方公里)	Area of Islands	(10 000 sq.km)	3.87
气候		**Climate**		
热量分布	(积温≥0℃)	Distribution of Heat	(Accumulated Temperature≥0℃)	
黑龙江北部及青藏高原		Northern Heilongjiang and Tibet Plateau		2000-2500
东北平原		Northeast Plain		3000-4000
华北平原		North China Plain		4000-5000
长江流域及以南地区		Changjiang (Yangtze) River Drainage Area and the Area to the south of it		5800-6000
南岭以南地区		Area to the South of Nanling Mountain		7000-8000
降水量	(毫米)	Precipitation	(mm)	
台湾中部山区		Mid-Taiwan Mountain Area		>=4000
华南沿海		Southern China Coastal Area		1600-2000
长江流域		Changjiang River Valley		1000-1500
华北、东北		Northern and Northeastern Area		400-800
西北内陆		Northwestern Inland		100-200
塔里木盆地、吐鲁番盆地和柴达木盆地		Tarim Basin, Turpan Basin and Qaidam Basin		<=25
气候带面积比例	(国土面积=100)	Percentage of Climatic Zones to Total Area of Territory		
湿润地区	(干燥度<1.0)	Humid Zone	(aridity<1.0)	32
半湿润地区	(干燥度=1.0-1.5)	Semi-Humid Zone	(aridity 1.0-1.5)	15
半干旱地区	(干燥度=1.5-2.0)	Semi-Arid Zone	(aridity 1.5-2.0)	22
干旱地区	(干燥度>2.0)	Arid Zone	(aridity>2.0)	31

注:1.气候资料为多年平均值。

2.岛屿面积未包括香港、澳门特别行政区和台湾省。

a) The climate data refer to the average figures in many years.

b) Island area does not include that of Hong Kong Special Administrative Region, Macao Special Administrative Region and Taiwan Province.

1-3 自 然 资 源

Natural Resources

项 目		Item		2003
土地资源	**（万公顷）**	**Land Resources**	**(10 000 hectares)**	
耕地面积		Area of Cultivated Land		13004
荒地面积		Area of Undeveloped Land		10800
#宜农荒地		Useable for Agricultural Production		3535
林业用地面积		Area of Afforested Land		26329
#宜林荒山荒地（含宜林沙荒）		Undeveloped Land Usable for Afforestation		5393
草原面积		Area of Grassland		40000
#可利用面积		Utilizable Area		31333
林木资源		**Forest Resources**		
活立木总蓄积量	（亿立方米）	Total Standing Stock Volume	(100 million cu.m)	124.9
森林面积	（万公顷）	Forest Area	(10 000 hectares)	15894
森林蓄积量	（亿立方米）	Stock Volume of the Forest	(100 million cu.m)	112.7
森林覆盖率	（%）	Forest-coverage Rate	(%)	16.55
水利资源		**Water Resources**		
大陆		Land		
水资源总量	（亿立方米）	Total Water Resources Volume	(100 million cu.m)	28124
地表水资源量（河川径流量）		Surface Water Volume		27115
#冰川融水量		Melt-Water Volume of Glaciers		563
地下水资源量		Ground Water Volume		8288
水力资源蕴藏量	（亿千瓦）	Hydropower Resources	(100 million kw)	6.76
#可开发量		Developable Resources		3.79
内陆水域总面积	（万公顷）	Inland Water Area	(10 000 hectares)	1747
#可养殖面积		Cultivatable Area		675
#已养殖面积		Cultivated Area		467
海洋		Sea		
海洋能源理论蕴藏量	（亿千瓦）	Theoretical Sea-energy Reserves	(100 million kw)	6.3
海岸带面积	（万平方公里）	Coastal Area	(10 000 sq.km)	28
滩涂面积	（万平方公里）	Sea-beach Area	(10 000 sq.km)	2.08
海水可养殖面积	（万公顷）	Cultivatable Area in Marine Areas	(10 000 hectares)	260.01
#已养殖面积	（万公顷）	Cultivated Area	(10 000 hectares)	109.49
浅海滩涂可养殖面积	（万公顷）	Cultivable Area in Shallow Sea and Sea-beaches	(10 000 hectares)	242
#已养殖面积	（万公顷）	Cultivated Area	(10 000 hectares)	89.37

注：1.土地资源为以前清查数，有待进一步勘测；耕地面积为1996年农业普查数据，草原面积为1991年调查数，林业用地面积和林木资源为1994-1998年清查数；水利资源为1985年评价数。

2.水资源总量等于地表水资源量加地下水资源量减两者之间的重复计算水量7279亿立方米。

a) Figures on land resources in the table were obtained from surveys in previous years. The figures are subject to further verification. Figures on area of cultivated land were taken from the 1996's agricultural census. The area of grassland was the figure of 1991's survey. Figures on area of afforested land and forest resources were taken from the Third Forest Census (1994-1998). Water Resources were the estimated figures in 1985.

b) Total amount of water resources is equal to surface water plus ground water and minus the repeat-calculated part between them.

1-4 土 地 状 况
Land Characteristics

项 目	Item	面积 Area	占总面积(%) Percentage to Total Area
总面积 （万平方公里）	**Total Land Area (10 000 sq.km)**	**960**	**100.00**
按地形分: （万平方公里）	**By Topographic Feature (10 000 sq.km)**		
山地	Mountains	320	33.33
高原	Plateaus	250	26.04
盆地	Basins	180	18.75
平原	Plains	115	11.98
丘陵	Hills	95	9.90
按地高分: （万平方公里）	**By Altitude (10 000 sq.km)**		
500米以下	Under 500m	241.7	25.18
500-1000米	500-1000m	162.5	16.93
1000-2000米	1000-2000m	239.9	24.99
2000-3000米	2000-3000m	67.6	7.04
3000米以上	Above 3000m	248.3	25.86
按特征分: （万公顷）	**By Land Use (10 000 hectares)**		
耕地	Cultivated Land	13004	13.54
森林	Forests	15894	16.56
内陆水域面积	Water Area in Land	1747	1.82
草地	Area of Grassland	40000	41.67
#可利用草地	Useable Area	31333	32.64
其他	Others	25355	26.41

注：本表数字多为过去清查数。
a) Most figures in this table were obtained from surveys in previous years.

1-5 主要山脉基本情况
Main Mountain Ranges

名 称	Mountain Range	山峰高程（米） Height of Mountain Peak (m)	雪线高程（米） Height of Snow Line (m)	冰川面积（平方公里） Glacier Area (sq.km)
阿尔泰山	Altay Mountains	4374	3000--3200	287
天山	Tianshan Mountains	7435	3600--4400	9548
祁连山	Qilian Mountains	5826	4300--5240	2063
帕米尔	Pamirs	7579		2258
昆仑山	Kunlun Mountains			11639
喀喇昆仑山	Karakorum Mountain	8611	5100--5400	3265
唐古拉山	Tanggula Mountains	6137		2082
羌塘高原	Qiangtang Plateau	6596		3566
念青塘古拉山	Nyainqentanglha Mountains	7111	4500--5700	7536
横断山	Hengduan Mountains	7556	4600--5500	1456
喜玛拉雅山	The Himalayas	8848	4300--6200	11055
冈底斯山	Gangdisi Mountains	7095	5800--6000	2188

1-6 主要河流基本情况
Major Rivers

名称	River	流域面积（平方公里） Drainage Area (sq.km)	河长（公里） Length (km)	年径流量（亿立方米） Annual Flow (100 million cu.m)
长 江	Changjiang River (Yangtze River)	1808500	6300	9513
黄 河	Huanghe River (Yellow River)	752443	5464	661
松花江	Songhuajiang River	557180	2308	762
辽 河	Liaohe River	228960	1390	148
珠 江	Zhujiang River (Pear River)	453690	2214	3338
海 河	Haihe River	263631	1090	228
淮 河	Huaihe River	269283	1000	622

1-7 河流流域面积
Drainage Area of Rivers

流域名称	River	流域面积（平方公里） Drainage Area (sq.km)	占外流河、内陆河流域面积合计 Percentage to Total (%)
合计	**Total of Out-flowing Rivers and Inland Rivers**	**9559370**	**100.00**
外流河	**Out-flowing Rivers**	**6114728**	**63.97**
黑龙江及绥芬河	Heilongjiang River and Suifenhe River	875342	9.16
辽河、鸭绿江及沿海诸河	Liaohe, Yalujiang and Related Coastal Rivers	345207	3.61
海滦河	Haihe River and luanhe River	318161	3.33
黄河	Huanghe River (Yellow River)	752443	7.87
淮河及山东沿海诸河	Huaihe and Related Coastal Rivers in Shandong Province	329211	3.44
长江	Changjiang River (Yangtze River)	1808500	18.92
浙闽台诸河	Rivers in Zhejiang, Fujian and Taiwan Provinces	239803	2.51
珠江及沿海诸河	Zhujiang River (Pear Rive) and Related Coastal River	580640	6.07
元江及澜仓江	Yuanjiang River and Lancang River	240652	2.52
怒江及滇西诸河	Nujiang River and West Yunnan Rivers	157156	1.64
雅鲁藏布江及藏南诸河	Brahmaputra and Southern Tibet Rivers	396258	4.15
藏西诸河	Western Tibet Rivers	57340	0.60
额尔齐斯河	Ertix River	50000	0.52
内陆河	**Inland Rivers**	**3408659**	**35.66**
内蒙内陆河	Rivers in Inner Mongolia	300067	3.14
河西内陆河	Rivers in Huanghe Upper Reach Area	488301	5.11
准噶尔内陆河	Rivers in Zhunger Basin	316530	3.31
中亚细亚内陆河	Rivers in Central Asia	93130	0.97
塔里木内陆河	Rivers in Tarim Basin	1074810	11.24
青海内陆河	Rivers in Qinghai Province	316285	3.31
羌唐内陆河	Rivers in Qiangtang	721182	7.54
松花江、黄河、藏南闭流区	Blind Drainage Areas of Songhua River, Huanghe River and Southern Tibet	90353	0.95

注：本表所列面积系水利部门量算初步汇总数，有待进一步核实。

a) Figures in the table are obtained from preliminary measurements and tabulated data by water conservancy departments, and are subject to further verification.

1-8 内陆水面面积

Inland Water Area

单位：千公顷 (1 000 hectares)

水 域	Water Area	总水面 Total Water Area	#可养殖水面 Cultivatable Area	#已养殖水面 Cultivated Area	#尚可利用水面 Utilizable Area
总 计	**Total**	**17471**	**6749**	**4669**	**2080**
池 塘	Pool	1922	1922	1858	64
湖 泊	Lake	7524	2151	824	1327
水 库	Reservoir	2302	1884	1516	368
河 沟	Brook	5278	766	347	419
其 他	Others	445	26	124	

1-9 海区海域及渔场面积

Sea Area and Areas of Fishing Ground

名 称	Sea	海域总面积（千公顷） Sea Area (1 000 hectares)	大陆架渔场面积（千公顷） Area of Fishing Ground of Continental Shelf (1 000 hectares)	深 度（米） Depth (m)	
				平 均 Average	最 大 Maximum
总 计	**Total**	**472700**	**280000**		
渤 海	Bohai Sea	7700	7700	18	70
黄 海	Huanghai Sea	38000	35300	44	140
东 海	Donghai Sea	77000	54900	370	2719
南 海	Nanhai Sea	350000	182100	1212	5559

1-10 浅海滩涂海湾可养殖面积

Seashore Land Area for Cultivation

单位：千公顷 (1 000 hectares)

地 区	Region	海水可养殖面积 Cultivatable Marine Area	浅 海 Shallow Sea	滩 涂 Sea-beach	港 湾 Harbor
全 国	**National Total**	**2600.11**	**1622.56**	**797.00**	**180.55**
北 京	Beijing	0.44		0.44	
天 津	Tianjin	18.49	10.00	8.49	
河 北	Hebei	111.37	49.66	61.70	
辽 宁	Liaoning	725.84	590.44	92.45	42.95
上 海	Shanghai	3.22		3.22	
江 苏	Jiangsu	139.00	7.87	130.96	0.17
浙 江	Zhejiang	101.46	36.30	57.39	7.77
福 建	Fujian	184.94	77.39	100.76	6.79
山 东	Shandong	358.21	131.68	173.41	53.12
广 东	Guangdong	835.67	664.00	120.00	51.67
广 西	Guangxi	31.95	6.78	22.09	3.08
海 南	Hainan	89.52	48.43	26.09	15.00

1-11 主要矿产基础储量

Major Mineral Basic Reserves

项 目		Item		2003
石油	（万吨）	Petroleum	(10 000 tons)	243193.6
天然气	（亿立方米）	Natural Gas	(100 million cu.m)	22288.7
煤炭	（亿吨）	Coal	(100 million tons)	3342.0
铁矿	（矿石，亿吨）	Iron	(Ore, 100 million tons)	212.4
锰矿	（矿石，万吨）	Manganese	(Ore, 10 000 tons)	20709.0
铬矿	（矿石，万吨）	Chromite	(Ore, 10 000 tons)	549.8
铜矿	（铜，万吨）	Copper	(Metal, 10 000 tons)	3003.0
铅矿	（铅，万吨）	Lead	(Metal, 10 000 tons)	1248.0
锌矿	（锌，万吨）	Zinc	(Metal, 10 000 tons)	3762.5
铝土矿	（矿石，万吨）	Bauxite	(Ore, 10 000 tons)	69453.7
镍矿	（镍，万吨）	Nickel	(Metal, 10 000 tons)	293.7
钨矿	（WO_3，万吨）	Tungsten	(WO_3, 10 000 tons)	286.6
锡矿	（锡，万吨）	Tin	(Metal, 10 000 tons)	178.6
钼矿	（钼，万吨）	Molybdenum	(Metal, 10 000 tons)	345.5
锑矿	（锑，万吨）	Antimony	(Metal, 10 000 tons)	87.5
金矿	（金，吨）	Gold	(Metal, tons)	1981.0
银矿	（银，吨）	Silver	(Metal, tons)	38214.0
稀土矿	（氧化物，万吨）	Rare Earths	(REO, 10 000 tons)	2099.3
菱镁矿	（矿石，万吨）	Magnesite Ore	(Ore, 10 000 tons)	150149.8
普通萤石	（萤石，万吨）	Fluorspar Mineral	(Mineral, 10 000 tons)	3052.9
硫铁矿	（矿石，万吨）	Pyrite Ore	(Ore, 10 000 tons)	196018.2
磷矿	（矿石，万吨）	Phosphorus Ore	(Ore, 10 000 tons)	390177.0
钾盐	（KCl，万吨）	Potassium KCl	(KCl, 10 000 tons)	27323.2
盐矿	（NaCl，亿吨）	Sodium Salt NaCl	(NaCl, 100 million tons)	1866.4
芒硝	（Na_2SO_4，亿吨）	Mirabilite	(Na_2SO_4, 100 million tons)	98.9
重晶石	（矿石，万吨）	Barite Ore	(Ore, 10 000 tons)	9852.1
玻璃硅质原料	（矿石，万吨）	Silicon Materials For Glass Ore	(Ore, 10 000 tons)	117003.3
石墨	（矿物，万吨）	Graphite Mineral (Crystal)	(Mineral, 10 000 tons)	5235.4
滑石	（矿石，万吨）	Talc Ore	(Ore, 10 000 tons)	9447.6
高岭土	（矿石，万吨）	Kaolin Ore	(Ore, 10 000 tons)	54644.7

注：本表资料由国土资源部提供。其中，石油和天然气的数据为剩余可采储量(下表同)。

a) The data in the table are provided by the Ministry of Land and Resources. The data for petroleum and natural gas are proved remaining reserves. The same as the following table.

1-12 各地区主要矿产基础储量（2003年）

Basic Reserves of Major Mineral by Region (2003)

地 区	Region	石 油（万吨）Petroleum (10 000 tons)	天然气（亿立方米）Natural Gas (100 million cu.m)	煤 炭（亿吨）Coal (100 million tons)	铁 矿（矿石,亿吨）Iron (100 million tons)	锰 矿（矿石,万吨）Manganese (10 000 tons)	铜 矿（万吨）Copper (10 000 tons)	菱镁矿（矿石,万吨）Magnesite (10 000 tons)	硫铁矿（矿石,万吨）Pyrite (10 000 tons)	玻璃硅质原料（矿石,万吨）Glass Silicon Materials (10 000 tons)
全 国	**National Total**	**243193.6**	**22288.7**	**3342.0**	**212.4**	**20709.0**	**3003.0**	**150149.8**	**196018.2**	**117003.3**
北 京	Beijing	9.0		5.8	3.0					176.0
天 津	Tianjin	3778.2	347.3	3.0						
河 北	Hebei	12762.8	182.1	89.0	40.3		16.4	1396.4	1976.8	3956.0
山 西	Shanxi			1045.3	6.4	12.9	158.5		1996.8	1861.0
内蒙古	Inner Mongolia	3950.8	3967.2	734.4	12.1	14.0	92.1		8600.7	4673.3
辽 宁	Liaoning	18414.3	228.2	48.2	61.0	1110.0	15.7	121912.2	2847.4	21491.0
吉 林	Jilin	14479.8	171.3	15.3	1.8	0.4	65.3		1457.2	3275.0
黑龙江	Heilongjiang	59881.9	467.8	95.9	0.5		121.7		48.2	407.0
上 海	Shanghai									
江 苏	Jiangsu	2305.2	24.5	25.8	2.4		7.0		1204.0	2606.0
浙 江	Zhejiang			0.5	0.1		9.5		986.8	4267.0
安 徽	Anhui	109.7	0.0	131.9	11.6		263.1		43676.2	3504.9
福 建	Fujian			4.4	3.7	103.9	97.6		1249.5	6301.0
江 西	Jiangxi			8.1	1.2		833.7		15576.6	6343.0
山 东	Shandong	31853.3	285.5	91.1	8.7		31.6		392.0	18344.0
河 南	Henan	6105.1	173.7	121.7	2.0		10.2		12632.6	2341.8
湖 北	Hubei	1053.1	40.9	2.4	5.2	878.2	234.6		2214.4	1604.8
湖 南	Hunan			20.1	0.8	5237.8	39.4		6923.5	4610.0
广 东	Guangdong	9.0	0.3	1.9	2.2	202.7	67.4		33655.4	636.0
广 西	Guangxi	135.7	8.6	8.3	1.0	6776.7	15.4		5169.2	86.0
海 南	Hainan	64.0	13.8	0.9	0.5		1.8			14940.0
重 庆	Chongqing		1043.3	16.3	0.0	1791.9			1907.1	1592.0
四 川	Sichuan	215.9	2032.8	45.2	31.2	26.3	85.7	26667.8	39058.6	3718.6
贵 州	Guizhou		11.1	149.2	0.5	2433.4	0.4		5460.3	2176.5
云 南	Yunnan	10.5	15.0	157.0	4.7	1268.5	262.5		8212.4	1204.0
西 藏	Tibet			0.1	0.3		220.5	123.5		
陕 西	Shaanxi	15104.4	3611.7	285.6	4.2	360.8	16.6		663.8	2597.0
甘 肃	Gansu	6716.1	67.3	48.9	4.1	18.4	203.0		4.0	899.0
青 海	Qinghai	3579.2	1260.2	17.4	0.1		50.8		96.8	1949.0
宁 夏	Ningxia	91.6	0.7	68.4						727.0
新 疆	Xinjiang	36362.5	5554.8	100.0	2.9	473.1	82.8	49.9	7.9	716.4
海 域	Ocean	26201.5	2780.7							

1-13 主要城市平均气温(2003年)

Monthly Average Temperature of Major Cities (2003)

单位: 摄氏度 (℃)

城市	City	1月 Jan.	2月 Feb.	3月 Mar.	4月 Apr.	5月 May	6月 June	7月 July	8月 Aug.	9月 Sept.	10月 Oct.	11月 Nov.	12月 Dec.	年平均 Annual Average
北京	Beijing	-3.2	0.8	6.2	15.2	20.9	24.6	26.0	26.1	20.5	13.1	3.4	0.2	12.8
天津	Tianjin	-3.6	0.3	6.4	15.5	21.2	24.2	26.1	25.5	20.8	13.1	3.9	-0.7	12.7
石家庄	Shijiazhuang	-1.7	2.3	7.4	15.4	21.1	25.9	26.2	25.1	21.2	14.4	4.7	1.5	13.6
太原	Taiyuan	-5.4	0.1	4.6	11.5	18.9	21.4	22.9	21.6	17.4	9.3	2.3	-3.3	10.1
呼和浩特	Hohhot	-12.9	-5.2	1.4	8.6	16.8	19.7	21.8	20.9	16.6	7.0	-1.3	-8.8	7.1
沈阳	Shenyang	-10.9	-4.1	1.8	11.9	18.7	21.9	23.7	23.5	18.5	10.2	0.7	-7.4	9.0
大连	Dalian	-4.2	-0.5	3.9	11.4	17.0	20.5	22.5	23.5	20.7	14.0	5.5	0.4	11.2
长春	Changchun	-13.7	-6.5	0.1	10.6	17.2	20.7	22.8	21.2	16.9	7.6	-2.9	-10.6	7.0
哈尔滨	Harbin	-15.7	-9.1	0.1	9.9	16.6	21.2	22.1	20.8	15.9	7.3	-5.3	-13.1	5.9
上海	Shanghai	3.6	6.8	9.8	15.4	19.8	24.5	29.5	29.2	26.1	18.7	13.9	6.4	17.0
南京	Nanjing	2.3	5.6	9.6	15.3	20.5	25.1	28.2	27.6	24.7	16.9	11.5	4.6	16.0
杭州	Hangzhou	4.2	7.5	10.6	16.3	21.0	24.9	30.9	29.3	26.0	18.4	12.9	6.3	17.4
合肥	Hefei	3.0	6.0	10.2	15.7	21.7	26.4	28.4	27.5	24.4	16.6	10.8	4.4	16.3
福州	Fuzhou	10.9	13.0	14.2	19.9	23.1	26.0	31.4	30.0	27.6	22.5	19.5	12.9	20.9
南昌	Nanchang	5.9	8.8	11.3	17.8	22.6	26.0	31.5	30.1	26.6	19.7	13.9	7.8	18.5
济南	Jinan	-1.4	3.0	7.7	15.2	21.3	25.7	25.8	24.8	21.3	14.7	6.7	1.2	13.8
青岛	Qingdao	-0.9	2.1	5.2	11.5	16.2	20.4	22.0	24.0	21.5	15.9	8.6	2.6	12.4
郑州	Zhengzhou	1.0	3.9	8.5	15.5	21.2	25.6	26.0	24.0	21.2	14.8	7.7	3.0	14.4
武汉	Wuhan	5.1	7.0	10.9	16.7	22.3	27.2	29.7	29.0	25.1	17.9	12.1	5.7	17.4
长沙	Changsha	5.5	7.8	10.7	16.8	21.4	26.2	31.2	28.9	24.3	18.4	12.9	6.6	17.6
广州	Guangzhou	13.8	17.8	18.5	23.9	27.3	27.5	30.3	29.2	27.4	24.2	20.3	14.6	22.9
南宁	Nanning	12.5	17.1	18.3	23.4	26.7	27.2	28.7	28.2	26.0	22.9	19.4	13.3	22.0
海口	Haikou	17.8	21.3	22.6	27.3	28.6	29.3	29.6	28.8	27.5	26.1	23.5	19.5	25.2
桂林	Guilin	9.0	11.6	13.3	19.6	23.1	26.0	30.0	28.9	25.8	20.5	15.8	10.3	19.5
重庆	Chongqing	8.3	12.5	14.4	19.5	22.7	24.5	28.1	29.5	24.3	17.6	14.5	9.3	18.8
成都	Chengdu	7.0	10.9	12.9	17.8	21.7	23.8	26.4	25.3	22.4	17.4	12.8	8.1	17.2
贵阳	Guiyang	5.0	8.8	10.1	15.9	18.4	20.4	23.3	23.6	20.5	14.6	11.5	5.6	14.8
昆明	Kunming	9.1	11.5	14.7	19.6	20.4	19.8	21.2	21.4	18.8	17.1	13.0	10.2	16.4
拉萨	Lhasa	-0.5	1.4	5.2	9.3	11.5	14.2	15.7	16.9	14.0	10.8	5.0	0.5	8.7
西安	Xi'an	0.4	5.4	9.2	15.1	21.7	26.5	26.6	23.4	21.0	13.8	6.5	2.3	14.3
兰州	Lanzhou	-3.2	2.4	7.2	12.3	17.3	21.4	22.6	21.6	17.6	9.8	3.4	-2.4	10.8
西宁	Xining	-6.7	-2.5	2.3	8.4	11.9	14.8	16.6	16.5	12.4	5.7	-0.3	-6.7	6.0
银川	Yinchuan	-7.1	-1.3	4.3	12.1	17.9	22.2	23.4	22.1	18.3	9.6	0.6	-6.2	9.7
乌鲁木齐	Urumqi	-10.6	-8.6	-2.2	6.9	15.3	22.7	21.0	21.9	17.1	10.0	-3.3	-10.3	6.7

1-14 主要城市平均相对湿度（2003年）

Average Relative Humidity of Major Cities (2003)

单位: % (%)

城市	City	1月 Jan.	2月 Feb.	3月 Mar.	4月 Apr.	5月 May	6月 June	7月 July	8月 Aug.	9月 Sept.	10月 Oct.	11月 Nov.	12月 Dec.	年平均 Annual Average
北京	Beijing	45	45	50	45	60	53	68	64	71	52	56	36	54
天津	Tianjin	67	66	61	49	62	62	74	74	77	61	66	54	64
石家庄	Shijiazhuang	61	61	59	55	68	52	71	74	77	58	71	47	63
太原	Taiyuan	60	58	58	52	53	59	70	73	81	68	65	48	62
呼和浩特	Hohhot	70	59	52	47	46	46	59	58	61	58	54	53	55
沈阳	Shenyang	64	52	49	40	45	62	72	68	67	58	57	59	58
大连	Dalian	57	57	53	52	61	66	80	77	69	62	58	53	62
长春	Changchun	68	51	39	31	36	60	73	72	62	63	63	70	57
哈尔滨	Harbin	74	68	48	36	39	63	79	76	68	62	63	78	63
上海	Shanghai	74	82	76	77	77	76	76	73	73	68	75	68	75
南京	Nanjing	65	77	67	71	71	68	81	81	77	71	73	67	72
杭州	Hangzhou	67	76	70	77	73	71	68	72	72	67	74	63	71
合肥	Hefei	70	82	73	79	73	68	83	85	80	75	78	73	77
福州	Fuzhou	68	78	73	79	76	76	66	72	70	65	68	63	71
南昌	Nanchang	71	80	78	81	77	80	69	72	70	64	71	60	73
济南	Jinan	50	51	52	48	56	50	75	79	71	55	61	50	58
青岛	Qingdao	57	65	68	67	75	79	91	87	78	65	68	61	72
郑州	Zhengzhou	54	68	61	59	66	60	82	87	83	64	70	53	67
武汉	Wuhan	68	80	74	76	73	70	73	74	72	69	72	70	73
长沙	Changsha	77	81	81	80	83	78	64	74	77	69	74	72	76
广州	Guangzhou	66	75	79	77	75	79	71	78	77	63	70	56	72
南宁	Nanning	78	83	80	81	82	82	80	82	82	75	73	67	79
海口	Haikou	83	85	83	78	81	76	76	81	86	75	81	75	80
桂林	Guilin	69	78	78	79	81	79	67	73	71	64	65	53	71
重庆	Chongqing	82	74	69	70	74	80	74	64	75	84	81	83	76
成都	Chengdu	76	69	69	70	71	73	77	81	80	76	75	74	74
贵阳	Guiyang	82	77	76	77	82	81	79	74	71	82	78	79	78
昆明	Kunming	63	53	53	43	58	75	72	73	75	75	66	70	65
拉萨	Lhasa	30	30	32	35	42	60	60	58	60	40	28	31	42
西安	Xi'an	64	69	59	62	56	49	68	81	80	75	75	61	67
兰州	Lanzhou	43	42	41	41	48	41	55	59	59	67	64	51	51
西宁	Xining	32	37	41	43	53	56	64	69	65	64	59	51	53
银川	Yinchuan	56	46	49	36	47	45	59	61	57	53	62	55	52
乌鲁木齐	Urumqi	72	78	73	44	40	39	50	41	41	38	64	77	55

1-15 主要城市降水量(2003年)

Monthly Precipitation of Major Cities (2003)

单位: 毫米 (millimeters)

城市	City	1月 Jan.	2月 Feb.	3月 Mar.	4月 Apr.	5月 May	6月 June	7月 July	8月 Aug.	9月 Sept.	10月 Oct.	11月 Nov.	12月 Dec.	全年 Annual Total
北京	Beijing	9.6	2.9	32.8	13.0	30.6	66.1	57.7	34.1	87.9	66.8	42.9	0.1	444.5
天津	Tianjin	1.0	1.7	7.6	8.0	59.1	123.1	161.2	77.6	41.1	165.8	21.8		668.0
石家庄	Shijiazhuang	2.6	2.9	17.3	56.9	103.5	27.9	131.5	115.9	37.4	94.7	50.4	0.1	641.1
太原	Taiyuan	3.7	9.6	20.0	17.7	7.6	72.4	126.9	62.1	116.3	50.3	38.8		525.4
呼和浩特	Hohhot	1.0	7.0	45.9	50.7	56.5	35.7	146.6	118.5	132.2	51.6	6.5	0.9	653.1
沈阳	Shenyang	5.9	3.1	19.4	38.2	25.9	89.7	182.7	85.7	57.9	103.6	22.4	8.5	643.0
大连	Dalian	9.7	9.8	0.6	82.5	18.2	59.9	106.0	82.1	91.8	44.5	10.6	5.5	521.2
长春	Changchun	3.9	0.4	5.0	2.4	41.8	105.6	129.9	114.7	17.3	80.6	13.4	2.2	517.2
哈尔滨	Harbin	2.2	1.0	7.5	15.0	18.8	93.2	143.7	110.5	64.4	35.8	17.1	3.9	513.1
上海	Shanghai	51.7	72.2	95.8	81.5	29.9	99.0	77.7	114.2	26.4	44.6	40.7	23.2	756.9
南京	Nanjing	39.2	69.8	120.6	176.5	32.4	205.1	495.9	128.7	184.2	92.1	57.0	22.0	1623.5
杭州	Hangzhou	52.3	134.0	167.9	111.7	88.4	116.1	81.2	49.2	42.9	32.4	43.6	28.0	947.7
合肥	Hefei	40.9	67.1	134.2	147.5	66.9	185.4	349.5	128.2	53.8	95.2	116.3	28.4	1413.4
福州	Fuzhou	58.9	23.3	68.8	133.7	128.9	134.3	17.1	110.8	59.4	23.5	16.5	1.4	776.6
南昌	Nanchang	82.0	140.4	136.2	264.6	365.6	521.9	84.2	23.4	13.9	21.5	72.1	17.1	1742.9
济南	Jinan	5.1	8.9	15.9	104.4	34.6	50.7	291.6	185.1	124.8	108.0	45.9	10.2	985.2
青岛	Qingdao	10.8	35.9	24.1	63.6	64.8	147.6	152.9	109.3	106.7	36.4	40.0	17.5	809.6
郑州	Zhengzhou	7.5	24.9	32.7	17.7	36.7	149.9	119.2	313.2	125.9	132.4	34.5	16.0	1010.6
武汉	Wuhan	36.3	98.0	188.5	163.7	97.7	195.7	301.7	93.7	47.9	61.2	79.9	21.0	1385.3
长沙	Changsha	80.1	99.4	132.8	190.0	280.3	116.1	5.3	39.4	39.6	13.9	34.7	33.5	1065.1
广州	Guangzhou	33.1	7.6	65.1	59.7	189.4	329.8	61.0	189.0	367.7	3.2	30.9	1.7	1338.2
南宁	Nanning	64.8	26.1	45.1	154.7	193.7	175.1	245.0	146.5	236.2		2.6	6.9	1296.7
海口	Haikou	30.6	4.8	38.8	34.9	149.4	98.0	248.2	234.4	467.6	21.1	92.8	0.8	1421.4
桂林	Guilin	117.7	71.7	87.1	192.1	462.4	303.5	29.2	48.2	145.0	48.9	28.0	20.0	1553.8
重庆	Chongqing	13.4	9.7	20.0	77.1	222.8	378.0	130.6	34.3	68.0	32.6	55.5	23.7	1065.7
成都	Chengdu	1.4	1.8	19.4	57.5	104.7	50.6	82.9	352.3	29.8	28.0	6.6	6.1	741.1
贵阳	Guiyang	18.4	5.0	39.8	169.7	236.3	163.6	107.8	17.3	40.6	58.7	19.9	47.7	924.8
昆明	Kunming	51.1	8.8	9.3	2.5	89.6	162.1	155.2	158.0	99.4	57.1	5.8	33.5	832.4
拉萨	Lhasa	1.3	2.9	2.9	3.1	29.3	197.7	90.6	121.2	95.2	3.3			547.5
西安	Xi'an	16.1	20.7	33.9	30.3	49.7	46.9	136.5	179.6	195.5	133.9	32.9	6.8	882.8
兰州	Lanzhou	0.1		5.8	21.5	50.8	64.6	38.1	84.0	28.9	23.6	5.6	0.1	324.1
西宁	Xining	0.2		10.0	36.7	87.4	100.8	125.0	114.5	53.1	27.4	5.5	3.4	564.0
银川	Yinchuan	0.6	0.4	5.3	1.9	25.3	40.5	25.6	51.2	29.4	13.8	7.6		201.6
乌鲁木齐	Urumqi	13.3	8.2	11.8	37.7	59.1	35.2	68.7	48.3	52.0	0.1	27.0	8.0	369.4

1-16 主要城市日照时数(2003年)

Monthly Sunshine Hours of Major Cities (2003)

单位: 小时 (hours)

城市	City	1月 Jan.	2月 Feb.	3月 Mar.	4月 Apr.	5月 May	6月 June	7月 July	8月 Aug.	9月 Sept.	10月 Oct.	11月 Nov.	12月 Dec.	全年 Annual Total
北京	Beijing	193	176	158	210	215	240	156	214	158	212	122	205	2260
天津	Tianjin	181	140	150	188	208	202	150	199	138	178	93	168	1994
石家庄	Shijiazhuang	169	110	94	131	105	158	90	197	155	215	98	203	1724
太原	Taiyuan	191	148	154	198	226	226	175	184	158	190	128	158	2135
呼和浩特	Hohhot	122	164	193	228	264	188	188	307	241	244	156	180	2474
沈阳	Shenyang	137	179	137	185	164	179	131	257	187	195	109	137	1996
大连	Dalian	207	187	213	249	272	183	166	203	176	202	132	180	2371
长春	Changchun	179	209	233	230	239	219	191	259	218	200	157	167	2500
哈尔滨	Harbin	142	167	224	214	198	185	166	206	187	162	133	104	2089
上海	Shanghai	155	100	154	124	107	133	171	185	178	161	121	126	1714
南京	Nanjing	157	77	148	110	157	161	157	135	175	176	131	135	1719
杭州	Hangzhou	112	76	119	106	123	133	249	197	184	178	120	130	1726
合肥	Hefei	152	79	157	101	140	171	169	119	161	167	150	126	1693
福州	Fuzhou	141	91	107	114	133	128	322	218	165	200	107	176	1902
南昌	Nanchang	150	69	112	126	164	161	341	249	235	205	173	215	2197
济南	Jinan	183	137	143	180	241	200	160	162	139	183	120	170	2017
青岛	Qingdao	183	159	165	177	191	144	103	112	164	192	163	174	1925
郑州	Zhengzhou	142	95	123	150	147	165	104	50	99	139	69	109	1392
武汉	Wuhan	128	65	126	112	110	143	212	177	172	138	153	92	1628
长沙	Changsha	77	56	111	101	77	140	283	165	140	124	120	76	1470
广州	Guangzhou	163	68	52	91	103	96	242	153	160	216	161	238	1742
南宁	Nanning	135	84	76	111	149	144	277	180	169	190	153	165	1833
海口	Haikou	112	98	114	165	192	198	263	205	152	224	138	141	2002
桂林	Guilin	105	56	68	84	83	113	285	205	198	145	140	148	1630
重庆	Chongqing	9	51	98	94	83	69	149	155	105	30	34	11	888
成都	Chengdu	44	61	83	94	77	101	111	66	68	51	27	36	819
贵阳	Guiyang	51	93	69	103	68	42	119	117	117	33	85	19	915
昆明	Kunming	223	241	268	283	203	100	156	170	118	141	213	180	2295
拉萨	Lhasa	251	215	254	246	274	227	219	259	206	277	277	248	2953
西安	Xi'an	99	88	132	164	223	203	205	86	134	138	95	91	1657
兰州	Lanzhou	188	183	194	226	255	267	230	204	182	172	144	169	2414
西宁	Xining	215	185	186	218	218	248	215	171	204	171	174	170	2375
银川	Yinchuan	202	190	195	210	258	275	241	222	215	241	141	179	2569
乌鲁木齐	Urumqi	139	105	171	215	269	297	308	319	256	256	120	95	2550

主要统计指标解释

行政区划 指国家对行政区域的划分。根据宪法规定，我国的行政区域划分如下：(1)全国分为省、自治区、直辖市；(2)省、自治区分为自治州、县、自治县、市；(3)自治州分为县、自治县、市；(4)县、自治县分为乡、民族乡、镇；(5)直辖市和较大的市分为区、县；(6)国家在必要时设立的特别行政区。

国土 指中华人民共和国国家管辖下的领土、领海和领空。

气候 指地球与大气之间长期能量交换与质量交换所形成的一种自然环境状态，它是多种因素综合作用的结果。气候既是人类生活和生产的环境要素之一，又是供给人类生活和生产的重要资源。气温、降水、湿度等气象要素的多年平均值是用来描述一个地区气候状况的主要参数，而各种气象要素某年、某月的平均值(或总量)则可以反映出该时期天气气候状况的重要特征。

自然资源 指人类可以直接从自然界获得，并用于生产和生活的物质资源。自然资源一般可以分成可再生资源和非再生资源两大类。可再生资源指在较短时间内可以再生、可以循环利用的资源，包括土地资源、水资源、气候资源、生物资源和海洋资源等。非再生资源指在使用后不能再生的资源，包括矿产资源和地热能源。

土地资源 土地指陆地的表层部分，它主要由岩石、岩石的风化物和土壤构成。土地资源按利用类型可以分为农用地、建筑用地和未利用地。农用地包括耕地、园地、林地、牧草地和水面。建筑用地包括居民点及工矿用地、交通用地和水利设施用地。未利用地指农用地和建筑用地以外的土地，包括滩涂、荒漠、戈壁、冰川和石山等。

耕地面积 指经过开垦用以种植农作物并经常进行耕耘的土地面积。包括种有作物的土地面积、休闲地、新开荒地和抛荒未满三年的土地面积。

林业用地面积 指生长乔木、竹类、灌木、沿海红树林等林木的土地面积，包括有林地、灌木林、疏林地、未成林造林地、迹地、苗圃等。

草地面积 指牧区和农区用于放牧牲畜或割草，植被盖度在5%以上的草原、草坡、草山等面积。包括天然的和人工种植或改良的草地面积。

森林资源 指森林、林木、林地以及依托森林、林木、林地生存的野生动物、植物和微生物。林木指树木和竹子。森林指以乔木为主体的植物群落，是集生的乔木及与其共同作用的植物、动物、微生物和土壤、气候等的总体。

活立木总蓄积量 指一定范围内土地上全部树木蓄积的总量，包括森林蓄积、疏林蓄积、散生木蓄积和四旁树蓄积。

森林面积 指由乔木树种构成，郁闭度0.2以上(含0.2)的林地或冠幅宽度10米以上的林带的面积，即有林地面积。森林面积包括天然起源和人工起源的针叶林面积、阔叶林面积、针阔混交林面积和竹林面积，不包括灌木林地面积和疏林地面积。

森林蓄积量 指一定森林面积上存在着的林木树干部分的总材积。它是反映一个国家或地区森林资源总规模和水平的基本指标之一，也是反映森林资源的丰富程度、衡量森林生态环境优劣的重要依据。

森林覆盖率 指一个国家或地区森林面积占土地总面积的百分比。森林覆盖率是反映森林资源的丰富程度和生态平衡状况的重要指标。在计算森林覆盖率时，森林面积包括郁闭度0.2以上的乔木林地面积和竹林地面积，国家特别规定的灌木林地面积、农田林网以及四旁(村旁、路旁、水旁、宅旁)林木的覆盖面积。计算公式为：

$$森林覆盖率（\%）=\frac{森林面积}{土地总面积}\times 100\%$$

水资源 水在自然界中以固体、液体和气态三种聚集状态存在，分布于海洋、陆地(包括土壤)以及大气之中，通过水循环形成水资源。水资源包括经人类控制并直接可供灌溉、发电、给水、航运、养殖等用途的地表水和地下水，以及江河、湖泊、井、泉、潮汐、港湾和养殖水域等。水资源是发展国民经济不可缺少的重要自然资源。

地表水和地下水 陆地上的水因空间分布不同，分为地表水和地下水。地表水指分别存在于河流、湖泊、沼泽、冰川和冰盖等水体中水分的总称，又称陆地水。地下水指储存在地面以下饱和岩土孔隙、裂隙及溶洞中的水。

内陆水域总面积 指江、河、湖泊、池塘、塘堰、水库等各种流水或蓄水的水面占地面积。

海洋 是海和洋的统称。洋为地球表面上相连接的广大咸水水体的主体部分。海为地球表面相连接的广大咸水水体被陆地、岛礁、半岛包围或分隔的边缘部分。

海水可养殖面积 指利用滩涂、浅海、港湾进行鱼、虾、蟹、贝、藻等海水经济动植物的人工养殖的水面面积。

径流 指陆地上接受降水后扣除损耗外，从地表和地下向流域出口断面汇集的水流。径流可分为地表径流、地下径流和壤中流。地表径流指沿地表向河流、湖泊、沼泽、海洋等汇集的水流；地下径流指沿潜水层或隔水层间的含水层，向河流、湖泊、沼泽、海洋等汇集的地下水水流。

径流量 指在一定时段内通过河流某一过水断面的水量，用以反映一个国家或地区水资源的丰歉程度。计算公式为：

径流量=降水量-蒸发量

矿产资源 矿产指由地质作用形成，富集于地壳中或出露于地表达到工农业利用要求的有用矿物。矿产是一种重要的自然资源，是社会发展的重要物质基础。

矿产基础储量 基础储量是查明矿产资源的一部分。它能满足现行采矿和生产所需的指标要求，是控制的、探明的并通过可行性或预可行性研究认为属于经济的、边界经济的部分，用未扣除设计、采矿损失的数量表示。

流域 每条河流都有自己的干流和支流，干支流共同组成这条河流的水系。每条河流都有自己的集水区域，这个集水区域就称为该河流的流域。

外流河 指直接或间接流入海洋的河流。供给外流河河水的区域称为外流区域。

内陆河 指在陆地内部干燥地区，河水沿途消失于沙漠或注入内陆湖泊的河流。供给内陆河河水的区域称为内陆区域。

大陆架 指沿海国家的领海以外，依其陆地领土的全部自然延伸，扩展到大陆边缘的，其宽度依据《联合国海洋法公约》规定的海底区域的海床和底土。大陆架海区水产资源丰富，海底多蕴藏石油、天然气以及其他矿产资源，这些自然资源属沿海国家所有。我国的大陆架为我国领海以外依本国陆地领土的全部自然延伸，扩展到大陆边外缘的海底区域的海床和底土；如果从测算领海宽度的基线量起至大陆边外缘的距离不足200海里，则扩展到200海里。

浅海养殖 指在可养殖的浅海中进行海水经济动植物养殖。

滩涂养殖 指利用位于海边潮间带的软泥或砂泥地带加以平整，筑堤、建坝等进行海水养殖。

港湾养殖 指利用港、湾，或在海边、河口附近的滩涂、洼地拦闸筑堤进行海水养殖。

气温 指空气的温度，我国一般以摄氏度(℃)为单位表示。气象观测的温度表是放在离地面约1.5米处通风良好的百叶箱里测量的，因此，通常说的气温指的是离地面1.5米处百叶箱中的温度。其统计计算方法为：

月平均气温是将全月各日的平均气温相加，除以该月的天数而得。

年平均气温是将12个月的月平均气温累加后除以12而得。

相对湿度 指空气中实际所含水蒸气密度和同温度下饱和水蒸气密度的百分比值。其统计方法与气温相同。

降水量 指从天空降落到地面的液态或固态(经融化后)水，未经蒸发、渗透、流失而在地面上积聚的深度。其统计计算方法为：

月降水量是将全月各日的降水量累加而得。

年降水量是将12个月的月降水量累加而得。

日照时数 指太阳实际照射地面的时间。其统计方法与降水量相同。

Explanatory Notes on Main Statistical Indicators

Administrative Division refers to the division of administrative areas by the state. The Constitution of the People's Republic of China stipulates that the administrative areas in China are divided as: 1) The whole country is divided into provinces, autonomous regions and municipalities directly under the central government; 2) Provinces and autonomous regions are divided into autonomous prefectures, counties, autonomous counties and cities; 3) Autonomous prefectures are divided into counties, autonomous counties and cities; 4) Counties and autonomous counties are divided into townships, nationality townships and towns; 5) Municipalities and large cities are divided into districts and counties, 6) The state shall, when necessary, establish special administrative regions.

Territory refers to territorial land, sea and air space under the administration of the People's Republic of China.

Climate refers to the natural environmental status formed by the long-term exchange of energy and mass between the earth and the air, and is the results of interaction of many factors. Climate is both one of the environment factors and the important resources for the living and production activities of the human being. The average values across several years of meteorological factors such as temperature, rainfall and humidity are used as important parameters to describe the climate of a region, while the average values (or total values) of a given year or month of meteorological factors reflect the key characteristics of climate for that period of time.

Natural Resources refer to material resources that could be obtained from the nature by human being and used for production and living. Natural resources in general can be classified as renewable resources and non-renewable resources. Renewable resources refer to resources that could be renewed and recycled during a relatively short period of time, including land resource, water resource, climate resource, biology resource and marine resource. Non-renewable resources include resources that could not be renewed, such as minerals and geothermal resource.

Land Resource Land refers to the surface of the earth, consisting of mainly rocks and its whethering and earth. Land resource can be classified, by its utilization, as land for agriculture, land for construction and unused land. Land for agriculture includes cultivated land, plantation land, forestland, grassland and waters. Land for construction includes land for residential purpose, for manufacturing and mining, for transportation and for water-conservancy projects. Unused land refers to land other than land for agriculture and construction, including beaches, deserts, Gobi, glaciers and rock mountains.

Area of Cultivated Land refers to area of land reclaimed for the regular cultivation of various farm crops, including crop-cover land, fallow, newly reclaimed land and land laid idle for less than 3 years.

Area of Afforested Land refer to land for trees bamboo, bushes and mangrove, including forest-cover land, bush-covered land, sparse forest land, land planned for afforestation and nurseries of young trees.

Area of Grassland refers to areas of grassland, grass-slopes and grass-covered hills with a vegetation-covering rate of over 5% that are used for animal husbandry or harvesting of grass. It includes natural, cultivated and improved grassland areas.

Forest Resource refers to forests, trees, forestland and wild animals, plants and microorganism that live on forest and trees. Trees include trees and bamboo. Forest refers to the population of clusters of trees and other plants, animals and microorganism as well as the earth and climate that have interactions with the trees.

Total Standing Stock Volume refers to the total stock volume of trees growing in land, including trees in forest, tress in sparse forest, scattered trees and trees planted by the side of villages, farm houses and along roads and rivers.

Forest Area refers to the area of forest where trees and bamboo grow with canopy density above 0.2, including land of natural woods and planted woods, but excluding bush land and thin forest land. It reflects the total areas of afforestation.

Stock Volume of Forest refers to total stock volume of wood growing in forest area, which shows the total size and level of forest resources of a country or a region. It is also an important indicator illustrating the richness of forest resource and the status of forest ecological environment.

Forest Coverage Rate refers to the ratio of area of afforested land to total land area. It is a very important indicator that reflects the status of abundance of forest resource and ecosystem balance. Forest area includes the area of trees and bamboo grow with canopy density above 0.2, the area of shrubby tree according to regulations of the government, the area of forest land inside farm land and the area of trees planted by the side of villages, farm houses and along roads and rivers. The formula for calculating forest coverage rate is as follows:

Forestry coverage rate (%)= (Area of Afforested Land/Area of Total Land)× 100%

Water Resource Water exists in the nature in solid, liquid and gaseous states, is distributed in the ocean, land (including earth) and air, and constitutes the water resource through the circulation of water. Water resource includes the surface water and underground water that is controlled by the human being for irrigation, power-generation, water supply, navigation and cultivation. It also includes rivers, lakes, wells, springs, tides, gulf and water area for cultivation. Water resource as an important natural resource is indispensable for the development of the national economy.

Surface Water and Underground Water Water on earth can be divided into surface water and underground water according to its distribution. Surface water refers to moisture exists in rivers, lakes, swamps, glaciers, icecaps and so on. It is also called land water. The underground water refers to water deposited underground in the cranny and the hole of saturated rock soil and in the water-eroded cave.

Inland Water Area refers to water area of rivers, lakes, ponds, reservoir, etc.

Ocean is the general name for sea and ocean. Ocean refers to the main body of large salt water connected with the earth. Sea refers to the edge areas of the salt water on the earth that are comparted or surrounded by land, island, reef or peninsula.

Marine Cultivatable Areas refer to water areas in beach, shallow sea and lough that are used to breed marine cash propagation, such as fish, shrimp, crab, shellfish, alga and so on.

Runoff refers to the water gathered at the way out of the cross section of drainage area either from the surface or underground after deducting the wastage of the precipitation on the land. Runoff can be divided into surface runoff, underground runoff and within soil runoff. Surface runoff refers to water flow to the rivers, lakes, swamps, and seas on the surface of the earth. Underground runoff refers to water flow to rivers, lakes, swamps, and seas through the water-bearing stratum of confined layer or unconfined layer.

Volume of Runoff refers to the total volume of water running through a certain cross section of a river during a certain period of time, reflecting the water resource condition in a country or a region. The formula for calculating volume or runoff is as follows:

Runoff =Precipitation-Evaporation

Mineral Resources refer to useful minerals that can be used for industrial or agricultural purposes enriched in lithosphere or on earth due to the geological process. Minerals are important natural resources, and important material base for social development.

Ensured Mineral Reserves refer to the actual mineral reserves, which equal to the proven mineral reserves (including industrial reserves and prospective reserves) minus extracted parts and underground losses.

Drainage Area Each river has its own main stream and branches to form the water system of the river. Each river has its own catchment area, which is also called as the drainage area of the river.

Out-flowing Rivers refer to rivers directly or indirectly flowing into the sea. The area providing water to the out-flowing rivers is called as out-flowing area.

Inland Rivers refer to rivers in inland dry areas that die away in desert on the way or infuse into inland lakes. The area providing water to the inland rivers is called as inland area.

Continental Shelf refers to seabed and subsoil of sea floor area that beyond the marginal sea of the coastal countries which stretches naturally of its land territory to continent edge, and its width is defined by the United Nations Marine Convention. The continental shelf area is rich in aquatic products, and its seabed contains petroleum, natural gas and other mineral resources, which belong to the coastal countries. The continental shelf of our country is the natural stretch of its land territory to the continent edge besides the marginal sea of our country. It expands to the seabed and subsoil of the sea floor area to the edge of the continent. If the distance from the baseline of the marginal sea to the continent edge is less than 200 nautical miles, it can be expanded to 200 nautical miles.

Shallow Sea Cultivation refers to the breeding of marine cash propagation in the cultivatable shallow sea.

Sea-breaches Cultivation refers to the level off the ooze and mud in tideland to bank up and build dam to conduct marine cultivation.

Harbor Cultivation refers to marine cultivation conducted in harbors, bays, or the sea-beaches or marshes around seaside and bayou by blocking the gate and banking up the dam.

Temperature refers to the air temperature. China uses centigrade as the unit. The thermometry used for weather observation is put in a breezy shutter, which is 1.5 meters high from the ground. Therefore, the commonly used temperature refers to the temperature in the breezy shutter 1.5 meters away from the ground. The calculation method is as follows:

Monthly average temperature is the summation of average daily temperature of one month divided by the actual days of that particular month.

Annual average temperature is the summation of monthly average of a year divided by 12 months.

Relative Humidity refers to the ratio of actual water vapor pressure to the saturation water vapor density under the current temperature. The statistical method is the same as that of temperature.

Volume of Precipitation refers to the deepness of liquid state or solid state (thawed) water falling from the sky to the ground that has not been evaporated, infiltrated or run off. The calculation method is as follows:

Monthly precipitation is the summation of daily precipitation of a month.

Annual precipitation is the summation of 12 months precipitation of a year.

Sunshine Hours refer to the actual hours of sun irradiating the earth. The calculation method is the same as that of the precipitation.

二、综合

General Survey

简要说明

一、本篇内容主要包括国民经济综合资料和民族自治地方社会经济发展情况资料两部分。分别由国家统计局综合司和国家民族事务委员会经济发展司编辑整理。

二、国民经济综合资料是抽取全书的精华，通过对各篇章主要统计指标及其速度、结构、比例和效益等的加工计算，来反映国民经济和社会发展的总体情况。

三、民族自治地方及少数民族统计资料由两部分组成：

一是以地域为主体进行的统计调查。即根据国家民委和国家统计局联合布置的民族自治地方国民经济和社会发展统计报表制度，由有民族自治地方的20个省、自治区、直辖市民委和统计局共同组织实施。统计范围是5个民族自治区、30个自治州、120个自治县（旗）辖区内的全部单位，全国汇总时不重复计算。统计调查方法为全面调查。另外，全国民族自治地方卫生情况由卫生部提供。民族自治地方行政区划资料是根据民政部编辑的《行政区划简册》汇总整理。

二是以民族成分为主体进行的统计调查，主要反映全国少数民族社会发展情况。其中全国少数民族教职员工、学生数据由教育部提供；全国少数民族优秀运动员、教练员数据由国家体育总局提供；全国少数民族文字出版物数据由新闻出版署提供。

四、从1998年年报开始执行国家统计局和国家工行政管理局共同制定的《关于划分企业登记注册类型的规定》。

Brief Introduction

I. This chapter consists of two parts: summary data on the national economy and data on the social and economic development of the minority national autonomous areas, which are compiled by the Department of Integrated Statistics of the National Bureau of Statistics and by the State Commission on Ethnic Affairs respectively.

II. The summary data on the national economy highlight the overall situation of the economic and social development by presenting key statistics including growth, structure, ratio and efficiency data derived from other chapters.

III. Data on the minority nationality autonomous areas and the minority nationalities are composed of two parts:

(1) Data collected from the surveys conducted by areas. A statistical reporting system on the economic and social development in the minority nationality autonomous areas has been assigned jointly by the State Commission on Ethnic Affairs and the National Bureau of Statistics and implemented by the ethnic affairs commissions and the statistical bureaus of 20 provinces and autonomous regions. The reporting system covers all units under the jurisdiction of the 5 minority nationality autonomous regions, 30 autonomous prefectures and 119 autonomous counties. Duplicated counts are excluded in the national tabulation. In addition, data on the public health of the minority nationality autonomous areas are provided by the Ministry of Public Health, and data on the divisions of administrative areas of the minority nationality autonomous areas are tabulated and prepared in accordance with the *Concise Edition of the Divisions of Administrative Areas* compiled by the Ministry of Civil Affairs.

(2) Data collected from the surveys mainly on the minority nationalities. They chiefly show the social development of the minority nationalities. Among them, data on the students and teaching staff of the minority nationalities are provided by the Ministry of Education; data on the excellent athletes and coaches are provided by the State Sports Administration; and data on the publications of the minority nationality languages are provided by the Press and Publication Administration.

IV. The *Regulation on the Classification of the Registration Status of Enterprises*, jointly developed by the National Bureau of Statistics and the State Industry and Commerce Administration, has been in use in compiling the annual statistics since 1998.

2-1 各部门机构数

Grassroots Units in Various Sectors

部门	Sector	机构数 Grassroots Units 2002	2003	2003年比上年增长(%) Increase Rate in 2003 over 2002(%)
农村基层单位 （万个）	**Rural Grassroots Units (10 000 units)**			
基层组织	Basic Units			
乡政府	Township Governments	1.92	1.84	-4.2
镇政府	Town Governments	1.98	1.96	-1.0
村民委员会	Village Committees	69.45	67.86	-2.3
乡村户数	Numbers of Rural Households	24569	24793	0.9
国营农场 （个）	**State-owned Farms (unit)**	**1945**	**1967**	**1.1**
国有及规模以上非国有工业企业 （万个）	**State-owned and Non-state-owned above Designated Size Industrial Enterprises (10 000 units)**	**18.16**	**19.62**	**8.0**
内资企业	Domestic Funded Enterprises	14.71	15.76	7.1
国有企业	State-owned Industry	2.94	2.32	-21.1
集体企业	Collective-owned Industry	2.75	2.25	-18.2
股份合作企业	Cooperative Enterprises	1.02	0.93	-8.8
联营企业	Joint Ownership Enterprises	0.20	0.17	-15.0
有限责任公司	Limited Liability Corporations	2.25	2.66	18.2
股份有限公司	Share Holding Enterprises	0.60	0.63	5.0
私营企业	Private Enterprises	4.92	6.76	37.4
其他企业	Other Enterprises	0.03	0.04	33.3
港澳台商投资企业	Enterprises with Funds from Hong Kong, Macao and Taiwan	1.95	2.12	8.7
外商投资企业	Foreign Funded Enterprises	1.49	1.74	16.8
建筑业企业 （个）	**Construction Enterprises and Units (unit)**	**47820**	**48688**	**1.8**
国有企业	Construction Enterprises	7536	6638	-11.9
集体企业	Collective-owned Industry	13177	10425	-20.9
港澳台商投资企业	Enterprises with Funds from Hong Kong, Macao and Taiwan	632	535	-15.3
外商投资企业	Foreign Funded Enterprises	279	287	2.9
其他企业	Other Enterprises	26196	30803	17.6
邮电业 （个）	**Establishments of Postal and Telecommunications (unit)**			
邮政局所	Post and Telecommunications Offices	76358	63555	-16.8
卫生事业 （个）	**Health Care (unit)**	**306038**	**291323**	**-4.8**
#医院、卫生院	Urban and Township Hospitals	63858	62968	-1.4
疗养院	Sanatoriums	365	305	-16.4
门诊部、所	Clinics	219907	204468	-7.0
专科防治所、站	Specialized Prevention & Treatment Stations	1839	1749	-4.9
疾病预防控制中心	CDC (Epidemic Prevention Station)	3580	3584	0.1
妇幼保健院（所、站）	Maternity and Child Care Centers	3067	3033	-1.1
社会福利 （个）	**Social Welfare Establishments (unit)**			
社会福利事业单位	Social Welfare Institutions	89766	87052	-3.0
#收养性福利事业单位	Adopting Social Welfare Institutions	38200	37294	-2.4
社会福利企业	Social Welfare Enterprises	35758	33976	-5.0
社区服务单位	Community Services Units	7898	7520	-4.8

2-1 续表 Continued

部门	Sector	机构数 Grassroots Units 2002	2003	2003年比上年增长(%) Increase Rate in 2003 over 2002 (%)
教育事业	**Education**			
普通高等学校 (所)	Regular Institutions of Higher Education (unit)	1396	1552	11.2
普通中等学校 (万所)	Secondary Schools (10 000 units)	9.40	8.94	-4.9
#普通中学	Regular Secondary Schools	8.01	7.95	-0.7
小学 (万所)	Primary Schools (10 000 units)	45.69	42.58	-6.8
幼儿园 (万所)	Kindergartens (10 000 units)	11.18	11.64	4.1
特殊教育 (所)	Special Schools (unit)	1540	1551	0.7
科技机构 (个)	**Science and Technology Institution (unit)**	**27862**	**25433**	**-8.7**
艺术事业 (个)	**Art Institutions (unit)**	**4416**	**5123**	**16.0**
#艺术表演团体	Art Performance Troupes	2587	2618	1.2
艺术表演场所	Art Show Centers	1829	1912	4.5
#剧场、影剧院	Theaters	1794	1869	4.2
公共图书馆 (个)	**Public Libraries (unit)**	**2697**	**2709**	**0.4**
群众文化事业 (个)	**Mass Cultural Establishments (unit)**	**42516**	**41816**	**-1.6**
群众艺术馆	Mass Art Centers	389	382	-1.8
文化馆	Cultural Centers	2854	2846	-0.3
文化站	Cultural Stations	39273	38588	-1.7
#乡文化站	Township Cultural Centers	36054	35138	-2.5
艺术教育事业 (个)	**Arts Education Establishments (unit)**	**205**	**195**	**-4.9**
其他文化事业 (个)	**Other Cultural Establishments (unit)**	**255769**	**295903**	**15.7**
艺术创作机构	Art Creation Institutions	433	404	-6.7
艺术研究机构	Art Research Institutions	184	185	0.5
艺术展览机构	Art Exhibition Institutions	51	53	3.9
文化艺术经纪与代理业	Brokers and Agents for Cultural and Arts Activities	421	584	38.7
出版、发行事业 (个)	**Publishing and Distribution Establishments (unit)**	**14222**	**13722**	**-3.5**
书刊出版社	Publishing Houses	568	570	0.4
国家定点书刊印刷厂	Pointed Printing Houses	286	285	-0.3
书店	Book Stores	13368	12867	-3.7
文物事业 (个)	**Cultural Relic Establishments (unit)**	**3867**	**3903**	**0.9**
博物馆	Museums	1511	1515	0.3
文物机构	Cultural Relic Agencies	2241	2275	1.5
文物商店	Cultural Relic Shops	115	113	-1.7
广播电视台站 (座)	**Broadcasting and Television Stations (unit)**			
广播电台	Radio Stations	306	277	-9.5
电视台	Television Stations	368	317	-13.9
县级广播电视台	Number of Wire Broadcasting and Television Stations in County Level	1526	1308	-14.3
金融业 (个)	**Financial Intermediation (unit)**	**108675**	**97864**	**-9.9**
银行系统合计	Sub-total of Banking System	108631	97802	-10.0
保险系统总公司合计	Sub-total of Insurance System	44	62	40.9

注：卫生机构数从2002年起为登记注册数。

a) Number of health institutions since 2002 are the number of registration.

2-2 平均每天主要社会经济活动

Selected Indicators on Average Daily Social and Economic Activities

指标	Item	1978	1989	1997	2003
每天创造的财富	**Daily Production**				
国内生产总值 (亿元)	Gross Domestic Product (100 million yuan)	9.9	46.3	204.0	321.2
第一产业	Primary Industry	2.8	11.6	38.9	46.8
第二产业	Secondary Industry	4.8	19.9	102.0	167.9
#工业	Industry	4.4	17.8	88.8	145.5
建筑业	Construction	0.4	2.2	13.2	22.4
第三产业	Tertiary Industry	2.4	14.8	63.1	106.5
#交通运输仓储和邮电通信业	Transport, Storage, Post & Telecommunication Services	0.5	2.2	10.4	18.4
批发和零售贸易餐饮业	Wholesale and Retail Trade & Catering Services	0.7	4.6	16.9	25.3
财政收入 (亿元)	Government Revenue (100 million yuan)	3.1	7.3	23.7	59.5
财政支出 (亿元)	Government Expenditures (100 million yuan)	3.1	7.7	25.3	67.5
粮食 (万吨)	Grain (10 000 tons)	83.5	111.7	135.4	118.0
棉花 (万吨)	Cotton (10 000 tons)	0.6	1.0	1.3	1.3
油料 (万吨)	Oil-bearing Crops (10 000 tons)	1.4	3.5	5.9	7.7
肉类 (万吨)	Meat (10 000 tons)			14.4	19.0
水产品 (万吨)	Aquatic Products (10 000 tons)	1.3	3.2	9.9	12.9
布 (万米)	Cloth (10 000 m)	3022	5184	6816	9685
原 煤 (万吨)	Coal (10 000 tons)	169	289	376	457
发电量 (亿千瓦小时)	Electricity (100 million kwh)	7.0	16.0	31.1	52.3
原 油 (万吨)	Crude Oil (10 000 tons)	28.5	37.7	44.0	46.5
钢 (万吨)	Steel (10 000 tons)	8.7	16.9	29.8	60.9
成品钢材 (万吨)	Steel Products (10 000 tons)	6.0	13.3	27.3	66.0
水 泥 (万吨)	Cement (10 000 tons)	17.9	57.6	140.2	236.2
每天消费量	**Daily National Consumption**				
最终消费 (亿元)	Final Consumption Expenditure (100 million yuan)	6.1	28.9	119.4	184.8
居民消费	Resident Consumption	4.8	23.4	95.5	144.3
农村居民	Rural Household	3.0	13.5	47.8	59.8
城镇居民	Urban Household	1.8	9.9	47.7	84.5
政府消费	Government Consumption Expenditure	1.3	5.6	23.9	40.4
能源消费量 (万吨标准煤)	Energy Consumption (10 000 tons of SCE)	156.6	265.6	377.5	459.7
社会消费品零售总额 (亿元)	Total Retail Sales of Consumer Goods (100 million yuan)	4.3	22.2	74.8	125.6
每天其他经济活动	**Other Daily Economic Activities**				
资本形成总额 (亿元)	Gross Capital Formation (100 million yuan)	3.8	16.7	78.0	140.8
固定资产形成	Fixed Capital Formation	2.9	11.9	68.9	140.4
存货增加	Changes in Stock	0.8	4.8	9.1	0.4
城镇新建住宅面积(万平方米)	Residential Buildings Completed in Urban Areas (10 000 sq.m)	10.4	54.0	111.2	150.7
农民新建房屋面积(万平方米)	Private Buildings Completed in Rural Areas (10 000 sq.m)	27.4	185.2	220.8	206.0
客运量 (万人)	Passenger Traffic (10 000 persons)	696	2168	3633	4349
货运量 (万吨)	Freight Traffic (10 000 tons)	682	2708	3502	4278
沿海主要港口货物吞吐量(万吨)	Cargo Handled at Principal Seaports (10 000 tons)	54.3	134.3	248.8	551.0
邮电业务总量 (亿元)	Business Volume of Postal and Telecommunications Services (100 million yuan)	0.1	0.3	4.9	19.2
进出口总额 (亿美元)	Total Value of Imports and Exports (USD 100 million)	0.6	3.1	8.9	23.3
出口总额	Total Exports	0.3	1.4	5.0	12.0
进口总额	Total Imports	0.3	1.6	3.9	11.3
实际利用外资额 (亿美元)	Foreign Capital Actually Used (USD 100 million)		0.3	1.8	1.5
过夜旅游者人数 (万人次)	Tourists (Overnight Visitors) (10 000 person-times)	0.2	2.6	6.5	9.0
居民新增储蓄额 (亿元)	Outstanding Amount of Savings Deposit (100 million yuan)	0.1	3.8	21.3	45.6
每天人口变动和婚姻	**Daily Population Changes and Marriages**				
出 生 (万人)	Births (10 000 persons)	4.8	6.7	5.6	4.4
死 亡 (万人)	Deaths (10 000 persons)	1.6	2.0	2.2	2.3
结 婚 (万对)	Marriages (10 000 couples)	1.6	2.6	2.5	2.2
离 婚 (对)	Divorces (couples)	781	2063	3282	3647

注:本表价值指标除邮电业务总量按不变价格计算外，其余均按当年价格计算。邮电业务总量2000年及以前按1990年不变价格计算，2001年起按2000年不变价格计算。

a) Figures in value terms in this table are at current prices, except that on the business transaction of post and telecommunications service which is at 1990 constant prices before 2000 and at 2000 constant prices since 2000.

2-3 国民经济和社会发展总量与速度指标

指标		Item		1978
人口与就业		**Population and Employment**		
人口	**（万人）**	**Population**	**(10 000 persons)**	
年底总人口		Population at the Year-end		96259
城镇人口		Urban		17245
乡村人口		Rural		79014
男性人口		Male		49567
女性人口		Female		46692
就业	**（万人）**	**Employment**	**(10 000 persons)**	
就业人员数		Employment		40152
#职工人数		Staff and Workers		9499
城镇登记失业人数		Urban Registeration Unemployment		530
宏观经济		**Macroeconomic Indicator**		
国民经济核算	**（亿元）**	**National Accounting**	**(100 million yuan)**	
国民总收入		Gross National Income		3624.1
国内生产总值		Gross Domestic Product		3624.1
第一产业		Primary Industry		1018.4
第二产业		Secondary Industry		1745.2
第三产业		Tertiary Industry		860.5
支出法国内生产总值		Gross Domestic Expenditures		3605.6
最终消费		Total Consumption		2239.1
居民消费		Resident Consumption		1759.1
政府消费		Public Consumption		480.0
资本形成总额		Total Investment		1377.9
固定资本形成		Fixed Assets		1073.9
存货增加		Stock		304.0
货物和服务净出口		Net Export of Good and Service		-11.4
固定资产投资	**（亿元）**	**Investment in Fixed Assets**	**(100 million yuan)**	
全社会固定资产投资总额		Total Investment in Fixed Assets		
#国有单位		State-Owned Units		
集体单位		Collective-Owned Units		
个体经济		Individuals		
财政	**（亿元）**	**Public Finance**	**(100 million yuan)**	
国家财政收入		Government Revenue		1132.3
中　央		Central Government		175.8
地　方		Local Governments		956.5
国家财政支出		Government Expenditures		1122.1
中　央		Central Government		532.1
地　方		Local Governments		590.0
物价总指数	**（上年=100）**	**Price Indices**	**(preceding year=100)**	
居民消费价格指数		Consumer Price Index		
商品零售价格指数		Retail Price Index		100.7
农产品生产价格指数		General Price Index of Produce		
工业品出厂价格指数		Ex-Factory Price Indices of Industrial Products		
原材料、燃料、动力购进价格指数		Purchasing Price Indices of Raw Material, Fuel and Power		
固定资产投资价格指数		Price Indices of Investment in Fixed Assets		
实际利用外资额	**（亿美元）**	**Utilization of Foreign Capital**	**(USD 100 million)**	
外商直接投资		Foreign Direct Investments		
外商其他投资		Other Foreign Investments		
能源生产与消费	**（万吨标准煤）**	**Production and Consumption of Energy**	**(10 000 tons of SCE)**	
能源生产总量		Total Energy Production		62770
能源消费总量		Total Energy Consumption		57144

Principal Aggregate Indicators on National Economic and Social Development and Their Related Indices and Growth Rates

总量指标 Aggregate Data				速度指标(%) Indices and Growth Rates (%)						
				指数 Index (2003为以下各年) (2003 as percentage of the following years)				平均增长速度 Average Annual Growth Rate		
1989	1997	2002	2003	1978	1989	1997	2002	1979-2003	1990-2003	1998-2003
112704	123626	128453	129227	134.2	114.7	104.5	100.6	1.2	1.0	0.7
29540	39449	50212	52376	303.7	177.3	132.8	104.3	4.5	4.2	4.8
83164	84177	78241	76851	97.3	92.4	91.3	98.2	-0.1	-0.6	-1.5
58099	63131	66115	66556	134.3	114.6	105.4	100.7	1.2	1.0	0.9
54605	60495	62338	62671	134.2	114.8	103.6	100.5	1.2	1.0	0.6
55329	69820	73740	74432	185.4	134.5	106.6	100.9	2.5	2.1	1.1
13742	14668	10558	10492	110.5	76.3	71.5	99.4	0.4	-1.9	-5.4
378	577	770	800	150.9	211.7	138.7	103.9	1.7	5.5	5.6
16917.8	73142.7	103935.3	116603.2	937.5	345.3	160.8	110.0	9.4	9.3	8.2
16909.2	74462.6	105172.3	117251.9	940.1	346.5	158.7	109.3	9.4	9.3	8.0
4228.0	14211.2	16117.3	17092.1	300.4	169.1	118.2	102.5	4.5	3.8	2.8
7278.0	37222.7	52980.2	61274.1	1450.7	492.1	172.8	112.7	11.3	12.1	9.5
5403.2	23028.7	36074.8	38885.7	1095.5	308.8	159.4	107.3	10.0	8.4	8.1
16466.0	74894.2	107897.6	121511.4							
10556.5	43579.4	62798.5	67442.5							
8523.5	34854.6	48881.6	52678.5							
2033.0	8724.8	13916.9	14764.0							
6095.0	28457.6	42304.9	51382.7							
4339.0	25154.2	41918.3	51248.3							
1756.0	3303.4	386.6	134.4							
-185.5	2857.2	2794.2	2686.2							
4410.4	24941.1	43499.9	55566.6		1259.9	222.8	127.7		21.1	12.1
2808.1	13091.7	18877.4	21661.0		771.4	165.5	114.7		18.2	8.6
570.0	3850.9	5987.4	8009.5		1405.2	208.0	133.8		22.7	9.9
1032.3	3429.4	6519.2	7720.1		747.9	225.1	118.4		15.1	13.1
2664.9	8651.1	18903.6	21715.3	1917.8	814.9	251.0	114.9	12.5	16.2	16.6
822.5	4226.9	10388.6	11865.3	6749.3	1442.6	280.7	114.2	18.4	21.0	18.8
1842.4	4424.2	8515.0	9850.0	1029.8	534.6	222.6	115.7	9.8	12.7	14.3
2823.8	9233.6	22053.2	24650.0	2196.8	872.9	267.0	111.8	13.2	16.7	17.8
888.8	2532.5	6771.7	7420.1	1394.5	834.8	293.0	109.6	11.1	16.4	19.6
1935.0	6701.1	15281.5	17229.9	2920.3	890.4	257.1	112.8	14.5	16.9	17.0
118.0	102.8	99.2	101.2							
117.8	100.8	98.7	99.9							
		99.7	104.37							
118.6	99.7	97.8	102.3							
126.4	101.3	97.7	104.8							
	101.7	100.2	102.2							
33.9	452.6	527.4	535.0		1577.4	118.2	101.4		21.8	2.8
3.8	71.3	22.7	26.4		691.6	37.0	116.2		14.8	-15.3
101639	132410	138369	160300	255.4	157.7	121.1	115.8	3.8	3.3	3.2
96934	137798	148222	167800	293.6	173.1	121.8	113.2	4.4	4.0	3.3

2-3 续表 1

指 标	Item	1978
产 业	**Industry**	
农业	**Agriculture**	
农林牧渔业从业人员 (万人)	Employed Persons of Farming, Forestry, Animal Husbandry and Fishery (10 000 persons)	28455.6
农林牧渔业总产值 (亿元)	Gross Output Value of Farming Forestry, Animal Husbandry and Fishery (100 million yuan)	1397.0
主要农产品产量 (万吨)	Output of Major Farm Products (10 000 tons)	
粮 食	Grain	30476.5
棉 花	Cotton	216.7
油 料	Oil-bearing Crops	521.8
甘 蔗	Sugar Cane	2111.6
甜 菜	Beet Roots	270.2
茶 叶	Tea	26.8
水 果	Fruits	657.0
肉 类	Meat	
水产品	Aquatic Products	465.4
工业	**Industry**	
主要工业产品产量	Output of Major Industrial Products	
布 (亿米)	Cloth (100 million m)	110
机制纸及纸板 (万吨)	Machine-Made Paper and Paperboards (10 000 tons)	439
糖 (万吨)	Sugar (10 000 tons)	227
家用电冰箱 (万台)	Household Refrigerators (10 000 units)	2.80
彩色电视机 (万台)	Color Television Sets (10 000 units)	0.38
家用洗衣机 (万台)	Household Washing Machines (10 000 units)	0.04
房间空调器 (万台)	Room Air-conditioning (10 000 units)	0.02
原 油 (万吨)	Crude Oil (10 000 tons)	10405
发电量 (亿千瓦小时)	Electricity (100 million kwh)	2566
钢 (万吨)	Steel (10 000 tons)	3178
成品钢材 (万吨)	Steel Products (10 000 tons)	2208
水 泥 (万吨)	Cement (10 000 tons)	6524
国有及限额以上非国有工业企业主要指标	Principal Indicators of Industrial Enterprises of State Ownership and Non-state-owned Above Designated Size	
工业总产值 (亿元)	Gross industrial Output Value (100 million yuan)	
固定资产原价 (亿元)	Original Value of Fixed Assets (100 million yuan)	
固定资产净值年平均余额 (亿元)	Annual Average Balance of Net Value of Fixed Assets (100 million yuan)	
利润总额 (亿元)	Profits (100 million yuan)	
建筑业	**Construction**	
建筑业企业从业人员 (万人)	Number of Employed Persons (10 000 persons)	
建筑业总产值 (亿元)	Gross Output Value (100 million yuan)	
施工房屋面积 (万平方米)	Floor Space of Buildings under Construction (10 000 sq.m)	
竣工房屋面积 (万平方米)	Floor Space of Buildings Completed (10 000 sq.m)	
交通运输	**Transportation**	
客运量 (万人)	Passenger Traffic (10 000 persons)	253993
铁 路	Railways	81491
公 路	Highways	149229
水 运	Waterways	23042
民 航	Civil Aviation	231
货运量 (万吨)	Freight Traffic (10 000 tons)	248946
铁 路	Railways	110119
公 路	Highways	85182
水 运	Waterways	43292
管 道	Pipelines	10347
民 航	Civil Aviation	6
沿海主要港口货物吞吐量 (万吨)	Volume of Freight Handled at Major Coastal Ports(10 000 tons)	19834

Continued

总量指标 Aggregate Data				速度指标(%) Indices and Growth Rates						
				指数 Index（2003为以下各年）(2003 as percentage of the following years)				平均增长速度 Average Annual Growth Rate		
1989	1997	2002	2003	1978	1989	1997	2002	1979-2003	1990-2003	1998-2003
32440.5	32434.9	31990.6	31259.6	109.9	96.4	96.4	97.7	0.4	-0.3	-0.6
6534.7	23788.4	27390.8	29691.8	444.8	234.8	130.5	103.9	6.2	6.3	4.5
40754.9	49417.1	45705.8	43069.5	141.3	105.7	87.2	94.2	1.4	0.4	-2.3
378.8	460.3	491.6	486.0	224.3	128.3	105.6	98.9	3.3	1.8	0.9
1295.2	2157.4	2897.2	2811.0	538.7	217.0	130.3	97.0	7.0	5.7	4.5
4879.5	7889.7	9010.7	9023.5	427.3	184.9	114.4	100.1	6.0	4.5	2.3
924.3	1496.8	1282.0	618.2	228.8	66.9	41.3	48.2	3.4	-2.8	-13.7
53.5	61.3	74.5	76.8	286.6	143.6	125.2	103.1	4.3	2.6	3.8
1831.9	5089.3	6952.0	14517.4	2209.8	792.5	285.3	208.8	13.2	15.9	19.1
	5268.8	6586.5	6932.9			131.6	105.3			4.7
1151.7	3601.8	4564.5	4704.6	1011.0	408.5	130.6	103.1	9.7	10.6	4.6
189	249	322	354	320.5	186.8	142.1	109.7	4.8	4.6	6.0
1333	2733	4667	4849	1104.6	363.8	177.4	103.9	10.1	9.7	10.0
501	703	926	1084	477.5	216.4	154.3	117.1	6.5	5.7	7.5
671	1044	1599	2243	80091	334.3	214.7	140.3	30.7	9.0	13.6
940	2711	5155	6541	1721421	695.9	241.3	126.9	47.7	14.9	15.8
825	1254	1596	1964	4911150	238.0	156.6	123.1	54.0	6.4	7.8
37	974	3135	4821	24104300	12865.9	494.9	153.8	64.2	41.5	30.5
13764	16074	16700	16960	163.0	123.2	105.5	101.6	2.0	1.5	0.9
5848	11356	16540	19106	744.6	326.7	168.3	115.5	8.4	8.8	9.1
6159	10894	18237	22234	699.6	361.0	204.1	121.9	8.1	9.6	12.6
4859	9979	19252	24108	1091.8	496.2	241.6	125.2	10.0	12.1	15.8
21029	51174	72500	86208	1321.4	409.9	168.5	118.9	10.9	10.6	9.1
		110776	142271				125.5			
		93888	105557				112.4			
		59483	66068				111.1			
		5784	8337				144.1			
1005	2102	2245	2414		240.3	114.9	107.5		6.5	2.3
1283	9126	18527	23084		1799.2	252.9	124.6		22.9	16.7
40650	128680	215609	259377		638.1	201.6	120.3		14.2	12.4
19723	62244	110217	122828		622.8	197.3	111.4		14.0	12.0
791376	1326094	1608150	1587497	625.0	200.6	119.7	98.7	7.6	5.1	3.0
113807	93308	105606	97260	119.4	85.5	104.2	92.1	0.7	-1.1	0.7
644508	1204583	1475257	1464335	981.3	227.2	121.6	99.3	9.6	6.0	3.3
31778	22573	18693	17142	74.4	53.9	75.9	91.7	-1.2	-4.3	-4.5
1283	5630	8594	8759	3791.8	682.7	155.6	101.9	15.7	14.7	7.6
988435	1278218	1483446	1561422	627.2	158.0	122.2	105.3	7.6	3.3	3.4
151489	172149	204955	221178	200.9	146.0	128.5	107.9	2.8	2.7	4.3
733781	976536	1116324	1159957	1361.7	158.1	118.8	103.9	11.0	3.3	2.9
87493	113406	141832	158070	365.1	180.7	139.4	111.4	5.3	4.3	5.7
15641	16002	20133	21997	212.6	140.6	137.5	109.3	3.1	2.5	5.4
31	125	202	219	3421.9	706.5	175.6	108.4	15.2	15.0	9.8
49025	90822	166628	201126	1014.0	410.3	221.5	120.7	9.7	10.6	14.2

指　　标		Item	1978
邮电通信业		**Post and Telecommunications**	
邮电业务总量	(亿元)	Total Business Revenue (100 million yuan)	34.1
函　件	(亿件)	Number of Letters Delivered (10 000 pieces)	28.4
报刊期发数	(万份)	Number of Newspapers and Magazines Distributed(10 000 copies)	11250
本地电话局用交换机容量	(万门)	Capacity of Local Office Telephone Exchanges (10 000 lines)	406
本地电话年末用户	(万户)	Number of Subscribers of Local Telephone at Year-end (10 000 subscriber)	193
城市		Urban Telephone Subscribers	119
乡村		Rural Telephone Subscribers	73
公用电话	(万户)	Public Telephone (10 000 Subscribers)	1.2
移动电话用户	(万户)	Number of Mobile Telephone Subscribers(10 000 subscribers)	
国内商业		**Domestic Trade**	
社会消费品零售总额	(亿元)	Total Retail Sales of Consumer Goods (100 million yuan)	1559
对外贸易		**Foreign Trade**	
进出口总额	(亿美元)	Total Exports and Imports (USD 100 million)	206.4
出口额		Exports	97.5
进口额		Imports	108.9
国际旅游		**International Tourism**	
入境旅游过夜者人数	(万人次)	Number of Tourists (Overnight Visitors) (10 000 person-times)	72
旅游外汇收入	(亿美元)	Foreign Exchange Earnings from Tourism (USD 100 million)	2.6
金融业		**Finanical Intermediation**	
金融机构人民币各项存款余额	(亿元)	Deposits of National Banking System (100 million yuan)	1135
金融机构人民币各项贷款余额	(亿元)	Loans of National Banking System (100 million yuan)	1850
股票筹资额	(亿元)	Raised Capital (100 million yuan)	
保险公司保费金额	(亿元)	Insurance Premium of Insurance Companies (100 million yuan)	
保险公司赔款及给付金额	(亿元)	Indemnity Expenditure and Payment of Insurance Companies (100 million yuan)	
教育、科技、文化		**Education, Science and Technology and Culture**	
教育		**Education**	
专任教师数	(万人)	Full-time Teachers (10 000 persons)	
普通高等学校		Institutions of Higher Education	20.6
普通中等学校		Secondary Schools	328.1
小　学		Primary Schools	522.6
在校学生数	(万人)	Students Enrollment (10 000 persons)	
普通高等学校		Institutions of Higher Education	85.6
普通中等学校		Secondary Schools	6637.2
小　学		Primary Schools	14624.0
教育经费支出	(亿元)	Government Expenditures on Education (100 million yuan)	
科技		**Science and Technology**	
科学家、工程师数	(万人)	Number of Scientists and Engineers (10 000 persons)	
研究与试验发展经费支出	(亿元)	Expenditures on Research and Development(100 million yuan)	
技术市场成交额	(亿元)	Volume of Transaction in Technical Markets (100 million yuan)	
文化		**Culture**	
出版数量		Publications	
图　书	(亿册.张)	Number of Books Published (100 million copies)	37.7
杂　志	(亿册)	Number of Magazines Issued (100 million copies)	7.6
报　纸	(亿份)	Number of Newspapers Issued (100 million copies)	127.8
故事影片产量	(部)	Production of Feature Films (film)	46
电视节目制作时间	(万小时)	Time for TV Programs Production (10 000 hours)	

Continued

总量指标 Aggregate Data				速度指标(%) Indices and Growth Rates						
				指数 Index (2003为以下各年) (2003 as percentage of the following years)				平均增长速度 Average Annual Growth Rate		
1989	1997	2002	2003	1978	1989	1997	2002	1979-2003	1990-2003	1998-2003
123.5	1773.3	5695.8	7019.8	26275.3	7255.2	505.1	123.2	25.0	35.8	31.0
57.3	68.6	106.0	103.8	365.5	181.2	151.3	97.9	5.3	4.3	7.1
17704	21875	17620	16594	147.5	93.7	75.9	94.2	1.6	-0.5	-4.5
1035	11269	28657	35082	8643.0	3390.6	311.3	122.4	19.5	28.6	20.8
568	7031	21422	26275	13649	4625.8	373.7	122.7	21.7	31.5	24.6
440	5244	13579	17110	14354	3892.0	326.3	126.0	22.0	29.9	21.8
128	1787	7843	9165	12486	7136.7	513.0	116.9	21.3	35.6	31.3
4.0	193.9	985.5	1561.4	130117	39132.8	805.3	158.4	33.2	53.2	41.6
1.0	1323.3	20600.5	26995.3		2754622	2040.0	131.0		107.6	65.3
8101	27299	42027	45842	2941.2	565.9	167.9	109.1	14.5	13.2	9.0
1116.8	3251.6	6207.7	8509.9	4123.0	762.0	261.7	137.1	16.0	15.6	17.4
525.4	1827.9	3256.0	4382.3	4494.6	834.1	239.7	134.6	16.4	16.4	15.7
591.4	1423.7	2951.7	4127.6	3790.3	697.9	289.9	139.8	15.7	14.9	19.4
936	2377	3680	3297	4604.7	352.2	138.7	89.6	16.6	9.4	5.6
18.6	120.7	203.9	174.1	6618.3	935.8	144.2	85.4	18.3	17.3	6.3
10786	82390	170917	208056	18339.0	1928.9	252.5	121.7	23.2	23.5	16.7
14360	74914	131294	158996	8594.4	1107.2	212.2	121.1	19.5	18.7	13.4
	1294	962	1358			104.9	141.2			0.8
139	773	3054	3880		2796.2	502.1	127.0		26.9	30.9
55	247	707	841		1539.7	340.3	119.0		21.6	22.6
39.7	40.5	61.8	72.5	351.9	182.6	179.0	117.3	5.2	4.4	10.2
342.3	418.6	489.4	502.5	153.2	146.8	120.0	102.7	1.7	2.8	3.1
554.4	579.4	577.9	570.3	109.1	102.9	98.4	98.7	0.3	0.2	-0.3
208.2	317.4	903.4	1108.6	1295.1	532.5	349.3	122.7	10.8	12.7	23.2
5054.0	6995.2	9255.7	9613.8	144.8	190.2	137.4	103.9	1.5	4.7	5.4
12373.1	13995.4	12156.7	11689.7	79.9	94.5	83.5	96.2	-0.9	-0.4	-3.0
	2531.7	5480.0								
	166.8	217.2	225.5			135.2	103.8			5.2
	509.2	1287.6	1539.6			302.4	119.6			20.3
	351.4	884.2	1084.7			308.7	122.7			20.7
58.6	73.1	68.7	66.7	176.9	113.8	91.2	97.1	2.3	0.9	-1.5
18.4	24.4	29.5	29.5	388.2	160.3	120.9	100.0	5.6	3.4	3.2
207.0	287.6	367.8	383.1	299.8	185.1	133.2	104.2	4.5	4.5	4.9
136	88	100	140	304.3	102.9	159.1	140.0	4.6	0.2	8.0
	61.6	107.3	118.6			192.3	110.5			11.5

2-3 续表 3

指标	Item	1978
家庭、生活、环境	**Family, People's Livelihood and Environment**	
家庭	**Family**	
家庭总户数 (万户)	Total Number of Households (10 000 households)	20641
城镇居民平均每户家庭人口 (人)	Average Household Size in Urban Areas (person)	
农村居民平均每户家庭人口 (人)	Average Household Size in Rural Areas (person)	
婚姻	**Marriages and Divorces**	
结婚登记总数 (万对)	Register Number of Marriages (10 000 couples)	597.8
离婚数 (万对)	Number of Divorces (10 000 couples)	28.5
居住	**Housing**	
城市人均住宅建筑面积 (平方米)	Per Capita Gross Living Space in Cities (sq.m)	6.7
农村居民人均住房面积 (平方米)	Per Capita Net Floor Space of Rural Residents (sq.m)	8.1
生活	**People's Livelihood**	
城镇居民人均可支配收入 (元)	Per Capita Annual Disposable Income of Urban Households (yuan)	343
农村居民人均纯收入 (元)	Per Capita Net Income of Rural Residents (yuan)	134
城乡人民币储蓄存款余额 (亿元)	Outstanding Amount of Saving Deposits in Urban and Rural Areas (100 million yuan)	211
工资	**Wages and Welfare**	
工资总额 (亿元)	Total Wages (100 million yuan)	569
职工平均工资 (元)	Average Wage of Staff and Workers (yuan)	615
离休、退休、退职费 (亿元)	Pensions for Retired Staff and Workers (100 million yuan)	17
卫生	**Health Care**	
医院、卫生院 (个)	Number of Hospitals	64309
医生 (万人)	Number of Doctors (10 000 persons)	103.3
医院、卫生院床位数 (万张)	Number of Hospital Beds (10 000 units)	184.7
市政建设	**City Construction**	
自来水供应量 (亿吨)	Volume of Tap Water Supply (100 million tons)	78.8
城市煤气和天然气供气量 (亿立方米)	Volume of Coal Gas and Natural Gas Supply in Urban Areas (10 000 cu.m)	19.5
排水管道长度 (万公里)	Length of Sewer Pipelines (10 000 km)	2.0
铺装道路长度 (万公里)	Length of Paved Roads (10 000 km)	2.7
公共汽(电)车运营数 (辆)	Total Number of Public Buses and Trolley Buses (unit)	25839
园林绿地面积 (万公顷)	Areas of Green Land (10 000 hectare)	8
环境、灾害	**Environment and Disaster**	
污染治理项目本年完成投资额(亿元)	Actual Investment in Implementation of the Project for Pollution Treatment in the Year (100 million yuan)	
环境污染与破坏事故次数 (起)	Number of Pollution Accidents (times)	
环境污染直接经济损失 (万元)	Losses Converted into Cash (10 000 yuan)	
环境污染事故赔罚款金额 (万元)	Amount of Reparations and Fines (10 000 yuan)	
火灾发生数 (起)	Number of Fire Disasters	
火灾损失 (万元)	Fire Loss (10 000 yuan)	
交通事故发生数 (起)	Number of Traffic Accidents	
交通事故损失 (万元)	Loss of Traffic Accidents (10 000 yuan)	

注：1.本表价值指标除邮电业务总量按不变价格计算外，其余均按当年价格计算。邮电业务总量2000年及以前按1990年不变价格计算，以后按2000年不变价格计算。

2.本表速度指标中，国民总收入、国内生产总值及三次产业增加值、物价指数、农林牧渔业总产值、工业总产值、邮电业务总量、城乡居民收入和平均工资指标均按可比价格计算。固定资产投资平均增长速度按累计法计算。

3.职工人数1997年及以前为全部职工人数，以后为在岗职工人数，两者不可比。

4.2000年及以后保险业务包括外资公司。

Continued

总量指标 Aggregate Data				速度指标(%) Indices and Growth Rates						
				指数 Index（2003为以下各年）(2003 as percentage of the following years)				平均增长速度 Average Annual Growth Rate		
1989	1997	2002	2003	1978	1989	1997	2002	1979-2003	1990-2003	1998-2003
27078	32890	35874	36198	175.4	133.7	110.1	100.9	2.3	2.1	1.6
3.55	3.19	3.04	3.01		84.8	94.4	99.0		-1.2	-1.0
4.86	4.35	4.13	4.10		84.4	94.3	99.3		-1.2	-1.0
937.2	914.1	786.2	811.4	135.7	86.6	88.8	103.2	1.2	-1.0	-2.0
75.3	119.8	117.7	133.1		176.8	111.1	113.1	6.4	4.2	1.8
13.5	17.8	22.8	23.7		175.6	133.1	103.9	5.2	4.1	4.9
17.2	22.5	26.5	27.2	335.8	158.1	120.9	102.6	5.0	3.3	3.2
1374	5160	7703	8472	514.6	282.0	165.0	109.0	6.8	7.7	8.7
602	2090	2476	2622	550.7	180.1	125.9	104.3	7.1	4.3	3.9
5196	46280	86911	103618	49201.3	1994.0	223.9	119.2	28.1	23.8	14.4
2619	9405	13161	14744	2591.7	563.1	156.8	112.0	13.9	13.1	7.8
1935	6470	12422	14040	438.9	305.9	201.1	112.0	6.1	8.3	12.3
319	1791	3659	4149	23982.7	1299.0	231.7	113.4	24.5	20.1	15.0
61613	67479	63858	62968	97.9	102.2	93.3	98.6	-0.1	0.2	-1.1
171.8	198.5	184.4	186.8	180.8	108.7	94.1	101.3	2.4	0.6	-1.0
253.7	286.9	290.7	295.5	160.0	116.5	103.0	101.7	1.9	1.1	0.5
393.7	476.8	466.5	475.3	603.2	120.7	99.7	101.9	7.5	1.4	-0.1
143.2	193.2	324.8	343.7	1762.6	240.0	177.9	105.8	12.2	6.5	10.1
5.5	12.0	17.3	19.9	1015.8	364.4	165.9	114.8	9.7	9.7	8.8
9.6	13.9	19.1	20.8	771.5	216.5	150.1	108.7	8.5	5.7	7.0
59671	169121	246129	264338	1023.0	443.0	156.3	107.4	9.7	11.2	7.7
38	68	107	121	1480.4	317.5	177.4	112.9	11.4	8.6	10.0
	502.4	1367.2	1627.7			324.0	119.1			21.6
3332	1992	1921	1843		55.3	92.5	95.9		-4.1	-1.3
	8366	4641	3375			40.3	72.7			-14.0
	3050	3141	2392			78.4	76.1			-4.0
	140280	258315	253932			181.0	98.3			10.4
	154141	154446	159089			103.2	103.0			0.5
	304217	773137	667507			219.4	86.3			14.0
	184616	332438	336915			182.5	101.3			10.5

a) Figures in value terms in this table are at current prices, except that on the business transaction of post and telecommunications service which is at 1990 constant prices before 2000 and at 2000 constant prices since 2000.

b) The indices and growth rates of the follow indicators are calculated at comparable prices: gross national income, gross domestic product, value-added of the tertiary industry, price indices, gross output value of farming, forestry, animal husbandry and fishery, gross output value of industry, business volume of post and telecommunications, per capita income of urban and rural residents, average wages and welfare. The average annual growth rate of total investment in fixed assets are calculated at the accumulate method.

c) Figures before 1998 on workers and staff refer to all workers and staff, while figures since 1998 refer to fully employed workers and staff. So, the data are not comparable.

d) Insurance business include foreign insurance company since 2000.

2-4 国民经济和社会发展结构指标

Structural Indicators on National Economic and Social Development

单位：% (%)

指 标	Item	1978	1989	1997	2003
人口与就业	**Population and Employment**				
人口	**Population**				
城乡结构	Urban and Rural Structure				
城镇	Urban	17.9	26.2	31.9	40.5
乡村	Rural	82.1	73.8	68.1	59.5
性别结构	Sexual Structure				
男	Male	51.5	51.6	51.1	51.5
女	Female	48.5	48.4	48.9	48.5
就业	**Employment**				
产业结构	Industrial Structure				
第一产业	Primary Industry	70.5	60.1	49.9	49.1
第二产业	Secondary Industry	17.3	21.6	23.7	21.6
第三产业	Tertiary Industry	12.2	18.3	26.4	29.3
宏观经济	**Macro Economy**				
国民经济核算	**National Accounting**				
国内生产总值产业结构	Industrial Structure				
第一产业	Primary Industry	28.1	25.0	19.1	14.6
第二产业	Secondary Industry	48.2	43.0	50.0	52.2
第三产业	Tertiary Industry	23.7	32.0	30.9	33.2
投资	**Investment**				
全社会固定资产投资结构	Structure of Total Investment in Fixed Assets				
基本建设	Capital Construction		35.2	39.8	41.2
更新改造	Innovation		17.9	15.7	15.5
房地产开发	Real Estate Development		6.2	12.7	18.3
其他投资	Other Investment		40.7	31.8	25.0
资金来源结构	Structure of Funded Sources				
国家预算内资金	State Budgetary Appropriation		8.3	2.8	4.6
国内贷款	Domestic Loans		17.3	18.9	20.5
利用外资	Foreign Investment		6.6	10.6	4.4
自筹和其他投资	Fundraising and Others Investment		67.8	67.7	70.5
财政	**Government Finance**				
财政收入结构	Structure of Government Revenue				
中央	Central Government	15.5	30.9	48.9	54.6
地方	Local Governments	84.5	69.1	51.1	45.4
财政支出结构	Structure of Government Expenditures				
中央	Central Government	47.4	31.5	27.4	30.1
地方	Local Governments	52.6	68.5	72.6	69.9
利用外资	**Utilization of Foreign Capital**				
实际利用外资结构	Structure of Foreign Capital Actually Utilized				
对外借款	Loans from Abroad		62.5	18.7	
外商直接投资	Direct Investment by Foreign Entrepreneurs		33.7	70.3	95.3
外商其他投资	Other Investment by Foreign Entrepreneurs		3.8	11.1	4.7
能源	**Energy**				
能源生产总量结构	Structure of Total Energy Production				
原煤	Coal	70.3	74.1	74.1	74.2
原油	Petroleum Crude Oil	23.7	19.3	17.3	15.2
天然气	Natural Gas	2.9	2.0	2.1	2.9
水电	Hydropower	3.1	4.6	6.5	7.7
能源消费总量结构	Structure of Total Energy Consumption				
煤炭	Coal	70.7	76.0	71.7	67.1
石油	Petroleum Oil	22.7	17.1	20.4	22.7
天然气	Natural Gas	3.2	2.1	1.7	2.8
水电	Hydropower	3.4	4.7	6.2	7.4

2-4 续表 1 Continued

单位: % (%)

指 标	Item	1978	1989	1997	2003
产 业	**Industrial**				
农业	**Agriculture**				
农林牧渔业产值结构	Structure of Gross Output Value of Agriculture				
#农业	Farming	80.0	62.8	58.2	50.1
林业	Forestry	3.4	4.4	3.4	4.2
牧业	Animal Husbandry	15.0	27.5	28.8	32.1
渔业	Fishery	1.6	5.3	9.6	10.6
工业	**Industry**				
工业总产值规模结构	Structure of Gross Output Value of Industry				
大型企业	Large Enterprises			41.3	34.4
中型企业	Medium-sized Enterprises			14.1	33.1
小型企业	Small Enterprises			44.6	32.5
建筑业	**Construction**				
建筑业总产值结构	Structure of Gross Output Value of Construction Industry				
国有企业	State-owned Enterprise		68.5	49.6	26.3
集体企业	Collective-owned Enterprises		31.5	43.0	14.2
港澳台商投资企业	Enterprise with Funds from Hong Kong, Macao &			0.7	0.5
外商投资企业	Foreign Funded Enterprise			0.8	0.5
其他	Other Enterprise			5.9	58.5
交通运输业	**Transportation**				
货运量结构	Structure of Freight Traffic				
铁 路	Railways	44.2	15.3	13.5	14.2
公 路	Highways	34.2	74.2	76.4	74.3
水 运	Waterways	17.4	8.9	8.9	10.1
民 航	Civil Aviation	…	…	…	…
管道输油(气)	Pipelines	4.2	1.6	1.3	1.4
国内商业	**Domestic Trade**				
社会消费品零售总额构成	Composition of Retail Sales of Consumer Goods				
市	Cities	32.4	45.3	61.0	65.0
县	Counties	24.4	16.4	12.8	11.4
县以下	Below Counties	43.2	38.3	26.2	23.6
对外经济贸易	**Foreign Trade**				
出口商品结构	Structure of Exports				
初级产品	Primary Goods	53.5	28.7	13.1	7.9
工业制成品	Manufactured Goods	46.5	71.3	86.9	92.1
进口商品结构	Structure of Imports				
初级产品	Primary Goods		19.9	20.1	17.6
工业制成品	Manufactured Goods		80.1	79.9	82.4
国际旅游	**International Tourism**				
来华旅游人数结构	Structure of Tourists				
外国人	Foreigners	12.7	6.0	12.9	12.4
港澳同胞	Hong Kong and Macao Compatriots	}86.3	}93.8	83.3	84.6
台湾同胞	Taiwan Compatriots			3.7	3.0
金融业	**Financial Intermediation**				
金融机构资金来源结构	Structure of Sources of Funds in State Banks				
各项存款	Deposits			86.7	92.3
金融债券	Bonds			…	1.0
对国际金融机构负债	Liability to International Finance Institutions			0.2	0.2
流通中现金	Currency in Circulation			10.7	8.8
其他	Others			2.3	-2.3
金融机构资金运用结构	Structure of Fund Uses in State Banks				
各项贷款	Loans			78.9	70.6
有价证券及投资	Securities and Investment			3.9	13.4
在国际金融机构资产	Capital in International Finance Institutions			0.6	0.4
金银占款	Purchase of Gold and Silver			…	0.1
外汇占款	Purchase of Foreign Exchanges			14.2	15.5
财政借款	Government Debt			1.7	
教育、科技、文化	**Education, Science and Culture**				
教育	**Education**				
在校学生结构	Structure of Student Enrollment				
大学生	College and University Students	0.4	1.2	1.5	4.9
中学生	Secondary School Students	31.1	28.7	32.8	42.9
小学生	Primary School Students	68.5	70.1	65.7	52.2

注：工业总产值规模结构1997年为1998年数据。
a) Structure of gross output value of industry in 1997 are the data in 1998.

2-4 续表 2 Continued

单位: % (%)

指 标	Item	1978	1989	1997	2003
专任教师结构	Full-time Teachers by Type				
大学	College and Universities	2.4	4.2	3.9	6.3
中学	Secondary Schools	37.6	36.6	40.3	43.9
小学	Primary Schools	60.0	59.2	55.8	49.8
科技	**Science and Technology**				
科技经费筹集额结构	Structure of Funding for Scientific and Technological Outlay				
#政府资金	Government Fund			26.2	24.3
企业资金	Enterprises Fund			44.6	59.4
金融机构贷款	Loans from Banks			13.1	7.5
科技经费内部支出结构	Structure of Internal Expenditures on Scientific and Technological Activities				
#劳务费	Service Fees			19.9	24.1
固定资产购建	Purchases of Fixed Assets			27.5	27.3
#研究与发展经费支出	Research and Development Expenses			45.2	49.3
生活、环境	**People's Livelihood and Environment**				
生活	**People's Livelihood**				
城镇居民消费结构	Consumption Structure of Urban Residents				
食品类	Food	57.5	54.5	46.6	37.1
衣着类	Clothing	13.6	12.3	12.5	9.8
用品及其他	Articles for Daily Use and Others	}28.9	}33.2	31.5	42.4
居住	Residence			9.4	10.7
农村居民消费结构	Consumption Structure of Rural Residents				
食品类	Food	67.7	54.8	55.1	45.6
衣着类	Clothing	12.7	8.3	6.8	5.7
用品及其他	Articles for Daily Use and Others	9.3	17.2	23.7	32.8
居住	Residence	10.3	19.7	14.4	15.9
福利	**Social Welfare**				
离退休退职人员结构	Structure of Retired and Resigned Persons				
离休人员	Retired Veterans		7.9	5.5	3.1
退休人员	Retired Persons		88.2	91.8	95.1
退职人员	Resigned Persons		3.9	2.7	1.8
离退休退职人员保险福利费结构	Structure of Insurance Contribution and Welfare Funds of Retired and Resigned Persons				
离休金	Pensions for Retired Veterans			8.0	6.2
退休金	Pensions for Retired Persons			69.7	82.4
退职生活费	Resignation Allowances for Living Expenses			1.1	0.9
医疗卫生费	Expenses for Medical Care			13.6	6.2
其他	Others			7.6	4.3
卫生	**Health Care**				
卫生技术人员结构	Doctors by Types				
#医生	Doctors	41.9	45.1	45.1	39.3
护师、护士	Nurses	16.5	24.2	27.2	26.6
医院床位结构	Hospital Beds by Area				
市医院	Hospitals at City Level	38.6	52.0	63.5	67.9
县医院	Hospitals at County Level	61.4	48.0	36.5	32.1
环境、灾害	**Environment and Disasters**				
治理污染资金使用结构	Uses of Funds in Pollution Treatment				
治理废水	Waste Water Treatment			62.5	39.4
治理废气	Waste Gas Treatment			24.7	41.5
治理固体废物	Solid Wastes Treatment			5.4	7.3
治理噪声	Noise Abatement			0.7	0.5
其他	Others			6.7	11.3
火灾事故损失额结构	Structure of Fire Losses Converted into Cash				
特大	Extraordinarily Serious Fires			23.7	7.5
重大	Serious Fires			14.5	8.4
一般	Ordinary Fires			61.8	84.1
交通事故损失额结构	Structure of Losses of Traffic Accidents Converted into Cash				
特大	Extraordinarily Serious Fires			12.8	10.1
重大	Serious Fires			21.1	17.3
一般	Ordinary Fires			66.1	72.6

2-5 国民经济和社会发展比例和效益指标

Indicators on Proportions and Efficiency in National Economic and Social Development

指标	Item	1978	1989	1997	2003
人口与就业	**Population and Employment**				
人口	**Population**				
出生率 (‰)	Birth Rate (‰)	18.25	21.58	16.57	12.41
死亡率 (‰)	Death Rate (‰)	6.25	6.54	6.51	6.40
自然增长率 (‰)	Natural Growth Rate (‰)	12.00	15.04	10.06	6.01
就业	**Employment**				
就业者负担人口	Dependency Ratio	1.40	1.04	0.77	0.74
三次产业就业者比例 (以第一产业为100)	Employment Ratio by Type of Industry (Employment in primary industry=100)				
第一产业	Primary Industry	100.0	100.0	100.0	100.0
第二产业	Secondary Industry	24.5	36.0	47.5	44.0
第三产业	Tertiary Industry	17.3	30.5	52.9	59.7
城镇登记失业率 (%)	Unemployment Rate in Urban Areas (%)	5.3	2.6	3.1	4.3
宏观经济	**Macro Economy**				
国民经济核算	**National Accounting**				
三次产业增加值比例 (以第一产业为100)	Ratio of Value-added by Type of Industry (Value added in primary industry=100)				
第一产业	Primary Industry	100.0	100.0	100.0	100.0
第二产业	Secondary Industry	171.4	172.1	261.9	358.5
第三产业	Tertiary Industry	84.5	127.8	162.0	227.5
全社会劳动生产率 (元/人)	Overall Labor Productivity (yuan/person)	911	354	2752	1863
第一产业	Primary Industry	3084	1292	6033	5387
第二产业	Secondary Industry	10732	4080	22731	12667
第三产业	Tertiary Industry	15826	4656	38468	18129
人均国内生产总值 (元)	Per Capita GDP (yuan)	379	1512	6054	9101
固定资产投资	**Investment in Fixed Assets**				
全社会固定资产投资相当于国内生产总值比例 (%)	Proportion of Investment in fixed Assets to GDP (%)		26.1	33.5	47.4
全社会房屋建筑面积竣工率 (%)	Rate of Total Floor Space of Buildings Completed in Construction (%)		77.9	72.0	59.0
基本建设固定资产交付使用率 (%)	Rate of Fixed Assets Completed in Capital Construction and Put into Use (%)	74.3	76.0	75.1	59.4
基本建设项目建成投产率 (%)	Rate of Projects Completed in Capital Construction and Put into Use (%)	26.0	53.3	56.9	51.0
财政	**Finance**				
国家财政收入相当于国内生产总值比例(%)	Proportion of Government Revenue to GDP (%)	31.2	15.8	11.6	18.5
国家财政支出相当于国内生产总值比例(%)	Proportion of Government Expenditures to GDP (%)	31.0	16.7	12.4	21.0
地方财政收入相当于中央财政收入比例(%)	Proportion of Local Government Revenue to Central Government Revenue (%)	544.2	224.0	104.7	83.0
地方财政支出相当于中央财政支出比例(%)	Proportion of Local Government Expenditure to Central Government Expenditure (%)	110.9	217.7	264.6	232.2
预算外资金收入相当于国家财政收入比例 (%)	Proportion of Extra-budgetary Receipt to Government Revenue (%)	30.7	99.8	32.7	23.7
利用外资	**Utilization of Foreign Capital**				
实际利用外商直接投资额相当于合同利用外商直接投资额比例 (%)	Proportion of Actually Foreign Direct Investment for Foreign Direct Investment (%)		60.6	88.7	46.5
能源	**Energy**				
能源生产弹性系数	Elasticity Ratio of Energy Production		1.48		1.70
能源消费弹性系数	Elasticity Ratio of Energy Consumption		1.02		1.42
每万元国内生产总值消耗的能源 (吨)	Energy Consumption per 10 000 yuan GDP (ton)	15.8	5.7	1.9	1.4

2-5 续表 1 Continued

指标	Item	1978	1989	1997	2003
产业	**Industries**				
农业	**Agriculture**				
每一农林牧渔业从业人员生产量(公斤)	Output of Farm Corps Per Agricultural Laborer (kg)				
粮食	Grain		1276	1528	1362
棉花	Cotton		11.9	14.2	15.4
油料	Oil-bearing Crops		40.5	66.7	88.9
猪牛羊肉	Pork, Beef and Mutton			131.4	174.1
水产品	Aquatic Products		36.0	111.3	148.8
每公顷播种面积农产品产量 (公斤)	Output of Farm Crops per Hectare of Sown Area (kg)				
粮食	Grain	2527	3632	4377	3765
棉花	Cotton	445	728	1025	951
油料	Oil-bearing Crops	839	1233	1743	1875
工业	**Industry**				
总资产贡献率 (%)	Ratio of Total Assets to Industrial Output Value (%)			7.12	10.50
资产负债率 (%)	Assets-Liability Ratio (%)			63.74	58.96
成本费用利润率 (%)	Ratio of Profits to Industrial Cost (%)			2.35	6.25
流动资产周转次数 (次/年)	Number of Times of Annual of Turnover Circulating Funds (times/year)			1.41	2.00
全员劳动生产率 (元/人) (按增加值计算)	Overall Labor Productivity (yuan/person) (in terms of value-added per employee)			31347	73045
建筑业	**Construction**				
技术装备率 (元/人)	Value of Machinery per Laborer (yuan/person)		2341	4729	9957
产值利税率 (%)	Ratio of Per-tax Profits to Gross Output Value (%)		5.8	4.2	5.5
全员劳动生产率 (元/人) (按增加值计算)	Overall Labor Productivity (yuan/person) (in terms of value-added per employee)			12089	17476
交通运输业	**Transportation**				
客运量弹性系数	Elasticity of Passenger Traffic			0.74	
货运量弹性系数	Elasticity of Freight Traffic		0.15		0.57
铁路网密度 (公里/万平方公里)	Railway Density (km/10000 sq.km)	54	59	69	76
公路网密度 (公里/万平方公里)	Highway Density (km/10000 sq.km)	927	1057	1278	1885
铁路货运密度 (吨/公里)	Railway Freight Traffic Density (ton/km)	21300	26624	26063	30298
公路货运密度 (吨/公里)	Highway Freight Traffic Density (ton/km)	957	7234	7963	6409
平均每一沿海港口泊位货物吞吐量 (万吨)	Cargo Handled at Seaports per Berth (10 000 tons)		55	68	90
邮电通信业	**Post and Communications**				
邮电业务总量弹性系数	Elasticity of Postal and Telecommunications Services		4.88	3.65	2.50
电话普及率(含移动电话) (部/百人)	Access to Telephones (include mobile phone) (set/100 persons)			8.1	42.2
移动电话普及率 (部/百人)	Access to Mobile Phones (set/100 persons)			1.1	21.0
国内商业	**Domestic Trade**				
人均社会消费品零售额 (元)	Per Capita Retail Sales of Consumer Goods (yuan)	163	724	2219	3558
对外贸易	**Foreign Trade**				
进出口总额相当于国内生产总值比例 (%)	Proportion of Total Imports & Exports to GDP (%)	9.8	24.6	36.2	60.1
国际旅游	**International Tourism**				
每一来华游客花费 (美元)	Expenditure per International Tourist in China (USD)		76	210	190
金融业	**Financial Intermediation**				
金融机构存款相当于国内生产总值比例 (%)	Bank Deposits as Percentage of GDP (%)	31.3	63.8	110.6	177.4
金融机构贷款相当于国内生产总值比例 (%)	Bank Loans as Percentage of GDP (%)	51.0	84.9	100.6	135.6
金融机构现金支出相当于收入比例 (%)	Proportion of Cash Outlay to Cash Receipt in Bank (%)	101.2	101.4	101.0	100.5

2-5 续表 2 Continued

指 标	Item	1978	1989	1997	2003
教育、科技、文化	**Education, Science and Technology and Culture**				
教育	**Education**				
学龄儿童入学率 (%)	Rate of School-age Children Enrollment (%)	95.5	97.4	98.9	98.7
小学毕业生升学率 (%)	Rate of Graduates of Primary Schools Entering Junior Secondary Schools (%)	87.7	71.5	93.7	97.9
初中毕业生升学率 (%)	Rate of Graduates of Junior Secondary Schools Entering Senior Secondary Schools (%)	40.9	38.3	51.5	60.2
学校教师负担系数 (%)	Student-teacher Ratio (in percentage) (%)				
高等学校	Colleges and Universities	4.2	5.2	7.8	15.3
中等学校	Secondary Schools	20.2	14.8	16.7	18.9
小学学校	Primary Schools	28.0	22.3	24.2	20.5
科技	**Science and Technology**				
研究与试验发展经费支出相当于国内生产总值比例 (%)	R&D Expenditures as Percentage of GDP (%)			0.65	1.31
文化 (个)	**Culture** (unit)				
每百万人有艺术表演团体	Number of Troupes per Million Persons	3.27	2.53	2.15	2.03
每百万人有公共图书馆	Number of Public Libraries per Million Persons	1.27	2.23	2.13	2.10
每百万人有博物馆	Number of Museums per Million Persons	0.36	0.86	1.04	1.17
家庭、生活、环境	**Family, People's Livelihood and Environment**				
家庭	**Family**				
少儿抚养比 (%)	Dependency Ratio of Children (%)	54.63	41.53	39.58	31.39
老年抚养比 (%)	Dependency Ratio of the Aged (%)	7.97	8.40	9.23	10.65
婚姻	**Marriages and Divorces**				
离婚率 (‰)	Divorce Rate (‰)		1.3	1.9	2.1
生活	**People's Livelihood**				
城镇与农村居民收入增长率比例(以农村居民收入指数为1) (1978=100)	Proportion of Growth Rate of Annual Income of Urban Residents to the Growth Rate of Annual Net Income of Rural Residents (1978=100)		0.40	0.63	0.92
福利	**Welfare**				
离退休退职费相当于工资总额比例 (%)	Pensions for Retired Veterans, Retired and Resigned Persons as Percentage of Total Wages (%)		12.2	19.0	28.1
离退休退职人员相当于在职人员比例 (%)	Proportion of the Number of Workers Who Have Retired or Resigned to the Number of Employed Ones (%)		16.0	22.8	43.1
卫生	**Health Care**				
每万人医生数 (人)	Number of Doctors per 10 000 Persons (person)	10.7	15.2	16.1	14.8
每万人医院、卫生院床位数 (张)	Number of Hospital Beds per 10 000 Persons (unit)	19.3	22.8	23.5	23.4
医疗机构病床使用率 (%)	Utilization Rate of Beds in Health Institution (%)		81.7	61.7	58.7
市政建设	**City Construction**				
用水普及率 (%)	Percentage of Households with Access to Tap Water (%)		47.4	61.2	86.2
燃气普及率 (%)	Percentage of Households with Access to Tap Gas (%)		17.8	40.0	76.7
人均公共绿地面积 (平方米)	Per Capita Public Green Areas (sq.m)		1.7	2.9	6.5
环境、灾害	**Environment and Disasters**				
平均每起火灾损失 (元)	Average Loss of per Fire Disaster (yuan)			10988	6265
平均每起交通事故损失 (元)	Average Loss of per Traffic Accident (yuan)			6069	5047
平均每起环境污染事故直接经济损失 (元)	Average Loss per Pollution Accident (yuan)			41998	18312

注：1.预算外资金收入相当于国家财政收入比例2003年为2002年数据。
2.工业企业效益1997年为1998年数据。
3.少儿抚养比和老年抚养比1978年、1989年和1997年分别为1982年、1990年和1995年数据。

a) Data on proportion of extra-budgetary receipt to government revenue in 2003 are the data in 2002.
b) Economic efficiency of industry in 1997 were the data in 1998.
c) Figures of dependency ratio of children and the aged in 1978, 1989 and 1997 were the 1982's, 1990's and 1995's data.

2-6 人均主要工农业产品产量

Per Capita Output of Major Industrial and Agricultural Products

年份 Year	粮食(公斤) Grain (kg)	棉花(公斤) Cotton (kg)	油料(公斤) Oil-bearing Crops (kg)	糖料(公斤) Sugar Crops (kg)	茶叶(公斤) Tea (kg)	水果(公斤) Fruits (kg)	猪牛羊肉(公斤) Pork, Beef and Mutton (kg)	水产品(公斤) Aquatic Products (kg)
1978	318.74	2.27	5.46	24.91	0.28	6.87		4.87
1980	326.69	2.76	7.84	29.67	0.31	6.92		4.59
1985	360.70	3.94	15.02	57.53	0.41	11.07		6.71
1986	367.00	3.32	13.82	54.86	0.43	12.63		7.72
1987	371.74	3.92	14.09	51.20	0.47	15.39		8.81
1988	357.72	3.77	11.98	56.17	0.49	15.12		9.63
1989	364.32	3.39	11.58	51.88	0.48	16.38		10.30
1990	393.10	3.97	14.21	63.55	0.48	16.51		10.90
1991	378.26	4.93	14.24	73.16	0.47	18.91		11.74
1992	379.97	3.87	14.09	75.61	0.48	20.95		13.37
1993	387.37	3.17	15.31	64.70	0.51	25.55		15.47
1994	373.46	3.64	16.69	61.63	0.49	29.36		17.98
1995	387.28	3.96	18.67	64.96	0.49	34.98		20.89
1996	414.39	3.45	18.16	68.66	0.49	38.21	30.35	27.01
1997	401.74	3.74	17.54	76.31	0.50	41.37	34.55	29.28
1998	412.42	3.62	18.63	78.82	0.54	43.90	37.02	31.45
1999	405.55	3.05	20.76	66.48	0.54	49.76	37.99	32.91
2000	366.04	3.50	23.40	60.47	0.54	49.30	38.32	33.89
2001	355.89	4.19	22.53	68.05	0.55	52.35	39.52	34.44
2002	356.97	3.84	22.63	80.39	0.58	54.30	40.83	35.64
2003	334.29	3.77	21.82	74.83	0.60	112.68	42.74	36.51

注:本表计算中所使用的人口数字为年平均人口数（下表同）；2003年水果产量含果用瓜。

a) Population data calculated in the table refer to the annual average population. The same as the following tables. Fruit products in 2003 include fruit melon.

2-6 续表 Continued

年份 Year	布(米) Cloth (m)	机制纸及纸板(公斤) Machine-made Paper and Paperboard (kg)	纱(公斤) Yarn (kg)	原煤(吨) Coal (ton)	原油(公斤) Crude Oil (kg)	发电量(千瓦小时) Electricity (kwh)	钢(公斤) Steel (kg)	水泥(公斤) Cement (kg)
1978	11.54	4.59	2.49	0.65	108.82	268.36	33.24	68.23
1980	13.73	5.45	2.98	0.63	107.98	306.35	37.83	81.39
1985	13.96	8.67	3.36	0.83	118.83	390.76	44.52	138.86
1986	15.44	9.36	3.73	0.84	122.51	421.36	48.93	155.66
1987	15.96	10.53	4.03	0.86	123.74	458.75	51.92	171.81
1988	17.06	11.53	4.23	0.89	124.41	494.90	53.95	190.75
1989	16.92	11.92	4.26	0.94	123.04	522.78	55.05	187.99
1990	16.63	12.08	4.07	0.95	121.84	547.22	58.45	184.74
1991	15.79	12.85	4.00	0.94	122.52	588.77	61.70	219.51
1992	16.37	14.81	4.31	0.96	121.97	647.18	69.47	264.57
1993	17.23	16.24	4.26	0.98	123.25	712.34	76.00	312.18
1994	17.73	17.94	4.11	1.04	122.57	778.72	77.70	353.39
1995	21.59	23.34	4.50	1.13	124.54	835.81	79.15	394.74
1996	17.17	21.67	4.21	1.15	129.22	888.10	83.15	403.42
1997	20.23	22.22	4.55	1.12	130.68	923.16	88.57	416.02
1998	19.40	17.11	4.36	1.01	129.61	939.48	93.05	431.50
1999	19.94	17.22	4.52	0.83	127.63	988.60	99.12	457.09
2000	21.94	19.70	5.20	0.79	129.09	1073.62	101.77	472.82
2001	22.80	29.70	5.98	0.91	128.91	1164.29	119.22	519.75
2002	25.18	36.45	6.64	1.08	130.43	1291.78	142.43	566.23
2003	27.44	37.64	7.63	1.29	131.64	1482.91	172.57	669.11

2-7 西部12省(区、市)和东北3省国民经济和社会发展主要指标(2003年)

Main Indicators of National Economic and Social Development of 12 Western Provinces and 3 Northeastern Provinces (2003)

指标	Item	全国总计 National Total	西部12省(区、市) 12 Western Provinces	东北3省 3 North-eastern Provinces	占全国比重(%) Percentage to National Total (%) 西部12省(区、市) 12 Western Provinces	东北3省 3 North-eastern Provinces
自然资源	**Natural Resources**					
土地面积 (万平方公里)	Area of Land (10 000 sq.km)	960.0	686.7	78.8	71.5	8.2
人口	**Population**					
年底总人口 (万人)	Population at the Year-end (10 000 persons)	129227	36923	10729	28.8	8.4
劳动就业	**Employment**					
年底就业人员 (万人)	Employment At the Year-end (10 000 persons)	74432	18796	4528	29.0	7.0
#城镇	Urban Area	25639	3628	1907	22.8	12.0
年末城镇登记失业率(%)	Registered Unemployment Rate in Urban Area (%)	4.3	3.9	5.2		
国民经济核算	**National Accounting**					
国内(地区)生产总值(亿元)	Gross Domestic Product (100 million yuan)	117251.9	22954.7	12955.2	16.9	9.6
第一产业	Primary Industry	17092.1	4450.4	1603.5	25.9	9.3
第二产业	Secondary Industry	61274.1	9836.1	6574.7	14.8	9.9
#工业	Industry	53092.9	7537.9	5734.7	13.3	10.1
第三产业	Tertiary Industry	38885.7	8668.2	4776.9	16.7	9.2
人均国内(地区)生产总值 (元)	Per Capita Gross Domestic Product (yuan)	9101	6306	12078		
固定资产投资	**Investment in Fixed Assets**					
全社会固定资产投资总额 (亿元)	Total Investment in Fixed Assets (100 million yuan)	55566.6	10843.5	4211.6	19.9	7.7
#基本建设	Capital Construction	22908.6	5604.7	1710.1	25.5	7.8
更新改造	Innovation	8624.9	1653.0	905.9	19.2	10.5
房地产开发	Real Estate Development	10153.8	1626.6	788.9	16.0	7.8
财政	**Government Finance**					
地方财政收入 (亿元)	Local Government Revenue (100 million yuan)	9850.0	1649.5	849.9	16.7	8.6
地方财政支出 (亿元)	Local Government Expenditure (100 million yuan)	17229.9	4344.8	1758.5	25.2	10.2
对外贸易	**Foreign Trade**					
进出口总额 (亿美元)	Imports and Exports (100 million USD)	8509.9	279.3	379.9	3.3	4.5
出口额	Exports	4382.3	162.4	196.4	3.7	4.5
进口额	Imports	4127.6	116.9	183.5	2.8	4.4
实际利用外商直接投资 (亿美元)	Actually Used Amount of Foreign Direct Investment (100 million USD)	535.0	17.2	33.4	3.3	6.3
物价	**Price Indices**					
居民消费价格总指数 (上年=100)	Consumer Price Index (last year=100)	101.2	101.4	101.3		
农业	**Agriculture**					
主要农产品产量 (万吨)	Output of Major Farm Products (10 000 tons)					
粮食	Grain	43069.5	12529.1	6270.2	29.1	14.6
棉花	Cotton	486.0	177.1	0.4	36.5	0.1
油料	Oil-bearing Corps	2811.0	697.2	163.2	24.8	5.8

2-7 续表 Continued

指 标	Item	全国总计 National Total	西部12省（区、市） 12 Western Provinces	东北3省 3 North -eastern Provinces	占全国比重（%） Percentage to National Total (%) 西部12省（区、市） 12 Western Provinces	东北3省 3 North -eastern Provinces
工业	**Industry**					
主要工业产品产量	Output of Major Industrial Products					
布 （亿米）	Cloth (100 million m)	353.5	34.2	6.3	9.7	1.8
原煤 （亿吨）	Coal (100 million tons)	16.7	4.0	1.5	30.3	11.0
原油 （万吨）	Crude Oil (10 000 tons)	16960.0	3703.5	6648.7	21.8	39.2
发电量（亿千瓦小时）	Electricity (100 million kwh)	19105.8	4574.0	1669.7	23.9	8.7
钢 （万吨）	Steel (10 000 tons)	22233.6	2917.3	2775.1	13.1	12.5
水泥 （万吨）	Cement (10 000 tons)	86208.1	18396.9	4673.3	21.3	5.4
交通运输业	**Transportation**					
铁路营业里程 （公里）	Length of Railways in Operation (km)	73002	26722	13219	36.6	18.1
公路里程 （公里）	Length of Highways (km)	1809828	739513	158997	40.9	8.8
#高速公路	Expressway	29745	7069	2592	23.8	8.7
旅客周转量（亿人公里）	Total Passenger-kilometer (100 million person-km)	13810.5	2900.4	1042.6	23.1	8.3
货物周转量（亿吨公里）	Total Freight Ton-kilometer (10 million ton-km)	53859.2	6939.1	3907.6	14.0	7.9
邮电通信业	**Post and Telecommunication Services**					
邮电业务总量 （亿元）	Total Business Revenue (100 million yuan)	7019.8	1318.2	670.8	18.9	9.6
国内商业	**Domestic Trade**					
社会消费品零售总额 （亿元）	Total Retail Sales of Consumer Goods (100 million yuan)	45842.0	7783.0	4817.5	16.3	10.1
教育	**Education**					
普通高等学校	Institutions of Higher Education					
学校数 （个）	Number of Institution (unit)	1552	378	164	24.4	10.6
招生数 （万人）	New Student Enrollment (10 000 persons)	382.2	81.9	39.3	21.4	10.3
在校学生数 （万人）	Student Enrollment (10 000 persons)	1108.6	235.4	122.6	21.2	11.1
毕业生数 （万人）	Number of Graduates (10 000 persons)	187.7	38.5	22.1	20.5	11.7
卫生	**Health Care**					
卫生机构数 （个）	Number of Hospital (unit)	291323	103055	28697	35.4	9.9
#医院、卫生院	Hospital and Health Center	62968	24065	5249	38.2	8.3
卫生技术人员 （万人）	Medical Technical Personnel (10 000 persons)	430.6	109.2	48.9	25.3	11.4
#医生	Doctor	186.8	50.1	21.4	26.8	11.4
卫生机构床位数（万张）	Number of Hospital Beds (10 000 beds)	314.4	82.8	37.2	26.3	11.8
#医院、卫生院	Hospital and Health Center	295.5	78.3	34.8	26.5	11.8
人民生活	**People's Livelihood**					
城镇居民可支配收入(元)	Per Capita Disposable Income of Urban Households (yuan)	8472	7205	6981		
农村居民人均纯收入(元)	Per Capita Net Income of Rural Households (yuan)	2622	1966	2681		

注：本表中涉及分地区数据相加不等于全国总计的指标，在计算西部12省（区、市）和东北3省占全国的比重时，分母为31个省（区、市）相加的合计数。

a) As the sum of some indicators by region is different to the national total, while calculating the percentage of 12 western provinces (autonomous regions, municipality) or 3 northeastern provinces to all country, the denominator is the sum of 31 provinces.

2-8 民族自治地方自然资源

Natural Resources in Minority Nationality Autonomous Areas

项　　目	Item	2003	占全国比重(%) Percentage to All Country
总面积　(万平方公里)	**Total Area　(10 000 sq.km)**	**611.73**	**63.72**
牧区、半农半牧区草原面积（万公顷）	Area of Grasslands in Pastoral and Semi-pastoral Areas　(10 000 hectares)	30000.00	75.0
森林面积　(万公顷)	Area of Forest　(10 000 hectares)	5648.00	42.2
森林蓄积量　(亿立方米)	Stock Volume of the Forest (100 million cu.m)	52.49	51.8
水力资源蕴藏量　(亿千瓦)	Hydropower Resources　(100 million kw)	4.46	66.0

注：除总面积外，其它资源为以前清查数，有待进一步勘测。

a) The figures of resources, except total area, were obtained from surveys in previous year, and are subject to further verification.

2-9 民族自治地方行政区划和人口（2003年）

Administrative Division and Population of Minority Nationality Autonomous Areas (2003)

省级单位名称	Provinces and Autonomous Regions	地级区划数（个） Number of Prefectures (unit)	#地级市 Cities at Prefecture Level	县级区划数（个） Number of Counties (unit)	#县级市 Cities at County Level	总人口（万人） Total Population in Minority Areas (10 000 persons)	#少数民族人口 Minority Population	少数民族人口占自治地方总人口比重(%) Minority Population as Percentage to Total Population in Minority Areas (%)
全　国	**National Total**	**77**	**31**	**699**	**66**	**17214.12**	**8016.96**	**46.57**
河　北	Hebei			6		194.59	113.12	58.13
内蒙古	Inner Mongolia	12	9	101	11	2379.61	505.77	21.25
辽　宁	Liaoning			8		334.57	167.79	50.15
吉　林	Jilin	1		11	6	331.25	115.00	34.72
黑龙江	Heilongjiang			1		24.88	5.22	21.00
浙　江	Zhejiang			1		17.93	1.78	9.94
湖　北	Hubei	1		10	2	443.35	239.81	54.09
湖　南	Hunan	1		15	1	481.93	352.60	73.16
广　东	Guangdong			3		47.16	17.52	37.16
广　西	Guangxi	14	14	109	7	4857.00	1854.00	38.17
海　南	Hainan			6		152.23	77.07	50.63
重　庆	Chongqing			4		249.36	167.22	67.06
四　川	Sichuan	3		51	1	639.71	354.23	55.37
贵　州	Guizhou	3		46	4	1556.35	915.87	58.85
云　南	Yunnan	8		78	7	2097.86	1141.40	54.41
西　藏	Tibet	7	1	73	1	259.21	248.67	95.93
甘　肃	Gansu	2		21	2	318.02	180.65	56.81
青　海	Qinghai	6		35	2	314.97	190.23	60.41
宁　夏	Ningxia	5	5	21	2	580.19	206.08	35.52
新　疆	Xinjiang	14	2	99	20	1933.95	1162.85	60.13

注：从2001年起人口为公安部门数。

a) Population since 2001 is from the public security department statistics.

2-10 民族自治地方国民经济和社会发展主要指标

指　　标	Item	1990
人口与就业	**Population and Employment**	
人口　（万人）	**Population　(10 000 persons)**	
年底总人口	Population at the Year-end	15296
#少数民族人口	Minority Population	6880
就业	**Employment**	
就业人员数　（万人）	Employment　(10 000 persons)	7406.44
宏观经济	**Macroeconomic Indicator**	
地区生产总值　（亿元）	**Gross Regional Product(100 million yuan)**	
第一产业	Primary Industry	
第二产业	Secondary Industry	
第三产业	Tertiary Industry	
固定资产	**Investment in Fixed Assets**	
全社会固定资产投资总额（亿元）	Total Investment in Fixed Assets (100 million yuan)	
#国有单位	State-owned Units	259
财政	**Government Finance**	
地方财政收入　（亿元）	Local Governments Revenue (100 million yuan)	167
地方财政支出　（亿元）	Local Governments Expenditures (100 million yuan)	304
产　　业	**Industry**	
农业	**Agriculture**	
耕地面积　（万公顷）	Cultivated Areas (10 000 hectares)	1763
灌溉面积　（万公顷）	Irrigated Areas (10 000 hectares)	764
农林牧渔总产值　（亿元）	Gross Output Value of Farming Forestry, Animal Husbandry and Fishery (100 million yuan)	
主要农产品产量	Output of Major Farm Products	
粮食产量　（万吨）	Grain Output　(10 000 tons)	5373
棉花产量　（万吨）	Cotton Output(10 000 tons)	47
油料产量　（万吨）	Oil-bearing Crops Output (10 000 tons)	208
大牲畜年底头数　（万头）	Large Domestic Animals　(10 000 heads)	5286
羊年底头数　（万只）	Goats and Sheep　(10 000 heads)	11362
猪年底头数　（万头）	Hogs　(10 000 heads)	5668
工业	**Industry**	
工业总产值　（亿元）	Gross Industrial Output Value (100 million yuan)	
主要工业产品产量	Output of Major Industrial Products	
布　（亿米）	Cloth (100 million m)	7.4
机制纸及纸板　（万吨）	Machine-Made Paper and Paperboards(10 000 tons)	94.1
糖　（万吨）	Sugar　(10 000 tons)	222.6
原煤　（亿吨）	Coal　(100 million tons)	1.2
原油　（万吨）	Crude Oil　(10 000 tons)	1265
发电量　（亿千瓦小时）	Electricity　(100 million kwh)	738.8
钢　（万吨）	Steel　(10 000 tons)	368.3
生铁　（万吨）	Pig Iron　(10 000 tons)	417.0
水泥　（万吨）	Cement　(10 000 tons)	1957.8
木材　（万立方米）	Timber　(10 000 cu.m)	1761

注：2001年及以后人口为公安部门数，与前几年抽样调查数据不可比。

Principal Aggregate Indicators on National Economic and Social Development of Minority Nationality Autonomous Areas

总量指标 Aggregate Data				速度指标(%) Indices and Growth Rates						
				指数 Index（2003为以下各年）(2003 as percentage of the following years)				平均增长速度 Average Annual Growth Rate		
1995	2000	2002	2003	1990	1995	2000	2002	1991-2003	1996-2003	2001-2003
16044	16818	17051	17214	112.5	107.3	102.4	101.0	0.9	0.9	0.8
7232	7767	7930	8017	116.5	110.9	103.2	101.1	1.2	1.3	1.1
7869.62	8308.89	8441.66	8634.40	116.6	109.7	103.9	102.3	1.2	1.2	1.3
4901	7486	9015	10381		205.9	133.5	111.9		9.4	10.1
1629	2022	2200	2456		151.2	115.1	105.9		5.3	4.8
1747	2834	3439	4164		242.3	143.9	117.2		11.7	12.9
1526	2629	3376	3762		219.8	136.7	110.2		10.3	11.0
1444	2477	3542	4734		327.8	191.1	133.6		16.0	24.1
983	1553	2188	2653	1022.6	270.0	170.8	121.2	19.6	13.2	19.5
248	476	595	674	404.3	271.7	141.7	113.3	11.3	13.3	12.3
595	1173	1927	2109	692.9	354.4	179.8	109.5	16.1	17.1	21.6
1508	2086	2007	1968	111.6	130.5	94.3	98.1	0.8	3.4	-1.9
838	936	983	975	127.7	116.4	104.3	99.2	1.9	1.9	1.4
2537	3200	3501	4015	200.9	156.3	119.4	105.8	5.5	5.7	6.1
5801	6381	6587	6480	120.6	111.7	101.5	98.4	1.5	1.4	0.5
95	146	148	161	342.2	170.0	110.0	108.5	9.9	6.9	3.2
264	353	355	359	172.7	136.1	101.7	101.1	4.3	3.9	0.6
5618	5566	5570	5798	109.7	103.2	104.2	104.1	0.7	0.4	1.4
11906	13076	13940	14800	130.3	124.3	113.2	106.2	2.1	2.8	4.2
7240	8201	8062	7729	136.4	106.8	94.2	95.9	2.4	0.8	-2.0
	3923.5	4524.3	5665.7			152.3	121.7			15.1
6.9	5.0	3.7	3.0	40.5	43.4	59.8	81.0	-6.7	-9.9	-15.7
191.2	175.5	178.0	219.7	233.4	114.9	125.2	123.4	6.7	1.8	7.8
239.5	498.2	669.1	824.0	370.1	344.0	165.4	123.1	10.6	16.7	18.3
1.7	1.5	1.6	1.9	155.5	113.3	128.7	119.6	3.5	1.6	8.8
1610	2292	2460	2597	205.3	161.3	113.3	105.6	5.7	6.2	4.3
1186.5	1712.5	1957.0	2243.2	303.6	189.1	131.0	114.6	8.9	8.3	9.4
699.6	647.1	899.8	1082.3	293.9	154.7	167.3	120.3	8.6	5.6	18.7
554.7	724.8	988.0	1156.9	277.4	208.6	159.6	117.1	8.2	9.6	16.9
4295.9	5703.1	6552.6	6700.8	342.3	156.0	117.5	102.3	9.9	5.7	5.5
3257	1052	1023	1097	62.3	33.7	104.2	107.2	-3.6	-12.7	1.4

a) Population since 2001 is from the public security department statistics, so it is incomparable with the data of sampling survey in the past years.

2-10 续表

指 标	Item	1990
建筑业	**Construction**	
建筑业企业人数（万人）	Number of Employed Persons (10 000 persons)	
建筑业总产值 （亿元）	Gross Output Value (100 million yuan)	
施工房屋面积 （万平方米）	Floor Space of Buildings Under Construction	
竣工房屋面积 （万平方米）	Floor Space of Buildings Completed (10 000 sq.m)	
邮电运输	**Transportation, Post and telecommunication**	
铁路营业里程 （万公里）	Railways in Operation (10 000 km)	1.3
公路通车里程 （万公里）	Highways (10 000 km)	29.4
邮电业务总量 （亿元）	Business Volume of Post and Telecommunications	8.6
邮路及农村投递线路总长度（万公里）	Postal Routes (10 000km)	88.0
国内商业	**Domestic Trade**	
社会消费品零售总额（亿元）	Total Value of Retail Sales (100 million yuan)	681.8
对外贸易	**Foreign Trade**	
进出口总额 （亿美元）	Total Exports and Imports (USD 100 million)	
出口额	Exports	
进口额	Imports	
国际旅游	**International Tourism**	
国际旅游人数 （万人次）	Number of Foreign Tourists(10 000 persons)	
旅游外汇收入 （亿美元）	Foreign Exchange Earning from Tourism (USD 100 million yuan)	
金融	**Finance**	
金融机构各项存款 （亿元）	Deposits of National Banking System(100 million yuan)	
金融机构各项贷款 （亿元）	Loans of National Banking System(100 million yuan)	
教育、文化、卫生	**Education, Culture and Public Health**	
教育	**Education**	
在校学生数 （万人）	Students Enrollment (10 000 persons)	2476.1
高等学校	Institutions of Higher Education	13.6
中等学校	Secondary Schools	609.6
小学	Primary Schools	1852.9
各类专任教师数 （万人）	Full-time Teachers(10 000 persons)	129.1
高等学校	Institutions of Higher Education	2.8
中等学校	Secondary Schools	41.5
小学	Primary Schools	84.8
文化	**Culture**	
出版数量	Publications	
图书 （万册）	Number of Books Published(10 000 copies)	30166
杂志 （万册）	Number of Magazines Issued(10 000 copies)	7866
报纸 （万份）	Number of Newspapers Issued(10 000 copies)	79120
卫生	**Public Health**	
卫生机构 （万个）	Number of Health Institutions(10 000 units)	3.2
卫生机构床位 （万张）	Number of Hospitals and Sanatorium Beds	35.9
卫生技术人员 （万人）	Medical Personnel (10 000 persons)	48.9

注：1. 2000年及以后铁路营业里程为国家铁路营业里程。

2. 工业总产值统计范围为全部国有和年销售收入500万元以上的非国有工业企业。

Continued

总量指标 Aggregate Data				速度指标(%) Indices and Growth Rates						
				指数 Index (2003为以下各年) (2003 as percentage of the following years)				平均增长速度 Average Annual Growth Rate		
1995	2000	2002	2003	1990	1995	2000	2002	1991–2003	1996–2003	2001–2003
	131.6	138.7	138.1			104.9	99.6			1.6
	754.3	1064.5	1227.2			162.7	115.3			17.6
	9232	11547	13420			145.4	116.2			13.3
	5326	6481	7223			135.6	111.4			10.7
1.7	1.4	1.4	1.5			106.0	105.4			2.0
33.2	42.4	52.7	54.8	186.5	164.9	129.3	103.9	4.9	6.5	8.9
78.0	296.9	428.7	524.8	6102.4	672.8	176.8	122.4	37.2	26.9	20.9
106.8	109.5	100.4	108.5	123.3	101.6	99.1	108.1	1.6	0.2	-0.3
1692.3	2569.8	2832.0	3109.0	456.0	183.7	121.0	109.8	12.4	7.9	6.6
	85.6	101.1	135.7			158.5	134.3			16.6
	49.7	46.0	78.4			157.8	170.3			16.4
	36.0	55.0	57.3			159.4	104.2			16.8
	348.2	678.3	215.1			61.8	31.7			-14.8
	7.5	9.2	6.0			79.4	65.1			-7.4
	7905.8	10238.6	11749.9			148.6	114.8			14.1
	6548.0	8039.7	9339.8			142.6	116.2			12.6
2629.2	2898.5	2967.6	2942.8	118.8	111.9	101.5	99.2	1.3	1.4	0.5
18.6	34.2	57.8	69.5	511.3	373.9	203.3	120.4	13.4	17.9	26.7
721.1	978.3	1096.5	1135.0	186.2	157.4	116.0	103.5	4.9	5.8	5.1
1889.5	1886.0	1813.3	1738.2	93.8	92.0	92.2	95.9	-0.5	-1.0	-2.7
138.4	148.1	155.9	154.1	119.4	111.4	104.1	98.9	1.4	1.4	1.3
3.7	3.6	4.2	4.9	174.3	131.9	134.1	115.7	4.4	3.5	10.3
48.9	54.5	62.0	61.5	148.3	125.8	112.9	99.3	3.1	2.9	4.1
85.8	89.9	89.7	87.7	103.4	102.2	97.5	97.8	0.3	0.3	-0.8
42275	42310	45564	43215	143.3	102.2	102.1	94.8	2.8	0.3	0.7
7881	8332	9085	9982	126.9	126.7	119.8	109.9	1.8	3.0	6.2
94985	123277	139467	163732	206.9	172.4	132.8	117.4	5.8	7.0	9.9
2.9	1.6	1.5	1.5	47.4	52.4	94.8	99.1	-5.6	-7.8	-1.8
38.7	38.2	36.2	38.0	105.7	98.1	99.5	104.9	0.4	-0.2	-0.2
52.7	35.5	46.0	46.3	94.8	87.9	130.4	100.7	-0.4	-1.6	9.3

a) The length of railway in operation since 2000 is national railways.

b) The statistical coverage of gross industrial output value is all state-owned industrial owned industrial enterprises and the non-state-enterprises with an annual sales income of over 5 million yuan.

2-11 少数民族分布的主要地区

Geographic Distribution of Minority Nationalities

人口数为2000年人口普查机器汇总数据。

Figures of population are obtained from the Population Census in 2000.

民族	Nationality	分布的主要地区	Main Geographic Distribution	人口数(人) Population (person)
蒙古族	Mongolian	内蒙古、辽宁、吉林、河北、黑龙江、新疆	Inner Mongolia, Liaoning, Jilin, Hebei, Heilongjiang and Xinjiang	5813947
回族	Hui	宁夏、甘肃、河南、新疆、青海、云南、河北、山东、安徽、辽宁、北京、内蒙古、天津、黑龙江、陕西、贵州、吉林、江苏、四川	Ningxia, Gansu, Henan, Xinjiang, Qinghai, Yunnan, Hebei, Shandong, Anhui, Liaoning, Beijing, Inner Mongolia, Tianjin, Heilongjiang, Shaanxi, Guizhou, Jilin, Jiangsu and Sichuan	9816805
藏族	Tibetan	西藏、四川、青海、甘肃、云南	Tibet, Sichuan, Qinghai, Gansu and Yunnan	5416021
维吾尔族	Uygur	新疆	Xinjiang	8399393
苗族	Miao	贵州、湖南、云南、广西、重庆湖北、四川	Guizhou, Hunan, Yunnan, Guangxi, Chongqing, Hubei and Sichuan	8940116
彝族	Yi	云南、四川、贵州	Yunnan, Sichuan and Guizhou	7762272
壮族	Zhuang	广西、云南、广东	Guangxi, Yunnan and Guangdong	16178811
布依族	Bouyei	贵州	Guizhou	2971460
朝鲜族	Korean	吉林、黑龙江、辽宁	Jilin, Heilongjiang and Liaoning	1923842
满族	Manchu	辽宁、河北、黑龙江、吉林、内蒙古、北京	Liaoning, Hebei, Heilongjiang, Jilin, Inner Mongolia and Beijing	10682262
侗族	Dong	贵州、湖南、广西	Guizhou, Hunan and Guangxi	2960293
瑶族	Yao	广西、湖南、云南、广东	Guangxi, Hunan, Yunnan and Guangdong	2637421
白族	Bai	云南、贵州、湖南	Yunnan, Guizhou and Hunan	1858063
土家族	Tujia	湖南、湖北、重庆、贵州	Hunan, Hubei, Chongqing and Guizhou	8028133
哈尼族	Hani	云南	Yunnan	1439673
哈萨克族	Kazak	新疆	Xinjiang	1250458
傣族	Dai	云南	Yunnan	1158989
黎族	Li	海南	Hainan	1247814
傈僳族	Lisu	云南、四川	Yunnan and Sichuan	634912
佤族	Va	云南	Yunnan	396610
畲族	She	福建、浙江、江西、广东	Fujian, Zhejiang, Jiangxi and Guangdong	709592
高山族	Gaoshan	台湾、福建	Taiwan and Fujian	4461
拉祜族	Lahu	云南	Yunnan	453705
水族	Shui	贵州、广西	Guizhou and Guangxi	406902
东乡族	Dongxiang	甘肃、新疆	Gansu and Xinjiang	513805
纳西族	Naxi	云南	Yunnan	308839
景颇族	Jingpo	云南	Yunnan	132143
柯尔克孜族	Kirgiz	新疆	Xinjiang	160823
土族	Tu	青海、甘肃	Qinghai and Gansu	241198
达斡尔族	Daur	内蒙古、黑龙江	Inner Mongolia and Heilongjiang	132394
仫佬族	Mulam	广西	Guangxi	207352
羌族	Qiang	四川	Sichuan	306072
布朗族	Blang	云南	Yunnan	91882
撒拉族	Salar	青海	Qinghai	104503
毛南族	Maonan	广西	Guangxi	107166
仡佬族	Gelao	贵州	Guizhou	579357
锡伯族	Xibe	辽宁、新疆	Liaoning and Xinjiang	188824
阿昌族	Achang	云南	Yunnan	33936
普米族	Pumi	云南	Yunnan	33600
塔吉克族	Tajik	新疆	Xinjiang	41028
怒族	Nu	云南	Yunnan	28759
乌孜别克族	Ozbek	新疆	Xinjiang	12370
俄罗斯族	Russian	新疆、黑龙江	Xinjiang and Heilongjiang	15609
鄂温克族	Ewenki	内蒙古	Inner Mongolia	30505
德昂族	De'ang	云南	Yunnan	17935
保安族	Bonan	甘肃	Gansu	16505
裕固族	Yugur	甘肃	Gansu	13719
京族	Jing	广西	Guangxi	22517
塔塔尔族	Tatar	新疆	Xinjiang	4890
独龙族	Drung	云南	Yunnan	7426
鄂伦春族	Oroqen	黑龙江、内蒙古	Heilongjiang and Inner Mongolia	8196
赫哲族	Hezhen	黑龙江	Heilongjiang	4640
门巴族	Moinba	西藏	Tibet	8923
珞巴族	Lhoba	西藏	Tibet	2965
基诺族	Jino	云南	Yunnan	20899

主要统计指标解释

可比价格 指计算各种总量指标所采用的扣除了价格变动因素的价格，可进行不同时期总量指标的对比。按可比价格计算总量指标有两种方法：一种是直接用产品产量乘某一年的不变价格计算；另一种是用价格指数进行缩减。

不变价格 指以同类产品某年的平均价格作为固定价格，用于计算各年的产品价值。按不变价格计算的产品价值消除了价格变动因素，不同时期对比可以反映生产的发展速度。新中国成立后，随着工农业产品价格水平的变化，国家统计局先后五次制定了全国统一的工业产品不变价格和农业产品不变价格。从1952年到1957年使用1952年工(农)业产品不变价格，从1957年到1970年使用1957年不变价格，从1971年到1980年使用1970年不变价格，从1981年到1990年使用1980年不变价格，从1991年开始使用1990年不变价格。

平均增长速度 我国计算平均增长速度有两种方法：一种是习惯上经常使用的“水平法”，又称几何平均法，是以间隔期最后一年的水平同基期水平对比来计算平均每年增长(或下降)速度；另一种是“累计法”，又称代数平均法或方程法，是以间隔期内各年水平的总和同基期水平对比来计算平均每年增长(或下降)速度。在一般正常情况下，两种方法计算的平均每年增长速度比较接近；但在经济发展不平衡、出现大起大落时，两种方法计算的结果差别较大。

本《年鉴》内所列的平均增长速度，除固定资产投资用“累计法”计算外，其余均用“水平法”计算。从某年到某年平均增长速度的年份，均不包括基期年在内。如建国四十三年以来的平均增长速度是以1949年为基期计算的，则写为1950–1992年平均增长速度，其余类推。

国民经济行业分类 自2003年定期报表开始使用新的《国民经济行业分类》（GB/T4754–2002）该分类是由国家统计局组织修订，经国家质量监督检验检疫总局批准，于2002年5月10日发布实施。这次修订是在1994年分类标准的基础上，参照联合国《全部经济活动的国际标准产业分类》（ISIC/Rev.3）进行的。修订后的《国民经济行业分类》（GB/T4754–2002）共有门类20个，大类95个，中类396个，小类913个。新增门类4个，大类增加3个，中类增加28个，小类增加67个。

企业(单位)登记注册类型 是以在工商行政管理机关登记注册的各类企业为划分对象，以工商行政管理部门对企业登记注册的类型为依据，将企业登记注册类型分为内资企业、港澳台商投资企业和外商投资企业三大类。内资企业包括国有企业、集体企业、股份合作企业、联营企业、有限责任公司、股份有限公司、私营公司和其他企业；港澳台商投资企业和外商投资企业分别包括合资经营企业、合作经营企业、独资经营企业和股份有限公司。对不在工商行政管理部门进行登记注册的行政机关、事业单位和社会团体，主要按其经费来源和管理方式进行划分。

国有企业 指企业全部资产归国家所有，并按《中华人民共和国企业法人登记管理条例》规定登记注册的非公司制的经济组织。不包括有限责任公司中的国有独资公司。

集体企业 指企业资产归集体所有，并按《中华人民共和国企业法人登记管理条例》规定登记注册的经济组织。

股份合作企业 指以合作制为基础，由企业职工共同出资入股，吸收一定比例的社会资产投资组建，实行自主经营，自负盈亏，共同劳动，民主管理，按劳分配与按股分红相结合的一种集体经济组织。

联营企业 指两个及两个以上相同或不同所有制性质的企业法人或事业单位法人，按自愿、平等、互利的原则，共同投资组成的经济组织。联营企业包括国有联营企业、集体联营企业、国有与集体联营企业和其他联营企业。

有限责任公司 指根据《中华人民共和国公司登记管理条例》规定登记注册，由两个以上、五十个以下的股东共同出资，每个股东以其所认缴的出资额对公司承担有限责任，公司以其全部资产对其债务承担责任的经济组织。有限责任公司包括国有独资公司以及其他有限责任公司。

股份有限公司 指根据《中华人民共和国公司登记管理条例》规定登记注册，其全部注册资本由等额股份构成并通过发行股票筹集资本，股东以其认购的股份对公司承担有限责任，公司以其全部资产对其债务承担责任的经济组织。

私营企业 指由自然人投资设立或由自然人控股，以雇佣劳动为基础的营利性经济组织。包括按照《公司法》、《合伙企业法》、《私营企业暂行条例》规定登记注册的私营有限责任公司、私营股份有限公司、私营合伙企业和私营独资企业。

其他企业 指上述企业之外的其他内资经济组织。

与港澳台商合资经营企业 指港澳台地区投资者与内地企业依照《中华人民共和国中外合资经营企业法》及有关法律的规定，按合同规定的比例投资设立、分享利润和分担风险的企业。

与港澳台商合作经营企业 指港澳台地区投资者与内地企业依照《中华人民共和国中外合作经营企业法》及有关法律的规定，依照合作合同的约定进行投资或提供条件设立、分配利润和分担风险的企业。

港澳台商独资经营企业 指依照《中华人民共和国外资企业法》及有关法律的规定，在内地由港澳台地区投资者全额投资设立的企业。

港澳台商投资股份有限公司 指根据国家有关规定，经原外经贸部依法批准设立，其中港、澳、台商的股本占公司注册资本的比例达25% 以上的股份有限公司。凡其中港、澳、台商的股本占公司注册资本的比例小于25%的，属于内资企业中的股份有限公司。

中外合资经营企业 指外国企业或外国人与中国内地企业依照《中华人民共和国中外合资经营企业法》及有关法律的规定，按合同规定的比例投资设立、分享利润和分担风险的企业。

中外合作经营企业 指外国企业或外国人与中国内地企

业依照《中华人民共和国中外合作经营企业法》及有关法律的规定，依照合作合同的约定进行投资或提供条件设立、分配利润和分担风险的企业。

外资企业 指依照《中华人民共和国外资企业法》及有关法律的规定，在中国内地由外国投资者全额投资设立的企业。

外商投资股份有限公司 指根据国家有关规定，经原外经贸部依法批准设立，其中外资的股本占公司注册资本的比例达25%以上的股份有限公司。凡其中外资股本占公司注册资本的比例小于25%的，属于内资企业中的股份有限公司。

行政机关、事业单位和社会团体 参照企业登记注册类型，主要按其经费来源和管理方式划分。具体规定如下：

(1)行政机关：包括国家机关和政党机关，原则上均列为“国有”。但有特殊规定的，如供销社等，则列为“集体”。

(2)事业单位：包括经国家机构编制部门和有关业务主管部门批准成立的各类事业单位，不包括实行企业化管理的事业单位。事业单位的划分办法如下：

①由国家财政预算拨款或列入财政预算外资金管理以及经费主要来源于国有主管部门或国有上级单位的事业单位，列为“国有”。

②经费主要来源于集体单位的事业单位，列为“集体”。

③公民个人(或个人合伙)开办的事业单位，列为“私营”。

④上述以外的其他事业单位，如果其经费来源不明确，按管理方式进行归类。

(3)社会团体：包括经民政部门批准成立以及未纳入社会团体管理条例范围的工会、妇联等各类社会团体。社会团体的划分办法如下：

①未纳入民政部社会团体管理条例范围的工会、妇联、共青团、青联、工商联、科协、侨联等社会团体，国家拨款设立的基金会或基金管理组织以及经费主要来源于国有业务主管部门或国有上级单位的社会团体，列为“国有”。

②经费主要来源于集体单位的社会团体，列为“集体”。

③公民个人(或个人合伙)开办的社会团体，划为“私营”。

④上述以外的其他社会团体，如果其经费来源不明确，改按管理方式进行归类。

Explanatory Notes on Main Statistical Indicators

Comparable Prices refer to prices that are used to remove the factors of price change in calculating economic aggregates, so as to facilitate comparison of aggregates over time. Two methods are used for calculating economic aggregates at comparable prices: 1) Multiplying the output of products by their constant prices of certain year; 2) Deflating data at current prices by relevant price indices.

Constant Price refers to the average price of a given product in certain year, which is used for comparison of output value over time. As the output value at constant prices removes the factor of price changes, it reflects the trend of production development over time. Since 1949, with the changes in general price level, National Bureau of Statistics has issued nationally unified constant prices five times: the 1952 constant prices for 1949-1957; the 1957 constant prices for 1957-1971; the 1970 constant prices for 1971-1981; the 1980 constant prices for 1981-1990; and the 1990 constant prices have been used since 1991.

Average Annual Growth Rate Two methods for calculating average annual growth rate are applied in China, one is often called level approach, or the method of calculating geometric average, which is derived by comparing the level of the last year of the interval with that of the beginning year; the other is called accumulative approach or algebraic average or equation method, which is derived by the summation of the actual figure of each year in the interval divided by the figure in the base year.

Usually the results calculated by the two methods are fairly close, but they differed sharply when uneven economic development occurred with striking fluctuations in growth.

The average annual growth rates listed in this statistical yearbook are calculated by level approach except for the growth rate of investment in fixed assets. The base years are not listed when the years are listed for average annual growth rates. For instance, the average annual growth rate of 43 years since 1949 is listed as average annual growth rate of 1950-1992 without listing the base year 1949. And the analogy of this is also the same for the rest of the years.

Industrial Classification of the National Economy The new *Industrial Classification of the National Economy* (GB/T 4754-2002) is introduced starting from the compilation of 2003 annual statistics. The revision of the 1994 classification was organized by the National Bureau of Statistics taking into consideration of the *International Standards of the Industrial Classification of All Economic Activities* (ISIC/Rev.3) of the United Nations, and the new *Classification* was promulgated by the National Administration of Quality Supervision, Inspection and Quarantine on May 10, 2002. The revised version of the *Industrial Classification of the National Economy* (GB/T 4754-2002) is composed of 20 major divisions, 95 divisions, 396 major groups and 913 groups, including 4 new major divisions, 3 new divisions, 28 major groups and 67 groups.

Registration Status of Enterprises Enterprises are classified into 3 categories, namely domestic-funded enterprises, enterprises with investment from Hong Kong, Macau and Taiwan, and enterprises with foreign investment, in the light of the registration status of an enterprise in industrial and commercial administration agencies. Domestic-funded enterprises include state-owned enterprises, collective-owned enterprises, cooperative enterprises, joint ownership enterprises, limited liability corporations, share-holding corporations Ltd., private enterprises and other enterprises. Included in the enterprises with investment from Hong Kong, Macau and Taiwan and enterprises with foreign investment are joint-venture enterprises, cooperative enterprises, sole investment enterprises and share-holding corporations Ltd. For government agencies, institutions and social organizations which are not requested to be registered in industrial and commercial administration agencies, they are classified mainly by their sources of funds and way of management.

State-owned Enterprises refer to non-corporation economic units where the entire assets are owned by the state and which have registered in accordance with the *Regulation of the People's Republic of China on the Management of Registration of Corporate Enterprises*. Excluded from this category are sole state-funded corporations in the limited liability corporations.

Collective-owned Enterprises refer to economic units where the assets are owned collectively and which have registered in accordance with the *Regulation of the People's Republic of China on the Management of Registration of Corporate Enterprises.*

Cooperative Enterprises refer to a form of collective economic units (enterprises) where capitals come mainly from employees as their shares, with certain proportion of capital from the outside, where production is organized on the basis of independent operation, independent accounting for profits and losses, joint work, democratic management, and a distribution system that integrates remuneration according to work with dividend according to capital share.

Joint Ownership Enterprises refer to economic units established by two or more corporate enterprises or corporate institutions of the same or different ownership, through joint investment on the basis of equality, voluntary participation and mutual benefits. They include state joint ownership enterprises, collective joint ownership enterprises, joint state-collective enterprises, other joint ownership enterprises.

Limited Liability Corporations refer to economic units established with investment from 2-50 investors and registered in accordance with the *Regulation of the People's Republic of China on the Management of Registration of Corporations*, each investor bearing limited liability to the corporation depending on its share of investment, and the corporation bearing liability to its debt to the maximum of its total assets. Limited liability corporations include exclusive state-funded limited liability corporations and other limited liability corporations.

Share-holding Corporations Ltd. refer to economic units

registered in accordance with the *Regulation of the People's Republic of China on the Management of Registration of Corporations*, with total registered capitals divided into equal shares and raised through issuing stocks. Each investor bears limited liability to the corporation depending on the holding of shares, and the corporation bears liability to its debt to the maximum of its total assets.

Private Enterprises refer to profit-making economic units invested and established by natural persons, or controlled by natural persons using employed labour. Included in this category are private limited liability corporations, private share-holding corporations Ltd., private partnership enterprises and private-funded enterprises registered in accordance with the *Corporation Law*, *Partnership Enterprises Law* and *Interim Regulations on Private Enterprises* .

Other Domestic-funded Enterprises refer to domestic-funded economic units other than those mentioned above.

Cooperative Enterprises with Funds from Hong Kong Macau and Taiwan established by investors from Hong Kong, Macau and Taiwan with enterprises in the mainland of China in accordance with the *Law of the People's Republic of China on Sino-foreign Cooperative Enterprises* and other relevant laws, where the investment or provision of facilities, and the share of profits and risks is stipulated in the cooperative contract.

Enterprises with Sole (exclusive) Investment from Hong Kong, Macau and Taiwan refer to enterprises established in the mainland of China with exclusive investment from investors from Hong Kong, Macau and Taiwan in accordance with the *Law of the People's Republic of China on Foreign-Funded Enterprises* and other relevant laws.

Share-holding Corporations Ltd. with Investment from Hong Kong, Macau and Taiwan refer to share-holding corporations Ltd. established with the approval from the former Ministry of Foreign Trade and Economic Relations in line with relevant state regulations, where the share of investment from Hong Kong, Macau or Taiwan businessmen exceeds 25% of the total registered capital of the corporation. In case the share of investment from Hong Kong, Macau or Taiwan is less than 25% of the total registered capital, the enterprise is to be classified as domestic-funded share-holding corporation Ltd.

Joint-venture Enterprises with Foreign Investment refer to enterprises jointly established by foreign enterprises or foreigners with enterprises in the mainland of China in accordance with the *Law of the People's Republic of China on Sino-foreign Joint Venture Enterprises* and other relevant laws, where the share of investment, profits and risks is stipulated in the contract.

Cooperation Enterprises with Foreign Investment refer to enterprises jointly established by foreign enterprises or foreigners with enterprises in the mainland of China in accordance with the *Law of the People's Republic of China on Sino-foreign Cooperative Enterprises* and other relevant laws, where the investment or provision of facilities, and the share of profits and risks is stipulated in the cooperative contract.

Enterprises with Sole (exclusive) Foreign Investment refer to enterprises established in the mainland of China with exclusive investment from foreign investors in accordance with the *Law of the People's Republic of China on Foreign-Funded Enterprises* and other relevant laws.

Share-holding Corporations Ltd. with Foreign Investment refer to share-holding corporations Ltd. established with the approval from the Ministry of Foreign Trade and Economic Relations in line with relevant state regulations, where the share of investment from foreign investors exceeds 25% of the total registered capital of the corporation. In case the share of foreign investment is less than 25% of the total registered capital, the enterprise is to be classified as domestic-funded share-holding corporation Ltd.

Government Agencies, Institutions and Social Organizations are classified into following categories by source of funds and way of management taking reference of the registration status of enterprises:

(1) Government agencies: include state and party agencies, classified in principle as state-owned. There are exceptions, such as supply and marketing cooperatives which are classified as collective-owned.

(2) Institutions: include institutions of various types established with the approval by organization and staffing departments of the government, but exclude institutions where enterprise management system is introduced. Institutions are further classified as follows:

(a) Institutions whose main budget is listed in the government budget appropriations or extra-budget funds, or allocated from the budget of their competent government agencies. Such institutions are classified as state-owned.

(b) Institutions whose budget mainly comes from collective units. Such institutions are classified as collective-owned.

(c) Institutions other than those mentioned above whose source of budget is not clear. Such institutions are classified by way of management.

(3) Social organizations: include social organizations established with the approval from the Ministry of Civil Affairs, and organizations that are not covered by social organization management regulations such as trade unions, womens federations etc.. Social organizations are further classified as follows:

(a) Social organizations that are not covered by social organization management regulations of the Ministry of Civil Affairs such as trade unions, womens federations, communist youth leagues, youth associations, industrial and commerce associations, scientists associations, overseas Chinese associations, etc., foundations and fund management organizations established with funds from the state, and social organizations whose funds mainly come from the budget of their competent government agencies. Such institutions are classified as state-owned.

(b) Social organizations whose budget mainly comes from collective units. Such institutions are classified as collective-owned.

(c) Social organizations established by individual or a group of citizens, which are classified as private.

(d) Social organizations other than those mentioned above whose source of budget is not clear. Such organizations are classified by way of management.

三、国民经济核算

National Accounts

简要说明

国民经济核算资料主要包括国内生产总值、投入产出表、资金流量表及国际收支概况四个部分。

一、国内生产总值

国内生产总值数据是由国家统计局国民经济核算司根据不同产业部门、不同支出构成的特点和资料来源情况而采用不同方法计算的。国民总收入是在国内生产总值的基础上加上来自国外的净要素收入求得的。

本年鉴公布的国民经济核算资料，最后一年数据不是最终数，还会发生变动；如果遇到普查年，在能够获得更详细的基础资料的情况下，国内生产总值的历史数据也会发生变动。1995年，根据第一次全国第三产业普查结果，对国内生产总值的历史数据做了调整，本年鉴中的数据是调整以后的数据。

本年鉴所列分地区的数据来自各省、自治区、直辖市统计局的国民经济核算资料。由于采取分级核算，各地区数据相加不等于全国总计。

二、投入产出表

中国2000年投入产出表是由国家统计局国民经济核算司编制的。

投入产出表也称部门联系平衡表或产业关联表，它是根据国民经济各部门生产中的投入来源和使用去向纵横交叉组成的一张棋盘式平衡表。它可以用来揭示部门间经济技术的相互依存、相互制约的数量关系。

三、资金流量表

我国资金流量表表式与国际上通用的表式相似，是机构部门与交易项目的矩阵表式。主栏为交易项目，主要反映分配方式和融资工具；宾栏按机构部门分类。机构部门分类是根据机构单位具有的基本特征所进行的部门分类。资金流量表把参与资金活动的主体分为非金融企业、金融机构、一般政府、住户和国外五个部门。每一部门下设资金来源与资金运用两栏。现行的资金流量表分为两大部分，上半部分为实物交易部分，由国家统计局国民经济核算司编制；下半部分为金融交易部分，由中国人民银行调查统计司编制。

四、国际收支平衡表

国际收支平衡表由国家外汇管理局国际收支司依据国际货币基金组织编写的《国际收支统计手册》第五版编制。

Brief Introduction

Statistics on national accounts include mainly four components, namely, gross domestic product, input-output table, flow of fund table and balance of payment.

I. Gross Domestic Product

Data on GDP are calculated by the Department of National Economic Accounting, National Bureau of Statistics (NBS) with various approaches in the light of the features of various sectors, various expenditure structures and the data sources. The gross national product can be calculated on the base of GDP and the net factor income from abroad.

Data on the national accounts of the latest year published in the yearbook are not final and are subject to changes. When it happens to be a census year, the data of GDP of the past years may also be revised. In 1995, the GDP figures of the past years were adjusted in accordance with the result of the first tertiary industry census. Data published in this yearbook are the adjusted data.

Regional data in this yearbook are prepared according to the data of national accounts provided by the statistical bureaus of the provinces, autonomous regions and municipalities directly under the central government. The sum of the regional data is not equal to the national total due to the decentralized accounting approach.

II. Input-output Table

The 2000 input-output table of China included in this chapter is compiled by the Department of National Accounts of the National Bureau of Statistics.

Reflecting the sources of the input into, and the utilization of the output from production by various industries of the national economy, the input-output table is used to reveal, in quantitative terms, the interrelated and mutually dependent economic and technological relations between industries.

III. Flow of Fund Table

Similar to internationally accepted format, the flow of fund table of China constitutes a matrix of institutional sectors by transactions. Items of transactions are expressed as row headings representing forms of distribution and methods of financing. Institutional sectors are shown as column headings, grouped by the characteristics of the transactors. There are 5 groups of institutional sectors in the flow of fund table, namely, non-financial corporations, financial institutions, general governments, households, and the rest of the world. Under each sector there are 2 headings: source of fund and utilization of fund. The current flow of fund table is composed of two parts: the first part is the physical (real) transactions compiled by the National Accounts Department of the National Bureau of Statistics, and the second part is the financial transactions compiled by the Survey and Statistics Department of the People's Bank of China.

IV. Balance of Payment Table

The balance of payment table is compiled by the Balance of Payment Department of the State Administration of Foreign Exchanges in accordance with the 5th edition of the *Manual on Balance of Payment* prepared by the International Monetary Fund.

3-1 国 内 生 产 总 值

Gross Domestic Product

本表按当年价格计算。

Data in this table are calculated at current prices.

单位: 亿元 (100 million yuan)

年 份 Year	国民总收入 Gross National Income	国内生产总值 Gross Domestic Product	第一产业 Primary Industry	第二产业 Secondary Industry	工 业 Industry	建筑业 Construc-tion	第三产业 Tertiary Industry	#交通运输仓储邮电通信业 Transport, Post and Telecommunication Services	#批发和零售贸易餐饮业 Wholesale, Retail Trade & Catering Services	人均国内生产总值(元/人) Per Capita GDP (yuan/person)
1978	3624.1	3624.1	1018.4	1745.2	1607.0	138.2	860.5	172.8	265.5	379
1979	4038.2	4038.2	1258.9	1913.5	1769.7	143.8	865.8	184.2	220.2	417
1980	4517.8	4517.8	1359.4	2192.0	1996.5	195.5	966.4	205.0	213.6	460
1981	4860.3	4862.4	1545.6	2255.5	2048.4	207.1	1061.3	211.1	255.7	489
1982	5301.8	5294.7	1761.6	2383.0	2162.3	220.7	1150.1	236.7	198.6	525
1983	5957.4	5934.5	1960.8	2646.2	2375.6	270.6	1327.5	264.9	231.4	580
1984	7206.7	7171.0	2295.5	3105.7	2789.0	316.7	1769.8	327.1	412.4	692
1985	8989.1	8964.4	2541.6	3866.6	3448.7	417.9	2556.2	406.9	878.4	853
1986	10201.4	10202.2	2763.9	4492.7	3967.0	525.7	2945.6	475.6	943.2	956
1987	11954.5	11962.5	3204.3	5251.6	4585.8	665.8	3506.6	544.9	1159.3	1104
1988	14922.3	14928.3	3831.0	6587.2	5777.2	810.0	4510.1	661.0	1618.0	1355
1989	16917.8	16909.2	4228.0	7278.0	6484.0	794.0	5403.2	786.0	1687.0	1512
1990	18598.4	18547.9	5017.0	7717.4	6858.0	859.4	5813.5	1147.5	1419.7	1634
1991	21662.5	21617.8	5288.6	9102.2	8087.1	1015.1	7227.0	1409.7	2087.0	1879
1992	26651.9	26638.1	5800.0	11699.5	10284.5	1415.0	9138.6	1681.8	2735.0	2287
1993	34560.5	34634.4	6882.1	16428.5	14143.8	2284.7	11323.8	2123.2	3090.7	2939
1994	46670.0	46759.4	9457.2	22372.2	19359.6	3012.6	14930.0	2685.9	4050.4	3923
1995	57494.9	58478.1	11993.0	28537.9	24718.3	3819.6	17947.2	3054.7	4932.3	4854
1996	66850.5	67884.6	13844.2	33612.9	29082.6	4530.5	20427.5	3494.0	5560.3	5576
1997	73142.7	74462.6	14211.2	37222.7	32412.1	4810.6	23028.7	3797.2	6159.9	6054
1998	76967.2	78345.2	14552.4	38619.3	33387.9	5231.4	25173.5	4121.3	6579.1	6308
1999	80579.4	82067.5	14472.0	40557.8	35087.2	5470.6	27037.7	4460.3	6910.3	6551
2000	88254.0	89468.1	14628.2	44935.3	39047.3	5888.0	29904.6	5408.6	7316.0	7086
2001	95727.9	97314.8	15411.8	48750.0	42374.6	6375.4	33153.0	5968.3	7918.8	7651
2002	103935.3	105172.3	16117.3	52980.2	45975.2	7005.0	36074.8	6420.3	8476.7	8214
2003	116603.2	117251.9	17092.1	61274.1	53092.9	8181.3	38885.7	6715.6	9238.1	9101

注:1980年以后国民总收入(原称国民生产总值)与国内生产总值的差额为国外净要素收入。

a) Since 1980, the difference between the Gross Domestic Product and the Gross National Income (formly, the Gross National Product) has been the net factor income from abroad.

3-2 国内生产总值构成

Composition of Gross Domestic Product

本表按当年价格计算。

Data in this table are calculated at current prices.

单位: % (%)

年份 Year	国内生产总值 Gross Domestic Product	第一产业 Primary Industry	第二产业 Secondary Industry	工业 Industry	建筑业 Construction	第三产业 Tertiary Industry	#交通运输仓储邮电通信业 Transport, Post and Telecommunication Services	#批发和零售贸易餐饮业 Wholesale, Retail Trade & Catering Services
1978	100.0	28.1	48.2	44.4	3.8	23.7	4.8	7.3
1979	100.0	31.2	47.4	43.8	3.6	21.4	4.6	5.5
1980	100.0	30.1	48.5	44.2	4.3	21.4	4.5	4.7
1981	100.0	31.8	46.4	42.1	4.3	21.8	4.3	5.3
1982	100.0	33.3	45.0	40.8	4.2	21.7	4.5	3.8
1983	100.0	33.0	44.6	40.0	4.6	22.4	4.5	3.9
1984	100.0	32.0	43.3	38.9	4.4	24.7	4.6	5.8
1985	100.0	28.4	43.1	38.5	4.6	28.5	4.5	9.8
1986	100.0	27.1	44.0	38.9	5.1	28.9	4.7	9.2
1987	100.0	26.8	43.9	38.3	5.6	29.3	4.6	9.7
1988	100.0	25.7	44.1	38.7	5.4	30.2	4.4	10.8
1989	100.0	25.0	43.0	38.3	4.7	32.0	4.6	10.0
1990	100.0	27.1	41.6	37.0	4.6	31.3	6.2	7.7
1991	100.0	24.5	42.1	37.4	4.7	33.4	6.5	9.7
1992	100.0	21.8	43.9	38.6	5.3	34.3	6.3	10.3
1993	100.0	19.9	47.4	40.8	6.6	32.7	6.1	8.9
1994	100.0	20.2	47.9	41.4	6.5	31.9	5.7	8.7
1995	100.0	20.5	48.8	42.3	6.5	30.7	5.2	8.4
1996	100.0	20.4	49.5	42.8	6.7	30.1	5.1	8.2
1997	100.0	19.1	50.0	43.5	6.5	30.9	5.1	8.3
1998	100.0	18.6	49.3	42.6	6.7	32.1	5.3	8.4
1999	100.0	17.6	49.4	42.8	6.6	33.0	5.4	8.4
2000	100.0	16.4	50.2	43.6	6.6	33.4	6.0	8.2
2001	100.0	15.8	50.1	43.5	6.6	34.1	6.1	8.1
2002	100.0	15.3	50.4	43.7	6.7	34.3	6.1	8.1
2003	100.0	14.6	52.2	45.3	6.9	33.2	5.7	7.9

3-3 国内生产总值指数

Indices of Gross Domestic Product

本表按可比价格计算。

Data in this table are calculated at comparable prices.

(上年=100) (preceding year=100)

年份 Year	国民总收入 Gross National Income	国内生产总值 Gross Domestic Product	第一产业 Primary Industry	第二产业 Secondary Industry	工业 Industry	建筑业 Construction	第三产业 Tertiary Industry	#交通运输仓储邮电通信业 Transport, Post and Telecommunication Services	#批发和零售贸易餐饮业 Wholesale, Retail Trade & Catering Services	人均国内生产总值 Per Capita GDP
1978	111.7	111.7	104.1	115.0	116.4	99.4	113.7	108.9	123.1	110.2
1979	107.6	107.6	106.1	108.2	108.7	102.0	107.8	107.7	108.8	106.1
1980	107.8	107.8	98.5	113.6	112.7	126.7	105.9	105.7	98.7	106.5
1981	105.2	105.2	107.0	101.9	101.7	103.2	110.4	101.9	130.0	103.9
1982	109.3	109.1	111.5	105.6	105.8	103.4	113.0	111.7	103.9	107.5
1983	111.1	110.9	108.3	110.4	109.7	117.1	115.2	110.0	121.9	109.3
1984	115.3	115.2	112.9	114.5	114.9	110.9	119.4	115.0	121.5	113.7
1985	113.2	113.5	101.8	118.6	118.2	122.2	118.3	113.5	128.9	111.9
1986	108.5	108.8	103.3	110.2	109.6	115.9	112.1	112.8	110.6	107.2
1987	111.5	111.6	104.7	113.7	113.2	117.9	114.4	110.0	113.5	109.8
1988	111.3	111.3	102.5	114.5	115.3	108.0	113.2	113.3	114.3	109.5
1989	104.2	104.1	103.1	103.8	105.1	91.6	105.4	104.7	91.7	102.5
1990	104.2	103.8	107.3	103.2	103.4	101.2	102.3	108.6	95.2	102.3
1991	109.1	109.2	102.4	113.9	114.4	109.6	108.8	111.2	104.5	107.7
1992	114.1	114.2	104.7	121.2	121.2	121.0	112.4	110.5	113.1	112.8
1993	113.1	113.5	104.7	119.9	120.1	118.0	110.7	112.4	106.6	112.2
1994	112.6	112.6	104.0	118.4	118.9	113.7	109.6	109.5	107.7	111.4
1995	109.0	110.5	105.0	113.9	114.0	112.4	108.4	112.0	105.9	109.3
1996	109.8	109.6	105.1	112.1	112.5	108.5	107.9	111.4	105.4	108.4
1997	108.6	108.8	103.5	110.5	111.3	102.6	109.1	110.8	108.5	107.7
1998	107.8	107.8	103.5	108.9	108.9	109.0	108.3	110.6	107.7	106.8
1999	107.2	107.1	102.8	108.1	108.5	104.3	107.7	111.3	107.2	106.2
2000	108.4	108.0	102.4	109.4	109.8	105.7	108.1	111.5	108.2	107.1
2001	107.2	107.5	102.8	108.4	108.7	106.8	108.4	109.5	107.5	106.7
2002	108.9	108.3	102.9	109.8	110.0	108.8	108.7	107.9	108.1	107.6
2003	110.0	109.3	102.5	112.7	112.8	112.1	107.3	107.0	109.1	108.7

3-4 国内生产总值指数

Indices of Gross Domestic Product

本表按可比价格计算。

Data in this table are calculated at comparable prices.

(1978年=100) (year of 1978=100)

年 份 Year	国民总收入 Gross National Income	国内生产总值 Gross Domestic Product	第一产业 Primary Industry	第二产业 Secondary Industry	工业 Industry	建筑业 Construc-tion	第三产业 Tertiary Industry	#交通运输仓储邮电通信业 Transport, Post and Tele-communications Services	#批发和零售贸易餐饮业 Wholesale, Retail Trade & Catering Services	人均国内生产总值 Per Capita GDP
1978	100.0	100.0	100.0	100.0	100.0	100.0	100.0	100.0	100.0	100.0
1979	107.6	107.6	106.1	108.2	108.7	102.0	107.8	107.7	108.8	106.1
1980	116.0	116.0	104.6	122.9	122.4	129.2	114.2	113.8	107.4	113.0
1981	122.0	122.1	111.9	125.2	124.5	133.3	126.2	116.0	139.6	117.5
1982	133.3	133.1	124.8	132.1	131.7	137.9	142.6	129.5	145.1	126.2
1983	148.2	147.6	135.1	145.8	144.5	161.4	164.3	142.5	176.8	137.9
1984	170.9	170.0	152.6	166.9	166.0	179.0	196.1	163.8	214.8	156.8
1985	193.5	192.9	155.4	197.9	196.2	218.7	231.9	185.9	276.8	175.5
1986	209.9	210.0	160.5	218.2	215.2	253.4	260.0	209.7	306.1	188.2
1987	234.1	234.3	168.1	248.1	243.6	298.7	297.4	230.7	347.3	206.6
1988	260.5	260.7	172.3	284.1	280.8	322.5	336.7	261.5	396.9	226.3
1989	271.5	271.3	177.6	294.8	295.0	295.3	354.8	273.8	363.8	231.9
1990	283.0	281.7	190.7	304.1	304.9	298.8	363.0	297.2	346.5	237.3
1991	308.8	307.6	195.2	346.3	348.8	327.4	395.0	330.5	362.1	255.6
1992	352.2	351.4	204.4	419.5	422.6	396.2	444.0	365.2	409.4	288.4
1993	398.4	398.8	214.0	502.8	507.5	467.5	491.3	410.5	436.4	323.6
1994	448.7	449.3	222.6	595.2	603.5	531.5	538.3	449.5	469.9	360.4
1995	489.1	496.5	233.7	677.7	688.2	597.4	583.4	503.4	497.6	394.0
1996	536.8	544.1	245.6	759.8	774.3	648.2	629.4	561.1	524.3	427.1
1997	582.9	592.2	254.2	839.4	861.9	665.2	687.1	621.4	568.8	460.3
1998	628.4	638.5	263.1	914.2	938.6	725.2	744.1	687.5	612.7	491.5
1999	673.5	684.1	270.5	988.6	1018.6	756.2	801.6	765.0	656.9	521.8
2000	730.0	738.8	277.0	1081.5	1118.4	799.3	866.5	853.0	710.8	559.2
2001	782.6	794.2	284.8	1172.3	1215.7	853.7	939.3	934.0	764.1	596.7
2002	852.3	860.1	293.1	1287.2	1337.3	928.8	1021.0	1007.8	826.0	642.0
2003	937.5	940.1	300.4	1450.7	1508.5	1041.2	1095.5	1078.3	901.2	697.9

3-5 第三产业增加值

Value Added of the Tertiary Industry

本表按当年价格计算。

Data in this table are calculated at current prices.

单位: 亿元 (100 million yuan)

行业	Sector	1997	1998	1999	2000	2001	2002
总计	**Total**	**23028.7**	**25173.5**	**27037.7**	**29904.6**	**33153.0**	**36074.9**
农、林、牧、渔服务业	Services for Farming, Forestry, Animal Husbandry and Fishery	177.3	199.6	221.9	228.5	265.1	298.5
地质勘查业水利管理业	Geological Prospecting and Water Conservancy	302.3	302.1	316.2	328.6	343.1	356.8
交通运输、仓储及邮电通信业	Transport, Storage, Post and Telecommunications	3797.2	4121.3	4460.3	5408.5	5968.3	6420.3
交通运输和仓储业	Transport and Storage	2689.6	2886.2	3058.1	3413.3	3597.9	3705.5
邮电通信业	Post and Telecommunications	1107.6	1235.1	1402.2	1995.3	2370.4	2714.8
批发和零售贸易餐饮业	Wholesale and Retail Trade and Catering Services	6159.9	6579.1	6910.3	7316.0	7918.8	8476.7
金融、保险业	Finance and Insurance	4534.6	4672.6	4847.3	5217.0	5585.9	5948.9
房地产业	Real Estate	1258.8	1452.6	1528.4	1690.4	1885.4	2098.2
社会服务业	Social Services	2177.9	2649.3	2893.7	3249.8	3855.7	4366.4
卫生体育和社会福利业	Health Care, Sports and Social Welfare	617.1	687.2	742.7	826.1	986.3	1068.4
教育、文化艺术及广播电影电视业	Education, Culture and Arts, Radio, Film and Television	1573.2	1823.9	2098.0	2391.2	2768.7	3090.5
科学研究和综合技术服务业	Scientific Research and Polytechnic Services	434.1	470.8	556.6	626.1	702.7	802.1
国家机关、政党机关和社会团体	Government Agencies, Parties Agencies and Social Organizations	1763.9	1969.1	2201.2	2347.8	2584.6	2844.5
其他行业	Others	232.4	245.9	261.2	274.5	288.4	303.8

3-6 第三产业增加值构成

Composition of Value Added of the Tertiary Industry

本表按当年价格计算。

Data in this table are calculated at current prices.

单位: % (%)

行业	Sector	1997	1998	1999	2000	2001	2002
总计	**Total**	**100.0**	**100.0**	**100.0**	**100.0**	**100.0**	**100.0**
农、林、牧、渔服务业	Services for Farming, Forestry, Animal Husbandry and Fishery	0.8	0.8	0.8	0.8	0.8	0.8
地质勘查业水利管理业	Geological Prospecting and Water Conservancy	1.3	1.2	1.2	1.1	1.0	1.0
交通运输、仓储及邮电通信业	Transport, Storage, Post and Telecommunications	16.5	16.4	16.5	18.1	18.0	17.8
交通运输和仓储业	Transport and Storage	11.7	11.5	11.3	11.4	10.9	10.3
邮电通信业	Post and Telecommunications	4.8	4.9	5.2	6.7	7.1	7.5
批发和零售贸易餐饮业	Wholesale and Retail Trade and Catering Services	26.7	26.1	25.6	24.5	23.9	23.5
金融、保险业	Finance and Insurance	19.7	18.6	17.9	17.4	16.8	16.5
房地产业	Real Estate	5.5	5.8	5.6	5.7	5.7	5.8
社会服务业	Social Services	9.4	10.5	10.7	10.9	11.6	12.1
卫生体育和社会福利业	Health Care, Sports and Social Welfare	2.7	2.7	2.7	2.8	3.0	3.0
教育、文化艺术及广播电影电视业	Education, Culture and Arts, Radio, Film and Television	6.8	7.2	7.8	8.0	8.4	8.6
科学研究和综合技术服务业	Scientific Research and Polytechnic Services	1.9	1.9	2.1	2.1	2.1	2.2
国家机关、政党机关和社会团体	Government Agencies, Parties Agencies and Social Organizations	7.7	7.8	8.1	7.9	7.8	7.9
其他行业	Others	1.0	1.0	1.0	0.9	0.9	0.8

3-7 第三产业增加值指数

Indices of Value Added of the Tertiary Industry

本表按可比价格计算。

Data in this table are calculated at comparable prices.

(上年=100) (preceding year=100)

行业	Sector	1997	1998	1999	2000	2001	2002
总计	**Total**	**109.1**	**108.3**	**107.7**	**108.1**	**108.4**	**108.7**
农、林、牧、渔服务业	Services for Farming, Forestry, Animal Husbandry and Fishery	132.5	113.4	106.3	103.0	111.7	112.0
地质勘查业水利管理业	Geological Prospecting and Water Conservancy	104.3	100.7	106.2	104.1	103.7	104.8
交通运输、仓储及邮电通信业	Transport, Storage, Post and Telecommunications	110.8	110.6	111.3	111.5	109.5	107.9
交通运输和仓储业	Transport and Storage	105.3	102.0	105.6	105.0	104.8	104.5
邮电通信业	Post and Telecommunications	123.1	127.4	120.1	120.4	117.5	112.9
批发和零售贸易餐饮业	Wholesale and Retail Trade and Catering Services	108.5	107.7	107.2	108.2	107.5	108.1
金融、保险业	Finance and Insurance	108.5	104.9	104.8	106.5	106.4	106.9
房地产业	Real Estate	104.1	107.7	105.9	107.1	111.0	109.9
社会服务业	Social Services	107.9	110.6	108.1	108.7	110.9	111.2
卫生体育和社会福利业	Health Care, Sports and Social Welfare	108.1	107.8	104.6	106.3	111.6	109.2
教育、文化艺术及广播电影电视业	Education, Culture and Arts, Radio, Film and Television	114.8	110.2	107.2	105.3	108.6	111.0
科学研究和综合技术服务业	Scientific Research and Polytechnic Services	112.1	110.8	110.5	106.9	107.4	112.1
国家机关、政党机关和社会团体	Government Agencies, Parties Agencies and Social Organizations	107.0	108.3	108.6	107.7	107.3	108.4
其他行业	Others	110.2	108.1	106.5	105.6	104.4	105.7

3-8 三次产业贡献率

Contributing Rate of the Three Industries

本表按可比价格计算。

Data in this table are calculated at comparable prices.

单位：% (%)

年份 Year	国内生产总值 Gross Domestic Product	第一产业 Primary Industry	第二产业 Secondary Industry	#工业 Industry	第三产业 Tertiary Industry
1990	100.0	41.9	41.0	39.7	17.1
1991	100.0	7.1	62.8	58.0	30.1
1992	100.0	8.4	64.5	57.6	27.2
1993	100.0	8.1	67.7	61.1	24.2
1994	100.0	6.8	70.5	65.0	22.7
1995	100.0	9.4	67.4	61.3	23.2
1996	100.0	10.0	66.4	61.7	23.6
1997	100.0	7.1	63.8	62.2	29.1
1998	100.0	7.7	62.3	56.7	30.0
1999	100.0	6.5	62.9	59.9	30.7
2000	100.0	4.8	66.0	62.6	29.2
2001	100.0	6.1	56.5	50.5	37.4
2002	100.0	5.4	59.6	52.7	35.0
2003	100.0	4.0	69.8	61.3	26.2

注：产业贡献率指各产业增加值增量与GDP增量之比。

a) Industrial contributing rate refers to the proportion of the increment of every industrial value added to the increment of GDP.

3-9 三次产业拉动率

Pulling Rate of the Three Industries

本表按可比价格计算。

Data in this table are calculated at comparable prices.

单位：% (%)

年份 Year	国内生产总值 Gross Domestic Product	第一产业 Primary Industry	第二产业 Secondary Industry	#工业 Industry	第三产业 Tertiary Industry
1990	3.8	1.6	1.6	1.5	0.7
1991	9.2	0.6	5.8	5.3	2.8
1992	14.2	1.2	9.2	8.2	3.9
1993	13.5	1.1	9.1	8.3	3.3
1994	12.6	0.9	8.9	8.2	2.9
1995	10.5	1.0	7.1	6.4	2.4
1996	9.6	1.0	6.4	5.9	2.3
1997	8.8	0.6	5.6	5.5	2.6
1998	7.8	0.6	4.9	4.4	2.3
1999	7.1	0.5	4.5	4.3	2.2
2000	8.0	0.4	5.3	5.0	2.3
2001	7.5	0.5	4.2	3.8	2.8
2002	8.3	0.5	4.9	4.4	2.9
2003	9.3	0.4	6.5	5.7	2.4

注：产业拉动率指GDP增长速度与各产业贡献率之乘积。

a) The industrial pulling rate to GDP growth refers to the growth rate of GDP multiplys the industrial contributing rate.

3-10 各地区生产总值和指数

Gross Domestic Product and Its Indices by Region

本表绝对数按当年价格计算，指数按可比价格计算。

Absolute figures in this table are calculated at current prices while indices are calculated at comparable prices.

地 区	Region	地区生产总值 (亿元) Gross Regional Product (100 million yuan)				指 数 (上年=100) Indices (preceding year=100)			
		2000	2001	2002	2003	2000	2001	2002	2003
北 京	Beijing	2478.76	2845.65	3212.71	3663.10	111.0	111.2	110.4	110.7
天 津	Tianjin	1639.36	1840.10	2051.16	2447.66	110.8	112.0	112.5	114.8
河 北	Hebei	5088.96	5577.78	6122.53	7098.56	109.5	108.7	109.6	111.6
山 西	Shanxi	1643.81	1779.97	2017.54	2456.59	107.8	108.4	111.7	113.9
内蒙古	Inner Mongolia	1401.01	1545.79	1756.29	2150.41	109.7	109.6	112.1	116.8
辽 宁	Liaoning	4669.06	5033.08	5265.66	6002.54	108.9	109.0	110.2	111.5
吉 林	Jilin	1821.19	2032.48	2246.12	2522.62	109.2	109.3	109.5	110.2
黑龙江	Heilongjiang	3253.00	3561.00	3882.16	4430.00	108.2	109.3	110.3	110.3
上 海	Shanghai	4551.15	4950.84	5408.76	6250.81	110.8	110.2	110.9	111.8
江 苏	Jiangsu	8582.73	9511.91	10631.75	12460.83	110.6	110.2	111.6	113.6
浙 江	Zhejiang	6036.34	6748.15	7796.00	9395.00	111.0	110.5	112.5	114.4
安 徽	Anhui	3038.24	3290.13	3553.56	3972.38	108.3	108.3	108.9	109.2
福 建	Fujian	3920.07	4253.68	4682.01	5232.17	109.5	109.0	110.5	111.6
江 西	Jiangxi	2003.07	2175.68	2450.48	2830.46	108.0	108.8	110.5	113.0
山 东	Shandong	8542.44	9438.31	10552.06	12435.93	110.5	110.1	111.6	113.7
河 南	Henan	5137.66	5640.11	6168.73	7048.59	109.4	109.1	109.5	110.8
湖 北	Hubei	4276.32	4662.28	4830.98	5401.71	109.3	109.1	109.1	109.4
湖 南	Hunan	3691.88	3983.00	4140.94	4638.73	109.0	109.0	109.0	109.6
广 东	Guangdong	9662.23	10647.71	11735.64	13625.87	110.8	109.6	111.4	114.3
广 西	Guangxi	2050.14	2231.19	2455.36	2735.13	107.3	108.2	110.5	110.2
海 南	Hainan	518.48	545.96	597.50	670.93	108.8	108.9	109.3	110.5
重 庆	Chongqing	1589.34	1749.77	1971.30	2250.56	108.5	109.0	110.3	111.5
四 川	Sichuan	4010.25	4421.76	4875.12	5456.32	109.0	109.2	110.6	111.8
贵 州	Guizhou	993.53	1084.90	1185.04	1356.11	108.7	108.8	109.1	110.1
云 南	Yunnan	1955.09	2074.71	2232.32	2465.29	107.1	106.5	108.2	108.6
西 藏	Tibet	117.46	138.73	161.42	184.50	109.4	112.8	112.9	112.1
陕 西	Shaanxi	1660.92	1844.27	2101.60	2398.58	109.0	109.1	109.7	110.9
甘 肃	Gansu	983.36	1072.51	1161.43	1304.60	108.7	109.4	109.4	110.1
青 海	Qinghai	263.59	300.95	341.11	390.21	109.0	112.0	112.4	112.1
宁 夏	Ningxia	265.57	298.38	329.28	385.34	109.8	110.1	110.2	112.2
新 疆	Xinjiang	1364.36	1485.48	1598.28	1877.61	108.2	108.1	108.1	110.8

3-11　各地区生产总值(2003年)

Gross Domestic Product by Region (2003)

本表绝对数按当年价格计算，指数按可比价格计算。

Absolute figures in this table are calculated at current prices while indices are calculated at comparable prices.

单位: 亿元　　(100 million yuan)

地　区	Region	地区生产总值 Gross Regional Product	第一产业 Primary Industry	第二产业 Secondary Industry	工　业 Industry	建筑业 Construction	第三产业 Tertiary Industry	农林牧渔服务业 Services for Farming, Forestry, Animal Husbandry and Fishery	地质勘查业水利管理业 Geological Prospecting and Water Conservancy
北　京	Beijing	3663.10	95.64	1311.86	1032.03	279.83	2255.60	2.66	5.95
天　津	Tianjin	2447.66	89.66	1245.29	1136.24	109.05	1112.71	2.54	13.60
河　北	Hebei	7098.56	1064.33	3657.19	3212.96	444.23	2377.04	32.23	29.28
山　西	Shanxi	2456.59	215.19	1389.33	1192.74	196.59	852.07	12.76	17.15
内蒙古	Inner Mongolia	2150.41	420.10	973.94	721.59	252.35	756.38	6.12	8.94
辽　宁	Liaoning	6002.54	615.80	2898.89	2556.82	342.07	2487.85	20.10	9.66
吉　林	Jilin	2522.62	486.90	1143.39	929.28	214.11	892.33	4.52	4.98
黑龙江	Heilongjiang	4430.00	500.80	2532.45	2248.59	283.86	1396.75	12.00	16.68
上　海	Shanghai	6250.81	90.64	3130.72	2865.85	264.87	3029.45	2.34	10.85
江　苏	Jiangsu	12460.83	1106.35	6787.11	6004.65	782.46	4567.37	56.10	33.29
浙　江	Zhejiang	9395.00	728.00	4941.00	4381.00	560.00	3726.00	8.88	13.16
安　徽	Anhui	3972.38	732.81	1780.60	1445.60	335.00	1458.97	31.00	28.23
福　建	Fujian	5232.17	692.94	2492.73	2147.00	345.73	2046.50	9.01	8.13
江　西	Jiangxi	2830.46	560.00	1227.38	849.32	378.06	1043.08	8.25	9.04
山　东	Shandong	12435.93	1480.67	6656.85	5860.63	796.22	4298.41	28.38	28.22
河　南	Henan	7048.59	1239.70	3551.94	3034.14	517.80	2256.95	41.00	38.49
湖　北	Hubei	5401.71	798.35	2580.58	2254.50	326.08	2022.78	10.29	11.56
湖　南	Hunan	4638.73	886.47	1794.21	1452.86	341.35	1958.05	15.14	14.60
广　东	Guangdong	13625.87	1093.52	7307.08	6532.98	774.10	5225.27	24.65	33.45
广　西	Guangxi	2735.13	652.28	1007.96	813.81	194.15	1074.89	7.31	4.85
海　南	Hainan	670.93	248.33	151.16	102.52	48.64	271.44	3.02	3.32
重　庆	Chongqing	2250.56	336.36	977.30	768.37	208.93	936.90	5.51	4.06
四　川	Sichuan	5456.32	1128.61	2266.06	1771.41	494.65	2061.65	19.37	16.02
贵　州	Guizhou	1356.11	298.37	579.31	457.12	122.19	478.43	5.34	3.01
云　南	Yunnan	2465.29	502.84	1069.29	872.14	197.15	893.16	12.61	6.52
西　藏	Tibet	184.50	40.62	47.99	13.77	34.22	95.89	1.51	2.54
陕　西	Shaanxi	2398.58	320.03	1133.56	834.76	298.80	944.99	14.34	5.02
甘　肃	Gansu	1304.60	236.61	607.62	449.81	157.81	460.37	6.39	12.00
青　海	Qinghai	390.21	46.15	184.26	120.77	63.49	159.80	2.32	5.72
宁　夏	Ningxia	385.34	55.50	192.00	143.31	48.69	137.84	1.99	3.72
新　疆	Xinjiang	1877.61	412.90	796.84	571.00	225.84	667.87	13.33	13.43

3-11 续表

单位: 亿元

地区	Region	交通运输仓储及邮电通信业 Transport, Storage, Post and Telecommunication Services	批发零售贸易及餐饮业 Wholesale, Retail Trade and Catering Services	金融、保险业 Finance and Insurance	房地产业 Real Estate	社会服务业 Social Services	卫生体育和社会福利业 Health Care, Sports and Social Welfare	教育、文化艺术及广播电影电视业 Education, Culture, Arts, Radio, Film and Television	科学研究和综合技术服务事业 Scientific Research and Polytechnic Services
北京	Beijing	253.80	279.69	537.32	190.55	365.40	63.10	242.66	197.73
天津	Tianjin	244.48	215.89	107.02	125.43	166.28	39.30	100.03	31.52
河北	Hebei	611.96	603.20	205.04	136.85	178.50	70.05	170.97	26.15
山西	Shanxi	203.77	173.93	88.82	37.45	67.34	34.58	88.22	10.11
内蒙古	Inner Mongolia	216.76	180.79	27.84	24.92	64.33	38.18	75.83	8.99
辽宁	Liaoning	495.67	803.21	145.38	188.49	386.12	89.50	157.38	41.35
吉林	Jilin	152.27	327.67	20.40	66.09	64.71	37.52	80.63	39.96
黑龙江	Heilongjiang	278.32	424.51	37.46	123.24	148.70	59.10	114.91	23.01
上海	Shanghai	420.53	649.11	624.74	463.93	345.46	103.44	215.95	85.50
江苏	Jiangsu	821.48	1204.61	537.77	549.50	424.97	156.97	354.10	58.79
浙江	Zhejiang	700.88	1159.25	416.97	238.50	396.49	167.64	311.08	35.27
安徽	Anhui	254.32	405.49	126.31	166.66	129.64	70.74	132.04	14.10
福建	Fujian	532.04	492.59	252.01	158.21	221.45	58.49	147.04	16.75
江西	Jiangxi	261.11	243.06	82.15	138.02	69.38	28.82	79.52	9.51
山东	Shandong	724.62	1161.55	514.54	490.88	364.06	153.81	331.09	42.90
河南	Henan	561.17	578.37	135.32	201.17	216.28	97.91	177.70	25.42
湖北	Hubei	334.59	558.52	283.37	148.95	221.02	82.12	171.66	31.08
湖南	Hunan	359.83	465.83	157.40	137.71	193.86	113.69	219.99	23.28
广东	Guangdong	1207.67	1246.24	418.57	731.57	767.02	158.02	264.50	47.21
广西	Guangxi	248.22	344.78	56.15	81.67	66.13	47.10	95.65	11.08
海南	Hainan	58.19	83.68	37.76	12.45	30.07	6.62	19.37	1.95
重庆	Chongqing	136.56	199.27	85.00	87.79	144.84	33.40	91.41	47.69
四川	Sichuan	381.25	575.13	229.25	187.36	183.23	78.25	174.53	33.65
贵州	Guizhou	93.11	101.86	41.58	38.85	41.02	28.36	55.58	4.94
云南	Yunnan	172.52	221.42	86.02	90.04	63.29	54.36	94.04	13.18
西藏	Tibet	19.21	20.41	4.69	4.35	6.77	4.34	10.64	1.46
陕西	Shaanxi	226.01	152.07	40.81	117.37	74.98	42.91	118.01	21.46
甘肃	Gansu	70.91	142.73	61.82	33.40	23.22	16.56	33.40	13.00
青海	Qinghai	32.58	28.42	16.86	5.94	10.10	6.40	17.53	2.22
宁夏	Ningxia	27.84	27.96	15.73	8.66	8.81	6.04	16.44	1.83
新疆	Xinjiang	121.24	155.60	65.43	24.67	58.18	26.04	72.80	6.11

注：人均地区生产总值，北京、天津、上海、重庆、四川5地采用户籍人口计算，其他地区采用常住人口计算。

continued

(100 million yuan)

国家机关、政党机关和社会团体 Government Agencies, Parties Agencies and Social Organizations	其 他 行 业 Others	构 成 (%) Composition (%)			指 数 (上年=100) Indices (preceding year=100)				人均地区生产总值 (元/人) Per Capita Gross Regional Product (yuan/person)
		第一产业 Primary Industry	第二产业 Secondary Industry	第三产业 Tertiary Industry	地区生产总值 Gross Regional Product	第一产业 Primary Industry	第二产业 Secondary Industry	第三产业 Tertiary Industry	
96.52	20.22	2.6	35.8	61.6	110.7	103.3	111.9	110.3	32061
59.69	6.93	3.6	50.9	45.5	114.8	106.1	118.0	111.8	26532
247.68	65.13	15.0	51.5	33.5	111.6	106.1	114.3	110.0	10513
113.85	4.09	8.8	56.6	34.7	113.9	106.9	116.0	112.8	7435
85.46	18.22	19.5	45.3	35.2	116.8	105.9	127.9	111.2	8975
150.99		10.3	48.3	41.4	111.5	107.2	112.3	111.7	14258
73.69	19.89	19.3	45.3	35.4	110.2	105.9	114.3	107.7	9338
118.80	40.02	11.3	57.2	31.5	110.3	102.4	111.9	110.1	11615
91.41	16.19	1.5	50.1	48.4	111.8	99.8	116.1	108.0	46718
315.49	54.30	8.9	54.5	36.6	113.6	99.9	117.2	111.9	16809
244.62	33.26	7.7	52.6	39.7	114.4	103.6	116.7	113.8	20147
93.44	7.00	18.5	44.8	36.7	109.2	97.8	112.6	111.4	6455
139.51	11.27	13.3	47.6	39.1	111.6	103.3	116.0	109.6	14979
111.20	3.02	19.8	43.4	36.8	113.0	102.7	124.3	107.4	6678
375.58	82.78	11.9	53.5	34.6	113.7	105.6	117.0	112.0	13661
208.41	16.71	17.6	50.4	32.0	110.8	97.5	117.0	109.9	7570
165.90	3.72	14.8	47.8	37.4	109.4	105.8	110.2	109.7	9011
228.04	28.68	19.1	38.7	42.2	109.6	103.6	112.4	109.7	7554
263.16	63.19	8.0	53.6	38.4	114.3	102.3	120.0	109.5	17213
97.30	14.65	23.8	36.9	39.3	110.2	104.0	114.6	109.9	5969
14.58	0.43	37.0	22.5	40.5	110.5	109.0	119.0	107.7	8316
101.37		15.0	43.4	41.6	111.5	104.2	116.0	109.4	7209
170.25	13.36	20.7	41.5	37.8	111.8	105.5	116.5	110.1	6418
58.46	6.32	22.0	42.7	35.3	110.1	104.6	113.3	110.2	3603
72.11	7.05	20.4	43.4	36.2	108.6	105.5	110.5	108.3	5662
19.97		22.0	26.0	52.0	112.1	103.4	134.7	106.9	6871
96.38	35.63	13.3	47.3	39.4	110.9	105.1	114.8	108.5	6480
35.59	11.35	18.1	46.6	35.3	110.1	105.4	112.2	109.8	5022
29.33	2.38	11.8	47.2	41.0	112.1	103.8	116.4	109.7	7277
14.32	4.50	14.4	49.8	35.8	112.2	102.4	118.8	108.4	6691
103.48	7.56	22.0	42.4	35.6	110.8	108.2	112.1	110.5	9700

(a) Per capita gross regional products of Beijing, Tianjin, Shanghai, Chongqing, and Sichuan are calculated by the population of permanent registered residence, others by de facto population.

3-12 各地区生产总值项目结构(2003年)

Structure of Gross Domestic Product by Region (2003)

本表按当年价格计算。

Data in this table are calculated at current prices.

单位:亿元 (100 million yuan)

地区	Region	地区生产总值 Gross Regional Product	劳动者报酬 Compensation of Employees	固定资产折旧 Depreciation of Fixed Assets	生产税净额 Net Taxes on Production	营业盈余 Operating Surplus
北京	Beijing	3663.10	1508.87	573.08	442.35	1138.80
天津	Tianjin	2447.66	1052.94	440.20	410.51	544.01
河北	Hebei	7098.56	3423.30	1012.98	682.68	1979.60
山西	Shanxi	2456.59	1051.25	373.38	382.64	649.32
内蒙古	Inner Mongolia	2150.41	1329.94	274.71	176.75	369.01
辽宁	Liaoning	6002.54	2669.34	1088.27	797.23	1447.70
吉林	Jilin	2522.62	1628.07	419.98	185.48	289.09
黑龙江	Heilongjiang	4430.00	2083.32	708.91	635.52	1002.25
上海	Shanghai	6250.81	2174.62	941.10	1587.79	1547.30
江苏	Jiangsu	12460.83	6093.45	1907.20	1592.07	2868.11
浙江	Zhejiang	9395.00	4375.29	1152.81	1399.18	2467.72
安徽	Anhui	3972.38	2078.52	555.46	557.21	781.19
福建	Fujian	5232.17	2537.00	745.23	550.16	1399.78
江西	Jiangxi	2830.46	1561.17	569.71	377.01	322.57
山东	Shandong	12435.93	5943.47	2701.85	1831.57	1959.04
河南	Henan	7048.59	4185.51	984.51	906.24	972.33
湖北	Hubei	5401.71	2918.08	890.28	930.84	662.51
湖南	Hunan	4638.73	2803.70	717.99	596.35	520.69
广东	Guangdong	13625.87	6130.77	2073.56	2255.77	3165.77
广西	Guangxi	2735.13	1706.99	339.38	334.79	353.97
海南	Hainan	670.93	382.03	108.37	76.90	103.63
重庆	Chongqing	2250.56	1174.44	279.55	317.96	478.61
四川	Sichuan	5456.32	3082.20	920.20	644.83	809.09
贵州	Guizhou	1356.11	750.33	172.53	212.72	220.53
云南	Yunnan	2465.29	1141.51	385.56	546.98	391.24
西藏	Tibet	184.50	112.51	36.31	9.97	25.71
陕西	Shaanxi	2398.58	1300.86	438.28	389.63	269.81
甘肃	Gansu	1304.60	639.55	274.10	209.12	181.83
青海	Qinghai	390.21	228.64	68.39	43.66	49.52
宁夏	Ningxia	385.34	219.71	79.82	48.73	37.08
新疆	Xinjiang	1877.61	973.31	317.77	229.78	356.75

3-13 支出法国内生产总值

Gross Domestic Product by Expenditure Approach

本表按当年价格计算。

Data in value terms in this table are calculated at current prices.

年 份 Year	支出法国内生产总值（亿元） Gross Domestic Product by Expenditure Approach (100 million yuan)				资本形成率（投资率）(%) Capital Formation Rate (%)	最终消费率（消费率）(%) Final Consumption Rate (%)
		最终消费 Final Consumption Expenditure	资本形成总额 Gross Capital Formation	货物和服务净出口 Net Export of Goods and Services		
1978	3605.6	2239.1	1377.9	-11.4	38.2	62.1
1979	4074.0	2619.4	1474.2	-19.6	36.2	64.3
1980	4551.3	2976.1	1590.0	-14.8	34.9	65.4
1981	4901.4	3309.1	1581.0	11.3	32.3	67.5
1982	5489.2	3637.9	1760.2	91.1	32.1	66.3
1983	6076.3	4020.5	2005.0	50.8	33.0	66.2
1984	7164.4	4694.5	2468.6	1.3	34.5	65.5
1985	8792.1	5773.0	3386.0	-366.9	38.5	65.7
1986	10132.8	6542.0	3846.0	-255.2	38.0	64.6
1987	11784.7	7451.2	4322.0	11.5	36.7	63.2
1988	14704.0	9360.1	5495.0	-151.1	37.4	63.7
1989	16466.0	10556.5	6095.0	-185.5	37.0	64.1
1990	18319.5	11365.2	6444.0	510.3	35.2	62.0
1991	21280.4	13145.9	7517.0	617.5	35.3	61.8
1992	25863.7	15952.1	9636.0	275.6	37.3	61.7
1993	34500.7	20182.1	14998.0	-679.4	43.5	58.5
1994	46690.7	26796.0	19260.6	634.1	41.3	57.4
1995	58510.5	33635.0	23877.0	998.5	40.8	57.5
1996	68330.4	40003.9	26867.2	1459.3	39.3	58.5
1997	74894.2	43579.4	28457.6	2857.2	38.0	58.2
1998	79003.3	46405.9	29545.9	3051.5	37.4	58.7
1999	82673.1	49722.7	30701.6	2248.8	37.1	60.1
2000	89340.9	54600.9	32499.8	2240.2	36.4	61.1
2001	98592.9	58927.4	37460.8	2204.7	38.0	59.8
2002	107897.6	62798.5	42304.9	2794.2	39.2	58.2
2003	121511.4	67442.5	51382.7	2686.2	42.3	55.5

注：支出法国内生产总值不等于国内生产总值是由于计算误差的影响。

a)The gross domestic production by expenditure approach is not equal to gross domestic product due to statistical discrepancies.

3-14 支出法国内生产总值结构

Structure of Gross Domestic Product by Expenditure Approach

本表按当年价格计算。

Data in value terms in this table are calculated at current prices.

年份 Year	最终消费 Final Consumption Expenditure								资本形成总额 Gross Capital Formation			
	绝对数（亿元） Absolute Figure (100 million yuan)				构成 Composition				绝对数（亿元） Absolute Figure (100million yuan)		构成（资本形成总额=100） Composition (Gross Capital Formation=100)	
					最终消费=100 Final Consumption Expenditure=100		居民消费=100 Household Consumption=100					
	居民消费 House-hold Consumption Expenditure	农村居民 Rural Households	城镇居民 Urban Households	政府消费 Government Consumption Expenditure	居民消费 Household Consumption Expenditure	政府消费 Government Consumption Expenditure	农村居民 Rural Households	城镇居民 Urban Households	固定资本形成总额 Gross Fixed Capital Formation	存货增加 Changes in Inventories	固定资本形成总额 Gross Fixed Capital Formation	存货增加 Changes in Inventories
1978	1759.1	1092.4	666.7	480.0	78.6	21.4	62.1	37.9	1073.9	304.0	77.9	22.1
1979	2005.4	1259.7	745.7	614.0	76.6	23.4	62.8	37.2	1151.2	323.0	78.1	21.9
1980	2317.1	1427.3	889.8	659.0	77.9	22.1	61.6	38.4	1318.0	272.0	82.9	17.1
1981	2604.1	1630.8	973.3	705.0	78.7	21.3	62.6	37.4	1253.0	328.0	79.3	20.7
1982	2867.9	1826.5	1041.4	770.0	78.8	21.2	63.7	36.3	1493.2	267.0	84.8	15.2
1983	3182.5	2063.4	1119.1	838.0	79.2	20.8	64.8	35.2	1709.0	296.0	85.2	14.8
1984	3674.5	2385.7	1288.8	1020.0	78.3	21.7	64.9	35.1	2125.6	343.0	86.1	13.9
1985	4589.0	2921.5	1667.5	1184.0	79.5	20.5	63.7	36.3	2641.0	745.0	78.0	22.0
1986	5175.0	3210.0	1965.0	1367.0	79.1	20.9	62.0	38.0	3098.0	748.0	80.6	19.4
1987	5961.2	3630.1	2331.1	1490.0	80.0	20.0	60.9	39.1	3742.0	580.0	86.6	13.4
1988	7633.1	4473.2	3159.9	1727.0	81.5	18.5	58.6	41.4	4624.0	871.0	84.1	15.9
1989	8523.5	4919.8	3603.7	2033.0	80.7	19.3	57.7	42.3	4339.0	1756.0	71.2	28.8
1990	9113.2	5129.1	3984.1	2252.0	80.2	19.8	56.3	43.7	4732.0	1712.0	73.4	26.6
1991	10315.9	5639.8	4676.1	2830.0	78.5	21.5	54.7	45.3	5940.0	1577.0	79.0	21.0
1992	12459.8	6571.6	5888.2	3492.3	78.1	21.9	52.7	47.3	8317.0	1319.0	86.3	13.7
1993	15682.4	7867.2	7815.2	4499.7	77.7	22.3	50.2	49.8	12980.0	2018.0	86.5	13.5
1994	20809.8	10308.3	10501.5	5986.2	77.7	22.3	49.5	50.5	16856.3	2404.3	87.5	12.5
1995	26944.5	13247.1	13697.4	6690.5	80.1	19.9	49.2	50.8	20300.5	3576.5	85.0	15.0
1996	32152.3	16398.0	15754.3	7851.6	80.4	19.6	51.0	49.0	23336.1	3531.1	86.9	13.1
1997	34854.6	17436.8	17417.8	8724.8	80.0	20.0	50.0	50.0	25154.2	3303.4	88.4	11.6
1998	36921.1	17667.2	19253.9	9484.8	79.6	20.4	47.9	52.1	27630.8	1915.1	93.5	6.5
1999	39334.4	18147.6	21186.8	10388.3	79.1	20.9	46.1	53.9	29475.5	1226.1	96.0	4.0
2000	42895.6	19196.9	23698.7	11705.3	78.6	21.4	44.8	55.2	32623.8	-124.0	100.4	-0.4
2001	45898.1	20307.4	25590.7	13029.3	77.9	22.1	44.2	55.8	36813.3	647.5	98.3	1.7
2002	48881.6	21265.7	27615.9	13916.9	77.8	22.2	43.5	56.5	41918.3	386.6	99.1	0.9
2003	52678.5	21819.3	30859.2	14764.0	78.1	21.9	41.4	58.6	51248.3	134.4	99.7	0.3

3-15 支出法地区生产总值（2003年）

Gross Regional Product by Expenditure Approach (2003)

本表按当年价格计算。

Data in value terms in this table are calculated at current prices.

地　区	Region	支出法地区生产总值（亿元） Gross Regional Product by Expenditure Approach (100 million yuan)	最终消费 Final Consumption Expenditure	资本形成总额 Gross Capital Formation	货物和服务净流出 Net Outflow of Goods and Services	资本形成率（投资率）(%) Capital Formation Rate (%)	最终消费率（消费率）(%) Final Consumption Rate (%)
北　京	Beijing	3663.10	1967.87	2293.93	-598.70	62.6	53.7
天　津	Tianjin	2447.66	1134.69	1320.47	-7.50	53.9	46.4
河　北	Hebei	7098.56	3259.52	3128.80	710.24	44.1	45.9
山　西	Shanxi	2516.38	1374.17	1230.34	-88.13	48.9	54.6
内蒙古	Inner Mongolia	2171.47	1218.20	1299.27	-346.00	59.8	56.1
辽　宁	Liaoning	6002.54	3102.51	2333.67	566.36	38.9	51.7
吉　林	Jilin	2598.74	1678.60	1102.87	-182.73	42.4	64.6
黑龙江	Heilongjiang	4233.15	2465.29	1307.86	460.00	30.9	58.2
上　海	Shanghai	6250.81	2769.74	2957.20	523.87	47.3	44.3
江　苏	Jiangsu	12460.83	5484.04	6182.38	794.41	49.6	44.0
浙　江	Zhejiang	9395.00	4368.50	4639.06	387.44	49.4	46.5
安　徽	Anhui	3973.02	2520.31	1455.21	-2.50	36.6	63.4
福　建	Fujian	5161.95	2682.76	2396.91	82.28	46.4	52.0
江　西	Jiangxi	2838.40	1515.64	1354.99	-32.23	47.7	53.4
山　东	Shandong	12435.93	5787.76	5788.53	859.64	46.5	46.5
河　南	Henan	7048.59	3975.53	2874.67	198.39	40.8	56.4
湖　北	Hubei	5377.30	3042.34	2141.90	193.06	39.8	56.6
湖　南	Hunan	4638.73	2886.03	1738.27	14.43	37.5	62.2
广　东	Guangdong	13625.87	7566.13	5259.48	800.26	38.6	55.5
广　西	Guangxi	2735.13	1850.81	1030.40	-146.08	37.7	67.7
海　南	Hainan	671.43	355.22	315.66	0.55	47.0	52.9
重　庆	Chongqing	2327.08	1415.31	1314.20	-402.43	56.5	60.8
四　川	Sichuan	5456.32	3155.90	2295.26	5.16	42.1	57.8
贵　州	Guizhou	1356.11	942.97	759.63	-346.49	56.0	69.5
云　南	Yunnan	2465.29	1597.60	1147.12	-279.43	46.5	64.8
西　藏	Tibet	184.50	168.06	104.58	-88.14	56.7	91.1
陕　西	Shaanxi	2398.58	1188.41	1447.73	-237.56	60.4	49.5
甘　肃	Gansu	1304.60	750.45	610.83	-56.68	46.8	57.5
青　海	Qinghai	389.76	250.98	294.25	-155.47	75.5	64.4
宁　夏	Ningxia	385.34	277.05	320.43	-212.14	83.2	71.9
新　疆	Xinjiang	1877.60	1037.59	1119.21	-279.20	59.6	55.3

3-16 各地区资本形成总额及构成(2003年)

Gross Capital Formation and Its Composition by Region (2003)

本表按当年价格计算。

Data in value terms in this table are calculated at current prices.

地区	Region	资本形成总额（亿元）Gross Capital Formation (100 million yuan)	固定资本形成总额 Gross Fixed Capital Formation	存货增加 Changes in Inventories	构成(资本形成总额=100) Composition (Total=100) 固定资本形成总额 Gross Fixed Capital Formation	存货增加 Changes in Inventories
北京	Beijing	2293.93	2211.56	82.37	96.4	3.6
天津	Tianjin	1320.47	1180.54	139.93	89.4	10.6
河北	Hebei	3128.80	2654.03	474.77	84.8	15.2
山西	Shanxi	1230.34	1113.18	117.16	90.5	9.5
内蒙古	Inner Mongolia	1299.27	1209.46	89.81	93.1	6.9
辽宁	Liaoning	2333.67	2102.10	231.57	90.1	9.9
吉林	Jilin	1102.87	998.10	104.77	90.5	9.5
黑龙江	Heilongjiang	1307.86	1267.10	40.76	96.9	3.1
上海	Shanghai	2957.20	2648.40	308.80	89.6	10.4
江苏	Jiangsu	6182.38	5480.80	701.58	88.7	11.3
浙江	Zhejiang	4639.06	4455.21	183.85	96.0	4.0
安徽	Anhui	1455.21	1362.18	93.03	93.6	6.4
福建	Fujian	2396.91	1752.48	644.43	73.1	26.9
江西	Jiangxi	1354.99	1303.23	51.76	96.2	3.8
山东	Shandong	5788.53	5275.17	513.36	91.1	8.9
河南	Henan	2874.67	2466.51	408.16	85.8	14.2
湖北	Hubei	2141.90	1875.78	266.12	87.6	12.4
湖南	Hunan	1738.27	1613.12	125.15	92.8	7.2
广东	Guangdong	5259.48	4934.87	324.61	93.8	6.2
广西	Guangxi	1030.40	990.71	39.69	96.1	3.9
海南	Hainan	315.66	262.97	52.69	83.3	16.7
重庆	Chongqing	1314.20	1244.83	69.37	94.7	5.3
四川	Sichuan	2295.26	2174.76	120.50	94.8	5.2
贵州	Guizhou	759.63	774.73	-15.10	102.0	-2.0
云南	Yunnan	1147.12	1031.39	115.73	89.9	10.1
西藏	Tibet	104.58	100.97	3.61	96.5	3.5
陕西	Shaanxi	1447.73	1390.28	57.45	96.0	4.0
甘肃	Gansu	610.83	530.68	80.15	86.9	13.1
青海	Qinghai	294.25	290.49	3.76	98.7	1.3
宁夏	Ningxia	320.43	318.21	2.22	99.3	0.7
新疆	Xinjiang	1119.21	1079.24	39.97	96.4	3.6

3-17 各地区最终消费及构成(2003年)

Final Consumption Expenditure and Its Composition by Region (2003)

本表按当年价格计算。

Data in value terms in this table are calculated at current prices.

地 区	Region	最终消费(亿元) Final Consumption Expenditure (100 million yuan)	居民消费 Household Consumption	农村居民 Rural Households	城镇居民 Urban Households	政府消费 Government Consumption	最终消费=100 Final Consumption Expenditure=100: 居民消费 Household Consumption	政府消费 Government Consumption	居民消费=100 Household Consumption Expenditure=100: 农村居民 Rural Households	城镇居民 Urban Households
北 京	Beijing	1967.87	1209.27	163.18	1046.09	758.60	61.5	38.5	13.5	86.5
天 津	Tianjin	1134.69	722.86	162.93	559.93	411.83	63.7	36.3	22.5	77.5
河 北	Hebei	3259.52	2331.08	1182.85	1148.23	928.44	71.5	28.5	50.7	49.3
山 西	Shanxi	1374.17	969.27	312.14	657.13	404.90	70.5	29.5	32.2	67.8
内蒙古	Inner Mongolia	1218.20	896.64	251.25	645.39	321.56	73.6	26.4	28.0	72.0
辽 宁	Liaoning	3102.51	2172.06	487.16	1684.90	930.45	70.0	30.0	22.4	77.6
吉 林	Jilin	1678.60	1231.20	284.20	947.00	447.40	73.3	26.7	23.1	76.9
黑龙江	Heilongjiang	2465.29	1771.63	405.63	1365.98	693.66	71.9	28.1	22.9	77.1
上 海	Shanghai	2769.74	2122.90	250.66	1872.24	646.84	76.6	23.4	11.8	88.2
江 苏	Jiangsu	5484.04	3909.55	1440.63	2468.92	1574.49	71.3	28.7	36.8	63.2
浙 江	Zhejiang	4368.50	3008.27	1622.25	1386.02	1360.23	68.9	31.1	53.9	46.1
安 徽	Anhui	2520.31	2038.10	1086.61	951.50	482.21	80.9	19.1	53.3	46.7
福 建	Fujian	2682.76	1859.60	1186.19	673.41	823.16	69.3	30.7	63.8	36.2
江 西	Jiangxi	1515.64	1161.01	628.50	532.51	354.63	76.6	23.4	54.1	45.9
山 东	Shandong	5787.76	3992.22	1873.07	2119.15	1795.54	69.0	31.0	46.9	53.1
河 南	Henan	3975.53	2913.36	1298.20	1615.16	1062.17	73.3	26.7	44.6	55.4
湖 北	Hubei	3042.34	2388.96	927.31	1461.65	653.38	78.5	21.5	38.8	61.2
湖 南	Hunan	2886.03	2016.88	1067.23	949.65	869.15	69.9	30.1	52.9	47.1
广 东	Guangdong	7566.13	4900.01	1416.37	3483.64	2666.12	64.8	35.2	28.9	71.1
广 西	Guangxi	1850.81	1244.70	663.06	581.64	606.11	67.3	32.7	53.3	46.7
海 南	Hainan	355.22	264.27	141.32	122.95	90.95	74.4	25.6	53.5	46.5
重 庆	Chongqing	1415.31	1004.38	381.26	623.12	410.93	71.0	29.0	38.0	62.0
四 川	Sichuan	3155.90	2413.60	1303.26	1110.34	742.30	76.5	23.5	54.0	46.0
贵 州	Guizhou	942.97	665.97	388.68	277.29	277.00	70.6	29.4	58.4	41.6
云 南	Yunnan	1597.60	1086.23	664.71	421.52	511.37	68.0	32.0	61.2	38.8
西 藏	Tibet	168.06	75.85	27.40	48.45	92.21	45.1	54.9	36.1	63.9
陕 西	Shaanxi	1188.41	943.19	389.34	553.85	245.22	79.4	20.6	41.3	58.7
甘 肃	Gansu	750.45	564.06	244.86	319.20	186.39	75.2	24.8	43.4	56.6
青 海	Qinghai	250.98	155.23	57.47	97.76	95.75	61.8	38.2	37.0	63.0
宁 夏	Ningxia	277.05	168.55	66.48	102.07	108.50	60.8	39.2	39.4	60.6
新 疆	Xinjiang	1037.59	617.26	202.68	414.58	420.33	59.5	40.5	32.8	67.2

3-18 居民消费水平

Household Consumption

本表绝对数按当年价格计算，指数按可比价格计算。

Absolute figures in this table are calculated at current prices, while indices are calculated at comparable prices.

地区 年份	Region Year	绝对数(元) Value (yuan) 全国居民 All Households	农村居民 Rural Households	城镇居民 Urban Households	城乡消费水平对比(农村居民=1) Urban/Rural Consumption Ratio (Urban Households=1)	指数(上年=100) Index(Preceding year=100) 全国居民 All Households	农村居民 Rural Households	城镇居民 Urban Households	指数(1978=100) Index (1978=100) 全国居民 All Households	农村居民 Rural Households	城镇居民 Urban Households
	1978	184	138	405	2.9	104.1	104.3	103.3	100.0	100.0	100.0
	1980	236	178	496	2.8	108.7	108.8	106.3	115.8	115.5	111.9
	1985	437	347	802	2.3	113.1	114.1	108.2	181.3	194.4	147.5
	1989	762	553	1568	2.8	99.5	99.2	98.4	213.8	218.8	184.4
	1990	803	571	1686	3.0	103.4	100.3	107.5	221.0	219.5	198.1
	1995	2236	1434	4874	3.4	107.5	108.2	104.6	327.7	308.7	289.6
	1996	2641	1768	5430	3.1	109.1	114.0	102.5	357.5	351.9	296.7
	1997	2834	1876	5796	3.1	104.2	103.3	103.5	372.4	363.6	307.0
	1998	2972	1895	6217	3.3	105.5	101.8	108.3	393.1	370.2	332.4
	1999	3138	1927	6796	3.5	107.9	104.7	111.3	424.2	387.6	370.0
	2000	3397	2037	7402	3.6	108.3	104.8	110.1	459.4	406.2	407.4
	2001	3609	2156	7761	3.6	105.3	104.5	104.4	483.7	424.5	425.3
	2002	3818	2269	8047	3.6	106.2	105.7	104.0	513.7	448.7	442.3
	2003	4089	2361	8471	3.6	106.3	102.7	104.9	546.1	460.8	464.0
北京	Beijing	10584	5041	12775	2.5	111.5	115.1	109.6			
天津	Tianjin	7836	4321	10266	2.4	108.0	106.8	107.9			
河北	Hebei	3452	2305	7082	3.1	110.7	106.6	104.8			
山西	Shanxi	2934	1535	5173	3.4	111.3	113.0	106.6			
内蒙古	Inner Mongolia	3742	1667	7263	4.4	105.6	105.1	103.6			
辽宁	Liaoning	5159	2630	7147	2.7	105.3	109.1	103.6			
吉林	Jilin	4557	2161	6830	3.2	116.2	107.0	109.4			
黑龙江	Heilongjiang	4645	2008	7614	3.8	108.0	103.6	108.1			
上海	Shanghai	15866	8141	18175	2.2	109.4	106.0	109.0			
江苏	Jiangsu	5274	3293	8126	2.5	109.9	107.2	100.9			
浙江	Zhejiang	6451	4665	11688	2.5	113.8	112.4	109.3			
安徽	Anhui	3312	2572	4933	1.9	108.0	104.7	109.8			
福建	Fujian	5324	4358	8731	2.0	108.5	106.3	111.6			
江西	Jiangxi	2739	1964	5127	2.6	102.9	104.0	99.6			
山东	Shandong	4385	2943	7740	2.6	109.1	107.5	106.7			
河南	Henan	3129	1897	6544	3.4	108.7	104.7	108.1			
湖北	Hubei	3985	2179	8402	3.9	109.7	102.4	113.3			
湖南	Hunan	3284	2227	7040	3.2	106.4	102.4	108.7			
广东	Guangdong	6190	3086	10471	3.4	109.0	102.2	96.5			
广西	Guangxi	2567	1678	6843	4.1	104.2	100.2	107.2			
海南	Hainan	3275	2400	5642	2.4	106.5	106.5	105.4			
重庆	Chongqing	3217	1599	8447	5.3	111.5	103.5	113.8			
四川	Sichuan	2839	1926	6404	3.3	108.1	107.0	106.0			
贵州	Guizhou	1770	1213	4964	4.1	103.3	102.1	104.4			
云南	Yunnan	2495	1821	5979	3.3	103.0	100.6	105.7			
西藏	Tibet	2825	1272	9112	7.2	111.8	92.4	109.2			
陕西	Shaanxi	2548	1395	6080	4.4	104.6	102.5	104.0			
甘肃	Gansu	2171	1211	5542	4.6	108.7	110.8	102.8			
青海	Qinghai	2895	1529	6102	4.0	107.2	105.0	107.6			
宁夏	Ningxia	2927	1695	5558	3.3	111.3	118.1	100.9			
新疆	Xinjiang	3237	1619	6330	3.9	101.0	103.9	99.0			

注:城乡消费水平对比，没有剔除城乡价格不可比的因素。

a)The effect of price differentials between urban and rural areas has not been removed in the calculation of the urban/rural consumption ratio.

3-19　2000年投入产出基本流量表(中间使用部分)

Intermediate Use Part of 2000 Input-Output Table

按当年生产者价格计算。

Data are calculated at producers' prices of 2000.

单位: 万元　　(10 000 yuan)

产　出 Output / 投　入 Input	农　业 Agriculture	采掘业 Mining and Quarrying	食品制造业 Foodstuff	纺织、缝纫及皮革产品制造业 Textile, Sewing Leather and Furs Products	其他制造业 Other Manufacturing
总投入合计 Total Input	**264482670**	**80837464**	**146508103**	**170892098**	**89257895**
中间投入合计 Intermediate Input	**111522265**	**34038340**	**100399413**	**125946715**	**59293735**
农　业 Agriculture	40355500	422434	59862700	14297790	4191934
采掘业 Mining and Quarrying	439177	3231715	518939	387774	996271
食品制造业 Foodstuff	15108300	20526	15770000	2431180	61861
纺织、缝纫及皮革产品制造业 Textile, Sewing, Leather and Furs Products	797955	557094	334723	72946931	6249883
其他制造业 Other Manufacturing	818887	651831	3974829	1462123	19243383
电力及蒸汽、热水生产和供应业 Production and Supply of Electric Power, Steam and Hot Water	3065830	5895331	1527740	1470560	3885102
炼焦、煤气及石油加工业 Coking, Gas and Petroleum Refining	3703100	2863437	394563	357705	582084
化学工业 Chemical Industry	24747300	3685135	4083860	14821590	7550987
建筑材料及其他非金属矿物制品业 Building Materials and Non-metal Mineral Products	509764	611922	734792	169959	579731
金属产品制造业 Metal Products	723666	2574132	947917	464741	3449912
机械设备制造业 Machinery and Equipment	4241720	6928553	1274015	2321156	2777540
建筑业 Construction	569970	150563	82608	115378	93094
运输邮电业 Transportation, Post and Telecommunications	3689724	2207226	1982753	2610251	2025888
商业饮食业 Commerce and Catering Trade	5026066	1829778	5867276	9104068	5319528
公用事业及居民服务业 Public Utilities and Resident Services	1405700	706874	1964982	1405785	1046135
金融保险业 Banking and Insurance	1522460	1023784	901546	1407194	895595
其他服务业 Other Services	4797146	678005	176170	172520	344808
增加值合计 Total Value-added	**152960405**	**46799124**	**46108690**	**44945383**	**29964160**
固定资产折旧 Depreciation of Fixed Assets	5968377	9589377	7041765	8593985	4006315
劳动者报酬 Compensation for Laborers	134431208	16610584	18150701	20351218	11742337
生产税净额 Net Taxes on Production	4150516	6777065	11616866	8570928	3379951
营业盈余 Operating Surplus	8410304	13822098	9299359	7429253	10835556

3–19 续表

单位：万元

投入 Input ＼ 产出 Output	电力及蒸汽、热水生产和供应业 Production and Supply of Electric Power, Steam and Hot Water	炼焦、煤气及石油加工业 Coking, Gas and Petroleum Refining	化学工业 Chemical Industry	建筑材料及其他非金属矿物制品业 Building Materials and Non-metal Mineral Products	金属产品制造业 Metal Products
总投入合计 Total Input	**85232150**	**83211417**	**215871883**	**62751302**	**157266045**
中间投入合计 Intermediate Input	**50622180**	**62494043**	**163668775**	**44195400**	**125877337**
农业 Agriculture	6456	342	7994920	216072	42590
采掘业 Mining and Quarrying	11167802	44976992	5744500	4032530	10850059
食品制造业 Foodstuff			2224590	59127	
纺织、缝纫及皮革产品制造业 Textile, Sewing, Leather and Furs Products	192046	115305	8013176	1071655	621704
其他制造业 Other Manufacturing	543024	247168	3928271	4398649	6415187
电力及蒸汽、热水生产和供应业 Production and Supply of Electric Power, Steam and Hot Water	5640620	2064048	19396300	4900150	15079780
炼焦、煤气及石油加工业 Coking, Gas and Petroleum Refining	11573106	6404800	7456845	2753838	8784425
化学工业 Chemical Industry	530640	1248344	81222900	4673320	3660110
建筑材料及其他非金属矿物制品业 Building Materials and Non-metal Mineral Products	273304	243572	1201500	5542450	2414982
金属产品制造业 Metal Products	352935	293547	2156161	3648620	52084702
机械设备制造业 Machinery and Equipment	9882520	2035874	4872407	3205812	7301837
建筑业 Construction	172100	61824	183998	57951	136175
运输邮电业 Transportation, Post and Telecommunications	2655863	1635608	5297666	3396887	6854492
商业饮食业 Commerce and Catering Trade	4677723	2024022	8106910	4371929	5664359
公用事业及居民服务业 Public Utilities and Resident Services	869258	434936	2823798	670078	1788855
金融保险业 Banking and Insurance	1756350	587042	2573590	1063380	3673830
其他服务业 Other Services	328434	120621	471243	132953	504249
增加值合计 Total Value-added	**34609970**	**20717374**	**52203108**	**18555902**	**31388708**
固定资产折旧 Depreciation of Fixed Assets	10595008	3800949	9979577	3659215	6612112
劳动者报酬 Compensation for Laborers	8405425	5991479	20160948	9726873	13739275
生产税净额 Net Taxes on Production	7609706	6274443	12663820	3261846	7027359
营业盈余 Operating Surplus	7999831	4650504	9398762	1907968	4009962

continued

(10 000 yuan)

机械设备制造业 Machinery and Equipment	建筑业 Construction	运输邮电业 Trans-portation, Post and Telecommuni-cations	商业饮食业 Commerce and Catering Trade	公用事业及居民服务业 Public Utilities & Resident Services	金融保险业 Banking and Insurance	其他服务业 Other Services	中间使用合计 Total Intermediate Use
416297688	**221570467**	**105707979**	**169342750**	**110427373**	**51651590**	**144218958**	**2575527831**
316494113	**162139831**	**51245687**	**95807995**	**59819524**	**13224801**	**75268910**	**1652059065**
101903	857150	126774	9102805	546504		1712843	139838717
1992402	2136107	388500	189162	469503	17183	795726	88334343
4396	128106	483231	14369000	2116972	6252	763199	53546741
2495449	695655	555077	2225673	2058057	85554	1446164	100462100
5855303	3501516	1700366	5843087	4379128	1172750	7038734	71174236
5646931	2426690	2520127	2063585	1518666	218178	2932270	80251908
3606135	17254243	11542864	3664433	3557676	143604	1617664	86260522
37294993	6216160	1426581	3358018	3325262	95516	10190589	208131306
4514651	35053100	247507	871393	1488516	41455	1026294	55524892
60529836	31417450	526232	650553	734754	55396	1245461	161856014
161245585	21408658	17182136	13503216	11008763	1723641	9033471	279946914
409796	132635	2081578	733634	3887340	622106	4134665	13625413
8072906	15390851	4130580	5328326	6130059	1525555	12442872	85377507
14260571	14412425	2097770	14618017	4252891	847051	6980000	109460384
5040607	6592904	3845842	11503534	8649647	3959280	7668631	60376844
4320328	1656930	1617536	6974741	4615162	2474000	2243318	39306786
1102320	2859251	772985	808820	1080624	237280	3997009	18584438
99803575	**59430636**	**54462291**	**73534755**	**50607849**	**38426789**	**68950047**	**923468767**
17599117	4498838	19920752	5441584	16125731	3208592	9413798	146055093
44696374	39053239	22579368	40165853	23663282	15506897	54220863	499195924
16238911	5471364	3381509	18537801	4716820	12413825	2031553	134124281
21269173	10407195	8580662	9389516	6102016	7297475	3283833	144093468

3-20 2000年投入产出基本流量表(最终使用部分)

按当年生产者价格计算。

单位: 万元

产出 Output / 投入 Input	最终使用 Final Use				
	最终消费 Final Consumption Expenditure				
	居民最终消费 Household Consumption Expenditure			政府消费 Government Consumption Expenditure	合计 Total Consumption
	农村居民 Agricultural Households	城镇居民 Non-agricultural Households	小计 Subtotal		
总投入合计 Total Input					
中间投入合计 Intermediate Input	**197681306**	**246034170**	**443715476**	**117053000**	**560768477**
农业 Agriculture	64185461	45369909	109555370		109555370
采掘业 Mining and Quarrying	792333	418295	1210628		1210628
食品制造业 Foodstuff	40425924	47853460	88279385		88279385
纺织、缝纫及皮革产品制造业 Textile, Sewing, Leather and Furs Products	12596969	21502204	34099173		34099173
其他制造业 Other Manufacturing	4968867	9894089	14862955		14862955
电力及蒸汽、热水生产和供应业 Production and Supply of Electric Power, Steam and Hot Water	2131847	4918184	7050031		7050031
炼焦、煤气及石油加工业 Coking, Gas and Petroleum Refining	477819	2864860	3342679		3342679
化学工业 Chemical Industry	7748718	9148718	16897436		16897436
建筑材料及其他非金属矿物制品业 Building Materials and Non-metal Mineral Products	1971901	5242760	7214661		7214661
金属产品制造业 Metal Products	1705712	2044900	3750612		3750612
机械设备制造业 Machinery and Equipment	14883423	20269641	35153064		35153064
建筑业 Construction					
运输邮电业 Transportation, Post and Telecommunications	6563144	9963689	16526832		16526832
商业饮食业 Commerce and Catering Trade	11563065	23167656	34730721		34730721
公用事业及居民服务业 Public Utilities and Resident Services	14860589	15008690	29869279	12046369	41915648
金融保险业 Banking and Insurance	5712306	9047171	14759477		14759477
其他服务业 Other Services	7093228	19319945	26413174	105006631	131419805

Final Use Part of 2000 Input-Output Table

Data are calculated at producers' prices of 2000

(10 000 yuan)

最终使用 Final Use					进口 Import	其他 Other	总产出 Total Output
资本形成总额 Capital Formation			出口 Export	最终使用合计 Total of Final Use			
固定资本形成总额 Gross Fixed Capital Formation	存货增加 Changes in Inventories	资本形成总额 Subtotal					
326238000	**-1240000**	**324998000**	**231989481**	**1117755958**	**-196815422**	**2528230**	**2575527831**
7239836	3848221	11088056	5847008	126490434	-5430393	3583911	264482670
	1526456	1526456	4006230	6743314	-15957450	1717257	80837464
	-2541879	-2541879	9312852	95050357	-5811356	3722361	146508103
	-1980676	-1980676	44588472	76706969	-11301475	5024504	170892098
2188984	-1334132	854851	13063715	28781521	-12020919	1323056	89257895
				7050031		-2069788	85232150
	-1517860	-1517860	2261226	4086045	-5084281	-2050869	83211417
	902690	902690	19190633	36990759	-26909947	-2340234	215871883
	-50600	-50600	3936231	11100292	-2314497	-1559386	62751301
2165857	-1942471	223386	14507201	18481199	-20526429	-2544739	157266045
88229099	1930978	90160077	81562196	206875336	-81031306	10506744	416297688
216877094		216877094	249235	217126329	-411470	-8769804	221570467
771846	-17219	754627	7615012	24896471	-1575754	-2990245	105707979
3721585	-63507	3658077	14987157	53375955	-694552	7200963	169342750
5043700		5043700	10039062	56998410	-5215049	-1732832	110427373
			156396	14915872	-2045593	-525476	51651590
			666858	132086663	-484951	-5967192	144218958

3-21 投入产出直接消耗系数表（2000年）

产出 Output / 投入 Input	农业 Agriculture	采掘业 Mining and Quarrying	食品制造业 Foodstuff	纺织、缝纫及皮革产品制造业 Textile, Sewing Leather and Furs Products	其他制造业 Other Manufacturing
总投入合计 Total Input	**1.0000000**	**1.0000000**	**1.0000000**	**1.0000000**	**1.0000000**
中间投入合计 Intermediate Input	**0.4216619**	**0.4210713**	**0.6852823**	**0.7369955**	**0.6642968**
农业 Agriculture	0.1525828	0.0052257	0.4085965	0.0836656	0.0469643
采掘业 Mining and Quarrying	0.0016605	0.0399779	0.0035421	0.0022691	0.0111617
食品制造业 Foodstuff	0.0571240	0.0002539	0.1076391	0.0142264	0.0006931
纺织、缝纫及皮革产品制造业 Textile, Sewing, Leather and Furs Products	0.0030170	0.0068915	0.0022847	0.4268596	0.0700205
其他制造业 Other Manufacturing	0.0030962	0.0080635	0.0271304	0.0085558	0.2155931
电力及蒸汽、热水生产和供应业 Production and Supply of Electric Power, Steam and Hot Water	0.0115918	0.0729282	0.0104277	0.0086052	0.0435267
炼焦、煤气及石油加工业 Coking, Gas and Petroleum Refining	0.0140013	0.0354222	0.0026931	0.0020932	0.0065214
化学工业 Chemical Industry	0.0935687	0.0455870	0.0278746	0.0867307	0.0845974
建筑材料及其他非金属矿物制品业 Building Materials and Non-metal Mineral Products	0.0019274	0.0075698	0.0050154	0.0009945	0.0064950
金属产品制造业 Metal Products	0.0027362	0.0318433	0.0064701	0.0027195	0.0386511
机械设备制造业 Machinery and Equipment	0.0160378	0.0857097	0.0086959	0.0135826	0.0311181
建筑业 Construction	0.0021550	0.0018625	0.0005638	0.0006751	0.0010430
运输邮电业 Transportation, Post and Telecommunications	0.0139507	0.0273045	0.0135334	0.0152743	0.0226970
商业饮食业 Commerce and Catering Trade	0.0190034	0.0226353	0.0400475	0.0532738	0.0595973
公用事业及居民服务业 Public Utilities and Resident Services	0.0053149	0.0087444	0.0134121	0.0082262	0.0117204
金融保险业 Banking and Insurance	0.0057564	0.0126647	0.0061536	0.0082344	0.0100338
其他服务业 Other Services	0.0181378	0.0083873	0.0012025	0.0010095	0.0038631
增加值合计 Total Value-added	**0.5783381**	**0.5789287**	**0.3147177**	**0.2630045**	**0.3357032**
固定资产折旧 Depreciation of Fixed Assets	0.0225662	0.1186254	0.0480640	0.0502890	0.0448847
劳动者报酬 Compensation for Laborers	0.5082798	0.2054813	0.1238887	0.1190881	0.1315552
生产税净额 Net Taxes on Production	0.0156930	0.0838357	0.0792916	0.0501540	0.0378672
营业盈余 Operating Surplus	0.0317991	0.1709863	0.0634733	0.0434734	0.1213961

Direct Input Coefficient of Input-Output Table (2000)

电力及蒸汽热水生产和供应业 Production and Supply of Electric Power, Steam and Hot Water	炼焦、煤气及石油加工业 Coking, Gas and Petroleum Refining	化学工业 Chemical Industry	建筑材料及其他非金属矿物制品业 Building Materials and Non-metal Mineral Products	金属产品制造业 Metal Products	机械设备制造业 Machinery and Equipment	建筑业 Construction
1.0000000	**1.0000000**	**1.0000000**	**1.0000000**	**1.0000000**	**1.0000000**	**1.0000000**
0.5939329	**0.7510273**	**0.7581755**	**0.7042946**	**0.8004101**	**0.7602591**	**0.7317755**
0.0000757	0.0000041	0.0370355	0.0034433	0.0002708	0.0002448	0.0038685
0.1310280	0.5405147	0.0266107	0.0642621	0.0689917	0.0047860	0.0096408
0.0000000	0.0000000	0.0103051	0.0009422	0.0000000	0.0000106	0.0005782
0.0022532	0.0013857	0.0371201	0.0170778	0.0039532	0.0059944	0.0031397
0.0063711	0.0029704	0.0181972	0.0700965	0.0407919	0.0140652	0.0158032
0.0661795	0.0248049	0.0898510	0.0780884	0.0958871	0.0135646	0.0109522
0.1357833	0.0769702	0.0345429	0.0438850	0.0558571	0.0086624	0.0778725
0.0062258	0.0150021	0.3762551	0.0744737	0.0232734	0.0895873	0.0280550
0.0032066	0.0029271	0.0055658	0.0883241	0.0153560	0.0108448	0.1582029
0.0041409	0.0035277	0.0099882	0.0581441	0.3311885	0.1454004	0.1417944
0.1159483	0.0244663	0.0225708	0.0510876	0.0464298	0.3873324	0.0966223
0.0020192	0.0007430	0.0008523	0.0009235	0.0008659	0.0009844	0.0005986
0.0311603	0.0196561	0.0245408	0.0541325	0.0435853	0.0193921	0.0694626
0.0548821	0.0243239	0.0375543	0.0696707	0.0360177	0.0342557	0.0650467
0.0101987	0.0052269	0.0130809	0.0106783	0.0113747	0.0121082	0.0297553
0.0206067	0.0070548	0.0119218	0.0169459	0.0233606	0.0103780	0.0074781
0.0038534	0.0014496	0.0021830	0.0021187	0.0032063	0.0026479	0.0129045
0.4060671	**0.2489727**	**0.2418245**	**0.2957054**	**0.1995899**	**0.2397409**	**0.2682245**
0.1243076	0.0456782	0.0462292	0.0583130	0.0420441	0.0422753	0.0203043
0.0986180	0.0720031	0.0933931	0.1550067	0.0873633	0.1073664	0.1762565
0.0892821	0.0754036	0.0586636	0.0519805	0.0446845	0.0390079	0.0246936
0.0938593	0.0558878	0.0435386	0.0304052	0.0254980	0.0510913	0.0469701

3-21 续表 continued

产出 Output / 投入 Input	运输邮电业 Transportation, Post and Telecommunications	商业饮食业 Commerce and Catering Trade	公用事业及居民服务业 Public Utilities & Resident Services	金融保险业 Banking and Insurance	其他服务业 Other Services
总投入合计 Total Input	**1.0000000**	**1.0000000**	**1.0000000**	**1.0000000**	**1.0000000**
中间投入合计 Intermediate Input	**0.4847854**	**0.5657638**	**0.5417092**	**0.2560386**	**0.5219072**
农业 Agriculture	0.0011993	0.0537537	0.0049490	0.0000000	0.0118767
采掘业 Mining and Quarrying	0.0036752	0.0011170	0.0042517	0.0003327	0.0055175
食品制造业 Foodstuff	0.0045714	0.0848516	0.0191707	0.0001210	0.0052919
纺织、缝纫及皮革产品制造业 Textile, Sewing, Leather and Furs Products	0.0052510	0.0131430	0.0186372	0.0016564	0.0100276
其他制造业 Other Manufacturing	0.0160855	0.0345045	0.0396562	0.0227050	0.0488059
电力及蒸汽、热水生产和供应业 Production and Supply of Electric Power, Steam and Hot Water	0.0238405	0.0121858	0.0137526	0.0042240	0.0203321
炼焦、煤气及石油加工业 Coking, Gas and Petroleum Refining	0.1091958	0.0216391	0.0322173	0.0027803	0.0112167
化学工业 Chemical Industry	0.0134955	0.0198297	0.0301127	0.0018492	0.0706605
建筑材料及其他非金属矿物制品业 Building Materials and Non-metal Mineral Products	0.0023414	0.0051457	0.0134796	0.0008026	0.0071162
金属产品制造业 Metal Products	0.0049782	0.0038416	0.0066537	0.0010725	0.0086359
机械设备制造业 Machinery and Equipment	0.1625434	0.0797390	0.0996923	0.0333705	0.0626372
建筑业 Construction	0.0196918	0.0043322	0.0352027	0.0120443	0.0286694
运输邮电业 Transportation, Post and Telecommunications	0.0390754	0.0314647	0.0555121	0.0295355	0.0862776
商业饮食业 Commerce and Catering Trade	0.0198450	0.0863221	0.0385130	0.0163993	0.0483986
公用事业及居民服务业 Public Utilities and Resident Services	0.0363818	0.0679305	0.0783288	0.0766536	0.0531735
金融保险业 Banking and Insurance	0.0153019	0.0411871	0.0417936	0.0478978	0.0155549
其他服务业 Other Services	0.0073125	0.0047762	0.0097858	0.0045938	0.0277149
增加值合计 Total Value-added	**0.5152146**	**0.4342362**	**0.4582908**	**0.7439614**	**0.4780928**
固定资产折旧 Depreciation of Fixed Assets	0.1884508	0.0321336	0.1460302	0.0621199	0.0652743
劳动者报酬 Compensation for Laborers	0.2136014	0.2371867	0.2142882	0.3002211	0.3759621
生产税净额 Net Taxes on Production	0.0319892	0.1094691	0.0427142	0.2403377	0.0140866
营业盈余 Operating Surplus	0.0811733	0.0554468	0.0552582	0.1412827	0.0227698

3-22 投入产出完全消耗系数表（2000年）

Total Input Coefficients of Input-Output Table (2000)

产出 Output / 投入 Input	农业 Agriculture	采掘业 Mining and Quarrying	食品制造业 Foodstuff	纺织、缝纫及皮革产品制造业 Textile, Sewing Leather and Furs Products	其他制造业 Other Manufacturing
农业 Agriculture	0.2420106	0.0300494	0.5867482	0.2341326	0.1289126
采掘业 Mining and Quarrying	0.0485274	0.1254948	0.0504144	0.0603614	0.0923983
食品制造业 Foodstuff	0.0890797	0.0122568	0.1711815	0.0628715	0.0306803
纺织、缝纫及皮革产品制造业 Textile, Sewing, Leather and Furs Products	0.0302606	0.0360520	0.0346615	0.7830293	0.1902769
其他制造业 Other Manufacturing	0.0261608	0.0371748	0.0634951	0.0500977	0.3116301
电力及蒸汽、热水生产和供应业 Production and Supply of Electric Power, Steam and Hot Water	0.0537290	0.1275759	0.0581273	0.0738022	0.1238479
炼焦、煤气及石油加工业 Coking, Gas and Petroleum Refining	0.0492089	0.0893669	0.0452082	0.0523330	0.0693031
化学工业 Chemical Industry	0.2265609	0.1487559	0.1857744	0.3323647	0.2792807
建筑材料及其他非金属矿物制品业 Building Materials and Non-metal Mineral Products	0.0093293	0.0185075	0.0146121	0.0116521	0.0207129
金属产品制造业 Metal Products	0.0376867	0.1160453	0.0499609	0.0548977	0.1330570
机械设备制造业 Machinery and Equipment	0.0939608	0.2394307	0.1035982	0.1388117	0.1863279
建筑业 Construction	0.0062677	0.0064697	0.0061345	0.0068272	0.0074255
运输邮电业 Transportation, Post and Telecommunications	0.0411837	0.0617691	0.0493035	0.0635261	0.0728490
商业饮食业 Commerce and Catering Trade	0.0581102	0.0691600	0.0947439	0.1491081	0.1430776
公用事业及居民服务业 Public Utilities and Resident Services	0.0247359	0.0319087	0.0399231	0.0453046	0.0482131
金融保险业 Banking and Insurance	0.0204835	0.0326710	0.0262398	0.0374754	0.0397758
其他服务业 Other Services	0.0260533	0.0138834	0.0157544	0.0106517	0.0128838

3-22 续表

产出 Output / 投入 Input	电力及蒸汽、热水生产和供应业 Production and Supply of Electric Power, Steam and Hot Water	炼焦、煤气及石油加工业 Coking, Gas and Petroleum Refining	化学工业 Chemical Industry	建筑材料及其他非金属矿物制品业 Building Materials and Non-metal Mineral Products	金属产品制造业 Metal Products
农业 Agriculture	0.0276629	0.0277291	0.1224812	0.0547089	0.0394701
采掘业 Mining and Quarrying	0.2857317	0.6797891	0.1584287	0.1949355	0.2527605
食品制造业 Foodstuff	0.0158769	0.0132419	0.0434491	0.0252202	0.0195202
纺织、缝纫及皮革产品制造业 Textile, Sewing, Leather and Furs Products	0.0304654	0.0323630	0.1323513	0.0801777	0.0512087
其他制造业 Other Manufacturing	0.0400498	0.0355999	0.0692680	0.1387172	0.1154951
电力及蒸汽、热水生产和供应业 Production and Supply of Electric Power, Steam and Hot Water	0.1334307	0.1177658	0.2060212	0.1717881	0.2241441
炼焦、煤气及石油加工业 Coking, Gas and Petroleum Refining	0.2067569	0.1535800	0.1271914	0.1298052	0.1714146
化学工业 Chemical Industry	0.1133656	0.1374317	0.7128931	0.2458404	0.1709487
建筑材料及其他非金属矿物制品业 Building Materials and Non-metal Mineral Products	0.0167302	0.0176711	0.0211667	0.1118799	0.0393195
金属产品制造业 Metal Products	0.1020026	0.0958837	0.0897077	0.1796438	0.5893478
机械设备制造业 Machinery and Equipment	0.3261589	0.2196166	0.2002855	0.2541604	0.2863077
建筑业 Construction	0.0079455	0.0065995	0.0079780	0.0083670	0.0091597
运输邮电业 Transportation, Post and Telecommunications	0.0753424	0.0692479	0.0832282	0.1127225	0.1180838
商业饮食业 Commerce and Catering Trade	0.1138870	0.0836461	0.1255267	0.1527318	0.1273560
公用事业及居民服务业 Public Utilities and Resident Services	0.0411152	0.0342433	0.0535083	0.0504132	0.0552115
金融保险业 Banking and Insurance	0.0467851	0.0343042	0.0459886	0.0508445	0.0665902
其他服务业 Other Services	0.0113736	0.0115468	0.0119616	0.0109583	0.0135929

continued

机械设备制造业 Machinery and Equipment	建筑业 Construction	运输邮电业 Trans-portation, Post and Telecommuni-cations	商业饮食业 Commerce and Catering Trade	公用事业及居民服务业 Public Utilities & Resident Services	金融保险业 Banking and Insurance	其他服务业 Other Services
0.0460993	0.0469173	0.0282522	0.1499864	0.0517408	0.0142006	0.0553551
0.1241118	0.1682647	0.1245985	0.0622692	0.0814487	0.0250460	0.0734861
0.0220279	0.0240491	0.0178944	0.1239407	0.0403288	0.0083692	0.0259462
0.0623923	0.0506518	0.0360397	0.0556673	0.0673722	0.0188665	0.0558425
0.0814942	0.0858124	0.0516619	0.0803109	0.0877518	0.0465131	0.0974618
0.1257639	0.1146713	0.0776837	0.0594880	0.0678751	0.0244347	0.0773967
0.0971328	0.1720665	0.1669175	0.0680002	0.0882467	0.0259865	0.0694906
0.3273225	0.1877586	0.1223092	0.1382083	0.1517594	0.0451851	0.2072065
0.0362854	0.1916639	0.0182326	0.0181329	0.0334425	0.0090561	0.0245211
0.4129330	0.3256050	0.1098053	0.0770743	0.1001276	0.0379838	0.0896935
0.7860565	0.3396671	0.3717619	0.2388895	0.2856213	0.1144430	0.2295781
0.0085398	0.0096656	0.0259944	0.0125763	0.0442454	0.0181174	0.0375185
0.0895238	0.1388097	0.0796901	0.0725190	0.1014791	0.0512420	0.1313791
0.1300887	0.1541403	0.0731961	0.1463656	0.0989661	0.0419856	0.1076251
0.0572813	0.0739013	0.0653965	0.1062536	0.1166086	0.0988656	0.0892005
0.0511047	0.0456704	0.0381393	0.0679384	0.0689125	0.0623182	0.0408107
0.0122732	0.0224604	0.0137755	0.0131911	0.0174592	0.0082358	0.0356041

3-23 资金流量表(实物交易，2001年)

单位: 亿元

机构部门 交易项目	Institutional Sector Transaction	非金融企业部门 Non-financial Enterprises		金融机构部门 Financial Institutions		政府部门 Governments	
		运用 Utilization	来源 Source	运用 Utilization	来源 Source	运用 Utilization	来源 Source
1.净出口	Net Exports						
2.增加值	Value Added		56017.42		2460.70		9814.02
3.劳动者报酬	Compensation of Laborers	20005.22		883.04		9176.62	
(1)工资及工资性收入	Wages and Related Income						
(2)单位社会保险付款	Employer's Contribution of Social Securities						
4.生产税净额	Taxes on Production, Net	14940.08		782.95		63.80	17281.3
(1)生产税	Taxes on Production						
(2)生产补贴	Subsidies to Production						
5.财产收入	Income from Properties	6804.71	2607.66	4777.94	4447.70	572.18	290.64
(1)利息	Interest	4751.22	2571.81	4727.48	4392.86	572.18	290.64
(2)红利	Dividend	2053.49	12.10		54.84		
(3)土地租金	Rent on Land Use						
(4)其他	Others		23.75	50.46			
6.初次分配总收入	Total Income from Primary Distribution		16875.07		464.47		17573.36
7.经常转移	Current Transfer	2794.76	227.76	622.96	449.54	3463.14	6221.55
(1)收入税	Taxes on Income	1952.51		173.42			3122.12
(2)社会保险缴款	Payment to Social Security						3088.00
(3)社会保险福利	Social Security Welfare					2738.00	
(4)社会补助	Allowances	70.05				708.19	
(5)其他	Others	772.20	227.76	449.54	449.54	16.95	11.43
8.可支配总收入	Total Disposable Income		14308.07		291.05		20331.77
9.最终消费	Final Consumption Expenditure					13029.30	
(1)居民消费	Household Consumption						
(2)政府消费	Government Consumption					13029.30	
10.总储蓄	Savings		14308.07		291.05		7302.47
11.资本转移	Capital Transfer		6053.83		2.00	6055.83	
(1)投资性补助	Investment Allowances						
(2)其他	Other						
12.资本形成总额	Gross Capital Formation	28064.38		169.17		3666.58	
(1)固定资本形成总额	Gross Fixed Capital Formation	27247.98		169.17		3666.58	
(2)存货增加	Changes in Inventories	816.40					
13.其他非金融资产获得减处置	Minus Items from Other Non-financial Capital						
14.净金融投资	Net Financial Investment	-7702.48		123.88		-2419.94	
15.统计误差	Statistical Discrepancy	1977.48		-2505.75		1351.34	

3-24 资金流量表(金融交易，2001年)

单位: 亿元

机构部门 交易项目	Institutional Sector Transaction	非金融企业部门 Non-financial Enterprises		金融机构部门 Financial Institutions		政府部门 Governments	
		运用 Utilization	来源 Source	运用 Utilization	来源 Source	运用 Utilization	来源 Source
净金融投资	Net Financial Investment	-5725.00		-2381.87		-1068.60	
资金运用合计	Total Utilization	8077.03		21559.05		1999.61	
资金来源合计	Total Sources		13802.03		23940.92		3068.21
通货	Currency in Circulation	93.25		0.01	1036.15	20.72	
存款	Savings Deposits	7096.34		215.17	19135.64	2024.82	
贷款	Loans	-5.40	9413.60	11772.07	-133.14		123.57
证券	Securities		1398.94	2796.22	1151.20	-22.86	2598.00
保险准备金	Reserves for Insurance Business	63.95			938.27		281.62
结算资金	Settlement Funds	316.63			281.91		
金融机构往来	Flow Between Financial Institutions			-1312.67	-952.63		
准备金	Reserve Funds			2082.65	1983.01		
库存现金	Cash			-52.13	-102.97		
中央银行贷款	Loans from the Central Bank			288.24	305.45		
其他（净）	Other(net)	806.49			350.88	-23.07	
直接投资	Foreign Investment	569.89	3661.76				
其他对外债权债务	Other Claims or Liabilities on Abroad	-864.12	-222.12	1852.48	-52.85		65.03
国际储备资产	Assets in International Serves			3917.01			
国际收支错误与遗漏	Errors and Omission of Balance of Payment		-450.16				

Flow of Funds Table (Physical Transaction, 2001)

(100 million yuan)

住户部门 Households		国内合计 Total of Domestic Sectors		国外部门 Rest of the World		合 计 Total	
运 用 Utilization	来 源 Source	运 用 Utilization	来 源 Source	运 用 Utilization	来 源 Source	运 用 Utilization	来 源 Source
					-2204.70		-2204.70
	29022.66		97314.80				97314.80
26898.42	56917.43	56963.30	56917.43	24.62	70.49	56987.92	56987.92
1494.47		17281.30	17281.30			17281.3	17281.30
81.00	3347.83	12235.83	10693.83	752.55	2294.42	12988.38	12988.25
81.00	3101.76	10131.88	10357.07	740.46	515.13	10872.34	10872.20
	219.36	2053.49	286.30	12.09	1779.29	2065.58	2065.59
	26.71	50.46	50.46			50.46	50.46
	60814.03		95726.93				95726.93
4119.61	4804.79	11000.47	11703.64	755.53	52.36	11756.00	11756.00
996.19		3122.12	3122.12			3122.12	3122.12
3088.00		3088.00	3088.00			3088.00	3088.00
	2738.00	2738.00	2738.00			2738.00	2738.00
	778.24	778.24	778.24			778.24	778.24
35.42	1288.55	1274.11	1977.28	755.53	52.36	2029.64	2029.64
	61499.21		96430.10				96430.10
45898.10		58927.40				58927.40	
45898.10		45898.10				45898.10	
		13029.30				13029.30	
	15601.11		37502.70		-1320.13		36182.57
4.00		6059.83	6055.83		4.00	6059.83	6059.83
5560.67		37460.80				37460.80	
5729.57		36813.30				36813.30	
-168.90		647.50				647.50	
10036.44		37.90		-1316.13		-1278.23	
574.68		1397.76		-119.53		1278.23	

Flow of Funds Table (Financial Transaction, 2001)

(100 million yuan)

住户部门 Households		国内合计 Total of Domestic Sectors		国外部门 Rest of the World		合 计 Total	
运 用 Utilization	来 源 Source	运 用 Utilization	来 源 Source	运 用 Utilization	来 源 Source	运 用 Utilization	来 源 Source
10611.12		1435.66		-1435.66			
14117.90		45753.59		3038.13		48791.73	
	3506.78		44317.94		4473.79		48791.73
873.87		987.86	1036.15	48.30		1036.16	1036.15
9973.25		19309.58	19135.64	41.23	215.17	19350.81	19350.81
	3506.78	11766.67	12910.82	-123.33	-1267.47	11643.34	11643.34
1907.66		4681.02	5148.14	70.27		4751.29	5148.14
1155.93		1219.88	1219.88			1219.88	1219.88
-34.73		281.91	281.91			281.91	281.91
		-1312.67	-952.63			-1312.67	-952.63
		2082.65	1983.01			2082.65	1983.01
		-52.13	-102.97		50.84	-52.13	-52.13
		288.24	305.45			288.24	305.45
241.91		1025.33	350.88			1025.33	350.88
		569.89	3661.76	3661.76	569.89	4231.65	4231.65
		988.35	-209.94	-209.94	988.35	778.41	778.41
		3917.01			3917.01	3917.01	3917.01
			-450.16	-450.16		-450.16	-450.16

3-25 国际收支平衡表(2003年)
Balance of Payments (2003)

单位: 万美元 (USD 10 000)

项目	Item	差额 Balance	贷方 Credit	借方 Debit
一.经常项目	**Current Account**	**4587481**	**51958039**	**47370557**
A.货物和服务	Goods and Service	3607898	48500322	44892424
a.货物	Goods	4465163	43826960	39361797
b.服务	Service	-857265	4673362	5530627
1.运输	Transportation	-1032643	790641	1823283
2.旅游	Tourism	221873	1740600	1518727
3.通讯服务	Communication Service	21103	63841	42738
4.建筑服务	Construction Service	10642	128966	118324
5.保险服务	Insurance Service	-425143	31278	456422
6.金融服务	Financial Service	-8057	15196	23252
7.计算机和信息服务	Computer and Information Service	6636	110218	103581
8.专有权利使用费和特许费	Fee for Patent or Royalty	-344115	10698	354813
9.咨询	Consultation	-156459	188495	344954
10.广告、宣传	Advertisement and Publicity	2838	48626	45788
11.电影、音像	Movies and Audio-video Products	-3609	3344	6954
12.其它商业服务	Other Commercial Service	859199	1505583	646384
13. 别处未提及的政府服务	Government Service not Elsewhere Classified	-9530	35878	45408
B.收益	Income and Profit	-783836	1609469	2393305
1.职工报酬	Compensation of Staff and Workers	16236	128259	112023
2.投资收益	Profit from Investment	-800072	1481210	2281282
C.经常转移	Current Transfer	1763420	1848248	84828
1.各级政府	Governments	804	11377	10574
2.其它部门	Other Departments	1762616	1836870	74255
二.资本和金融项目	**Capital and Finance Account**	**5272594**	**21963061**	**16690467**
A.资本项目	Capital Account	-4808	0	4808
B. 金融项目	Financial Account	5277402	21963061	16685659
1. 直接投资	Direct Investments	4722899	5550712	827813
1.1 我国在外直接投资	Chinese Direct Investments Abroad	15227	200212	184984
1.2 外国在华直接投资	Foreign Direct Investments in China	4707672	5350500	642828
2. 证券投资	Securities	1142676	1230668	87993
2.1 资产	Assets	298312	300016	1704
2.1.1 股本证券	Capital Stock	0	0	0
2.1.2 债务证券	Liability Stock	298312	300016	1704
2.1.2.1 (中)长期债券	(Metaphase) Long-term Bonds	298312	300016	1704
2.1.2.2 货币市场工具	Money Market Tools	0	0	0
2.2 负债	Liabilities	844364	930652	86288
2.2.1 股本证券	Capital Stock	772900	772900	0
2.2.2 债务证券	Liability Stock	71464	157752	86288
2.2.2.1 (中)长期债券	(Metaphase) Long-term Bonds	71679	153057	81378
2.2.2.2 货币市场工具	Money Market Tools	-215	4695	4910
3. 其它投资	Other Investments	-588173	15181681	15769854
3.1 资产	Assets	-1792152	5198558	6990709
3.1.1 贸易信贷	Trade Credit	-146499	0	146499
长期	Long Term	0	0	0
短期	Short Term	-146499	0	146499
3.1.2 贷款	Loans	1392740	2170081	777341
长期	Long Term	-69300	0	69300
短期	Short Term	1462040	2170081	708041
3.1.3 货币和存款	Currencies and Deposits	-655211	66287	721498
3.1.4 其它资产	Other Assets	-2383182	2962190	5345372
长期	Long Term	-4500000	0	4500000
短期	Short Term	2116818	2962190	845372
3.2 负债	Liabilities	1203979	9983124	8779145
3.2.1 贸易信贷	Trade Credit	472030	472030	0
长期	Long Term	0	0	0
短期	Short Term	472030	472030	0
3.2.2 贷款	Loans	661431	7887434	7226004
长期	Long Term	-535588	1749928	2285516
短期	Short Term	1197019	6137507	4940488
3.2.3 货币和存款	Currencies and Deposits	74244	879506	805262
3.2.4 其它负债	Other Liabilities	-3726	744153	747879
长期	Long Term	-101580	393013	494593
短期	Short Term	97854	351140	253286
三. 储备资产	**Reserve Assets**	**-11702310**	**0**	**11702310**
3.1 货币黄金	Gold Reserves	0	0	0
3.2 特别提款权	SDR (Special Drawing Rights)	-9000	0	9000
3.3 在基金组织的储备头寸	China's Reserve in IMF (International Monetary Fund)	-8900	0	8900
3.4 外汇	Foreign Exchange	-11684410	0	11684410
3.5 其它债权	Other Creditor's rights	0	0	0
四.净误差与遗漏	**Net Error and Omission**	**1842235**	**1842235**	**0**

注: 1.本表贸易数据来自海关统计。
2.本表直接投资贷方数据来自商务部统计和间接申报中的“与土地有关的土地批租和租赁”;借方数据来自间接申报统计。
3.本表其余数据来自间接申报统计。

a) Trade data in the table are from customs statistics.
b) Credit data on direct investment in the table are from statistics and from "Approved Leasing of Land" in indirect reporting, both collected by the Ministry of Commerce, and debit data are from indirect reporting.
c) Other data in the table are from indirect reporting.

主要统计指标解释

国内生产总值(GDP) 指按市场价格计算的一个国家(或地区)所有常住单位在一定时期内生产活动的最终成果。国内生产总值有三种表现形态，即价值形态、收入形态和产品形态。从价值形态看，它是所有常住单位在一定时期内生产的全部货物和服务价值超过同期投入的全部非固定资产货物和服务价值的差额，即所有常住单位的增加值之和；从收入形态看，它是所有常住单位在一定时期内创造并分配给常住单位和非常住单位的初次收入之和；从产品形态看，它是所有常住单位在一定时期内最终使用的货物和服务价值减去货物和服务进口价值。在实际核算中，国内生产总值有三种计算方法，即生产法、收入法和支出法。三种方法分别从不同的方面反映国内生产总值及其构成。

国民总收入(GNI) 即国民生产总值，指一个国家(或地区)所有常住单位在一定时期内收入初次分配的最终结果。一国常住单位从事生产活动所创造的增加值在初次分配中主要分配给该国的常住单位，但也有一部分以生产税及进口税(扣除生产和进口补贴)、劳动者报酬和财产收入等形式分配给非常住单位；同时，国外生产所创造的增加值也有一部分以生产税及进口税(扣除生产和进口补贴)、劳动者报酬和财产收入等形式分配给该国的常住单位，从而产生了国民总收入的概念。它等于国内生产总值加上来自国外的净要素收入。与国内生产总值不同，国民总收入是个收入概念，而国内生产总值是个生产概念。

三次产业 三产业的划分是世界上较为常用的产业结构分类，但各国的划分不尽一致。我国的三次产业划分是：

第一产业是指农、林、牧、渔业。

第二产业是指采矿业，制造业，电力、煤气及水的生产和供应业，建筑业。

第三产业是指除第一、二产业以外的其他行业。

劳动者报酬 指劳动者因从事生产活动所获得的全部报酬。包括劳动者获得的各种形式的工资、奖金和津贴，既包括货币形式的，也包括实物形式的，还包括劳动者所享受的公费医疗和医药卫生费、上下班交通补贴、单位支付的社会保险费、住房公积金等。对于个体经济来说，其所有者所获得的劳动报酬和经营利润不易区分，这两部分统一作为劳动者报酬处理。

生产税净额 指生产税减生产补贴后的余额。生产税指政府对生产单位从事生产、销售和经营活动以及因从事生产活动使用某些生产要素(如固定资产、土地、劳动力)所征收的各种税、附加费和规费。生产补贴与生产税相反，指政府对生产单位的单方面转移支出，因此视为负生产税，包括政策亏损补贴、价格补贴等。

固定资产折旧 指一定时期内为弥补固定资产损耗按照规定的固定资产折旧率提取的固定资产折旧，或按国民经济核算统一规定的折旧率虚拟计算的固定资产折旧。它反映了固定资产在当期生产中的转移价值。各类企业和企业化管理的事业单位的固定资产折旧是指实际计提的折旧费；不计提折旧的政府机关、非企业化管理的事业单位和居民住房的固定资产折旧是按照统一规定的折旧率和固定资产原值计算的虚拟折旧。原则上，固定资产折旧应按固定资产的重置价值计算，但是目前我国尚不具备对全社会固定资产进行重估价的基础，所以暂时只能采用上述办法。

营业盈余 指常住单位创造的增加值扣除劳动者报酬、生产税净额和固定资产折旧后的余额。它相当于企业的营业利润加上生产补贴，但要扣除从利润中开支的工资和福利等。

支出法国内生产总值 是从最终使用的角度反映一个国家(或地区)一定时期内生产活动最终成果的一种方法，包括最终消费、资本形成总额及货物和服务净出口三部分。计算公式为：

支出法国内生产总值=最终消费+资本形成总额+货物和服务净出口

最终消费 指常住单位为满足物质、文化和精神生活的需要，从本国经济领土和国外购买的货物和服务的支出。它不包括非常住单位在本国经济领土内的消费支出。最终消费分为居民消费和政府消费。

居民消费 指常住住户在一定时期内对于货物和服务的全部最终消费支出。居民消费除了直接以货币形式购买的货物和服务的消费支出外，还包括以其他方式获得的货物和服务的消费支出，即所谓的虚拟消费支出。居民虚拟消费支出包括如下几种类型：单位以实物报酬及实物转移的形式提供给劳动者的货物和服务；住户生产并由本住户消费了的货物和服务，其中的服务仅指住户的自有住房服务和付酬的家庭雇员提供的家庭和个人服务；金融机构提供的金融媒介服务；保险公司提供的保险服务。

政府消费 指政府部门为全社会提供的公共服务的消费支出和免费或以较低的价格向居民住户提供的货物和服务的净支出，前者等于政府服务的产出价值减去政府单位所获得的经营收入的价值，后者等于政府部门免费或以较低价格向居民住户提供的货物和服务的市场价值减去向住户收取的价值。

资本形成总额 指常住单位在一定时期内获得减去处置的固定资产和存货的净额，包括固定资本形成总额和存货增加两部分。

固定资本形成总额 指生产者在一定时期内获得的固定资产减处置的固定资产的价值总额。固定资产是通过生产活动生产出来的，且其使用年限在一年以上、单位价值在规定标准以上的资产，不包括自然资产。可分为有形固定资本形成总额和无形固定资本形成总额。有形固定资本形成总额包括一定时期内完成的建筑工程、安装工程和设备工器具购置(减处置)价值，以及土地改良、新增役、种、奶、毛、娱乐用牲畜和新增经济林木价值。无形固定资本形成总额包括矿藏的勘探、计算机软件等获得减处置。

存货增加 指常住单位在一定时期内存货实物量变动的市场价值，即期末价值减期初价值的差额，再扣除当期由于价格变动而产生的持有收益。存货增加可以是正值，也可以是负值，正值表示存货上升，负值表示存货下降。存货包括生产单位购进的原材料、燃料和储备物资等存货，以及生产单位生产的产成品、在制品和半成品等存货。

货物和服务净出口 指货物和服务出口减货物和服务进口的差额。出口包括常住单位向非常住单位出售或无偿转让的各种货物和服务的价值；进口包括常住单位从非常住单位购买或无偿得到的各种货物和服务的价值。由于服务活动的提供与使用同时发生，一般把常住单位从非常住单位得到的服务作为进口，非常住单位从常住单位得到的服务作为出口。货物的出口和进口都按离岸价格计算。

直接消耗系数 也称为投入系数，记为$a_{ij}(ij=1,2,...,n)$它是指在生产经营过程中第j产品(或产业)部门的单位总产出所直接消耗的第i产品部门货物或服务的价值量，将各产品(或产业)部门的直接消耗系数用表的形式表现出来，就是直接消耗系数表或直接消耗系数矩阵，通常用字母A表示。

完全消耗系数 指第j产品部门每提供一个单位最终使用时，对第i产品部门货物或服务的直接消耗和间接消耗之和。将各产品部门的完全消耗系数用表的形式表现出来，就是完全消耗系数表或完全消耗系数矩阵，通常用字母B表示。

机构单位 指有权拥有资产和承担负债，能够独立地从事经济活动并与其他实体进行交易的经济实体。

机构部门 将相同性质的机构单位归并在一起，就形成机构部门。资金流量核算将常住机构单位划分为以下四个机构部门：非金融企业部门、金融机构部门、政府部门、住户部门。与常住单位发生经济往来关系的非常住单位组成国外部门，在资金流量核算中也视同机构部门。

非金融企业与非金融企业部门 非金融企业指主要从事市场货物生产和提供非金融市场服务的常住企业，它主要包括从事上述活动的各类法人企业。所有非金融企业归并在一起，就形成非金融企业部门。

金融机构与金融机构部门 金融机构指主要从事金融媒介以及与金融媒介密切相关的辅助金融活动的常住单位，它主要包括中央银行、商业银行和政策性银行、非银行信贷机构和保险公司。所有金融机构归并在一起，就形成金融机构部门。

政府单位与政府部门 政府单位指在我国境内通过政治程序建立的、在一特定区域内对其他机构单位拥有立法、司法和行政权的法律实体及其附属单位。政府单位的主要职能是利用征税和其他方式获得的资金向社会和公众提供公共服务。通过转移支付，对社会收入和财产进行再分配。它主要包括各种行政单位和非营利性事业单位。所有政府单位归并在一起，就形成政府部门。

住户与住户部门 住户指共享同一生活设施、部分或全部收入和财产集中使用、共同消费住房、食品和其他消费品与消费服务的常住个人或个人群体。所有住户归并在一起，就形成住户部门。

非常住单位与国外部门 所有不具有常住性的机构单位都是非常住单位。将所有与我国常住单位发生交易的非常住单位归并在一起，就形成国外部门。

初次分配总收入 初次分配是生产活动形成的净成果在参与生产活动的生产要素的所有者及政府之间的分配。生产活动的净成果是增加值。生产要素包括劳动力、土地、资本。劳动力所有者因提供劳动而获得劳动报酬；土地所有者因出租土地而获得地租；资本的所有者因资本的形态不同而获得不同形式的收入：借贷资本所有者获得利息收入；股权所有者获得红利或未分配利润；政府因直接或间接介入生产过程而获得生产税或支付补贴。初次分配的结果形成各个机构部门的初次分配总收入。各部门的初次分配总收入之和就等于国民总收入，亦即国民生产总值。

经常转移 转移是一个机构单位向另一个机构单位提供货物、服务或资产，而同时并没有从后一机构单位获得任何货物、服务或资产作为回报的一种交易。经常转移包括扣除资本转移外的所有转移。其形式有收入税、社会保险付款、社会补助和其他经常转移。

可支配总收入 在初次分配总收入的基础上，通过经常转移的形式对初次分配总收入进行再次分配。再分配的结果形成各个机构部门的可支配总收入。各部门的可支配总收入之和称为国民可支配总收入。

总储蓄 指可支配总收入用于最终消费后的余额。各部门的总储蓄之和称为国民总储蓄。

资本转移 指一个部门无偿地向另一个部门支付用于非金融投资的资金，是一种不从对方获取任何对应物作为回报的交易。资本转移具有不同于经常转移的两个特征，一是转移的目的是用于投资，而不是用于消费；二是资本转移其实物形式往往涉及除存货和现金以外资产所有权的转移；其现金形式往往涉及除存货以外的资产的处置。资本转移包括投资性补助和其他资本转移。

净金融投资 它反映机构部门或经济总体资金富余或短缺的状况。从实物交易角度看，它是指总储蓄加资本转移收入减资本转移支出减非金融投资后的差额。从金融交易角度看，它是金融资产的增加额减金融负债的增加额之后的差额。

通货 指以现金形式存在于市场流通中的货币，包括本币和外币。

存款 指金融机构接受客户存入的货币款项，存款人可随时或按约定时间支取款项的信用业务。包括活期存款、定期存款、住户储蓄存款、财政存款、外汇存款和其他存款等。

贷款 指金融机构将其所吸收的资金，按一定的利率贷放给客户并约期归还的信用业务。包括短期贷款、中长期贷款、财政贷款、外汇贷款和其他贷款。

证券(不含股票) 由债券购买者承购的或因销售产品而拥有的，可在金融市场上交易并代表一定债权的书面证明。包括政府债券、金融债券、企业债券、商业票据、支付固定收入但不提供法人企业残余价值分享权的优先股等。

股票及其他股权 指股票购买者及直接投资者对其投资企业净资产所拥有的权益。股票是股份公司签发的证明股东投资并按其所持股份享有权益和承担义务的权益性证券。其他股权是机构单位以直接投资的方式用除股票、债权性证券以外的土地、房屋及建筑物、机器设备、存货、资源资产等实物资产，商标、专利权、土地使用权、特许使用权、商誉等无形资产及货币资金直接向其他单位进行的投资。通常以股权证、出资证明书、参与证或类似的单据为凭证。

保险准备金 指对人寿保险准备金和养恤基金的净权益、保险费预付款和未结索赔准备金。

结算资金 指金融机构用于结算目的汇兑在途的资金。

金融机构往来 指各金融机构之间的资金往来，包括同业存放款和同业拆借款。

准备金 指各金融机构在中央银行的存款及缴存中央银行的法定准备金。

中央银行贷款 指中央银行向各金融机构的贷款。

经常项目 包括货物、服务、收益及经常性转移。

货物进出口 指通过我国海关进出口的货物。货物的进出口值都按离岸价格估价。离岸价格可视为进口商在出口商边境领取货物时支付的购买者价格。当进口商领取该货物时，该货物已装载到进口商自己的运载工具或其他运载工具，出口商已为该货物支付了出口税或获得了出口退税。

服务进出口 指常住单位与非常住单位之间相互提供的服务。包括运输服务、旅游服务、通讯服务、建筑服务、保险服务、金融服务、计算机和信息服务、咨询服务、广告、宣传服务、电影音像服务、专有权力使用费和特许费、其他商务服务、政府服务。

收益 指常住单位与非常住单位之间因相互提供生产要素而产生的收入，包括劳动者报酬和投资收益。其中投资收益包括直接投资、证券投资和其他投资的收益和支出，以及直接投资收益的再投资。

资本项目 包括移民转移、债务减免等资本性转移。

金融项目 包括直接投资、证券投资和其他投资。

直接投资 指外国、港澳台地区在我国和我国在外国、港澳台地区以独资、合资、合作及合作勘探开发方式进行的投资。

证券投资 指我国对外国、港澳台地区发行的股票、债券等有价证券和我国购买外国、港澳台地区发行的股票、债券等有价证券。

其他投资 指除直接投资和证券投资以外的所有对外金融资产与负债交易项目。包括外国提供给我国和我国提供给外国的贸易信贷、贷款、货币和存款以及其他资产。

储备资产增减额 指我国在黄金储备、外汇储备、在国际货币基金组织的储备头寸、特别提款权、使用基金信贷等方面本年末与上年末余额之间的差额。负号表示储备资产增加，正号表示储备资产减少。

Explanatory Notes on Main Statistical Indicators

Gross Domestic Product (GDP) refers to the final products at market prices produced by all resident units in a country (or a region) during a certain period of time. Gross domestic product is expressed in three different forms, i.e. value, income, and products respectively. GDP in its value form refers to the total value of all goods and services produced by all resident units during a certain period of time, minus the total value of input of goods and services of the nature of non-fixed assets; in order term, it is the sum of the value-added of all resident units. GDP in the form of income includes the income created by all resident units and distributed to resident and non-resident units. GDP in the form of products refers to the value of all goods and services for final consumption by all resident units minus the net exports of goods and services during a given period of time. In the practice of national accounting, gross domestic product is calculated with three approaches, i.e. production approach, income approach and expenditure approach, which reflect gross domestic product and its composition from different aspects.

Gross National Income (GNI) also known as gross national product, refers to the final result of the primary distribution of the income created by all the resident units of a country (or a region) during a certain period of time. The value-added created by the resident units of a country engaged in production activities is distributed, during the primary distribution, mainly to the resident units of that country, while part of it is distributed to the non-resident units in the form of production tax and import duties (minus subsidies to production and import), remuneration for the labourers and property income. At the meantime, a part of the value-added created abroad is distributed to the resident units of the country in the form of production tax and import duties (minus subsidies to production and import), remuneration for the labourers and property income. The concept of gross national income is thus developed, which equals to the gross domestic product plus the net factor income from abroad. Unlike the gross domestic product which is a concept of production, the gross national income is a concept of income.

Three Industries Classification of economic activities into three branches of industries is a common practice in the world, although the grouping varies to some extent form country to country. In China economic activities are categorized into following industries:

Primary industry: refers to agriculture, forestry, animal husbandry and fishery.

Secondary industry: refers to mining and quarrying, manufacturing, production and supply of electricity, water and gas, and construction.

Tertiary industry: refers to all other economic activities not included in primary or secondary industry.

Labourers Remuneration refers to the whole payment of various forms earned by the labourers from the productive activities they are engaged in. It includes wages, bonuses and allowances the labourers earned in monetary form and in kind. It also includes the free medical services provided to the labourers and the medicine expenses, traffic subsidies and social insurance, housing fund paid by the employers. As the individual economy is concerned, since the labourers remuneration is not easily distinguished from the operating profit, both are treated as labourers remuneration.

Net Taxes on Production refers to the difference of the taxes on production minus the subsidies on production. The taxes on production refers to the various taxes, extra charges and fees levied on the production units on their production, sale and business activities as well as on the use of some factors of production, such as fixed assets, land and labour force in the production activities they are engaged in. In contrast to the taxes on production, the subsidies on production refer to the unilateral government transfer to the production units and are therefore regarded as negative taxes on production. They include subsidies on the loss due to implementation of government policies, price subsidies, etc.

Depreciation of Fixed Assets refers to the depreciation of fixed assets of a given period, drawn in accordance with the stipulated depreciation rate for the purpose of compensating the wear loss of the fixed assets or the depreciation of fixed assets calculated in a fictitious way in accordance with the stipulated unified depreciation rate in the national economic accounting system. It reflects the value of transfer of the fixed assets in the production of the current period. The depreciation of fixed assets in various enterprises and institutions managed as enterprises refers to the depreciation expenses actually drawn. In government agencies and institutions not managed as enterprises which do not draw the depreciation expenses, as well as for the houses of residents, the depreciation of fixed assets is the imputed depreciation, which is calculated in accordance with the stipulated unified depreciation rate. In principle, the depreciation of fixed assets should be calculated on the basis of the re-purchased value of the fixed assets. However, there is no actual condition to re-evaluate all the fixed assets in China. Therefore, the above-mentioned methods are temporarily adopted at present.

Operating Surplus refers to the balance of the value added created by the resident units deducting the labourers remuneration, net taxes on production and the depreciation of fixed assets. It is equivalent to the business profit of the enterprises plus subsidies on production, but the wages and welfare expenses paid from the profits should be deducted.

GDP by Expenditure Approach refers to the method of measuring the final results of production activities of a country (region) during a given period from the perspective of final use. It includes final consumption, total capital formation and net export of goods and services, i.e.:

GDP by expenditure approach = final consumption + total capital formation + net export of goods and services

Final Consumption refers to the total expenditure of resident units for purchases of goods and services from domestic economic territory and abroad to meet the requirements of material, cultural and spiritual life. It excludes the expenditure of non-resident units on consumption in the economic territory of the country. The final consumption is broken down into household consumption and government consumption.

Households Consumption refers to the total expenditure of resident households on the final consumption of goods and services. In addition to the consumption of goods and services bought by the households directly with money, the households consumption also includes expenditure on goods and services obtained by the households in other ways, i.e. the so-called imputed consumption expenditure, which includes the following: (a) the goods and services provided to the households by the employer in the form of payment in kind and transfer in kind; (b) goods and services produced and consumed by the households themselves, in which the services refer only to the owner-occupied housing and domestic and individual services provided by the paid household workers; (c) financial intermediate services provided by financial institutions; (d) insurance services provided by insurance companies.

Government Consumption refers to the expenditure on the consumption of the public services provided by the government to the whole society and the net expenditure on the goods and services provided by the government to the households free of charge or at low prices. The former equals to the output value of the government services minus the value of operating income obtained by the government departments. The latter equals to the market value of the goods and services provided by the government free of charge or at low prices to the households minus the value received by the government from the households.

Total Capital Formation refers to the fixed assets acquired minus those disposed of and the net value of inventory, including the total fixed capital formation and the increase in inventory.

Total Fixed Capital Formation refers to the value of fixed assets acquired minus those disposed of during a given period. Fixed assets are the assets produced through production activities with specified unit value which could be used for over one year, excluding natural assets. Total fixed capital formation can be categorized into total tangible capital formation and total intangible capital formation. The total tangible capital formation include the value of the construction projects, installation projects completed and the equipment, apparatus and instruments purchased as well as the value of land improved, the value of draught animals, breeding stock, animals for milk, wool and for recreational purpose, and the newly increased forest with economic value during a given period. The total intangible capital formation includes the prospecting of minerals, the acquisition of computer software minus the disposal of them.

Increase in Inventory refers to the market value of the change in inventory of resident units during a given period, i.e. the difference of value between the beginning and the end of the period minus the current gains due to the change in prices. The increase in inventory can be positive or negative. A positive value indicates the increase in inventory while a negative value indicates the decrease in stock. The inventory includes the raw materials, fuels and reserve materials purchased by the production units as well as the inventory of finished products, semi-finished products, work-in-progress, etc.

Net Export of Goods and Services refers to the difference of the exports of goods and services minus the imports of goods and services. The imports include the value of various goods and services sold or gratuitously transferred by the resident units to the non-resident units. The imports include the value of various goods and services purchased or gratuitously acquired by the resident units from the non-resident units. Because the provision of services and the use of them happen simultaneously, the acquisition of services by the resident units from abroad is usually treated as import while the acquisition of services by non-resident units in this country is usually treated as export. The export and import of goods are calculated at FOB.

Direct Input Coefficient refers to the volume of products and services of industry *i*, which is consumed directly by industry *j* in the course of its production or business, recorded as a_{ij} (i,j=1, 2, … ,n). The direct input coefficient table or direct input coefficient matrix, usually denoted as A, is a table that presents direct input coefficients of all industries.

Total Input Coefficient refers to the volume of products and services of industry *i* which is consumed directly and indirectly by industry *j* in producing each unit of final use. The total input coefficient table or total input coefficient matrix, usually denoted as B, is a table that presents total input coefficients of all industries.

Institutional Units refer to economic entities that are in a position to own assets and incur liabilities, to engage independently in economic activities, and to conduct transactions with other entities.

Institutional Sectors refer groups of institutional units that are homogenous in nature. Following 4 institutional sectors are identified in the flow of fund accounts: non-financial corporations, financial institutions, governments and households. Also treated as an institutional sector is the rest of the world, which is composed of non-resident units that have economic relations with the resident units.

Non-Financial Corporations and the Sector of Non-Financial Corporations Non-financial corporations refer to resident corporations that are engaged in the production of goods and the provision of non financial services in the market, mainly covering corporate enterprises of various types engaged in the abovementioned activities. All non-financial corporations make up the sector of non-financial corporations.

Financial Institutions and the Sector of Financial Institutions Financial institutions refer to resident institutions that are engaged in the financial intermediate services or auxiliary financial activities that are closed related with financial intermediate services, mainly covering central banks, commercial banks, policy-related banks, non-banking credit institutions and insurance companies. All financial institutions make up the sector of financial institutions.

Government Units and the Sector of Governments Government units refer to legal entities and their auxiliary units within the territory of China that are established through political process and are empowered with legislative, administrative or judicial rights over other institutional units in a given region. The main function of government units is to acquire funds through taxation or other means, to provide public services to the society and households, and to conduct redistribution of income and properties of the society through transfer payment. Government units cover mainly administrative and non-profit institutional units of various types. All government units make up the sector of governments.

Households and the Sector of Households Households refer to resident individuals or groups of resident individuals who share common living facilities, pool together entire or part of their income and properties at their common disposal, and share their housing, food and other consumer goods and services. All households make up the sector of households.

Non-resident Units and the Rest of the World Non-resident units refer to of units that are of a non-resident nature. All non-resident units that have transactions with resident units make up the sector the rest of the world.

Total Income of Primary Distribution Primary distribution refers to the distribution of net results from production activities among the owners of factors of production and the governments. Factors of production include labour force, land and capitals. Owners of labour force gain remuneration by providing labour. Owners of land receive rents from leasing of land. Owners of capitals get income of various forms depending on the type of capitals: bankers receive income from interest and share holders receive dividends or non-distributed profits. Governments either gain production tax or pay for subsidies by participating directly or indirectly in the production process. Results of primary distribution generate the total income of primary distribution of each sector, and the sum of the total income of primary distribution of all sectors make up the gross national income, or the gross national product.

Current Transfers Transfer refers to the transaction of provision of goods, services or assets by an institutional unit to another institutional unit without receiving any goods, services or assets in return from the recipient. Current transfers refer to all kinds of transfers other than capital transfers, including income tax, payment to social securities, social allowances and other current transfers.

Total Disposable Income Total income of primary distribution is re-distributed through current transfer, resulting in the total disposable income of various institutional sectors. The sum of total disposable income of all institutional sectors makes up the total national disposable income.

Total Savings refer to the total disposable income minus the final consumption. Total savings of all sectors make up the total national savings.

Capital Transfer refers to the free payment from one sector to another sector for non-financial capital formation, and is a transaction that seeks no return from the recipient. The capital transfer differs from the current transfer in 2 aspects: 1) The purpose of the capital transfer is investment rather than consumption. 2) The capital transfer features the transfer of the ownership of the assets other than inventory and cash, and the capital transfer in its monetary form involves the disposal of assets other than inventory. Capital transfer includes investment subsidies and other capital transfers.

Net Financial Investment reflects the surplus or shortage of capitals of institutional sectors or of the economy in general. It refers to total savings plus the income from capital transfer minus payment for capital transfer and the non-financial investment from the point of view of physical transaction. In terms of monetary transaction, it is the difference between the increase in financial assets minus the increase of the financial liabilities.

Currency in Circulation refers to currency that is in circulation in the market, including local and foreign currencies.

Deposits refer to credit transactions by which financial institutions accept deposits from clients who could withdraw their deposit at any time or by agreed time frame. They include current deposit, fixed deposit, household savings deposit, government deposit, foreign exchange deposit and other deposits.

Loans refer to credit transactions by which financial institutions lend their capital to clients at certain level of interest rates, which the latter will repay by agreed time frame. They include short-term loans, medium and long-term loans, government loans, foreign exchange loans and other loans.

Securities (excluding stocks) refer to written certificates representing creditors' rights, purchased by bond holders or owned by selling products, which can be transacted at the financial markets. They include government bonds, financial bonds, corporation bonds, commercial drafts, preferential stocks that provide fixed income without the right to share the residual value of corporations, etc.

Stocks and Other Holding Rights refer to the rights by stockholders and direct investors on the net assets of corporations they invested in. Stocks refer to negotiable securities on creditor's rights, issued by stock companies certifying the investment by stockholders and their rights and duties depending on their stocks. Other holding rights refer to the direct investment by institutional units to other units in forms other than stocks and negotiable securities on creditor's rights, including tangible assets such as land, buildings, machines and equipment, inventory, resources, etc., and intangible assets such as trade marks, patents, rights on land use, licenses, commodity credit, and the capitals. Documents on holding rights usually include certificates on creditor's right, certificates on investment or on participation, etc.

Insurance Reserve Funds refer to reserve fund for life insurance, the net pension fund, advance payment of premium and non-claimed reserves.

Settlement Fund refers to bank fund of financial institutions for settlement that is in the process of remittance.

Transactions Between Financial Institutions refer to flow of capital between financial institutions, including inter-bank deposits and loans.

Reserve Funds refer to savings of financial institutions in the central bank and designated reserves to the central bank.

Loans from the Central Bank refer to loans from the central bank to financial institutions.

Current Account includes goods, services, earnings and current transfers.

Import and Export of Goods refer to imported or exported goods through Chinese customs. Both import and export of goods are valued at free on board (f.o.b.) prices. Free on board prices can be regarded as the purchaser's prices paid by importers when claiming goods at the boarder of the exporters. When the importer claim the imported goods, the goods have been loaded in importer's carriers or other carriers, and the exporter has paid export duty or received export redeem.

Import and Export of Services refers services provided between resident and non-resident units, including services on transportation, tourism, communications, construction, insurance, banking, computer and information, consultation, advertisements and publicity, as well as film, audio and video services, royalty for patents, trademarks and other special rights, other commercial services, and government services.

Earnings refers income from provision of factors of production between resident and non-resident units, including compensation of labours and earnings from investment. Earnings from investment include earnings from and expenses on direct investment, security investment and other investment, as well as reinvestment of earnings from direct investment.

Capital Account includes capital transfers such as immigration transfer, reduction or exemption of debts, etc..

Financial Account includes direct investment, security investment and other investments.

Direct Investment refers to investment by foreign investors or investors from Hong Kong, Macao and Taiwan in China, or by Chinese investors in foreign countries or in Hong Kong, Macao and Taiwan, in forms of exclusive investment, joint investment, contracted operation and cooperative development,.

Security Investment refers to the issue of stocks and securities by China in foreign countries or in Hong Kong, Macao and Taiwan, and the purchase by Chinese units of stocks and securities issued in foreign countries or in Hong Kong, Macao and Taiwan.

Other Investment refers to all external transactions on financial assets and liabilities other than direct investment and security investment, including trade credits, loans, currency, savings and other assets, provided by foreign countries to China and by China to foreign countries.

Reserve Assets, Net Increase refers to the net balance between the end of the reference year and the end of the previous year, in the gold reserve, foreign exchange reserve, special drawing rights in the International Monetary Fund, and the use of the Funds credits. The increase in the reserve assets is expressed in negative figure and the decrease in the reserve assets is expressed in positive figure.

四、人口

Population

简要说明

一、本篇资料的主要内容

本篇资料反映我国2003年及历年人口方面的基本情况，包括全国及31个省、自治区、直辖市的主要人口统计数据，如：全国历年人口总数、城镇人口、乡村人口；2003年各地区总人口、出生率、死亡率、自然增长率、人口负担系数、家庭户规模、人口受教育程度等。另外，我们还对建国以来进行的五次全国人口普查主要数据进行了比较。

二、本篇的资料来源

本篇资料由国家统计局人口和社会科技统计司整理。其中表4-1、4-2 中1982-1989年的数据根据1982年、1990年两次全国人口普查数据进行了调整；1990-2000年的数据根据2000年全国人口普查数据进行了调整；2001-2003年数据为人口变动情况抽样调查推算数；其余年份为户籍统计数据。表4-3为2003年人口变动情况抽样调查推算数据。表4-4为五次全国人口普查主要数据。表4-6至4-16为2003年人口变动情况抽样调查数据。表4-5是根据1990年和2000年全国人口普查数据计算的。

三、2003年人口变动情况抽样调查是以全国为总体，各省、自治区、直辖市为次总体，采用分层、等距、整群概率比例抽样方法，在全国31个省、自治区、直辖市抽取了990个县(市、区)、3734个乡(镇、街道)、6544个调查小区的126万人。经加权后汇总，2003年全国人口出生率为12.41‰，死亡率为6.40‰，自然增长率为6.01‰。按此推算，2003年末全国总人口为129227万人，出生人口为1599万人，死亡人口为825万人，净增人口为774万人。

Brief Introduction

I. Main Content

Data in this chapter show the basic condition of population in 2003 and in previous years of the whole nation and of 31 provinces, autonomous regions and municipalities directly under the central government, such as the national population, urban population and rural population over the years; population, birth rates, death rates, natural growth rates, dependency ratio, household size and education attainment of population by province. In addition, a comparison is made among the data from the five population censuses undertaken after the founding of the People's Republic of China.

II. Source of Data

Data in this chapter are prepared by the Department of Population, Social and Science Statistics of the National Bureau of Statistics. In tables 4-1 and 4-2, figures for 1982-1989 have been adjusted in line with the data from the population censuses of 1982 and 1990, and figures for 1990-2000 have been adjusted on the basis of the 2000 population census, figures for 2001-2003 are estimates from the annual national sample survey on population changes, while figures for other years are statistics derived from household registration. Data in Table 4-3 are estimates from the annual national sample survey on population changes in 2003. Data in Table 4-4 present the main results from the five national population censuses. Data in tables 4-6 to 4-16 are the results of the annual national sample survey on population changes in 2003. Data in Table 4-5 are compiled from the 1990 and 2000 population censuses.

III. The annual national sample survey on population changes in 2003 was conducted with a multi-stage systematic PPS cluster sampling scheme, taking the whole nation as the population and each province, autonomous region or municipality as the sub-population. A total of 1.26 million people were selected as the sample from 6,544 survey districts in 3,734 townships (towns and urban neighborhood committees) in 990 counties (cities and districts) of the 31 provinces, autonomous regions and municipalities. The weighted estimation procedure suggested that the birth rate was 12.41 per thousand, the death rate was 6.40 per thousand and the natural growth rate was 6.01 per thousand for China in 2003. Based on these rates, it was further estimated that China had a total population of 1,292.27 million at the end of 2003, with 15.99 million births, 8.25 million deaths and a net increase of 7.74 million people during the year.

4-1 人口数及构成

Population and Its Composition

本表各年人口未包括香港、澳门特别行政区和台湾省的人口数据。

Data in this table exclude the population of Hong Kong SAR, Macao SAR and Taiwan Province.

单位：万人 (10 000 persons)

年份 Year	年底总人口 Total Population (year-end)	按性别分 By Sex 男 Male 人口数 Population	男 Male 比重(%) Proportion	女 Female 人口数 Population	女 Female 比重(%) Proportion	按城乡分 By Residence 城镇总人口 Urban 人口数 Population	城镇 Urban 比重(%) Proportion	乡村总人口 Rural 人口数 Population	乡村 Rural 比重(%) Proportion
1978	96259	49567	51.49	46692	48.51	17245	17.92	79014	82.08
1980	98705	50785	51.45	47920	48.55	19140	19.39	79565	80.61
1985	105851	54725	51.70	51126	48.30	25094	23.71	80757	76.29
1989	112704	58099	51.55	54605	48.45	29540	26.21	83164	73.79
1990	114333	58904	51.52	55429	48.48	30195	26.41	84138	73.59
1991	115823	59466	51.34	56357	48.66	31203	26.94	84620	73.06
1992	117171	59811	51.05	57360	48.95	32175	27.46	84996	72.54
1993	118517	60472	51.02	58045	48.98	33173	27.99	85344	72.01
1994	119850	61246	51.10	58604	48.90	34169	28.51	85681	71.49
1995	121121	61808	51.03	59313	48.97	35174	29.04	85947	70.96
1996	122389	62200	50.82	60189	49.18	37304	30.48	85085	69.52
1997	123626	63131	51.07	60495	48.93	39449	31.91	84177	68.09
1998	124761	63940	51.25	60821	48.75	41608	33.35	83153	66.65
1999	125786	64692	51.43	61094	48.57	43748	34.78	82038	65.22
2000	126743	65437	51.63	61306	48.37	45906	36.22	80837	63.78
2001	127627	65672	51.46	61955	48.54	48064	37.66	79563	62.34
2002	128453	66115	51.47	62338	48.53	50212	39.09	78241	60.91
2003	129227	66556	51.50	62671	48.50	52376	40.53	76851	59.47

注：1.1982年以前数据为户籍统计数，1982—1989年数据根据1990年人口普查数据有所调整，1990-2000年数据根据2000年人口普查数据进行了调整，2001-2003年数据为人口变动情况抽样调查推算数(下表同)。

2.总人口和按性别分人口中包括中国人民解放军现役军人，按城乡分人口中现役军人计入城镇人口。

a) Data before 1982 were taken from the annual reports of the Ministry of Public Security. Data in 1982-1989 were adjusted on the basis of the 1990 national population censuses. Data in 1990-2000 were adjusted on the basis of the estimated on the basis of the 2000 national population censuses. Data in 2001-2003 have been estimated on the basis of the annual national sample surveys on population changes. (the next table is the same).

b) Total population and population by sex include the military personnel of Chinese People's Liberation Army, the military personnel are classified as urban population in the item of population by residence.

4-2 人口出生率、死亡率和自然增长率

Birth Rate, Death Rate and Natural Growth Rate of Population

单位：‰ (‰)

年份 Year	出生率 Birth Rate	死亡率 Death Rate	自然增长率 Natural Growth Rate	年份 Year	出生率 Birth Rate	死亡率 Death Rate	自然增长率 Natural Growth Rate
1978	18.25	6.25	12.00	1992	18.24	6.64	11.60
1980	18.21	6.34	11.87	1993	18.09	6.54	11.45
1981	20.91	6.36	14.55	1994	17.70	6.49	11.21
1982	22.28	6.60	15.68	1995	17.12	6.57	10.55
1983	20.19	6.90	13.29	1996	16.98	6.56	10.42
1984	19.90	6.82	13.08	1997	16.57	6.51	10.06
1985	21.04	6.78	14.26	1998	15.64	6.50	9.14
1986	22.43	6.86	15.57	1999	14.64	6.46	8.18
1987	23.33	6.72	16.61	2000	14.03	6.45	7.58
1988	22.37	6.64	15.73	2001	13.38	6.43	6.95
1989	21.58	6.54	15.04	2002	12.86	6.41	6.45
1990	21.06	6.67	14.39	2003	12.41	6.40	6.01
1991	19.68	6.70	12.98				

4-3 各地区总人口和出生率、死亡率、自然增长率（2003年）

Total Population and Birth Rate, Death Rate and Natural Growth Rate by Region (2003)

地区	Region	年底总人口（万人） Total Population (year-end) (10 000 persons)	出生率 Birth Rate (‰)	死亡率 Death Rate (‰)	自然增长率 Natural Growth Rate (‰)
全　国	**National Total**	**129227**	**12.41**	**6.40**	**6.01**
北　京	Beijing	1456	5.10	5.20	-0.10
天　津	Tianjin	1011	7.14	6.04	1.10
河　北	Hebei	6769	11.43	6.27	5.16
山　西	Shanxi	3314	12.26	6.04	6.22
内蒙古	Inner Mongolia	2380	9.24	6.17	3.07
辽　宁	Liaoning	4210	6.90	5.83	1.07
吉　林	Jilin	2704	7.25	5.64	1.61
黑龙江	Heilongjiang	3815	7.48	5.45	2.03
上　海	Shanghai	1711	4.85	6.20	-1.35
江　苏	Jiangsu	7406	9.04	7.03	2.01
浙　江	Zhejiang	4680	9.66	6.38	3.28
安　徽	Anhui	6410	11.15	5.20	5.95
福　建	Fujian	3488	11.43	5.58	5.85
江　西	Jiangxi	4254	14.07	5.98	8.09
山　东	Shandong	9125	11.42	6.64	4.78
河　南	Henan	9667	12.10	6.46	5.64
湖　北	Hubei	6002	8.26	5.94	2.32
湖　南	Hunan	6663	11.82	6.87	4.95
广　东	Guangdong	7954	13.66	5.31	8.35
广　西	Guangxi	4857	13.86	6.57	7.29
海　南	Hainan	811	14.68	5.52	9.16
重　庆	Chongqing	3130	9.89	7.20	2.69
四　川	Sichuan	8700	9.18	6.06	3.12
贵　州	Guizhou	3870	15.91	6.87	9.04
云　南	Yunnan	4376	17.00	7.20	9.80
西　藏	Tibet	270	17.40	6.30	11.10
陕　西	Shaanxi	3690	10.67	6.38	4.29
甘　肃	Gansu	2603	12.58	6.46	6.12
青　海	Qinghai	534	16.94	6.09	10.85
宁　夏	Ningxia	580	15.68	4.73	10.95
新　疆	Xinjiang	1934	16.01	5.23	10.78

注：1.全国总人口包括现役军人数，分地区数字中未包括。

2.全国数据未包括香港、澳门特别行政区和台湾省的人口数据。

3.全国数据根据抽样误差和调查误差进行了修正。

a)The military personnel were included in the national total population, but excluded in the regional total population.

b)The national total population excluded the population of Hong Kong, Macao and Taiwan.

c)The national total population was adjusted according to the sampling error and investigation error.

4-4 五次全国人口普查人口基本情况

Basic Statistics on National Population Census in 1953, 1964, 1982, 1990 and 2000

本表未包括香港、澳门特别行政区及台湾省数据。

Data in this table excluded the population of Hong Kong , Macao and Taiwan.

指 标	Item	1953	1964	1982	1990	2000
总人口 （万人）	**Total Population (10 000 persons)**	**59435**	**69458**	**100818**	**113368**	**126583**
男	Male	30799	35652	51944	58495	65355
女	Female	28636	33806	48874	54873	61228
性别比（以女性为100）	Sex Ratio (female=100)	107.56	105.46	106.30	106.60	106.74
家庭户规模 （人/户）	**Average Family Size (person/household)**	**4.33**	**4.43**	**4.41**	**3.96**	**3.44**
各年龄组人口 （%）	**Population by Age Group (%)**					
0-14岁	0-14	36.28	40.69	33.59	27.69	22.89
15-64岁	15-64	59.31	55.75	61.50	66.74	70.15
65岁及以上	65 and Over	4.41	3.56	4.91	5.57	6.96
民族人口	**Nationality Population**					
汉族 （万人）	Han Nationality (10 000 persons)	54728	65456	94088	104248	115940
占总人口比重 （%）	Percentage to Total Population (%)	93.94	94.24	93.32	91.96	91.59
少数民族 （万人）	Minority Nationalities (10 000 persons)	3532	4002	6730	9120	10643
占总人口比重 （%）	Percentage to Total Population (%)	6.06	5.76	6.68	8.04	8.41
每十万人拥有的各种受教育程度人口 （人）	**Population with Various Education Attainments Per 100 000 Persons (person)**					
大专及以上	Junior College and Above		416	615	1422	3611
高中和中专	Senior Secondary/Secondary Technical School		1319	6779	8039	11146
初中	Junior Secondary School		4680	17892	23344	33961
小学	Primary School		28330	35237	37057	35701
文盲人口及文盲率	**Illiterate Population and Illiterate Rate**					
文盲人口 （万人）	Illiterate Population (10 000 persons)		23327	22996	18003	8507
文盲率 （%）	Illiterate Rate (%)		33.58	22.81	15.88	6.72
城乡人口 （万人）	**Population by Residence (10 000 persons)**					
城镇人口	Urban Population	7726	12710	21082	29971	45844
乡村人口	Rural Population	50534	56748	79736	83397	80739

注：1.历次普查总人口数据中包括了中国人民解放军现役军人。在城乡人口中，中国人民解放军现役军人列为城镇人口统计。

2.1953年总人口数据中包括了间接调查人口，而民族人口、城乡人口中未包括。

3.1964年文盲人口为13岁及13岁以上不识字人口，1982、1990、2000年文盲人口为15岁及15岁以上不识字或识字很少的人。

a) Total population from population censuses includes the military personnel. Military personnel is listed as urban population in population by residence.

b) Total population of 1953 census includes the population from indirect survey, but excludes in the nationality population and urban/rural population.

c) Illiterate population of 1964 census referred to people of 13 years old and over who could not read. Illiterate population of 1982, 1990 and 2000 censuses referred to people of 15 years old and over who could not read or could read very little.

4-5 各地区人口平均预期寿命

Population Life Expectancy by Region

单位:岁 (years old)

地 区	Region	1990年预期寿命 Life Expectancy in 1990	男 Male	女 Female	2000年预期寿命 Life Expectancy in 2000	男 Male	女 Female
全 国	**National Total**	**68.55**	**66.84**	**70.47**	**71.40**	**69.63**	**73.33**
北 京	Beijing	72.86	71.07	74.93	76.10	74.33	78.01
天 津	Tianjin	72.32	71.03	73.73	74.91	73.31	76.63
河 北	Hebei	70.35	68.47	72.53	72.54	70.68	74.57
山 西	Shanxi	68.97	67.33	70.93	71.65	69.96	73.57
内蒙古	Inner Mongolia	65.68	64.47	67.22	69.87	68.29	71.79
辽 宁	Liaoning	70.22	68.72	71.94	73.34	71.51	75.36
吉 林	Jilin	67.95	66.65	69.49	73.10	71.38	75.04
黑龙江	Heilongjiang	66.97	65.50	68.73	72.37	70.39	74.66
上 海	Shanghai	74.90	72.77	77.02	78.14	76.22	80.04
江 苏	Jiangsu	71.37	69.26	73.57	73.91	71.69	76.23
浙 江	Zhejiang	71.78	69.66	74.24	74.70	72.50	77.21
安 徽	Anhui	69.48	67.75	71.36	71.85	70.18	73.59
福 建	Fujian	68.57	66.49	70.93	72.55	70.30	75.07
江 西	Jiangxi	66.11	64.87	67.49	68.95	68.37	69.32
山 东	Shandong	70.57	68.64	72.67	73.92	71.70	76.26
河 南	Henan	70.15	67.96	72.55	71.54	69.67	73.41
湖 北	Hubei	67.25	65.51	69.23	71.08	69.31	73.02
湖 南	Hunan	66.93	65.41	68.70	70.66	69.05	72.47
广 东	Guangdong	72.52	69.71	75.43	73.27	70.79	75.93
广 西	Guangxi	68.72	67.17	70.34	71.29	69.07	73.75
海 南	Hainan	70.01	66.93	73.28	72.92	70.66	75.26
重 庆	Chongqing				71.73	69.84	73.89
四 川	Sichuan	66.33	65.06	67.70	71.20	69.25	73.39
贵 州	Guizhou	64.29	63.04	65.63	65.96	64.54	67.57
云 南	Yunnan	63.49	62.08	64.98	65.49	64.24	66.89
西 藏	Tibet	59.64	57.64	61.57	64.37	62.52	66.15
陕 西	Shaanxi	67.40	66.23	68.79	70.07	68.92	71.30
甘 肃	Gansu	67.24	66.35	68.25	67.47	66.77	68.26
青 海	Qinghai	60.57	59.29	61.96	66.03	64.55	67.70
宁 夏	Ningxia	66.94	65.95	68.05	70.17	68.71	71.84
新 疆	Xinjiang	62.59	61.95	63.26	67.41	65.98	69.14

注：2000年各省人口平均预期寿命是根据各省1990年以来人口变动调查公布的死亡率对2000年人口普查死亡数据修正后计算的。

a) Life expectancy in 2000 by region is calculated by the death data of 2000's Population Census, which modified by the mortality rates from the annual national sample surveys on population changes since 1990.

4-6 按年龄和性别分人口数

Population by Age and Sex

本表是2003年人口变动情况抽样调查样本数据，抽样比为0.982‰.

Data in this table are obtained from the Sample Survey of Population Changes in 2003. The sampling fraction is 0.982‰.

年 龄 Age	人口数（人） Population (person)			占总人口比重（%） Percentage to Total Population (%)			性别比 （女=100） Sex Ratio (female=100)
	合计 Total	男 Male	女 Female	合计 Total	男 Male	女 Female	
总计 Total	**1260498**	**643400**	**617098**	**100.00**	**51.05**	**48.95**	**104.26**
0-4	62977	34509	28468	5.03	2.73	2.30	121.22
5-9	81127	44193	36934	6.55	3.55	3.00	119.66
10-14	112240	59219	53021	8.75	4.61	4.15	111.69
15-19	104716	54997	49720	8.37	4.36	4.00	110.61
20-24	80596	40027	40569	6.79	3.41	3.39	98.67
25-29	93892	46629	47263	7.60	3.79	3.81	98.66
30-34	123497	61870	61628	9.71	4.88	4.83	100.39
35-39	123252	61929	61323	9.61	4.86	4.75	100.99
40-44	91467	46740	44727	7.41	3.81	3.60	104.50
45-49	94314	47753	46561	7.49	3.78	3.70	102.56
50-54	81679	41095	40584	6.32	3.18	3.15	101.26
55-59	57472	29401	28071	4.42	2.23	2.18	104.74
60-64	46023	23345	22678	3.62	1.82	1.80	102.94
65-69	41710	20974	20737	3.29	1.65	1.64	101.14
70-74	31484	15833	15650	2.46	1.24	1.22	101.17
75-79	19310	9033	10277	1.47	0.70	0.77	87.89
80-84	9832	4137	5695	0.75	0.32	0.42	72.64
85-89	3687	1330	2357	0.27	0.10	0.17	56.43
90-94	1026	323	703	0.08	0.03	0.05	45.98
95+	197	63	134	0.02	0.00	0.01	46.88

4-7 各地区户数、人口数、性别比和户规模

Household, Population and Sex Ratio by Region

本表是2003年人口变动情况抽样调查样本数据，抽样比为0.982‰。

Data in this table are obtained from the Sample Survey on Population Changes in 2003. The sampling fraction is 0.982 ‰.

地 区	Region	户数（户） Number of Households (household)	家庭户 Family Household	集体户 Non-family Household	人口数（人） Population (person)	男 Male	女 Female	性别比（女=100） Sex Ratio (female=100)
全 国	**National Total**	**370919**	**367550**	**3369**	**1260498**	**643400**	**617098**	**104.26**
北 京	Beijing	4769	4614	156	14070	7242	6827	106.08
天 津	Tianjin	3228	3208	19	9956	4914	5043	97.44
河 北	Hebei	19231	19203	28	66569	33965	32604	104.17
山 西	Shanxi	8854	8832	21	32558	16677	15881	105.01
内蒙古	Inner Mongolia	7381	7356	25	23510	12006	11505	104.36
辽 宁	Liaoning	13376	13319	57	41549	20779	20770	100.05
吉 林	Jilin	8113	8070	43	26684	13387	13297	100.67
黑龙江	Heilongjiang	12010	11985	25	37693	19172	18521	103.52
上 海	Shanghai	5702	5669	33	16061	8024	8038	99.82
江 苏	Jiangsu	22908	22685	223	72967	36113	36854	97.99
浙 江	Zhejiang	15662	15374	288	45934	23239	22695	102.40
安 徽	Anhui	18217	18053	164	62652	32243	30409	106.03
福 建	Fujian	10333	9939	394	34261	17516	16745	104.61
江 西	Jiangxi	12053	11927	126	41741	21396	20345	105.16
山 东	Shandong	29112	28889	223	89775	44983	44793	100.42
河 南	Henan	26966	26799	167	95029	49199	45830	107.35
湖 北	Hubei	17796	17586	210	59184	30286	28897	104.81
湖 南	Hunan	18981	18746	235	65521	34082	31438	108.41
广 东	Guangdong	20105	19550	555	77676	39703	37973	104.55
广 西	Guangxi	12858	12834	24	47661	24948	22714	109.84
海 南	Hainan	1983	1958	25	7939	4217	3721	113.33
重 庆	Chongqing	8954	8941	13	30713	15625	15088	103.56
四 川	Sichuan	25825	25758	67	85739	43493	42246	102.95
贵 州	Guizhou	10372	10348	24	37933	19663	18270	107.63
云 南	Yunnan	10866	10822	44	42836	22374	20462	109.34
西 藏	Tibet	538	537	1	2638	1266	1372	92.25
陕 西	Shaanxi	10166	10101	65	36314	18617	17697	105.20
甘 肃	Gansu	6412	6384	28	25628	13146	12483	105.31
青 海	Qinghai	1335	1329	6	5225	2666	2559	104.15
宁 夏	Ningxia	1515	1503	12	5650	2871	2779	103.29
新 疆	Xinjiang	5298	5229	69	18834	9591	9243	103.77

注：由于各地区数据采用加权汇总的方法，人口变动情况抽样调查样本数据合计与各分项相加略有误差。

a) Because data by region are calculated by the weighted sum method, total data of the sample survey on population changes is not equal to the sum of each items.

4-7 续表 continued

地 区	Region	家庭户人口数（人） Family Household Population (person)	男 Male	女 Female	集体户人口数（人） Non-Family Household Population (person)	男 Male	女 Female	平均家庭户规模（人/户） Average Family Size (person/household)
全 国	**National Total**	**1242389**	**632263**	**610126**	**18109**	**11137**	**6972**	**3.38**
北 京	Beijing	12664	6190	6473	1406	1052	354	2.74
天 津	Tianjin	9883	4877	5006	73	37	37	3.08
河 北	Hebei	66421	33870	32551	148	94	53	3.46
山 西	Shanxi	32441	16580	15861	117	97	20	3.67
内蒙古	Inner Mongolia	23417	11942	11475	93	64	29	3.18
辽 宁	Liaoning	41320	20617	20702	229	162	67	3.10
吉 林	Jilin	26392	13374	13018	292	13	279	3.27
黑龙江	Heilongjiang	37601	19118	18484	92	54	37	3.14
上 海	Shanghai	15954	7944	8010	107	79	28	2.81
江 苏	Jiangsu	72210	35594	36616	757	520	238	3.18
浙 江	Zhejiang	44948	22680	22268	986	559	426	2.92
安 徽	Anhui	60993	31277	29717	1659	966	693	3.38
福 建	Fujian	32376	16368	16008	1885	1148	736	3.26
江 西	Jiangxi	41038	20880	20158	703	515	187	3.44
山 东	Shandong	88966	44535	44431	809	448	361	3.08
河 南	Henan	94277	48631	45645	752	568	185	3.52
湖 北	Hubei	57727	29455	28272	1457	832	625	3.28
湖 南	Hunan	63640	32881	30758	1881	1201	680	3.39
广 东	Guangdong	74822	38096	36726	2853	1607	1247	3.83
广 西	Guangxi	47591	24903	22688	70	44	26	3.71
海 南	Hainan	7786	4112	3674	153	105	48	3.98
重 庆	Chongqing	30649	15585	15064	64	40	24	3.43
四 川	Sichuan	85388	43290	42098	350	202	148	3.32
贵 州	Guizhou	37852	19610	18242	81	53	28	3.66
云 南	Yunnan	42641	22248	20393	195	126	69	3.94
西 藏	Tibet	2625	1256	1369	13	10	3	4.89
陕 西	Shaanxi	35947	18373	17574	367	244	123	3.56
甘 肃	Gansu	25409	13065	12345	219	81	138	3.98
青 海	Qinghai	5189	2639	2550	36	27	9	3.91
宁 夏	Ningxia	5615	2851	2764	34	20	15	3.74
新 疆	Xinjiang	18606	9421	9184	228	170	59	3.56

4-8 各地区分性别各种户口状况人口

Residence Status of Population by Region and by Sex

本表是2003年人口变动情况抽样调查样本数据，抽样比为0.982‰。

Data in this table are obtained from the Sample Survey on Population Changes in 2003. The sampling fraction is 0.982 ‰.

单位:人 (person)

地 区	Region	合 计 Total			住本调查小区，户口在本乡、镇、街道 Population with Residence Registered in this Township, Town or Subdistrict and Actually Residing in this Enumeration Area		
		小 计 Sub-total	男 Male	女 Female	小 计 Sub-total	男 Male	女 Female
全 国	**National Total**	**1260498**	**643400**	**617098**	**1148379**	**586608**	**561770**
北 京	Beijing	14070	7242	6827	9659	4884	4776
天 津	Tianjin	9956	4914	5043	8623	4281	4342
河 北	Hebei	66569	33965	32604	62672	32010	30661
山 西	Shanxi	32558	16677	15881	29276	14973	14303
内蒙古	Inner Mongolia	23510	12006	11505	20666	10615	10050
辽 宁	Liaoning	41549	20779	20770	36955	18542	18413
吉 林	Jilin	26684	13387	13297	25088	12636	12452
黑龙江	Heilongjiang	37693	19172	18521	34693	17634	17059
上 海	Shanghai	16061	8024	8038	14300	7212	7088
江 苏	Jiangsu	72967	36113	36854	66048	32713	33335
浙 江	Zhejiang	45934	23239	22695	38440	19523	18916
安 徽	Anhui	62652	32243	30409	57166	29275	27891
福 建	Fujian	34261	17516	16745	26990	13749	13241
江 西	Jiangxi	41741	21396	20345	37263	19077	18186
山 东	Shandong	89775	44983	44793	81353	40653	40699
河 南	Henan	95029	49199	45830	89623	46271	43351
湖 北	Hubei	59184	30286	28897	54526	27848	26678
湖 南	Hunan	65521	34082	31438	61371	31975	29396
广 东	Guangdong	77676	39703	37973	65701	33604	32097
广 西	Guangxi	47661	24948	22714	45550	23944	21607
海 南	Hainan	7939	4217	3721	7095	3789	3306
重 庆	Chongqing	30713	15625	15088	29367	14969	14398
四 川	Sichuan	85739	43493	42246	81369	41443	39926
贵 州	Guizhou	37933	19663	18270	35169	18354	16815
云 南	Yunnan	42836	22374	20462	40659	21249	19410
西 藏	Tibet	2638	1266	1372	2635	1264	1371
陕 西	Shaanxi	36314	18617	17697	34207	17528	16679
甘 肃	Gansu	25628	13146	12483	24746	12769	11977
青 海	Qinghai	5225	2666	2559	4913	2507	2406
宁 夏	Ningxia	5650	2871	2779	5178	2626	2552
新 疆	Xinjiang	18834	9591	9243	17079	8691	8387

4-8 续表 continued

单位:人 (person)

地区	Region	住本调查小区半年以上，户口在外乡、镇、街道 Population with Residence Registered in Other Township Town or Subdistrict, but Having Actually Resided in This Enumeration Area for More Than Half Year			住本调查小区不满半年，离开户口登记地半年以上 Population Having Left Place of Residence Registration More Than Half Year and Having Resided in This Enumeration Area for Less Than Half Year			住本调查小区，户口待定 Pcpulation with Residence Registration in This Enumeration Area Not Yet Settled		
		小计 Sub-total	男 Male	女 Female	小计 Sub-total	男 Male	女 Female	小计 Sub-total	男 Male	女 Female
全国	**National Total**	**97273**	**49017**	**48255**	**8585**	**4621**	**3964**	**6262**	**3153**	**3109**
北京	Beijing	3983	2145	1838	379	189	190	48	24	23
天津	Tianjin	1235	587	648	64	31	33	34	14	20
河北	Hebei	3541	1752	1789	161	88	73	196	114	81
山西	Shanxi	2709	1383	1326	249	155	94	324	166	158
内蒙古	Inner Mongolia	2443	1181	1261	201	111	90	201	99	103
辽宁	Liaoning	4223	2056	2166	221	115	107	150	66	84
吉林	Jilin	1504	699	805	66	41	24	26	11	15
黑龙江	Heilongjiang	2562	1299	1263	218	118	99	221	121	99
上海	Shanghai	1656	763	893	51	22	29	54	27	27
江苏	Jiangsu	6011	2908	3103	499	297	202	408	195	213
浙江	Zhejiang	6924	3445	3479	349	169	180	221	102	119
安徽	Anhui	4522	2351	2170	669	461	209	295	156	139
福建	Fujian	5992	3104	2888	1033	563	471	245	100	145
江西	Jiangxi	3909	2030	1879	253	126	127	316	163	153
山东	Shandong	7661	3946	3716	518	280	238	243	103	140
河南	Henan	4864	2621	2243	313	179	134	229	128	101
湖北	Hubei	4356	2268	2088	121	57	63	180	112	68
湖南	Hunan	3582	1820	1762	319	174	145	249	114	134
广东	Guangdong	9814	5013	4801	1287	646	642	874	440	434
广西	Guangxi	1644	752	891	234	130	104	233	121	112
海南	Hainan	725	368	356	51	25	26	68	35	33
重庆	Chongqing	1085	518	567	189	99	90	73	39	34
四川	Sichuan	3710	1709	2001	313	165	148	346	175	171
贵州	Guizhou	2347	1109	1238	195	90	104	222	109	113
云南	Yunnan	1836	934	902	94	58	37	246	133	113
西藏	Tibet	1	1					3	1	2
陕西	Shaanxi	1855	959	897	72	33	39	180	98	82
甘肃	Gansu	541	246	295	234	74	160	107	56	51
青海	Qinghai	215	108	107	36	20	16	61	31	31
宁夏	Ningxia	374	192	182	30	17	13	68	35	33
新疆	Xinjiang	1451	748	704	165	90	75	139	62	76

4-9 各地区人口年龄构成和抚养比

Age Composition and Dependency Ratio of Population by Region

本表是2003年人口变动情况抽样调查样本数据，抽样比为0.982‰。

Data in this table are obtained from the Sample Survey on Population Changes in 2003. The sampling fraction is 0.982‰.

地区	Region	人口数（人）Population (person)	0-14岁 Age 0-14	15-64岁 Age 15-64	65岁及以上 Age 65 and Over	总抚养比（%）Gross Dependency Ratio (%)	少年儿童抚养比 Children Dependency Ratio	老年人口抚养比 Old People Dependency Ratio
全国	**National Total**	**1260498**	**256344**	**896908**	**107246**	**40.54**	**28.58**	**11.96**
北京	Beijing	14070	1486	11008	1576	27.82	13.50	14.32
天津	Tianjin	9956	1390	7478	1088	33.15	18.60	14.55
河北	Hebei	66569	12778	48760	5031	36.52	26.21	10.32
山西	Shanxi	32558	7476	22769	2313	42.99	32.84	10.16
内蒙古	Inner Mongolia	23510	4288	17427	1796	34.91	24.60	10.30
辽宁	Liaoning	41549	6108	31409	4032	32.28	19.45	12.84
吉林	Jilin	26684	4067	20736	1881	28.68	19.61	9.07
黑龙江	Heilongjiang	37693	5971	29217	2505	29.01	20.44	8.58
上海	Shanghai	16061	1415	12017	2630	33.66	11.77	21.88
江苏	Jiangsu	72967	12418	52271	8278	39.59	23.76	15.84
浙江	Zhejiang	45934	7400	33254	5280	38.13	22.25	15.88
安徽	Anhui	62652	13669	43853	5131	42.87	31.17	11.70
福建	Fujian	34261	7326	24211	2724	41.51	30.26	11.25
江西	Jiangxi	41741	9696	29140	2905	43.24	33.27	9.97
山东	Shandong	89775	16475	65164	8137	37.77	25.28	12.49
河南	Henan	95029	21465	65920	7644	44.16	32.56	11.60
湖北	Hubei	59184	12511	42002	4671	40.91	29.79	11.12
湖南	Hunan	65521	12686	46950	5885	39.56	27.02	12.53
广东	Guangdong	77676	20593	50799	6283	52.91	40.54	12.37
广西	Guangxi	47661	10284	33038	4339	44.26	31.13	13.13
海南	Hainan	7939	1913	5405	621	46.88	35.39	11.49
重庆	Chongqing	30713	5768	22113	2832	38.89	26.08	12.81
四川	Sichuan	85739	17170	61129	7439	40.26	28.09	12.17
贵州	Guizhou	37933	9822	25233	2878	50.33	38.93	11.40
云南	Yunnan	42836	10550	29274	3012	46.32	36.04	10.29
西藏	Tibet	2638	711	1767	160	49.31	40.26	9.05
陕西	Shaanxi	36314	7589	25911	2814	40.15	29.29	10.86
甘肃	Gansu	25628	5889	18029	1710	42.15	32.67	9.49
青海	Qinghai	5225	1288	3630	307	43.92	35.47	8.46
宁夏	Ningxia	5650	1487	3841	322	47.10	38.71	8.39
新疆	Xinjiang	18834	4656	13155	1023	43.17	35.40	7.78

4-10 各地区按性别和婚姻状况分的人口

Population by Sex, Marital Status and Region

本表是2003年人口变动情况抽样调查样本数据，抽样比为0.982‰。

Data in this table are obtained from the Sample Survey on Population Changes in 2003. The sampling fraction is 0.982‰.

单位：人 (person)

地区	Region	15岁及以上人口 Population Aged 15 and Over	男 Male	女 Female	未婚 Never Married	男 Male	女 Female	初婚有配偶 First Married	男 Male	女 Female
全国	**National Total**	**1004154**	**505478**	**498676**	**196717**	**115776**	**80941**	**721846**	**357524**	**364322**
北京	Beijing	12583	6472	6111	2828	1600	1228	8731	4511	4219
天津	Tianjin	8566	4201	4365	1577	839	738	6274	3101	3173
河北	Hebei	53791	27172	26620	11679	6608	5071	38424	19057	19367
山西	Shanxi	25082	12755	12327	4681	2804	1877	18392	9190	9203
内蒙古	Inner Mongolia	19223	9815	9408	3519	2136	1383	14135	7073	7062
辽宁	Liaoning	35441	17632	17809	6150	3461	2689	25878	12876	13002
吉林	Jilin	22617	11259	11358	4628	2423	2205	16159	8066	8094
黑龙江	Heilongjiang	31722	16004	15718	5823	3380	2442	23083	11505	11578
上海	Shanghai	14646	7304	7342	2929	1741	1188	10184	5044	5140
江苏	Jiangsu	60549	29480	31069	8597	5041	3556	46169	22444	23725
浙江	Zhejiang	38534	19292	19242	6185	3656	2529	28874	14419	14455
安徽	Anhui	48983	24798	24186	9923	5989	3934	35195	17374	17821
福建	Fujian	26935	13505	13430	5913	3486	2426	18860	9322	9538
江西	Jiangxi	32045	16118	15927	5749	3390	2359	23794	11835	11959
山东	Shandong	73300	36226	37074	13017	7245	5772	54563	27033	27529
河南	Henan	73564	37159	36405	14324	8288	6036	53463	26659	26803
湖北	Hubei	46673	23525	23148	9500	5715	3785	33319	16297	17022
湖南	Hunan	52835	27187	25647	10813	6560	4253	37567	18859	18709
广东	Guangdong	57083	28411	28672	14018	7913	6105	38930	19197	19732
广西	Guangxi	37377	19275	18102	10001	6229	3772	24185	11888	12297
海南	Hainan	6026	3121	2905	1586	981	606	4017	1995	2022
重庆	Chongqing	24945	12503	12442	3968	2424	1543	18391	9065	9326
四川	Sichuan	68569	34325	34244	11450	6945	4505	50432	24751	25681
贵州	Guizhou	28111	14350	13760	5904	3629	2275	19533	9635	9898
云南	Yunnan	32286	16808	15478	6800	4419	2381	22521	11160	11361
西藏	Tibet	1927	890	1036	596	313	284	1148	530	618
陕西	Shaanxi	28725	14531	14194	5768	3405	2363	20705	10253	10453
甘肃	Gansu	19739	10066	9673	4110	2401	1708	14161	7057	7104
青海	Qinghai	3937	1981	1957	769	460	309	2765	1370	1395
宁夏	Ningxia	4163	2094	2069	852	480	372	3030	1507	1523
新疆	Xinjiang	14178	7220	6957	3059	1812	1246	8964	4451	4512

4-10 续表　continued

单位：人 (person)

地 区	Region	再婚有配偶 Re-married	男 Male	女 Female	离 婚 Divorced	男 Male	女 Female	丧 偶 Widowed	男 Male	女 Female
全 国	**National Total**	**17293**	**8146**	**9147**	**10805**	**6415**	**4389**	**57493**	**17617**	**39876**
北 京	Beijing	244	122	122	187	89	98	593	150	444
天 津	Tianjin	130	65	65	102	51	51	483	144	339
河 北	Hebei	608	288	320	499	298	201	2581	920	1661
山 西	Shanxi	528	229	299	232	160	72	1249	373	876
内蒙古	Inner Mongolia	377	161	216	236	146	90	956	299	657
辽 宁	Liaoning	724	360	364	783	415	368	1906	519	1387
吉 林	Jilin	387	189	198	422	226	196	1020	354	666
黑龙江	Heilongjiang	786	385	401	542	294	248	1489	440	1048
上 海	Shanghai	272	135	137	338	184	154	923	200	723
江 苏	Jiangsu	1063	440	624	540	375	165	4180	1180	2999
浙 江	Zhejiang	723	305	417	441	273	168	2311	639	1672
安 徽	Anhui	666	305	362	422	249	173	2776	881	1895
福 建	Fujian	348	166	182	223	127	97	1590	403	1187
江 西	Jiangxi	490	247	243	282	175	107	1729	471	1258
山 东	Shandong	1275	546	730	374	230	144	4071	1172	2899
河 南	Henan	1015	426	589	593	410	183	4170	1376	2794
湖 北	Hubei	668	338	330	401	261	141	2784	914	1871
湖 南	Hunan	813	372	441	464	310	155	3177	1087	2090
广 东	Guangdong	491	254	238	360	222	138	3284	825	2459
广 西	Guangxi	454	241	213	342	218	125	2395	699	1696
海 南	Hainan	70	37	32	46	29	18	307	79	228
重 庆	Chongqing	637	285	351	413	230	183	1537	499	1038
四 川	Sichuan	1495	684	811	857	502	354	4336	1442	2893
贵 州	Guizhou	538	275	263	406	243	163	1729	569	1161
云 南	Yunnan	569	285	284	299	168	131	2096	776	1320
西 藏	Tibet	7	4	3	34	8	26	141	36	105
陕 西	Shaanxi	434	205	229	249	155	94	1569	514	1054
甘 肃	Gansu	205	106	99	182	116	67	1080	386	694
青 海	Qinghai	98	50	48	78	37	41	227	62	164
宁 夏	Ningxia	67	36	31	43	22	20	170	47	123
新 疆	Xinjiang	1109	605	504	413	193	220	634	159	474

4-11 各地区按性别和受教育程度分的人口

Population by Sex, Educational Level and Region

本表是2003年人口变动情况抽样调查样本数据，抽样比为0.982‰。

Data in this table are obtained from the Sample Survey on Population Changes in 2003. The sampling fraction is 0.982‰.

单位：人 (person)

地区	Region	6岁及6岁以上人口 Population Aged 6 and Over	男 Male	女 Female	不识字或识字很少 Illterate	男 Male	女 Female	小学 Primary	男 Male	女 Female
全 国	**National Total**	**1182247**	**600593**	**581653**	**114500**	**33359**	**81141**	**395118**	**193215**	**201903**
北 京	Beijing	13595	6989	6606	594	134	460	2001	925	1076
天 津	Tianjin	9550	4702	4848	564	134	430	2149	1023	1125
河 北	Hebei	62686	31800	30887	4080	1212	2868	18837	9124	9713
山 西	Shanxi	30367	15507	14860	1550	476	1074	9108	4326	4782
内蒙古	Inner Mongolia	22221	11354	10867	2733	907	1825	6815	3366	3449
辽 宁	Liaoning	39692	19802	19891	1795	474	1322	10161	4816	5346
吉 林	Jilin	25568	12799	12769	1022	383	639	7695	3689	4006
黑龙江	Heilongjiang	35942	18212	17730	1934	592	1342	10424	4911	5513
上 海	Shanghai	15698	7840	7858	887	171	716	2112	933	1179
江 苏	Jiangsu	69585	34335	35250	8951	2270	6681	21505	10382	11123
浙 江	Zhejiang	43420	21904	21516	5217	1532	3684	14520	7264	7256
安 徽	Anhui	58913	30153	28760	6810	1988	4822	19469	9357	10112
福 建	Fujian	32243	16393	15850	3754	887	2867	11770	5670	6100
江 西	Jiangxi	38534	19662	18871	2731	715	2017	12776	5901	6875
山 东	Shandong	83824	41811	42013	10243	2753	7490	23462	10925	12536
河 南	Henan	88402	45453	42949	6925	1985	4940	26922	13022	13900
湖 北	Hubei	56338	28633	27705	5596	1392	4204	18440	8938	9502
湖 南	Hunan	61285	31681	29604	4567	1279	3288	21357	10588	10769
广 东	Guangdong	71928	36389	35539	4800	1170	3629	27565	12960	14605
广 西	Guangxi	44290	23111	21179	3570	983	2587	17143	8488	8656
海 南	Hainan	7371	3886	3485	605	158	447	2377	1163	1214
重 庆	Chongqing	28968	14658	14310	2230	630	1600	11818	5953	5865
四 川	Sichuan	80344	40564	39780	8509	2656	5853	32491	16490	16000
贵 州	Guizhou	34629	17857	16771	5846	1887	3959	14108	7400	6708
云 南	Yunnan	38942	20304	18639	7254	2482	4772	20218	10714	9503
西 藏	Tibet	2426	1154	1272	1089	423	666	993	542	451
陕 西	Shaanxi	34371	17532	16839	3542	1161	2381	10443	5090	5353
甘 肃	Gansu	23934	12258	11676	4176	1503	2673	8589	4289	4300
青 海	Qinghai	4781	2429	2352	1015	327	688	1683	910	773
宁 夏	Ningxia	5131	2600	2530	778	240	538	1815	906	909
新 疆	Xinjiang	17268	8823	8445	1134	454	679	6354	3150	3204

4-11 续表 continued

单位: 人 (person)

地区	Region	初中 Junior Secondary School	男 Male	女 Female	高中 Senior Secondary School	男 Male	女 Female	大专以上 College and Higher Level	男 Male	女 Female
全国	**National Total**	**449693**	**246547**	**203146**	**158060**	**89289**	**68771**	**64875**	**38183**	**26692**
北京	Beijing	4796	2698	2098	3446	1726	1720	2758	1506	1252
天津	Tianjin	3597	1868	1729	2204	1114	1090	1037	562	474
河北	Hebei	27200	14522	12678	8433	4666	3766	4138	2276	1861
山西	Shanxi	14220	7633	6588	3855	2178	1676	1634	893	740
内蒙古	Inner Mongolia	8396	4729	3666	3062	1683	1380	1214	668	545
辽宁	Liaoning	17990	9333	8658	6185	3234	2951	3561	1945	1614
吉林	Jilin	10822	5643	5178	4389	2184	2205	1642	900	742
黑龙江	Heilongjiang	16778	8974	7804	5042	2738	2305	1762	996	766
上海	Shanghai	5521	2832	2689	4560	2383	2177	2617	1520	1097
江苏	Jiangsu	25753	13742	12012	9922	5813	4109	3454	2129	1326
浙江	Zhejiang	15031	8276	6756	5973	3237	2736	2679	1596	1084
安徽	Anhui	22841	12993	9847	6899	4089	2810	2894	1725	1170
福建	Fujian	10879	6260	4619	4336	2580	1756	1504	997	509
江西	Jiangxi	14360	7810	6550	6245	3668	2577	2421	1569	853
山东	Shandong	34149	18826	15323	11370	6498	4871	4601	2806	1793
河南	Henan	41081	22551	18529	10646	6215	4431	2829	1680	1149
湖北	Hubei	21441	11967	9473	7799	4509	3290	3063	1828	1236
湖南	Hunan	23521	12810	10711	8959	5270	3688	2881	1734	1147
广东	Guangdong	26240	14239	12001	9679	5792	3887	3645	2229	1417
广西	Guangxi	16581	9556	7025	4996	2864	2132	2000	1219	780
海南	Hainan	2754	1528	1226	1209	749	461	426	289	138
重庆	Chongqing	10657	5754	4903	3219	1710	1509	1045	611	433
四川	Sichuan	27761	14864	12897	8580	4742	3838	3004	1811	1192
贵州	Guizhou	9841	5818	4024	3003	1665	1338	1831	1089	742
云南	Yunnan	8856	5563	3294	1902	1136	767	712	409	302
西藏	Tibet	258	146	111	66	33	34	20	10	10
陕西	Shaanxi	12419	6730	5689	5775	3237	2538	2192	1314	878
甘肃	Gansu	7128	4012	3115	2980	1797	1183	1062	657	405
青海	Qinghai	1311	768	542	530	284	246	242	139	102
宁夏	Ningxia	1594	918	676	660	370	290	284	168	117
新疆	Xinjiang	5920	3184	2735	2135	1125	1010	1726	909	817

4-12 各地区按性别分15岁及15岁以上文盲半文盲人口

Illiterate and Semi-Literate Population Aged 15 and Over by Sex and Region

本表是2003年人口变动情况抽样调查样本数据，抽样比为0.982‰。

Data in this table are obtained from the Sample Survey on Population Changes in 2003. The sampling fraction is 0.982‰.

单位：人、%　　(person, %)

地 区	Region	15岁及15岁以上人口 Population Aged 15 and Over	男 Male	女 Female	文盲、半文盲人口 Illiterate and Semi-literate	男 Male	女 Female	文盲半文盲占15岁及以上人口的比重 % to Total Aged 15 and Over	男 Male	女 Female
全 国	**National Total**	**1004154**	**505478**	**498676**	**109955**	**30912**	**79043**	**10.95**	**6.12**	**15.85**
北 京	Beijing	12583	6472	6111	580	127	453	4.61	1.96	7.41
天 津	Tianjin	8566	4201	4365	545	125	420	6.36	2.97	9.62
河 北	Hebei	53791	27172	26620	3955	1150	2805	7.35	4.23	10.54
山 西	Shanxi	25082	12755	12327	1452	425	1026	5.79	3.34	8.32
内蒙古	Inner Mongolia	19223	9815	9408	2628	857	1771	13.67	8.73	18.82
辽 宁	Liaoning	35441	17632	17809	1680	419	1261	4.74	2.38	7.08
吉 林	Jilin	22617	11259	11358	880	302	578	3.89	2.68	5.09
黑龙江	Heilongjiang	31722	16004	15718	1835	538	1298	5.79	3.36	8.26
上 海	Shanghai	14646	7304	7342	861	157	705	5.88	2.14	9.60
江 苏	Jiangsu	60549	29480	31069	8753	2168	6585	14.46	7.35	21.19
浙 江	Zhejiang	38534	19292	19242	5096	1459	3638	13.23	7.56	18.90
安 徽	Anhui	48983	24798	24186	6694	1925	4769	13.67	7.76	19.72
福 建	Fujian	26935	13505	13430	3650	826	2825	13.55	6.11	21.03
江 西	Jiangxi	32045	16118	15927	2644	662	1982	8.25	4.11	12.44
山 东	Shandong	73300	36226	37074	10020	2626	7394	13.67	7.25	19.94
河 南	Henan	73564	37159	36405	6773	1907	4866	9.21	5.13	13.37
湖 北	Hubei	46673	23525	23148	5522	1357	4165	11.83	5.77	17.99
湖 南	Hunan	52835	27187	25647	4476	1227	3249	8.47	4.51	12.67
广 东	Guangdong	57083	28411	28672	4308	869	3439	7.55	3.06	12.00
广 西	Guangxi	37377	19275	18102	3309	826	2483	8.85	4.28	13.72
海 南	Hainan	6026	3121	2905	549	126	423	9.11	4.05	14.56
重 庆	Chongqing	24945	12503	12442	2095	552	1543	8.40	4.42	12.40
四 川	Sichuan	68569	34325	34244	8046	2424	5622	11.73	7.06	16.42
贵 州	Guizhou	28111	14350	13760	5533	1718	3815	19.68	11.97	27.72
云 南	Yunnan	32286	16808	15478	6941	2327	4614	21.50	13.84	29.81
西 藏	Tibet	1927	890	1036	1057	408	649	54.86	45.82	62.63
陕 西	Shaanxi	28725	14531	14194	3421	1092	2329	11.91	7.51	16.41
甘 肃	Gansu	19739	10066	9673	4013	1429	2584	20.33	14.20	26.71
青 海	Qinghai	3937	1981	1957	924	280	643	23.45	14.15	32.88
宁 夏	Ningxia	4163	2094	2069	731	220	511	17.57	10.52	24.69
新 疆	Xinjiang	14178	7220	6957	984	384	600	6.94	5.32	8.62

注：本表"文盲、半文盲人口"指15岁及15岁以上不识字及识字很少人口。

a) Illiterate and semi-illiterate population in this table refers to the population aged 15 and over, who are unable or very difficult to read.

4-13 各地区按家庭户规模分的户数

Number and Size of Family Households by Region

本表是2003年人口变动情况抽样调查样本数据，抽样比为0.982‰。

Data in this table are obtained from the Sample Survey on Population Changes in 2003. The sampling fraction is 0.982‰.

单位：户 (household)

地区	Region	户数合计 Total Number of Household	一人户 One Person	二人户 Two Persons	三人户 Three Persons	四人户 Four Persons	五人户 Five Persons	六人户 Six Persons	七人户 Seven Persons	八人户 Eight Persons	九人户 Nine Persons	十人及以上户 Ten Persons and Over
全 国	**National Total**	**367550**	**28112**	**70068**	**116558**	**83688**	**42188**	**17341**	**5733**	**2344**	**841**	**676**
北 京	Beijing	4614	670	1241	1789	560	261	67	16	7	2	1
天 津	Tianjin	3208	193	677	1455	560	240	63	18	3		
河 北	Hebei	19203	1217	3271	5872	5121	2366	945	302	83	15	13
山 西	Shanxi	8832	474	1291	2356	2599	1222	593	193	69	22	15
内蒙古	Inner Mongolia	7356	429	1615	2848	1529	641	221	52	14	4	3
辽 宁	Liaoning	13319	844	2954	5760	2182	1131	305	91	45	4	3
吉 林	Jilin	8070	385	1467	3411	1672	816	223	63	24	7	3
黑龙江	Heilongjiang	11985	629	2611	5170	2164	1033	273	67	31	5	3
上 海	Shanghai	5669	583	1448	2583	648	329	58	16	3		1
江 苏	Jiangsu	22685	1951	5520	7311	4033	2673	846	191	110	30	22
浙 江	Zhejiang	15374	1801	4071	5336	2540	1104	391	95	28	6	2
安 徽	Anhui	18053	1331	3339	5650	4468	2087	784	237	104	31	23
福 建	Fujian	9939	1072	1992	2938	2190	1090	440	135	50	16	17
江 西	Jiangxi	11927	831	2057	3881	2982	1240	570	194	94	35	44
山 东	Shandong	28889	2304	6747	10645	5970	2307	710	138	41	18	9
河 南	Henan	26799	2160	4314	7312	7067	3721	1479	445	148	103	51
湖 北	Hubei	17586	1400	3488	5631	4325	1804	629	190	91	14	14
湖 南	Hunan	18746	1443	3488	5478	4977	2043	871	258	116	47	25
广 东	Guangdong	19550	2095	2890	4017	4226	3008	1762	831	395	146	179
广 西	Guangxi	12834	923	1854	3265	3388	1872	919	333	179	61	40
海 南	Hainan	1958	140	248	450	447	326	182	92	40	16	16
重 庆	Chongqing	8941	393	1592	3164	2330	897	343	124	60	22	16
四 川	Sichuan	25758	2195	5109	8321	5482	2866	1159	400	131	48	46
贵 州	Guizhou	10348	672	1760	2742	2574	1598	671	224	67	26	15
云 南	Yunnan	10822	626	1172	2122	3480	1922	1010	314	112	41	23
西 藏	Tibet	537	23	35	84	120	96	73	45	26	17	19
陕 西	Shaanxi	10101	549	1728	2943	2615	1381	605	184	61	22	12
甘 肃	Gansu	6384	267	754	1597	1679	1044	629	262	92	34	24
青 海	Qinghai	1329	73	182	352	319	196	108	46	25	14	12
宁 夏	Ningxia	1503	79	242	411	351	224	120	49	20	6	2
新 疆	Xinjiang	5229	361	913	1662	1092	653	292	128	74	30	25

4-14　家庭户人数和户主的年龄、性别构成

Population of Family Households, Age and Sex Composition of Household Head

本表是2003年人口变动情况抽样调查样本数据,抽样比为0.982‰.

Data in this table are obtained from the Sample Survey of Population Changes in 2003.The sampling fraction is 0.982‰.

年　龄 Age	家庭户人口数(人) Population of Family Household (person)			户　主(人) Household Head (person)			户　主　率(%) Household Head Rate (%)		
	合计 Total	男 Male	女 Female	合计 Total	男 Male	女 Female	合计 Total	男 Male	女 Female
总计　Total	**1242389**	**632263**	**610126**	**367550**	**309213**	**58337**	**29.34**	**48.33**	**9.69**
14岁及以下 under 15	**255784**	**137615**	**118169**	**1636**	**923**	**714**	**0.47**	**0.50**	**0.44**
15-19	**100660**	**52857**	**47803**	**1395**	**861**	**534**	**1.24**	**1.45**	**1.01**
15	23981	12574	11407	290	176	114	0.92	1.05	0.77
16	25010	13056	11954	293	179	113	0.92	1.04	0.79
17	20438	10732	9707	218	129	89	1.06	1.22	0.89
18	16711	8911	7800	278	179	99	1.56	1.89	1.18
19	14520	7585	6935	317	198	118	2.11	2.49	1.69
20-24	**75926**	**37565**	**38361**	**4993**	**3701**	**1293**	**6.84**	**10.31**	**3.40**
20	14223	7300	6923	400	264	136	3.00	3.88	2.07
21	15833	8052	7782	591	389	203	3.94	5.19	2.62
22	14669	7198	7471	790	544	247	5.87	8.42	3.39
23	14714	7104	7610	1266	972	294	8.83	14.15	3.84
24	16488	7911	8577	1946	1532	414	12.16	19.90	4.84
25-29	**91293**	**44932**	**46361**	**20732**	**17556**	**3176**	**22.83**	**39.56**	**6.60**
25	16911	8258	8653	2600	2125	475	15.56	26.38	5.21
26	15670	7759	7911	2974	2500	474	19.15	32.67	6.01
27	18739	9301	9438	4281	3632	649	22.97	39.57	6.66
28	19113	9369	9745	4846	4103	743	25.50	44.55	7.23
29	20860	10246	10614	6031	5195	836	29.23	51.29	7.62
30-34	**121508**	**60490**	**61018**	**45644**	**39891**	**5752**	**37.37**	**66.02**	**8.92**
30	22651	11284	11368	7328	6369	959	32.37	56.97	8.00
31	22847	11343	11504	8079	7053	1026	35.46	62.70	8.47
32	24637	12269	12369	9191	8036	1156	36.96	65.39	8.85
33	26640	13225	13415	10652	9331	1320	39.76	70.49	9.33
34	24732	12370	12362	10394	9103	1291	41.71	73.44	9.84

4-14 续表 continued

年 龄 Age	家庭户人口数(人) Population of Family Household (person)			户 主(人) Household Head (person)			户 主 率(%) Household Head Rate (%)		
	合计 Total	男 Male	女 Female	合计 Total	男 Male	女 Female	合计 Total	男 Male	女 Female
35-39	**121757**	**60846**	**60911**	**55943**	**49264**	**6679**	**45.63**	**80.31**	**10.70**
35	27415	13617	13798	11895	10481	1414	43.27	76.24	10.22
36	21573	10720	10853	9662	8513	1149	44.48	78.68	10.37
37	24355	12206	12149	11336	10021	1316	46.22	81.52	10.45
38	24374	12325	12049	11634	10268	1366	47.37	82.68	11.00
39	24040	11978	12062	11416	9981	1435	46.97	82.69	11.50
40-44	**90569**	**46064**	**44505**	**45060**	**39599**	**5460**	**49.54**	**84.92**	**12.57**
40	29065	14741	14324	14200	12445	1755	48.59	83.54	12.36
41	20932	10550	10382	10347	9144	1203	49.34	85.37	11.98
42	12214	6252	5963	6141	5391	750	49.89	84.89	12.75
43	14660	7470	7189	7317	6438	878	49.93	85.18	12.93
44	13698	7051	6646	7055	6182	874	51.04	86.81	13.35
45-49	**93637**	**47242**	**46395**	**48130**	**41981**	**6149**	**51.21**	**87.92**	**14.02**
45	17831	9051	8780	9095	7961	1134	50.59	87.07	13.41
46	19551	9903	9648	10059	8763	1296	51.31	87.43	14.32
47	18173	9064	9109	9157	8032	1125	50.59	87.92	13.00
48	19165	9750	9415	9980	8728	1252	51.76	88.39	14.37
49	18917	9474	9442	9839	8496	1343	51.75	88.81	14.93
50-54	**81274**	**40774**	**40500**	**42186**	**36084**	**6102**	**51.71**	**87.49**	**15.82**
50	18493	9113	9379	9496	8143	1353	51.10	88.42	14.89
51	17694	8852	8841	9119	7871	1248	51.38	87.87	14.76
52	15388	7870	7518	8145	7008	1137	52.34	87.52	16.22
53	14927	7473	7454	7730	6544	1187	51.73	86.59	16.83
54	14772	7465	7307	7695	6518	1177	52.22	86.77	16.85
55-59	**57243**	**29214**	**28029**	**29559**	**24926**	**4633**	**51.32**	**84.68**	**17.36**
55	12868	6485	6383	6638	5629	1009	51.45	86.21	16.56
56	12481	6477	6004	6450	5497	953	51.03	84.18	16.54
57	11414	5848	5565	5988	5050	938	52.08	85.43	17.75
58	10491	5328	5162	5380	4498	882	51.08	84.16	17.79
59	9990	5075	4914	5103	4253	850	50.90	83.05	18.53
60-64	**45887**	**23238**	**22649**	**23272**	**18828**	**4444**	**50.62**	**80.34**	**20.73**
60	10041	5047	4994	5123	4170	953	51.06	82.16	20.25
61	9254	4698	4557	4719	3838	881	50.66	80.17	20.47
62	9555	4853	4703	4852	3965	887	50.62	80.88	19.77
63	9028	4670	4358	4628	3731	897	51.24	79.46	22.15
64	8009	3970	4038	3950	3124	826	49.31	78.63	21.14
65岁及以上 65 and over	**106851**	**51427**	**55424**	**48999**	**35598**	**13400**	**46.93**	**69.42**	**25.79**

4-15 各地区15-49岁妇女活产和存活子女状况

Live Births and Surviving Children of Women Aged 15-49 by Region

本表是2003年人口变动情况抽样调查样本数据，抽样比为0.982‰。

Data in this table are obtained from the Sample Survey on Population Changes in 2003. The sampling fraction is 0.982‰.

单位:人 (person)

地区	Region	15-49岁妇女人数 Number of Women Aged 15-49	活产子女 人数 Number of Live Births	男 Male	女 Female	存活子女 人数 Number of Surviving Children	男 Male	女 Female	妇女平均活产子女数 Average Number of Live Births per Women	妇女平均存活子女数 Average Number of Surviving Children per Women
全国	**National Total**	**351789**	**410327**	**217093**	**193235**	**406099**	**214961**	**191138**	**1.17**	**1.15**
北京	Beijing	4128	2947	1529	1418	2933	1522	1411	**0.71**	**0.71**
天津	Tianjin	2903	2519	1302	1217	2499	1289	1210	0.87	0.86
河北	Hebei	19322	22117	11712	10405	21995	11652	10342	1.14	1.14
山西	Shanxi	9090	12012	6357	5655	11927	6307	5620	1.32	1.31
内蒙古	Inner Mongolia	6891	8216	4228	3988	8166	4201	3964	1.19	1.19
辽宁	Liaoning	12320	10899	5638	5261	10833	5592	5241	0.88	0.88
吉林	Jilin	8428	7479	3779	3699	7449	3760	3689	0.89	0.88
黑龙江	Heilongjiang	11551	11635	6128	5507	11564	6085	5479	1.01	1.00
上海	Shanghai	4276	2947	1514	1434	2934	1506	1429	0.69	0.69
江苏	Jiangsu	20022	20690	10952	9738	20488	10855	9632	1.03	1.02
浙江	Zhejiang	12986	13516	7175	6341	13411	7118	6293	1.04	1.03
安徽	Anhui	17204	20401	10687	9714	20196	10579	9617	1.19	1.17
福建	Fujian	10002	12719	6877	5841	12595	6830	5765	1.27	1.26
江西	Jiangxi	11810	15634	8344	7291	15435	8239	7197	1.32	1.31
山东	Shandong	25743	27793	14475	13318	27588	14401	13187	1.08	1.07
河南	Henan	25779	31671	16945	14726	31494	16840	14655	1.23	1.22
湖北	Hubei	16349	19448	10278	9171	19277	10190	9088	1.19	1.18
湖南	Hunan	17960	21546	11295	10252	21238	11140	10098	1.20	1.18
广东	Guangdong	21031	30175	16349	13826	30026	16264	13762	1.43	1.43
广西	Guangxi	12543	15715	8583	7132	15594	8530	7064	1.25	1.24
海南	Hainan	2135	2897	1621	1276	2874	1609	1265	1.36	1.35
重庆	Chongqing	8311	8696	4648	4048	8563	4578	3985	1.05	1.03
四川	Sichuan	23505	24759	13136	11623	24480	13018	11463	1.05	1.04
贵州	Guizhou	9640	13766	7289	6477	13438	7121	6317	1.43	1.39
云南	Yunnan	11469	16642	8707	7935	16179	8468	7710	1.45	1.41
西藏	Tibet	790	1017	524	493	989	508	482	1.29	1.25
陕西	Shaanxi	10106	12201	6472	5729	12097	6430	5666	1.21	1.20
甘肃	Gansu	7041	9043	4757	4286	8971	4731	4240	1.28	1.27
青海	Qinghai	1466	1931	1013	918	1896	994	902	1.32	1.29
宁夏	Ningxia	1580	2342	1214	1128	2305	1194	1111	1.48	1.46
新疆	Xinjiang	5408	6954	3564	3389	6666	3412	3254	1.29	1.23

4-16 育龄妇女分年龄、孩次的生育状况

Age-specific Fertility Rate of Childbearing Women by Age of Mother and Birth Order (2002.11.1-2003.10.31)

本表是2003年人口变动情况抽样调查样本数据,抽样比为0.982‰.

Data in this table are obtained from the Sample Survey of Population Changes in 2003. The sampling fraction is 0.982‰.

年 龄 Age	平均育龄妇女人数（人） Average Number of Childbearing Woman (person)	出生人数（人） Births (person)	一孩 1st Births	二孩 2nd Births	三孩及以上 3rd Births and over	生育率（‰） Fertility Rate (‰)	一孩 1st Births	二孩 2nd Births	三孩及以上 3rd Births and over
总计 Total	**350677**	**13328**	**9159**	**3541**	**628**	**38.01**	**26.12**	**10.1**	**1.79**
15-19	**47631**	**250**	**238**	**9**	**3**	**5.25**	**4.99**	**0.20**	**0.06**
15	11978	6	6			0.51	0.51		
16	11210	10	8	1		0.85	0.75	0.09	
17	9154	22	21	1		2.40	2.28	0.12	
18	7833	57	55	1	1	7.27	7.07	0.10	0.10
19	7456	155	147	7	2	20.84	19.72	0.87	0.25
20-24	**41296**	**5066**	**4614**	**373**	**78**	**122.67**	**111.73**	**9.04**	**1.90**
20	7913	446	420	22	4	56.42	53.13	2.77	0.51
21	8134	830	786	37	7	102.05	96.58	4.59	0.89
22	7924	1097	1021	63	12	138.40	128.89	7.99	1.51
23	8423	1292	1160	108	24	153.35	137.67	12.82	2.87
24	8902	1401	1227	143	31	157.39	137.86	16.04	3.49
25-29	**48555**	**4974**	**3440**	**1344**	**190**	**102.44**	**70.86**	**27.68**	**3.91**
25	8496	1234	1030	175	29	145.19	121.19	20.54	3.45
26	8846	1082	824	224	34	122.37	93.17	25.30	3.90
27	9763	1018	706	270	42	104.29	72.28	27.66	4.35
28	10330	872	508	325	39	84.42	49.18	31.43	3.81
29	11119	768	373	351	44	69.04	33.53	31.56	3.96
30-34	**62838**	**2405**	**743**	**1431**	**232**	**38.28**	**11.82**	**22.78**	**3.68**
30	11576	678	278	347	53	58.57	23.98	30.00	4.60
31	12080	580	193	339	48	48.00	15.96	28.08	3.97
32	13015	485	128	314	43	37.25	9.81	24.13	3.31
33	12986	379	86	249	45	29.21	6.58	19.16	3.47
34	13180	283	59	182	42	21.50	4.49	13.80	3.20
35-39	**61568**	**533**	**106**	**331**	**95**	**8.65**	**1.73**	**5.37**	**1.55**
35	12429	206	47	130	30	16.61	3.81	10.42	2.37
36	11585	123	27	75	20	10.58	2.32	6.49	1.77
37	12164	90	14	57	19	7.43	1.17	4.68	1.57
38	12119	70	12	42	16	5.77	1.01	3.45	1.30
39	13271	43	6	27	11	3.26	0.42	2.05	0.79
40-44	**41927**	**74**	**12**	**42**	**21**	**1.77**	**0.28**	**1.00**	**0.49**
40	12422	33	3	22	8	2.63	0.26	1.76	0.61
41	8216	21	4	12	4	2.51	0.47	1.50	0.55
42	6603	9	2	3	4	1.37	0.28	0.47	0.63
43	6945	6	1	2	3	0.90	0.18	0.30	0.42
44	7742	6	2	3	2	0.74	0.20	0.32	0.21
45-49	**46862**	**26**	**6**	**11**	**10**	**0.56**	**0.12**	**0.23**	**0.21**
45	9252	5	1	2	2	0.52	0.11	0.17	0.24
46	9418	6	1	3	2	0.68	0.14	0.30	0.24
47	9294	6	1	4	2	0.69	0.08	0.40	0.21
48	9459	4	1	1	2	0.43	0.10	0.13	0.21
49	9439	4	2	1	1	0.47	0.20	0.14	0.13

主要统计指标解释

人口数 指一定时点、一定地区范围内有生命的个人总和。

年度统计的年末人口数指每年12月31日24时的人口数。年度统计的全国人口总数内未包括香港、澳门特别行政区和台湾省以及海外华侨人数。

城镇人口和乡村人口的划分 城镇人口是指居住在城镇范围内的全部人口；乡村人口是除上述人口以外的全部人口。

历年城乡人口数据是按照当时国家《关于统计上划分城乡的规定》计算的。

三次普查之间年份的城乡人口根据1990年和2000年人口普查数据进行了调整。

出生率(又称粗出生率) 指在一定时期内(通常为一年)一定地区的出生人数与同期内平均人数(或期中人数)之比，用千分率表示。本资料中的出生率指年出生率，其计算公式为：

$$出生率=\frac{年出生人数}{年平均人数}\times 1000‰$$

式中：出生人数指活产婴儿，即胎儿脱离母体时(不管怀孕月数)，有过呼吸或其他生命现象。年平均人数指年初、年底人口数的平均数，也可用年中人口数代替。

死亡率(又称粗死亡率) 指在一定时期内(通常为一年)一定地区的死亡人数与同期内平均人数(或期中人数)之比，用千分率表示。本资料中的死亡率指年死亡率，其计算公式为：

$$死亡率=\frac{年死亡人数}{年平均人数}\times 1000‰$$

人口自然增长率 指在一定时期内(通常为一年)人口自然增加数(出生人数减死亡人数)与该时期内平均人数(或期中人数)之比，用千分率表示。计算公式为：

$$人口自然增长率=\frac{本年出生人数-本年死亡人数}{年平均人数}\times 1000‰$$
$$=人口出生率-人口死亡率$$

总抚养比 也称总负担系数。指人口总体中非劳动年龄人口数与劳动年龄人口数之比。通常用百分比表示。说明每100名劳动年龄人口大致要负担多少名非劳动年龄人口。用于从人口角度反映人口与经济发展的基本关系。计算公式为：

$$GDR=\frac{P_{0\sim14}+P_{65^+}}{P_{15\sim64}}\times 100\%$$

其中：GDP为总抚养比；

$P_{0\sim14}$为0～14岁少年儿童人口数；

P_{65^+}为65岁及65岁以上的老年人口数；

$P_{15\sim64}$为15～64岁劳动年龄人口数。

老年人口抚养比 也称老年人口抚养系数。指某一人口中老年人口数与劳动年龄人口数之比。通常用百分比表示。用以表明每100名劳动年龄人口要负担多少名老年人。老年人口抚养比是从经济角度反映人口老化社会后果的指标之一。计算公式为：

$$ODR=\frac{P_{65^+}}{P_{15\sim64}}\times 100\%$$

其中：ODR为老年人口抚养比；

P_{65^+}为65岁及65岁以上的老年人口数；

$P_{15\sim64}$为15～64岁的劳动年龄人口数。

少年儿童抚养比 也称少年儿童抚养系数。指某一人口中少年儿童人口数与劳动年龄人口数之比。通常用百分比表示。以反映每100名劳动年龄人口要负担多少名少年儿童。计算公式为：

$$CDR=\frac{P_{0\sim14}}{P_{15\sim64}}\times 100\%$$

其中：CDR为少年儿童抚养比；

$P_{0\sim14}$为0～14岁少年儿童人口数；

$P_{15\sim64}$为15～64岁劳动年龄人口数。

Explanatory Notes on Main Statistical Indicators

Total Population refers to the total number of people alive at a certain point of time within a given area.

The annual statistics on total population is taken at midnight, the 3lst of December, not including residents in Taiwan province, Hong Kong and Macao and overseas Chinese.

Urban Population and Rural Population Urban population refer to all people residing in cities and towns, while rural population refer to population other than urban population.

Statistics on urban and rural population over the years are compiled in line with the regulations of statistical classification on urban and rural population stipulated by the government, which were in effect at different times.

Figures on urban/rural population for the years between the 3 censuses are adjusted in accordance with the 1990 and 2000 population census data.

Birth Rate or (Crude Birth Rate) refers to the ratio of the number of births to the average population (or mid-period population) during a certain period of time (usually a year), expressed in‰. Birth rate in the chapter refers to annual birth rate. The following formula is used:

Birth Rate = (Number of Births/Average Number of Population)×1000%

Number of births in the formula refers to live births, i.e. when a baby has breathed or showed any vital phenomena regardless of the length of pregnancy.

Annual average number of population is the average of the number of population at the beginning of the year and that at the end of the year. Sometimes it is substituted by the mid-year population.

Death Rate (or Crude Death Rate) refers to the ratio of the number of deaths to the average population (or mid-period population) during a certain period of time (usually a year), expressed in‰. Death rate in the chapter refers to annual death rate. The following formula is used:

Death Rate= (Number of Deaths/Annual Average Number of Population)×1000%

Natural Growth Rate of Population refers to the ratio of natural increase in population (number of births minus number of deaths) in a certain period of time (usually a year) to the average population (or mid-period population) of the same period, expressed in ¡ë. The following formula is applied:

Natural Growth Rate of Population = [(Number of Births-Number of Deaths)/Average Number of Population]×1000%

Natural Growth Rate of Population = Birth Rate-Death Rate

Gross Dependency Ratio also called gross dependency coefficient, refers to the ratio of non-working-age population to the working-age population, express in %. Describing in general the number of non-working-age population that every 100 people at working ages will take care of, this indicator reflects the basic relation between population and economic development from the demographic perspective. The gross dependency ratio is calculated with the following formula:

$$GDR=\frac{P_{0-14}+P_{65+}}{P_{15-64}}\times 100\%$$

Where: GDR is the gross dependency ratio

P_{0-14} is the population of children aged 0-14

P_{65+} is the elderly population aged 65 and over, and

P_{15-64} is the working-age population aged 15-64

Old Dependency Ratio also called old dependency coefficient, refers to the ratio of the elderly population to the working-age population, express in %. It describes the number of the elderly population that every 100 people at working ages will take care of. Old dependency ratio is one of the indicators reflecting the social implication of population aging from the economic perspective. The old dependency ratio is calculated with the following formula:

$$ODR=\frac{P_{65+}}{P_{15-64}}\times 100\%$$

Where:ODR is the old dependency ratio

P_{65+} is the elderly population aged 65 and over, and

P_{15-64} is the working-age population aged 15-64

Children Dependency Ratio also called children dependency coefficient, refers to the ratio of the children population to the working-age population, express in %. It describes the number of children population that every 100 people at working ages will take care of. The children dependency ratio is calculated with the following formula:

$$CDR=\frac{P_{0-14}}{P_{15-64}}\times 100\%$$

Where: CDR is the children dependency ratio

P_{0-14} is the children population aged 0-14, and

P_{15-64} is the working-age population aged 15-64

五、就业人员和职工工资

Employment and Wages

简要说明

一、本篇资料的主要内容

本篇资料反映我国劳动经济方面的基本情况，包括31个省、自治区、直辖市的主要劳动统计数据。如：经济活动人口数，就业人员及职工人数，城镇登记失业人数，职工工资总额，平均工资及指数变化情况等。

二、本篇资料的统计范围

《劳动统计报表制度》的调查范围为全部独立核算单位；《人口变动情况抽样调查方案》的调查范围为全国人口，统计范围为16岁及以上人口；《乡村社会经济调查方案》的调查范围为全国乡镇以下农村地区；《培训、就业统计报表制度》的调查范围为全国的城镇人口；私营企业及个体工商业统计范围为全社会。1990年及以后的经济活动人口、就业人员、城镇和乡村就业人员资料，是根据第五次全国人口普查资料调整的，因此分地区、分类型、分行业的资料相加不等于总计。1998年及以后城镇单位就业人员、职工人数及相关指标统计口径有调整。

三、本篇的资料来源

1.就业基本情况及分组资料(5-1至5-15表)、职工工资总额等资料(5-20至5-34表)，是国家统计局人口和社会科技统计司根据其《劳动统计报表制度》、《人口变动情况抽样调查方案》及《乡村社会经济调查方案》加工整理。

2.职业介绍服务机构及劳动力交流情况、城镇登记失业人数（5-35、5-36表)，是劳动和社会保障部根据其《培训、就业统计报表制度》整理提供。

3.私营企业及个体工商业就业人员(5-16至5-19表)，由国家工商行政管理总局提供。

四、本篇的统计调查方法

劳动统计采用全面调查方法，由各级统计部门逐级上报；人口变动情况抽样调查采用多阶段、分层、整群抽样方法；培训、就业统计及私营企业和个体工商业统计利用行政登记资料加工整理。

五、自1989年始，国家统计局与劳动和社会保障部每年度联合出版《中国劳动统计年鉴》，提供了比本篇更为详细的资料。

Brief Introduction

I. Main Content

Data in this chapter show the basic conditions of China's labour economy, including the main data of labour statistics of the whole country and 31 provinces, autonomous regions and municipalities under the direct leadership of the central government, such as the economically active population, number of the employed persons and staff and workers, number of persons employed in the urban and rural private enterprises and self-employed persons in industry and commerce, number of registered unemployed persons in urban areas, total wages and average wages of the staff and workers and the changes in index, etc.

II. Coverage of Statistics

The Comprehensive Labour Statistics Reporting System covers all independent accounting units. *The Sample Survey on the Population Changes* covers the population aged 16 and over of the whole country. *The Rural Social and Economic Survey* covers all rural areas below township level in China. *The Statistical Reporting System on Training and Employment* covers all urban population of China. The Statistical Reports on Private Enterprises and Individual Industrial and Commercial Business cover the whole society. Data on economically active population, total employed population and employed population by urban and rural areas are adjusted on the basis of the 2000 population census, therefore the breakdown of these data by province, by type of ownership and by industry do not add up to the totals. Adjustments are also made with regard to the definition of urban employed population, total number of workers and staff and other related statistics since 1998.

III. Source of Data

(1) Data on basic conditions of employment (tables 5-1 to 5-15), total wage bill of workers and staff (tables 5-20 to 5-34) are collected and compiled through the *Comprehensive Labour Statistics Reporting System, the Sample Survey on the Population Changes*, and the *Rural Social and Economic Survey* by the Department of Population, Social and Science Statistics of the National Bureau of Statistics.

(2) Data on the career services and the exchanges of labour force and on the urban registered unemployed persons (tables 5-35 and 5-36) are collected through the Statistical Reporting System on Training and Employment and provided by the Ministry of Labour and Social Security.

(3) Data on the number of persons employed in the urban and rural private enterprises and self-employed persons in industry and commerce (tables 5-16 to 5-19) are provided by the State Administration for Industry and Commerce.

IV. Survey Methodology

A complete reporting from lower levels to higher levels is used in the labour statistics reporting system. The sample surveys on population changes are conducted with a multi-stage stratified cluster sampling scheme. Statistics on training, employment, private enterprises and self-employed individuals are collected and compiled on basis of administrative records.

V. Since 1989, *China Labour Statistical Yearbook* has been jointly published by the National Bureau of Statistics and the Ministry of Labour and Social Security, which provides more detailed data than those in this chapter.s

5-1 就业基本情况

Employment

项　目	Item	2000	2001	2002	2003
经济活动人口　（万人）	**Economically Active Population (10 000 persons)**	**73992**	**74432**	**75360**	**76075**
就业人员合计　（万人）	**Total Number of Employed Persons (10 000 persons)**	**72085**	**73025**	**73740**	**74432**
第一产业	Primary Industry	36043	36513	36870	36546
第二产业	Secondary Industry	16219	16284	15780	16077
第三产业	Tertiary Industry	19823	20228	21090	21809
就业人员构成(合计=100)	**Composition of Employed Persons (total=100)**				
第一产业	Primary Industry	50.0	50.0	50.0	49.1
第二产业	Secondary Industry	22.5	22.3	21.4	21.6
第三产业	Tertiary Industry	27.5	27.7	28.6	29.3
按城乡分就业人员(万人)	**Number of Employed Persons by Urban and Rural Areas (10 000 persons)**				
城镇就业人员	Urban Employed Persons	23151	23940	24780	25639
#国有单位	State-owned Units	8102	7640	7163	6876
城镇集体单位	Urban Collective-owned Units	1499	1291	1122	1000
股份合作单位	Cooperative Units	155	153	161	173
联营单位	Joint Ownership Units	42	45	45	44
有限责任公司	Limited Liability Corporations	687	841	1083	1261
股份有限公司	Share-holding Corporations Ltd.	457	483	538	592
私营企业	Private Enterprises	1268	1527	1999	2545
港澳台商投资单位	Units with Funds from Hong Kong, Macao & Taiwan	310	326	367	409
外商投资单位	Foreign Funded Units	332	345	391	454
个体	Self-employed Individuals	2136	2131	2269	2377
乡村就业人员	Rural Employed Persons	48934	49085	48960	48793
#乡镇企业	Township and Village Enterprises	12820	13086	13288	13573
私营企业	Private Enterprises	1139	1187	1411	1754
个体	Self-employed Individuals	2934	2629	2474	2260
在岗职工人数　（万人）	**Number of Staff and Workers (10 000 persons)**	**11259**	**10792**	**10558**	**10492**
国有单位	State-owned Units	7878	7409	6924	6621
城镇集体单位	Urban Collective-owned Units	1447	1241	1071	951
其他单位	Units of Other Types of Ownership	1935	2142	2563	2920
城镇登记失业人数(万人)	**Number of Registered Unemployed Persons in Urban Areas (10 000 persons)**	**595**	**681**	**770**	**800**
城镇登记失业率　（%）	**Registered Unemployment Rate in Urban Areas (%)**	**3.1**	**3.6**	**4.0**	**4.3**

注：1990年至2000年，就业人员总计、城镇和乡村就业人员小计资料根据第五次全国人口普查资料重新调整，2001年及以后资料根据人口变动抽样调查资料推算，因此分地区、分类型、分行业的分项资料相加不等于总计（下表同）。

a) From 1990 to 2000, the total number of employed persons, the sub-total of urban and rural employed persons have been adjusted in accordance with the data obtained from the 5th National Population Census. Since 2001, these data are calculated by the annual population sampling survey. As a result, the sum of the data by region, by ownship and by sector is not equal to the total. The same as in the following tables.

5-2 按三次产业分就业人员数（年底数）

Number of Employed Persons at the Year-end by Three Industries

年份 Year	经济活动人口（万人） Economically Active Population (10 000 persons)	就业人员（万人） Total Employed Persons (10 000 persons)	第一产业 Primary Industry	第二产业 Secondary Industry	第三产业 Tertiary Industry	构成（合计=100） Composition in Percentage 第一产业 Primary Industry	第二产业 Secondary Industry	第三产业 Tertiary Industry
1952	21106	20729	17317	1531	1881	83.5	7.4	9.1
1957	23971	23771	19309	2142	2320	81.2	9.0	9.8
1962		25910	21276	2059	2575	82.1	8.0	9.9
1965		28670	23396	2408	2866	81.6	8.4	10.0
1970		34432	27811	3518	3103	80.8	10.2	9.0
1975		38168	29456	5152	3560	77.2	13.5	9.3
1978	40682	40152	28318	6945	4890	70.5	17.3	12.2
1979	41592	41024	28634	7214	5177	69.8	17.6	12.6
1980	42903	42361	29122	7707	5532	68.7	18.2	13.1
1981	44165	43725	29777	8003	5945	68.1	18.3	13.6
1982	45674	45295	30859	8346	6090	68.1	18.4	13.5
1983	46707	46436	31151	8679	6606	67.1	18.7	14.2
1984	48433	48197	30868	9590	7739	64.0	19.9	16.1
1985	50112	49873	31130	10384	8359	62.4	20.8	16.8
1986	51546	51282	31254	11216	8811	60.9	21.9	17.2
1987	53060	52783	31663	11726	9395	60.0	22.2	17.8
1988	54630	54334	32249	12152	9933	59.3	22.4	18.3
1989	55707	55329	33225	11976	10129	60.1	21.6	18.3
1990	65323	64749	38914	13856	11979	60.1	21.4	18.5
1991	66091	65491	39098	14015	12378	59.7	21.4	18.9
1992	66782	66152	38699	14355	13098	58.5	21.7	19.8
1993	67468	66808	37680	14965	14163	56.4	22.4	21.2
1994	68135	67455	36628	15312	15515	54.3	22.7	23.0
1995	68855	68065	35530	15655	16880	52.2	23.0	24.8
1996	69765	68950	34820	16203	17927	50.5	23.5	26.0
1997	70800	69820	34840	16547	18432	49.9	23.7	26.4
1998	72087	70637	35177	16600	18860	49.8	23.5	26.7
1999	72791	71394	35768	16421	19205	50.1	23.0	26.9
2000	73992	72085	36043	16219	19823	50.0	22.5	27.5
2001	74432	73025	36513	16284	20228	50.0	22.3	27.7
2002	75360	73740	36870	15780	21090	50.0	21.4	28.6
2003	76075	74432	36546	16077	21809	49.1	21.6	29.3

5-3 各地区按三次产业分就业人员数（2003年底）

Number of Employed Persons at the Year-end by Three Industries and Region (2003)

地 区	Region	就业人员（万人）Total Employed Persons (10 000 persons)	第一产业 Primary Industry	第二产业 Secondary Industry	第三产业 Tertiary Industry	构成（合计=100）Composition in Percentage 第一产业 Primary Industry	第二产业 Secondary Industry	第三产业 Tertiary Industry
全 国	**National Total**	**74432.0**	**36546.0**	**16077.0**	**21809.0**	**49.1**	**21.6**	**29.3**
北 京	Beijing	858.6	66.9	280.2	511.5	7.8	32.6	59.6
天 津	Tianjin	419.7	82.3	168.1	169.3	19.6	40.0	40.4
河 北	Hebei	3389.5	1670.1	936.9	782.5	49.3	27.6	23.1
山 西	Shanxi	1469.5	650.6	360.3	458.7	44.3	24.5	31.2
内蒙古	Inner Mongolia	1005.2	548.7	152.5	303.9	54.6	15.2	30.2
辽 宁	Liaoning	1861.3	696.7	457.4	707.1	37.4	24.6	38.0
吉 林	Jilin	1044.6	523.8	181.9	338.9	50.1	17.4	32.4
黑龙江	Heilongjiang	1622.4	827.7	316.9	477.8	51.0	19.5	29.4
上 海	Shanghai	771.5	73.7	316.5	381.3	9.6	41.0	49.4
江 苏	Jiangsu	3610.3	1250.0	1239.5	1120.8	34.6	34.3	31.0
浙 江	Zhejiang	2961.9	877.6	1092.4	991.9	29.6	36.9	33.5
安 徽	Anhui	3416.0	1875.2	647.4	893.3	54.9	19.0	26.2
福 建	Fujian	1756.7	745.8	488.3	522.6	42.5	27.8	29.8
江 西	Jiangxi	1972.3	988.8	351.1	632.4	50.1	17.8	32.1
山 东	Shandong	4850.6	2276.9	1272.5	1301.3	46.9	26.2	26.8
河 南	Henan	5535.7	3331.9	1083.6	1120.3	60.2	19.6	20.2
湖 北	Hubei	2537.3	1144.1	473.9	919.3	45.1	18.7	36.2
湖 南	Hunan	3515.9	2017.1	546.6	952.2	57.4	15.5	27.1
广 东	Guangdong	4119.5	1559.6	1149.9	1410.1	37.9	27.9	34.2
广 西	Guangxi	2601.4	1556.6	279.3	765.5	59.8	10.7	29.4
海 南	Hainan	353.8	210.6	34.8	108.5	59.5	9.8	30.7
重 庆	Chongqing	1659.5	816.3	310.3	532.9	49.2	18.7	32.1
四 川	Sichuan	4449.6	2426.6	749.6	1273.4	54.5	16.8	28.6
贵 州	Guizhou	2118.4	1327.1	204.3	587.0	62.6	9.6	27.7
云 南	Yunnan	2349.6	1709.3	209.6	430.7	72.7	8.9	18.3
西 藏	Tibet	130.7	85.0	11.9	33.7	65.1	9.1	25.8
陕 西	Shaanxi	1911.3	996.7	315.7	598.9	52.1	16.5	31.3
甘 肃	Gansu	1304.0	769.9	177.5	356.7	59.0	13.6	27.4
青 海	Qinghai	254.3	137.6	40.3	76.4	54.1	15.8	30.1
宁 夏	Ningxia	290.6	150.6	63.2	76.9	51.8	21.8	26.4
新 疆	Xinjiang	721.3	397.2	95.7	228.4	55.1	13.3	31.7

5-4 按城乡分就业人员数（年底数）

单位：万人

年份 Year 地区 Region	合计 Total	城镇 小计 Sub-total	#国有单位 State-owned Units	#集体单位 Collective-owned Units	#股份合作单位 Cooperative Units	#联营单位 Joint Ownership Units	#有限责任公司 Limited Liability Corporations	#股份有限公司 Share Holding Corporations Ltd.
1978	40152	9514	7451	2048				
1980	42361	10525	8019	2425				
1985	49873	12808	8990	3324		38		
1989	55329	14390	10108	3502		82		
1990	64749	17041	10346	3549		96		
1991	65491	17465	10664	3628		49		
1992	66152	17861	10889	3621		56		
1993	66808	18262	10920	3393		66		164
1994	67455	18653	11214	3285		52		292
1995	68065	19040	11261	3147		53		317
1996	68950	19922	11244	3016		49		363
1997	69820	20781	11044	2883		43		468
1998	70637	21616	9058	1963	136	48	484	410
1999	71394	22412	8572	1712	144	46	603	420
2000	72085	23151	8102	1499	155	42	687	457
2001	73025	23940	7640	1291	153	45	841	483
2002	73740	24780	7163	1122	161	45	1083	538
2003	74432	25639	6876	1000	173	44	1261	592
北京 Beijing	858.6	689.0	212.8	30.0	15.5	3.8	102.3	33.4
天津 Tianjin	419.7	245.9	90.7	14.0	1.3	1.8	24.8	9.0
河北 Hebei	3389.5	641.4	373.6	42.9	6.3	0.4	37.7	19.7
山西 Shanxi	1469.5	456.7	254.7	39.0	3.3	0.2	44.7	11.1
内蒙古 Inner Mongolia	1005.2	352.9	169.2	15.8	2.0	0.3	40.2	12.0
辽宁 Liaoning	1861.3	845.0	317.8	50.2	6.4	0.5	57.4	25.6
吉林 Jilin	1044.6	375.6	207.6	28.2	2.5	0.2	22.8	20.5
黑龙江 Heilongjiang	1622.4	686.3	342.7	55.9	17.3	1.9	38.0	36.8
上海 Shanghai	771.5	521.5	163.7	21.1	5.3	2.3	34.8	31.2
江苏 Jiangsu	3610.3	961.2	317.4	55.1	12.4	2.6	75.2	47.5
浙江 Zhejiang	2961.9	742.0	179.0	32.2	16.9	1.8	89.4	29.9
安徽 Anhui	3416.0	554.2	222.0	43.2	4.4	0.6	49.9	23.7
福建 Fujian	1756.7	473.0	152.5	24.4	4.5	3.8	23.1	11.5
江西 Jiangxi	1972.3	383.9	204.4	21.1	3.9	0.2	17.8	9.2
山东 Shandong	4850.6	1132.3	496.7	75.6	12.1	1.6	80.0	40.2
河南 Henan	5535.7	840.7	398.6	116.5	7.6	2.0	120.5	39.0
湖北 Hubei	2537.3	704.8	341.2	40.1	4.4	1.7	44.4	27.8
湖南 Hunan	3515.9	601.5	313.2	34.4	3.6	0.5	24.4	18.4
广东 Guangdong	4119.5	1295.0	376.5	78.5	13.3	6.1	67.5	31.3
广西 Guangxi	2601.4	385.1	200.9	23.0	2.0	1.0	24.3	10.5
海南 Hainan	353.8	113.5	58.6	4.1	0.4	1.1	3.6	2.3
重庆 Chongqing	1659.5	319.3	124.4	19.4	4.1	5.8	38.2	11.6
四川 Sichuan	4449.6	690.0	327.8	50.9	7.4	1.1	68.9	35.2
贵州 Guizhou	2118.4	243.5	148.4	14.4	1.6	0.4	21.0	9.4
云南 Yunnan	2349.6	346.9	187.7	16.0	3.6	0.3	25.2	12.1
西藏 Tibet	130.7	27.1	16.1	0.5	…	0.1	0.4	0.3
陕西 Shaanxi	1911.3	515.1	254.4	24.8	3.8	0.6	27.7	14.2
甘肃 Gansu	1304.0	253.5	159.6	15.8	4.6	0.9	7.0	3.2
青海 Qinghai	254.3	73.7	34.5	2.5	0.9	0.1	2.8	1.7
宁夏 Ningxia	290.6	82.2	40.0	2.3	1.2	0.1	12.9	3.5
新疆 Xinjiang	721.3	339.0	188.9	8.0	0.6	0.3	34.3	10.1

Number of Employed Persons at the Year-end in Urban and Rural Areas

(10 000 persons)

Urban Area				乡 村 Rural Area			
#私营企业 Private Enterprises	#港澳台商投资单位 Units with Funds from Hong Kong, Macao and Taiwan	#外商投资单位 Foreign Funded Units	#个体 Self-employed individuals	小计 Sub-total	#乡镇企业 Township and Village Enterprises	#私营企业 Private Enterprises	#个体 Self-employed Individuals
			15	30638	2827		
			81	31836	3000		
		6	450	37065	6979		
	4	43	648	40939	9367		
57	4	62	614	47708	9265	113	1491
68	69	96	692	48026	9609	116	1616
98	83	138	740	48291	10625	134	1728
186	155	133	930	48546	12345	187	2010
332	211	195	1225	48802	12017	316	2551
485	272	241	1560	49025	12862	471	3054
620	265	275	1709	49028	13508	551	3308
750	281	300	1919	49039	13050	600	3522
973	294	293	2259	49021	12537	737	3855
1053	306	306	2414	48982	12704	969	3827
1268	310	332	2136	48934	12820	1139	2934
1527	326	345	2131	49085	13086	1187	2629
1999	367	391	2269	48960	13288	1411	2474
2545	409	454	2377	48793	13573	1754	2260
160.6	17.3	31.5	37.2	169.6	120.8	106.8	21.6
42.5	11.4	34.2	12.5	173.8	139.3	23.7	13.5
58.4	6.5	10.0	83.8	2748.0	903.9	123.3	172.8
72.7	2.0	1.3	27.1	1012.8	349.5	37.7	48.8
35.7	1.7	2.5	72.8	652.3	194.0	15.6	35.6
152.3	8.8	30.0	192.5	1016.3	507.4	54.6	114.3
31.9	2.3	6.4	51.8	669.0	197.9	9.2	22.7
52.5	3.5	3.5	118.5	936.1	159.3	23.7	87.0
158.1	26.7	55.0	21.2	250.1	167.8	159.9	10.2
236.3	33.1	49.0	116.4	2649.1	1044.3	231.7	89.8
218.3	21.8	21.3	130.9	2219.9	1082.8	265.7	167.4
70.8	2.5	5.0	128.9	2861.7	512.5	48.0	157.5
75.5	76.7	45.2	52.9	1283.7	595.2	30.8	39.5
42.7	4.1	2.5	73.5	1588.4	346.1	50.6	69.4
203.0	14.6	54.4	150.8	3718.4	1529.8	163.5	196.3
41.0	8.5	5.6	98.0	4695.0	965.8	39.5	160.2
71.0	6.0	5.3	131.4	1832.5	663.2	34.3	117.3
82.6	3.2	3.4	117.3	2914.4	794.4	26.6	80.5
276.9	141.3	65.5	237.0	2824.5	1227.8	82.5	153.0
35.8	4.4	4.2	77.6	2216.3	352.5	13.5	71.5
23.5	1.8	1.6	16.6	240.3	30.2	4.8	9.5
56.3	2.6	3.2	52.8	1340.3	179.0	30.2	48.0
81.4	3.2	5.8	102.9	3759.6	678.2	68.9	121.5
18.8	0.9	1.2	27.2	1874.9	216.3	10.7	34.4
26.6	2.0	1.4	67.0	2002.7	318.1	30.1	56.7
2.8			6.8	103.6	2.5	0.4	1.7
122.5	1.1	2.0	62.3	1396.2	393.1	37.7	96.0
25.9	0.5	1.5	32.3	1050.5	184.6	10.4	29.4
14.3	0.1		16.7	180.6	24.4	6.2	7.7
12.3	0.1	0.9	8.3	208.5	57.1	6.3	7.2
42.3	0.6	0.7	52.0	382.3	88.1	6.8	18.7

5-5 各地区按行业分城镇单位就业人员数（2003年底）

Number of Employed Persons in Urban Units at the Year-end by Sector and Region (2003)

单位: 万人 (10 000 persons)

地 区	Region	合 计 Total	农、林、牧、渔业 Agriculture, Forestry, Animal Husbandry and Fishing	采矿业 Mining	制造业 Manufacturing	电力、燃气及水的生产和供应业 Production and Distribution of Electricity, Gas and Water	建筑业 Construction	交通运输、仓储和邮政业 Transport, Storage and Post
全国总计	**National Total**	**10969.7**	**484.5**	**488.3**	**2980.5**	**297.6**	**833.7**	**636.5**
北 京	Beijing	491.2	2.9	2.5	102.2	3.8	65.1	30.7
天 津	Tianjin	191.0	1.0	7.0	77.1	3.5	9.9	13.5
河 北	Hebei	499.2	9.1	28.1	126.7	16.8	33.1	27.1
山 西	Shanxi	356.9	4.1	56.9	76.1	11.5	20.9	21.8
内蒙古	Inner Mongolia	244.4	32.3	16.9	45.0	8.9	13.0	16.5
辽 宁	Liaoning	500.2	26.8	30.7	151.1	17.0	30.9	33.7
吉 林	Jilin	291.9	20.9	15.0	73.9	8.1	16.5	25.6
黑龙江	Heilongjiang	515.3	89.7	38.7	113.7	15.6	40.6	32.6
上 海	Shanghai	342.1	1.7	…	127.0	5.6	14.1	34.8
江 苏	Jiangsu	608.5	18.1	16.6	225.5	12.7	26.4	34.5
浙 江	Zhejiang	392.8	2.7	1.7	111.5	9.0	51.9	19.7
安 徽	Anhui	354.6	12.2	29.6	79.5	8.7	29.2	17.1
福 建	Fujian	344.6	7.8	3.6	153.9	8.1	26.4	14.2
江 西	Jiangxi	267.7	16.6	9.8	60.7	9.3	18.1	16.3
山 东	Shandong	778.5	9.4	60.8	272.0	20.5	38.7	30.8
河 南	Henan	701.7	9.6	48.7	159.9	23.1	61.7	32.9
湖 北	Hubei	502.4	30.5	11.2	149.1	12.7	30.1	31.8
湖 南	Hunan	401.6	18.1	12.2	80.0	11.4	31.2	25.5
广 东	Guangdong	781.1	13.2	4.0	283.8	19.6	54.6	43.7
广 西	Guangxi	271.7	14.1	4.8	57.6	8.3	16.8	17.5
海 南	Hainan	73.5	20.5	1.2	7.0	2.0	4.5	3.6
重 庆	Chongqing	210.2	2.5	7.1	54.9	5.8	31.0	14.6
四 川	Sichuan	505.7	11.3	19.2	119.4	15.6	72.4	22.5
贵 州	Guizhou	197.5	4.4	9.0	42.4	6.0	18.6	10.0
云 南	Yunnan	253.3	17.6	5.9	46.9	7.1	17.3	14.6
西 藏	Tibet	17.4	0.5	0.2	1.0	0.7	0.8	0.8
陕 西	Shaanxi	330.3	6.6	17.3	88.6	8.5	20.4	20.4
甘 肃	Gansu	195.4	8.7	7.8	48.1	7.1	15.6	12.5
青 海	Qinghai	42.7	2.3	1.9	6.8	1.7	2.9	2.9
宁 夏	Ningxia	61.6	4.4	6.2	12.0	3.1	4.4	3.2
新 疆	Xinjiang	244.7	65.2	13.9	26.9	5.6	16.5	11.1

5-5 续表 1 continued

单位: 万人 (10 000 persons)

地 区	Region	信息传输、计算机服务和软件业 Information Transmission, Computer Service and Software	批发和零售业 Wholesale and Retail Trade	住宿和餐饮业 Hotel and Restaurants	金融业 Financial Intermediation	房地产业 Real Estate	租赁和商务服务业 Leasing and Business Services
全国总计	**National Total**	**116.8**	**628.1**	**172.1**	**353.3**	**120.2**	**183.5**
北 京	Beijing	17.8	37.6	21.2	14.0	18.9	37.6
天 津	Tianjin	1.5	11.9	3.5	5.2	1.9	4.0
河 北	Hebei	3.8	33.2	4.8	17.8	2.4	3.4
山 西	Shanxi	2.7	25.3	3.7	11.7	1.4	3.9
内蒙古	Inner Mongolia	2.5	8.4	2.6	7.6	1.5	3.7
辽 宁	Liaoning	4.8	19.7	6.1	18.8	6.2	8.2
吉 林	Jilin	2.6	14.7	2.8	9.6	2.8	3.4
黑龙江	Heilongjiang	4.0	31.4	4.8	11.7	4.4	4.9
上 海	Shanghai	4.2	26.7	8.5	14.8	8.3	15.0
江 苏	Jiangsu	5.7	37.9	7.9	21.5	6.7	8.1
浙 江	Zhejiang	4.8	20.7	8.8	18.3	5.0	10.3
安 徽	Anhui	2.7	22.7	3.6	11.9	2.5	3.5
福 建	Fujian	3.7	12.4	4.2	9.5	3.5	3.6
江 西	Jiangxi	2.5	13.7	2.2	8.6	2.0	1.7
山 东	Shandong	5.8	43.1	9.2	25.4	5.2	7.9
河 南	Henan	5.3	58.9	9.8	21.1	4.6	8.3
湖 北	Hubei	3.7	29.5	10.1	13.3	4.4	8.5
湖 南	Hunan	4.8	19.5	5.5	14.1	3.2	5.7
广 东	Guangdong	11.7	40.9	19.9	28.2	14.5	15.6
广 西	Guangxi	2.7	14.9	5.1	8.0	2.3	5.0
海 南	Hainan	0.6	3.4	3.1	1.9	1.1	1.0
重 庆	Chongqing	1.9	10.3	2.5	6.6	3.1	1.8
四 川	Sichuan	4.7	20.7	4.6	16.1	4.2	3.4
贵 州	Guizhou	1.1	11.7	2.4	4.9	2.5	3.3
云 南	Yunnan	3.1	15.5	4.2	7.1	1.7	2.2
西 藏	Tibet	0.2	0.7	0.5	0.6	…	0.1
陕 西	Shaanxi	2.9	21.2	4.7	9.8	1.5	2.9
甘 肃	Gansu	2.0	9.5	1.9	5.3	1.3	1.7
青 海	Qinghai	0.7	1.8	0.5	1.5	0.2	0.5
宁 夏	Ningxia	0.6	2.5	0.8	2.3	0.6	0.6
新 疆	Xinjiang	1.5	8.1	2.8	6.1	2.2	3.7

5-5 续表 2 continued

单位: 万人 (10 000 persons)

地 区	Region	科学研究、技术服务和地质勘查业 Scientific Research, Technical Services, and Geological Prospecting	水利、环境和公共设施管理业 Water Management of Conservancy, Environment and Public Facilities	居民服务和其他服务业 Services to Households and Other Services	教育 Education	卫生、社会保障和社会福利业 Health, Social Securities and Social Welfare	文化、体育和娱乐业 Culture, Sports and Entertainment	公共管理和社会组织 Public Management and Social Organization
全国总计	**National Total**	**221.9**	**172.5**	**52.8**	**1442.8**	**485.8**	**127.8**	**1171.0**
北 京	Beijing	36.3	6.1	9.2	32.9	13.6	11.9	27.0
天 津	Tianjin	5.3	3.3	3.2	16.9	6.8	2.1	13.2
河 北	Hebei	7.3	8.0	2.7	81.6	21.9	5.1	66.4
山 西	Shanxi	5.5	4.9	3.1	45.0	13.6	4.1	40.8
内蒙古	Inner Mongolia	3.9	5.4	0.9	32.2	10.3	3.1	29.6
辽 宁	Liaoning	9.1	10.5	1.9	52.3	22.0	5.5	44.9
吉 林	Jilin	6.0	6.5	1.2	35.9	13.9	4.5	27.9
黑龙江	Heilongjiang	8.8	7.6	3.7	44.4	17.0	3.7	38.1
上 海	Shanghai	10.3	5.5	4.1	25.0	14.3	4.8	17.1
江 苏	Jiangsu	8.4	10.7	2.0	80.0	28.7	5.4	51.7
浙 江	Zhejiang	7.1	5.3	0.9	49.7	22.4	4.5	38.4
安 徽	Anhui	5.1	6.2	1.2	55.9	16.8	4.3	42.1
福 建	Fujian	3.7	3.2	1.3	42.5	11.3	3.1	28.7
江 西	Jiangxi	4.9	4.2	1.0	43.1	13.0	3.3	36.7
山 东	Shandong	7.5	10.5	1.2	104.6	34.9	5.5	85.4
河 南	Henan	10.7	10.4	1.6	103.8	31.8	7.0	92.3
湖 北	Hubei	9.8	8.7	1.3	63.7	24.7	5.9	53.3
湖 南	Hunan	6.8	6.9	0.7	65.7	23.0	6.5	60.9
广 东	Guangdong	9.3	11.2	3.0	92.4	34.6	7.0	73.9
广 西	Guangxi	4.5	4.6	0.7	54.3	15.5	3.0	32.2
海 南	Hainan	1.4	1.6	…	8.4	2.9	1.2	8.2
重 庆	Chongqing	5.9	2.3	0.4	29.9	8.5	1.7	19.5
四 川	Sichuan	11.0	7.1	2.4	77.8	26.1	5.1	62.0
贵 州	Guizhou	2.8	2.3	0.5	35.9	8.8	2.0	29.0
云 南	Yunnan	6.2	3.8	0.7	46.2	12.3	4.0	37.0
西 藏	Tibet	0.5	0.1	…	2.9	1.1	0.5	6.2
陕 西	Shaanxi	11.8	4.9	1.8	47.9	13.2	5.0	40.9
甘 肃	Gansu	4.8	3.5	0.3	27.7	7.5	3.8	26.3
青 海	Qinghai	1.9	1.2	0.2	6.1	2.2	0.6	6.7
宁 夏	Ningxia	1.2	1.7	…	7.5	2.6	0.8	7.0
新 疆	Xinjiang	4.1	4.1	1.7	30.7	10.5	2.6	27.5

5-6 按行业分就业人员数（年底数）
Number of Employed Persons at the Year-end by Sector

单位: 万人 (10 000 persons)

年份 Year	合计 Total	农、林、牧、渔业 Farming, Forestry, Animal Husbandry and Fishery	采掘业 Mining and Quarrying	制造业 Manufacturing	电力、煤气及水的生产和供应业 Production and Supply of Electricity Gas and Water	建筑业 Construction	地质勘查业水利管理业 Geological Prospecting and Water Conservancy	交通运输仓储和邮电通信业 Transport, Storage, Post & Telecommunication Services
1978	40152	28318	652	5332	107	854	178	750
1980	42361	29122	697	5899	118	993	188	805
1985	49873	31130	795	7412	142	2035	197	1279
1989	55329	33225	842	8547	180	2407	199	1522
1990	64749	34117	882	8624	192	2424	197	1566
1991	65491	34956	905	8839	203	2482	199	1617
1992	66152	34795	898	9106	215	2660	202	1674
1993	66808	33966	932	9295	240	3050	144	1688
1994	67455	33386	915	9613	246	3188	139	1864
1995	68065	33018	932	9803	258	3322	135	1942
1996	68950	32910	902	9763	273	3408	129	2013
1997	69820	33095	868	9612	283	3449	129	2062
1998	70637	33232	721	8319	283	3327	116	2000
1999	71394	33493	667	8109	285	3412	111	2022
2000	72085	33355	597	8043	284	3552	110	2029
2001	73025	32974	561	8083	288	3669	105	2037
2002	73740	32487	558	8307	290	3893	98	2084

5-6 续表 continued

单位: 万人 (10 000 persons)

年份 Year	批发零售贸易和餐饮业 Wholesale and Retail Trade & Catering Services	金融、保险业 Finance and Insurance	房地产业 Real Estate	社会服务业 Social Services	卫生体育和社会福利业 Health Care, Sports & Social Welfare	教育、文化艺术和广播电影电视业 Education, Culture and Arts, Radio, Film and Television	科学研究和综合技术服务业 Scientific Research and Polytechnic Services	国家机关、政党机关和社会团体 Government Agencies, Party Agencies and Social Organizations	其他 Others
1978	1140	76	31	179	363	1093	92	467	521
1980	1363	99	37	276	389	1147	113	527	588
1985	2306	138	36	401	467	1273	144	799	1319
1989	2770	205	43	550	518	1426	165	1022	1709
1990	2839	218	44	594	536	1457	173	1079	1798
1991	2998	234	48	604	553	1497	179	1136	1910
1992	3209	248	54	643	565	1520	183	1148	2313
1993	3459	270	66	543	416	1210	173	1030	3740
1994	3921	264	74	626	434	1436	178	1033	4155
1995	4292	276	80	703	444	1476	182	1042	4484
1996	4511	292	84	747	458	1513	183	1093	4563
1997	4795	308	87	810	471	1557	186	1093	4862
1998	4645	314	94	868	478	1573	178	1097	5118
1999	4751	328	96	923	482	1568	173	1102	4969
2000	4686	327	100	921	488	1565	174	1104	5643
2001	4737	336	107	976	493	1568	165	1101	5852
2002	4969	340	118	1094	493	1565	163	1075	6245

5-7 按行业分职工人数（年底数）

Number of Staff and Workers at the Year-end by Sector

单位: 万人 (10 000 persons)

年 份 Year	合 计 Total	农、林、牧、渔业 Farming, Forestry, Animal Husbandry and Fishery	采掘业 Mining and Quarrying	制造业 Manufacturing	电力、煤气及水的生产和供应业 Production and Supply of Electricity Gas and Water	建筑业 Construction	地质勘查业水利管理业 Geological Prospecting and Water Conservancy	交通运输仓储和邮电通信业 Transport, Storage, Post & Telecommunication Services
1978	9499	830	652	3595	107	623	178	669
1980	10444	788	697	3947	118	710	188	714
1985	12358	777	795	4620	142	900	197	823
1989	13742	782	842	5206	180	900	199	874
1990	14059	780	882	5304	192	896	197	895
1991	14508	769	905	5443	203	940	199	916
1992	14792	758	898	5508	215	995	202	921
1993	14849	708	925	5469	232	1153	144	826
1994	14849	680	904	5434	244	1072	137	835
1995	14908	660	914	5439	257	1053	134	824
1996	14845	617	886	5293	272	1035	128	830
1997	14668	612	851	5083	282	1004	128	824
1998	12337	546	702	3769	281	846	115	701
1999	11773	519	650	3496	283	778	110	682
2000	11259	494	581	3240	282	744	109	659
2001	10792	458	544	3010	284	733	104	629
2002	10558	430	537	2907	285	756	96	613

5-7 续表 continued

单位: 万人 (10 000 persons)

年 份 Year	批发零售贸易和餐饮业 Wholesale and Retail Trade & Catering Services	金融、保险业 Finance and Insurance	房地产业 Real Estate	社会服务业 Social Services	卫生体育和社会福利业 Health Care, Sports & Social Welfare	教育、文化艺术和广播电影电视业 Education, Culture and Arts, Radio, Film and Television	科学研究和综合技术服务业 Scientific Research and Polytechnic Services	国家机关、政党机关和社会团体 Government Agencies, Party Agencies and Social Organizations	其 他 Others
1978	1079	65	31	166	247	736	92	430	
1980	1239	89	37	218	287	817	105	490	
1985	1518	126	36	271	342	962	131	718	
1989	1675	184	43	327	382	1117	147	885	
1990	1715	195	44	344	392	1143	152	929	
1991	1786	208	48	369	410	1181	156	974	
1992	1844	223	54	386	421	1212	159	996	
1993	1796	239	66	422	416	1205	166	1030	55
1994	1833	261	72	447	428	1249	174	1017	63
1995	1828	273	77	449	438	1291	178	1027	66
1996	1807	288	82	458	451	1345	176	1075	103
1997	1774	298	84	480	464	1403	179	1080	125
1998	1256	301	89	451	469	1451	168	1084	108
1999	1110	300	90	453	473	1480	165	1088	96
2000	977	294	93	457	476	1500	164	1091	99
2001	840	292	97	463	481	1512	154	1088	104
2002	733	287	107	483	480	1517	151	1056	120

注:1998年及以后为在岗职工数(以下各表同)。

a) Data since 1998 are the figures of on-post staff and workers. The same as in the following tables.

5-8 各地区按行业分职工人数（2003年底）

Number of Staff and Workers at the Year-end by Sector and Region (2003)

单位: 万人 (10 000 persons)

地 区	Region	合 计 Total	农、林、牧、渔业 Agriculture, Forestry, Animal Husbandry and Fishing	采矿业 Mining	制造业 Manufacturing	电力、燃气及水的生产和供应业 Production and Distribution of Electricity, Gas and Water	建筑业 Construction	交通运输、仓储和邮政业 Transport, Storage and Post
全国总计	**National Total**	**10492.0**	**459.7**	**481.0**	**2898.9**	**292.3**	**773.5**	**609.7**
北 京	Beijing	436.3	2.8	2.4	95.2	3.7	59.0	28.4
天 津	Tianjin	174.9	1.0	6.3	72.5	3.4	9.1	12.2
河 北	Hebei	486.8	9.1	28.1	125.1	15.8	30.3	26.5
山 西	Shanxi	347.9	4.0	56.4	75.0	11.4	20.2	21.5
内蒙古	Inner Mongolia	240.3	32.3	16.6	44.7	8.9	12.6	16.1
辽 宁	Liaoning	483.5	26.6	30.5	147.5	16.8	29.8	33.1
吉 林	Jilin	286.8	20.8	14.9	72.9	8.1	16.1	25.2
黑龙江	Heilongjiang	487.8	75.1	38.6	110.4	15.4	39.0	31.9
上 海	Shanghai	279.2	1.0	…	107.0	5.5	12.1	29.2
江 苏	Jiangsu	579.1	17.7	16.5	216.8	12.5	24.3	33.1
浙 江	Zhejiang	373.2	2.6	1.7	109.0	8.8	48.5	18.7
安 徽	Anhui	337.8	11.7	29.3	77.3	8.5	25.3	16.5
福 建	Fujian	334.1	7.3	3.5	152.1	7.8	24.5	13.6
江 西	Jiangxi	256.7	16.1	9.6	59.2	9.0	16.4	15.1
山 东	Shandong	762.3	9.3	60.3	270.1	20.4	37.5	30.4
河 南	Henan	682.5	9.5	48.0	157.5	22.9	56.8	32.3
湖 北	Hubei	486.1	29.5	10.8	146.7	12.6	27.6	31.1
湖 南	Hunan	379.4	17.1	11.7	77.4	11.2	25.3	23.9
广 东	Guangdong	763.5	12.9	4.0	281.6	19.5	52.4	42.6
广 西	Guangxi	255.7	13.1	4.6	55.6	8.1	14.7	16.1
海 南	Hainan	71.6	20.2	1.1	6.7	1.9	4.3	3.5
重 庆	Chongqing	205.6	2.5	7.0	54.1	5.8	30.7	14.3
四 川	Sichuan	486.7	11.0	18.9	117.4	15.3	67.0	21.7
贵 州	Guizhou	188.7	4.2	8.8	41.2	5.8	17.2	9.2
云 南	Yunnan	244.0	15.9	5.8	46.1	6.9	16.9	14.2
西 藏	Tibet	14.5	0.3	0.1	0.7	0.6	0.4	0.7
陕 西	Shaanxi	319.4	6.4	16.9	86.8	8.3	19.2	19.8
甘 肃	Gansu	189.0	8.5	7.5	47.4	7.0	14.5	12.3
青 海	Qinghai	41.1	2.2	1.9	6.7	1.7	2.7	2.8
宁 夏	Ningxia	59.4	4.4	6.1	11.7	3.1	3.9	3.1
新 疆	Xinjiang	237.9	64.7	13.0	26.6	5.5	15.4	10.6

5-8 续表 1 continued

单位：万人 (10 000 persons)

地 区	Region	信息传输、计算机服务和软件业 Information Transmission, Computer Service and Software	批发和零售业 Wholesale and Retail Trade	住宿和餐饮业 Hotel and Restaurants	金融业 Financial Intermediation	房地产业 Real Estate	租赁和商务服务业 Leasing and Business Services
全国总计	**National Total**	**104.0**	**592.0**	**159.4**	**286.2**	**108.3**	**167.6**
北 京	Beijing	15.6	32.1	17.9	8.3	15.0	33.3
天 津	Tianjin	1.5	10.1	2.8	3.6	1.6	3.6
河 北	Hebei	3.5	32.7	4.7	14.7	2.4	3.3
山 西	Shanxi	2.5	24.5	3.6	9.3	1.3	3.8
内蒙古	Inner Mongolia	2.4	8.3	2.6	6.9	1.5	3.3
辽 宁	Liaoning	4.3	19.0	5.8	14.4	5.8	7.9
吉 林	Jilin	2.5	14.5	2.8	8.5	2.7	3.3
黑龙江	Heilongjiang	3.8	29.7	4.6	10.0	4.1	4.7
上 海	Shanghai	3.1	17.5	5.4	11.7	5.0	10.3
江 苏	Jiangsu	5.1	36.1	7.1	15.9	6.0	7.4
浙 江	Zhejiang	4.2	19.5	8.4	14.7	4.6	9.7
安 徽	Anhui	2.3	21.5	3.4	8.4	2.4	3.2
福 建	Fujian	3.0	11.7	4.0	8.1	3.3	3.4
江 西	Jiangxi	2.1	13.1	2.1	7.1	1.9	1.6
山 东	Shandong	5.2	42.4	8.8	18.9	5.0	7.8
河 南	Henan	4.4	57.4	9.5	17.1	4.5	8.1
湖 北	Hubei	3.5	28.3	9.8	12.0	4.3	8.3
湖 南	Hunan	4.3	18.4	5.1	11.3	3.1	4.4
广 东	Guangdong	10.7	39.9	19.2	25.0	14.1	15.3
广 西	Guangxi	2.3	13.8	4.8	7.3	2.2	4.6
海 南	Hainan	0.6	3.2	3.1	1.8	1.0	1.0
重 庆	Chongqing	1.8	10.1	2.5	5.0	2.9	1.6
四 川	Sichuan	4.1	19.9	4.4	12.9	4.0	3.2
贵 州	Guizhou	1.0	11.0	2.4	4.3	2.3	3.1
云 南	Yunnan	2.9	14.9	4.1	6.8	1.5	2.1
西 藏	Tibet	0.2	0.6	0.3	0.6	…	…
陕 西	Shaanxi	2.6	20.5	4.5	8.8	1.5	2.8
甘 肃	Gansu	1.8	9.2	1.8	4.9	1.2	1.6
青 海	Qinghai	0.7	1.7	0.5	1.3	0.2	0.4
宁 夏	Ningxia	0.6	2.4	0.8	1.8	0.6	0.5
新 疆	Xinjiang	1.5	8.0	2.7	4.9	2.0	3.6

5-8 续表 2 continued

单位: 万人 (10 000 persons)

地 区	Region	科学研究、技术服务和地质勘查业 Scientific Research, Technical Services, and Geological Prospecting	水利、环境和公共设施管理业 Water Management of Conservancy, Environment and Public Facilities	居民服务和其他服务业 Services to Households and Other Services	教育 Education	卫生、社会保障和社会福利业 Health, Social Securities and Social Welfare	文化、体育和娱乐业 Culture, Sports and Entertainment	公共管理和社会组织 Public Management and Social Organization
全国总计	**National Total**	**206.3**	**163.9**	**47.5**	**1401.7**	**471.7**	**122.0**	**1146.3**
北 京	Beijing	29.7	5.8	7.8	30.1	13.1	10.6	25.6
天 津	Tianjin	4.8	3.0	2.9	16.1	6.6	2.0	11.9
河 北	Hebei	7.2	7.9	2.7	80.5	21.6	5.0	65.9
山 西	Shanxi	5.3	4.8	3.1	43.4	13.4	4.0	40.4
内蒙古	Inner Mongolia	3.9	5.2	0.9	31.7	10.2	3.1	29.1
辽 宁	Liaoning	8.6	10.1	1.8	51.0	21.3	5.2	44.1
吉 林	Jilin	5.8	6.3	1.2	35.7	13.7	4.3	27.5
黑龙江	Heilongjiang	8.4	6.8	3.6	43.9	16.7	3.6	37.4
上 海	Shanghai	9.1	4.7	2.9	22.9	12.9	3.9	15.0
江 苏	Jiangsu	7.8	10.0	1.7	78.6	27.5	5.2	49.8
浙 江	Zhejiang	6.4	4.9	0.8	47.8	21.6	4.3	37.0
安 徽	Anhui	4.9	5.8	1.1	54.9	16.2	4.2	40.9
福 建	Fujian	3.5	3.1	1.3	41.7	10.9	3.0	28.2
江 西	Jiangxi	4.9	3.8	0.9	42.2	12.5	3.2	35.9
山 东	Shandong	7.2	10.3	1.2	102.9	34.3	5.4	85.0
河 南	Henan	10.5	10.1	1.5	102.7	31.3	6.9	91.4
湖 北	Hubei	9.3	8.2	1.2	60.9	24.1	5.6	52.1
湖 南	Hunan	6.4	6.5	0.7	64.3	22.4	6.3	59.9
广 东	Guangdong	8.9	11.0	2.9	89.4	33.8	6.9	73.4
广 西	Guangxi	4.2	4.2	0.6	50.4	14.9	2.8	31.3
海 南	Hainan	1.4	1.6	…	8.2	2.8	1.2	8.0
重 庆	Chongqing	5.8	2.3	0.4	29.6	8.3	1.6	19.3
四 川	Sichuan	10.7	6.7	2.4	75.8	25.3	5.0	60.9
贵 州	Guizhou	2.7	2.1	0.4	34.3	8.4	2.0	28.2
云 南	Yunnan	5.0	3.6	0.6	44.8	11.9	3.8	36.2
西 藏	Tibet	0.5	0.1	…	2.5	0.9	0.5	5.4
陕 西	Shaanxi	11.6	4.7	1.6	45.5	12.8	4.9	40.1
甘 肃	Gansu	4.7	3.4	0.3	26.0	7.4	3.7	25.9
青 海	Qinghai	1.7	1.0	0.2	6.0	2.1	0.6	6.5
宁 夏	Ningxia	1.2	1.7	…	7.4	2.5	0.8	6.8
新 疆	Xinjiang	4.0	4.1	0.7	30.4	10.3	2.6	27.3

5-9 按登记注册类型和细行业分职工人数（2003年底）

Number of Staff and Workers at the Year-end by Status of Registration and Sector in Detail (2003)

单位: 万人 (10 000 persons)

项目	Item	合计 Total	国有单位 State-owned Units	城镇集体单位 Urban Collective-owned Units	其他单位 Units of Other Types of Ownership
全国总计	**National Total**	**10492.0**	**6621.3**	**950.5**	**2920.3**
按企、事业和机关分组	**Grouped by Enterprises, Institutions and Agencies**				
企业	Enterprises	6796.8	3066.7	819.9	2910.2
事业	Institutions	2643.7	2508.2	126.8	8.7
机关	Agencies & Organizations	1050.1	1046.4	3.7	
按国民经济行业分组	**Grouped by Sector**				
农、林、牧、渔业	**Farming, Forestry, Animal Husbandry and Fishing**	**459.7**	**433.9**	**13.9**	**11.9**
农业	Farming	221.2	216.9	1.3	3.0
林业	Forestry	115.7	113.4	0.7	1.5
畜牧业	Animal Husbandry	25.8	22.4	0.5	2.9
渔业	Fishing	8.2	6.4	0.4	1.5
农、林、牧、渔服务业	Services	88.8	74.7	11.0	3.1
采矿业	**Mining**	**481.0**	**259.7**	**27.0**	**194.3**
制造业	**Manufacturing**	**2898.9**	**854.2**	**287.4**	**1757.4**
电力、燃气及水的生产和供应业	**Production and Distribution of Electricity, Gas and Water**	**292.3**	**220.1**	**6.8**	**65.4**
建筑业	**Construction**	**773.5**	**278.7**	**201.1**	**293.8**
房屋和土木工程建筑业	Construction of Buildings and Civil Engineering	676.0	241.6	180.4	254.0
建筑安装业	Building Installation	68.4	29.3	15.4	23.7
建筑装饰业	Building Decoration	18.3	3.3	2.9	12.1
其他建筑业	Other Construction	10.9	4.5	2.4	4.0
交通运输、仓储和邮政业	**Transport, Storage and Post**	**609.7**	**474.4**	**36.6**	**98.7**
铁路运输业	Railway Transport	172.8	165.1	3.2	4.4
道路运输业	Road Transport	162.5	114.4	13.9	34.1
城市公共交通业	Urban Public Transport	88.9	55.6	3.0	30.2
水上运输业	Water Transport	57.0	38.4	5.9	12.7
航空运输业	Air Transport	17.9	11.7	0.1	6.1
管道运输业	Transport Via Pipelines	2.1	1.8	0.1	0.3
装卸搬运和其他运输服务业	Loading, Unloading and Other Transport Services	27.7	13.8	8.9	5.0
仓储业	Storage	36.7	31.1	1.0	4.6
邮政业	Post	44.2	42.6	0.4	1.2
信息传输、计算机服务和软件业	**Information Transmission, Computer Services and Software**	**104.0**	**63.9**	**1.7**	**38.4**
电信和其他信息传输服务业	Telecommunications and Other Information Transmission Services	81.3	60.4	1.0	19.9
计算机服务业	Computer Services	8.4	2.1	0.5	5.7
软件业	Software	14.3	1.4	0.2	12.7
批发和零售业	**Wholesale and Retail Trade**	**592.0**	**286.3**	**122.4**	**183.3**
批发业	Wholesale Trade	324.4	192.7	54.4	77.3
零售业	Retail Trade	267.6	93.6	68.0	105.9
住宿和餐饮业	**Hotel and Restaurants**	**159.4**	**69.2**	**15.2**	**75.0**
住宿业	Hotels	106.3	56.3	9.1	40.9
餐饮业	Restaurants	53.1	13.0	6.0	34.1
金融业	**Financial Intermediation**	**286.2**	**176.3**	**63.7**	**46.2**
银行业	Banks	244.1	158.2	62.9	23.0

5-9 续表 continued

单位：万人 (10 000 persons)

项目	Item	合计 Total	国有单位 State-owned Units	城镇集体单位 Urban Collective-owned Units	其他单位 Units of Other Types of Ownership
证券业	Security Activities	6.3	1.7	0.1	4.6
保险业	Insurance	32.0	14.3	0.1	17.7
其他金融活动	Other Financial Activities	3.7	2.1	0.7	0.9
房地产业	**Real Estate**	**108.3**	**48.8**	**6.8**	**52.6**
#房地产开发经营	Development and Management of Real Estate	54.7	19.3	4.1	31.4
物业管理	Property Management	39.1	17.8	2.3	19.0
房地产中介服务	Agency Services for Real Estate	4.3	2.6	0.1	1.5
租赁和商务服务业	**Leasing and Business Services**	**167.6**	**98.7**	**28.4**	**40.6**
租赁业	Leasing	3.2	1.4	0.5	1.3
商务服务业	Business Services	164.4	97.3	27.8	39.2
科学研究、技术服务和地质勘查业	**Scientific Research, Technical Service and Geologic Prospecting**	**206.3**	**176.7**	**3.4**	**26.2**
研究与实验发展	Research and Experimental Development	61.1	59.2	0.2	1.6
专业技术服务业	Professional Technical Services	94.5	72.0	2.1	20.4
科技交流和推广服务业	services of Science and Technology Exchanges and Promotion	19.6	15.5	0.8	3.3
地质勘查业	Geologic Prospecting	31.1	30.0	0.2	0.9
水利、环境和公共设施管理业	**Management of Water Conservancy, Environment and Public Facilities**	**163.9**	**147.9**	**9.8**	**6.1**
水利管理业	Management of Water Conservancy	47.4	46.2	1.0	0.2
环境管理业	Environmental Management	66.1	57.2	7.2	1.7
公共设施管理业	Management of Public Facilities	50.4	44.5	1.7	4.2
居民服务和其他服务业	**Services to Households and Other Services**	**47.5**	**19.9**	**14.0**	**13.6**
居民服务业	Services to Households	21.9	11.9	3.9	6.0
其他服务业	Other Services	25.6	8.0	10.1	7.6
教育	**Education**	**1401.7**	**1340.1**	**55.6**	**6.1**
#初等教育	Junior Education	605.7	563.8	41.1	0.8
中等教育	Secondary Education	590.6	576.4	11.2	3.0
高等教育	Senior Education	136.8	135.8	0.2	0.8
卫生、社会保障和社会福利业	**Health, Social Security and Social Welfare**	**471.7**	**419.1**	**49.3**	**3.3**
卫生	Health	451.1	399.5	48.5	3.1
社会保障业	Social Security	9.3	9.1	0.2	0.1
社会福利业	Social Welfare	11.3	10.5	0.6	0.1
文化、体育和娱乐业	**Culture, Sports and Entertainment**	**122.0**	**112.4**	**3.0**	**6.6**
新闻出版业	Journalism and Publishing Activities	21.6	20.9	0.2	0.6
广播、电影、电视和音像业	Broadcasting, Movies, Televisions and Audiovisual Activities	46.9	45.3	0.7	0.9
文化艺术业	Cultural and Art Activities	38.6	36.4	1.5	0.6
体育	Sports Activities	8.3	7.8	…	0.5
娱乐业	Entertainment	6.6	2.0	0.6	4.1
公共管理和社会组织	**Public Management and Social Organization**	**1146.3**	**1141.1**	**4.5**	**0.7**
#中国共产党机关	Organs of Communist Party of China	46.8	46.8		
国家机构	Government Agencies	1060.3	1056.9	3.3	
人民政协和民主党派	People's Political Consultative Conference and Democratic Parties	8.5	8.5	…	
群众社团、社会团体和宗教组织	Non-Governmental Institutions, Social Organizations and Religion Organizations	18.1	17.2	0.7	0.2

5-10 按行业分国有单位职工人数（年底数）

Number of Staff and Workers in State-owned Units at the Year-end by Sector

单位: 万人 (10 000 persons)

年份 Year	合计 Total	农、林、牧、渔业 Farming, Forestry, Animal Husbandry and Fishery	采掘业 Mining and Quarrying	制造业 Manufacturing	电力、煤气及水的生产和供应业 Production and Supply of Electricity Gas and Water	建筑业 Construction	地质勘查业水利管理业 Geological Prospecting and Water Conservancy	交通运输仓储和邮电通信业 Transport, Storage, Post & Telecommunication Services
1978	7451	774	588	2449	102	447	177	465
1980	8019	740	621	2601	112	475	187	498
1985	8990	726	706	2975	134	545	196	585
1989	10109	736	757	3344	172	541	199	640
1990	10346	737	786	3395	183	538	194	660
1991	10664	727	797	3482	193	557	196	682
1992	10889	717	792	3526	203	577	199	693
1993	10920	672	834	3444	220	663	142	664
1994	10890	653	820	3321	230	629	135	677
1995	10955	634	834	3326	237	605	132	677
1996	10949	592	809	3218	250	595	126	684
1997	10766	588	772	3011	257	577	125	681
1998	8809	525	596	1883	242	444	113	584
1999	8336	500	525	1648	239	399	108	568
2000	7878	475	448	1415	233	372	107	549
2001	7409	440	402	1194	229	336	102	518
2002	6924	410	347	979	220	302	94	498

5-10 续表 continued

单位: 万人 (10 000 persons)

年份 Year	批发零售贸易和餐饮业 Wholesale and Retail Trade & Catering Services	金融、保险业 Finance and Insurance	房地产业 Real Estate	社会服务业 Social Services	卫生体育和社会福利业 Health Care, Sports & Social Welfare	教育、文化艺术和广播电影电视业 Education, Culture and Arts, Radio, Film and Television	科学研究和综合技术服务业 Scientific Research and Polytechnic Services	国家机关、政党机关和社会团体 Government Agencies, Party Agencies and Social Organizations	其他 Others
1978	907	42	28	107	183	674	91	417	
1980	1005	63	33	130	217	757	104	476	
1985	800	93	32	181	272	925	129	691	
1989	923	136	38	221	314	1086	144	859	
1990	947	145	40	236	323	1112	148	903	
1991	993	154	43	251	340	1151	151	946	
1992	1037	166	48	269	356	1183	153	969	
1993	1014	182	55	293	356	1180	153	1014	34
1994	1054	196	59	308	368	1227	165	1007	40
1995	1061	203	61	315	379	1265	167	1019	42
1996	1055	208	63	329	390	1322	166	1068	74
1997	1037	210	64	345	402	1362	167	1074	95
1998	694	208	63	322	410	1408	155	1079	84
1999	608	205	61	319	415	1433	153	1084	72
2000	531	200	60	314	419	1447	147	1086	76
2001	447	193	59	310	425	1455	137	1084	80
2002	365	184	57	311	427	1452	133	1053	91

5-11 各地区按行业分国有单位职工人数（2003年底）

Number of Staff and Workers in State-owned Units at the Year-end by Sector and Region (2003)

单位: 万人 (10 000 persons)

地区	Region	合计 Total	农、林、牧、渔业 Agriculture, Forestry, Animal Husbandry and Fishing	采矿业 Mining	制造业 Manufacturing	电力、燃气及水的生产和供应业 Production and Distribution of Electricity, Gas and Water	建筑业 Construction	交通运输、仓储和邮政业 Transport, Storage and Post
全国总计	**National Total**	**6621.3**	**433.9**	**259.7**	**854.2**	**220.1**	**278.7**	**474.4**
北京	Beijing	197.6	1.4	0.2	22.0	1.9	14.0	15.3
天津	Tianjin	85.8	0.9	0.9	15.3	2.6	3.6	9.4
河北	Hebei	367.3	8.6	22.2	59.3	13.6	13.7	23.8
山西	Shanxi	248.8	3.7	36.9	30.3	9.2	12.5	19.2
内蒙古	Inner Mongolia	166.1	31.0	6.3	5.7	6.2	4.1	14.5
辽宁	Liaoning	310.2	25.8	18.8	46.6	12.1	12.0	28.1
吉林	Jilin	204.4	20.0	7.5	27.5	6.4	8.2	21.6
黑龙江	Heilongjiang	321.3	73.8	3.2	39.8	12.2	15.1	28.7
上海	Shanghai	140.7	0.7	…	30.0	3.7	6.2	14.5
江苏	Jiangsu	305.0	15.5	11.6	37.5	8.6	8.5	21.9
浙江	Zhejiang	170.4	2.3	0.5	8.1	6.2	3.5	11.3
安徽	Anhui	212.2	10.6	2.9	25.5	6.5	9.6	12.0
福建	Fujian	147.1	6.7	2.1	7.9	5.9	7.1	10.7
江西	Jiangxi	196.1	15.8	7.3	23.2	7.5	7.1	13.7
山东	Shandong	487.5	6.5	49.9	88.6	17.1	14.8	23.4
河南	Henan	388.0	7.0	13.3	46.3	16.5	21.1	27.2
湖北	Hubei	330.2	28.2	7.3	60.9	9.5	11.6	24.8
湖南	Hunan	297.5	16.4	9.3	39.7	9.6	12.3	19.9
广东	Guangdong	365.6	11.6	2.3	23.1	13.3	13.1	26.9
广西	Guangxi	189.9	12.3	2.8	22.8	7.1	4.7	12.2
海南	Hainan	57.3	19.9	1.1	2.4	1.3	2.6	2.6
重庆	Chongqing	121.9	1.8	4.4	21.7	3.7	5.5	11.3
四川	Sichuan	315.9	9.4	11.5	42.9	8.9	22.7	16.0
贵州	Guizhou	141.7	4.1	5.4	18.2	5.4	9.3	8.5
云南	Yunnan	181.8	15.3	3.8	18.0	4.1	7.8	11.8
西藏	Tibet	13.7	0.3	0.1	0.4	0.6	0.2	0.7
陕西	Shaanxi	246.4	5.9	14.4	46.4	7.2	12.0	18.5
甘肃	Gansu	155.1	8.1	5.7	31.8	6.7	7.2	11.3
青海	Qinghai	33.3	2.1	1.1	3.0	1.6	1.9	2.6
宁夏	Ningxia	38.7	4.4	0.6	2.6	2.6	1.6	2.8
新疆	Xinjiang	184.0	63.9	6.2	6.7	2.4	5.1	9.1

5-11 续表 1 continued

单位: 万人 (10 000 persons)

地 区	Region	信息传输、计算机服务和软件业 Information Transmission, Computer Service and Software	批发和零售业 Wholesale and Retail Trade	住宿和餐饮业 Hotel and Restaurants	金融业 Financial Intermediation	房地产业 Real Estate	租赁和商务服务业 Leasing and Business Services
全国总计	**National Total**	**63.9**	**286.3**	**69.2**	**176.3**	**48.8**	**98.7**
北 京	Beijing	2.2	9.0	5.7	5.3	3.7	19.2
天 津	Tianjin	0.8	3.2	0.9	2.2	0.5	2.4
河 北	Hebei	2.7	19.7	3.4	9.1	1.8	2.1
山 西	Shanxi	2.2	14.0	2.4	5.6	1.0	2.7
内蒙古	Inner Mongolia	2.3	4.7	1.4	4.8	1.1	2.5
辽 宁	Liaoning	2.8	7.8	2.0	8.6	3.5	4.6
吉 林	Jilin	1.9	9.2	1.5	5.3	1.7	2.0
黑龙江	Heilongjiang	2.9	15.6	3.0	6.2	2.6	2.4
上 海	Shanghai	1.5	5.8	2.5	4.3	2.0	4.6
江 苏	Jiangsu	2.4	11.3	3.5	10.0	2.8	4.6
浙 江	Zhejiang	2.1	4.6	2.5	8.4	1.7	4.8
安 徽	Anhui	1.9	11.6	1.7	5.4	1.5	1.6
福 建	Fujian	1.9	5.9	1.6	5.8	1.1	2.4
江 西	Jiangxi	1.7	9.0	1.5	4.6	1.4	1.3
山 东	Shandong	4.5	20.7	5.5	11.3	3.3	4.1
河 南	Henan	3.0	31.6	5.0	9.5	2.2	5.0
湖 北	Hubei	2.6	13.3	1.8	7.8	2.0	4.1
湖 南	Hunan	2.9	10.8	2.9	6.9	2.0	3.2
广 东	Guangdong	6.5	17.4	5.2	15.0	5.0	9.1
广 西	Guangxi	1.6	7.9	2.6	4.9	1.2	3.0
海 南	Hainan	0.3	1.7	0.9	1.4	0.5	0.6
重 庆	Chongqing	1.4	4.6	1.0	2.9	0.9	0.7
四 川	Sichuan	3.4	10.6	1.8	7.8	1.4	2.1
贵 州	Guizhou	0.9	6.9	1.1	2.8	0.6	2.3
云 南	Yunnan	2.0	6.8	1.8	4.6	0.6	1.1
西 藏	Tibet	0.2	0.4	0.3	0.5	…	…
陕 西	Shaanxi	1.5	11.6	2.3	5.8	0.9	1.7
甘 肃	Gansu	1.5	5.4	1.3	3.5	0.9	1.2
青 海	Qinghai	0.6	1.1	0.4	1.0	0.1	0.2
宁 夏	Ningxia	0.5	1.3	0.3	1.3	0.2	0.4
新 疆	Xinjiang	1.0	2.7	1.5	3.5	0.9	2.5

5-11 续表 2 continued

单位: 万人 (10 000 persons)

地 区	Region	科学研究、技术服务和地质勘查业 Scientific Research, Technical Services, and Geological Prospecting	水利、环境和公共设施管理业 Water Management of Conservancy, Environment and Public Facilities	居民服务和其他服务业 Services to Households and Other Services	教育 Education	卫生、社会保障和社会福利业 Health, Social Securities and Social Welfare	文化、体育和娱乐业 Culture, Sports and Entertainment	公共管理和社会组织 Public Management and Social Organization
全国总计	**National Total**	**176.7**	**147.9**	**19.9**	**1340.1**	**419.1**	**112.4**	**1141.1**
北 京	Beijing	16.6	4.6	1.4	28.9	11.8	8.8	25.5
天 津	Tianjin	3.6	2.8	0.9	15.9	6.3	1.9	11.8
河 北	Hebei	7.0	7.5	2.2	80.4	20.1	4.5	65.7
山 西	Shanxi	5.2	4.5	0.9	43.1	11.2	3.8	40.2
内蒙古	Inner Mongolia	3.7	4.9	0.5	31.4	8.8	3.0	29.1
辽 宁	Liaoning	7.8	9.6	0.9	50.8	19.6	4.8	44.0
吉 林	Jilin	5.5	5.7	0.8	35.5	12.7	4.2	27.4
黑龙江	Heilongjiang	7.9	6.5	1.0	43.7	16.0	3.6	37.3
上 海	Shanghai	7.9	4.1	0.9	22.6	11.0	3.5	14.8
江 苏	Jiangsu	6.7	8.1	0.7	77.2	19.9	4.6	49.3
浙 江	Zhejiang	5.1	3.4	0.5	46.6	18.0	4.0	36.8
安 徽	Anhui	4.8	5.4	0.4	54.6	11.7	4.0	40.7
福 建	Fujian	3.2	2.7	0.8	41.5	8.8	2.7	28.2
江 西	Jiangxi	4.9	3.5	0.7	42.1	11.8	3.2	35.8
山 东	Shandong	6.7	9.7	0.7	102.1	28.9	5.0	84.8
河 南	Henan	9.7	9.8	0.9	52.9	29.6	6.4	90.7
湖 北	Hubei	8.9	7.5	0.5	59.6	23.2	5.5	51.2
湖 南	Hunan	5.9	5.9	0.5	63.9	19.8	5.9	59.7
广 东	Guangdong	7.5	9.0	0.9	88.5	32.5	5.3	73.2
广 西	Guangxi	4.0	4.1	0.2	50.1	14.7	2.6	31.1
海 南	Hainan	1.3	1.4	…	7.9	2.4	0.9	7.9
重 庆	Chongqing	2.6	2.0	0.3	29.5	6.7	1.6	19.2
四 川	Sichuan	10.5	6.1	0.7	75.4	19.4	4.8	60.7
贵 州	Guizhou	2.5	1.6	0.1	34.0	8.0	1.9	28.2
云 南	Yunnan	4.5	3.3	0.2	44.7	11.8	3.5	36.1
西 藏	Tibet	0.5	0.1	…	2.5	0.9	0.5	5.4
陕 西	Shaanxi	11.1	4.6	1.1	45.1	11.6	4.7	39.9
甘 肃	Gansu	4.6	3.4	0.3	26.0	7.0	3.5	25.7
青 海	Qinghai	1.7	0.6	0.1	5.9	2.1	0.6	6.5
宁 夏	Ningxia	1.1	1.5	…	7.4	2.5	0.8	6.8
新 疆	Xinjiang	3.8	3.9	0.7	30.3	10.2	2.5	27.3

5-12 按行业分城镇集体单位职工人数（年底数）

Number of Staff & Workers in Urban Collective-owned Units at the Year-end by Sector

单位: 万人 (10 000 persons)

年份 Year	合计 Total	农、林、牧、渔业 Farming, Forestry, Animal Husbandry and Fishery	采掘业 Mining and Quarrying	制造业 Manufacturing	电力、煤气及水的生产和供应业 Production and Supply of Electricity Gas and Water	建筑业 Construction	地质勘查业水利管理业 Geological Prospecting and Water Conservancy	交通运输仓储和邮电通信业 Transport, Storage, Post & Telecommunication Services
1978	2048	56	64	1146	5	176	0.5	204
1980	2425	48	76	1346	6	235	1.0	216
1985	3324	51	89	1608	8	354	1.0	237
1989	3502	45	84	1754	7	357	0.4	232
1990	3549	42	95	1773	8	357	3.3	232
1991	3628	41	107	1782	9	380	3.4	232
1992	3621	39	105	1747	10	414	3.2	226
1993	3393	34	89	1595	8	479	2.1	154
1994	3211	24	81	1515	9	427	2.0	149
1995	3076	23	77	1417	9	427	2.0	138
1996	2954	22	72	1346	11	412	2.0	134
1997	2817	20	72	1244	11	393	3.0	125
1998	1900	16	49	742	11	311	2.0	79
1999	1652	14	42	622	10	278	1.9	67
2000	1447	14	35	519	9	261	1.9	56
2001	1241	12	30	425	8	243	1.5	47
2002	1071	11	30	346	7	218	1.4	39

5-12 续表 continued

单位: 万人 (10 000 persons)

年份 Year	批发零售贸易和餐饮业 Wholesale and Retail Trade & Catering Services	金融、保险业 Finance and Insurance	房地产业 Real Estate	社会服务业 Social Services	卫生体育和社会福利业 Health Care, Sports & Social Welfare	教育、文化艺术和广播电影电视业 Education, Culture and Arts, Radio, Film and Television	科学研究和综合技术服务业 Scientific Research and Polytechnic Services	国家机关、政党机关和社会团体 Government Agencies, Party Agencies and Social Organizations	其他 Others
1978	172	23	3	59	64	62	1	13	
1980	234	26	4	88	70	60	1	14	
1985	716	33	4	87	70	37	2	27	
1989	748	49	4	94	68	32	3	26	
1990	762	51	4	93	69	32	3	26	
1991	786	54	5	98	70	30	4	28	
1992	796	57	4	96	65	28	5	27	
1993	744	55	5	101	60	24	9	15	20
1994	716	62	6	102	59	21	7	9	22
1995	693	67	6	94	59	26	8	8	23
1996	667	73	7	86	60	22	7	7	27
1997	637	76	7	87	62	40	8	6	27
1998	414	71	7	68	58	41	7	5	20
1999	345	70	7	65	57	45	6	5	18
2000	285	68	6	61	56	49	5	5	16
2001	216	66	6	56	54	53	3	4	16
2002	167	64	7	49	51	56	2	3	19

5-13 各地区按行业分城镇集体单位职工人数（2003年底）

Number of Staff and Workers in Urban Collective-owned Units at the Year-end by Sector and Region (2003)

单位：万人 (10 000 persons)

地 区	Region	合 计 Total	农、林、牧、渔业 Agriculture, Forestry, Animal Husbandry and Fishing	采矿业 Mining	制造业 Manufacturing	电力、燃气及水的生产和供应业 Production and Distribution of Electricity, Gas and Water	建筑业 Construction	交通运输、仓储和邮政业 Transport, Storage and Post
全国总计	**National Total**	**950.5**	**13.9**	**27.0**	**287.4**	**6.8**	**201.1**	**36.6**
北 京	Beijing	26.1	0.2	0.1	6.2	…	9.9	0.7
天 津	Tianjin	11.8	…	0.3	4.6	0.1	1.3	0.7
河 北	Hebei	41.1	0.5	0.9	14.3	0.1	8.3	1.0
山 西	Shanxi	37.4	0.3	2.8	12.1	0.5	3.9	0.9
内蒙古	Inner Mongolia	15.5	0.4	1.3	4.2	0.1	2.7	0.5
辽 宁	Liaoning	48.5	0.3	1.7	21.2	0.6	10.6	1.8
吉 林	Jilin	27.6	0.2	0.7	13.2	0.1	4.3	1.8
黑龙江	Heilongjiang	55.2	0.9	2.7	22.2	0.4	13.2	1.9
上 海	Shanghai	15.5	0.1	…	3.8	0.1	0.6	0.9
江 苏	Jiangsu	52.6	1.2	0.8	16.9	0.5	6.0	2.6
浙 江	Zhejiang	30.5	0.2	…	6.5	0.4	8.7	1.0
安 徽	Anhui	40.7	0.8	5.0	8.3	0.2	8.8	2.4
福 建	Fujian	23.1	…	0.1	6.2	0.2	7.7	0.9
江 西	Jiangxi	20.0	0.2	0.3	5.4	…	7.2	0.9
山 东	Shandong	74.1	1.9	3.8	28.2	0.3	11.2	1.9
河 南	Henan	113.7	2.0	0.8	18.2	0.2	12.0	2.8
湖 北	Hubei	38.3	0.7	1.4	14.2	0.2	7.2	2.6
湖 南	Hunan	31.3	0.6	0.4	8.7	0.2	7.2	2.3
广 东	Guangdong	77.0	0.2	0.3	27.7	1.6	21.7	2.4
广 西	Guangxi	20.1	0.1	0.3	5.1	0.2	5.0	1.5
海 南	Hainan	3.9	0.1	…	0.5	…	1.2	0.1
重 庆	Chongqing	18.9	0.6	0.2	6.4	0.2	6.0	1.0
四 川	Sichuan	48.7	1.3	0.9	10.1	0.3	17.6	1.8
贵 州	Guizhou	13.7	…	0.2	3.2	0.1	4.8	0.3
云 南	Yunnan	14.6	0.1	0.3	4.2	0.1	3.1	0.5
西 藏	Tibet	0.4	…	…	0.2		0.1	…
陕 西	Shaanxi	23.3	0.4	0.3	7.2	…	4.7	0.6
甘 肃	Gansu	14.7	0.1	1.0	5.2	0.1	3.5	0.5
青 海	Qinghai	2.4	…	…	0.7	…	0.5	0.1
宁 夏	Ningxia	2.2	…	…	0.7		0.5	…
新 疆	Xinjiang	7.6	0.3	0.1	1.7	0.1	1.5	0.1

5-13 续表 1 continued

单位: 万人 (10 000 persons)

地区	Region	信息传输、计算机服务和软件业 Information Transmission, Computer Service and Software	批发和零售业 Wholesale and Retail Trade	住宿和餐饮业 Hotel and Restaurants	金融业 Financial Intermediation	房地产业 Real Estate	租赁和商务服务业 Leasing and Business Services
全国总计	**National Total**	**1.7**	**122.4**	**15.2**	**63.7**	**6.8**	**28.4**
北京	Beijing	0.1	2.7	1.1	…	0.6	1.2
天津	Tianjin	0.1	2.1	0.2	0.5	0.1	0.5
河北	Hebei	…	7.6	0.4	4.3	…	0.9
山西	Shanxi	…	7.2	0.7	2.7	0.2	0.9
内蒙古	Inner Mongolia	…	1.5	0.3	1.9	…	0.6
辽宁	Liaoning	0.2	3.5	0.6	2.8	0.2	2.2
吉林	Jilin	…	2.1	0.2	2.4	0.1	0.4
黑龙江	Heilongjiang	…	5.9	0.5	1.9	0.5	1.4
上海	Shanghai	0.1	3.0	0.3	…	0.2	3.2
江苏	Jiangsu	0.3	8.3	0.6	2.8	0.3	1.5
浙江	Zhejiang	0.1	2.4	0.8	3.4	0.2	1.3
安徽	Anhui	…	5.9	0.4	2.2	0.2	0.4
福建	Fujian	0.1	2.6	0.5	1.6	0.2	0.5
江西	Jiangxi	…	2.4	0.1	1.8	0.1	0.1
山东	Shandong	…	11.1	1.0	4.9	0.3	2.2
河南	Henan	0.2	15.3	1.9	5.3	0.5	2.1
湖北	Hubei	…	4.4	0.6	2.4	0.3	0.8
湖南	Hunan	0.1	3.9	0.3	3.3	0.2	0.5
广东	Guangdong	0.1	7.1	1.6	5.6	1.4	3.1
广西	Guangxi	…	3.5	0.5	1.9	0.1	1.1
海南	Hainan	…	0.7	0.2	0.3	0.1	0.1
重庆	Chongqing	…	1.4	0.1	0.8	0.1	0.1
四川	Sichuan	0.1	3.3	0.5	4.0	0.2	0.4
贵州	Guizhou	…	2.1	0.3	1.1	0.2	0.5
云南	Yunnan	0.1	3.0	0.5	1.6	0.1	0.4
西藏	Tibet		0.1	…			
陕西	Shaanxi	…	4.7	0.5	1.7	0.1	1.0
甘肃	Gansu	0.1	2.1	0.1	1.0	0.1	0.1
青海	Qinghai		0.2	…	0.3	…	0.2
宁夏	Ningxia	…	0.3	0.1	0.3	…	0.1
新疆	Xinjiang	…	1.9	0.2	0.8	0.1	0.4

5-13 续表 2 continued

单位: 万人 (10 000 persons)

地 区	Region	科学研究、技术服务和地质勘查业 Scientific Research, Technical Services, and Geological Prospecting	水利、环境和公共设施管理业 Water Management of Conservancy, Environment and Public Facilities	居民服务和其他服务业 Services to Households and Other Services	教育 Education	卫生、社会保障和社会福利业 Health, Social Securities and Social Welfare	文化、体育和娱乐业 Culture, Sports and Entertainment	公共管理和社会组织 Public Management and Social Organization
全国总计	**National Total**	**3.4**	**9.8**	**14.0**	**55.6**	**49.3**	**3.0**	**4.5**
北 京	Beijing	0.6	0.2	0.9	0.5	1.0	0.2	0.1
天 津	Tianjin	0.2	0.1	0.8	0.2	0.2	…	…
河 北	Hebei	…	0.2	0.4	0.1	1.5	0.2	0.2
山 西	Shanxi	0.1	0.3	2.2	0.2	2.1	0.2	0.2
内蒙古	Inner Mongolia	…	0.2	0.3	…	1.3	…	…
辽 宁	Liaoning	0.2	0.3	0.5	0.2	1.4	…	0.1
吉 林	Jilin	0.1	0.5	0.3	0.1	1.0	0.1	0.1
黑龙江	Heilongjiang	0.2	0.3	2.2	0.1	0.7	…	0.1
上 海	Shanghai	0.1	0.3	0.6	0.1	1.9	0.1	0.2
江 苏	Jiangsu	0.3	1.5	0.6	0.9	6.6	0.3	0.5
浙 江	Zhejiang	0.2	1.2	0.1	0.5	3.4	0.1	…
安 徽	Anhui	…	0.2	0.6	0.3	4.4	0.2	0.2
福 建	Fujian	0.1	0.2	0.2	…	2.1	0.1	…
江 西	Jiangxi	…	0.3	0.2	…	0.6	…	0.2
山 东	Shandong	0.1	0.4	0.3	0.7	5.3	0.2	0.2
河 南	Henan	0.3	0.1	0.4	49.1	1.4	0.4	0.6
湖 北	Hubei	0.1	0.5	0.1	0.9	0.9	…	0.7
湖 南	Hunan	0.1	0.4	0.1	0.1	2.5	0.1	0.2
广 东	Guangdong	0.2	1.3	0.5	0.6	1.1	0.2	0.1
广 西	Guangxi	0.1	0.1	0.3	0.1	0.1	…	…
海 南	Hainan	…	…	…	…	0.4	…	0.1
重 庆	Chongqing	…	0.2	…	0.1	1.6	…	…
四 川	Sichuan	0.1	0.5	1.6	0.1	5.8	0.1	0.2
贵 州	Guizhou	…	0.3	0.1	0.2	0.1	…	0.1
云 南	Yunnan	0.1	0.2	0.1	…	0.1	…	0.1
西 藏	Tibet			…			…	
陕 西	Shaanxi	…	…	0.4	0.2	1.2	0.2	0.2
甘 肃	Gansu	…	…	0.1	…	0.4	0.2	0.1
青 海	Qinghai		…	0.1	…	0.1		0.1
宁 夏	Ningxia	…	…	…	…	…	…	…
新 疆	Xinjiang	…	0.1	…	…	0.1	…	…

5-14 各地区按行业分其他单位职工人数（2003年底）

Number of Staff and Workers in Units of Other Types of Ownership at the Year-end by Sector and Region (2003)

单位: 万人 (10 000 persons)

地区 Region	合计 Total	农、林、牧、渔业 Agriculture, Forestry, Animal Husbandry and Fishing	采矿业 Mining	制造业 Manufacturing	电力、燃气及水的生产和供应业 Production and Distribution of Electricity, Gas and Water	建筑业 Construction	交通运输、仓储和邮政业 Transport, Storage and Post
全国总计 National Total	**2920.3**	**11.9**	**194.3**	**1757.4**	**65.4**	**293.8**	**98.7**
北京 Beijing	212.7	1.2	2.1	67.0	1.8	35.2	12.5
天津 Tianjin	77.4	0.1	5.1	52.6	0.8	4.2	2.0
河北 Hebei	78.4	…	4.9	51.5	2.2	8.3	1.7
山西 Shanxi	61.7	0.1	16.7	32.6	1.6	3.8	1.4
内蒙古 Inner Mongolia	58.7	0.9	9.0	34.8	2.6	5.7	1.0
辽宁 Liaoning	124.9	0.5	10.0	79.7	4.1	7.2	3.2
吉林 Jilin	54.8	0.6	6.7	32.3	1.7	3.6	1.9
黑龙江 Heilongjiang	111.2	0.4	32.7	48.4	2.9	10.6	1.3
上海 Shanghai	123.0	0.2	…	73.2	1.7	5.2	13.7
江苏 Jiangsu	221.5	1.0	4.0	162.4	3.5	9.8	8.5
浙江 Zhejiang	172.3	0.1	1.2	94.4	2.2	36.3	6.5
安徽 Anhui	84.8	0.3	21.3	43.6	1.8	6.9	2.0
福建 Fujian	163.9	0.6	1.3	138.0	1.7	9.6	2.0
江西 Jiangxi	40.6	…	1.9	30.6	1.4	2.1	0.5
山东 Shandong	200.8	0.9	6.6	153.3	3.0	11.5	5.0
河南 Henan	180.8	0.4	33.9	92.9	6.2	23.7	2.3
湖北 Hubei	117.6	0.5	2.1	71.6	2.8	8.8	3.7
湖南 Hunan	50.6	0.1	2.0	28.9	1.3	5.8	1.6
广东 Guangdong	320.9	1.1	1.4	230.8	4.6	17.6	13.3
广西 Guangxi	45.8	0.7	1.5	27.8	0.8	5.0	2.3
海南 Hainan	10.5	0.2	…	3.8	0.5	0.5	0.8
重庆 Chongqing	64.8	…	2.4	25.9	1.9	19.2	2.0
四川 Sichuan	122.1	0.3	6.6	64.4	6.1	26.7	3.9
贵州 Guizhou	33.2	…	3.3	19.8	0.4	3.1	0.4
云南 Yunnan	47.6	0.5	1.6	23.9	2.6	6.0	1.9
西藏 Tibet	0.4	…	…	0.1		0.1	…
陕西 Shaanxi	49.7	0.1	2.3	33.2	1.1	2.5	0.7
甘肃 Gansu	19.2	0.2	0.8	10.4	0.3	3.7	0.6
青海 Qinghai	5.4	…	0.7	3.1	0.1	0.3	0.1
宁夏 Ningxia	18.5	…	5.5	8.3	0.5	1.8	0.3
新疆 Xinjiang	46.4	0.5	6.7	18.2	3.1	8.8	1.4

5-14 续表 1 continued

单位: 万人 (10 000 persons)

地 区	Region	信息传输、计算机服务和软件业 Information Transmission, Computer Service and Software	批发和零售业 Wholesale and Retail Trade	住宿和餐饮业 Hotel and Restaurants	金融业 Financial Intermediation	房地产业 Real Estate	租赁和商务服务业 Leasing and Business Services
全国总计	**National Total**	**38.4**	**183.3**	**75.0**	**46.2**	**52.6**	**40.6**
北 京	Beijing	13.3	20.4	11.0	3.0	10.8	12.9
天 津	Tianjin	0.6	4.8	1.7	0.9	1.1	0.7
河 北	Hebei	0.7	5.4	0.9	1.3	0.6	0.3
山 西	Shanxi	0.2	3.3	0.6	1.0	0.2	0.1
内蒙古	Inner Mongolia	0.2	2.2	0.9	0.2	0.3	0.2
辽 宁	Liaoning	1.4	7.7	3.2	2.9	2.2	1.2
吉 林	Jilin	0.5	3.2	1.0	0.8	1.0	0.9
黑龙江	Heilongjiang	0.9	8.2	1.1	1.8	1.1	1.0
上 海	Shanghai	1.5	8.7	2.6	7.4	2.8	2.6
江 苏	Jiangsu	2.4	16.5	2.9	3.0	2.9	1.3
浙 江	Zhejiang	2.1	12.5	5.1	2.9	2.7	3.6
安 徽	Anhui	0.3	3.9	1.3	0.8	0.7	1.3
福 建	Fujian	1.0	3.3	2.0	0.7	2.0	0.5
江 西	Jiangxi	0.3	1.7	0.4	0.7	0.4	0.2
山 东	Shandong	0.7	10.6	2.3	2.7	1.4	1.6
河 南	Henan	1.1	10.5	2.7	2.2	1.8	0.9
湖 北	Hubei	0.9	10.6	7.4	1.9	1.9	3.4
湖 南	Hunan	1.3	3.8	1.9	1.1	0.9	0.6
广 东	Guangdong	4.2	15.3	12.4	4.4	7.7	3.1
广 西	Guangxi	0.7	2.4	1.7	0.5	0.9	0.6
海 南	Hainan	0.3	0.7	2.0	0.1	0.5	0.3
重 庆	Chongqing	0.4	4.0	1.3	1.3	1.9	0.8
四 川	Sichuan	0.7	6.0	2.1	1.1	2.5	0.7
贵 州	Guizhou	0.1	2.1	1.0	0.4	1.5	0.3
云 南	Yunnan	0.8	5.0	1.9	0.6	0.9	0.6
西 藏	Tibet		0.1	…	…	…	…
陕 西	Shaanxi	1.1	4.3	1.7	1.2	0.5	0.1
甘 肃	Gansu	0.2	1.7	0.4	0.4	0.2	0.2
青 海	Qinghai	0.1	0.4	0.1	…	…	…
宁 夏	Ningxia	…	0.7	0.4	0.3	0.4	0.1
新 疆	Xinjiang	0.5	3.3	1.1	0.5	1.0	0.7

5-14 续表 2 continued

单位: 万人 (10 000 persons)

地 区	Region	科学研究、技术服务和地质勘查业 Scientific Research, Technical Services, and Geological Prospecting	水利、环境和公共设施管理业 Water Management of Conservancy, Environment and Public Facilities	居民服务和其他服务业 Services to Households and Other Services	教 育 Education	卫生、社会保障和社会福利业 Health, Social Securities and Social Welfare	文化、体育和娱乐业 Culture, Sports and Entertainment	公共管理和社会组织 Public Management and Social Organization
全国总计	**National Total**	**26.2**	**6.1**	**13.6**	**6.1**	**3.3**	**6.6**	**0.7**
北 京	Beijing	12.6	1.0	5.4	0.7	0.3	1.6	…
天 津	Tianjin	1.0	0.1	1.2	…	…	0.1	0.1
河 北	Hebei	0.2	0.2	0.1	…	…	0.3	
山 西	Shanxi	…		…	0.1	0.1	…	…
内蒙古	Inner Mongolia	0.1	0.1	0.1	0.3	…	0.1	
辽 宁	Liaoning	0.6	0.1	0.3	0.1	0.3	0.3	
吉 林	Jilin	0.3	0.1	…	0.1	0.1	0.1	
黑龙江	Heilongjiang	0.4	0.1	0.3	0.1	…	0.1	
上 海	Shanghai	1.0	0.4	1.4	0.2	…	0.3	
江 苏	Jiangsu	0.8	0.4	0.4	0.5	1.0	0.2	…
浙 江	Zhejiang	1.1	0.3	0.2	0.8	0.1	0.1	0.1
安 徽	Anhui	0.1	0.2	0.2	…	…	0.1	…
福 建	Fujian	0.2	0.2	0.3	0.2	0.1	0.3	
江 西	Jiangxi	…	…	…	0.1	0.1	…	
山 东	Shandong	0.5	0.2	0.1	0.1	…	0.1	…
河 南	Henan	0.5	0.2	0.2	0.7	0.3	0.2	0.1
湖 北	Hubei	0.3	0.1	0.7	0.3	0.1	0.1	0.2
湖 南	Hunan	0.3	0.2	0.1	0.2	…	0.3	
广 东	Guangdong	1.2	0.7	1.5	0.3	0.1	1.3	…
广 西	Guangxi	0.1	0.1	0.1	0.2	0.1	0.2	0.2
海 南	Hainan	0.1	0.1	…	0.2	…	0.2	
重 庆	Chongqing	3.2	0.1	0.1	0.1	…	…	
四 川	Sichuan	0.1	0.2	0.2	0.3	0.1	0.1	
贵 州	Guizhou	0.1	0.2	0.2	0.1	0.2	…	
云 南	Yunnan	0.4	0.1	0.3	0.1	…	0.4	…
西 藏	Tibet							
陕 西	Shaanxi	0.5	…	0.1	0.2	…	…	…
甘 肃	Gansu	0.1	…	…	…	…	…	…
青 海	Qinghai	…	0.4	…				
宁 夏	Ningxia	0.1	0.1	…	…	…		
新 疆	Xinjiang	0.2	0.1	…	0.1	…	0.1	

5-15 各地区按行业分城镇单位专业技术人员数（2003年底）

Number of Scientific and Technical Personnel in Urban Collective-owned Units by Sector and Region at the Year-end (2003)

单位: 万人 (10 000 persons)

地区	Region	合计 Total	农、林、牧、渔业 Agriculture, Forestry, Animal Husbandry and Fishing	采矿业 Mining	制造业 Manufacturing	电力、燃气及水的生产和供应业 Production and Distribution of Electricity, Gas and Water	建筑业 Construction	交通运输、仓储和邮政业 Transport, Storage and Post
全国总计	**National Total**	**3113.0**	**78.2**	**66.5**	**431.6**	**68.3**	**160.9**	**90.0**
北京	Beijing	147.0	0.7	0.4	20.7	1.0	15.0	2.8
天津	Tianjin	47.5	0.3	2.3	9.2	0.6	2.8	2.5
河北	Hebei	159.4	1.7	4.6	18.2	3.6	7.6	4.0
山西	Shanxi	93.4	1.2	7.6	12.5	2.7	4.9	2.7
内蒙古	Inner Mongolia	72.9	6.0	2.4	7.5	2.5	2.6	2.0
辽宁	Liaoning	137.2	2.7	3.5	22.7	3.6	6.1	5.1
吉林	Jilin	88.6	4.9	2.6	11.4	2.1	3.5	2.9
黑龙江	Heilongjiang	116.0	11.2	5.0	13.9	3.5	5.1	3.8
上海	Shanghai	76.7	0.3		18.4	1.1	3.9	4.0
江苏	Jiangsu	165.4	2.2	2.3	32.0	2.9	6.3	5.6
浙江	Zhejiang	114.6	1.1	0.3	14.1	2.8	7.3	3.1
安徽	Anhui	102.6	1.8	3.5	10.6	2.1	5.2	2.3
福建	Fujian	88.0	1.3	0.4	15.2	2.0	5.3	1.9
江西	Jiangxi	83.3	2.1	1.3	9.9	2.0	3.1	2.5
山东	Shandong	231.6	3.0	7.9	36.3	5.4	7.9	5.8
河南	Henan	191.5	1.4	6.0	23.6	4.3	9.9	3.1
湖北	Hubei	132.0	3.3	0.9	20.2	3.0	6.3	6.9
湖南	Hunan	129.3	1.7	1.7	14.3	2.4	5.3	3.5
广东	Guangdong	198.2	1.8	0.7	31.9	4.2	10.1	6.5
广西	Guangxi	91.7	2.6	0.9	8.4	2.0	3.4	2.4
海南	Hainan	17.7	2.6	0.2	0.9	0.4	0.7	0.6
重庆	Chongqing	62.1	1.1	1.0	9.8	1.3	6.9	2.0
四川	Sichuan	157.5	4.2	2.5	20.5	3.5	12.7	3.1
贵州	Guizhou	62.5	1.5	1.6	7.1	1.4	3.0	1.1
云南	Yunnan	86.0	4.4	0.8	8.1	1.8	3.3	2.4
西藏	Tibet	4.0	0.1	…	0.1	0.1	0.1	0.1
陕西	Shaanxi	101.9	2.0	2.4	19.3	1.9	4.7	3.1
甘肃	Gansu	53.2	1.7	1.2	7.6	1.7	2.5	1.5
青海	Qinghai	13.8	0.7	0.3	1.1	0.4	0.8	0.6
宁夏	Ningxia	17.3	0.8	0.2	1.7	0.7	1.0	0.4
新疆	Xinjiang	70.1	7.8	2.2	4.2	1.3	3.8	1.8

5-15 续表 1 continued

单位: 万人 (10 000 persons)

地 区	Region	信息传输、计算机服务和软件业 Information Transmission, Computer Service and Software	批发和零售业 Wholesale and Retail Trade	住宿和餐饮业 Hotel and Restaurants	金融业 Financial Intermediation	房地产业 Real Estate	租赁和商务服务业 Leasing and Business Services
全国总计	**National Total**	**41.1**	**101.0**	**17.5**	**159.5**	**29.3**	**36.4**
北 京	Beijing	9.6	7.9	2.6	6.4	4.3	8.8
天 津	Tianjin	0.6	1.9	0.3	2.5	0.4	0.5
河 北	Hebei	1.4	5.3	0.6	8.3	0.6	0.8
山 西	Shanxi	0.9	3.7	0.3	5.1	0.3	0.9
内蒙古	Inner Mongolia	0.9	1.4	0.3	3.8	0.4	0.7
辽 宁	Liaoning	1.7	4.2	0.9	9.2	1.7	1.9
吉 林	Jilin	1.0	2.7	0.3	5.0	0.7	1.0
黑龙江	Heilongjiang	1.5	4.1	0.3	5.2	0.8	1.0
上 海	Shanghai	1.4	3.0	0.5	5.7	1.3	1.5
江 苏	Jiangsu	1.7	4.6	0.5	8.5	1.5	1.8
浙 江	Zhejiang	1.6	4.6	1.0	9.1	1.7	2.4
安 徽	Anhui	0.8	2.8	0.4	4.3	0.7	0.5
福 建	Fujian	1.1	2.3	0.4	4.8	0.9	0.8
江 西	Jiangxi	0.7	2.4	0.3	4.1	0.5	0.3
山 东	Shandong	1.7	8.8	1.1	10.5	2.0	1.9
河 南	Henan	1.3	7.0	1.1	7.5	1.1	1.3
湖 北	Hubei	1.3	3.5	0.6	5.7	1.2	1.2
湖 南	Hunan	1.4	3.7	0.6	6.0	0.9	1.1
广 东	Guangdong	3.7	7.7	1.9	14.4	3.0	2.9
广 西	Guangxi	1.0	2.9	0.5	4.4	0.7	0.9
海 南	Hainan	0.2	0.4	0.3	0.9	0.2	0.2
重 庆	Chongqing	0.3	1.7	0.3	2.4	0.9	0.3
四 川	Sichuan	1.3	3.1	0.5	7.0	1.0	0.7
贵 州	Guizhou	0.4	1.5	0.2	2.4	0.7	0.6
云 南	Yunnan	1.1	2.7	0.4	4.6	0.4	0.5
西 藏	Tibet	0.1	…	…	0.4	…	…
陕 西	Shaanxi	0.9	3.2	0.5	4.4	0.3	0.5
甘 肃	Gansu	0.6	1.1	0.2	2.3	0.2	0.3
青 海	Qinghai	0.2	0.3	0.1	0.8	…	0.1
宁 夏	Ningxia	0.2	0.4	0.1	1.1	0.2	0.1
新 疆	Xinjiang	0.6	1.8	0.5	2.7	0.5	0.9

5-15 续表 2 continued

单位: 万人 (10 000 persons)

地 区	Region	科学研究、技术服务和地质勘查业 Scientific Research, Technical Services, and Geological Prospecting	水利、环境和公共设施管理业 Water Management of Conservancy, Environment and Public Facilities	居民服务和其他服务业 Services to Households and Other Services	教育 Education	卫生、社会保障和社会福利业 Health, Social Securities and Social Welfare	文化、体育和娱乐业 Culture, Sports and Entertainment	公共管理和社会组织 Public Management and Social Organization
全国总计	**National Total**	**112.8**	**26.3**	**7.1**	**1154.2**	**349.3**	**60.1**	**122.8**
北 京	Beijing	18.4	0.8	1.8	22.6	10.0	5.8	7.5
天 津	Tianjin	2.7	0.5	0.3	12.8	5.2	1.1	0.9
河 北	Hebei	3.7	1.4	0.9	70.3	15.8	2.2	8.4
山 西	Shanxi	2.8	0.7	0.2	34.4	10.0	1.9	0.5
内蒙古	Inner Mongolia	2.1	0.9	0.1	26.9	7.8	1.8	2.8
辽 宁	Liaoning	5.1	1.6	0.4	43.6	16.1	2.6	4.4
吉 林	Jilin	3.6	1.1	0.1	30.0	10.3	2.1	3.4
黑龙江	Heilongjiang	3.4	1.1	0.3	36.8	12.5	1.8	4.6
上 海	Shanghai	4.3	0.6	0.3	17.4	10.1	1.7	1.2
江 苏	Jiangsu	4.5	1.9	0.2	61.1	20.7	2.5	4.7
浙 江	Zhejiang	4.3	0.9	0.1	41.0	16.3	2.2	0.5
安 徽	Anhui	2.6	0.9	0.1	45.3	11.9	2.5	4.4
福 建	Fujian	2.0	0.5	0.3	36.7	8.0	1.4	2.7
江 西	Jiangxi	2.2	0.6	0.1	36.7	9.4	1.6	3.6
山 东	Shandong	4.3	2.3	0.2	88.6	27.0	2.8	14.1
河 南	Henan	5.0	1.2	0.2	83.0	20.8	2.5	11.3
湖 北	Hubei	5.0	1.4	0.2	46.0	17.3	2.3	5.9
湖 南	Hunan	3.2	1.1	0.1	53.2	16.6	3.8	8.6
广 东	Guangdong	5.1	1.1	0.3	73.7	24.3	2.4	2.7
广 西	Guangxi	2.5	0.7	0.1	41.6	11.1	1.4	4.2
海 南	Hainan	0.4	0.1	…	6.5	2.1	0.5	0.5
重 庆	Chongqing	2.2	0.2	…	23.6	6.0	0.6	1.6
四 川	Sichuan	5.8	0.8	0.2	63.1	18.0	2.3	6.9
贵 州	Guizhou	1.5	0.3	…	28.8	6.1	1.1	3.2
云 南	Yunnan	3.1	0.7	0.1	37.2	9.4	1.9	2.9
西 藏	Tibet	0.3	…	…	1.6	0.5	0.2	0.4
陕 西	Shaanxi	6.4	1.0	0.3	35.3	9.4	2.5	4.0
甘 肃	Gansu	2.2	0.5	…	20.3	5.1	2.0	2.2
青 海	Qinghai	0.8	0.2	…	4.9	1.6	0.3	0.6
宁 夏	Ningxia	0.6	0.3	…	6.4	1.9	0.5	0.5
新 疆	Xinjiang	2.5	1.0	0.2	24.8	8.0	1.6	3.8

5-16 按行业分私营企业和个体就业人数

Number of Employed Persons in Private Enterprises and Self-employed Individuals by Sector

单位: 万人 (10 000 persons)

年份 Year 地区 Region	合计 Total	农、林、牧、渔业 Farming, Forestry, Animal Husbandry & Fishery	采掘业 Mining and Quarrying	制造业 Manufacturing	建筑业 Construction	交通运输仓储和邮电通信业 Transport, Storage, Post & Telecommunication Services	批发零售贸易和餐饮业 Wholesale & Retail Trade & Catering Services	社会服务业 Social Services	其他 Others
1989	2142.0	2.6		441.4	24.8	165.0	1272.6	214.3	21.3
1990	2274.3	0.6		469.2	23.3	182.0	1321.0	251.9	26.3
1991	2491.5	0.4		549.9	27.3	200.5	1446.2	244.4	22.7
1992	2699.5			578.8	26.9	207.1	1592.2	283.9	10.6
1993	3312.0		35.7	691.4	35.0	254.6	1926.6	334.4	34.3
1994	4424.2	57.0		1003.6	50.5	360.9	2481.0	412.2	59.1
1995	5569.5	119.5	61.4	1253.5	69.5	419.4	3020.4	552.3	73.5
1996	6188.2	183.5	66.5	1388.3	77.5	468.6	3300.0	612.6	91.2
1997	6791.1	255.0	68.1	1518.5	85.9	501.2	3585.6	680.6	96.3
1998	7823.5	362.1	80.6	1774.7	115.3	559.9	4013.5	795.0	122.4
1999	8262.5	416.2	78.7	1932.3	129.3	564.7	4161.6	853.8	125.9
2000	7476.5	339.0	69.2	1932.9	144.8	445.7	3621.7	776.0	147.1
2001	7474.1	246.1	67.9	1975.2	166.6	417.4	3617.2	808.5	175.3
2002	8152.2	224.4	71.9	2135.4	213.2	402.9	3813.9	917.1	373.5
2003	8935.7	189.8	87.7	2531.7	270.5	389.8	4060.5	1029.2	376.4
北 京 Beijing	326.2	8.1	0.7	90.2	11.4	4.2	124.6	48.3	38.6
天 津 Tianjin	92.1	0.6	0.1	28.9	2.6	2.8	37.7	9.5	9.8
河 北 Hebei	438.3	5.7	13.0	166.2	17.4	23.1	172.6	34.3	6.1
山 西 Shanxi	186.3	2.5	1.6	30.2	5.1	7.4	98.7	15.8	25.1
内蒙古 Inner Mongolia	159.7	6.3	3.7	24.8	5.2	11.2	80.2	22.9	5.4
辽 宁 Liaoning	513.7	28.6	5.4	109.7	16.1	49.0	233.3	54.5	17.1
吉 林 Jilin	115.6	1.9	1.1	16.2	3.2	6.9	65.6	16.3	4.4
黑龙江 Heilongjiang	281.7	28.5	1.6	46.8	5.2	21.6	137.5	34.2	6.2
上 海 Shanghai	349.5	1.2	…	95.5	17.6	5.9	152.3	47.5	29.6
江 苏 Jiangsu	674.2	5.2	1.5	326.0	30.0	15.7	221.8	57.2	16.7
浙 江 Zhejiang	782.3	7.8	3.2	406.7	15.5	23.0	244.4	72.4	9.3
安 徽 Anhui	405.1	8.7	2.1	85.9	9.0	26.0	208.8	55.2	9.4
福 建 Fujian	198.6	5.2	1.7	61.6	4.0	3.2	89.4	25.8	7.9
江 西 Jiangxi	236.2	4.3	5.4	64.7	8.8	11.3	106.6	29.7	5.5
山 东 Shandong	713.5	20.3	3.1	269.3	21.0	25.0	297.9	66.1	10.7
河 南 Henan	338.6	4.6	4.1	73.2	5.5	24.0	177.1	42.3	7.8
湖 北 Hubei	354.0	9.2	2.8	72.2	10.4	24.1	179.9	46.2	9.2
湖 南 Hunan	307.0	2.8	2.9	59.7	8.6	15.1	171.2	37.9	8.8
广 东 Guangdong	749.3	5.3	3.5	206.2	8.0	13.3	359.1	77.4	76.7
广 西 Guangxi	198.4	4.7	3.0	33.1	2.4	13.8	112.7	23.9	4.9
海 南 Hainan	54.3	3.9	0.5	3.2	2.3	3.6	26.7	9.7	4.5
重 庆 Chongqing	187.3	2.1	3.0	40.4	13.4	6.2	92.6	23.4	6.2
四 川 Sichuan	374.8	5.2	5.8	77.3	11.2	15.7	191.5	56.9	11.2
贵 州 Guizhou	91.2	1.6	2.5	16.5	1.9	3.6	49.5	12.1	3.4
云 南 Yunnan	180.4	3.6	6.8	33.1	8.6	7.9	96.3	20.1	4.0
西 藏 Tibet	11.8	0.3	0.1	0.6	1.4	0.5	6.6	1.9	0.5
陕 西 Shaanxi	318.5	5.0	4.8	45.4	10.7	13.4	162.1	51.0	26.0
甘 肃 Gansu	98.0	1.5	0.8	16.6	4.7	1.9	58.7	11.9	1.8
青 海 Qinghai	45.0	2.3	0.8	7.2	4.4	1.9	22.4	4.7	1.2
宁 夏 Ningxia	34.1	0.9	0.2	6.9	1.8	1.4	18.2	4.0	0.7
新 疆 Xinjiang	119.8	1.9	2.1	17.5	3.2	7.1	64.5	15.9	7.6

5-17 按行业分城镇私营企业和个体就业人数

Number of Employed Persons in Urban Private Enterprises and Self-employed Individuals at the Year-end by Sector

单位: 万人 (10 000 persons)

年份 Year / 地区 Region	合计 Total	农、林、牧、渔业 Farming, Forestry, Animal Husbandry and Fishery	采掘业 Mining and Quarrying	制造业 Manufacturing	建筑业 Construction	交通运输仓储和邮电通信业 Transport, Storage, Post & Telecommunication Services	批发零售贸易和餐饮业 Wholesale & Retail Trade and Catering Services	社会服务业 Social Services	其他 Others
1978	15.0			3.0	1.0	1.0	9.0	1.0	
1980	81.4	0.2		9.5	0.4	0.8	57.1	13.4	
1985	450.1	1.9		51.4	5.1	22.3	325.0	44.4	
1989	648.2	2.6		84.5	4.9	34.1	443.1	79.0	
1990	670.5	0.6		91.3	4.6	36.4	431.2	106.4	
1991	759.5	0.4		128.0	7.9	46.1	489.0	78.2	9.9
1992	837.9			129.6	5.9	47.5	550.7	93.6	10.6
1993	1115.7		6.7	175.4	10.8	62.3	714.9	132.8	12.8
1994	1557.4	5.4		271.8	17.9	95.7	973.5	167.2	26.0
1995	2045.0	13.4	10.2	339.0	28.1	111.0	1265.8	241.9	35.6
1996	2328.8	17.7	10.3	400.1	33.9	131.8	1419.1	274.5	41.4
1997	2669.0	31.8	10.8	450.6	38.8	153.6	1617.7	315.7	50.1
1998	3231.9	43.4	13.9	563.9	55.2	190.3	1896.2	397.2	71.8
1999	3466.9	44.0	12.4	601.7	64.9	202.3	2024.7	447.2	69.7
2000	3404.0	40.5	12.3	632.7	79.7	178.4	1924.3	438.5	97.6
2001	3658.0	39.4	13.2	716.6	97.8	180.4	1997.9	484.9	127.7
2002	4267.5	41.4	15.8	821.1	130.8	185.3	2197.8	572.7	302.5
2003	4922.1	46.5	18.4	1085.1	166.4	194.4	2464.8	662.6	284.0
北京 Beijing	197.8	4.4	0.4	50.9	6.5	2.6	75.9	30.9	26.2
天津 Tianjin	54.9	0.1	…	10.8	1.6	2.1	25.1	7.2	8.0
河北 Hebei	142.2	0.8	1.4	41.3	3.9	7.1	69.1	15.9	2.8
山西 Shanxi	99.8	0.5	0.1	6.2	1.4	1.1	62.8	7.0	20.7
内蒙古 Inner Mongolia	108.5	2.0	1.6	17.1	3.6	8.2	56.3	16.1	3.7
辽宁 Liaoning	344.8	2.6	0.5	63.8	11.8	28.2	178.1	44.1	15.5
吉林 Jilin	83.7	0.4	0.3	10.7	2.7	5.4	47.0	13.4	3.7
黑龙江 Heilongjiang	171.0	3.2	0.4	27.6	4.1	14.6	93.2	23.2	4.6
上海 Shanghai	179.4	0.3	…	36.4	9.2	4.0	83.6	26.9	19.0
江苏 Jiangsu	352.7	1.6	0.2	143.7	17.8	7.6	134.8	37.5	9.5
浙江 Zhejiang	349.2	1.9	0.4	130.5	9.1	8.6	144.9	47.7	6.0
安徽 Anhui	199.6	2.4	0.3	36.0	6.0	13.6	105.6	31.4	4.3
福建 Fujian	128.4	2.1	0.5	33.3	3.1	2.3	62.0	18.9	6.2
江西 Jiangxi	116.2	0.9	0.7	30.1	3.6	5.8	58.3	14.8	2.0
山东 Shandong	353.8	2.9	0.6	105.5	12.9	9.0	173.4	42.5	7.1
河南 Henan	139.0	1.0	0.7	22.9	2.8	6.5	83.3	18.2	3.4
湖北 Hubei	202.4	2.9	0.7	37.7	6.5	11.8	106.0	29.4	7.5
湖南 Hunan	199.9	1.3	1.2	31.3	6.4	7.6	118.0	27.7	6.3
广东 Guangdong	513.9	2.9	0.7	114.4	6.0	7.5	252.7	58.0	71.6
广西 Guangxi	113.4	1.5	1.0	17.2	1.9	8.0	63.8	16.4	3.7
海南 Hainan	40.0	2.8	0.3	1.8	1.7	2.4	19.0	8.1	3.8
重庆 Chongqing	109.1	0.6	0.2	20.3	10.2	3.6	54.8	14.8	4.5
四川 Sichuan	184.3	1.4	0.9	28.4	8.0	7.2	101.9	30.8	5.7
贵州 Guizhou	46.0	0.6	0.5	8.5	1.4	2.0	23.5	7.4	2.3
云南 Yunnan	93.6	1.5	1.1	13.7	4.2	3.0	55.1	12.6	2.5
西藏 Tibet	9.7	0.2	0.1	0.5	1.0	0.5	5.3	1.7	0.4
陕西 Shaanxi	184.8	1.2	2.5	17.2	7.6	4.6	95.1	33.3	23.4
甘肃 Gansu	58.1	0.5	0.2	7.6	3.3	1.3	36.2	7.6	1.4
青海 Qinghai	31.0	0.5	0.2	4.0	3.8	1.3	16.9	3.6	0.7
宁夏 Ningxia	20.6	0.3	0.1	3.7	1.3	0.7	11.3	2.6	0.6
新疆 Xinjiang	94.3	1.1	0.7	11.9	2.8	6.1	52.0	12.6	7.0

5-18 各地区私营企业就业人数（2003年底）

Number of Employed Persons in Private Enterprises at the Year-end by Region (2003)

单位: 万户、万人 (10 000 enterprises, 10 000 persons)

地 区	Region	户数 Number of Enterprises	就业人数 Number of Employed Persons	# 投资者 Employers	城镇就业人数 Number of Employed Persons in Urban Areas	# 投资者 Employers	乡村就业人数 Number of Employed Persons in Rural Areas	# 投资者 Employers
全 国	**National Total**	**300.6**	**4299.1**	**772.8**	**2545.2**	**520.0**	**1754.0**	**252.9**
北 京	Beijing	18.7	267.3	48.1	160.6	34.7	106.8	13.5
天 津	Tianjin	5.9	66.2	14.7	42.5	10.0	23.7	4.6
河 北	Hebei	8.6	181.7	21.3	58.4	8.9	123.3	12.4
山 西	Shanxi	4.3	110.4	10.6	72.7	5.3	37.7	5.3
内蒙古	Inner Mongolia	3.5	51.4	10.3	35.7	7.2	15.6	3.1
辽 宁	Liaoning	11.4	207.0	24.6	152.3	19.9	54.6	4.7
吉 林	Jilin	3.8	41.2	8.4	31.9	7.0	9.2	1.5
黑龙江	Heilongjiang	5.1	76.2	13.5	52.5	9.8	23.7	3.7
上 海	Shanghai	29.2	318.1	62.4	158.1	33.4	159.9	29.0
江 苏	Jiangsu	34.4	468.0	81.4	236.3	39.4	231.7	42.0
浙 江	Zhejiang	30.2	484.0	69.7	218.3	39.0	265.7	30.6
安 徽	Anhui	7.5	118.8	18.8	70.8	11.9	48.0	7.0
福 建	Fujian	8.8	106.2	19.4	75.5	14.6	30.8	4.8
江 西	Jiangxi	4.9	93.3	11.3	42.7	6.8	50.6	4.5
山 东	Shandong	22.9	366.5	60.1	203.0	42.2	163.5	17.9
河 南	Henan	8.1	80.5	19.1	41.0	11.7	39.5	7.4
湖 北	Hubei	8.6	105.3	20.5	71.0	14.7	34.3	5.8
湖 南	Hunan	5.7	109.1	28.9	82.6	25.1	26.6	3.8
广 东	Guangdong	32.3	359.4	74.4	276.9	62.2	82.5	12.2
广 西	Guangxi	3.5	49.3	9.2	35.8	7.2	13.5	1.9
海 南	Hainan	2.6	28.3	6.9	23.5	5.8	4.8	1.1
重 庆	Chongqing	5.5	86.4	15.4	56.3	10.6	30.2	4.8
四 川	Sichuan	11.0	150.3	28.8	81.4	17.1	68.9	11.7
贵 州	Guizhou	2.8	29.5	7.2	18.8	4.7	10.7	2.5
云 南	Yunnan	4.4	56.7	12.2	26.6	5.6	30.1	6.6
西 藏	Tibet	0.2	3.3	0.4	2.8	0.4	0.4	…
陕 西	Shaanxi	8.1	160.2	50.5	122.5	44.0	37.7	6.5
甘 肃	Gansu	2.6	36.3	6.8	25.9	5.5	10.4	1.4
青 海	Qinghai	0.9	20.6	2.3	14.3	1.9	6.2	0.4
宁 夏	Ningxia	1.5	18.6	4.1	12.3	3.1	6.3	1.0
新 疆	Xinjiang	3.7	49.2	11.3	42.3	10.2	6.8	1.1

5-19 各地区个体就业人数（2003年底）

Number of Self-employed Individuals at the Year-end by Region (2003)

单位: 万户、万人 (10 000 households, 10 000 persons)

地区	Region	个体户数 Number of Enterprises	个体就业人数 Number of Employed Persons	城镇 Urban Employed Persons	乡村 Rural Employed Persons
全国	**National Total**	**2353.2**	**4636.5**	**2377.0**	**2259.6**
北京	Beijing	44.7	58.8	37.2	21.6
天津	Tianjin	18.9	25.9	12.5	13.5
河北	Hebei	103.6	256.6	83.8	172.8
山西	Shanxi	40.6	75.9	27.1	48.8
内蒙古	Inner Mongolia	55.6	108.4	72.8	35.6
辽宁	Liaoning	140.9	306.7	192.5	114.3
吉林	Jilin	40.5	74.5	51.8	22.7
黑龙江	Heilongjiang	94.2	205.5	118.5	87.0
上海	Shanghai	26.8	31.4	21.2	10.2
江苏	Jiangsu	140.1	206.2	116.4	89.8
浙江	Zhejiang	158.5	298.3	130.9	167.4
安徽	Anhui	120.1	286.3	128.9	157.5
福建	Fujian	46.4	92.4	52.9	39.5
江西	Jiangxi	59.4	142.9	73.5	69.4
山东	Shandong	158.6	347.0	150.8	196.3
河南	Henan	121.2	258.2	98.0	160.2
湖北	Hubei	104.9	248.7	131.4	117.3
湖南	Hunan	94.0	197.9	117.3	80.5
广东	Guangdong	185.5	389.9	237.0	153.0
广西	Guangxi	99.0	149.1	77.6	71.5
海南	Hainan	13.1	26.0	16.6	9.5
重庆	Chongqing	47.7	100.8	52.8	48.0
四川	Sichuan	143.4	224.5	102.9	121.5
贵州	Guizhou	41.5	61.6	27.2	34.4
云南	Yunnan	72.8	123.7	67.0	56.7
西藏	Tibet	5.2	8.6	6.8	1.7
陕西	Shaanxi	76.5	158.3	62.3	96.0
甘肃	Gansu	33.2	61.7	32.3	29.4
青海	Qinghai	12.3	24.4	16.7	7.7
宁夏	Ningxia	8.8	15.5	8.3	7.2
新疆	Xinjiang	45.0	70.7	52.0	18.7

5-20 职工工资总额和指数

Total Wages of Staff and Workers and Related Index

年份 Year 地区 Region	工资总额（亿元）Total Wages (100 million yuan)				指数（上年=100）Indices (preceding year=100)			
	合计 Total	国有单位 State-owned Units	城镇集体单位 Urban Collective-owned Units	其他单位 Units of Other Types of Ownership	合计 Total	国有单位 State-owned Units	城镇集体单位 Urban Collective-owned Units	其他单位 Units of Other Types of Ownership
1978	568.9	468.7	100.2		110.5	110.1	112.5	
1980	772.4	627.9	144.5		119.4	118.6	123.3	
1985	1383.0	1064.8	312.3	5.9	122.0	121.6	123.0	163.9
1989	2618.5	2050.2	534.4	33.9	113.1	113.5	109.6	157.7
1990	2951.1	2324.1	581.0	46.0	112.7	113.4	108.7	135.7
1991	3323.9	2594.9	658.6	70.4	112.6	111.7	113.4	153.0
1992	3939.2	3090.4	743.2	105.6	118.5	119.1	112.8	150.0
1993	4916.2	3812.7	849.9	253.6	124.8	123.4	114.4	240.2
1994	6656.4	5177.4	1023.3	455.6	135.4	135.8	120.4	179.7
1995	8100.0	6080.2	1182.0	637.8	121.7	117.4	115.5	140.0
1996	9080.0	6792.7	1241.0	761.4	112.1	111.7	105.0	119.4
1997	9405.3	7211.0	1253.4	940.8	103.6	106.2	101.0	123.6
1998	9296.5	6812.5	1021.6	1462.4	100.2	95.8	83.1	156.9
1999	9875.5	7160.8	962.7	1752.0	106.2	105.1	94.2	119.8
2000	10656.2	7612.9	919.0	2124.3	107.9	106.3	95.5	121.3
2001	11830.9	8355.6	864.6	2610.7	111.0	109.8	94.1	122.9
2002	13161.1	8948.6	828.1	3384.4	111.2	107.1	95.8	129.6
2003	14743.5	9693.8	829.4	4220.3	112.0	108.3	100.2	124.7
北京 Beijing	1098.9	565.5	35.0	498.4	115.6	111.1	87.5	124.0
天津 Tianjin	325.4	168.4	13.7	143.3	111.9	106.0	97.0	121.7
河北 Hebei	548.2	434.4	29.2	84.6	108.8	107.5	98.7	120.1
山西 Shanxi	371.5	277.8	24.8	68.9	112.7	110.0	105.0	128.5
内蒙古 Inner Mongolia	272.3	198.8	11.6	62.0	114.7	111.0	103.1	131.6
辽宁 Liaoning	648.5	432.7	38.9	176.9	107.4	104.2	94.9	119.8
吉林 Jilin	321.6	229.9	22.5	69.2	107.0	102.1	107.2	127.1
黑龙江 Heilongjiang	535.4	352.8	30.0	152.6	109.4	103.3	97.6	130.4
上海 Shanghai	768.7	408.5	27.0	333.1	109.6	106.6	96.0	115.0
江苏 Jiangsu	917.3	540.6	53.5	323.2	112.8	106.8	88.6	131.1
浙江 Zhejiang	784.8	462.1	48.7	274.1	120.4	118.2	105.3	127.5
安徽 Anhui	361.0	241.1	26.5	93.4	107.1	104.1	93.0	121.2
福建 Fujian	468.9	242.6	25.9	200.4	114.6	108.0	98.0	126.7
江西 Jiangxi	271.1	216.2	13.8	41.2	111.2	108.0	103.1	135.9
山东 Shandong	954.8	679.1	63.2	212.4	109.9	107.7	106.3	119.1
河南 Henan	720.5	436.3	88.5	195.7	115.8	109.0	109.5	138.6
湖北 Hubei	520.1	391.1	27.2	101.8	110.5	108.4	96.9	124.8
湖南 Hunan	465.0	376.9	26.7	61.3	107.6	106.6	96.4	121.1
广东 Guangdong	1515.6	841.0	83.5	591.0	116.0	114.0	104.1	121.0
广西 Guangxi	305.3	234.5	15.8	55.0	108.9	107.9	103.9	114.9
海南 Hainan	75.4	59.7	2.8	13.0	107.8	107.4	101.8	111.1
重庆 Chongqing	254.0	166.6	16.0	71.4	115.6	109.6	100.4	138.3
四川 Sichuan	604.5	441.3	42.3	120.9	112.1	108.4	109.0	129.5
贵州 Guizhou	209.3	163.0	10.3	36.0	113.6	109.6	109.9	137.0
云南 Yunnan	315.0	246.2	12.3	56.4	104.7	100.4	93.4	132.9
西藏 Tibet	38.8	37.6	0.3	0.9	106.7	106.9	62.6	128.2
陕西 Shaanxi	366.3	292.1	16.1	58.1	109.9	107.7	105.2	124.2
甘肃 Gansu	230.9	198.2	11.2	21.5	109.7	109.0	94.6	128.4
青海 Qinghai	63.5	55.8	2.0	5.6	103.4	102.4	91.3	120.7
宁夏 Ningxia	79.4	53.5	2.1	23.9	112.3	99.1	75.4	170.2
新疆 Xinjiang	331.5	249.7	7.7	74.1	113.7	112.9	82.8	121.3

注:1998年及以后工资总额为在岗职工工资总额,1998年及以后指数按可比口径计算（以下各表同）。

a) Data on total wages since 1998 refer to wages of fully employed staff and workers, and the indices since 1998 was calculated on the basis of comparable coverage. (Similarly in the following tables).

5-21 职工平均工资及指数

Average Wage of Staff and Workers and Related Indices

年份 Year / 地区 Region	平均货币工资（元）Average Money Wage (yuan)				指数（上年=100）Indices (preceding year=100) 货币工资 Average Money Wage				实际工资 Average Real Wage			
	合计 Total	国有单位 State-owned Units	城镇集体单位 Urban Collective-owned Units	其他单位 Units of Other Types of Ownership	合计 Total	国有单位 State-owned Units	城镇集体单位 Urban Collective-owned Units	其他单位 Units of Other Types of Ownership	合计 Total	国有单位 State-owned Units	城镇集体单位 Urban Collective-owned Units	其他单位 Units of Other Types of Ownership
1978	615	644	506		106.8	107.0	105.9		106.0	106.2	105.1	
1980	762	803	623		114.1	113.9	114.9		106.1	106.0	106.9	
1985	1148	1213	967	1436	117.9	117.3	119.2	137.0	105.3	104.8	106.6	122.5
1989	1935	2055	1557	2707	110.8	110.9	109.2	113.6	95.2	95.4	93.9	97.7
1990	2140	2284	1681	2987	110.6	111.1	108.0	110.3	109.2	109.7	106.6	108.9
1991	2340	2477	1866	3468	109.3	108.5	111.0	116.1	104.0	103.2	105.6	110.5
1992	2711	2878	2109	3966	115.9	116.2	113.0	114.4	106.7	107.0	104.1	105.3
1993	3371	3532	2592	4966	124.3	122.7	122.9	125.2	107.1	105.7	105.9	107.9
1994	4538	4797	3245	6303	134.6	135.8	125.2	126.9	107.7	108.7	100.2	101.5
1995	5500	5625	3931	7463	121.2	117.3	121.1	118.4	103.8	100.4	103.7	101.4
1996	6210	6280	4302	8261	112.9	111.6	109.4	110.7	103.8	102.6	100.6	101.7
1997	6470	6747	4512	8789	104.2	107.4	104.9	106.4	101.1	104.2	101.7	103.2
1998	7479	7668	5331	8972	106.6	106.1	102.5	97.7	107.2	106.7	103.1	98.3
1999	8346	8543	5774	9829	111.6	111.4	108.3	109.6	113.1	112.9	109.7	111.0
2000	9371	9552	6262	10984	112.3	111.8	108.5	111.8	111.4	110.9	107.6	110.9
2001	10870	11178	6867	12140	116.0	117.0	109.7	110.5	115.2	116.2	108.9	109.7
2002	12422	12869	7667	13212	114.3	115.1	111.6	108.8	115.5	116.3	112.7	109.9
2003	14040	14577	8678	14574	113.0	113.3	113.2	110.3	112.0	112.3	112.2	109.3
北京 Beijing	25312	28464	13580	23769	115.8	119.8	113.2	110.9	114.8	118.7	112.2	109.9
天津 Tianjin	18648	19352	11285	19026	114.7	113.4	120.7	114.0	113.7	112.4	119.6	113.0
河北 Hebei	11189	11783	6919	10701	111.5	111.4	109.1	112.2	110.5	110.4	108.1	111.2
山西 Shanxi	10729	11213	6629	11276	114.7	112.9	120.0	116.5	113.7	111.9	118.9	115.5
内蒙古 Inner Mongolia	11279	11929	7620	10391	116.5	116.0	118.5	118.4	115.5	115.0	117.4	117.3
辽宁 Liaoning	13008	13603	7629	13665	111.6	111.1	107.5	111.9	110.6	110.1	106.5	110.9
吉林 Jilin	11081	11124	8018	12471	110.9	107.3	125.1	116.9	109.9	106.3	124.0	115.9
黑龙江 Heilongjiang	11038	11034	5425	13871	111.2	111.2	106.4	104.8	110.2	110.2	105.5	103.9
上海 Shanghai	27304	28406	16973	27354	114.0	114.9	114.3	112.0	113.0	113.9	113.3	111.0
江苏 Jiangsu	15712	17502	9836	14656	116.3	116.4	113.9	116.0	115.3	115.4	112.9	115.0
浙江 Zhejiang	21367	27293	16058	16344	113.7	119.7	113.7	108.7	112.7	118.6	112.7	107.7
安徽 Anhui	10581	11220	6407	10999	113.8	112.6	110.3	115.8	112.8	111.6	109.3	114.8
福建 Fujian	14310	16460	11386	12719	107.5	109.5	112.5	106.1	106.5	108.5	111.5	105.2
江西 Jiangxi	10521	10918	6905	10359	113.6	113.7	117.8	109.7	112.6	112.7	116.7	108.7
山东 Shandong	12567	13975	8442	10680	110.5	109.4	118.4	111.7	109.5	108.4	117.3	110.7
河南 Henan	10749	11397	7894	11160	117.2	115.5	118.5	119.5	116.2	114.5	117.4	118.4
湖北 Hubei	10692	11806	7137	8698	111.2	113.5	109.2	106.3	110.2	112.5	108.2	105.4
湖南 Hunan	12221	12604	8546	12226	111.4	110.8	110.9	113.8	110.4	109.8	109.9	112.8
广东 Guangdong	19986	22944	10836	18782	112.2	116.5	109.7	106.7	111.2	115.5	108.7	105.7
广西 Guangxi	11953	12331	7962	12118	110.9	111.2	112.4	108.2	109.9	110.2	111.4	107.2
海南 Hainan	10397	10305	7029	12130	109.7	110.0	106.3	107.9	108.7	109.0	105.4	106.9
重庆 Chongqing	12425	13586	8552	11316	113.4	115.7	112.6	109.5	112.4	114.7	111.6	108.5
四川 Sichuan	12441	13923	8723	10038	111.3	112.4	118.0	108.7	110.3	111.4	116.9	107.7
贵州 Guizhou	11037	11390	7504	10975	112.5	112.2	114.3	113.4	111.5	111.2	113.3	112.4
云南 Yunnan	12870	13471	8519	11886	107.4	108.4	107.2	103.9	106.4	107.4	106.2	103.0
西藏 Tibet	26931	27611	9348	20475	108.7	107.5	95.8	130.5	107.7	106.5	94.9	129.3
陕西 Shaanxi	11461	11833	6858	11794	110.7	110.6	112.8	109.2	109.7	109.6	111.8	108.2
甘肃 Gansu	12307	12929	7573	11010	110.4	109.7	108.7	115.4	109.4	108.7	107.7	114.4
青海 Qinghai	15356	16692	8306	10341	106.1	105.5	115.2	107.9	105.2	104.6	114.2	106.9
宁夏 Ningxia	12981	13721	8924	12009	111.5	111.0	117.9	115.5	110.5	110.0	116.8	114.5
新疆 Xinjiang	13255	13199	9966	13937	114.2	115.4	106.6	109.2	113.2	114.4	105.6	108.2

5-22 按行业分职工工资总额

Total Wages of Staff and Workers by Sector

单位: 亿元 (100 million yuan)

年 份 Year	合 计 Total	农、林、牧、渔业 Farming, Forestry, Animal Husbandry and Fishery	采掘业 Mining and Quarrying	制造业 Manufacturing	电力、煤气及水的生产和供应业 Production and Supply of Electricity Gas and Water	建筑业 Construction	地质勘查业水利管理业 Geological Prospecting and Water Conservancy	交通运输仓储和邮电通信业 Transport, Storage, Post & Telecommunication Services
1978	568.9	39.0	44.1	214.8	9.1	43.6	12.6	46.4
1980	772.4	48.9	58.4	289.7	11.9	59.7	16.7	58.8
1985	1383.0	68.7	103.4	504.0	17.1	120.0	27.7	103.0
1989	2618.5	109.1	199.0	983.8	40.0	196.2	44.3	192.0
1990	2951.1	120.3	234.3	1089.3	49.4	211.5	48.8	214.6
1991	3323.9	128.0	262.9	1230.2	57.7	244.5	53.6	243.3
1992	3939.2	139.6	289.3	1443.0	70.9	300.2	64.6	286.0
1993	4916.2	143.0	337.7	1796.3	96.5	433.4	53.5	346.4
1994	6656.4	191.5	417.0	2292.3	146.5	527.1	75.9	470.9
1995	8100.0	230.1	516.2	2760.4	197.0	609.8	79.8	565.6
1996	9080.0	246.4	565.2	2939.5	234.8	647.5	83.9	645.7
1997	9405.3	262.8	574.3	2993.4	268.8	673.3	91.7	702.8
1998	9296.5	249.9	513.9	2724.3	293.4	635.0	92.2	693.5
1999	9875.5	252.9	494.9	2758.9	324.1	633.4	97.5	753.0
2000	10656.2	260.1	496.0	2882.6	361.2	669.6	107.5	820.4
2001	11830.9	268.2	528.2	2990.6	414.2	713.4	114.6	897.9
2002	13161.1	278.1	593.2	3219.0	467.4	790.3	117.5	990.1

5-22 续表 continued

单位: 亿元 (100 million yuan)

年 份 Year	批发零售贸易和餐饮业 Wholesale and Retail Trade & Catering Services	金融、保险业 Finance and Insurance	房地产业 Real Estate	社会服务业 Social Services	卫生体育和社会福利业 Health Care, Sports & Social Welfare	教育、文化艺术和广播电影电视业 Education, Culture and Arts, Radio, Film and Television	科学研究和综合技术服务业 Scientific Research and Polytechnic Services	国家机关、政党机关和社会团体 Government Agencies, Party Agencies and Social Organizations	其 他 Others
1978	59.4	3.6	1.8	9.2	13.7	38.6	5.9	27.0	
1980	83.0	5.9	2.8	14.5	19.9	55.6	8.7	37.9	
1985	149.7	13.8	4.1	29.3	37.7	109.3	16.3	78.7	
1989	275.3	33.3	8.3	62.0	73.8	207.3	30.8	163.3	
1990	308.2	39.7	9.7	72.7	85.1	238.6	36.0	192.9	
1991	346.8	45.5	11.7	86.8	95.3	260.7	39.5	217.5	
1992	400.0	60.6	15.8	107.5	116.5	323.9	49.1	272.3	
1993	468.7	85.1	26.9	147.1	139.5	389.7	63.4	357.7	18.3
1994	637.0	170.1	44.1	220.2	216.8	607.4	106.8	500.2	32.3
1995	758.1	197.9	54.9	264.3	253.8	690.8	121.4	559.5	40.4
1996	823.0	240.4	66.3	305.5	303.2	812.2	141.9	672.1	67.6
1997	848.5	288.0	75.1	357.4	348.1	931.1	161.9	744.0	84.1
1998	746.6	319.6	89.7	374.3	395.3	1070.5	172.6	835.4	90.3
1999	722.3	359.3	103.0	418.8	453.5	1244.9	192.4	971.0	95.5
2000	718.9	399.7	116.5	472.8	517.0	1410.3	224.5	1090.4	108.7
2001	703.0	476.9	136.1	548.4	618.5	1718.1	253.9	1317.7	131.0
2002	703.9	550.4	164.8	646.6	706.2	2002.2	289.5	1474.0	167.8

5-23 各地区按行业分职工工资总额（2003年）

Total Wages of Staff and Workers by Sector and Region (2003)

单位: 亿元 (100 million yuan)

地区	Region	合计 Total	农、林、牧、渔业 Agriculture, Forestry, Animal Husbandry and Fishing	采矿业 Mining	制造业 Manufacturing	电力、燃气及水的生产和供应业 Production and Distribution of Electricity, Gas and Water	建筑业 Construction	交通运输、仓储和邮政业 Transport, Storage and Post
全国总计	**National Total**	**14743.5**	**322.6**	**655.6**	**3621.4**	**547.6**	**905.2**	**980.7**
北京	Beijing	1098.9	4.2	4.7	193.9	14.3	98.5	56.3
天津	Tianjin	325.4	1.3	15.0	116.7	8.9	18.7	29.3
河北	Hebei	548.2	4.4	39.8	128.1	27.7	28.9	34.1
山西	Shanxi	371.5	3.1	71.6	67.1	14.1	18.4	29.7
内蒙古	Inner Mongolia	272.3	22.0	14.9	44.5	15.9	13.4	22.1
辽宁	Liaoning	648.5	13.3	42.5	188.7	31.3	32.6	50.3
吉林	Jilin	321.6	11.6	18.6	82.3	12.1	15.2	27.8
黑龙江	Heilongjiang	535.4	39.2	48.4	110.7	24.4	42.0	41.3
上海	Shanghai	768.7	2.0	0.1	275.9	17.9	30.5	76.5
江苏	Jiangsu	917.3	13.5	24.1	294.4	31.6	32.9	57.1
浙江	Zhejiang	784.8	4.4	2.4	151.2	30.7	76.0	42.5
安徽	Anhui	361.0	7.0	38.8	75.9	11.6	21.4	15.8
福建	Fujian	468.9	5.9	3.9	179.5	16.0	32.3	24.7
江西	Jiangxi	271.1	9.0	9.3	57.3	11.5	15.0	21.4
山东	Shandong	954.8	8.1	107.8	267.9	35.7	37.9	49.1
河南	Henan	720.5	5.8	67.6	147.1	32.9	51.0	40.2
湖北	Hubei	520.1	15.6	12.4	149.7	17.9	27.4	37.3
湖南	Hunan	465.0	9.1	10.7	88.9	16.9	22.7	30.4
广东	Guangdong	1515.6	11.7	5.3	436.1	56.4	77.4	110.0
广西	Guangxi	305.3	9.0	5.1	61.7	14.1	15.8	22.3
海南	Hainan	75.4	9.8	1.0	7.0	3.0	4.1	5.4
重庆	Chongqing	254.0	2.2	7.2	64.4	9.5	29.4	18.2
四川	Sichuan	604.5	10.1	20.2	131.8	23.4	60.9	29.1
贵州	Guizhou	209.3	3.6	10.1	43.6	10.9	15.3	12.2
云南	Yunnan	315.0	15.8	6.5	59.8	12.6	16.2	20.3
西藏	Tibet	38.8	0.6	0.1	0.8	1.4	0.8	1.7
陕西	Shaanxi	366.3	5.3	20.8	89.8	13.2	19.3	28.8
甘肃	Gansu	230.9	7.6	9.1	53.2	12.2	14.3	18.2
青海	Qinghai	63.5	2.4	2.8	8.1	3.7	3.1	5.1
宁夏	Ningxia	79.4	3.7	8.8	12.5	6.0	5.9	4.7
新疆	Xinjiang	331.5	61.3	26.1	32.5	9.9	27.9	18.9

5-23 续表 1 continued

单位: 亿元 (100 million yuan)

地 区	Region	信息传输、计算机服务和软件业 Information Transmission, Computer Service and Software	批发和零售业 Wholesale and Retail Trade	住宿和餐饮业 Hotel and Restaurants	金融业 Financial Intermediation	房地产业 Real Estate	租赁和商务服务业 Leasing and Business Services
全国总计	**National Total**	**331.3**	**660.5**	**175.3**	**646.8**	**184.0**	**271.7**
北 京	Beijing	80.5	74.0	29.0	50.3	38.2	83.3
天 津	Tianjin	4.8	15.8	3.5	9.5	3.3	4.7
河 北	Hebei	8.2	22.6	3.9	22.6	2.5	3.0
山 西	Shanxi	4.5	15.1	2.3	14.1	1.2	3.2
内蒙古	Inner Mongolia	4.2	6.5	1.9	9.8	1.6	4.0
辽 宁	Liaoning	15.2	21.2	6.1	29.5	8.0	9.5
吉 林	Jilin	5.3	10.1	2.4	13.3	3.1	3.9
黑龙江	Heilongjiang	10.3	25.9	3.0	18.6	4.6	4.3
上 海	Shanghai	19.0	45.6	11.8	47.9	16.4	23.3
江 苏	Jiangsu	15.9	43.5	8.6	38.6	10.2	11.7
浙 江	Zhejiang	18.4	39.5	11.2	46.1	10.1	19.1
安 徽	Anhui	4.3	14.3	2.5	12.4	2.6	2.2
福 建	Fujian	9.8	15.8	4.2	21.6	5.4	4.8
江 西	Jiangxi	3.5	10.5	1.7	11.3	1.9	1.7
山 东	Shandong	12.4	34.6	8.2	37.9	7.0	9.9
河 南	Henan	8.2	40.5	7.4	28.0	4.9	8.2
湖 北	Hubei	5.7	19.5	6.6	17.7	4.5	8.3
湖 南	Hunan	9.0	19.7	4.9	20.9	4.0	5.8
广 东	Guangdong	46.6	74.9	28.5	84.6	30.8	32.2
广 西	Guangxi	5.5	12.1	3.9	12.8	2.7	4.9
海 南	Hainan	1.8	2.9	2.6	3.8	1.3	1.1
重 庆	Chongqing	4.5	10.7	2.3	11.2	3.6	1.8
四 川	Sichuan	9.4	20.7	4.1	26.8	5.1	4.0
贵 州	Guizhou	1.9	9.8	2.0	7.2	2.3	3.6
云 南	Yunnan	5.5	17.3	3.6	10.3	1.9	3.0
西 藏	Tibet	1.0	0.8	0.4	1.9	0.1	0.1
陕 西	Shaanxi	6.9	15.0	3.4	15.1	1.6	2.8
甘 肃	Gansu	2.3	6.9	1.3	6.9	1.4	1.6
青 海	Qinghai	1.8	1.8	0.6	2.5	0.3	0.5
宁 夏	Ningxia	1.4	2.3	0.6	3.5	0.6	0.6
新 疆	Xinjiang	3.4	10.4	2.8	10.1	2.7	4.5

5-23 续表 2 continued

单位: 亿元 (100 million yuan)

地 区	Region	科学研究、技术服务和地质勘查业 Scientific Research, Technical Services, and Geological Prospecting	水利、环境和公共设施管理业 Water Management of Conservancy, Environment and Public Facilities	居民服务和其他服务业 Services to Households and Other Services	教育 Education	卫生、社会保障和社会福利业 Health, Social Securities and Social Welfare	文化、体育和娱乐业 Culture, Sports and Entertainment	公共管理和社会组织 Public Management and Social Organization
全国总计	**National Total**	**427.7**	**197.6**	**60.1**	**2007.3**	**767.6**	**210.3**	**1770.5**
北 京	Beijing	102.6	13.3	12.6	85.8	44.0	36.7	76.7
天 津	Tianjin	11.6	5.4	3.9	30.9	13.4	3.9	24.7
河 北	Hebei	12.0	8.0	3.9	88.8	25.2	6.0	78.5
山 西	Shanxi	6.9	3.8	2.0	50.3	14.6	4.3	45.2
内蒙古	Inner Mongolia	5.5	5.0	0.7	42.1	13.6	4.3	40.3
辽 宁	Liaoning	15.6	10.8	1.7	69.6	30.2	8.0	64.6
吉 林	Jilin	8.2	5.7	1.4	46.1	16.1	5.1	33.3
黑龙江	Heilongjiang	13.8	6.7	2.2	60.3	21.9	5.0	52.9
上 海	Shanghai	28.1	11.7	5.1	61.4	36.8	12.6	45.9
江 苏	Jiangsu	18.6	15.1	2.8	129.8	51.4	10.2	107.2
浙 江	Zhejiang	18.0	9.2	1.6	121.3	62.1	11.5	109.4
安 徽	Anhui	6.6	5.4	0.9	62.7	19.0	4.7	52.7
福 建	Fujian	7.0	4.0	1.9	62.4	17.9	5.1	46.6
江 西	Jiangxi	6.2	3.3	0.7	46.1	15.8	3.8	41.0
山 东	Shandong	12.5	11.8	1.4	136.3	51.5	8.8	115.9
河 南	Henan	15.6	9.9	1.4	109.7	35.5	7.3	99.5
湖 北	Hubei	13.6	7.4	1.1	73.4	29.2	6.5	66.0
湖 南	Hunan	9.5	6.4	0.7	85.5	33.6	9.5	76.7
广 东	Guangdong	29.0	17.9	5.1	181.2	84.3	17.7	185.9
广 西	Guangxi	6.3	4.3	0.7	56.7	20.4	3.6	43.4
海 南	Hainan	1.6	1.5	…	10.8	4.2	1.7	11.9
重 庆	Chongqing	8.4	2.1	0.4	37.8	11.2	2.6	26.7
四 川	Sichuan	21.2	6.6	3.2	96.7	37.4	7.0	86.9
贵 州	Guizhou	3.8	1.8	0.4	36.1	10.1	2.2	32.3
云 南	Yunnan	7.4	3.9	0.7	59.8	18.0	5.1	47.3
西 藏	Tibet	1.6	0.2	…	6.9	2.8	1.4	16.5
陕 西	Shaanxi	17.4	4.4	1.5	57.0	14.3	5.4	44.1
甘 肃	Gansu	6.7	4.0	0.3	34.9	10.2	4.6	35.2
青 海	Qinghai	4.0	1.1	0.3	9.8	3.7	0.9	11.1
宁 夏	Ningxia	1.7	2.0	…	11.1	3.5	1.1	9.3
新 疆	Xinjiang	6.5	5.0	1.3	46.0	15.8	3.8	42.7

5-24 按行业分职工平均工资
Average Wage of Staff and Workers by Sector

单位：元 (yuan)

年 份 Year	合 计 Total	农、林、牧、渔业 Farming, Forestry, Animal Husbandry and Fishery	采 掘 业 Mining and Quarrying	制 造 业 Manufacturing	电力、煤气及水的生产和供应业 Production and Supply of Electricity Gas and Water	建 筑 业 Construction	地质勘查业水利管理业 Geological Prospecting and Water Conservancy	交通运输仓储和邮电通信业 Transport, Storage, Post & Telecommunication Services
1978	615	470	676	597	850	714	708	694
1980	762	616	854	752	1035	855	895	832
1985	1148	878	1324	1112	1239	1362	1406	1275
1989	1935	1389	2378	1900	2241	2166	2199	2197
1990	2140	1541	2718	2073	2656	2384	2465	2426
1991	2340	1652	2942	2289	2922	2649	2707	2686
1992	2711	1828	3209	2635	3392	3066	3222	3114
1993	3371	2042	3711	3348	4319	3779	3717	4273
1994	4538	2819	4679	4283	6155	4894	5450	5690
1995	5500	3522	5757	5169	7843	5785	5962	6948
1996	6210	4050	6482	5642	8816	6249	6581	7870
1997	6470	4311	6833	5933	9649	6655	7160	8600
1998	7479	4528	7242	7064	10478	7456	7951	9808
1999	8346	4832	7521	7794	11513	7982	8821	10991
2000	9371	5184	8340	8750	12830	8735	9622	12319
2001	10870	5741	9586	9774	14590	9484	10957	14167
2002	12422	6398	11017	11001	16440	10279	12303	16044

5-24 续表 continued

单位：元 (yuan)

年 份 Year	批发零售贸易和餐饮业 Wholesale and Retail Trade & Catering Services	金融、保险业 Finance and Insurance	房地产业 Real Estate	社 会 服务业 Social Services	卫生体育和社会福利业 Health Care, Sports & Social Welfare	教育、文化艺术和广播电影电视业 Education, Culture and Arts, Radio, Film and Television	科学研究和综合技术服务业 Scientific Research and Polytechnic Services	国家机关、政党机关和社会团体 Government Agencies, Party Agencies and Social Organizations	其 他 Others
1978	551	610	548	392	573	545	669	655	
1980	692	720	694	475	718	700	851	800	
1985	1007	1154	1028	777	1124	1166	1272	1127	
1989	1660	1867	1925	1926	1959	1883	2118	1874	
1990	1818	2097	2243	2170	2209	2117	2403	2113	
1991	1981	2255	2507	2431	2370	2243	2573	2275	
1992	2204	2829	3106	2844	2812	2715	3115	2768	
1993	2679	3740	4320	3588	3413	3278	3904	3505	3371
1994	3537	6712	6288	5026	5126	4923	6162	4962	5213
1995	4248	7376	7330	5982	5860	5435	6846	5526	6295
1996	4661	8406	8337	6778	6790	6144	8048	6340	7184
1997	4845	9734	9190	7553	7599	6759	9049	6981	6838
1998	5865	10633	10302	8333	8493	7474	10241	7773	8481
1999	6417	12046	11505	9263	9664	8510	11601	8978	10068
2000	7190	13478	12616	10339	10930	9482	13620	10043	11098
2001	8192	16277	14096	11869	12933	11452	16437	12142	12590
2002	9398	19135	15501	13499	14795	13290	19113	13975	14215

5-25 各地区按行业分职工平均工资（2003年）

Average Wage of Staff and Workers by Sector and Region (2003)

单位：元 (yuan)

地 区	Region	合 计 Total	农、林、牧、渔业 Agriculture, Forestry, Animal Husbandry and Fishing	采矿业 Mining	制造业 Manufacturing	电力、燃气及水的生产和供应业 Production and Distribution of Electricity, Gas and Water	建筑业 Construction	交通运输、仓储和邮政业 Transport, Storage and Post
全国总计	**National Total**	**14040**	**6969**	**13682**	**12496**	**18752**	**11478**	**15973**
北 京	Beijing	25312	14980	18858	20059	37112	16730	19977
天 津	Tianjin	18648	13347	23605	16179	26085	19609	23748
河 北	Hebei	11189	4857	14057	10139	17582	9098	12777
山 西	Shanxi	10729	7787	12871	8944	12468	9169	13894
内蒙古	Inner Mongolia	11279	6832	9760	10050	17942	8297	13604
辽 宁	Liaoning	13008	4960	13756	12206	18559	9660	14688
吉 林	Jilin	11081	5512	11859	11129	15206	8716	10909
黑龙江	Heilongjiang	11038	5373	13466	10063	15702	10641	12784
上 海	Shanghai	27304	18706	44197	25477	32330	24591	25903
江 苏	Jiangsu	15712	7468	14530	13512	25000	13167	17031
浙 江	Zhejiang	21367	16583	13994	14267	34733	15982	22718
安 徽	Anhui	10581	5985	12699	9701	13563	8531	9473
福 建	Fujian	14310	7974	10858	12217	20562	13779	18181
江 西	Jiangxi	10521	5534	9421	9626	12707	9220	14011
山 东	Shandong	12567	8643	17802	10000	17681	10028	16124
河 南	Henan	10749	6155	14339	9550	14570	9370	12556
湖 北	Hubei	10692	5340	11556	10145	14247	9926	11827
湖 南	Hunan	12221	5357	9189	11312	15022	9328	12565
广 东	Guangdong	19986	8997	12961	15763	28574	14608	25936
广 西	Guangxi	11953	6796	10865	11156	17571	10604	13999
海 南	Hainan	10397	4762	8264	9929	15928	9190	15571
重 庆	Chongqing	12425	8877	9725	11883	16372	10028	12506
四 川	Sichuan	12441	8988	10613	11172	15303	9255	13171
贵 州	Guizhou	11037	8563	11556	10291	18801	8942	13280
云 南	Yunnan	12870	9803	10861	12645	18490	10475	13810
西 藏	Tibet	26931	19113	16284	11916	23092	17805	22759
陕 西	Shaanxi	11461	8230	12534	10281	16218	9926	14506
甘 肃	Gansu	12307	8971	12205	11635	17544	9303	14843
青 海	Qinghai	15356	10836	14930	12193	21364	10694	18227
宁 夏	Ningxia	12981	8297	14573	10424	18793	10893	15341
新 疆	Xinjiang	13255	9005	19978	12181	17724	11619	17767

5-25 续表 1 continued

单位：元 (yuan)

地区	Region	信息传输、计算机服务和软件业 Information Transmission, Computer Service and Software	批发和零售业 Wholesale and Retail Trade	住宿和餐饮业 Hotel and Restaurants	金融业 Financial Intermediation	房地产业 Real Estate	租赁和商务服务业 Leasing and Business Services
全国总计	**National Total**	**32244**	**10939**	**11083**	**22457**	**17182**	**16501**
北京	Beijing	53010	23088	16530	61713	26064	25742
天津	Tianjin	33785	15606	12430	26295	21253	13514
河北	Hebei	23494	6824	7900	15237	10832	9225
山西	Shanxi	17953	6178	6250	15103	9472	8353
内蒙古	Inner Mongolia	17367	7867	7516	14060	10858	12511
辽宁	Liaoning	35486	10466	10123	20171	13394	11915
吉林	Jilin	21777	6935	8357	15559	11596	11824
黑龙江	Heilongjiang	26318	8400	8528	18407	11142	9069
上海	Shanghai	62821	25038	21168	42544	32802	22990
江苏	Jiangsu	32533	11452	11869	24173	16897	15931
浙江	Zhejiang	44263	20288	13516	31578	22692	20137
安徽	Anhui	19158	6163	7302	14475	11128	8483
福建	Fujian	33158	13375	10333	26245	16582	14538
江西	Jiangxi	16831	7782	8313	15390	9873	10783
山东	Shandong	24660	8006	9249	19924	14269	12805
河南	Henan	19377	7169	7917	16595	11159	10321
湖北	Hubei	16517	6923	7134	14539	10616	9943
湖南	Hunan	21361	10337	9638	18159	12959	13380
广东	Guangdong	42966	18296	14778	33426	22312	21306
广西	Guangxi	23783	8558	8001	17341	12596	10396
海南	Hainan	27898	8810	8352	19979	12017	10607
重庆	Chongqing	25298	10497	9412	22300	12174	10805
四川	Sichuan	23069	10055	9192	20550	12688	12559
贵州	Guizhou	18426	8630	8581	16121	10396	11884
云南	Yunnan	19343	11068	8793	15133	12694	14861
西藏	Tibet	45446	14036	13251	32525	20670	15988
陕西	Shaanxi	26772	7290	7654	17032	10931	9853
甘肃	Gansu	13104	7397	7461	13991	11178	10345
青海	Qinghai	24594	9986	11811	19235	14024	12874
宁夏	Ningxia	26867	9268	7918	19532	10678	11282
新疆	Xinjiang	23338	13082	10337	20680	13327	12666

5-25 续表 2 continued

单位: 元 (yuan)

地 区	Region	科学研究、技术服务和地质勘查业 Scientific Research, Technical Services, and Geological Prospecting	水利、环境和公共设施管理业 Water Management of Conservancy, Environment and Public Facilities	居民服务和其他服务业 Services to Households and Other Services	教育 Education	卫生、社会保障和社会福利业 Health, Social Securities and Social Welfare	文化、体育和娱乐业 Culture, Sports and Entertainment	公共管理和社会组织 Public Management and Social Organization
全国总计	**National Total**	**20636**	**12095**	**12900**	**14399**	**16352**	**17268**	**15533**
北 京	Beijing	34898	22357	17433	28565	34173	35006	30279
天 津	Tianjin	24545	17325	14492	19226	20426	19838	21363
河 北	Hebei	16699	10021	14647	11100	11681	12012	11954
山 西	Shanxi	13109	7969	6714	11648	10915	10826	11239
内蒙古	Inner Mongolia	14060	10235	7257	13383	13353	13664	13886
辽 宁	Liaoning	17600	10623	9804	13704	14073	15327	14650
吉 林	Jilin	14140	8758	12335	12950	11771	11542	12274
黑龙江	Heilongjiang	14084	9898	6330	13808	13066	13977	14097
上 海	Shanghai	30928	24850	18542	26601	28531	32090	30748
江 苏	Jiangsu	23744	14964	16735	16549	18729	19550	21498
浙 江	Zhejiang	28627	18908	19269	25677	29366	27060	29785
安 徽	Anhui	13348	9328	7600	11436	11845	11167	12915
福 建	Fujian	19913	12948	15009	15029	16589	16919	16567
江 西	Jiangxi	12804	8736	8152	10986	12614	11888	11484
山 东	Shandong	17264	11685	11633	13342	15106	16325	13723
河 南	Henan	14986	9942	9217	10774	11474	10818	11031
湖 北	Hubei	14610	9131	8941	12098	12121	11697	12616
湖 南	Hunan	14853	9890	11274	13309	15122	15082	12818
广 东	Guangdong	32963	16257	17832	20449	25157	25901	25642
广 西	Guangxi	14944	10166	12021	11344	13800	12926	13912
海 南	Hainan	11709	9465	12538	13353	15329	14726	14785
重 庆	Chongqing	14478	9359	12920	12865	13472	15537	14003
四 川	Sichuan	19913	9859	13180	12825	14861	13779	14532
贵 州	Guizhou	14090	8724	8455	10597	12120	11437	11472
云 南	Yunnan	14827	10848	10954	13391	15094	13284	13191
西 藏	Tibet	31626	16053	29909	28138	29897	28485	30687
陕 西	Shaanxi	14977	9528	9076	12598	11129	11067	11030
甘 肃	Gansu	14470	11678	10629	13534	13859	12789	13677
青 海	Qinghai	21917	10930	13188	16473	17172	15071	16971
宁 夏	Ningxia	13876	12007	10566	15115	14119	13910	13757
新 疆	Xinjiang	16201	12091	13860	15167	15327	14966	15680

5-26 按细行业分职工平均工资（2003年）

Average Wage of Staff and Workers by Sector in Detail (2003)

单位：元 (yuan)

项　目	Item	合 计 Total	国有单位 State-owned Units	城镇集体单位 Urban Collective-owned Units	其他单位 Units of Other Types of Ownership
全国总计	**National Total**	**14040**	**14577**	**8678**	**14574**
按企、事业和机关分组	**Grouped by Enterprises, Institutions and Agencies**				
企业	Enterprises	13578	14028	8401	14575
事业	Institutions	14564	14770	10448	15147
机关	Agencies & Organizations	15736	15757	9742	
按国民经济行业分组	**Grouped by Sector**				
农、林、牧、渔业	**Farming, Forestry, Animal Husbandry and Fishing**	**6969**	**6912**	**6125**	**10022**
农业	Farming	6360	6328	5969	8904
林业	Forestry	6139	6126	4072	8130
畜牧业	Animal Husbandry	6585	5854	6233	12380
渔业	Fishing	9489	9224	7172	11319
农、林、牧、渔服务业	Services	9453	9930	6247	9233
采矿业	**Mining**	**13682**	**13888**	**7178**	**14321**
制造业	**Manufacturing**	**12496**	**12601**	**7600**	**13263**
电力、燃气及水的生产和供应业	**Production and Distribution of Electricity, Gas and Water**	**18752**	**18226**	**14911**	**20923**
建筑业	**Construction**	**11478**	**12739**	**8375**	**12345**
房屋和土木工程建筑业	Construction of Buildings and Civil Engineering	11036	12306	8079	11872
建筑安装业	Building Installation	15253	15723	11736	16923
建筑装饰业	Building Decoration	12282	11854	7592	13568
其他建筑业	Other Construction	13214	15679	9714	12597
交通运输、仓储和邮政业	**Transport, Storage and Post**	**15973**	**16234**	**8212**	**17621**
铁路运输业	Railway Transport	18140	18091	12367	24044
道路运输业	Road Transport	11157	11293	7595	12183
城市公共交通业	Urban Public Transport	13977	13922	9393	14549
水上运输业	Water Transport	22506	24078	7171	24966
航空运输业	Air Transport	33377	30791	14060	38739
管道运输业	Transport Via Pipelines	25761	25343	23619	28854
装卸搬运和其他运输服务业	Loading, Unloading and Other Transport Services	14695	16298	7430	23119
仓储业	Storage	10359	9446	9650	16932
邮政业	Post	18907	18953	14221	18995
信息传输、计算机服务和软件业	**Information Transmission, Computer Services and Software**	**32244**	**26572**	**12484**	**42867**
电信和其他信息传输服务业	Telecommunications and Other Information Tıansmission Services	30481	27096	14867	41715
计算机服务业	Computer Services	41722	14470	8297	55406
软件业	Software	36873	22568	12221	38981
批发和零售业	**Wholesale and Retail Trade**	**10939**	**11064**	**6593**	**13710**
批发业	Wholesale Trade	12295	12167	7277	16214
零售业	Retail Trade	9277	8786	6045	11856
住宿和餐饮业	**Hotel and Restaurants**	**11083**	**10525**	**8342**	**12179**
住宿业	Hotels	11524	10891	8828	13003
餐饮业	Restaurants	10200	8996	7613	11167
金融业	**Financial Intermediation**	**22457**	**23075**	**14370**	**31370**
银行业	Banks	21783	23088	14398	32994

5-26 续表 continued

单位: 元 (yuan)

项　目	Item	合 计 Total	国有单位 State-owned Units	城镇集体单位 Urban Collective-owned Units	其他单位 Units of Other Types of Ownership
证券业	Security Activities	42582	43647	10661	42548
保险业	Insurance	22576	19213	9047	25399
其他金融活动	Other Financial Activities	31651	31518	12580	47526
房地产业	**Real Estate**	**17182**	**16064**	**12228**	**18898**
#房地产开发经营	Development and Management of Real Estate	17514	16418	10840	19069
物业管理	Property Management	16799	15814	14608	18038
房地产中介服务	Agency Services for Real Estate	19242	15693	15173	25634
租赁和商务服务业	**Leasing and Business Services**	**16501**	**15378**	**11042**	**23281**
租赁业	Leasing	13196	13229	9495	14633
商务服务业	Business Services	16566	15409	11071	23582
科学研究、技术服务和地质勘查业	**Scientific Research, Technical Service and Geologic Prospecting**	**20636**	**19975**	**14541**	**26061**
研究与实验发展	Research and Experimental Development	22391	22307	12551	27057
专业技术服务业	Professional Technical Services	22046	21111	15553	26211
科技交流和推广服务业	Services of Science and Technology Exchanges and Promotion	16877	15190	12962	25981
地质勘查业	Geologic Prospecting	15277	15111	11765	21427
水利、环境和公共设施管理业	**Management of Water Conservancy, Environment and Public Facilities**	**12095**	**12104**	**10380**	**14560**
水利管理业	Management of Water Conservancy	11322	11338	10534	11368
环境管理业	Environmental Management	11255	11316	9952	14572
公共设施管理业	Management of Public Facilities	13885	13875	12108	14683
居民服务和其他服务业	**Services to Households and Other Services**	**12900**	**15075**	**8713**	**14046**
居民服务业	Services to Households	13009	14916	7751	12653
其他服务业	Other Services	12806	15315	9097	15161
教育	**Education**	**14399**	**14602**	**9308**	**16163**
#初等教育	Junior Education	12223	12465	8858	13995
中等教育	Secondary Education	14415	14484	10166	17261
高等教育	Senior Education	23639	23675	20044	18232
卫生、社会保障和社会福利业	**Health, Social Security and Social Welfare**	**16352**	**16922**	**11685**	**14102**
卫生	Health	16389	16980	11692	14031
社会保障业	Social Security	15729	15718	16750	13859
社会福利业	Social Welfare	15396	15743	9284	15630
文化、体育和娱乐业	**Culture, Sports and Entertainment**	**17268**	**17544**	**9429**	**16121**
新闻出版业	Journalism and Publishing Activities	26917	26809	17083	34087
广播、电影、电视和音像业	Broadcasting, Movies, Televisions and Audiovisual Activities	15098	15065	9618	21180
文化艺术业	Cultural and Art Activities	14919	15154	8690	16465
体育	Sports Activities	18934	19158	8985	16065
娱乐业	Entertainment	12875	14553	8991	12588
公共管理和社会组织	**Public Management and Social Organization**	**15533**	**15557**	**10748**	**8765**
#中国共产党机关	Organs of Communist Party of China	15456	15458		
国家机构	Government Agencies	15517	15533	10582	
人民政协和民主党派	People's Political Consultative Conference and Democratic Parties	17327	17333	5000	
群众社团、社会团体和宗教组织	Non-Governmental Institutions, Social Organizations and Religion Organizations	17481	17849	11621	7370

5-27 按行业分国有单位职工平均工资

Average Wage of Staff and Workers in State-owned Units by Sector

单位：元 (yuan)

年份 Year	合计 Total	农、林、牧、渔业 Farming, Forestry, Animal Husbandry and Fishery	采掘业 Mining and Quarrying	制造业 Manufacturing	电力、煤气及水的生产和供应业 Production and Supply of Electricity Gas and Water	建筑业 Construction	地质勘查业水利管理业 Geological Prospecting and Water Conservancy	交通运输仓储和邮电通信业 Transport, Storage, Post & Telecommunication Services
1978	644	482	704	663	873	760	712	720
1980	803	628	891	821	1073	924	895	902
1985	1213	892	1384	1190	1272	1532	1408	1383
1989	2055	1401	2449	2081	2248	2419	2199	2423
1990	2284	1559	2763	2289	2648	2667	2463	2697
1991	2477	1665	2982	2505	2883	2924	2718	2967
1992	2878	1845	3239	2889	3354	3406	3235	3452
1993	3532	2043	3856	3562	4317	4182	3729	4604
1994	4797	2821	4863	4508	6124	5498	5476	6212
1995	5625	3527	5944	5352	7734	6512	5987	7572
1996	6280	4038	6709	5798	8701	6992	6610	8546
1997	6747	4304	7091	6008	9541	7388	7180	9303
1998	7668	4522	7499	6981	10324	8171	7968	10302
1999	8543	4813	7732	7611	11239	8734	8843	11345
2000	9552	5132	8283	8554	12458	9512	9651	12613
2001	11178	5702	9446	9590	14132	10299	11005	14318
2002	12869	6326	10601	10876	15799	11231	12296	16030

5-27 续表 continued

单位：元 (yuan)

年份 Year	批发零售贸易和餐饮业 Wholesale and Retail Trade & Catering Services	金融、保险业 Finance and Insurance	房地产业 Real Estate	社会服务业 Social Services	卫生体育和社会福利业 Health Care, Sports & Social Welfare	教育、文化艺术和广播电影电视业 Education, Culture and Arts, Radio, Film and Television	科学研究和综合技术服务业 Scientific Research and Polytechnic Services	国家机关、政党机关和社会团体 Government Agencies, Party Agencies and Social Organizations	其他 Others
1978	569	650	630	607	605	566	670	661	
1980	716	754	758	795	751	722	853	807	
1985	1087	1234	1170	1208	1164	1184	1268	1133	
1989	1851	1960	1992	2028	1999	1899	2123	1875	
1990	2028	2200	2247	2307	2263	2134	2411	2115	
1991	2201	2355	2476	2547	2417	2257	2580	2277	
1992	2478	2967	3082	3008	2883	2732	3130	2774	
1993	2933	3885	4278	3661	3494	3292	3898	3512	3793
1994	3856	7017	5997	5098	5267	4944	6212	4967	5744
1995	4568	7595	6884	5949	6009	5457	6835	5528	6854
1996	4940	8679	7897	6695	6967	6161	7984	6344	7643
1997	5134	10012	8570	7425	7794	6810	8974	6985	6891
1998	6150	10898	9441	8136	8704	7537	10146	7776	8258
1999	6678	12249	10475	9054	9899	8590	11543	8982	9762
2000	7414	13729	11626	9847	11234	9599	13221	10048	10198
2001	8220	16605	13111	11254	13340	11591	16218	12152	11488
2002	9444	19648	14465	12239	15281	13473	19006	13987	13559

5-28 各地区按行业分国有单位职工平均工资（2003年）

Average Wage of Staff and Workers in State-owned Units by Sector and Region (2003)

单位: 元 (yuan)

地区	Region	合计 Total	农、林、牧、渔业 Agriculture, Forestry, Animal Husbandry and Fishing	采矿业 Mining	制造业 Manufacturing	电力、燃气及水的生产和供应业 Production and Distribution of Electricity, Gas and Water	建筑业 Construction	交通运输、仓储和邮政业 Transport, Storage and Post
全国总计	**National Total**	**14577**	**6912**	**13888**	**12601**	**18226**	**12739**	**16234**
北京	Beijing	28464	16635	12280	20285	43375	22010	24410
天津	Tianjin	19352	12627	25261	13941	24385	19634	22774
河北	Hebei	11783	4835	13664	11086	16602	11320	13071
山西	Shanxi	11213	8152	12436	8392	12798	10118	14617
内蒙古	Inner Mongolia	11929	6858	9138	9430	16216	9154	14495
辽宁	Liaoning	13603	4727	14658	13293	17892	11084	15249
吉林	Jilin	11124	5522	8023	11676	14832	8839	10942
黑龙江	Heilongjiang	11034	5406	7511	9590	14903	12190	13260
上海	Shanghai	28406	18849	47948	26415	30494	26229	28056
江苏	Jiangsu	17502	7439	14577	14500	24454	16219	18593
浙江	Zhejiang	27293	16419	13482	19126	35862	20896	24476
安徽	Anhui	11220	6030	14675	9365	14272	11021	10862
福建	Fujian	16460	7859	10161	16025	20420	15458	18233
江西	Jiangxi	10918	5519	9664	9810	12224	11902	14774
山东	Shandong	13975	9615	19290	10637	17286	11212	16479
河南	Henan	11397	6497	15458	9434	14397	9790	13583
湖北	Hubei	11806	5314	13424	13151	13902	12479	12462
湖南	Hunan	12604	5333	8970	11951	14547	9735	13343
广东	Guangdong	22944	8132	12603	17949	27283	18588	25789
广西	Guangxi	12331	6742	9750	11217	17130	11518	14999
海南	Hainan	10305	4725	8224	8962	12368	10274	15617
重庆	Chongqing	13586	9200	10072	13325	18257	11038	13620
四川	Sichuan	13923	9196	11952	13217	16523	11848	14393
贵州	Guizhou	11390	8601	11325	9821	19186	10394	13319
云南	Yunnan	13471	9864	11396	15601	18345	11045	14513
西藏	Tibet	27611	19221	17131	11872	23092	12623	23166
陕西	Shaanxi	11833	8356	12937	10291	16184	11558	14847
甘肃	Gansu	12929	8992	12019	12462	17440	10277	15381
青海	Qinghai	16692	10849	16746	15631	21413	12071	19116
宁夏	Ningxia	13721	8269	11992	10386	19462	11677	15842
新疆	Xinjiang	13199	9019	18883	11287	17887	11716	19088

5-28 续表 1 continued

单位：元 (yuan)

地　区	Region	信息传输、计算机服务和软件业 Information Transmission, Computer Service and Software	批发和零售业 Wholesale and Retail Trade	住宿和餐饮业 Hotel and Restaurants	金融业 Financial Intermediation	房地产业 Real Estate	租赁和商务服务业 Leasing and Business Services
全国总计	**National Total**	**26572**	**11064**	**10525**	**23075**	**16064**	**15378**
北　京	Beijing	45775	31473	16986	59874	26842	20249
天　津	Tianjin	30212	18180	12177	26290	19852	11302
河　北	Hebei	23840	7490	7782	16469	11294	10142
山　西	Shanxi	18402	6808	6982	15944	9847	8921
内蒙古	Inner Mongolia	16943	8630	7479	15026	11528	13903
辽　宁	Liaoning	32811	10781	9228	21280	12808	11935
吉　林	Jilin	20722	6858	8201	17889	11312	12350
黑龙江	Heilongjiang	26357	8156	6911	19457	11536	9325
上　海	Shanghai	63249	27589	22104	44327	31258	20288
江　苏	Jiangsu	26867	12061	11359	23794	19677	16679
浙　江	Zhejiang	42018	29744	13893	31234	26906	21519
安　徽	Anhui	19213	6531	7663	15697	11634	11251
福　建	Fujian	30493	15588	10629	28827	17869	14631
江　西	Jiangxi	14299	8279	8137	16069	10132	11732
山　东	Shandong	24717	8551	9170	21683	14385	14226
河　南	Henan	16676	7652	7904	18708	10954	10855
湖　北	Hubei	17419	7009	7284	14483	11210	10375
湖　南	Hunan	21112	10911	9320	18785	13190	13350
广　东	Guangdong	38323	18725	14316	35354	20320	19913
广　西	Guangxi	24378	9217	7879	18865	12995	11251
海　南	Hainan	29686	9236	7743	22275	11600	11691
重　庆	Chongqing	24422	12039	9135	21427	12706	11763
四　川	Sichuan	23607	11521	10167	23010	15014	14099
贵　州	Guizhou	18361	9527	8484	17138	11266	13280
云　南	Yunnan	19290	12854	8687	15805	12496	14231
西　藏	Tibet	45446	15048	13780	32849	21925	14512
陕　西	Shaanxi	18249	7810	7578	16933	10882	10771
甘　肃	Gansu	13460	7830	7796	14310	11340	10969
青　海	Qinghai	24987	11331	13057	21160	15940	15538
宁　夏	Ningxia	27885	9886	8276	19933	9273	12331
新　疆	Xinjiang	25635	13927	10414	22153	14998	12822

5-28 续表 2 continued

单位：元 (yuan)

地区	Region	科学研究、技术服务和地质勘查业 Scientific Research, Technical Services, and Geological Prospecting	水利、环境和公共设施管理业 Water Management of Conservancy, Environment and Public Facilities	居民服务和其他服务业 Services to Households and Other Services	教育 Education	卫生、社会保障和社会福利业 Health, Social Securities and Social Welfare	文化、体育和娱乐业 Culture, Sports and Entertainment	公共管理和社会组织 Public Management and Social Organization
全国总计	**National Total**	**19975**	**12104**	**15075**	**14602**	**16922**	**17544**	**15557**
北京	Beijing	37387	23163	24560	28942	34724	37569	30297
天津	Tianjin	24617	17146	17650	19363	20768	20188	21490
河北	Hebei	16851	10080	15758	11101	12028	12579	11959
山西	Shanxi	13230	8172	9781	11660	11720	11293	11243
内蒙古	Inner Mongolia	14267	10424	8763	13430	14191	13877	13888
辽宁	Liaoning	17726	10682	11918	13716	14630	15435	14669
吉林	Jilin	14164	8738	10804	12952	12025	11532	12274
黑龙江	Heilongjiang	14277	9912	9750	13797	13251	13961	14102
上海	Shanghai	29963	25395	22257	26764	28582	33330	30828
江苏	Jiangsu	23183	15736	17001	16642	20757	20529	21575
浙江	Zhejiang	29838	20768	24115	25814	31305	27715	29841
安徽	Anhui	13479	9322	10777	11432	13382	11346	12923
福建	Fujian	20168	13010	16677	15006	17511	17604	16573
江西	Jiangxi	12816	8937	8593	10986	12829	11925	11498
山东	Shandong	17367	11866	13510	13368	15969	16484	13730
河南	Henan	14858	9969	10748	12450	11641	11155	11053
湖北	Hubei	14865	9121	12079	12170	12316	11755	12713
湖南	Hunan	15046	9926	12333	13314	15992	14712	12825
广东	Guangdong	32959	16606	26119	20481	25469	28549	25662
广西	Guangxi	14887	10288	18479	11350	13774	13310	13960
海南	Hainan	11724	9655	18381	13394	16053	16223	14937
重庆	Chongqing	19253	9575	14053	12879	14344	15741	14010
四川	Sichuan	20010	9963	14618	12809	16451	13962	14535
贵州	Guizhou	14280	8822	10678	10563	12028	11471	11470
云南	Yunnan	14355	10852	12360	13370	15131	13668	13192
西藏	Tibet	31626	16053	33828	28138	29897	28592	30687
陕西	Shaanxi	14733	9538	10155	12544	11461	11275	11040
甘肃	Gansu	14543	11693	11946	13533	14093	13025	13705
青海	Qinghai	22032	12027	18323	16494	17230	15071	17095
宁夏	Ningxia	14025	12156	13552	15128	14196	13951	13753
新疆	Xinjiang	16166	12220	14219	15172	15318	15115	15680

5-29 按行业分城镇集体单位职工平均工资

Average Wage of Staff and Workers in Urban Collective-owned Units by Sector

单位: 元 (yuan)

年份 Year	合计 Total	农、林、牧、渔业 Farming, Forestry, Animal Husbandry and Fishery	采掘业 Mining and Quarrying	制造业 Manufacturing	电力、煤气及水的生产和供应业 Production and Supply of Electricity Gas and Water	建筑业 Construction	地质勘查业水利管理业 Geological Prospecting and Water Conservancy	交通运输仓储和邮电通信业 Transport, Storage, Post & Telecommunication Services
1978	506	304	443	503	333	594	600	632
1980	623	458	548	619	333	716	700	676
1985	967	725	852	963	667	1101	900	1009
1989	1557	1178	1433	1523	1625	1763	1000	1575
1990	1681	1238	1844	1622	2133	1935	1212	1661
1991	1866	1366	1960	1798	2588	2216	1765	1854
1992	2109	1487	2000	2017	2737	2554	2188	2070
1993	2592	1887	2327	2469	3539	3182	2843	2711
1994	3245	2510	2793	3076	5734	3936	3692	3110
1995	3931	2927	3680	3717	7461	4677	4294	3584
1996	4302	3814	3968	4007	8324	5092	4784	3961
1997	4512	3945	4164	4120	9064	5466	6342	4057
1998	5331	4358	4567	5016	9470	5941	7017	5163
1999	5774	4878	4545	5327	9834	6296	7636	5707
2000	6262	5536	4857	5722	10707	6873	7509	5816
2001	6867	5654	5517	6088	12250	7260	7605	6322
2002	7667	6415	6067	6749	13051	7745	9599	6940

5-29 续表 continued

单位: 元 (yuan)

年份 Year	批发零售贸易和餐饮业 Wholesale and Retail Trade & Catering Services	金融、保险业 Finance and Insurance	房地产业 Real Estate	社会服务业 Social Services	卫生体育和社会福利业 Health Care, Sports & Social Welfare	教育、文化艺术和广播电影电视业 Education, Culture and Arts, Radio, Film and Television	科学研究和综合技术服务业 Scientific Research and Polytechnic Services	国家机关、政党机关和社会团体 Government Agencies, Party Agencies and Social Organizations	其他 Others
1978	453	526	467	451	484	317	500	455	
1980	584	640	638	584	618	433	571	538	
1985	912	945	1050	806	975	779	1052	1046	
1989	1417	1597	1967	1521	1774	1352	1710	1860	
1990	1548	1806	1969	1638	1956	1533	1997	2042	
1991	1691	1965	2432	1905	2135	1689	2120	2206	
1992	1827	2428	2763	2082	2416	1987	2392	2565	
1993	2213	3182	4006	2727	2935	2539	3474	3071	2547
1994	2823	5625	5290	3754	4238	3548	4719	4411	4067
1995	3449	6407	6706	4707	4890	4291	6046	5314	4935
1996	3818	6857	6820	5032	5603	4949	7206	5686	5675
1997	3873	7634	7687	5663	6294	4955	7749	6244	5780
1998	4517	8144	9144	5990	6883	5192	8116	7033	7048
1999	4802	9088	10516	6621	7826	5750	8771	7985	8135
2000	5089	9754	10371	7269	8521	5854	10434	8899	9044
2001	5428	10914	10658	7950	9638	7304	12137	9487	9621
2002	5983	12540	11504	8957	10738	8036	12976	10456	10038

5-30 各地区按行业分城镇集体单位职工平均工资（2003年）

Average Wage of Staff and Workers in Urban Collective-owned Units by Sector and Region (2003)

单位：元 (yuan)

地区	Region	合计 Total	农、林、牧、渔业 Agriculture, Forestry, Animal Husbandry and Fishing	采矿业 Mining	制造业 Manufacturing	电力、燃气及水的生产和供应业 Production and Distribution of Electricity, Gas and Water	建筑业 Construction	交通运输、仓储和邮政业 Transport, Storage and Post
全国总计	**National Total**	**8678**	**6125**	**7178**	**7600**	**14911**	**8375**	**8212**
北京	Beijing	13580	10329	11310	10886	11417	12962	11328
天津	Tianjin	11285	9049	13184	9461	11921	15099	11158
河北	Hebei	6919	5000	5193	6368	7120	7190	7451
山西	Shanxi	6629	3164	8196	6063	11984	5781	6282
内蒙古	Inner Mongolia	7620	4571	6379	6902	13813	8217	5288
辽宁	Liaoning	7629	8314	6367	6907	10410	7595	6923
吉林	Jilin	8018	4153	5435	6609	8756	8521	15280
黑龙江	Heilongjiang	5425	2478	5912	5008	14994	5054	5500
上海	Shanghai	16973	22095	9333	13458	36963	15609	12009
江苏	Jiangsu	9836	6545	7001	8375	12544	9133	8992
浙江	Zhejiang	16058	21454	12294	11480	18105	14183	13831
安徽	Anhui	6407	4676	7196	6357	7166	6340	4525
福建	Fujian	11386	8044	11929	9409	23699	12526	10713
江西	Jiangxi	6905	5917	5613	6200	8160	7009	5376
山东	Shandong	8442	5671	7825	8440	8787	8017	8308
河南	Henan	7894	4683	7230	6755	8994	7761	5957
湖北	Hubei	7137	5970	7284	6778	10053	7356	7104
湖南	Hunan	8546	5140	6768	7889	12817	7990	5907
广东	Guangdong	10836	9148	6903	9106	20228	9154	11525
广西	Guangxi	7962	7990	7520	7160	22021	8272	7964
海南	Hainan	7029	4518	8679	6533	4450	6101	7744
重庆	Chongqing	8552	7662	4856	7799	8852	8802	7800
四川	Sichuan	8723	7545	6597	8075	14619	7588	7331
贵州	Guizhou	7504	7742	8076	6953	5697	6637	7746
云南	Yunnan	8519	5789	7896	8237	16671	8171	9734
西藏	Tibet	9348	8394	8207	9459		13000	7174
陕西	Shaanxi	6858	5980	6744	6479	4872	6761	6957
甘肃	Gansu	7573	7947	8958	7622	8848	6423	10862
青海	Qinghai	8306	12752	7545	5567	33164	7545	6545
宁夏	Ningxia	8924	8939	6212	7037		9023	4134
新疆	Xinjiang	9966	5979	9512	9574	10230	9591	11944

5-30 续表 1 continued

单位: 元 (yuan)

地 区	Region	信息传输、计算机服务和软件业 Information Transmission, Computer Service and Software	批发和零售业 Wholesale and Retail Trade	住宿和餐饮业 Hotel and Restaurants	金融业 Financial Intermediation	房地产业 Real Estate	租赁和商务服务业 Leasing and Business Services
全国总计	**National Total**	**12484**	**6593**	**8342**	**14370**	**12228**	**11042**
北 京	Beijing	22017	14734	11528	49522	14307	15554
天 津	Tianjin	13531	9636	9873	20935	14259	14776
河 北	Hebei	15435	4973	6044	11705	10433	7173
山 西	Shanxi	2027	5131	4752	13314	9077	6705
内蒙古	Inner Mongolia	9148	6224	6721	11663	10852	6609
辽 宁	Liaoning	16615	6310	7231	13249	11269	10486
吉 林	Jilin	5307	5815	5816	10815	11655	9069
黑龙江	Heilongjiang	8961	3980	5192	11300	11171	6265
上 海	Shanghai	31905	15183	11930	21184	19108	17544
江 苏	Jiangsu	12033	7005	9966	16614	18774	11028
浙 江	Zhejiang	16852	12605	12138	28038	18224	19962
安 徽	Anhui	5492	3899	4877	10834	6583	7649
福 建	Fujian	12884	7518	9921	16699	16066	10514
江 西	Jiangxi	6124	5261	6355	11234	8691	7914
山 东	Shandong	17157	5886	8806	14160	12282	8275
河 南	Henan	6258	5477	7815	11316	8905	8495
湖 北	Hubei	8436	4962	8163	10340	6577	9330
湖 南	Hunan	7203	7362	8550	15440	8990	8462
广 东	Guangdong	19753	9566	10346	19386	14531	13876
广 西	Guangxi	7761	5778	7253	12745	9655	6905
海 南	Hainan	4267	4989	7479	9710	10861	9533
重 庆	Chongqing	11364	6664	7110	16467	5989	11378
四 川	Sichuan	7802	6600	7289	15098	9983	7399
贵 州	Guizhou	10208	5880	7316	13286	9079	7858
云 南	Yunnan	9138	6783	7353	12102	9784	8085
西 藏	Tibet		4906	9175			
陕 西	Shaanxi	6989	5471	4936	11402	6572	7821
甘 肃	Gansu	6966	5706	5066	11173	12726	8678
青 海	Qinghai		6358	7551	12111	8467	10080
宁 夏	Ningxia	6500	6977	6823	17230	4177	6098
新 疆	Xinjiang	12709	9209	10179	13510	9932	9535

5-30 续表 2 continued

单位: 元 (yuan)

地区	Region	科学研究、技术服务和地质勘查业 Scientific Research, Technical Services, and Geological Prospecting	水利、环境和公共设施管理业 Water Management of Conservancy, Environment and Public Facilities	居民服务和其他服务业 Services to Households and Other Services	教育 Education	卫生、社会保障和社会福利业 Health, Social Securities and Social Welfare	文化、体育和娱乐业 Culture, Sports and Entertainment	公共管理和社会组织 Public Management and Social Organization
全国总计	**National Total**	**14541**	**10380**	**8713**	**9308**	**11685**	**9429**	**10748**
北京	Beijing	19526	18683	12062	16162	29929	10954	25335
天津	Tianjin	16329	8809	11057	8973	12350	11582	16108
河北	Hebei	12347	7275	9411	10173	7180	6742	10072
山西	Shanxi	7828	5000	5561	10394	6735	3996	10145
内蒙古	Inner Mongolia	14043	5463	5062	9375	7870	6050	12633
辽宁	Liaoning	9918	7607	6815	8222	6614	7627	7088
吉林	Jilin	10149	8780	16559	10589	8346	12317	12196
黑龙江	Heilongjiang	9972	9936	4453	16889	8792	14096	11680
上海	Shanghai	19838	17574	14720	15733	27779	19690	23432
江苏	Jiangsu	16847	10871	16652	11322	13920	10554	13134
浙江	Zhejiang	22391	14609	12602	17089	19378	21280	18320
安徽	Anhui	8734	7853	5815	10508	7785	7618	11179
福建	Fujian	16608	14834	8797	12973	12877	8432	12620
江西	Jiangxi	9248	6610	6244	6638	8843	5194	8117
山东	Shandong	12813	8151	7894	9342	10455	10507	10380
河南	Henan	12038	7837	6033	8952	8022	5458	7742
湖北	Hubei	10693	9780	7384	8237	7554	7785	7519
湖南	Hunan	7449	7808	8784	11571	8437	8390	10478
广东	Guangdong	17199	11772	11792	16613	16678	15540	16943
广西	Guangxi	15272	6166	9192	8946	10320	8811	7210
海南	Hainan	12810	6550	7429	12967	10827	7186	6191
重庆	Chongqing	13040	7366	8216	7274	9795	9313	10626
四川	Sichuan	15954	8384	12941	10930	9608	8305	13601
贵州	Guizhou	8543	8019	7137	14350	9015	12750	12026
云南	Yunnan	10511	9523	11122	11191	9209	7518	13052
西藏	Tibet			1500			3667	
陕西	Shaanxi	6025	9508	5333	13061	7931	5026	9172
甘肃	Gansu	7406	10685	4594	13500	9480	7870	8607
青海	Qinghai		13747	6255	12619	14761		4916
宁夏	Ningxia	9909	14707	6744	2667	8914	8576	17360
新疆	Xinjiang	11658	7292	8837	13675	17002	11037	14371

5-31 按行业分其他单位职工平均工资

Average Wage of Staff and Workers in Other Ownership Units by Sector

单位：元 (yuan)

年份 Year	合计 Total	农、林、牧、渔业 Farming, Forestry, Animal Husbandry and Fishery	采掘业 Mining and Quarrying	制造业 Manufacturing	电力、煤气及水的生产和供应业 Production and Supply of Electricity Gas and Water	建筑业 Construction	地质勘查业水利管理业 Geological Prospecting and Water Conservancy	交通运输仓储和邮电通信业 Transport, Storage, Post & Telecommunication Services
1985	1436	1519	1270	1328	1270	1000		2429
1989	2707	2938	2427	2889	3232	5000		3846
1990	2987	3778	2270	3055	3088	3571	5714	3667
1991	3468	3760	3855	3626	3333	4641	4615	5500
1992	3966	4069	3579	4154	4238	5061	5263	5955
1993	4966	3905	3423	4874	6309	4464	7441	6450
1994	6303	5394	4233	6096	8005	5766	4362	8713
1995	7463	6992	5174	7245	10746	6798	5408	10492
1996	8261	7389	5217	7945	12030	6937	6464	11931
1997	8789	7061	5385	8367	12127	7517	5770	13734
1998	8972	5685	6749	8556	12158	8983	6909	11858
1999	9829	6740	7651	9316	13856	9540	8439	14241
2000	10984	8519	9842	10192	15486	10391	13064	16173
2001	12140	8473	11246	11074	17256	11139	11892	18737
2002	13212	9553	12870	12027	19271	11358	18553	20864

5-31 续表 continued

单位：元 (yuan)

年份 Year	批发零售贸易和餐饮业 Wholesale and Retail Trade & Catering Services	金融、保险业 Finance and Insurance	房地产业 Real Estate	社会服务业 Social Services	卫生体育和社会福利业 Health Care, Sports & Social Welfare	教育、文化艺术和广播电影电视业 Education, Culture and Arts, Radio, Film and Television	科学研究和综合技术服务业 Scientific Research and Polytechnic Services	其他 Others
1985	1955	2107		1904		3184	1728	
1989	2882	4376	1776	3202	2945	3604	3241	
1990	3284	5565	2517	3463	5430	4022	3425	
1991	3585	6041	4923	4004	4817	4560	3906	
1992	4368	9761	5561	4545	5461	5107	5033	
1993	4975	6073	4940	5934	3665	5289	5645	4953
1994	6460	10400	9610	8013	7051	8360	7882	9691
1995	7190	12949	10746	9274	8668	8968	9678	10502
1996	7862	15818	11801	10820	11014	10172	13358	13508
1997	8051	17970	13249	11812	11863	10017	14370	16423
1998	8320	16255	13636	12027	15124	11687	14847	20393
1999	9001	18648	14693	12785	16618	12871	15671	20548
2000	10250	21538	15485	14544	17883	12027	20299	26677
2001	11584	25662	16621	16142	17045	15951	19506	28156
2002	12202	27788	17630	18518	14548	17008	21017	27741

5-32 各地区按行业分其他单位职工平均工资（2003年）

Average Wage of Staff and Workers in Other Ownership Units by Sector and Region (2003)

单位: 元　　(yuan)

地 区	Region	合 计 Total	农、林、牧、渔业 Agriculture, Forestry, Animal Husbandry and Fishing	采矿业 Mining	制造业 Manufacturing	电力、燃气及水的生产和供应业 Production and Distribution of Electricity, Gas and Water	建筑业 Construction	交通运输、仓储和邮政业 Transport, Storage and Post
全国总计	**National Total**	**14574**	**10022**	**14321**	**13263**	**20923**	**12345**	**17621**
北 京	Beijing	23769	13704	20054	20866	30478	15721	14826
天 津	Tianjin	19026	20580	23880	17540	32349	21096	32783
河 北	Hebei	10701	8616	17391	10105	23947	7646	12020
山 西	Shanxi	11276	8018	14629	10528	10746	9587	8333
内蒙古	Inner Mongolia	10391	6935	10629	10544	22088	7842	5334
辽 宁	Liaoning	13665	15652	13389	12967	21809	10151	14347
吉 林	Jilin	12471	5630	17320	12502	16868	8676	6476
黑龙江	Heilongjiang	13871	5676	14820	12728	19260	15350	12729
上 海	Shanghai	27354	16279	30600	25712	36157	23719	24537
江 苏	Jiangsu	14656	8962	16002	13833	27943	12809	15643
浙 江	Zhejiang	16344	12409	14258	14031	34729	15909	20984
安 徽	Anhui	10999	7685	13812	10544	11824	7809	7051
福 建	Fujian	12719	9348	11997	12114	20692	13466	21288
江 西	Jiangxi	10359	8412	9095	10110	15455	7075	8934
山 东	Shandong	10680	7708	12759	9924	20637	10454	17538
河 南	Henan	11160	7573	14065	10161	15198	9810	8386
湖 北	Hubei	8698	5860	7888	8234	15754	8554	10871
湖 南	Hunan	12226	10466	10659	11444	18776	10178	12427
广 东	Guangdong	18782	18060	15091	16352	35048	17972	28971
广 西	Guangxi	12118	7628	13753	11860	20492	11920	12533
海 南	Hainan	12130	8499	9939	10915	24739	11016	16160
重 庆	Chongqing	11316	16013	9531	11658	13493	10095	8644
四 川	Sichuan	10038	8781	8731	10250	13526	8065	10893
贵 州	Guizhou	10975	5056	12133	11294	16175	8058	15742
云 南	Yunnan	11886	8738	10111	11200	18804	10889	10792
西 藏	Tibet	20475	19375	10468	15874		27237	13773
陕 西	Shaanxi	11794	8453	10110	11098	16499	8154	12033
甘 肃	Gansu	11010	8715	17021	11321	22511	9966	7523
青 海	Qinghai	10341	6530	12190	10389	14286	8602	7020
宁 夏	Ningxia	12009	12936	14914	10725	14998	10871	10805
新 疆	Xinjiang	13937	8814	21209	12790	17718	11782	9862

5-32 续表 1 continued

单位: 元 (yuan)

地 区	Region	信息传输、计算机服务和软件业 Information Transmission, Computer Service and Software	批发和零售业 Wholesale and Retail Trade	住宿和餐饮业 Hotel and Restaurants	金融业 Financial Intermediation	房地产业 Real Estate	租赁和商务服务业 Leasing and Business Services
全国总计	**National Total**	**42867**	**13710**	**12179**	**31370**	**18898**	**23281**
北 京	Beijing	54481	20245	16771	64964	26472	35460
天 津	Tianjin	40929	16556	12975	28964	22407	20599
河 北	Hebei	22383	7084	9085	17947	9200	9480
山 西	Shanxi	15700	5815	4900	15028	7687	8596
内蒙古	Inner Mongolia	24300	7220	7846	12812	8688	11579
辽 宁	Liaoning	44401	12074	11312	23352	14507	14302
吉 林	Jilin	26779	7905	9402	14610	12081	11872
黑龙江	Heilongjiang	26923	11785	13073	22338	10222	12225
上 海	Shanghai	63681	26734	21529	41447	35145	34483
江 苏	Jiangsu	41262	13369	12956	32929	13747	18668
浙 江	Zhejiang	47596	18243	13543	36752	20329	18289
安 徽	Anhui	20786	8468	7621	16124	11350	2496
福 建	Fujian	39309	13973	10179	25546	15908	18113
江 西	Jiangxi	32100	8801	9746	21664	9211	7091
山 东	Shandong	24573	9213	9626	22952	14497	15403
河 南	Henan	30386	8198	8014	20345	11992	11688
湖 北	Hubei	14278	7662	7007	19995	10656	9574
湖 南	Hunan	22785	11696	10334	21976	13168	17873
广 东	Guangdong	51122	22001	15553	45045	25078	33172
广 西	Guangxi	22988	10482	8408	19193	12554	12185
海 南	Hainan	26200	11646	8726	20338	12558	8569
重 庆	Chongqing	29294	10045	9777	28199	12320	9742
四 川	Sichuan	21620	9385	8899	22598	11583	10931
贵 州	Guizhou	19264	8391	9067	16603	10269	8202
云 南	Yunnan	20303	11035	9289	18474	13031	20633
西 藏	Tibet		14823	12357	26997	12571	24521
陕 西	Shaanxi	38228	7840	8533	25351	12009	12907
甘 肃	Gansu	11875	8046	7165	18629	9178	7848
青 海	Qinghai	20948	8411	9120	21855	8293	12340
宁 夏	Ningxia	12022	9101	7848	20212	11648	11573
新 疆	Xinjiang	18361	14629	10259	22307	12094	14221

5-32 续表 2 continued

单位: 元 (yuan)

地 区	Region	科学研究、技术服务和地质勘查业 Scientific Research, Technical Services, and Geological Prospecting	水利、环境和公共设施管理业 Water Management of Conservancy, Environment and Public Facilities	居民服务和其他服务业 Services to Households and Other Services	教育 Education	卫生、社会保障和社会福利业 Health, Social Securities and Social Welfare	文化、体育和娱乐业 Culture, Sports and Entertainment	公共管理和社会组织 Public Management and Social Organization
全国总计	**National Total**	**26061**	**14560**	**14046**	**16163**	**14102**	**16121**	**8765**
北 京	Beijing	32214	19379	16229	21708	24931	23104	26474
天 津	Tianjin	25611	23691	13571	4692	9220	12456	4243
河 北	Hebei	10460	10410	7472	11774	10644	7466	
山 西	Shanxi	9445		3861	7909	7980	5775	7824
内蒙古	Inner Mongolia	8312	9061	7354	7770	9510	7691	
辽 宁	Liaoning	19732	13071	8944	21621	13118	14723	
吉 林	Jilin	15089	10188	7633	13718	15350	11474	
黑龙江	Heilongjiang	11225	8311	8853	14371	12267	14816	
上 海	Shanghai	39993	23899	17569	14222	46884	23011	
江 苏	Jiangsu	30403	15011	16407	11786	10827	11600	26644
浙 江	Zhejiang	24284	15125	13572	22523	23292	11789	12781
安 徽	Anhui	9050	10746	6916	22557	8943	9011	20833
福 建	Fujian	17230	10836	14848	21704	10239	12588	
江 西	Jiangxi	9950	7394	16190	11304	10372	6024	
山 东	Shandong	16664	10056	10153	16273	11462	19439	19350
河 南	Henan	18924	10059	9210	12871	11108	9488	10155
湖 北	Hubei	9228	6970	6902	9911	6031	9892	7023
湖 南	Hunan	14636	12496	8641	12497	9638	25178	
广 东	Guangdong	36260	20562	15041	18885	21393	16622	14658
广 西	Guangxi	16598	9391	8495	11155	18632	8137	6476
海 南	Hainan	11513	8220	6531	11571	16257	8874	
重 庆	Chongqing	10572	8462	13161	11728	12941	11063	
四 川	Sichuan	15220	9776	8878	17258	12399	10233	
贵 州	Guizhou	12082	8973	7969	12934	16852	9044	
云 南	Yunnan	20815	12290	10198	26255	14328	10091	11281
西 藏	Tibet							
陕 西	Shaanxi	21473	7386	12707	23985	10862	10133	6417
甘 肃	Gansu	9089	9889	5860	16041	10122	8400	7120
青 海	Qinghai	16256	8907	6418				
宁 夏	Ningxia	13014	9484	6288	9355	8667		
新 疆	Xinjiang	16984	10944	8822	14246	9790	7950	

5-33 按登记注册类型分其他单位职工平均工资

Average Wage of Staff and Workers in Units of Other Types of Ownership by Registration Status

单位: 元 (yuan)

年份 Year / 地区 Region	合计 Total	股份合作单位 Cooperative Units	联营单位 Joint Ownership Units	有限责任公司 Limited Liability Corporations	股份有限公司 Share-Holding Corporations Ltd.	其他 Others	港、澳、台商投资单位 Units with Funds from Hong Kong, Macao & Taiwan	外商投资单位 Foreign Funded Units
1993	4966		3741		5171	3279	5147	5315
1994	6303		4982		6383	4954	6376	6533
1995	7463		6056		7277	6494	7484	8058
1996	8261		6856		7623	7131	8334	9383
1997	8789		7310		7693	7063	9329	10361
1998	8972	6054	8431	7750	8833	6133	10027	11767
1999	9829	6709	9501	8632	9720	8425	10991	12951
2000	10984	7473	10663	9766	11131	10223	11914	14372
2001	12140	8398	11887	10993	12385	11621	12544	16101
2002	13212	9484	12451	11997	13850	10242	13756	17892
2003	14574	10575	13531	13392	15857	10572	14691	19366
北京 Beijing	23769	13282	15642	22191	24417	14465	28517	44653
天津 Tianjin	19026	17556	16860	19226	24272	10126	16385	19278
河北 Hebei	10701	8461	12310	10945	10757	6489	12414	10978
山西 Shanxi	11276	6121	8161	11977	10848	4942	9033	10898
内蒙古 Inner Mongolia	10391	6495	10356	10410	12078	6931	6691	8530
辽宁 Liaoning	13665	8685	8810	12839	16165	8422	13846	15060
吉林 Jilin	12471	7470	8151	11214	13648	7904	10342	17323
黑龙江 Heilongjiang	13871	12360	10488	9918	20531	10106	11634	11846
上海 Shanghai	27354	18091	21930	25327	27084	20674	22061	32674
江苏 Jiangsu	14656	9887	11949	13813	15129	12279	14748	17921
浙江 Zhejiang	16344	12533	16829	15771	20976	17408	16016	15788
安徽 Anhui	10999	7145	9130	10694	13136	5569	8912	12107
福建 Fujian	12719	12005	13779	13267	15910	10536	11845	13277
江西 Jiangxi	10359	8405	11361	10347	13327	8149	8058	10448
山东 Shandong	10680	8131	11048	10753	10663	7991	10881	11246
河南 Henan	11160	9228	8689	10930	12093	8645	12175	13240
湖北 Hubei	8698	7066	8074	8837	9182	7355	9209	14282
湖南 Hunan	12226	10631	10013	11562	13316	9534	12217	13614
广东 Guangdong	18782	13512	21072	22429	24810	15147	15259	20748
广西 Guangxi	12118	7243	14110	12154	12452	11522	8711	16828
海南 Hainan	12130	14618	11465	11446	15427	9829	8835	13401
重庆 Chongqing	11316	9791	9710	10254	14831	13267	12779	14529
四川 Sichuan	10038	9018	10359	9319	11001	8925	12354	13518
贵州 Guizhou	10975	8562	7285	10792	12236	8163	9821	10365
云南 Yunnan	11886	8761	15062	11899	13722	8625	13243	14409
西藏 Tibet	20475	21264	16554	24306	13603	19375		
陕西 Shaanxi	11794	7048	10688	11083	13539	10262	14730	18074
甘肃 Gansu	11010	12765	8696	8273	13342	10348	11477	16037
青海 Qinghai	10341	10086	19558	9802	10731	10500	14244	
宁夏 Ningxia	12009	8839	10405	12434	11579	9492	12299	13240
新疆 Xinjiang	13937	9371	10839	12434	21496	8782	11946	13439

5-34 各地区国有及国有控股企业就业人数和劳动报酬（2003年）

Employed Persons at the Year-end and Earnings in State-owned and State-controlling Enterprises by Region (2003)

地区	Region	就业人员（万人） Number of Employed Persons (10 000 persons)	# 女性 Female	职工（万人） Staff and Workers (10 000 persons)	# 专业技术人员 Technical Personnel	就业人员劳动报酬（亿元） Earnings of Employed Persons (10 000 yuan)	职工工资总额（亿元） Wages of Staff and Workers (10 000 yuan)	职工平均工资（元） Average Wage of Staff and Workers (yuan)
全国	**National Total**	**4692.5**	**1639.7**	**4461.4**	**1050.0**	**6818.5**	**6562.5**	**14558**
北京	Beijing	190.4	62.2	169.3	51.5	511.7	467.6	27372
天津	Tianjin	73.0	23.7	68.8	19.2	148.4	142.6	20236
河北	Hebei	216.7	74.3	211.7	44.4	267.9	263.2	12308
山西	Shanxi	185.1	55.3	180.5	35.7	209.9	206.4	11484
内蒙古	Inner Mongolia	115.2	39.9	113.0	23.5	125.4	123.5	10935
辽宁	Liaoning	375.7	137.2	364.9	117.0	529.9	519.9	13816
吉林	Jilin	135.2	45.1	132.7	29.0	158.9	156.1	11507
黑龙江	Heilongjiang	233.1	77.0	213.3	39.2	218.5	206.0	9824
上海	Shanghai	164.8	52.4	133.7	32.7	445.4	401.5	29144
江苏	Jiangsu	233.4	84.2	221.5	50.3	378.4	364.7	16091
浙江	Zhejiang	95.3	35.1	88.3	24.8	226.2	215.0	24324
安徽	Anhui	136.5	46.1	127.9	27.2	152.1	145.7	11155
福建	Fujian	74.1	25.5	70.0	16.0	129.4	124.8	17637
江西	Jiangxi	124.0	42.6	117.7	29.4	130.3	125.9	10523
山东	Shandong	309.6	112.6	301.7	59.9	425.0	417.0	13812
河南	Henan	275.5	99.5	264.8	49.5	311.2	303.9	11656
湖北	Hubei	225.1	87.3	217.4	47.8	250.6	244.8	11181
湖南	Hunan	190.4	65.3	176.3	41.7	227.3	215.4	12106
广东	Guangdong	220.7	79.2	213.2	50.8	530.7	515.5	23896
广西	Guangxi	112.8	42.3	106.0	26.1	139.0	134.8	12619
海南	Hainan	38.8	15.7	37.9	6.3	33.1	32.5	8377
重庆	Chongqing	136.8	48.3	133.9	47.5	186.1	183.1	13609
四川	Sichuan	192.4	65.0	183.8	44.0	259.4	249.5	13486
贵州	Guizhou	81.4	26.1	77.8	16.3	98.4	95.5	12263
云南	Yunnan	108.7	38.7	104.1	26.7	142.7	140.0	13148
西藏	Tibet	8.5	2.9	6.8	1.7	17.4	16.1	23814
陕西	Shaanxi	154.7	52.0	150.0	35.4	182.3	178.9	11894
甘肃	Gansu	102.8	35.1	99.9	23.0	131.1	129.2	12856
青海	Qinghai	17.3	5.8	16.5	4.4	29.0	28.4	16950
宁夏	Ningxia	29.0	9.7	27.8	4.8	39.4	38.1	13499
新疆	Xinjiang	135.4	53.6	130.6	24.1	183.3	176.9	12896

5-35 各地区职业介绍工作情况（2003年）

单位：万人

地 区	Region	本年末职业介绍机构个数（个） Number of Careers Service (unit)	本年末职业介绍机构人数 Staff and Workers in Careers Service	本年登记招聘人数 Total Registered Job Vacancies This Year	本年登记求职人数 Total Registered Job-seekers This Year	#女 性 Female	#下岗职工 Laid-off Workers
全 国	**National Total**	**31109**	**9.7**	**3832.0**	**3060.2**	**1356.3**	**386.8**
北 京	Beijing	413	0.3	58.2	87.8	42.2	2.4
天 津	Tianjin	158	0.1	43.1	125.4	55.0	46.2
河 北	Hebei	1729	0.5	119.9	126.7	61.4	9.6
山 西	Shanxi	941	0.3	21.0	29.4	9.0	5.6
内蒙古	Inner Mongolia	1410	0.3	38.9	56.3	20.3	5.2
辽 宁	Liaoning	1542	0.4	127.1	153.4	76.7	26.5
吉 林	Jilin	1243	0.3	39.6	46.9	23.2	13.0
黑龙江	Heilongjiang	1266	0.3	77.3	93.5	42.6	34.4
上 海	Shanghai	424	0.5	132.6	110.6	48.5	13.9
江 苏	Jiangsu	2351	0.7	1194.0	179.2	88.1	7.9
浙 江	Zhejiang	2128	0.5	335.3	305.6	113.4	19.3
安 徽	Anhui	2136	0.6	93.6	116.2	47.2	13.6
福 建	Fujian	847	0.2	111.3	119.4	57.7	5.6
江 西	Jiangxi	649	0.2	55.8	61.4	31.1	15.4
山 东	Shandong	1616	0.6	212.7	227.7	116.9	13.0
河 南	Henan	1151	0.4	107.1	132.2	60.4	35.9
湖 北	Hubei	887	0.3	108.7	116.2	54.8	24.8
湖 南	Hunan	815	0.2	59.6	90.3	45.5	29.6
广 东	Guangdong	1560	0.8	505.5	438.3	178.4	12.8
广 西	Guangxi	237	0.1	46.4	68.7	24.8	3.0
海 南	Hainan	43		5.0	13.8	7.8	0.9
重 庆	Chongqing	281	0.1	30.4	32.4	13.5	3.6
四 川	Sichuan	1439	0.5	101.1	98.1	46.5	16.4
贵 州	Guizhou	408	0.1	17.9	19.9	9.2	4.1
云 南	Yunnan	1662	0.3	38.9	45.0	20.0	3.7
西 藏	Tibet	19		0.6	1.0	0.7	
陕 西	Shaanxi	2258	0.6	53.3	63.4	25.6	10.1
甘 肃	Gansu	557	0.1	14.9	17.8	8.6	4.0
青 海	Qinghai	282	0.1	35.5	36.8	8.9	1.8
宁 夏	Ningxia	207	0.1	17.9	11.0	5.3	1.1
新 疆	Xinjiang	450	0.1	28.7	35.7	13.1	3.4

Situations of Careers Service by Region (2003)

(10 000 persons)

#失业人员 Unemployment	#获得职业资格人员 Person with Certificates	本年职业指导人数 Person-times of Vocational Guidance	本年介绍成功人数 Placed Job-seekers	#女性 Female	#下岗职工 Laid-off Workers	#失业人员 Unemployment	#获得职业资格人员 Person with Certificates
1049.9	**460.4**	**1611.0**	**1586.0**	**730.5**	**194.0**	**574.4**	**306.6**
22.7	9.0	35.1	32.2	14.2	1.2	12.1	6.2
28.6	6.3	41.8	64.9	25.3	12.1	16.5	3.3
27.2	32.5	83.7	66.6	31.5	5.0	15.3	25.8
6.3	1.4	13.7	17.9	6.3	3.6	4.4	1.3
26.8	2.6	19.4	30.2	11.0	3.7	17.3	2.2
80.8	20.2	111.9	84.2	40.4	12.9	45.2	9.3
18.8	7.5	33.4	28.2	13.2	7.9	12.2	5.0
33.1	7.3	43.1	52.2	23.5	19.3	17.8	4.7
55.7	7.9	78.8	38.7	18.5	6.7	20.3	7.5
94.3	45.3	88.0	95.5	57.8	3.2	52.6	27.3
71.5	41.6	108.0	156.2	57.5	9.9	37.9	25.2
26.4	8.9	57.4	64.7	29.6	8.1	16.5	6.4
23.5	6.7	48.7	49.3	26.5	3.0	12.9	4.6
24.8	7.2	33.0	39.9	19.7	8.3	11.4	4.1
63.9	25.5	117.0	132.1	63.9	8.8	40.4	14.6
24.7	18.9	66.0	75.9	29.3	19.5	17.2	11.9
48.2	24.4	79.4	74.1	35.1	14.9	28.7	17.7
45.0	28.0	55.1	35.1	17.7	12.1	18.4	18.2
163.7	102.0	162.5	200.2	104.0	6.7	81.0	67.4
23.5	5.9	30.9	34.6	17.3	1.6	15.5	3.3
1.0	0.4	7.4	3.3	1.7	0.5	0.3	0.1
16.4	5.5	21.3	16.1	8.3	2.3	9.5	3.6
48.3	15.7	102.6	57.1	25.3	8.0	29.9	11.8
7.5	1.6	13.1	10.5	4.9	2.1	4.5	1.2
17.4	6.9	43.1	28.1	12.1	1.5	11.5	4.0
0.7	0.1	0.7	0.8	0.6		0.6	0.1
16.8	11.6	39.1	32.8	13.8	5.0	7.1	7.3
7.7	2.3	14.3	10.1	4.6	2.6	3.8	1.2
5.8	1.8	33.1	33.3	7.5	1.0	3.7	7.0
4.2	0.9	9.4	5.0	2.3	0.6	2.8	0.9
14.6	4.3	20.0	16.6	6.9	1.9	7.2	3.2

5-36 各地区城镇登记失业人员及失业率

Urban Registered Unemployment and Unemployment Rate by Region

地区	Region	失业人员(万人) Unemployment (10 000 persons)			失业率(%) Unemployment Rate (%)		
		1990	2002	2003	1990	2002	2003
北京	Beijing	1.7	6.0	7.0	0.4	1.4	1.4
天津	Tianjin	8.1	12.9	12.0	2.7	3.9	3.8
河北	Hebei	7.7	22.2	25.7	1.1	3.6	3.9
山西	Shanxi	5.5	14.5	13.1	1.2	3.4	3.0
内蒙古	Inner Mongolia	15.2	16.3	17.6	3.8	4.1	4.5
辽宁	Liaoning	23.7	75.6	72.0	2.2	6.5	6.5
吉林	Jilin	10.5	23.8	28.4	1.9	3.6	4.3
黑龙江	Heilongjiang	20.4	41.6	35.0	2.2	4.9	4.2
上海	Shanghai	7.7	28.8	30.1	1.5	4.8	4.9
江苏	Jiangsu	22.5	42.2	41.8	2.4	4.2	4.1
浙江	Zhejiang	11.2	27.7	28.3	2.2	4.2	4.2
安徽	Anhui	15.2	22.6	25.1	2.8	4.0	4.1
福建	Fujian	9.0	15.0	14.6	2.6	4.2	4.1
江西	Jiangxi	10.3	17.8	21.6	2.4	3.4	3.6
山东	Shandong	26.2	39.7	41.3	3.2	3.6	3.6
河南	Henan	25.1	25.4	26.3	3.3	2.9	3.1
湖北	Hubei	12.7	44.7	49.3	1.7	4.3	4.3
湖南	Hunan	15.9	30.4	37.1	2.7	4.0	3.8
广东	Guangdong	19.2	36.5	35.5	2.2	3.1	2.9
广西	Guangxi	13.9	14.7	14.9	3.9	3.7	3.6
海南	Hainan	3.5	4.0	3.6	3.0	3.1	3.4
重庆	Chongqing		16.2	16.2		4.1	4.1
四川	Sichuan	38.0	33.8	33.1	3.7	4.5	4.4
贵州	Guizhou	10.7	11.1	11.2	4.1	4.1	4.0
云南	Yunnan	7.8	9.8	12.1	2.5	4.0	4.1
西藏	Tibet		1.3			4.9	
陕西	Shaanxi	11.2	13.5	13.9	2.8	3.3	3.5
甘肃	Gansu	12.5	8.7	9.3	4.9	3.2	3.4
青海	Qinghai	4.2	2.9	3.1	5.6	3.6	3.8
宁夏	Ningxia	4.0	3.5	3.8	5.4	4.4	4.4
新疆	Xinjiang	9.6	9.9	9.9	3.0	3.7	3.5

主要统计指标解释

经济活动人口 指在16岁以上，有劳动能力，参加或要求参加社会经济活动的人口。包括就业人员和失业人员。

就业人员 指从事一定社会劳动并取得劳动报酬或经营收入的人员，包括在岗职工、再就业的离退休人员、私营业主、个体户主、私营和个体就业人员、乡镇企业就业人员、农村就业人员、其他就业人员(包括民办教师、宗教职业者、现役军人等)。这一指标反映了一定时期内全部劳动力资源的实际利用情况，是研究我国基本国情国力的重要指标。

各单位的就业人员 指在各级国家机关、政党机关、社会团体及企业、事业单位中工作，取得工资或其他形式的劳动报酬的全部人员。包括在岗职工、再就业的离退休人员、民办教师以及在各单位中工作的外方人员和港澳台方人员、兼职人员、借用的外单位人员和第二职业者。不包括离开本单位仍保留劳动关系的职工。各单位的就业人员反映了各单位实际参加生产或工作的全部劳动力。

城镇私营和个体就业人员 城镇私营就业人员指在工商管理部门注册登记，其经营地址设在县城关镇(含县城关镇)以上的私营企业就业人员，包括私营企业投资者和雇工。城镇个体就业人员指在工商管理部门注册登记，并持有城镇户口或在城镇长期居住，经批准从事个体工商经营的就业人员，包括个体经营者和在个体工商户劳动的家庭帮工和雇工。

城镇登记失业人员 指有非农业户口，在一定的劳动年龄内(16岁以上及男50岁以下、女45岁以下)，有劳动能力，无业而要求就业，并在当地就业服务机构进行求职登记的人员。

城镇登记失业率 城镇登记失业人员与城镇单位就业人员(扣除使用的农村劳动力、聘用的离退休人员、港澳台及外方人员)、城镇单位中的不在岗职工、城镇私营业主、个体户主、城镇私营企业和个体就业人员、城镇登记失业人员之和的比。计算公式为:

$$\text{城镇登记失业率}=\frac{\text{城镇登记失业人数}}{\text{（城镇单位就业人员-使用的农村劳动力-聘用的离退休人员-聘用的港澳台及外方人员）+不在岗职工+城镇私营业主+城镇个体户主+城镇私营企业及个体就业人员+城镇登记失业人数}}\times 100\%$$

职工 指在国有、城镇集体、联营、股份制、外商和港、澳、台投资、其他单位及其附属机构工作，并由其支付工资的各类人员。不包括下列人员：(1)乡镇企业就业人员；(2)私营企业就业人员；(3)城镇个体劳动者；(4)离休、退休、退职人员；(5)再就业的离、退休人员；(6)民办教师；(7)在城镇单位中工作的外方及港、澳、台人员；(8)其他按有关规定不列入职工统计范围的人员。(1998年及以后的数据均为在岗职工数据，其他相关指标如职工工资总额，职工平均工资等指标也从1998年按此口径进行了相应调整)。

国有单位 指资产归国家所有的经济组织。包括按《中华人民共和国企业法人登记管理条例》规定登记注册的非公司制的经济组织，以及中央、地方各级国家机关、事业单位和社会团体。

集体单位 指生产资料归集体所有，并按《中华人民共和国企业法人登记管理条例》规定登记注册的经济组织。

其他单位 包括股份合作单位、联营单位、有限责任公司、股份有限公司、港澳台商投资单位以及外商投资单位等其他登记注册类型单位。

在岗职工 指在本单位工作并由单位支付工资的人员，以及有工作岗位，但由于学习、病伤产假等原因暂未工作，仍由单位支付工资的人员。

工资总额 指各单位在一定时期内直接支付给本单位全部职工的劳动报酬总额。工资总额的计算原则应以直接支付给职工的全部劳动报酬为根据。各单位支付给职工的劳动报酬以及其他根据有关规定支付的工资，不论是计入成本的还是不计入成本的，不论是按国家规定列入计征奖金税项目的，还是未列入计征奖金税项目的，不论是以货币形式支付的还是以实物形式支付的，均包括在工资总额内。

平均工资 指企业、事业、机关单位的职工在一定时期内平均每人所得的货币工资额。它表明一定时期职工工资收入的高低程度，是反映职工工资水平的主要指标。计算公式为:

$$\text{平均工资}=\frac{\text{报告期实际支付的全部职工工资总额}}{\text{报告期全部职工平均人数}}$$

平均工资指数 指报告期职工平均工资与基期职工平均工资的比率，是反映不同时期职工货币工资水平变动情况的相对数。计算公式为:

$$\text{平均工资指数}=\frac{\text{报告期职工平均工资}}{\text{基期职工平均工资}}\times 100\%$$

平均实际工资指数 职工平均实际工资指扣除物价变动因素后的职工平均工资。职工平均实际工资指数是反映实际工资变动情况的相对数，表明职工实际工资水平提高或降低的程度。计算公式为:

$$\text{平均实际工资指数}=\frac{\text{报告期职工平均工资指数}}{\text{报告期城镇居民消费价格指数}}\times 100\%$$

专业技术人员 指从事专业技术工作的人员以及从事专业技术管理工作且已在1983年以前评定了专业技术职称或在1984年以后聘任了专业技术职务的人员。

专业技术人员具体指工程技术人员、农业技术人员、科研人员(自然科学研究、社会科学研究及实验技术人员)、卫生技术人员、教学人员(含高等院校、中等专业学校、技工学校、中学、小学)、民用航空飞行技术人员、船舶技术人员、经济人员、会计人员、统计人员、翻译人员、图书资料、档案、文博人员、新闻、出版人员、律师、公证人员、广播电视播音人员、工艺美术人员、体育人员、艺术人员及政工人员。

专业技术管理人员具体指企业、事业单位的领导；企业、事业单位下设的职能机构、企业的生产车间和辅助车间(或附属辅助生产单位)中从事生产、技术、经济管理和政治工作人员。

按照公务员管理或参照公务员管理的人员不统计为专业技术人员。

Explanatory Notes on Main Statistical Indicators

Economically Active Population refers to the population aged 16 and over who are capable to work, are participating in or willing to participate in economic activities, including employed persons and unemployed persons.

Employed Persons refer to the persons who are engaged in social working and receive remuneration payment or earn business income, including total staff and workers, re-employed retirees, employers of private enterprises, self-employed workers, employees in private enterprises and individual economy, employees in township enterprises, employed persons in the rural areas, and other employed persons (including teachers in the schools run by the local people, people engaged in religious profession and the servicemen, etc.). This indicator reflects the actual utilization of total labour force during a certain period of time and is often used for the research on China's economic situation and national power.

Persons Employed in Various Units refer to all the persons working in government agencies of various levels, political and party organizations, social organizations, enterprises and institutions, and receiving wages or other forms of payment. They include fully-employed staff and workers, re-employed retirees, teachers in schools run by the local people, foreigners and Chinese compatriots from Hong Kong, Macao, and Taiwan working in various units, part-time employees, employees of other units working temporarily at current posts, and employees holding the second job, but exclude staff and workers who have left their working units while keeping their labour contract (employment relation) unchanged. This indicator reflects the total number of laborers actually engaged in production or other operations in various units.

Persons Employed in Private Enterprises and Self-Employed Individuals in Urban Areas Persons employed in private enterprises refer to the persons employed in the private enterprises which have been registered at the departments of industrial and commercial administration and are situated at a county town (i.e. a town where the county government is located) for business operation or at urban areas with the level higher than a county town. The self-employed individuals in urban areas refer to persons who hold the certificates of residence in urban areas or have resided in the urban areas for a long time and have been registered at the departments of industrial and commercial administration and approved to be engaged in individual industrial or commercial business, including self-employed persons as well as helpers and hired labourers who work in the individual households engaged in industrial or commercial business.

Registered Urban Unemployed Persons refer to the persons with non-agricultural household registration at certain working ages (16-50 years for male and 16-45 years for females), who are capable of work, unemployed and willing to work, and have been registered at the local employment service agencies to apply for a job.

Registered Urban Unemployment Rate refers to the ratio of the number of the registered unemployed persons to the sum of the number of persons employed in various units (minus the rural labour force, retirees, and Hong Kong, Macao, Taiwan or foreign employees they employ) laid-off workers in urban units, owners and employees in urban private enterprises, urban self-employed individuals and the registered urban unemployed persons. The formula is as follows:

Registered urban unemployment rate = number of registered urban unemployed persons ÷ (number of persons employed in urban units - rural labour force employed – retirees employed - Hong Kong, Macao, Taiwan or foreign employees employ + laid-off workers + owners and employees in urban private enterprises + self-employed individuals in urban areas + registered urban unemployed persons) × 100%.

Staff and Workers refer to persons working in, and receive payment from units of state ownership, collective ownership, joint ownership, share holding ownership, foreign ownership, and ownership by entrepreneurs from Hong Kong, Macao, and Taiwan, and other types of ownership and their affiliated units. They do not include 1) persons employed in township enterprises, 2) persons employed in private enterprises, 3) urban self-employed persons, 4) retirees, 5) re-employed retirees, 6) teachers in the schools run by the local people, 7) foreigners and persons from Hong Kong, Macao and Taiwan who work in urban units, and 8) other persons not to be included by relevant regulations. (Data of 1998 and afterward refer to fully employed staff and workers. Other related statistics such as total wage bill and average wage are adjusted since 1998 accordingly).

State-owned Units refer to economic units whose assets are owned by the state. Included are non-corporation units registered according to *Regulation of the People's Republic of China on the Registration of Enterprises and Corporations*, state organs, institutions and social organizations at the central and local levels.

Collective Units refer to economic units registered according to *Regulation of the People's Republic of China on the Registration of Enterprises and Corporations* where the means of production are collectively owned.

Units of Other Types of Ownership refer to units registered with other types of ownership, including cooperative units, joint ownership units, limited companies, share holding corporations, units invested by entrepreneurs from Hong Kong, Macao, and Taiwan, and foreign-invested units.

Fully Employed Staff and Workers refer to persons who work in, and receive wages from their working units, as well as persons who have their work posts, but are temporarily absent from work for reasons of study or on sick, injury or maternal leave and still receive wages from their working units.

Total Wages Bill refer to the total remuneration payment to staff and workers in various units during a certain period of time. The calculation of total wages is based on the total remuneration payment to the staff and workers. Therefore, all the wages and salaries and other payments to staff and workers are included in the total wages regardless of their sources, category, and forms (in kind or cash). (Total wages of staff and workers in this yearbook include only total wages of fully employed staff and workers, excluding the living allowances distributed to those who have left their working units while keeping their labour contract/employment relation unchanged).

Average Wage refers to the average wage in money terms per person during a certain period of time for staff and workers in enterprises, institutions, and government agencies, which reflects the general level of wage income during a certain period of time and is calculated as follows:

Average Wage = Total Wages of Staff and Workers at Reference Time /Average Number of Staff and Workers at Reference Time.

Average Wage Indices refers to the ratio of average wage of staff and workers in the report period to that in the base period, which reflects the change of wage of staff and workers at the different period. It is calculated as follows:

Average Wage Indices = Average Wage of Staff and Workers at Reference Time / Average Wage of Staff and Workers at Base Period x 100%

Average Real Wage Indices average real wage of staff and workers refers to the average wage of staff and workers after removing the effects of the price changes and average real wage indices of staff and workers refers to the change of real wage, which reflects the relative increasing or decreasing level of real wage of staff and workers, which is calculated as follows:

Average Real Wage Indices = Average Wage Indices of Staff and Workers at the Reference Time / Urban Consumer Price Indices at Reference Time x 100%

Professional Personnel refers to the persons who are engaged in special professional work or in professional management who got the titles of a professional post before 1983 or who were appointed to professional positions since 1984.

Professional personnel specifically refers to engineering professionals, agricultural professionals, scientific research professionals (natural science researchers, social science researchers and laboratory technicians), health professionals, teaching professionals (including institutions of higher education, specialized secondary schools, technical schools, regular secondary schools, and primary schools), civil aviation professionals, nautical professionals, economic professionals, accounting professionals, statistical professionals, interpretation professionals, library professionals, archives professionals, professionals of culture, arts and cultural relics, newsman and publishing professionals, lawyers, notary professionals, radio and television announcers, industrial arts professionals, sports professionals, artists and political professionals.

Professional management personnel specifically refers to the managers of enterprises and institutions, the personnel engaged in the management of production, techniques, economic and political aspects in the functional departments under the enterprise and institution, production workshops and accessorial workshops (or accessorial production units) under the enterprises.

Professional personnel excluded the personnel managed by or according to the system of civil servants.

六、固定资产投资

Investment in Fixed Assets

简要说明

一、本篇资料的主要内容

本篇资料通过对一定时期全社会建造和购置固定资产活动的数量方面的描述，反映报告期内固定资产投资的规模和速度、固定资产投资的结构和比例关系、固定资产投资的资金来源及固定资产投资的效果等。

二、本篇资料的统计范围

固定资产投资统计的范围包括：基本建设投资，更新改造投资，房地产开发投资，国有其他固定资产投资，城镇集体固定资产投资，农村集体固定资产投资，城镇和工矿区私人建房投资，农村个人固定资产投资。从1999年起，城镇私营和个体投资纳入固定资产投资统计范围。

三、本篇的资料来源

跨省、区项目资料来自国务院各部门；农村集体和农村个人固定资产投资资料来自国家统计局农村经济调查总队的乡村社会经济调查；除此以外的固定资产投资统计资料均来自国家统计局固定资产投资统计司统计调查。

四、本篇的统计调查方法

除农村集体和农村个人固定资产投资统计采用抽样调查方法外，其他均为全面统计报表。

五、自1997年起，除房地产开发投资、农村集体投资、个人投资及城镇和工矿区私人建房投资外，基本建设、更新改造和其他固定资产投资的统计起点由5万元提高到50万元。为便于比较，对1996年的相应数据作了全面调整，括号内的数为原口径数。

Brief Introduction

I. Main Content

Statistics in this chapter describe activities on the construction and purchase of fixed assets of the whole society during a given period of time, and reflect the size, growth, structure, finance and results of the investment in fixed assets during the reference period.

II. Coverage of Statistics

Statistics on the investment in fixed assets cover the investment in capital construction, the investment in innovation, the investment in real estate development, the investment in other state-owned fixed assets, the investment in fixed assets by urban collective units, the investment in fixed assets by rural collective units, the housing investment by urban individuals and the investment in fixed assets by rural individuals. Starting from 1999, investment statistics also include investment in fixed assets by urban private units and individuals.

III. Sources of Data

Data on the trans-regional projects are provided by the various departments under the State Council. Data on the investment in fixed assets in collective units and by individuals in rural areas are provided by the Rural Socio-economic Survey Organization of NBS through its rural social and economic survey. Other data on the investment in fixed assets are from the surveys conducted by the Department of Statistics of Investment in Fixed Assets, NBS.

IV. Method of Data Collection

All data on the investment in fixed assets are collected by the statistical reporting system with complete enumeration, except data on the investment in fixed assets in collective units and by individuals in rural areas, which are collected through sample surveys.

V. Since 1997, the cut-off point of projects to be covered in the investment statistics are modified from an investment of 50, 000 yuan to 500,000 yuan in the statistics of investment in capital construction, investment in innovation and other investments, while the cut-off point of projects in the statistics of investment in real estate development, rural collective investment and individual investment remain unchanged. For the convenience of comparison, relevant data of 1996 are adjusted accordingly, and figures in brackets are compiled on the basis of the old coverage.

6-1 全社会固定资产投资

Total Investment in Fixed Assets

指 标	Item	2002	2003	2003年比上年增长(%) Increase Rate in 2003 over 2002 (%)
投资总额 （亿元）	**Total Investment (100 million yuan)**	**43499.91**	**55566.61**	**27.7**
按经济类型分	Grouped by Ownership			
国有经济	State-owned Units	18877.35	21661.00	14.7
集体经济	Collective-owned Units	5987.43	8009.48	33.8
#农 村	Rural	4887.91	6553.95	34.1
个体经济	Individuals Economy	6519.19	7720.10	18.4
#农 村	Rural	3123.23	3200.96	2.5
联营经济	Joint Ownership Economic Units	138.19	187.96	36.0
股份制经济	Share Holding Economic Units	8328.81	12733.58	52.9
外商投资经济	Foreign Funded Economic Units	1685.42	2533.71	50.3
港澳台商投资经济	Economic Units with Funds from Hong Kong, Macao and Taiwan	1765.33	2375.08	34.5
其他经济	Others	198.19	345.69	74.4
按管理渠道分	Grouped by Channel of Management			
基本建设	Capital Construction	17666.62	22908.60	29.7
更新改造	Innovation	6750.55	8624.86	27.8
房地产开发	Real Estate Development	7790.92	10153.80	30.3
其他投资	Others	11291.82	13879.35	22.9
按资金来源分	Grouped by Source of Funds			
国家预算内资金	State Budgetary Appropriation	3160.96	2687.82	-15.0
国内贷款	Domestic Loans	8859.07	12044.36	36.0
利用外资	Foreign Investment	2084.98	2599.35	24.7
自筹资金	Fundraising	22813.69	31449.82	37.9
其他资金	Others	8128.22	9834.94	21.0
按构成分	Grouped by Use of Funds			
建筑安装工程	Construction and Installation	26578.89	33447.17	25.8
设备工具器具购置	Purchase of Equipment and Instruments	9884.47	12681.90	28.3
其他费用	Others	7036.55	9437.54	34.1
房屋建筑面积 （万平方米）	**Floor Space of Buildings (10 000 sq.m)**			
施工面积	Floor Space under Construction	304428.15	343741.65	12.9
竣工面积	Floor Space Completed	196737.87	202643.73	3.0
#住宅	Residential Buildings	134002.10	130160.75	-2.9

注：1.按资金来源分组为财务拨款数，各项相加不等于投资总额。
2.增长速度未扣除价格因素（以下各表同）。

a) Total investment grouped by source of funds refers to financial appropriation, and the subentry figures do not add up to the total.

b) The growth rates are calculated without removing the factor of price. The same as in the following tables.

6-2 按经济类型分全社会固定资产投资

Total Investment in Fixed Assets by Ownership

指 标 Item	总 计 Total	国有经济 State-owned Units	集体经济 Collective-owned Units	个体经济 Individuals Economy	其他经济 Other Types of Ownership
投资额（亿元） Investment (100 million yuan)					
1980	910.9	745.9	46.0	119.0	
1985	2543.2	1680.5	327.5	535.2	
1986	3120.6	2079.4	391.8	649.4	
1987	3791.7	2448.8	547.0	795.9	
1988	4753.8	3020.0	711.7	1022.1	
1989	4410.4	2808.1	570.0	1032.3	
1990	4517.0	2986.3	529.5	1001.2	
1991	5594.5	3713.8	697.8	1182.9	
1992	8080.1	5498.7	1359.4	1222.0	
1993	13072.3	7925.9	2317.3	1476.2	1352.9
1994	17042.1	9615.0	2758.9	1970.6	2697.6
1995	20019.3	10898.2	3289.4	2560.2	3271.3
1996	(22974.0)	(12056.2)	(3660.6)	(3211.2)	(4046.0)
	22913.5	12006.2	3651.5	3211.2	4044.7
1997	24941.1	13091.7	3850.9	3429.4	4569.1
1998	28406.2	15369.3	4192.2	3744.4	5100.3
1999	29854.7	15947.8	4338.6	4195.7	5372.7
2000	32917.7	16504.4	4801.5	4709.4	6902.5
2001	37213.5	17607.0	5278.6	5429.6	8898.4
2002	43499.9	18877.4	5987.4	6519.2	12115.9
2003	55566.6	21661.0	8009.5	7720.1	18176.0
增长速度（上年=100） Growth Rate (previous year=100)					
1981	5.5	-10.5	150.4	49.8	
1985	38.8	41.8	37.2	30.9	
1986	22.7	23.7	19.6	21.3	
1987	21.5	17.8	39.6	22.6	
1988	25.4	23.3	30.1	28.4	
1989	-7.2	-7.0	-19.9	1.0	
1990	2.4	6.3	-7.1	-3.0	
1991	23.9	24.4	31.7	18.1	
1992	44.4	48.1	94.8	3.3	
1993	61.8	44.1	70.5	20.8	
1994	30.4	21.3	19.1	33.5	99.4
1995	17.5	13.3	19.2	29.9	21.3
1996	14.8	10.6	11.3	25.4	23.7
1997	8.8	9.0	5.5	6.8	13.0
1998	13.9	17.4	8.9	9.2	11.6
1999	5.1	3.8	3.5	12.1	5.3
2000	10.3	3.5	10.7	12.2	28.5
2001	13.0	6.7	9.9	15.3	28.9
2002	16.9	7.2	13.4	20.1	36.2
2003	27.7	14.7	33.8	18.4	50.0

注:1.其他经济类型包括联营经济、股份制经济、外商投资经济、港澳台商投资经济等国有、集体和个体经济以外的经济成份。
2.根据1994年房地产快速调查结果，对1990年至1994年的全社会固定资产投资数据进行了调整。
3.自1997年起,除房地产投资、农村集体投资、个人投资外,基本建设、更新改造和其他固定资产投资的统计起点由5万元提高到50万元。为便于比较，对1996年的相应数据作了全面调整，括号内的数据为原口径数，未加括号的为调整后的新口径数（以下有关各表同）。

a) Other types of ownership refer to the types of ownership other than state-owned units, collective-owned units and individuals economy, including joint ownership economic units, share holding economic units, foreign funded economic units, and economic units with funds from Hong Kong, Macao and Taiwan, etc.

b) The data of the total investment in fixed assets from 1990 to 1994 have been adjusted in accordance with the data obtained from the fast survey on the real estates in 1994.

c) In 1997, the cut-off point of investment statistics to be included in statistical surveys on capital construction, on technical transformation and other investment statistics was changed from a minimum of 50,000 yuan to the minimum of 500,000 yuan , except statistics on investment in housing, rural collective investment and individual investment. For the convenience of comparison, relevant data of 1996 in this table were adjusted accordingly. Data before adjustment were based on the old coverage and data after the adjustment were based on the new coverage. Data in parenthesis were based on the old coverage. Data without parethesis are based on the new standard. The relative tables in the chapter are the same.

6-3 按资金来源和构成分全社会固定资产投资

Total Investment in Fixed Assets by Source of Funds and Use of Funds

年 份 Year	按资金来源分 Grouped by Source of Funds				按构成分 Grouped by Use of Funds		
	国家预算内资金 State Budgetary Appropriation	国内贷款 Domestic Loans	利用外资 Foreign Investment	自筹和其他资金 Fundraising and Others	建筑安装工程 Construction and Installation	设备工具器具购置 Purchase of Equipment and Instruments	其他费用 Others
投资额（亿元） Investment (100 million yuan)							
1981	269.76	122.00	36.36	532.89	689.83	223.64	47.54
1982	279.26	176.12	60.51	714.51	871.12	291.41	67.87
1983	339.71	175.50	66.55	848.30	993.32	358.31	78.43
1984	421.00	258.47	70.66	1082.74	1217.58	509.23	106.06
1985	407.80	510.27	91.48	1533.64	1655.46	718.08	169.65
1986	455.62	658.46	137.31	1869.19	2059.66	851.95	208.99
1987	496.64	871.98	181.97	2241.11	2475.65	1038.78	277.26
1988	431.96	977.84	275.31	2968.69	3099.66	1305.37	348.77
1989	366.05	762.98	291.08	2990.28	2994.59	1115.81	299.98
1990	393.03	885.45	284.61	2954.41	3008.72	1165.54	342.74
1991	380.43	1314.73	318.89	3580.44	3647.68	1460.19	486.63
1992	347.46	2214.03	468.66	5049.95	5163.37	2125.14	791.58
1993	483.67	3071.99	954.28	8562.36	8201.21	3315.92	1555.18
1994	529.57	3997.64	1768.95	11530.96	10786.52	4328.26	1928.08
1995	621.05	4198.73	2295.89	13409.19	13173.33	4262.46	2583.48
1996	(629.72)	(4576.53)	(2747.41)	(15465.35)	(15153.41)	(4940.79)	(2879.83)
	625.88	4573.69	2746.60	15412.40	15109.29	4925.98	2878.28
1997	696.74	4782.55	2683.89	17096.49	15614.03	6044.84	3282.25
1998	1197.39	5542.89	2617.03	19359.61	17874.53	6528.53	4003.10
1999	1852.14	5725.93	2006.78	20169.80	18795.93	7053.04	4005.74
2000	2109.45	6727.27	1696.24	22577.14	20536.26	7785.62	4595.85
2001	2546.42	7239.79	1730.73	26470.04	22954.88	8833.79	5424.83
2002	3160.96	8859.07	2084.98	30941.91	26578.89	9884.47	7036.55
2003	2687.82	12044.36	2599.35	41284.76	33447.17	12681.90	9437.54
构成(%) Percentage							
1981	28.1	12.7	3.8	55.4	71.8	23.3	4.9
1982	22.7	14.3	4.9	58.1	70.8	23.7	5.5
1983	23.8	12.3	4.7	59.2	69.5	25.1	5.4
1984	23.0	14.1	3.9	59.0	66.4	27.8	5.8
1985	16.0	20.1	3.6	60.3	65.1	28.2	6.7
1986	14.6	21.1	4.4	59.9	66.0	27.3	6.7
1987	13.1	23.0	4.8	59.1	65.3	27.4	7.3
1988	9.3	21.0	5.9	63.8	65.2	27.5	7.3
1989	8.3	17.3	6.6	67.8	67.9	25.3	6.8
1990	8.7	19.6	6.3	65.4	66.6	25.8	7.6
1991	6.8	23.5	5.7	64.0	65.2	26.1	8.7
1992	4.3	27.4	5.8	62.5	63.9	26.3	9.8
1993	3.7	23.5	7.3	65.5	62.7	25.4	11.9
1994	3.0	22.4	9.9	64.7	63.3	25.4	11.3
1995	3.0	20.5	11.2	65.3	65.8	21.3	12.9
1996	2.7	19.6	11.8	66.0	66.0	21.5	12.5
1997	2.8	18.9	10.6	67.7	62.6	24.2	13.2
1998	4.2	19.3	9.1	67.4	62.9	23.0	14.1
1999	6.2	19.2	6.7	67.8	63.0	23.6	13.4
2000	6.4	20.3	5.1	68.2	62.4	23.7	13.9
2001	6.7	19.1	4.6	69.6	61.7	23.7	14.6
2002	7.0	19.7	4.6	68.7	61.1	22.7	16.2
2003	4.6	20.5	4.4	70.5	60.2	22.8	17.0

注：1993年及以后的资金来源为财务拔款数（基本建设和更新改造资金来源表同）。

a) Since 1993, the source of funds refers to financial appropriation. The sources of investment in capital construction and innovation are same.

6-4 按经济类型分全社会固定资产投资（2003年）

指标	Item	总计 Total	国有经济 State-owned Units	集体经济 Collective-owned Units	#农村 Rural
投资总额（亿元）	**Total Investment (100 million yuan)**	**55566.61**	**21661.00**	**8009.48**	**6553.95**
按资金来源分	Grouped by Source of Funds				
国家预算内资金	State Budgetary Appropriations	2687.82	2248.30	337.89	327.68
国内贷款	Domestic Loans	12044.36	5547.35	927.10	695.03
利用外资	Foreign Investment	2599.35	338.72	402.14	387.60
自筹资金	Fundraising	31449.82	10965.02	5819.68	4899.71
其他资金	Others	9834.94	2507.61	636.02	243.93
按构成分	Grouped by Use of Funds				
建筑安装工程	Construction and Installation	33447.17	14331.11	4276.94	3288.54
设备、工具、器具购置	Purchase of Equipment and Instruments	12681.90	3701.85	2895.99	2671.04
其他费用	Others	9437.54	3628.04	836.56	594.37
房屋建筑面积（万平方米）	**Floor Space of Buildings (10 000 sq.m)**				
施工面积	Floor Space under Construction	343741.65	66758.04	54118.84	41359.86
竣工面积	Floor Space Completed	202643.73	28636.15	39666.68	33845.45
#住宅	Residential Buildings	130160.75	13936.88	9176.86	5448.14
按地区分投资总额（亿元）	**Total Investment by Region (100 million yuan)**				
北京	Beijing	2169.26	728.91	204.18	151.86
天津	Tianjin	1039.39	472.19	111.46	89.73
河北	Hebei	2477.98	831.38	596.70	505.73
山西	Shanxi	1100.86	463.65	76.52	48.71
内蒙古	Inner Mongolia	1174.66	607.02	33.05	21.88
辽宁	Liaoning	2076.36	712.22	229.49	200.68
吉林	Jilin	969.03	416.44	33.22	25.10
黑龙江	Heilongjiang	1166.18	573.63	31.76	17.72
上海	Shanghai	2499.14	785.47	331.09	247.11
江苏	Jiangsu	5233.00	1998.18	1244.54	1030.36
浙江	Zhejiang	4740.27	1381.43	1405.04	1330.37
安徽	Anhui	1418.69	594.45	126.97	84.09
福建	Fujian	1496.37	512.73	207.66	170.67
江西	Jiangxi	1303.22	596.36	123.61	103.91
山东	Shandong	5315.14	1595.62	1177.01	855.21
河南	Henan	2262.97	941.62	292.32	260.50
湖北	Hubei	1809.45	823.82	157.23	132.15
湖南	Hunan	1590.32	695.07	199.59	174.83
广东	Guangdong	4813.20	1422.17	616.49	450.40
广西	Guangxi	921.30	442.40	43.28	28.81
海南	Hainan	280.02	91.57	18.12	14.57
重庆	Chongqing	1161.51	458.84	91.26	71.86
四川	Sichuan	2336.34	873.04	354.54	324.56
贵州	Guizhou	748.12	451.37	39.20	27.32
云南	Yunnan	1000.12	528.59	64.72	52.77
西藏	Tibet	133.96	125.76	0.52	
陕西	Shaanxi	1200.68	685.87	62.78	30.91
甘肃	Gansu	619.82	377.23	46.74	28.46
青海	Qinghai	255.62	151.37	13.22	9.32
宁夏	Ningxia	317.99	152.35	35.70	31.64
新疆	Xinjiang	973.39	472.35	41.50	32.71
不分地区	Not Classified by Region	962.22	697.89		

Total Investment in Fixed Assets by Ownership (2003)

个体经济 Individuals Economy	#农　村 Rural	联营经济 Joint Ownership Economic Units	股份制经济 Share Holding Economic Units	外商投资经济 Foreign Funded Economic Units	港澳台商投资经济 Economic Units with Funds From Hong Kong, Macao and Taiwan	其他经济 Others Ownership
7720.10	**3200.96**	**187.96**	**12733.58**	**2533.71**	**2375.08**	**345.69**
1.74		0.95	89.97	3.37	1.00	4.60
895.04	125.44	22.57	3526.99	490.08	596.03	39.04
20.49		1.87	183.49	989.64	656.51	6.49
5086.40	2932.76	122.18	7334.02	965.52	936.70	220.46
2300.72	142.76	59.02	3257.05	314.99	676.41	83.12
5059.43	2067.31	118.50	7110.84	1068.98	1267.38	213.98
1251.32	710.19	42.49	2909.97	1115.60	690.23	74.44
1409.35	423.46	26.96	2712.76	349.13	417.47	57.28
129378.44	81123.66	853.68	67847.91	9096.82	13688.67	1999.25
101152.76	75683.58	327.48	25125.30	2881.66	3897.87	955.84
88147.85	69741.10	175.34	15271.88	967.38	2110.82	373.74
137.56	17.48	3.63	811.21	147.29	129.52	6.96
89.78	17.93	2.21	253.56	75.03	30.30	4.87
316.42	199.45	23.77	524.40	53.75	91.64	39.93
137.72	53.32	13.98	381.57	10.50	8.95	7.97
138.78	55.68	0.43	373.12	8.47	6.42	7.36
335.16	104.45	1.29	608.67	114.62	60.52	14.39
157.91	71.03	0.96	309.38	36.01	11.30	3.81
152.71	78.98	1.14	381.00	13.21	9.36	3.37
297.02	6.49	16.80	616.30	309.25	132.91	10.31
574.15	191.05	10.19	678.45	444.93	272.05	10.50
511.53	211.39	3.52	1129.02	176.22	110.01	23.50
277.20	150.09	1.80	350.19	30.03	26.75	11.29
209.26	96.42	4.29	224.25	150.36	179.79	8.03
256.85	100.21	2.86	220.82	43.12	50.98	8.61
740.29	296.03	33.89	1322.91	245.06	168.47	31.90
457.07	325.30	1.41	418.32	69.95	54.58	27.70
246.49	103.57	10.76	429.19	50.80	63.15	28.02
290.38	180.23	7.52	313.35	21.81	51.63	10.96
751.04	217.68	19.54	842.40	379.68	756.43	25.45
204.93	101.24	2.71	163.80	30.03	28.18	5.97
32.87	19.20	1.01	97.16	28.85	8.60	1.84
233.85	49.01	3.02	301.89	30.86	33.63	8.17
385.61	176.71	3.18	658.51	23.24	28.18	10.06
119.61	52.88	3.15	119.10	6.98	6.45	2.26
182.93	108.13	7.31	179.25	6.41	23.99	6.94
3.21		0.07	3.80			0.60
198.96	98.73	2.91	212.78	14.69	9.48	13.22
72.10	37.64	2.07	105.58	4.17	4.81	7.13
23.36	9.36	0.75	62.55	2.23	1.34	0.81
60.22	23.22	1.44	60.67	4.44	1.97	1.21
125.15	48.08	0.36	316.06	1.73	13.70	2.55
			264.33			

6-5 国有经济固定资产投资

Investment in Fixed Assets of State-owned Units

指　　标	Item	1995	1998	2000	2002	2003
投资总额　　（亿元）	**Total Investment　(100 million yuan)**	**10898.24**	**15369.30**	**16504.44**	**18877.35**	**21661.00**
按资金来源分	Grouped by Source of Funds					
国家预算内资金	State Budgetary Appropriation	544.98	1080.62	1719.10	2639.39	2248.30
国内贷款	Domestic Loans	2578.19	3578.07	4160.24	4520.09	5547.46
利用外资	Foreign Investment	859.38	665.89	398.69	407.43	338.72
自筹资金	Fundraising	5307.15	7664.69	7478.66	8860.47	10964.91
其他资金	Others	1731.82	2247.46	2177.55	2106.47	2507.61
按构成分	Grouped by Use of Funds					
建筑安装工程	Construction and Installation	6604.61	9594.45	10413.97	12194.13	14331.11
设备、工具、器具购置	Purchase of Equipment and Instruments	2750.51	3315.78	3720.27	3592.29	3701.85
其他费用	Others	1543.12	2459.07	2370.20	3090.94	3628.04
按建设性质分	Grouped by Type of Construction					
#新建	New Construction	3362.17	5507.37	6133.01	7793.52	10217.00
扩建	Expansion	3722.60	4984.90	4732.19	4862.26	5543.05
改建	Reconstruction	1986.23	3058.98	3052.76	3495.50	3499.03
按产业分	Grouped by Type of Industry					
第一产业	Primary Industry	73.64	201.32	303.80	499.50	382.13
第二产业	Secondary Industry	4692.72	4874.79	4820.51	4938.10	5701.68
第三产业	Tertiary Industry	6131.88	10293.19	11380.13	13439.75	15577.19
按主要行业分	Grouped by Main Sector					
#农业	Agriculture	93.40	237.08	357.42	564.54	382.13
工业	Industry	4526.20	4703.30	4578.68	4667.13	5360.65
#能源工业	Energy	2025.28	2862.10	2839.58	2626.16	2876.71
新增固定资产(亿元)	**Newly Increased Fixed Assets (100 million yuan)**	**7390.14**	**11471.31**	**12924.63**	**13014.40**	**13830.42**
房屋建筑面积(万平方米)	**Floor Space of Buildings　(10000 sq.m)**					
施工面积	Floor Space under Construction	70420	73606	67586	63875	66758
竣工面积	Floor Space Completed	31829	33907	33954	29536	28636
#住宅	Residential Buildings	17714	20288	20282	15010	13937

注：1.改建投资1998年及以前数据含单纯建造生活设施投资。

2.按国民经济行业分、按建设性质分不含房地产投资，其他统计分组则包含房地产投资（以下各表同）。

3.根据新国民经济核算标准，对第一产业投资进行了调整。

a) The investment in reconstruction before 1998 includes the investment in construction of facilities simply for the improvement of residents' life.

b) The total investment grouped by main sector and by type of construction exclude the investment in the real estate development, and total investment grouped by others include that. The same as in the following tables.

c) Data on the investment in primary industry has been adjusted according to the new classification standards of national economic accounting.

6-6 按管理渠道分全社会固定资产投资

Total Investment in Fixed Assets by Channel of Management

指 标 Item	基本建设 Capital Construction	更新改造 Innvation	房地产开发 Real Estate Development	其他投资 Others
投资额（亿元） Investment (100 million yuan)				
1980	558.9	137.4		214.6
1985	1074.4	449.1		1019.7
1986	1176.1	619.2	101.0	1224.3
1987	1343.1	758.6	149.9	1540.2
1988	1574.3	980.6	257.2	1941.7
1989	1551.7	788.8	272.7	1797.2
1990	1703.8	830.2	253.3	1729.7
1991	2115.8	1023.2	336.2	2119.3
1992	3012.7	1461.1	731.2	2875.2
1993	4615.5	2195.9	1937.5	4323.5
1994	6436.7	2918.6	2554.1	5132.7
1995	7403.6	3299.4	3149.0	6167.3
1996	(8610.8)	(3622.7)	(3216.4)	(7524.1)
	8570.8	3615.0	3216.4	7511.3
1997	9917.0	3921.9	3178.4	7923.8
1998	11916.4	4516.8	3614.2	8358.8
1999	12455.3	4485.1	4103.2	8811.2
2000	13427.3	5107.6	4984.1	9398.8
2001	14820.1	5923.8	6344.1	10125.5
2002	17666.6	6750.6	7790.9	11291.8
2003	22908.6	8624.9	10153.8	13879.4
增长速度（上年=100） Growth Rate (previous year=100)				
1980	6.8			
1985	44.6	45.2		30.7
1986	9.5	37.9		20.1
1987	14.2	22.5	48.5	25.8
1988	17.2	29.3	71.6	26.1
1989	-1.4	-19.6	6.0	-7.4
1990	9.8	5.2	-7.1	-3.8
1991	24.2	23.3	32.7	22.5
1992	42.4	42.8	117.5	35.7
1993	53.2	50.3	165.0	50.4
1994	39.5	32.9	31.8	18.7
1995	15.0	13.0	23.3	20.2
1996	16.3	9.8	2.1	22.0
1997	15.7	8.5	-1.2	5.5
1998	20.2	15.2	13.7	5.5
1999	4.5	-0.7	13.5	5.4
2000	7.8	13.9	21.5	6.7
2001	10.4	16.0	27.3	7.7
2002	19.2	14.0	22.8	11.5
2003	29.7	27.8	30.3	22.9

6-7 按资金来源和隶属关系分基本建设投资

Investment in Capital Construction by Source of Funds and Administrative Relationship

单位: 亿元 (100 million yuan)

年份 地区	Year Region	按资金来源分 By Source of Funds					按隶属关系分 By Administrative Relationship	
		国家预算内资金 State Budgetary Appropriations	国内贷款 Domestic Loans	利用外资 Foreign Investment	自筹资金 Fund-Raising	其他资金 Others	中央项目 Central Government Projects	地方项目 Local Projects
	1978	389.21		28.16	83.62		266.43	234.56
	1980	300.11	41.22	53.65	163.90		292.61	266.28
	1985	381.18	187.92	73.52	339.99	91.76	575.24	499.13
	1989	323.33	293.00	221.45	495.03	218.92	837.71	714.03
	1990	363.59	378.62	224.05	529.92	207.62	919.15	784.67
	1991	348.45	527.07	239.96	746.73	253.59	1060.44	1055.37
	1992	307.87	831.48	334.15	1242.92	296.24	1341.69	1670.96
	1993	431.76	1117.55	456.15	1991.25	697.25	1834.90	2780.60
	1994	434.57	1583.45	912.03	2820.48	616.36	2430.75	4005.99
	1995	491.67	1646.24	1055.42	3121.86	932.14	2970.67	4432.95
	1996	(524.38)	(1938.86)	(1235.43)	(3778.83)	(1064.76)	(3379.33)	(5231.50)
		521.11	1937.76	1234.84	3752.32	1056.61	3376.28	5194.50
	1997	574.51	2239.88	1351.92	4432.24	1111.61	3858.22	6058.80
	1998	1021.32	2814.36	1445.78	4870.26	1461.22	4122.92	7793.51
	1999	1478.88	2972.04	1064.15	4857.15	1467.25	4046.79	8408.49
	2000	1594.07	3586.35	852.18	5233.10	1396.78	4290.92	9136.35
	2001	2052.31	3637.15	898.13	6231.09	1443.09	4399.47	10420.63
	2002	2533.60	4412.39	1031.19	7654.07	1582.42	4528.49	13138.13
	2003	2103.24	6140.95	1236.86	11252.49	2087.33	4147.48	18761.12
北京	Beijing	75.50	155.89	16.02	312.92	22.54	160.48	398.30
天津	Tianjin	13.68	185.69	24.12	258.66	17.45	113.22	388.15
河北	Hebei	35.45	149.67	23.61	532.22	105.57	92.75	753.15
山西	Shanxi	33.72	146.79	17.33	224.44	43.43	97.67	400.58
内蒙古	Inner Mongolia	99.15	166.70	6.13	355.01	62.09	79.42	671.31
辽宁	Liaoning	71.77	150.69	27.72	380.78	46.51	99.38	583.78
吉林	Jilin	34.04	59.81	6.11	250.97	73.47	64.58	369.30
黑龙江	Heilongjiang	60.86	79.36	9.56	354.74	57.16	145.07	448.00
上海	Shanghai	28.42	248.07	138.09	451.71	33.35	115.78	783.49
江苏	Jiangsu	81.02	564.71	156.29	1024.54	60.66	238.66	1679.45
浙江	Zhejiang	72.57	523.67	89.72	863.44	103.85	163.03	1480.90
安徽	Anhui	47.64	131.68	13.60	258.19	73.89	18.67	531.32
福建	Fujian	62.13	136.85	39.47	191.69	32.33	15.63	456.21
江西	Jiangxi	61.27	181.33	33.83	222.23	62.18	28.34	538.51
山东	Shandong	74.46	297.90	90.56	1128.78	185.34	142.29	1652.78
河南	Henan	72.32	336.62	20.36	468.72	83.33	111.24	860.33
湖北	Hubei	137.78	184.11	53.52	353.58	288.51	217.28	611.25
湖南	Hunan	55.48	157.66	26.77	290.00	63.86	53.88	545.86
广东	Guangdong	53.97	420.46	260.87	1107.64	62.98	207.18	1621.21
广西	Guangxi	65.58	164.15	14.57	184.21	43.02	96.50	364.40
海南	Hainan	16.07	34.56	41.19	64.02	32.23	27.80	151.86
重庆	Chongqing	98.55	164.89	8.88	197.66	79.35	45.64	522.94
四川	Sichuan	53.26	300.25	28.82	469.09	92.34	84.62	864.92
贵州	Guizhou	31.44	135.16	5.82	175.82	17.25	122.71	257.36
云南	Yunnan	49.33	188.98	9.78	176.76	37.69	74.66	418.46
西藏	Tibet	79.76	5.31		27.68	20.15	89.61	28.70
陕西	Shaanxi	81.35	150.04	18.44	235.66	112.72	84.31	542.83
甘肃	Gansu	60.77	88.24	3.89	84.86	49.10	71.18	236.08
青海	Qinghai	36.76	16.12	1.53	67.15	22.62	31.08	133.69
宁夏	Ningxia	25.86	56.40	1.04	45.98	17.08	29.20	133.46
新疆	Xinjiang	131.69	121.97	8.20	265.79	61.77	289.06	332.53
不分地区	Not Classified by Region	201.59	437.22	41.02	227.54	23.51	936.56	

6-8 按构成和建设性质分基本建设投资

Investment in Capital Construction by Use of Funds and Type of Construction

单位：亿元 (100 million yuan)

年份 地区	Year Region	投资额 Total	按构成分 By Use of Funds			按建设性质分 By Type of Construction		
			建筑安装工程 Construction and Installation	设备、工器具购置 Purchase of Equipment and Instruments	其他费用 Others	#新建 New Construction	#扩建 Expansion	#改建 Reconstruction
	1978	500.99	300.85	165.78	34.36	286.62	187.58	
	1980	558.89	381.07	136.53	41.29	290.24	237.49	
	1985	1074.37	726.71	217.39	130.27	481.42	350.29	171.60
	1989	1551.74	998.73	380.94	172.07	708.49	569.54	159.49
	1990	1703.81	1045.37	453.76	204.69	822.96	610.99	175.28
	1991	2115.80	1308.83	521.22	285.76	983.06	778.86	230.39
	1992	3012.65	1889.39	667.34	455.92	1484.57	1003.45	351.45
	1993	4615.50	3018.74	899.55	697.22	2400.13	1472.47	296.78
	1994	6436.74	4123.89	1402.84	910.01	3523.90	1898.03	383.41
	1995	7403.62	4641.13	1635.04	1127.44	3971.94	2348.01	443.32
	1996	(8610.84)	(5345.27)	(1861.15)	(1404.42)	(4600.81)	(2797.68)	(521.42)
		8570.79	5310.07	1857.29	1403.43	4590.02	2782.24	516.56
	1997	9917.02	6215.22	2060.60	1641.20	5513.98	3030.69	611.36
	1998	11916.42	7695.75	2101.83	2118.84	6765.24	3204.87	1032.42
	1999	12455.28	8543.60	2132.30	1779.39	6775.46	3241.87	1250.68
	2000	13427.27	8936.81	2457.88	2032.59	7324.86	3368.07	1685.57
	2001	14820.10	10154.63	2473.29	2192.18	8168.22	3939.30	1646.89
	2002	17666.62	11865.82	2780.18	3020.62	10361.51	4217.45	2018.33
	2003	22908.60	15426.44	3495.78	3986.38	14786.53	5012.38	2111.72
北京	Beijing	558.78	329.20	53.37	176.21	253.71	259.13	25.14
天津	Tianjin	501.37	355.62	51.40	94.35	363.70	113.49	13.70
河北	Hebei	845.90	584.52	145.18	116.21	635.63	120.17	56.01
山西	Shanxi	498.25	329.07	111.33	57.85	315.85	118.80	37.15
内蒙古	Inner Mongolia	750.73	543.09	115.55	92.10	466.95	161.57	96.88
辽宁	Liaoning	683.16	453.35	122.68	107.13	413.39	178.93	55.24
吉林	Jilin	433.88	348.81	43.42	41.64	234.26	81.35	99.90
黑龙江	Heilongjiang	593.08	442.46	77.39	73.23	403.05	132.60	32.19
上海	Shanghai	899.27	484.94	192.26	222.07	736.91	78.86	64.74
江苏	Jiangsu	1918.11	1235.17	298.04	384.91	1179.46	538.92	188.37
浙江	Zhejiang	1643.92	1046.65	166.52	430.76	1156.65	288.01	146.16
安徽	Anhui	549.99	409.33	60.31	80.35	406.81	78.24	49.09
福建	Fujian	471.84	330.28	41.92	99.65	387.99	58.72	19.24
江西	Jiangxi	566.85	446.71	66.17	53.96	380.31	121.58	54.18
山东	Shandong	1795.07	1276.47	327.86	190.74	1072.78	549.65	101.27
河南	Henan	971.56	661.06	161.46	149.04	635.87	190.23	113.89
湖北	Hubei	828.53	503.72	110.77	214.04	556.07	143.34	99.37
湖南	Hunan	599.75	440.64	54.63	104.48	401.04	114.31	66.67
广东	Guangdong	1828.39	1182.49	298.26	347.63	1402.04	312.89	57.79
广西	Guangxi	460.91	304.71	64.95	91.25	303.18	91.23	51.28
海南	Hainan	179.66	92.27	65.57	21.81	105.97	42.35	6.89
重庆	Chongqing	568.58	387.85	63.60	117.12	369.44	81.39	66.14
四川	Sichuan	949.54	613.95	109.22	226.36	564.17	180.62	169.50
贵州	Guizhou	380.08	256.11	56.97	67.00	254.22	80.54	34.12
云南	Yunnan	493.12	357.59	48.47	87.06	320.31	90.74	64.25
西藏	Tibet	118.31	109.55	6.79	1.97	69.14	16.36	29.20
陕西	Shaanxi	627.13	467.70	69.65	89.78	382.12	138.25	57.89
甘肃	Gansu	307.26	243.66	32.87	30.73	214.94	51.74	22.56
青海	Qinghai	164.77	135.86	17.28	11.64	121.72	29.00	10.79
宁夏	Ningxia	162.67	124.64	22.07	15.95	91.00	38.98	22.02
新疆	Xinjiang	621.59	472.70	79.31	69.57	173.68	239.47	174.49
不分地区	Not Classified by Region	936.56	456.28	360.50	119.79	414.18	290.94	25.62

注：1980年及以前按建设性质分的扩建中含改建。

a) Before 1980, investment in expansion by type of construction include investment in reconstruction.

6-9 各行业按建设性质分基本建设投资（2003年）

Investment in Capital Construction by Type of Construction and Sector (2003)

单位: 亿元 (100 million yuan)

行业	Sector	投资额 Investment	#新建 New Construction	#扩建 Expansion	#改建 Reconstruction
全国总计	**National Total**	**22908.60**	**14786.53**	**5012.38**	**2111.72**
农、林、牧、渔业	**Agriculture, Forestry, Animal Husbandry and Fishing**	**416.78**	**258.24**	**103.36**	**43.32**
农业	Agriculture	109.49	72.25	18.39	10.97
林业	Forestry	126.53	70.97	45.67	9.12
畜牧业	Animal Husbandry	63.37	43.43	14.96	4.38
渔业	Fishing	13.81	9.96	2.84	0.97
农、林、牧、渔服务业	Service Activities for Agriculture, Forestry, Animal Husbandry and Fishing	103.58	61.63	21.50	17.87
采矿业	**Mining**	**894.15**	**375.16**	**435.64**	**68.51**
煤炭开采和洗选业	Mining and Washing of Coal	193.10	164.17	20.93	3.67
石油和天然气开采业	Extraction of Petroleum and Natural Gas	639.81	169.96	398.98	63.84
黑色金属矿采选业	Mining and Processing of Ferrous Metal Ores	15.35	11.70	1.60	0.06
有色金属矿采选业	Mining and Processing of Non-Ferrous Metal Ores	27.32	15.57	10.03	0.81
非金属矿采选业	Mining and Processing of Nonmetal Ores	17.26	12.47	4.08	0.13
其他采矿业	Mining of Other Ores	1.31	1.29		
制造业	**Manufacturing**	**3639.36**	**2818.37**	**595.02**	**73.97**
农副食品加工业	Processing of Food from Agricultural Products	148.94	118.77	19.61	2.68
食品制造业	Manufacture of Foods	99.32	79.27	12.56	1.73
饮料制造业	Manufacture of Beverages	66.98	51.94	11.67	1.23
烟草制品业	Manufacture of Tobacco	11.00	4.46	3.57	1.07
纺织业	Manufacture of Textile	177.42	143.45	28.38	1.01
纺织服装、鞋、帽制造业	Manufacture of Textile Wearing Apparel, Footware, and Caps	74.18	59.21	12.29	0.39
皮革毛皮羽毛(绒)及其制品业	Manufacture of Leather, Fur, Feather and Related Products	38.34	32.59	5.18	0.16
木材加工及木竹藤棕草制品业	Processing of Timber, Manufacture of Wood, Bamboo, Rattan, Palm, and Straw Products	37.87	30.30	5.51	1.23
家具制造业	Manufacture of Furniture	34.09	28.88	4.45	0.17
造纸及纸制品业	Manufacture of Paper and Paper Products	87.04	64.61	21.48	0.25
印刷业和记录媒介的复制	Printing,Reproduction of Recording Media	37.62	28.25	3.61	0.08
文教体育用品制造业	Manufacture of Articles for Culture, Education and Sport Activity	14.35	10.71	3.50	0.04
石油加工、炼焦及核燃料加工业	Processing of Petroleum, Coking, Processing of Nuclear Fuel	82.75	58.82	20.90	0.19
化学原料及化学制品制造业	Manufacture of Raw Chemical Materials and Chemical Products	503.10	402.75	87.40	3.76
医药制造业	Manufacture of Medicines	161.16	125.38	23.83	2.04
化学纤维制造业	Manufacture of Chemical Fibers	31.69	13.70	17.23	0.04
橡胶制品业	Manufacture of Rubber	35.49	18.82	15.36	0.38
塑料制品业	Manufacture of Plastics	86.58	75.27	9.26	0.65
非金属矿物制品业	Manufacture of Non-metallic Mineral Products	253.48	207.94	33.84	2.16
黑色金属冶炼及压延加工业	Smelting and Pressing of Ferrous Metals	318.39	220.80	59.07	35.97
有色金属冶炼及压延加工业	Smelting and Pressing of Non-ferrous Metals	183.99	146.01	35.92	0.96
金属制品业	Manufacture of Metal Products	105.82	86.92	14.36	0.53
通用设备制造业	Manufacture of General Purpose Machinery	110.53	81.57	15.72	2.29
专用设备制造业	Manufacture of Special Purpose Machinery	132.43	98.20	19.34	4.33
交通运输设备制造业	Manufacture of Transport Equipment	187.47	128.37	37.20	5.95
电气机械及器材制造业	Manufacture of Electrical Machinery and Equipment	98.67	78.70	12.47	1.37
通信设备、计算机及其他电子设备制造业	Manufacture of Communication Equipment, Computers and Other Electronic Equipment	338.87	276.95	32.23	1.45
仪器仪表文化办公用机械制造业	Manufacture of Measuring Instruments and Machinery for Cultural Activity and Office Work	44.23	33.36	6.96	1.27
工艺品及其他制造业	Manufacture of Artwork and Other Manufacturing	135.43	110.78	21.91	0.61
废弃资源和废旧材料回收加工业	Recycling and Disposal of Waste	2.12	1.60	0.20	
电力燃气水的生产供应业	**Production and Distribution of Electricity, Gas and Water**	**2964.73**	**2054.55**	**671.85**	**219.01**
电力、热力的生产和供应业	Production and Distribution of Electric Power and Heat Power	2567.09	1767.72	581.01	203.10
燃气生产和供应业	Production and Distribution of Gas	114.30	93.32	17.63	2.03
水的生产和供应业	Production and Distribution of Water	283.35	193.51	73.20	13.89
建筑业	**Construction**	**381.41**	**233.28**	**80.32**	**42.26**
房屋和土木工程建筑业	Construction of Buildings and Civil Engineering	350.55	212.11	72.99	41.76
建筑安装业	Building Installation	12.76	8.38	2.89	0.28
建筑装饰业	Buidling Decoration	6.00	3.07	2.82	0.10
其他建筑业	Other Construction	12.09	9.72	1.62	0.12

6-9 续表 continued

单位: 亿元 (100 million yuan)

行 业	Sector	投资额 Investment	#新 建 New Construction	#扩 建 Expansion	#改 建 Reconstruction
交通运输、仓储和邮政业	**Transport, Storage and Post**	**4892.71**	**3025.49**	**770.38**	**791.93**
铁路运输业	Railway Transport	616.38	301.51	100.93	37.10
道路运输业	Road Transport	3162.01	2090.88	318.65	702.53
城市公共交通业	Urban Public Transport	360.13	304.72	22.25	21.88
水上运输业	Water Transport	299.11	162.02	121.30	11.33
航空运输业	Air Transport	180.73	61.84	60.92	1.92
管道运输业	Transport Via Pipelines	139.52	19.02	118.42	
装卸搬运和其他运输服务业	Loading, Unloading and Other Transport Services	29.36	13.35	2.79	13.06
仓储业	Storage	84.88	62.56	16.71	3.14
邮政业	Post	20.57	9.59	8.41	0.98
信息传输、计算机服务和软件业	**Information Transmission, Computer Services and Software**	**506.93**	**304.26**	**176.51**	**15.47**
电信和其他信息传输服务业	Telecommunications and Other Information Transmission Services	479.07	283.33	170.39	15.20
计算机服务业	Computer Services	5.13	4.32	0.71	0.02
软件业	Software	22.74	16.61	5.42	0.25
批发和零售业	**Wholesale and Retail Trade**	**516.58**	**359.38**	**106.51**	**35.74**
批发业	Wholesale Trade	204.28	137.46	44.07	13.02
零售业	Retail Trade	312.30	221.92	62.44	22.72
住宿和餐饮业	**Hotel and Restaurants**	**205.53**	**138.41**	**44.26**	**19.90**
住宿业	Hotels	163.75	111.21	37.86	12.88
餐饮业	Restaurants	41.78	27.20	6.40	7.02
金融业	**Financial Intermediation**	**58.24**	**32.29**	**14.75**	**2.25**
银行业	Banks	49.48	26.28	13.08	1.73
证券业	Security Activities	0.79	0.43	0.01	0.08
保险业	Insurance	4.70	2.50	1.50	0.44
其他金融活动	Other Financial Activities	3.27	3.08	0.15	
房地产业	**Real Estate**	**326.27**	**247.94**	**27.13**	**19.28**
租赁和商务服务业	**Leasing and Business Services**	**252.58**	**178.38**	**51.35**	**4.51**
租赁业	Leasing	0.69	0.57	0.06	
商务服务业	Business Services	251.89	177.82	51.29	4.51
科学研究、技术服务和地质勘查业	**Scientific Research, Technical Service and Geologic Prospecting Geologic Prospecting**	**244.29**	**146.80**	**66.76**	**13.04**
研究与试验发展	Research and Experimental Development	111.06	56.33	39.49	5.30
专业技术服务业	Professional Technical Services	78.95	56.45	14.44	4.31
科技交流和推广服务业	Services of Science and Technology Exchanges and Promotion	29.17	14.56	9.23	3.00
地质勘查业	Geologic Prospecting	25.10	19.47	3.61	0.43
水利、环境和公共设施管理业	**Management of Water Conservancy, Environment and Public Facilities**	**3863.24**	**2441.27**	**793.43**	**588.36**
水利管理业	Management of Water Conservancy	680.94	389.46	121.97	160.52
环境管理业	Environmental Management	222.80	135.23	56.92	24.59
公共设施管理业	Management of Public Facilities	2959.50	1916.58	614.55	403.25
居民服务和其他服务业	**Services to Households and Other Services**	**46.24**	**36.21**	**4.80**	**1.78**
居民服务业	Services to Households	37.39	29.13	3.69	1.61
其他服务业	Other Services	8.85	7.08	1.11	0.16
教育	**Education**	**1364.96**	**685.86**	**526.78**	**47.26**
卫生、社会保障和社会福利业	**Health, Social Security and Social Welfare**	**299.02**	**121.87**	**131.61**	**17.46**
卫生	Health	280.15	108.60	128.72	16.73
社会保障业	Social Security	**3.36**	**1.96**	**0.22**	**0.21**
社会福利业	Social Welfare	15.51	11.31	2.67	0.53
文化、体育和娱乐业	**Culture, Sports and Entertainment**	**425.82**	**338.40**	**55.08**	**15.31**
新闻出版业	Journalism and Publishing Activities	21.67	12.73	5.81	0.42
广播、电视、电影和音像业	Broadcasting, Movies, Televisions and Audiovisual Activities	67.30	45.52	16.40	2.33
文化艺术业	Cultural and Art Activities	119.94	92.65	15.63	7.05
体育	Sports Activities	100.59	83.05	10.41	1.89
娱乐业	Entertainment	116.33	104.45	6.83	3.62
公共管理和社会组织	**Public Management and Social Organization**	**1609.49**	**990.08**	**356.85**	**92.36**
中国共产党机关	Organs of Communist Party of China	28.92	13.30	10.82	2.05
国家机构	Government Agencies	1509.45	943.06	323.04	87.78
人民政协和民主党派	People's Political Consultative Conference and Democratic Parties	5.97	3.80	1.36	0.18
群众团体、社会团体和宗教组织	Non-Governmental Institutions, Social Organizaitons and Religion Organizations	24.61	11.26	10.49	0.69
基层群众自治组织	Grass Roots Self-governing Organizations	40.55	18.65	11.14	1.65
国际组织	**International Organizations**	**0.29**	**0.29**		

注： 改建不含单纯建造生活设施投资。

a) Investment in reconstruction excludes that only for human services.

6-10 按行业分基本建设投资
Investment in Capital Construction by Sector

单位: 亿元　　　　(100 million yuan)

年　份 Year	合　计 Total	农、林、牧、渔业 Farming, Forestry, Animal Husbandry and Fishery	采掘业 Mining and Quarrying	制造业 Manufacturing	电力、煤气及水的生产和供应业 Production and Supply of Electricity Gas and Water	建筑业 Construction	地质勘查业水利管理业 Geological Prospecting and Water Conservancy	交通运输仓储和邮电通信业 Transport, Storage, Post & Telecommu-nication Services
1978	500.99	17.95		273.16		8.84	46.33	68.04
1980	558.89	24.96		275.61		11.22	29.56	62.34
1985	1074.37	17.89	101.56	223.33	121.60	22.00	25.27	178.10
1989	1551.74	20.20	170.68	361.41	290.40	13.84	35.62	170.03
1990	1703.81	26.57	204.64	382.03	365.93	10.41	45.41	211.01
1991	2115.80	33.46	243.31	477.96	425.94	12.60	59.03	340.18
1992	3012.65	43.51	303.22	599.31	555.78	23.25	79.54	457.58
1993	4615.50	46.22	351.32	884.52	768.61	115.02	98.38	901.24
1994	6436.74	56.77	394.55	1216.33	1150.79	138.35	120.61	1372.94
1995	7403.62	76.59	437.77	1540.08	1258.49	145.55	165.83	1587.53
1996	(8610.84)	(111.30)	(498.75)	(1681.22)	(1546.83)	(183.70)	(228.46)	(1847.12)
	8570.79	109.40	498.56	1679.71	1545.97	183.36	227.90	1844.62
1997	9917.02	153.88	648.57	1532.05	1938.89	150.95	277.42	2197.45
1998	11916.42	225.38	540.52	1484.08	2144.55	158.28	433.16	3252.19
1999	12455.28	299.01	474.19	1182.72	2193.18	223.65	556.56	3429.28
2000	13427.27	360.93	589.36	1175.11	2479.80	197.47	596.64	3641.94
2001	14820.10	434.59	644.56	1509.02	2196.30	189.24	569.99	4116.43
2002	17666.62	587.80	679.93	2097.83	2458.61	268.97	720.41	4393.98

6-10 续表 continued

单位: 亿元　　　　(100 million yuan)

年　份 Year	批发零售贸易和餐饮业 Wholesale and Retail Trade & Catering Services	金融、保险业 Finance and Insurance	房地产业 Real Estate	社会服务业 Social Services	卫生体育和社会福利业 Health Care, Sports & Social Welfare	教育、文化艺术和广播电影电视业 Education, Culture and Arts, Radio, Film and Television	科学研究和综合技术服务业 Scientific Research and Polytechnic Services	国家机关、政党机关和社会团体 Government Agencies, Party Agencies and Social Organizations	其　他 Others
1978	15.29			15.39		22.49		33.50	
1980	28.57			33.81		44.83		47.99	
1985	39.85	7.13	62.32	55.60	23.10	78.12	20.82	49.63	48.08
1989	41.62	15.59	39.55	72.44	28.30	100.33	21.98	58.33	111.43
1990	38.93	15.09	15.04	66.65	35.28	102.52	21.03	62.10	101.18
1991	63.78	18.80	27.89	93.90	32.83	119.39	23.13	87.75	55.85
1992	136.50	32.21	56.40	154.01	45.56	151.34	31.56	141.65	201.24
1993	203.45	66.67	140.90	301.73	66.23	204.45	48.65	301.44	116.66
1994	254.73	96.06	316.34	417.45	93.66	261.53	52.76	376.58	117.29
1995	249.37	125.50	183.19	490.01	105.05	352.69	68.28	474.08	143.60
1996	(254.61)	(136.24)	(139.82)	(609.10)	(125.02)	(430.29)	(65.78)	(591.64)	(160.98)
	251.05	135.14	139.64	607.79	122.50	418.31	65.29	580.89	160.70
1997	265.00	142.79	146.47	820.36	148.51	529.21	68.17	715.99	181.33
1998	295.37	148.28	186.18	1123.87	184.54	615.56	75.82	888.00	160.63
1999	279.23	126.63	184.85	1355.52	198.70	711.65	88.56	1006.19	145.35
2000	292.59	90.26	151.71	1611.52	218.36	823.37	103.10	878.18	216.94
2001	342.45	92.70	168.47	1965.16	265.74	951.36	126.21	1006.19	241.70
2002	397.45	65.47	201.62	2588.06	339.43	1164.56	139.13	1353.42	209.95

6-11 各地区按行业分基本建设投资（2003年）

Investment in Capital Construction by Sector (2003)

单位: 亿元 (100 million yuan)

地 区	Region	合 计 Total	农、林、牧、渔业 Agriculture, Forestry, Animal Husbandry and Fishing	采矿业 Mining	制造业 Manufacturing	电力、燃气及水的生产和供应业 Production and Distribution of Electricity, Gas and Water	建筑业 Construction	交通运输、仓储和邮政业 Transport, Storage and Post
全国总计	**National Total**	**22908.60**	**416.78**	**894.15**	**3639.36**	**2964.73**	**381.41**	**4892.71**
北 京	Beijing	558.78	1.96	0.15	48.13	23.47	4.17	112.97
天 津	Tianjin	501.37	1.91	87.01	38.70	24.98	3.67	93.10
河 北	Hebei	845.90	25.32	7.78	205.71	88.53	23.65	114.21
山 西	Shanxi	498.25	7.74	33.69	105.16	128.78	1.62	100.47
内蒙古	Inner Mongolia	750.73	35.09	23.20	125.38	146.68	2.36	183.36
辽 宁	Liaoning	683.16	15.92	37.92	137.44	55.63	5.97	102.69
吉 林	Jilin	433.88	10.47	24.13	61.89	38.06	16.34	62.58
黑龙江	Heilongjiang	593.08	31.68	91.77	65.99	46.11	18.84	89.40
上 海	Shanghai	899.27	2.55	2.46	321.99	75.40	0.27	170.99
江 苏	Jiangsu	1918.11	9.88	6.38	327.73	305.13	8.36	382.19
浙 江	Zhejiang	1643.92	6.40	0.05	265.91	187.19	24.28	272.22
安 徽	Anhui	549.99	8.42	24.69	65.90	30.78	40.05	116.88
福 建	Fujian	471.84	6.07	1.23	66.27	48.20	5.00	134.90
江 西	Jiangxi	566.85	3.53	2.65	73.63	38.99	0.24	160.98
山 东	Shandong	1795.07	19.59	131.21	521.49	154.14	65.99	144.41
河 南	Henan	971.56	21.49	20.17	158.67	150.42	4.21	263.66
湖 北	Hubei	828.53	21.23	8.23	87.33	206.48	7.94	186.35
湖 南	Hunan	599.75	8.05	1.28	48.37	87.22	7.80	167.18
广 东	Guangdong	1828.39	7.91	10.11	451.43	212.36	64.84	345.00
广 西	Guangxi	460.91	8.15	3.23	44.98	98.83	1.30	98.40
海 南	Hainan	179.66	12.15	0.84	48.21	9.35	5.52	34.12
重 庆	Chongqing	568.58	12.28	2.08	69.12	66.73	34.81	86.72
四 川	Sichuan	949.54	18.00	7.16	93.42	129.47	1.48	176.45
贵 州	Guizhou	380.08	2.81	5.75	17.69	127.34	0.98	89.02
云 南	Yunnan	493.12	8.91	4.46	26.24	101.79	0.56	157.03
西 藏	Tibet	118.31	5.71	0.16	3.01	17.28	0.96	45.01
陕 西	Shaanxi	627.13	26.47	33.11	77.99	58.02	5.57	138.21
甘 肃	Gansu	307.26	16.79	10.37	18.73	57.27	11.96	73.53
青 海	Qinghai	164.77	10.88	11.10	17.68	30.41	8.04	39.46
宁 夏	Ningxia	162.67	7.90	1.08	11.63	33.05	0.93	25.81
新 疆	Xinjiang	621.59	41.54	162.82	33.57	46.26	3.68	97.72
不分地区	Not Classified by Region	936.56		137.90		140.40		627.68

6-11　续表 1 continued

单位: 亿元 (100 million yuan)

地区	Region	信息传输、计算机服务和软件业 Information Transmission, Computer Service and Software	批发和零售业 Wholesale and Retail Trade	住宿和餐饮业 Hotel and Restaurants	金融业 Financial Intermediation	房地产业 Real Estate	租赁和商务服务业 Leasing and Business Services	科学研究、技术服务和地质勘查业 Scientific Research, Technical Services, and Geological Prospecting
全国总计	**National Total**	**506.93**	**516.58**	**205.53**	**58.24**	**326.27**	**252.58**	**244.29**
北　京	Beijing	11.15	11.52	13.82	2.46	3.78	20.20	34.56
天　津	Tianjin	9.48	6.24	1.20	0.15	32.03	2.76	1.20
河　北	Hebei	11.90	38.43	10.65	2.50	34.47	14.76	23.27
山　西	Shanxi	8.07	8.64	1.49	1.43	1.37	0.61	0.90
内蒙古	Inner Mongolia	5.02	13.72	4.83	1.59	8.05	1.50	4.33
辽　宁	Liaoning	18.89	30.58	8.33	2.83	6.75	6.84	13.51
吉　林	Jilin	9.92	15.36	6.92	1.86	1.88	2.16	3.48
黑龙江	Heilongjiang	20.35	20.00	1.94	3.15	4.51	11.32	4.76
上　海	Shanghai	28.51	5.79	6.46	0.61	13.64	1.39	6.45
江　苏	Jiangsu	22.54	31.29	8.67	1.47	10.45	12.12	21.93
浙　江	Zhejiang	18.77	20.00	13.20	3.27	25.55	31.21	10.28
安　徽	Anhui	4.29	12.01	9.07	1.43	11.09	6.78	2.73
福　建	Fujian	4.61	7.27	3.18	0.68	13.58	10.70	2.99
江　西	Jiangxi	20.36	12.67	8.51	1.67	5.37	2.94	2.60
山　东	Shandong	27.11	69.50	8.19	7.41	26.83	16.38	20.37
河　南	Henan	30.64	19.21	5.49	2.37	6.82	8.88	6.06
湖　北	Hubei	15.26	28.17	9.95	2.62	8.16	11.38	7.15
湖　南	Hunan	5.54	25.85	8.27	2.18	8.62	17.38	4.16
广　东	Guangdong	72.33	19.56	11.83	2.56	21.62	23.94	27.19
广　西	Guangxi	28.14	7.29	5.32	1.18	1.51	6.26	2.07
海　南	Hainan	2.20	0.94	17.51	0.80	2.96	3.48	0.49
重　庆	Chongqing	7.51	11.45	7.29	1.28	22.73	4.21	3.60
四　川	Sichuan	40.09	19.86	8.96	1.71	16.79	5.33	10.65
贵　州	Guizhou	8.41	5.26	1.44	1.51	2.75	1.96	0.78
云　南	Yunnan	15.62	8.53	3.11	1.98	2.90	1.47	2.44
西　藏	Tibet	3.13	1.18	1.14	0.37	0.03	0.04	1.29
陕　西	Shaanxi	16.19	21.72	5.67	2.79	10.21	21.96	14.05
甘　肃	Gansu	4.32	9.29	1.47	0.92	5.37	2.64	2.40
青　海	Qinghai	4.64	3.26	1.40	0.38	0.31	0.16	0.88
宁　夏	Ningxia	2.91	6.15	3.49	0.55	12.44	0.11	0.55
新　疆	Xinjiang	29.03	25.84	6.69	2.51	3.72	1.74	4.77
不分地区	Not Classified by Region							2.42

6-11 续表 2 continued

单位: 亿元 (100 million yuan)

地 区	Region	水利、环境和公共设施管理业 Water Management of Conservancy, Environment and Public Facilities	居民服务和其他服务业 Services to Households and Other Services	教 育 Education	卫生、社会保障和社会福利业 Health, Social Securities and Social Welfare	文化、体育和娱乐业 Culture, Sports and Entertainment	公共管理和社会组织 Public Management and Social Organization	国际组织 International Organizations
全国总计	**National Total**	**3863.24**	**46.24**	**1364.96**	**299.02**	**425.82**	**1609.49**	**0.29**
北 京	Beijing	120.23	1.85	46.80	15.19	24.53	61.83	
天 津	Tianjin	116.16	0.07	30.00	13.55	25.70	13.45	
河 北	Hebei	82.86	1.72	51.31	11.34	15.83	81.67	
山 西	Shanxi	51.62	0.06	19.90	5.12	7.49	14.08	
内蒙古	Inner Mongolia	114.94	1.42	21.86	7.51	8.68	41.21	
辽 宁	Liaoning	73.14	0.74	41.75	7.44	13.81	102.97	
吉 林	Jilin	71.47	0.28	34.22	5.46	9.18	58.23	
黑龙江	Heilongjiang	59.68	0.88	43.31	6.16	13.62	59.60	
上 海	Shanghai	157.87	1.57	38.21	10.42	36.15	18.56	
江 苏	Jiangsu	503.81	5.04	130.96	16.49	29.93	83.76	
浙 江	Zhejiang	505.88	12.31	112.83	26.22	33.15	75.20	
安 徽	Anhui	61.89	1.00	41.38	6.36	5.36	99.89	
福 建	Fujian	63.82	1.08	38.72	7.79	6.45	49.32	
江 西	Jiangxi	120.06	0.81	32.57	21.67	6.94	50.67	
山 东	Shandong	188.53	3.65	125.58	20.91	25.07	218.72	
河 南	Henan	131.80	1.20	62.34	11.57	11.03	55.53	
湖 北	Hubei	104.80	1.14	49.95	11.62	8.91	51.87	
湖 南	Hunan	76.89	1.46	34.22	12.09	21.98	60.96	0.26
广 东	Guangdong	287.63	2.36	121.10	17.62	39.71	89.28	
广 西	Guangxi	99.55	0.31	22.34	8.10	5.78	18.17	
海 南	Hainan	16.39	0.17	6.43	1.49	9.06	7.55	
重 庆	Chongqing	145.65	1.01	31.38	6.34	8.57	45.83	
四 川	Sichuan	270.93	1.60	83.88	12.40	17.31	34.06	
贵 州	Guizhou	65.21	0.31	16.71	6.51	5.77	19.88	
云 南	Yunnan	83.96	1.02	20.68	5.34	6.36	40.74	
西 藏	Tibet	16.94	0.47	5.17	1.87	1.70	12.87	
陕 西	Shaanxi	69.37	0.80	54.03	6.10	13.44	51.40	0.03
甘 肃	Gansu	23.66	0.23	16.83	4.10	4.20	43.17	
青 海	Qinghai	14.48	0.12	2.96	1.47	0.71	16.44	
宁 夏	Ningxia	39.83	0.38	5.47	1.72	1.51	7.17	
新 疆	Xinjiang	96.05	1.19	22.09	9.07	7.90	25.39	
不分地区	Not Classified by Region	28.17						

6-12 按项目规模分基本建设投资及项目个数

Number of Capital Construction Projects by Project Size

年份 地区	Year Region	项目投资(亿元) Investment in Projects (100 million yuan) 大中型 Large and Medium Sized	小型 Small Sized	施工项目(个) Number of Projects under Construction (unit)	#大中型 Large and Medium Sized	全部建成投产项目(个) Number of Projects Completed and Put into Use (unit)	#大中型 Large and Medium Sized
	1978	243.94	233.92	45261	1723	11762	99
	1980	215.98	330.67	67618	1106	24823	82
	1985	394.17	627.67	87766	961	44477	121
	1989	729.70	686.59	66382	969	35370	95
	1990	896.16	702.56	67842	1059	36502	152
	1991	1058.23	935.54	77704	1053	41783	148
	1992	1322.43	1528.32	90609	1153	50633	158
	1993	1946.31	2543.70	90954	1340	51886	186
	1994	2738.13	3562.00	88841	1412	49021	224
	1995	3196.29	4053.07	88685	1408	50512	238
	1996	(3615.88)	(4751.59)	(93997)	(1266)	(55434)	(200)
		3615.88	4714.14	77954	1266	42008	200
	1997	4042.57	5634.40	84480	1240	48102	184
	1998	4539.21	7192.94	99665	1308	54950	175
	1999	3743.71	8332.93	97084	1135	57090	174
	2000	3771.38	9251.13	91252	1245	52645	241
	2001	3707.08	10671.94	91316	1257	51042	248
	2002	4497.93	12725.65	97488	1381	52465	253
	2003	5186.00	17373.92	111290	1977	56784	359
北京	Beijing	99.87	457.67	1046	17	360	2
天津	Tianjin	195.18	301.17	835	59	423	21
河北	Hebei	132.18	711.58	4959	59	2655	9
山西	Shanxi	161.89	336.19	2260	31	1126	3
内蒙古	Inner Mongolia	176.91	572.59	4385	71	2942	17
辽宁	Liaoning	92.61	582.49	2640	35	1458	4
吉林	Jilin	43.41	385.01	1971	35	1216	16
黑龙江	Heilongjiang	74.41	512.46	3126	88	2170	34
上海	Shanghai	412.38	480.54	1261	137	452	30
江苏	Jiangsu	185.49	1730.59	4819	14	2713	2
浙江	Zhejiang	204.36	1435.85	5995	52	2302	4
安徽	Anhui	77.07	466.71	3584	31	1459	3
福建	Fujian	118.03	352.92	2315	54	777	10
江西	Jiangxi	137.07	423.04	3368	52	1799	5
山东	Shandong	161.95	1624.63	7412	50	3148	7
河南	Henan	182.29	782.42	5179	70	2750	9
湖北	Hubei	257.62	564.51	4959	35	3245	4
湖南	Hunan	59.38	538.99	4441	34	2274	6
广东	Guangdong	687.69	1129.46	6173	425	2004	79
广西	Guangxi	74.18	385.01	6071	42	2962	7
海南	Hainan	60.49	98.76	973	51	529	5
重庆	Chongqing	60.82	503.97	3335	67	1890	23
四川	Sichuan	137.35	797.69	5953	94	2644	8
贵州	Guizhou	114.07	261.71	3200	25	1752	2
云南	Yunnan	72.20	418.39	4467	45	2306	5
西藏	Tibet	27.42	90.86	1918	29	1366	3
陕西	Shaanxi	159.55	467.15	3867	79	2060	9
甘肃	Gansu	80.60	224.80	3521	92	1602	20
青海	Qinghai	32.54	131.86	1971	13	1083	2
宁夏	Ningxia	20.04	142.62	1179	3	666	
新疆	Xinjiang	156.26	462.21	4037	20	2646	5
不分地区	Not Classified by Region	730.67	0.08	70	68	5	5

6-13 基本建设房屋建筑面积

Floor Space of Buildings Through Capital Construction

单位: 万平方米 (10 000 sq.m)

年份 地区	Year Region	施工面积 Floor Space of under Construction	#住宅 Residential Buildings	竣工面积 Floor Space of Completed	#住宅 Residential Buildings
	1978	18484.90	7314.33	9010.92	3752.47
	1980	27537.60	14817.40	14499.90	8230.30
	1985	37029.20	18893.90	17161.20	9565.10
	1989	24744.18	9749.94	11611.55	5064.20
	1990	23236.54	9259.90	11245.93	4824.78
	1991	27262.61	11309.23	12604.48	5687.92
	1992	32709.19	13399.25	15133.72	6919.15
	1993	39535.76	15016.40	17070.05	7993.44
	1994	42749.88	16981.97	18644.05	8955.12
	1995	41948.29	16739.06	19929.32	9249.25
	1996	(43661.23)	(17269.40)	(21256.63)	(9824.79)
		42786.07	16974.08	20544.83	9589.36
	1997	44206.26	18065.42	21439.12	10091.49
	1998	52023.11	24529.90	24685.04	12552.44
	1999	52833.80	25642.02	28620.79	16033.23
	2000	50968.27	21559.64	26292.93	13145.97
	2001	51787.04	19824.75	25471.80	11653.52
	2002	58144.95	18650.80	27395.33	10417.13
	2003	69931.51	20458.60	29473.65	10155.82
北京	Beijing	1965.60	614.77	566.87	225.72
天津	Tianjin	841.00	77.14	255.47	19.59
河北	Hebei	3253.66	1218.56	1466.41	509.50
山西	Shanxi	1329.18	569.79	646.46	299.32
内蒙古	Inner Mongolia	1929.75	651.79	1091.66	439.45
辽宁	Liaoning	1987.58	527.91	948.66	350.88
吉林	Jilin	1645.26	542.32	897.53	305.30
黑龙江	Heilongjiang	2298.53	782.65	1292.34	559.00
上海	Shanghai	1156.61	75.46	354.01	26.74
江苏	Jiangsu	3570.89	791.18	1472.62	262.68
浙江	Zhejiang	5295.38	792.82	1766.22	293.29
安徽	Anhui	2121.23	721.29	913.71	278.94
福建	Fujian	1349.37	186.56	566.59	88.01
江西	Jiangxi	1614.56	343.76	824.14	246.00
山东	Shandong	5926.95	1530.26	2381.84	620.92
河南	Henan	3872.56	1092.88	1586.93	540.59
湖北	Hubei	2176.83	679.31	1221.59	473.27
湖南	Hunan	2535.49	699.17	987.49	314.90
广东	Guangdong	6656.95	665.17	1705.17	269.01
广西	Guangxi	1477.81	498.70	600.06	245.96
海南	Hainan	586.42	178.98	224.52	113.33
重庆	Chongqing	2515.49	1196.58	1319.86	684.47
四川	Sichuan	3413.03	1315.99	1332.14	601.22
贵州	Guizhou	1160.25	413.09	538.44	210.12
云南	Yunnan	1903.87	1028.30	777.56	366.44
西藏	Tibet	270.80	78.20	171.32	35.40
陕西	Shaanxi	2651.87	1204.80	1249.12	599.93
甘肃	Gansu	1453.27	765.51	507.07	287.05
青海	Qinghai	326.85	110.23	119.70	39.57
宁夏	Ningxia	609.97	263.27	312.49	162.47
新疆	Xinjiang	1912.40	833.47	1287.68	678.57
不分地区	Not Classified by Region	122.08	8.67	87.97	8.17

6-14 按行业分基本建设新增固定资产

Newly Increased Fixed Assets though Capital Construction by Sector

单位: 亿元 (100 million yuan)

年份 Year	合计 Total	农、林、牧、渔业 Farming, Forestry, Animal Husbandry and Fishery	采掘业 Mining and Quarrying	制造业 Manufacturing	电力、煤气及水的生产和供应业 Production and Supply of Electric Power, Gas and Water	建筑业 Construction	地质勘查业水利管理业 Geological Prospecting and Water Conservancy	交通运输仓储和邮电通信业 Transport, Storage, Postal and Telecom-munication Services
1985	733.16	11.91	68.04	133.16	86.13	14.01	23.69	132.73
1989	1179.03	15.20	169.49	240.59	194.25	12.41	26.48	129.60
1990	1362.61	18.09	203.36	295.31	238.78	9.54	30.92	160.23
1991	1498.73	22.41	163.33	343.67	317.10	10.01	34.96	203.15
1992	1975.00	27.30	195.59	381.85	398.90	20.86	47.91	261.00
1993	2758.93	34.83	193.82	588.30	452.20	62.17	54.01	491.22
1994	3729.78	34.85	212.79	757.62	667.43	65.50	76.55	710.00
1995	4712.67	46.90	285.53	878.89	816.90	67.80	110.14	1099.05
1996	(6168.14)	(63.08)	(281.64)	(1361.73)	(1029.85)	(100.12)	(109.91)	(1414.87)
	6129.65	61.30	281.46	1360.26	1029.04	99.81	109.38	1412.52
1997	7443.15	82.53	480.14	1407.61	1207.22	125.87	146.28	1809.58
1998	8499.82	109.64	348.18	1272.65	1774.65	115.17	200.50	1784.80
1999	9519.30	208.99	451.96	1327.96	1719.39	131.55	308.71	2090.66
2000	10431.66	212.98	510.91	1028.28	2092.12	111.82	378.08	2897.78
2001	10112.67	189.64	507.22	1069.96	1650.88	146.69	328.34	2654.08
2002	11989.69	238.99	483.40	1418.11	1802.77	177.95	411.14	3393.80

6-14 续表 continued

年份 Year	批发零售贸易和餐饮业 Wholesale & Retail Trade and Catering Services	金融、保险业 Banking and Insurance	房地产业 Real Estate	社会服务业 Social Services	卫生体育和社会福利业 Health Care, Sports and Social Welfare	教育、文化艺术和广播电影电视业 Education, Culture, Arts, Radio, Film and Television	科学研究和综合技术服务业 Scientific Research and Polytech-nical Services	国家机关、政党机关和社会团体 Governments, Parties and Social Organizations	其他行业 Others
1985	24.77	4.54	43.01	36.12	15.49	57.60	13.70	34.40	33.85
1989	37.41	14.61	38.08	34.97	22.65	81.96	17.46	54.18	89.70
1990	32.43	12.59	13.28	46.66	40.08	98.25	21.61	57.55	83.93
1991	48.44	15.61	13.53	77.73	30.11	102.14	19.75	68.16	28.63
1992	79.18	24.15	30.12	100.33	35.02	120.40	18.79	102.34	131.27
1993	124.63	42.93	65.41	172.16	42.14	148.84	27.19	195.29	63.81
1994	162.96	63.86	122.38	228.69	64.90	191.57	35.25	264.38	71.06
1995	162.44	76.75	84.06	272.23	69.16	275.97	49.75	355.78	61.33
1996	(190.09)	(100.10)	(100.65)	(356.06)	(98.65)	(356.06)	(43.86)	(449.13)	(112.34)
	186.58	99.02	100.47	354.84	96.22	344.37	43.42	438.86	112.10
1997	219.70	114.17	100.77	479.43	111.95	418.11	50.00	543.39	146.40
1998	256.88	152.56	135.68	826.72	132.22	501.52	57.22	717.21	114.22
1999	231.85	118.82	124.07	1006.28	168.03	619.58	73.95	833.86	103.65
2000	262.26	86.98	84.04	986.56	163.72	685.47	64.38	755.48	110.81
2001	252.76	82.03	107.87	1170.50	202.83	724.83	72.06	813.11	139.87
2002	275.50	46.65	121.32	1436.87	229.83	812.97	93.39	923.74	123.24

6-15 各地区按行业分基本建设新增固定资产（2003年）

Newly Increased Fixed Assets through Capital Construction by Setor (2003)

单位: 亿元　　　　(100 million yuan)

地区	Region	合计 Total	农、林、牧、渔业 Agriculture, Forestry, Animal Husbandry and Fishing	采矿业 Mining	制造业 Manufacturing	电力、燃气及水的生产和供应业 Production and Distribution of Electricity, Gas and Water	建筑业 Construction	交通运输、仓储和邮政业 Transport, Storage and Post
全国总计	**National Total**	**13604.54**	**294.11**	**706.39**	**2050.27**	**1731.01**	**235.15**	**2945.11**
北京	Beijing	358.54	2.76	0.14	26.33	52.39	4.42	9.71
天津	Tianjin	284.09	1.69	68.48	22.51	16.53	0.54	74.44
河北	Hebei	479.89	17.80	4.60	116.81	39.89	15.25	62.52
山西	Shanxi	317.56	5.46	16.96	67.85	41.69	1.04	113.68
内蒙古	Inner Mongolia	508.31	26.87	17.50	82.46	124.36	1.48	92.61
辽宁	Liaoning	440.78	11.91	31.98	79.41	28.54	4.03	43.71
吉林	Jilin	283.35	7.51	17.06	46.70	22.03	15.32	32.59
黑龙江	Heilongjiang	427.30	21.23	88.71	47.04	30.34	15.66	36.62
上海	Shanghai	408.89	0.86		133.27	38.55	0.10	35.94
江苏	Jiangsu	1038.38	7.19	3.16	189.86	125.54	4.04	137.57
浙江	Zhejiang	865.35	3.05	0.02	120.22	49.36	10.34	198.82
安徽	Anhui	245.41	5.34	4.68	39.68	9.92	20.58	29.08
福建	Fujian	207.76	2.78	0.15	33.63	28.40	2.48	36.93
江西	Jiangxi	377.84	3.67	8.72	50.41	51.66	0.19	109.45
山东	Shandong	1131.67	11.76	114.38	317.37	129.55	37.15	138.68
河南	Henan	539.95	13.91	17.40	99.98	73.09	3.41	131.63
湖北	Hubei	675.49	15.07	7.68	93.68	238.13	6.80	85.16
湖南	Hunan	414.11	5.99	0.93	23.58	74.17	1.43	140.79
广东	Guangdong	852.72	6.40	12.45	189.71	129.65	42.90	183.79
广西	Guangxi	289.12	4.86	2.84	39.13	50.87	0.95	87.26
海南	Hainan	118.37	11.07	0.94	17.89	9.02	3.38	31.03
重庆	Chongqing	283.51	8.67	1.23	34.17	22.38	19.01	41.37
四川	Sichuan	493.88	9.25	2.78	47.38	66.20	1.33	122.32
贵州	Guizhou	206.84	1.93	1.35	7.16	41.03	0.44	62.76
云南	Yunnan	358.60	8.68	5.62	16.25	63.18	0.42	142.56
西藏	Tibet	78.99	3.97		1.15	5.35	0.78	33.08
陕西	Shaanxi	369.95	18.97	35.59	49.97	35.72	3.27	42.01
甘肃	Gansu	195.51	6.68	6.69	16.30	32.71	6.81	55.12
青海	Qinghai	60.89	8.46	1.75	4.67	5.12	5.85	2.54
宁夏	Ningxia	106.76	5.03	0.20	8.18	29.55	2.31	0.31
新疆	Xinjiang	442.92	35.31	111.21	27.53	45.85	3.46	52.98
不分地区	Not Classified by Region	741.85		121.17		20.24		578.04

6-15 续表 1 continued

单位: 亿元 (100 million yuan)

地 区 Region	信息传输、计算机服务和软件业 Information Transmission, Computer Service and Software	批发和零售业 Wholesale and Retail Trade	住宿和餐饮业 Hotel and Restaurants	金融业 Financial Intermediation	房地产业 Real Estate	租赁和商务服务业 Leasing and Business Services	科学研究、技术服务和地质勘查业 Scientific Research, Technical Services, and Geological Prospecting
全国总计 National Total	**332.79**	**333.29**	**119.42**	**46.44**	**164.25**	**141.06**	**125.96**
北 京 Beijing	9.72	4.65	4.64	0.25	1.65	22.15	12.51
天 津 Tianjin	6.92	5.63	0.44	0.36	6.80	0.25	0.44
河 北 Hebei	8.82	22.71	4.83	1.61	18.35	7.95	16.66
山 西 Shanxi	3.33	5.16	1.14	1.19	0.49	0.09	1.23
内蒙古 Inner Mongolia	3.98	10.02	3.07	1.82	5.53	1.01	2.22
辽 宁 Liaoning	18.11	16.63	9.13	3.86	5.85	5.15	6.00
吉 林 Jilin	10.19	11.04	3.61	1.37	1.58	1.26	3.03
黑龙江 Heilongjiang	14.91	13.23	1.91	2.87	3.26	12.92	4.62
上 海 Shanghai	1.80	1.74	8.46		16.70	0.45	4.14
江 苏 Jiangsu	24.22	17.01	6.01	0.95	2.01	6.92	12.27
浙 江 Zhejiang	17.33	15.19	7.56	0.33	10.71	13.68	4.01
安 徽 Anhui	3.82	9.89	3.09	0.68	6.81	1.66	1.39
福 建 Fujian	6.70	4.64	1.22	0.42	1.80	2.27	1.67
江 西 Jiangxi	7.38	9.86	5.20	2.05	2.01	0.86	0.97
山 东 Shandong	11.89	43.84	5.84	5.57	15.08	8.15	8.40
河 南 Henan	27.33	11.29	2.17	2.40	2.31	1.83	4.32
湖 北 Hubei	11.23	21.12	9.10	1.24	3.80	9.25	3.98
湖 南 Hunan	5.02	16.49	4.75	1.34	1.71	4.95	1.07
广 东 Guangdong	28.59	12.69	4.53	0.99	8.13	11.79	12.94
广 西 Guangxi	14.08	4.87	2.54	0.72	0.74	8.87	0.76
海 南 Hainan	1.75	0.61	10.85	0.13	2.12	3.49	0.49
重 庆 Chongqing	6.67	6.80	2.53	1.39	11.73	1.22	0.40
四 川 Sichuan	29.33	8.24	3.99	4.95	9.25	2.22	8.01
贵 州 Guizhou	8.04	2.31	0.44	2.31	2.72	0.32	0.66
云 南 Yunnan	8.58	6.54	2.03	1.98	3.30	0.88	1.67
西 藏 Tibet	1.27	1.16	0.68	0.04	0.03	0.02	1.54
陕 西 Shaanxi	9.13	15.86	3.96	2.09	5.07	7.97	5.92
甘 肃 Gansu	3.14	5.02	0.71	0.48	1.87	2.20	0.50
青 海 Qinghai	3.98	1.98	0.57	0.20	0.19	0.08	0.27
宁 夏 Ningxia	1.92	5.04	0.37	0.52	9.58	0.11	0.54
新 疆 Xinjiang	23.61	22.01	4.08	2.34	3.08	1.12	3.34
不分地区 Not Classified by Region							

6-15 续表 2 continued

单位: 亿元 (100 million yuan)

地区	Region	水利、环境和公共设施管理业 Water Management of Conservancy, Environment and Public Facilities	居民服务和其他服务业 Services to Households and Other Services	教育 Education	卫生、社会保障和社会福利业 Health, Social Securities and Social Welfare	文化、体育和娱乐业 Culture, Sports and Entertainment	公共管理和社会组织 Public Management and Social Organization	国际组织 International Organizations
全国总计	**National Total**	**2004.15**	**28.71**	**916.53**	**211.10**	**186.22**	**1032.27**	**0.29**
北京	Beijing	109.93	0.15	39.46	4.98	1.87	50.82	
天津	Tianjin	41.15	0.00	22.59	3.41	1.92	9.99	
河北	Hebei	47.53	1.43	32.26	7.19	6.19	47.49	
山西	Shanxi	26.71	0.04	15.87	3.52	2.82	9.30	
内蒙古	Inner Mongolia	77.27	1.27	15.06	5.03	2.53	34.24	
辽宁	Liaoning	45.32	0.80	32.62	4.75	10.26	82.72	
吉林	Jilin	38.07	0.55	25.66	4.77	2.38	38.63	
黑龙江	Heilongjiang	35.91	0.63	35.05	3.97	5.00	53.42	
上海	Shanghai	133.25		18.34	7.03	2.55	5.71	
江苏	Jiangsu	322.27	1.11	91.94	17.31	18.37	50.63	
浙江	Zhejiang	214.77	8.74	106.07	19.96	14.93	50.25	
安徽	Anhui	26.23	0.39	29.24	3.71	2.06	47.16	
福建	Fujian	28.93	0.42	20.12	7.41	2.12	25.68	
江西	Jiangxi	56.57	0.54	16.21	19.27	3.08	29.72	
山东	Shandong	80.78	2.12	63.19	15.74	17.71	104.48	
河南	Henan	61.64	1.19	33.33	7.38	8.37	36.97	
湖北	Hubei	71.08	1.08	39.29	12.12	5.73	39.93	
湖南	Hunan	51.43	0.97	25.93	6.02	9.81	37.48	0.26
广东	Guangdong	79.56	2.13	58.95	7.83	16.08	43.59	
广西	Guangxi	35.97	1.68	16.13	4.78	2.02	10.06	
海南	Hainan	9.66	0.01	3.87	0.96	5.99	5.12	
重庆	Chongqing	55.74	0.68	23.96	7.00	5.53	33.06	
四川	Sichuan	98.07	0.98	41.87	8.04	9.76	19.92	
贵州	Guizhou	40.69	0.27	12.49	5.75	5.55	10.60	
云南	Yunnan	35.36	0.23	16.09	4.66	8.71	31.86	
西藏	Tibet	10.77	0.09	4.03	1.90	1.44	11.69	
陕西	Shaanxi	31.31	0.33	40.44	4.83	3.96	53.52	0.03
甘肃	Gansu	18.38	0.23	10.46	1.54	2.04	24.61	
青海	Qinghai	14.14	0.07	1.70	1.19	0.44	7.69	
宁夏	Ningxia	31.52	0.31	3.77	1.27	2.35	3.89	
新疆	Xinjiang	51.72	0.29	20.53	7.80	4.65	22.04	
不分地区	Not Classified by Region	22.40						

6-16 基本建设施工、投产项目个数和新增固定资产

Number of Capital Construction Projects under Construction and Put into Use and Newly Increased Fixed Assets

年份 地区	Year Region	施工项目(个) Number of Projects under Construction (unit)	全部建成投产项目(个) Number of Projects Completed and Put into Use (unit)	项目建成投产率(%) Rate of Projects Completed and Put into Use (%)	新增固定资产(亿元) Newly Increased Fixed Assets (100 million yuan)	固定资产交付使用率(%) Rate of Fixed Assets Put into Use (%)
1978		45261	11762	26.0	372.30	74.3
1980		67618	24823	36.7	442.06	79.1
1985		87766	44477	50.7	733.16	68.2
1989		66382	35370	53.3	1179.03	76.0
1990		67842	36502	53.8	1362.61	80.0
1991		77704	41783	53.8	1498.73	70.8
1992		90609	50633	55.9	1975.00	65.6
1993		90954	51886	57.0	2758.93	59.8
1994		88841	49021	55.2	3729.78	57.9
1995		88685	50512	57.0	4712.67	63.7
1996		(93997)	(55434)	(59.0)	(6168.14)	(71.6)
		77954	42008	53.9	6129.65	71.5
1997		84480	48102	56.9	7443.15	75.1
1998		99665	54950	55.1	8499.82	71.3
1999		97084	57090	58.8	9519.30	76.4
2000		91252	52645	57.7	10431.66	77.7
2001		91316	51042	55.9	10112.67	68.2
2002		97488	52465	53.8	11989.69	67.9
2003		111290	56784	51.0	13604.54	59.4
北　京	Beijing	1046	360	34.4	358.54	64.2
天　津	Tianjin	835	423	50.7	284.09	56.7
河　北	Hebei	4959	2655	53.5	479.89	56.7
山　西	Shanxi	2260	1126	49.8	317.56	63.7
内蒙古	Inner Mongolia	4385	2942	67.1	508.31	67.7
辽　宁	Liaoning	2640	1458	55.2	440.78	64.5
吉　林	Jilin	1971	1216	61.7	283.35	65.3
黑龙江	Heilongjiang	3126	2170	69.4	427.30	72.0
上　海	Shanghai	1261	452	35.8	408.89	45.5
江　苏	Jiangsu	4819	2713	56.3	1038.38	54.1
浙　江	Zhejiang	5995	2302	38.4	865.35	52.6
安　徽	Anhui	3584	1459	40.7	245.41	44.6
福　建	Fujian	2315	777	33.6	207.76	44.0
江　西	Jiangxi	3368	1799	53.4	377.84	66.7
山　东	Shandong	7412	3148	42.5	1131.67	63.0
河　南	Henan	5179	2750	53.1	539.95	55.6
湖　北	Hubei	4959	3245	65.4	675.49	81.5
湖　南	Hunan	4441	2274	51.2	414.11	69.0
广　东	Guangdong	6173	2004	32.5	852.72	46.6
广　西	Guangxi	6071	2962	48.8	289.12	62.7
海　南	Hainan	973	529	54.4	118.37	65.9
重　庆	Chongqing	3335	1890	56.7	283.51	49.9
四　川	Sichuan	5953	2644	44.4	493.88	52.0
贵　州	Guizhou	3200	1752	54.8	206.84	54.4
云　南	Yunnan	4467	2306	51.6	358.60	72.7
西　藏	Tibet	1918	1366	71.2	78.99	66.8
陕　西	Shaanxi	3867	2060	53.3	369.95	59.0
甘　肃	Gansu	3521	1602	45.5	195.51	63.6
青　海	Qinghai	1971	1083	54.9	60.89	37.0
宁　夏	Ningxia	1179	666	56.5	106.76	65.6
新　疆	Xinjiang	4037	2646	65.5	442.92	71.3
不分地区	Not Classified by Region	70	5	7.1	741.85	79.2

6-17 按行业分基本建设施工、投产项目个数（2003年）

Number of Capital Construction Projects under Construction and Put into Use by Sector (2003)

单位: 亿元 (100 million yuan)

行业	Sector	施工项目（个）Number of Projects under Construction (unit)	#新开工 Started This Year	全部建成投产项目（个）Number of Projects Completed and Put into Use (unit)	项目建成投产率(%) Rate of Projects Completed & Put into Use (%)
全国总计	**National Total**	**111290**	**77528**	**56784**	**51.0**
农、林、牧、渔业	**Agriculture, Forestry, Animal Husbandry and Fishing**	**5676**	**4503**	**3593**	**63.3**
农业	Agriculture	1503	1196	938	62.4
林业	Forestry	1469	1169	991	67.5
畜牧业	Animal Husbandry	866	716	520	60.0
渔业	Fishing	151	111	73	48.3
农、林、牧、渔服务业	Service Activities for Agriculture, Forestry, Animal Husbandry and Fishing	1687	1311	1071	63.5
采矿业	**Mining**	**1142**	**832**	**560**	**49.0**
煤炭开采和洗选业	Mining and Washing of Coal	483	295	202	41.8
石油和天然气开采业	Extraction of Petroleum and Natural Gas	110	76	54	49.1
黑色金属矿采选业	Mining and Processing of Ferrous Metal Ores	121	99	61	50.4
有色金属矿采选业	Mining and Processing of Non-Ferrous Metal Ores	161	124	85	52.8
非金属矿采选业	Mining and Processing of Nonmetal Ores	256	228	153	59.8
其他采矿业	Mining of Other Ores	11	10	5	45.5
制造业	**Manufacturing**	**17243**	**13150**	**7511**	**43.6**
农副食品加工业	Processing of Food from Agricultural Products	1147	947	587	51.2
食品制造业	Manufacture of Foods	708	551	332	46.9
饮料制造业	Manufacture of Beverages	419	320	217	51.8
烟草制品业	Manufacture of Tobacco	64	32	32	50.0
纺织业	Manufacture of Textile	1054	860	504	47.8
纺织服装、鞋、帽制造业	Manufacture of Textile Wearing Apparel, Footware, and Caps	564	418	252	44.7
皮革毛皮羽毛(绒)及其制品业	Manufacture of Leather, Fur, Feather and Related Products	274	195	116	42.3
木材加工及木竹藤棕草制品业	Processing of Timber, Manufacture of Wood, Bamboo, Rattan, Palm, and Straw Products	449	385	254	56.6
家具制造业	Manufacture of Furniture	283	230	117	41.3
造纸及纸制品业	Manufacture of Paper and Paper Products	382	317	194	50.8
印刷业和记录媒介的复制	Printing,Reproduction of Recording Media	290	220	127	43.8
文教体育用品制造业	Manufacture of Articles For Culture, Education and Sport Activity	140	106	49	35.0
石油加工、炼焦及核燃料加工业	Processing of Petroleum, Coking, Processing of Nuclear Fuel	255	205	114	44.7
化学原料及化学制品制造业	Manufacture of Raw Chemical Materials and Chemical Products	1300	964	563	43.3
医药制造业	Manufacture of Medicines	823	568	248	30.1
化学纤维制造业	Manufacture of Chemical Fibers	62	48	25	40.3
橡胶制品业	Manufacture of Rubber	164	130	77	47.0
塑料制品业	Manufacture of Plastics	696	559	312	44.8
非金属矿物制品业	Manufacture of Non-metallic Mineral Products	1483	1215	742	50.0
黑色金属冶炼及压延加工业	Smelting and Pressing of Ferrous Metals	618	522	238	38.5
有色金属冶炼及压延加工业	Smelting and Pressing of Non-ferrous Metals	285	205	120	42.1
金属制品业	Manufacture of Metal Products	854	696	350	41.0
通用设备制造业	Manufacture of General Purpose Machinery	947	725	461	48.7
专用设备制造业	Manufacture of Special Purpose Machinery	889	656	375	42.2
交通运输设备制造业	Manufacture of Transport Equipment	897	617	358	39.9
电气机械及器材制造业	Manufacture of Electrical Machinery and Equipment	719	524	259	36.0
通信设备、计算机及其他电子设备制造业	Manufacture of Communication Equipment, Computers and Other Electronic Equipment	762	467	244	32.0
仪器仪表文化办公用机械制造业	Manufacture of Measuring Instruments and Machinery for Cultural Activity and Office Work	253	146	83	32.8
工艺品及其他制造业	Manufacture of Artwork and Other Manufacturing	441	308	156	35.4
废弃资源和废旧材料回收加工业	Recycling and Disposal of Waste	21	14	5	23.8
电力燃气水的生产供应业	**Production and Distribution of Electricity, Gas and Water**	**7065**	**4188**	**2986**	**42.3**
电力、热力的生产和供应业	Production and Distribution of Electric Power and Heat Power	4758	2879	2070	43.5
燃气生产和供应业	Production and Distribution of Gas	463	255	136	29.4
水的生产和供应业	Production and Distribution of Water	1844	1054	780	42.3
建筑业	**Construction**	**2761**	**2043**	**1420**	**51.4**
房屋和土木工程建筑业	Construction of Buildings and Civil Engineering	2563	1893	1327	51.8
建筑安装业	Building Installation	82	58	43	52.4
建筑装饰业	Buidling Decoration	39	29	17	43.6
其他建筑业	Other Construction	77	63	33	42.9

6-17 续表 continued

单位: 亿元 (100 million yuan)

行业	Sector	施工项目(个) Number of Projects under Construc-tion (unit)	# 新开工 Started This Year	全部建成投产项目(个) Number of Projects Completed and Put into Use (unit)	项目建成投产率(%) Rate of Projects Completed & Put into Use (%)
交通运输、仓储和邮政业	**Transport, Storage and Post**	**10599**	**7052**	**5174**	**48.8**
铁路运输业	Railway Transport	184	94	65	35.3
道路运输业	Road Transport	8065	5591	4008	49.7
城市公共交通业	Urban Public Transport	634	379	265	41.8
水上运输业	Water Transport	364	162	110	30.2
航空运输业	Air Transport	125	49	34	27.2
管道运输业	Transport Via Pipelines	25	14	4	16.0
装卸搬运和其他运输服务业	Loading, Unloading and Other Transport Services	161	133	98	60.9
仓储业	Storage	696	444	403	57.9
邮政业	Post	345	186	187	54.2
信息传输、计算机服务和软件业	**Information Transmission, Computer Services and Software**	**2250**	**1539**	**1314**	**58.4**
电信和其他信息传输服务业	Telecommunications and Other Information Transmission Services	2133	1468	1276	59.8
计算机服务业	Computer Services	49	29	18	36.7
软件业	Software	68	42	20	29.4
批发和零售业	**Wholesale and Retail Trade**	**4624**	**3395**	**2647**	**57.2**
批发业	Wholesale Trade	2171	1562	1202	55.4
零售业	Retail Trade	2453	1833	1445	58.9
住宿和餐饮业	**Hotel and Restaurants**	**1539**	**1094**	**794**	**51.6**
住宿业	Hotels	1097	731	521	47.5
餐饮业	Restaurants	442	363	273	61.8
金融业	**Financial Intermediation**	**947**	**635**	**570**	**60.2**
银行业	Banks	811	548	485	59.8
证券业	Security Activities	7	4	4	57.1
保险业	Insurance	104	60	69	66.3
其他金融活动	Other Financial Activities	25	23	12	48.0
房地产业	**Real Estate**	**1626**	**1107**	**711**	**43.7**
租赁和商务服务业	**Leasing and Business Services**	**973**	**654**	**409**	**42.0**
租赁业	Leasing	19	16	9	47.4
商务服务业	Business Services	954	638	400	41.9
科学研究、技术服务和地质勘查业	**Scientific Research, Technical Service and Geologic Prospecting Geologic Prospecting**	**1572**	**944**	**653**	**41.5**
研究与试验发展	Research and Experimental Development	687	359	266	38.7
专业技术服务业	Professional Technical Services	532	337	225	42.3
科技交流和推广服务业	Services of Science and Technology Exchanges and Promotion	198	142	77	38.9
地质勘查业	Geologic Prospecting	155	106	85	54.8
水利、环境和公共设施管理业	**Management of Water Conservancy, Environment and Public Facilities**	**15591**	**10545**	**7388**	**47.4**
水利管理业	Management of Water Conservancy	4685	3053	2381	50.8
环境管理业	Environmental Management	1122	665	450	40.1
公共设施管理业	Management of Public Facilities	9784	6827	4557	46.6
居民服务和其他服务业	**Services to Households and Other Services**	**477**	**326**	**244**	**51.2**
居民服务业	Services to Households	385	251	200	51.9
其他服务业	Other Services	92	75	44	47.8
教育	**Education**	**13347**	**9320**	**8248**	**61.8**
卫生、社会保障和社会福利业	**Health, Social Security and Social Welfare**	**3997**	**2664**	**2066**	**51.7**
卫生	Health	3509	2314	1786	50.9
社会保障业	Social Security	65	43	45	69.2
社会福利业	Social Welfare	423	307	235	55.6
文化、体育和娱乐业	**Culture, Sports and Entertainment**	**2534**	**1569**	**1107**	**43.7**
新闻出版业	Journalism and Publishing Activities	99	59	44	44.4
广播、电视、电影和音像业	Broadcasting, Movies, Televisions and Audiovisual Activities	607	339	305	50.2
文化艺术业	Cultural and Art Activities	976	620	419	42.9
体育	Sports Activities	418	231	156	37.3
娱乐业	Entertainment	434	320	183	42.2
公共管理和社会组织	**Public Management and Social Organization**	**17325**	**11967**	**9388**	**54.2**
中国共产党机关	Organs of Communist Party of China	356	211	168	47.2
国家机构	Government Agencies	16121	11138	8726	54.1
人民政协和民主党派	People's Political Consultative Conference and Democratic Parties	85	54	53	62.4
群众团体、社会团体和宗教组织	Non-Governmental Institutions, Social Organizaitons and Religion Organizations	325	208	178	54.8
基层群众自治组织	Grass Roots Self-governing Organizations	438	356	263	60.0
国际组织	**International Organizations**	**2**	**1**	**1**	**50.0**

6-18 按行业分基本建设投资和新增固定资产（2003年）

Investment in Capital Construction and Newly Increased Fixed Assets by Sector (2003)

行业	Sector	投资额(亿元) Investment (100 million yuan)	新增固定资产(亿元) Newly Increased Fixed Assets (100 million yuan)	固定资产交付使用率(%) Rate of Fixed Assets Put into Use (%)
全国总计	**National Total**	**22908.60**	**13604.54**	**59.4**
农、林、牧、渔业	**Agriculture, Forestry, Animal Husbandry and Fishing**	**416.78**	**294.11**	**70.6**
农业	Agriculture	109.49	80.08	73.1
林业	Forestry	126.53	85.82	67.8
畜牧业	Animal Husbandry	63.37	44.22	69.8
渔业	Fishing	13.81	9.38	67.9
农、林、牧、渔服务业	Service Activities for Agriculture, Forestry, Animal Husbandry and Fishing	103.58	74.62	72.0
采矿业	**Mining**	**894.15**	**706.39**	**79.0**
煤炭开采和洗选业	Mining and Washing of Coal	193.10	140.21	72.6
石油和天然气开采业	Extraction of Petroleum and Natural Gas	639.81	522.61	81.7
黑色金属矿采选业	Mining and Processing of Ferrous Metal Ores	15.35	9.84	64.1
有色金属矿采选业	Mining and Processing of Non-Ferrous Metal Ores	27.32	21.51	78.7
非金属矿采选业	Mining and Processing of Nonmetal Ores	17.26	11.93	69.2
其他采矿业	Mining of Other Ores	1.31	0.30	22.7
制造业	**Manufacturing**	**3639.36**	**2050.27**	**56.3**
农副食品加工业	Processing of Food from Agricultural Products	148.94	88.68	59.5
食品制造业	Manufacture of Foods	99.32	56.99	57.4
饮料制造业	Manufacture of Beverages	66.98	50.15	74.9
烟草制品业	Manufacture of Tobacco	11.00	9.60	87.3
纺织业	Manufacture of Textile	177.42	111.10	62.6
纺织服装、鞋、帽制造业	Manufacture of Textile Wearing Apparel, Footware, and Caps	74.18	43.00	58.0
皮革毛皮羽毛(绒)及其制品业	Manufacture of Leather, Fur, Feather and Related Products	38.34	23.04	60.1
木材加工及木竹藤棕草制品业	Processing of Timber, Manufacture of Wood, Bamboo, Rattan, Palm, and Straw Products	37.87	24.46	64.6
家具制造业	Manufacture of Furniture	34.09	16.29	47.8
造纸及纸制品业	Manufacture of Paper and Paper Products	87.04	54.91	63.1
印刷业和记录媒介的复制	Printing,Reproduction of Recording Media	37.62	22.59	60.1
文教体育用品制造业	Manufacture of Articles For Culture, Education and Sport Activity	14.35	7.33	51.1
石油加工、炼焦及核燃料加工业	Processing of Petroleum, Coking, Processing of Nuclear Fuel	82.75	52.90	63.9
化学原料及化学制品制造业	Manufacture of Raw Chemical Materials and Chemical Products	503.10	161.54	32.1
医药制造业	Manufacture of Medicines	161.16	82.40	51.1
化学纤维制造业	Manufacture of Chemical Fibers	31.69	23.93	75.5
橡胶制品业	Manufacture of Rubber	35.49	16.07	45.3
塑料制品业	Manufacture of Plastics	86.58	53.23	61.5
非金属矿物制品业	Manufacture of Non-metallic Mineral Products	253.48	153.44	60.5
黑色金属冶炼及压延加工业	Smelting and Pressing of Ferrous Metals	318.39	168.58	52.9
有色金属冶炼及压延加工业	Smelting and Pressing of Non-ferrous Metals	183.99	131.74	71.6
金属制品业	Manufacture of Metal Products	105.82	62.78	59.3
通用设备制造业	Manufacture of General Purpose Machinery	110.53	66.26	59.9
专用设备制造业	Manufacture of Special Purpose Machinery	132.43	88.69	67.0
交通运输设备制造业	Manufacture of Transport Equipment	187.47	117.70	62.8
电气机械及器材制造业	Manufacture of Electrical Machinery and Equipment	98.67	56.50	57.3
通信设备、计算机及其他电子设备制造业	Manufacture of Communication Equipment, Computers and Other Electronic Equipment	338.87	226.96	67.0
仪器仪表文化办公用机械制造业	Manufacture of Measuring Instruments and Machinery for Cultural Activity and Office Work	44.23	27.27	61.6
工艺品及其他制造业	Manufacture of Artwork and Other Manufacturing	135.43	51.22	37.8
废弃资源和废旧材料回收加工业	Recycling and Disposal of Waste	2.12	0.93	43.9
电力燃气水的生产供应业	**Production and Distribution of Electricity, Gas and Water**	**2964.73**	**1731.01**	**58.4**
电力、热力的生产和供应业	Production and Distribution of Electric Power and Heat Power	2567.09	1499.97	58.4
燃气生产和供应业	Production and Distribution of Gas	114.30	79.62	69.7
水的生产和供应业	Production and Distribution of Water	283.35	151.42	53.4
建筑业	**Construction**	**381.41**	**235.15**	**61.7**
房屋和土木工程建筑业	Construction of Buildings and Civil Engineering	350.55	218.76	62.4
建筑安装业	Building Installation	12.76	7.09	55.6
建筑装饰业	Buidling Decoration	6.00	3.38	56.3
其他建筑业	Other Construction	12.09	5.93	49.0

6-18 续表 continued

行业	Sector	投资额（亿元） Investment (100 million yuan)	新增固定资产（亿元） Newly Increased Fixed Assets (100 million yuan)	固定资产交付使用率（%） Rate of Fixed Assets Put into Use (%)
交通运输、仓储和邮政业	**Transport, Storage and Post**	**4892.71**	**2945.11**	**60.2**
铁路运输业	Railway Transport	616.38	495.20	80.3
道路运输业	Road Transport	3162.01	1854.52	58.7
城市公共交通业	Urban Public Transport	360.13	155.85	43.3
水上运输业	Water Transport	299.11	129.89	43.4
航空运输业	Air Transport	180.73	98.22	54.3
管道运输业	Transport Via Pipelines	139.52	118.52	85.0
装卸搬运和其他运输服务业	Loading, Unloading and Other Transport Services	29.36	14.64	49.9
仓储业	Storage	84.88	59.89	70.6
邮政业	Post	20.57	18.37	89.3
信息传输、计算机服务和软件业	**Information Transmission, Computer Services and Software**	**506.93**	**332.79**	**65.6**
电信和其他信息传输服务业	Telecommunications and Other Information Transmission Services	479.07	316.53	66.1
计算机服务业	Computer Services	5.13	3.57	69.5
软件业	Software	22.74	12.70	55.8
批发和零售业	**Wholesale and Retail Trade**	**516.58**	**333.29**	**64.5**
批发业	Wholesale Trade	204.28	138.80	67.9
零售业	Retail Trade	312.30	194.49	62.3
住宿和餐饮业	**Hotel and Restaurants**	**205.53**	**119.42**	**58.1**
住宿业	Hotels	163.75	94.58	57.8
餐饮业	Restaurants	41.78	24.84	59.5
金融业	**Financial Intermediation**	**58.24**	**46.44**	**79.8**
银行业	Banks	49.48	37.70	76.2
证券业	Security Activities	0.79	0.51	63.9
保险业	Insurance	4.70	7.82	166.3
其他金融活动	Other Financial Activities	3.27	0.41	12.7
房地产业	**Real Estate**	**326.27**	**164.25**	**50.3**
租赁和商务服务业	**Leasing and Business Services**	**252.58**	**141.06**	**55.8**
租赁业	Leasing	0.69	0.58	84.7
商务服务业	Business Services	251.89	140.48	55.8
科学研究、技术服务和地质勘查业	**Scientific Research, Technical Service and Geologic Prospecting Geologic Prospecting**	**244.29**	**125.96**	**51.6**
研究与试验发展	Research and Experimental Development	111.06	58.27	52.5
专业技术服务业	Professional Technical Services	78.95	37.96	48.1
科技交流和推广服务业	Services of Science and Technology Exchanges and Promotion	29.17	11.82	40.5
地质勘查业	Geologic Prospecting	25.10	17.91	71.4
水利、环境和公共设施管理业	**Management of Water Conservancy, Environment and Public Facilities**	**3863.24**	**2004.15**	**51.9**
水利管理业	Management of Water Conservancy	680.94	407.99	59.9
环境管理业	Environmental Management	222.80	79.17	35.5
公共设施管理业	Management of Public Facilities	2959.50	1516.99	51.3
居民服务和其他服务业	**Services to Households and Other Services**	**46.24**	**28.71**	**62.1**
居民服务业	Services to Households	37.39	24.73	66.1
其他服务业	Other Services	8.85	3.98	45.0
教育	**Education**	**1364.96**	**916.53**	**67.1**
卫生、社会保障和社会福利业	**Health, Social Security and Social Welfare**	**299.02**	**211.10**	**70.6**
卫生	Health	280.15	197.10	70.4
社会保障业	Social Security	**3.36**	**3.28**	**97.5**
社会福利业	Social Welfare	15.51	10.72	69.1
文化、体育和娱乐业	**Culture, Sports and Entertainment**	**425.82**	**186.22**	**43.7**
新闻出版业	Journalism and Publishing Activities	21.67	11.47	53.0
广播、电视、电影和音像业	Broadcasting, Movies, Televisions and Audiovisual Activities	67.30	32.83	48.8
文化艺术业	Cultural and Art Activities	**119.94**	**45.00**	**37.5**
体育	Sports Activities	100.59	38.62	38.4
娱乐业	Entertainment	116.33	58.29	50.1
公共管理和社会组织	**Public Management and Social Organization**	**1609.49**	**1032.27**	**64.1**
中国共产党机关	Organs of Communist Party of China	28.92	20.78	71.9
国家机构	Government Agencies	1509.45	957.66	63.4
人民政协和民主党派	People's Political Consultative Conference and Democratic Parties	5.97	5.07	85.0
群众团体、社会团体和宗教组织	Non-Governmental Institutions, Social Organizaitons and Religion Organizations	24.61	24.91	101.3
基层群众自治组织	Grass Roots Self-governing Organizations	40.55	23.85	58.8
国际组织	**International Organizations**	**0.29**	**0.29**	**100.0**

6-19 基本建设新增主要产品生产能力

Newly Increased Production Capacity through Capital Construction

能力名称	Item	1999	2000	2001	2002	2003
铁矿开采（原矿）(万吨/年)	Iron-Ore Mining (10 000 tons/year)	913	12	110	90	466
烧结铁矿 (万吨/年)	Sintering of Iron-Ore (10 000 tons/year)	498		21	29	79
生铁 (万吨/年)	Iron Smelting (10 000 tons/year)	180	5	22	77	363
炼钢 (万吨/年)	Steel-making (10 000 tons/year)	456		2	14	655
初轧 (万吨/年)	Rough Rolling (10 000 tons/year)					3
铁合金 (万吨/年)	Iron Alloy, Electric Furnace (10 000 tons/year)		1	12	16	39
铜选矿	Copper Ore Dressing					
处理原矿 (万吨/年)	Crude Ore Dressing (10 000 tons/year)	38	25	50		79
铜含量 (吨/年)	Copper Content in Concentrate Ore (ton/year)					8000
原煤开采 (万吨/年)	Coal Mining (10 000 tons/year)	2347	2255	1488	1819	4014
天然原油开采 (万吨/年)	Petroleum Extraction (10 000 tons/year)	950	920	1563	2233	1465
硫酸 (万吨/年)	Sulfuric Acid (10 000 tons/year)		10	43	20	2
纯碱 (万吨/年)	Soda Ash (10 000 tons/year)	20	20			
烧碱 (万吨/年)	Caustic Soda (10 000 tons/year)		8	2	5	
合成氨 (万吨/年)	Synthetic Ammonia (10 000 tons/year)	68	90	42	59	33
化肥 (万吨/年)	Chemical Fertilizer (10 000 tons/year)	136	62	105	28	68
乙烯 (吨/年)	Ethylene (ton/year)	80000			182690	3125
塑料 (吨/年)	Plastics (ton/year)	325400	16700	183250	145110	61382
轮胎 (万条/年)	Tires (10 000 /year)					
内胎	Inner Tube	416			1500	58
外胎	Tire (Cover)	179		50	27	122
发电机组容量 (万千瓦)	Capacity of Power Generating Sets (10 000 kw/year)	2052	2012	1587	1193	2759
#火电	Thermal Power	1424	1560	1297	808	1557
水电	Hydropower	629	452	290	148	1199
汽车制造 (辆/年)	Motor Vehicles (unit/year)	30000	119000	75000	125400	158800
#载重汽车制造	Trucks			25000		
拖拉机制造 (混合台/年)	Tractors (unit/year)				160	
#手扶拖拉机制造 (混合台/年)	Walking Tractors (unit/year)				160	
蒸汽锅炉制造 (台/年)	Steam Boilers (unit/year)				20	2
蒸汽锅炉蒸发量(小时吨/年)	Evaporative Capacity of Steam Boilers (hr.tons/year)					1335
交流电动机制造(万千瓦/年)	Electric Motors (10 000 kw/year)		2000		50	12
金属切削机床制造 (台/年)	Metal-Cutting Machine Tools (unit/year)	50		480	125	1622
民用钢质船舶制造 (综合吨/年)	Civilian Ships (ton/year)					105
胶合板 (万立方米/年)	Plywood (10 000 cu.m/year)	2	12	8	71	141

6-19 续表 continued

能 力 名 称	Item	1999	2000	2001	2002	2003
水泥 (万吨/年)	Cement (10 000 tons/year)	231	490	310	479	1275
化学纤维 (吨/年)	Chemical Fiber (ton/year)	117524	97080	132070	19290	67466
棉纺锭 (万锭)	Cotton Spindles (10 000 units)	1	2		14	179
棉布织机 (台)	Cotton Loom (unit)			240	204	12956
棉印染布 (万米/年)	Printed and Dyed Cloth (10 000 m/year)	5409	3000	1980	13394	19925
毛纺锭 (锭)	Wool Spindles			2500		14700
机制糖	Machine-processed Sugar					
年生产 (万吨)	Annual Production Capacity(10000 tons)	3.0	4.2		1.3	64.3
日处理原料 (吨)	Raw Materials Processing (ton/day)	1776	3000		1000	2340
卷烟 (万箱/年)	Cigarettes (10 000 cases/year)					
酒 (万吨/年)	Liquors (10 000 tons/year)	14	16	9	25	42
糖果 (吨/年)	Candy (ton/year)		4700	300		930
奶粉 (吨/年)	Milk Powder (ton/year)			1901	4560	51690
原盐 (万吨/年)	Raw Salt (10 000 tons/year)	2	2		10	
机制纸及纸板 (万吨/年)	Machine-made Paper and Paperboards (10 000 tons/year)	87	8	78	97	105
肥皂 (万箱/年)	Soap (10 000 cases/year)		1			
合成洗涤剂 (万吨/年)	Synthetic Detergent (10 000 tons/year)	3		1		46
鞣制皮革 (万张/年)	Tanning (10 000 pcs/year)	1				450
皮鞋 (万双/年)	Leather Shoes (10 000 pairs/year)	906	85	1789	2277	5186
日用搪瓷制品 (万件/年)	Daily-use Enamelware (10 000 pcs/year)					20
日用陶瓷器 (万件/年)	Daily-use Ceramics (10 000 pcs/year)	300	400	700	5702	11733
保温瓶 (万个/年)	Thermos Bottles (10 000 units/year)				800	
灯泡 (万只/年)	Bulbs (10 000 units/year)			28000	40	3010
自行车 (万辆/年)	Bicycles (10 000 units/year)			18	20	74
家用电冰箱 (万台/年)	Refrigerators (10 000 units/year)					
电视机 (万台/年)	Television Sets (10 000 set/year)	6	46	20		27
录放音机 (万部/年)	Tape Recorders (10 000/year)					
家用洗衣机 (万台/年)	Washing Machines (10 000/year)			20		2
新建铁路主线正线交付营业里程 (公里)	Length of Newly Built Railways Put into Operation (km)	1242	655	1246	1994	929
新(扩)建港口码头	Newly Built or Expanded Ports					
年吞吐量 (万吨)	Annual Handling Capacity (10 000 tons)	3542	4665	6935	4959	8375
泊位 (个)	Number of Berths (unit)	95	84	97	128	58
新建公路 (公里)	Length of New Highways (km)	41978	48069	35855	47465	25021
改建公路 (公里)	Length of Reconstructed Highways (km)	57255	43133	53218	77376	50387
商业石油库 (万立方米)	Commercial Petroleum Depot (10 000cu.m)	44	8	62	50	50
物资储备石油库(万立方米)	Petroleum Tanks in Materials Warehouse System (10 000 cu.m)	2	5	15	31	3
商业冷藏库 (万吨)	Commercial Freezers (10 000 tons)	25	2413	2	13	66
粮食仓库 (万平方米)	Grain Storehouses (10 000 sq.m)	249	237	204	232	69
粮食仓库 (万公斤)	Grain Storehouses (10 000 kg)	1001811	1018885	820206	953895	244076
高等院校学生席位 (个)	Students Capacity of Universities and Colleges	180886	406072	572990	702983	730454
医院病床床位 (张)	Number of Hospital Beds	64670	61490	56620	55583	71425
城市自来水供水能力(万吨/日)	Tap Water Supply Capacity (10 000tons/day)	758	555	1288	692	783

6-20 按资金来源和隶属关系分更新改造投资

Investment on Innovation by Source of Funds and Administrative Relationship

单位: 亿元 (100 million yuan)

年份 地区	Year Region	按资金来源分 By Source of Funds					按隶属关系分 By Administrative Relationship	
		国家预算内资金 State Budgetary Appropriations	国内贷款 Domestic Loans	利用外资 Foreign Investment	自筹资金 Fundraising	其他资金 Others	中央项目 Central Government Projects	地方项目 Local Projects
	1980	24.18	33.66		79.54		23.80	113.58
	1985	19.69	186.75	5.55	226.08	11.07	104.82	344.32
	1989	14.15	233.21	26.73	440.69	74.01	205.99	582.79
	1990	17.56	269.55	33.85	455.37	53.87	228.46	601.73
	1991	17.36	411.22	36.49	508.62	49.53	279.37	743.86
	1992	20.11	604.56	53.15	722.56	60.73	370.46	1090.65
	1993	31.31	800.71	84.97	1227.57	106.60	633.31	1562.54
	1994	30.60	830.11	212.85	1675.08	151.10	909.26	2009.35
	1995	38.32	803.55	321.11	1929.77	157.89	1081.46	2217.89
	1996	(29.58)	(831.26)	(353.97)	(2191.19)	(166.72)	(1250.29)	(2372.45)
		29.31	830.45	353.90	2185.05	166.24	1249.49	2365.51
	1997	36.48	796.09	272.35	2522.36	185.72	1407.73	2514.20
	1998	60.96	845.29	219.29	3019.81	226.19	1739.79	2776.96
	1999	107.48	933.06	237.11	2883.76	214.55	1581.91	2903.18
	2000	155.31	1041.22	217.65	3449.94	220.10	1861.89	3245.71
	2001	165.18	1081.56	246.81	4195.00	222.26	2130.80	3792.96
	2002	167.21	1219.53	312.25	4856.33	266.80	1953.46	4797.09
	2003	191.91	1587.97	380.32	6220.94	322.07	1915.96	6708.90
北京	Beijing	2.90	7.15	2.71	186.75	0.54	68.46	147.81
天津	Tianjin	0.74	33.94	32.52	122.20	4.78	36.58	172.04
河北	Hebei	7.74	69.96	6.48	415.52	14.47	54.28	457.61
山西	Shanxi	3.35	37.74	0.93	206.44	12.08	43.94	208.41
内蒙古	Inner Mongolia	5.30	29.80	0.81	129.40	8.84	33.80	139.80
辽宁	Liaoning	7.41	66.74	15.57	349.24	16.02	139.52	322.50
吉林	Jilin	1.95	34.11	4.23	180.76	13.38	76.43	135.70
黑龙江	Heilongjiang	7.87	33.01	4.35	182.56	7.10	135.96	95.73
上海	Shanghai	4.74	72.07	18.35	283.82	4.18	114.99	273.03
江苏	Jiangsu	8.92	137.10	79.64	442.82	9.23	111.14	580.82
浙江	Zhejiang	2.09	77.67	8.43	263.22	9.62	88.61	268.10
安徽	Anhui	12.40	103.01	7.04	241.39	15.89	35.39	319.83
福建	Fujian	1.14	43.10	15.01	159.26	8.53	31.25	195.54
江西	Jiangxi	4.78	32.15	13.07	134.36	11.94	20.88	174.74
山东	Shandong	12.78	187.94	48.13	651.05	47.10	132.93	777.59
河南	Henan	9.82	80.05	5.06	259.04	13.87	72.85	296.87
湖北	Hubei	11.62	73.51	4.68	269.12	22.29	96.00	287.16
湖南	Hunan	8.87	53.90	8.00	222.90	13.21	58.76	243.11
广东	Guangdong	17.03	76.44	87.15	470.11	15.26	102.07	556.70
广西	Guangxi	2.62	33.70	5.54	97.25	9.50	30.45	116.39
海南	Hainan	0.46	2.21	0.16	7.87	2.41	0.24	12.57
重庆	Chongqing	4.62	28.18	1.89	80.53	7.65	56.92	65.09
四川	Sichuan	8.36	70.26	3.46	287.29	11.16	75.43	293.69
贵州	Guizhou	8.78	35.63	1.45	96.50	4.98	60.66	79.40
云南	Yunnan	3.79	40.05	0.91	99.48	4.96	50.29	98.07
西藏	Tibet	2.83	0.38		4.38	2.01	7.15	2.14
陕西	Shaanxi	14.72	43.64	1.69	108.52	10.47	26.62	146.61
甘肃	Gansu	7.07	27.61	1.18	118.15	6.55	42.01	119.79
青海	Qinghai	1.33	6.70	1.20	19.35	7.56	18.45	22.12
宁夏	Ningxia	1.31	12.99	0.47	26.50	0.91	7.58	33.19
新疆	Xinjiang	4.56	37.22	0.22	79.50	5.62	60.67	66.74
不分地区	Not Classified by Region				25.66		25.66	

6-21 按构成和建设性质分更新改造投资

Investment in Innovation by Use of Funds and Type of Construction

单位: 亿元 (100 million yuan)

年份、地区 Year Region		投资额 Total	按构成分 By Use of Funds 建筑安装工程 Construction and Installation	设备、工器具购置 Purchase of Equipment and Instruments	其他费用 Others	按建设性质分 By Type of Construction #新建 New Construction	#扩建 Expansion	#改建 Reconstruction
	1980	137.38	74.21	59.65	3.52			
	1985	449.14	196.23	224.94	27.97	23.06	194.45	191.16
	1989	788.78	377.25	355.89	55.64	38.87	345.54	363.49
	1990	830.19	372.91	397.36	59.92	45.62	370.35	364.57
	1991	1023.23	426.33	513.35	83.54	42.82	460.91	448.46
	1992	1461.10	620.64	715.34	125.12	71.63	659.72	642.35
	1993	2195.85	945.27	1070.93	179.65	140.31	1069.26	888.40
	1994	2918.61	1258.72	1419.79	240.09	189.95	1486.20	1076.44
	1995	3299.35	1343.62	1682.20	273.53	288.19	1640.28	1179.86
	1996	(3622.74)	(1396.77)	(1900.50)	(325.47)	(349.02)	(1818.44)	(1190.99)
		3615.00	1394.07	1895.69	325.24	347.03	1816.62	1188.12
	1997	3921.94	1540.77	2033.74	347.43	381.82	1947.48	1298.31
	1998	4516.75	1681.38	2445.24	390.13	452.61	2324.42	1407.51
	1999	4485.08	1667.61	2465.70	351.77	364.83	2206.87	1531.27
	2000	5107.60	1943.25	2776.41	387.93	455.86	2506.31	1746.58
	2001	5923.76	2206.06	3297.88	419.82	585.06	2958.56	1943.73
	2002	6750.55	2598.03	3635.32	517.19	845.32	3208.70	2202.77
	2003	8624.86	3420.13	4460.51	744.22	1339.20	4345.75	2408.92
北京	Beijing	216.27	70.35	115.27	30.66	4.18	106.22	78.27
天津	Tianjin	208.62	97.82	97.36	13.45	69.11	75.85	38.02
河北	Hebei	511.90	190.29	272.31	49.29	79.51	230.81	168.50
山西	Shanxi	252.35	109.40	117.79	25.16	39.57	135.76	74.19
内蒙古	Inner Mongolia	173.59	72.41	87.13	14.05	33.53	105.25	32.63
辽宁	Liaoning	462.03	208.42	207.56	46.04	37.75	228.63	164.89
吉林	Jilin	212.13	93.14	104.01	14.98	36.72	93.70	73.97
黑龙江	Heilongjiang	231.69	99.18	123.77	8.75	72.20	93.78	55.92
上海	Shanghai	388.01	141.29	215.79	30.93	64.57	101.94	169.20
江苏	Jiangsu	691.96	275.15	362.12	54.69	93.63	367.36	195.76
浙江	Zhejiang	356.71	107.64	211.70	37.36	65.84	192.52	77.36
安徽	Anhui	355.22	125.30	199.58	30.34	79.85	162.68	103.10
福建	Fujian	226.80	74.59	139.44	12.78	31.26	135.32	27.22
江西	Jiangxi	195.61	76.13	104.59	14.89	61.46	63.28	63.63
山东	Shandong	910.52	369.24	454.53	86.75	131.55	582.63	170.75
河南	Henan	369.72	175.04	163.71	30.98	72.51	199.49	85.04
湖北	Hubei	383.16	119.82	220.85	42.50	40.93	183.46	133.26
湖南	Hunan	301.87	130.37	141.85	29.64	66.88	125.64	100.86
广东	Guangdong	658.77	256.67	360.95	41.15	69.64	360.25	138.70
广西	Guangxi	146.84	49.96	84.84	12.04	22.99	82.10	30.84
海南	Hainan	12.81	5.25	5.99	1.57	0.52	5.00	3.42
重庆	Chongqing	122.01	50.45	60.73	10.83	3.44	83.44	23.42
四川	Sichuan	369.11	140.50	191.77	36.85	72.54	178.18	107.88
贵州	Guizhou	140.06	59.28	69.45	11.33	16.54	75.45	43.81
云南	Yunnan	148.35	51.55	86.88	9.92	5.63	91.56	45.61
西藏	Tibet	9.29	3.76	5.34	0.19	0.47	2.80	5.82
陕西	Shaanxi	173.23	76.40	77.67	19.17	10.70	93.70	61.50
甘肃	Gansu	161.80	75.79	72.60	13.41	16.73	86.32	53.97
青海	Qinghai	40.57	25.08	14.15	1.34	13.60	16.16	9.76
宁夏	Ningxia	40.76	21.34	15.86	3.57	9.81	20.64	8.64
新疆	Xinjiang	127.41	50.04	70.93	6.44	15.53	65.85	37.35
不分地区	Not Classified by Region	25.66	18.49	4.00	3.17			25.66

6-22 各行业按建设性质分更新改造投资（2003年）

Investment in Innovation by Type of Construction and Sector (2003)

单位: 亿元 (100 million yuan)

行业	Sector	投资额 Investment	#新建 New Construction	#扩建 Expansion	#改建 Reconstruction
全国总计	**National Total**	**8624.86**	**1339.20**	**4345.75**	**2408.92**
农、林、牧、渔业	**Agriculture, Forestry, Animal Husbandry and Fishing**	**31.80**	**5.64**	**16.81**	**7.89**
农业	Agriculture	7.88	1.78	3.40	2.17
林业	Forestry	5.26	0.24	4.09	0.91
畜牧业	Animal Husbandry	7.00	1.14	4.81	0.85
渔业	Fishing	0.83	0.04	0.62	0.10
农、林、牧、渔服务业	Service Activities for Agriculture, Forestry, Animal Husbandry and Fishing	10.83	2.45	3.89	3.86
采矿业	**Mining**	**531.72**	**62.38**	**298.86**	**167.16**
煤炭开采和洗选业	Mining and Washing of Coal	194.59	12.56	79.76	100.74
石油和天然气开采业	Extraction of Petroleum and Natural Gas	261.79	39.75	176.76	45.00
黑色金属矿采选业	Mining and Processing of Ferrous Metal Ores	21.95	3.57	12.35	5.49
有色金属矿采选业	Mining and Processing of Non-Ferrous Metal Ores	34.10	2.66	21.63	9.40
非金属矿采选业	Mining and Processing of Nonmetal Ores	19.13	3.85	8.20	6.52
其他采矿业	Mining of Other Ores	0.16		0.16	
制造业	**Manufacturing**	**5147.09**	**872.82**	**2649.43**	**1354.51**
农副食品加工业	Processing of Food from Agricultural Products	155.85	32.96	92.20	25.51
食品制造业	Manufacture of Foods	128.17	24.50	79.47	19.79
饮料制造业	Manufacture of Beverages	117.53	20.82	68.47	24.10
烟草制品业	Manufacture of Tobacco	73.82	1.59	34.30	22.46
纺织业	Manufacture of Textile	286.89	39.45	154.02	69.64
纺织服装、鞋、帽制造业	Manufacture of Textile Wearing Apparel, Footware, and Caps	47.48	7.53	29.16	6.04
皮革毛皮羽毛(绒)及其制品业	Manufacture of Leather, Fur, Feather and Related Products	22.54	4.33	10.46	5.09
木材加工及木竹藤棕草制品业	Processing of Timber, Manufacture of Wood, Bamboo, Rattan, Palm, and Straw Products	46.08	15.87	15.28	13.62
家具制造业	Manufacture of Furniture	15.16	2.81	8.05	2.61
造纸及纸制品业	Manufacture of Paper and Paper Products	153.45	26.61	99.45	21.48
印刷业和记录媒介的复制	Printing,Reproduction of Recording Media	55.56	10.32	24.50	9.54
文教体育用品制造业	Manufacture of Articles For Culture, Education and Sport Activity	11.02	3.26	6.00	1.00
石油加工、炼焦及核燃料加工业	Processing of Petroleum, Coking, Processing of Nuclear Fuel	190.28	36.31	96.44	55.57
化学原料及化学制品制造业	Manufacture of Raw Chemical Materials and Chemical Products	463.52	69.51	258.15	124.65
医药制造业	Manufacture of Medicines	282.18	63.70	115.61	81.15
化学纤维制造业	Manufacture of Chemical Fibers	76.29	22.88	43.22	8.61
橡胶制品业	Manufacture of Rubber	70.06	5.51	49.76	14.12
塑料制品业	Manufacture of Plastics	104.34	34.89	46.97	13.22
非金属矿物制品业	Manufacture of Non-metallic Mineral Products	368.01	87.40	186.43	83.33
黑色金属冶炼及压延加工业	Smelting and Pressing of Ferrous Metals	966.65	90.06	461.10	408.39
有色金属冶炼及压延加工业	Smelting and Pressing of Non-ferrous Metals	238.32	36.19	143.13	55.62
金属制品业	Manufacture of Metal Products	83.19	17.44	42.04	17.34
通用设备制造业	Manufacture of General Purpose Machinery	166.57	23.64	83.44	40.41
专用设备制造业	Manufacture of Special Purpose Machinery	139.21	22.53	57.04	39.85
交通运输设备制造业	Manufacture of Transport Equipment	458.36	70.00	231.67	126.87
电气机械及器材制造业	Manufacture of Electrical Machinery and Equipment	130.83	23.15	69.45	21.15
通信设备、计算机及其他电子设备制造业	Manufacture of Communication Equipment, Computers and Other Electronic Equipment	243.36	65.10	118.51	34.86
仪器仪表文化办公用机械制造业	Manufacture of Measuring Instruments and Machinery for Cultural Activity and Office Work	31.77	8.52	14.23	5.48
工艺品及其他制造业	Manufacture of Artwork and Other Manufacturing	20.08	5.91	10.49	2.89
废弃资源和废旧材料回收加工业	Recycling and Disposal of Waste	0.53	0.04	0.37	0.13
电力燃气水的生产供应业	**Production and Distribution of Electricity, Gas and Water**	**718.64**	**90.77**	**307.05**	**305.57**
电力、热力的生产和供应业	Production and Distribution of Electric Power and Heat Power	640.35	74.25	277.76	273.85
燃气生产和供应业	Production and Distribution of Gas	24.54	7.38	7.64	9.11
水的生产和供应业	Production and Distribution of Water	53.76	9.14	21.64	22.61
建筑业	**Construction**	**54.23**	**4.14**	**8.21**	**19.97**
房屋和土木工程建筑业	Construction of Buildings and Civil Engineering	48.43	3.30	7.05	17.59
建筑安装业	Building Installation	2.86	0.71	0.58	0.81
建筑装饰业	Buidling Decoration	1.90	0.11	0.08	1.44
其他建筑业	Other Construction	1.03	0.03	0.50	0.13

6-22 续表 continued

单位: 亿元 (100 million yuan)

行业	Sector	投资额 Investment	#新建 New Construction	#扩建 Expansion	#改建 Reconstruction
交通运输、仓储和邮政业	**Transport, Storage and Post**	**432.25**	**23.87**	**79.70**	**200.90**
铁路运输业	Railway Transport	89.31	9.00	10.09	65.84
道路运输业	Road Transport	151.65	5.17	27.51	95.07
城市公共交通业	Urban Public Transport	59.36	1.37	5.11	4.28
水上运输业	Water Transport	59.55	1.30	23.52	21.35
航空运输业	Air Transport	39.07	1.32	2.79	2.93
管道运输业	Transport Via Pipelines	3.93	0.38	0.38	3.00
装卸搬运和其他运输服务业	Loading, Unloading and Other Transport Services	4.10	0.05	1.26	2.32
仓储业	Storage	18.77	3.97	6.36	4.25
邮政业	Post	6.53	1.30	2.69	1.86
信息传输、计算机服务和软件业	**Information Transmission, Computer Services and Software**	**1120.85**	**204.76**	**803.42**	**101.90**
电信和其他信息传输服务业	Telecommunications and Other Information Transmission Services	1110.09	199.71	799.05	100.91
计算机服务业	Computer Services	2.33	1.44	0.25	0.64
软件业	Software	8.43	3.62	4.13	0.35
批发和零售业	**Wholesale and Retail Trade**	**76.36**	**12.86**	**30.99**	**25.34**
批发业	Wholesale Trade	35.91	6.74	15.87	9.20
零售业	Retail Trade	40.46	6.12	15.12	16.14
住宿和餐饮业	**Hotel and Restaurants**	**27.92**	**1.14**	**13.11**	**12.78**
住宿业	Hotels	12.66	0.23	5.08	7.07
餐饮业	Restaurants	15.26	0.91	8.04	5.71
金融业	**Financial Intermediation**	**17.78**	**0.32**	**0.86**	**4.62**
银行业	Banks	16.40	0.32	0.68	4.58
证券业	Security Activities	0.52		0.10	0.02
保险业	Insurance	0.70		0.09	0.01
其他金融活动	Other Financial Activities	0.15			
房地产业	**Real Estate**	**11.55**	**2.26**	**0.99**	**3.39**
租赁和商务服务业	**Leasing and Business Services**	**12.43**	**3.00**	**5.08**	**3.00**
租赁业	Leasing	0.14		0.07	
商务服务业	Business Services	12.29	3.00	5.01	3.00
科学研究、技术服务和地质勘查业	**Scientific Research, Technical Service and Geologic Prospecting Geologic Prospecting**	**30.04**	**6.09**	**13.91**	**5.50**
研究与试验发展	Research and Experimental Development	19.31	4.41	9.99	3.16
专业技术服务业	Professional Technical Services	8.87	1.24	3.77	1.79
科技交流和推广服务业	Services of Science and Technology Exchanges and Promotion	1.21	0.44	0.15	0.54
地质勘查业	Geologic Prospecting	0.64			0.02
水利、环境和公共设施管理业	**Management of Water Conservancy, Environment and Public Facilities**	**246.84**	**36.23**	**64.01**	**142.88**
水利管理业	Management of Water Conservancy	31.41	0.74	6.87	22.82
环境管理业	Environmental Management	30.37	4.04	5.34	20.36
公共设施管理业	Management of Public Facilities	185.06	31.45	51.79	99.70
居民服务和其他服务业	**Services to Households and Other Services**	**2.71**	**0.39**	**0.70**	**1.48**
居民服务业	Services to Households	2.16		0.65	1.41
其他服务业	Other Services	0.55	0.39	0.05	0.07
教育	**Education**	**38.10**	**2.55**	**14.76**	**7.37**
卫生、社会保障和社会福利业	**Health, Social Security and Social Welfare**	**35.25**	**3.46**	**6.84**	**4.81**
卫生	Health	32.82	1.62	6.59	4.51
社会保障业	Social Security	**2.19**	**1.84**	**0.15**	**0.20**
社会福利业	Social Welfare	0.24		0.11	0.09
文化、体育和娱乐业	**Culture, Sports and Entertainment**	**19.75**	**0.63**	**4.90**	**9.19**
新闻出版业	Journalism and Publishing Activities	1.72	0.08	0.01	0.20
广播、电视、电影和音像业	Broadcasting, Movies, Televisions and Audiovisual Activities	11.31	0.48	2.83	5.14
文化艺术业	Cultural and Art Activities	1.74	0.02	0.21	1.05
体育	Sports Activities	1.48	0.03	0.24	1.21
娱乐业	Entertainment	3.51	0.02	1.61	1.58
公共管理和社会组织	**Public Management and Social Organization**	**69.55**	**5.88**	**26.12**	**30.66**
中国共产党机关	Organs of Communist Party of China	0.77	0.00	0.30	0.08
国家机构	Government Agencies	67.05	5.76	25.59	29.74
人民政协和民主党派	People's Political Consultative Conference and Democratic Parties	0.08			
群众团体、社会团体和宗教组织	Non-Governmental Institutions, Social Organizaitons and Religion Organizations	0.78	0.11	0.14	0.24
基层群众自治组织	Grass Roots Self-governing Organizations	0.87		0.08	0.59
国际组织	**International Organizations**				

6-23 更新改造施工、投产项目个数和新增固定资产

Number of Innovation Projects Under Construction and Put into Use and Newly Increased Fixed Assets

年份 Year / 地区 Region		施工项目 (个) Number of Projects under Construction (unit)	全部建成投产项目 (个) Number of Projects Completed and Put into Use (unit)	项目建成投产率 (%) Rate of Projects Completed and Put into Use (%)	新增固定资产 (亿元) Newly Increased Fixed Assets (100 million yuan)	固定资产交付使用率 (%) Rate of Fixed Assets Put into Use (%)
	1980	46152	23105	50.1	92.58	67.4
	1985	77604	43149	55.6	316.79	70.5
	1989	60146	31805	52.9	636.88	80.7
	1990	56825	31537	55.5	722.94	87.1
	1991	64574	36770	56.9	858.30	83.9
	1992	69781	40574	58.1	1105.05	75.6
	1993	64670	35932	55.6	1531.93	69.8
	1994	59089	33091	56.0	2192.57	75.1
	1995	55242	35267	63.8	2524.87	76.5
	1996	(57501)	(36534)	(63.5)	(3002.69)	(82.9)
		55235	34580	62.6	2995.31	82.9
	1997	51576	33590	65.1	3250.55	82.9
	1998	51054	33407	65.4	3690.36	81.7
	1999	52484	34319	65.4	3644.67	81.3
	2000	53641	33093	61.7	4111.51	80.5
	2001	55061	35782	65.0	4411.49	74.5
	2002	55217	33484	60.6	4693.16	69.5
	2003	54359	30870	56.8	5643.19	65.4
北京	Beijing	566	361	63.8	112.94	52.2
天津	Tianjin	668	380	56.9	101.11	48.5
河北	Hebei	3169	1671	52.7	345.81	67.6
山西	Shanxi	1640	954	58.2	138.65	54.9
内蒙古	Inner Mongolia	1694	1159	68.4	121.52	70.0
辽宁	Liaoning	3571	2493	69.8	342.68	74.2
吉林	Jilin	1463	1025	70.1	140.29	66.1
黑龙江	Heilongjiang	1382	1124	81.3	207.55	89.6
上海	Shanghai	1975	92	4.7	258.76	66.7
江苏	Jiangsu	3079	1948	63.3	437.97	63.3
浙江	Zhejiang	2527	1413	55.9	227.35	63.7
安徽	Anhui	2077	1073	51.7	193.43	54.5
福建	Fujian	2081	1239	59.5	172.78	76.2
江西	Jiangxi	792	342	43.2	79.77	40.8
山东	Shandong	3270	1656	50.6	583.86	64.1
河南	Henan	1630	1000	61.3	247.58	67.0
湖北	Hubei	2634	1770	67.2	256.47	66.9
湖南	Hunan	3161	1958	61.9	193.11	64.0
广东	Guangdong	3884	1653	42.6	402.95	61.2
广西	Guangxi	2178	1433	65.8	95.92	65.3
海南	Hainan	242	180	74.4	9.89	77.2
重庆	Chongqing	810	537	66.3	97.75	80.1
四川	Sichuan	2500	1223	48.9	258.13	69.9
贵州	Guizhou	1391	664	47.7	85.80	61.3
云南	Yunnan	1109	576	51.9	91.08	61.4
西藏	Tibet	127	88	69.3	5.38	58.0
陕西	Shaanxi	1106	573	51.8	131.01	75.6
甘肃	Gansu	1810	969	53.5	135.35	83.7
青海	Qinghai	241	126	52.3	11.58	28.5
宁夏	Ningxia	272	172	63.2	26.90	66.0
新疆	Xinjiang	1305	1013	77.6	107.18	84.1
不分地区	Not Classified by Region	5	5	100.0	22.63	88.2

6-24 按行业分更新改造投资

Investment in Innovation by Sector

单位: 亿元 (100 million yuan)

年份 Year	合计 Total	农、林、牧、渔业 Farming, Forestry, Animal Husbandry and Fishery	采掘业 Mining and Quarrying	制造业 Manufacturing	电力、煤气及水的生产和供应业 Production and Supply of Electricity Gas and Water	建筑业 Construction	地质勘查业水利管理业 Geological Prospecting and Water Conservancy	交通运输仓储和邮电通信业 Transport, Storage, Post & Telecommunication Services
1980	137.38	1.21	34.55	73.72	5.62	1.07	0.14	12.17
1985	449.14	5.56	44.09	289.71	17.25	6.97	0.79	41.49
1989	788.78	8.40	87.83	500.12	35.23	7.66	3.34	65.28
1990	830.19	7.32	85.49	518.20	43.79	7.69	3.15	81.32
1991	1023.23	13.16	92.96	646.29	43.98	8.51	3.53	113.67
1992	1461.10	14.77	90.13	920.59	65.96	14.20	5.23	192.77
1993	2195.85	17.83	141.69	1298.33	99.31	32.98	7.04	361.47
1994	2918.61	19.64	171.02	1606.03	150.99	31.47	5.50	576.95
1995	3299.35	18.83	206.67	1775.84	217.64	45.80	8.26	680.73
1996	(3622.74)	(23.22)	(228.29)	(1843.01)	(259.21)	(34.17)	(10.35)	(875.97)
	3615.00	22.91	228.09	1839.23	258.93	33.98	10.31	875.19
1997	3921.94	27.21	244.37	1866.24	275.43	47.91	25.10	1050.13
1998	4516.75	27.11	308.78	1797.30	344.52	30.04	33.48	1542.25
1999	4485.08	26.33	251.66	1796.07	463.86	31.28	30.52	1420.67
2000	5107.60	26.35	373.86	2104.15	481.67	65.82	24.89	1553.60
2001	5923.76	21.04	413.78	2662.76	483.15	42.57	25.49	1825.32
2002	6750.55	22.86	473.03	3523.77	582.48	66.44	31.01	1530.25

6-24 续表 continued

单位: 亿元 (100 million yuan)

年份 Year	批发零售贸易和餐饮业 Wholesale and Retail Trade & Catering Services	金融、保险业 Finance and Insurance	房地产业 Real Estate	社会服务业 Social Services	卫生体育和社会福利业 Health Care, Sports & Social Welfare	教育、文化艺术和广播电影电视业 Education, Culture and Arts, Radio, Film and Television	科学研究和综合技术服务业 Scientific Research and Polytechnic Services	国家机关、政党机关和社会团体 Government Agencies, Party Agencies and Social Organizations	其他 Others
1980	4.02	0.06	2.28		0.23	0.50	0.43	0.99	0.39
1985	10.37	0.97	3.05	17.41	1.78	2.91	2.35	3.24	1.49
1989	22.46	2.07	8.95	27.49	2.83	4.31	2.35	6.19	4.26
1990	22.10	1.72	8.54	27.68	3.16	4.65	2.18	7.05	6.14
1991	27.83	2.11	8.90	34.74	3.22	5.62	2.29	9.22	7.20
1992	48.12	2.42	13.02	52.93	4.22	6.08	3.16	12.81	14.69
1993	65.47	3.73	33.80	78.68	6.04	9.37	3.18	21.22	15.73
1994	101.04	3.63	59.79	120.03	4.47	10.07	5.02	27.38	25.58
1995	97.30	2.85	56.57	108.50	5.93	15.27	6.29	29.94	22.93
1996	(70.93)	(8.11)	(41.76)	(131.30)	(10.38)	(13.38)	(5.77)	(37.47)	(29.42)
	70.38	8.07	41.75	131.01	10.17	12.98	5.64	36.93	29.42
1997	61.06	11.77	56.92	151.47	10.77	17.95	4.85	37.55	33.21
1998	52.64	12.86	25.54	189.48	11.64	20.41	5.83	49.86	64.99
1999	46.03	6.89	35.51	228.33	15.31	26.77	18.89	54.87	32.09
2000	57.74	6.22	32.25	225.13	19.67	33.67	34.35	50.19	18.05
2001	55.72	16.53	17.96	199.15	23.92	43.74	33.10	35.94	23.57
2002	78.29	19.77	8.69	225.39	35.12	45.22	28.65	48.24	31.35

6-25 各地区按行业分更新改造投资（2003年）

Investment in Innovation by Sector (2003)

单位: 亿元 (100 million yuan)

地区	Region	合计 Total	农、林、牧、渔业 Agriculture, Forestry, Animal Husbandry and Fishing	采矿业 Mining	制造业 Manufacturing	电力、燃气及水的生产和供应业 Production and Distribution of Electricity, Gas and Water	建筑业 Construction	交通运输、仓储和邮政业 Transport, Storage and Post
全国总计	**National Total**	**8624.86**	**31.80**	**531.72**	**5147.09**	**718.64**	**54.23**	**432.25**
北京	Beijing	216.27	0.29	1.93	78.33	15.19	1.37	12.33
天津	Tianjin	208.62	0.09	1.76	127.84	17.32	5.63	2.78
河北	Hebei	511.90	3.80	18.86	302.58	50.79	7.59	32.99
山西	Shanxi	252.35	0.52	48.08	154.18	13.15	1.00	4.54
内蒙古	Inner Mongolia	173.59	1.15	17.59	98.59	30.14		7.00
辽宁	Liaoning	462.03	0.95	43.00	274.72	37.81	2.78	23.13
吉林	Jilin	212.13	0.34	13.25	177.71	9.15	0.80	3.37
黑龙江	Heilongjiang	231.69	1.62	36.63	102.34	27.48	0.25	8.69
上海	Shanghai	388.01		0.03	225.35	27.67	5.63	38.58
江苏	Jiangsu	691.96	0.53	20.77	474.63	65.54	1.01	17.86
浙江	Zhejiang	356.71	0.67	0.93	221.42	35.72	1.07	18.42
安徽	Anhui	355.22	1.54	25.28	253.69	20.41	1.86	13.69
福建	Fujian	226.80	0.36	0.97	143.14	13.05	0.54	10.30
江西	Jiangxi	195.61	0.77	5.78	119.97	9.78	0.23	12.43
山东	Shandong	910.52	1.97	102.15	597.79	61.22	4.90	34.21
河南	Henan	369.72	2.35	53.50	210.91	40.79	0.46	19.91
湖北	Hubei	383.16	0.64	10.56	259.69	29.05	3.23	16.47
湖南	Hunan	301.87	0.47	5.91	212.17	22.85	0.32	11.72
广东	Guangdong	658.77	0.62	12.22	224.51	55.69	9.28	72.25
广西	Guangxi	146.84	0.62	1.37	97.91	17.89	0.04	7.90
海南	Hainan	12.81	1.61		3.97	1.86		1.06
重庆	Chongqing	122.01	0.06	3.46	56.58	17.23	0.40	3.89
四川	Sichuan	369.11	0.57	12.25	282.48	22.21	0.35	11.11
贵州	Guizhou	140.06	0.05	7.89	71.34	27.51	0.61	3.92
云南	Yunnan	148.35	0.44	6.02	74.35	7.01		10.77
西藏	Tibet	9.29	0.15	0.19	0.53	3.91	0.04	0.46
陕西	Shaanxi	173.23	0.72	28.54	79.72	13.21	1.37	7.86
甘肃	Gansu	161.80	2.69	9.62	109.10	12.53	0.83	7.16
青海	Qinghai	40.57	0.17	6.86	27.67	1.45	0.41	1.74
宁夏	Ningxia	40.76	0.04	4.02	29.29	1.57	0.09	0.74
新疆	Xinjiang	127.41	6.00	10.32	54.58	9.46	2.14	11.26
不分地区	Not Classified by Region	25.66		21.95				3.71

6-25 续表 1 continued

单位: 亿元 (100 million yuan)

地 区	Region	信息传输、计算机服务和软件业 Information Transmission, Computer Service and Software	批发和零售业 Wholesale and Retail Trade	住宿和餐饮业 Hotel and Restaurants	金融业 Financial Intermediation	房地产业 Real Estate	租赁和商务服务业 Leasing and Business Services	科学研究、技术服务和地质勘查业 Scientific Research, Technical Services, and Geological Prospecting
全国总计	**National Total**	**1120.85**	**76.36**	**27.92**	**17.78**	**11.55**	**12.43**	**30.04**
北 京	Beijing	73.89	0.62	0.78			0.10	0.60
天 津	Tianjin	23.90	1.60	0.40	0.62		1.59	0.27
河 北	Hebei	50.42	6.89	0.40	0.77	4.25	2.58	1.40
山 西	Shanxi	25.42	0.54					0.10
内蒙古	Inner Mongolia	14.62		0.07		1.17	0.08	
辽 宁	Liaoning	38.09	17.23	10.90	1.31	0.45	2.87	0.42
吉 林	Jilin	3.54	0.32				0.21	0.21
黑龙江	Heilongjiang	53.85	0.20		0.01			
上 海	Shanghai	47.68	4.05	1.55	0.01	1.76	0.36	2.38
江 苏	Jiangsu	65.08	1.97	1.42	0.05	0.56	0.44	4.61
浙 江	Zhejiang	69.42	0.73	0.76	0.78		0.01	0.08
安 徽	Anhui	30.22	2.25	0.32	0.06	0.08	0.38	0.23
福 建	Fujian	54.34	0.30	0.05		0.10	0.18	0.29
江 西	Jiangxi	32.72	0.52	0.16	0.59	0.19		0.02
山 东	Shandong	59.22	4.61	0.69	0.04	0.35	1.13	1.65
河 南	Henan	17.56	1.38	0.23		0.83	0.10	1.41
湖 北	Hubei	39.72	4.70	0.32	1.59	0.35	0.26	0.70
湖 南	Hunan	34.87	3.36	2.87	0.13		0.45	0.48
广 东	Guangdong	180.61	6.69	3.51	9.46	0.40	1.07	8.42
广 西	Guangxi	18.37	0.72	0.11	0.07			0.01
海 南	Hainan	2.84			0.01			
重 庆	Chongqing	33.94	0.90	0.03	0.86	0.26		0.29
四 川	Sichuan	29.61	2.41	0.32		0.68	0.34	2.83
贵 州	Guizhou	25.18	0.78	0.05	0.02	0.01	0.03	0.25
云 南	Yunnan	38.35	0.53	0.85	0.03	0.07	0.12	0.09
西 藏	Tibet	3.72		0.02	0.01			
陕 西	Shaanxi	14.98	2.71	0.44			0.01	2.52
甘 肃	Gansu	12.67	4.21	0.10			0.01	0.42
青 海	Qinghai	0.35	0.12	0.02				0.05
宁 夏	Ningxia	4.57	0.07				0.10	
新 疆	Xinjiang	21.11	5.97	1.55	1.38	0.04	0.03	0.30
不分地区	Not Classified by Region							

6-25 续表 2 continued

单位: 亿元 (100 million yuan)

地 区	Region	水利、环境和公共设施管理业 Water Management of Conservancy, Environment and Public Facilities	居民服务和其他服务业 Services to Households and Other Services	教 育 Education	卫生、社会保障和社会福利业 Health, Social Securities and Social Welfare	文化、体育和娱乐业 Culture, Sports and Entertainment	公共管理和社会组织 Public Management and Social Organization	国际组织 International Organizations
全国总计	**National Total**	**246.84**	**2.71**	**38.10**	**35.25**	**19.75**	**69.55**	
北 京	Beijing	20.67		1.10	0.52	0.10	8.45	
天 津	Tianjin	22.59	0.13	0.52	0.17	0.14	1.26	
河 北	Hebei	17.00	0.29	4.29	1.89	1.40	3.70	
山 西	Shanxi	3.91		0.15	0.59	0.14		
内蒙古	Inner Mongolia	1.98		0.03	0.38	0.01	0.79	
辽 宁	Liaoning	2.62	0.27	1.12	0.32	2.63	1.40	
吉 林	Jilin	0.17	0.41	0.10	0.33	0.10	2.13	
黑龙江	Heilongjiang	0.02		0.24	0.05	0.09	0.23	
上 海	Shanghai	24.70	0.02	2.87	1.75	0.78	2.86	
江 苏	Jiangsu	32.03	0.17	1.72	1.31	0.68	1.59	
浙 江	Zhejiang	2.49	0.04	0.42	2.41	0.56	0.80	
安 徽	Anhui	1.57		0.16	0.79	0.41	2.30	
福 建	Fujian	1.13		0.01	0.69	0.67	0.65	
江 西	Jiangxi	1.43	0.10	5.13	3.05	0.94	1.80	
山 东	Shandong	23.36	0.02	0.40	1.30	1.84	13.66	
河 南	Henan	14.87	0.05	1.08	1.20	0.48	2.63	
湖 北	Hubei	5.31	0.02	5.21	2.33	1.38	1.64	
湖 南	Hunan	3.05	0.03	0.24	1.64	0.68	0.62	
广 东	Guangdong	31.80	1.11	9.07	9.49	4.70	17.88	
广 西	Guangxi	1.06		0.12	0.45	0.18	0.02	
海 南	Hainan	0.61		0.01	0.14	0.17	0.56	
重 庆	Chongqing	0.15	0.01	1.07	2.06	0.15	0.67	
四 川	Sichuan	1.99	0.02	0.25	0.81	0.60	0.30	
贵 州	Guizhou	1.79	0.01	0.25	0.23	0.08	0.08	
云 南	Yunnan	7.37		0.86	0.50	0.33	0.66	
西 藏	Tibet	0.01		0.03		0.02	0.18	
陕 西	Shaanxi	19.28		0.35	0.20	0.31	0.98	
甘 肃	Gansu	0.82		0.05	0.15	0.06	1.37	
青 海	Qinghai	1.13		0.50		0.01	0.10	
宁 夏	Ningxia	0.10			0.13	0.03		
新 疆	Xinjiang	1.81	0.02	0.76	0.35	0.09	0.24	
不分地区	Not Classified by Region							

6-26 按行业分更新改造施工、投产项目个数（2003年）

Number of Innovation Projects under Construction and Put into Use by Sector (2003)

行业	Sector	施工项目（个）Number of Projects under Construction (unit)	#新开工 Started This Year	全部建成投产项目（个）Number of Projects Completed and Put into Use (unit)	项目建成投产率（%）Rate of Projects Completed & Put into Use (%)
全国总计	**National Total**	**54359**	**39830**	**30870**	**56.8**
农、林、牧、渔业	**Agriculture, Forestry, Animal Husbandry and Fishing**	**608**	**527**	**444**	**73.0**
农业	Agriculture	157	136	109	69.4
林业	Forestry	137	110	99	72.3
畜牧业	Animal Husbandry	66	51	33	50.0
渔业	Fishing	16	14	12	75.0
农、林、牧、渔服务业	Service Activities for Agriculture, Forestry, Animal Husbandry and Fishing	232	216	191	82.3
采矿业	**Mining**	**2893**	**2441**	**1787**	**61.8**
煤炭开采和洗选业	Mining and Washing of Coal	1930	1678	1210	62.7
石油和天然气开采业	Extraction of Petroleum and Natural Gas	141	105	81	57.4
黑色金属矿采选业	Mining and Processing of Ferrous Metal Ores	171	137	94	55.0
有色金属矿采选业	Mining and Processing of Non-Ferrous Metal Ores	338	257	200	59.2
非金属矿采选业	Mining and Processing of Nonmetal Ores	312	263	201	64.4
其他采矿业	Mining of Other Ores	1	1	1	100.0
制造业	**Manufacturing**	**28768**	**20465**	**14730**	**51.2**
农副食品加工业	Processing of Food from Agricultural Products	1347	1126	778	57.8
食品制造业	Manufacture of Foods	897	691	490	54.6
饮料制造业	Manufacture of Beverages	814	599	457	56.1
烟草制品业	Manufacture of Tobacco	388	178	191	49.2
纺织业	Manufacture of Textile	1808	1390	1055	58.4
纺织服装、鞋、帽制造业	Manufacture of Textile Wearing Apparel, Footware, and Caps	469	369	245	52.2
皮革毛皮羽毛(绒)及其制品业	Manufacture of Leather, Fur, Feather and Related Products	227	184	117	51.5
木材加工及木竹藤棕草制品业	Processing of Timber, Manufacture of Wood, Bamboo, Rattan, Palm, and Straw Products	466	409	300	64.4
家具制造业	Manufacture of Furniture	151	123	84	55.6
造纸及纸制品业	Manufacture of Paper and Paper Products	774	597	391	50.5
印刷业和记录媒介的复制	Printing,Reproduction of Recording Media	327	246	190	58.1
文教体育用品制造业	Manufacture of Articles For Culture, Education and Sport Activity	154	114	85	55.2
石油加工、炼焦及核燃料加工业	Processing of Petroleum, Coking, Processing of Nuclear Fuel	957	607	514	53.7
化学原料及化学制品制造业	Manufacture of Raw Chemical Materials and Chemical Products	3588	2723	2045	57.0
医药制造业	Manufacture of Medicines	1857	1098	726	39.1
化学纤维制造业	Manufacture of Chemical Fibers	189	116	95	50.3
橡胶制品业	Manufacture of Rubber	254	191	126	49.6
塑料制品业	Manufacture of Plastics	652	461	354	54.3
非金属矿物制品业	Manufacture of Non-metallic Mineral Products	2377	1890	1346	56.6
黑色金属冶炼及压延加工业	Smelting and Pressing of Ferrous Metals	2783	1945	1371	49.3
有色金属冶炼及压延加工业	Smelting and Pressing of Non-ferrous Metals	1140	772	598	52.5
金属制品业	Manufacture of Metal Products	696	507	335	48.1
通用设备制造业	Manufacture of General Purpose Machinery	1279	894	612	47.8
专用设备制造业	Manufacture of Special Purpose Machinery	1129	807	554	49.1
交通运输设备制造业	Manufacture of Transport Equipment	1725	997	691	40.1
电气机械及器材制造业	Manufacture of Electrical Machinery and Equipment	969	635	447	46.1
通信设备、计算机及其他电子设备制造业	Manufacture of Communication Equipment, Computers and Other Electronic Equipment	874	505	333	38.1
仪器仪表文化办公用机械制造业	Manufacture of Measuring Instruments and Machinery for Cultural Activity and Office Work	223	112	98	43.9
工艺品及其他制造业	Manufacture of Artwork and Other Manufacturing	243	169	96	39.5
废弃资源和废旧材料回收加工业	Recycling and Disposal of Waste	11	10	6	54.5
电力燃气水的生产供应业	**Production and Distribution of Electricity, Gas and Water**	**5543**	**3697**	**3060**	**55.2**
电力、热力的生产和供应业	Production and Distribution of Electric Power and Heat Power	4766	3207	2736	57.4
燃气生产和供应业	Production and Distribution of Gas	120	77	51	42.5
水的生产和供应业	Production and Distribution of Water	657	413	273	41.6
建筑业	**Construction**	**325**	**255**	**200**	**61.5**
房屋和土木工程建筑业	Construction of Buildings and Civil Engineering	262	207	164	62.6
建筑安装业	Building Installation	29	22	20	69.0
建筑装饰业	Buidling Decoration	20	16	11	55.0
其他建筑业	Other Construction	14	10	5	35.7

6-26 续表 continued

行业	Sector	施工项目 (个) Number of Projects under Construction (unit)	#新开工 Started This Year	全部建成投产项目 (个) Number of Projects Completed and Put into Use (unit)	项目建成投产率 (%) Rate of Projects Completed & Put into Use (%)
交通运输、仓储和邮政业	**Transport, Storage and Post**	**3320**	**2373**	**2019**	**60.8**
铁路运输业	Railway Transport	1171	879	844	72.1
道路运输业	Road Transport	1151	870	722	62.7
城市公共交通业	Urban Public Transport	107	59	49	45.8
水上运输业	Water Transport	476	314	216	45.4
航空运输业	Air Transport	55	34	27	49.1
管道运输业	Transport Via Pipelines	7	3	3	42.9
装卸搬运和其他运输服务业	Loading, Unloading and Other Transport Services	35	23	18	51.4
仓储业	Storage	103	77	49	47.6
邮政业	Post	215	114	91	42.3
信息传输、计算机服务和软件业	**Information Transmission, Computer Services and Software**	**7728**	**6336**	**5738**	**74.2**
电信和其他信息传输服务业	Telecommunications and Other Information Transmission Services	7652	6287	5705	74.6
计算机服务业	Computer Services	18	12	6	33.3
软件业	Software	58	37	27	46.6
批发和零售业	**Wholesale and Retail Trade**	**917**	**759**	**589**	**64.2**
批发业	Wholesale Trade	534	452	362	67.8
零售业	Retail Trade	383	307	227	59.3
住宿和餐饮业	**Hotel and Restaurants**	**306**	**231**	**208**	**68.0**
住宿业	Hotels	134	85	67	50.0
餐饮业	Restaurants	172	146	141	82.0
金融业	**Financial Intermediation**	**64**	**51**	**27**	**42.2**
银行业	Banks	59	49	24	40.7
证券业	Security Activities	2	1	1	50.0
保险业	Insurance	3	1	2	66.7
其他金融活动	Other Financial Activities				
房地产业	**Real Estate**	**149**	**108**	**95**	**63.8**
租赁和商务服务业	**Leasing and Business Services**	**83**	**46**	**39**	**47.0**
租赁业	Leasing	2	2	2	100.0
商务服务业	Business Services	81	44	37	45.7
科学研究、技术服务和地质勘查业	**Scientific Research, Technical Service and Geologic Prospecting Geologic Prospecting**	**213**	**116**	**53**	**24.9**
研究与试验发展	Research and Experimental Development	142	78	33	23.2
专业技术服务业	Professional Technical Services	51	24	16	31.4
科技交流和推广服务业	Services of Science and Technology Exchanges and Promotion	17	13	3	17.6
地质勘查业	Geologic Prospecting	3	1	1	33.3
水利、环境和公共设施管理业	**Management of Water Conservancy, Environment and Public Facilities**	**1824**	**1223**	**899**	**49.3**
水利管理业	Management of Water Conservancy	519	218	173	33.3
环境管理业	Environmental Management	145	109	84	57.9
公共设施管理业	Management of Public Facilities	1160	896	642	55.3
居民服务和其他服务业	**Services to Households and Other Services**	**54**	**45**	**43**	**79.6**
居民服务业	Services to Households	44	36	37	84.1
其他服务业	Other Services	10	9	6	60.0
教育	**Education**	**501**	**380**	**344**	**68.7**
卫生、社会保障和社会福利业	**Health, Social Security and Social Welfare**	**228**	**176**	**146**	**64.0**
卫生	Health	207	163	134	64.7
社会保障业	Social Security	10	3	5	50.0
社会福利业	Social Welfare	11	10	7	63.6
文化、体育和娱乐业	**Culture, Sports and Entertainment**	**230**	**150**	**124**	**53.9**
新闻出版业	Journalism and Publishing Activities	4	2	1	25.0
广播、电视、电影和音像业	Broadcasting, Movies, Televisions and Audiovisual Activities	129	91	78	60.5
文化艺术业	Cultural and Art Activities	39	24	18	46.2
体育	Sports Activities	27	11	9	33.3
娱乐业	Entertainment	31	22	18	58.1
公共管理和社会组织	**Public Management and Social Organization**	**605**	**451**	**325**	**53.7**
中国共产党机关	Organs of Communist Party of China	6	4	2	33.3
国家机构	Government Agencies	552	413	289	52.4
人民政协和民主党派	People's Political Consultative Conference and Democratic Parties	2	1		
群众团体、社会团体和宗教组织	Non-Governmental Institutions, Social Organizaitons and Religion Organizations	19	13	13	68.4
基层群众自治组织	Grass Roots Self-governing Organizations	26	20	21	80.8
国际组织	**International Organizations**				

6-27 按行业分更新改造新增固定资产

Newly Increased Fixed Assets though Investment in Innovation by Sector

单位: 亿元 (100 million yuan)

年 份 Year	合 计 Total	农、林、牧、渔业 Farming, Forestry, Animal Husbandry and Fishery	采掘业 Mining and Quarrying	制造业 Manufacturing	电力、煤气及水的生产和供应业 Production and Supply of Electricity Gas and Water	建筑业 Construction	地质勘查业水利管理业 Geological Prospecting and Water Conservancy	交通运输仓储和邮电通信业 Transport, Storage, Post & Telecommunication Services
1980	92.58	0.90	21.91	49.59	3.53	0.94	0.09	9.15
1985	316.79	4.30	32.13	196.46	11.95	6.40	0.67	33.24
1989	636.88	7.15	67.58	399.22	27.48	7.07	2.50	49.23
1990	722.94	7.14	67.81	460.33	33.12	6.69	2.41	68.48
1991	858.30	11.43	75.91	542.84	38.30	8.05	3.93	98.28
1992	1105.05	12.71	72.22	684.00	49.34	12.82	2.46	154.62
1993	1531.93	15.23	110.63	876.43	68.59	27.27	4.28	285.30
1994	2192.57	17.12	145.08	1210.46	103.14	18.72	5.00	473.56
1995	2524.87	17.37	164.06	1381.19	146.54	29.86	6.38	563.74
1996	(3002.69)	(21.10)	(187.10)	(1512.97)	(218.13)	(30.27)	(7.39)	(739.95)
	2995.31	20.87	186.92	1509.36	217.86	30.10	7.34	739.21
1997	3250.55	23.36	219.23	1504.22	230.45	41.85	12.83	884.03
1998	3690.36	22.51	242.82	1518.86	284.26	24.82	15.42	1210.86
1999	3644.67	20.24	217.48	1527.02	324.89	25.82	16.37	1109.86
2000	4111.51	20.44	284.27	1660.99	351.38	61.12	16.22	1317.75
2001	4411.49	18.66	296.06	1920.06	342.94	36.99	24.77	1387.25
2002	4693.16	17.85	356.69	2268.07	458.88	55.71	20.51	1137.13

6-27 续表 continued

单位: 亿元 (100 million yuan)

年 份 Year	批发零售贸易和餐饮业 Wholesale and Retail Trade & Catering Services	金融、保险业 Finance and Insurance	房地产业 Real Estate	社会服务业 Social Services	卫生体育和社会福利业 Health Care, Sports & Social Welfare	教育、文化艺术和广播电影电视业 Education, Culture and Arts, Radio, Film and Television	科学研究和综合技术服务业 Scientific Research and Polytechnic Services	国家机关、政党机关和社会团体 Government Agencies, Party Agencies and Social Organizations	其 他 Others
1980	3.00	0.03	1.53		0.16	0.38	0.27	0.76	0.34
1985	7.91	0.77	2.54	11.13	1.67	2.47	1.93	2.33	0.90
1989	21.34	2.23	8.29	26.31	2.72	3.82	2.12	5.46	4.36
1990	23.05	1.45	8.16	25.26	3.05	3.53	1.58	5.48	5.41
1991	21.32	1.85	7.97	26.03	2.86	4.96	1.50	7.12	5.95
1992	34.44	2.03	9.14	39.88	3.49	5.36	2.81	10.05	9.68
1993	36.62	2.82	18.31	51.72	4.21	5.40	1.89	14.63	8.58
1994	50.30	2.47	31.24	91.29	3.95	5.90	3.09	20.09	11.16
1995	49.92	2.32	38.80	69.34	4.60	11.23	3.00	21.19	15.33
1996	(65.07)	(6.28)	(36.99)	(100.87)	(7.79)	(10.23)	(5.76)	(28.51)	(24.28)
	64.53	6.24	36.98	100.60	7.60	9.82	5.63	27.99	24.26
1997	36.10	9.15	57.87	137.14	10.31	13.46	5.98	33.81	30.76
1998	64.86	12.86	26.41	157.94	10.39	16.39	4.91	42.91	34.15
1999	54.22	6.16	32.32	189.42	13.02	20.95	16.20	43.18	27.51
2000	48.69	6.17	30.00	186.59	17.37	27.68	30.51	37.56	14.75
2001	45.25	14.07	8.64	188.81	23.39	38.36	24.96	29.30	11.98
2002	64.92	17.23	2.87	163.38	29.98	35.19	18.23	32.53	13.99

6-28 各地区按行业分更新改造新增固定资产（2003年）

Newly Increased Fixed Assets through Investment in Innovation by Sector (2003)

单位: 亿元 (100 million yuan)

地区	Region	合计 Total	农、林、牧、渔业 Agriculture, Forestry, Animal Husbandry and Fishing	采矿业 Mining	制造业 Manufacturing	电力、燃气及水的生产和供应业 Production and Distribution of Electricity, Gas and Water	建筑业 Construction	交通运输、仓储和邮政业 Transport, Storage and Post
全国总计	**National Total**	**5643.19**	**20.55**	**384.85**	**3308.92**	**445.88**	**44.24**	**339.83**
北京	Beijing	112.94	0.09	2.52	37.02	16.23	0.81	10.78
天津	Tianjin	101.11		1.65	58.93	6.57	4.93	1.88
河北	Hebei	345.81	2.77	10.24	208.24	25.36	5.43	17.60
山西	Shanxi	138.65		35.68	78.84	5.14	1.02	2.73
内蒙古	Inner Mongolia	121.52	0.37	14.03	63.63	20.27		6.18
辽宁	Liaoning	342.68	0.70	34.06	214.94	21.89	2.61	9.66
吉林	Jilin	140.29	0.34	9.63	117.09	6.16	0.34	2.74
黑龙江	Heilongjiang	207.55	0.99	34.00	87.69	24.83	0.25	8.12
上海	Shanghai	258.76			172.52	22.21	4.27	33.63
江苏	Jiangsu	437.97	0.44	11.87	286.94	30.68	0.96	15.11
浙江	Zhejiang	227.35	0.56	1.00	152.09	23.67	0.82	11.51
安徽	Anhui	193.43	0.92	12.55	123.18	17.82	1.47	8.94
福建	Fujian	172.78	0.37	0.22	102.83	9.40	0.10	6.39
江西	Jiangxi	79.77	0.60	5.32	51.52	5.83	0.04	4.53
山东	Shandong	583.86	1.42	71.08	353.64	39.48	4.06	42.90
河南	Henan	247.58	0.15	49.25	132.28	22.81	0.45	16.97
湖北	Hubei	256.47	0.59	9.25	164.14	21.02	2.80	14.12
湖南	Hunan	193.11	0.25	5.29	134.03	13.29	0.24	8.30
广东	Guangdong	402.95	0.31	1.40	178.48	34.64	7.81	56.60
广西	Guangxi	95.92	0.58	0.65	65.30	4.20	0.04	8.19
海南	Hainan	9.89	1.45		1.93	1.69		0.82
重庆	Chongqing	97.75	0.16	2.64	37.82	8.51	0.37	3.41
四川	Sichuan	258.13	0.16	8.63	207.72	7.56	0.34	6.94
贵州	Guizhou	85.80	0.10	5.45	38.83	9.96	0.61	4.58
云南	Yunnan	91.08	0.29	2.28	31.13	2.53		8.36
西藏	Tibet	5.38	0.01	0.23	0.40	1.86	0.03	0.57
陕西	Shaanxi	131.01	0.61	21.59	54.54	15.17	1.37	6.47
甘肃	Gansu	135.35	0.50	4.15	93.57	16.76	0.53	5.35
青海	Qinghai	11.58	0.01	1.20	6.54	1.64	0.33	0.93
宁夏	Ningxia	26.90	0.04	2.91	18.82	2.25	0.06	0.60
新疆	Xinjiang	107.18	5.77	6.99	34.29	6.45	2.14	11.36
不分地区	Not Classified by Region	22.63		19.07				3.56

6-28 续表 1 continued

单位: 亿元 (100 million yuan)

地区	Region	信息传输、计算机服务和软件业 Information Transmission, Computer Service and Software	批发和零售业 Wholesale and Retail Trade	住宿和餐饮业 Hotel and Restaurants	金融业 Financial Intermediation	房地产业 Real Estate	租赁和商务服务业 Leasing and Business Services	科学研究、技术服务和地质勘查业 Scientific Research, Technical Services, and Geological Prospecting
全国总计	**National Total**	**709.71**	**48.66**	**19.84**	**15.17**	**8.58**	**8.15**	**15.23**
北京	Beijing	28.63	0.17	0.51			0.19	0.43
天津	Tianjin	12.26	2.08	0.15	0.27		1.09	0.31
河北	Hebei	46.95	3.54	0.37	0.01	3.54	1.58	1.27
山西	Shanxi	11.11	0.10					0.02
内蒙古	Inner Mongolia	12.99		0.07		1.25		
辽宁	Liaoning	32.34	8.78	9.13	1.25	0.10	1.85	0.32
吉林	Jilin	2.36	0.32				0.21	0.21
黑龙江	Heilongjiang	50.78	0.32		0.01			
上海	Shanghai	0.17	2.42	0.99		1.42	0.29	1.29
江苏	Jiangsu	56.92	1.58	0.83	0.05	0.39	0.41	1.10
浙江	Zhejiang	31.33	0.71	0.24	0.68			0.02
安徽	Anhui	23.44	1.12	0.17	0.05	0.03		0.12
福建	Fujian	50.67	0.18	0.05			0.35	0.29
江西	Jiangxi	0.93	0.47	0.06	0.43	0.06		0.01
山东	Shandong	41.51	3.75	0.53	0.04	0.32	0.02	0.29
河南	Henan	16.24	0.70	0.19		0.03	0.10	0.16
湖北	Hubei	25.15	2.32	0.29	1.14	0.27	0.03	0.46
湖南	Hunan	24.51	1.81	0.97	0.13		0.19	0.02
广东	Guangdong	43.48	6.36	2.48	8.75	0.18	0.90	6.43
广西	Guangxi	15.07	0.52	0.08	0.07			0.02
海南	Hainan	2.65			0.01			
重庆	Chongqing	38.78	0.61		0.86	0.26		0.29
四川	Sichuan	21.42	0.89	0.12			0.19	1.56
贵州	Guizhou	23.58	0.70	0.02	0.02	0.01		0.25
云南	Yunnan	38.15	0.51	0.74	0.03	0.68	0.60	0.03
西藏	Tibet	2.02		0.02	0.01			
陕西	Shaanxi	13.86	1.45	0.33			0.01	0.01
甘肃	Gansu	7.69	5.51	0.05				
青海	Qinghai	0.30	0.10					0.03
宁夏	Ningxia	1.92	0.05				0.10	
新疆	Xinjiang	32.48	1.60	1.44	1.38	0.04	0.03	0.30
不分地区	Not Classified by Region							

6-28 续表 2 continued

单位: 亿元 (100 million yuan)

地区	Region	水利、环境和公共设施管理业 Water Management of Conservancy, Environment and Public Facilities	居民服务和其他服务业 Services to Households and Other Services	教育 Education	卫生、社会保障和社会福利业 Health, Social Securities and Social Welfare	文化、体育和娱乐业 Culture, Sports and Entertainment	公共管理和社会组织 Public Management and Social Organization	国际组织 International Organizations
全国总计	**National Total**	**151.62**	**1.48**	**30.81**	**33.11**	**13.87**	**42.70**	
北京	Beijing	13.60		0.15	0.84	0.09	0.88	
天津	Tianjin	8.96	0.28	0.47	0.13	0.17	0.97	
河北	Hebei	10.75	0.26	2.69	1.19	1.09	2.93	
山西	Shanxi	3.71		0.15	0.08	0.09		
内蒙古	Inner Mongolia	1.57			0.38	0.01	0.78	
辽宁	Liaoning	1.45	0.27	0.62	0.30	1.17	1.22	
吉林	Jilin	0.17	0.06	0.10	0.03	0.01	0.53	
黑龙江	Heilongjiang	0.02		0.24	0.05	0.03	0.23	
上海	Shanghai	15.64	0.02	2.26	0.71	0.34	0.58	
江苏	Jiangsu	27.61	0.17	0.11	1.08	0.52	1.21	
浙江	Zhejiang	1.09	0.05	0.23	2.40	0.42	0.52	
安徽	Anhui	0.88		0.16	0.73	0.03	1.84	
福建	Fujian	0.51		0.01	0.43	0.69	0.26	
江西	Jiangxi	1.32	0.10	4.88	2.29	0.83	0.53	
山东	Shandong	15.11	0.02	0.18	1.14	1.44	6.94	
河南	Henan	3.71	0.02	1.06	1.21	0.13	2.11	
湖北	Hubei	5.03	0.02	5.21	2.33	1.37	0.92	
湖南	Hunan	1.69	0.03	0.12	1.18	0.47	0.59	
广东	Guangdong	14.71	0.12	8.26	12.21	3.42	16.41	
广西	Guangxi	0.47		0.15	0.40	0.16	0.02	
海南	Hainan	0.61		0.01	0.14	0.16	0.43	
重庆	Chongqing	0.06	0.01	1.28	2.12	0.14	0.42	
四川	Sichuan	1.38	0.02	0.10	0.46	0.34	0.31	
贵州	Guizhou	1.15	0.01	0.25	0.14	0.07	0.08	
云南	Yunnan	3.80		0.92	0.50	0.17	0.36	
西藏	Tibet	0.01		0.03			0.18	
陕西	Shaanxi	14.13		0.35	0.14	0.31	0.66	
甘肃	Gansu	0.55			0.15	0.06	0.49	
青海	Qinghai	0.28		0.07		0.04	0.10	
宁夏	Ningxia	0.12				0.03		
新疆	Xinjiang	1.51	0.02	0.76	0.33	0.08	0.22	
不分地区	Not Classified by Region							

6-29 按行业分更新改造投资和新增固定资产（2003年）

Investment in Innovation and Newly Increased Fixed Assets by Sector (2003)

行 业	Sector	投资额（亿元） Investment (100 million yuan)	新 增 固定资产（亿元） Newly Increased Fixed Assets (100 million yuan)	固定资产交付使用率（%） Rate of Fixed Assets Put into Use (%)
全 国 总 计	**National Total**	**8624.86**	**5643.19**	**65.4**
农、林、牧、渔业	**Agriculture, Forestry, Animal Husbandry and Fishing**	**31.80**	**20.55**	**64.6**
农业	Agriculture	7.88	5.32	67.5
林业	Forestry	5.26	3.90	74.2
畜牧业	Animal Husbandry	7.00	3.46	49.3
渔业	Fishing	0.83	0.53	63.9
农、林、牧、渔服务业	Service Activities for Agriculture, Forestry, Animal Husbandry and Fishing	10.83	7.34	67.8
采矿业	**Mining**	**531.72**	**384.85**	**72.4**
煤炭开采和洗选业	Mining and Washing of Coal	194.59	129.52	66.6
石油和天然气开采业	Extraction of Petroleum and Natural Gas	261.79	197.64	75.5
黑色金属矿采选业	Mining and Processing of Ferrous Metal Ores	21.95	19.17	87.4
有色金属矿采选业	Mining and Processing of Non-Ferrous Metal Ores	34.10	24.64	72.3
非金属矿采选业	Mining and Processing of Nonmetal Ores	19.13	13.72	71.7
其他采矿业	Mining of Other Ores	0.16	0.16	100.0
制造业	**Manufacturing**	**5147.09**	**3308.92**	**64.3**
农副食品加工业	Processing of Food from Agricultural Products	155.85	102.31	65.6
食品制造业	Manufacture of Foods	128.17	91.34	71.3
饮料制造业	Manufacture of Beverages	117.53	80.30	68.3
烟草制品业	Manufacture of Tobacco	73.82	50.30	68.1
纺织业	Manufacture of Textile	286.89	196.18	68.4
纺织服装、鞋、帽制造业	Manufacture of Textile Wearing Apparel, Footware, and Caps	47.48	28.60	60.2
皮革毛皮羽毛(绒)及其制品业	Manufacture of Leather, Fur, Feather and Related Products	22.54	16.16	71.7
木材加工及木竹藤棕草制品业	Processing of Timber, Manufacture of Wood, Bamboo, Rattan, Palm, and Straw Products	46.08	30.35	65.9
家具制造业	Manufacture of Furniture	15.16	9.97	65.8
造纸及纸制品业	Manufacture of Paper and Paper Products	153.45	91.79	59.8
印刷业和记录媒介的复制	Printing,Reproduction of Recording Media	55.56	42.49	76.5
文教体育用品制造业	Manufacture of Articles For Culture, Education and Sport Activity	11.02	6.05	54.9
石油加工、炼焦及核燃料加工业	Processing of Petroleum, Coking, Processing of Nuclear Fuel	190.28	134.67	70.8
化学原料及化学制品制造业	Manufacture of Raw Chemical Materials and Chemical Products	463.52	278.63	60.1
医药制造业	Manufacture of Medicines	282.18	187.10	66.3
化学纤维制造业	Manufacture of Chemical Fibers	76.29	39.20	51.4
橡胶制品业	Manufacture of Rubber	70.06	51.17	73.0
塑料制品业	Manufacture of Plastics	104.34	81.87	78.5
非金属矿物制品业	Manufacture of Non-metallic Mineral Products	368.01	229.87	62.5
黑色金属冶炼及压延加工业	Smelting and Pressing of Ferrous Metals	966.65	588.49	60.9
有色金属冶炼及压延加工业	Smelting and Pressing of Non-ferrous Metals	238.32	154.49	64.8
金属制品业	Manufacture of Metal Products	83.19	51.29	61.7
通用设备制造业	Manufacture of General Purpose Machinery	166.57	109.97	66.0
专用设备制造业	Manufacture of Special Purpose Machinery	139.21	90.37	64.9
交通运输设备制造业	Manufacture of Transport Equipment	458.36	255.44	55.7
电气机械及器材制造业	Manufacture of Electrical Machinery and Equipment	130.83	92.87	71.0
通信设备、计算机及其他电子设备制造业	Manufacture of Communication Equipment, Computers and Other Electronic Equipment	243.36	177.01	72.7
仪器仪表文化办公用机械制造业	Manufacture of Measuring Instruments and Machinery for Cultural Activity and Office Work	31.77	26.73	84.2
工艺品及其他制造业	Manufacture of Artwork and Other Manufacturing	20.08	13.55	67.5
废弃资源和废旧材料回收加工业	Recycling and Disposal of Waste	0.53	0.35	66.0
电力燃气水的生产供应业	**Production and Distribution of Electricity, Gas and Water**	**718.64**	**445.88**	**62.0**
电力、热力的生产和供应业	Production and Distribution of Electric Power and Heat Power	640.35	397.22	62.0
燃气生产和供应业	Production and Distribution of Gas	24.54	15.40	62.8
水的生产和供应业	Production and Distribution of Water	53.76	33.26	61.9
建筑业	**Construction**	**54.23**	**44.24**	**81.6**
房屋和土木工程建筑业	Construction of Buildings and Civil Engineering	48.43	40.38	83.4
建筑安装业	Building Installation	2.86	2.15	75.2
建筑装饰业	Buidling Decoration	1.90	0.66	34.8
其他建筑业	Other Construction	1.03	1.05	101.5

6-29 续表 continued

行 业	Sector	投资额（亿元） Investment (100 million yuan)	新增固定资产（亿元） Newly Increased Fixed Assets (100 million yuan)	固定资产交付使用率（%） Rate of Fixed Assets Put into Use (%)
交通运输、仓储和邮政业	**Transport, Storage and Post**	**432.25**	**339.83**	**78.6**
铁路运输业	Railway Transport	89.31	68.60	76.8
道路运输业	Road Transport	151.65	110.36	72.8
城市公共交通业	Urban Public Transport	59.36	55.98	94.3
水上运输业	Water Transport	59.55	45.90	77.1
航空运输业	Air Transport	39.07	36.87	94.4
管道运输业	Transport Via Pipelines	3.93	3.14	79.8
装卸搬运和其他运输服务业	Loading, Unloading and Other Transport Services	4.10	2.85	69.7
仓储业	Storage	18.77	12.26	65.3
邮政业	Post	6.53	3.86	59.1
信息传输、计算机服务和软件业	**Information Transmission, Computer Services and Software**	**1120.85**	**709.71**	**63.3**
电信和其他信息传输服务业	Telecommunications and Other Information Transmission Services	1110.09	705.66	63.6
计算机服务业	Computer Services	2.33	0.81	34.6
软件业	Software	8.43	3.24	38.4
批发和零售业	**Wholesale and Retail Trade**	**76.36**	**48.66**	**63.7**
批发业	Wholesale Trade	35.91	21.50	59.9
零售业	Retail Trade	40.46	27.16	67.1
住宿和餐饮业	**Hotel and Restaurants**	**27.92**	**19.84**	**71.1**
住宿业	Hotels	12.66	7.07	55.8
餐饮业	Restaurants	15.26	12.77	83.7
金融业	**Financial Intermediation**	**17.78**	**15.17**	**85.3**
银行业	Banks	16.40	13.80	84.1
证券业	Security Activities	0.52	0.52	100.0
保险业	Insurance	0.70	0.69	98.9
其他金融活动	Other Financial Activities	0.15	0.15	100.0
房地产业	**Real Estate**	**11.55**	**8.58**	**74.3**
租赁和商务服务业	**Leasing and Business Services**	**12.43**	**8.15**	**65.5**
租赁业	Leasing	0.14	0.07	45.8
商务服务业	Business Services	12.29	8.08	65.8
科学研究、技术服务和地质勘查业	**Scientific Research, Technical Service and Geologic Prospecting Geologic Prospecting**	**30.04**	**15.23**	**50.7**
研究与试验发展	Research and Experimental Development	19.31	6.87	35.6
专业技术服务业	Professional Technical Services	8.87	7.19	81.0
科技交流和推广服务业	Services of Science and Technology Exchanges and Promotion	1.21	0.67	55.5
地质勘查业	Geologic Prospecting	0.64	0.50	78.5
水利、环境和公共设施管理业	**Management of Water Conservancy, Environment and Public Facilities**	**246.84**	**151.62**	**61.4**
水利管理业	Management of Water Conservancy	31.41	18.76	59.7
环境管理业	Environmental Management	30.37	22.38	73.7
公共设施管理业	Management of Public Facilities	185.06	110.48	59.7
居民服务和其他服务业	**Services to Households and Other Services**	**2.71**	**1.48**	**54.6**
居民服务业	Services to Households	2.16	1.28	59.1
其他服务业	Other Services	0.55	0.20	36.9
教育	**Education**	**38.10**	**30.81**	**80.9**
卫生、社会保障和社会福利业	**Health, Social Security and Social Welfare**	**35.25**	**33.11**	**93.9**
卫生	Health	32.82	30.91	94.2
社会保障业	Social Security	2.19	2.03	92.7
社会福利业	Social Welfare	0.24	0.16	69.5
文化、体育和娱乐业	**Culture, Sports and Entertainment**	**19.75**	**13.87**	**70.2**
新闻出版业	Journalism and Publishing Activities	1.72	1.56	90.8
广播、电视、电影和音像业	Broadcasting, Movies, Televisions and Audiovisual Activities	11.31	8.31	73.5
文化艺术业	Cultural and Art Activities	1.74	1.05	60.3
体育	Sports Activities	1.48	1.13	76.6
娱乐业	Entertainment	3.51	1.82	51.9
公共管理和社会组织	**Public Management and Social Organization**	**69.55**	**42.70**	**61.4**
中国共产党机关	Organs of Communist Party of China	0.77	0.46	59.6
国家机构	Government Agencies	67.05	40.78	60.8
人民政协和民主党派	People's Political Consultative Conference and Democratic Parties	0.08	0.09	108.5
群众团体、社会团体和宗教组织	Non-Governmental Institutions, Social Organizaitons and Religion Organizations	0.78	0.60	77.2
基层群众自治组织	Grass Roots Self-governing Organizations	0.87	0.78	89.1
国际组织	**International Organizations**			

6-30 各地区限额以上更新改造项目个数、投资和新增固定资产(2003年)

Number of Innovation Projects, Investment and Newly Increased Fixed Assets above Designated Size by Region (2003)

地 区	Region	施工项目 (个) Number of Projects under Construction (unit)	全部建成投产项目 (个) Number of Projects Completed and Put into Use (unit)	项目建成投产率 (%) Rate of Projects Completed and Put into Use (%)	投资完成额 Investment 绝对数 (亿元) Value (100 million yuan)	投资完成额 Investment 比重 (%) Percentage (%)	新增固定资产 (亿元) Newly Increased Fixed Assets (100 million yuan)	固定资产交付使用率 (%) Rate of Fixed Assets Put into Use (%)
全国总计	**National Total**	**2886**	**774**	**26.8**	**2587.27**	**100.0**	**1506.36**	**58.2**
北 京	Beijing	115	21	18.3	185.44	7.2	85.70	46.2
天 津	Tianjin	61	12	19.7	72.66	2.8	17.15	23.6
河 北	Hebei	162	45	27.8	179.90	7.0	113.65	63.2
山 西	Shanxi	16	3	18.8	25.58	1.0	8.18	32.0
内蒙古	Inner Mongolia	149	45	30.2	73.48	2.8	42.63	58.0
辽 宁	Liaoning	170	35	20.6	167.34	6.5	103.80	62.0
吉 林	Jilin	68	21	30.9	74.22	2.9	44.72	60.3
黑龙江	Heilongjiang	100	28	28.0	89.87	3.5	78.84	87.7
上 海	Shanghai	302	92	30.5	225.64	8.7	142.69	63.2
江 苏	Jiangsu	98	34	34.7	91.27	3.5	55.19	60.5
浙 江	Zhejiang	61	30	49.2	49.29	1.9	48.87	99.1
安 徽	Anhui	126	25	19.8	145.37	5.6	44.43	30.6
福 建	Fujian	64	19	29.7	50.80	2.0	34.27	67.5
江 西	Jiangxi	30	8	26.7	36.88	1.4	15.94	43.2
山 东	Shandong	75	14	18.7	186.90	7.2	107.26	57.4
河 南	Henan	47	13	27.7	61.61	2.4	33.60	54.5
湖 北	Hubei	72	21	29.2	52.86	2.0	22.56	42.7
湖 南	Hunan	40	15	37.5	58.61	2.3	35.51	60.6
广 东	Guangdong	206	58	28.2	165.88	6.4	72.69	43.8
广 西	Guangxi	84	22	26.2	67.74	2.6	40.24	59.4
海 南	Hainan	3	1	33.3	3.70	0.1	2.40	64.8
重 庆	Chongqing	14	4	28.6	14.45	0.6	4.15	28.7
四 川	Sichuan	375	101	26.9	208.69	8.1	144.93	69.4
贵 州	Guizhou	149	27	18.1	76.47	3.0	35.65	46.6
云 南	Yunnan	59	10	16.9	41.59	1.6	7.84	18.9
西 藏	Tibet							
陕 西	Shaanxi	113	26	23.0	66.94	2.6	46.81	69.9
甘 肃	Gansu	71	30	42.3	34.09	1.3	66.84	196.1
青 海	Qinghai	17	3	17.6	21.65	0.8	2.67	12.3
宁 夏	Ningxia	7	1	14.3	11.38	0.4	2.95	26.0
新 疆	Xinjiang	27	5	18.5	21.30	0.8	21.58	101.3
不分地区	Not Classified by Region	5	5	100.0	25.66	1.0	22.63	88.2

6-31 按行业分限额以上更新改造施工、投产项目个数(2003年)

Number of Innovation Projects above Designated Size under Construction or Completed and Put into Use by Sector (2003)

行业	Sector	施工项目 (个) Number of Projects under Construction (unit)	#新开工 Started This Year	全部建成投产项目 (个) Number of Projects Completed and Put into Use (unit)	项目建成投产率 (%) Rate of Projects Completed & Put into Use (%)
全国总计	**National Total**	**2886**	**1304**	**774**	**26.8**
农、林、牧、渔业	**Agriculture, Forestry, Animal Husbandry and Fishing**	**6**	**5**		
农业	Agriculture	2	2		
林业	Forestry	1			
畜牧业	Animal Husbandry	2	2		
渔业	Fishing				
农、林、牧、渔服务业	Service Activities for Agriculture, Forestry, Animal Husbandry and Fishing	1	1		
采矿业	**Mining**	**94**	**53**	**33**	**35.1**
煤炭开采和洗选业	Mining and Washing of Coal	49	29	10	20.4
石油和天然气开采业	Extraction of Petroleum and Natural Gas	15	9	10	66.7
黑色金属矿采选业	Mining and Processing of Ferrous Metal Ores	9	7	5	55.6
有色金属矿采选业	Mining and Processing of Non-Ferrous Metal Ores	7	2	2	28.6
非金属矿采选业	Mining and Processing of Nonmetal Ores	14	6	6	42.9
其他采矿业	Mining of Other Ores				
制造业	**Manufacturing**	**2192**	**1002**	**588**	**26.8**
农副食品加工业	Processing of Food from Agricultural Products	59	47	15	25.4
食品制造业	Manufacture of Foods	60	36	23	38.3
饮料制造业	Manufacture of Beverages	67	33	27	40.3
烟草制品业	Manufacture of Tobacco	31	7	4	12.9
纺织业	Manufacture of Textile	85	41	28	32.9
纺织服装、鞋、帽制造业	Manufacture of Textile Wearing Apparel, Footware, and Caps	8	3	2	25.0
皮革毛皮羽毛(绒)及其制品业	Manufacture of Leather, Fur, Feather and Related Products	6	4	1	16.7
木材加工及木竹藤棕草制品业	Processing of Timber, Manufacture of Wood, Bamboo, Rattan, Palm, and Straw Products	8	6	3	37.5
家具制造业	Manufacture of Furniture	1	1		
造纸及纸制品业	Manufacture of Paper and Paper Products	60	27	14	23.3
印刷业和记录媒介的复制	Printing,Reproduction of Recording Media	17	8	4	23.5
文教体育用品制造业	Manufacture of Articles For Culture, Education and Sport Activity	6	3	1	16.7
石油加工、炼焦及核燃料加工业	Processing of Petroleum, Coking, Processing of Nuclear Fuel	66	38	20	30.3
化学原料及化学制品制造业	Manufacture of Raw Chemical Materials and Chemical Products	211	94	64	30.3
医药制造业	Manufacture of Medicines	198	75	42	21.2
化学纤维制造业	Manufacture of Chemical Fibers	25	11	10	40.0
橡胶制品业	Manufacture of Rubber	26	10	8	30.8
塑料制品业	Manufacture of Plastics	37	16	14	37.8
非金属矿物制品业	Manufacture of Non-metallic Mineral Products	134	71	42	31.3
黑色金属冶炼及压延加工业	Smelting and Pressing of Ferrous Metals	357	201	98	27.5
有色金属冶炼及压延加工业	Smelting and Pressing of Non-ferrous Metals	119	48	29	24.4
金属制品业	Manufacture of Metal Products	24	6	10	41.7
通用设备制造业	Manufacture of General Purpose Machinery	83	26	10	12.0
专用设备制造业	Manufacture of Special Purpose Machinery	64	22	15	23.4
交通运输设备制造业	Manufacture of Transport Equipment	247	96	35	14.2
电气机械及器材制造业	Manufacture of Electrical Machinery and Equipment	65	24	24	36.9
通信设备、计算机及其他电设备制造业	Manufacture of Communication Equipment, Computers and Other Electronic Equipment	103	40	35	34.0
仪器仪表文化办公用机械制造业	Manufacture of Measuring Instruments and Machinery for Cultural Activity and Office Work	20	5	8	40.0
工艺品及其他制造业	Manufacture of Artwork and Other Manufacturing	5	3	2	40.0
废弃资源和废旧材料回收加工业	Recycling and Disposal of Waste				
电力燃气水的生产供应业	**Production and Distribution of Electricity, Gas and Water**	**229**	**95**	**53**	**23.1**
电力、热力的生产和供应业	Production and Distribution of Electric Power and Heat Power	174	73	45	25.9
燃气生产和供应业	Production and Distribution of Gas	11	5		
水的生产和供应业	Production and Distribution of Water	44	17	8	18.2
建筑业	**Construction**	**12**	**6**	**2**	**16.7**
房屋和土木工程建筑业	Construction of Buildings and Civil Engineering	12	6	2	16.7
建筑安装业	Building Installation				
建筑装饰业	Buidling Decoration				
其他建筑业	Other Construction				

6-31 续表 continued

行业	Sector	施工项目(个) Number of Projects under Construction (unit)	#新开工 Started This Year	全部建成投产项目(个) Number of Projects Completed and Put into Use (unit)	项目建成投产率(%) Rate of Projects Completed & Put into Use (%)
交通运输、仓储和邮政业	**Transport, Storage and Post**	**83**	**33**	**11**	**13.3**
铁路运输业	Railway Transport	7	5	4	57.1
道路运输业	Road Transport	37	12	4	10.8
城市公共交通业	Urban Public Transport	3	2		
水上运输业	Water Transport	25	7	2	8.0
航空运输业	Air Transport				
管道运输业	Transport Via Pipelines	1		1	100.0
装卸搬运和其他运输服务业	Loading, Unloading and Other Transport Services	1			
仓储业	Storage	9	7		
邮政业	Post				
信息传输、计算机服务和软件业	**Information Transmission, Computer Services and Software**	**111**	**50**	**39**	**35.1**
电信和其他信息传输服务业	Telecommunications and Other Information Transmission Services	100	45	34	34.0
计算机服务业	Computer Services	3	3		
软件业	Software	8	2	5	62.5
批发和零售业	**Wholesale and Retail Trade**	**14**	**10**	**5**	**35.7**
批发业	Wholesale Trade	8	6	3	37.5
零售业	Retail Trade	6	4	2	33.3
住宿和餐饮业	**Hotel and Restaurants**	**2**			
住宿业	Hotels	2			
餐饮业	Restaurants				
金融业	**Financial Intermediation**				
银行业	Banks				
证券业	Security Activities				
保险业	Insurance				
其他金融活动	Other Financial Activities				
房地产业	**Real Estate**	**5**	**2**	**2**	**40.0**
租赁和商务服务业	**Leasing and Business Services**	**1**			
租赁业	Leasing				
商务服务业	Business Services	1			
科学研究、技术服务和地质勘查业	**Scientific Research, Technical Service and Geologic Prospecting Geologic Prospecting**	**32**	**10**	**8**	**25.0**
研究与试验发展	Research and Experimental Development	19	6	2	10.5
专业技术服务业	Professional Technical Services	12	3	6	50.0
科技交流和推广服务业	Services of Science and Technology Exchanges and Promotion	1	1		
地质勘查业	Geologic Prospecting				
水利、环境和公共设施管理业	**Management of Water Conservancy, Environment and Public Facilities**	**82**	**31**	**28**	**34.1**
水利管理业	Management of Water Conservancy	18	3	5	27.8
环境管理业	Environmental Management	8	4	4	50.0
公共设施管理业	Management of Public Facilities	56	24	19	33.9
居民服务和其他服务业	**Services to Households and Other Services**	**2**	**1**		
居民服务业	Services to Households	1			
其他服务业	Other Services	1	1		
教育	**Education**	**3**	**2**		
卫生、社会保障和社会福利业	**Health, Social Security and Social Welfare**	**5**	**1**	**2**	**40.0**
卫生	Health	5	1	2	40.0
社会保障业	Social Security				
社会福利业	Social Welfare				
文化、体育和娱乐业	**Culture, Sports and Entertainment**	**2**			
新闻出版业	Journalism and Publishing Activities				
广播、电视、电影和音像业	Broadcasting, Movies, Televisions and Audiovisual Activities	2			
文化艺术业	Cultural and Art Activities				
体育	Sports Activities				
娱乐业	Entertainment				
公共管理和社会组织	**Public Management and Social Organization**	**11**	**3**	**3**	**27.3**
中国共产党机关	Organs of Communist Party of China				
国家机构	Government Agencies	11	3	3	27.3
人民政协和民主党派	People's Political Consultative Conference and Democratic Parties				
群众团体、社会团体和宗教组织	Non-Governmental Institutions, Social Organizaitons and Religion Organizations				
基层群众自治组织	Grass Roots Self-governing Organizations				
国际组织	**International Organizations**				

6-32 更新改造新增主要产品生产能力

Newly Increased Production Capacity Through Investment in Innovation

能力名称	Item	1999	2000	2001	2002	2003
铁矿开采（原矿）(万吨/年)	Iron-Ore Mining (10 000 tons/year)	47	185	220	180	103
烧结铁矿 (万吨/年)	Sintering of Iron-Ore (10 000 tons/year)	1176	284	596	344	1077
生铁 (万吨/年)	Iron Smelting (10 000 tons/year)	189	333	405	760	1801
炼钢 (万吨/年)	Steel-making (10 000 tons/year)	376	338	187	495	1625
初轧 (万吨/年)	Rough Rolling (10 000 tons/year)		120	95	71	100
铁合金 (万吨/年)	Iron Alloy, Electric Furnace (10 000 tons/year)	3	55	24	26	80
铜选矿:	Copper Ore Dressing					
处理原矿 (万吨/年)	Crude Ore Dressing (10 000 tons/year)	8	42	29	75	21
铜含量 (吨/年)	Copper Content in Concentrate Ore (ton/year)	4700	1790	1000		2865
原煤开采 (万吨/年)	Coal Mining (10 000 tons/year)	901	614	741	1353	2745
天然原油开采 (万吨/年)	Petroleum Extraction (10 000 tons/year)	35	340	236	277	195
硫酸 (万吨/年)	Sulfuric Acid (10 000 tons/year)	109	83	123	106	174
纯碱 (万吨/年)	Soda Ash (10 000 tons/year)	26	4	18	29	27
烧碱 (万吨/年)	Caustic Soda (10 000 tons/year)	15	58	26	23	34
合成氨 (万吨/年)	Synthetic Ammonia (10 000 tons/year)	141	142	49	67	103
化肥 (万吨/年)	Chemical Fertilizer (10 000 tons/year)	232	216	268	186	379
乙烯 (吨/年)	Ethylene (ton/year)	137500	42500	310000	317500	65200
塑料 (吨/年)	Plastics (ton/year)	512603	440801	758520	604929	541507
轮胎: (万条/年)	Tyres (10 000 tyres/year)					
内胎	Inner Tube	120	304	48	30	27
外胎	Tire (Cover)	792	406	208	779	1137
发电机组容量 (万千瓦)	Capacity of Power Generating Sets (10 000 kw/year)	132	41	132	240	468
#火电	Thermal Power	132	41	132	240	436
水电	Hydropower					23
汽车制造 (辆/年)	Motor Vehicles (unit/year)	143000	144120	113700	704445	624750
#载重汽车制造	Trucks	9500	800	50900	80845	37800
拖拉机制造 (混合台/年)	Tractors (unit/year)	90499	64400	2550	5000	40000
#手扶拖拉机制造 (混合台/年)	Walking Tractors (unit/year)	3000	50000	1200		
蒸汽锅炉制造 (台/年)	Steam Boilers (unit/year)	231	2	1		2
蒸汽锅炉蒸发量(小时吨/年)	Evaporative Capacity of Steam Boilers (hour.tons/year)			2000		1040
交流电动机制造(万千瓦/年)	Electric Motors (10 000 kw/year)	34	256	56	319	220
金属切削机床制造 (台/年)	Metal-Cutting Machine Tools (unit/year)	2803	4042	647	1425	3550
民用钢质船舶制造 (综合吨/年)	Civilian Ships (ton/year)	65011	330000	560000	170000	15000
胶合板 (万立方米/年)	Plywood (10 000 cu.m/year)	12	28	61	39	38
水泥 (万吨/年)	Cement (10 000 tons/year)	1834	1616	2165	1587	5591

6-32 续表 continued

能力名称	Item	1999	2000	2001	2002	2003
化学纤维 (吨/年)	Chemical Fiber (ton/year)	112000	191393	159086	165974	732823
棉纺锭 (万锭)	Cotton Spindles (10 000 units)	15	31	28	104	147
棉布织机 (台)	Cotton Loom (unit)	2747	3370	6436	6184	3024
棉印染布 (万米/年)	Printed and Dyed Cloth (10 000 m/year)	11952	23271	25810	27116	38950
毛纺锭 (锭)	Wool Spindles (ingot)	15200	5442	11700	2180	23314
机制糖	Machine-processed Sugar					
年生产 (万吨)	Annual Production Capacity(10000 tons)	21	6	11	57	36
日处理原料 (吨/天)	Raw Materials Processing (ton/day)	18250	14260	13194	53047	12983
卷烟 (万箱/年)	Cigarettes (10 000 cases/year)	95	51	68	19	44
酒 (万吨/年)	Liquors (10 000 tons/year)	5730	300	267	243	242
糖果 (吨/年)	Candy (ton/year)	7010	11724	2000	1280	1780
奶粉 (吨/年)	Milk Powder (ton/year)	36910	2000	50140	315770	39982
原盐 (万吨/年)	Raw Salt (10 000 tons/year)	25	80	2	161	76
机制纸及纸板 (万吨/年)	Machine-made Paper and Paperboards (10 000 tons/year)	159	174	544	397	246
肥皂 (万箱/年)	Soap (10 000 cases/year)	2	1	14	11	
合成洗涤剂 (万吨/年)	Synthetic Detergent (10 000 tons/year)	20	7	14	14	11
鞣制皮革 (万张/年)	Tanning (10 000 pcs/year)	157	9	100	241	179
皮鞋 (万双/年)	Leather Shoes (10 000 pairs/year)	370	826	1428	1101	1461
日用搪瓷制品 (万件/年)	Daily-use Enamelware (10 000 pcs/year)	1				12
日用陶瓷器 (万件/年)	Daily-use Ceramics (10 000 pcs/year)	14647	11382	9008	27371	17929
保温瓶 (万个/年)	Thermos Bottles (10 000 units/year)	1000	84	460		
灯泡 (万只/年)	Bulbs (10 000 units/year)	17083	24660	10791	11500	8370
自行车 (万辆/年)	Bicycles (10 000 units/year)	70	20	1	60	6
家用电冰箱 (万台/年)	Refrigerators (10 000 sets/year)	275	45	71		76
电视机 (万台/年)	Television Sets (10 000 sets/year)	336	80	90	273	185
录放音机 (万部/年)	Tape Recorders (10 000 sets/year)		248			82
家用洗衣机 (万台/年)	Washing Machines (10 000 sets/year)	60	156	225	90	211
商业石油库 (万立方米)	Commercial Petroleum Depot (10 000cu.m)	19	6	25	11	2
物资储备石油库(万立方米)	Petroleum Tanks in Materials Warehouse System (10 000 cu.m)		2		2	5
商业冷藏库 (万吨)	Commercial Freezers (10 000 tons)	1	123	2	2	17
粮食仓库 (万平方米)	Grain Storehouses (10 000 sq.m)	17	11	6	2	4
粮食仓库 (万公斤)	Grain Storehouses (10 000 kg)	48591	30461	42632	8338	4790
高等院校学生席位 (个)	Students Capacity of Universities and Colleges			10450	1080	970
医院病床床位 (张)	Number of Hospital Beds (unit)	3360	2641	1454	1479	1868
城市自来水供水能力(万吨/日)	Tap Water Supply Capacity (10 000tons/day)	162	183	127	121	204

6-33 按用途分更新改造投资和房屋建筑面积

Investment on Innovation by Purpose and Floor Space of Buildings

年份 Year	按用途分的更新改造投资（亿元） Investment on Innovation by Purpose (100 million yuan)							房屋建筑面积（万平方米） Floor Space of Buildings (10 000 sq.m)			
	增产 Increasing Production	节约能源 Energy Saving	其他节约 Other Saving Measures	增加品种 Increasing Product Variety	提高产品质量 Improving Product Quality	三废治理 Environmental Protection	其他 Others	施工面积 Under Construction	#住宅 Residential Buildings	竣工面积 Completed	#住宅 Residential Buildings
1980	77.87	4.71	2.44		6.57	3.42	42.37	4019.90	1206.10	2133.00	683.80
1981	93.20	7.79	1.61		7.08	2.65	82.97	6305.80	2429.20	3603.60	1439.50
1982	87.01	11.98	2.15	15.70	11.46	4.12	117.95	8963.50	3531.40	5047.40	2108.50
1983	106.46	13.27	2.62	17.66	15.22	4.37	131.53	9363.60	3701.70	5358.70	2271.90
1984	106.83	17.35	2.09	23.80	17.50	6.11	135.60	8105.90	2652.32	4454.66	1554.78
1985	160.35	17.37	1.50	61.30	26.58	9.08	172.96	8784.45	2447.56	4596.04	1434.01
1986	211.20	22.75	2.10	97.88	39.16	11.78	234.34	10515.85	3591.34	5741.57	2070.70
1987	273.25	25.90	1.93	108.61	42.82	14.33	291.75	12318.43	4398.89	6330.23	2328.10
1988	394.78	30.55	2.93	140.12	48.38	16.79	347.00	13963.02	4820.65	6930.15	2467.93
1989	303.08	25.25	2.32	119.00	39.38	14.99	284.76	10616.70	3825.33	5403.15	1995.63
1990	291.95	27.28	2.65	130.10	52.00	14.76	311.45	9179.22	3386.48	4738.65	1771.70
1991	359.48	33.49	4.43	165.75	73.48	19.56	367.04	9270.12	3306.25	4793.31	1694.35
1992	496.47	41.38	5.16	225.97	107.66	23.33	561.13	10815.77	3530.70	5208.79	1750.73
1993	797.79	49.57	9.19	334.88	142.04	32.13	830.25	11337.62	3663.37	5282.45	1748.54
1994	1026.45	79.93	14.94	381.76	177.04	45.67	1192.81	11998.32	4373.66	5638.70	2031.18
1995	1222.17	92.86	10.53	409.58	196.93	47.47	1319.82	10691.39	3886.85	5360.98	1991.92
1996	(1301.97)	(80.84)	(14.95)	(434.35)	(201.79)	(61.35)	(1527.49)	(9619.27)	(3449.37)	(4799.24)	(1847.04)
	1299.96	80.66	14.90	433.54	201.20	61.24	1523.49	9580.36	3441.55	4764.94	1840.50
1997	1389.54	102.19	20.34	417.93	214.77	64.63	1712.54	8470.86	3263.66	4409.81	1771.22
1998	1426.53	103.11	32.46	422.79	245.17	71.17	2215.51	7467.81	2990.87	3861.51	1570.83
1999	1422.22	148.83	35.05	407.54	280.35	89.08	2102.02	6099.82	2270.36	3587.06	1516.71
2000	1707.78	163.66	55.15	440.37	392.33	120.41	2227.91	5595.94	1284.61	2913.96	802.06
2001	1948.16	198.13	56.98	620.08	422.64	111.49	2566.30	5359.39	649.87	2827.44	435.34
2002	2491.95	229.28	36.38	814.72	546.87	111.66	2519.69	6711.48	535.18	3371.10	280.57
2003								8888.80	518.98	4375.62	283.52

6-34 按行业分城镇集体单位固定资产投资和新增固定资产（2003年）

Investment in Fixed Assets of Urban Collective-owned Units by Sector (2003)

单位: 亿元 (100 million yuan)

行业	Sector	投资额 Investment	新增固定资产 Newly Increased Fixed Assets	固定资产交付使用率(%) Rate of Fixed Assets Put into Use (%)
全国总计	**National Total**	**1455.53**	**1018.95**	**70.0**
农、林、牧、渔业	Farming, Forestry, Animal Husbandry and Fishing	12.20	7.94	65.1
采矿业	Mining	21.67	11.83	54.6
制造业	Manufacturing	376.77	246.20	65.3
电力、燃气及水的生产和供应业	Production and Supply of Electric Power, Gas and Water	44.40	13.22	29.8
建筑业	Construction	39.08	30.11	77.0
交通运输、仓储及邮政业	Transport, Storage and Post	36.18	18.16	50.2
信息传输、计算机服务和软件业	Information Transmission, Computer Services and Software	3.71	2.06	55.5
批发和零售业	Wholesale and Retail Trade	77.12	59.61	77.3
住宿和餐饮业	Hotel and Restaurants	19.69	17.39	88.3
金融业	Financial Intermediation	8.83	6.18	70.0
房地产业	Real Estate	575.04	444.26	77.3
租赁和商务服务业	Leasing and Business Services	28.81	20.82	72.2
科学研究、技术服务和地质勘查业	Scientific Research, Technical Service and Geologic Prospecting	2.15	2.18	101.6
水利、环境和公共设施管理业	Management of Water Conservancy, Environment and Public Facilities	60.35	34.97	57.9
居民服务和其他服务业	Services to Households and Other Services	5.85	4.57	78.2
教育	Education	21.85	13.46	61.6
卫生、社会保障和社会福利业	Health, Social Security and Social Welfare	6.54	5.24	80.2
文化、体育和娱乐业	Culture, Sports and Entertainment	7.77	4.08	52.5
公共管理和社会组织	Public Management and Social Organization	107.52	76.66	71.3
国际组织	International Organizations			

6-35 按构成分城镇集体单位固定资产投资和房屋建筑面积

Investment in Fixed Assets of Urban Collective-owned Units by Use of Funds and Floor Space of Buildings by Region

年份 地区	Year Region	合计（亿元） Total Investment (100 million yuan)	建筑安装工程 Construction and Installation	设备工具器具购置 Purchase of and Equipment Instruments	其他费用 Others	房屋建筑面积（万平方米）Floor Space of Buildings(10 000 sq.m) 施工面积 Under Construction	#住宅 Residential Buildings	竣工面积 Completed	#住宅 Residential Buildings
	1985	128.23	71.28	51.20	5.75	5087.10	1606.90	2746.30	896.60
	1989	185.63	98.95	72.27	14.41	4323.38	1256.99	2477.69	701.80
	1990	163.38	84.81	69.18	9.39	3357.93	1085.76	1970.45	636.17
	1991	203.83	106.51	84.84	12.48	3828.53	1110.36	2112.81	639.00
	1992	364.49	182.52	159.91	22.05	5412.32	1418.52	2766.74	752.62
	1993	686.12	381.97	253.44	50.71	6318.01	2176.48	3342.14	1129.77
	1994	770.27	455.89	270.06	44.32	5060.25	1842.81	3086.87	1128.89
	1995	921.74	616.06	167.08	138.61	12229.83	7677.71	5459.69	3286.38
	1996	(858.31)	(565.92)	(176.52)	(115.87)	(10999.99)	(6650.62)	(5059.03)	(2966.39)
		849.24	560.71	172.91	115.62	10879.67	6615.88	4958.59	2939.13
	1997	795.23	543.82	141.18	110.23	10094.11	6277.70	4927.40	3012.26
	1998	958.93	654.10	165.31	139.52	11205.85	7085.82	5542.54	3492.10
	1999	995.42	680.17	174.97	140.28	11466.58	7487.48	5856.91	3739.26
	2000	1009.83	693.18	166.99	149.67	11519.24	7766.26	5910.57	3846.65
	2001	1042.85	721.08	157.69	164.08	11330.50	7640.78	5662.39	3721.22
	2002	1099.52	747.89	179.84	171.79	10952.69	7129.10	5421.24	3426.47
	2003	1455.53	988.40	224.95	242.19	12758.98	8048.45	5821.23	3728.72
北京	Beijing	52.31	35.01	1.85	15.45	533.09	430.44	198.36	172.80
天津	Tianjin	21.73	10.06	3.80	7.88	151.44	85.05	86.71	50.98
河北	Hebei	90.97	61.56	17.06	12.35	572.62	348.86	291.99	163.43
山西	Shanxi	27.81	16.47	8.09	3.26	179.75	103.09	93.79	63.47
内蒙古	Inner Mongolia	11.16	7.92	1.62	1.62	102.68	47.25	63.50	34.38
辽宁	Liaoning	28.81	17.10	8.51	3.20	189.16	102.11	137.82	79.10
吉林	Jilin	8.12	5.77	1.72	0.64	46.16	24.12	40.59	20.90
黑龙江	Heilongjiang	14.04	9.38	3.35	1.32	115.65	59.44	87.70	46.20
上海	Shanghai	83.98	56.26	4.99	22.72	723.48	548.32	315.79	234.92
江苏	Jiangsu	214.18	151.85	27.03	35.30	1516.92	1101.44	690.93	465.38
浙江	Zhejiang	74.67	44.56	3.72	26.39	718.58	459.23	265.49	178.14
安徽	Anhui	42.88	25.07	8.57	9.24	293.33	145.90	156.15	77.60
福建	Fujian	36.99	30.52	1.84	4.63	423.30	328.19	153.64	114.31
江西	Jiangxi	19.70	12.22	3.14	4.35	216.99	137.43	105.87	66.45
山东	Shandong	321.79	219.92	70.93	30.94	2471.68	1350.82	1237.97	686.74
河南	Henan	31.82	19.23	8.59	3.99	248.19	150.51	126.82	69.17
湖北	Hubei	25.07	14.97	6.38	3.72	214.69	158.83	112.28	77.14
湖南	Hunan	24.76	18.13	1.93	4.70	273.64	189.76	88.47	65.97
广东	Guangdong	166.10	124.54	15.73	25.82	1971.40	1076.88	793.59	527.75
广西	Guangxi	14.47	9.48	2.71	2.29	183.39	130.52	76.99	52.25
海南	Hainan	3.54	2.82	0.21	0.51	31.54	18.42	7.57	6.29
重庆	Chongqing	19.40	12.63	2.83	3.94	228.02	151.93	115.34	74.41
四川	Sichuan	29.98	20.66	1.95	7.37	380.49	277.58	168.90	131.28
贵州	Guizhou	11.88	7.05	2.79	2.04	121.52	76.84	45.89	30.24
云南	Yunnan	11.94	7.80	2.63	1.52	116.25	79.18	60.21	45.40
西藏	Tibet	0.52	0.50	0.02		3.86		3.37	
陕西	Shaanxi	31.86	20.67	7.19	4.00	303.79	188.12	129.41	86.75
甘肃	Gansu	18.28	14.04	2.40	1.84	269.95	192.29	69.99	49.47
青海	Qinghai	3.90	2.95	0.66	0.29	33.57	20.55	18.90	10.61
宁夏	Ningxia	4.06	3.43	0.06	0.57	62.01	38.47	43.07	28.72
新疆	Xinjiang	8.79	5.86	2.64	0.28	61.84	26.89	34.13	18.45

6-36 各地区按行业分城镇集体单位固定资产投资（2003年）

Investment in Fixed Assets of Urban Collective-owned Units by Sector and Region (2003)

单位: 亿元 (100 million yuan)

地 区	Region	合 计 Total	农、林、牧、渔业 Agriculture, Forestry, Animal Husbandry and Fishing	采矿业 Mining	制造业 Manufacturing	电力、燃气及水的生产和供应业 Production and Distribution of Electricity, Gas and Water	建筑业 Construction	交通运输、仓储和邮政业 Transport, Storage and Post
全国总计	**National Total**	**1455.53**	**12.20**	**21.67**	**376.77**	**44.40**	**39.08**	**36.18**
北 京	Beijing	52.31			3.29		1.20	
天 津	Tianjin	21.73	0.20	0.03	5.84		0.24	6.22
河 北	Hebei	90.97	0.87	0.24	32.32	0.27	7.70	0.77
山 西	Shanxi	27.81	0.82	6.84	11.49		0.12	0.14
内蒙古	Inner Mongolia	11.16	0.33	0.50	2.86	0.53	0.05	0.47
辽 宁	Liaoning	28.81	0.91	0.84	11.34	0.87	0.40	1.70
吉 林	Jilin	8.12	0.24	0.14	4.07	0.05	0.70	0.01
黑龙江	Heilongjiang	14.04	0.20	0.57	5.54	0.06	1.69	0.09
上 海	Shanghai	83.98	0.23		17.50	0.15	0.25	4.42
江 苏	Jiangsu	214.18	0.75	0.04	55.88	6.87	2.76	2.15
浙 江	Zhejiang	74.67	0.05		9.03	0.74	0.76	1.04
安 徽	Anhui	42.88	0.32	1.12	13.47	0.40	0.64	6.46
福 建	Fujian	36.99	0.61		2.43	0.37	0.23	0.64
江 西	Jiangxi	19.70	0.61	0.11	4.29	0.68	0.04	0.30
山 东	Shandong	321.79	1.66	6.23	110.68	14.14	12.59	2.29
河 南	Henan	31.82	0.62	0.85	15.57	0.01	0.49	0.29
湖 北	Hubei	25.07	1.04	0.46	7.94	1.24	0.51	0.69
湖 南	Hunan	24.76	0.22	0.23	3.79	2.38	0.34	2.38
广 东	Guangdong	166.10	0.38	0.05	27.89	3.03	3.70	2.67
广 西	Guangxi	14.47	0.09	0.14	2.79	0.71	0.19	0.74
海 南	Hainan	3.54	0.05		0.84	0.14	0.01	0.01
重 庆	Chongqing	19.40	0.22	0.20	4.56	0.91	1.15	1.62
四 川	Sichuan	29.98	0.16	0.26	2.22	1.30	0.33	0.12
贵 州	Guizhou	11.88	0.02	0.87	3.33	0.54	0.02	0.02
云 南	Yunnan	11.94	0.45	0.22	2.85	2.34	0.40	0.35
西 藏	Tibet	0.52		0.03	0.13			
陕 西	Shaanxi	31.86	0.18	0.51	5.69	5.29	0.31	0.24
甘 肃	Gansu	18.28	0.61	0.31	5.19	0.47	1.91	0.09
青 海	Qinghai	3.90		0.04	0.94	0.26	0.06	0.06
宁 夏	Ningxia	4.06	0.05		0.36	0.01	0.12	0.14
新 疆	Xinjiang	8.79	0.31	0.86	2.66	0.61	0.19	0.05

6-36 续表 1 continued

单位: 亿元 (100 million yuan)

地区	Region	信息传输、计算机服务和软件业 Information Transmission, Computer Service and Software	批发和零售业 Wholesale and Retail Trade	住宿和餐饮业 Hotel and Restaurants	金融业 Financial Intermediation	房地产业 Real Estate	租赁和商务服务业 Leasing and Business Services	科学研究、技术服务和地质勘查业 Scientific Research, Technical Services, and Geological Prospecting
全国总计	**National Total**	**3.71**	**77.12**	**19.69**	**8.83**	**575.04**	**28.81**	**2.15**
北京	Beijing	0.04	1.01	0.12	0.91	41.92	1.71	0.01
天津	Tianjin	0.05	1.30	0.02		5.20	0.15	0.02
河北	Hebei	0.02	12.46	2.38	0.53	11.56	1.29	0.22
山西	Shanxi		1.86	0.03	0.17	3.79	0.68	
内蒙古	Inner Mongolia		0.64	0.09	0.32	2.58	0.03	
辽宁	Liaoning	0.04	1.89	0.83	0.17	5.93	0.77	0.18
吉林	Jilin		0.49	0.11	0.32	1.08	0.49	0.32
黑龙江	Heilongjiang	1.21	1.14		0.16	2.25	0.50	
上海	Shanghai		2.40	0.79		52.69	0.14	0.24
江苏	Jiangsu	1.25	7.53	1.72	0.27	94.43	1.83	0.24
浙江	Zhejiang	0.10	2.13	0.66	0.66	49.02	3.92	
安徽	Anhui	0.07	0.81	1.26	0.16	13.88	0.16	0.22
福建	Fujian		0.65	0.82	0.06	29.44	0.24	0.13
江西	Jiangxi	0.03	1.18	0.44	0.12	9.64	0.60	
山东	Shandong	0.05	17.78	3.83	0.31	75.63	4.69	0.06
河南	Henan	0.01	3.40	0.23	0.76	3.59	0.28	0.32
湖北	Hubei	0.03	1.32	1.43	0.21	7.12	0.14	
湖南	Hunan		0.84	1.18	0.02	11.89	0.20	0.07
广东	Guangdong	0.47	5.44	0.55	1.42	87.31	8.64	0.03
广西	Guangxi	0.27	0.91	0.11	0.04	7.36	44.00	
海南	Hainan		0.14	0.67		0.97	0.18	0.01
重庆	Chongqing	0.04	1.38	0.09	0.38	7.04	0.04	0.06
四川	Sichuan		1.05	0.45	0.24	22.32	0.27	
贵州	Guizhou		1.30	0.01	0.62	4.47	0.09	
云南	Yunnan		0.66	0.76	0.46	2.39	0.14	
西藏	Tibet		0.20	0.07				
陕西	Shaanxi	0.04	1.81	0.45	0.15	12.01	0.53	0.02
甘肃	Gansu		3.35	0.13	0.12	3.86	0.50	
青海	Qinghai		0.56	0.23	0.03	1.16	0.01	
宁夏	Ningxia		0.25	0.00	0.01	2.78	0.01	
新疆	Xinjiang		1.24	0.24	0.20	1.73	0.57	

6-36 续表 2 continued

单位: 亿元 (100 million yuan)

地区	Region	水利、环境和公共设施管理业 Water Management of Conservancy, Environment and Public Facilities	居民服务和其他服务业 Services to Households and Other Services	教育 Education	卫生、社会保障和社会福利业 Health, Social Securities and Social Welfare	文化、体育和娱乐业 Culture, Sports and Entertainment	公共管理和社会组织 Public Management and Social Organization	国际组织 International Organizations
全国总计	**National Total**	**60.35**	**5.85**	**21.85**	**6.54**	**7.77**	**107.52**	
北京	Beijing	0.45	0.44	0.54			0.67	
天津	Tianjin	1.43	0.09	0.89	0.05	0.01		
河北	Hebei	1.16	2.44	1.80	0.78	0.97	13.18	
山西	Shanxi	0.78		0.67	0.03		0.41	
内蒙古	Inner Mongolia	0.13		0.09	0.02	0.58	1.95	
辽宁	Liaoning	0.67	0.14	0.84	0.17	0.57	0.54	
吉林	Jilin	0.06			0.02		0.01	
黑龙江	Heilongjiang	0.05		0.02	0.19	0.02	0.34	
上海	Shanghai	3.33		1.26	0.16	0.12	0.30	
江苏	Jiangsu	24.13	0.60	2.02	0.92	1.39	9.40	
浙江	Zhejiang	4.54		0.81	0.60	0.07	0.54	
安徽	Anhui	1.38		0.62	0.28	0.05	1.56	
福建	Fujian	0.30	0.13	0.38	0.05	0.25	0.27	
江西	Jiangxi		0.06	0.67	0.07		0.87	
山东	Shandong	6.76	0.53	2.74	0.55	2.80	58.48	
河南	Henan	1.03	0.13	1.08	0.61	0.16	2.37	
湖北	Hubei	1.32	0.12	0.02	0.07	0.05	1.35	
湖南	Hunan	0.21	0.10	0.02	0.04	0.09	0.80	
广东	Guangdong	10.88	0.47	2.16	0.83	0.05	10.14	
广西	Guangxi	0.60	0.01	0.30	0.02		0.19	
海南	Hainan	0.20		0.28	0.03	0.02		
重庆	Chongqing	0.02	0.03	0.21	0.61	0.19	0.67	
四川	Sichuan	0.38		0.39	0.12	0.16	0.20	
贵州	Guizhou	0.04	0.25	0.19	0.04	0.03	0.02	
云南	Yunnan	0.17	0.05	0.38	0.04	0.03	0.24	
西藏	Tibet						0.09	
陕西	Shaanxi	0.29	0.16	2.10	0.10	0.12	1.87	
甘肃	Gansu	0.03	0.01	1.04	0.10		0.55	
青海	Qinghai			0.20		0.03	0.34	
宁夏	Ningxia		0.09	0.09		0.01	0.12	
新疆	Xinjiang			0.02	0.05		0.06	

6-37 城镇和工矿区个人建房

Building Construction by Individuals in Cities and Towns and in Industrial and Mining Areas

年份 Year 地区 Region	城镇工矿区个数(个) Number of Cities, Towns, Industrial and Mining Areas (unit)	建房户数(户) Number of Households with Building Construction (unit)	竣工房屋建筑面积(万平方米) Floor Space of Buildings Completed (10 000 sq.m)	#住宅 Residential Buildings	竣工房屋价值(万元) Value of Buildings Completed (10 000 yuan)	#住宅 Residential Buildings
1985	5941	910362	7081.36	6306.80	567917	493872
1989	8590	945178	8565.38	7822.55	1402278	1260234
1990	8304	775011	7180.55	6492.93	1247034	1103317
1991	8637	773083	7554.40	6808.24	1403230	1250861
1992	9367	919069	9673.43	8586.22	2164663	1897651
1993	10170	1052853	11463.44	9812.95	3385002	2804212
1994	11728	1234606	14098.18	12268.36	4513203	3870038
1995	12189	1279426	15194.84	13333.90	5523894	4770290
1996	13214	1294859	16556.86	14518.78	6552198	5629097
1997	21218	1338976	17570.24	15165.03	7041112	5938633
1998	14943	1552136	20781.49	18227.39	8485630	7272165
1999	15262	1490469	21830.37	19246.43	9175357	7818281
2000	13910	1440145	21763.53	18929.01	9529931	8120255
2001	14125	1435477	22315.32	19473.45	9891467	8356750
2002	14596	1393897	22282.58	19442.79	9991320	8467054
2003	14145	1372495	22444.14	19474.51	10186387	8644673
北京 Beijing						
天津 Tianjin	39	4745	33.62	31.39	22264	19976
河北 Hebei	656	94449	1300.74	1034.77	768781	563459
山西 Shanxi	460	19283	216.58	196.87	110891	99921
内蒙古 Inner Mongolia	403	34368	352.30	281.91	180946	132623
辽宁 Liaoning	86	12027	109.90	96.85	67298	57385
吉林 Jilin	495	70531	709.32	574.25	450426	338345
黑龙江 Heilongjiang	397	64320	637.36	560.68	324845	297844
上海 Shanghai		2546	17.35	17.26	20724	20690
江苏 Jiangsu	776	75159	1318.67	1081.27	591271	526187
浙江 Zhejiang	534	57804	1373.50	1260.76	729034	653942
安徽 Anhui	935	82971	906.43	759.63	361563	291935
福建 Fujian	469	39769	1011.86	965.68	478659	456713
江西 Jiangxi	748	53132	1165.67	1035.22	408064	366746
山东 Shandong	192	35290	454.13	323.76	257359	171773
河南 Henan	162	59757	1188.40	964.26	604300	483163
湖北 Hubei	792	86841	1384.84	1217.26	560749	488208
湖南 Hunan	716	60017	1537.72	1350.36	580867	512890
广东 Guangdong	388	47146	1422.75	1293.77	834757	753956
广西 Guangxi	856	156620	2346.77	2263.13	830886	802953
海南 Hainan	164	8732	160.70	136.72	129909	98633
重庆 Chongqing	594	40428	597.17	526.49	226151	187669
四川 Sichuan	1752	88561	1588.44	1294.31	602107	488413
贵州 Guizhou	722	51712	753.04	659.05	220771	193620
云南 Yunnan	386	30929	661.40	574.83	286400	217306
西藏 Tibet	179	2421	55.01	38.19	27748	19634
陕西 Shaanxi	727	39705	617.23	511.55	286447	227678
甘肃 Gansu	238	21493	193.65	161.88	70238	58032
青海 Qinghai	83	5394	52.22	42.63	24888	20656
宁夏 Ningxia	20	1971	22.47	19.28	10396	8632
新疆 Xinjiang	176	24374	254.91	200.53	117648	85691

6-38 农村个人固定资产投资和建房

Individual Investment in Fixed Assets and Building Construction in Rural Areas

年份 Year / 地区 Region		投资总额 (亿元) Total Investment (100 million yuan)	#竣工房屋投资 Investment in Buildings Completed 小计 Subtotal	#住宅 Residential Buildings	施工房屋建筑面积 (万平方米) Floor Space of Buildings under Construction (10 000 sq.m)	竣工房屋建筑面积 (万平方米) Floor Space of Buildings Completed (10 000 sq.m) 总计 Total	#住宅 Residential Buildings	竣工房屋造价 (元/平方米) Cost of Buildings Completed (yuan/sq.m) 总计 Total	#住宅 Residential Buildings
	1985	478.43	350.13	313.15		78973	69542	44	45
	1989	892.03	794.15	641.68	74906	71026	66134	112	97
	1990	876.47	777.14	649.78	76819	71136	67812	109	96
	1991	1042.56	912.48	759.25	85405	79501	74193	115	102
	1992	1005.52	937.51	678.52	83392	65338	60442	143	112
	1993	1137.73	1015.37	760.26	57432	56012	46129	181	165
	1994	1519.24	1315.92	1002.73	72283	65390	57646	201	174
	1995	2007.85	1709.41	1349.85	78192	73522	66230	233	204
	1996	2544.03	2250.87	1766.40	96115	87277	79531	258	222
	1997	2691.16	2405.80	1890.65	89309	85888	77287	280	245
	1998	2681.52	2402.24	1907.23	89099	83864	77031	286	248
	1999	2779.59	1908.20	1799.10	89050	83244	76758	229	234
	2000	2904.26	1969.32	1846.85	88232	81270	75515	242	245
	2001	2976.56	1908.17	1775.04	81048	74517	68799	256	258
	2002	3123.23	1956.47	1858.08	80345	75126	69841	260	266
	2003	3200.96	2053.21	1926.91	81124	75684	69741	271	276
北京	Beijing	17.48	13.30	11.63	347	310	269	429	433
天津	Tianjin	17.93	13.06	11.50	288	243	216	537	532
河北	Hebei	199.45	113.69	105.01	4098	3660	3348	311	314
山西	Shanxi	53.32	33.28	32.05	1295	1152	1023	289	313
内蒙古	Inner Mongolia	55.68	22.03	19.58	1109	1018	848	216	231
辽宁	Liaoning	104.45	68.02	61.72	2135	2122	2043	321	302
吉林	Jilin	71.03	11.53	11.26	315	314	307	367	367
黑龙江	Heilongjiang	78.98	22.39	21.34	749	693	633	323	337
上海	Shanghai	6.49	6.20	6.20	77	77	77	800	800
江苏	Jiangsu	191.05	118.48	114.79	3154	3146	3022	377	380
浙江	Zhejiang	211.39	164.54	156.31	3989	3638	3448	452	453
安徽	Anhui	150.09	96.86	94.50	4968	4804	4613	202	205
福建	Fujian	96.42	53.64	50.13	1750	1429	1336	375	375
江西	Jiangxi	100.21	54.01	50.85	2718	2186	2131	247	239
山东	Shandong	296.03	193.71	182.68	6521	6409	5932	302	308
河南	Henan	325.30	212.56	193.55	9156	8989	8023	236	241
湖北	Hubei	103.57	81.94	79.32	3038	2911	2790	281	284
湖南	Hunan	180.23	123.09	117.88	5345	5091	4825	242	244
广东	Guangdong	217.68	125.80	124.74	4141	3051	3014	412	414
广西	Guangxi	101.24	74.98	74.03	3349	3211	3167	233	234
海南	Hainan	19.20	8.26	8.05	248	212	204	390	395
重庆	Chongqing	49.01	43.00	39.72	2484	2267	2118	190	188
四川	Sichuan	176.71	91.53	81.79	5961	5736	4868	160	168
贵州	Guizhou	52.88	31.83	29.11	1804	1612	1487	197	196
云南	Yunnan	108.13	71.58	63.11	3889	3792	3033	189	208
西藏	Tibet								
陕西	Shaanxi	98.73	60.63	55.55	2604	2495	2380	243	233
甘肃	Gansu	37.64	113.69	105.01	4098	3660	3348	311	314
青海	Qinghai	9.36	3.82	3.45	234	218	197	176	175
宁夏	Ningxia	23.22	11.79	10.02	320	320	268	369	374
新疆	Xinjiang	48.08	13.98	12.01	940	917	774	152	155

6-39 房地产开发企业(单位)主要指标

Main Indicators of Real Estate Development

指　标	Item	2000	2001	2002	2003
企业个数（个）	**Number of Enterprises (unit)**	**27303**	**29552**	**32618**	**37123**
内资	Domestic Funded	23277	25509	28657	33107
#国有	State-owned Enterprises	6641	5862	5015	4558
集体	Collective-owned Enterprises	3492	2991	2488	2205
港、澳、台投资	Enterprises with Funds from Hong Kong, Macao and Taiwan	2899	2959	2884	2840
外商投资	Foreign Funded	1127	1084	1077	1176
平均从业人数（万人）	**Average Number of Employed Persons (10 000 persons)**	**97.19**	**106.23**	**113.40**	**120.54**
内资	Domestic Funded	86.22	94.96	101.43	108.69
#国有	State-owned Enterprises	29.23	25.77	20.87	17.96
集体	Collective-owned Enterprises	11.64	10.98	8.97	7.24
港、澳、台投资	Enterprises with Funds from Hong Kong, Macao and Taiwan	7.91	8.17	8.54	7.94
外商投资	Foreign Funded	3.06	3.11	3.43	3.90
土地开发及购置（万平方米）	**Land Development and Purchase (10 000 sq.m)**				
本年土地开发面积	Land Space Developed This Year	11666.1	15315.8	19416.0	22166.3
本年土地购置面积	Land Space Purchased This Year	16905.2	23409.0	31356.8	35696.5
本年完成投资额（亿元）	**Investment Completed This Year (100 million yuan)**	**4984.1**	**6344.1**	**7790.9**	**10153.8**
#住宅	Residential Buildings	3312.0	4216.7	5227.8	6776.7
#经济适用房屋	Economical Houses	542.4	599.7	589.0	622.0
资金来源小计（亿元）	**Source of Funds (100 million yuan)**	**5997.6**	**7696.4**	**9750.0**	**13196.9**
#国内贷款	Domestic Loans	1385.1	1692.2	2220.3	3138.3
利用外资	Foreign Investment	168.7	135.7	157.2	170.0
自筹资金	Fundraising	1614.2	2184.0	2738.5	3770.7
房屋建筑面积（万平方米）	**Floor Space of Buildings (10 000 sq.m)**				
施工面积	Floor Space under Construction	65896.9	79411.7	94104.0	117526.0
竣工面积	Floor Space Completed	25104.9	29867.4	34975.8	41464.1
本年新开工面积	Floor Space Started This Year	29582.6	37394.2	42800.5	54707.5
#住宅	Residential Buildings	24401.2	30532.7	34719.3	43853.9
#经济适用房屋	Economical Houses	5313.3	5796.0	5279.7	5330.6
商品房屋销售面积（万平方米）	**Floor Space of Selling House (10 000 sq.m)**	**18637.1**	**22411.9**	**26808.3**	**33717.6**
#住宅	Residential Buildings	16570.3	19938.7	23702.3	29778.8
#经济适用房屋	Economical Houses	3760.1	4021.5	4003.6	4018.9
商品房屋销售价格（元/平方米）	**Selling Price of House (yuan/sq.m)**	**2112**	**2170**	**2250**	**2359**
#住宅	Residential Buildings	1948	2017	2092	2197
#经济适用房屋	Economical Houses	1202	1240	1283	1380
实收资本合计（亿元）	**Total Capital Hold (100 million yuan)**	**5302.9**	**6019.9**	**6750.9**	**8471.0**
#国家资本金	State Capital	215.6	471.7	325.6	408.3
资产负债率 (%)	**Ratio of Liabilities to Assets (%)**	**75.6**	**75.0**	**74.9**	**75.8**
经营总收入（亿元）	**Total Revenue (100 million yuan)**	**4515.7**	**5471.7**	**7077.9**	**9137.3**
#土地转让收入	Land Transferred	129.6	189.0	225.1	279.7

6-40 房地产开发企业(单位)个数

Number of Enterprises for Real Estate Development

单位：个 (unit)

年份 地区	Year Region	企业个数 Number of Enterprises	内资企业 Domestic Funded Enterprises	#国有 State-owned Enterprises	#集体 Collective-owned Enterprises	港、澳、台投资企业 Enterprises with Funds from Hong Kong Macao and Taiwan	外商投资企业 Foreign Funded Enterprises
	1997	21286	17202			1989	2095
	1998	24378	19960	7958	4538	3214	1204
	1999	25762	21422	7370	4127	3167	1173
	2000	27303	23277	6641	3492	2899	1127
	2001	29552	25509	5862	2991	2959	1084
	2002	32618	28657	5015	2488	2884	1077
	2003	37123	33107	4558	2205	2840	1176
北京	Beijing	1056	849	111	30	146	61
天津	Tianjin	761	701	148	37	37	23
河北	Hebei	749	705	108	14	30	14
山西	Shanxi	711	688	141	28	16	7
内蒙古	Inner Mongolia	687	685	45	10	1	1
辽宁	Liaoning	1800	1629	116	41	93	78
吉林	Jilin	457	438	55	4	14	5
黑龙江	Heilongjiang	776	734	144	21	25	17
上海	Shanghai	2199	1945	282	136	161	93
江苏	Jiangsu	2580	2311	373	264	186	83
浙江	Zhejiang	2301	2199	189	110	57	45
安徽	Anhui	1388	1303	218	83	53	32
福建	Fujian	1900	1235	253	96	455	210
江西	Jiangxi	1217	1035	172	53	114	68
山东	Shandong	2152	1986	330	227	120	46
河南	Henan	1430	1320	200	78	74	36
湖北	Hubei	1309	1145	222	53	107	57
湖南	Hunan	1157	1038	178	43	88	31
广东	Guangdong	4171	3370	487	536	692	109
广西	Guangxi	749	641	132	46	81	27
海南	Hainan	186	154	22	5	23	9
重庆	Chongqing	1597	1486	81	36	78	33
四川	Sichuan	2014	1936	148	92	58	20
贵州	Guizhou	1157	1095	91	46	45	17
云南	Yunnan	393	374	67	7	15	4
西藏	Tibet	4	4	2			
陕西	Shaanxi	622	592	103	32	20	10
甘肃	Gansu	721	654	91	58	37	30
青海	Qinghai	170	162	13	3	4	4
宁夏	Ningxia	217	213	3	10	2	2
新疆	Xinjiang	492	480	33	6	8	4

6-41 房地产开发企业(单位)从业人员数

Number of Employed Persons in Enterprises for Real Estate Development

单位：人 (person)

年份 地区	Year Region	平均从业人数 Number of Employed Persons	内资企业 Domestic Funded Enterprises	#国有 State-owned Enterprises	#集体 Collective-owned Enterprises	港、澳、台投资企业 Enterprises with Funds from Hong Kong Macao and Taiwan	外商投资企业 Foreign Funded Enterprises
	1997	683217	578927			50000	54290
	1998	825888	708738	332834	134939	83784	33366
	1999	880257	767187	312240	127370	80216	32854
	2000	971942	862245	292252	116416	79066	30631
	2001	1062319	949580	257695	109826	81668	31071
	2002	1134009	1014254	208722	89739	85449	34306
	2003	1205355	1086923	179614	72400	79397	39035
北京	Beijing	52269	41180	8124	1661	7419	3670
天津	Tianjin	20126	18275	4357	744	998	853
河北	Hebei	30892	29453	5529	346	1127	312
山西	Shanxi	24967	24144	6712	866	619	204
内蒙古	Inner Mongolia	17594	17533	1007	123	16	45
辽宁	Liaoning	49497	45890	4199	1055	1697	1910
吉林	Jilin	15331	14570	2191	82	389	372
黑龙江	Heilongjiang	27465	26773	4029	679	307	385
上海	Shanghai	73322	60423	10685	3772	7243	5656
江苏	Jiangsu	65913	60069	14024	6759	3928	1916
浙江	Zhejiang	54035	51217	5275	2188	1264	1554
安徽	Anhui	40289	37782	6917	2333	1535	972
福建	Fujian	39641	26720	6193	2098	8569	4352
江西	Jiangxi	36589	32140	8263	1559	3255	1194
山东	Shandong	83454	78402	19951	9263	3453	1599
河南	Henan	43698	39544	7405	1285	2716	1438
湖北	Hubei	59504	54597	10497	2865	3283	1624
湖南	Hunan	41700	38417	7499	1651	2141	1142
广东	Guangdong	126518	105841	13913	19693	17379	3298
广西	Guangxi	22750	19372	4209	1040	2009	1369
海南	Hainan	5560	4238	1378	96	468	854
重庆	Chongqing	54148	49072	2903	964	4075	1001
四川	Sichuan	103331	101044	7608	6731	1533	754
贵州	Guizhou	30160	28861	3127	1296	939	360
云南	Yunnan	14659	13274	3283	150	395	990
西藏	Tibet	398	398	87			
陕西	Shaanxi	25957	24885	5039	1188	677	395
甘肃	Gansu	19461	17903	3548	1448	1051	507
青海	Qinghai	5464	5231	688	60	78	155
宁夏	Ningxia	6627	6498	44	250	55	74
新疆	Xinjiang	14036	13177	930	155	779	80

6-42 房地产开发企业（单位）土地开发及购置

Land Development and Purchase of Enterprises for Real Estate Development

单位：万平方米 (10 000 sq.m)

年 份 地 区	Year Region	本年完成开发土地面积 Land Space Developed This Year	土地购置费用（亿元） Total Value of Land Purchased (100 million yuan)	待开发的土地面积 Land Space Needed to Development	本年购置土地面积 Land Space Purchased This Year
	1997	7371.3	247.6	17670.1	6641.7
	1998	7730.1	375.4	13530.7	10109.3
	1999	9319.6	500.0	13505.2	11958.9
	2000	11666.1	733.9	14754.8	16905.2
	2001	15315.8	1038.8	14582.1	23409.0
	2002	19416.0	1445.8	19178.7	31356.8
	2003	22166.3	2055.2	21782.6	35696.5
北 京	Beijing	1084.4	213.2	1957.3	1391.3
天 津	Tianjin	740.4	30.2	436.8	1093.3
河 北	Hebei	559.6	38.2	266.6	1040.3
山 西	Shanxi	196.4	14.1	118.2	364.3
内蒙古	Inner Mongolia	284.0	15.6	7.6	521.3
辽 宁	Liaoning	1062.9	102.4	721.9	1668.7
吉 林	Jilin	241.1	18.9	7.0	356.3
黑龙江	Heilongjiang	416.4	26.6	202.4	494.4
上 海	Shanghai	605.5	173.3	205.9	1469.1
江 苏	Jiangsu	1600.3	220.7	2060.2	3219.3
浙 江	Zhejiang	1790.9	339.0	1509.3	3407.9
安 徽	Anhui	776.5	55.8	827.6	1607.4
福 建	Fujian	1019.8	70.7	669.7	1519.4
江 西	Jiangxi	772.2	38.6	432.0	1504.4
山 东	Shandong	2010.5	105.5	1582.1	3661.9
河 南	Henan	553.7	38.6	363.1	1081.8
湖 北	Hubei	774.7	40.5	1271.8	1536.4
湖 南	Hunan	980.8	39.7	1066.0	1550.6
广 东	Guangdong	2714.0	214.5	4148.0	2468.1
广 西	Guangxi	414.0	21.1	479.0	599.8
海 南	Hainan	13.8	5.2	1.5	98.8
重 庆	Chongqing	842.4	47.4	1622.9	1637.2
四 川	Sichuan	703.9	87.5	225.9	87.2
贵 州	Guizhou	375.2	14.6	386.9	624.2
云 南	Yunnan	426.7	23.4	117.1	749.7
西 藏	Tibet	7.2	0.1	40.6	8.0
陕 西	Shaanxi	393.9	29.8	315.6	594.5
甘 肃	Gansu	219.0	7.3	137.9	263.6
青 海	Qinghai	108.8	3.0	40.6	118.0
宁 夏	Ningxia	94.8	6.4	110.4	295.2
新 疆	Xinjiang	382.4	13.3	450.5	664.3

6-43 房地产开发企业(单位)建设投资总规模及完成投资

General Scale of and Actually Completed Investment in Real Estate Development

单位：亿元 (100 million yuan)

年份 地区	Year Region	实际需要总投资 Total Investment Actually Needed	自开始建设至本年底累计完成投资 Accumulative Investment Actually Made Since Starting of Construction up to the End of This Year	#本年完成投资 Investment Made This Year	全部建成尚需投资 Further Investment Required for the Completion of Construction
	1997	17685.72	9109.72	3178.37	8576.00
	1998	19623.04	10515.44	3614.23	9107.60
	1999	20207.68	11509.43	4103.20	8698.25
	2000	22664.18	12816.37	4984.05	9847.82
	2001	27552.59	15580.22	6344.11	11972.36
	2002	33953.72	18998.76	7790.92	14954.97
	2003	40055.27	22691.60	10153.80	17363.67
北京	Beijing	5024.83	2760.08	1202.48	2264.75
天津	Tianjin	783.33	437.19	211.39	346.13
河北	Hebei	705.27	409.48	251.27	295.79
山西	Shanxi	328.85	199.98	95.07	128.86
内蒙古	Inner Mongolia	185.92	122.97	90.79	62.95
辽宁	Liaoning	1759.78	1002.34	486.39	757.44
吉林	Jilin	354.65	195.87	139.24	158.79
黑龙江	Heilongjiang	390.31	244.78	163.28	145.53
上海	Shanghai	4601.94	3040.75	901.24	1561.19
江苏	Jiangsu	2431.39	1430.60	809.96	1000.79
浙江	Zhejiang	3346.05	1896.91	980.05	1449.13
安徽	Anhui	873.56	407.48	240.65	466.08
福建	Fujian	1620.94	864.72	362.07	756.21
江西	Jiangxi	540.40	288.68	177.47	251.71
山东	Shandong	2035.51	1003.45	581.88	1032.06
河南	Henan	718.45	365.15	185.56	353.29
湖北	Hubei	1068.03	585.73	239.04	482.29
湖南	Hunan	804.42	436.27	230.03	368.16
广东	Guangdong	6753.16	4046.14	1233.52	2707.02
广西	Guangxi	504.33	291.60	120.31	212.73
海南	Hainan	126.18	59.88	36.61	66.30
重庆	Chongqing	1543.38	681.42	327.89	861.95
四川	Sichuan	1322.18	725.26	450.87	596.91
贵州	Guizhou	471.36	218.48	104.95	252.88
云南	Yunnan	411.90	250.11	114.97	161.79
西藏	Tibet	7.04	2.82	2.00	4.22
陕西	Shaanxi	672.77	347.18	188.31	325.60
甘肃	Gansu	211.47	98.65	50.80	112.82
青海	Qinghai	78.44	40.71	22.31	37.73
宁夏	Ningxia	83.31	63.63	50.91	19.68
新疆	Xinjiang	296.12	173.26	102.49	122.86

6-44 按用途分房地产开发企业(单位)投资完成额

Actually Completed Investment of Enterprises for Real Estate Development by Use

单位：万元 (10 000 yuan)

年份 地区	Year Region	本年完成投资额 Investment Made This Year	住宅 Residential Buildings	#别墅、高档公寓 Villas, High-grade Apartments	#经济适用房屋 Economical Houses	办公楼 Office Buildings	商业营业用房 Houses for Business Use	其他 Other
	1997	31783702	15393805	1562955	1854959	3889819	4258452	8241626
	1998	36142292	20815647	1818526	2708523	4337956	4758297	6230392
	1999	41032024	26384794	1786233	4370211	3385973	4843349	6417908
	2000	49840529	33119839	2700142	5424365	2978511	5799927	7942252
	2001	63441107	42166760	3699241	5996464	3079470	7553018	10641859
	2002	77909223	52277560	5169632	5890445	3810018	9336107	12485538
	2003	101538009	67766861	6329872	6219833	5083372	13023473	15664303
北京	Beijing	12024763	6329718	995141	686695	1427491	613455	3654099
天津	Tianjin	2113876	1509252	176977	434000	77808	242564	284252
河北	Hebei	2512674	1642136	34416	288197	87301	348012	435225
山西	Shanxi	950740	473991	2110	160506	53641	211630	211478
内蒙古	Inner Mongolia	907881	514832	8373	75702	55181	258169	79699
辽宁	Liaoning	4863947	3434716	151660	234820	131670	866730	430831
吉林	Jilin	1392394	977740	3590	143422	60698	291525	62431
黑龙江	Heilongjiang	1632806	886210	2630	259567	63710	351126	331760
上海	Shanghai	9012427	6762825	1066623		666736	678172	904694
江苏	Jiangsu	8099636	5966854	622235	407726	275428	1092992	764362
浙江	Zhejiang	9800514	7158355	600408	367706	481362	1454305	706492
安徽	Anhui	2406505	1656236	79178	161681	78679	439252	232338
福建	Fujian	3620657	2376658	118573	68852	106394	382660	754945
江西	Jiangxi	1774707	1085084	36311	134782	25820	316210	347593
山东	Shandong	5818758	4088581	191406	311485	186966	765754	777457
河南	Henan	1855555	1350953	52682	215342	52989	235413	216200
湖北	Hubei	2390412	1719094	87411	226013	81061	176634	413623
湖南	Hunan	2300324	1457959	173471	480846	73970	479640	288755
广东	Guangdong	12335231	8274350	871841	152244	440832	1369168	2250881
广西	Guangxi	1203112	732095	41615	29314	17572	159421	294024
海南	Hainan	366131	298856	63465	29301	9586	31619	26070
重庆	Chongqing	3278881	1774341	116952	163154	118569	508227	877744
四川	Sichuan	4508670	3269725	530376	230457	137719	789550	311676
贵州	Guizhou	1049510	565984	7213	107116	51155	151162	281209
云南	Yunnan	1149688	815444	175397	155670	33316	88964	211964
西藏	Tibet	20005	16461	6317	10144	200	2378	966
陕西	Shaanxi	1883082	1234696	71986	227873	146057	245935	256394
甘肃	Gansu	508029	343764	13705	121278	16702	67793	79770
青海	Qinghai	223121	154551	2097	53411	21610	21251	25709
宁夏	Ningxia	509065	347630	5501	38878	21652	96866	42917
新疆	Xinjiang	1024908	547770	20212	243651	81497	286896	108745

6-45 房地产开发企业(单位)资金来源

Source of Funds of Enterprises for Real Estate Development

单位：万元 (10 000 yuan)

年份 地区	Year Region	本年资金来源小计 Total Funds This Year	国家预算内资金 State Budgetary Appropriation	国内贷款 Domestic Loans	债券 Bonds	利用外资 Foreign Investment	#外商直接投资 Direct Foreign Investment	自筹资金 Fundraising	其他资金来源 Others
	1997	38170650	124789	9111902	48691	4608565	3279010	9728831	14547872
	1998	44149422	149480	10531712	62319	3617581	2588698	11669821	18118509
	1999	47959012	100457	11115664	98703	2566022	1804807	13446210	20631956
	2000	59976309	68720	13850756	34760	1687046	1348026	16142122	28192905
	2001	76963877	136291	16921968	3425	1357044	1061150	21839587	36705562
	2002	97499536	118044	22203357	22439	1572284	1241285	27384451	46198961
	2003	131969224	113631	31382699	5460	1700040	1162667	37706891	61060503
北京	Beijing	18713885		5868594		332107	99981	3758456	8754728
天津	Tianjin	3224137		911374		38315	30463	900460	1373988
河北	Hebei	2631696	7644	384960		23715	23715	1131948	1083429
山西	Shanxi	1198252	1250	278140		1000	1000	468939	448923
内蒙古	Inner Mongolia	839988	600	83040		375	375	554774	201199
辽宁	Liaoning	5582992	3388	1332891		55561	46434	2273464	1917688
吉林	Jilin	1366796		171010		1500	510	790184	404102
黑龙江	Heilongjiang	1607981	350	260166		4050	4050	870635	472780
上海	Shanghai	12947692		2827047		341438	171810	3139075	6640132
江苏	Jiangsu	9604457		2565988		74815	62230	2585426	4378228
浙江	Zhejiang	13841274	200	3941332	850	45555	45555	2534602	7318735
安徽	Anhui	3002227	4472	568264		15038	15038	985305	1429148
福建	Fujian	5131384	18491	986461	1000	121847	119243	1252934	2750651
江西	Jiangxi	1841081		339321		65347	61059	753751	682662
山东	Shandong	6792940		1355450		70733	67774	2464375	2902382
河南	Henan	2155250	60	397800		10841	8941	764412	982137
湖北	Hubei	3080076	41782	673144		18406	12114	995289	1351455
湖南	Hunan	2537745	13620	561418	119	66913	60310	971465	924210
广东	Guangdong	16836826	4012	3708234	1000	307852	232805	4240624	8575104
广西	Guangxi	1591269		369154		23017	19910	421576	777522
海南	Hainan	401828		65455		6172	4677	159983	170218
重庆	Chongqing	4223263	1000	949504		41458	41208	1371847	1859454
四川	Sichuan	5432113	150	1026278		6627	6527	1801966	2597092
贵州	Guizhou	1313854		260061		7414	6994	451268	595111
云南	Yunnan	1553014	89	403185		10415	10415	385852	753473
西藏	Tibet	45946		9000				27159	9787
陕西	Shaanxi	1979864	14185	564856		4352	4352	708451	688020
甘肃	Gansu	622337	2193	145674	391	300	300	224966	248813
青海	Qinghai	230688		41998	2100	3550	3550	97984	85056
宁夏	Ningxia	520710	145	124552		1327	1327	171280	223406
新疆	Xinjiang	1117659		208348				448441	460870

6-46 房地产开发企业(单位)建设房屋建筑面积和造价

Floor Space of Buildings and their Cost in Real Estate Development

年 份 地 区	Year Region	施工房屋面积 (万平方米) Floor Space of Buildings under Construction (10 000 sq.m)	竣工房屋面积 (万平方米) Floor Space of Buildings Completed (10 000 sq.m)	房屋建筑面积竣工率 (%) Rate of Floor Space of Buildings Completed (%)	竣工房屋价值 (万 元) Value of Buildings Completed (10 000 yuan)	竣工房屋造价 (元/平方米) Cost of Buildings Completed (yuan/sq.m)
	1997	44985.5	15819.7	35.2	18592458	1175
	1998	50770.1	17566.6	34.6	21391927	1218
	1999	56857.6	21410.8	37.7	24675822	1152
	2000	65896.9	25104.9	38.1	28593463	1139
	2001	79411.7	29867.4	37.6	33694469	1128
	2002	94104.0	34975.8	37.2	41416949	1184
	2003	117526.0	41464.1	35.3	52799528	1273
北 京	Beijing	9070.7	2593.6	28.6	4618258	1781
天 津	Tianjin	2314.4	911.3	39.4	1199770	1317
河 北	Hebei	2908.7	1207.3	41.5	1314185	1089
山 西	Shanxi	1294.6	482.6	37.3	544055	1127
内蒙古	Inner Mongolia	1176.0	615.9	52.4	530759	862
辽 宁	Liaoning	5314.1	2139.7	40.3	2301203	1075
吉 林	Jilin	1437.7	711.0	49.5	820176	1154
黑龙江	Heilongjiang	1900.0	883.5	46.5	869686	984
上 海	Shanghai	8267.5	2491.8	30.1	7452427	2991
江 苏	Jiangsu	8924.7	3120.2	35.0	3261003	1045
浙 江	Zhejiang	10804.8	3214.9	29.8	4781533	1487
安 徽	Anhui	3140.1	1326.2	42.2	1094037	825
福 建	Fujian	4891.0	1363.0	27.9	1517270	1113
江 西	Jiangxi	2577.9	1055.5	40.9	782784	742
山 东	Shandong	7246.8	2688.8	37.1	2799368	1041
河 南	Henan	3210.3	1005.5	31.3	859132	854
湖 北	Hubei	3252.2	1332.5	41.0	1434262	1076
湖 南	Hunan	3118.9	1142.3	36.6	1114571	976
广 东	Guangdong	12855.0	4383.7	34.1	7301472	1666
广 西	Guangxi	1929.8	558.7	29.0	426733	764
海 南	Hainan	459.1	115.0	25.0	192314	1673
重 庆	Chongqing	5287.8	1677.0	31.7	1572467	938
四 川	Sichuan	6837.9	2864.1	41.9	2321414	811
贵 州	Guizhou	2104.0	655.4	31.1	545722	833
云 南	Yunnan	1363.2	586.6	43.0	602198	1027
西 藏	Tibet	17.4	12.6	72.3	16115	1283
陕 西	Shaanxi	2274.4	709.5	31.2	861591	1214
甘 肃	Gansu	997.8	260.7	26.1	257506	988
青 海	Qinghai	412.1	157.0	38.1	152522	972
宁 夏	Ningxia	754.9	407.3	54.0	344124	845
新 疆	Xinjiang	1382.1	791.1	57.2	910871	1151

6-47 按用途分房地产开发企业(单位)新开工房屋面积

Floor Space Started in Real Estate Development by Use

单位：万平方米 (10 000 sq.m)

年份 地区	Year Region	本年新开工房屋面积 Floor Space Started This Year	住宅 Residential Buildings	#别墅、高档公寓 Villas, High-grade Apartments	#经济适用房屋 Economical Houses	办公楼 Office Buildings	商业营业用房 Houses for Business Use	其他 Other
	1997	14026.98	10996.64	469.72	1720.57	872.44	1462.45	695.44
	1998	20387.90	16637.50	638.60	3466.40	871.50	1938.65	940.25
	1999	22579.41	18797.94	594.06	3970.36	690.29	2198.56	892.62
	2000	29582.64	24401.15	1169.09	5313.32	898.81	3034.77	1247.91
	2001	37394.18	30532.72	1456.69	5795.97	1072.98	4105.40	1683.08
	2002	42800.52	34719.35	2278.17	5279.68	1254.24	4926.48	1900.45
	2003	54707.53	43853.88	2349.29	5330.58	1466.89	6706.80	2679.96
北京	Beijing	3433.75	2503.46	233.15	341.14	259.09	226.04	445.16
天津	Tianjin	838.17	721.51	62.20	220.15	17.94	59.98	38.74
河北	Hebei	1529.49	1304.54	8.73	254.92	22.50	176.20	26.26
山西	Shanxi	685.33	524.41	3.90	157.72	27.25	120.12	13.54
内蒙古	Inner Mongolia	795.91	544.73	6.58	71.91	20.82	203.26	27.10
辽宁	Liaoning	2617.63	2116.05	19.41	183.41	60.49	347.54	93.55
吉林	Jilin	960.28	765.78	2.07	133.13	31.64	139.84	23.02
黑龙江	Heilongjiang	1110.41	761.29	16.79	215.11	22.90	262.07	64.14
上海	Shanghai	3134.53	2613.19	335.54		86.10	248.37	186.88
江苏	Jiangsu	5143.31	4296.32	276.66	377.13	108.93	536.80	201.26
浙江	Zhejiang	4988.70	3981.71	249.52	244.30	160.79	534.45	311.75
安徽	Anhui	1655.56	1298.32	41.65	101.77	40.59	271.94	44.71
福建	Fujian	1903.00	1571.39	51.65	76.85	22.09	194.19	115.33
江西	Jiangxi	1484.17	1128.22	19.85	166.50	12.46	287.24	56.25
山东	Shandong	4039.93	3382.17	102.29	368.75	59.87	503.11	94.78
河南	Henan	1486.47	1284.54	21.95	192.81	35.98	147.39	18.57
湖北	Hubei	1542.34	1340.02	34.75	210.07	32.86	110.14	59.33
湖南	Hunan	1476.75	1110.45	79.70	354.84	45.09	259.19	62.03
广东	Guangdong	4328.19	3417.99	254.94	113.68	122.39	462.48	325.33
广西	Guangxi	1058.18	872.21	32.40	38.76	15.92	117.45	52.60
海南	Hainan	170.67	154.69	29.30	6.74	0.17	13.16	2.65
重庆	Chongqing	2098.24	1580.04	50.44	187.75	50.22	312.31	155.67
四川	Sichuan	3646.77	2925.80	254.57	225.02	62.03	523.91	135.04
贵州	Guizhou	902.94	715.09	10.32	125.75	19.53	130.83	37.49
云南	Yunnan	701.23	600.10	81.23	194.03	6.66	67.06	27.41
西藏	Tibet	17.37	14.66	4.93	9.72	0.07	2.63	
陕西	Shaanxi	944.09	783.34	13.02	215.64	48.79	93.18	18.79
甘肃	Gansu	462.45	379.80	37.83	148.19	6.17	69.22	7.26
青海	Qinghai	236.34	185.34		69.04	17.00	30.84	3.15
宁夏	Ningxia	532.55	419.46	4.08	65.31	17.67	80.14	15.28
新疆	Xinjiang	782.78	557.28	9.83	260.43	32.88	175.73	16.89

6-48 商品房屋销售情况

Selling of Commercial Houses

年 份 地 区	Year Region	房屋销售面积（万平方米）Floor Space Sold (10 000 sq.m)	# 住宅 Residential Buildings	个人购买商品住宅（万平方米）Commercial Houses Purchased by Individuals (10 000 sq.m)	商品房销售额（万元）Total Sales of Commercial Houses (10 000 yuan)	# 住宅 Residential Buildings
	1991	3025.46	2745.17	926.55	2378597	2075979
	1992	4288.86	3812.21	1456.01	4265938	3798493
	1993	6687.91	6035.19	2943.39	8637141	7291913
	1994	7230.35	6118.03	3344.53	10184950	7305208
	1995	7905.94	6787.03	3344.81	12577269	10240705
	1996	7900.41	6898.46	3666.82	14271292	11069006
	1997	9010.17	7864.30	5233.72	17994763	14075553
	1998	12185.30	10827.10	7792.62	25133027	20068676
	1999	14556.53	12997.87	10408.53	29878734	24137347
	2000	18637.13	16570.28	14464.38	39354423	32286046
	2001	22411.90	19938.75	18250.77	48627517	40211543
	2002	26808.29	23702.31	22793.69	60323413	49578501
	2003	33717.63	29778.85	28714.61	79556627	65434492
北 京	Beijing	1895.77	1771.05	1720.14	8979571	7891587
天 津	Tianjin	786.50	720.64	709.17	1980448	1724256
河 北	Hebei	939.43	838.02	779.62	1374568	1125134
山 西	Shanxi	359.60	299.43	272.73	579177	378205
内蒙古	Inner Mongolia	547.97	433.97	432.18	696144	467570
辽 宁	Liaoning	1499.08	1320.29	1275.55	3434521	2813999
吉 林	Jilin	501.14	436.32	415.66	788764	631448
黑龙江	Heilongjiang	814.64	673.11	654.92	1465500	1091465
上 海	Shanghai	2376.40	2224.47	2181.91	12163398	11098649
江 苏	Jiangsu	2721.57	2364.32	2342.21	5979054	4768819
浙 江	Zhejiang	2781.84	2356.78	2309.24	7613003	5776372
安 徽	Anhui	1093.27	906.35	884.43	1654143	1219565
福 建	Fujian	1250.10	1083.79	1038.42	2871627	2224564
江 西	Jiangxi	865.83	693.53	683.37	1047243	668583
山 东	Shandong	2251.52	2005.03	1870.78	3823732	3255188
河 南	Henan	862.71	795.78	748.10	1197375	1025863
湖 北	Hubei	1073.48	1015.04	929.63	1616159	1473462
湖 南	Hunan	848.47	725.28	675.57	1198667	861836
广 东	Guangdong	3061.32	2739.60	2627.41	9781005	8201276
广 西	Guangxi	505.31	451.67	443.79	951643	767366
海 南	Hainan	112.64	108.95	107.43	237092	219783
重 庆	Chongqing	1316.83	1132.95	1076.78	2102260	1499915
四 川	Sichuan	2457.85	2181.82	2138.62	3493680	2681965
贵 州	Guizhou	554.34	494.45	481.90	727889	564928
云 南	Yunnan	521.97	480.52	464.66	982134	853008
西 藏	Tibet	10.32	10.20	10.20	18088	17794
陕 西	Shaanxi	580.05	531.98	495.23	890059	739693
甘 肃	Gansu	224.77	208.87	195.68	286528	245323
青 海	Qinghai	83.51	70.34	65.46	122365	94398
宁 夏	Ningxia	232.38	187.81	187.59	434150	284466
新 疆	Xinjiang	587.02	516.48	496.25	1066640	768012

6-49 按用途分商品房屋实际销售面积

Floor Space of Commercial Houses Actually Sold by Use

单位：万平方米 (10 000 sq.m)

年份 地区	Year Region	房屋销售面积 Floor Space Sold	住宅 Residential Buildings	#别墅、高档公寓 Villas, High-grade Apartments	#经济适用房屋 Economical Houses	办公楼 Office Buildings	商业营业用房 Houses for Business Use	其他 Other
	1997	9010.17	7864.30	254.25	1211.85	341.43	634.06	170.38
	1998	12185.30	10827.10	345.30	1666.50	400.60	810.80	146.80
	1999	14556.53	12997.87	435.74	2701.31	403.43	1003.17	152.06
	2000	18637.13	16570.28	640.72	3760.07	436.98	1399.31	230.56
	2001	22411.90	19938.75	878.19	4021.47	502.57	1696.15	274.44
	2002	26808.29	23702.31	1241.26	4003.61	538.92	2218.58	348.47
	2003	33717.63	29778.85	1449.87	4018.87	630.49	2833.10	475.19
北　京	Beijing	1895.77	1771.05	131.90	320.02	38.12	50.82	35.78
天　津	Tianjin	786.50	720.64	39.29	214.65	15.72	28.89	21.25
河　北	Hebei	939.43	838.02	11.35	139.59	11.01	82.20	8.20
山　西	Shanxi	359.60	299.43	0.71	93.28	16.94	41.77	1.46
内蒙古	Inner Mongolia	547.97	433.97	0.06	87.14	9.72	100.09	4.19
辽　宁	Liaoning	1499.08	1320.29	14.79	110.40	25.96	133.58	19.25
吉　林	Jilin	501.14	436.32	0.21	99.80	12.26	46.03	6.53
黑龙江	Heilongjiang	814.64	673.11	2.23	233.84	14.66	115.44	11.43
上　海	Shanghai	2376.40	2224.47	217.66		45.18	78.05	28.70
江　苏	Jiangsu	2721.57	2364.32	121.68	195.69	60.78	259.64	36.84
浙　江	Zhejiang	2781.84	2356.78	92.74	100.97	61.94	272.79	90.33
安　徽	Anhui	1093.27	906.35	28.64	129.98	22.83	148.47	15.62
福　建	Fujian	1250.10	1083.79	66.37	39.80	34.64	104.86	26.81
江　西	Jiangxi	865.83	693.53	7.28	99.06	6.09	155.52	10.70
山　东	Shandong	2251.52	2005.03	64.75	215.78	24.93	200.84	20.73
河　南	Henan	862.71	795.78	14.40	168.39	9.63	51.85	5.47
湖　北	Hubei	1073.48	1015.04	42.15	186.72	16.45	32.36	9.63
湖　南	Hunan	848.47	725.28	65.80	234.95	11.84	100.86	10.50
广　东	Guangdong	3061.32	2739.60	218.92	106.46	53.53	207.34	60.85
广　西	Guangxi	505.31	451.67	20.80	28.13	16.19	29.45	8.00
海　南	Hainan	112.64	108.95	12.64	20.91	2.17	1.28	0.24
重　庆	Chongqing	1316.83	1132.95	26.12	126.69	32.00	135.93	15.94
四　川	Sichuan	2457.85	2181.82	162.06	233.21	26.50	236.85	12.68
贵　州	Guizhou	554.34	494.45	3.28	78.52	10.57	46.31	2.99
云　南	Yunnan	521.97	480.52	56.00	156.22	5.54	32.69	3.22
西　藏	Tibet	10.32	10.20	2.08	8.12		0.12	
陕　西	Shaanxi	580.05	531.98	11.26	264.36	16.06	29.57	2.44
甘　肃	Gansu	224.77	208.87	4.68	37.20	2.57	12.63	0.70
青　海	Qinghai	83.51	70.34	2.91	20.99	4.14	8.27	0.75
宁　夏	Ningxia	232.38	187.81	2.70	34.98	7.24	35.16	2.17
新　疆	Xinjiang	587.02	516.48	4.42	233.02	15.30	53.44	1.80

6-50 按用途分商品房屋平均销售价格
Average Selling Price of Commercial Houses by Use

单位：元/平方米 (yuan/sq.m)

年份 地区	Year Region	房屋平均销售价格 Average Selling Price of Houses	住宅 Residential Buildings	#别墅、高档公寓 Villas, High-grade Apartments	#经济适用房屋 Economical Houses	办公楼 Office Buildings	商业营业用房 Houses for Business Use	其他 Other
	1997	1997	1790	5382	1097	4677	3090	2129
	1998	2063	1854	4596	1035	5552	3170	1837
	1999	2053	1857	4503	1093	5265	3333	1804
	2000	2112	1948	4288	1202	4751	3260	1864
	2001	2170	2017	4348	1240	4588	3274	2033
	2002	2250	2092	4154	1283	4336	3489	1919
	2003	2359	2197	4145	1380	4196	3675	2241
北京	Beijing	4737	4456	7416	2846	10645	10189	4596
天津	Tianjin	2518	2393	4052	2233	6287	4141	1777
河北	Hebei	1463	1343	2233	1122	2288	2637	915
山西	Shanxi	1611	1263	2000	966	4085	3135	587
内蒙古	Inner Mongolia	1270	1077	1860	1007	1302	2104	1277
辽宁	Liaoning	2291	2131	3226	1679	3363	3657	2323
吉林	Jilin	1574	1447	3440	1415	2361	2413	2651
黑龙江	Heilongjiang	1799	1622	3636	1442	3025	2618	2406
上海	Shanghai	5118	4989	6539		9711	6462	4240
江苏	Jiangsu	2197	2017	3240	1439	4136	3487	1448
浙江	Zhejiang	2737	2451	4276	2123	3525	5190	2241
安徽	Anhui	1513	1346	1942	1134	2212	2455	1257
福建	Fujian	2297	2053	3344	1384	2899	4823	1524
江西	Jiangxi	1210	964	1419	667	2028	2255	1460
山东	Shandong	1698	1624	3448	1070	2150	2443	1173
河南	Henan	1388	1289	1276	910	2081	2756	1571
湖北	Hubei	1506	1452	2555	1172	2476	2759	1316
湖南	Hunan	1413	1188	1960	874	2015	3006	933
广东	Guangdong	3195	2994	4293	1498	5281	5475	2659
广西	Guangxi	1883	1699	2381	1391	2170	4534	1951
海南	Hainan	2105	2017	2846	1315	3914	6737	878
重庆	Chongqing	1596	1324	3361	890	2478	3661	1589
四川	Sichuan	1421	1229	2893	1147	1725	3154	1504
贵州	Guizhou	1313	1143	2684	833	2553	2857	1213
云南	Yunnan	1882	1775	2522	1294	2572	3194	3250
西藏	Tibet	1753	1745	2505	1550		2496	
陕西	Shaanxi	1534	1390	3502	1098	4111	2729	1493
甘肃	Gansu	1275	1175	1390	1154	2356	2523	4713
青海	Qinghai	1465	1342	1629	1246	2126	2276	451
宁夏	Ningxia	1868	1515	2948	992	2701	3610	1466
新疆	Xinjiang	1817	1487	2759	1315	4587	4202	2159

6-51 房地产开发企业(单位)资产负债

Asset Balance of Enterprises for Real Estate Development

单位：万元 (10 000 yuan)

年 份 地 区	Year Region	实收资本 合 计 Total Capital Hold	#国 家 资本金 State Capital	资产总计 Total Assets	累计折旧 Total Depreciation	#本年折旧 Depreciation This Year	负债总计 Total Liabilities	所有者权益 Creditors' Equity	资产负债率 (%) Ratio of Liabilities to Assets
	1997	38120741	2443003	164169597	1756884	410656	125154596	39015001	76.2
	1998	57787310	8418989	195261772	1910386	390176	148572535	46689237	76.1
	1999	45208800	3024487	187448042	2087894	398180	142638782	44809260	76.1
	2000	53029071	2155664	251859857	2992816	577153	190321015	61538842	75.6
	2001	60198577	4717344	285668126	3544631	674683	214357160	71310966	75.0
	2002	67509145	3255888	330431260	3905332	817353	247645673	82785587	74.9
	2003	84710226	4082557	404864877	4508222	968337	306985556	97879321	75.8
北 京	Beijing	8312715	562812	57038522	404198	101164	46691607	10346915	81.9
天 津	Tianjin	2535110	139652	11185740	114693	20143	8203420	2982320	73.3
河 北	Hebei	842334	23604	4315288	60067	18608	3339524	975764	77.4
山 西	Shanxi	761357	31157	2885712	47924	8363	2068570	817142	71.7
内蒙古	Inner Mongolia	419701	8558	1557572	20856	5005	1063707	493865	68.3
辽 宁	Liaoning	3084611	238463	16167966	227282	47510	13121864	3046102	81.2
吉 林	Jilin	628942	23426	3042905	42229	8374	2340331	702574	76.9
黑龙江	Heilongjiang	1189064	42082	4973235	65822	12201	3787027	1186208	76.1
上 海	Shanghai	16626838	1162839	70243992	551438	113120	49781553	20462439	70.9
江 苏	Jiangsu	7946750	284000	24833778	197567	39534	20183408	4650370	81.3
浙 江	Zhejiang	4172708	99907	32362708	176753	47079	27093839	5268869	83.7
安 徽	Anhui	1644394	36764	5877267	76841	19996	4096093	1781174	69.7
福 建	Fujian	3794572	44020	15725909	185687	30921	11375776	4350133	72.3
江 西	Jiangxi	984170	28142	2595427	33599	12831	1699858	895569	65.5
山 东	Shandong	3071876	65847	14807523	188464	41143	11313769	3493754	76.4
河 南	Henan	1455042	42641	5510446	102740	19951	4038378	1472068	73.3
湖 北	Hubei	2393068	135675	8230872	130759	18862	5852668	2378204	71.1
湖 南	Hunan	1882443	48650	6751863	108075	50346	4114324	2637539	60.9
广 东	Guangdong	11839072	711672	67872403	890978	161437	51557439	16314964	76.0
广 西	Guangxi	867679	31184	4170909	42586	9164	3247403	923506	77.9
海 南	Hainan	484964		1702798	34023	3780	1347173	355625	79.1
重 庆	Chongqing	2895894	121331	12968949	206505	42805	9257357	3711592	71.4
四 川	Sichuan	2717345	49905	12115331	298546	56015	8326672	3788659	68.7
贵 州	Guizhou	893982	49191	3322298	58911	20910	2442491	879807	73.5
云 南	Yunnan	497803	17097	3127228	62227	20950	2484467	642761	79.4
西 藏	Tibet	13800		48890	525	148	40677	8213	83.2
陕 西	Shaanxi	1205042	18628	4486674	66220	15384	3292541	1194133	73.4
甘 肃	Gansu	570089	12426	1935812	38051	5718	1337161	598651	69.1
青 海	Qinghai	130100	10608	321307	8827	1254	184704	136603	57.5
宁 夏	Ningxia	255150	22949	1214750	20320	4328	929885	284865	76.5
新 疆	Xinjiang	593611	19327	3470803	45509	11293	2371870	1098933	68.3

6-52 房地产开发企业(单位)经营情况

Real Estate Development and Management

单位：万元 (10 000 yuan)

年份 地区	Year Region	经营总收入 Total Revenue	土地转让收入 Land Transferred	商品房屋销售收入 Commercial Houses Sold	房屋出租收入 Houses Leased	其他收入 Others	经营税金及附加 Business Tax and Extra Charges	营业利润 Operating Surplus
	1991	2840325	153810	2378597	39221	268697	205551	275239
	1992	5285565	427420	4265938	59617	532590	414435	635196
	1993	11359074	839281	8637141	106348	1776304	965917	1559223
	1994	12881866	959357	10184950	172817	1564742	951029	1674350
	1995	17316624	1943981	12582817	257927	2531899	903047	1434087
	1996	19687850	1203378	15337647	299899	2846926	927779	179805
	1997	22184557	1032847	17552061	387878	3211770	1042143	-103462
	1998	29512078	1322454	24084097	493192	3612325	1388134	-106565
	1999	30260108	1032492	25550245	627408	3049963	1453611	-350926
	2000	45157119	1296054	38968215	953237	3939613	2145704	732836
	2001	54716555	1889894	47294194	1173453	4359014	2734549	1254738
	2002	70778478	2251311	61457990	1445728	5623449	3701458	2529148
	2003	91372734	2797200	81536881	1643335	5395318	4937227	4303655
北京	Beijing	9005234	499302	7923321	385244	197367	529889	89590
天津	Tianjin	2130358	62295	1854575	27783	185705	98512	120860
河北	Hebei	1409743	10617	1201363	2437	195326	70408	23029
山西	Shanxi	552574	15781	465074	5207	66512	24167	-14019
内蒙古	Inner Mongolia	701717	2459	688429	1816	9013	32391	1217
辽宁	Liaoning	3675534	43475	3518507	15173	98379	217110	-30147
吉林	Jilin	926212	90	783755	1168	141199	44169	846
黑龙江	Heilongjiang	1202999	1462	1177070	3417	21050	61544	-23284
上海	Shanghai	15539532	785285	12272310	586598	1895339	773887	1518009
江苏	Jiangsu	6765976	349411	6226388	56421	133756	368109	443566
浙江	Zhejiang	8317021	40285	8054015	21397	201324	451698	688717
安徽	Anhui	1658421	23753	1530878	10953	92837	93388	44145
福建	Fujian	3183222	55978	2869595	20932	236717	201931	59861
江西	Jiangxi	857459	28676	815100	999	12684	45495	12618
山东	Shandong	4350857	68114	4152972	16226	113545	240766	165689
河南	Henan	1455785	21397	1368253	18096	48039	76469	-32181
湖北	Hubei	1579605	14434	1439571	15652	109948	82747	13256
湖南	Hunan	1330404	105646	1159731	11273	53754	71762	-2358
广东	Guangdong	14705884	435521	13287783	299798	682782	811515	1066154
广西	Guangxi	995439	66252	840738	36676	51773	66196	28322
海南	Hainan	230178	10530	181920	2451	35277	11061	-18274
重庆	Chongqing	2469860	37242	1914342	43603	474673	128979	56159
四川	Sichuan	3801311	76880	3576630	15053	132748	201764	145645
贵州	Guizhou	718363	7996	639360	10515	60492	37535	-161250
云南	Yunnan	1031761	12337	964364	8785	46275	55210	39171
西藏	Tibet	17948		17868	80		736	1991
陕西	Shaanxi	850467	19981	783870	5273	41343	46364	-8880
甘肃	Gansu	302309	529	284706	7254	9820	14393	-464
青海	Qinghai	117130		112345	681	4104	4975	-7242
宁夏	Ningxia	414250	319	377835	960	35136	20466	11322
新疆	Xinjiang	1075181	1153	1054213	11414	8401	53591	71587

6-53 按规模分房地产开发企业(单位)完成投资

Actually Completed Investment of Enterprises for Real Estate Development by Size of Enterprise

单位：万元 (10 000 yuan)

年 份 Year 地 区 Region		500万元以下 below 5 million yuan	500-1000万元 5-10 million yuan	1000-3000万元 10-30 million yuan	3000-5000万元 30-50 million yuan
	2001	490789	1249780	6016181	5175316
	2002	431143	1208124	6176178	5876400
	2003	384991	1206793	6646676	6624730
北 京	Beijing	2013	4338	59895	98492
天 津	Tianjin	698	5018	81620	118377
河 北	Hebei	7773	24971	215139	203457
山 西	Shanxi	8295	16903	111602	108998
内蒙古	Inner Mongolia	22443	59859	226567	123769
辽 宁	Liaoning	11936	50312	324164	303300
吉 林	Jilin	8327	24766	174428	146077
黑龙江	Heilongjiang	2983	24400	172096	167579
上 海	Shanghai	2615	13149	108579	156792
江 苏	Jiangsu	24285	79872	477292	669023
浙 江	Zhejiang	10048	36331	298227	409574
安 徽	Anhui	24187	66857	342056	275749
福 建	Fujian	9144	36560	239467	230503
江 西	Jiangxi	19557	71361	279831	232388
山 东	Shandong	14226	62894	510795	629088
河 南	Henan	17773	49291	212691	209130
湖 北	Hubei	29843	71672	268306	173294
湖 南	Hunan	18173	54542	263043	217332
广 东	Guangdong	35991	109955	463020	409391
广 西	Guangxi	10311	27400	137789	123531
海 南	Hainan	340	4230	34867	50689
重 庆	Chongqing	10221	40126	245147	325745
四 川	Sichuan	27444	94982	602486	559580
贵 州	Guizhou	24617	61104	222954	132198
云 南	Yunnan	8368	15844	68496	95742
西 藏	Tibet				1200
陕 西	Shaanxi	8691	31783	131899	111800
甘 肃	Gansu	10222	21238	100516	76932
青 海	Qinghai	457	3788	48104	28250
宁 夏	Ningxia	5043	15365	88860	94487
新 疆	Xinjiang	8967	27882	136740	142263

6-53 续表 continued

单位：万元 (10 000 yuan)

年 份 地 区	Year Region	5000万-1亿元 50-100 million yuan	1-5亿元 100-500 million yuan	5-10亿元 500-1000 million yuan	10亿元以上 1 billion yuan
	2001	9609580	22835419	7377710	10686332
	2002	11306026	29614623	9576046	13720683
	2003	13634361	40638179	14216639	18185640
北 京	Beijing	361067	3887497	2545686	5065775
天 津	Tianjin	268853	920334	287171	431805
河 北	Hebei	444815	1324967	237104	54448
山 西	Shanxi	225748	382454	61720	35020
内蒙古	Inner Mongolia	168868	265495	40880	
辽 宁	Liaoning	608060	2005092	731168	829915
吉 林	Jilin	282826	509394	55336	191240
黑龙江	Heilongjiang	304557	479925	165926	315340
上 海	Shanghai	571814	3706302	2224411	2228765
江 苏	Jiangsu	1304917	3877292	1004127	662828
浙 江	Zhejiang	1109355	4500946	1856388	1579645
安 徽	Anhui	484681	933274	256526	23175
福 建	Fujian	640867	1664452	510746	288918
江 西	Jiangxi	352124	561828	146296	111322
山 东	Shandong	1183263	2621268	459265	337959
河 南	Henan	410414	758366	137506	60384
湖 北	Hubei	284353	887798	226150	448996
湖 南	Hunan	471022	1100545	91433	84234
广 东	Guangdong	973396	4342514	1994018	4006946
广 西	Guangxi	287616	532918	68214	15333
海 南	Hainan	92745	163663	11607	7990
重 庆	Chongqing	577218	1288453	351679	440292
四 川	Sichuan	950336	1617886	182050	473906
贵 州	Guizhou	270208	276674	55435	6320
云 南	Yunnan	220763	501377	166309	72789
西 藏	Tibet	4343	14462		
陕 西	Shaanxi	333130	701746	251773	312260
甘 肃	Gansu	112285	150820	24000	12016
青 海	Qinghai	42285	92533	7704	
宁 夏	Ningxia	103335	165659	36316	
新 疆	Xinjiang	189097	402245	29695	88019

6-54 房地产开发企业(单位)建设成套住宅和其他类房屋竣工情况

Sets of Residential Houses and Floor Space of Other Houses Completed by Enterprises for Real Estate Development

年 份 地 区	Year Region	住宅竣工套数合计(套) Total Sets of Residential Houses (sets)	#别 墅、高档公寓 Villas, High-grade Apartments	#经济适用房 屋 Economical Houses	其他类房屋竣工面积(平方米) Floor Space of Other Houses (sq.m)	#拆迁还建 Rebuilding on the Place of House-breaking	#统建代建 United-Building or Deputized-Building
	1999	1946358	44025	484978	35150720	18636811	13793008
	2000	2139702	59880	603573	35299728	19509189	13148350
	2001	2414392	72207	604788	35259087	18841753	13223046
	2002	2629616	97751	538486	36126156	19376106	12527211
	2003	3021134	108525	447678	40911789	21815285	14789307
北 京	Beijing	193270	7497	27790	4759489	2418562	500425
天 津	Tianjin	78954	3914	26441	708466	128586	541044
河 北	Hebei	84787	946	16258	949221	353632	569822
山 西	Shanxi	34321	35	13232	981560	552848	372953
内蒙古	Inner Mongolia	47689	3	5034	763666	514827	186298
辽 宁	Liaoning	182464	3403	17297	3235474	1663443	1327097
吉 林	Jilin	56079	311	11309	731235	349930	334842
黑龙江	Heilongjiang	74099	334	23105	633030	444226	185103
上 海	Shanghai	168338	11920		322451	64961	162789
江 苏	Jiangsu	218232	8162	29182	4419318	3202275	1096174
浙 江	Zhejiang	192040	5719	13994	3251578	1849659	1090223
安 徽	Anhui	101500	1953	14333	1583490	1022160	427765
福 建	Fujian	91302	2397	3257	1563399	992050	519271
江 西	Jiangxi	65383	1494	12461	671223	385448	164780
山 东	Shandong	212253	6183	27559	3002733	1423308	1428925
河 南	Henan	74297	2339	15605	532526	229628	282946
湖 北	Hubei	91942	3293	16278	729403	254123	380640
湖 南	Hunan	76655	5827	32580	1702482	253389	1393416
广 东	Guangdong	334499	16586	13335	1272233	877188	96751
广 西	Guangxi	41578	1040	3703	185173	36614	78529
海 南	Hainan	8117	1108	2242			
重 庆	Chongqing	111026	1837	12418	2408933	1231704	1001983
四 川	Sichuan	212712	12877	29237	2740032	1834207	753822
贵 州	Guizhou	46323	477	6896	475225	255052	219552
云 南	Yunnan	39952	5102	12097	453375	86070	351749
西 藏	Tibet	728	55	624			
陕 西	Shaanxi	52682	2080	15783	765648	409344	299594
甘 肃	Gansu	22149	624	9732	310155	103617	187174
青 海	Qinghai	13024		4069	549196	94059	455137
宁 夏	Ningxia	30740	233	4862	776713	593081	168646
新 疆	Xinjiang	63999	776	26965	434362	191294	211857

6-55 35个大中城市主要指标完成情况(2003年)

Main Indicators of Real Estate in 35 Large-scale and Medium-scale Cities (2003)

城市	City	本年完成投资(万元) Investment Completed This Year (1 000 yuan)	#住宅 Residential Buildings	#办公楼 Office Buildings	#商业营业用房 Houses for Business Use	施工房屋面积(万平方米) Floor Space of Buildings under Construction (10 000 sq.m)	竣工房屋面积(万平方米) Floor Space of Buildings Completed (10 000 sq.m)	#住宅 Residential Buildings
总计	**Total**	**64122726**	**42527573**	**4062880**	**6571019**	**65151.8**	**20559.6**	**16842.0**
北京	Beijing	12024763	6329718	1427491	613455	9070.7	2593.6	2080.7
天津	Tianjin	2113876	1509252	77808	242564	2314.4	911.3	750.7
石家庄	Shijiazhuang	620931	361086	19913	36173	431.3	136.6	130.9
太原	Taiyuan	429703	170857	39368	97252	521.1	165.3	105.5
呼和浩特	Hohhot	273982	123772	34230	92725	342.0	131.8	110.1
沈阳	Shenyang	1773283	1306195	33572	323564	1738.8	585.9	494.3
长春	Changchun	700020	482072	19703	167914	529.1	254.4	185.6
哈尔滨	Harbin	1060366	500947	49064	201327	1039.6	418.1	302.7
上海	Shanghai	9012427	6762825	666736	678172	8267.5	2491.8	2140.0
南京	Nanjing	1838038	1293320	132705	136919	1553.8	390.9	334.9
杭州	Hangzhou	2588452	1940139	151832	307904	2449.9	701.4	554.0
合肥	Hefei	900136	641047	38402	167748	939.6	329.4	264.5
福州	Fuzhou	1670394	1136397	55807	146290	1936.8	492.0	423.7
南昌	Nanchang	600118	445574	13555	72110	660.3	134.0	103.7
济南	Jinan	897967	740877	53687	64109	818.7	295.4	254.3
郑州	Zhengzhou	742644	641296	30919	38557	1277.6	303.6	277.6
武汉	Wuhan	1695468	1248271	64501	99110	1955.5	682.6	600.2
长沙	Changsha	1108269	757746	45971	158339	1140.9	439.7	369.0
广州	Guangzhou	4194802	3172112	223030	433728	4350.4	1139.5	903.0
南宁	Nanning	394830	229928	8335	32151	726.5	215.0	179.2
海口	Haikou	277007	226977	7036	26613	402.2	89.4	81.2
重庆	Chongqing	3278881	1774341	118569	508227	5287.8	1677.0	1231.7
成都	Chengdu	2453696	1889675	83080	300990	2712.3	1016.1	895.7
贵阳	Guiyang	603621	300351	39058	67759	1072.5	276.5	213.1
昆明	Kunming	700700	521439	27885	23792	749.0	313.5	286.8
西安	Xi'an	1248177	783868	129362	164846	1343.1	339.7	289.6
兰州	Lanzhou	301456	198156	13526	36728	636.2	116.5	97.0
西宁	Xining	188950	127259	21050	16261	350.4	135.3	120.6
银川	Yinchuan	393550	279647	19354	58898	569.6	314.3	251.6
乌鲁木齐	Urumqi	484927	238920	64811	103057	665.2	390.1	318.3
大连	Dalian	1511363	1035736	45428	245167	1396.6	579.2	469.2
青岛	Qingdao	1277969	938646	49476	145146	1747.1	546.6	456.5
宁波	Ningbo	1842589	1368423	76782	200473	2026.8	635.5	529.8
厦门	Xiamen	792737	548790	30308	90038	1290.2	297.3	219.6
深圳	Shenzhen	4126634	2501914	150526	472913	2838.2	1020.3	816.6

6-55 续表 continued

城市	City	房屋销售面积（万平方米）Floor Space Sold (10 000 sq.m)	#住宅 Residential Buildings	房屋销售价格（元/平方米）Selling Price of House (yuan/sq.m)	#住宅 Residential Buildings	本年购置土地面积（万平方米）Land Space Purchased This Year (10 000 sq.m)	本年开发土地面积（万平方米）Land Space Developed This Year (10 000 sq.m)
总计	**Total**	**16591.6**	**14975.2**	**3225**	**3033**	**16101.9**	**9763.0**
北京	Beijing	1895.8	1771.1	4737	4456	1391.3	1084.4
天津	Tianjin	786.5	720.6	2518	2393	1093.3	740.4
石家庄	Shijiazhuang	118.1	114.6	1581	1570	134.6	142.0
太原	Taiyuan	84.3	57.7	3165	2204	122.6	82.8
呼和浩特	Hohhot	137.4	113.0	1552	1277	179.9	169.7
沈阳	Shenyang	324.8	291.6	2916	2753	607.4	219.2
长春	Changchun	185.2	167.2	2155	1973	225.6	96.2
哈尔滨	Harbin	390.8	325.5	2353	2183	299.3	227.4
上海	Shanghai	2376.4	2224.5	5118	4989	1469.1	605.5
南京	Nanjing	444.5	400.2	3148	2888	459.5	257.1
杭州	Hangzhou	555.5	471.1	3939	3657	681.0	275.0
合肥	Hefei	290.0	248.2	2088	1889	536.6	198.4
福州	Fuzhou	452.1	410.6	2347	2178	542.1	283.6
南昌	Nanchang	135.1	109.4	2367	2079	235.2	208.8
济南	Jinan	256.2	241.3	2327	2307	314.8	178.4
郑州	Zhengzhou	269.3	256.9	2045	1955	203.9	119.1
武汉	Wuhan	542.8	512.1	2072	2023	964.3	511.5
长沙	Changsha	327.5	291.2	2040	1786	681.5	475.4
广州	Guangzhou	815.5	755.2	4211	3999	334.7	503.7
南宁	Nanning	192.2	169.3	2252	2169	103.6	90.4
海口	Haikou	95.7	92.1	2092	1989	47.8	
重庆	Chongqing	1316.8	1133.0	1596	1324	1637.2	842.4
成都	Chengdu	966.3	897.3	2096	1908	55.3	16.9
贵阳	Guiyang	229.0	212.1	1949	1735	356.1	204.6
昆明	Kunming	317.4	298.4	2233	2131	385.6	211.0
西安	Xi'an	252.7	230.3	2148	1921	339.5	271.7
兰州	Lanzhou	86.1	81.0	1858	1673	124.7	99.4
西宁	Xining	57.9	50.7	1644	1499	97.8	92.8
银川	Yinchuan	170.3	135.9	2139	1728	168.4	3.8
乌鲁木齐	Urumqi	303.8	271.4	2361	1864	89.1	113.9
大连	Dalian	498.1	446.7	2921	2699	358.8	334.9
青岛	Qingdao	462.7	407.9	2406	2297	776.9	507.5
宁波	Ningbo	548.6	463.3	2865	2541	721.3	359.0
厦门	Xiamen	294.4	245.6	3371	3077	100.6	64.4
深圳	Shenzhen	411.7	358.1	6256	5793	262.2	171.7

6-56 在建大型项目基本情况（2003年）

单位：万元

单位名称	Name of Enterprise	项目名称
首都机场	Beijing Capital Airport	机场改造
北京地铁五号线投资有限责任公司	Beijing Subway Line No.5 Investment Co. Ltd.	地铁五号线
北京地铁建设管理有限责任公司	Beijing Subway Group Co., Ltd.	地铁四号线
北京地铁建设管理有限责任公司	Beijing Subway Group Co., Ltd.	地铁十号线
中海石油（中国）有限公司天津分公司	Tianjin Branch of China National Offshore	油气田勘探开发建设
天津市滨海市政建设发展有限公司	Tianjin Binhai Municipal Engineering Construction and Development Co., Ltd.	快速路系统工程
东方希望包头稀土铝业有限责任公司	Baotou Rear Earth Metal & Aluminium Co., Ltd. of East Hope Group	铝电一体化工程
一汽-大众汽车有限公司	FAW-Volkswager Automobile Co., Ltd	PQ35项目
大庆油田有限责任公司	Daqing Oilfield Company Ltd.	产能建设工程
外高桥电厂第二发电有限公司	No.2 Power Generation Co., Ltd., Shanghai Waigaoqiao Power Plant	外高桥电厂二期工程
宝钢集团上海一钢公司	Shanghai No.1 Iron and Steel Co., Ltd., Bao Steel Group	不锈钢板卷工程
上海赛科石油化工有限责任公司	Shanghai SECCO Petrochemical Company Ltd.	上海赛科90万吨/年乙烯工程
上海轨道交通杨浦线发展有限公司	Shanghai Rail Transport, Yangpu Line Development Co., Ltd.	轨道交通8号线（杨浦线）
上海轨道交通申松线发展有限公司	Shanghai Rail Transport, Shensong Line Development Co., Ltd	轨道交通9号线（申松线）
上海同盛投资（集团）有限公司	Shanghai Tongsheng Investment (Group) Co., Ltd.	洋山深水港区一期工程
上海磁悬浮交通发展有限公司	Shanghai Maglev Transport Development Co., Ltd.	上海磁浮快速列车示范运营线
扬子巴斯夫石油化工有限责任公司	Yangtze-BASF Petro-chemical Co., Ltd.	扬巴一体化石化基地
启东大唐吕四火力发电有限公司	Qidong Datang Lusi Themo-power Co., Ltd.	大唐火力发电一期工程
杭州杭千高速公路发展有限公司	Hangzhou-Qiandaohu Expressway Development C., Ltd.	杭千高速公路
杭州湾大桥工程指挥部	Hangzhouwan Bay Bridge Construction Headquarters	杭州湾跨海大桥
浙江嘉华发电有限责任公司	Zhejiang Jiahua Power Generation Co., Ltd	嘉兴电厂二期
嵊泗县洋山同盛有限公司	Zhejiang Shengsi Yangshan Tongsheng Co., Ltd	洋山深水港集装箱项目一期工程
福建省高速公路建设指挥部	Fujian Expressway Construction Headquarters	三福高速公路
河南鑫旺电力有限公司	Henan Xinwang Power Co., Ltd	火力发电
湖北清江水电开发有限责任公司	Qingjiang Hydro-power Development Co., Ltd., Hubei	清江水布垭
广州市地下铁道总公司	Guangzhou City Subway General Co.	广州地铁三号线工程
广州科学城	Guandzhou Science Park	广州科学城基础设施建设
广州大学城建设指挥部办公室	Project Office of Guangzhou University Park	广州大学城
广州白云国际机场有限公司	Guangzhou International Airport Co., Ltd.	白云国际机场迁建工程
佛山市地下铁道有限公司	Foshan Municipal Subway Co., Ltd	广佛轻轨工程
惠州中海壳牌石油化工有限公司	CNOOC Huizhou Shell Petro-chemical Co., Ltd	中海壳牌石化项目
龙滩水电开发有限公司	Longtan Hydro-power Development Co., Ltd	龙滩水电站
贵州乌江水电开发有限责任公司	Guizhou Wujiang Hydro-power Development Co., Ltd	构皮滩水电站
景洪电站建设指挥部	Jinghong Power Station Construction Headquarters	景洪电站
云南小湾电站工程建设前期筹备处	Preparation Office of Yunnan Xiaowan Power Station Project	小湾水电站
铁道部	Ministry of Railways	宁西线西安至合肥段
铁道部	Ministry of Railways	渝怀线
铁道部	Ministry of Railways	青藏线（格拉段）
铁道部	Ministry of Railways	浙赣电化
中国石油天然气股份有限公司	PetroChina Company Ltd.	西气东输基建项目

Basic Conditions of Large Projects Being Constructed (2003)

(10 000 yuan)

Name of Project	开工时间 Starting Time	计划总投资 Total Planned Investment	累计完成投资 Accumulated Investment Completed	累计新增固定资产 Accumulated Newly Increased Fixed Assets
Transformation of Airport	2002.01	1719258	153297	12232
Subway Line No.5	2000.09	1200000	138377	
Subway Line No.4	2003.12	1480000	16946	
Subway Line No.10	2003.12	1572000	9285	
Exploration and Development of Oil and Gas Fields	2000.01	1457240	1536033	1536033
Rapid-trans System	2003.07	1730000	144680	
Integrated Aluminium-power Project	2002.11	1000000	356500	350000
PQ35 Project	2003.07	1253000	44124	
Production Capacity-building Project	2003.03	1003423	811567	811567
Phase II of Waigaoqiao Power Plant	2001.07	1066589	580277	
Stainless Steel Rolling Project	2001.11	1178000	869621	250090
Shanghai Saike 900,000-ton/year Ethylene Project	2002.03	2239030	319051	2631
Line No. 8 of Rail-transport System (Yangpu Line)	2001.12	1376500	364545	
Line No. 9 of Rail-transport System (Shensong Line)	2002.10	1201699	71646	
Phase I of Yangshan Deep Water Port	2002.06	1430976	573595	
Demonstration Line of Shanghai Maglev High-speed Train	2001.03	1002990	1002993	
Integrated Petro-chemical Base	2001.09	2200000	1156342	
Phase I Datang Themo-power Plant	2003.11	1100000	3000	
Hangzhou-Qiandaohu Expressway	2003.03	1138223	50612	
Hangzhouwan Bay Bridge	2003.03	1176000	60000	
Phase II of Jiaxing Power Plant	2002.01	1028153	426130	
Phase I of Container Pier of Yangshan Deep Water Port	2002.07	1000000	332316	
Sanming-Fuzhon Expressway	2000.08	1155642	929158	
Themo-power Project	2003.12	1100000	16170	
Qingjiang Shuibuya Project	2002.02	1061707	337568	63492
Guangzhou Subway Line No.3	2001.12	1529500	189428	
Infrastructure for Guandzhou Science Park	2000.01	1000000	491335	234
Guangzhou University Park	2003.03	3000000	485840	222620
Guangzhou New International Airport Project	2000.04	1486200	1218968	
Guangzhou-Foshan Light-rail Transport System	2002.12	1470000	8000	
CNOOC Shell Petro-chemical Project	2002.06	3330000	949139	949139
Longtan Hydro-power Station	2001.07	2429105	510486	1110
Goupitan Hydro-power Station	2003.11	1386700	129796	886
Jinghong Power Station	2003.06	1030000	25000	
Xiaowan Hydro-power Station	2002.01	2773200	411974	
Hefei-Xi'an Section of Nanjing-Xi'an Railway	2000.05	2402799	1928000	31369
Chongqing-Huaihua Railway	2000.12	1979085	1455000	
Qinghai-Tibet Railway (Geermu-Lhasa Section)	2001.06	2621524	1300000	
Zhejiang-Jiangxi Electric Railway	2003.12	1050000	35000	
Capital Construction Project of West-East Gas Pipeline	2002.01	4350000	4350000	1165461

主要统计指标解释

全社会固定资产投资 以货币形式表现的在一定时期内全社会建造和购置固定资产的工作量以及与此有关的费用的总称。该指标是反映固定资产投资规模、结构和发展速度的综合性指标,又是观察工程进度和考核投资效果的重要依据。全社会固定资产投资按登记注册类型可分为国有、集体、个体、联营、股份制、外商、港澳台商、其他等。按照管理渠道，可分为基本建设、更新改造、房地产开发投资和其他固定资产投资四个部分。

基本建设投资 基本建设指企业、事业、行政单位以扩大生产能力(或新增工程效益)为主要目的的新建、扩建工程及有关工作。其综合范围为总投资50万元以上(含50万元，下同)的基本建设项目。具体包括：(1)列入中央和各级地方本年基本建设计划的建设项目，以及虽未列入本年基本建设计划，但使用以前年度基建计划内结转投资(包括利用基建库存设备材料)在本年继续施工的建设项目；(2)本年基本建设计划内投资与更新改造计划内投资结合安排的新建项目和新增生产能力(或工程效益)达到大中型项目标准的扩建项目，以及为改变生产力布局而进行的全厂性迁建项目；(3)国有经济中既未列入基建计划，也未列入更新改造计划的总投资在50万元以上的新建、扩建、恢复项目和为改变生产力布局而进行的全厂性迁建项目，以及行政、事业单位增建业务用房和行政单位增建生活福利设施的项目。

更新改造投资 更新改造一般是指企业、事业单位对原有设施进行技术改造（包括固定资产更新）以及相应配套的辅助性生产、生活福利设施等工程和有关的工作。其综合范围为总投资50万元以上的更新改造单位(或项目)。具体包括：(1)列入中央和各级地方本年更新改造计划的投资单位(或项目)以及虽未列入本年更新改造计划，但使用上年更新改造计划内结转的投资在本年继续施工的单位(或项目)；(2)本年更新改造计划内投资与基本建设计划内投资结合安排的对企、事业单位原有设施进行技术改造或更新的项目和增建主要生产车间、分厂等其新增生产能力(或工程效益)未达到大中型项目标准的项目，以及由于城市环境保护和安全生产的需要而进行的迁建工程；(3)国有经济中既未列入基建计划也未列入更新改造计划，总投资在50万元以上的属于改建或更新改造性质的项目，以及由于城市环境保护和安全生产的需要而进行的迁建工程。

房地产开发投资 指各种登记注册类型的房地产开发公司、商品房建设公司及其他房地产开发法人单位和附属于其他法人单位实际从事房地产开发或经营活动的单位统一开发的包括统代建、拆迁还建的住宅、厂房、仓库、饭店、宾馆、度假村、写字楼、办公楼等房屋建筑物和配套的服务设施，土地开发工程（如道路、给水、排水、供电、供热、通讯、平整场地等基础设施工程）的投资；不包括单纯的土地交易活动。

其他固定资产投资 指全社会固定资产投资中未列入基本建设、更新改造和房地产开发投资的总投资在50万元以上的城镇范围内建造和购置固定资产的活动，以及城镇私人建房和农村企业、事业、行政单位和农村个人固定资产投资活动。具体包括：

(1)国有单位未纳入基本建设计划和更新改造计划管理，计划总投资（或实际需要总投资）在50万元以上的以下工程：①用油田维护费和石油开发基金进行的油田维护和开发工程；②煤炭、铁矿、森工等采掘采伐业用维简费进行的开拓延伸工程；③交通部门用公路养路费对原有公路、桥梁进行改建的工程；④商业部门用简易建筑费建造的仓库工程。

(2)城镇集体固定资产投资：指所有隶属直辖市、省辖市、县级市和县城所在地城关镇区域范围内的集体经济单位（乡镇企业局管理的除外）建造和购置固定资产其计划总投资（或实际需要总投资）在50万元及50万元以上，未列入基本建设和更新改造计划的单位(项目)投资。

(3)除上述以外的其他各种登记注册类型的企、事业单位(包括城镇私营企、事业单位和个体户)建造和购置固定资产总投资在50万元及50万元以上、未列入基本建设计划和更新改造计划的单位(项目)。其中个体经营户只统计50万元以上非建房投资。

(4)城镇和工矿区私人建房投资：包括市、县城、城关镇、工矿区所辖范围内的全部私人建房，不论其房主是否系本地的常住户口均应包括。

(5)农村投资：包括农村区域范围内进行固定资产投资活动的企业、事业、行政单位及农村个人投资。

固定资产投资的资金来源 根据固定资产投资的资金来源不同，分为国家预算内资金、国内贷款、利用外资、自筹资金和其他资金来源。

(1)国家预算内资金：分为财政拨款和财政安排的贷款两部分。包括中央财政的基本建设基金(分经营性基金和非经营性基金两部分)、专项支出(如煤代油专项等)、收回再贷、贴息资金，财政安排的挖潜改造和新产品试制支出、城建支出、商业部门简易建筑支出、不发达地区发展基金等资金中用于固定资产投资的资金；地方财政中由国家统筹安排的资金等。

(2)国内贷款：指报告期固定资产投资单位向银行及非银行金融机构借入的用于固定资产投资的各种国内借款，包括银行利用自有资金及吸收的存款发放的贷款、上级主管部门拨入的国内贷款、国家专项贷款(包括煤代油贷款、劳改煤矿专项贷款等)、地方财政专项资金安排的贷款、国内储备贷款、周转贷款等。

(3)利用外资：指报告期收到的用于固定资产建造和购置的国外资金(包括设备、材料、技术在内)。包括对外借款(外国政府、国际金融组织贷款、出口信贷、外国银行商业贷款、对外发行债券和股票)、外商直接投资及外商其他投资。不包括我国自有外汇资金(国家外汇、地方外汇、留成外汇、调剂外汇和中国银行自有资金发行的外汇贷款等)。计算利用外资时，需要折算成人民币，折算中所使用的外汇汇率按现汇计算，即按使用外汇时的汇率计算。

(4)自筹资金：指固定资产投资单位报告期收到的，由各地区、各部门及企、事业单位筹集用于固定资产投资的预算外资金，包括中央各部门、各级地方和企、事业单位的自筹资金。

(5)其他资金来源：指在报告期收到的除以上各种资金之外其他用于固定资产投资的资金，包括企业或金融机构通过发行各种债券筹集到的资金、群众集资、个人资金、无偿捐赠的资金及其他单位拨入的资金等。

固定资产投资按国民经济行业分 建设项目归哪个行业，按其建成投产后的主要产品或主要用途及社会经济活动性质来确定。基本建设按建设项目划分国民经济行业，更新改造、其他固定资产投资根据整个企业、事业单位所属的行业来划分。一般情况下，一个建设项目或一个企业、事业单位只能属于一种国民经济行业。为了更准确地反映国民经济各行业之间的比例关系，联合企业(总厂)所属分厂属于不同行业的，原则上按分厂划分行业。

固定资产投资按建设性质分 建设项目的性质一般分为新建、扩建、改建、迁建、恢复。房地产开发单位、农村投资、城镇工矿区私人建房投资不划分建设性质。基本建设按建设项目划分建设性质，更新改造、国有经济中其他固定资产投资及城镇集体投资等按整个企业、事业单位的建设情况确定建设性质。

(1)新建：一般指从无到有"平地起家"开始建设的企业、事业和行政单位或独立的工程。现有企业、事业、行政单位一般不属于新建。但如有的单位原有基础很小，经过建设后新增的固定资产价值超过该企、事业、行政单位原有固定资产价值(原值)三倍以上的也应作为新建。

(2)扩建：指在厂内或其他地点，为扩大原有产品的生产能力(或效益)或增加新的产品生产能力，而增建主要的生产车间(或主要工程)、分厂、独立的生产线。行政、事业单位在原单位增建业务用房(如学校增建教学用房、医院增建门诊部、病房等)也作为扩建。

现有企、事业单位为扩大原有主要产品生产能力或增加新的产品生产能力，增建一个或几个主要生产车间(或主要工程)、分厂，同时进行一些更新改造工程的，也应作为扩建。

(3)改建：指对原有设施进行技术改造或更新(包括相应配套的辅助性生产、生活福利设施)，没有增建主要生产车间、分厂等。现有企、事业单位为适应市场变化的需要，而改变企业的主要产品种类(如军工企业转产民品等)，或原有产品生产作业线由于各工序(车间)之间能力不平衡，为填平补齐充分发挥原有生产能力而增建不增加本企业主要产品设计能力的车间，也应作为改建。

固定资产投资按构成分 固定资产投资活动按其工作内容和实现方式分为建筑安装工程，设备、工具、器具购置，其他费用三个部分。

(1)建筑安装工程(建筑安装工作量)：指各种房屋、建筑物的建造工程和各种设备、装置的安装工程。包括各种房屋建造工程，各种用途设备基础和各种工业窑炉的砌筑工程及金属结构工程；为施工而进行的各种准备工作和临时工程以及完工后的清理工作等；铁路、道路的铺设，矿井的开凿及石油管道的架设等；水利工程；防空地下建筑等特殊工程；列入房屋工程预算内的暖气、卫生、通风、照明、煤气等设备的价值及装设油饰工程；列入建筑工程预算内的各种管道(蒸汽、压缩空气、石油、给排水等管道)、电力、电讯电缆导线等的敷设工程；以及各种机械设备的安装工程；为测定安装工程质量，对设备进行的试运工作；房地产开发单位进行的商品房屋开发建设工程、土地开发工程。在安装工程中，不包括被安装设备本身的价值。

(2)设备、工具、器具购置：指建设单位或企、事业单位购置或自制的，达到固定资产标准的设备、工具、器具的价值。新建单位及扩建单位的新建车间，按照设计或计划要求购置或自制的全部设备、工具、器具，不论是否达到固定资产标准均计入"设备、工具、器具购置"中。

(3)其他费用：指在固定资产建造和购置过程中发生的，除上述几项内容以外的各种应分摊计入固定资产的费用。

基本建设项目按大中小型划分 基本建设划分大中小型项目原则上应按照上级批准的设计任务书或初步设计所确定的总规模或总投资划分，没有正式批准设计任务书或初步设计的，按国家或省、自治区、直辖市年度基本建设投资计划中所列的总规模或总投资划分。上述两条均不具备的，按本年计划施工工程的建设总规模或总投资划分。生产单一产品的工业项目，按产品的设计能力划分；生产多种产品的工业项目，按其主要产品的设计能力划分。品种繁多，难以按生产能力划分的，按全部计划总投资划分。划分标准以国家颁发的《大中小型建设项目划分标准》为依据。国家曾在1953年、1962年、1972年、1977年和1979年先后五次修订《大中小型建设项目划分标准》，因此各历史时期的大中型项目数不完全可比。

施工项目 指报告期内进行过建筑或安装施工活动的项目。凡是报告期内施过工的建设项目，不论施工时间长短，均作为施工项目统计。施工项目个数可以反映一定时期固定资产投资的实际规模，与同期建成投产的建设项目个数相比，可以从建设速度的角度反映固定资产投资的效果。根据建设项目施工活动的不同性质，施工项目又分为：本年正式施工项目、本年收尾项目和以前年度全部停缓建项目。

全部建成投产项目 工业项目指设计文件规定形成生产能力的主体工程及其相应配套的辅助设施全部建成，经负荷试运转，证明具备生产设计规定合格产品的条件，并经过验收鉴定合格或达到竣工验收标准，与生产性工程配套的生活福利设施可以满足近期正常生产的需要，正式移交生产的建设项目。非工业项目指设计文件规定的主体工程和相应的配套工程全部建成，能够发挥设计规定的全部效益，经验收鉴定合格或达到竣工验收标准，正式移交使用的建设项目。

新增生产能力(或工程效益) 指通过固定资产投资活动而增加的设计能力(或工程效益)，该指标是以实物形态表现的反映固定资产投资成果的指标，也是考核投资经济效果的重要依据之一。

新增生产能力(或工程效益)一般有以下几种表现形式：

(1)用产品数量表示，以工程在单位时间内(一般是一年)所能生产的产品数量(即年产量)表示。如原煤开采用万吨／年表示，化学农药用吨／年表示，拖拉机制造用台／年表示等。某些化工产品由于含量差别较大，按其设计含量计算折合量表示，如硫酸、纯碱、烧碱等。

(2)用单位时间内所能处理的原料数量表示，以工程每天(或小时)所能处理原料的数量表示。如机制糖工程日处理原料吨，食用植物油日处理原料吨，城市污水处理能力用万吨／日表示等。

(3)用新增加的主要设备的数量或容量表示，如新增棉布织机、丝织机等台数，毛纺锭等锭数，发电厂新增发电机组容量用千瓦表示等。

(4)以节约的原材料、燃料、动力实物量表示，适用于反映更新改造节约项目的效益。

(5)用建筑物容积、容量、面积、长度表示，是非工业项目或工程新增效益的一种表现形式。如铁路里程、公路里程、水库容量、仓库容量、房屋建筑面积、学校学生席位、医院病床、灌区灌溉面积等。

根据工程的特点，有时需要用两种或两种以上的复合计量单位表示新增生产能力(或工程效益)，如新增内燃机生产能力同时用年产台数、千瓦数表示等。

为了规范新增生产能力(或工程效益)的名称和计算单位，国家统计局制订了《新增生产能力(或工程效益)目录》和《节约原材料、燃料、动力目录》，各固定资产投资单位在统计新增生产能力(或工程效益)时，必须按目录中规定的名称和计量单位填报。

房屋建筑面积 指房屋建筑物勒脚以上外墙外围的水平截面面积，包括房屋建筑物的有效面积和结构面积。该指标是从实物形态上反映建设规模和建设成果的重要指标之一，也是检查工程形象进度、计算工程造价、分析投资效果、研究施工任务和建筑材料之间平衡情况的重要依据。

住宅建筑面积 指施工和竣工房屋建筑面积中供居住用的房屋建筑面积。

施工面积 指报告期内施工的全部房屋建筑面积。包括本期新开工的面积和上期开工跨入本期继续施工的房屋面积，以及上期已停建在本期恢复施工的房屋面积。本期竣工和本期施工后又停缓建的房屋，其建筑面积仍计入本期房屋施工面积中。

竣工面积 指在报告期内房屋建筑按照设计要求已经全部完工，达到住人和使用条件，经验收鉴定合格(或达到竣工验收标准)，正式移交使用单位的各栋房屋建筑面积的总和。

房屋建筑面积竣工率 指一定时期内房屋竣工面积占同期房屋施工面积的比率。该指标从房屋建筑施工速度的角度反映投资效果的指标。

新增固定资产 指报告期内已经完成建造和购置过程，并已交付生产或使用单位的固定资产价值。该指标是表示固定资产投资成果的价值指标，也是反映建设进度，计算固定资产投资效果的重要指标。

建设项目投产率 指一定时期内全部建成投产项目个数与同期施工项目个数的比率。该指标是从建设单位建设速度的角度反映投资效果的指标。

固定资产交付使用率 指一定时期新增固定资产与同期完成投资额的比率。该指标是反映固定资产动用速度，衡量建设过程中宏观投资效果的综合指标。由于新增固定资产是较长时期内形成的结果，而投资额则是当年完成的，因此，该指标一般适宜于反映较长时期内固定资产的动用情况。

竣工房屋住宅套数 指报告期内按照设计要求全部完工，经验收合格，达到居住和使用条件并正式交付使用的成套住宅数量。包括独立厨房、独立卫生间、若干卧室、室内走廊等设施在内的供一户居住和使用的房屋。该指标可以反映住宅建设的产业化程度和城市化进程以及人民居住水平提高的情况。

别墅、高档公寓 指建筑造价和销售价格明显高于一般商品住宅的商品住宅。别墅一般指地处郊区，独立成栋的商品住宅；高档公寓一般指地处市内高尚社区，高层或多层的商品住宅。别墅、高档公寓的确定标准：一是经有房地产投资计划审批权的主管部门审批建设的别墅、高档公寓开发项目；二是销售价格高于当地同等地段商品住宅平均销售价格一倍以上的别墅、公寓开发项目。该指标可以分析房地产投资结构，反映高收入家庭商品住宅的供求平衡情况。

经济适用房 指根据国家经济适用房计划安排建设的政策性住宅。经济是指房屋建筑造价和销售价格低于一般商品住宅；适用是指适合中低收入家庭购买使用。经济适用房主要是由国家统一下达投资计划，房地产公司开发，对外销售；用地一般采用行政划拨或招标投标方式，免收土地出让金；对各种经批准的收费减半征收，开发利润不超过3%；销售价格实行政府指导价。该指标可以分析房地产投资结构，反映中低收入家庭商品住宅的供求平衡情况。

Explanatory Notes on Main Statistical Indicators

Total Investment in Fixed Assets in the Whole Country refers to the volume of activities in construction and purchases of fixed assets and related fees, expressed in monetary terms. It is a comprehensive indicator which shows the size, structure and growth of the investment in fixed assets, providing basis for observing the progress of construction projects and evaluating results of investment. Total investment in fixed assets in the whole country includes, by type of ownership, the investment by the state-owned units, collective units, individuals, joint ownership units, share-holding units, as well as investment by businessmen from foreign countries and from Hong Kong, Macau and Taiwan, and by other units. According to China's current management system, the investment in fixed assets is classified into the following four parts: investment in capital construction, investment in innovation, investment in real estates development and other investment in fixed assets.

Investment in Capital Construction Capital construction refers to the new construction projects or extension projects and the related activities of the enterprises, institutions or administrative units mainly for the purpose of expanding production capacity (or improving project efficiency), covering only projects each with a total investment of 500,000 RMB yuan and over. It includes: (1) projects listed in the capital construction plan of the current year of the central government and the local governments at various levels as well as the projects, though not listed in the capital construction plan of the current year, but continued to be constructed in this year, using the investment listed in the plan of capital construction of previous years and carried forward to this year (also using the equipment and materials kept in stock of the capital construction); (2) new construction projects arranged both in the plan of capital construction and the plan of innovation; extension projects with the newly increased production capacity (or project efficiency) up to the standard of a large and medium-sized project; and the projects of moving the whole factory to a new site so as to improve the distribution of productive forces; (3) new construction projects, extension projects or restoration projects with the total investment of 500,000 RMB yuan and over by the state-owned units, though listed neither in the plan of capital construction nor in the plan of innovation; the projects in the state-owned units of moving the whole factory to a new site so as to improve the distribution of productive forces; and the projects of building additional business houses by the administrative units and institutions and building welfare facilities by the administrative units.

Investment in Innovation Innovation refers in general to the technological innovation of the original facilities (including renewal of fixed assets) by the enterprises and institutions as well as the corresponding supplementary projects for production or welfare facilities and the related activities, covering only projects each with a total investment of 500,000 RMB yuan and over. It includes: (1) projects listed in the innovation plan of the current year of the central government and the local governments at various levels as well as the projects, though not listed in the innovation plan of the current year, but continued to be constructed in this year, using the investment listed in the plan of innovation of previous years and carried forward to this year; (2) projects of technological innovation or renewal of the original facilities, arranged both in the plan of innovation and in the plan of capital construction; extension projects (main workshops or a branch of the factory) with the newly increased production capacity (or project efficiency) not up to the standard of a large and medium-sized project; and the projects of moving the whole factory to a new site so as to meet the requirements of urban environmental protection or safe production; (3) projects of reconstruction or technological innovation with the total investment of 500,000 RMB yuan and over by the state-owned units, though listed neither in the plan of capital construction nor in the plan of innovation; the projects in the state-owned units of moving the whole factory to a new site so as to meet the requirements of urban environmental protection or safe production.

Investment in Real Estate Development It includes the investment by the real estate development companies, commercial buildings construction companies and other real estate development units of various types of ownership in the construction of house buildings, such as residential buildings, factory buildings, warehouses, hotels, guesthouses, holiday villages, office buildings, and the complementary service facilities and land development projects, such as roads, water supply, water drainage, power supply, heating, telecommunications, land leveling and other projects of infrastructure. It excludes the activities in simple land transactions.

Other Investment in Fixed Assets refers to the construction and purchases of fixed assets with an investment of over 500, 000 yuan which are not listed in the investment in capital construction, investment in innovation and investment in real estate development, as well as urban private housing projects and investment in fixed assets by enterprises, institutions and individuals in rural areas. It includes:

1) The following projects of the state-owned units with the total planned (or actually needed) investment of over 500,000 yuan, which are not included in the plan of capital construction and the plan of innovation: (1) projects of oil fields maintenance and exploitation with the oil fields maintenance funds and petroleum development funds; (2) opening and extending projects with the maintenance funds in coal, ore and other mining enterprises and logging enterprises; (3) project of reconstruction of the original highways and bridges with the highway maintenance funds in the department of communication; (4) projects of construction of warehouses with the funds of simple construction in the commercial department.

2) The investment in fixed assets by urban collective units: refer to projects of construction and purchases of fixed assets

with the planned total investment of 500,000 yuan and over by all collective units in areas under the jurisdiction of cities and county towns (excluding investment by collective units under township enterprise administration offices).

3) The projects of construction and purchases of fixed assets by the enterprises, institutions (including urban private enterprises or institutions) or individuals other than those mentioned above with total investment of 500,000 yuan and over, which are not included in the plan of capital construction and the plan of innovation. For individual investment, only the investment in non-housing projects is to be included.

4) The private investment in housing construction in the urban areas and in industrial and mining areas: including all private housing construction under the jurisdiction of cities, county towns and industrial and mining areas, no matter whether the owner of the house is registered as the permanent resident in the locality or not.

5) The investment in rural areas: including investment in fixed assets by enterprises, institutions and individuals in the rural areas.

Sources of Funds for Investment in Fixed Assets include fund from state budget, domestic loans, foreign investment, self-raised funds, and others depending on the source of investment.

(1) Fund from state budget consists of budgetary appropriation and loans from state budget. More specifically, it includes, from the budget of the central government, capital construction fund (operation fund and non-operational fund), special expenses (e.g. expenses on substituting petroleum with coal), loans from repayment, discount fund, expenses on innovation and trial production of new products, expenses on urban construction, expenses on temporary construction by trade departments, development fund for less developed areas, as well as local budgetary fund transferred from the central budget.

(2) Domestic loans refer to loans of various forms borrowed by investing units from banks and non-bank financial institutions during the reference period for the purpose of investment in fixed assets, including loans issued by banks from their self-owned funds and deposit, loans appropriated by higher responsible authorities, special loans by government (including loan for substituting petroleum with coal, special loan for reform-through-labour coal mines), loans arranged by local government from special funds, domestic reserve loan, and working loan, etc..

(3) Foreign Investment refers to foreign funds received during the reference period for the construction and purchase of investment in fixed assets (covering equipment, materials and technology), including foreign borrowings (loans from foreign governments and international financial institutions, export credit, commercial loans from foreign banks, issue of bonds and stocks overseas), foreign direct investment and other foreign investment. Excluded in this category are capitals in foreign exchanges owned by China (foreign exchanges owned by the central and local governments, foreign exchanges retained by enterprises, foreign exchanges by enterprises through regulating mechanism, loans in foreign exchanges issued by the Bank of China with its own fund, etc.). In calculating the utilization of foreign capitals, foreign currencies are converted into Chinese Renminbi applying the current exchange rate when the foreign capitals are actually used.

(4) Self-raised funds refer to extra-budgetary funds for investment in fixed assets received by investing units from central government ministries, local governments, enterprises and institutions, including their self-raised funds.

(5) Others refer to funds for investment in fixed assets received from the sources other than those listed above, including capitals raised through issuing bonds by enterprises or financial institutions, funds raised from individuals and through donations, and funds transferred from other units.

Investment in Fixed Assets by Sector The classification of construction projects by sector is determined by the major products or the purpose of the projects when they are put into production or use, and by the nature of their social economic activities. The investment in capital construction is classified into different sectors of the national economy by the nature of construction projects, while investment in innovation and other investment are classified according to the sector to which the whole enterprise or institution belongs. In general, one project or one enterprise or institution can only be classified into one sector. In order to reflect more accurately the relation among various sectors, the branch factories of an integrated complex are classified into different sectors according to the economic activities of the branch factories.

Investment in Fixed Assets by Type of Construction The construction projects in general can be classified, by the type of construction, into new construction, expansion, reconstruction, moving and restoration. However, investment by type of construction is not applied to investment by real-estate development units, investment in rural areas and investment in housing by urban individuals. In capital construction, the type of construction is determined by the nature of the project. In investment in innovation, in other investment by state-owned units and investment by collective-owned units, the type of construction is determined by the condition of the whole enterprise or institutions.

(1) New construction in general refers to newly constructed enterprises, institutions, administrative agencies or independent projects from scratch. Construction in the existing enterprises, institutions or agencies is not considered as new construction. In case the assets of the existing unit is quite small, and the value of newly added fixed assets exceeds the original value of assets by three times, the expansion will be considered as new construction.

(2) Expansion refers to construction of new major production workshop, branch factory or independent production line within a factory or in other locations, for the purpose of increasing the production capacity (or improving efficiency) of the original products. Newly constructed houses for the operation of institutions and administrative organizations (such as the newly constructed buildings for teaching in schools, buildings for clinics or wards in hospitals, etc.) are also classified as expansion.

Also included in the expansion are investments by existing enterprises or institutions in building major production line(s) or branch factory(ies) along with some work on innovation, for the purpose of expending the production capacity of original products or producing new products.

(3) Reconstruction refers to innovation or technical transformation of the existing facilities (including auxiliary production equipment and welfare facilities), without building major new workshops or branch factories. Also considered as reconstruction is the construction of new workshops by the existing enterprises or institutions for improving the existing production capacity (improving or changing the variety of products to meet the market demand), rather than increasing the designed capacity of the main products.

Investment in Fixed Assets by Structure By their contents, investment activities are classified into 3 categories, i.e. construction and installation, purchase of equipment and instrument, and other expenses.

(1) Construction and installation (work volume of construction and installation) refers to the construction of various houses and buildings and installation of various kinds of equipment and instruments. They include construction of various houses; equipment foundations, industrial kilns and stoves, and metal structure work; preparation works for project construction, and clearing up works post project construction; pavement of railways and roads, drilling of mines and putting up of oil pipes; construction of projects of water conservancy; construction of underground air-raid shelters and construction of other special projects; value of equipment for heating, sanitation, ventilation, lighting, gas, painting, etc. that are covered by the budget of housing projects; laying out of various pipelines (for steam, compressed air, petroleum, tap water and sewage) and lines for electric power and for communications; installation of various machinery equipment, testing operation for pre-testing the quality of installation projects, and land and other development work conducted by real estate developers for commercial housing. The value of equipment installed is not included in the value of installation projects.

(2) Purchase of equipment and instruments refers to the total value of equipment, tools, and instruments purchased or self-produced which come up to standards for fixed assets by the construction units or investing enterprises or institutions. Equipment, tools and instruments purchased or self-produced for new workshops by newly established or expanded units are categorized as "purchase of equipment and instruments" no matter whether they come up to the standards for fixed assets.

(3) Other expenses refer to expenses occurring during the construction or purchase of fixed assets other than those mentioned above.

Capital Construction Projects by Size The classification of size of capital construction projects should be determined according to the total scale or total investment set in the approved construction plan by higher responsible authorities or in the tentative design, otherwise according to the total scale or total investment set in the current capital construction plan of the state, provinces, autonomous regions, and municipalities directly under central government. Industrial projects which produce unitary products are classified according to its design capacity of products; projects which produce multi-products are classified by the design capacity of the major product or by the total planned investment. Standards for the Classification of Construction Projects into large, medium-sized and small ones issued by the government are the base for size division of construction projects, which was revised five times in 1958, 1962, 1972, 1977, and 1979 respectively and therefore, data on projects by size are not entirely comparable from year to year.

Projects under Construction refer to projects with construction and installation activities undertaken in the reference period. All projects that have construction activities undertaken during the reference period are reported as projects under construction irrespective of the length of construction work. The number of projects under construction can reflect the actual size of investment in fixed assets during a given period, and when compared with the number of projects completed and put into use during the same period, it demonstrates the results of investment in fixed assets. Depending on the nature of construction activities, projects under construction can also be classified into projects under construction in current year, winding-up projects in current year and stopped or suspended projects in previous years (with preservation work in current year).

Projects Completed and Put into Use Industrial projects refer to the major projects and accessory facilities completed which result in forming production capacity and have been checked and accepted while the living and welfare facilities have been completed and can ensure normal production and formally put into production. Non-industrial projects refer to the major projects and accessory facilities completed which possess the designed capacity and have been checked, accepted and formally put into production.

Newly Increased Production Capacity (or Project Efficiency) refers to the increase of designed capacity (or project efficiency) through investment in fixed assets, which reflects the accomplishment of investment in fixed assets in kind and serves as important basis for evaluating the economic efficiency of investment.

The newly increased production capacity (project efficiency) are usually expressed in one of the following forms:

(1) output of products, i.e. the output that the project can produce during a given period (usually a year). For instance, the capacity in coal mining is expressed in 10,000 tons/year, the capacity in producing chemical pesticides expressed in ton/year, the capacity in producing tractors in tractor/year, etc. For some chemical products where the effective contents differ significantly, the production capacity is expressed as the designed effective content equivalent, such as in the case of sulphuric acid, soda ash, caustic soda, etc;

(2) raw materials processing capacity, i.e. the volume of raw materials that could be processed by the project per day (or per hour), such as tons of materials processed per day by a sugar refining project or edible vegetable oil project, or tons of urban sewage processed per day;

(3) number or capacity of major equipment increased, such as number of cotton or silk looms increased, wool spindles increased, or capacity (in kilowatts) of power generators increased;

(4) saved raw materials, fuels or power, which are mainly

used for the efficiency of innovation and transformation projects; and

(5) physical measures (volume, capacity, area, and length) of construction, which is typical for non-industrial projects, for instance, the length of new railways or highways, the capacity of reservoirs, the floor space of housing projects, capacity for new students in schools or beds in hospitals, areas under new irrigation project, etc.

Features of projects sometimes call for combined use of two or more measurement to reflect the increased production capacity (or project efficiency), for instance, the new capacity for the production of internal combustion engines are expressed in sets per year and kilowatts per year simultaneously.

To standardize the nomenclature and unit of measurement for new production capacity (or project efficiency), the National Bureau of Statistics has developed *Nomenclature for New Production Capacity (Project Efficiency)* and *Nomenclature for Saving Raw Materials, Fuels and Power*. All reporting units with investment activities are required to follow these two nomenclatures in reporting statistics on new production capacity (project efficiency).

Floor Space of Buildings under Construction and Completed refers to total floor space of the horizontal section of outer walls above the plinth of the building, including the effective area and the area occupied by the structure. This indicator is one of the important indicators in physical terms to reflect the scale and accomplishment of the construction industry, and important basis for monitoring the progress, calculating the cost, analyzing the efficiency and studying the supply of building materials in relation with the construction projects.

Floor Space of Residential Buildings refers to the floor space of the residential buildings among the total space of buildings under construction or completed.

Floor Space under Construction refers to total floor space of all buildings under construction during the reference period, including floor space of newly started buildings during the reference period, floor space of construction extended from the previous period to the current period, and floor space of construction suspended during the previous period and resumed in the current period. Floor space of construction completed in the current period, and floor space of construction started and then suspended in the current period are also included in the floor space under construction of the current year.

Floor Space of Buildings Completed refers to the floor space of all buildings completed in the reference period, which have been appraised and accepted (or come up to the designed standards) and have been transferred to the owners for use.

Completion Rate of Floor Space of Buildings refers to the ratio of the floor space of buildings completed in certain period of time to the floor space of buildings under construction in the same period. This indicator reflects the investment result from the perspective of the speed of construction.

Newly Increased Fixed Assets refer to the newly increased value of fixed assets, constructed or purchased, that have been transferred to the investors. This is an indicator that demonstrates the results of investment in fixed assets in monetary terms, and an important indicator to reflect the speed of construction and to calculate the efficiency of investment.

Rate of Construction Projects Completed and Put into Use refers to the ratio of the number of construction projects completed and put into use in certain period of time to the number of projects under construction in the same period. This reflects the investment efficiency from the perspective of the speed of projects construction.

Rate of Projects of Fixed Assets Completed and Put into Operation refers to the ratio of the newly increased fixed assets to the total investment made in the same period. This is a comprehensive indicator reflecting the speed of the employment of fixed assets and the investment efficiency at the macro-level. As the newly increase fixed assets is the result of a long period while the investment is completed in the current year, this indicator is expected to be used to reflect the employment of fixed assets over a long period of time.

Number of Flats in Completed Residential Buildings refers to total number of flats completed during the reference period, appraised and accepted as meeting the standards for living, and transferred for use. A flat includes separate kitchen and bathroom, several bedrooms and corridor, suitable for one household. This indicator reflects the degree of industrialization of the residential building construction, the process of urbanization and the improvement of the living standard of people.

Villas, High-Grade Apartments refers to commercial houses whose construction costs and marketing prices are significantly higher than ordinary housing. Villas are independent structures generally located in the suburbs; high-grade apartments are multi-story buildings located in elegant urban neighborhoods. Criteria for villas and high-grade apartments include: 1) projects for the construction of villas or high-grade apartments have to be approved by competent departments in charge of real estate development and investment plans, and 2) prices for projects on villas or high-grade apartments are higher by over 100% compared with the average prices of ordinary commercial housing projects in similar location. This indicator helps to analyze the investment structure of the real estate industry and the demand and supply of housing for high-income households.

Economically Affordable Housing refers to housing constructed according to the state plan for economically affordable housing. Houses of this category featured in low cost in construction and low prices, and therefore are affordable to mid-income or low income households. Economically affordable housing projects are developed by real estate companies under the state investment plan, with the land provided through government allocation or tendering procedures. Developers are exempted from land utilization fees and enjoy another 50% exemption of all other legitimate fees, while their profits are limited to less than 3%, and the completed houses are sold under the government-guided prices. This indicator helps to analyze the investment structure of the real estate industry and the demand and supply of housing for mid or low income households.

七、能源

Energy

简要说明

一、本篇资料的主要内容

本篇包括的主要内容有能源生产、消费及品种构成，能源生产和消费弹性系数，综合能源平衡表和主要能源品种的单项平衡表，分行业分主要能源品种的消费量，能源加工转换效率及生活用能源消费量等。

二、本篇资料的统计范围为全社会。

三、本篇的资料来源

7-1表数据来自工业产品产量统计，并以此为依据计算；7-14表数据来自电力企业联合会；其它表的数据均来自历年能源平衡表。

四、关于数据口径与计算的说明

1.一次能源生产量与工业统计数字一致。

2.能源生产与消费弹性系数分别以能源生产、消费增长速度与国内生产总值增长速度相比求得。

3.能源平衡表中，进口量和出口量采用海关统计数据。进口量中包括我国轮船、飞机在国外加油量，出口量中包括外国轮船、飞机在我国加油量。电力折算标准煤系数按平均发电煤耗计算。

4.能源加工转换效率表中，电力折算标准煤系数采用当量值计算，每千瓦小时折0.1229千克标准煤。

Brief Introduction

I. Main Contents

Data in this chapter cover mainly the energy production and consumption and their composition, the elasticity ratio of energy production and consumption, the overall balance of energy and the balance by different types of energy, the consumption of energy by sector and by types of energy, efficiency of energy conversion and the consumption of energy for non-production uses.

II. Data in this chapter cover the whole society.

III. Source of Data

Data in Table 7-1 are calculated on the basis of statistics on output of industrial products, data in Table 7-14 come from the Association of Power Generation Enterprises, and data in other tables in this chapter are from the energy balance sheets over the years.

IV. Notes on Coverage and Calculation of Data:

(1) The data on the production of primary energy are the same as the concerned data of the industrial statistics.

(2) The elasticity ratio of energy production is calculated as the quotient of the growth rate of energy production divided by the growth rate of GDP; and the elasticity ratio of energy consumption is calculated as the quotient of the growth rate of energy consumption divided by the growth rate of GDP.

(3) In the energy balance, the data on the imports and exports are data from the customs statistics. The refueling by Chinese ships and airplanes abroad is included in the imports. The refueling by foreign ships and airplanes in China is included in the exports. The coefficient for conversion of electric power into the standard coal equivalent is calculated according to the average consumption of coal for generating electricity.

(4) In the table on the efficiency of energy conversion, the coefficient for conversion of electric power into the standard coal equivalent is calculated on the basis of heat value equivalent. One kwh is equal to 0.1229 kg SCE.

7-1 能源生产总量及构成

Total Production of Energy and Its Composition

年 份 Year	能源生产总量（万吨标准煤）Total Energy Production (10 000 tons of SCE)	占能源生产总量的比重(%) As Percentage of Total Energy Production			
		原 煤 Coal	原 油 Crude Oil	天然气 Natural Gas	水 电 Hydro-power
1978	62770	70.3	23.7	2.9	3.1
1980	63735	69.4	23.8	3.0	3.8
1985	85546	72.8	20.9	2.0	4.3
1989	101639	74.1	19.3	2.0	4.6
1990	103922	74.2	19.0	2.0	4.8
1991	104844	74.1	19.2	2.0	4.7
1992	107256	74.3	18.9	2.0	4.8
1993	111059	74.0	18.7	2.0	5.3
1994	118729	74.6	17.6	1.9	5.9
1995	129034	75.3	16.6	1.9	6.2
1996	132616	75.2	17.0	2.0	5.8
1997	132410	74.1	17.3	2.1	6.5
1998	124250	71.9	18.5	2.5	7.1
1999	109126	68.3	21.0	3.1	7.6
2000	106988	66.6	21.8	3.4	8.2
2001	120900	68.6	19.4	3.3	8.7
2002	138369	71.2	17.3	3.1	8.4
2003	160300	74.2	15.2	2.9	7.7

注：电力折算标准煤的系数根据当年平均发电煤耗计算(下表同)。

a)The coefficient for conversion of electric power into SCE (standard coal equivalent) is calculated on the basic of the data on the average coal consumption in generating electric power in the same year. The same as in the following tables.

7-2 能源消费总量及构成

Total Consumption of Energy and Its Composition

年 份 Year	能源消费总量（万吨标准煤）Total Energy Consumption (10 000 tons of SCE)	占能源消费总量的比重(%) As Percentage of Total Energy Consumption			
		煤 炭 Coal	石 油 Crude Oil	天然气 Natural Gas	水 电 Hydro-power
1978	57144	70.7	22.7	3.2	3.4
1980	60275	72.2	20.7	3.1	4.0
1985	76682	75.8	17.1	2.2	4.9
1989	96934	76.1	17.1	2.1	4.7
1990	98703	76.2	16.6	2.1	5.1
1991	103783	76.1	17.1	2.0	4.8
1992	109170	75.7	17.5	1.9	4.9
1993	115993	74.7	18.2	1.9	5.2
1994	122737	75.0	17.4	1.9	5.7
1995	131176	74.6	17.5	1.8	6.1
1996	138948	74.7	18.0	1.8	5.5
1997	137798	71.7	20.4	1.7	6.2
1998	132214	69.6	21.5	2.2	6.7
1999	130119	68.0	23.2	2.2	6.6
2000	130297	66.1	24.6	2.5	6.8
2001	134914	65.3	24.3	2.7	7.7
2002	148222	65.6	24.0	2.6	7.8
2003	167800	67.1	22.7	2.8	7.4

注:2003年能源消费量为估算数。

a)Data on energy consumption in 2003 were estimated figures.

7-3 综合能源平衡表

Overall Energy Balance Sheet

单位：万吨标准煤 (10 000 tons of SCE)

项目	Item	1990	1995	2000	2001	2002
可供消费的能源总量	**Total Energy Available for Consumption**	**96138**	**129535**	**115150**	**125310**	**144319**
一次能源生产量	Primary Energy Output	103922	129034	106988	120900	138369
回收能	Recovery of Energy		2312	1760	1859	1908
进口量	Imports	1310	5456	14331	13471	15769
出口量(-)	Exports (-)	5875	6776	9026	11145	11017
年初年末库存差额	Stock Changes in the Year	-3219	-491	1097	225	-710
能源消费总量	**Total Energy Consumption**	**98703**	**131176**	**130297**	**134915**	**148222**
在总量中:	Consumption by Sector					
1.农、林、牧、渔、水利业	1.Farming,Forestry,Animal Husbandry, Fishery and Water Conservancy	4852	5505	5787	6233	6514
2.工　业	2.Industry	67578	96191	89634	92347	102181
3.建筑业	3.Construction	1213	1335	1433	1453	1610
4.交通运输、仓储及邮电通讯业	4.Transport, Storage, Post and Telecommunication Services	4541	5863	9916	10257	11087
5.批发和零售贸易餐饮业	5.Wholesale and Retail Trade and Catering Services	1247	2018	2893	3165	3464
6.其他	6.Others	3473	4519	5722	6034	6333
7.生活消费	7.Residential Consumption	15799	15745	14912	15427	17033
在总量中:	Consumption by Usage					
(一) 终端消费	(I)Final Consumption	94289	124252	124032	128951	140847
#工业	Industry	63239	89473	83707	86711	95143
(二) 加工转换损失量	(II)Losses in Processing and Transformation	2264	3634	2372	2011	2612
#炼焦	Coking	905		487	387	322
炼油	Petroleum Refining	326		781	636	1015
(三) 损失量	(III)Other Losses	2150	3289	3893	3953	4763
平衡差额	**Balance**	**-2565**	**-1641**	**-15147**	**-9605**	**-3903**

注：1.电力、热力按等价热值折算,因此加工转换损失量中不包括发电、供热损失量。村办工业包括在工业中(下表同)。

2.进口量包括我国飞机、轮船在国外加油量;出口量包括外国飞机、轮船在我国加油量。

a) Electric power and heat are converted on the basic of equal caloric value. Therefore, losses in processing and transformation exclude losses in power generation and heating. Energy consumption of industry include that of village industry. The same as in the following tables.

b) Data on imports include the petroleum consumed by the Chinese airplanes and ships in refueling abroad. Data on exports include the petroleum consumed by the foreign airplanes and ships in refueling in China.

7-4 石油平衡表

Petroleum Balance Sheet

单位: 万吨　　(10 000 tons)

项　　目	Item	1990	1995	2000	2001	2002
可供量	**Total Energy Available for Consumption**	**11435.0**	**16072.7**	**22631.8**	**23204.7**	**24925.1**
生产量	Output	13830.6	15005.0	16300.0	16395.9	16700.0
进口量	Imports	755.6	3673.2	9748.5	9118.2	10269.3
出口量(-)	Exports (-)	3110.4	2454.5	2172.1	2046.7	2139.2
年初年末库存差额	Stock Changes in the Year	-40.8	-151.0	-1244.6	-262.7	94.9
消费量	**Total Energy Consumption**	**11485.6**	**16064.9**	**22439.3**	**22838.3**	**24779.8**
在消费量中:	Consumption by Sector					
1.农、林、牧、渔、水利业	1.Farming,Forestry,Animal Husbandry, Fishery and Water Conservancy	1033.6	1203.2	1496.7	1568.5	1674.1
2.工　业	2.Industry	7321.6	9349.3	11404.7	11388.6	12489.6
3.建筑业	3.Construction	327.3	242.8	344.3	372.3	410.4
4.交通运输、仓储及邮电通讯业	4.Transport, Storage, Post and Telecommunication Services	1683.2	2863.6	5509.4	5692.9	6156.6
5.批发和零售贸易餐饮业	5.Wholesale and Retail Trade and Catering Services	77.6	333.9	545.0	567.4	593.0
6.其他	6.Others	757.8	1390.3	1882.7	1953.7	1978.6
7.生活消费	7.Residential Consumption	284.5	682.0	1256.5	1294.8	1477.5
在消费量中:	Consumption by Usage					
(一) 终端消费	(I)Final Consumption	9304.7	13676.3	19893.5	20357.0	21982.8
#工　业	Industry	5180.4	7095.5	9016.2	9059.9	9854.5
(二) 中间消费 (用于加工转换)	(II)Intermediate Consumption (Consumed in Transformation)	1630.4	2230.0	2352.8	2292.0	2606.8
发　电	Power Generation	1234.4	1358.5	1178.2	1213.6	1275.6
供　热	Heating	356.3	399.9	427.0	438.7	420.7
制　气	Gas Production	39.7	51.6	25.9	22.8	18.9
(三) 炼油损失量	(III) Losses in Petroleum Refining	295.8	420.1	721.8	617.0	891.6
(四) 损失量	(Ⅳ) Other Losses	254.7	158.6	192.9	189.3	190.2
平衡差额	**Balance**	**-50.6**	**7.8**	**192.5**	**366.4**	**145.3**

注: 1.生产量为原油产量。

2.进口量包括我国飞机、轮船在国外加油量;出口量包括外国飞机、轮船在我国加油量。

a) Data on output refer to the output of crude oil.

b) Data on imports include the petroleum consumed by the Chinese airplanes and ships in refueling abroad. Data on exports include the petroleum consumed by the foreign airplanes and ships in refueling in China.

7-5 煤炭平衡表

Coal Balance Sheet

单位: 万吨 (10 000 tons)

项目	Item	1990	1995	2000	2001	2002
可供量	**Total Energy Available for Consumption**	**102221.0**	**133461.7**	**98176.1**	**108480.0**	**129604.8**
生产量	Output	107988.3	136073.1	99800.0	116078.0	138000.0
进口量	Imports	200.3	163.5	217.9	266.0	1125.8
出口量(-)	Exports (-)	1729.0	2861.7	5506.5	9012.9	8389.6
年初年末库存差额	Stock Changes in the Year	-4238.5	86.8	3664.7	1148.9	-1131.4
消费量	**Total Energy Consumption**	**105523.0**	**137676.5**	**124537.4**	**126211.3**	**136605.5**
在消费量中:	Consumption by Sector					
1.农、林、牧、渔、水利业	1.Farming,Forestry,Animal Husbandry, Fishery and Water Conservancy	2095.2	1856.7	1647.7	1599.6	1622.9
2.工业	2.Industry	81090.9	117570.7	111730.0	113608.0	124195.4
3.建筑业	3.Construction	437.6	439.8	536.8	538.0	553.5
4.交通运输、仓储及邮电通讯业	4.Transport, Storage, Post and Telecommunication Services	2160.9	1315.1	1139.9	1050.9	1055.0
5.批发和零售贸易餐饮业	5.Wholesale and Retail Trade and Catering Services	1058.3	977.4	814.6	809.9	809.1
6.其他	6.Others	1980.4	1986.7	761.2	774.7	767.0
7.生活消费	7.Residential Consumption	16699.7	13530.1	7907.2	7830.3	7602.6
在消费量中:	Consumption by Usage					
(一) 终端消费	(I)Final Consumption	60205.9	66156.1	46086.8	43891.3	42692.4
#工业	Industry	35773.8	46050.3	33279.7	31287.9	30282.2
(二) 中间消费 (用于加工转换)	(II)Intermediate Consumption (Consumed in Transformation)	41257.8	69487.6	78450.6	82320.1	93913.1
发电	Power Generation	27204.3	44440.2	54611.2	57687.9	65600.0
供热	Heating	2995.5	5887.3	6692.1	6961.5	7473.7
炼焦	Coking	10697.6	18396.4	15000.4	15436.4	18209.7
制气	Gas Production	360.4	763.7	810.0	893.8	973.2
(三) 洗选损耗	(III) Losses in Coal Washing and Dressing	4059.3	2032.8	1441.2	1450.5	1717.5
平衡差额	**Balance**	**-3302.0**	**-4214.8**	**-26361.3**	**-17731.3**	**-7000.8**

注:生产量为原煤产量。

a)Data on output refer to the output of raw coal.

7-6 电力平衡表

Electricity Balance Sheet

单位: 亿千瓦小时 (100 million kwh)

项目	Item	1990	1995	2000	2001	2002
可供量	**Total Energy Available for Consumption**	**6230.4**	**10023.4**	**13472.7**	**14632.6**	**16330.7**
生产量	Output	6212.0	10077.3	13556.0	14716.6	16404.7
水电	Hydropower	1267.2	1905.8	2224.1	2774.3	2879.7
火电	Thermal Power	4944.8	8043.2	11164.5	11767.5	13273.8
核电	Nuclear Power		128.3	167.4	174.7	251.2
进口量	Imports	19.3	6.4	15.5	18.0	23.0
出口量(-)	Exports (-)	0.9	60.3	98.8	101.9	97.0
消费量	**Total Energy Consumption**	**6230.4**	**10023.4**	**13471.4**	**14633.5**	**16331.5**
在消费量中:	Consumption by Sector					
1.农、林、牧、渔、水利业	1.Farming,Forestry,Animal Husbandry, Fishery and Water Conservancy	426.8	582.4	673.0	762.4	776.2
2.工业	2.Industry	4873.3	7659.8	9653.6	10444.7	11793.2
3.建筑业	3.Construction	65.0	159.6	154.8	144.9	164.1
4.交通运输、仓储及邮电通讯业	4.Transport, Storage, Post and Telecommunication Services	105.9	182.3	281.2	309.3	338.0
5.批发和零售贸易餐饮业	5.Wholesale and Retail Trade and Catering Services	76.2	199.5	393.6	444.9	500.0
6.其他	6.Others	202.4	234.2	643.2	688.1	758.6
7.生活消费	7.Residential Consumption	480.8	1005.6	1672.0	1839.2	2001.4
在消费量中:	Consumption by Usage					
(一) 终端消费	(I)Final Consumption	5795.8	9278.9	12534.7	13600.0	15162.8
#工业	Industry	4438.7	6915.3	8716.9	9411.2	10624.5
(二) 输配电损失量	(II)Losses in Transmission	434.6	744.5	936.7	1033.5	1168.7

7-7 能源生产弹性系数

Elasticity Ratio of Energy Production

年 份 Year	能源生产比上年增长（%） Growth Rate of Energy Production over Preceding Year (%)	电力生产比上年增长（%） Growth Rate of Electricity Production over Preceding Year (%)	国内生产总值比上年增长（%） Growth Rate of Gross Domestic Product(GDP) over Preceding Year (%)	能源生产弹性系数 Elasticity Ratio of Energy Production	电力生产弹性系数 Elasticity Ratio of Electricity Production
1985	9.9	8.9	13.5	0.73	0.66
1989	6.1	7.3	4.1	1.48	1.78
1990	2.2	6.2	3.8	0.58	1.63
1991	0.9	9.1	9.2	0.10	1.00
1992	2.3	11.3	14.2	0.16	0.80
1993	3.6	15.3	13.5	0.31	1.13
1994	6.9	10.7	12.6	0.55	0.85
1995	8.7	8.6	10.5	0.83	0.82
1996	2.8	7.2	9.6	0.29	0.75
1997	-0.2	5.0	8.8	-	0.57
1998	-6.2	2.9	7.8	-	0.37
1999	-12.2	6.3	7.1	-	0.89
2000	-2.0	9.4	8.0	-	1.18
2001	13.0	8.6	7.5	1.73	1.15
2002	14.4	11.5	8.3	1.73	1.34
2003	15.8	16.5	9.3	1.70	1.77

注：国内生产总值增长速度按可比价格计算(下表同)。

a)The growth rates of GDP are calculated at comparable prices. The same as in the following tables.

7-8 能源消费弹性系数

Elasticity Ratio of Energy Consumption

年 份 Year	能源消费比上年增长（%） Growth Rate of Energy Consumption over Preceding Year (%)	电力消费比上年增长（%） Growth Rate of Electricity Consumption over Preceding Year (%)	国内生产总值比上年增长（%） Growth Rate of Gross Domestic Product(GDP),over Preceding Year (%)	能源消费弹性系数 Elasticity Ratio of Energy Consumption	电力消费弹性系数 Elasticity Ratio of Electricity Consumption
1985	8.1	9.0	13.5	0.60	0.67
1989	4.2	7.3	4.1	1.02	1.78
1990	1.8	6.2	3.8	0.47	1.63
1991	5.1	9.2	9.2	0.55	1.00
1992	5.2	11.5	14.2	0.37	0.81
1993	6.3	11.0	13.5	0.21	0.70
1994	5.8	9.9	12.6	0.46	0.79
1995	6.9	8.2	10.5	0.66	0.78
1996	5.9	7.4	9.6	0.62	0.77
1997	-0.8	4.8	8.8	-	0.55
1998	-4.1	2.8	7.8	-	0.36
1999	-1.6	6.1	7.1	-	0.86
2000	0.1	9.5	8.0	0.02	1.19
2001	3.5	8.6	7.5	0.47	1.15
2002	9.9	11.6	8.3	1.19	1.40
2003	13.2	16.5	9.3	1.42	1.77

注:2003年为估算数。

a) The data in 2003 were estimated figures.

7-9 按行业分能源消费量（2002年）

行　业	Sector	能源消费总量（万吨标准煤）Total Energy Consumption (10 000 tons of SCE)	煤炭消费量（万吨）Coal Consumption (10 000 tons)
消费总量	**Total Consumption**	**148221.13**	**136605.53**
农、林、牧、渔业	**Farming, Forestry, Animal Husbandry, Fishery and Water Conservancy**	**6514.29**	**1622.89**
工业	**Industry**	**102181.18**	**124195.37**
采掘业	**Mining and Quarrying**	**10406.15**	**8921.14**
煤炭采选业	Coal Mining and Dressing	4242.42	7273.82
石油和天然气开采业	Petroleum and Natural Gas Extraction	4517.70	898.34
黑色金属矿采选业	Ferrous Metals Mining and Dressing	399.76	60.71
有色金属矿采选业	Nonferrous Metals Mining and Dressing	427.46	82.57
非金属矿采选业	Nonmetal Minerals Mining and Dressing	654.54	505.23
其他矿采选业	Other Minerals Mining and Dressing	38.23	2.00
木材及竹材采运业	Logging and Transport of Wood and Bamboo	126.04	98.47
制造业	**Manufacturing**	**79532.95**	**48996.36**
食品加工业	Food Processing	1604.63	1337.05
食品制造业	Food Production	947.38	572.51
饮料制造业	Beverage Production	662.64	571.03
烟草加工业	Tobacco Processing	259.27	124.74
纺织业	Textile Industry	2984.43	1266.89
服装及其他纤维制品制造	Garments and Other Fiber Products	355.20	107.88
皮革毛皮羽绒及其制品业	Leather, Furs, Down and Related Products	209.77	62.85
木材加工及竹藤棕草制品业	Timber Processing, Bamboo, Cane, Palm Fiber & Straw Products	324.27	204.31
家具制造业	Furniture Manufacturing	87.95	38.82
造纸及纸制品业	Papermaking and Paper Products	2180.54	1747.30
印刷业记录媒介的复制	Printing and Record Medium Reproduction	197.46	46.72
文教体育用品制造业	Cultural, Educational and Sports Articles	154.52	10.32
石油加工及炼焦业	Petroleum Processing and Coking	8478.69	9843.29
化学原料及制品制造业	Raw Chemical Materials and Chemical Products	14507.73	7530.93
医药制造业	Medical and Pharmaceutical Products	845.44	483.20
化学纤维制造业	Chemical Fiber	1942.76	720.23
橡胶制品业	Rubber Products	643.59	251.72
塑料制品业	Plastic Products	702.84	104.16
非金属矿物制品业	Nonmetal Mineral Products	10624.64	8868.88
黑色金属冶炼及压延加工业	Smelting and Pressing of Ferrous Metals	19327.49	11845.42
有色金属冶炼及压延加工业	Smelting and Pressing of Nonferrous Metals	4372.95	1307.05
金属制品业	Metal Products	1481.75	217.27
普通机械制造业	Ordinary Machinery	1325.07	330.34
专用设备制造业	Equipment for Special Purposes	782.46	266.83
交通运输设备制造业	Transportation Equipment	1555.65	679.60
电气机械及器材制造业	Electric Equipment and Machinery	725.47	159.39
电子及通信设备制造业	Electronic and Telecommunications Equipment	798.87	57.73
仪器仪表文化办公用机械	Instruments, Meters, Cultural and Office Machinery	169.42	24.77
其他制造业	Other Manufacturing Industry	1280.07	215.13
电力煤气及水生产供应业	**Electric Power, Gas and Water Production and Supply**	**12242.08**	**66277.87**
电力蒸汽热水生产供应业	Production and Supply of Electric Power, Steam and Hot Water	11150.53	65173.60
煤气的生产和供应业	Production and Supply of Gas	547.72	1068.69
自来水的生产和供应业	Production and Supply of Tap Water	543.83	35.58
建筑业	**Construction**	**1610.13**	**553.54**
交通运输、仓储及邮电通信业	**Transportation, Storage, Post and Telecommunication Services**	**11086.49**	**1054.95**
批发和零售贸易餐饮业	**Wholesale, Retail Trade and Catering Services**	**3464.02**	**809.08**
其他行业	**Others**	**6333.27**	**767.06**
生活消费	**Residential Consumption**	**17031.75**	**7602.64**

注：工业分行业数字中不包括其他石油制品和其他焦化产品，但工业合计中包括。

Consumption of Energy by Sector (2002)

焦炭消费量 (万吨) Coke Consumption (10 000 tons)	原油消费量 (万吨) Crude Oil Consumption (10 000 tons)	汽油消费量 (万吨) Gasoline Consumption (10 000 tons)	煤油消费量 (万吨) Kerosene Consumption (10 000tons)	柴油消费量 (万吨) Diesel Oil Consumption (10 000tons)	燃料油消费量 (万吨) Fuel Oil Consumption (10 000 tons)	天然气消费量 (亿立方米) Natural Gas Consumption (100 million cu.m)	电力消费量 (亿千瓦小时) Electricity Consumption (100 million kwh)
12343.69	**22541.05**	**3749.70**	**919.19**	**7667.89**	**3873.87**	**291.84**	**16331.45**
140.98		**187.93**	**1.40**	**1484.31**	**0.41**		**776.23**
11977.83	**22357.50**	**632.14**	**87.35**	**1732.08**	**2950.86**	**227.53**	**11793.16**
165.77	**3378.87**	**104.10**	**8.15**	**317.02**	**197.44**	**79.98**	**1127.86**
47.73	1.18	30.10	5.99	54.80			498.82
5.00	3377.69	39.10	0.40	187.36	196.30	79.97	349.51
52.15		6.18	0.03	15.52			75.55
28.12		4.87	1.31	13.72	0.11		88.00
32.62		8.57	0.42	34.11	1.03	0.01	95.55
0.03		0.28		1.01			9.40
0.12		15.00		10.50			11.03
11780.00	**18909.36**	**499.79**	**78.66**	**1150.46**	**1851.46**	**138.67**	**8011.57**
14.23	0.30	30.66	0.29	33.07	8.38	0.15	195.19
14.00	0.43	13.18	0.07	19.84	9.11	0.10	113.69
3.30	0.59	8.46	0.08	11.84	8.08	0.02	67.81
1.26		30.54	0.10	4.55	1.47	0.12	31.23
4.54	0.05	35.44	4.34	43.94	65.16	0.81	454.11
2.17	0.12	8.06	0.51	15.35	14.67		58.97
1.53		4.81	0.15	14.05	3.35		35.70
1.55		3.00	0.10	6.09	3.04		37.59
1.14		3.87	0.05	3.29	0.74		11.21
1.73	0.50	15.65	2.93	29.73	21.85	0.27	284.97
0.26		6.51	5.96	7.89	1.65	0.10	33.80
1.70	0.09	2.86	1.20	15.68	1.14		32.05
67.69	16317.92	15.98	17.00	76.51	479.59	15.30	330.62
1169.03	1876.95	55.03	10.25	125.34	370.39	102.02	1355.56
0.72		10.65	0.10	6.81	4.63	0.98	97.93
25.56	646.40	3.64	0.37	10.55	87.72		206.46
2.37	0.06	8.29	0.05	7.34	12.40		108.87
5.13	0.50	11.68	0.49	40.55	9.17	0.10	143.53
371.71	49.61	55.70	1.72	301.64	339.18	3.50	879.64
9319.68	13.47	31.22	6.46	81.10	263.11	2.30	1323.10
233.22	1.00	11.02	0.63	42.81	69.30	0.66	823.81
152.57	0.04	19.78	2.17	43.63	12.76	0.82	282.10
227.49	0.09	22.14	3.53	31.83	8.41	0.22	201.52
69.34	0.25	27.48	1.18	11.18	9.79	2.22	102.86
43.37	0.05	19.79	6.64	42.20	11.93	1.79	258.58
10.46	0.50	18.19	0.32	27.44	12.19	1.02	129.98
0.49		9.70	0.25	60.94	15.49	4.83	150.15
5.68		3.03	0.33	11.46	0.14	0.03	32.04
28.08	0.44	13.43	11.39	23.81	6.62	1.31	228.50
32.06	**69.27**	**28.25**	**0.54**	**264.60**	**901.96**	**8.88**	**2653.73**
	69.27	24.34	0.50	251.24	883.38	6.93	2476.90
32.06		1.47	0.00	11.00	18.56	1.93	36.95
		2.44	0.04	2.36	0.02	0.02	139.88
23.38	**4.20**	**122.32**	**0.00**	**251.99**	**19.10**	**0.68**	**164.14**
11.44	**177.94**	**1503.00**	**616.74**	**2964.80**	**872.10**	**6.37**	**338.00**
42.60	**0.12**	**224.22**	**13.00**	**280.79**	**12.30**	**6.10**	**500.00**
12.34	**1.29**	**916.29**	**140.00**	**870.00**	**19.10**	**0.00**	**758.50**
135.12		**163.80**	**60.70**	**83.92**		**51.16**	**2001.42**

a) The consumption of other petroleum products and other coking products (such as benzene etc.) is included in the total consumption of the industrial sector, but not included in consumption of the various industrial branches.

7-10 能源加工转换效率

Efficiency of Energy Conversion

单位: %　　　　(%)

年 份 Year	总效率 Total Efficiency	发电及电站供热 Electricity Generation and Heating by Power Stations	炼 焦 Coking	炼 油 Petroleum Refining
1983	69.93	36.94	91.18	99.16
1984	69.16	36.95	90.08	99.17
1985	68.29	36.85	90.79	99.10
1986	68.32	36.69	90.63	99.04
1987	67.48	36.75	90.46	98.81
1988	66.54	36.34	90.77	98.76
1989	66.51	36.74	90.30	98.57
1990	67.20	37.34	91.28	97.90
1991	65.90	37.60	89.90	98.10
1992	66.00	37.80	92.70	96.80
1993	67.32	39.90	98.05	98.49
1994	65.20	39.35	89.62	97.48
1995	71.05	37.31	91.99	97.67
1996	71.50	38.30	94.07	97.46
1997	69.23	35.89	92.08	97.37
1998	69.44	37.06	94.97	97.42
1999	70.45	38.99	95.80	97.51
2000	70.96	39.91	96.28	97.32
2001	70.41	39.40	97.17	97.83
2002	69.78	39.41	97.96	96.71

7-11 平均每天能源消费量

Average Daily Energy Consumption by Variety

能源品种	Item	1990	1995	1999	2000	2001	2002
合计（万吨标准煤）	**Total (10 000 tons of SCE)**	**270.4**	**359.4**	**356.5**	**357.0**	**369.6**	**406.1**
煤炭 (万吨)	Coal (10 000 tons of SCE)	289.1	377.2	346.2	341.2	345.8	374.3
焦炭 (万吨)	Coke (10 000 tons of SCE)	18.9	29.4	28.6	28.6	30.1	33.8
原油 (万吨)	Crude Oil (10 000 tons of SCE)	32.2	40.8	51.9	58.2	58.5	61.8
燃料油 (万吨)	Fuel Oil (10 000 tons of SCE)	9.2	10.2	10.8	10.6	11.0	10.6
汽油 (万吨)	Gasoline (10 000 tons of SCE)	5.2	8.0	9.3	9.6	9.9	10.3
煤油 (万吨)	Kerosene (10 000 tons of SCE)	1.0	1.4	2.3	2.4	2.4	2.5
柴油 (万吨)	Diesel Oil (10 000 tons of SCE)	7.4	11.8	17.1	18.6	19.5	21.0
天然气 (亿立方米)	Natural Gas (100 million cu.m)	0.4	0.5	0.6	0.7	0.8	0.8
电力 (亿千瓦小时)	Electricity (100 million kwh)	17.1	27.5	33.7	36.9	40.1	44.7

7-12 生活能源消费量

Average Annual Energy Consumption for Non-Production Purpose

能源品种	Item	1990	1995	1999	2000	2001	2002
合计 （万吨标准煤）	**Total (10 000 tons of SCE)**	**15800**	**15745**	**14552**	**14912**	**15427**	**17032**
煤炭 （万吨）	Coal (10 000 tons)	16700	13530	8408	7907	7830	7603
煤油 （万吨）	Kerosene (10 000 tons)	105	64	71	72	75	61
液化石油气 （万吨）	Liquefied Petroleum Gas (10 000 tons)	159	534	878	988	1006	1169
天然气 （亿立方米）	Natural Gas (100 million cu.m)	19	19	26	32	44	51
煤气 （亿立方米）	Gas (100 million cu.m)	29	57	81	89	119	125
热力 （万百万千焦）	Heat (10 billion kilo-joule)	8972	12637	20127	23234	23369	26613
电力 （亿千瓦小时）	Electricity (100 million kwh)	481	1006	1481	1672	1839	2001

7-13 人均生活能源消费量

Annual Per Capita Energy Consumption for Non-Production Purpose

年 份 Year	平均每人生活消费能源 （千克标准煤） Annual Per Capita Consumption for Non-production Purpose (Kg of SCE)	煤 炭 （千克） Coal (kg)	电 力 （千瓦小时） Electricity (kwh)	煤 油 （千克） Kerosene (kg)	液化石油气 （千克） Liquefied Petroleum Gas (kg)	天然气 （立方米） Natural Gas (cu.m)	煤 气 （立方米） Gas (cu.m)
1983	106.6	127.7	13.4	1.2	0.6	0.1	1.5
1984	113.5	134.9	15.3	1.4	0.6	0.5	1.5
1985	127.5	149.6	21.3	1.2	0.9	0.4	1.3
1986	127.3	148.3	23.2	1.3	1.1	0.7	1.3
1987	132.1	152.1	26.4	1.2	1.1	0.7	1.6
1988	141.0	159.1	31.2	1.1	1.2	1.4	1.5
1989	139.3	152.4	35.3	1.1	1.4	1.5	2.4
1990	139.2	147.1	42.4	0.9	1.4	1.6	2.5
1991	138.1	142.0	46.9	0.8	1.7	1.6	3.1
1992	133.4	126.1	54.6	0.7	2.0	1.8	4.4
1993	130.6	120.5	61.2	0.6	2.5	1.4	4.5
1994	129.3	109.5	72.7	0.6	3.2	1.7	6.3
1995	130.8	112.3	83.5	0.5	4.4	1.6	4.7
1996	145.5	118.3	93.1	0.5	5.8	1.6	3.9
1997	133.1	99.5	101.8	0.5	6.0	1.7	4.9
1998	115.9	71.5	106.6	0.5	6.2	1.9	6.0
1999	116.1	67.1	118.1	0.6	7.0	2.1	9.3
2000	118.1	62.6	132.4	0.6	7.8	2.6	10.0
2001	121.3	61.6	144.6	0.6	7.9	3.5	9.4
2002	133.0	59.4	156.3	0.4	9.1	4.0	9.8

注：按年平均人口数计算。

a) Data in the table are calculated with the data on the annual average population in each year.

7-14 各地区电力消费量

Electricity Consumption by Region

单位：亿千瓦小时 (100 million kwh)

地 区	Region	1995	1999	2000	2001	2002	2003
北 京	Beijing	261.74	344.13	384.43	399.94	439.96	467.61
天 津	Tianjin	178.99	211.19	234.05	247.94	274.39	305.64
河 北	Hebei	602.68	745.72	809.34	867.55	965.83	1099.00
山 西	Shanxi	399.16	459.34	501.99	557.58	628.82	725.20
内蒙古	Inner Mongolia	186.83	236.77	254.21	280.89	320.43	416.44
辽 宁	Liaoning	622.81	756.11	748.89	764.77	809.45	907.91
吉 林	Jilin	267.60	295.46	291.37	295.08	306.29	338.70
黑龙江	Heilongjiang	409.38	422.58	442.28	456.86	468.45	493.37
上 海	Shanghai	403.27	501.20	559.45	592.98	645.71	745.97
江 苏	Jiangsu	684.80	848.74	971.34	1078.44	1245.14	1505.11
浙 江	Zhejiang	439.59	611.67	738.05	848.40	1010.72	1232.54
安 徽	Anhui	288.97	312.96	338.93	359.59	389.94	445.42
福 建	Fujian	261.28	355.26	401.51	439.19	496.83	585.74
江 西	Jiangxi	181.21	193.91	208.15	222.28	246.57	299.53
山 东	Shandong	741.07	805.47	1000.71	1104.53	1241.74	1395.72
河 南	Henan	571.48	672.09	718.52	808.41	916.25	1041.89
湖 北	Hubei	414.99	487.65	503.02	526.02	561.96	629.20
湖 南	Hunan	374.76	376.74	406.12	439.78	477.49	545.83
广 东	Guangdong	787.66	1086.24	1334.58	1458.42	1687.83	2031.29
广 西	Guangxi	220.77	289.06	314.44	331.92	356.95	415.83
海 南	Hainan	32.00	38.65	38.37	42.96	49.00	56.62
重 庆	Chongqing		303.86	307.61	220.54	248.01	269.26
四 川	Sichuan	582.85	462.26	521.23	589.57	660.51	759.80
贵 州	Guizhou	203.70	274.22	287.78	335.19	366.63	399.57
云 南	Yunnan	223.71	296.70	273.58	320.75	353.20	370.31
陕 西	Shaanxi	239.68	273.63	292.76	321.54	355.97	404.11
甘 肃	Gansu	241.06	291.58	295.33	306.09	339.66	398.34
青 海	Qinghai	69.02	107.24	109.10	111.90	125.51	150.16
宁 夏	Ningxia	92.38	115.32	136.17	151.81	178.76	212.12
新 疆	Xinjiang	119.67	169.30	182.98	197.92	214.60	236.10

注：2000年及以后为电力公司数。

a) Data from 2000 are obtained from State Power Company.

主要统计指标解释

能源生产总量 指一定时期内全国一次能源生产量的总和。该指标是观察全国能源生产水平、规模、构成和发展速度的总量指标。一次能源生产量包括原煤、原油、天然气、水电、核能及其他动力能(如风能、地热能等)发电量，不包括低热值燃料生产量、生物质能、太阳能等的利用和由一次能源加工转换而成的二次能源产量。

能源消费总量 指一定时期内全国物质生产部门、非物质生产部门和生活消费的各种能源的总和。该指标是观察能源消费水平、构成和增长速度的总量指标。能源消费总量包括原煤和原油及其制品、天然气、电力，不包括低热值燃料、生物质能和太阳能等的利用。能源消费总量分为终端能源消费量、能源加工转换损失量和能源损失量三部分。

(1)终端能源消费量：指一定时期内全国生产和生活消费的各种能源在扣除了用于加工转换二次能源消费量和损失量以后的数量。

(2)能源加工转换损失量：指一定时期内全国投入加工转换的各种能源数量之和与产出各种能源产品之和的差额。该指标是观察能源在加工转换过程中损失量变化的指标。

(3)能源损失量：指一定时期内能源在输送、分配、储存过程中发生的损失和由客观原因造成的各种损失量，不包括各种气体能源放空、放散量。

能源生产弹性系数 研究能源生产增长速度与国民经济增长速度之间关系的指标。计算公式为：

$$能源生产弹性系数=\frac{能源生产总量年平均增长速度}{国民经济年平均增长速度}$$

国民经济年平均增长速度，可根据不同的目的或需要，用国民生产总值、国内生产总值等指标来计算，本年鉴是采用国内生产总值指标计算的。

电力生产弹性系数 研究电力生产增长速度与国民经济增长速度之间关系的指标。一般来说，电力的发展应当快于国民经济的发展，也就是说电力应超前发展。计算公式为：

$$电力生产弹性系数=\frac{电力生产量年平均增长速度}{国民经济年平均增长速度}$$

能源消费弹性系数 反映能源消费增长速度与国民经济增长速度之间比例关系的指标。计算公式为：

$$能源消费弹性系数=\frac{能源消费量年平均增长速度}{国民经济年平均增长速度}$$

电力消费弹性系数 反映电力消费增长速度与国民经济增长速度之间比例关系的指标。计算公式为：

$$电力消费弹性系数=\frac{电力消费量年平均增长速度}{国民经济年平均增长速度}$$

能源加工转换效率 指一定时期内能源经过加工、转换后，产出的各种能源产品的数量与同期内投入加工转换的各种能源数量的比率。该指标是观察能源加工转换装置和生产工艺先进与落后、管理水平高低等的重要指标。计算公式为：

$$能源加工转换效率=\frac{能源加工转换产出量}{能源加工转换投入量}\times 100\%$$

Explanatory Notes on Main Statistical Indicators

Total Energy Production refers to the total production of primary energy by all energy producing enterprises in the country in a given period of time. It is a comprehensive indicator to show the capacity, scale, composition and development of energy production of the country. The production of primary energy includes that of coal, crude oil, natural gas, hydro-power and electricity generated by nuclear energy and other means such as wind power and geothermal power. However, it excludes the production of fuels of low calorific value, bio-energy, solar energy and the secondary energy converted from the primary energy.

Total Domestic Energy Consumption refers to the total consumption of energy of various kinds by material production sectors, non material production sectors and households in the country in a given period of time. It is a comprehensive indicator to show the scale, composition and development of energy consumption. The total energy consumption includes that of coal, crude oil and their products, natural gas and electricity, However, it excludes the consumption of fuel of low calorific value, bio-energy and solar energy. Total domestic energy consumption can be divided into three parts: final energy consumption, loss during the process of energy conversion, and energy loss.

(1)Final Energy Consumption: It refers to the total energy consumption by material production sectors, non material production sectors and households in the country (region) in a given period of time, but excludes the consumption in conversion of the primary energy into the secondary energy and the loss in the process of energy conversion.

(2)Loss During the Process of Energy Conversion: It refers to the total input of various kinds of energy for conversion, minus the total output of various kinds of energy in the country in a given period of time. It is an indicator to show the loss that occurs during the process of energy conversion.

(3)Energy Loss: It refers to the total of the loss of energy during the course of energy transport, distribution and storage and the loss caused by any objective reason in a given period of time. The loss of various kinds of gas due to gas discharges and stocktaking is excluded.

Elasticity Ratio of Energy Production is an indicator to show the relationship between the growth rate of energy production and the growth rate of the national economy. The formula is:

Elasticity Ratio of Energy Production = Average Annual Growth Rate of Energy Production / Average Annual Growth Rate of National Economy

The average annual growth rate of the national economy can be shown by the gross national product, gross domestic product and other indicators, depending upon the purposes or needs. The gross domestic product is used in calculation of the ratio in this chapter.

Elasticity Ratio of Electricity Production is an indicator to show the relationship between the growth rate of electricity production and the growth rate of the national economy. Generally speaking, the growth rate of electricity production should be higher than that of the national economy.

Its formula is:

Elasticity Ratio of Electricity Production = Average Annual Growth Rate of Electricity Production /Average Annual Growth Rate of National Economy

Elasticity Ratio of Energy Consumption is an indicator to show the relationship between the growth rate of energy consumption and the growth rate of the national economy. The formula is:

Elasticity Ratio of Energy Consumption = Average Annual Growth Rate of Energy Consumption /Average Annual Growth Rate of National Economy

Elasticity Ratio of Electricity Consumption is an indicator to show the relationship between the growth rate of electricity consumption and the growth rate of the national economy. The formula is:

Elasticity Ratio of Electricity Consumption = Average Annual Growth Rate of Electricity /Average Annual Growth Rate of National Economy

Efficiency of Energy Processing and Conversion refers to the ratio of the total output of energy products of various kinds after processing and conversion and the total input of energy of various kinds for processing and conversion in the same reference period. It is an important indicator to show the current conditions of energy processing and conversion equipment, production technique and management. The formula is:

Efficiency of Energy Processing & Conversion = (Output of Energy After Processing & Conversion / Input of Energy for Processing & Conversion)×100%

八、财政

Government Finance

简要说明

一、本篇反映国家财政收支状况，资料来源于财政部门，资料基础为国家财政决算、预算外资金收支决算和有关财务报表。

国家财政决算由中央级决算和地方总决算组成。省(自治区、直辖市)级决算及其所属州、县(市)总决算汇总组成省(自治区、直辖市)总决算；各省(自治区、直辖市)总决算汇总成地方总决算。

中央级决算、省(自治区、直辖市)级决算和县(市)总决算，由同级主管部门汇总的行政事业单位决算、企业财务决算、基本建设财务决算和金库年报、税收年报等组成。

为了保证决算数据的准确和完整，年度终了以前，各级财政总预算之间，财政总预算和部门单位预算之间，部门单位预算和所属单位预算之间，都对上下级之间的全年预算数据进行核对。年终后各级财政部门、国家金库会同预算缴款单位将决算收入数据进行核对一致，填制对帐单办理签证后，分别按系统上报。

为保持决算口径的一致，财政部每年要制定和颁发各省(自治区、直辖市)总决算表格和中央单位决算表格。各级财政部门和中央主管部门也要结合本部门的具体情况下达有关决算表格。决算表格按国家决算的组成，分为各级财政部门适用的总决算表格和各级主管部门、单位预算机关适用的单位决算表格，决算表数据根据总预算或单位预算会计帐簿填报。

有关财政收支方面的资料，是根据决算收支总表、决算收入明细表、决算支出明细表的数据加工整理编制。

预算外资金收支决算和有关财务报表的编报与国家决算的编报基本相同。

二、针对历年财政收入、财政支出以及各项财政收支之间由于财政体制、预算编列方法的改变，而存在口径不统一的情况，本年鉴对有关数据进行了调整，使各年之间基本可比。主要调整的项目有：

1.财政收入：将1993年及以前各年的国内外债务收入从财政收入中剔除，不再作为财政收入。将1978–1985年财政价格补贴由冲减财政收入改列财政支出。相应地，“国家财政分项目收入”中取消债务收入一项。

2.财政支出：将1993年及以前各年的国内外债务还本付息支出和利用国外借款安排的基本建设支出从财政支出中剔除，不再作为财政支出。将1978–1985年财政价格补贴由冲减财政收入改列财政支出。相应地，“国家财政分项目支出”、“国家财政分费用类别支出”取消债务支出一项，“国家财政分项目支出”中的基本建设支出不再包括利用国外借款安排的基本建设支出，“国家财政分费用类别支出”中的有关项目也进行了调整。从2000年起，财政支出中包括国内外债务付息支出。

3.中央财政和地方财政收支：根据上述财政收入和财政支出的调整，中央财政收支也相应进行了调整，地方支出个别年份有所调整。“中央财政和地方财政收支总额”表，反映的是按当年的财政体制划分的中央、地方财政组织的收入和负责安排的支出状况，由于财政体制的变化和企业隶属关系的变化对中央、地方财政收支的影响未做调整。此外，中央与地方财政之间还存在着上解、补助和税收返还的关系。因此，“中央财政和地方财政收支总额”表不反映各级财力情况。

预算外资金从1982年开始建立统计制度，预算外收入和预算外支出项目几经变化。1993年由于实施新的财务通则和会计准则，预算外收支范围又一次做了较大调整，国营企业更新改造资金、大修理基金等不再作为预算外资金，因此1992年以前年度与1993年以后年度的预算外资金收支不可比。从1997年起，预算外资金收支不包括纳入预算内管理的政府性基金（收费），与以前各年也不可比。

Brief Introduction

I. The data in this chapter show the government revenue and expenditure. The data come from the departments of finance. The data are based on the final state financial accounts, the final accounts of extra-budgetary revenue and expenditure and the concerned financial reports.

The final state financial accounts are composed of the final accounts at the level of central government and the total final accounts at the level of local governments. The total final accounts at the level of local governments are composed of the total final accounts of the governments of provinces, autonomous regions and municipalities directly under the central government. The total final accounts at the provincial (autonomous region, municipality directly under the central government) level are composed of the final accounts at the provincial level and the total final accounts at the level of governments of prefectures and counties (cities).

The final accounts at the central level, at the provincial level and at the county (city) level are respectively composed of the final accounts of the administrative and institutional units, the final financial accounts of enterprises, final financial accounts of capital construction, annual reports on treasury and annual reports on tax revenue, pooled together by the responsible departments at the same level.

In order to ensure the accuracy and completeness of the data of final accounts, the financial departments at different levels should check the budgetary data of the higher and lower levels of the whole year before the end of the year, including the related figures of the total government budgets between different levels, the related figures between the government total budget and the budgets of the departments and the related figures between the budget of the departments and the budgets of the subordinate units. After the end of the year, the financial departments of different levels and the state treasury should check the data of the revenue in the final accounts together with the units which hand over the budget, filled out the accounts checking sheet, made signatures and reported to the higher authorities respectively.

In order to ensure the consistency in the coverage of the final accounts, the Ministry of Finance works out and issues the final accounts forms for the provinces, autonomous regions and municipalities directly under the central government and the final accounts forms for the departments at the central level. The financial departments at various levels and the central government departments should also work out and issue the final accounts forms in the light of the specific conditions of the department to the departments or units at the lower level. The final account forms are designed in accordance with the composition of the state final account and are composed of the total final accounts forms suitable for the financial departments of different levels and the unit final accounts forms suitable for the budgetary agencies of the responsible departments or units. The data for the final accounts are filled out in accordance with the data in the account books of the total budget or unit budget.

Data on the government revenue and expenditure are compiled on the basis of information from the total final accounts table of the revenue and expenditure, the subsidiary table of the final accounts of the revenue, and the subsidiary table of the final accounts of the expenditure.

The procedures for the compilation of the extra-budgetary revenue and expenditure and the related financial tables are basically the same as those for the compilation of the state final accounts.

II. Owing to the changes in financial system and in the methods of compiling and listing the items of the budget, the coverage of the government revenue and expenditure and their breakdowns are not consistent over the years. In view of the above situation, the concerned data in this yearbook have been adjusted so as to make them basically comparable over the years. The main adjusted items are as follows:

(1) Government revenue. The revenues from the domestic and foreign debts in 1993 and the previous years are deducted from the government revenue and no longer listed as the component of the government revenue. The financial subsidies for the price adjustment in 1978-1985 were listed formerly as an item to eat up part of the government revenue and are now listed as an item of government expenditure. Correspondingly, the original item revenue from debtsunder the government revenue by itemis cancelled

(2) Government expenditure. The expenditures for repayment of the principal and interest of the domestic and foreign debts in 1993 and the previous years are deducted from the government expenditure and no longer listed as the component of the government expenditure. The financial subsidies on the price adjustment in 1978-1985 were listed formerly as an item to eat up part of the government revenue and are now listed as an item of government expenditure. Correspondingly, the original item expenditure for debts under the government expenditure by account item and the government expenditure by general categories is canceled; the expenditure for capital construction under the government expenditure by account item no longer includes the expenditure for capital construction as a result of the utilization of the foreign loans; the related items under the government expenditure by general categories have also been adjusted. Total government expenditures include the payment for capital and its interest of domestic and foreign debts since 2000.

(3) Revenue and expenditure of the central government and local governments. According to the above-mentioned adjustments in the government revenue and expenditure, adjustments are also made in the revenue and expenditure of the central government correspondingly and in the revenue and expenditure of the local governments in a few years. The table on Total Revenue and Total Expenditure of the Central Government and Local Governments show the revenues and expenditures of the central government and local governments at the current years. The changes in the financial structure and in the subordinate relationship of the enterprises have the impact on the revenues and expenditures of the central government and local governments. However, no adjustments have been made in the data of the past years. In addition, there are also appropriate adaptations made in the specific conditions in the relationship between the central government and local governments: Sometimes some local governments hand certain amount of their funds over to the central government; Sometimes the central government pays subsidies to the difficult provinces and autonomous regions or send back parts of the tax revenue to the local government. Therefore the table on Total Revenue and Total Expenditure of the Central Government and Local Governments does not show the real financial strengths of the governments at different levels.

Data on the extra-budgetary funds have been collected in accordance with the statistical reporting scheme since 1982. Changes have been made in the items in the extra-budgetary revenue and the extra-budgetary expenditure several times. In 1993, new financial general rules and accounting standards were implemented. As a result, significant changes have been made again in the scope of extra-budgetary revenue and extra-budgetary expenditure. The innovation fund and the major repair fund in the state-owned enterprises were no longer listed as the extra-budgetary funds. Therefore the extra-budgetary revenues and the extra-budgetary expenditures in the years before 1993 and since 1993 are not comparable. Starting from 1997, government funds (revenue from fees) were reclassified into budget management and were not included in the extra-budgetary revenues. Therefore, figures since 1997 were not comparable with earlier figures.

8-1 国家财政收支总额及增长速度

Government Revenue and Expenditure and Their Increase Rates

年份 Year	财政收入（亿元） Government Revenue (100 million yuan)	财政支出（亿元） Government Expenditure (100 million yuan)	收支差额（亿元） Balance (100 million yuan)	增长速度（%）Increase Rates (%) 财政收入 Government Revenue	财政支出 Government Expenditure	财政收入占国内生产总值的比重(%) Percentage of Government Revenue to GDP (%)
1978	1132.26	1122.09	10.17	29.5	33.0	31.2
1980	1159.93	1228.83	-68.90	1.2	-4.1	25.7
1985	2004.82	2004.25	0.57	22.0	17.8	22.4
1989	2664.90	2823.78	-158.88	13.1	13.3	15.8
1990	2937.10	3083.59	-146.49	10.2	9.2	15.8
1991	3149.48	3386.62	-237.14	7.2	9.8	14.6
1992	3483.37	3742.20	-258.83	10.6	10.5	13.1
1993	4348.95	4642.30	-293.35	24.8	24.1	12.6
1994	5218.10	5792.62	-574.52	20.0	24.8	11.2
1995	6242.20	6823.72	-581.52	19.6	17.8	10.7
1996	7407.99	7937.55	-529.56	18.7	16.3	10.9
1997	8651.14	9233.56	-582.42	16.8	16.3	11.6
1998	9875.95	10798.18	-922.23	14.2	16.9	12.6
1999	11444.08	13187.67	-1743.59	15.9	22.1	13.9
2000	13395.23	15886.50	-2491.27	17.0	20.5	15.0
2001	16386.04	18902.58	-2516.54	22.3	19.0	16.8
2002	18903.64	22053.15	-3149.51	15.4	16.7	18.0
2003	21715.25	24649.95	-2934.70	14.9	11.8	18.5

注：1.在国家财政收支中，价格补贴1985年以前冲减财政收入，1986年以后列为财政支出。为了可比，本表将1985年以前冲减财政收入的价格补贴改列在财政支出中。

2.从2000年起,财政支出中包括国内外债务付息支出，以下各表中涉及财政支出和中央财政支出数据的均为此口径。

a) Government price subsidies were listed as negative revenue items prior to 1986, but they have been listed as expenditure items in government accounts since 1986. For comparison purpose, budgetary price subsidies before 1985 were adjusted，and listed as expenditure items.

b) Government expenditures include the payment for interest of domestic and foreign debts from 2000, and other tables which concern the government expenditure of the central government are consistent with this definition.

8-2 国家财政分项目收入

Government Revenue by Item

单位: 亿元 (100 million yuan)

年份 Year	收入合计 Total Government Revenue	各项税收 Taxes	企业收入 Revenue from Enterprises	企业亏损补贴 Subsidies to Loss-making Enterprises	能源交通重点建设基金收入 Revenue Raised from Funds for Key Construction Projects in Energy Industry and Transportation	预算调节基金收入 Revenue Raised from Budget Adjustment Fund	教育费附加收入 Revenue from Extra-charges for Education	其他收入 Other Revenue
1978	1132.26	519.28	571.99					40.99
1980	1159.93	571.70	435.24					152.99
1985	2004.82	2040.79	43.75	-507.02	146.79			280.51
1989	2664.90	2727.40	63.60	-598.88	202.18	91.19		179.41
1990	2937.10	2821.86	78.30	-578.88	185.08	131.21		299.53
1991	3149.48	2990.17	74.69	-510.24	188.22	138.53	28.01	240.10
1992	3483.37	3296.91	59.97	-444.96	157.11	117.47	31.72	265.15
1993	4348.95	4255.30	49.49	-411.29	117.72	102.46	44.23	191.04
1994	5218.10	5126.88		-366.22	53.96	59.10	64.20	280.18
1995	6242.20	6038.04		-327.77	17.42	34.92	83.40	396.19
1996	7407.99	6909.82		-337.40	3.78	11.09	96.04	724.66
1997	8651.14	8234.04		-368.49			103.29	682.30
1998	9875.95	9262.80		-333.49			113.34	833.30
1999	11444.08	10682.58		-290.03			126.10	925.43
2000	13395.23	12581.51		-278.78			147.52	944.98
2001	16386.04	15301.38		-300.04			166.60	1218.10
2002	18903.64	17636.45		-259.60			198.05	1328.74
2003	21715.25	20017.31		-226.38			232.39	1691.93

注：国家财政收入中不包括国内外债务收入。

a) Government revenue from both domestic and foreign borrowings are excluded in this table.

8-3 各项税收

Tax

单位: 亿元 (100 million yuan)

年份 Year	合计 Total	#增值税 Value-added Tax	#营业税 Business Tax	#消费税 Consumption Tax	#关税 Tariffs	#农业各税 Agricultural and Related Tax	#企业所得税 Company Income Tax
1978	519.28				28.76	28.40	
1980	571.70				33.53	27.67	
1985	2040.79	147.70	211.07		205.21	42.05	696.06
1989	2727.40	430.83	487.30		181.54	84.94	700.43
1990	2821.86	400.00	515.75		159.01	87.86	716.00
1991	2990.17	406.36	564.00		187.28	90.65	731.13
1992	3296.91	705.93	658.67		212.75	119.17	720.78
1993	4255.30	1081.48	966.09		256.47	125.74	678.60
1994	5126.88	2308.34	670.02	487.40	272.68	231.49	708.49
1995	6038.04	2602.33	865.56	541.48	291.83	278.09	878.44
1996	6909.82	2962.81	1052.57	620.23	301.84	369.46	968.48
1997	8234.04	3283.92	1324.27	678.70	319.49	397.48	963.18
1998	9262.80	3628.46	1575.08	814.93	313.04	398.80	925.54
1999	10682.58	3881.87	1668.56	820.66	562.23	423.50	811.41
2000	12581.51	4553.17	1868.78	858.29	750.48	465.31	999.63
2001	15301.38	5357.13	2064.09	929.99	840.52	481.70	2630.87
2002	17636.45	6178.39	2450.33	1046.32	704.27	717.85	3082.79
2003	20017.31	7236.54	2844.45	1182.26	923.13	871.77	2919.51

注：农业各税包括农业税、牧业税、耕地占用税、农业特产税和契税。

a) The agricultural and retail taxes include the agricultural tax, the animal husbandry tax, the tax on the use of cultivated land, the tax on special agricultural products and the contract tax.

8-4 国家财政主要支出项目

Government Expenditure by Main Item

单位: 亿元 (100 million yuan)

年份 Year	基本建设支出 Expenditure for Capital Construction	增拨企业流动资金 Additional Appropriation for Circulating Capital of Enterprises	挖潜改造资金和科技三项费用 Innovation Funds and Science and Technology Promotion Funds	地质勘探费 Geological Prospecting Expenses	工、交、流通部门事业费 Operating Expenses of the Departments of Industry, Transport and Commerce	支农支出 Expenditure for Supporting Agricultural Production
1978	451.92	66.60	63.24	20.15	17.79	76.95
1980	346.36	36.71	80.45	22.57	22.85	82.12
1985	554.56	14.30	103.42	29.58	35.16	101.04
1989	481.70	12.09	146.30	33.16	45.01	197.12
1990	547.39	10.90	153.91	36.19	46.93	221.76
1991	559.62	13.08	180.81	38.34	52.41	243.55
1992	555.90	10.63	223.62	44.07	64.58	269.04
1993	591.93	18.48	421.38	49.06	76.22	323.42
1994	639.72	17.33	415.13	64.13	100.77	399.70
1995	789.22	34.80	494.45	66.32	102.76	430.22
1996	907.44	42.93	523.02	68.56	120.41	510.07
1997	1019.50	52.20	643.20	73.37	136.41	560.77
1998	1387.74	42.36	641.18	83.13	121.56	626.02
1999	2116.57	56.41	766.05	83.69	128.07	677.46
2000	2094.89	71.06	865.24	88.12	150.07	766.89
2001	2510.64	22.71	991.56	99.01	200.12	917.96
2002	3142.98	18.97	968.38	102.89	232.38	1102.70
2003	3429.30	11.95	1092.99	106.94	285.23	1134.86

注：行政管理费中包括公检法司支出和外交外事支出。

a) Administrative expenses includes the expenditure for public security, judicial expenditure, law court expenditure, procuratorial expenditure and expenditure for foreign affairs.

8-4 续表 continued

单位: 亿元 (100 million yuan)

年份 Year	文教、科学、卫生支出 Expenses on Culture, Education, Science and Public Health	抚恤和社会福利救济费 Expenditure for Pension and Social Welfare	国防支出 Expenditure for National Defense	行政管理费 Administrative Expenses	政策性补贴支出 Expenditure on Policy-related Subsidies
1978	112.66	18.91	167.84	49.09	11.14
1980	156.26	20.31	193.84	66.79	117.71
1985	316.70	31.15	191.53	130.58	261.79
1989	553.33	49.60	251.47	261.86	373.35
1990	617.29	55.04	290.31	303.10	380.80
1991	708.00	67.32	330.31	343.60	373.77
1992	792.96	66.45	377.86	424.58	321.64
1993	957.77	75.27	425.80	535.77	299.30
1994	1278.18	95.14	550.71	729.43	314.47
1995	1467.06	115.46	636.72	872.68	364.89
1996	1704.25	128.03	720.06	1040.80	453.91
1997	1903.59	142.14	812.57	1137.16	551.96
1998	2154.38	171.26	934.70	1326.77	712.12
1999	2408.06	179.88	1076.40	1525.68	697.64
2000	2736.88	213.03	1207.54	1787.58	1042.28
2001	3361.02	266.68	1442.04	2197.52	741.51
2002	3979.08	372.97	1707.78	2979.42	645.07
2003	4505.51	498.82	1907.87	3437.68	617.28

8-5 国家财政按功能性质分类的支出

Government Expenditure by Function

单位: 亿元 (100 million yuan)

年份 Year	支出合计 Total Government Expenditure	经济建设费 Economic Construction	社会文教费 Social, Cultural and Educational Development	国防费 National Defense	行政管理费 Administrative Expenses	其他支出 Other Expenditure
1978	1122.09	718.98	146.96	167.84	52.90	35.41
1980	1228.83	715.46	199.01	193.84	75.53	44.99
1985	2004.25	1127.55	408.43	191.53	171.06	105.68
1989	2823.78	1291.19	668.44	251.47	386.26	226.42
1990	3083.59	1368.01	737.61	290.31	414.56	273.10
1991	3386.62	1428.47	849.65	330.31	414.01	364.18
1992	3742.20	1612.81	970.12	377.86	463.41	318.00
1993	4642.30	1834.79	1178.27	425.80	634.26	569.18
1994	5792.62	2393.69	1501.53	550.71	847.68	499.01
1995	6823.72	2855.78	1756.72	636.72	996.54	577.96
1996	7937.55	3233.78	2080.56	720.06	1185.28	717.87
1997	9233.56	3647.33	2469.38	812.57	1358.85	945.43
1998	10798.18	4179.51	2930.78	934.70	1600.27	1152.92
1999	13187.67	5061.46	3638.74	1076.40	2020.60	1390.47
2000	15886.50	5748.36	4384.51	1207.54	2768.22	1777.87
2001	18902.58	6472.56	5213.23	1442.04	3512.49	2262.26
2002	22053.15	6673.70	5924.58	1707.78	4101.32	3645.77
2003	24649.95	7410.87	6469.37	1907.87	4691.26	4170.58

8-6 国家财政用于农业的支出

Government Expenditure For Agriculture

单位:亿元 (100 million yuan)

年份 Year	合计 Total	支农支出 Expenditure for Supporting Agricultural Production	农业基本建设支出 Expenditure for Capital Construction	农业科技三项费用 Science & Technology Promotion Funds	农村救济费 Rural Relief Funds	其他 Others	用于农业支出占财政支出的比重(%) Percentage to Total Government Expenditure
1978	150.66	76.95	51.14	1.06	6.88	14.63	13.43
1980	149.95	82.12	48.59	1.31	7.26	10.67	12.20
1985	153.62	101.04	37.73	1.95	12.90		7.66
1989	265.94	197.12	50.64	2.48	15.70		9.42
1990	307.84	221.76	66.71	3.11	16.26		9.98
1991	347.57	243.55	75.49	2.93	25.60		10.26
1992	376.02	269.04	85.00	3.00	18.98		10.05
1993	440.45	323.42	95.00	3.00	19.03		9.49
1994	532.98	399.70	107.00	3.00	23.28		9.20
1995	574.93	430.22	110.00	3.00	31.71		8.43
1996	700.43	510.07	141.51	4.94	43.91		8.82
1997	766.39	560.77	159.78	5.48	40.36		8.30
1998	1154.76	626.02	460.70	9.14	58.90		10.69
1999	1085.76	677.46	357.00	9.13	42.17		8.23
2000	1231.54	766.89	414.46	9.78	40.41		7.75
2001	1456.73	917.96	480.81	10.28	47.68		7.71
2002	1580.76	1102.70	423.80	9.88	44.38		7.17
2003	1754.45	1134.86	527.36	12.43	79.80		7.12

注：从1998年开始，"农业基本建设支出"包括增发国债安排的支出。

a) Expenditure for agricultural capital construction since 1998 included the expenditure funded from additional issuing national debt.

8-7 国家财政用于科学研究的支出

Government Expenditure for Science and Research

单位: 亿元 (100 million yuan)

年份 Year	合计 Total	科技三项费用 Expense on S&T Promotion	科学支出 Expenditure for Sciences	科研基建费 Expenses on Capital Construction of S&T Institutes	其他科研事业费 Other S&T Operating Expenses
1978	52.89	25.47	15.46	6.66	5.30
1980	64.59	27.57	19.63	11.27	6.12
1985	102.59	44.35	32.00	18.83	7.41
1989	127.87	59.13	38.45	17.91	12.38
1990	139.12	63.48	44.44	17.47	13.73
1991	160.69	73.32	54.15	18.40	14.82
1992	189.26	89.41	57.16	24.55	18.14
1993	225.61	106.56	65.59	33.95	19.51
1994	268.25	114.22	87.90	36.06	30.07
1995	302.36	136.02	96.86	38.00	31.48
1996	348.63	155.01	109.66	48.55	35.41
1997	408.86	189.97	127.12	42.74	49.03
1998	438.60	189.90	151.92	47.28	49.50
1999	543.85	272.80	168.06	52.89	50.10
2000	575.62	277.22	189.03	61.52	47.85
2001	703.26	359.64	223.08	63.37	57.17
2002	816.22	398.60	269.85	69.99	77.78
2003	975.54	416.64	300.79	111.06	147.05

8-8 国家财政用于抚恤和社会福利的支出
Government Expenditure for Pension and Social Welfare

单位：亿元 (100 million yuan)

年 份 Year	合 计 Total	抚恤支出 Pension for Disable and Bereaved Families	离退休费 Expenditure on Retirees	社会救济福利费 Social Welfare and Relief Funds	救灾支出 Expenses on Disaster Relief	其 他 Others
1978	18.91	2.93	2.34	4.62	9.02	
1980	20.31	4.51	3.41	5.36	7.03	
1985	31.15	7.13	4.88	7.71	10.25	1.18
1989	49.60	14.43	8.56	10.80	12.88	2.93
1990	55.04	16.61	9.60	12.07	13.33	3.43
1991	67.32	17.21	10.32	13.18	22.51	4.10
1992	66.45	18.45	12.40	14.36	15.89	5.35
1993	75.27	20.78	14.09	17.01	15.40	7.99
1994	95.14	24.78	20.12	20.55	19.42	10.27
1995	115.46	29.11	22.78	24.19	27.27	12.11
1996	128.03	32.78	10.67	28.98	39.06	16.54
1997	142.14	37.62	13.51	36.57	34.51	19.93
1998	171.26	40.38	16.24	35.29	52.32	27.03
1999	179.88	54.57	19.68	48.52	34.05	23.06
2000	213.03	59.72	23.72	59.71	28.73	41.15
2001	266.68	69.86	30.26	89.99	35.17	41.40
2002	372.97	60.03	41.28	141.63	32.93	97.10
2003	498.82	99.15	42.19	217.69	55.71	84.08

注:1.从1996年起离退休费不包括已划入行政事业单位离退休经费支出类中的由民政部门管理的地方离退休费。
2.从1976年起救灾支出中包括抗震救灾费。

a) Since 1996, the pension for retires and excluded the local pension for retires which had been transferred to the pension of administration operation and run by the department of civil affairs.

b) Since 1976, expense on disaster relief include the expense on earthquake relief.

8-9 政策性补贴支出
Budgetary Expenditure for Price Subsidies

单位：亿元 (100 million yuan)

年份 Year	合计 Total	粮棉油价格补贴 Subsidies on Price Increases in Grain, Cotton and Edible Oil	平抑物价等补贴 Subsidies on Curbing Price Increase	肉食品价格补贴 Subsidies on Increase in Meat Price	其他价格补贴 Other Price Subsidies
1978	11.14	11.14			
1980	117.71	102.80			14.91
1985	261.79	198.66		33.52	29.61
1989	373.55	262.52		41.29	69.74
1990	380.80	267.61		41.78	71.41
1991	373.77	267.03		42.46	64.28
1992	321.64	224.35		38.54	58.75
1993	299.30	224.75		29.86	44.69
1994	314.47	202.03	41.25	25.41	45.78
1995	364.89	228.91	50.17	24.17	61.64
1996	453.91	311.39	53.38	27.46	61.68
1997	551.96	413.67	43.20	28.25	66.84
1998	712.12	565.04	28.10	26.09	92.89
1999	697.64	492.29	14.25	20.55	170.55
2000	1042.28	758.74	17.71	19.39	246.44
2001	741.51	605.44	16.74	4.55	114.78
2002	645.07	535.24	5.32	1.60	102.91
2003	617.28	550.15	5.15	1.28	60.70

注：政策性补贴支出，1985年以前冲减财政收入，1986年以后作为支出项目列在财政支出中。

a) The government expenditure for price subsidies were listed as a negative revenue item prior to 1986, but they have been listed as a government expenditure item since 1986.

8-10 国家财政债务发行情况
Government Debts Issuance

单位:亿元 (100 million yuan)

年 份 Year	合 计 Total	国内债务 Domestic Debts	国外借款 Foreign Borrowing	国内其他债务 Other Domestic Debts
1985	89.85	60.61	29.24	
1986	138.25	62.51	75.74	
1987	223.55	63.07	106.48	54.00
1988	270.78	92.17	138.61	40.00
1989	407.97	56.07	144.06	207.84
1990	375.45	93.46	178.21	103.78
1991	461.40	199.30	180.13	81.97
1992	669.68	395.64	208.91	65.13
1993	739.22	314.78	357.90	66.54
1994	1175.25	1028.57	146.68	
1995	1549.76	1510.86	38.90	
1996	1967.28	1847.77	119.51	
1997	2476.82	2412.03	64.79	
1998	3310.93	3228.77	82.16	
1999	3715.03	3702.13		12.90
2000	4180.10	4153.59	23.10	3.41
2001	4604.00	4483.53	120.47	
2002	5679.00	5660.00		19.00
2003	6153.53	6029.24	120.68	3.61

注：从1999年开始，国内其他债务项目为债务收入大于支出部分增列的偿债基金。

a) Since 1999, other domestic debts were the sinking fund which come from the excessive part of the revenue from borrowings minus the expenditure for debts.

8-11 国家财政债务还本付息支出
Government Payment for the Principal and Interest of Debts

单位:亿元 (100 million yuan)

年份 Year	合 计 Total	国内债务还本付息 Payment for the Principal and Interest of Domestic Debts	国外债务还本付息 Payment for the Principal and Interest of Foreign Debts	归还向人民银行借款的利息 Payment of the Interest of Loans from People's Bank	债务收入大于支出部分增列偿债基金 Sinking Fund from the Excessive Part of the Revenue from Borrowings minus the Expenditure for Debts.
1980	28.58		24.40	4.18	
1985	39.56		32.59	6.97	
1989	72.37	19.30	45.84	7.23	
1990	190.07	113.42	68.21	8.44	
1991	246.80	156.69	80.22	9.89	
1992	438.57	342.42	80.26	15.89	
1993	336.22	224.30	89.22	22.70	
1994	499.36	364.96	107.17	27.23	
1995	882.96	784.06	71.69	27.21	
1996	1355.03	1266.29	60.76	27.98	
1997	1918.37	1820.40	70.76	27.21	
1998	2352.92	2245.79	76.60	30.53	
1999	1910.53	1792.33	90.99	27.21	12.90
2000	1579.82	1552.21	27.61		3.41
2001	2007.73	1923.42	84.31		
2002	2563.13	2467.71	95.42		19.00
2003	2952.24	2876.58	75.66		3.61

注：从2000年开始，表中数据均为债务还本支出。

a) Since 2000, expenditure in this table refers to payment for the principal of debts.

8-12 外 债 余 额
Balance of Foreign Debts

债务类型	Type of Debts	1998	1999	2000	2001	2002	2003
总计 （亿美元）	**Total (USD 100 million)**	**1460.43**	**1518.30**	**1457.30**	**1701.10**	**1713.60**	**1936.34**
按债务类型分	**By Type of Debt**						
外国政府贷款	Loans from Foreign Governments	224.06	265.60	246.10	237.00	244.23	254.20
国际金融组织贷款	Loans from International Financial Institutions	229.54	251.39	263.50	275.70	277.02	264.67
国际商业贷款	International Commercial Loans	682.22	653.80	947.70	972.30	929.10	1051.73
贸易信贷	Trade Loans				216.10	263.23	365.74
按偿还期限分	**By Repayment Terms**						
长期债务余额	Balance of Long-term Debts	1287.00	1366.50	1326.50	1195.30	1155.60	1165.90
短期债务余额	Balance of Short-term Debts	173.40	151.80	130.80	505.80	558.00	770.44
构成 （%）	**Percentage (%)**	**100.0**	**100.0**	**100.0**	**100.0**	**100.0**	**100.0**
按债务类型分	**By Type of Debt**						
外国政府贷款	Loans from Foreign Governments	15.4	17.5	16.9	13.9	14.5	13.1
国际金融组织贷款	Loans from International Financial Institutions	15.7	16.5	18.1	16.2	16.4	13.7
国际商业贷款	International Commercial Loans	46.7	43.1	65.0	57.2	53.5	54.3
贸易信贷	Trade Loans				12.7	15.6	18.9
按偿还期限分	**By Repayment Terms**						
长期债务余额	Balance of Long Term Debts	88.1	90.0	91.0	70.3	67.4	60.2
短期债务余额	Balance of Short Term of Debts	11.9	10.0	9.0	29.7	32.6	39.8

注：2001年及以后外债余额按新口径统计，比2000年及以前的登记债务余额增加了3个月以内贸易项下的对外融资余额。

a) Foreign debts since 2001 are collected by the new standard, the figures increase the foreign loans under the item of international trade loans within 3 months than the debts before 2001.

8-13 外 债 风 险 指 标
Risk Indicators on Foreign Debts

单位：% (%)

年份 Year	偿债率 Debt Service Ratio	负债率 Liability Ratio	债务率 Foreign Debt Ratio
1985	2.7	5.2	56.0
1986	15.4	7.3	72.1
1987	9.0	9.4	77.1
1988	6.5	10.0	87.1
1989	8.3	9.2	86.4
1990	8.7	13.5	91.6
1991	8.5	14.9	91.9
1992	7.1	14.4	87.9
1993	10.2	13.9	96.5
1994	9.1	17.1	78.0
1995	7.6	15.2	72.4
1996	6.0	14.2	67.7
1997	7.3	14.5	63.2
1998	10.9	15.2	70.4
1999	11.3	15.3	69.5
2000	9.2	13.5	52.1
2001	7.5	14.7	56.8
2002	7.9	13.6	46.1
2003	6.9	13.7	39.9

注：1.本表资料由国家外汇管理局提供。
2.偿债率指偿还外债本息与当年贸易和非贸易外汇收入(国际收支口径)之比。
3.负债率指外债余额与当年国内生产总值之比。
4.债务率指外债余额与当年贸易和非贸易外汇收入(国际收支口径)之比。

a) The table is provided by State Administration of Foreign Exchange.
b) Debt service ratio refers to the ratio of the payment of principal and interest of foreign debts to the foreign exchange receipts from foreign trade and non-trade services of the current year.
c) Liability ratio refers to the ratio of the balance of foreign debts to the gross domestic product of the current year.
d) Foreign debt ratio refers to the ratio of the balance of foreign debts to the foreign exchange receipts from foreign trade and non-trade services of the current year.

8-14 各地区财政收入(2003年)

Final Statement of Government Revenue by Region (2003)

单位: 万元 (10 000 yuan)

地 区	Region	收入合计 Total Revenue	增值税 Value-added Tax	营业税 Operation tax	企业所得税 Enterprises' Income Tax	企业所得税退税 Return for Enterprises' Income Tax	个人所得税 Individual Income Tax	资源税 Resources Tax
地方合计	**Region Total**	**98499846**	**18109890**	**27675640**	**10435041**	**-1403**	**5672469**	**832961**
北 京	Beijing	5925388	752553	2636946	937007		572106	2848
天 津	Tianjin	2045295	451925	643231	238022	-6	125347	3755
河 北	Hebei	3358263	687193	653546	286917	-1	181460	58092
山 西	Shanxi	1860547	513574	366306	142312	-2	85860	80305
内蒙古	Inner Mongolia	1387157	225940	363318	71615	-5	54288	20144
辽 宁	Liaoning	4470490	854907	1190908	359313	-38	235562	61245
吉 林	Jilin	1540033	306877	350192	118021	-72	78070	14776
黑龙江	Heilongjiang	2488643	586400	461394	107808	-2	109793	144485
上 海	Shanghai	8862277	1701998	3323140	1461501		718127	
江 苏	Jiangsu	7981065	1814325	2072215	926878		401547	17731
浙 江	Zhejiang	7065607	1550060	2200657	1065165		457895	6338
安 徽	Anhui	2207487	369517	459731	190470	-29	82408	26472
福 建	Fujian	3047095	543961	847298	368133	-63	212552	14501
江 西	Jiangxi	1681670	230683	431628	97435	-7	72763	12664
山 东	Shandong	7137877	1260824	1447077	664382		260262	104760
河 南	Henan	3380535	579478	753089	291370	-49	156041	35884
湖 北	Hubei	2597636	456411	574219	213471		114805	18995
湖 南	Hunan	2686469	361183	602304	134574		121622	9089
广 东	Guangdong	13155151	2336835	4158122	1700183		947674	15274
广 西	Guangxi	2036578	286917	479121	130545		103496	11294
海 南	Hainan	513205	63637	160617	26044		27801	5494
重 庆	Chongqing	1615618	246601	466392	87694		78711	20172
四 川	Sichuan	3365917	480965	896047	247547		143575	29744
贵 州	Guizhou	1245552	194261	314589	84133	-828	54412	9731
云 南	Yunnan	2289992	391100	451702	214963	-3	83851	14585
西 藏	Tibet	81499	9364	40160	7160	-1	2851	1999
陕 西	Shaanxi	1773300	316393	510441	127942		68506	26337
甘 肃	Gansu	876561	181230	240705	53111	-31	36776	12331
青 海	Qinghai	240411	52503	73079	12177	-1	7831	6252
宁 夏	Ningxia	300310	50424	108953	16846		13021	1301
新 疆	Xinjiang	1282218	251851	398513	52302	-265	63456	46363

8-14 续表 1 continued

单位: 万元 (10 000 yuan)

地区	Region	固定资产投资方向调节税 Tax on the Adjustment of the Investment in the Fixed Assets	城市维护建设税 Tax on City Maintenance and Construction	房产税 Tax on Real Estates	印花税 Stamp Tax	城镇土地使用税 Tax on the Use of Urban Land	土地增值税 Land Value Added Tax	车船使用和牌照税 Tax on the Use of Vehicles and Ships
地方合计	**Region Total**	**48158**	**5467076**	**3238610**	**911130**	**915681**	**372812**	**321492**
北京	Beijing	631	288542	307915	73524	32911	30689	25763
天津	Tianjin	91	107987	71989	20708	7510		6262
河北	Hebei	281	187733	90009	23300	39235	2380	7608
山西	Shanxi	541	129631	52527	17682	21206	100	3494
内蒙古	Inner Mongolia	1996	69675	58620	12052	41839	3688	5760
辽宁	Liaoning	3502	257669	207190	47453	75689	27589	14154
吉林	Jilin	77	93277	63792	14564	18876	3833	3920
黑龙江	Heilongjiang	1921	210205	90352	12362	32298	1630	8783
上海	Shanghai	168	356155	224086	131908	22519	16609	12497
江苏	Jiangsu	2609	463216	231595	79339	38232	26544	19880
浙江	Zhejiang	836	421743	172580	64799	16313	29836	16666
安徽	Anhui	12	133121	59682	16674	33547	11088	7091
福建	Fujian	69	139206	131463	34770	20168	9874	9804
江西	Jiangxi	49	82215	35392	9698	16267	5494	3760
山东	Shandong	24299	444019	244706	46613	198074	54899	48420
河南	Henan	59	205386	91636	16398	24270	2095	6747
湖北	Hubei		173749	82399	24721	46881	5970	9975
湖南	Hunan	3	163264	65418	18550	23111	4317	5601
广东	Guangdong	1976	477462	455607	141344	58690	84434	65869
广西	Guangxi	659	95192	59819	8728	23805	19106	4385
海南	Hainan		27447	26268	4439	3745	1371	2621
重庆	Chongqing		86520	42134	12939	11890	4104	1775
四川	Sichuan	-33	206002	94439	23067	25196	19089	8678
贵州	Guizhou	127	86919	36655	5653	14558	2755	2184
云南	Yunnan	6381	235834	69915	16015	28732	2468	11440
西藏	Tibet		3168		482		182	
陕西	Shaanxi	1506	122833	65942	12825	25646	701	4568
甘肃	Gansu	72	70085	34316	6754	5358	22	1709
青海	Qinghai	25	15483	8401	1538	883	8	365
宁夏	Ningxia	4	18485	12012	2482	3417	364	507
新疆	Xinjiang	297	94853	51751	9749	4814	1573	1206

8-14 续表 2 continued

单位: 万元 (10 000 yuan)

地 区	Region	屠宰税 Slaughter Tax	筵席税 Banquet Tax	农业税 Agricultural Tax	农业特产税 Tax on Special Agricultural Products	牧业税 Tax on the Animal Husbandry	耕地占用税 Tax on The Occupancy of Cultivated Land	契税 Contract Tax
地方合计	**Region Total**	**22892**	**42**	**3365576**	**896001**	**14865**	**898968**	**3580454**
北 京	Beijing	39		5609	906		17589	203975
天 津	Tianjin	70		3595	138		12474	82543
河 北	Hebei	1		249978	8306		18644	59877
山 西	Shanxi	709		39350	941		5807	15613
内蒙古	Inner Mongolia	25	41	70152	10450	1576	26132	28108
辽 宁	Liaoning	2401		72322	30935		15921	156920
吉 林	Jilin			101705	20622		20485	48553
黑龙江	Heilongjiang			162802	16652		12302	55374
上 海	Shanghai			1186			32059	634831
江 苏	Jiangsu			265992			143228	402796
浙 江	Zhejiang	19		54442	14		199110	478227
安 徽	Anhui			266789	166		39974	71027
福 建	Fujian	601		11785	37141		20931	115484
江 西	Jiangxi			156977	3181		3808	68503
山 东	Shandong	28		424030	120176		86975	153276
河 南	Henan	56		377052	27121		18329	59071
湖 北	Hubei			231984	26792		15902	57511
湖 南	Hunan	20		181682	80452		39369	55541
广 东	Guangdong	6710		79777	13801		66007	485211
广 西	Guangxi	2752		67753	111904		13740	45355
海 南	Hainan	1145		4816	35025		1006	13949
重 庆	Chongqing			62348	13848		16641	41920
四 川	Sichuan			211223	18501	125	21182	116586
贵 州	Guizhou	4		51639	49668		10425	17562
云 南	Yunnan	6438		47912	200736		21670	40530
西 藏	Tibet						22	
陕 西	Shaanxi	18	1	66480	42066	5	13680	25364
甘 肃	Gansu	2		52691	11092	3238	2541	10432
青 海	Qinghai	6		5043	2703	6242	919	2814
宁 夏	Ningxia			7438	42		831	8046
新 疆	Xinjiang	1848		31024	12622	3679	1265	25455

8-14 续表 3 continued

单位: 万元 (10 000 yuan)

地 区	Region	国有资产经营收益 State-downed Assets Profit	国有企业计划亏损补贴 Planning Subsidies to Loss-suffering Stated-owned Enterprises	行政性收费收入 Income from Administrative Fees	罚没收入 Penalty and confiscatory income	海域场地矿区使用费收入 Income from Use of Sea Area, Field and Diggings	专项收入 Expert Project Income	其他收入 Other Income
地方合计	**Region Total**	**1354356**	**-1940433**	**7141324**	**4312379**	**51664**	**3417288**	**1384913**
北 京	Beijing	6992	-510546	181240	102177	13756	215243	26973
天 津	Tianjin	5000	-30000	147274	59786	1538	60031	26025
河 北	Hebei	37565	-15560	294368	259740	3315	166549	57726
山 西	Shanxi	12170	-17987	134890	122860	3	109097	23558
内蒙古	Inner Mongolia	60521	-6149	123014	61011		51762	31584
辽 宁	Liaoning	91424	-33307	378573	204765	4716	180998	29679
吉 林	Jilin	24076	-62948	150066	96015	264	60639	14353
黑龙江	Heilongjiang	48254	-21795	151960	105347	4	140902	49412
上 海	Shanghai		-361866	227976	141381		197772	20230
江 苏	Jiangsu	27265	-73058	508231	349877	1134	234098	27391
浙 江	Zhejiang	7451	-472124	203224	312889	694	259011	19762
安 徽	Anhui	24154	-22920	229728	103739		76418	28628
福 建	Fujian	25143	-2944	214450	165018	1442	82689	43619
江 西	Jiangxi	30404	-2192	182076	133723		49309	57840
山 东	Shandong	207506	-48894	757389	251479	6592	285982	95003
河 南	Henan	78914	-17060	300409	191958	282	141795	40204
湖 北	Hubei	12736	-42408	243369	192457	357	76810	60530
湖 南	Hunan	52136	-39804	348640	228507	228	99509	131153
广 东	Guangdong	207825	-28582	876579	448339	12774	335068	208172
广 西	Guangxi	92251	-15372	220037	141645	1482	65425	66539
海 南	Hainan	14978		47247	25144	3009	13822	3580
重 庆	Chongqing	36510	-23319	259343	79978		48764	20653
四 川	Sichuan	91972	-27401	422951	179529		111470	45463
贵 州	Guizhou	19503	-5369	117114	67559		52411	59887
云 南	Yunnan	17793	-23597	123962	111629		88781	127155
西 藏	Tibet	872	-9186	6318	2928	28	2580	12572
陕 西	Shaanxi	90440	-13006	102627	74630	40	67904	19411
甘 肃	Gansu	7343	-12904	57503	31427	6	49334	21418
青 海	Qinghai	4885	-40	12467	5798		14557	6473
宁 夏	Ningxia	5904	-11	20394	12942		11846	5062
新 疆	Xinjiang	12369	-84	97905	48102		66712	4858

8-15　各地区财政支出(2003年)

Final Statement of Government Expenditure by Region (2003)

单位: 万元　　　　(10 000 yuan)

地　区	Region	支出合计 Total Expenditure	基本建设 Expenditure for Capital Construction	企业挖潜改造资金 Expenditure for Innovation Enterprises	地质勘探费 Expenditure for Geological Prospecting	科技三项费用 Expenditure for Science and Technology Promotion	流动资金 Expenditure for Circulating Funds	农业支出 Expenditure for Agriculture	林业支出 Expenditure for Forestry
地方合计	**Region Total**	**172298463**	**19065287**	**6342499**	**813625**	**1903799**	**13984**	**5740503**	**1956940**
北　京	Beijing	7348043	719875	458741	9140	63736		178125	46295
天　津	Tianjin	3120771	524274	293732	11241	78023		55028	7194
河　北	Hebei	6467439	415300	99938	20805	54058		190704	56367
山　西	Shanxi	4156866	368678	68039	17523	29874	2399	154706	63263
内蒙古	Inner Mongolia	4472566	781312	147553	36051	30112		159636	148624
辽　宁	Liaoning	7843764	680144	156750	40867	162423		281979	70974
吉　林	Jilin	4092265	318364	104058	32987	30797		116888	67086
黑龙江	Heilongjiang	5649080	387665	127258	22600	57873		206589	184849
上　海	Shanghai	10884386	2447362	1545172	1614	15383		138058	49758
江　苏	Jiangsu	10476812	759687	511946	22230	135056		415909	29157
浙　江	Zhejiang	8967740	633046	489049	27185	195284		402093	49748
安　徽	Anhui	5074398	474481	148824	35359	27109		169118	34848
福　建	Fujian	4523010	374593	143434	13097	58128	315	172527	38754
江　西	Jiangxi	3820981	338935	68589	56914	17248		154592	41412
山　东	Shandong	10106395	636760	462915	21837	140670	2684	425229	68101
河　南	Henan	7165978	502569	166891	25856	57218		210074	53144
湖　北	Hubei	5404356	307235	123936	21727	61746	4323	175539	43405
湖　南	Hunan	5737453	513964	101835	53731	49090		226221	65871
广　东	Guangdong	16956324	2408689	220378	30684	364417	3095	416297	114954
广　西	Guangxi	4436023	399988	126696	28202	28805	682	167211	62568
海　南	Hainan	1053984	134463	1917	3171	5881		38686	16011
重　庆	Chongqing	3415775	640685	72583	6609	27969		91157	57025
四　川	Sichuan	7322993	750182	232608	41255	61228	486	268650	134181
贵　州	Guizhou	3323547	316396	54909	31141	23103		145073	57591
云　南	Yunnan	5873475	705029	176823	27641	45658		257792	144157
西　藏	Tibet	1459054	594347	2233	14544	3603		40011	12770
陕　西	Shaanxi	4182008	462523	93786	46292	28706		141922	83160
甘　肃	Gansu	3000070	329959	63887	42937	12759		99521	64337
青　海	Qinghai	1220438	295285	10488	13216	7490		41566	21169
宁　夏	Ningxia	1057793	203563	39719	11236	7500		51442	18157
新　疆	Xinjiang	3684676	639934	27812	45933	22852		148160	52010

8-15 续表 1 continued

单位: 万元　　(10 000 yuan)

地区	Region	农林水利气象等部门事业费 Expenditure for Operating Expenses of Agriculture, Forestry, Water Conservancy and Meteorology	工业交通部门事业费 Expenditure for Operating Expenses of Departments of Industry & Transportation	流通部门事业费 Expenditure for Operating Expenses of Department of Commerce	文体广播事业费 Expenditure for Operating Expenses of Departments of Culture, Sport & Broadcasting	教育事业费 Expenditure for Operating Expenses of Education	科学事业费 Expenditure for Operating Expenses of Department of Science	卫生经费 Expenditure for Public Health
地方合计	**Region Total**	**2295271**	**1714485**	**292702**	**4346507**	**26971435**	**1098015**	**7559834**
北京	Beijing	37401	41309	2429	164145	988222	107629	496358
天津	Tianjin	18141	16272	220	71864	475804	19403	153135
河北	Hebei	58528	106779	10785	170256	1190712	26922	348275
山西	Shanxi	43964	45436	7153	114282	674140	15867	203272
内蒙古	Inner Mongolia	47227	38046	5970	105711	543525	16572	170878
辽宁	Liaoning	84706	88672	16125	144850	983397	37469	251624
吉林	Jilin	33628	57391	13379	105212	535908	20429	161382
黑龙江	Heilongjiang	53342	83421	23912	141932	810979	35049	230611
上海	Shanghai	49585	39850	1533	169554	1313724	113439	364420
江苏	Jiangsu	214275	99016	10326	256666	1790766	55235	555684
浙江	Zhejiang	146709	165706	11293	276526	1642075	71680	453797
安徽	Anhui	122420	34324	5677	118748	845575	18204	170815
福建	Fujian	60077	70220	11364	137180	929670	42527	207211
江西	Jiangxi	38953	50577	9799	92796	644665	18547	150613
山东	Shandong	124786	89036	14466	307350	1791484	58375	396107
河南	Henan	97693	59539	8146	238910	1311582	30337	301893
湖北	Hubei	64675	45475	16048	139234	890687	21776	242474
湖南	Hunan	70006	58892	18599	155101	900570	22267	168303
广东	Guangdong	428841	117926	39310	381087	2652474	152589	735442
广西	Guangxi	69446	30280	4066	135794	790977	35027	210155
海南	Hainan	15454	5291	1211	23079	147959	3887	46470
重庆	Chongqing	21642	10871	3229	74597	429462	8666	108218
四川	Sichuan	82962	62928	15786	177801	1089036	38508	314235
贵州	Guizhou	44006	41009	8215	115871	601258	19641	172994
云南	Yunnan	87938	64409	16884	138045	931733	42628	327463
西藏	Tibet	9806	30864	484	35893	130664	2545	52805
陕西	Shaanxi	65651	80227	11951	121122	663304	17968	167206
甘肃	Gansu	42650	23529	1769	88750	475673	16739	118002
青海	Qinghai	12148	13799	299	25618	126319	3756	52972
宁夏	Ningxia	16798	11915	1361	31619	137830	5771	44812
新疆	Xinjiang	31813	31476	913	86914	530261	18563	182208

8-15 续表 2 continued

单位: 万元 (10 000 yuan)

地　区	Region	其他部门的事业费 Expenditure for Operating Expenses of Other Departments	抚恤和社会福利救济费 Expenditure for Pensions and Relief Funds for Social Welfare	行政事业单位离退休经费 Expenditure for Retired Persons in Administrative Department	社会保障补助支出 Expenditure on Subsidies to Social Security Programs	国防支出 Expenditure for National Defense	行政管理费 Expenditure for Government Administration	外交外事支出 Expenditure for Foreign Affairs	武装警察部队支出 Expenditure for Armed Police Troops
地方合计	**Region Total**	**8866225**	**4936860**	**8056373**	**11177192**	**225773**	**16577202**	**98712**	**242441**
北　京	Beijing	315935	228318	339052	128102	3354	390900	1335	7
天　津	Tianjin	81941	59350	11029	275049	1815	175505	4404	1486
河　北	Hebei	481874	190083	355094	560816	8983	670410	6789	3076
山　西	Shanxi	198278	132787	262100	468907	7532	454411	1089	3776
内蒙古	Inner Mongolia	258935	109468	302696	244960	5603	456517	1037	10524
辽　宁	Liaoning	416685	307939	384032	1276451	17261	622468	15725	9368
吉　林	Jilin	229029	160270	287777	495632	5581	312315	3588	8441
黑龙江	Heilongjiang	383160	188269	169275	620253	8035	489551	2726	13997
上　海	Shanghai	391940	155024	61114	331291	2681	447886	8130	
江　苏	Jiangsu	536722	265957	363917	339492	10342	1071724	5383	12219
浙　江	Zhejiang	664839	180694	73186	220311	9163	952162	6958	15306
安　徽	Anhui	178608	208102	322677	491158	7250	512911	3372	3901
福　建	Fujian	250683	96399	273823	84712	10497	366675	1933	14026
江　西	Jiangxi	220192	134785	141237	414471	2064	359542	623	4594
山　东	Shandong	523771	281244	444158	345457	10982	1123337	3971	6728
河　南	Henan	398718	241193	506498	536876	7383	831015	669	
湖　北	Hubei	331140	251717	239215	485471	10856	570864	972	4475
湖　南	Hunan	332605	218603	339042	478624	9982	591494	1651	6563
广　东	Guangdong	908202	304539	837492	370069	20588	1754697	6057	53898
广　西	Guangxi	325073	112174	193680	220779	10794	463286	6858	5856
海　南	Hainan	69272	31048	51076	87269	2238	105078	1402	3801
重　庆	Chongqing	73557	128237	240926	339682	4841	368357	670	10409
四　川	Sichuan	242844	254623	465885	535911	16409	945994	2960	13371
贵　州	Guizhou	131443	88755	27572	197285	4685	433298	1351	2547
云　南	Yunnan	274399	172517	452154	423004	11972	554288	2870	16789
西　藏	Tibet	13980	21094	17490	36360	710	200566	430	2509
陕　西	Shaanxi	254390	155448	202954	413506	4306	469146	1367	2248
甘　肃	Gansu	122209	80088	178269	370725	3454	313176	2065	1947
青　海	Qinghai	37836	35463	131365	107051	1379	111201	707	1300
宁　夏	Ningxia	37186	26717	53414	88764	1621	77326	969	1343
新　疆	Xinjiang	180779	115955	328174	188754	3412	381102	651	7936

8-15 续表 3 continued

单位: 万元 (10 000 yuan)

地区	Region	公检法司支出 Expenditure for Public Security Agency, Procuratorial Agency and Court of Justice	城市维护费 Expenditure for City Maintenance	政策性补贴支出 Expenditure for Price Subsidies	支援不发达地区支出 Expenditure for Supporting Underdeveloped Areas	海域开发建设和场地使用费支出 Expenditure for Developing Land and Sea Area	债务利息支出 Expenditure for Interest of Debts	专项支出 Expenditure for Special Items	其他支出 Other Expenditure
地方合计	**Region Total**	**12305865**	**7618222**	**3797871**	**1559906**	**23868**	**86826**	**3096970**	**13513271**
北　京	Beijing	562899	361534	44901		400		238454	1419447
天　津	Tianjin	208891	276061	31147	39	1738		55272	212713
河　北	Hebei	478509	212357	216263	51674	1870	43	147568	332601
山　西	Shanxi	258890	117745	92200	55251	12	782	85525	208985
内蒙古	Inner Mongolia	229631	185405	198437	66952	43	8213	45247	117681
辽　宁	Liaoning	521892	480929	259170	32410	2215	1153	154099	341987
吉　林	Jilin	252775	118799	415377	30787	677	19783	49094	103831
黑龙江	Heilongjiang	379659	250618	446546	34312	13		141288	155298
上　海	Shanghai	644892	447399	10092				199818	1934667
江　苏	Jiangsu	851484	926665	142070	8358	1044	15442	209398	860642
浙　江	Zhejiang	781618	596096	51750	33121	673	1000	225035	591637
安　徽	Anhui	304227	141734	216787	48315	252	1027	69203	359372
福　建	Fujian	351761	128797	68662	29845	1002	2312	77689	505097
江　西	Jiangxi	277990	129612	111274	50103	60		45097	245697
山　东	Shandong	666962	685165	194468	13790	4279		259129	1003154
河　南	Henan	482008	220220	277590	70896	304	3013	124616	401127
湖　北	Hubei	371613	178897	154425	46019	373	2369	80879	516791
湖　南	Hunan	395958	234149	140698	62699	98	3645	89750	427442
广　东	Guangdong	1696994	634956	124757	91898	2341	275	305155	1778223
广　西	Guangxi	365876	187385	53162	83635	917	2552	56899	257200
海　南	Hainan	67134	35434	13867	21282	665	53	11574	109311
重　庆	Chongqing	235683	198820	53581	39372		905	47287	120735
四　川	Sichuan	521760	241893	154624	103376	260	16878	95074	441285
贵　州	Guizhou	237561	85189	29988	106567	72	2484	48255	295288
云　南	Yunnan	385311	181702	42685	142495	118		59086	187885
西　藏	Tibet	63372	5020	18151	29242			4620	114941
陕　西	Shaanxi	252287	152771	53043	68647	46	231	51779	116021
甘　肃	Gansu	134915	66241	53501	99131	50	1984	40769	151034
青　海	Qinghai	52951	12089	11371	43244		2682	8521	39153
宁　夏	Ningxia	51587	27957	19375	34583	65		10940	44223
新　疆	Xinjiang	218775	96583	97909	61863	4281		59850	119803

8-16 中央和地方财政收入及比重

Government Revenue and Ratio of the Central and Local Government

年份 Year	全国(亿元) Total Revenue (100 million yuan)	中央 Central Government	地方 Local Government	比重(%) Ratio (%) 中央 Central Government	地方 Local Government
1978	1132.26	175.77	956.49	15.5	84.5
1980	1159.93	284.45	875.48	24.5	75.5
1985	2004.82	769.63	1235.19	38.4	61.6
1989	2664.90	822.52	1842.38	30.9	69.1
1990	2937.10	992.42	1944.68	33.8	66.2
1991	3149.48	938.25	2211.23	29.8	70.2
1992	3483.37	979.51	2503.86	28.1	71.9
1993	4348.95	957.51	3391.44	22.0	78.0
1994	5218.10	2906.50	2311.60	55.7	44.3
1995	6242.20	3256.62	2985.58	52.2	47.8
1996	7407.99	3661.07	3746.92	49.4	50.6
1997	8651.14	4226.92	4424.22	48.9	51.1
1998	9875.95	4892.00	4983.95	49.5	50.5
1999	11444.08	5849.21	5594.87	51.1	48.9
2000	13395.23	6989.17	6406.06	52.2	47.8
2001	16386.04	8582.74	7803.30	52.4	47.6
2002	18903.64	10388.64	8515.00	55.0	45.0
2003	21715.25	11865.27	9849.98	54.6	45.4

注:1.中央、地方财政收入均为本级收入。
　2.本表数字不包括国内外债务收入。

a) The revenue of the central and local governments refers to revenue actually collected by the central and local governments.
b) Revenue in this table does not include revenue from domestic and foreign borrowings.

8-17 中央和地方财政支出及比重

Government Expenditure and Ratio of Central and Local Government

年份 Year	全国(亿元) Total Expenditure (100 million yuan)	中央 Central Government	地方 Local Government	比重(%) Ratio (%) 中央 Central Government	地方 Local Government
1978	1122.09	532.12	589.97	47.4	52.6
1980	1228.83	666.81	562.02	54.3	45.7
1985	2004.25	795.25	1209.00	39.7	60.3
1989	2823.78	888.77	1935.01	31.5	68.5
1990	3083.59	1004.47	2079.12	32.6	67.4
1991	3386.62	1090.81	2295.81	32.2	67.8
1992	3742.20	1170.44	2571.76	31.3	68.7
1993	4642.30	1312.06	3330.24	28.3	71.7
1994	5792.62	1754.43	4038.19	30.3	69.7
1995	6823.72	1995.39	4828.33	29.2	70.8
1996	7937.55	2151.27	5786.28	27.1	72.9
1997	9233.56	2532.50	6701.06	27.4	72.6
1998	10798.18	3125.60	7672.58	28.9	71.1
1999	13187.67	4152.33	9035.34	31.5	68.5
2000	15886.50	5519.85	10366.65	34.7	65.3
2001	18902.58	5768.02	13134.56	30.5	69.5
2002	22053.15	6771.70	15281.45	30.7	69.3
2003	24649.95	7420.10	17229.85	30.1	69.9

注: 1.中央、地方财政支出均为本级支出。
　2.本表数字2000年以前不包括国内外债务还本付息支出和利用国外借款收入安排的基本建设支出。从2000年起,全国财政支出和中央财政支出中包括国内外债务付息支出。

a) The expenditure of the central and local governments refers to expenditure actually collected by the central and local governments.
b) Expenditure in this table does not include the payment of the principal and interest of domestic and foreign debts and the expenditure for capital construction using foreign loans.

8-18 中央和地方财政主要收入项目(2003年)

Main Items of Government Revenue of the Central Government and Local Government (2003)

单位:亿元 (100 million yuan)

项目	Item	国家财政收入 Total Government Revenue	中央 Central Government	地方 Local Government
一、各项税收	**Total Taxes**	**20017.31**	**11604.04**	**8413.27**
消费税	Consumption Tax	1182.26	1182.26	
增值税	Value Added Tax	7236.54	5425.55	1810.99
营业税	Business Tax	2844.45	76.89	2767.56
进口产品消费税、增值税	Consumption Tax and Value Added Tax on Imports	2788.59	2788.59	
资源税	Resource Tax	83.30		83.30
城市维护建设税	Urban Maintenance and Development Tax	550.01	3.30	546.71
企业所得税	Company Income Tax	2919.51	1740.71	1178.80
个人所得税	Personal Income Tax	1418.04	850.79	567.25
城镇土地使用税	Urban Land Using Tax	91.57		91.57
其他各税	Other Tax	491.49		491.49
关税	Tariffs	923.13	923.13	
船舶吨税	Cargo Tax	9.38	9.38	
农业税	Agriculture and Related Taxes	423.82		423.82
契税	Tax on Contracts	358.05		358.05
耕地占用税	Tax on the Use of Arable Land	89.90		89.90
外贸企业出口退税	Tax Rebate to Foreign Trade Company	-1988.59	-1988.59	
证券交易印花税	Stamp Tax on Security Exchange	127.70	123.87	3.83
车辆购置税	Vehicle Purchase Tax	468.16	468.16	
二、企业亏损补贴	**Subsidies for the Losses of the State-owned Enterprises**	**-226.38**	**-32.34**	**-194.04**
工业企业	Industry Enterprises	-51.46	-21.69	-29.77
商业企业	Commercial Enterprises	-4.74		-4.74
粮食企业	Grain Enterprises	-42.27		-42.27
外贸企业	Foreign Trade Enterprises	-5.57	-5.09	-0.48
农林、水产、气象企业	Agriculture, Forest, Aquaculture and Meteorology Enterprises	-2.72	-2.04	-0.68
其它企业	Other Enterprises	-119.62	-3.52	-116.10
三、征收排污费和城市水资源费收入	**Fee on Sewage Treatment and Fee on Urban Water Resource**	**93.40**		**93.40**
四、其他收入	**Other Revenues**	**1598.53**	**291.73**	**1306.80**
五、教育费附加收入	**Extra-charges for Education**	**232.39**	**1.84**	**230.55**

8-19 中央和地方财政主要支出项目(2003年)

Main Items of Budgetary Expenditure of Central and Local Governments (2003)

单位:亿元 (100 million yuan)

项目	Item	国家财政支出 Total Expenditure	中央 Central Government	地方 Local Government
一、基本建设支出	**Expenditure for Capital Construction**	**3429.30**	**1522.77**	**1906.53**
二、挖潜改造和科技三项费用	**Innovation Funds and Science & Technology Promotion Funds**	**1092.99**	**268.36**	**824.63**
企业挖潜改造资金	Enterprises Innovation Funds	676.35	42.10	634.25
科技三项费用	Science and Technology Promotion Funds	416.64	226.26	190.38
三、增拨企业流动资金	**Additional Appropriation for Enterprises' Circulating Capital**	**11.95**	**10.55**	**1.40**
四、地质勘探费	**Geological Prospecting Expenses**	**106.94**	**25.58**	**81.36**
五、工业、交通、流通部门事业费	**Operating Expenses of Department of Industry, Transportation and Commerce**	**285.23**	**84.51**	**200.72**
六、支农支出	**Expenditure for Supporting Agricultural Production**	**1134.86**	**135.59**	**999.27**
农、林、水利和气象支出	Expenses of Agriculture, Forest, Irrigation and Meteorology	979.18	108.85	870.33
农业综合开发支出	Expenses of Agriculture Comprensive Development	155.68	26.74	128.94
七、城市维护建设支出	**Urban Maintenance and Construction Expenditure**	**850.78**		**850.78**
城市维护建设费	Urban Maintenance and Construction Expense	761.82		761.82
环境保护和城市水资源建设支出	Environmental Protection and Urban Water Resources Construction Expenses	88.96		88.96
八、文教、科学、卫生事业费	**Operating Expenses for Culture, Education, Science and Health Care**	**4505.51**	**507.94**	**3997.57**
教育事业费	Operating Expenses for Education	2937.34	240.20	2697.14
科学事业费	Operating Expenses for Science	300.79	190.99	109.80
卫生事业费	Operating Expenses for Health	778.05	22.07	755.98
文体广播事业费	Operating Expenses for Culture, Sports and Broadcast	489.33	54.68	434.65
九、抚恤和社会福利救济费	**Pensions and Relief Funds for Social Welfare**	**498.82**	**5.13**	**493.69**
十、社会保障补助支出	**Social Security Subsidiary Expenses**	**1262.12**	**144.40**	**1117.72**
十一、国防支出	**Expenditure for National Defense**	**1907.87**	**1885.29**	**22.58**
十二、行政管理费	**Expenditure for Government Administration**	**2058.35**	**400.63**	**1657.72**
十三、公检法司支出	**Expenditure for Public Security Agency, Procuratorial Agency and Court of Justice**	**1301.33**	**70.74**	**1230.59**
十四、武装警察部队支出	**Expenditure for Armed Police Troops**	**264.21**	**239.97**	**24.24**
十五、外交外事支出	**Expenditure for Diplomacy**	**78.00**	**68.13**	**9.87**
十六、对外援助支出	**Expenditure for External Assistance**	**52.23**	**52.23**	
十七、支援经济不发达地区支出	**Expenditure for Supporting Undeveloped Areas**	**164.37**	**8.38**	**155.99**
十八、政策性补贴支出	**Expenditure for Price Subsidies**	**617.28**	**237.49**	**379.79**
粮、棉、油价格补贴	Subsidies on Price Increases in Grain, Cotton and Edible Oil	550.15	219.88	330.27
平抑物价和储备糖等补贴	Subsidies on Stabilizing Price Level and Sugar Reserve	5.15	3.17	1.98
肉食价格补贴	Subsidies on Price Increase in Meats	1.28		1.28
其他价格补贴	Other Price Subsidies	60.70	14.44	46.26
十九、税务等部门事业费	**Operating Expenses in Tax and Other Department**	**937.14**	**50.52**	**886.62**
二十、其他支出	**Other Expenditures**	**1560.75**	**192.03**	**1368.72**
廿一、中央预备费	**Central Government Reserve**			
廿二、地方预备费	**Local Government Reserve**			
廿三、教育费附加支出	**Expenditure on Education Surcharge**	**202.92**	**0.15**	**202.77**
廿四、行政事业单位离退休经费	**Expenditure for Retired Persons in Administrative Department**	**894.97**	**89.33**	**805.64**
廿五、用车购税收入安排的支出	**Expenditure by Using the Vehicle Purchase Tax**	**468.16**	**465.19**	**2.97**
廿六、预算外资金改革支出	**Expenditure for the Off-budget administrative reform**			
廿七、国内外债务付息支出	**Interest Payment for the Domestic and Foreign Debts**	**963.87**	**955.19**	**8.68**
国内债务付息支出	Interest Payment for the Domestic Debts	899.29	892.85	6.44
归还向人民银行借款利息	Interest Payment for the Loans from PBC	27.21	27.21	
国外借款付息支出	Interest Payment for the Foreign Debts	37.37	35.13	2.24

8-20 预算外资金分项目收入

Extra-budgetary Revenue by Item

单位：亿元 (100 million yuan)

年份 Year	合计 Total	行政事业性收费 Revenue of Administrative and Institutional Units	政府性基金收入 Revenue of Funds	乡镇自筹、统筹资金 Revenue form Fundraising Programs of Township Governments	地方财政收入 Revenue of Local Governments	国有企业和主管部门收入 Revenue of State-owned Enterprises and Its Governing Department	其他收入 Other Revenue
1978	347.11	63.41			31.09	252.61	
1980	557.40	74.44			40.85	442.11	
1985	1530.03	233.22			44.08	1252.73	
1989	2658.83	500.66			54.36	2103.81	
1990	2708.64	576.95			60.59	2071.10	
1991	3243.30	697.00			68.77	2477.53	
1992	3854.92	885.45			90.88	2878.59	
1993	1432.54	1317.83			114.71		
1994	1862.53	1722.50			140.03		
1995	2406.50	2234.85			171.65		
1996	3893.34	3395.75		272.90	224.69		
1997	2826.00	2414.32		295.78	115.90		
1998	3082.29	1981.92	478.41	337.31		54.67	229.98
1999	3385.17	2354.28	396.51	358.86		50.11	225.41
2000	3826.43	2654.54	383.51	403.34		59.22	325.81
2001	4300.00	3090.00	380.00	410.00		60.00	360.00
2002	4479.00	3238.00	376.00	272.00		72.00	521.00

注：1993-1995年和1996年的预算外资金收入范围分别有所调整，与以前各年不可比。从1997年起，预算外资金收入不包括纳入预算内管理的政府性基金（收费），与以前各年也不可比。

a) Since adjustment on the coverage of extra-budgetary revenues from 1993 to 1995 and in 1998 has made, the figures are not comparable with the previous years. Since 1997, the extra-budgetary revenues do not include the intra-budgetary government fund (fee), the figures are not comparable with the previous years.

8-21 预算外资金分项目支出

Extra-budgetary Expenditure by Item

单位:亿元 (100 million yuan)

年份 Year	合计 Total	基本建设支出 Capital Construction	专项支出 Special Expenditure	行政事业费支出 Operating and Administrative Expenses	城市维护费支出 Urban Maintenance Expenses	乡镇自筹、统筹支出 Expenditure by Township Governments	其他支出 Other Expenses
1996	3838.32	1490.23	307.27	1254.36		136.39	650.07
1997	2685.54	502.03	311.59	1280.19		288.69	303.04
1998	2918.31	393.98	423.60	1588.28		335.26	177.19
1999	3139.14	539.82		1816.13	127.45	350.34	305.40
2000	3529.01	426.20		2225.09	146.38	387.39	343.96
2001	3850.00	350.00		2500.00	150.00	400.00	450.00
2002	3831.00	260.00		2655.00	160.00	268.00	488.00

注：1996年预算外资金支出范围有所调整，与以前各年不可比。从1997年起，预算外资金支出不包括纳入预算内管理的政府性基金(收费)，与以前各年也不可比。

a) Because adjustment on the coverage of extra-budgetary expenditures in 1998 has made, the figures are not comparable with the previous years. Since 1997, the extra-budgetary expenditures do not include the intra-budgetary government fund (fee), the figures are not comparable with the previous years.

8-22 中央和地方预算外资金收支及比重

Total Extra-budgetary Revenues and Expenditures and Ratio of the Central Government and Local Government

项 目 Item	全国(亿元) Total (100 million yuan)	中央 Central Government	地方 Local Government	比重(%) Ratio (%) 中央 Central Government	地方 Local Government
一、收 入 Revenue					
1986	1737.31	716.63	1020.68	41.2	58.8
1987	2028.80	828.03	1200.77	40.8	59.2
1988	2360.77	907.15	1453.62	38.4	61.6
1989	2658.83	1072.28	1586.55	40.3	59.7
1990	2708.64	1073.28	1635.36	39.6	60.4
1991	3243.30	1381.10	1862.20	42.6	57.4
1992	3854.92	1707.73	2147.19	44.3	55.7
1993	1432.54	245.90	1186.64	17.2	82.8
1994	1862.53	283.32	1579.21	15.2	84.8
1995	2406.50	317.57	2088.93	13.2	86.8
1996	3893.34	947.66	2945.68	24.3	75.7
1997	2826.00	145.08	2680.92	5.1	94.9
1998	3082.29	164.15	2918.14	5.3	94.7
1999	3385.17	230.45	3154.72	6.8	93.2
2000	3826.43	247.63	3578.79	6.5	93.5
2001	4300.00	347.00	3953.00	8.1	91.9
2002	4479.00	440.00	4039.00	9.8	90.2
二、支 出 Expenditure					
1986	1578.37	640.94	937.43	40.6	59.4
1987	1840.75	741.61	1099.14	40.3	59.7
1988	2145.27	842.86	1302.41	39.3	60.7
1989	2503.10	975.87	1527.23	39.0	61.0
1990	2707.06	1037.69	1669.37	38.3	61.7
1991	3092.26	1263.27	1828.99	40.9	59.1
1992	3649.90	1592.81	2057.09	43.6	56.4
1993	1314.30	198.87	1115.43	15.1	84.9
1994	1710.39	225.02	1485.37	13.2	86.8
1995	2331.26	351.38	1979.88	15.1	84.9
1996	3838.32	1034.92	2803.40	27.0	73.0
1997	2685.54	143.91	2541.63	5.4	94.6
1998	2918.31	139.74	2778.57	4.8	95.2
1999	3139.14	164.82	2974.32	5.3	94.7
2000	3529.01	210.74	3318.28	6.0	94.0
2001	3850.00	258.13	3591.87	6.7	93.3
2002	3831.00	259.00	3572.00	6.8	93.2

注：1993-1995年和1996年的预算外资金收支范围分别有所调整，与以前各年不可比。从1997年起，预算外资金收支不包括纳入预算内管理的政府性基金（收费），与以前各年也不可比。

a) Because adjustment on the coverage of extra-budgetary revenues and expenditures from 1993 to 1995 and in 1998 has made, the figures are not comparable with the previous years. Since 1997, the extra-budgetary revenues and expenditures do not include the intra-budgetary government fund (fee), the figures are not comparable with the previous years.

主要统计指标解释

财政收入 指国家财政参与社会产品分配所取得的收入，是实现国家职能的财力保证。财政收入所包括的内容几经变化，目前主要包括：

(1)各项税收：包括增值税、营业税、消费税、土地增值税、城市维护建设税、资源税、城市土地使用税、企业所得税、个人所得税、关税、证券交易印花税、车辆购置税、农牧业税和耕地占用税等。

(2)专项收入：包括排污费收入、城市水资源费收入、矿产资源补偿费收入、教育费附加收入等。

(3)其他收入：包括利息收入、基本建设贷款归还收入、基本建设收入、捐赠收入等。

(4)国有企业亏损补贴：此项为负收入，冲减财政收入。主要包括对工业企业、商业企业、粮食企业的补贴。

财政支出 国家财政将筹集起来的资金进行分配使用，以满足经济建设和各项事业的需要，主要包括：

(1)基本建设支出：指按国家有关规定，属于基本建设范围内的基本建设有偿使用、拨款、资本金支出以及经国家批准对专项和政策性基建投资贷款，在部门的基建投资额中统筹支付的贴息支出。

(2)企业挖潜改造资金：指国家预算内拨给的用于企业挖潜、革新和改造方面的资金。包括各部门企业挖潜改造资金和企业挖潜改造贷款资金，为农业服务的县办“五小”企业技术改造补助，挖潜改造贷款贴息资金。

(3)地质勘探费用：指国家预算用于地质勘探单位的勘探工作费用，包括地质勘探管理机构及其事业单位经费、地质勘探经费。

(4)科技三项费用：指国家预算用于科技支出的费用，包括新产品试制费、中间试验费、重要科学研究补助费。

(5)支援农村生产支出：指国家财政支援农村集体(户)各项生产的支出。包括对农村举办的小型农田水利和打井、喷灌等的补助费，对农村水土保持措施的补助费，对农村举办的小水电站的补助费，特大抗旱的补助费，农村开荒补助费，扶持乡镇企业资金，支援农村合作生产组织资金、农村农技推广和植保补助费，农村草场和畜禽保护补助费，农村造林和林木保护补助费，农村水产补助费，发展粮食生产专项资金。

(6)农林水利气象等部门的事业费用：指国家财政用于农垦、农场、农业、畜牧、农机、林业、森工、水利、水产、气象、乡镇企业的技术推广、良种推广(示范)、动植物(畜禽、森林)保护、水质监测、勘探设计、资源调查、干部训练等项费用，园艺特产场补助费，中等专业学校经费，飞播牧草试验补助费，营林机构、气象机构经费，渔政费以及农业管理事业费等。

(7)工业交通商业等部门的事业费：指国家预算支付给工交商各部门用于事业发展的人员和公用经费支出，包括勘探设计费、中等专业学校经费、技术学校经费、干部训练费。

(8)文教科学卫生事业费：指国家预算用于文化、出版、文物、教育、卫生、中医、公费医疗、体育、档案、地震、海洋、通讯、电影电视、计划生育、党政群干部训练、自然科学、社会科学、科协等项事业的人员和公用经费支出以及高技术研究专项经费。主要包括工资、补助工资、福利费、离退休费、助学金、公务费、设备购置费、修缮费、业务费、差额补助费。

(9)抚恤和社会福利救济费：指国家预算用于抚恤和社会福利救济事业的经费。包括由民政部门开支的烈士家属和牺牲病残人员家属的一次性、定期抚恤金，革命伤残人员的抚恤金，各种伤残补助费，烈军属、复员退伍军人生活补助费，退伍军人安置费，优抚事业单位经费，烈士纪念建筑物管理、维修费，自然灾害救济事业费和特大自然灾害灾后重建补助费等。

(10)行政事业单位离退休支出：指实行归口管理的行政事业单位离退休经费。

(11)社会保障补助支出：指国家预算用于社会保障的补助支出，包括对社会保险基金的补助、促进就业补助、国有企业下岗职工补助、补充全国社会保障基金等。

(12)国防支出：指国家预算用于国防建设和保卫国家安全的支出，包括国防费、国防科研事业费、民兵建设以及专项工程支出等。

(13)行政管理费：包括行政管理支出，党派团体补助支出，外交支出，公安安全支出，司法支出，法院支出，检察院支出和公检法办案费用补助。

(14)政策性补贴支出：指经国家批准，由国家财政拨给用于粮棉油等产品的价格补贴支出。主要包括粮、棉、油差价补贴，平抑物价和储备糖补贴，农业生产资料价差补贴，粮食风险基金，副食品风险基金，地方煤炭风险基金等。

(15)债务利息支出：指国家预算中用于偿还国内外债务利息的支出。

中央财政收入和地方财政收入 指按现行分税制财政体制划分的中央本级收入和地方本级收入。1994年实行分税制财政体制以后，属于中央财政的收入包括关税、海关代征消费税和增值税，消费税，中央企业所得税，地方银行和外资银行及非银行金融企业所得税，铁道部门、各银行总行、各保险总公司等集中缴纳的营业税、利润和城市维护建设税，车辆购置税，船舶吨税，增值税的75%部分，证券交易税(印花税)94%部分，个人所得税中的利息所得税，利息所得税之外的个人所得税中央分享的部分，海洋石油资源税。属于地方财政的收入包括营业税，地方企业所得税，利息所得税之外的个人所得税地方分享的部分，城镇土地使用税，固定资产投资方向调节税，城镇维护建设税，房产税，车船使用税，印花税，屠宰税，农牧业税，农业特产税，耕地占用税，契税，土地增值税、国有土地有偿使用收入，增值税25%部分，证券交易税(印花税)6%部分和除海洋石油资源税以外的其他资源税。

中央财政支出和地方财政支出 指根据政府在经济和社

会活动中的不同职责，划分中央和地方政府的责权，按照政府的责权划分确定的支出。中央财政支出包括国防支出，武装警察部队支出，中央级行政管理费和各项事业费，重点建设支出以及中央政府调整国民经济结构、协调地区发展、实施宏观调控的支出。地方财政支出主要包括地方行政管理和各项事业费，地方统筹的基本建设、技术改造支出，支援农村生产支出，城市维护和建设经费，价格补贴支出等。

预算外资金收支 预算外资金指国家机关、事业单位和社会团体为履行或代行政府职能，依据国家法律、法规和具有法律效力的规章而收取、提取和安排使用的未纳入国家预算管理的各种财政性资金。其范围主要包括：法律、法规规定的行政事业性收费、政府性基金和附加收入等；国务院或省级人民政府及其财政、计划（物价）部门审批的行政事业性收费；国务院及财政部审批建立的政府性基金、附加收入等；主管部门所属单位集中上缴资金；用于乡镇政府开支的乡自筹和乡统筹资金；其他未纳入预算管理的财政性资金。社会保障基金在国家财政尚未建立社会保障预算制度以前，先按预算外资金管理制度进行管理，专款专用。财政部门在银行开设统一的专户，用于预算外资金收入和支出管理。部门和单位的预算外收入必须上缴同级财政专户，支出由同级财政按预算外资金收支计划和单位财务收支计划统筹安排，从财政专户中拨付，实行收支两条线管理。

债务收入 国家以信用形式筹措的资金，包括财政部对国内商业银行和其他投资者发行的各种政府债券、财政部在国际资金市场发行的外币债券以及国家财政“统借统还”的其他政府外债。

债务还本支出 指国家财政用于偿还国内、国外债务本金支出。

中央财政赤字 指当年中央财政总支出大于中央财政总收入的差额。

Explanatory Notes on Main Statistical Indicators

Government Revenue refers to the revenue of the government finance by means of participating in the distribution of the social products, which is the financial resources for ensuring the government to function. The contents of government revenue have been changed several times. Now it includes the following main items:

(1) Various tax revenues, including value added tax, business tax, consumption tax, land value added tax, tax on city maintenance and construction, resources tax, tax on use of urban land, enterprise income tax, personal income tax, tariff, stamp tax on security transactions, tax on purchase of motor vehicles, tax on agriculture and animal husbandry and tax on occupancy of cultivated land, etc.

(2) Special revenues, including revenues from the fee on sewage treatment, fee on urban water resources, fee for the compensation of mineral resources and extra-charges for education, etc.

(3) Other revenues, including revenue from interest, revenue from the repayment of capital construction loan, revenue from capital construction projects, and donations and grants.

(4) Subsidies for the losses of the state-owned enterprises. This is an item of negative revenue, consisting of subsidies to industrial, commercial and grain purchasing and supply enterprises.

Government Expenditure refers to the distribution and use of the funds the government finance has raised, so as to meet the needs of economic construction and various causes. It includes the following main items:

(1) Expenditure for capital construction: It refers to the non-gratuitous use and appropriation of funds for capital construction in the range of capital construction, outlay of capital as well as the loans on capital construction approved by the government for special purpose or policy purpose and the expenditure with discount paid in an overall way within the amount of the funds appropriated to the departments for capital construction.

(2) Innovation funds of the enterprises: They refer to the funds appropriated from the government budget for the enterprises to tap the latent power, upgrade the technology and carry out innovation, including the innovation fund of the departments, loan of the enterprises for innovation, subsidies on the innovation of the small fertilizer plant, small cement plant, small coal mines, small machinery plant and small steel plant, the expenditure of interest for the loan for innovation.

(3) Geological prospecting expenses: They refer to the expenses appropriated from the government budget to the geological prospecting units for the expenditure of the prospecting work, including the expenditures of the administrative agencies for geological prospecting and their institutional units as well as the geological prospecting expenditure.

(4) expenditures for science and technology promotion: They refer to the expenses appropriated from the government budget for the scientific and technological expenditure, including new products development expenditure, expenditure for intermediate trial and subsidies on important scientific researches.

(5) Expenditure for supporting rural production: It refers to the expenditures appropriated from the government budget for supporting the various expenditures of the rural collective units or households for production, including the subsidies to the small water conservancy projects and well drilling, sprinkling irrigation projects run by the villages; subsidies on the rural water and soil conserving measures; subsidies to the small power stations run by the villages; subsidies to the expenditure for fighting against particularly severe draughts; subsidies on the rural waste land exclamation; fund for supporting the township enterprises; fund for supporting rural cooperative production organizations, subsidies to the expenditure for popularization of the agricultural technologies and plant protection in the rural areas; subsidies to the expenditure for the protection of grasslands and cattle and fowls; subsidies on afforestation and forest protection in rural areas; subsidies on the rural aquatic products industry; special fund for developing grain production.

(6) Operating expenses of the departments of farming, forestry, water conservancy and meteorology etc.: They refer to the expenses appropriated from the government budget for the expenditures of agricultural exclamation, farms, agriculture, animal husbandry, agricultural machinery, forestry, timber industry, water conservancy, aquatic products industry, meteorology, technology popularization in township enterprises, popularization (demonstration) of improved varieties, plant (cattle and fowls, forest) protection, water quality monitoring, prospecting and designing, resources investigation, cadres training, subsidies to horticulture gardens, expenditure of specialized secondary schools, subsidies on the experiments of sowing herbage seeds by flights, expenditures of afforestation agencies and meteorology agencies, expenses for fishery administration and operating expenses for agricultural administration, etc.

(7) Operating expenses of the departments of industry, transport and commerce: They refer to the expenses appropriated from the government budget to cover the expenditure on salaries and operational expenditure of the departments of industry, transport and commerce for the expenditure of business development, in-

cluding expenses for prospecting and designing, expenditures of specialized secondary schools, expenditures of the technical training schools and expenditures for cadres training, etc.

(8) Operating expenses of the departments of culture, education, science and public health: They refer to the expenses appropriated from the government budget for the expenditures on salaries and operational expenditure of the causes of culture, publication, cultural relics, education, public health, traditional Chinese medical science, free medical services, sports, archives, earthquake, ocean, communications, broadcasting, film and television, family planning; expenditure for training of cadres of government, party and mass organization; expenditures for natural sciences, social sciences, associations for science and technology and the special expenditure for the high-tech researches. They include mainly wages, extra wages, welfare funds, pension for the retirees, stipend, expenses for official business, expenses for equipment purchases, expenses for repairs, business expenses and subsidies to the units which are unable to support their expenditures by their own earnings.

(9) Pension for the disabled or for the families of the bereaved and relief funds for social welfare: They refer to the funds appropriated from the government budget for the expenditures of pension for the disabled or for the families of the bereaved and relief funds for social welfare, including the lump-sum or regular pension paid by the departments of civil affairs to the members of martyrs families and families of those who died for the public interest, pension to the revolutionary disabled, subsidies for permanent disability of various kinds, subsidies to the military martyrs dependents and the demobilized servicemen, expenditure for settling down the demobilized servicemen, operating expenses of the consoling institutions, expenses for management and repair of the commemorative buildings for the martyrs, the expenses managed by the departments of civil affairs for the retirees and those who have quitted their work, expenses for social relief in rural and urban areas, operating expenses for providing relief to the areas of natural calamity and subsidies on the reconstruction after the particularly severe natural calamities, etc.

(10) Expenditure on retirees: It refers to the expenditure on retirees of government agencies and institutions that are covered by the state budget.

(11) Expenses on subsidies to social security system: It refers to expenditure from the state budget for subsidies to social security system, including subsidies to the social insurance fund, subsidies to promoting employment, subsidies to laid-off workers of state-owned enterprises, supplement to national social security funds, etc.

(12) Expenditures for national defence: They refer to the funds appropriated from the government budget for the expenditures for building up national defence and safeguarding national security, including expenses of national defence, expenses of scientific researches on national defence, expenses for building up peoples militia and expenditure for special projects, etc.

(13) Administrative expenses: They include expenditure for administration, subsidies to the parties and mass organizations, diplomatic expenditure, expenditure for public security, judicial expenditure, law court expenditure, procuratorial expenditure and subsidies to the expenses for treating the cases by the public security departments, procuratorial organs and law courts.

(14) Expenditure on policy-related subsidies: It refers to the expenditure appropriated, with the approval of the government, from the state budget for price subsidies on such products as grain, cotton and edible oil. More specifically, it includes subsidies to the difference between the selling prices and purchasing prices of grains, cotton and edible oil, subsidies for curtaining prices and for sugar reserve, subsidies to the difference between the selling prices and purchasing prices of means pf agricultural production, risk fund for grains, risk fund for non-staple food, risk fund for local production of coal, etc.

(15) Expenditure on interest of debts: It refers to expenses from the state budget on paying interest of domestic and foreign debts.

Revenue of the central government and revenue of the local governments: refers to the revenue of the central government and that of the local governments as defined by the decentralized taxation system starting from 1994. In accordance with this system, the revenue of the central government includes tariff, consumption tax and value added tax levied by the customs, consumption tax, income tax of the enterprises subordinate to the central government, income taxes of the local banks, foreign-funded banks and non-bank financial institutions, business tax and profits of railways, head offices of banks, head office of insurance company , which are handed over to the government in a centralized way, tax on city maintenance and construction, tax on purchasing motor vehicles, tonnage tax of ships, 75% of the value added tax, 94% of the tax on stock dealing (stamp tax), interest income tax in the personal income tax, proportion of the personal income tax (other that interest income tax) to be shared by the central government, and tax on ocean petroleum resources,. The revenue of the local governments includes business tax, income tax of the enterprises subordinate to the local government, proportion of the personal income tax (other that interest income tax) to be shared by the central government, tax on the use of urban land, tax on the adjustment of the investment in fixed assets, tax on town maintenance and construction, tax on real estates, tax on the use of vehicles and ships, stamp tax, slaughter tax, tax on agriculture and animal husbandry, tax on special agricultural products, tax on the occupancy of cultivated land, contract tax, value-added tax on land, income from charges on use of state-owned land, 25% of the value added tax, 6% of the tax on stock dealing (stamp tax) and tax on resources other than the ocean petroleum resources.

Expenditure of the central government and expenditure of the local governments: according to the different functions of the central government and local governments in the economic and social activities, the rights of affairs administration are classified between the central government and local governments; and the classification of the expenditure between the central government and local governments are made on the basis of the classification of the rights of affairs administration between them. The expenditure of the central government includes the expenditure for national defence, expenditure for armed police forces, the administrative expenses and various operating expenses at the level of central government, expenditure for key projects and the expenditure of the central government for adjusting the national economic structure, coordinating the development among different regions and exercising the macro-economic regulation and control. The expenditure of the local governments includes mainly the administrative expenses and various operating expenses at the level of local governments, the expenditure for capital construction and technological innovation with the funds raised by the local government, expenditure for supporting rural production, expenditure for city maintenance and construction and expenditure for price subsidies, etc.

Extra-budgetary revenue and expenditure Extra-budgetary fund refers to financial fund of various types not covered by the regular government budgetary management, which is collected, allocated or arranged by government agencies, institutions and social organizations while performing duties delegated to them or on behalf of the government in accordance with laws, rules and regulations. It mainly covers following items: administrative and institutional fees, governmental funds and extra charges that are stipulated by laws and regulations; administrative and institutional fees approved by the State Council and provincial governments and their financial and planning (price management) departments; governmental funds and extra charges established by the State Council and the Ministry of Finance; funds turned over to competent departments by their subordinate institutions; self-raised and collected funds by township governments for their own expenditure; and other financial funds that are not covered in budgetary management. Social security funds are treated as extra-budget fund and managed for its exclusive use, given the circumstance that separate government budgetary system for social security is yet to be designed. Special accounts are opened by the financial departments in banks for the management of revenue and expenditure of extra-budgetary fund. Extra-budgetary revenue and expenditure is managed separately, namely, revenue of institutions and departments must enter into the special accounts of the financial departments at the same administrative level, and their extra-budgetary expenditure is arranged in line with the extra-budget plans and appropriated from these accounts.

Revenue from debts refers to fund raised by the state in credit forms, including various domestic government bonds issued by the Ministry of Finance to commercial banks and other investors, bonds in foreign currencies issued by the Ministry of Finance at the international capital market, and other foreign debts borrowed and to be repaid centrally by the government finance.

Expenditure on repayment of principal of debts refers to the expenditure from government finance on the repayment of principal of domestic and foreign debts.

Deficit of central government finance refers to the difference between the total expenditure and the total revenue of the central government.

九、价格指数

Price Indices

简要说明

一、本篇资料的主要内容

本篇价格指数资料，反映生产、消费与投资等环节的价格变动趋势和变动幅度。主要包括居民消费价格指数、商品零售价格指数、农业生产资料价格指数、工业品出厂价格指数(生产者价格指数)、原材料、燃料和动力购进价格指数、固定资产投资价格指数和房地产价格指数。

二、本篇的资料来源

价格指数统计由国家统计局城市社会经济调查总队组织实施。由各省、自治区、直辖市及抽选出的市、县城市社会经济调查队依据国家统计局统一制定的价格统计调查制度向基层采集原始数据汇总后上报。

三、居民消费、商品零售价格指数

编制居民消费、商品零售价格指数的资料采用分层抽样调查方法取得，即在全国选择不同经济区域和分布合理的地区、以及有代表性的商品作为样本，对其市场价格进行经常性的调查，以样本推断总体。目前，国家一级抽选出的调查市、县226个。编制过程按下列几个步骤进行：

1.选择调查地区和调查点。调查地区按照经济区域和地区分布合理等原则，选出具有代表性的大、中、小城市和县作为国家的调查地区；在此基础上选定经营规模大、商品种类多的商场(包括集市)作为调查点。

2.选择代表商品和代表规格品。代表商品是选择那些消费量大、价格变动有代表性的商品；代表规格品的确定是根据商品零售资料和4万户城市居民、6.7万户农村居民的消费支出记帐资料，按照有关规定筛选的。筛选原则：(1)与社会生产和人民生活关系密切；(2)销售数量(金额)大；(3)市场供应稳定；(4)价格变动趋势有代表性；(5)所选的代表规格品之间差异大。

目前，居民消费价格调查按用途划分为8大类，251个基本分类，各地每月调查600-700种规格产品价格；商品零售价格按用途划分为16个大类，225个基本分类，各地每月调查500种以上的规格产品价格。

3.价格调查方式。采用派员直接到调查点登记调查，同时全国聘请近万名辅助调查员协助登记调查。

4.权数的确定。商品零售价格指数的计算权数根据社会商品零售额统计确定，居民消费价格指数的计算权数根据10万多户城乡居民家庭消费支出构成确定。

四、工业品出厂价格指数

工业品出厂价格是工业品第一次出售时的出厂价格。该项调查采用重点调查与典型调查相结合的调查方法。重点调查对象为年销售收入500万元以上的工业企业，典型调查对象为年销售收入500万元以下的工业企业。

1.选择代表企业的原则：(1)按工业行业选择调查企业，各中类行业原则上都要有调查企业；(2)大型企业应尽量都选上(或占相当大比重)；(3)选择生产正常、稳定的企业作为调查对象；(4)选择企业时要兼顾不同所有制形式。

2.选择代表产品的原则：(1)按工业行业选择代表产品；(2)选择对国计民生影响大的产品；(3)选择生产较为稳定的产品；(4)选择有发展前景的产品；(5)选择具有地方特色的产品。

目前《工业品价格调查目录》包括2700种工业出厂产品(5700个规格)。上述代表产品所代表的行业销售额占当年全国工业品销售总额的90%以上。

3.价格调查方式。采用企业报表形式，每月4.5万家工业企业上报数据资料。

4.权数的确定。编制工业品出厂价格指数所用的权数，用工业品销售额计算。计算资料来源于工业普查数据。若近期没有工业普查数据时，采用工业统计资料和部门统计资料来推算。权数一般五年更换一次。

五、固定资产投资价格指数

固定资产投资价格调查采用重点调查与典型调查相结合的方法。固定资产投资价格调查所涉及的价格是构成固定资产投资额实体的实际购进价格或结算价格。调查的内容包括构成当年建筑工程实体的钢材、木材、水泥、地方材料(如砖、瓦、灰、沙、石等)、化工材料(如油漆等)等主要建筑材料价格；作为活劳动投入的劳动力价格（单位工资）和建筑机械使用费用；设备工器具购置和其他费用投资价格。

1.选择建筑安装工程调查点的原则：(1)样本单位应具有一定覆盖面；(2)投资经济活动代表性强；(3)兼顾不同经济类型；(4)选择重点工程；(5)兼顾国民经济各门类及不同工程类别。

2.选择其他费用调查点的原则：在选择其他费用调查点时，所遵循的原则与建筑安装工程调查点的原则基本相同，特别是要注意选择那些投资额大的工程。但由于其他费用不易取得，所以在实际操作过程中，应同时在建设单位、施工单位开展重点调查，并辅以典型调查(从管理部门取得资料)。

3.价格调查方式。采用企业报表和调查员走访相结合的方式。

4.权数的确定。固定资产投资价格指数的计算权数是建筑安装工程、设备工器具购置和其他费用三者前三年的平均比重。

六、房地产价格指数

从广义上讲，房地产是房产与地产的总称。因此房地产价格调查的内容主要包括以下几个部分：

1.房屋销售价格。从进入房地产市场的渠道看，房屋销售价格包括商品房销售价格、公房销售价格和私房销售价格三部分。

2.房屋租赁价格。房屋租赁价格包括住宅、办公用房、商业用房和厂房仓库四部分。

3.土地交易价格。土地交易价格包括居民住宅用地、工业用地、商业旅游娱乐用地和其他用地四部分。

房地产价格调查采用重点调查与典型调查相结合的方法。调查方式采用报表与走访相结合的方式。

目前我国房地产价格调查在三十五个大中城市开展，调查样本约为8000个。

Brief Introduction

I. Main Content

Data on the price indices in this chapter show the changing trend and the change rates in production, consumption and investment, including mainly consumer price indices of residents, retail price indices, price indices of agricultural means of production, purchasing price indices of farm products, producers' price indices of industrial products, purchasing price indices of raw materials, fuels and power, price indices of investment in fixed assets, and real estate price indices.

II. Source of Data

Statistical surveys for price indices are organized by the Urban Socio-economic Survey Organization, NBS. The urban socio-economic survey organizations of the provinces, autonomous regions and municipalities and of the selected cities and counties collect data from the grassroots units in accordance with the scheme of price survey stipulated by the NBS, tabulate them and report them to the higher agencies.

III. Consumer Price Indices of Residents and Retail Price Indices

Data for calculation of the consumer price indices of residents and the retail price indices in China are collected with the stratified sampling method. Areas distributed in different economic regions are selected as the sample areas and the representative commodities are selected as the sample commodities. Regular surveys are conducted to collect the data on the market prices. The data on the population are estimated on the basis of the sample. At present, 226 cities and counties have been selected for this purpose. Following are major steps in the process of calculation of the price indices:

(1) The selection of the areas and places for survey: Based on such principles as regional economic features and reasonable geographic distribution, representative sample areas for the national survey are selected which include large, medium and small cities and counties. When the sample areas are selected, large-scale shops and markets (including fairs) with great varieties of commodities are selected as the survey places.

(2) The selection of the representative commodities and their specifications or varieties: The representative commodities are the commodities consumed in large quantity and representative in price changes. The representative specifications or varieties are determined according to the data on the retail sales of commodities and the account data of the residents of 40,000 urban households and 67,000 rural households, following the related instructions for selection. In principle, only those specifications or varieties of the commodities can be selected: (a) They are closely related to the social production and people's livelihood; (b) They are sold in large quantities (or big values); (c) The market supply is stable; (d) The changes of their prices are representative in trend; (e) There is great difference among the specifications or varieties selected.

At present, data are collected on about 600-700 specifications each month under 251 basic headings in 8 categories in the consumer price surveys. For the retail price surveys, data are collected on more than 500 specifications each month under 225 basic headings in 16 categories

(3) Data collection: Enumerators are sent to the survey places to take the records of the prices. Nearly 10 thousand assistant enumerators are invited to assist the survey work.

(4) The determination of the weights: The weights for calculation of the retail price indices are determined according to the total retail sales of commodities. The weights for calculation of the consumer price indices are determined according to the composition of the consumption expenditures of more than 100,000 urban and rural households.

IV. Producers' Prices of Industrial Products

Producers' prices of industrial products refer to the first sale price of industrial products when they leave factories. The survey ways include the key units survey and typical units survey. The key units refer to the industrial enterprises with annual sale revenue above 5 million yuan. The typical units refer to the industrial enterprises with annual sale revenue below 5 million yuan.

(1) Principle in selecting the representative enterprises:

(a) Enterprises to be covered in the survey are selected by industrial sectors. In principle, every branch should have enterprises selected; (b) All (or a majority of) large-sized enterprises should be selected; (c) Enterprises with normal and stable production are to be selected; (d) Different types of ownership should be considered in selecting enterprises.

(2) The principle to select the representative products:

(a) The products are selected by industrial sectors; (b) The selected products should have great impact on the national economy and the people's livelihood; (c) The production of the products selected are stable; (d) The foreground of products is representative in trend; (e) The products are typical and with local color.

The present List of Industrial Products for the survey includes 2,700 products (including 5,700 specifications or varieties). The industrial sales value of the industries represented by these products accounts for more than 90 percent of total industrial sales value.

(3) Data collection: Reports by enterprises are adopted. About 45,000 industrial enterprises report price data every month.

(4) The determination of the weights: The weights for calculation of the producers' price indices of industrial products are determined according to the total sales value of industrial products. Data from the industrial census are used for the calculation. If industrial census data are not available for the reference year, industrial statistical data and statistical data from other agencies will be used to estimate the weights. The weights are replaced every five years.

V. Price Indices for Investment in Fixed Assets

Data on prices of investment in fixed assets are collected by the survey on key units and typical units. The prices of the survey of investment in fixed assets are the actual purchasing prices or balancing prices of entity of investment in fixed assets. The survey content includes the prices of main construction materials that composing the architecture engineering entity in the year, such as steel, timber, cement, local construction materials (such as brick, tile, calcareousness, sand, stone, etc.), chemical materials (such as oil paint, etc.), the price of labor force as input (wages), prices for renting of building machinery and equipment, the purchasing price of equipment, tools and instruments and the prices of others investments.

The following principle to select the sample of price survey of investment in fixed assets should be followed.

(1) The principle to select the prices survey point of construction and installation: (a) Sample units should be a certain coverage; (b) The economic activity of investment is great representative; (c) Different economic types of ownership should be considered; (d) The key projects need to be selected; (e) Give attention to both various branches and types of project.

(2) The principle to select the prices survey point of others investments: The principle to select the prices survey point of others fees is general the same as that of construction and installation, especially to select the projects with great investment value. Since it is not easy to obtain the other fees, it should do the key survey on the construction owner units and building units assisted with typical survey (gotten from the administration department), in the actual operation.

(3) Price survey way: Enterprises reporting system is used together with the enumerators visiting method.

(4) The determination of the weights: The weights for calculation of the price indices of investment in fixed assets are determined according to the average proportion of construction and installation, purchase of equipment, tools and instruments and others investment in the 3 previous years.

VI. Price Indices for Real Estate

The real estate in broad sense refers to the property in terms of buildings and land. Therefore, the price survey on real estate covers the following items:

1) Prices for selling houses and buildings. In terms of the types of houses sold at the market, prices for selling houses in-

clude the prices for commercial houses, for houses built or purchased by various units and for privately owned houses.

2) Prices for renting houses and buildings. Included in this category are prices for renting residential housing, office buildings, commercial buildings and warehouses.

3) Prices for land transaction. Included in this category are prices for the transaction of land used for residential housing, for industrial purposes, for commercial or recreational purposes and for other uses.

Survey on real estate prices employed a combination of survey of key units and survey of typical cases. Data are collected through reporting forms supplemented by interviews.

The survey on real estate prices at present is conducted in 35 large and medium cities, with a sample of 8,000 units.

9-1 各种价格指数

Price Indices

(上年=100) (preceding year=100)

年份 Year	居民消费价格指数 Consumer Price Index	城市居民消费价格指数 Urban Areas	农村居民消费价格指数 Rural Areas	商品零售价格指数 Retail Price Index	工业品出厂价格指数 Ex-Factory Price Indices of Industrial Products	原材料、燃料、动力购进价格指数 Purchasing Price Indices of Raw Material, Fuel and Power	固定资产投资价格指数 Investment in Fixed Assets Price Index
1978		100.7		100.7			
1980		107.5		106.0			
1985	109.3	111.9	107.6	108.8	108.7		
1989	118.0	116.3	119.3	117.8	118.6	126.4	
1990	103.1	101.3	104.5	102.1	104.1	105.6	
1991	103.4	105.1	102.3	102.9	106.2	109.1	109.5
1992	106.4	108.6	104.7	105.4	106.8	111.0	115.3
1993	114.7	116.1	113.7	113.2	124.0	135.1	126.6
1994	124.1	125.0	123.4	121.7	119.5	118.2	110.4
1995	117.1	116.8	117.5	114.8	114.9	115.3	105.9
1996	108.3	108.8	107.9	106.1	102.9	103.9	104.0
1997	102.8	103.1	102.5	100.8	99.7	101.3	101.7
1998	99.2	99.4	99.0	97.4	95.9	95.8	99.8
1999	98.6	98.7	98.5	97.0	97.6	96.7	99.6
2000	100.4	100.8	99.9	98.5	102.8	105.1	101.1
2001	100.7	100.7	100.8	99.2	98.7	99.8	100.4
2002	99.2	99.0	99.6	98.7	97.8	97.7	100.2
2003	101.2	100.9	101.6	99.9	102.3	104.8	102.2

9-2 各种价格定基指数

Fixed-base Price Indices

年份 Year	居民消费价格指数 Consumer Price Index (1985=100)	城市居民消费价格指数 Urban Areas (1978=100)	农村居民消费价格指数 Rural Areas (1985=100)	商品零售价格指数 Retail Price Index (1978=100)	工业品出厂价格指数 Ex-factory Price Indices of Industrial Products (1985=100)	原材料、燃料、动力购进价格指数 Purchasing Price Indices of Raw Material, Fuel and Power (1990=100)	固定资产投资价格指数 Investment in Fixed Assets Price Index (1991=100)
1978		100.0		100.0			
1980		109.5		108.1			
1985	100.0	134.2	100.0	128.1	100.0		
1989	160.2	219.2	157.9	203.4	152.8	96.1	
1990	165.2	222.0	165.1	207.7	159.0	100.0	
1991	170.8	233.3	168.9	213.7	168.9	109.1	100.0
1992	181.7	253.4	176.8	225.2	180.4	121.1	115.3
1993	208.4	294.2	201.0	254.9	223.7	163.6	145.9
1994	258.6	367.8	248.0	310.2	267.3	193.4	161.1
1995	302.8	429.6	291.4	356.1	307.1	222.9	170.6
1996	327.9	467.4	314.4	377.8	316.0	231.6	177.4
1997	337.1	481.9	322.3	380.8	315.0	234.6	180.4
1998	334.4	479.0	319.1	370.9	302.1	224.7	180.0
1999	329.7	472.8	314.3	359.8	294.8	217.3	179.3
2000	331.0	476.6	314.0	354.4	303.1	228.4	181.3
2001	333.3	479.9	316.5	351.6	299.2	227.9	182.0
2002	330.6	475.1	315.2	347.0	292.6	222.7	182.4
2003	334.6	479.4	320.2	346.7	299.3	233.4	186.4

9-3 居民消费价格分类指数（2003年）

Consumer Price Indices by Category (2003)

（上年=100） (preceding year=100)

项　目	Item	全国 National Indices	城市 Urban Indices	农村 Rural Indices
居民消费价格指数	**Consumer Price Index**	**101.2**	**100.9**	**101.6**
食品	**Food**	**103.4**	**103.4**	**103.4**
粮食	Grain	102.3	102.3	102.2
#大米	Rice	103.1	103.2	102.9
面粉	Flour	101.8	101.6	102.0
淀粉及薯类	Starches and Tubers	100.6	100.4	100.9
干豆类及豆制品	Bean and Its Products	106.5	106.3	106.7
油脂	Oil or Fat	112.6	112.0	113.4
肉禽及其制品	Meal, Poultry and Their Products	103.3	102.8	104.2
蛋	Eggs	98.6	98.3	99.0
水产品	Aquatic Products	100.3	100.5	99.9
菜	Vegetables	117.7	119.2	113.4
#鲜菜	Fresh Vegetables	120.5	121.1	118.0
调味品	Flavoring	100.1	99.5	100.8
糖	Carbohydrate	97.5	98.9	95.5
茶及饮料	Tea and Beverages	99.2	99.2	98.9
茶	Tea	99.7	99.5	99.9
饮料	Beverages	98.9	99.1	98.2
干鲜瓜果	Dried and Fresh Melons and Fruits	103.0	102.6	104.2
#鲜果	Fresh Fruits	101.8	101.6	102.5
糕点饼干面包	Cake, Biscuit and Bread	99.3	99.2	99.6
奶及奶制品	Milk and Its Products	99.2	99.2	99.0
在外用膳食品	Outward Dinner	100.1	100.1	100.2
其它食品及加工服务费	Other Foods and Manufacturing Services	99.1	99.0	99.2
烟酒及用品	**Tobacco, Liquor and Articles**	**99.8**	**99.8**	**99.9**
烟草	Tobacco	99.8	99.7	99.9
酒	Liquor	100.1	100.2	100.1
吸烟、饮酒用品	Articles for Smoking and Drinking	99.3	99.2	99.4
衣着	**Clothing**	**97.8**	**97.4**	**98.6**
服装	Garments	97.6	97.3	98.5
衣着材料	Clothing Material	99.2	98.7	99.8
鞋袜帽	Footgear and Hats	97.7	97.4	98.4
衣着加工服务费	Clothing Manufacturing Services	100.1	99.9	100.8
家庭设备用品及服务	**Household Facilities, Articles and Services**	**97.4**	**97.0**	**98.3**
耐用消费品	Durable Consumer Goods	95.8	95.3	97.1
家具	Furniture	97.9	97.5	98.5
家庭设备	Household Facilities	94.6	94.3	95.8

9-3 续表 continued

(上年=100) (preceding year=100)

项　目	Item	全国 National Indices	城市 Urban Indices	农村 Rural Indices
室内装饰品	Interior Decorations	98.8	98.6	99.3
床上用品	Bed Articles	98.4	97.9	99.5
家庭日用杂品	Daily Use Household Articles	98.3	98.0	98.7
家庭服务及加工维修服务费	Other Household Service and Manufacturing Upkeep	101.1	101.1	101.1
医疗保健和个人用品	**Health Cares & Personal Articles**	**100.9**	**99.8**	**102.5**
医疗保健	Medical Appliances and Articles	101.2	99.8	103.5
医疗器具及用品	Medical Instrument and Articles	101.0	100.8	101.2
中药材及中成药	Traditional Chinese Medicine	105.0	104.0	107.4
西药	Western Medicine	94.5	94.1	95.2
保健器具及用品	Health Care Appliances and Articles	98.2	98.2	98.2
医疗保健服务	Health Care Services	108.9	107.6	110.0
个人用品及服务	Personal Articles and Services	100.2	100.0	100.4
化妆美容用品	Cosmetic	99.5	99.7	98.9
卫生用品	Sanitation Article	97.1	96.3	98.4
个人饰品	Personal Decorations	102.9	104.5	101.2
个人服务	Personal Service	100.8	100.2	101.2
交通和通信	**Transportation and Communication**	**97.8**	**97.4**	**98.6**
交通	Transportation	99.5	99.6	99.4
交通工具	Transportation Facility	95.9	95.5	96.2
车用燃料及零配件	Fuels and Parts	108.3	108.8	107.4
车辆使用及维修费	Using and Upkeeping Fare	98.9	99.5	97.8
市内公共交通费	Incity Traffic Fare	100.6	100.6	100.6
城市间交通费	Intercity Traffic Fare	101.4	100.2	102.6
通信	Telecommunication	96.1	95.7	97.4
通信工具	Telecommunication Facility	82.1	79.8	87.6
通信服务	Telecommunication Service	99.4	99.1	100.1
娱乐教育文化	**Recreation, Education and Culture Articles**	**101.3**	**100.5**	**102.8**
文娱用耐用消费品及服务	Durable Consumer Goods for Recreational Use	92.7	92.0	94.1
教育	Education	104.3	103.9	104.8
教材及参考书	Teaching Materials and Reference Books	101.7	102.0	101.0
学杂托幼费	Tuition and Children Care	104.5	104.1	105.0
文化娱乐用品	Cultural and Recreational Articles	101.3	101.7	99.6
文化用品	Cultural Articles	98.7	98.7	98.7
书报杂志	Newspapers and Magazines	100.4	100.5	100.1
文娱费	Expenditure of Entertainment	104.6	105.0	101.5
旅游及外出	Touring and Outgoing	95.4	95.1	99.0
居住	**Residence**	**102.1**	**102.8**	**101.0**
建房及装修材料	Building and Building Decoration Materials	99.5	99.2	99.7
租房	Rent	103.5	103.8	101.5
自有住房	Private Housing	99.1	98.8	100.1
水电燃料	Water, Electricity and Fuels	105.7	106.5	103.9

9-4 商品零售价格分类指数（2003年）

Retail Price Indices by Category (2003)

(上年=100) (preceding year=100)

项　目	Item	全国 National Indices	城市 Urban Indices	农村 Rural Indices
商品零售价格总指数	**Retail Price Index**	**99.9**	**99.6**	**100.5**
食品类	**Food**	**103.4**	**103.2**	**103.7**
粮食	Grain	102.2	102.0	102.6
油脂	Oil or Fat	112.5	111.6	113.5
肉禽及其制品	Meat, Poultry and Their Products	103.0	102.5	103.9
蛋	Eggs	98.5	98.6	98.3
水产品	Aquatic Products	100.3	100.8	99.2
菜	Vegetables	116.3	116.4	116.1
调味品	Flavoring	100.3	100.0	100.7
食糖	Sugar	91.1	93.2	88.9
糖果	Candy	103.1	103.9	102.3
干鲜瓜果	Dried and Fresh, Melon and Fruits	102.2	102.4	101.8
糕点	Cake	99.8	99.8	99.8
奶及奶制品	Milk and Its Products	99.7	99.4	100.7
在外用膳食品	Outward Dinner Food	100.0	100.0	100.2
主食	Staple Food	100.7	100.7	100.7
炒菜	Fried Dishes	99.7	99.7	99.6
地方小吃	Local Snack	100.3	100.1	100.8
其它食品	Other Foods	99.2	99.3	99.1
饮料、烟酒	**Beverages, Tobacco and Liquor**	**99.9**	**99.8**	**99.9**
茶及饮料	Tea and Beverages	99.3	99.5	99.0
烟草	Tobacco	99.8	99.6	100.1
酒	Liquor	100.3	100.3	100.2
服装、鞋帽	**Garments, Shoes and Hats**	**97.5**	**97.0**	**98.5**
服装	Garments	97.5	96.9	98.6
鞋袜帽	Footgear and Hats	97.4	96.8	98.5
纺织品	**Textiles**	**99.3**	**98.9**	**99.8**
棉布	Cotton Cloth	99.9	98.7	101.1
棉花化纤混纺布	Blend Cloth	99.6	98.9	100.1
化纤布	Chemical Fiber Cloth	100.2	99.6	100.7
毛织品	Wool	98.5	98.8	98.0
丝织品	Silk	99.2	99.1	99.3
家用电器及音像器材	**Household Appliances, Music and Video Equipments**	**94.2**	**93.7**	**95.2**
文化办公用品	**Cultural and Office Appliances**	**95.8**	**95.3**	**97.0**
日用品	**Articles for Daily Use**	**98.5**	**98.2**	**98.9**
日用百货	General Merchandise for Daily Use	98.0	97.7	98.7
日用杂品	Grocery for Daily Use	99.7	100.0	99.3
体育娱乐用品	**Sports and Recreation Articles**	**98.1**	**97.6**	**99.1**
交通、通信用品	**Transportation and Communication Appliances**	**91.1**	**90.8**	**91.8**
家具	**Fornitures**	**97.8**	**97.6**	**98.4**
化妆品	**Cosmetics**	**98.9**	**98.8**	**99.3**
金银珠宝	**Gold, Silver and Jewelry**	**108.6**	**108.9**	**108.0**
中西药品及医疗保健用品	**Traditional Chinese and Western Medicines and Health Care Articles**	**98.4**	**98.2**	**98.8**
医疗器具及用品	Medical Apparatus and Article	100.6	100.5	100.7
中药材及中成药	Tradtional Chinese Medicinal Materials and Medicines	104.4	104.0	105.2
西药	Western Medicines	94.3	94.2	94.4
书报杂志及电子出版物	**Books, Newspapers, Magazines and Electronic Publications**	**100.3**	**100.4**	**100.2**
燃料	**Fuels**	**109.3**	**109.2**	**109.5**
建筑材料及五金电料	**Building Materials and Hardware**	**99.7**	**99.4**	**100.1**
建筑装潢材料	Building Decoration Materials	99.7	99.4	100.1
五金电料	Hardware	99.7	99.5	100.0

9-5 居民消费价格指数和商品零售价格指数

Consumer Price Indices and Retail Price Indices

(上年=100) (preceding year=100)

年份 地区	Year Region	居民消费价格指数 Consumer Price Index			商品零售价格指数 Retail Price Index		
		全省（区、市） Province	城市 Urban Areas	农村 Rural Areas	全省（区、市） Province	城市 Urban Areas	农村 Rural Areas
	1994	124.1	125.0	123.4	121.7	120.9	122.9
	1995	117.1	116.8	117.5	114.8	113.5	116.4
	1996	108.3	108.8	107.9	106.1	105.8	106.4
	1997	102.8	103.1	102.5	100.8	100.8	100.7
	1998	99.2	99.4	99.0	97.4	97.4	97.6
	1999	98.6	98.7	98.5	97.0	97.0	97.1
	2000	100.4	100.8	99.9	98.5	98.5	98.5
	2001	100.7	100.7	100.8	99.2	98.9	99.6
	2002	99.2	99.0	99.6	98.7	98.5	99.1
	2003	101.2	100.9	101.6	99.9	99.6	100.5
北京	Beijing	100.2	100.2		98.2	98.2	
天津	Tianjin	101.0	101.0		97.4	97.4	
河北	Hebei	102.2	102.3	102.0	100.2	100.1	100.4
山西	Shanxi	101.8	101.6	102.5	100.3	100.2	100.6
内蒙古	Inner Mongolia	102.2	101.5	103.5	99.6	99.6	99.6
辽宁	Liaoning	101.7	101.2	103.7	98.9	98.4	101.3
吉林	Jilin	101.2	101.1	101.5	100.5	100.4	101.1
黑龙江	Heilongjiang	100.9	100.8	101.2	99.7	99.2	101.1
上海	Shanghai	100.1	100.1		99.0	99.0	
江苏	Jiangsu	101.0	100.9	101.2	99.8	99.6	100.2
浙江	Zhejiang	101.9	100.5	102.9	99.6	99.4	99.9
安徽	Anhui	101.7	101.8	101.7	101.3	100.8	101.7
福建	Fujian	100.8	100.7	101.0	99.1	98.7	99.5
江西	Jiangxi	100.8	100.9	100.6	100.1	99.4	100.7
山东	Shandong	101.1	100.7	101.5	100.2	99.6	101.0
河南	Henan	101.6	101.7	101.4	101.3	101.2	101.4
湖北	Hubei	102.2	102.6	101.3	101.2	101.4	100.8
湖南	Hunan	102.4	101.4	104.1	100.6	100.1	101.1
广东	Guangdong	100.6	100.7	100.4	100.0	99.7	100.6
广西	Guangxi	101.1	100.9	101.3	100.2	99.6	100.8
海南	Hainan	100.1	99.4	100.9	100.4	100.2	100.8
重庆	Chongqing	100.6	100.6		99.5	99.5	
四川	Sichuan	101.7	101.9	100.9	100.1	100.1	100.1
贵州	Guizhou	101.2	100.9	102.0	100.0	99.2	101.1
云南	Yunnan	101.2	101.3	101.0	99.9	100.5	99.3
西藏	Tibet	100.9	100.8	100.9	99.4	99.1	100.0
陕西	Shaanxi	101.7	100.8	103.5	100.5	100.2	101.0
甘肃	Gansu	101.1	100.9	101.4	100.2	100.0	100.6
青海	Qinghai	102.0	101.8	102.5	100.8	101.2	100.1
宁夏	Ningxia	101.7	101.5	102.0	99.5	99.2	100.1
新疆	Xinjiang	100.4	100.5	100.2	99.2	99.1	99.5

9-6 各地区居民消费价格分类指数(2003年)
Consumer Price Indices by Category and by Region (2003)

(上年=100) (preceding year=100)

地　区	Region	总指数 General Index	食　品 Food	#粮食 Grain	#油脂 Oil or Fat	#肉禽及其制品 Meal, and Poultry	#蛋 Eggs	#水产品 Aquatic Products	#菜 Vegetables	#鲜菜 Fresh Vegetables
全　国	**National**	**101.2**	**103.4**	**102.3**	**112.6**	**103.3**	**98.6**	**100.3**	**117.7**	**120.5**
北　京	Beijing	100.2	103.2	99.1	114.1	100.9	96.9	102.5	139.8	145.4
天　津	Tianjin	101.0	103.3	102.1	111.5	102.2	102.0	111.0	121.6	123.8
河　北	Hebei	102.2	104.5	102.4	113.1	104.3	98.6	97.6	122.8	128.8
山　西	Shanxi	101.8	104.7	101.5	110.3	106.9	98.0	100.1	129.4	134.7
内蒙古	Inner Mongolia	102.2	102.8	100.2	105.3	101.8	94.1	94.4	125.1	131.6
辽　宁	Liaoning	101.7	105.3	99.0	125.5	103.5	96.5	101.5	128.0	131.7
吉　林	Jilin	101.2	104.0	98.5	113.3	102.2	95.1	100.7	125.1	127.5
黑龙江	Heilongjiang	100.9	103.3	99.9	112.6	101.7	97.1	96.6	124.9	129.1
上　海	Shanghai	100.1	101.3	100.8	106.1	101.7	101.0	105.6	99.2	98.9
江　苏	Jiangsu	101.0	103.3	102.1	112.8	104.5	99.2	97.7	117.9	120.2
浙　江	Zhejiang	101.9	102.8	103.2	112.9	105.3	98.4	100.2	107.4	107.9
安　徽	Anhui	101.7	106.0	104.5	116.8	108.1	100.6	99.5	126.3	128.7
福　建	Fujian	100.8	102.0	106.7	110.5	101.7	96.5	100.1	100.9	101.1
江　西	Jiangxi	100.8	102.9	103.6	115.4	103.5	99.8	97.8	112.8	116.6
山　东	Shandong	101.1	104.9	105.2	113.1	106.3	99.6	102.1	128.3	131.5
河　南	Henan	101.6	104.7	103.5	119.2	105.0	98.0	98.4	123.7	129.5
湖　北	Hubei	102.2	104.3	107.1	115.0	104.9	101.4	98.4	118.2	120.2
湖　南	Hunan	102.4	105.8	103.4	113.7	109.4	100.5	98.5	118.4	120.4
广　东	Guangdong	100.6	102.3	101.9	108.6	100.6	99.8	101.3	109.7	111.7
广　西	Guangxi	101.1	102.9	106.8	113.1	101.9	99.2	97.9	109.4	111.1
海　南	Hainan	100.1	102.9	101.8	103.6	103.2	98.0	101.7	105.9	106.6
重　庆	Chongqing	100.6	104.3	100.5	114.2	99.2	98.3	104.7	120.6	122.8
四　川	Sichuan	101.7	102.7	101.5	107.5	100.7	97.3	97.0	124.9	130.0
贵　州	Guizhou	101.2	103.2	103.6	108.9	102.1	99.8	96.5	114.0	116.2
云　南	Yunnan	101.2	101.7	100.5	107.9	100.3	95.6	99.6	106.0	106.5
西　藏	Tibet	100.9	100.5	98.0	96.1	102.1	95.8	94.5	100.3	100.5
陕　西	Shaanxi	101.7	105.2	105.0	110.3	103.9	98.1	100.5	133.0	137.0
甘　肃	Gansu	101.1	103.0	101.6	108.1	100.0	96.1	100.2	120.9	128.5
青　海	Qinghai	102.0	104.1	101.5	112.1	104.5	98.6	101.2	121.1	123.8
宁　夏	Ningxia	101.7	104.5	101.1	106.2	102.5	98.2	99.2	124.7	127.7
新　疆	Xinjiang	100.4	102.5	96.7	114.8	98.1	97.8	93.0	129.1	131.2

9-6 续表 1 continued

(上年=100) (preceding year=100)

地 区	Region	#干鲜瓜果 Dried and Fresh Melons and Fruits	#鲜 果 Fresh Fruits	#在外用膳食品 Outward Dinner	烟酒及用品 Tobacco, Liquor and Articles	#烟 草 Tobacco	#酒 Liquor	衣 着 Clothing	服 装 Garments	衣着材料 Clothing Material
全 国	**National**	**103.0**	**101.8**	**100.1**	**99.8**	**99.8**	**100.1**	**97.8**	**97.6**	**99.2**
北 京	Beijing	109.0	111.4	98.1	100.2	99.7	101.1	97.1	98.3	99.0
天 津	Tianjin	99.8	95.5	100.0	98.8	98.4	99.1	88.1	87.6	100.2
河 北	Hebei	98.0	95.1	99.8	100.1	99.7	100.5	97.8	98.0	98.4
山 西	Shanxi	94.9	92.4	101.7	100.7	100.3	102.4	97.5	97.2	98.5
内蒙古	Inner Mongolia	107.8	108.6	99.1	99.4	98.9	100.0	98.7	98.6	97.0
辽 宁	Liaoning	100.8	98.7	99.1	98.6	97.2	100.6	97.8	98.1	98.9
吉 林	Jilin	102.0	97.2	101.3	100.4	100.3	100.4	99.6	99.8	100.6
黑龙江	Heilongjiang	101.9	101.1	99.3	98.8	98.7	99.2	98.4	98.3	98.0
上 海	Shanghai	97.2	94.0	100.8	99.8	99.3	100.3	97.5	97.9	98.5
江 苏	Jiangsu	101.0	98.5	100.9	99.5	99.2	99.9	99.0	98.8	99.5
浙 江	Zhejiang	103.0	98.3	99.9	101.2	101.6	100.7	96.7	96.9	99.0
安 徽	Anhui	100.8	98.4	100.0	99.9	100.0	99.8	97.3	97.9	98.4
福 建	Fujian	108.8	109.1	99.7	100.4	100.9	99.8	96.5	96.3	98.8
江 西	Jiangxi	101.7	97.4	99.4	99.8	99.6	99.9	97.2	96.6	99.8
山 东	Shandong	96.7	95.5	100.7	99.6	98.8	100.3	96.9	96.1	100.2
河 南	Henan	96.7	92.7	100.7	100.3	100.6	100.1	98.0	97.6	100.0
湖 北	Hubei	102.3	101.4	100.6	99.8	99.8	100.0	101.0	101.1	100.3
湖 南	Hunan	111.2	114.2	99.4	99.8	100.5	98.1	98.8	99.0	99.4
广 东	Guangdong	106.9	107.8	99.9	101.4	101.7	100.9	97.7	97.6	100.6
广 西	Guangxi	105.1	104.9	99.5	100.0	98.5	102.3	98.5	96.3	98.0
海 南	Hainan	114.8	116.7	101.3	100.1	100.4	100.4	95.9	95.2	101.8
重 庆	Chongqing	122.6	130.5	101.3	98.2	97.0	101.1	94.2	93.9	103.1
四 川	Sichuan	104.8	103.3	100.2	100.2	99.5	101.3	98.5	98.5	100.5
贵 州	Guizhou	110.4	108.9	98.6	99.6	100.0	99.7	97.6	98.7	102.1
云 南	Yunnan	103.0	100.0	103.7	99.9	99.9	100.4	97.2	97.0	96.1
西 藏	Tibet	105.2	106.8	99.6	103.0	104.4	100.6	101.5	101.3	105.0
陕 西	Shaanxi	98.8	97.2	100.5	99.6	99.3	100.0	99.0	97.8	98.7
甘 肃	Gansu	99.7	98.4	101.1	99.8	101.1	99.4	98.4	98.3	101.9
青 海	Qinghai	108.7	110.2	99.7	99.0	98.8	98.9	101.9	102.2	97.0
宁 夏	Ningxia	109.2	109.5	100.0	101.1	101.6	99.3	99.4	98.6	98.0
新 疆	Xinjiang	104.8	104.5	100.3	99.8	99.7	99.8	99.2	99.2	99.5

9-6 续表 2 continued

(上年=100) (preceding year=100)

地　区	Region	鞋袜帽 Footgear and Hats	衣着加工服务费 Clothing Manufacturing Service	家庭设备用品及服务 Household Facilities and Articles	耐用消费品 Durable Consumer Goods	室内装饰品 Interior Decorations	床上用品 Bed Articles	家庭日用杂品 Daily Use Household Articles	家庭服务及加工维修服务费 Other Household Service and Manufacturing Upkeep
全　国	**National**	**97.7**	**100.1**	**97.4**	**95.8**	**98.8**	**98.4**	**98.3**	**101.1**
北　京	Beijing	93.3	109.0	97.7	95.8	98.6	99.8	97.5	107.6
天　津	Tianjin	86.0	100.0	96.5	95.9	100.6	90.7	95.0	103.0
河　北	Hebei	97.1	100.3	97.0	95.7	98.9	99.1	98.4	100.5
山　西	Shanxi	98.3	100.6	98.8	98.1	98.2	101.9	98.3	102.1
内蒙古	Inner Mongolia	99.5	96.5	98.1	98.4	98.4	96.0	97.5	100.2
辽　宁	Liaoning	96.8	99.1	96.4	94.0	97.1	100.9	97.6	100.6
吉　林	Jilin	98.9	99.5	97.9	96.8	99.3	99.0	97.6	99.9
黑龙江	Heilongjiang	98.7	97.2	97.0	95.4	98.8	99.3	97.7	97.7
上　海	Shanghai	95.9	100.1	98.4	98.9	99.1	99.6	96.3	98.9
江　苏	Jiangsu	98.8	105.4	96.6	94.7	99.1	99.4	97.7	100.9
浙　江	Zhejiang	95.8	100.6	96.9	94.6	97.8	95.8	99.9	100.9
安　徽	Anhui	95.6	100.0	97.7	95.9	99.3	98.1	98.5	101.2
福　建	Fujian	96.7	102.0	97.3	95.3	99.1	96.3	99.1	100.8
江　西	Jiangxi	98.1	103.2	97.5	95.0	95.9	99.3	99.1	102.5
山　东	Shandong	97.5	100.2	98.0	96.6	99.4	99.7	98.8	101.9
河　南	Henan	98.6	99.6	97.7	96.6	98.4	99.0	98.0	100.2
湖　北	Hubei	101.0	99.9	97.3	95.1	100.2	99.6	99.0	101.7
湖　南	Hunan	97.8	101.4	97.2	95.4	99.8	99.4	99.3	99.9
广　东	Guangdong	97.1	99.9	98.0	96.2	99.8	98.7	98.1	102.6
广　西	Guangxi	104.0	99.4	97.4	94.6	97.2	100.1	97.7	106.2
海　南	Hainan	97.1	101.3	98.1	98.7	98.4	97.9	98.8	93.6
重　庆	Chongqing	94.3	98.9	95.5	94.2	99.6	99.0	94.0	99.8
四　川	Sichuan	98.1	98.6	98.3	96.4	99.7	99.0	99.7	101.8
贵　州	Guizhou	94.6	102.5	97.2	96.3	99.4	93.8	98.6	99.8
云　南	Yunnan	97.5	100.8	98.4	97.9	100.6	98.5	99.0	96.8
西　藏	Tibet	100.9	101.1	101.4	100.5	99.9	102.8	103.4	100.3
陕　西	Shaanxi	102.0	99.7	97.1	95.3	96.8	98.8	99.2	99.5
甘　肃	Gansu	97.7	97.4	98.5	97.6	98.5	99.4	98.6	101.8
青　海	Qinghai	103.3	98.6	100.1	99.2	105.7	101.0	98.6	104.0
宁　夏	Ningxia	101.9	99.2	95.7	92.6	97.9	91.6	100.5	103.0
新　疆	Xinjiang	99.1	100.4	98.9	98.3	98.5	99.4	99.5	99.9

9-6 续表 3 continued

(上年=100) (preceding year=100)

地 区	Region	医疗保健和个人用品 Health Care & Personal Articles	医疗保健 Health Care	医疗器具及用品 Medical Appliances and Articles	中药材及中成药 Traditional Chinese Medicine	西药 Western Medicine	保健器具及用品 Health Care Appliances and Articles	医疗保健服务 Health Care Services	个人用品及服务 Personal Articles and Personal Service
全 国	**National**	**100.9**	**101.2**	**101.0**	**105.0**	**94.5**	**98.2**	**108.9**	**100.2**
北 京	Beijing	100.1	99.9	100.3	99.3	100.4	99.6	100.0	100.7
天 津	Tianjin	94.0	92.1	103.1	96.4	84.9	95.2	100.0	100.0
河 北	Hebei	106.0	108.8	92.8	108.2	94.5	98.3	144.9	100.5
山 西	Shanxi	99.0	97.9	100.3	103.4	93.0	97.8	101.3	101.3
内蒙古	Inner Mongolia	98.9	97.9	101.9	100.0	93.2	98.7	104.8	101.0
辽 宁	Liaoning	103.5	104.9	100.2	106.1	95.2	99.0	131.5	99.4
吉 林	Jilin	101.8	101.9	97.8	108.9	95.6	99.7	106.4	101.3
黑龙江	Heilongjiang	99.4	98.6	95.8	98.0	93.5	93.4	110.9	102.3
上 海	Shanghai	100.0	99.1	104.8	103.7	96.3	98.1	99.1	102.3
江 苏	Jiangsu	100.3	99.9	100.5	106.4	94.4	98.6	101.9	101.1
浙 江	Zhejiang	100.1	100.1	98.0	113.9	91.4	98.6	101.0	100.1
安 徽	Anhui	99.9	99.8	101.5	108.9	93.8	98.8	103.5	99.9
福 建	Fujian	98.7	98.2	106.8	104.9	91.3	97.9	100.2	99.6
江 西	Jiangxi	97.8	96.6	101.9	99.2	90.5	96.4	100.5	99.7
山 东	Shandong	100.3	101.0	102.7	109.8	95.6	98.8	101.9	98.8
河 南	Henan	102.5	103.2	110.3	110.8	96.5	100.4	104.2	100.9
湖 北	Hubei	99.6	99.4	96.0	104.5	95.2	102.5	100.5	100.2
湖 南	Hunan	105.9	108.6	92.8	101.4	93.9	99.4	143.2	100.2
广 东	Guangdong	100.4	100.6	102.5	104.1	97.5	98.4	102.0	100.1
广 西	Guangxi	102.8	103.9	102.0	106.6	97.1	98.0	114.2	100.8
海 南	Hainan	100.1	101.2	102.6	103.1	97.5	101.0	103.8	97.8
重 庆	Chongqing	99.3	99.2	104.7	97.2	97.7	98.7	104.3	99.8
四 川	Sichuan	102.9	103.8	100.1	107.8	98.0	97.1	111.2	100.8
贵 州	Guizhou	104.3	107.3	96.8	100.0	97.6	99.4	132.9	100.7
云 南	Yunnan	99.3	98.6	101.2	101.2	95.7	100.4	100.7	101.1
西 藏	Tibet	101.0	100.9	98.4	103.3	99.7	99.3	101.7	101.3
陕 西	Shaanxi	106.6	108.2	104.9	106.5	89.9	97.7	139.4	101.3
甘 肃	Gansu	101.9	101.6	105.5	107.8	97.2	101.2	102.2	102.4
青 海	Qinghai	104.8	106.4	94.0	100.8	96.1	98.7	138.9	100.5
宁 夏	Ningxia	100.2	99.3	99.7	103.9	95.9	99.5	100.7	103.2
新 疆	Xinjiang	94.8	92.3	100.9	100.2	82.7	91.8	101.6	100.2

9-6 续表 4 continued

(上年=100) (preceding year=100)

地 区	Region	化妆美容用品 Cosmetics	卫生用品 Health Articles	个人饰品 Individual Decorations	个人服务 Individual Service	交通和通信 Transportation and Communication	交通 Transportation	交通工具 Transportation Facility
全 国	**National**	**99.5**	**97.1**	**102.9**	**100.8**	**97.8**	**99.5**	**95.9**
北 京	Beijing	99.2	94.2	108.7	100.9	97.8	101.0	91.9
天 津	Tianjin	98.0	101.1	99.5	100.3	97.0	99.2	98.2
河 北	Hebei	99.7	97.1	101.2	101.6	98.1	99.4	97.2
山 西	Shanxi	97.2	97.0	105.8	101.5	98.2	99.2	96.9
内蒙古	Inner Mongolia	104.0	96.8	100.1	103.5	97.3	98.7	93.9
辽 宁	Liaoning	97.5	95.9	101.7	100.4	97.7	101.5	98.9
吉 林	Jilin	98.0	96.7	108.0	102.2	97.9	99.8	96.3
黑龙江	Heilongjiang	104.3	95.7	107.7	101.1	98.5	99.7	95.9
上 海	Shanghai	99.6	97.3	108.9	100.5	96.3	99.1	96.4
江 苏	Jiangsu	99.7	96.4	106.5	101.6	97.4	98.6	95.8
浙 江	Zhejiang	99.2	97.2	102.7	99.9	95.1	95.4	91.0
安 徽	Anhui	100.9	96.2	102.9	100.3	97.9	99.8	98.1
福 建	Fujian	98.2	97.2	100.8	101.0	97.3	98.8	95.8
江 西	Jiangxi	99.7	97.1	101.9	100.6	99.3	101.6	95.5
山 东	Shandong	99.3	95.5	99.3	100.1	98.8	100.0	97.6
河 南	Henan	99.9	99.1	104.4	100.5	99.2	100.2	96.2
湖 北	Hubei	99.9	98.7	100.9	101.7	98.5	100.7	99.0
湖 南	Hunan	99.1	99.0	103.9	100.0	98.0	100.5	97.0
广 东	Guangdong	99.7	98.0	102.8	100.5	97.9	99.0	96.1
广 西	Guangxi	102.0	96.6	101.8	103.6	96.4	97.9	92.7
海 南	Hainan	99.9	94.1	102.5	98.8	91.8	99.1	93.6
重 庆	Chongqing	96.3	97.2	108.3	100.0	98.7	100.2	97.5
四 川	Sichuan	100.0	98.8	102.3	101.3	99.8	102.1	98.6
贵 州	Guizhou	100.4	97.1	97.0	105.8	100.2	105.4	98.2
云 南	Yunnan	103.2	95.4	102.3	102.3	98.6	100.9	97.8
西 藏	Tibet	100.5	102.2	97.8	105.8	100.1	100.1	99.8
陕 西	Shaanxi	99.8	100.3	103.0	101.1	95.6	99.3	97.4
甘 肃	Gansu	100.0	99.4	102.4	105.6	98.7	102.7	97.4
青 海	Qinghai	99.3	98.7	103.5	99.3	98.7	99.9	99.1
宁 夏	Ningxia	98.5	97.3	111.8	105.2	98.1	100.6	96.7
新 疆	Xinjiang	98.8	96.4	102.1	104.8	99.1	100.2	97.4

9-6 续表 5 continued

(上年=100) (preceding year=100)

地 区	Region	车用燃料及零配件 Fuels and Parts	车辆使用及维修费 Using and Upkeep Fare	市内公共交通费 Incity Traffic Fare	城市间交通费 Intercity Traffic Fare	通信 Communication	通信工具 Communication Facility	通信服务 Communication Services
全 国	**National**	**108.3**	**98.9**	**100.6**	**101.4**	**96.1**	**82.1**	**99.4**
北 京	Beijing	104.6	112.2	100.0	101.0	95.5	79.2	99.8
天 津	Tianjin	104.4	100.6	100.0	96.1	95.3	73.7	99.6
河 北	Hebei	112.8	99.8	101.3	101.5	96.9	82.2	99.8
山 西	Shanxi	107.7	95.0	100.5	101.8	97.5	83.8	99.8
内蒙古	Inner Mongolia	116.3	98.2	99.3	101.5	95.6	86.3	98.3
辽 宁	Liaoning	106.2	102.6	101.0	103.3	95.4	73.2	99.8
吉 林	Jilin	105.5	101.8	100.3	99.5	95.9	78.0	98.6
黑龙江	Heilongjiang	103.6	101.7	100.0	100.2	97.5	80.0	99.8
上 海	Shanghai	105.8	98.5	100.0	99.8	93.7	70.4	100.0
江 苏	Jiangsu	107.2	95.3	101.6	102.9	96.2	76.5	100.0
浙 江	Zhejiang	105.3	94.9	100.3	100.2	94.8	81.4	99.9
安 徽	Anhui	106.4	98.2	100.9	99.6	96.2	82.2	99.5
福 建	Fujian	108.6	95.6	99.7	101.1	96.2	77.6	100.2
江 西	Jiangxi	107.7	101.2	102.1	105.8	97.2	83.1	99.9
山 东	Shandong	112.4	98.1	101.0	100.7	97.5	83.9	101.0
河 南	Henan	108.5	100.1	101.6	102.8	98.1	86.7	99.8
湖 北	Hubei	104.1	100.5	100.4	102.2	95.0	80.7	97.2
湖 南	Hunan	106.2	99.5	99.7	103.6	95.8	88.4	98.2
广 东	Guangdong	108.4	98.2	98.9	98.3	96.7	84.1	99.7
广 西	Guangxi	105.3	98.5	100.1	100.6	94.4	81.6	97.7
海 南	Hainan	107.0	98.6	100.0	100.2	82.2	84.2	81.7
重 庆	Chongqing	111.2	96.9	99.2	102.2	97.7	78.6	100.0
四 川	Sichuan	106.1	101.0	106.5	101.3	97.9	90.2	100.1
贵 州	Guizhou	107.8	102.8	102.1	125.5	94.8	91.7	95.7
云 南	Yunnan	109.8	96.5	98.7	106.2	97.1	89.7	99.2
西 藏	Tibet	102.0	100.7	96.3	99.9	100.4	87.3	103.0
陕 西	Shaanxi	107.1	99.1	99.5	99.9	91.8	81.5	93.9
甘 肃	Gansu	104.2	100.0	110.9	101.2	95.0	83.9	97.5
青 海	Qinghai	109.9	99.3	100.8	99.8	97.2	83.2	100.0
宁 夏	Ningxia	106.3	100.0	99.6	105.6	96.1	80.9	99.8
新 疆	Xinjiang	106.5	99.1	100.5	100.4	97.8	89.2	99.4

9-6 续表 6 continued

(上年=100) (preceding year=100)

地区	Region	娱乐教育文化 Recreation, Education & Culture	文娱用耐用消费品及服务 Durable Consumer Goods and Service for Recreational Use	教育 Education	教材及参考书 Teaching Materials and Reference Books	学杂托幼费 Tuition and Child Care	文化娱乐用品 Cultural and Recreational Articles	文化用品 Cultural Articles
全 国	**National**	**101.3**	**92.7**	**104.3**	**101.7**	**104.5**	**101.3**	**98.7**
北 京	Beijing	98.3	89.5	99.7	95.0	100.0	103.1	97.6
天 津	Tianjin	110.7	93.2	118.5	97.0	120.4	121.4	100.1
河 北	Hebei	100.7	92.1	102.5	102.8	102.5	101.5	99.2
山 西	Shanxi	100.4	94.0	102.4	107.7	102.0	98.9	96.7
内蒙古	Inner Mongolia	112.0	95.9	117.7	102.6	118.2	103.0	98.8
辽 宁	Liaoning	99.6	89.2	102.8	100.7	103.0	99.6	96.9
吉 林	Jilin	99.2	93.8	100.1	105.5	99.3	100.9	99.3
黑龙江	Heilongjiang	101.9	90.7	104.2	101.1	104.4	100.8	99.2
上 海	Shanghai	100.3	92.4	104.6	101.2	105.1	102.8	98.9
江 苏	Jiangsu	102.5	90.0	105.9	103.8	106.0	100.3	97.5
浙 江	Zhejiang	111.2	92.2	120.7	98.8	121.6	101.1	98.9
安 徽	Anhui	100.9	94.1	102.3	111.0	102.1	99.9	99.0
福 建	Fujian	104.3	92.3	110.0	109.5	110.0	100.7	99.1
江 西	Jiangxi	100.1	92.9	101.1	101.9	101.1	101.5	99.1
山 东	Shandong	100.1	95.3	101.3	103.0	101.3	100.4	99.2
河 南	Henan	99.4	94.8	100.4	100.6	100.3	100.7	99.5
湖 北	Hubei	102.7	92.5	105.3	104.8	105.3	102.1	99.5
湖 南	Hunan	100.4	95.2	102.5	101.2	102.5	101.1	98.0
广 东	Guangdong	98.0	92.1	100.2	101.4	100.0	100.8	99.5
广 西	Guangxi	100.6	87.8	104.8	95.2	105.5	100.9	99.0
海 南	Hainan	98.7	94.9	101.1	97.9	101.0	100.5	98.6
重 庆	Chongqing	99.6	93.0	102.2	103.9	102.0	98.8	99.4
四 川	Sichuan	100.7	95.0	102.8	103.1	102.7	100.9	99.8
贵 州	Guizhou	100.7	92.3	102.2	104.1	102.0	103.6	98.7
云 南	Yunnan	106.4	95.8	115.2	100.9	115.9	98.2	96.7
西 藏	Tibet	99.7	98.7	99.4	100.0	99.3	100.1	99.0
陕 西	Shaanxi	98.9	91.0	101.3	96.0	101.8	100.3	99.6
甘 肃	Gansu	100.5	92.9	101.5	101.9	101.5	100.9	97.8
青 海	Qinghai	100.9	89.1	105.0	99.6	105.1	98.1	99.0
宁 夏	Ningxia	105.6	89.8	117.1	104.9	119.4	99.1	97.6
新 疆	Xinjiang	99.1	95.8	100.6	100.0	100.6	100.7	99.5

9-6 续表 7 continued

(上年=100) (preceding year=100)

地区	Region	书报杂志 Newspapers and Magazines	文娱费 Cultural and Recreation	旅游及外出 Touring and Outgoing	居住 Residence	建房及装修材料 Building Decoration Materials	租房 Rent	自有住房 Private Housing	水电燃料 Water, Electricity and Fuels
全国	**National**	**100.4**	**104.6**	**95.4**	**102.1**	**99.5**	**103.5**	**99.1**	**105.7**
北京	Beijing	100.0	109.4	95.9	101.6	92.5	100.0	97.8	109.2
天津	Tianjin	102.0	164.6	83.5	101.7	98.8	104.6	99.0	102.7
河北	Hebei	100.5	108.3	96.5	104.5	100.1	108.8	99.5	108.9
山西	Shanxi	100.0	100.4	96.8	106.7	98.4	100.5	99.0	116.1
内蒙古	Inner Mongolia	102.0	109.1	100.0	99.7	97.9	100.6	98.2	101.5
辽宁	Liaoning	100.3	102.4	94.4	101.7	95.8	100.3	98.3	107.8
吉林	Jilin	99.3	103.9	97.8	100.4	98.1	105.2	97.0	102.4
黑龙江	Heilongjiang	98.7	103.6	100.5	101.2	100.4	101.1	97.4	102.5
上海	Shanghai	100.2	104.8	91.0	101.1	100.9	100.0	98.4	102.7
江苏	Jiangsu	100.4	103.9	97.0	101.0	98.7	107.5	98.9	104.6
浙江	Zhejiang	101.6	102.8	92.2	101.2	100.9	104.2	99.2	102.1
安徽	Anhui	100.5	100.6	93.9	100.7	99.8	104.8	98.6	102.7
福建	Fujian	100.4	102.3	96.8	102.8	98.9	100.6	98.8	107.6
江西	Jiangxi	101.2	104.7	95.7	102.1	100.9	102.7	100.0	105.1
山东	Shandong	100.8	101.7	97.8	101.0	99.1	101.0	98.7	104.2
河南	Henan	100.4	103.3	97.5	102.3	99.9	103.0	98.7	107.0
湖北	Hubei	100.0	105.4	98.9	103.5	99.5	103.5	100.7	108.6
湖南	Hunan	99.2	105.6	95.2	103.1	100.1	100.5	101.0	108.1
广东	Guangdong	101.5	101.5	94.7	103.1	101.4	105.3	100.0	104.7
广西	Guangxi	103.6	100.7	98.1	102.3	99.9	108.7	99.4	105.0
海南	Hainan	100.4	101.6	87.6	101.7	100.8	118.1	98.7	102.5
重庆	Chongqing	97.3	99.3	98.7	102.2	100.0	99.9	98.5	106.1
四川	Sichuan	100.4	102.3	93.9	102.9	99.0	103.1	99.8	109.4
贵州	Guizhou	100.8	110.2	96.5	101.0	98.2	100.0	98.1	104.4
云南	Yunnan	100.3	98.4	102.9	101.9	101.0	101.1	98.0	105.3
西藏	Tibet	99.7	101.8	101.4	98.8	99.1	99.5	98.6	98.5
陕西	Shaanxi	99.6	101.6	90.0	101.0	99.0	100.5	97.5	107.8
甘肃	Gansu	100.4	104.7	107.0	101.5	97.6	100.1	98.7	107.0
青海	Qinghai	99.9	97.2	99.5	99.9	96.3	100.2	98.7	104.5
宁夏	Ningxia	100.2	100.4	99.5	100.0	94.3	101.7	101.3	106.0
新疆	Xinjiang	100.6	101.9	93.3	104.2	101.1	98.7	98.9	112.3

9-7 商品零售价格分类指数

Retail Price Indices by Category of Commodities

(上年=100) (preceding year=100)

年份 地区	Year Region	总指数 General Index	食品 Food	#粮食 Grain	#油脂 Oil or Fat	#肉禽及其制品 Meat, Poultry and Their Products	#蛋 Eggs	#水产品 Aquatic Products	#菜 Vegetables	#干鲜瓜果 Fresh and Dried Fruits
	1994	121.7	135.2	148.7	161.4			120.7		
	1995	114.8	124.7	134.4	116.3			114.2		
	1996	106.1	107.7	107.5	92.1			105.6		
	1997	100.8	99.8	92.1	101.6			101.2		
	1998	97.4	96.8	96.9	100.7			94.2		
	1999	97.0	95.8	96.4	94.4			93.6		
	2000	98.5	97.5	90.1	86.2			102.7		
	2001	99.2	100.6	101.5	89.3			96.3		
	2002	98.7	99.9	98.6	100.1			96.2		
	2003	99.9	103.4	102.2	112.5	103.0	98.5	100.3	116.3	102.2
北京	Beijing	98.2	103.0	99.1	114.1	100.8	97.0	102.6	137.1	108.2
天津	Tianjin	97.4	103.7	102.1	111.5	102.0	102.1	111.0	123.7	100.3
河北	Hebei	100.2	103.9	102.4	113.8	104.3	96.2	99.3	120.4	96.7
山西	Shanxi	100.3	105.0	101.9	111.1	106.6	98.3	100.0	128.8	95.8
内蒙古	Inner Mongolia	99.6	102.5	100.2	104.2	101.8	95.8	96.2	118.3	105.9
辽宁	Liaoning	98.9	104.0	98.2	123.0	102.0	96.1	101.0	122.2	102.6
吉林	Jilin	100.5	103.4	99.1	111.7	102.2	95.1	100.5	119.3	97.4
黑龙江	Heilongjiang	99.7	103.6	99.5	115.0	101.6	96.9	96.4	124.5	100.0
上海	Shanghai	99.0	101.5	100.5	106.8	101.7	101.0	103.9	101.5	97.6
江苏	Jiangsu	99.8	103.5	102.0	112.7	103.9	99.0	98.9	117.0	102.6
浙江	Zhejiang	99.6	102.7	102.4	111.7	105.5	99.1	99.4	109.6	103.2
安徽	Anhui	101.3	106.0	100.5	115.3	107.6	100.8	99.4	129.3	102.3
福建	Fujian	99.1	101.9	106.2	109.2	101.5	96.7	100.6	101.3	109.2
江西	Jiangxi	100.1	103.5	104.0	112.5	105.0	99.8	97.1	111.4	100.3
山东	Shandong	100.2	105.6	105.6	115.5	106.1	100.4	101.0	125.9	95.8
河南	Henan	101.3	105.2	104.8	118.6	105.0	97.6	97.5	122.1	99.8
湖北	Hubei	101.2	104.7	106.9	113.0	105.5	101.2	98.3	116.1	99.8
湖南	Hunan	100.6	104.2	102.2	110.5	106.0	99.8	97.9	117.2	108.2
广东	Guangdong	100.0	102.0	101.1	108.9	100.6	99.4	100.8	108.2	105.9
广西	Guangxi	100.2	103.1	107.1	111.1	102.2	99.0	98.0	109.8	107.2
海南	Hainan	100.4	102.9	102.2	103.0	103.0	98.9	101.8	108.4	111.2
重庆	Chongqing	99.5	104.4	100.5	114.2	99.2	98.3	104.6	120.7	122.6
四川	Sichuan	100.1	102.7	101.2	107.9	100.4	97.1	97.4	124.0	103.5
贵州	Guizhou	100.0	103.5	103.9	108.2	102.6	98.9	97.0	113.4	112.1
云南	Yunnan	99.9	101.9	100.7	108.2	100.3	95.2	98.9	104.5	103.3
西藏	Tibet	99.4	101.9	98.8	97.8	103.3	102.1	97.8	107.2	103.8
陕西	Shaanxi	100.5	105.2	104.9	110.3	104.5	98.0	100.4	129.9	99.1
甘肃	Gansu	100.2	102.5	101.2	108.1	100.1	96.5	98.7	117.2	97.0
青海	Qinghai	100.8	104.0	101.7	112.5	103.6	98.1	100.5	120.3	106.6
宁夏	Ningxia	99.5	104.3	101.1	106.1	102.2	97.6	99.1	122.8	109.8
新疆	Xinjiang	99.2	99.9	97.1	119.1	96.5	96.2	92.8	103.2	101.3

9-7 续表 1 continued

(上年=100) (preceding year=100)

年 份 地 区	Year Region	饮料烟酒 Beverages, Tobacco and Liquor	服装鞋帽 Clothing, Shoes and Hats	纺织品 Textiles	家用电器及音像器材 Household Appliances, Music and Video Equipments	文化办公用品 Cultural and Office Appliances	日用品 Articles for Daily Use	体育娱乐用品 Sports and Recreation Articles	交通、通信用品 Transportation and Communication Appliances
	1994	111.3	119.6	114.7			113.9		
	1995	107.8	116.8	115.4			109.7		
	1996	105.1	108.5	106.4			105.3		
	1997	101.2	103.5	101.9			102.3		
	1998	98.8	99.3	99.1			99.0		
	1999	97.3	97.3	98.0			97.9		
	2000	98.0	99.2	98.6			98.1		
	2001	99.5	98.9	99.1			98.3		
	2002	99.9	97.9	99.4			98.7		
	2003	99.9	97.5	99.3	94.2	95.8	98.5	98.1	91.1
北 京	Beijing	100.7	97.1	99.5	94.6	93.0	93.4	98.7	92.7
天 津	Tianjin	98.8	87.4	95.3	90.9	98.1	96.8	99.2	90.0
河 北	Hebei	100.2	97.8	99.0	94.0	98.0	98.6	98.0	90.9
山 西	Shanxi	100.4	97.6	99.7	94.7	96.2	98.0	98.5	90.2
内蒙古	Inner Mongolia	99.6	98.9	96.9	97.0	98.7	98.7	100.0	92.3
辽 宁	Liaoning	98.4	95.3	99.9	90.1	95.7	96.0	94.4	87.8
吉 林	Jilin	100.3	99.2	100.4	94.7	97.9	99.4	99.4	89.3
黑龙江	Heilongjiang	99.2	98.8	98.5	93.0	96.3	98.2	99.2	88.0
上 海	Shanghai	99.5	96.7	99.8	95.8	93.7	99.1	97.4	91.2
江 苏	Jiangsu	99.7	99.5	99.6	93.2	93.6	98.7	96.4	87.3
浙 江	Zhejiang	100.6	96.6	97.6	94.1	95.7	98.3	98.3	92.4
安 徽	Anhui	99.7	98.3	99.0	95.0	95.5	99.5	100.4	92.9
福 建	Fujian	100.5	96.2	97.2	92.9	94.5	98.8	98.5	90.4
江 西	Jiangxi	99.3	96.8	99.7	94.6	97.3	98.9	98.4	90.9
山 东	Shandong	99.8	96.8	99.6	94.9	94.4	98.7	98.2	91.6
河 南	Henan	99.8	98.2	100.0	95.7	97.3	98.1	99.3	93.4
湖 北	Hubei	99.5	99.0	100.9	95.4	99.3	99.7	97.9	89.3
湖 南	Hunan	99.5	99.4	99.3	94.6	98.0	99.4	98.9	93.4
广 东	Guangdong	100.6	97.1	99.0	94.0	94.8	99.1	98.3	90.2
广 西	Guangxi	99.6	99.6	98.9	91.8	93.4	98.1	99.0	88.9
海 南	Hainan	99.4	95.7	99.4	97.4	99.1	99.0	99.8	92.8
重 庆	Chongqing	98.6	94.0	100.5	93.5	98.2	94.9	98.9	90.8
四 川	Sichuan	100.3	98.6	100.0	95.2	95.0	99.6	98.6	94.1
贵 州	Guizhou	99.9	98.8	94.6	95.4	99.1	98.9	98.6	92.4
云 南	Yunnan	98.8	96.6	96.5	95.7	97.2	100.4	98.0	93.7
西 藏	Tibet	103.8	102.0	101.8	98.1	97.8	98.6	95.8	89.7
陕 西	Shaanxi	99.8	99.8	100.8	93.0	98.5	98.3	97.1	92.4
甘 肃	Gansu	100.6	98.1	100.4	96.7	97.6	99.1	98.8	89.8
青 海	Qinghai	99.2	102.0	99.0	94.6	93.6	99.6	97.4	94.7
宁 夏	Ningxia	100.2	99.5	94.4	91.3	94.3	98.0	97.5	89.4
新 疆	Xinjiang	99.1	99.7	99.5	97.8	98.9	99.3	100.0	94.9

9-7 续表 2 continued

(上年=100) (preceding year=100)

年 份 地 区	Year Region	家 具 Fornitures	化妆品 Cosmetics	金银珠宝 Gold, Silver and Jewelry	中西药品及医疗保健用品 Traditional Chinese and Western Medicines and Health Care Articles	书报杂志及电子出版物 Books, Newspapers, Magazines and Electronic Publications	燃料 Fuels	建筑材料及五金电料 Building Materials and Hardware
	1994		116.4				115.1	
	1995		109.9				107.4	
	1996		105.0				105.0	
	1997		102.3				107.3	
	1998		100.5				96.1	
	1999		99.6				100.4	
	2000		98.9				117.7	
	2001		98.8				102.4	
	2002		98.4				102.0	
	2003	97.8	98.9	108.6	98.4	100.3	109.3	99.7
北 京	Beijing	97.5	98.6	108.6	99.9	97.2	109.9	94.2
天 津	Tianjin	99.2	99.2	115.5	90.1	99.5	109.9	99.1
河 北	Hebei	98.6	100.6	109.7	98.6	101.6	108.6	99.7
山 西	Shanxi	99.4	96.7	107.5	97.1	103.3	114.8	98.8
内蒙古	Inner Mongolia	99.3	98.9	108.6	97.5	101.2	104.8	98.2
辽 宁	Liaoning	94.8	96.9	108.8	98.6	99.0	108.3	94.9
吉 林	Jilin	95.9	98.2	112.8	99.8	101.4	106.7	98.6
黑龙江	Heilongjiang	97.3	97.3	107.6	94.7	100.1	106.2	99.6
上 海	Shanghai	99.5	100.4	106.5	98.3	98.3	108.6	100.8
江 苏	Jiangsu	98.2	99.4	112.5	100.8	99.7	110.0	99.3
浙 江	Zhejiang	97.1	99.2	109.3	97.4	99.8	108.8	100.6
安 徽	Anhui	97.6	99.0	107.1	98.9	102.6	109.3	99.4
福 建	Fujian	98.8	97.5	103.8	98.3	103.3	109.6	99.9
江 西	Jiangxi	97.9	98.2	108.8	94.4	101.1	108.7	101.5
山 东	Shandong	96.6	98.2	104.9	99.1	101.0	108.9	99.2
河 南	Henan	97.8	99.6	109.3	104.0	100.3	108.9	100.4
湖 北	Hubei	99.4	99.0	110.0	99.4	101.6	108.6	101.4
湖 南	Hunan	98.1	99.9	110.0	94.0	99.5	109.2	100.9
广 东	Guangdong	98.7	99.6	108.9	100.4	100.4	113.1	101.3
广 西	Guangxi	99.1	98.9	105.8	101.5	99.6	112.5	100.1
海 南	Hainan	97.9	96.5	107.8	98.1	99.4	109.5	100.6
重 庆	Chongqing	98.2	97.1	110.5	97.8	100.2	105.3	100.1
四 川	Sichuan	99.0	99.3	108.3	101.2	102.2	104.3	99.2
贵 州	Guizhou	95.9	101.0	106.4	98.0	101.3	107.6	98.6
云 南	Yunnan	99.9	100.2	108.4	98.0	98.4	108.3	99.9
西 藏	Tibet	96.6	96.7	98.5	99.7	99.6	95.0	100.0
陕 西	Shaanxi	93.9	99.7	106.8	95.7	97.3	109.9	99.9
甘 肃	Gansu	97.5	99.7	106.1	102.0	99.3	107.2	98.0
青 海	Qinghai	98.0	100.0	101.5	97.3	100.2	107.6	97.4
宁 夏	Ningxia	92.6	100.0	111.6	98.2	100.9	106.3	97.8
新 疆	Xinjiang	98.0	99.7	104.4	93.7	99.4	105.7	97.6

9-8 各地区农业生产资料价格分类指数（2003年）

Price Indices of Agricultural Means of Production by Category and by Region (2003)

(上年=100) (preceding year=100)

地区	Region	总指数 General Index	小农具 Small Farm Tools	饲料 Forage	产品畜 Production Livestocks	役畜 Labour Livestocks	半机械化农具 Semi-mechanized Farm Tools
全国平均	**National**	**101.4**	**99.3**	**102.0**	**102.9**	**106.6**	**99.4**
河北	Hebei	99.8	99.8	101.6	101.3	103.9	94.8
山西	Shanxi	98.4	100.5	86.9	109.0	103.1	99.6
内蒙古	Inner Mongolia	101.2	96.5	95.4	99.5	108.8	98.3
辽宁	Liaoning	98.4	74.9	101.4	105.4	121.9	107.7
吉林	Jilin	101.0	101.0	100.8	99.2	110.9	94.7
黑龙江	Heilongjiang	101.8	108.1	100.7	95.3	104.7	98.9
江苏	Jiangsu	101.9	97.0	105.3	105.3	115.6	99.4
浙江	Zhejiang	102.9	101.5	103.3	112.3	103.6	100.8
安徽	Anhui	100.2	95.8	100.5	97.9	111.4	99.6
福建	Fujian	101.8	102.5	101.8	103.3	108.5	101.7
江西	Jiangxi	102.5	101.1	104.0	108.0	109.7	98.8
山东	Shandong	102.4	100.7	104.6	104.1	104.3	101.0
河南	Henan	101.9	102.0	103.4	104.0	101.5	96.1
湖北	Hubei	100.8	95.8	106.0	99.3	103.4	100.5
湖南	Hunan	102.6	103.1	101.0	110.2	109.5	102.1
广东	Guangdong	99.6	97.2	99.1	105.0	101.8	100.5
广西	Guangxi	102.4	100.4	98.8	102.7	103.4	99.8
海南	Hainan	104.8	96.6	115.9	93.5	103.2	98.5
四川	Sichuan	100.8	102.5	103.6	94.0	105.7	99.4
贵州	Guizhou	104.1	99.1	100.8	107.4	107.9	95.2
云南	Yunnan	101.9	95.8	106.0	97.3	109.1	98.4
西藏	Tibet	102.8	100.0	99.9	96.0	99.9	100.0
陕西	Shaanxi	102.3	99.1	104.8	102.9	114.6	99.4
甘肃	Gansu	101.8	98.9	98.0	97.2	109.6	101.0
青海	Qinghai	101.1	97.4	99.9	95.7	100.0	100.9
宁夏	Ningxia	99.4	100.1	92.7	94.4	110.4	101.0
新疆	Xinjiang	101.1	105.4	100.6	105.9	104.2	98.8

9-8 续表 continued

(上年=100) (preceding year=100)

地区	Region	机械化农具 Mechnized Farm Machinery	化学肥料 Chemical Fertilizer	农药及农药械 Pesticide and Its Appliances	农用机油 Oil for Farm Machinery	其他农业生产资料 Other Agricultural Means of Production
全国平均	**National**	**98.5**	**101.6**	**99.9**	**107.8**	**97.0**
河北	Hebei	97.8	100.8	98.5	109.7	85.9
山西	Shanxi	98.4	100.3	95.3	106.4	86.1
内蒙古	Inner Mongolia	102.5	104.7	97.6	104.0	96.2
辽宁	Liaoning	98.6	96.4	99.6	100.8	94.4
吉林	Jilin	93.3	104.1	98.0	111.3	89.5
黑龙江	Heilongjiang	92.0	103.3	103.4	104.9	107.2
江苏	Jiangsu	100.3	101.6	100.7	109.9	96.6
浙江	Zhejiang	100.5	102.3	99.1	107.2	101.4
安徽	Anhui	101.0	101.3	98.6	108.8	91.8
福建	Fujian	98.8	102.4	98.4	110.6	98.0
江西	Jiangxi	99.5	102.6	99.9	108.2	99.6
山东	Shandong	98.8	101.9	100.7	111.4	97.2
河南	Henan	99.3	102.4	98.6	111.7	96.0
湖北	Hubei	97.5	100.1	99.3	109.0	102.1
湖南	Hunan	99.5	100.5	101.8	104.2	107.0
广东	Guangdong	97.6	97.4	100.6	106.1	104.4
广西	Guangxi	98.4	101.1	109.8	111.8	105.6
海南	Hainan	100.0	108.3	101.5	114.7	97.8
四川	Sichuan	97.6	103.1	99.9	102.7	93.9
贵州	Guizhou	89.3	107.4	104.6	114.0	98.4
云南	Yunnan	99.0	104.2	95.9	97.6	99.8
西藏	Tibet	100.8	119.7	96.8	101.1	99.8
陕西	Shaanxi	99.5	102.9	101.0	107.6	92.5
甘肃	Gansu	100.0	99.4	100.6	109.5	105.2
青海	Qinghai	96.5	101.8	101.9	108.3	100.5
宁夏	Ningxia	97.9	99.6	99.9	116.9	94.4
新疆	Xinjiang	97.6	102.9	97.6	101.4	98.8

9-9 农产品生产价格指数

Price Indices of Farm Produce

(上年＝100) (preceding year=100)

指　标	Item	2002	2003
农产品生产价格总指数	**General Price Index of Farm Produce**	**99.7**	**104.4**
农业产品	**Agriculture Produce**	**100.0**	**107.4**
谷物	Cereal	95.8	102.3
#小麦	Wheat	98.1	103.0
稻谷	Rice	97.2	99.9
玉米	Corn	91.5	104.6
大豆	Beans	98.9	120.6
油料	Oil-bearing Crops	104.8	119.4
棉花	Cotton	103.4	135.3
糖料	Sugar	86.0	90.5
蔬菜	Vegetable	95.1	110.4
水果	Fruit	109.9	102.0
林业产品	**Forestry Produce**	**98.3**	**107.0**
牧业产品	**Animal Husbandry Produce**	**100.2**	**101.8**
猪（毛重）	Pig (gross weight)	98.0	102.9
牛（毛重）	Cattle and Buffaloes (gross weight)	91.4	101.7
羊（毛重）	Sheep and Goats (gross weight)	140.0	96.3
家禽（毛重）	Poultry (gross weight)	106.1	101.0
蛋类	Eggs	102.8	101.1
奶类	Milk	99.7	103.7
渔业产品	**Fishing Produce**	**95.9**	**100.3**
海水鱼类	Seawater Fish	104.9	104.0
淡水鱼类	Freshwater Fish	93.1	98.7

9-10 各地区工业品出厂价格指数

Ex-Factory Price Indices of Industrial Products by Region

(上年=100) (preceding year=100)

地 区	Region	1997	1998	1999	2000	2001	2002	2003
全 国	**National**	**99.7**	**95.9**	**97.6**	**102.8**	**98.7**	**97.8**	**102.3**
北 京	Beijing	100.6	95.1	97.8	102.5	99.4	96.6	101.5
天 津	Tianjin	98.3	94.7	96.4	102.8	95.9	95.9	102.5
河 北	Hebei	98.8	94.4	95.9	105.3	99.9	99.4	107.1
山 西	Shanxi	102.2	97.5	95.3	100.9	100.3	103.6	112.2
内蒙古	Inner Mongolia	101.5	98.0	100.4	102.8	100.1	99.3	103.2
辽 宁	Liaoning	100.1	95.8	102.0	108.8	98.6	97.8	103.6
吉 林	Jilin	101.4	96.9	100.1	105.1	100.3	98.6	102.5
黑龙江	Heilongjiang	102.3	97.7	107.4	122.9	95.9	97.8	111.9
上 海	Shanghai	98.9	93.9	97.6	102.5	96.7	96.4	101.4
江 苏	Jiangsu	97.9	94.5	96.1	101.1	99.1	97.6	102.3
浙 江	Zhejiang	99.2	96.0	96.8	101.1	98.3	96.9	100.6
安 徽	Anhui	99.4	96.4	92.9	98.9	98.6	99.8	103.5
福 建	Fujian	100.3	95.7	96.6	100.5	98.1	97.2	100.7
江 西	Jiangxi	101.7	98.4	96.1	101.0	98.1	98.5	104.0
山 东	Shandong	101.1	96.0	97.2	105.9	99.1	98.8	103.5
河 南	Henan	100.6	95.3	95.4	104.0	100.5	98.6	105.0
湖 北	Hubei	98.6	96.2	97.8	101.7	99.0	98.2	103.5
湖 南	Hunan	99.2	95.9	98.5	102.9	99.8	99.2	102.6
广 东	Guangdong	100.1	94.8	97.7	103.4	98.5	96.5	99.3
广 西	Guangxi	97.7	95.4	95.6	105.5	106.3	95.6	102.8
海 南	Hainan						98.7	99.5
重 庆	Chongqing		94.6	97.7	98.6	98.1	97.6	100.6
四 川	Sichuan	101.2	97.3	97.0	98.1	100.4	97.7	100.5
贵 州	Guizhou	101.2	98.2	99.7	100.4	102.2	98.9	103.4
云 南	Yunnan	100.7	97.2	98.2	101.2	99.9	98.2	101.4
西 藏	Tibet							
陕 西	Shaanxi	103.7	96.6	97.9	101.5	100.4	100.7	105.7
甘 肃	Gansu	104.9	95.2	98.1	107.2	98.5	97.9	110.0
青 海	Qinghai	104.3	100.7	102.8	108.1	93.7	97.6	105.5
宁 夏	Ningxia	100.3	97.7	98.4	103.6	100.3	99.7	103.9
新 疆	Xinjiang	104.9	95.8	100.2	129.4	96.3	97.3	115.1

9-11 按行业分工业品出厂价格指数
Ex-Factory Price Indices of Industrial Products by Sector

(上年=100) (preceding year=100)

年份 Year	总指数 General Index	冶金工业 Metallurgical Industry	电力工业 Power Industry	煤炭工业 Coal Industry	石油工业 Petroleum Industry	化学工业 Chemical Industry	机械工业 Machine Building Industry	建筑材料工业 Building Materials Industry
1980	100.5	106.2	98.4	106.4	102.1	98.2	97.5	102.5
1985	108.7	114.3	103.4	117.6	107.2	102.9	111.8	115.4
1989								
1990	104.1	110.3	107.4	106.2	107.1	101.6	102.8	99.6
1991	106.2	114.2	116.9	113.1	118.8	102.4	102.8	106.1
1992	106.8	114.2	108.8	116.1	115.3	102.7	106.6	111.1
1993	124.0	157.7	135.9	139.7	171.3	108.3	119.7	142.8
1994	119.5	106.8	139.5	122.2	148.7	115.4	109.5	107.6
1995	114.9	105.5	109.5	111.3	121.2	126.2	106.3	106.4
1996	102.9	97.7	113.1	113.7	104.6	103.4	101.6	104.3
1997	99.7	97.3	114.0	108.0	107.4	95.5	98.1	99.6
1998	95.9	93.1	105.5	96.6	93.0	92.9	97.0	96.6
1999	97.6	95.8	100.9	94.8	109.6	96.5	97.0	97.7
2000	102.8	103.3	102.4	98.1	144.3	101.0	97.4	99.6
2001	98.7	98.6	102.3	106.5	99.1	97.1	96.8	99.0
2002	97.8	97.6	100.8	111.6	95.2	97.6	96.2	97.8
2003	102.3	106.8	100.9	107.0	115.6	102.3	97.0	99.6

9-11 续表 continued

(上年=100) (preceding year=100)

年份 Year	森林工业 Timber Industry	食品工业 Food Industry	纺织工业 Textile Industry	缝纫工业 Tailoring Industry	皮革工业 Leather Industry	造纸工业 Paper Industry	文教艺术用品工业 Cultural, Educational & Handicrafts Articles
1980	104.5	101.2	101.6	100.8	102.4	100.5	101.6
1985	114.9	105.5	104.3	105.1	112.1	113.7	103.2
1989							
1990	94.6	101.0	107.2	109.1	106.3	102.3	107.3
1991	100.4	103.3	104.1	109.0	109.0	102.9	105.8
1992	105.9	106.2	99.3	100.8	112.8	102.7	102.3
1993	131.8	113.5	103.8	117.9	111.8	108.9	110.6
1994	106.9	123.4	136.8	116.1	121.9	106.6	109.1
1995	99.5	123.2	117.3	116.5	121.7	144.5	111.4
1996	98.2	104.2	96.0	108.2	111.3	116.1	101.5
1997	99.3	99.6	98.0	103.9	98.3	94.5	100.0
1998	95.4	98.6	94.1	97.7	98.3	94.1	94.4
1999	100.1	96.7	96.0	98.0	96.8	95.9	93.6
2000	99.2	95.8	104.7	99.4	100.2	99.9	99.2
2001	99.6	100.5	98.7	99.2	100.8	99.7	97.9
2002	98.6	99.6	94.7	98.7	99.3	97.9	97.4
2003	99.3	101.1	102.2	99.9	99.8	98.7	98.6

9-12 工业品出厂价格分类指数

Ex-Factory Price Indices of Industrial Products

(上年=100) (preceding year=100)

类 别	Item	1997	1998	1999	2000	2001	2002	2003
全部工业品	**Total Industry Products**	**99.7**	**95.9**	**97.6**	**102.8**	**98.7**	**97.8**	**102.3**
生产资料	**Means of Production**	**99.7**	**95.4**	**98.3**	**105.1**	**98.8**	**97.7**	**103.6**
采掘工业	Mining & Quarrying Industry	105.5	98.4	104.5	124.9	100.1	101.9	113.3
原材料工业	Raw Materials Industry	100.0	93.4	98.2	108.4	99.7	98.0	106.7
加工工业	Manufacturing Industry	98.1	96.8	97.1	98.6	98.1	96.9	100.2
生活资料	**Consumer Goods**	**99.6**	**96.9**	**96.4**	**97.8**	**98.5**	**97.9**	**98.9**
食品类	Food	100.8	98.9	97.4	96.0	100.5	99.7	100.9
衣着类	Clothing	101.1	96.2	96.1	100.6	99.0	98.8	99.8
一般日用品	Articles for Daily Use	98.3	96.7	96.0	98.0	98.3	97.9	99.5
耐用消费品	Durable Consumer Goods	94.9	94.0	95.6	96.4	95.3	94.7	95.6

9-13 原材料、燃料、动力购进价格指数

Purchasing Price Indices of Raw Material, Fuel and Power

(上年=100) (preceding year=100)

年 份 Year	总指数 General Index	燃料、动力类 Fuel and Power	黑色金属材料类 Ferrous Metals	有色金属材料类 Nonferrous Metals	化工原料类 Raw Chemical Materials	木材及纸浆类 Timber and Paper Pulp	建材类 Building Materials	农副产品类 Agricultural Products	纺织原料类 Textile Materials
1989	126.4	124.7	130.3	127.6	124.4	111.4	122.7	128.9	128.5
1990	105.6	110.7	103.9	97.2	95.6	99.4	115.2	107.8	107.4
1991	109.1	112.9	112.5	101.2	99.8	105.6	101.2	106.8	108.9
1992	111.0	116.4	114.5	112.4	102.6	102.0	118.8	103.4	100.5
1993	135.1	136.7	174.1	115.8	114.3	128.6	140.9	112.2	107.1
1994	118.2	118.0	103.8	110.7	111.7	115.1	114.3	148.3	139.6
1995	115.3	108.7	98.2	128.3	127.2	115.8	102.6	143.1	123.6
1996	103.9	110.2	99.3	92.4	98.0	101.9	102.5	114.7	94.5
1997	101.3	109.3	97.4	96.2	97.1	100.9	99.7	102.0	94.7
1998	95.8	99.1	95.1	88.3	93.6	96.7	98.6	94.5	94.3
1999	96.7	100.9	94.7	98.9	97.6	100.4	98.8	89.8	96.8
2000	105.1	115.4	100.9	110.3	105.6	99.8	101.5	99.9	102.4
2001	99.8	100.2	100.5	95.6	98.4	100.4	98.6	101.2	99.7
2002	97.7	100.1	98.2	96.5	97.5	98.7	98.2	95.7	97.1
2003	104.8	107.4	107.9	105.3	102.9	100.3	99.7	106.7	101.4

9-14 各地区固定资产投资价格指数

Price Indices of Investment in Fixed Assets by Region

(上年=100) (preceding year=100)

地 区	Region	2002				2003			
		固定资产投 资 Investment in Fixed Assets	建筑安装工 程 Construction and Installation	设 备 工、器具 Purchase of Equipment, Tools and Instruments	其 他 费 用 Others	固定资产投 资 Investment in Fixed Assets	建筑安装工 程 Construction and Installation	设 备 工、器具 Purchase of Equipment, Tools and Instruments	其 他 费 用 Others
全 国	**National Total**	**100.2**	**101.0**	**97.0**	**101.2**	**102.2**	**104.2**	**97.0**	**101.6**
北 京	Beijing	100.4	101.2	93.7	100.7	102.2	104.3	95.6	100.8
天 津	Tianjin	99.5	100.7	94.9	100.2	102.6	104.9	97.8	100.4
河 北	Hebei	99.5	100.0	98.0	100.3	102.3	104.2	98.5	101.4
山 西	Shanxi	100.5	101.2	97.8	101.2	102.9	103.9	99.5	102.3
内蒙古	Inner Mongolia	101.0	101.5	99.7	100.4	102.6	103.7	100.2	100.5
辽 宁	Liaoning	100.7	101.0	99.3	101.7	102.5	104.8	97.7	101.2
吉 林	Jilin	101.2	101.9	98.6	103.2	101.1	102.3	98.1	101.3
黑龙江	Heilongjiang	100.2	101.1	96.9	101.5	102.3	102.7	100.8	103.0
上 海	Shanghai	100.3	101.9	96.7	100.3	102.4	105.2	97.5	101.4
江 苏	Jiangsu	101.7	102.4	99.6	103.2	104.3	107.7	97.6	103.6
浙 江	Zhejiang	100.5	101.3	96.4	102.1	103.5	106.1	98.2	101.7
安 徽	Anhui	101.1	102.1	98.7	100.4	103.5	105.8	98.3	101.1
福 建	Fujian	99.7	100.5	96.2	103.0	101.4	104.2	95.4	101.2
江 西	Jiangxi	100.0	100.4	97.6	103.3	105.1	107.5	99.8	102.9
山 东	Shandong	101.1	102.3	97.3	104.1	102.9	104.7	98.5	104.2
河 南	Henan	98.7	99.5	95.9	100.2	103.8	105.8	99.2	102.1
湖 北	Hubei	99.8	100.6	97.1	101.2	103.3	105.9	98.1	102.5
湖 南	Hunan	100.3	100.9	99.0	98.6	102.8	104.4	97.7	101.8
广 东	Guangdong	99.7	101.2	94.6	100.7	102.2	104.3	96.8	100.5
广 西	Guangxi	100.3	100.8	98.4	100.1	101.8	103.5	96.9	100.3
海 南	Hainan	98.2	97.8	98.7	98.4	103.2	105.7	99.2	100.5
重 庆	Chongqing	100.7	101.9	96.2	100.4	102.9	104.7	96.7	101.3
四 川	Sichuan	100.5	102.0	96.1	99.9	102.2	103.8	97.7	101.8
贵 州	Guizhou	100.2	100.8	98.3	100.0	102.3	103.9	98.7	99.9
云 南	Yunnan	100.0	100.9	96.7	100.8	102.2	103.1	99.4	102.4
西 藏	Tibet								
陕 西	Shaanxi	102.0	102.7	99.7	101.0	101.7	102.1	98.6	103.0
甘 肃	Gansu	100.2	100.9	98.8	98.5	101.7	102.9	99.1	100.4
青 海	Qinghai	103.2	104.7	97.3	101.5	102.0	102.9	97.8	102.5
宁 夏	Ningxia	100.7	102.1	97.0	100.0	102.3	103.7	96.9	103.2
新 疆	Xinjiang	100.2	99.8	100.5	102.0	103.4	104.0	100.6	100.9

9-15 房地产价格指数

Price Indices of Real Estate

(上年=100) (preceding year=100)

项　目	Item	1999	2000	2002	2003
房屋销售价格指数	**Selling Price Indices of Houses**	**100.0**	**101.1**	**103.7**	**104.8**
商品房	Commercial Houses	100.3	100.8	103.4	105.0
住宅	Residential Buildings	100.4	101.4	104.0	105.7
经济适用房	Economical Houses	102.0	101.4	101.8	102.6
普通住宅	General Residential Buildings	100.2	101.5	104.3	106.2
多层住宅	Multilayer Buildings	101.2	102.3	105.5	106.8
高层住宅	High-layer Buildings	100.6	102.4	103.0	106.1
豪华住宅	Luxury Residential Buildings	98.9	101.3	101.7	104.0
别墅	Villas	99.2	101.4	102.1	104.3
高档公寓	High-grade Apartment	98.6	101.1	101.5	103.8
非住宅	Non-Residential Buildings	99.9	98.7	101.3	102.7
写字楼	Office Buildings	97.6	98.1	99.8	103.4
商业用房	Houses for Business Use	101.0	99.6	102.4	102.3
其他	Others	100.6	96.9	102.1	103.7
公房	State-owned Houses	98.9	100.9	101.9	100.4
#住宅	Residential Buildings	95.0	103.4	101.9	100.4
私房	Private-owned Houses	99.9	102.7	105.9	105.2
住宅	Residential Buildings	101.5	101.0	108.6	105.8
非住宅	Non-Residential Buildings	94.4	106.8	101.1	104.1
土地交易价格指数	**Transactions Price Indices of Land**	**100.0**	**100.2**	**106.9**	**108.3**
居民住宅用地	Land for Residential Building Use	99.9	101.0	107.7	112.4
豪华住宅用地	Luxury Residential Buildings	100.1	101.6	101.9	105.9
普通住宅用地	General Residential Buildings	99.6	100.9	108.4	113.0
工业用地	Land for Industry Use	100.0	98.6	100.4	101.3
商业、旅游、娱乐用地	Land for Business Tour and Entertainment	100.0	100.4	107.0	104.9
其他用地	Land for Other	100.2	99.8	106.9	104.4
房屋租赁价格指数	**Renting Price Indices of Houses**	**98.5**	**102.4**	**100.8**	**101.9**
住宅	Residential Buildings	102.4	114.2	102.0	107.5
公房	State-owned Houses	104.4	114.2	101.9	101.1
私房	Private-owned Houses	95.7	114.1	102.3	113.9
办公用房	Office Buildings	95.2	96.2	99.5	99.9
高标准写字楼	High-grade Office Buildings	89.2	95.2	101.1	100.2
普通办公用房	General Office Buildings	99.3	96.9	98.6	99.7
商业用房	Houses for Business	99.0	99.0	100.2	99.6
厂房仓库	Workshops and Storehouses	99.0	99.6	100.7	100.5
工业厂房	Industry Workshops	97.1	98.8	101.3	102.0
仓库	Storehouses	101.5	100.5	100.2	98.7

9-16 全国和35个大中城市房地产价格指数

Price Indices of Real Estate in China and 35 Large-scale and Medium-scale Cities

(上年=100) (preceding year=100)

地区	Region	房屋销售价格指数 Selling Price Indices of Houses			土地交易价格指数 Transactions Price Indices of Land			房屋租赁价格指数 Renting Price Indices of Houses		
		2000	2002	2003	2000	2002	2003	2000	2002	2003
总计	**Total**	**101.1**	**103.7**	**104.8**	**100.2**	**106.9**	**108.3**	**102.4**	**100.8**	**101.9**
北京	Beijing	99.5	100.3	100.3	100.0	100.0	100.6	166.6	107.6	108.5
天津	Tianjin	100.0	101.6	104.1	100.5	102.2	103.0	100.1	106.0	100.7
石家庄	Shijiazhuang	101.8	101.4	100.3	107.7	99.7	99.4	102.2	100.4	99.3
太原	Taiyuan	101.1	103.3	102.8	100.0	126.7	121.9	105.6	106.1	102.3
呼和浩特	Hohhot	102.0	102.3	100.7	102.5	103.4	102.4	97.1	102.7	98.5
沈阳	Shenyang	103.0	100.1	107.6	101.8	83.1	116.1	102.3	99.5	101.4
大连	Dalian	100.2	98.4	100.7	100.0	100.0	103.5	105.4	98.1	100.0
长春	Changchun	106.6	97.2	100.2	100.2	113.7	103.7	106.4	104.6	104.0
哈尔滨	Harbin	101.8	101.1	100.2	101.1	100.0	101.6	101.0	100.0	98.6
上海	Shanghai	98.6	107.3	120.1	91.9	106.3	115.1	95.8	99.0	102.2
南京	Nanjing	101.6	103.0	109.8	101.9	103.9	104.7	101.1	100.6	104.4
杭州	Hangzhou	104.9	106.9	106.1	103.2	125.0	138.1	103.3	103.0	106.7
宁波	Ningbo	105.5	116.4	116.6	100.4	109.2	113.2	92.5	102.8	106.0
合肥	Hefei	100.0	104.0	104.1	100.3	103.7	107.0	99.1	102.0	102.3
福州	Fuzhou	100.3	101.1	101.1	100.0	106.0	107.7	99.5	98.6	98.7
厦门	Xiamen	100.1	103.0	102.8	100.0	101.7	102.3	96.2	98.0	100.3
南昌	Nanchang	103.2	111.6	104.8	103.0	125.2	110.1	113.2	104.2	103.3
济南	Jinan	102.8	102.5	103.1	102.3	102.1	103.5	101.6	103.2	100.0
青岛	Qingdao	102.3	107.6	114.6	100.4	104.3	101.8	95.8	94.4	99.4
郑州	Zhengzhou	99.5	101.9	102.0	102.1	101.4	101.0	103.7	103.0	99.1
武汉	Wuhan	101.5	101.9	103.8	100.1	100.7	103.7	97.3	98.6	98.5
长沙	Changsha	99.6	101.1	100.5	102.7	101.4	100.9	99.1	101.6	101.0
广州	Guangzhou	97.3	99.6	99.3	99.9	100.0	100.0	98.0	102.0	99.9
深圳	Shenzhen	99.2	100.4	102.2	101.5	100.0	102.0	95.7	100.2	100.0
南宁	Nanning	99.3	102.5	102.1	66.7	106.0	101.4	102.1	99.5	102.3
海口	Haikou	99.4	101.9	102.7	97.1	100.5	100.4	92.7	94.6	92.6
成都	Chengdu	101.3	101.3	102.9	101.9	106.4	109.1	99.3	100.9	100.3
贵阳	Guiyang	103.9	101.6	101.3	100.3	100.6	100.3	104.1	98.0	101.6
昆明	Kunming	100.2	100.0	99.1	100.0	100.0	100.0	97.8	98.4	100.4
重庆	Chongqing	101.8	102.1	106.1	100.0	101.7	115.5	95.1	97.5	100.3
西安	Xi'an	101.3	101.1	101.4	100.0	100.5	100.7	101.2	100.6	98.9
兰州	Lanzhou	100.5	104.3	101.8	100.0	100.0	100.0	100.0	100.3	97.8
西宁	Xining	101.1	102.2	101.9	100.4	102.7	106.2	114.3	107.3	103.1
银川	Yinchuan	102.2	103.6	102.1	103.6	102.9	103.4	118.0	106.4	99.8
乌鲁木齐	Urumqi	102.4	99.2	99.9	99.4	102.3	101.0	99.2	100.1	99.9

主要统计指标解释

居民消费价格指数 是反映一定时期内城乡居民所购买的生活消费品价格和服务项目价格变动趋势和程度的相对数，是对城市居民消费价格指数和农村居民消费价格指数进行综合汇总计算的结果。该指数可以观察和分析消费品的零售价格和服务价格变动对城乡居民实际生活费支出的影响程度。

城市居民消费价格指数 是反映一定时期内城市居民家庭所购买的生活消费品价格和服务项目价格变动趋势和程度的相对数。该指数可以观察和分析消费品的零售价格和服务项目价格变动对职工货币工资的影响，作为研究职工生活和确定工资政策的依据。

农村居民消费价格指数 是反映一定时期内农村居民家庭所购买的生活消费品价格和服务项目价格变动趋势和程度的相对数。该指数可以观察农村消费品的零售价格和服务项目价格变动对农村居民生活消费支出的影响，直接反映农民生活水平的实际变化情况，为分析和研究农村居民生活问题提供依据。

商品零售价格指数 是反映一定时期内城乡商品零售价格变动趋势和程度的相对数。商品零售物价的变动直接影响到城乡居民的生活支出和国家的财政收入，影响居民购买力和市场供需的平衡，影响到消费与积累的比例关系。因此，该指数可以从一个侧面对上述经济活动进行观察和分析。

农业生产资料价格指数 指反映一定时期内农业生产资料价格变动趋势和程度的相对数。农业生产资料价格指数分为小农具、饲料、幼禽家畜、半机械化农具、机械化农具、化学肥料、农药及农药械、农机用油等八大类。其编制目的是了解农业生产中物质资料投入价格的变动状况，服务于国民经济核算。1994年以前，农业生产资料价格指数仅仅是商品零售价格指数的一个类别，此后，从商品零售价格指数中分离出来，单独编制。

农产品生产价格指数 是反映一定时期内，农产品生产者出售农产品价格水平变动趋势及幅度的相对数。该指数可以客观反映全国农产品生产价格水平和结构变动情况，满足农业与国民经济核算需要。其中某代表品生产价格指数是通过对全部有出售该产品行为的调查单位的个体指数进行几何平均求得的，类价格指数是通过对其所属的类（或代表品）的价格指数进行加权平均求得的。季度累计价格指数的计算方法与分季指数的计算方法相同。

工业品出厂价格指数 是反映一定时期内全部工业产品出厂价格总水平的变动趋势和程度的相对数，包括工业企业售给本企业以外所有单位的各种产品和直接售给居民用于生活消费的产品。该指数可以观察出厂价格变动对工业总产值及增加值的影响。

原材料、燃料和动力购进价格指数 是反映工业企业作为生产投入，而从物资交易市场和能源、原材料生产企业购买原材料、燃料和动力产品时，所支付的价格水平变动趋势和程度的统计指标，是扣除工业企业物质消耗成本中的价格变动影响的重要依据。

目前，我国编制的原材料、燃料和动力购进价格指数所调查的产品包括燃料动力、黑色金属、有色金属、化工、建材等九大类的900多种产品。

固定资产投资价格指数 是反映一定时期内固定资产投资品及项目的价格变动趋势和程度的相对数。固定资产投资额是由建筑安装工程投资完成额、设备工器具购置投资完成额和其他费用投资完成额三部分组成的。编制固定资产投资价格指数应首先分别编制上述三部分投资的价格指数，然后采用加权算术平均法求出固定资产投资价格总指数。

该指数可以准确地反映固定资产投资中涉及的各类投资品和取费项目价格变动趋势和变动幅度，消除按现价计算的固定资产投资指标中的价格变动因素，真实地反映固定资产投资的规模、速度、结构和效益，为国家科学地制定、检查固定资产投资计划并提高宏观调控水平，为完善国民经济核算体系提供科学的、可靠的依据。

房地产价格指数 是反映一定时期内房地产价格变动趋势和程度的相对数，包括房屋销售价格指数、房屋租赁价格指数和土地交易价格指数。这三套指数的计算方法相似，均采用由下到上逐级汇总的方法。

Explanatory Notes on Main Statistical Indicators

Retail Price Indices reflect the trend and degree of change in retail prices of commodities during a given period. The change in retail prices of commodities directly affect the living expenditure of urban and rural residents, government revenue, purchasing power of residents and the equilibrium of market supply and demand, and the ratio of consumption to accumulation. Therefore, the retail price indices are useful to analyze the changes of the above economic activities.

Consumer Price Indices reflect the trend and degree of changes in prices of consumer goods and services purchased by urban and rural residents, and is a composite indices derived from the urban consumer price indices and the rural consumer price indices. Consumer price indices can be used to analyze the impact of consumer price change on actual expenditure for living cost of urban and rural residents.

Urban Consumer Price Indices reflect the trend and degree of changes in prices of consumer goods and services purchased by urban households during a given period. It can be used to observe and analyze the impact of price changes in consumer goods and services on wages (in monetary terms) of staff and workers, and provide basis for policy-making concerning the living cost and wages of staff and workers.

Rural Consumer Price Indices reflect the trend and degree of changes in prices of consumer goods and services purchased by rural households during a given period. It can be used to observe the impact of change in retail prices of consumer goods and service prices in rural areas on living expenditure of rural households, and to show the changes in the living standard of peasants. It provides basis for analysis and research on condition of life in rural areas.

Price Indices of Means of Agricultural Production reflect the trend and degree of changes in prices of means of agricultural production during a given period. Price indices of means of agricultural production are composed of 8 categories including small farm tools, feeds, young domestic animals and poultries, semi-mechanized farm machinery, mechanized farm machinery, chemical fertilizers, pesticides and spraying machinery, fuels for farm machinery. Compilation of these indices help to understand the changes in prices of input into agricultural production and facilitate the compilation of national account statistics. Before 1994, price indices of means of agricultural production was a subcategory in the in the retail price indices of commodities, and it has been compiled separately since 1994.

Indices of Producers' Prices for Farm Products reflect the trend and degree of changes in producers' prices received by farmers when they sell farm products during a given period. These indices depict the change in the level and structure of producers' prices of farm products of the country and meet the needs of agriculture statistics and national account statistics. The producers' price index of a given product is calculated through geometrical mean of individual indices of all surveyed units who sell such product, and the indices of a product category is obtained through weighted mean of price indices of all products in the category. Method for calculating accumulative quarterly indices is the same as for calculating the distinctive quarterly indices.

Ex-factory Price Indices of Industrial Products reflect the trend and degree of changes in general ex-factory prices of all industrial products during a given period, including sales of industrial products by an industrial enterprise to all units outside the enterprise, as well as sales of consumer goods to residents. It can be used to analyze the impact of ex-factory prices on gross output value and value-added of the industrial sector.

Indices of Purchasing Prices of Raw Materials, Fuels and Power reflect changes in the level and degree of prices paid by industrial enterprises when they purchase production input such as raw materials, fuels and power from the market or from other energy or raw materials producing enterprises. These indices provide important basis for measuring the material consumption of industrial enterprises after removing influence of price changes.

At present, over 900 products in 9 categories, including fuels and power, ferrous metals, non-ferrous metals, chemicals, building materials, are covered in China for the survey to produce indices of purchasing prices of raw materials, fuels and power.

Price Indices of Investment in Fixed Assets reflect the trend and degree of changes in prices of investment goods and projects in fixed assets during a given period. The investment in fixed assets consists of three components, namely the investment in construction and installation, the investment in purchases of equipment and instrument, and the investment in other items.

Price indices of investment in fixed assets are calculated as the weighted arithmetic mean of the price indices of the three components of investment in fixed assets.

Removing the factor of price change in the aggregates of investment at current prices, this indicator shows the changes in the prices of commodities and fees involved in the investment of fixed assets, and can be used to observe the actual size, growth, structure, and efficiency of investment in fixed assets and provides reliable and scientific data for government planning, management, decision-making, and further improving the current national accounting system.

Price Indices for Real Estate reflect the trend and degree of changes in prices of real estate during a given period, including price indices for selling houses and buildings, price indices for leasing houses and buildings and price indices for land transaction. The methods for the compilation of the three sets of indices are similar in that they all use bottom-up approach under which data are reported from lower level to higher level.

十、人民生活

People's Livelihood

简要说明

一、本篇资料的主要内容

本篇资料反映我国人民生活现状及变化情况，分为城镇居民生活和农村居民生活两部分。

二、城镇居民生活资料来源

城镇居民生活状况的数据来源于国家统计局城市社会经济调查总队的城镇住户调查，是对城镇居民家庭抽样调查汇总的结果。主要内容包括家庭人口及其构成、家庭现金收支、主要商品购买数量及支出金额、劳动就业状况、居住状况和耐用消费品的拥有量等。

三、城镇居民生活调查方法

城镇住户调查是由国家统计局城市社会经济调查总队组织实施，各省、自治区、直辖市城调队及抽中城市及县的城调队依据国家统计局统一制定的城镇住户调查方案，收集资料并逐级汇总上报。

调查对象在2001年以前为全国非农业住户，2002年以后改为全国城市市区和县城关镇区住户。

城镇住户调查采用固定样本户进行连续记帐的调查方式，每一调查期为3年，每年轮换三分之一。调查户是按“二阶段”、“划类选点”、“等距抽样”随机抽选的。

第一阶段，在全国范围内划类选点直接抽选调查城市。把全国市、县按人口规模划分为特大、大、中、小城市和县城五种类型，然后在此基础上按六大行政区分组。每一行政区内又按城市职工平均工资水平高低排列，再把各城市的职工人数累计起来进行等距抽样，每隔100万职工抽取一个样本城市，作为调查城市。

第二阶段，在抽中的城市内采用多阶段和二相抽样相结合的方法抽取调查户。特大、大城市采用三阶段抽选一相调查样本，即先抽选调查街道，从抽中街道再抽调查居委会、最后从抽中居委会抽选调查户；中小城市及县城采用二阶段抽选一相调查样本，即直接抽选居委会，再从中抽选调查户。第二相样本是在一相样本基础上，采取分层等比例抽选经常性调查户。

按上述办法国家统计局共抽选出调查市、县226个，调查户25000户。加上各地根据同一方案抽选的地方点调查户，共有50000余户。

四、农村居民生活资料来源

农村居民生活状况的数据来源于国家统计局农村经济调查总队的农村居民住户调查，是对农村居民家庭抽样调查汇总的结果。主要内容包括农村居民家庭基本情况、人均总收入和纯收入、生活消费支出、主要消费品消费量、耐用消费品拥有量等。

五、农村居民生活调查方法

农村居民住户调查是以各省(区、直辖市)为总体，直接抽选调查村，在抽中村中抽选调查户。综合运用多种抽样方法确定住户调查网点。农村住户调查网点分布在全国7100多个村、68000多个农户中。

农村居民住户调查在95%的概率把握程度下要求抽样误差不得超过±3%。为保证农村居民住户调查资料的准确性，国家统计局农村经济调查总队为调查户设置了现金和实物两本帐，并聘请了近万名辅助调查员帮助做好记帐工作，及时核实、汇总住户调查资料。

为解决调查户的厌烦情绪及样本老化问题，增强抽样调查网点的代表性，更加准确、及时地反映农村社会经济情况，国家统计局农村经济调查总队对农村住户调查网点实行样本轮换制度，每五年为一个周期。

Brief Introduction

I. Main Content

Data in this chapter show the conditions of people's livelihood in China. Consisting of two parts on the life of urban (i.e.: city and town) residents and of rural residents respectively.

II. Source of Data on the Livelihood of Urban Residents

Data on the livelihood of the urban residents in this chapter come from the data collected through samples survey on the urban households conducted by the Urban Socio-economic Survey Organization, NBS. The main content of the survey includes the population in the household and its composition, the cash income and expenditure of the household, the quantity of, and the expenditure on major commodities purchased, the employment of the household members, the housing condition and the possession of the durable consumer goods.

III. Methodology for Urban Household Survey

The survey on the urban households is organized by the Urban Socio-economic Survey Organization, NBS. The urban socio-economic survey organizations of the provinces, autonomous regions and municipalities directly under the central government as well as the urban socio-economic survey organizations of the selected cities and counties collect the data in accordance with the survey scheme stipulated by NBS and report them to the higher organization.

Until 2001, the survey covered only non-agricultural households. Starting from 2002, it covers all households in urban areas and county towns.

The survey on the urban households is conducted in such a way that households selected by sampling method keep accounts for successive three years and be interviewed by the enumerators. By a rotation sampling scheme, one third of the old sample households should be replaced by the new sample households every year. The respondent households are selected by the two-stage stratified systematic random sampling scheme.

At the first stage, the cities and counties are firstly classified into 5 categories by their population size, namely the particularly large cities, large cities, medium-sized cities, small cities and counties. Secondly, they are grouped into the 6 administrative regions (northeastern region, north region, eastern region, central region, northwestern region and southwestern region). In each administrative region, the cities and counties are arranged in the order of the average wages of their staff and workers in the urban areas. Thirdly, the number of the staff and workers of the cities are accumulated and the sample cities or counties are selected by a systematic sampling scheme; the sampling interval is one million staff and workers.

At the second stage, the sample households are selected by the multi-stage and two-phase sampling scheme. In the particularly large and large cities, the first phase sample is selected by three-stage sampling method: Firstly, the sample sub-districts are selected; Secondly, the sample residents committees are selected from the sample sub-districts; Thirdly, the sample households are selected from the sample residents committees. In the medium-sized and small cities and counties, the first phase sample is selected by two-stage sampling method: Firstly, the sample residents committees are directly selected; Secondly, the sample households are selected from the sample residents committees. The second phase sample is composed of the sample households which are surveyed in a regular way and these households are selected with stratified sampling method from the households in the first phase sample.

In total, 25,000 households in 226 cities and counties are selected by the National Bureau of Statistics in the above-mentioned approach. Additional local samples are selected by local statistical offices by the same sample design, making the total sample size to reach over 50,000 households.

IV. Source of Data on the Livelihood of Rural Residents

Data on the livelihood of the rural residents come from the data collected through the sample survey on the rural households, which is organized by the Rural Socio-economic Survey Organization, NBS. The main content of the survey includes the basic condition of the rural households, the per capita total income and net income, the expenditure for the residential consumption, the consumption of major consumer goods and the quantity of durable consumer goods owned.

V. Methodology for Rural Household Survey

The sample survey on the rural households is conducted by first selecting sample villages and then selecting households in the selected villages in each province, with all rural households in the province as the population. A combination of various sampling approaches are used to identify a total of 68,000 households selected from 7,100 villages throughout the whole country.

It is required that the sampling error should not exceed to ±3%, with confidence of probability as 95%. In order to ensure the accuracy of the data of the survey on the rural households, two accounts are designed for the respondent households by the Rural Socio-economic Survey Organization, NBS, the cash account and the account on goods in kind. Nearly 10 thousand assistant enumerators have been invited to help the households to keep good accounts and check and tabulate the data of the survey.

In order to overcome the boring feeling of the respondent households and solve the problem of aging samples to make the sample more representative of the population and able to reflect the rural social and economic situation more accurately and timely, a rotation sampling scheme is implemented by the Rural Socio-economic Survey Organization, NBS in selecting the rural sample households, with the cycle of complete rotation being 5 years.

10-1 人民生活基本情况

People's Life

指标名称	Item	1989	1997	2002	2003
就业	**Employment**				
城镇居民家庭每户就业人口 (人)	Average Number of Employed Persons per City Household (person)	2.00	1.83	1.58	1.58
农村居民家庭每户整半劳动力 (人)	Average Number of Able-bodied and Semi-able-bodied Laborers per Rural Household (person)	2.94	2.79	2.76	2.80
城镇居民家庭每一就业者负担人数(人)	Number of Dependents per Employee of City Household (person)	1.78	1.74	1.92	1.91
农村居民家庭每一劳动力负担人数(人)	Number of Dependents per Laborer of Rural Household (person)	1.65	1.56	1.50	1.47
城镇登记失业人数 (万人)	Urban Registration Unemployment (10 000 persons)	378	577	770	800
城镇登记失业率 (%)	Urban Registration Unemployment Rate (%)	2.6	3.1	4.0	4.3
本年职业介绍服务机构 (个)	Number of Career Service Organization at the Year-end (unit)		34286	26158	31109
本年登记求职人数 (万人)	Total Registered Job-seekers This Year (10 000 persons)		1162	2684	3060
收入与支出	**Income and Expenditure**				
城镇人均可支配收入 (元)	Annual Per Capita Disposable Income of City Residents (yuan)	1374	5160	7703	8472
农村人均纯收入 (元)	Annual Per Capita Disposable Income of Rural Residents (yuan)	602	2090	2476	2622
城镇人均消费性支出 (元)	Annual Per Capita Consumption Expenditure of City Household (yuan)	1211	4186	6030	6511
农村人均生活消费支出 (元)	Annual Per Capita Living Expenditure of Rural Household (yuan)	535	1617	1834	1943
人均储蓄存款余额 (元)	Per Capita Balance of Saving Deposit (yuan)	461	3744	6766	8018
生活质量	**Life Quality**				
居民家庭恩格尔系数 (%)	Household's Engle Coefficient (%)				
城镇	Urban	54.5	46.6	37.7	37.1
农村	Rural	54.8	55.1	46.2	45.6
居住条件	Residence Condition				
城市人均住宅建筑面积 (平方米)	Per Capita Building Space in City Areas (sq.m)	13.5	17.8	22.8	23.7
农村人均住房面积 (平方米)	Per Capita Living Space in Rural Areas (sq.m)	17.2	22.5	26.5	27.2
交通条件	Traffic Condition				
城市每万人拥有公交车辆 (标台)	Number of Public Transportation Vehicles per 10 000 Population in Cities (unit)	2.1	4.5	6.7	7.7
城市人均拥有铺路面积 (平方米)	Per Capita Area of Paved Roads (sq.m)	3.2	5.2	7.9	9.3
农村通公路行政村比重 (%)	Percentage of Administrative Village Access to Highway (%)	75.0	85.8	92.3	91.9
城镇每百户拥有家用汽车 (辆)	Number of Family Vehicles Per 100 City Household (unit)		0.19	0.88	1.36
农村每百户拥有摩托车 (辆)	Number of Motor Cycles Per 100 Rural Households (unit)	0.95	10.89	28.07	31.80
通信条件	Communication Condition				
电话普及率 (部/百人)	Mobile Telephone Popularization Rate (set/100 persons)	0.98	8.11	33.60	42.16
移动电话普及率 (部/百人)	Mobile Telephone Popularization Rate (set/100 persons)	…	1.07	16.10	21.02
每千人拥有公用电话数 (部)	Per 1 000 Person Public Telephone (Sets)	0.04	1.57	7.67	12.08
城市公用设施普及占有率	City Public Utility				
用水普及率 (%)	Rate of Access to Tap Water (%)	47.4	61.2	77.9	86.2
燃气普及率 (%)	Rate of Access to Gas (%)	17.8	40.0	67.2	76.7
人均公共绿地面积 (平方米)	Per Capita Green Area (sq.m)	1.7	2.9	5.4	6.5
每万人拥有公共厕所 (座)	Number of Public Toilet per 10 000 Persons (unit)	3.1	3.0	3.2	3.2
人均国内旅游花费 (元)	Per Capita Domestic Expenditure on Tour (yuan)		328.1	441.8	395.7
城镇	Urban		599.8	739.7	684.9
农村	Rural		145.7	209.1	200.0

10-1 续表 continued

指标名称	Item	1989	1997	2002	2003
文化、教育和卫生	**Culture, Education and Sport**				
文化	Culture				
广播人口覆盖率 (%)	Broadcast Covering Rate of Population (%)	73.0	86.0	93.3	93.7
电视人口覆盖率 (%)	TV Covering Rate of Population (%)	77.9	87.6	94.6	95.0
每百户彩色电视机拥有量 (部/百户)	Number of Colour TV per 100 Households (set)				
城镇	Urban	51.5	100.5	126.4	130.5
农村	Rural	3.6	27.3	60.5	67.8
每百户家用电脑拥有量 (部/百户)	Number of Computer per 100 Households (set)				
城镇	Urban		2.6	20.6	27.8
农村	Rural			1.1	1.4
居民家庭文教娱乐支出比重 (%)	Percentage of Household Expenditure on Education, Culture and Entertainment (%)				
城镇	Urban	11.1	10.7	15.0	14.4
农村	Rural	5.7	9.2	11.5	12.1
教育	Education				
升学率 (%)	Rate of Entering the Higher School (%)				
小学升中学	Entering Middle School from Elementary School	71.5	93.7	97.0	97.9
初中升高级中学	Entering Senior Secondary School from Junior Secomdary School	38.3	51.5	58.3	60.2
高中升高等教育	Entering College and University from Senior Secondary School	24.6	45.1	83.5	83.4
每万人口在校学生数 (人)	Number of Student per 10 000 Population (person)				
大学生数	College and University Student	18.5	25.7	70.3	86.3
中学生数	Secondary School Student	448	566	733	763
小学生数	Elementary School Student	1098	1132	946	910
平均每一学生占有预算内教育事业费支出 (元)	Budgetary Educational Fund per Student (yuan)				
#普通高校	Regular Institutions of Higher Education		6522.9	6178.0	
普通高中	Regular Senior School		1155.4	1565.3	
普通初中	Regular Junior School		591.4	960.5	
小学	Primary School		333.8	813.1	
卫生	Health				
每万人口医院、卫生院床位数 (张)	Number of Hospital Beds per 10 000 Population (bed)	22.8	23.5	23.2	23.4
每万人口医生数 (人)	Number of Doctor per 10 000 Population (person)	15.2	16.1	14.7	14.8
人均卫生总费用支出 (元)	Per Capita Expenditure for Public Health (yuan)	76.7	186.4	442.5	
居民家庭医疗保健支出比重 (%)	Percentage of Resident Expenditure on Health Care (%)				
城镇	Urban	1.3	4.3	7.1	7.3
农村	Rural	3.1	3.9	5.7	6.0
社会保障和社区服务	**Social Security and Social Service**				
社会保障	Social Security				
参加基本养老保险职工人数 (万人)	Number of Employee Joining Basic Endowment Insurance (10 000 persons)	4817	8671	11129	11647
参加基本养老保险离退休退职人数 (万人)	Number of Retiree Joining Basic Endowment Insurance (10 000 persons)	893	2533	3608	3860
参加失业保险职工人数 (万人)	Number of Person Joining Unemployment Insurance (10 000 persons)		7961	10182	10373
参加基本医疗保险人数 (万人)	Number of Person Joining Basic Medical Care System (10 000 persons)		1762	9401	10902
参加农村养老保险人数 (万人)	Number of Person Joining Rural Endowment Insurance (10 000 persons)			5462	5428
人均离退休退职费 (元)	Per Capita Retirement Pension (yuan)	1478	5458	8881	9485
社区服务	Social Service				
城镇社区服务设施 (万个)	Number of Urban Community Welfare Facilities (10 000 units)	7.1	13.3	19.9	19.6
城镇便民利民服务网点 (万个)	Number of Urban Community Service Points for Civilian		30.7	62.3	66.8

注：1.城市人均住宅建筑面积、城市交通状况、城市公用事业资料由建设部提供。
2.城镇居民家庭文教娱乐支出比重1989年为1990年数据。
3.人均卫生总费用支出1989年和1997年分别为1991年和1995年数据。

a) Data of urban per capita residence floor space, traffic, and city public utility are provided by the Ministry of Construction.
b) The percentage of urban household expenditure on education, culture and entertainment in 1989 is the data in 1990.
c) The figures of per capita expenditure for public health in 1989 and 1997 are the data in 1991 and 1995.

10-2 城乡居民家庭人均收入及恩格尔系数

Per Capita Annual Income and Engle Coefficient of Urban and Rural Households

年份 Year	农村居民家庭人均纯收入 Per Capital Annual Net Income of Rural Households		城镇居民家庭人均可支配收入 Per Capital Annual Disposable Income of Urban Households		农村居民家庭恩格尔系数（%）Engle Coefficient of Rural Households (%)	城镇居民家庭恩格尔系数（%）Engle Coefficient of City Households (%)
	绝对数（元）Value (yuan)	指数（1978=100）Index	绝对数（元）Value (yuan)	指数（1978=100）Index		
1978	133.6	100.0	343.4	100.0	67.7	57.5
1980	191.3	139.0	477.6	127.0	61.8	56.9
1985	397.6	268.9	739.1	160.4	57.8	53.3
1989	601.5	305.7	1373.9	182.5	54.8	54.5
1990	686.3	311.2	1510.2	198.1	58.8	54.2
1991	708.6	317.4	1700.6	212.4	57.6	53.8
1992	784.0	336.2	2026.6	232.9	57.6	53.0
1993	921.6	346.9	2577.4	255.1	58.1	50.3
1994	1221.0	364.4	3496.2	276.8	58.9	50.0
1995	1577.7	383.7	4283.0	290.3	58.6	50.1
1996	1926.1	418.2	4838.9	301.6	56.3	48.8
1997	2090.1	437.4	5160.3	311.9	55.1	46.6
1998	2162.0	456.2	5425.1	329.9	53.4	44.7
1999	2210.3	473.5	5854.0	360.6	52.6	42.1
2000	2253.4	483.5	6280.0	383.7	49.1	39.4
2001	2366.4	503.8	6859.6	416.3	47.7	38.2
2002	2475.6	528.0	7702.8	472.1	46.2	37.7
2003	2622.2	550.7	8472.2	514.6	45.6	37.1

10-3 城乡居民人民币储蓄存款

Savings Deposit in Urban and Rural Areas

单位: 亿元 (100 million yuan)

年份 Year	年底余额 Outstanding Amount			年增加额 Increased Amount		
	总计 Total	定期 Time Deposits	活期 Demand Deposits	总计 Total	定期 Time Deposits	活期 Demand Deposits
1978	210.6	128.9	81.7	29.0	17.2	11.8
1980	399.5	304.9	94.6	118.5	138.5	-20.0
1985	1622.6	1225.2	397.4	407.9	324.3	83.6
1989	5196.4	4215.4	981.0	1374.2	1366.9	7.3
1990	7119.8	5911.2	1208.6	1923.4	1695.8	227.6
1991	9241.6	7691.7	1549.9	2121.8	1780.5	341.3
1992	11759.4	9425.2	2334.2	2517.8	1733.5	784.3
1993	15203.5	11971.0	3232.5	3444.1	2545.8	898.3
1994	21518.8	16838.7	4680.1	6315.3	4867.7	1447.6
1995	29662.3	23778.2	5884.1	8143.5	6939.5	1204.0
1996	38520.8	30873.4	7647.4	8858.5	7095.2	1763.3
1997	46279.8	36226.7	10053.1	7759.0	5353.3	2405.7
1998	53407.5	41791.6	11615.9	7615.4	5473.7	2141.7
1999	59621.8	44955.1	14666.7	6253.0	3198.5	3054.5
2000	64332.4	46141.7	18190.7	4976.7	1310.3	3666.4
2001	73762.4	51434.9	22327.6	9457.6	4144.5	5313.2
2002	86910.6	58788.9	28121.7	13233.2	7432.0	5801.2
2003	103617.7	68498.7	35119.0	16631.9	9674.5	6957.4

10-4 各地区城乡居民人民币储蓄存款(年底余额)

Savings Deposit of Urban and Rural Household by Region at the Year-end

单位：亿元 (100 million yuan)

地区	Region	城乡储蓄 Total Savings		城镇储蓄 Savings of Urban Household		农户储蓄 Savings of Rural Household	
		2001	2002	2001	2002	2001	2002
全 国	**National Total**	**73762.4**	**86910.6**	**59941.1**	**71504.8**	**13821.4**	**15405.8**
总 行	Head Office	0.1	2.5	0.1	2.5		
北 京	Beijing	3536.3	4389.7	3253.9	4073.1	282.5	316.6
天 津	Tianjin	1285.0	1486.4	1117.3	1308.3	167.6	178.1
河 北	Hebei	4364.5	4808.3	2973.3	3317.5	1391.2	1490.8
山 西	Shanxi	1979.7	2307.3	1522.5	1768.7	457.2	538.6
内蒙古	Inner Mongolia	986.7	1137.9	834.8	959.0	152.0	178.9
辽 宁	Liaoning	4131.6	4665.0	3584.4	4070.5	547.1	594.5
吉 林	Jilin	1676.1	1878.5	1465.2	1643.3	210.9	235.1
黑龙江	Heilongjiang	2578.5	2915.7	2341.3	2654.5	237.2	261.1
上 海	Shanghai	3001.9	3891.5	2781.8	3638.9	220.1	252.6
江 苏	Jiangsu	5172.8	6276.2	4217.9	5333.8	954.9	942.4
浙 江	Zhejiang	4262.4	5212.7	3178.0	3935.4	1084.4	1277.3
安 徽	Anhui	1700.5	2047.5	1322.0	1609.1	378.5	438.4
福 建	Fujian	2030.9	2430.5	1792.8	2157.1	238.1	273.4
江 西	Jiangxi	1429.5	1706.6	1157.3	1397.2	272.2	309.5
山 东	Shandong	5063.4	5803.5	3764.7	4355.2	1298.7	1448.3
河 南	Henan	3634.5	4196.0	2746.7	3211.7	887.9	984.3
湖 北	Hubei	2287.4	2754.5	1947.7	2364.7	339.7	389.9
湖 南	Hunan	2183.7	2576.4	1620.8	1947.5	562.9	628.9
广 东	Guangdong	9930.1	11813.3	7986.6	9633.5	1943.5	2179.9
广 西	Guangxi	1538.6	1733.5	1289.9	1453.0	248.7	280.5
海 南	Hainan	427.3	483.5	378.1	427.4	49.3	56.2
重 庆	Chongqing	1317.2	1582.3	1040.5	1260.6	276.7	321.8
四 川	Sichuan	3123.4	3665.2	2403.5	2886.2	719.9	779.0
贵 州	Guizhou	641.7	758.7	551.4	646.6	90.3	112.1
云 南	Yunnan	1298.5	1499.8	1074.8	1243.5	223.7	256.3
西 藏	Tibet	50.2	70.4	50.2	70.4		
陕 西	Shaanxi	1768.5	2108.1	1436.5	1737.9	332.0	370.2
甘 肃	Gansu	920.7	1042.4	799.5	898.1	121.2	144.3
青 海	Qinghai	188.5	222.4	174.2	206.3	14.3	16.1
宁 夏	Ningxia	258.0	306.8	227.9	269.3	30.1	37.5
新 疆	Xinjiang	994.3	1137.6	905.4	1024.2	88.9	113.5

10-5 城镇居民家庭基本情况

Basic Conditions of Urban Households

项 目	Item	1990	1995	2000	2002	2003
调查户数 (户)	**Number of Households Surveyed (household)**	**35660**	**35520**	**42220**	**45317**	**48028**
平均每户家庭人口 (人)	**Average Household Size (person)**	**3.50**	**3.23**	**3.13**	**3.04**	**3.01**
平均每户就业人口 (人)	**Average Number of Employed Persons per Household (persons)**	**1.98**	**1.87**	**1.68**	**1.58**	**1.58**
平均每户就业面 (%)	**Percentage of Employment per Household (%)**	**56.57**	**57.89**	**53.67**	**51.97**	**52.49**
平均每一就业者负担人数（包括就业者本人）(人)	**Number of Persons Supported by Each Employee (including the employee himself or herself) (person)**	**1.77**	**1.73**	**1.86**	**1.92**	**1.91**
平均每人全部年收入（元）	**Per Capita Annual Income (yuan)**	**1516.21**	**4279.02**	**6295.91**	**8177.40**	**9061.22**
工薪收入	Income of Wages and Salaries	1149.70	3390.21	4480.50	5739.96	6410.22
经营净收入	Net Income from Management	22.50	72.62	246.24	332.16	403.82
财产性收入	Property Income	15.60	90.43	128.38	102.12	134.98
转移性收入	Transfer Income	328.41	725.76	1440.78	2003.16	2112.20
#可支配收入	Disposable Income	1510.16	4282.95	6279.98	7702.80	8472.20
平均每人消费性支出（元）	**Per Capita Annual Living Expenditures for Consumption (yuan)**	**1278.89**	**3537.57**	**4998.00**	**6029.88**	**6510.94**
食 品	Food	693.77	1771.99	1971.32	2271.84	2416.92
衣 着	Clothing	170.90	479.20	500.46	590.88	637.72
家庭设备用品及服务	Household Facilities, Articles and Service	108.45	263.36	374.49	388.68	410.34
医疗保健	Medicine and Medical Service	25.67	110.11	318.07	430.08	475.98
交通通信	Transport, Post and Communication Services	40.51	183.22	426.95	626.04	721.12
教育文化娱乐服务	Education, Cultural and Recreation Services	112.26	331.01	669.58	902.28	934.38
居住	Residence	60.86	283.76	565.29	624.36	699.38
杂项商品与服务	Miscellaneous Commodities and Services	66.57	114.92	171.83	195.84	215.10
平均每人消费性支出构成（人均消费性支出=100）	**Composition of Per Capita Annual Living Expenditures for Consumption (%)**					
食 品	Food	54.25	50.09	39.44	37.68	37.12
衣 着	Clothing	13.36	13.55	10.01	9.80	9.79
家庭设备用品及服务	Household Facilities, Articles and Service	10.14	7.44	7.49	6.45	6.30
医疗保健	Medicine and Medical Service	2.01	3.11	6.36	7.13	7.31
交通通信	Transport, Post and Communication Services	1.20	5.18	8.54	10.38	11.08
教育文化娱乐服务	Education，Cultural and Recreation Services	11.12	9.36	13.40	14.96	14.35
居住	Residence	6.98	8.02	11.31	10.35	10.74
杂项商品与服务	Miscellaneous Commodities and Services	0.94	3.25	3.44	3.25	3.30

注：1.本表至10-17表为城镇居民家庭收支抽样调查资料。

2.从2002年起，城镇住户调查对象由原来的非农业人口改为城市市区和县城关镇区；本篇章相关资料均按新口径计算，历史数据作了相应调整。

a) Data from the table to 10-17 are obtained from the sample survey on income and expenditures of urban households.

b) Since 2002, the objects of urban households survey are the permanent residents of city districts and county towns. The relative data in the chapter are calculated according to the new standard, and historical data have been adjusted accordingly.

10-6 城镇居民家庭基本情况（2003年）

项　目	Item	全　国 National
调查户数　（户）	Number of Households Surveyed (household)	48028
调查户比重　（%）	Proportion (%)	100.00
平均每户家庭人口　（人）	Average Household Size (person)	3.01
平均每户就业人口　（人）	Average Number of Employees per Household (person)	1.58
平均每户就业面　（%）	Percentage of Employed Persons per Household (%)	52.49
平均每一就业者负担人数（包括就业者本人）（人）	Number of Persons Supported by Each Employee (including the employee himself or herself) (person)	1.91
平均每人全部年收入（元）	Per Capita Annual Income (yuan)	9061.22
平均每人可支配收入（元）	Per Capita Disposable Income (yuan)	8472.20
平均每人消费性支出（元）	Per Capita Annual Living Expenditure (yuan)	6510.94

10-7 城镇居民家庭平均每人全年消费性支出（2003年）

项　目	Item	总平均 Average	最低收入户 Lowest Income Households (first decile)	# 困难户 Poor Households (first five percent)
消费性支出　（元）	**Total Living Expenditures (yuan)**	**6510.94**	**2562.36**	**2237.27**
食品	Food	2416.92	1222.76	1087.20
#粮食	Grain	194.15	170.66	166.58
肉禽及其制品	Meat, Poultry and Related Products	473.19	283.09	248.75
蛋类	Eggs	60.97	45.44	42.17
水产品	Aquatic Products	170.31	60.57	50.72
奶及奶制品	Milk and Dairy Products	124.70	38.31	29.61
衣着	Clothing	637.73	198.71	157.02
#服装	Garments	455.32	127.93	98.68
家庭设备用品及服务	Household Facilities, Articles and Services	410.34	91.99	76.85
#耐用消费品	Durable Consumer Goods	213.57	24.79	17.32
医疗保健	Medicine and Medical Services	475.98	175.77	144.97
交通通信	Transport, Post and Communication Services	721.13	174.17	137.67
教育文化娱乐服务	Education，Cultural and Recreation Services	934.38	327.71	293.00
#文娱用品	Consumer Goods for Recreational Use	264.47	39.58	31.11
居住	Residence	699.39	309.01	286.93
#住房	Housing	256.45	56.79	53.49
杂项商品与服务	Miscellaneous Commodities and Services	215.10	62.25	53.62
消费性支出构成 (%)	**Total Living Expenditures (%)**			
食品	Food	37.12	47.72	48.59
衣着	Clothing	9.79	7.75	7.02
家庭设备用品及服务	Household Facilities, Articles and Services	6.30	3.59	3.43
医疗保健	Medicine and Medical Services	7.31	6.86	6.48
交通通信	Transport, Post and Communication Services	11.08	6.80	6.15
教育文化娱乐服务	Education，Cultural and Recreation Services	14.35	12.79	13.10
居住	Residence	10.74	12.06	12.83
杂项商品与服务	Miscellaneous Commodities and Services	3.30	2.43	2.40

Basic Condition of Urban Households (2003)

按收入等级分							
(Grouped by Percentile of Households)							
最低收入户 Lowest Income Households (first decile)	# 困难户 Poor Households (first five percent)	低收入户 Low Income Households (second decile)	中等偏下户 Lower Middle Income Households (second quintile)	中等收入户 Middle Income Households (third quintile)	中等偏上户 Upper Middle Income Households (fourth quintile)	高收入户 High Income Households (ninth decile)	最高收入户 Highest Income Households (tenth decile)
4783	2383	4849	9691	9663	9615	4767	4660
9.96	4.96	10.10	20.18	20.12	20.02	9.92	9.70
3.40	3.46	3.28	3.13	3.03	2.87	2.76	2.68
1.35	1.25	1.53	1.58	1.65	1.61	1.57	1.62
39.71	36.13	46.65	50.48	54.46	56.10	56.88	60.45
2.52	2.77	2.14	1.98	1.84	1.78	1.76	1.65
2762.43	2278.29	4209.16	5705.67	7753.86	10463.66	14076.07	23483.95
2590.17	2098.92	3970.03	5377.25	7278.75	9763.37	13123.08	21837.32
2562.36	2237.27	3549.28	4557.82	5848.02	7547.31	9627.58	14515.68

Per Capita Annual Living Expenditure of Urban Households (2003)

低收入户 Low Income Households (second decile)	中等偏下户 Lower Middle Income Households (second quintile)	中等收入户 Middle Income Households (third quintile)	中等偏上户 Upper Middle Income Households (fourth quintile)	高收入户 High Income Households (ninth decile)	最高收入户 Highest Income Households (tenth decile)
3549.28	**4557.82**	**5848.02**	**7547.31**	**9627.58**	**14515.68**
1594.67	1926.06	2293.98	2762.75	3337.82	4332.62
178.47	188.56	190.53	202.68	213.74	220.08
364.71	419.32	477.16	538.63	597.80	651.98
53.72	60.31	60.88	65.72	70.05	68.84
85.57	114.88	154.27	201.02	268.90	377.10
66.24	95.63	122.90	153.33	189.32	228.01
329.15	456.14	617.54	791.36	945.33	1276.08
219.17	314.44	438.10	566.91	688.59	956.63
156.26	228.41	343.06	472.55	687.17	1172.69
57.49	104.45	177.56	249.21	389.11	657.34
236.76	325.14	415.13	560.89	757.57	1070.24
300.65	427.79	598.16	826.32	1106.03	2081.14
454.53	605.57	811.91	1102.89	1482.57	2208.97
75.28	132.59	206.49	334.04	493.44	757.35
387.88	459.56	588.75	779.81	965.22	1794.64
77.48	98.85	165.42	286.49	389.00	1012.43
89.41	129.17	179.54	250.79	345.91	579.33
44.93	42.26	39.23	36.61	34.67	29.85
9.27	10.01	10.56	10.49	9.82	8.79
4.40	5.01	5.87	6.26	7.14	8.08
6.67	7.13	7.10	7.43	7.87	7.37
8.47	9.39	10.23	10.95	11.49	14.34
12.81	13.29	13.88	14.61	15.40	15.22
10.93	10.08	10.07	10.33	10.03	12.36
2.52	2.83	3.07	3.32	3.59	3.99

10-8 西部12省(区、市)城镇居民家庭基本情况

项　目	Item	1990 西部12省（区、市） 12 Western Provinces	1990 西部12省（区、市）占全国比例（全国=1） Ratio of 12 Western Provinces to National Total (National Total=1)
调查户数　（户）	**Number of Households Surveyed (household)**	**10000**	**0.28**
平均每户家庭人口　（人）	**Average Household Size (person)**	**3.67**	**-**
平均每户就业人口　（人）	**Average Number of Employed Persons per Household (persons)**	**1.91**	**-**
平均每户就业面　(%)	**Percentage of Employment per Household (%)**	**52.12**	**-**
平均每一就业者负担人数（包括就业者本人）（人）	**Number of Persons Supported by Each Employee (including the employee himself or herself) (person)**	**1.92**	**-**
平均每人全部年收入（元）	**Per Capita Annual Income (yuan)**	**1401.74**	**0.92**
#可支配收入	Disposable Income	1388.70	0.92
平均每人消费性支出（元）	**Per Capita Annual Living Expenditures for Consumption (yuan)**	**1156.42**	**0.90**
食　品	Food	618.13	0.89
衣　着	Clothing	159.33	0.93
家庭设备用品及服务	Household Facilities, Articles and Service		
医疗保健	Medicine and Medical Service		
交通通信	Transport, Post and Communication Services		
教育文化娱乐服务	Education, Cultural and Recreation Services		
居住	Residence		
杂项商品与服务	Miscellaneous Commodities and Services		
平均每人消费性支出构成（人均消费性支出=100）	**Composition of Per Capita Annual Living Expenditures for Consumption (%)**		
食　品	Food	53.45	-
衣　着	Clothing	13.78	-
家庭设备用品及服务	Household Facilities, Articles and Service		-
医疗保健	Medicine and Medical Service		-
交通通信	Transport, Post and Communication Services		-
教育文化娱乐服务	Education，Cultural and Recreation Services		-
居住	Residence		-
杂项商品与服务	Miscellaneous Commodities and Services		-

注：本表1990-2001年各项指标暂缺西藏数据。

Basic Conditions of Urban Households in 12 Western Provinces (Autonomous Regions, Municipality)

1995		2000		2002		2003	
西部12省（区、市） 12 Western Provinces	西部12省（区、市）占全国比例（全国=1） Ratio of 12 Western Provinces to National Total (National Total=1)	西部12省（区、市） 12 Western Provinces	西部12省（区、市）占全国比例（全国=1） Ratio of 12 Western Provinces to National Total (National Total=1)	西部12省（区、市） 12 Western Provinces	西部12省（区、市）占全国比例（全国=1） Ratio of 12 Western Provinces to National Total (National Total=1)	西部12省（区、市） 12 Western Provinces	西部12省（区、市）占全国比例（全国=1） Ratio of 12 Western Provinces to National Total (National Total=1)
10320	**0.29**	**11520**	**0.27**	**12759**	**0.28**	**12926**	**0.27**
3.23	**-**	**3.10**	**-**	**3.07**	**-**	**3.04**	**-**
1.81	**-**	**1.62**	**-**	**1.52**	**-**	**1.53**	**-**
56.13	**-**	**52.17**	**-**	**49.62**	**-**	**50.20**	**-**
1.79	**-**	**1.92**	**-**	**2.02**	**-**	**2.00**	**-**
3773.52	**0.88**	**5516.95**	**0.87**	**7067.26**	**0.86**	**7742.68**	**0.85**
3765.06	0.88	5486.21	0.87	6674.82	0.87	7235.39	0.85
3191.03	**0.90**	**4534.69**	**0.91**	**5470.95**	**0.91**	**5859.54**	**0.90**
1604.49	0.91	1779.71	0.90	2043.43	0.90	2227.84	0.92
438.07	0.91	489.30	0.98	614.04	1.04	656.09	1.03
233.76	0.89	342.85	0.92	351.61	0.90	353.42	0.86
114.13	1.04	288.44	0.91	369.97	0.86	413.90	0.87
169.41	0.92	369.73	0.87	583.38	0.93	653.81	0.91
307.73	0.93	614.83	0.92	780.83	0.87	781.14	0.84
206.86	0.73	472.35	0.84	539.36	0.86	567.62	0.81
116.59	0.96	177.48	0.97	188.32	0.96	205.73	0.96
50.28	-	39.25	-	37.35	-	38.02	-
13.73	-	10.79	-	11.22	-	11.20	-
7.33	-	7.56	-	6.43	-	6.03	-
3.58	-	6.36	-	6.76	-	7.06	-
5.31	-	8.15	-	10.66	-	11.16	-
9.64	-	13.56	-	14.27	-	13.33	-
6.48	-	10.42	-	9.86	-	9.69	-
3.65	-	3.91	-	3.44	-	3.51	-

a) All indicators of Tibet from 1990 to 2001 in the table are not available.

10-9 西部12省(区、市)城镇居民家庭平均每人全年购买的主要商品数量

项 目	Item	1990 西部12省（区、市） 12 Western Provinces	1990 西部12省（区、市）占全国比例（全国=1） Ratio of 12 Western Provinces to National Total (National Total=1)	1995 西部12省（区、市） 12 Western Provinces	1995 西部12省（区、市）占全国比例（全国=1） Ratio of 12 Western Provinces to National Total (National Total=1)
粮 食 （千克）	Grain (kg)	144.52	1.11	100.95	1.04
鲜 菜 （千克）	Fresh Vegetables (kg)	137.70	0.99	120.20	1.03
食用植物油 （千克）	Edible Vegetable Oil (kg)	6.94	1.08	7.46	1.05
猪 肉 （千克）	Pork (kg)	17.74	0.96	18.06	1.05
牛 羊 肉 （千克）	Beef and Mutton (kg)	6.31	1.92	4.34	1.78
家 禽 （千克）	Poultry (kg)	2.99	0.87	4.18	1.05
鲜 蛋 （千克）	Fresh Eggs (kg)	4.22	0.58	6.64	0.68
水 产 品 （千克）	Aquatic Products (kg)	3.96	0.51	4.93	0.54
鲜 奶 （千克）	Milk (kg)	5.73	1.24	6.04	1.31
水 果（瓜果）（千克）	Fresh Melons and Fruits (kg)	43.01	1.05	44.03	0.98
坚果及果仁类 （千克）	Nuts and Kernels (kg)	3.23	1.01	3.17	1.04
酒 （千克）	Liquor (kg)	5.60	0.61	5.91	0.60
煤 炭 （千克）	Coal (kg)	204.05	0.99	93.74	0.72

注：本表2002年以前各项指标暂缺西藏数据。

10-10 西部12省(区、市)城镇居民家庭平均每百户年底耐用消费品拥有量

项 目	Item	1990 西部12省（区、市） 12 Western Provinces	1990 西部12省（区、市）占全国比例（全国=1） Ratio of Western Provinces to National Total (National Total=1)	1995 西部12省（区、市） 12 Western Provinces	1995 西部12省（区、市）占全国比例（全国=1） Ratio of Western Provinces to National Total (National Total=1)
摩托车 （辆）	Motorcycle (unit)	2.78	1.44	4.85	0.77
自行车 （辆）	Bicycle (unit)	175.73	0.93	160.19	0.82
家用汽车 （辆）	Automobile (unit)				
洗衣机 （台）	Washing Machine (set)	82.60	1.05	91.28	1.03
电风扇 （台）	Electric Fan (set)	74.95	0.55	105.95	0.63
电冰箱 （台）	Refrigerator (set)	29.28	0.69	60.31	0.91
彩色电视机 （台）	Color Television Set (set)	62.50	1.06	90.13	1.00
家用电脑 （台）	Computer (set)				
组合音响 （套）	Hi-Fi Stereo Component System (set)			8.68	0.83
录音机 （台）	Tape Recorder (set)	72.00	1.03	26.49	0.96
照相机 （架）	Camera (set)	18.14	0.94	29.50	0.97
空调 （台）	Air conditioner (unit)	0.35	1.03	4.54	0.56
排油烟机 （台）	Smoke Absorber (unit)			28.19	0.82
移动电话机 （部）	Mobile Telephone (unit)				

注：本表2002年以前各项指标暂缺西藏数据。

Per Capita Annual Purchases of Major Commodities of Urban Households in 12 Western Provinces (Autonomous Regions, Municipality)

2000		2002		2003	
西部12省（区、市） 12 Western Provinces	西部12省（区、市）占全国比例（全国=1） Ratio of 12 Western Provinces to National Total (National Total=1)	西部12省（区、市） 12 Western Provinces	西部12省（区、市）占全国比例（全国=1） Ratio of 12 Western Provinces to National Total (National Total=1)	西部12省（区、市） 12 Western Provinces	西部12省（区、市）占全国比例（全国=1） Ratio of 12 Western Provinces to National Total (National Total=1)
80.04	0.97	77.30	0.98	82.83	1.04
107.03	0.93	110.12	0.95	116.22	0.98
7.90	0.97	8.51	1.00	9.68	1.05
16.88	1.01	18.68	0.92	19.53	0.96
5.57	1.67	6.12	2.04	6.56	1.98
5.84	1.07	8.39	0.91	9.21	1.00
8.25	0.74	7.83	0.74	8.88	0.79
5.11	0.52	6.14	0.47	6.72	0.50
11.57	1.16	16.24	1.03	20.26	1.09
54.12	0.94	55.86	0.99	56.78	1.00
3.12	0.94	2.57	0.93	2.55	0.94
6.21	0.62	6.13	0.67	7.49	0.80
115.97	0.91	96.80	0.96	101.06	0.97

a) All indicators of Tibet before 2002 in the table are not available.

Number of Major Durable Consumer Goods Owned Per 100 Urban Households in 12 Western Provinces (Autonomous Regions, Municipality) at the Year-end

2000		2002		2003	
西部12省（区、市） 12 Western Provinces	西部12省（区、市）占全国比例（全国=1） Ratio of Western Provinces to National Total (National Total=1)	西部12省（区、市） 12 Western Provinces	西部12省（区、市）占全国比例（全国=1） Ratio of Western Provinces to National Total (National Total=1)	西部12省（区、市） 12 Western Provinces	西部12省（区、市）占全国比例（全国=1） Ratio of Western Provinces to National Total (National Total=1)
13.47	0.72	15.05	0.68	15.92	0.66
128.88	0.79	120.50	0.84	120.52	0.84
0.50	0.98	0.66	0.75	0.95	0.70
93.31	1.03	92.66	1.00	94.14	1.00
111.28	0.66	104.54	0.57	104.04	0.57
78.43	0.98	83.50	0.96	84.07	0.95
114.57	0.98	119.89	0.95	124.17	0.95
6.55	0.67	12.97	0.63	18.23	0.66
24.00	1.08	24.97	0.99	26.98	1.00
43.17	0.90	45.42	0.95	46.80	0.96
36.71	0.95	39.61	0.90	40.26	0.89
14.46	0.47	20.33	0.40	25.87	0.42
50.41	0.93	53.55	0.88	57.25	0.90
12.81	0.66	55.03	0.87	81.50	0.90

a) All indicators of Tibet before 2002 in the table are not available.

10-11 城镇居民家庭平均每人全年购买主要商品数量

Per Capita Annual Purchases of Major Commodities of Urban Households

项　目	Item	1990	1995	1999	2000	2002	2003
粮　　食　（千克）	Grain (kg)	130.72	97.00	84.91	82.31	78.48	79.52
鲜　　菜　（千克）	Fresh Vegetables (kg)	138.70	116.47	114.94	114.74	116.52	118.34
食用植物油　（千克）	Edible Vegetable Oil (kg)	6.40	7.11	7.78	8.16	8.52	9.20
猪　　肉　（千克）	Pork (kg)	18.46	17.24	16.91	16.73	20.28	20.43
牛　羊　肉　（千克）	Beef and Mutton (kg)	3.28	2.44	3.09	3.33	3.00	3.31
家　　禽　（千克）	Poultry (kg)	3.42	3.97	4.92	5.44	9.24	9.20
鲜　　蛋　（千克）	Fresh Eggs (kg)	7.25	9.74	10.92	11.21	10.56	11.19
水　产　品　（千克）	Aquatic Products (kg)	7.69	9.20	10.34	11.74	13.20	13.35
鲜　　奶　（千克）	Milk (kg)	4.63	4.62	7.88	9.94	15.72	18.62
水果（瓜果）（千克）	Fresh Melons and Fruits (kg)	41.11	44.96	54.21	57.48	56.52	57.79
坚果及果仁类（千克）	Nuts and Kernels (kg)	3.21	3.04	3.26	3.30	2.76	2.70
酒　　　（千克）	Liquor (kg)	9.25	9.93	9.61	10.01	9.12	9.39
煤　　炭　（千克）	Coal (kg)	206.04	129.52	115.46	128.07	101.28	104.71

10-12 城镇居民家庭平均每百户年底耐用消费品拥有量

Number of Major Durable Consumer Goods Owned Per 100 Urban Households at the Year-end

项　目	Item	1990	1995	1999	2000	2002	2003
摩托车　（辆）	Motorcycle (unit)	1.94	6.29	15.12	18.80	22.19	24.00
洗衣机　（台）	Washing Machine (set)	78.41	88.97	91.44	90.50	92.90	94.41
电冰箱　（台）	Refrigerator (set)	42.33	66.22	77.74	80.10	87.38	88.73
彩色电视机　（台）	Color Television Set (set)	59.04	89.79	111.57	116.60	126.38	130.50
录放像机　（台）	Video-recorder (set)		18.19	21.73	20.10	18.43	17.91
组合音响　（套）	Hi-Fi Stereo Component System (set)		10.52	19.66	22.20	25.16	26.89
照相机　（架）	Camera (set)	19.22	30.56	38.11	38.40	44.08	45.36
空调器　（台）	Air Conditioner (unit)	0.34	8.09	24.48	30.80	51.10	61.79
淋浴热水器　（台）	Shower (unit)		30.05	45.49	49.10	62.42	66.61
排油烟机　（台）	Smoke Absorber (unit)		34.47	48.62	54.10	60.67	63.55
影碟机　（台）	Video Disc Player (set)			24.71	37.50	52.57	58.69
家用电脑　（台）	Computer (set)			5.91	9.70	20.63	27.81
摄相机　（架）	Pickup Camera (set)			1.06	1.30	1.92	2.45
微波炉　（台）	Oven (unit)			12.15	17.60	30.91	36.96
健身器材　（套）	Healthy Equipment (set)			3.83	3.50	3.74	4.07
移动电话　（部）	Mobile Telephone (unit)			7.14	19.50	62.89	90.07
家用汽车　（辆）	Automobile (unit)			0.34	0.50	0.88	1.36

10-13 按收入等级分城镇居民家庭平均每人全年购买主要商品数量（2003年）

Per Capita Annual Purchases of Major Commodities of Urban Households by Level of Income (2003)

项　目	Item	总平均 Average	最低收入户 Lowest Income Households	#困难户 Poor Households	低收入户 Low Income Households	中等偏下户 Lower Middle Income Households	中等收入户 Middle Income Households	中等偏上户 Upper Middle Income Households	高收入户 High Income Households	最高收入户 Highest Income Households
粮　食（千克）	Grain (kg)	79.52	84.08	84.28	82.63	82.94	78.49	78.67	77.49	69.65
淀粉及薯类（千克）	Starches and Tubers (kg)	10.14	11.28	11.82	10.49	10.51	9.92	9.89	10.05	8.79
食用植物油（千克）	Edible Vegetable Oil (kg)	9.20	8.69	8.45	9.36	9.60	9.20	9.39	9.05	8.49
食用动物油（千克）	Edible Animal Oil (kg)	0.39	0.64	0.58	0.55	0.44	0.36	0.33	0.25	0.15
猪　肉（千克）	Pork (kg)	20.43	16.38	15.17	18.48	19.91	20.69	21.77	22.78	22.57
牛　肉（千克）	Beef (kg)	1.98	1.24	1.13	1.66	1.90	2.09	2.30	2.33	2.14
羊　肉（千克）	Mutton (kg)	1.33	0.86	0.77	1.05	1.27	1.43	1.57	1.59	1.34
家　禽（千克）	Poultry (kg)	9.20	5.42	4.65	7.08	8.20	9.34	10.42	11.54	12.77
鲜　蛋（千克）	Fresh Eggs (kg)	11.19	9.06	8.49	10.46	11.49	11.23	11.78	12.20	11.40
鱼　（千克）	Fish (kg)	9.79	6.27	5.57	7.68	8.60	9.74	10.79	12.43	14.05
虾　（千克）	Shrimp (kg)	1.33	0.39	0.31	0.63	0.91	1.25	1.65	2.15	2.72
鲜　菜（千克）	Fresh Vegetables (kg)	118.34	105.03	103.04	110.25	116.33	117.40	124.09	129.91	124.97
白　酒（千克）	Liquor (kg)	2.40	2.29	2.08	2.46	2.65	2.43	2.48	2.27	1.78
果　酒（千克）	Fruit Wine (kg)	0.29	0.13	0.13	0.16	0.25	0.30	0.35	0.39	0.49
啤　酒（千克）	Beer (kg)	6.12	3.50	2.87	5.22	5.87	6.51	7.16	6.98	6.78
茶　叶（千克）	Tea (kg)	0.23	0.16	0.15	0.20	0.20	0.22	0.26	0.30	0.27
鲜瓜果（千克）	Fresh Melons & Fruits (kg)	56.57	32.07	26.65	44.36	51.26	58.06	64.39	70.84	75.08
糕　点（千克）	Cake (kg)	4.18	2.04	1.65	2.97	3.69	4.29	4.93	5.58	5.74
鲜　奶（千克）	Milk (kg)	18.62	6.71	5.23	10.85	15.51	18.94	23.43	26.82	28.29
奶　粉（千克）	Milk Powder (kg)	0.56	0.31	0.30	0.46	0.57	0.61	0.62	0.62	0.63
酸　奶（千克）	Yogurt (kg)	2.53	0.68	0.46	1.35	2.01	2.57	3.11	3.92	4.33
男士服装（件）	Men's Clothing (piece)	2.64	1.23	1.04	1.79	2.22	2.60	3.07	3.58	4.32
女士服装（件）	Women's Clothing (piece)	3.56	1.59	1.33	2.28	2.83	3.52	4.16	5.04	6.09
儿童服装（件）	Children's Clothing (piece)	1.02	0.61	0.54	0.83	0.92	1.07	1.13	1.21	1.41
鞋　类（双）	Shoes (pair)	2.58	1.71	1.55	2.15	2.39	2.60	2.84	3.08	3.38

10-14 按收入等级分城镇居民家庭平均每百户年底耐用消费品拥有量（2003年）

Number of Durable Consumer Goods Owned Per 100 Urban Households at Year-end by Level of Income (2003)

项 目		Item		总平均 Average	最低收入户 Lowest Income Households	#困难户 Poor Households	低收入户 Low Income Households	中等偏下户 Lower Middle Income Households	中等收入户 Middle Income Households	中等偏上户 Upper Middle Income Households	高收入户 High Income Households	最高收入户 Highest Income Households
成套家具	(套)	Composite Furniture	(set)	73.04	52.13	49.16	63.47	68.10	72.73	77.51	80.69	93.46
摩托车	(辆)	Motorcycle	(unit)	24.00	13.35	12.89	18.46	22.07	25.17	25.29	29.66	31.66
自行车	(辆)	Bicycle	(unit)	143.55	130.76	119.65	146.25	146.82	148.78	144.27	143.23	135.17
助力车	(辆)	Helping Hand Car	(unit)	4.25	1.63	1.36	1.93	2.78	3.96	4.99	6.90	7.84
家用汽车	(辆)	Automobile	(unit)	1.36	0.20	0.11	0.25	0.42	0.62	1.00	1.97	6.57
洗衣机	(台)	Washing Machine	(unit)	94.41	79.59	76.85	87.06	92.11	95.44	98.03	100.14	103.72
电风扇	(台)	Electric Fan	(unit)	181.58	148.80	142.47	168.97	174.05	182.59	185.33	198.04	210.08
电冰箱	(台)	Refrigerator	(unit)	88.73	60.58	55.43	75.46	84.50	91.29	96.37	99.20	103.32
冰柜	(台)	Freezer	(set)	6.97	6.91	6.27	5.76	6.46	6.42	7.15	8.23	8.53
彩色电视机	(台)	Color Television Set	(set)	130.50	102.39	98.42	113.25	119.22	128.11	138.32	146.52	165.16
影碟机	(台)	Video Disc Player	(set)	58.69	34.56	31.38	46.32	52.57	61.25	64.15	68.33	77.43
录音机	(台)	Tape Recorder	(set)	48.55	34.80	31.09	40.09	44.36	48.56	51.86	56.75	61.52
录放像机	(台)	Video-recorder	(set)	17.91	5.34	4.51	9.93	13.91	16.73	21.05	25.00	32.66
家用电脑	(台)	Computer	(set)	27.81	3.33	2.53	8.36	14.78	23.44	35.25	48.26	64.76
组合音响	(套)	Hi-Fi Stereo Component System	(set)	26.89	10.35	9.63	16.08	20.95	27.51	30.75	35.08	45.50
摄像机	(架)	Pickup Camera	(set)	2.45	0.29	0.21	0.65	0.96	1.37	2.40	3.98	9.27
照相机	(架)	Camera	(set)	45.36	14.07	12.78	23.82	32.68	42.96	53.81	65.43	84.16
钢琴	(架)	Piano	(set)	1.91	0.30	0.08	0.93	0.85	1.28	2.43	2.94	5.28
其他中高档乐器	(件)	Other Medium and High Grade Musical Instrument	(unit)	6.88	1.55	0.92	3.05	4.69	6.91	8.66	9.10	13.44
微波炉	(台)	Oven	(unit)	36.96	7.10	4.78	13.10	22.86	35.36	46.72	58.66	73.75
空调器	(台)	Air Conditioner	(unit)	61.79	10.63	9.44	22.47	36.62	54.16	72.33	98.35	146.75
取暖器	(台)	Room Heater	(unit)	32.26	11.92	9.75	21.43	25.16	33.96	38.66	43.50	46.47
电炊具	(台)	Electric Cooking Appliances	(unit)	101.19	74.51	73.32	83.64	88.97	98.65	109.37	117.41	136.06
淋浴热水器	(台)	Shower	(unit)	66.61	30.40	26.71	44.94	55.81	68.32	77.21	85.18	96.00
排油烟机	(台)	Smoke Absorber	(unit)	63.55	30.88	26.22	47.34	56.79	65.75	71.90	77.38	85.47
消毒碗柜	(台)	Disinfection Cupboard	(unit)	12.94	2.96	2.74	6.42	7.06	11.10	14.47	20.17	31.81
洗碗机	(台)	Dishwasher	(unit)	0.59	0.13	0.04	0.21	0.24	0.49	0.57	1.08	1.75
饮水机	(台)	Drinking Machine	(unit)	31.94	10.52	8.91	18.55	24.29	32.47	38.48	44.21	51.30
吸尘器	(台)	Dust Catcher	(unit)	12.66	1.98	1.51	3.94	6.88	10.03	15.53	21.39	31.38
健身器材	(套)	Healthy Equipment	(unit)	4.07	0.38	0.42	0.82	1.57	3.21	4.75	6.55	12.68
普通电话	(部)	Telephone	(unit)	95.41	77.29	72.70	88.76	94.18	97.01	98.74	101.53	104.02
移动电话	(部)	Mobile Telephone	(unit)	90.07	24.64	18.79	45.28	64.64	89.73	110.05	129.03	158.89
传真机	(部)	Fax-Machine	(unit)	0.72	0.10	0.15	0.16	0.20	0.32	0.70	1.25	3.02

10-15 各地区城镇居民平均每人全年家庭收入来源（2003年）

Per Capita Annual Income of Urban Residents by Source and by Region (2003)

单位: 元 (yuan)

地 区	Region	可支配收入 Disposable Income	总收入 Total Income	工薪收入 Income of Wages and Salaries	经营净收入 Net Income from Management	财产性收入 Property Income	转移性收入 Transfer Income
全 国	**National Average**	**8472.20**	**9061.22**	**6410.22**	**403.82**	**134.98**	**2112.20**
北 京	Beijing	13882.62	14959.30	10152.14	314.19	174.67	4318.30
天 津	Tianjin	10312.91	10971.57	6663.54	468.96	96.41	3742.66
河 北	Hebei	7239.06	7608.43	4924.32	279.23	118.82	2286.06
山 西	Shanxi	7005.03	7446.89	5527.89	302.37	87.23	1529.41
内蒙古	Inner Mongolia	7012.90	7351.58	5235.96	614.22	83.73	1417.66
辽 宁	Liaoning	7240.58	7832.70	5204.18	314.61	63.26	2250.65
吉 林	Jilin	7005.17	7311.23	4828.31	575.10	100.76	1807.06
黑龙江	Heilongjiang	6678.90	6968.01	4489.37	511.68	38.03	1928.94
上 海	Shanghai	14867.49	16380.24	11525.99	376.71	130.05	4347.49
江 苏	Jiangsu	9262.46	9912.14	6091.04	638.82	151.13	3031.10
浙 江	Zhejiang	13179.53	14295.38	9692.52	1171.51	373.97	3057.39
安 徽	Anhui	6778.03	7155.91	4878.30	371.10	114.37	1792.14
福 建	Fujian	9999.54	10816.32	7499.01	547.79	285.75	2483.78
江 西	Jiangxi	6901.42	7153.65	5108.21	366.43	63.76	1615.26
山 东	Shandong	8399.91	9057.58	7418.42	227.91	109.78	1301.47
河 南	Henan	6926.12	7245.00	4757.86	362.92	84.64	2039.58
湖 北	Hubei	7321.98	7745.77	5847.66	238.62	85.03	1574.45
湖 南	Hunan	7674.20	8145.07	5984.74	356.17	100.65	1703.50
广 东	Guangdong	12380.43	13451.13	10413.47	621.51	307.52	2108.62
广 西	Guangxi	7785.04	8293.90	6149.78	402.44	169.18	1572.50
海 南	Hainan	7259.25	7605.69	5020.58	243.14	288.08	2053.90
重 庆	Chongqing	8093.67	8671.91	6288.55	114.13	80.80	2188.43
四 川	Sichuan	7041.87	7488.49	4910.82	351.14	183.45	2043.09
贵 州	Guizhou	6569.23	6746.36	4668.50	379.61	55.12	1643.14
云 南	Yunnan	7643.57	8202.58	5854.39	286.92	86.43	1974.84
西 藏	Tibet	8765.45	9696.79	9466.39		7.15	223.25
陕 西	Shaanxi	6806.35	7314.44	5170.32	139.83	138.06	1866.22
甘 肃	Gansu	6657.24	7132.82	5269.23	269.66	41.40	1552.53
青 海	Qinghai	6745.32	7155.13	4493.36	276.19	50.87	2334.70
宁 夏	Ningxia	6530.48	6991.26	4670.76	441.47	82.48	1796.54
新 疆	Xinjiang	7173.54	7866.85	6219.72	291.63	76.01	1279.49

10-16 各地区城镇居民家庭平均每人全年消费性支出（2003年）

Per Capita Annual Living Expenditure of Urban Residents by Region (2003)

单位: 元 (yuan)

地 区	Region	消费性支出 Living Expenditure	食 品 Food	粮 食 Grain	淀粉及薯类 Starches and Tubers	干豆类及豆制品 Beans and Bean Products	油脂类 Oil and Fats	肉禽及制品 Meat, Poultry and Related Products	蛋 类 Eggs
全 国	**National Average**	**6510.94**	**2416.92**	**194.15**	**17.08**	**31.40**	**78.46**	**473.19**	**60.97**
北 京	Beijing	11123.84	3522.69	224.11	26.12	38.15	81.63	575.01	71.80
天 津	Tianjin	7867.53	2963.85	217.41	24.71	28.05	79.46	479.36	93.27
河 北	Hebei	5439.77	1912.42	182.83	18.41	25.51	95.31	340.73	75.09
山 西	Shanxi	5105.38	1712.13	230.78	20.58	28.26	57.89	251.76	66.27
内蒙古	Inner Mongolia	5419.14	1705.56	211.98	17.48	18.74	50.55	344.86	47.33
辽 宁	Liaoning	6077.92	2394.98	213.62	30.52	36.61	88.06	420.19	82.87
吉 林	Jilin	5492.10	1957.92	198.23	26.14	36.17	74.39	347.02	60.38
黑龙江	Heilongjiang	5015.19	1783.95	200.55	21.57	29.22	72.44	326.64	57.12
上 海	Shanghai	11040.34	4102.65	195.77	23.26	56.63	84.27	618.80	65.73
江 苏	Jiangsu	6708.58	2566.89	167.89	20.32	44.03	70.87	516.47	63.82
浙 江	Zhejiang	9712.89	3558.41	182.99	12.62	45.10	63.42	474.87	47.89
安 徽	Anhui	5064.34	2238.91	181.91	11.08	34.54	85.65	468.93	84.59
福 建	Fujian	7356.26	3104.80	248.98	17.22	37.48	83.28	662.66	71.91
江 西	Jiangxi	4914.55	1979.83	178.03	5.57	33.68	104.01	444.81	48.14
山 东	Shandong	6069.35	2051.30	178.71	15.54	24.69	48.95	347.85	75.71
河 南	Henan	4941.60	1662.30	200.32	19.87	27.74	63.48	317.97	65.96
湖 北	Hubei	5963.25	2279.64	184.20	13.04	31.98	95.94	430.47	50.47
湖 南	Hunan	6082.62	2179.40	194.50	8.42	34.10	94.64	465.63	44.59
广 东	Guangdong	9636.27	3583.72	230.24	11.45	25.89	86.17	846.22	44.85
广 西	Guangxi	5763.50	2305.98	170.07	11.21	30.06	80.44	715.98	41.78
海 南	Hainan	5502.43	2463.03	165.84	6.85	14.23	75.46	679.38	25.83
重 庆	Chongqing	7118.06	2702.34	168.39	18.15	33.55	104.50	616.57	71.53
四 川	Sichuan	5759.21	2240.65	174.46	18.87	26.97	91.77	535.32	58.15
贵 州	Guizhou	4948.98	1968.22	157.29	7.17	21.13	71.30	450.80	43.65
云 南	Yunnan	6023.56	2506.62	199.98	12.66	30.78	48.87	469.94	53.42
西 藏	Tibet	8045.34	3542.89	286.21	22.50	9.63	115.51	685.55	59.00
陕 西	Shaanxi	5666.54	1960.29	189.43	21.87	29.17	67.10	259.99	46.74
甘 肃	Gansu	5298.91	1908.10	185.20	10.55	17.93	80.16	290.95	45.87
青 海	Qinghai	5400.24	1986.54	226.36	12.15	15.06	66.85	385.55	41.73
宁 夏	Ningxia	5330.34	1919.42	204.07	21.43	22.44	74.53	332.80	40.12
新 疆	Xinjiang	5540.61	1987.42	189.65	18.64	20.16	74.14	412.76	43.54

10-16 续表 1 continued

单位: 元 (yuan)

地 区	Region	水产品类 Aquatic Products	菜 类 Vegetables	调味品 Condiments	糖 类 Sugar	烟草类 Tobacco	酒和饮料 Liquor and Beverages	干鲜瓜果类 Dried and Fresh Melons and Fruits	坚果及果仁 Nuts and Kernels
全 国	**National Average**	**170.31**	**236.44**	**35.22**	**26.51**	**122.19**	**120.11**	**174.89**	**26.14**
北 京	Beijing	160.94	266.62	67.06	44.56	100.04	246.46	313.01	64.42
天 津	Tianjin	271.92	249.97	56.18	24.24	112.77	170.61	241.72	55.12
河 北	Hebei	98.93	224.11	31.40	33.50	108.85	157.93	154.31	18.03
山 西	Shanxi	36.37	191.68	25.80	17.97	123.69	83.29	125.95	17.68
内蒙古	Inner Mongolia	43.24	156.04	27.23	16.00	86.29	97.69	136.80	20.68
辽 宁	Liaoning	189.75	288.17	39.97	35.64	147.80	150.99	234.66	23.07
吉 林	Jilin	102.10	221.99	36.16	26.76	85.17	100.90	198.27	18.52
黑龙江	Heilongjiang	84.99	175.80	30.44	22.71	76.17	94.65	165.07	19.65
上 海	Shanghai	534.09	336.30	49.59	54.21	226.21	212.17	294.26	49.93
江 苏	Jiangsu	234.46	245.06	38.04	23.54	158.04	119.15	154.20	30.48
浙 江	Zhejiang	547.10	311.38	36.33	28.42	254.58	173.46	255.48	39.21
安 徽	Anhui	112.94	218.83	34.62	21.58	171.14	176.93	128.42	20.26
福 建	Fujian	581.56	271.53	44.37	21.91	132.14	131.54	207.43	24.71
江 西	Jiangxi	110.71	262.94	26.33	19.10	81.03	74.36	145.80	20.89
山 东	Shandong	120.79	179.91	25.60	18.07	60.59	125.60	156.02	26.77
河 南	Henan	39.28	189.63	29.04	15.51	75.92	102.39	111.50	19.29
湖 北	Hubei	119.35	257.12	35.13	20.04	145.22	101.80	123.08	22.28
湖 南	Hunan	100.92	238.90	23.39	27.09	109.79	80.53	186.42	23.66
广 东	Guangdong	359.79	287.91	36.21	36.32	93.14	106.87	225.50	28.20
广 西	Guangxi	191.51	216.11	24.85	23.23	52.75	65.82	153.57	17.05
海 南	Hainan	353.23	236.65	35.73	18.68	69.20	51.43	126.88	5.82
重 庆	Chongqing	110.75	255.26	54.09	35.83	160.42	103.63	183.14	29.75
四 川	Sichuan	68.47	236.66	43.29	28.34	134.99	100.83	137.70	22.71
贵 州	Guizhou	43.50	211.95	29.29	31.74	134.90	95.87	142.63	20.72
云 南	Yunnan	78.42	262.13	32.71	27.75	246.60	70.91	168.07	17.91
西 藏	Tibet	88.98	404.27	51.28	118.32	484.22	380.27	246.17	3.48
陕 西	Shaanxi	45.72	184.89	31.60	19.51	122.87	91.19	140.21	26.50
甘 肃	Gansu	41.67	221.60	31.23	18.51	123.58	115.05	152.44	24.78
青 海	Qinghai	51.58	184.21	31.52	22.52	113.79	134.50	134.52	18.17
宁 夏	Ningxia	43.06	203.69	29.76	21.19	112.05	78.80	171.87	29.00
新 疆	Xinjiang	54.72	182.13	21.59	29.32	67.28	81.25	177.18	34.41

10-16 续表 2 continued

单位: 元 (yuan)

地 区	Region	糕点类 Cake	奶及奶制品 Milk and Dairy Products	其他食品 Other Food	在外用餐 Dining Out	食品加工服务费 Food Processing Service Fees	衣 着 Clothing	服 装 Garments	衣着材料 Clothing Materials
全 国	**National Average**	**53.46**	**124.70**	**58.37**	**438.24**	**1.22**	**637.73**	**455.32**	**11.88**
北 京	Beijing	125.94	255.99	95.37	829.68	0.19	906.21	612.99	19.97
天 津	Tianjin	84.08	139.08	77.94	612.07	1.00	579.70	402.09	15.54
河 北	Hebei	43.98	117.51	18.90	184.06	1.06	587.60	403.94	16.73
山 西	Shanxi	43.65	128.45	29.31	249.92	0.52	725.81	520.37	19.00
内蒙古	Inner Mongolia	28.56	109.24	60.15	252.18	1.20	793.53	548.32	16.05
辽 宁	Liaoning	47.56	129.81	35.21	221.84	1.71	637.40	439.38	13.88
吉 林	Jilin	33.87	86.59	53.93	268.71	1.16	666.49	463.85	9.44
黑龙江	Heilongjiang	33.88	101.37	44.86	245.20	1.29	696.24	483.90	9.43
上 海	Shanghai	118.82	241.82	93.77	896.85	0.11	750.81	542.05	16.78
江 苏	Jiangsu	52.94	141.95	86.23	428.30	1.59	587.86	422.89	12.39
浙 江	Zhejiang	62.58	139.17	94.71	827.63	0.67	830.03	627.83	11.23
安 徽	Anhui	50.76	117.20	41.46	297.85	0.47	558.07	400.85	10.19
福 建	Fujian	49.23	153.00	43.35	346.64	0.56	576.18	445.12	4.26
江 西	Jiangxi	42.92	94.30	64.08	243.00	1.02	480.86	342.20	11.60
山 东	Shandong	64.24	149.65	71.92	386.43	1.04	790.60	563.64	18.79
河 南	Henan	42.15	91.96	38.99	229.79	0.80	602.64	435.93	13.70
湖 北	Hubei	50.14	90.27	47.66	482.43	1.29	669.30	480.02	10.56
湖 南	Hunan	37.63	87.65	75.96	367.46	1.79	621.33	449.03	8.60
广 东	Guangdong	73.05	124.01	71.50	924.09	0.49	559.90	417.80	2.28
广 西	Guangxi	36.89	85.31	52.68	352.76	0.96	373.60	272.85	8.25
海 南	Hainan	42.81	68.98	24.27	466.56	1.02	279.60	216.66	2.19
重 庆	Chongqing	50.72	178.21	53.62	501.55	2.43	735.01	526.98	7.07
四 川	Sichuan	38.04	130.10	39.18	374.42	3.08	536.46	378.18	9.52
贵 州	Guizhou	41.96	82.48	69.60	331.68	1.27	524.90	363.82	7.40
云 南	Yunnan	55.39	67.73	57.25	623.81	0.20	594.50	449.78	8.62
西 藏	Tibet	46.58	333.64		205.64	5.12	1129.49	785.89	1.82
陕 西	Shaanxi	54.57	103.81	58.07	492.96	0.61	559.07	394.62	13.51
甘 肃	Gansu	30.20	115.57	86.31	333.99	7.29	645.19	437.52	21.72
青 海	Qinghai	33.54	96.29	97.19	338.77	0.42	612.75	402.89	12.69
宁 夏	Ningxia	32.21	103.70	73.26	354.02	0.42	585.24	410.05	18.96
新 疆	Xinjiang	47.36	110.10	60.18	396.65	0.76	783.54	550.10	17.82

10-16 续表 3 continued

单位: 元 (yuan)

地区	Region	鞋类 Shoes	衣着加工服务费 Tailoring and Laundering Service Fees	家庭设备用品及服务 Household Facilities, Articles and Services	耐用消费品 Durable Consumer Goods	室内装饰品 Room Decorations	床上用品 Bed Articles	家庭日用杂品 Household Articles for Daily Use	家具材料 Furniture Materials
全国	**National Average**	**138.67**	**6.80**	**410.34**	**213.57**	**15.58**	**29.40**	**120.89**	**3.12**
北京	Beijing	216.93	17.12	704.17	354.28	28.56	45.49	217.37	6.83
天津	Tianjin	122.02	10.05	467.03	261.65	24.71	26.87	121.74	3.99
河北	Hebei	136.27	8.25	365.37	224.61	16.15	27.80	77.62	4.73
山西	Shanxi	150.93	3.00	314.34	180.81	13.65	15.12	86.85	0.60
内蒙古	Inner Mongolia	171.57	11.21	297.69	140.60	20.92	20.66	98.40	1.86
辽宁	Liaoning	152.78	6.83	257.41	97.42	21.23	26.72	90.54	9.05
吉林	Jilin	157.78	5.32	245.62	105.97	11.44	21.62	90.62	2.72
黑龙江	Heilongjiang	171.16	7.89	217.00	92.17	11.60	20.85	75.88	1.50
上海	Shanghai	150.54	11.27	792.51	433.95	29.31	57.88	193.03	1.72
江苏	Jiangsu	117.50	8.74	452.06	228.16	10.21	37.17	138.29	1.98
浙江	Zhejiang	158.93	9.69	592.61	320.29	23.85	47.89	140.61	13.21
安徽	Anhui	124.69	2.88	257.19	140.66	7.06	13.15	77.21	4.15
福建	Fujian	108.26	3.68	440.43	227.58	9.97	31.11	132.37	5.53
江西	Jiangxi	102.09	4.92	351.50	191.96	9.15	24.89	102.32	4.85
山东	Shandong	163.36	10.08	461.09	275.66	17.59	25.61	124.73	1.79
河南	Henan	127.41	5.61	345.68	196.16	9.95	27.52	91.96	1.86
湖北	Hubei	147.91	7.18	383.40	207.37	8.85	21.02	129.82	1.53
湖南	Hunan	137.60	5.74	420.19	208.98	13.21	33.33	132.77	1.20
广东	Guangdong	115.34	3.74	658.04	316.89	24.30	46.54	189.69	1.78
广西	Guangxi	76.88	3.82	376.86	199.45	13.76	31.34	112.11	0.75
海南	Hainan	49.79	1.51	318.99	137.37	12.64	19.86	124.75	0.20
重庆	Chongqing	169.38	4.47	475.36	253.06	16.54	37.67	131.50	2.69
四川	Sichuan	121.33	5.89	399.60	217.25	9.93	26.14	119.74	0.95
贵州	Guizhou	132.56	3.05	286.62	100.69	9.96	21.28	127.67	6.21
云南	Yunnan	118.20	1.62	269.57	123.74	12.50	40.47	81.76	0.10
西藏	Tibet	323.96	3.37	444.00	204.37	11.69	99.84	117.94	0.48
陕西	Shaanxi	122.47	6.65	383.48	204.40	13.36	23.07	119.42	3.36
甘肃	Gansu	138.34	7.54	302.66	139.68	18.72	20.18	105.19	2.66
青海	Qinghai	144.52	6.76	370.93	185.07	33.88	26.46	109.04	4.35
宁夏	Ningxia	128.00	6.39	363.09	205.31	22.21	19.92	96.05	0.20
新疆	Xinjiang	166.47	11.44	271.14	113.71	22.06	20.06	95.36	2.84

10-16 续表 4 continued

单位: 元 (yuan)

地 区	Region	家务服务 Household Services	医疗保健 Medicine and Medical Services	交通和通信 Transport and Communication Services	交 通 Transport	通 信 Communication	教育文化娱乐服务 Education, Cultural and Recreation Services	文化娱乐用品 Recreation Articles	教 育 Education
全 国	**National Average**	**27.79**	**475.98**	**721.13**	**297.11**	**424.01**	**934.38**	**264.47**	**514.00**
北 京	Beijing	51.65	994.01	1688.08	924.31	763.77	1964.19	581.85	971.00
天 津	Tianjin	28.08	697.76	721.28	296.11	425.18	1083.91	318.63	638.40
河 北	Hebei	14.46	550.90	607.75	259.11	348.65	660.58	214.20	361.99
山 西	Shanxi	17.31	367.47	478.09	145.30	332.79	799.35	247.45	467.46
内蒙古	Inner Mongolia	15.25	425.88	596.21	226.74	369.47	770.50	230.85	432.52
辽 宁	Liaoning	12.45	534.30	631.14	219.69	411.45	747.41	198.09	476.16
吉 林	Jilin	13.25	462.12	550.17	202.52	347.66	742.15	190.66	471.74
黑龙江	Heilongjiang	15.00	456.29	499.69	174.45	325.24	644.49	153.22	396.55
上 海	Shanghai	76.61	602.73	1258.72	621.22	637.50	1833.79	587.06	936.67
江 苏	Jiangsu	36.24	493.80	686.47	349.15	337.32	971.91	269.04	549.97
浙 江	Zhejiang	46.76	738.49	1223.95	639.93	584.02	1486.63	389.31	801.66
安 徽	Anhui	14.96	318.20	502.72	183.74	318.98	536.20	159.81	300.98
福 建	Fujian	33.87	348.81	867.82	294.28	573.54	898.57	288.52	472.05
江 西	Jiangxi	18.34	264.89	465.83	126.40	339.43	664.32	173.23	371.16
山 东	Shandong	15.72	444.04	638.22	272.44	365.78	931.46	334.59	500.30
河 南	Henan	18.22	443.27	533.86	127.15	406.72	629.91	188.07	332.79
湖 北	Hubei	14.81	397.49	571.93	197.33	374.60	843.66	198.49	524.78
湖 南	Hunan	30.70	391.29	680.21	261.18	419.03	993.94	246.26	545.95
广 东	Guangdong	78.84	616.81	1272.78	551.98	720.80	1437.07	377.40	678.88
广 西	Guangxi	19.46	322.68	608.27	281.66	326.61	797.81	217.69	442.08
海 南	Hainan	24.17	413.95	601.92	284.82	317.10	630.05	146.63	382.17
重 庆	Chongqing	33.90	459.69	790.26	293.58	496.68	1025.99	250.24	565.07
四 川	Sichuan	25.58	425.13	586.79	239.16	347.63	823.72	237.20	450.63
贵 州	Guizhou	20.81	291.82	561.22	212.99	348.23	714.30	199.29	378.23
云 南	Yunnan	11.01	545.76	763.59	311.88	451.71	735.88	254.52	334.36
西 藏	Tibet	9.68	310.44	1183.87	375.80	808.07	596.91	134.34	430.70
陕 西	Shaanxi	19.87	491.17	528.62	175.00	353.62	950.85	213.54	627.11
甘 肃	Gansu	16.24	434.80	531.19	209.26	321.93	793.19	223.48	455.10
青 海	Qinghai	12.14	451.31	509.37	182.43	326.94	713.27	218.33	366.69
宁 夏	Ningxia	19.41	450.70	585.42	203.50	381.92	644.72	219.47	320.56
新 疆	Xinjiang	17.12	357.64	601.13	239.48	361.65	806.53	212.25	504.87

10-16 续表 5 continued

单位: 元 (yuan)

地区	Region	文化娱乐服务 Recreation Services	居住 Residence	住房 Housing	水电燃料及其他 Water, Electricity, Fuels and Others	杂项商品和服务 Miscellaneous Commodities and Services	杂项商品 Miscellaneous Commodities	服务 Services
全国	**National Average**	**155.91**	**699.39**	**256.45**	**412.73**	**215.10**	**134.57**	**80.53**
北京	Beijing	411.33	955.77	489.50	438.58	388.73	261.06	127.66
天津	Tianjin	126.88	1095.61	463.13	610.58	258.39	154.69	103.69
河北	Hebei	84.40	595.24	149.23	426.32	159.90	89.22	70.68
山西	Shanxi	84.44	561.49	228.40	305.12	146.69	76.53	70.17
内蒙古	Inner Mongolia	107.13	618.18	181.58	357.29	212.76	129.17	83.59
辽宁	Liaoning	73.17	630.86	182.71	433.29	244.42	112.92	131.51
吉林	Jilin	79.75	669.32	217.33	429.18	198.30	118.18	80.12
黑龙江	Heilongjiang	94.72	539.50	145.70	367.85	178.05	106.96	71.09
上海	Shanghai	310.07	1280.43	641.36	551.82	418.71	281.94	136.77
江苏	Jiangsu	152.89	715.98	297.20	398.08	233.61	136.85	96.76
浙江	Zhejiang	295.66	953.10	427.60	491.92	329.68	196.44	133.24
安徽	Anhui	75.41	487.37	140.79	332.85	165.69	82.53	83.15
福建	Fujian	138.00	878.94	289.71	558.13	240.72	129.33	111.39
江西	Jiangxi	119.93	573.38	231.80	332.72	133.94	86.87	47.08
山东	Shandong	96.58	551.75	174.50	359.86	200.89	139.45	61.44
河南	Henan	109.06	566.30	187.85	350.65	157.63	98.30	59.33
湖北	Hubei	120.38	655.00	216.60	419.30	162.83	114.07	48.76
湖南	Hunan	201.72	586.90	214.21	355.61	209.35	136.73	72.63
广东	Guangdong	380.78	1196.40	443.72	661.90	311.55	209.84	101.70
广西	Guangxi	138.05	801.15	363.77	419.49	177.15	112.08	65.07
海南	Hainan	101.25	604.72	184.05	383.06	190.18	122.04	68.14
重庆	Chongqing	210.68	741.60	249.19	451.61	187.81	149.94	37.87
四川	Sichuan	135.90	580.47	224.92	333.00	166.39	115.36	51.03
贵州	Guizhou	136.77	422.05	88.61	314.32	179.85	112.23	67.63
云南	Yunnan	147.00	445.46	151.14	277.88	162.18	94.49	67.69
西藏	Tibet	31.86	468.49	74.44	374.47	369.26	160.53	208.73
陕西	Shaanxi	110.19	609.05	264.52	328.77	184.01	112.11	71.90
甘肃	Gansu	114.62	505.60	164.60	322.54	178.17	105.04	73.14
青海	Qinghai	128.25	559.33	206.83	314.02	196.74	123.29	73.45
宁夏	Ningxia	104.69	560.53	196.73	335.44	221.23	141.93	79.30
新疆	Xinjiang	89.41	499.93	115.31	352.54	233.28	160.23	73.05

10-17 各地区城镇居民家庭平均每百户耐用消费品拥有量(2003年底)

Number of Major Durable Consumer Goods Owned Per 100 Urban Households at the Year-end by Region (2003)

地区	Region	成套家具（套）Composite Furniture (sets)	摩托车（辆）Motorcycle (unit)	自行车（辆）Bicycle (unit)	助力车（辆）Helping Hand Car (unit)	家用汽车（辆）Automobile (unit)	洗衣机（台）Washing Machine (set)	电风扇（台）Electric Fan (set)	电冰箱（台）Refrigerator (set)
全国	**National Average**	**73.04**	**24.00**	**143.55**	**4.25**	**1.36**	**94.41**	**181.58**	**88.73**
北京	Beijing	88.58	5.59	202.06	4.61	6.60	99.25	143.05	100.40
天津	Tianjin	91.87	8.87	228.53	4.40	2.20	96.33	119.93	98.47
河北	Hebei	81.14	34.62	221.91	3.85	1.96	99.21	163.00	93.70
山西	Shanxi	74.70	26.00	182.45	2.35	1.16	97.22	89.93	78.96
内蒙古	Inner Mongolia	66.72	29.08	196.97	2.09	1.33	93.41	66.04	78.96
辽宁	Liaoning	41.15	6.97	131.76	2.31	0.58	89.26	76.99	87.05
吉林	Jilin	25.16	13.38	139.02	0.59	0.57	95.10	69.77	79.19
黑龙江	Heilongjiang	39.77	8.76	101.13	0.25	1.07	89.65	57.16	73.30
上海	Shanghai	92.20	3.80	125.40	17.80	1.80	94.00	205.00	102.00
江苏	Jiangsu	71.74	27.58	172.89	13.22	1.50	97.65	205.09	90.29
浙江	Zhejiang	80.26	25.53	176.55	15.89	2.98	92.69	258.44	98.60
安徽	Anhui	61.80	17.65	134.15	3.57	0.18	93.20	248.68	88.54
福建	Fujian	81.54	42.37	143.91	2.81	0.73	97.74	242.40	96.23
江西	Jiangxi	72.81	18.13	139.92	1.81	0.21	93.92	253.70	84.97
山东	Shandong	87.57	46.12	192.24	7.82	1.28	92.13	180.76	90.52
河南	Henan	69.44	25.65	204.56	4.82	0.54	95.94	218.43	83.69
湖北	Hubei	85.56	13.91	116.08	2.22	0.21	94.85	233.89	94.44
湖南	Hunan	82.98	14.75	67.61	2.01	0.27	95.25	253.57	87.06
广东	Guangdong	75.72	75.18	133.11	1.75	4.37	97.71	299.98	92.56
广西	Guangxi	82.37	46.87	186.62	4.08	0.82	90.68	290.34	85.47
海南	Hainan	17.03	63.71	113.59		2.25	77.16	189.37	70.21
重庆	Chongqing	92.00	2.00	4.00	0.33	1.33	97.67	194.33	98.00
四川	Sichuan	93.01	6.62	86.67	1.78	0.88	94.01	217.22	91.16
贵州	Guizhou	68.93	7.74	21.51	0.41	0.46	95.58	98.82	84.71
云南	Yunnan	64.83	28.34	139.43	2.77	2.20	93.16	34.73	77.09
西藏	Tibet	86.00	6.00	126.00		2.00	91.00	11.00	84.00
陕西	Shaanxi	68.95	15.69	138.32	0.82	0.44	94.94	131.59	81.47
甘肃	Gansu	77.79	10.97	161.56	1.90	0.11	96.39	54.73	85.71
青海	Qinghai	44.49	7.09	71.02	1.24	0.81	99.10	12.81	78.45
宁夏	Ningxia	28.11	16.24	176.64	1.73	0.52	91.82	77.88	79.53
新疆	Xinjiang	65.00	14.34	137.44	0.94	0.51	91.93	58.94	84.33

10-17 续表 1 continued

地 区	Region	冰 柜（台）Freezer (set)	彩色电视机（台）Color TV Set (set)	影碟机（台）Video Disc Player (set)	录音机（台）Tape Recorder (set)	录放像机（台）Video Recorder (set)	家用电脑（台）Computer (set)	组合音响（套）Hi-Fi Stereo Component System (set)	摄像机（架）Pickup Camera (set)
全 国	**National Average**	**6.97**	**130.50**	**58.69**	**48.55**	**17.91**	**27.81**	**26.89**	**2.45**
北 京	Beijing	14.03	146.99	60.42	71.99	51.27	68.31	37.61	11.31
天 津	Tianjin	16.73	134.53	49.60	56.80	30.33	34.07	26.80	3.40
河 北	Hebei	15.27	125.22	45.70	56.68	17.78	18.34	21.33	2.14
山 西	Shanxi	9.63	114.40	43.22	49.30	12.61	18.01	15.97	1.68
内蒙古	Inner Mongolia	13.78	113.97	44.07	57.22	10.51	12.07	13.33	1.01
辽 宁	Liaoning	9.33	121.57	44.63	50.55	22.02	23.12	22.09	2.81
吉 林	Jilin	9.07	120.41	50.13	51.91	15.54	14.07	12.17	1.50
黑龙江	Heilongjiang	12.10	110.44	43.22	49.61	15.24	13.77	14.46	2.70
上 海	Shanghai	3.20	167.60	73.80	60.20	33.40	60.40	39.60	5.80
江 苏	Jiangsu	3.90	142.52	54.84	41.21	19.13	27.91	25.04	3.13
浙 江	Zhejiang	4.52	159.39	63.19	51.46	20.42	40.23	28.11	2.76
安 徽	Anhui	5.72	124.17	52.24	40.55	14.70	16.98	18.59	0.88
福 建	Fujian	2.24	147.35	72.58	38.46	16.34	39.35	28.39	1.58
江 西	Jiangxi	3.22	130.37	50.55	36.81	10.10	16.05	22.85	1.85
山 东	Shandong	14.55	119.60	55.87	64.53	20.90	31.43	21.39	2.72
河 南	Henan	7.99	124.19	49.25	48.81	10.27	19.19	18.39	1.64
湖 北	Hubei	6.24	128.34	67.63	39.28	14.32	27.68	31.61	1.28
湖 南	Hunan	6.65	124.82	61.20	37.91	12.96	26.67	34.52	1.31
广 东	Guangdong	0.84	152.52	81.24	54.93	17.81	56.02	51.47	3.79
广 西	Guangxi	2.23	126.84	69.04	40.65	11.66	23.36	33.04	1.37
海 南	Hainan	2.54	117.86	54.97	51.74	11.36	15.61	22.44	0.25
重 庆	Chongqing	1.00	150.67	70.67	28.00	20.67	34.67	35.33	3.67
四 川	Sichuan	2.99	131.89	67.90	37.69	14.55	21.29	30.17	1.23
贵 州	Guizhou	4.52	122.11	70.00	26.84	14.71	17.51	38.31	1.47
云 南	Yunnan	1.79	124.57	72.46	50.95	20.17	18.61	34.65	2.26
西 藏	Tibet	9.00	132.00	73.00	59.00	45.00	16.00	33.00	5.00
陕 西	Shaanxi	3.19	123.15	58.35	48.26	15.88	18.86	22.04	1.55
甘 肃	Gansu	5.47	119.32	52.49	51.81	16.00	14.40	22.39	1.38
青 海	Qinghai	8.30	119.25	59.70	54.54	13.71	13.27	21.51	0.77
宁 夏	Ningxia	3.53	113.83	50.00	42.62	9.15	12.86	20.27	0.72
新 疆	Xinjiang	3.14	112.39	55.12	64.02	16.07	15.81	19.68	1.09

10-17 续表 2 continued

地 区	Region	照相机（架）Camera (set)	钢 琴（架）Piano (set)	其他中高档乐器（件）Other Medium and High Grade Musical Instrument (unit)	微波炉（台）Oven (unit)	空调器（台）Air Conditioner (unit)	取暖器（台）Room Heater (unit)	电炊具（台）Electric Cooking Appliances (unit)	淋浴热水器（台）Shower (unit)
全 国	**National Average**	**45.36**	**1.91**	**6.88**	**36.96**	**61.79**	**32.26**	**101.19**	**66.61**
北 京	Beijing	103.33	3.74	13.76	79.20	119.31	32.88	107.79	85.42
天 津	Tianjin	56.27	1.40	4.13	61.40	90.87	21.80	101.13	82.73
河 北	Hebei	45.58	1.18	6.52	26.93	55.91	14.83	65.23	66.47
山 西	Shanxi	38.78	1.22	5.69	14.63	18.17	10.27	38.95	31.06
内蒙古	Inner Mongolia	33.73	0.90	6.83	14.49	3.01	5.79	148.45	33.50
辽 宁	Liaoning	48.10	2.46	5.97	31.39	11.21	16.83	94.74	57.74
吉 林	Jilin	36.01	1.50	6.83	20.38	3.31	9.03	128.23	34.52
黑龙江	Heilongjiang	31.12	1.28	4.77	16.06	4.89	9.20	165.50	26.69
上 海	Shanghai	70.00	3.20	6.80	87.60	135.80	73.20	154.40	80.60
江 苏	Jiangsu	41.74	1.67	4.18	63.52	90.94	50.21	108.68	72.76
浙 江	Zhejiang	50.72	2.00	6.50	51.21	105.23	44.09	112.09	82.98
安 徽	Anhui	33.62	1.29	7.09	28.18	61.75	44.28	90.99	61.69
福 建	Fujian	43.47	2.03	7.28	56.88	99.88	13.70	125.31	94.90
江 西	Jiangxi	32.11	1.52	7.41	23.04	46.01	64.44	77.43	69.22
山 东	Shandong	54.17	3.06	8.67	31.89	52.31	28.85	82.48	65.83
河 南	Henan	37.03	1.95	7.39	20.37	73.07	33.46	69.63	41.54
湖 北	Hubei	42.81	1.68	7.09	37.99	77.75	60.55	110.46	67.96
湖 南	Hunan	38.70	1.47	6.65	30.81	55.38	68.59	57.90	64.02
广 东	Guangdong	60.18	2.89	8.79	54.64	141.99	10.20	107.49	104.89
广 西	Guangxi	39.36	1.16	6.36	33.02	46.82	21.08	124.94	94.00
海 南	Hainan	21.78	0.76	4.98	16.77	29.66		144.14	76.11
重 庆	Chongqing	48.33	1.33	3.00	58.67	126.67	35.67	70.33	92.00
四 川	Sichuan	37.57	1.44	6.22	32.10	56.21	44.04	107.08	82.06
贵 州	Guizhou	30.50	2.07	4.71	28.09	4.58	55.47	106.31	46.25
云 南	Yunnan	49.85	1.39	6.13	32.21	0.10	26.54	151.06	48.98
西 藏	Tibet	51.00		2.00	24.00	4.00	43.00	20.00	22.00
陕 西	Shaanxi	41.42	1.26	5.62	30.59	59.34	18.51	87.05	58.49
甘 肃	Gansu	40.79	2.57	8.70	17.64	1.96	9.16	73.71	49.17
青 海	Qinghai	45.26	1.19	6.92	26.76	0.29	22.73	50.37	29.65
宁 夏	Ningxia	25.37	0.87	5.64	20.63	2.58	8.11	136.37	50.88
新 疆	Xinjiang	39.93	2.37	13.57	12.96	4.92	8.68	86.02	61.83

10-17 续表 3 continued

地 区	Region	排油烟机（台）Smoke Absorber (unit)	消毒碗柜（台）Disinfection Cupboard (unit)	洗碗机（台）Dishwasher (unit)	饮水机（台）Drinking Machine (unit)	吸尘器（台）Dust Catcher (unit)	健身器材（套）Health Equipment (set)	普通电话（部）Telephone (unit)	移动电话（部）Mobile Telephone (unit)	传真机（部）Fax Machine (unit)
全 国	**National Average**	**63.55**	**12.94**	**0.59**	**31.94**	**12.66**	**4.07**	**95.41**	**90.07**	**0.72**
北 京	Beijing	81.32	6.24	0.75	42.32	36.39	10.94	102.30	133.68	1.78
天 津	Tianjin	82.40	1.40	0.20	31.33	24.33	5.40	97.67	77.80	1.00
河 北	Hebei	69.90	2.53	0.49	25.68	12.71	6.19	92.54	65.81	0.30
山 西	Shanxi	58.11	1.34	0.29	27.83	6.53	2.44	92.17	61.72	0.26
内蒙古	Inner Mongolia	55.18	0.83	0.24	21.18	10.32	1.90	87.92	74.64	0.44
辽 宁	Liaoning	75.64	3.92	0.55	20.21	23.50	2.92	93.38	74.50	0.60
吉 林	Jilin	74.78	2.68	0.27	19.00	13.22	3.61	95.81	80.80	0.20
黑龙江	Heilongjiang	69.97	2.69	0.47	20.56	13.52	2.10	89.12	55.58	0.40
上 海	Shanghai	76.80	11.20	1.40	55.60	43.40	6.80	102.00	133.00	3.40
江 苏	Jiangsu	73.49	5.07	0.41	47.33	15.09	4.02	98.65	99.73	1.27
浙 江	Zhejiang	83.34	16.08	0.99	45.04	18.85	5.68	100.10	130.64	2.03
安 徽	Anhui	55.42	2.32	0.52	23.98	8.55	3.10	95.58	69.84	0.25
福 建	Fujian	62.74	27.96	0.99	28.82	5.39	6.95	105.37	121.05	1.33
江 西	Jiangxi	39.14	6.87	0.31	24.08	4.15	2.13	94.65	78.06	0.17
山 东	Shandong	82.61	5.21	0.89	56.92	16.22	4.89	97.32	97.48	0.26
河 南	Henan	49.10	5.80	0.32	30.63	4.59	3.38	95.05	66.27	0.51
湖 北	Hubei	47.43	10.89	0.46	22.26	7.44	3.15	94.11	74.98	0.46
湖 南	Hunan	35.68	17.85	0.44	23.35	4.26	2.64	92.36	102.66	0.17
广 东	Guangdong	79.24	76.49	1.25	31.66	10.13	7.08	102.04	150.66	2.15
广 西	Guangxi	56.81	39.72	0.34	22.80	4.72	3.46	95.04	75.76	0.68
海 南	Hainan	53.23	48.88		16.79	0.51	3.49	93.50	73.56	
重 庆	Chongqing	41.00	8.67	1.00	33.33	14.67	4.67	97.67	95.67	
四 川	Sichuan	37.63	6.99	0.44	26.69	5.90	2.79	91.37	82.37	0.13
贵 州	Guizhou	41.20	25.76	0.26	46.13	5.41	2.08	92.00	81.50	0.46
云 南	Yunnan	73.06	8.13	0.64	40.29	8.39	3.55	93.65	85.94	0.24
西 藏	Tibet	34.00	7.00	2.00	30.00	7.00	1.00	87.00	107.00	
陕 西	Shaanxi	61.56	3.80	0.23	32.64	6.12	2.02	89.81	82.94	0.42
甘 肃	Gansu	74.75	1.75	0.78	32.67	5.91	2.21	90.28	70.63	0.23
青 海	Qinghai	78.03	3.30		27.95	8.96	1.20	88.46	75.98	0.27
宁 夏	Ningxia	57.40	1.26		27.75	6.09	0.87	92.91	73.20	0.15
新 疆	Xinjiang	76.36	3.82	0.36	24.97	17.30	3.22	92.73	72.36	0.07

10-18 农村居民家庭基本情况

Basic Conditions of Rural Households

项 目	Item	2000 全国 National Total	2000 西部12省(区、市) 12 Western Provinces	2002 全国 National Total	2002 西部12省(区、市) 12 Western Provinces	2003 全国 National Total	2003 西部12省(区、市) 12 Western Provinces
调查户数 (户)	**Number of Households Surveyed (household)**	**68116**	**21986**	**68190**	**22060**	**68190**	**22060**
调查户人口 (人)	**Number of Residents Surveyed (person)**						
常住人口	Number of Permanent Residents in the Households Surveyed	286162	98712	281674	97122	279536	96422
平均每户常住人口	Average Number of Permanent Residents per Household	4.20	4.49	4.13	4.40	4.10	4.37
平均每户整半劳力	Average Number of Able-bodied and Semi-able-bodied Laborers per Household	2.76	2.83	2.76	2.82	2.80	2.86
平均每个劳动力负担人口(含本人)	Average Number of Persons Supported by a Laborer (including the laborer himself or herself)	1.52	1.59	1.50	1.56	1.47	1.53
平均每人年收入(元)	**Per Capita Annual Income (yuan)**						
总收入	Total Revenue	3146.21	2496.42	3448.62	2718.13	3582.42	2836.72
工资性收入	Wages Income	702.30	390.93	840.22	483.87	918.38	540.93
家庭经营收入	Household Business Income	2251.28	1976.01	2380.51	2076.21	2454.96	2148.46
财产性收入	Property Income	45.04	31.23	50.68	30.80	65.75	41.85
转移性收入	Transfer Income	147.59	98.25	177.21	127.25	143.33	105.49
现金收入	Cash Income	2381.60	1722.50	2712.95	1928.18	2929.47	2100.78
工资性收入	Wages Income	700.41	390.31	839.17	483.44	916.65	540.42
家庭经营收入	Household Business Income	1498.81	1210.64	1653.65	1293.51	1822.11	1430.80
财产性收入	Property Income	38.89	26.18	47.65	28.57	53.96	34.33
转移性收入	Transfer Income	143.49	95.37	172.48	122.66	136.75	95.23
平均每人年支出(元)	**Per Capita Annual Expenditures (yuan)**						
总支出	Total Expenditure	2652.42	2211.35	2923.60	2412.11	3024.99	2514.20
家庭经营费用支出	Expenditure for Household Business	654.27	643.57	731.01	707.20	755.38	733.48
购置生产性固定资产	Purchasing Productive Fixed Assets	63.90	63.64	85.50	93.43	101.64	113.10
税费支出	Expenditure for Tax and Fee	95.52	79.45	78.70	57.36	67.31	49.14
生活消费支出	Expenditure for Consumption	1670.13	1325.85	1834.31	1438.90	1943.30	1524.22
转移性和财产性支出	Expenditure for Transfer and Property	168.60	98.84	194.08	115.22	157.36	94.27
现金支出	Cash Expenditure	2140.37	1621.29	2437.72	1833.06	2537.42	1918.62
家庭经营费用支出	Expenditure for Household Business	544.49	483.47	617.41	532.83	638.40	548.21
购买生产性固定资产	Purchasing Productive Fixed Assets	63.91	63.64	85.50	93.43	101.64	113.10
税费支出	Expenditure for Tax and Fee	89.81	74.40	75.58	53.98	65.99	47.35
生活消费支出	Expenditure for Consumption	1284.74	907.03	1467.62	1039.43	1576.64	1117.09
转移性和财产性支出	Expenditure for Transfer and Property	157.42	92.75	191.61	113.39	154.74	92.87
平均每人年纯收入(元)	**Per Capita Annual Net Income (yuan)**	**2253.42**	**1661.03**	**2475.63**	**1820.87**	**2622.24**	**1936.01**
工资性收入	Wages Income	702.30	390.93	840.22	483.87	918.38	540.93
家庭经营纯收入	Household Business Income	1427.27	1182.43	1486.54	1230.52	1541.28	1276.60
财产性收入	Property Income	45.04	31.23	50.68	30.97	65.75	41.85
转移性收入	Transfer Income	78.81	56.44	98.19	75.50	96.83	76.64

注:本表至10-34表为农村住户抽样调查资料。

a) Data from Tables 10-17 to 10-34 are obtained from the sample surveys on rural households.

10-19　农村居民按纯收入分组的户数占调查户比重
Percentage of Rural Households Grouped by Per Capita Annual Net Income

项　目	Item	1990	1995	2000	2002	2003
按纯收入分组户数	**Percentage of Households Grouped by**					
占调查户比重 (%)	**Per Capita Annual Net Income (%)**					
100元以下	100 Yuan and below	0.30	0.21	0.31	0.40	0.49
100-200 (元)	100-200 Yuan	1.78	0.36	0.20	0.19	0.18
200-300 (元)	200-300 Yuan	6.56	0.78	0.43	0.28	0.31
300-400 (元)	300-400 Yuan	12.04	1.47	0.69	0.50	0.52
400-500 (元)	400-500 Yuan	14.37	2.30	1.01	0.79	0.78
500-600 (元)	500-600 Yuan	13.94	3.37	1.37	1.25	1.19
600-800 (元)	600-800 Yuan	20.80	9.54	4.44	3.62	3.25
800-1000 (元)	800-1000 Yuan	12.49	11.63	5.72	4.98	4.87
1000-1200 (元)	1000-1200 Yuan		11.83	6.75	6.16	5.52
1200-1300 (元)	1200-1300 Yuan	12.25	5.38	3.75	3.25	2.97
1300-1500 (元)	1300-1500 Yuan		9.74	7.42	6.89	6.39
1500-1700 (元)	1500-1700 Yuan	3.48	7.92	7.48	6.89	6.45
1700-2000 (元)	1700-2000 Yuan		9.39	10.45	9.89	9.39
2000-2500 (元)	2000-2500 Yuan		10.29	14.54	14.31	13.79
2500-3000 (元)	2500-3000 Yuan		5.89	10.29	10.45	10.81
3000-3500 (元)	3000-3500 Yuan		3.49	7.11	7.79	8.02
3500-4000 (元)	3500-4000 Yuan	1.99	1.95	4.76	5.61	5.84
4000-4500 (元)	4000-4500 Yuan		1.34	3.44	3.83	4.20
4500-5000 (元)	4500-5000 Yuan		0.86	2.40	2.84	3.16
5000元以上	5000 Yuan and over		2.26	7.45	10.09	11.85

10-20　农村居民家庭平均每人纯收入
Per Capita Annual Net Income of Rural Households

单位: 元　　(yuan)

项　目	Item	1990	1995	2000	2002	2003
纯收入	**Net Income**	**686.31**	**1577.74**	**2253.42**	**2475.63**	**2622.24**
按收入来源分	**By Source**					
工资性收入	Wages Income	138.80	353.70	702.30	840.22	918.38
家庭经营纯收入	Net Income from Household Business	518.55	1125.79	1427.27	1486.54	1541.28
农业收入	Farming	344.59	799.44	833.93	866.67	885.70
林业收入	Forestry	7.53	13.52	22.44	25.53	29.28
牧业收入	Animal Husbandry	96.81	127.81	207.35	210.62	245.68
渔业收入	Fishery	7.11	15.69	26.95	32.17	34.92
工业收入	Industry	9.15	13.63	52.67	63.29	60.49
建筑业收入	Construction	12.18	34.53	46.73	45.28	48.12
交通、运输、邮电业收入	Transport, Post and Telecommunication Services	13.45	27.76	63.63	69.38	68.91
批发.零售贸易及餐饮业	Wholesale and Retail Trade and Catering Services	12.69	34.26	78.54	85.56	89.05
社会服务业收入	Social Services	6.55	17.18	28.09	31.36	30.97
文教卫生业收入	Culture, Education and Health Care			6.86	7.99	8.76
其他收入	Others	8.49	41.97	60.08	48.68	39.38
转移性和财产性收入	Transfer Income and Property Income	28.96	98.25	123.85	148.87	162.58

10-21 各地区农村居民家庭平均每人纯收入

Per Capita Net Income of Rural Households by Region

单位：元 (yuan)

地 区	Region	1990	1995	2000	2001	2002	2003
全 国	**National Average**	**686.31**	**1577.74**	**2253.42**	**2366.40**	**2475.63**	**2622.24**
北 京	Beijing	1297.05	3223.65	4604.55	5025.50	5398.48	5601.55
天 津	Tianjin	1069.04	2406.38	3622.39	3947.72	4278.71	4566.01
河 北	Hebei	621.67	1668.73	2478.86	2603.60	2685.16	2853.38
山 西	Shanxi	603.51	1208.30	1905.61	1956.05	2149.82	2299.17
内蒙古	Inner Mongolia	607.15	1208.38	2038.21	1973.37	2086.02	2267.65
辽 宁	Liaoning	836.17	1756.50	2355.58	2557.93	2751.34	2934.44
吉 林	Jilin	803.52	1609.60	2022.50	2182.22	2300.99	2530.41
黑龙江	Heilongjiang	759.86	1766.27	2148.22	2280.28	2405.24	2508.94
上 海	Shanghai	1907.32	4245.61	5596.37	5870.87	6223.55	6653.92
江 苏	Jiangsu	959.06	2456.86	3595.09	3784.71	3979.79	4239.26
浙 江	Zhejiang	1099.04	2966.19	4253.67	4582.34	4940.36	5389.04
安 徽	Anhui	539.16	1302.82	1934.57	2020.04	2117.56	2127.48
福 建	Fujian	764.41	2048.59	3230.49	3380.72	3538.83	3733.89
江 西	Jiangxi	669.90	1537.36	2135.30	2231.60	2306.45	2457.53
山 东	Shandong	680.18	1715.09	2659.20	2804.51	2947.65	3150.49
河 南	Henan	526.95	1231.97	1985.82	2097.86	2215.74	2235.68
湖 北	Hubei	670.80	1511.22	2268.59	2352.16	2444.06	2566.76
湖 南	Hunan	664.24	1425.16	2197.16	2299.46	2397.92	2532.87
广 东	Guangdong	1043.03	2699.24	3654.48	3769.79	3911.90	4054.58
广 西	Guangxi	639.45	1446.14	1864.51	1944.33	2012.60	2094.51
海 南	Hainan	696.22	1519.71	2182.26	2226.47	2423.20	2588.06
重 庆	Chongqing			1892.44	1971.18	2097.58	2214.55
四 川	Sichuan	557.76	1158.29	1903.60	1986.99	2107.64	2229.86
贵 州	Guizhou	435.14	1086.62	1374.16	1411.73	1489.91	1564.66
云 南	Yunnan	540.86	1010.97	1478.60	1533.74	1608.64	1697.12
西 藏	Tibet	649.71	1200.31	1330.81	1404.01	1462.27	1690.76
陕 西	Shaanxi	530.80	962.89	1443.86	1490.80	1596.25	1675.66
甘 肃	Gansu	430.98	880.34	1428.68	1508.61	1590.30	1673.05
青 海	Qinghai	559.78	1029.77	1490.49	1557.32	1668.94	1794.13
宁 夏	Ningxia	578.13	998.75	1724.30	1823.05	1917.36	2043.30
新 疆	Xinjiang	683.47	1136.45	1618.08	1710.44	1863.26	2106.19

10-22 各地区按来源分农村居民家庭纯收入(2003年)

Per Capita Net Income of Rural Households by Source and by Region (2003)

单位: 元 (yuan)

地 区	Region	纯收入 Net Income	工资性收入 Wage Income	家庭经营纯收入 Family Business Income	财产性收入 Property Income	转移性收入 Transfer Income
全 国	**National Average**	**2622.24**	**918.38**	**1541.28**	**65.75**	**96.83**
北 京	Beijing	5601.55	3480.30	1450.82	305.92	364.51
天 津	Tianjin	4566.01	2152.55	2162.87	140.74	109.85
河 北	Hebei	2853.38	1072.33	1645.17	75.31	60.57
山 西	Shanxi	2299.17	897.50	1316.55	24.16	60.96
内蒙古	Inner Mongolia	2267.65	344.60	1818.78	51.66	52.62
辽 宁	Liaoning	2934.44	1056.59	1709.99	66.33	101.52
吉 林	Jilin	2530.41	425.51	1991.17	66.40	47.34
黑龙江	Heilongjiang	2508.94	394.24	1950.17	139.07	25.46
上 海	Shanghai	6653.92	5251.58	813.08	236.21	353.05
江 苏	Jiangsu	4239.26	2189.06	1794.28	94.29	161.63
浙 江	Zhejiang	5389.04	2574.85	2332.11	250.41	231.68
安 徽	Anhui	2127.48	818.92	1199.94	36.21	72.41
福 建	Fujian	3733.89	1353.79	2015.36	78.38	286.37
江 西	Jiangxi	2457.53	1022.14	1357.37	28.93	49.09
山 东	Shandong	3150.49	1095.45	1874.45	63.92	116.67
河 南	Henan	2235.68	635.59	1487.82	38.58	73.69
湖 北	Hubei	2566.76	706.79	1785.27	15.76	58.95
湖 南	Hunan	2532.87	988.35	1427.21	32.34	84.97
广 东	Guangdong	4054.58	1965.78	1761.02	184.36	143.42
广 西	Guangxi	2094.51	784.60	1229.88	16.77	63.26
海 南	Hainan	2588.06	329.87	2122.12	53.28	82.79
重 庆	Chongqing	2214.55	858.50	1185.12	34.17	136.76
四 川	Sichuan	2229.86	765.76	1347.09	31.26	85.75
贵 州	Guizhou	1564.66	458.84	988.48	36.77	80.59
云 南	Yunnan	1697.12	318.22	1242.65	67.21	69.04
西 藏	Tibet	1690.76				
陕 西	Shaanxi	1675.66	615.92	919.69	49.19	90.85
甘 肃	Gansu	1673.05	488.73	1108.52	16.98	58.81
青 海	Qinghai	1794.13	454.06	1200.32	51.49	88.27
宁 夏	Ningxia	2043.30	592.30	1255.35	68.76	126.88
新 疆	Xinjiang	2106.19	140.27	1875.03	58.91	31.99

10-23 不同收入组农户家庭基本情况（2003年）

Basic Conditions of Rural Households by Level of Income (2003)

项　目	Item	低收入户 Low Income Households	中低收入户 Lower Middle Income Households	中等收入户 Middle Income Households	中高收入户 Upper Middle Income Households	高收入户 High Income Households
平均每户常住人口（人）	Average Number of Permanent Residents per Household	4.61	4.34	4.11	3.90	3.54
平均每户整半劳动力（人）	Average Number of Able-bodied and Semi-able-bodied Laborers per Household	2.92	2.86	2.81	2.76	2.63
平均每个劳动力负担人口（人）	Average Number of Persons Supported by a Laborer (including self)	1.58	1.52	1.46	1.41	1.34
平均每人总收入（元）	Per Capita Annual Income (yuan)	1573.40	2327.99	3123.12	4219.52	7999.28
＃现金收入	Cash Income	1082.48	1691.36	2443.48	3491.18	7229.34
平均每人总支出（元）	Per Capita Annual Expenditures (yuan)	1803.31	2148.59	2668.13	3336.13	5763.72
＃现金支出	Cash Expenditures	1344.39	1646.60	2164.93	2826.85	5298.58
平均每人纯收入（元）	Per Capita Annual Net Income (yuan)	865.90	1606.53	2273.13	3206.79	6346.86
工资性收入	Wages Income	233.15	483.24	795.44	1218.07	2574.73
家庭经营纯收入	Household Business Income	590.52	1057.51	1380.06	1833.93	3238.28
财产性收入	Property Income	14.66	22.48	34.52	54.28	245.94
转移性收入	Transfer Income	27.57	43.30	63.11	100.52	287.90

10-24 不同收入组农户平均每人生活消费支出（2003年）

Per Capita Living Expenditure of Rural Households by Level of Income (2003)

单位：元　　(yuan)

项　目	Item	低收入户 Low Income Households	中低收入户 Lower Middle Income Households	中等收入户 Middle Income Households	中高收入户 Upper Middle Income Households	高收入户 High Income Households
生活消费总支出	**Living Expenditure**	**1064.76**	**1377.56**	**1732.74**	**2189.27**	**3755.57**
食品	Food	575.66	714.11	840.82	999.23	1429.05
衣着	Clothing	59.47	77.69	97.70	125.64	214.06
居住	Residence	141.56	180.85	240.93	339.43	726.39
家庭设备用品及服务	Household Facilities, Articles and Services	39.35	51.55	66.33	90.53	181.74
医疗保健	Medicines and Medical Services	63.83	81.70	104.25	124.85	228.51
交通通讯	Transport, Post and Telecommunications	56.91	84.09	128.85	183.21	412.72
文教娱乐用品及服务	Cultural, Educational and Recreational Articles and Services	109.94	161.37	218.34	276.81	465.45
其他商品及服务	Other Commodities and Services	18.03	26.21	35.52	49.56	97.65
生活消费现金支出	**Consumption Paid in Cash**	**737.49**	**1004.16**	**1348.63**	**1797.81**	**3393.49**
食品	Food	277.45	372.72	490.39	642.21	1097.20
衣着	Clothing	58.78	77.07	96.78	124.53	213.63
居住	Residence	113.80	149.98	208.68	307.97	696.98
家庭设备用品及服务	Household Facilities, Articles and Services	39.25	51.45	66.17	89.05	181.62
医疗保健	Medicines and Medical Services	63.83	81.70	104.25	124.85	228.51
交通通讯	Transport, Post and Telecommunications	56.91	84.09	128.85	183.21	412.72
文教娱乐用品及服务	Cultural, Educational and Recreational Articles and Services	109.94	161.37	218.34	276.81	465.45
其他商品及服务	Other Commodities and Services	17.52	25.78	35.16	49.17	97.39

10-25 农村居民家庭平均每人生活消费支出构成

Composition of Per Capita Living Expenditure of Rural Households

单位: % (%)

指 标	Item	1990	1995	2000	2002	2003
生活消费总支出	**Living Expenditure**	**100.00**	**100.00**	**100.00**	**100.00**	**100.00**
食品	Food	58.80	58.62	49.13	46.25	45.59
衣着	Clothing	7.77	6.85	5.75	5.72	5.67
居住	Residence	17.34	13.91	15.47	16.36	15.87
家庭设备用品及服务	Household Facilities, Articles and Services	5.29	5.23	4.52	4.38	4.20
医疗保健	Medicines and Medical Services	3.25	3.24	5.24	5.67	5.96
交通通讯	Transport, Post and Telecommunications	1.44	2.58	5.58	7.01	8.36
文教娱乐用品及服务	Cultural, Educational and Recreational Articles and Services	5.37	7.81	11.18	11.47	12.13
其他商品及服务	Other Commodities and Services	0.74	1.76	3.14	3.14	2.21
生活消费现金支出	**Consumption Paid in Cash**	**100.00**	**100.00**	**100.00**	**100.00**	**100.00**
食品	Food	41.59	41.10	36.14	34.82	34.96
衣着	Clothing	11.75	10.32	7.41	7.12	6.95
居住	Residence	21.66	17.20	17.98	18.50	17.64
家庭设备用品及服务	Household Facilities, Articles and Services	8.20	7.92	5.79	5.46	5.16
医疗保健	Medicines and Medical Services	5.06	4.94	6.82	7.08	7.34
交通通讯	Transport, Post and Telecommunications	2.24	3.92	7.25	8.76	10.31
文教娱乐用品及服务	Cultural, Educational and Recreational Articles and Services	8.36	11.91	14.53	14.33	14.95
其他商品及服务	Other Commodities and Services	1.13	2.68	4.08	3.93	2.70

10-26 各地区农村居民家庭平均每人生活消费支出(2003年)

Per Capita Living Expenditure of Rural Households by Region (2003)

单位：元 (yuan)

地 区	Region	生活消费支出合计 Living Expenditure	食 品 Food	衣 着 Clothing	居 住 Residence	家庭设备及服务 Household Facilities, Articles and Services	医疗保健 Medicines and Health Care	交通和通讯 Transport, and Communi-cation	文教、娱乐用品及服务 Cultural, Educational and Recreational Articles and Services	其他商品及服务 Other Commo-dities and Services
全 国	**National Average**	**1943.30**	**886.03**	**110.27**	**308.38**	**81.65**	**115.75**	**162.53**	**235.68**	**43.01**
北 京	Beijing	4147.30	1331.69	288.25	787.84	216.25	356.31	393.35	691.39	82.22
天 津	Tianjin	2319.52	887.14	183.28	377.55	76.96	167.67	198.50	379.44	48.97
河 北	Hebei	1600.10	639.10	114.97	311.46	71.65	101.63	149.52	186.48	25.28
山 西	Shanxi	1434.40	620.62	149.73	169.55	55.03	81.22	119.00	213.15	26.09
内蒙古	Inner Mongolia	1770.56	731.12	121.81	246.85	65.73	124.42	192.00	256.17	32.46
辽 宁	Liaoning	1884.08	813.66	147.72	289.86	68.42	132.63	170.60	218.99	42.20
吉 林	Jilin	1815.57	799.16	118.08	253.45	57.63	153.75	173.82	221.70	37.98
黑龙江	Heilongjiang	1661.70	676.14	119.05	309.48	48.63	135.20	157.90	188.22	27.08
上 海	Shanghai	5669.57	2004.14	250.30	1436.72	296.51	332.77	587.02	675.56	86.55
江 苏	Jiangsu	2704.37	1118.55	140.56	441.87	137.74	142.11	268.53	379.15	75.86
浙 江	Zhejiang	4285.13	1635.64	229.47	774.99	206.69	306.31	496.08	531.11	104.84
安 徽	Anhui	1596.27	734.75	79.55	281.28	74.96	87.14	126.07	184.64	27.87
福 建	Fujian	2715.50	1222.23	144.58	398.15	146.66	128.95	278.43	296.65	99.85
江 西	Jiangxi	1907.57	986.07	99.85	264.12	62.68	91.98	141.69	223.80	37.39
山 东	Shandong	2133.20	891.82	134.30	341.69	92.17	138.80	187.03	291.33	56.07
河 南	Henan	1508.70	726.57	96.36	238.44	63.32	91.39	100.17	160.94	31.49
湖 北	Hubei	1801.63	930.98	80.19	223.41	73.00	95.55	122.05	223.92	52.53
湖 南	Hunan	2139.15	1111.27	106.16	271.97	79.63	105.23	146.85	270.54	47.51
广 东	Guangdong	2927.35	1402.04	117.68	469.48	121.85	137.43	286.66	305.86	86.35
广 西	Guangxi	1751.23	899.07	61.12	323.28	63.69	74.81	121.45	175.55	32.26
海 南	Hainan	1644.79	947.10	52.59	147.69	75.80	96.05	107.80	158.32	59.44
重 庆	Chongqing	1583.31	831.63	70.49	212.38	76.68	89.42	102.40	180.28	20.03
四 川	Sichuan	1747.02	941.70	85.94	224.80	64.85	91.36	105.19	202.27	30.92
贵 州	Guizhou	1185.17	674.71	54.46	170.56	41.51	46.62	49.59	128.13	19.59
云 南	Yunnan	1405.70	744.58	57.27	257.65	51.42	79.93	59.54	131.49	23.82
西 藏	Tibet	1030.13	669.91	114.66	85.99	53.34	21.27	37.06	32.22	15.68
陕 西	Shaanxi	1455.39	572.67	85.15	236.33	63.52	106.66	97.33	267.87	25.86
甘 肃	Gansu	1336.85	586.38	74.02	201.57	57.45	96.18	109.34	191.83	20.08
青 海	Qinghai	1563.15	775.89	113.88	192.17	60.94	115.73	145.85	131.71	26.98
宁 夏	Ningxia	1637.13	680.15	109.19	286.09	56.09	116.31	170.52	178.34	40.44
新 疆	Xinjiang	1465.31	667.11	135.65	254.63	50.92	116.48	99.04	112.93	28.54

10-27 各地区农村居民家庭平均每人生活消费现金支出(2003年)

Per Capita Living Expenditure in Cash of Rural Households by Region (2003)

单位: 元 (yuan)

地区	Region	生活消费现金支出合计 Living Expenditure in Cash	食品 Food	衣着 Clothing	居住 Residence	家庭设备及服务 Household Facilities, Articles and Services	医疗保健 Medicines and Medical Services	交通和通讯 Transport, and Communication Services	文教、娱乐用品及服务 Cultural, Educational and Recreational Articles and Services	其他商品及服务 Other Commodities and Services
全国	**National Average**	**1576.64**	**551.21**	**109.51**	**278.07**	**81.28**	**115.75**	**162.53**	**235.68**	**42.61**
北京	Beijing	4081.96	1271.63	288.12	786.46	216.25	356.31	393.35	691.39	78.46
天津	Tianjin	2220.24	788.31	182.83	377.55	76.96	167.67	198.50	379.44	48.97
河北	Hebei	1388.48	427.62	114.85	311.46	71.65	101.63	149.52	186.48	25.27
山西	Shanxi	1205.69	399.03	149.67	162.74	54.86	81.22	119.00	213.15	26.01
内蒙古	Inner Mongolia	1417.27	426.65	120.84	205.07	65.73	124.42	192.00	256.17	26.39
辽宁	Liaoning	1581.45	530.38	147.69	271.00	68.36	132.63	170.60	218.99	41.81
吉林	Jilin	1490.10	549.50	118.07	177.64	57.63	153.75	173.82	221.70	37.98
黑龙江	Heilongjiang	1404.44	497.33	119.05	231.09	48.58	135.20	157.90	188.22	27.07
上海	Shanghai	5385.90	1720.50	250.30	1436.72	296.49	332.77	587.02	675.56	86.55
江苏	Jiangsu	2292.94	727.88	140.49	421.18	137.74	142.11	268.53	379.15	75.86
浙江	Zhejiang	4018.13	1379.59	229.03	764.53	206.64	306.31	496.08	531.11	104.84
安徽	Anhui	1223.00	437.42	79.41	205.64	74.96	87.14	126.07	184.64	27.73
福建	Fujian	2460.16	1002.98	144.50	362.42	146.66	128.95	278.43	296.65	99.56
江西	Jiangxi	1423.41	550.49	99.27	216.66	62.57	91.98	141.69	223.80	36.95
山东	Shandong	1827.57	596.26	133.13	332.79	92.17	138.80	187.03	291.33	56.07
河南	Henan	1093.84	366.60	96.22	187.92	59.15	91.39	100.17	160.94	31.45
湖北	Hubei	1264.55	430.72	79.30	187.90	72.94	95.55	122.05	223.92	52.17
湖南	Hunan	1692.34	672.05	106.09	265.80	79.60	105.23	146.85	270.54	46.18
广东	Guangdong	2528.14	1056.87	116.09	417.49	121.40	137.43	286.66	305.86	86.35
广西	Guangxi	1354.81	547.74	61.05	278.46	63.66	74.81	121.45	175.55	32.10
海南	Hainan	1214.25	549.87	52.59	114.39	75.80	96.05	107.80	158.32	59.42
重庆	Chongqing	1111.06	376.75	70.49	195.52	76.20	89.42	102.40	180.28	20.00
四川	Sichuan	1194.64	440.40	85.20	174.66	64.69	91.36	105.19	202.27	30.87
贵州	Guizhou	745.20	248.73	54.46	157.49	41.40	46.62	49.59	128.13	18.79
云南	Yunnan	970.27	343.29	57.22	223.94	51.05	79.93	59.54	131.49	23.80
西藏	Tibet	614.31	267.70	106.62	80.95	52.99	21.27	37.06	32.22	15.50
陕西	Shaanxi	1245.41	379.96	84.87	219.35	63.52	106.66	97.33	267.87	25.86
甘肃	Gansu	1001.48	273.00	73.98	180.09	57.45	96.18	109.34	191.83	19.62
青海	Qinghai	1081.33	312.55	110.50	177.99	60.07	115.73	145.85	131.71	26.93
宁夏	Ningxia	1273.04	323.90	109.11	278.33	56.09	116.31	170.52	178.34	40.44
新疆	Xinjiang	1108.04	331.60	125.23	244.27	49.94	116.48	99.04	112.93	28.54

10-28 各地区农村居民家庭平均每人主要食品消费量（2003年）

Per Capita Consumption of Major Food in Rural Households by Region (2003)

单位：公斤 (kg)

地区	Region	粮食 Grain	蔬菜 Vegetables	食油 Edible Oil	猪牛羊肉 Pork, Beef and Mutton	家禽 Poultry	蛋类及其制品 Eggs and Related Products	水产品 Aquatic Products	食糖 Sugar	酒 Liquor
全国	**National Average**	**222.44**	**107.40**	**6.27**	**15.04**	**3.20**	**4.81**	**4.65**	**1.24**	**7.67**
北京	Beijing	134.05	92.78	9.15	14.60	2.17	10.13	4.25	2.92	14.42
天津	Tianjin	150.20	69.99	10.00	11.07	0.84	10.80	8.35	0.72	10.14
河北	Hebei	216.72	55.97	6.59	7.10	0.54	6.36	2.25	0.65	7.29
山西	Shanxi	218.91	80.87	5.72	5.36	0.24	6.15	0.47	1.15	2.59
内蒙古	Inner Mongolia	207.30	70.77	2.79	21.18	1.41	3.82	1.45	1.34	10.77
辽宁	Liaoning	194.39	178.59	5.90	16.45	2.51	9.59	4.49	0.73	10.80
吉林	Jilin	255.99	115.20	6.27	11.42	3.23	8.64	3.60	0.75	13.64
黑龙江	Heilongjiang	195.08	111.70	7.62	7.85	2.61	6.26	3.35	0.90	15.09
上海	Shanghai	189.44	76.60	8.59	16.37	7.40	7.51	16.11	2.12	16.77
江苏	Jiangsu	251.98	109.12	8.27	12.05	4.50	6.72	9.09	1.30	8.82
浙江	Zhejiang	208.46	83.91	5.81	16.42	6.03	5.33	14.64	2.13	24.15
安徽	Anhui	228.35	80.97	6.87	9.07	4.27	5.04	5.43	1.42	10.61
福建	Fujian	198.27	99.92	5.19	16.51	5.14	3.55	13.30	2.35	16.84
江西	Jiangxi	264.80	144.22	8.77	13.24	3.31	3.50	5.19	1.13	7.31
山东	Shandong	229.06	118.19	6.96	8.09	2.70	11.61	4.01	1.00	10.81
河南	Henan	236.97	100.11	4.22	6.48	1.23	8.01	1.35	1.13	4.23
湖北	Hubei	227.39	159.76	9.40	19.86	2.74	3.86	8.10	0.92	7.29
湖南	Hunan	247.21	149.44	8.35	17.51	3.89	3.28	6.89	1.13	4.02
广东	Guangdong	233.75	130.22	6.73	22.27	10.40	2.83	13.30	2.16	3.33
广西	Guangxi	205.65	108.94	4.92	14.44	7.33	1.12	3.57	1.18	6.14
海南	Hainan	236.31	86.61	5.70	15.40	9.77	1.31	14.75	1.24	3.88
重庆	Chongqing	215.31	154.70	3.34	28.06	2.21	3.98	1.93	2.44	7.98
四川	Sichuan	223.81	180.65	5.21	28.05	3.59	4.73	1.91	1.37	6.43
贵州	Guizhou	201.36	130.67	3.85	28.01	1.18	1.20	0.33	0.84	5.18
云南	Yunnan	195.37	90.80	3.03	26.41	2.67	1.56	1.21	1.21	5.36
西藏	Tibet	266.09	15.27	3.22	11.31	0.02	0.41		1.36	1.65
陕西	Shaanxi	193.30	50.69	5.83	6.63	0.32	2.29	0.29	0.92	2.24
甘肃	Gansu	235.23	40.02	4.95	10.80	1.11	2.14	0.24	0.85	3.31
青海	Qinghai	219.54	53.93	8.25	30.44	0.55	0.77	0.53	1.37	2.71
宁夏	Ningxia	224.23	84.38	7.22	11.33	2.81	2.74	0.51	1.62	2.02
新疆	Xinjiang	236.50	75.12	9.37	11.88	1.51	1.27	0.40	0.40	1.27

10-29 全国和西部12省(区、市)农村居民家庭平均每人主要消费品消费量

Per Capita Consumption of Major Consumer Goods in Rural Households of National and 12 Western Provinces (Autonomous Regions, Municipality) at the Year-end

品名		Item		2000 全国 National Total	2000 西部12省(区、市) 12 Western Provinces	2002 全国 National Total	2002 西部12省(区、市) 12 Western Provinces	2003 全国 National Total	2003 西部12省(区、市) 12 Western Provinces
粮食(原粮)	(公斤)	Grain (Unprocessed)	(kg)	250.23	240.77	236.50	228.22	222.44	214.47
#小麦		Wheat		80.27	84.95	76.31	79.19	73.23	76.60
稻谷		Rice		126.82	105.75	123.11	105.75	119.31	105.20
豆类及豆制品	(公斤)	Soybeans and Related Products	(kg)	5.49	3.98	5.76	4.87	5.28	4.10
#大豆		Soybean		2.53	1.59	2.20	1.51	2.05	1.43
蔬菜	(公斤)	Fresh Vegetable	(kg)	111.98	103.02	110.55	98.72	107.40	100.75
食油	(公斤)	Edible Oil	(kg)	7.06	6.18	7.53	6.53	6.27	4.94
#植物油		Vegetable Oil		5.45	4.36	5.77	4.71	5.31	4.08
肉禽及制品	(公斤)	Meats, Poultry and Related Products	(kg)	18.30	20.15	18.60	20.81	19.68	23.24
#猪肉		Pork		13.28	15.79	13.70	16.13	13.78	17.23
牛肉		Beef		0.52	0.75	0.52	0.74	0.50	0.86
羊肉		Mutton		0.61	1.34	0.65	1.41	0.76	1.77
家禽		Poultry		2.81	1.98	2.91	2.21	3.20	2.45
蛋及制品	(公斤)	Eggs and Related Products	(kg)	4.77	2.24	4.66	2.25	4.81	2.41
奶及制品	(公斤)	Milk and Related Products	(kg)	1.06	2.30	1.19	2.01	1.71	2.87
水产品	(公斤)	Aquatic Product	(kg)	3.92	1.07	4.36	1.19	4.65	1.25
食糖	(公斤)	Sugar	(kg)	1.28	1.20	1.64	1.46	1.24	1.18
酒	(公斤)	Liquor	(kg)	7.02	4.72	7.50	4.94	7.67	5.12
水果及制品	(公斤)	Fruits and Related Products	(kg)	18.31	14.79	18.77	16.61	17.54	14.69
坚果及制品	(公斤)	Nuts and Related Product	(kg)	0.74	0.50	0.78	0.65	0.72	0.59

10-30 全国和西部12省(区、市)农村居民家庭平均每百户年底耐用消费品拥有量

Number of Durable Consumer Goods Owned Per 100 Rural Households of National and 12 Western Provinces (Autonomous Regions, Municipality) at the Year-end

品名		Item		2000 全国 National Total	2000 西部12省(区、市) 12 Western Provinces	2002 全国 National Total	2002 西部12省(区、市) 12 Western Provinces	2003 全国 National Total	2003 西部12省(区、市) 12 Western Provinces
洗衣机	(台)	Washing Machine	(unit)	28.58	18.49	31.80	21.07	34.27	23.11
电风扇	(台)	Electric Fan	(unit)	122.62	64.97	134.26	72.29	138.08	76.18
电冰箱	(台)	Refrigerator	(unit)	12.31	4.63	14.83	6.08	15.89	6.68
空调机	(台)	Air Conditioner	(unit)	1.32	0.09	2.29	0.15	3.45	0.22
抽油烟机	(台)	Exhaust Fan	(unit)	2.75	0.51	3.58	0.63	4.11	0.66
自行车	(辆)	Bicycle	(unit)	120.48	77.20	121.32	76.33	118.50	75.16
摩托车	(辆)	Motorcycle	(unit)	21.94	12.33	28.07	17.26	31.80	20.53
电话机	(部)	Telephone Set	(set)	26.38	10.37	40.77	20.67	49.06	28.14
移动电话	(部)	Mobile Telephone	(set)	4.32	1.09	13.67	6.27	23.68	13.55
组合音响	(台)	Hi-Fi Stereo Component System	(unit)	7.76	5.32	9.73	6.90	10.46	7.84
寻呼机	(台)	Beep-pager	(unit)	7.74	3.66	5.45	3.90	3.02	2.31
黑白电视机	(台)	Black and White TV Set	(unit)	52.97	50.86	48.14	46.12	42.80	41.59
彩色电视机	(台)	Color TV Set	(unit)	48.74	36.60	60.45	47.98	67.80	55.76
录放像机	(台)	Video-recorder	(unit)	3.30	1.84	3.32	2.01	3.51	2.42
收录机	(台)	Radio Cassette Player	(unit)	21.58	25.14	20.41	24.71	18.70	23.48
照相机	(架)	Camera	(set)	3.12	1.76	3.34	2.02	3.36	1.99

10-31 各地区农村居民家庭平均每百户主要耐用消费品拥有量（2003年底）

Number of Durable Consumer Goods Owned Per 100 Rural Households by Region at the Year-end (2003)

地 区	Region	大型家具（件）Large Furniture (unit)	洗衣机（台）Washing Machine (unit)	电风扇（台）Electric Fan (unit)	电冰箱（台）Refrigerator (unit)	空调机（台）Air Conditioner (unit)	抽油烟机（台）Exhaust Fan (unit)	自行车（辆）Bicycle (unit)
全 国	**National Average**	**285.82**	**34.27**	**138.08**	**15.89**	**3.45**	**4.11**	**118.50**
北 京	Beijing	261.07	94.00	159.47	96.93	35.07	29.47	212.80
天 津	Tianjin	172.67	84.17	151.00	57.17	16.00	11.50	197.50
河 北	Hebei	202.10	68.17	161.24	26.83	3.07	2.98	191.02
山 西	Shanxi	267.33	56.67	52.05	12.29	0.67	2.05	130.86
内蒙古	Inner Mongolia	154.81	29.90	11.07	10.05		0.44	80.24
辽 宁	Liaoning	144.55	58.52	51.53	18.31	0.32	2.80	125.87
吉 林	Jilin	92.31	58.75	18.63	7.19	0.19	0.63	86.44
黑龙江	Heilongjiang	73.79	54.20	16.88	10.98	0.31	2.10	84.42
上 海	Shanghai	320.50	75.00	341.00	81.17	37.00	44.50	210.67
江 苏	Jiangsu	296.82	56.32	232.18	27.15	13.32	8.82	184.56
浙 江	Zhejiang	402.07	43.11	292.19	53.11	20.37	28.44	168.70
安 徽	Anhui	300.61	17.58	192.29	12.61	0.84	0.68	135.32
福 建	Fujian	232.14	42.14	184.67	26.26	7.58	8.02	83.79
江 西	Jiangxi	288.29	5.39	161.92	6.29	0.41	0.82	119.14
山 东	Shandong	296.98	24.67	164.93	20.90	1.79	4.36	177.00
河 南	Henan	262.52	36.83	156.29	7.55	1.64	0.52	152.14
湖 北	Hubei	257.15	20.12	169.39	8.52	1.15	1.06	103.48
湖 南	Hunan	548.48	20.73	187.00	9.03	0.51	0.76	80.30
广 东	Guangdong	369.30	28.28	304.38	18.95	7.07	11.45	145.47
广 西	Guangxi	162.60	3.59	202.08	3.42	0.04	0.30	119.48
海 南	Hainan	267.08	4.86	114.15	5.56	0.97	0.97	48.56
重 庆	Chongqing	403.78	15.89	141.61	8.89	0.39	0.33	16.94
四 川	Sichuan	460.25	22.45	143.40	7.09	0.65	0.43	48.23
贵 州	Guizhou	365.67	17.41	30.40	3.48		0.04	7.59
云 南	Yunnan	107.79	21.00	10.79	4.17	0.25	1.67	44.21
西 藏	Tibet	428.33	3.54		3.13			55.42
陕 西	Shaanxi	251.04	40.36	81.80	6.31	0.36	0.63	133.47
甘 肃	Gansu	305.78	34.33	24.56	5.44		1.11	127.22
青 海	Qinghai	383.50	23.17	3.00	6.50		0.33	55.83
宁 夏	Ningxia	439.83	44.33	26.67	8.83		1.33	164.67
新 疆	Xinjiang	215.23	24.90	16.06	14.19	0.06	1.42	120.06

10-31 续表 continued

地 区	Region	摩托车 (辆) Motorcycle (unit)	电话机 (部) Telephone Set (unit)	黑白电视机 (台) Black and White TV Set (unit)	彩色电视机 (台) Color TV Set (unit)	录放像机 (台) Video-recorder (unit)	收录机 (台) Radio Cassette Player (unit)	照相机 (架) Camera (unit)
全 国	**National Average**	**31.80**	**49.06**	**42.80**	**67.80**	**3.51**	**18.70**	**3.36**
北 京	Beijing	41.87	100.67	9.47	116.67	15.07	29.47	30.53
天 津	Tianjin	45.50	73.67	15.67	105.50	7.33	19.00	6.00
河 北	Hebei	43.83	57.60	40.71	79.64	2.71	17.36	4.33
山 西	Shanxi	32.67	35.33	37.71	74.10	3.29	24.48	2.90
内蒙古	Inner Mongolia	37.57	22.91	36.80	65.19	1.07	32.28	2.86
辽 宁	Liaoning	33.39	71.38	26.30	86.93	5.29	17.41	4.76
吉 林	Jilin	32.56	53.44	25.13	81.63	1.75	19.31	2.44
黑龙江	Heilongjiang	24.11	53.53	29.87	77.59	2.23	13.21	2.63
上 海	Shanghai	87.67	108.83	48.33	125.17	11.17	33.17	12.83
江 苏	Jiangsu	40.09	80.26	55.68	75.09	6.65	20.08	4.91
浙 江	Zhejiang	47.56	84.15	39.89	109.67	10.19	25.19	7.93
安 徽	Anhui	17.10	58.75	60.32	59.00	2.39	16.19	2.13
福 建	Fujian	63.30	86.70	30.00	88.57	7.09	10.71	4.73
江 西	Jiangxi	27.84	42.45	65.92	52.04	2.53	11.18	1.59
山 东	Shandong	51.33	74.52	42.64	71.05	3.45	17.10	5.07
河 南	Henan	21.14	39.57	53.14	56.00	1.24	11.64	1.38
湖 北	Hubei	25.01	31.39	55.00	56.27	1.18	9.82	1.79
湖 南	Hunan	17.49	41.35	57.86	49.59	2.08	10.86	1.35
广 东	Guangdong	71.41	70.20	16.95	92.27	5.82	17.97	4.34
广 西	Guangxi	32.34	31.08	57.19	47.66	1.26	13.38	1.21
海 南	Hainan	65.00	32.36	10.28	64.58	6.39	18.29	1.81
重 庆	Chongqing	7.78	43.72	49.06	53.33	2.50	5.89	1.50
四 川	Sichuan	15.48	23.15	52.30	56.05	2.40	12.05	1.30
贵 州	Guizhou	9.64	17.10	32.95	39.20	1.21	9.78	1.16
云 南	Yunnan	8.08	19.30	25.33	57.55	2.67	16.38	3.29
西 藏	Tibet	2.29	4.79	6.46	26.46	7.50	72.29	0.83
陕 西	Shaanxi	22.16	45.74	42.75	65.95	1.04	22.52	1.85
甘 肃	Gansu	24.17	36.72	33.11	69.44	2.61	38.28	3.06
青 海	Qinghai	33.83	21.50	33.00	56.83	0.67	56.50	2.00
宁 夏	Ningxia	45.50	38.17	28.33	84.33	0.17	37.17	3.00
新 疆	Xinjiang	27.48	25.94	53.55	45.68	8.97	58.52	2.45

10-32 城乡新建住宅面积和居民住房情况

Floor Space Completed and Housing Conditions of Urban and Rural Residents

年份 Year	城镇新建住宅面积 (亿平方米) Floor Space of New Residential Buildings in Urban Areas (100 million sq.m)	农村新建住宅面积 (亿平方米) Floor Space of New Residential Buildings in Rural Areas (100 million sq.m)	城市人均住宅建筑面积 (平方米) Per Capita Floor Space of Residentail Building in Urban Areas (sq.m)	农村人均住房面积 (平方米) Per Capita Floor Space in Rural Areas (sq.m)
1978	0.38	1.00	6.7	8.1
1980	0.92	5.00	7.2	9.4
1985	1.88	7.22	10.0	14.7
1986	2.22	9.84	12.4	15.3
1987	2.23	8.84	12.7	16.0
1988	2.40	8.45	13.0	16.6
1989	1.97	6.76	13.5	17.2
1990	1.73	6.91	13.7	17.8
1991	1.92	7.54	14.2	18.5
1992	2.40	6.19	14.8	18.9
1993	3.08	4.81	15.2	20.7
1994	3.57	6.18	15.7	20.2
1995	3.75	6.99	16.3	21.0
1996	3.95	8.28	17.0	21.7
1997	4.06	8.06	17.8	22.5
1998	4.76	8.00	18.7	23.3
1999	5.59	8.34	19.4	24.2
2000	5.49	7.97	20.3	24.8
2001	5.75	7.29	20.8	25.7
2002	5.98	7.42	22.8	26.5
2003	5.50	7.52	23.7	27.2

注:城市人均住宅建筑面积由建设部提供。

a)Data on the per capital floor space of residential buildings in urban areas are provided by the Ministry of Construction.

10-33 农村居民家庭住房情况

Housing Conditions of Rural Households

本表为农村住户抽样调查资料。

Data in this table are obtained from the sample surveys on rural households.

项目	Item	1990	1995	2000	2002	2003
本年新建房屋	**Rooms Newly Built within the Year**					
面积 (平方米/人)	Per Capita Floor Space of Houses (sq.m/person)	0.82	0.78	0.87	0.86	0.79
价值 (元/平方米)	Value of Houses (yuan/sq.m)	92.32	200.30	260.23	295.62	303.77
住房结构 (平方米/人)	Structure of House (sq.m/person)					
#钢筋混凝土结构	Reinforced Concrete Structure	0.23	0.33	0.47	0.51	0.47
砖木结构	Brick and Wood Structure	0.47	0.37	0.36	0.30	0.28
年末住房情况	**House at the End of Year**					
住房面积 (平方米/人)	Per Capita Floor Space of Houses (sq.m/person)	17.83	21.01	24.82	26.53	27.24
住房价值 (元/平方米)	Value of Houses (yuan/sq.m)	44.60	101.64	187.41	202.78	217.07
住房结构 (平方米/人)	Structure of House (sq.m/person)					
#钢筋混凝土结构	Reinforced Concrete Structure	1.22	3.10	6.15	7.69	8.53
砖木结构	Brick and Wood Structure	9.84	11.91	13.61	13.88	14.12

10–34 各地区农村居民家庭住房情况（2003年底）

Housing Conditions of Rural Households at the Year-end by Region (2003)

地 区	Region	住房面积（平方米/人） Per Capita Floor Space of Houses (sq.m/person)	住房价值（元/平方米） Value of Houses (yuan/sq.m)	住房结构（平方米/人） House Structures (sq.m/person)	
				钢筋混凝土结构 Reinforced Concrete Structure	砖木结构 Brick and Wood Structure
全 国	**National Average**	**27.24**	**217.07**	**8.53**	**14.12**
北 京	Beijing	32.99	578.03	5.76	27.18
天 津	Tianjin	23.30	538.94	1.75	21.39
河 北	Hebei	25.55	246.17	3.79	20.61
山 西	Shanxi	22.94	209.60	4.06	16.06
内蒙古	Inner Mongolia	18.33	157.68	0.04	10.30
辽 宁	Liaoning	23.69	278.91	2.68	20.77
吉 林	Jilin	19.75	261.08	0.41	16.39
黑龙江	Heilongjiang	19.61	257.47	0.43	13.06
上 海	Shanghai	59.03	519.06	45.74	13.27
江 苏	Jiangsu	35.87	300.58	14.41	20.99
浙 江	Zhejiang	50.73	326.76	27.30	21.69
安 徽	Anhui	24.50	196.18	10.41	13.23
福 建	Fujian	36.02	290.04	17.67	11.51
江 西	Jiangxi	30.55	151.84	13.72	13.45
山 东	Shandong	26.53	226.87	5.54	19.05
河 南	Henan	25.41	171.49	8.06	16.28
湖 北	Hubei	32.44	144.49	13.95	15.59
湖 南	Hunan	35.09	167.67	11.80	21.00
广 东	Guangdong	24.79	304.62	16.34	6.73
广 西	Guangxi	26.08	150.26	12.76	8.29
海 南	Hainan	19.51	229.07	4.54	14.53
重 庆	Chongqing	31.45	145.32	8.27	16.55
四 川	Sichuan	28.99	140.68	7.36	12.47
贵 州	Guizhou	21.62	116.10	3.96	12.28
云 南	Yunnan	23.45	156.12	3.88	4.76
西 藏	Tibet	21.42	156.79		0.03
陕 西	Shaanxi	26.11	182.78	8.66	11.33
甘 肃	Gansu	17.60	165.69	0.74	6.44
青 海	Qinghai	16.86	104.36	0.42	1.27
宁 夏	Ningxia	20.12	146.84	0.71	9.20
新 疆	Xinjiang	18.62	138.88	0.77	4.87

主要统计指标解释

一、城镇住户

城镇家庭人口 指居住在一起，经济上合在一起共同生活的家庭成员。凡计算为家庭人口的成员其全部收支都包括在本家庭中。

城镇就业面 指就业人口占家庭人口的百分比。

城镇就业者负担人数 指家庭人口与就业人口之比。

城镇家庭总收入 指家庭成员得到的工薪收入、经营净收入、财产性收入、转移性收入之和，不包括出售财物收入和借贷收入。

城镇家庭可支配收入 指家庭成员得到可用于最终消费支出和其它非义务性支出以及储蓄的总和，即居民家庭可以用来自由支配的收入。它是家庭总收入扣除交纳的所得税、个人交纳的社会保障支出以及记账补贴后的收入。计算公式为：

$$\text{可支配收入}=\text{家庭总收入}-\text{交纳所得税}-\text{个人交纳的社会保障支出}-\text{记帐补贴}$$

城镇家庭总支出 指除借贷支出以外的全部家庭支出。包括消费性支出、购房建房支出、转移性支出、财产性支出、社会保障支出。

城镇家庭消费性支出 指家庭用于日常生活的支出，包括食品、衣着、家庭设备用品及服务、医疗保健、交通和通信、娱乐教育文化服务、居住、杂项商品和服务等八大类支出。

城镇家庭服务性消费支出 指家庭用于支付社会提供的各种非商品性服务费用。

城镇家庭收入分组方法 将所有调查户依户人均可支配收入由低到高排队，按10%，10%，20%，20%，20%，10%，10%的比例依次分成：最低收入户、低收入户、中等偏下收入户、中等收入户、中等偏上收入户、高收入户、最高收入户等七组。总体中最低5%的户为困难户。

恩格尔系数 指食物支出金额在生活消费总支出金额中所占的比例。计算公式为：

$$\text{恩格尔系数}=\frac{\text{食品支出金额}}{\text{生活消费总支出金额}}\times 100\%$$

二、农村住户

农村住户 指农村常住户。农村常住户指长期(一年以上)居住在乡镇(不包括城关镇)行政管理区域内的住户，以及长期居住在城关镇所辖行政村范围内的农村住户。户口不在本地而在本地居住一年及以上的住户也包括在本地农村常住户范围内；有本地户口，但举家外出谋生一年以上的住户，无论是否保留承包耕地都不包括在本地农村住户范围内。

常住人口 指全年经常在家或在家居住6个月以上，而且经济和生活与本户连成一体的人口。外出从业人员在外居住时间虽然在6个月以上，但收入主要带回家中，经济与本户连为一体，仍视为家庭常住人口；在家居住，生活和本户连成一体的国家职工、退休人员也为家庭常住人口。但是现役军人、中专及以上(走读生除外)的在校学生、以及常年在外(不包括探亲、看病等)且已有稳定的职业与居住场所的外出从业人员，不算家庭常住人口。家庭常住人口主要作为计算农村住户平均每人收入、消费和积累水平及分析家庭人口状况的依据。

整、半劳动力 整劳动力指男子18周岁到50周岁，女子18周岁到45周岁；半劳动力指男子16周岁到17周岁，51周岁到60周岁；女子16周岁到17周岁，46周岁到55周岁，同时具有劳动能力的人。虽然在劳动年龄之内，但已丧失劳动能力的人，不应算为劳动力；超过劳动年龄，但能经常参加劳动，计入半劳动力数内。常住人口中的职工，若这些职工为劳动力，就包括在本户的整半劳动力中。

总收入 指调查期内农村住户和住户成员从各种来源渠道得到的收入总和。按收入的性质划分为工资性收入、家庭经营收入、财产性收入和转移性收入。

工资性收入 指农村住户成员受雇于单位或个人，靠出卖劳动而获得的收入。

家庭经营收入 指农村住户以家庭为生产经营单位进行生产筹划和管理而获得的收入。农村住户家庭经营活动按行业划分为农业、林业、牧业、渔业、工业、建筑业、交通运输业邮电业、批发和零售贸易餐饮业、社会服务业、文教卫生业和其他家庭经营。

财产性收入 指金融资产或有形非生产性资产的所有者向其他机构单位提供资金或将有形非生产性资产供其支配，作为回报而从中获得的收入。

转移性收入 指农村住户和住户成员无须付出任何对应物而获得的货物、服务、资金或资产所有权等，不包括无偿提供的用于固定资本形成的资金。一般情况下，是指农村住户在二次分配中的所有收入。

现金收入 指农村住户和住户成员在调查期内得到以现金形态表现的收入。按来源分成工资性收入、家庭经营现金收入、财产性收入、转移性收入。

纯收入 指农村住户当年从各个来源得到的总收入相应地扣除所发生的费用后的收入总和。计算方法：

$$\text{纯收入}=\text{总收入}-\text{家庭经营费用支出}-\text{税费支出}-\text{生产性固定资产折旧}-\text{调查补贴}-\text{赠送农村外部亲友支出}$$

纯收入主要用于再生产投入和当年生活消费支出，也可用于储蓄和各种非义务性支出。“农民人均纯收入”按人口平均的纯收入水平，反映的是一个地区或一个农户农村居民的平均收入水平。

总支出 指农村住户用于生产、生活和再分配的全部支出。家庭经营费用支出、购置生产性固定资产支出、生产性固定资产折旧、税费支出、生活消费支出、财产性支出和转移性支出。

家庭经营费用支出 指农村住户以家庭为基本生产经营单位从事生产经营活动而消费的商品和服务、自产自用产品。所消费的未计算为住户收入的自产自用产品，不计算为费用支出；库存的化肥、农药也不计算为本期费用支出。

购置生产性固定资产支出 指农村住户用于建造和购置生产性固定资产所支出的费用。

税费支出 指农村住户以现金和实物形式缴纳的从事生产经营活动的各种税费、附加费、村提留、乡统筹、一事一议费和各种集资摊派费用。在已进行税费改革的地区一般表现为农业税、特产税、两税附加、一事一议费和从事非农业生产经营活动所缴纳的各种税费，还包括除按国家规定所收取的税费外，地方额外增加的各种费用；在未进行税费改革的地区一般表现为从事生产经营活动的各种税费、村提留、乡统筹和各种集资摊派费用。

生活消费支出 指农村住户用于物质生活和精神生活方面的支出。生活消费支出包括食品，衣着，居住，家庭设备、用品及服务，医疗保健，交通和通讯，文化教育娱乐用品及服务，其他商品和服务等消费支出。

财产性支出 为获得其他住户财产(包括无形资产)的使用权而支付的各种费用。

转移性支出 指农村住户和住户成员没有获得任何对应物而支出的货物、服务、资金或资产所有权等，不包括无偿提供的用于固定资本形成的资金。一般情况下，是指农村住户在二次分配中的所有支出。

现金支出 指农村住户在调查期内用于生产、生活和再分配所支付的现金。包括家庭经营费用支出、缴纳的税费、购买生产性固定资产、生活消费、财产性和转移性支出。

Explanatory Notes on Main Statistical Indicators

I. Urban Households

Population of urban households refer to members of the household living and sharing economically together. All income and expenditure of the population of the household are included in the income and expenditure of the household.

Proportion of urban employment refer to the proportion of employed population to the population of urban households.

Number of dependents per urban employee refers to the ratio between number of persons in urban households and the number of dependents.

Total Income of Urban Households refers to the sum of wage and salary, net business income, income from properties, and income from transfers of members of the households, excluding income from selling of properties and income from borrowings.

Disposable Income of Urban Households refers to the actual income at the disposal of members of the households which can be used for final consumption, other non-compulsory expenditure and savings. This equals to total income minus income tax, personal contribution to social security and sample household subsidy for keeping dairies. Following formula is used:

Disposable income = total household income - income tax - personal contribution to social security - sample household subsidy for keeping dairies

Total expenditure of Urban Households refer to all expenditure of the households except expenditure on leading. It includes expenditure on consumption, on purchasing or building houses, on transfers, on properties and on social security.

Consumption Expenditure of Urban Households refers to total expenditure of the sample households for consumption in daily life, including expenditure on eight categories such as food, clothing, household appliances and services, health care and medical services, transport and communications, recreation, education and cultural services, housing, miscellaneous goods and services.

Expenditure of Urban Households on Consumption of Services refers to expenditure of households on services of various kinds provided by the society.

Urban Households by Income Group All households in the sample are grouped, by per capita disposable income of the household, into groups of lowest income, low income, lower middle income, middle income, upper middle income, high income and highest income, each group consisting of 10%, 10%, 20%, 20%, 20%, 10% and 10% of all households respectively. The lowest 5% of households are also referred to as poor households.

Engel Coefficient refers to the percentage of expenditure on food in the total consumption expenditure, using the following formula:

Engel Coefficient = (expenditure on food / total consumption expenditure) x 100%

II. Rural Households

Rural Households refer to resident households in rural areas. Resident households in rural areas are the households residing for more than one year in the areas under the jurisdiction of administration of township governments (excluding county towns), and in the areas under the jurisdiction of administration of villages in county towns. Migrated households residing in the current addresses for over one year with their household registration in other places are included in the resident households of their current addresses. For households with their household registration in one place but all members of the households moving away for living in another place for over one year, they will not be included in the rural households of the area where they are registered, irrespective of whether they still keep their contracted land.

Resident Population refers to population staying at home permanently or for over 6 months during a year and sharing life economically with the household. Members of the household staying away from the household for over 6 months but keeping a close economic relation with the household by sending the majority of income to the household are regarded as resident population of the household. Government staff and workers or retirees living as close members of the household are also considered as resident population. However, servicemen, students of secondary technical schools or schools of higher education and persons with stable jobs and residence outside the household (excluding those visiting relatives or seeking medical service) are not included as resident population of the household. Resident population is used in calculating income, consumption, accumulation on per capita basis of rural households and in analyzing composition of rural households.

Full/Semi Labour Force Full labour force refers to persons capable of work, aged 18-50 for males and 18-45 for females. Semi labour force refers to persons capable of work, aged 16-17 and 51-60 for males and 16-17 and 46-55 for females. Persons at their working ages but not capable of work are not to be included as labour force. Persons not at working ages but participating regularly in work are included in semi labour force. For staff and workers as resident population of the household, they are included as full or semi labour force of the household if they are in the labour force.

Total Income refers to the sum of income earned from various sources by the rural households and their members during the reference period, and is classified as income from wages and salaries, income from household operations, income from properties and income from transfers.

Income from Wages and Salaries refers to income from labour earned by the members of rural households employed by other units or individuals.

Income from Household Operations refers to income by the rural households as units of production and operations. Operations by rural households are classified by economic activities as agriculture, forestry, animal husbandry, fishery, manufacturing, construction, transportation, post and telecommunications, wholesale, retail and catering, social service, culture, education, health, and other household operations.

Income from Properties refers to the income received as returns by owners of financial assets or tangible non-productive assets by providing capitals or tangible non-productive assets to other institutional units.

Income from Transfers refers to the receipt by rural households and their members of goods, services, capitals or rights of assets without giving or repaying accordingly, excluding capitals provided to them for the formation of fixed assets. In general, it refers to all income received by rural households through redistribution.

Cash Income refers to income received by rural households and their members in the form of cash during the reference period. It is classified, by source of income, into income from wages and salaries, cash income from household operations, income from properties and income from transfers

Net Income refers to the total income of rural households from all sources minus all corresponding expenses. The formula for calculation is as follows:

Net income = total income – household operation expenses – taxes and fees – depreciation of fixed assets for production – subsidy for participating in household survey – gifts to non-rural relatives

Net income is mainly used as input for reproduction and as consumption expenditure of the year, and also used for savings and non-compulsory expenses of various forms. "Per capita net income of farmers" is the level of net income averaged by population which reflects the average income level of rural households in a given area.

Total Expenditure refers to total expenses of rural households on production, consumption and redistribution, including expenditure on household operations, on purchase of productive fixed assets, depreciation of productive fixed assets, taxes and fees, expenses on household consumption, expenses on properties and expenses on transfers.

Expenditure on Household Operations refers expenditure by rural households on goods and services consumed (including own-produced goods) in household-based production or operations. Consumption of own-produced goods which are not included as household income is not considered as expenditure. Chemical fertilizers and pesticides in stock are not included as expenditure of the current period.

Expenditure on Purchase of Productive Fixed Assets refers to expenses by rural households on building or purchase of productive fixed assets.

Expenditure on Taxes and Fees refers to taxes and fees of various forms, surcharges, fees retained by villages and townships, ad hoc fees, and various apportions and contributions to fund-raising, which are paid by rural households, in cash and in kind, in relation with their production and operations. In areas where reform on taxes and fees is introduced, they are collected in the form of agriculture tax, tax on special products, surcharges of agriculture tax and tax on special products, ad hoc fee and other taxes and fees related to non-agriculture activities and operations, as well as various local fees in addition to those collected in line with state regulations. In areas where reform on taxes and fees is not introduced, they are collected in the form of various taxes and fees in relation to production and operations, fees retained by villages and townships, and apportions and contributions to fund-raising.

Expenditure on Household Consumption refers to expenditure by rural households on their material and cultural life, including expenditure on food; clothing; housing; household appliances, articles and services; health and medical service; transportation and communications; articles and services on culture, education and recreation; and other goods and services.

Expenditure on Properties refers to expenses on the right for other properties (including intangible assets) of the households.

Expenditure on Transfers refers to the provision of goods, services, capitals or rights of assets by rural households and their members without receiving anything accordingly, excluding capitals provided by them for the formation of fixed assets. In general, it refers to all expenditure by rural households through redistribution.

Cash Expenditure refers to cash expenditure by rural households for production, consumption and redistribution during the reference period, including cash expenses on household operations, taxes and fees, purchase of productive fixed assets, household consumption, and expenses on properties and transfers.

十一、城市概况

General Survey of Cities

简要说明

一、本篇资料的主要内容

本篇资料反映我国城市社会、经济发展和城市建设的规模、速度、效益及综合水平等基本情况，主要内容有五部分：

1.全国城市分布情况；

2.沿海开放城市和经济特区城市社会经济主要指标；

3.省会城市和计划单列市主要经济指标；

4.地级及以上城市国民经济和社会发展主要指标；

5.城市房屋及公用设施指标。

二、本篇的资料来源

前四部分全国城市分布情况、沿海开放城市和经济特区城市社会经济主要指标、省会城市和计划单列市主要经济指标、地级及以上城市国民经济和社会发展主要指标由各省、自治区、直辖市统计局及城市社会经济调查队依据国家统计局制定的《市、县社会经济基本情况统计报表制度》收集整理提供。

“城市概况”中的有关城市面积、房屋及公用设施方面的资料均是建设部根据其《城市、县城建设统计报表制度》和《房地产统计报表制度》汇总整理提供的。

Brief Introduction

I. Main Content

Data in this chapter show the social and economic development as well as the scale, growth rate, economic efficiency, overall level and other basic conditions of China's cities. The main content is composed of the following 5 parts:

(1) Distribution of the cities in China;

(2) Main indicators on the social and economic development of the open coastal cities and the cities in special economic zones;

(3) Main indicators on the social and economic development of the provincial capitals and the important cities separately listed in the national plan;

(4) Main indicators on the social and economic development of cities at and above prefecture level

(5) Indicators on the urban residential buildings and public facilities.

II. Source of Data

Data of the first 4 parts (distribution of the cities in China, main indicators on the social and economic development of the open coastal cities and the cities in special economic zones, main indicators on the social and economic development of the provincial capitals and the important cities separately listed in the national plan, and main indicators on the social and economic development of cities at and above prefecture level) are collected and prepared by the statistical bureaus of the provinces, autonomous regions and municipalities directly under the central government and urban socio-economic survey organizations of these bureaus in accordance with the *Statistical Reporting System on the Basic Social and Economic Situation of the Cities and Counties*, which is stipulated by the NBS.

Data on the areas, buildings and public facilities of the cities in the General Survey of Cities are collected, prepared and provided by the Ministry of Construction in line with its *Statistical Reporting System of Construction in Cities and Counties* and *Statistical Reporting System on Real Estate Development*.

11-1 城 市 数（2003年）

Number of Cities (2003)

单位：个 (unit)

地区	Region	合计 Total	按城市市辖区总人口分组 Grouped by Population in Urban Districts					
			400万以上 4 million and over	200-400万 2 million-4 million	100-200万 1 million-2 million	50-100万 0.5 million-1 million	20-50万 0.2 million-0.5 million	20万以下 under 0.2 million
全 国	**National Total**	**660**	**11**	**22**	**141**	**274**	**172**	**40**
北 京	Beijing	1	1					
天 津	Tianjin	1	1					
河 北	Hebei	33		2	2	18	11	
山 西	Shanxi	22		1	1	7	13	
内蒙古	Inner Mongolia	20			3	2	8	7
辽 宁	Liaoning	31	1	1	4	22	3	
吉 林	Jilin	28		1	3	7	15	2
黑龙江	Heilongjiang	31		1	2	16	8	4
上 海	Shanghai	1	1					
江 苏	Jiangsu	40	1	4	15	17	3	
浙 江	Zhejiang	33		2	9	18	4	
安 徽	Anhui	22			6	13	3	
福 建	Fujian	23		1	5	7	10	
江 西	Jiangxi	21			3	11	5	2
山 东	Shandong	48		4	17	26	1	
河 南	Henan	38		1	9	19	8	1
湖 北	Hubei	36	1	1	11	18	5	
湖 南	Hunan	29			7	13	8	1
广 东	Guangdong	44	2	2	18	12	10	
广 西	Guangxi	21			5	8	5	3
海 南	Hainan	8			1	4	2	1
重 庆	Chongqing	5	1		3	1		
四 川	Sichuan	32	1		11	15	5	
贵 州	Guizhou	13			2	4	7	
云 南	Yunnan	17		1	1	4	8	3
西 藏	Tibet	2						2
陕 西	Shaanxi	13	1			8	4	
甘 肃	Gansu	15			2	1	8	4
青 海	Qinghai	3				1		2
宁 夏	Ningxia	7				1	6	
新 疆	Xinjiang	22			1	1	12	8

11-2 沿海开放城市和经济特区城市社会经济指标（2003年）

Main Social and Economic Indicators of Open Coastal Cities and Cities in Special Economic Zones (2003)

指标	Item	沿海开放城市合计 Total of Open Coastal Cities		经济特区城市合计 Total of Cities in Special Economic Zones	
		包括市辖县 Counties Included	不包括市辖县 Counties Excluded	包括市辖县 Counties Included	不包括市辖县 Counties Excluded
土地面积 （万平方公里）	**Total Area (10 000 sq.km)**	**14.03**	**3.25**	**0.73**	**0.72**
人口与就业	**Population and Employment**				
年底人口数 （万人）	Population (year-end) (10 000 persons)	9442.9	4303.2	859.4	852.1
#非农业人口	Non-agricultural Population	4314.8	3189.2	768.2	765.5
在岗职工人数	Staff and Workers	1264.1	969.9	230.0	229.1
地区生产总值 （亿元）	**Gross Regional Product (100 million yuan)**	**24521.1**	**17612.0**	**4655.3**	**4648.8**
第一产业	Primary Industry	1555.3	428.4	99.8	97.8
第二产业	Secondary Industry	12268.8	8725.8	2694.2	2692.1
第三产业	Tertiary Industry	10697.0	8457.9	1861.3	1859.0
固定资产投资	**Investment in Fixed Assets**				
固定资产投资额 （亿元）	Total Investment in Fixed Assets (100 million yuan)	7867.1	6441.2	1299.9	1296.9
#房地产开发投资额 （亿元）	Total Investment in Real Estate Development (100 million yuan)	2522.8	2251.2	545.8	545.8
#住宅	Residential Buildings	1838.6	1639.9	342.9	342.9
全年用电量（亿千瓦小时）	**Annual Electricity Consumption (100 million kwh)**	**2536.2**	**1992.9**	**505.4**	**437.7**
农业	**Agriculture**				
主要农产品产量 （万吨）	Output of Major Agricultural Products (10 000 tons)				
蔬菜	Vegetable	4406.4		251.5	
水果	Fruit	1105.0		27.5	
肉类	Meat	443.4		27.3	
水产品	Aquatic Products	1461.8		72.7	
限额以上工业企业主要指标	**Main Indicators of Industrial Enterprises above Designated Size**				
工业企业单位数 （个）	Number of Industrial Enterprises above Designated Size (unit)	41633.0	28083.0	5106.0	5089.0
#内资企业	Domestic Funded Enterprises	28542.0	17885.0	1788.0	1773.0
工业总产值 （当年价格，亿元）	Gross Industrial Output Value (at current prices, 100 million yuan)	33395.0	25443.2	8035.4	8033.1
#内资企业	Domestic Funded Enterprises	17860.8	12070.0	1925.4	1923.7
产品销售收入 （亿元）	Product Sales (100 million yuan)	33377.7	26166.5	7986.9	7984.4
利税总额 （亿元）	Pre-tax Profits (100 million yuan)	3590.5	2963.1	765.2	765.1
资产总额 （亿元）	Total Assets (100 million yuan)	27218.1	22697.1	5996.1	5991.1
每百元资产提供利税 （元）	Pre-tax Profits per 100 Yuan Assets (yuan)	13.2	13.1	12.8	12.8

11-2 续表 continued

指标	Item	沿海开放城市合计 Total of Open Coastal Cities		经济特区城市合计 Total of Cities in Special Economic Zones	
		包括市辖县 Counties Included	不包括市辖县 Counties Excluded	包括市辖县 Counties Included	不包括市辖县 Counties Excluded
运输邮电	**Transport, Post and Telecommunication Services**				
客运量 (亿人)	Passenger Traffic (sent) (100 million persons)	16.2		2.0	
货运量 (亿吨)	Freight Traffic (sent) (100 million tons)	25.0		1.6	
年底邮政局所数 (个)	Number of Post and Telecommunications Offices at the year-end (unit)	8598.0	5528.0	1070.0	1067.0
年末固定电话用户数 (万户)	Number of Telephone Sets (year-end) (10 000 households)	3548.2	2362.6	623.5	495.9
年末移动电话用户 (万户)	Number of Cell Phones (year-end) (10 000 households)	4658.1	3518.4	1237.7	1058.8
国内贸易	**Domestic Trade**				
社会消费品零售总额 (亿元)	Total Retail Sales of Consumer Goods (100 million yuan)	8654.4	6237.7	1445.8	1441.1
限额以上批发零售贸易业商品销售总额 (亿元)	Total Wholesales and Retail Sales of Consumer Goods (100 million yuan)	13027.6	12280.4	2496.1	2490.5
实际利用外资金额(亿美元)	**Amount of Foreign Capital Actually Utilized (USD 100 million)**	**227.0**	**174.4**	**60.1**	**60.0**
在校学生数 (万人)	**Student Enrollment (10 000 persons)**				
普通高等学校	Number of Regular Institutes of Higher Education	183.6	178.3	8.8	8.8
中等职业学校	Number of Specialized Secondary Schools	127.9	97.0	4.7	4.7
普通中学	Number of Regular Secondary Schools	626.6	270.2	67.0	66.4
小学	Number of Primary Schools	748.0	306.3	145.2	144.3
成人高等学校	Number of Schools of Higher Education for Adults	83.6	80.7	6.0	6.0
卫生	**Public Health**				
医院、卫生院数 (个)	Number of Hospitals (unit)	3910.0	1783.0	250.0	246.0
医院、卫生院床位数(万张)	Number of Beds in Hospitals (10 000 beds)	32.0	23.0	2.9	2.9
医生数 (万人)	Number of Doctors (10 000 persons)	18.1	12.7	2.0	2.0
在岗职工工资总额 (亿元)	**Total Wages of Staff and Workers (100 million yuan)**	**2598.7**	**2209.2**	**539.1**	**538.4**
城乡储蓄存款年底余额 (亿元)	**Outstanding Amount of Savings Deposit in Urban and Rural Areas (year-end) (100 million yuan)**	**19697.1**	**15424.1**	**3515.3**	**3512.0**

注：沿海开放城市系指上海、天津、大连、秦皇岛、青岛、烟台、威海、连云港、南通、宁波、温州、福州、广州、湛江、北海共15个城市；经济特区城市系指深圳、珠海、汕头和厦门4个城市。

a) Open coastal cities refer to following 15 cities: Shanghai, Tianjin, Dalian, Qinhuangdao, Qingdao, Yantai, Weihai, Lianyungang, Nantong, Ningbo, Wenzhou, Fuzhou, Guangzhou, Zhanjiang and Beihai. Cities in special economic zones refer to following 4 cities: Shenzhen, Zhuhai, Shantou and Xiamen.

11-3 省会城市和计划单列市主要经济指标（2003年）

Main Social and Economic Indicators of Provincial Capitals and Separate Planning Cities (2003)

包括市辖县。

Counties under the jurisdiction of city governments are included.

城市名称	City	年底总人口（万人）Total Population (year-end) (10 000 persons)	地区生产总值（当年价格）（万元）Gross Regional Product (Current Prices) (10 000 yuan)	工业总产值（万元）Gross Industrial Output Value (10 000 yuan)	客运量（万人）Passenger Traffic (10 000 persons)	货运量（万吨）Freight Traffic (10 000 tons)
北京	Beijing	1148.82	36631000	38103630	30520	30671
天津	Tianjin	926.00	24476600	40496103	3507	34679
石家庄	Shijiazhuang	910.51	13779438	11981505	11843	10008
太原	Taiyuan	327.40	5157089	5183200	2975	15248
呼和浩特	Hohhot	213.89	4062029	2407794	3508	4155
沈阳	Shenyang	689.10	16033795	10643612	6612	14636
大连	Dalian	560.16	16325900	15468641	11001	21081
长春	Changchun	718.23	13380369	15115270	6999	10892
哈尔滨	Harbin	954.31	14147991	7215089	6458	9518
上海	Shanghai	1341.77	62508100	103428195	7212	63861
南京	Nanjing	572.23	15763300	25093816	16790	14805
杭州	Hangzhou	642.78	20997744	32025226	21349	16815
宁波	Ningbo	549.07	17868542	26302862	24938	13797
合肥	Hefei	456.60	4849623	5348605	6034	4641
福州	Fuzhou	604.86	13476759	12889573	9680	8250
厦门	Xiamen	141.76	7596934	13201500	4441	3055
南昌	Nanchang	450.77	6410248	4149169	5728	4454
济南	Jinan	582.56	13653256	13185425	5810	14354
青岛	Qingdao	720.68	17804200	25588695	14666	30553
郑州	Zhengzhou	661.07	11022770	9270494	10709	7847
武汉	Wuhan	781.19	16621797	13344938	11882	16610
长沙	Changsha	601.76	9294858	5339304	10609	10631
广州	Guangzhou	725.19	34968787	40178324	29751	28859
深圳	Shenzhen	150.93	28954070	52451037	10989	6793
南宁	Nanning	614.67	5025271	2083763	7016	5893
海口	Haikou	139.19	2288595	2025643	13284	3304
重庆	Chongqing	3130.10	22505600	15889928	58290	32450
成都	Chengdu	1044.31	18708046	9700976	72793	28798
贵阳	Guiyang	344.86	3809191	3569419	18511	5318
昆明	Kunming	500.79	8120121	5809573	5126	12338
西安	Xi'an	716.58	9416000	6386627	11413	9392
兰州	Lanzhou	304.36	4400803	5215490	2209	5581
西宁	Xining	204.97	1448328	1148959	2788	2037
银川	Yinchuan	133.01	1567845	1464867	2146	2127
乌鲁木齐	Urumqi	181.53	4085834	3110943	2188	12754

注：工业总产值的统计范围为全部国有及年销售收入500万元以上的非国有工业企业。

a) The gross industrial output value is covered all state-owned industrial enterprises and non-state-owned industrial enterprises of annual sale above 5 million yuan.

11-3 续表 continued

城市名称	City	地方财政预算内收入(万元) Budgetary Revenue of Local Governments (10 000 yuan)	固定资产投资总额(万元) Total Investment in Fixed Assets (10 000 yuan)	城乡居民年底储蓄余额(万元) Outstanding Amount of Savings Deposit of Urban and Rural Residents (year-end) (10 000 yuan)	在岗职工人数(万人) Number of Fully-employed Staff and Workers (10 000 persons)	在岗职工工资总额(万元) Total Wages of Fully-employed Staff and Workers (10 000 yuan)
北京	Beijing	5925388	19999107	64413910	434.2	10989365
天津	Tianjin	2045295	9338629	18253200	174.5	3254148
石家庄	Shijiazhuang	493429	4155500	10444919	86.7	1067432
太原	Taiyuan	333473	1973167	6601300	74.6	945212
呼和浩特	Hohhot	205779	1821221	2554496	28.9	407963
沈阳	Shenyang	810889	5568516	14229575	101.7	1521548
大连	Dalian	1105405	4065425	13101986	82.1	1442215
长春	Changchun	459709	2936937	8313564	89.7	1244167
哈尔滨	Harbin	763600	4229569	11536951	168.8	2102165
上海	Shanghai	8992850	22735547	60546000	281.5	7686511
南京	Nanjing	1364788	7944136	11336202	87.9	1950742
杭州	Hangzhou	1503888	7169624	14664200	75.7	1867776
宁波	Ningbo	1394162	5546918	10596339	59.9	1418635
合肥	Hefei	358694	2445667	3592488	37.9	526577
福州	Fuzhou	674522	3755708	8762245	71.3	1073262
厦门	Xiamen	701456	2375028	3971559	54.8	1042111
南昌	Nanchang	314094	2097382	4828029	49.8	692717
济南	Jinan	761054	4293567	7583525	78.4	1256160
青岛	Qingdao	1201398	5475526	9084693	104.6	1603305
郑州	Zhengzhou	658737	3733908	10484859	84.0	1137056
武汉	Wuhan	804368	6228215	12855341	136.1	1868350
长沙	Changsha	598930	4339489	7048500	60.0	1019924
广州	Guangzhou	2747707	10885608	37273276	182.2	5247087
深圳	Shenzhen	2908370	8753965	21994500	105.0	3259900
南宁	Nanning	362435	1699199	4514961	50.8	668976
海口	Haikou	122541	992462	2843664	23.0	340392
重庆	Chongqing	1615618	11868146	18965569	203.8	2535070
成都	Chengdu	895752	7880037	14944197	124.0	1894496
贵阳	Guiyang	403855	2309086	3449487	54.5	664234
昆明	Kunming	601101	3416701	7085278	73.3	1045469
西安	Xi'an	648037	4457381	12105607	113.7	1535896
兰州	Lanzhou	205660	2028339	4683830	54.9	740661
西宁	Xining	84397	761128	1749293	20.6	301364
银川	Yinchuan	122605	1336232	1930771	29.1	393035
乌鲁木齐	Urumqi	409119	1803200	4203000	47.4	782873

11-4 地级及以上城市国民经济和社会发展主要指标（2003年）

Main Indicators of National Economic and Social Development of Cities at Prefecture Level (2003)

指　　标	Item	全国总计 National Total	地级城市合　计（市辖区）Prefecture Cities (Districts under City)	地级城市合计占全国比重（%）Percentage of Prefecture Cities to National Total (%)
自然资源	**Natural Resources**			
土地面积　(万平方公里)	Area of Land　(10 000 sq.km)	960.0	56.5	5.9
人口	**Population**			
年末总人口　(万人)	Population at the Year-end　(10 000 persons)	129227.0	34197.0	26.5
国民经济核算	**National Accounting**			
地区生产总值　(亿元)	Gross Regional Product　(100 million yuan)	117251.9	76151.6	64.9
第一产业	Primary Industry	17092.1	3424.3	20.0
第二产业	Secondary Industry	61274.1	39298.9	64.1
#工业	Industry	53092.9	33580.4	63.2
第三产业	Tertiary Industry	38885.7	33428.4	86.0
固定资产投资	**Investment in Fixed Assets**			
固定资产投资总额　(亿元)	Total Investment in Fixed Assets　(100 million yuans)	55566.6	28891.4	52.0
#房地产开发	Real Estate Development	10153.8	8547.6	84.2
财政	**Government Finance**			
地方财政收入　(亿元)	Local Government Revenue　(100 million yuans)	9850.0	5794.9	58.8
地方财政支出　(亿元)	Local Government Expenditure　(100 million yuans)	17229.9	7845.2	45.5
进出口	**Imports and Exports**			
进出口总额　(亿美元)	Total Value of Imports and Exports (100 million USD)	8509.9	5229.1	61.4
出口额	Exports	4382.3	2708.2	61.8
进口额	Imports	4127.6	2520.9	61.1
工业	**Industry**			
规模以上工业企业数　(个)	Number of Industrial Enterprises above Designated Size　(unit)	196222	100472	51.2
内资企业	Domestic Funded Enterprises	157641	73829	46.8
港澳台投资企业	Enterprises with Funds from Hong Kong, Macao and Taiwan	21152	14486	68.5
外商投资企业	Foreign Funded Enterprises	17429	12145	69.7
工业总产值　(亿元)	Gross Industrial Output Value　(100 million yuans)	142271.2	96285.4	67.7
内资企业	Domestic Funded Enterprises	97913.4	60506.9	61.8
港澳台投资企业	Enterprises with Funds from Hong Kong, Macao and Taiwan	17425.6	13161.3	75.5
外商投资企业	Foreign Funded Enterprises	26932.2	22604.6	83.9
固定资产净值年平均余额　(亿元)	Annual Average Balance of Net Value of Fixed Assets　(100 million yuans)	66068.4	45094.7	68.3
产品销售收入　(亿元)	Sale Revenue　(100 million yuans)	143171.5	96857.3	67.7
本年应交增值税　(亿元)	Value Added Tax Payable　(100 million yuans)	5487.7	3840.8	70.0
利润总额　(亿元)	Total Profits　(100 million yuans)	8337.2	5958.7	71.5
邮电通信业　(亿元)	**Post and Telecommunication Services (100 million yuan)**			
邮政业务总量	Business Volume of Post	541.0	308.8	57.1
电信业务总量	Business Volume of Telecommunication	6478.8	3103.2	47.9
国内商业	**Domestic Trade**			
社会消费品零售额　(亿元)	Total Retail Sales of Consumer Goods　(100 million yuans)	45842.0	28133.4	61.4
教育	**Education**			
高等学校	Institutions of Higher Education			
学校数　(个)	Number of Institution　(unit)	1552	1524	98.2
在校学生数　(万人)	Student Enrollment　(10 000 persons)	1108.6	1101.0	99.3
卫生	**Health Care**			
医院、卫生院数　(个)	Hospital and Health Center　(unit)	62968	21451	34.1
医生数　(万人)	Doctors　(10 000 persons)	186.8	83.7	44.8
医院、卫生机构床位数(万张)	Number of Hospital Beds　(10 000 beds)	295.5	157.5	53.3

注:进出口总额系35个大中城市资料。

a) Total value of imports and exports are the data of 35 large-sized and medium-sized cities.

11-5 城市公用事业基本情况

Basic Statistics on Urban Public Utilities

本表各项指标按全社会范围计算。

Data have covered the public utilities of all urban units

项目	Item	1990	1995	2000	2002	2003
城市及建筑物面积	**Cities Areas and Floor Space of Buildings**					
建成区面积 (平方公里)	Developed Areas (sq.m)	12856	19264	22439	25973	28308
城市人口密度 (人/平方公里)	Population Density of Urban Districts (persons/sq.km)	279	322	442	754	847
年末实有房屋建筑面积 (亿平方米)	Total Floor Space of Buildings (year-end) (100 million sq.m)	39.8	57.3	76.6	131.8	140.9
年末实有住宅建筑面积 (亿平方米)	Total Floor Space of Residential Buildings (year-end) (100 million sq.m)	20.0	31.0	44.1	81.8	89.1
供水、供气及供热	**Water Supply, Gas Supply and Heating**					
年供水总量 (亿吨)	Annual Supply of Tap Water (100 million tons)	382.3	481.6	469.0	466.5	475.3
#生活用水量	Water Consumption for Residential use	100.1	158.1	200.0	213.2	224.7
人均生活用水 (吨)	Per Capita Water Consumption for Residential Use (ton)	67.9	71.3	95.5	77.8	77.1
用水普及率 (%)	Percentage of Population with Access to Tap Water (%)	48.0	58.7	63.9	77.9	86.2
人工煤气供气量 (亿立方米)	Coal Gas Supply (100 million cu.m)	174.7	126.7	152.4	198.9	202.1
#家庭用量	Consumption of Coal Gas for Residential Use	27.4	45.7	63.1	49.0	58.4
天然气供气量 (亿立方米)	Natural Gas Supply (100 million cu.m)	64.2	67.3	82.1	125.9	141.6
#家庭用量	Consumption of Coal Gas for Residential Use	11.6	16.4	24.8	35.0	37.5
液化石油气供气量 (万吨)	Liquefied Petroleum Gas (10 000 ton)	219.0	488.7	1053.7	1136.4	1126.3
#家庭用量 (万吨)	Consumption of Liquefied Gas for Residential Use (10 000 ton)	142.8	370.2	532.3	656.2	781.7
供气管道长度 (万公里)	Length of Gas Pipelines (10 000 km)	2.4	4.4	8.9	11.4	13.0
燃气普及率 (%)	Percentage of Population with Access to Gas (%)	19.1	34.3	45.4	67.2	76.7
集中供热面积 (亿平方米)	Heated Area (100 million sq.m)	2.1	6.5	11.1	15.6	18.9
市政设施	**Municipal Infra-structure**					
道路长度 (万公里)	Length of Roads (10 000 km)	9.5	13.0	16.0	19.1	20.8
每万人拥有道路长度 (公里)	Length of Roads per 10 000 Population (km)	3.1	3.8	4.1	5.4	6.2
道路面积 (亿平方米)	Area of Roads (100 million sq.m)	8.9	13.6	19.0	27.7	31.6
人均拥有道路面积 (平方米)	Area of Roads per 10 000 Population (sq.m)	3.1	4.4	6.1	7.9	9.3
排水管道长度 (万公里)	Length of Sewer Pipelines (10 000 km)	5.8	11.0	14.2	17.3	19.9
排水管道密度(公里/平方公里)	Density of Sewer Pipelines (km/sq.m)	4.5	5.7	6.3	6.7	7.0
公共交通	**Public Traffic**					
公共汽(电)车运营车数 (万辆)	Number of Public Vehicles for Business Transportation (Buses and Trolley Buses, etc.) (10 000 units)	6.2	13.7	22.6	24.6	26.4
每万人拥有公交车辆 (标台)	Number of Public Transportation Vehicles per 10 000 Population (unit)	2.2	3.6	5.3	6.7	7.7
出租汽车数量 (万辆)	Taxi (10 000 units)	11.1	50.4	82.5	88.4	90.3
城市绿化	**Afforestation in Cities**					
园林绿地面积 (万公顷)	Public Green Areas (10 000 hectare)	47.5	67.8	86.5	107.2	121.2
人均公共绿地面积 (平方米)	Public Green Areas per 10 000 Population (sq.m)	1.8	2.5	3.7	5.4	6.5
公园个数 (个)	Number of Park and Zoo (unit)	1970	3619	4455	5178	5832
公园面积 (万公顷)	Area of Park and Zoo (10 000 hectare)	3.9	7.3	8.2	10.0	11.3
环境卫生	**Environmental Sanitation**					
清运垃圾 (万吨)	Volume of Garbage Disposal (10 000 tons)	6767	10671	11819	13650	14857
清运粪便 (万吨)	Volume of Disposal of Excrement and Urine (10 000 tons)	2385	3066	2829	3160	3475
每万人拥有公厕 (座)	Number of Public Lavatories per 10 000 Population	3.0	3.0	2.7	3.2	3.2

注：人均和普及率指标均按城市人口计算，城市人口指市区（不包括市辖县）有常住户口的人。

a) Per capita data and popularization data are calculated by city population, which refers to population permanently registrated in urban districts exluded counties.

11-6 各地区城市房屋建筑及住房情况（2003年）

Basic Statistics on Building Construction and Housing Condition in Cities by Region (2003)

地 区	Region	建成区面积 (平方公里) Developed Areas (sq.km)	征用土地面积 (平方公里) Land Put in Requisition for State Construction Projects (sq.km)	城市人口密度 (人/平方公里) Population Density of Urban Districts (persons/sq.km)	年末全市实有房屋建筑面积 (万平方米) Total Floor Space of Buildings (year-end) (10 000 sq.m)	年末全市实有住宅建筑面积 (万平方米) Total Floor Space of Residential Buildings (year-end) (10 000 sq.m)
全 国	**National Total**	**28308.0**	**1605.6**	**847**	**1409091.4**	**891114.6**
北 京	Beijing	1180.1	56.6	2128	43121.5	23847.5
天 津	Tianjin	487.5		841	19324.1	12575.4
河 北	Hebei	1171.0	50.7	2057	66359.1	42375.3
山 西	Shanxi	678.7	13.5	860	38828.6	27172.6
内蒙古	Inner Mongolia	679.3	2.6	537	28011.5	17308.7
辽 宁	Liaoning	1694.6	36.6	1244	67315.8	40488.0
吉 林	Jilin	850.5	9.8	756	34192.9	22239.0
黑龙江	Heilongjiang	1362.5	19.5	355	56876.5	36803.1
上 海	Shanghai	549.6	88.1	1971	51375.0	30560.0
江 苏	Jiangsu	2119.5	310.6	1332	130639.9	75239.7
浙 江	Zhejiang	1397.0	209.5	1117	76756.9	50449.6
安 徽	Anhui	1044.2	52.9	1524	33897.5	22480.6
福 建	Fujian	598.4	66.0	1025	36363.9	25075.5
江 西	Jiangxi	598.5	96.4	2582	33887.5	22411.6
山 东	Shandong	2195.4	111.4	901	99112.1	60591.8
河 南	Henan	1345.9	97.4	3706	60091.0	35576.2
湖 北	Hubei	1415.6	23.5	619	60716.8	39255.5
湖 南	Hunan	959.4	60.0	1123	81863.6	52421.6
广 东	Guangdong	2546.9	84.2	1779	123771.5	80755.3
广 西	Guangxi	685.4	16.6	583	33058.7	21398.7
海 南	Hainan	176.7	2.1	851	7695.5	4747.8
重 庆	Chongqing	523.7	51.5	1057	26778.5	16879.4
四 川	Sichuan	1357.4	43.1	237	76077.6	49999.8
贵 州	Guizhou	348.1	11.1	1037	14786.0	11280.5
云 南	Yunnan	410.5	16.5	375	23863.3	15587.7
西 藏	Tibet	72.4	0.4	1137	977.3	781.9
陕 西	Shaanxi	508.3	30.7	2217	28825.9	19954.0
甘 肃	Gansu	478.3	7.0	3929	22849.0	13315.9
青 海	Qinghai	101.8	1.0	1930	3684.0	2674.8
宁 夏	Ningxia	206.1	22.7	281	6714.9	4070.0
新 疆	Xinjiang	564.8	13.7	211	21275.2	12797.5

11-7 各地区城市供水情况（2003年）

Basic Statistics on Tap Water Supply in Cities by Region (2003)

地 区	Region	年末供水综合生产能力（万立方米/日）Production Capacity of Tap Water (year-end) (10 000 tons/day)	年末供水管道长度（公里）Length of Water Supply Pipelines (year-end) (km)	全年供水总量（万立方米）Total Annual Volume of Water Supply (10 000 tons)	#生活用水 For Residential Use	#生产用水 For Productive Use	用水人口（万人）Number of Residents with Access to Tap Water (10 000 persons)	人均日生活用水量（升）Per Capita Daily Consumption of Tap Water for Residential Use (liter)
全 国	**National Total**	**23967.1**	**333288.8**	**4752548**	**2246665**	**2069345**	**29124.5**	**210.9**
北 京	Beijing	1265.0	15896.0	128823	87153	38139	962.7	248.0
天 津	Tianjin	343.1	6822.0	64537	29829	24889	623.9	131.0
河 北	Hebei	882.9	10771.2	160132	69981	77788	1243.8	154.2
山 西	Shanxi	375.6	5669.3	77525	33844	41372	776.7	119.4
内蒙古	Inner Mongolia	309.4	5635.5	59276	22529	33742	495.8	124.5
辽 宁	Liaoning	1346.5	21999.0	280510	94322	131973	1779.7	145.2
吉 林	Jilin	698.5	6384.9	159570	44603	99066	804.4	151.9
黑龙江	Heilongjiang	685.1	9065.9	153387	66717	73218	1099.9	166.2
上 海	Shanghai	1493.6	22098.8	308309	160992	115615	1278.2	330.6
江 苏	Jiangsu	1835.0	36632.4	380395	171830	174834	2167.7	217.2
浙 江	Zhejiang	1179.4	24126.9	235535	111291	102757	1290.2	236.3
安 徽	Anhui	1026.5	7389.4	204128	72313	121167	928.1	213.5
福 建	Fujian	697.9	6270.4	118512	57841	51587	598.8	264.6
江 西	Jiangxi	620.1	5094.7	143240	59203	76629	618.6	262.2
山 东	Shandong	1351.5	26073.9	259782	118767	125612	2321.8	140.1
河 南	Henan	996.0	11405.6	185092	80943	87600	1384.8	160.1
湖 北	Hubei	1406.9	15668.6	257787	154130	95119	1584.1	266.6
湖 南	Hunan	1213.9	9341.8	262691	99211	134226	872.1	311.7
广 东	Guangdong	2429.9	35728.8	568949	319004	199712	2969.4	294.3
广 西	Guangxi	634.6	6923.1	134412	67162	58766	600.2	306.6
海 南	Hainan	140.4	1726.7	20241	14784	2010	182.2	222.4
重 庆	Chongqing	389.0	6082.7	71077	35390	28311	624.6	155.2
四 川	Sichuan	867.7	12251.3	165632	102616	55430	1266.6	222.0
贵 州	Guizhou	247.2	3275.3	45198	25846	11603	381.7	185.5
云 南	Yunnan	249.9	5208.5	52742	27781	13281	407.2	186.9
西 藏	Tibet	18.1	364.9	5363	3860	1001	20.6	513.4
陕 西	Shaanxi	386.5	4270.0	73580	42452	24967	714.5	162.8
甘 肃	Gansu	334.4	5010.0	62127	21560	36359	423.9	139.3
青 海	Qinghai	68.3	893.0	14390	7641	4804	93.1	224.9
宁 夏	Ningxia	123.7	1538.2	22921	8788	11458	131.6	182.9
新 疆	Xinjiang	350.7	3670.2	76685	34282	16310	477.9	196.5

11-8 各地区城市燃气情况（2003年）

Basic Statistics on Supply of Gas in Cities by Region (2003)

地 区	Region	人工煤气生产能力（万立方米/日） Production Capacity of Coal Gas (10 000 cu.m/day)	管道长度（公里） Length of Gas Pipelines (km)			全年供气总量 Total Gas Supply			用气人口(万人) Population with Access to Gas (10 000 persons)		
			人工煤气 Coal Gas	液化石油气 Liquefied Petroleum Gas	天然气 Natural Gas	人工煤气（万立方米） Coal Gas (10 000 cu.m)	液化石油气（万吨） Liquefied Petroleum Gas (10 000 tons)	天然气（万立方米） Natural Gas (10 000 cu.m)	人工煤气 Coal Gas	液化石油气 Liquefied Petroleum Gas	天然气 Natural Gas
全 国	**National Total**	**4912.9**	**57017.4**	**15349.1**	**57845.3**	**2020883.2**	**1126.4**	**1416415.3**	**4792.1**	**16833.9**	**4320.2**
北 京	Beijing		194.7	229.0	6772.6	27286.6	38.4	238471.0	26.0	397.0	538.0
天 津	Tianjin	185.0	1423.0	157.4	5380.0	25896.0	8.0	48004.0	96.3	117.8	391.5
河 北	Hebei	161.1	3304.7	120.0	1739.9	70347.5	33.7	12059.3	360.5	707.7	86.7
山 西	Shanxi	188.1	3451.9	0.5	205.7	89706.1	4.9	3874.3	370.1	174.8	31.4
内蒙古	Inner Mongolia	190.4	824.0	39.0	250.0	9043.0	13.4	33.0	74.1	260.3	28.0
辽 宁	Liaoning	230.5	4871.0	290.2	4286.0	69121.2	43.2	30338.0	541.6	734.4	456.5
吉 林	Jilin	72.4	1925.0	101.9	2141.2	20562.2	20.3	19109.0	158.6	437.8	123.3
黑龙江	Heilongjiang	218.0	2200.7	153.2	1109.3	36183.3	22.2	18175.0	256.0	583.6	84.4
上 海	Shanghai	1134.3	8561.0		3628.2	250873.6	42.9	49682.3	592.5	505.6	180.2
江 苏	Jiangsu	220.3	5994.8	2765.5	714.5	802429.5	135.8	1676.9	405.8	1673.5	9.9
浙 江	Zhejiang	91.7	2381.0	2212.0	92.0	33721.0	118.5	1008.0	156.5	1103.5	11.9
安 徽	Anhui	44.8	2204.0	329.5	215.8	20147.8	33.3	31.6	203.1	517.3	3.4
福 建	Fujian	4.0	261.5	1710.1		1257.4	30.1		8.9	573.4	
江 西	Jiangxi	195.3	1663.4	92.6	61.1	39984.3	15.0	0.2	138.7	356.5	0.1
山 东	Shandong	146.3	6167.5	737.2	3812.1	47187.4	54.5	83720.8	422.0	1614.3	225.6
河 南	Henan	205.5	1520.1	69.4	3708.8	84775.5	17.5	43136.4	139.3	507.7	283.4
湖 北	Hubei	161.2	2263.5	1340.1	392.5	15592.6	31.3	892.0	137.2	1230.0	6.8
湖 南	Hunan	159.2	1141.0	625.6		43529.7	23.1		100.5	571.8	
广 东	Guangdong	141.4	2101.3	3691.5	398.0	128836.1	33.4	2178.1	246.8	2702.3	18.0
广 西	Guangxi	10.6	315.0	509.6		3903.4	25.0		23.2	466.6	
海 南	Hainan			3.5	356.0		8.0	2308.5		110.8	41.6
重 庆	Chongqing	2.0	132.0	5.0	7228.9	336.0	6.3	110438.0	1.8	46.1	438.0
四 川	Sichuan	355.0	411.0	112.8	10944.8	120233.0	14.2	559451.5	31.5	137.8	862.5
贵 州	Guizhou	80.8	1489.3	14.4	17.5	14411.0	5.7	6199.0	100.3	184.6	1.7
云 南	Yunnan	76.0	1413.0	25.7	98.0	17330.0	9.4	14500.0	144.3	174.7	4.5
西 藏	Tibet						0.1			12.5	
陕 西	Shaanxi		147.0		1754.9	1258.0	10.7	50336.0	15.2	336.6	240.3
甘 肃	Gansu	15.0	280.6		375.0	3433.1	5.5	9687.0	24.8	191.6	86.4
青 海	Qinghai				370.2		1.5	38126.0		35.5	7.8
宁 夏	Ningxia		314.0		429.9	2848.0	2.2	50464.2	10.5	81.8	16.6
新 疆	Xinjiang	624.0	61.3	13.4	1362.6	40650.0	17.2	22515.4	5.9	286.2	142.0

11-9 各地区城市集中供热情况（2003年）

Basic Statistics on Heating in Cities by Region (2003)

地 区	Region	供应能力 Heating Capacity		供热总量 Volume Supplied		管道长度(公里) Length of Pipelines(km)		供热面积 (万平方米) Heated Area (10 000 sq.m)
		蒸汽 (吨/小时) Steam (ton/hour)	热水 (兆瓦) Hot Water (Mega Watts)	蒸汽 (万吉焦) Steam (10 000 gigajoules)	热水 (万吉焦) Hot Water (10 000 gigajoules)	蒸汽 Steam	热水 Hot Water	
全 国	**National Total**	**92590**	**59136**	**171472**	**128950**	**11939**	**58028**	**188955.6**
北 京	Beijing	3816	3406	22646	11565	245	4419	25107.8
天 津	Tianjin	3234	1486	9390	6191	439	6948	10786.9
河 北	Hebei	6881	6119	11218	7882	922	4712	15309.0
山 西	Shanxi	3397	929	5642	4753	560	1828	7105.6
内蒙古	Inner Mongolia	874	532	9536	7557	97	2977	7907.2
辽 宁	Liaoning	10975	3999	30874	19719	1707	10927	29669.4
吉 林	Jilin	4450	1570	17478	11555	399	4557	15872.9
黑龙江	Heilongjiang	5993	2524	20493	20814	532	7451	19944.3
上 海	Shanghai							
江 苏	Jiangsu	13372	9637	68	2	1273	17	2156.5
浙 江	Zhejiang	3333	2969	388	242	415	76	4006.4
安 徽	Anhui	1798	2325			152	15	123.6
福 建	Fujian			13	76		17	234.0
江 西	Jiangxi							
山 东	Shandong	18754	9636	22663	17472	3163	5870	20430.2
河 南	Henan	3899	2348	1494	1115	697	1037	4365.0
湖 北	Hubei	1404	596	78	16	128	7	460.0
湖 南	Hunan	105	5			8		250.0
广 东	Guangdong							
广 西	Guangxi							
海 南	Hainan							
重 庆	Chongqing							
四 川	Sichuan	160	134			42		4000.0
贵 州	Guizhou							
云 南	Yunnan							
西 藏	Tibet							
陕 西	Shaanxi	2258	1711	1494	1266	338	397	3087.2
甘 肃	Gansu	5845	8113	4777	5808	519	3195	5655.6
青 海	Qinghai			158	70		70	102.4
宁 夏	Ningxia	646	241	4111	4247	132	897	3443.2
新 疆	Xinjiang	1396	856	8951	8600	171	2611	8938.6

11-10 各地区城市市政设施（2003年）

Basic Statistics on Municipal Infra-structure in Cities by Region (2003)

地 区	Region	年末实有道路长度（公里）Length of Roads (year-end) (km)	年末实有道路面积（万平方米）Area of Roads (year-end) (10 000 sq.m)	城市桥梁（座）Number of Bridges (unit)	城市排水管道长度（公里）Length of Sewer Pipelines (km)	城市污水日处理能力（万立方米）Daily Disposal Capacity of Sewage (10 000 cu.m)	城市路灯（盏）Number of Street Lights (unit)
全 国	**National Total**	**208052.0**	**315645.2**	**50732**	**198645.0**	**6626.4**	**8731143**
北 京	Beijing	7947.7	10569.8	1666	6649.3	216.1	256032
天 津	Tianjin	4084.1	5489.0	490	9123.7	76.0	178826
河 北	Hebei	7736.7	14133.8	1259	8911.3	242.3	286120
山 西	Shanxi	4421.0	6371.1	744	2858.4	91.9	204034
内蒙古	Inner Mongolia	3393.1	5344.4	250	3785.1	88.8	193870
辽 宁	Liaoning	10203.6	14885.0	1326	9120.3	376.0	634979
吉 林	Jilin	4485.9	6950.5	468	4713.6	139.8	171797
黑龙江	Heilongjiang	8839.1	10654.5	637	5465.0	252.8	337943
上 海	Shanghai	9802.0	15933.0	7225	5882.0	519.6	237623
江 苏	Jiangsu	25540.8	31859.1	12256	20342.5	906.6	970896
浙 江	Zhejiang	10341.7	16743.2	5915	15331.2	501.7	565675
安 徽	Anhui	6931.2	11355.4	1045	5982.0	292.1	231452
福 建	Fujian	4355.0	6091.6	1152	4957.3	162.5	219511
江 西	Jiangxi	3430.5	5466.0	410	2952.6	74.0	255084
山 东	Shandong	20915.2	34165.7	4251	18152.6	462.5	550687
河 南	Henan	5987.0	12409.6	993	7801.3	231.1	351287
湖 北	Hubei	13837.6	18815.0	1798	8314.7	412.0	277892
湖 南	Hunan	5368.9	7980.8	541	4404.0	223.0	224858
广 东	Guangdong	18408.7	30323.8	3226	23321.0	489.3	844968
广 西	Guangxi	4268.4	6326.9	483	3430.5	206.7	271357
海 南	Hainan	1074.8	2184.1	120	1822.3	41.2	64122
重 庆	Chongqing	3278.8	4784.1	618	3267.5	71.0	165155
四 川	Sichuan	7840.0	13295.8	1896	8282.2	116.4	505575
贵 州	Guizhou	1804.1	2079.3	302	1988.9	8.0	84032
云 南	Yunnan	2430.8	3270.9	474	2557.2	146.8	144560
西 藏	Tibet	407.9	429.0	32	220.2		11085
陕 西	Shaanxi	2909.1	4686.4	408	2801.6	48.8	111729
甘 肃	Gansu	2967.5	5281.7	294	2591.4	61.1	100579
青 海	Qinghai	514.3	843.5	62	485.0	8.5	20322
宁 夏	Ningxia	1044.6	1797.3	103	669.7	37.0	100513
新 疆	Xinjiang	3482.0	5124.8	288	2460.5	122.8	158580

11-11 各地区城市公共交通情况（2003年）

Basic Statistics on Public Transportation in Cities by Region (2003)

地区	Region	年末公共汽(电)车运营数(辆) Number of Public Vehicles of Bus, Trolley Bus at the year-end (unit)	公共汽车 Buses	电车 Trolley	地铁 Subways	公共汽(电)车客运总量(万人次) Number of Passengers Carried of Bus, Trolley Bus (10 000 person-times)	公共汽车 Buses	电车 Trolley	地铁 Subways	出租汽车(辆) Number of Taxi (unit)
全国	**National Total**	**264338**	**259339**	**3086**	**1913**	**3813505**	**3607696**	**105449**	**100360**	**903381**
北京	Beijing	19991	18084	583	1324	426682	350573	28861	47248	65984
天津	Tianjin	6066	6066			62048	62048			31939
河北	Hebei	8913	8913			69819	69819			42006
山西	Shanxi	3832	3713	119		48030	45592	2438		26849
内蒙古	Inner Mongolia	2849	2849			25334	25334			30789
辽宁	Liaoning	16324	16161	157	6	338884	329585	8850	449	83730
吉林	Jilin	8293	8256	25	12	97467	96235	799	433	50249
黑龙江	Heilongjiang	10254	10210	44		112088	111809	279		56719
上海	Shanghai	19070	18102	523	445	313690	260000	13086	40604	48672
江苏	Jiangsu	17822	17822			233586	233586			40073
浙江	Zhejiang	13244	13027	217		198120	184168	13951		27671
安徽	Anhui	7817	7817			101568	101568			35013
福建	Fujian	6628	6628			117111	117111			13612
江西	Jiangxi	4678	4586	92		64722	60827	3895		9510
山东	Shandong	16117	15853	264		168930	163225	5705		47058
河南	Henan	11193	11019	174		109678	105331	4347		54117
湖北	Hubei	17199	16983	216		200403	195752	4651		26290
湖南	Hunan	8995	8995			117634	117634			22715
广东	Guangdong	15010	14470	414	126	280481	258759	10096	11626	32132
广西	Guangxi	4148	4148			75444	75444			11140
海南	Hainan	1342	1342			12565	12565			3407
重庆	Chongqing	5333	5250	83		90407	84133	6274		17233
四川	Sichuan	9717	9717			181664	181664			23406
贵州	Guizhou	4802	4802			65615	65615			8016
云南	Yunnan	4772	4772			55491	55351	140		15013
西藏	Tibet	1249	1249			590	590			1341
陕西	Shaanxi	5786	5711	75		77139	75459	1681		20881
甘肃	Gansu	3190	3090	100		49741	49345	396		17660
青海	Qinghai	1428	1428			25476	25476			7258
宁夏	Ningxia	1011	1011			9215	9215			9476
新疆	Xinjiang	7265	7265			83881	83881			23422

11-12 各地区城市园林和绿地(2003年)

Basic Statistics on Parks, Gardens and Green Areas in Cities by Region (2003)

地 区	Region	城市园林绿地面积(公顷) Total Area of Parks, Gardens and Green Areas in Cities (hectare)	# 公共绿地 Public Green Areas	公 园(个) Number of Parks (unit)	公园面积(公顷) Area of Parks (hectare)	年游人量(万人次) Number of Visitors to Parks and Zoos in the Year (10 000 person-times)
全 国	**National Total**	**1211742.1**	**219514.4**	**5832**	**113462.0**	**141925.4**
北 京	Beijing	48495.7	10825.7	222	5662.2	9970.5
天 津	Tianjin	13238.8	4161.3	196	2829.4	3934.0
河 北	Hebei	37950.2	8153.9	318	4664.3	5744.4
山 西	Shanxi	14496.7	3976.9	103	2233.4	551.8
内蒙古	Inner Mongolia	17731.5	3875.7	71	2282.2	989.1
辽 宁	Liaoning	65211.2	12653.9	225	6945.7	5078.0
吉 林	Jilin	24606.0	5699.9	67	2338.2	1446.6
黑龙江	Heilongjiang	38022.9	8997.4	145	4406.1	6373.3
上 海	Shanghai	24286.1	9400.2	134	1468.6	9621.7
江 苏	Jiangsu	145956.0	18742.5	446	7317.1	8443.5
浙 江	Zhejiang	42875.1	9879.9	525	4119.1	7763.7
安 徽	Anhui	36500.4	5958.5	120	3154.1	4372.7
福 建	Fujian	23093.1	4638.8	245	3593.3	5140.1
江 西	Jiangxi	21689.1	4305.7	112	1785.6	1768.4
山 东	Shandong	80384.7	20085.1	402	9050.7	7674.2
河 南	Henan	32619.1	10100.1	337	4318.2	6207.3
湖 北	Hubei	54290.4	12143.0	191	5323.2	5633.6
湖 南	Hunan	34254.8	5116.3	129	3513.4	3102.0
广 东	Guangdong	261358.7	26952.4	890	17095.5	24667.1
广 西	Guangxi	25541.9	4234.1	99	2966.7	2779.0
海 南	Hainan	5574.5	1683.3	32	893.7	2005.8
重 庆	Chongqing	12125.0	2523.0	71	1249.8	1202.5
四 川	Sichuan	63163.2	8961.9	304	4873.4	4792.0
贵 州	Guizhou	26633.5	2586.4	51	2585.6	3848.0
云 南	Yunnan	11577.7	3714.3	98	2924.8	3538.1
西 藏	Tibet	14.3	14.2	2	52.0	60.0
陕 西	Shaanxi	13392.0	3248.4	82	1622.1	2680.0
甘 肃	Gansu	8655.0	2245.3	69	1250.2	879.1
青 海	Qinghai	1909.7	587.3	14	289.7	248.8
宁 夏	Ningxia	5554.5	924.6	23	466.5	638.4
新 疆	Xinjiang	20540.3	3124.6	109	2187.3	771.7

11-13 各地区城市环境卫生情况（2003年）

Basic Statistics on Urban Sanitation in Cities by Region (2003)

地 区	Region	清扫保洁面积（万平方米）Area under Cleaning Program (10 000 sq.m)	生活垃圾清运量（万吨）Volume of Garbage Disposal (10 000 tons)	粪便清运量（万吨）Volume of Excrement and Urine Disposal (10 000 tons)	市容环卫专用车辆总数（台）Number of Special Vehicles for Environmental Sanitation (unit)	公共厕所（座）Number of Public Lavatories (unit)	#水冲式 Water-Closet
全 国	**National Total**	**247879.6**	**14856.5**	**3474.9**	**56068**	**107949**	**58996**
北 京	Beijing	8547.5	454.5	233.6	4763	5662	4341
天 津	Tianjin	4376.0	171.8	25.2	1151	2430	1932
河 北	Hebei	11262.6	713.1	169.2	2693	6342	1859
山 西	Shanxi	6162.6	601.5	157.7	1331	3902	862
内蒙古	Inner Mongolia	4566.3	391.5	95.0	1077	3574	623
辽 宁	Liaoning	18590.0	791.0	143.8	2920	9529	1103
吉 林	Jilin	7440.8	580.6	113.8	1967	5667	551
黑龙江	Heilongjiang	9438.1	1042.9	256.1	3304	10369	901
上 海	Shanghai	7989.0	585.3	251.1	4025	2356	2086
江 苏	Jiangsu	20874.4	774.5	405.5	4456	10660	8771
浙 江	Zhejiang	12591.1	674.7	112.4	2572	4283	4074
安 徽	Anhui	6621.8	406.8	44.7	1046	3537	1955
福 建	Fujian	5192.8	265.4	33.3	1353	1442	1402
江 西	Jiangxi	4143.4	236.6	19.7	629	1311	950
山 东	Shandong	23874.6	1182.9	151.5	3581	4249	3253
河 南	Henan	12514.5	651.2	85.6	1995	4912	2948
湖 北	Hubei	11451.3	813.4	116.8	2527	5192	4065
湖 南	Hunan	5402.1	443.9	64.1	867	2538	1919
广 东	Guangdong	24921.4	1447.0	587.3	5242	4714	4527
广 西	Guangxi	4926.4	225.3	21.0	876	1216	1121
海 南	Hainan	2288.9	85.4	9.3	286	262	222
重 庆	Chongqing	3637.7	215.3	57.9	924	2263	1552
四 川	Sichuan	11473.6	544.1	77.6	2066	3699	2859
贵 州	Guizhou	1854.7	187.1	9.5	508	928	845
云 南	Yunnan	2708.0	197.6	60.2	997	1092	883
西 藏	Tibet	262.0	38.0	0.7	18	81	38
陕 西	Shaanxi	4565.2	350.7	16.0	929	1257	820
甘 肃	Gansu	2982.4	275.8	97.0	647	1163	616
青 海	Qinghai	1001.1	55.9	43.3	191	299	186
宁 夏	Ningxia	1428.8	118.8	7.6	245	973	339
新 疆	Xinjiang	4790.4	333.9	8.4	882	2047	1393

11-14 各地区城市设施水平（2003年）

Level of Public Facilities in Cities by Region (2003)

地 区	Region	人均住宅建筑面积（平方米） Per Capita Floor Space of Residential Buildings (sq.m)	城市用水普及率（%） Percentage of with Access to Tap Water (%)	城市燃气普及率（%） Percentage of Population with Access to Gas (%)	每万人拥有公共交通车辆(标台) Number of Public Transportation Vehicles per 10 000 Persons (set)	人均拥有道路面积（平方米） Per Capita Area of Roads (sq.m)	人均公共绿地面积（平方米） Per Capita Public Green Areas (sq.m)	每万人拥有公共厕所（座） Number of Public Lavatories per 10 000 Population
全 国	**National Average**	**23.67**	**86.15**	**76.74**	**7.66**	**9.34**	**6.49**	**3.19**
北 京	Beijing	24.77	100.00	99.82	26.37	9.60	11.25	5.88
天 津	Tianjin	23.10	100.00	97.07	9.38	8.80	6.67	3.89
河 北	Hebei	23.17	99.86	92.73	6.65	11.35	6.55	5.09
山 西	Shanxi	23.00	81.16	60.22	4.12	6.66	4.16	4.08
内蒙古	Inner Mongolia	20.05	80.04	58.51	4.03	8.63	6.26	5.77
辽 宁	Liaoning	20.24	87.88	85.55	8.18	7.35	6.25	4.71
吉 林	Jilin	20.71	78.51	70.25	7.13	6.78	5.56	5.53
黑龙江	Heilongjiang	20.49	80.01	67.21	6.70	7.75	6.54	7.54
上 海	Shanghai	29.35	100.00	100.00	16.78	12.46	7.35	1.84
江 苏	Jiangsu	24.44	91.93	88.60	7.22	13.51	7.95	4.52
浙 江	Zhejiang	31.02	98.24	96.85	9.91	12.75	7.52	3.26
安 徽	Anhui	20.75	79.93	62.32	6.20	9.78	5.13	3.05
福 建	Fujian	30.30	92.11	89.57	9.43	9.37	7.14	2.22
江 西	Jiangxi	22.62	92.26	73.87	6.79	8.15	6.42	1.96
山 东	Shandong	24.48	71.61	69.76	4.92	10.54	6.19	1.31
河 南	Henan	20.20	90.44	60.76	6.54	8.10	6.60	3.21
湖 北	Hubei	22.90	73.61	63.85	6.78	8.74	5.64	2.41
湖 南	Hunan	24.43	86.36	66.58	7.50	7.90	5.07	2.51
广 东	Guangdong	24.93	90.75	90.68	5.10	9.27	8.24	1.44
广 西	Guangxi	24.17	65.92	53.80	4.39	6.95	4.65	1.34
海 南	Hainan	23.43	83.63	69.95	4.36	10.03	7.73	1.20
重 庆	Chongqing	25.72	76.48	59.50	6.16	5.86	3.09	2.77
四 川	Sichuan	26.36	97.28	79.25	7.35	10.21	6.88	2.84
贵 州	Guizhou	18.19	78.72	59.10	8.92	4.29	5.33	1.91
云 南	Yunnan	24.93	81.45	64.71	8.68	6.54	7.43	2.18
西 藏	Tibet	19.93	69.01	41.88	26.00	14.37	0.48	2.71
陕 西	Shaanxi	21.75	93.78	77.71	7.36	6.15	4.26	1.65
甘 肃	Gansu	21.11	82.21	58.70	5.67	10.24	4.35	2.26
青 海	Qinghai	19.11	100.00	46.52	13.73	9.06	6.31	3.21
宁 夏	Ningxia	22.26	63.59	52.61	4.12	8.68	4.47	4.70
新 疆	Xinjiang	20.78	96.71	87.84	12.75	10.37	6.32	4.14

主要统计指标解释

供水综合生产能力 指按供水设施取水、净化、送水、出厂输水干管等环节设计能力计算的综合生产能力。包括在原设计能力的基础上，经挖、革、改增加的生产能力。计算时，以四个环节中最薄弱的环节为主确定能力。

年末供水管道长度 指从送水泵至用户水表之间所有管道的长度。不包括新安装尚未使用的管道。

全年供水总量 指报告期供水企业(单位)供出的全部水量。包括有效供水量和漏损水量。

生活用水量 包括公共服务用水和居民家庭用水。公共服务用水指为城市社会公共生活服务的用水。包括行政事业单位、部队营区和公共设施服务、社会服务业、批发零售贸易业、旅馆饮食业以及其他公共服务业等单位的用水。居民家庭用水指城市范围内所有居民家庭的日常生活用水。包括城市居民、农民家庭、公共供水站用水。

用水普及率 指城市用水人口数与城市人口总数的比率。计算公式：

$$用水普及率=\frac{城市用水人口数}{城市人口总数}\times 100\%$$

人工煤气生产能力 指报告期末人工煤气生产厂制气、净化、输送等环节的综合生产能力，不包括备用设备能力。一般按设计能力计算，如果实际生产能力大于设计能力时，应按实际测定的生产能力计算。测定时应以制气、净化、输送三个环节中最薄弱的环节为主。

供气管道长度 指报告期末从气源厂压缩机的出口或门站出口至各类用户引入管之间的全部已经通气投入使用的管道长度。不包括煤气生产厂、输配站、液化气储存站、灌瓶站、储配站、气化站、混气站、供应站等厂(站)内的管道。

全年供气总量 指全年燃气企业(单位)向用户供应的燃气数量。包括销售量和损失量。

用气普及率 指报告期末使用燃气的城市人口数与城市人口总数的比率。计算公式为：

$$用气普及率=\frac{城市用气人口数}{城市人口总数}\times 100\%$$

城市供热能力 指供热企业(单位)向城市热用户输送热能的设计能力。

城市供热总量 指在报告期供热企业(单位)向城市热用户输送全部蒸汽和热水的总热量。

城市供热管道长度 指从各类热源到热用户建筑物接入口之间的全部蒸汽和热水的管道长度。不包括各类热源厂内部的管道长度。

年末道路长度 指年末道路长度和与道路相通的广场、桥梁、隧道的长度，按车行道中心线计算。在统计时只统计路面宽度在3.5米(含3.5米)以上的各种铺装道路，包括开放型工业区和住宅区道路在内。

城市桥梁 指为跨越天然或人工障碍物而修建的构筑物。包括跨河桥、立交桥、人行天桥以及人行地下通道等。包括永久性桥和半永久性桥。

城市排水管道长度 指所有排水总管、干管、支管、检查井及连接井进出口等长度之和。

城市污水日处理能力 指污水处理厂(或处理装置)每昼夜处理污水量的设计能力。

年末运营车数 指年末公交企业(单位)用于运营业务的全部车辆数。以企业(单位)固定资产台帐中已投入运营的车辆数为准。

城市园林绿地面积 指报告期末用作园林和绿化的各种绿地面积。包括公共绿地、居住区绿地、单位附属绿地、防护绿地、生产绿地、道路绿地和风景林地面积。

不包括：

1.屋顶绿化、垂直绿化、阳台绿化和室内绿化。

2.以物质生产为主的林地、耕地、牧草地、果园和竹园等。

3.城市总体规划中不列入绿地的水域。

公共绿地 指向公众开放的市级、区级、居住区级各类公园、街旁游园，包括其范围内的水域。其中居住区级公园应不小于1万平方米，街旁游园的宽度不小于8米，面积不小于400平方米。

Explanatory Notes on Main Statistical Indicators

Production Capacity of Water Supply refers to the designed comprehensive production capacity of water facilities, covering the 4 links of water collection, purification, conveyance, and outflow through trunk pipelines. Increase capacity through transformation and innovation projects are included as well. The capacity is determined mainly on the weakest of the above-mentioned 4 links.

Length of Water Supply Pipelines at the Year-end refers to the total length of all the pipelines between the water pumps and the user's water meters, excluding pipelines newly installed but not used yet.

Annual Volume of Water Supply refers to the total volume of water supplied by water-works (units) during the reference period, including both the effective water supply and loss during the water supply.

Consumption of Water for Residential Use refers to the water consumption of households for daily life and the water consumption of public service facilities. The latter refers to water consumption for urban public services, including the consumption of government agencies and public institutions, military barracks, public facilities, wholesale and retail outlets, restaurants, hotels, and other units providing public services. Household water consumption refers to consumption of water for daily life of all households in the boundary of cities, including households of urban residents and farmers, and public water supply stations.

Percentage of Urban Population with Access to Tap Water refers to the ratio of the urban population with access to tap water to the total urban population. The formula is:

Percentage of population with access to tap water= (Urban population with access to tap water) / (Urban population)×100%

Production Capacity of Gaswork Gas refers to the comprehensive production capacity of the urban gasworks in gas generation, purification and delivery at the end of the reference period, excluding capacity of the reserved facilities. In general, it is determined by the designed capacity, and when actual production capacity is larger than the designed capacity, the capacity is determined by the actual measurement on the weakest link in the production, purification and delivery.

Length of Gas Pipelines refers to the total length of pipelines in use between the outlet of the compressor of gas-work or outlet of gas stations and the leading pipe of users, excluding pipelines within gasworks, delivery stations, LPG storage stations, refilling stations, gas-mixing stations and supply stations.

Volume of Gas Supply refers to the total volume of gas provided to users by gas-producing enterprises (units) in a year, including the volume sold and the volume lost.

Percentage of Urban Population with Access to Gas refers to the ratio of the urban population with access to gas to the total urban population at the end of the reference period. The formula is:

Percentage of population with access to gas = (Urban population with access to gas / Urban population) x 100%

Heating Capacity in Urban Area refers to the designed capacity of heating enterprises (units) in supplying heating energy to urban users during the reference period.

Quantity of Heat Supplied in Urban Area refers to the total quantity of heat from steam and hot water supplied to urban users by heating enterprises (units) during the reference period.

Length of Heating Pipelines refers to the total length of steam or hot water pipelines for sources of heat to the leading pipelines of the buildings of the users, excluding internal pipelines in heat generating enterprises.

Length of Paved Roads at the Year-end refers to the length of roads with paved surface including squares bridges and tunnels connected with roads by the end of the year. Length of the roads is measured by the central lines for vehicles for paved roads with a width of 3.5 meters and over, including roads in open-ended factory compounds and residential quarters.

Urban Bridges refer to bridges built to cross over natural or man-made barriers, including bridges over rivers, overpasses for traffic and for pedestrian, underpasses for pedestrian, etc. Both permanent and semi-permanent bridges are included.

Length of Urban Sewage Pipes refers to the total length of general drainage, trunks. branch and inspection wells, connection wells, inlets and outlets, etc.

Daily Disposal Capacity of Urban Sewage refers to the designed 24 hour capacity of sewage disposal by the sewage treatment works or facilities.

Number of Vehicles under Operation at the Year-end refers to the total number of vehicles under operation by public transport enterprises (units) at the end of the year, based on the records of operational vehicles by the enterprises (units).

Area of Urban Gardens and Green Areas refers to the total area occupied for green projects at the end of the reference period, including public green land, green land in residential quarters, green land attached to institutions, protection green land, production green land, roadside green land and forest in scenic spots. It does not include the following:

(1)Greenery and plants on roofs, balconies, indoors and vertical green areas;

(2)Forest, cultivated land, grassland, orchards and bamboo grooves that are for production purpose; and

(3)Water areas that are not included in urban master plan as green land.

Public Green Area refers to green areas open to the public such as municipal, community and neighborhood parks and roadside parks, including waters within parks. Neighborhood parks should occupy an area larger than 10,000 square meters, and the width of roadside parks should occupy an area larger than 400 square meters, with a width of more that 8 meters.

十二、环境保护

Enviornment Protections

简要说明

本篇主要反映我国环境保护事业发展情况。主要内容包括水环境、大气环境、固体废物、声环境、生态环境、自然灾害和环境污染治理投资等内容。

主要反映我国总的水资源、供水、用水情况以及工业废水和生活污水的排放及治理情况；城市空气质量，废气排放及处理情况；工业固体废物的产生、处理及利用情况以及城市生活垃圾清运及处理情况；我国国控城市道路交通和区域环境噪声监测情况；我国的土地利用、耕地变动、森林资源、造林及其自然保护基本情况；地质、地震、海洋、森林灾害及环境污染与破坏事故情况；环境污染治理投资等情况。

一、涉及环境污染与治理情况即反映各地区工业"三废"（废水、废气、固体废物）和生活污染物排放及处理情况由国家环境保护总局提供。统计调查、范围如下：

1．统计范围：各地区有污染物排放的工业企业、城镇生活及其他排污单位等。

2．调查方法：1.工业企业污染排放及处理利用情况对重点调查工业企业单位逐个发表填报汇总，对非重点调查工业企业的排污情况实行整体估算。

重点调查单位指筛选出的排污量占各地区全部工业污染源排污总量85%以上的工业企业单位。非重点调查单位数据的估算方法为对占各地区排污总量15%的非重点工业企业，按废水、化学需氧量、氨氮、二氧化硫、烟尘、粉尘、固体废物等项目的排放进行测算，汇总生成非重点调查数据。以上两方面的数据汇总成为各地区工业污染排放数据。

3．生活及其他污染情况，依据相关基础数据和技术参数进行估算。

此外，涉及声环境、工业污染治理投资、排污费征收情况由国家环境保护总局提供。

二、涉及水资源、城市生活垃圾清运及处理、土地利用和耕地变动、森林资源、海洋灾害等情况分别由水利部、建设部、国土资源部、国家林业局、国家海洋局提供。

Brief Introduction

This chapter contain information that reflect the development of environment protection in China, including total water resources, water supply and utilization, discharge and treatment of industrial and other waste water; urban air quality, emission and treatment of waste gas; production, treatment and utilization of industrial solid wastes, collection and disposal of consumption wastes in cities; national monitoring of road traffic noise and urban environmental noise in key cities; land use, change in cultivated land, forest resources, afforestation, and forest protection; cases of geological, seismic, marine and forest disasters, environmental pollution or destruction accidents; investment in environment pollution treatment, etc.

I. Data on environment pollution and treatment of "three-wastes" from industrial sources and pollutants from consumption by region are provided by the State Administration of Environment Protection. The coverage of statistics and survey methodology is as follows:

1)Coverage of statistics: industrial enterprises and other urban units which discharge pollutants.

2)Survey methodology for discharge and treatment of industrial pollutants: comprehensive survey is conducted on all key industrial enterprises, while overall estimation is carried out for ordinary enterprises.

Key enterprises refer to those enterprises which discharged more than 85% of all pollutants in the region. For ordinary enterprises whose discharge is less than 15% in the total of the region, estimation is made for the volume of their discharge of waste water, oxygen required substances, ammonia and nitrogen, sulphur dioxide, industrial soot and dust, and solid wastes. Data on discharge of pollutants of key and ordinary enterprises make up the total discharge of the region.

3)Data on pollution from consumption and other sources are estimated using relevant statistics and technical parameters.

Data on noise monitoring, investment in the treatment of industrial pollution and collection of fees on discharge of pollutants are provided by the State Administration of Environment Protection.

II. Data on water resources, collection and disposal of urban consumption wastes, land use and change in cultivated land, forest resources, marine disasters, etc. are provided respectively by Ministry of Water Conservancy, Ministry of Construction, Ministry of Land and Resources, State Forestry Administration and State Oceanic Administration.

12-1 环境保护基本情况

Basic Statistics on Environmental Protection

指 标	Item	1999	2000	2001	2002	2003
水环境	**Water**					
水资源总量 (亿立方米)	Water Resources (100 million cu.m)	28195.7	27700.8	26867.8	28261.3	27460.2
#地表水	Surface Water	27203.8	26561.9	25933.4	27243.3	26250.7
地下水	Groundwater	8386.7	8501.9	8390.1	8697.2	8299.3
人均水资源量(立方米/人)	Per Captia Water Resources (cu.m/person)	2250.7	2193.9	2112.5	2207.2	2131.3
供水总量 (亿立方米)	Water Supply (100 million cu.m)	5613.3	5530.7	5567.4	5497.3	5320.4
#地表水	Surface Water	4514.2	4440.4	4450.7	4404.4	4286.0
地下水	Groundwater	1074.6	1069.2	1094.9	1072.4	1018.1
用水总量 (亿立方米)	Water Use (100 million cu.m)	5590.9	5497.6	5567.4	5497.3	5320.4
#农业	Agriculture	3869.2	3783.5	3825.7	3736.2	3432.8
工业	Industry	1159.0	1139.1	1141.8	1142.4	1177.2
生活	Consumption	562.8	574.9	599.9	618.7	630.9
废水排放总量 (亿吨)	Waste Water Discharge (100 million tons)	401	415	433	439	459
#工业废水排放量 (亿吨)	Industry	197	194	203	207	212
生活污水排放量 (亿吨)	Consumption	204	221	230	232	247
工业废水排放达标量(亿吨)	Industrial Waste Water Meeting Discharge Standards (100 million tons)	132	149	173	183	189
工业废水排放达标率 (%)	Percentage of Industrial Waste Water Meeting Discharge Standards (%)	66.7	76.9	85.2	88.3	89.2
化学需氧量排放量 (万吨)	Discharge Amount of COD (10 000 tons)	1389	1445	1405	1367	1333
#工业	Industry	692	705	608	584	512
生活	Consumption	697	740	797	783	821
氨氮排放量 (万吨)	Ammonia Nitrogen Discharge (10 000 tons)			125	129	129
#工业	Industry			41	42	40
生活	Consumption			84	87	89
大气环境	**Atmosphere Environment**					
工业废气排放量 (亿标立方米)	Industrial Waste Gas Emission (100 million cu.m)	126807	138145	160863	175257	198906
#燃料燃烧	Fuels Combustion	75919	81970	93526	103776	116447
生产工艺	Process of Industrial Production	50887	56032	67337	71481	82459
二氧化硫排放量 (万吨)	Sulphur Dioxide Emission (10 000 tons)	1857	1995	1948	1927	2159
#工业	Industry	1460	1612	1567	1562	1792
生活	Consumption	397	383	381	365	367
烟尘排放量 (万吨)	Soot Emission (10 000 tons)	1159	1165	1070	1012	1048
#工业	Industry	953	953	852	804	846
生活	Consumption	206	212	218	208	202
工业粉尘排放量 (万吨)	Industrial Dust Emission (10 000 tons)	1175	1092	991	941	1021
工业二氧化硫去除量(万吨)	Industrial Sulphur Dioxide Removed (10 000 tons)	501	575	565	698	749
工业烟尘去除量 (万吨)	Industrial Soot Removed (10 000 tons)	9894	10717	12317	13998	15649
工业粉尘去除量 (万吨)	Industrial Dust Romoved (10 000 tons)	4336	4480	5322	5570	5995
建成城市烟尘控制区数(个)	Number of Soot Control Zones Established (unit)	1952	2981	3203	3369	3599
烟尘控制区面积(万平方公里)	Area of Soot Control Zones (10 000 sq.km)	1.4	2.0	2.2	2.6	3.3

12-1 续表 1 continued

指 标	Item	1999	2000	2001	2002	2003
固体废物	**Solid Wastes**					
工业固体废物产生量（万吨）	Industrial Solid Wastes Produced (10 000 tons)	78442	81608	88746	94509	100428
#危险废物	Hazardous Wastes	1015	830	952	1000	1170
工业固体废物综合利用量（万吨）	Industrial Solid Wastes Utilized (10 000 tons)	35756	37451	47285	50061	56040
工业固体废物综合利用率(%)	Ratio of Industrial Solid Wastes Utilized (%)	45.6	45.9	52.1	51.9	54.8
工业固体废物排放量(万吨)	Industrial Solid Wastes Discharged (10 000 tons)	3880	3186	2894	2635	1941
“三废”综合利用产品产值（亿元）	Output Value of Products Made from Waste Gas, WasteWater & Solid Wastes (100 million yuan)	257	311	345	386	441
噪声	**Noise**					
建成城市环境噪声达标区数（个）	Developed Districts of Environmental Noise Meeting National Standard (unit)	1778	2463	3111	3128	3573
城市环境噪声达标区面积（万平方公里）	Area of Urban Environmental Noise Meeting National Standard (10 000 sq.km)	0.8	1.3	1.5	1.6	2.0
生态环境	**Eco-Environment Protection**					
森林面积（万公顷）	Area of Forest (10 000 hectares)					15894.1
森林覆盖率（%）	Forest Coverage (%)					16.55
当年造林面积（万公顷）	Area of Reforestation of the Year (10 000 hectares)	490	511	495	777	912
自然保护区数（个）	Number of Nature Reserves (unit)	1146	1227	1551	1757	1999
#国家级	National Level	155	155	171	188	226
自然保护区面积（万公顷）	Area of Nature Reserves (10 000 hectares)	8815	9821	12989	13295	14398
自然保护区面积占辖区面积比重（%）	Area of Nature Reserves in Regions (%)	8.8	9.9	12.9	13.2	14.4
生态示范区数（个）	Number of Demonstration Zones of Ecology (unit)	222	220	215	322	484
#国家级	National Level	154	158	82	82	82
湿地面积（万公顷）	Area of Wetland (10 000 hectares)					3848.6
湿地面积占国土面积比重(%)	Area of Wetland out of National Surface Area (%)					4.0
自然灾害	**Natural Disaster**					
发生地质灾害起数（次）	Geological Disaster (unit)	13446	19653	5793	40246	15489
#滑坡	Landslide	8625	13431	3034	31247	10240
崩塌	Collapse	2683	2945	583	3097	2604
泥石流	Mudflow	889	1958	1539	4976	1549
发生地震灾害次数（次）	Seismic Disaster (unit)	15	10	12	5	21
#5.0级以上	Magnitude above 5 Richter scale	14	9	11	4	17
海洋赤潮发生次数（次）	Red Tide (unit)	16	28	77	79	119
森林火灾次数（次）	Forest Fire (unit)	6847	5934	4933	7527	10463
#重大	Serious	27	60	17	24	14
特大	Extraordinarily Serious		8	3	7	7
森林火灾受灾面积（万公顷）	Fire-Affected Forest Area (10 000 hectares)	4.4	8.8	4.6	4.8	45.1
森林病虫害发生面积（万公顷）	Forest Area Affected by Disease and Pests (10 000 hectares)	766.1	851.9	839.0	841.2	888.7
森林病虫害防治面积（万公顷）	Forest Area Provented and Cured from Disease and Pests (10 000 hectares)	541.5	574.2	587.3	572.0	582.9
森林病虫害防治率（%）	Rate of Prevention and Cure (%)	71	67	70	68	66

12-1 续表 2 continued

指 标	Item	1999	2000	2001	2002	2003
环境污染	**Pollution**					
环境污染与破坏事故次数（次）	Pollution Accidents (unit)	1614	2411	1842	1921	1843
#水污染	Water Pollution	888	1138	1096	1097	1042
大气污染	Air Pollution	582	864	576	597	654
固体废物污染	Solid Wastes Pollution	80	103	39	109	56
噪声与震动危害	Noise and Vibration Pollution	40	266	80	97	50
其他	Other	24	40	51	21	41
污染直接经济损失 （万元）	Direct Economic Loss Due to Pollution (10 000 yuan)	5710.6	17807.9	12272.4	4640.9	3374.9
污染事故赔款总额 （万元）	Reparations for Pollution Incidents (10 000 yuan)	2116.0	3144.9	2948.7	2629.7	1999.0
污染事故罚款总额 （万元）	Fines to Pollution Incidents (10 000 yuan)	290.7	537.7	315.2	511.0	392.0
环境污染治理投资	**Investment in Pollution Treatment**					
环境污染治理投资总额（亿元）	Investment in Pollution Treatment (100 million yuan)	823.2	1014.9	1106.7	1367.2	1627.7
#城市环境基础设施建设投资	Urban Environmental Infrastructure	478.9	515.5	595.8	789.1	1072.4
工业污染源治理投资	Urban Environmental Infrastructure	152.7	239.4	174.5	188.0	221.8
建设项目“三同时”环保投资	Urban Environmental Infrastructure	191.6	260.0	336.4	389.7	333.5
环境污染治理投资总额占国内生产总值比重 （%）	Investment in Pollution Treatment Out of GDP (%)	1.00	1.13	1.14	1.30	1.39
城市环境基础设施建设投资额 （亿元）	Investment in Urban Environment Infrastructure (100 million yuan)		515.5	595.8	789.1	1072.4
#燃气	Gas Supply		70.9	75.5	88.4	133.5
集中供热	Central Heating		67.8	82.0	121.4	145.8
排水	Sewerage Projects		149.3	224.5	275.0	375.2
园林绿化	Landscape and Greening		143.2	163.2	239.5	321.9
市容环境卫生	Sanitation		84.3	50.6	64.8	96.0
污染治理项目当年投资来源总额 （亿元）	Investment in Pollution Treatment Projects of the Year, by Source (100 million yuan)	152.7	239.4	174.5	188.0	221.8
#国家预算内资金	State Budget	32.4	49.6	36.3	42.0	18.8
环保专项资金	Special Funds for Environmental Protection	13.2	19.3	15.8	14.8	12.4
其他资金	Other Sources	107.1	170.5	122.3	131.6	190.7
工业污染治理项目及投资情况	Industrial Pollution Treatment Projects					
当年施工污染治理项目数（个）	Projects under Construction of the Year (unit)	19866	27243	11640	11557	11292
污染治理项目本年完成投资 （亿元）	Investment Completed in Pollution Treatment Projects (100 million yuan)	152.7	239.4	174.5	188.4	221.8
#治理废水	Waste Water	68.8	109.6	72.9	71.5	87.4
治理废气	WasteGas	51.0	90.9	65.8	69.8	92.1
治理固体废物	Solid Wastes	8.3	11.5	18.7	16.1	16.2
治理噪声	Noise Pollution	0.9	6.0	0.6	1.0	1.0
治理其他	Others	23.7	21.4	16.5	29.9	25.1
实际执行“三同时”项目环保投资总额 （亿元）	Investment in "Three Simultaneity" Projects (100 million yuan)	191.6	260.0	336.4	389.7	333.5
#新建	New Projects	109.0	145.6	238.2	238.0	220.1
扩建	Expansion	52.1	64.7	52.1	67.0	56.7
改建	Technical Improvement	29.6	39.4	46.5	84.7	56.7

12-2 水资源情况

Water Resource

地区	Region	水资源总量（亿立方米）Total Amount of Water Resource (100 million cu.m)	地表水资源量 Surface Water	地下水资源量 Ground Water	地下水与地下水资源重复量 Duplicated Measurement Between Surface Water and Groundwater	人均水资源量（立方米/人）Per Capita Water Resources (cu.m/person)
	2000	27700.8	26561.9	8501.9	7363.0	2193.9
	2001	26867.8	25933.4	8390.1	7455.7	2112.5
	2002	28261.3	27243.3	8697.2	7679.2	2207.2
	2003	27460.2	26250.7	8299.3	7089.9	2131.3
北京	Beijing	18.4	6.1	14.8	2.5	127.8
天津	Tianjin	10.6	6.2	4.8	0.4	105.1
河北	Hebei	153.1	46.5	135.8	29.3	226.7
山西	Shanxi	134.9	89.2	86.0	40.3	408.2
内蒙古	Inner Mongolia	495.6	355.6	239.2	99.3	2082.7
辽宁	Liaoning	220.0	179.4	102.4	61.8	522.9
吉林	Jilin	326.5	265.7	109.9	49.1	1208.7
黑龙江	Heilongjiang	826.8	694.1	291.7	159.0	2167.8
上海	Shanghai	15.1	15.1	8.6	8.6	90.6
江苏	Jiangsu	619.1	499.8	138.3	19.0	837.3
浙江	Zhejiang	574.5	564.0	161.3	150.8	1231.9
安徽	Anhui	1083.0	1038.1	252.3	207.4	1699.1
福建	Fujian	806.6	805.4	284.4	283.2	2319.9
江西	Jiangxi	1362.7	1345.5	339.9	322.7	3215.4
山东	Shandong	489.7	349.3	247.4	107.0	537.9
河南	Henan	697.7	540.9	263.0	106.2	723.8
湖北	Hubei	1234.1	1205.4	312.8	284.1	2058.6
湖南	Hunan	1799.2	1790.9	416.4	408.1	2707.2
广东	Guangdong	1458.4	1448.7	404.8	395.1	1844.6
广西	Guangxi	1901.0	1901.0	575.3	575.3	3928.1
海南	Hainan	291.8	288.4	69.3	66.0	3615.9
重庆	Chongqing	590.7	590.7	109.9	109.9	1894.3
四川	Sichuan	2589.8	2588.2	596.4	594.8	2981.5
贵州	Guizhou	915.5	915.5	247.8	247.8	2375.7
云南	Yunnan	1699.4	1699.4	592.2	592.2	3902.5
西藏	Tibet	4757.1	4757.1	1081.0	1081.0	177174.7
陕西	Shaanxi	574.6	537.6	173.1	136.1	1560.6
甘肃	Gansu	247.2	237.3	136.9	126.9	951.6
青海	Qinghai	634.7	616.6	273.9	255.8	11940.9
宁夏	Ningxia	12.3	10.0	25.4	23.2	212.7
新疆	Xinjiang	920.1	863.2	604.3	547.4	4793.6

12-3 供水用水情况

Water Supply and Water Used

地 区	Region	供水总量 (亿立方米) Water Supply (100 million cu.m)	地表水 Surface Water	地下水 Ground Water	其 他 Others	用水总量 (亿立方米) Water Used (100 million cu.m)	农 业 Agricul -ture	生 产 Produc -tion	生 活 Consump -tion	生 态 Ecology	人均用水量 (立方米) Per Capita Water Used (cu.m/person)
	2000	5530.7	4440.4	1069.2	21.1	5497.6	3783.5	1139.1	574.9		435.4
	2001	5567.4	4450.7	1094.9	21.9	5567.4	3825.7	1141.8	599.9		437.7
	2002	5497.3	4404.4	1072.4	20.5	5497.3	3736.2	1142.4	618.7		429.3
	2003	5320.4	4286.0	1018.1	16.3	5320.4	3432.8	1177.2	630.9	79.5	412.9
北 京	Beijing	35.0	8.3	25.4	1.3	35.0	12.9	7.6	13.5	1.0	243.1
天 津	Tianjin	20.5	13.4	7.1	0.0	20.5	11.2	4.9	4.2	0.3	203.5
河 北	Hebei	199.8	33.7	165.5	0.6	199.8	149.6	26.2	23.7	0.3	295.9
山 西	Shanxi	56.2	19.9	35.8	0.5	56.2	33.3	14.1	8.5	0.3	170.2
内蒙古	Inner Mongolia	166.9	85.9	80.7	0.3	166.9	146.1	10.1	10.0	0.7	701.4
辽 宁	Liaoning	128.3	60.3	67.9	0.1	128.3	83.5	21.9	22.9		305.1
吉 林	Jilin	104.0	63.1	40.9		104.0	67.5	22.2	14.3		385.0
黑龙江	Heilongjiang	245.8	149.9	95.9		245.8	171.4	52.5	18.9	3.0	644.5
上 海	Shanghai	109.0	108.0	1.0		109.0	16.3	72.2	18.3	2.1	653.4
江 苏	Jiangsu	433.5	422.5	11.0		433.5	223.1	155.8	39.9	14.6	586.3
浙 江	Zhejiang	206.0	197.1	8.5	0.4	206.0	110.2	55.3	29.1	11.5	441.7
安 徽	Anhui	178.6	161.5	16.5	0.6	178.6	93.8	63.1	21.3	0.4	280.1
福 建	Fujian	182.8	177.4	4.2	1.1	182.8	101.0	60.1	20.6	1.1	525.7
江 西	Jiangxi	172.5	163.3	9.2		172.5	104.1	46.7	20.6	1.1	407.0
山 东	Shandong	219.4	104.1	114.0	1.3	219.4	157.0	31.6	29.3	1.4	241.0
河 南	Henan	187.6	73.9	113.7	0.1	187.6	113.3	39.9	32.0	2.4	194.6
湖 北	Hubei	245.1	236.6	6.9	1.6	245.1	136.2	80.7	28.0	0.1	408.8
湖 南	Hunan	318.8	295.3	22.1	1.5	318.8	209.4	68.4	39.4	1.6	479.8
广 东	Guangdong	457.5	436.5	20.6	0.4	457.5	242.6	130.4	79.5	5.0	578.7
广 西	Guangxi	278.4	265.5	11.5	1.4	278.4	205.4	37.0	32.7	3.2	575.2
海 南	Hainan	46.3	42.4	3.9		46.3	35.7	4.1	5.9	0.6	573.9
重 庆	Chongqing	63.2	60.9	1.9	0.3	63.2	20.7	26.9	15.3	0.3	202.6
四 川	Sichuan	209.9	195.7	12.8	1.4	209.9	121.7	56.1	30.4	1.7	241.6
贵 州	Guizhou	93.7	85.5	8.0	0.2	93.7	52.2	26.4	14.8	0.4	243.2
云 南	Yunnan	146.1	139.3	6.2	0.6	146.1	109.6	17.4	18.3	0.8	335.5
西 藏	Tibet	25.3	23.9	1.4		25.3	22.6	0.3	1.9	0.4	940.6
陕 西	Shaanxi	75.1	40.6	32.9	1.6	75.1	50.7	13.0	11.3	0.1	203.9
甘 肃	Gansu	121.6	93.1	28.1	0.4	121.6	96.4	16.3	8.6	0.2	467.9
青 海	Qinghai	29.0	23.9	5.1		29.0	21.7	4.2	3.0	0.2	545.8
宁 夏	Ningxia	64.0	57.6	6.5		64.0	58.4	3.5	1.7	0.4	1111.5
新 疆	Xinjiang	500.7	447.0	53.1	0.6	500.7	454.9	8.3	13.1	24.4	2608.3

注:生态用水仅包括河湖人工补水和城市环境用水。

a) Water used in ecology only includes artficial supplement of river & lake and city entironment.

12-4 各地区废水排放及处理情况（2003年）

Discharge and Treatment of Industrial Waste Water by Region (2003)

单位：万吨 (10 000 tons)

地区	Region	汇总工业企业数(个) Number of Industrial Enterprises (unit)	废水治理设施数(套) Number of Facilities for Treatment of Waste Water (set)	工业废水排放总量 Total Volume of Waste Water Discharged	#直接排入海 Volume of Waste Water Direct Discharge into Sea	工业废水排放达标量 Industrial Waste Water Meeting Discharge Standards
全国	**National Total**	**69904**	**65128**	**2122527**	**115032**	**1892891**
北京	Beijing	927	568	13107		13015
天津	Tianjin	1503	833	21605	1899	21571
河北	Hebei	2674	3687	108324	3415	102609
山西	Shanxi	3263	2456	30929		26939
内蒙古	Inner Mongolia	959	585	23577		15076
辽宁	Liaoning	2574	2131	89186	30348	81704
吉林	Jilin	888	643	31365		24071
黑龙江	Heilongjiang	1517	1234	50286		47353
上海	Shanghai	1655	1730	61112	14830	58020
江苏	Jiangsu	5604	3989	247524	803	241765
浙江	Zhejiang	5629	5491	168088	5131	163387
安徽	Anhui	1669	1450	63525		60908
福建	Fujian	3140	4856	98388	42328	95633
江西	Jiangxi	1062	1130	50135		41642
山东	Shandong	5040	4014	115933	11247	112590
河南	Henan	4083	3387	114224	475	104480
湖北	Hubei	2342	1984	96498	1845	80848
湖南	Hunan	3102	2942	124132		99127
广东	Guangdong	6873	8234	148867		123453
广西	Guangxi	1731	2188	119291		103212
海南	Hainan	285	270	7181		6741
重庆	Chongqing	1406	1167	81973		73663
四川	Sichuan	3849	3557	120160		98313
贵州	Guizhou	2574	1519	16815		9411
云南	Yunnan	1500	1707	34655		24172
西藏	Tibet	24	10	612		
陕西	Shaanxi	1856	1775	33526		29138
甘肃	Gansu	1091	762	20899		15901
青海	Qinghai	206	82	3453		2067
宁夏	Ningxia	272	334	10740		6288
新疆	Xinjiang	606	413	16417		9794

12-4 续表 continued

地区	Region	工业废水中化学需氧量排放量(吨) COD Discharge from Industrial Waste Water (ton)	工业废水中氨氮排放量(吨) Ammonia Nitrogen Discharge from Industrial Waste Water (ton)	生活污水排放量(万吨) Comsumption Waste Water Discharge (10 000 tons)	生活污水中化学需氧量排放量(吨) COD Discharge from Consumption Waste Water (ton)	生活污水中氨氮排放量(吨) Ammonia Nitrogen Discharge from Consumption Waste Water (ton)
全国	**National Total**	**5118062.8**	**403600.8**	**2470115**	**8211402**	**892199**
北京	Beijing	10424.7	1057.1	80646	123649	14899
天津	Tianjin	40994.5	4557.3	24724	89443	11175
河北	Hebei	353467.9	29592.3	72906	282606	35089
山西	Shanxi	156832.6	12418.8	61577	201502	28391
内蒙古	Inner Mongolia	134754.3	9076.2	27213	139610	19600
辽宁	Liaoning	185483.7	11431.0	102655	360964	55012
吉林	Jilin	136999.3	3987.7	51126	234727	28708
黑龙江	Heilongjiang	134003.6	4256.1	68461	376465	44169
上海	Shanghai	43849.0	3385.5	129885	294592	24951
江苏	Jiangsu	281141.1	17646.3	172546	486118	51871
浙江	Zhejiang	256441.7	37996.4	102174	305582	30431
安徽	Anhui	123237.9	19490.7	77735	289184	30933
福建	Fujian	78587.7	8567.3	66234	272822	35295
江西	Jiangxi	86621.1	4587.5	61823	335467	26183
山东	Shandong	406347.7	25911.8	129849	423156	51544
河南	Henan	341561.3	32747.9	125542	365857	46939
湖北	Hubei	188307.3	28655.1	134080	446116	48187
湖南	Hunan	251580.8	35784.6	111645	562512	49960
广东	Guangdong	211105.7	8230.6	397563	770797	85033
广西	Guangxi	625361.2	31313.5	95523	301558	23595
海南	Hainan	12189.8	421.1	18870	55335	4619
重庆	Chongqing	110027.7	11004.9	51988	150590	15293
四川	Sichuan	461548.2	28826.1	108254	474758	40900
贵州	Guizhou	25422.9	2547.0	38727	194866	16042
云南	Yunnan	92805.2	2610.3	33526	192372	15094
西藏	Tibet	1158.7	2.5	467	6745	726
陕西	Shaanxi	121518.6	2653.7	37239	199600	21538
甘肃	Gansu	40636.8	13253.4	26994	117816	12190
青海	Qinghai	2927.4	37.9	7857	28960	3571
宁夏	Ningxia	76419.0	9327.7	12798	25143	3353
新疆	Xinjiang	126305.4	2222.5	39488	102492	16908

12-5 工业按行业分废水排放及处理情况（2003年）
Discharge and Treatment of Waste Water by Sector (2003)

行 业	Sector	汇总工业企业数（个） Number of Industrial Enterprises (unit)	工业废水排放总量（万吨） Total Volume of Industrial Waste Water Discharge (10 000 tons)	工业废水排放达标量（万吨） Volume of Industrial Waste Water Meeting Discharge Standards (10 000 tons)	废水治理设施数（套） Number of Facilities for Treatment of Waste Water (set)
煤炭采选业	Coal Mining and Dressing	2379	53168	47873	2317
石油和天然气开采业	Petroleum and Natural Gas Extraction	186	10644	10145	676
黑色金属矿采选业	Ferrous Metals Mining and Dressing	512	13031	11438	853
有色金属矿采选业	Nonferrous Metals Mining and Dressing	1074	22855	19182	1535
非金属矿采选业	Nonmetal Minerals Mining and Dressing	486	8609	7964	515
其他矿采选业	Other Mining and Dressing	46	756	711	47
木材及竹材采运业	Logging and Transport of Timber and Bamboo				
食品加工业	Food Processing	3475	96383	76423	3079
食品制造业	Food Manufacturing	2234	31230	25769	1588
饮料制造业	Beverage Manufacturing	2048	33366	28987	1618
烟草加工业	Tobacco Processing	185	4438	2921	152
纺织业	Textile Industry	5906	141264	131449	5153
服装及其他纤维制品制造	Garments and Other Fiber Products	602	5266	4987	420
皮革毛皮羽绒及其制品业	Leather, Furs, Down and Related Products	854	13106	11831	889
木材加工及竹藤棕草制品业	Timber Processing, Bamboo, Cane, Palm Fiber and Straw Products	646	6851	6036	458
家具制造业	Furniture Manufacturing	181	386	355	101
造纸及纸制品业	Papermaking and Paper Products	4217	318336	273333	5561
印刷业记录媒介的复制	Printing and Record Medium Reproduction	445	1569	1488	125
文教体育用品制造业	Cultural, Educational and Sports Goods	188	694	535	81
石油加工及炼焦业	Petroleum Processing and Coking	924	53762	51947	1382
化学原料及制品制造业	Raw Chemical Materials and Chemical Products	6541	312825	284602	8636
医药制造业	Medical and Pharmaceutical Products	1998	35874	32997	1668
化学纤维制造业	Chemical Fiber	228	48847	44154	362
橡胶制品业	Rubber Products	571	6865	6695	342
塑料制品业	Plastic Products	723	2344	2243	265
非金属矿物制品业	Nonmetal Mineral Products	12642	47181	43479	6318
#水泥制造业	Concrete Machinery	4844	27718	25915	1441
黑色金属冶炼及压延加工业	Smelting and Pressing of Ferrous Metals	1884	177456	167125	2816
有色金属冶炼及压延加工业	Smelting and Pressing of Nonferrous Metals	1466	31761	25361	1560
金属制品业	Metal Products	4153	15910	14810	4007
普通机械制造业	Ordinary Machinery	2391	13467	12493	1236
专用设备制造业	Special Purpose Equipment	1195	14038	12024	878
交通运输设备制造业	Transport Equipment	1683	40805	39312	2040
电气机械及器材制造业	Electric Equipment and Machinery	789	10253	9804	702
电子及通信设备制造业	Electronic and Telecommunications Equipment	916	13214	12656	853
仪器仪表文化办公用机械	Instruments, Meters, Cultural and Office Machinery	710	9291	8733	2038
其他制造业	Other Machinery	396	1933	1816	381
电力蒸汽热水生产供应业	Production and Supply of Electric Power, Steam and Hot Water	1904	604	507	139
#火力发电业	Firepower Generator	1157	228797	221169	2186
煤气的生产和供应业	Production and Supply of Gas	82	3895	3183	96
自来水的生产和供应业	Production and Supply of Tap Water	142	15783	14905	62
其它行业	Other Branches	2409	32360	28672	1405

12-6 全海域海水水质评价结果(2003年)

Ambient Sea Water Quality (2003)

单位：万平方公里 (10 000 sq.km)

海区 Sea Area	较清洁海域面积 Clean Area	轻度污染海域面积 Lightly Polluted Area	中度污染海域面积 Moderately Polluted Area	严重污染海域面积 Heavily Polluted Area	首要超标污染物 Principal Pollutants
全国 National Total	**8.05**	**2.20**	**1.49**	**2.40**	无机氮、磷酸盐、铅 Inorganic Nitrogen, Phosphate, Lead
渤海 Bohai Sea	1.53	0.38	0.09	0.15	无机氮、磷酸盐、铅 Inorganic Nitrogen, Phosphate, Lead
黄海 Yellow Sea	1.44	0.57	0.35	0.32	无机氮、磷酸盐、铅 Inorganic Nitrogen, Phosphate, Lead
东海 The East China Sea	3.24	0.54	0.86	1.72	无机氮、磷酸盐、铅 Inorganic Nitrogen, Phosphate, Lead
南海 South China Sea	1.84	0.71	0.20	0.28	无机氮、磷酸盐、铅 Inorganic Nitrogen, Phosphate, Lead

12-7 主要城市空气质量指标 (2003年)

Ambient Air Quality in Main Cities (2003)

单位:毫克/立方米 (milligram/cu.m)

城市 City	可吸入颗粒物 (PM_{10}) Paticulate Matters	二氧化硫 (SO_2) Sulphur Dioxide	二氧化氮 (NO_2) Nitrogen Dioxide	空气质量达到及好于二级的天数（天） Days of Air Quality Equal to or Above Grade II (days)
北京 Beijing	0.141	0.061	0.072	224
天津 Tianjin	0.133	0.074	0.052	264
石家庄 Shijiazhuang	0.175	0.152	0.044	211
太原 Taiyuan	0.172	0.099	0.031	181
呼和浩特 Hohhot	0.116	0.039	0.046	286
沈阳 Shenyang	0.135	0.052	0.036	298
长春 Dalian	0.098	0.012	0.022	342
哈尔滨 Harbin	0.121	0.043	0.065	297
上海 Shanghai	0.097	0.043	0.057	325
南京 Nanjing	0.120	0.030	0.049	297
杭州 Hangzhou	0.119	0.049	0.056	293
合肥 Hefei	0.100	0.012	0.025	287
福州 Fuzhou	0.080	0.008	0.034	344
南昌 Nanchang	0.100	0.051	0.034	315
济南 Jinan	0.149	0.064	0.046	214
郑州 Zhengzhou	0.107	0.050	0.033	308
武汉 Wuhan	0.133	0.049	0.052	246
长沙 Changsha	0.135	0.081	0.038	245
广州 Guangzhou	0.099	0.059	0.072	314
南宁 Nanning	0.072	0.047	0.032	348
海口 Haikou	0.030	0.009	0.013	365
重庆 Chongqing	0.147	0.115	0.046	237
成都 Chengdu	0.118	0.052	0.046	312
贵阳 Guiyang	0.104	0.089	0.019	351
昆明 Kunming	0.086	0.045	0.033	363
拉萨 Lhasa	0.065	0.002	0.029	353
西安 Xi'an	0.136	0.057	0.035	252
兰州 Lanzhou	0.174	0.086	0.050	207
西宁 Xining	0.139	0.031	0.031	261
银川 Yinchuan	0.132	0.063	0.037	291
乌鲁木齐 Urumqi	0.127	0.097	0.055	282

12-8 工业按行业分废气排放及处理情况（2003年）

行业	Sector	废气治理设施数(套) Number of Facilities for Treatment of Waste Gas (set)	工业废气排放总量(亿标立方米) Total Volume of Waste Gas Emission (100 million cu.m)	燃料燃烧过程中废气排放量 Volume of Waste Gas from Fuel Burning
煤炭采选业	Coal Mining and Dressing	4431	1782	1235
石油和天然气开采业	Petroleum and Natural Gas Extraction	717	828	810
黑色金属矿采选业	Ferrous Metals Mining and Dressing	856	796	97
有色金属矿采选业	Nonferrous Metals Mining and Dressing	1001	577	162
非金属矿采选业	Nonmetal Minerals Mining and Dressing	650	378	235
其他矿采选业	Other Mining and Dressing	19	14	8
木材及竹材采运业	Logging and Transport of Timber and Bamboo			
食品加工业	Food Processing	3303	1884	1724
食品制造业	Food Manufacturing	2173	1419	1281
饮料制造业	Beverage Manufacturing	2266	800	796
烟草加工业	Tobacco Processing	724	317	158
纺织业	Textile Industry	8646	2428	2356
服装及其他纤维制品制造	Garments and Other Fiber Products	539	184	119
皮革毛皮羽绒及其制品业	Leather, Furs, Down and Related Products	849	119	100
木材加工及竹藤棕草制品业	Timber Processing, Bamboo, Cane, Palm Fiber and Straw Products	1473	492	297
家具制造业	Furniture Manufacturing	253	155	65
造纸及纸制品业	Papermaking and Paper Products	5280	3357	2966
印刷业记录媒介的复制	Printing and Record Medium Reproduction	241	88	56
文教体育用品制造业	Cultural, Educational and Sports Goods	179	54	12
石油加工及炼焦业	Petroleum Processing and Coking	1409	7381	2682
化学原料及制品制造业	Raw Chemical Materials and Chemical Products	11898	11989	6888
医药制造业	Medical and Pharmaceutical Products	2261	1615	1573
化学纤维制造业	Chemical Fiber	612	2724	969
橡胶制品业	Rubber Products	1038	479	329
塑料制品业	Plastic Products	623	188	91
非金属矿物制品业	Nonmetal Mineral Products	43707	39615	10669
#水泥制造业	Concrete Machinery	35376	32302	6100
黑色金属冶炼及压延加工业	Smelting and Pressing of Ferrous Metals	7798	33841	8437
有色金属冶炼及压延加工业	Smelting and Pressing of Nonferrous Metals	3695	9939	1595
金属制品业	Metal Products	1894	431	225
普通机械制造业	Ordinary Machinery	3378	536	373
专用设备制造业	Special Purpose Equipment	2057	506	379
交通运输设备制造业	Transport Equipment	5950	1746	582
电气机械及器材制造业	Electric Equipment and Machinery	1583	591	244
电子及通信设备制造业	Electronic and Telecommunications Equipment	1624	664	216
仪器仪表文化办公用机械	Instruments, Meters, Cultural and Office Machinery	1070	654	134
其他制造业	Other Machinery	410	79	28
电力蒸汽热水生产供应业	Production and Supply of Electric Power, Steam and Hot Water	8134	68008	67477
#火力发电业	Firepower Generator	3941	62144	61638
煤气的生产和供应业	Production and Supply of Gas	578	531	164
自来水的生产和供应业	Production and Supply of Tap Water	83	15	15
其它行业	Other Branches	3044	1841	1143

Emission and Treatment of Waste Gas by Sector (2003)

生产工艺过程中废气排放量 Volume of Waste Gas from Production Process	工业二氧化硫排放量 (吨) Volume of Sulphur Dioxide Emission (ton)	工业二氧化硫去除量 (吨) Volume of Sulphur Dioxide Removed (ton)	工业烟尘排放量 (吨) Volume of Industrial Soot Emission (ton)	工业烟尘去除量 (吨) Volume of Industrial Soot Removed (ton)	工业粉尘排放量 (吨) Volume of Industrial Soot Emission (ton)	工业粉尘去除量 (吨) Volume of Industrial Dust Removed (ton)
547	155244	66213	1043837	133507	89206	52103
19	23538	90742	82460	13119	1748	1410
700	32266	2152	125025	22530	431909	20500
415	48819	63705	181338	14549	393655	17814
142	47834	15561	215499	25141	227183	50435
6	2374	2183	3281	2884	497	2785
160	168189	48530	671663	236263	29298	15380
138	70705	34566	283917	37574	23208	2178
3	105958	27567	381131	82718	181	625
159	14709	6774	52556	7961	20657	1600
72	246467	77336	847244	101021	5316	1930
66	9496	3368	44056	4779	914	176
19	13832	3377	33657	7901	66	62
195	34955	9439	123833	44038	63477	16525
90	3170	762	34988	2233	10030	898
390	362882	120405	2237309	225425	87595	22545
33	3203	17421	10960	2023	162	439
42	1176	231	2161	993	535	620
4698	442085	621136	1399785	301506	160652	157806
5101	832677	598708	5402432	432200	629803	131696
42	68333	24121	305162	42742	4172	999
1755	127620	29069	1140854	36876	12542	3183
150	41060	20378	178652	16516	2874	1096
97	9546	2362	24426	3582	787	221
28947	1553792	325711	3013029	1222744	38016606	5119539
26202	915072	251822	2374501	385357	36514452	4596558
25405	832359	200858	4931892	419397	15644539	913299
8344	581653	3851456	2089435	175675	2968693	157461
206	23552	15775	45198	16618	7773	8887
163	39550	11512	101353	29223	29664	20155
127	36237	13969	190447	24603	36261	12565
1164	70041	15525	421133	61823	117702	59522
346	18086	5271	59616	10066	3583	1397
447	18053	7393	62032	8575	67165	3329
520	9841	3338	26599	4564	2061	488
51	3263	1093	9900	2416	1514	3293
531	8619462	1075885	127569284	3369721	70404	29090
506	8026038	969172	120816025	3128735	57963	27489
367	28568	9136	149892	20882	412232	32552
	2754	450	2579	645	5	6
698	165996	14607	1182811	81310	154641	19899

12-9 各地区废气排放及处理情况（2003年）

Emission and Treatment of Industrial Waste Gas by Region (2003)

地 区	Region	工业废气排放总量（亿标立方米） Total Volume of Industrial Waste Gas Emission (100 million cu.m)	燃料燃烧过程中废气排放量 Volume of Waste Gas from Process of Fuel Burning	生产工艺过程中废气排放量 Volume of Waste Gas from Process of Production	废气治理设施数(套) Number of Facilities for Treatment of Waste Gas (set)
全 国	**National Total**	**198906**	**116447**	**82459**	**137204**
北 京	Beijing	3005	1825	1179	2285
天 津	Tianjin	4360	3467	893	3131
河 北	Hebei	15768	8147	7621	9476
山 西	Shanxi	12849	7191	5659	7139
内蒙古	Inner Mongolia	7961	5273	2687	3256
辽 宁	Liaoning	12774	6814	5960	6872
吉 林	Jilin	3869	2456	1413	2959
黑龙江	Heilongjiang	4841	3943	898	3986
上 海	Shanghai	7799	3377	4422	3001
江 苏	Jiangsu	14633	8981	5652	7510
浙 江	Zhejiang	10432	7208	3224	10354
安 徽	Anhui	5383	3281	2102	3275
福 建	Fujian	4189	2379	1810	4995
江 西	Jiangxi	3202	1812	1390	1994
山 东	Shandong	16139	10314	5826	9868
河 南	Henan	11992	7093	4899	8562
湖 北	Hubei	6707	3248	3459	5868
湖 南	Hunan	4603	2497	2105	4703
广 东	Guangdong	11075	6934	4141	9985
广 西	Guangxi	6636	2937	3699	5024
海 南	Hainan	533	294	239	399
重 庆	Chongqing	2277	1341	936	2045
四 川	Sichuan	6634	3384	3250	5066
贵 州	Guizhou	3477	1822	1656	2183
云 南	Yunnan	4197	1978	2220	3806
西 藏	Tibet	14	9	4	19
陕 西	Shaanxi	3861	2505	1355	3841
甘 肃	Gansu	4033	2292	1742	2407
青 海	Qinghai	1002	312	690	463
宁 夏	Ningxia	1727	1022	705	939
新 疆	Xinjiang	2934	2311	623	1793

12-9 续表 1 continued

地 区	Region	工业二氧化硫排放量(吨) Volume of Sulphur Dioxide Emission by Industry (ton)	生活二氧化硫排放量(吨) Volume of Sulphur Dioxide Emission by Consumption (ton)	工业二氧化硫去除量(吨) Volume of Industry Sulphur Dioxide Removed (ton)	工业烟尘排放量(吨) Volume of Industrial Soot Emission (ton)	生活烟尘排放量(吨) Volume of Consumption Soot Emission (ton)
全 国	**National Total**	**17915620**	**3669379**	**7492125**	**8460745**	**2024527**
北 京	Beijing	114012	68768	23902	29218	41565
天 津	Tianjin	230171	29158	43821	86525	16121
河 北	Hebei	1194954	227186	211798	539146	160327
山 西	Shanxi	1033339	330040	265141	878266	218752
内蒙古	Inner Mongolia	1137818	150431	140197	328872	150613
辽 宁	Liaoning	637265	185587	670233	405124	182550
吉 林	Jilin	188434	83469	49713	201309	87167
黑龙江	Heilongjiang	285306	70643	17594	416688	91317
上 海	Shanghai	315611	134676	48551	49671	65760
江 苏	Jiangsu	1178402	62269	332250	370633	17214
浙 江	Zhejiang	707271	27040	346933	193839	10911
安 徽	Anhui	405353	49500	572693	224511	35075
福 建	Fujian	293073	10649	59436	95506	8448
江 西	Jiangxi	391746	45495	667084	188715	7813
山 东	Shandong	1540090	295609	565022	503374	120285
河 南	Henan	901694	137234	260416	633713	58378
湖 北	Hubei	542834	65737	333528	267776	25614
湖 南	Hunan	671389	176969	503180	411019	72235
广 东	Guangdong	1054256	20900	151959	219347	9510
广 西	Guangxi	830469	43080	364055	521262	8388
海 南	Hainan	22442	475	4527	10826	592
重 庆	Chongqing	613139	153227	293913	119817	90704
四 川	Sichuan	1050542	156044	219756	744441	89766
贵 州	Guizhou	570254	752655	120706	222135	169130
云 南	Yunnan	380683	71884	496559	131379	39029
西 藏	Tibet	749			936	
陕 西	Shaanxi	651036	115024	91550	277291	68273
甘 肃	Gansu	441105	52804	563522	132213	43883
青 海	Qinghai	50522	9758		38697	21039
宁 夏	Ningxia	258372	34948	26679	109040	17217
新 疆	Xinjiang	223289	108121	47407	109456	96851

12-9 续表 2 continued

地 区	Region	工业烟尘去除量(吨) Volume of Industrial Soot Removed (ton)	工业粉尘排放量(吨) Volume of Industrial Dust Emission (ton)	工业粉尘去除量(吨) Volume of Industrial Dust Romoved (ton)	建成烟尘控制区数(个) Number of Soot Control Zones Established (unit)	建成烟尘控制区面积(平方公里) Area of Soot Control Zones (sq.km)
全 国	**National Total**	**156493712**	**10213064**	**59949356**	**3599**	**33333.7**
北 京	Beijing	1748442	32145	883572	54	825.3
天 津	Tianjin	3588363	21981	229802	60	557.3
河 北	Hebei	11770211	654747	4010551	143	1521.0
山 西	Shanxi	10093379	635025	2852476	183	575.5
内蒙古	Inner Mongolia	5922401	324259	1163886	70	460.6
辽 宁	Liaoning	9246873	347380	3718927	64	1433.9
吉 林	Jilin	5825941	115655	2683202	365	1172.5
黑龙江	Heilongjiang	8069435	109669	956599	280	1047.5
上 海	Shanghai	4028884	16974	3480215	127	821.6
江 苏	Jiangsu	12538350	449971	3449002	285	2907.6
浙 江	Zhejiang	6027637	368357	3404234	153	3084.2
安 徽	Anhui	4529596	442309	1891396	162	761.9
福 建	Fujian	2937774	165117	1971085	110	829.3
江 西	Jiangxi	4543237	333253	1857601	65	516.8
山 东	Shandong	13272448	760652	4976636	223	2512.4
河 南	Henan	10927795	733777	4002183	160	1397.2
湖 北	Hubei	4527293	334926	2518965	110	4450.9
湖 南	Hunan	3172762	702011	2073246	194	1122.3
广 东	Guangdong	7563224	438387	3010190	174	2912.6
广 西	Guangxi	3345719	502940	3493974	77	992.8
海 南	Hainan	334964	12592	165103	16	116.5
重 庆	Chongqing	1569948	222312	406016	54	344.0
四 川	Sichuan	3526343	465302	1769880	151	1007.3
贵 州	Guizhou	3930620	253374	1059988	79	267.4
云 南	Yunnan	3305204	121854	1348091	22	211.9
西 藏	Tibet	152	1796	156		
陕 西	Shaanxi	3655387	319656	927950	87	583.0
甘 肃	Gansu	2127447	155492	673953	43	398.2
青 海	Qinghai	618626	58506	132371		
宁 夏	Ningxia	2270283	180617	253108	30	150.3
新 疆	Xinjiang	1474974	158028	584998	58	351.9

12-10 各地区工业固体废物产生及处理利用情况（2003年）

Production, Treatment and Utilization of Industrial Solid Wastes by Region (2003)

地 区	Region	工业固体废物产生量（万吨） Volume of Industrial Solid Wastes Produced (10 000 tons)	#危险废物 Hazardous Wastes	工业固体废物综合利用量（万吨） Volume of Industrial Solid Wasts Utilized (10 000 tons)	工业固体废物贮存量（万吨） Volume of Industrial Solid Wastes in Stocks (10 000 tons)	工业固体废物处置量（万吨） Volume of Industrial Solid Wastes Treated (10 000 tons)	工业固体废物排放量（吨） Volume of Industrial Solid Wastes Discharged (ton)	#危险废物 Hazardous Wastes	"三废"综合利用产品产值（万元） Output Value of Products Made from Utilization of Waste Gas, Water & Solid Wastes (10 000 yuan)
全 国	**National Total**	**100428**	**1170**	**56040**	**27667**	**17751**	**19409096**	**2798**	**4410121.0**
北 京	Beijing	1186	4	876	99	367	99281		64518.3
天 津	Tianjin	644	6	619	…	57	321		41775.8
河 北	Hebei	8975	32	4467	2650	2023	462215		188107.6
山 西	Shanxi	9252	8	3700	1172	3893	6288789		193569.0
内蒙古	Inner Mongolia	3647	31	1196	2083	337	645343		36429.3
辽 宁	Liaoning	8250	58	3398	2247	2708	142135		133004.9
吉 林	Jilin	1736	7	937	764	93	5727		67172.2
黑龙江	Heilongjiang	3097	13	2243	453	424	4639		114778.6
上 海	Shanghai	1659	31	1643	1	47	102		71347.7
江 苏	Jiangsu	3894	85	3861	215	135	92		409334.1
浙 江	Zhejiang	1976	15	1722	34	222	44436		423460.1
安 徽	Anhui	3522	9	2800	409	487	688	48	123441.9
福 建	Fujian	2981	5	1889	81	1021	42053		87935.0
江 西	Jiangxi	6182	3	1368	4534	590	95540		100654.4
山 东	Shandong	6786	68	6054	670	350	10176		551148.0
河 南	Henan	4467	22	3115	815	829	35903		202559.0
湖 北	Hubei	3112	11	2277	764	91	94855		375174.9
湖 南	Hunan	2754	44	1750	718	247	894969	984	153129.3
广 东	Guangdong	2246	62	1881	163	326	178124	921	210894.5
广 西	Guangxi	3224	55	1997	955	190	1087106		146624.7
海 南	Hainan	91	…	56	31	19	1		6287.7
重 庆	Chongqing	1336	46	968	232	74	1416885		71512.2
四 川	Sichuan	5145	214	2511	2186	342	1328699	10	194881.3
贵 州	Guizhou	3772	156	1105	1094	1325	3184825	800	102214.3
云 南	Yunnan	3418	12	1369	1365	732	1216723	…	150530.7
西 藏	Tibet	6		6		2			
陕 西	Shaanxi	2948	3	663	1693	558	533558	21	41366.2
甘 肃	Gansu	2073	45	662	1294	68	575379	15	44778.7
青 海	Qinghai	379	74	78	292	15	75619		2823.3
宁 夏	Ningxia	582	…	289	255	98	62990		21062.1
新 疆	Xinjiang	1087	51	540	397	81	881923		79605.2

12-11 按行业分工业固体废物产生及处理利用情况（2003年）

Production, Treatment and Utilization of Industrial Solid Wastes by Sector (2003)

行 业	Sector	工业固体废物产生量（万吨）Volume of Industrial Solid Wastes Produced (10 000 tons)	#危险废物产生量 Hazardous Wastes	工业固体废物综合利用量（万吨）Volume of Industrial Solid Wastes Utilized (10 000 tons)	工业固体废物贮存量（万吨）Volume of Industrial Wastes in Stocks (10 000 tons)
煤炭采选业	Coal Mining and Dressing	13746	2.69	7893	2440
石油和天然气开采业	Petroleum and Natural Gas Extraction	138	10.83	70	13
黑色金属矿采选业	Ferrous Metals Mining and Dressing	8893		1072	3563
有色金属矿采选业	Nonferrous Metals Mining and Dressing	10543	158.00	3160	5136
非金属矿采选业	Nonmetal Minerals Mining and Dressing	1007	71.33	484	354
其他矿采选业	Other Mining and Dressing	45		16	8
木材及竹材采运业	Logging and Transport of Timber and Bamboo	1205	0.07	1133	15
食品加工业	Food Processing	340	0.14	295	26
食品制造业	Food Manufacturing	567	0.01	539	14
饮料制造业	Beverage Manufacturing	45	…	32	4
烟草加工业	Tobacco Processing	529	5.49	492	1
纺织业	Textile Industry	33	0.38	30	…
服装及其他纤维制品制造	Garments and Other Fiber Products	44	2.72	34	…
皮革毛皮羽绒及其制品业	Leather, Furs, Down and Related Products	137	0.04	131	3
木材加工及竹藤棕草制品业	Timber Processing, Bamboo, Cane, Palm Fiber and Straw Products	9	0.19	8	…
家具制造业	Furniture Manufacturing	1003	9.05	891	40
造纸及纸制品业	Papermaking and Paper Products	45	0.36	20	23
印刷业记录媒介的复制	Printing and Record Medium Reproduction	2	0.05	2	…
文教体育用品制造业	Cultural, Educational and Sports Goods	1519	53.84	1011	138
石油加工及炼焦业	Petroleum Processing and Coking	7442	626.05	5249	1248
化学原料及制品制造业	Raw Chemical Materials and Chemical Products	259	20.12	235	3
医药制造业	Medical and Pharmaceutical Products	288	16.05	258	17
化学纤维制造业	Chemical Fiber	81	0.05	76	…
橡胶制品业	Rubber Products	34	3.72	33	1
塑料制品业	Plastic Products	2457	3.42	2290	131
非金属矿物制品业	Nonmetal Mineral Products	1424	…	1381	93
#水泥制造业	Concrete Machinery	15317	29.12	10861	2930
黑色金属冶炼及压延加工业	Smelting and Pressing of Ferrous Metals	3436	98.62	1117	1379
有色金属冶炼及压延加工业	Smelting and Pressing of Nonferrous Metals	87	8.00	62	15
金属制品业	Metal Products	180	2.75	141	1
普通机械制造业	Ordinary Machinery	249	3.19	172	3
专用设备制造业	Special Purpose Equipment	375	8.42	298	15
交通运输设备制造业	Transport Equipment	62	3.31	50	…
电气机械及器材制造业	Electric Equipment and Machinery	63	13.69	57	1
电子及通信设备制造业	Electronic and Telecommunications Equipment	61	15.20	51	…
仪器仪表文化办公用机械	Instruments, Meters, Cultural and Office Machinery	9	0.17	8	…
其他制造业	Other Machinery	10	0.75	9	…
电力蒸汽热水生产供应业	Production and Supply of Electric Power, Steam and Hot Water	19026	1.46	13418	4823
#火力发电业	Firepower Generator	17217	1.24	12021	4525
煤气的生产和供应业	Production and Supply of Gas	132	0.25	98	32
自来水的生产和供应业	Production and Supply of Tap Water	5	0.03	4	
其它行业	Other Branches	509	1.33	464	61

12-11 续表 continued

行业	Sector	工业固体废物处置量（万吨）Volume of Industrial Solid Wastes Treated (10 000 tons)	工业固体废物排放量（万吨）Volume of Industrial Solid Wastes Discharged (10 000 tons)	#危险废物排放量 Hazardous Wastes	“三废”综合利用产品产值（万元）Output Value of Products Made from Utilization of Waste Gas, Waste Water & Solid Wastes (10 000 yuan)
煤炭采选业	Coal Mining and Dressing	3569	532		131391.0
石油和天然气开采业	Petroleum and Natural Gas Extraction	63	…		95523.0
黑色金属矿采选业	Ferrous Metals Mining and Dressing	4050	226		15655.1
有色金属矿采选业	Nonferrous Metals Mining and Dressing	2605	177	…	14295.4
非金属矿采选业	Nonmetal Minerals Mining and Dressing	140	31		18870.4
其他矿采选业	Other Mining and Dressing	20	…		1129.9
木材及竹材采运业	Logging and Transport of Timber and Bamboo	36	23		173891.8
食品加工业	Food Processing	10	9		62011.8
食品制造业	Food Manufacturing	7	8		110644.1
饮料制造业	Beverage Manufacturing	7	2		4013.1
烟草加工业	Tobacco Processing	32	5	…	27297.8
纺织业	Textile Industry	4	…		1366.0
服装及其他纤维制品制造	Garments and Other Fiber Products	9	1		15451.0
皮革毛皮羽绒及其制品业	Leather, Furs, Down and Related Products	2	1		16940.2
木材加工及竹藤棕草制品业	Timber Processing, Bamboo, Cane, Palm Fiber and Straw Products	1			689.1
家具制造业	Furniture Manufacturing	57	18		208443.4
造纸及纸制品业	Papermaking and Paper Products	2	…	…	2997.0
印刷业记录媒介的复制	Printing and Record Medium Reproduction	…	…		217.3
文教体育用品制造业	Cultural, Educational and Sports Goods	310	63		215375.7
石油加工及炼焦业	Petroleum Processing and Coking	1263	111	…	537990.2
化学原料及制品制造业	Raw Chemical Materials and Chemical Products	15	6	…	39784.7
医药制造业	Medical and Pharmaceutical Products	11	1		45888.1
化学纤维制造业	Chemical Fiber	4	1		8185.8
橡胶制品业	Rubber Products	2	…		11126.1
塑料制品业	Plastic Products	68	82		1077743.7
非金属矿物制品业	Nonmetal Mineral Products	18	23		848479.8
#水泥制造业	Concrete Machinery	1351	234		843395.2
黑色金属冶炼及压延加工业	Smelting and Pressing of Ferrous Metals	1046	65	0.08	213810.9
有色金属冶炼及压延加工业	Smelting and Pressing of Nonferrous Metals	12	2	0.07	36803.0
金属制品业	Metal Products	16	23		43936.7
普通机械制造业	Ordinary Machinery	72	4	0.10	12558.4
专用设备制造业	Special Purpose Equipment	54	8	…	50043.8
交通运输设备制造业	Transport Equipment	11	1	…	14898.4
电气机械及器材制造业	Electric Equipment and Machinery	5	1		19793.6
电子及通信设备制造业	Electronic and Telecommunications Equipment	9	1	0.03	11293.3
仪器仪表文化办公用机械	Instruments, Meters, Cultural and Office Machinery	1	…		797.4
其他制造业	Other Machinery	1	…		53801.0
电力蒸汽热水生产供应业	Production and Supply of Electric Power, Steam and Hot Water	1470	73	…	238133.1
#火力发电业	Firepower Generator	1361	68		217393.5
煤气的生产和供应业	Production and Supply of Gas	2	…		7010.8
自来水的生产和供应业	Production and Supply of Tap Water	…	1		60.1
其它行业	Other Branches	30	9	0.01	21806.5

12-12 各地区城市生活垃圾清运和处理情况（2003年）

Collection, Transport and Disposal of Consumption Wastes in Cities by Region (2003)

地区	Region	生活垃圾清运量（万吨）Consumption Wastes Collected and Transported (10 000 tons)	无害化处理厂数（座）Number of Factories for Wastes Treatment (unit)	#卫生填埋 Landfill	#堆肥 Piling	#焚烧 Burning	无害化处理能力（吨/日）Treatment Capacity (ton/day)	#卫生填埋 Landfill	#堆肥 Piling	#焚烧 Burning
全国	**National Total**	**14856.5**	**575**	**457**	**70**	**47**	**219607**	**187092**	**16511**	**15000**
北京	Beijing	454.5	15	11	1	3	9400	8280	900	220
天津	Tianjin	171.8	3	3			3800	3800		
河北	Hebei	713.1	16	10	4	2	8774	6764	1550	460
山西	Shanxi	601.5	23	18	3	2	4591	3379		1212
内蒙古	Inner Mongolia	391.5	8	8			3474	3417	50	7
辽宁	Liaoning	791	9	7	1	1	11534	10334	800	400
吉林	Jilin	580.6	18	16	1		8233	7929	300	
黑龙江	Heilongjiang	1042.9	32	25	3	4	7374	5949	835	590
上海	Shanghai	585.3	4	1	1	2	4400	400	1000	2000
江苏	Jiangsu	774.5	66	57	6	3	20728	19158	1090	480
浙江	Zhejiang	674.7	52	42		10	18337	14380		3957
安徽	Anhui	406.8	14	11	2	1	4848	4408	420	20
福建	Fujian	265.4	15	11	3	1	6436	5270	726	440
江西	Jiangxi	236.6	9	9			3151	3151		
山东	Shandong	1182.9	93	78	14	1	23597	20374	2543	680
河南	Henan	651.2	40	24	16		11907	8702	3205	
湖北	Hubei	813.4	43	42	1		13605	13505	100	
湖南	Hunan	443.9	2	2			2762	2762		
广东	Guangdong	1447	18	11		7	16597	13297		3300
广西	Guangxi	225.3	9	6	3		4010	3000	850	160
海南	Hainan	85.4	5	3	2		2208	1699	509	
重庆	Chongqing	215.3	5	4		1	1450	1330		120
四川	Sichuan	544.1	22	12	4	6	7755	6130	750	875
贵州	Guizhou	187.1	6	4	1	1	3216	2930	250	36
云南	Yunnan	197.6	16	12	3	1	4161	3840	283	38
西藏	Tibet	38								
陕西	Shaanxi	350.7	4	4			3725	3725		
甘肃	Gansu	275.8	14	14			3375	3375		
青海	Qinghai	55.9	2	2			1400	1400		
宁夏	Ningxia	118.8	2	1	1		1350	1000	350	
新疆	Xinjiang	333.9	10	9		1	3409	3404		5

12-12 续表 continued

地区	Region	无害化处理量（万吨） Volume of Wastes Disposed (10 000 tons)	#卫生填埋 Landfill	#堆肥 Piling	#焚烧 Burning	简易处理量（万吨） Volume of Wastes Disposed in a Simple Way (10 000 tons)	粪便清运量（万吨） Collection and Transport of Excrement and Urine (10 000 tons)	粪便处理量（万吨） Disposal of Excrement and Urine (10 000 tons)	生活垃圾无害化处理率（%） Treatment Rate of Consumption Wastes (%)
全国	**National Total**	**7544.7**	**6404.0**	**716.8**	**369.9**	**4631.8**	**3474.9**	**2492.3**	**50.8**
北京	Beijing	334.3	294.2	32.0	8.1	120.2	233.6	92.9	73.6
天津	Tianjin	104.1	104.1			67.0	25.2	25.2	60.6
河北	Hebei	292.4	256.9	31.3	4.2	199.3	169.2	159.9	41.0
山西	Shanxi	200.6	171.9	28.7		117.0	157.7	59.0	33.3
内蒙古	Inner Mongolia	126.4	126.3		0.1	72.3	95.0	26.3	32.3
辽宁	Liaoning	368.2	324.2	29.2	14.8	296.9	143.8	19.3	46.5
吉林	Jilin	284.1	273.2	11.0		211.2	113.8	64.0	48.9
黑龙江	Heilongjiang	286.6	240.9	24.5	13.0	419.6	256.1	153.2	27.5
上海	Shanghai	69.3	18.1	18.4	32.8	516.0	251.1	251.1	11.8
江苏	Jiangsu	695.0	655.8	22.6	16.6	35.0	405.5	365.9	89.7
浙江	Zhejiang	572.5	471.3		101.2	37.5	112.4	106.2	84.9
安徽	Anhui	147.1	117.8	14.5	0.8	143.5	44.7	32.2	36.2
福建	Fujian	203.6	181.0	12.8	9.8	54.6	33.3	27.8	76.7
江西	Jiangxi	117.0	117.0			109.5	19.7	17.7	49.5
山东	Shandong	1020.4	733.2	277.5	9.8	108.3	151.5	150.1	86.3
河南	Henan	423.8	289.6	127.0		157.2	85.6	50.0	65.1
湖北	Hubei	510.7	506.3	4.4		123.3	116.8	71.9	62.8
湖南	Hunan	100.0	100.0			328.8	64.1	61.2	22.5
广东	Guangdong	612.3	464.1		126.3	505.5	587.3	578.2	42.3
广西	Guangxi	136.4	113.3	22.8	0.4	62.2	21.0	11.3	60.5
海南	Hainan	62.5	56.8	5.7		22.5	9.3	7.7	73.2
重庆	Chongqing	31.5	27.1		4.4	181.6	57.9	46.8	14.6
四川	Sichuan	236.5	190.7	19.2	24.0	116.4	77.6	4.2	43.5
贵州	Guizhou	48.8	38.7	9.1	1.0	96.8	9.5	6.2	26.1
云南	Yunnan	139.2	124.2	13.6	1.4	30.5	60.2	50.0	70.5
西藏	Tibet						0.7		
陕西	Shaanxi	135.2	135.2			173.3	16.0	1.9	38.5
甘肃	Gansu	96.7	96.7			134.7	97.0	50.5	35.0
青海	Qinghai	47.9	47.9			3.0	43.3		85.7
宁夏	Ningxia	36.2	23.5	12.7		15.6	7.6	1.1	30.5
新疆	Xinjiang	105.6	104.3		1.3	172.6	8.4	0.5	31.6

12-13 主要城市道路交通噪声监测情况(2003年)

Monitoring of Urban Road Traffic Noise in Key Cities (2003)

城市	City	路段总长度(米) Total Length of Roads (m)	超标路段(米) Roads with Excess Noise (m)	路段超标率(%) Percentage of Roads with Excess Noise (%)	路段平均宽度(米) Average Width of Roads (m)	平均车流量(辆/小时) Average Traffic Volume (cars/hour)	噪声均值(LeqdBA) Average Noise Value (LeqdBA)
北　京	Beijing	596.1	260.0	43.6	36.0	5822	69.7
天　津	Tianjin	270.7	46.0	17.0	26.0	2214	68.2
石家庄	Shijiazhuang	179.4	38.2	21.3	28.8	1513	67.8
太　原	Taiyuan	137.6	32.5	23.6	23.0	2154	67.8
呼和浩特	Hohhot	82.6	26.4	32.0	29.3	2016	69.3
沈　阳	Shenyang	144.0	3.2	2.2	33.7	2048	67.8
长　春	Changchun	123.6	29.4	23.8	29.8	2670	68.4
哈尔滨	Harbin	91.8	14.4	15.7	17.0	2120	68.3
上　海	Shanghai	213.9	112.5	52.6	20.0	2319	70.4
南　京	Nanjing	169.8	40.8	24.0	29.4	1678	68.9
杭　州	Hangzhou	193.9	38.4	19.8	16.3	2078	67.9
合　肥	Hefei	94.0	2.9	3.1	38.9	1933	67.7
福　州	Fuzhou	111.2	18.5	16.6	22.9	2393	68.4
南　昌	Nanchang	67.5	41.6	61.7	29.3	2809	69.9
济　南	Jinan	206.6	64.0	31.0	46.9	2117	68.7
郑　州	Zhengzhou	84.1	10.7	12.7	43.5	2019	68.0
武　汉	Wuhan	223.4	123.8	55.4	18.7	2205	69.9
长　沙	Changsha	95.8	50.2	52.4	28.3	2552	70.0
广　州	Guangzhou	237.1	65.2	27.5	23.0	3421	68.4
南　宁	Nanning	102.0	54.1	53.0	19.8	3276	69.7
海　口	Haikou	107.3	20.4	19.0	34.2	2679	67.9
重　庆	Chongqing	331.4	90.1	27.2	14.4	1461	67.5
成　都	Chengdu	313.2	58.3	18.6	44.7	2543	68.0
贵　阳	Guiyang	52.3	28.2	53.9	23.7	2466	70.2
昆　明	Kunming	91.5	40.9	44.7	30.0	2044	70.5
拉　萨	Lhasa	52.9	11.5	21.8	17.5	622	67.4
西　安	Xi'an	195.1	69.7	35.7	23.6	2673	68.0
兰　州	Lanzhou	125.4	47.6	38.0	19.7	1550	69.1
西　宁	Xining	85.7	47.6	55.6	19.0	2247	70.6
银　川	Yinchuan	94.6	15.0	15.9	29.1	1502	68.0
乌鲁木齐	Urumqi	112.5	63.2	56.2	40.0	1549	70.0

12-14 国控主要城市区域环境噪声监测情况（2003年）
Monitoring of Urban Environment Noise in Key Cities under National Control Programme (2003)

城 市	City	网格长度（米）Grid Length (m)	网格宽度（米）Grid Width (m)	网格总数（个）Total number of Grids (unit)	等效声级LeqdB(A) Sound Level LeqdB(A)
北 京	Beijing	1000	1000	428	53.6
天 津	Tianjin	1000	1000	205	55.0
石家庄	Shijiazhuang	500	500	240	54.0
太 原	Taiyuan	750	750	232	53.8
呼和浩特	Hohhot	400	400	204	54.0
沈 阳	Shenyang	750	750	240	53.5
长 春	Changchun	500	500	204	57.0
哈尔滨	Harbin	700	700	216	56.1
上 海	Shanghai	1414	1414	204	56.7
南 京	Nanjing	1000	1000	210	54.3
杭 州	Hangzhou	500	500	235	56.0
合 肥	Hefei	500	500	250	52.5
福 州	Fuzhou	500	500	220	56.3
南 昌	Nanchang	500	500	201	55.8
济 南	Jinan	1000	1000	426	48.6
郑 州	Zhengzhou	500	500	235	55.9
武 汉	Wuhan	1000	1000	210	55.1
长 沙	Changsha	500	500	288	53.8
广 州	Guangzhou	1000	1000	202	54.5
南 宁	Nanning	550	550	200	56.2
海 口	Haikou	400	400	203	56.1
重 庆	Chongqing	500	500	661	55.0
成 都	Chengdu	900	900	215	54.8
贵 阳	Guiyang	500	500	220	55.8
昆 明	Kunming	800	800	223	54.6
拉 萨	Lhasa				55.6
西 安	Xi'an	500	500	212	55.6
兰 州	Lanzhou	375	375	224	58.0
西 宁	Xining	500	500	200	51.3
银 川	Yinchuan	750	750	209	51.1
乌鲁木齐	Urumqi	1000	1000	428	53.4

12-15 各地区土地利用情况（2003年）

Land Use by Region (2003)

单位:万公顷 (10 000 hectares)

地区	Region	土地调查面积 Area under Land Survey	农用地 Land for Agriculture Use	#园地 Garden Land	#牧草地 Grazing and Pasture Land	建设用地 Land for Construction	居民点及工矿用地 Land for Living Quarters, Mining and Manufacturing Sites	交通用地 Land for Transport Facilities	水利设施用地 Land for Water Conservancy Facilities
全国	**National Total**	**95067.99**	**65706.14**	**1108.16**	**26311.18**	**3106.47**	**2535.42**	**214.52**	**356.53**
北京	Beijing	164.11	111.81	11.92	0.20	30.85	25.74	2.48	2.62
天津	Tianjin	119.17	72.00	3.68	0.06	31.41	23.53	1.46	6.42
河北	Hebei	1884.31	1302.79	57.54	81.50	169.14	146.98	10.03	12.13
山西	Shanxi	1567.11	1010.22	28.56	65.44	82.75	73.88	5.66	3.21
内蒙古	Inner Mongolia	11451.21	9508.83	7.33	6622.21	139.57	116.90	13.71	8.96
辽宁	Liaoning	1480.64	1125.00	60.70	36.99	132.65	110.43	8.03	14.20
吉林	Jilin	1911.24	1640.10	11.59	104.74	104.21	82.60	6.14	15.47
黑龙江	Heilongjiang	4526.45	3780.16	6.04	228.08	146.22	114.13	11.33	20.76
上海	Shanghai	82.39	38.53	1.08	0.00	22.68	20.74	1.75	0.19
江苏	Jiangsu	1067.42	683.88	29.57	0.51	174.44	144.48	10.17	19.80
浙江	Zhejiang	1053.97	866.28	56.82	0.15	87.42	66.70	6.34	14.38
安徽	Anhui	1401.26	1123.30	34.31	3.77	159.87	128.37	8.62	22.88
福建	Fujian	1240.16	1077.81	61.43	0.27	56.42	44.17	6.32	5.93
江西	Jiangxi	1668.94	1419.14	26.99	0.38	88.90	62.37	6.17	20.35
山东	Shandong	1570.54	1162.42	102.38	4.14	233.56	193.60	14.93	25.03
河南	Henan	1655.36	1229.09	32.08	1.45	212.44	183.25	11.04	18.16
湖北	Hubei	1858.88	1466.65	42.57	5.46	134.44	96.92	7.79	29.73
湖南	Hunan	2118.55	1792.80	50.25	10.51	132.22	104.11	8.81	19.31
广东	Guangdong	1797.57	1497.05	84.95	2.82	165.26	133.34	10.82	21.10
广西	Guangxi	2375.58	1790.15	47.01	73.83	87.66	65.56	7.31	14.79
海南	Hainan	353.54	282.35	53.02	1.94	29.09	21.74	1.33	6.02
重庆	Chongqing	822.69	695.39	21.00	23.84	54.00	45.66	3.93	4.40
四川	Sichuan	4840.56	4243.71	69.52	1373.43	153.34	131.18	12.35	9.81
贵州	Guizhou	1761.52	1529.55	11.32	162.18	52.51	43.80	5.22	3.50
云南	Yunnan	3831.94	3173.51	78.12	78.48	74.91	58.52	8.85	7.54
西藏	Tibet	12020.72	7760.43	0.17	6444.58	5.98	3.80	2.09	0.09
陕西	Shaanxi	2057.95	1847.49	65.10	315.99	78.83	69.07	5.84	3.92
甘肃	Gansu	4040.91	2385.96	19.38	1264.78	96.01	87.12	6.07	2.82
青海	Qinghai	7174.81	4367.49	0.77	4038.57	31.03	23.95	2.69	4.39
宁夏	Ningxia	519.54	420.72	3.38	233.39	18.69	16.66	1.52	0.51
新疆	Xinjiang	16648.97	6301.54	29.58	5131.49	119.96	96.12	5.76	18.08

12-16 各地区森林资源情况

Forest Resources by Region

地区	Region	林业用地面积 (万公顷) Area of Afforested Land (10 000 hectares)	森林面积 (万公顷) Forest Area (10 000 hectares)	#人工林 Man-made Forest	森林覆盖率 (%) Forest Coverage Rate (%)	活立木总蓄积量 (万立方米) Total Standing Forest Stock (10 000 cu.m)	森林蓄积量 (万立方米) Stock Volume of Forest (10 000 cu.m)
全国	**National Total**	**26329.47**	**15894.09**	**4708.95**	**16.55**	**1248786.39**	**1126659.14**
北京	Beijing	93.06	33.74	22.97	18.93	1115.25	685.82
天津	Tianjin	13.30	8.58	8.21	7.47	250.46	160.25
河北	Hebei	631.22	336.13	199.73	18.08	7856.82	5948.19
山西	Shanxi	676.47	183.58	83.02	11.72	8009.04	5643.97
内蒙古	Inner Mongolia	3181.95	1474.85	185.23	12.73	116859.43	98163.48
辽宁	Liaoning	567.43	451.05	211.75	30.95	17362.63	16136.90
吉林	Jilin	829.74	706.98	138.38	37.43	82753.39	78656.81
黑龙江	Heilongjiang	2131.24	1760.31	192.38	38.72	156615.58	141069.30
上海	Shanghai	2.33	2.18	2.18	3.66	133.67	23.93
江苏	Jiangsu	59.26	46.24	43.68	4.51	3633.57	865.77
浙江	Zhejiang	639.66	517.18	238.34	50.80	12660.40	11122.00
安徽	Anhui	418.65	317.05	171.38	22.95	10441.14	8295.77
福建	Fujian	901.83	735.37	348.27	60.52	41763.62	36490.99
江西	Jiangxi	1045.32	889.78	270.12	53.37	27695.69	22308.38
山东	Shandong	263.84	191.52	182.08	12.58	6022.19	1480.99
河南	Henan	378.64	209.01	109.70	12.52	13167.55	5258.50
湖北	Hubei	764.09	482.84	133.12	25.98	14759.04	13223.82
湖南	Hunan	1173.66	823.97	339.41	38.90	23147.09	19890.46
广东	Guangdong	1034.70	815.02	440.89	45.81	21325.15	19726.70
广西	Guangxi	1269.19	816.66	371.34	34.37	31027.39	27699.92
海南	Hainan	169.96	134.93	82.65	39.56	7281.49	6613.03
重庆	Chongqing						
四川	Sichuan	2657.91	1330.15	324.47	23.50	154520.65	144621.65
贵州	Guizhou	740.71	367.31	143.12	20.81	17022.35	14050.18
云南	Yunnan	2380.79	1287.32	181.84	33.64	142391.06	128364.94
西藏	Tibet	1260.66	408.15	0.11		126789.71	125337.41
陕西	Shaanxi	1197.49	592.03	133.40	28.74	33407.95	30265.74
甘肃	Gansu	720.87	217.41	64.29	4.83	19224.52	17201.76
青海	Qinghai	337.95	30.88	3.04	0.43	3728.46	3270.36
宁夏	Ningxia	100.40	14.64	10.40	2.20	674.17	585.26
新疆	Xinjiang	476.91	178.37	31.19	1.08	28998.52	25401.95

注：1.本表为第五次全国森林资源清查（1994-1998）资料。
2.全国总计数包括台湾省和西藏实际控制线外部分，不包括香港、澳门特别行政区数据。
3.重庆市数据含在四川省内。

a) Data in the table are the figures of the Fifith National Forestry Survey (1994-1998).

b) National total include forest resources in Taiwan provice and Tibet, but exclude forest resource in Hong Kong SAR and Macao SAR.

c) Sichuan data include Chongqing's data.

12-17 造林面积

Area of Afforestation

单位：公顷 (hectare)

年份 地区	Year Region	造林总面积 Total area of Afforestation	按造林方式分 By Approach 人工造林 Manual Planting	飞机播种 Airplane Planting	按林种用途分 By Function of Forest 用材林 Timber Forests	经济林 By-product Forests	防护林 Protection Forests	薪炭林 Fuel Forests	特种用途林 Forests for Special Purpose
	2000	5105138	4345008	760130	1218461	1350277	2430834	82338	23228
	2001	4953038	3977324	975714	905518	1068540	2913538	45611	19831
	2002	7770971	6896041	874930	898736	964211	5828810	59144	20070
	2003	9118894	8432486	686408	1175812	797318	7087319	37070	21374
北京	Beijing	47168	35616	11552	5907	11581	26818	66	2796
天津	Tianjin	6894	6894		3127	1617	2150		
河北	Hebei	624215	560881	63334	91136	35645	495464	1580	390
山西	Shanxi	507681	418546	89135	7249	24386	476046		
内蒙古	Inner Mongolia	836123	699373	136750	17202	4852	813389	680	
辽宁	Liaoning	195150	195150		23262	24637	140768	6483	
吉林	Jilin	167924	167924		19775	4315	140225	3574	35
黑龙江	Heilongjiang	277980	277980		88883	9773	169710	2760	6854
上海	Shanghai	16457	16457		3004	7857	3016		2580
江苏	Jiangsu	112413	112413		30900	16972	64541		
浙江	Zhejiang	22114	22114		1771	4525	14758	972	88
安徽	Anhui	194508	194508		4145	12073	177389	793	108
福建	Fujian	16581	16581		6740	2756	6860	199	25
江西	Jiangxi	219745	219745		21301	24462	172982	554	446
山东	Shandong	344078	344078		192652	92130	57709	1039	548
河南	Henan	320124	300168	19956	97518	52682	168162	1208	554
湖北	Hubei	315476	315476		101788	41081	168879	3674	54
湖南	Hunan	409578	409578		52338	45066	307389	47	4738
广东	Guangdong	48020	48020		25774	3656	16970	1260	360
广西	Guangxi	277969	277969		125359	48385	103616	466	143
海南	Hainan	75206	75206		4480	11846	58437	267	176
重庆	Chongqing	352619	331886	20733	27884	31464	292431	840	
四川	Sichuan	723215	601086	122129	73099	54717	592063	2971	365
贵州	Guizhou	377939	360283	17656	3972	13030	360937		
云南	Yunnan	495135	431426	63709	83737	90962	318492	1010	934
西藏	Tibet	23233	23233				23233		
陕西	Shaanxi	727978	625590	102388	46452	34476	644296	2724	30
甘肃	Gansu	582243	565044	17199		21377	560798		68
青海	Qinghai	96908	96908				96908		
宁夏	Ningxia	319625	307758	11867	158	3671	314283	1513	
新疆	Xinjiang	352328	342328	10000	10388	65654	273814	2390	82
大兴安岭	Great Xingan Mountains	5811	5811		5811				

注：2003年全国合计造林面积中包括军事管理区26456公顷人工造林，其中经济林1670公顷，防护林24786公顷。

a) Total area of afforestation in 2003 include 26456 hectares afforested in the military precinct, of which, including 1670 hectares by-product forests and 24786 hectares protection forests.

12-18 林业重点工程造林面积

Area of Key Afforestation Projects

单位:万公顷 (10 000 hectares)

年份 地区	Year Region	造林总面积 Total Area of Afforestation	天然林保护工程 Preserve of Natural Forests	退耕还林工程 Grain for Green Projects	三北及长江流域等防护林建设工程 Protection Forests in North China and Yangtze River Basin	京津风沙源治理工程 Projects on Harnessing Source of Sand and Dust in Beijing and Tianjin	速生丰产用材林基地建设工程 Projects on Fast-growing Timber Forest Bases
	2000	334.59	42.64	68.36	28.03	170.88	24.69
	2001	317.33	94.81	89.03	21.73	102.87	8.89
	2002	677.74	85.61	442.36	67.64	77.56	4.57
	2003	826.28	68.83	619.61	82.44	53.35	2.04
北京	Beijing	3.58			2.46	1.12	
天津	Tianjin	0.69			0.12	0.57	
河北	Hebei	58.68		21.07	32.63	4.51	0.48
山西	Shanxi	48.17	6.11	28.04	10.23	3.79	
内蒙古	Inner Mongolia	81.89	10.37	34.02	37.01	0.49	
辽宁	Liaoning	19.52		17.47		2.04	
吉林	Jilin	14.81		12.95		1.86	
黑龙江	Heilongjiang	25.99		23.68		2.31	
上海	Shanghai	0.16				0.16	
江苏	Jiangsu	1.77				1.77	
浙江	Zhejiang	1.16				1.15	0.01
安徽	Anhui	18.37		16.17		2.20	
福建	Fujian	1.07				0.63	0.44
江西	Jiangxi	21.85		21.33		0.52	
山东	Shandong	1.92				1.92	
河南	Henan	28.66		25.33		3.33	
湖北	Hubei	30.96	0.16	28.05		2.39	0.37
湖南	Hunan	40.65		39.25		0.84	0.56
广东	Guangdong	0.80				0.80	
广西	Guangxi	26.09		24.91		1.00	0.18
海南	Hainan	7.34		6.92		0.42	
重庆	Chongqing	35.26	2.07	33.19			
四川	Sichuan	71.40	23.51	47.89			
贵州	Guizhou	37.79	1.77	34.66		1.36	
云南	Yunnan	44.53	9.03	33.66		1.83	0.01
西藏	Tibet	2.00	0.03	1.33		0.64	
陕西	Shaanxi	69.21	11.37	56.24		1.59	
甘肃	Gansu	58.09	3.09	52.61		2.38	
青海	Qinghai	9.46	0.12	8.82		0.53	
宁夏	Ningxia	31.96	1.19	27.08		3.70	
新疆	Xinjiang	32.45		24.95		7.50	

12-19 各地区湿地面积（2003年）

Area of Wetlands by Region (2003)

地区	Region	湿地面积（千公顷） Area of Wetlands (1 000 hectares)	天然湿地 Natural Wetlands	近岸及海岸 Coasts and Seashores	河流 Rivers	湖泊 Lakes	沼泽 Marshland	人工湿地 Man-made Wetlands	湿地面积占国土面积比重(%) Proportion of Wetlands in Total Area of Territory (%)
全国	**National Total**	**38485.5**	**36200.6**	**5941.7**	**8207.0**	**8351.6**	**13700.3**	**2285.0**	**4.01**
北京	Beijing	34.4	5.0		5.0			29.4	1.93
天津	Tianjin	171.8	133.7	58.1	55.1	12.3	8.2	38.1	14.95
河北	Hebei	1081.9	1042.3	278.8	319.3	307.2	136.9	39.6	5.82
山西	Shanxi	499.9	462.2		454.1	8.1		37.7	3.19
内蒙古	Inner Mongolia	4245.0	4200.8		607.5	495.2	3098.1	44.3	3.66
辽宁	Liaoning	1219.6	1106.8	738.1	252.2	6.3	110.2	112.9	8.37
吉林	Jilin	1203.4	1016.4	5.8	581.4	74.5	354.7	187.0	6.37
黑龙江	Heilongjiang	4314.8	4182.8		460.7	401.9	3320.3	132.0	9.49
上海	Shanghai	319.7	319.4	305.4	7.2	6.8		0.3	53.68
江苏	Jiangsu	1674.7	1651.1	843.5	203.3	604.2		23.6	16.32
浙江	Zhejiang	802.2	695.9	574.3	118.5	3.0	0.1	106.3	7.88
安徽	Anhui	653.9	590.0		239.5	350.5		63.9	4.73
福建	Fujian	443.0	421.2	370.6	31.1	19.5		21.8	3.65
江西	Jiangxi	998.8	872.9		314.9	443.2	114.8	125.9	5.99
山东	Shandong	1784.1	1681.4	1210.9	301.1	165.5	3.9	102.7	11.72
河南	Henan	624.1	482.2		472.7	2.6	6.9	141.9	3.74
湖北	Hubei	927.3	730.5		377.4	294.7	58.4	196.9	4.99
湖南	Hunan	1226.9	1047.5		683.1	359.3	5.1	179.5	5.79
广东	Guangdong	1398.1	1252.0	1017.8	231.7	1.5	1.0	146.0	7.86
广西	Guangxi	656.1	567.5	348.4	219.1	0.0		88.6	2.76
海南	Hainan	311.5	256.6	190.0	38.3	17.3	11.0	54.9	9.13
重庆	Chongqing	43.2	31.9		31.6	0.3		11.3	0.52
四川	Sichuan	961.7	919.5		563.9	13.4	342.3	42.1	1.98
贵州	Guizhou	79.4	65.9		58.0	2.3	5.7	13.5	0.45
云南	Yunnan	235.3	220.3		119.8	96.5	4.0	15.0	0.61
西藏	Tibet	5232.0	5231.5		231.1	2538.6	2461.7	0.5	4.26
陕西	Shaanxi	292.9	277.2		252.1	7.3	17.8	15.7	1.42
甘肃	Gansu	1258.1	1131.4		565.6	44.3	521.5	126.7	2.80
青海	Qinghai	4126.0	4087.7		107.5	1232.0	2748.1	38.3	5.72
宁夏	Ningxia	255.6	252.4		104.1	148.3		3.2	3.85
新疆	Xinjiang	1410.2	1264.6		200.2	694.9	369.5	145.5	0.86

注：本表为中国首次湿地调查资料,不包括台湾省、香港和澳门特别行政区；湿地面积不包括水稻田湿地。

a) Data in the table is the figures of China First Wetlands Survey, excluding the wetlands of Taiwan province, Hong Kong SAR, Macao SAR. Area of wetlands excludes the wetland of paddyfield.

12-20 红树林各地类面积

Site Classification and Area of Sharpleaf Mangrove (Rhizophora Apiculata)

单位:公顷 (hectare)

地区	Region	红树林各地类总面积 Total Site Area of Sharpleaf Mangrove	现有面积 Established	未成林面积 Unestablished	宜林地面积 Suitable for Planting
全国	**National Total**	**82757.2**	**22024.9**	**1884.1**	**58848.2**
浙江	Zhejiang	5452.3	20.6	236.1	5195.6
福建	Fujian	13410.1	615.1	286.4	12508.6
广东	Guangdong	32325.9	9084.0	981.3	22260.6
广西	Guangxi	18029.2	8374.9	380.3	9274.0
海南	Hainan	13539.7	3930.3		9609.4

注:本表数据为2002年全国红树林资源调查资料。

a) Data in the table are the figures of National Sharpleaf Mangrove Survey in 2002.

12-21 各地区自然保护基本情况(2003年)

Basic Situation of Natural Protection by Region (2003)

地区	Region	自然保护区 Nature Reserves 个数(个) Number of Nature Reserves (unit)	面积(万公顷) Area of Nature Reserves (10 000 hectares)	占辖区面积比重(%) Percentage of Nature Reserves in the Region (%)	珍稀濒危动物繁殖场(个) Number of Farms to Breed Rare or Endangered Animals (unit)	珍稀植物引种栽培场(个) Cultivating Farms of Rare Plants (unit)	生态示范区建设试点地区和单位(个) Number of Experimental Units and Region of Ecological Demonstration Zones(unit)	已批准国家级生态示范区(个) Number of Approved the National-level Ecological Demonstration Zones (unit)
全国	**National Total**	**1999**	**14398.1**	**14.4**	**641**	**211**	**484**	**82**
北京	Beijing	18	10.9	6.5	7		5	2
天津	Tianjin	9	15.6	13.7			7	1
河北	Hebei	24	35.9	1.9			26	1
山西	Shanxi	39	105.9	6.8		2	24	1
内蒙古	Inner Mongolia	183	1489.0	12.6	4	2	13	2
辽宁	Liaoning	81	287.6	11.3	50	89	20	5
吉林	Jilin	32	217.8	12.1	4	4	10	2
黑龙江	Heilongjiang	151	382.8	8.4	58	20	23	9
上海	Shanghai	4	9.4	14.8			1	1
江苏	Jiangsu	25	65.0	6.3	10	2	51	14
浙江	Zhejiang	49	26.3	2.6	2	3	23	6
安徽	Anhui	31	53.1	4.1	6	4	30	6
福建	Fujian	79	47.9	2.9	7	2	13	3
江西	Jiangxi	126	76.0	4.6	4	5	27	4
山东	Shandong	65	81.4	4.9			34	6
河南	Henan	25	49.5	3.0	16	3	20	3
湖北	Hubei	35	84.5	4.5	8	13	12	3
湖南	Hunan	82	95.4	4.5	2	4	28	2
广东	Guangdong	209	317.2	4.3	31	5	13	1
广西	Guangxi	67	148.1	6.1	380	5	11	2
海南	Hainan	66	272.1	5.1	14	1	1	1
重庆	Chongqing	46	86.6	10.5			2	
四川	Sichuan	120	707.7	14.5	8	11	27	3
贵州	Guizhou	107	80.9	4.6			12	1
云南	Yunnan	186	355.0	9.0	14	21	17	1
西藏	Tibet	15	4087.3	34.1			2	
陕西	Shaanxi	32	67.7	3.3	2	4	17	
甘肃	Gansu	47	878.6	19.3	12	8	2	
青海	Qinghai	8	2060.8	28.6			2	
宁夏	Ningxia	12	49.2	9.5		2	3	1
新疆	Xinjiang	26	2152.9	13.5	2	1	7	1

12-22 地质灾害及防治情况

Prevention of Geological Disasters

年份 地区	Year Region	发生地质灾害起数（次） Geological Disasters (case)	#滑坡 Land-slide	#崩塌 Collapse	#泥石流 Mud-rock Flow	#地面塌陷 Land Subside	人员伤亡（人） Casualties (person)	#死亡人数 Deaths
	2000	19653	13431	2945	1958	347	27697	1179
	2001	5793	3034	583	1539	554	1675	788
	2002	40246	31247	3097	4976	521	2759	853
	2003	15489	10240	2604	1549	574	1333	767
北京	Beijing	1		1				
天津	Tianjin							
河北	Hebei	18	3	1	3	1		
山西	Shanxi	112	8	12	7	17	52	52
内蒙古	Inner Mongolia	23	4	4	5	10	2	2
辽宁	Liaoning	7	2	2		3	8	4
吉林	Jilin	47	2	8	33	4		
黑龙江	Heilongjiang	17	2		14	1		
上海	Shanghai	1				1		
江苏	Jiangsu	154	151			3	4	1
浙江	Zhejiang	62	44	14	2	2	1	1
安徽	Anhui	670	93	557	11	9		
福建	Fujian	124	104	17	2	1	15	9
江西	Jiangxi	56	34	12	2	8	19	11
山东	Shandong	44	2	4		34		
河南	Henan	146	85	44	5	12	22	20
湖北	Hubei	561	405	88	6	56	46	29
湖南	Hunan	1499	1247	138	73	41	129	82
广东	Guangdong	60	27	14		19	54	36
广西	Guangxi	658	70	567	5	16	34	33
海南	Hainan	1		1				
重庆	Chongqing	2679	2282	321	36	40	95	41
四川	Sichuan	1808	1463	134	77	104	305	129
贵州	Guizhou	436	240	90	66	18	69	69
云南	Yunnan	1691	1234	173	220	62	96	61
西藏	Tibet	289	111	45	131		28	18
陕西	Shaanxi	4150	2571	338	820	43	225	94
甘肃	Gansu	111	22	12	13	64	86	59
青海	Qinghai	13	8	1	3	1	14	1
宁夏	Ningxia	1		1			2	2
新疆	Xinjiang	50	26	5	15	4	27	13

12-22 续表 continued

年份 地区	Year Region	直接经济损失（万元） Direct Economic Loss (10 000 yuan)	地质灾害防治项目 Project of Prevention of Geological Disasters 项目数（个） Projects (unit)	投资（万元） Investment (10 000 yuan)	滑坡、泥石流治理面积(公顷) Area Covered by Landslide and Mud-rock Flow Harnessing Projects (hectare)
	2000	494201	429	33197	52848
	2001	348699	999	44639	25714
	2002	509740	1595	110022	29696
	2003	504325	1815	166514	14450
北　京	Beijing	2			
天　津	Tianjin		1		
河　北	Hebei	332	3	453	
山　西	Shanxi	18471	19	380	
内蒙古	Inner Mongolia	953	11	4894	19
辽　宁	Liaoning	3086			
吉　林	Jilin	3533	3	2040	200
黑龙江	Heilongjiang	3940	3	602	27
上　海	Shanghai		30	800	
江　苏	Jiangsu	3950	12	1000	2
浙　江	Zhejiang	455	98	6062	88
安　徽	Anhui	6075	33	843	41
福　建	Fujian	1140	169	4577	315
江　西	Jiangxi	1631	65	1514	
山　东	Shandong	1913	46	4141	93
河　南	Henan	13985	103	3204	815
湖　北	Hubei	46856	193	37289	849
湖　南	Hunan	93980	141	3515	968
广　东	Guangdong	10656	32	12500	250
广　西	Guangxi	1582	11	610	10
海　南	Hainan	1	2	107	
重　庆	Chongqing	36421	299	66233	14
四　川	Sichuan	27673			
贵　州	Guizhou	29443	38	3675	1000
云　南	Yunnan	35998	291	5205	9096
西　藏	Tibet	2990	3		
陕　西	Shaanxi	137800	202	6665	663
甘　肃	Gansu	15262			
青　海	Qinghai	3905			
宁　夏	Ningxia	40	1	40	
新　疆	Xinjiang	2252	6	165	

12-23 森林火灾情况

Forest Fires

年份 地区	Year Region	森林火灾次数（次） Forest Fires (case)	森林火警 Fire Alarms	一般火灾 Ordinary Fires	重大火灾 Major Fires	特大火灾 Severe Fires	火场总面积（公顷） Total Area of Fires (hectare)	受灾森林面积（公顷） Destructed Forest Area (hectare)	#天然林 Natural Forest	#人工林 Man-made Forest	伤亡人数（人） Casualties (person)	#死亡人数 Deaths	经济损失（万元） Economic Loss (10 000 yuan)
	2000	5934	2722	3144	60	8	167098	88390	46960	40529	178	81	3069
	2001	4933	2984	1929	17	3	192734	46181	32289	11721	58	20	7409
	2002	7527	4450	3046	24	7	131823	47631	17031	17123	98	48	3610
	2003	10463	5582	4860	14	7	1123751	451020	294271	33531	142	72	37000
北京	Beijing	4	4				6	1		1			
天津	Tianjin	2	2				1	1		1			
河北	Hebei	19	19				166	3		1			0
山西	Shanxi	5	3	2			11	8		8			2
内蒙古	Inner Mongolia	151	105	40	2	4	212455	122295	19	1078			2
辽宁	Liaoning	323	257	66			574	328	119	190	3	3	141
吉林	Jilin	86	79	7			139	48	4	19			23
黑龙江	Heilongjiang	232	149	79	1	3	799307	287408	287408		1	1	25352
上海	Shanghai												
江苏	Jiangsu	97	85	12			219	112	1	111			10
浙江	Zhejiang	866	210	652	4		11120	5258	2317	2941	18	10	245
安徽	Anhui	67	46	21			308	151		151			52
福建	Fujian	522	87	435			7905	4634	219	4343	1		48
江西	Jiangxi	882	316	566			12108	6408	437	5971	2	1	2065
山东	Shandong	41	30	11			204	144	1	143			31
河南	Henan	40	36	4			141	17		17			8
湖北	Hubei	244	183	61			1823	571	61	366	4	3	8
湖南	Hunan	1839	787	1048	4		13596	9089	1482	7575	22	19	3208
广东	Guangdong	258	99	159			3199	1633	23	1611			246
广西	Guangxi	1015	492	522	1		18974	4807	100	4187	19	16	409
海南	Hainan	185	113	72			962	439	100	339	1	1	
重庆	Chongqing	154	137	16	1		713	334	19	315	4	1	64
四川	Sichuan	378	302	76			5919	826	482	343	12		101
贵州	Guizhou	2154	1441	713			14919	3251	650	2479	29	4	766
云南	Yunnan	786	533	253			15484	2168	68	1102	9	3	152
西藏	Tibet	11	6	5			414	84					108
陕西	Shaanxi	36	13	23			272	129		129	17	10	34
甘肃	Gansu	30	27	2	1		2354	724	715	9			3913
青海	Qinghai	8	4	4			21	6	1	5			4
宁夏	Ningxia	3	1	2			68	16		16			
新疆	Xinjiang	25	16	9			370	129	47	83			8

12-24 森林病虫害防治情况

Prevention of Forest Diseases and Pests

年份 Year / 地区 Region		合计 Total			森林病害 Forest Diseases		
		发生面积（公顷）Area of Occurrence (hectare)	防治面积（公顷）Area of Prevention (hectare)	防治率（%）Prevention Rate (%)	发生面积（公顷）Area of Occurrence (hectare)	防治面积（公顷）Area of Prevention (hectare)	防治率（%）Prevention Rate (%)
	2000	8518580	5741860	67	934520	619450	66
	2001	8390270	5872910	70	804950	582850	72
	2002	8412496	5719588	68	744980	571240	77
	2003	8887362	5829187	66	757456	552461	73
北京	Beijing	33444	31039	93	5087	3735	73
天津	Tianjin	18293	16676	91	948	948	100
河北	Hebei	395559	325742	82	35286	21186	60
山西	Shanxi	407196	146690	36	770	425	55
内蒙古	Inner Mongolia	720660	512664	71	22885	17883	78
辽宁	Liaoning	589786	480576	81	40170	31673	79
吉林	Jilin	257343	179749	70	49511	48269	97
黑龙江	Heilongjiang	595132	513438	86	52028	40408	78
上海	Shanghai	18660	31171	100	3428	7058	100
江苏	Jiangsu	79919	87412	100	30650	19381	63
浙江	Zhejiang	77155	74133	96	27750	27211	98
安徽	Anhui	271741	225799	83	30357	27639	91
福建	Fujian	174603	60498	35	6544	2247	34
江西	Jiangxi	215863	135140	63	29225	18882	65
山东	Shandong	431788	294624	68	92945	64948	70
河南	Henan	485229	348422	72	59576	44574	75
湖北	Hubei	246379	123987	50	15202	5306	35
湖南	Hunan	256009	87066	34	3089	1946	63
广东	Guangdong	644562	40777	6	21790	20549	94
广西	Guangxi	205744	93088	45	44407	9096	20
海南	Hainan	24026	16000	67	8921	5559	62
重庆	Chongqing	135821	115735	85	10408	7768	75
四川	Sichuan	709027	673768	95	56801	51608	91
贵州	Guizhou	215358	166998	78	16974	14625	86
云南	Yunnan	314619	257304	82	24652	19120	78
西藏	Tibet						
陕西	Shaanxi	404432	276955	68	20251	14978	74
甘肃	Gansu	182801	136326	75	19727	9346	47
青海	Qinghai	267662	122354	46	21267	8981	42
宁夏	Ningxia	291372	75876	26	1066	1067	100
新疆	Xinjiang	217179	179180	83	5741	6045	100

12-24 续表 continued

年份 Year 地区 Region		森林虫害 Forest Pest Plague			森林鼠害 Forest Rat Plague		
		发生面积(公顷) Area of Occurrence (hectare)	防治面积(公顷) Area of Prevention (hectare)	防治率(%) Prevention Rate (%)	发生面积(公顷) Area of Occurrence (hectare)	防治面积(公顷) Area of Prevention (hectare)	防治率(%) Prevention Rate (%)
	2000	6692820	4565910	68	891240	556500	62
	2001	6683790	4592690	69	901530	697370	77
	2002	6792324	4512293	66	875192	636056	73
	2003	7184617	4633348	64	945289	643378	68
北　京	Beijing	28357	27304	96			
天　津	Tianjin	17345	15728	91			
河　北	Hebei	356589	302256	85	3684	2300	62
山　西	Shanxi	393814	142246	36	12612	4019	32
内蒙古	Inner Mongolia	632728	428923	68	65047	65858	100
辽　宁	Liaoning	547354	447144	82	2262	1759	78
吉　林	Jilin	199503	123529	62	8329	7951	95
黑龙江	Heilongjiang	262219	214247	82	280885	258783	92
上　海	Shanghai	15232	24113	100			
江　苏	Jiangsu	49269	68031	100			
浙　江	Zhejiang	49405	46922	95			
安　徽	Anhui	241248	198067	82	136	93	68
福　建	Fujian	168059	58251	35			
江　西	Jiangxi	186638	116258	62			
山　东	Shandong	338843	229676	68			
河　南	Henan	425653	303848	71			
湖　北	Hubei	228244	118681	52	2933		
湖　南	Hunan	252920	85120	34			
广　东	Guangdong	622772	20228	3			
广　西	Guangxi	161337	83992	52			
海　南	Hainan	14630	10348	71	475	93	20
重　庆	Chongqing	105346	94767	90	20067	13200	66
四　川	Sichuan	618728	590008	95	33498	32152	96
贵　州	Guizhou	191057	148491	78	7327	3882	53
云　南	Yunnan	281587	230639	82	8380	7545	90
西　藏	Tibet						
陕　西	Shaanxi	334182	226643	68	49999	35334	71
甘　肃	Gansu	95607	65379	68	67467	61601	91
青　海	Qinghai	137345	51840	38	109050	61533	56
宁　夏	Ningxia	56308	14007	25	233998	60802	26
新　疆	Xinjiang	172298	146662	85	39140	26473	68

12-25 环境污染与破坏事故情况

Environment Pollution and Destruction Accidents

地区	Region	环境污染与破坏事故次数(次) Number of Pollution and Destruction Accidents (time)	水污染 Water Pollution	大气污染 Air Pollution	固体废物污染 Solid Wastes Pollution	噪声与振动危害 Noise and Vibration Pollution	其他 Others	污染直接经济损失(万元) Direct Economic Losses (10 000 yuan)	污染事故赔、罚款总额(万元) Reparations and Fines on Pollution Accidents (10 000 yuan)
	2000	2411	1138	864	103	266	40	17807.9	3682.6
	2001	1842	1096	576	39	80	51	12272.4	3263.9
	2002	1921	1097	597	109	97	21	4640.9	3140.7
	2003	1843	1042	654	56	50	41	3374.9	2391.5
北　京	Beijing								
天　津	Tianjin	2		2				6.7	14.0
河　北	Hebei	8	2	5		1		40.2	56.4
山　西	Shanxi	9	4	5				10.9	2.9
内蒙古	Inner Mongolia	10	7	3				55.7	11.5
辽　宁	Liaoning	17	8	5	1	3		45.2	15.3
吉　林	Jilin	7	4	2		1		9.6	15.0
黑龙江	Heilongjiang	84	81	1	1	1		34.4	40.4
上　海	Shanghai	10	6	4				59.0	4.4
江　苏	Jiangsu	30	20	7	3			28.4	7.8
浙　江	Zhejiang	229	176	49	1		3	357.5	355.1
安　徽	Anhui	68	39	24	1	4		158.0	57.1
福　建	Fujian	22	12	8			2	65.6	47.3
江　西	Jiangxi	96	81	14		1		81.5	70.6
山　东	Shandong	34	10	20			4	112.3	55.9
河　南	Henan	18	3	15				28.3	27.0
湖　北	Hubei	25	18	5	2			46.5	31.3
湖　南	Hunan	314	134	127	11	29	13	662.5	615.2
广　东	Guangdong	49	25	17	2		5	148.9	69.1
广　西	Guangxi	406	181	213	5	5	2	636.5	336.7
海　南	Hainan	4	2	2				1.6	0.8
重　庆	Chongqing	6	4	2				18.6	1.3
四　川	Sichuan	103	48	48	4	1	2	271.9	260.1
贵　州	Guizhou	32	18	12	1		1	43.3	24.1
云　南	Yunnan	115	59	44	11		1	153.6	135.5
西　藏	Tibet	16	7	5			4	6.3	23.8
陕　西	Shaanxi	119	87	14	12	4	2	132.4	98.7
甘　肃	Gansu	1	1					1.1	…
青　海	Qinghai	2	1	1				2.2	2.2
宁　夏	Ningxia	7	4		1		2	156.2	12.0
新　疆	Xinjiang								

12-26 地震灾害情况

Earthquake Disasters

年 份 地 区	Year Region	地震次数（次） Number of Earthquakes (case)	5.0-5.9级 5.0-5.9 Richter scale	6.0-6.9级 6.0-6.9 Richter scale	7.0级以上 Over 7.0 Richter scale	人员伤亡（人） Casualties (person)	#死亡人数 Deaths	经济损失（万元） Direct Economic Loss (10 000 yuan)
	2000	10	7	2		2987	10	146792
	2001	12	8	2	1	750	9	148449
	2002	5	4			362	2	14774
	2003	21	10	6	1	7465	319	466040
山 西	Shanxi	1				11		55
内蒙古	Inner Mongolia	1	1			1068	4	80649
四 川	Sichuan	3	1			9		2927
云 南	Yunnan	4	2	2		991	23	129240
西 藏	Tibet	1	1			16	2	4342
陕 西	Shaanxi	1				1		1302
甘 肃	Gansu	2	1	1		190	11	63010
青 海	Qinghai	1		1				7324
新 疆	Xinjiang	5	4	1		5125	269	151529
中俄边境	China-Russia Border	1			1			7636
中哈边境	China-Kazakhstan Border	1		1		54	10	18026

12-27 主要海洋灾害情况(2003年)

Major Marine Disasters (2003)

灾 种	Disaster Categories	发生次数（次） Occurrence (case)	灾害次数（次） Disasters (case)	人员伤亡、失踪（人） Casualties and Missing People (person)	经济损失（亿元） Economic Loss (100 million yuan)
合 计	**Total**			**128**	**80.52**
风暴潮	Stormy Tides	14	5	25	78.77
赤 潮	Red Tides	119	14		0.43
巨 浪	Huge Waves	34	10	103	1.15
溢 油	Leak of Oil	5	2		0.17

12-28 环境污染治理投资

Investment in Environment Pollution Harnessing Projects

指 标	Item	2000	2001	2002	2003
环境污染治理投资总额(亿元)	**Total Investment in Environment Pollution Harnessing Projects (100 million yuan)**	**1014.9**	**1106.7**	**1367.2**	**1627.7**
#城市环境基础设施建设投资	Investment in Urban Environment Infrastructure Facilities	515.5	595.8	789.1	1072.4
#燃气	Gas	70.9	75.5	88.4	133.5
集中供热	Central Heating	67.8	82.0	121.4	145.8
排水	Drainage Works	149.3	224.5	275.0	375.2
园林绿化	Gardening and Greenary	143.2	163.2	239.5	321.9
市容环境卫生	Environmental Sanitation	84.3	50.6	64.8	96.0
工业污染源治理投资	Investment in Harnessing Sources of Industrial Pollution	239.4	174.5	188.4	221.8
建设项目“三同时”环保投资	Investment in Environment Protection Facilities Designed Concurrently with Construction Projects	260.0	336.4	389.7	333.5
环境污染治理投资总额占国内生产总值比重(%)	**Investment in Environment Pollution Harnessing Projects as Percent of GDP (%)**	**1.13**	**1.14**	**1.30**	**1.39**

12-29 工业污染治理投资来源

Source of Investment in Industrial Pollution Harnessing Projects

年 份 Year 地 区 Region	污染治理项目当年投资来源总额(亿元) Source of Current Investment in Pollution Harnessing Projects (100 million yuan)	国家预算内资金 State Budgetary Appropriations	环保专项资金 Special Funds for Enviromental Protection	其他资金 Other Funds	#国内贷款 Domestic Loans	#利用外资 Foreign Investment	#企业自筹 Enterprise Fundraising
2000	239.40	49.60	19.30	170.50			
2001	174.50	36.30	15.80	122.30			
2002	188.40	42.00	14.80	131.60	43.60	7.20	
2003	221.80	18.75	12.38	190.66	25.10	6.78	141.94
北 京 Beijing	6.40	0.22	4.43	1.75	0.06		
天 津 Tianjin	8.70	1.10	0.14	7.48	1.40	0.35	4.64
河 北 Hebei	9.90	1.01	1.14	7.72	1.44	0.08	6.02
山 西 Shanxi	6.40	0.14	0.36	5.95	0.42	0.24	5.25
内蒙古 Inner Mongolia	2.80	0.24		2.50	0.22	1.18	0.87
辽 宁 Liaoning	15.40	2.83	0.98	11.62	1.47	0.20	9.75
吉 林 Jilin	2.60	0.14	0.01	2.49	0.08	…	2.37
黑龙江 Heilongjiang	4.90	1.29	0.07	3.53	0.45		3.05
上 海 Shanghai	2.80	…	…	2.77	0.32	…	2.43
江 苏 Jiangsu	15.00	0.04	0.96	14.03	1.35	1.03	11.62
浙 江 Zhejiang	10.50	0.51	0.27	9.67	2.28	0.14	6.63
安 徽 Anhui	5.80	0.39	0.34	5.07	0.97	1.08	2.37
福 建 Fujian	12.90	0.53	0.27	12.09	0.26	0.11	11.01
江 西 Jiangxi	0.90	…	…	0.84	0.08		0.75
山 东 Shandong	35.20	1.33	0.86	32.96	5.01	0.26	24.57
河 南 Henan	9.50	…	0.41	9.04	1.24	0.10	3.17
湖 北 Hubei	9.40	0.64	0.37	8.42	0.79	0.56	7.07
湖 南 Hunan	3.40	0.09	0.19	3.12	1.21	…	1.64
广 东 Guangdong	25.10	6.97	0.31	17.79	2.12	1.22	13.95
广 西 Guangxi	2.40	0.09	0.17	2.15	0.37		1.73
海 南 Hainan	0.30	…	…	0.27			0.26
重 庆 Chongqing	1.40	…	0.14	1.28	…	…	1.13
四 川 Sichuan	9.90	0.11	0.24	9.55	1.19	0.06	7.63
贵 州 Guizhou	2.50	0.02	0.09	2.42	0.27	…	2.08
云 南 Yunnan	4.50	0.10	0.11	4.28	0.36		3.72
西 藏 Tibet							
陕 西 Shaanxi	5.53	0.22	0.19	5.12	0.53	0.06	4.50
甘 肃 Gansu	3.57	0.31	0.12	3.15	0.64		1.78
青 海 Qinghai	0.24	0.07	…	0.17			0.16
宁 夏 Ningxia	1.17		…	1.16	0.32		0.84
新 疆 Xinjiang	2.65	0.27	0.11	2.27	0.23		0.95

12-30 工业污染治理投资完成情况

Completed Investment in Industrial Pollution Harnessing Projects

地区	Region	污染治理项目 本年完成投资（万元） Investment Completed in Pollution Hanessing Projects (10 000 yuan)	治理废水 Treatment of Waste Water	治理废气 Treatment of Waste Gas	治理固体废物 Treatment of Solid Waste	治理噪声 Treatment of Noise Pollution	治理其他 Treatment of Other Pollution	本年竣工项目数（个） Number of Projects Completed (unit)
	2000	2394390.8	1095897.4	909241.6	114673.0	60188.5	214390.3	21070
	2001	1745280.0	729214.3	657940.4	186967.2	6424.4	164733.7	10277
	2002	1883662.8	714935.1	697864.3	161287.3	10463.5	299112.6	9733
	2003	2218281.0	873747.7	921222.4	161763.4	10139.2	251408.3	9568
北京	Beijing	64065.5	4800.9	58033.6	851.8	192.3	186.9	171
天津	Tianjin	87152.2	28611.8	45626.9	6586.7	718.8	5608.0	182
河北	Hebei	98682.8	33438.3	53370.1	6214.9	1170.5	4489.0	264
山西	Shanxi	64411.7	10667.3	35434.4	12440.3	339.8	5529.9	412
内蒙古	Inner Mongolia	27697.9	20040.7	6021.9	1157.4	37.0	440.9	69
辽宁	Liaoning	154297.9	45716.0	29449.5	6141.4	103.0	72888.0	274
吉林	Jilin	26395.9	15466.3	8355.2	801.1	336.1	1437.2	172
黑龙江	Heilongjiang	48911.0	21035.6	16282.2	4496.2	476.5	6620.5	174
上海	Shanghai	28087.8	15910.9	9149.4	101.6	175.4	2750.5	164
江苏	Jiangsu	150278.8	74340.7	68671.9	2444.0	333.6	4488.6	654
浙江	Zhejiang	104529.7	60943.0	25028.7	3125.5	688.2	14744.3	683
安徽	Anhui	58087.0	16320.2	32355.7	3520.5	359.5	5531.1	189
福建	Fujian	128844.9	21707.9	86948.2	2033.3	182.4	17973.1	414
江西	Jiangxi	9181.4	1827.4	6054.8	1010.8	46.0	242.4	155
山东	Shandong	351545.0	161083.3	75459.1	61117.7	510.0	53374.9	860
河南	Henan	94855.3	35696.6	49609.8	4914.2	267.2	4367.5	665
湖北	Hubei	94314.3	29743.2	55718.8	724.5	239.3	7888.5	320
湖南	Hunan	34059.6	14262.5	12331.1	5569.9	439.0	1457.1	326
广东	Guangdong	250649.8	96041.9	111792.1	16591.7	1588.8	24635.3	1054
广西	Guangxi	24029.8	15405.8	5052.4	676.4	67.0	2828.2	322
海南	Hainan	2699.0	2214.5	295.5			189.0	28
重庆	Chongqing	14192.1	7907.5	6154.0	21.3	97.0	12.3	172
四川	Sichuan	99053.5	55190.2	31042.6	9864.4	436.8	2519.5	657
贵州	Guizhou	25371.9	11792.1	11863.5	1287.3	7.0	422.0	194
云南	Yunnan	44830.0	14276.1	26507.0	2444.7	116.0	1486.2	349
西藏	Tibet	390.0		390.0				
陕西	Shaanxi	55267.8	31715.4	18414.1	1673.2	1061.0	2404.1	297
甘肃	Gansu	35739.6	13262.6	18984.8	866.7	47.0	2578.5	170
青海	Qinghai	2403.0	602.0	1753.0	48.0			19
宁夏	Ningxia	11747.0	4429.3	5557.8	172.9	83.0	1504.0	64
新疆	Xinjiang	26508.8	9297.7	9514.3	4865.0	21.0	2810.8	94

12-31 林业系统营林固定资产投资资金来源

Source of Funds of Investment in Fixed Assets for Silviculture Performance in Forest System

单位:万元 (10 000 yuan)

年份 地区	Year Region	合计 Source of Funds This Year	上年底结余资金 Unspent Capitals from Last Year	国家预算内资金 State Budgetary Approp-riations	#国债资金 National Debts	#中央财政专项资金 Central Funds Earmarked for Environment Protection	国内贷款 Domestic Loans	利用外资 Foreign Capitals	自筹资金 Enterprise Fundraising	其他资金 Other Funds
	2000	1614486	91197	1099858	377841	431435	49052	34453	271273	68653
	2001	2015639	106744	1502046	533967	723542	55248	19971	221322	110308
	2002	3082417	147963	2472167	788071	1417855	68610	30893	246913	115871
	2003	3963491	146493	3033522	935756	1758212	86305	46065	428001	223105
北京	Beijing	87823	695	56131	10786	4426		189	29828	980
天津	Tianjin	6900		4085	3500	212	900			1915
河北	Hebei	172104	490	131885	59839	65189	7733	1852	16071	14073
山西	Shanxi	172906	2013	162986	60336	88291	350	6436	598	523
内蒙古	Inner Mongolia	336540	2298	319751	91962	215812	1033	5380	5554	2524
辽宁	Liaoning	66581		57479	24418	10343		786	7764	552
吉林	Jilin	159359	3194	131675	23251	107087	2000	25	1293	21172
黑龙江	Heilongjiang	293913	424	261986	45449	214737	195		13753	17555
上海	Shanghai	137870		68056		40	12700		34959	22155
江苏	Jiangsu	126241		5218	4114	285	390	300	103793	16540
浙江	Zhejiang	14531	4305	7787	3497	13	50		1613	776
安徽	Anhui	83017	462	56082	27001	26771	5936	2539	11835	6163
福建	Fujian	29384	54	9775	5210	1096	7331	415	8872	2937
江西	Jiangxi	45345	502	38226	17662	15711	743	141	1804	3929
山东	Shandong	97004		19875	7575	7100	6026	2978	49840	18285
河南	Henan	92778	505	70539	29684	33266	4341	1819	5694	9880
湖北	Hubei	102569	1474	71860	36803	29365	586	1004	9741	17904
湖南	Hunan	83754		32058	30106			346	49251	2099
广东	Guangdong	24201	3121	12154	4419	703	1000		4811	3115
广西	Guangxi	119679	6274	62152	27480	27016	7284	2549	28791	12629
海南	Hainan	33348	5499	11355	6433	3457	1700	5043	1827	7924
重庆	Chongqing	184652	897	177421	32971	125532	1445	499	422	3968
四川	Sichuan	463632	34292	408368	81394	299730	865	2132	5491	12484
贵州	Guizhou	204583	16593	182212	41488	133656	442	850	260	4226
云南	Yunnan	184760	22402	137889	53662	71609	3731	1036	7292	12410
西藏	Tibet	6775		6775	6775					
陕西	Shaanxi	164987	12572	143997	65754	66123		6929	775	714
甘肃	Gansu	205415		197232	58864	135065	6907	312	781	183
青海	Qinghai	70761	665	68815	18158	46832		1044	117	120
宁夏	Ningxia	38420		33150	22854	9398		1461	3809	
新疆	Xinjiang	94704	1338	64824	34311	19347	2217		21342	4983

12-32 林业系统营林固定资产投资完成情况

Completed Investment in Fixed Assets for Silviculture Performance in Forest System

年份 地区	Year Region	本年完成投资(万元) Completed Investment During the Year (10 000 yuan)	#国家投资 State Investment	#国债资金 National Debt	本年新增固定资产(万元) New Increased Fixed Assets (10 000 yuan)	本年施工项目数(个) Number of Projects During the Year (unit)
	2000	1510541	1103624	365907	425135	2456
	2001	1919835	1516932	509195	409064	3635
	2002	2976388	2479492	778882	797275	4670
	2003	3892793	3098907	945705	1283847	4130
北京	Beijing	88885	57784	11242	1872	20
天津	Tianjin	4349	2765	1520		
河北	Hebei	170365	130895	59308	73620	158
山西	Shanxi	172522	164066	60568	217	5
内蒙古	Inner Mongolia	338416	321079	92859	77436	149
辽宁	Liaoning	66581	57479	24418	29356	219
吉林	Jilin	158049	135029	23280	44979	93
黑龙江	Heilongjiang	293891	261986	45449	22712	206
上海	Shanghai	137870	68056		123314	22
江苏	Jiangsu	129191	5302	4114	3483	49
浙江	Zhejiang	10904	8491	5015	2092	47
安徽	Anhui	84494	59510	25219	64922	327
福建	Fujian	29303	9663	5225	16372	222
江西	Jiangxi	43210	37198	16689	11771	134
山东	Shandong	97004	19875	7575	19024	41
河南	Henan	91687	76977	29103	56001	220
湖北	Hubei	106246	73085	37605	52127	200
湖南	Hunan	83754	32058	30106	42189	219
广东	Guangdong	20139	10689	4791	6102	92
广西	Guangxi	116420	65214	28518	36096	364
海南	Hainan	33348	11355	6433	33348	28
重庆	Chongqing	185812	182282	32081	61590	81
四川	Sichuan	456043	440930	83183	31615	83
贵州	Guizhou	176124	169365	41533	149133	215
云南	Yunnan	168232	147248	58074	31268	269
西藏	Tibet	6775	6775	6775	6775	18
陕西	Shaanxi	165391	157661	71417	104976	236
甘肃	Gansu	206878	198870	59246	85278	184
青海	Qinghai	70761	69480	18208	53222	
宁夏	Ningxia	38420	33150	22854		4
新疆	Xinjiang	108611	54823	33297	31481	117

主要统计指标解释

水资源总量　一定区域内的水资源总量指当地降水形成的地表和地下产水量，即地表径流量与降水入渗补给量之和，不包括过境水量。

地表水资源量　指河流、湖泊、冰川等地表水体中由当地降水形成的、可以逐年更新的动态水量，即天然河川径流量。

地下水资源量　指当地降水和地表水对饱水岩土层的补给量。

地表水与地下水资源重复计算量　指地表水和地下水相互转化的部分，即在河川径流量中包括一部分地下水排泄量，地下水补给量中包括一部分来源于地表水的入渗量。

供水总量　指各种水源工程为用户提供的包括输水损失在内的毛供水量。

地表水源供水量　指地表水体工程的取水量，按蓄、引、提、调四种形式统计。从水库、塘坝中引水或提水，均属蓄水工程供水量；从河道或湖泊中自流引水的，无论有闸或无闸，均属引水工程供水量；利用扬水站从河道或湖泊中直接取水的，属提水工程供水量；跨流域调指水资源一级区或独立流域之间的跨流域调配水量，不包括在蓄、引、提水量中。

地下水源供水量　指水井工程的开采量，按浅层谈水、深层承压水和微咸水分别统计。城市地下水源供水量包括自来水厂的开采量和工矿企业自备井的开采量。

其他水源供水量　包括污水处理再利用、集雨工程、海水淡化等水源工程的供水量。

用水总量　指分配给用户的包括输水损失在内的毛用水量。按用户特性分为农业、工业、生活和生态用水四大类。

农业用水　包括农田灌溉和林牧渔业用水。林牧渔业用水指林果地灌溉、草地灌溉和鱼塘补水。

工业用水　按新水取用量计，不包括企业内部的重复利用水量。

生活用水　包括城镇生活用水和农村生活用水。城镇生活用水由居民用水和公共用水（含服务业、商饮业、货运邮电业及建筑业等用水）组成；农村生活用水除居民生活用水外，还包括畜用水在内。

生态用水　仅包括河湖人工补水和城市环境用水。

工业废水排放量　指经过企业厂区所有排放口排到企业外部的工业废水量。包括生产废水、外排的直接冷却水、超标排放的矿井地下水和与工业废水混排的厂区生活污水，不包括外排的间接冷却水(清污不分流的间接冷却水应计算在内)。

直接排入海的　指经企业位于海边的排放口，直接排入海的废水量。直接排放指废水经过工厂的排污口直接排入海，而未经过城市下水道或其他中间体，也不受其他水体的影响。

工业废水排放达标量　指报告期内废水中各项污染物指标都达到国家或地方排放标准的外排工业废水量，包括未经处理外排达标的，经废水处理设施处理后达标排放的，以及经污水处理厂处理后达标排放的。

工业废水排放达标率　指工业废水排放达标量占工业废水排放量的百分率，计算公式为：

$$\text{工业废水排放达标率}=\frac{\text{工业废水排放达标量}}{\text{工业废水排放量}}\times 100\%$$

城镇生活污水排放量　指城镇居民每年排放的生活污水。用人均系数法测算。测算公式为：

$$\begin{matrix}\text{城镇生活}\\\text{污水排放量}\end{matrix}=\begin{matrix}\text{城镇生活}\\\text{污水排放系数}\end{matrix}\times\begin{matrix}\text{市镇非}\\\text{农业人口}\end{matrix}\times 365$$

城镇生活污水中化学需氧量(COD)产生量　指城镇居民每年排放的生活污水中的COD的产生量。用人均系数法测算。测算公式为：

$$\begin{matrix}\text{城镇生活污水}\\\text{中}COD\text{产生量}\end{matrix}=\begin{matrix}\text{城镇生活污水中}\\COD\text{产生系数}\end{matrix}\times\begin{matrix}\text{市镇非}\\\text{农业人口}\end{matrix}\times 365$$

化学需氧量(COD)　测量有机和无机物质化学所消耗氧的质量浓度的水污染指数。

工业废气排放量　指报告期内企业厂区内燃料燃烧和生产工艺过程中产生的各种排入大气的含有污染物的气体的总量，以标准状态(273K，101325Pa)计算。测算公式为：

$$\begin{matrix}\text{工业废气}\\\text{排放量}\end{matrix}=\begin{matrix}\text{燃料燃烧过程}\\\text{中废气排放量}\end{matrix}+\begin{matrix}\text{生产工艺过程中}\\\text{废气排放量}\end{matrix}$$

生活及其他SO_2排放量　以生活及其他煤炭消费量和其含硫量为基础，根据以下公式计算：

$$\begin{matrix}\text{生活及其他}\\SO_2\text{排放量}\end{matrix}=\begin{matrix}\text{生活及其他}\\\text{煤炭消费量}\end{matrix}\times\text{含硫量}\times 0.8\times 2$$

工业SO_2排放量　指报告期内企业在燃料燃烧和生产工艺过程中排入大气的SO_2总量，计算公式为：

$$\begin{matrix}\text{工业}SO_2\\\text{排放量}\end{matrix}=\begin{matrix}\text{燃料燃烧过程中}\\SO_2\text{排放量}\end{matrix}+\begin{matrix}\text{生产工艺过程中}\\SO_2\text{排放量}\end{matrix}$$

工业烟尘排放量　指企业厂区内燃料燃烧过程中产生的烟气中夹带的颗粒物排放量。

生活及其他烟尘排放量　指除工业生产活动以外的所有社会、经济活动及公共设施的经营活动中燃烧所排放的烟尘纯重量。以生活及其他煤炭消费量为基础进行测算。

工业粉尘排放量　指企业在生产工艺过程中排放的能在空气中悬浮一定时间的固体颗粒物排放量。如钢铁企业的耐火材料粉尘、焦化企业的筛焦系统粉尘、烧结机的粉尘、石灰窑的粉尘、建材企业的水泥粉尘等。不包括电厂排入大气的烟尘。

工业固体废物产生量　指报告期内企业在生产过程中产

生的固体状、半固体状和高浓度液体状废弃物的总量，包括危险废物、冶炼废渣、粉煤灰、炉渣、煤矸石、尾矿、放射性废物和其他废物等；不包括矿山开采的剥离废石和掘进废石(煤矸石和呈酸性或碱性的废石除外)。酸性或碱性废石指采掘的废石其流经水、雨淋水的pH值小于4或pH值大于10.5者。

危险废物 指列入国家危险废物名录或根据国家规定的危险废物鉴别标准和鉴别方法认定的，具有爆炸性、易燃性、易氧化性、毒性、腐蚀性、易传染疾病等危险特性之一的废物。

工业固体废物综合利用量 指报告期内企业通过回收、加工、循环、交换等方式，从固体废物中提取或者使其转化为可以利用的资源、能源和其他原材料的固体废物量(包括当年利用往年的工业固体废物贮存量)，如用作农业肥料、生产建筑材料、筑路等。综合利用量由原产生固体废物的单位统计。

工业固体废物综合利用率 指工业固体废物综合利用量占工业固体废物产生量(包括综合利用往年贮存量)的百分率。计算公式为：

$$\text{工业固体废物综合利用率}=\frac{\text{工业固体废物综合利用量}}{\text{工业固体废物产生量}+\text{综合利用往年贮存量}}\times 100\%$$

工业固体废物贮存量 指报告期内企业以综合利用或处置为目的，将固体废物暂时贮存或堆存在专设的贮存设施或专设的集中堆存场所内的数量。专设的固体废物贮存场所或贮存设施必须有防扩散、防流失、防渗漏、防止污染大气、水体的措施。

工业固体废物处置量 指报告期内企业将固体废物焚烧或者最终置于符合环境保护规定要求的场所，并不再回取的工业固体废物量(包括当年处置往年的工业固体废物贮存量)。处置方式有填埋(其中危险废物应安全填埋)、焚烧、专业贮存场(库)封场处理、深层灌注、回填矿井及海洋处置(经海洋管理部门同意投海处置)等。

工业固体废物排放量 指报告期内企业将所产生的固体废物排到固体废物污染防治设施、场所以外的数量，不包括矿山开采的剥离废石和掘进废石(煤矸石和呈酸性或碱性的废石除外)。

“三废”综合利用产品产值 指报告期内利用“三废”作为主要原料生产的产品价值(现行价)；已经销售或准备销售的应计算产品价值，留作生产自用的不应计算产品价值。

生活垃圾清运量 指报告期内收集和运送到垃圾处理厂(场)的生活垃圾数量。生活垃圾指城市日常生活或为城市日常生活提供服务的活动中产生的固体废物以及法律行政规定的视为城市生活垃圾的固体废物。包括：居民生活垃圾、商业垃圾、集市贸易市场垃圾、街道清扫垃圾、公共场所垃圾和机关、学校、厂矿等单位的生活垃圾。

生活垃圾无害化处理率 指报告期生活垃圾无害化处理量与生活垃圾产生量比率。在统计上，由于生活垃圾产生量不易取得，可用清运量代替。计算公式为：

$$\text{生活垃圾无害化处理率}=\frac{\text{生活垃圾无害化处理量}}{\text{生活垃圾产生量}}\times 100\%$$

土地调查面积 指行政区域内的土地调查总面积，包括农用地、建设用地和未利用地。

农用地 指直接用于农业生产的土地，包括耕地、园地、林地、牧草地及其他农用地。

人工林面积 指由人工播种、植苗或扦插造林形成的生长稳定，(一般造林3-5年后或飞机播种5-7年后)每公顷保存株数大于或等于造林设计植树株数80%或郁闭度0.20以上(含02.0)的林分面积。

造林总面积 指报告期内在荒山、荒地、沙丘、退耕地等一切可以造林的土地上，采用人工播种、飞机播种、植苗造林、分植造林等方法新植成片乔木林和灌木林，经过检查验收符合《造林技术规程》要求的单位面积株数，并按《中华人民共和国森林法实施条例》规定，成活率达85%以上(含85%，年降雨量在400毫米以下且无浇灌条件的地区造林成活率达70%以上)的总面积。四旁植树如一侧在四行以上，连片面积0.066公顷(一亩)以上，应统计在造林面积内。造林面积，通常按所有制(国有、国有集体合作、集体和个人)、造林方式(人工、飞机播种)、主要林种用途(用材林、经济林、防护林、薪炭林、特种用途林)分组进行统计。

用材林 指以生产木材为主要目的的森林和林木，包括以生产竹材为主要目的的竹林。

速生丰产林 指在凡具备一定条件的宜林地，经过科学规划设计，相对集中连片，采取集约经营方式，以达到高速度、高质量、高标准地提供林木产品的基地上，选用生长快、成材早、材质好、经济价值高的速生优良树种，通过各项技术措施培育，以缩短林木生长周期，提高林木生长量和木材质量，并达到部颁标准(每亩年生长量0.6立方米以上)或省颁标准而营造的森林。

经济林 指以生产果品，食用油料、饮料、调料，工业原料和药材为主要目的的林木。经济林是人们为了取得林木的果实、叶片、皮层、胶液等产品作为工业原料或者供食用所营造的林木，如油茶、油桐、核桃、樟树、花椒、茶、桑、果等。

防护林 指以防护为主要目的的森林、林木和灌木丛。包括水源涵养林，水土保持林，防风固沙林，农田、牧场防护林，护岸林，护路林等。

薪炭林 指以生产燃料为主要目的的林木。

特种用途林 指以国防、环境保护、科学实验等为主要目的的森林和林木。包括国防林、实验林、母树林、环境保护林、风景林，名胜古迹和革命纪念地的林木，自然保护区的森林。

天然林保护工程 是我国林业的“天”字号工程、一号工程,也是投资最大的生态工程。具体包括三个层次:全面停止长江上游、黄河上中游地区天然林采伐；大幅度调减东北、内蒙古等重点国有林区的木材产量；同时保护好其他地区的天然林资源。主要解决这些区域天然林资源的休养生息和恢复发展问题。

退耕还林还草工程 是我国林业建设上涉及面最广、政策性最强、工序最复杂、群众参与度最高的生态建设工程。主要解决重点地区的水土流失问题。

三北和长江流域等重点防护林体系建设工程 三北和长江中下游地区等重点防护林体系建设工程,是我国涵盖面最大、内容最丰富的防护林体系建设工程。具体包括三北防护林四期工程、长江中下游及淮河太湖流域防护林二期工程、沿海防护林二期工程、珠江防护林二期工程、太行山绿化二期工程和平原绿化二期工程。主要解决三北地区的防沙治沙问题和其他区域各不相同的生态问题。

京津风沙源治理工程 环北京地区防沙治沙工程,是首都乃至中国的"形象工程",也是环京津生态圈建设的主体工程。虽然规模不大,但是意义特殊。主要解决首都周围地区的风沙危害问题。

野生动植物保护及自然保护区建设工程 野生动植物保护及自然保护区建设工程,是一个面向未来,着眼长远,具有多项战略意义的生态保护工程,也是呼应国际大气候、树立中国良好国际形象的"外交工程"。主要解决基因保存、生物多样性保护、自然保护、湿地保护等问题。

重点地区速生丰产用材林基地建设工程 重点地区以速生丰产用材林为主的林业产业基地建设工程,是我国林业产业体系建设的骨干工程,也是增强林业实力的"希望工程"。主要解决我国木材和林产品的供应问题。

湿地 指天然或人工、长久或暂时性的沼泽地、泥炭地或水域地带，包括静止或流动、淡水、半咸水、咸水体，低潮时水深不超过6米的水域以及海岸地带地区的珊瑚滩和海草床、滩涂、红树林、河口、河流、淡水沼泽、沼泽森林、湖泊、盐沼及盐湖。

红树林 指生长在热带、亚热带低能海岸潮间带上部，受周期性潮水浸淹，以红树植物为主体的常绿灌木或乔木组成的潮滩湿地木本生物群落。

自然保护区 指对有代表性的自然生态系统、珍稀濒危野生动植物物种的天然分布区、水源涵养区、有特殊意义的自然历史遗迹等保护对象所在的陆地、陆地水体或海域，依法划出一定面积进行特殊保护和管理的区域。以县及县以上各级人民政府正式批准建立的自然保护区为准(包括"六五"以前由部门或"革委会"批准且现仍存在的自然保护区)。风景名胜区、文物保护区不计在内。

生态示范区 指省级以上环境保护行政主管部门批准，以省、地、县政府为主按批准的生态示范区建设规划实施的行政区域。包括已经过国家或省级环境保护行政主管部门验收的和正在开展试点工作的。

滑坡 指斜坡上不稳定的岩土体在重力作用下沿一定软面(或滑动带)整体向下滑动的物理地质现象。地表水和地下水的作用以及人为的不合理工程活动对斜坡岩、土体稳定性的破坏，经常是促使滑坡发生的主要因素。在露天采矿、水利、铁路、公路等工程中，滑坡往往造成严重危害。

崩塌 指陡坡上大块的岩土体在重力作用下突然脱离母体崩落的物理地质现象。它可因多裂隙的岩体经强烈的物理风化、雨水渗入或地震而造成，往往毁坏建筑物，堵塞河道或交通路线。

泥石流 指山地突然爆发的包含大量泥沙、石块的特殊洪流，多见于半干旱山地高原地区。其形成条件是地形陡峻，松散堆积物丰富，有特大暴雨或大量冰融水的流出。

地面塌陷 指地表岩、土体在自然或人为因素作用下向下陷落，并在地面形成塌陷坑(洞)的一种动力地质现象。由于其发育的地质条件和作用因素的不同，地面塌陷可分为：岩溶塌陷、非岩溶塌陷。

环境污染与破坏事故 指由于违反环境保护法规的经济、社会活动与行为，以及意外因素的影响或不可抗拒的自然灾害等原因，致使环境受到污染，国家重点保护的野生动植物、自然保护区受到破坏，人体健康受到危害，社会经济和人民财产受到损失，造成不良社会影响的突发性事件。

环境污染治理投资 指在工业污染源治理和城市环境基础设施建设的资金投入中，用于形成固定资产的资金。包括工业新老污染源治理工程投资、建设项目"三同时"环保投资，以及城市环境基础设施建设所投入的资金。

营林固定资产投资 指在报告期内进行的营林基本建设和营林更新改造活动投资。

上年末结余资金 指在上年资金来源中没有形成固定资产投资额而结余的资金。包括尚未用到工程上去的材料价值、未开始安装的需要安装设备价值及结存的现金和银行存款等。

本年完成投资 指从本年1月1日起至本年最后一天止完成的全部投资额。本年完成投资是反映本年的实际投资规模，计算有关投资效果，进行年度国民经济平衡分析的重要指标。

Explanatory Notes on Main Statistical Indicators

Total Water Resources refers to total volume of water resources measured as run-off for surface water from rainfall and recharge for groundwater in a given area, excluding transit water.

Surface Water Resources refers to total renewable resources which exist in rivers, lakes, glaciers and other collectors from rainfall and are measured as run-off of rivers.

Groundwater Resources refers to replenishment of aquifers with rainfall and surface water.

Duplicated Measurement Between Surface Water and Groundwater refers to mutual exchange between surface water and groundwater, i.e. run-off of rivers includes some depletion with groundwater while groundwater includes some replenishment with surface water.

Water Supply refers to gross water supply by supply systems from sources to consumers, including losses during distribution.

Surface Water Supply refers to withdrawals by surface water supply system, broken down with storage, flow, pumping and transfer. Supply from storage projects includes withdrawals from reservoirs£» supply from flow includes withdrawals from rivers and lakes with natural flows no matter if there are locks or not; supply from pumping projects includes withdrawals from rivers or lakes with pumping stations; and supply from transfer refers to water supplies transferred from first-level regions of water resources or independent river drainage areas to others, and should not be covered under supplies of storage, flow and pumping.

Ground Water Supply refers to withdrawals from supplying wells, broken down with shallow layer freshwater, deep layer freshwater and slightly brackish water. Groundwater supply for urban areas includes water mining by both waterworks and own wells of enterprises.

Other Water Supply Sources include supplies by wastewater treatment, rain collection, seawater desalinization and other water projects.

Water Use refers to gross water use distributed to users, including loss during transportation, broken down with use by agriculture, industry, living consumption and biological protection.

Water Use by Agriculture includes uses of water by irrigation of farming fields and by forestry, animal husbandry and fishing. Water use by forestry, animal husbandry and fishing includes irrigation of forestry and orchards, irrigation of grassland and replenishment of fishing pools.

Water Use by Industry refers to new withdrawals of water, excluding reuse of water within enterprises.

Water Use by Living Consumption includes use of water for living consumption in both urban and rural areas. Urban water use by living consumption is composed of household use and public use (including services, commerce, restaurants, cargo transportation, posts, telecommunication and construction). Rural water use by living consumption includes both households and animals.

Water Use by Biological Protection includes replenishment of rivers and lakes and use for urban environment.

Waste Water Discharged by Industry refers to the volume of waste water discharged by industrial enterprises through all their outlets, including waste water from production process, directly cooled water, groundwater from mining wells which does not meet discharge standards and sewage from households mixed with waste water produced by industrial activities, but excluding indirectly cooled water discharged (It should be included if the discharge is not separated with waste water).

Waste Water Directly Discharged into Sea refers to the volume of waste water directly discharged into sea through outlets of enterprises situated by sea without going through municipal sewerage networks or any other intermediates or being affected by any other water bodies.

Industrial Waste Water Meeting Discharge Standards refers to volume of industrial waste water discharge which, with or without treatment, reaches national or local standards.

Ratio of Industrial Waste Water Meeting Discharge Standards refers to percentage of industrial waste water meeting discharge standards over total industrial waste water discharge. Its calculation formula is:

$$\text{Ratio}=\frac{\text{industrial waste water meeting discharge standards}}{\text{total industrial waste water discharge}}\times 100\%$$

Urban Consumption Waste Water Discharge refers to annual discharge of consumption waste water by urban households. Its calculation formula is:

$$\text{Discharge}=\text{discharge of consumption wastewater by urban households}\times\text{urban non-agricultural population}\times 365$$

COD Generated by Urban Consumption Waster Water refers to chemical oxygen demand generated by annual consumption waste water by urban households. Its formula is:

$$\text{COD Generated}=\begin{array}{c}\text{coefficient of COD generated}\\ \text{by annual consumption waste}\\ \text{water by urban households}\end{array}\times\frac{\text{urban non-agricultural}}{\text{population}}\times 365$$

Chemical Oxygen Demand (COD) refers to index of water pollution measuring the mass concentration of oxygen consumed by the chemical breakdown of organic and inorganic matter.

Industrial Waste Air Emission refers to discharge into atmosphere of waste air containing pollutants generated from fuel burning and production process in enterprises within a given period of time. It is converted into standard (273K, 101325Pa) with the following formula:

$$\text{Emission}=\begin{array}{c}\text{waste air emission}\\ \text{from fuel burning}\end{array}+\begin{array}{c}\text{waste air emission}\\ \text{from production process}\end{array}$$

SO_2 Emission by Consumption and Others is calculated on the basis of consumption of coal by households and others and sulphur content of coal with the following formula:

$$\text{Emission}=\begin{array}{c}\text{consumption of coal by}\\ \text{households and others}\end{array}\times\begin{array}{c}\text{sulphur content}\\ \text{of coal}\end{array}\times 0.8\times 2$$

Industrial SO_2 Emission refers to volume of sulphur dioxide emission from fuel burning and production process in premises of enterprises for a given period of time. Its calculation formula is:

$$\text{Emission}=\begin{array}{c}SO_2\text{ Emission}\\ \text{from fuel burning}\end{array}+\begin{array}{c}SO_2\text{ Emission from}\\ \text{production process}\end{array}$$

Industrial Soot Emission refers to volume of soot in smoke emitted in process of fuel burning in premises of enterprises.

Soot Emission by Consumption and Others refers to net volume of soot emitted by fuel burning from all social and economic activities and operation of public facilities other than industrial activities. It is calculated on the basis of coal consumption by households and others.

Industrial Dust Emission refers to volume of dust emitted by production process of enterprises and suspended in the air for a given period of time, including dust from refractory material of iron and steel works, dust from coke-screening systems and sintering machines of coke plants, dust from lime kilns and dust from cement production in building material enterprises, but excluding soot and dust emitted from power plants.

Industrial Solid Wastes Produced refers to total volume of solid, semi-solid and high concentration liquid residues produced by industrial enterprises from production process in a given period of time, including hazardous wastes, slag, coal ash, gangue, tailings, radioactive residues and other wastes, but excluding stones stripped or dug out in mining (gangue and acid or alkaline stones not included). A stone is acid or alkaline depending on the pH value of the water below 4 or above 10.5 when the stone is in, or soaked by, the water.

Hazardous Wastes refers to those included in the national hazardous wastes catalogue or specified as any one of the following properties in the national hazardous wastes identification standards: explosive, ignitable, oxidizable, toxic, corrosive or liable to cause infectious diseases or lead to other dangers.

Industrial Solid Wastes Utilized refers to volume of solid wastes from which useful materials can be extracted or which can be converted into usable resources, energy or other materials by means of reclamation, processing, recycling and exchange (including utilizing in the year the stocks of industrial solid wastes of the previous year). Examples of such utilizations include fertilizers, building materials and road materials. The information shall be collected by the producing units of the wastes.

Ratio of Industrial Solid Wastes Utilized refers to the percentage of industrial solid wastes utilized over industrial solid wastes produced (including stocks of the previous year). Its calculation formula is:

$$\text{Ratio}=\frac{\text{industrial solid wastes utilized}}{\begin{array}{c}\text{industrial solid wastes produced}\\ \text{+stocks of previous year utilized}\end{array}}\times 100\%$$

Stocks of Industrial Solid Wastes refers to volume of solid wastes placed in special facilities or special sites for purposes of utilization or disposal. The sites or facilities should take measures against dispersion, loss, seepage, and air and water contamination.

Industrial Solid Wastes Disposed refers to quantity of industrial solid wastes which are burnt or placed ultimately in the sites meeting the requirements for environmental protection and not salvaged or recycled (including disposition in the year of those wastes of previous years). The disposition includes landfill (Safe landfills should be conducted for hazardous wastes), incineration, containment spaces, deep underground disposal, backfill in mining pits and disposal at sea.

Industrial Solid Wastes Discharged refers to volume of industrial solid wastes discharged by producing enterprises to disposal facilities or to other sites. The wastes exclude stones stripped or dug from mining (gangue and acid or alkaline waste stones not included).

Output Value of Products Made from Waste Gas, Waste Water and Solid Wastes refers current value of products with waste gas, waste water and solid wastes as main materials of production. Products sold and ready to sell shall be included while those produced for own use shall not be included.

Consumption Wastes Transported refers to volume of consumption wastes collected and transported to disposal factories or sites. Consumption wastes are solid wastes produced from urban households or from service activities for urban households, and solid wastes regarded by laws and regulations as urban consumption wastes, including those from households, commercial activities, markets, cleaning of streets, public sites, offices, schools, factories, mining units and other sources.

Ratio of Consumption Wastes Treated refers to consumption wastes treated over that produced. In practical statistics, as it is difficult to estimate, the volume of consumption wastes produced is replaced with that transported. Its calculation formula is:

$$\text{Ratio}=\frac{\text{consumption wastes treated}}{\text{consumption wastes produced}}\times 100\%$$

Area under Land Survey refers to the total area of land, under the land survey, within the jurisdiction of the administrative region, including land for agriculture use, land for construction and unused land.

Land for Agriculture Use refers to land directly used for agriculture production, including land for cultivation, gardening, forests, herbage and other agriculture activities.

Area of Man-made Forests refer to the area of stable growing forests, planted manually or by airplanes, with a survival rate of 80% or higher of the designed number of trees per hectare, or with a canopy density of or above 0.20 after 3-5 years of manual planting or 5-7 years of airplane planting.

Total Area of Afforestation refers to the total area of land suitable for afforestation, including barren hills, idle land, sand dunes, "grain for green" land, on which acres of arbores or bushes are planted through manual planting, airplane planting, plant seedlings, etc. in accordance with the required density standards of the Technical Procedures of Afforestation, and with a survival rate of over 85% in line with the Implementing Rules of the Forest Law of the People's Republic of China (or a survival rate of 75% in areas with less that 400 mm of annual rainfall and without irrigation facilities). Included in the this category are trees planted alone the roadsides, riversides, or next to houses that occupy an area over 0.066 hectares, or where more than 4 lines of trees are planted. Total area of afforestation is further classified by ownership (state-owned, state-collective, collective or private), by approach of planting (manual, airplane), and by type of forests (timber, by-products, protection, fuel, special use, etc.).

Timber Forests refer to forests which is mainly for the production of timber, including bamboo groves planted to harvest bamboos.

Fast-growing Timber Forests refer to forests intensively planted and managed through scientific planning to produce fast-growing, high quality timber product. In these forest bases, Superior species of trees with shorter growing span, good quality and high economic value are planted and grow under various technological measures so as to meet the standards set by the Ministry of Forest (annual growth of over 0.6 cubic metres per 0.066 hectares of trees) of by the provincial authorities.

By-product Forests refer to forests that mainly produce fruits, nuts, edible oil, beverages, indigents, raw materials and medicine materials. By-product forests are planted to harvest the fruits, leaves, bark or liquid of trees, and consume them as food or raw materials for the manufacturing industry, such as tea-oil trees, tung oil trees, walnut trees, camphor trees, tea bushes, mulberry trees, fruit trees, etc.

Protection Forests refer to forests, trees and bushes planted mainly for protection or preservation purpose, including water resource conservation forests, water and soil conservation forests, windbreak and dune-fixing forests, farmland and pasture protection forests, riverside protection forests, roadside protection forests, etc.

Fuel Forests refer to forests planted mainly for fuels.

Forests for Special Purpose refer to forests planted mainly for national defence, environment protection or scientific experiments, including national defence forests, experimental forests, mother-tree forests, environment protection forests, scenery forests, trees in historical or scenic spots, forests in natural reserves.

Project on Preservation of Natural Forests is the Number One ecological project in China's forest industry that involves the largest investment. It consists of 3 components: 1) Complete halt of all cutting and logging activities in the natural forests at the upper stream of Yangtze River and the upper and middle streams of the Yellow River. 2) Significant reduction of timber production of key state forest zones in northeast provinces and in Inner Mongolia. 3) Better protection of natural forests in other regions through rehabilitation programmes.

Projects on Converting Cultivated Land to Forests and Grassland (Grain for Green Projects) aiming at preventing soil erosion in key regions, these projects are ecological construction projects in the development of forest industry that have the widest coverage and most sophisticated procedures, with strong policy implications and most active participation of the people.

Projects on Protection Forests in North China and Yangtze River Basin covering the widest areas in China with a rich variety of contents, these projects aim at solving the problem of sand and dust in northeastern China, northern China and northwestern China and the ecological issues in other areas. More specifically, they include phase IV of project on North China protection forests, phase II of project on protection forests at the middle and lower streams of Yangtze River and at the Huihe River and Taihu Lake valley, phase II of project on coastal protection forests, phase II of project on Pearl River protection forests, phase II project on greenery of Taihang Mountain and phase II projects on greenery of plains.

Projects on Harnessing Source of Sand and Dust in Beijing and Tianjin these Beijing-ring projects aim at harnessing the sand and dust weather around Beijing and its vicinities. As the key to the development of Beijing-Tianjin ecological zone, these projects are of particular importance as it concerns the image of China's capital city and the whole country.

Projects on Preserving Wild Animals and Plants and on Construction of Nature Reserves aiming at gene preservation and protection of bio-diversity, nature and wetlands, these projects look into the future with strategic perspective and are integrated with international trends.

Projects on Fast-growing Timber Forests Bases in Key Regions these are key projects for the forest industry to strengthen its capacity in supplying more timber and forest by-products.

Wetlands refer to marshland and peat bog, whether natural or man-made, permanent or temporary; water covered areas, whether stagnant or flowing, with fresh or semi-fresh or salty water that is less than 6 metres deep at low tide; as well as coral beach, weed beach, mud beach, mangrove, river outlet, rivers, fresh-water marshland, marshland forests, lakes, salty bog and salt lakes along the coastal areas.

Mangrove refer to evergreen woody plants or plant communities in tropical or sub-tropical zones which live between the sea and the land in areas which are inundated by tides.

Nature Reserves refer to certain areas of land, waters or sea that are representative in natural ecological systems, or are natural habitats for rare or endangered wild animals or plants, or water conservation zones, or the location of important natural or historic relics, which are demarked by law and put under special protection and management. Nature reserves are designated by the formal approval of governments at and above county level (including those approved by relevant departments or "revolutionary committees" before 1980). Scenic spots and cultural preservation zones are not included.

Ecological Demonstration Zones refer to administrative areas approved by the environment protection agencies of central and provincial governments and established by provincial, prefecture or county governments in line with the approved programme for ecological demonstration zones. They include those evaluated and accepted by the environment protection agencies of central and provincial governments and those under pilot development stage.

Landslides refer to the geological phenomenon of unstable rocks and earth on slopes sliding down along certain soft surface as a result of gravitational force. Role of surface water and underground water, and destruction of the stability of slopes by irrational construction work are usually main factors triggering the landslides. Several damages are often caused by landslides in open mining, in water conservancy projects, and in the construction of railways and highways.

Collapse refers to the geological phenomenon of large mass of rocks or earth suddenly collapsing from the mountain or cliff as a result of gravitational force. Usually caused by weathering of rocks, permeance of rain or earthquakes, collapse often destructs buildings and blocks river course or transport routes.

Mud-rock Flow refers to the sudden rush of flood torrents containing large amount of mud and rocks in mountainous areas. It is found mostly in semi-arid hills or plateaus. High and precipitous topographic features, loose soil mass, heavy rains or melting water contribute to the mud-rock flow.

Land Subside refers to the geological phenomenon of surface rocks or earth subsiding into holes or pits as a result of natural or human factors. Land subside can be classified as karst subside and non-karst subside.

Environment Pollution and Destruction Accidents refer to sudden accidents, due to economic or social activities that are in contrast to environment protection laws or due to unforeseen factors or natural disasters, that lead to the environment pollution, the destruction of protected wild animals, plants or nature reserves, the damage to human health, the economic and property losses, and the negative impact on the society.

Investment in Environment Pollution Harnessing Projects refers to the proportion of investment in fixed assets in the total investment in harnessing industrial pollution and in the construction of urban environment infrastructure facilities. It includes investment in harnessing sources of industrial pollution, investment in environment protection facilities designed concurrently with construction projects, and investment in urban environment infrastructure facilities.

Investment in Fixed Assets for Silviculture Performance refers to the investment in capital construction and updating projects in afforestation during the reference period.

Unspent Capitals from Last Year refer to capitals from the last year that have not been invested in the fixed assets, including value of materials that have not been used yet, the value of equipment yet to be installed, as well as cash in hand and bank deposits.

Completed Investment during the Year reflecting the actual size of investment completed during January 1 and December 31 of the reference year, this indicator is important in estimating investment efficiency and in making annual analysis of the performance of the national economy.

十三、农业

Agriculture

简要说明

一、本篇资料反映我国农业生产和农村经济的基本情况，内容主要包括乡村从业人员、耕地、农业机械拥有量、农林牧渔业产值、主要农产品产量、水利设施与除涝治碱、农村居民家庭拥有生产性固定资产、国营农场基本情况等方面的统计资料。

农业统计范围包括全社会除军马生产及农业科研机构进行的农业生产以外的所有农业生产活动。即农村各种经济组织和农户经营的农林牧渔业生产活动；各种专业性农、林、牧、渔场的农业生产活动；国家各级机关、团体、学校、部队进行的农业生产活动；集体所有制的乡、镇、村办农场的农业生产活动；以及工矿企业经营的农、林、牧、渔业生产活动。

1.农业：指对各种农作物的种植活动。包括谷物、豆类、薯类、棉花、油料、糖料、麻类、烟叶、蔬菜、园艺作物、水果、坚果、饮料和香料作物、中草药及其它作物的种植。

2.林业：包括林木的栽培(不包括茶园、桑园和果园的栽培、管理和收获等活动)、木材和竹材的采运、林产品的采集。

3.畜牧业：包括牲畜饲养和放牧、家禽饲养以及野生动物的捕猎和饲养。

4.渔业：包括水生动物和海藻类植物的养殖和捕捞。

农村社会经济统计范围包括除县城关镇以外所有乡镇的社会经济活动。

二、本篇资料来源及调查方法

1.农村基层组织、乡村从业人员和农业生产基本情况等（13-1至13-8表、13-15至13-22表），由国家统计局农村社会经济调查总队根据《农林牧渔业统计报表制度》、《农业产值综合统计报表制度》、《乡村社会经济调查方案》和《农产量抽样调查制度》的有关资料整理提供。

《农林牧渔业统计报表制度》是各省、自治区、直辖市统计局上报国家统计局的全面报表，由各级统计部门根据当地实际情况，采取抽样调查、重点调查或全面调查的办法搜集资料并逐层上报；或利用同级业务部门统计资料。如农业生产条件中的部分指标及林业生产情况、渔业生产情况等指标取自同级业务部门的统计资料。

《农产量抽样调查制度》是国家统计局为取得高质量的农产品产量等相关指标数据，在全国范围内统一抽选样本调查、推算，并由直属调查队伍实施的抽样调查制度。主要以农业普查资料作为有关标识编制抽样框，采取综合运用多阶段、多相、分层、系统随机抽样等多种方法确定调查网点选取样本，利用了多目标与规模成比例的概率抽样确定样本容量，开展多主题调查。全国共抽选了约2万个村，13万个样本地块进行实割实测调查，并运用这些样本科学地推算全国粮食产量数据，在95%的概率把握程度下，误差系数不超过±2%。农产量抽样调查实行样本轮换制度，五年为一个周期。粮食产量、播种面积、主要畜产品产量等指标来源于《农产量抽样调查制度》。

《乡村社会经济调查方案》是国家统计局为了解乡镇社会经济基本情况、农村劳动力总量规模和转移情况、以及农村固定资产投资情况等内容而专门设置的统计调查制度。制度规定对乡镇和村基本情况每三年进行一次全面调查；其他内容采用抽样调查方法，调查网点包括乡镇级调查网点、村级调查网点和住户调查网点，前两套网点分别是以全省乡镇一级单位编制抽样框和以全省村一级单位编制抽样框，抽选样本进行直接调查，住户调查网点与农村住户调查网点相同。

2.农村家庭固定资产、经营耕地及农产品出售情况（13-12至13-14表、13-25表、13-26表），由国家统计局农村社会经济调查总队根据《农村住户调查方案》的有关资料整理提供。《农村住户调查方案》的说明见本年鉴“十、人民生活”部分。

3.国营农场基本情况资料主要取材于农业部农垦局汇总的统计报表。其调查范围涉及全国除西藏外的30个省、自治区、直辖市。统计方法为逐级上报、全面汇总。指标设置及统计口径均与国家统计局一致。

4.灌溉、水库和除涝、治水、治碱情况及各地区水利设施和除涝、治碱面积资料，主要来源于水利部汇总的统计报表。其统计范围包括各省、自治区、直辖市。资料收集以县为基本统计单位，采取逐级汇总上报的方式。有些特殊指标如灌区数、大型水库、跨县的中小型水库，由地区直接统计，上报省水利厅。

5.受灾面积和成灾面积是与民政部、水利部、国家气象局等部门共同核定的数据。

Brief Introduction

I. Main Content

The data in this chapter show the basic conditions of agricultural production and rural economy, including mainly rural employed labour force, cultivated land, quantity of agricultural machinery, output of farming, forestry, animal husbandry and fishery, output of major products, facilities of water conservancy and efforts to eliminate water-logging and combat alkalinity, productive fixed assets owned by the rural households, basic conditions of the state-owned farms, and basic conditions of township enterprises.

Statistics on agriculture cover all agricultural production activities except horse raising for military purpose and activities undertaken by agriculture research institutions. Included in agriculture statistics are production activities in crop cultivation, forestry, animal husbandry and fishery undertaken by rural economic units of various types and by rural households, production activities of farms specializing in crop cultivation, forestry, animal husbandry and fishery; production activities undertaken by government agencies, institutions, schools and military units; production activities in agriculture undertaken by collective farms run by townships and villages; and production activities in crop cultivation, forestry, animal husbandry and fishery undertaken by manufacturing and mining enterprises.

(1) Agriculture: refers to cultivation of farms crops, including cereals, beans, tuber crops, cotton, oil-bearing crops, sugar crops, hemp, tobacco leaves, vegetables, gardening plants, fruits, nuts, crops for beverages and for perfumes, medicinal herbs and other farm crops.

(2) Forestry: includes the planting of trees (excluding the operation on tea plantations, mulberry fields and orchards), felling and transport of timber and bamboo and collection of forest products.

(3) Animal husbandry: includes the raising and grazing of domestic animals and poultry, and the hunting and raising of wild animals.

(4) Fishery: includes cultivation and catching of aquatic animals and seaweed.

The rural social and economic statistics cover social and economic activities in all townships except that taking place in county towns.

II. Source of Data and Survey Methodology

(1) Data on rural grassroots units, employed labour force and agricultural production (tables 13-1 to 13-8, tables 13-15 to 13-22) are provided by the Rural Socio-economic Survey Organization, NBS using data from the *Comprehensive Statistical Reporting on Farming, Forestry, Animal Husbandry and Fishery*, the *Comprehensive Statistical Reporting on Agricultural Output*, the *Rural Social and Economic Survey*, and the *Sample Survey of Farm Crops*.

Comprehensive Statistical Reporting on Farming, Forestry, Animal Husbandry and Fishery is a comprehensive reporting program reported by provincial statistical bureaus to the National Bureau of Statistics. Data required in this reporting program are collected by statistical offices at all levels by means of sample surveys, surveys of key units or full enumeration depending on the local circumstances, or estimated by using information from other government agencies at the same level or from the sample survey of farm crops and rural household survey conducted by NBS. For instance, some data on condition of agriculture production and on forestry and fishery are obtained from statistics collected by other government agencies at the same level.

Sample Survey of Farm Crops is a nation-wide survey designed by NBS and implemented by sample survey teams throughout China with unified sample selection and estimation procedure, in order to obtain high quality data on grain production and related statistics. Using data from the agriculture census as sampling frame, a total of 130,000 sample plots are selected from some 20,000 villages in the country through a comprehensive multi-stage and multi-phase stratified systematic sampling programme. Actual crop cutting and measuring is conducted on these plots to estimate the national production. The survey is characterized by a multi-purpose probability proportional to size sample design that keeps sampling error to ±2% with the confidence probability as 95%. A rotation scheme is used in the sample survey on farm crops with the cycle of a complete rotation being 5 years. Data on crop production, crop planting acreage and production of major animal husbandry products are collected are from the *Sample Survey of Farm Crops*.

Rural Social and Economic Survey is a special survey designed by the NBS to understand the basic condition of social and economic activities at township level, the size and transfer of total rural labour force and investment in fixed assets in rural areas. Under this survey program, a complete enumeration is conducted every 3 years to collect information on basic condition of social and economic activities at township and village levels, while sample survey is used to collect information on other items with the same sampling units as in the Rural Household Survey.

(2) Data on the fixed assets, cultivated land and sales of farm products of rural households (tables 13-12 to 13-14, tables 13-25 to 13-26) are collected and compiled by the Rural Socio-economic Survey Organization, NBS through the *Rural Household Survey Programme*. Please refer to Chapter 10 (People's Livelihood) of the Yearbook for description of the *Rural Household Survey Programme.*

(3) Data on the basic conditions of the state-owned farms come from the statistical reports tabulated by the Bureau of Reclamation, Ministry of Agriculture. The statistical coverage includes 30 provinces, autonomous regions and municipalities directly under the central government; except Tibet. Data are collected from the grassroots units in accordance with the statistical reporting scheme and tabulated and reported level by level. The content of indicators and calculation methods are consistent with those stipulated by the National Bureau of Statistics.

(4) Data on irrigation and reservoirs, the data on the efforts to eliminate water-logging, prevent floods by water control and combat alkalinity as well as the data on the facilities of water conservancy and the area of water-logging eliminated and the improved area of saline-alkaline land come mainly from statistical reports of the Ministry of Water Conservancy. The statistical coverage includes provinces, autonomous regions and municipalities directly under the central government. County is the basic statistical unit. The data are collected from the counties in accordance with the statistical reporting scheme and tabulated and reported level by level. Data on some special indicators such as the number of irrigated areas, large reservoirs and the medium-sized and small reservoirs that cut across counties are collected directly by the prefectures and reported to the water conservancy departments of the provinces.

(6)Data on disaster-covered areas and disaster-affected areas are figures jointly confirmed by NBS in consultation with Ministry of Civil affairs, Ministry of Water Conservancy and National Bureau of Meteorology.

13-1 农村基层组织和农业基本情况

Basic Conditions of Rural Grassroots Units and Agriculture

指　　标	Item	1999	2000	2002	2003
乡镇数 (个)	Number of Township and Town Governments (unit)	44741	43735	39054	38028
#镇数	Number of Town Governments	19184	19692	19811	19588
村民委员会 (个)	Number of Villagers' Committees (unit)	737429	734715	694515	678589
乡村户数 (万户)	Number of Rural Households (10 000 units)	23810.5	24148.7	24569.4	24793.1
乡村从业人员 (万人)	Number of Rural Laborers (10 000 persons)	46896.5	47962.1	48526.9	48971.0
男	Male	24995.7	25517.8	25850.1	26121.0
女	Female	21900.8	22444.3	22676.7	22850.0
按行业分乡村从业人员 (万人)	Number of Rural Laborers by Sector (10 000 persons)	46896.5	47962.1	48526.9	48971.0
农林牧渔业	Farming, Forestry, Animal Husbandry & Fishery	32911.8	32797.5	31990.6	31259.6
工业	Industry	3953.0	4108.6	4505.6	4937.1
建筑业	Construction	2531.9	2691.7	2959.0	3201.0
交通运输业、仓储及邮电通信业	Transport, Storage, Post and Telecommunication Services	1115.8	1170.6	1259.1	1328.2
批发零售贸易业餐饮业	Wholesale, Retail Trade and Catering Services	1584.6	1751.8	1996.8	2059.1
其他非农行业	Other Non-agricultural Trades	4799.3	5441.9	5815.8	6186.0
农业机械总动力 (万千瓦)	Total Agricultural Machinery Power (10 000 kw)	48996.1	52573.6	57929.9	60386.5
农用大中型拖拉机 (台)	Number of Large and Medium Agricultural Tractors (unit)	784216	974547	911670	980560
农用大中型拖拉机动力 (万千瓦)	Capacity of Large and Medium Agricultural Tractors (10 000 kw)	2772.8	3161.1	3073.4	3229.8
小型拖拉机 (万台)	Number of Mini-tractors (10 000 unit)	1200.3	1264.4	1339.4	1377.7
小型拖拉机动力 (万千瓦)	Capacity of Mini-tractors (10 000 kw)	11008.9	11663.9	12695.0	13060.2
大中型拖拉机配套农具 (万部)	Number of Large and Medium Tractor Towing Farm Machinery (10 000 unit)	132.0	140.0	157.9	169.8
小型拖拉机配套农具 (万部)	Mini-Tractor Towing Farm Machinery (10 000 unit)	1621.0	1788.8	2003.4	2117.2
农用排灌柴油机 (万台)	Number of Diesel Engines (10 000 unit)	645.0	688.1	750.6	749.6
农用排灌柴油机动力 (万千瓦)	Capacity of Diesel Engines (10 000 kw)	4934.6	5232.6	5667.9	5592.8
渔用机动船 (艘)	Number of Motorized Fishing Boats (unit)	417379	459888	485693	478123
渔用机动船动力 (万千瓦)	Capacity of Motorized Fishing Boats (10 000 kw)	1253.1	1338.7	1381.2	1425.9
有效灌溉面积 (千公顷)	Irrigated Area (1 000 hectares)	53158	53820	54355	54014
化肥施用量 (万吨)	Consumption of Chemical Fertilizers (10 000tons)	4124.3	4146.4	4339.4	4411.6
乡村办水电站个数 (个)	Number of Hydropower Stations in Rural Areas (unit)	31678	29962	27633	26696
乡村办水电站发电能力 (万千瓦)	Generating Capacity of Hydropower Station in Rural Areas (10 000 kw)	664.1	698.5	812.2	862.3
农村用电量 (亿千瓦小时)	Electricity Consumed in Rural Areas(100 million kwh)	2173.4	2421.3	2993.4	3432.9
农作物总播种面积 (千公顷)	Total Sown Area (1 000 hectares)	156373	156300	154636	152415
粮食	Grain Crops	113161	108463	103891	99410
谷物	Cereal	91617	85264	81466	76810
#稻谷	Rice	31284	29962	28202	26508
小麦	Wheat	28855	26653	23908	21997
玉米	Corn	25904	23056	24634	24068
豆类	Beans	11190	12660	12543	12898
薯类	Tubers	10355	10538	9881	9702
油料	Oil-bearing Crops	13906	15400	14766	14990
棉花	Cotton	3726	4041	4184	5111
麻类	Fiber Crops	205	262	338	337
糖料	Sugar Crops	1644	1514	1818	1657
烟叶	Tobacco	1374	1437	1328	1264
蔬菜	Vegetables	13347	15237	17353	17954
茶园面积 (千公顷)	Area of Tea Plantations (1 000 hectares)	1130	1089	1134	1207
果园面积 (千公顷)	Area of Orchards (1 000 hectares)	8667	8932	9098	9437

注：2003年大中型拖拉机中不含变形拖拉机，2002年数据相应做了调整。

a) Number of large and medium agricultural tractors excluded the transfiguration tractors in 2003, the data in 2002 were adjusted accordingly.

13-2 主要农牧渔业生产情况

Output of Farming, Animal Husbandry and Fishery

指 标	Item	1999	2000	2001	2002	2003
农产品产量 (万吨)	Yield of Farm Crops (10 000 tons)					
粮食	Grain	50838.6	46217.5	45263.7	45705.8	43069.5
谷物	Cereal	45304.1	40522.4	39648.2	39798.7	37428.7
#稻谷	Rice	19848.7	18790.8	17758.0	17453.9	16065.6
小麦	Wheat	11388.0	9963.6	9387.3	9029.0	8648.8
玉米	Corn	12808.6	10600.0	11408.8	12130.8	11583.0
豆类	Beans	1894.0	2010.0	2052.8	2241.2	2127.5
薯类	Tubers	3640.6	3685.2	3563.1	3665.9	3513.3
油料	Oil-bearing Crops	2601.2	2954.8	2864.9	2897.2	2811.0
#花生	Peanuts	1263.9	1443.7	1441.6	1481.8	1342.0
油菜籽	Rapeseeds	1013.2	1138.1	1133.1	1055.2	1142.0
芝麻	Sesame	74.3	81.1	80.4	89.5	59.3
棉花	Cotton	382.9	441.7	532.4	491.6	486.0
麻类	Fiber Crops	47.2	52.9	68.1	96.4	85.3
#黄红麻	Jute and Ambary Hemp	16.4	12.6	10.6	15.9	10.0
甘蔗	Sugarcane	7470.3	6828.0	7566.3	9010.7	9023.5
甜菜	Beetroots	863.9	807.3	1088.9	1282.0	618.2
烟叶	Tobacco	246.9	255.2	235.0	244.7	225.7
#烤烟	Flue-Cured Tobacco	218.5	223.8	204.5	213.5	201.5
蚕茧	Silkworm Cocoons	48.5	54.8	65.5	69.8	66.7
#桑蚕茧	Mulberry Silkworm Cocoons	44.7	50.1	60.2	64.5	61.1
茶叶	Tea	67.6	68.3	70.2	74.5	76.8
水果	Fruits	6237.6	6225.1	6658.0	6952.0	14517.4
农产品单位面积产量 (公斤/公顷)	Yield of Farm Crops per Hectare (kg/hectare)					
谷物	Cereal	4945	4753	4800	4885	4873
棉花	Cotton	1028	1093	1107	1175	951
花生	Peanuts	2961	2973	2888	3011	2654
油菜籽	Rapeseeds	1469	1519	1597	1477	1582
芝麻	Sesames	1066	1034	1061	1180	863
黄红麻	Jute and Ambary Hemp	2531	2516	2046	2868	2462
甘蔗	Sugarcane	57338	57626	60625	64663	64023
甜菜	Beetroots	25335	24518	26807	30232	24925
烤烟	Flue-Cured Tobacco	1797	1763	1732	1792	1768
大牲畜年底头数(万头)	Number of Large Animals (year-end,10 000 heads)	15024.8	15151.5	14995.9	15189.3	15500.1
#牛	Cattle and Buffaloes	12698.3	12866.3	12824.2	13084.8	13467.2
马	Horses	891.4	876.6	826.0	808.8	790.0
驴	Donkeys	934.8	922.7	881.5	849.9	820.7
骡	Mules	467.3	453.0	436.2	419.4	395.7
骆驼	Camels	33.0	32.6	27.9	26.4	26.5
肉猪出栏头数 (万头)	Number of Slaughtered Fattened Hogs (10000 heads)	50749.0	52673.3	54936.7	56684.0	59200.5
猪年底头数 (万头)	Number of Hogs (year-end,10 000 heads)	43144.2	44681.5	45743.0	46291.5	46601.7
羊年底只数 (万只)	Number of Sheep and Goats (year-end,10 000 heads)	27925.8	29031.9	29826.4	31655.2	34053.7
山羊	Goats	14816.3	15715.9	16129.2	17275.9	18320.7
绵羊	Sheep	13109.5	13316.0	13697.2	14379.3	15733.0
肉类产量 (万吨)	Output of Meat (10 000 tons)	5820.7	6125.4	6333.9	6586.5	6932.9
#猪牛羊肉	Pork Beef and Mutton	4647.4	4838.2	5026.0	5227.9	5506.3
猪肉	Pork	3890.7	4031.4	4184.5	4326.6	4518.6
牛肉	Beef	505.4	532.8	548.8	584.6	630.4
羊肉	Mutton	251.3	274.0	292.7	316.7	357.2
奶类 (万吨)	Milk (10 000 tons)	806.9	919.1	1122.9	1400.4	1848.6
#牛奶	Cow Milk	717.6	827.4	1025.5	1299.8	1746.3
绵羊毛 (吨)	Sheep Wool (ton)	283152	292502	298254.2	307588	338058
山羊毛 (吨)	Goat Wool (ton)	31849	33266	34240.5	35459	36692
羊绒 (吨)	Cashmere (ton)	10180	11057	10967.7	11765	13528
禽蛋 (万吨)	Poultry Eggs (10 000 tons)	2134.7	2243.3	2336.7	2462.7	2606.7
水产品总产量 (万吨)	Total Aquatic Products (10 000 tons)	4122.4	4278.5	4381.3	4564.5	4704.6
海水产品	Seawater Aquatic Products	2471.9	2538.7	2571.7	2646.3	2685.8
淡水产品	Freshwater Aquatic Products	1650.5	1739.7	1809.6	1918.2	2018.8

注：2003年水果产量包括瓜果类产量.

a) Output of fruits in 2003 includes yield of melon and fruit.

13-3 农村基层组织情况

Basic Conditions of Rural Grassroot Unit

年份 地区	Year Region	乡镇数(个) Number of Township and Town Government (unit)	#镇数 Town Government	村民委员会(个) Number of Villager' Committee (unit)	乡村户数(万户) Number of Household (10 000 households)	乡村人口数(万人) Rural Population (10 000 persons)	乡村从业人员(万人) Number of Rural Laborer (10 000 persons)	男 Male	女 Female
	1978	52781		690000	17347.0	80320.0	30638.0	16548.4	14089.6
	1980	54183		709820	17673.0	81096.0	31835.7	17379.7	14456.2
	1985	91138	7956	940617	19077.0	84419.7	37065.1	20153.2	16911.9
	1989	55764	11060	746432	21504.0	87831.0	40938.8	22218.0	18721.0
	1990	55838	11392	743278	22237.0	89590.3	42009.5	22551.8	19457.7
	1991	55542	11882	804153	22566.0	90525.1	43092.5	23121.9	19970.6
	1992	48250	14135	806032	22849.0	91154.4	43801.6	23449.9	20351.7
	1993	48179	15223	802352	22984.0	91333.5	44255.7	23653.1	20602.6
	1994	48075	16433	802052	23165.0	91526.2	44654.1	23854.1	20800.1
	1995	47136	17282	740150	23282.0	91674.6	45041.8	24037.4	21004.4
	1996	45484	17998	740128	23437.6	91941.0	45288.0	24154.9	21133.1
	1997	44689	18402	739447	23406.2	91524.7	45962.1	24500.6	21462.1
	1998	45462	19060	739980	23678.0	91960.1	46432.3	24733.1	21699.2
	1999	44741	19184	737429	23810.5	92216.3	46896.5	24995.7	21900.8
	2000	43735	19692	734715	24148.7	92819.7	47962.1	25517.8	22444.3
	2001	40161	19555	709257	24432.2	93382.9	48228.9	25685.4	22543.5
	2002	39054	19811	694515	24569.4	93502.5	48526.9	25850.1	22676.7
	2003	38028	19588	678589	24793.1	93750.6	48971.0	26121.0	22850.0
北京	Beijing	190	143	4003	131.1	360.6	169.6	87.9	81.7
天津	Tianjin	140	120	3825	115.1	391.4	173.8	94.7	79.1
河北	Hebei	1971	937	49752	1436.1	5383.0	2748.0	1470.8	1277.3
山西	Shanxi	1191	477	28745	630.1	2335.5	1012.8	560.6	452.2
内蒙古	Inner Mongolia	1138	427	12269	351.0	1358.1	652.3	366.3	286.0
辽宁	Liaoning	1011	617	13720	692.1	2325.6	1016.3	566.2	450.1
吉林	Jilin	774	457	9569	377.9	1439.4	669.0	385.3	283.7
黑龙江	Heilongjiang	904	452	9018	479.1	1895.6	936.1	535.8	400.3
上海	Shanghai	127	124	1991	114.1	355.9	250.1	130.1	120.0
江苏	Jiangsu	1259	1133	19520	1551.4	5209.7	2649.1	1372.5	1276.6
浙江	Zhejiang	1334	791	38322	1168.7	3712.1	2219.9	1186.7	1033.3
安徽	Anhui	1739	970	28852	1320.6	5142.7	2861.7	1530.0	1331.8
福建	Fujian	960	608	14894	679.4	2675.8	1283.7	691.7	592.0
江西	Jiangxi	1449	768	17955	776.1	3244.9	1588.4	831.2	757.2
山东	Shandong	1476	1180	86666	2043.1	7044.4	3718.4	1975.2	1743.1
河南	Henan	2014	771	48442	2005.8	7936.1	4695.0	2483.5	2211.5
湖北	Hubei	964	739	27634	997.9	3958.0	1832.5	970.7	861.8
湖南	Hunan	2357	1098	50195	1468.7	5425.9	2914.4	1579.1	1335.3
广东	Guangdong	1395	1379	22574	1487.4	6174.8	2824.5	1479.2	1345.4
广西	Guangxi	1325	747	14601	950.2	4088.7	2216.3	1170.8	1045.4
海南	Hainan	200	180	2633	108.7	511.4	240.3	124.3	116.0
重庆	Chongqing	1183	642	14357	718.7	2436.5	1340.3	715.1	625.2
四川	Sichuan	5008	1931	54742	1967.2	6872.1	3759.6	1992.6	1767.1
贵州	Guizhou	1381	621	22245	762.5	3201.5	1874.9	992.9	882.0
云南	Yunnan	1406	467	13308	885.3	3510.8	2002.7	1041.5	961.2
西藏	Tibet	685	142	6047	39.0	221.2	103.6	52.7	51.0
陕西	Shaanxi	1544	862	28956	698.2	2770.6	1396.2	764.0	632.2
甘肃	Gansu	1523	442	17491	457.1	2055.7	1050.5	555.9	494.6
青海	Qinghai	392	107	4133	73.8	347.3	180.6	94.6	86.0
宁夏	Ningxia	189	89	2685	92.2	407.6	208.5	109.0	99.5
新疆	Xinjiang	799	167	9445	214.8	957.8	382.3	210.6	171.6

注：本表乡村人口数是指户口在乡村的常住人口，具体范围按1964年建镇标准划分，包括后来的新建制镇人口，口径大于人口篇的乡村总人口。

a)Total rural population refers to persons residing and registered in rural areas. This indicator is calculated on the basis of the town classification standards of 1964 which includes rural population in what are now established towns. Therefore, the statistical coverage in the table are larger than the rural population shown in Chapter 4.

13-4 乡村从业人员(年底数)

Rural Laborers at the Year-end

本表分行业从业人员是按从事的主行业划分的，如以农业为主、兼营商业的，仍作为农林牧渔业从业人员。

The number of laborers by sector in this table is classified by main economic activity. For example, those engaged primarily in agriculture and secondarily in commerce are classified as the laborers under farming, forestry, animal husbandry and fishery.

单位: 万人 (10 000 persons)

年份 地区	Year Region	农林牧渔业 Farming, Forestry, Animal Husbandry and Fishery	工业 Industry	建筑业 Construction	交通运输业、仓储及邮电通信业 Transport Storage, Post and Communication Services	批发零售贸易业餐饮业 Wholesale, Retail Trade and Catering Services	其他非农行业 Other Nonagricultural Trades
	1978	28455.6					
	1980	29808.4	916.3				
	1985	30351.5	2741.0	1130.1	434.1	462.6	1945.8
	1989	32440.5	3255.6	1501.8	614.2	652.4	2474.3
	1990	33336.4	3228.7	1522.8	635.3	693.2	2593.1
	1991	34186.3	3267.9	1533.8	655.0	722.8	2726.7
	1992	34037.0	3468.2	1658.8	706.3	813.7	3117.6
	1993	33258.2	3659.0	1886.8	799.9	948.8	3703.1
	1994	32690.3	3849.5	2057.3	908.3	1084.3	4064.5
	1995	32334.5	3970.7	2203.6	983.0	1170.4	4379.7
	1996	32260.4	4018.5	2304.3	1027.6	1261.5	4415.7
	1997	32434.9	4031.3	2372.7	1057.8	1381.5	4683.9
	1998	32626.4	3928.6	2453.5	1087.9	1461.9	4874.0
	1999	32911.8	3953.0	2531.9	1115.8	1584.6	4799.3
	2000	32797.5	4108.6	2691.7	1170.6	1751.8	5441.9
	2001	32451.0	4296.0	2797.4	1205.4	1864.5	5614.6
	2002	31990.6	4505.6	2959.0	1259.1	1996.8	5815.8
	2003	31259.6	4937.1	3201.0	1328.2	2059.1	6186.0
北京	Beijing	59.5	32.5	16.4	16.1	18.9	26.2
天津	Tianjin	81.2	45.1	12.9	11.9	14.7	8.0
河北	Hebei	1660.2	441.9	243.7	101.0	124.9	176.3
山西	Shanxi	646.0	129.8	57.5	56.6	41.6	81.4
内蒙古	Inner Mongolia	514.4	21.3	25.3	12.6	19.3	59.5
辽宁	Liaoning	667.3	85.8	65.7	39.8	55.0	102.7
吉林	Jilin	502.5	25.2	29.3	16.9	22.5	72.6
黑龙江	Heilongjiang	734.8	40.5	35.7	22.1	35.5	67.5
上海	Shanghai	71.7	112.5	11.7	7.1	14.3	32.8
江苏	Jiangsu	1230.3	509.3	287.3	93.9	119.9	408.3
浙江	Zhejiang	873.0	647.4	130.9	79.6	191.2	297.9
安徽	Anhui	1860.6	228.8	229.5	72.8	122.4	347.8
福建	Fujian	735.9	174.5	85.0	38.8	68.4	181.1
江西	Jiangxi	971.3	132.6	86.1	30.5	46.5	321.4
山东	Shandong	2264.6	431.1	330.3	133.5	192.1	366.7
河南	Henan	3321.2	432.0	331.6	126.9	210.4	272.9
湖北	Hubei	1110.7	112.6	113.3	48.3	73.2	374.3
湖南	Hunan	1997.7	224.9	148.0	62.0	99.5	382.3
广东	Guangdong	1543.4	467.0	199.7	74.4	149.8	390.3
广西	Guangxi	1541.0	78.1	93.7	38.5	62.4	402.5
海南	Hainan	187.3	8.3	8.1	6.3	11.1	19.3
重庆	Chongqing	813.2	78.3	102.5	22.6	36.0	287.7
四川	Sichuan	2414.0	216.0	269.6	65.3	137.2	657.5
贵州	Guizhou	1322.1	73.7	44.2	23.0	43.4	368.5
云南	Yunnan	1690.2	54.3	59.2	38.2	39.6	121.3
西藏	Tibet	84.4	1.9	5.8	2.3	2.2	7.0
陕西	Shaanxi	989.0	64.8	88.8	40.4	49.1	164.1
甘肃	Gansu	760.8	34.7	53.0	22.3	27.6	152.1
青海	Qinghai	134.8	8.9	10.0	5.1	5.6	16.1
宁夏	Ningxia	145.8	12.8	19.7	9.6	10.6	10.0
新疆	Xinjiang	330.9	10.5	6.9	9.9	14.4	9.8

注：工业从业人员中包括村及村以下办的工业从业人员。

a) Number of employed persons of industry includes those working in enterprises at village and lower levels.

13-5 各地区耕地面积

Area of Cultivated Land by Region

地 区	Region	耕地面积（总资源）（千公顷） Cultivated Land (Total Area) (1 000 hectares)	占全国比重 (%) Percentage to Total Area (%)
全国总计	**National Total**	**130039.2**	**100.00**
北 京	Beijing	343.9	0.26
天 津	Tianjin	485.6	0.37
河 北	Hebei	6883.3	5.29
山 西	Shanxi	4588.6	3.53
内蒙古	Inner Mongolia	8201.0	6.31
辽 宁	Liaoning	4174.8	3.21
吉 林	Jilin	5578.4	4.29
黑龙江	Heilongjiang	11773.0	9.05
上 海	Shanghai	315.1	0.24
江 苏	Jiangsu	5061.7	3.89
浙 江	Zhejiang	2125.3	1.63
安 徽	Anhui	5971.7	4.59
福 建	Fujian	1434.7	1.10
江 西	Jiangxi	2993.4	2.30
山 东	Shandong	7689.3	5.91
河 南	Henan	8110.3	6.24
湖 北	Hubei	4949.5	3.81
湖 南	Hunan	3953.0	3.04
广 东	Guangdong	3272.2	2.52
广 西	Guangxi	4407.9	3.39
海 南	Hainan	762.1	0.59
四 川	Sichuan	9169.1	7.05
贵 州	Guizhou	4903.5	3.77
云 南	Yunnan	6421.6	4.94
西 藏	Tibet	362.6	0.28
陕 西	Shaanxi	5140.5	3.95
甘 肃	Gansu	5024.7	3.86
青 海	Qinghai	688.0	0.53
宁 夏	Ningxia	1268.8	0.98
新 疆	Xinjiang	3985.7	3.07

注：本表数据来源于国土资源部、国家统计局、全国农业普查办公室“关于土地利用现状调查数据成果的公报”，耕地面积（总资源）数据为1996年10月31日时点数。据国家统计局初步测算，2001年耕地总资源为127082千公顷，其中：常用耕地面积为105826千公顷，临时性耕地面积为21256千公顷。

a) Data come from the "*Communique of Main Data on Land Use Survey*" issued by the Ministry of Land and Resources, National Bureau of Statistics, and National Agricultural Census Office of China. The cultivated areas is the data at Oct. 31, 1996. According to the estimation by National Bureau of Statistics, area of cultivated land (total area) in 2001 is 127 082 000 hectares, of which, regularly cultivated land is 105 826 000 hectares, and temporarily cultivated land is 21 256 000 hectares.

13-6 农、林、牧、渔业总产值及指数

Gross Output Value of Farming, Forestry, Animal Husbandry and Fishery and Related Indices

本表绝对数按当年价格计算，指数按可比价格计算。2003年执行新国民经济行业分类标准，总产值包括农林牧渔服务业产值.

Data in value terms in this table are calculated at current prices, while the indices are calculated at comparable prices.

年 份 地 区	Year Region	绝对数（亿元） Gross Output Value of Farming, Forestry, Animal Husbandry and Fishery (100 million yuan)					指 数（上年=100） Indices of Gross Output of Farming, Forestry, Animal Husbandry and Fishery (preceding year=100)				
		农林牧渔业总产值 Total	#农 业 Farming	#林 业 Forestry	#牧 业 Animal Husbandry	#渔 业 Fishery	农林牧渔业总产值 Total	#农 业 Farming	#林 业 Forestry	#牧 业 Animal Husbandry	#渔 业 Fishery
	1978	1397.0	1117.5	48.1	209.3	22.1					
	1980	1922.6	1454.1	81.4	354.2	32.9	101.4	99.7	112.2	107.0	107.7
	1985	3619.5	2506.4	188.7	798.3	126.1	103.4	99.8	104.5	117.2	118.9
	1989	6534.7	4100.6	284.9	1800.4	348.8	103.1	102.4	100.4	105.5	107.2
	1990	7662.1	4954.3	330.3	1967.0	410.6	107.6	108.0	103.1	107.0	110.0
	1991	8157.0	5146.4	367.9	2159.2	483.5	103.7	100.9	108.0	108.8	107.6
	1992	9084.7	5588.0	422.6	2460.5	613.5	106.4	104.2	107.7	108.8	115.3
	1993	10995.5	6605.1	494.0	3014.4	882.0	107.8	105.2	108.0	110.8	118.4
	1994	15750.5	9169.2	611.1	4672.0	1298.2	108.6	103.2	108.9	116.7	120.0
	1995	20340.9	11884.6	709.9	6045.0	1701.3	110.9	107.9	105.0	114.8	119.4
	1996	22353.7	13539.8	778.0	6015.5	2020.4	109.4	107.8	105.7	111.4	114.0
	1997	23788.4	13852.5	817.8	6835.4	2282.7	106.7	104.5	103.3	110.1	111.5
	1998	24541.9	14241.9	851.3	7025.8	2422.9	106.0	104.9	102.9	107.4	108.8
	1999	24519.1	14106.2	886.3	6997.6	2529.0	104.7	104.3	103.2	104.6	107.2
	2000	24915.8	13873.6	936.5	7393.1	2712.6	103.6	101.4	105.4	106.3	106.5
	2001	26179.6	14462.8	938.8	7963.1	2815.0	104.2	103.6	99.3	106.3	103.9
	2002	27390.8	14931.5	1033.5	8454.6	2971.1	104.9	103.9	107.1	106.0	106.1
	2003	29691.8	14870.1	1239.9	9538.8	3137.6	103.9	100.5	106.9	107.3	105.3
北 京	Beijing	246.8	88.8	13.5	125.5	10.2	104.1	98.2	116.1	108.5	104.6
天 津	Tianjin	213.9	88.2	1.6	77.2	26.4	106.9	100.0	103.8	113.6	106.7
河 北	Hebei	1956.9	958.3	41.3	820.6	57.7	106.3	105.6	111.7	107.3	99.4
山 西	Shanxi	403.6	249.5	20.4	111.9	2.0	104.7	104.0	79.7	110.1	106.3
内蒙古	Inner Mongolia	666.4	336.0	47.9	267.1	4.9	106.2	94.8	112.9	122.0	87.2
辽 宁	Liaoning	1215.0	497.3	38.4	422.0	224.0	107.1	104.2	114.2	109.0	107.1
吉 林	Jilin	792.1	438.3	33.8	298.4	13.6	106.3	105.0	102.4	108.6	106.4
黑龙江	Heilongjiang	903.3	502.9	59.1	294.2	23.1	103.0	96.5	102.5	115.4	106.0
上 海	Shanghai	247.3	98.2	13.1	81.1	49.2	101.1	92.9	133.4	95.0	123.0
江 苏	Jiangsu	1952.2	981.2	31.5	458.9	371.6	101.0	94.3	120.0	102.8	106.6
浙 江	Zhejiang	1184.0	529.4	65.7	233.0	337.1	104.2	105.0	102.7	102.0	103.0
安 徽	Anhui	1305.4	617.9	73.4	443.5	129.7	94.0	83.3	95.0	109.2	99.7
福 建	Fujian	1151.2	466.8	79.3	237.3	351.9	103.7	102.6	101.5	105.4	104.8
江 西	Jiangxi	841.6	383.7	70.5	254.0	118.5	102.7	99.5	107.0	103.6	107.9
山 东	Shandong	2902.5	1599.3	53.7	831.3	370.0	105.5	106.5	107.6	105.7	101.7
河 南	Henan	2193.1	1137.7	69.1	835.9	23.3	98.0	90.4	103.8	106.9	108.3
湖 北	Hubei	1342.1	733.4	34.8	383.7	170.4	105.3	101.8	107.9	104.4	105.5
湖 南	Hunan	1453.0	671.7	81.7	575.1	97.0	103.7	102.7	104.0	104.1	107.3
广 东	Guangdong	1908.7	851.7	55.7	482.8	432.7	103.8	102.5	97.2	107.0	104.3
广 西	Guangxi	1030.9	500.8	53.8	342.8	115.5	104.3	100.0	114.8	109.2	106.9
海 南	Hainan	380.0	152.7	53.3	64.8	103.1	109.0	107.5	107.8	107.0	112.7
重 庆	Chongqing	488.6	270.1	14.6	177.6	18.3	106.7	103.5	119.6	104.8	106.8
四 川	Sichuan	1784.5	804.7	59.3	832.3	53.3	106.2	101.9	109.7	109.2	118.4
贵 州	Guizhou	466.7	275.5	25.9	139.5	6.1	105.4	104.9	101.0	108.8	106.4
云 南	Yunnan	799.3	433.9	73.2	242.5	16.6	106.6	104.7	114.4	107.2	113.7
西 藏	Tibet	58.6	25.3	5.3	27.1		105.0	96.0	187.2	101.4	42.0
陕 西	Shaanxi	535.0	334.4	26.8	145.6	4.5	106.4	104.3	107.1	111.3	106.6
甘 肃	Gansu	400.8	275.8	19.8	93.9	1.0	105.9	103.2	148.4	107.4	97.2
青 海	Qinghai	76.9	29.7	2.6	40.7	0.1	103.0	102.3	82.7	106.1	73.6
宁 夏	Ningxia	103.4	54.1	7.5	36.4	2.6	106.0	101.2	156.1	106.1	106.1
新 疆	Xinjiang	688.3	482.8	13.7	162.0	3.2	106.3	105.2	120.7	108.7	101.7

13-7 主要农业机械拥有量（年底数）

Agricultural Machinery and Machinery For Processing Farm Products at the Year-end

年份 地区	Year Region	农业机械总动力（万千瓦） Total Power of Agricultural Machinery (10 000 kw)	农用大中型拖拉机 Large and Medium Agricultural Tractors		小型拖拉机 Mini-Tractors		大中型拖拉机配套农具（部） Number of Large and Medium Tractor Towing Farm Machinery (unit)
			数量（台） Number (unit)	动力（万千瓦） Capacity (10 000 kw)	数量（台） Number (unit)	动力（万千瓦） Capacity (10 000 kw)	
	1978	11749.9	557358	1756.2	1373000	1172.0	1192000
	1980	14745.7	744865	2369.3	1874000	1615.5	1369000
	1985	20912.5	852357	2743.6	3824000	3367.0	1128000
	1989	28067.0	848220	2814.0	6543000	5848.0	991000
	1990	28707.7	813521	2745.5	6981000	6231.4	974000
	1991	29388.6	784466	2682.4	7304000	6528.6	991000
	1992	30308.4	758904	2630.2	7507000	6720.0	1044000
	1993	31816.6	721216	2532.5	7883000	7042.7	1001000
	1994	33802.5	693154	2463.5	8237000	7399.7	980000
	1995	36118.1	671846	2404.0	8646266	7848.0	991220
	1996	38546.9	670848	2415.1	9189200	8385.2	1049900
	1997	42015.6	689051	2486.5	10484813	9337.2	1157316
	1998	45207.7	725215	2587.9	11220551	10031.5	1203687
	1999	48996.1	784216	2772.8	12002509	11008.9	1320429
	2000	52573.6	974547	3161.1	12643696	11663.9	1399886
	2001	55172.1	829900	2901.7	13050840	12257.9	1469355
	2002	57929.9	911670	3073.4	13393884	12695.0	1578861
	2003	60386.5	980560	3229.8	13777056	13060.2	1698436
北京	Beijing	365.9	10998	44.2	20073	23.4	29884
天津	Tianjin	601.7	9290	37.5	35820	35.2	10560
河北	Hebei	7764.5	73400	280.8	1337894	1344.1	143412
山西	Shanxi	1928.2	22792	85.9	192658	189.2	46736
内蒙古	Inner Mongolia	1616.6	42270	160.3	498816	554.8	57022
辽宁	Liaoning	1542.3	34630	135.6	168738	168.7	47675
吉林	Jilin	1230.6	48749	132.3	465259	459.8	100160
黑龙江	Heilongjiang	1807.7	99462	351.8	695446	691.4	201096
上海	Shanghai	112.6	5395	20.2	7989	7.3	14232
江苏	Jiangsu	3029.1	40500	131.1	874587	778.4	78421
浙江	Zhejiang	2039.7	4600	12.9	218178	173.5	3489
安徽	Anhui	3544.7	20700	68.3	1924968	1538.6	43081
福建	Fujian	951.9	1602	6.4	110800	105.6	380
江西	Jiangxi	1220.5	10800	24.5	91300	83.0	5100
山东	Shandong	8336.7	188553	586.7	1641632	1409.4	371590
河南	Henan	6953.2	87200	285.4	2598500	2717.9	169500
湖北	Hubei	1661.8	65925	144.6	282271	204.3	62133
湖南	Hunan	2664.5	6000	17.0	175603	167.3	6827
广东	Guangdong	1788.8	4600	18.9	320129	254.3	7382
广西	Guangxi	1696.3	23200	62.7	324590	265.9	12816
海南	Hainan	221.6	4547	12.2	32128	24.7	2209
重庆	Chongqing	695.7	2868	7.4	9300	11.1	1600
四川	Sichuan	1891.1	4700	16.7	122469	141.1	8802
贵州	Guizhou	762.0	10800	33.4	51810	49.3	4530
云南	Yunnan	1542.9	25300	75.5	305106	307.1	9051
西藏	Tibet	181.2	3200	15.9	50600	66.2	2507
陕西	Shaanxi	1228.1	29353	89.9	183756	208.8	46876
甘肃	Gansu	1255.4	12997	47.2	358402	372.3	18893
青海	Qinghai	292.4	2700	12.5	200714	177.2	3595
宁夏	Ningxia	486.3	7100	21.1	167005	167.1	9516
新疆	Xinjiang	972.7	76329	291.2	310515	363.3	179361

注：2002年及以后大中型拖拉机中不包括变形拖拉机，2001年数据相应做了调整。

a) Number of large and medium agricultural tractors excluded the transfiguration tractors since 2002. The data in 2001 were adjusted accordingly.

13-7 续表 continued

年 份 Year 地 区 Region	小型拖拉机配套农具(部) Number of Mini-Tractor Towing Farm Machinery (unit)	农用排灌柴油机 Diesel Engines		渔用机动船 Motorized Fishing Boats	
		数 量 (台) Number (unit)	动 力 (万千瓦) Capacity (10 000 kw)	数 量 (台) Number (unit)	动 力 (万千瓦) Capacity (10 000 kw)
1978	1454000	2657000	2521.6	47176	213.7
1980	2191000	2899000	2717.7	61022	258.5
1985	3202000	2865000	2567.8	172582	367.2
1989	6043000	3867000	3207.0	289205	609.0
1990	6488000	4111000	3348.5	320927	696.0
1991	7327000	4330000	3447.1	329843	733.4
1992	8308000	4377000	3441.6	335875	786.1
1993	8657000	4554275	3613.1	334656	804.4
1994	8662000	4711516	3731.0	351327	831.0
1995	9579774	4912068	3839.0	376813	965.7
1996	10911500	5092934	3984.9	358869	864.1
1997	12530020	5461235	4292.4	398788	1080.4
1998	14378324	5816118	4499.0	411322	1174.4
1999	16210408	6449528	4934.6	417379	1253.1
2000	17887868	6881174	5232.6	459888	1338.1
2001	18821829	7285693	5580.0	480125	1379.7
2002	20033634	7506066	5667.9	485693	1381.2
2003	21171505	7495652	5592.8	478123	1425.9
北 京 Beijing	11524	1672	1.2	2	…
天 津 Tianjin	34430	36570	28.1		
河 北 Hebei	1706313	1302060	1139.1	12687	42.7
山 西 Shanxi	230476	18783	21.7	19	…
内蒙古 Inner Mongolia	624173	148554	135.9	78	0.3
辽 宁 Liaoning	204707	127736	117.9	40825	111.9
吉 林 Jilin	1172776	264467	180.0	1049	1.3
黑龙江 Heilongjiang	762596	188788	171.6	4109	3.4
上 海 Shanghai	8043	9	…	2530	16.7
江 苏 Jiangsu	1457021	177448	145.8	65072	122.0
浙 江 Zhejiang	217232	82350	41.5	55569	427.5
安 徽 Anhui	4259831	328972	242.0	13663	14.2
福 建 Fujian	60970	77360	49.6	76400	173.6
江 西 Jiangxi	117300	292100	181.7	16800	11.1
山 东 Shandong	2471959	1724822	1396.0	44241	131.6
河 南 Henan	4555000	518700	488.3	801	1.0
湖 北 Hubei	490320	197207	159.3	13128	7.5
湖 南 Hunan	49199	871023	415.3	21755	26.8
广 东 Guangdong	295026	199829	117.4	67988	223.5
广 西 Guangxi	565104	263127	133.3	13435	47.8
海 南 Hainan	5369	75574	34.2	16607	54.7
重 庆 Chongqing	6000	74100	46.5	2000	1.3
四 川 Sichuan	112357	310430	187.4	7300	3.7
贵 州 Guizhou	10170	85100	60.4	1120	2.0
云 南 Yunnan	171968	64327	33.9	258	0.3
西 藏 Tibet	15252	4675	4.3		
陕 西 Shaanxi	244466	31748	28.3	296	0.2
甘 肃 Gansu	603209	15505	16.2	9	…
青 海 Qinghai	132230	815	1.3	71	0.1
宁 夏 Ningxia	162597	3568	2.9	145	0.7
新 疆 Xinjiang	413887	8233	11.9	166	0.2

13-8 有效灌溉面积、农用化肥施用量、农村水电站及用电量

Irrigated Area, Consumption of Chemical Fertilizers, Number of Hydropower Stations and Electricity Consumption in Rural Areas

年份 地区	Year Region	有效灌溉面积（千公顷） Irrigated Area (1 000 hectares)	化肥施用量（万吨） Consumption of Chemical Fertilizer (10 000 tons)	氮肥 Nitrogenous Fertilizer	磷肥 Phosphate Fertilizer	钾肥 Potash Fertilizer	复合肥 Compound Fertilizer	乡村办水电站 Hydropower Station in Rural Areas: 个数 Number	发电能力（万千瓦） Generating Capacity (10 000 kw)	农村用电量（亿千瓦时） Electricity Consumed in Rural Area (100 million kwh)
	1978	44965.0	884.0					82387	228.4	253.1
	1980	44888.1	1269.4	934.2	273.3	34.6	27.2	80319	304.1	320.8
	1985	44035.9	1775.8	1204.9	310.9	80.4	179.6	55754	380.2	508.9
	1989	44917.2	2357.1	1536.8	418.9	120.5	280.9	50862	416.8	790.5
	1990	47403.1	2590.3	1638.4	462.4	147.9	341.6	52387	428.8	844.5
	1991	47822.1	2805.1	1726.1	499.6	173.9	405.5	49644	456.9	963.2
	1992	48590.1	2930.2	1756.1	515.7	196.0	462.4	48082	478.6	1106.9
	1993	48727.9	3151.9	1835.1	575.1	212.3	529.4	45153	481.7	1244.8
	1994	48759.1	3317.9	1882.0	600.7	234.8	600.6	48722	503.7	1473.9
	1995	49281.2	3593.7	2021.9	632.4	268.5	670.8	40699	519.5	1655.7
	1996	50381.4	3827.9	2145.3	658.4	289.6	734.7	37743	533.7	1812.7
	1997	51238.5	3980.7	2171.7	689.1	322.0	798.1	36117	562.4	1980.1
	1998	52295.6	4083.7	2233.3	682.5	345.7	822.0	33185	634.8	2042.1
	1999	53158.4	4124.3	2180.9	697.8	365.6	880.0	31678	664.1	2173.4
	2000	53820.3	4146.4	2161.6	690.5	376.5	917.9	29962	698.5	2421.3
	2001	54249.4	4253.8	2164.1	705.7	399.6	983.7	29183	896.6	2610.8
	2002	54354.8	4339.4	2157.3	712.2	422.4	1040.4	27633	812.2	2993.4
	2003	54014.2	4411.6	2149.9	713.9	438.0	1109.8	26696	862.3	3432.9
北京	Beijing	178.9	14.3	7.7	1.3	0.6	4.7	34	1.5	36.3
天津	Tianjin	354.1	17.8	9.3	2.3	1.0	5.2			42.3
河北	Hebei	4404.0	283.3	148.0	45.5	21.1	68.6	85	2.6	216.8
山西	Shanxi	1095.3	89.9	39.8	18.6	6.5	25.0	94	3.6	58.1
内蒙古	Inner Mongolia	2568.5	93.2	50.5	15.6	5.7	21.4	3	0.1	24.6
辽宁	Liaoning	1512.8	112.6	62.9	11.4	8.4	30.0	134	20.9	136.0
吉林	Jilin	1545.5	122.3	61.9	6.3	9.2	44.9	67	3.4	23.1
黑龙江	Heilongjiang	2111.5	125.7	50.4	28.3	13.8	33.2	11	1.1	30.7
上海	Shanghai	257.3	15.9	9.7	1.5	0.5	4.1			89.7
江苏	Jiangsu	3841.0	334.7	183.4	48.7	19.6	83.0	2		529.5
浙江	Zhejiang	1403.8	90.4	53.9	12.2	7.6	16.7	2592	154.9	409.0
安徽	Anhui	3285.4	281.3	120.2	46.8	28.0	86.3	530	10.9	57.5
福建	Fujian	940.0	120.3	51.4	16.3	23.8	28.7	3998	144.6	118.5
江西	Jiangxi	1873.2	111.0	44.4	22.2	18.9	25.5	1849	43.4	39.7
山东	Shandong	4760.8	432.7	182.0	54.5	41.3	154.8	13	0.4	272.2
河南	Henan	4792.2	467.9	215.8	103.8	43.3	105.0	445	6.0	144.6
湖北	Hubei	2043.7	270.3	136.9	61.6	21.2	50.7	646	32.8	63.1
湖南	Hunan	2675.3	188.3	97.6	23.5	31.3	36.0	3912	49.7	53.8
广东	Guangdong	1315.9	199.6	97.6	18.9	39.4	43.8	4937	171.5	714.3
广西	Guangxi	1516.7	183.7	58.7	24.5	44.8	55.7	908	18.9	31.2
海南	Hainan	177.3	33.9	11.6	2.5	4.1	15.8	57	8.4	3.0
重庆	Chongqing	649.7	71.6	43.9	16.6	3.1	8.1	623	31.1	36.7
四川	Sichuan	2503.2	208.4	117.5	41.9	11.6	37.5	2715	80.4	99.9
贵州	Guizhou	682.7	74.9	44.7	10.2	5.6	14.5	786	20.5	16.0
云南	Yunnan	1457.0	129.2	74.5	21.5	10.4	22.8	953	25.3	37.1
西藏	Tibet	156.3	3.2	1.7	0.6	0.2	0.8	239	2.1	0.4
陕西	Shaanxi	1271.9	142.7	77.8	15.8	9.0	40.2	642	9.0	75.5
甘肃	Gansu	994.4	69.6	34.1	14.3	4.0	17.1	223	5.0	31.7
青海	Qinghai	181.7	6.9	3.1	1.6	0.3	1.9	52	4.2	2.9
宁夏	Ningxia	413.2	25.4	14.0	3.3	0.7	7.4			8.6
新疆	Xinjiang	3051.0	90.7	45.0	22.3	3.0	20.5	146	10.0	29.9

13-9 农村水电建设和发电量

Rural Hydropower Construction and Amount of Electric Power Generation

年 份 地 区	Year Region	本年完成投资额（万元） Amount of Investment Finished This Year (10 000 yuan)	年末发电设备容量（千瓦） Capability of Electricity Generation Equipment at the Year-end (kw)	#本年新增发电设备容量 Newly Increased Capability of Electricity Generation Equipment	在建电站规模（千瓦） Scale of Constructing Electric Power Plant (kw)	#当年新开工电站规模 Scale of New Start Electric Power Station This Year	发电量（万千瓦时） Amount of Electric Power Generation (10 000 kwh)
	1990	348848	13978100	791000			4181100
	1991	476529	14942700	1009100			4066800
	1992	594081	15728195	964769	4170000		4818494
	1993	792747	16622781	995124	9600000		5841049
	1994	1020937	17566675	1163873	10500000		5771834
	1995	1321689	18721073	1207854	10760000		6316247
	1996	1442828	20095552	1408342			6496723
	1997	1452004	21771773	1780352			7221270
	1998	1585787	23390300	1741631			7560916
	1999	1833853	25562760	2344285	8717000	386000	7715124
	2000	2220993	27487791	2060127	7459500	2384000	8755014
	2001	2133741	28787476	1714454	3547500	1462800	9490187
	2002	2393195	31044576	1883648	5680800	1419000	10366868
	2003	3006249	34157792	2702834	10850143	6385500	10966512
北 京	Beijing	86	42920				2224
天 津	Tianjin		5000				866
河 北	Hebei	3003	323934	4812	55670	48525	28640
山 西	Shanxi	2350	150930		22130		27991
内蒙古	Inner Mongolia	265	49530	160	11000		9317
辽 宁	Liaoning	91927	340180	136360	3360		49242
吉 林	Jilin	70792	325708	9025	109360	22520	78544
黑龙江	Heilongjiang	10625	183835		34000	10000	50814
上 海	Shanghai						
江 苏	Jiangsu		34451	2905			4071
浙 江	Zhejiang	229973	2297783	268900	433355		400854
安 徽	Anhui	29187	504097	14895	64000	64000	129265
福 建	Fujian	363666	4150808	349791	883980	740830	1114077
江 西	Jiangxi	98030	1380076	148114	310000	260000	335580
山 东	Shandong	14	66449				6276
河 南	Henan	7149	326598	4720	11610	3130	77393
湖 北	Hubei	172532	2172317	107580	773436	460710	785241
湖 南	Hunan	210693	2812594	322845	1149482	810000	1007222
广 东	Guangdong	380204	4741531	497352	450000	210000	1316587
广 西	Guangxi	305379	2164700	178742	1212255	756885	822490
海 南	Hainan	527	229443	7335	13800	1200	73247
重 庆	Chongqing	152251	1058002	81650	112375	85215	411992
四 川	Sichuan	308902	4569287	220837	2000000	700000	1877062
贵 州	Guizhou	53660	1055772	38370	357290	245995	423936
云 南	Yunnan	247475	2815362	160005	2004700	1697100	1141713
西 藏	Tibet		158798				18300
陕 西	Shaanxi	60211	512362	41064	210000	29750	146286
甘 肃	Gansu	166309	563494	78327	484450	150380	208008
青 海	Qinghai	16053	275125	26450	138000	86000	124839
宁 夏	Ningxia		3200				800
新 疆	Xinjiang	16747	583259	2595	2630		183973
新疆兵团	Xinjiang PC Corps	8239	153647		3260	3260	58806
水利部直属	Directly under The Ministry of Water Resources		106600				50856

注:本表由水利部农村水电及电气化发展局提供。农村水电是指国家、集体和个人兴建，直接为农村经济社会发展提供电力的水电站及电网。

a) The table are provided by the Bureau of Rural Electrification, the Ministry of Water Resources. Rural hydropower refers to the water electric power station and power grid, which built by the state, collectivity and individual and directly serves for rural economic and social development.

13-10 灌溉、水库和除涝、治水、治碱情况

Irrigation, Reservoirs, Flood Prevention, Water and Soil Conservation and Improvement of Saline-Alkaline Land

项　目	Item	1990	1995	2000	2002	2003
年底灌区数　(处)	Number of Irrigation Areas at the year-end (set)	5363	5562	5683	5691	5729
3.3万公顷以上	33 000 Hectares and Over	72	74	101	110	112
2.0-3.3万公顷	20 000-33 000 Hectares	76	99	141	168	169
灌区有效灌溉面积(万公顷)	Effective Irrigated Areas (10 000 hectares)	2123.1	2249.9	2449.3	2503.0	2524.4
3.3万公顷以上	33 000 Hectares and Over	604.7	631.4	788.3	915.8	938.1
2.0-3.3万公顷	20 000-33 000 Hectares	189.6	244.4	344.0	407.2	408.4
水库　(座)	Number of Reservoirs	83387	84775	85120	85288	85153
大型水库	Large	366	387	420	445	453
中型水库	Medium-sized	2499	2593	2704	2781	2827
小型水库	Small	80522	81795	81996	82062	81873
水库库容量　(亿立方米)	Capacity of Reservoirs (100 million cu.m)	4660	4797	5184	5595	5658
大型水库	Large	3397	3493	3842	4229	4278
中型水库	Medium-sized	690	719	746	767	783
小型水库	Small	573	585	594	597	597
节水灌溉面积　(万公顷)	Water-saving Irrigated Area (10 000 hectares)			1638.9	1862.7	1944.3
除涝面积　(万公顷)	Flooded or Waterlogged Area (10 000 hectares)	1933.7	2006.5	2098.9	2109.7	2113.9
水土流失治理面积(万公顷)	Area of Soil Erosion under Control (10 000 hectares)	5300	6690	8096	8541	8971
治碱面积　(万公顷)	Improved Area of Saline-Alkaline Land (10 000 hectares)	499.5	543.4	584.1	528.3	586.5
堤防长度　(万公里)	Total Length of Dikes (10 000 km)	22.0	24.7	27.0	27.4	27.8
堤防保护面积　(万公顷)	Area of Land Protected by Dikes (10 000 hectares)	3200.0	3060.9	3960.0	4286.2	4387.5

注：大型水库库容：1亿立方米以上；中型水库库容：1千万至1亿立方米；小型水库库容：10万至1千万立方米。

a) The capacity of the large reservoirs is over 100 million cubic meters, while that of the medium ones is from 10 million to 100 million cubic meters, and that of the small ones is from 100 000 to 10 million cubic meters.

13-11 各地区水利设施和除涝、治碱面积（2003年）

Water Conservancy Facilities and Area with Flood Prevention Measures and Improved Area of Saline-Alkaline Land by Region (2003)

地区	Region	水库数（座） Number of Reservoirs (unit)	水库总库容量（亿立方米） Capacity of Reservoirs (100 million cu.m)	除涝面积（千公顷） Area with Flood Prevention Measures (1 000 hectares)	治碱面积（千公顷） Improved Area of Saline-alkaline Land (1 000 hectares)	水土流失治理面积（千公顷） Area of Soil Erosion under Control (1 000 hectares)
全国	**National Total**	**85153**	**5658.4**	**21139.0**	**5864.6**	**89713.6**
北京	Beijing	85	94.0	149.8		672.6
天津	Tianjin	141	27.5	401.9	211.9	34.5
河北	Hebei	1102	158.3	1642.5	833.7	5791.7
山西	Shanxi	732	52.7	89.1	211.1	4548.9
内蒙古	Inner Mongolia	466	77.8	275.7	299.8	8391.8
辽宁	Liaoning	951	331.0	995.1	304.4	5533.4
吉林	Jilin	1317	308.2	1002.7	135.8	3213.3
黑龙江	Heilongjiang	622	85.1	3220.8	196.8	3764.9
上海	Shanghai			61.0	28.6	
江苏	Jiangsu	919	189.1	2779.1	691.7	817.5
浙江	Zhejiang	3934	380.0	485.5	2.7	2145.0
安徽	Anhui	4861	194.8	2185.1	101.6	1884.1
福建	Fujian	2690	116.9	161.1	38.8	1154.9
江西	Jiangxi	9448	283.1	345.8		3320.8
山东	Shandong	5555	194.2	2578.8	936.1	3645.8
河南	Henan	2348	396.2	1864.2	676.2	3986.2
湖北	Hubei	5825	549.0	1126.9	3.4	4426.3
湖南	Hunan	13295	366.6	464.7		2427.0
广东	Guangdong	6616	583.3	503.1		1267.1
广西	Guangxi	4367	296.0	202.3	112.8	1327.7
海南	Hainan	1015	94.0	9.9		27.6
重庆	Chongqing	2753	41.3	14.3		1729.9
四川	Sichuan	6673	100.3	88.0	0.3	4755.7
贵州	Guizhou	1950	74.8	49.3		2484.0
云南	Yunnan	5298	103.1	226.4	5.1	3746.2
西藏	Tibet	16	8.5	36.2	0.1	358.3
陕西	Shaanxi	1024	66.4	129.3	56.1	8657.8
甘肃	Gansu	289	87.0	12.5	66.3	7241.2
青海	Qinghai	152	299.9		9.9	707.3
宁夏	Ningxia	206	18.9		95.8	1530.7
新疆	Xinjiang	503	80.3	38.1	845.4	121.5

13-12 农村居民家庭生产性固定资产原值(年底数)

Original Value of Productive Fixed Assets of Rural Household at the End of Year

本表为农村住户抽样调查资料。

Data in this table are obtained from the sample surveys on rural households.

单位:元/户 (yuan/household)

年份 地区	Year Region	固定资产原值合计 Total	农业 Agriculture	工业 Industry	建筑业 Construction	交通运输及邮电业 Transport, Post and Telecommunication Services	批发零售贸易及餐饮业 Wholesale and Retail Trade and Catering Services	社会服务业 Social Services	文教卫生业 Education, Culture, and Health Care	其他 Others
	1985	792.53	603.34	42.28		112.84				34.07
	1989	1126.07	800.51	72.37		198.22				54.97
	1990	1258.06	898.93	82.56		215.82				60.45
	1995	2774.27	2088.23	182.73		444.73				58.57
	1999	4045.48	2915.49	274.45		638.02				217.53
	2000	4676.98	3321.66	334.79	29.02	621.04	149.24	60.16	12.86	144.30
	2001	4883.80	3544.09	349.89	27.78	630.31	134.85	49.67	16.41	129.05
	2002	5221.33	3741.01	418.20	34.38	662.36	153.65	56.83	19.96	135.01
	2003	5586.34	4152.75	345.61	41.13	640.47	201.85	58.85	23.55	122.12
北京	Beijing	5146.29	2034.75	334.67		2153.73	359.40	137.33	26.67	99.75
天津	Tianjin	7050.93	4231.56	180.00	14.83	1142.77	490.27	44.17	88.33	859.00
河北	Hebei	7273.40	4841.45	874.41	69.00	928.83	357.73	87.24	19.17	95.58
山西	Shanxi	4172.69	2316.81	135.86	80.27	1214.30	236.00	68.43	6.76	114.26
内蒙古	Inner Mongolia	12319.41	11622.02	61.75		322.02	117.14	4.71	20.58	171.20
辽宁	Liaoning	5488.40	4268.18	253.24	3.76	651.38	229.87	44.60	30.42	6.96
吉林	Jilin	8528.88	8285.52	7.80	0.00	198.06	6.88	18.75	0.00	11.88
黑龙江	Heilongjiang	8536.23	8174.45	54.82	6.70	131.13	76.47	22.83	20.36	49.48
上海	Shanghai	2479.10	1687.35	41.33	58.25	310.00	182.50	82.17	58.33	59.17
江苏	Jiangsu	5623.79	3290.26	853.33	62.32	990.48	218.49	133.05	3.97	71.89
浙江	Zhejiang	9222.73	3738.95	2568.73	55.20	1437.00	1097.69	212.56	40.58	72.02
安徽	Anhui	4621.83	3908.28	90.29	28.77	359.91	125.01	51.72	16.52	41.33
福建	Fujian	4832.47	2958.61	409.67	83.98	781.73	271.07	159.62	66.91	100.88
江西	Jiangxi	3115.30	2398.19	71.51	3.20	470.24	74.54	45.94	31.16	20.51
山东	Shandong	6255.04	4733.43	295.00	76.12	732.58	228.55	46.67	46.25	96.44
河南	Henan	5487.30	4654.29	266.30	38.05	295.17	125.65	59.02	24.49	24.33
湖北	Hubei	2989.82	2431.10	104.13	32.70	292.48	69.61	13.82	6.42	39.55
湖南	Hunan	3165.65	2191.09	183.66	36.59	492.69	138.05	58.63	18.59	46.36
广东	Guangdong	4030.46	2166.27	417.57	101.89	680.39	240.18	26.52	16.12	381.53
广西	Guangxi	3139.39	2305.27	187.68	6.49	376.39	116.68	30.47	9.99	106.42
海南	Hainan	5334.57	4289.36	21.46	59.54	423.21	228.04	58.43	103.75	150.78
重庆	Chongqing	2531.71	2036.18	36.98	3.11	315.34	73.33	31.57	1.69	33.51
四川	Sichuan	3840.19	3092.48	63.33	15.48	437.85	130.32	19.66	11.58	69.50
贵州	Guizhou	3443.99	2714.07	147.17	55.73	347.11	80.58	24.45	8.13	66.76
云南	Yunnan	5389.67	4056.21	233.45	19.25	431.96	88.00	15.92	30.00	514.88
西藏	Tibet	18058.70	14902.32	21.94		2801.85	90.63	70.21	34.79	136.96
陕西	Shaanxi	4254.10	2601.01	224.38	108.45	962.24	114.80	61.59	34.72	146.91
甘肃	Gansu	5355.20	4279.27	162.25	38.00	456.25	187.83	102.61	53.22	75.76
青海	Qinghai	8604.52	6859.20	115.63		929.18	73.00	57.50	38.33	531.67
宁夏	Ningxia	13058.17	7925.36	554.65	1.11	2388.79	381.87	85.35	7.83	1713.22
新疆	Xinjiang	9756.94	8901.92	87.52	51.61	545.52	150.90	2.03	1.61	15.83

13-13 农村居民家庭平均每百户拥有主要生产性固定资产数量(年底数)

Number of Major Productive Fixed Assets Per 100 Rural Households at the End of Year

本表为农村住户抽样调查资料。

Data in this table are obtained from the sample surveys on rural households.

年份 地区 Year Region	汽车 (辆) Motor Vehicles (set)	大中型拖拉机 (台) Large and Medium Tractors (set)	小型和手扶拖拉机 (台) Mini and Walking Tractors (set)	机动脱粒机 (台) Motorized Threshing Machines (set)	胶轮大车 (辆) Carts with Rubber Tyres (set)	农用水泵 (台) Pumps (unit)	役畜 (头) Draught Animals (unit)	产品畜 (头) Commodity Animals (unit)
1985	0.25	0.35	2.71	1.91	5.49	1.69	57.15	32.12
1989	0.28	0.47	4.84	2.61	7.68	3.81	58.67	34.63
1990	0.28	0.45	5.30	3.55	7.89	3.86	57.27	30.91
1991	0.24	0.51	6.61	3.85	8.24	4.73	53.93	28.73
1992	0.28	0.55	7.25	4.16	8.67	5.48	52.95	30.07
1993	0.33	0.64	8.40	5.30	9.60	8.54	59.98	53.15
1994	0.40	0.79	8.77	5.15	9.32	7.90	58.79	56.70
1995	0.51	0.77	9.93	6.33	9.29	9.07	55.99	50.72
1996	0.78	0.99	12.46	6.87	8.78	10.97	54.99	56.26
1997	0.82	1.39	14.26	7.41	8.83	12.12	55.58	52.72
1998	1.01	1.22	14.34	8.58	8.52	13.73	48.39	52.20
1999	1.09	1.44	16.28	8.35	7.87	14.02	45.02	54.08
2000	1.32	1.41	16.72	9.59	13.26	17.73	41.75	41.56
2001	1.20	1.50	17.41	9.28	14.52	19.92	39.67	54.65
2002	1.29	1.53	18.48	9.62	14.31	21.53	39.38	56.43
2003	1.40	1.79	18.93	10.06	13.71	21.12	35.52	58.62
北京 Beijing	5.33	0.93	13.33	0.13	1.33	1.07	0.67	621.33
天津 Tianjin	5.83	1.83	22.33	2.69	7.17	18.67	10.08	15.17
河北 Hebei	2.51	2.20	35.50	5.43	10.91	30.62	18.15	38.52
山西 Shanxi	2.60	2.38	17.42	1.29	7.79	5.90	29.43	32.14
内蒙古 Inner Mongolia	2.06	2.50	44.08	4.56	38.01	36.36	81.31	240.00
辽宁 Liaoning	1.75	1.96	12.12	3.65	31.11	39.23	50.37	47.46
吉林 Jilin	0.81	4.88	29.75	7.02	31.19	29.84	60.63	51.81
黑龙江 Heilongjiang	0.45	5.57	43.83	5.83	8.84	19.89	32.23	47.72
上海 Shanghai	0.67	0.33	1.50	5.36		2.50		4.50
江苏 Jiangsu	1.32	0.85	19.60	25.95	24.62	16.94	4.89	22.56
浙江 Zhejiang	2.21	1.52	4.89	27.45	10.69	21.70	2.99	14.00
安徽 Anhui	0.63	1.97	35.18	21.18	11.76	47.56	15.06	20.41
福建 Fujian	1.26	0.93	3.08	8.04	4.23	7.09	11.20	23.57
江西 Jiangxi	0.82	0.41	2.41	19.11	10.96	14.99	45.53	16.18
山东 Shandong	1.63	2.94	26.66	3.24	25.32	42.85	23.26	29.50
河南 Henan	0.95	4.01	44.60	13.08	17.32	40.01	20.28	31.40
湖北 Hubei	0.68	1.18	10.72	2.59	14.92	17.64	29.46	12.84
湖南 Hunan	0.80	0.46	2.72	17.10	4.00	16.11	22.37	19.92
广东 Guangdong	1.31	0.16	7.89	13.48	4.86	11.99	29.51	20.62
广西 Guangxi	0.40	0.43	8.40	12.60	4.24	12.46	56.94	35.97
海南 Hainan	0.56	0.42	8.82	8.79	3.47	13.42	73.49	66.39
重庆 Chongqing	0.67		0.11	9.89	0.39	8.00	19.16	31.84
四川 Sichuan	0.90	0.30	1.03	13.65	0.98	27.38	32.02	47.12
贵州 Guizhou	0.76	0.49	0.98	3.97	3.39	3.97	74.74	29.06
云南 Yunnan	1.29	0.67	7.50	5.63	6.71	4.10	65.01	55.13
西藏 Tibet	2.50	0.83	37.71	4.58	12.29		261.46	705.42
陕西 Shaanxi	1.62	2.70	16.33	3.60	18.92	12.35	20.53	35.45
甘肃 Gansu	1.33	2.89	26.00	1.83	20.11	6.78	71.39	62.06
青海 Qinghai	3.67	1.83	55.58	3.28	21.50	1.00	89.50	135.50
宁夏 Ningxia	4.17	0.50	59.00	2.00	5.83	14.08	60.08	32.17
新疆 Xinjiang	1.74	4.97	23.29	2.39	51.87	3.03	93.10	404.77

13-14 各地区农村居民家庭土地经营情况（2003年底）

Area of Land Managed by Rural Households at the Year-end by Region (2003)

本表为农村住户抽样调查资料。

Data in this table are obtained from the sample surveys on rural households.

单位：亩/人 (mu/person)

地区	Region	经营耕地面积 Area of Cultivated Land under Management	经营山地面积 Hilly Area under Management	园地面积 Area of Garden Plot	牧草地面积 Area of Grassland	养殖水面面积 Water Area for Breeding Aquatics
全国	**National Total**	**1.96**	**0.19**	**0.07**	**4.40**	**0.02**
北京	Beijing	0.69	0.01	0.22	0.01	
天津	Tianjin	1.29		0.07		
河北	Hebei	1.75	0.07	0.07	0.02	
山西	Shanxi	2.24	0.04	0.16	0.04	
内蒙古	Inner Mongolia	7.50	0.51	0.01	132.37	
辽宁	Liaoning	3.11	0.35	0.08		0.03
吉林	Jilin	5.29		0.07		
黑龙江	Heilongjiang	9.43		0.01		
上海	Shanghai	0.68		0.02		
江苏	Jiangsu	1.16		0.02		0.07
浙江	Zhejiang	0.72	0.39	0.11		0.03
安徽	Anhui	1.44	0.04	0.03		0.02
福建	Fujian	0.74	0.12	0.21	0.01	0.03
江西	Jiangxi	1.30	0.61	0.04		0.02
山东	Shandong	1.48	0.01	0.07		
河南	Henan	1.45		0.03		0.04
湖北	Hubei	1.49	0.34	0.04		0.08
湖南	Hunan	1.08	0.34	0.06	0.03	0.03
广东	Guangdong	0.65	0.46	0.11		0.10
广西	Guangxi	1.34	0.43	0.11	0.01	0.04
海南	Hainan	1.01	0.16	0.29		0.02
重庆	Chongqing	0.95	0.04	0.09	0.03	0.01
四川	Sichuan	0.94	0.14	0.04	0.01	0.01
贵州	Guizhou	1.06	0.16	0.01	0.01	
云南	Yunnan	1.39	0.18	0.05		
西藏	Tibet	2.23		0.01	0.05	
陕西	Shaanxi	1.62	0.12	0.22	0.07	
甘肃	Gansu	2.35	0.44	0.06	0.06	
青海	Qinghai	1.91		0.01	49.80	
宁夏	Ningxia	3.65	0.30	0.04	0.28	0.01
新疆	Xinjiang	3.74		0.10	0.24	

13-15 农作物总播种面积

Total Sown Areas of Farm Crops

单位: 千公顷 (1 000 hectares)

年份 Year 地区 Region	农作物总播种面积 Total Sown Area	粮食作物播种面积 Sown Area of Grain Crops	谷物 Cereal	#稻谷 Rice	#小麦 Wheat	#玉米 Corn	豆类 Soybeans
1978	150105	120587		34421	29183	19961	
1980	146381	117234		33879	28844	20087	
1985	143626	108845		32070	29218	17694	
1989	146554	112205		32700	29841	20353	
1990	148363	113466		33064	30753	21401	
1991	149586	112314	94073	32590	30948	21574	9163
1992	149008	110560	92520	32090	30496	21044	8983
1993	147741	110509	88912	30355	30235	20694	12377
1994	148241	108544	87537	30171	28981	21152	12736
1995	149879	110060	89310	30744	28860	22776	11232
1996	152381	112548	92208	31406	29611	24498	10543
1997	153969	112912	91964	31765	30057	23775	11164
1998	155706	113787	92117	31214	29774	25239	11671
1999	156373	113161	91617	31284	28855	25904	11190
2000	156300	108463	85264	29962	26653	23056	12660
2001	155708	106080	82596	28812	24664	24282	13268
2002	154636	103891	81466	28202	23908	24634	12543
2003	152415	99410	76810	26508	21997	24068	12898
北　京 Beijing	308.8	141.3	116.7	1.6	35.8	75.2	19.2
天　津 Tianjin	501.5	258.1	224.0	7.0	78.3	124.9	32.3
河　北 Hebei	8638.5	5944.0	5183.5	75.6	2192.9	2488.8	384.0
山　西 Shanxi	3708.0	2833.6	2114.0	3.1	720.6	915.5	355.0
内蒙古 Inner Mongolia	5752.8	4051.5	2433.6	67.0	317.6	1591.2	1081.8
辽　宁 Liaoning	3719.1	2743.3	2250.9	500.6	20.1	1434.9	343.9
吉　林 Jilin	4716.8	4013.8	3318.5	541.0	22.1	2627.2	607.7
黑龙江 Heilongjiang	9802.7	8114.7	3867.1	1290.9	229.6	2053.8	3813.0
上　海 Shanghai	419.2	148.3	139.3	106.2	21.7	4.6	8.5
江　苏 Jiangsu	7681.5	4659.5	4135.5	1840.9	1620.5	451.9	389.7
浙　江 Zhejiang	2834.4	1427.8	1136.2	979.4	71.5	51.9	193.3
安　徽 Anhui	9124.7	6157.2	4708.0	1972.4	2012.0	627.4	1011.5
福　建 Fujian	2518.9	1471.1	1016.9	962.6	8.8	36.9	120.5
江　西 Jiangxi	4997.4	3051.1	2729.0	2685.3	20.6	17.5	184.4
山　东 Shandong	10885.3	6415.4	5691.8	112.6	3105.1	2405.9	323.9
河　南 Henan	13684.4	8923.3	7840.8	503.0	4804.6	2386.7	612.5
湖　北 Hubei	7138.3	3557.8	2820.5	1805.1	603.2	341.1	324.9
湖　南 Hunan	7731.2	4529.8	3835.9	3410.0	86.3	289.8	293.5
广　东 Guangdong	4883.4	2771.9	2286.7	2130.6	5.8	135.7	106.3
广　西 Guangxi	6279.1	3470.0	2914.8	2356.3	12.3	531.1	287.1
海　南 Hainan	906.7	541.8	366.4	343.1		19.9	15.5
重　庆 Chongqing	3365.8	2469.0	1578.0	750.5	322.7	455.5	209.0
四　川 Sichuan	9384.5	6387.3	4763.9	2040.3	1318.7	1161.3	521.6
贵　州 Guizhou	4634.2	3021.3	1952.0	720.5	474.3	686.3	321.1
云　南 Yunnan	5756.0	4068.4	2999.8	1043.1	567.4	1066.9	463.4
西　藏 Tibet	233.7	185.9	175.6	1.0	42.2	3.3	9.9
陕　西 Shaanxi	4055.8	3122.8	2438.4	139.5	1233.3	948.3	379.9
甘　肃 Gansu	3620.9	2499.5	1772.2	4.8	961.3	490.5	230.7
青　海 Qinghai	466.8	248.0	142.6		107.0		39.7
宁　夏 Ningxia	1129.5	805.3	607.3	46.7	319.3	176.3	110.3
新　疆 Xinjiang	3535.0	1377.2	1250.3	67.2	661.5	467.9	104.4

13-15 续表 1 continued

单位：千公顷 (1 000 hectares)

年份 Year / 地区 Region		薯类 Tubers	油料 Oil-bearing Crops	#花生 Peanuts	#油菜籽 Rapeseeds	棉花 Cotton	麻类 Fiber Crops	#黄红麻 Jute and Ambary Hemp	糖料 Sugar Crops
	1978	11796	6222	1768	2599	4867	751	412	879
	1980	10153	7929	2339	2844	4920	667	314	922
	1985	8572	11800	3319	4494	5141	1230	991	1524
	1989	9097	10504	2946	4993	5203	563	286	1528
	1990	9121	10900	2907	5503	5588	495	300	1679
	1991	9078	11530	2880	6133	6538	453	270	1947
	1992	9057	11489	2976	5976	6835	434	277	1906
	1993	9220	11142	3379	5300	4985	420	274	1687
	1994	9270	12081	3776	5783	5528	372	176	1755
	1995	9519	13101	3809	6907	5422	376	147	1820
	1996	9798	12556	3616	6734	4722	350	147	1846
	1997	9785	12381	3722	6475	4491	327	162	1923
	1998	10000	12919	4039	6527	4459	224	93	1984
	1999	10355	13906	4268	6899	3726	205	65	1644
	2000	10538	15400	4855	7494	4041	262	50	1514
	2001	10217	14631	4991	7095	4810	323	52	1654
	2002	9881	14766	4921	7143	4184	338	55	1818
	2003	9702	14990	5057	7221	5111	337	41	1657
北京	Beijing	5.4	13.8	13.3		3.2			
天津	Tianjin	1.8	15.8	3.5		70.6	…	…	
河北	Hebei	376.5	634.0	489.5	28.3	581.4	2.1	1.9	11.5
山西	Shanxi	364.7	323.0	17.7	10.7	91.5	0.9		2.9
内蒙古	Inner Mongolia	536.1	723.4	12.6	279.7	5.0	4.7		37.4
辽宁	Liaoning	148.5	334.5	271.6	1.7	4.2	0.6		1.1
吉林	Jilin	87.6	301.8	110.5		0.6	1.3		2.6
黑龙江	Heilongjiang	434.6	463.3	22.7	2.5		112.9		118.8
上海	Shanghai	0.6	39.4	1.6	37.9	0.8			3.2
江苏	Jiangsu	134.2	911.0	214.5	683.0	369.5	1.8	0.3	6.3
浙江	Zhejiang	98.2	250.9	17.5	229.5	17.6	0.6	0.4	19.2
安徽	Anhui	437.7	1412.6	273.0	1014.5	390.0	14.3	7.4	7.8
福建	Fujian	333.7	123.5	108.3	13.8	0.1	0.2	0.1	18.3
江西	Jiangxi	137.7	632.7	166.8	428.1	65.5	8.9	0.6	24.4
山东	Shandong	399.8	1013.0	988.2	19.6	881.7	1.8	1.6	0.1
河南	Henan	470.0	1569.9	963.4	384.6	926.7	14.8	14.1	4.9
湖北	Hubei	412.4	1506.0	201.1	1174.6	355.0	25.8	3.0	17.2
湖南	Hunan	400.5	867.8	145.9	711.1	139.0	57.2	1.3	28.6
广东	Guangdong	378.9	334.5	325.8	7.0		0.8	0.8	156.1
广西	Guangxi	268.1	301.2	228.0	61.1	1.4	5.6	5.1	708.6
海南	Hainan	159.8	49.8	45.5			0.2	0.2	69.1
重庆	Chongqing	682.0	236.7	48.3	176.9	0.4	7.1	0.2	2.8
四川	Sichuan	1102.1	1086.9	270.0	805.6	31.2	31.8	3.5	32.0
贵州	Guizhou	748.2	501.8	43.2	451.4	1.6	1.8	0.1	19.2
云南	Yunnan	605.3	189.8	41.1	133.0	0.8	9.7		292.3
西藏	Tibet	0.4	21.6	…	21.6				
陕西	Shaanxi	304.7	285.6	29.5	165.8	65.1	0.5	…	0.3
甘肃	Gansu	496.6	335.0	1.3	154.2	52.2	3.4		5.3
青海	Qinghai	65.7	152.1		149.2		0.1		
宁夏	Ningxia	87.7	132.5	…	1.1		…		
新疆	Xinjiang	22.5	226.4	2.4	74.5	1055.5	28.4		67.3

13-15 续表 2 continued

单位: 千公顷 (1 000 hectares)

年份 Year 地区 Region		# 甘蔗 Sugarcane	# 甜菜 Beetroots	烟叶 Tobacco	# 烤烟 Flue-cured Tobacco	蔬菜 Vegetables	茶园面积 Area of Tea Plantations at Year-end	果园面积 Area of Orchards at Year-end
	1978	549	331	784	613	3331	1048	1657
	1980	479	443	512	397	3163	1041	1783
	1985	965	561	1313	1077	4753	1077	2736
	1989	959	569	1798	1503	6290	1065	5372
	1990	1009	670	1593	1342	6338	1061	5179
	1991	1164	783	1804	1562	6546	1060	5318
	1992	1246	660	2093	1849	7031	1084	5818
	1993	1088	599	2089	1835	8084	1171	6432
	1994	1057	698	1490	1302	8921	1135	7264
	1995	1125	695	1470	1309	9515	1115	8098
	1996	1208	638	1853	1683	10491	1103	8553
	1997	1312	612	2353	2161	11288	1076	8648
	1998	1401	583	1361	1200	12293	1057	8535
	1999	1303	341	1374	1216	13347	1130	8667
	2000	1185	329	1437	1269	15237	1089	8932
	2001	1248	406	1340	1181	16402	1141	9043
	2002	1393	424	1328	1192	17353	1134	9098
	2003	1409	248	1264	1139	17954	1207	9437
北京	Beijing			…		116.3		87.5
天津	Tianjin					134.6		41.1
河北	Hebei		11.5	4.7	3.1	1068.5		1075.0
山西	Shanxi		2.9	2.8	2.7	278.5		278.2
内蒙古	Inner Mongolia		37.4	6.6	5.5	192.1		48.3
辽宁	Liaoning		1.1	13.7	11.7	468.5		318.2
吉林	Jilin		2.6	21.0	10.7	269.1		95.3
黑龙江	Heilongjiang		118.8	36.6	32.6	399.6		41.4
上海	Shanghai	3.2				150.4		24.8
江苏	Jiangsu	6.0	0.3	0.9		1341.7	22.7	178.3
浙江	Zhejiang	19.2		2.2		700.8	142.8	286.7
安徽	Anhui	7.8	0.1	11.7	11.0	654.9	113.1	100.5
福建	Fujian	18.3		59.6	58.6	613.8	138.6	554.4
江西	Jiangxi	24.4		11.6	9.7	548.3	34.0	262.4
山东	Shandong		0.1	42.9	42.3	2027.1	11.8	797.1
河南	Henan	4.9		134.0	133.9	1526.2	24.6	374.1
湖北	Hubei	17.2		55.1	39.5	1086.9	119.4	227.9
湖南	Hunan	28.6		94.1	87.1	964.3	74.0	378.3
广东	Guangdong	156.1		29.9	25.0	1194.9	38.7	917.1
广西	Guangxi	708.6		16.1	9.8	1006.8	42.9	821.3
海南	Hainan	69.1		0.1	0.1	161.9	1.9	159.2
重庆	Chongqing	2.8		57.2	46.6	387.0	23.4	164.8
四川	Sichuan	31.9	0.1	66.6	44.3	1006.2	124.7	418.2
贵州	Guizhou	19.1	0.1	207.2	188.8	414.9	48.1	103.1
云南	Yunnan	292.1	0.2	343.7	333.2	437.7	192.2	217.8
西藏	Tibet					13.6	0.2	0.8
陕西	Shaanxi	0.1	0.3	31.5	30.9	276.8	50.9	750.5
甘肃	Gansu		5.3	13.4	12.2	268.7	3.3	320.1
青海	Qinghai			0.1		24.1		5.1
宁夏	Ningxia			0.1	0.1	55.7		44.9
新疆	Xinjiang		67.3	1.1	…	163.8		344.2

13-16 主要农作物种植结构

Planting Structure of Major Farm Crops

单位：% (%)

项　目	Item	1995	2000	2001	2002	2003
农作物总播种面积	**Total Sown Areas of Farm Crops**	**100.00**	**100.00**	**100.00**	**100.00**	**100.00**
粮食作物	**Grain Crops**	**73.43**	**69.39**	**68.13**	**67.18**	**65.22**
谷物	Cereal	59.59	54.55	53.05	52.68	50.40
稻谷	Rice	20.51	19.17	18.50	18.24	17.39
小麦	Wheat	19.26	17.05	15.84	15.46	14.43
玉米	Corn	15.20	14.75	15.59	15.93	15.79
谷子	Millet	1.02	0.80	0.74	0.74	0.67
高粱	Jowar	0.81	0.57	0.50	0.55	0.47
其它谷物	Other Cereal	2.80	2.21	1.87	1.77	1.63
豆类	Soybeans	7.49	8.10	8.52	8.11	8.46
#大豆	Soja	5.42	5.95	6.09	5.64	6.11
杂豆	Miscellaneous Beans	2.07	2.15	2.43	2.47	2.35
薯类	Tubers	6.35	6.74	6.56	6.39	6.37
#马铃薯	Potato	2.29	3.02	3.03	3.02	2.97
油料作物	**Oil-bearing Crops**	**8.74**	**9.85**	**9.40**	**9.55**	**9.83**
#花生	Peanuts	2.54	3.11	3.21	3.18	3.32
油菜籽	Rapeseeds	4.61	4.79	4.56	4.62	4.74
芝麻	Sesame	0.43	0.50	0.49	0.49	0.45
胡麻籽	Benne	0.41	0.32	0.26	0.29	0.29
向日葵	Helianthus	0.54	0.79	0.65	0.73	0.77
棉花	**Cotton**	**3.62**	**2.59**	**3.09**	**2.71**	**3.35**
麻类	**Fiber Crops**	**0.25**	**0.17**	**0.21**	**0.22**	**0.22**
#黄红麻	Jute and Ambary Hemp	0.10	0.03	0.03	0.04	0.03
苎　麻	Ramee	0.06	0.06	0.07	0.08	0.08
大　麻	Hemp		0.01	0.01	0.01	0.01
亚　麻	Flax	0.08	0.06	0.09	0.09	0.10
糖料	**Sugar Crops**	**1.21**	**0.97**	**1.06**	**1.18**	**1.09**
甘蔗	Sugarcane	0.75	0.76	0.80	0.90	0.92
甜菜	Beetroots	0.46	0.21	0.26	0.27	0.16
烟叶	**Tobacco**	**0.98**	**0.92**	**0.86**	**0.86**	**0.83**
#烤烟	Flue-cured Tobacco	0.87	0.81	0.76	0.77	0.75
药材	**Medicinal Materials**	**0.19**	**0.43**	**0.53**	**0.62**	**0.82**
蔬菜、瓜类	**Vegetables and Melon**	**7.08**	**11.06**	**11.99**	**12.74**	**13.32**
#蔬菜	Vegetables	6.35	9.75	10.53	11.22	11.78
其他农作物	**Other Farm Crops**	**4.49**	**4.70**	**4.74**	**4.94**	**5.31**
#青饲料	Succulence	1.22	1.37	1.66	1.95	2.33

13-17 主要农产品单位面积产量

Yield of Major Farm Crops Per Hectare

单位: 公斤/公顷 (kg/hectare)

年 份 地 区	Year Region	谷 物 Cereals	棉 花 Cotton	花 生 Peanuts	油菜籽 Rapeseeds	芝 麻 Sesame	黄红麻 Jute and Ambary Hemp	甘 蔗 Sugar-cane	甜 菜 Beet-roots	烤 烟 Flue-cured Tobacco
	1978		445	1344	720	503	2641	38496	8175	1725
	1980		550	1545	840	330	3497	47565	14250	1815
	1985		807	2010	1245	660	4165	53430	15898	1920
	1989		728	1815	1095	465	2310	50850	16245	1605
	1990		807	2190	1260	705	2415	57120	21660	1680
	1991	4206	868	2189	1215	645	1905	58350	20790	1710
	1992	4342	660	2000	1281	692	2233	58605	22832	1687
	1993	4557	750	2492	1309	747	2449	59012	20124	1654
	1994	4500	785	2564	1296	794	2020	57671	17936	1491
	1995	4659	879	2687	1416	908	2534	58136	20132	1584
	1996	4894	890	2804	1367	969	2491	56471	24150	1750
	1997	4823	1025	2592	1479	919	2649	60158	24475	1809
	1998	4953	1009	2943	1272	1042	2677	59549	24806	1740
	1999	4945	1028	2961	1469	1066	2531	57338	25335	1797
	2000	4753	1093	2973	1519	1034	2516	57626	24518	1763
	2001	4800	1107	2888	1597	1061	2046	60625	26807	1732
	2002	4885	1175	3011	1477	1180	2868	64663	30232	1792
	2003	4873	951	2654	1582	863	2462	64023	24925	1768
北 京	Beijing	4455	1077	2446		589				
天 津	Tianjin	5001	1341	2973		1072	867			
河 北	Hebei	4256	898	3026	1362	853	3102		19105	1431
山 西	Shanxi	3818	1002	2201	1238	948			39296	2320
内蒙古	Inner Mongolia	4489	1055	1875	903	1048			26581	2536
辽 宁	Liaoning	6042	829	2019	1586	769			30058	1956
吉 林	Jilin	6074		2484		1263			27001	1810
黑龙江	Heilongjiang	4634		1781	1191	1331			6012	1379
上 海	Shanghai	6895	1429	2805	1565			41161		
江 苏	Jiangsu	5567	787	2404	2134	1505	3103	56280	25745	
浙 江	Zhejiang	6166	1193	2630	1682	1438	3492	64516		
安 徽	Anhui	4134	618	2543	1507	708	2108	33557	11840	1919
福 建	Fujian	5315	854	2240	1175	1066	2564	64722		1728
江 西	Jiangxi	5024	1162	2208	852	682	2544	48423		1590
山 东	Shandong	5403	994	3599	2301	1477	3912		3482	2221
河 南	Henan	4279	407	2369	1815	507	2189	42892		1624
湖 北	Hubei	6000	915	3400	1593	1313	4191	44064		1589
湖 南	Hunan	5802	1173	2091	1320	1206	2935	49684		2029
广 东	Guangdong	5385		2478	1456	1051	2636	72660		1917
广 西	Guangxi	4687	503	2112	1041	897	2016	68608		1503
海 南	Hainan	4105		2042		776	5975	58197		1175
重 庆	Chongqing	5065	579	1780	1612	855	923	40092		1467
四 川	Sichuan	5212	812	2218	1935	1203	2066	53508	22000	1860
贵 州	Guizhou	4427	358	1729	1418	658	1352	39561	1881	1522
云 南	Yunnan	4043	378	1300	1711	647		58037	12291	1911
西 藏	Tibet	5298		3333	2285					
陕 西	Shaanxi	3540	811	2340	1631	968		38904	19248	1576
甘 肃	Gansu	3387	1660	1726	1466				37922	2261
青 海	Qinghai	3485			1723					
宁 夏	Ningxia	3935			1569					4383
新 疆	Xinjiang	5872	1516	1860	2071	3800			56700	2500

13-18 主要农产品产量

Yield of Major Farm Crops

单位：万吨 (10 000 tons)

年份 地区	Year Region	粮食 Grain	谷物 Cereal	#稻谷 Rice	#小麦 Wheat	#玉米 Corn	豆类 Beans	薯类 Tubers	油料 Oil-bearing Crops
	1978	30476.5		13693.0	5384.0	5594.5		3174.0	521.8
	1980	32055.5		13990.5	5520.5	6260.0		2872.5	769.1
	1985	37910.8		16856.9	8580.5	6382.6		2603.6	1578.4
	1989	40754.9		18013.0	9080.7	7892.8		2730.4	1295.2
	1990	44624.0		18933.1	9822.9	9681.9		2743.2	1613.2
	1991	43529.0	39566.3	18381.3	9595.3	9877.3	1247.1	2715.9	1638.3
	1992	44265.8	40169.6	18622.2	10158.7	9538.3	1252.0	2844.2	1641.2
	1993	45648.8	40517.4	17751.4	10639.0	10270.4	1950.4	3181.1	1803.9
	1994	44510.1	39389.1	17593.3	9929.7	9927.5	2095.6	3025.4	1989.6
	1995	46661.8	41611.6	18522.6	10220.7	11198.6	1787.5	3262.6	2250.3
	1996	50453.5	45127.1	19510.3	11056.9	12747.1	1790.3	3536.0	2210.6
	1997	49417.1	44349.3	20073.5	12328.9	10430.9	1875.5	3192.3	2157.4
	1998	51229.5	45624.7	19871.3	10972.6	13295.4	2000.6	3604.2	2313.9
	1999	50838.6	45304.1	19848.7	11388.0	12808.6	1894.0	3640.6	2601.2
	2000	46217.5	40522.4	18790.8	9963.6	10600.0	2010.0	3685.2	2954.8
	2001	45263.7	39648.2	17758.0	9387.3	11408.8	2052.8	3563.1	2864.9
	2002	45705.8	39798.7	17453.9	9029.0	12130.8	2241.2	3665.9	2897.2
	2003	43069.5	37428.7	16065.6	8648.8	11583.0	2127.5	3513.3	2811.0
北京	Beijing	58.0	52.0	1.0	18.4	32.2	3.1	2.9	3.3
天津	Tianjin	119.3	112.0	5.7	35.9	64.8	6.2	1.0	3.1
河北	Hebei	2387.8	2205.9	41.1	1018.8	1073.6	60.6	121.3	163.1
山西	Shanxi	958.9	807.1	1.2	256.0	477.0	48.7	103.1	36.4
内蒙古	Inner Mongolia	1360.7	1092.3	45.0	79.0	888.7	93.9	174.5	102.3
辽宁	Liaoning	1498.3	1360.1	351.4	6.2	907.2	71.0	67.2	61.4
吉林	Jilin	2259.6	2015.6	318.2	6.0	1615.3	191.1	52.9	57.1
黑龙江	Heilongjiang	2512.3	1792.0	842.8	39.7	830.9	616.1	104.2	44.7
上海	Shanghai	98.8	96.0	82.2	7.4	3.2	2.2	0.5	6.4
江苏	Jiangsu	2471.9	2302.2	1404.6	608.7	197.3	95.3	74.3	199.5
浙江	Zhejiang	793.4	700.6	646.9	20.8	21.5	41.7	51.1	43.8
安徽	Anhui	2214.8	1946.2	963.7	642.8	260.6	120.4	148.2	231.4
福建	Fujian	713.2	540.5	523.4	2.8	11.6	25.2	147.5	26.0
江西	Jiangxi	1450.3	1371.1	1360.5	2.9	6.3	26.8	52.5	76.0
山东	Shandong	3435.5	3075.4	77.9	1565.0	1411.0	82.3	277.8	361.8
河南	Henan	3569.5	3355.3	240.2	2292.5	766.3	72.7	141.5	309.9
湖北	Hubei	1921.0	1692.2	1341.3	165.4	167.5	67.1	161.8	272.7
湖南	Hunan	2442.7	2225.6	2070.2	16.5	128.6	56.1	161.0	125.7
广东	Guangdong	1430.4	1231.4	1170.5	1.6	53.1	21.8	177.1	81.9
广西	Guangxi	1465.1	1366.0	1202.7	1.7	159.7	39.2	59.9	55.7
海南	Hainan	204.6	150.4	143.4		6.1	3.3	50.9	9.6
重庆	Chongqing	1087.1	799.3	497.1	83.8	207.0	32.2	255.7	38.3
四川	Sichuan	3054.1	2483.0	1471.9	426.2	517.3	113.9	457.4	217.1
贵州	Guizhou	1104.3	864.2	459.3	74.6	319.9	39.3	200.8	72.3
云南	Yunnan	1471.0	1212.9	635.9	124.4	399.9	85.8	172.3	29.7
西藏	Tibet	96.6	93.0	0.6	27.2	1.6	3.4	0.2	4.9
陕西	Shaanxi	968.4	863.3	75.5	395.5	373.2	24.6	80.5	41.3
甘肃	Gansu	789.3	600.3	3.6	272.5	244.4	39.0	150.1	46.0
青海	Qinghai	86.8	49.7		36.8		8.9	28.2	26.2
宁夏	Ningxia	270.2	239.0	37.0	75.6	119.9	8.6	22.6	13.2
新疆	Xinjiang	775.5	734.1	50.7	344.1	317.3	27.0	14.3	50.1

13-18 续表 1 continued

单位: 万吨 (10 000 tons)

年 份 地 区	Year Region				棉 花 Cotton	麻 类 Fiber Crops		甘 蔗 Sugarcane	甜 菜 Beetroots
		# 花 生 Peanuts	# 油菜籽 Rapeseeds	# 芝 麻 Sesame			# 黄红麻 Jute and Ambary Hemp		
	1978	237.7	186.8	32.2	216.7	135.1	108.8	2111.6	270.2
	1980	360.0	238.4	25.9	270.7	143.6	109.8	2280.7	630.5
	1985	666.4	560.7	69.1	414.7	444.8	411.9	5154.9	891.9
	1989	536.3	543.6	33.8	378.8	112.4	66.0	4879.5	924.3
	1990	636.8	695.8	46.9	450.8	109.7	72.6	5762.0	1452.5
	1991	630.3	743.6	43.5	567.5	88.4	51.3	6789.8	1628.9
	1992	595.3	765.3	51.6	450.8	93.8	61.9	7301.1	1506.9
	1993	842.1	693.9	56.3	373.9	96.0	67.2	6419.4	1204.8
	1994	968.2	749.2	54.8	434.1	74.7	35.5	6092.7	1252.5
	1995	1023.5	977.7	58.3	476.8	89.7	37.1	6542.0	1398.4
	1996	1013.8	920.1	57.5	420.3	79.5	36.5	6818.7	1541.5
	1997	964.8	957.8	56.6	460.3	74.9	43.0	7889.7	1496.8
	1998	1188.6	830.1	65.6	450.1	49.5	24.8	8343.8	1446.6
	1999	1263.9	1013.2	74.3	382.9	47.2	16.4	7470.3	863.9
	2000	1443.7	1138.1	81.1	441.7	52.9	12.6	6828.0	807.3
	2001	1441.6	1133.1	80.4	532.4	68.1	10.6	7566.3	1088.9
	2002	1481.8	1055.2	89.5	491.6	96.4	15.9	9010.7	1282.0
	2003	1342.0	1142.0	59.3	486.0	85.3	10.0	9023.5	618.2
北 京	Beijing	3.3		…	0.3				
天 津	Tianjin	1.0		0.1	9.5	…	…		
河 北	Hebei	148.1	3.8	1.6	52.2	0.6	0.6		22.0
山 西	Shanxi	3.9	1.3	0.8	9.2	0.1			11.4
内蒙古	Inner Mongolia	2.4	25.3	0.9	0.5	1.2			99.4
辽 宁	Liaoning	54.8	0.3	1.0	0.3	0.1			3.4
吉 林	Jilin	27.4		7.0	0.1	0.4			7.0
黑龙江	Heilongjiang	4.0	0.3	1.1		28.3			71.4
上 海	Shanghai	0.4	5.9		0.1			13.1	
江 苏	Jiangsu	51.6	145.7	1.9	29.1	0.5	0.1	33.7	0.7
浙 江	Zhejiang	4.6	38.6	0.6	2.1	0.2	0.1	123.9	
安 徽	Anhui	69.4	152.9	8.8	24.1	2.8	1.6	26.0	0.1
福 建	Fujian	24.2	1.6	0.1	…	…	…	118.1	
江 西	Jiangxi	36.8	36.5	2.5	7.6	1.2	0.2	118.2	
山 东	Shandong	355.6	4.5	0.4	87.7	0.6	0.6		…
河 南	Henan	228.2	69.8	11.0	37.7	3.3	3.1	21.2	
湖 北	Hubei	68.4	187.1	16.3	32.5	5.7	1.2	76.0	
湖 南	Hunan	30.5	93.9	1.1	16.3	13.5	0.4	142.3	
广 东	Guangdong	80.7	1.0	0.2		0.2	0.2	1134.1	
广 西	Guangxi	48.1	6.4	0.5	0.1	1.1	1.0	4861.8	
海 南	Hainan	9.3		0.3		0.1	0.1	402.1	
重 庆	Chongqing	8.6	28.5	0.6	…	1.0	…	11.3	
四 川	Sichuan	59.9	155.9	0.5	2.5	5.0	0.7	170.5	0.3
贵 州	Guizhou	7.5	64.0	…	0.1	0.2	…	75.7	…
云 南	Yunnan	5.3	22.7	…	…	4.5	…	1695.0	0.3
西 藏	Tibet	…	4.9						
陕 西	Shaanxi	6.9	27.0	1.9	5.3	0.1	…	0.3	0.5
甘 肃	Gansu	0.2	22.6		8.7	1.1			19.9
青 海	Qinghai		25.7			0.1			
宁 夏	Ningxia	…	0.2			…			…
新 疆	Xinjiang	0.4	15.4	0.1	160.0	13.3			381.6

13-18 续表 2 continued

单位: 万吨 (10 000 tons)

年 份 Year / 地 区 Region		烟 叶 Tobacco	#烤 烟 Flue-cured Tobacco	蚕 茧 Silkworm Cocoons	#桑蚕茧 Mulberry Silkworm Cocoons	茶 叶 Tea	水 果 Fruits	#苹 果 Apples	#柑 桔 Citrus	#梨 Pears	#葡 萄 Grapes	#香 蕉 Bananas
	1978	124.2	105.2	22.8	17.3	26.8	657.0	227.5	38.3	151.7	10.4	8.5
	1980	84.5	71.7	32.6	25.0	30.4	679.3	236.3	71.3	146.6	11.0	6.1
	1985	242.5	207.5	37.1	33.6	43.2	1163.9	361.4	180.8	213.7	36.1	63.1
	1989	283.0	240.5	48.8	43.5	53.5	1831.9	449.9	456.1	256.5	87.4	140.4
	1990	262.7	225.9	53.4	48.0	54.0	1874.4	431.9	485.5	235.3	85.9	145.6
	1991	303.1	267.0	58.4	55.1	54.2	2176.1	454.0	633.3	249.8	91.6	198.1
	1992	349.9	311.9	69.2	66.0	56.0	2440.1	655.6	516.0	284.6	112.5	245.1
	1993	345.1	303.6	75.7	71.2	60.0	3011.2	907.0	656.1	321.7	135.5	270.1
	1994	223.8	194.0	81.3	77.7	58.8	3499.8	1112.9	680.5	404.3	152.2	289.8
	1995	231.4	207.2	80.0	76.0	58.9	4214.6	1400.8	822.5	494.2	174.2	312.5
	1996	323.4	294.6	50.8	47.1	59.3	4652.8	1704.7	845.7	580.7	188.3	253.6
	1997	425.1	390.8	46.9	42.3	61.3	5089.3	1721.9	1010.2	641.5	203.3	289.2
	1998	236.4	208.8	52.6	47.5	66.5	5452.9	1948.1	859.0	727.5	235.8	351.8
	1999	246.9	218.5	48.5	44.7	67.6	6237.6	2080.2	1078.7	774.2	270.8	419.4
	2000	255.2	223.8	54.8	50.1	68.3	6225.1	2043.1	878.3	841.2	328.2	494.1
	2001	235.0	204.5	65.5	60.2	70.2	6658.0	2001.5	1160.7	879.6	368.0	527.2
	2002	244.7	213.5	69.8	64.5	74.5	6952.0	1924.1	1199.0	930.9	447.9	555.7
	2003	225.7	201.5	66.7	61.1	76.8	14517.4	2110.2	1345.4	979.8	517.6	590.3
北 京	Beijing	…		…	…		114.2	13.5		13.1	6.3	
天 津	Tianjin						84.3	6.8		2.6	14.0	
河 北	Hebei	1.1	0.4	0.1	0.1		1270.7	200.3		282.1	80.3	
山 西	Shanxi	0.6	0.6	0.4	0.4		328.8	180.2		15.5	11.2	
内蒙古	Inner Mongolia	1.6	1.4	0.3	…		123.3	5.2		9.3	2.1	
辽 宁	Liaoning	2.6	2.3	4.4	…		396.9	109.0		51.6	58.6	
吉 林	Jilin	5.0	1.9	0.1			253.2	19.0		12.0	10.7	
黑龙江	Heilongjiang	4.6	4.5	0.3			356.7	16.9		3.5	1.9	
上 海	Shanghai			…	…		114.5	…	17.4	1.8	2.8	
江 苏	Jiangsu	0.2		10.7	10.7	1.2	601.9	49.5	5.4	50.2	14.1	
浙 江	Zhejiang	0.5		7.9	7.9	13.3	568.4	0.1	176.7	24.4	17.3	
安 徽	Anhui	2.2	2.1	2.6	2.6	5.1	609.1	22.1	1.1	58.3	16.2	
福 建	Fujian	10.3	10.1	…	…	15.0	522.0	…	194.4	13.0	5.6	83.8
江 西	Jiangxi	1.8	1.5	0.8	0.8	1.3	273.2		62.0	4.5	0.4	
山 东	Shandong	9.6	9.4	6.8	6.7	0.4	2526.0	611.9		98.3	76.1	
河 南	Henan	21.8	21.7	1.4	1.1	1.0	1318.5	251.0	3.0	43.3	33.1	
湖 北	Hubei	9.3	6.3	1.2	1.2	7.2	611.6	1.3	124.1	56.4	5.7	
湖 南	Hunan	18.7	17.7	0.2	0.2	6.1	512.4		172.8	7.1	3.7	
广 东	Guangdong	6.0	4.8	5.2	5.2	4.1	836.9		135.1	3.9		301.8
广 西	Guangxi	2.6	1.5	8.7	8.7	2.1	641.2		152.1	8.2	9.4	103.6
海 南	Hainan	…	…			0.1	193.5		1.5			84.2
重 庆	Chongqing	8.6	6.8	2.8	2.8	1.4	128.6	0.6	75.2	14.3	1.7	0.1
四 川	Sichuan	13.4	8.2	9.3	9.3	7.2	464.9	22.5	186.2	54.8	14.4	1.4
贵 州	Guizhou	31.2	28.7	0.1	0.1	1.8	78.8	0.9	15.0	9.8	1.6	0.9
云 南	Yunnan	65.5	63.7	1.3	1.3	8.6	126.2	11.3	13.3	17.6	4.3	14.6
西 藏	Tibet	…				…	1.1	0.6		…		
陕 西	Shaanxi	5.0	4.9	1.9	1.9	0.8	730.9	461.8	9.9	69.0	9.0	
甘 肃	Gansu	3.1	2.8	…	…	…	247.7	83.0	0.3	28.6	6.3	
青 海	Qinghai	0.1					2.4	0.8		0.4	…	
宁 夏	Ningxia	0.1	0.1	…	…		71.2	15.5		1.2	4.1	
新 疆	Xinjiang	0.3	…	0.1	0.1		408.3	26.3		25.0	106.6	

注：2003年水果产量包括瓜果类产量。

a) Output of fruits in 2003 includes yield of melon and fruit.

13-19 主要林产品产量

Output of Major Forest Products

单位: 吨 (ton)

年份 地区	Year Region	橡胶 Rubber	松脂 Pine Resin	生漆 Lacquer	油桐籽 Tung-oil Seeds	油茶籽 Tea-oil Seeds	核桃 Walnuts
	1978	101600	337600	2200	391150	478900	118650
	1980	112945	420750	2450	303350	490350	118900
	1985	187901	343946	2168	378770	619229	121917
	1989	242766	486837	2951	334757	667245	160053
	1990	264243	435244	2683	350770	523313	149560
	1995	424025	548133	2976	404929	623128	230867
	1996	402450	580819	3740	407744	696633	237989
	1997	451970	701183	4416	453535	856868	249834
	1998	462344	543156	4577	438680	722846	265121
	1999	489991	571477	5314	448323	792690	274246
	2000	480248	551057	5279	453461	823224	309875
	2001	477437	563689	4925	406716	824731	252347
	2002	527413	563388	6360	389024	854624	340174
	2003	565045	625757	8664	372645	779492	393529
北京	Beijing						10364
天津	Tianjin						389
河北	Hebei						32746
山西	Shanxi						40777
内蒙古	Inner Mongolia						
辽宁	Liaoning						17069
吉林	Jilin						1638
黑龙江	Heilongjiang						
上海	Shanghai						
江苏	Jiangsu				195	16	4
浙江	Zhejiang		2697	15	122	33035	
安徽	Anhui		4075	214	2579	8544	327
福建	Fujian	49	67732	228	19237	64606	108
江西	Jiangxi		54758	107	12681	163191	252
山东	Shandong						12391
河南	Henan		240	978	42223	6898	18364
湖北	Hubei		5479	2438	10650	11245	1578
湖南	Hunan		17399	153	37713	339716	3945
广东	Guangdong	24527	125591	…	4935	30928	
广西	Guangxi	1074	254299	46	53998	92714	201
海南	Hainan	316041	6068				
重庆	Chongqing		7	654	19853	2104	2787
四川	Sichuan		3738	1319	50299	11854	77004
贵州	Guizhou		5682	1221	89857	9307	7578
云南	Yunnan	223354	76592	310	18118	4548	76118
西藏	Tibet						
陕西	Shaanxi		200	962	9634	198	43114
甘肃	Gansu		1200	19	551	588	28293
青海	Qinghai						83
宁夏	Ningxia						182
新疆	Xinjiang						18217

13-20 牲畜饲养情况

Number of Livestock

单位: 万头、万只 (10 000 heads)

年份 地区	Year Region	大牲畜年底头数 Large Animals (year-end)	牛 Cattle and Buffaloes	马 Horses	驴 Donkeys	骡 Mules	骆驼 Camels
	1996	13360.6	11031.8	871.5	944.4	478.0	34.5
	1997	14541.8	12182.2	891.2	952.8	480.6	35.0
	1998	14803.2	12441.9	898.1	955.8	473.9	33.5
	1999	15024.8	12698.3	891.4	934.8	467.3	33.0
	2000	15151.5	12866.3	876.6	922.7	453.0	32.6
	2001	14995.9	12824.2	826.0	881.5	436.2	27.9
	2002	15189.3	13084.8	808.8	849.9	419.4	26.4
	2003	15500.1	13467.2	790.0	820.7	395.7	26.5
北京	Beijing	33.0	29.8	0.5	1.8	0.9	
天津	Tianjin	48.8	42.9	0.6	3.8	1.5	
河北	Hebei	944.3	737.1	36.8	121.1	49.3	
山西	Shanxi	294.1	218.3	4.7	35.5	35.5	
内蒙古	Inner Mongolia	615.4	409.7	72.0	78.6	47.5	7.6
辽宁	Liaoning	455.0	301.9	33.3	91.9	28.0	
吉林	Jilin	599.4	500.0	64.4	18.3	16.7	
黑龙江	Heilongjiang	592.3	526.4	53.0	7.7	5.2	
上海	Shanghai	6.3	6.3				
江苏	Jiangsu	74.1	66.4	0.9	6.0	0.9	
浙江	Zhejiang	38.9	38.9				
安徽	Anhui	496.3	492.6	1.0	2.1	0.6	
福建	Fujian	109.9	109.9				
江西	Jiangxi	358.6	358.6				
山东	Shandong	1143.9	1040.2	16.9	72.5	14.3	
河南	Henan	1469.5	1396.0	21.6	34.5	17.4	
湖北	Hubei	404.0	401.5	1.7	0.7	0.2	
湖南	Hunan	560.3	556.2	3.4	0.5	0.2	
广东	Guangdong	398.4	398.3	0.1	…		
广西	Guangxi	802.7	760.6	38.7	0.1	3.3	
海南	Hainan	147.0	147.0				
重庆	Chongqing	173.2	169.9	2.2	0.2	0.8	
四川	Sichuan	1175.9	1078.0	81.5	8.2	8.2	
贵州	Guizhou	801.9	721.7	77.9	0.1	2.2	
云南	Yunnan	941.5	762.6	81.2	32.6	65.1	
西藏	Tibet	647.8	591.4	43.1	11.8	1.5	
陕西	Shaanxi	322.4	285.6	1.5	25.1	10.3	
甘肃	Gansu	599.1	390.4	26.4	117.5	62.4	2.4
青海	Qinghai	455.9	405.6	26.8	8.4	14.3	0.9
宁夏	Ningxia	95.8	70.5	0.7	17.6	7.0	0.1
新疆	Xinjiang	694.5	453.1	99.4	124.0	2.5	15.6

13-20 续表 continued

单位: 万头、万只 (10 000 heads)

年 份 地 区	Year Region	肉猪出栏头数 Slaughtered Fattened Hogs	猪年底头数 Hogs (year-end)	羊年底只数 Sheep and Goats (year-end)	山 羊 Goats	绵 羊 Sheep
	1996	41225.1	36283.6	23728.3	12315.8	11412.5
	1997	46483.7	40034.8	25575.7	13480.1	12095.6
	1998	50215.1	42256.3	26903.5	14168.3	12735.2
	1999	50749.0	43144.2	27925.8	14816.3	13109.5
	2000	52673.3	44681.5	29031.9	15715.9	13316.0
	2001	54936.7	45743.0	29826.4	16129.2	13697.2
	2002	56684.0	46291.5	31655.2	17275.9	14379.3
	2003	59200.5	46601.7	34053.7	18320.7	15733.0
北 京	Beijing	467.0	248.5	183.0	57.9	125.0
天 津	Tianjin	412.9	245.1	106.5	39.3	67.2
河 北	Hebei	3875.1	2763.4	2209.7	911.1	1298.6
山 西	Shanxi	610.2	462.5	1015.8	415.4	600.4
内蒙古	Inner Mongolia	791.9	647.7	4450.2	1617.2	2832.9
辽 宁	Liaoning	1712.8	1275.4	1076.9	471.1	605.8
吉 林	Jilin	1127.1	523.9	392.0	60.0	332.0
黑龙江	Heilongjiang	1174.2	1046.2	1029.5	403.0	626.5
上 海	Shanghai	410.0	195.0	62.0	53.5	8.5
江 苏	Jiangsu	3009.1	1993.0	1205.1	1184.8	20.3
浙 江	Zhejiang	1792.0	1132.4	262.9	138.5	124.4
安 徽	Anhui	2557.2	2019.3	1049.9	1047.0	2.9
福 建	Fujian	1603.1	1180.8	123.8	123.8	
江 西	Jiangxi	1858.8	1301.2	103.7	88.3	15.4
山 东	Shandong	4016.2	2975.2	3133.7	2443.9	689.8
河 南	Henan	4850.0	3914.0	3315.8	2921.9	393.9
湖 北	Hubei	3000.7	2123.3	327.1	326.3	0.8
湖 南	Hunan	5905.8	4108.7	588.4	588.3	0.1
广 东	Guangdong	3269.7	1961.1	27.8	27.8	
广 西	Guangxi	2555.1	2637.7	246.6	246.6	
海 南	Hainan	346.3	346.6	93.9	93.9	
重 庆	Chongqing	1818.4	1719.6	245.1	244.9	0.2
四 川	Sichuan	6236.9	5564.9	1370.2	1030.8	339.4
贵 州	Guizhou	1398.2	1867.5	391.9	369.8	22.1
云 南	Yunnan	2384.5	2554.1	809.6	716.2	93.4
西 藏	Tibet	13.9	25.2	1779.0	644.4	1134.6
陕 西	Shaanxi	816.4	722.1	877.2	681.3	195.9
甘 肃	Gansu	675.9	630.2	1236.3	303.9	932.4
青 海	Qinghai	105.4	101.0	1761.7	315.7	1446.0
宁 夏	Ningxia	165.1	125.1	474.4	97.0	377.4
新 疆	Xinjiang	240.7	191.2	4104.3	657.2	3447.2

13-21 畜产品产量

Output of Livestock Products

年份 Year 地区 Region		肉类产量（万吨）Output of Meat (10000 tons)	#猪牛羊肉 Output of Pork, Beef and Mutton	猪肉 Pork	牛肉 Beef	羊肉 Mutton	奶类（万吨）Milk (10 000 tons)	#牛奶 Cow Milk
	1996	4584.0	3694.7	3158.0	355.7	181.0	735.8	629.4
	1997	5268.8	4249.9	3596.3	440.9	212.8	681.1	601.1
	1998	5723.8	4598.2	3883.7	479.9	234.6	745.4	662.9
	1999	5820.7	4647.4	3890.7	505.4	251.3	806.9	717.6
	2000	6125.4	4838.2	4031.4	532.8	274.0	919.1	827.4
	2001	6333.9	5026.0	4184.5	548.8	292.7	1122.9	1025.5
	2002	6586.5	5227.9	4326.6	584.6	316.7	1400.4	1299.8
	2003	6932.9	5506.3	4518.6	630.4	357.2	1848.6	1746.3
北　京	Beijing	70.3	42.6	32.7	5.2	4.7	63.7	63.3
天　津	Tianjin	53.4	40.7	32.2	5.4	3.1	43.2	43.2
河　北	Hebei	502.4	397.9	290.3	78.6	29.0	207.6	197.9
山　西	Shanxi	66.5	60.7	46.8	6.7	7.2	55.6	53.2
内蒙古	Inner Mongolia	162.7	140.6	71.3	24.0	45.3	312.2	308.0
辽　宁	Liaoning	280.1	186.9	147.9	33.9	5.1	46.4	42.7
吉　林	Jilin	218.5	128.5	84.5	40.3	3.8	23.3	22.7
黑龙江	Heilongjiang	151.5	122.2	85.6	29.9	6.7	303.9	300.5
上　海	Shanghai	50.8	25.5	24.6	0.1	0.9	27.1	27.1
江　苏	Jiangsu	354.8	244.4	221.2	5.6	17.6	50.0	49.8
浙　江	Zhejiang	153.9	122.2	117.2	1.4	3.6	24.7	24.7
安　徽	Anhui	329.6	259.6	209.7	34.9	15.1	9.0	9.0
福　建	Fujian	146.2	120.6	116.4	2.5	1.6	19.5	19.2
江　西	Jiangxi	195.2	151.1	142.7	7.0	1.4	10.9	10.9
山　东	Shandong	662.1	445.2	332.6	79.7	32.9	148.4	124.4
河　南	Henan	603.6	521.0	386.0	93.0	42.0	52.6	49.6
湖　北	Hubei	301.1	258.4	238.6	14.9	4.9	11.1	11.1
湖　南	Hunan	503.8	444.8	419.3	16.1	9.4	5.3	5.3
广　东	Guangdong	359.6	240.8	234.5	5.8	0.6	10.8	10.6
广　西	Guangxi	227.1	195.5	179.8	12.9	2.8	3.8	3.8
海　南	Hainan	47.0	32.3	28.4	2.7	1.3	0.1	0.1
重　庆	Chongqing	160.6	140.1	132.1	5.3	2.7	9.1	9.1
四　川	Sichuan	581.8	504.6	461.6	25.6	17.4	45.8	45.4
贵　州	Guizhou	152.5	141.6	126.9	10.1	4.5	3.38	3.38
云　南	Yunnan	253.7	234.5	208.8	17.6	8.2	23.4	21.7
西　藏	Tibet	19.0	19.0	0.9	10.8	7.4	25.1	19.6
陕　西	Shaanxi	92.1	80.4	62.0	10.5	7.9	107.1	74.2
甘　肃	Gansu	75.9	69.9	48.7	10.7	10.6	22.6	22.2
青　海	Qinghai	23.7	23.0	7.4	7.1	8.5	23.5	22.1
宁　夏	Ningxia	23.4	19.9	10.7	3.7	5.5	38.7	38.6
新　疆	Xinjiang	110.0	91.7	17.4	28.8	45.5	120.8	113.0

13-21 续表 continued

年份 地区	Year Region	绵羊毛 (吨) Sheep Wool (ton)	#细羊毛 Fine Wool	#半细羊毛 Semi-Fine Wool	山羊毛 (吨) Goat Wool (ton)	羊绒 (吨) Cashmere (ton)	禽蛋 (万吨) Poultry Eggs (10 000 tons)	蜂蜜 (万吨) Honey (10 000 tons)
	1996	298102	121020	74099	35284	9585	1965.2	18.30
	1997	255059	116054	55683	25865	8626	1897.1	21.10
	1998	277545	115752	68775	31417	9799	2021.3	20.70
	1999	283152	114103	73700	31849	10180	2134.7	22.99
	2000	292502	117386	84921	33266	11057	2243.3	24.60
	2001	298254	114651	88075	34241	10968	2336.7	25.16
	2002	307588	112193	102419	35459	11765	2462.7	26.46
	2003	338058	120263	110249	36692	13528	2606.7	28.9
北京	Beijing	1245	42	1203	397	153	16.2	0.3
天津	Tianjin	1186	81	1105	95	1	24.2	…
河北	Hebei	30004	4345	12614	4075	958	415.2	0.6
山西	Shanxi	8401	1724	972	1715	672	50.3	0.3
内蒙古	Inner Mongolia	69255	38240	13990	5793	5338	34.4	0.3
辽宁	Liaoning	10587	4385	5572	1393	719	169.5	0.1
吉林	Jilin	24453	19507	3504	401	50	90.0	0.6
黑龙江	Heilongjiang	20606	7452	13154	713	393	90.3	0.7
上海	Shanghai	45		45	131		15.1	0.1
江苏	Jiangsu	646	398	248	10	8	188.2	0.6
浙江	Zhejiang	1671		1671	71		42.2	8.1
安徽	Anhui	126	14	112	93	4	119.8	1.2
福建	Fujian				10		42.4	0.7
江西	Jiangxi						37.1	1.0
山东	Shandong	19761	4553	15208	8791	916	424.7	1.0
河南	Henan	10680	1674	6195	2639	394	326.2	3.8
湖北	Hubei	20			452		117.4	0.8
湖南	Hunan	3	3		10		64.6	0.9
广东	Guangdong				11		32.5	1.3
广西	Guangxi						15.0	0.6
海南	Hainan						2.6	0.1
重庆	Chongqing	5	5		11		35.4	0.6
四川	Sichuan	5059	456	2254	412	21	133.6	3.3
贵州	Guizhou	347	63	284	27	1	9.1	0.1
云南	Yunnan	1758	338	937	100	6	14.4	0.7
西藏	Tibet	8746	196	3324	1181	853	0.2	…
陕西	Shaanxi	4187	1872	450	1148	765	49.0	0.3
甘肃	Gansu	16976	5709	4013	1646	370	13.4	0.1
青海	Qinghai	16483	450	3873	866	319	1.4	…
宁夏	Ningxia	7389	469	1784	843	444	8.7	0.1
新疆	Xinjiang	78419	28287	17737	3658	1143	23.6	0.4

13-22 水 产 品 产 量

Output of Aquatic Products

单位: 万吨 (10 000 tons)

年份 地区	Year Region	水产品总产量 Total Aquatic Products	海水产品 Seawater Aquatic Products	天然生产 Naturally Grown	人工养殖 Artificially Cultured	鱼类 Fish	虾蟹类 Shrimps, Prawns and Crabs	贝类 Shell-fish	藻类 Algae	其他 Others
	1978	465.4	359.5	314.5	45.0	256.1	50.6	26.8	26.0	
	1980	449.7	325.7	281.3	44.4	234.1	42.1	23.4	26.2	
	1985	705.2	419.8	348.5	71.2	274.5	70.6	47.3	27.3	
	1989	1151.7	661.2	503.6	157.6	382.9	105.7	137.5	30.0	5.0
	1990	1237.0	713.3	550.9	162.4	423.1	107.0	147.3	27.5	8.2
	1991	1350.8	800.1	609.6	190.5	466.2	119.4	158.6	40.0	15.9
	1992	1557.1	933.7	691.2	242.4	517.6	127.4	204.4	56.8	27.5
	1993	1823.0	1076.0	767.3	308.7	557.4	138.7	288.6	69.4	22.0
	1994	2143.2	1241.5	895.8	345.7	647.4	170.9	323.6	74.5	25.1
	1995	2517.2	1439.1	1026.8	412.3	758.1	184.8	392.3	74.9	29.0
	1996	3288.1	2012.9	1249.0	763.9	823.5	204.7	852.7	92.9	39.1
	1997	3601.8	2176.4	1385.4	791.0	964.2	225.7	824.2	98.0	64.4
	1998	3906.5	2356.7	1496.7	860.0	1056.0	258.6	870.1	104.1	68.0
	1999	4122.4	2471.9	1497.6	974.3	1057.9	277.1	959.3	119.4	58.2
	2000	4278.5	2538.7	1477.5	1061.3	1033.0	297.1	1038.7	122.2	47.8
	2001	4381.3	2571.7	1440.6	1131.1	1014.7	302.5	1078.1	124.9	51.3
	2002	4564.5	2646.3	1433.5	1212.8	1022.3	310.6	1119.3	133.3	60.8
	2003	4704.6	2685.8	1432.4	1253.3	1028.4	298.2	1109.6	141.3	108.2
北京	Beijing	7.1								
天津	Tianjin	29.8	5.1	4.2	0.9	1.8	1.3	0.7		1.3
河北	Hebei	86.3	49.0	31.1	17.9	17.8	9.0	18.1		4.0
山西	Shanxi	3.1								
内蒙古	Inner Mongolia	7.3								
辽宁	Liaoning	382.0	330.8	148.0	182.9	83.8	32.6	165.2	33.0	16.2
吉林	Jilin	10.9								
黑龙江	Heilongjiang	41.9								
上海	Shanghai	35.5	13.3	13.1	0.3	9.8	1.7	1.4		0.4
江苏	Jiangsu	342.9	98.2	57.2	40.9	36.3	12.1	41.5	1.4	6.8
浙江	Zhejiang	482.8	406.0	314.2	91.9	208.5	82.1	103.5	3.9	8.1
安徽	Anhui	165.3								
福建	Fujian	572.8	507.9	221.2	286.7	179.0	37.3	234.2	41.7	15.6
江西	Jiangxi	146.1								
山东	Shandong	706.2	604.2	268.1	336.1	186.7	48.4	284.8	53.6	30.6
河南	Henan	39.0								
湖北	Hubei	286.8								
湖南	Hunan	156.6								
广东	Guangdong	648.5	379.2	181.9	197.3	158.7	39.7	170.3	3.6	6.9
广西	Guangxi	264.6	168.7	85.1	83.6	60.5	20.1	83.9	0.1	4.2
海南	Hainan	123.1	104.5	89.6	15.0	76.9	13.9	5.9	4.0	3.8
重庆	Chongqing	22.5								
四川	Sichuan	76.4								
贵州	Guizhou	8.0								
云南	Yunnan	20.4								
西藏	Tibet	…								
陕西	Shaanxi	6.7								
甘肃	Gansu	1.4								
青海	Qinghai	0.1								
宁夏	Ningxia	5.0								
新疆	Xinjiang	6.7								
中国水产总公司	China Aquatic Company	18.8	18.8	18.8		8.6	0.1			10.2

13-22 续表 continued

单位:万吨 (10 000 tons)

年份 地区	Year Region	淡水产品 Freshwater Aquatic Products	天然生产 Naturally Grown	人工养殖 Artificially Cultured	鱼类 Fish	虾蟹类 Shrimps, Prawns and Crabs	贝类 Shell-fish	其他 Others
	1978	105.9	29.6	76.2	99.7	3.8	2.4	
	1980	124.0	33.9	90.2	116.3	5.2	2.5	
	1985	285.4	47.6	237.8	276.5	5.5	3.4	
	1989	490.5	73.5	417.0	472.8	9.5	7.3	
	1990	523.7	78.3	445.4	504.9	9.5	7.6	1.8
	1991	550.7	91.5	459.2	530.4	10.7	8.5	1.0
	1992	623.5	90.1	533.4	598.4	12.4	10.5	2.2
	1993	747.0	102.9	644.1	710.6	13.3	16.3	6.7
	1994	901.7	116.7	785.0	859.3	20.3	15.3	6.8
	1995	1078.1	137.3	940.8	1018.6	27.3	20.5	11.6
	1996	1275.2	176.3	1099.0	1177.8	36.3	48.4	12.7
	1997	1425.4	188.6	1236.7	1324.9	47.8	36.4	16.3
	1998	1549.8	228.4	1321.4	1425.2	60.4	45.8	18.3
	1999	1650.5	227.8	1422.7	1517.1	70.7	43.0	19.7
	2000	1739.7	226.4	1513.4	1573.1	88.3	46.3	32.1
	2001	1809.6	214.6	1595.0	1629.0	100.8	52.6	27.2
	2002	1918.2	225.2	1693.0	1710.2	122.4	56.7	28.9
	2003	2018.8	246.8	1772.0	1795.2	138.8	54.1	30.7
北京	Beijing	7.1		7.1	7.1	0.1		
天津	Tianjin	24.7	1.1	23.7	22.9	1.5	0.2	0.1
河北	Hebei	37.3	7.2	30.1	34.0	2.6	0.6	0.1
山西	Shanxi	3.1	…	3.1	3.1	…		…
内蒙古	Inner Mongolia	7.3	2.8	4.5	6.9	0.3	…	0.1
辽宁	Liaoning	51.1	3.1	48.1	46.9	3.0	0.4	0.8
吉林	Jilin	10.9	1.9	8.9	10.7	…	0.1	
黑龙江	Heilongjiang	41.9	4.8	37.1	41.6	0.3	…	…
上海	Shanghai	22.1	0.6	21.5	15.1	6.6	0.1	0.3
江苏	Jiangsu	244.8	36.1	208.6	185.8	45.7	9.9	3.4
浙江	Zhejiang	76.8	8.6	68.3	54.3	10.1	4.5	8.0
安徽	Anhui	165.3	40.5	124.8	133.5	18.8	10.4	2.6
福建	Fujian	64.9	8.4	56.5	55.3	3.3	4.5	1.8
江西	Jiangxi	146.1	23.1	123.0	133.6	5.2	5.1	2.2
山东	Shandong	102.1	10.1	92.0	95.1	5.3	1.3	0.3
河南	Henan	39.0	2.6	36.3	37.6	1.0	…	0.3
湖北	Hubei	286.8	40.4	246.3	270.9	10.4	3.8	1.7
湖南	Hunan	156.6	17.6	139.0	150.1	2.4	2.5	1.6
广东	Guangdong	269.3	13.1	256.3	237.9	19.1	7.4	4.9
广西	Guangxi	95.9	10.5	85.3	91.9	1.3	2.1	0.5
海南	Hainan	18.6	2.3	16.3	16.9	0.4	0.3	1.0
重庆	Chongqing	22.5	1.2	21.3	22.0	0.1	0.2	0.1
四川	Sichuan	76.4	5.7	70.7	74.6	0.5	0.6	0.8
贵州	Guizhou	8.0	0.9	7.0	7.8	0.2		…
云南	Yunnan	20.4	2.4	18.0	19.8	0.5	0.1	0.1
西藏	Tibet	…	…	…	…			
陕西	Shaanxi	6.7	0.3	6.4	6.6	…	…	…
甘肃	Gansu	1.4	0.1	1.3	1.4			…
青海	Qinghai	0.1	…	0.1	0.1			
宁夏	Ningxia	5.0	…	5.0	5.0	…		…
新疆	Xinjiang	6.7	1.3	5.4	6.6			0.1
中国水产总公司	China Aquatic Company							

13-23 主要农产品人均占有量

Output of Major Farm Corps Per Capita

单位：公斤 (kg)

年份 地区	Year Region	粮食 Grain	棉花 Cotton	油料 Oil-bearing Corps	猪牛羊肉 Pork, Beef and Mutton	水产品 Total Aquatic Products	牛奶 Milk
	1980	327	2.8	7.8		4.6	1.2
	1985	361	3.9	15.0		6.7	2.4
	1989	364	3.4	11.6		10.3	3.4
	1990	393	4.0	14.2		10.9	3.7
	1995	387	4.0	18.7		20.9	4.6
	1997	402	3.7	17.5	34.6	29.3	5.4
	2000	366	3.5	23.4	38.3	33.9	6.6
	2001	356	4.2	22.5	39.5	34.4	8.1
	2002	357	3.8	22.6	40.8	35.6	10.2
	2003	334	3.8	21.8	42.7	36.5	13.6
北京	Beijing	40	0.2	2.3	29.6	4.9	44.0
天津	Tianjin	118	9.4	3.1	40.4	29.6	42.8
河北	Hebei	354	7.7	24.2	58.9	12.8	29.3
山西	Shanxi	290	2.8	11.0	18.4	0.9	16.1
内蒙古	Inner Mongolia	572	0.2	43.0	59.1	3.1	129.5
辽宁	Liaoning	356	0.1	14.6	44.4	90.8	10.1
吉林	Jilin	836	0.0	21.1	47.6	4.0	8.4
黑龙江	Heilongjiang	659		11.7	32.0	11.0	78.8
上海	Shanghai	59	0.1	3.8	15.3	21.3	16.2
江苏	Jiangsu	334	3.9	27.0	33.1	46.4	6.7
浙江	Zhejiang	170	0.5	9.4	26.2	103.5	5.3
安徽	Anhui	347	3.8	36.3	40.7	25.9	1.4
福建	Fujian	205	…	7.5	34.7	164.7	5.5
江西	Jiangxi	342	1.8	17.9	35.6	34.5	2.6
山东	Shandong	377	9.6	39.7	48.9	77.6	13.7
河南	Henan	370	3.9	32.1	54.0	4.0	5.1
湖北	Hubei	320	5.4	45.5	43.1	47.8	1.8
湖南	Hunan	368	2.5	18.9	66.9	23.6	0.8
广东	Guangdong	181		10.4	30.5	82.0	1.3
广西	Guangxi	303	…	11.5	40.4	54.7	0.8
海南	Hainan	254		11.9	40.1	152.5	0.1
重庆	Chongqing	349	0.0	12.3	44.9	7.2	2.9
四川	Sichuan	352	0.3	25.0	58.1	8.8	5.2
贵州	Guizhou	287	…	18.8	36.7	2.1	0.9
云南	Yunnan	338	…	6.8	53.9	4.7	5.0
西藏	Tibet	360		18.4	70.8	…	73.1
陕西	Shaanxi	263	1.4	11.2	21.8	1.8	20.2
甘肃	Gansu	304	3.3	17.7	26.9	0.6	8.5
青海	Qinghai	163		49.3	43.3	0.2	41.7
宁夏	Ningxia	469		22.9	34.6	8.7	67.0
新疆	Xinjiang	404	83.4	26.1	47.8	3.5	58.9

13-24 平均每一农林牧渔业从业人员主要农产品生产量

Output of Major Farm Corps Per Agricultural Laborer

单位：公斤 (kg)

年份 地区	Year Region	粮食 Grain	棉花 Cotton	油料 Oil-bearing Corps	猪牛羊肉 Pork, Beef and Mutton	水产品 Total Aquatic Products	牛奶 Milk
	1985	1222	13.4	50.8		22.7	8.1
	1989	1276	11.9	40.5		36.0	11.9
	1990	1357	13.4	47.9		36.7	12.6
	1995	1435	14.7	69.2		77.4	17.7
	1997	1528	14.2	66.7	131.4	111.3	18.6
	2000	1407	13.4	89.9	147.3	130.2	25.2
	2001	1387	16.3	87.8	154.0	134.3	31.4
	2002	1419	15.3	89.9	162.3	141.7	40.3
	2003	1362	15.4	88.9	174.1	148.8	55.2
北京	Beijing	939	5.5	53.3	688.5	115.3	1023.8
天津	Tianjin	1478	117.3	38.2	504.7	369.5	535.5
河北	Hebei	1442	31.5	98.5	240.2	52.1	119.5
山西	Shanxi	1470	14.1	55.8	93.0	4.8	81.6
内蒙古	Inner Mongolia	2592	1.0	194.8	267.8	13.9	586.7
辽宁	Liaoning	2259	0.5	92.6	281.8	575.9	64.4
吉林	Jilin	4467	0.1	112.9	254.1	21.5	44.8
黑龙江	Heilongjiang	3393		60.4	165.0	56.6	405.8
上海	Shanghai	1289	1.4	83.4	333.4	463.2	353.2
江苏	Jiangsu	1913	22.5	154.3	189.1	265.4	38.5
浙江	Zhejiang	880	2.3	48.6	135.6	535.7	27.4
安徽	Anhui	1168	12.7	122.1	136.9	87.2	4.8
福建	Fujian	956	…	34.9	161.5	767.5	25.7
江西	Jiangxi	1484	7.8	77.7	154.6	149.4	11.1
山东	Shandong	1482	37.8	156.1	192.1	304.7	53.7
河南	Henan	1063	11.2	92.3	155.2	11.6	14.8
湖北	Hubei	1714	29.0	243.3	230.5	255.8	9.9
湖南	Hunan	1216	8.1	62.6	221.4	78.0	2.6
广东	Guangdong	923		52.9	155.4	418.6	6.8
广西	Guangxi	946	…	36.0	126.2	170.8	2.5
海南	Hainan	1109		52.1	175.3	667.1	0.3
重庆	Chongqing	1305	…	45.9	168.2	27.0	10.9
四川	Sichuan	1242	1.0	88.3	205.2	31.1	18.5
贵州	Guizhou	825	…	54.0	105.8	5.9	2.5
云南	Yunnan	869	…	17.5	138.5	12.1	12.8
西藏	Tibet	1115		57.1	219.5	0.1	226.6
陕西	Shaanxi	976	5.3	41.7	81.0	6.7	74.8
甘肃	Gansu	1053	11.6	61.4	93.2	1.9	29.6
青海	Qinghai	640		193.1	169.6	0.9	163.2
宁夏	Ningxia	1823		88.9	134.4	34.0	260.4
新疆	Xinjiang	2361	487.2	152.6	279.3	20.5	344.1

13-25 农村居民家庭平均每人出售主要农产品

Per Capita Main Farm Produce Sold by Rural Households by Region

本表为农村住户抽样调查资料。

Data in this table are obtained from the sample surveys on rural households.

单位：公斤 (kg)

年份 地区	Year Region	粮食 Grain	棉花 Cotton	油料 Oil-bearing Corps	麻类 Fiber Corps	烟叶 Tobacco	蔬菜 Vegetables	水果 Fruits
	1985	123.49	4.13	14.37	2.80	2.25	53.76	6.78
	1989	154.27	3.48	10.70	1.28	2.78	64.05	11.93
	1990	180.24	4.31	12.87	1.56	2.67	65.07	13.17
	1991	179.44	5.54	13.22	1.32	3.17	68.70	15.74
	1992	165.89	4.16	11.27	1.18	3.58	75.58	16.92
	1993	159.35	3.26	10.48	0.86	3.19	77.73	19.60
	1994	188.53	4.01	10.68	0.50	2.02	72.68	22.64
	1995	179.20	4.31	12.02	0.73	2.21	79.96	24.28
	1996	203.47	3.90	11.64	0.83	3.07	97.00	29.78
	1997	228.01	5.12	11.13	0.57	4.45	106.22	36.21
	1998	227.53	5.10	12.39	0.41	2.33	108.72	38.51
	1999	243.34	4.43	15.59	0.28	2.42	111.66	43.17
	2000	264.74	5.59	18.43	0.47	2.73	132.07	46.43
	2001	268.04	7.05	18.31	0.44	2.42	132.94	48.21
	2002	281.15	6.94	18.47	0.64	2.59	143.77	49.06
	2003	294.35	16.77	19.22	0.71	2.62	147.56	48.83
北京	Beijing	152.40	0.71	2.55			132.53	217.86
天津	Tianjin	225.38	90.37	3.66			527.56	17.59
河北	Hebei	249.72	48.14	12.08	0.21	0.01	158.74	101.26
山西	Shanxi	133.20	11.28	10.44	0.02	0.04	154.38	125.75
内蒙古	Inner Mongolia	606.12		101.06	0.04		121.42	8.06
辽宁	Liaoning	786.25	0.32	17.52		2.14	255.86	78.32
吉林	Jilin	1785.46		22.07	1.08	0.41	120.79	1.46
黑龙江	Heilongjiang	1672.23		8.68	3.78	4.92	220.06	1.32
上海	Shanghai	108.63	0.01	7.85			123.31	16.17
江苏	Jiangsu	328.89	12.58	20.96	0.02		86.99	2.99
浙江	Zhejiang	92.68	1.17	3.87		0.13	309.44	90.47
安徽	Anhui	260.74	13.59	36.82	0.53	0.19	60.19	1.27
福建	Fujian	69.56		1.75	0.05	5.75	154.05	109.08
江西	Jiangxi	317.11	5.59	11.02	0.20	1.41	71.10	11.94
山东	Shandong	393.95	33.48	25.25	0.05	1.27	330.07	92.57
河南	Henan	280.35	15.29	21.53	2.21	1.93	113.38	33.13
湖北	Hubei	299.98	33.83	58.96	2.15	1.65	145.02	54.72
湖南	Hunan	145.42	10.61	5.60	1.58	5.84	84.51	33.91
广东	Guangdong	97.69		4.68		1.73	256.92	29.63
广西	Guangxi	87.09		2.18	0.62	0.47	92.70	43.29
海南	Hainan	85.38		9.69	0.02	0.01	224.40	77.13
重庆	Chongqing	71.67	0.03	5.27	0.06	4.08	69.98	25.67
四川	Sichuan	76.84	0.06	18.05	0.61	1.83	123.26	29.37
贵州	Guizhou	62.97		17.82		11.41	50.36	4.72
云南	Yunnan	92.31		4.81	1.53	22.04	131.39	29.14
西藏	Tibet	31.78		6.33	0.02		1.66	1.35
陕西	Shaanxi	142.53	8.85	9.41	0.02	0.95	105.11	136.16
甘肃	Gansu	120.37	36.04	14.78		0.67	97.19	27.49
青海	Qinghai	32.69		52.67	0.60		69.43	8.47
宁夏	Ningxia	325.11		18.64			243.08	40.18
新疆	Xinjiang	321.80	177.87	34.37	2.68	0.96	152.95	94.99

13-26 农村居民家庭平均每人出售主要畜产品及水产品

Sales of Livestock, Poultry, Small Animals and Fishery Per Capita Rural Household

本表为农村住户抽样调查资料。

Data in this table are obtained from the sample surveys on rural households.

单位：公斤 (kg)

年 份 地 区	Year Region	猪 肉 (公斤) Pork	牛 肉 (公斤) Beef	羊 肉 (公斤) Mutton	家 禽 (公斤) Poultry	蛋 类 (公斤) Poultry Eggs	牛羊奶 (公斤) Milk	蚕 茧 (公斤) Silkworm Cocoons	水产品 (公斤) Aquatic Products
	1985	16.27	0.52	0.57	1.00	2.21	1.02	0.36	1.74
	1989	16.79	0.51	0.66	1.59	2.01	1.44	0.51	2.18
	1990	17.84	0.55	0.71	1.45	1.89	1.68	0.58	2.05
	1991	20.07	0.76	0.90	2.18	2.65	1.91	0.65	2.92
	1992	21.17	0.72	0.86	2.23	2.90	1.85	0.70	3.21
	1993	23.80			2.41	2.89	1.76	0.74	3.10
	1994				2.30	3.35	1.81	0.83	2.97
	1995				2.42	3.54	1.90	0.79	2.94
	1996				2.45	2.58	2.55	0.50	3.27
	1997	26.08	2.33	1.76	2.99	3.76	2.76	0.54	4.50
	1998	23.04	1.04	1.67	2.42	3.57	2.60	0.65	4.31
	1999	28.41	1.86	1.85	3.41	4.07	3.00	0.62	6.20
	2000	30.19	2.40	2.06	4.60	6.32	2.67	0.64	5.82
	2001	30.86	2.76	2.31	5.03	5.96	3.65	0.80	6.53
	2002	32.30	2.73	2.50	6.01	6.54	4.87	0.77	8.04
	2003	38.31	3.70	4.08	6.67	7.06	7.29	0.76	7.47
北 京	Beijing	16.99	0.17	4.93	1.87	4.99	16.85		2.32
天 津	Tianjin	77.79	5.69	4.40	22.96	32.44	21.28		5.95
河 北	Hebei	21.85	3.56	2.41	7.16	11.25	9.67		1.68
山 西	Shanxi	16.83	2.00	4.48	1.34	15.20	11.28	0.25	
内蒙古	Inner Mongolia	18.30	18.26	57.27	1.45	1.49	57.13		
辽 宁	Liaoning	68.13	7.71	1.46	12.94	31.92		3.86	9.67
吉 林	Jilin	37.81	13.97	1.29	3.45	5.91	1.81	0.01	0.32
黑龙江	Heilongjiang	41.50	8.38	4.72	10.12	12.05	37.07		1.58
上 海	Shanghai	8.39		0.50	0.73	1.58			3.87
江 苏	Jiangsu	39.18	0.63	1.23	13.14	14.04	4.42	1.18	19.52
浙 江	Zhejiang	28.62	0.12	0.65	8.46	4.52	3.62	4.04	6.95
安 徽	Anhui	33.81	4.71	1.77	4.32	4.56		0.91	1.48
福 建	Fujian	35.04	0.53	0.28	5.65	3.27	0.70	0.01	15.51
江 西	Jiangxi	41.58	0.36	0.07	2.48	5.85	2.30	0.32	5.85
山 东	Shandong	39.96	9.09	3.03	23.73	12.35	8.13	1.57	2.04
河 南	Henan	48.16	3.83	2.95	3.28	9.76	0.11	0.02	2.80
湖 北	Hubei	40.18	0.72	0.54	1.48	7.23		0.10	28.84
湖 南	Hunan	66.92	0.30	0.43	4.38	1.45			6.41
广 东	Guangdong	37.11	0.47	0.03	17.79	0.55	0.05	1.34	36.41
广 西	Guangxi	61.04	1.52	0.68	5.22	0.19		2.98	6.13
海 南	Hainan	24.73	3.29	1.06	10.00	6.50	0.02		62.58
重 庆	Chongqing	59.49	0.85	0.38	4.69	1.32		1.68	5.07
四 川	Sichuan	77.96	1.29	1.06	9.32	4.05	0.76	1.23	3.27
贵 州	Guizhou	36.37	1.59	0.75	2.60	0.67			0.07
云 南	Yunnan	37.18	2.94	1.02	1.57	0.33	10.64	0.35	0.33
西 藏	Tibet	0.99	9.85	1.54	0.14	0.28	0.53		
陕 西	Shaanxi	22.84	0.67	1.70	2.41	12.20	11.86	0.49	0.06
甘 肃	Gansu	7.00	1.67	3.12	0.66	3.48	1.24		
青 海	Qinghai	5.13	7.12	27.27	0.23	0.04	6.69		6.86
宁 夏	Ningxia	12.08	6.04	9.20	5.78	19.98	96.63		3.11
新 疆	Xinjiang	2.70	12.53	19.47	1.42	6.56	14.51	0.13	

注：1992年及以前，蛋类不包括蛋制品，水产品出售量仅指鱼虾出售量。

a) Sales of poultry eggs before 1992 exclude egg product, and sales of aquatic products only referred to the sales of fish and shrimp.

13-27 主要农产品产量与解放前最高年产量比较

Output of Major Agricultural Products in Comparison with Peak Year Prior to 1949

产品名称	Item	解放前最高年 Peak Year prior to 1949		指数(以解放前最高年为100) Indices (peak year prior to 1949=100)		
		年份 Year	产量 Output	1949	1952	2003
种植业 （万吨）	**Planting (10 000 tons)**					
粮食	Grain	1936	15000	75.5	109.3	287.1
#稻谷	Rice	1936	5735	84.8	119.3	280.1
小麦	Wheat	1936	2330	59.3	77.8	371.2
玉米	Corn	1936	1010		166.8	1146.8
大豆	Soybeans	1936	1130	45.0	84.3	136.2
薯类	Tubers	1936	635	155.1	257.2	553.3
棉花	Cotton	1936	84.9	52.3	153.6	572.4
花生	Peanuts	1933	317	40.0	73.0	423.2
油菜籽	Rapeseeds	1934	191	38.5	48.9	598.8
芝麻	Sesame	1933	99.1	32.9	48.5	90.1
黄红麻	Jute and Ambary Hemp	1945	5.5	34.6	278.2	181.8
桑蚕茧	Mulberry Silkworm Cocoons	1931	22.1	14.0	28.1	302.0
茶叶	Tea	1932	22.5	18.2	36.4	341.3
甘蔗	Sugarcane	1940	565	46.7	125.9	1596.5
甜菜	Beetroots	1939	32.9	58.1	145.6	1879.0
烤烟	Flue-cured Tobacco	1948	17.9	24.0	124.0	1125.7
苹果	Apples	1926	12.1		97.5	17439.7
柑桔	Citrus	1926	40.1		51.6	3355.1
香蕉	Bananas	1927	10.3		106.8	5731.1
畜牧业（万头、万只）	**Animal Husbandry (10 000 head)**					
大牲畜年底头数	Large Animals (year-end)	1935	7151	83.9	106.9	216.8
牛	Cattle and Buffaloes	1935	4827	91.0	117.3	279.0
马	Horses	1935	649	75.1	94.5	121.7
驴	Donkeys	1935	1215	78.1	97.2	67.5
骡	Mules	1935	460	32.0	35.6	86.0
猪年底头数	Hogs (year-end)	1934	7853	73.5	114.3	593.4
羊年底只数	Sheep and Goats (year-end)	1937	6252	67.7	98.8	544.7
渔业						
水产品 （万吨）	Aquatic Products (10 000 tons)	1936	150	30.0	111.3	3136.4

13-28 受灾面积和成灾面积

Areas Covered and Affected by Natural Disaster

单位: 千公顷 (1 000 hectares)

年份 地区	Year Region	受灾面积 Areas Covered	成灾面积 Areas Affected	成灾面积占受灾面积比重(%) Percentage of Disaster Areas Affected to Areas Covered (%)	水灾 Flood		旱灾 Drought	
					受灾面积 Areas Covered	成灾面积 Areas Affected	受灾面积 Areas Covered	成灾面积 Areas Affected
	1978	50790	24457	48.2	2850	2012	40170	17970
	1980	44526	29777	66.9	9146	6070	26111	14174
	1985	44365	22705	51.2	14197	8949	22989	10063
	1989	46991	24449	52.0	11328	5917	29358	15262
	1990	38474	17819	46.3	11804	5605	18175	7805
	1991	55472	27814	50.1	24596	14614	29414	10559
	1992	51333	25859	50.4	9423	4464	32980	17049
	1993	48829	23133	47.4	16387	8611	21098	8657
	1994	55043	31383	57.0	17329	10744	30425	17049
	1995	45821	22267	48.6	12731	7630	23455	10401
	1996	46989	21233	45.2	18146	10855	20151	6247
	1997	53429	30309	56.7	11414	5840	33514	20250
	1998	50145	25181	50.2	22292	13785	14236	5060
	1999	49981	26731	53.5	9020	5071	30156	16614
	2000	54688	34374	62.9	7323	4321	40541	26784
	2001	52215	31793	60.9	6042	3614	38472	23698
	2002	47119	27319	58.0	12378	7474	22207	13247
	2003	54506	32516	59.8	19208	12289	24852	14470
北京	Beijing	59	25	42.4			49	24
天津	Tianjin	143	95	66.2			120	80
河北	Hebei	2998	1947	64.9	198	160	1782	1183
山西	Shanxi	829	345	41.6	273	98	287	73
内蒙古	Inner Mongolia	3227	2312	71.6	362	255	2372	1673
辽宁	Liaoning	1169	1026	87.8	58	31	1049	941
吉林	Jilin	1905	768	40.3	65	46	1510	521
黑龙江	Heilongjiang	6659	4160	62.5	1346	1023	4544	2636
上海	Shanghai	1			1			
江苏	Jiangsu	2864	1677	58.6	2676	1595		
浙江	Zhejiang	613	344	56.2	55	24	542	311
安徽	Anhui	3747	2619	69.9	2416	1746	399	173
福建	Fujian	1097	509	46.4	34	20	906	389
江西	Jiangxi	1823	1328	72.8	595	380	1057	853
山东	Shandong	2632	1250	47.5	1530	928	857	173
河南	Henan	4965	2739	55.2	3204	2208	494	69
湖北	Hubei	3099	1883	60.8	1575	956	995	690
湖南	Hunan	2741	1737	63.4	825	548	1676	1072
广东	Guangdong	1194	498	41.7	25	6	131	105
广西	Guangxi	1831	1134	61.9	315	128	755	415
海南	Hainan	277	149	53.8			99	38
重庆	Chongqing	959	603	62.9	480	291	431	283
四川	Sichuan	2743	1264	46.1	1409	814	882	360
贵州	Guizhou	1060	579	54.6	252	148	594	323
云南	Yunnan	1493	810	54.3	227	119	864	491
西藏	Tibet	4			4			
陕西	Shaanxi	2136	1160	54.3	946	524	1000	533
甘肃	Gansu	1051	757	72.0	210	154	736	534
青海	Qinghai	174	103	59.4	14	11.3	141	80
宁夏	Ningxia	245	179	72.9	31	22	183	131
新疆	Xinjiang	768	516	67.2	82	53	397	316

13-29 国营农场基本情况

Basic Statistics on State Farms

本表为农垦系统数据。

Data in this table cover those of the land reclamation department.

指标	Item	2000	2001	2002	2003
农场数 （个）	**Number of Farms (unit)**	**2026**	**1961**	**1945**	**1967**
职工人数 （万人）	**Number of Staff and Workers (10 000 persons)**	**391.9**	**366.0**	**355.7**	**353.7**
耕地面积 （千公顷）	**Cultivated Area (1 000 hectares)**	**4801.0**	**4814.6**	**4740.7**	**4690.1**
农业机械总动力 （亿瓦）	**Total Power of Agricultural Machinery (100 million watts)**	**115.9**	**120.1**	**124.4**	**129.9**
农业机械拥有量 （台.辆）	**Ownership of Agricultural Machinery (unit)**				
大中型农用拖拉机	Large and Medium Agricultural Tractors	66562	67302	72000	70000
小型及手扶拖拉机	Mini and Walking Agricultural Tractors	214000	216000	232000	245000
农用排灌动力机械	Machinery for Agricultural Drainage and Irrigation	139000	157000	168600	177000
联合收割机	Combine Harvesters	15000	15000	16300	18000
农用载重汽车	Trucks for Agricultural Use	12524	13000	46000	50000
农用化肥施用量 （万吨）	**Consumption of Chemical Fertilizers(10 000 tons)**	**131.7**	**133.7**	**134.2**	**143.9**
农业总产值 （亿元）	**Gross Agricultural Output Value (100 million yuan)**	**644.0**	**652.8**	**726.4**	**846.3**
农作物总播种面积（千公顷）	**Sown Area of Farm Crops (1 000 hectares)**	**4755.8**	**4750.4**	**4792.6**	**4674.7**
粮食作物	Grain	3163.9	3096.0	3073.7	2831.1
棉 花	Cotton	527.3	605.4	571.6	627.6
油 料	Oil-bearing Crops	461.2	354.6	405.4	446.9
糖 料	Sugar Crops	103.6	138.4	148.9	115.1
麻 类	Fiber Crops	9.4	37.6	44.1	67.0
年底实有茶园面积	Area of Tea Plantations (year-end)	34.1	32.7	31.2	29.6
年底实有桑园面积	Area of Mulberry Plantations (year-end)	3.9	3.9	2.3	2.6
年底实有果园面积	Area of Orchards (year-end)	193.6	210.9	230.0	224.4
年底实有橡胶园面积	Area of Rubber Plantations (year-end)	382.3	383.6	385.3	404.3
主要农产品产量	**Yield of Major Farm Crops**				
粮食作物 （万吨）	Grain (10 000 tons)	1465.2	1480.2	1498.9	1342.6
棉 花 （万吨）	Cotton (10 000 tons)	83.2	84.9	99.0	103.4
油 料 （万吨）	Oil-bearing Crops (10 000 tons)	71.2	52.8	67.3	71.9
糖 料 （万吨）	Sugar Crops (10 000 tons)	589.5	824.9	913.3	721.7
麻 类 （万吨）	Fiber Crops (10 000 tons)	3.0	12.0	18.0	19.4
茶 叶 （万吨）	Tea (10 000 tons)	3.9	3.9	4.7	3.8
桑蚕茧 （吨）	Mulberry Silkworm Cocoons (ton)				
水 果 （万吨）	Fruits (10 000 tons)	118.6	127.6	147.8	146.4
干 胶 （万吨）	Rubber (10 000 tons)	34.7	34.7	37.8	39.5
畜牧业、渔业生产	**Production of Animal Husbandry and Fishery**				
大牲畜年底头数 （万头）	Number of Large Animals (year-end) (10 000 heads)	214.6	217.4	232.6	260.2
猪年底头数 （万头）	Number of Hogs (10 000 heads)	478.1	500.0	569.8	588.3
羊年底只数 （万只）	Number of Sheep and Goats (10 000 heads)	1104.7	1119.9	1240.0	1509.6
#绵 羊	Sheep	888.4	890.2	945.5	431.8
畜产品产量 （万吨）	**Output of Livestock Products (10 000 tons)**				
猪牛羊肉	Pork, Beef and Mutton	68.3	72.4	78.5	87.7
#猪 肉	Pork	51.4	54.4	58.6	64.2
牛 奶	Milk	116.5	134.4	159.2	176.8
禽 蛋	Poultry Eggs	20.4	19.5	19.9	21.3
羊 毛	Sheep Wool	2.1	2.1	2.1	2.4
水产品总产量 （万吨）	**Total output of Aquatic Products (10 000 tons)**	**49.1**	**55.3**	**63.1**	**65.7**

主要统计指标解释

农林牧渔业总产值 指以货币表现的农、林、牧、渔业全部产品和对农林牧渔业生产活动进行的各种支持性服务活动的价值总量，它反映一定时期内农林牧渔业生产总规模和总成果。1957年以前的农林牧渔业总产值中包括了厩肥和农民自给性手工业(如农民自制衣服、鞋、袜，自己从事粮食初步加工等)。1958年及以后，林业中增加了村及村以下竹木采伐产值；牧业中取消了厩肥产值；副业中取消了农民自给性手工业产值，增加了村及村以下办的工业产值；渔业中增加了海洋捕捞水产品产值。1980年及以后，在副业中增加了农民家庭兼营工业商品部分的产值。从1984年起村及村以下工业产值划归工业。从1993年起取消副业，将野生动物的捕猎划入牧业、野生植物采集和农民家庭兼营商品性工业划归农业。从2003年起，执行新的国民经济行业分类标准，农林牧渔业总产值中包括了农林牧渔服务业产值。林业中增加了森林采运业产值。农业中取消了家庭兼营商品性工业产值，将野生林产品的采集划归林业。第一次农业普查以后，由于畜牧业产品年报数据与普查数据之间存在一定的差距，国家统计局农调总队对畜牧业年报数据与普查数据进行衔接，相应的畜牧业产值进行调整。

农林牧渔业总产值的计算方法通常是按农、林、牧、渔业产品及其副产品的产量分别乘以各自单位产品价格求得；少数生产周期较长，当年没有产品或产品产量不易统计的，则采用间接方法匡算其产值；然后将四业产品产值相加即为农林牧渔业总产值。

粮食产量 指全社会的产量。包括国有经济经营的、集体统一经营的和农民家庭经营的粮食产量，还包括工矿企业办的农场和其他生产单位的产量。粮食除包括稻谷、小麦、玉米、高粱、谷子及其他杂粮外，还包括薯类和豆类。其产量计算方法，豆类按去豆荚后的干豆计算；薯类(包括甘薯和马铃薯，不包括芋头和木薯)1963年以前按每4公斤鲜薯折1公斤粮食计算，从1964年开始改为按5公斤鲜薯折1公斤粮食计算。城市郊区作为蔬菜的薯类(如马铃薯等)按鲜品计算，并且不作粮食统计。其他粮食一律按脱粒后的原粮计算。1989年以前全国粮食产量数据主要靠全面报表取得，1989年开始使用抽样调查数据。

棉花产量 指全社会的产量。包括春播棉和夏播棉。产量按皮棉计算。3公斤籽棉折1公斤皮棉，不包括木棉。

油料产量 指全部油料作物的生产量。包括花生、油菜籽、芝麻、向日葵籽、胡麻籽（亚麻籽）和其他油料。不包括大豆、木本油料和野生油料。花生以带壳干花生计算。

水产品产量 指人工养殖的水产品和天然生长的水产品的捕捞量。包括海水的鱼类、虾蟹类、贝类和藻类以及内陆水域的鱼类、虾蟹类和贝类，不包括淡水生植物。水产品产量是通过各级水产和统计部门逐级上报取得数据。1995年及以前，贝类中牡蛎按鲜肉计算；蚶、蛤、蛏按 5 斤鲜品折 1 斤计算。1996年以后则统一按鲜品计算。

猪、牛、羊肉产量 指当年出栏并已屠宰、除去头蹄下水后带骨肉(即胴体重)的重量。包括全社会范围内的产量。1996年前为各级逐级上报数据。1996年第一次农业普查以后，由于畜牧业产品年报数据与普查数据之间存在一定的差距，国家统计局农调总队对畜牧业年报数据与普查数据进行衔接。1999年以后，国家统计局开展了猪、牛、羊、禽等主要畜禽品种的抽样调查，并用抽样数据作为国家定案数据使用。未开展抽样调查的品种，仍使用各级统计部门逐级上报数据。

期初(末)畜禽存栏头(只)数 指报告期初(末)农村各种合作经济组织和国营农场、农民个人、机关、团体、学校、工矿企业、部队等单位以及城镇居民饲养的大牲畜、猪、羊、家禽等畜禽的存栏数。数据上报方式及数据调整情况同猪、牛、羊肉产量。

常用耕地 是指耕地总资源中专门种植农作物并经常进行耕种、能够正常收获的土地。包括当年实际耕种的熟地；弃耕、休闲不满三年，随时可以复耕的地；开荒利用三年以上的土地。在统计口径上包括南方小于1米、北方小于2米宽的沟、渠、路和田塄。不包括临时种植农作物的坡度在25度以上的陡坡地；在河套、湖畔、库区临时开发的成片或零星土地；也不包括已列为国家和省（区、市）退耕计划但临时耕种的土地。常用耕地是国家需要重点保护的耕地，是反映我国农业综合生产能力的一个重要指标。

农作物播种面积 指实际播种或移植有农作物面积。凡是实际种植有农作物的面积，不论种植在耕地上还是种植在非耕地上，均包括在农作物播种面积中。在播种季节基本结束后，因遭灾而重新改种和补种的农作物面积，也包括在内。它是反映我国耕地面积利用情况的一个重要指标。目前，农作物播种面积主要包括粮食、棉花、油料、糖料、麻类、烟叶、蔬菜和瓜类、药材和其它农作物九大类。

有效灌溉面积 指具有一定的水源，地块比较平整，灌溉工程或设备已经配套，在一般年景下当年能够进行正常灌溉的耕地面积。在一般情况下，有效灌溉面积应等于灌溉工程或设备已经配备，能够进行正常灌溉的水田和水浇地面积之和。它是反映我国耕地抗旱能力的一个重要指标。

农用化肥施用量 指本年内实际用于农业生产的化肥数量，包括氮肥、磷肥、钾肥和复合肥。化肥施用量要求按折纯量计算数量。折纯量是指把氮肥、磷肥、钾肥分别按含氮、含五氧化二磷、含氧化钾的百分之百成份进行折算后的数量。复合肥按其所含主要成分折算。公式为：

折纯量= 实物量 × 某种化肥有效成份含量的百分比

农业机械总动力 指主要用于农、林、牧、渔业的各种动力机械的动力总和。包括耕作机械、排灌机械、收获机械、农用运输机械、植物保护机械、牧业机械、林业机械、渔业机械和其他农业机械〔内燃机按引擎马力折成瓦(特)计算、电动机按功率折成瓦(特)计算〕。不包括专门用于乡、镇、村、组办工业、基本建设、非农业运输、科学试验和教学等非农业生产方面用的动力机械与作业机械。这个指标的统计数据主要来源于农机部门。

乡村从业人员 指乡村人口中劳动年龄在16周岁以上实际参加生产经营活动并取得实物或货币收入的人员，包括劳动年龄内经常参加劳动的人员，也包括超过劳动年龄但经常参加劳动的人员，但不包括户口在家的在外学生、现役军人和丧失劳动能力的人，也不包括待业人员和家务劳动者。从业人员按从事主业时间最长（时间相同按收入）分为农业从业人员、工业从业人员、建筑业从业人员、交运仓储及邮电业从业人员、批零贸易及餐饮业从业人员、其它从业人员。

Explanatory Notes on Main Statistical Indicators

Gross Output Value of Farming, Forestry, Animal Husbandry and Fishery refers to the total value of products of farming, forestry, animal husbandry and fishery, and total value of services rendered to support farming, forestry, animal husbandry and fishery activities. It reflects the total scale and results of agricultural production during a given period. Prior to 1957, Chinas gross agricultural output value included barnyard manure and handicraft products for self-consumption (clothes, shoes, stockings, and initial grain processing undertaken by peasants). Since 1958, cutting and felling of bamboo and trees by villages and other cooperative organizations under villages have been included in forestry; value of barnyard manure has been excluded from animal husbandry; self consumed handicrafts has been excluded from sideline occupations, while the output value of industries run by villages and cooperative organizations under village had been included in sideline occupations and the output value of fish catches by motor fishing boats has been added to fishery. Since 1980, the value of handicraft products made for sale by individuals in households had been added to sideline occupations. Since 1984, industries run by villages and under villages have been included in the sector of industry. Since 1993, the subdivision of sideline occupations has been canceled, and the hunting of wild animals has been classified into animal husbandry, and the gathering of wild plants and commodity industry run by rural household have been included in farming. A new industrial classification of economic activities was introduced in 2003. Under the new classification, value of services to farming, forestry, animal husbandry and fishery is included in the gross output value of agriculture, value of wood felling and transport is included in forestry, value of industrial output by rural households is not included in agriculture, and the collection of wild forest products is taken from agriculture and included in the forestry. The first agriculture census of China revealed some discrepancy between the production of animal products from the annual reports and that from the census. Efforts were made by the Rural Socio-economic Survey Organization of NBS to adjust the output value of animal husbandry to make the figures from the annual reports consistent with the census data.

Gross output value of agriculture is obtained by first multiplying the output of each product or by product by its price, resulting in the output value of each single item. For a small number of products, annual output of which is not available or difficult to get due to the long production growing process involved, the output value is estimated through an indirect approach. The sum of output value of all products of farming, forestry, animal husbandry, and fishery is then equal to the gross output value of agriculture.

Grain Output refers to the total output in the whole country including grains produced by state farms, collective units, rural households, as well as by farms affiliated to industrial and mining enterprises and other production units. Grain includes rice, wheat, corn, sorghum, millet and other miscellaneous grains as well as tubers and bean. Output of beans refers to dry beans without pods. The output of tubers (sweet potatoes and potatoes, not including taros and cassava) was converted into that of grain at the ratio 4:1, i.e. 4 kilograms of fresh tubers was equivalent to 1 kilogram of grain up to 1963. Since 1964 the ratio for conversion has been 5:1. Tubers supplied as vegetables (such as potatoes) in cities and suburbs are calculated as fresh vegetables and their output is not included in the output of grain. Output of all other grains refers to husked grain. Data on grain production before 1989 were obtained through Comprehensive Statistical Reporting System. Since 1989, data from sample surveys are used.

Cotton Output refers to the cotton production in the whole country including cotton sown in spring and in autumn. Output is measured as the weight of ginned cotton. Three kilograms of seed-cotton are equivalent to 1 kilogram of ginned cotton, excluding ceiba.

Output of Oil-bearing Crops refers to the total production of oil-bearing crops of various kinds, including peanuts, (dry, in shell) rapeseeds, sesame, sunflower seeds, flax seeds, and other oil-bearing crops. Soybeans, oil-bearing woody plants, and wild oil-bearing crops are not included.

Output of Aquatic Products refers to catches of both artificially cultured and naturally grown aquatic products, including fish, shrimps, crabs and shellfish in sea and inland water as well as seaweed. Freshwater plants are not included. Data on output of aquatic products are reported by aquatic product and statistical agencies level by level. Before 1995, among the shellfish, the oyster was counted as fresh meat; 5 kilograms of ark shell, clams and frogs are equivalent to 1 kilogram of fresh aquatic products; they are all counted as fresh aquatic products since 1996.

Output of Pork, Beef, and Mutton refers to the meat of slaughtered hogs, cattle, sheep and goats with head, feet, and offal taken away. Data refers to the production of the whole country. The first agriculture census of China in 1996 revealed some discrepancy between the production of animal products from the annual reports and that from the census. Efforts were made by the Rural Socio-economic Survey Organization of NBS to adjust the output value of animal husbandry to make the figures from the annual reports consistent with the census data. Since 1999, NBS conducted sample survey for the major animal husbandry products, such as hogs, cattle, sheep and goats and fowls, and the data from sample surveys are used as national finalized data. Those products, which are not covered by the sample survey, are still reported by statistical agencies level by level.

Number of Livestock or Poultry in Stock at Beginning (or End) refers to the total number of large animals, pigs, sheep, fowls, etc. raised by rural cooperative organizations, state farms, rural individuals, government agencies, schools, industrial and mining enterprises, army, and urban residents at the beginning (or end) of the reference period. Data reporting system and data adjustment are the same as that in the output of pork, beef and mutton.

Regularly Cultivated Land refers to farmland among the total land resources, which is exclusively used for farming and is under regular cultivation with harvest in normal years. Included are currently cultivated land, land that has been abandoned or put in idle for less than 3 years and could be re-used for cultivation at any time, and new-claimed land that has been put into cultivation for more than 3 years. According to statistical coverage, it includes the gouges, dykes, roads and ridges of field with 1 meter wide in Southern areas and 2 meters wide in Northern areas. Excluded under this category are steep slope land over 25 degrees under temporary cultivation, land (large or small plots) that is claimed along river bends, lake sides or banks of reservoirs, as well as land that has been designated under the "Green for Grain" programmes of the state and provincial governments but is still temporarily under cultivation. The regularly cultivated land is the key protection land of the nation, an important indicator reflecting the comprehensive productivity of agriculture of China.

Sown Area of Crops refers to area of land sown or transplanted with crops regardless of being in cultivated area or non-cultivated area. Area of land re-sown due to natural disasters is also included. This is an important indicator that can reflect the utilization condition of the cultivated land in China. At present, the sown area of crops mainly include the following 9 categories of crops: grain, cotton, oil-bearing crops, sugar crops, fiber crops, Tobacco, Vegetables and melons, medicinal materials and other farm crops.

Irrigated Area refers to areas that are effectively irrigated, i.e. level land, which has water source and complete sets of irrigation facilities to lift and move adequate water for irrigation purpose under normal conditions. Under normal conditions, irrigated area is the sum of watered fields and irrigated fields where irrigation systems or equipment have been installed for regular irrigation purpose. This important indicator reflects drought resistance capacity of the cultivated land in China.

Consumption of Chemical Fertilizers in Agriculture refers to the quantity of chemical fertilizers applied in agriculture in the year, including nitrogenous fertilizer, phosphate fertilizer, potash fertilizer, and compound fertilizer. The consumption of chemical fertilizers is required in calculation to convert the gross weight into weight containing 100% effective component (e.g. 100% nitrogen content in nitrogenous fertilizer, 100% phosphorous pent oxide contents in phosphate fertilizer, 100% potassium oxide contents in potash fertilizer). Compound fertilizer is converted with its major component. The formula is :

Volume of effective component= physical quantity × effective component of certain chemical fertilizer(%)

Total Power of Farm Machinery refers to total mechanical power of machinery used in farming, forestry, animal husbandry, and fishery, including ploughing, irrigation and drainage, harvesting, transport, plant protection, stock breeding, forestry and fishery. The power of internal combustion engines is required to convert horsepower into watts and the power of electric motors is required to be converted into watts. Machinery employed for non-agricultural purposes, such as the machines used in township run and village-run industry, construction, non-agricultural transport, scientific experiments and teaching, is excluded. Data are mainly from agricultural machinery agencies.

Rural Employed Persons refer to rural labor forces aged over 16 years old who are engaged in real production and management activities and receive payment in kind or wages, including those covered within the age frame and regularly participating in production activities, and those who are out of the range of age frame and also participating in production activities regularly. Excluding students studying in other places with their permanent residence registered in local areas, servicemen and persons incapable of working; also excluding those who are waiting for jobs and those engaged in household work. Persons employed are classified as rural employed persons; industrial employed persons; construction industry employed persons; transport, storage and telecommunications industries employed persons; whole sales and retail sales trade and catering industry employed persons and others according to the longest period of persons engaged in major activities (or using income indicator when periods are the same).

十四、工业

Industry

简要说明

一、本篇资料的主要内容

本篇资料反映我国工业经济方面的基本情况，包括31个省、自治区、直辖市的主要工业经济统计数据。

1.全部国有及规模以上非国有工业企业单位数和总产值；

2.全部国有及规模以上非国有工业企业按登记注册类型、轻重工业、企业规模、工业行业大类和按地区分组的主要经济指标和经济效益指标。指标包括：工业总产值、工业增加值、实收资本、资产总计、负债合计、流动资产、固定资产、流动负债、长期负债、所有者权益、产品销售收入、销售成本、销售税金及附加、利润总额、应交增值税、工业增加值率、总资产贡献率、资产负债率、成本费用利润率、流动资产周转次数、全员劳动生产率、产品销售率；

3.国有及国有控股工业企业按工业行业大类和按地区分组的主要经济指标和经济效益指标；

4.外商投资和港澳台商投资工业企业按工业行业大类和按地区分组的主要经济指标和经济效益指标；

5.大中型工业企业按工业行业大类和按地区分组的主要经济指标和经济效益指标；

6.主要工业产品产量；

7.重点工业企业主要产品生产能力；

8.按主要登记注册类型分组的工业企业经济效益指标。

二、本篇的统计范围

工业统计调查范围为我国境内（除港、澳、台）的全部工业企业。1997年以前，我国工业的统计范围按隶属关系划分，分为乡及乡以上独立核算工业企业和非独立核算生产单位、村办工业、城镇合作工业、农村合作工业、城镇个体工业、农村个体工业六大部分。（1984年以前村办工业不在工业统计范围内）

1998年及以后年份，工业统计调查范围由按隶属关系划分，改变为按企业规模划分，分为全部国有及年产品销售收入在500万元以上非国有工业企业和年产品销售收入在500万元以下非国有工业企业两部分。

本篇资料为全部国有及年产品销售收入在500万元以上的非国有工业企业范围。简称全部国有及规模以上非国有工业企业。

本篇资料中工业行业分类按2002年《国民经济行业分类标准》划分；企业大中小型划分按2003年《统计上大中小型企业划分办法（暂行）》标准执行。

三、数据来源和调查方法

本篇工业企业统计数据是根据工业统计年度报表中有关资料整理汇总的。工业统计年度报表是全国各省、自治区、直辖市统计局上报给国家统计局的全面报表，由各级统计部门根据当地实际情况采取全面调查的方法布置、收集。

本篇《主要工业产品生产能力》，内容包括2002年41种主要工业产品生产能力。资料来自有关部门、行业协会、总公司。是其系统内的重点企业范围。

Brief Introduction

I. Main Content

Data in this chapter reflect the basic condition of industrial sector including main industrial economic indicators of 31 provinces, autonomous regions and municipalities.

(1) The number of industrial enterprises, and the gross industrial output value of all state-owned industrial enterprises and the non-state enterprises that are above designated size;

(2) Main economic indicators and efficiency indicators of all state-owned industrial enterprises, and of non-state enterprises above designated size classified by type of registration, light and heavy industries, size of the enterprises, branch of industrial enterprises and regions. Those indicators include gross industrial output value, industrial value-added, total capital hold, total assets, total liabilities, working capital (circulating assets), fixed assets, liquid liabilities, long-term liabilities, creditors equity, sales income, sales cost, sales tax and extra-charges, total profits, value-added tax payable, ratio of value-added to gross industrial output value, ratio of profits, taxes and interests to average assets, ratio of debts to assets, ratio of profits to cost and charges, turnover of working capital and overall labour productivity, sales ratio of industrial products;

(3) Main economic indicators and efficiency indicators of the state-owned industrial enterprises and enterprises where the state holds the majority of shares, classified by region and by branch of industry;

(4) Major indicators of foreign-funded industrial enterprises and enterprises funded by entrepreneurs from Hong Kong, Macao and Taiwan are classified by region and by branch of industry;

(5) Major indicators of large and medium scale industrial enterprises by region and by branch of industry;

(6) Output of key industrial products;

(7) Production capacity of main products by key industrial enterprises;

(8) Economic efficiency indicators of industrial enterprises by main status of registration.

II. Coverage of Statistics

Industrial statistics covers all industrial enterprises within the territory (excluding Hong Kong, Macao and Taiwan). Before 1997, the industrial statistics was based on types of ownership, consisting of following six parts: industrial enterprises at and above county level with independent accounting system and production units with dependant accounting system, village industrial enterprise, urban joint industrial enterprises, rural joint industrial enterprise, urban individual industrial enterprises, and rural industrial enterprises (village industrial enterprises were not included in this part before 1984).

Since 1998, the coverage of industrial statistics was changed from types of ownership to the size of enterprises, they are: all state-owned industrial enterprises and those non-state industrial enterprises with annual sales over 5 million yuan, and non-state industrial enterprises with annual sales below 5 million yuan.

Data in this chapter cover the all state-owned industrial enterprises and those non-state-owned industrial enterprises with annual sales over 5 million yuan. The shortened description is all state-owned industrial enterprises and non-state enterprises above designated size.

Data by industries in this chapter are based on the 2002 *National Industrial Classification of all Economic Activities*, and data by size of enterprises are based on the *Preliminary Standards of Enterprises by Size*.

III. Source of Data and Survey Methodology

The industrial enterprises statistics in this chapter are collected from Year Report of Industrial Statistics, which are provided by statistical bureaus of all provinces, autonomous regions and municipalities through Comprehensive Reports to NBS. Statistical agencies at various levels arrange and collect data through comprehensive reporting system basing of real situation in local areas.

The table on Production Capacity of Major Industrial Products in this chapter includes 41 main industrial products in 2002. Sources of data are mainly from departments concerned, guild and corporations, which are main enterprises within the sector.

14-1 按类型分全部国有及规模以上非国有工业企业单位数和总产值

Number of All State-owned and Non-state-owned above Designated Size Industrial Enterprises and Their Gross Output Value by Type

项 目	Item	2002		2003	
		企业单位数 (个) Number of Enterprises (unit)	工业总产值 (亿元) Gross Industrial Output Value (100 million yuan)	企业单位数 (个) Number of Enterprises (unit)	工业总产值 (亿元) Gross Industrial Output Value (100 million yuan)
全国总计	**National Total**	**181557**	**110776.48**	**196222**	**142271.22**
按注册登记类型分	**Grouped by Status of Registration**				
内资企业	Domestic Funded Enterprises	147091	78317.20	157641	97913.42
国有企业	State-owned Industry	29449	17271.09	23228	18479.40
集体企业	Collective-owned Industry	27477	9618.95	22478	9458.43
股份合作企业	Cooperative Enterprises	10193	3202.94	9283	3250.90
联营企业	Joint Ownership Enterprises	1964	941.90	1689	948.67
#国有联营	State Joint Ownership Enterprises	330	331.25	296	394.72
集体联营	Collective Joint Ownership Enterprises	546	176.90	486	173.24
国有与集体联营	Joint State-collective Ownership Enterprises	733	318.76	549	231.93
有限责任公司	Limited Liability Corporations	22486	20069.77	26606	26583.94
#国有独资公司	Sole State-funded Corporations	1349	6215.53	1330	7073.68
股份有限公司	Share Holding Enterprises	5998	14119.03	6313	18017.06
私营企业	Private Enterprises	49176	12950.86	67607	20980.23
其他企业	Other Enterprises	348	142.64	437	194.79
港澳台商投资企业	Enterprises with Funds from Hong Kong, Macao and Taiwan	19546	13668.81	21152	17425.62
外商投资企业	Foreign Funded Enterprises	14920	18790.47	17429	26932.18
#国有及国有控股	State-owned and State-holding Enterprises	41125	45178.96	34280	53407.90
按轻重工业分	**Grouped by Light & Heavy Industry**				
轻工业	Light Industry	92525	43355.74	92712	50497.50
重工业	Heavy Industry	89032	67420.74	103510	91773.72
按大中小型分	**Grouped by Size of Enterprises**				
大型工业企业	Large Industrial Enterprises	8752	51128.32	1984	48914.24
中型工业企业	Medium-sized Industrilal Enterprises	14571	14189.19	21647	47065.22
小型工业企业	Small Industrilal Enterprises	158234	45458.97	172591	46291.76

注：1.全部国有及规模以上非国有工业企业是指全部国有工业企业及年产品销售收入在500万元以上的非国有的工业企业(以下表同)。

2.工业总产值按当年价格计算。

3. 2003年大中小型分组按新标准划分。

a) All state-owned and non-state-owned industrial enterprises above designated size refer to all state-owned industrial enterprises and the non-state-owned industrial enterprises with an annual sales income of over 5 million yuan. The same as following tables.

b) The gross industrial output value is calculated at current prices.

c) The categories of the large, medium and small scale enterprises are divided by the new criterion in 2003.

14-2 全部国有及规模以上非国有工业企业单位数和工业总产值

Number of All State-owned and Non-state-owned above Designated Size Industrial Enterprises and Their Gross Output Value

单位: 个、亿元 (unit) (100 million yuan)

年份 Year 地区 Region		全部国有及规模以上非国有 All States-owned and Non-state-owned above Designated Size			# 国有及国有控股企业 State-owned and State-holding Enterprises		
		企业单位数 Number of Enterprise	总产值 Gross Output Value		企业单位数 Number of Enterprise	总产值 Gross Output Value	
			1990年不变价格 At 1990 Constant Prices	当年价格 At Current Prices		1990年不变价格 At 1990 Constant Prices	当年价格 At Current Prices
1998		165080	57574.61	67737.14	64737	26794.56	33621.04
1999		162033	64776.75	72707.04	61301	29151.63	35571.18
2000		162885	75710.69	85673.66	53489	31958.43	40554.37
2001		171256	86772.70	95448.98	46767	34466.50	42408.49
2002		181557	102568.84	110776.48	41125	37278.08	45178.96
2003		196222	128716.25	142271.22	34280	42538.14	53407.90
北京	Beijing	4019	3740.73	3810.36	1362	1897.69	2051.79
天津	Tianjin	5341	4050.70	4049.61	1625	1070.26	1456.51
河北	Hebei	7923	4506.08	5708.76	1675	1680.45	2360.39
山西	Shanxi	3613	1643.35	2439.30	1354	907.59	1381.77
内蒙古	Inner Mongolia	1653	1022.24	1355.70	591	536.46	798.51
辽宁	Liaoning	6842	4953.76	6112.96	1334	2326.73	3552.29
吉林	Jilin	2284	2424.86	2662.27	969	1809.69	2017.7
黑龙江	Heilongjiang	2567	1696.18	2909.98	970	1167.25	2311.94
上海	Shanghai	11098	10755.43	10342.82	1606	4549.57	4466.43
江苏	Jiangsu	23862	14833.26	18036.74	1242	3021.28	3422.44
浙江	Zhejiang	25526	13840.79	12864.23	861	1458.39	1686.99
安徽	Anhui	4158	2352.08	2610.03	747	1061.81	1438.88
福建	Fujian	9208	4933.23	4953.74	888	982.86	1125.72
江西	Jiangxi	3051	1199.27	1472.33	1071	757.46	946.60
山东	Shandong	16177	12248.09	15379.54	1961	3823.03	5148.72
河南	Henan	9091	3769.7	5365.65	2253	1931.29	2718.98
湖北	Hubei	6271	3628.36	4030.11	1617	1921.52	2287.46
湖南	Hunan	5967	2064.75	2611.45	1642	1001.34	1391.74
广东	Guangdong	24494	23379.18	21513.46	2103	3849.43	3949.03
广西	Guangxi	2871	1348.01	1436.43	1252	716.71	797.95
海南	Hainan	619	282.95	333.46	346	172.03	213.56
重庆	Chongqing	2241	1671.04	1588.00	570	870.84	852.72
四川	Sichuan	5448	3404.28	3387.43	1065	1673.77	1609.79
贵州	Guizhou	2129	802.68	977.64	1037	509.8	667.75
云南	Yunnan	1995	988.58	1557.17	943	631.02	1145.91
西藏	Tibet	325	9.76	21.39	199	6.86	16.76
陕西	Shaanxi	2493	1497.51	1879.26	1235	1087.92	1392.06
甘肃	Gansu	2884	733.35	1147.52	706	491.76	880.76
青海	Qinghai	400	143.08	247.90	206	107.12	195.01
宁夏	Ningxia	418	262.18	352.81	154	138.79	211.74
新疆	Xinjiang	1254	530.81	1113.14	696	377.43	909.99

14-2 续表 1 continued

单位: 个、亿元 (unit) (100 million yuan)

年份 Year / 地区 Region	# 集体企业 Collective-owned Enterprises			# 股份有限公司 Share-holding Corporation Ltd.			# 外商投资企业 Foreign Funded Enterprises		
	企业单位数 Number of Enterprise	总产值 Gross Output Value		企业单位数 Number of Enterprise	总产值 Gross Output Value		企业单位数 Number of Enterprise	总产值 Gross Output Value	
		1990年不变价格 At 1990 Constant Prices	当年价格 At Current Prices		1990年不变价格 At 1990 Constant Prices	当年价格 At Current Prices		1990年不变价格 At 1990 Constant Prices	当年价格 At Current Prices
1998	47745	11307.61	13179.67	4120	3873.88	4334.46	10717	8455.16	8458.43
1999	42585	11456.85	12414.11	4480	4981.14	5247.08	11054	10282.75	9960.23
2000	37841	11007.85	11907.92	5086	7606.76	10090.29	11955	13662.07	12890.25
2001	31018	9226.69	10052.49	5692	10039.85	12698.34	13166	17005.69	15373.72
2002	27477	8688.51	9618.95	5998	11690.55	14119.03	14920	20857.77	18790.47
2003	22478	8402.42	9458.43	6313	13662.5	18017.06	17429	29625.62	26932.18
北京 Beijing	555	125.18	134.49	150	513.65	582.84	633	1448.91	1134.53
天津 Tianjin	1220	321.71	384.05	83	272.51	514.08	956	2191.23	1633.98
河北 Hebei	1174	501.92	542.01	390	443.48	753.07	499	322.97	391.25
山西 Shanxi	607	113.46	175.24	150	147.49	209.26	54	60.36	90.65
内蒙古 Inner Mongolia	102	18.26	22.10	137	234.33	326.11	61	86.37	94.36
辽宁 Liaoning	959	257.71	285.24	282	542.99	1248.51	1082	1189.35	1158.66
吉林 Jilin	242	77.22	83.29	181	379.60	562.53	142	738.65	736.52
黑龙江 Heilongjiang	257	53.13	65.30	206	403.99	1345.98	121	119.78	129.92
上海 Shanghai	1344	313.36	361.16	95	584.81	646.02	2576	6156.44	5043.03
江苏 Jiangsu	1690	983.24	1124.85	587	1163.25	1626.85	2626	3300.29	4050.46
浙江 Zhejiang	1089	751.26	690.81	296	1269.76	1221.88	1761	1628.83	1382.58
安徽 Anhui	430	117.24	99.95	199	343.19	443.83	220	310.32	299.22
福建 Fujian	732	155.16	171.78	167	260.64	217.54	1189	1200.00	1231.77
江西 Jiangxi	201	35.48	40.04	78	71.27	72.75	92	125.30	125.39
山东 Shandong	2136	2243.75	2526.39	700	1308.80	1804.98	2113	1573.10	1862.74
河南 Henan	2694	648.82	931.77	400	388.15	572.31	186	108.49	170.26
湖北 Hubei	784	218.96	244.86	449	683.75	725.58	203	458.42	401.23
湖南 Hunan	905	143.05	184.64	303	357.75	454.58	124	214.44	140.72
广东 Guangdong	2513	831.55	849.63	324	2236.27	1818.65	2070	7482.08	5971.94
广西 Guangxi	301	65.54	69.36	109	177.46	182.08	125	245.19	231.19
海南 Hainan	22	4.29	4.79	27	23.73	37.85	41	38.75	40.92
重庆 Chongqing	208	53.75	52.03	83	316.41	232.58	97	173.72	176.34
四川 Sichuan	368	102.21	113.27	432	496.66	517.77	191	202.10	186.85
贵州 Guizhou	194	24.57	26.64	84	133.27	121.62	43	34.31	32.43
云南 Yunnan	176	50.33	63.43	116	142.42	171.76	61	48.98	55.80
西藏 Tibet	81	1.98	3.67	11	1.77	5.74	6	0.03	0.03
陕西 Shaanxi	274	58.56	63.89	148	229.75	336.4	81	114.91	102.89
甘肃 Gansu	1113	114.37	121.04	26	178.20	391.43	13	12.07	13.70
青海 Qinghai	22	2.40	2.98	52	72.49	145.12	7	2.32	1.90
宁夏 Ningxia	28	4.04	4.83	14	34.98	41.73	21	26.95	26.07
新疆 Xinjiang	57	9.92	14.91	34	249.71	685.64	35	10.96	14.86

14-2 续表 2 continued

单位: 个、亿元 (unit) (100 million yuan)

年份 地区	Year Region	#港澳台商投资企业 Enterprises with Funds from Hong Kong, Macao & Taiwan			轻工业 Enterprises of Light Industry			重工业 Enterprises of Heavy Industry		
		企业单位数 Number of Enterprises	总产值 Gross Output Value		企业单位数 Number of Enterprises	总产值 Gross Output Value		企业单位数 Number of Enterprises	总产值 Gross Output Value	
			1990年不变价格 At 1990 Constant Prices	当年价格 At Current Prices		1990年不变价格 At 1990 Constant Prices	当年价格 At Current Prices		1990年不变价格 At 1990 Constant Prices	当年价格 At Current Prices
	1998	15725	7618.37	8299.47	83738	26314.90	29081.79	81342	31259.71	38655.35
	1999	15783	8937.05	8994.00	81820	29276.13	30514.98	80213	35500.62	42192.06
	2000	16490	10323.03	10574.30	81902	33090.19	34094.51	80983	42620.51	51579.15
	2001	18257	11657.83	11847.18	86705	37205.50	37636.93	84551	49567.20	57812.05
	2002	19546	13832.08	13668.81	92525	43550.54	43355.74	89032	59018.30	67420.74
	2003	21152	17408.59	17425.62	92712	50003.72	50497.50	103510	78712.52	91773.72
北 京	Beijing	327	538.64	418.65	1792	741.01	809.19	2227	2999.72	3001.18
天 津	Tianjin	389	230.93	262.07	2378	1257.43	1095.39	2963	2793.27	2954.22
河 北	Hebei	340	273.89	351.18	3124	1620.96	1619.10	4799	2885.11	4089.66
山 西	Shanxi	47	50.44	48.47	756	205.84	215.72	2857	1437.50	2223.58
内蒙古	Inner Mongolia	48	63.38	57.50	653	388.12	428.77	1000	634.12	926.94
辽 宁	Liaoning	406	299.90	292.35	2278	1179.18	1017.99	4564	3774.58	5094.97
吉 林	Jilin	64	47.78	44.72	917	532.45	507.19	1367	1892.40	2155.07
黑龙江	Heilongjiang	59	43.84	49.61	1117	601.38	586.11	1450	1094.80	2323.88
上 海	Shanghai	1714	1303.01	1383.72	5164	3048.67	2931.93	5934	7706.76	7410.89
江 苏	Jiangsu	2173	1658.42	1956.96	11000	5454.97	6580.10	12862	9378.28	11456.64
浙 江	Zhejiang	1914	1326.93	1203.23	14281	7357.34	6660.98	11245	6483.45	6203.25
安 徽	Anhui	157	227.22	148.32	1857	923.45	860.82	2301	1428.63	1749.21
福 建	Fujian	2715	2125.70	1894.49	5663	2272.59	2300.35	3545	2660.64	2653.39
江 西	Jiangxi	144	47.64	53.03	1365	381.03	435.88	1686	818.24	1036.46
山 东	Shandong	812	486.39	620.50	7842	5569.29	6274.20	8335	6678.79	9105.35
河 南	Henan	216	163.93	192.41	3951	1391.91	1776.19	5140	2377.79	3589.46
湖 北	Hubei	261	183.41	176.56	2789	1192.46	1257.23	3482	2435.89	2772.88
湖 南	Hunan	181	91.17	108.81	2045	612.13	833.92	3922	1452.62	1777.53
广 东	Guangdong	8549	7792.71	7709.39	14834	11063.56	9919.03	9660	12315.62	11594.43
广 西	Guangxi	152	78.00	77.00	1218	540.32	532.84	1653	807.68	903.59
海 南	Hainan	56	16.01	17.83	322	142.08	153.99	297	140.87	179.47
重 庆	Chongqing	65	97.08	106.59	946	666.61	567.18	1295	1004.43	1020.82
四 川	Sichuan	147	100.96	99.39	2035	1478.69	1235.04	3413	1925.59	2152.39
贵 州	Guizhou	38	7.73	7.08	718	250.45	284.62	1411	552.23	693.02
云 南	Yunnan	78	38.32	39.10	687	363.32	719.73	1308	625.26	837.45
西 藏	Tibet	1	0.01	0.01	141	3.84	7.51	184	5.92	13.88
陕 西	Shaanxi	52	78.76	57.09	984	412.98	430.79	1509	1084.53	1448.47
甘 肃	Gansu	26	21.23	26.44	1048	140.50	174.18	1836	592.85	973.33
青 海	Qinghai	6	4.92	5.54	124	14.67	22.26	276	128.41	225.65
宁 夏	Ningxia	5	5.37	8.34	134	61.00	70.75	284	201.18	282.06
新 疆	Xinjiang	10	4.87	9.26	549	135.45	188.52	705	395.35	924.63

14-2 续表 3 continued

单位: 个、亿元 (unit) (100 million yuan)

年份 Year / 地区 Region	大型企业 Large Enterprises			中型企业 Medium-sized Enterprises			小型企业 Small Enterprises		
	企业单位数 Number of Enterprises	总产值 Gross Output Value		企业单位数 Number of Enterprises	总产值 Gross Output Value		企业单位数 Number of Enterprises	总产值 Gross Output Value	
		1990年不变价格 At 1990 Constant Prices	当年价格 At Current Prices		1990年不变价格 At 1990 Constant Prices	当年价格 At Current Prices		1990年不变价格 At 1990 Constant Prices	当年价格 At Current Prices
1998	7558	23125.92	27977.62	15850	8665.78	9574.72	141672	25782.91	30184.80
1999	7864	27152.99	31582.21	14371	9209.14	9857.20	139798	28414.63	31267.62
2000	7983	31838.39	38303.21	13741	9989.02	10689.81	141161	33883.28	36680.64
2001	8589	40285.89	44815.99	14398	11716.19	12542.41	148269	34770.62	38090.58
2002	8752	47185.68	51128.32	14571	13203.67	14189.19	158234	42179.50	45458.97
2003	1984	43363.52	48914.24	21647	43684.50	47065.22	172591	41668.22	46291.76
北京 Beijing	44	1227.77	1493.24	407	1476.85	1257.17	3568	1036.11	1059.96
天津 Tianjin	46	1747.38	1576.77	435	1242.83	1238.04	4860	1060.48	1234.81
河北 Hebei	101	1374.51	2047.72	917	1420.39	1818.35	6905	1711.17	1842.69
山西 Shanxi	57	637.54	1011.24	550	597.36	866.52	3006	408.44	561.55
内蒙古 Inner Mongolia	31	379.27	511.10	224	358.23	457.25	1398	284.74	387.35
辽宁 Liaoning	95	2065.10	3040.87	715	1525.24	1645.16	6032	1363.42	1426.93
吉林 Jilin	31	1442.12	1613.13	314	561.86	607.49	1939	420.87	441.64
黑龙江 Heilongjiang	49	933.40	1976.16	330	378.73	497.64	2188	384.05	436.18
上海 Shanghai	74	4546.83	4152.16	1105	3245.29	2957.19	9919	2963.32	3233.46
江苏 Jiangsu	207	3934.66	5141.52	2448	5305.20	6226.07	21207	5593.39	6669.16
浙江 Zhejiang	122	2560.46	2300.14	2227	5396.66	4903.18	23177	5883.67	5660.92
安徽 Anhui	59	830.64	1081.98	494	868.50	884.08	3605	652.94	643.96
福建 Fujian	40	1232.67	1053.09	814	1880.54	1982.91	8354	1820.01	1917.74
江西 Jiangxi	25	427.11	583.14	301	389.10	440.26	2725	383.07	448.93
山东 Shandong	264	4177.33	5264.31	2311	3977.34	4938.80	13602	4093.41	5176.44
河南 Henan	111	1354.05	1823.47	908	1062.17	1537.34	8072	1353.48	2004.84
湖北 Hubei	66	1139.05	1410.17	637	1117.05	1181.87	5568	1372.26	1438.07
湖南 Hunan	56	689.31	892.36	478	593.14	719.20	5433	782.30	999.90
广东 Guangdong	182	8304.82	6204.03	3110	8144.19	8149.50	21202	6930.17	7159.93
广西 Guangxi	25	348.60	370.13	374	573.72	604.86	2472	425.69	461.44
海南 Hainan	2	73.42	79.62	54	97.24	117.46	563	112.29	136.38
重庆 Chongqing	43	640.62	602.53	356	637.92	600.21	1842	392.50	385.26
四川 Sichuan	68	1382.81	1226.13	775	1077.23	1169.78	4605	944.24	991.51
贵州 Guizhou	23	239.64	317.62	201	317.61	367.89	1905	245.43	292.13
云南 Yunnan	26	296.64	615.37	339	402.73	583.88	1630	289.20	357.93
西藏 Tibet				12	3.58	9.80	313	6.18	11.59
陕西 Shaanxi	63	645.13	915.51	357	538.29	610.18	2073	314.09	353.57
甘肃 Gansu	30	330.93	641.31	153	188.31	259.49	2701	214.11	246.71
青海 Qinghai	9	72.11	143.00	47	40.53	62.53	344	30.43	42.37
宁夏 Ningxia	14	102.13	158.12	83	103.90	126.04	321	56.15	68.65
新疆 Xinjiang	21	227.46	668.30	171	162.72	245.08	1062	140.62	199.76

14-3 按行业分全部国有及规模以上非国有工业企业主要指标（2003年）

单位：亿元

项　　目	Item	企业单位数（个）Number of Enterprises (unit)	工业总产值 Gross Industrial Output Value
全 国 总 计	**National Total**	**196222**	**142271.22**
按注册登记类型分	**Grouped by status of registration**		
在总计中	Of the Total:		
国有及国有控股企业	State-owned and State-holding Enterprises	34280	53407.90
在总计中	Of the Total:		
集体企业	Collective-owned Enterprises	22478	9458.43
股份有限公司	Share-holding Corporations Ltd.	6313	18017.06
外商投资企业	Foreign Funded	17429	26932.18
港澳台商投资企业	Enterprises with Funds from Hong Kong, Macao and Taiwan	21152	17425.62
按轻重工业分	**Grouped by Light & Heavy Industry**		
轻工业	Light Industry	92712	50497.50
重工业	Heavy Industry	103510	91773.72
按企业规模分：大型企业	**Grouped by Size of Enterprises:** Large	1984	48914.24
中型企业	Medium-sized	21647	47065.22
小型企业	Small	172591	46291.76
按行业分	**Grouped by Sector**		
煤炭开采和洗选业	Mining and Washing of Coal	3139	2459.38
石油和天然气开采业	Extraction of Petroleum and Natural Gas	112	3479.02
黑色金属矿采选业	Mining and Processing of Ferrous Metal Ores	913	350.93
有色金属矿采选业	Mining and Processing of Non-Ferrous Metal Ores	1276	573.28
非金属矿采选业	Mining and Processing of Nonmetal Ores	1827	486.75
其他采矿业	Mining of Other Ores	13	7.46
农副食品加工业	Processing of Food from Agricultural Products	11192	6152.32
食品制造业	Manufacture of Foods	4636	2290.07
饮料制造业	Manufacture of Beverages	3194	2233.22
烟草制品业	Manufacture of Tobacco	255	2235.81
纺织业	Manufacture of Textile	14863	7725.20
纺织服装、鞋、帽制造业	Manufacture of Textile Wearing Apparel, Footware, and Caps	9717	3426.02
皮革、毛皮、羽毛(绒)及其制品业	Manufacture of Leather, Fur, Feather and Related Products	4518	2274.05
木材加工及木、竹、藤、棕、草制品业	Processing of Timber, Manufacture of Wood, Bamboo, Rattan, Palm, and Straw Products	3501	992.79
家具制造业	Manufacture of Furniture	2046	719.97
造纸及纸制品业	Manufacture of Paper and Paper Products	5570	2526.05
印刷业和记录媒介的复制	Printing,Reproduction of Recording Media	4084	1027.22
文教体育用品制造业	Manufacture of Articles For Culture, Education and Sport Activity	2516	965.90
石油加工、炼焦及核燃料加工业	Processing of Petroleum, Coking, Processing of Nuclear Fuel	1323	6235.26
化学原料及化学制品制造业	Manufacture of Raw Chemical Materials and Chemical Products	13803	9244.86
医药制造业	Manufacture of Medicines	4063	2889.98
化学纤维制造业	Manufacture of Chemical Fibers	937	1448.40
橡胶制品业	Manufacture of Rubber	2016	1312.90
塑料制品业	Manufacture of Plastics	8382	3063.83
非金属矿物制品业	Manufacture of Non-metallic Mineral Products	16245	5653.25
黑色金属冶炼及压延加工业	Smelting and Pressing of Ferrous Metals	4119	10007.37
有色金属冶炼及压延加工业	Smelting and Pressing of Non-ferrous Metals	3367	3564.07
金属制品业	Manufacture of Metal Products	9746	3857.40
通用设备制造业	Manufacture of General Purpose Machinery	12546	5711.21
专用设备制造业	Manufacture of Special Purpose Machinery	7129	3831.65
交通运输设备制造业	Manufacture of Transport Equipment	8281	11214.05
电气机械及器材制造业	Manufacture of Electrical Machinery and Equipment	10400	7916.19
通信设备、计算机及其他电子设备制造业	Manufacture of Communication Equipment, Computers and Other Electronic Equipment	5856	15839.76
仪器仪表及文化、办公用机械制造业	Manufacture of Measuring Instruments and Machinery for Cultural Activity and Office Work	2515	1636.72
工艺品及其他制造业	Manufacture of Artwork and Other Manufacturing	4259	1306.62
废弃资源和废旧材料回收加工业	Recycling and Disposal of Waste	107	49.94
电力、热力的生产和供应业	Production and Distribution of Electric Power and Heat Power	4998	6858.60
燃气生产和供应业	Production and Distribution of Gas	352	272.64
水的生产和供应业	Production and Distribution of Water	2406	431.09

Main Indicators of All State-owned and Non-state-owned Above Designed Size Industrial Enterprises by Industrial Sector (2003)

(100 million yuan)

工业增加值 Value-added of Industry	实收资本 Paid-up Capital	资产总计 Total Assets	流动资产合计 Circulating Funds	流动资产年平均余额 Annual Average Balance of Circulating Funds	固定资产原价 Original Value of Fixed Assets	固定资产净值年平均余额 Annual Average Balance of Net Value of Fixed Assets
41990.23	**43479.56**	**168807.70**	**76163.74**	**71487.80**	**105557.09**	**66068.38**
18837.60	23018.04	94519.79	36125.14	34327.98	69701.11	42118.40
2551.67	1526.29	6902.34	3635.90	3505.07	3329.28	2204.83
6203.66	5187.98	22259.11	8726.44	8336.13	17175.49	9522.67
6919.15	7792.85	23041.69	12745.23	11612.59	12459.69	7977.27
4680.49	5423.97	16218.57	8744.62	8253.55	9359.24	5745.06
14352.50	13056.46	49128.09	25133.25	23765.65	24412.35	16147.20
27637.73	30423.10	119679.61	51030.50	47722.15	81144.74	49921.18
15137.87	15034.03	66277.25	27443.66	25532.73	46364.00	27483.62
13935.56	15200.93	58854.47	26824.72	25172.75	36033.76	23028.70
12916.80	13244.59	43675.98	21895.36	20782.32	23159.33	15556.05
1152.04	1689.69	5433.01	1979.12	1862.85	4080.52	2599.44
2388.22	1805.12	4944.97	967.91	996.40	7149.85	3361.56
146.19	173.66	472.65	185.22	173.44	252.78	161.92
177.65	155.82	614.19	226.96	217.77	412.75	260.86
162.88	228.54	712.43	257.80	245.26	454.68	325.08
2.36	5.80	44.76	16.84	16.41	18.02	10.11
1466.42	1045.35	4141.82	2098.89	1966.88	1994.07	1411.75
667.09	707.94	2307.29	1108.42	1031.86	1183.35	801.90
795.97	889.45	3192.52	1465.55	1424.04	1737.23	1149.80
1573.48	367.06	2799.51	1698.18	1598.70	1085.50	602.45
1906.70	1963.65	7801.29	3757.61	3510.81	4355.41	2850.02
916.54	672.33	2377.25	1414.83	1345.65	956.78	637.29
591.35	376.19	1334.26	824.80	793.97	511.98	360.07
265.72	296.38	906.91	403.37	395.87	520.61	379.14
182.96	190.22	616.18	331.77	312.08	263.94	186.45
681.42	854.46	3293.45	1346.34	1264.41	1980.43	1416.13
334.46	438.19	1370.88	643.78	621.65	858.21	527.63
249.93	241.93	711.59	430.22	414.85	321.96	204.47
1287.45	1282.88	3978.98	1432.28	1385.42	3733.94	2123.70
2464.88	3020.49	10704.09	4407.04	4317.29	7144.28	4414.44
1024.74	1160.54	4316.45	2132.19	2057.66	1675.70	1156.56
295.25	423.46	1595.13	586.42	559.54	1192.33	762.39
369.95	379.07	1423.82	714.23	673.23	763.54	473.44
763.20	970.12	2959.67	1510.38	1436.68	1565.05	1020.96
1749.08	2160.11	7583.31	3219.27	3056.82	4749.08	3102.84
2824.01	2744.67	12021.24	5011.00	4487.98	8200.62	4807.42
902.13	1041.33	4042.55	1800.30	1673.73	2368.79	1508.39
971.00	918.76	3256.63	1918.33	1804.21	1419.86	936.59
1590.39	1628.48	6604.64	4061.46	3699.82	2747.60	1687.59
1008.19	1138.94	4816.05	2804.33	2608.56	2029.88	1256.86
2896.97	2814.27	11916.41	6891.40	6296.83	4756.76	2935.98
2023.48	1770.51	7373.50	4589.62	4282.49	2679.65	1677.96
3482.50	2728.00	12086.97	7994.09	7344.39	4346.83	2690.32
445.03	424.19	1524.04	953.72	895.71	583.10	364.87
347.74	269.82	884.52	520.66	499.47	361.18	244.96
10.67	6.36	26.03	19.04	16.95	6.95	4.11
3606.13	5462.82	25651.02	5707.29	5478.50	24659.59	16013.09
75.34	324.57	818.72	246.24	245.57	585.85	395.71
190.74	708.37	2149.02	486.86	474.04	1848.45	1244.14

14-3 续表

单位: 亿元

项目	Item	流动负债合计 Liquid Liabilities	长期负债合计 Long-term Liabilities
全国总计	**National Total**	**73413.53**	**24859.83**
按注册登记类型分	**Grouped by status of registration**		
在总计中	Of the Total:		
国有及国有控股企业	State-owned and State-holding Enterprises	36430.98	18926.33
在总计中	Of the Total:		
集体企业	Collective-owned Enterprises	3506.92	632.21
股份有限公司	Share-holding Corporations Ltd.	8087.63	3021.52
外商投资企业	Foreign Funded	10885.53	1735.24
港澳台商投资企业	Enterprises with Funds from Hong Kong, Macao and Taiwan	7580.97	1309.96
按轻重工业分	**Grouped by Light & Heavy Industry**		
轻工业	Light Industry	23772.57	4139.53
重工业	Heavy Industry	49640.96	20720.30
按企业规模分: 大型企业	**Grouped by Size of Enterprises:** Large	26105.87	10229.44
中型企业	Medium-sized	26186.89	9410.26
小型企业	Small	21120.77	5220.13
按行业分	**Grouped by Sector**		
煤炭开采和洗选业	Mining and Washing of Coal	2045.55	977.75
石油和天然气开采业	Extraction of Petroleum and Natural Gas	1112.52	643.25
黑色金属矿采选业	Mining and Processing of Ferrous Metal Ores	199.71	40.66
有色金属矿采选业	Mining and Processing of Non-Ferrous Metal Ores	265.72	100.20
非金属矿采选业	Mining and Processing of Nonmetal Ores	273.70	123.70
其他采矿业	Mining of Other Ores	19.12	3.27
农副食品加工业	Processing of Food from Agricultural Products	2316.71	351.68
食品制造业	Manufacture of Foods	1112.00	196.49
饮料制造业	Manufacture of Beverages	1495.35	231.04
烟草制品业	Manufacture of Tobacco	1099.31	84.01
纺织业	Manufacture of Textile	3994.70	877.05
纺织服装、鞋、帽制造业	Manufacture of Textile Wearing Apparel, Footware, and Caps	1228.83	106.63
皮革、毛皮、羽毛(绒)及其制品业	Manufacture of Leather, Fur, Feather and Related Products	729.33	51.71
木材加工及木、竹、藤、棕、草制品业	Processing of Timber, Manufacture of Wood, Bamboo, Rattan, Palm, and Straw Products	401.03	118.01
家具制造业	Manufacture of Furniture	300.47	33.25
造纸及纸制品业	Manufacture of Paper and Paper Products	1508.43	522.45
印刷业和记录媒介的复制	Printing,Reproduction of Recording Media	606.93	106.95
文教体育用品制造业	Manufacture of Articles For Culture, Education and Sport Activity	355.18	23.59
石油加工、炼焦及核燃料加工业	Processing of Petroleum, Coking, Processing of Nuclear Fuel	1504.29	463.11
化学原料及化学制品制造业	Manufacture of Raw Chemical Materials and Chemical Products	4557.53	1496.46
医药制造业	Manufacture of Medicines	1903.58	370.49
化学纤维制造业	Manufacture of Chemical Fibers	671.72	256.06
橡胶制品业	Manufacture of Rubber	706.12	165.29
塑料制品业	Manufacture of Plastics	1357.37	230.72
非金属矿物制品业	Manufacture of Non-metallic Mineral Products	3470.90	1081.69
黑色金属冶炼及压延加工业	Smelting and Pressing of Ferrous Metals	5318.79	1623.90
有色金属冶炼及压延加工业	Smelting and Pressing of Non-ferrous Metals	1954.22	631.19
金属制品业	Manufacture of Metal Products	1737.82	202.74
通用设备制造业	Manufacture of General Purpose Machinery	3728.87	445.74
专用设备制造业	Manufacture of Special Purpose Machinery	2712.01	415.92
交通运输设备制造业	Manufacture of Transport Equipment	6253.42	914.96
电气机械及器材制造业	Manufacture of Electrical Machinery and Equipment	3962.74	389.26
通信设备、计算机及其他电子设备制造业	Manufacture of Communication Equipment, Computers and Other Electronic Equipment	6738.22	670.35
仪器仪表及文化、办公用机械制造业	Manufacture of Measuring Instruments and Machinery for Cultural Activity and Office Work	767.83	85.26
工艺品及其他制造业	Manufacture of Artwork and Other Manufacturing	439.66	43.24
废弃资源和废旧材料回收加工业	Recycling and Disposal of Waste	17.51	0.25
电力、热力的生产和供应业	Production and Distribution of Electric Power and Heat Power	5771.64	10255.21
燃气生产和供应业	Production and Distribution of Gas	262.23	131.37
水的生产和供应业	Production and Distribution of Water	512.45	394.93

continued

(100 million yuan)

所有者权益 Creditors' Equity	产品销售收入 Sales Revenue	产品销售成本 Cost of Sales	产品销售税金及附加 Sales Tax and Extra Charges	利润总额 Total Profits	本年应交增值税 Value Added Tax Payable	全部从业人员年平均人数（万人） Annual Average Employed Persons (10 000 persons)
69129.56	**143171.53**	**118638.47**	**2049.21**	**8337.24**	**5487.73**	**5748.57**
38381.02	58027.15	45987.63	1589.87	3836.20	3025.57	2162.87
2659.96	8767.07	7524.37	70.66	449.75	267.84	479.93
10921.82	17698.86	13699.00	297.33	1914.71	818.02	452.30
10253.21	26853.80	22305.38	163.15	1851.42	740.32	558.49
7220.10	16753.83	14298.71	60.51	926.01	448.69	700.18
20813.56	48347.67	39598.40	1192.26	2354.73	1636.82	2418.92
48316.01	94823.85	79040.08	856.95	5982.51	3850.91	3329.64
29543.50	52552.29	42743.87	1045.43	3835.93	2196.98	1306.68
22753.72	47157.78	38701.86	724.86	2687.05	1868.13	1917.63
16832.35	43461.46	37192.75	278.92	1814.26	1422.62	2524.27
2320.74	2474.70	1714.83	36.05	140.07	186.00	376.6
3177.03	3372.07	1658.95	84.45	1221.46	306.52	72.68
227.52	353.93	271.11	6.98	26.20	17.73	27.39
238.97	550.33	422.67	5.13	52.58	16.07	41.37
307.86	458.87	347.74	9.43	23.56	21.16	45.61
22.33	12.97	10.58	0.08	1.04	0.56	1.74
1437.34	5851.13	5261.23	21.12	173.17	91.05	181.66
983.11	2168.36	1680.74	10.51	113.09	89.09	101.07
1433.72	2117.23	1410.92	126.03	149.04	127.70	89
1614.42	2217.50	859.19	854.69	275.57	245.84	21.22
2873.04	7495.51	6727.34	31.36	248.20	195.55	499.16
1008.26	3239.42	2803.51	13.35	132.57	83.96	289.19
541.25	2139.19	1904.62	8.04	79.86	47.74	165.37
376.89	945.28	830.11	5.60	33.58	25.99	63.83
270.65	693.83	588.84	4.07	28.90	15.09	43.39
1235.91	2432.38	2066.48	11.15	117.05	99.76	113.95
646.89	980.31	792.61	4.54	73.86	45.72	59.41
325.98	917.27	793.23	2.69	36.45	15.54	87.14
1933.51	6341.81	5620.24	228.15	123.41	203.47	59.66
4541.33	9016.97	7403.82	65.19	472.63	337.95	311.33
1986.96	2750.68	1765.18	18.81	259.64	168.42	115.4
661.47	1413.09	1266.23	5.17	58.00	41.39	34.22
544.97	1214.21	1006.85	16.78	57.92	38.08	62.24
1349.40	2954.96	2569.90	10.62	130.94	77.58	140.91
2966.81	5314.38	4368.25	41.79	290.31	256.30	396.22
5039.54	10234.93	8712.01	55.35	609.55	503.58	255.91
1427.58	3534.93	3101.37	14.58	154.72	112.47	106.6
1279.31	3703.88	3206.75	16.04	168.41	95.67	171.24
2398.51	5418.43	4442.74	25.71	299.63	195.54	283.49
1644.03	3665.64	3021.64	14.80	173.46	113.26	205.31
4696.24	11028.57	9071.24	180.54	777.04	376.87	311.77
2926.30	7487.04	6241.24	24.00	374.48	211.48	265.12
4606.38	15876.27	14103.56	15.29	617.19	230.46	273.46
657.21	1607.26	1341.27	7.24	86.83	38.45	71.96
394.11	1223.55	1069.37	6.35	48.75	29.00	103.22
8.23	50.89	48.09	0.13	0.84	0.85	1.36
9392.82	11113.24	9466.78	59.91	699.26	791.93	238.41
420.99	391.99	357.55	1.98	6.47	11.68	14.67
1211.95	408.51	309.69	5.51	1.51	22.23	46.27

14-4 按行业分全部国有及规模以上非国有工业企业主要经济效益指标（2003年）

行业	Sector	工业增加值率 (%) Ratio of Value Added to Gross Industrial Output Value (%)	总资产贡献率 (%) Ratio of Total Assets to Industrial Output Value (%)
全国总计	**National Total**	**29.51**	**10.50**
按轻重工业分	**Grouped by Light & Heavy Industry**		
轻工业	Light Industry	28.42	11.61
重工业	Heavy Industry	30.12	10.05
按行业分	**Grouped by Sector**		
煤炭开采和洗选业	Mining and Washing of Coal	46.84	7.67
石油和天然气开采业	Extraction of Petroleum and Natural Gas	68.65	33.08
黑色金属矿采选业	Mining and Processing of Ferrous Metal Ores	41.66	11.79
有色金属矿采选业	Mining and Processing of Non-Ferrous Metal Ores	30.99	13.47
非金属矿采选业	Mining and Processing of Nonmetal Ores	33.46	8.53
其他采矿业	Mining of Other Ores	31.59	4.36
农副食品加工业	Processing of Food from Agricultural Products	23.84	8.31
食品制造业	Manufacture of Foods	29.13	10.26
饮料制造业	Manufacture of Beverages	35.64	13.53
烟草制品业	Manufacture of Tobacco	70.38	49.98
纺织业	Manufacture of Textile	24.68	7.43
纺织服装、鞋、帽制造业	Manufacture of Textile Wearing Apparel, Footware, and Caps	26.75	10.59
皮革、毛皮、羽毛(绒)及其制品业	Manufacture of Leather, Fur, Feather and Related Products	26.00	11.15
木材加工及木、竹、藤、棕、草制品业	Processing of Timber, Manufacture of Wood, Bamboo, Rattan, Palm, and Straw Products	26.77	8.38
家具制造业	Manufacture of Furniture	25.41	8.73
造纸及纸制品业	Manufacture of Paper and Paper Products	26.98	8.51
印刷业和记录媒介的复制	Printing,Reproduction of Recording Media	32.56	9.90
文教体育用品制造业	Manufacture of Articles For Culture, Education and Sport Activity	25.88	8.38
石油加工、炼焦及核燃料加工业	Processing of Petroleum, Coking, Processing of Nuclear Fuel	20.65	14.99
化学原料及化学制品制造业	Manufacture of Raw Chemical Materials and Chemical Products	26.66	9.45
医药制造业	Manufacture of Medicines	35.46	11.44
化学纤维制造业	Manufacture of Chemical Fibers	20.38	8.11
橡胶制品业	Manufacture of Rubber	28.18	9.18
塑料制品业	Manufacture of Plastics	24.91	8.37
非金属矿物制品业	Manufacture of Non-metallic Mineral Products	30.94	9.01
黑色金属冶炼及压延加工业	Smelting and Pressing of Ferrous Metals	28.22	10.84
有色金属冶炼及压延加工业	Smelting and Pressing of Non-ferrous Metals	25.31	8.47
金属制品业	Manufacture of Metal Products	25.17	9.62
通用设备制造业	Manufacture of General Purpose Machinery	27.85	8.87
专用设备制造业	Manufacture of Special Purpose Machinery	26.31	7.34
交通运输设备制造业	Manufacture of Transport Equipment	25.83	11.88
电气机械及器材制造业	Manufacture of Electrical Machinery and Equipment	25.56	9.20
通信设备、计算机及其他电子设备制造业	Manufacture of Communication Equipment, Computers and Other Electronic Equipment	21.99	7.71
仪器仪表及文化、办公用机械制造业	Manufacture of Measuring Instruments and Machinery for Cultural Activity and Office Work	27.19	9.34
工艺品及其他制造业	Manufacture of Artwork and Other Manufacturing	26.61	10.45
废弃资源和废旧材料回收加工业	Recycling and Disposal of Waste	21.37	8.06
电力、热力的生产和供应业	Production and Distribution of Electric Power and Heat Power	52.58	7.62
燃气生产和供应业	Production and Distribution of Gas	27.63	3.14
水的生产和供应业	Production and Distribution of Water	44.25	2.12

Main Indicators on Economic Benefit of All State-owned and Non-state-owned Industrial Enterprises by Industrial Sector (2003)

资产负债率 (%) Assets-Liability Ratio (%)	流动资产周转次数（次/年） Number of Times of Annual of Turnover Circulating Funds (times/year)	工业成本费用利润率 (%) Ratio of Profits to Industrial Cost (%)	全员劳动生产率（元/人.年） Overall Labor Productivity (yuan/person-year)	产品销售率 (%) Proportion of Products Sold (%)
58.96	**2.00**	**6.25**	**73045**	**98.02**
57.63	2.03	5.23	59334	97.44
59.51	1.99	6.77	83005	98.34
55.89	1.33	6.04	30590	98.14
35.64	3.38	64.13	328613	100.12
51.86	2.04	8.20	53383	98.27
61.09	2.53	10.55	42938	98.52
56.79	1.87	5.51	35710	98.20
50.11	0.79	8.61	13528	106.78
65.30	2.97	3.06	80721	97.32
57.39	2.10	5.52	66002	96.95
55.08	1.49	8.04	89435	98.32
42.33	1.39	24.62	741392	100.02
63.17	2.13	3.42	38198	97.86
57.59	2.41	4.28	31693	97.20
59.43	2.69	3.89	35758	97.94
58.44	2.39	3.69	41633	97.37
56.08	2.22	4.40	42164	97.93
62.40	1.92	5.06	59798	98.28
52.81	1.58	8.07	56294	97.60
54.19	2.21	4.15	28682	97.57
51.28	4.58	2.07	215798	99.60
57.49	2.09	5.53	79172	97.82
53.94	1.34	10.38	88803	94.06
58.53	2.53	4.27	86271	98.09
61.72	1.80	5.07	59441	97.46
54.41	2.06	4.64	54161	97.91
60.88	1.74	5.77	44144	97.11
58.06	2.28	6.39	110353	99.30
64.69	2.11	4.59	84629	98.05
60.71	2.05	4.77	56703	97.81
63.68	1.46	5.83	56100	97.00
65.86	1.41	4.92	49106	97.21
60.41	1.75	7.59	92919	98.21
60.31	1.75	5.25	76323	96.75
61.82	2.16	4.03	127349	97.99
56.88	1.79	5.69	61844	98.22
55.44	2.45	4.16	33691	97.65
68.37	3.00	1.69	78338	99.61
63.31	2.03	6.73	151258	99.89
48.58	1.60	1.59	51367	100.63
43.60	0.86	0.36	41226	97.22

14-5 全部国有及规模以上非国有工业企业主要指标
Main Indicators of All State-owned and Non-state-owned above Designated Size Industrial Enterprises

单位：亿元 (100 million yuan)

年份 Year / 地区 Region	企业单位数（个）Number of Enterprises (unit)	工业总产值 Gross Industrial Output Value	工业增加值 Value-added of Industry	实收资本 Paid-up Capital	资产总计 Total Assets	流动资产合计 Total Circulating Funds
1998	165080	67737.14	19421.93	26676.62	108821.87	46600.87
1999	162033	72707.04	21564.74	28983.26	116968.89	49630.23
2000	162885	85673.66	25394.80	32940.45	126211.24	54338.15
2001	171256	95448.98	28329.37	36217.11	135402.49	57804.97
2002	181557	110776.48	32994.75	39155.63	146217.78	63468.46
2003	196222	142271.22	41990.23	43479.56	168807.70	76163.74
北京 Beijing	4019	3810.36	1012.53	1478.68	5177.98	2492.33
天津 Tianjin	5341	4049.61	1074.78	1283.41	4626.67	2175.95
河北 Hebei	7923	5708.76	1801.75	1742.34	6975.54	2861.39
山西 Shanxi	3613	2439.30	908.71	1103.92	4565.20	1786.74
内蒙古 Inner Mongolia	1653	1355.70	516.72	716.92	2439.08	835.37
辽宁 Liaoning	6842	6112.96	1715.92	2417.98	9180.58	3843.47
吉林 Jilin	2284	2662.27	814.83	864.49	3674.95	1552.98
黑龙江 Heilongjiang	2567	2909.98	1363.10	1458.64	4499.00	1767.77
上海 Shanghai	11098	10342.82	2832.88	3603.22	11608.99	6019.42
江苏 Jiangsu	23862	18036.74	4670.58	3981.84	16308.67	8415.52
浙江 Zhejiang	25526	12864.23	3097.62	2809.33	12526.66	6482.10
安徽 Anhui	4158	2610.03	881.47	1037.97	3719.19	1544.88
福建 Fujian	9208	4953.74	1448.50	1545.65	4902.48	2306.49
江西 Jiangxi	3051	1472.33	446.78	551.87	2268.75	942.48
山东 Shandong	16177	15379.54	4701.10	3207.54	14461.60	6319.19
河南 Henan	9091	5365.65	1740.11	1586.27	6575.13	2790.32
湖北 Hubei	6271	4030.11	1364.76	1615.44	6843.02	2407.20
湖南 Hunan	5967	2611.45	888.56	841.37	3642.69	1430.33
广东 Guangdong	24494	21513.46	5718.14	5318.53	19126.47	10061.23
广西 Guangxi	2871	1436.43	446.48	496.57	2190.37	823.88
海南 Hainan	619	333.46	96.31	161.55	455.38	195.33
重庆 Chongqing	2241	1588.00	447.63	616.80	2363.33	1087.21
四川 Sichuan	5448	3387.43	1165.69	1344.59	6023.49	2476.34
贵州 Guizhou	2129	977.64	346.49	545.77	1958.60	783.10
云南 Yunnan	1995	1557.17	745.97	644.10	3033.50	1268.41
西藏 Tibet	325	21.39	12.39	50.90	91.53	26.68
陕西 Shaanxi	2493	1879.26	674.35	786.39	3672.72	1487.87
甘肃 Gansu	2884	1147.52	388.10	595.67	2191.88	821.16
青海 Qinghai	400	247.90	95.23	227.74	871.48	259.42
宁夏 Ningxia	418	352.81	109.41	172.58	736.10	280.46
新疆 Xinjiang	1254	1113.14	463.36	671.49	2096.68	618.73

14-5 续表 1 continued

单位: 亿元 (100 million yuan)

年 份 Year / 地 区 Region	流动资产年平均余额 Annual Average Balance of Circulating Funds	固定资产原价合计 Original Value of Fixed Assets	固定资产净值年平均余额 Annual Average Balance of Net Value of Fixed Assets	流动负债合计 Total Liquid Liabilities	长期负债合计 Long-term Liabilities	所有者权益合计 Creditors' Equity
1998	45420.55	64832.05	44136.87	47773.02	20987.01	39445.40
1999	47643.44	71847.09	47281.43	50070.19	21552.58	44618.80
2000	51910.37	78646.30	51792.33	53052.64	22825.72	49406.88
2001	56486.77	86293.10	55437.43	56138.72	22807.25	55424.40
2002	60798.36	93887.95	59482.66	61663.06	23328.50	60242.01
2003	71487.80	105557.09	66068.38	73413.53	24859.83	69129.56
北 京 Beijing	2298.67	2755.96	1629.76	2115.64	618.55	2424.00
天 津 Tianjin	1991.12	3036.78	1793.13	2072.17	571.32	1908.36
河 北 Hebei	2715.09	4787.11	3028.91	3044.61	1177.59	2673.05
山 西 Shanxi	1651.64	3139.78	2020.25	1800.27	1082.91	1613.07
内蒙古 Inner Mongolia	783.54	1908.73	1155.90	847.49	571.32	994.16
辽 宁 Liaoning	3758.78	6813.89	3940.30	4003.90	1369.75	3776.27
吉 林 Jilin	1463.60	2409.52	1520.51	1691.55	602.55	1373.25
黑龙江 Heilongjiang	1644.42	4052.93	2245.32	1842.03	650.24	1945.16
上 海 Shanghai	5528.44	6788.95	3875.12	4886.01	840.13	5842.10
江 苏 Jiangsu	7794.45	8663.48	5591.40	8394.62	1671.67	6205.14
浙 江 Zhejiang	5988.82	6017.68	4024.45	5927.96	1242.38	5356.33
安 徽 Anhui	1417.91	2358.26	1556.96	1572.64	688.34	1441.34
福 建 Fujian	2095.48	2979.24	2019.14	2007.11	636.56	2230.96
江 西 Jiangxi	888.23	1426.27	923.40	1028.56	455.96	742.60
山 东 Shandong	5857.73	8947.82	5555.95	6480.89	1964.69	5875.50
河 南 Henan	2617.74	4558.61	2783.97	3076.44	1132.24	2348.06
湖 北 Hubei	2381.97	4577.29	3276.54	2205.39	1636.09	2793.99
湖 南 Hunan	1327.44	2510.77	1558.18	1471.89	798.85	1314.10
广 东 Guangdong	9732.67	10768.77	6666.84	8678.68	1932.65	8318.24
广 西 Guangxi	792.77	1489.55	983.38	938.03	438.16	759.14
海 南 Hainan	181.59	299.92	180.36	155.08	87.25	210.47
重 庆 Chongqing	1030.56	1343.02	838.63	1119.26	326.23	917.83
四 川 Sichuan	2346.04	3658.81	2370.74	2418.37	1187.22	2326.96
贵 州 Guizhou	752.22	1215.52	759.68	789.44	438.32	722.33
云 南 Yunnan	1125.47	1843.08	1143.97	1105.25	559.61	1368.64
西 藏 Tibet	26.26	63.75	47.38	18.48	6.15	66.90
陕 西 Shaanxi	1376.05	2503.21	1601.84	1518.32	790.86	1306.74
甘 肃 Gansu	791.93	1544.63	1017.53	866.11	531.10	771.79
青 海 Qinghai	259.95	615.29	423.16	268.71	317.21	276.94
宁 夏 Ningxia	266.00	503.85	333.73	317.37	165.32	253.41
新 疆 Xinjiang	601.23	1974.60	1201.95	751.26	368.61	972.74

14-5 续表 2 continued

单位: 亿元 (100 million yuan)

年份 地区	Year Region	产品销售收入 Sales Revenue	产品销售成本 Cost of Sales	产品销售税金及附加 Sales Tax and Extra Charges	利润总额 Total Profits	本年应交增值税 Value Added Tax Payable	全部从业人员年平均人数(万人) Annual Average Employed Persons (10 000 persons)
	1998	64148.86	52797.54	1236.79	1458.11	2827.02	6195.81
	1999	69851.73	57339.52	1307.65	2288.24	3105.92	5805.05
	2000	84151.75	68653.95	1434.17	4393.48	3685.20	5559.36
	2001	93733.34	77259.89	1553.82	4733.43	4018.09	5441.43
	2002	109485.77	90243.76	1761.61	5784.48	4476.01	5520.66
	2003	143171.53	118638.47	2049.21	8337.24	5487.73	5748.57
北 京	Beijing	3885.65	3203.24	36.13	235.29	147.57	100.81
天 津	Tianjin	4202.02	3546.84	39.29	237.62	124.44	115.28
河 北	Hebei	5920.88	4947.98	63.17	386.76	246.94	270.24
山 西	Shanxi	2465.30	1901.32	29.63	135.07	165.74	182.49
内蒙古	Inner Mongolia	1357.52	1105.36	17.94	64.97	71.45	72.15
辽 宁	Liaoning	6340.92	5321.37	84.67	235.95	245.58	241.99
吉 林	Jilin	2638.91	2147.99	67.83	159.75	110.16	101.48
黑龙江	Heilongjiang	2941.92	1967.05	63.91	575.56	209.60	133.14
上 海	Shanghai	10982.62	9020.10	139.34	805.65	384.14	220.01
江 苏	Jiangsu	18020.17	15631.30	135.62	793.98	542.86	569.33
浙 江	Zhejiang	13002.63	11070.55	139.08	793.63	468.06	481.96
安 徽	Anhui	2620.12	2077.00	65.92	168.52	125.08	148.94
福 建	Fujian	4822.24	4019.59	60.42	314.40	143.80	221.35
江 西	Jiangxi	1494.28	1226.17	34.08	51.41	71.10	96.12
山 东	Shandong	14932.21	12575.68	153.72	920.27	531.74	595.42
河 南	Henan	5284.81	4399.48	83.83	255.91	208.00	317.32
湖 北	Hubei	3993.99	3191.20	78.25	194.40	172.31	198.60
湖 南	Hunan	2604.98	2042.49	106.88	111.25	127.54	158.44
广 东	Guangdong	21566.93	18384.94	157.46	1075.41	618.03	741.17
广 西	Guangxi	1418.18	1137.05	25.27	66.42	81.79	82.93
海 南	Hainan	312.05	247.26	6.81	17.66	14.12	12.00
重 庆	Chongqing	1595.07	1283.11	31.34	85.97	73.78	84.47
四 川	Sichuan	3482.36	2759.31	65.63	153.08	164.61	201.62
贵 州	Guizhou	974.30	745.51	41.07	37.52	57.28	65.53
云 南	Yunnan	1537.37	1036.95	207.08	108.06	123.90	66.36
西 藏	Tibet	19.96	13.16	0.52	2.97	1.73	2.77
陕 西	Shaanxi	1843.33	1360.80	50.08	158.62	101.88	112.12
甘 肃	Gansu	1160.05	939.54	29.60	30.35	57.30	77.82
青 海	Qinghai	275.36	215.26	4.27	12.16	15.99	14.24
宁 夏	Ningxia	378.33	320.01	4.58	8.92	16.23	22.80
新 疆	Xinjiang	1097.06	800.88	25.82	139.71	64.95	39.66

14-6 全部国有及规模以上非国有工业企业主要经济效益指标

Main Indicators on Economic Benefit of All State-owned and Non-state-owned above Designated Size Industrial Enterprises

年 份 Year 地 区 Region	工业增加值率(%) Ratio of Value Added to Gross Industrial Output Value (%)	总资产贡献率(%) Ratio of Total Assets to Industrial Output Value (%)	资产负债率(%) Assets-Liability Ratio (%)	流动资产周转次数(次/年) Number of Times of Turnover of Circulating Fund (times/year)	工业成本费用利润率(%) Ratio of Profits to Industrial Cost (%)	全员劳动生产率(元/人.年) Overall Labor Productivity (yuan-person-year)	产品销售率(%) Proportion of Products Sold (%)
1998	28.67	7.12	63.74	1.41	2.35	31347	96.52
1999	29.66	7.45	61.83	1.47	3.42	37148	97.15
2000	29.64	9.00	60.81	1.62	5.56	45679	97.67
2001	29.68	8.91	58.97	1.66	5.35	52062	97.63
2002	29.78	9.45	58.72	1.80	5.62	59766	98.02
2003	29.51	10.50	58.96	2.00	6.25	73045	98.02
北 京 Beijing	26.57	8.79	53.13	1.69	6.34	100439	97.86
天 津 Tianjin	26.54	9.63	58.75	2.11	6.03	93235	98.88
河 北 Hebei	31.56	11.39	61.68	2.18	7.03	66671	98.52
山 西 Shanxi	37.25	8.79	63.79	1.49	5.86	49796	97.75
内蒙古 Inner Mongolia	38.11	7.71	59.24	1.73	5.09	71616	98.55
辽 宁 Liaoning	28.07	7.31	58.76	1.69	3.92	70910	98.09
吉 林 Jilin	30.61	10.19	62.51	1.80	6.53	80297	97.62
黑龙江 Heilongjiang	46.84	19.81	55.79	1.79	25.13	102382	98.11
上 海 Shanghai	27.39	12.01	49.68	1.99	7.93	128764	99.02
江 苏 Jiangsu	25.89	10.06	61.95	2.31	4.63	82037	97.86
浙 江 Zhejiang	24.08	12.44	57.24	2.17	6.52	64272	97.63
安 徽 Anhui	33.77	10.78	61.24	1.85	7.04	59183	98.51
福 建 Fujian	29.24	11.64	54.34	2.30	7.07	65439	97.59
江 西 Jiangxi	30.35	8.33	66.23	1.68	3.65	46481	98.01
山 东 Shandong	30.57	12.34	59.37	2.55	6.62	78954	97.93
河 南 Henan	32.43	9.99	64.29	2.02	5.15	54838	98.52
湖 北 Hubei	33.86	7.40	59.17	1.68	5.24	68719	98.45
湖 南 Hunan	34.03	10.67	63.92	1.96	4.69	56082	99.83
广 东 Guangdong	26.58	10.42	56.51	2.22	5.28	77150	97.27
广 西 Guangxi	31.08	9.29	65.35	1.79	4.96	53836	97.82
海 南 Hainan	28.88	9.42	53.78	1.72	6.13	80226	96.46
重 庆 Chongqing	28.19	9.46	61.16	1.55	5.71	52990	97.83
四 川 Sichuan	34.41	7.84	61.37	1.48	4.68	57815	98.80
贵 州 Guizhou	35.44	8.17	63.12	1.30	4.11	52871	97.08
云 南 Yunnan	47.91	15.75	54.88	1.37	8.62	112418	99.36
西 藏 Tibet	57.91	5.80	26.91	0.76	16.78	44687	94.02
陕 西 Shaanxi	35.88	9.77	63.94	1.34	9.71	60144	97.59
甘 肃 Gansu	33.82	6.48	64.79	1.46	2.83	49871	97.88
青 海 Qinghai	38.41	4.97	68.22	1.06	4.72	66860	97.14
宁 夏 Ningxia	31.01	5.76	65.57	1.42	2.41	47978	96.71
新 疆 Xinjiang	41.63	12.01	53.61	1.82	14.92	116833	98.25

14-7 按行业分国有及国有控股工业企业主要指标（2003年）

单位：亿元

行　　业	Sector	企业单位数（个）Number of Enterprises (unit)	工业总产值 Gross Industrial Output Value
全国总计	**National Total**	**34280**	**53407.90**
煤炭开采和洗选业	Mining and Washing of Coal	1008	1893.11
石油和天然气开采业	Extraction of Petroleum and Natural Gas	81	3208.67
黑色金属矿采选业	Mining and Processing of Ferrous Metal Ores	126	107.07
有色金属矿采选业	Mining and Processing of Non-Ferrous Metal Ores	389	236.29
非金属矿采选业	Mining and Processing of Nonmetal Ores	390	142.05
其他采矿业	Mining of Other Ores	5	6.30
农副食品加工业	Processing of Food from Agricultural Products	2346	1080.96
食品制造业	Manufacture of Foods	1012	410.56
饮料制造业	Manufacture of Beverages	841	850.36
烟草制品业	Manufacture of Tobacco	210	2206.97
纺织业	Manufacture of Textile	1449	1193.16
纺织服装、鞋、帽制造业	Manufacture of Textile Wearing Apparel, Footware, and Caps	370	118.36
皮革、毛皮、羽毛(绒)及其制品业	Manufacture of Leather, Fur, Feather and Related Products	138	41.38
木材加工及木、竹、藤、棕、草制品业	Processing of Timber, Manufacture of Wood, Bamboo, Rattan, Palm, and Straw Products	358	118.52
家具制造业	Manufacture of Furniture	149	24.91
造纸及纸制品业	Manufacture of Paper and Paper Products	571	516.74
印刷业和记录媒介的复制	Printing,Reproduction of Recording Media	1448	278.20
文教体育用品制造业	Manufacture of Articles For Culture, Education and Sport Activity	128	34.05
石油加工、炼焦及核燃料加工业	Processing of Petroleum, Coking, Processing of Nuclear Fuel	235	5325.12
化学原料及化学制品制造业	Manufacture of Raw Chemical Materials and Chemical Products	2271	3596.09
医药制造业	Manufacture of Medicines	1001	1063.45
化学纤维制造业	Manufacture of Chemical Fibers	113	390.68
橡胶制品业	Manufacture of Rubber	234	335.02
塑料制品业	Manufacture of Plastics	543	210.97
非金属矿物制品业	Manufacture of Non-metallic Mineral Products	2556	1068.66
黑色金属冶炼及压延加工业	Smelting and Pressing of Ferrous Metals	485	5947.73
有色金属冶炼及压延加工业	Smelting and Pressing of Non-ferrous Metals	481	1451.22
金属制品业	Manufacture of Metal Products	730	356.12
通用设备制造业	Manufacture of General Purpose Machinery	1921	1761.72
专用设备制造业	Manufacture of Special Purpose Machinery	1687	1467.11
交通运输设备制造业	Manufacture of Transport Equipment	1977	6958.38
电气机械及器材制造业	Manufacture of Electrical Machinery and Equipment	1062	989.29
通信设备、计算机及其他电子设备制造业	Manufacture of Communication Equipment, Computers and Other Electronic Equipment	932	3464.25
仪器仪表及文化、办公用机械制造业	Manufacture of Measuring Instruments and Machinery for Cultural Activity and Office Work	505	189.54
工艺品及其他制造业	Manufacture of Artwork and Other Manufacturing	207	70.54
废弃资源和废旧材料回收加工业	Recycling and Disposal of Waste	7	0.90
电力、热力的生产和供应业	Production and Distribution of Electric Power and Heat Power	3933	5749.81
燃气生产和供应业	Production and Distribution of Gas	231	183.10
水的生产和供应业	Production and Distribution of Water	2150	360.52

Main Indicators of State-owned and State-holding Industrial Enterprises by Industrial Sector (2003)

(100 million yuan)

工业增加值 Value-added of Industry	实收资本 Paid-up Capital	资产总计 Total Assets	流动资产合计 Circulating Funds	流动资产年平均余额 Annual Average Balance of Circulating Funds	固定资产原价 Original Value of Fixed Assets	固定资产净值年平均余额 Annual Average Balance of Net Value of Fixed Assets
18837.60	**23018.04**	**94519.79**	**36125.14**	**34327.98**	**69701.11**	**42118.40**
923.72	1556.02	4929.50	1739.22	1641.99	3815.93	2410.24
2242.70	1747.61	4802.28	934.06	968.65	7060.71	3286.53
48.66	125.97	279.03	93.65	87.55	164.92	95.47
77.65	94.40	388.89	138.91	133.06	270.41	160.61
57.86	162.63	491.28	152.66	143.85	335.29	238.93
2.02	5.61	43.59	16.27	15.84	17.34	9.71
243.90	261.11	1080.78	496.60	495.53	580.52	398.95
118.44	157.96	671.56	300.89	285.14	317.00	219.72
331.78	304.29	1526.13	705.11	697.44	758.15	511.85
1562.18	355.87	2764.07	1679.48	1580.09	1066.60	591.10
309.05	458.85	2042.10	948.57	906.54	1200.01	747.36
36.17	38.48	148.00	82.72	81.23	67.89	45.28
10.95	15.28	58.73	34.04	34.48	25.27	15.40
36.49	78.98	262.44	90.12	86.44	186.37	131.24
6.88	17.85	51.39	23.05	22.17	22.23	15.50
145.88	250.17	1182.37	431.52	399.46	717.50	506.79
115.73	168.33	523.72	209.95	209.86	356.58	205.63
11.14	21.95	70.58	39.23	40.84	28.73	16.92
1041.12	1086.16	3174.45	1036.10	1023.40	3365.17	1854.38
920.05	1670.57	5936.30	1948.90	2039.66	4804.10	2852.37
377.07	467.18	2019.37	969.74	953.15	766.27	502.46
78.55	177.46	702.59	236.73	220.77	598.37	366.03
91.77	103.74	488.13	238.50	226.43	259.76	154.18
54.01	117.45	447.37	188.69	183.17	265.67	176.11
360.47	680.89	2624.38	1045.32	1004.11	1676.04	1075.96
1850.10	2085.21	8827.52	3304.93	3001.87	6887.56	3845.32
428.32	635.53	2491.13	979.64	916.67	1666.89	1019.21
95.93	145.49	569.38	311.33	296.75	273.30	173.10
497.92	673.38	3104.90	1960.84	1745.41	1273.51	735.97
365.91	599.68	2664.17	1450.43	1366.44	1261.40	752.79
1863.14	1905.66	8391.05	4804.91	4388.97	3446.83	2058.85
265.16	364.37	1845.74	1086.59	1040.71	682.70	414.80
879.09	785.84	3940.55	2496.32	2357.73	1231.08	724.35
58.95	116.30	453.44	264.62	256.40	178.88	106.33
18.54	18.39	79.13	43.23	41.06	35.91	21.26
0.20	0.31	0.51	0.29	0.31	0.37	0.18
3088.44	4621.25	22828.34	5014.11	4816.97	21854.95	14215.37
57.36	292.68	720.39	208.96	208.67	529.06	352.37
164.31	649.15	1894.53	418.88	409.16	1651.84	1109.76

14-7 续表

单位: 亿元

行业	Sector	流动负债合计 Liquid Liabilities	长期负债合计 Long-term Liabilities
全国总计	**National Total**	**36430.98**	**18926.33**
煤炭开采和洗选业	Mining and Washing of Coal	1812.93	923.49
石油和天然气开采业	Extraction of Petroleum and Natural Gas	1083.83	641.24
黑色金属矿采选业	Mining and Processing of Ferrous Metal Ores	102.12	25.63
有色金属矿采选业	Mining and Processing of Non-Ferrous Metal Ores	176.26	69.44
非金属矿采选业	Mining and Processing of Nonmetal Ores	180.10	106.30
其他采矿业	Mining of Other Ores	18.29	3.23
农副食品加工业	Processing of Food from Agricultural Products	652.51	116.79
食品制造业	Manufacture of Foods	334.10	73.66
饮料制造业	Manufacture of Beverages	691.91	102.80
烟草制品业	Manufacture of Tobacco	1082.12	80.12
纺织业	Manufacture of Textile	1113.06	354.45
纺织服装、鞋、帽制造业	Manufacture of Textile Wearing Apparel, Footware, and Caps	82.91	13.70
皮革、毛皮、羽毛(绒)及其制品业	Manufacture of Leather, Fur, Feather and Related Products	43.27	6.67
木材加工及木、竹、藤、棕、草制品业	Processing of Timber, Manufacture of Wood, Bamboo, Rattan, Palm, and Straw Products	105.87	60.55
家具制造业	Manufacture of Furniture	23.84	4.84
造纸及纸制品业	Manufacture of Paper and Paper Products	497.38	255.32
印刷业和记录媒介的复制	Printing,Reproduction of Recording Media	207.19	57.45
文教体育用品制造业	Manufacture of Articles For Culture, Education and Sport Activity	35.25	4.85
石油加工、炼焦及核燃料加工业	Processing of Petroleum, Coking, Processing of Nuclear Fuel	1101.33	389.98
化学原料及化学制品制造业	Manufacture of Raw Chemical Materials and Chemical Products	2312.79	1086.48
医药制造业	Manufacture of Medicines	917.67	181.77
化学纤维制造业	Manufacture of Chemical Fibers	271.78	129.06
橡胶制品业	Manufacture of Rubber	235.36	78.07
塑料制品业	Manufacture of Plastics	192.00	61.27
非金属矿物制品业	Manufacture of Non-metallic Mineral Products	1214.26	478.10
黑色金属冶炼及压延加工业	Smelting and Pressing of Ferrous Metals	3571.60	1342.22
有色金属冶炼及压延加工业	Smelting and Pressing of Non-ferrous Metals	1158.16	499.09
金属制品业	Manufacture of Metal Products	316.81	61.77
通用设备制造业	Manufacture of General Purpose Machinery	1911.40	274.98
专用设备制造业	Manufacture of Special Purpose Machinery	1595.97	309.73
交通运输设备制造业	Manufacture of Transport Equipment	4384.64	711.47
电气机械及器材制造业	Manufacture of Electrical Machinery and Equipment	1036.48	162.27
通信设备、计算机及其他电子设备制造业	Manufacture of Communication Equipment, Computers and Other Electronic Equipment	2022.50	291.43
仪器仪表及文化、办公用机械制造业	Manufacture of Measuring Instruments and Machinery for Cultural Activity and Office Work	245.12	52.52
工艺品及其他制造业	Manufacture of Artwork and Other Manufacturing	45.85	11.76
废弃资源和废旧材料回收加工业	Recycling and Disposal of Waste	0.20	
电力、热力的生产和供应业	Production and Distribution of Electric Power and Heat Power	5017.04	9419.45
燃气生产和供应业	Production and Distribution of Gas	214.80	121.49
水的生产和供应业	Production and Distribution of Water	422.32	362.91

continued

(100 million yuan)

所有者权益 Creditors' Equity	产品销售收入 Sales Revenue	产品销售成本 Cost of Sales	产品销售税金及附加 Sales Tax and Extra Charges	利润总额 Total Profits	本年应交增值税 Value-added Tax Payable	全部从业人员年平均人数(万人) Annual Average Employed Persons (10 000 persons)
38381.02	**58027.15**	**45987.63**	**1589.87**	**3836.20**	**3025.57**	**2162.87**
2109.60	1930.92	1311.70	25.35	88.31	152.21	308.49
3065.03	3225.37	1614.54	76.54	1150.07	293.34	72.01
148.58	119.69	87.29	3.00	2.69	6.81	12.49
137.25	229.10	164.59	1.55	18.53	7.74	23.19
203.01	144.25	99.42	4.31	3.89	9.22	21.99
22.08	11.85	9.80	0.04	0.99	0.51	1.62
300.32	1061.86	950.42	3.79	17.89	21.89	43.42
260.08	388.58	304.00	2.27	13.42	17.20	24.08
714.29	836.18	523.33	65.67	79.87	57.15	38.02
1600.05	2190.77	840.60	852.01	274.00	243.66	19.97
552.43	1246.22	1121.59	4.30	0.70	39.37	131.67
49.13	110.31	95.59	0.61	0.90	2.76	14.57
8.13	37.40	33.05	0.11	-0.83	1.00	3.92
91.61	113.68	96.03	0.96	1.53	5.01	12.65
22.06	26.01	21.65	0.17	0.10	0.72	2.44
415.49	509.36	417.62	2.22	21.01	26.50	25.14
251.93	262.99	197.66	1.76	21.20	17.10	20.9
29.88	35.90	28.23	0.11	1.27	1.32	3.37
1612.59	5436.50	4861.90	217.46	76.78	162.48	36.86
2475.06	3628.39	3062.91	29.04	113.66	140.46	143.64
903.86	1117.26	720.30	7.99	102.39	67.91	48.08
301.12	389.38	330.64	1.59	16.52	17.00	13.53
171.65	309.76	254.45	6.55	8.59	11.90	15.54
187.08	225.58	190.78	0.78	6.88	7.76	10.89
916.26	1038.91	816.12	7.44	35.17	66.39	98.91
3899.06	6227.60	5078.89	40.43	420.22	381.32	160.28
819.03	1502.64	1237.75	6.67	85.09	62.78	58.56
187.37	362.76	300.96	1.54	10.06	13.06	19.72
910.51	1700.94	1365.62	6.65	61.01	69.75	100.42
746.99	1443.48	1195.40	5.59	23.26	41.56	108.54
3257.68	6987.84	5669.50	140.68	513.11	258.51	170.18
599.30	958.77	774.61	3.87	14.92	34.84	47.69
1599.43	3296.19	2818.27	5.97	119.07	59.52	58.92
153.33	188.24	139.83	0.83	5.27	8.71	16.75
20.79	65.36	57.69	0.40	0.89	1.16	3.88
0.31	0.82	0.70	0.01	0.02	0.02	0.07
8177.57	10038.06	8669.09	55.04	531.64	687.70	213.85
380.10	289.32	263.92	1.63	3.80	10.11	13.06
1080.96	338.91	261.20	4.93	-7.71	19.14	43.58

14-8 按行业分国有及国有控股工业企业主要经济效益指标（2003年）

行　业	Sector	工业增加值率 (%) Ratio of Value Added to Gross Industrial Output Value (%)	总资产贡献率 (%) Ratio of Total Assets to Industrial Output Value (%)
全国总计	**National Total**	**35.27**	**10.09**
煤炭开采和洗选业	Mining and Washing of Coal	48.79	6.36
石油和天然气开采业	Extraction of Petroleum and Natural Gas	69.90	32.12
黑色金属矿采选业	Mining and Processing of Ferrous Metal Ores	45.45	5.27
有色金属矿采选业	Mining and Processing of Non-Ferrous Metal Ores	32.86	8.56
非金属矿采选业	Mining and Processing of Nonmetal Ores	40.74	4.40
其他采矿业	Mining of Other Ores	32.02	4.13
农副食品加工业	Processing of Food from Agricultural Products	22.56	5.53
食品制造业	Manufacture of Foods	28.85	6.05
饮料制造业	Manufacture of Beverages	39.02	14.16
烟草制品业	Manufacture of Tobacco	70.78	50.38
纺织业	Manufacture of Textile	25.90	3.55
纺织服装、鞋、帽制造业	Manufacture of Textile Wearing Apparel, Footware, and Caps	30.56	3.74
皮革、毛皮、羽毛(绒)及其制品业	Manufacture of Leather, Fur, Feather and Related Products	26.45	1.36
木材加工及木、竹、藤、棕、草制品业	Processing of Timber, Manufacture of Wood, Bamboo, Rattan, Palm, and Straw Products	30.79	3.91
家具制造业	Manufacture of Furniture	27.62	2.77
造纸及纸制品业	Manufacture of Paper and Paper Products	28.23	5.85
印刷业和记录媒介的复制	Printing,Reproduction of Recording Media	41.60	8.42
文教体育用品制造业	Manufacture of Articles For Culture, Education and Sport Activity	32.71	5.12
石油加工、炼焦及核燃料加工业	Processing of Petroleum, Coking, Processing of Nuclear Fuel	19.55	15.33
化学原料及化学制品制造业	Products	25.58	6.14
医药制造业	Manufacture of Medicines	35.46	9.98
化学纤维制造业	Manufacture of Chemical Fibers	20.10	6.51
橡胶制品业	Manufacture of Rubber	27.39	7.00
塑料制品业	Manufacture of Plastics	25.60	4.71
非金属矿物制品业	Manufacture of Non-metallic Mineral Products	33.73	5.39
黑色金属冶炼及压延加工业	Smelting and Pressing of Ferrous Metals	31.11	10.63
有色金属冶炼及压延加工业	Smelting and Pressing of Non-ferrous Metals	29.51	7.78
金属制品业	Manufacture of Metal Products	26.94	5.43
通用设备制造业	Manufacture of General Purpose Machinery	28.26	5.45
专用设备制造业	Manufacture of Special Purpose Machinery	24.94	3.91
交通运输设备制造业	Manufacture of Transport Equipment	26.78	11.48
电气机械及器材制造业	Manufacture of Electrical Machinery and Equipment	26.80	4.13
通信设备、计算机及其他电子设备制造业	Manufacture of Communication Equipment, Computers and Other Electronic Equipment	25.38	5.52
仪器仪表及文化、办公用机械制造业	Manufacture of Measuring Instruments and Machinery for Cultural Activity and Office Work	31.10	4.34
工艺品及其他制造业	Manufacture of Artwork and Other Manufacturing	26.28	4.47
废弃资源和废旧材料回收加工业	Recycling and Disposal of Waste	21.84	8.45
电力、热力的生产和供应业	Production and Distribution of Electric Power and Heat Power	53.71	7.14
燃气生产和供应业	Production and Distribution of Gas	31.33	2.82
水的生产和供应业	Production and Distribution of Water	45.58	1.57

Main Indicators on Economic Benefit of State-owned and State-holding Industrial Enterprises by Industrial Sector (2003)

资产负债率 (%) Assets-Liability Ratio (%)	流动资产周转次数 (次/年) Number of Times of Annual of Turnover Circulating Funds (times/year)	工业成本费用利润率 (%) Ratio of Profits to Industrial Cost (%)	全员劳动生产率 (元/人.年) Overall Labor Productivity (yuan/person-year)	产品销售率 (%) Proportion of Products Sold (%)
59.24	**1.69**	**7.25**	**87095**	**98.87**
55.67	1.18	4.81	29943	97.75
36.06	3.33	62.01	311441	100.21
46.75	1.37	2.40	38957	99.58
64.71	1.72	8.74	33486	98.96
58.68	1.00	2.79	26312	99.39
49.35	0.75	8.93	12484	108.06
72.21	2.14	1.71	56174	97.79
61.27	1.36	3.54	49184	97.46
53.20	1.20	11.31	87265	99.17
42.11	1.39	24.98	782234	100.03
72.95	1.37	0.06	23472	99.59
66.80	1.36	0.82	24826	90.33
86.16	1.08	-2.15	27892	100.72
65.09	1.32	1.34	28853	98.25
57.08	1.17	0.40	28237	96.71
64.64	1.28	4.29	58030	98.76
51.89	1.25	8.58	55361	97.20
57.67	0.88	3.57	33083	98.56
49.04	5.31	1.50	282483	99.62
58.17	1.78	3.23	64052	99.03
55.24	1.17	9.96	78419	95.39
57.13	1.76	4.43	58046	99.11
64.84	1.37	2.88	59054	98.45
58.18	1.23	3.09	49610	98.71
65.09	1.03	3.45	36444	98.35
55.81	2.07	7.33	115430	99.81
67.12	1.64	6.08	73141	98.53
67.07	1.22	2.85	48652	99.92
70.68	0.97	3.68	49585	97.61
71.96	1.06	1.60	33713	98.00
60.91	1.59	7.93	109483	98.66
67.53	0.92	1.56	55597	97.82
59.18	1.40	3.68	149189	96.37
66.19	0.73	2.78	35200	95.86
73.73	1.59	1.36	47731	99.41
38.55	2.66	1.84	29451	100.00
64.10	2.08	5.61	144420	100.09
47.24	1.39	1.24	43939	100.88
42.94	0.83	-2.15	37703	97.01

14-9 国有及国有控股工业企业主要指标

Main Indicators of State-owned and State-holding Industrial Enterprises

单位: 亿元 (100 million yuan)

年 份 Year 地 区 Region	企业单位数 (个) Number of Enterprises (unit)	工业总产值 Gross Industrial Output Value	工业增加值 Value Added of Industry	实收资本 Paid-up Capital	资产总计 Total Assets	流动资产合计 Total Circulating Funds
1998	64737	33621.04	11076.90	16424.73	74916.27	29559.03
1999	61301	35571.18	12132.41	17839.85	80471.69	31042.81
2000	53489	40554.37	13777.68	20156.14	84014.94	32628.81
2001	46767	42408.49	14652.05	21780.70	87901.54	33239.63
2002	41125	45178.96	15935.03	22268.48	89094.60	33468.77
2003	34280	53407.90	18837.60	23018.04	94519.79	36125.14
北 京 Beijing	1362	2051.79	548.47	956.97	3388.12	1376.25
天 津 Tianjin	1625	1456.51	470.20	675.96	2715.27	1019.27
河 北 Hebei	1675	2360.39	850.60	1088.41	4377.65	1565.25
山 西 Shanxi	1354	1381.77	558.79	820.11	3341.94	1193.53
内蒙古 Inner Mongolia	591	798.51	307.60	558.02	1807.38	544.22
辽 宁 Liaoning	1334	3552.29	1038.54	1480.78	6277.99	2360.65
吉 林 Jilin	969	2017.70	610.43	648.78	2931.20	1198.65
黑龙江 Heilongjiang	970	2311.94	1181.65	1221.48	3703.92	1366.18
上 海 Shanghai	1606	4466.43	1468.64	1760.52	6320.43	2792.32
江 苏 Jiangsu	1242	3422.44	999.37	1139.06	5055.70	2190.18
浙 江 Zhejiang	861	1686.99	604.88	569.65	2688.42	1031.78
安 徽 Anhui	747	1438.88	532.98	694.47	2572.42	973.54
福 建 Fujian	888	1125.72	413.39	385.52	1629.27	576.86
江 西 Jiangxi	1071	946.60	283.52	388.40	1782.95	738.39
山 东 Shandong	1961	5148.72	1799.18	1675.55	7488.79	2891.55
河 南 Henan	2253	2718.98	946.47	1088.97	4705.00	1891.37
湖 北 Hubei	1617	2287.46	807.82	1210.44	5438.98	1778.16
湖 南 Hunan	1642	1391.74	523.60	513.20	2564.22	969.27
广 东 Guangdong	2103	3949.03	1440.71	1456.96	6328.47	2505.41
广 西 Guangxi	1252	797.95	268.61	306.74	1485.76	512.07
海 南 Hainan	346	213.56	63.78	113.60	323.47	121.99
重 庆 Chongqing	570	852.72	272.40	449.49	1697.64	723.97
四 川 Sichuan	1065	1609.79	591.99	819.35	3846.39	1455.26
贵 州 Guizhou	1037	667.75	256.35	458.28	1664.53	621.42
云 南 Yunnan	943	1145.91	620.25	488.77	2447.02	1007.89
西 藏 Tibet	199	16.76	9.48	43.18	78.12	22.73
陕 西 Shaanxi	1235	1392.06	508.84	601.50	2971.38	1172.95
甘 肃 Gansu	706	880.76	305.64	496.82	1848.10	664.39
青 海 Qinghai	206	195.01	76.90	199.78	775.33	222.00
宁 夏 Ningxia	154	211.74	69.27	128.45	548.97	198.16
新 疆 Xinjiang	696	909.99	407.23	578.83	1714.95	439.47

14-9 续表 1 continued

单位: 亿元 (100 million yuan)

年份 地区	Year Region	流动资产年平均余额 Annual Average Balance of Circulating Funds	固定资产原价合计 Original Value of Fixed Assets	固定资产净值年平均余额 Annual Average Balance of Net Value of Fixed Assets	流动负债合计 Total Liquid Liabilities	长期负债合计 Long-term Liabilities	所有者权益合计 Creditors' Equity
	1998	36122.72	47913.25	31891.43	30625.48	17122.90	26759.22
	1999	29885.62	53146.30	33938.96	31828.59	17666.42	30566.88
	2000	31485.38	57294.96	36886.64	32237.41	18456.43	32714.81
	2001	32575.86	61782.45	38638.22	33144.47	18322.40	35741.27
	2002	32625.56	64521.95	39728.29	34009.59	18295.55	36139.17
	2003	34327.98	69701.11	42118.40	36430.98	18926.33	38381.02
北京	Beijing	1294.38	2111.56	1213.73	1236.26	516.26	1622.35
天津	Tianjin	956.63	2070.16	1222.46	1128.27	501.11	1061.23
河北	Hebei	1526.95	3521.11	2118.17	1791.13	936.90	1617.16
山西	Shanxi	1125.11	2544.91	1575.83	1189.59	941.28	1153.60
内蒙古	Inner Mongolia	507.44	1539.52	938.08	595.26	480.88	709.94
辽宁	Liaoning	2375.25	5178.07	2871.65	2585.38	1145.19	2532.50
吉林	Jilin	1135.99	2030.77	1245.33	1321.27	529.98	1075.17
黑龙江	Heilongjiang	1265.31	3638.86	1948.64	1421.44	581.70	1647.45
上海	Shanghai	2631.59	4311.12	2348.84	2231.66	582.59	3492.53
江苏	Jiangsu	2099.77	3262.88	2006.74	2214.75	831.43	1999.28
浙江	Zhejiang	996.47	1929.96	1194.91	873.15	497.21	1318.05
安徽	Anhui	886.54	1759.68	1128.39	1014.79	546.61	999.76
福建	Fujian	533.31	1279.40	821.36	567.66	394.25	652.57
江西	Jiangxi	691.44	1182.66	736.97	818.42	409.92	522.23
山东	Shandong	2672.69	5519.79	3184.83	3066.73	1308.63	3054.38
河南	Henan	1745.26	3506.03	2074.36	2202.52	928.79	1564.61
湖北	Hubei	1748.62	3883.61	2786.10	1635.07	1487.28	2183.02
湖南	Hunan	915.97	1901.90	1148.50	1043.49	642.68	831.82
广东	Guangdong	2430.01	4603.66	2804.35	2165.91	1218.32	2873.00
广西	Guangxi	492.93	1103.25	715.45	597.53	337.99	499.05
海南	Hainan	116.75	237.49	139.85	101.18	75.33	144.88
重庆	Chongqing	704.58	1057.17	642.49	761.47	270.62	665.55
四川	Sichuan	1395.57	2627.61	1659.82	1470.03	944.29	1396.23
贵州	Guizhou	606.92	1091.15	668.73	628.01	411.91	619.56
云南	Yunnan	885.25	1500.01	918.76	825.64	464.39	1156.99
西藏	Tibet	22.76	57.63	42.47	15.82	5.63	56.67
陕西	Shaanxi	1085.36	2134.03	1354.15	1227.99	660.59	1038.36
甘肃	Gansu	631.96	1358.58	884.72	699.81	502.91	634.48
青海	Qinghai	224.47	566.87	384.29	227.03	306.31	237.69
宁夏	Ningxia	188.01	408.15	266.74	215.91	139.68	193.38
新疆	Xinjiang	434.68	1783.52	1071.68	557.77	325.66	827.55

14-9 续表 2 continued

单位: 亿元 (100 million yuan)

年份 地区	Year Region	产品销售收入 Sales Revenue	产品销售成本 Cost of Sales	产品销售税金及附加 Sales Tax and Extra Charges	利润总额 Total Profits	本年应交增值税 Value-added Tax Payable	全部从业人员年平均人数(万人) Annual Average Employed Persons (10 000 persons)
	1998	33566.11	27092.45	993.53	525.14	1852.36	3747.78
	1999	35950.70	28919.13	1062.21	997.86	2019.03	3394.58
	2000	42203.12	33473.62	1150.28	2408.33	2320.36	2995.25
	2001	44443.52	35522.47	1250.18	2388.56	2408.97	2675.11
	2002	47844.21	38048.00	1401.82	2632.94	2580.51	2423.63
	2003	58027.15	45987.63	1589.87	3836.20	3025.57	2162.87
北京	Beijing	2065.90	1726.52	30.43	118.60	84.79	51.86
天津	Tianjin	1667.86	1363.90	31.71	107.13	69.94	45.21
河北	Hebei	2753.84	2237.65	44.19	161.92	151.67	130.22
山西	Shanxi	1468.35	1106.95	18.46	75.18	106.49	111.73
内蒙古	Inner Mongolia	826.95	681.26	13.85	28.89	50.72	45.18
辽宁	Liaoning	3887.28	3262.95	65.65	115.97	169.12	128.55
吉林	Jilin	2073.42	1698.10	62.53	122.97	91.79	71.09
黑龙江	Heilongjiang	2375.96	1504.05	58.16	555.53	185.45	96.53
上海	Shanghai	4855.86	3864.39	127.02	472.78	228.77	70.88
江苏	Jiangsu	3886.92	3249.26	78.48	160.57	164.03	104.87
浙江	Zhejiang	2147.09	1777.22	78.26	110.43	114.24	38.12
安徽	Anhui	1527.98	1164.79	56.92	111.31	83.92	75.99
福建	Fujian	1120.55	857.84	41.11	89.00	57.35	29.59
江西	Jiangxi	998.00	821.15	28.90	26.29	52.48	56.51
山东	Shandong	5662.93	4543.93	99.38	397.63	264.88	201.28
河南	Henan	2855.49	2336.05	64.96	111.96	138.09	174.11
湖北	Hubei	2404.62	1891.44	61.52	132.15	123.98	103.17
湖南	Hunan	1499.44	1132.21	93.13	52.68	85.98	81.27
广东	Guangdong	4717.48	3867.37	91.59	307.28	224.61	75.20
广西	Guangxi	815.45	638.50	20.96	38.14	54.87	44.25
海南	Hainan	209.04	168.85	5.73	11.60	9.23	7.82
重庆	Chongqing	898.97	701.44	23.64	53.68	51.40	43.85
四川	Sichuan	1761.94	1369.91	47.60	67.58	101.21	93.67
贵州	Guizhou	706.36	529.71	38.22	28.16	45.23	47.02
云南	Yunnan	1129.97	696.75	204.50	87.92	102.11	41.75
西藏	Tibet	16.27	11.54	0.39	2.02	1.40	1.99
陕西	Shaanxi	1389.05	1010.06	44.66	128.15	79.11	83.90
甘肃	Gansu	929.93	747.82	26.91	22.54	49.86	53.49
青海	Qinghai	229.01	177.76	3.70	9.93	13.88	10.41
宁夏	Ningxia	248.51	211.38	3.13	2.67	11.85	14.87
新疆	Xinjiang	896.73	636.85	24.19	125.54	57.13	28.47

14-10 国有及国有控股工业企业主要经济效益指标

Main Indicators on Economic Benefit of State-owned and State-holding Industrial Enterprises

年份 Year 地区 Region	工业增加值率(%) Ratio of Value-added to Gross Industrial Output Value (%)	总资产贡献率(%) Ratio of Total Assets to Industrial Output Value (%)	资产负债率(%) Assets-Liability Ratio (%)	流动资产周转次数(次/年) Number of Times of Turnover of Circulating Fund (times/year)	工业成本费用利润率(%) Ratio of Profits to Industrial Cost (%)	全员劳动生产率(元/人.年) Overall Labor Productivity (yuan-person-year)	产品销售率(%) Proportion of Products Sold (%)
1998	32.95	6.51	64.26	0.93	1.61	29054	97.41
1999	34.11	6.77	61.98	1.20	2.89	35741	98.15
2000	33.97	8.43	60.99	1.34	6.15	45998	98.88
2001	34.55	8.17	59.19	1.36	5.75	54772	98.65
2002	35.27	8.71	59.30	1.47	5.93	65749	98.98
2003	35.27	10.09	59.24	1.69	7.25	87095	98.87
北京 Beijing	26.73	7.72	52.03	1.60	5.96	105759	98.43
天津 Tianjin	32.28	8.81	60.92	1.74	6.98	104007	99.92
河北 Hebei	36.04	9.60	63.06	1.80	6.31	65319	98.88
山西 Shanxi	40.44	7.53	64.29	1.31	5.45	50010	98.02
内蒙古 Inner Mongolia	38.52	6.61	60.72	1.63	3.70	68078	98.41
辽宁 Liaoning	29.24	6.76	59.51	1.64	3.14	80786	98.76
吉林 Jilin	30.25	10.48	63.18	1.83	6.38	85865	98.21
黑龙江 Heilongjiang	51.11	22.47	54.33	1.88	31.64	122408	98.64
上海 Shanghai	32.88	13.68	44.74	1.85	10.89	207207	99.30
江苏 Jiangsu	29.20	8.98	60.46	1.85	4.41	95292	99.16
浙江 Zhejiang	35.86	12.37	50.97	2.15	5.58	158698	99.51
安徽 Anhui	37.04	10.81	61.13	1.72	8.16	70135	99.52
福建 Fujian	36.72	12.62	59.47	2.10	8.97	139685	98.63
江西 Jiangxi	29.95	7.55	69.39	1.44	2.76	50174	98.79
山东 Shandong	34.94	11.39	59.21	2.12	7.71	89385	98.75
河南 Henan	34.81	8.31	66.75	1.64	4.15	54360	98.97
湖北 Hubei	35.32	6.66	59.86	1.38	5.96	78302	99.46
湖南 Hunan	37.62	10.17	67.56	1.64	3.94	64428	100.51
广东 Guangdong	36.48	10.88	54.60	1.94	7.05	191590	97.44
广西 Guangxi	33.66	8.95	66.41	1.65	4.97	60701	98.64
海南 Hainan	29.86	9.28	55.21	1.79	6.06	81537	97.92
重庆 Chongqing	31.95	9.05	60.80	1.28	6.33	62117	98.55
四川 Sichuan	36.77	7.20	63.70	1.26	4.10	63203	99.91
贵州 Guizhou	38.39	7.99	62.78	1.16	4.29	54521	98.60
云南 Yunnan	54.13	17.39	52.72	1.28	10.22	148557	99.78
西藏 Tibet	56.59	4.98	27.46	0.71	13.76	47720	91.83
陕西 Shaanxi	36.55	9.76	64.50	1.28	10.53	60649	98.18
甘肃 Gansu	34.70	6.51	65.67	1.47	2.63	57138	99.57
青海 Qinghai	39.43	4.80	69.34	1.02	4.66	73900	96.86
宁夏 Ningxia	32.72	4.93	64.77	1.32	1.09	46575	98.27
新疆 Xinjiang	44.75	12.99	51.75	2.06	16.86	143018	98.88

14-11 按行业分“三资”工业企业主要指标（2003年）

单位: 亿元

行业	Sector	企业单位数(个) Number of Enterprises (unit)	工业总产值 Gross Industrial Output Value
全国总计	**National Total**	**38581**	**44357.81**
煤炭开采和洗选业	Mining and Washing of Coal	15	7.35
石油和天然气开采业	Extraction of Petroleum and Natural Gas	3	253.40
黑色金属矿采选业	Mining and Processing of Ferrous Metal Ores	11	2.50
有色金属矿采选业	Mining and Processing of Non-Ferrous Metal Ores	20	5.78
非金属矿采选业	Mining and Processing of Nonmetal Ores	85	25.39
其他采矿业	Mining of Other Ores		
农副食品加工业	Processing of Food from Agricultural Products	1589	1653.61
食品制造业	Manufacture of Foods	1081	883.19
饮料制造业	Manufacture of Beverages	512	711.58
烟草制品业	Manufacture of Tobacco	7	12.36
纺织业	Manufacture of Textile	3115	1827.15
纺织服装、鞋、帽制造业	Manufacture of Textile Wearing Apparel, Footware, and Caps	4035	1589.51
皮革、毛皮、羽毛(绒)及其制品业	Manufacture of Leather, Fur, Feather and Related Products	1848	1160.14
木材加工及木、竹、藤、棕、草制品业	Processing of Timber, Manufacture of Wood, Bamboo, Rattan, Palm, and Straw Products	688	263.03
家具制造业	Manufacture of Furniture	616	358.95
造纸及纸制品业	Manufacture of Paper and Paper Products	825	793.17
印刷业和记录媒介的复制	Printing,Reproduction of Recording Media	611	345.16
文教体育用品制造业	Manufacture of Articles For Culture, Education and Sport Activity	1196	572.90
石油加工、炼焦及核燃料加工业	Processing of Petroleum, Coking, Processing of Nuclear Fuel	110	632.09
化学原料及化学制品制造业	Manufacture of Raw Chemical Materials and Chemical Products	2041	2175.20
医药制造业	Manufacture of Medicines	701	636.00
化学纤维制造业	Manufacture of Chemical Fibers	194	290.79
橡胶制品业	Manufacture of Rubber	422	482.50
塑料制品业	Manufacture of Plastics	2439	1310.29
非金属矿物制品业	Manufacture of Non-metallic Mineral Products	1773	959.28
黑色金属冶炼及压延加工业	Smelting and Pressing of Ferrous Metals	267	874.23
有色金属冶炼及压延加工业	Smelting and Pressing of Non-ferrous Metals	346	471.99
金属制品业	Manufacture of Metal Products	1929	1345.41
通用设备制造业	Manufacture of General Purpose Machinery	1714	1429.30
专用设备制造业	Manufacture of Special Purpose Machinery	1029	768.71
交通运输设备制造业	Manufacture of Transport Equipment	1319	4535.61
电气机械及器材制造业	Manufacture of Electrical Machinery and Equipment	2333	2787.82
通信设备、计算机及其他电子设备制造业	Manufacture of Communication Equipment, Computers and Other Electronic Equipment	2937	12209.21
仪器仪表及文化、办公用机械制造业	Manufacture of Measuring Instruments and Machinery for Cultural Activity and Office Work	834	1105.73
工艺品及其他制造业	Manufacture of Artwork and Other Manufacturing	1517	543.93
废弃资源和废旧材料回收加工业	Recycling and Disposal of Waste	20	8.93
电力、热力的生产和供应业	Production and Distribution of Electric Power and Heat Power	309	1238.80
燃气生产和供应业	Production and Distribution of Gas	59	70.27
水的生产和供应业	Production and Distribution of Water	31	16.85

Main Indicators of Foreign Funded Enterprises by Industrial Sector (2003)

(100 million yuan)

工业增加值 Value-added of Industry	实收资本 Paid-up Capital	资产总计 Total Assets	流动资产合计 Circulating Funds	流动资产年平均余额 Annual Average Balance of Circulating Funds	固定资产原价 Original Value of Fixed Assets	固定资产净值年平均余额 Annual Average Balance of Net Value of Fixed Assets
11599.65	**13216.82**	**39260.26**	**21489.84**	**19866.14**	**21818.93**	**13722.33**
2.08	3.38	12.43	8.52	8.11	4.30	3.71
133.47	43.99	107.70	21.52	19.45	61.20	60.55
0.87	1.60	3.27	1.30	1.24	2.06	1.37
1.83	2.13	6.39	3.75	3.69	2.78	1.76
6.28	9.57	22.85	11.61	11.52	12.16	8.25
386.04	355.52	1161.70	654.25	601.50	579.73	372.00
275.87	371.85	856.98	443.37	419.15	503.96	314.48
257.33	426.12	942.59	395.92	369.91	659.49	412.17
7.03	7.73	18.66	11.18	11.32	13.00	6.08
460.74	736.92	1884.28	972.05	917.45	1103.32	698.84
431.78	367.91	1065.22	674.15	633.33	462.03	287.61
299.91	232.56	726.71	460.29	448.72	300.84	200.87
69.54	116.22	288.66	138.18	140.39	174.40	121.37
88.94	103.63	313.16	178.73	164.24	133.14	91.84
215.75	391.79	1159.69	465.23	434.10	777.40	566.09
107.56	180.63	457.67	239.10	225.58	289.32	176.74
150.73	177.38	449.94	279.80	266.45	216.95	134.53
149.81	140.96	493.73	180.84	171.92	422.71	244.73
617.81	813.86	2106.03	1059.64	971.35	1198.25	799.28
244.68	289.89	772.60	427.28	398.31	352.10	238.23
67.62	162.68	352.82	114.26	112.47	290.86	187.13
139.98	200.48	600.20	286.34	270.52	365.18	217.09
336.70	593.94	1399.68	726.16	689.17	818.68	512.83
295.99	625.22	1478.43	620.86	586.93	992.40	649.46
205.29	263.03	900.08	470.54	418.20	420.68	305.37
103.06	171.56	455.39	227.64	207.54	254.95	178.39
326.35	443.65	1197.08	720.51	674.42	599.21	375.72
436.32	554.75	1515.80	952.75	863.35	709.43	446.78
211.71	251.67	795.95	522.01	476.42	288.47	179.75
1291.03	1062.66	3534.99	2158.74	1926.50	1572.89	957.19
713.12	823.65	2362.54	1470.66	1359.73	1075.72	652.73
2424.52	1911.11	7645.07	5191.63	4746.91	3119.81	1909.07
286.03	231.49	709.39	470.72	431.94	301.86	182.55
149.09	150.62	388.24	233.47	227.22	171.22	114.40
1.45	2.34	8.50	6.38	4.90	1.32	0.98
685.41	921.35	2892.22	641.38	605.10	3457.36	2026.19
11.94	28.85	81.46	32.16	30.34	46.91	36.76
6.01	44.13	92.17	16.91	16.75	62.85	49.44

14-11 续表

单位: 亿元

行业	Sector	流动负债合计 Liquid Liabilities	长期负债合计 Long-term Liabilities
全国总计	**National Total**	**18466.50**	**3045.20**
煤炭开采和洗选业	Mining and Washing of Coal	7.80	0.29
石油和天然气开采业	Extraction of Petroleum and Natural Gas	14.70	0.04
黑色金属矿采选业	Mining and Processing of Ferrous Metal Ores	1.30	
有色金属矿采选业	Mining and Processing of Non-Ferrous Metal Ores	3.25	0.14
非金属矿采选业	Mining and Processing of Nonmetal Ores	9.85	2.07
其他采矿业	Mining of Other Ores		
农副食品加工业	Processing of Food from Agricultural Products	678.05	72.63
食品制造业	Manufacture of Foods	409.83	46.99
饮料制造业	Manufacture of Beverages	430.37	71.58
烟草制品业	Manufacture of Tobacco	8.35	
纺织业	Manufacture of Textile	880.20	120.50
纺织服装、鞋、帽制造业	Manufacture of Textile Wearing Apparel, Footware, and Caps	546.08	27.59
皮革、毛皮、羽毛(绒)及其制品业	Manufacture of Leather, Fur, Feather and Related Products	396.91	19.31
木材加工及木、竹、藤、棕、草制品业	Processing of Timber, Manufacture of Wood, Bamboo, Rattan, Palm, and Straw Products	125.01	41.94
家具制造业	Manufacture of Furniture	155.52	9.76
造纸及纸制品业	Manufacture of Paper and Paper Products	529.30	153.67
印刷业和记录媒介的复制	Printing,Reproduction of Recording Media	192.91	23.09
文教体育用品制造业	Manufacture of Articles For Culture, Education and Sport Activity	219.32	9.56
石油加工、炼焦及核燃料加工业	Processing of Petroleum, Coking, Processing of Nuclear Fuel	165.09	67.61
化学原料及化学制品制造业	Manufacture of Raw Chemical Materials and Chemical Products	874.85	189.56
医药制造业	Manufacture of Medicines	345.56	51.01
化学纤维制造业	Manufacture of Chemical Fibers	119.79	54.65
橡胶制品业	Manufacture of Rubber	283.30	69.27
塑料制品业	Manufacture of Plastics	600.87	87.47
非金属矿物制品业	Manufacture of Non-metallic Mineral Products	564.18	195.82
黑色金属冶炼及压延加工业	Smelting and Pressing of Ferrous Metals	407.04	124.92
有色金属冶炼及压延加工业	Smelting and Pressing of Non-ferrous Metals	228.17	46.99
金属制品业	Manufacture of Metal Products	608.68	48.78
通用设备制造业	Manufacture of General Purpose Machinery	745.59	53.56
专用设备制造业	Manufacture of Special Purpose Machinery	380.87	33.84
交通运输设备制造业	Manufacture of Transport Equipment	1585.36	152.52
电气机械及器材制造业	Manufacture of Electrical Machinery and Equipment	1198.68	57.58
通信设备、计算机及其他电子设备制造业	Manufacture of Communication Equipment, Computers and Other Electronic Equipment	4537.60	354.94
仪器仪表及文化、办公用机械制造业	Manufacture of Measuring Instruments and Machinery for Cultural Activity and Office Work	356.87	13.58
工艺品及其他制造业	Manufacture of Artwork and Other Manufacturing	182.34	8.60
废弃资源和废旧材料回收加工业	Recycling and Disposal of Waste	6.30	
电力、热力的生产和供应业	Production and Distribution of Electric Power and Heat Power	594.87	815.32
燃气生产和供应业	Production and Distribution of Gas	47.82	5.18
水的生产和供应业	Production and Distribution of Water	23.70	14.86

continued

(100 million yuan)

所有者权益 Creditors' Equity	产品销售收入 Sales Revenue	产品销售成本 Cost of Sales	产品销售税金及附加 Tax and Sales Extra Charges	利润总额 Total Profits	本年应交增值税 Value Added Tax Payable	全部从业人员年平均人数(万人) Annual Average Employed Persons (10 000 persons)
17473.30	**43607.63**	**36604.09**	**223.65**	**2777.44**	**1189.01**	**1258.67**
4.34	7.89	5.23	0.02	0.02	0.46	0.36
92.97	130.14	35.27	7.65	66.29	11.71	0.05
1.96	2.30	1.99	0.05	0.03	0.12	0.20
3.00	5.55	3.95	0.02	0.86	0.20	0.25
10.69	25.67	19.76	0.38	1.16	0.92	1.01
404.36	1617.00	1451.38	1.67	46.61	23.23	35.03
396.58	858.15	617.10	1.61	53.16	44.56	28.16
427.40	672.56	425.42	23.08	45.64	46.52	16.83
10.31	13.16	7.00	2.44	1.82	1.55	0.37
867.78	1749.35	1562.75	2.80	61.15	32.45	93.36
480.87	1531.52	1323.33	3.35	60.06	32.85	144.83
304.35	1091.08	982.67	2.30	30.34	18.94	102.02
119.38	250.20	220.19	0.53	6.45	6.29	13.58
138.98	349.70	297.71	0.32	14.79	6.02	21.68
474.98	795.51	654.73	0.87	51.15	35.88	20.77
239.76	336.34	273.27	0.25	31.33	14.89	14.87
216.12	550.09	479.61	0.66	20.13	5.31	56.82
260.34	646.21	557.20	11.21	35.22	24.15	3.73
1019.35	2114.98	1547.28	12.45	197.67	95.73	29.87
370.39	576.69	326.99	2.67	69.30	43.81	16.92
177.60	281.29	246.96	0.50	17.05	8.88	4.71
246.48	473.29	382.04	7.16	26.06	12.54	19.03
706.85	1279.04	1105.23	1.26	60.75	29.51	58.84
709.74	921.07	740.03	2.30	59.43	39.54	41.64
366.44	876.49	773.32	0.99	61.72	30.51	10.84
177.61	453.04	408.56	0.25	16.78	7.61	7.43
532.49	1335.33	1154.50	1.61	68.78	24.13	46.20
709.63	1381.22	1099.48	1.32	124.61	41.65	36.29
362.98	765.65	607.73	0.98	65.28	22.61	20.46
1777.59	4456.75	3437.40	120.36	523.38	185.32	50.43
1074.96	2689.75	2231.93	2.38	166.43	56.91	90.34
2708.39	12426.48	11289.98	2.97	443.59	139.02	177.56
336.82	1098.86	948.14	4.20	60.00	16.63	31.99
193.92	518.46	449.03	1.19	22.04	8.69	48.79
2.00	8.86	8.49		-0.04	0.12	0.11
1463.84	1192.59	814.26	1.67	263.30	118.07	12.05
28.45	106.09	101.11	0.17	1.03	0.57	0.75
53.57	19.29	13.04	0.01	4.07	1.09	0.53

14-12 按行业分“三资”工业企业主要经济效益指标（2003年）

行　业	Sector	工业增加值率 (%) Ratio of Value Added to Gross Industrial Output Value (%)
全国总计	**National Total**	**26.15**
煤炭开采和洗选业	Mining and Washing of Coal	28.36
石油和天然气开采业	Extraction of Petroleum and Natural Gas	52.67
黑色金属矿采选业	Mining and Processing of Ferrous Metal Ores	34.90
有色金属矿采选业	Mining and Processing of Non-Ferrous Metal Ores	31.70
非金属矿采选业	Mining and Processing of Nonmetal Ores	24.73
其他采矿业	Mining of Other Ores	
农副食品加工业	Processing of Food from Agricultural Products	23.35
食品制造业	Manufacture of Foods	31.24
饮料制造业	Manufacture of Beverages	36.16
烟草制品业	Manufacture of Tobacco	56.90
纺织业	Manufacture of Textile	25.22
纺织服装、鞋、帽制造业	Manufacture of Textile Wearing Apparel, Footware, and Caps	27.16
皮革、毛皮、羽毛(绒)及其制品业	Manufacture of Leather, Fur, Feather and Related Products	25.85
木材加工及木、竹、藤、棕、草制品业	Processing of Timber, Manufacture of Wood, Bamboo, Rattan, Palm, and Straw Products	26.44
家具制造业	Manufacture of Furniture	24.78
造纸及纸制品业	Manufacture of Paper and Paper Products	27.20
印刷业和记录媒介的复制	Printing,Reproduction of Recording Media	31.16
文教体育用品制造业	Manufacture of Articles For Culture,Education and Sport Activity	26.31
石油加工、炼焦及核燃料加工业	Processing of Petroleum, Coking, Processing of Nuclear Fuel	23.70
化学原料及化学制品制造业	Manufacture of Raw Chemical Materials and Chemical Products	28.40
医药制造业	Manufacture of Medicines	38.47
化学纤维制造业	Manufacture of Chemical Fibers	23.25
橡胶制品业	Manufacture of Rubber	29.01
塑料制品业	Manufacture of Plastics	25.70
非金属矿物制品业	Manufacture of Non-metallic Mineral Products	30.86
黑色金属冶炼及压延加工业	Smelting and Pressing of Ferrous Metals	23.48
有色金属冶炼及压延加工业	Smelting and Pressing of Non-ferrous Metals	21.83
金属制品业	Manufacture of Metal Products	24.26
通用设备制造业	Manufacture of General Purpose Machinery	30.53
专用设备制造业	Manufacture of Special Purpose Machinery	27.54
交通运输设备制造业	Manufacture of Transport Equipment	28.46
电气机械及器材制造业	Manufacture of Electrical Machinery and Equipment	25.58
通信设备、计算机及其他电子设备制造业	Manufacture of Communication Equipment,Computers and Other Electronic Equipment	19.86
仪器仪表及文化、办公用机械制造业	Manufacture of Measuring Instruments and Machinery for Cultural Activity and Office Work	25.87
工艺品及其他制造业	Manufacture of Artwork and Other Manufacturing	27.41
废弃资源和废旧材料回收加工业	Recycling and Disposal of Waste	16.20
电力、热力的生产和供应业	Production and Distribution of Electric Power and Heat Power	55.33
燃气生产和供应业	Production and Distribution of Gas	16.99
水的生产和供应业	Production and Distribution of Water	35.65

Main Indicators on Economic Benefit of Foreign Funded Industrial Enterprises by Industrial Sector (2003)

总资产贡献率 (%) Ratio of Total Assets to Industrial Output Value (%)	资产负债率 (%) Assets-Liability Ratio (%)	流动资产周转次数（次/年） Number of Times of Annual of Turnover Circulating Funds (times/year)	工业成本费用利润率 (%) Ratio of Profits to Industrial Cost (%)	全员劳动生产率 (元/人.年) Overall Labor Productivity (yuan/person-year)	产品销售率 (%) Proportion of Products Sold (%)
11.46	**55.43**	**2.20**	**6.83**	**92158**	**98.17**
5.81	65.05	0.97	0.29	57681	106.01
80.24	13.68	6.69	167.88	26325266	99.33
6.52	39.95	1.85	1.31	44290	98.53
17.39	53.01	1.50	18.33	74376	97.73
11.47	53.20	2.23	4.88	62218	99.27
					0.00
7.34	65.19	2.69	2.98	110189	97.00
12.21	53.72	2.05	6.64	97949	97.40
13.03	54.66	1.82	7.58	152879	98.88
32.21	44.74	1.16	20.02	191153	106.28
6.04	53.95	1.91	3.61	49352	97.39
9.74	54.86	2.42	4.10	29813	97.92
7.84	58.12	2.43	2.86	29398	98.16
5.58	58.64	1.78	2.63	51216	97.69
7.37	55.62	2.13	4.46	41019	98.98
9.02	59.04	1.83	6.85	103885	99.63
10.79	47.61	1.49	10.20	72349	97.84
6.27	51.97	2.06	3.80	26527	97.83
15.66	47.27	3.76	5.88	401843	99.89
15.42	51.60	2.18	10.32	206847	96.69
15.86	52.06	1.45	13.55	144631	92.46
8.73	49.66	2.50	6.38	143445	96.71
8.78	58.93	1.75	5.93	73564	98.42
7.20	49.50	1.86	4.99	57221	98.43
7.75	51.99	1.57	6.90	71087	96.95
11.41	59.29	2.10	7.60	189324	99.42
6.87	61.00	2.18	3.83	138727	97.76
8.63	55.52	1.98	5.42	70646	99.57
11.64	53.18	1.60	9.84	120235	97.36
11.74	54.40	1.61	9.30	103460	97.71
23.74	49.26	2.31	13.67	255996	98.34
10.14	54.50	1.98	6.59	78936	97.74
8.07	64.47	2.62	3.69	136547	98.68
11.64	52.52	2.54	5.77	89407	98.42
8.82	50.05	2.28	4.45	30561	97.98
2.47	76.46	1.81	-0.49	134798	98.92
15.24	49.39	1.97	28.18	568891	99.78
2.72	65.07	3.50	0.97	160124	100.00
6.23	41.88	1.15	24.45	114224	98.92

14-13 "三资"工业企业主要指标

Main Indicators of Foreign Funded Industrial Enterprises

单位：亿元 (100 million yuan)

年份 Year / 地区 Region		企业单位数(个) Number of Enterprises (unit)	工业总产值 Gross Industrial Output Value	工业增加值 Value Added of Industry	实收资本 Total Capital Hold	资产总计 Total Assets	流动资产合计 Total Circulating Funds
	1998	26442	16757.90	4055.07	7538.86	21326.95	9971.87
	1999	26837	18954.23	4850.92	8181.30	23018.92	11127.85
	2000	28445	23464.55	6090.35	9080.11	25714.06	12849.54
	2001	31423	27220.91	7128.11	10256.78	28354.46	14029.75
	2002	34466	32459.28	8573.10	11447.28	31513.76	16237.04
	2003	38581	44357.81	11599.65	13216.82	39260.26	21489.84
北京	Beijing	960	1553.18	401.54	481.42	1337.13	846.26
天津	Tianjin	1345	1896.06	424.76	608.93	1558.16	920.21
河北	Hebei	839	742.43	227.58	286.06	881.64	390.23
山西	Shanxi	101	139.12	51.15	76.84	251.58	82.37
内蒙古	Inner Mongolia	109	151.86	53.43	44.87	197.32	117.79
辽宁	Liaoning	1488	1451.01	388.90	595.48	1611.20	830.92
吉林	Jilin	206	781.23	221.64	127.62	517.35	292.94
黑龙江	Heilongjiang	180	179.53	60.74	76.67	268.53	131.87
上海	Shanghai	4290	6426.75	1584.66	2149.79	5973.25	3498.35
江苏	Jiangsu	4799	6007.42	1573.41	1754.24	5167.13	2722.83
浙江	Zhejiang	3675	2585.81	630.09	728.93	2399.27	1395.80
安徽	Anhui	377	447.54	141.19	174.88	481.65	226.27
福建	Fujian	3904	3126.26	863.91	930.62	2693.51	1431.09
江西	Jiangxi	236	178.42	50.09	45.02	182.69	85.02
山东	Shandong	2925	2483.24	730.01	664.60	2238.73	1048.05
河南	Henan	402	362.68	114.01	128.41	480.06	244.95
湖北	Hubei	464	577.79	200.95	224.03	587.88	242.07
湖南	Hunan	305	249.53	73.94	122.86	298.58	117.49
广东	Guangdong	10619	13681.32	3400.86	3407.72	10466.16	6045.36
广西	Guangxi	277	308.19	82.10	104.35	314.27	145.00
海南	Hainan	97	58.74	14.14	30.34	68.66	38.60
重庆	Chongqing	162	282.93	83.12	108.80	337.67	155.08
四川	Sichuan	338	286.23	93.23	136.69	395.70	196.03
贵州	Guizhou	81	39.51	10.22	29.43	60.80	33.68
云南	Yunnan	139	94.91	29.74	63.90	138.93	64.12
西藏	Tibet	7	0.04	0.01	0.47	0.73	0.25
陕西	Shaanxi	133	159.97	63.73	69.01	198.64	110.28
甘肃	Gansu	39	40.14	12.59	16.60	56.18	28.57
青海	Qinghai	13	7.43	2.11	3.16	10.62	3.59
宁夏	Ningxia	26	34.41	8.97	12.75	47.88	24.50
新疆	Xinjiang	45	24.12	6.81	12.33	38.35	20.29

14-13 续表 1 continued

单位: 亿元 (100 million yuan)

年 份 Year / 地 区 Region	流动资产年平均余额 Annual Average Balance of Circulating Funds	固定资产原价合计 Original Value of Fixed Assets	固定资产净值年平均余额 Annual Average Balance of Net Value of Fixed Assets	流动负债合计 Total Liquid Liabilities	长期负债合计 Long-term Liabilities	所有者权益合计 Creditors' Equity
1998	9671.91	11439.70	8313.98	9507.28	2855.06	8844.84
1999	10606.05	12747.02	9062.95	10407.35	2680.68	9730.41
2000	11926.66	14318.30	9808.74	11616.67	2861.93	11054.36
2001	13750.96	16700.30	11111.58	12466.43	2935.75	12794.29
2002	15174.60	18726.88	12097.09	14146.01	2864.80	14359.94
2003	19866.14	21818.93	13722.33	18466.50	3045.20	17473.30
北 京 Beijing	770.07	565.34	328.41	669.41	66.97	597.18
天 津 Tianjin	841.99	851.05	499.57	713.86	63.43	764.30
河 北 Hebei	370.00	561.31	391.46	354.93	149.33	367.49
山 西 Shanxi	73.49	190.72	150.02	82.01	77.91	90.86
内蒙古 Inner Mongolia	120.02	69.75	50.61	62.22	37.71	96.01
辽 宁 Liaoning	767.74	1047.77	645.54	720.53	131.33	757.07
吉 林 Jilin	251.53	275.24	162.33	233.97	40.05	243.33
黑龙江 Heilongjiang	127.35	168.80	115.80	160.31	25.75	81.00
上 海 Shanghai	3131.65	3186.90	1848.72	2789.34	298.96	2863.60
江 苏 Jiangsu	2450.29	2876.39	1914.11	2662.51	385.07	2109.25
浙 江 Zhejiang	1280.85	1124.38	745.85	1220.76	149.25	1029.27
安 徽 Anhui	206.75	300.59	199.85	198.14	75.31	208.08
福 建 Fujian	1281.24	1500.85	1022.80	1201.14	215.22	1262.00
江 西 Jiangxi	82.43	99.04	68.82	69.97	22.12	71.73
山 东 Shandong	981.05	1351.68	908.46	995.29	250.39	978.45
河 南 Henan	238.40	321.12	180.49	250.05	40.58	188.06
湖 北 Hubei	236.49	363.38	262.73	223.34	72.63	255.70
湖 南 Hunan	102.43	225.59	142.50	117.79	52.85	127.30
广 东 Guangdong	5787.17	5704.86	3412.12	5056.07	662.24	4654.91
广 西 Guangxi	133.60	197.18	134.34	133.87	42.63	137.08
海 南 Hainan	34.73	36.63	23.62	29.82	5.05	33.79
重 庆 Chongqing	137.49	261.20	153.22	117.92	72.01	147.74
四 川 Sichuan	189.79	200.46	142.32	155.58	41.60	172.51
贵 州 Guizhou	30.05	28.32	19.02	38.23	5.45	17.03
云 南 Yunnan	61.21	95.90	64.26	50.51	17.92	70.49
西 藏 Tibet	0.60	0.47	0.40	0.06	0.07	0.60
陕 西 Shaanxi	104.02	128.85	76.94	83.95	20.85	93.07
甘 肃 Gansu	28.62	33.10	20.65	29.15	8.24	18.70
青 海 Qinghai	3.63	7.54	5.52	4.62	1.20	4.77
宁 夏 Ningxia	22.30	20.50	16.43	25.11	7.13	15.64
新 疆 Xinjiang	19.14	24.01	15.40	16.06	5.96	16.31

14-13 续表 2 continued

单位: 亿元 (100 million yuan)

年 份 地 区	Year Region	产品销售收入 Sales Revenue	产品销售成本 Cost of Sales	产品销售税金及附加 Sales Tax and Extra Charges	利润总额 Total Profits	本年应交增值税 Value-added Tax Payable	全部从业人员年平均人数(万人) Annual Average Employed Persons (10 000 Persons)
	1998	15604.60	13023.55	98.64	418.61	521.06	775.19
	1999	17966.55	14824.32	111.51	753.93	590.79	791.86
	2000	22545.74	18583.27	129.76	1282.48	738.88	852.96
	2001	26022.08	21677.74	134.78	1442.95	876.37	938.98
	2002	31189.27	25907.35	151.87	1877.22	960.87	1054.34
	2003	43607.63	36604.09	223.65	2777.44	1189.01	1258.67
北 京	Beijing	1623.70	1310.52	8.51	122.02	56.12	23.02
天 津	Tianjin	1914.01	1631.31	8.16	92.43	41.06	34.53
河 北	Hebei	708.90	575.93	2.42	66.86	29.76	23.13
山 西	Shanxi	132.65	99.05	0.59	9.40	9.12	4.62
内蒙古	Inner Mongolia	155.58	122.27	0.04	14.24	4.83	4.45
辽 宁	Liaoning	1417.35	1180.02	11.39	81.65	41.16	39.01
吉 林	Jilin	724.58	569.32	29.35	80.92	23.44	6.77
黑龙江	Heilongjiang	170.22	123.80	3.15	7.11	9.07	7.45
上 海	Shanghai	6727.60	5508.54	48.06	483.68	192.05	103.78
江 苏	Jiangsu	5926.59	5152.14	10.77	314.96	132.41	137.66
浙 江	Zhejiang	2534.88	2132.46	5.68	179.07	79.35	93.36
安 徽	Anhui	412.54	332.24	3.17	33.93	17.92	11.49
福 建	Fujian	3005.74	2530.40	11.43	214.05	68.70	129.95
江 西	Jiangxi	169.29	132.74	1.61	11.15	7.14	8.91
山 东	Shandong	2317.61	1970.10	7.72	143.74	70.38	94.25
河 南	Henan	341.57	277.14	1.97	24.15	12.89	11.64
湖 北	Hubei	539.53	428.95	7.08	27.88	21.62	14.45
湖 南	Hunan	232.96	183.19	1.15	19.93	10.50	8.37
广 东	Guangdong	13281.27	11368.03	51.40	753.69	297.42	463.47
广 西	Guangxi	294.51	236.83	1.80	17.83	14.50	9.42
海 南	Hainan	52.24	38.45	0.67	2.98	2.28	1.91
重 庆	Chongqing	271.54	208.80	3.35	24.56	16.58	5.91
四 川	Sichuan	292.55	225.15	1.64	20.14	12.77	9.64
贵 州	Guizhou	35.27	27.20	0.08	0.48	1.19	2.05
云 南	Yunnan	93.86	72.89	0.50	7.28	4.81	2.58
西 藏	Tibet	0.07	0.02	0.00	0.03	0.00	0.04
陕 西	Shaanxi	137.15	91.12	0.92	18.85	9.28	3.20
甘 肃	Gansu	32.14	25.43	0.42	1.28	0.97	1.47
青 海	Qinghai	8.68	7.00	0.01	0.73	0.35	0.18
宁 夏	Ningxia	31.16	25.75	0.44	0.75	0.64	1.11
新 疆	Xinjiang	21.89	17.29	0.19	1.68	0.70	0.88

14-14 "三资"工业企业主要经济效益指标

Main Indicators on Economics Benefit of Foreign Funded Industrial Enterprises

年份 Year / 地区 Region	工业增加值率 (%) Ratio of Value-added to Gross Industrial Output Value (%)	总资产贡献率 (%) Ratio of Total Assets to Industrial Output Value (%)	资产负债率 (%) Assets-Liability Ratio (%)	流动资产周转次数（次/年） Number of Times of Annual of Turnover Circulating Funds (times/year)	成本费用利润率 (%) Ratio of Profits to Industrial Cost (%)	全员劳动生产率（元/人.年） Overall Labor Productivity (yuan/person-year)	产品销售率 (%) Proportion of Products Sold (%)
1998	24.20	6.76	58.52	1.61	2.75	52311	96.82
1999	25.59	7.93	57.73	1.69	4.39	61260	97.18
2000	25.96	9.76	57.01	1.89	6.03	71403	97.74
2001	26.19	9.83	54.87	1.89	5.85	75913	97.64
2002	26.41	10.46	54.38	2.06	6.40	81313	98.28
2003	26.15	11.46	55.43	2.20	6.83	92158	98.17
北 京 Beijing	25.85	14.51	55.34	2.11	8.11	174451	97.73
天 津 Tianjin	22.40	9.73	50.95	2.27	5.07	123020	99.59
河 北 Hebei	30.65	12.71	58.32	1.92	10.42	98397	99.85
山 西 Shanxi	36.77	10.05	63.88	1.81	7.68	110781	96.60
内蒙古 Inner Mongolia	35.19	11.07	51.34	1.30	10.32	120042	102.74
辽 宁 Liaoning	26.80	9.29	53.01	1.85	6.15	99702	97.57
吉 林 Jilin	28.37	26.27	52.97	2.88	13.03	327273	96.26
黑龙江 Heilongjiang	33.83	8.71	69.83	1.34	4.69	81496	95.50
上 海 Shanghai	24.66	12.59	52.06	2.15	7.76	152700	99.03
江 苏 Jiangsu	26.19	9.65	59.18	2.42	5.61	114295	98.13
浙 江 Zhejiang	24.37	12.00	57.10	1.98	7.59	67489	97.35
安 徽 Anhui	31.55	12.82	56.80	2.00	8.99	122845	98.22
福 建 Fujian	27.63	11.91	52.86	2.35	7.69	66483	97.53
江 西 Jiangxi	28.07	11.93	51.91	2.05	7.13	56229	96.63
山 东 Shandong	29.40	11.06	56.29	2.36	6.60	77456	98.00
河 南 Henan	31.44	9.60	60.83	1.43	7.64	97913	97.23
湖 北 Hubei	34.78	10.68	56.50	2.28	5.59	139100	100.70
湖 南 Hunan	29.63	11.98	57.37	2.27	9.40	88328	99.52
广 东 Guangdong	24.86	11.06	55.52	2.29	6.05	73378	98.07
广 西 Guangxi	26.64	12.39	56.38	2.20	6.46	87161	97.07
海 南 Hainan	24.07	9.12	50.79	1.50	6.11	73960	99.10
重 庆 Chongqing	29.38	14.57	56.25	1.97	10.11	140767	97.42
四 川 Sichuan	32.57	9.89	56.40	1.54	7.40	96675	97.56
贵 州 Guizhou	25.87	4.00	71.99	1.17	1.31	49933	90.52
云 南 Yunnan	31.34	9.89	49.26	1.53	8.44	115410	95.90
西 藏 Tibet	34.30	4.25	17.94	0.11	66.01	3084	112.49
陕 西 Shaanxi	39.84	15.81	53.15	1.32	15.95	199126	97.18
甘 肃 Gansu	31.37	5.94	66.72	1.12	4.36	85786	93.37
青 海 Qinghai	28.35	12.13	55.12	2.39	9.13	119332	117.56
宁 夏 Ningxia	26.07	5.94	67.34	1.40	2.46	81066	96.65
新 疆 Xinjiang	28.24	8.04	57.47	1.14	8.27	77474	96.75

14-15 按行业分大中型工业企业主要指标（2003年）

单位: 亿元

行业	Sector	企业单位数 (个) Number of Enterprises (unit)	工业总产值 Gross Industrial Output Value
全国总计	**National Total**	**23631**	**95979.46**
煤炭开采和洗选业	Mining and Washing of Coal	467	1984.30
石油和天然气开采业	Extraction of Petroleum and Natural Gas	53	3190.31
黑色金属矿采选业	Mining and Processing of Ferrous Metal Ores	96	181.94
有色金属矿采选业	Mining and Processing of Non-Ferrous Metal Ores	165	298.79
非金属矿采选业	Mining and Processing of Nonmetal Ores	109	157.30
其他采矿业	Mining of Other Ores	1	5.91
农副食品加工业	Processing of Food from Agricultural Products	788	2605.43
食品制造业	Manufacture of Foods	495	1357.84
饮料制造业	Manufacture of Beverages	527	1591.63
烟草制品业	Manufacture of Tobacco	146	2177.15
纺织业	Manufacture of Textile	2087	4437.92
纺织服装、鞋、帽制造业	Manufacture of Textile Wearing Apparel, Footware, and Caps	770	1414.11
皮革、毛皮、羽毛(绒)及其制品业	Manufacture of Leather, Fur, Feather and Related Products	467	1169.44
木材加工及木、竹、藤、棕、草制品业	Processing of Timber, Manufacture of Wood, Bamboo, Rattan, Palm, and Straw Products	187	334.00
家具制造业	Manufacture of Furniture	189	327.89
造纸及纸制品业	Manufacture of Paper and Paper Products	538	1352.41
印刷业和记录媒介的复制	Printing,Reproduction of Recording Media	262	415.41
文教体育用品制造业	Manufacture of Articles For Culture, Education and Sport Activity	281	463.62
石油加工、炼焦及核燃料加工业	Processing of Petroleum, Coking, Processing of Nuclear Fuel	267	5638.19
化学原料及化学制品制造业	Manufacture of Raw Chemical Materials and Chemical Products	1549	5519.75
医药制造业	Manufacture of Medicines	712	1920.63
化学纤维制造业	Manufacture of Chemical Fibers	184	1130.34
橡胶制品业	Manufacture of Rubber	291	927.26
塑料制品业	Manufacture of Plastics	607	1210.08
非金属矿物制品业	Manufacture of Non-metallic Mineral Products	1643	2522.38
黑色金属冶炼及压延加工业	Smelting and Pressing of Ferrous Metals	689	8509.96
有色金属冶炼及压延加工业	Smelting and Pressing of Non-ferrous Metals	490	2318.25
金属制品业	Manufacture of Metal Products	694	1545.99
通用设备制造业	Manufacture of General Purpose Machinery	1288	3143.02
专用设备制造业	Manufacture of Special Purpose Machinery	899	2418.10
交通运输设备制造业	Manufacture of Transport Equipment	1421	9368.94
电气机械及器材制造业	Manufacture of Electrical Machinery and Equipment	1410	5161.47
通信设备、计算机及其他电子设备制造业	Manufacture of Communication Equipment, Computers and Other Electronic Equipment	1467	13952.99
仪器仪表及文化、办公用机械制造业	Manufacture of Measuring Instruments and Machinery for Cultural Activity and Office Work	332	1072.85
工艺品及其他制造业	Manufacture of Artwork and Other Manufacturing	244	420.04
废弃资源和废旧材料回收加工业	Recycling and Disposal of Waste	1	11.58
电力、热力的生产和供应业	Production and Distribution of Electric Power and Heat Power	1569	5322.20
燃气生产和供应业	Production and Distribution of Gas	84	153.56
水的生产和供应业	Production and Distribution of Water	162	246.47

Main Indicators of Large-scale and Medium-scale Industrial Enterprises by Industrial Sector (2003)

(100 million yuan)

工业增加值 Value-added of Industry	实收资本 Paid-up Capital	资产总计 Total Assets	流动资产合计 Circulating Funds	流动资产年平均余额 Annual Average Balance of Circulating Funds	固定资产原价 Original Value of Fixed Assets	固定资产净值年平均余额 Annual Average Balance of Net Value of Fixed Assets
29073.42	**30234.97**	**125131.72**	**54268.38**	**50705.48**	**82397.76**	**50512.33**
964.44	1554.73	4984.58	1784.32	1678.82	3811.08	2409.39
2228.60	1741.72	4757.49	921.81	950.58	6999.74	3251.47
82.48	137.96	344.75	126.76	118.61	187.22	112.95
93.33	95.37	418.11	143.54	137.34	287.20	176.68
57.76	150.54	456.87	142.51	133.32	306.68	223.55
1.89	5.40	42.72	15.79	15.38	16.84	9.40
620.02	446.56	2059.27	1021.63	953.00	982.50	677.43
406.69	356.97	1400.27	680.08	622.85	692.71	456.11
592.12	579.14	2288.82	1047.64	1022.43	1274.39	820.96
1541.08	347.42	2711.53	1649.84	1553.03	1043.13	574.16
1093.96	1180.91	5215.51	2451.98	2257.95	2943.76	1868.58
378.18	297.39	1216.42	693.85	643.72	485.28	319.20
312.45	188.45	721.24	449.55	424.04	272.06	189.61
89.66	118.94	404.12	174.34	173.78	239.79	169.37
80.41	89.51	327.64	177.10	163.48	134.33	94.55
373.95	540.07	2232.10	821.57	763.62	1405.91	1012.82
146.79	186.67	588.52	264.68	258.18	379.95	224.67
121.02	122.86	388.75	228.38	218.03	183.59	114.44
1123.22	1155.57	3588.76	1224.04	1195.07	3562.22	1999.05
1493.11	2002.77	7576.14	2781.31	2784.20	5596.29	3367.24
688.82	663.13	2916.50	1439.26	1415.25	1108.95	745.76
225.64	327.82	1289.45	452.65	436.81	1007.32	635.67
261.84	270.49	1103.49	532.91	498.66	611.98	375.27
294.38	370.10	1332.63	646.84	605.95	701.97	458.66
827.07	1161.02	4406.92	1770.12	1660.59	2810.65	1773.50
2467.78	2492.35	11044.92	4462.48	3987.37	7782.38	4496.19
623.77	825.99	3255.57	1349.86	1252.83	2043.29	1277.61
386.99	356.18	1423.78	839.71	777.20	591.53	384.34
866.41	961.57	4225.79	2641.06	2363.57	1721.76	1023.05
607.36	722.77	3307.40	1886.20	1744.18	1410.37	855.26
2405.94	2274.24	10087.43	5818.23	5290.04	4023.54	2435.76
1311.33	1078.52	4982.27	3086.60	2877.28	1818.83	1107.72
2998.82	2113.44	10075.58	6667.29	6127.48	3716.79	2276.25
281.75	225.32	894.29	551.16	510.57	372.85	233.01
112.63	90.71	360.04	204.13	189.43	148.30	97.74
2.02	0.20	3.75	2.97	2.56	0.88	0.48
2749.90	4305.42	20739.63	4656.84	4437.27	20050.62	13166.32
46.31	250.47	605.81	173.04	177.70	454.08	301.17
113.52	446.31	1352.85	286.29	283.30	1217.03	796.93

14-15 续表

单位: 亿元

行 业	Sector	流动负债合计 Liquid Liabilities	长期负债合计 Long-term Liabilities
全国总计	**National Total**	**52292.76**	**19639.70**
煤炭开采和洗选业	Mining and Washing of Coal	1835.02	924.63
石油和天然气开采业	Extraction of Petroleum and Natural Gas	1081.17	628.11
黑色金属矿采选业	Mining and Processing of Ferrous Metal Ores	135.35	29.06
有色金属矿采选业	Mining and Processing of Non-Ferrous Metal Ores	179.37	64.23
非金属矿采选业	Mining and Processing of Nonmetal Ores	160.37	96.53
其他采矿业	Mining of Other Ores	17.75	3.22
农副食品加工业	Processing of Food from Agricultural Products	1166.88	174.86
食品制造业	Manufacture of Foods	666.45	124.59
饮料制造业	Manufacture of Beverages	1030.44	151.91
烟草制品业	Manufacture of Tobacco	1055.39	70.17
纺织业	Manufacture of Textile	2559.14	658.73
纺织服装、鞋、帽制造业	Manufacture of Textile Wearing Apparel, Footware, and Caps	593.84	68.16
皮革、毛皮、羽毛(绒)及其制品业	Manufacture of Leather, Fur, Feather and Related Products	384.53	27.64
木材加工及木、竹、藤、棕、草制品业	Processing of Timber, Manufacture of Wood, Bamboo, Rattan, Palm, and Straw Products	176.81	58.46
家具制造业	Manufacture of Furniture	159.37	17.29
造纸及纸制品业	Manufacture of Paper and Paper Products	966.94	434.31
印刷业和记录媒介的复制	Printing,Reproduction of Recording Media	238.90	45.33
文教体育用品制造业	Manufacture of Articles For Culture, Education and Sport Activity	187.90	14.90
石油加工、炼焦及核燃料加工业	Processing of Petroleum, Coking, Processing of Nuclear Fuel	1311.06	439.56
化学原料及化学制品制造业	Manufacture of Raw Chemical Materials and Chemical Products	3049.44	1232.55
医药制造业	Manufacture of Medicines	1263.95	240.39
化学纤维制造业	Manufacture of Chemical Fibers	517.25	212.68
橡胶制品业	Manufacture of Rubber	541.93	144.77
塑料制品业	Manufacture of Plastics	580.46	123.03
非金属矿物制品业	Manufacture of Non-metallic Mineral Products	1902.56	703.10
黑色金属冶炼及压延加工业	Smelting and Pressing of Ferrous Metals	4765.28	1551.52
有色金属冶炼及压延加工业	Smelting and Pressing of Non-ferrous Metals	1511.83	572.77
金属制品业	Manufacture of Metal Products	747.65	92.22
通用设备制造业	Manufacture of General Purpose Machinery	2369.00	295.10
专用设备制造业	Manufacture of Special Purpose Machinery	1847.35	324.94
交通运输设备制造业	Manufacture of Transport Equipment	5237.36	790.94
电气机械及器材制造业	Manufacture of Electrical Machinery and Equipment	2671.95	261.53
通信设备、计算机及其他电子设备制造业	Manufacture of Communication Equipment, Computers and Other Electronic Equipment	5696.30	547.97
仪器仪表及文化、办公用机械制造业	Manufacture of Measuring Instruments and Machinery for Cultural Activity and Office Work	451.02	48.34
工艺品及其他制造业	Manufacture of Artwork and Other Manufacturing	174.86	21.33
废弃资源和废旧材料回收加工业	Recycling and Disposal of Waste	3.53	
电力、热力的生产和供应业	Production and Distribution of Electric Power and Heat Power	4615.73	8130.08
燃气生产和供应业	Production and Distribution of Gas	170.97	95.52
水的生产和供应业	Production and Distribution of Water	267.64	219.21

continued

(100 million yuan)

所有者权益 Creditors' Equity	产品销售收入 Sales Revenue	产品销售成本 Cost of Sales	产品销售税金及附加 Sales Tax and Extra Charges	利润总额 Total Profits	本年应交增值税 Value-added Tax Payable	全部从业人员年平均人数（万人） Annual Average Employed Persons (10 000 persons)
52297.22	**99710.07**	**81445.72**	**1770.28**	**6522.98**	**4065.11**	**3224.3**
2141.38	2021.02	1368.13	26.45	107.39	157.22	303.96
3036.04	3207.54	1608.16	76.32	1140.84	292.31	72.06
177.42	196.71	148.01	4.15	13.01	10.48	16.03
167.98	289.04	213.31	2.38	27.89	9.25	23.32
197.09	161.12	111.85	4.27	8.21	9.24	17.88
21.75	11.50	9.60	0.04	0.96	0.48	1.53
711.47	2524.02	2252.07	7.64	95.11	45.59	75.99
603.69	1300.51	972.15	5.24	81.47	59.25	49.98
1091.14	1552.98	982.70	104.60	125.50	103.14	55.91
1584.67	2175.79	829.11	852.30	272.97	243.22	18.81
1968.26	4403.87	3936.05	15.21	162.11	118.22	276.48
536.47	1348.83	1141.88	4.99	77.59	34.59	92.27
303.25	1101.29	969.99	3.10	48.98	22.52	76.82
163.32	332.47	291.34	1.52	13.47	9.59	18.88
144.13	326.55	275.07	0.85	15.68	6.11	18.82
819.42	1337.56	1112.37	4.34	73.84	62.55	51.22
299.23	408.90	317.53	1.62	42.99	20.91	19.77
181.98	449.90	385.04	0.91	22.75	5.15	39.19
1763.75	5793.10	5148.18	223.42	95.68	181.76	48.35
3214.56	5514.16	4443.48	43.19	305.99	223.81	180.45
1371.51	1944.14	1208.63	12.78	207.29	125.68	69.59
555.36	1107.33	985.07	3.89	51.76	35.02	24.86
414.03	862.44	708.29	14.50	41.56	26.26	36.21
622.42	1203.67	1039.85	2.95	66.33	28.08	49.1
1774.71	2447.98	1949.73	16.41	174.27	131.54	151.69
4710.02	8834.09	7420.47	48.65	576.00	469.78	209.38
1150.20	2344.10	1997.68	9.44	125.31	82.18	75.69
570.57	1509.05	1283.99	5.14	84.43	35.90	60.89
1552.06	3060.17	2465.71	11.03	191.12	110.71	130.36
1105.84	2353.73	1949.10	8.05	106.60	67.47	120.87
4025.35	9283.65	7594.35	170.67	688.36	319.95	213.66
1977.26	4916.35	4058.76	12.64	249.98	134.23	149.23
3785.63	13815.39	12349.49	10.53	535.73	185.34	201.41
390.11	1068.29	908.72	5.04	56.95	19.50	37.52
161.64	395.43	340.81	1.77	20.50	7.55	28.68
0.21	12.82	12.50	0.01	0.11	0.05	0.18
7825.22	9628.66	8262.79	49.41	609.49	647.35	178.3
337.16	231.48	208.98	1.43	5.02	9.69	10.8
840.93	234.43	184.77	3.42	-0.27	13.42	18.15

14-16 按行业分大中型工业企业主要经济效益指标（2003年）

行 业	Sector	工业增加值率 (%) Ratio of Value-added to Gross Industrial Output Value (%)	总资产贡献率 (%) Ratio of Total Assets to Industrial Output Value (%)
全国总计	**National Total**	**30.29**	**10.99**
煤炭开采和洗选业	Mining and Washing of Coal	48.60	6.82
石油和天然气开采业	Extraction of Petroleum and Natural Gas	69.86	32.18
黑色金属矿采选业	Mining and Processing of Ferrous Metal Ores	45.33	8.92
有色金属矿采选业	Mining and Processing of Non-Ferrous Metal Ores	31.24	10.91
非金属矿采选业	Mining and Processing of Nonmetal Ores	36.72	5.58
其他采矿业	Mining of Other Ores	32.00	4.07
农副食品加工业	Processing of Food from Agricultural Products	23.80	8.66
食品制造业	Manufacture of Foods	29.95	11.46
饮料制造业	Manufacture of Beverages	37.20	15.45
烟草制品业	Manufacture of Tobacco	70.78	51.29
纺织业	Manufacture of Textile	24.65	7.11
纺织服装、鞋、帽制造业	Manufacture of Textile Wearing Apparel, Footware, and Caps	26.74	10.64
皮革、毛皮、羽毛(绒)及其制品业	Manufacture of Leather, Fur, Feather and Related Products	26.72	11.37
木材加工及木、竹、藤、棕、草制品业	Processing of Timber, Manufacture of Wood, Bamboo, Rattan, Palm, and Straw Products	26.85	7.33
家具制造业	Manufacture of Furniture	24.52	7.85
造纸及纸制品业	Manufacture of Paper and Paper Products	27.65	8.05
印刷业和记录媒介的复制	Printing,Reproduction of Recording Media	35.34	12.08
文教体育用品制造业	Manufacture of Articles For Culture, Education and Sport Activity	26.10	8.11
石油加工、炼焦及核燃料加工业	Processing of Petroleum, Coking, Processing of Nuclear Fuel	19.92	14.99
化学原料及化学制品制造业	Manufacture of Raw Chemical Materials and Chemical Products	27.05	8.92
医药制造业	Manufacture of Medicines	35.86	12.95
化学纤维制造业	Manufacture of Chemical Fibers	19.96	8.68
橡胶制品业	Manufacture of Rubber	28.24	8.81
塑料制品业	Manufacture of Plastics	24.33	8.34
非金属矿物制品业	Manufacture of Non-metallic Mineral Products	32.79	8.64
黑色金属冶炼及压延加工业	Smelting and Pressing of Ferrous Metals	29.00	11.04
有色金属冶炼及压延加工业	Smelting and Pressing of Non-ferrous Metals	26.91	8.19
金属制品业	Manufacture of Metal Products	25.03	9.95
通用设备制造业	Manufacture of General Purpose Machinery	27.57	8.42
专用设备制造业	Manufacture of Special Purpose Machinery	25.12	6.69
交通运输设备制造业	Manufacture of Transport Equipment	25.68	12.33
电气机械及器材制造业	Manufacture of Electrical Machinery and Equipment	25.41	8.91
通信设备、计算机及其他电子设备制造业	Manufacture of Communication Equipment, Computers and Other Electronic Equipment	21.49	7.84
仪器仪表及文化、办公用机械制造	Manufacture of Measuring Instruments and Machinery for Cultural Activity and Office Work	26.26	9.75
工艺品及其他制造业	Manufacture of Artwork and Other Manufacturing	26.81	9.24
废弃资源和废旧材料回收加工业	Recycling and Disposal of Waste	17.42	6.11
电力、热力的生产和供应业	Production and Distribution of Electric Power and Heat Power	51.67	7.89
燃气生产和供应业	Production and Distribution of Gas	30.16	3.31
水的生产和供应业	Production and Distribution of Water	46.06	1.76

Main Indicators on Economic Benefit of Large-scale and Medium-scale Industrial Enterprises by Industrial Sector (2003)

资产负债率 (%) Assets-Liability Ratio (%)	流动资产周转次数（次/年） Number of Times of Annual of Turnover Circulating Funds (times/year)	工业成本费用利润率 (%) Ratio of Profits to Industrial Cost (%)	全员劳动生产率（元/人.年） Overall Labor Productivity (yuan/person-year)	产品销售率 (%) Proportion of Products Sold (%)
58.09	**1.97**	**7.10**	**90170**	**98.37**
55.52	1.20	5.63	31729	97.96
36.07	3.37	61.79	309278	100.19
48.54	1.66	7.31	51453	98.62
59.82	2.10	10.55	40020	98.75
56.86	1.21	5.45	32303	99.44
49.10	0.75	8.86	12347	108.63
65.45	2.65	3.92	81590	97.07
56.89	2.09	6.70	81368	97.24
52.33	1.52	9.41	105913	99.13
41.56	1.40	25.23	819384	100.04
62.26	1.95	3.80	39567	98.31
55.90	2.10	6.09	40985	96.80
57.95	2.60	4.66	40673	98.13
59.59	1.91	4.19	47492	97.95
56.01	2.00	5.10	42722	98.35
63.17	1.75	5.83	73002	98.95
49.16	1.58	11.56	74258	97.50
53.19	2.06	5.33	30879	97.52
50.71	4.85	1.76	232306	100.02
57.46	1.98	5.87	82744	98.25
52.93	1.37	11.84	98984	95.12
56.92	2.54	4.89	90760	98.52
62.48	1.73	5.14	72304	97.55
53.29	1.99	5.82	59961	97.84
59.73	1.47	7.59	54523	97.46
57.34	2.22	7.04	117861	99.52
64.67	1.87	5.69	82411	98.38
59.92	1.94	5.92	63555	98.10
63.27	1.29	6.61	66460	97.14
66.56	1.35	4.68	50248	97.82
59.88	1.75	8.02	112605	98.34
60.31	1.71	5.34	87872	96.57
62.34	2.25	4.01	148893	97.97
56.38	2.09	5.63	75090	99.17
55.11	2.09	5.45	39275	97.93
94.34	5.00	0.87	110412	99.98
62.18	2.17	6.77	154233	99.91
44.35	1.30	2.05	42868	101.03
37.84	0.83	-0.11	62551	97.98

14-17 大中型工业企业主要指标

Main Indicators of Large-scale and Medium-scale Industrial Enterprises

单位：亿元 (100 million yuan)

年 份 Year 地 区 Region	企业单位数（个）Number of Enterprises (unit)	工业总产值 Gross Industrial Output Value	工业增加值 Value-added of Industry	实收资本 Total Capital Hold	资产总计 Total Assets	流动资产合计 Total Circulating Funds
1998	23408	37552.34	11766.31	17177.06	76095.76	30719.90
1999	22235	41439.42	13279.95	18924.67	82143.59	32711.77
2000	21724	48993.02	15747.32	21409.53	87309.83	35282.86
2001	22987	57358.40	18133.44	24841.86	97372.22	39102.67
2002	23323	65317.51	20841.19	26445.82	103516.44	41911.77
2003	23631	95979.46	29073.42	30234.97	125131.72	54268.38
北 京 Beijing	451	2750.41	713.58	1010.06	3723.07	1633.18
天 津 Tianjin	481	2814.80	762.57	842.96	3167.31	1434.82
河 北 Hebei	1018	3866.07	1266.07	1261.05	5433.29	2136.74
山 西 Shanxi	607	1877.75	717.43	916.31	3815.24	1431.58
内蒙古 Inner Mongolia	255	968.35	354.46	536.09	1736.97	630.55
辽 宁 Liaoning	810	4686.03	1288.13	1763.21	6879.72	2771.05
吉 林 Jilin	345	2220.62	666.25	668.01	3003.89	1253.73
黑龙江 Heilongjiang	379	2473.80	1209.67	1231.55	3780.99	1416.50
上 海 Shanghai	1179	7109.36	1988.53	2483.99	8386.89	4005.40
江 苏 Jiangsu	2655	11367.58	3012.87	2687.72	11755.15	5776.48
浙 江 Zhejiang	2349	7203.32	1752.16	1575.83	7340.05	3853.51
安 徽 Anhui	553	1966.06	694.04	827.40	3053.94	1214.30
福 建 Fujian	854	3036.00	877.04	792.37	3079.27	1445.21
江 西 Jiangxi	326	1023.41	303.91	380.36	1717.73	711.10
山 东 Shandong	2575	10203.11	3225.06	2401.21	11542.82	4816.65
河 南 Henan	1019	3360.81	1060.33	1210.32	5242.82	2152.56
湖 北 Hubei	703	2592.04	873.49	1259.77	5640.56	1920.33
湖 南 Hunan	534	1611.55	571.04	532.60	2585.82	1044.68
广 东 Guangdong	3292	14353.53	3858.66	3135.60	13008.58	6766.04
广 西 Guangxi	399	974.99	304.93	313.28	1513.71	560.16
海 南 Hainan	56	197.08	51.03	92.64	247.20	108.98
重 庆 Chongqing	399	1202.74	347.72	483.39	1889.53	853.69
四 川 Sichuan	843	2395.92	843.29	959.10	4707.48	1943.03
贵 州 Guizhou	224	685.51	259.81	420.14	1531.72	602.61
云 南 Yunnan	365	1199.24	615.75	447.77	2349.44	1001.02
西 藏 Tibet	12	9.80	5.65	12.33	32.11	12.82
陕 西 Shaanxi	420	1525.69	555.45	606.78	3045.31	1204.70
甘 肃 Gansu	183	900.80	311.19	494.52	1824.96	671.58
青 海 Qinghai	56	205.53	79.96	195.15	779.51	226.67
宁 夏 Ningxia	97	284.16	90.44	141.67	625.64	229.85
新 疆 Xinjiang	192	913.38	412.93	551.77	1690.98	438.83

14-17 续表 1 continued

单位: 亿元 (100 million yuan)

年份 地区	Year Region	流动资产年平均余额 Annual Average Balance of Circulating Funds	固定资产原价合计 Original Value of Fixed Assets	固定资产净值年平均余额 Annual Average Balance of Net Value of Fixed Assets	流动负债合计 Total Liquid Liabilities	长期负债合计 Long-term Liabilities	所有者权益合计 Creditors' Equity
	1998	30074.66	47898.94	31712.58	31076.11	16401.71	28246.56
	1999	31428.90	53515.04	34031.40	32270.98	16778.93	32684.52
	2000	33763.10	58348.15	37293.79	33935.97	17584.07	35165.58
	2001	38325.79	66145.71	41393.89	37602.83	18183.04	40898.91
	2002	40411.83	71606.08	44085.34	40870.32	18500.80	43524.43
	2003	50705.48	82397.76	50512.33	52292.76	19639.70	52297.22
北京	Beijing	1493.57	2246.46	1308.00	1421.09	532.18	1759.27
天津	Tianjin	1310.22	2346.88	1350.31	1354.01	393.23	1379.59
河北	Hebei	2020.08	3947.26	2417.37	2270.36	1012.11	2107.39
山西	Shanxi	1328.31	2745.47	1728.42	1413.08	983.67	1358.04
内蒙古	Inner Mongolia	590.47	1341.86	806.52	613.21	363.04	754.49
辽宁	Liaoning	2726.92	5432.53	3279.89	2924.72	937.82	2999.36
吉林	Jilin	1174.93	2031.43	1238.26	1357.28	495.33	1144.94
黑龙江	Heilongjiang	1305.70	3662.67	1956.78	1462.99	538.58	1728.14
上海	Shanghai	3681.04	5370.97	2990.88	3285.31	705.91	4380.12
江苏	Jiangsu	5333.58	6540.63	4172.66	5801.60	1358.98	4560.90
浙江	Zhejiang	3525.49	3344.98	2152.33	3476.69	497.96	3365.41
安徽	Anhui	1111.68	1995.75	1298.16	1239.59	596.31	1205.56
福建	Fujian	1290.63	1901.67	1240.11	1259.87	468.67	1335.28
江西	Jiangxi	666.21	1109.31	693.20	767.00	370.75	550.90
山东	Shandong	4448.95	7511.40	4534.66	4969.15	1746.61	4739.36
河南	Henan	1992.07	3834.85	2262.39	2391.39	943.32	1901.28
湖北	Hubei	1901.15	3941.70	2820.71	1736.11	1442.63	2322.62
湖南	Hunan	971.92	1781.23	1046.65	1033.60	592.92	916.08
广东	Guangdong	6437.59	7447.72	4540.98	5790.84	1393.48	5700.72
广西	Guangxi	539.93	1058.48	679.07	623.84	303.09	539.03
海南	Hainan	104.60	172.82	106.59	83.88	43.11	118.20
重庆	Chongqing	806.34	1102.46	675.87	861.23	270.92	757.38
四川	Sichuan	1833.70	2910.60	1839.89	1874.30	967.34	1821.40
贵州	Guizhou	579.85	976.22	602.09	564.92	352.21	611.20
云南	Yunnan	887.33	1399.11	828.93	814.14	391.97	1143.32
西藏	Tibet	12.20	15.00	9.40	8.21	4.39	19.51
陕西	Shaanxi	1107.35	2174.28	1369.80	1181.78	679.26	1140.14
甘肃	Gansu	641.82	1312.46	854.84	680.89	485.92	650.27
青海	Qinghai	229.67	567.89	385.36	232.49	305.07	236.22
宁夏	Ningxia	219.57	440.50	289.44	256.27	147.23	222.14
新疆	Xinjiang	432.63	1733.20	1032.74	542.91	315.65	828.96

14-17 续表 2 continued

单位: 亿元 (100 million yuan)

年份 地区	Year Region	产品销售收入 Sales Revenue	产品销售成本 Cost of Sales	产品销售税金及附加 Sales Tax and Extra Charges	利润总额 Total Profits	本年应交增值税 Value-added Tax Payable	全部从业人员年平均人数(万人) Annual Average Employed Persons (10 000 persons)
	1998	37130.61	29949.73	1003.18	881.94	1956.72	3412.76
	1999	41405.57	33254.65	1075.24	1588.58	2175.16	3110.13
	2000	50120.30	39768.89	1173.45	3183.28	2566.15	2880.60
	2001	58480.45	47033.65	1294.65	3440.56	2843.54	2782.72
	2002	66977.14	53839.14	1471.01	4008.97	3109.76	2710.20
	2003	99710.07	81445.72	1770.28	6522.98	4065.11	3224.30
北京	Beijing	2820.26	2355.59	32.92	160.74	107.95	57.16
天津	Tianjin	3042.24	2567.46	34.22	174.19	88.30	58.84
河北	Hebei	4230.07	3502.21	51.24	296.70	201.44	164.72
山西	Shanxi	1960.29	1499.36	21.64	116.20	133.51	126.00
内蒙古	Inner Mongolia	967.10	786.67	14.24	48.49	49.87	46.68
辽宁	Liaoning	4751.49	3937.53	76.37	194.97	189.26	155.51
吉林	Jilin	2262.34	1840.97	64.60	145.32	96.29	67.58
黑龙江	Heilongjiang	2553.46	1640.05	60.02	568.05	193.55	95.84
上海	Shanghai	7501.09	6112.50	132.79	606.40	282.14	110.01
江苏	Jiangsu	11723.00	10082.36	104.05	566.93	350.87	290.24
浙江	Zhejiang	7656.80	6422.77	105.89	510.49	268.32	205.90
安徽	Anhui	2015.27	1558.15	61.75	151.25	103.89	93.17
福建	Fujian	2984.41	2443.82	46.46	237.53	89.24	94.87
江西	Jiangxi	1082.10	884.37	29.56	40.63	56.03	51.13
山东	Shandong	10467.99	8688.04	124.26	705.00	392.62	367.73
河南	Henan	3568.85	2932.15	68.84	169.11	163.29	192.25
湖北	Hubei	2715.80	2130.31	65.54	157.42	137.17	110.43
湖南	Hunan	1717.43	1305.27	93.98	85.79	93.51	73.80
广东	Guangdong	14860.39	12602.29	120.63	840.67	431.54	383.71
广西	Guangxi	978.44	768.82	21.16	56.62	60.31	40.77
海南	Hainan	194.73	155.44	5.84	10.12	8.66	4.87
重庆	Chongqing	1229.44	972.32	28.35	73.89	59.89	52.34
四川	Sichuan	2528.89	1970.90	57.57	122.44	129.67	125.64
贵州	Guizhou	741.22	551.88	38.01	38.47	46.54	37.48
云南	Yunnan	1199.12	753.22	204.77	103.18	104.29	40.40
西藏	Tibet	10.68	6.49	0.17	1.99	0.96	0.73
陕西	Shaanxi	1529.26	1106.90	45.58	157.97	89.36	76.14
甘肃	Gansu	959.82	774.20	27.29	26.84	50.39	47.12
青海	Qinghai	237.47	185.18	4.00	11.08	14.28	9.85
宁夏	Ningxia	316.67	268.31	4.11	7.30	14.13	17.49
新疆	Xinjiang	903.97	640.18	24.43	137.20	57.84	25.89

14-18 大中型工业企业主要经济效益指标

Main Indicators on Economics Benefit of Large-scale and Medium-scale Industrial Enterprises

年份 Year 地区 Region	工业增加值率 (%) Ratio of Value-added to Gross Industrial Output Value (%)	总资产贡献率 (%) Ratio of Total Assets to Industrial Output Value (%)	资产负债率 (%) Assets-Liability Ratio (%)	流动资产周转次数 (次/年) Number of Times of Annual of Turnover Circulating Funds (times/year)	成本费用利润率 (%) Ratio of Profits to Industrial Cost (%)	全员劳动生产率 (元/人.年) Overall Labor Productivity (yuan/person-year)	产品销售率 (%) Proportion of Products Sold (%)
1998	31.33	7.06	62.86	1.23	2.46	34477	97.53
1999	32.05	7.60	60.18	1.32	4.04	42699	98.03
2000	32.14	9.40	59.65	1.48	6.88	54667	98.64
2001	31.61	9.10	57.86	1.53	6.31	65164	98.45
2003	31.91	9.57	57.84	1.66	6.45	76899	98.77
2003	30.29	10.99	58.09	1.97	7.10	90170	98.37
北京 Beijing	25.94	8.85	52.67	1.89	5.97	124840	97.83
天津 Tianjin	27.09	10.42	56.44	2.32	6.13	129604	99.12
河北 Hebei	32.75	11.53	61.21	2.09	7.60	76864	98.77
山西 Shanxi	38.21	8.72	63.36	1.48	6.36	56938	98.32
内蒙古 Inner Mongolia	36.60	8.02	56.56	1.64	5.29	75935	99.33
辽宁 Liaoning	27.49	7.88	56.26	1.74	4.36	82833	98.37
吉林 Jilin	30.00	11.21	61.73	1.93	6.95	98580	97.98
黑龙江 Heilongjiang	48.90	22.68	53.13	1.96	29.72	126224	98.48
上海 Shanghai	27.97	12.74	47.77	2.04	8.85	180766	99.04
江苏 Jiangsu	26.50	9.75	61.20	2.20	5.12	103807	98.41
浙江 Zhejiang	24.32	13.40	54.15	2.17	7.19	85096	98.09
安徽 Anhui	35.30	11.46	60.52	1.81	8.37	74493	99.16
福建 Fujian	28.89	13.10	56.39	2.31	8.77	92445	97.95
江西 Jiangxi	29.70	8.87	66.55	1.62	3.98	59442	98.35
山东 Shandong	31.61	11.83	58.94	2.35	7.29	87702	98.26
河南 Henan	31.55	9.34	63.74	1.79	5.04	55154	99.10
湖北 Hubei	33.70	7.21	58.82	1.43	6.29	79099	99.15
湖南 Hunan	35.43	11.65	64.57	1.77	5.62	77373	100.29
广东 Guangdong	26.88	11.41	56.18	2.31	6.03	100561	97.25
广西 Guangxi	31.27	10.43	64.39	1.81	6.22	74789	97.71
海南 Hainan	25.89	10.96	52.19	1.86	5.65	104768	97.90
重庆 Chongqing	28.91	9.96	59.92	1.52	6.43	66436	98.11
四川 Sichuan	35.20	8.07	61.31	1.38	5.20	67120	99.17
贵州 Guizhou	37.90	9.30	60.10	1.28	5.65	69320	97.71
云南 Yunnan	51.34	18.75	51.34	1.35	11.30	152411	99.83
西藏 Tibet	57.67	9.96	39.24	0.88	21.77	76922	95.73
陕西 Shaanxi	36.41	10.90	61.98	1.38	11.90	72950	98.42
甘肃 Gansu	34.55	6.86	64.37	1.50	3.04	66038	99.61
青海 Qinghai	38.90	5.03	69.70	1.03	5.01	81148	97.29
宁夏 Ningxia	31.83	5.82	64.49	1.44	2.36	51701	97.61
新疆 Xinjiang	45.21	13.95	50.98	2.09	18.46	159515	98.91

14-19 按注册登记主要类型分工业企业经济效益指标

Main Indicators on Economic Benefit of Industrial Enterprises by Status of Registration

注册登记类型	Status of Registration	总资产贡献率(%) Ratio of Total Assets to Industrial Output Value (%)	资产负债率(%) Assets-Liability Ratio (%)	流动资产周转次数(次/年) Number of Times of Annual Turnover of Circulating Funds (times /year)	全员劳动生产率(元/人、年) Overall Labor Productivity (yuan/person-year)
全国总计	**National Total**				
1999	1999	7.45	61.83	1.47	37148
2000	2000	9.00	60.81	1.62	45679
2001	2001	8.91	58.97	1.66	52062
2002	2002	9.45	58.72	1.80	59766
2003	2003	10.50	58.96	2.00	73045
内资企业	Domestic Funded				
1999	1999	7.33	62.84	1.40	33340
2000	2000	8.80	61.78	1.54	41017
2001	2001	8.67	60.05	1.58	47088
2002	2002	9.17	59.91	1.72	54680
2003	2003	10.21	60.03	1.93	67687
国有及控股	State-owned and Control Section				
1999	1999	6.77	61.98	1.20	35741
2000	2000	8.43	60.99	1.34	45998
2001	2001	8.17	59.19	1.36	54772
2002	2002	8.71	59.30	1.47	65749
2003	2003	10.09	59.24	1.69	87095
集体企业	Collective-owned Enterprises				
1999	1999	10.39	66.62	2.04	31577
2000	2000	10.98	65.59	2.14	35581
2001	2001	10.93	64.24	2.16	38916
2002	2002	11.77	63.54	2.30	43556
2003	2003	12.76	61.46	2.50	53168
联营企业	Joint Ownership Enterprises				
1999	1999	6.68	64.95	1.62	36521
2000	2000	8.50	63.61	1.73	46465
2001	2001	9.52	58.95	1.77	53156
2002	2002	9.52	57.75	1.83	64185
2003	2003	10.21	59.77	1.92	77090
有限责任公司	Limited Liability Corporations				
1999	1999	5.58	64.20	1.19	29950
2000	2000	6.63	63.53	1.31	36140
2001	2001	7.17	61.57	1.37	43338
2002	2002	7.40	60.98	1.50	50744
2003	2003	8.36	61.57	1.67	63038
股份有限公司	Share-holding Corporations Limited				
1999	1999	8.84	52.57	1.26	48231
2000	2000	14.41	49.41	1.74	89639
2001	2001	12.85	49.72	1.73	103293
2002	2002	12.59	50.47	1.80	112362
2003	2003	14.65	50.90	2.12	137158
港澳台商投资企业	Enterprises with Funds from Hong Kong, Macao & Taiwan				
1999	1999	7.34	59.13	1.64	49267
2000	2000	8.89	57.83	1.80	58102
2001	2001	8.68	56.07	1.80	59139
2002	2002	9.35	55.23	1.95	62508
2003	2003	9.68	55.44	2.00	66847
外商投资企业	Foreign Funded Enterprises				
1999	1999	8.46	56.45	1.75	79046
2000	2000	10.52	56.30	1.97	89976
2001	2001	10.74	53.91	1.97	98413
2002	2002	11.30	53.73	2.14	106075
2003	2003	12.71	55.43	2.31	123891

14-20 主要工业产品产量

Output of Major Industrial Products

年份 地区	Year Region	化学纤维 (万吨) Chemical Fiber (10 000 tons)	纱 (万吨) Yarn (10 000 tons)	布 (亿米) Cloth (100 million m)	丝 (万吨) Silk (10 000 tons)	机制纸及纸板 (万吨) Machine-made Paper and Paperboards (10 000 tons)	原盐 (万吨) Salt (10 000 tons)	糖 (万吨) Sugar (10 000 tons)
	1978	28.46	238.20	110.30	2.97	439.00	1953.00	227.00
	1980	45.03	292.60	134.70	3.54	535.00	1728.00	257.00
	1985	94.78	353.50	146.70	4.22	911.00	1479.00	451.00
	1989	148.09	476.70	189.20	5.22	1333.00	2829.00	501.00
	1990	165.42	462.60	188.80	5.66	1372.00	2023.00	582.00
	1991	191.03	460.80	181.70	6.07	1479.00	2410.00	640.00
	1992	213.04	501.70	190.70	7.42	1725.00	2838.00	829.00
	1993	237.37	501.50	203.00	9.40	1914.00	2943.00	771.00
	1994	280.33	489.50	211.30	10.64	2138.00	2996.00	592.00
	1995	341.17	542.20	260.18	11.34	2812.30	2977.72	558.64
	1996	375.45	512.21	209.10	9.49	2638.20	2903.57	640.20
	1997	471.62	559.83	248.79	8.25	2733.20	3082.66	702.58
	1998	510.00	542.00	241.00	6.77	2125.63	2242.52	826.00
	1999	600.00	567.00	250.00	7.02	2159.30	2812.36	861.00
	2000	694.00	657.00	277.00	7.33	2486.94	3128.00	700.00
	2001	841.38	760.68	290.00	8.73	3777.07	3410.51	653.10
	2002	991.20	850.00	322.39	9.82	4666.99	3602.43	926.00
	2003	1181.15	983.58	353.52	11.10	4849.33	3437.70	1083.94
北京	Beijing	0.06	3.82	0.99		15.63		0.03
天津	Tianjin	30.02	7.82	2.53	0.04	35.50	221.07	
河北	Hebei	15.44	50.14	19.73		370.58	418.11	3.21
山西	Shanxi	2.17	10.61	3.35	0.02	38.67		0.13
内蒙古	Inner Mongolia	0.36	2.26	0.47	0.02	18.92	148.72	14.74
辽宁	Liaoning	26.74	15.78	4.01	0.21	63.58	185.05	5.38
吉林	Jilin	18.68	6.80	1.00		41.06		1.47
黑龙江	Heilongjiang	20.88	5.94	1.29		75.03		27.45
上海	Shanghai	54.17	12.39	2.93	0.03	51.69		
江苏	Jiangsu	307.76	201.00	67.10	2.58	398.91	318.13	
浙江	Zhejiang	407.57	60.93	71.28	4.20	657.73	11.81	
安徽	Anhui	14.36	35.13	6.80	0.32	117.65	45.25	
福建	Fujian	60.23	41.52	14.13		166.16	52.94	8.68
江西	Jiangxi	11.97	15.32	3.18	0.10	27.21	15.28	1.74
山东	Shandong	70.40	195.95	51.22	0.78	858.28	911.57	8.25
河南	Henan	39.20	86.91	17.90	0.16	469.37	90.47	
湖北	Hubei	14.35	88.03	20.11	0.13	102.22	316.58	1.26
湖南	Hunan	8.31	22.49	3.56		137.92	78.94	3.49
广东	Guangdong	46.54	28.72	28.11	0.11	664.56	25.77	115.07
广西	Guangxi	1.36	11.10	0.47	0.22	96.47	11.04	601.41
海南	Hainan	5.70		0.11		1.89	17.98	39.78
重庆	Chongqing	1.47	7.43	13.54	0.60	30.77	46.41	0.15
四川	Sichuan	15.66	19.81	6.46	1.40	135.16	341.82	13.56
贵州	Guizhou	0.36	1.49	0.52	0.01	8.15		2.18
云南	Yunnan	1.35	1.37	0.26	0.04	26.30	47.79	189.65
西藏	Tibet							
陕西	Shaanxi	1.58	19.82	10.53	0.13	166.88	10.12	0.01
甘肃	Gansu	1.87	2.23	0.48		11.03	3.65	0.87
青海	Qinghai		0.01			0.42	66.45	
宁夏	Ningxia	0.30				37.44		
新疆	Xinjiang	2.29	28.76	1.46	0.01	24.15	52.74	45.43

注:糖产量1998年以前包括土糖,1998年及以后为机制糖。

a) Data on sugar before 1998 include home-made sugar, and data since 1998 refer to machine-made sugar.

14-20 续表 1 continued

年份 Year 地区 Region	啤酒 (万吨) Beer (10 000 tons)	卷烟 (万箱) Cigarettes (10 000 cases)	家用电冰箱 (万台) Household Refrigerators (10 000 units)	房间空调器 (万台) Air-conditioners for Room (10 000 units)	家用洗衣机 (万台) Household Washing Machines (10 000 units)	彩色电视机 (万台) Color Television Sets (10 000 units)	原煤 (亿吨) Coal (100 million tons)
1978	40.00	1182.00	2.80	0.02	0.04	0.38	6.18
1980	69.00	1520.00	4.90	1.32	24.53	3.21	6.20
1985	310.00	2370.00	144.81	12.35	887.20	435.28	8.72
1989	643.00	3195.00	670.79	37.47	825.40	940.02	10.54
1990	692.00	3298.00	463.06	24.07	662.68	1033.04	10.80
1991	838.00	3226.00	469.94	63.03	687.17	1205.06	10.87
1992	1021.00	3285.00	485.76	158.03	707.93	1333.08	11.16
1993	1192.00	3376.00	596.66	346.41	895.85	1435.76	11.50
1994	1415.00	3432.00	768.12	393.42	1094.24	1689.15	12.40
1995	1568.82	3485.02	918.54	682.56	948.41	2057.74	13.61
1996	1681.91	3401.92	979.65	786.21	1074.72	2537.60	13.97
1997	1888.94	3377.42	1044.43	974.01	1254.48	2711.33	13.73
1998	1987.67	3374.00	1060.00	1156.87	1207.31	3497.00	12.50
1999	2098.77	3340.00	1210.00	1337.64	1342.17	4262.00	10.45
2000	2231.32	3397.00	1279.00	1826.67	1442.98	3936.00	9.98
2001	2288.93	3402.10	1351.26	2333.64	1341.61	4093.70	11.61
2002	2402.70	3467.08	1598.87	3135.11	1595.76	5155.00	13.80
2003	2540.48	3580.86	2242.56	4820.86	1964.46	6541.40	16.67
北京 Beijing	123.51	22.88	22.73	15.23	23.14		0.08
天津 Tianjin	17.33	22.00	29.64	242.33		112.41	
河北 Hebei	114.79	117.05		0.10			0.66
山西 Shanxi	17.14	25.00		0.60		16.07	2.95
内蒙古 Inner Mongolia	43.54	30.50				134.30	1.20
辽宁 Liaoning	149.38	41.33	109.73	88.14	3.76	451.41	0.59
吉林 Jilin	81.54	58.57	5.35	1.61	3.92	78.55	0.20
黑龙江 Heilongjiang	202.33	71.65	4.86			61.00	0.67
上海 Shanghai	43.40	145.66	34.46	312.49	141.86	158.41	
江苏 Jiangsu	115.90	132.55	243.83	436.71	338.39	474.73	0.28
浙江 Zhejiang	201.68	112.95	129.98	419.13	525.85	94.04	0.01
安徽 Anhui	122.02	180.09	274.92	296.67	188.24	265.25	0.67
福建 Fujian	137.27	107.81				252.66	0.08
江西 Jiangxi	45.31	60.44	29.95	0.78		64.10	0.10
山东 Shandong	321.70	235.19	499.00	460.33	400.92	553.29	1.47
河南 Henan	112.55	285.51	145.91	23.90	36.26	158.37	1.19
湖北 Hubei	113.33	198.97		98.42	69.94		0.04
湖南 Hunan	42.21	251.63	44.73				0.24
广东 Guangdong	213.79	193.51	564.89	2194.46	179.06	2527.64	0.02
广西 Guangxi	40.33	98.90		0.11	2.51		0.04
海南 Hainan	5.82	11.80					
重庆 Chongqing	45.10	77.50		135.81	14.10	60.30	0.15
四川 Sichuan	90.12	134.12	33.39	93.94	22.78	899.89	0.31
贵州 Guizhou	12.00	183.19	50.39			42.69	0.78
云南 Yunnan	18.67	614.70					0.14
西藏 Tibet	3.29						
陕西 Shaanxi	53.72	110.86	17.33	0.09	8.00	136.23	0.74
甘肃 Gansu	23.85	42.00	1.47		5.73	0.06	0.26
青海 Qinghai	0.19						0.03
宁夏 Ningxia	6.29	2.00					0.20
新疆 Xinjiang	22.38	12.50		0.01			0.18

14-20 续表 2 continued

年份 地区	Year Region	原油 (万吨) Crude Oil (10 000 tons)	天然气 (亿立方米) Natural Gas (100 million cu.m)	发电量 (亿千瓦小时) Electricity (100 million kwh)	#水电 Hydropower	生铁 (万吨) Pig Iron (10 000 tons)	钢 (万吨) Steel (10 000 tons)	成品钢材 (万吨) Steel Products (10 000 tons)	水泥 (万吨) Cement (10000 tons)
	1978	10405.00	137.30	2566.00	446.00	3479.00	3178.00	2208.00	6524.00
	1980	10595.00	142.70	3006.00	582.00	3802.00	3712.00	2716.00	7986.00
	1985	12490.00	129.30	4107.00	924.00	4384.00	4679.00	3693.00	14595.00
	1989	13764.00	150.50	5848.00	1183.00	5820.00	6159.00	4859.00	21029.00
	1990	13831.00	152.98	6212.00	1267.00	6238.00	6635.00	5153.00	20971.00
	1991	14099.00	160.73	6775.00	1247.00	6765.00	7100.00	5638.00	25261.00
	1992	14210.00	157.88	7539.00	1307.00	7589.00	8094.00	6697.00	30822.00
	1993	14524.00	167.65	8395.00	1518.00	8739.00	8956.00	7716.00	36788.00
	1994	14608.00	175.59	9281.00	1674.00	9741.00	9261.00	8428.00	42118.00
	1995	15004.95	179.47	10070.30	1905.77	10529.27	9535.99	8979.80	47560.59
	1996	15733.39	201.14	10813.10	1879.66	10722.50	10124.06	9338.02	49118.90
	1997	16074.14	227.03	11355.53	1959.83	11511.41	10894.17	9978.93	51173.80
	1998	16100.00	232.79	11670.00	1988.90	11863.67	11559.00	10737.80	53600.00
	1999	16000.00	251.98	12393.00	1965.80	12539.24	12426.00	12109.78	57300.00
	2000	16300.00	272.00	13556.00	2224.14	13101.48	12850.00	13146.00	59700.00
	2001	16395.87	303.29	14808.02	2774.32	15554.25	15163.44	16067.61	66103.99
	2002	16700.00	326.61	16540.00	2879.74	17084.60	18236.61	19251.59	72500.00
	2003	16959.98	350.15	19105.75	2836.81	21366.68	22233.60	24108.01	86208.11
北京	Beijing			192.16	6.52	788.17	816.41	785.28	999.00
天津	Tianjin	1316.30	8.49	320.07		342.65	565.95	1083.50	451.00
河北	Hebei	511.01	6.34	1088.34	3.01	4227.34	4065.06	3729.37	6811.40
山西	Shanxi		2.50	965.01	19.29	2572.16	1002.69	823.52	1949.00
内蒙古	Inner Mongolia	5.00		647.73	7.07	606.90	576.83	560.36	947.86
辽宁	Liaoning	1332.22	13.28	837.11	22.97	2062.45	2227.77	2359.35	2439.74
吉林	Jilin	476.40	2.32	338.83	40.80	318.74	381.62	369.05	1119.13
黑龙江	Heilongjiang	4840.12	20.96	493.78	11.72	136.70	165.69	141.43	1114.43
上海	Shanghai	38.02	4.97	687.63		1302.80	1728.80	1779.78	744.67
江苏	Jiangsu	166.35	0.33	1336.77	4.00	784.83	1742.21	2961.49	7825.14
浙江	Zhejiang			1101.74	125.00	173.27	334.24	527.03	7194.10
安徽	Anhui			557.15	15.60	697.65	692.68	720.14	3072.96
福建	Fujian			610.70	188.99	225.24	257.85	461.98	2400.20
江西	Jiangxi			320.94	47.64	497.08	599.53	664.14	2524.18
山东	Shandong	2665.51	8.10	1396.97	0.20	1381.28	1415.41	1437.74	9935.00
河南	Henan	549.77	20.14	1025.10	54.00	740.38	873.90	744.68	4722.60
湖北	Hubei	77.53	0.94	780.46	380.64	1034.59	1254.30	1126.25	3445.81
湖南	Hunan			537.76	242.97	575.61	592.18	562.01	3135.00
广东	Guangdong	1275.70	26.88	1882.68	180.02	351.69	599.79	846.32	7530.01
广西	Guangxi	3.28		362.91	192.63	249.80	206.20	228.84	2665.19
海南	Hainan	7.57		58.59	13.22	6.40	0.19	10.82	397.84
重庆	Chongqing		2.23	204.11	46.19	207.44	225.20	242.28	2037.66
四川	Sichuan	13.92	113.43	849.26	480.15	792.67	738.92	827.30	4059.85
贵州	Guizhou		0.52	640.98	208.25	217.35	206.16	193.07	1590.98
云南	Yunnan		0.24	474.80	280.90	512.38	294.75	286.54	2052.79
西藏	Tibet								124.91
陕西	Shaanxi	1267.43	52.86	419.16	46.75	163.47	180.20	132.98	1828.00
甘肃	Gansu	73.44	0.21	404.87	108.07	239.03	223.89	245.58	1160.82
青海	Qinghai	220.02	15.57	130.48	66.60		47.73	40.30	307.00
宁夏	Ningxia			206.13	7.28	14.72	13.33	12.68	494.13
新疆	Xinjiang	2120.39	49.84	233.53	36.33	143.89	204.12	204.20	1127.71

14-20 续表 3 continued

年份 Year 地区 Region		平板玻璃(万重量箱) Plate Glass (10 000 weight cases)	木材(万立方米) Timber (10 000 cu.m)	硫酸(万吨) Sulfuric Acid (10 000 tons)	纯碱(万吨) Soda Ash (10 000 tons)	烧碱(万吨) Caustic Soda (10 000 tons)	农用氮、磷、钾化肥(万吨) Chemical Fertilizer (10 000 tons)	化学农药(万吨) Chemical Pesticide (10 000 tons)
	1978	1784.00	5162.00	661.00	132.90	164.00	869.30	53.30
	1980	2466.00	5359.00	764.30	161.30	192.30	1232.10	53.70
	1985	4942.00	6323.00	676.40	201.10	235.30	1322.20	21.10
	1989	8442.00	5802.00	1153.30	304.20	321.10	1802.50	20.80
	1990	8067.00	5571.00	1196.90	379.50	335.40	1879.70	22.80
	1991	8712.00	5807.00	1332.90	393.60	354.10	1979.50	25.50
	1992	9359.00	6174.00	1408.70	455.00	379.50	2047.90	28.10
	1993	11086.00	6390.00	1336.50	534.90	395.40	1956.30	25.70
	1994	11925.00	6615.00	1536.50	581.40	429.60	2272.80	29.00
	1995	15731.71	6766.86	1811.00	597.71	531.82	2548.14	41.65
	1996	16069.37	6710.27	1883.57	669.29	573.78	2809.04	44.75
	1997	16630.70	6394.79	2036.87	725.76	574.40	2820.96	52.67
	1998	17194.03	5966.20	2171.00	744.00	539.37	3010.00	55.90
	1999	17419.79	5236.80	2356.00	766.00	580.14	3251.00	62.50
	2000	18352.20	4723.97	2427.00	834.00	667.88	3186.00	60.70
	2001	20964.12	4552.03	2696.32	914.37	787.96	3383.01	78.72
	2002	23445.56	4436.07	3050.40	1033.15	877.97	3791.00	92.90
	2003	27702.60	4758.87	3371.22	1133.56	945.27	3881.31	76.72
北京	Beijing	666.12	2.57	4.76		13.56	1.30	
天津	Tianjin	262.77		10.96	82.97	79.95	16.12	2.25
河北	Hebei	4681.91	38.61	99.78	135.35	41.73	236.36	4.65
山西	Shanxi	304.62	4.60	58.27	5.52	23.28	193.13	0.18
内蒙古	Inner Mongolia	852.49	327.92	21.29	60.84	19.19	50.93	0.57
辽宁	Liaoning	1361.50	130.08	108.47	80.02	48.52	105.31	2.14
吉林	Jilin	339.34	376.51	6.03	0.06	7.57	9.63	0.61
黑龙江	Heilongjiang	247.67	709.26	8.46		16.36	44.31	0.07
上海	Shanghai	790.25		40.25		41.44	4.90	2.25
江苏	Jiangsu	3807.27	38.24	301.92	181.32	113.69	206.19	19.49
浙江	Zhejiang	1677.02	204.24	60.00	11.82	54.25	55.55	12.45
安徽	Anhui	418.15	278.83	188.36	17.15	16.40	197.50	3.07
福建	Fujian	511.85	518.33	40.80	16.20	24.67	56.69	2.87
江西	Jiangxi	575.00	354.24	103.29		20.06	51.88	0.97
山东	Shandong	2252.27	42.59	353.82	184.31	165.37	469.60	7.71
河南	Henan	3129.23	60.01	91.83	108.85	52.11	314.52	3.07
湖北	Hubei	1086.62	107.00	310.25	69.46	23.07	276.68	4.58
湖南	Hunan	764.56	412.10	139.61	15.90	25.57	178.27	4.53
广东	Guangdong	739.33	308.24	143.90	28.81	19.73	19.33	0.61
广西	Guangxi	452.17	444.84	129.13	2.13	21.36	68.57	1.48
海南	Hainan		70.65	1.09			33.45	0.18
重庆	Chongqing	147.02	0.27	99.33	9.89	10.26	94.35	0.73
四川	Sichuan	915.27	50.76	282.63	66.06	61.17	318.13	1.99
贵州	Guizhou	77.44	29.25	224.36		5.84	189.60	0.05
云南	Yunnan	336.43	179.77	340.49	9.78	3.09	258.93	0.07
西藏	Tibet		20.00					
陕西	Shaanxi	864.52	14.93	70.99	15.95	9.70	105.82	0.09
甘肃	Gansu	270.37	0.70	102.70	15.50	5.89	74.20	0.02
青海	Qinghai	84.47	2.19	7.32	6.08	0.99	89.97	
宁夏	Ningxia	18.61	0.14	12.60		9.04	74.79	0.02
新疆	Xinjiang	68.32	32.00	8.53	9.59	11.41	85.30	0.03

14-20 续表 4 continued

年份 Year 地区 Region	塑料 (万吨) Plastics (10 000 tons)	金属切削机床 (万台) Metal-cutting Machine Tools (10 000 units)	汽车 (万辆) Motor Vehicles (10 000 units)	#轿车 Cars	大中型拖拉机 (万台) Tractors (10 000 units)	微型电子计算机 (万部) Micro-Computers (10 000 units)	集成电路 (万块) Integrated Circuit (10 000 units)
1978	67.9	18.32	14.91		11.35		3041
1980	89.8	13.36	22.23	0.54	9.77		1684
1985	123.4	16.72	43.72	0.90	4.50		6385
1989	200.8	17.87	58.35	3.58	3.98	7.54	13156
1990	227.0	13.45	51.40	3.50	3.94	8.21	10838
1991	283.0	16.39	71.42	6.87	5.27	16.25	17049
1992	330.8	22.87	106.67	16.17	5.70	12.62	16099
1993	359.9	26.20	129.85	22.29	3.77	14.66	20101
1994	401.4	20.65	136.69	26.87	4.67	24.57	48462
1995	516.9	20.34	145.27	33.70	6.33	83.57	551686
1996	576.9	17.74	147.52	38.29	8.37	138.83	388987
1997	685.8	18.65	158.25	48.60	8.24	206.55	255455
1998	692.6	11.91	163.00	50.71	6.78	291.40	262577
1999	871.1	14.22	183.20	57.10	6.54	405.00	415000
2000	1087.5	17.66	207.00	60.70	4.10	672.00	588000
2001	1288.7	25.58	234.17	70.36	3.82	877.65	636288
2002	1455.7	30.86	325.10	109.20	4.54	1463.51	963101
2003	1652.1	30.58	444.39	202.01	4.88	3216.70	1483101
北京 Beijing	123.0	0.44	34.91	7.33		470.58	46892
天津 Tianjin	101.2	0.12	17.25	17.25	0.56	0.42	36937
河北 Hebei	64.1	0.11	11.17				
山西 Shanxi	4.7	0.19	0.07				
内蒙古 Inner Mongolia	10.0		0.27			5.06	
辽宁 Liaoning	119.1	5.65	13.00	3.39		178.30	135
吉林 Jilin	51.3	0.04	64.07	35.07			
黑龙江 Heilongjiang	82.5	0.38	20.00	3.24	0.02	3.95	3
上海 Shanghai	166.9	1.90	58.73	57.43	0.69	739.46	401872
江苏 Jiangsu	279.2	5.62	21.26	8.42	0.51	605.59	368617
浙江 Zhejiang	47.1	3.87	8.19	2.01	0.34	7.40	109582
安徽 Anhui	14.1	1.21	20.63	12.48	0.02	15.80	
福建 Fujian	30.7	0.11	8.67	3.57		241.74	13389
江西 Jiangxi	14.3	0.40	18.52		0.06	10.56	
山东 Shandong	122.9	4.91	7.49	3.80	1.43	48.55	45
河南 Henan	57.5	0.30	2.77		1.10	0.50	
湖北 Hubei	29.7	0.33	36.89	17.16	0.09	2.02	
湖南 Hunan	26.2	0.10	4.38	0.58			8
广东 Guangdong	172.7	2.03	18.88	11.72		881.05	393381
广西 Guangxi	5.7	0.43	18.06	0.05		0.01	52
海南 Hainan			5.50	4.26			
重庆 Chongqing	0.4	0.32	40.45	12.06		1.04	
四川 Sichuan	39.8	0.59	4.76		0.05	2.52	56
贵州 Guizhou		0.05	0.13	0.13			3334
云南 Yunnan	1.4	0.44	4.05	0.05			
西藏 Tibet							
陕西 Shaanxi	4.4	0.74	4.27	2.01		2.15	
甘肃 Gansu	33.8	0.08	0.02				108799
青海 Qinghai		0.05					
宁夏 Ningxia	1.0	0.20					
新疆 Xinjiang	48.5				0.01		

14-21 工业产品产量

Output of Industrial Products

产品名称	Item	2002	2003
化学纤维 (万吨)	Chemical Fiber (10 000 tons)	991.20	1181.15
纱 (万吨)	Yarn (10 000 tons)	850.00	983.58
布 (亿米)	Cloth (100 million m)	322.39	353.52
#纯棉布	Pure Cotton Cloth	172.54	200.86
针棉织品折用纱线量(万吨)	Cotton Knitwear (10 000 tons)	116.52	91.45
绒线（毛线） (万吨)	Knitting Wool (10 000 tons)	51.50	65.74
丝 (万吨)	Silk (10 000 tons)	9.82	11.10
呢绒 (万米)	Woolen Piece Goods (10 000 m)	32691.21	44294.58
机制纸及纸板 (万吨)	Machine-made Paper and Paperboard (10 000 tons)	4666.99	4849.33
家用电冰箱 (万台)	Home Refrigerators (10 000 sets)	1598.87	2242.56
冷冻箱 (万台)	Freezers (10 000 sets)	464.85	567.32
家用洗衣机 (万台)	Home Washing Machines (10 000 sets)	1595.76	1964.46
吸尘器 (万台)	Vacuum Cleaners (10 000 sets)	1611.16	2185.35
电风扇 (万台)	Electric Fans (10 000 sets)	10761.33	12980.92
房间空调器 (万台)	Air Conditioners (10 000 sets)	3135.11	4820.86
排油烟机 (万台)	Smoke Absorbers (10 000 sets)	426.46	477.25
日用陶瓷 (亿件)	Household Ceramics (100 million pcs)	164.67	96.20
合成洗涤剂 (万吨)	Synthetic Detergents (10 000 tons)	348.32	386.79
原盐 (万吨)	Salt (10 000 tons)	3602.43	3437.70
糖 (万吨)	Sugar (10 000 tons)	926.00	1083.94
卷烟 (万箱)	Cigarettes (10 000 cases)	3467.08	3580.86
罐头 (万吨)	Canned Food (10 000 tons)	375.17	436.38
白酒 (万吨)	Liquor (10 000 tons)	739.57	647.49
啤酒 (万吨)	Beer (10 000 tons)	2402.70	2540.48
食用植物油 (万吨)	Edible Vegetable Oil (10 000 tons)	1531.22	1584.29
中成药 (万吨)	Traditional Chinese Medicine (10 000 tons)	94.32	70.91
化学原料药 (万吨)	Chemical Medicine (10 000 tons)	73.93	99.42
彩色电视机 (万台)	Color Television Sets (10 000 sets)	5155.00	6541.40
录像机 (万部)	Video Recorders (10 000 sets)	1562.02	2029.47
组合音响 (万部)	Hi-Fi Stereo Component Players (10 000 sets)	4835.70	5541.82
照相机 (万架)	Cameras (10 000 sets)	5309.61	6198.14
农用氮、磷、钾化肥(万吨)	Chemical Fertilizers (10 000 tons)	3791.00	3881.31
#氮肥 (万吨)	Nitrogen Fertilizers (10 000 tons)	2808.48	2814.52
磷肥 (万吨)	Phosphate Fertilizers (10 000 tons)	801.03	978.08
化学农药 (万吨)	Chemical Pesticide (10 000 tons)	92.90	76.72
塑料树脂及共聚物 (万吨)	Plastics (10 000 tons)	1455.67	1652.08
合成橡胶 (万吨)	Synthetic Rubber (10 000 tons)	136.21	134.83
轮胎外胎 (万条)	Tires (10 000 tires)	16306.59	19311.96
矿山设备 (万吨)	Mining Equipment (10 000 tons)	84.04	79.08
化工设备 (万吨)	Equipment for Chemical Industry (10 000 tons)	28.12	29.28
发电设备 (万千瓦)	Power Generating Equipment (10 000 kw)	2120.84	3700.62
金属切削机床 (万台)	Metal-cutting Machine Tools (10 000 units)	30.86	30.58
汽车 (万辆)	Motor Vehicles (10 000 sets)	325.10	444.39
#载货汽车 (万辆)	Trucks (10 000 sets)	109.20	112.44
客车 (万辆)	Buses (10 000 sets)	86.47	99.78
轿车 (万辆)	Cars (10 000 sets)	109.20	202.01
摩托车 (万辆)	Motorcycles (10 000 sets)	1198.80	1461.34
自行车 (万辆)	Bicycles (10 000 sets)	3957.52	5451.70
大中型拖拉机 (万台)	Large and Medium Tractors (10 000 sets)	4.54	4.88
内燃机 (万千瓦)	Internal Combustion Engines (10 000 kw)	28505.75	31851.30
铁路客车 (辆)	Railway Passenger Coaches (unit)	2856	1525
铁路货车 (万辆)	Railway Freight Wagons (10 000 units)	3.13	3.12
载波通信设备 (万部)	Carrier Wave Communication Equipment (10 000 units)	0.42	0.48
移动电话机 (万部)	Mobile Telephone (10 000 units)	12146.35	18231.37

14-21 续表 continued

产品名称		Item		2002	2003
电话单机	(万部)	Telephone Sets	(10 000 units)	11892.42	12935.90
传真机	(万部)	Fax Machines	(10 000 units)	297.29	746.58
磁带（折6.30毫米）	(亿米)	Tape (converted into 6.30mm)	(100 million m)	258.38	238.70
软磁盘	(亿片)	Floppy Disks	(100 million pcs)	7.18	6.71
电子计算机	(部)	Computers	(units)	26622	50910
微型电子计算机	(万部)	Micro-computers	(10 000 units)	1463.51	3216.70
大规模半导体集成电路	(亿块)	Large Semiconductor Integrated Circuit	(100 000 000 pcs)	41.32	68.63
复印机械	(万台)	Copying Machines	(10 000 units)	207.39	264.17
原煤	(亿吨)	Coal	(100 million tons)	13.80	16.67
原油	(万吨)	Crude Petroleum Oil	(10 000 tons)	16700.00	16959.98
汽油	(万吨)	Gasoline	(10 000 tons)	4320.76	4790.86
柴油	(万吨)	Diesel Oil	(10 000 tons)	7706.10	8532.78
天然气	(亿立方米)	Natural Gas	(100 million cu.m)	326.61	350.15
发电量	(亿千瓦小时)	Electricity	(100 million kwh)	16540.00	19105.75
#水电		Hydropower		2879.74	2836.81
生铁	(万吨)	Pig Iron	(10 000 tons)	17084.60	21366.68
钢	(万吨)	Steel	(10 000 tons)	18236.61	22233.60
成品钢材	(万吨)	Steel Products	(10 000 tons)	19251.59	24108.01
#重轨		Heavy Rail		135.65	122.46
普通大型钢材		Ordinary Rolled-steel, Large		267.82	309.31
普通中型钢材		Ordinary Rolled-steel, Medium		731.56	729.77
普通小型钢材		Ordinary Rolled-steel, Small		5093.32	6779.35
优质型钢材		High Quality Section Steel		1128.56	1377.41
线材		Wire Rod		3562.35	4026.73
特厚钢板		Heavy Steel Plate		103.53	132.99
中厚钢板		Medium Steel Plate		2460.31	3281.42
薄钢板		Steel Sheet		2244.50	2396.21
硅钢片		Silicon Steel Sheet		184.52	193.22
无缝钢管		Seamless Steel Pipe		608.30	699.90
焦炭	(万吨)	Coke	(10 000 tons)	14279.81	17775.71
水泥	(万吨)	Cement	(10 000 tons)	72500.00	86208.11
平板玻璃	(万重量箱)	Plain Glass	(10 000 weight cases)	23445.56	27702.60
木材	(万立方米)	Timber	(10 000 cu.m)	4436.07	4758.87
硫酸	(万吨)	Sulfuric Acid	(10 000 tons)	3050.40	3371.22
碳酸钠（纯碱）	(万吨)	Soda Ash	(10 000 tons)	1033.15	1133.56
氢氧化钠（烧碱）	(万吨)	Caustic Soda	(10 000 tons)	877.97	945.27
合成氨	(万吨)	Synthetic Ammonia	(10 000 tons)	3675.25	3822.65

注:1.纱包括纯棉纱、棉混纺纱、纯化纤纱，不包括棉线、代用纤维纱和手工纺纱。
2.布包括纯棉布、棉混纺布、纯化纤布，不包括代用纤维布、手工织布。
3.针棉织品为折用棉纱量。
4.农用化肥按有效成分100%计算。
5.发电设备指500千瓦以上的,包括水轮发电机组、汽轮发电机和燃气轮发电机。
6.金属切削机床不包括台钻、 砂轮机、抛光机。
7.拖拉机是指14.7千瓦及以上的轮式和履带式拖拉机。用本厂自产的拖拉机装配的推土机，只计推土机产量，不计拖拉机产量。
8.原煤包括无烟煤、烟煤、褐煤,不包括石煤。
9.原油包括天然原油和人造原油。
10.成品钢材已剔除重复加工的钢材。

a) Yarn includes pure and blended cotton yarn, pure chemical-fiber yarn, but excludes cotton thread, substitute fiber yarn and hand-made yarn.
b) Cloth includes pure and blended cotton cloth, pure chemical-fiber cloth and canvas, but excludes substitute fiber cloth, hand-woven cloth and cord fabric.
c) Knitwear refers to cotton yarn substitutes.
d) The output of chemical fertilizers is calculated on the basis of 100 % effective content.
e) Power generating equipment refers to units with a generating capacity of 500 kw and over, including hydroturbine generating units, steam turbine generating units and gas turbine generating units.
f) Metal-cutting machine tools exclude bench drills, grinders and polishing machines.
g) Tractors refer to both wheel and crawler tractors with a haulage capacity of 14.7 kw and over. The tractors which are refitted into bulldozers by the same tractor factories are deducted.
h) Coal includes anthracite, bituminous coal and lignite, but excludes stone coal.
i) Crude oil includes natural and synthetic crude oil.
j) The output of rolled steel final products excludes the steel products reprocessed.

14-22 重点工业企业主要工业产品生产能力(2002年)

Production Capacity of Major Industrial Products of Key Industry Enterprises (2002)

产品名称		Item		2002
原煤	(万吨)	Coal	(10 000 tons)	83499
发电设备容量总计	(万千瓦)	Power Generating Equipment	(10 000 kw)	35657.09
卷烟综合生产能力	(亿支)	Cigarettes	(10 000 cases)	30633.9
化学纤维	(万吨)	Chemical Fiber	(10 000 tons)	1165.53
棉印染布	(亿米)	Printing and Dyeing Cotton Cloth	(100 million meters)	226.38
棉纺锭(棉纺企业年末安装数)	(万锭)	Cotton Hasp	(10 000 ingots)	4906.91
毛纺锭(毛纺企业年末安装数)	(万锭)	Woolen Hasp	(10 000 ingots)	358.29
锯材	(万立方米)	Saw Timber	(10 000 cu.m)	349.2
胶合板	(万立方米)	Plywood	(10 000 cu.m)	104.3
纤维板	(万立方米)	Fiberboard	(10 000 cu.m)	182
生铁	(万吨)	Pig Iron	(10 000 tons)	17650.93
钢	(万吨)	Steels	(10 000 tons)	19734.98
#电炉钢	(万吨)	Electric Steel	(10 000 tons)	4035.26
转炉钢	(万吨)	Convertor Steel	(10 000 tons)	15696.6
连铸坯	(万吨)	Continuous Casting	(10 000 tons)	18081.44
钢材	(万吨)	Steels	(10 000 tons)	21350.16
工业锅炉	(万蒸吨)	Industry Boiler	(10 000 tons)	6.4
内燃机	(万台)	Internal Combustion Engines	(10 000 units)	815.58
金属切削机床	(万台)	Metal-cutting Machine Tools	(10 000 units)	13.4
#数控机床	(万台)	Numerical Control Tool	(10 000 units)	1.02
起重机械	(万台)	Lift	(10 000 units)	19.9
叉车	(万台)	Forklift Truck	(10 000 units)	2.91
运输设备	(万台)	Transport Equipment	(10 000 units)	7.46
装载机	(万台)	Loading Machine	(10 000 units)	2.71
炼油化工设备	(万台)	Chemical Equipment for Oil Refining	(10 000 units)	10.59
泵	(万台)	Pump	(10 000 units)	94.49
风机	(万台)	Wind Machine	(10 000 units)	9.56
汽车	(万辆)	Motor Vehicle	(10 000 units)	263.17
载货汽车	(万辆)	Truck	(10 000 units)	110.89
客车	(万辆)	Passenger Vehicle	(10 000 units)	62.71
#轿车	(万辆)	Car	(10 000 units)	73
移动通信手持机	(万部)	Mobile Phone	(10 000 units)	21914
移动通信基站设备	(万信道)	Mobile Communication Equipment for Base Station	(10 000 channels)	1098.63
移动交换机	(万线)	Mobile Switchyard	(10 000 lines)	4050
台式个人电脑	(万台)	Personal Computers	(10 000 units)	2525
服务器	(万台)	Computer Servers	(10 000 units)	48
笔记本电脑	(万台)	Notebook Computer	(10 000 units)	165
显像管	(万只)	Kinescope	(10 000 units)	7750
#彩色显像管	(万只)	Color Kinescope	(10 000 units)	5380
电视机	(万台)	Television Sets	(10 000 units)	9350
#彩色电视机	(万台)	Color Television Sets	(10 000 units)	8796

主要统计指标解释

工业指从事自然资源的开采，对采掘品和农产品进行加工和再加工的物质生产部门。具体包括：(1)对自然资源的开采，如采矿、晒盐等(但不包括禽兽捕猎和水产捕捞)；(2)对农副产品的加工、再加工，如粮油加工、食品加工、缫丝、纺织、制革等；(3)对采掘品的加工、再加工，如炼铁、炼钢、化工生产、石油加工、机器制造、木材加工等，以及电力、自来水、煤气的生产和供应等；(4)对工业品的修理、翻新，如机器设备的修理、交通运输工具(包括小卧车)的修理等。

1984年以前农村的村及村以下办工业归属农业，1984年以后划归工业。

工业统计调查单位为独立核算法人工业企业。

独立核算法人工业企业指从事工业生产经营活动的单位。独立核算法人工业企业应同时具备以下条件：①依法成立，有自己的名称、组织机构和场所，能够承担民事责任；②独立拥有和使用资产，承担负债，有权与其他单位签订合同；③独立核算盈亏，并能够编制资产负债表。

本年鉴中涉及的企业登记注册类型：

国有及国有控股企业 指国有企业加上国有控股企业。国有企业(即原全民所有制工业或国营工业)指企业全部资产归国家所有，并按《中华人民共和国企业法人登记管理条例》规定登记注册的非公司制的经济组织。包括国有企业、国有独资公司和国有联营企业。1957年以前的公私合营和私营工业，后均改造为国营工业，1992年改为国有工业，这部分工业的资料不单独分列时，均包括在国有企业内。国有控股企业是对混合所有制经济的企业进行的"国有控股"分类。它是指这些企业的全部资产中国有资产(股份)相对其他所有者中的任何一个所有者占资(股)最多的企业。该分组反映了国有经济控股情况。

集体企业 指企业资产归集体所有，并按《中华人民共和国企业法人登记管理条例》规定登记注册的经济组织。是社会主义公有制经济的组成部分。包括城乡所有使用集体投资举办的企业，以及部分个人通过集资自愿放弃所有权并依法经工商行政管理机关认定为集体所有制的企业。

股份合作企业 指以合作制为基础，由企业职工共同出资入股，吸收一定比例的社会资产投资组建，实行自主经营，自负盈亏，共同劳动，民主管理，按劳分配与按股分红相结合的一种集体经济组织。

联营企业 指两个及两个以上相同或不同所有制性质的企业法人或事业单位法人，按自愿、平等、互利的原则，共同投资组成的经济组织。联营企业包括：

国有联营企业指国有企业与国有企业间的联营；

集体联营企业指集体企业与集体企业间的联营；

国有与集体联营企业指国有企业与集体企业间的联营。

有限责任公司 指根据《中华人民共和国公司登记管理条例》规定登记注册，由两个以上，五十个以下的股东共同出资，每个股东以其所缴的出资额对公司承担有限责任，公司以其全部资产对其债务承担责任的经济组织。

有限责任公司包括国有独资公司以及其他有限责任公司。

股份有限公司 指根据《中华人民共和国企业法人登记管理条例》规定登记注册，其全部注册资本由等额股份构成并通过发行股票筹集资本，股东以其认购的股份对公司承担有限责任，公司以其全部资产对其债务承担责任的经济组织。

私营企业 指由自然人投资设立或由自然人控股，以雇佣劳动为基础的营利性经济组织。包括按照《公司法》、《合伙企业法》、《私营企业暂行条例》规定登记注册的私营有限责任公司、私营股份有限公司、私营合伙企业和私营独资企业。

港、澳、台商投资企业 指企业注册登记类型中的港、澳、台资合资、合作、独资经营企业和股份有限公司之和。

外商投资企业 指企业注册登记类型中的中外合资、合作经营企业、外资企业和外商投资股份有限公司之和。

“三资”企业系指港、澳、台商投资企业和外资企业的简称。

轻工业 指主要提供生活消费品和制作手工工具的工业。按其所使用的原料不同，可分为两大类：(1)以农产品为原料的轻工业，是指直接或间接以农产品为基本原料的轻工业。主要包括食品制造、饮料制造、烟草加工、纺织、缝纫、皮革和毛皮制作、造纸以及印刷等工业；(2)以非农产品为原料的轻工业，是指以工业品为原料的轻工业。主要包括文教体育用品、化学药品制造、合成纤维制造、日用化学制品、日用玻璃制品、日用金属制品、手工工具制造、医疗器械制造、文化和办公用机械制造等工业。

重工业 指为国民经济各部门提供物质技术基础的主要生产资料的工业。按其生产性质和产品用途，可以分为下列三类：(1)采掘(伐)工业，是指对自然资源的开采，包括石油开采、煤炭开采、金属矿开采、非金属矿开采等工业；(2)原材料工业，指向国民经济各部门提供基本材料、动力和燃料的工业。包括金属冶炼及加工、炼焦及焦炭、化学、化工原料、水泥、人造板以及电力、石油和煤炭加工等工业；(3)加工工业，是指对工业原材料进行再加工制造的工业。包括装备国民经济各部门的机械设备制造工业、金属结构、水泥制品等工业，以及为农业提供的生产资料如化肥、农药等工业。

根据上述划分原则，修理业中以重工业产品为修理作业对象的划为重工业，反之划为轻工业。

工业总产值

(1)定义：工业总产值是以货币形式表现的，工业企业在一定时期内生产的工业最终产品或提供工业性劳务活动的总价值量。它反映一定时间内工业生产的总规模和总水平。

(2)计算原则：

工业生产的原则，即凡是企业在报告期生产的经检验合格的产品，不管是否在报告期销售，均包括在内。

最终产品的原则，即凡是计入工业总产值的产品，必须是本企业生产的经检验合格的，不需要再进行任何加工的最终产品。如果企业有中间产品(半成品)对外销售，则对外销售的中间产品应视为企业的最终产品。

工厂法原则，即工业总产值是以工业企业作为基本计算(核算)单位，即按企业的最终产品计算工业总产值。按这种方法计算的工业总产值，不允许同一产品价值在企业内部重复计算，不能把企业内部各个车间(分厂)生产的成果相加，但允许企业间的重复计算。

(3)内容及计算方法：1995年全国工业普查对工业总产值(原规定)的内容及计算原则和方法做了某些修订，修订后的工业总产值(新规定)包括三项内容：即本期生产成品价值、对外加工费收入、在制品半成品期末期初差额价值三部分。

本期生产成品价值：指企业本期生产，并在报告期内不再进行加工，经检验、包装入库的全部工业成品(半产品)价值合计，包括企业生产的自制设备及提供给本企业在建工程、其他非工业部门和福利部门等单位使用的成品价值。本期生产成品价值为按自备原材料生产的产品的数量乘以本期不含增值税(销项税额)的产品实际销售平均单价计算；会计核算中按成本价格转帐的自制设备和自产自用的成品，按成本价格计算生产成品价值。生产成品价值中不包括用定货者来料加工的成品(半产品)价值。

对外加工费收入：指企业在报告期内完成的对外承接的工业品加工(包括用定货者来料加工产品)的加工费收入和对外工业修理作业所取得的加工费收入。对外加工费收入按不含增值税(销项税额)的价格计算，可根据会计“产品销售收入”科目的有关资料取得。

对于本企业对内非工业部门提供的加工修理、设备安装的劳务收入，如果企业会计核算基础较好，能取得这部分资料，而且这部分价值所占比重较大，应包括在对外加工费收入中。

自制半成品在制品期末期初差额价值：指企业报告期在制品期末减期初的差额价值，本指标一般可以从会计核算资料中取得。如果会计产品成本核算中不计算半成品、在制品的成本，则总产值中也不包括这部分价值，反之则包括。

(4)工业总产值统计范围变化和计算方法修订情况：

1984年以前工业总产值不包括村办工业，村办工业总产值划归农业。1984年以后工业总产值包括村办工业。 1995年工业普查对工业总产值计算方法做了修订，即从1995年始按新修订(新规定)方法计算工业总产值。新规定与原规定的区别如下：

全价与加工费的计算原则不同：新规定为凡自备原材料，不论其生产繁简程度如何，一律按全价计算工业总产值；凡来料加工，允许按加工费计算工业总产值。原规定则视生产加工的繁简程度不同，规定哪些行业按全价，哪些行业按加工费计算工业总产值。

自制半成品、在产品期末期初差额价值的计算原则不同：新规定要求，凡会计产品成本核算时计算了成本的差额价值，总产值中就应包括，否则可不包括；原规定则按生产周期六个月的界限区分，凡生产周期六个月以上的企业，总产值计算中应包括这部分差额价值，否则可不包括。

计算价格不同：新规定按不含增值税(销项税额)的价格计算；原规定则按含增值税(销项税额)的价格计算。

工业增加值 指工业企业在报告期内以货币表现的工业生产活动的最终成果。

工业增加值有两种计算方法：一是生产法，即工业总产出减去工业中间投入加上应交增值税；二是收入法，即从收入的角度出发，根据生产要素在生产过程中应得到的收入份额计算，具体构成项目有固定资产折旧、劳动者报酬、生产税净额、营业盈余，这种方法也称要素分配法。本年鉴中的工业增加值是以生产法计算的。

生产法工业增加值的计算方法为：

工业增加值=工业总产出-工业中间投入+应交增值税

(1)工业总产出：指工业企业在一定时期内工业生产活动的总成果。工业总产出包括：成品生产价值，对外加工费收入，自制半成品、在产品期末期初差额价值。1995年后用新规定计算的工业总产值代替。

(2)工业中间投入：指工业企业在工业生产活动中消耗的外购物质产品和对外支付的服务费用。服务费用包括支付给物质生产部门(工业、农业、批发零售贸易业、建筑业、运输邮电业)的服务费用和支付给非物质生产部门(如保险、金融、文化教育、科学研究、医疗卫生、行政管理等)的服务费用。工业中间投入的确定须遵循以下原则：必须从外部购入的，并已计入工业总产出的产品和服务价值；必须是本期投入生产，并一次性消耗掉(包括本期摊销的低值易耗品等)的产品和服务价值。

工业中间投入包括直接材料费用、制造费用中的工业中间投入、管理费用中的工业中间投入、销售费用中的工业中间投入和利息支出五部分。

实收资本 指企业实际收到投资者的可作为长期周转使用的经营资金。根据现行会计制度规定，实收资本按投资主体分为：国家资本、集体资本、法人资本、个人资本、港澳台资本和外商资本。

国家资本：指有权代表国家投资的政府部门或者机构以国有资产投入企业形成的资本。

集体资本：指有权代表国家投资的集体部门或者机构以国有资产投入企业形成的资本。

法人资本：指其他法人单位以其依法可以支配的资产投入企业形成的资本。

个人资本：指社会个人或者本企业内部职工以个人合法财产投放到企业形成的资本。

港澳台资本：指我国香港、澳门和台湾地区投资者以各种形式的资产进行投资形成的资本。

外商资本：指外国投资者对企业投资形成的资本。

资产总计 指企业拥有或控制的能以货币计量的经济资源，包括各种财产、债权和其他权利。资产按流动性分为流动资产、长期投资、固定资产、无形资产、递延资产和其他资产。该指标根据企业会计“资产负债表”中“资产总计”项目的期末数增列。

流动资产合计 指可以在一年或者超过一年的一个营业周期内变现或者耗用的资产，包括现金及各种存款、短期投资、应收及预付货款、存款等。

流动资产平均余额 指企业在报告期内全部流动资产的平均余额。

固定资产原价 指企业在建造、购置、安装、改建、扩建、技术改造某项固定资产时所支出的全部货币总额。它一般包括买价、包装费、运杂费和安装费等。

固定资产净值年平均余额 指固定资产净值在报告期内余额的平均数。计算公式为：

$$\text{固定资产净值年平均余额} = \frac{\text{1至12月各月月初、月末固定资产净值之和}}{24}$$

该指标根据“资产负债表”中“固定资产原价”、“累计折旧”指标的期初、期末数计算填列。

固定资产净值指固定资产原价减去历年已提折旧额后的净额。计算公式为：

固定资产净值=固定资产原价-累计折旧

流动负债合计 指将在一年或超过一年的一个营业周期内偿还的债务。流动负债包括短期负债、应付票据、应付帐款、预收帐款、应付工资、应付福利费、应交税金、应付利润、其他应付款、预提费用等。

流动负债具有偿还期限短，在债权人提出要求时即期偿付，或在一年内必须偿还的特点。该指标根据“资产负债表”中“流动负债”项的期末数填列。

长期负债合计 指偿还期在一年或超过一年的一个营业周期以上的债务，它是除了投资人投入企业的资本以外，企业向债权人筹集、可供企业长期使用的资金，是企业必须以资产或劳务偿还的经济责任，包括长期借款、应付债款、长期应付款、其他长期负债等。与流动负债相比，长期负债具有为数较大、偿还期限较长的特点，且对投资者来说可带来更大的利益。指标根据“资产负债表”中“长期负债合计”项的期末数填列。

所有者权益 指企业投资人对企业净资产的所有权。企业净资产等于企业全部资产减去全部负债后的余额，包括企业投资人对企业的最初投入的实际到位的资产及资本公积金、盈余公积金和未分配利润。所有者权益合计数小于零，表示企业资不抵债。

产品销售收入 指企业在报告期内生产的成品、自制半成品和工业性劳务取得的收入。

产品销售成本 指企业在报告期内销售本企业生产的成品、自制半成品和工业性劳务等的实际成本。

产品销售税金及附加 指企业在报告期内销售产品、提供的劳务等主要经营业务应负担的城市维护建设税、消费税、资源税和教育费附加等。

利润总额 指企业生产经营活动的最终成果，是企业在一定时期内实现的盈亏相抵后的利润总额(亏损以“-”号表示)，它等于营业利润加上补贴收入加上投资收益加上营业外净收入再加上以前年度损益调整。

本年应交增值税 指企业在报告期内应交纳的增值税额。它等于本年销项税额加上出口退税加上进项税额转出数减去本年进项税额。小规模纳税企业直接按全年计税销售额乘以征收率计算取得。

年末从业人员平均人数 从业人员是指在企业工作并取得劳动报酬的全部人员数。包括在岗职工、再就业的离退休人员、民办教师及在企业工作的外方人员和港澳台方人员、兼职人员、借用的外单位人员和第二职业者。不包括离开本单位但仍保留劳动关系的职工。

从业人员平均人数是指报告期内每天拥有的从业人员人数。其计算公式为：

$$\text{月平均人数}=\frac{\text{报告月内每天实有人数之和}}{\text{报告月日历日数}}$$

$$\text{季平均人数}=\frac{\text{季内各月平均人数之和}}{3}$$

$$\text{年平均人数}=\frac{\text{年内各月平均人数之和}}{12}$$

总资产贡献率 反映企业全部资产的获利能力，是企业经营业绩和管理水平的集中体现，是评价和考核企业盈利能力的核心指标。计算公式为：

$$\text{总资产贡献率（\%）}=\frac{\text{利润总额+税金总额+利息支出}}{\text{平均资金总额}}\times 100\%$$

公式中：税金总额为产品销售税金及附加与应交增值税之和；平均资产总额为期初期末资产之和的算术平均值。

资产负债率 该指标既反映企业经营风险的大小，也反映企业利用债权人提供的资金从事经营活动的能力。计算公式为：

$$\text{资产负债率（\%）}=\frac{\text{负债总额}}{\text{资产总额}}\times 100\%$$

资产与负债均为报告期期末数。

流动资产周转次数 指一定时期内流动资产完成的周转次数，反映投入工业企业流动资金的周转速度。计算公式为：

$$\text{流动资产周转资转}=\frac{\text{产品销售收入}}{\text{全部流动资产平均余额}}$$

公式中：全部流动资产平均余额为期初和期末的流动资产之和的算术平均值。

成本费用利润率 反映企业投入的生产成本及费用的经济效益，同时也反映企业降低成本所取得的经济效益。计算公式为：

$$\text{成本费用利润（\%）}=\frac{\text{利润总额}}{\text{成本费用总额}}\times 100\%$$

公式中：成本费用总额为产品销售成本、销售费用、管理费用、财务费用之和。

全员劳动生产率 该指标反映企业的生产效率和劳动投入的经济效益。计算公式为：

$$\text{全员劳动生产率（元/人）}=\frac{\text{工业增加值}}{\text{全部从业人员平均人数}}$$

产品销售率 该指标反映工业产品已实现销售的程度，是分析工业产销衔接情况、研究工业产品满足社会需求的指标。计算公式为：

$$\text{产品销售率（\%）}=\frac{\text{工业销售产值}}{\text{工业总产值（现价）}}\times 100\%$$

Explanatory Notes on Main Statistical Indicators

Industry refers to the material production sector which is engaged in extraction of natural resources and processing and reprocessing of minerals and agricultural products, including (1) extraction of natural resources, such as mining, salt production (but not including hunting and fishing); (2) processing and reprocessing of farm and sideline produces, such as rice husking, flour milling, wine making, oil pressing, silk reeling, spinning and weaving, and leather making; (3) manufacture of industrial products, such as steel making, iron smelting, chemicals manufacturing, petroleum processing, machine building, timber processing; water and gas production and electricity generation and supply; (4)repairing of industrial products such as the repairing of machinery and means of transport (including cars).

Prior to 1984, the rural industry run by villages and cooperative organizations under village was classified into agriculture. Since 1984, it has been grouped into industry.

Units of industrial statistics survey corporate industrial enterprises with independent accounting system.

Corporate industrial enterprises with independent accounting system refer to enterprises engaging in industrial production activities, which meet the following requirements: ①They are established legally, having their own names, organizations, location, able to take civil liability; ②They possess and use their assets independently, assume liabilities, and are entitled to sign contracts with other units; ③They are financially independent and compile their own balance sheets.

Enterprises covered in the industrial statistics in the Yearbook include following categories by their registration:

State-owned Enterprises refer to industrial enterprises where the means of production or income are owned by the state. Joint state-private industries and private industries, which existed before 1957, have been transformed into state industries. Statistics on these enterprises has been included in the state-owned industries since 1957 when separation of data was no longer necessary.

Collective-owned Enterprises refer to industrial enterprises where the means of production are owned collectively, including urban and rural enterprises invested by collectives and some enterprises which were formerly owned privately but have been registered in industrial and commercial administration agency as collective units through raising fund from the public.

Share-holding Cooperative Enterprises refer to economic units set up on cooperative basis, with funding partly from members of the enterprise and partly from outside investment, where the operation and management is decided by the members who also participate in the production, and the distribution of income is based both on work (labour input) and on shares (capital input).

Joint-operation enterprises refer to economic units that are established by joint investment by two or more corporate enterprises or institutions of the same or different types of ownership on voluntary, equal and mutual-beneficial basis. They include:

a) state-owned joint-operation enterprises (joint operation between state-owned enterprises);

b) collective joint-operation enterprises (joint operation between collective enterprises; and

c) state-collective joint-operation enterprises (joint operation between state and collective enterprises).

Limited Liability Corporations refer to economic units registered in accordance with the Regulation of the People's Republic of China on the Management of Registration of Corporations, with capitals from 2 to 49 investors, each investor bears limited liability to the corporation depending on his/her holding of shares, and the corporation bears liability to its debt to the maximum of its total assets.

Share-holding Corporations Ltd. refer to economic units registered in accordance with the Regulation of the People's Republic of China on the Management of Registration of Corporate Enterprises, with total registered capitals divided into equal shares and raised through issuing stocks. Each investor bears limited liability to the corporation depending on the holding of shares, and the corporation bears liability to its debt to the maximum of its total assets.

Private Enterprises refer to economic units invested or controlled (by holding the majority of the shares) by natural persons who hire labours for profit-making activities. Included in this category are private limited liability corporations, private share-holding corporations Ltd., private partnership enterprises and private sole investment enterprises registered in accordance with the Corporation Law, Partnership Enterprise Law and Tentative Regulation on Private Enterprises.

Enterprises with Funds form Hong Kong, Macao and Taiwan refers to all industrial enterprises registered as the joint-venture, cooperative, sole (exclusive) investment industrial enterprises and limited liability corporations with funds from Hong Kong, Macao and Taiwan.

Foreign Funded Enterprises refers to all industrial enterprises registered as the joint-venture, cooperative, sole (exclusive) investment industrial enterprises and limited liability corporations with foreign funds.

Light Industry refers to the industry that produces consumer goods and hand tools. It consists of two categories, depending on the materials used:

(1) Industries using farm products as raw materials. These are branches of light industry which directly or indirectly use farm products as basic raw materials, including the manufacture of food and beverages, tobacco processing, textile, clothing, fur and leather manufacturing, paper making, printing, etc.

(2) Industries using non farm products as raw materials. These are branches of light industry which use manufactured goods as raw materials, including the manufacture of cultural, educational articles and sports goods, chemicals, synthetic fiber, chemical products for daily use, glass products for daily use, metal products for daily use, hand tools, medical apparatus and instruments, and the manufacture of cultural and clerical machinery.

Heavy Industry refers to the industry which produces capital goods, and provides various sectors of the national economy with necessary material and technical basis. It consists of the following three branches according to the purpose of production or the use of products:

(1) Mining, quarrying and logging industry refers to the industry that extracts natural resources, including extraction of petroleum, coal, metal and non-metal ores.

(2) Raw materials industry refers to the industry that provides various sectors of the national economy with raw materials, fuels and power. It includes smelting and processing of metals, coking and coke chemistry, chemical materials and building materials such as cement, plywood, and power, petroleum refining and coal dressing.

(3) Manufacturing industry refers to the industry that processes raw materials. It includes machine building industry which equips sectors of the national economy, industries of metal structure and cement products, industries producing means of agricultural production, such as chemical fertilizers and pesticides. According to the above principle of classification, the repairing trades which are engaged primarily in repairing products of heavy industry are classified into heavy industry while these engaged in repairing products of light industry are classified into light industry.

Gross Industrial Output Value

(1) Definition: Gross industrial output value is the total volume of final industrial products produced and industrial services provided during a given period. It reflects the total achievements and overall scale of industrial production during a given period.

(2) Principles for calculation:

Statistics on industrial production follow the principle that all products produced by the enterprises and accepted during the reference period are to be included no matter whether they are sold or not during the reference period.

Determination of final products follow the principle that all products that are included in the calculation of grow industrial output value are the final products of the enterprise which have been accepted through quality check and require no further processing. If an enterprise has intermediate (semi-finished) products to sell, these intermediate products are considered as the final products of the enterprise.

Gross industrial output value is calculated following the principle of factory approach, i.e. industrial enterprise is used as the basic accounting unit in calculating the gross industrial output value. By this approach, value of the same product is not to be double counted, and the output value of different workshops (branch factories) should not be added. However, this approach does not exclude the possibility of double counting between enterprises.

(3) Content and calculation method: The old definition of gross industrial output value was modified during the national industrial census in 1995. The revised (new) definition of gross industrial output value consists of 3 components: value of the finished products during the reference period, income from external processing, and value of change in semi-finished products at the end and at the beginning of the reference period.

Value of the finished products during the reference period: refers to the value of all finished (semi-finished) industrial products that are produced during the reference period without the need for further processing, checked for acceptance, packed and put into the warehouse of the enterprise, including the value of own-produced equipment and the value of products provided to the projects under construction of the enterprise, and to other non-industrial or welfare units. Value of finished products during the reference period is calculated by the quantity of products produced using own materials multiplied by the average unit prices at which products are sold (excluding value-added tax). Own-produced equipment and products produced for own use are value at cost prices as in the case of enterprise accounting. Value of finished products does not include the value of finished products (semi-finished products) that are produced using the materials from the clients who make the orders.

Income from external processing: refers to income from contracted external processing of industrial products (including processing of industrial products using materials from the clients), and the income from industrial repairing work provided to other units. Income from external processing is calculated using information from the item "products sales income" in the enterprise accounting at the prices excluding value-added tax.

For income from services such as processing, repairing and

installation of equipment provided to non-industrial units within the enterprise, if the accounting work of the enterprise is good enough to separate it from other records, and the share of such services is significant, it should also be included in the income from external processing.

Value of change in semi-finished products at the end and at the beginning of the reference period: refers to the value of change in semi-finished products at the end and at the beginning of the reference period, which generally can be obtained from accounting records of enterprises. If the enterprise accounting excludes the cost of semi-finished products, then it should not be included in the gross industrial output value, and vice versa.

(4) Changes in the coverage and method of calculation of gross industrial output value

Prior to 1984, the value of rural industry run by villages was classified into agriculture instead of industry. Since 1984, it has been included in the gross industrial output value.

Method of calculation for the gross industrial output value was modified in the industrial census in 1995. The difference in the new method as compared with the old one is outlined below:

Principle in using full value vs. processing fee: The new method stipulates that all products produced using own materials are to be calculated with full value in reporting the gross industrial output value irrespective of sophistication of production, and for external processing, it allows calculation using processing fee. In the old method, however, the use of full value or processing fee was determined by the degree of sophistication of production in different branches of industries.

Principle in determining the value of change in semi-finished products: The new method requires that value of the change in semi-finished products should be included in the gross industrial output value if it is included in the accounting record of the enterprise, otherwise it should not be included. By the old method, it is determined by the type of enterprises in terms of production cycle. If the production cycle is over 6 months, the value of change in semi-finished products is included in the gross industrial output value, otherwise it is excluded.

Difference in prices: The new method uses prices excluding value-added tax in the calculation of gross industrial output value, while the old method used prices including value-added tax.

Value-added of Industry refers to the final results of industrial production of industrial enterprises in money terms during the reference period.

Industrial value-added can be calculated by two approaches: the production approach, i.e. gross industrial output value minus intermediate input plus value-added tax, and the income approach, i.e. income for various factors used in the course of production, including depreciation of fixed assets, remuneration of labourers, net of production tax, and operating surplus. Value-added of industry in the Yearbook is calculated by production approach as following:

Value-added of industry = gross industrial output – industrial intermediate input + value-added tax

(1) Gross industrial output: refers to the total achievements of industrial production during a given period. Gross industrial output includes value of finished products, income from external processing, and value of change in semi-finished products at the end and at the beginning of the reference period. Since 1995, it was substituted by the gross industrial output value by new method.

(2) Industrial intermediate input: refers to purchased goods and paid services consumed during the industrial production of enterprises. Fees paid for services include fees paid for the services provided by material production sectors (industry, agriculture, wholesale and retail trade, construction, transport, post and telecommunications) and by non-material production sectors (insurance, banking, culture, education, scientific research, health and medical care, public administration, etc.). The determination of industrial intermediate input follows the principle that the goods and services must be purchased from outside and included in the gross industrial output, and that the goods and services are inputted into production and consumed (include low-value consumables) during the reference period.

Industrial intermediate input includes 5 components, namely direct consumption of materials, industrial intermediate input in manufacturing cost, industrial intermediate input in management cost, industrial intermediate input in marketing cost and expenditure on interest.

Capitals Obtained refers to capital actually received by the enterprise from investors that could be used as operational capitals for a long period. According to the current accounting system, capitals obtained can be classified by investors as state capital, collective capital, corporate capital, individual capital, capital from Hong Kong, Macau and Taiwan and foreign capital.

State capital: refers to capital which is formed through state-owned investment into the enterprise by government agencies or institutions that could represent the state in the investment.

Collective capital: refers to capital which is formed through state-owned investment into the enterprise by collective institutions or units that could represent the state in the investment.

Corporate capital: refers to capital which is formed through investment by other corporate units using assets which is at their disposal by law.

Individual capital: refers to capital which is formed through investment by individuals outside the enterprise or employees of the enterprise using their personal legal properties.

Capital from Hong Kong, Macau and Taiwan: refers to capital which is formed through investment by investors from

Hong Kong, Macau and Taiwan of China using their assets of various forms.

Foreign capital: refers to capital which is formed through investment by foreign investors.

Total Assets refer to all economic resources, in monetary terms, that is owned or controlled by enterprises, including properties, creditors equity and other economic rights of all forms. Classified by the degree of equitability, total assets include circulating assets, long-term investment, fixed assets, intangible assets and deferred assets, and other assets. Data on this indicator can be obtained by the year-end figures of total assets in the *Assets and Liability Table* of accounting records of enterprises.

Total of Working Capitals refer to capitals which can be cashed in or spent or consumed in an operating cycle of one year or over one year, including cash, all kinds of deposits, short term investment, receivable and payable payment for goods or deposits.

Average Value of Working Capitals refers to the average value of all working capitals of the enterprise during the reference period.

Original Value of Fixed Assets refers to the value of payment by the enterprise in building, purchasing installing reconstructing, expending or transforming a particular item of fixed assets. In general, it includes value of purchase, cost for packaging, transportation, installation, etc.

Annual Average of Net Value of Fixed Assets refer to average of the net value of fixed assets during the reference period, calculated with the following formula:

Annual Average of Net Value of Fixed Assets = sum of net value of fixed assets at the beginning and at the end of each month from January to December / 24.

Information on this indicator can be obtained from the beginning and ending figures of the original value of fixed assets and cumulative depreciation from the *Assets and Liability Table* of enterprises.

Net value of fixed assets refers to the original value of fixed assets minus depreciation over the years, i.e.:

Net value of fixed assets = original value of fixed assets – cumulative depreciation

Total Liquid Liabilities refer to enterprises' total debt payable within an operating cycle of one year or over one year, including short-term loans, notes and accounts payable, advance payments received, wages and welfare funds payable, taxes and profit payable, other payables, fees received by advance payment, etc.

Liquid liabilities feature in the short term of payment, immediate payment at the request of creditors, or payable within one year. Data on this item can be obtained from the ending figures on liquid liabilities from the *Assets and Liability Table* of enterprises.

Total Long-term Liabilities refers to the debt payable within an operating cycle of one year or over one year. It is the capital that enterprises raised from creditors for the long-term use of enterprises in addition to capitals put into the enterprise by investors, and constitutes the economic liabilities that enterprises have to repay by assets or labour services, including long-term loans, payable liabilities, long-term payable, other long-term liabilities, etc. Compared with the liquid liabilities, the long-term liabilities feature in large volume, longer term for repayment, and larger benefits for investors. Data on this item can be obtained from the ending figures on long-term liabilities from the *Assets and Liability Table* of enterprises.

Creditors' Equity refers to investors ownership of net assets of the enterprise, which is equal to the total assets of the enterprise minus its total liabilities, including the primary input actually received at the enterprise from investors, capital accumulation fund, surplus accumulation fund and undistributed profit. When the total of creditors' equity is less than zero, that indicates the liability of the enterprise is larger that its assets.

Sales Revenue of Industrial Products refers to the revenue from the sales of finished and semi-finished products and from rendering of industrial services by industrial enterprises during the reference period.

Cost of Industrial Products Sold refers to the actual cost of finished and semi-finished products sold and industrial services rendered by industrial enterprises during the reference period.

Tax and Extra Charges on Sales of Products refer to the tax on city maintenance and construction, consumption tax, resources tax and extra charges for education, which should be borne by the enterprises in selling products and providing industrial services during the reference period.

Total Profits refer to the final achievements of production and operation of the enterprises, represented by the total profits after deducting losses (loss is expressed by the negative figure). It is the sum of profits from operation, income from subsidies, investment earnings, net income from activities other than operation, and adjustment of profits and losses of previous years.

Value-added Tax Payable refers to the amount of the value-added tax which should be paid by the enterprises during the reference period. It is the sum of tax on sales, export rebate, and transferred tax on purchases of the current year, minus the tax on purchases of the current year. Value-added tax payable of small-size enterprises is determined by the taxable sales of the year multiplied by the tax rate.

Average Annual Number of Employed Persons Employed persons refer to all those who are employed in enterprises and receive remunerations therefrom, including currently working employees, retirees who are re-employed, teachers of local-run schools, as well as foreigners, staff from Hong Kong,

Macau and Taiwan, part-time employees and persons with second job who are employed by the enterprise, and employees of other units temporarily working in the enterprises, but excluding former employees who left the enterprise with their employment records still kept by the enterprises.

Average number of employed persons refers to the number of employees everyday during the reference period, calculated with the following fomula:

Monthly average number = sum of actual employees everyday in reference month/number of calendar dates in reference month

Quarterly average number = sum of monthly average number in reference quarter/3

Annual average number = sum of monthly average number in reference year/12

Ratio of Profits, Taxes and Interests to Average Assets reflects the profit-making capability of all assets of the enterprise and is a key indicator manifesting the performance and management and evaluating the profit-making potential of the enterprise. It is calculated as follows:

Ratio of Profits, Taxes and Interests to Average Assets (%) = [(total profits + total taxes + interest payment) / average assets] ×100%

In the above formula, total taxes is the sum of tax and extra charges on the sales of products and value-added tax payable; and average assets is the arithmetic mean of the sum of beginning assets and ending assets.

Ratio of Debts to Assets reflect both the operation risk and the capability of the enterprise in making use of the capital from the creditors. It is calculated as follows:

Ratio of Debts to Assets (%) = (total debts / total assets) ×100%

Both assets and debts are figures at the end of the reference period.

Turnover of Working Capital refers to the number of times of turnover of working capital in a given period of time, which reflects the speed of the turnover of working capital of industrial enterprises, and is calculated as follows:

Turnover of Working Capital=(sales revenue of products) / (average balance of total working capital)

In the above formula, average balance of total working capital refers to the arithmetic mean of the sum of working capital at the beginning and at the end of the reference period.

Ratio of Profits to Total Industrial Costs refers to the ratio of profits realized in a given period to the total costs in the same period, which reflects the economic efficiency of input cost and is calculated as follows:

Ratio of Profits to Total Industrial Cost(%)=(total profits/ total costs)×100%

Total costs in the above formula is the sum of cost of products sold, marketing cost, management cost and financial cost.

Overall Labour Productivity of Industrial Enterprises reflects efficiency of production and economic results of labour input of enterprises. The formula used is:

Overall Labour Productivity=(value added of industry) / (average number of staff and workers)

Ratio of Sales to Gross Output Value reflects the degree at which industrial products are sold. It helps to analyze the linkage between production and sales and the extent of the needs of the society that has been met by the supply of industrial products. It is calculated as follows:

Ratio of Sales to Gross Output Value=(Industrial sales / Gross industrial output value at current prices) ×100%

十五、建筑业

Construction

简要说明

一、本篇资料的主要内容

本篇资料反映我国建筑业概况和发展情况。包括建筑业企业基本情况和生产经营情况，主要指标有企业个数、从业人员数、建筑业总产值、建筑业增加值、房屋建筑面积、机械设备、资产负债、企业总收入、利润税金、劳动生产率、技术装备率等。此外，还包括勘察设计机构和人员情况主要指标。

二、本篇的统计范围

根据建筑业发展的实际情况，建筑业统计范围从2002年年报起由原具有建筑业资质等级四级及四级以上的独立核算的建筑业企业调整为具有建筑业资质的独立核算建筑业企业。

三、本篇的资料来源及调查方法

本篇建筑业企业统计数据是根据国家统计局制定的《建筑业统计报表制度》中有关资料整理汇总。建筑业统计年度报表是各级统计部门根据当地实际情况采取全面调查的方法布置、收集，由各省、自治区、直辖市统计局上报的全面报表。

勘察设计机构和人员表依据建设部制定的《勘察设计报表制度》中有关年报资料编制，由建设部提供。

Brief Introduction

I. Main Content

Data in this chapter show the general situation and the development of the construction in China. They cover the situation of production and management of the enterprises of construction, including the number of enterprises, number of employed persons, gross output value and value added of construction industry, floor space of the buildings, machinery and equipment, assets and liabilities, total revenue of enterprises, profits and taxes of enterprises, labour productivity, per capita machinery, etc. They also cover the situation of prospecting and designing institutions and the personnel.

II. Coverage of Statistics

According to the development of construction industry, starting from 2002, the coverage of construction statistics has been adjusted to include all the construction enterprises of various types of ownership with qualification certificates and with independent accounting system, instead of the original criteria that required construction enterprises of various types of ownership to have qualification certificates at or above Class 4 with independent accounting system.

III. Source of Data and Survey Methodology

Data on construction enterprises are collected in accordance with the *Reporting System of Construction Statistics* stipulated by the National Bureau of Statistics. The annual reports on construction statistics are assigned and collected by statistical bureaus at various levels through comprehensive reporting system, and provided by statistical bureaus of each province, autonomous region and municipality.

Data on prospecting and designing institutions and the personnel are provided by the Ministry of Construction, based on prospecting and designing statistical reporting scheme stipulated by the Ministry of Construction.

15-1 建筑业企业概况

Main Indicators on Construction Enterprises

年 份 Year	总 计 Total	国有企业 State-owned	集体企业 Collective-owned	港澳台商投资企业 Funded from Hong Kong, Macao and Taiwan	外商投资企业 Foreign Funded	其 他 Others
企业单位数（个） Number of Enterprises						
1980	6604	1996	4608			
1985	11150	3385	7765			
1989	13106	3927	9179			
1990	13327	4275	9052			
1995	24133	7531	15348	329	312	613
1996	41364	9109	29044	417	388	2406
1997	44017	9650	29872	491	454	3550
1998	45634	9458	28410	629	337	6800
1999	47234	9394	27197	664	341	9638
2000	47518	9030	24756	635	319	12778
2001	45893	8264	19096	622	274	17637
2002	47820	7536	13177	632	279	26196
2003	48688	6638	10425	535	287	30803
从业人员（万人） Number of Persons Employed (10 000 persons)						
1980	648.0	481.8	166.2			
1985	911.5	576.7	334.8			
1989	1004.8	614.7	390.1			
1990	1010.7	621.0	389.7			
1995	1497.9	824.3	631.9	5.0	5.4	31.3
1996	2121.9	855.9	1171.4	8.7	8.6	77.3
1997	2101.5	828.6	1148.2	8.2	9.6	106.9
1998	2030.0	738.4	1057.3	9.3	5.1	219.9
1999	2020.1	690.6	993.1	11.5	6.1	318.9
2000	1994.3	635.6	887.5	8.2	4.4	458.6
2001	2110.7	590.7	739.9	7.7	4.3	768.1
2002	2245.2	543.8	579.2	7.4	4.5	1110.4
2003	2414.3	524.3	505.6	7.0	6.0	1371.3
建筑业总产值（亿元） Gross Output Value (100 million yuan)						
1980	286.93	220.90	66.03			
1985	675.10	474.51	200.59			
1989	1282.98	878.57	404.41			
1990	1345.01	935.19	409.82			
1995	5793.75	3670.25	1899.47	33.60	33.19	157.24
1996	8282.25	4160.21	3695.68	46.85	50.51	329.00
1997	9126.48	4526.52	3925.81	63.72	70.49	539.94
1998	10061.99	4571.44	4012.01	91.94	62.52	1324.08
1999	11152.86	4861.38	4081.79	91.97	64.43	2053.29
2000	12497.60	5053.79	4035.84	99.18	67.49	3241.30
2001	15361.56	5362.81	3775.89	102.55	73.06	6047.25
2002	18527.18	5582.86	3338.50	113.87	91.38	9400.57
2003	23083.87	6060.23	3270.73	123.71	129.39	13499.81

注：1.本表1980年至1992年数据为全民和集体所有制建筑业企业数据；1993年至1995年数据为各种经济成分的建制镇以上建筑业企业数据；1996年至2001年数据为资质等级(旧资质)四级及四级以上建筑业企业数据；2002年及以后数据为所有具有资质等级的施工总承包、专业承包建筑业企业（不含劳务分包建筑业企业）数据，与以前各年不可比（以下各表同）。

2.从业人员数1993年至1997年为年平均人数。

a) Data from 1980 to 1992 are the figures of state-owned and collective-owned construction enterprises. Data from 1993 to 1995 are the figures of all economic types of construction enterprises above towns. The statistical coverage from 1996 to 2001 included the fourth and higher grades construction enterprises (old classification of grades), and that since 2002 included all grades construction enterprises, both general constructing contractors and professional contractors (excluding the construction enterprises of work subcontractors). Therefore the data were not comparable with the data of the previous years. The same as in the following table.

b) The number of employed persons refers to the annual average number from 1993 to 1997.

15-2 按登记注册类型分建筑业企业主要经济指标（2003年）

指 标		Item		合 计 Total
企业单位数	（个）	Number of Construction Enterprises	(unit)	48688
从业人员	（万人）	Number of Employed Persons	(10 000 persons)	2414.27
自有固定资产原价	（亿元）	Fixed Assets Owned (original value)	(100 million yuan)	6548.74
自有固定资产净价	（亿元）	Fixed Assets Owned (net value)	(100 million yuan)	4453.22
自有机械设备年末总台数	（万台）	Number of Machinery and Equipment Owned	(10 000 set)	800.18
自有机械设备年末净值	（亿元）	Net Value of Machinery and Equipment Owned	(100 million yuan)	2403.96
自有机械设备年末总功率	（万千瓦）	Total Power of Machinery and Equipment Owned	(10 000 kw)	11712.38
建筑业总产值	（亿元）	Gross Output Value of Construction	(100 million yuan)	23083.87
建筑业增加值	（亿元）	Value Added of Construction	(100 million yuan)	4654.71
#本年固定资产折旧		Depreciation of Fixed Assets		332.76
应付工资		Wages Payable		2618.46
应付福利费		Welfare Expenses Payable		302.45
工程结算税金及附加		Taxes and Extra Charges on Project Settle Accounts		720.29
管理费用中的税金		Taxes in Management Expenses		38.36
营业利润		Profits of Business		501.76
房屋建筑施工面积	（万平方米）	Floor Space of Buildings under Construction	(10 000 sq.m)	259377.13
房屋建筑竣工面积	（万平方米）	Floor Space of Buildings Completed	(10 000 sq.m)	122827.61
利润总额	（亿元）	Total Profits	(100 million yuan)	519.87
税金总额	（亿元）	Total Tax	(100 million yuan)	758.65
劳动生产率		Overall Labor Productivity		
按总产值计算	（元/人）	In Terms of Gross Output Value	(yuan/person)	86666
按增加值计算	（元/人）	In Terms of Value-added	(yuan/person)	17476
技术装备率	（元/人）	Value of Machines per Laborer	(yuan/person)	9957
动力装备率	（千瓦/人）	Power of Machines per Laborer	(kw/person)	4.9
房屋建筑面积竣工率	(%)	Rate of Floor Space of Buildings Completed	(%)	47.4
产值利润率	(%)	Ratio of Profit to Gross Output Value	(%)	2.3
产值利税率	(%)	Ratio of Pre-tax Profit to Gross Output Value	(%)	5.5

Main Economic Indicators on Construction Enterprises by Registration Status (2003)

内资企业 Domestic Funded	#国有 State-owned	#集体 Collective-owned	港澳台商投资企业 Funded from Hong Kong, Macao and Taiwan	#港澳台商独资企业 Solely Owned	外商投资企业 Foreign Funded	#外商独资企业 Solely Owned
47866	6638	10425	535	46	287	18
2401.20	524.32	505.57	7.04	0.36	6.04	0.13
6482.94	2389.09	916.04	34.70	1.76	31.10	0.97
4412.73	1511.59	662.28	21.09	1.11	19.41	0.55
793.48	164.98	187.96	4.08	0.13	2.62	0.09
2386.92	692.08	377.10	8.14	0.45	8.90	0.22
11646.69	3493.75	2040.02	35.99	1.36	29.69	0.94
22830.77	6060.23	3270.73	123.71	3.90	129.39	3.18
4613.41	1133.42	720.62	20.54	0.90	20.75	0.47
328.86	119.60	36.45	2.29	0.11	1.62	0.07
2597.67	607.95	435.85	10.25	0.48	10.55	0.20
300.71	81.78	47.96	0.98	0.03	0.75	0.02
712.78	190.69	104.37	3.32	0.12	4.19	0.07
37.98	11.46	7.17	0.23	0.01	0.15	
495.53	49.28	77.27	3.07	0.15	3.16	0.10
258189.61	46803.66	50488.91	463.99	22.44	723.53	37.31
122277.79	18774.06	26727.64	181.39	17.56	368.44	36.66
514.07	54.03	78.58	2.88	0.16	2.92	0.11
750.76	202.15	111.54	3.56	0.13	4.34	0.08
86326	100409	62670	134876	90466	134181	190209
17444	18779	13808	22394	20942	21523	28242
9941	13200	7459	11570	12284	14733	17037
4.9	6.7	4.0	5.1	3.7	4.9	7.3
47.4	40.1	52.9	39.1	78.3	50.9	98.3
2.3	0.9	2.4	2.3	4.1	2.3	3.5
5.5	4.2	5.8	5.2	7.4	5.6	5.8

15-3 建筑业企业主要经济指标

Main Economic Indicators on Construction Enterprises

指　标	Item	2002	2003	2003年比上年增长(%) Growth Rate of 2003 to 2002 (%)
企业单位数 （个）	Number of Construction Enterprises (unit)	47820	48688	1.8
从业人员 （万人）	Number of Employed Persons (10 000 persons)	2245.19	2414.27	7.5
自有固定资产原价 （亿元）	Original Value of Fixed Assets Owned (100 million yuan)	6183.80	6548.74	5.9
自有固定资产净价 （亿元）	Net Value of Fixed Assets Owned (100 million yuan)	4273.18	4453.22	4.2
自有机械设备年末总台数 （万台）	Total Number of Machinery and Equipment Owned (10 000 set)	754.00	800.18	6.1
自有机械设备年末净值（亿元）	Net Value of Machinery and Equipment Owned (100 million yuan)	2172.29	2403.96	10.7
自有机械设备年末总功率 （万千瓦）	Total Power of Machinery and Equipment Owned (10 000 kw)	11022.52	11712.38	6.3
建筑业总产值 （亿元）	Gross Output Value of Construction (100 million yuan)	18527.18	23083.87	24.6
建筑业增加值 （亿元）	Value Added of Construction (100 million yuan)	3822.42	4654.71	21.8
#本年固定资产折旧	Depreciation of Fixed Assets	301.05	332.76	10.5
应付工资	Wages Payable	2176.41	2618.46	20.3
应付福利费	Welfare Expenses Payable	248.49	302.45	21.7
工程结算税金及附加	Taxes and Extra Charges on Project Settle Accounts	566.76	720.29	27.1
管理费用中的税金	Taxes in Management Expenses	32.67	38.36	17.4
营业利润	Profits of Business	369.00	501.76	36.0
房屋建筑施工面积（万平方米）	Floor Space of Buildings under Construction (10 000 sq.m)	215609	259377	20.3
房屋建筑竣工面积（万平方米）	Floor Space of Buildings Completed (10 000 sq.m)	110217	122828	11.4
利润总额 （亿元）	Total Profits (100 million yuan)	370.35	519.87	40.4
税金总额 （亿元）	Total Tax (100 million yuan)	599.43	758.65	26.6
劳动生产率	Overall Labor Productivity			
按总产值计算 （元/人）	In Terms of Gross Output Value (yuan/person)	76171	86666	13.8
按增加值计算 （元/人）	In Terms of Value-added (yuan/person)	15715	17476	11.2
技术装备率 （元/人）	Value of Machines per Laborer (yuan/person)	9675	9957	2.9
动力装备率 （千瓦/人）	Power of Machines per Laborer (kw/person)	4.9	4.9	
房屋建筑面积竣工率 (%)	Rate of Floor Space of Buildings Completed (%)	51.1	47.4	
产值利润率 (%)	Ratio of Profit to Gross Output Value (%)	2.0	2.3	
产值利税率 (%)	Ratio of Pre-tax Profit to Gross Output Value (%)	5.2	5.5	

注：自2003年起，建筑业增加值核算口径有所调整。为便于比较，此表中2002年数据已做相应调整。

a) Since 2003, the statistical coverage of value added of construction have been adjusted. In order to compare, the data in 2002 have been adjusted accordingly.

15-4 各地区总承包建筑业企业主要经济指标（2003年）

Main Economic Indicators on Construction Enterprises of General Contractors by Region (2003)

地区	Region	企业单位数（个）Number of Enterprises (unit)	从业人员（人）Number of Employed Persons (person)	建筑业总产值（万元）Gross Output Value of Construction (100 million yuan)	利税总额（万元）Total Pre-Tax Profits (100 million yuan)	按增加值计算的劳动生产率（元/人）Overall Labor Productivity by Added-Value (yuan/person)
全国	**National Total**	**29359**	**21064589**	**197435733**	**10419867**	**16937**
北京	Beijing	674	451598	10643294	572931	19045
天津	Tianjin	236	167428	4021856	158058	20510
河北	Hebei	1106	864976	6774134	361023	14430
山西	Shanxi	644	513133	4895150	201580	16064
内蒙古	Inner Mongolia	549	247316	2359944	140933	15532
辽宁	Liaoning	1195	757398	8186717	386426	15593
吉林	Jilin	517	255897	3068513	134725	13665
黑龙江	Heilongjiang	958	379251	3868858	194519	14871
上海	Shanghai	927	379135	9097954	576936	24674
江苏	Jiangsu	2170	2358880	23317313	1018147	19714
浙江	Zhejiang	1645	2138429	27242585	1437563	25543
安徽	Anhui	1014	754385	5198654	264752	14243
福建	Fujian	723	476306	4727721	235254	20358
江西	Jiangxi	729	518951	3027643	155907	14104
山东	Shandong	2737	1842752	13167792	752684	12867
河南	Henan	1305	835605	5518765	249463	12757
湖北	Hubei	1221	907455	7676865	456642	17627
湖南	Hunan	1285	1035622	7506718	407909	15551
广东	Guangdong	1822	1213155	11370921	872179	21352
广西	Guangxi	631	327889	2575912	130686	16599
海南	Hainan	87	56505	362676	27412	12064
重庆	Chongqing	1265	759247	5365296	293328	14944
四川	Sichuan	2332	1891459	11043730	577303	12733
贵州	Guizhou	443	274998	2025434	107971	16744
云南	Yunnan	917	491021	3686981	197947	13821
西藏	Tibet	148	34912	284773	30108	16703
陕西	Shaanxi	634	381737	4110085	164342	14670
甘肃	Gansu	561	411922	1940046	99063	10732
青海	Qinghai	232	87579	655067	31631	13312
宁夏	Ningxia	251	69839	925588	40468	13648
新疆	Xinjiang	401	179809	2788748	141977	19371

15-5 各地区专业承包建筑业企业主要经济指标（2003年）

Main Economic Indicators on Construction Enterprises of Professional Contractors by Region (2003)

地 区	Region	企业单位数（个）Number of Enterprises (unit)	从业人员（人）Number of Employed Persons (person)	建筑业总产值（万元）Gross Output Value of Construction (100 million yuan)	利税总额（万元）Total Pre-Tax Profits (100 million yuan)	按增加值计算的劳动生产率（元/人）Overall Labor Productivity by Added-Value (yuan/person)
全 国	**National Total**	**19329**	**3078131**	**33402930**	**2365393**	**21198**
北 京	Beijing	1407	118169	2055227	126529	24751
天 津	Tianjin	648	71529	1186546	91775	29053
河 北	Hebei	478	124341	1025179	90741	20574
山 西	Shanxi	483	78143	506129	24892	13358
内蒙古	Inner Mongolia	105	18637	216631	7695	20250
辽 宁	Liaoning	1373	209392	1984077	127387	17592
吉 林	Jilin	269	47940	400768	20354	15538
黑龙江	Heilongjiang	499	62267	533020	37693	14590
上 海	Shanghai	1082	126050	2860080	223627	38956
江 苏	Jiangsu	2077	368126	4632041	283348	23137
浙 江	Zhejiang	1747	290923	4030194	339435	27911
安 徽	Anhui	683	156306	1028419	66319	15783
福 建	Fujian	720	77305	765720	71546	24646
江 西	Jiangxi	329	55754	565713	37057	18313
山 东	Shandong	1497	229778	1645826	123993	13563
河 南	Henan	422	97296	826452	48158	17552
湖 北	Hubei	525	141308	1053093	90842	19986
湖 南	Hunan	300	83484	681684	43114	17316
广 东	Guangdong	1545	279665	3792321	271354	24839
广 西	Guangxi	261	25811	242554	21249	19442
海 南	Hainan	18	4705	31377	3034	18210
重 庆	Chongqing	455	58750	496799	36261	18916
四 川	Sichuan	1068	179075	1209644	85544	16570
贵 州	Guizhou	98	18312	97473	7175	13633
云 南	Yunnan	298	31449	280976	16732	13561
西 藏	Tibet	14	1681	8654	1044	14049
陕 西	Shaanxi	119	28574	294277	12731	16117
甘 肃	Gansu	225	37487	296814	15132	20038
青 海	Qinghai	105	13922	92258	4332	10384
宁 夏	Ningxia	180	18386	154958	9421	17300
新 疆	Xinjiang	299	23566	408026	26879	23802

15-6 各地区建筑业总产值

Total Output Value of Construction by Region

单位: 万元 (10 000 yuan)

地 区	Region	1997	1998	1999	2000	2001	2002	2003
全 国	**National Total**	**91264777**	**100619922**	**111528640**	**124975961**	**153615626**	**185271753**	**230838663**
北 京	Beijing	5192363	6230089	6814102	7274774	8879099	10550535	12698521
天 津	Tianjin	1909999	2111208	2227406	2380991	2886808	4061628	5208402
河 北	Hebei	3760962	3935044	4321432	4921005	6145010	7111712	7799313
山 西	Shanxi	1920095	2178150	2397739	2393974	3114390	4469457	5401279
内蒙古	Inner Mongolia	963852	1017600	1168732	1367309	1782561	2200194	2576575
辽 宁	Liaoning	4291256	4189831	4893444	5980933	7611747	8393428	10170794
吉 林	Jilin	1369882	1460359	1713517	2391840	2740726	2926017	3469281
黑龙江	Heilongjiang	2435310	2739532	2996115	3340903	3723204	4079097	4401878
上 海	Shanghai	5524161	5859020	5683036	6223565	7215808	8222730	11958034
江 苏	Jiangsu	10716094	11962007	13299853	15388416	18218039	21995164	27949354
浙 江	Zhejiang	8773546	9425292	11282810	13837658	17684490	22829906	31272779
安 徽	Anhui	2359972	2356154	2773364	3028240	4215500	5282183	6227073
福 建	Fujian	2268855	2446658	2511292	2711420	3690460	4026874	5493441
江 西	Jiangxi	856436	893804	1022296	1164115	1691530	2450718	3593356
山 东	Shandong	6479717	7001115	7672600	8170949	9842204	11511730	14813618
河 南	Henan	2946903	3049638	3169845	3573425	4524908	5367328	6345217
湖 北	Hubei	3059698	3436527	3990201	4541767	5290240	6365491	8729958
湖 南	Hunan	2965005	3273222	3338963	3544202	4897879	5955616	8188402
广 东	Guangdong	6747406	7886723	8719500	8919834	11320549	13417808	15163242
广 西	Guangxi	1275627	1344209	1491385	1509158	1802891	2211684	2818466
海 南	Hainan	279923	308507	333933	302139	353453	415089	394053
重 庆	Chongqing	2440552	2896198	3175927	3486579	4368169	5006543	5862095
四 川	Sichuan	5206436	5977644	6495237	7138102	8228676	10725229	12253374
贵 州	Guizhou	767046	831976	966508	1090571	1502008	1811244	2122907
云 南	Yunnan	2189844	2517439	3114900	3092645	3439350	3582375	3967957
西 藏	Tibet	79519	94455	134958	168178	186832	216949	293427
陕 西	Shaanxi	1642493	1879804	2183009	2423046	2797388	3465727	4404362
甘 肃	Gansu	1056249	1133752	1187695	1251202	1473057	1923798	2236860
青 海	Qinghai	309340	355576	396528	447162	542130	733550	747325
宁 夏	Ningxia	334919	393603	482827	562352	703722	839121	1080546
新 疆	Xinjiang	1141318	1434787	1569486	2349506	2742800	3122828	3196774

15-7 各地区建筑业增加值

Value-added of Construction by Region

单位: 万元 (10 000 yuan)

地 区	Region	1997	1998	1999	2000	2001	2002	2003
全 国	**National Total**	**25405426**	**27837909**	**30222586**	**33410864**	**40235718**	**38224156**	**46547067**
北 京	Beijing	1424872	1787588	1809631	1861649	2215886	1710390	1945971
天 津	Tianjin	508102	580644	599298	596889	665186	638907	795963
河 北	Hebei	1058799	1026622	1176002	1255840	1595275	1495270	1688931
山 西	Shanxi	571361	619820	623871	659211	775992	784804	951478
内蒙古	Inner Mongolia	309691	352602	387728	415530	530331	508817	666669
辽 宁	Liaoning	1331824	1271822	1458714	1650483	2013803	1731074	1968475
吉 林	Jilin	428432	410049	477403	648043	828044	573885	622364
黑龙江	Heilongjiang	720763	796891	838384	901381	1012242	855445	959828
上 海	Shanghai	1209914	1311338	1224694	1381463	1432718	1414863	2153664
江 苏	Jiangsu	2620881	2915897	3212848	3700633	4346794	4387544	5609752
浙 江	Zhejiang	2212090	2431151	2861430	3521692	4368676	4672740	6342032
安 徽	Anhui	680801	703797	783765	837832	1195204	1185951	1359808
福 建	Fujian	618988	738348	662526	710129	954305	815704	1063081
江 西	Jiangxi	256353	262760	303880	324209	448780	553425	739617
山 东	Shandong	1894007	2020712	2162466	2269464	2740505	2579653	3157332
河 南	Henan	795700	875188	915452	1006563	1184251	1070946	1273423
湖 北	Hubei	951010	1063379	1208960	1346062	1438777	1423250	1914661
湖 南	Hunan	836320	876333	909667	965511	1307676	1279692	1724388
广 东	Guangdong	1964243	2230076	2492533	2509568	3212604	2932624	3281041
广 西	Guangxi	378210	436240	463926	495053	536363	524687	611761
海 南	Hainan	73788	67747	77185	68036	78689	89284	88847
重 庆	Chongqing	677742	783224	870648	912266	1207981	1139108	1287202
四 川	Sichuan	1593421	1776678	1855648	2073881	2442159	2528302	2678743
贵 州	Guizhou	230913	244071	276657	313945	411845	411619	486887
云 南	Yunnan	613405	678146	857556	819742	884943	761495	791021
西 藏	Tibet	33468	41089	40991	45811	42524	58839	66508
陕 西	Shaanxi	508819	509819	557333	591203	683851	622949	697852
甘 肃	Gansu	347624	380112	388427	402912	459363	483668	549941
青 海	Qinghai	97950	117884	137154	162241	161192	150146	158293
宁 夏	Ningxia	110707	120438	145697	173888	204157	191314	249257
新 疆	Xinjiang	345229	407445	442113	789737	855600	647761	662277

注：自2003年起，建筑业增加值核算口径有所调整。为便于比较，本表按新口径对2002年的数据进行了调整。

a) Since 2003, the statistical coverage of value added of construction have been adjusted. In order to compare, the data in 2002 have been adjusted accordingly.

15-8 各地区建筑业企业利税总额

Total Pre-Tax Profits of Construction Enterprises by Region

单位: 万元 (10 000 yuan)

地 区	Region	1997	1998	1999	2000	2001	2002	2003
全 国	**National Total**	**3815831**	**4192554**	**4944082**	**5792206**	**7934252**	**9697797**	**12785260**
北 京	Beijing	253878	305450	341341	385714	465129	584471	699460
天 津	Tianjin	71020	82554	80172	96435	121086	191909	249833
河 北	Hebei	166060	165394	207616	224663	416927	381119	451764
山 西	Shanxi	54660	59524	72317	93678	119342	178827	226472
内蒙古	Inner Mongolia	29568	39201	51242	58719	81525	113728	148628
辽 宁	Liaoning	126853	89493	183582	255827	388175	406326	513813
吉 林	Jilin	28550	30355	54198	88242	136570	128794	155079
黑龙江	Heilongjiang	71737	90084	109410	134863	168938	176265	232212
上 海	Shanghai	264634	273404	278825	342818	386166	480415	800563
江 苏	Jiangsu	369130	416444	443934	585377	740637	936746	1301495
浙 江	Zhejiang	425246	476539	571252	740235	1009064	1284708	1776998
安 徽	Anhui	81957	80036	105523	126076	217112	275184	331071
福 建	Fujian	109996	129438	120981	141997	236135	231295	306800
江 西	Jiangxi	29593	30587	37586	44866	72464	134489	192964
山 东	Shandong	359251	379508	416839	419264	561028	666717	876677
河 南	Henan	112364	113707	132961	148742	202791	245271	297621
湖 北	Hubei	123314	151995	190966	216898	278040	390134	547484
湖 南	Hunan	122324	115843	121018	153028	255126	319042	451023
广 东	Guangdong	350041	424246	522531	543688	800994	888679	1143533
广 西	Guangxi	53428	65467	63830	64151	85386	125653	151935
海 南	Hainan	16135	9686	17655	14801	19191	30539	30446
重 庆	Chongqing	100613	117637	133598	152870	236729	262773	329589
四 川	Sichuan	209659	229653	268304	318422	415125	569936	662847
贵 州	Guizhou	24536	26509	32956	47008	71097	95505	115146
云 南	Yunnan	106361	119929	154874	160638	159381	167754	214679
西 藏	Tibet	6225	6745	8358	12805	16876	26030	31152
陕 西	Shaanxi	49080	50480	67403	84901	111932	144683	177073
甘 肃	Gansu	48910	55147	61307	67918	71882	103144	114195
青 海	Qinghai	8849	9832	8921	18312	25542	36704	35963
宁 夏	Ningxia	9886	10074	19804	29994	35175	37429	49889
新 疆	Xinjiang	31970	37597	64778	19257	28688	83528	168856

15-9 各地区建筑业企业利润总额

Total Profits of Construction Enterprises by Region

单位: 万元 (10 000 yuan)

地 区	Region	1997	1998	1999	2000	2001	2002	2003
全 国	**National Total**	**1099170**	**1173285**	**1547982**	**1920635**	**2943904**	**3703532**	**5198716**
北 京	Beijing	104320	123744	135595	163561	187424	251894	299739
天 津	Tianjin	21445	29350	21991	27993	37517	73614	97029
河 北	Hebei	48968	40479	62006	67370	126382	146051	180629
山 西	Shanxi	-828	-10161	-882	-514	17683	37332	47523
内蒙古	Inner Mongolia	-5999	3241	13076	14561	19053	40988	55627
辽 宁	Liaoning	-8711	-42535	30962	66730	148186	127030	165123
吉 林	Jilin	-15110	-16523	790	17339	36912	29628	23497
黑龙江	Heilongjiang	3122	10870	23741	31070	53572	45741	54530
上 海	Shanghai	126383	130723	141889	184252	191779	235432	409236
江 苏	Jiangsu	113507	138139	121082	206569	258129	353159	547982
浙 江	Zhejiang	170603	194607	235308	318850	458497	606604	832163
安 徽	Anhui	10221	774	15904	28127	72552	90671	110443
福 建	Fujian	28436	26052	25773	25831	89109	91740	115820
江 西	Jiangxi	-1710	-2548	3395	6157	15635	40478	58418
山 东	Shandong	161762	162328	176337	182235	262288	312306	410531
河 南	Henan	26029	21442	37901	31281	58802	75985	94049
湖 北	Hubei	16076	38036	51890	58425	88285	129633	190795
湖 南	Hunan	29655	19488	17230	43938	86497	111240	154992
广 东	Guangdong	131085	153969	199092	203926	373276	373902	571518
广 西	Guangxi	8418	16059	13227	9147	22519	43171	47095
海 南	Hainan	4868	295	6439	3907	6709	14339	14343
重 庆	Chongqing	27203	33093	41582	49310	90786	99587	137489
四 川	Sichuan	51222	58555	76014	100995	150604	213687	259289
贵 州	Guizhou	-286	638	1775	9855	17334	25997	45525
云 南	Yunnan	34195	35929	53070	58350	46654	46553	80134
西 藏	Tibet	4858	4392	5033	7385	11402	14307	18879
陕 西	Shaanxi	3517	-3552	5799	14497	24786	34906	46895
甘 肃	Gansu	10906	14455	16917	19977	19906	22434	33042
青 海	Qinghai	-797	-1555	-3873	3812	5249	13780	13601
宁 夏	Ningxia	157	-622	5559	13722	13863	12354	15575
新 疆	Xinjiang	-4347	-5875	13359	-48022	-47485	-11011	67205

15-10 各地区建筑业劳动生产率

Labor Productivity of Construction Enterprises by Region

按建筑业增加值计算。

Calculated in terms of value-added of construction.

单位: 元/人 (yuan/person)

地 区	Region	1997	1998	1999	2000	2001	2002	2003
全 国	**National Average**	**12089**	**13350**	**14451**	**15929**	**17621**	**15715**	**17476**
北 京	Beijing	17736	21203	21900	22553	26435	19100	19916
天 津	Tianjin	17364	19791	20875	21765	25736	18562	22475
河 北	Hebei	10785	10807	12360	13070	15023	13352	15169
山 西	Shanxi	12101	14249	15071	16824	18118	13638	15705
内蒙古	Inner Mongolia	9529	11716	11753	11913	13509	12029	15802
辽 宁	Liaoning	11883	12163	13948	15062	16867	14737	15966
吉 林	Jilin	12059	11988	13355	16594	21197	13709	13900
黑龙江	Heilongjiang	11220	12917	13462	13991	15559	13157	14835
上 海	Shanghai	20666	23038	21488	24375	23565	23005	27720
江 苏	Jiangsu	12683	12904	14540	16793	18823	17455	20185
浙 江	Zhejiang	15863	17059	19013	21228	23593	23291	25842
安 徽	Anhui	10080	10902	11195	11738	13259	13375	14501
福 建	Fujian	12835	17159	16826	17061	22417	19102	20956
江 西	Jiangxi	7566	8749	10455	11240	13428	13089	14578
山 东	Shandong	10889	12026	12615	12517	13555	12522	12943
河 南	Henan	8501	10228	11656	12766	13628	11577	13257
湖 北	Hubei	12499	12869	14105	16268	17315	15535	17932
湖 南	Hunan	10297	10594	11787	12697	14987	14337	15700
广 东	Guangdong	14396	16332	17523	19829	22559	19978	22056
广 西	Guangxi	10578	12537	13273	15308	15449	14606	16816
海 南	Hainan	8198	9463	12660	11868	11821	12685	12482
重 庆	Chongqing	9826	10245	11656	12859	14526	13636	15246
四 川	Sichuan	10331	11163	11589	13118	14223	12897	13062
贵 州	Guizhou	9780	11386	12296	14311	16162	15169	16548
云 南	Yunnan	11432	12717	14653	15531	16089	14717	13803
西 藏	Tibet	19937	23931	16375	17105	16676	19987	16593
陕 西	Shaanxi	10644	11827	13599	14559	15160	13090	14769
甘 肃	Gansu	8207	10728	11203	11701	12594	10998	11520
青 海	Qinghai	10241	12030	13505	15348	15508	12325	12930
宁 夏	Ningxia	10486	10448	11699	13895	15211	13036	14177
新 疆	Xinjiang	11739	13545	15660	25209	26411	17966	19854

注: 自2003年起，建筑业增加值核算口径有所调整,相应的按增加值计算的劳动生产率口径也发生了变化。为便于比较，本表按新口径对2002年的数据进行了调整。

a) Since 2003, the statistical standard of value added of construction has been adjusted, the labor productivity of value added have been changed accordingly. In order to compare, the 2002's data in the table have been adjusted by the new statistical standard correspondingly.

15-11 各地区按登记注册类型分建筑业企业单位数（2003年）

Number of Construction Enterprises by Registration Status and Region (2003)

单位: 个 (unit)

地 区	Region	合 计 Total	内资企业 Domestic Funded	#国 有 State-owned	#集 体 Collective-owned	港澳台商投资企业 Funded from Hong Kong, Macao and Taiwan	#港澳台商独资企业 Solely Owned	外商投资企 业 Foreign Funded	#外商独资企业 Solely Owned
全 国	**National Total**	**48688**	**47866**	**6638**	**10425**	**535**	**46**	**287**	**18**
北 京	Beijing	2081	1988	260	366	55	1	38	
天 津	Tianjin	884	861	151	192	15		8	
河 北	Hebei	1584	1577	242	295	4	1	3	
山 西	Shanxi	1127	1114	211	194	11		2	
内蒙古	Inner Mongolia	654	650	37	30	2	1	2	
辽 宁	Liaoning	2568	2490	391	603	32		46	2
吉 林	Jilin	786	775	226	154	7	1	4	1
黑龙江	Heilongjiang	1457	1450	237	266	2	1	5	
上 海	Shanghai	2009	1859	196	304	105	1	45	
江 苏	Jiangsu	4247	4181	380	737	39		27	1
浙 江	Zhejiang	3392	3358	163	329	20	1	14	2
安 徽	Anhui	1697	1682	222	445	9	2	6	2
福 建	Fujian	1443	1385	125	305	44	5	14	2
江 西	Jiangxi	1058	1043	205	343	10	2	5	2
山 东	Shandong	4234	4172	431	1141	42	10	20	2
河 南	Henan	1727	1715	385	470	8		4	
湖 北	Hubei	1746	1730	402	366	7	2	9	
湖 南	Hunan	1585	1580	273	537	5	1		
广 东	Guangdong	3367	3279	541	728	72	7	16	1
广 西	Guangxi	892	886	181	343	3		3	
海 南	Hainan	105	101	43	28	2		2	1
重 庆	Chongqing	1720	1707	124	288	7	1	6	1
四 川	Sichuan	3400	3379	334	773	15	6	6	
贵 州	Guizhou	541	539	141	176	2			
云 南	Yunnan	1215	1206	120	315	8	1	1	1
西 藏	Tibet	162	161	37	69	1	1		
陕 西	Shaanxi	753	753	147	252				
甘 肃	Gansu	786	784	153	201	1		1	
青 海	Qinghai	337	335	76	66	2	1		
宁 夏	Ningxia	431	429	84	47	2			
新 疆	Xinjiang	700	697	120	62	3			

15-12 各地区按登记注册类型分建筑业企业从业人员（2003年）

Number of Staff and Workers in Construction Enterprises by Registration Status and Region (2003)

单位：人 (person)

地 区	Region	合 计 Total	内资企业 Domestic Funded	#国 有 State-owned	#集 体 Collective-owned	港澳台商投资企业 Funded from Hong Kong, Macao and Taiwan	#港澳台商独资企业 Solely Owned	外商投资企业 Foreign Funded	#外商独资企业 Solely Owned
全 国	**National Total**	**24142720**	**24011967**	**5243158**	**5055656**	**70362**	**3626**	**60391**	**1286**
北 京	Beijing	569767	560816	167641	113587	3607	23	5344	
天 津	Tianjin	238957	237090	74372	57480	1446		421	
河 北	Hebei	989317	988668	211856	160377	186	30	463	
山 西	Shanxi	591276	587933	192435	98992	2658		685	
内蒙古	Inner Mongolia	265953	265528	20991	6468	255	7	170	
辽 宁	Liaoning	966790	950451	234442	221808	3369		12970	45
吉 林	Jilin	303837	302474	126955	44544	750	15	613	20
黑龙江	Heilongjiang	441518	439999	115644	59646	60	56	1459	
上 海	Shanghai	505185	490656	91228	56786	8911	5	5618	
江 苏	Jiangsu	2727006	2712028	300169	531438	8382		6596	115
浙 江	Zhejiang	2429352	2417538	113200	263700	3726	24	8088	152
安 徽	Anhui	910691	907115	200738	279715	1734	613	1842	268
福 建	Fujian	553611	546727	98128	146733	4231	247	2653	178
江 西	Jiangxi	574705	573274	165476	179484	1091	50	340	40
山 东	Shandong	2072530	2061192	315780	597983	5321	482	6017	145
河 南	Henan	932901	930797	288922	193922	1756		348	
湖 北	Hubei	1048763	1045719	342050	183772	763	153	2281	
湖 南	Hunan	1119106	1116757	303758	317664	2349	246		
广 东	Guangdong	1492820	1475954	361418	424003	14026	908	2840	211
广 西	Guangxi	353700	353083	163237	104734	276		341	
海 南	Hainan	61210	60951	34037	13522	199		60	20
重 庆	Chongqing	817997	814741	96864	121318	2673	64	583	40
四 川	Sichuan	2070534	2068567	538412	417915	1402	552	565	
贵 州	Guizhou	293310	293242	175904	50544	68			
云 南	Yunnan	522470	521896	116646	131760	522	25	52	52
西 藏	Tibet	36593	36522	10078	15706	71	71		
陕 西	Shaanxi	410311	410311	139414	94601				
甘 肃	Gansu	449409	449353	104619	131675	14		42	
青 海	Qinghai	101501	101326	38859	18705	175	55		
宁 夏	Ningxia	88225	88026	28130	7629	199			
新 疆	Xinjiang	203375	203233	71755	9445	142			

15-13 建筑业企业技术装备情况

Number and Power of Machinery and Equipment Owned by Construction Enterprises

年份 地区	Year Region	自有机械设备年末总台数（台） Number of Machinery and Equipment Owned (set)	自有机械设备年末总功率（万千瓦） Total Power of Machinery and Equipment Owned (10 000 kw)	#施工机械功率 Power of Construction Machines	自有机械设备年末净值（万元） Net Value of Machinery and Equipment Owned (10 000yuan)	技术装备率（元/人） Value of Machines per Laborer (yuan/person)	动力装备率（千瓦/人） Power of Machines per Laborer (kw/person)
	1991	2528110	4250.2	2780.6	2722151	2572	4.0
	1992	2531578	4431.9	3006.6	3147398	2719	3.8
	1993	2608091	4948.9	3349.6	4671699	4105	4.3
	1994	2952629	5712.7	4012.5	4981982	3446	4.0
	1995	3482784	7056.5	4399.4	6386383	4264	4.7
	1996	5649612	9804.8	6448.9	8814352	4154	4.6
	1997	5604603	8668.5	6782.4	9938659	4729	4.1
	1998	5833748	8656.5	6641.1	10407189	5127	4.3
	1999	6110175	9077.8	6973.0	11628317	5756	4.5
	2000	6259885	9228.1	7100.1	12572317	6304	4.6
	2001	7022174	10251.7	8017.5	15062491	7136	4.9
	2002	7540011	11022.5	8664.0	21722927	9675	4.9
	2003	8001782	11712.4	9156.4	24039576	9957	4.9
北京	Beijing	230085	511.6	392.5	715296	12554	9.0
天津	Tianjin	105602	227.2	163.5	580864	24308	9.5
河北	Hebei	443997	575.4	416.0	1046003	10573	5.8
山西	Shanxi	215962	318.1	247.4	644556	10901	5.4
内蒙古	Inner Mongolia	102345	182.0	149.1	364427	13703	6.8
辽宁	Liaoning	294589	612.5	461.8	1188941	12298	6.3
吉林	Jilin	101530	216.5	168.0	410691	13517	7.1
黑龙江	Heilongjiang	172595	390.6	310.1	825358	18694	8.9
上海	Shanghai	162748	255.8	219.8	682087	13502	5.1
江苏	Jiangsu	726169	1030.9	875.4	2163835	7935	3.8
浙江	Zhejiang	630150	779.7	682.0	1858867	7652	3.2
安徽	Anhui	351747	381.6	310.0	721914	7927	4.2
福建	Fujian	185389	250.1	205.0	509383	9201	4.5
江西	Jiangxi	123928	200.0	148.3	379249	6599	3.5
山东	Shandong	549491	740.1	596.0	1486019	7170	3.6
河南	Henan	398267	504.9	357.6	1015098	10881	5.4
湖北	Hubei	426493	561.0	418.6	1251645	11934	5.4
湖南	Hunan	386375	521.2	430.0	988198	8830	4.7
广东	Guangdong	668101	860.6	672.9	1627471	10902	5.8
广西	Guangxi	187732	238.8	177.1	365119	10323	6.8
海南	Hainan	16973	30.3	22.8	51472	8409	4.9
重庆	Chongqing	201606	276.8	224.6	667199	8156	3.4
四川	Sichuan	484080	744.9	585.5	1802446	8705	3.6
贵州	Guizhou	68367	117.5	85.9	227425	7754	4.0
云南	Yunnan	224232	308.1	213.3	647840	12400	5.9
西藏	Tibet	7244	16.0	10.3	45820	12522	4.4
陕西	Shaanxi	155839	255.7	163.1	530978	12941	6.2
甘肃	Gansu	188275	240.4	184.2	482617	10739	5.4
青海	Qinghai	42820	72.2	54.4	176329	17372	7.1
宁夏	Ningxia	48138	85.5	68.4	186564	21146	9.7
新疆	Xinjiang	100913	206.5	142.9	395865	19465	10.2

15-14 国有建筑业企业技术装备情况

Number and Power of Machinery and Equipment of State-owned Construction Enterprises

年份 Year 地区 Region		自有机械设备年末总台数（台）Number of Machinery and Equipment Owned (set)	自有机械设备年末总功率（万千瓦）Total Power of Machinery and Equipment Owned (10 000 kw)	#施工机械功率 Power of Construction Machinery	自有机械设备年末净值（万元）Net Value of Machinery and Equipment Owned (10 000yuan)	技术装备率（元/人）Value of Machinery per Laborer (yuan/person)	动力装备率（千瓦/人）Power of Machinery per Laborer (kw/person)
	1991	1519637	3248.9	2036.3	2213621	3465	5.1
	1992	1410064	3314.6	2137.4	2464943	3618	4.9
	1993	1309360	3323.8	2149.6	2848367	4335	5.1
	1994	1476295	3900.2	2555.7	3567576	4361	4.8
	1995	1637276	3984.6	2780.5	4161384	5048	4.8
	1996	1870826	4213.3	2995.3	4692164	5482	4.9
	1997	1865910	4419.9	3222.3	5211213	6289	5.3
	1998	1818321	4343.2	3157.3	5180338	7016	5.9
	1999	1876329	4405.0	3189.1	5548440	8035	6.4
	2000	1822716	4150.8	2996.3	5485356	8631	6.5
	2001	1831423	4008.7	2928.1	5561988	9417	6.8
	2002	1710768	3663.2	2711.6	6811241	12527	6.7
	2003	1649774	3493.8	2571.8	6920800	13200	6.7
北京	Beijing	57505	177.2	121.5	252916	15087	10.6
天津	Tianjin	35425	86.0	62.4	208231	27999	11.6
河北	Hebei	79429	142.4	98.1	262434	12387	6.7
山西	Shanxi	56345	98.5	66.5	184876	9607	5.1
内蒙古	Inner Mongolia	8436	24.0	20.4	64344	30653	11.4
辽宁	Liaoning	74120	217.8	158.5	437486	18661	9.3
吉林	Jilin	46249	105.2	75.7	172122	13558	8.3
黑龙江	Heilongjiang	44986	116.3	93.5	188415	16293	10.1
上海	Shanghai	29886	66.5	52.5	149074	16341	7.3
江苏	Jiangsu	107142	216.7	170.0	414709	13816	7.2
浙江	Zhejiang	32185	69.8	54.7	169458	14970	6.2
安徽	Anhui	60366	114.6	89.4	201851	10055	5.7
福建	Fujian	23186	50.5	38.7	104046	10603	5.2
江西	Jiangxi	35489	101.7	67.2	175746	10621	6.1
山东	Shandong	76201	174.0	136.3	351096	11118	5.5
河南	Henan	125977	210.7	148.1	424163	14681	7.3
湖北	Hubei	132851	234.1	173.5	530247	15502	6.8
湖南	Hunan	91220	186.5	146.9	325343	10711	6.1
广东	Guangdong	169158	260.4	208.6	473240	13094	7.2
广西	Guangxi	44625	102.3	75.1	165822	10158	6.3
海南	Hainan	7227	18.4	15.1	28074	8248	5.4
重庆	Chongqing	22039	45.2	33.0	109133	11267	4.7
四川	Sichuan	93141	212.2	159.5	631513	11729	3.9
贵州	Guizhou	32354	69.3	50.1	140461	7985	3.9
云南	Yunnan	30020	82.2	43.9	142784	12241	7.1
西藏	Tibet	2541	7.7	3.6	13823	13716	7.6
陕西	Shaanxi	39050	83.2	53.1	156033	11192	6.0
甘肃	Gansu	37239	84.3	58.1	157343	15040	8.1
青海	Qinghai	15535	35.3	28.0	92897	23906	9.1
宁夏	Ningxia	12989	28.6	22.6	52210	18560	10.2
新疆	Xinjiang	26858	72.1	47.3	140910	19638	10.1

15-15 各地区建筑业总产值（2003年）

Total Output Value of Construction by Region (2003)

单位：万元 (10 000 yuan)

地 区	Region	建筑业总产值 Total Output Value	建筑工程产值 Output Value of Construction	安装工程产值 Output Value of Installation	其 他 Others
全 国	**National Total**	**230838663**	**195087179**	**25764020**	**9987464**
北 京	Beijing	12698521	11053775	1321891	322855
天 津	Tianjin	5208402	4305105	743489	159808
河 北	Hebei	7799313	6674726	877957	246630
山 西	Shanxi	5401279	4447468	571813	381998
内蒙古	Inner Mongolia	2576575	2224610	301201	50764
辽 宁	Liaoning	10170794	8200795	1647527	322472
吉 林	Jilin	3469281	2911903	425335	132043
黑龙江	Heilongjiang	4401878	3556538	702789	142551
上 海	Shanghai	11958034	9497197	1705448	755389
江 苏	Jiangsu	27949354	23906977	2621444	1420933
浙 江	Zhejiang	31272779	26845397	3268934	1158448
安 徽	Anhui	6227073	5271049	619029	336995
福 建	Fujian	5493441	4685345	622960	185136
江 西	Jiangxi	3593356	3101774	315244	176338
山 东	Shandong	14813618	12264332	2006307	542979
河 南	Henan	6345217	5237707	825421	282089
湖 北	Hubei	8729958	7653788	518761	557409
湖 南	Hunan	8188402	6904174	594925	689303
广 东	Guangdong	15163242	12518142	2210432	434668
广 西	Guangxi	2818466	2427466	277609	113391
海 南	Hainan	394053	361312	29083	3658
重 庆	Chongqing	5862095	5268331	421868	171896
四 川	Sichuan	12253374	10224002	1203240	826132
贵 州	Guizhou	2122907	1754241	311704	56962
云 南	Yunnan	3967957	3512085	310567	145305
西 藏	Tibet	293427	238109	44307	11011
陕 西	Shaanxi	4404362	4025666	306197	72499
甘 肃	Gansu	2236860	1755107	404701	77052
青 海	Qinghai	747325	622176	91853	33296
宁 夏	Ningxia	1080546	929613	125449	25484
新 疆	Xinjiang	3196774	2708269	336535	151970

15-16 各地区按登记注册类型分建筑业总产值（2003年）

Total Output Value of Construction by Registration Status and Region (2003)

单位：万元 (10 000 yuan)

地区	Region	合计 Total	内资企业 Domestic Funded	#国有 State-owned	#集体 Collective-owned	港澳台商投资企业 Funded from Hong Kong, Macao and Taiwan	#港澳台商独资企业 Solely Owned	外商投资企业 Foreign Funded	#外商独资企业 Solely Owned
全　国	**National Total**	**230838663**	**228307659**	**60602331**	**32707323**	**1237133**	**38991**	**1293871**	**31803**
北　京	Beijing	12698521	12381683	4687770	1553928	103388	254	213450	
天　津	Tianjin	5208402	5146992	1976613	566917	41028		20382	
河　北	Hebei	7799313	7794134	2383363	891609	673	204	4506	
山　西	Shanxi	5401279	5378380	1779430	308499	14418		8481	
内蒙古	Inner Mongolia	2576575	2571697	363435	69186	3678	20	1200	
辽　宁	Liaoning	10170794	9817204	3095257	1493295	65716		287874	1022
吉　林	Jilin	3469281	3448325	1340345	267291	7785	620	13171	153
黑龙江	Heilongjiang	4401878	4353777	1207479	518959	1088	900	47013	
上　海	Shanghai	11958034	11462516	2303917	1304581	342481	28	153037	
江　苏	Jiangsu	27949354	27677315	3593289	4423057	111385		160654	6617
浙　江	Zhejiang	31272779	31037435	1793672	2701990	117623	183	117721	2297
安　徽	Anhui	6227073	6203736	1851883	1247544	14496	5895	8841	467
福　建	Fujian	5493441	5402028	1569278	1058277	49277	1466	42136	10515
江　西	Jiangxi	3593356	3577149	1549165	992374	13488	458	2719	341
山　东	Shandong	14813618	14657859	3629272	3319385	46661	3206	109098	951
河　南	Henan	6345217	6323782	2667597	885343	15077		6358	
湖　北	Hubei	8729958	8716276	3336842	900662	2998	1299	10684	
湖　南	Hunan	8188402	8172288	3097194	1747798	16114	2296		
广　东	Guangdong	15163242	14874297	4489568	2822297	229302	16578	59643	8924
广　西	Guangxi	2818466	2806789	1586648	589562	861		10816	
海　南	Hainan	394053	390201	243122	75527	1932		1920	214
重　庆	Chongqing	5862095	5836081	916546	749038	19358	258	6656	172
四　川	Sichuan	12253374	12235888	3624607	2017665	10283	4151	7203	
贵　州	Guizhou	2122907	2122514	1527831	234933	393			
云　南	Yunnan	3967957	3965996	1275186	660468	1831	637	130	130
西　藏	Tibet	293427	293069	104398	72864	358	358		
陕　西	Shaanxi	4404362	4404362	2021271	452396				
甘　肃	Gansu	2236860	2236485	839912	492137	197		178	
青　海	Qinghai	747325	745985	436592	70417	1340	180		
宁　夏	Ningxia	1080546	1078901	365480	74272	1645			
新　疆	Xinjiang	3196774	3194515	945369	145052	2259			

15-17 各地区按行业分建筑业总产值（2003年）

Total Output Value of Construction by Branch and Region (2003)

单位：万元 (10 000 yuan)

地区	Region	建筑业总产值 Total Output Value of Construction	房屋和土木工程建筑业 Building and Civil Engineering	房屋工程建筑 Building	土木工程建筑 Civil Engineering	建筑安装业 Construction Installation	建筑装饰业 Construction Decoration	其他建筑业 Other Construction
全国	**National Total**	**230838663**	**201385904**	**143168458**	**58217446**	**18402815**	**8091824**	**2958120**
北京	Beijing	12698521	10435684	8057795	2377889	1351905	796961	113971
天津	Tianjin	5208402	4267202	1814471	2452731	716208	162491	62501
河北	Hebei	7799313	6991708	5458254	1533454	577155	134241	96209
山西	Shanxi	5401279	5010169	1523715	3486454	225892	87715	77503
内蒙古	Inner Mongolia	2576575	2445579	1610510	835069	108553	14138	8305
辽宁	Liaoning	10170794	8399122	5073352	3325770	1157791	528109	85772
吉林	Jilin	3469281	3218801	2320245	898556	193781	48475	8224
黑龙江	Heilongjiang	4401878	3566468	2430821	1135647	738088	86427	10895
上海	Shanghai	11958034	9517513	6664647	2852866	1157545	1033512	249464
江苏	Jiangsu	27949354	23971249	18709098	5262151	2415489	1067286	495330
浙江	Zhejiang	31272779	27923071	21672418	6250653	1978029	996223	375456
安徽	Anhui	6227073	5575966	4062184	1513782	351572	199497	100038
福建	Fujian	5493441	4689126	3447554	1241572	479388	236782	88145
江西	Jiangxi	3593356	3227637	2149397	1078240	254113	100639	10967
山东	Shandong	14813618	12869314	10399311	2470003	1516965	311424	115915
河南	Henan	6345217	5633373	3346899	2286474	534623	102572	74649
湖北	Hubei	8729958	7920378	4944041	2976337	388280	129075	292225
湖南	Hunan	8188402	7691784	5644029	2047755	391028	77925	27665
广东	Guangdong	15163242	12148059	9052419	3095640	1510589	1286242	218352
广西	Guangxi	2818466	2431054	1725214	705840	272633	52082	62697
海南	Hainan	394053	357108	291786	65322	21335	14938	672
重庆	Chongqing	5862095	5382569	4778661	603908	291620	144872	43034
四川	Sichuan	12253374	11322844	8280515	3042329	574272	236043	120215
贵州	Guizhou	2122907	1927197	978855	948342	173658	15115	6937
云南	Yunnan	3967957	3616737	2325792	1290945	214734	102198	34288
西藏	Tibet	293427	287016	151925	135091	5505	786	120
陕西	Shaanxi	4404362	4222933	1896817	2326116	127184	30352	23893
甘肃	Gansu	2236860	1926672	1399951	526721	257304	29551	23333
青海	Qinghai	747325	605965	266816	339149	109449	15208	16703
宁夏	Ningxia	1080546	1029153	597832	431321	28083	21471	1839
新疆	Xinjiang	3196774	2774453	2093134	681319	280044	29474	112803

15-18 各地区按资质等级分总承包建筑业总产值（2003年）

Total Output Value of Construction of General Contractor by Qualification Criteria and by Region (2003)

单位：万元 (10 000 yuan)

地区	Region	合计 Total	特级 Special Grade	一级 First Grade	二级 Second Grade	三级及以下 Third Grade and below
全国	**National Total**	**197435733**	**18425446**	**76392700**	**55705402**	**46912185**
北京	Beijing	10643294	2036732	5960284	1943908	702370
天津	Tianjin	4021856	970179	2075197	690239	286241
河北	Hebei	6774134	405685	2798941	2145880	1423628
山西	Shanxi	4895150	2204471	1428717	610931	651031
内蒙古	Inner Mongolia	2359944	148796	644476	749366	817306
辽宁	Liaoning	8186717	816530	3168405	1992121	2209661
吉林	Jilin	3068513	509189	1380911	542631	635782
黑龙江	Heilongjiang	3868858	547145	1293585	1220385	807743
上海	Shanghai	9097954	1007732	2977954	2960163	2152105
江苏	Jiangsu	23317313	1668009	8587154	6705852	6356298
浙江	Zhejiang	27242585	1918407	12284913	7897458	5141807
安徽	Anhui	5198654	815530	1236001	1509395	1637728
福建	Fujian	4727721	71433	1810032	1756648	1089608
江西	Jiangxi	3027643		1150116	732092	1145435
山东	Shandong	13167792	328654	4828376	3612590	4398172
河南	Henan	5518765	94913	2343407	1750822	1329623
湖北	Hubei	7676865	1940486	1955346	1837992	1943041
湖南	Hunan	7506718	396965	2892203	2117911	2099639
广东	Guangdong	11370921	745098	4493615	3363056	2769152
广西	Guangxi	2575912	162659	929556	852806	630891
海南	Hainan	362676		183121	123619	55936
重庆	Chongqing	5365296		1457974	2410977	1496345
四川	Sichuan	11043730	364467	3468307	3819976	3390980
贵州	Guizhou	2025434	96097	1111784	487563	329990
云南	Yunnan	3686981	248117	1324369	1044601	1069894
西藏	Tibet	284773		7112	191915	85746
陕西	Shaanxi	4110085	772432	1968591	777933	591129
甘肃	Gansu	1940046		697295	781991	460760
青海	Qinghai	655067		326709	148305	180053
宁夏	Ningxia	925588		311799	263884	349905
新疆	Xinjiang	2788748	155720	1296450	662392	674186

15-19 各地区按资质等级分专业承包建筑业总产值（2003年）

Total Output Value of Construction of Professional Contractors by Qualification Criteria and by Region (2003)

单位：万元 (10 000 yuan)

地区	Region	合计 Total	一级 First Grade	二级 Second Grade	三级及以下 Third Grade and below
全国	**National Total**	**33402930**	**10742470**	**11293617**	**11366843**
北京	Beijing	2055227	765251	692238	597738
天津	Tianjin	1186546	478268	294439	413839
河北	Hebei	1025179	370096	455069	200014
山西	Shanxi	506129	141540	197149	167440
内蒙古	Inner Mongolia	216631	94166	60437	62028
辽宁	Liaoning	1984077	590370	680017	713690
吉林	Jilin	400768	20764	239084	140920
黑龙江	Heilongjiang	533020	132476	277938	122606
上海	Shanghai	2860080	1237706	892238	730136
江苏	Jiangsu	4632041	1306804	1285716	2039521
浙江	Zhejiang	4030194	1112794	1342356	1575044
安徽	Anhui	1028419	191767	401171	435481
福建	Fujian	765720	208531	330766	226423
江西	Jiangxi	565713	260135	166862	138716
山东	Shandong	1645826	267743	590116	787967
河南	Henan	826452	419390	269278	137784
湖北	Hubei	1053093	388246	436356	228491
湖南	Hunan	681684	214062	232094	235528
广东	Guangdong	3792321	1590409	907994	1293918
广西	Guangxi	242554	20560	118631	103363
海南	Hainan	31377	11180	16196	4001
重庆	Chongqing	496799	141637	195189	159973
四川	Sichuan	1209644	334718	506775	368151
贵州	Guizhou	97473	9264	47407	40802
云南	Yunnan	280976	47948	167876	65152
西藏	Tibet	8654		1618	7036
陕西	Shaanxi	294277	135057	124238	34982
甘肃	Gansu	296814	133106	102222	61486
青海	Qinghai	92258	30992	22463	38803
宁夏	Ningxia	154958	38305	45609	71044
新疆	Xinjiang	408026	49185	194075	164766

15-20 各地区建筑业增加值（2003年）

Value-added of Construction by Region (2003)

单位：万元 (10 000 yuan)

地 区	Region	建筑业增加值 Total Value-added of Construction	本年提取的固定资产折旧 Depreciation of Fixed Assets of the Year	应付工资 Wages Payable	应付福利费 Welfare Expenses Payable	工程结算税金及附加 Taxes and Extra Charges on Project Settlement Accounts	营业利润 Profits of Business	管理费用中的税金 Taxes in Management Expenses	管理费用中的劳动、待业保险费 Labor and Unemployment Insurance in Management Expenses
全 国	**National Total**	**46547067**	**3327636**	**26184579**	**3024450**	**7202940**	**5017609**	**383604**	**1406249**
北 京	Beijing	1945971	158882	920561	101943	386322	245216	13399	119648
天 津	Tianjin	795963	92066	365519	48844	141869	92958	10935	43772
河 北	Hebei	1688931	128778	922019	116813	257423	176294	13712	73892
山 西	Shanxi	951478	120429	484925	62903	171224	53891	7725	50381
内蒙古	Inner Mongolia	666669	45585	401017	42378	86154	60629	6847	24059
辽 宁	Liaoning	1968475	161727	1105809	135839	332797	141710	15893	74700
吉 林	Jilin	622364	60984	320534	45779	127619	32471	3963	31014
黑龙江	Heilongjiang	959828	88424	539784	75046	172058	50013	5624	28879
上 海	Shanghai	2153664	226154	1046996	95221	380524	344760	10803	49206
江 苏	Jiangsu	5609752	262687	3543835	412016	727645	531691	25868	106010
浙 江	Zhejiang	6342032	227214	3865185	409393	913192	814027	31643	81378
安 徽	Anhui	1359808	91519	791254	99424	208214	108969	12414	48014
福 建	Fujian	1063081	49754	628501	53872	184134	111557	6846	28417
江 西	Jiangxi	739617	46326	433801	46418	119026	59305	15520	19221
山 东	Shandong	3157332	215282	1791287	203989	431951	408895	34195	71733
河 南	Henan	1273423	112999	685256	118658	187941	100302	15631	52636
湖 北	Hubei	1914661	159034	984466	138953	335351	199079	21338	76440
湖 南	Hunan	1724388	134517	984853	113197	278008	156640	18023	39150
广 东	Guangdong	3281041	255019	1662850	182551	540817	518648	31198	89958
广 西	Guangxi	611761	44053	355896	35854	98696	45459	6144	25659
海 南	Hainan	88847	7291	46589	3937	15557	13895	546	1032
重 庆	Chongqing	1287202	76175	775119	84215	182562	137509	9538	22084
四 川	Sichuan	2678743	205387	1547736	170151	375483	263774	28075	88137
贵 州	Guizhou	486887	33820	274568	31072	65067	59280	4554	18526
云 南	Yunnan	791021	84262	417481	42354	125693	81032	8852	31347
西 藏	Tibet	66508	4957	25623	2003	10582	20889	1691	763
陕 西	Shaanxi	697852	78415	352574	50013	124003	46061	6175	40611
甘 肃	Gansu	549941	47145	316806	39823	73653	42993	7500	22021
青 海	Qinghai	158293	25223	79654	7696	20794	13876	1568	9482
宁 夏	Ningxia	249257	22193	153066	17003	32490	16286	1824	6395
新 疆	Xinjiang	662277	61335	361015	37092	96091	69500	5560	31684

15-21 各地区按登记注册类型分建筑业增加值（2003年）

Value Added of Construction by Registration Status and Region (2003)

单位: 万元 (10 000 yuan)

地 区	Region	合 计 Total	内资企业 Domestic Funded	#国 有 State-owned	#集 体 Collective-owned	港澳台商投资企业 Funded from Hong Kong, Macao and Taiwan	#港澳台商独资企业 Solely Owned	外商投资企业 Foreign Funded	#外商独资企业 Solely Owned
全 国	**National Total**	**46547067**	**46134116**	**11334155**	**7206234**	**205407**	**9026**	**207544**	**4722**
北 京	Beijing	1945971	1910163	650841	286817	12929	-3	22879	
天 津	Tianjin	795963	792093	277068	114355	2220		1650	
河 北	Hebei	1688931	1687467	424067	255130	138	-59	1326	
山 西	Shanxi	951478	947364	323640	78129	3544		570	
内蒙古	Inner Mongolia	666669	665299	83219	18688	925	5	445	
辽 宁	Liaoning	1968475	1915683	553830	345283	13266		39526	115
吉 林	Jilin	622364	618352	235990	58106	1342	148	2670	41
黑龙江	Heilongjiang	959828	949668	239879	111225	498	471	9662	
上 海	Shanghai	2153664	2080581	479766	188886	47443	-8	25640	
江 苏	Jiangsu	5609752	5557116	670332	892860	18899		33737	436
浙 江	Zhejiang	6342032	6306894	351790	595049	16406	53	18732	458
安 徽	Anhui	1359808	1355075	347579	330926	2700	754	2033	262
福 建	Fujian	1063081	1044593	268584	214391	8507	322	9981	1753
江 西	Jiangxi	739617	735707	295196	224327	3127	41	783	79
山 东	Shandong	3157332	3134135	728178	738258	7778	937	15419	166
河 南	Henan	1273423	1268283	511266	201328	4371		769	
湖 北	Hubei	1914661	1909255	731146	220947	1578	335	3828	
湖 南	Hunan	1724388	1721692	519756	424438	2696	634		
广 东	Guangdong	3281041	3219833	916863	621495	47936	4588	13272	1106
广 西	Guangxi	611761	609750	342355	126954	126		1885	
海 南	Hainan	88847	87673	49588	22715	911		263	73
重 庆	Chongqing	1287202	1282250	181076	159839	3917	72	1035	48
四 川	Sichuan	2678743	2675758	713360	458738	1718	399	1267	
贵 州	Guizhou	486887	486820	342374	62170	67			
云 南	Yunnan	791021	790329	212684	143854	507	65	185	185
西 藏	Tibet	66508	66269	20776	24354	239	239		
陕 西	Shaanxi	697852	697852	305878	104975				
甘 肃	Gansu	549941	549958	191814	118270	-4		-13	
青 海	Qinghai	158293	158115	94329	15012	178	33		
宁 夏	Ningxia	249257	248654	81769	20542	603			
新 疆	Xinjiang	662277	661435	189162	28173	842			

15-22 各地区按登记注册类型分建筑业企业实收资本（2003年）

Paid-up Capitals of Construction Enterprises by Registration Status and Region (2003)

单位: 万元 (10 000 yuan)

地区	Region	合计 Total	内资企业 Domestic Funded	#国有 State-owned	#集体 Collective-owned	港澳台商投资企业 Funded from Hong Kong, Macao and Taiwan	#港澳台商独资企业 Solely Owned	外商投资企业 Foreign Funded	#外商独资企业 Solely Owned
全　国	**National Total**	**65407983**	**64384557**	**17415883**	**9959581**	**604163**	**32617**	**419263**	**14125**
北　京	Beijing	3381070	3223104	1096350	407569	79295	1242	78671	
天　津	Tianjin	1375719	1350129	634824	161146	18231		7359	
河　北	Hebei	2590389	2585802	750633	290249	863	153	3724	
山　西	Shanxi	1920221	1899378	840304	137196	19041		1802	
内蒙古	Inner Mongolia	882095	878477	95769	25131	2546	518	1072	
辽　宁	Liaoning	3050211	2934376	857083	484740	29000		86835	1415
吉　林	Jilin	1023735	1013199	373766	93983	3608	668	6928	100
黑龙江	Heilongjiang	2124403	2109948	468993	220315	2373	800	12082	
上　海	Shanghai	3003572	2814559	659359	261777	130031	29	58982	
江　苏	Jiangsu	5319921	5249039	844020	812092	41529		29353	1654
浙　江	Zhejiang	4237240	4200537	292012	411186	20497	100	16206	453
安　徽	Anhui	1977828	1965468	526101	410763	7115	1207	5245	1738
福　建	Fujian	1984457	1920161	488492	382054	44274	5004	20022	1994
江　西	Jiangxi	1191017	1177967	481818	287240	10167	2820	2883	792
山　东	Shandong	4263245	4208513	796544	967021	18359	3565	36373	593
河　南	Henan	2368794	2359643	856936	394748	6418		2733	
湖　北	Hubei	2816790	2795114	958828	378511	7980	1561	13696	
湖　南	Hunan	2335226	2322017	701929	578414	13209	698		
广　东	Guangdong	4883318	4752920	1557668	840293	109072	5226	21326	2464
广　西	Guangxi	1133480	1128625	537134	298498	1263		3592	
海　南	Hainan	206347	204735	66151	53626	887		725	225
重　庆	Chongqing	2119920	2103977	296503	242038	12675	434	3268	129
四　川	Sichuan	4910819	4889918	1211385	709667	17325	7213	3576	
贵　州	Guizhou	654431	651421	344065	125768	3010			
云　南	Yunnan	1639619	1635158	417193	316971	1893	239	2568	2568
西　藏	Tibet	232736	232206	62817	86542	530	530		
陕　西	Shaanxi	1142370	1142370	400570	211728				
甘　肃	Gansu	1010021	1009073	308756	238419	706		242	
青　海	Qinghai	349365	348262	137480	44283	1103	610		
宁　夏	Ningxia	444107	443904	133909	37286	203			
新　疆	Xinjiang	835517	834557	218491	50327	960			

15-23 各地区建筑业企业资产（2003年）

Assets of Construction Enterprises by Region (2003)

单位：万元 (10 000 yuan)

地区	Region	资产合计 Total Assets	# 流动资产 Circulating Funds	# 固定资产 Fixed Assets	# 无形及递延资产 Intangible and Deferred Assets
全国	**National Total**	**235419044**	**166034099**	**51447123**	**5832396**
北京	Beijing	17537485	13819104	2125103	203607
天津	Tianjin	5732065	4111629	1202545	72733
河北	Hebei	7629880	4877814	2130612	339619
山西	Shanxi	6310377	3990472	1772504	115800
内蒙古	Inner Mongolia	2641549	1751844	723563	86120
辽宁	Liaoning	10153341	7105583	2490570	225886
吉林	Jilin	4051415	2898304	975163	87887
黑龙江	Heilongjiang	5959309	4069601	1589211	82552
上海	Shanghai	15448088	11785940	2207470	162024
江苏	Jiangsu	22271265	17191831	3881238	352312
浙江	Zhejiang	18286813	13888036	3318552	258630
安徽	Anhui	5898281	3922480	1544838	250967
福建	Fujian	6311243	4601406	1139472	93705
江西	Jiangxi	3578780	2289759	964982	135102
山东	Shandong	16020947	11610381	3292024	510353
河南	Henan	6563213	4097697	2025057	251817
湖北	Hubei	9086246	5765622	2600375	453324
湖南	Hunan	6753249	4285756	1975541	238638
广东	Guangdong	22264911	16720907	3643661	410638
广西	Guangxi	3859770	2287232	1255339	109188
海南	Hainan	529727	287833	168501	46473
重庆	Chongqing	5035697	3303249	1351964	153346
四川	Sichuan	13156812	8287017	3403536	557167
贵州	Guizhou	2459632	1718463	561315	92035
云南	Yunnan	4823107	2954787	1330463	170524
西藏	Tibet	420166	165506	191872	3999
陕西	Shaanxi	4211310	2847484	1144384	105320
甘肃	Gansu	2815863	1773835	923736	44386
青海	Qinghai	958230	527520	350713	27945
宁夏	Ningxia	1275081	804285	375131	24950
新疆	Xinjiang	3375192	2292722	787688	165349

15-24 各地区按登记注册类型分建筑业企业资产（2003年）

Assets of Construction Enterprises by Registration Status and Region (2003)

单位: 万元 (10 000 yuan)

地区	Region	合计 Total	内资企业 Domestic Funded	#国有 State-owned	#集体 Collective-owned	港澳台商投资企业 Funded from Hong Kong, Macao and Taiwan	#港澳台商独资企业 Solely Owned	外商投资企业 Foreign Funded	#外商独资企业 Solely Owned
全国	**National Total**	**235419044**	**232360971**	**78456638**	**30412613**	**1663245**	**89050**	**1394828**	**52043**
北京	Beijing	17537485	17129632	7335698	1823558	154321	2814	253532	
天津	Tianjin	5732065	5649221	2499247	599374	66719		16125	
河北	Hebei	7629880	7618045	2855700	709045	2106	533	9729	
山西	Shanxi	6310377	6272737	2882267	363912	30735		6905	
内蒙古	Inner Mongolia	2641549	2632885	319869	65333	6281	1803	2383	
辽宁	Liaoning	10153341	9786803	3387967	1473506	73306		293232	6070
吉林	Jilin	4051415	4024815	1740858	269606	11306	2377	15294	312
黑龙江	Heilongjiang	5959309	5924370	1628204	562825	4174	2600	30765	
上海	Shanghai	15448088	14881698	4250619	1634300	356741	228	209649	
江苏	Jiangsu	22271265	22052199	4282617	3090062	116125		102941	4382
浙江	Zhejiang	18286813	18125547	1558004	1806805	111962	230	49304	4264
安徽	Anhui	5898281	5854876	1974671	1100513	29045	2744	14360	1789
福建	Fujian	6311243	6162237	1942961	1116963	90863	11390	58143	10081
江西	Jiangxi	3578780	3548342	1685670	890867	26003	8330	4435	1864
山东	Shandong	16020947	15847071	4454591	3199623	55926	6014	117950	3938
河南	Henan	6563213	6533970	2956226	896440	21330		7913	
湖北	Hubei	9086246	9044245	4274463	700436	18461	1970	23540	
湖南	Hunan	6753249	6728519	3023221	1268796	24730	784		
广东	Guangdong	22264911	21757650	8091008	3333970	373972	20912	133289	15356
广西	Guangxi	3859770	3846705	2361585	730979	2926		10139	
海南	Hainan	529727	524360	222862	88453	2916		2451	916
重庆	Chongqing	5035697	5006822	1053663	527212	22581	599	6294	132
四川	Sichuan	13156812	13090835	4686391	1717407	42969	22811	23008	
贵州	Guizhou	2459632	2453709	1742258	265842	5923			
云南	Yunnan	4823107	4815956	1808071	680042	4212	694	2939	2939
西藏	Tibet	420166	419174	156849	132821	992	992		
陕西	Shaanxi	4211310	4211310	2097701	523248				
甘肃	Gansu	2815863	2814132	1160894	517416	1223		508	
青海	Qinghai	958230	956017	560010	93603	2213	1225		
宁夏	Ningxia	1275081	1274444	420951	82065	637			
新疆	Xinjiang	3375192	3372645	1041542	147591	2547			

15-25 各地区建筑业企业负债及所有者权益（2003年）

Liabilities and Creditors' Equity of Construction Enterprises by Region (2003)

单位：万元 (10 000 yuan)

地区	Region	负债合计 Total Liabilities	流动负债 Liquid Liabilities	长期负债 Long-term Liabilities	所有者权益 Creditors' Equity	# 实收资本 Paid-up Capitals
全国	**National Total**	**149924251**	**141812876**	**8111375**	**85494793**	**65407983**
北京	Beijing	12978637	12368429	610208	4558848	3381070
天津	Tianjin	4052644	3792194	260450	1679421	1375719
河北	Hebei	4453951	4232939	221012	3175929	2590389
山西	Shanxi	4188262	3733473	454789	2122115	1920221
内蒙古	Inner Mongolia	1572208	1487933	84275	1069341	882095
辽宁	Liaoning	6250665	5951555	299110	3902676	3050211
吉林	Jilin	2724512	2653008	71504	1326903	1023735
黑龙江	Heilongjiang	3532544	3372525	160019	2426765	2124403
上海	Shanghai	10464163	9970915	493248	4983925	3003572
江苏	Jiangsu	15401204	14985334	415870	6870061	5319921
浙江	Zhejiang	12071187	11726823	344364	6215626	4237240
安徽	Anhui	3501226	3309637	191589	2397055	1977828
福建	Fujian	3887518	3791502	96016	2423725	1984457
江西	Jiangxi	2163710	2020865	142845	1415070	1191017
山东	Shandong	10516876	9980230	536646	5504071	4263245
河南	Henan	3783881	3616461	167420	2779332	2368794
湖北	Hubei	5199466	4635270	564196	3886780	2816790
湖南	Hunan	3794797	3519188	275609	2958452	2335226
广东	Guangdong	15113318	14224666	888652	7151593	4883318
广西	Guangxi	2210812	1961588	249224	1648958	1133480
海南	Hainan	242166	216461	25705	287561	206347
重庆	Chongqing	2522918	2327690	195228	2512779	2119920
四川	Sichuan	6690513	6255688	434825	6466299	4910819
贵州	Guizhou	1632156	1499817	132339	827476	654431
云南	Yunnan	2820724	2513211	307513	2002383	1639619
西藏	Tibet	122367	104833	17534	297799	232736
陕西	Shaanxi	2771643	2581697	189946	1439667	1142370
甘肃	Gansu	1612713	1511687	101026	1203150	1010021
青海	Qinghai	533867	502102	31765	424363	349365
宁夏	Ningxia	786286	758808	27478	488795	444107
新疆	Xinjiang	2327317	2206347	120970	1047875	835517

15-26 各地区按登记注册类型分建筑业企业所有者权益（2003年）

Creditors' Equity of Construction Enterprises by Registration Status and Region (2003)

单位: 万元 (10 000 yuan)

地 区	Region	合 计 Total	内资企业 Domestic Funded	#国 有 State-owned	#集 体 Collective-owned	港澳台商投资企业 Funded from Hong Kong, Macao and Taiwan	#港澳台商独资企业 Solely Owned	外商投资企业 Foreign Funded	#外商独资企业 Solely Owned
全 国	**National Total**	**85494793**	**84265763**	**23678872**	**12752811**	**697711**	**38492**	**531319**	**22038**
北 京	Beijing	4558848	4402130	1755139	555433	80692	640	76026	
天 津	Tianjin	1679421	1658744	614686	239213	12504		8173	
河 北	Hebei	3175929	3170313	863162	364073	992	153	4624	
山 西	Shanxi	2122115	2101217	866689	159836	19428		1470	
内蒙古	Inner Mongolia	1069341	1065855	114594	30458	2368	340	1118	
辽 宁	Liaoning	3902676	3739802	1148346	610033	37065		125809	1167
吉 林	Jilin	1326903	1313873	465795	113943	4604	668	8426	103
黑龙江	Heilongjiang	2426765	2404593	511031	257915	2774	1200	19398	
上 海	Shanghai	4983925	4769162	1600739	483820	147020	29	67743	
江 苏	Jiangsu	6870061	6783670	1172289	1032999	50763		35628	1892
浙 江	Zhejiang	6215626	6163122	448807	596568	33347	147	19157	1971
安 徽	Anhui	2397055	2383482	593593	506742	7829	1228	5744	1738
福 建	Fujian	2423725	2351655	649942	462339	47595	5130	24475	4800
江 西	Jiangxi	1415070	1399473	557063	346792	12705	3388	2892	801
山 东	Shandong	5504071	5426872	1040979	1268186	21964	4230	55235	1189
河 南	Henan	2779332	2769654	969442	469488	7173		2505	
湖 北	Hubei	3886780	3862443	1533743	457423	9166	1852	15171	
湖 南	Hunan	2958452	2945120	900645	704622	13332	744		
广 东	Guangdong	7151593	6972095	2137584	1140638	140329	9382	39169	5030
广 西	Guangxi	1648958	1642559	857226	402038	1278		5121	
海 南	Hainan	287561	284520	109234	65440	1588		1453	650
重 庆	Chongqing	2512779	2493438	335321	280654	16061	434	3280	129
四 川	Sichuan	6466299	6442457	1873888	890530	17950	7379	5892	
贵 州	Guizhou	827476	824403	455052	147435	3073			
云 南	Yunnan	2002383	1997839	539796	380102	1976	239	2568	2568
西 藏	Tibet	297799	297100	107773	93539	699	699		
陕 西	Shaanxi	1439667	1439667	551237	261335				
甘 肃	Gansu	1203150	1202202	374317	275981	706		242	
青 海	Qinghai	424363	423260	182166	49649	1103	610		
宁 夏	Ningxia	488795	488564	127413	46341	231			
新 疆	Xinjiang	1047875	1046479	221181	59246	1396			

15-27 各地区按登记注册类型分建筑业企业负债（2003年）

Liabilities of Construction Enterprises by Registration Status and Region (2003)

单位: 万元　　(10 000 yuan)

地 区	Region	合 计 Total	内资企业 Domestic Funded	#国 有 State-owned	#集 体 Collective-owned	港澳台商投资企业 Funded from Hong Kong, Macao and Taiwan	#港澳台商独资企业 Solely Owned	外商投资企业 Foreign Funded	#外商独资企业 Solely Owned
全 国	**National Total**	**149924251**	**148095208**	**54777766**	**17659802**	**965534**	**50558**	**863509**	**30005**
北 京	Beijing	12978637	12727502	5580559	1268125	73629	2174	177506	
天 津	Tianjin	4052644	3990477	1884561	360161	54215		7952	
河 北	Hebei	4453951	4447732	1992538	344972	1114	380	5105	
山 西	Shanxi	4188262	4171520	2015578	204076	11307		5435	
内蒙古	Inner Mongolia	1572208	1567030	205275	34875	3913	1463	1265	
辽 宁	Liaoning	6250665	6047001	2239621	863473	36241		167423	4903
吉 林	Jilin	2724512	2710942	1275063	155663	6702	1709	6868	209
黑龙江	Heilongjiang	3532544	3519777	1117173	304910	1400	1400	11367	
上 海	Shanghai	10464163	10112536	2649880	1150480	209721	199	141906	
江 苏	Jiangsu	15401204	15268529	3110328	2057063	65362		67313	2490
浙 江	Zhejiang	12071187	11962425	1109197	1210237	78615	83	30147	2293
安 徽	Anhui	3501226	3471394	1381078	593771	21216	1516	8616	51
福 建	Fujian	3887518	3810582	1293019	654624	43268	6260	33668	5281
江 西	Jiangxi	2163710	2148869	1128607	544075	13298	4942	1543	1063
山 东	Shandong	10516876	10420199	3413612	1931437	33962	1784	62715	2749
河 南	Henan	3783881	3764316	1986784	426952	14157		5408	
湖 北	Hubei	5199466	5181802	2740720	243013	9295	118	8369	
湖 南	Hunan	3794797	3783399	2122576	564174	11398	40		
广 东	Guangdong	15113318	14785555	5953424	2193332	233643	11530	94120	10326
广 西	Guangxi	2210812	2204146	1504359	328941	1648		5018	
海 南	Hainan	242166	239840	113628	23013	1328		998	266
重 庆	Chongqing	2522918	2513384	718342	246558	6520	165	3014	3
四 川	Sichuan	6690513	6648378	2812503	826877	25019	15432	17116	
贵 州	Guizhou	1632156	1629306	1287206	118407	2850			
云 南	Yunnan	2820724	2818117	1268275	299940	2236	455	371	371
西 藏	Tibet	122367	122074	49076	39282	293	293		
陕 西	Shaanxi	2771643	2771643	1546464	261913				
甘 肃	Gansu	1612713	1611930	786577	241435	517		266	
青 海	Qinghai	533867	532757	377844	43954	1110	615		
宁 夏	Ningxia	786286	785880	293538	35724	406			
新 疆	Xinjiang	2327317	2326166	820361	88345	1151			

15-28 各地区建筑业企业总收入（2003年）

Total Income of Construction Enterprises by Region (2003)

单位：万元 (10 000 yuan)

地　区	Region	企业总收入 Total Income of Enterprises	工程结算收入 Revenue of Project Settlement Accounts	#工程结算成本 Costs of Project Settlement Accounts	#工程结算利润 Profits of Project Settlement Accounts	其他业务收入 Other Revenue from Business	#其他业务利润 Other Profit from Business
全　国	**National Total**	**220372689**	**214935842**	**190992216**	**16740685**	**5436847**	**954564**
北　京	Beijing	13344478	12839608	11371088	1082198	504870	93272
天　津	Tianjin	5325230	5159802	4617473	400460	165428	10201
河　北	Hebei	7933457	7780884	6809625	713835	152573	21072
山　西	Shanxi	5235875	5042419	4483424	387771	193456	27621
内蒙古	Inner Mongolia	2543457	2510153	2209291	214708	33304	8786
辽　宁	Liaoning	10094085	9879561	8785768	760996	214524	36589
吉　林	Jilin	3421774	3371344	3005186	238539	50430	10088
黑龙江	Heilongjiang	4571841	4497320	3990445	334817	74521	6891
上　海	Shanghai	13865136	13359661	12017703	961434	505475	90484
江　苏	Jiangsu	21542959	20805944	18550227	1528072	737015	103494
浙　江	Zhejiang	26753336	26403606	23820921	1669493	349730	74765
安　徽	Anhui	6098641	5939173	5257627	473332	159468	25442
福　建	Fujian	5428946	5277613	4739298	354181	151333	22284
江　西	Jiangxi	3430755	3378677	3013012	246639	52078	9377
山　东	Shandong	13392431	13345673	11722331	1191391	46758	46757
河　南	Henan	5983766	5863468	5201036	474491	120298	24334
湖　北	Hubei	9445963	9189787	8026421	828015	256176	28242
湖　南	Hunan	7682464	7563464	6739295	546161	119000	23125
广　东	Guangdong	16845992	16290994	14342711	1407466	554998	113476
广　西	Guangxi	2760296	2676224	2372151	205377	84072	17482
海　南	Hainan	371224	370393	320976	33860	831	475
重　庆	Chongqing	5156178	5037625	4466646	388417	118553	16334
四　川	Sichuan	11419252	11167319	9821031	970805	251933	43788
贵　州	Guizhou	2030888	1952343	1736522	150754	78545	20360
云　南	Yunnan	3779502	3712577	3292968	293916	66925	12267
西　藏	Tibet	289888	288080	244457	33041	1808	1036
陕　西	Shaanxi	4571414	4440549	4038416	278130	130865	19541
甘　肃	Gansu	2128718	2065321	1809455	182213	63397	11746
青　海	Qinghai	675545	658381	573117	64470	17164	4604
宁　夏	Ningxia	1052408	1001841	897709	71642	50567	8940
新　疆	Xinjiang	3196790	3066038	2715886	254061	130752	21691

15-29　各地区按登记注册类型分建筑业企业总收入（2003年）

Total Income of Construction by Registration Status and Region (2003)

单位: 万元　　　　(10 000 yuan)

地　区	Region	合　计 Total	内资企业 Domestic Funded	#国　有 State-owned	#集　体 Collective-owned	港澳台商投资企业 Funded from Hong Kong, Macao and Taiwan	#港澳台商独资企业 Solely Owned	外商投资企　业 Foreign Funded	#外商独资企业 Solely Owned
全　国	**National Total**	**220372689**	**217707103**	**64106255**	**28747770**	**1315110**	**38026**	**1350476**	**37512**
北　京	Beijing	13344478	12955312	5275113	1351040	125190	643	263976	
天　津	Tianjin	5325230	5236067	2036911	552143	68521		20642	
河　北	Hebei	7933457	7927816	2454471	1178696	671	204	4970	
山　西	Shanxi	5235875	5220842	1777156	229274	7873		7160	
内蒙古	Inner Mongolia	2543457	2540588	347758	71556	1670	20	1199	
辽　宁	Liaoning	10094085	9728489	3166108	1467516	73181		292415	1022
吉　林	Jilin	3421774	3407414	1289139	265708	6935	620	7425	153
黑龙江	Heilongjiang	4571841	4523383	1243378	458897	1388	1200	47070	
上　海	Shanghai	13865136	13296643	2970382	1318165	359319	89	209174	
江　苏	Jiangsu	21542959	21320843	3743241	2914209	100130		121986	1208
浙　江	Zhejiang	26753336	26546135	1776234	2337539	111712	167	95489	2327
安　徽	Anhui	6098641	6077579	1776308	1225615	12639	5895	8423	503
福　建	Fujian	5428946	5327264	1620308	959426	48714	1485	52968	20639
江　西	Jiangxi	3430755	3417104	1538393	912959	10743	201	2908	531
山　东	Shandong	13392431	13237776	3684322	2666172	50046	3973	104609	898
河　南	Henan	5983766	5961215	2666923	787946	13389		9162	
湖　北	Hubei	9445963	9413768	3693965	928494	10639	1851	21556	
湖　南	Hunan	7682464	7670880	2918299	1655896	11584	2296		
广　东	Guangdong	16845992	16523953	5953514	2481346	264804	14746	57235	8791
广　西	Guangxi	2760296	2750879	1650548	507546	514		8903	
海　南	Hainan	371224	365549	230856	65737	3755		1920	214
重　庆	Chongqing	5156178	5135599	897528	622071	16813	258	3766	172
四　川	Sichuan	11419252	11405584	3729774	1783433	7359	3271	6309	
贵　州	Guizhou	2030888	2030601	1475853	212494	287			
云　南	Yunnan	3779502	3776631	1237730	593104	1817	672	1054	1054
西　藏	Tibet	289888	289530	106562	75132	358	358		
陕　西	Shaanxi	4571414	4571414	2246168	415029				
甘　肃	Gansu	2128718	2128364	829118	454018	197		157	
青　海	Qinghai	675545	674308	417500	54556	1237	77		
宁　夏	Ningxia	1052408	1051032	390686	62736	1376			
新　疆	Xinjiang	3196790	3194541	962009	139317	2249			

15-30 各地区建筑业企业利税总额（2003年）

Total Pre-Tax Profits of Construction Enterprises by Region (2003)

地区	Region	利税总额合计（万元）Total Pre-tax Profits (10 000 yuan)	利润总额 Total Profits	工程结算税金及附加 Taxes and Extra Charges on Project Settlement Accounts	管理费用中的税金 Taxes in Management Expenses	产值利税率（%）Ratio of Pre-tax Profits to Output Value (%)	资产利税率（%）Ratio of Pre-tax Profits to Assets (%)
全　国	**National Total**	**12785260**	**5198716**	**7202940**	**383604**	**5.5**	**5.4**
北　京	Beijing	699460	299739	386322	13399	5.5	4.0
天　津	Tianjin	249833	97029	141869	10935	4.8	4.4
河　北	Hebei	451764	180629	257423	13712	5.8	5.9
山　西	Shanxi	226472	47523	171224	7725	4.2	3.6
内蒙古	Inner Mongolia	148628	55627	86154	6847	5.8	5.6
辽　宁	Liaoning	513813	165123	332797	15893	5.1	5.1
吉　林	Jilin	155079	23497	127619	3963	4.5	3.8
黑龙江	Heilongjiang	232212	54530	172058	5624	5.3	3.9
上　海	Shanghai	800563	409236	380524	10803	6.7	5.2
江　苏	Jiangsu	1301495	547982	727645	25868	4.7	5.8
浙　江	Zhejiang	1776998	832163	913192	31643	5.7	9.7
安　徽	Anhui	331071	110443	208214	12414	5.3	5.6
福　建	Fujian	306800	115820	184134	6846	5.6	4.9
江　西	Jiangxi	192964	58418	119026	15520	5.4	5.4
山　东	Shandong	876677	410531	431951	34195	5.9	5.5
河　南	Henan	297621	94049	187941	15631	4.7	4.5
湖　北	Hubei	547484	190795	335351	21338	6.3	6.0
湖　南	Hunan	451023	154992	278008	18023	5.5	6.7
广　东	Guangdong	1143533	571518	540817	31198	7.5	5.1
广　西	Guangxi	151935	47095	98696	6144	5.4	3.9
海　南	Hainan	30446	14343	15557	546	7.7	5.7
重　庆	Chongqing	329589	137489	182562	9538	5.6	6.5
四　川	Sichuan	662847	259289	375483	28075	5.4	5.0
贵　州	Guizhou	115146	45525	65067	4554	5.4	4.7
云　南	Yunnan	214679	80134	125693	8852	5.4	4.5
西　藏	Tibet	31152	18879	10582	1691	10.6	7.4
陕　西	Shaanxi	177073	46895	124003	6175	4.0	4.2
甘　肃	Gansu	114195	33042	73653	7500	5.1	4.1
青　海	Qinghai	35963	13601	20794	1568	4.8	3.8
宁　夏	Ningxia	49889	15575	32490	1824	4.6	3.9
新　疆	Xinjiang	168856	67205	96091	5560	5.3	5.0

15-31 各地区按登记注册类型分建筑业企业税金总额（2003年）

Tax of Construction Enterprises by Registration Status and by Region (2003)

单位: 万元 (10 000 yuan)

地区	Region	合计 Total	内资企业 Domestic Funded	#国有 State-owned	#集体 Collective-owned	港澳台商投资企业 Funded from Hong Kong, Macao and Taiwan	#港澳台商独资企业 Solely Owned	外商投资企业 Foreign Funded	#外商独资企业 Solely Owned
全国	**National Total**	**7586544**	**7507570**	**2021522**	**1115438**	**35553**	**1259**	**43421**	**757**
北京	Beijing	399721	388712	147110	47156	3502	19	7507	
天津	Tianjin	152804	150659	56600	21554	1643		502	
河北	Hebei	271135	270943	78506	42853	40	6	152	
山西	Shanxi	178949	178296	63211	12868	439		214	
内蒙古	Inner Mongolia	93001	92844	13390	3189	55	1	102	
辽宁	Liaoning	348690	333581	103293	53557	2128		12981	31
吉林	Jilin	131582	129707	47698	9265	214	22	1661	11
黑龙江	Heilongjiang	177682	176110	39461	15390	81	75	1491	
上海	Shanghai	391327	380085	82247	38098	7731	3	3511	
江苏	Jiangsu	753513	746420	108078	109450	3167		3926	94
浙江	Zhejiang	944835	939980	54436	83716	2243	5	2612	69
安徽	Anhui	220628	219730	62024	48201	639	185	259	16
福建	Fujian	190980	188048	53261	36738	1341	85	1591	237
江西	Jiangxi	134546	134084	60867	35617	375	6	87	19
山东	Shandong	466146	460578	119006	105698	2078	120	3490	27
河南	Henan	203572	203003	86042	32380	266		303	
湖北	Hubei	356689	355895	132963	39915	301	23	493	
湖南	Hunan	296031	295663	101848	67338	368	69		
广东	Guangdong	572015	562475	165492	112078	7731	442	1809	192
广西	Guangxi	104840	104528	53242	25893	19		293	
海南	Hainan	16103	15929	10232	2371	120		54	7
重庆	Chongqing	192100	191436	32900	23946	531	8	133	5
四川	Sichuan	403558	403140	116767	67986	222	74	196	
贵州	Guizhou	69621	69607	46611	9153	14			
云南	Yunnan	134545	134432	37849	24075	64	20	49	49
西藏	Tibet	12273	12179	4493	3894	94	94		
陕西	Shaanxi	130178	130178	60425	15550				
甘肃	Gansu	81153	81146	27585	18458	2		5	
青海	Qinghai	22362	22326	12606	1980	36	2		
宁夏	Ningxia	34314	34284	12531	2445	30			
新疆	Xinjiang	101651	101572	30748	4626	79			

15-32 各地区按登记注册类型分建筑业企业利润总额（2003年）

Total Profits of Construction Enterprises by Registration Status and Region (2003)

单位: 万元 (10 000 yuan)

地 区	Region	合 计 Total	内资企业 Domestic Funded	# 国 有 State-owned	# 集 体 Collective-owned	港澳台商投资企业 Funded from Hong Kong, Macao and Taiwan	# 港澳台商独资企业 Solely Owned	外商投资企业 Foreign Funded	# 外商独资企业 Solely Owned
全 国	**National Total**	**5198716**	**5140731**	**540339**	**785771**	**28756**	**1617**	**29229**	**1100**
北 京	Beijing	299739	300076	35549	66143	-327	-197	-10	
天 津	Tianjin	97029	101076	12958	19343	-4200		153	
河 北	Hebei	180629	180201	12710	28156	-78	-130	506	
山 西	Shanxi	47523	48141	3952	1886	-420		-198	
内蒙古	Inner Mongolia	55627	55345	6822	839	266	-26	16	
辽 宁	Liaoning	165123	156055	12022	25836	1442		7626	-15
吉 林	Jilin	23497	23837	-17094	3930	-1	-18	-339	-1
黑龙江	Heilongjiang	54530	53091	2613	5088	45	52	1394	
上 海	Shanghai	409236	395317	34221	33419	10789		3130	
江 苏	Jiangsu	547982	540130	40903	72755	2647		5205	10
浙 江	Zhejiang	832163	824155	35351	84110	5778	8	2230	14
安 徽	Anhui	110443	110039	11640	26203	180	7	224	2
福 建	Fujian	115820	112126	15438	15290	1414	-108	2280	949
江 西	Jiangxi	58418	58160	18035	14690	336	-15	-78	10
山 东	Shandong	410531	403536	53237	96404	1627	246	5368	-102
河 南	Henan	94049	92358	23791	19808	1754		-63	
湖 北	Hubei	190795	190246	33163	27632	310	162	239	
湖 南	Hunan	154992	154916	24566	36955	76	46		
广 东	Guangdong	571518	563048	69016	71333	7182	1667	1288	248
广 西	Guangxi	47095	46918	13665	11044	-76		253	
海 南	Hainan	14343	14529	3304	8045	-152		-34	-37
重 庆	Chongqing	137489	137166	13848	12264	143		180	
四 川	Sichuan	259289	259516	33223	39008	-101	-35	-126	
贵 州	Guizhou	45525	45579	23325	11681	-54			
云 南	Yunnan	80134	80181	537	15878	-69		22	22
西 藏	Tibet	18879	18857	6216	7193	22	22		
陕 西	Shaanxi	46895	46895	12512	8275				
甘 肃	Gansu	33042	33142	-4598	13903	-63		-37	
青 海	Qinghai	13601	13661	7380	1379	-60	-64		
宁 夏	Ningxia	15575	15576	1393	2212	-1			
新 疆	Xinjiang	67205	66858	641	5069	347			

15-33 各地区按资质等级分总承包建筑业企业利润总额（2003年）

Total Profits of Construction of General Contractors by Qualification Criteria and by Region (2003)

单位：万元 (10 000 yuan)

地 区	Region	合计 Total	特 级 Special Grade	一 级 First Grade	二 级 Second Grade	三级及以下 Third Grade and below
全 国	**National Total**	**3936230**	**281576**	**1048254**	**1371527**	**1234873**
北 京	Beijing	236663	39152	119681	54089	23741
天 津	Tianjin	42151	10132	14514	7586	9919
河 北	Hebei	135661	1968	33076	54475	46142
山 西	Shanxi	40086	15148	9968	4940	10030
内蒙古	Inner Mongolia	55734	366	6362	27866	21140
辽 宁	Liaoning	116119	11626	30596	26394	47503
吉 林	Jilin	15962	5074	-1182	5148	6922
黑龙江	Heilongjiang	35347	6223	6598	13158	9368
上 海	Shanghai	272276	19287	50955	110105	91929
江 苏	Jiangsu	387907	27154	115023	130799	114931
浙 江	Zhejiang	618842	44867	228263	183319	162393
安 徽	Anhui	81832	5246	10412	23980	42194
福 建	Fujian	72368	468	19434	27705	24761
江 西	Jiangxi	40706		7251	10827	22628
山 东	Shandong	338714	11804	72342	117457	137111
河 南	Henan	73919	2780	11813	30191	29135
湖 北	Hubei	143859	14566	14203	52634	62456
湖 南	Hunan	139502	758	37432	47147	54165
广 东	Guangdong	430178	40452	107725	170764	111237
广 西	Guangxi	33874	1732	7004	12337	12801
海 南	Hainan	12847		765	11526	556
重 庆	Chongqing	118224		28590	61137	28497
四 川	Sichuan	217464	10387	37039	90501	79537
贵 州	Guizhou	41562	680	18602	17506	4774
云 南	Yunnan	72509	-1385	22777	18728	32389
西 藏	Tibet	18310		485	11905	5920
陕 西	Shaanxi	41772	7688	11290	10854	11940
甘 肃	Gansu	26844		-3210	17624	12430
青 海	Qinghai	11503		5779	112	5612
宁 夏	Ningxia	11309		1788	4281	5240
新 疆	Xinjiang	52186	5403	22879	16432	7472

15-34 各地区按资质等级分专业承包建筑业企业利润总额（2003年）

Total Profits of Construction of General Contractors by Qualification Criteria and by Region (2003)

单位: 万元 (10 000 yuan)

地区	Region	合计 Total	一级 First Grade	二级 Second Grade	三级及以下 Third Grade and below
全国	**National Total**	**1262486**	**307312**	**410904**	**544270**
北京	Beijing	63076	15660	26174	21242
天津	Tianjin	54878	27163	10686	17029
河北	Hebei	44968	19054	15947	9967
山西	Shanxi	7437	-339	4601	3175
内蒙古	Inner Mongolia	-107	-2616	1078	1431
辽宁	Liaoning	49004	16620	15824	16560
吉林	Jilin	7535	-1049	5569	3015
黑龙江	Heilongjiang	19183	3873	13587	1723
上海	Shanghai	136960	40700	38316	57944
江苏	Jiangsu	160075	32975	43906	83194
浙江	Zhejiang	213321	37956	63515	111850
安徽	Anhui	28611	4393	9858	14360
福建	Fujian	43452	13099	14786	15567
江西	Jiangxi	17712	4740	7558	5414
山东	Shandong	71817	9691	27215	34911
河南	Henan	20130	8902	6501	4727
湖北	Hubei	46936	8756	18734	19446
湖南	Hunan	15490	3144	5025	7321
广东	Guangdong	141340	38367	31257	71716
广西	Guangxi	13221	1268	7974	3979
海南	Hainan	1496	916	511	69
重庆	Chongqing	19265	9357	5775	4133
四川	Sichuan	41825	6900	16001	18924
贵州	Guizhou	3963	12	1980	1971
云南	Yunnan	7625	448	4171	3006
西藏	Tibet	569		194	375
陕西	Shaanxi	5123	2039	2094	990
甘肃	Gansu	6198	2542	2970	686
青海	Qinghai	2098	103	384	1611
宁夏	Ningxia	4266	-164	2609	1821
新疆	Xinjiang	15019	2802	6104	6113

15-35 各地区按登记注册类型分建筑业企业工程结算利润（2003年）
Profits of Project Settlement Accounts of Construction Enterprises by Registration Status and Region (2003)

单位: 万元 (10 000 yuan)

地 区	Region	合 计 Total	内资企业 Domestic Funded	#国 有 State-owned	#集 体 Collective-owned	港澳台商投资企业 Funded from Hong Kong, Macao and Taiwan	#港澳台商独资企业 Solely Owned	外商投资企业 Foreign Funded	#外商独资企业 Solely Owned
全 国	**National Total**	**16740685**	**16479606**	**4416532**	**2316727**	**128671**	**6733**	**132408**	**4219**
北 京	Beijing	1082198	1051383	321448	150679	11309	57	19506	
天 津	Tianjin	400460	393617	136328	54705	5514		1329	
河 北	Hebei	713835	712403	180314	192044	136	6	1296	
山 西	Shanxi	387771	387122	121869	18731	607		42	
内蒙古	Inner Mongolia	214708	214007	26827	5142	405	12	296	
辽 宁	Liaoning	760996	714630	224139	108452	7471		38895	269
吉 林	Jilin	238539	237476	87966	22092	905	56	158	22
黑龙江	Heilongjiang	334817	329571	83845	32120	195	175	5051	
上 海	Shanghai	961434	911708	160130	83142	29993	21	19733	
江 苏	Jiangsu	1528072	1503401	244316	227374	10379		14292	71
浙 江	Zhejiang	1669493	1653828	152424	150117	11123	22	4542	280
安 徽	Anhui	473332	471879	117959	89655	773	126	680	53
福 建	Fujian	354181	344718	96888	47171	4948	188	4515	2119
江 西	Jiangxi	246639	245008	112864	50991	1490	31	141	72
山 东	Shandong	1191391	1176277	284884	249145	4969	593	10145	187
河 南	Henan	474491	469761	197413	66593	3202		1528	
湖 北	Hubei	828015	824362	314300	77225	1848	326	1805	
湖 南	Hunan	546161	544617	196292	101702	1544	505		
广 东	Guangdong	1407466	1373732	345588	206607	27436	4112	6298	879
广 西	Guangxi	205377	204658	114513	35647	107		612	
海 南	Hainan	33860	32971	11731	11176	434		455	102
重 庆	Chongqing	388417	386173	56395	37938	1647	31	597	22
四 川	Sichuan	970805	969663	297938	132439	825	254	317	
贵 州	Guizhou	150754	150646	107121	16453	108			
云 南	Yunnan	293916	293530	81799	46404	243	162	143	143
西 藏	Tibet	33041	32940	10560	11092	101	101		
陕 西	Shaanxi	278130	278130	123471	36011				
甘 肃	Gansu	182213	182177	68201	34343	4		32	
青 海	Qinghai	64470	64351	43234	4885	119	-45		
宁 夏	Ningxia	71642	71516	19885	5077	126			
新 疆	Xinjiang	254061	253351	75890	11575	710			

15-36 各地区建筑业劳动生产率（2003年）

Labor Productivity of Construction by Region (2003)

单位：元/人 (yuan/person)

地区	Region	按建筑业总产值计算的劳动生产率 Overall Labor Productivity in Terms of Total Output Value	#国有 State-owned	#集体 Collective-owned	按建筑业增加值计算的劳动生产率 Overall Labor Productivity in Terms of Added-Value	#国有 State-owned	#集体 Collective-owned
全国	**National Average**	**86666**	**100409**	**62670**	**17476**	**18779**	**13808**
北京	Beijing	129961	141993	109842	19916	19714	20274
天津	Tianjin	147063	171624	84315	22475	24057	17007
河北	Hebei	70048	109051	49893	15169	19403	14277
山西	Shanxi	89151	95579	35211	15705	17384	8917
内蒙古	Inner Mongolia	61074	92200	38533	15802	21112	10408
辽宁	Liaoning	82496	103366	59031	15966	18495	13649
吉林	Jilin	77486	78590	50494	13900	13837	10977
黑龙江	Heilongjiang	68033	73439	62641	14835	14589	13425
上海	Shanghai	153910	141709	163746	27720	29509	23708
江苏	Jiangsu	100569	114488	85362	20185	21358	17232
浙江	Zhejiang	127430	152666	102060	25842	29942	22476
安徽	Anhui	66407	86385	44705	14501	16214	11859
福建	Fujian	108288	148481	84085	20956	25413	17034
江西	Jiangxi	70826	90561	55856	14578	17256	12626
山东	Shandong	60728	80061	50840	12943	16064	11307
河南	Henan	66056	87189	44605	13257	16711	10143
湖北	Hubei	81761	93576	49126	17932	20504	12051
湖南	Hunan	74553	107602	57131	15700	18057	13874
广东	Guangdong	101932	122414	68856	22056	24999	15163
广西	Guangxi	77472	94984	56558	16816	20495	12179
海南	Hainan	55361	55357	54552	12482	11291	16407
重庆	Chongqing	69432	84901	59089	15246	16773	12609
四川	Sichuan	59748	70851	49686	13062	13944	11297
贵州	Guizhou	72152	85408	47268	16548	19139	12509
云南	Yunnan	69238	86003	49838	13803	14344	10855
西藏	Tibet	73205	95271	44505	16593	18960	14875
陕西	Shaanxi	93212	115392	44801	14769	17462	10396
甘肃	Gansu	46857	72496	35507	11520	16556	8533
青海	Qinghai	61046	87432	36240	12930	18890	7726
宁夏	Ningxia	61459	69396	42641	14177	15526	11794
新疆	Xinjiang	95835	100658	92958	19854	20141	18055

15-37 建筑业房屋建筑面积

Floor Space of Building Construction of Construction Enterprises

单位：万平方米 (10 000 sq.m)

年份 Year 地区 Region	房屋建筑面积 Floor Space of Building Construction		#国有 State-owned		#集体 Collective-owned	
	施工面积 Floor Space under Construction	竣工面积 Floor Space Completed	施工面积 Floor Space under Construction	竣工面积 Floor Space Completed	施工面积 Floor Space under Construction	竣工面积 Floor Space Completed
1985	35491.8	17072.7	19295.8	8563.1	16196.0	8509.6
1989	40649.9	19723.4	21399.0	9143.3	19250.9	10580.1
1990	37923.0	19552.5	20303.2	9361.7	17619.7	10190.9
1991	41054.2	20256.3	21395.4	9566.2	19658.8	10690.1
1992	51885.4	24045.5	25896.1	10968.0	25989.3	13077.5
1993	65374.2	28684.8	32118.1	12085.4	32724.1	16379.0
1994	78032.2	32383.3	39445.8	14143.0	37004.4	17674.0
1995	89862.8	35666.3	44562.9	15182.4	41829.5	19262.0
1996	129087.0	60047.9	48372.8	17491.3	74668.4	39827.3
1997	128680.3	62244.0	48830.1	18507.5	70795.3	39859.3
1998	137593.6	65682.6	45866.9	17577.4	71597.6	39338.0
1999	147262.5	73924.9	47055.7	19868.6	70590.4	39949.1
2000	160141.1	80714.9	46237.5	20145.0	68112.3	38515.5
2001	188328.7	97699.0	46627.5	20338.2	61239.2	36115.1
2002	215608.7	110217.1	44567.3	19628.2	52564.4	30071.3
2003	259377.1	122827.6	46803.7	18774.1	50488.9	26727.6
北 京 Beijing	11971.8	4254.8	3908.2	1312.9	1596.0	703.1
天 津 Tianjin	3395.9	1465.8	1252.6	503.2	497.5	292.5
河 北 Hebei	8914.6	4748.3	1507.3	692.6	1291.7	754.1
山 西 Shanxi	3119.1	1313.3	1305.3	511.4	434.6	239.6
内蒙古 Inner Mongolia	2494.8	1450.7	72.5	34.8	112.4	69.7
辽 宁 Liaoning	8198.1	3957.1	1292.9	550.6	1583.0	926.3
吉 林 Jilin	2538.8	1626.8	973.3	573.9	244.3	193.8
黑龙江 Heilongjiang	3743.4	2181.3	929.2	510.3	617.2	336.1
上 海 Shanghai	9978.6	3609.2	1680.3	506.5	1177.2	459.2
江 苏 Jiangsu	33950.0	17730.0	1948.0	899.2	6010.9	3513.8
浙 江 Zhejiang	39473.4	16183.9	600.4	237.0	3660.1	1552.9
安 徽 Anhui	7357.7	4017.6	1490.7	672.3	2258.5	1296.9
福 建 Fujian	6440.1	2952.1	1487.6	533.1	1725.7	776.3
江 西 Jiangxi	5145.1	2750.9	1466.9	683.6	2245.1	1167.3
山 东 Shandong	18714.4	9139.8	3267.8	1111.3	5179.5	2818.4
河 南 Henan	8026.1	3433.6	2163.1	898.3	1899.1	956.6
湖 北 Hubei	8933.4	4840.8	2598.4	1145.8	1663.3	1027.6
湖 南 Hunan	10052.0	4969.7	2482.2	905.2	3047.4	1687.3
广 东 Guangdong	20059.5	8105.0	4687.7	1690.2	5886.2	2614.9
广 西 Guangxi	3791.7	1721.6	1660.9	663.0	1287.8	661.6
海 南 Hainan	457.4	121.5	291.2	71.7	80.3	35.9
重 庆 Chongqing	9754.1	4939.6	941.7	434.3	1318.5	740.6
四 川 Sichuan	15561.4	8784.6	3178.7	1399.1	3234.4	2010.5
贵 州 Guizhou	2519.8	980.3	1460.9	447.0	482.4	254.1
云 南 Yunnan	3646.7	2248.7	920.8	424.1	890.7	625.0
西 藏 Tibet	131.1	121.3	35.6	31.6	44.5	43.9
陕 西 Shaanxi	3897.2	1580.0	1508.8	534.4	965.1	403.0
甘 肃 Gansu	2715.4	1327.2	688.7	311.9	767.8	393.6
青 海 Qinghai	556.6	242.9	112.5	49.8	86.4	38.8
宁 夏 Ningxia	1119.9	578.7	381.5	176.9	109.9	64.6
新 疆 Xinjiang	2719.2	1450.8	507.9	258.4	91.8	69.9

15-38 各地区劳务分包建筑业企业主要指标（2003年）

Main Indicators of Construction Enterprises of Work Subcontractors by Region (2003)

地区	Region	企业单位数（个）Number of Enterprises (unit)	从业人数（人）Number of Persons Employed (person)	企业总收入（万元）Total Revenue (10 000 yuan)	#劳务收入 Work Revenue	税金（万元）Tax (10 000 yuan)	利润总额（万元）Total Profits (10 000 yuan)	从业人员劳动报酬(万元) Earnings of Employed Persons (10 000 yuan)
全国	**National Total**	**2021**	**571979**	**1105124**	**871319**	**27713**	**39168**	**613735**
北京	Beijing	47	4301	27358	17707	802	2767	5148
天津	Tianjin	85	4253	19083	9904	884	653	3466
河北	Hebei	104	39453	72724	57531	907	3926	48401
山西	Shanxi	46	8243	7261	5067	198	134	10771
内蒙古	Inner Mongolia	10	617	1456	1371	38		456
辽宁	Liaoning	136	14411	30229	20441	1012	-3090	5607
吉林	Jilin	8	344	851	715	24	-44	307
黑龙江	Heilongjiang	23	1087	2115	1588	61	-9	832
上海	Shanghai	51	3990	41238	37767	859	830	7968
江苏	Jiangsu	505	142332	335321	289897	8152	8850	196831
浙江	Zhejiang	122	17195	44920	39210	1472	2067	20936
安徽	Anhui	96	85392	131944	95955	2020	4074	71910
福建	Fujian	71	46317	79653	43076	1661	1010	65987
江西	Jiangxi	23	2277	4698	3905	153	181	1260
山东	Shandong	204	17553	45244	31605	1799	2508	11657
河南	Henan	95	17499	21425	18515	597	638	11647
湖北	Hubei	38	22386	32670	30353	324	1468	19100
湖南	Hunan	86	25852	31129	26733	1710	2279	20378
广东	Guangdong	12	1246	3476	2823	119	-47	1130
广西	Guangxi	6	529	3932	1769	188	268	735
海南	Hainan							
重庆	Chongqing	29	29299	35782	29612	762	2052	21757
四川	Sichuan	98	79251	97073	90272	2810	8330	75456
贵州	Guizhou							
云南	Yunnan	3	336	1735	1588	57	91	274
西藏	Tibet							
陕西	Shaanxi	14	1026	5333	947	159	119	837
甘肃	Gansu	29	1538	3021	1006	121	152	1220
青海	Qinghai							
宁夏	Ningxia	12	533	856	734	31	13	298
新疆	Xinjiang	68	4719	24597	11228	793	-52	9366

15-39 勘察设计机构和人员数（2003年）

Number of Prospecting and Designing Institutions and Their Staff and Workers (2003)

地 区	Region	单位数（个）Number of Institutions (unit)	年底职工人数（人）Number of Staff & Workers at Year-end (person)	高级职称 Senior Title	中级职称 Middle Title	初级职称 Junior Title	其他人员 Others
全 国	**National Total**	**12373**	**831543**	**196997**	**280097**	**178809**	**175640**
北 京	Beijing	558	63929	20992	18415	12358	12164
天 津	Tianjin	201	21806	6507	6472	4036	4791
河 北	Hebei	472	33658	8327	11055	6524	7752
山 西	Shanxi	330	23962	4902	8183	4830	6047
内蒙古	Inner Mongolia	206	13261	3086	4838	3088	2249
辽 宁	Liaoning	784	42127	11480	15423	8545	6679
吉 林	Jilin	364	22572	5796	7385	4652	4739
黑龙江	Heilongjiang	343	19172	5889	6819	3362	3102
上 海	Shanghai	325	31675	7539	9980	6134	8022
江 苏	Jiangsu	420	26818	7221	9815	5820	3962
浙 江	Zhejiang	427	22616	6091	7759	4959	3807
安 徽	Anhui	541	33108	7194	11545	8416	5953
福 建	Fujian	556	36080	3723	8570	7721	16066
江 西	Jiangxi	348	17587	3641	6406	4353	3187
山 东	Shandong	1101	55766	13272	18636	12102	11756
河 南	Henan	518	40699	8029	12988	7976	11706
湖 北	Hubei	511	45552	10996	15912	9483	9161
湖 南	Hunan	424	29024	6910	10904	6074	5136
广 东	Guangdong	856	50062	9311	18454	13539	8758
广 西	Guangxi	294	16129	3863	6037	3870	2359
海 南	Hainan	96	5145	1093	1701	1251	1100
重 庆	Chongqing	218	15320	4319	5744	2870	2387
四 川	Sichuan	906	55246	12107	19184	12751	11204
贵 州	Guizhou	285	16285	3122	6059	3719	3385
云 南	Yunnan	173	12234	2339	4068	3421	2406
西 藏	Tibet	40	2205	283	631	487	804
陕 西	Shaanxi	439	32461	8512	10522	6242	7185
甘 肃	Gansu	220	19522	3707	6684	3907	5224
青 海	Qinghai	89	4110	789	1520	914	887
宁 夏	Ningxia	69	2994	717	978	903	396
新 疆	Xinjiang	216	15168	3577	5457	3720	2414

主要统计指标解释

建筑业统计单位 指从事房屋、构筑物建造和设备安装活动的法人企业。建筑业法人企业应具有建筑业资质并能够独立核算；同时应具备以下条件：①依法成立，有自己的名称、组织机构和场所，能够承担民事责任；②独立拥有和使用资产，承担负债，有权与其他单位签订合同；③独立核算盈亏，能够编制资产负债表。

建筑业总产值 是以货币形式表现的建筑业企业在一定时期内生产的建筑业产品和提供的服务的总和。建筑业总产值包括：

⑴建筑工程产值：指列入建筑工程预算内的各种工程价值。

⑵安装工程产值：指设备安装工程价值，不包括被安装设备本身的价值。

⑶其他产值：建筑业总产值中除建筑工程、安装工程以外的产值。包括房屋构筑物修理产值、非标准设备制造产值、总包企业向分包企业收取的管理费以及不能明确划分的施工活动所完成的产值。

a.房屋构筑物修理产值：指房屋和构筑物修理所完成的产值，但不包括被修理房屋、构筑物本身价值和生产设备的修理产值。

b.非标准设备制造产值：指加工制造没有定型的非标准生产设备的加工费和原材料价值(如化工厂、炼油厂用的各种罐、槽，矿井生产统一使用的各种漏斗、三角槽、阀门等)以及附属加工厂为本企业承建工程制作的非标准设备的价值。

建筑业增加值 指建筑业企业在报告期内以货币形式表现的建筑业生产经营活动的最终成果。目前建筑业增加值采用分配法(收入法)计算，即从收入的角度出发，根据生产要素在生产过程中应得的收入份额计算。具体计算公式为：

建筑业增加值=本年提取的固定资产折旧+应付工资+应付福利费+管理费用中的劳动待业保险费、税金+工程结算税金及附加+营业利润

房屋建筑施工面积 指在报告期内施过工的全部房屋建筑面积，包括本期新开工的房屋面积、上期施工跨入本期继续施工的房屋面积、上期停缓建在本期恢复施工的房屋面积、本期竣工的房屋面积及本期施工后又停缓建的房屋面积。

房屋建筑竣工面积 指在报告期内房屋建筑按照设计要求全部完工，达到了使用条件，经验收鉴定合格，正式移交使用单位的房屋建筑面积。

自有机械设备年末总台数 指归本企业所有，属于本企业固定资产的生产性机械设备年末总台数。包括施工机械、生产设备、运输设备以及其他设备。

自有机械设备年末总功率 指本企业自有施工机械、生产设备、运输设备以及其他设备等列为在册固定资产的生产性机械设备年末总功率，按设定能力或查定能力计算。包括机械本身的动力和为该机械服务的单独动力设备，如电动机等。计算单位用千瓦，动力换算可按1马力＝0.735千瓦折合成千瓦数。电焊机、变压器、锅炉不计算动力。

工程结算收入 指企业承包工程实现的工程价款结算收入，以及向发包单位收取的除工程价款以外的按规定列作营业收入的各种款项，如临时设施费、劳动保险费、施工机械调迁费等以及向发包单位收取的各种索赔款。

工程结算利润 指已结算工程实现的利润，如亏损以"–"号表示。计算公式为：

工程结算利润=工程结算收入–工程结算成本–工税结算税金及附加

企业总收入 指与企业生产经营直接有关的各项收入，包括工程结算收入和其他业务收入。计算公式为：

企业总收入=工程结算收入+其他业务收入

Explanatory Notes on Main Statistical Indicators

Statistical Unit in Construction refers to corporate enterprise engaged in the construction of buildings and structures and in the installation of equipment. A corporate construction enterprise should have qualification certificates with independent accounting system, and should meet the following 3 requirements: ①being set up in line with relevant legal basis, having its full name, organization and location, and capable of taking civil liabilities; ② independently possessing and using its assets and assuming its liabilities, and entitled to sign contracts with other institutions; and ③ making independent accounts of its profits and losses, and capable of compiling its own balance sheet.

Gross Output Value of Construction refers to total of construction products and services, expressed in money terms, produced or rendered by construction and installation enterprises during a given period of time. It includes:

(1) Output value of construction projects, that is the value of projects covered by the project budgets;

(2) Output value of installation projects, that is the value of the installation of equipment, (excluding the value of the equipment to be installed);

(3) Output value of others, that is the output value of construction industry excluding that of construction projects and installation projects. It includes: output value of repair of buildings and structures; output value of non-standard equipment manufacturing; overhead expenses received by contracted enterprises to the sub-contracted enterprises and the completed output value of construction activities that have no clear definition.

a. Output value of repair of buildings and structures, that is the value created through the repairs of buildings or structures, but does not include the value of buildings or structures being repaired and the value of the repair of production equipment;

b. Output value of manufactured non-standard equipment, that is the value of non-standard production equipment including raw materials and manufacturing cost made for the construction project (i.e., chemical plant; kettles or tanks used by refineries; various fillers, triangle tanks, valves used by mines), and the output value of equipment manufactured by subsidiary workshops.

Value-added of Construction refers to the final result of the activities of production and management of construction industry in monetary terms in the reference period. At present, the value-added of construction is calculated with the income approach, that is to say, it is the sum of income of various production factors in the production process. The formula is as follows:

Value-added of Construction=depreciation of fixed assets in the year + wages payable + welfare expenses payable + insurance premium and tax for waiting for employment in the administrative expenses + taxes and surcharges on project settlement + profit.

Floor Space of Buildings Under Construction refers to floor space of buildings under construction during the reference period, including newly started buildings, buildings started earlier and continued during the reference period, and buildings suspended earlier but restarted during the reference period, buildings completed during the reference period, and buildings under construction and then suspended during the reference period.

Floor Space of Buildings Completed refers to the floor space of buildings that are completed in the reference period in accordance with the requirements of the design, up to the standard for putting them into use, and have been checked and accepted by concerned departments as qualified ones.

Total Number of Machinery and Equipment Owned by the End of Year refers to the number of machines and equipment owned by the enterprises, and listed as the fixed assets of the enterprises by the end of the year, including machinery and equipment for construction, production and transportation and other equipment.

Total Power of Machinery and Equipment Owned by the End of Year refers to the total power of machinery and equipment owned by the enterprises, and listed as the fixed assets of the enterprises by the end of the year, including machinery and equipment for construction, production and transportation and other equipment. The power of the machinery is calculated on basis of the designed or verified capacity, covering the power of the machinery/equipment and the separate power equipment serving the machinery/equipment (such as electric motors), but excluding welders, transformers and boilers. The unit used for the calculation of power is kilowatt, with horsepower converted to kilowatt by 1 horsepower=0.735 kilowatt.

Income from Settlement of Projects refers to the income received by the construction enterprise from the contracted project through settlement procedures, and other charges to the contractee as operational costs in addition to the value of the project, such as temporary facility fee, labour insurance premium, moving cost of construction equipment, as well as various types of claims to the contractee.

Profit from Settlement of Projects refers to profit realized through settled projects. It is calculated with the following formula:

Profit from Settlement of Projects=Income from Settlement of Projects - Settled Cost - Settled Taxes and Other Cost

Total Revenue of Enterprises refers to the sum of income from production and operation of enterprises, including income from settlement of projects and other operational income, namely:

Total Revenue of Enterprises=Income from Settlement of Projects + Other Operational Income

十六、运输和邮电

Transport, Post and Telecommunication Services

简要说明

一、本篇资料的主要内容

本篇资料反映我国交通运输业和邮政、通信业发展的基本状况。

交通运输业资料主要包括：五种运输方式的线路里程、运输设备拥有量、技术质量情况，各种运输方式完成的货物运输量和旅客运输量，铁路运输的固定资产构成及财务主要情况，主要港口码头长度及泊位情况，沿海主要港口货物吞吐量。

邮电通信业资料主要包括：全国邮政局(所)及邮路情况，邮电通信主要电路及设备拥有量，主要的邮电业务完成情况，邮电通信发展水平等资料。

二、各部分资料的调查范围及统计单位

1.铁路资料：包括国家铁路、地方铁路和合资铁路运营情况，不含军用铁路及由厂矿企事业单位自建的铁路专用线和专用铁道。国家铁路和合资铁路运营资料来源于各铁路局下属分局及所属运输企业(公司)。地方铁路运营概况资料来源于各省地方铁路管理部门。

2.公路、水运、港口资料：(1)公路和水路线路里程为年末通车和通航里程数，不含在建和未正式投入使用的公路和航道里程；(2)民用汽车拥有量及机动车和汽车驾驶员人数，根据公安部交通管理局所属各省车管部门登记注册的车辆资料和驾驶员资料整理，不含军用车辆；(3)公路运输汽车拥有量，根据交通部门所属各省道路运输管理部门登记注册的从事公路运输的营业性和非营业性运输车辆资料整理，属于民用汽车的一部分；(4)民用运输船舶拥有量，根据交通部所属各省水上航运管理部门登记注册的船舶资料整理，不含渔船、水上施工作业船和军用船舶；(5)公路、水路客货运输量资料，按照交通部和国家统计局1992年联合发布的《公路、水路运输全行业统计工作规定》的要求，由交通部和国家统计局分工负责收集整理；(6)公路、水路运输全行业统计以全面调查和非全面调查两种方式进行，统计范围包括在我国注册从事公路、水路客、货运输的全部企事业单位和私人(包括个体联户)；(7)沿海、内河主要港口的生产能力及吞吐量，根据各地港务管理部门注册的港口企业和从事港口生产活动单位的资料整理。

3.管道运输资料：包括输原油、输成品油、输天然气、输其他气体的管线长度、输送能力及完成的运输量。具体包括：油气田企业直接通向炼油厂、化工厂、电站等用户及装车站、油码头的管道，炼油厂通向用户(包括商业石油公司油库)的成品油气管道，独立核算的管道运输企业通向用户及装车(站)栈桥、油码头的管道。管道运输统计数据主要来源于中国石油天然气集团公司和中国石油化工集团公司所属的管道运输企业，由两家集团公司分别负责收集审核本部门统计数据。

4.民航运输资料：统计对象为在我国境内注册从事民用航空运输飞行和通用飞行的航空运输企业和民用航空机场，不包括在我国境内运输飞行的外国航空公司。统计范围为各航空公司从事国内运输、港澳台运输、国际运输的定期航班航线条数及里程、运输量及飞机构成和运营情况、通用飞行完成情况、民用航空机场航班起降架次和客货吞吐量等。

5.邮电通信资料：包括全社会通信和邮政运营企业为社会公众提供的各类通信和邮政服务，不含专用网业务资料。邮电业务量按业务种类分为通信业务量和邮政业务量；按业务范围分为国内业务量和国际及港澳业务量(对台业务量统计在港澳中)。

三、本篇的资料来源

本篇资料由国家统计局工业交通司负责整理、编辑。有关交通运输资料分别来源于铁道部、交通部、民航总局、公安部、中国石油天然气集团公司、中国石油化工集团公司和各省、自治区、直辖市统计局。邮电通信业资料来源于信息产业部、国家邮政局。

Brief Introduction

I. Main Content

Data in this chapter cover mainly the basic conditions of the development of transportation, post and telecommunications in China.

Data of transport cover mainly the length of the routes of five means of transportation, the possession of the transport equipment, the technological quality, the freight traffic and passenger traffic accomplished by various means of transportation, the composition of the fixed assets and main financial conditions in the railway transport, the length of major ports and the situation of berths, and cargo handled at principal sea ports.

Data of post and telecommunication cover mainly the situation of post and telecommunication offices and postal routes, the telephone lines, telegraph lines and the possession of the telecommunication facilities, the complete business volume of post and telecommunication services, and the development of the post and telecommunication services, etc.

II. Coverage and Statistical Units

Data on railway transportation: including the operation and management of the national, local and joint-venture railways, not including the railways for military purpose, industrial lines and special railways. The data on the operation and management of the national railways and joint-venture railways come from the railway sub-bureaus and the transport enterprises subordinate to them. The data on the operation and management of local railways come from the provincial administrative departments of the local railways.

Data on highways, waterways and ports: (1) The length of highways and waterways refer to the length open to traffic or navigation at the end of the year, not including the highways and waterways under construction or not officially put into used ones. (2) The data on the possession of civil motor vehicles and number of drivers are provided by the divisions of vehicle management under the provincial departments of public security, subordinate to the Traffic Management Bureau, Ministry of Public Security, not including those for military use. (3) The data on possession of highway vehicles are provided by the divisions of vehicle management under the provincial departments of public security, subordinate to the Traffic Management Bureau, Ministry of Public Security, including vehicles for business use and non-business use. It is part of the civil motor vehicles. (4) The data on the possession of ships are provided by the divisions of navigation or ports management under the provincial departments of communications, subordinate to the Ministry of Communications, not including fishermen, ships for constructions in water and ships for military use. (5) The data on the passenger traffic and freight traffic by highways and waterways are collected and prepared separately by the Ministry of Communications and the National Bureau of Statistics in accordance with the "Provisions on the Statistical Work of the Whole Trades of Highway and Waterway Transport", jointly issued by the Ministry of Communications and the National Bureau of Statistics in 1992. (6) The data on highway and waterway transportation are collected through comprehensive reporting system and non-comprehensive reporting system. The statistical coverage is all the enterprises and institutional units and individuals (including joint-households) registered in the People's Republic of China and engaged in highway or waterway freight or passenger transport business. (7) The data on production capacity and handling capacity of the seaports and inland river ports are from the administrative record of local seaport management offices, with those registered enterprises and production units engaged in this field.

Data on the pipeline transport: The data on pipeline transport cover the length, transport capacity and the volume transported of the petroleum (crude oil) pipelines, petroleum products pipelines, natural gas pipelines and other gas pipelines. The coverage of statistics of pipeline transport includes the pipelines leading directly from the enterprises of oil fields or gas fields to the users such as refineries, chemical plants, power stations, etc. and to the loading stations and ports or piers, the petroleum products pipelines leading from the refineries to the users (including the oil depots of the commercial oil companies) and the pipelines leading from the enterprises engaged in pipeline transport with independent accounting system to the users and causeways and ports or piers. The data sources of the pipeline transport statistics are mainly the enterprises engaged in the pipeline transport subordinate to the China National Petroleum and Natural Gas Corporation Group and China Petrochemical Corporation Group. The two corporations collect and examine the statistical data from the units subordinate to them respectively.

Data on the civil aviation transport: The civil aviation transport includes the enterprises engaged in the civil aviation transport flights, flights for general purpose and airports for civil aviation, excluding foreign companies' flights within Chinese territory. The statistical data cover the air lines, length, and transport volume of the domestic transport, the transport between China mainland and Hong Kong, Macao and Taiwan, and the international transport engaged by the air companies as well as the composition of aircraft; the statistical data also cover the data on the operation and performance of the civil aviation, and condition of flights for general purpose.

Data on post and telecommunications: Data in this category include telecommunications and post services rendered to the public by telecommunications and postal enterprises, but exclude services provided through dedicated networks. The business volume of post and telecommunications is classified by nature into telecommunication service and postal service, and by customers into the domestic service, international service, and service between the mainland and Hong Kong, Macao (business volume of the service to Taiwan is covered in that for Hong Kong and Macao).III. Sources of Data

Data in this chapter are arranged and compiled by Department of Industrial and Transportation Statistics of NBS. Data on transportation are from Ministry of Railway, Ministry of Communication, Civil Aviation Administration of China, Ministry of Public Security, China Petroleum and Natural Gas Corporation Group, China Petrochemical Corporation Group, and statistical bureaus of provinces, autonomous regions and municipalities directly under the central government. Data on post and telecommunication services come from Ministry of Information Industry and National Postal Office.

16-1 各地区交通运输、邮电通信业职工人数（2003年底）

Number of Staff and Employed Workers in Transport, Post and Telecommunication Services by Region (End of 2003)

单位：人 (person)

地区	Region	铁路运输业 Railway Transport	道路运输业 Road Transport	城市公共交通业 Urban Public Transport	水上运输业 Water Transport	航空运输业 Air Transport	管道运输业 Transport Via Pipelines	装卸搬运和其他运输服务业 Loading, Unloading and Other Transport Services	邮政业 Post	电信和其他信息传输服务业 Telecommunications and Other Information Transmission Services
全　国	**National Total**	**1727735**	**1624952**	**888518**	**570463**	**178820**	**21439**	**277122**	**441626**	**812511**
北　京	Beijing	50683	22089	152131	32	17805	114	14483	18954	44594
天　津	Tianjin	33485	15481	16106	27580	2754		9890	4887	11139
河　北	Hebei	86672	85502	19562	22251	1163	3780	12004	19129	33299
山　西	Shanxi	112977	52184	16718	120	3518		5587	14865	23362
内蒙古	Inner Mongolia	85616	33692	11173	49	2761		3884	11120	23967
辽　宁	Liaoning	106344	70771	45251	33877	11094	3477	24280	16758	36571
吉　林	Jilin	83710	39824	17575	750	3342	900	16189	14085	20775
黑龙江	Heilongjiang	116337	69570	29462	5994	3907	541	12206	21858	34056
上　海	Shanghai	33215	18358	120885	60219	19467		10402	16959	20550
江　苏	Jiangsu	61167	87206	37414	86528	4674	8756	12915	22042	43670
浙　江	Zhejiang	26230	67309	29253	25391	6205	16	8041	20423	37414
安　徽	Anhui	29136	59242	23851	21586	2139		6587	14009	22227
福　建	Fujian	26881	33459	20682	15737	7900		11047	15944	25744
江　西	Jiangxi	62349	45165	11477	6745	2015		4571	13525	19415
山　东	Shandong	61819	103097	36965	48340	6437	1232	10493	23429	50276
河　南	Henan	111382	122755	30721	2860	1526	94	13984	20645	36580
湖　北	Hubei	82585	101759	36521	39621	4928	569	17832	16026	27532
湖　南	Hunan	78847	74580	23232	12727	4270	10	15547	22122	32109
广　东	Guangdong	58822	114582	74754	87837	21712	315	15353	37082	93527
广　西	Guangxi	46504	53611	11964	19525	3219		9292	10151	21362
海　南	Hainan	1811	9145	1705	10247	6956		1545	2580	5613
重　庆	Chongqing	34950	35095	18933	30782	3858	134	5634	10321	17191
四　川	Sichuan	42324	88410	31611	8520	11873	809	8197	18109	37702
贵　州	Guizhou	32947	28804	9854	2253	2561		2483	8913	9287
云　南	Yunnan	48507	57816	9603	589	5555	128	6163	10330	25991
西　藏	Tibet		4800	200	11	612			1551	2164
陕　西	Shaanxi	93163	45428	19138	187	7385	32	9661	13872	16548
甘　肃	Gansu	57239	28969	15064	83	2616	80	6462	6151	13939
青　海	Qinghai	14845	9765	621	19	237		77	2071	6544
宁　夏	Ningxia	14128	10869	1797	3	397		1003	2169	5179
新　疆	Xinjiang	33060	35615	14295		5934	452	1310	11546	14184

16-2 交通运输业基本情况

Basic Conditions of Transport

指　　标	Item	2000	2001	2002	2003
运输线路长度　（万公里）	**Length of Transport Routes　(10 000 km)**				
铁路营业里程	Railways in Operation	6.87	7.01	7.19	7.30
#国家铁路电气化里程	National Electrified Railways	1.49	1.69	1.74	1.81
公路	Highways	140.27	169.80	176.52	180.98
#高速公路	Expressway	1.63	1.94	2.51	2.97
内河	Navigable Inland Waterways	11.93	12.15	12.16	12.40
民航	Total Civil Aviation Routes	150.29	155.36	163.77	174.95
#国际航线	International Routes	50.84	51.69	57.45	71.53
管道	Petroleum and Gas Pipelines	2.47	2.76	2.98	3.26
客运量总计　（万人）	**Total Passenger Traffic　(10 000 persons)**	**1478573**	**1534122**	**1608150**	**1587497**
铁路	Railways	105073	105155	105606	97260
国家	National Railways	101847	101680	101741	93634
地方	Local Railways	519	558	516	412
合资	Joint-venture Railways	2707	2917	3349	3214
公路	Highways	1347392	1402798	1475257	1464335
水运	Waterways	19386	18645	18693	17142
民用航空	Civil Aviation	6722	7524	8594	8759
旅客周转量总计（亿人公里）	**Total Passenger-Kilometers (100 million passenger-km)**	**12261.0**	**13155.1**	**14125.7**	**13810.5**
铁路	Railways	4532.6	4766.8	4969.4	4788.6
国家	National Railways	4414.7	4636.6	4803.1	4622.8
地方	Local Railways	4.6	5.2	5.3	4.0
合资	Joint-venture Railways	113.3	125.1	161.1	161.8
公路	Highways	6657.4	7207.1	7805.8	7695.6
水运	Waterways	100.5	89.9	81.8	63.1
民用航空	Civil Aviation	970.5	1091.4	1268.7	1263.2
货运量总计　（万吨）	**Total Freight Traffic　(10 000 tons)**	**1358682**	**1401786**	**1483446**	**1561422**
铁路	Railways	178581	193189	204955	221178
国家	National Railways	166056	179201	187578	199814
地方	Local Railways	8369	9542	11241	13064
合资	Joint-venture Railways	4156	4446	6136	8300
公路	Highways	1038813	1056312	1116324	1159957
水运	Waterways	122391	132675	141832	158070
民用航空	Civil Aviation	196.7	171.0	202.1	219.0
管道	Petroleum and Gas Pipelines	18700	19439	20133	21997
货物周转量　（亿吨公里）	**Total Freight Ton-kilometers (100 million ton-km)**	**44321**	**47710**	**50686**	**53859**
铁路	Railways	13771	14694	15658	17247
国家	National Railways	13444	14369	15219	16476
地方	Local Railways	44	55	63	69
合资	Joint-venture Railways	283	270	377	702
公路	Highways	6129	6330	6782	7099
水运	Waterways	23734	25989	27511	28716
民用航空	Civil Aviation	50.3	43.7	51.6	57.9
管道	Petroleum and Gas Pipelines	636	653	683	739
民用汽车拥有量　（万辆）	**Number of Civil Motor Vehicles Owned (10 000 units)**	**1608.91**	**1802.04**	**2053.17**	**2382.93**
#载客汽车	Number of Buses and Cars	853.73	993.96	1202.37	1478.81
载货汽车	Number of Trucks	716.32	765.24	812.22	853.51
#运输汽车	Number of Transport Vehicles	702.82	764.39	826.34	924.64
#私人汽车	Number of Private-owned Motor Vehicles	625.33	770.78	968.98	1219.23
其他机动车拥有量　（万辆）	**Number of Other Motor Vehicles　(10 000 units)**	**4168.06**	**4724.05**	**6174.09**	**7108.90**
民用运输船舶拥有量　（艘）	**Number of Civil Transport Vessels　(unit)**				
机动船	Motor Vessels	185018	169329	165936	163813
驳船	Barges	44658	41457	37041	40457
#私人运输船舶拥有量	Number of Private-owned Transport Vessels (unit)				
机动船	Motor Vessels	128654	111633	105697	97837
驳船	Barges	13463	10088	9411	16460
沿海主要港口货物吞吐量（万吨）	**Volume of Freight Handled in Major Coastal Ports (10 000 tons)**	**125603**	**142634**	**166628**	**201126**

16-3 各地区运输线路长度（2003年底）

Length of Transport Routes by Region (End of 2003)

单位: 公里 (km)

地 区	Region	铁路营业里程 Length of Railways in Operation	内河航道里程 Length of Navigable Inland Waterways	公路里程 Total Length of Highways	等级路 Expressway and Class I to IV Highway	#高速 Expressway	#一级 First Class	#二级 Second Class	等外路 Highway Below Class IV
全 国	**National Total**	**73002.0**	**123964**	**1809828**	**1438738**	**29745**	**29903**	**211929**	**371090**
北 京	Beijing	1136.1		14453	14139	499	420	1845	314
天 津	Tianjin	666.3	89	10168	9901	517	420	1468	267
河 北	Hebei	4744.0		65391	55682	1681	2169	10582	9709
山 西	Shanxi	3137.5	485	63122	60838	1211	781	9407	2284
内蒙古	Inner Mongolia	6202.6	2403	74135	65157	329	341	6604	8978
辽 宁	Liaoning	4173.9	413	50095	49845	1637	1100	11378	250
吉 林	Jilin	3561.8	1444	43779	41362	542	1258	5625	2417
黑龙江	Heilongjiang	5483.7	5130	65123	59599	413	925	6623	5524
上 海	Shanghai	256.5	2223	6484	6322	240	468	1534	162
江 苏	Jiangsu	1393.6	24793	65565	56300	2004	3316	11287	9265
浙 江	Zhejiang	1249.9	9892	46193	43436	1438	2251	5948	2757
安 徽	Anhui	2219.7	5586	69560	63374	1070	301	8198	6186
福 建	Fujian	1453.9	3245	54876	42222	727	312	5723	12654
江 西	Jiangxi	2298.2	5590	61233	37791	1040	330	7372	23442
山 东	Shandong	3150.5	1012	76266	76170	3018	3945	20764	96
河 南	Henan	3654.2	1208	73831	68739	1418	44	17853	5092
湖 北	Hubei	2388.5	8155	87813	69914	1074	876	12268	17899
湖 南	Hunan	2977.2	11551	85233	39689	1218	468	5173	45544
广 东	Guangdong	2112.5	11843	110253	99733	2303	6543	15926	10520
广 西	Guangxi	2738.0	5413	58451	45284	1011	482	5351	13167
海 南	Hainan	221.7	343	20877	11894	626	172	1386	8983
重 庆	Chongqing	718.2	4103	31407	22562	580	168	3624	8845
四 川	Sichuan	2961.8	10720	112543	75290	1501	1516	9190	37253
贵 州	Guizhou	1900.1	3502	45304	32352	323	87	2616	12952
云 南	Yunnan	2340.3	2540	166133	109300	1064	230	2677	56833
西 藏	Tibet			41302	9107			611	32195
陕 西	Shaanxi	2892.3	1065	50019	44422	844	187	5335	5597
甘 肃	Gansu	2312.5	860	40293	30947	342	154	4176	9346
青 海	Qinghai	1091.8	330	24377	21568	118	144	3187	2809
宁 夏	Ningxia	791.4	26	11916	11770	526	142	1998	146
新 疆	Xinjiang	2773.3		83633	64029	431	353	6200	19604

16-4 运输线路长度

Length of Transportation Routes

单位:万公里 (10 000 km)

年 份 Year	铁路营业里程 Length of Railways in Operation	# 国家铁路电气化里程 National Electrified Railways	公路 Length of Highways	#高速公路 Expressway	内河 Length of Navigable Inland Waterways	民航 Length of Civil Aviation Routes	# 国际航线 International Routes	管道 Length of Petroleum and Gas Pipelines
1978	5.17	0.10	89.02		13.60	14.89	5.53	0.83
1980	5.33	0.17	88.33		10.85	19.53	8.12	0.87
1981	5.39	0.17	89.75		10.87	21.83	8.28	0.97
1982	5.29	0.18	90.70		10.86	23.27	9.99	1.04
1983	5.41	0.23	91.51		10.89	22.91	9.99	1.08
1984	5.45	0.30	92.67		10.93	26.02	10.74	1.10
1985	5.50	0.42	94.24		10.91	27.72	10.60	1.17
1986	5.57	0.44	96.28		10.94	32.43	10.76	1.30
1987	5.58	0.46	98.22		10.98	38.91	14.89	1.38
1988	5.61	0.57	99.96	0.01	10.94	37.38	12.83	1.43
1989	5.69	0.64	101.43	0.03	10.90	47.19	16.64	1.51
1990	5.78	0.69	102.83	0.05	10.92	50.68	16.64	1.59
1991	5.78	0.78	104.11	0.06	10.97	55.91	17.74	1.62
1992	5.81	0.84	105.67	0.07	10.97	83.66	30.30	1.59
1993	5.86	0.89	108.35	0.11	11.02	96.08	27.87	1.64
1994	5.90	0.90	111.78	0.16	10.27	104.56	35.19	1.68
1995	5.97	0.97	115.70	0.21	11.06	112.90	34.82	1.72
1996	6.49	1.01	118.58	0.34	11.08	116.65	38.63	1.93
1997	6.60	1.20	122.64	0.48	10.98	142.50	50.44	2.04
1998	6.64	1.30	127.85	0.87	11.03	150.58	50.44	2.31
1999	6.74	1.40	135.17	1.16	11.65	152.22	52.33	2.49
2000	6.87	1.49	140.27	1.63	11.93	150.29	50.84	2.47
2001	7.01	1.69	169.80	1.94	12.15	155.36	51.69	2.76
2002	7.19	1.74	176.52	2.51	12.16	163.77	57.45	2.98
2003	7.30	1.81	180.98	2.97	12.40	174.95	71.53	3.26

16-5 运输线路质量

Quality of Transport Routes

指 标	Item	1990	1995	2000	2002	2003
国家铁路营业里程 (公里)	**Length of National Railways in Operation (km)**	**53378**	**54616**	**58656**	**59530**	**60446**
#复线里程 (公里)	Double-Tracking Length (km)	13024	16909	21408	23058	23702
复线里程比重 (%)	Proportion (%)	24.4	31.0	36.5	38.7	39.2
#自动闭塞里程 (公里)	Automatic Blocking Length (km)	10370	12910	18318	20682	21920
自动闭塞里程比重 (%)	Proportion (%)	19.4	23.6	31.2	34.7	36.3
公路线路里程 (公里)	**Length of Highways (km)**	**1028348**	**1157009**	**1402698**	**1765222**	**1809828**
#等级公路里程 (公里)	Expressway and Class I to IV Highway (km)	741040	910754	1216013	1382926	1438738
等级公路里程比重 (%)	Proportion (%)	72.1	78.7	86.7	78.3	79.5
内河航道里程 (公里)	**Length of Navigable Inland Waterways (km)**	**109192**	**110562**	**119325**	**121557**	**123964**
#等级航道里程 (公里)	Standard Waterways (km)		56587	61367	63597	60865
等级航道里程比重 (%)	Proportion (%)		51.2	51.4	52.3	49.1

16-6 客 运 量

Passenger Traffic

单位: 万人 (10 000 persons)

年 份 Year	客运量总计 Total	铁 路 Railways	国 家 National Railways	地 方 Local Railways	合 资 Joint-venture Railways	公 路 Highways	水 运 Waterways	民用航空 Civil Aviation
1978	253993	81491	80729	762		149229	23042	231
1980	341785	92204	91246	958		222799	26439	343
1985	620206	112110	110913	1197		476486	30863	747
1989	791376	113807	112798	1009		644508	31778	1283
1990	772682	95712	94888	824		648085	27225	1660
1991	806048	95080	94208	872		682681	26109	2178
1992	860855	99693	98788	905		731774	26502	2886
1993	996634	105458	104580	878		860719	27074	3383
1994	1092883	108738	108009	729		953940	26165	4038
1995	1172596	102745	102081	664		1040810	23924	5117
1996	1245356	94796	93550	612	634	1122110	22895	5555
1997	1326094	93308	91919	659	730	1204583	22573	5630
1998	1378717	95085	92991	629	1465	1257332	20545	5755
1999	1394413	100164	97725	528	1911	1269004	19151	6094
2000	1478573	105073	101847	519	2707	1347392	19386	6722
2001	1534122	105155	101680	558	2917	1402798	18645	7524
2002	1608150	105606	101741	516	3349	1475257	18693	8594
2003	1587497	97260	93634	412	3214	1464335	17142	8759

16-7 旅 客 周 转 量

Passenger-Kilometers

单位: 亿人公里 (100 million passenger-km)

年 份 Year	旅客周转量总计 Total	铁 路 Railways	国 家 National Railways	地 方 Local Railways	合 资 Joint-venture Railways	公 路 Highways	水 运 Waterways	民用航空 Civil Aviation
1978	1743.1	1093.2	1090.8	2.4		521.3	100.6	27.9
1980	2281.3	1383.2	1380.4	2.8		729.5	129.1	39.6
1985	4436.4	2416.1	2412.5	3.6		1724.9	178.7	116.7
1989	6074.6	3037.4	3034.4	3.0		2662.1	188.3	186.8
1990	5628.3	2612.6	2610.1	2.5		2620.3	164.9	230.5
1991	6178.4	2828.1	2824.8	3.2		2871.7	177.2	301.3
1992	6949.4	3152.2	3148.3	4.0		3192.6	198.4	406.1
1993	7858.1	3483.3	3479.4	3.9		3700.7	196.5	477.6
1994	8591.4	3636.1	3632.8	3.2		4220.3	183.5	551.6
1995	9001.9	3545.7	3542.6	3.1		4603.1	171.8	681.3
1996	9164.8	3347.6	3322.0	3.4	22.2	4908.8	160.6	747.8
1997	10055.5	3584.9	3543.5	4.7	36.6	5541.4	155.7	773.5
1998	10636.7	3773.4	3691.0	5.0	77.4	5942.8	120.3	800.2
1999	11299.8	4136.0	4046.3	4.4	85.3	6199.2	107.3	857.3
2000	12261.0	4532.6	4414.7	4.6	113.3	6657.4	100.5	970.5
2001	13155.1	4766.8	4636.6	5.2	125.1	7207.1	89.9	1091.4
2002	14125.7	4969.4	4803.1	5.3	161.1	7805.8	81.8	1268.7
2003	13810.5	4788.6	4622.8	4.0	161.8	7695.6	63.1	1263.2

16-8 货 运 量

Freight Traffic

单位：万吨　　　　(10 000 tons)

年 份 Year	货运量 总计 Total	铁 路 Railways	国 家 National Railways	地 方 Local Railways	合 资 Joint-venture Railways	公 路 Highways	水 运 Waterways	民用航空 Civil Aviation	管道输 油(气)量 Petroleum and Gas Pipelines
1978	248946	110119	107492	2627		85182	43292	6.4	10347
1980	546537	111279	108584	2695		382048	42676	8.9	10525
1985	745763	130709	127516	3193		538062	63322	19.5	13650
1989	988435	151489	146804	4685		733781	87493	31.0	15641
1990	970602	150681	146209	4472		724040	80094	37.0	15750
1991	985793	152893	147898	4995		733907	83370	45.2	15578
1992	1045899	157627	152317	5310		780941	92490	57.5	14783
1993	1115902	162794	156791	6003		840256	97938	69.4	14845
1994	1180396	163216	157278	5938		894914	107091	82.9	15092
1995	1234937	165982	159473	6509		940387	113194	101.1	15274
1996	1298421	171024	161787	7125	2112	983860	127430	115.0	15992
1997	1278218	172149	162010	7854	2285	976536	113406	124.7	16002
1998	1267427	164309	153435	8035	2839	976004	109555	140.1	17419
1999	1293008	167554	157239	7296	3019	990444	114608	170.0	20232
2000	1358682	178581	166056	8369	4156	1038813	122391	196.7	18700
2001	1401786	193189	179201	9542	4446	1056312	132675	171.0	19439
2002	1483446	204955	187578	11241	6136	1116324	141832	202.1	20133
2003	1561422	221178	199814	13064	8300	1159957	158070	219.0	21997

注：1.从1979年起，公路运输包括社会车辆完成数量，从1984年起，还包括私营运输完成的数量(下表同)。
　　2.1993年及以后年份铁路货物运输指标口径有调整，增加了行包运量(下表同)。

a) Since 1979, the freight traffic by highways has included the quantities transported by trucks of non-highway departments. Since 1984, it has also included the quantities transported by private trucks. The same as the following table.

b) The indicator standard of railways freight has been adjusted since 1993, increased freight of package. The same as the following table.

16-9 货 物 周 转 量

Freight Ton-Kilometers

单位：亿吨公里　　　　(100 million ton-km)

年 份 Year	货物周转量 总计 Total	铁 路 Railways	国 家 National Railways	地 方 Local Railways	合 资 Joint-venture Railways	公 路 Highways	水 运 Waterways	民用航空 Civil Aviation	管道输 油(气)量 Petroleum and Gas Pipelines
1978	9829	5345.2	5333.5	11.7		274.1	3779.2	0.97	430
1980	12026	5716.9	5707.3	9.6		764.0	5052.8	1.41	491
1985	18365	8125.7	8111.6	14.1		1903.2	7729.3	4.15	603
1989	25591	10394.2	10373.0	21.2		3374.8	11186.8	6.90	629
1990	26207	10622.4	10601.2	21.2		3358.1	11591.9	8.20	627
1991	27986	10972.0	10948.1	23.9		3428.0	12955.4	10.10	621
1992	29218	11575.6	11548.5	27.0		3755.4	13256.2	13.42	617
1993	30525	11968.9	11937.7	31.2		4070.5	13860.8	16.61	608
1994	33275	12471.4	12440.0	31.4		4486.3	15686.6	18.59	612
1995	35909	13049.5	13015.3	34.2		4694.9	17552.2	22.30	590
1996	36590	13106.2	12935.0	48.6	122.5	5011.2	17862.5	24.93	585
1997	38385	13269.9	13063.0	50.7	156.2	5271.5	19235.0	29.10	579
1998	38089	12560.1	12304.5	50.7	204.8	5483.4	19405.8	33.45	606
1999	40568	12910.3	12649.8	37.6	222.9	5724.3	21263.0	42.30	628
2000	44321	13770.5	13444.0	43.6	282.9	6129.4	23734.2	50.27	636
2001	47710	14694.1	14368.8	55.4	270.0	6330.4	25988.9	43.72	653
2002	50686	15658.4	15219.1	62.8	376.5	6782.5	27510.6	51.55	683
2003	53859	17246.7	16475.6	69.0	702.1	7099.5	28715.8	57.90	739

16-10 旅客运输平均运距
Average Transport Distance of Passengers

单位: 公里 (km)

年份 Year	总计 Total	铁路 Railways	公路 Highways	水运 Waterways	民用航空 Civil Aviation
1978	69	134	35	44	1208
1980	67	150	33	49	1153
1985	72	216	36	58	1563
1989	77	267	41	59	1456
1990	73	273	40	61	1388
1991	77	297	42	68	1383
1992	81	316	44	75	1407
1993	79	330	43	73	1412
1994	79	334	44	70	1366
1995	77	345	44	72	1331
1996	74	353	44	70	1346
1997	76	384	46	69	1374
1998	77	406	47	59	1391
1999	82	413	49	56	1407
2000	83	431	49	52	1444
2001	86	453	51	48	1450
2002	88	471	53	44	1476
2003	87	492	53	37	1442

16-11 货物运输平均运距
Average Transport Distance of Freight

单位: 公里 (km)

年份 Year	总计 Total	铁路 Railways	公路 Highways	水运 Waterways	管道 Petroleum and Gas Pipelines	民用航空 Civil Aviation
1978	395	485	32	873	416	1521
1980	220	514	20	1184	467	1573
1985	243	636	31	1216	442	2128
1989	259	686	46	1279	402	2228
1990	270	705	46	1447	398	2218
1991	284	718	46	1554	399	2234
1992	279	734	48	1433	417	2330
1993	274	735	48	1415	409	2393
1994	282	791	50	1465	406	2241
1995	289	807	50	1551	386	2206
1996	282	766	51	1402	366	2168
1997	300	770	54	1696	362	2334
1998	300	763	56	1771	348	2388
1999	313	768	58	1855	310	2482
2000	326	767	59	1939	340	2556
2001	340	757	60	1959	336	2557
2002	341	760	61	1940	339	2551
2003	345	780	61	1817	336	2644

16-12 各地区客运量(2003年)

Passenger Traffic by Region (2003)

单位: 万人 (10 000 persons)

地区	Region	合计 Total	铁路 Railways	国家铁路 National Railways	地方铁路 Local Railways	合资铁路 Joint-venture Railways	公路 Highways	水运 Waterways
全国	**National Total**	**1587497**	**97260**	**93634**	**412**	**3214**	**1464335**	**17142**
北京	Beijing	29300	4360	4359	1		24940	
天津	Tianjin	3403	1291	1291			2109	3
河北	Hebei	65209	4442	4442			60767	
山西	Shanxi	37225	2861	2861			34328	36
内蒙古	Inner Mongolia	23599	2768	2722		46	20831	
辽宁	Liaoning	50349	8731	8719	12		41076	542
吉林	Jilin	24505	4306	4306			20112	87
黑龙江	Heilongjiang	47842	8319	8212	107		39347	176
上海	Shanghai	6481	3391	3391			2052	1038
江苏	Jiangsu	123297	5104	5104			118046	147
浙江	Zhejiang	141148	5197	4080		1117	133968	1983
安徽	Anhui	62727	2987	2821	6	160	59544	196
福建	Fujian	47766	1576	1356		220	45483	707
江西	Jiangxi	36909	3325	3325			33196	388
山东	Shandong	77212	3343	3272	71		72754	1115
河南	Henan	81228	4864	4726	138		76301	63
湖北	Hubei	61961	3017	3009		8	58371	573
湖南	Hunan	96207	5061	4907		154	90353	793
广东	Guangdong	131199	7237	6315	11	911	122265	1697
广西	Guangxi	42932	1623	1561	39	23	40524	785
海南	Hainan	24787	13	13			24037	737
重庆	Chongqing	58159	1069	1069			55673	1417
四川	Sichuan	141148	4233	3812	2	419	133782	3133
贵州	Guizhou	55074	1796	1796			52695	583
云南	Yunnan	34785	1364	1245	26	93	33039	382
西藏	Tibet	125					125	
陕西	Shaanxi	30977	2497	2435		62	28159	321
甘肃	Gansu	14961	989	989			13732	240
青海	Qinghai	4265	395	395			3870	
宁夏	Ningxia	5856	251	251			5605	
新疆	Xinjiang	18103	852	852			17251	
不分地区	Not Classified by Region	8759						

注:不分地区合计为民航完成数。

a) The total passenger traffic not classified by region is that completed by civil aviation.

16-13　各地区旅客周转量（2003年）

Passenger-kilometers by Region (2003)

单位: 亿人公里　　　　　　　　　　　　　　　　　　　　　　　　(100 million passenger-km)

地　区	Region	合　计 Total	铁　路 Railways	国家铁路 National Railways	地方铁路 Local Railways	合资铁路 Joint-venture Railways	公　路 Highways	水　运 Waterways
全　国	**National Total**	**13810.5**	**4788.6**	**4622.8**	**4.0**	**161.8**	**7695.6**	**63.1**
北　京	Beijing	131.8	62.5	62.5	…		69.3	
天　津	Tianjin	91.7	70.1	70.1			21.6	…
河　北	Hebei	780.5	383.8	383.8			396.7	
山　西	Shanxi	246.8	84.6	84.6			162.2	…
内蒙古	Inner Mongolia	204.8	82.7	79.8		2.9	122.1	
辽　宁	Liaoning	480.8	309.5	309.5	…		164.1	7.2
吉　林	Jilin	206.9	122.4	122.4			84.4	0.1
黑龙江	Heilongjiang	354.9	151.2	149.3	1.9		203.4	0.3
上　海	Shanghai	100.8	38.1	38.1			58.0	4.7
江　苏	Jiangsu	957.6	183.0	183.0			774.1	0.5
浙　江	Zhejiang	718.4	181.0	151.3		29.8	531.6	5.7
安　徽	Anhui	620.9	223.8	215.2	…	8.6	396.7	0.4
福　建	Fujian	334.0	75.3	68.4		6.9	257.5	1.1
江　西	Jiangxi	482.1	299.9	299.2		0.8	181.3	0.8
山　东	Shandong	623.2	220.2	219.2	0.9	0.2	397.7	5.2
河　南	Henan	812.3	462.1	461.3	0.8		350.0	0.2
湖　北	Hubei	545.4	232.3	231.5		0.8	309.4	3.7
湖　南	Hunan	817.9	430.8	413.0		17.9	384.7	2.4
广　东	Guangdong	1262.8	267.1	197.1	…	70.1	987.8	7.9
广　西	Guangxi	463.4	93.7	93.2	0.2	0.4	367.4	2.3
海　南	Hainan	78.2	0.1	0.1			76.2	1.8
重　庆	Chongqing	235.7	34.8	34.8			187.5	13.5
四　川	Sichuan	547.9	145.3	127.7	…	17.6	400.1	2.4
贵　州	Guizhou	248.6	112.1	112.1			135.3	1.2
云　南	Yunnan	229.5	35.8	32.1	0.1	3.5	192.9	0.9
西　藏	Tibet	5.5					5.5	
陕　西	Shaanxi	382.6	207.8	205.3		2.5	174.3	0.5
甘　肃	Gansu	243.6	156.2	156.2			87.2	0.2
青　海	Qinghai	38.0	16.3	16.3			21.7	
宁　夏	Ningxia	51.0	17.5	17.5			33.5	
新　疆	Xinjiang	249.8	88.5	88.5			161.3	
不分地区	Not Classified by Region	1263.2						

注:不分地区合计为民航完成数。

a) The total passenger-kilometers not classified by region is that completed by civil aviation.

16-14 各地区货运量（2003年）

Freight Traffic by Region (2003)

单位: 万吨 (10 000 tons)

地区	Region	合计 Total	铁路 Railways	国家铁路 National Railways	地方铁路 Local Railways	合资铁路 Joint-venture Railways	公路 Highways	水运 Waterways
全国	**National Total**	**1561422**	**221178**	**199814**	**13064**	**8300**	**1159957**	**158070**
北京	Beijing	30729	2368	2265	103		28361	
天津	Tianjin	32014	5664	2658	3006		20072	6278
河北	Hebei	77089	14347	12831	1486	30	61570	1172
山西	Shanxi	106720	39020	36704	259	2057	67671	29
内蒙古	Inner Mongolia	50820	12288	11547	522	219	38532	
辽宁	Liaoning	83515	13885	13135	750		65981	3649
吉林	Jilin	31436	6153	6019	134		25211	72
黑龙江	Heilongjiang	54350	14267	13842	425		39031	1052
上海	Shanghai	58507	1208	1208			30678	26621
江苏	Jiangsu	92845	5204	4567	637		64321	23320
浙江	Zhejiang	103833	3328	2525	83	720	70907	29598
安徽	Anhui	54643	8744	7886	688	170	39918	5981
福建	Fujian	34415	4207	3207		1000	23884	6324
江西	Jiangxi	27709	4784	4131	653		21047	1878
山东	Shandong	117051	14009	12981	1026	2	97977	5065
河南	Henan	69688	12925	11852	1073		56100	663
湖北	Hubei	41261	4718	4436	259	23	30348	6195
湖南	Hunan	60306	5570	5217	63	290	51136	3600
广东	Guangdong	100565	6391	4899	497	995	73087	21087
广西	Guangxi	31525	4587	3290	468	829	24164	2774
海南	Hainan	8008	368	348		20	5689	1951
重庆	Chongqing	32563	1943	1812	120	11	28406	2214
四川	Sichuan	57527	7278	6840	353	85	47467	2782
贵州	Guizhou	18224	4971	4920		51	12886	367
云南	Yunnan	58170	4146	3854	155	137	53864	160
西藏	Tibet	266					266	
陕西	Shaanxi	34961	6686	5053		1633	28165	110
甘肃	Gansu	24539	3783	3783			20713	43
青海	Qinghai	5653	858	858			4795	
宁夏	Ningxia	7344	2296	1992	304		5048	
新疆	Xinjiang	27078	4416	4416			22662	
不分地区	Not Classified by Region	28070	768	738	…	30		5085

注:不分地区合计中,包括民航、管道、铁路行包运量及中国远洋运输集团总公司海外公司完成数。

a) The freight traffic not classified by region includes that completed by enterprises directly under the departments of civil aviation, pipelines，railway baggage freight and abroad companies under China Ocean Shipping (Group) Company.

16-15 各地区货物周转量(2003年)

Freight Ton-kilometers by Region (2003)

单位: 亿吨公里 (100 million ton-km)

地 区	Region	合计 Total	铁路 Railways	国家铁路 National Railways	地方铁路 Local Railways	合资铁路 Joint-venture Railways	公路 Highways	水运 Waterways
全 国	**National Total**	**53859.2**	**17246.7**	**16475.6**	**69.0**	**702.1**	**7099.5**	**28715.8**
北 京	Beijing	462.5	383.5	383.3	0.2		79.0	
天 津	Tianjin	6521.1	319.8	303.8	12.4	3.6	68.2	6133.1
河 北	Hebei	3223.2	2019.4	1776.0	7.7	235.8	591.6	612.2
山 西	Shanxi	1259.1	922.9	846.1	0.8	75.9	336.2	…
内蒙古	Inner Mongolia	1160.3	918.4	831.4	3.3	83.7	241.9	
辽 宁	Liaoning	2385.2	1028.1	1026.4	1.7		226.5	1130.6
吉 林	Jilin	531.0	440.2	440.0	0.3		90.6	0.2
黑龙江	Heilongjiang	991.4	808.9	804.3	4.6		163.1	19.4
上 海	Shanghai	8492.3	38.4	38.4			68.8	8385.1
江 苏	Jiangsu	1772.6	412.2	405.4	6.8		365.0	995.3
浙 江	Zhejiang	2047.2	252.7	212.0	0.1	40.5	313.7	1480.9
安 徽	Anhui	1328.6	810.3	798.9	3.2	8.3	318.4	199.9
福 建	Fujian	1222.9	194.3	166.2		28.2	193.5	835.1
江 西	Jiangxi	768.6	556.1	551.8	1.4	2.9	162.1	50.5
山 东	Shandong	3908.9	1039.1	995.2	5.3	38.6	527.6	2342.2
河 南	Henan	1891.6	1463.2	1452.4	10.8		405.2	23.2
湖 北	Hubei	1212.6	611.7	610.1	1.0	0.6	223.9	377.0
湖 南	Hunan	1350.6	773.4	748.7	0.1	24.6	455.5	121.7
广 东	Guangdong	3158.0	286.2	203.2	2.3	80.8	553.4	2318.4
广 西	Guangxi	863.4	527.2	500.2	2.6	24.4	217.1	119.1
海 南	Hainan	250.7	2.2	2.2		…	45.5	203.0
重 庆	Chongqing	367.7	102.7	102.1	0.4	0.2	107.3	157.7
四 川	Sichuan	768.3	533.6	522.9	1.2	9.4	219.6	15.1
贵 州	Guizhou	547.0	465.9	464.0		1.9	76.6	4.5
云 南	Yunnan	612.2	253.0	246.7	0.7	5.5	357.6	1.5
西 藏	Tibet	27.1					27.1	
陕 西	Shaanxi	849.1	668.0	633.4		34.6	180.8	0.3
甘 肃	Gansu	738.7	614.9	614.9			123.7	0.1
青 海	Qinghai	124.2	81.4	81.4			42.8	
宁 夏	Ningxia	244.5	181.4	179.3	2.1		63.1	
新 疆	Xinjiang	636.6	382.7	382.7			253.9	
不分地区	Not Classified by Region	4141.9	154.9	152.2	…	2.7		3189.8

注:不分地区合计中,包括民航、管道、铁路行包运量及中国远洋运输集团总公司海外公司完成数。

a) The freight ton-kilometers not classified by region includes that completed by enterprises directly under the departments of civil aviation, pipelines, railway baggage freight and abroad companies under China Ocean Shipping (Group) Company.

16-16 国家营业铁路基本情况
Basic Statistics on National Railways in Operation

项目	Item	1985	1990	1995	2000	2002	2003
营业里程 (公里)	**Length of Railways in Operation (km)**	**52119**	**53378**	**54616**	**58656**	**59530**	**60446**
正式营业	In Formal Operation	49433	50310	50866	51262	54422	56238
临时营业	In Temporary Operation	2686	3068	3750	7394	5108	4208
正式营业里程比重 (%)	Proportion of the Length in Formal Operation	94.8	94.3	93.1	87.4	91.4	93.0
复线里程 (公里)	**Double-Tracking Length (km)**	**9989**	**13024**	**16909**	**21408**	**23058**	**23702**
占营业里程比重 (%)	As Percentage of the Length of Railways in Operation	19.2	24.4	31.0	36.5	38.7	39.2
电气化线路里程 (公里)	**Length of Electrified Railways (km)**	**4151**	**6941**	**9703**	**14864**	**17409**	**18060**
占营业里程比重 (%)	As Percentage of Railways in Operation	8.0	13.0	17.8	25.3	29.2	29.9
内燃机牵引线路里程(公里)	**Length of Diesel Engine Routes (km)**	**10822**	**16097**	**24749**	**39497**	**42121**	**42387**
占营业里程比重 (%)	As Percentage of Railways in Operation	20.8	30.2	45.3	67.3	70.8	70.1
调度集中里程 (公里)	**Length under Centralized Traffic Control (km)**	**1307**	**1169**	**1226**	**1200**	**1401**	**1842**
占营业里程比重 (%)	As Percentage of Railways in Operation	2.5	2.2	2.2	2.0	2.4	3.1
自动闭塞里程 (公里)	**Automatic Blocking Length (km)**	**6921**	**10370**	**12910**	**18318**	**20682**	**21920**
占营业里程比重 (%)	As Percentage of Railways in Operation	13.3	19.4	23.6	31.2	34.7	36.3
半自动闭塞里程 (公里)	**Semi-automatic Blocking Length (km)**	**42625**	**38832**	**40859**	**41695**	**39990**	**39522**
占营业里程比重 (%)	As Percentage of Railways in Operation	81.8	72.7	74.8	71.1	67.2	65.4
无缝线路里程 (公里)	**Length of Continuous Welded Rail (km)**	**10439**	**14644**	**21854**	**29975**	**35967**	**39497**
占正线里程比重 (%)	As Percentage of the Trunk Lines	16.7	21.7	40.0	51.1	42.7	46.0
有电气集中的车站 (个)	**Number of Stations with Electric Interlocking (unit)**	**2320**	**3535**	**4587**	**5232**	**5278**	**5204**
占营业车站比重 (%)	As Percentage of Railways Stations in Operation	46.9	62.9	73.9	90.4	91.8	92.9

16-17 铁路机车拥有量
Number of Railway Locomotives

单位: 台 (unit)

项目	Item	1985	1990	1995	2000	2002	2003
国家铁路	**Number of Locomotives Owned by National Railways**	**11772**	**13592**	**15146**	**14472**	**15159**	**15456**
蒸汽机车	Steam Locomotives	7674	6279	4347	601	109	94
#前进型	Qianjin Model	4429	4188	2985	261	31	24
建设型	Jianshe Model	1216	1644	1329	340	78	70
内燃机车	Diesel Locomotives	3511	5680	8282	10355	10752	10778
#东风4型	Dongfeng Model IV	955	2351	4362	5623	6373	6411
电力机车	Electric Locomotives	587	1633	2517	3516	3876	4584
#韶山1型	Shaoshan Model I	505	816	814	800	749	707
地方铁路	**Number of Locomotives Owned by Local Railways**	**368**	**378**	**398**	**327**	**357**	**359**
蒸汽机车	Steam Locomotives	239	253	260	159	141	131
内燃机车	Diesel Locomotives	129	125	129	168	216	228
合资铁路	**Number of Locomotives Owned by Joint-venture Railways**				**454**	**510**	**505**
蒸汽机车	Steam Locomotives				151	124	118
内燃机车	Diesel Locomotives				303	344	349
电力机车	Electric Locomotives					42	38

16-18 国家铁路客、货车拥有量

Number of National Railway Passenger Coaches and Freight Cars Owned

项　目	Item	1985	1990	1995	2000	2002	2003
客　车　（辆）	**Passenger Coaches (coach)**	**20872**	**27261**	**32404**	**35989**	**37942**	**38972**
软卧车	Soft Berth Coaches	679	1061	1537	2055	2421	2621
硬卧车	Hard Berth Coaches	2633	4351	7607	10139	11738	11920
软座车	Soft Seat Coaches	260	330	574	764	676	746
硬座车	Hard Seat Coaches	13700	17503	18076	17571	17148	17210
软硬座车	Soft and Hard Seat Coaches	114	63	35	25	5	5
餐　车	Dining Cars	1221	1520	1695	1847	2008	1983
行李邮政车	Luggage and Post Cars	1498	1686	1949	2144	2237	2226
公务车	Business Cars	87	77	87	69	62	71
简易及代用客车	Simple and Substitute Cars	79	42	9			
其　他	Others	601	628	835	1375	1647	2190
货　车　（辆）	**Freight Cars (coach)**	**300886**	**364966**	**432731**	**439943**	**446707**	**503868**
按车型分	Grouped by Type of Car						
棚　车	Covered Cars	52667	66668	80437	92569	91835	95678
敞　车	Open Cars	185684	232999	268179	252977	257642	308578
平　车	Flat Cars	18753	18726	27461	24685	28028	29115
毒品车	Hazardous Materials Cars		1229	1580	1578	1956	2056
罐　车	Tank Cars	31837	33646	37119	37778	39258	40495
保温车	Refrigerator Cars	3991	5150	7030	7909	7711	7696
其　他	Others	7944	6548	10925	22447	20277	20250
按载重量分	Grouped by Capacity of Car						
20吨及以下	20 Tons and Under	1476	949	1458			
25-40吨	25-40 Tons	21520	8699	8786	7765①	8546	8525
50吨	50 Tons	104456	92442	48287	15799	3607	3590
51-59吨	51-59 Tons	16544	15500	27951		54218	54452
60吨	60 Tons	153198	238680	342086	307521	233327	268063
65吨	65 Tons	1571	6825	3546	103431②	138624	159620
73吨及以上	73 Tons and Over	306	329	385	5427③	796	2029
其他	Others	1815	1542	232			
货车总标记载重量（万吨）	**Total Loading Capacity of Freight Cars (10 000 tons)**	**1612.5**	**2055.3**	**2502.9**	**2619.9**	**2686.2**	**3040.9**
平均每辆车标记载重量（吨）	**Average Marked Loading Capacity per Car (ton)**	**53.9**	**56.6**	**57.9**	**59.6**	**60.1**	**60.4**

注：1997年起货车按标记载重量统计，分组与以前年份相比有所调整。带①号的数据含20吨及以下货车。带②号的数据是载重量61吨货车。带③号的数据是载重量70吨及以上货车（以后各年相同）。

a) Statistics on freight cars are based on marked loading capacity of cars since 1997, resulting in the adjustment of grouping of cars. Data marked ① refer to cars with a loading capacity of 20 tons and less, data marked ② refer to cars with a loading capacity of 61 tons, and ③ refer to cars with a loading capacity of 70 tons and over. The same as in the following years.

16-19 国家铁路运输固定资产

Fixed Assets of National Railway Transport

单位: 亿元 (100 million yuan)

项　目	Item	1990	1995	2000	2002	2003
固定资产原值	**Original Value of Fixed Assets**	**1253.9**	**3613.6**	**5268.8**	**7133.4**	**7872.3**
#生产用	Fixed Assets for Productive Purpose	1116.1	3526.0	5205.7	7053.0	7784.0
#机车车辆	Locomotives, Coaches and Freight Cars	312.1	776.9	816.8	1650.7	1818.3
线　路	Lines	545.2	1850.7	2854.4	3355.9	3691.2
通信线路	Communications Lines	19.5	43.2	0.2		
通信信号设备	Communications & Signaling Equipment	35.4	80.8	153.6		
房屋及建筑物	Buildings	107.4	489.9	683.1	823.1	902.9
机械动力设备	Machinery and Power Equipment	47.7	84.0	143.6	197.2	221.6
传导设备	Conduction Equipment	34.6	72.5	153.4	201.0	117.4
非生产用	Fixed Assets for Non-productive Purposes	106.8				
未使用	Unused Fixed Assets	24.5	73.2	56.3	70.2	73.8
不需用	Non-required Fixed Assets	1.0	2.1	1.4	3.5	5.8
封存及租出的	Sealed-up for Safekeeping and Leased	4.4	12.3	5.3	6.7	8.7
土　地	Land	0.3				
固定资产净值	**Net Value of Fixed Assets**	**889.3**	**2409.4**	**3830.1**	**5105.1**	**5658.3**
固定资产折旧	**Depreciation of Fixed Assets**	**364.6**	**1204.1**	**1438.7**	**2028.3**	**2214.0**

注:1995年起生产用固定资产统计口径变更为在用固定资产，原非生产用固定资产和土地包括其中。

a) Since 1995, the fixed assets for productive purposes have changed to be the fixed assets in use, and included land and the fixed assets for non-productive purpose.

16-20 按货类分国家铁路货物运输量

National Railway Freight Traffic by Category of Cargo

项　目	Item	2002 货运量(万吨) Freight Traffic (10 000 tons)	2002 货物周转量(百万吨公里) Freight Ton-kilometers (million ton-kilometers)	2002 平均运距(公里) Average Transport Distance (km)	2003 货运量(万吨) Freight Traffic (10 000 tons)	2003 货物周转量(百万吨公里) Freight Ton-kilometers (million ton-kilometers)	2003 平均运距(公里) Average Transport Distance (km)
总　计	**Total**	**186894**	**1507817**	**807**	**199076**	**1632341**	**820**
煤	Coal	81852	463886	567	88132	505540	574
焦　炭	Coke	5613	48755	869	7124	63789	895
石　油	Petroleum	10299	97316	945	10765	102934	956
钢　铁	Steel and Iron	14123	147046	1041	15280	165545	1083
金属矿石	Metal Ores	16777	92098	549	18082	103868	574
非金属矿石	Nonmetal Ores	8176	49840	610	7945	50799	639
矿建材料	Mineral Building Materials	8599	42808	498	7664	36500	476
水　泥	Cement	3596	14908	415	3652	15347	420
木　材	Timber	3149	55393	1759	3054	53866	1764
化肥和农药	Chemical Fertilizers and Pesticides	5942	73348	1234	5660	72312	1278
粮　食	Grain	8282	114500	1383	10138	136651	1348
棉　花	Cotton	243	8361	3441	218	7334	3366
盐	Salt	1256	9525	758	1263	10031	794
其　他	Others	18987	290033	1528	20099	307825	1532

16-21 国家铁路平均每日装车数

Daily Average Number of Freight Car Loading

单位：车 (car)

年份 Year	合计 Total	#煤 Coal	#石油 Petroleum	#钢铁 Steel and Iron	#矿物性建筑材料 Mineral Building Materials	#粮食 Grain
1978	62234	21595	3641	3425	9301	1335
1980	61298	21627	3294	3399	8256	1590
1985	67228	25333	3448	3963	7765	2247
1989	72919	28479	3785	4010	6936	2490
1990	72368	29323	3811	4165	5858	2530
1991	72911	29103	3823	4127	5628	2878
1992	74109	29523	3880	4146	5564	2919
1993	76306	30039	4059	4756	5959	3022
1994	75664	30183	3969	4636	5168	3430
1995	76416	30754	4230	4406	4818	2985
1996	76895	32720	4195	4426	4533	2670
1997	76948	31876	4419	4630	4570	3196
1998	72429	28757	4455	4700	4581	2529
1999	74038	28987	4893	4849	4666	2950
2000	77645	30582	5220	5352	4325	3591
2001	83693	34213	5382	5999	4403	3225
2002	87457	36511	5594	6613	3919	3797
2003	93040	39397	5792	7156	3515	4658

16-22 国家铁路货车平均静载重

Average Static Load of Freight Cars

单位：吨/车 (ton/car)

年份 Year	合计 Total	#煤 Coal	#石油 Petroleum	#钢铁 Steel and Iron	#矿物性建筑材料 Mineral Building Materials	#粮食 Grain
1978	46.9	50.6	46.3	47.5	49.9	50.3
1980	48.0	52.5	46.3	49.0	52.6	54.2
1985	51.6	55.7	46.2	51.9	55.3	54.6
1989	54.8	58.3	46.8	54.6	57.6	42.2
1990	55.0	58.5	47.0	55.0	57.9	58.3
1991	55.2	58.7	46.7	55.6	58.0	58.5
1992	55.8	59.1	47.1	56.4	58.3	58.9
1993	56.1	59.3	47.4	57.1	58.5	59.1
1994	56.6	59.6	47.6	57.8	59.0	59.3
1995	56.8	59.9	47.6	58.2	59.2	59.4
1996	57.1	60.0	47.5	58.5	59.4	59.6
1997	57.3	60.2	48.0	58.6	59.4	59.6
1998	57.6	60.8	48.6	58.9	59.7	59.7
1999	57.7	61.1	49.2	59.1	59.9	59.6
2000	57.9	61.1	49.8	58.9	59.7	59.7
2001	58.1	61.1	50.2	58.8	59.8	59.6
2002	58.2	61.2	50.6	58.7	59.6	59.5
2003	58.3	61.1	51.0	58.6	59.6	59.4

16–23 铁路主要干线客货运输量（2003年）

Passenger and Freight Traffic of Principal Trunk Railways (2003)

线路名称	Name	客运量（万人）Passenger Traffic (10 000 persons)	旅客周转量（百万人公里）Passenger-kilometers (million passenger-km)
京沪线	Beijing-Shanghai	8946	48516
新石线	Xinjiang-Rizhao	284	1209
沪杭、浙赣线	Shanghai-Hangzhou, Hangzhou-Ganzhou	5222	33262
鹰厦线	Yingtan-Xiamen	644	5984
京九线	Beijing-Kowloon	3717	32849
京广线	Beijing-Guangzhou	11510	86203
石太线	Shijiazhuang-Taiyuan	698	1663
石德线	Shijiazhuang-Dezhou	453	1713
焦柳线	Jiaozuo-Liuzhou	1601	8224
京包线	Bingjing-Baotou	1404	6171
包兰线	Baotou-Lanzhou	614	2277
北同蒲线	Taiyuan-Datong	489	1328
南同蒲线	Fenglingdu-Taiyuan	1166	3758
陇海线	Lianyungang-Lanzhou	4507	34521
宝中线	Baoji-Zhongwei	78	1518
兰新线	Lanzhou-Urumqi	958	15588
兰青、青藏线	Lanzhou-Qinghai, Qinghai-Tibet	393	1873
湘黔线	Zhuzhou-Guiyang	1317	13380
宝成、成渝线	Baoji-Chengdu, Chengdu-Chongqing	2037	10752
襄渝线	Xiangfan-Chongqing	1583	10336
贵昆线	Guiyang-Kunming	978	3520
南昆线	Nanning-Kunming	408	625
成昆线	Chengdu-Kunming	1159	4652
京秦线	Beijing-Qinhuangdao	661	3156
大秦线	Datong-Qinhuangdao	47	264
京哈线	Beijing-Harbin	7561	36225

线路名称	Name	货运量（万吨）Freight Traffic (10 000 tons)	货物周转量（百万吨公里）Freight Ton-kilometers (million ton-km)
京沈线	Beijing-Shenyang	3181	84877
哈大线	Harbin-Dalian	3263	68007
津沪线	Tianjin-Shanghai	5396	107517
沪杭线	Shanghai-Hangzhou	209	6046
京广线	Beijing-Guangzhou	6998	133799
南北同蒲线	Datong-Taiyuan-Fenglingdu	12389	33862
太焦柳线	Taiyuan-Jiaozuo-Liuzhou	8280	62638
京九线	Beijing-Kowloon	3265	57538
兰新线	Lanzhou-Urumqi	3558	68275
滨洲线	Harbin-Manzhouli	3464	23073
滨绥线	Harbin-Suifenhe	1245	17468
京包线	Bingjing-Baotou	5859	59645
石太线	Shijiazhuang-Taiyuan	3974	22636
石德线	Shijiazhuang-Dezhou	373	11423
浙赣线	Hangzhou-Ganzhou	2673	48625
陇海线	Lianyungang-Lanzhou	6677	109857
胶济线	Qingdao-Jinan	1890	25015
京秦线	Beijing-Qinhuangdao	352	9877
新石线	Xinjiang-Rizhao	2955	20472
宝成线	Baoji-Chengdu	1254	22731
成昆线	Chengdu-Kunming	1981	28773
大秦线	Datong-Qinhuangdao	347	67727
湘黔线	Zhuzhou-Guiyang	2167	38734
贵昆线	Guiyang-Kunming	2072	21396
包兰线	Baotou-Lanzhou	4278	28033
青藏线	Qinghai-Tibet	764	6189

16-24 铁路主要车站旅客发送量

Number of Passengers Dispatched from Principal Railway Stations

单位: 万人 (10 000 persons)

车站名称	Railway Station	1996	1997	1998	1999	2000	2001	2002	2003
哈尔滨	Harbin	1286	1301	1346	1371	1252	1342	1345	1249
沈阳	Shenyang	1399	1280	1217	1168	1168	1303	1235	1077
长春	Changchun	952	932	925	973	1062	1085	1069	793
鞍山	Anshan	854	682	293	300	295	309	306	288
本溪	Benxi	854	682	599	569	574	685	617	585
锦州	Jinzhou	438	401	416	436	421	429	424	371
吉林	Jilin	405	400	396	438	397	443	417	373
北京	Beijing	1541	1656	1691	1868	1997	2115	2163	1795
北京南	Southern Beijing	566	443	403	366	382	438	436	374
北京西	Western Beijing						1652	2102	1896
天津	Tianjin	876	876	925	1006	1004	1019	1005	855
石家庄	Shijiazhuang	657	722	732	817	864	927	956	877
太原	Taiyuan	700	684	642	661	679	767	798	719
郑州	Zhengzhou	992	1095	1170	1291	1333	1440	1548	1475
武昌	Wuchang	719	747	748	772	821	864	883	826
洛阳	Luoyang	298	303	318	339	353	397	375	335
西安	Xi'an	959	1023	1031	1096	1063	1211	1245	1196
济南	Jinan	549	597	645	658	702	728	707	673
徐州	Xuzhou	371	619	653	674	632	680	647	611
南京	Nanjing	766	776	787	918	897	932	995	940
蚌埠	Bangbu	358	351	358	406	412	442	433	406
镇江	Zhenjiang	313	310	309	333	327	342	352	323
常州	Changzhou	439	460	465	516	4524	560	581	558
无锡	Wuxi	743	662	633	702	704	768	802	785
苏州	Suzhou	671	636	625	685	703	776	843	859
上海	Shanghai	2492	2516	2430	2536	2595	2860	3118	3031
杭州	Hangzhou	815	395	1008	1074	1061	1025	1192	1129
南昌	Nanchang	508	666	747	807	795	943	1013	968
广州	Guangzhou	1465	1469	1576	1728	1776	1838	2001	2005
深圳	Shenzhen	812	644	718	817	758	902	966	940
柳州	Liuzhou	380	386	366	360	335	323	271	246
成都	Chengdu	809	803	845	960	1042	1141	1282	1107
重庆	Chongqing	440	560	581	695	651	776	754	708
贵阳	Guiyang	540	557	571	627	598	610	614	553
兰州	Lanzhou	368	387	408	439	444	515	523	477
乌鲁木齐	Urumqi	312	352	403	411	399	398	410	359

16-25 铁路主要车站货物发送量

Volume of Freight Dispatched from Principal Railway Stations

单位: 万吨 (10 000 tons)

车站名称	Name of Railway Station	1996	1997	1998	1999	2000	2001	2002	2003
七台河	Qitaihe	1143	1289	1273	1317	1338	1333	1314	1304
恒　山	Hengshan	561	481	386	374	371	441	519	614
竣　德	Junde	550	584	404	526	418	478	538	572
鹤　岗	Hegang	649	821	656	725	822	787	803	843
双鸭山	Shuangyashan	560	669	621	722	751	831	832	1011
大官屯	Daguantun	767	653	643	689	657	683	670	662
灵　山	Lingshan	1008	910	909	957	999	956	935	907
甘井子	Ganjingzi	489	488	502	470	464	389	270	327
本　溪	Benxi	410	384	377	356	405	391	518	483
阜　新	Fuxin	640	686	602	503	531	571	573	529
白云鄂博	Baiyun'ebo	939	969	860	808	739	794	850	918
石景山南	Southern Shijingshan	419	517	564	522	602	572	537	517
古　冶	Guye	896	970	837	847	866	849	873	843
唐　山	Tangshan	406	429	418	394	404	381	357	351
沙河驿镇	Shaheyizhen	883	895	920	826	877	887	829	827
秦皇岛南	Southern Qinhuangdao	408	331	406	381	398	489	473	515
白羊墅	Baiyangshu	1025	1029	856	959	986	1082	1090	1052
云　岗	Yungang	573	557	436	438	458	517	603	618
云岗西	Western Yungang	1051	1087	839	752	846	919	1020	1158
新高山	Xingaoshan	1198	1040	905	868	942	1076	1160	1225
介　休	Jiexiu	540	504	522	488	574	634	587	653
鹤壁北	Northern Hebi	292	289	261	316	331	407	408	409
晋城北	Northern Jincheng	1259	1100	1168	1265	1293	1471	1381	1279
长治北	Northern Changzhi	684	947	939	947	952	1032	1038	1155
蜜　县	Mixian	645	452	370	342	345	368	394	446
平顶山东	Eastern Pindingshan	2174	2119	2013	1953	1984	2146	2309	2453
武昌东	Eastern Wuchang	549	553	532	454	429	463	428	469
邹　县	Zouxian	532	525	650	704	691	983	1139	1155
青龙山	Qinglongshan	470	386	380	455	502	532	533	516
茂　名	Maoming	415	461	433	388	544	525	579	684

16-26 国家铁路运输主要财务指标

Financial Indicators of National Railway Transport

单位: 亿元 (100 million yuan)

指　标	Item	1990	1995	2000	2002	2003
运输总收入	**Total Transport Revenue**	**411.1**	**632.1**	**1097.4**	**1420.5**	**1483.4**
客运收入	Revenue from Passenger Traffic	110.9	201.5	369.3	496.8	476.7
货运收入	Revenue from Freight Traffic	272.1	357.6	566.6	704.7	784.3
行李包裹收入	Revenue from Luggage	8.6	15.8	38.1	42.3	44.3
邮运收入	Revenue from Postal Delivery	1.0	1.9	3.5	3.8	3.8
其他收入	Other Revenue	18.4	55.2	119.9	173.0	174.3
营运成本	**Operation Cost**	**253.9**	**640.6**	**951.1**	**1120.5**	**1186.4**
工　资	Wages and Salaries	42.8	139.6	197.4	272.7	276.6
材　料	Materials	32.6	85.5	76.9	113.3	115.6
燃　料	Fuel	38.5	101.1	140.8	145.7	165.3
电　力	Electricity	9.0	32.2	61.7	87.0	100.1
折　旧	Depreciation	108.8	73.7	351.4	223.2	201.6
其　他	Other Costs	22.3	208.5	122.9	278.6	327.2
营业外收支净额	**Non-operating Net Revenue or Expenditure**	**24.1**	**33.4**	**47.1**	**58.5**	**60.2**
应缴税金	**Taxes Payable**	**21.6**	**32.3**	**37.8**	**59.5**	**48.3**
实现利润	**Profits**	**113.1**	**-64.1**	**33.8**	**24.7**	**18.5**

16-27 国家铁路运输主要技术经济指标

Principal Economic and Technical Indicators of National Railway Transport

指　　标	Item	1999	2000	2001	2002	2003
货运机车日产量　(万吨公里)	Average Daily Ton-kilometers of Freight Locomotives (10 000 ton-km)	97.0	99.4	99.9	102.2	105.8
蒸汽机车	Steam Locomotives	42.0	42.3	40.0	23.7	19.3
内燃机车	Diesel Locomotives	98.8	101.1	100.7	99.3	101.4
电力机车	Electric Locomotives	99.5	99.6	100.7	106.8	112.8
货运机车平均牵引总重　(吨)	Average Total Tonnage of Freight Locomotives (ton)	2654	2676	2760	2789	2829
蒸汽机车	Steam Locomotives	1720	1712	1775	944	824
内燃机车	Diesel Locomotives	2596	2608	2668	2648	2679
电力机车	Electric Locomotives	2870	2869	2985	3028	3071
货运机车日车公里　(公里)	Daily Distance per Freight Locomotive (km)	438	443	437	445	450
客运机车日车公里　(公里)	Daily Distance per Passenger Locomotive (km)	520	521	533	557	562
蒸汽机车每万吨公里耗煤 (公斤)	Coal Consumption of Steam Locomotives (kg/10 000 ton-km)	206.6	207.8	195.0	421.3	330.5
内燃机车每万吨公里耗油 (公斤)	Oil Consumption of Diesel Locomotives (kg/10 000 ton-km)	26.2	25.8	25.7	25.9	25.4
电力机车每万吨公里耗电 (千瓦小时)	Electricity Consumption of Electric Locomotives (kwh/10 000 ton-km)	113.6	113.2	113.1	110.8	110
货物列车出发正点率　(%)	Punctuality Rate of Freight Trains at Departure (%)	96.8	97.2	97.2	97.3	96.9
货物列车运行正点率　(%)	Punctuality Rate of Freight Trains in Running (%)	96.6	96.8	96.8	96.7	96.5
旅客列车出发正点率　(%)	Punctuality Rate of Passenger Trains at Departure (%)	99.8	99.8	99.8	99.8	99.7
旅客列车运行正点率　(%)	Punctuality Rate of Passenger Trains in Running (%)	97.3	97.1	96.9	97.6	96.5
旅客列车技术速度(公里/小时)	Technical Speed of Passenger Trains (km/hr)	65.7	66.6	69.5	71.4	71.7
旅客列车旅行速度(公里/小时)	Traveling Speed of Passenger Trains (km/hr)	56.0	56.8	60.5	62.0	62.2
客运密度　(万人公里/公里)	Density of Passenger Transport (10 000 passenger-km/km)	699.0	753.0	785.0	807.0	765.0
货物列车技术速度(公里/小时)	Technical Speed of Freight Trains (km/hr)	46.5	46.4	46.7	47.1	47.1
货物列车旅行速度(公里/小时)	Running Speed of Freight Trains (km/hr)	31.6	31.8	39.5	32.4	32.8
货运密度　(万吨公里/公里)	Density of Freight Transport (10 000 ton-km/km)	2172	2274	2412	2533	2726
货车周转时间　(天)	Turning Around Time of Freight Cars (day)	5.50	5.39	5.08	5.10	5.10
一次货物作业时间　(小时)	Handling Time of Freight (hour)	23.4	23.1	22.0	21.2	20.9
货车中转停留时间　(小时)	Transfer Waiting Time per Car (hour)	4.9	4.7	4.6	4.6	4.5
货车静载重(准轨)　(吨)	Static Load of Freight Cars (Standard Gauge) (ton)	57.7	57.9	58.1	58.2	58.3
货车载重力利用率　(%)	Utilization Rate of Loading Capacity of Freight Cars (%)	96.8	97.1	97.3	96.7	96.5

16-28 民用汽车拥有量

Number of Civil Vehicles Owned

年份 地区	Year Region	民用汽车总计（万辆）Total (10 000 units)	载客汽车（万辆）Passenger Vehicles (10 000 units)	大型 Large	中型 Medium	小型 Small	微型 Minicar	载货汽车（万辆）Trucks (10 000 units)
	1978	135.84	25.90					100.17
	1980	178.29	35.08					129.90
	1985	321.12	79.45					223.20
	1989	511.32	146.43					346.37
	1990	551.36	162.19					368.48
	1991	606.11	185.24					398.62
	1992	691.74	226.16					441.45
	1993	817.58	285.98					501.00
	1994	941.95	349.74					560.33
	1995	1040.00	417.90					585.43
	1996	1100.08	488.02					575.03
	1997	1219.09	580.56					601.23
	1998	1319.30	654.83					627.89
	1999	1452.94	740.23					676.95
	2000	1608.91	853.73					716.32
	2001	1802.04	993.96					765.24
	2002	2053.17	1202.37	75.48	104.80	789.74	232.34	812.22
	2003	2382.93	1478.81	75.76	115.96	1017.21	269.88	853.51
北京	Beijing	163.07	141.41	3.25	10.59	106.73	20.84	18.59
天津	Tianjin	53.78	38.24	1.38	2.97	22.78	11.11	14.09
河北	Hebei	155.61	87.39	2.85	2.15	59.02	23.37	63.59
山西	Shanxi	73.82	40.67	1.37	2.28	26.30	10.72	31.89
内蒙古	Inner Mongolia	49.85	28.65	1.27	1.84	19.67	5.87	20.23
辽宁	Liaoning	103.54	64.59	5.20	4.91	48.08	6.39	35.94
吉林	Jilin	53.07	34.91	1.64	1.33	26.90	5.04	17.63
黑龙江	Heilongjiang	76.17	48.00	2.75	2.71	35.69	6.85	26.67
上海	Shanghai	71.90	54.03	3.30	6.87	39.89	3.97	17.87
江苏	Jiangsu	131.77	87.33	4.04	8.76	59.49	15.03	41.79
浙江	Zhejiang	135.82	84.84	2.94	6.42	61.49	13.99	48.30
安徽	Anhui	64.73	31.92	2.92	3.95	18.42	6.64	30.17
福建	Fujian	52.08	29.40	1.45	3.25	20.97	3.73	21.43
江西	Jiangxi	35.56	18.08	1.37	1.57	12.43	2.71	16.61
山东	Shandong	175.74	104.20	3.86	7.55	64.85	27.94	66.56
河南	Henan	119.75	69.29	4.22	6.29	41.38	17.40	46.97
湖北	Hubei	72.86	41.87	3.40	3.71	32.15	2.61	29.25
湖南	Hunan	65.08	36.79	2.81	2.37	27.78	3.82	27.40
广东	Guangdong	257.96	159.74	8.08	16.77	128.76	6.13	93.79
广西	Guangxi	43.44	25.32	2.08	1.60	14.06	7.58	17.01
海南	Hainan	12.58	7.47	0.76	0.17	6.49	0.05	4.91
重庆	Chongqing	34.25	18.00	1.67	0.86	13.61	1.85	15.36
四川	Sichuan	113.87	73.42	4.50	3.64	34.43	30.85	39.26
贵州	Guizhou	32.46	17.84	0.98	2.20	7.06	7.60	14.46
云南	Yunnan	77.09	44.30	1.44	2.62	27.64	12.60	32.32
西藏	Tibet	6.06	3.74	0.13	0.40	3.04	0.16	2.30
陕西	Shaanxi	54.01	34.99	2.25	5.22	18.62	8.89	17.88
甘肃	Gansu	27.39	15.02	1.26	1.38	9.56	2.82	11.79
青海	Qinghai	10.47	5.78	0.40	0.54	4.14	0.69	4.49
宁夏	Ningxia	12.39	5.96	0.48	0.45	4.12	0.91	5.97
新疆	Xinjiang	46.76	25.64	1.69	0.58	21.65	1.72	18.99

16-28 续表 continued

年 份 Year 地 区 Region		载货汽车（万辆） Trucks（10 000 units） 重型 Heavy	中型 Middle	轻型 Light	微型 Mini	其他汽车（万辆） Others（10 000 units）	机动车驾驶员（万人） Number of Motor Drivers（10 000 persons）	#汽车驾驶员 Automobile Drivers
	1978							192.45
	1980							245.23
	1985							462.44
	1989						1577.99	722.32
	1990						1635.85	790.96
	1991						1791.57	859.44
	1992						2017.83	969.55
	1993						2359.42	1112.97
	1994						2812.12	1269.23
	1995						3501.52	1673.39
	1996						4275.26	2100.74
	1997						5206.79	2619.25
	1998						5944.58	2974.06
	1999						6727.49	3361.12
	2000						7655.56	3746.51
	2001						8455.04	4462.68
	2002	148.28	218.69	360.58	84.66	38.58	9362.03	4827.08
	2003	136.79	243.70	390.79	82.22	50.61	10611.04	5368.07
北 京	Beijing	2.60	3.72	11.74	0.53	3.07	308.01	290.11
天 津	Tianjin	2.34	2.28	7.79	1.68	1.44	143.59	112.93
河 北	Hebei	19.67	10.08	29.85	3.99	4.63	629.14	324.12
山 西	Shanxi	7.36	9.45	11.00	4.08	1.27	216.49	139.48
内蒙古	Inner Mongolia	7.04	6.12	6.10	0.97	0.98	281.48	107.82
辽 宁	Liaoning	10.36	8.72	15.84	1.02	3.01	359.45	238.06
吉 林	Jilin	3.79	4.76	8.69	0.39	0.54	239.77	172.54
黑龙江	Heilongjiang	4.70	9.48	10.50	1.99	1.49	204.01	151.97
上 海	Shanghai	2.28	7.12	6.52	1.95		222.59	160.71
江 苏	Jiangsu	3.29	19.74	15.88	2.87	2.65	814.56	257.77
浙 江	Zhejiang	1.87	13.75	26.04	6.64	2.68	549.20	277.37
安 徽	Anhui	3.53	13.62	10.82	2.21	2.64	308.23	163.79
福 建	Fujian	0.93	4.99	11.74	3.78	1.24	350.54	119.01
江 西	Jiangxi	6.24	3.35	6.35	0.67	0.87	235.47	106.78
山 东	Shandong	5.59	16.22	37.50	7.24	4.98	991.64	353.30
河 南	Henan	14.13	10.91	15.15	6.78	3.49	555.75	274.72
湖 北	Hubei	1.89	12.76	11.09	3.52	1.75	394.74	210.78
湖 南	Hunan	3.78	11.01	11.06	1.55	0.89	307.09	168.02
广 东	Guangdong	9.36	14.31	66.63	3.50	4.43	1345.93	575.29
广 西	Guangxi	2.50	5.40	5.19	3.92	1.12	448.45	142.61
海 南	Hainan	1.81	0.23	2.77	0.10	0.20	88.14	43.49
重 庆	Chongqing	3.34	3.72	7.94	0.36	0.89	122.13	91.78
四 川	Sichuan	1.22	15.96	15.34	6.74	1.20	520.63	282.04
贵 州	Guizhou	0.23	4.81	5.97	3.44	0.16	121.35	94.84
云 南	Yunnan	3.91	10.72	10.84	6.85	0.47	288.87	162.55
西 藏	Tibet	1.77	0.29	0.20	0.04	0.02	9.38	8.20
陕 西	Shaanxi	2.36	7.42	5.42	2.68	1.15	216.32	128.17
甘 肃	Gansu	1.39	4.70	4.89	0.80	0.58	106.80	61.96
青 海	Qinghai	0.68	1.80	1.58	0.42	0.20	44.32	23.00
宁 夏	Ningxia	0.84	2.28	2.41	0.44	0.46	49.63	25.01
新 疆	Xinjiang	6.02	3.98	7.93	1.07	2.13	137.36	99.84

注：1.小轿车包括在载客汽车中（下表同）。

2.从2002年起，载客汽车和载货汽车的其中分项、其他汽车统计口径有调整与以前年份不可比（下表同）。

a) Cars are included in passenger vehicles. The same as in the following table.

b) Since 2002, the statistical standard of detail item of passenger vehicles and trucks, other vehicles have been adjusted, the data are not comparable with the previous years. The same as in the following table.

16-29 私人汽车拥有量

Number of Private-owned Vehicles

单位：万辆 (10 000 units)

年份 地区	Year Region	汽车总计 Total	载客汽车 Passenger Vehicles	大型 Large	中型 Medium	小型 Small	微型 Minicar
	1985	28.49	1.93				
	1989	73.12	20.28				
	1990	81.62	24.07				
	1991	96.04	30.36				
	1992	118.20	41.78				
	1993	155.77	59.85				
	1994	205.42	78.62				
	1995	249.96	114.15				
	1996	289.67	143.04				
	1997	358.36	191.27				
	1998	423.65	230.65				
	1999	533.88	304.09				
	2000	625.33	365.09				
	2001	770.78	469.85				
	2002	968.98	623.76	9.89	35.87	408.49	169.51
	2003	1219.23	845.87	7.36	42.51	586.90	209.10
北京	Beijing	107.09	98.40	0.11	5.39	73.49	19.41
天津	Tianjin	30.96	24.81	0.12	1.24	14.13	9.33
河北	Hebei	95.12	66.08	0.65	1.03	42.79	21.60
山西	Shanxi	34.15	22.86	0.19	0.90	14.29	7.48
内蒙古	Inner Mongolia	31.33	18.76	0.29	1.01	12.58	4.88
辽宁	Liaoning	35.31	26.23	0.35	1.19	21.88	2.81
吉林	Jilin	24.46	18.83	0.20	0.47	14.19	3.97
黑龙江	Heilongjiang	33.93	24.40	0.36	1.13	17.73	5.17
上海	Shanghai	22.44	22.13	0.01	1.96	17.91	2.25
江苏	Jiangsu	58.72	45.81	0.09	2.45	31.81	11.47
浙江	Zhejiang	75.87	53.14	0.09	1.69	39.74	11.62
安徽	Anhui	24.68	14.45	0.52	1.56	7.50	4.89
福建	Fujian	28.78	16.75	0.08	0.89	12.80	2.98
江西	Jiangxi	10.59	6.22	0.21	0.23	4.10	1.68
山东	Shandong	89.86	60.49	0.38	2.38	35.90	21.84
河南	Henan	57.20	36.45	0.83	2.65	21.01	11.96
湖北	Hubei	29.44	18.19	0.37	1.32	14.54	1.97
湖南	Hunan	36.01	19.14	0.46	0.93	14.55	3.20
广东	Guangdong	160.72	107.64	0.48	8.75	92.76	5.65
广西	Guangxi	21.83	13.14	0.32	0.50	6.37	5.94
海南	Hainan	4.78	2.30	0.12	0.09	2.08	0.00
重庆	Chongqing	12.89	7.99	0.02	0.07	6.49	1.42
四川	Sichuan	67.02	45.46	0.13	1.05	20.28	24.00
贵州	Guizhou	11.40	5.47	0.03	0.41	2.18	2.84
云南	Yunnan	44.04	24.56	0.14	0.79	14.23	9.40
西藏	Tibet	1.68	0.31	0.01	0.03	0.26	0.02
陕西	Shaanxi	29.51	20.72	0.26	1.31	11.95	7.20
甘肃	Gansu	10.36	5.61	0.30	0.58	3.06	1.67
青海	Qinghai	4.10	2.37	0.05	0.16	1.64	0.53
宁夏	Ningxia	5.76	3.19	0.07	0.19	2.22	0.71
新疆	Xinjiang	19.20	13.95	0.14	0.18	12.42	1.21

16-29 续表 continued

单位：万辆 (10 000 units)

年 份 Year / 地 区 Region		载货汽车 Trucks	重型 Heavy	中型 Middle	轻型 Light	微型 Mini	其他汽车 Others
	1985	26.48					
	1989	52.50					
	1990	57.48					
	1991	65.61					
	1992	76.15					
	1993	94.00					
	1994	123.29					
	1995	131.83					
	1996	142.78					
	1997	163.19					
	1998	192.03					
	1999	228.68					
	2000	259.09					
	2001	298.95					
	2002	341.29	48.27	84.40	158.67	49.95	3.94
	2003	367.35	44.47	95.20	176.58	51.09	6.00
北 京	Beijing	8.35	0.94	1.41	5.57	0.43	0.34
天 津	Tianjin	5.97	0.62	0.74	3.33	1.29	0.18
河 北	Hebei	28.15	6.58	4.27	14.43	2.87	0.89
山 西	Shanxi	11.23	1.20	3.40	4.15	2.48	0.07
内蒙古	Inner Mongolia	12.29	3.98	3.87	3.68	0.78	0.28
辽 宁	Liaoning	8.91	2.25	1.22	5.14	0.30	0.17
吉 林	Jilin	5.57	1.05	1.44	2.85	0.23	0.05
黑龙江	Heilongjiang	9.41	1.12	3.40	3.59	1.30	0.12
上 海	Shanghai	0.31	0.01	0.05	0.20	0.05	
江 苏	Jiangsu	12.59	1.02	5.25	4.94	1.38	0.32
浙 江	Zhejiang	22.45	0.69	4.89	12.67	4.20	0.28
安 徽	Anhui	10.10	0.52	4.28	4.17	1.14	0.12
福 建	Fujian	11.95	0.31	2.75	6.25	2.63	0.08
江 西	Jiangxi	4.33	1.72	0.53	1.76	0.32	0.04
山 东	Shandong	28.44	2.06	6.12	15.51	4.75	0.93
河 南	Henan	20.27	4.32	4.08	7.78	4.09	0.48
湖 北	Hubei	11.11	0.44	4.56	4.09	2.02	0.13
湖 南	Hunan	16.75	2.05	7.07	6.53	1.10	0.12
广 东	Guangdong	52.59	4.21	8.13	37.38	2.86	0.49
广 西	Guangxi	8.61	1.17	2.58	2.29	2.57	0.08
海 南	Hainan	2.45	0.92	0.17	1.34	0.03	0.03
重 庆	Chongqing	4.87	1.26	0.46	2.94	0.21	0.03
四 川	Sichuan	21.45	0.37	7.87	8.29	4.93	0.11
贵 州	Guizhou	5.88	0.05	1.90	2.30	1.64	0.04
云 南	Yunnan	19.41	1.69	6.50	6.89	4.33	0.07
西 藏	Tibet	1.36	1.05	0.24	0.06	0.01	0.00
陕 西	Shaanxi	8.41	0.67	3.28	2.48	1.98	0.39
甘 肃	Gansu	4.71	0.62	2.25	1.53	0.31	0.04
青 海	Qinghai	1.71	0.20	0.73	0.58	0.19	0.02
宁 夏	Ningxia	2.53	0.26	0.94	1.05	0.29	0.04
新 疆	Xinjiang	5.18	1.13	0.81	2.82	0.42	0.07

16-30 新注册民用汽车数量

New Registration Statistics on Civil Vehicles

单位：辆 (unit)

地 区	Region	民用汽车 总 计 Total	载客汽车 Passenger Vehicles	大 型 Large	中 型 Medium	小 型 Small	微 型 Minicar
	2002	3371951	2294649	97200	145062	1491479	560908
	2003	4337485	3160859	100284	157523	2421951	481101
北 京	Beijing	339344	319251	3151	20248	281177	14675
天 津	Tianjin	77851	65914	2262	2281	56487	4884
河 北	Hebei	554245	337134	9211	7775	216565	103583
山 西	Shanxi	200825	127360	2932	5215	83403	35810
内蒙古	Inner Mongolia	54734	38337	975	1047	26656	9659
辽 宁	Liaoning	122268	93139	3463	7466	74108	8102
吉 林	Jilin	57566	46286	1807	1617	33519	9343
黑龙江	Heilongjiang	70235	45641	2522	2023	32869	8227
上 海	Shanghai	138079	117150	4509	11984	99812	845
江 苏	Jiangsu	286603	222633	5592	11560	180651	24830
浙 江	Zhejiang	373359	289371	5471	12194	239714	31992
安 徽	Anhui	89214	50499	2414	4234	33722	10129
福 建	Fujian	101675	72897	1935	3413	60802	6747
江 西	Jiangxi	53788	32289	1580	1999	21243	7467
山 东	Shandong	296504	216227	4702	6563	155801	49161
河 南	Henan	225882	157999	8662	7939	99055	42343
湖 北	Hubei	100890	74865	3511	5147	58840	7367
湖 南	Hunan	90878	64960	3768	6483	48536	6173
广 东	Guangdong	460665	350588	12044	20386	310997	7161
广 西	Guangxi	43632	33373	1653	947	25447	5326
海 南	Hainan	18268	13156	1400	941	10414	401
重 庆	Chongqing	56729	32444	2471	1744	26865	1364
四 川	Sichuan	160912	130326	4544	2437	86690	36655
贵 州	Guizhou	44628	26343	1301	630	16934	7478
云 南	Yunnan	90837	57607	1374	2702	37631	15900
西 藏	Tibet	9914	5750	206	412	4185	947
陕 西	Shaanxi	92587	61493	1662	3655	40373	15803
甘 肃	Gansu	33181	21209	1454	1130	16233	2392
青 海	Qinghai	12354	7776	630	535	5452	1159
宁 夏	Ningxia	16052	8613	467	504	6571	1071
新 疆	Xinjiang	63786	40229	2611	2312	31199	4107

16-30 续表 continued

单位：辆 (unit)

地 区	Region	载货汽车 Trucks	重 型 Heavy	中 型 Middle	轻 型 Light	微 型 Mini	其他汽车 Others
	2002	993761	186498	220969	501985	84309	83541
	2003	1075692	168363	259173	576073	72083	100934
北 京	Beijing	15174	2582	2572	10017	3	4919
天 津	Tianjin	9778	929	1157	7271	421	2159
河 北	Hebei	200636	51985	28687	103466	16498	16475
山 西	Shanxi	70296	16343	20736	26886	6331	3169
内蒙古	Inner Mongolia	14688	6352	2062	5709	565	1709
辽 宁	Liaoning	26452	5978	9296	8893	2285	2677
吉 林	Jilin	9888	2144	1825	5307	612	1392
黑龙江	Heilongjiang	19570	7416	3002	7692	1460	5024
上 海	Shanghai	20929	1137	10054	9347	391	
江 苏	Jiangsu	56238	6822	21145	27112	1159	7732
浙 江	Zhejiang	76778	5705	14188	50730	6155	7210
安 徽	Anhui	33178	4908	11948	15488	834	5537
福 建	Fujian	27027	690	4082	20367	1888	1751
江 西	Jiangxi	20167	2812	8599	7775	981	1332
山 东	Shandong	68739	6978	8336	50037	3388	11538
河 南	Henan	63915	10644	21501	26826	4944	3968
湖 北	Hubei	23896	2879	7535	11524	1958	2129
湖 南	Hunan	25148	1561	11219	12092	276	770
广 东	Guangdong	101180	3235	16594	77440	3911	8897
广 西	Guangxi	8962	1062	2257	5224	419	1297
海 南	Hainan	4824	518	1209	2578	519	288
重 庆	Chongqing	22726	1534	10472	10688	32	1559
四 川	Sichuan	28802	1465	9770	15942	1625	1784
贵 州	Guizhou	18040	131	3204	5617	9088	245
云 南	Yunnan	32502	3359	13664	13720	1759	728
西 藏	Tibet	4162	1976	1133	852	201	2
陕 西	Shaanxi	28588	6172	6162	14906	1348	2506
甘 肃	Gansu	11189	1809	2445	6536	399	783
青 海	Qinghai	4342	1097	618	2299	328	236
宁 夏	Ningxia	6712	1811	683	3859	359	727
新 疆	Xinjiang	21166	6329	3018	9873	1946	2391

16-31 运输汽车拥有量

Number of Transport Vehicles

年份 地区	Year Region	汽车总计(万辆) Total (10 000 units)	载客汽车 Passenger Vehicles 辆数(万辆) Number (10 000 units)	载客汽车 Passenger Vehicles 客位(万客位) Number of Seats (10 000 seats)	载货汽车 Trucks 辆数(万辆) Number (10 000 units)	载货汽车 Trucks #普通载货汽车 Ordinary Trucks	载货汽车 Trucks 吨位(万吨) Capacity (10 000 tons)	载货汽车 Trucks #普通载货汽车 Ordinary Trucks
	1990	31.30	10.76	468.92	20.22	19.82	131.61	127.06
	1991	31.67	11.53	497.35	19.83	19.36	132.02	126.54
	1992	30.87	12.70	528.87	18.17	17.59	125.91	118.42
	1993	28.96	12.85	509.56	16.15	15.53	116.20	108.37
	1994	27.97	13.05	493.94	14.87	14.22	109.80	101.21
	1995	27.49	13.73	480.61	13.75	13.12	103.13	94.56
	1996	28.81	15.41	499.58	13.40	12.74	102.08	91.83
	1997	29.89	17.01	519.10	12.88	12.22	95.31	85.09
	1998	31.88	19.40	536.43	12.48	11.81	90.02	79.51
	1999	501.77	92.14	1409.86	409.62	401.28	1481.02	1406.00
	2000	702.82	216.81	2524.45	486.02	475.24	1667.70	1573.73
	2001	764.39	255.12	2701.68	509.27	496.65	1733.58	1621.40
	2002	826.34	289.55	2972.32	536.78	520.27	1808.45	1674.79
	2003	924.64	352.19	3430.64	572.45	553.23	1941.52	1788.86
北　京	Beijing	11.97	0.40	14.03	11.57	10.89	47.92	41.13
天　津	Tianjin	6.22	0.58	15.32	5.64	4.58	25.56	17.82
河　北	Hebei	65.53	23.98	194.01	41.56	40.59	181.18	174.59
山　西	Shanxi	23.04	6.04	56.82	17.00	16.76	83.77	82.53
内蒙古	Inner Mongolia	25.38	13.08	90.49	12.31	12.12	57.61	56.31
辽　宁	Liaoning	29.14	1.85	46.99	27.29	25.99	105.08	91.78
吉　林	Jilin	21.95	8.00	90.82	13.95	13.60	49.65	46.90
黑龙江	Heilongjiang	38.16	20.67	157.72	17.49	17.25	66.66	64.86
上　海	Shanghai	19.91	3.55	41.48	16.37	15.05	67.82	55.64
江　苏	Jiangsu	90.13	56.54	486.71	33.59	31.99	123.04	110.60
浙　江	Zhejiang	111.57	69.91	471.81	41.66	40.63	92.38	82.08
安　徽	Anhui	22.27	4.17	64.07	18.10	17.69	65.09	62.33
福　建	Fujian	14.68	3.16	42.69	11.53	10.72	33.11	25.36
江　西	Jiangxi	10.99	1.84	35.25	9.15	9.06	28.87	28.40
山　东	Shandong	60.73	18.04	168.56	42.68	40.69	153.07	137.95
河　南	Henan	25.72	3.95	81.40	21.77	21.30	88.26	85.11
湖　北	Hubei	23.65	6.10	76.57	17.54	16.68	58.61	52.70
湖　南	Hunan	23.23	7.14	96.87	16.09	15.88	50.59	49.09
广　东	Guangdong	74.16	5.61	124.05	68.55	66.46	161.22	140.84
广　西	Guangxi	14.46	3.65	58.95	10.81	10.62	35.11	33.27
海　南	Hainan	2.84	0.86	15.85	1.98	1.96	6.21	6.01
重　庆	Chongqing	33.36	18.00	260.32	15.36	14.92	38.09	35.30
四　川	Sichuan	32.92	7.61	112.67	25.31	25.10	60.72	59.23
贵　州	Guizhou	18.31	9.09	79.04	9.22	9.15	24.07	23.66
云　南	Yunnan	62.15	39.53	341.68	22.63	22.38	71.14	68.66
西　藏	Tibet	2.91	0.93	8.19	1.98	1.93	12.36	12.08
陕　西	Shaanxi	13.63	4.01	50.69	9.61	9.28	33.16	31.66
甘　肃	Gansu	13.86	5.37	54.38	8.49	7.98	31.22	29.45
青　海	Qinghai	6.10	2.58	23.90	3.52	3.45	13.98	13.36
宁　夏	Ningxia	7.67	2.33	24.13	5.34	5.22	15.54	14.51
新　疆	Xinjiang	17.98	3.61	45.19	14.37	13.29	60.44	55.65

注：1.小轿车包括在载客汽车中。

2.1999年以前数据仅为公路部门营运汽车，1999年为全国营运汽车。2000年起为全国运输汽车(含营运和非营运汽车)。

a) Passenger vehicles include cars.

b) Before 1999, number of vehicles for business transportation only included those owned by the department of highway transportation. That referred to all working vehicles for business transportation in 1999, and all vehicles for business transportation, including working and non-working vehicles since 2000.

16-32 民用运输船舶拥有量

Number of Civil Transport Vessels Owned

年份 地区	Year Region	机动船 Motor Vessels 艘数(艘) Number (unit)	净载重量(吨) Dead Weight Tonnage (ton)	载客量(客位) Passenger Capacity (seat)	拖船功率(千瓦) Drawing Power (kw)	驳船 Barges 艘数(艘) Number (unit)	净载重量(吨) Dead Weight Tonnage (ton)	载客量(客位) Passenger Capacity (seat)
	1980	64307	12789410	545042	1514998	119464	5951401	100312
	1985	260296	20898230	877963	1665030	132682	8670224	99643
	1989	351450	27290103	1095018	1759366	88903	8958617	52459
	1990	325858	29090082	1138937	1750351	82482	9066738	62926
	1991	307127	29959203	1169982	1845705	78410	9588216	61526
	1992	302313	31225749	1177035	1844101	71255	9437823	46337
	1993	307285	34682035	1124114	1734606	65196	8891435	43801
	1994	293472	39591864	1065140	1678066	59913	8898065	26335
	1995	299717	40940087	979985	1707115	57998	9449652	17722
	1996	269879	39774235	988046	1616585	56128	9315335	15148
	1997	215814	38749289	1022970	1468612	49983	9064891	13879
	1998	212093	38896576	983630	1584601	48115	9019417	14914
	1999	194590	38911462	929138	1494500	47453	8981998	10306
	2000	185018	42640605	1014013	1439743	44658	8640504	18258
	2001	169329	45526726	1048915	1370221	41457	8968670	27902
	2002	165936	48372587	945387	1433547	37041	8683075	33405
	2003	163813	60745234	971514	1269607	40457	9871079	30631
北京	Beijing							
天津	Tianjin	210	3027590	3894	28145	33	37741	
河北	Hebei	41	1502274		465	1	1308	
山西	Shanxi	154	2145	895				
内蒙古	Inner Mongolia							
辽宁	Liaoning	629	2321532	21008	15530	22	6704	
吉林	Jilin	544	5789	11845	2931	30	13440	
黑龙江	Heilongjiang	1027	44229	13613	52275	397	226960	150
上海	Shanghai	2309	9904592	79445	91264	663	290801	
江苏	Jiangsu	38076	6352836	20903	359167	15687	3726218	735
浙江	Zhejiang	30756	6715360	60304	52857	2858	269314	557
安徽	Anhui	23875	6716383	20705	62535	3282	745616	
福建	Fujian	2589	2316028	27034	3384	21	10100	
江西	Jiangxi	4408	524362	15851	9744	173	48276	
山东	Shandong	3070	2888680	17150	150596	9458	2090680	
河南	Henan	3690	1104321	6338	4630	396	69259	
湖北	Hubei	4153	890844	36611	205150	1751	1529491	56
湖南	Hunan	8676	532624	73866	16135	353	77982	1167
广东	Guangdong	13258	5838700	79194	49123	145	99995	
广西	Guangxi	8352	1388701	95688	1687	20	9440	
海南	Hainan	636	482256	15269	8979	5	5548	
重庆	Chongqing	2933	635881	134842	120638	787	481426	
四川	Sichuan	9246	200894	147530	24120	3606	99498	17341
贵州	Guizhou	1945	36235	33759	6706	152	23242	
云南	Yunnan	1143	29012	22409	1755	21	4827	
西藏	Tibet							
陕西	Shaanxi	1235	7721	19048	167	361	1065	3260
甘肃	Gansu	348	1938	9423		42	413	1575
青海	Qinghai	82		1405				
宁夏	Ningxia	278	291	3485	1624	193	1735	5790
新疆	Xinjiang							
不分地区	Not Classified by Region	150	7274016					

注：不分地区数据为中国远洋运输集团总公司海外公司数。

a) Number of civil transport vessels not classified by region is the number of abroad companies under China Ocean Shipping (Group) Company.

16-33 私人运输船舶拥有量

Number of Private-Owned Transport Vessels

年 份 Year 地 区 Region	机动船 Motor Vessels				驳船 Barges		
	艘数（艘）Number	净载重量（吨）Dead Weight Tonnage (ton)	载客量（客位）Passenger Capacity (seat)	拖船功率（千瓦）Drawing Power (kw)	艘数（艘）Number	净载重量（吨）Dead Weight Tonnage (ton)	载客量（客位）Passenger Capacity (seat)
1985	133165	2139297	140722	52736	12253	417664	2267
1989	228988	4654767	298174	67638	13021	581523	12308
1990	206589	4257594	283248	70250	10927	586650	3352
1991	200357	4517888	312280	54028	11673	519506	9075
1992	190262	3976814	326587	60481	9192	503787	11622
1993	190820	5961873	302898	85806	9458	636200	3103
1994	198241	7112807	261908	59848	7379	506187	5116
1995	182060	6942745	276555	78867	7964	749329	180
1996	157370	4821091	289402	55129	6533	657652	1240
1997	147415	6714642	347405	115168	9944	879692	1948
1998	127130	6547095	328884	98537	7290	794618	1850
1999	113359	6070634	343208	85615	7262	775881	606
2000	128654	8244485	387405	168099	13463	1523260	13682
2001	111633	8190264	443140	114209	10088	1142822	20293
2002	105697	8913536	428614	112152	9411	1178379	21346
2003	97837	11668873	409915	187186	16460	2779120	20399
北 京 Beijing							
天 津 Tianjin	15	649	576	99	1	101	
河 北 Hebei	2	76500					
山 西 Shanxi	130	1853	414				
内蒙古 Inner Mongolia							
辽 宁 Liaoning	245	4113					
吉 林 Jilin	458	5036	5839	1560	23	12800	
黑龙江 Heilongjiang	676	8246	5412	14048	76	30620	
上 海 Shanghai	256	17500					
江 苏 Jiangsu	22950	3147533	3275	92656	8985	1831798	358
浙 江 Zhejiang	26758	2562852	707	9057	797	68176	
安 徽 Anhui	10930	3256393	12004	6599	262	56919	
福 建 Fujian							
江 西 Jiangxi	2747	123996	10292				
山 东 Shandong	792	178699		28606	2237	621355	
河 南 Henan							
湖 北 Hubei	2668	324001	15304	20075	262	86995	56
湖 南 Hunan	7299	311129	62521	1974	16	3720	
广 东 Guangdong	2610	875524	1902	1029	3	591	
广 西 Guangxi	4080	327822	65425				
海 南 Hainan	439	10519	4397				
重 庆 Chongqing	1825	212225	28000	874	38	6889	
四 川 Sichuan	8600	166438	125597	10488	3345	54560	15302
贵 州 Guizhou	1771	31352	29129		27	2617	
云 南 Yunnan	1003	17117	14924	121	6	537	
西 藏 Tibet							
陕 西 Shaanxi	1041	7473	14913		340	1029	3108
甘 肃 Gansu	341	1612	7563		42	413	1575
青 海 Qinghai	37		555				
宁 夏 Ningxia	164	291	1166				
新 疆 Xinjiang							

16-34 沿海主要港口分货类吞吐量

Volume of Freight Handled in Major Coastal Ports by Type of Freight

单位：万吨　　(10 000 tons)

货物种类	Type of Freight	2002			2003		
		合计 Total	出港 Out-port	进港 In-port	合计 Total	出港 Out-port	进港 In-port
总计	**Total**	**166628**	**79736**	**86891**	**201126**	**96344**	**104782**
煤炭	Coal	40282	25063	15219	46872	30477	16395
石油	Petroleum	25775	10584	15190	30438	12125	18313
金属矿石	Metal Ores	18238	4283	13955	24285	5721	18564
钢铁	Steel and Iron	6205	2514	3691	8416	3428	4988
矿建材料	Mineral Building Materials	12570	5109	7461	14689	5697	8992
水泥	Cement	1203	406	797	1622	560	1062
木材	Timber	1152	412	740	1294	440	855
非金属矿石	Nonmetal Ores	3161	2023	1138	3198	1997	1201
化肥和农药	Chemical Fertilizers and Pesticides	2221	610	1610	1995	748	1247
盐	Salt	658	243	415	686	257	428
粮食	Grain	5564	2966	2599	7465	3876	3589
其他	Others	49600	25524	24076	60166	31018	29148

16-35 沿海主要港口货物吞吐量

Volume of Freight Handled in Major Coastal Ports

单位：万吨　　(10 000 tons)

港口	Seaport	1985	1990	1995	1999	2000	2001	2002	2003
总计	**Total**	**31154**	**48321**	**80166**	**105162**	**125603**	**142634**	**166628**	**201126**
大连	Dalian	4381	4952	6417	8505	9084	10047	10851	12602
营口	Yingkou	98	237	1156	1945	2268	2520	3127	4009
秦皇岛	Qinhuangdao	4419	6945	8382	8261	9743	11302	11167	12562
天津	Tianjin	1856	2063	5787	7298	9566	11369	12906	16182
烟台	Yantai	689	668	1361	1646	1774	2190	2689	2936
青岛	Qingdao	2611	3034	5103	7257	8636	10398	12213	14090
日照	Rizhao		925	1452	2003	2674	2933	3136	4507
连云港	Lianyungang	929	1137	1716	2017	2708	3058	3316	3752
上海	Shanghai	11291	13959	16567	18641	20440	22099	26384	31621
宁波	Ningbo	1040	2554	6853	9660	11547	12852	15398	18543
汕头	Shantou	201	279	716	1191	1284	1309	1380	1470
广州	Guangzhou	1772	4163	7299	10157	11128	12823	15324	17187
湛江	Zhanjiang	1231	1557	1885	1751	2038	2205	2627	2866
海口	Haikou	170	288	468	674	808	888	1073	1329
八所	Basuo	388	431	275	380	378	342	343	425
三亚	Sanya	78	37	42	27	48	71	49	61
其他港口	Other Ports		5092	14687	23749	31479	36228	44645	56984

16-36 沿海主要港口码头泊位数（2003年底）
Number of Berths in Major Coastal Ports (End of 2003)

名称	Name	总计 Total			生产用 For Productive Use			非生产用 For Nonproductive Use	
		码头长度（米）Length of Quay Line (m)	泊位个数（个）Number of Berths (unit)	#万吨级 10 000 Ton Class	码头长度（米）Length of Quay Line (m)	泊位个数（个）Number of Berths (unit)	#万吨级 10 000 Ton Class	码头长度（米）Length of Quay Line (m)	泊位个数（个）Number of Berths (unit)
总计	**Total**	**280756**	**2562**	**650**	**256748**	**2238**	**650**	**24008**	**324**
#大连	Dalian	29207	206	55	24611	175	55	4596	31
营口	Yingkou	4929	30	16	4848	27	16	81	3
秦皇岛	Qinhuangdao	8335	52	27	7017	31	27	1318	21
天津	Tianjin	14443	76	52	13544	68	52	899	8
烟台	Yantai	6608	37	21	6225	34	21	383	3
青岛	Qingdao	12457	54	36	11539	47	36	918	7
日照	Rizhao	5514	34	17	5194	27	17	320	7
连云港	Lianyungang	6493	36	26	6023	31	26	470	5
上海	Shanghai	25604	215	82	21433	137	82	4171	78
宁波	Ningbo	8877	76	23	7480	46	23	1397	30
汕头	Shantou	8777	88	13	8521	82	13	256	6
广州	Guangzhou	12395	122	32	10518	92	32	1877	30
湛江	Zhanjiang	7285	43	25	6057	32	25	1228	11
海口	Haikou	1719	15	2	1719	15	2		
八所	Basuo	1412	8	6	1412	8	6		
三亚	Sanya	602	5		602	5			

16-37 内河主要港口码头泊位数（2003年底）
Number of Berths in Major Ports of Inland Rivers (End of 2003)

名称	Name	总计 Total			生产用 For Productive Use			非生产用 For Nonproductive Use	
		码头长度（米）Length of Quay Line (m)	泊位个数（个）Number of Berths (unit)	#万吨级 10 000 Ton Class	码头长度（米）Length of Quay Line (m)	泊位个数（个）Number of Berths (unit)	#万吨级 10 000 Ton Class	码头长度（米）Length of Quay Line (m)	泊位个数（个）Number of Berths (unit)
总计	**Total**	**283699**	**5887**	**121**	**275026**	**5759**	**121**	**8673**	**128**
#重庆	Chongqing	4067	77		4067	77			
万州	Wanzhou	9655	73		7405	56		2250	17
宜昌	Yichang	1140	21		920	16		220	5
枝城	Zhicheng	1205	25		989	20		216	5
城陵矶	Chenglingji	712	11		712	11			
武汉	Wuhan	20085	315		19495	307		590	8
黄石	Huangshi	3256	68		3151	66		105	2
九江	Jiujiang	1020	13		890	11		130	2
安庆	Anqing	2340	35		1979	27		361	8
池州	Chizhou	1210	20		1210	20			
铜陵	Tongling	921	14		856	13		65	1
芜湖	Wuhu	2420	39		2175	35		245	4
马鞍山	Maanshan	1999	30		1775	26		224	4
南京	Nanjing	6088	66	17	5169	50	17	919	16
镇江	Zhenjiang	2744	23	10	2744	23	10		
泰州	Taizhou	5179	45	6	5155	44	6	24	1
扬州	Yangzhou	2478	49	3	2478	49	3		
江阴	Jiangyin	5046	44	11	5046	44	11		
常州	Changzhou	4461	124	1	4461	124	1		
南通	Nantong	10436	85	30	10189	81	30	247	4

16-38 民用航空航线及飞机架数

Number of Civil Aviation Routes and Civil Aircrafts

指标	Item	1990	1995	2000	2002	2003
民用航空航线条数（条）	**Number of Civil Aviation Routes (line)**	**437**	**797**	**1165**	**1176**	**1155**
国际航线	International Routes	44	85	133	161	194
国内航线	Domestic Routes	385	694	1032	1015	961
地区航线	Regional Routes	8	18	42	44	43
民用航空航线里程（公里）	**Length of Civil Aviation Routes (km)**	**506762**	**1128961**	**1502887**	**1637708**	**1749545**
国际航线	International Routes	166350	348175	508405	574470	715269
国内航线	Domestic Routes	329493	750794	994482	1063238	1034276
地区航线	Regional Routes	10919	29992	55759	61626	62874
民用航班飞行机场（个）	**Number of Civil Airports (unit)**	**94**	**139**	**139**	**141**	**126**
民用飞机期末架数（架）	**Number of Civil Aircraft (unit)**	**499**	**852**	**982**	**1112**	**1160**
#运输飞机	Aero transport			527	602	664
大中型飞机	Air bus			462	525	580
#波音747	Boeing 747	11	16	19	20	19
波音737	Boeing 737	21	115	186	234	264
波音757	Boeing 757	9	44	48	54	55
波音767	Boeing 767	6	17	16	18	22
MD90	MD-90			22	22	22
MD82	MD-82	25	39	27	26	26
A310	Airbus A310	2	3	3	3	3
A320	Airbus A320			60	65	76
图154	Tupolov 154	20	33	10		
Bae-146	BB-146	10	14	7	2	7
小型飞机	Puddle-jumper			65	77	84
#运7	Yun 7	45	67	22	11	7
通用飞机	General Aircraft			301	335	343

注:1.1997年以前，民航机场和飞机架数为民航总局直属企业数，1997年起为民航全行业数字(下表同)。

2.1997年以前，地区航线含民航至香港、澳门航线,与国内航线、国际航线并列。1997年起，民航至香港航线统计在国内航线中，航线里程及运输量统计口径也做同样调整。1999年起，地区航线为国内航线的其中项，仍含民航至香港、澳门航线及运量(下表同)。

3.民用飞机合计中含教学校验用飞机。

a) Before 1997, the number of civil airports and aircrafts refers to those owned by enterprises directly under CAAC. Since 1997, it refers to those owned by all enterprises of civil aviation. The same as in the following table.

b) Before 1997, regional routes includes the routes to and from Hong Kong, Macao, and are taken as the parataxis item as the item of domestic routes and international routes. Since 1997, regional routes to and from Hong Kong are taken as domestic routes, and adjustment are also made on the length of aviation routes and traffic volume accordingly. Since 1999, regional routes are taken as a part of domestic routes, and include the aviation routes to and from Hong Kong, Macao. The same as in the following table.

c) Number of civil aircrafts include the teaching aircrafts and check aircrafts.

16–39 民用航空运输量及通用飞行时间

Civil Aviation Traffic and Flying Time of General Aviation

指　　标	Item	1990	1995	2000	2002	2003
客运量　（万人）	**Passenger Traffic (10 000 persons)**	**1660**	**5117**	**6722**	**8594**	**8759**
国际航线	International Routes	114	368	690	838	682
国内航线	Domestic Routes	1346	4419	6031	7756	8078
地区航线	Regional Routes	200	330	403	438	341
旅客周转量	**Passenger-tons**					
（万人公里）	**(10 000 person-km)**	**2304797**	**6813036**	**9705437**	**12687022**	**12631853**
国际航线	International Routes	516910	1149710	2328154	2967177	2483542
国内航线	Domestic Routes	1576554	5287232	7377283	9719846	10148311
地区航线	Regional Routes	211333	376094	502405	567557	450344
货(邮)运量　（吨）	**Freight Traffic (ton)**	**369722**	**1011145**	**1967123**	**2020620**	**2190416**
国际航线	International Routes	81102	229632	492356	425321	514163
国内航线	Domestic Routes	239467	702557	1474767	1595299	1676253
地区航线	Regional Routes	49153	78956	135442	96836	106906
货邮周转量	**Freight Ton-kilometers**					
（万吨公里）	**(10 000 ton-km)**	**81825**	**222981**	**502683**	**515515**	**578976**
国际航线	International Routes	43830	115894	291550	283064	335820
国内航线	Domestic Routes	31647	96604	211133	232451	243156
地区航线	Regional Routes	6348	10483	19495	14856	16451
总周转量	**Total Air Traffic Ton-kilometers**					
（万吨公里）	**(10 000 ton-km)**	**249950**	**714385**	**1225007**	**1649267**	**1707946**
国际航线	International Routes	82595	201250	465190	548619	557794
国内航线	Domestic Routes	145156	474660	759818	1100647	1150153
地区航线	Regional Routes	22199	38475	56878	65578	56684
通用飞行时间(小时)	**Flying Time of General Aviation (hr)**	**34919**	**39485**	**48707**	**57577**	**63504**
农林业航空作业	Flight for Agriculture and Forestry	22540	16838	22922	25266	25486
#航空护林	Forest Protection Service	3573	2410	3927	5795	7115
播种造林	Afforestation	4605	1713	4060	5465	3043
工业航空作业	Flight for Industry	12379	22647	24116	23685	28525

16-40 输油(气)管道长度和运输量（2003年底）

Length and Traffic of Petroleum and Gas Pipelines (End of 2003)

本表是中国石油天然气集团公司和中国石油化工集团公司数据。

Data in this table are provided by China National Petroleum Corporation and China Petro-chemical Corporation.

项目	Item	输油(气)管道里程(公里) Length of Pipelines (km)	输油(气)能力(万吨) Capacity of Pipeline Traffic (10 000 tons)	输油(气)量(万吨或千万立方米) Pipeline Traffic (10 000 tons or 10 million cu.m)	输油(气)周转量(万吨公里或千万立方米公里) Ton-kilometer or Cubic Meter-kilometers (10 000 ton-km or 10 million cu.m-km)
总　计	**Total**	**32592**	**42550.7**	**21997.5**	**7393936.8**
#输油管	Petroleum Pipelines	15737	39273.9	19684.2	6338705.8
输气管	Gas Pipelines	16855	3276.8	2313.3	1055230.9
输原油管道	**Crude Oil Pipelines**	**12443**	**31595.9**	**17162.3**	**5951655.3**
管道分公司	Pipelines Subsidiary Company	3327	7100.0	4073.8	3193799.0
大庆油田有限责任公司	Daqing Oil Fields Limited Corporation	298	1547.0	1221.3	45814.0
新疆油田分公司	Xinjiang Oil Fields Subsidiary Company	1127	1850.0	1004.2	206523.0
胜利油田有限公司	Shengli Oil Fields Limited Co.	347	1595.0	653.6	49663.2
吉林油田分公司	Jilin Oil Fields Subsidiary Company	19	612.0	426.6	1746.0
华北油田分公司	North China Oil Fields Subsidiary Company	636	1207.0	250.6	27894.0
大港油田分公司	Dagang Oil Fields Subsidiary Company	40	877.0	337.5	3641.0
玉门油田分公司	Yumen Oil Fields Subsidiary Company	69	879.0	67.6	1144.0
辽河油田分公司	Liaohe Oil Fields Subsidiary Company	494	1425.0	915.9	96050.0
青海油田分公司	Qinghai Oil Fields Subsidiary Company	435	200.0	207.2	90072.0
江汉分公司	Jianghan Subsidiary Company	42	113.9	85.1	2298.2
天津分公司	Tianjin Subsidiary Company	45	450.0		
河南油田分公司	Henan Oil Fields Subsidiary Company	93	400.0	151.4	4470.9
茂名石油化工公司	Maoming Petrochemical Co.	170	2000.0	1176.0	86179.5
长庆油田分公司	Changqing Oil Fields Subsidiary Company	1084	1385.0	637.0	180930.0
塔里木油田分公司	Tarim Oil Fields Subsidiary Company	472	415.0	293.1	72599.0
锦州石化分公司	Jinzhou Petrochemical Subsidiary Company	58	600.0	519.0	13649.0
锦西石化分公司	Jinxi Petrochemical Subsidiary Company	30	300.0		
长岭炼化有限责任公司	Changling Refinery & Petrochemical Corporation	48	905.0	455.7	6512.1
吉林石化分公司	Jilin Petrochemical Subsidiary Company	150	400.0	418.0	62700.0
石化集团管道储运分公司	China Petrochemical Corporation Pipeline Transport Subsidiary Company	2640	4815.0	2850.9	1701029.0
石家庄炼化股份有限公司	Shijiazhuang Refinery & Petrochemical Limited Co.	155	350.0	131.5	20378.2
荆门分公司	Jingmen Subsidiary Company	210	350.0	150.3	31563.0
天津石化公司	Tianjin Petrochemical Co.	48	100.0		
金陵分公司	Jinling Subsidiary Company	23	500.0	342.3	7872.0
西北分公司	Northwest Subsidiary Company	150	340.0	201.5	13148.3
济南分公司	Jinan Subsidiary Company	70	330.0	262.2	18354.0
青岛石油化工厂	Qingdao Petrochemical Factory	60	300.0	183.0	10980.0
巴陵石油化工公司	Baling Petrochemical Co.	18	200.0	147.0	2646.0
保定石油化工厂	Baoding Petrochemical Factory	84	50.0		
输成品油管道	**Refined Oil Pipelines**	**3294**	**7678.0**	**2521.9**	**387048.5**
燕山石化有限公司	Yanshan Petrochemical Ltd.	26	469.0	53.0	344.8
天津石油化工公司	Tianjin Petrochemical Co.	3	22.0		
抚顺石化分公司	Fushun Petrochemical Subsidiary Company	268	435.0	255.2	62891.0
锦州石化分公司	jimson Petrochemical Subsidiary Company	126	240.0	155.0	6510.0
锦西石化分公司	Jinxi Petrochemical Subsidiary Company	64	337.6	141.0	4230.0
鞍山炼油厂	Anshan Refinery	52	352.0	7.6	153.0
大连石化分公司	Dalian Petrochemical Subsidiary Company	11	80.0	5.5	28.0
中国石化长岭分公司	China Petrochemical Corporation Changling Subsidiary Company	99	77.1	1.6	19.6
大庆石化分公司	Daqing Petrochemical Subsidiary Company	52	188.0	25.6	50.0
天津分公司	Tianjin Subsidiary Company	17	335.0	52.7	158.0
沧州分公司	Cangzhou Subsidiary Company	10	50.9	9.0	37.8
镇海炼化股份有限公司	Zhenhai Refinery & Petrochemical Limited Co.	46	109.4	61.1	589.5
九江分公司	Jiujiang Subsidiary Company	19	259.5	10.3	47.5
荆门分公司	Jingmen Subsidiary Company	12	56.0	4.6	10.8
武汉石油化工厂	Wuhan Petrochemical Factory	15	349.0	28.4	100.9
安庆分公司	Anqing Subsidiary Company	2	10.5	19.3	19.2

16-40 续表 continued

项　　目	Item	输油(气)管道里程(公里) Length of Pipelines (km)	输油(气)能力(万吨) Capacity of Pipeline Traffic (10 000 tons)	输油(气)量(万吨或千万立方米) Pipeline Traffic (10 000 tons or 10 million cu.m)	输油(气)周转量(万吨公里或千万立方米公里) Ton-kilometer or Cubic Meter-kilometers (10 000 ton-km or 10 million cu.m-km)
中国石化广州分公司	China Petrochemical Corporation Guangzhou Subsidiary Company	67	568.0	428.2	1839.6
茂名炼化股份有限公司	Maoming Refinery & Petrochemical Limited Co.	201	828.0	368.2	7975.4
茂名石油化工公司	Maoming Petrochemical Industrial Co.	230	650.0	279.7	7769.5
齐鲁分公司	Qilu Subsidiary Company	3	60.0	4.6	13.8
管道分公司	Pipelines Subsidiary Company	1261	800.0	305.1	287182.0
大庆油田有限责任公司	Daqing Oil Fields Limited Corporation	36	98.0		
新疆油田分公司	Xinjiang Oil Fields Subsidiary Company	291	130.0		
吉林油田分公司	Jilin Oil Fields Subsidiary Company	11	20.0		
哈尔滨石化分公司	Harbin Petrochemical Subsidiary Company	71	50.0	12.3	312.0
高桥分公司	Gaoqiao Subsidiary Company	42	150.0	100.0	4200.0
巴陵石油化工公司	Baling Petrochemical Company	123	250.0	50.6	890.7
金陵石油化工公司	Jinling Petrochemical Company	123	423.0	96.2	970.4
青岛石油化工厂	Qingdao Petrochemical Company	15	280.0	47.0	705.0
输天然气管道	**Natural Gas Pipelines**	**16539**	**2873.0**	**2217.4**	**1054194.9**
管道分公司	Pipelines Subsidiary Company	2130	355.0	160.9	90631.0
西南油气分公司	Southwest Oil & Gas Subsidiary Company	6417		877.0	509329.0
大庆油田有限责任公司	Daqing Oil Fields Limited Corporation	209	195.5	71.1	1075.0
胜利油田有限公司	Shengli Oil Fields Limited Corporation	143	40.0	7.7	1093.7
华北油田分公司	North China Oil Fields Subsidiary Company	87	28.9	25.4	1778.0
辽河油田分公司	Liaohe Oil Fields Subsidiary Company	788	247.8	45.0	595.0
大港油田分公司	Dagang Oil Fields Subsidiary Company	188	91.3	40.6	3946.0
中原油气高新股份有限公司	Sinopec Zhongyuan Petroleum Co., LTD	150	14.6	15.6	2334.0
南方勘探开发分公司	Southern Prospecting & Exploiture Subsidiary	6	62.3	3.9	2.0
江汉油田分公司	Jianghan Oil Fields Subsidiary Company	58	14.0	2.5	43.7
新疆油田分公司	Xinjiang Oil Fields Subsidiary Company	626	187.8	159.9	22847.0
青海油田分公司	Qinghai Oil Fields Subsidiary Company	896	146.5	58.4	12360.0
长庆油田分公司	Changqing Oil Fields Subsidiary Company	188	253.3	243.4	7579.0
塔里木油田分公司	Tarim Oil Fields Subsidiary Company	455	107.0	50.9	3825.0
吉林油田分公司	Jilin Oil Fields Subsidiary Company	239	36.0	6.4	582.0
西气东输管道公司	Gas from West to East Pipeline Transport Company	1581	120.0	8.9	2824.0
北京华油天然气有限公司	Beijing Oil and Natural Gas Co.	1090	300.0	273.6	295543.0
中原油田分公司	Zhongyuan Oil Fields Subsidiary Company	274	5.0	9.7	2651.4
东北分公司	Northeast Subsidiary Company	269	110.0	0.1	4.1
华北分公司	North China Subsidiary Company	138	21.9	0.6	85.6
西南分公司	Southwest Subsidiary Company	609	536.0	156.0	95066.4
输其他气体管道	**Other Gas pipelines**	**316**	**403.8**	**95.9**	**1037.0**
大庆油田有限责任公司	Daqing Oil Fields Limited Corporation	9	1.3		
锦西石化分公司	Jinxi Petrochemical Subsidiary Company	1	10.0		
燕山石化有限公司	Yanshan Petrochemical Co.	3	21.0	3.7	11.2
天津石油化工公司	Tianjin Petrochemical Co.	2	5.0		
沧州分公司	Cangzhong Subsidiary Company	1	9.9	0.6	0.3
金陵分公司	Jinling Subsidiary Company	16	6.4	5.9	94.1
镇海炼化股份有限公司	Zhenhai Refinery & Petrochemical Limited Co.	29	62.5	18.0	69.5
武汉石油化工厂	Wuhan Petrochemical Factory	23	16.0	7.6	109.6
荆门分公司	Jingmen Subsidiary company	3	1.2	0.1	0.4
石家庄炼化股份有限公司	Shijiazhuang Refinery & Petrochemical Limited Co.	37	34.0	3.9	85.1
中国石化广州分公司	China Petrochemical Corporation Guangzhou Subsidiary Company	5	9.8	6.5	30.4
茂名炼化股份有限公司	Maoming Refinery & Petrochemical Limited Co.	53	55.6	37.2	399.8
中国石化长岭分公司	China Petrochemical Corporation Changling Subsidiary Company	39	20.0		
天津分公司	Tianjin Subsidiary Company	35	67.0	6.0	69.4
锦州石化分公司	Jinzhou Petrochemical Subsidiary Company	45	32.0	2.0	90.0
巴陵石油化工公司	Baling Petrolchemical Co.	18	52.0	4.4	77.3

注：管道输气量按一千立方米折一吨计算。

a) Gas transport though pipelines is converted from volume to tonnage using the conversion ratio of 1000 cubic meters equal to one ton.

16-41 邮电业务基本情况

Basic Conditions of Post and Telecommunication Services

指标	Item	1999	2000	2001	2002	2003
邮电业务总量 (亿元)	Business Volume of Post and Telecommunications Service (100 million yuan)	3330.82	4792.70	4556.26	5695.80	7019.79
函件 (亿件)	Number of Letters (100 million pcs)	60.52	77.71	86.93	106.01	103.84
特快专递 (万件)	Pieces of Express Mail Services (10 000 pcs)	9091.3	11031.4	12652.7	14036.2	17237.8
报刊期发数 (万份)	Number of Newspapers and Magazines Circulation (10 000 copies)	25035.2	20089.7	21811.1	17620.0	16594.4
集邮业务 (万枚)	Philately Business (10 000 pcs)	522475	453500	344114	244159	183421
长途电话 (亿次)	Number of Long-distance Calls (100 million times)	178.25	210.75	219.98	192.79	196.03
年末无线寻呼用户 (万户)	Number of Subscribers of Pagering Service at Year-end (10 000 subscribers)	4674.5	4884.3	3606.4	1872.1	1057.6
年末移动电话用户 (万户)	Number of Mobile Telephone Subscribers at Year-end (10 000 subscribers)	4329.6	8453.3	14522.2	20600.5	26995.3
本地电话年末用户 (万户)	Local Telephone Subscribers of at Year-end (10 000 subscribers)	10871.6	14482.9	18036.8	21422.2	26274.7
城市电话用户 (万户)	Local (Urban) Telephone Subscribers at Year-end (10 000 subscribers)	7463.3	9311.6	11193.7	13579.1	17109.7
#住宅电话用户	Residential Telephone Subscribers	5894.4	7219.4	8535.3	10196.7	12533.9
乡村电话用户 (万户)	Number of Rural Telephones Subscribers at Year-end (10 000 subscribers)	3408.4	5171.3	6843.1	7843.1	9165.0
#住宅电话用户	Residential Telephone Subscribers	2949.2	4597.8	6197.7	7183.8	8389.7
邮政局所 (处)	Number of Post & Telecommunications Offices (unit)	66649	58437	57136	76358	63555
邮路及农村投递路线总长度 (万公里)	Length of Postal Routes and Rural Delivery Routes (10 000 km)	632.71	643.78	659.53	659.22	680.20
长途光缆线路长度 (万公里)	Length of Long-distance Optical Cable Lines (10 000 km)	23.97	28.66	39.91	48.77	59.43
长途电话交换机容量(万路端)	Capacity of automatic toll switching systems (10 000 lines)	503.20	563.55	703.58	773.01	869.40
局用交换机容量 (万门)	Capacity of C.O. switches (10000 lines)	15346	17826	25566	28657	35082
用户交换机容量 (万门)	Capacity of PBXs (10000 lines)	1672.2	1587.6	1514.5	1370.5	1294.1
移动电话交换机容量 (万户)	Capacity of Mobile Telephone Exchanges (10 000 subscribers)	8136.0	13985.6	21926.3	27400.3	33698.4
电话机 (万部)	Number of Telephone Sets (10 000 units)	17567.4	25606.6	35334.7	42972.2	54155.3
固定电话	Number of Fixed Telephones	13237.8	17153.3	20812.5	22371.7	27160.0
移动电话	Number of Mobile Telephones	4329.6	8453.3	14522.2	20600.5	26995.3

注:1.邮电业务总量2000年及以前按1990年不变价格计算，2001年是按2000年不变价格计算，按可比价格比上年增长27.6%。

2.邮政局所数1998年及以前为邮电局所；从2002年起统计口径为邮政营销网点，含邮政局所和邮政代办点(下表同)。

a) The business volume of post and telecommunication services before 2000 was calculated at 1990's constant prices and that in 2001 was calculated at 2000's constant prices. The increase rate at comparable price in 2001 was 27.6 %.

b) Number of postal and telecommunications offices refers to number of postal offices before 1998. That refers to the postal marketing station, including the postal offices and the postal deputy station, since 2002. The same as the following table.

16-42 邮电业务量

Post and Telecommunication Services

年份 Year 地区 Region		邮电业务总量（亿元）Business Volume of Post and Telecommunications (100 million yuan)	邮政业务总量 Business Volume of Post	电信业务总量 Business Volume of Telecommunications	函件（亿件）Number of Letters (100 million pcs)	特快专递（万件）Pieces of Express Mail Services (10 000 pcs)	报刊期发数（万份）Newspapers and Magazines Circulation (10 000 copies)
	1978	34.09			28.35		11250
	1980	39.03			33.13		16431
	1985	62.21			46.78		30172
	1989	123.46			57.28	247.3	17704
	1990	155.54	45.95	109.59	54.87	343.3	20078
	1991	204.39	52.75	151.63	52.11	566.7	23277
	1992	290.94	64.36	226.57	57.18	959.2	25104
	1993	462.71	80.26	382.45	68.70	2156.2	25511
	1994	688.19	95.89	592.30	76.50	4019.5	24096
	1995	988.85	113.34	875.51	79.55	5562.7	21689
	1996	1342.04	133.29	1208.75	78.68	7096.6	21157
	1997	1773.29	144.34	1628.95	68.55	6878.9	21875
	1998	2431.21	166.28	2264.94	65.51	7331.8	22989
	1999	3330.82	198.44	3132.38	60.52	9091.3	25035
	2000	4792.70	232.80	4559.90	77.71	11031.4	20090
	2001	4556.26	457.42	4098.84	86.93	12652.7	21811
	2002	5695.80	494.69	5201.12	106.01	14036.2	17620
	2003	7019.79	541.04	6478.75	103.84	17237.8	16594
北 京	Beijing	287.29	31.32	255.96	8.38	1188.8	803
天 津	Tianjin	113.93	8.97	104.96	2.20	321.5	191
河 北	Hebei	293.18	21.02	272.17	4.01	651.0	777
山 西	Shanxi	144.51	12.12	132.38	1.16	199.9	567
内蒙古	Inner Mongolia	108.36	8.51	99.85	1.37	191.7	249
辽 宁	Liaoning	296.01	19.05	276.97	1.60	619.8	352
吉 林	Jilin	152.90	11.30	141.61	1.72	330.1	198
黑龙江	Heilongjiang	221.92	20.48	201.43	1.53	339.6	413
上 海	Shanghai	292.35	31.47	260.88	7.34	1148.7	847
江 苏	Jiangsu	441.71	44.46	397.25	8.30	1302.9	1268
浙 江	Zhejiang	493.41	27.72	465.69	7.49	1014.2	1014
安 徽	Anhui	169.37	18.81	150.57	3.11	426.3	692
福 建	Fujian	307.19	22.36	284.83	5.46	682.1	539
江 西	Jiangxi	139.58	13.70	125.88	2.21	351.9	325
山 东	Shandong	382.36	36.08	346.28	5.82	1089.4	1152
河 南	Henan	290.46	26.42	264.04	3.59	944.9	880
湖 北	Hubei	210.91	22.31	188.60	5.68	671.3	721
湖 南	Hunan	227.01	21.17	205.84	5.06	563.4	835
广 东	Guangdong	1160.41	54.33	1106.08	13.07	2180.1	1043
广 西	Guangxi	162.26	10.36	151.90	2.31	414.6	455
海 南	Hainan	40.41	3.45	36.96	0.34	84.2	66
重 庆	Chongqing	121.31	8.49	112.82	2.05	271.4	217
四 川	Sichuan	252.50	19.05	233.44	3.36	939.2	915
贵 州	Guizhou	100.02	5.50	94.51	0.79	253.3	274
云 南	Yunnan	153.05	8.52	144.54	1.00	199.6	329
西 藏	Tibet	9.81	0.93	8.88	0.06	28.0	22
陕 西	Shaanxi	163.66	13.82	149.84	2.81	335.3	312
甘 肃	Gansu	81.72	6.41	75.32	0.76	196.0	469
青 海	Qinghai	22.14	1.54	20.61	0.38	47.7	41
宁 夏	Ningxia	28.52	2.12	26.40	0.26	52.1	43
新 疆	Xinjiang	114.88	7.20	107.68	0.60	198.8	587
不分地区	Not Classified by Region	36.65	2.06	34.59			

注：邮电业务总量2000年及以前按1990年不变价格计算，以后按2000年不变价格计算。2001年按可比价格比上年增长27.6%。

a) The business volumes of post and telecommunications before 2000 were calculated at 1990's constant prices and these since 2000 were calculated at 2000's constant prices. The increase rate at comparable price in 2001 was 27.6%.

16-42 续表 1 continued

年份 地区	Year Region	集邮业务 (万枚) Philately (10 000 pieces)	长途电话 (万次) Number of Long Distance Telephone Calls (10 000 times)	无线寻呼用户 (万户) Number of Subscribers of Pagering Services (10 000 subscribers)	移动电话用户 (万户) Number of Mobile Telephone Subscribers (10 000 subscribers)	互联网上网人数 (万人) Number of Users of Internet Services (10 000 persons)
	1978		18574			
	1980		21404			
	1985		38254			
	1989		78462	23.7	1.0	
	1990	71233	116292	43.7	1.8	
	1991	123523	172921	87.4	4.8	
	1992	167303	287380	222.0	17.7	
	1993	210885	506853	561.4	63.9	
	1994	236849	757639	1033.0	156.8	
	1995	239250	1013966	1739.2	362.9	
	1996	303436	1273951	2536.2	685.3	
	1997	451729	1554026	3254.6	1323.3	
	1998	502850	1825941	3908.2	2386.3	
	1999	522475	1782529	4674.5	4329.6	
	2000	453500	2107542	4884.3	8453.3	
	2001	344114	2199823	3606.4	14522.2	
	2002	244159	1927910	1872.1	20600.5	
	2003	183421	1960283	1057.6	26995.3	7950
北京	Beijing	13387	78849	11.8	1108.9	398
天津	Tianjin	6794	33147	9.6	383.4	144.6
河北	Hebei	6460	81617	29.8	1253.2	289.1
山西	Shanxi	3249	39785	28.6	600.9	148.8
内蒙古	Inner Mongolia	3082	21648	10.4	479.1	74.9
辽宁	Liaoning	4413	104078	61.7	1080.3	291.5
吉林	Jilin	2792	40059	31.2	633.2	146.5
黑龙江	Heilongjiang	4869	34146	102.3	856.5	226
上海	Shanghai	4041	76872	24.4	1098.6	431.6
江苏	Jiangsu	13708	160462	16.4	1926.3	610.9
浙江	Zhejiang	10847	160690	30.9	1955.2	451.2
安徽	Anhui	13711	57424	8.1	697.9	183.5
福建	Fujian	5410	66589	71.1	946.5	318.2
江西	Jiangxi	2605	47513	27.6	532.1	169.4
山东	Shandong	7002	109007	67.1	1510.2	626.6
河南	Henan	9159	101394	63.2	1072.6	225.7
湖北	Hubei	15782	50249	35.1	874.2	380.9
湖南	Hunan	5161	46543	61.6	846.2	265.4
广东	Guangdong	8076	311756	103.8	4007.0	950.2
广西	Guangxi	3068	32496	31.7	649.8	228.6
海南	Hainan	770	5852	14.7	136.3	39.7
重庆	Chongqing	1842	23408	6.7	619.4	176.6
四川	Sichuan	5204	74896	108.4	1195.4	424.3
贵州	Guizhou	1031	20298	12.8	331.1	83.1
云南	Yunnan	2701	26946	11.5	628.4	166.4
西藏	Tibet	250	6897	0.0	33.1	8.6
陕西	Shaanxi	5537	56385	24.6	617.6	196.7
甘肃	Gansu	2876	19996	6.7	277.7	122.4
青海	Qinghai	515	7336	0.9	100.0	19.5
宁夏	Ningxia	1842	6359	3.2	123.0	33.3
新疆	Xinjiang	3113	38988	41.4	421.2	117.8
不分地区	Not Classified by Region	14125.5	18595			

16-42 续表 2 continued

年份 地区	Year Region	本地电话年末用户(万户) Number of Subscribers of Local Telephone at Year-end (10 000subscribers)	城市电话用户 Number of Urban Telephone Subscribers	# 住宅电话 Residential Telephone Subscribers	乡村电话用户 Rural Telephone Subscribers	# 住宅电话 Residential Telephone Subscribers	公用电话(万户) Public Telephone (10 000 subscribers)
	1978	192.5	119.2		73.4		1.2
	1980	214.1	134.2		79.9		1.4
	1985	312.0	219.0	4.1	93.1	2.0	2.7
	1989	568.0	439.6	89.6	128.4	21.3	4.0
	1990	685.0	538.4	152.7	146.6	30.7	4.6
	1991	845.1	670.8	239.0	174.2	49.5	5.4
	1992	1146.9	920.6	415.4	226.3	79.0	8.4
	1993	1733.2	1407.4	800.4	325.8	139.5	15.8
	1994	2729.5	2246.8	1489.4	482.7	274.9	38.7
	1995	4070.6	3263.6	2358.4	807.0	551.4	85.0
	1996	5494.7	4277.8	3224.6	1216.9	907.3	138.0
	1997	7031.0	5244.4	4057.2	1786.6	1406.6	193.9
	1998	8742.1	6259.8	4911.1	2482.3	2070.7	259.5
	1999	10871.6	7463.3	5894.4	3408.4	2949.2	297.4
	2000	14482.9	9311.6	7219.4	5171.3	4597.8	352.0
	2001	18036.8	11193.7	8535.3	6843.1	6197.7	346.2
	2002	21422.2	13579.1	10196.7	7843.1	7183.8	985.5
	2003	26274.7	17109.7	12533.9	9165.0	8389.7	1561.4
北京	Beijing	683.7	602.3	432.6	81.4	81.3	35.9
天津	Tianjin	360.1	358.5	237.9	1.6	1.6	24.1
河北	Hebei	1339.0	731.5	558.7	607.5	582.5	43.4
山西	Shanxi	674.3	463.6	361.1	210.7	195.1	48.1
内蒙古	Inner Mongolia	427.7	342.8	260.1	85.0	76.5	16.1
辽宁	Liaoning	1278.7	907.4	618.9	371.3	354.0	73.7
吉林	Jilin	594.6	417.2	354.6	177.4	169.6	23.3
黑龙江	Heilongjiang	874.4	658.1	563.6	216.3	208.0	41.8
上海	Shanghai	733.9	733.9	536.3			26.3
江苏	Jiangsu	2043.9	1175.4	876.2	868.5	799.2	95.7
浙江	Zhejiang	1656.5	937.3	616.7	719.2	626.9	100.5
安徽	Anhui	997.9	472.1	377.3	525.8	508.0	29.6
福建	Fujian	1122.7	695.9	483.6	426.8	390.8	71.7
江西	Jiangxi	630.3	387.1	292.2	243.2	226.4	37.9
山东	Shandong	2088.8	1004.2	814.4	1084.5	1028.6	89.0
河南	Henan	1362.6	752.7	576.0	609.9	573.0	89.2
湖北	Hubei	889.8	640.5	483.5	249.3	222.7	79.5
湖南	Hunan	941.9	541.3	408.2	400.6	367.5	72.1
广东	Guangdong	2567.0	1759.5	1144.4	807.5	647.1	241.0
广西	Guangxi	638.5	429.2	309.9	209.2	190.8	40.1
海南	Hainan	162.8	114.4	75.9	48.4	41.6	14.4
重庆	Chongqing	533.4	343.8	249.8	189.6	176.7	30.5
四川	Sichuan	1128.2	804.9	581.4	323.3	293.9	64.5
贵州	Guizhou	332.4	234.8	175.2	97.5	88.0	20.9
云南	Yunnan	483.2	359.9	260.1	123.3	105.3	29.7
西藏	Tibet	27.4	26.1	18.0	1.3	0.8	1.2
陕西	Shaanxi	671.9	446.1	318.8	225.8	206.5	42.7
甘肃	Gansu	399.8	284.9	204.6	115.0	101.5	31.3
青海	Qinghai	76.4	64.2	47.4	12.3	10.9	2.6
宁夏	Ningxia	100.3	72.2	53.1	28.1	25.7	4.6
新疆	Xinjiang	412.0	311.1	231.6	100.9	88.6	28.2
不分地区	Not Classified by Region	40.6	36.7	11.7	3.9	0.4	11.6

注：2002年及以后年份，公用电话用户中包括安装在街道等公共场所的智能网专线接入终端用户，与以前年度的统计口径不同。

a) Number of subscribers of public telephone since 2002 included the smart net special end-users which were installed at the public spatial, such as stree
The data are not comparable with the previous years.

16-43　邮政局所数及邮递线路(年底数)

Post and Telecommunication Services Facilities (Year-end)

年　份 地　区	Year Region	邮政局所(处) Number of Post and Telecommunication Offices (unit)	信筒信箱(处) Number of Post Boxes (unit)	邮路总长度(公里) Length of Postal Routes (km)	# 汽车邮路 Highway Routes	# 铁路邮路 Railway Routes	农村投递线路(公里) Rural Delivery Routes (km)
	1978	49623	156398	4863282	572204	150249	4266291
	1980	49471	159009	4737124	582058	150819	4138879
	1985	53107	174678	1416303	663016	182178	3565758
	1989	53092	178289	1526073	675352	196178	3389374
	1990	53629	181877	1618200	676747	191313	3364861
	1991	54006	181939	1603344	685759	185872	3371424
	1992	54891	183289	1646931	712367	189359	3374556
	1993	57005	187966	1760506	727380	189704	3377769
	1994	60447	193902	1781787	757931	187871	3364730
	1995	61898	203011	1886082	819412	183036	3345848
	1996	72496	217235	2118940	917151	183884	3358051
	1997	79273	231337	2363108	873688	186382	3402946
	1998	102225	234716	2853942	930622	189652	3361484
	1999	66649	232674	2979007	989122	190056	3348054
	2000	58437	239356	3073331	1070304	184925	3364498
	2001	57136	225846	3102558	1074092	180399	3492761
	2002	76358	217541	3080989	1112806	177685	3511190
	2003	63555	275962	3270209	1137480	191351	3531832
北　京	Beijing	874	3459	367731	44552	29369	17263
天　津	Tianjin	364	1649	19986	9395	5071	16438
河　北	Hebei	2487	8088	52827	42929	7851	155408
山　西	Shanxi	1633	3594	104201	23650	5427	102385
内蒙古	Inner Mongolia	1686	3022	62344	42799	5764	111636
辽　宁	Liaoning	1643	7622	118248	32629	4282	93475
吉　林	Jilin	1374	5502	69201	23816	7687	90993
黑龙江	Heilongjiang	2165	6990	105874	35912	15786	120685
上　海	Shanghai	601	4392	189100	32336	14720	28279
江　苏	Jiangsu	3216	11220	109008	68570	4790	252724
浙　江	Zhejiang	2453	16968	116277	41537	3466	118614
安　徽	Anhui	2700	8465	70671	38871	2087	137047
福　建	Fujian	1654	14595	136627	32962	1216	78661
江　西	Jiangxi	1979	7583	90867	41182	7063	119295
山　东	Shandong	4410	34979	156848	49946	7025	240162
河　南	Henan	2828	6009	87167	49714	4104	186332
湖　北	Hubei	2644	53929	93627	45729	5216	192869
湖　南	Hunan	4353	15965	96018	53427	3267	219859
广　东	Guangdong	4532	16788	301873	87804	7733	196480
广　西	Guangxi	1707	7147	67425	43223	4007	108050
海　南	Hainan	536	953	41939	16053		22858
重　庆	Chongqing	2440	6101	83392	24092	3067	66607
四　川	Sichuan	6250	8183	171346	53799	5058	186899
贵　州	Guizhou	1729	2028	67472	26693	6848	67990
云　南	Yunnan	1965	4487	136365	52855	4638	165196
西　藏	Tibet	128	249	18544	17190		42677
陕　西	Shaanxi	1899	5503	92825	29148	8223	126685
甘　肃	Gansu	1383	6482	68399	27852	5318	106200
青　海	Qinghai	210	600	24107	8857	2923	12728
宁　夏	Ningxia	378	801	18310	6040	2498	10766
新　疆	Xinjiang	1334	2609	131590	33918	6847	136571

注：邮路总长度1980年及以前是邮路及农村投递线路总长度之和。

a) Length of postal routes before 1981 included the length of postal routes and rural delivery routes.

16-44 电信主要通信能力（年底数）

Main Communication Capacity of Telecommunications (Year-end)

年份 Year / 地区 Region	长途自动交换机容量（路端）Capacity of Long-distance Telephone Exchanges (circuit)	本地电话局用交换机容量（万门）Capacity of Local Office Telephone Exchanges (10 000 line)	移动电话交换机容量（万户）Capacity of Mobile Telephone Exchanges (10 000 subscribers)	长途光缆线路长度（公里）Length of Long Distance Optical Cable Lines (km)	长途微波线路长度（公里）Length of Long Distance Microwave Lines (km)
1978	1863	405.9			13958
1980	1969	443.2			13958
1985	11522	613.4			17275
1989	103269	1034.7	3.7	1851	26338
1990	161370	1231.8	5.1	3334	33626
1991	286325	1492.2	10.5	6490	39282
1992	521885	1915.1	45.3	14388	54418
1993	1206091	3040.8	156.1	38666	64368
1994	2416296	4926.2	371.6	73290	
1995	3518781	7203.6	796.7	106882	79634
1996	4162009	9291.2	1536.2	130159	71503
1997	4368305	11269.2	2585.7	150754	65013
1998	4491595	13823.7	4706.7	194100	66518
1999	5032026	15346.1	8136.0	239735	65228
2000	5635498	17825.6	13985.6	286642	121947
2001	7035769	25566.3	21926.3	399082	164052
2002	7730133	28656.8	27400.3	487684	193636
2003	8693998	35082.5	33698.4	594303	119886
北京 Beijing	219155	992.8	1351.0	3984	266
天津 Tianjin	145580	512.6	515.0	2077	5045
河北 Hebei	221375	1730.5	1350.0	13889	4642
山西 Shanxi	142841	792.5	698.2	16624	3631
内蒙古 Inner Mongolia	146900	624.8	545.4	28440	8442
辽宁 Liaoning	309628	1707.7	1366.8	15285	3423
吉林 Jilin	123014	870.1	767.1	14635	5143
黑龙江 Heilongjiang	223384	1177.7	1037.8	30256	5381
上海 Shanghai	235000	872.5	1547.0	4215	313
江苏 Jiangsu	512399	2671.8	2380.8	19361	4368
浙江 Zhejiang	440981	2193.8	2492.3	20464	3416
安徽 Anhui	349825	1272.5	827.0	20042	3378
福建 Fujian	310569	1409.1	1173.9	19186	5006
江西 Jiangxi	269847	843.4	681.3	13836	2825
山东 Shandong	390687	2817.4	1814.7	17715	4080
河南 Henan	280830	1703.6	1184.5	23198	1565
湖北 Hubei	249936	1274.6	1118.2	18148	4010
湖南 Hunan	335125	1232.2	1050.8	23813	8165
广东 Guangdong	1414646	3356.5	5328.1	41333	7007
广西 Guangxi	270964	843.5	803.5	28549	2574
海南 Hainan	71966	240.9	158.0	1180	985
重庆 Chongqing	108097	727.3	686.2	8829	3966
四川 Sichuan	565500	1520.1	1470.9	25481	2384
贵州 Guizhou	193740	465.4	495.3	20800	9202
云南 Yunnan	197478	684.6	788.0	18031	4229
西藏 Tibet	46000	50.8	48.0	6542	225
陕西 Shaanxi	216010	922.2	785.2	25387	3323
甘肃 Gansu	133550	527.7	372.0	20703	1807
青海 Qinghai	62640	101.7	123.8	11575	633
宁夏 Ningxia	46502	168.9	172.3	6519	883
新疆 Xinjiang	174561	624.2	565.3	32144	9570
不分地区 Not Classified by Region	285268	148.9		42060	

注:电话交换机容量中不包括用户交换机容量。

a)The capacity of exchanges in this table excludes the capacity of exchanges owned by users.

16-45 邮电通信服务水平

Level of Post and Telecommunication Services

指　　标	Item	1999	2000	2001	2002	2003
一、邮政通信水平	**Post and Communication Level**					
平均每一邮政局所服务面积（平方公里）	Average Area Served by Every Post Office (sq.km)	144.0	135.3	168.0	123.8	148.8
平均每一邮政局所服务人口　（万人）	Average People Served by Every Post office (10 000 persons)	1.87	1.70	2.20	1.70	2.02
平均每人每年发函件数　（件）	Annual Average Number of Letters Mailed per Capita (piece)	4.90	6.40	6.90	8.30	8.08
平均每百人每年订报刊数　（份）	Annual Average Number of Newspaper and Magazine Subscribed per 100 Persons (piece)	20.0	16.4	17.2	13.9	12.9
设有邮政局、所的乡(镇)比重　(%)	Percentage of Townships with Post and Telecommunication Offices (%)	79.4	78.7	77.6	81.9	82.8
已通邮的行政村比重　(%)	Percentage of Administrative Village with Post Communication (%)			94.45	97.80	97.98
二、电信通信水平	**Communication Level of Telecommunications**					
移动电话（GSM）网络覆盖县（市）	Number of County (City) Covered by GSM				2025	2813
移动电话（CDMA）网络覆盖县（市）	Number of County (City) Covered by CDMA				2012	2142
移动电话漫游国家和地区　（个）	Number of Country (Territory) Roamed through Mobile Telephone (unit)			90	116	155
电话普及率（包括移动电话）（部/百人）	Popularization Rate of Telephone (include mobile telephone) (sets/100 persons)	13.00	20.10	25.90	33.60	42.16
移动电话普及率　（部/百人）	Popularization Rate of Mobile Telephone (sets/100 persons)	3.50	6.77	11.20	16.10	21.02
每千人拥有公用电话数　（部）	Per 1 000 Person Public Telephone (Sets)	2.36	2.78	2.71	7.67	12.08
已通固定电话的行政村比重　(%)	Percentage of Administrative Village with Telephone (%)		82.90	85.30	87.90	89.94

主要统计指标解释

铁路营业里程 又称营业长度(包括正式营业和临时营业里程)，指办理客货运输业务的铁路正线总长度。凡是全线或部分建成双线及以上的线路，以第一线的实际长度计算；复线、站线、段管线、岔线和特殊用途线以及不计算运费的联络线都不计算营业里程。该指标可以反映铁路运输业基础设施的发展水平，也是计算客货周转量、运输密度和机车车辆运用效率等指标的基础资料。

铁路电气化里程 指在全部铁路营业里程中已安装了供电线路及设备，可以供电力机车牵引列车运行的区段的总里程。

铁路自动、半自动闭塞里程 指装有列车自动或人工完成闭塞状态的铁路设备里程。为保证列车安全运行，在一个区间、同一时间内，一般只允许一列列车运行，这种保证列车在这个区间安全间隔运行的技术方法称为“闭塞”。自动或半自动闭塞里程占铁路营业里程的比重是反映铁路现代化的重要标志之一。

公路里程 指在一定时期内实际达到《公路工程[WTBZ]技术标准JTJ01-88》规定的等级公路，并经公路主管部门正式验收交付使用的公路里程数。包括大中城市的郊区公路以及通过小城镇街道部分的公路里程和桥梁、渡口的长度，不包括大中城市的街道、厂矿、林区生产用道和农业生产用道的里程。两条或多条公路共同经由同一路段，只计算一次，不得重复计算里程长度。该指标可以反映公路建设的发展规模，也是计算运输网密度等指标的基础资料。

内河航道里程 也称内河通航里程，指在一定时期内，能通航运输船舶及排筏的天然河流、湖泊水库、运河及通航渠道的长度。包括全年季节性通航累计三个月以上的航道，不包括仅供零散流放竹、木排的河道。该指标可以反映内河水运网的规模、水平和发展情况。

民用航空航线里程 指民航运输定期班机飞行的航线长度的总和。航线长度按机场之间的距离计算，通常有两种计算方法：一是将每条航线长度相加称为重复计算航线里程；一是将两线或两条以上航线经过同一区段里程，只计算一次航线长度称为不重复计算航线里程。一般常用的是后者，该指标可以确切反映民航运输网的规模，是表明民航事业为国民经济服务和方便人民生活程度的主要指标。

输油(气)管道长度 也称输油(气)里程，指油品(或天然气)的实际输送距离，一般按输油(气)管道的单线长度计算。若包括复线和备用线长度则称为输油(气)管道延展长度，是指管道铺设的实际长度。我们通常使用的是不包括复线的“输油(气)管道里程”，该指标可以反映管道运输的发展规模和水平。

货(客)运量 指在一定时期内，各种运输工具实际运送的货物(旅客)数量。该指标是反映运输业为国民经济和人民生活服务的数量指标，也是制定和检查运输生产计划、研究运输发展规模和速度的重要指标。货运按吨计算，客运按人计算。货物不论运输距离长短、货物类别，均按实际重量统计。旅客不论行程远近或票价多少，均按一人一次客运量统计；半价票、小孩票也按一人统计。

货(客)运密度 指在一定时期内某种运输方式在营运线路的某一区段平均每公里线路通过的货物(旅客)运输周转量。计算公式为：

$$货（客）运密度=\frac{货物（旅客）周转量}{营业线路长度}$$

该指标可以反映交通运输线路上的货物(旅客)运输量运输繁忙程度，是平衡运输线路运输能力和通过能力，规划线路建设及改造、配备技术设备，研究运输网布局的重要依据。

货物(旅客)周转量 指在一定时期内，由各种运输工具运送的货物(旅客)数量与其相应运输距离的乘积之总和。该指标可以反映运输业生产的总成果，也是编制和检查运输生产计划，计算运输效率、劳动生产率以及核算运输单位成本的主要基础资料。计算货物周转量通常按发出站与到达站之间的最短距离，也就是计费距离计算。计算公式为：

$$货物（旅客）周转量=\sum 货物（旅客）运输量\times 运输距离$$

铁路货车平均静载重 指铁路货车在始发站静止状态下平均每车装载的货物重量，用以分析货车完成装车时车辆载重力的利用情况。计算公式为：

$$货车平均静载量=\frac{货物发送吨数}{装车数}$$

静载重的多少取决于运送货物的性质、种类、车辆的类型和装载技术的高低。根据货车的平均标记载重与静载重进行对比，可以反映货车载重能力的利用程度。计算公式为：

$$货车载重力利用率（\%）=\frac{货车平均静载重}{货车平均标记载重}\times 100\%$$

铁路货运机车日产量 指在一定时期内，平均每台货运机车在一昼夜内所完成的总重吨公里数，包括载运货物的重量和车辆本身的自重。该指标从时间和牵引能力两方面反映了机车运用效率。计算公式为：

$$货运机车平均日产量=\frac{货运总重吨公里数}{货运机车台日数}$$

沿海主要港口货物吞吐量 指经水运进出沿海主要港区范围，并经过装卸的货物数量，包括邮件及办理托运手续的行李、包裹以及补给运输船舶的燃、物料和淡水。货物吞吐量按货物流向分为进口、出口吞吐量，按货物交流性质分为外贸货物吞吐量和国内贸易货物吞吐量。货物吞吐量的货类构成及其流向，是衡量港口生产能力大小的重要指标。

民用汽车拥有量 指报告期末，在公安交通管理部门按照《机动车注册登记工作规范》，已注册登记领有民用车辆牌照的全部汽车数量。汽车拥有量统计的主要分类：根据汽车结构分为载客汽车、载货汽车及其他汽车；根据汽车所有者不同分为个人(私人)汽车、单位汽车；根据汽车的使用性质分为营运汽车、非营运汽车和特种汽车；根据汽车大小规格不同载客汽车分为大型、中型、小型和微型，载货汽车分为重型、中型、轻型和微型。

邮电业务总量 指以价值量形式表现的邮电通信企业为社会提供各类邮电通信服务的总数量。邮电业务量按专业分类包括函件、包件、汇票、报刊发行、邮政快件、特快专递、邮政储蓄、集邮、公众电报、用户电报、传真、长途电话、出租电路、无线寻呼、移动电话、分组交换数据通信、出租代维等。计算方法为各类产品乘以相应的平均单价(不变价)之和，再加上出租电路和设备、代用户维护电话交换机和线路等的服务收入。该指标综合反映了一定时期邮电业务发展的总成果，是研究邮电业务量构成和发展趋势的重要指标。计算公式为：

邮电业务总量=∑（各类邮电业务量×不变单价）

+出租代维及其他业务收入

=邮电业务总量+电信业务总量

无线寻呼用户 无线寻呼是指电话用户通过无线寻呼中心，在规定范围内向携带小型寻呼机的用户发出声音、数字或文字显示信息。在寻呼台办理登记手续携带小型寻呼机的用户，称为无线寻呼用户。

移动电话用户 指通过移动电话交换机进入移动电话网、占用移动电话号码的各类电话用户。包括签约用户和智能网预付费用户。一个移动电话号码统计为一户。

互联网上网人数 指平均每周使用互联网至少1小时的中国公民人数。

本地电话用户 指接入本地电信运营商固定电话网上的电话用户。包括：住宅用户、单位用户、公用电话用户等。按电话用户位置又分为市内电话用户和农村电话用户。1997年以前，“市内电话用户”是指接入县城及县以上城市的电话网上的电话用户；“农村电话用户”是指接入县邮电局农话台及县以下农村电话交换点，以县城为中心(除市话用户外)联通县、乡(镇)、行政村、村民小组的用户。从1997年起，电话用户数分组调整为以用户所在区域划分为“城市电话用户”和“乡村电话用户”，与过去的按市内电话和农村电话划分方法不同。而电话用户总数、电话机总部数统计范围不变。

城市电话用户 指直辖市、省辖市、地级市、县级市的市区、市郊区及县城(包括县人民政府所在地的县城关区或行政建制相当于县人民政府所在地的镇)范围内接入局用交换机的电话用户数，包括分布在农村地区的独立工矿区、林区、驻军等电话用户数。

乡村电话用户 指按行政区划属于城市范围以外的乡(镇)、村的电话用户数。

住宅电话用户 指安装在居民住宅或农民家里并按照住宅电话用户登记注册和收费的电话用户。包括私人付费、单位付费和按规定免费安装的住宅电话用户。

长途电话交换机容量 指用于接入长途电话网的电话交换机设备的额定容量，包括国际电话交换机容量。

局用交换机容量 指安装在电信运营企业内用于接续本地固定电话的电话交换机容量，包括现用和备用的人工或自动交换机的全部容量。不包括用户交换机容量。

移动电话交换机容量 指移动电话交换机根据一定话务模型和交换机处理能力计算出来的最大同时服务用户的数量。

Explanatory Notes on Main Statistical Indicators

Length of Railways in Operation refers to the total length of the trunk line under passenger and freight transportation (including both full operation and temporary operation). The calculation is based on the actual length of the first line even if this line has a full or partial double track or more tracks, excluding double tracks, station sidings, tracks under the charge of stations, branch lines, special-purpose lines and the non-payable connecting lines. The length of railways in operation is an important indicator to show the development of the infrastructure for the railway transport, and also the essential data to calculate volume of passenger freight transport, traffic density and utilization efficiency of the locomotives and carriages.

Length of Electrified Railways refers to the length of the section of railways in operation in which the power supply lines and other equipment are installed for the running of electrified locomotives. The proportion of the length of electrified railways to the total length of railways in operation is an important indicator to show the modernization of railways.

Automatic-blocking and Semi-automatic-blocking Length of Railways refer to length of railways installed with equipment to perform automatic or manual blocking of trains. Blocking is a spacing technique by which a section of the railway only allows one train to pass at a time in the aim of ensuring the traffic safety. the proportion of automatic/semi-automatic blocking length to the total length of railways in operation is an important indicator to show the modernization of railways.

Length of Highways refers to the length of highways which are built in conformity with the grades specified by the highway engineering standard formulated by the Ministry of Communications, and have been formally checked and accepted by the departments of highways and put into use. The length of highways includes that of the suburb highways at large and medium-sized cities, highways passing through streets at small cities and towns, and also the length of bridges and ferries. It does not include the length of streets in big and medium-sized cities and highways built for the production purpose at factories, mines, forest areas and agricultural areas. If two or more highways go the same section of the way, the length of the section is only calculated for once and no duplication is allowed. The length of highways is an important indicator to show the development of the highway construction and to provide essential information to calculate the transport network density.

Length of Navigable Inland Waterways it is an indicator reflecting the size and development of inland water network, it refers to the length of the natural rivers, lakes, reservoirs, canals, and ditches open to navigation during a given period, which enables the transport by ships and rafts. It includes the channels open to navigation for over an accumulative 3 months in a year, yet this does not include the river courses, which are only used to float odd logs and bamboo rafts. This indicator can reflect the scale, level and development situation of the inland waterway network.

Length of Civil Aviation Routes refers to the length of all routes for regular civil aviation flights. There are usually two ways to calculate the distance between airports connected by the route length: One is to put the length of all air routes together, called duplicated calculation of the length of the routes; the other is not to allow the duplication in calculation when two or more routes passing the same section of aviation routes. The latter is usually used, as it can precisely show the size of the civil aviation network and indicate the extent of civil aviation serving the national economy and the people.

Length of Oil (Gas) Pipelines used as an indicator to show the development, scale and level of the pipeline transportation, it refers to the actual transport distance of oil (or gas) products, and is in general calculated in the length of single pipeline. If the length of the double pipelines and alternate pipeline are included, it is called the extension length of the oil (gas) pipelines, which indicates the actual length of the pipelines built, excluding double pipelines.

Freight (Passenger) Traffic refers to the volume of freight (passenger) transported with various means. Freight transport is calculated in tons and passenger traffic is calculated in the number of persons. Despite the type of freight and traveling distance, the freight transport is calculated in the actual weight of the goods: and despite the traveling distance and ticket price, the passenger traffic is calculated by the principle that one person can be counted only once in one travel. The passengers who travel with a half price ticket or a child ticket is also calculated as one person. The freight (passenger) traffic provides a quantitative measure to show how the transport industry serves the national economy and people, and is also an important indicator for planning the transport industry and for studying the development scale and speed of the transport industry.

Freight (Passenger) Traffic Density refers to the freight (passenger) traffic volume carried by a particular means of transportation during a given period through one kilometer of a specific section of transportation route. The formula is as follows:

Freight (Passenger) traffic density=[freight ton-kilometers (passenger-kilometers)] / (length of route in operation)

Freight (passenger) traffic density reflects the degree of business of freight (passenger) traffic on transportation routes, and therefore provides important information for balancing transport capability, planning construction and upgrading of transport routes and studying the distribution of transport network.

Freight Ton-kilometers (Passenger-kilometers) refer to the sum of the products of the volume of transported cargo (passengers) multiplying by the transport distance. It is an important indicator to reflect the achievement of transportation industry. Normally, the shortest distance between the departure station and the destination station (i.e., the payable distance) is the basis to calculate the freight ton-kilometers. This is an important indicator to show the total results of the transport industry, to prepare and examine the transport plan and to measure the efficiency, the labour productivity and the unit cost of transport.

The formula is as follows:

Freight ton-kilometers (passenger-kilometers) = Σ {freight (passenger) traffic x distance of transportation}

Static Load of Freight Cars refers to the average cargo weight as loaded by each freight car under the static condition at the departure station. It is used to show the utilization extent of the loading capacity of the freight cars. The formula is:

Static load (ton) of freight car=(tonnage of goods dispatched) / (number of freight cars loaded)

The static load of freight cars is determined by the nature and type of goods loaded, the type of vehicles, and the technique of loading. The difference between the average marked load and the static load of freight cars reflects the utilization of loading capacity of freight cars. For its calculation the following formula is applied:

Utilization rate of capacity of freight cars(%)=[(Average static load) / (Average marked load)] × 100%

Average Daily Haul of Freight Locomotives refers to the average total ton-kilometers accomplished by each freight transport locomotive over day and night during a given period of time. It includes both the weight of the goods carried and the dead weight of the train itself. It is a comprehensive indicator reflecting the locomotive efficiency in terms of both time and the pulling force.

Average daily haul of freight transport locomotive (ton-kilometer)=(Total ton/kilometers of freight) / (Daily number of freight transport locomotive)

Volume of Freight Handled in Major Coastal Ports refers to the volume of cargo passing in and out the harbor area of the major coastal ports and having been loaded and unloaded. The volume includes that of the postal matters, registered luggage and fuels, materials and fresh water as supplies of the ships. The volume of freight handled may be classified by direction of flow as freight for import and freight for export, or by nature of cargo as freight for domestic trade and freight for foreign trade. As an important indicator, the volume of freight handled by type of cargo and by main flow direction reflects the production capacity of ports.

Possession of Civil Motor Vehicles: refer to the total numbers of vehicles that are registered and received vehicles' license tags according to the Work Standard for Motor Vehicles Registration formulated by transport management office under department of public security at the end of reference period. They are divided into following categories according to the structure of motor vehicles: passenger vehicles, trucks and others; and private vehicles and vehicles for units use according to ownerships; working vehicles, non-working vehicles and special motor vehicles according to kind of usage; large passenger vehicles, medium passenger vehicles and small passenger vehicles, heavy trucks, light-heavy trucks and light trucks according to sizes of vehicles.

Business Volume of Post and Telecommunications refers to the total amount of post and telecommunication services, expressed in value terms, provided by the post and telecommunications departments for the society. Post and telecommunication services can be classified as letters, parcels, remittance, issue of newspapers and magazines, fast mail service, express mail service, savings deposits, stamps for collection, public and individual telegraph service, facsimiles, long-distance telephone service, leasing of telephone lines, urban paging service, mobile telephone service, data transfer and transmission, etc. The accounting approach is to multiply the service products of all types with their average unit price (constant price) to get sum of business value, plus income from other services such as leasing of telephone lines and equipment, maintenance of telephone switchboards and lines on behalf of customers. This indicator reflects the overall results of post and telecommunications service during a given period, and is important to study the composition of business service and the development of post and telecommunications service.

The formula is as follows:

Business volume of post and telecommunications= Σ (Transaction of post and telecommunication service x constant price) + Income from leasing, maintenance and other services

Subscribers of Wireless Paging Services Wireless paging service refers the service by which telephone users send audio, digital or character signals to persons carrying small-size pagers within the designated areas through wireless paging centers. The page carriers who have registered in paging centers are counted as paging subscribers.

Mobile Telephone Subscribers refer to the persons who own mobile telephone numbers and are connected with the mobile telephone communication network through the mobile telephone switchboards, including contracted subscribers and prepaid subscribers for intelligent network. One mobile telephone is taken as a subscriber.

Internet Users refer to the number of Chinese citizens who use Internet at least for one hour each week.

Local Telephone Subscribers refer to subscribers that are connected to the local telecommunication service provider through fix line network, including household subscribers, institutional subscribers and public telephones. They are also classified as city subscribers and rural subscribers according to locations. Before 1997, city subscribers referred to those connected to city telephone networks in county towns and cities, while village subscribers referred to those connected to village telephone stations at and below counties. Since 1997, the classification of telephone subscribers was modified on the basis of physical location of the subscribers as urban telephone subscribers and rural telephone subscribers, which is different from the previous classification of categorizing local telephones and rural telephones, while the definition of total subscribers and total number of telephones remain unchanged.

Urban Telephone Subscribers refer to number of telephone subscribers, located at municipalities, cities under the jurisdiction of province, cities at prefecture level, downtown and suburb of city at county level town and county towns (including country towns where county government located, and towns of county level according to the administrative organizational system), that are connected to the public line telephone network, including rural mineral area, forest area, military area.

Rural Telephone Subscribers refer to telephone subscribers, located at counties (towns) and villages outside the range of cities according to administrative jurisdiction.

Household Telephone Subscribers refer to telephone sets installed in the dwelling units of urban or rural residents, and registered as residence subscribers for payment, including 3 types of payment for the service: private payment, public payment and free service.

Capacity of Long Distance Telephone Exchanges: refers to the rated capacity of telephone exchanges to connect long distance telephone network, including capacity of international telephone exchanges.

Capacity of Office Telephone Exchanges refers to the capacity (measured in gate) of telephone exchanges installed in the offices of telecommunication service providers for communication between fixed telephones. It includes the capacity of both manual and automatic exchanges in use and for stand-by purpose, excluding the capacity of subscribers' exchanges.

Capacity of Mobile Telephone Exchanges: refers to the capacity of the maximum services provided to subscribers at one time basing on a certain model and transacting capacity of the mobile telephone exchanges.

十七、国内贸易

Domestic Trade

简要说明

一、本篇资料的主要内容

反映中国国内市场的发展和批发零售贸易业、餐饮业商品经营情况。主要内容有限额以上批发零售贸易业、餐饮业基本情况、商品流转、财务状况；社会消费品零售总额；亿元商品交易市场；连锁零售业、餐饮业经营情况以及全国消费品市场交易情况等。

二、本篇的统计范围

全国批发零售贸易业、餐饮业，亿元商品交易市场，连锁零售业、餐饮业经营情况以及全国消费品交易市场。

社会消费品零售总额指标在1993年、1997年和2003年做了较大调整。1993年及以后不包括农业生产资料；1997年及以后不包括居民购买住房；2003年及以后不包括由各种经济类型的制造业法人企业、产业活动单位和个体工业，直接售给城乡居民（包括本企业职工）和社会集团的商品和农民在田间地头出售的农产品

限额以上批发零售贸易业、餐饮业统计限额标准：批发业，年末从业人员20人及以上，年销售额2000万元以上；零售业，年末从业人员60人及以上，年销售额500万元以上；餐饮业，年末从业人员40人及以上，年销售额200万元以上。

三、本篇的资料来源

本篇资料是国家统计局贸易外经司根据批发零售贸易、餐饮业统计报表制度进行搜集和加工整理而得，全国消费品交易市场情况由国家工商行政管理总局提供。

四、本篇的统计调查方法

本篇资料中限额以上批发、零售贸易业法人企业和餐饮业法人企业基本情况、商品流转、财务状况报表采用全面调查的方法，逐级汇总上报。限额以下的小型企业及个体户资料采用抽样调查方法推算。

五、本篇资料中各地区社会消费品零售总额相加不等于全国总计，原因是全国总计根据相关核算资料和部门资料进行了修正和调整。

Brief Introduction

I. Main Content

Data in this chapter reflect the development of China's domestic market and the operational and managerial condition of wholesale and retail sale trades as well as catering trade, including the basic condition, the circulation of commodities and the financial condition in the wholesale and retail sale trades above designated size; total retail sales of consumer goods; large commodity transaction markets (with transaction over 100 million yuan); development of chain stores of retail and catering trades; and transaction markets of consumer goods in the country.

II. Coverage of Statistics

National wholesale and retail sale trades, catering industry, large commodity transaction markets, chain stores of retail and catering trades and national transactions of consumer goods.

Major adjustments were made for total retail sales of consumer goods in 1993 and 1997. Starting from 1993, this indicator does not include means of agricultural production; starting from 1997, this indicator does not include purchase of houses by residents. Since 2003, this indicator does not include commodities sold to urban and rural households (including their own employees) and institutions directly by manufacturing corporations, establishments and individual manufacturers, nor farm products sold by farmers in the fields.

Criteria for wholesale and retail sale trades and catering industry above designated size is as follows: wholesale trade, having 20 or more employees at year-end with annual sales over 20 million yuan; retail sale trade, having 60 or more employees at year-end with annual sales over 5 million yuan; catering industry, having 40 or more employees with annual sales over 2 million yuan.

III. Sources of Data

Data in this chapter are collected and processed in accordance with the statistical reporting scheme on wholesale and retail sale trades as well as catering trade by the Department of Trade and External Economic Relations of the National Bureau of Statistics. Data on transaction markets of consumer goods are provided by State Administration for Industry and Commerce.

IV. Survey Methodology

Data on basic conditions, circulation of goods and financial conditions for all corporate enterprises of wholesale, retail and catering trades above the designated size are collected through comprehensive reporting systems and data are reported level by level. Data on small-size enterprises and individual enterprises below the designated size are collected through sample surveys.

V. In this chapter, the sum of total retail sales of consumer goods of all provinces is not equal to the national total, as the national total has been adjusted and modified in line with national accounts data and data from other departments.

17-1 国内贸易基本情况

Basic Conditions of Domestic Trade

指 标	Item	1998	2000	2001	2002	2003
法人机构 (个)	**Number of Corporation Unit (unit)**					
批发零售贸易业	Wholesale and Retail Trades		25567	25543	26605	27340
餐饮业	Catering Services		3508	4132	5021	5935
产业活动单位 (个)	**Number of Economic Active Unit (unit)**					
批发零售贸易业	Wholesale and Retail Trades		42438	47099	60019	57237
餐饮业	Catering Services		5363	6386	7424	8908
从业人员 (万人)	**Persons Employed (10 000 persons)**					
批发零售贸易业	Wholesale and Retail Trades		448.5	404.6	419.1	406.8
餐饮业	Catering Services		66.5	77.9	97.8	113.3
批发零售贸易业	**Wholesale and Retail Trade**					
商品购进总额 (亿元)	Total Purchases (100 million yuan)	24297.4	29784.1	32489.0	36885.9	45383.9
商品销售总额 (亿元)	Total Sales (100 million yuan)	56437.7	66359.5	72415.2	81266.2	99446.1
商品库存总额 (亿元)	Total Inventory (100 million yuan)	3789.7	3569.9	3618.0	3577.9	3898.2
社会消费品零售总额 (亿元)	**Total Retail Sales of Consumer Goods (100 million yuan)**	**29152.5**	**34152.6**	**37595.2**	**42027.1**	**45842.0**
按销售单位所在地分	By Location of Establishments					
市	City	17825.2	21110.3	23543.4	26986.3	29777.3
县	County	3681.9	4217.2	4583.2	4860.0	5247.8
县以下	Under County Level	7645.4	8825.1	9468.6	10180.8	10816.9
按行业分	By Sector					
批发零售贸易业	Wholesale and Retail Trade	19185.8	23042.3	25510.8	34514.2	37692.5
餐饮业	Catering Services	2816.4	3752.6	4368.9	5433.3	6065.7
其他行业	Others	7150.3	7357.7	7715.5	2079.6	2083.8

注：1.批发零售贸易业商品购进、库存总额为限额以上批发零售贸易业数据。
2.社会消费品零售总额不含居民购买住房；2002年及以后不包括由各种登记注册类型的制造业法人企业、产业活动单位和个体工业直接售给城乡居民和社会集团的商品和农业生产者出售的农产品(下表同)。
3.法人机构、产业活动单位和从业人员为限额以上企业。

a) Figures on purchase, sales and inventory by wholesale and retail trade refer to units above designated size.

b) Data on total retail sales of consumer goods exclude purchase of commodity housing by households, and since 2002, that excludes the sales of commodity, which directly sold to urban and rural households and social groups by the various types of registration of manufacturing enterprises, economic active units and individual industries, and farmer produce, which sold by agricultural producer. Similarly in the following tables.

c) Number of corporation unit, economic active units and persons employed refer to those enterprises above designated size.

17-2 消费品市场交易情况

Trade of Consumable Markets in Urban and Rural Areas

项 目	Item	1990	2000	2001	2002	2003
消费品市场数 (个)	**Number of Free Markets (unit)**	**72579**	**88811**	**87418**	**82498**	**81017**
城市市场	Urban Areas	13106	26395	27663	26529	27006
农村市场	Rural Areas	59473	62416	59755	55969	54011
消费品市场成交额(亿元)	**Transaction Value (100 million yuan)**	**2168.2**	**24279.6**	**24949.4**	**25975.7**	**26497.5**
城市市场	Urban Areas	837.8	13800.4	14319.7	15140.1	15447.5
农村市场	Rural Areas	1330.4	10479.2	10629.7	10835.6	11050.0
在成交额中	**Of the Transaction Value:**					
#粮油类	Grain and Oil	146.8	1959.5	1868.5	2095.5	2324.9
肉禽蛋类	Meat, Poultry and Eggs	618.8	4201.9	4185.3	4468.0	4541.4
水产品类	Aquatic Products	182.4	2073.4	2076.8	2205.4	2246.0
蔬菜类	Vegetables	264.2	2661.8	2695.2	2887.7	2938.1
干鲜果类	Dried and Fresh Fruits	183.5	1546.2	1584.4	1692.2	1708.8

注：本表资料由国家工商行政管理总局提供。

a) Data in this table were obtained from the State Administration for Industry & Commerce.

17-3 社会消费品零售总额

Total Retail Sale of Consumer Goods

单位: 亿元 (100 million yuan)

年份 Year 地区 Region		社会消费品零售总额 Total Retail Sales of Consumer Goods	按销售单位所在地分			按行业分		
			市 City	县 County	县以下 Under County Level	批发零售贸易业 Wholesale and Retail Trade	餐饮业 Catering Services	其他行业 Others
	1978	1558.6	505.2	380.4	673.0	1363.7	54.8	140.1
	1980	2140.0	733.6	399.4	1007.0	1768.0	80.0	292.0
	1985	4305.0	1874.5	737.2	1693.3	3272.2	196.9	835.9
	1989	8101.4	3666.8	1329.5	3105.1	6009.5	405.1	1686.8
	1990	8300.1	3888.6	1337.4	3074.1	6127.4	419.8	1752.9
	1991	9415.6	4529.8	1491.2	3394.6	6903.9	492.0	2019.7
	1992	10993.7	5470.3	1689.8	3833.6	7922.2	589.7	2481.8
	1993	12462.1	7224.9	2039.5	3197.7	8726.9	800.1	2935.1
	1994	16264.7	9661.2	2407.2	4196.3	11039.7	1175.1	4049.9
	1995	20620.0	12376.7	2919.6	5323.7	13801.3	1579.2	5239.5
	1996	24774.1	14951.2	3280.0	6542.9	16205.1	2024.9	6544.1
	1997	27298.9	16650.4	3500.1	7148.4	18108.3	2433.3	6757.3
	1998	29152.5	17825.2	3681.9	7645.4	19185.8	2816.4	7150.3
	1999	31134.7	19091.6	3892.5	8150.6	20551.8	3199.6	7383.3
	2000	34152.6	21110.3	4217.2	8825.1	23042.3	3752.6	7357.7
	2001	37595.2	23543.4	4583.2	9468.6	25510.8	4368.9	7715.5
	2002	42027.1	26986.3	4860.0	10180.8	34514.2	5433.3	2079.6
	2003	45842.0	29777.3	5247.8	10816.9	37692.5	6065.7	2083.8
北京	Beijing	1916.7	1535.8	88.8	292.2	1611.2	121.4	184.1
天津	Tianjin	922.3	859.2	35.3	27.8	727.1	109.9	85.3
河北	Hebei	2177.9	1064.4	421.1	692.4	1894.8	233.5	49.6
山西	Shanxi	729.3	471.3	135.2	122.8	614.2	81.7	33.4
内蒙古	Inner	726.8	449.5	166.5	110.8	592.2	99.2	35.3
辽宁	Liaoning	2330.8	1963.7	112.0	255.2	1935.6	338.9	56.3
吉林	Jilin	1110.3	857.7	76.8	175.8	951.0	153.8	5.4
黑龙江	Heilongjiang	1376.5	1019.4	186.6	170.4	1191.9	152.3	32.2
上海	Shanghai	2220.6	1905.9	17.6	297.1	1990.2	214.8	15.6
江苏	Jiangsu	3566.5	2516.3	217.8	832.3	3072.6	434.4	59.4
浙江	Zhejiang	3157.1	1999.9	329.5	827.7	2696.4	358.9	101.8
安徽	Anhui	1331.2	666.6	285.6	379.0	1143.7	159.4	28.2
福建	Fujian	1740.4	1057.5	218.3	464.6	1423.1	211.2	106.2
江西	Jiangxi	923.2	455.3	206.6	261.3	812.0	85.3	25.9
山东	Shandong	3936.5	2525.6	396.4	1014.5	3251.7	497.2	187.6
河南	Henan	2426.4	1234.8	494.2	697.4	2009.7	343.1	73.6
湖北	Hubei	2358.7	1603.3	222.9	532.5	1884.7	298.3	175.7
湖南	Hunan	1816.3	997.1	332.5	486.7	1558.4	224.6	33.3
广东	Guangdong	5606.0	3718.3	269.4	1618.3	4681.1	877.3	47.6
广西	Guangxi	857.7	458.5	169.7	229.5	716.8	115.3	25.6
海南	Hainan	191.6	128.1	16.6	46.9	150.5	31.0	10.1
重庆	Chongqing	835.5	482.3	112.7	240.5	719.1	107.3	9.1
四川	Sichuan	2091.1	1004.2	357.3	729.6	1621.5	349.4	120.2
贵州	Guizhou	458.8	272.0	85.8	101.0	374.3	75.5	9.0
云南	Yunnan	782.5	425.3	180.5	176.7	635.4	124.6	22.4
西藏	Tibet	58.3	26.1	25.0	7.2	46.6	8.2	3.6
陕西	Shaanxi	853.2	565.6	149.1	138.5	646.3	184.3	22.6
甘肃	Gansu	474.6	308.0	76.2	90.4	388.3	66.9	19.5
青海	Qinghai	102.7	66.1	24.7	11.8	83.4	16.4	2.8
宁夏	Ningxia	120.8	81.5	20.8	18.5	98.8	19.6	2.3
新疆	Xinjiang	421.2	311.3	49.2	60.6	341.9	60.6	18.6

注：1.1992年及以前为社会商品零售总额。
2.各地区相加不等于全国总计，原因是全国数据进行了修正。

a) Figures before 1992 refer to retail sales of commodities.
b) The sum of provincial figures do not add up to the national total, as the national total was adjusted.

17-4 按登记注册类型分限额以上批发零售贸易、餐饮业基本情况（2003年）

Basic Conditions of Enterprises above Designated Size in Wholesale and Retail Trade, Catering Services by Types of Registration (2003)

指标	Item	法人企业（个）Number of Corporation Unit	产业活动单位数（个）Number of Economic Active Unit	从业人数（人）Persons Employed (person)
总计	**Total**	**33275**	**66145**	**5200497**
批发业合计	**Wholesale Trade**	**14937**	**27856**	**1786669**
内资企业	**Domestic Funded Enterprises**	**14406**	**27181**	**1741806**
国有企业	State-owned Enterprises	5712	10029	847948
集体企业	Collective-owned Enterprises	1238	1898	144120
股份合作企业	Cooperative Enterprises	279	346	24199
联营企业	Joint Ownership Enterprises	178	207	9886
国有联营企业	State Joint Ownership Enterprises	91	117	5801
集体联营企业	Collective Joint Ownership Enterprises	11	11	431
国有与集体联营企业	Joint State-collective Enterprises	33	33	1740
其他联营企业	Other Joint Ownership Enterprises	43	46	1914
有限责任公司	Limited Liability Corporations	3605	8505	351206
国有独资公司	State Sole Funded Corporations	241	591	47311
其他有限责任公司	Other Limited Liability Corporations	3364	7914	303895
股份有限公司	Share-holding Corporations Ltd.	1033	3479	255971
私营企业	Private Enterprises	2343	2699	106450
私营独资企业	Private-funded Enterprises	104	139	5742
私营合伙企业	Private Partnership Enterprises	45	45	2056
私营有限责任公司	Private Limited Liability Corporations	2086	2388	93140
私营股份有限公司	Private Share-holding Corporations Ltd.	108	127	5512
其他企业	Other Enterprises	18	18	2026
港、澳、台商投资企业	**Enterprises with Funds from Hong Kong, Macao and Taiwan**	**199**	**259**	**16577**
合资经营企业	Joint-venture Enterprises	53	66	4221
合作经营企业	Cooperative Enterprises	16	20	2563
独资经营企业	Enterprises with Sole Investment	121	162	7987
投资股份有限公司	Share-holding Corporations Ltd. with Investment	9	11	1806
外商投资企业	**Foreign Funded Enterprises**	**332**	**416**	**28286**
中外合资经营企业	Joint-venture Enterprises	43	103	8193
中外合作经营企业	Cooperation Enterprises	6	12	897
外资企业	Enterprises with Sole Foreign Investment	282	298	18611
外商投资股份有限公司	Share-holding Corporations Ltd. with Foreign Investment	1	3	585
零售业合计	**Retail Trade**	**12403**	**29381**	**2281095**
内资企业	**Domestic Funded Enterprises**	**12149**	**28500**	**2140069**
国有企业	State-owned Enterprises	3166	6062	495369
集体企业	Collective-owned Enterprises	1632	2520	166921
股份合作企业	Cooperative Enterprises	412	753	55778
联营企业	Joint Ownership Enterprises	114	132	15201
国有联营企业	State Joint Ownership Enterprises	48	57	5492
集体联营企业	Collective Joint Ownership Enterprises	10	12	644
国有与集体联营企业	Joint State-collective Enterprises	30	35	3898
其他联营企业	Other Joint Ownership Enterprises	26	28	5167
有限责任公司	Limited Liability Corporations	2925	9459	625223
国有独资公司	State Sole Funded Corporations	98	231	28665
其他有限责任公司	Other Limited Liability Corporations	2827	9228	596558
股份有限公司	Share-holding Corporations Ltd.	968	4797	439955

注：批发业限额以上是指年末从业人员20人及以上，年销售额2000万元及以上；零售贸易业限额以上是指年末从业人员60人及以上，年销售额500万元及以上；餐饮业限额以上是指年末从业人员40人及以上，年营业额200万元及以上。

a) Enterprise above designated size in wholesale trade refers to that the employed person is more than 20 persons and above and annual sale value is 20 million yuans and above. Enterprise above designated size in retail trade refers to that the employed person is more than 60 persons and above and annual sale value is 5 million yuans and above. Enterprise above designated size in catering services refers to that the employed person is more than 40 persons and above and annual turnover is 2 million yuans and above.

17-4 续表 continued

指 标	Item	法人企业（个） Number of Corporation Unit	产业活动单位数（个） Number of Economic Active Unit	从业人数（人） Persons Employed (person)
私营企业	Private Enterprises	2903	4730	337434
私营独资企业	Private-funded Enterprises	266	924	31693
私营合伙企业	Private Partnership Enterprises	94	102	11561
私营有限责任公司	Private Limited Liability Corporations	2344	3429	270543
私营股份有限公司	Private Share-holding Corporations Ltd.	199	275	23637
其他企业	Other Enterprises	29	47	4188
港、澳、台商投资企业	**Enterprises with Funds from Hong Kong, Macao and Taiwan**	**107**	**403**	**49626**
合资经营企业	Joint-venture Enterprises	58	89	34021
合作经营企业	Cooperative Enterprises	21	160	7609
独资经营企业	Enterprises with Sole Funds	27	152	7614
投资股份有限公司	Share-holding Corporations Ltd. with Funds	1	2	382
外商投资企业	**Foreign Funded Enterprises**	**147**	**478**	**91400**
中外合资经营企业	Joint-venture Enterprises	85	254	58144
中外合作经营企业	Cooperation Enterprises	33	128	15678
外资企业	Enterprises with Sole Foreign Investment	26	92	16159
外商投资股份有限公司	Share-holding Corporations Ltd. with Foreign Investment	3	4	1419
餐饮业合计	**Catering Services**	**5935**	**8908**	**1132733**
内资企业	**Domestic Funded Enterprises**	**5277**	**7363**	**871863**
国有企业	State-owned Enterprises	723	1294	192960
集体企业	Collective-owned Enterprises	516	825	73672
股份合作企业	Cooperative Enterprises	266	351	30555
联营企业	Joint Ownership Enterprises	32	52	6545
国有联营企业	State Joint Ownership Enterprises	10	22	2883
集体联营企业	Collective Joint Ownership Enterprises	5	9	1335
国有与集体联营企业	Joint State-collective Enterprises	2	2	466
其他联营企业	Other Joint Ownership Enterprises	15	19	1861
有限责任公司	Limited Liability Corporations	875	1274	168449
国有独资公司	State Sole Funded Corporations	5	17	2966
其他有限责任公司	Other Limited Liability Corporations	870	1257	165483
股份有限公司	Share-holding Corporations Ltd.	184	371	46747
私营企业	Private Enterprises	2626	3125	345953
私营独资企业	Private-funded Enterprises	848	966	89203
私营合伙企业	Private Partnership Enterprises	191	221	20802
私营有限责任公司	Private Limited Liability Corporations	1473	1800	218854
私营股份有限公司	Private Share-holding Corporations Ltd.	114	138	17094
其他企业	Other Enterprises	55	71	6982
港、澳、台商投资企业	**Enterprises with Funds from Hong Kong, Macao and Taiwan**	**385**	**829**	**130095**
合资经营企业	Joint-venture Enterprises	192	375	58216
合作经营企业	Cooperative Enterprises	80	149	33993
独资经营企业	Enterprises with Sole Funds	106	292	35432
投资股份有限公司	Share-holding Corporations Ltd. with Funds	7	13	2454
外商投资企业	**Enterprises With Foreign Investment**	**273**	**716**	**130775**
中外合资经营企业	Joint-venture Enterprises	133	276	56344
中外合作经营企业	Cooperation Enterprises	53	144	23607
外资企业	Enterprises with Sole Foreign Funds	83	287	49955
外商投资股份有限公司	Share-holding Corporations Ltd. with Foreign Investment	4	9	869

17-5 限额以上批发零售贸易、餐饮业法人企业数

Number of Corporation Units above Designated Size in Wholesale and Retail Trade, Catering Services

单位:个 (unit)

年 份 Year 地 区 Region	合 计 Total	批发业 Wholesale Trade	零售业 Retail Trade	餐饮业 Catering Service
1999	30381	16382	10733	3266
2000	29075	15393	10174	3508
2001	29675	15258	10285	4132
2002	31626	15262	11343	5021
2003	33275	14937	12403	5935
北 京 Beijing	2479	997	1120	362
天 津 Tianjin	916	559	250	107
河 北 Hebei	1062	576	389	97
山 西 Shanxi	802	312	382	108
内蒙古 Inner Mongolia	495	177	177	141
辽 宁 Liaoning	1427	607	520	300
吉 林 Jilin	397	156	200	41
黑龙江 Heilongjiang	607	285	212	110
上 海 Shanghai	1280	758	280	242
江 苏 Jiangsu	2231	821	827	583
浙 江 Zhejiang	2645	1481	763	401
安 徽 Anhui	686	388	243	55
福 建 Fujian	2143	1060	769	314
江 西 Jiangxi	478	241	188	49
山 东 Shandong	2594	865	1179	550
河 南 Henan	2249	686	1341	222
湖 北 Hubei	945	372	377	196
湖 南 Hunan	932	414	358	160
广 东 Guangdong	3761	1722	986	1053
广 西 Guangxi	711	335	278	98
海 南 Hainan	222	87	83	52
重 庆 Chongqing	681	286	243	152
四 川 Sichuan	878	327	340	211
贵 州 Guizhou	302	152	84	66
云 南 Yunnan	827	497	266	64
西 藏 Tibet	22	12	10	
陕 西 Shaanxi	369	197	124	48
甘 肃 Gansu	392	180	139	73
青 海 Qinghai	71	32	27	12
宁 夏 Ningxia	153	61	59	33
新 疆 Xinjiang	518	294	189	35

17-6 限额以上批发零售贸易、餐饮业产业活动单位数

Number of Economic Active Units above Designated Size in Wholesale and Retail Trade, Catering Services

单位:个 (unit)

年份 地区	Year Region	合计 Total	批发业 Wholesale Trade	零售业 Retail Trade	餐饮业 Catering Services
	1999	47906	23720	19220	4966
	2000	47801	23956	18482	5363
	2001	53485	25227	21872	6386
	2002	67443	31268	28751	7424
	2003	66145	27856	29381	8908
北京	Beijing	2573	1032	1154	387
天津	Tianjin	923	565	251	107
河北	Hebei	1074	577	389	108
山西	Shanxi	802	312	382	108
内蒙古	Inner Mongolia	530	184	184	162
辽宁	Liaoning	1518	626	539	353
吉林	Jilin	479	171	209	99
黑龙江	Heilongjiang	1572	1030	394	148
上海	Shanghai	15492	4602	9962	928
江苏	Jiangsu	4733	1702	2357	674
浙江	Zhejiang	8313	4606	2862	845
安徽	Anhui	3460	2112	1195	153
福建	Fujian	2329	1078	789	462
江西	Jiangxi	564	260	198	106
山东	Shandong	2916	974	1239	703
河南	Henan	2328	703	1365	260
湖北	Hubei	1238	426	535	277
湖南	Hunan	3047	1309	1411	327
广东	Guangdong	4221	1759	1027	1435
广西	Guangxi	866	398	297	171
海南	Hainan	222	87	83	52
重庆	Chongqing	832	302	266	264
四川	Sichuan	927	336	345	246
贵州	Guizhou	324	156	92	76
云南	Yunnan	3036	1689	1194	153
西藏	Tibet	81	22	59	
陕西	Shaanxi	445	227	151	67
甘肃	Gansu	406	186	144	76
青海	Qinghai	83	33	29	21
宁夏	Ningxia	201	70	71	60
新疆	Xinjiang	610	322	208	80

17-7 限额以上批发零售贸易、餐饮业从业人数

Number of Persons Employed in Enterprises above Designated Size in Wholesale and Retail Trade, Catering Services

单位:人 (person)

年份 地区	Year Region	合计 Total	批发业 Wholesale Trade	零售业 Retail Trade	餐饮业 Catering Services
	1999	5583021	2543600	2378571	660850
	2000	5150084	2319248	2166087	664749
	2001	4825325	1982927	2063028	779370
	2002	5169139	1944793	2246303	978043
	2003	5200497	1786669	2281095	1132733
北京	Beijing	280286	80989	144910	54387
天津	Tianjin	105019	38691	47752	18576
河北	Hebei	198310	76292	104858	17160
山西	Shanxi	135326	46736	66813	21777
内蒙古	Inner Mongolia	62402	21850	26765	13787
辽宁	Liaoning	199557	57921	103884	37752
吉林	Jilin	92377	37362	40405	14610
黑龙江	Heilongjiang	114565	46713	56437	11415
上海	Shanghai	324465	99628	174932	49905
江苏	Jiangsu	461865	123105	247060	91700
浙江	Zhejiang	279326	103939	92750	82637
安徽	Anhui	124925	58672	51698	14555
福建	Fujian	172847	65323	58646	48878
江西	Jiangxi	80025	34743	31481	13801
山东	Shandong	440796	130585	220388	89823
河南	Henan	300659	118419	149221	33019
湖北	Hubei	239598	100054	90990	48554
湖南	Hunan	180774	59459	76561	44754
广东	Guangdong	579179	164578	164899	249702
广西	Guangxi	109640	39735	47181	22724
海南	Hainan	21582	5873	6026	9683
重庆	Chongqing	139452	51267	48410	39775
四川	Sichuan	159564	48491	71023	40050
贵州	Guizhou	58458	26899	19675	11884
云南	Yunnan	98665	53354	34722	10589
西藏	Tibet	3253	1136	2117	
陕西	Shaanxi	83560	28872	42177	12511
甘肃	Gansu	48499	18087	19970	10442
青海	Qinghai	14788	6400	5785	2603
宁夏	Ningxia	23444	7019	10531	5894
新疆	Xinjiang	67291	34477	23028	9786

17-8 按行业分限额以上批发零售贸易业商品购、销、存总额(2003年)

Total Purchases, Sales and Inventory of Enterprise above Designated Size in Wholesale and Retail Trade by Sector (2003)

单位：亿元　　(100 million yuan)

指　标	Item	购进总额 Total Purchases	销售总额 Total Sales	批　发 Wholesale Trade	零　售 Retail Trade	年末库存总　额 Inventory (year-end)
总　计	**Total**	**45383.9**	**48613.2**	**37974.3**	**10638.9**	**3898.2**
批发业合计	**Wholesale Trade**	**36696.4**	**38924.3**	**36364.8**	**2559.5**	**2865.0**
农畜产品批发业	Wholesale of Farm Produce and Livestock Product	1177.7	1324.6	1310.3	14.3	441.9
食品、饮料及烟草制品批发业	Wholesale of Food, Beverages and Tobaccos	6355.1	7140.8	6968.2	172.7	539.6
#米、面制品及食用油批发业	Wholesale of Rice, Flour and Edible Oil	651.5	691.8	677.8	14.0	137.3
烟草制品批发业	Whole of Tobaccos	4550.5	5126.3	5046.4	79.9	322.5
纺织、服装及日用品批发业	Wholesale of Textiles, Garments and Daily Consumer Articles	3133.7	3452.5	3392.4	60.0	156.5
#服装批发业	Wholesale of Garments	1037.5	1139.7	1126.0	13.7	56.9
文化、体育用品及器材批发业	Wholesale of Culture, Sports Appliances and Equipments	723.2	728.9	688.3	40.6	115.9
医药及医疗器材批发业	Wholesale of Medicines and Medical Appliances	1837.8	1997.2	1398.5	598.7	250.4
矿产品、建材及化工产品批发业	Wholesale of Mineral Products, Building Material and Chemical Products	15639.1	16066.6	15061.7	1004.9	747.6
#煤炭及制品批发业	Wholesale of Coal and Related Products	693.8	891.9	875.0	16.9	33.6
石油及制品批发业	Wholesale of Petrolem and Related Products	7959.3	7961.7	7122.9	838.7	198.8
金属及金属矿批发业	Wholesale of Metal Materials	4380.2	4510.0	4432.7	77.4	313.1
建材批发业	Wholesale of Building Materials	506.4	517.6	473.4	44.2	37.8
化肥批发业	Wholesale of Chemical Fertilizer	648.1	681.8	671.0	10.8	80.3
机械设备、五金交电及电子产品批发	Wholesale of Machinery, Hardware and Electronic Equipment	6128.1	6322.9	5668.0	654.9	476.2
#汽车、摩托车及零配件批发业	Wholesale of Motor Vehicles, Motorcycles and Parts	2225.0	2258.5	1767.3	491.2	152.8
家用电器批发业	Wholesale of Household Electrical Appliances	638.5	670.1	626.3	43.8	67.6
计算机、软件及辅助设备批发业	Wholesale of Computer, Software and Assistant Appliances	344.0	356.2	331.1	25.0	17.6
贸易经纪与代理	Trade Broker and Agency	650.0	796.9	794.4	2.5	86.4
其他批发业	Other Wholesale not Classified Elsewhere	1051.6	1094.0	1083.0	11.0	50.6
零售业合计	**Retail Trade**	**8687.5**	**9688.9**	**1609.5**	**8079.4**	**1033.2**
综合零售业	Integrated Retail	4211.7	4981.8	564.8	4416.9	493.1
#百货零售业	Retail of General Merchandise	2544.4	3031.0	272.2	2758.8	286.8
超级市场零售业	Retail of Supermarkets	1517.2	1776.7	247.2	1529.5	190.1
食品、饮料及烟草制品专门零售业	Retail of Food, Beverages and Tobaccos	233.0	264.1	76.0	188.1	53.3
纺织、服装及日用品专门零售业	Special Retail of Textiles, Garments and Daily Consumer Articles	218.3	259.3	58.6	200.7	41.6
#服装零售业	Retail of Garments	101.7	117.2	29.5	87.7	16.1
文化、体育用品及器材专门零售业	Retail of Culture, Sports Appliances and Equipments	386.2	385.0	80.7	304.2	101.9
#体育用品零售业	Retail of Sports Goods	5.8	6.9	2.7	4.2	0.4
图书零售业	Retail of Books	281.7	270.6	35.7	234.9	83.6
医药及医疗器材专门零售业	Retail of Medicines and Medical Appliances	403.0	443.9	129.9	314.0	71.6
#药品零售业	Retail of Medicines	385.5	423.1	126.0	297.1	68.6
汽车、摩托车、燃料及零配件专门零售业	Retail of Motor Vehicles, Motorcycles, Fuel and Parts	2014.1	2056.0	395.1	1660.9	136.7
#汽车零售业	Retail of Motor Vehicles	1401.5	1404.6	207.3	1197.3	103.5
机动车燃料零售业	Retail of Fuel of Motor Vehicles	482.0	515.8	159.9	355.9	19.0
家用电器及电子产品专门零售业	Special Retail of Household Electric Appliances and Electronic Products	976.2	1022.9	227.0	795.9	104.7
#家用电器零售业	Retail of Household Electric Appliances	732.8	769.5	125.2	644.3	78.3
计算机、软件及辅助设备零售业	Retail of Computer, Software and Assistant Appliances	139.0	142.5	61.2	81.3	13.8
通讯设备零售业	Retail of Communication Equipments	91.6	96.4	30.8	65.6	10.3
五金、家具及室内装修材料专门零售业	Special Retail of Hardware, Furniture and Decoration Materials	159.7	175.4	45.5	129.8	22.5
无店铺及其他零售业	Non-shop and Other Retails	85.2	100.7	31.8	68.9	7.9
#邮购及电子销售业	Distribution of Post and E-commerce	1.1	4.7	0.3	4.5	0.1

17-9 限额以上批发零售贸易业商品购、销、存总额

Total Purchases, Sales and Inventory of Enterprise above Designated Size in Wholesale and Retail Sale Trades

单位: 亿元 (100 million yuan)

年份 Year / 地区 Region		购进总额 Total Goods Purchase	销售总额 Total Sales	批发 Wholesale Trade	零售 Retail Trade	年末库存总额 Inventory (year-end)
	1998	24297.4	27146.8	22090.8	5056.1	3789.7
	1999	24580.8	27448.3	22055.8	5392.5	3629.7
	2000	29784.1	32265.5	25977.9	6287.6	3569.9
	2001	32489.1	35153.3	28131.1	7022.1	3618.0
	2002	36885.9	40090.3	31591.9	8498.4	3577.9
	2003	45383.9	48613.2	37974.3	10638.9	3898.2
北京	Beijing	4387.3	4509.9	3504.4	1005.5	462.2
天津	Tianjin	1858.6	1915.5	1678.9	236.6	107.9
河北	Hebei	880.4	984.9	707.7	277.2	78.2
山西	Shanxi	505.6	573.6	391.8	181.8	117.7
内蒙古	Inner Mongolia	300.4	329.3	233.5	95.8	37.2
辽宁	Liaoning	2365.2	2476.5	2006.3	470.2	160.0
吉林	Jilin	487.0	547.4	351.4	196.0	82.1
黑龙江	Heilongjiang	571.2	639.7	463.6	176.1	106.7
上海	Shanghai	4840.0	5287.7	4181.7	1106.0	375.1
江苏	Jiangsu	3619.1	3846.3	2848.7	997.6	259.1
浙江	Zhejiang	5069.5	5220.0	4390.1	829.9	310.5
安徽	Anhui	950.8	1024.1	825.8	198.3	71.8
福建	Fujian	1582.2	1775.3	1445.2	330.1	139.9
江西	Jiangxi	517.8	579.3	449.3	130.0	32.6
山东	Shandong	2720.9	2915.9	2033.9	882.0	250.4
河南	Henan	1126.9	1239.9	923.8	316.1	119.3
湖北	Hubei	1204.4	1385.4	1007.7	377.7	97.9
湖南	Hunan	975.8	1038.2	784.4	253.8	98.1
广东	Guangdong	5745.2	6162.7	4945.0	1217.7	353.7
广西	Guangxi	498.1	521.2	354.8	166.4	35.4
海南	Hainan	146.8	153.3	126.5	26.8	12.3
重庆	Chongqing	738.9	811.2	580.5	230.7	68.3
四川	Sichuan	939.5	1022.7	739.8	282.9	71.5
贵州	Guizhou	291.5	314.5	258.9	55.6	39.3
云南	Yunnan	1148.4	1289.9	1133.9	156.0	161.3
西藏	Tibet	12.5	21.3	14.0	7.3	3.3
陕西	Shaanxi	533.7	570.2	419.6	150.6	52.0
甘肃	Gansu	524.1	526.7	431.2	95.5	37.8
青海	Qinghai	52.7	59.6	40.1	19.5	12.5
宁夏	Ningxia	88.7	94.8	56.7	38.1	14.6
新疆	Xinjiang	700.9	776.4	645.2	131.2	129.5

17-10 限额以上批发零售贸易业主要商品分类销售额
Total Sales of Enterprises above Designated Size in Wholesale and Retail Trade by Category of Main Commodities

单位：亿元 (100 million yuan)

项目	Item	销售合计 Total		批发 Wholesale Trade		零售 Retail Trade	
		2002	2003	2002	2003	2002	2003
食品、饮料、烟酒类	Food, Beverages, Tobacco and Liquor	7565.1	8821.5	6009.6	6951.4	1555.5	1870.1
肉禽蛋类	Meat, Poultry and Eggs	441.7	465.3	235.9	230.3	205.8	235.0
其他食品类	Other Food	2123.3	2720.6	1286.9	1683.4	836.4	1037.2
饮料类	Beverages	272.8	326.2	107.7	124.9	165.1	201.3
烟酒类	Tobacco and Liquor	4727.3	5309.3	4379.0	4912.8	348.3	396.5
服装鞋帽、针、纺织品类	Clothing, Shoes, Hats and Textiles	3236.5	3627.3	2075.7	2306.7	1160.8	1320.7
服装类	Clothing	1786.1	2101.3	1045.6	1252.9	740.5	848.4
鞋帽类	Shoes and Hats	422.6	475.1	208.4	229.5	214.3	245.6
针、纺织品类	Knitwear and Textiles	1027.8	1051.0	821.7	824.2	206.1	226.7
化妆品类	Cosmetics	243.2	278.3	67.7	71.4	175.5	206.9
金银珠宝类	Gold, Silver and Jewelry	181.6	190.9	36.0	28.2	145.6	162.7
日用品类	Articles for Daily Use	992.6	1124.5	525.1	591.4	467.5	533.1
#洗涤用品类	Washing Articles	215.0	259.1	89.5	97.9	125.5	161.2
儿童玩具类	Children Toys	51.0	58.1	25.8	29.4	25.3	28.7
五金、电料类	Hardware and Electrical Materials	324.8	359.0	260.5	288.9	64.3	70.0
体育、娱乐用品类	Sports and Recreation Articles	119.8	145.3	57.2	66.4	62.6	78.9
书报杂志类	Newspapers and Magazines	609.3	677.4	349.8	382.1	259.5	295.4
电子出版物及音像制品类	E-journal and Video Products	36.4	41.9	14.6	16.3	21.8	25.6
家用电器和音像器材类	Household Appliances and Video Appliances	1842.6	2185.4	889.6	1058.2	953.0	1127.2
中西药品类	Traditional Chinese and Western Medicines	1853.3	2275.6	1042.8	1380.8	810.5	894.7
#西药	Western Medicines	1271.0	1566.0	705.1	939.2	565.9	626.8
中草药及中成药	Traditional Chinese Medicines	488.3	597.6	277.8	368.4	210.5	229.2
文化办公用品类	Cultural and Official Goods	474.9	639.0	314.6	451.2	160.3	187.8
家具类	Furniture	104.9	135.3	43.1	56.1	61.8	79.2
通讯器材类	Communication Appliances	591.8	756.6	468.5	546.0	123.2	210.6
煤炭及制品类	Coal and Related Products	649.6	800.3	637.7	786.7	11.9	13.6
木材及制品类	Wood and Wooden Products	78.6	98.4	74.9	93.0	3.6	5.3
石油及制品类	Petroleum and Related Products	6705.8	8665.1	5840.9	7468.8	864.9	1196.3
化工材料及制品类	Raw Chemical Materials	1805.0	2128.6	1790.2	2110.8	14.7	17.9
#化肥类	Fertilizer	664.3	708.4	664.3	708.4		
金属材料类	Metal Materials	2374.4	3832.5	2352.9	3806.4	21.5	26.1
建筑及装潢材料类	Building and Decoration Materials	245.3	360.6	175.3	265.6	70.0	95.0
机电产品及设备类	Mechanical and Electrical Products	4015.4	5127.1	3032.8	3534.7	982.6	1592.4
#农机类	Agricultural Machinery	138.6	120.9	138.6	120.9		
汽车类	Automobile	2549.5	3359.4	1670.0	1877.5	879.6	1481.9
种子饲料类	Seed and Feedstuff	62.7	73.7	62.7	73.7		
棉麻类	Cotton, Hemp	428.5	582.8	428.5	582.8		
其他类	Others	2133.2	2396.1	1942.5	2186.0	190.7	210.1

17-11 限额以上批发零售贸易业商品销售数量

Total Sales Number of Enterprises above Designated Size in Wholesale and Retail Trade by Commodities

项目	Item	销售合计 Total		批发 Wholesale Trade		零售 Retail Trade	
		2002	2003	2002	2003	2002	2003
粮食 (万吨)	Grain (10 000 ton)	4797.3	6550.8	4479.0	6201.7	318.3	349.1
食用植物油 (万吨)	Edible Vegetable Oil (10 000 ton)	319.5	439.4	251.7	357.7	67.9	81.7
食糖 (万吨)	Sugar (10 000 ton)	262.3	306.8	246.8	287.3	15.5	19.5
卷烟 (亿支)	Cigarettes(100 million piece)		42698.1		41579.2		1118.9
酒 (万吨)	Liquor wine(10 000 ton)		549.2		401.9		147.3
#白酒 (万吨)	Distilled Spirit (10 000 ton)		138.1		79.7		58.4
啤酒 (万吨)	Beer (10 000 ton)		310.2		273.9		36.3
棉花 (万吨)	Cotton (10 000 ton)	417.9	534.8	415.9	533.3	2.0	1.5
布 (亿米)	Cloth (100 million meter)	38.6	35.8	37.7	34.9	0.9	0.9
各种服装 (亿件)	Clothing (100 million piece)		37.1		29.9		7.2
#童装 (亿件)	Children Clothing (100 million piece)		2.5		1.7		0.8
鞋 (亿双)	Shoes (100 million pair)	11.0	13.3	8.7	10.3	2.3	3.0
照相机 (万台)	Camera (10 000 units)		260.5		116.5		144.0
数码照相 (万台)	Digital Camera (10 000 units)		37.4		13.5		23.9
彩色电视机 (万台)	Television Set (10 000 units)	2373.6	2590.7	1322.6	1457.1	1051.0	1133.6
组合音响 (万台)	Hi-Fi Stereo Component System (10 000 units)	151.4	188.7	47.9	59.6	103.4	129.1
摄像机 (万台)	Pickup Camera (10 000 units)	20.3	34.8	2.7	8.1	17.6	26.7
影碟机 (万台)	Video Disc Player (10 000 units)	598.7	773.7	132.3	218.3	466.4	555.4
家用电冰箱 (万台)	Household Refrigerator (10 000 units)	1053.6	1201.5	563.3	623.1	490.3	578.4
家用洗衣机 (万台)	Household Washing Machine (10 000 units)	977.0	1235.4	470.8	587.4	506.2	648.0
房间空调器 (万台)	Room Air Conditioner (10 000 units)	1408.0	1865.0	834.3	1087.2	573.7	777.8
微波炉 (万台)	Micro-oven (10 000 units)	633.3	742.1	256.7	316.3	376.6	425.8
微型计算机 (万台)	Personal Computer (10 000 units)	187.9	298.9	105.8	159.4	82.1	139.5
普通电话机 (万台)	Telephone (10 000 units)	1132.0	1460.1	562.0	861.5	570.0	598.6
移动电话机 (万台)	Hand Telephone (10 000 units)	3017.7	3897.7	2407.1	2731.7	610.6	1166.0
化学肥料 (万吨)	Chemical Fertilizers (10 000 ton)	5383.8	5451.2	5383.8	5451.2		
化学农药 (万吨)	Chemical Pesticide (10 000 ton)	58.3	111.7	58.3	111.7		
农用薄膜 (万吨)	Farming Pellicle (10 000 ton)	28.8	26.1	28.8	26.1		
煤炭 (万吨)	Coal (10 000 ton)	24787.3	29320.8	24212.6	28828.3	574.7	492.5
木材 (万立方米)	Wood (10 000 cu.m)	335.3	466.4	331.6	460.4	3.7	6.0
汽油 (万吨)	Gasoline (10 000 ton)	8015.5	8562.6	6829.4	7047.3	1186.1	1515.3
煤油 (万吨)	Kerosene (10 000 ton)	1142.6	1187.0	1122.1	1170.2	20.5	16.8
柴油 (万吨)	Diesel Oil (10 000 ton)	15983.6	16810.7	14770.0	15175.6	1213.6	1635.1
钢材 (万吨)	Steel Products (10 000 ton)	6875.9	11644.3	6815.4	11566.2	60.5	78.1
铜 (万吨)	Copper (10 000 ton)	96.8	110.7	96.8	110.7		
铝 (万吨)	Aluminum (10 000 ton)	62.8	85.5	62.8	85.5		
水泥 (万吨)	Cement (10 000 ton)	974.1	1290.6	959.2	1285.9	14.9	4.7
汽车 (万辆)	Motor Vehicles (10 000 units)	220.3	264.4	146.8	154.3	73.5	110.1
#轿车 (万辆)	Car (10 000 units)	124.7	151.5	83.8	81.9	40.9	69.6
摩托车 (万辆)	Motor (10 000 units)	262.5	315.0	182.2	223.4	80.3	91.6
拖拉机 (万台)	Tractors (10 000 units)	37.7	20.7	37.7	20.7		

17-12 各地区餐饮业营业收入

Business Revenue of Catering Services by Region

单位: 亿元 (100 million yuan)

指 标	Item	1999	2000	2001	2002	2003
总　计	**Total**	**3554.8**	**4123.3**	**4748.7**	**5555.1**	**6325.9**
按限额标准分	**By Size of Enterprises**					
限额以上企业	Above Designated Size	442.6	528.5	618.7	740.3	896.2
限额以下企业	Below Designated Size	3112.2	3594.8	4130.0	4814.8	5429.7
北　京	Beijing	82.4	90.6	98.4	113.0	124.2
天　津	Tianjin	69.9	82.9	94.7	103.2	110.7
河　北	Hebei	179.1	184.1	207.1	241.1	256.4
山　西	Shanxi	51.5	54.0	62.0	86.4	92.4
内蒙古	Inner Mongolia	43.1	52.6	58.9	69.5	101.6
辽　宁	Liaoning	198.4	234.4	268.0	312.0	344.7
吉　林	Jilin	76.5	101.9	126.8	149.2	160.4
黑龙江	Heilongjiang	83.7	101.2	115.8	137.3	157.7
上　海	Shanghai	111.3	139.9	146.4	184.6	214.8
江　苏	Jiangsu	220.5	264.0	306.3	382.2	462.2
浙　江	Zhejiang	188.8	235.6	283.5	322.1	369.1
安　徽	Anhui	97.0	110.9	125.7	137.0	156.8
福　建	Fujian	146.9	158.1	197.4	175.8	178.0
江　西	Jiangxi	60.7	68.5	73.5	89.4	93.4
山　东	Shandong	269.0	311.8	358.8	407.5	524.6
河　南	Henan	184.3	211.8	250.9	295.4	343.4
湖　北	Hubei	155.4	191.2	240.0	272.5	308.2
湖　南	Hunan	136.8	155.3	175.7	214.1	243.5
广　东	Guangdong	576.0	654.8	739.6	810.1	873.9
广　西	Guangxi	88.1	102.8	123.2	133.8	140.5
海　南	Hainan	21.9	24.2	27.0	29.0	31.6
重　庆	Chongqing	50.7	56.2	68.4	71.8	110.7
四　川	Sichuan	197.2	242.0	268.5	322.9	383.4
贵　州	Guizhou	33.3	43.8	53.2	67.6	77.6
云　南	Yunnan	54.5	51.2	67.4	90.0	117.6
西　藏	Tibet	8.3	6.6	7.4	15.0	
陕　西	Shaanxi	61.9	71.7	74.4	172.0	178.4
甘　肃	Gansu	45.2	46.9	51.5	58.5	63.5
青　海	Qinghai	11.6	12.2	12.8	14.8	16.5
宁　夏	Ningxia	12.4	11.5	14.8	17.2	23.3
新　疆	Xinjiang	38.4	50.7	50.9	60.1	66.9

17-13 按登记注册类型分限额以上批发、零售贸易企业资产及负债（2003年）

Assets and Liability of Enterprises above Designated Size in Wholesale and Retail Trade by Types of Registration (2003)

单位: 亿元 (100 million yuan)

指标	Item	资产合计 Total Assets	#流动资产 Circulating Funds	#固定资产 Fixed Asset	负债合计 Total Liabilities	所有者权益合计 Total Creditors' Equity
批发零售贸易企业总计	**Total**	**23380.5**	**16195.4**	**4190.2**	**17519.5**	**5861.0**
批发企业合计	**Wholesale Trade**	**17827.6**	**13139.9**	**2385.8**	**13452.2**	**4375.4**
内资企业	**Domestic Funded Enterprises**	**17124.5**	**12541.4**	**2341.9**	**12922.4**	**4202.2**
国有企业	State-owned Enterprises	8002.1	5841.0	1167.4	6079.7	1922.4
集体企业	Collective-owned Enterprises	1178.8	974.9	105.1	1088.1	90.7
股份合作企业	Cooperative Enterprises	126.0	94.7	19.0	97.1	28.9
联营企业	Joint Ownership Enterprises	144.1	115.9	10.2	111.7	32.4
国有联营企业	State Joint Ownership Enterprises	75.6	65.5	4.9	57.7	17.9
集体联营企业	Collective Joint Ownership Enterprises	14.9	10.1	0.4	14.0	0.9
国有与集体联营企业	Joint State-collective Enterprises	18.7	12.0	2.0	12.8	6.0
其他联营企业	Other Joint Ownership Enterprises	34.9	28.4	3.0	27.3	7.6
有限责任公司	Limited Liability Corporations	4140.3	3202.3	414.2	3129.6	1010.7
国有独资公司	State Sole Funded Corporations	928.2	648.0	101.3	651.0	277.2
其他有限责任公司	Other Limited Liability Corporations	3212.1	2554.3	312.9	2478.6	733.6
股份有限公司	Share-holding Corporations Ltd.	2462.7	1399.8	542.9	1573.6	889.1
私营企业	Private Enterprises	1062.0	905.3	82.3	835.2	226.8
私营独资企业	Private-funded Enterprises	49.3	39.9	4.3	36.9	12.3
私营合伙企业	Private Partnership Enterprises	10.4	8.7	0.7	7.4	2.9
私营有限责任公司	Private Limited Liability Corporations	942.7	804.9	73.2	741.3	201.4
私营股份有限公司	Private Share-holding Corporations Ltd.	59.7	51.9	4.1	49.6	10.1
其他企业	Other Enterprises	8.5	7.5	0.7	7.4	1.1
港、澳、台商投资企业	**Enterprises with Funds from Hong Kong, Macao and Taiwan**	**212.0**	**162.8**	**16.5**	**154.4**	**57.7**
合资经营企业	Joint-venture Enterprises	42.3	27.8	8.1	31.5	10.8
合作经营企业	Cooperative Enterprises	20.0	13.9	2.1	14.2	5.8
独资经营企业	Enterprises with Sole Funds	111.3	106.3	3.2	94.3	17.0
投资股份有限公司	Share-holding Corporations Ltd. with Funds	38.4	14.8	3.1	14.4	24.1
外商投资企业	**Foreign Funded Enterprises**	**491.0**	**435.7**	**27.4**	**375.5**	**115.5**
中外合资经营企业	Joint-venture Enterprises	108.6	90.6	12.8	84.9	23.7
中外合作经营企业	Cooperation Enterprises	4.0	2.4	0.6	5.7	-1.8
外资企业	Enterprises with Sole Foreign Funds	378.3	342.6	14.1	284.8	93.5
外商投资股份有限公司	Share-holding Corporations Ltd. with Foreign Funds	0.1	0.1		0.1	0.1

17-13 续表 continued

单位: 亿元 (100 million yuan)

指 标	Item	资产合计 Total Assets	#流动资产 Circulating Funds	#固定资产 Fixed Asset	负债合计 Total Liabilities	所有者权益合计 Total Creditors' Equity
零售企业合计	**Retail Trade**	**5553.0**	**3055.5**	**1804.4**	**4067.3**	**1485.6**
内资企业	**Domestic Funded Enterprises**	**5061.0**	**2807.1**	**1636.6**	**3691.0**	**1370.0**
国有企业	State-owned Enterprises	1018.4	499.4	430.3	765.8	252.6
集体企业	Collective-owned Enterprises	243.6	138.6	81.9	186.3	57.4
股份合作企业	Cooperative Enterprises	110.3	65.0	31.5	84.6	25.8
联营企业	Joint Ownership Enterprises	63.0	37.1	14.9	44.1	19.0
国有联营企业	State Joint Ownership Enterprises	21.2	12.9	3.9	15.2	6.0
集体联营企业	Collective Joint Ownership Enterprises	2.7	1.1	0.4	2.0	0.7
国有与集体联营企业	Joint State-collective Enterprises	25.0	15.6	6.4	16.7	8.3
其他联营企业	Other Joint Ownership Enterprises	14.2	7.6	4.3	10.2	4.0
有限责任公司	Limited Liability Corporations	1484.1	914.3	389.5	1166.5	317.6
国有独资公司	State Sole Funded Corporations	93.4	51.2	32.1	77.3	16.1
其他有限责任公司	Other Limited Liability Corporations	1390.7	863.2	357.4	1089.2	301.5
股份有限公司	Share-holding Corporations Ltd.	1407.0	611.2	551.7	874.3	532.7
私营企业	Private Enterprises	728.3	536.4	136.2	564.7	163.6
私营独资企业	Private-funded Enterprises	49.4	33.4	11.3	40.0	9.5
私营合伙企业	Private Partnership Enterprises	14.8	10.9	3.2	11.1	3.7
私营有限责任公司	Private Limited Liability Corporations	616.4	459.4	111.5	477.7	138.7
私营股份有限公司	Private Share-holding Corporations Ltd.	47.7	32.8	10.2	36.0	11.7
其他企业	Other Enterprises	6.3	4.9	0.6	4.8	1.5
港、澳、台商投资企业	**Enterprises with Funds from Hong Kong, Macao and Taiwan**	**176.9**	**85.3**	**65.9**	**139.2**	**37.7**
合资经营企业	Joint-venture Enterprises	116.4	55.0	41.2	88.2	28.2
合作经营企业	Cooperative Enterprises	34.8	18.7	12.6	31.1	3.7
独资经营企业	Enterprises with Sole Funds	25.5	11.4	12.1	19.7	5.9
投资股份有限公司	Share-holding Corporations Ltd. with Funds	0.1	0.1		0.2	
外商投资企业	**Foreign Funded Enterprises**	**315.4**	**163.4**	**101.9**	**237.5**	**77.9**
中外合资经营企业	Joint-venture Enterprises	191.1	95.6	60.0	131.3	59.8
中外合作经营企业	Cooperation Enterprises	47.2	23.1	15.6	35.5	11.7
外资企业	Enterprises with Sole Foreign Funds	73.6	43.6	24.4	67.1	6.5
外商投资股份有限公司	Share-holding Corporations Ltd. with Foreign Funds	3.6	1.0	2.0	3.6	-0.1

17-14 按行业分限额以上批发、零售贸易企业资产及负债(2003年)

Assets and Liability of Enterprises above Designated Size in Wholesale and Retail Trade by Sector (2003)

单位: 亿元 (100 million yuan)

指 标	Item	资产合计 Total Assets	#流动资产 Circula-ting Funds	#固定资产 Fixed Asset	负债合计 Total Liabilities	所有者权益合计 Total Creditors' Equity
总 计	**Total**	**23380.5**	**16195.4**	**4190.2**	**17519.5**	**5861.0**
批发业合计	**Wholesale Trade**	**17827.6**	**13139.9**	**2385.8**	**13452.2**	**4375.4**
农畜产品批发业	Wholesale of Farm Produce and Livestock Product	1878.5	1536.1	175.2	1798.4	80.1
食品、饮料及烟草制品批发业	Wholesale of Food, Beverages and Tobaccos	3106.4	2160.0	589.0	1918.0	1188.5
#米、面制品及食用油批发业	Wholesale of Rice, Flour and Edible Oil	688.0	530.2	88.7	589.4	98.6
烟草制品批发业	Whole of Tobaccos	1663.8	1139.5	348.5	797.7	866.1
纺织、服装及日用品批发业	Wholesale of Textiles, Garments and Daily Consumer Articles	1823.6	1506.7	153.8	1435.1	388.4
#服装批发业	Wholesale of Garments	606.5	463.3	44.2	439.1	167.4
文化、体育用品及器材批发业批发业	Wholesale of Culture, Sports Appliances and Equipments	484.4	321.1	78.7	335.3	149.1
医药及医疗器材批发业	Wholesale of Medicines and Medical Appliances	983.7	737.9	136.8	774.6	209.1
矿产品、建材及化工产品批发业	Wholesale of Mineral Products, Building Material and Chemical Products	5820.2	3845.9	966.6	4184.0	1636.2
#煤炭及制品批发业	Wholesale of Coal and Related Products	391.0	292.2	63.7	278.9	112.0
石油及制品批发业	Wholesale of Petrolem and Related Products	2003.5	825.9	639.7	1199.1	804.4
金属及金属矿批发业	Wholesale of Metal Materials	2103.9	1712.2	133.9	1652.4	451.5
建材批发业	Wholesale of Building Materials	314.4	219.8	34.5	244.8	69.6
化肥批发业	Wholesale of Chemical Fertilizer	416.8	348.4	38.3	351.7	65.2
机械设备、五金交电及电子产品批发	Wholesale of Machinery, Hardware and Electronic Equipment	2850.9	2308.7	222.4	2311.7	539.2
#汽车、摩托车及零配件批发业	Wholesale of Motor Vehicles, Motorcycles and Parts	734.7	596.1	62.6	594.9	139.7
家用电器批发业	Wholesale of Household Electrical Appliances	237.1	213.2	15.1	209.1	28.1
计算机、软件及辅助设备批发业	Wholesale of Computer, Software and Assistant Appliances	130.0	93.4	6.7	88.6	41.3
贸易经纪与代理	Trade Broker and Agency	403.7	365.2	21.5	321.1	82.6
其他批发业	Other Wholesale not Classified Elsewhere	476.1	358.2	41.8	374.0	102.1
零售业合计	**Retail Trade**	**5553.0**	**3055.5**	**1804.4**	**4067.3**	**1485.6**
综合零售业	Integrated Retail	3251.6	1541.3	1219.9	2376.1	875.5
#百货零售业	Retail of General Merchandise	2271.4	971.2	952.0	1612.9	658.6
超级市场零售业	Retail of Supermarkets	871.1	512.3	230.3	679.1	192.0
食品、饮料及烟草制品专门零售业	Retail of Food, Beverages and Tobaccos	215.7	123.9	67.6	174.7	41.0
纺织、服装及日用品专门零售业	Special Retail of Textiles, Garments and Daily Consumer Articles	158.0	87.3	54.7	123.1	34.9
#服装零售业	Retail of Garments	83.5	41.7	33.7	66.7	16.9
文化、体育用品及器材专门零售业	Retail of Culture, Sports Appliances and Equipments	287.7	160.8	104.7	168.9	118.8
#体育用品零售业	Retail of Sports Goods	5.4	3.6	1.6	4.4	0.9
图书零售业	Retail of Books	219.0	119.6	85.1	124.3	94.7
医药及医疗器材专门零售业	Retail of Medicines and Medical Appliances	233.3	161.8	47.8	177.4	56.0
#药品零售业	Retail of Medicines	219.8	152.1	45.2	167.1	52.7
汽车、摩托车、燃料及零配件专门零售业	Retail of Motor Vehicles, Motorcycles, Fuel and Parts	736.3	519.2	147.5	531.5	204.8
#汽车零售业	Retail of Motor Vehicles	525.5	421.1	60.1	398.2	127.2
机动车燃料零售业	Retail of Fuel of Motor Vehicles	154.0	54.5	79.5	89.4	64.6
家用电器及电子产品专门零售业	Special Retail of Household Electric Appliances and Electronic Products	462.3	358.6	80.8	370.4	91.9
#家用电器零售业	Retail of Household Electric Appliances	339.4	281.8	45.5	289.8	49.6
计算机、软件及辅助设备零售业	Retail of Computer, Software and Assistant Appliances	49.7	40.4	5.0	39.0	10.7
通讯设备零售业	Retail of Communication Equipments	67.7	31.6	30.0	37.1	30.5
五金、家具及室内装修材料专门零售业	Special Retail of Hardware, Furniture and Decoration Materials	105.8	63.3	28.7	85.2	20.6
无店铺及其他零售业	Non-shop and Other Retails	102.3	39.3	52.6	60.1	42.2
#邮购及电子销售业	Distribution of Post and E-commerce	1.9	1.7		1.2	0.6

17-15 限额以上批发零售贸易企业资产及负债

Assets and Liability of Enterprises above Designated Size in Wholesale and Retail Trade

单位: 亿元 (100 million yuan)

年 份 Year 地 区 Region	资产合计 Total Assets	#流动资产 Circulating Funds	#固定资产 Fixed Asset	负债合计 Total Liabilities	所有者权益合计 Total Creditors' Equity
1998	18272.1	12248.4	3915.8	14615.1	3657.0
1999	18285.2	11999.8	3866.2	14615.8	3669.4
2000	19092.2	12705.4	3852.3	15219.2	3873.0
2001	19219.8	12478.0	3845.2	14682.6	4537.2
2002	20992.6	14163.2	4063.5	15924.7	5067.8
2003	23380.5	16195.4	4190.2	17519.5	5861.0
北 京 Beijing	3525.4	2586.1	311.8	2573.3	952.1
天 津 Tianjin	703.0	530.0	104.4	553.2	149.8
河 北 Hebei	531.9	340.7	150.9	429.0	102.9
山 西 Shanxi	367.6	234.0	107.1	276.2	91.4
内蒙古 Inner Mongolia	162.2	108.6	43.1	123.3	38.8
辽 宁 Liaoning	1059.6	783.6	233.9	883.1	176.5
吉 林 Jilin	355.2	245.1	79.1	318.2	37.0
黑龙江 Heilongjiang	389.5	295.2	101.7	312.8	76.7
上 海 Shanghai	2220.4	1499.6	329.4	1505.8	714.5
江 苏 Jiangsu	1577.9	1097.1	301.9	1169.5	408.4
浙 江 Zhejiang	1905.5	1409.3	281.3	1352.7	552.7
安 徽 Anhui	404.5	287.9	82.2	317.4	87.1
福 建 Fujian	835.4	600.6	139.2	539.3	296.0
江 西 Jiangxi	189.0	123.2	49.7	143.4	45.6
山 东 Shandong	1385.3	912.8	298.6	1111.2	274.1
河 南 Henan	653.2	456.1	153.8	567.8	85.4
湖 北 Hubei	681.1	440.6	151.3	538.2	142.9
湖 南 Hunan	553.1	331.2	132.6	432.6	120.5
广 东 Guangdong	2555.5	1695.8	421.9	1875.1	680.4
广 西 Guangxi	230.5	134.3	73.4	168.1	62.4
海 南 Hainan	76.7	42.2	23.2	44.3	32.5
重 庆 Chongqing	351.1	240.9	78.7	279.6	71.5
四 川 Sichuan	461.0	295.4	97.9	331.5	129.5
贵 州 Guizhou	193.8	134.9	47.8	158.4	35.4
云 南 Yunnan	768.3	527.6	135.2	539.1	229.2
西 藏 Tibet	20.8	11.7	5.7	12.5	8.2
陕 西 Shaanxi	282.7	182.5	64.5	230.8	52.0
甘 肃 Gansu	197.0	114.5	58.6	151.4	45.6
青 海 Qinghai	33.9	18.1	11.9	22.4	11.5
宁 夏 Ningxia	51.2	33.8	14.8	34.4	16.7
新 疆 Xinjiang	658.4	482.2	104.5	524.9	133.5

17-16 限额以上批发贸易企业资产及负债

Assets and Liability of Enterprises above Designated Size in Wholesale Trade

单位: 亿元 (100 million yuan)

年份 地区	Year Region	资产合计 Total Assets	#流动资产 Circulating Funds	#固定资产 Fixed Asset	负债合计 Total Liabilities	所有者权益合计 Total Creditors' Equity
	1998	14561.0	10455.7	2419.5	11947.0	2614.0
	1999	14540.4	10233.0	2350.8	11891.0	2649.4
	2000	15141.7	10807.2	2303.3	12336.3	2805.4
	2001	15122.5	10471.0	2279.2	11726.7	3395.8
	2002	16356.8	11775.4	2398.0	12573.5	3783.3
	2003	17827.6	13139.9	2385.8	13452.2	4375.4
北 京	Beijing	2923.1	2217.8	167.1	2170.2	752.8
天 津	Tianjin	552.1	449.3	59.7	449.5	102.6
河 北	Hebei	369.5	259.3	83.3	304.0	65.4
山 西	Shanxi	230.2	165.8	48.8	175.1	55.1
内蒙古	Inner Mongolia	103.6	78.2	18.9	82.3	21.3
辽 宁	Liaoning	762.0	643.3	113.1	664.0	98.0
吉 林	Jilin	246.2	191.9	33.8	236.8	9.4
黑龙江	Heilongjiang	292.4	252.8	51.2	240.9	51.5
上 海	Shanghai	1655.7	1218.0	148.6	1122.5	533.2
江 苏	Jiangsu	1083.4	819.7	149.7	790.4	293.0
浙 江	Zhejiang	1612.4	1235.3	195.1	1147.0	465.3
安 徽	Anhui	325.4	244.7	53.6	256.2	69.2
福 建	Fujian	692.0	506.8	99.3	445.4	246.7
江 西	Jiangxi	144.2	97.0	35.2	111.8	32.4
山 东	Shandong	910.0	647.6	137.7	737.8	172.2
河 南	Henan	450.0	334.2	90.8	385.7	64.2
湖 北	Hubei	469.0	345.2	68.0	382.5	86.5
湖 南	Hunan	416.5	266.6	77.6	337.4	79.1
广 东	Guangdong	2045.6	1373.4	296.5	1486.5	559.1
广 西	Guangxi	143.1	87.4	41.0	109.5	33.6
海 南	Hainan	53.1	29.2	14.5	27.4	25.7
重 庆	Chongqing	248.2	175.0	48.1	198.1	50.1
四 川	Sichuan	314.2	203.8	57.4	223.8	90.4
贵 州	Guizhou	155.7	113.3	36.4	126.0	29.6
云 南	Yunnan	669.6	480.4	109.3	458.0	211.6
西 藏	Tibet	11.1	7.4	2.4	7.9	3.2
陕 西	Shaanxi	187.1	134.8	29.8	167.7	19.4
甘 肃	Gansu	140.8	92.3	29.2	110.8	30.0
青 海	Qinghai	21.5	13.0	5.6	13.0	8.5
宁 夏	Ningxia	28.1	17.4	7.5	20.8	7.4
新 疆	Xinjiang	571.7	439.1	76.6	462.8	108.9

17-17 限额以上零售贸易企业资产及负债

Assets and Liability of Enterprises above Designated Size in Retail Trade

单位: 亿元 (100 million yuan)

年 份 Year / 地 区 Region		资产合计 Total Assets	#流动资产 Circulating Funds	#固定资产 Fixed Asset	负债合计 Total Liabilities	所有者权益合计 Total Creditors' Equity
	1998	3711.1	1792.7	1496.3	2668.1	1043.0
	1999	3744.8	1766.7	1515.4	2724.7	1020.0
	2000	3950.5	1898.2	1549.1	2882.9	1067.6
	2001	4097.3	2007.0	1566.0	2955.9	1141.4
	2002	4635.7	2387.8	1665.4	3351.2	1284.5
	2003	5553.0	3055.5	1804.4	4067.3	1485.6
北 京	Beijing	602.4	368.3	144.8	403.1	199.3
天 津	Tianjin	150.9	80.7	44.8	103.6	47.2
河 北	Hebei	162.4	81.4	67.6	124.9	37.5
山 西	Shanxi	137.4	68.2	58.3	101.0	36.3
内蒙古	Inner Mongolia	58.6	30.4	24.2	41.0	17.6
辽 宁	Liaoning	297.6	140.3	120.8	219.0	78.5
吉 林	Jilin	109.0	53.1	45.3	81.4	27.6
黑龙江	Heilongjiang	97.1	42.4	50.5	71.9	25.2
上 海	Shanghai	564.7	281.6	180.8	383.3	181.4
江 苏	Jiangsu	494.5	277.4	152.2	379.1	115.4
浙 江	Zhejiang	293.1	174.0	86.2	205.7	87.4
安 徽	Anhui	79.1	43.3	28.5	61.2	17.9
福 建	Fujian	143.3	93.8	39.9	94.0	49.4
江 西	Jiangxi	44.8	26.2	14.4	31.6	13.2
山 东	Shandong	475.3	265.2	161.0	373.4	101.9
河 南	Henan	203.2	121.9	63.0	182.0	21.2
湖 北	Hubei	212.1	95.4	83.3	155.7	56.4
湖 南	Hunan	136.7	64.6	55.0	95.3	41.4
广 东	Guangdong	509.9	322.4	125.4	388.6	121.4
广 西	Guangxi	87.4	46.8	32.4	58.5	28.8
海 南	Hainan	23.6	13.0	8.6	16.8	6.8
重 庆	Chongqing	102.9	65.9	30.6	81.5	21.4
四 川	Sichuan	146.8	91.6	40.6	107.7	39.2
贵 州	Guizhou	38.1	21.6	11.4	32.4	5.8
云 南	Yunnan	98.7	47.2	25.9	81.1	17.6
西 藏	Tibet	9.6	4.2	3.3	4.6	5.0
陕 西	Shaanxi	95.6	47.8	34.7	63.1	32.5
甘 肃	Gansu	56.2	22.2	29.5	40.5	15.6
青 海	Qinghai	12.4	5.1	6.3	9.4	3.0
宁 夏	Ningxia	23.0	16.4	7.3	13.7	9.4
新 疆	Xinjiang	86.7	43.0	27.9	62.1	24.6

17-18 按登记注册类型和行业分限额以上餐饮企业资产及负债(2003年)

Assets and Liability of Enterprises above Designated Size in Catering Services by Types of Registration and by Sector (2003)

单位: 亿元

(100 million yuan)

指 标	Item	资产合计 Total Assets	#流动资产 Circulating Funds	#固定资产 Fixed Asset	负债合计 Total Liabilities	所有者权益合计 Total Creditors' Equity
总　计	**Total**	**1110.8**	**306.0**	**620.0**	**745.0**	**365.8**
按登记注册类型分	**By Types of Registration**					
内资企业	**Domestic Funded Enterprises**	**813.5**	**234.4**	**459.7**	**523.3**	**290.1**
国有企业	State-owned Enterprises	189.3	43.0	120.1	119.3	69.9
集体企业	Collective-owned Enterprises	65.8	17.0	42.2	39.5	26.3
股份合作企业	Cooperative Enterprises	20.0	7.5	9.6	14.0	6.0
联营企业	Joint Ownership Enterprises	4.9	1.6	2.9	4.2	0.7
国有联营企业	State Joint Ownership Enterprises	2.8	0.8	1.7	1.9	0.9
集体联营企业	Collective Joint Ownership Enterprises	1.2	0.2	0.9	1.8	-0.6
国有与集体联营企业	Joint State-collective Enterprises	0.8	0.6	0.1	0.5	0.3
其他联营企业	Other Joint Ownership Enterprises	0.5	0.3	0.2	0.4	0.2
有限责任公司	Limited Liability Corporations	200.1	52.5	116.7	137.9	62.2
国有独资公司	State Sole Funded Corporations	4.1	0.5	1.4	1.4	2.7
其他有限责任公司	Other Limited Liability Corporations	196.0	52.0	115.3	136.5	59.4
股份有限公司	Share-holding Corporations Ltd.	50.4	13.8	31.5	32.4	18.0
私营企业	Private Enterprises	282.6	99.3	136.1	176.0	106.6
私营独资企业	Private-funded Enterprises	50.2	16.6	26.7	26.9	23.2
私营合伙企业	Private Partnership Enterprises	18.1	5.8	9.1	8.7	9.4
私营有限责任公司	Private Limited Liability Corporations	201.4	72.3	93.1	132.5	68.9
私营股份有限公司	Private Share-holding Corporations Ltd.	12.9	4.6	7.2	7.9	5.0
其他企业	Other Enterprises	1.8	0.6	1.0	0.9	1.0
港、澳、台商投资企业	**Enterprises with Funds from Hong Kong, Macao and Taiwan**	**138.9**	**37.0**	**73.6**	**116.4**	**22.5**
合资经营企业	Joint-venture Enterprises	73.7	17.6	45.2	64.2	9.5
合作经营企业	Cooperative Enterprises	35.9	9.5	16.9	30.8	5.2
独资经营企业	Enterprises with Sole Investment	27.1	9.5	9.7	19.2	7.9
投资股份有限公司	Share-holding Corporations Ltd. with Investment	2.2	0.3	1.9	2.3	
外商投资企业	**Foreign Funded Enterprises**	**158.4**	**34.6**	**86.6**	**105.2**	**53.2**
中外合资经营企业	Joint-venture Enterprises	88.1	14.8	55.9	61.0	27.1
中外合作经营企业	Cooperation Enterprises	27.9	10.4	12.2	17.1	10.9
外资企业	Enterprises with Sole Foreign Funds	41.6	9.1	18.3	26.8	14.8
外商投资股份有限公司	Share-holding Corporations Ltd. with Foreign Investment	0.8	0.3	0.3	0.4	0.5
按国民经济行业分	**By Sector**					
正餐服务业	Dinner	1006.0	278.4	580.8	683.6	322.5
快餐服务业	Snack	88.6	22.9	31.9	52.2	36.3
饮料及冷饮服务业	Beverages and Cold Drinks	1.6	0.5	0.6	1.2	0.4
其他餐饮服务业	Others	14.6	4.1	6.8	8.0	6.7

17-19 限额以上餐饮企业资产及负债

Assets and Liability of Enterprises above Designated Size in Catering Services

单位: 亿元 (100 million yuan)

年份 Year 地区 Region		资产合计 Total Assets	#流动资产 Circulating Funds	#固定资产 Fixed Asset	负债合计 Total Liabilities	所有者权益合计 Total Creditors' Equity
	1998	578.3	152.0	326.9	375.9	202.4
	1999	714.3	176.2	414.1	479.2	235.1
	2000	764.3	180.8	457.2	508.6	255.7
	2001	797.9	208.9	448.0	527.6	270.4
	2002	891.4	243.1	503.3	584.4	307.0
	2003	1110.8	306.0	620.0	745.0	365.9
北京	Beijing	62.4	21.9	22.7	42.2	20.3
天津	Tianjin	20.2	6.0	8.2	14.1	6.1
河北	Hebei	24.2	5.4	16.4	17.6	6.6
山西	Shanxi	18.9	6.5	9.8	14.2	4.6
内蒙古	Inner Mongolia	20.3	4.7	14.5	13.5	6.8
辽宁	Liaoning	58.6	14.9	35.9	36.7	21.9
吉林	Jilin	3.9	1.5	2.3	2.9	1.0
黑龙江	Heilongjiang	8.9	3.1	4.9	3.7	5.2
上海	Shanghai	50.5	15.7	21.9	32.9	17.6
江苏	Jiangsu	153.0	42.8	88.1	96.4	56.7
浙江	Zhejiang	77.0	21.8	41.0	49.5	27.5
安徽	Anhui	5.5	2.0	2.2	3.3	2.1
福建	Fujian	43.6	11.7	20.9	23.4	20.2
江西	Jiangxi	3.9	1.2	2.0	2.0	1.9
山东	Shandong	117.9	24.9	78.8	78.6	39.3
河南	Henan	23.4	6.2	14.6	17.6	5.9
湖北	Hubei	45.0	8.5	29.4	31.9	13.2
湖南	Hunan	26.2	6.7	16.5	17.0	9.2
广东	Guangdong	205.0	59.8	108.2	150.4	54.6
广西	Guangxi	9.9	2.7	6.4	8.6	1.3
海南	Hainan	20.6	4.3	14.6	18.6	2.0
重庆	Chongqing	15.5	4.6	8.5	10.1	5.4
四川	Sichuan	45.4	12.5	25.1	25.8	19.7
贵州	Guizhou	4.6	1.6	2.3	2.9	1.7
云南	Yunnan	13.0	3.6	8.0	8.9	4.2
西藏	Tibet					
陕西	Shaanxi	16.0	6.5	6.5	10.8	5.2
甘肃	Gansu	9.2	2.6	5.6	6.4	2.8
青海	Qinghai	1.3	0.4	0.8	0.8	0.5
宁夏	Ningxia	3.0	0.8	1.9	1.9	1.1
新疆	Xinjiang	4.1	1.3	2.1	2.7	1.4

17-20 按登记注册类型分限额以上批发零售贸易企业主要财务指标(2003年)

Main Financial Indicators of Enterprises above Designated Size in Wholesale and Retail Trade by Registration (2003)

单位:亿元 (100 million yuan)

指标	Item	商品销售收入净额 Sales Revenue	商品销售成本 Cost of Sales	经营费用 Management Cost	商品销售税金及附加 Sales Tax and Extra Changes	商品销售利润 Sales Profit
批发零售贸易业总计	**Total**	**41889.2**	**38514.5**	**1595.3**	**62.7**	**1714.7**
批发企业合计	**Wholesale Trade**	**33689.9**	**31211.0**	**1068.8**	**39.2**	**1368.8**
内资企业	**Domestic Funded Enterprises**	**31671.2**	**29421.9**	**960.9**	**37.2**	**1249.2**
国有企业	State-owned Enterprises	12667.4	11575.9	375.3	18.8	696.3
集体企业	Collective-owned Enterprises	1255.2	1189.9	30.7	1.1	33.6
股份合作企业	Cooperative Enterprises	318.3	301.4	9.4	0.3	7.2
联营企业	Joint Ownership Enterprises	329.9	312.6	8.7	0.2	8.3
国有联营企业	State Joint Ownership Enterprises	210.8	200.1	5.2	0.1	5.3
集体联营企业	Collective Joint Ownership Enterprises	16.6	15.1	0.9		0.5
国有与集体联营企业	Joint State-collective Enterprises	45.8	43.7	1.2		1.0
其他联营企业	Other Joint Ownership Enterprises	56.6	53.7	1.4		1.5
有限责任公司	Limited Liability Corporations	8389.1	7866.0	270.3	7.6	245.2
国有独资公司	State Sole Funded Corporations	1290.9	1201.6	54.1	1.0	34.2
其他有限责任公司	Other Limited Liability Corporations	7098.2	6664.3	216.2	6.7	211.0
股份有限公司	Share-holding Corporations Ltd.	6029.2	5626.6	194.7	6.6	200.4
私营企业	Private Enterprises	2658.0	2527.2	70.9	2.4	57.5
私营独资企业	Private-funded Enterprises	131.3	122.8	3.6	0.1	4.8
私营合伙企业	Private Partnership Enterprises	29.4	28.0	0.8		0.6
私营有限责任公司	Private Limited Liability Corporations	2391.4	2276.5	63.5	2.0	49.4
私营股份有限公司	Private Share-holding Corporations Ltd.	105.9	99.9	3.0	0.3	2.7
其他企业	Other Enterprises	24.1	22.3	1.1		0.6
港、澳、台商投资企业	**Enterprises with Funds from Hong Kong, Macao and Taiwan**	**462.9**	**417.3**	**23.1**	**0.2**	**22.3**
合资经营企业	Joint-venture Enterprises	87.4	81.1	4.0		2.3
合作经营企业	Cooperative Enterprises	66.9	60.4	4.3		2.2
独资经营企业	Enterprises with Sole Investment	291.7	264.8	10.9	0.1	15.9
投资股份有限公司	Share-holding Corporations Ltd. with Funds	16.9	11.0	3.9		2.0
外商投资企业	**Foreign Funded Enterprises**	**1555.8**	**1371.8**	**84.8**	**1.9**	**97.3**
中外合资经营企业	Joint-venture Enterprises	733.5	671.5	29.2		32.7
中外合作经营企业	Cooperation Enterprises	12.4	11.5	0.8		0.2
外资企业	Enterprises with Sole Foreign Funds	808.9	688.2	54.7	1.8	64.2
外商投资股份有限公司	Share-holding Corporations Ltd. with Foreign Funds	0.9	0.7	0.1		0.1

17-20 续表 continued

单位: 亿元 (100 million yuan)

指 标	Item	商品销售收入净额 Sales Revenue	商品销售成本 Cost of Sales	经营费用 Management Cost	商品销售税金及附加 Sales Tax and Extra Changes	商品销售利润 Sales Profit
零售企业合计	**Retail Trade**	**8199.4**	**7303.5**	**526.5**	**23.5**	**345.9**
内资企业	**Domestic Funded Enterprises**	**7412.2**	**6633.9**	**436.5**	**22.3**	**319.4**
国有企业	State-owned Enterprises	1091.2	944.4	70.6	4.0	72.2
集体企业	Collective-owned Enterprises	341.4	308.1	16.4	1.2	15.6
股份合作企业	Cooperative Enterprises	195.1	177.0	9.7	0.7	7.8
联营企业	Joint Ownership Enterprises	141.2	132.4	5.4	0.2	3.2
国有联营企业	State Joint Ownership Enterprises	37.1	33.9	2.0		1.1
集体联营企业	Collective Joint Ownership Enterprises	5.8	5.1	0.6		0.1
国有与集体联营企业	Joint State-collective Enterprises	80.2	77.3	1.2		1.6
其他联营企业	Other Joint Ownership Enterprises	18.1	16.1	1.6	0.1	0.4
有限责任公司	Limited Liability Corporations	2465.0	2221.9	159.0	6.1	78.0
国有独资公司	State Sole Funded Corporations	111.2	98.0	5.9	0.4	6.9
其他有限责任公司	Other Limited Liability Corporations	2353.8	2123.9	153.0	5.7	71.1
股份有限公司	Share-holding Corporations Ltd.	1633.6	1425.6	92.6	6.4	108.9
私营企业	Private Enterprises	1533.4	1414.1	82.3	3.6	33.3
私营独资企业	Private-funded Enterprises	92.7	81.6	8.0	0.4	2.8
私营合伙企业	Private Partnership Enterprises	32.9	29.7	1.9	0.2	1.2
私营有限责任公司	Private Limited Liability Corporations	1312.4	1214.6	67.8	2.8	27.2
私营股份有限公司	Private Share-holding Corporations Ltd.	95.4	88.3	4.7	0.3	2.2
其他企业	Other Enterprises	11.3	10.4	0.5		0.3
港、澳、台商投资企业	**Enterprises with Funds from Hong Kong, Macao and Taiwan**	**219.4**	**177.5**	**25.4**	**0.6**	**15.8**
合资经营企业	Joint-venture Enterprises	153.8	126.2	17.4	0.3	9.9
合作经营企业	Cooperative Enterprises	39.2	30.8	4.3	0.2	3.8
独资经营企业	Enterprises with Sole Investment	26.2	20.3	3.7	0.1	2.1
投资股份有限公司	Share-holding Corporations Ltd. with Funds	0.2	0.2			
外商投资企业	**Foreign Funded Enterprises**	**567.8**	**492.0**	**64.6**	**0.5**	**10.7**
中外合资经营企业	Joint-venture Enterprises	307.2	261.0	37.1	0.4	8.7
中外合作经营企业	Cooperation Enterprises	98.0	81.4	10.3	0.1	6.1
外资企业	Enterprises with Sole Foreign Funds	158.1	145.9	16.9		-4.8
外商投资股份有限公司	Share-holding Corporations Ltd. with Foreign Funds	4.5	3.7	0.2		0.6

17-21 按行业分限额以上批发零售贸易企业主要财务指标(2003年)

Main Financial Indicators of Enterprises above Designated Size in Wholesale and Retail Trade by Sector (2003)

单位: 亿元 (100 million yuan)

指 标	Item	商品销售收入净额 Sales Revenue	商品销售成本 Cost of Sales	经营费用 Management Cost	商品销售税金及附加 Sales Tax and Extra Changes	商品销售利润 Sales Profit
总 计	**Total**	**41889.2**	**38514.5**	**1595.3**	**62.7**	**1714.7**
批发业合计	**Wholesale Trade**	**33689.9**	**31211.0**	**1068.8**	**39.2**	**1368.8**
农畜产品批发业	Wholesale of Farm Produce and Livestock Product	1288.8	1234.8	52.8	0.9	0.3
食品、饮料及烟草制品批发业	Wholesale of Food, Beverages and Tobaccos	5905.1	5132.6	197.9	13.3	561.3
#米、面制品及食用油批发业	Wholesale of Rice, Flour and Edible Oil	634.6	609.2	23.9	0.2	1.2
烟草制品批发业	Whole of Tobaccos	4228.3	3586.6	118.3	10.6	512.8
纺织、服装及日用品批发业	Wholesale of Textiles, Garments and Daily Consumer Articles	3265.8	3058.7	102.7	1.4	103.0
#服装批发业	Wholesale of Garments	1071.9	991.8	37.7	0.5	41.9
文化、体育用品及器材批发业	Wholesale of Culture, Sports Appliances and Equipments	583.7	522.4	25.1	1.0	35.1
医药及医疗器材批发业	Wholesale of Medicines and Medical Appliances	1752.6	1604.1	73.1	2.1	73.2
矿产品、建材及化工产品批发业	Wholesale of Mineral Products, Building Material and Chemical Products	13857.9	13084.0	394.4	14.1	363.5
#煤炭及制品批发业	Wholesale of Coal and Related Products	772.3	695.7	50.9	1.3	24.4
石油及制品批发业	Wholesale of Petrolem and Related Products	6629.2	6215.5	207.5	6.9	197.3
金属及金属矿批发业	Wholesale of Metal Materials	3924.8	3773.7	65.8	3.2	82.1
建材批发业	Wholesale of Building Materials	458.0	435.0	12.7	0.6	9.7
化肥批发业	Wholesale of Chemical Fertilizer	677.6	643.7	19.5	0.2	14.3
机械设备、五金交电及电子产品批发	Wholesale of Machinery, Hardware and Electronic Equipment	5314.2	5001.5	160.5	3.8	148.4
#汽车、摩托车及零配件批发业	Wholesale of Motor Vehicles, Motorcycles and Parts	2032.3	1919.7	52.5	1.1	59.1
家用电器批发业	Wholesale of Household Electrical Appliances	551.2	516.2	27.4	0.5	7.0
计算机、软件及辅助设备批发业	Wholesale of Computer, Software and Assistant Appliances	265.4	253.6	5.7	0.2	5.9
贸易经纪与代理	Trade Broker and Agency	730.4	623.9	41.4	2.1	63.1
其他批发业	Other Wholesale not Classified Elsewhere	991.5	948.9	21.0	0.7	20.8
零售业合计	**Retail Trade**	**8199.4**	**7303.5**	**526.5**	**23.5**	**345.9**
综合零售业	Integrated Retail	4102.8	3569.4	334.8	14.5	184.1
#百货零售业	Retail of General Merchandise	2400.0	2062.2	150.6	10.7	176.5
超级市场零售业	Retail of Supermarkets	1571.7	1393.4	169.3	3.4	5.6
食品、饮料及烟草制品专门零售业	Retail of Food, Beverages and Tobaccos	221.5	193.8	17.1	1.1	9.6
纺织、服装及日用品专门零售业	Special Retail of Textiles, Garments and Daily Consumer Articles	184.6	144.8	23.8	1.1	14.9
#服装零售业	Retail of Garments	94.0	72.2	13.0	0.5	8.3
文化、体育用品及器材专门零售业	Retail of Culture, Sports Appliances and Equipments	324.8	252.4	29.8	1.9	40.7
#体育用品零售业	Retail of Sports Goods	6.0	5.0	0.4		0.5
图书零售业	Retail of Books	227.2	169.1	23.2	1.0	33.9
医药及医疗器材专门零售业	Retail of Medicines and Medical Appliances	355.3	308.5	24.9	0.8	21.1
#药品零售业	Retail of Medicines	337.3	292.7	23.7	0.8	20.1
汽车、摩托车、燃料及零配件专门零售业	Retail of Motor Vehicles, Motorcycles, Fuel and Parts	1838.9	1742.4	41.9	1.9	52.7
#汽车零售业	Retail of Motor Vehicles	1302.5	1247.5	21.6	1.1	32.3
机动车燃料零售业	Retail of Fuel of Motor Vehicles	412.2	377.2	17.3	0.6	17.0
家用电器及电子产品专门零售业	Special Retail of Household Electric Appliances and Electronic Products	928.4	877.9	32.8	1.5	16.1
#家用电器零售业	Retail of Household Electric Appliances	686.1	650.6	23.9	0.9	10.7
计算机、软件及辅助设备零售业	Retail of Computer, Software and Assistant Appliances	140.9	133.3	4.8	0.1	2.7
通讯设备零售业	Retail of Communication Equipments	90.0	83.3	3.6	0.5	2.6
五金、家具及室内装修材料专门零售业	Special Retail of Hardware, Furniture and Decoration Materials	154.6	135.1	15.8	0.6	3.1
无店铺及其他零售业	Non-shop and Other Retails	88.6	79.2	5.5	0.2	3.6
#邮购及电子销售业	Distribution of Post and E-commerce	4.6	4.4			0.1

17-22 限额以上批发零售贸易企业主要财务指标

Main Financial Indicators of Enterprises above Designated Size in Wholesale and Retail Trade

单位: 亿元 (100 million yuan)

年份 地区	Year Region	商品销售收入净额 Sales Revenue	商品销售成本 Cost of Sales	经营费用 Management Cost	商品销售税金及附加 Sales Tax and Extra Changes	商品销售利润 Sales Profit
	1998	23260.8	21005.8	929.4	70.6	950.7
	1999	24042.3	21860.9	923.0	53.6	982.8
	2000	28591.9	26141.1	1007.9	54.2	1127.9
	2001	30302.7	27775.6	1137.2	55.6	1103.1
	2002	35126.6	32305.5	1331.8	58.4	1430.8
	2003	41889.2	38514.5	1595.3	62.7	1714.7
北　京	Beijing	3883.5	3583.9	161.3	4.9	133.4
天　津	Tianjin	1603.4	1523.0	46.8	1.2	32.5
河　北	Hebei	856.0	787.7	33.7	1.3	33.3
山　西	Shanxi	542.1	493.0	22.7	1.6	24.8
内蒙古	Inner Mongolia	265.4	239.6	12.0	0.7	13.1
辽　宁	Liaoning	2068.0	1939.5	74.9	2.3	51.2
吉　林	Jilin	491.2	468.7	26.8	0.5	-4.8
黑龙江	Heilongjiang	600.7	543.1	28.3	1.2	26.0
上　海	Shanghai	4810.9	4343.0	231.5	7.2	229.2
江　苏	Jiangsu	3218.4	2935.9	121.7	4.7	156.1
浙　江	Zhejiang	4593.3	4282.4	125.0	5.8	180.0
安　徽	Anhui	857.5	784.4	28.8	1.2	43.0
福　建	Fujian	1631.5	1511.8	55.5	2.3	61.9
江　西	Jiangxi	435.3	394.0	18.4	1.0	21.9
山　东	Shandong	2220.6	2053.7	73.2	2.9	90.9
河　南	Henan	1021.2	942.9	35.4	1.9	41.0
湖　北	Hubei	1166.5	1073.7	37.4	2.4	53.0
湖　南	Hunan	910.0	824.0	34.5	1.7	49.9
广　东	Guangdong	5574.7	5178.1	205.1	7.3	184.3
广　西	Guangxi	418.9	376.6	18.6	1.2	22.6
海　南	Hainan	138.5	124.5	6.6	0.2	7.1
重　庆	Chongqing	625.4	568.0	27.5	1.7	28.3
四　川	Sichuan	902.1	813.8	35.5	1.6	51.2
贵　州	Guizhou	258.1	219.7	14.6	0.8	23.0
云　南	Yunnan	1092.3	953.8	47.4	2.7	88.4
西　藏	Tibet	21.5	14.0	0.9		6.6
陕　西	Shaanxi	444.9	407.9	18.3	0.7	18.0
甘　肃	Gansu	489.3	454.9	22.3	0.7	11.4
青　海	Qinghai	59.1	51.4	2.6	0.1	5.0
宁　夏	Ningxia	72.3	64.9	3.4	0.1	3.9
新　疆	Xinjiang	616.4	562.7	24.5	1.0	28.3

17-23 限额以上批发贸易企业主要财务指标

Main Financial Indicators of Enterprises above Designated Size in Wholesale Trades

单位: 亿元 (100 million yuan)

年份 地区	Year Region	商品销售收入净额 Sales Revenue	商品销售成本 Cost of Sales	经营费用 Management Cost	商品销售税金及附加 Sales Tax and Extra Changes	商品销售利润 Sales Profit
	1998	19268.7	17630.4	693.8	53.9	712.4
	1999	20099.9	18469.8	692.3	37.8	740.4
	2000	24184.1	22365.0	751.2	37.6	862.4
	2001	25133.0	23293.3	816.8	38.0	820.4
	2002	28665.9	26598.2	920.8	35.4	1111.5
	2003	33689.9	31211.0	1068.8	39.2	1368.8
北京	Beijing	3007.0	2803.7	98.1	2.8	102.4
天津	Tianjin	1417.5	1357.3	32.2	0.8	27.3
河北	Hebei	694.6	645.7	23.6	0.7	24.6
山西	Shanxi	397.7	362.1	15.8	1.0	18.8
内蒙古	Inner Mongolia	195.5	176.5	8.6	0.4	10.0
辽宁	Liaoning	1695.3	1607.3	56.6	1.1	30.3
吉林	Jilin	350.8	339.4	21.4	0.2	-10.2
黑龙江	Heilongjiang	489.6	446.8	21.3	0.6	18.8
上海	Shanghai	3827.9	3492.2	135.8	4.3	195.6
江苏	Jiangsu	2394.9	2199.7	73.2	2.6	119.5
浙江	Zhejiang	4057.3	3799.6	97.1	4.5	156.2
安徽	Anhui	739.4	680.5	22.0	0.8	36.1
福建	Fujian	1355.2	1263.2	39.9	1.4	50.7
江西	Jiangxi	363.2	329.6	14.9	0.7	18.0
山东	Shandong	1501.7	1396.5	44.0	1.5	59.6
河南	Henan	775.4	717.8	24.5	1.1	32.0
湖北	Hubei	903.2	841.8	24.5	1.3	35.5
湖南	Hunan	749.4	685.6	23.3	1.0	39.5
广东	Guangdong	4649.5	4352.3	132.3	5.0	159.9
广西	Guangxi	306.6	276.8	12.9	0.8	16.2
海南	Hainan	112.7	101.6	5.1	0.2	5.8
重庆	Chongqing	439.5	402.2	18.3	0.6	18.3
四川	Sichuan	670.2	606.3	20.4	1.1	42.4
贵州	Guizhou	214.8	181.9	11.0	0.6	21.3
云南	Yunnan	968.3	844.3	38.4	2.4	83.2
西藏	Tibet	10.8	5.6	0.6		4.7
陕西	Shaanxi	349.1	325.0	11.5	0.3	12.3
甘肃	Gansu	435.2	407.0	18.9	0.5	8.7
青海	Qinghai	47.4	41.2	1.9	0.1	4.2
宁夏	Ningxia	48.5	43.7	2.2	0.1	2.6
新疆	Xinjiang	521.6	478.0	18.3	0.7	24.6

17-24 限额以上零售贸易企业主要财务指标

Main Financial Indicators of Enterprises above Designated Size in Retail Trades

单位: 万元　　(10 000 yuan)

年份 地区	Year Region	商品销售收入净额 Sales Revenue	商品销售成本 Cost of Sales	经营费用 Management Cost	商品销售税金及附加 Sales Tax and Extra Changes	商品销售利润 Sales Profit
	1998	3992.1	3375.3	235.6	16.7	238.3
	1999	3942.4	3391.2	230.7	15.8	242.4
	2000	4407.7	3776.1	256.7	16.6	265.5
	2001	5169.7	4482.3	320.5	17.6	282.7
	2002	6460.6	5707.3	411.0	23.0	319.3
	2003	8199.4	7303.5	526.5	23.5	345.9
北　京	Beijing	876.5	780.2	63.2	2.1	31.0
天　津	Tianjin	185.9	165.7	14.5	0.4	5.3
河　北	Hebei	161.3	142.0	10.1	0.6	8.7
山　西	Shanxi	144.4	131.0	7.0	0.5	5.9
内蒙古	Inner Mongolia	69.9	63.2	3.4	0.2	3.1
辽　宁	Liaoning	372.7	332.2	18.3	1.2	21.0
吉　林	Jilin	140.4	129.3	5.4	0.2	5.4
黑龙江	Heilongjiang	111.1	96.3	7.1	0.5	7.2
上　海	Shanghai	983.1	850.8	95.7	2.9	33.6
江　苏	Jiangsu	823.4	736.2	48.5	2.1	36.6
浙　江	Zhejiang	536.0	482.9	27.9	1.3	23.9
安　徽	Anhui	118.1	104.0	6.8	0.4	7.0
福　建	Fujian	276.2	248.6	15.6	1.0	11.1
江　西	Jiangxi	72.1	64.5	3.4	0.3	3.9
山　东	Shandong	719.0	657.2	29.1	1.4	31.3
河　南	Henan	245.8	225.2	10.9	0.7	9.0
湖　北	Hubei	263.3	231.9	12.9	1.1	17.4
湖　南	Hunan	160.7	138.3	11.3	0.7	10.4
广　东	Guangdong	925.2	825.7	72.8	2.3	24.4
广　西	Guangxi	112.3	99.8	5.6	0.4	6.4
海　南	Hainan	25.8	22.9	1.5	0.1	1.3
重　庆	Chongqing	186.0	165.8	9.1	1.0	10.0
四　川	Sichuan	231.9	207.4	15.2	0.5	8.9
贵　州	Guizhou	43.3	37.8	3.6	0.2	1.7
云　南	Yunnan	124.0	109.5	9.0	0.4	5.1
西　藏	Tibet	10.7	8.4	0.4		1.9
陕　西	Shaanxi	95.8	82.9	6.8	0.4	5.7
甘　肃	Gansu	54.1	47.9	3.4	0.2	2.7
青　海	Qinghai	11.7	10.2	0.7		0.8
宁　夏	Ningxia	23.8	21.2	1.1	0.1	1.4
新　疆	Xinjiang	94.8	84.6	6.2	0.3	3.6

17-25 按登记注册类型和行业分限额以上餐饮企业主要财务指标(2003年)

Main Financial Indicators of Enterprises above Designated Size in Catering Services by Types of Registration and by Sector (2003)

单位: 亿元 (100 million yuan)

指 标	Item	营业收入 Sales Revenue	营业成本 Cost of Sales	营业费用 Management Cost	营业税金及附加 Sales Tax and Extra Changes	经营利润 Profits
总 计	**Total**	**747.0**	**361.7**	**239.7**	**35.1**	**110.4**
按登记注册类型分	**By Types of Registration**					
内资企业	**Domestic Funded Enterprises**	**526.0**	**271.8**	**156.7**	**26.2**	**71.3**
国有企业	State-owned Enterprises	69.6	31.5	23.1	3.0	12.0
集体企业	Collective-owned Enterprises	37.0	18.5	11.6	1.8	5.2
股份合作企业	Cooperative Enterprises	21.9	11.8	6.8	1.0	2.3
联营企业	Joint Ownership Enterprises	3.3	1.4	1.1	0.2	0.5
国有联营企业	State Joint Ownership Enterprises	1.0	0.4	0.3		0.2
集体联营企业	Collective Joint Ownership Enterprises	0.2	0.1	0.1		
国有与集体联营企业	Joint State-collective Enterprises	0.8	0.3	0.3		0.2
其他联营企业	Other Joint Ownership Enterprises	1.2	0.6	0.4	0.1	0.1
有限责任公司	Limited Liability Corporations	105.9	52.3	31.8	5.1	16.6
国有独资公司	State Sole Funded Corporations	0.7	0.2	0.3		0.1
其他有限责任公司	Other Limited Liability Corporations	105.2	52.1	31.5	5.1	16.5
股份有限公司	Share-holding Corporations Ltd.	24.5	11.2	7.5	1.1	4.7
私营企业	Private Enterprises	260.4	142.9	74.1	13.8	29.7
私营独资企业	Private-funded Enterprises	57.7	33.5	15.2	3.3	5.8
私营合伙企业	Private Partnership Enterprises	20.3	11.6	5.9	0.9	1.9
私营有限责任公司	Private Limited Liability Corporations	170.6	91.4	50.0	9.0	20.3
私营股份有限公司	Private Share-holding Corporations Ltd.	11.7	6.4	3.0	0.6	1.7
其他企业	Other Enterprises	3.4	2.2	0.8	0.2	0.2
港、澳、台商投资企业	**Enterprises with Funds from Hong Kong, Macao and Taiwan**	**82.6**	**35.6**	**31.3**	**3.5**	**12.2**
合资经营企业	Joint-venture Enterprises	31.3	13.5	10.7	1.3	5.9
合作经营企业	Cooperative Enterprises	16.5	7.1	6.3	0.6	2.4
独资经营企业	Enterprises with Sole Funds	34.1	14.7	14.1	1.5	3.8
投资股份有限公司	Share-holding Corporations Ltd. with Funds	0.6	0.2	0.2	0.1	0.1
外商投资企业	**Foreign Funded Enterprises**	**138.4**	**54.4**	**51.7**	**5.4**	**26.9**
中外合资经营企业	Joint-venture Enterprises	59.3	23.4	21.7	2.3	11.9
中外合作经营企业	Cooperation Enterprises	24.3	10.4	8.9	0.8	4.2
外资企业	Enterprises with Sole Foreign Funds	53.8	20.3	20.7	2.3	10.5
外商投资股份有限公司	Share-holding Corporations Ltd. with Foreign Funds	1.1	0.3	0.4	0.1	0.3
按国民经济行业分	**By Sector**					
正餐服务业	Dinner	585.3	295.6	177.9	28.9	83.0
快餐服务业	Snack	145.1	58.6	56.7	5.5	24.2
饮料及冷饮服务业	Beverages and Cold Drinks	1.8	0.7	0.8	0.1	0.2
其他餐饮服务业	Other	14.7	6.8	4.4	0.6	3.0

17-26 限额以上餐饮企业主要财务指标

Main Financial Indicators of Enterprises above Designated Size of Catering Services

单位: 亿元 (100 million yuan)

年份 Year 地区 Region		营业收入 Sales Revenue	营业成本 Cost of Sales	营业费用 Management Cost	营业税金及附加 Sales Tax and Extra Changes	经营利润 Profits
	1998	302.9	145.4	104.0	14.9	38.3
	1999	352.0	166.7	118.5	18.4	48.4
	2000	405.2	194.6	132.2	21.0	57.5
	2001	489.9	237.2	156.8	26.5	69.5
	2002	624.2	299.3	203.0	34.3	87.5
	2003	747.0	361.7	239.7	35.1	110.4
北　京	Beijing	64.1	28.0	23.7	2.2	10.2
天　津	Tianjin	18.0	9.0	6.0	0.8	2.2
河　北	Hebei	7.7	4.1	2.7	0.3	0.6
山　西	Shanxi	11.3	5.8	3.3	0.5	1.7
内蒙古	Inner Mongolia	7.8	3.3	2.3	0.4	1.8
辽　宁	Liaoning	34.2	16.4	10.3	2.3	5.2
吉　林	Jilin	2.5	1.4	0.7	0.1	0.2
黑龙江	Heilongjiang	9.1	5.4	2.3	0.6	0.8
上　海	Shanghai	63.0	28.5	21.3	3.0	10.2
江　苏	Jiangsu	78.3	37.3	23.1	3.3	14.6
浙　江	Zhejiang	57.7	28.5	17.1	2.9	9.3
安　徽	Anhui	6.6	3.9	1.8	0.3	0.5
福　建	Fujian	32.5	17.3	9.5	1.7	3.9
江　西	Jiangxi	6.2	3.6	1.5	0.3	0.9
山　东	Shandong	51.2	25.0	14.2	2.7	9.3
河　南	Henan	14.8	8.6	3.8	0.6	1.7
湖　北	Hubei	26.8	13.1	8.8	1.4	3.5
湖　南	Hunan	16.1	8.3	4.8	0.8	2.2
广　东	Guangdong	164.1	77.6	59.1	7.2	20.2
广　西	Guangxi	5.1	2.4	1.6	0.2	0.8
海　南	Hainan					
重　庆	Chongqing	3.6	1.5	1.2	0.2	0.6
四　川	Sichuan	11.1	5.8	3.1	0.5	1.8
贵　州	Guizhou	20.8	9.8	7.0	1.0	3.1
云　南	Yunnan	5.1	2.8	1.3	0.3	0.7
西　藏	Tibet	6.2	2.9	2.0	0.3	1.0
陕　西	Shaanxi	10.6	5.0	3.4	0.4	1.7
甘　肃	Gansu	6.7	3.3	2.1	0.4	0.8
青　海	Qinghai	0.9	0.6	0.2		0.1
宁　夏	Ningxia	2.3	1.3	0.6	0.1	0.3
新　疆	Xinjiang	2.5	1.2	0.9	0.2	0.2

17-27　按业态分限额以上连锁零售企业基本情况

Basic Conditions of Enterprises Above Designated Size of Chain Store by Business Categries

指　标	Indicator	合计 Total 2002	合计 Total 2003	直营店 Direct Sale Shop 2002	直营店 Direct Sale Shop 2003	加盟店 League Shop 2002	加盟店 League Shop 2003
门店总数　　（个）	**Number of Stores (unit)**	**30746**	**39089**	**22157**	**26686**	**8589**	**12403**
＃百货店	Department Store	1550	2090	1143	1272	407	818
超级市场	Supermarket	10281	13494	7443	9358	2838	4136
专业店	Professional Shop	12177	15410	8766	10321	3411	5089
专卖店	Regie Shop	2901	3105	1403	1597	1498	1508
便利店	Neighbourhood Market	3324	4447	2911	3625	413	822
其他	Others	513	543	491	513	22	30
营业面积（万平方米）	**Operational Area (10 000 sq.m)**	**1733.0**	**2150.2**	**1510.2**	**1832.6**	**222.7**	**317.6**
＃百货店	Department Store	334.6	443.0	311.0	414.2	23.6	28.7
超级市场	Supermarket	930.5	1127.8	818.7	967.7	111.8	160.1
专业店	Professional Shop	352.6	420.6	281.5	317.5	71.1	103.1
专卖店	Regie Shop	34.2	43.8	24.6	32.5	9.6	11.2
便利店	Neighbourhood Market	43.5	62.6	37.1	48.5	6.3	14.1
其他	Others	37.6	52.5	37.3	52.1	0.3	0.5
从业人数　　（万人）	**Employed Person (10 000 person)**	**63.32**	**79.21**	**52.63**	**63.31**	**10.69**	**15.90**
＃百货店	Department Store	10.87	12.02	10.53	11.44	0.34	0.58
超级市场	Supermarket	31.01	38.60	24.84	29.65	6.17	8.95
专业店	Professional Shop	14.86	21.12	11.77	16.06	3.09	5.07
专卖店	Regie Shop	2.32	2.50	1.49	1.65	0.83	0.85
便利店	Neighbourhood Market	2.81	3.45	2.58	3.02	0.23	0.43
其他	Others	1.45	1.51	1.43	1.48	0.02	0.03
销售总额　　（亿元）	**Total Revenue of Sales (100 million yuan)**	**2658.3**	**3434.4**	**2295.9**	**2960.2**	**362.4**	**474.2**
＃百货店	Department Store	484.7	603.0	445.4	556.6	39.3	46.3
超级市场	Supermarket	1318.2	1726.5	1105.9	1446.8	212.3	279.7
专业店	Professional Shop	657.5	860.4	567.0	737.8	90.4	122.6
专卖店	Regie Shop	85.5	100.1	72.9	85.5	12.7	14.6
便利店	Neighbourhood Market	49.2	66.9	41.9	56.3	7.2	10.5
其他	Others	63.3	77.6	62.8	77.1	0.4	0.4
零售额　　（亿元）	**Retail Sails (100 million yuan)**	**2209.0**	**2890.3**	**1875.9**	**2450.1**	**333.0**	**440.3**
＃百货店	Department Store	431.9	533.7	395.0	492.3	36.8	41.4
超级市场	Supermarket	1098.1	1442.6	886.7	1163.6	211.4	279.0
专业店	Professional Shop	502.2	693.4	431.8	592.0	70.4	101.5
专卖店	Regie Shop	71.7	84.9	63.1	75.4	8.6	9.4
便利店	Neighbourhood Market	45.4	62.0	40.0	53.5	5.4	8.5
其他	Others	59.6	73.8	59.2	73.3	0.4	0.4

17-27 续 countinued

指 标	Indicator	合计 Total 2002	合计 Total 2003	直营店 Direct Sale Shop 2002	直营店 Direct Sale Shop 2003	加盟店 League Shop 2002	加盟店 League Shop 2003
利润总额 (亿元)	**Total Profits (100 million yuan)**	**23.1**	**31.3**	**23.1**	**31.3**		
#百货店	Department Store	8.0	5.9	8.0	5.9		
超级市场	Supermarket	4.9	11.0	4.9	11.0		
专业店	Professional Shop	8.8	14.0	8.8	14.0		
专卖店	Regie Shop	1.2	2.6	1.2	2.6		
便利店	Neighbourhood Market	-1.2	-2.3	-1.2	-2.3		
其他	Others	1.4	0.2	1.4	0.2		
资产总额 (亿元)	**Total Assets (100 million yuan)**	**937.1**	**1177.9**	**937.1**	**1177.9**		
#百货店	Department Store	231.6	275.2	231.6	275.2		
超级市场	Supermarket	408.3	513.6	408.3	513.6		
专业店	Professional Shop	207.7	272.4	207.7	272.4		
专卖店	Regie Shop	34.0	42.7	34.0	42.7		
便利店	Neighbourhood Market	17.5	26.5	17.5	26.5		
其他	Others	37.9	47.4	37.9	47.4		
负债总额 (亿元)	**Total Liabilities (100 million yuan)**	**703.5**	**891.8**	**703.5**	**891.8**		
#百货店	Department Store	167.3	206.1	167.3	206.1		
超级市场	Supermarket	318.8	411.8	318.8	411.8		
专业店	Professional Shop	149.9	193.9	149.9	193.9		
专卖店	Regie Shop	24.3	30.4	24.3	30.4		
便利店	Neighbourhood Market	14.8	19.1	14.8	19.1		
其他	Others	28.3	30.4	28.3	30.4		
配送中心数 (个)	**Number of Distribution Center (unit)**	**1202**	**1346**				
#百货店	Department Store	70	70				
超级市场	Supermarket	557	600				
专业店	Professional Shop	409	499				
专卖店	Regie Shop	90	90				
便利店	Neighbourhood Market	55	61				
其他	Others	21	26				
统一配送比重 (%)	**Proportion of Unification Distribution (%)**	**74.5**	**73.4**	**63.7**	**70.6**	**42.0**	**45.5**
#百货店	Department Store	40.4	45.7	39.6	45.6	40.3	32.1
超级市场	Supermarket	85.6	82.2	66.2	78.2	38.8	38.9
专业店	Professional Shop	75.0	78.8	77.7	79.0	49.5	66.3
专卖店	Regie Shop	57.7	60.8	56.3	57.9	50.8	49.7
便利店	Neighbourhood Market	92.8	91.5	85.5	84.1	38.7	34.6
其他	Others	40.4	33.7	40.2	33.5	25.1	21.5
自有配送比重 (%)	**Proportion of Owned Distribution (%)**	**50.4**	**49.2**	**43.6**	**48.1**	**30.8**	**34.1**
#百货店	Department Store	38.2	42.8	37.4	42.8	39.4	29.7
超级市场	Supermarket	49.7	43.4	37.8	42.5	22.3	22.0
专业店	Professional Shop	64.1	67.1	66.0	66.2	46.1	63.2
专卖店	Regie Shop	42.4	45.3	42.6	44.3	34.2	35.8
便利店	Neighbourhood Market	77.7	78.7	68.8	69.6	38.1	33.9
其他	Others	9.6	8.3	9.5	8.2	25.1	21.5
非自有配送比重 (%)	**Proportion of Non-owned Distribution (%)**	**24.0**	**24.0**	**19.9**	**22.3**	**11.2**	**11.5**
#百货店	Department Store	2.2	2.2	2.2	2.0	0.9	2.3
超级市场	Supermarket	35.8	38.7	28.2	35.6	16.6	16.9
专业店	Professional Shop	10.8	11.7	11.7	12.8	3.3	3.1
专卖店	Regie Shop	15.3	15.5	13.6	13.6	16.7	13.9
便利店	Neighbourhood Market	14.7	12.5	16.1	14.2	0.6	0.6
其他	Others	30.7	25.3	30.7	25.2		

17-28 按登记注册类型分限额以上连锁零售企业基本情况

Basic Conditions of Enterprises above Designated Size in Chain Store by Status of Registration

单位：亿元 (100 millon yuan)

登记注册类型	Status of Registration	资产总额 Total Assets		负债总额 Total Liablities	
		2002	2003	2002	2003
合　　计	**Total**	**937.1**	**1177.9**	**703.5**	**891.8**
内资企业	**Domestic Funded Enterprises**	**749.2**	**951.3**	**554.9**	**705.7**
国有企业	State-owned Enterprises	77.1	90.1	59.2	71.4
集体企业	Collective-owned Enterprises	17.8	20.6	11.2	12.8
股份合作企业	Cooperative Enterprises	15.9	16.5	11.4	12.1
联营企业	Joint Ownedship Enterprises	25.3	30.8	16.6	9.6
国有联营企业	State Joint Ownedship Enterprises	6.3	10.5	4.6	8.3
集体联营企业	Collective Joint Ownedship Enterprises				
国有与集体联营企业	Joint State-collective Enterprises	19.0	20.3	12.0	1.3
其他联营企业	Other Joint Ownership Enterprises				
有限责任公司	Limited Liability Coporations	237.0	308.3	181.3	241.4
国有独资公司	State Sole Funded Coporations	5.0	4.7	3.0	3.7
其他有限责任公司	Other Limited Liability Coporations	227.3	297.0	175.3	233.2
股份有限公司	Share-holding Coporations Ltd.	264.9	323.9	186.2	226.5
私营企业	Private Enterprises	109.6	158.7	87.5	129.7
私营独资企业	Private-funded Enterprises	4.8	6.3	3.2	4.5
私营合伙企业	Private Partetrship Enterprises	0.2	0.2	0.1	0.1
私营有限责任公司	Private Limited Liability Coporations	93.3	139.5	75.4	113.5
私营股份有限公司	Private Share-holding Coporations Ltd.	11.3	12.6	8.8	11.6
其他企业	Other Enterprises	1.7	2.3	1.6	2.2
港、澳、台商投资企业	**Enterprises with Funds from Hong Kong, Macao and Taiwan**	**78.4**	**95.4**	**62.1**	**78.1**
港、澳、台商合资经营企业	Joint-venture Enterprises	68.8	85.3	52.9	69.6
港、澳、台商合作经营企业	Cooperative Enterprises	0.7	0.9	0.4	0.4
港、澳、台商独资经营企业	Enterprises with Sole Investment	0.3	0.5	0.2	0.4
港、澳、台商投资股份有限公司	Share-holding Coporations Ltd. with Investment	8.5	8.8	8.5	7.8
外商投资企业	**Foreign Funded Enterprises**	**109.6**	**131.2**	**86.5**	**108.0**
中外合资经营企业	Joint-venture Enterprises	43.7	52.6	33.8	40.6
中外合作经营企业	Cooperative Enterprises	60.3	74.8	48.7	64.2
外资企业	Enterprises with Sole Foreign Investment	5.5	3.9	4.1	3.2
外商投资股份有限公司	Share-holdoing Coporations Ltd. with Foreign Investment				

17-28 续 continued

单位：亿元 (100 million yuan)

登记注册类型	Status of Registration	销售总额 Total Sales		#零售额 Retail		利润总额 Total Profits	
		2002	2003	2002	2003	2002	2003
合　计	**Total**	**2658.3**	**3434.4**	**2209.0**	**2890.3**	**23.1**	**31.3**
内资企业	**Domestic Funded Enterprises**	**2233.7**	**2866.7**	**1824.7**	**2384.2**	**24.0**	**32.0**
国有企业	State-owned Enterprises	157.7	190.5	135.7	163.4		-0.6
集体企业	Collective-owned Enterprises	36.8	48.6	34.5	45.6	1.1	1.3
股份合作企业	Cooperative Enterprises	25.5	29.8	22.8	27.0	-0.2	-0.2
联营企业	Joint Ownership Enterprises	87.8	91.1	54.5	66.7	0.7	0.6
国有联营企业	State Joint Ownership Enterprises	3.5	5.4	3.2	5.0		
集体联营企业	Collective Joint Ownership Enterprises						
国有与集体联营企业	Joint State-collective Enterprises	84.3	85.7	51.2	61.6	0.7	0.6
其他联营企业	Other Joint Ownership Enterprises						
有限责任公司	Limited Liability Corporations	731.3	959.9	607.2	797.2	6.4	8.0
国有独资公司	State Sole Funded Corporations	9.0	8.8	4.8	4.7		-0.2
其他有限责任公司	Other Limited Liability Corporations	711.2	935.4	595.4	782.1	6.3	7.1
股份有限公司	Share-holding Corporations Ltd.	898.9	1151.7	693.4	913.8	15.4	20.4
私营企业	Private Enterprises	290.2	388.7	271.4	364.5	0.5	2.4
私营独资企业	Private-funded Enterprises	9.2	11.3	7.5	9.5		0.1
私营合伙企业	Private Partnership Enterprises	1.6	1.4	0.8	0.7		
私营有限责任公司	Private Limited Liability Corporations	249.5	337.7	234.8	317.6	0.6	2.6
私营股份有限公司	Private Share-holding Corporations Ltd.	29.9	38.4	28.3	36.6	-0.2	-0.4
其他企业	Other Enterprises	5.5	6.4	5.2	6.0		0.1
港、澳、台商投资企业	**Enterprises with Funds from Hong Kong, Macao and Taiwan**	**170.6**	**229.5**	**169.9**	**228.8**	**-0.2**	**-2.1**
港、澳、台商合资经营企业	Joint-venture Enterprises	149.9	206.7	149.3	206.0	-0.3	-2.3
港、澳、台商合作经营企业	Cooperative Enterprises	1.0	1.1	1.0	1.1		
港、澳、台商独资经营企业	Enterprises with Sole Investment	1.1	1.7	1.1	1.6		
港、澳、台商投资股份有限公司	Share-holding Corporations Ltd. with Investmen	18.6	20.1	18.6	20.1		0.2
外商投资企业	**Foreign Funded Enterprises**	**254.0**	**338.2**	**214.3**	**277.3**	**-0.7**	**1.4**
中外合资经营企业	Joint-venture Enterprises	67.6	85.8	66.4	81.3	1.2	1.5
中外合作经营企业	Cooperative Enterprises	176.7	237.2	138.3	180.8	-1.5	
外资企业	Enterprises with Sole Foreign Investment	9.6	15.2	9.6	15.2	-0.5	-0.1
外商投资股份有限公司	Share-holding Corporations Ltd. with Foreign Investment						

17-29 亿元以上商品交易市场基本情况（2003年）

Basic Statistics on Commodity Exchange Markets of Turnover above 100 Million Yuan (2003)

市　　场	Market	市场数量（个）Nomber of Market (unit)	摊位数（个）Nmber of Booth (unit)	营业面积（万平方米）Operating Area (10 000 sq.m)	成交额（亿元）Turnover (100 million yuan)
全　　国	**National Total**	**3265**	**2148866**	**10984.0**	**21514.5**
综合市场	**Comprehensive Markets**	**1591**	**1315771**	**4430.9**	**8069.4**
工业品综合市场	Industrial Products Comprehensive Markets	415	500431	1834.1	3873.7
农产品综合市场	Farmer Produces Comprehensive Markets	820	488108	1415.9	3007.1
其他综合市场	Others Comprehensive Markets	356	327232	1180.9	1188.7
专业市场	**Special Markets**	**1664**	**825039**	**6534.0**	**13399.4**
纺织品服装鞋帽市场	Textile, Garments, Footgear, and Hats Markets	255	253027	823.7	2799.7
食品饮料烟酒市场	Food, Beverages, Tobacco, and Liquor Markets	115	45954	276.4	759.2
药材药品及医疗器材市场	Medicinal Materials, Medicine and Medical Instruments Markets	11	12929	66.8	114.9
家具市场	Furniture Markets	58	24724	340.6	233.9
小商品市场	Merchandise Markets	64	64068	147.3	482.9
文化音像书报杂志市场	Culture, Video Books, Newspapers and Magazines Markets	42	11430	42.3	185.5
旧货市场	Second Hand Markets	15	6863	33.6	34.5
机动车市场	Motor Vehicle Markets	104	12792	306.1	1071.7
金属材料市场	Metal Materials Markets	128	27626	476.2	2399.7
煤炭市场	Coal and Charcoal Markets	12	1421	926.2	43.1
木材市场	Wood Markets	30	4987	318.6	159.5
建材装饰材料市场	Buliding and Decoration Materials Markets	213	74789	885.9	1033.3
粮油市场	Grain and Oil Markets	42	6323	75.8	188.9
干鲜果品市场	Dried and Fresh Melons and Fruits Markets	65	20076	182.0	278.1
水产品市场	Aquatic Products Markets	64	27170	139.6	443.8
蔬菜市场	Vegetables Markets	152	104099	511.3	656.6
肉食禽蛋市场	Meat, Poultry and Eggs Markets	32	3490	42.8	99.1
土畜产品市场	Local and Livestock Products Markets	23	14886	51.2	86.0
农业生产资料市场	Agricultural Productions Markets	8	3729	18.1	33.0
其他专业市场	Other Specialty Markets	231	104656	869.6	2296.1
其他市场	**Others Markets**	**10**	**8056**	**19.1**	**45.7**

17-30 亿元以上商品交易市场摊位分类情况（2003年）

Classification of Commodity Exchange Markets of Turnover above 100 Million Yuan (2003)

单位：亿元 (100 million yuan)

类别	Classification	摊位数（个）Number of Booth (unit)	成交额 Turnover	批发 Wholesale Trade	零售 Retail Trade
全国	**National Total**	**2148866**	**21514.5**	**16832.6**	**4681.9**
食品、饮料、烟酒类	Food, Beverages, Tobacco and Liquor	795707	6077.4	4231.6	1845.7
#粮油果菜类	Grain, Oil, Fruit and Vegetable	487475	2988.7	1993.7	995.0
服装鞋帽、针、纺织品类	Garments, Footgear, Hats, Knitgoods and Textiles	657688	4583.0	3886.2	696.8
化妆品类	Cosmetics	29856	211.0	169.9	41.1
日用品类	Articles for Daily Use	150588	919.0	736.6	182.3
五金、电料类	Hardware & Electrical Materials	47141	421.3	355.3	65.9
体育、娱乐用品类	Sports & Recreational Articles	10548	65.8	59.4	6.5
书报杂志类	Newspapers and Magazines	3817	27.1	23.8	3.2
电子出版物及音像制品类	E-journal and Video Products	7068	62.1	47.6	14.6
家用电器和音像器材类	Household Appliances and Video Equipments	29441	380.9	293.1	87.8
中西药品类	Chinese Traditional Medicine and Western Medicine	16879	155.5	49.3	106.2
#中草药及中成药类	Chinese Herbal Medicine and Chinese Nostrum	15696	133.8	46.3	87.5
文化办公用品类	Cultural office Articles	33249	405.3	229.7	175.6
家具类	Furnitures	40402	378.3	208.8	169.5
煤炭及制品类	Coal and Related Products	1782	41.6	37.4	4.2
木材及制品类	Wood and Wooden Products	17827	428.9	368.2	60.7
化工材料及制品类	Raw Chemical Materials and Their Products	12970	830.4	818.0	12.3
金属材料类	Metal Materials	37096	2691.8	2484.6	207.2
建筑及装潢材料类	Building and Decoration Materials	68633	944.6	702.3	242.4
机电产品及设备类	Mechanical & Electrical Products	43218	1534.6	1031.4	503.3
#农机类	Agricultural Machinery	3144	76.1	73.0	3.1
汽车类	Automobile	16378	1037.0	596.4	440.6
其他类	Others	144956	1356.0	1099.5	256.5
#旧货类	Second Hand	11491	84.5	63.1	21.4

主要统计指标解释

社会消费品零售总额 指批发和零售业、餐饮业、新闻出版业、邮政业和其他服务业等，售予城乡居民用于生活消费的商品和社会集团用于公共消费的商品之总量。社会消费品零售总额包括：

一、批发和零售业企业（单位）：

1.售予城乡居民的各种生活消费品；

2.售予入境旅游的外国人、华侨、港澳台同胞的各类商品；

3.售予行政事业单位、社会团体、军队和武警等机构的商品，以及以零售方式售予各类企业的商品。具体包括：用于非生产和社会交往的办公用品，如通讯设备、计算器具和设备、电讯网络设备、文印设备、音像视听器材和设备、纸张、本册、文具及装订文印材料、家具、日用电器、针纺织品、清洁卫生用品、文体用品、奖品、纪念品、礼品等；供内部人员乘坐的交通工具和燃料；用于办公设施修缮的各类配件、材料、工具等；用于取暖和防暑降温的设备、燃料、材料及食品等；专用于教学的用品和设备；非营利医疗机构的中、西药品、中药材和医疗设备器材；非专用的劳动保护用品；不对外营业的内部食堂用的餐具、炊具、设备、清洁卫生工具和食品、燃料等；军队、武警用于其人员生活的衣着品和个人用品；其他各类非生产性设备和用品。

二、餐饮业出售的主食、菜肴、烟酒饮料和其他商品。

三、新闻出版业、邮政业售予城乡居民、企事业单位、军队和武警等机构的书报杂志、音像制品、邮品等。

四、其他服务业出售的食品、烟酒饮料、服装鞋帽、日常生活用品、医药保健用品、艺术品、工艺美术品、玩具、殡葬用品以及其他消费品。

批发零售贸易业商品购、销、存总额 指各种登记注册类型的批发、零售业企业(单位)以本企业(单位)为总体的，从国内、国外市场购进的商品总量，销售和出口的商品总量、库存商品总量等情况。该指标可以反映商品流转过程中商品的购进、销售、库存之间的比例关系和存在的问题。

商品购进总额 指从本企业(单位)以外的单位和个人购进(包括从境外直接进口)作为转卖或加工后转卖的商品总额。它反映批发零售贸易业从国内、国外市场上购进商品的总量。商品购进总额包括：(1)从工农业生产者购进的商品；(2)从出版社、报社的出版发行部门购进的图书、杂志和报纸；(3)从各种登记注册类型的批发零售贸易企业(单位)购进的商品；(4)从其他单位购进的商品，如从机关、团体、企业等单位购进的剩余物资，从餐饮业、服务业购进的商品，从海关、市场管理部门购进的缉私和没收的商品，从居民手中收购的废旧商品等；(5)从国(境)外直接进口的商品。不包括企业(单位)为自身经营用和未通过买卖行为而收入的商品以及销售退回、商品升溢等。

商品销售总额 指对本企业(单位)以外的单位和个人出售(包括对境外直接出口)的商品总额。它反映批发零售贸易业在国内市场上销售商品以及出口商品的总量。商品销售总额包括：(1)售给城乡居民和社会集团消费用的商品；(2)售给工业、农业、建筑业、运输邮电业、批发零售贸易业、餐饮业、服务业等作为生产、经营使用的商品；(3)售给批发零售贸易业作为转卖或加工后转卖的商品；(4)对国(境)外直接出口的商品。不包括出售本企业(单位)自用的废旧包装用品；未通过买卖行为付出的商品；经本单位介绍，由买卖双方直接结算，本单位只收取手续费的业务；购货退出的商品以及商品损耗和损失等。

批发零售贸易业库存 指报告期末各种登记注册类型的批发零售贸易企业(单位)已取得所有权的商品。它反映批发零售贸易企业(单位)的商品库存情况和对市场商品供应的保证程度。期末库存包括：(1)存放在批发零售贸易业经营单位(如门市部、批发站、经营处)仓库、货场、货柜和货架中的商品；(2)挑选、整理、包装中的商品；(3)已记入购进而尚未运到本单位的商品，即发货单或银行承兑凭证已到而货未到的部分；(4)寄放他处的商品，如因购货方拒绝承付而暂时存放在购货方的商品和已办完加工成品收回手续而未提回的商品；(5)委托其他单位代销(未作销售或调出)尚未售出的商品；(6)代其他单位购进尚未交付的商品。不包括所有权不属于本单位的商品、拨付除批发零售贸易业以外的其他行业所属独立核算加工厂等加工生产尚未收回成品的商品、代国家物资储备部门保管的商品等。

库存总额采用的计算价格是：农副产品采购单位按购进价计算；批发单位按进货价计算； 零售单位按核算价格计算，即按什么价格核算就按什么价格计算。

餐饮业营业收入 指餐饮企业、产业活动单位或个体户的全部营业额，包括商品零售额和其他服务性收入。其主要反映餐饮企业、活动单位或个体户的经营情况及发展变化趋势。

餐饮业商品零售额 指餐饮企业、产业活动单位或个体户直接对居民和社会集团零售的各种商品。包括：(1)经烹饪、调制加工后出售的各种食品，如主食、炒菜、凉拌菜等；(2)不经加工直接转卖的各种外购商品，如卷烟、酒、饮料、熟食、水果等；(3)附设非独立核算的专门销售商品的小卖部出售的各种食品及其他商品。

消费品市场成交额 指在全国消费品交易市场成交的全部商品金额。消费品市场包括农副产品市场和工业消费品市场。

亿元商品交易市场成交额 指年销售额达到亿元以上，经工商部门批准、专门从事商品批发、零售业务活动的市场。其市场所有摊位销售总额称为商品交易市场成交额。

连锁企业（或称连锁店、连锁公司） 指在核心企业或总店的领导下，由分散的、经营同类商品或服务的企业或活动单位，采取共同方针，实行集中采购和分散销售的有机结合，通过规范化经营，实现规模效益的经济联合组织形式。一般连锁店应由若干个分店组成。其经营特征：（1）经营同类商品；（2）使用统一商号；（3）统一采购配送，采购与销售相分离（部分商品可根据物流合理和保质保鲜原则，由供应商直接送货到门店，其余均由总部统一配送）。

连锁门店包括下列两种形式：

直营连锁：指正规连锁。连锁门店均由总部独资或控股开设，在总部的直接领导下统一经营。

加盟连锁：指特许连锁。各连锁门店（被特许人）通过合同形式，取得使用总部（特许人）商标、商号、经营技术和销售总部开发的商品的特许权，各加盟连锁门店为独立法人，在总部指导下统一经营。

Explanatory Notes on Main Statistical Indicators

Total Retail Sales of Consumer Goods refer to the sum of retail sales of commodities sold by wholesale, retail, catering, publishing, post and telecommunications and other service industries to urban and rural households for private consumption and to social institutions for public consumption. Retail sales of consumer goods include:

1)Sales by wholesale and retail units:

a)of consumer goods sold to urban and rural households

b)of commodities sold to foreigners, overseas Chinese and Chinese compatriots from Hong Kong, Macau and Taiwan visiting in China

c)of commodities sold to government agencies, institutions, social organizations, military and armed police units, and commodities sold to enterprises in the form of retail sales. More specifically, they include: office facilities and articles for non-production purposes such as communications equipment, computing equipment and instruments, TV and network equipment, printing and copying equipment, audio-visual equipment and instruments, paper, notebooks, stationeries, furniture, electric appliances, knitwear, sanitation and cleaning articles, cultural and sport articles, articles for prizes, souvenirs, etc.; transport vehicles and fuels for employees; materials, spare parts and tools for the maintenance of office facilities; equipment, fuels, materials and food for winter heating or summer cooling purposes; articles and equipment for teaching purpose; Chinese and western medicines and medical equipment and facilities purchased by non profit-making medical institutes; non-specialized work safety articles; cooking utensils, tableware, equipment, cleaning articles, food and fuels purchased by internal cafeterias; clothes and personal articles purchased by military or armed police units for their officials and soldiers; and other equipment and articles for non-production purposes.

2)Sales of stable food, cooked dishes, beverages, tobaccos and other articles by catering units.

3)Sales of books, newspapers, magazines, audio-visual products and post products by publishing, post and telecommunications departments to urban and rural households and to enterprises, institutions, military and armed police units.

4)Sales of food, beverages, tobaccos, clothing, hats, footwear, articles for daily use, medicines, medical and health articles, work of art, handicrafts, toys, funeral articles and other articles by other service industries.

Purchase, Sales and Stock of Commodities by Wholesale and Retail Trades refer to the total volume of commodities purchased, total volume of sales and exports, and the stock of commodities by wholesale and retail enterprises (establishments) of different status of registration from domestic and overseas markets. This indictor reflects the relationship among purchase, sales and stock of commodities in the circulation of goods and reveals the existing problems.

Total Purchases of Commodities refer to the total value of purchases of commodities by the enterprises (establishments) from other establishments or individuals (including direct import from abroad) for the purpose of re-selling, either with or without further processing of the commodities purchased. This indicator is used to show the total value of purchases of commodities by wholesale and retail establishments from domestic and overseas markets. The total purchases include: (1) agricultural and industrial products purchased from producers; (2) books, magazines and newspapers purchased from distribution departments of the publishers; (3) commodities purchased from wholesale and retail establishments of different status of registration; (4) commodities purchased from other units, such as surplus materials purchased from government agencies, enterprises or institutions, commodities purchased from catering and service establishments, confiscated goods purchased from customs authorities or market management agencies, second-hand goods and wastes purchased from residents; and (5) commodities directly imported from abroad. Excluded are commodities purchased by enterprises (establishments) for use in their own business operation, commodities obtained without buying or selling procedures, rejected commodities, etc.

Total Sales of Commodities refer to value of commodities sold by the establishments to other establishments and individuals (including direct export). This indicator is used to show the total value of sales of commodities at domestic markets and export. The total sales include: (1) commodities sold to urban and rural residents and social groups for their consumption; (2) commodities sold to establishments in industry, agriculture, construction, transportation, post and telecommunications, wholesale and retail trades, catering trade and public utility for their production and operation; (3) commodities sold to wholesale and retail establishments for re selling, with or without further processing; and (4)commodities for direct export to other countries. Excluded are selling of waste packaging materials used by the establishments (units) themselves, commodities transferred without buying or selling procedures, commission income from brokerage in transactions whose settlement is directly handled by buyers and sellers, rejected commodities in the purchase, loss in commodities, etc.

Commodity Stock of Wholesale and Retail Enterprises refers to total commodities possessed by wholesale and retail enterprises (units) of various types of registration status at the end of the reference period, which reflects the commodity stock level of various wholesale and retail enterprises and the potential for market supply. It includes: (1) commodities located in storage, garages, counters, and shelves of operating units (such as sale stores, wholesale centers, and operating offices) of wholesale and retail enterprises; (2) commodities in the process of selecting, sorting, and packing; (3) commodities not arrived but recorded as purchase in the account, i.e. commodities not arrived but payment receipts for the commodities from the sellers or the banks arrived; (4) commodities deposited in other places rather than places mentioned above, for instance: commodities in the hold of purchasers temporarily due to the refusal of payment and commodities not taken back after going through the formalities; (5) commodities entrusted to other units to sell but not sold yet; (6) commodities purchased for other units but not delivered yet. Commodities not included as stock are those not owned by the enterprises (units), those allocated to financially independent factories rather than wholesale and retail enterprises for processing but not taken back yet, and finally those put in stock by wholesale and retail enterprises on behalf of the state material reserves units.

For the calculation of the value of commodities stock, the value is calculated at purchasing prices in agricultural goods purchasing units and wholesale units, and at the accounting prices in retail units.

Business Income of Catering Industry: refer to the total turnover of catering businesses, establishments or individuals, including retail sales and other services income. It reflects the operational and managerial conditions and development trend of catering businesses, establishments and individuals in this sector.

Retail Sales of Commodities in Catering Industry: refer to retail sales to residents and social groups by catering enterprises, establishments and individual, including: (1) various food sold after cooking and processing, such as: staple food, cooked dishes, cold and dressed dishes and so on. (2) re-selling commodities without further processing, such as beverages, tobaccos, cooked food, fruits and so on. (3) food and other commodities sold in affiliated shops without independent accounting system.

Volume of Transaction at Consumer Goods Markets refers to the value of transaction of all goods at consumer goods markets in the country, including both markets for farm and sideline products and for industrial consumption goods.

Volume of Transaction at Large Commodity Markets (with transaction value over 100 million yuan) refers to markets approved by the industrial and commercial administration departments, which specialize in wholesale and retail of commodities with an annual sales of over 100 million yuan. The sum of sales of all sellers in the markets makes up the transaction value of the markets.

Chain Enterprises (also called chain stores or chain corporations) refer to a form of joint economic entities under which scattered enterprises or establishments engaged in providing homogeneous commodities or services, with the central leadership of core enterprise or headquarters and guided by common policies, conduct centralized purchase and distributed selling of commodities, in order to gain better efficiency through standardized operation. Consisting of a number of branch stores, the chain stores have in general following features: 1) homogeneous commodities, 2) unique name of stores, 3) centralized purchase and delivery which is separated from distributed selling operation (most commodities are delivered from the headquarters except some items which, from logistics, quality or freshness considerations, might be delivered by the suppliers directly).

Chain stores have two categories:

a) Chain stores under direct management: These are formal chain stores invested or controlled by the headquarters. They operate under the direct and unified management from the headquarters.

b) Chain stores through license arrangement: Through contracts, chain stores (their owners) obtain licenses from the headquarters to use designated trade marks, names, operation know-how, and to sell the commodity developed by the headquarters. Under this arrangement, each store in the chain is an independent legal entity and operates under the guidance from the headquarters.

十八、对外经济贸易

Foreign Trade and Economic Cooperation

简要说明

本篇资料综合反映中国的对外贸易、利用外资、对外经济合作的历年概况，重点反映对外经济贸易的近期发展状况。

一、对外贸易部分

对外贸易统计的主要内容包括：进出口货物的品种、数(重)量、金额、国别(地区)、经营单位、境内目的地、境内货源地、贸易方式、关别等项目。

对外贸易统计的范围是按照联合国的国际贸易统计原则制定的，即凡能引起中华人民共和国关境内物质资源存量增加或减少的进出口货物，除制度另有规定者外，均列入该项统计。

对外贸易统计的资料来源是海关总署，调查方法是全面调查。

特殊说明：1979年及以前为外贸业务统计数字，来源于原对外贸易经济合作部（现为商务部）；1980年及以后为海关进出口统计数字，来源于海关总署。

海关历年出口商品分类金额和海关历年进口商品分类金额按照联合国《国际贸易标准分类》(SITC)进行统计。海关进出口商品分类金额按照海关合作理事会制定的《商品名称及编码协调制度》(HS)目录进行统计。

我国对各国(地区)进出口总额表中，出口货物按中华人民共和国关境外最终目的国(地)，进口货物按中华人民共和国关境外原产国(地)统计。各地区进出口商品总值分别按境内经营单位所在地和目的地、货源地列示。经营单位所在地是指中华人民共和国关境内进出口企业报关注册的登记地；境内货源地是指出口货物在中华人民共和国关境内的产地或原始发货地；境内目的地则指进口货物在中华人民共和国关境内的消费、使用地或最终运抵地。

二、利用外资统计部分

利用外资统计的主要内容包括：对外借款、外商直接投资和外商其他投资，外商投资企业登记注册情况。

统计范围是凡经工商行政管理机关核准登记，在中华人民共和国境内所有利用外资的单位和部门，经批准设立的中外合资经营企业、合作经营企业、外资企业、外商投资股份制企业、合作开发项目等具有法人资格的独立核算企业(包括港澳台地区投资企业)，在华从事经营活动的外国及港澳台地区企业及外国公司在中国境内设立的分支机构。

利用外资统计的资料来源是商务部，其中，外商投资企业的登记注册情况资料来源于国家工商行政管理总局，调查方法是全面调查。

特殊说明：利用外资统计1985年及以前为政府统计部门的调查汇总数，1986年及以后全部来源于对外贸易经济合作部，现为商务部。

三、对外经济合作部分

对外经济合作统计的主要内容包括：对外承包工程、对外劳务合作、对外设计咨询的合同数、合同金额、完成营业额和按国别、地区分的对外经济合作完成营业额等。

统计范围是对外承包工程、对外劳务合作、对外设计咨询。

该制度统计单位是经各级商务部门批准的从事对外承包和劳务合作业务并具有法人地位的对外承包劳务企业。

资料来源是商务部，调查方法是全面调查。

四、其他

历年人民币对美元、日元、港币的年平均汇价，资料来源于国家外汇管理局，各年的年平均汇价是根据当年国家外汇管理局公布的每日汇价进行加权平均计算而得出的。

Brief Introduction

Data in this chapter show the summary data of Chinas foreign trade, utilization of foreign capital, contracted projects and labour cooperation with the foreign countries or territories over the years, focusing on the recent situation of foreign trade and economic cooperation.

I. Foreign Trade

Data on foreign trade include: varieties of imports and exports, amount (weight), value, countries (regions), imports and exports corporations, destination within territory, origin of goods within territory, means of trade, types of taxes and so on.

The coverage of foreign trade statistics are designed according to principle on international trade by United Nations, that is: all imports or exports that will lead to stock changes of material resources with the territory of People's Republic of China; excluding goods by escape clause.

Sources of data on foreign trade are from General Administration of Customs of the People's Republic of China through comprehensive reporting system.

Special notice: Data in the years prior to 1980 were statistical data of foreign trade and come from the former Ministry of Foreign Trade and Economic Cooperation (current Ministry of Commerce). Since 1980, the data have been the statistical data of customs on imports and exports and come from the General Administration of Customs.

Customs statistics on value term imports and exports by categories are using the UN Standard International Trade Classification (SITC). However, the Harmonized Commodity Description and Coding System (HS) stipulated by the Customs Cooperation Council is used in the classification of the import and export commodities.

In the table on China's total imports and exports with related countries and regions, the export commodities are calculated at the customs of the countries (regions) of destination and the import commodities are calculated at the customs of the countries (regions) of origin. The total values of the import and export commodities by region are calculated respectively at the provinces where the import or export corporations are situated and at the provinces of destination or provinces of origin within the boundary of the People's Republic of China. The province where the import or export corporations are situated refers to the province where the import or export corporations have applied to and have been registered at the customs. The province of origin within the boundary of the Peoples Republic of China refers to the province where the export commodities are produced or originally delivered. The province of destination within the boundary of the Peoples Republic of China refers to the province where the import commodities are consumed, used or transported to the destination.

II. Statistics on Utilization of Foreign Capitals

Utilization of foreign capitals includes: foreign loans, foreign direct investments and other foreign investments, and the basic condition of registration of foreign funded enterprises.

The statistics cover all the units and departments which have utilized foreign capital and all the Sino-foreign joint ventures, Sino-foreign cooperative enterprises, ventures exclusively with foreign investment, foreign-funded stock companies, Sino-foreign cooperative development projects and other corporate enterprises (including the enterprises funded by the entrepreneurs from Hong Kong, Macao and Taiwan) with independent accounting system which have been approved by the Chinese government to set up in the boundary of the People's Republic of China.

Data on utilization of foreign capitals are from Ministry of Commerce, of which, data on basic condition of registration of foreign funded enterprises are from State Administration for Industry and Commerce through comprehensive reporting system.

Special notice: data on utilization of foreign capitals before 1985 were survey results fro governmental statistical agencies, since 1986 all data are from Ministry of Commerce (former MOFTEC).

III. Foreign Economic Cooperation

Data on foreign economic cooperation include: contracted projects, labour services cooperation, design and consultation services, contracted volume, complete business turnover, business turnover by countries (regions) and so on.

The statistics cover contracted projects, labour services cooperation and design and consultation service with foreign countries.

The statistical unit in the scheme is the corporate enterprise engaged in contracted projects and labour services cooperation with foreign countries and has been approved by the departments commerce at various levels.

Data on foreign economic cooperation are from Ministry of Commerce through comprehensive reporting system.

IV. Others

The average exchange rates of RMB yuan to US dollar, Japanese yen and Hong Kong dollar over the years come from the State Administration of Exchange Control. The annual average exchange rate is calculated as the weighted mean of the daily exchange rates provided by the State Administration of Foreign Exchange in the year.

18-1 对外经济贸易基本情况
Foreign Trade and Economic Cooperation

指　标	Item	1999	2000	2001	2002	2003
进出口总额　（人民币亿元）	**Total Value of Imports and Exports (RMB 100 million yuan)**	**29896.2**	**39273.2**	**42183.6**	**51378.2**	**70483.5**
出口总额	Total Exports	16159.8	20634.4	22024.4	26947.9	36287.9
进口总额	Total Imports	13736.4	18638.8	20159.2	24430.3	34195.6
进出口差额	Balance	2423.4	1995.6	1865.2	2517.6	2092.3
进出口总额　（亿美元）	**Total Value of Imports and Exports (USD 100 million)**	**3606.3**	**4742.9**	**5096.5**	**6207.7**	**8509.9**
出口总额	Total Exports	1949.3	2492.0	2661.0	3256.0	4382.3
初级产品	Primary Goods	199.4	254.6	263.4	285.4	348.1
工业制成品	Manufactured Goods	1749.9	2237.4	2397.6	2970.6	4034.2
进口总额	Total Imports	1657.0	2250.9	2435.5	2951.7	4127.6
初级产品	Primary Goods	268.5	467.4	457.4	492.7	727.6
工业制成品	Manufactured Goods	1388.5	1783.5	1978.1	2459.0	3400.0
进出口差额	Balance	292.3	241.1	225.5	304.3	254.7
合同利用外资项目　（个）	**Number of Projects for Contracted Foreign Capital (unit)**	**17022**	**22347**	**26140**	**34171**	**41081**
对外借款	Foreign Loans	104				
外商直接投资	Foreign Direct Investments	16918	22347	26140	34171	41081
合同利用外资额　（亿美元）	**Total Amount of Contracted Foreign Capital (USD 100 million)**	**520.09**	**711.30**	**719.76**	**847.51**	**1169.01**
对外借款	Foreign Loans	83.60				
外商直接投资	Foreign Direct Investments	412.23	623.80	691.95	827.68	1150.70
外商其他投资	Other Foreign Investments	24.26	87.50	27.81	19.82	18.32
实际利用外资额　（亿美元）	**Total Amount of Foreign Capital Actually Utilized (USD 100 million)**	**526.59**	**593.56**	**496.72**	**550.11**	**561.40**
对外借款	Foreign Loans	102.12	100.00			
外商直接投资	Foreign Direct Investments	403.19	407.15	468.78	527.43	535.05
外商其他投资	Other Foreign Investments	21.28	86.41	27.94	22.68	26.35
外商投资企业基本情况	**Registered Foreign-funded Enterprises**					
年底登记户数　（户）	Number of Registered Enterprises (household)	212436	203208	202306	208056	226373
投资总额　（亿美元）	Total Investment (USD 100 million)	7785.68	8246.75	8750.11	9818.93	11173.51
注册资本　（亿美元）	Registered Capital (USD 100 million)	4635.49	4839.50	5057.93	5521.19	6226.41
#外方	Capital from Foreign Partners	3166.82	3371.99	3596.83	4020.00	4657.79
对外经济合作　（亿美元）	**Economic Cooperation with Foreign Countries & Territories (USD 100 million)**					
合同金额	Contracted Value	130.02	149.43	164.55	178.91	209.30
#对外承包工程	Contracted Projects	101.99	117.19	130.39	150.55	176.67
对外劳务合作	Labor Services	26.32	29.91	33.28	27.52	30.87
完成营业额	Value of Business Fulfilled	112.35	113.25	121.39	143.52	172.34
#对外承包工程	Contracted Projects	85.22	83.79	88.99	111.94	138.37
对外劳务合作	Labor Services	26.23	28.13	31.77	30.71	33.09

注：2000年至2003年合同利用外资数据中未包括对外借款；2001年至2003年实际利用外资额未包括对外借款（18-13、18-14表类同）。

a) Data of contracted foreign capital from 2000 to 2003 don't include foreign loans. Data of total amount of foreign capital actually utilized from 2001 to 2003 don't include foreign loans. Similarly in Table 18-13 and 18-14.

18-2 人民币对主要外币年平均汇价(中间价)

Average Exchange Rate of RMB Yuan Against Main Convertible Currencies (Middle Rate)

单位：人民币元 (RMB yuan)

年 份 Year	100美元 100 US Dollars	100日元 100 Japanese Yen	100港元 100 Hong Kong Dollars	100欧元 100 Euros
1985	293.66	1.2457	37.57	
1986	345.28	2.0694	44.22	
1987	372.21	2.5799	47.74	
1988	372.21	2.9082	47.70	
1989	376.51	2.7360	48.28	
1990	478.32	3.3233	61.39	
1991	532.33	3.9602	68.45	
1992	551.46	4.3608	71.24	
1993	576.20	5.2020	74.41	
1994	861.87	8.4370	111.53	
1995	835.10	8.9225	107.96	
1996	831.42	7.6352	107.51	
1997	828.98	6.8600	107.09	
1998	827.91	6.3488	106.88	
1999	827.83	7.2932	106.66	
2000	827.84	7.6864	106.18	
2001	827.70	6.8075	106.08	
2002	827.70	6.6237	106.07	800.58
2003	827.70	7.1466	106.24	936.13

注：欧元自2002年开始进入市场流通。

a) ECU enters the circulating market since 2002.

18-3 进出口贸易总额

Total Value of Imports and Exports

本表1978年为外贸业务统计数，1980年起为海关进出口统计数。

Data in 1978 were obtained from the Ministry of Foreign Trade, and the data since 1980 have been obtained from the customs statistics.

年 份 Year	人 民 币 (亿元) 100 million Yuan				美 元 (亿元) USD 100 million			
	进出口总额 Total Imports & Exports	出口总额 Total Exports	进口总额 Total Imports	差 额 Balance	进出口总额 Total Imports & Exports	出口总额 Total Exports	进口总额 Total Imports	差 额 Balance
1978	355.0	167.6	187.4	-19.8	206.4	97.5	108.9	-11.4
1980	570.0	271.2	298.8	-27.6	381.4	181.2	200.2	-19.0
1985	2066.7	808.9	1257.8	-448.9	696.0	273.5	422.5	-149.0
1989	4156.0	1956.1	2199.9	-243.8	1116.8	525.4	591.4	-66.0
1990	5560.1	2985.8	2574.3	411.5	1154.4	620.9	533.5	87.4
1991	7225.8	3827.1	3398.7	428.4	1357.0	719.1	637.9	81.2
1992	9119.6	4676.3	4443.3	233.0	1655.3	849.4	805.9	43.5
1993	11271.0	5284.8	5986.2	-701.4	1957.0	917.4	1039.6	-122.2
1994	20381.9	10421.8	9960.1	461.7	2366.2	1210.1	1156.1	54.0
1995	23499.9	12451.8	11048.1	1403.7	2808.6	1487.8	1320.8	167.0
1996	24133.8	12576.4	11557.4	1019.0	2898.8	1510.5	1388.3	122.2
1997	26967.2	15160.7	11806.5	3354.2	3251.6	1827.9	1423.7	404.2
1998	26849.7	15223.6	11626.1	3597.5	3239.5	1837.1	1402.4	434.7
1999	29896.2	16159.8	13736.4	2423.4	3606.3	1949.3	1657.0	292.3
2000	39273.2	20634.4	18638.8	1995.6	4742.9	2492.0	2250.9	241.1
2001	42183.6	22024.4	20159.2	1865.2	5096.5	2661.0	2435.5	225.5
2002	51378.2	26947.9	24430.3	2517.6	6207.7	3256.0	2951.7	304.3
2003	70483.5	36287.9	34195.6	2092.3	8509.9	4382.3	4127.6	254.7

注：进出口差额负数为入超。

a) A negative balance indicates an unfavourable balance of foreign trade.

18-4 海关历年出口商品分类金额

Value of Exports by Category of Commodities (Customs Statistics)

单位: 亿美元 (USD 100 million)

年份 Year	总额 Total	初级产品 Primary Goods	食品及主要供食用的活动物 Food and Live Animals Used Chiefly for Food	饮料及烟类 Beverages and Tobacco	非食用原料 Non-Edible Raw Materials	矿物燃料、润滑油及有关原料 Mineral Fuels, Lubricants and Related Materials	动、植物油脂及蜡 Animal and Vegetable Oils, Fats and Wax
1980	181.19	91.14	29.85	0.78	17.11	42.80	0.60
1985	273.50	138.28	38.03	1.05	26.53	71.32	1.35
1989	525.38	150.78	61.45	3.14	42.12	43.21	0.86
1990	620.91	158.86	66.09	3.42	35.37	52.37	1.61
1991	719.10	161.45	72.26	5.29	34.86	47.54	1.50
1992	849.40	170.04	83.09	7.20	31.43	46.93	1.39
1993	917.44	166.66	83.99	9.01	30.52	41.09	2.05
1994	1210.06	197.08	100.15	10.02	41.27	40.69	4.95
1995	1487.80	214.85	99.54	13.70	43.75	53.32	4.54
1996	1510.48	219.25	102.31	13.42	40.45	59.31	3.76
1997	1827.92	239.53	110.75	10.49	41.95	69.87	6.47
1998	1837.09	204.89	105.13	9.75	35.19	51.75	3.07
1999	1949.31	199.41	104.58	7.71	39.21	46.59	1.32
2000	2492.03	254.60	122.82	7.45	44.62	78.55	1.16
2001	2660.98	263.38	127.77	8.73	41.72	84.05	1.11
2002	3255.96	285.40	146.21	9.84	44.02	84.35	0.98
2003	4382.28	348.12	175.31	10.19	50.32	111.14	1.15

18-4 续表 continued

单位: 亿美元 (USD 100 million)

年份 Year	工业制成品 Manufactured Goods	化学品及有关产品 Chemicals and Related Products	轻纺产品、橡胶制品矿冶产品及其制品 Light and Textile Industrial Products, Rubber Products, Minerals Metal-lurgical Products	机械及运输设备 Machinery and Transport Equipment	杂项制品 Miscellaneous Products	未分类的其他商品 Products Not Otherwise Classified
1980	90.05	11.20	39.99	8.43	28.36	2.07
1985	135.22	13.58	44.93	7.72	34.86	34.13
1989	374.60	32.01	108.97	38.74	107.55	87.33
1990	462.05	37.30	125.76	55.88	126.86	116.25
1991	556.98	38.18	144.56	71.49	166.20	136.55
1992	679.36	43.48	161.35	132.19	342.34	
1993	750.78	46.23	163.92	152.82	387.81	
1994	1012.98	62.36	232.18	218.95	499.37	0.12
1995	1272.95	90.94	322.40	314.07	545.48	0.06
1996	1291.23	88.77	284.98	353.12	564.24	0.12
1997	1588.39	102.27	344.32	437.09	704.67	0.04
1998	1632.20	103.21	324.77	502.17	702.00	0.05
1999	1749.90	103.73	332.62	588.36	725.10	0.09
2000	2237.43	120.98	425.46	826.00	862.78	2.21
2001	2397.60	133.52	438.13	949.01	871.10	5.84
2002	2970.56	153.25	529.55	1269.76	1011.53	6.48
2003	4034.16	195.81	690.18	1877.73	1260.88	9.56

18-5 海关历年进口商品分类金额

Value of Imports by Category of Commodities (Customs Statistics)

单位: 亿美元 (USD 100 million)

年 份 Year	总 额 Total	初级产品 Primary Goods	食品及主要供食用的活动物 Food and Live Animals Chiefly for Food	饮料及烟类 Beverages and Tobacco	非食用原料 Non-edible Raw Materials	矿物燃料、润滑油及有关原料 Mineral Fuels, Lubricants and Related Materials	动、植物油脂及蜡 Animal and Vegetable Oils, Fats and Waxes
1980	200.17	69.59	29.27	0.36	35.54	2.03	2.39
1985	422.52	52.89	15.53	2.06	32.36	1.72	1.22
1989	591.40	117.54	41.92	2.02	48.35	16.50	8.75
1990	533.45	98.53	33.35	1.57	41.07	12.72	9.82
1991	637.91	108.34	27.99	2.00	50.03	21.13	7.19
1992	805.85	132.55	31.46	2.39	57.75	35.70	5.25
1993	1039.59	142.10	22.06	2.45	54.38	58.19	5.02
1994	1156.14	164.86	31.37	0.68	74.37	40.35	18.09
1995	1320.84	244.17	61.32	3.94	101.59	51.27	26.05
1996	1388.33	254.41	56.72	4.97	106.98	68.77	16.97
1997	1423.70	286.20	43.04	3.20	120.06	103.06	16.84
1998	1402.37	229.49	37.88	1.79	107.15	67.76	14.91
1999	1656.99	268.46	36.19	2.08	127.40	89.12	13.67
2000	2250.94	467.39	47.58	3.64	200.03	206.37	9.77
2001	2435.53	457.43	49.76	4.12	221.27	174.66	7.63
2002	2951.70	492.71	52.38	3.87	227.36	192.85	16.25
2003	4127.60	727.63	59.60	4.90	341.24	291.89	30.00

18-5 续表 continued

单位: 亿美元 (USD 100 million)

年 份 Year	工业制成品 Manufactured Goods	化学品及有关产品 Chemicals and Related Products	轻纺产品、橡胶制品矿冶产品及其制品 Light and Textile Industrial Products, Rubber Products, Minerals and Metallurgical Products	机械及运输设备 Machinery and Transport Equipment	杂项制品 Miscellaneous Products	未分类的其他商品 Products Not Otherwise Classified
1980	130.58	29.09	41.54	51.19	5.42	3.34
1985	369.63	44.69	118.98	162.39	19.02	24.55
1989	473.86	75.56	123.35	182.07	20.73	72.15
1990	434.92	66.48	89.06	168.45	21.03	89.90
1991	529.57	92.77	104.93	196.01	24.39	111.47
1992	673.30	111.57	192.73	313.12	55.88	
1993	897.49	97.04	285.27	450.23	64.95	
1994	991.28	121.30	280.84	514.67	67.68	6.79
1995	1075.67	172.99	287.72	526.42	82.61	6.93
1996	1133.92	181.06	313.91	547.63	84.86	6.46
1997	1137.50	192.97	322.20	527.74	85.50	9.09
1998	1172.88	201.58	310.75	568.45	84.56	7.54
1999	1388.53	240.30	343.17	694.53	97.01	13.52
2000	1783.55	302.13	418.07	919.31	127.51	16.53
2001	1978.10	321.04	419.38	1070.15	150.76	16.76
2002	2458.99	390.36	484.89	1370.10	198.01	15.64
2003	3399.96	489.75	639.02	1928.26	330.11	12.82

18-6 海关进出口商品分类金额

Value of Imports and Exports by Category of Commodities (Customs Statistics)

单位：亿美元 (USD 100 million)

商品类别	Categories of Commodities	2002 出口 Exports	2002 进口 Imports	2003 出口 Exports	2003 进口 Imports
总　　额	**Total Value**	**3255.96**	**2951.70**	**4382.28**	**4127.60**
活动物；动物产品	**Live Animals & Animal Products**	**47.30**	**27.09**	**52.71**	**33.08**
活动物	Live Animals	3.44	0.53	3.27	1.17
肉及食用杂碎	Meat and Edible Haslets	6.65	6.27	6.46	7.58
鱼、甲壳动物、软体动物及其他水生无脊椎动物	Fish; Shellfish; Molluscs and Other Aquatic Invertebrates	28.73	15.65	33.35	18.65
乳品；蛋品；天然蜂蜜；其他食用动物产品	Dairy Products; Eggs; Natural Honey;	1.94	2.72	2.22	3.50
植物产品	**Vegetables; Fruits and Cereals**	**58.61**	**40.63**	**75.79**	**71.74**
食用蔬菜、根及块茎	Edible Vegetables; Roots and Stem Tubers	18.83	1.94	21.80	2.42
食用水果及坚果;甜瓜或柑桔属水果的果皮	Edible Fruits and Nuts; Muskmelon and Orange Peels	5.55	3.78	7.52	4.96
咖啡、茶、马黛茶及调味香料	Coffee; Tea and Spices	5.52	0.23	6.24	0.28
谷物	Cereals	16.50	4.82	25.89	4.44
含油子仁及果实；杂项子仁及果实；工业用或药用植物；稻草、秸秆及饲料	Oil Seeds and Kernels and Oleaginous Fruits; Other Seeds and Kernels and Fruits; Plants for Industrial and Medicinal Use; Straws and Forage	9.40	27.77	11.25	56.60
动植物油脂及分解产品；精制食用油脂；动植物蜡	**Animal and Vegetable Oils; Fats and Wax; Refined Edible Oils and Fats**	**1.08**	**15.80**	**1.28**	**29.25**
食品、饮料、酒及醋；烟草及代用品的制品	**Food; Beverages; Liquor and Vinegar; Tobacco and Tobacco Substitutes**	**67.01**	**19.79**	**76.69**	**21.07**
肉鱼甲壳和软体动物及其他水生无脊椎动物制品	Meat; Fish and Shellfish Products Mollusks and Other Aquatic Products	23.27	0.19	26.79	0.27
糖及糖食	Sugar and Sugar Products	2.27	2.80	1.96	2.16
谷物、粮食粉、淀粉或乳的制品；糕饼点心	Cereals; Grain; Starches or Milk and Pastry Products	4.54	1.49	5.27	1.48
蔬菜水果坚果或植物其他部分的制品	Products of Vegetables; Fruits and Nuts	17.57	1.10	21.68	1.34
饮料、酒及醋	Beverages; Liquor and Vinegar	5.97	1.48	6.22	1.86
烟草、烟草及烟草代用品的制品	Tobacco; Products of Tobacco & Tobacco	4.33	2.43	4.93	3.07
矿产品	**Minerals**	**98.39**	**244.78**	**127.35**	**377.03**
盐；硫磺；泥土及石料；石膏料、石灰及水泥	Salt; Sulphur; Clay and Rock; Plaster Stone; Lime and Cement	12.23	8.76	13.68	12.81
矿砂、矿渣及矿灰	Ore; Slag and Mortar	1.81	42.81	2.53	71.75
矿物燃料、矿物油及蒸馏产品;沥青物质;矿物蜡	Mineral Fuels; Lubricants; Asphalt; Mineral Wax	84.35	193.21	111.14	292.48
化学工业及其相关工业的产品	**Chemicals and Related Products**	**146.14**	**243.02**	**185.27**	**317.89**
有机化学品	Organic Chemicals	55.67	111.56	71.31	160.06
药品	Medicinal and Pharmaceutical Products	7.90	11.30	9.18	13.92
肥料	Fertilizers	3.50	23.53	8.00	17.63
鞣料和染料浸膏;鞣酸及衍生物;染颜料及其他着色料;油漆清漆;油灰及类似胶粘剂；墨水、油墨	Tanning and Dyeing Extracts; Tannic Acid; and Dyeing Materials; Paint and Lacquer; Putty; Ink and Printing Ink	13.87	20.88	15.26	25.83
精油及香膏；芳香料制品及化妆盥洗品	Essential Oils and Perfumed Materials; Cosmetics	5.18	2.01	7.61	2.81
塑料及其制品；橡胶及其制品	**Plastics and Related Products; Rubber and Related Products**	**100.27**	**198.46**	**125.32**	**247.45**
塑料及其制品	Plastics and Related Products	80.36	173.78	99.78	210.30
橡胶及其制品	Rubber and Related Products	19.91	24.68	25.54	37.15
生皮、皮革、毛皮及制品；鞍具挽具;旅行用品、手提包及类似物品；动物肠线(蚕胶丝除外)制品	**Raw Hides; Leather; Furs and Related Products; Saddle; Travel Articles; Handbags and Similar Containers**	**93.33**	**35.38**	**115.73**	**41.22**
生皮(毛皮除外)及皮革	Raw Hides and Leather	9.65	32.61	11.49	37.66
皮革制品；鞍具挽具；旅行用品、手提包及类似容器；动物肠线制品	Leather Products; Saddle; Travel Articles; Handbags and Similar Containers	78.28	0.91	95.11	1.28
毛皮、人造毛皮及其制品	Furs; Artificial Furs and Related Products	5.40	1.86	9.12	2.28
木及木制品；木炭；软木及软木制品；稻草、秸秆、针茅或其他编结材料制品；篮筐及柳条编结品	**Wood and Wooden Products; Charcoal; Cork and Related Products; Straws; Plaited Products; Baskets and Wickerwork**	**35.66**	**41.69**	**43.59**	**46.67**
木浆及其他纤维状纤维素浆;纸及纸板的废碎品；纸、纸板及其制品	**Paper Pulp and Cellulose Pulp; Paper and Waste Paper; Paperboard and Related**	**23.39**	**73.74**	**30.30**	**86.30**
木浆及其他纤维状纤维素浆;纸及纸板的废碎品	Paper Pulp and Cellulose Pulp; Paper and Paper Board Waste	0.16	29.00	0.21	38.92
纸及纸板;纸浆、纸或纸板制品	Paper and Paperboard; Articles of Paper Pulp or Paper and Paperboard Products	17.08	41.37	23.06	43.93

18-6 续表 continued

单位: 亿美元 (USD 100 million)

商品类别	Categories of Commodities	2002		2003	
		出口 Exports	进口 Imports	出口 Exports	进口 Imports
纺织原料及纺织制品	**Textile Materials and Products**	**578.49**	**169.93**	**733.46**	**192.92**
蚕丝	Natural Silk	7.67	0.96	8.24	1.10
羊毛、动物细毛或粗毛；马毛纱线及其机织物	Wool; Wool Yarn and Woolen Woven Fabrics	10.69	18.31	13.17	16.83
棉花	Cotton	48.94	33.27	62.20	46.50
其他植物纺织纤维；纸纱线及其机织物	Other Textile Fiber; Yarn and Related Woven Fabrics	5.02	3.35	5.26	4.35
化学纤维长丝	Chemical Fiber; Continuous Filament	24.26	33.32	37.52	36.03
化学纤维短纤	Chemical Fiber; Staple Fiber	25.23	29.95	27.87	32.61
絮胎毡呢及无纺织物;特种纱线;线绳索缆及制品	Wadding; Felt and Adhesive-Bond Fabrics; Special Yarn; Thread; Rope; Cable and Related	3.65	4.34	4.69	5.25
地毯及纺织材料的其他铺地制品	Carpets and Related Products	5.57	0.35	6.38	0.47
特种机织物；簇绒织物；花边；装饰毯；装饰带；刺绣品	Special Woven Fabrics; Lace; Embroidery	11.55	6.47	15.55	7.07
浸渍、涂布、包覆或层压纺织物；工业用纺织制品	Coated Textiles; Textile Products for Industrial Use	6.24	11.95	8.26	12.25
针织物及钩编织物	Knitwear and Crocheted Fabrics	20.06	14.32	25.08	16.40
针织或钩编织的服装及衣着附件	Knitted or Crocheted Garments & Clothing Accessories	159.84	5.23	206.78	5.57
非针织或钩编织的服装及衣着附件	Garments Not Knitted or Crocheted	205.83	7.65	250.79	7.84
其他纺织制成品；成套物品；旧衣着旧纺织品；碎织物	Other Textile Products; Secondhand Garments	43.95	0.44	61.69	0.66
鞋、帽、伞、杖、鞭及其零件;已加工的羽毛及其制品;人造花;人发制品	**Footwear; Headgear; Umbrellas; Canes; Whips; Processed Feather; Artificial Flowers; Wigs**	**134.05**	**4.00**	**156.29**	**4.87**
鞋靴、护裙和类似品及其零件	Parts of Footwear; Gaiters	110.90	3.04	129.55	3.74
帽类及其零件	Headgear And Accessories	7.47	0.06	9.39	0.07
雨伞阳伞、手杖、鞭子马鞭及其零件	Umbrellas; Canes; Whips and Accessories	5.90	0.11	6.73	0.11
已加工羽毛、羽绒及其制品；人造花；人发制品	Processed Feathers and Related Products; Artificial Flowers; Wigs	9.78	0.78	10.62	0.95
石料石膏水泥石棉云母及类似材料的制品；陶瓷产品；玻璃及其制品	**Gypsum; Cement; Asbestos; Mica; Ceramic Glass**	**54.61**	**20.82**	**69.34**	**26.28**
石料、石膏、水泥、石棉、云母及类似材料制品	Gypsum; Cement; Asbestos; Mica and Related Products	13.14	2.69	16.13	3.42
陶瓷产品	Ceramics	23.33	1.47	29.58	2.24
玻璃及其制品	Glass and Glassware	18.14	16.67	23.63	20.63
天然或养殖珍珠、宝石或半宝石、贵金属、包贵金属及其制品;仿首饰硬币	**Natural or Cultivated Pearls; Precious or Semi-Stones; Jewelry of Precious Metal or Rolled Precious Metal; Artificial Jewelry; Coins**	**28.43**	**13.32**	**32.95**	**18.47**
贱金属及其制品	**Base Metals and Related Products**	**189.07**	**262.81**	**251.20**	**393.84**
钢铁	Iron and Steel	23.07	132.40	34.17	222.23
钢铁制品	Iron and Steel Products	72.62	27.71	94.47	33.73
铜及其制品	Copper and Related Products	7.52	56.68	9.52	71.66
镍及其制品	Nickel and Related Products	0.51	4.27	1.26	8.96
铝及其制品	Aluminium and Related Products	22.85	24.41	33.93	33.54
铅及其制品	Lead and Related Products	2.43	0.37	2.42	0.48
锌及其制品	Zinc and Related Products	4.92	3.12	5.26	4.18
锡及其制品	Tin and Related Products	1.66	1.11	1.91	1.34
机器、机械器具、电气设备及零件；录音机及放声机、电视图象声音的录制和重放设备及零附件	**Machinery; Electric Equipment and Accessories; Recorders; Video Recorder and Accessories**	**1159.21**	**1253.88**	**1723.34**	**1754.09**
车辆、航空器、船舶及有关运输设备	**Locomotives; Vehicles; Aircraft; Ship and Related Transportation Equipment**	**105.48**	**115.19**	**155.92**	**175.07**
铁道及电车道机车、车辆及零件；铁道及电车轨道固定装置及零附件;各种机械(电动);交通信号设备	Rail Locomotives; Tramcars and Accessories; Fixed Track Equipment; Signal Equipment for	23.92	3.86	40.34	4.48
车辆及其零件、附件；但铁道及电车道车辆除外	Vehicles and Related Parts and Accessories	57.93	64.74	80.97	117.87
航空器、航天器及零件	Aircraft; Spacecraft and Parts Thereof	4.39	40.52	4.39	44.61
船舶及浮动结构体	Ships and Related Products	19.25	6.07	30.22	8.12
光学、照相、电影、计量、检验、医疗或外科用仪器设备、精密仪器及设备;钟表;乐器;及其零附件	**Optical; Photographic; Film; Measuring and and Medical Instruments and Equipment; Instruments and Equipment; Clocks; Musical Instruments; Related Parts and Accessories**	**95.23**	**144.21**	**131.05**	**261.73**
其他	**Others**	**240.20**	**27.15**	**294.70**	**28.63**

18-7 我国同各国(地区)海关进出口总额

China's Foreign Trade with Related Countries and Regions (Customs Statistics)

单位：万美元 (USD 10 000)

国 别（地区）	Country (Region)	2002			2003		
		进出口总额 Total	出口总额 Exports	进口总额 Imports	进出口总额 Total	出口总额 Exports	进口总额 Imports
总　计	**Total**	**62076607**	**32559597**	**29517010**	**85098757**	**43822777**	**41275980**
亚洲	**Asia**	**36303033**	**17130288**	**19172745**	**49547835**	**22257956**	**27289879**
阿富汗	Afghanistan	1999	1991	8	2706	2645	61
巴林	Bahrain	10968	5792	5176	13528	8315	5213
孟加拉国	Bangladesh	109863	106627	3236	136806	133467	3339
不丹	Bhutan	64	62	2	198	197	1
文莱	Brunei	26283	2102	24181	34626	3389	31237
缅甸	Myanmar	86164	72475	13689	107974	91022	16952
柬埔寨	Cambodia	27611	25156	2455	32065	29465	2600
塞浦路斯	Cyprus	22591	22515	76	21948	21836	112
朝鲜	Korea Rep.	73823	46754	27069	102309	62774	39535
中国香港	Hong Kong, China	6918939	5846315	1072624	8739303	7627437	1111866
印度	India	494503	267116	227387	759461	334323	425138
印度尼西亚	Indonesia	793480	342645	450835	1022886	448189	574697
伊朗	Iran	373957	139330	234627	562252	231516	330736
伊拉克	Iraq	51706	42082	9624	5638	5606	33
以色列	Israel	141709	89944	51765	183130	114090	69040
日本	Japan	10189984	4843384	5346600	13355683	5940870	7414813
约旦	Jordan	35803	30476	5327	52481	46427	6054
科威特	Kuwait	72733	26298	46435	118824	67499	51325
老挝	Laos	6396	5431	965	10944	9824	1120
黎巴嫩	Lebanon	28027	27607	420	37010	36542	468
中国澳门	Macao, China	101839	87612	14227	146563	128009	18554
马来西亚	Malaysia	1427051	497421	929630	2012730	614089	1398641
马尔代夫	Maldives	298	298		335	334	1
蒙古	Mongolia	36345	14003	22342	43984	15589	28395
尼泊尔	Nepal	11035	10507	528	12736	12201	535
阿曼	Oman	150665	6018	144647	206772	8196	198575
巴基斯坦	Pakistan	179961	124211	55750	242993	185499	57494
巴勒斯坦	Palestine	448	439	9	693	670	23
菲律宾	Philippines	525940	204224	321716	939952	309269	630683
卡塔尔	Qatar	22355	4954	17401	35488	6180	29308
沙特阿拉伯	Saudi Arabia	510689	167154	343535	731912	214680	517232
新加坡	Singapore	1403078	698422	704656	1934862	886377	1048485
韩国	Republic of Korea	4410257	1553456	2856801	6322282	2009477	4312805
斯里兰卡	Sri Lanka	35109	33675	1434	52424	50444	1980
叙利亚	Syria	37108	35694	1414	50628	47992	2636
泰国	Thailand	855695	295735	559960	1265475	382791	882684
土耳其	Turkey	137783	108904	28879	259781	206514	53267
阿联酋	United Arab Emirates	389626	345090	44536	581046	503700	77346
也门共和国	Arab Republic of Yemen	73110	30523	42587	189923	35338	154585
越南	Vietnam	326427	214838	111589	463945	318274	145671
中华人民共和国	P. R. China	1498019		1498019	2509430		2509430
中国台湾	Taiwan, China	4464711	658572	3806139	5836447	900409	4936038
东帝汶	Timor Leste				107	107	
哈萨克	Kazakhstan	195475	60010	135465	329188	157190	171998
吉尔吉斯	Kirghizia	20188	14616	5572	31430	24516	6914
塔吉克	Tadzhikistan	1239	650	589	3882	2081	1801
土库曼	Turkmenistan	8752	8678	74	8292	7883	410
乌兹别克	Uzbekstan	13177	10437	2740	34703	14678	20025
亚洲其它国家（地区）	Other Countries (Regions) in Asia	56	46	10	60	38	22
非洲	**Africa**	**1238836**	**696121**	**542715**	**1854184**	**1018185**	**835999**
阿尔及利亚	Algeria	43381	35191	8190	74515	64594	9922
安哥拉	Angola	114836	6131	108705	235173	14579	220594
贝宁	Benin	43787	42086	1701	53946	47106	6840
博茨瓦那	Botswana	1899	1898	1	2495	2277	218
布隆迪	Burundi	272	223	49	519	345	174
喀麦隆	Cameroon	15863	4397	11466	18016	6494	11522
加那利群岛	Canary Is.	3024	3024		3753	3753	

18-7 续表 1 continued

单位: 万美元 (USD 10 000)

国 别（地区）	Country (Region)	2002			2003		
		进出口总额 Total	出口总额 Exports	进口总额 Imports	进出口总额 Total	出口总额 Exports	进口总额 Imports
佛得角	Cape Verde	184	184		260	260	
中非	Central Africa	195	69	126	444	213	231
塞卜泰(休达)	Ceuta	169	169		91	91	
乍得	Chad	324	171	153	452	168	284
科摩罗	Comoros	76	76		69	69	
刚果	Congo	29088	3961	25127	87455	5989	81466
吉布提	Djibouti	4983	4981	2	6601	6586	15
埃及	Egypt	94477	85292	9185	108958	93676	15282
赤道几内亚	Eq.Guinea	38602	329	38273	41694	505	41189
埃塞俄比亚	Ethiopia	10012	9643	369	15749	15275	474
加蓬	Gabon	23664	470	23194	30949	889	30060
冈比亚	Gambia	8190	8190		11752	11597	155
加纳	Ghana	21246	18231	3015	35610	32179	3431
几内亚	Guinea	5492	4338	1154	8374	7329	1045
几内亚(比绍)	Guinea-Bissau	450	450		1235	1235	
科特迪瓦共和国	Cote d'lvoir	23385	21972	1413	26498	22822	3676
肯尼亚	Kenya	18636	18056	580	25045	24171	874
利比里亚	Liberia	8570	3011	5559	6814	2619	4196
利比亚	Libya	11275	11153	122	21568	17474	4095
马达加斯加	Madagascar	5152	4020	1132	11865	11170	696
马拉维	Malawi	713	652	61	1079	1078	1
马里	Mali	2335	2162	173	6359	3520	2839
毛里塔尼亚	Mauritania	6177	5200	977	6419	5649	771
毛里求斯	Mauritius	9467	9000	467	11050	10737	313
摩洛哥	Morocco	57341	45126	12215	85676	69579	16097
莫桑比克	Mozambique	4851	2593	2258	7162	4503	2659
纳米比亚	Namibia	4911	2018	2893	7458	3762	3695
尼日尔	Niger	1474	1474		1934	1934	
尼日利亚	Nigeria	116846	104715	12131	185763	178597	7166
留尼汪	Reunion	874	874		1385	1385	
卢旺达	Rwanda	905	386	519	1065	353	712
圣多美和普林西比	Sao Tome & Principle	16	16		23	20	3
塞内加尔	Senegal	5875	5768	107	7913	7285	628
塞舌尔	Seychelles	147	146	1	182	179	3
塞拉利昂	Sierra Leone	1457	1441	16	1661	1661	
索马里	Somalia	339	183	156	1053	390	662
南非	South Africa	257941	131064	126877	386935	202936	183999
西撒哈拉	Western Sahara	37	37		56	56	
苏丹	Sudan	154998	39239	115759	192024	47842	144182
坦桑尼亚	Tanzania	12804	12142	662	21904	19147	2757
多哥	Togo	14382	13847	535	28465	26254	2211
突尼斯	Tunisia	18241	14411	3830	20089	18384	1705
乌干达	Uganda	3366	2806	560	5489	5139	350
布基纳法索	Burkina Faso	652	582	70	4405	1171	3234
民主刚果	Congo DR	3146	1899	1247	5166	2542	2624
赞比亚	Zambia	8328	3719	4609	8276	3488	4788
津巴布韦	Zimbabwe	19175	3216	15959	19735	3027	16708
莱索托	Lesotho	2451	2451		2488	2488	
梅利利亚	Melilla	84	84		215	215	
斯威士兰	Swaziland	1582	473	1109	2122	668	1453
厄立特里亚	Eritrea	604	603	1	547	547	
马约特岛	Mayotte				35	35	
非洲其它国家（地区）	Other Countries (Regions) in Africa	91	80	11	156	154	2
欧洲	**Europe**	**11024571**	**5827785**	**5196786**	**15786463**	**8816772**	**6969691**
比利时	Belgium	489790	287585	202205	670188	393370	276818
丹麦	Denmark	155378	91698	63680	245849	149434	96415
英国	United Kingdom	1139539	805943	333596	1439406	1082372	357034
德国	Germany	2778827	1137185	1641642	4173400	1744211	2429189
法国	France	832498	407186	425312	1339226	729353	609873
爱尔兰	Ireland	145959	77013	68946	234307	139158	95149
意大利	Italy	914691	482744	431947	1173290	665232	508058

单位: 万美元 (USD 10 000)

国别(地区)	Country (Region)	2002 进出口总额 Total	2002 出口总额 Exports	2002 进口总额 Imports	2003 进出口总额 Total	2003 出口总额 Exports	2003 进口总额 Imports
卢森堡	Luxembourg	10128	5130	4998	42700	31141	11558
荷兰	Netherlands	1067913	910756	157157	1543436	1350124	193312
希腊	Greece	78691	73185	5506	118827	111360	7467
葡萄牙	Portugal	38359	30088	8271	60087	40626	19461
西班牙	Spain	347823	257805	90018	525212	389079	136133
奥地利	Austria	137434	48142	89292	177864	67385	110479
芬兰	Finland	266641	115364	151277	346195	167351	178844
瑞典	Sweden	270105	91002	179103	416883	145293	271590
阿尔巴尼亚	Albania	1878	1869	9	3225	3219	6
安道尔	Andorra	29	28	1	87	87	
保加利亚	Bulgaria	11908	9760	2148	22520	16647	5873
直布罗陀	Gibraltar	79	79		2115	2115	
匈牙利	Hungary	161766	144883	16883	258765	228629	30136
冰岛	Iceland	3293	1850	1443	6830	4553	2278
列支敦士登	Liechtenstein	493	33	460	1173	217	957
马耳他	Malta	29525	11564	17961	35199	12444	22756
摩纳哥	Monaco	576	314	262	2173	1783	391
挪威	Norway	145039	52716	92323	176465	89927	86538
波兰	Poland	138327	116462	21865	197941	162025	35916
罗马尼亚	Romania	75290	36196	39094	97564	50554	47010
圣马力诺	San Marino	35	35		46	43	3
瑞士	Switzerland	267461	63782	203679	352224	83959	268265
爱沙尼亚	Estonia	17321	13716	3605	17001	13968	3033
拉脱维亚	Latvia	7275	6751	524	12983	11062	1921
立陶宛	Lithuania	11004	9823	1181	18778	17052	1726
格鲁吉亚	Georgia	1151	800	351	2812	1990	822
亚美尼亚	Armenia	860	194	666	649	471	178
阿塞拜疆	Azerbaijan	9549	9403	146	23816	20349	3467
白俄罗斯	Belorussia	8000	1622	6378	12895	3223	9672
摩尔多瓦	Moldavia	590	169	421	1474	672	802
俄罗斯联邦	Russia	1192743	352074	840669	1575800	602993	972807
乌克兰	Ukraine	123377	52745	70632	217462	92855	124607
塞尔维亚和黑山	Serbian				14947	13553	1393
斯洛文尼亚	Slovenia	12499	9544	2955	18732	15129	3603
克罗地亚	Croatia	11840	11265	575	17596	16915	681
捷克	Czech	96194	80733	15461	157881	128159	29722
斯洛伐克	Slovakia	12960	9173	3787	25919	13707	12212
前南斯拉夫马其顿	Macedonia of Former Yugoslavia	1792	1728	64	3886	2413	1473
波黑	Bosnia and Herzegovina	347	309	38	635	571	64
欧洲其它国家(地区)	Other Countries (Regions) in Europe				1	1	
拉丁美洲	**Latin America**	**1782440**	**948824**	**833616**	**2680681**	**1187743**	**1492938**
安提瓜和巴布达	Antigua and Barbuda	295	295		312	312	
阿根廷	Argentina	142483	18537	123946	317627	44719	272908
阿鲁巴岛	Aruba	280	276	4	224	222	3
巴哈马	Bahamas	6293	6287	6	12251	12172	78
巴巴多斯	Barbados	1037	1024	13	922	917	5
伯利兹	Belize	920	904	16	1126	1027	99
玻利维亚	Bolivia	2163	955	1208	1872	1184	688
巴西	Brazil	446940	146638	300302	798555	214326	584229
开曼群岛	Cayman Is.	210	210		388	388	
智利	Chile	256535	99826	156709	353160	128344	224816
哥伦比亚	Colombia	31638	28726	2912	45866	39820	6046
多米尼加	Dominica	4617	4543	74	3434	3358	76
哥斯达黎加	Costa Rica	26614	8165	18449	65942	9852	56090
古巴	Cuba	42635	31066	11569	35681	23630	12051
库腊索岛	Curacao	4129	4129		3904	3883	21
多米尼加共和国	Dominica Rep.	10729	10548	181	15166	14815	351
厄瓜多尔	Ecuador	20805	19448	1357	27902	23929	3973
法属圭亚那	French Guyana	67	67		86	85	1
格林纳达	Granada	29	29		74	43	31
瓜德罗普群岛	Guadeloupe Is.	159	159		246	246	
危地马拉	Guatemala	24525	24467	58	30744	30562	182

18-7 续表 3 continued

单位: 万美元 (USD 10 000)

国别（地区）	Country (Region)	2002 进出口总额 Total	2002 出口总额 Exports	2002 进口总额 Imports	2003 进出口总额 Total	2003 出口总额 Exports	2003 进口总额 Imports
圭亚那	Guyana	1772	1372	400	1842	1812	30
海地	Haiti	2347	2347		2640	2638	2
洪都拉斯	Honduras	5954	5877	77	8125	7787	338
牙买加	Jamaica	11476	6596	4880	20750	10204	10546
马提尼克岛	Martinique	79	79		114	114	
墨西哥	Mexico	397862	286366	111496	494377	326703	167674
蒙特塞拉特	Montserrat	1	1		57	3	54
尼加拉瓜	Nicaragua	4920	4917	3	6968	6931	37
巴拿马	Panama	127638	127266	372	150861	147999	2862
巴拉圭	Paraguay	8690	7903	787	13893	12619	1274
秘鲁	Peru	97825	24664	73161	111375	35374	76001
波多黎各	Puerto Rico	12776	10430	2346	23760	15953	7807
萨巴	Saba	1	1		5	5	
圣卢西亚	Saint Lucia	269	269		154	154	1
圣马丁岛	Saint Martin Is.	98	98		140	140	
圣文森特和格林纳丁斯	Saint Vincent & Grenadines	823	821	2	765	765	
萨尔瓦多	El Salvador	13447	13257	190	15962	15756	206
苏里南	Surinam	1772	1515	257	3586	1977	1609
特立尼达和多巴哥	Trinidad and Tobago	4715	4234	481	6876	5852	1024
特克斯和凯科斯群岛	Turks & Caicos Is.				4	2	2
乌拉圭	Uruguay	17302	9495	7807	20337	12762	7575
委内瑞拉	Venezuela	47763	33267	14496	74140	19924	54216
英属维尔京群岛	Virgin Is. (E)	1657	1601	56	7632	7632	
圣其茨-尼维斯	St. Kitts-Nevis	27	27		15	15	
荷属安地列斯群岛	Andreas Is. (N)				751	714	36
拉美其它国家（地区）	Other Countries (Regions) in Latin America	123	122	1	76	76	
北美洲	**North America**	**10514619**	**7426926**	**3087693**	**13639397**	**9813121**	**3826276**
加拿大	Canada	793034	430346	362688	1000667	563218	437449
美国	United States	9718343	6994579	2723764	12633286	9246677	3386609
格陵兰	Greenland	1253	14	1239	2274	57	2217
百慕大群岛	Bermuda	1959	1959		3163	3163	
北美洲其它国家（地区）	Other Countries (Regions) in North America	29	27	2	5	5	
大洋洲及太平洋群岛	**Oceanic and Pacific Islands**	**1212288**	**528920**	**683368**	**1588998**	**729001**	**859997**
澳大利亚	Australia	1043561	458504	585057	1356365	626358	730007
库克群岛	Cook Islands	20	7	13	58	50	8
斐济	Fiji	3197	3057	140	3132	2597	536
盖比群岛	Gambier Is.	15	15		34	33	1
马克萨斯群岛	Marquesas Is.				10	10	
瑙鲁	Nauru	42	42		5	5	
新喀里多尼亚	New Caledonia (Fr)	368	367	1	1380	763	617
瓦努阿图	Vanuatu	167	141	26	308	289	20
新西兰	New Zealand	139931	59597	80334	182609	80251	102358
诺福克岛	Norfolk Islands	12	12		39	38	1
巴布亚新几内亚	Papua New Guinea	18692	2725	15967	29203	6093	23111
社会群岛	Society Is.	274	274		323	323	1
所罗门群岛	Solomon Is.	1929	107	1822	3475	212	3264
汤加	Tonga	484	483	1	210	204	5
萨摩亚	Samoa	279	279		319	283	36
基里巴斯	Kiribati	49	49		89	89	
图瓦卢	Tuvalu				7	7	
密克罗尼西亚联邦	Micronesia Commonwealth	130	130		274	274	
马绍尔群岛共和国	Marshall. Is.	2371	2369	1	10026	10021	6
帕劳共和国	Republic of Palau	29	29		19	19	
法属波利尼西亚	Polynesia (F)				344	329	15
大洋州其它国家（地区）	Other Countries (Regions) in Oceanic	739	733	5	769	756	13
国别（地区）不详	**Others**	**822**	**734**	**88**	**1201**		**1201**

18-8 海关出口主要商品数量和金额

Main Export Commodities in Volume and Value (Customs Statistics)

金额单位：万美元 (USD 10 000)

品名		Item		2002		2003	
				数量 Volume	金额 Value	数量 Volume	金额 Value
活猪	(万头)	Live Hogs	(10 000 heads)	188	21337	188	21477
活家禽	(万只)	Live Poultry	(10 000 heads)	4280	8207	3908	6736
鲜、冻牛肉	(万吨)	Frozen，Fresh Beef	(10 000 tons)	1	1902	1	1488
鲜、冻猪肉	(万吨)	Frozen，Fresh Pork	(10 000 tons)	16	20946	21	26918
冻鸡	(万吨)	Frozen Chicken	(10 000 tons)	282423	36015	226984	27897
鲜、冻兔肉	(吨)	Frozen，Fresh Rabbit Meat	(ton)	9081	1135	4426	599
水海产品	(万吨)	Aquatic and Seawater Products	(10 000 tons)	163	287131	158	333246
鲜蛋	(百万个)	Fresh Eggs	(million units)	1001	2224	1292	3102
谷物及谷物粉	(万吨)	Cereals and Cereals Flour	(10 000 tons)	1482	171786	2194	265708
#稻谷和大米	(万吨)	Rice	(10 000 tons)	199	38501	262	50178
玉米	(万吨)	Maize	(10 000 tons)	1167	116751	1639	176718
蔬菜	(万吨)	Vegetables	(10 000 tons)	360	188773	432	219559
#鲜或冷藏蔬菜	(万吨)	Fresh Vegetables	(10 000 tons)	240	73718	296	90659
干豆	(万吨)	Dried Plusles	(10 000 tons)	86	31910	104	35869
橘、橙	(吨)	Mandarins and Oranges	(ton)	196641	5117	265438	6935
鲜苹果	(吨)	Apples	(ton)	438738	14943	609045	20978
核桃仁	(吨)	Walnut Meat	(ton)	6721	1987	8518	2584
栗子	(吨)	Chestnut	(ton)	33412	5162	34499	5297
白果	(吨)	Gingko Nuts	(ton)	3977	1098	3848	902
松子仁	(吨)	Pine Nut Kernels	(ton)	7015	4642	6080	5133
大豆	(万吨)	Soybean	(10 000 tons)	28	7668	27	8700
花生及花生仁	(万吨)	Peanuts	(10 000 tons)	52	26371	49	31788
食用植物油(含棕榈油)	(吨)	Edible Vegetable Oil	(ton)	97443	5821	59705	5967
食糖	(万吨)	Sugar	(10 000 tons)	325826	7971	103165	2956
天然蜂蜜	(吨)	Natural Honey	(ton)	76450	7794	84088	10314
茶叶	(吨)	Tea	(ton)	252272	33176	259917	36734
辣椒干	(吨)	Dried Chillies	(ton)	70870	4860	90518	7726
猪肉罐头	(吨)	Canned Pork	(ton)	49060	7061	52161	7506
蘑菇罐头	(吨)	Canned Mushroom	(ton)	210279	22210	262409	28264
啤酒	(万升)	Beer	(10 000 liters)	13042	6813	15180	7618
猪鬃	(吨)	Bristle	(ton)	11299	6381	10926	6306
肠衣	(吨)	Casings	(ton)	55012	28957	64724	39754
填充用羽毛；羽绒	(吨)	Feathers and Down for Stuffing	(ton)	41792	25684	36675	23504
药材	(吨)	Medical Materials	(ton)	144110	21585	163249	22626
烤烟	(吨)	Flue-cured Tobacco	(ton)	135138	18142	134545	18385
未硝整张毛皮	(吨)	Raw Complete Pieces of Fur Skins	(ton)	176	454	173	459
#水貂皮	(吨)	Raw Mink Skins	(ton)		6		
锯材	(立方米)	Wood Sawn	(cu.m)	430721	19005	523083	23385
生丝	(吨)	Raw Silk	(ton)	14701	24296	13893	21163
山羊绒	(吨)	Cashmere	(ton)	4140	23171	4638	25187
兔毛	(吨)	Rabbit Hair	(ton)	4722	4672	2815	2869
棉花（原棉）	(吨)	Cotton (Cotton Wool)	(ton)	149538	16959	112020	13257
苎麻	(吨)	Ramie	(ton)	1848	633	1480	530
天然石墨	(吨)	Natural Graphite	(ton)	321795	4614	339609	5352
天然碳酸镁；氧化镁	(万吨)	Natural Magnesium Carbonate, Magnesia	(10 000 tons)	201	24051	205	27861
萤石（氟石）	(万吨)	Fluorite	(10 000 tons)	101	10547	95	11126
天然硫酸钡(重晶石)	(万吨)	Barite	(10 000 tons)	171	5593	217	6744

18-8 续表 1 continued

金额单位: 万美元 (USD 10 000)

品 名		Item		2002		2003	
				数 量 Volume	金 额 Value	数 量 Volume	金 额 Value
滑石	(万吨)	Talcum	(10 000 tons)	73	6755	73	6990
铝矿砂及其精矿	(万吨)	Aluminum Ores	(10 000 tons)		10		7
煤	(万吨)	Coal	(10 000 tons)	8383	253209	9388	275032
焦炭、半焦炭	(万吨)	Coke and Semi-coke	(10 000 tons)	1357	95714	1472	167236
原油	(万吨)	Crude Oil	(10 000 tons)	766	129618	813	166122
成品油	(万吨)	Petroleum Products Refined	(10 000 tons)	1068	238463	1382	372066
石蜡	(万吨)	Paraffin Wax	(10 000 tons)	62	24840	62	27373
仲钨酸铵	(吨)	Tungstates	(ton)	6078	3049	8548	4173
氧化锌及过氧化锌	(吨)	Zinc Oxide and Zinc Peroxide	(ton)	87057	5694	96960	6561
糠醛	(吨)	Furfural	(ton)	27002	1321	22433	1174
合成有机染料	(吨)	Synthetic Organic Dyestuffs	(ton)	203042	57285	198669	54488
医药品	(吨)	Medical and Pharmaceutical Products	(ton)	261189	232389	303576	285812
#中式成药	(吨)	Medicaments of Chinese Type	(ton)	11739	10303	11960	10466
医用敷料	(吨)	Pharmaceutical Goods	(ton)	74699	29669	85595	35285
洗衣粉	(吨)	Detergent	(ton)	54951	3262	80526	4278
烟花、爆竹	(吨)	Fireworks and Firecrackers	(ton)	223475	27641	258679	31595
松香及树脂酸	(吨)	Resin and Resin Acids	(ton)	356334	15953	301173	13981
新的充气橡胶轮胎	(万条)	Rubber Tyres	(10 000 units)	13391	121838	15779	160782
纸及纸板(未切成形)	(万吨)	Paper and Paperboard in Rolls	(10 000 tons)	74	57317	114	86237
棉纱线	(吨)	Cotton Yarn	(ton)	388413	100674	504168	137823
亚麻及苎麻纱线	(吨)	Flax or Ramie Yarn	(ton)	39356	12236	33036	11379
丝绸	(万米)	Silk	(10 000 m)	15280	34746	19514	41159
棉机织物	(万米)	Cotton Cloth	(10 000 m)	457883	425692	559407	546331
亚麻及苎麻机织物	(万米)	Flax or Ramie Woven Fabric	(10 000 m)	22000	35149	23916	38186
合成短纤与棉混纺机织物	(万米)	Synthetic Short Fibre and Cotton-fibre Mixture Woven Fabric	(10 000 m)	196867	84932	182562	83782
人造纤维短纤机织物	(万米)	Short Rayon Woven Fabric	(10 000 m)	50248	21234	51573	23409
地毯	(万平方米)	Carpets	(10 000 sq.m)	6533	55704	9865	63761
棉浴巾	(万条)	Cotton Bath Towels	(10 000 units)	26721	29282	30670	35955
塑料编织袋（周转袋除外）	(万条)	Bags of PP or PE Strip (Except Turnover Bags)	(10 000 units)	136833	17501	184804	24213
水泥	(万吨)	Cement	(10 000 tons)	516	16431	533	17158
平板玻璃	(万平方米)	Plate Glass	(10 000 sq.m)	11335	24976	12427	28242
玻璃制品		Glass Products			74435		97457
家用陶瓷器皿	(吨)	Porcelain and Pottery Ware for Household Use	(ton)	1365240	88499	1614425	108063
生铁及镜铁	(万吨)	Pig Iron and Spiegeleise	(10 000 tons)	40	5189	71	12560
硅铁	(万吨)	Ferro-silicon	(10 000 tons)	54	24072	84	43361
钢坯及粗锻件	(万吨)	Billet and Crude Fougings	(10 000 tons)	133	29593	147	37532
钢材	(万吨)	Rolled Steel	(10 000 tons)	545	218279	696	310496
未锻造铜及合金	(吨)	Unwrought Copper and its Alloys	(ton)	81328	13119	67083	11870
铜材	(吨)	Rolled Copper	(ton)	171575	49631	232880	69022
未锻造铝及合金	(吨)	Unwrought Aluminum and its Alloys	(ton)	787341	109956	1249249	179257
铝材	(吨)	Rolled Aluminum	(ton)	188744	45652	273293	66774
未锻造的锌及锌合金	(吨)	Unwrought Zinc and Zinc Alloys	(ton)	495990	39342	484231	39658
未锻造的锡及锡合金	(吨)	Unwrought Tin and Tin Alloys	(ton)	42578	15553	41220	18041
未锻造的锑、粉末及废碎料	(吨)	Unwrought Antimony	(ton)	20276	2872	25243	5591
未锻造的锰	(吨)	Unwrought Manganese	(ton)	126757	9722	165458	16178
钢铁或铜制标准紧固件	(万吨)	Iron or Copper Nails, Bolts, etc.	(10 000 tons)	661783	58855	854814	81995
搪瓷器	(吨)	Enamelware	(ton)	112475	13945	123610	15626
手用或机用工具	(吨)	Hand Tools and Tools for Machines	(ton)	662159	141484	790616	176230

18-8 续表 2 continued

金额单位: 万美元 (USD 10 000)

品 名	Item	2002 数量 Volume	2002 金额 Value	2003 数量 Volume	2003 金额 Value
锁 (吨)	Locks (ton)	204866	48431	229563	56639
电扇 (万台)	Fans (10 000 sets)	21285	102070	35847	134633
纺织机械及零件	Textile Machinery		35649		51735
缝纫机(包括工业用) (万架)	Sewing Machines (Including Industrial Use) (10 000 sets)	1119	39052	1299	53187
金属加工机床 (万台)	Machine Tools (10 000 sets)	555	31280	623	37910
电子计算器 (万台)	Electric Calculator (10 000 sets)	47674	77711	43843	94140
轴承 (万套)	Bearings (10 000 units)	172097	60741	181869	65877
电动机及发电机 (万台)	Electric Motors and Generators (10 000 sets)	301744	218319	326211	243867
静止式变流器 (万个)	Static Converters (10 000 units)	93118	215918	122558	288467
原电池 (万个)	Primary Cells and Batteries (10 000 units)	1584982	68672	1881103	86438
蓄电池 (万个)	Electric Accumulators (10 000 units)	108813	139846	158868	209053
手电筒 (万个)	Flashlights (10 000 units)	56621	21806	68764	28655
有线电话机(包括无绳电话机) (万台)	Line Telephone Sets (10 000 sets)	16880	140457	19327	166613
扬声器 (万个)	Loudspeakers (10 000 units)	140862	115336	167197	140755
收录机及组合音响 (万台)	Sound Recording Apparatus (10 000 sets)	19537	296229	20583	313536
收音机 (万台)	Radio (10 000 sets)	21704	27201	26052	32309
电视机（包括整套散件）(万台)	TV Sets (including a Complete Set of Spare Parts) (10 000 sets)	3164	239627	4762	347159
电容器 (吨)	Electrical Capacitors (ton)	41800	83524	48078	98527
通断保护电路装置	Electrical Apparatus for Switching or Protecting Electrical Circuits		213860		283736
二极管及类似半导体器件(万个)	Diode and Semi Conductors (10 000 units)	8849800	133861	10641127	173320
电线电缆 (吨)	Insulated Wire or Cable (ton)	690096	208608	848326	266396
集装箱 (个)	Containers (unit)	1078009	221211	1773053	385412
汽车和汽车底盘 (辆)	Motor Vehicles and Chassis (unit)	43491	26728	133372	41765
汽车零件	Parts of Motor Vehicles		184172		241568
自行车 (万辆)	Bicycles (10 000 units)	4556	127897	5044	143250
船舶 (艘)	Ships (unit)	50423	189401	70674	298752
照相机 (万架)	Cameras (10 000 sets)	9156	77728	6121	56445
医疗仪器及器械	Medical Instruments and Appliances		76054		100290
手表 (万只)	Wrist Watches (10 000 units)	82413	77760	90781	95300
日用钟 (万只)	Clocks (10 000 sets)	43688	39811	43522	44412
家俱及其零件	Furniture		535936		729711
服装(针织、钩织的除外)	Garments (Excluding Knitwear and Crochet)		1925016		2332086
针织钩织服装	Garments, Knitted or Crocheted		1463510		1885949
皮鞋 (万双)	Leather Shoes (10 000 pairs)	95664	481594	103739	535606
橡胶或塑料底布鞋（包括球鞋） (万双)	Cloth Shoes With Outer of Rubber or Artificial Plastic Materials (including Gym Shoes) (10 000 pairs)	72649	140625	81875	159507
塑料制品 (万吨)	Plastic Articles (10 000 tons)	4598847	605164	5482683	731766
玩具	Toys		557408		597930
足球、篮球、排球 (万个)	Footballs, Basketballs and Volleyballs (10 000 units)	8277	10406	9657	12733
铅笔 (吨)	Pencils (ton)	35945	8609	40431	9840
伞 (万把)	Umbrellas (10 000 units)	61320	55572	68846	63322
竹编结品 (吨)	Bamboo Products (ton)	76892	13812	78160	15371
藤编结品 (吨)	Rattan Products (ton)	31725	7354	37968	9788
草编结品 (吨)	Straw Mats and Straw Products (ton)	34609	7124	36367	8920
柳编结品 (吨)	Wickerwork (ton)	89007	15624	102699	19983
鬃刷 (万把)	Bristle Brushes (10 000 units)	46075	6672	53865	7838
人造花 (吨)	Artificial Flowers (ton)	217347	53507	247945	54073
热水瓶 (万个)	Vacuum Flasks (10 000 units)	9325	14768	10137	15450
机电产品	Mechanical and Electrical Products		15706213		22745672

18-9 海关进口主要商品数量和金额

Main Import Commodities in Volume and Value (Customs Statistics)

金额单位: 万美元 (USD 10 000)

品名	Item	2002 数量 Volume	2002 金额 Value	2003 数量 Volume	2003 金额 Value
谷物及谷物粉 (万吨)	Cereals and Cereals Flour (10 000 tons)	285	49350	208	45487
#小麦 (万吨)	Wheat (10 000 tons)	63	11271	45	8552
稻谷和大米 (万吨)	Rice (10 000 tons)	24	8031	26	9718
大豆 (万吨)	Soybean (10 000 tons)	1131	248284	2074	541687
食用植物油 (万吨)	Edible Vegetable Oil (10 000 tons)	319	130965	541	257903
其他植物油 (万吨)	Other Vegetable Oils (10 000 tons)	25	10148	34	15749
食糖 (万吨)	Sugar (10 000 tons)	118	23846	78	17411
配制的动物饲料 (吨)	Prepared Feeding Stuff (ton)	95870	9106	133642	10631
天然橡胶（包括胶乳）(万吨)	Natural Rubber (including Latex) (10 000 tons)	96	69429	120	115474
合成橡胶（包括胶乳）(万吨)	Synthetic Rubber (including Latex) (10 000 tons)	92	93948	101	115191
原木 (万立方米)	Logs (10 000 cu.m)	2433	213826	2546	244731
纸浆 (万吨)	Paper Pulp (10 000 tons)	526	216767	603	266092
锯材 (立方米)	Wood Sawn (cu.m)	5395988	115910	5511711	119045
棉花(原棉) (万吨)	Cotton, not Carded or Combed (10 000 tons)	18	18644	87	116885
羊毛及条 (吨)	Wool and Wool Tops (ton)	237264	103777	194349	91335
纺织用合成纤维 (万吨)	Synthetic Fibers Suitable for Spinning (10 000 tons)	104	106286	106	124033
#聚酯纤维 (吨)	Polyester Fibers (ton)	600248	46585	577126	51780
聚丙烯腈纤维 (吨)	Polyacryolnitr Fibers (ton)	423051	55419	458385	66637
铁矿砂 (万吨)	Iron Ore (10 000 tons)	11149	276907	14813	485650
锰矿砂 (万吨)	Manganese Ores (10 000 tons)	208	15144	286	20498
铜矿砂 (万吨)	Copper Ores (10 000 tons)	207	80945	267	128819
铬矿砂 (万吨)	Chromium Ores (10 000 tons)	114	7891	178	15083
氧化铝 (万吨)	Aluminum Oxide (10 000 tons)	457	75295	561	137576
煤 (万吨)	Coal (10 000 tons)	1081	32846	1076	36430
原油 (万吨)	Crude Oil (10 000 tons)	6941	1275731	9112	1980873
成品油 (万吨)	Petroleum Products Refined (10 000 tons)	2034	379826	2824	586118
乙二醇 (万吨)	Ethylene Glycol (10 000 tons)	2145723	88620	2518956	158603
对苯二甲酸 (吨)	Telephthalic Acid (ton)	4296879	209943	4542054	256608
己内酰胺 (吨)	Carprolactam (ton)	320551	31285	376986	43060
碳酸钠（纯碱）(吨)	Soda Ash (ton)	293685	3029	301277	3141
合成有机染料 (吨)	Synthetic Organic Dyestuffs (ton)	60095	25718		
医药品 (吨)	Pharmaceutical Products (ton)	27155	143475	30257	170708
肥料(自然吨) (万吨)	Chemical Fertilizers, Manufactured (Actual Weight) (10 000 tons)	1682	235347	1213	176264

18-9 续表 continued

金额单位: 万美元 (USD 10 000)

品名	Item	2002 数量 Volume	2002 金额 Value	2003 数量 Volume	2003 金额 Value
#尿素 (万吨)	Urea (10 000 tons)	79	9183	13	1542
氮、磷、钾复合肥 (万吨)	Compound Fertilizers of Nitrogen, Phosphor and Kalium (10 000 tons)	282	45284	224	38069
磷酸氢二胺	Diammonium Phosphape (10 000 tons)	493	85946	261	50390
氯化钾 (万吨)	Potassium Chloride (10 000 tons)	665	76833	623	73942
原形聚乙烯 (万吨)	Polyethylene in primary Forms (10 000 tons)	4558882	269786	3591739	239889
原形聚丙烯 (万吨)	Polypropylene in Primary Forms (10 000 tons)	2441900	163529	2734202	202353
原形聚苯乙烯 (万吨)	Polystyrene in Primary Forms (10 000 tons)	3483033	320810	3587714	343275
#ABS树脂 (万吨)	ABS Copolymers (10 000 tons)	1637508	167675	1789595	188192
原形聚氯乙烯 (万吨)	Polyvinyl Chloride in Primary Forms (10 000 tons)	2251347	133569	291956	150152
聚酯切片 (万吨)	Slices or Chips of Polyethylene Terephthalate (10 000 tons)	175356	11475	171984	13763
农药 (吨)	Pesticides (ton)	27432	13609	28408	13399
纸及纸板(未切成形)(万吨)	Paper and Paperboard (Unchopped in Shape) (10 000 tons)	633	353959	636	372713
钢材 (万吨)	Rolled Steel (10 000 tons)	2449	1236555	3717	1991581
未锻造的铜及铜合金 (吨)	Copper and Copper Alloys (ton)	1330146	215418	1562152	281847
铜材 (吨)	Rolled Copper (ton)	917634	228239	1055765	278339
未锻造的铝及铝合 (吨)	Aluminum and Aluminum Alloys (ton)	581737	78263	880735	122710
铝材 (吨)	Rolled Aluminum (ton)	475648	127213	531477	149089
锅炉 (台)	Boilers (set)	945	4230	577	5049
制冷压缩机 (万台)	Compressors for Refrigerating Equipment	1274	66155	1483	87130
金属加工机床 (台)	Machine Tools (set)	122884	315000	125702	413088
阀门 (万套)	Valves (10 000 sets)	14342	80674	20627	123315
自动数据处理设备及其部件 (万台)	Automatic Data Processing Machines and Components (10 000 sets)	114792224	673333	202874779	1141457
有线电话或电报交换机 (台)	Line Telephonic or Telegraphic Switching Apparatus (set)	37674	4357	33170	7454
收录机及组合音响 (万台)	Sound Recording Apparatus (10 000 sets)	59	3378	130	7682
电视机 (万台)	TV Sets (10 000 sets)	17	3699	101	8553
电视显像管 (万只)	Cathode-ray TV Picture Tube (10 000 sets) (10 000 sets)	1349	77166	2415	108725
汽车和汽车底盘 (辆)	Motor Vehicles and Chassis (unit)	127367	317449	172339	520990
#小轿车(包括整套散件)(辆)	Cars (including a Complete Set of Spare Parts) (unit)	70326	161355	103017	308252
卡车(包括整套散件)(辆)	Trucks (including a Complete Set of Spare Parts) (unit)	6692	25970	9769	41703
自卸车(包括整套散件)(辆)	Dump Trucks (including a Complete Set of Spare Parts) (unit)	141	2442	93	918
装有引擎的底盘 (台)	Chassis with Engines (unit)	209	931	1014	3104
汽车零件	Parts of Motor Vehicles		299571		626382
飞机 (架)	Aircraft (unit)	170	284231	167	350064
船舶 (艘)	Ships (unit)	1135	36355	1248	28572
复印机 (台)	Photo or Thermos Copying Apparatus (sets)	112871	6251	94192	4895
医疗仪器及器械	Medical Instruments and Appliances		121457		165341
机电产品	Mechanical and Electrical Products		15556299		22498739

18-10 各地区按经营单位所在地分商品进出口总额

Total Value of Import and Export by Location of China's Foreign Trade Managing Units by Region

单位:万美元 (USD 10 000)

地区	Region	2000			2002			2003		
		进出口 Total	出口 Exports	进口 Imports	进出口 Total	出口 Exports	进口 Imports	进出口 Total	出口 Exports	进口 Imports
全国	**National Total**	**47429628**	**24920255**	**22509373**	**62076607**	**32559597**	**29517010**	**85098757**	**43822777**	**41275980**
北京	Beijing	4962189	1196813	3765376	5250529	1261386	3989142	6850017	1688682	5161335
天津	Tianjin	1715400	862578	852822	2281140	1163169	1117972	2934244	1434940	1499304
河北	Hebei	523862	371000	152862	666525	459411	207114	897825	592754	305071
山西	Shanxi	176438	123687	52751	231154	166161	64993	309013	227202	81811
内蒙古	Inner Mongolia	262205	97017	165188	243402	80667	162736	282902	115569	167333
辽宁	Liaoning	1903148	1085632	817516	2173965	1236656	937309	2650917	1457935	1192982
吉林	Jilin	257042	125683	131359	370248	176849	193398	614841	218228	396613
黑龙江	Heilongjiang	298637	145118	153519	434915	198665	236251	532940	287426	245514
上海	Shanghai	5470802	2535233	2935569	7262711	3203739	4058972	11233955	4845296	6388659
江苏	Jiangsu	4563636	2576683	1986953	7028854	3846512	3182342	11361740	5911302	5450438
浙江	Zhejiang	2783262	1944275	838987	4195576	2941068	1254508	6141081	4159497	1981584
安徽	Anhui	334684	217198	117486	418097	245313	172784	594781	306363	288418
福建	Fujian	2122046	1290607	831439	2839737	1737063	1102674	3532553	2113173	1419380
江西	Jiangxi	162405	119741	42664	169447	105198	64249	252806	150490	102315
山东	Shandong	2498976	1552884	946092	3393448	2110783	1282665	4463682	2655706	1807977
河南	Henan	228290	149578	78712	320316	211862	108454	471217	297929	173288
湖北	Hubei	322286	193555	128731	395314	209826	185488	510930	265537	245393
湖南	Hunan	251222	165271	85951	287584	179528	108055	373236	214585	158651
广东	Guangdong	17009888	9191770	7818118	22109631	11846274	10263357	28352477	15284823	13067654
广西	Guangxi	203379	148891	54488	243049	150746	92303	318675	196992	121683
海南	Hainan	128786	80289	48497	186680	81930	104749	227492	86620	140871
重庆	Chongqing	178590	99566	79024	179307	109101	70206	259476	158499	100977
四川	Sichuan	254520	139437	115083	446853	271163	175690	563429	320871	242558
贵州	Guizhou	65998	42056	23942	69147	44183	24964	98433	58798	39635
云南	Yunnan	181276	117509	63767	222676	142971	79705	266913	167659	99254
西藏	Tibet	13031	11334	1697	13037	8112	4925	15986	12126	3860
陕西	Shaanxi	214008	131005	83003	222403	137603	84800	278262	173414	104848
甘肃	Gansu	56953	41495	15458	87740	54891	32849	132714	87720	44994
青海	Qinghai	15973	11200	4773	19664	15100	4565	33914	27389	6525
宁夏	Ningxia	44292	32737	11555	44291	32818	11473	65323	51195	14128
新疆	Xinjiang	226404	120413	105991	269170	130850	138320	476986	254055	222931

18-11 各地区按境内目的地和货源地分商品进出口总额

Import and Export Value of Commodities by Places of Destination or Origin in China by Region

单位:万美元 (USD 10 000)

地区	Region	2000			2002			2003		
		进出口 Total	出口 Exports	进口 Imports	进出口 Total	出口 Exports	进口 Imports	进出口 Total	出口 Exports	进口 Imports
全国	**National Total**	**47429628**	**24920255**	**22509373**	**62076607**	**32559597**	**29517010**	**85098757**	**43822777**	**41275980**
北京	Beijing	2424378	766723	1657655	2670211	833685	1836527	3133411	995985	2137426
天津	Tianjin	1715625	767427	948198	2285020	1108387	1176633	3003040	1384932	1618109
河北	Hebei	548711	327814	220897	682908	415768	267139	968589	593993	374596
山西	Shanxi	279154	209094	70060	359739	275155	84584	517926	373515	144412
内蒙古	Inner Mongolia	238627	111400	127227	266538	103212	163326	322632	152567	170065
辽宁	Liaoning	2006747	1058947	947800	2342633	1205989	1136644	2986137	1504708	1481429
吉林	Jilin	298532	148693	149839	407432	186810	220622	673023	240856	432167
黑龙江	Heilongjiang	399259	242393	156866	468766	241239	227526	621514	372503	249011
上海	Shanghai	5470336	2463961	3006375	7225129	3101288	4123841	11051596	4583292	6468305
江苏	Jiangsu	4919437	2637694	2281743	7448888	3901482	3547407	12128389	5958671	6169718
浙江	Zhejiang	3152170	2048214	1103956	4635482	3156471	1479011	6631807	4438510	2193298
安徽	Anhui	368983	211942	157041	420473	232631	187842	567499	276877	290621
福建	Fujian	2295726	1362282	933444	3032918	1838727	1194191	3856262	2346763	1509499
江西	Jiangxi	205206	118837	86369	199678	105792	93887	295684	141502	154182
山东	Shandong	2824997	1609267	1215730	3736954	2150069	1586886	4941117	2769400	2171717
河南	Henan	312389	158683	153706	373042	233571	139471	558253	333074	225179
湖北	Hubei	389264	189977	199287	453214	207335	245879	580831	256564	324268
湖南	Hunan	299226	163190	136036	327337	180355	146981	469895	216386	253509
广东	Guangdong	17548753	9342792	8205961	22545138	11909156	10635982	28922994	15370992	13552002
广西	Guangxi	228496	164048	64448	260694	147665	113029	322168	177705	144463
海南	Hainan	109420	60853	48567	179312	67461	111851	191151	64842	126309
重庆	Chongqing	185107	106048	79059	202313	111615	90698	255927	148969	106958
四川	Sichuan	277752	143360	134392	446145	262983	183161	577991	302836	275156
贵州	Guizhou	85646	48166	37480	98029	56551	41478	155344	81182	74162
云南	Yunnan	188420	109271	79149	232758	129403	103355	272005	146961	125044
西藏	Tibet	14892	10902	3990	12521	6816	5705	14686	9908	4778
陕西	Shaanxi	238754	132693	106061	278413	157739	120674	355470	190697	164772
甘肃	Gansu	69155	42079	27076	103829	51047	52782	129211	74062	55150
青海	Qinghai	22645	13355	9290	23444	16228	7216	34277	22081	12196
宁夏	Ningxia	53211	35426	17785	49422	35938	13483	74464	53802	20662
新疆	Xinjiang	258610	114724	143886	308232	129029	179203	485462	238643	246819

18-12 各地区外商投资企业商品进出口总额

Value of Import and Export Goods of Foreign-funded Enterprises by Region

单位:万美元 (USD 10 000)

地 区	Region	2000			2002			2003		
		进出口 Total	出 口 Exports	进 口 Imports	进出口 Total	出 口 Exports	进 口 Imports	进出口 Total	出 口 Exports	进 口 Imports
全 国	**National Total**	**23671390**	**11944121**	**11727269**	**33023948**	**16998509**	**16025439**	**47216996**	**24030598**	**23186398**
北 京	Beijing	776847	287108	489739	877384	401640	475745	1180654	512473	668181
天 津	Tianjin	1369289	637925	731364	1831326	909006	922320	2328980	1141831	1187149
河 北	Hebei	158147	101240	56907	225227	143722	81504	305669	184636	121032
山 西	Shanxi	41876	15209	26667	24149	16089	8060	41227	26390	14836
内蒙古	Inner Mongolia	18157	13799	4358	25031	12489	12543	20930	14906	6024
辽 宁	Liaoning	1229698	624464	605234	1346998	720003	626996	1656935	874599	782336
吉 林	Jilin	112274	39197	73077	172414	40392	132022	270414	41056	229358
黑龙江	Heilongjiang	47353	26679	20674	64718	28162	36556	63223	29288	33935
上 海	Shanghai	3341054	1426102	1914952	4501428	1915697	2585731	7195227	3079445	4115782
江 苏	Jiangsu	3018082	1445340	1572742	4988156	2424878	2563278	8598191	4111856	4486335
浙 江	Zhejiang	938993	534851	404142	1458388	920127	538261	2193179	1305000	888179
安 徽	Anhui	94779	39993	54786	112891	46184	66708	153315	57917	95398
福 建	Fujian	1405740	759713	646027	1879764	1046590	833174	2367421	1346529	1020892
江 西	Jiangxi	31814	16298	15516	40650	18067	22583	67215	27706	39509
山 东	Shandong	1392569	792766	599803	1941081	1098793	842288	2435767	1376753	1059014
河 南	Henan	57695	30889	26806	67033	37201	29832	106329	53652	52676
湖 北	Hubei	104686	42956	61730	146268	66922	79346	201845	84242	117604
湖 南	Hunan	47717	18250	29467	66298	24304	41994	76867	33406	43461
广 东	Guangdong	9203696	4951011	4252685	12860694	6962505	5898189	17467761	9537313	7930449
广 西	Guangxi	55339	34112	21227	78204	30688	47515	103708	37732	65976
海 南	Hainan	45993	30464	15529	95336	35466	59871	82681	27756	54925
重 庆	Chongqing	32389	9666	22723	37812	9732	28080	61754	13695	48058
四 川	Sichuan	61524	24517	37007	66785	32046	34738	95710	45192	50518
贵 州	Guizhou	5690	4012	1678	12810	5423	7387	27763	11056	16708
云 南	Yunnan	19658	8113	11545	25382	13067	12315	26776	14403	12374
西 藏	Tibet	634	389	245	290	243	48	379	175	204
陕 西	Shaanxi	35433	11611	23822	40409	11453	28956	52999	15522	37478
甘 肃	Gansu	5657	3832	1825	13510	10000	3510	14162	10750	3412
青 海	Qinghai	925	202	723	1138	312	826	1411	1295	116
宁 夏	Ningxia	6125	4294	1831	9339	6153	3186	11913	7799	4114
新 疆	Xinjiang	11557	9119	2438	9847	6209	3638	14779	9382	5397

18-13 利用外资概况

Utilization of Foreign Capital

项目单位: 个;　金额单位: 亿美元　(unit) (USD 100 million)

年 份 Year	总 计 Total		对外借款 Foreign Loans		外商直接投资 Direct Foreign Investments		外商其他投资额 Other Foreign Investments
	项 目 Number of Projects	金 额 Value	项 目 Number of Projects	金 额 Value	项 目 Number of Projects	金 额 Value	
合同利用外资额 Total Amount of Contracted Foreign Capital							
1979-1984	3365	287.69	117	169.78	3248	103.93	13.98
1985	3145	98.67	72	35.34	3073	59.31	4.02
1989	5909	114.79	130	51.85	5779	56.00	6.94
1990	7371	120.86	98	50.99	7273	65.96	3.91
1995	37184	1032.05	173	112.88	37011	912.82	6.35
1996	24673	816.10	117	79.62	24556	732.77	3.71
1997	21138	610.58	137	58.72	21001	510.04	41.82
1998	19850	632.01	51	83.85	19799	521.02	27.14
1999	17022	520.09	104	83.60	16918	412.23	24.26
2000	22347	711.30			22347	623.80	87.50
2001	26140	719.76			26140	691.95	27.81
2002	34171	847.51			34171	827.68	19.82
2003	41081	1169.01			41081	1150.70	18.32
实际利用外资额 Total Amount of Foreign Capital Actually Utilized							
1979-1984		171.43		130.41		30.60	10.42
1985		44.62		25.06		16.58	2.98
1989		100.59		62.86		33.92	3.81
1990		102.89		65.34		34.87	2.68
1995		481.33		103.27		375.21	2.85
1996		548.04		126.69		417.25	4.10
1997		644.08		120.21		452.57	71.30
1998		585.57		110.00		454.63	20.94
1999		526.59		102.12		403.19	21.28
2000		593.56		100.00		407.15	86.41
2001		496.72				468.78	27.94
2002		550.11				527.43	22.68
2003		561.40				535.05	26.35
1979-2003		6795.58		1471.57		4997.60	326.41

18-14 按方式分外商投资额

Amount of Foreign Investment by Type

金额单位: 亿美元　(USD 100 million)

指 标	Item	2002 项目（个） Number of Projects	2002 合同金额 Contracted Value	2002 实际使用金额 Used Value	2003 项目（个） Number of Projects	2003 合同金额 Contracted Value	2003 实际使用金额 Used Value
总 计	**Total**	**34171**	**847.51**	**550.11**	**41081**	**1169.01**	**561.40**
外商直接投资	**Foreign Direct Investments**	**34171**	**827.68**	**527.43**	**41081**	**1150.70**	**535.05**
合资经营企业	Joint Ventures Enterprises	10380	185.02	149.92	12521	255.06	153.92
合作经营企业	Cooperative Operation Enterprises	1595	62.17	50.58	1547	74.79	38.36
外资企业	Foreign Investment Enterprises	22173	572.55	317.25	26943	816.09	333.84
外商投资股份制企业	Foreign Investment Share Enterprises	19	7.39	6.97	37	3.89	3.28
合作开发	Cooperative Development	4	0.55	2.72	8	0.86	0.32
其他	Others				25		5.31
外商其他投资	**Other Foreign Investment**		**19.82**	**22.68**		**18.32**	**26.35**
对外发行股票	Sale Share					0.42	2.75
国际租赁	International Lease		1.30	1.31		1.29	1.29
补偿贸易	Compensation Trade			0.04			0.07
加工装配	Processing and Assembly		18.52	21.33		16.61	22.25

18-15 按国别(地区)分实际外商投资额

Actually Foreign Investment by Country or Region

单位: 万美元 (USD 10 000)

国别(地区)	Country (Region)	2002		2003	
		外商直接投资 Foreign Direct Investment	外商其他投资 Foreign Other Investment	外商直接投资 Foreign Direct Investment	外商其他投资 Foreign Other Investment
总计	**Total**	**5274286**	**226823**	**5350467**	**263548**
亚洲	**Asia**	**3256997**	**196401**	**3410169**	**240559**
巴林	Bahrain			101	
孟加拉国	Bangladesh	48		306	
文莱	Brunei	1736		5260	275
缅甸	Myanmar	1676		351	
柬埔寨	Cambodia	1374		1252	
塞浦路斯	Cyprus	107		83	
朝鲜	Korea,DPR	374		238	
中国香港	Hong Kong, China	1786093	130902	1770010	181596
印度	India	3057		1593	
印度尼西亚	Indonesia	12164		15013	
伊朗	Iran	8		55	
伊拉克	Iraq	150		7	
以色列	Israel	952		1573	
日本	Japan	419009	16608	505419	8828
约旦	Jordan	49		622	
科威特	Kuwait	20		10	
老挝	Laos	515		40	
黎巴嫩	Lebanon	20		124	
中国澳门	Macao, China	46838	3335	41660	1550
马来西亚	Malaysia	36786		25103	21
蒙古	Mongolia	76	96	18	
阿曼	Oman	250		126	
巴基斯坦	Pakistan	137		343	
菲律宾	the Philippines	18600		22001	
沙特阿拉伯	Saudi Arabia	1314		355	
新加坡	Singapore	233720	214	205840	142
韩国	Republic of Korea	272073	793	448854	755
斯里兰卡	Sri Lanka	268		112	
叙利亚	Syria	4		39	
泰国	Thailand	18772		17352	385
土耳其	Turkey	243		1270	
阿联酋	United Arab Emirates	3230		6958	
也门	Republic of Yemen	16		26	
越南	Viet Nam	251		331	
中国台湾	Taiwan, China	397064	44453	337724	47007
亚洲其他国家	Other Countries in Asia	3			
非洲	**Africa**	**56462**	**3**	**61776**	
#阿尔及利亚	Algeria	108		183	
贝宁	Benin	1071		330	
博茨瓦纳	Botswana	12		137	
刚果	Congo			137	
埃及	Egypt	182		334	
加蓬	Gabon			12	
肯尼亚	Kenya	7			
马达加斯加	Madagascar	176		190	
毛里求斯	Mauritius	48369	3	52098	
摩洛哥	Morocco			76	
纳米比亚	Namibia	70		391	
尼日尔	Niger	140			

18-15 续表 1 continued

单位: 万美元 (USD 10 000)

国别(地区)	Country (Region)	2002		2003	
		外商直接投资 Foreign Direct Investment	外商其他投资 Foreign Other Investment	外商直接投资 Foreign Direct Investment	外商其他投资 Foreign Other Investment
尼日利亚	Nigeria	646		2083	
塞舌尔	Seychelles	597		246	
塞拉利昂	Sierra Leone	57		2	
南非	South Africa	2593		3245	
苏丹	Sudan	2			
坦桑尼亚	Tanzania			50	
多哥	Togo	15		210	
乌干达	Uganda	15			
赞比亚	Zambia	15		109	
津巴布韦	Zimbabwe	180			
利比亚	Libyan	16			
冈比亚	Gambia	1006			
利比里亚	Liberia	40		1124	
几内亚（比绍）	Guinea Bissau	75		20	
喀麦隆	Cameroon	16		73	
佛得角	Cape Verde	350		33	
卢旺达	Rwanda	4			
莱索托	Lesotho	200			
非洲其他国家	Other Countries in Africa	500		693	
欧洲	**Europe**	**404891**	**4240**	**427197**	**4132**
#比利时	Belgium	12428		11059	
丹麦	Denmark	7109	1	4282	1
英国	United Kingdom	89576	2089	74247	1146
德国	Germany	92796	16	85697	2942
法国	France	57560	2102	60431	
爱尔兰	Ireland	1322		1061	
意大利	Italy	17674		31670	
卢森堡	Luxembourg	1353		17543	
荷兰	Netherlands	57175		72549	
希腊	Greece	617		177	
葡萄牙	Portugal	976		415	
西班牙	Spain	9224		9181	
阿尔巴尼亚	Albania			65	
奥地利	Austria	6727		9450	
保加利亚	Bulgaria	214		234	
芬兰	Finland	6465		3239	
直布罗陀	Gibraltar	31		49	
匈牙利	Hungary	2073		2366	
冰岛	Iceland	28			
列支敦士登	Liechtenstein			229	
马耳他	Malta	133		113	
挪威	Norway	2899		1861	
波兰	Poland	367		364	
罗马尼亚	Romania	2059		1527	
圣马力诺	San Marino			450	
瑞典	Sweden	9980		12030	43
瑞士	Switzerland	19980	32	18134	
阿塞拜疆	Azerbaijan	53		25	
白俄罗斯	Belorussia	2		83	
哈萨克	Kazakhstan	276		70	
俄罗斯	Russia	3865		5430	
乌克兰	Ukraine	109		279	
乌兹别克斯坦	Uzbekstan	20			
南斯拉夫	Yugoslavia	12		190	
克罗地亚	Croatia	2		4	
捷克	Czech	1569		1245	
斯洛伐克	Slovakia	69		1175	
马其顿	Macedonia			6	

18-15 续表 2 continued

单位: 万美元 (USD 10 000)

国别(地区)	Country (Region)	2002		2003	
		外商直接投资 Foreign Direct Investment	外商其他投资 Foreign Other Investment	外商直接投资 Foreign Direct Investment	外商其他投资 Foreign Other Investment
吉尔吉斯	Kirghizia	25		90	
拉脱维亚	Latvia	10			
格鲁吉亚	Georgia	20			
欧洲其他国家	Other Countries in Europe	93		177	
拉丁美洲	**Latin America**	**754979**	**3720**	**690657**	**784**
阿根廷	Argentina	1030		1889	
巴哈马	Bahamas	8990		8787	
巴巴多斯	Barbados	1611		2446	
伯利兹	Belize	2502		1990	
玻利维亚	Bolivia	607		290	
巴西	Brazil	1536		1671	
开曼群岛	Cayman Islands	117954		86604	
智利	Chile	1189		801	
哥伦比亚	Colombia			47	
哥斯达黎加	Costa Rica	598			
古巴	Cuba			1407	
多米尼加联邦	Commonwealth of Dominica	38			
多米尼加共和国	Republic of Dominica	748		307	
厄瓜多尔	Ecuador	27		53	
危地马拉	Guatemala	147			
洪都拉斯	Honduras	106		69	
牙买加	Jamaica			10	
墨西哥	Mexico	731		555	
尼加拉瓜	Nicaragua			120	
巴拿马	Panama	4646		3283	
巴拉圭	Paraguay	107		60	
秘鲁	Peru	112		90	
波多黎各	Puerto Rico			10	
萨尔瓦多	El Salvador			34	
苏里南	Suriname			243	
特克斯和凯科斯岛	Turks and Caicos Islands	80		57	
委内瑞拉	Venezuela	203		128	
维尔京群岛	Virgin Islands	611739	3720	577696	784
圣其茨-尼维斯	St.Kitts-Nevis			1400	
拉美洲其他国家	Other Countries in Latin America	278		610	
北美洲	**North America**	**649032**	**13249**	**516135**	**17253**
#加拿大	Canada	58798		56351	
美国	United States	542392	13249	419851	17253
百慕大	Bermuda	47842		39820	
北美洲其他国家	Other Countries in North America			113	
大洋洲及太平洋岛屿	**Oceanic and Pacific Islands**	**141722**	**129**	**173119**	**305**
#澳大利亚	Australia	38070		59253	
库克群岛	Cook Islands	388	129	251	5
斐济	Fiji	32			
瑙鲁	Nauru	119		258	
新西兰	New Zealand	4616		6577	133
巴布亚新几内亚	Papua New Guinea			45	
汤加	Tonga	228		81	
萨摩亚	Samoan	87947		98572	167
图瓦卢	Tuvalu	200			
马绍尔群岛	Marshall Islands	668		1102	
基里巴斯	Kiribati	106		110	
东萨摩亚	East Samoan	6420			
贝劳共和国	Palau			5158	
其它太平洋岛屿	Other Pacific Islands	2322		1247	
大洋洲其他国家	Other Countries in Oceanic	606		465	
其他	**Others**	**10129**	**9084**	**71414**	**515**

注：外商其他投资的“其他”项中含当年对外发行股票额。

a) The "Others" item of foreign other investment include the stock issued in foreign countries at the same year.

18-16 按地区分实际外商投资额

Actually Foreign Investment by Region

单位: 万美元 (USD 10 000)

地区、部门	Region and Sector	2002		2003	
		外商直接投资 Foreign Direct Investment	外商其他投资 Foreign Other Investment	外商直接投资 Foreign Direct Investment	外商其他投资 Foreign Other Investment
总　计	**National Total**	**5274286**	**226826**	**5350467**	**263548**
省市合计	**Regional Total**	**5247126**	**5316336**	**5294028**	
北　京	Beijing	172464		219126	
天　津	Tianjin	158195		153473	
河　北	Hebei	78271	490	96405	13574
山　西	Shanxi	21164		21361	
内蒙古	Inner Mongolia	17701		8854	
辽　宁	Liaoning	341168		282410	
吉　林	Jilin	24468		19059	
黑龙江	Heilongjiang	35511		32180	
上　海	Shanghai	427229		546849	
江　苏	Jiangsu	1018960		1056365	
浙　江	Zhejiang	307610		498055	
安　徽	Anhui	38375		36720	
福　建	Fujian	383837		259903	
江　西	Jiangxi	108197		161202	
山　东	Shandong	473404	6606	601617	
河　南	Henan	40463		53903	
湖　北	Hubei	142665	21870	156886	22772
湖　南	Hunan	90022		101835	
广　东	Guangdong	1133400	197732	782294	227041
广　西	Guangxi	41726		41856	
海　南	Hainan	51196		42125	
重　庆	Chongqing	19576	128	26083	161
四　川	Sichuan	55583		41231	
贵　州	Guizhou	3821		4521	
云　南	Yunnan	11169		8384	
西　藏	Tibet				
陕　西	Shaanxi	36005		33190	
甘　肃	Gansu	6121		2342	
青　海	Qinghai	4726		2522	
宁　夏	Ningxia	2200		1743	
新　疆	Xinjiang	1899		1534	
部门合计	**Total of the Ministries and Other Departments**	**27160**		56439	

注：外商其他投资部门合计为当年对外发行股票额。

a) Total of the foreign other investment department is external issue .

18-17 按行业分合同外商直接投资额
Contracted Foreign Direct Investment by Sector

行 业	Sector	项 目(个) Number of Projects (unit)		金 额(万美元) Amount of Capital (USD 10 000)	
		2002	2003	2002	2003
总 计	**National Total**	**34171**	**41081**	**8276833**	**11506969**
农、林、牧、渔业	Farming, Forestry, Animal Husbandry and Fishery	975	1116	168804	227611
采掘业	Mining and Quarrying	164	211	38088	65566
制造业	Manufacturing	24930	29281	5926985	8074727
电力、煤气及水的生产和供应业	Electric Power, Gas and Water Production and Supply	185	333	147495	207321
建筑业	Construction	329	396	105761	167717
地质勘查业、水利管理业	Geological Prospecting and Water Conservancy	10	16	3088	5050
交通运输、仓储及邮电通信业	Transport, Storage, Post and Telecommunication Services	405	506	152902	501475
批发和零售贸易餐饮业	Wholesale & Retail Trade and Catering Services	1716	2207	166364	238389
金融、保险业	Banking and Insurance	17	23	46002	31880
房地产业	Real Estate Management	1316	1553	721713	910568
社会服务业	Social Services	3418	4242	498789	704220
卫生体育和社会福利业	Health Care, Sports and Social Welfare	50	85	25796	26941
教育、文化艺术和广播电影电视业	Education, Culture and Arts, Radio, Film and Television	48	70	10884	28201
科学研究和综合技术服务业	Scientific Research and Polytechnic Services	227	558	53365	75306
其他行业	Other Sectors	381	484	210797	241997

18-18 按行业分实际外商直接投资额
Foreign Direct Investment Actually Utilized by Sector

单位：万美元 (USD 10 000)

行 业	Sector	2000	2002	2003
总 计	**National Total**	**4071481**	**5274286**	**5350467**
农、林、牧、渔业	Farming, Forestry, Animal Husbandry and Fishery	67594	102764	100084
采掘业	Mining and Quarrying	58328	58106	33635
制造业	Manufacturing	2584417	3679998	3693570
电力、煤气及水的生产和供应业	Electric Power, Gas and Water Production and Supply	224212	137508	129538
建筑业	Construction	90542	70877	61176
地质勘查业、水利管理业	Geological Prospecting and Water Conservancy	481	696	1777
交通运输、仓储及邮电通信业	Transport, Storage, Post and Telecommunication Services	101188	91346	86737
批发和零售贸易餐饮业	Wholesale & Retail Trade and Catering Services	85781	93264	111604
金融、保险业	Banking and Insurance	7629	10665	23199
房地产业	Real Estate Management	465751	566277	523560
社会服务业	Social Services	218544	294345	316095
卫生体育和社会福利业	Health Care, Sports and Social Welfare	10588	12807	12737
教育、文化艺术和广播电影电视业	Education, Culture and Arts, Radio, Film and Television	5446	3779	5782
科学研究和综合技术服务业	Scientific Research and Polytechnic Services	5703	19752	25871
其他行业	Other Sectors	145277	132102	225102

18-19 按行业分外商投资企业年底注册登记情况

Sector Distribution Registered of Foreign Funded Enterprises at the Year-end

行业	Sector	企业数(户) Number of Enterprises (household)		投资总额(亿美元) Total Investment (100 million USD)		注册资本(亿美元) Registered Capital (100 million USD)		#外方 Capital Invested by Foreign Partner	
		2002	2003	2002	2003	2002	2003	2002	2003
合计	**National Total**	**208056**	**226373**	**9818.93**	**11173.51**	**5521.19**	**6226.41**	**4020.00**	**4657.79**
农、林、牧、渔业	Farming, Forestry, Animal Husbandry and Fishery	4640	4957	103.71	119.30	68.47	77.87	52.20	61.52
采掘业	Mining and Quarrying	957	903	36.58	39.29	25.20	27.02	16.91	18.49
制造业	Manufacturing	146515	159789	5727.61	6708.09	3393.40	3850.77	2482.96	2894.48
电力、煤气及水的生产和供应业	Electricity, Gas and Water Production and Supply	1185	1349	538.98	562.24	213.94	226.47	120.25	128.63
建筑业	Construction	4197	4098	229.37	255.49	123.67	139.89	78.60	91.85
地质勘查和水利管理业	Geological Prospecting and Water Conservancy	153	160	43.79	44.72	15.90	22.39	14.59	21.07
交通运输、仓储及邮电通信业	Transport, Storage, Post and Telecommunication Services	3540	3660	445.88	567.26	227.88	302.88	169.62	231.06
批发和零售贸易餐饮业	Wholesale and Retail Trade & Catering Services	12431	13578	262.94	285.92	161.21	176.95	116.89	131.56
金融、保险业	Finance and Insurance	87	119	25.30	36.03	23.72	33.51	16.26	21.50
房地产业	Real Estate	11850	12203	1480.33	1561.69	693.84	748.17	518.65	579.75
社会服务业	Social Services	16825	18330	589.56	639.20	356.65	381.67	249.97	279.02
卫生体育和社会福利业	Health Care, Sports and Social Welfare	468	505	32.35	37.59	18.18	21.18	12.99	14.82
教育、文化艺术及广播电影电视业	Education, Culture and Arts, Radio, Film and Television	443	435	12.65	13.21	9.15	9.79	6.55	7.24
科学研究和综合技术服务业	Scientific Research and Polytechnic Services	2705	3683	75.83	106.65	47.49	69.50	37.96	55.31
其他	Others	2060	2604	214.07	196.83	142.47	138.35	125.59	121.50

18-20 各地区外商投资企业年底注册登记情况

Basic Indicators of Registered Foreign Funded Enterprises by Region at the Year-end

地 区	Region	企业数(户) Number of Enterprises (household)		投资总额(亿美元) Total Investment (100USD)		注册资本(亿美元) Registered Capital (USD 10 000)		#外 方 Capital Invested by Foreign Partner	
		2002	2003	2002	2003	2002	2003	2002	2003
全 国	**National Total**	**208056**	**226373**	**9818.93**	**11173.51**	**5521.19**	**6226.41**	**4020.00**	**4657.79**
北 京	Beijing	9172	9185	454.95	463.28	252.10	256.03	178.92	182.59
天 津	Tianjin	9020	9792	365.29	415.55	203.43	245.20	160.18	195.50
河 北	Hebei	3396	3454	154.77	175.19	88.16	97.92	53.91	60.26
山 西	Shanxi	773	760	57.69	61.19	29.75	31.22	17.27	18.72
内蒙古	Inner Mongolia	805	923	24.23	38.36	16.99	22.05	9.50	13.79
辽 宁	Liaoning	13642	13814	664.08	735.01	430.02	386.88	279.56	282.22
吉 林	Jilin	2541	2690	179.12	182.65	54.57	56.79	33.96	35.71
黑龙江	Heilongjiang	2067	2243	74.68	81.23	43.94	49.43	25.39	29.42
上 海	Shanghai	20963	24133	1279.64	1508.16	691.61	804.10	516.33	615.14
江 苏	Jiangsu	22991	26925	1254.84	1500.14	623.53	747.26	495.51	600.45
浙 江	Zhejiang	12111	15140	432.02	612.26	243.37	346.47	162.81	242.37
安 徽	Anhui	1914	2034	96.22	116.44	59.57	69.63	36.94	42.05
福 建	Fujian	15563	16884	594.00	661.18	330.41	360.79	286.88	318.75
江 西	Jiangxi	2478	2939	98.69	136.67	48.35	70.65	35.69	50.79
山 东	Shandong	14741	17237	470.87	596.62	282.16	352.29	182.28	241.87
河 南	Henan	2437	2403	118.16	126.28	70.40	75.53	43.52	48.02
湖 北	Hubei	3705	4031	158.54	176.76	93.11	107.11	56.07	68.35
湖 南	Hunan	2152	2337	86.81	102.14	48.53	58.67	33.33	42.30
广 东	Guangdong	49875	51672	2363.54	2412.62	1349.49	1405.06	1045.33	1106.67
广 西	Guangxi	2509	2311	104.44	104.48	61.35	60.57	41.21	42.97
海 南	Hainan	2251	2366	98.51	89.00	50.22	55.96	37.45	42.59
重 庆	Chongqing	1388	1129	68.93	65.47	39.65	35.43	25.28	22.73
四 川	Sichuan	3913	4162	119.98	136.32	81.12	89.48	45.10	52.17
贵 州	Guizhou	639	595	18.91	21.00	12.34	13.78	8.16	9.39
云 南	Yunnan	1619	1666	60.55	73.09	36.69	40.70	22.28	24.55
西 藏	Tibet	94	107	3.49	3.59	1.98	2.03	1.25	1.27
陕 西	Shaanxi	2993	3179	106.25	116.00	64.07	72.02	41.23	47.59
甘 肃	Gansu	694	607	21.66	21.64	14.20	14.52	8.24	8.83
青 海	Qinghai	140	147	7.00	7.86	3.49	4.78	2.46	3.70
宁 夏	Ningxia	454	481	22.60	38.84	9.33	15.14	6.02	11.58
新 疆	Xinjiang	338	342	11.44	12.51	7.53	8.21	4.19	4.52
国家工商行政管理局	State Administration for Industry and Commerce	678	685	247.06	381.96	179.70	270.70	123.74	190.90

18-21 对外经济合作

Economic Cooperation with Foreign Countries or Regions

年份 Year	合同数 (份) Number of Contracts (unit)	合同金额 (亿美元) Contracted Value (100 million USD)	完成营业额 (亿美元) Value of Business Fulfilled (100 million USD)
总计 Total	**245448**	**1278.67**	**930.72**
1976-1988	7534	105.95	60.91
1989	3100	22.12	16.86
1990	5175	26.04	18.67
1991	8438	36.09	23.63
1992	9405	65.85	30.49
1993	11605	68.00	45.38
1994	17491	79.88	59.78
1995	19321	96.72	65.88
1996	24891	102.73	76.96
1997	28442	113.56	83.83
1998	25955	117.73	101.34
1999	21126	130.02	112.35
2000	23565	149.43	113.25
2001	39400	164.55	121.39
2002	34461	178.91	143.52
2003	42059	209.30	172.34
对外承包工程 Contracted Projects			
1976-1988	3449	89.00	49.70
1989	776	17.81	14.84
1990	920	21.25	16.44
1991	1171	25.24	19.70
1992	1164	52.51	24.03
1993	1393	51.89	36.68
1994	1702	60.28	48.83
1995	1558	74.84	51.08
1996	1634	77.28	58.21
1997	2085	85.16	60.36
1998	2322	92.43	77.69
1999	2527	101.99	85.22
2000	2597	117.19	83.79
2001	5836	130.39	88.99
2002	4036	150.55	111.94
2003	3708	176.67	138.37
对外劳务合作 Labor Cooperation			
1976-1988	4085	16.95	11.21
1989	2324	4.31	2.02
1990	4255	4.78	2.23
1991	7267	10.85	3.93
1992	8241	13.35	6.46
1993	10212	16.11	8.70
1994	15789	19.60	10.95
1995	17397	20.07	13.47
1996	22723	22.80	17.12
1997	25743	25.50	21.65
1998	23191	23.90	22.76
1999	18173	26.32	26.23
2000	20474	29.91	28.13
2001	33358	33.28	31.77
2002	30163	27.52	30.71
2003	38043	30.87	33.09
对外设计咨询 Design Consultation			
1995	366	1.81	1.33
1996	534	2.65	1.64
1997	614	2.90	1.82
1998	442	1.40	0.89
1999	426	1.71	0.90
2000	494	2.33	1.34
2001	206	0.88	0.63
2002	262	0.85	0.87
2003	308	1.76	0.88

18-22 按国别(地区)分对外经济合作完成营业额

Turnover of Economic Cooperation with Foreign Countries or Regions

单位：万美元 (USD 10 000)

国别(地区)	Country (Region)	2002				2003			
		合计 Total	承包工程 Contracted Projects	劳务合作 Labour Cooperation	设计咨询 Design Consultation	合计 Total	承包工程 Contracted Projects	劳务合作 Labour Cooperation	设计咨询 Design Consultation
合计	**Total**	**1435222**	**1119358**	**307141**	**8723**	**1723393**	**1383736**	**330881**	**8776**
亚洲	**Asia**	**780699**	**573791**	**203360**	**3548**	**903868**	**692664**	**208131**	**3073**
#阿富汗	Afghanistan					524	519		5
巴林	Bahrain	7		7		11	1	10	
孟加拉国	Bangladesh	41243	40024	582	637	35349	34882	370	97
文莱	Brunei	49	35	14		87		87	
缅甸	Myanmar	30020	28805	817	398	37878	37074	643	161
柬埔寨	Cambodia	7981	5756	2139	86	5266	3542	1435	289
塞浦路斯	Cyprus	1174	1028	146		2896	2796	100	
朝鲜	Korea, DPR	787	255	517	15	902	487	415	
中国香港	Hong Kong, China	231340	213750	17185	405	283751	263732	19803	216
印度	India	5984	5764	148	72	8954	8485	145	324
印度尼西亚	Indonesia	9742	8134	1600	8	16361	14414	1939	8
伊朗	Iran	38275	38208	27	40	33717	32844	442	431
伊拉克	Iraq	15325	14506	4	815	12995	12843		152
以色列	Israel	15230	1086	14144		11696	786	10910	
日本	Japan	59433	5004	54337	92	70461	2739	67680	42
约旦	Jordan	9008	5492	3504	12	7679	3426	4253	
科威特	Kuwait	1359	121	1235	3	2717	798	1919	
老挝	Laos	13951	13677	132	142	10331	10189	116	26
黎巴嫩	Lebanon	4		4		2274	2271	3	
中国澳门	Macao, China	18904	7934	10911	59	29223	17041	11830	352
马来西亚	Malaysia	15225	12827	2372	26	24918	23308	1587	23
马尔代夫	Maldives	210	79	128	3	35		35	
蒙古	Mongolia	6011	5485	506	20	17964	17073	807	84
尼泊尔	Nepal	2254	2243	10	1	2433	2424	9	
阿曼	Oman	179		179		1453	1011	442	
巴基斯坦	Pakistan	35732	35455	160	117	61758	61473	145	140
菲律宾	Philippines	7537	7348	189		10254	10082	167	5
卡塔尔	Qatar	2747	2621	126		1599	1482	117	
沙特阿拉伯	Saudi Arabia	6387	5323	1064		4745	3485	1260	
新加坡	Singapore	108637	54026	54611		92796	49933	42863	
韩国	Republic of Korea	21079	893	20168	18	31879	9101	22755	23
斯里兰卡	Sri Lanka	5641	5496	144	1	10684	10413	71	200
叙利亚	Syrian	2271	2260	11		689	684	5	
泰国	Thailand	19819	18428	1365	26	12423	11411	972	40
土耳其	Turkey	2512	2339	173		2109	1895	186	28

18-22 续表 1 continued

单位：万美元 (USD 10 000)

国别(地区)	Country (Region)	2002				2003			
		合　计 Total	承包工程 Contracted Projects	劳务合作 Labour Cooperation	设计咨询 Design Consultation	合　计 Total	承包工程 Contracted Projects	劳务合作 Labour Cooperation	设计咨询 Design Consultation
阿联酋	United Arab Emirates	8570	5823	2747		16289	13331	2958	
也门共和国	Republic of Yemen	6656	6513	143		5839	5644	185	10
越南	Vietnam	17636	14700	2413	523	19492	16148	2927	417
中国台湾	Taiwan, China	11465	2047	9398	20	13437	4897	8540	
非洲	**Africa**	**202295**	**181357**	**19579**	**1359**	**283269**	**260125**	**22256**	**888**
#阿尔及利亚	Algeria	22712	21158	1548	6	50026	47176	2846	4
安哥拉	Angola	524	408	116		3537	3407	71	59
贝宁	Benin	1560	1542	15	3	1260	1256	4	
博茨瓦纳	Botswana	4716	4522	194		13547	13336	206	5
布隆迪	Burundi	192	179	13		199	152	5	42
喀麦隆	Cameroon	1555	1270	159	126	1369	1124	245	
佛得角	Cape Verde	21	16		5	51	45	6	
中非	Central Africa	134	134			1535	1535		
科摩罗	Comoros	2			2	105	101	4	
刚果（布）	Congo(B)	524	400	22	102	1247	1220	15	12
吉布提	Djibouti	382	268	108	6	898	823	66	9
埃及	Egypt	3075	3022	49	4	2431	2374	50	7
赤道几内亚	Eq. Guinea	1198	1171	20	7	1117	1059	34	24
埃塞俄比亚	Ethiopia	16793	15656	1093	44	19650	18048	1574	28
加蓬	Gabon	419	324	51	44	743	704	27	12
冈比亚	Gambia	711	696	15		1326	1304	22	
加纳	Ghana	6877	6743	132	2	4164	4100	61	3
几内亚	Guinea	5949	5546	397	6	7162	6651	511	
几内亚(比绍)	Guinea Bissau	3342	3244	98		2767	2677	82	8
科特迪瓦	Cote d'Lvoire	1183	1127	30	26	744	692	39	13
肯尼亚	Kenya	3319	3293	26		3136	3126	9	1
利比里亚	Liberia	496		496		447		447	
利比亚	Libyan	2194	1478	716		16150	15503	647	
马达加斯加	Madagascar	783	526	257		4328	4052	275	1
马拉维	Malawi	991	991			1472	1472		
马里	Mali	6316	6254	62		8516	8462	54	
毛里塔尼亚	Mauritania	4221	3473	748		4797	3985	792	20
毛里求斯	Mauritius	11170	2204	8966		10548	1851	8697	
摩洛哥	Morocco	2845	2532	313		3743	3423	320	
莫桑比克	Mozambique	2527	2428	17	82	2657	2456	158	43
纳米比亚	Namibia	2420	2326	94		2359	2046	307	6
尼日尔	Niger	1170	1098	72		230	92	138	

18-22 续表 2 continued

单位：万美元 (USD 10 000)

国别(地区)	Country (Region)	2002				2003			
		合　计 Total	承包工程 Contracted Projects	劳务合作 Labour Cooperation	设计咨询 Design Consultation	合　计 Total	承包工程 Contracted Projects	劳务合作 Labour Cooperation	设计咨询 Design Consultation
尼日利亚	Nigeria	15613	14416	1172	25	27536	26428	1091	17
卢旺达	Rwanda	1203	1158	45		747	719	26	2
圣多美和普林西比	Sao Tome & Principe	26	26			24	24		
塞内加尔	Senegal	2537	2399	138		2860	2821	39	
塞舌尔	Seychelles	846	799	43	4	944	919	25	
塞拉利昂	Sierra Leone	2108	2052	44	12	2422	2348	74	
索马里	Somali	23	23			12	12		
南非	S. Africa	647	361	286		1924	1631	283	10
苏丹	Sudan	44032	43327	338	367	48854	47691	809	354
坦桑尼亚	Tanzania	4296	4108	178	10	6052	5865	177	10
多哥	Togo	286	200	82	4	500	415	81	4
突尼斯	Tunisia	3441	3430	11		2434	2429	5	
乌干达	Uganda	1900	1243	653	4	2208	2032	170	6
布基纳法索	Burkina Faso	1	1			19	19		
刚果（金）	Congo(J)	458	439	19		2313	2257	50	6
赞比亚	Zambia	3253	3189	13	51	2451	2395	56	
津巴布韦	Zimbabwe	7781	7382		399	4710	4564		146
莱索托	Lesotho	1958	1270	682	6	3760	2194	1560	6
斯威士兰	Swaziland	48		48		84		84	
厄立特里亚	Eritrea	1512	1505		7	1154	1110	14	30
欧洲	**Europe**	**110739**	**90931**	**17801**	**2007**	**141526**	**116053**	**25042**	**431**
#比利时	Belgium	2000	2000			51	51		
丹麦	Denmark	4		4		931	880	51	
英国	United Kingdom	7759	5479	537	1743	4675	3770	633	
德国	Germany	20653	15291	5306	56	24579	18569	6007	
法国	France	1108	1020	88		4409	4397	11	2
爱尔兰	Ireland	369		369		564	213	351	
意大利	Italy	9136	9116	20		5051	2783	2268	3
荷兰	Netherlands	39		39		51	51		1
希腊	Greece	2883	2245	638		7376	6960	416	
西班牙	Spain	4330	4035	295		1833	1621	212	
阿尔巴尼亚	Albania	200	59	4	137	200	192	6	
奥地利	Austria	8		8		20		20	272
保加利亚	Bulgaria	329		329		72		72	
芬兰	Finland	4		4		2999	2988	11	
匈牙利	Hungary	9		9		1579		1579	

18-22 续表 3 continued

单位：万美元 (USD 10 000)

国别(地区)	Country (Region)	2002 合计 Total	2002 承包工程 Contracted Projects	2002 劳务合作 Labour Cooperation	2002 设计咨询 Design Consultation	2003 合计 Total	2003 承包工程 Contracted Projects	2003 劳务合作 Labour Cooperation	2003 设计咨询 Design Consultation
冰岛	Iceland					84	84		
马耳他	Malta	189	160	26	3	41	33	8	
挪威	Norway	1226	567	659		3506	2559	947	
波兰	Poland	474	467	7		132	130	2	
罗马尼亚	Romania	105	5	100		10077	10024	53	
瑞典	Sweden	3015	3015			33	32	1	
瑞士	Switzerland	39		39		1452	1420	32	
拉脱维亚	Latvia	20		20		24		24	
格鲁吉亚	Georgia	1644	1642	2		1673	1671	2	
亚美尼亚	Armenia	72		72		246	56	190	
阿塞拜疆	Azerbaijan	55	50	5		678	676	2	3
白俄罗斯	Belorussia	67	64		3	879	871	8	
哈萨克	Kazakhstan	24305	24072	233		21269	21023	96	
吉尔吉斯	Kirghizia	1401	1265	136		10376	10363	13	
摩尔多瓦	Moldavia	3		3		2		2	150
俄罗斯	Russia	18559	9952	8552	55	20532	8671	11858	
塔吉克	Tadzhikistan	30	30			646	646		
乌克兰	Ukraine	196	118	78		524	451	73	
乌兹别克	Uzbekstan	2106	2063	43		6079	6068	11	
土库曼	Turkmenistan	6039	6027	12		7297	7290	7	
南斯拉夫	Yugoslavia	2131	2042	89		65		65	
斯洛文尼亚	Slovenia	160	147	13		71	67	4	
爱沙尼亚	Estonia					31	31		
捷克	Czech	5		5		157	152	5	
斯洛伐克共和国	Slovakia Republic	4		4		2		2	
马其顿	Macedonia					1260	1260		
波黑	Bosnia and Herzegovina	7		7					
拉丁美洲	**Latin America**	**40954**	**34722**	**6197**	**35**	**70917**	**64800**	**6090**	**27**
#安提瓜和巴布达	Antigua & Barbuda	655	624	20	11	957	846	102	9
阿根廷	Argentina	1951	1039	912		3014	2249	765	
巴哈马	Bahamas	3		3		1273	1260	13	
巴巴多斯	Barbados	1316	1207	109		757	636	120	1
伯利兹	Belize	121		121		690	602	86	2
玻利维亚	Bolivia	13	13			33	33		
巴西	Brazil	1439	1382	57		1340	1325	15	
智利	Chile	203	203			437	437	0	
哥伦比亚	Colombia	54	49	5		253	249	4	
哥斯达黎加	Costarica	7	7						
古巴	Cuba	7741	7475	266		8941	8876	65	
多米尼加共和国	Republic of Dominica	208	207	1		3367	3366	1	
厄瓜多尔	Ecuador	1195	1039	156		4946	4836	95	15
格林纳达	Grenada	85	85						

18-22 续表 4 continued

单位：万美元 (USD 10 000)

国别(地区)	Country (Region)	2002				2003			
		合计 Total	承包工程 Contracted Projects	劳务合作 Labour Cooperation	设计咨询 Design Consultation	合计 Total	承包工程 Contracted Projects	劳务合作 Labour Cooperation	设计咨询 Design Consultation
危地马拉	Guatemala	29		29					
圭亚那	Guyana	76	30	46		46	10	36	
洪都拉斯	Honduras	124		124		135		135	
牙买加	Jamaica	231		227	4	259		259	
墨西哥	Mexico	1459	604	855		25813	24756	1057	
尼加拉瓜	Nicaragua	415		415		428		428	
巴拿马	Panama	1058		1058		4105	3270	835	
巴拉圭	Paraguay	1		1					
秘鲁	Peru	1751	1587	157	7	3034	1326	1708	
圣卢西亚	Saint Lucia	906	789	117		177	147	30	
圣文森特和格林纳丁斯	Saint Vincent & Grenadines					33		33	
萨尔瓦多	EL Salvador	71		71		46		46	
苏里南	Suriname	2734	2275	457	2	1530	1304	226	
特立尼达和	Trinidad & Tobago	152	150	2		580	580		
乌拉圭	Uruguay	1064	153	911		66	35	31	
委内瑞拉	Venezuela	15892	15811	70	11	8657	8657		
北美洲	**North America**	**72192**	**57304**	**14423**	**465**	**30912**	**16105**	**14529**	**278**
加拿大	Canada	1467	1364	103		817	740	77	0
美国	United States	70725	55940	14320	465	30095	15365	14452	278
大洋洲及太平洋岛屿	**Oceanic & Pacific Islands**	**12216**	**9116**	**3057**	**43**	**8620**	**5564**	**2979**	**77**
#澳大利亚	Australia	3800	3703	91	6	1779	1726	49	4
库克群岛	Cook Islands					124	76		48
斐济	Fiji	2895	2464	431		2258	1588	670	
瓦努阿图	Vanuatu	4		4		37	33	4	
新西兰	New Zealand	465	216	249		338	3	335	
巴布亚新几内亚	Papua New Guinea	1388	1303	79	6	1239	1123	97	19
社会群岛	Society Islands	618		618		90		90	
汤加	Tonga	435	345	73	17	258	186	72	
萨摩亚	Samoa	224		224		636		636	
基里巴斯	Kiribati	9	6		3	135	129		6
密克罗尼西亚	Micronesia FS	1530	601	918	11	1206	595	611	
马绍尔群岛	Marshall Is.	12		12		12		12	
贝劳共和国	Palau	636	478	158		326	105	221	
瓦利斯群岛	Wallis Islands					2		2	
马克萨斯群岛	Marguesas Is.					180		180	
法属波利尼西亚	French Polynesia	20		20					
其它	**Others**	**20518**	**19025**	**1099**	**394**	**27670**	**27309**	**232**	**129**
国境内	**Inner Country**	**195609**	**153112**	**41625**	**872**	**256611**	**201116**	**51622**	**3873**

主要统计指标解释

进出口总额 指实际进出我国国境的货物总金额。包括对外贸易实际进出口货物，来料加工装配进出口货物，国家间、联合国及国际组织无偿援助物资和赠送品，华侨、港澳台同胞和外籍华人捐赠品，租赁期满归承租人所有的租赁货物，进料加工进出口货物，边境地方贸易及边境地区小额贸易进出口货物(边民互市贸易除外)，中外合资企业、中外合作经营企业、外商独资经营企业进出口货物和公用物品，到、离岸价格在规定限额以上的进出口货样和广告品(无商业价值、无使用价值和免费提供出口的除外)，从保税仓库提取在中国境内销售的进口货物，以及其他进出口货物。该指标可以观察一个国家在对外贸易方面的总规模。我国规定出口货物按离岸价格统计，进口货物按到岸价格统计。

商品经营单位所在地进、出口额 指所在地海关注册登记的有进出口经营权的企业实际进、出口额。

商品目的地进口额和商品货源地出口额 目的地进口额指进口货物的消费、使用或最终抵运地的实际进口额，货源地出口额指出口货物的产地或原始发货地的实际出口额。

利用外资 指我国各级政府、部门、企业和其他经济组织通过对外借款、吸收外商直接投资以及用其他方式筹措的境外现汇、设备、技术等。

对外借款 指通过对外正式签订借款协议，从境外筹措的资金，包括外国政府贷款、国际金融组织贷款、外国银行商业贷款、出口信贷以及对外发行债券等。1996年及以前还包括对外发行股票。该指标是我国利用外资的重要部分。

外商直接投资 指外国企业和经济组织或个人(包括华侨、港澳台胞以及我国在境外注册的企业)按我国有关政策、法规，用现汇、实物、技术等在我国境内开办外商独资企业、与我国境内的企业或经济组织共同举办中外合资经营企业、合作经营企业或合作开发资源的投资(包括外商投资收益的再投资)，以及经政府有关部门批准的项目投资总额内企业从境外借入的资金。

外商其他投资 指除对外借款和外商直接投资以外的各种利用外资的形式。包括企业在境内外股票市场公开发行的以外币计价的股票（目前主要是在香港证券市场发行的H股和在境内证券市场发行的B股）发行价总额，国际租赁进口设备的应付款，补偿贸易中外商提供的进口设备、技术、物料的价款，加工装配贸易中外商提供的进口设备、物料的价款。

对外承包工程 指各对外承包公司以招标议标承包方式承揽的下列业务：(1)承包国外工程建设项目；(2)承包我国对外经援项目；(3)承包我国驻外机构的工程建设项目；(4)承包我国境内利用外资进行建设的工程项目；(5)与外国承包公司合营或联合承包工程项目时我国公司分包部分；(6)对外承包兼营的房屋开发业务。对外承包工程的营业额是以货币表现的本期内完成的对外承包工程的工作量，包括以前年度签订的合同和本年度新签订的合同在报告期内完成的工作量。

对外劳务合作 指以收取工资的形式向业主或承包商提供技术和劳动服务的活动。我国对外承包公司在境外开办的合营企业，中国公司同时又提供劳务的，其劳务部分也纳入劳务合作统计。劳务合作营业额按报告期内向雇主提交的结算数(包括工资、加班费和奖金等)统计。

对外设计咨询 指以服务成果向业主收费的技术服务项目。包括承担地形地貌测绘，地质资源勘探与普查，建设区域规划，提供设计文件、图纸、生产工艺技术资料和工程技术经济咨询，工程项目的可行性考察、研究和评估，进行技术指导和培训人员等；也包括承担国(境)内利用外资建设工程项目中的设计咨询项目内收取外币部分。

Explanatory Notes on Main Statistical Indicators

Total Imports and Exports at Customs refer to the real value of commodities imported into and exported from the boundary of China. They include the actual imports and exports through foreign trade, imported and exported goods under the processing and assembling trades and materials, supplies and gifts as aid given gratis between governments and by the United Nations and other international organizations, and contributions donated by overseas Chinese, compatriots in Hong Kong and Macao and Chinese with foreign citizenship, leasing commodities owned by tenant at the expiration of leasing period, the imported and exported commodities processed with imported materials, commodities trading in border areas (excluding mutual exchange goods), the imported and exported commodities and articles for public use of the Sino-foreign joint ventures, cooperative enterprises and ventures exclusively with foreign own investment. Also included are import or export of samples and advertising goods for whose CIF or FOB value are beyond the permitted ceiling (excluding goods of no trading or use value and free commodities for export), imported goods sold in China from bonded warehouses and other imported or exported goods. The indicator of the total imports and exports at customs can be used to observe the total size of external trade in a country. In accordance with the stipulation of the Chinese government, imports are calculated at CIF, while exports are calculated at FOB

Import Export Value by Location of Chinas Foreign Trade Managing Units refers to actual value of imports and exports carried out by corporations which have been registered by the local customhouse and are vested with right to run import export business.

Import Value of Commodities by the Places of their Destination and Export Value of Commodities by the Places of their Origin in China: The former indicator refers to the value of import commodities of the places of their consumption, utilization or the places of their final destination. The latter indicator refers to the value of export commodities of the places of their origin or the places of the commodities dispatched.

Utilization of Foreign Capitals refers to remittance, equipment and technology financed from abroad, by loans, foreign direct investment and other forms undertaken by the Chinese governments at all levels, by various departments, enterprises and other economic units.

Foreign Borrowings refer to funds borrowed from abroad through formal signing of borrowing agreements with foreign institutions, including loans of foreign governments, loans of international financial institutions, commercial loans of foreign banks, export credit, and funds raised by Chinese bonds (and shares before 1996) issued abroad. It is an important part of China's utilization of foreign capitals.

Foreign Direct Investment refers to the investments inside China by foreign enterprises and economic organizations or individuals (including overseas Chinese, compatriots from Hong Kong, Macao and Taiwan, and Chinese enterprises registered abroad), following the relevant policies and laws of China, for the establishment of ventures exclusively with foreign own investment, Sino-foreign joint ventures and cooperative enterprises or for co-operative exploration of resources with enterprises or economic organizations in China. It includes the re investment of the foreign entrepreneurs with the profits gained from the investment and the funds that enterprises borrow from abroad in the total investment of projects which are approved by the relevant department of the government.

Other Investment by Foreign Entrepreneurs refers to all forms of utilization of foreign capitals other than foreign borrowings and foreign direct investment. It includes the total value of stock shares in foreign currencies issued by enterprises at domestic or foreign stock exchanges (now mainly consisting of H shares issued at Hong Kong Security Market and B shares issued at domestic security markets), rent payable for the imported equipment through international leasing arrangement, cost of imported equipment, technology and materials provided by foreign counterparts in compensation trade and processing and assembly trade.

Contracted Projects with Foreign Countries refer to projects undertaken by Chinese contractors (project contracting companies) through bidding process. They include: (1) overseas civil engineering construction projects financed by foreign investors; (2) overseas projects financed by the Chinese government through its foreign aid programs; (3) construction projects of Chinese diplomatic missions, trade offices and other institutions stationed abroad; (4)construction projects in China financed by foreign investment; (5) sub-contracted projects to be taken by Chinese contractors through a joint umbrella project with foreign contractor(s); (6) housing development projects. The business income from international contracted projects is the work volume of contracted projects completed during the reference period, expressed in monetary terms, including completed work on projects signed in previous years.

Service Cooperation with Foreign Countries refers to the activities of providing technology and labour services to employers or contractors in the forms of receiving salaries and wages. Labour services providing by contractual joint ventures of Chinese international contracting corporations should be included in the statistics of service co-operation with foreign countries. The business income of labour service cooperation is the income in the form of wages and salaries, overtime pay, bonuses and other remuneration received from the employers during the reference period.

Overseas Design and Consultation Service refers to projects with charges for technical services from overseas operators. It includes geographic and topographic mapping, geological resource prospecting and survey, planning of construction areas, provision of design documents, blueprints, materials on production process and techniques, as well as engineering, technical and economic consultation, and feasibility study, research and evaluation of projects. Also included under this category are the above-mentioned services of foreign-financed projects in China that are paid in foreign currencies.

十九、旅游

Tourism

简要说明

一、本篇资料的主要内容

旅游统计的主要内容包括：旅行社个数、旅行社职工人数、星级饭店个数、入境国际旅游者(外国人、华侨、港澳同胞和台湾同胞)人数、出境居民人数、国内居民(城镇和农村)旅游人数，以及国际、国内旅游收入等。

二、本篇资料的统计范围

包括国际旅游和国内旅游。

三、本篇的资料来源

本篇资料是国家统计局贸易外经司根据公安部和国家旅游局的资料编制的。资料来源：入境国际旅游人数和国内居民出境人数来自公安部出、入境管理资料；各地区接待国际旅游者人数、旅行社接待国际旅游者人数、国内旅游人数和国内旅游收入来自国家旅游局；国际旅游外汇收入1994年以前由国家统计局贸易外经司根据国际旅游者在华花费外汇券统计资料整理提供；1994年及以后由国家旅游局整理提供；旅行社、星级饭店基本情况来自国家旅游局。

四、本篇的统计调查方法

国际、国内旅游收入和国内出游人数等指标采取抽样调查方法，其余指标均为全面调查统计取得。

Brief Introduction

I. Main Content

Data on tourism mainly include: number of travel agencies, number of employees in travel agencies, number of star-hotels, total number of international tourists received (foreigners, overseas Chinese, Chinese compatriots from Hong Kong, Macao and Taiwan), Chinese residents going abroad, domestic tourists (from urban and from rural areas), number of domestic tourists (urban and rural areas), and income from international and domestic tourism.

II. Coverage of Statistics

Data in this chapter include both international and domestic tourism.

III. Sources of Data

Data in this chapter are compiled by the Department of Trade and Foreign Economic Relations of the National Bureau of Statistics on the basis of data from the Ministry of Public Security and State Tourism Administration. Sources of data are as follows: number of international tourists entering into China and Chinese residents going abroad is provided by the Frontier Administration of the Ministry of Public Security; number of international tourists received by province, number of international tourists received by travel agency, number of domestic tourists and earnings from domestic tourism are provided by the State Tourism Administration; figures on the earnings from international tourism before 1994 are provided by the Department of Trade and Foreign Economic Relations Statistics of the National Bureau of Statistics using data on the expenditure of Foreign Exchange Certificates by international tourists, and since 1994, by the State Tourism Administration; data on basic situation of travel agencies and tourist hotels are provided the State Tourism Administration.

IV. Survey Methodology

Data on the earnings from international and domestic tourism and domestic tourists are collected from sample surveys, while statistics on other items are from comprehensive reporting system.

19-1 旅游事业发展情况

Development of Tourism

指 标	Item	1999	2000	2001	2002	2003
旅行社数 （个）	**Total Number of Travel Agencies (unit)**	**7326**	**8993**	**10532**	**11552**	**13361**
国际旅行社	International Travel Agencies	1256	1268	1310	1349	1364
国内旅行社	Domestic Travel Agencies	6070	7725	9222	10203	11997
旅行社职工人数 （人）	**Number of Staff and Workers of Travel Agencies (person)**	**108830**	**164336**	**192408**	**229147**	**249802**
国际旅行社	International Travel Agencies	47153	68093	72801	89128	100742
国内旅行社	Domestic Travel Agencies	61677	96243	119607	140019	149060
星级饭店总数 （个）	**Total Number of Tourist Hotel (unit)**	**7035**	**10481**	**7358**	**8880**	**9751**
入境旅游人数 （万人次）	**Total Number of International Tourists Arrival to China (10 000 person-times)**	**7279.56**	**8344.39**	**8901.29**	**9790.83**	**9166.21**
外国人	Foreigners	843.23	1016.04	1122.64	1343.95	1140.29
华 侨	Overseas Chinese	10.81	7.55			
港澳同胞	Compatriots from Hong Kong and Macao	6167.06	7009.93	7434.45	8080.82	7752.73
台湾同胞	Compatriots from Taiwan	258.46	310.86	344.20	366.06	273.19
#过夜旅游者人数(万人次)	Tourists (Overnight Visitors) (10 000 person-times)	2704.66	3123.60	3316.67	3680.26	3297.05
国内居民出境人数(万人次)	**Total Number of Domestic Resident Outbound (10 000 person-times)**	**923.24**	**1047.26**	**1213.44**	**1660.23**	**2022.19**
#因私出境人数	For Private Purpose	426.61	563.09	694.67	1007.39	1481.09
国内旅游人数 （万人次）	**Total Number of Domestic Tourists (10 000 person-times)**	**71900**	**74400**	**78400**	**87800**	**87000**
旅游收入	**Tourism Earnings**					
国际旅游收入 （亿美元）	International Tourism Earnings (100 million USD)	140.99	162.24	177.92	203.85	174.06
国内旅游收入 （亿元）	Domestic Tourism Earnings (100 million yuan)	2831.92	3175.32	3522.36	3878.36	3442.27

注：2000年及以前的星级饭店总数为涉外饭店数。

a) Prior to 2000, the total number of tourist hotels is the number of hotels that concerning foreign affairs.

19-2 各地区旅行社数和职工人数（2003年底）

Number of Travel Agencies and Staff and Workers by Region (End of 2003)

地 区	Region	旅行社数（个）Total Number of Travel Agencies (unit)	国际旅行社 International Travel Agencies	国内旅行社 Domestic Travel Agencies	旅行社职工人数（人）Number of Staff and Workers of Travel Agencies (person)	国际旅行社 International Travel Agencies	国内旅行社 Domestic Travel Agencies
全 国	**National Total**	**13361**	**1364**	**11997**	**249802**	**100742**	**149060**
北 京	Beijing	554	166	388	15999	11081	4918
天 津	Tianjin	231	19	212	5270	1253	4017
河 北	Hebei	630	31	599	7658	1767	5891
山 西	Shanxi	406	23	383	6701	1724	4977
内蒙古	Inner Mongolia	205	28	177	2625	1166	1459
辽 宁	Liaoning	803	57	746	8763	2946	5817
吉 林	Jilin	239	42	197	3211	1459	1752
黑龙江	Heilongjiang	366	62	304	4839	2385	2454
上 海	Shanghai	588	41	547	17285	5846	11439
江 苏	Jiangsu	996	72	924	15702	5369	10333
浙 江	Zhejiang	855	46	809	14556	4181	10375
安 徽	Anhui	480	36	444	6404	1547	4857
福 建	Fujian	470	38	432	9598	3984	5614
江 西	Jiangxi	399	22	377	4970	998	3972
山 东	Shandong	1172	55	1117	14516	2684	11832
河 南	Henan	626	30	596	8727	2370	6357
湖 北	Hubei	460	30	430	9904	5097	4807
湖 南	Hunan	439	35	404	9213	3229	5984
广 东	Guangdong	680	176	504	27796	17891	9905
广 西	Guangxi	340	50	290	8635	3892	4743
海 南	Hainan	157	39	118	3923	1876	2047
重 庆	Chongqing	203	23	180	4252	1628	2624
四 川	Sichuan	498	50	448	9765	3831	5934
贵 州	Guizhou	142	12	130	2532	861	1671
云 南	Yunnan	422	40	382	10872	4047	6825
西 藏	Tibet	45	22	23	815	631	184
陕 西	Shaanxi	307	33	274	6286	2995	3291
甘 肃	Gansu	218	27	191	3305	1524	1781
青 海	Qinghai	101	11	90	1216	412	804
宁 夏	Ningxia	63	7	56	771	294	477
新 疆	Xinjiang	266	41	225	3693	1774	1919

19-3 各地区按经济类型分星级饭店数（2003年底）

Number of Tourist Hotels by Ownership and Regions (End of 2003)

单位：个 (unit)

地区	Region	星级饭店个数 Total Number of Tourist Hotels	国有 State-owned	集体 Collective owned	私营 Private	联营 Joint Ownership	有限责任 Ltd. Liability Co.	股份合作 Cooperative	股份有限 Shareholding Co.	其它内资 Other Domestic Funds	外商投资 Foreign Funded	港澳台投资 Funded from Hong Kong, Macao and Taiwan
全国	**National Total**	**9751**	**5622**	**909**	**189**	**95**	**860**	**359**	**635**	**404**	**411**	**267**
北京	Beijing	617	336	95	19	10	36	16	33	6	24	42
天津	Tianjin	87	46	9			9	3	4		5	11
河北	Hebei	313	298	3			2	1	2	3	2	2
山西	Shanxi	236	121	19	4	1	30	18	24	14	3	2
内蒙古	Inner Mongolia	132	114	6			8	2	2			
辽宁	Liaoning	379	183	31	5	1	43	24	30	5	32	25
吉林	Jilin	192	151	6	5		2	3	6	2	4	13
黑龙江	Heilongjiang	205	88	2	1		9	2	8	90	4	1
上海	Shanghai	338	151	31	8	9	58	21	18	10	19	13
江苏	Jiangsu	590	322	66	2	5	70	22	28	43	17	15
浙江	Zhejiang	733	298	57	45	5	149	48	98	22	11	
安徽	Anhui	298	186	25	3	2	27	15	17	5	8	10
福建	Fujian	305	119	33	7	6	35	9	45	4	30	17
江西	Jiangxi	187	155	4	5	1		3	3	4	6	6
山东	Shandong	482	305	46	9	5	33	23	33	2	11	15
河南	Henan	359	255	32	3	1	19	10	31	2	4	2
湖北	Hubei	540	404	57	3	3	17	15	18	11	12	
湖南	Hunan	356	247	33	1	4	18	9	19	3	18	4
广东	Guangdong	967	401	124	25	19	94	33	66	16	149	40
广西	Guangxi	293	139	30	3	5	43	11	29	4	22	7
海南	Hainan	199	73	21	13	8	30	16	15	4	9	10
重庆	Chongqing	147	96	6	1		15	3	7	12	3	4
四川	Sichuan	346	167	27	9	3	55	22	22	27	10	4
贵州	Guizhou	112	106		1		1	1		1	1	1
云南	Yunnan	572	249	89	11	6	38	18	46	100	5	10
西藏	Tibet	58	21	11	3			2	8	13		
陕西	Shaanxi	229	181	17		1	9	4	8		1	8
甘肃	Gansu	157	153				1	1				2
青海	Qinghai	50	27	2	2		3	1	14	1		
宁夏	Ningxia	33	33									
新疆	Xinjiang	239	197	27	1		6	3	1		1	3

19-4 各地区按规模分星级饭店数（2003年底）

Number of Tourist Hotels by Capacity and Regions (End of 2003)

单位：个 (unit)

地 区	Region	星级饭店个数 Total Number of Tourist Hotel	客房总数500间以上 with 500 Rooms and Over	客房总数300-499间 with 300-499 Rooms	客房总数200-299间 with 200-299 Rooms	客房总数100-199间 with 100-199 Rooms	客房总数99间以下 with Less than 100 Rooms
全 国	**National Total**	**9751**	**83**	**349**	**680**	**2324**	**6315**
北 京	Beijing	617	26	63	53	132	343
天 津	Tianjin	87	1	4	10	26	46
河 北	Hebei	313	1	4	18	111	179
山 西	Shanxi	236		1	9	65	161
内蒙古	Inner Mongolia	132	1		4	30	97
辽 宁	Liaoning	379	3	10	30	99	237
吉 林	Jilin	192	1	3	10	32	146
黑龙江	Heilongjiang	205		2	11	46	146
上 海	Shanghai	338	15	33	41	109	140
江 苏	Jiangsu	590	2	24	42	154	368
浙 江	Zhejiang	733	3	13	59	190	468
安 徽	Anhui	298		28	25	22	223
福 建	Fujian	305		10	19	63	213
江 西	Jiangxi	187		3	13	31	140
山 东	Shandong	482	3	14	37	138	290
河 南	Henan	359		8	27	111	213
湖 北	Hubei	540		10	20	99	411
湖 南	Hunan	356		4	11	44	297
广 东	Guangdong	967	15	37	62	198	655
广 西	Guangxi	293	2	14	28	88	161
海 南	Hainan	199	3	12	31	67	86
重 庆	Chongqing	147		7	15	44	81
四 川	Sichuan	346	1	9	31	122	183
贵 州	Guizhou	112		1	7	38	66
云 南	Yunnan	572	3	9	20	81	459
西 藏	Tibet	58		1	2	5	50
陕 西	Shaanxi	229	2	11	17	42	157
甘 肃	Gansu	157	1	5	11	44	96
青 海	Qinghai	50		2		15	33
宁 夏	Ningxia	33				13	20
新 疆	Xinjiang	239		7	17	65	150

19-5 国际旅游外汇收入及构成

Foreign Exchange Earnings and Its Composition

单位: 百万美元 (USD million)

指 标	Item	2002 数额 Value	2002 比重 Percentage (%)	2003 数额 Value	2003 比重 Percentage (%)
总计	**Total**	**20385**	**100.0**	**17406**	**100.0**
长途交通	Long Distance Transportation	5260	25.8	4438	25.5
民航	Air	3661	18.0	3090	17.7
铁路	Railway	465	2.3	392	2.3
汽车	Highway	874	4.3	737	4.2
轮船	Waterway	260	1.3	220	1.3
游览	Visiting	1431	7.0	1220	7.0
住宿	Accommodation	2565	12.6	2164	12.4
餐饮	Food and Beverage	1660	8.1	1431	8.2
商品销售	Shopping	4211	20.7	3620	20.8
娱乐	Entertainment	1525	7.5	1302	7.5
邮电通讯	Post and Communication Services	720	3.5	618	3.5
市内交通	Local Transportation	882	4.3	786	4.5
其他服务	Other Service	2131	10.5	1827	10.5

19-6 按性别、年龄和事由分外国入境旅游人数

Number of Foreigner Tourists by Sex, Age and Purpose

单位: 万人次 (10 000 person-times)

指 标	Item	2002 人数 Persons	2002 比重 Percentage (%)	2003 人数 Persons	2003 比重 Percentage (%)
总 计	**Total**	**1343.95**	**100.0**	**1140.29**	**100.0**
按性别分	**By Sex**				
男	Male	877.51	65.3	778.58	68.3
女	Female	466.44	34.7	361.71	31.7
按年龄分	**By Age**				
14岁及以下	14 and under	48.16	3.6	37.72	3.3
15至24岁	15-24	101.77	7.6	86.72	7.6
25至44岁	25-44	651.28	48.5	591.32	51.9
45至64岁	45-64	464.96	34.6	380.8	33.4
65岁以上	65 and over	77.78	5.8	43.73	3.8
按目的分类	**By Purpose**				
会议/商务	Meeting /Business	322.04	24.0	290.20	25.5
观光休闲	Sightseeing and Holiday	556.05	41.4	430.67	37.8
探亲访友	Visiting Relatives and Friends	41.25	3.1	24.73	2.2
服务	Services	153.33	11.4	152.51	13.4
其他	Others	271.28	20.2	242.17	21.2

19-7 按国别分外国入境旅游人数

Number of Foreigner Tourists by Country

单位：万人次 (10 000 person-times)

地　区	Region	1995	1997	1998	1999	2000	2001	2002	2003
总　计	**Total**	**588.67**	**742.80**	**710.77**	**843.23**	**1016.04**	**1122.64**	**1343.95**	**1140.29**
亚洲	**Asia**	**338.26**	**428.17**	**400.06**	**499.27**	**610.15**	**686.42**	**864.38**	**726.50**
#朝鲜	Korea, D.P.Rep.	6.64	7.14	6.12	6.98	7.64	7.71	7.93	7.71
印度	India	4.50	6.05	6.57	8.42	12.09	15.94	21.36	21.91
印度尼西亚	Indonesia	13.28	14.73	10.46	18.29	22.06	22.42	27.47	23.18
日本	Japan	130.52	158.17	157.21	185.52	220.15	238.57	292.56	225.48
马来西亚	Malaysia	25.18	36.13	30.01	37.29	44.10	46.86	59.24	43.01
蒙古	Mongolia	26.19	34.29	26.48	35.45	39.91	38.71	45.31	41.83
菲律宾	the Philippines	21.97	27.67	25.65	29.83	36.39	40.80	50.86	45.77
新加坡	Singapore	26.15	31.68	31.64	35.25	39.94	41.50	49.71	37.81
韩国	Republic of Korea	52.95	78.11	63.28	99.20	134.47	167.88	212.43	194.55
泰国	Thailand	17.33	16.85	14.43	20.64	24.11	29.84	38.63	27.54
非洲	**Africa**	**4.08**	**4.91**	**5.43**	**5.21**	**6.56**	**7.32**	**9.85**	**10.42**
欧洲	**Europe**	**159.06**	**201.83**	**181.33**	**211.27**	**248.90**	**268.38**	**282.58**	**259.76**
#英国	United Kingdom	18.49	22.79	24.29	25.89	28.39	30.25	34.30	28.83
德国	Germany	16.65	18.47	19.19	21.76	23.91	25.34	28.18	22.20
法国	France	11.85	13.13	13.80	15.56	18.50	19.95	22.21	15.61
意大利	Italy	6.37	6.51	7.25	7.22	7.78	7.77	9.17	6.58
荷兰	Netherlands	3.49	5.23	5.89	7.01	7.60	9.30	10.04	6.79
葡萄牙	Portugal	2.56	3.58	3.85	4.02	2.28	2.68	3.61	3.01
瑞典	Sweden	3.52	3.85	4.06	4.68	5.36	5.28	6.28	5.00
瑞士	Switzerland	3.43	3.03	2.84	2.99	3.07	3.08	3.24	2.37
哈萨克	Kazakhstan	9.92	9.49	9.60	6.87	6.71	6.93	6.57	
俄罗斯	Russia	48.93	81.37	69.20	83.30	108.02	119.62	127.16	138.07
拉丁美洲	**Latin America**	**5.37**	**7.66**	**7.46**	**7.59**	**8.29**	**7.45**	**9.71**	**8.01**
北美洲	**North America**	**64.36**	**79.05**	**87.33**	**95.01**	**113.28**	**120.31**	**141.25**	**105.28**
#加拿大	Canada	12.88	17.41	19.60	21.37	23.66	25.39	29.13	23.03
美国	United States	51.49	61.64	67.73	73.64	89.62	94.92	112.12	82.25
大洋洲及太平洋岛屿	**Oceanic and Pacific Islands**	**15.85**	**19.35**	**22.48**	**24.38**	**28.18**	**30.97**	**35.37**	**30.01**
#澳大利亚	Australia	12.94	15.68	18.64	20.35	23.41	25.51	29.13	24.54
新西兰	New Zealand	2.29	2.83	3.00	3.14	3.76	4.44	5.02	4.34
其他	**Others**	**1.69**	**1.83**	**0.68**	**0.50**	**0.68**	**1.79**	**0.81**	**0.30**

注:俄罗斯1990年的数据为前苏联数据。

a) The data of Russia in 1990 referred to the data of former USSR.

19-8 各地区国际旅游外汇收入

Foreign Exchange Earnings by Region

单位：百万美元 (USD million)

地　区	Region	1995	1997	1998	1999	2000	2001	2002	2003
北　京	Beijing	2182	2248	2384	2496	2768	2946	3115	1904
天　津	Tianjin	133	180	202	209	232	280	342	329
河　北	Hebei	42	97	100	124	142	157	167	85
山　西	Shanxi	21	37	38	43	50	59	75	36
内蒙古	Inner Mongolia	91	107	126	120	126	137	149	138
辽　宁	Liaoning	189	260	262	304	383	463	550	454
吉　林	Jilin	41	59	38	45	58	76	86	66
黑龙江	Heilongjiang	61	105	121	148	189	250	297	244
上　海	Shanghai	939	1317	1218	1364	1613	1808	2275	2053
江　苏	Jiangsu	260	408	529	620	724	822	1050	1132
浙　江	Zhejiang	236	345	361	410	514	699	928	873
安　徽	Anhui	31	64	51	67	86	106	124	83
福　建	Fujian	484	614	651	725	894	942	1100	915
江　西	Jiangxi	25	45	43	50	62	70	72	47
山　东	Shandong	154	204	220	265	315	382	472	370
河　南	Henan	60	95	101	114	124	133	145	63
湖　北	Hubei	73	170	88	105	146	201	284	136
湖　南	Hunan	65	140	156	185	221	271	311	46
广　东	Guangdong	2393	2801	2942	3272	4112	4484	5091	4267
广　西	Guangxi	121	178	156	202	307	301	321	164
海　南	Hainan	81	102	96	105	109	106	92	80
重　庆	Chongqing		105	88	97	138	163	218	113
四　川	Sichuan	125	79	84	97	122	166	200	150
贵　州	Guizhou	29	44	48	55	61	69	80	29
云　南	Yunnan	165	264	261	350	339	367	419	340
西　藏	Tibet	11	32	33	36	52	46	52	19
陕　西	Shaanxi	139	225	247	272	280	309	351	198
甘　肃	Gansu	21	28	30	37	55	45	54	21
青　海	Qinghai	2	3	3	4	7	9	10	5
宁　夏	Ningxia	1	1	1	2	3	3	2	1
新　疆	Xinjiang	74	71	82	86	95	99	99	49

19-9 各地区接待入境旅游人数

Number of International Tourists by Region

单位: 万人次 (10 000 person-times)

地区	Region	1995 总计 Total	1995 # 外国人 Foreigners	2000 总计 Total	2000 # 外国人 Foreigners	2002 总计 Total	2002 # 外国人 Foreigners	2003 总计 Total	2003 # 外国人 Foreigners
北 京	Beijing	206.87	166.52	282.09	237.96	310.38	266.45	185.12	152.66
天 津	Tianjin	20.06	16.27	35.62	32.14	50.60	45.32	48.90	45.61
河 北	Hebei	16.50	13.59	41.43	35.90	47.36	42.70	28.03	25.76
山 西	Shanxi	7.12	5.15	16.53	11.66	24.80	16.15	11.60	7.91
内蒙古	Inner Mongolia	30.09	29.46	39.19	38.74	43.94	43.45	41.36	41.02
辽 宁	Liaoning	26.38	21.46	61.22	50.05	92.94	79.42	77.89	66.81
吉 林	Jilin	15.61	14.49	22.27	19.19	29.40	25.94	21.17	18.52
黑龙江	Heilongjiang	16.23	13.94	55.17	50.47	71.74	66.95	58.71	54.63
上 海	Shanghai	136.79	107.54	181.40	143.90	272.53	215.94	244.71	199.00
江 苏	Jiangsu	76.77	48.68	160.95	98.15	222.63	138.97	223.16	143.45
浙 江	Zhejiang	67.27	36.65	112.59	64.75	204.10	121.08	180.83	106.93
安 徽	Anhui	14.29	7.28	31.84	16.79	45.91	23.88	28.08	16.40
福 建	Fujian	90.64	22.41	161.33	49.75	184.82	52.80	149.72	45.94
江 西	Jiangxi	7.36	2.34	16.31	5.54	24.09	6.57	16.56	4.48
山 东	Shandong	45.09	30.43	72.31	48.01	97.68	74.14	77.67	61.55
河 南	Henan	21.84	9.12	32.50	18.21	41.01	25.45	18.86	11.27
湖 北	Hubei	27.09	16.83	45.08	35.74	102.43	75.57	40.52	32.32
湖 南	Hunan	17.73	7.18	45.40	15.79	56.62	22.38	15.39	10.54
广 东	Guangdong	620.68	122.07	1198.94	212.85	1525.88	298.06	1196.96	245.76
广 西	Guangxi	41.85	30.74	122.91	50.80	136.34	65.93	65.02	32.93
海 南	Hainan	28.71	5.75	48.68	9.37	38.94	16.52	29.34	14.43
重 庆	Chongqing			26.61	19.29	46.15	31.09	23.45	18.17
四 川	Sichuan	37.67	24.51	46.20	19.97	66.72	41.15	45.17	24.40
贵 州	Guizhou	13.66	7.79	18.39	7.12	22.81	8.45	7.70	2.40
云 南	Yunnan	59.69	47.38	100.11	66.59	130.36	78.13	100.01	65.71
西 藏	Tibet	6.78	6.54	15.00	13.58	14.23	12.96	5.11	4.57
陕 西	Shaanxi	44.23	39.73	71.28	58.48	85.01	71.81	46.58	30.78
甘 肃	Gansu	9.09	7.07	21.31	14.34	23.68	16.27	10.18	6.79
青 海	Qinghai	1.33	0.87	3.26	1.46	4.35	1.91	1.77	0.77
宁 夏	Ningxia	0.37	0.28	0.78	0.58	0.60	0.41	0.30	0.22
新 疆	Xinjiang	20.36	18.55	25.61	20.84	27.54	23.37	17.05	14.99

19-10 各地区国际旅行社主要经济指标（2003年）
Main Economic Indicators of International Travel Services by Region (2003)

地 区	Region	固定资产原值（万元）Original Valued of Fixed Assets (10 000 yuan)	营业收入（万元）Takings (10 000 yuan)	税 金（万元）Taxes (10 000 yuan)	全员劳动生产率（万元／人）Overall Labor Productivity (10 000 yuan/person)	人均实现利税（万元／人）Realize Pre-tax Profits Per Labor (10 000 yuan/person)	人均固定资产原值（万元／人）Original Valued of Fixed Assets Per Labor (10 000 yuan/person)
全 国	**National Total**	**2564447.8**	**4006932.5**	**54019.6**	**39.8**	**0.6**	**25.5**
北 京	Beijing	809657.6	1007022.0	30814.5	90.9	2.5	73.1
天 津	Tianjin	18578.3	37853.2	107.9	30.2	…	14.8
河 北	Hebei	8809.4	20163.6	78.9	11.4	0.3	5.0
山 西	Shanxi	13722.7	23122.8	141.8	13.4	0.1	8.0
内蒙古	Inner Mongolia	13281.9	11345.1	207.0	9.7	0.3	11.4
辽 宁	Liaoning	29451.7	70690.1	1013.6	24.0	0.3	10.0
吉 林	Jilin	14378.6	19221.5	107.2	13.2	0.8	9.9
黑龙江	Heilongjiang	24400.7	55101.2	876.6	23.1	0.9	10.2
上 海	Shanghai	168042.7	291093.0	2179.3	49.8	0.5	28.7
江 苏	Jiangsu	82691.7	281242.5	768.5	52.4	0.6	15.4
浙 江	Zhejiang	69886.0	175077.4	705.7	41.9	0.4	16.7
安 徽	Anhui	19341.6	25369.5	109.2	16.4	0.3	12.5
福 建	Fujian	159396.8	143126.5	1268.8	35.9	0.1	40.0
江 西	Jiangxi	7799.8	19023.8	45.2	19.1	-0.6	7.8
山 东	Shandong	61033.6	70268.0	1308.4	26.2	0.3	22.7
河 南	Henan	39290.5	38923.2	262.4	16.4	0.3	16.6
湖 北	Hubei	93899.0	52780.7	521.7	10.4	-1.2	18.4
湖 南	Hunan	13423.5	56138.2	172.4	17.4	0.4	4.2
广 东	Guangdong	488113.1	870486.0	7954.9	48.7	1.0	27.3
广 西	Guangxi	48738.9	90911.7	1125.7	23.4	0.2	12.5
海 南	Hainan	61985.8	196520.2	721.5	104.8	1.6	33.0
重 庆	Chongqing	81732.5	68209.8	788.0	41.9	1.8	50.2
四 川	Sichuan	75415.4	105570.4	452.2	27.6	0.2	19.7
贵 州	Guizhou	6928.3	19187.8	53.7	22.3	0.1	8.0
云 南	Yunnan	48744.0	125751.5	812.1	31.1	…	12.0
西 藏	Tibet	17438.4	20998.8	190.7	33.3	-4.3	27.6
陕 西	Shaanxi	39369.1	52455.3	642.6	17.5	-0.6	13.1
甘 肃	Gansu	21308.3	14003.8	73.3	9.2	-0.4	14.0
青 海	Qinghai	4285.3	3923.0	16.8	9.5	1.0	10.4
宁 夏	Ningxia	1649.5	5360.3	14.5	18.2	0.1	5.6
新 疆	Xinjiang	21653.1	35991.9	484.6	20.3	0.5	12.2

19-11 国 内 旅 游 情 况
Statistics of Domestic Tourism

年 份 Year	旅游人数（百万人次）Domestic Tourists (million person-times)	城镇居民 Urban Residents	农村居民 Rural Residents	旅游收入（亿元）Tourism Earning (100 million yuan)	城镇居民 Urban Residents	农村居民 Rural Residents	人均花费（元）Per Capita Expenditure (yuan)	城镇居民 Urban Residents	农村居民 Rural Residents
1994	524	205	319	1023.5	848.2	175.3	195.3	414.7	54.9
1995	629	246	383	1375.7	1140.1	235.6	218.7	464.0	61.5
1996	640	256	383	1638.4	1368.4	270.0	256.2	534.1	70.5
1997	644	259	385	2112.7	1551.8	560.9	328.1	599.8	145.7
1998	695	250	445	2391.2	1551.1	876.1	345.0	607.0	197.0
1999	719	284	435	2831.9	1748.2	1083.7	394.0	614.8	249.5
2000	744	329	415	3175.5	2235.3	940.3	426.6	678.6	226.6
2001	784	375	409	3522.4	2651.7	870.7	449.5	708.3	212.7
2002	878	385	493	3878.4	2848.1	1030.3	441.8	739.7	209.1
2003	870	351	519	3442.3	2404.1	1038.2	395.7	684.9	200.0

主要统计指标解释

旅游者人数

(1)入境国际旅游者人数：指来中国参观、访问、旅行、探亲、访友、休养、考察、参加会议和从事经济、科技、文化、教育、宗教等活动的外国人、华侨、港澳同胞和台湾同胞的人数。不包括外国在我国的常驻机构，如使领馆、通讯社、企业办事处的工作人员；来我国常住的外国专家、留学生以及在岸逗留不过夜人员。

(2)出境居民人数：指大陆居民因公务活动或私人事务短期出境的人数。公务活动出境居民人数包括在国际交通工具上的中国服务员工，因私出境居民人数不包括在国际交通工具上的中国服务员工。

(3)国内旅游者人数：指我国大陆居民和在我国常住1年以上的外国人、华侨、港澳台同胞离开常住地在境内其他地方的旅游设施内至少停留一夜，最长不超过6个月的人数。

国际旅游(外汇)收入 指入境旅游的外国人、华侨、港澳同胞和台湾同胞在中国大陆旅游过程中发生的一切旅游支出，对于国家来说就是国际旅游(外汇)收入。

国际旅行社 指经营对外招徕并接待外国人、华侨、港澳同胞和台湾同胞来中国、归国或回内地旅游业务的旅行社。

国内旅行社 指负责经营招徕、组团、接待国内旅客的旅游业务，以及不对外招徕，负责经营接待国际旅行社或其它涉外部门组织的外国人、华侨、港澳同胞和台湾同胞来中国、归国或回内地的旅游业务的旅行社。

星级饭店 指已评定星级的饭店。

Explanatory Notes on Main Statistical Indicators

Number of Tourists

(1) International tourists refer to foreigners, overseas Chinese, Chinese compatriots from Hong Kong, Macao and Taiwan coming to China for sight-seeing, visits, tours, family reunions, vacations, study tours, conferences and other activities of a business, scientific and technological, cultural, educational and religious nature. It does not include representatives and employees of resident institutions of foreign countries in China such as embassies, consulates, news agencies and offices of foreign companies and organizations, nor does it include long-term foreign experts or students residing in China, or persons in transition without spending a night in China.

(2) Chinese residents going abroad refer to Chinese residents going abroad for short terms for either public business or private purposes. Chinese employees working on international transport carriers are included in those going abroad for public business purpose, not in those for private purpose.

(3) Domestic tourists refer to residents of the mainland of China who stay for one night at least but no more than 6 months at tourist facilities in other places than their permanent residence within the territory of the mainland China, including foreigners, overseas Chinese and Chinese compatriots from Hong Kong, Macao and Taiwan who have resided in China for over one year.

Foreign Exchange Earnings from International Tourism refer to the total expenditures of foreigners, overseas Chinese, Chinese compatriots from Hong Kong, Macao and Taiwan during their stay in the mainland of China, which are earnings of foreign exchange from international tourism from the point of view from China.

International Travel Agencies refer to travel agencies engaged in the promotion, solicitation, organization and reception of tours to the mainland of China by foreigners, overseas Chinese, Chinese compatriots from Hong Kong, Macao and Taiwan.

Domestic Travel Agencies refer to travel agencies engaged in the promotion, solicitation, organization and reception of domestic tourists, and in the reception of foreigners, overseas Chinese, Chinese compatriots from Hong Kong, Macao and Taiwan organized by international travel agencies or other departments concerned, without their own promotion and solicitation programmes.

Star-Hotels refer to hotels rated with stars.

二十、金融业

Financial Intermediation

简要说明

一、本篇资料的主要内容

本篇反映我国金融、证券和保险业发展情况。有以下五个部分：一是银行系统机构人员，二是金融机构金融活动情况，三是存贷款利率调整情况，四是直接融资情况，五是保险业务情况。

二、本篇各部分资料来源

1.反映金融机构人员情况的表是“20-1银行系统机构、人员数”，由中国人民银行总行人事部门根据有关的行政记录汇总和填报。

2.反映金融机构活动情况的资料包括：“20-2金融机构人民币信贷资金平衡表(资金来源)”，“20-3金融机构人民币信贷资金平衡表(资金运用)”，“20-4金融机构现金收入”，“20-5金融机构现金支出”，“20-6金融机构现金投放与回笼”，“20-7国家银行人民币信贷收支（年底余额）”，“20-8货币供应量（年底余额）”20-9货币供应量同比增长率”，“20-12黄金和外汇储备”，“20-13国有商业银行资产负债表（年底余额）”，“20-14外资银行资产负债表（年底余额）”。金融机构信贷资金平衡表及现金收支表的统计范围包括中国人民银行、国家政策性银行、国有商业银行、其他商业银行、城市信用合作社、农村信用合作社、外资银行、财务公司、信托投资公司、金融租赁公司、邮政储蓄机构。中国人民银行总行根据金融机构的基层单位全面填报、并按各自系统汇总的资料，进行归并和汇总，最后得到金融机构的信贷收支及现金收支表。黄金和外汇储备表中的资料取自于中国人民银行的资产负债表，由该行有关部门提供。

3.反映存贷款利率调整情况的“20-10金融机构法定存款利率”，“20-11金融机构法定贷款利率表”，数据来自中国人民银行总行规定的、并对外发布的存贷款利率。

4.反映直接融资情况的“20-15国内有价证券分类发行情况”，“20-16证券市场基本情况”，“20-17上市公司数量”，“20-18股票发行量和筹资额”“20-19股票交易情况”，资料取自中国证券监督管理委员会编制的《中国证券期货统计年鉴》。

5.反映保险业务情况的“20-20　保险系统机构、人员数”，“20-21保险公司业务经济技术指标”，数据取自中国保险监督管理委员会编制的保险统计资料。

Brief Introduction

I. Main Content

Data in this chapter show the development of China's banking, securities and insurance, in the following 5 aspects: (1) The number of the institutions and personnel in the banking system; (2) The financial activities of banking institutions; (3) The changes of the interest rates of the deposits and loans; (4) The direct financing; (5) The business of insurance.

II. Sources of Data:

(1) Table 20-1 showing the number of banking institutions and personnel are prepared by the personnel departments of the Headquarter of the People's Bank of China on the basis of the related administrative registers.

(2) Tables 20-2 to 20-9, and tables 20-12 to tables 20-14 show the banking activities of banks and rural credit cooperatives. The statistics cover the balance table of the credit funds (tables 20-2 and 20-3), cash revenue, expenditure and balance of the banking institutions (tables 20-4 to table 20-6, and tables 20-13, 20-14), source and use of credit funds of national banks, money supply (tables 20-8, 20-9), and gold and foreign exchange reserves (table 20-12), . Statistics in tables 20-2 to 20-9 and tables 20-12 to tables 20-14 cover the People's Bank of China, the state policy banks, the state-owned commercial banks, other commercial banks, urban and rural credit cooperatives, foreign banks, financing corporations, trust investment corporations, financing and leasing corporations, and savings deposit institutions under the postal offices. The grassroots units of the above banking institutions fill out the questionnaires and report to the higher authorities. The higher authorities tabulate the data level by level. Finally, the Department of Investigation and Statistics of the Head Office of the People's Bank of China tabulate the data and get the national total. The data in the table on the gold and foreign exchange reserves are extracted from the balance sheet of the People's Bank of China and provided by its concerned departments.

(3) Tables 20-10 and 20-11 show the changes of the interest rates of savings deposits and loans. Data are from the interest rates of deposits and loans stipulated and published by the Head Office of the People's Bank of China.

(4) Tables 20-15 to 20-19 show the direct fund raising. Data are from the *Statistical Yearbook on China's Securities and Futures* compiled by China Securities Regulatory Commission.

(5) Tables 20-20 and 20-25 show the business of insurance, with data coming from the insurance statistics compiled by China Insurance Regulatory Commission.

20-1 银行系统机构、人员数（2003年底）

Number of Institution and Employed Person in Finance System (Year-end of 2003)

项　　目	Item	机构数(个) Number of Institution (unit)	年末人数(人) Number of Staff and Workers (person)	#女性 Female
总　计	**Total**	**97802**	**1776776**	**763675**
中国人民银行	The People's Bank of China	2199	160020	50475
中国工商银行	Industrial and Commercial Bank of China	24129	389045	172948
中国农业银行	Agricultural Bank of China	36138	511425	216165
中国银行	Bank of China	11609	171777	76898
中国建设银行	Construction Bank of China	16613	342967	161170
中国农业发展银行	Agricultural Development Bank of China	2275	59487	18855
交通银行	Bank of Communications	2145	55510	26482
中国进出口银行	Export Import Bank of China	16	646	271
浦东发展银行	Shanghai Pudong Development Bank	329	7796	3699
国家开发银行	National Development Bank	37	4629	1209
中信实业银行	CITIC Industrial Bank	379	9457	4369
中国光大银行	China Everbright Bank	31	8569	4199
中国民生银行	China Minsheng Banking Corp., Ltd	185	5273	2751
华夏银行	China Huaxia Bank	220	6681	3183
招商银行	China Merchants Bank	400	15965	8078
广东发展银行	Guangdong Development Bank	526	12449	5879
福建兴业银行	Fujiang Industrial Bank	256	7259	3366
深圳发展银行	Shenzhen Development Bank Co., Ltd	241	6471	2977
恒丰银行	Hengfeng Bank	74	1350	701

20-2 金融机构人民币信贷资金平衡表(资金来源)

Credit Funds Balance Sheet of Financial Institutions (Sources of Funds)

(年底余额) 单位：亿元　　(year-end) (100 million yuan)

项　　目	Item	2002	2003
资金来源合计	**All Sources**	**184024.5**	**225313.3**
各项存款	Deposits	170917.4	208055.6
企业存款	Deposits of Enterprises	60028.6	72487.1
财政存款	Treasury Deposits	3481.9	5126.9
机关团体存款	Deposits of Government Agencies and Organizations	5184.5	6727.7
城乡储蓄存款	Urban and Rural Savings Deposits	86910.7	103617.7
农业存款	Agricultural Deposits	3764.2	4898.3
委托及信托类存款	Trusted Deposits	2414.4	2458.1
其他类存款	Other Deposits	9133.2	12740.0
金融债券	Bonds	90.3	2226.3
对国际金融机构负债	Liabilities to International Financial Institutions	423.1	483.0
流通中现金	Currency in Circulation	17278.0	19746.0
其他	Others	-4684.3	-5197.2

注：金融机构包括人民银行、政策性银行、国有独资商业银行、邮政储蓄机构、其他商业银行、城市合作银行、农村信用社、城市信用社、外资银行、信托投资公司、租赁公司、财务公司等。

a) Financial Institutions include banks, savings deposit agencies of postal offices, housing saving banks, urban credit cooperative banks, rural credit cooperatives, urban credit banks, foreign-funded banks, financial trust investment agencies and financial companies etc.

20-3 金融机构人民币信贷资金平衡表(资金运用)

Credit Funds Balance Sheet of Financial Institutions (Uses of Funds)

(年底余额) 单位: 亿元 (year-end) (100 million yuan)

项目	Item	2002	2003
资金运用合计	**All Uses**	**184024.5**	**225313.3**
各项贷款	Loans	131293.9	158996.2
短期贷款	Short-term Loans	74247.9	83661.2
工业贷款	Industrial Loans	20190.5	22756.0
商业贷款	Commercial Loans	17973.1	17994.4
建筑业贷款	Construction Loans	2748.0	3002.1
农业贷款	Agricultural Loans	6884.6	8411.4
乡镇企业贷款	Loans to Township Enterprises	6812.3	7661.6
私营企业及个体贷款	Loans to Private Enterprises and Individuals	1058.8	1461.6
三资企业贷款	Loans to Sino-foreign Joint Venture and Cooperative Enterprises and Foreign-funded Enterprises	2697.4	2569.4
其他短期贷款	Other Short-term Loans	15883.4	19804.7
中长期贷款	Medium-term & Long-term Loans	48642.0	63401.4
委托及信托类贷款	Credit Loans	2170.3	2281.3
其他类贷款	Other Loans	6233.7	9652.4
有价证券及投资	Securities & Investment	26789.7	30259.5
在国际金融机构资产	Assets in International Financial Institutions	798.2	873.4
金银占款	Purchase of Gold & Silver	337.2	337.2
外汇占款	Purchase of Foreign Exchanges	23223.3	34846.9
财政借款	Government Debt	1582.1	

20-4 金融机构现金收入

Cash Income of Financial Institutions

单位: 亿元 (100 million yuan)

项目	Item	2002	2003
收入总计	**Total Income**	**365593.0**	**455527.9**
商品销售收入	Income from Commodity Sales	40101.4	48545.9
服务业收入	Income from Service Trade	16848.9	19369.3
税款收入	Income from Taxes	2114.0	2513.7
城乡个体经营收入	Income from Urban and Rural Individual Business	12645.5	15458.1
储蓄存款收入	Income from Savings Deposits	252322.5	321577.8
其他金融机构收入	Income from Other Financial Institutions	2259.6	2272.2
居民归还贷款收入	Income from Repayment of Loans by Residents	6260.7	8062.8
汇兑收入	Income from Remittances	5900.6	5091.7
有价证券收入	Income from Securities	952.3	1124.3
其他收入	Other Income	26187.6	31512.1
#兑换外币收入	Income from Exchange of Foreign Currencies	115.9	164.9

20-5 金融机构现金支出

Cash Expenditures of Financial Institutions

单位: 亿元 (100 million yuan)

项目	Item	2002	2003
支出总计	**Total Expenditure**	**367182.2**	**457995.9**
工资性支出	Wages	23743.9	28641.0
农副产品采购支出	Purchases of Agricultural and Sideline Products	8340.3	10483.2
工矿及其他产品采购支出	Expenditure for Purchases of Industrial and Mineral Products	6328.7	8741.5
行政企事业管理费支出	Government and Enterprises Overhead	19997.2	23767.9
城乡个体经营支出	Expenditure for Individual Business	16779.5	20958.3
储蓄存款支出	Expenditure for Savings Deposits	251240.2	318132.0
其他金融机构支出	Expenditure for Other Financial Institutions	2339.6	2233.1
居民提取贷款支出	Expenditure for Loans by Residents	6362.4	8079.9
汇兑支出	Expenditure for Remittances	3930.5	3280.2
有价证券支出	Expenditure for Securities	941.2	1002.4
其他支出	Other Expenditure	27178.8	32676.5

20-6 金融机构现金投放与回笼

Cash Statistics of Financial Institutions

单位：亿元 (100 million yuan)

年 份 Year	现金收入 Cash Income	现金支出 Cash Expenditures	投 放 Currency Issuance
1957	516.7	512.2	-4.5
1962	633.2	614.0	-19.2
1965	675.7	686.5	10.8
1970	812.8	799.3	-13.5
1975	1128.2	1134.2	6.0
1978	1336.0	1352.6	16.6
1979	1626.4	1682.1	55.7
1980	2033.2	2111.7	78.5
1981	2402.2	2452.3	50.1
1982	2819.6	2862.4	42.8
1983	3428.7	3519.4	90.7
1984	4207.6	4469.9	262.3
1985	5499.1	5694.8	195.7
1986	6613.3	6843.9	230.6
1987	8779.6	9015.7	236.1
1988	12810.5	13490.0	679.5
1989	15057.6	15267.6	210.0
1990	17171.1	17471.4	300.4
1991	21465.1	21998.5	533.4
1992	31248.0	32406.2	1158.2
1993	48883.8	50412.5	1528.7
1994	71247.1	72671.0	1423.9
1995	96725.5	97322.3	596.8
1996	120263.3	121179.9	916.6
1997	141612.6	142988.3	1375.7
1998	203966.5	204993.1	1026.6
1999	233399.0	235650.4	2251.3
2000	277067.1	278264.3	1197.2
2001	321380.2	322416.3	1036.1
2002	365593.0	367182.2	1589.2
2003	455527.9	457995.9	2468.0

注：投放栏中的负数表示现金回笼。

a) The negative amount in currency issuance indicates the amount of cash withdrawn.

20-7 国家银行人民币信贷收支(年底余额)

Sources and Uses of Credit Funds of National Banks at the Year-end

单位：亿元 (100 million yuan)

项目	Item	2001	2002
资金来源总计	**Funds Sources**	**118424.2**	**137173.5**
各项存款	Total Deposits	97346.9	113452.3
企业存款	Deposits by Enterprises	33081.3	35980.1
活期存款	Demand Deposits	25192.8	27546.9
定期存款	Time Deposits	7888.5	8433.1
财政存款	Fiscal Deposits	3330.6	3447.9
机关团体存款	Deposits by Government Departments & Organizations	2493.6	4610.0
城镇储蓄存款	Urban and Rural Household Savings Deposits	54306.9	64024.5
活期储蓄	Demand Deposits	16626.6	20893.9
定期储蓄	Time Deposits	37680.2	43130.6
农业存款	Agricultural Deposits	409.7	465.7
其他类存款	Other Deposits	3724.8	4924.1
金融债券	Financial Bonds	0.8	0.5
同业往来	Inter-bank Credits	5870.9	5055.8
流通中现金	Currency in Circulation	15688.8	17278.0
对国际金融机构负债	Liabilities to International Financial Institutions	484.5	423.1
其他	Others	-967.7	963.9
资金运用总计	**Funds Uses**	**118424.2**	**137173.5**
各项贷款	Total Loans	80077.6	90892.6
短期贷款	Short-term Loans	43679.8	45800.7
工业贷款	Loans to Industial Sector	15763.2	16745.4
商业贷款	Loans to Commercial Sector	16463.5	15760.1
建筑业贷款	Loans to Construction Sector	1684.8	2168.0
农业贷款	Loans to Agricultural Sector	1272.3	1286.0
乡镇企业贷款	Loans to Township Enterprises	1450.5	1542.6
三资企业贷款	Loans to Enterprises with Foreign Funds	2392.2	1723.5
私营企业及个体贷款	Loans to Private Enterprises and Individuals	425.9	392.4
其他短期贷款	Other Short-term Loans	4227.4	6182.6
中长期贷款	Medium-term & Long-term Loans	34995.7	42317.2
其它类贷款	Other Loans	1402.1	2774.8
有价证券及投资	Portfolio Investment	16913.4	19488.4
同业往来	Inter-bank Debts	1153.7	1060.9
金银占款	Position for Bullion & Silver Purchase	256.0	337.2
外汇占款	Position for Foreign Exchanges	17687.3	23014.1
财政借款	Fiscal Debts	1582.1	1582.1
在国际金融机构资产	Assets with International Financial Institutions	754.2	798.2

注：1. 本表统计口径包括中国人民银行、政策性银行、国有独资商业银行、邮政储蓄机构。
2. 中国人民银行自2002年12月起对黄金储备和金银占款数据进行了调整。

a) The statistics coverage of the table includes the People's Bank of China, policy banks, state-owned commercial banks and agencies of postal saving.
b) Since December in 2002, the data of gold reserve and position for bullion & silver purchase have been adjusted by the People's Bank of China.

20-8 货币供应量（年底余额）

Money Supply at the Year-end

单位：亿元 (100 million yuan)

年份 Year	货币和准货币 (M_2) Money and Quasi-Money (M_2)	货币 (M_1) Money (M_1)	流通中现金 (M_0) Currency in Circulation (M_0)	活期存款 Demand Deposits	准货币 Quasi-Money	定期存款 Time Deposits	储蓄存款 Saving Deposits	其他存款 Other Deposits
1990	15293.4	6950.7	2644.4	4306.3	8342.7			
1991	19349.9	8633.3	3177.8	5455.5	10716.6			
1992	25402.2	11731.5	4336.0	7395.2	13670.7			
1993	34879.8	16280.4	5864.7	10415.7	18599.4	1247.9	15203.5	2148.0
1994	46923.5	20540.7	7288.6	13252.1	26382.8	1943.1	21518.4	2921.3
1995	60750.5	23987.1	7885.3	16101.8	36763.4	3324.2	29662.2	3777.0
1996	76094.9	28514.8	8802.0	19712.8	47580.1	5041.9	38520.8	4017.4
1997	90995.3	34826.3	10177.6	24648.7	56169.0	6738.5	46279.8	3150.7
1998	104498.5	38953.7	11204.2	27749.5	65544.9	8301.9	53407.5	3835.5
1999	119897.9	45837.3	13455.5	32381.8	74060.6	9476.8	59621.8	4962.0
2000	134610.4	53147.2	14652.7	38494.5	81463.2	11261.1	64332.4	5869.7
2001	158301.9	59871.6	15688.8	44182.8	98430.3	14180.1	73762.4	10487.8
2002	185007.0	70881.8	17278.0	53603.8	114125.2	16433.8	86910.7	10780.7
2003	221222.8	84118.6	19746.0	64372.6	137104.3	20940.4	103617.7	12546.2

注：2001年6月起，已将证券公司客户保证金计入货币供应量(M2),含在其他存款项内。

a) Since June in 2001, the consignment guarantee money of client at securities company had been calculated as the other deposit of M_2.

20-9 货币供应量同比增长率

Percentage Change of Money Supply Over the Last Corresponding Period

单位：% (%)

年份 Year	货币和准货币 (M_2) Money and Quasi-Money (M_2)	货币 (M_1) Money (M_1)	流通中现金 (M_0) Currency in Circulation (M_0)	活期存款 Demand Deposits	准货币 Quasi-Money	定期存款 Time Deposits	储蓄存款 Saving Deposits	其他存款 Other Deposits
1991	26.5	24.2	20.2	26.7	28.5			
1992	31.3	35.9	36.4	35.6	27.6			
1993								
1994	34.5	26.2	24.3	27.2	41.8	55.7	41.5	36.0
1995	29.5	16.8	8.2	21.5	39.3	71.1	37.9	29.3
1996	25.3	18.9	11.6	22.4	29.4	51.7	29.9	6.4
1997	19.6	22.1	15.6	25.0	18.1	33.7	20.1	-21.6
1998	14.8	11.9	10.1	12.6	16.7	23.2	15.4	21.7
1999	14.7	17.7	20.1	16.7	13.0	14.2	11.6	29.4
2000	12.3	16.0	8.9	18.9	10.0	18.8	7.9	18.3
2001	17.6	12.7	7.1	14.8	15.5	25.9	14.7	9.1
2002	16.8	16.8	10.1	19.2	16.8	21.8	17.8	2.8
2003	19.6	18.7	14.3	20.1	20.1	27.4	19.2	16.4

注：1.同期比增长率是按可比口径计算的。因1992年以前口径与1993年口径不一致，故1993年未计算增长率。

2.2001年6月起，已将证券公司客户保证金计入货币供应量(M_2)，含在其他存款内。

3.1997年初，中国人民银行对金融统计制度进行了调整，因此自1997年起的数据与历史数据不完全可比。

a) Percentage change over the last corresponding period is calculated by the comparable standard. Because the statistical standard before 1992 was no comparable with that in 1993, the change in 1993 was not calculated.

b) Since June of 2001, the consignment guarantee money of client at securities company had been calculated as the other deposit of M_2.

c) The People's Bank of China have been adjusted the system of financial statistics at the beginning of 1997, the data since 1997 are imperfectible comparable with the previous years.

20-10　金融机构法定存款利率

Nominal Interest Rates on Deposits of Financial Institutions

单位：年利率%　　　　(annual interest rate %)

项　目	Item	1998.3.25 Mar. 25, 1998	1998.7.1 Jul. 1, 1998	1998.12.7 Dec. 7, 1998	1999.6.10 Jun. 10,1999	2002.2.21 Feb. 21,2002
个人人民币储蓄存款	**Household Deposits**					
活期	Demand	1.71	1.44	1.44	0.99	0.72
定期	Time					
三个月	3 Months	2.88	2.79	2.79	1.98	1.71
半年	6 Months	4.14	3.96	3.33	2.16	1.89
一年	1 Year	5.22	4.77	3.78	2.25	1.98
二年	2 Year	5.58	4.86	3.96	2.43	2.25
三年	3 Year	6.21	4.95	4.14	2.70	2.52
五年	5 Year	6.66	5.22	4.50	2.88	2.79
企业单位	**Enterprises Deposits**					
活期	Demand	1.71	1.44	1.44	0.99	0.72
定期	Time					
三个月	3 Months	2.88	2.79	2.79	1.98	1.71
半年	6 Months	4.14	3.96	3.33	2.16	1.89
一年	1 Year	5.22	4.77	3.78	2.25	1.98
二年	2 Year	5.58	4.86	3.96	2.43	2.25
三年	3 Year	6.21	4.95	4.14	2.70	2.52
五年	5 Year	6.66	5.22	4.50	2.88	2.79
大额可转让定期存单	**CDs**					
1个月	1 month					
3个月	3 months	2.88	2.79	2.79		
6个月	6 months	4.14	3.96	3.33		
9个月	9 months					
12个月	12 months	5.22	4.77	3.78		

20-11　金融机构法定贷款利率

Nominal Interest Rates on Loans of Financial Institutions

单位：年利率%　　　　(annual interest rate %)

项　目	Item	1997.10.23 Oct. 23, 1997	1998.3.25 Mar. 25, 1998	1998.7.1 Jul. 1, 1998	1998.12.7 Dec. 7, 1998	1999.6.10 Jun. 10, 1999	2002.2.21 Jun. 10, 2000
短期贷款	**Shor-term**						
六个月	6 Months	7.65①	7.02①	6.57②	6.12②	5.58③	5.04③
一年	1 Year	8.64①	7.92①	6.93②	6.39②	5.85③	5.31③
中长期贷款	**Medium-and Long- term**						
一年以上至三年	3 Years or Less	9.36	9.00	7.11②	6.66②	5.94③	5.49③
三年以上至五年	5 Years or Less	9.90	9.72	7.65②	7.2②	6.03③	5.58③
五年以上	More than 5 Years	10.53	10.35	8.01②	7.56②	6.21③	5.76③

注：1. ①在法定贷款利率基础上可上浮10%，下浮10%。农村信用社贷款利率最高可上浮40%，下浮10%。
2. ②从1998年11月起，金融机构对小企业贷款利率可在法定贷款利率基础上上浮20%。大中企业上浮10%。农村信用社贷款利率最高可上浮50%；金融机构贷款最低下浮10%。
3. ③从1999年9月起，金融机构对中小企业贷款利率可在法定贷款利率基础上上浮30%，对大型企业贷款最高上浮10%；金融机构贷款最低下浮10%。

a)① The lending rate could be 10% higher or 10% lower than nominal interest rates;for rural credit cooperatives, the lending rate could be 40% higher or 10% lower than nominal interest rates.

b)② As of November 1998, the lending rate for small-sized entrprises could be 20% higher than nominal interest rates, and the lending rate for medium- and large- sized entrprises could be 10% higher than nominal interest rates. For all financial institutions, the lending rate could be 10% lower than nominal interest rates, whil, for rural credit cooperatives, the lending rate coould be 50% higher than nominal interest rates.

c)③ As of September 1999, the lending rate for medium- and small-sized entrprises could be 30% higher than nominal interest rates; for large-sized entrprises, the lending rate could be as much as 10% higher than nominal interest rates. For all financial institutions,the lending rate could be 10% lower than nominal interest rates.

20-12 黄金和外汇储备

Gold and Foreign Exchange Reserves

年份 Year	黄金储备（万盎司） Gold (10 000 fine troy ounce)	外汇储备（亿美元） Foreign Exchange Reserve (USD 100 million)	年份 Year	黄金储备（万盎司） Gold (10 000 fine troy ounce)	外汇储备（亿美元） Foreign Exchange Reserve (USD 100 million)
1978	1280	1.67	1991	1267	217.12
1979	1280	8.40	1992	1267	194.43
1980	1280	-12.96	1993	1267	211.99
1981	1267	27.08	1994	1267	516.20
1982	1267	69.86	1995	1267	735.97
1983	1267	89.01	1996	1267	1050.29
1984	1267	82.20	1997	1267	1398.90
1985	1267	26.44	1998	1267	1449.60
1986	1267	20.72	1999	1267	1546.75
1987	1267	29.23	2000	1267	1655.74
1988	1267	33.72	2001	1608	2121.65
1989	1267	55.50	2002	1929	2864.07
1990	1267	110.93	2003	1929	4032.51

20-13 国有商业银行资产负债表（年底余额）

Balance Sheet of Domestic Business Banks at the Year-end

单位：亿元 (100 million yuan)

项目	Item	2002	2003
总资产	**Total Assets**	**135496.0**	**156400.1**
国外资产	Overseas Assets	9594.9	8386.2
储备资产	Reserve Assets	11943.1	13507.5
准备金存款	Bank Reserve	11189.2	12673.4
库存现金	Cash on hand	753.9	834.1
央行债券	Claims on the Central Bank	586.4	2548.8
对政府债权	Claims on Government	8379.2	9013.1
对非金融机构债权	Claims on Non-financial Institutions	81548.6	96400.8
对特定存款机构债权	Claims on Special Depository Institutions	4385.8	5358.9
对其他金融机构债权	Claims on Other Financial Institutions	7623.7	11377.4
其他资产	Other Assets	11434.4	9807.4
总负债	**Total Liabilities**	**135496.0**	**156400.1**
对非金融机构负债	Liabilities to Non-financial Institutions	110251.9	127119.8
活期存款	Demand Deposits	32934.3	37797.0
定期存款	Time Deposits	8415.9	10038.1
储蓄存款	Savings Deposits	56655.4	66850.4
其他存款	Other Deposits	2851.5	3475.4
外币存款	Foreign Currency Deposits	9394.8	8958.8
对中央银行负债	Liabilities to Central Bank	3165.3	2610.7
对特定存款机构负债	Liabilities to Special Deposit Institutions	202.8	197.6
对其他金融机构负债	Liabilities to Other Financial Institutions	5420.4	5769.1
#计入广义货币的存款	Broad Sense Currency Deposits	1519.3	1244.1
国外负债	Overseas Liabilities	1884.7	1985.5
债券	Bonds	208.5	0.4
实收资本	Paid-up Capital	5082.3	6672.4
其他负债	Other Liabilities	9280.1	12044.6

20-14 外资银行资产负债表（年底余额）

Balance Sheet of Foreign Capital Banks at the Year-end

单位: 亿元 (100 million yuan)

项目	Item	2002	2003
总资产	**Total Assets**	**2881.0**	**3330.5**
国外资产	Overseas Assets	919.3	1103.5
储备资产	Reserve Assets	109.1	171.0
准备金	Bank Reserve	108.8	170.6
库存现金	Cash on hand	0.3	0.4
中央银行债券	Claims on the Central Bank		
对政府债权	Claims on Government	18.6	51.9
对非金融机构债权	Claims on Non-financial Institutions	1374.3	1476.2
对特定存款机构债权	Claims on Special Deposit Institutions	41.1	30.9
对其他金融机构债权	Claims on Other Financial Institutions	0.2	
其他资产	Other Assets	418.5	496.9
总负债	**Total Liabilities**	**2881.0**	**3330.5**
国外负债	Overseas Liabilities	1246.0	1620.8
对非金融机构负债	Liabilities to Non-financial Institutions	692.3	906.7
活期存款	Demand Deposits	118.9	189.3
定期存款	Time Deposits	93.1	199.1
储蓄存款	Savings Deposits	3.1	0.3
其他存款	Other Deposits		
外币存款	Foreign Currency Deposits	477.3	518.0
对中央银行负债	Liabilities to Central Bank		0.1
对特定存款机构负债	Liabilities to Special Deposit Institutions	10.3	2.6
对其他金融机构负债	Liabilities to Other Financial Institutions	23.6	30.1
#计入广义货币的存款	Broad Sense Currency Deposits		
债券	Bonds	5.0	4.7
实收资本	Paicl-up Capital	347.5	354.6
其他负债	Other Liabilities	556.2	411.0

20-15 国内有价证券分类发行情况（2003年）

Issuance of Domestic Securities (2003)

单位: 亿元 (100 million yuan)

种类	Kind	发行额 Total Value of Issued Securities	兑付额 Total Value of Redemption	年底余额 Balance (Year-end)
国债	National Debt	6280.1	2755.8	22603.6
#国库券	Treasury Bonds			
财政证券	Fiscal Bonds			
政策性金融债券	Policy Financial Bonds	4561.4	2505.3	11650.0
其他金融债	Other Financial Bonds			
企业债	Corporate Bonds	358.0		
国家投资债	Government Investment Bonds			
国家投资公司债	Bonds Issued by Government Investment Company			
股票	Shares	83.6	453.5	

注：股票是指A种股票(不含A股可转换债券)，股票兑付额是指筹资额。

a) Shares refer to A shares. The figure shown under the column "total value of redemption" for shares refers to the capital raised.

20-16 证券市场基本情况

General Statistics on Securities Markets

项　目	Item	2002	2003
境内上市公司数（A、B股）（家）	Number of Listed Companies (A and B Shares) in Mainland	1224	1287
境内上市外资股（B股）（家）	Number of Listed Companies of Foreign Fund (B Shares) in Mainland	111	110
境外上市公司数（H股）（家）	Number of Listed Companies (H Shares) Overseas	75	93
股票总发行股本（亿股）	Total Issued Capital (100 million shares)	5875.45	6428.46
#流通股本（亿股）	Negotiable Capital (100 million shares)	2036.90	2269.92
股票市价总值（亿元）	Total Market Capitalization (100 million yuan)	38329.12	42457.72
#股票流通市值（亿元）	Negotiable Market Capitalization (100 millon yuan)	12484.55	13178.52
股票成交量（百万股）	Stock Trading Volume (million shares)	301619.49	416308.40
股票成交金额（亿元）	Total Stock Turnover (100 million yuan)	27990.46	32115.27
上证综合指数（收盘）	Composite Index of Shanghai	1357.65	1497.04
深证综合指数（收盘）	Composite Index of Shenzhen	388.76	378.62
投资者开户数（万户）	Total Investors (10 000 accounts)	7202.16	7344.41
平均市盈率	Average P/E Ratio		
上海	Shanghai	34.43	36.54
深圳	Shenzhen	36.97	36.19
平均换手率（%）	Average Turnover Rate (%)		
上海	Shanghai	214.00	250.75
深圳	Shenzhen	198.79	214.18
国债发行额（亿元）	T-bonds Issued Volume (100 million yuans)	5934.30	6280.10
企业债发行额（亿元）	Enterprise Bonds Issued Volume (100 million yuans)	325.00	358.00
债券成交量（万手）	Bonds Trading Volume (10 000 pieces)	329252.26	620194.41
债券成交额（亿元）	Total Bonds Turnover (100 million yuans)	33249.53	62136.36
国债现货成交金额（亿元）	Turnover of T-bonds Spots (100 million yuans)	8708.68	5756.11
国债回购成交金额（亿元）	Turnover of T-bonds Repurchase (100 million yuans)	24419.64	52999.85
证券投资基金只数（只）	Number of Securities Investment Funds (unit)	71	95
证券投资基金规模（亿元）	Capital of Securities Investment Funds (100 million yuans)	1318.85	1614.67
证券投资基金成交金额（亿元）	Turnover of Securities Investment Funds (100 million yuans)	1166.58	682.65
期货总成交量（万手）	Future Trading Volume (10 000 pieces)	13943.37	27992.43
期货总成交额（亿元）	Total Future Turnover (100 million yuans)	39490.28	108396.59

注：换手率=全年成交金额/[（本年末流通市值+上年末流通市值）/2]*100%

a) Average Turnover Rate = [Total Stock Turnover/(Negotiable Market Capitalization at the year-end + Negotiable Market Capitalization at the previous year-end)/2]*100%

20-17 上 市 公 司 数 量

Summary for Number of Listed Companies

单位：个 (unit)

年　份 Year	全国合计 National	上交所 Shanghai Stock Exchange	深交所 Shenzhen Stock Exchange	仅发A股公司 A share Only	发A、H股公司 A&H Share	发A、B股公司 A&B Share	仅发B股公司 B Share Only
1990	10	8	2	10			
1991	14	8	6	14			
1992	53	29	24	53		18	
1993	183	106	77	183	3	34	6
1994	291	171	120	227	6	54	4
1995	323	188	135	242	11	58	12
1996	530	293	237	431	14	69	16
1997	745	383	362	627	17	76	25
1998	851	438	413	727	18	80	26
1999	949	484	465	822	19	82	26
2000	1088	572	516	955	19	86	28
2001	1160	646	514	1025	23	88	24
2002	1224	715	509	1085	28	87	24
2003	1287	780	507	1146	30	87	24

20-18 股票发行量和筹资额

Issued Share and Raised Capital

年 份 Year	股票发行量 (亿股) Issued Share (100 million shares)	A 股 A Shares	H股, N股 H,N Shares	B 股 B Shares	股票筹资额 (亿元) Raised Capital (100 million yuan)	A 股 A Shares	#配股 Rights Issued	H股,N股 H & N Shares	B 股 B Shares
1991	5.00	5.00			5.00	5.00			
1992	20.75	10.00		10.75	94.09	50.00			44.09
1993	95.79	42.59	40.41	12.79	375.47	276.41	81.58	60.93	38.13
1994	91.26	10.97	69.89	10.40	326.78	99.78	50.16	188.73	38.27
1995	31.60	5.32	15.38	10.90	150.32	85.51	62.83	31.46	33.35
1996	86.11	38.29	31.77	16.05	425.08	294.34	69.89	83.56	47.18
1997	267.63	105.65	136.88	25.10	1293.82	825.92	170.86	360.00	80.76
1998	105.56	86.30	12.86	9.90	841.52	778.02	334.97	37.95	25.55
1999	122.93	98.11	23.05	1.77	944.56	893.60	320.97	47.17	3.79
2000	512.03	145.68	359.26	7.10	2103.08	1527.03	519.46	562.21	13.99
2001	141.48	93.00	48.48		1252.34	1182.13	430.63	70.21	
2002	291.74	134.20	157.54		961.75	779.75	56.61	181.99	
2003	281.43	83.64	196.79	1.00	1357.75	819.56	74.79	534.65	3.54

20-19 股 票 交 易 情 况

Trading Summary for Stocks

项 目	Item	1995	1998	1999	2000	2001	2002	2003
会员总数	No. of Members	1085	659	628	631	547	437	382
上市公司数目（家）	No. of listed Companies	323	851	949	1088	1160	1224	1287
上市股票数目（只）	No. of listed Stocks	381	931	1029	1174	1240	1310	1372
A股	A Shares	311	825	921	1010	1130	1199	1261
B股	B Shares	70	106	108	114	110	111	111
股票总发行股本（亿股）	**Total Issued Capital (100 million share)**	**765.63**	**2345.35**	**2908.85**	**3613.39**	**4838.35**	**5462.99**	**5997.93**
A股	A Shares	704.08	2203.96	2757.88	3439.60	4650.45	5283.64	5808.31
B股	B Shares	61.55	141.37	150.96	173.79	187.90	179.34	189.62
流通股本 （亿股）	**Negotiable Shares (100 million share)**	**234.98**	**740.94**	**952.34**	**1233.32**	**1480.88**	**1679.94**	**1897.32**
A股	A Shares	178.98	607.01	810.45	1078.33	1315.21	1508.43	1717.93
B股	B Shares	45.99	133.91	141.88	154.99	165.67	171.51	179.39
股票市价总值(亿元)	**Total Market Capitalization (100 million yuan)**	**3474**	**19506**	**26471**	**48091**	**43522**	**38329**	**42458**
A股	A Shares	3311	19299	26168	47456	42246	37527	41520
B股	B Shares	164	206	304	635	1277	803	937
股票流通市值(亿元)	**Negotiable Market Capitalization (100 million yuan)**	**938**	**5746**	**8214**	**16088**	**14463**	**12485**	**13179**
A股	A Shares	791	5550	7937	15524	13345	11719	12306
B股	B Shares	147	196	276	563	1118	766	873
股票成交金额(亿元)	**Total Turnover (100 million yuan)**	**4036**	**23544**	**31320**	**60827**	**38305**	**27990**	**32115**
A股	A Shares	4319	23418	31050	60279	33242	27142	31270
B股	B Shares	78	127	270	548	5063	848	845
总成交股数 （亿股）	**Trading Volume (100 million share)**	**705.31**	**2154.11**	**2932.39**	**4758.36**	**3152.28**	**3016.19**	**4163.08**
A股	A Shares	681.07	2092.50	2809.75	4558.00	2463.41	2859.49	3992.28
B股	B Shares	24.24	61.60	122.64	200.36	688.88	156.70	170.80
深证综合指数	**Shenzhen Composite Index**							
最高	High	169.66	441.04	525.14	654.37	664.85	512.38	449.42
最低	Low	112.63	317.10	310.65	414.69	439.36	371.79	350.74
收盘	Close	113.24	343.85	402.18	635.73	475.94	388.76	378.63
上证综合指数	**Shanghai Composite Index**							
最高	High	926.41	1422.98	1756.18	2125.72	2245.44	1748.89	1649.60
最低	Low	524.43	1043.02	1047.83	1361.21	1514.86	1339.20	1307.40
收盘	Close	555.29	1146.70	1366.58	2073.48	1645.97	1357.65	1497.04

20-20 保险系统机构、人员数（2003年底）
Number of Institutions and Employed Persons in Insurance System (Year-end of 2003)

项目	Item	机构数（个） Number of Institution (unit)	职工人数（人） Employed Person (person)	# 女职工 Female
总计	**Total**	**62**	**199705**	**82687**
中资保险公司	**Domestic Funded Insurance Institutions**	**26**	**196370**	**80820**
国有公司	**State-owned**			
#总公司	National Corporations	10	1865	673
省级分公司	Provincial Branches	92	9234	3785
计划单列市	Branches at Separate Planning Cities	12	1644	753
省会城市营业部	Business Departments at Provincial Capitals	56	3421	1892
地市级分公司	Prefecture/City Branches	851	40550	16897
地市级营业部	Prefecture/City Business Departments	167	5414	1726
县级支公司	County Branches	4303	55488	20156
县级营业部	County Business Departments	533	5136	2126
办事处或营业部	Business Offices or Departments	1739	3642	706
保险院校	Colleges and Schools	4	367	166
其他	Others	29	517	180
股份制公司	**Share-holding Corporations**			
#总公司	National Corporations	16	7217	3078
一级分公司	First Level Filiales	188	29387	14236
二级分公司	Second Level Filiales	127	1026	513
支公司	Branches	415	27562	12007
办事处或营业部	Offices or Business Departments	508	3854	1893
其他	Others	6	46	33
中外合资公司、外资保险公司	**Joint-venture and Foreign Investment Insurance Institutions**	**36**	**3335**	**1867**
中外合资公司	Joint-venture Insurance Corporation	15	1346	741
外资分公司	Foreign Funded Insurance Branches	21	1989	1126

注：职工人数不包括营销、代理人员。
a) Number of employed persons exclude the marketing persons and agent persons.

20-21 保险公司业务经济技术指标(2003年)
Economic and Technical Indicators of Insurance Companies Funded with Chinese and Foreign Capital (2003)

项目	Item	保费（亿元） Premium (100 million yuan)	赔款及给付（亿元） Claim and Payment (100 million yuan)
合计	**Total**	**3880**	**841**
财产保险公司	**Property Insurance Companies**	**869**	**476**
企业财产保险	Enterprise Property Insurance	125	64
家庭财产保险	Family Property Insurance	19	4
机动车辆保险	Motor Vehicle Insurance	540	328
船舶保险	Ship Insurance	15	11
货物运输保险	Freight Transport Insurance	41	17
卫星及核能险	Satellite and Nuclear Energy Insurance	1	
建筑、安装工程保险及责任保险	Construction and Installation Projects Insurance and Related Liability Insurance	12	5
责任保险	Liability Insurance	35	20
保证保险	Guarantee Insurance	2	1
信用保险	Export Credit Insurance	8	8
农业保险	Agriculture Insurance	5	3
其他保险	Other Insurance	66	15
人寿保险公司	**Life Insurance Companies**	**3011**	**365**
寿险	Life Insurance	2669	264
健康险	Health Insurance	242	70
人身意外伤害险	Unforeseen Human Injury Insurance	100	31

主要统计指标解释

信贷资金 指金融机构以信用方式积聚和分配的货币资金。金融机构信贷资金的来源有各项存款、金融债券发行、应付及暂收款、对国际金融机构负债、流通中货币、各项准备、所有者权益和其他项目等；信贷资金的运用有各项贷款、有价证券及投资、应收及预付款、委托投资、金银占款、外汇占款、库存现金、财政借款及在国际金融机构中的资产等。

存款 指企业、机关、团体或居民根据资金必须收回的原则，把货币资金存入银行或其他信贷机构保管并取得一定利息的一种信用活动形式。根据存款对象或性质的不同可划分为企业存款、财政存款、机关团体存款、基本建设存款、储蓄存款、农村存款、委托存款、其他存款等科目。它是银行信贷资金的主要来源。

贷款 指银行或其他信贷机构根据资金必须归还的原则，按一定利率，为企业、个人等提供资金的一种信用活动形式。我国银行贷款分为短期贷款、中期流动资金贷款、中长期贷款、信托贷款、融资租赁、委托贷款、票据融资、各项垫款等。

保险公司 在中国境内的、经过保险监督管理部门批准设立，并依法登记注册的各类商业保险公司。

保险金额 指保险人承担赔偿或者给付保险金责任的最高限额。

保费 指投保人为取得保险人在约定范围内所承担赔偿责任而支付给保险人的费用。

赔款 指保险人根据保险合同的规定，向被保险人支付的赔偿保险责任损失的金额。

给付 包括死伤医疗给付和满期给付。死伤医疗给付是指保险人根据人寿保险及长期健康保险合同的规定，因被保险人在保险期内发生保险责任范围内的保险事故支付给被保险人(或受益人)的金额。满期给付是指被保险人生存期满，保险人按人寿保险合同规定支付给被保险人的满期保险金额。

Explanatory Notes on Main Statistical Indicators

Credit Funds refer to the funds issued as loans by banking institutions. The sources of credit funds of the banking institutions included deposits, issue of financial bonds, account-payable and temporary gathering, liabilities to international financial institutions, currency in circulation, various reserves, owners' rights and interests and other items. The credit funds can be used in forms of loans, securities and investment, account receivable and advance payment, entrusted investment, gold, foreign exchange, cash on hand, government debt and assets in the international financial institutions.

Deposit is a form of credit by which enterprises, institutions, organizations or households can put money into banks and other credit institutions for safekeeping and interest earning under the principle of free withdrawal. According to different depositors, deposits are divided into enterprise deposits, treasury deposits, deposits of government agencies and organizations, capital construction deposits, savings deposits, rural saving deposits, entrusted deposits and other deposits. Deposits are major sources of the credit funds of banks.

Loan is a form of credit by which banks and other credit institutions provide funds at certain interest rate to enterprises and individuals in the light of the principle of unconditional repayment. Loans from Chinese banks include circulating capital loans, fixed assets loans, loans to urban and rural individuals engaged in industrial and commercial business and agricultural loans.

Insurance Companies refer to commercial insurance companies of various forms registered by law and established in China with the approval of insurance regulatory agencies.

Amount Insured refers to the maximum that the insurant will get for the claim of the case insured.

Premium is the fee paid by the insurant to the insurer to obtain the obligation of compensation from the insurance within the agreed terms.

Settled Claim is the compensation paid by the insurer to the insurant in accordance with the insurance contract.

Payment includes payment for death, injury or medical treatment and mature payment. Payment for death, injury or medical treatment refers to the money paid to the insurant (or the beneficiary) in accordance with the life or health insurance contract when the insurant encounters accidents within the insured period covered in the contract. Mature payment refers to the mature payment to the insurant in accordance with the life insurance contract at the end of the insured period.

二十一、教育和科技

Education, Science and Technology

简要说明

本篇主要反映我国教育事业的发展情况和科学技术活动的基本情况。

一、教育统计资料包括研究生教育、普通高等教育(普通教育本专科)、普通中等教育(中等专业学校、技工学校、普通中学、职业中学和工读学校)、初等教育(小学)、幼儿教育、特殊教育(盲聋哑和弱智儿童学校等)、各级各类成人教育(成人高校、成人中等学校和成人初等学校)以及教育经费等资料。主要指标包括学校数、在校学生数、招生数、毕业生数、教职工数和专任教师数、教育经费总额及国家财政性教育经费等。

教育事业统计资料、教育经费统计资料由教育部提供；技工学校的资料由劳动和社会保障部提供。

详细资料分别见《中国教育事业统计年鉴》（教育部发展规划司编）和《全国教育经费执行情况统计公告》（教育部、国家统计局和财政部联合发文）。

二、科技统计资料主要内容包括：国有企事业单位专业技术人员情况；独立核算的科研机构、高校及各类企事业单位的科技活动人员、科技活动经费筹集及支出、研究与试验发展（R&D）活动、科技成果及奖励等情况；国内外职务及非职务专利申请和授权情况；全国技术市场技术合同成交情况；科协系统科技活动情况；高新技术产业开发区企业主要经济指标情况；综合技术服务部门业务机构及业务活动情况等。

统计范围：科技活动统计资料基本包括了全社会有科技活动的企事业单位，具体包括大中型工业企业、独立核算的科研机构、普通高等学校、规模以上小型工业企业、具有一级资质的建筑企业、地市及以上运输和通信企业、地市及以上农业和卫生业企事业单位、从事软件开发活动的企业、以及从事综合技术服务活动的单位等。

资料来源：全国综合资料、各类企业资料、医疗卫生机构和农业事业等单位资料由国家统计局调查提供；独立核算的科研机构资料、技术市场资料、高新技术产业开发区企业资料由科技部调查提供；高校科技活动资料由教育部调查提供；国防科研机构资料由国防科工委调查提供；专业技术人员资料由中组部和国家统计局调查提供；科协系统科技活动资料由中国科协调查提供；测绘、气象、地震、海洋、产品质量监督抽查、专利等资料，分别由国家测绘局、中国气象局、国家地震局、国家海洋局、国家技术监督及检验检疫局、国家知识产权局等部门调查提供。

统计调查方法：工业企业、独立核算的科研机构、高校的科技活动资料采用全数调查取得，其中大中型工业企业实施年报调查制度，规模以上小型工业企业实施双年报调查制度；科协、测绘、气象、地震、海洋、产品质量监督抽查、专利资料采用抽样等多种调查方法取得；建筑业、运输业、通信业、软件业、农业和卫生业采用五年为一周期的滚动调查制度。

科技活动统计资料口径变动说明：2000年以前科技活动统计资料只包括大中型工业企业、独立核算的科研机构、普通高等学校，2000年及以后年份扩大到了小型工业、建筑业、运输业、通信业、软件业、农业和卫生等行业企事业单位。

Brief Introduction

Data in this chapter show the development of China's education and the basic conditions of the activities of China's science and technology.

I. The data on education cover the situations on postgraduates, higher education (universities and colleges), secondary education (specialized secondary schools, regular secondary schools, vocational secondary schools and schools for juvenile delinquents), primary education (primary schools), kindergarten education, special education (schools for the blind, deaf-mutes, and the retarded), adult education of various levels and categories (adult universities and colleges, adult secondary schools, and adult primary schools), and expenditure on education. The main indicators cover the number of schools, the number of students enrolled, the number of new students enrolled, the number of graduates, the number of staff and workers, the number of full-time teachers, sources and outlay of education fund, education expenditure from the state budget.

The Ministry of Education mainly provides statistical data on education and education funds. Data on the technical training schools are provided by the Ministry of Labour and Social Security.

Detailed information can be found in "Statistical Yearbook on China Educational Undertakings" compiled by Department of Planning and Development, Ministry of Education; and the "Communiqué on the Implementation of National Education Funds" compiled jointly by Ministry of Education, National Bureau of Statistics and Ministry of Finance.

II. Data on technology mainly include: condition of professional scientific and technological personnel of state-owned enterprises and institutions; scientific and technological institutions with independent accounting system, scientific and technological personnel in universities and colleges and various enterprises or institutions, funds raising and expenditure on scientific and technological activities, activities of R&D and scientific and technological achievements and prizes; condition on applied and certified patent applications by services and non-services both domestically and overseas; the situation of signed technological contracts on technological market; scientific and technological activities within scientific and technological system; major economic indicators of high and new-tech industrial zones and the condition of comprehensive technological service agencies and their business activities.

Statistical scope: data on scientific and technological activities include all institutions of the society engaged in those activities, they are mainly: large and medium-sized industrial enterprises, scientific and technological institutions with independent accounting system, universities and colleges, small industrial enterprises above designated size, the construction enterprises with first grade, transportation and telecommunication enterprises at and above prefecture level, agricultural and health care institutions at and above prefecture level, enterprises engaged in software development, units engaged in scientific and technological services and so on.

Sources of data: data on national level, various enterprises, medical and health care institutions and agricultural undertakings are from National Bureau of Statistics; data on scientific and technologic research institutions, technological markets and high and new-tech industrial zones are from Ministry of Science and Technology; data on scientific and technological activities in universities and colleges are from Ministry of Education; data on scientific research institutions for defense are from Commission of Science, Technology and Industry for National Defense. Department of Organization of the Central Committee of the Communist Party of China and National Bureau of Statistics provide the data on the number of scientific and technological personnel. The China Association provides data on the scientific and technological activities of the associations for science and technology for Science and Technology. Data on the development of the mapping, meteorology, seismology, ocean, supervision and checking of the products quality and patents are provided separately by the National Bureau of Surveying and Mapping, China Meteorological Administration, China Seismological Bureau, National Bureau of Marine Administration, General Administration of Quality Supervision, Inspection and Quarantine and State Intellectual Property Office.

Statistical methodology: data on industrial enterprises, scientific and technological institutions with independent accounting system and scientific and technological activities of universities and colleges are collected through complete surveys, of which data on large and medium-sized industrial enterprises are following the scheme of annual reporting system, and that of small industrial enterprises above the designated size are reporting the data every other year. Data on scientific and technological association, mapping, meteorology, seismology, ocean, supervision and checking of the products quality and patent applications are through sample surveys and other surveys. Data on construction, transportation, telecommunication, software industry, agriculture and health care are from rolling survey system with 5 years as one cycle.

Changes of the statistical scope of data on scientific and technological activities: before 2000, data only included large and medium-sized industrial enterprises, scientific research institutions with independent accounting system, and universities and colleges. Since 2000 (inclusive), data include: small industrial enterprises, construction sector, transportation sector, telecommunication sector, software sector, agriculture and health care agencies.

21-1 教育事业基本情况
Basic Statistics on Education

指标	Item	1990	1995	2000	2002	2003
学校数（所）	**Number of Schools (unit)**					
普通高等学校	Regular Institutions of Higher Education	1075	1054	1041	1396	1552
普通中等学校	Secondary Schools	100777	95216	89763	90422	89398
普通中等专业学校	Specialized Secondary Schools	3982	4049	3646	2953	3065
普通中学	Regular Secondary Schools	87631	81020	77268	80067	79490
高中	Senior Secondary Schools	15678	13991	14564	15406	15779
初中	Junior Secondary Schools	71953	67029	62704	64661	63711
职业中学	Vocational Secondary Schools	9164	10147	8849	7402	6843
小学	Primary Schools	766072	668685	553622	456903	425846
特殊教育	Special Schools	746	1379	1539	1540	1551
幼儿园	Kindergartens	172322	180438	175836	111752	116390
专任教师（万人）	Number of Full-time Teachers (10 000 persons)					
普通高等学校	Regular Institutions of Higher Education	39.5	40.1	46.3	61.8	72.5
普通中等学校	Secondary Schools	349.2	388.3	458.1	489.4	502.5
普通中等专业学校	Specialized Secondary Schools	23.4	25.7	25.6	20.8	19.9
普通中学	Regular Secondary Schools	303.3	333.4	400.5	437.6	453.7
高中	Senior Secondary Schools	56.2	55.1	75.7	94.6	107.1
初中	Junior Secondary Schools	247.0	278.4	324.9	343.0	346.7
职业中学	Vocational Secondary Schools	22.4	29.2	32.0	31.0	28.9
小学	Primary Schools	558.2	566.4	586.0	577.9	570.3
特殊教育	Special Schools	1.4	2.5	3.2	3.0	3.0
幼儿园	Kindergartens	75.0	87.5	85.6	57.1	61.3
招生数（万人）	New Student Enrollment (10 000 persons)					
普通高等学校	Regular Institutions of Higher Education	60.9	92.6	220.6	320.5	382.2
普通中等学校	Secondary Schools	1815.8	2354.0	3051.3	3301.2	3353.4
普通中等专业学校	Specialized Secondary Schools	73.0	138.1	132.6	155.3	183.9
普通中学	Regular Secondary Schools	1619.6	2025.9	2736.0	2929.0	2947.4
高中	Senior Secondary Schools	249.8	273.7	472.7	676.7	752.1
初中	Junior Secondary Schools	1369.9	1752.3	2263.3	2252.3	2195.3
职业中学	Vocational Secondary Schools	123.2	190.0	182.7	216.9	222.1
小学	Primary Schools	2064.0	2531.8	1946.5	1952.8	1829.4
特殊教育	Special Schools	1.6	5.6	5.3	5.3	4.9
幼儿园	Kindergartens		1972.4	1531.1	1373.6	1316.8
在校学生数（万人）	Student Enrollment (10 000 persons)					
普通高等学校	Regular Institutions of Higher Education	206.3	290.6	556.1	903.4	1108.6
普通中等学校	Secondary Schools	5105.4	6191.5	8361.6	9255.7	9613.8
普通中等专业学校	Specialized Secondary Schools	224.4	372.2	489.5	456.4	502.4
普通中学	Regular Secondary Schools	4586.0	5371.0	7368.9	8287.9	8583.2
高中	Senior Secondary Schools	717.3	713.2	1201.3	1683.8	1964.8
初中	Junior Secondary Schools	3868.7	4657.8	6167.6	6604.1	6618.4
职业中学	Vocational Secondary Schools	295.0	448.3	503.2	511.5	528.2
小学	Primary Schools	12241.4	13195.2	13013.3	12156.7	11689.7
特殊教育	Special Schools	7.2	29.6	37.8	37.5	36.5
幼儿园	Kindergartens	1972.2	2711.2	2244.2	2036.0	2003.9
毕业生数（万人）	Graduates (10 000 persons)					
普通高等学校	Regular Institutions of Higher Education	61.4	80.5	95.0	133.7	187.7
普通中等学校	Secondary Schools	1497.5	1636.9	2235.6	2553.2	2737.7
普通中等专业学校	Specialized Secondary Schools	66.1	83.9	150.7	144.2	148.4
普通中学	Regular Secondary Schools	1342.1	1429.0	1908.6	2263.6	2453.7
高中	Senior Secondary Schools	233.0	201.6	301.5	383.8	458.1
初中	Junior Secondary Schools	1109.1	1227.4	1607.1	1879.9	1995.6
职业中学	Vocational Secondary Schools	89.3	124.0	176.3	145.4	135.5
小学	Primary Schools	1863.1	1961.5	2419.2	2351.9	2267.9
特殊教育	Special Schools	0.5	1.9	4.3	4.4	4.5

21-2 各级各类学校数

Number of Schools by Level and Type of School

单位: 所 (unit)

年份 Year	普通高等学校 Regular Institutions of Higher Education	普通中等学校 Secondary Schools	#中等专业学校 Specialized Secondary Schools	中等技术学校 Technical Secondary Schools	中等师范学校 Teacher Secondary Schools	#普通中学 Regular Secondary Schools	高中 Senior Secondary Schools	初中 Junior Secondary Schools	#职业中学 Vocational Secondary Schools	小学 Primary Schools	特殊教育学校 Special Schools	幼儿园 Kindergartens
1978	598	165105	2760	1714	1046	162345	49215	113130		949323	292	163952
1980	675	124760	3069	2052	1017	118377	31300	87077	3314	917316	292	170419
1985	1016	104848	3557	2529	1028	93221	17318	75903	8070	832309	375	172262
1986	1054	104936	3782	2741	1041	92967	17111	75856	8187	820846	423	173376
1987	1063	105151	3913	2854	1059	92857	16930	75927	8381	807406	504	176775
1988	1075	104468	4022	2957	1065	91492	16524	74968	8954	793261	577	171845
1989	1075	102732	3984	2940	1044	89575	16050	73525	9173	777244	662	172634
1990	1075	100777	3982	2956	1026	87631	15678	71953	9164	766072	746	172322
1991	1075	99348	3925	2977	948	85851	15243	70608	9572	729158	886	164465
1992	1053	97784	3903	2984	919	84021	14850	69171	9860	712973	1077	172506
1993	1065	96744	3964	3046	918	82795	14380	68415	9985	696681	1123	165197
1994	1080	96562	3987	3093	894	82358	14242	68116	10217	682588	1241	174657
1995	1054	95216	4049	3152	897	81020	13991	67029	10147	668685	1379	180438
1996	1032	94115	4099	3206	893	79967	13875	66092	10049	645983	1428	187324
1997	1020	92832	4143	3251	892	78642	13880	64762	10047	628840	1440	182485
1998	1022	92071	4109	3234	875	77888	13948	63940	10074	609626	1535	181368
1999	1071	95255	3962	3147	815	77213	14127	63086	9636	582291	1520	181136
2000	1041	93629	3646	2963	683	77268	14564	62704	8849	553622	1539	175836
2001	1225	95362	3260	2690	570	80432	14907	65525	7802	491273	1531	111706
2002	1396	90422	2953	2523	430	80067	15406	64661	7402	456903	1540	111752
2003	1552	89398	3065			79490	15779	63711	6843	425846	1551	116390

注: 1999年起中等学校包括技工学校和工读学校数（下表同）。

a) Number of secondary schools since 1999 include various technical schools and schools for juvenile delinquents. The same as in the following table.

21-3 各级各类学校教职工数

Number of Teachers and Staff by Level and Type of School

单位: 万人 (10 000 persons)

年份 Year	普通高等学校 Regular Institutions of Higher Education	普通中等学校 Secondary Schools	#中等专业学校 Specialized Secondary Schools	中等技术学校 Technical Secondary Schools	中等师范学校 Teacher Secondary Schools	#普通中学 Regular Secondary Schools	#职业中学 Vocational Secondary Schools	小学 Primary Schools	特殊教育学校 Special Schools	幼儿园 Kindergartens
1978	51.8	415.4	23.7	17.6	6.1	391.7		562.0	0.7	46.9
1980	63.2	423.6	29.8	22.3	7.5	389.7	4.1	605.4	0.8	61.0
1985	87.1	417.6	40.3	31.3	9.0	355.7	21.6	602.1	1.1	79.8
1986	93.1	437.7	43.6	33.9	9.7	368.9	25.2	606.5	1.3	88.1
1987	96.9	455.3	45.9	35.7	10.2	381.3	28.1	608.5	1.4	94.1
1988	99.4	468.1	47.6	37.0	10.6	389.7	30.8	614.2	1.6	97.9
1989	100.4	473.9	48.2	37.6	10.6	393.1	32.6	619.5	1.8	101.2
1990	100.6	482.6	49.2	38.5	10.7	399.1	34.3	624.0	2.0	105.2
1991	100.9	490.6	49.4	38.8	10.6	405.4	35.8	619.4	2.3	106.2
1992	101.4	499.2	50.3	39.7	10.6	411.3	37.6	619.9	2.7	112.1
1993	102.1	504.1	51.1	40.3	10.8	413.3	39.7	621.8	3.0	112.6
1994	104.0	512.3	51.7	40.7	11.0	419.1	41.5	627.1	3.3	114.9
1995	104.1	525.9	53.0	41.8	11.2	429.5	43.4	632.4	3.7	116.0
1996	103.6	541.9	54.3	43.0	11.3	442.4	45.2	638.6	4.0	117.4
1997	103.2	556.2	55.4	44.0	11.4	454.1	46.7	643.6	4.3	117.3
1998	103.0	564.6	54.7	43.5	11.2	462.1	47.8	644.6	4.2	115.8
1999	106.5	606.7	52.9	42.1	10.7	475.4	47.2	647.1	4.5	115.8
2000	111.3	611.8	48.8	39.8	9.0	491.1	44.7	645.5	4.4	114.4
2001	121.4	623.1	42.9	35.3	7.6	514.9	43.0	638.0	3.9	86.2
2002	130.4	636.9	38.2	32.0	6.1	533.5	43.0	634.0	4.0	90.3
2003	145.3	624.4	34.7			549.7	40.0	625.6	4.1	97.3

21-4 各级各类学校专任教师数

Number of Full-time Teachers by Level and Type of School

单位：万人 (10 000 persons)

年份 Year	普通高等学校 Regular Institutions of Higher Education	普通中等学校 Secondary Schools	#中等专业学校 Specialized Secondary Schools	中等技术学校 Technical Secondary Schools	中等师范学校 Teacher Secondary Schools	#普通中学 Regular Secondary Schools	高中 Senior Secondary Schools	初中 Junior Secondary Schools	#职业中学 Vocational Secondary Schools	小学 Primary Schools	特殊教育学校 Special Schools	幼儿园 Kinder-gartens
1978	20.6	328.1	9.9	6.9	3.0	318.2	74.1	244.1		522.6	0.4	27.7
1980	24.7	317.1	12.8	9.1	3.7	302.0	57.1	244.9	2.3	549.9	0.5	41.1
1985	34.4	296.7	17.4	12.8	4.6	265.2	49.2	216.0	14.1	537.7	0.7	55.0
1986	37.2	311.5	19.3	14.3	5.0	275.8	51.8	223.9	16.4	541.4	0.8	60.5
1987	38.5	326.6	21.0	15.6	5.4	287.0	54.4	232.7	18.5	543.4	0.9	65.1
1988	39.3	338.9	22.5	16.8	5.7	296.0	55.7	240.3	20.3	550.1	1.1	67.0
1989	39.7	342.3	22.9	17.1	5.8	298.0	55.4	242.7	21.4	554.4	1.2	70.9
1990	39.5	349.2	23.4	17.6	5.8	303.3	56.2	247.0	22.4	558.2	1.4	75.0
1991	39.1	355.7	23.2	17.5	5.7	309.0	57.3	251.7	23.5	553.2	1.6	76.9
1992	38.8	362.4	23.5	17.8	5.7	314.1	57.6	256.5	24.8	552.7	1.9	81.5
1993	38.8	366.8	23.9	18.1	5.8	316.7	55.9	260.8	26.2	555.2	2.0	83.6
1994	39.6	375.7	24.7	18.7	6.0	323.4	54.7	268.7	27.7	561.1	2.3	86.2
1995	40.1	388.3	25.7	19.5	6.2	333.4	55.1	278.4	29.2	566.4	2.5	87.5
1996	40.3	404.0	26.7	20.4	6.3	346.5	57.2	289.3	30.8	573.6	2.7	88.9
1997	40.5	418.6	27.6	21.2	6.4	358.7	60.5	298.2	32.2	579.4	2.9	88.4
1998	40.7	431.2	27.9	21.5	6.4	369.7	64.2	305.5	33.6	581.9	3.0	87.5
1999	42.6	459.6	27.4	21.2	6.2	384.1	69.2	314.8	33.6	586.1	3.1	87.2
2000	46.3	473.4	25.6	20.4	5.3	400.5	75.7	324.9	32.0	586.0	3.2	85.6
2001	53.2	486.6	23.0	18.4	4.6	418.8	84.0	334.8	30.6	579.8	2.9	63.0
2002	61.8	489.4	20.8	17.0	3.8	437.6	94.6	343.0	31.0	577.9	3.0	57.1
2003	72.5	502.5	19.9			453.7	107.1	346.7	28.9	570.3	3.0	61.3

21-5 各级各类学校在校学生数

Number of Students Enrollment by Level and Type of School

单位：万人 (10 000 persons)

年份 Year	普通高等学校 Regular Institutions of Higher Education	普通中等学校 Secondary Schools	#中等专业学校 Specialized Secondary Schools	中等技术学校 Technical Secondary Schools	中等师范学校 Teacher Secondary Schools	#普通中学 Regular Secondary Schools	高中 Senior Secondary Schools	初中 Junior Secondary Schools	#职业中学 Vocational Secondary Schools	小学 Primary Schools	特殊教育学校 Special Schools	幼儿园 Kinder-gartens
1978	85.6	6637.2	88.9	52.9	36.0	6548.3	1553.1	4995.2		14624.0	3.1	787.7
1980	114.4	5677.8	124.3	76.1	48.2	5508.1	969.8	4538.3	45.4	14627.0	3.3	1150.8
1985	170.3	5092.6	157.1	100.9	56.2	4706.0	741.1	3964.8	229.5	13370.2	4.2	1479.7
1986	188.0	5321.6	175.7	114.6	61.1	4889.9	773.4	4116.6	256.0	13182.5	4.7	1629.0
1987	195.9	5403.1	187.4	122.3	65.1	4948.1	773.7	4174.4	267.6	12835.9	5.3	1807.8
1988	206.6	5246.1	205.2	136.8	68.3	4761.5	746.0	4015.5	279.4	12535.8	5.8	1854.5
1989	208.2	5054.0	217.7	149.3	68.5	4554.0	716.1	3837.9	282.3	12373.1	6.4	1847.7
1990	206.3	5105.4	224.4	156.7	67.7	4586.0	717.3	3868.7	295.0	12241.4	7.2	1972.2
1991	204.4	5226.8	227.7	161.6	66.1	4683.5	722.9	3960.6	315.6	12164.2	8.5	2209.3
1992	218.4	5354.4	240.8	174.3	66.6	4770.8	704.9	4065.9	342.8	12201.3	13.0	2428.2
1993	253.6	5383.7	282.0	209.8	72.2	4739.1	656.9	4082.2	362.6	12421.2	16.9	2552.5
1994	279.9	5707.1	319.8	241.4	78.4	4981.7	664.9	4316.7	405.6	12822.6	21.1	2630.3
1995	290.6	6191.5	372.2	287.4	84.8	5371.0	713.2	4657.8	448.3	13195.2	29.6	2711.2
1996	302.1	6635.7	422.8	334.8	88.0	5739.7	769.3	4970.4	473.3	13615.0	32.1	2666.3
1997	317.4	6995.2	465.4	374.3	91.1	6017.9	850.1	5167.8	511.9	13995.4	34.1	2519.0
1998	340.9	7340.7	498.1	406.0	92.1	6301.0	938.0	5363.0	541.6	13953.8	35.8	2403.0
1999	413.4	8002.7	515.5	425.0	90.5	6771.3	1049.7	5721.6	533.9	13548.0	37.2	2326.3
2000	556.1	8518.5	489.5	412.5	77.0	7368.9	1201.3	6167.6	503.2	13013.3	37.8	2244.2
2001	719.1	8901.4	458.0	391.7	66.2	7836.0	1405.0	6431.1	466.4	12543.5	38.6	2021.8
2002	903.4	9255.7	456.4	396.2	60.1	8287.9	1683.8	6604.1	511.5	12156.7	37.5	2036.0
2003	1108.6	9613.8	502.4			8583.2	1964.8	6618.4	528.2	11689.7	36.5	2003.9

21-6 各级各类学校招生数

Number of New Students Enrollment by Level and Type of School

单位：万人 (10 000 persons)

年份 Year	普通高等学校 Regular Institutions of Higher Education	普通中等学校 Secondary Schools	#中等专业学校 Specialized Secondary Schools	中等技术学校 Technical Secondary Schools	中等师范学校 Teacher Secondary Schools	#普通中学 Regular Secondary Schools	高中 Senior Secondary Schools	初中 Junior Secondary Schools	#职业中学 Vocational Secondary Schools	小学 Primary Schools	特殊教育学校 Special Schools
1978	40.2	2743.6	44.7	26.8	17.9	2698.9	692.9	2006.0		3315.4	0.6
1980	28.1	2011.8	46.8	25.3	21.5	1934.3	383.4	1550.9	30.7	2942.3	0.6
1985	61.9	1789.8	66.8	45.2	21.6	1606.9	257.5	1349.4	116.1	2298.2	0.9
1986	57.2	1824.4	67.7	45.0	22.7	1643.9	257.3	1386.6	112.8	2258.2	1.1
1987	61.7	1834.2	71.5	48.5	23.0	1649.5	255.2	1394.3	113.2	2094.6	1.2
1988	67.0	1781.9	77.6	54.1	23.6	1584.8	244.3	1340.5	119.5	2123.3	1.2
1989	59.7	1743.3	73.5	50.8	22.7	1551.5	242.1	1309.4	118.3	2151.5	1.4
1990	60.9	1815.8	73.0	50.3	22.7	1619.6	249.8	1369.9	123.2	2064.0	1.6
1991	62.0	1871.0	78.0	55.1	22.9	1655.2	243.8	1411.3	137.8	2072.7	2.0
1992	75.4	1939.8	87.9	63.8	24.1	1699.7	234.7	1465.0	152.1	2183.2	3.0
1993	92.4	1983.7	114.9	86.5	28.4	1707.3	228.3	1479.0	161.5	2353.5	3.4
1994	90.0	2157.6	122.5	93.5	29.1	1859.8	243.4	1616.4	175.3	2537.0	4.0
1995	92.6	2354.1	138.1	107.3	30.8	2025.9	273.6	1752.3	190.1	2531.8	5.6
1996	96.6	2384.2	152.3	120.8	31.6	2042.9	282.2	1760.7	188.9	2524.7	4.8
1997	100.0	2501.5	162.1	129.6	32.5	2128.2	322.6	1805.6	211.2	2462.0	4.6
1998	108.4	2705.4	166.8	134.9	31.9	2321.0	359.6	1961.4	217.6	2201.4	4.9
1999	159.7	2963.3	163.4	134.3	29.1	2546.0	396.3	2149.7	194.1	2029.5	5.0
2000	220.6	3103.2	132.6	111.6	21.0	2736.0	472.7	2263.3	182.7	1946.5	5.3
2001	268.3	3179.4	127.7	108.2	19.5	2815.9	558.0	2257.9	185.0	1944.2	5.6
2002	320.5	3301.2	155.3	135.9	19.4	2929.0	676.7	2252.3	216.9	1952.8	5.3
2003	382.2	3353.4	183.9			2947.4	752.1	2195.3	222.1	1829.4	4.9

21-7 各级各类学校毕业生数

Number of Graduates by Level and Type of School

单位：万人 (10 000 persons)

年份 Year	普通高等学校 Regular Institutions of Higher Education	普通中等学校 Secondary Schools	#中等专业学校 Specialized Secondary Schools	中等技术学校 Technical Secondary Schools	中等师范学校 Teacher Secondary Schools	#普通中学 Regular Secondary Schools	高中 Senior Secondary Schools	初中 Junior Secondary Schools	#职业中学 Vocational Secondary Schools	小学 Primary Schools	特殊教育学校 Special Schools
1978	16.5	2398.5	23.2	11.9	11.3	2375.3	682.7	1692.6		2287.9	0.3
1980	14.7	1629.9	41.0	20.1	20.9	1581.0	616.2	964.7	7.9	2053.3	0.4
1985	31.6	1279.1	42.9	26.1	16.8	1194.9	196.6	998.3	41.3	1999.9	0.4
1986	39.3	1388.5	49.6	32.1	17.5	1281.0	224.0	1057.0	57.9	2016.1	0.5
1987	53.2	1496.9	57.8	38.9	18.9	1364.1	246.8	1117.3	75.0	2043.0	0.4
1988	55.3	1548.4	59.6	39.2	20.4	1407.8	250.6	1157.2	81.0	1930.3	0.5
1989	57.6	1520.9	59.1	36.5	22.6	1377.5	243.2	1134.3	86.3	1857.1	0.5
1990	61.4	1497.5	66.1	42.8	23.4	1342.1	233.0	1109.1	89.3	1863.1	0.5
1991	61.4	1477.0	74.0	49.6	24.4	1308.5	222.9	1085.5	94.5	1896.7	0.6
1992	60.4	1499.4	74.3	50.7	23.6	1328.4	226.1	1102.3	96.7	1872.4	0.9
1993	57.1	1541.9	73.6	50.7	22.8	1365.9	231.7	1134.2	102.5	1841.5	1.2
1994	63.7	1542.4	72.9	50.4	22.6	1361.9	209.3	1152.6	107.6	1899.6	1.4
1995	80.5	1636.9	83.9	59.4	24.5	1429.0	201.6	1227.4	124.0	1961.5	1.9
1996	83.9	1725.4	101.9	73.8	28.1	1484.0	204.9	1279.0	139.6	1934.1	2.4
1997	82.9	1929.8	115.7	86.3	29.4	1664.0	221.7	1442.4	150.1	1960.1	2.8
1998	83.0	2124.1	129.3	98.7	30.6	1832.0	251.8	1580.2	162.8	2117.4	3.5
1999	84.8	2229.2	140.2	109.3	30.9	1852.7	262.9	1589.8	167.8	2313.7	3.8
2000	95.0	2302.3	150.7	119.6	31.1	1908.6	301.5	1607.1	176.3	2419.2	4.3
2001	103.6	2429.3	150.3	122.5	27.8	2047.4	340.5	1707.0	166.5	2396.9	4.6
2002	133.7	2553.2	144.2	121.9	22.3	2263.6	383.8	1879.9	145.4	2351.9	4.4
2003	187.7	2737.7	148.4			2453.7	458.1	1995.6	135.5	2267.9	4.5

21-8 研究生和留学生数

Number of Postgraduates and Students Studying Abroad

单位: 人 (person)

年份 Year	研究生数 Number of Postgraduates			出国留学人员 Number of Students Studying Abroad	学成回国留学人员 Number of Returned Students
	在学人数 Student Enrollment	招生数 New Student Enrollment	毕业生数 Graduates		
1978	10934	10708	9	860	248
1980	21604	3616	476	2124	162
1985	87331	46871	17004	4888	1424
1986	110371	41310	16950	4676	1388
1987	120191	39017	27603	4703	1605
1988	112776	35645	40838	3786	3000
1989	101339	28569	37232	3329	1753
1990	93018	29649	35440	2950	1593
1991	88128	29679	32537	2900	2069
1992	94164	33439	25692	6540	3611
1993	106771	42145	28214	10742	5128
1994	127935	50864	28047	19071	4230
1995	145443	51053	31877	20381	5750
1996	163322	59398	39652	20905	6570
1997	176353	63749	46539	22410	7130
1998	198885	72508	47077	17622	7379
1999	233513	92225	54670	23749	7748
2000	301239	128484	58767	38989	9121
2001	393256	165197	67809	83973	12243
2002	500980	202611	80841	125179	17945
2003	651260	268925	111091	117307	20152

21-9 普通高等教育分科在校学生数

Student Enrollment in Institutions of Higher Education by Field of Study

单位: 人 (person)

项目	Item	2002			2003		
		合计 Total	本科 Regular College Course	专科 Specialized Subject (Three Years)	合计 Total	本科 Regular College Course	专科 Specialized Subject (Three Years)
合计	**Total**	**9033631**	**5270845**	**3762786**	**11085642**	**6292089**	**4793553**
哲学	Philosophy	6637	5624	1013	5974	5558	416
经济学	Economics	466433	284348	182085	604135	360683	243452
法学	Law	474846	264039	210807	560916	313131	247785
教育学	Education	470293	183528	286765	592123	223837	368286
文学	Literature	1368278	746090	622188	1719230	950274	768956
历史学	History	55565	40333	15232	56673	42543	14130
理学	Science	852238	600480	251758	1004506	723579	280927
工学	Engineering	3084999	1886996	1198003	3693401	2156584	1536817
农学	Agriculture	216040	140868	75172	249671	151756	97915
医学	Medicine	656560	424401	232159	814741	496136	318605
管理学	Management	1381742	694138	687604	1784272	868008	916264

21-10 普通高等教育分科招生数

New Student Enrollment in Institutions of Higher Education by Field of Study

单位: 人 (person)

项 目	Item	2002 合 计 Total	2002 本 科 Regular College Course	2002 专 科 Specialized Subject (Three Years)	2003 合 计 Total	2003 本 科 Regular College Course	2003 专 科 Specialized Subject (Three Years)
合 计	**Total**	**3204976**	**1587939**	**1617037**	**3821701**	**1825262**	**1996439**
哲 学	Philosophy	2175	1700	475	1520	1446	74
经济学	Economics	182416	94337	88079	221410	114545	106865
法 学	Law	160618	78519	82099	185999	91920	94079
教育学	Education	178223	59317	118906	218575	69682	148893
文 学	Literature	509315	243324	265991	612021	297002	315019
历史学	History	15351	10474	4877	16330	11496	4834
理 学	Science	294867	191997	102870	329656	220157	109499
工 学	Engineering	1057241	543447	513794	1242426	595398	647028
农 学	Agriculture	69247	37513	31734	81619	41637	39982
医 学	Medicine	207909	105815	102094	257681	119270	138411
管理学	Management	527614	221496	306118	654464	262709	391755

21-11 普通高等教育分科毕业生数

Graduates of Institutions of Higher Education by Field of Study

单位: 人 (person)

项 目	Item	2002 合 计 Total	2002 本 科 Regular College Course	2002 专 科 Specialized Subject (Three Years)	2003 合 计 Total	2003 本 科 Regular College Course	2003 专 科 Specialized Subject (Three Years)
合 计	**Total**	**1337309**	**655763**	**681546**	**1877492**	**929598**	**947894**
哲 学	Philosophy	1012	858	154	1196	1127	69
经济学	Economics	65942	37517	28425	88181	48878	39303
法 学	Law	79966	36332	43634	110416	52756	57660
教育学	Education	79812	22885	56927	117072	30977	86095
文 学	Literature	198535	77710	120825	286889	126087	160802
历史学	History	11683	7022	4661	13905	8791	5114
理 学	Science	131494	72526	58968	173031	103409	69622
工 学	Engineering	459842	252024	207818	644106	351537	292569
农 学	Agriculture	36284	22462	13822	50057	29758	20299
医 学	Medicine	79500	47320	32180	111356	55927	55429
管理学	Management	193239	79107	114132	281283	120351	160932

21-12 普通高等学校分科专任教师数（2003年）

Number of Full-time Teachers by Field of Study in Regular Higher Educational Institutions (2003)

单位: 人 (person)

项 目	Item	合 计 Total	正高级 Senior Title	副高级 Associate Title	中 级 Junior Title	初 级 Primary Title	无职称 Non-title
合 计	**Total**	**724658**	**70063**	**216161**	**240555**	**146092**	**51787**
哲 学	Philosophy	23157	2267	7966	8462	3318	1144
经济学	Economics	42705	3803	12110	15662	8253	2877
法 学	Law	27331	2248	7546	9965	5678	1894
教育学	Education	65307	2941	18400	23865	14813	5288
文 学	Literature	152301	9250	37332	51575	39453	14691
历史学	History	9735	1393	3282	3326	1306	428
理 学	Science	100976	12277	34957	30879	16912	5951
工 学	Engineering	197531	22116	61189	63272	37704	13250
农 学	Agriculture	21453	2857	7255	6964	3283	1094
医 学	Medicine	49666	7714	16166	14645	8654	2487
管理学	Management	34496	3197	9958	11940	6718	2683

注：现指标已无教授、副教授，只按职称分。

a) The indicators are not classified by professor and assorciate professor, these done by the technical or professinal title.

21-13 普通中等专业学校分科学生数(2003年)

Number of Students by Field of Study in Specialized Secondary Schools (2003)

单位: 人 (person)

项 目	Item	毕业生数 Graduates	招生数 New Student Enrollment	在校学生数 Student Enrollment
合 计	**Total**	**1484471**	**1838777**	**5023708**
农林类	Agriculture, Forestry	68620	47903	159020
资源与环境类	Resource and Environment	19623	12587	38159
能源类	Power	12147	15541	36942
土木水利工程类	Construction and Water Conservancy Engineering	69021	60196	164442
加工制造类	Machining and Manufacture	153563	245748	551768
交通运输类	Transport	26527	45119	106655
信息技术类	Information Technology	246046	320214	883427
医药卫生类	Health	189029	265965	788287
商贸与旅游类	Trade and Tour	94774	162107	431172
财经类	Finance and Economics	123212	106701	291985
文化艺术与体育类	Arts and Physical Culture	97287	99166	313814
社会公共事物类	Society Commonality Business	66493	55675	160799
师范类	Normal School	159653	152861	487899

21-14 技工学校数和学生数

Number of Technical Schools, Students, Staff and Teachers

年 份 Year	学校数 (所) Schools (unit)	在校学生数 (万人) Student Enrollment (10 000 persons)	毕业生数 (万人) Graduates (10 000 persons)	招生数 (万人) New Student Enrollment (10 000 persons)	教职工数 (万人) Staff and Teachers (10 000 persons)
1985	3548	74.2	22.6	35.5	21.5
1986	3765	89.2	23.3	39.4	24.4
1987	3952	103.1	26.5	42.3	26.2
1988	3996	116.1	31.1	46.1	28.0
1989	4102	125.8	36.8	47.0	29.6
1990	4184	133.2	41.3	50.6	30.8
1991	4269	142.2	45.4	54.4	32.5
1992	4392	155.6	45.7	60.2	33.6
1993	4477	171.7	49.7	66.4	33.5
1994	4430	187.1	55.7	71.4	34.0
1995	4521	188.6	68.1	74.0	33.7
1996	4467	191.8	68.1	72.7	33.5
1997	4395	193.1	69.9	73.4	31.0
1998	4362	181.3	68.2	59.4	31.0
1999	4098	156.0	66.2	51.5	26.9
2000	3792	140.1	64.6	50.4	24.0
2001	3470	134.7	47.7	55.1	22.0
2002	3075	153.0	45.4	73.3	20.3
2003	2970	193.1	45.3	91.6	20.2

21-15 各类技工学校情况(2003年)

Statistics on Various Technical Schools (2003)

指 标	Item	合 计 Total	国务院各部门 Ministries of the State Council	省、自治区、直辖市 Provinces, Autonomous Regions and Municipalities
学校数 (所)	Number of Schools (unit)	2970	200	2770
在校学生数 (万人)	Number of Students (10 000 persons)	193.1	10.3	183
教职工数 (万人)	Teachers and Staff (10 000 persons)	20.2	1.8	18
#文化技术理论课指导教师 (万人)	Classroom Teachers (10 000 persons)	9.6	0.7	9
生产实习课指导教师 (万人)	Practical Training Teachers (10 000 persons)	3.4	0.2	3

21-16 初中、小学毕业生升学率及小学学龄儿童入学率

Percentage of Graduates of Junior Secondary Schools and Primary Schools Entering Higher Level Schools, Percentage of School-Age Children Enrolled

年 份 Year	初中毕业生升学率 Percentage of Graduates of Junior Secondary Schools Entering Senior Secondary Schools			小学毕业生升学率 Percentage of Graduates of Primary Schools Entering Junior Secondary Schools			小学学龄儿童入学率 Percentage of School-age Children Enrolled		
	初中毕业生数(万人) Graduates of Junior Secondary Schools (10 000 persons)	高级中等学校招生数(万人) Students Entering Senior Secondary Schools (10 000 persons)	升学率(%) Percentage of Graduates of Junior Secondary Schools Entering Senior Secondary Schools	小学毕业生数(万人) Graduates of Primary Schools (10 000 persons)	初级中等学校招生数(万人) Students Entering Junior Secondary Schools (10 000 persons)	升学率(%) Percentage of Graduates of Primary Schools Entering Junior Secondary Schools	学龄儿童数(万人) School-Age Children (10 000 persons)	已入学学龄儿童数(万人) School-Age Children Enrolled in Schools (10 000 persons)	入学率(%) Enrollment Rate (%)
1978	1692.6	692.9	40.9	2287.9	2006.0	87.7	12131.3	11585.4	95.5
1980	964.7	442.8	45.9	2053.3	1557.6	75.9	12219.6	11478.2	93.9
1985	998.3	416.2	41.7	1999.9	1367.0	68.4	10362.3	9942.8	96.0
1986	1057.0	429.2	40.6	2016.1	1402.0	69.5	10067.5	9702.1	96.4
1987	1117.3	437.0	39.1	2043.0	1410.9	69.1	9750.9	9477.2	97.2
1988	1157.2	439.6	38.0	1930.3	1359.0	70.4	9623.9	9351.4	97.2
1989	1134.3	434.6	38.3	1857.1	1328.4	71.5	9699.1	9450.7	97.4
1990	1109.1	450.4	40.6	1863.1	1389.2	74.6	9740.7	9529.7	97.8
1991	1085.5	462.9	42.9	1896.7	1435.1	75.7	9806.6	9594.8	97.8
1992	1102.3	478.1	43.4	1872.4	1491.7	79.7	11156.2	10845.5	97.2
1993	1134.2	500.5	44.1	1841.5	1505.6	81.8	11432.0	11170.9	97.7
1994	1166.4	541.1	46.4	1899.6	1644.9	86.6	11949.6	11758.2	98.4
1995	1244.3	601.6	48.3	1961.5	1781.1	90.8	12375.4	12192.5	98.5
1996	1297.8	633.4	48.8	1934.1	1791.4	92.6	12876.5	12723.3	98.8
1997	1463.3	753.6	51.5	1960.1	1836.5	93.7	13346.7	13202.5	98.9
1998	1603.1	812.2	50.7	2117.4	1996.3	94.3	13369.3	13226.8	98.9
1999	1613.9	807.0	50.0	2313.7	2183.4	94.4	12991.4	12872.8	99.1
2000	1633.5	834.6	51.1	2419.2	2295.6	94.9	12445.3	12333.9	99.1
2001	1731.5	916.0	52.9	2396.9	2287.9	95.5	11766.4	11561.2	98.3
2002	1903.7	1109.7	58.3	2351.9	2281.8	97.0	11310.4	11150.0	98.6
2003	2018.5	1214.4	60.2	2267.9	2220.1	97.9	10908.3	10761.6	98.7

注:1994年起初中毕业生数中包括职业初中毕业生数。

a) The number of the graduates of junior secondary schools since 1994 has included the graduates of vocational schools.

21-17 平均每万人口在校学生数和大中小学学生构成

Student Enrollment per 10 000 Population and Composition of Students Enrolled

年 份 Year	各级在校学生数占全国人口比重(%) Students as Percentage of Total Population	平均每万人口中 Number of Students per 10 000 Population			大、中、小学学生占学生总数比重(%) Students of Different Level as Percentage of Total Students (%)		
		大学生(人) University and College Students	中学生(人) Secondary School Students	小学生(人) Primary School Students	大学生 University and College Students	中学生 Secondary School Students	小学生 Primary School Students
1978	22.2	8.9	690	1519	0.4	31.1	68.5
1980	20.7	11.6	575	1482	0.6	27.8	71.6
1985	17.6	16.1	481	1263	0.9	27.3	71.8
1989	15.7	18.5	448	1098	1.2	28.7	70.1
1990	15.4	18.0	447	1071	1.2	29.1	69.7
1991	15.2	17.6	451	1050	1.2	29.7	69.1
1992	15.2	18.6	457	1041	1.2	30.1	68.7
1993	15.2	21.4	454	1048	1.4	29.8	68.8
1994	15.7	23.4	476	1070	1.5	30.3	68.2
1995	16.3	24.0	511	1089	1.5	31.5	67.1
1996	17.0	24.7	542	1112	1.5	32.3	66.2
1997	17.2	25.7	566	1132	1.5	32.8	65.7
1998	17.3	27.3	588	1118	1.6	33.9	64.5
1999	17.3	32.8	621	1076	1.9	35.9	62.2
2000	17.3	43.9	660	1028	2.5	38.6	58.9
2001	17.4	56.3	697	983	3.2	40.2	56.6
2002	17.5	70.3	733	946	4.0	42.0	54.0
2003	17.7	86.3	763	910	4.9	42.9	52.2

注：“大学生”仅含普通高等学校学生。

a) "University and college Students" just includes regular institutions of higher education students.

21-18 各级学校专任教师负担学生数

Student-teacher Ratio by Level of School

年 份 Year	普通高等学校 Regular Institutions of Higher Education		普通中等学校 Regular Secondary Schools		小 学 Primary Schools	
	专任教师数(万人) Number of Full-time Teachers (10 000 persons)	平均每个专任教师负担学生数(人) Student-teacher Ratio	专任教师数(万人) Number of Full-time Teachers (10 000 persons)	平均每个专任教师负担学生数(人) Student-teacher Ratio	专任教师数(万人) Number of Full-time Teachers (10 000 persons)	平均每个专任教师负担学生数(人) Student-teacher Ratio
1978	20.6	4.2	328.1	20.2	522.6	28.0
1980	24.7	4.6	317.1	17.9	549.9	26.6
1985	34.4	5.0	296.7	17.2	537.7	24.9
1989	39.7	5.2	342.3	14.8	554.4	22.3
1990	39.5	5.2	349.2	14.6	558.2	21.9
1991	39.1	5.2	355.7	14.7	553.2	22.0
1992	38.8	5.6	362.4	14.8	552.7	22.1
1993	38.8	6.5	366.8	14.7	555.2	22.4
1994	39.6	7.1	375.7	15.2	561.1	22.9
1995	40.1	7.2	388.3	15.9	566.4	23.3
1996	40.3	7.5	404.0	16.4	573.6	23.7
1997	40.5	7.8	418.6	16.7	579.4	24.2
1998	40.7	8.4	431.2	17.0	581.9	23.9
1999	42.6	9.7	445.0	17.6	586.1	23.1
2000	46.3	12.0	458.2	18.2	586.0	22.2
2001	53.2	13.5	486.6	18.3	579.8	21.6
2002	61.8	14.6	489.4	18.7	577.9	21.0
2003	72.5	15.3	502.5	18.9	570.3	20.5

注：本表中等学校不包括技工学校和工读学校。

a) Secondary schools in this table don't include various technical schools and schools for juvenile delinquents.

21-19 各地区普通高等学校分类别学校数（2003年）

Number of Regular Institutions of Higher Education by Region and Type (2003)

单位: 所 (unit)

地区	Region	合计 Total	综合大学 Comprehensive Universities	理工院校 Science and Engineering	农业院校 Agriculture	林业院校 Forestry	医药院校 Medicine
全国	**National Total**	**1552**	**121**	**223**	**37**	**6**	**97**
北京	Beijing	**73**	7	17	2	1	3
天津	Tianjin	37	1	6	1		3
河北	Hebei	83	1	14	1		5
山西	Shanxi	45	2	4	1		4
内蒙古	Inner Mongolia	27	1	4	1		1
辽宁	Liaoning	70	5	17	2		6
吉林	Jilin	40	4	8	2		2
黑龙江	Heilongjiang	54	6	7	2	1	4
上海	Shanghai	56	2	12	1		2
江苏	Jiangsu	94	8	18	2	1	5
浙江	Zhejiang	64	3	8	1	1	3
安徽	Anhui	73	1	8	1		6
福建	Fujian	39	2	6	1		2
江西	Jiangxi	54	8	6	1		2
山东	Shandong	85	11	8	2		8
河南	Henan	71	2	14	3		3
湖北	Hubei	75	8	10	1		3
湖南	Hunan	73	5	10	1	1	3
广东	Guangdong	77	14	4	3		4
广西	Guangxi	45	1	5			5
海南	Hainan	11	1		1		1
重庆	Chongqing	34	4	6	1		1
四川	Sichuan	62	6	11	1		3
贵州	Guizhou	34	1	1			4
云南	Yunnan	34	3	2	1	1	3
西藏	Tibet	4	1				1
陕西	Shaanxi	57	7	13	1		2
甘肃	Gansu	31	2	3	1		4
青海	Qinghai	12	1				1
宁夏	Ningxia	12	1				1
新疆	Xinjiang	26	2	1	2		2

21-19 续表 continued

单位: 所 (unit)

地 区	Region	师范院校 Teacher Training	语言院校 Linguistics and Literacy	财经院校 Economics and Finance	政法院校 Politics and Law	体育院校 Physical Culture	艺术院校 Art Institutes	民族院校 Nationality Academy	职业技术学院 Short-cycle Vocational Colleges
全 国	**National Total**	**188**	**16**	**64**	**33**	**15**	**29**	**12**	**711**
北 京	Beijing	2	7	4	4	2	7	1	17
天 津	Tianjin	2	1	2		1	2		18
河 北	Hebei	11		3	2	1			45
山 西	Shanxi	7		2	1				24
内蒙古	Inner Mongolia	4	1	1					14
辽 宁	Liaoning	7	1	3	2	1	2	1	23
吉 林	Jilin	6	1	4	1	1	1		10
黑龙江	Heilongjiang	5		2		1			26
上 海	Shanghai	2	1	7	2	1	2		24
江 苏	Jiangsu	9		2	2	1	1		45
浙 江	Zhejiang	7	1	3	2		1		34
安 徽	Anhui	14		2					41
福 建	Fujian	7		1	1				19
江 西	Jiangxi	3		1	1				32
山 东	Shandong	8		2	1	1	2		42
河 南	Henan	14		4	2				28
湖 北	Hubei	5		3	1	1	2	2	39
湖 南	Hunan	7		3	1				42
广 东	Guangdong	4	1	3	1	1	2		40
广 西	Guangxi	10		3	1	1	1	1	17
海 南	Hainan	2							6
重 庆	Chongqing	3	1	1	1		1		15
四 川	Sichuan	8		2	1	1	1	1	27
贵 州	Guizhou	10		2				1	15
云 南	Yunnan	9		1	1		1	1	11
西 藏	Tibet				1			1	
陕 西	Shaanxi	6	1	1	1	1	2		22
甘 肃	Gansu	7		1	1			1	11
青 海	Qinghai	3						1	6
宁 夏	Ningxia	1						1	8
新 疆	Xinjiang	5		1	2		1		10

21-20 各地区高等学校教职工数（2003年）

Number of Teachers and Staff in Institutions of Higher Education by Region (2003)

单位：人 (person)

地区	Region	教职工总数 Total	校本部教职工 Number of Staff and Workers	专任教师 Full-time Teachers	教辅人员 Auxiliary Teaching Staff	行政人员 Administrative Personnel	工勤人员 Logistics Personnel
全国	**National Total**	**1452623**	**1271567**	**724658**	**160180**	**225725**	**161004**
北京	Beijing	108843	86026	41904	15012	16954	12156
天津	Tianjin	33371	29348	15553	4107	5657	4031
河北	Hebei	66560	58853	33617	6433	9973	8830
山西	Shanxi	38358	35317	20224	4194	6010	4889
内蒙古	Inner Mongolia	22592	21068	12153	2871	3830	2214
辽宁	Liaoning	75632	67425	38086	9093	11934	8312
吉林	Jilin	46950	42028	21824	5708	7870	6626
黑龙江	Heilongjiang	60609	51053	28525	6092	8410	8026
上海	Shanghai	63138	48782	24387	7959	9163	7273
江苏	Jiangsu	100684	86634	49810	10688	15510	10626
浙江	Zhejiang	53612	47972	29508	5805	8048	4611
安徽	Anhui	44395	41022	24744	4815	6092	5371
福建	Fujian	30699	27430	16171	3176	5189	2894
江西	Jiangxi	39794	35091	20560	3447	6524	4560
山东	Shandong	84393	76842	45457	9282	14076	8027
河南	Henan	59249	53726	33045	6006	8586	6089
湖北	Hubei	94215	82089	46947	10226	15099	9817
湖南	Hunan	66084	57484	33229	7459	10093	6703
广东	Guangdong	70009	62698	39897	7418	10683	4700
广西	Guangxi	24746	22943	14106	2810	3508	2519
海南	Hainan	5157	4719	2699	476	919	625
重庆	Chongqing	30678	27139	15790	3060	4771	3518
四川	Sichuan	62457	54734	31372	6953	8979	7430
贵州	Guizhou	20400	19020	11775	1977	3163	2105
云南	Yunnan	23662	21929	12236	2718	4261	2714
西藏	Tibet	1794	1749	972	194	353	230
陕西	Shaanxi	67527	57077	30696	6564	10953	8864
甘肃	Gansu	23012	20520	12274	2311	3285	2650
青海	Qinghai	5589	4684	2769	600	823	492
宁夏	Ningxia	6383	5866	3415	491	1107	853
新疆	Xinjiang	22031	20299	10913	2235	3902	3249

21-21 各地区中等专业学校教职工数（2003年）

Number of Teachers and Staff in Specialized Secondary Schools by Region (2003)

单位：人 (person)

地 区	Region	教职工总数 Total	校本部教职工 Number of Teachers and Staff in Central Campus	专任教师 Full-time Teachers	教辅人员 Auxiliary Teaching Staff	行政人员 Administrative Personnel	工勤人员 Logistics Personnel
全 国	**National Total**	**347013**	**330934**	**198550**	**55932**	**28314**	**48138**
北 京	Beijing	8001	7474	3775	1673	699	1327
天 津	Tianjin	6814	6539	3600	1379	450	1110
河 北	Hebei	14890	14399	7816	2631	1381	2571
山 西	Shanxi	10907	10480	5983	1945	898	1654
内蒙古	Inner Mongolia	7391	7265	4386	1115	762	1002
辽 宁	Liaoning	15615	15092	8521	2770	1488	2313
吉 林	Jilin	7558	7089	3966	1448	694	981
黑龙江	Heilongjiang	6592	6320	3302	1224	647	1147
上 海	Shanghai	11912	11003	5286	2197	1229	2291
江 苏	Jiangsu	17655	17223	11134	2524	1287	2278
浙 江	Zhejiang	6030	5760	3636	832	538	754
安 徽	Anhui	10193	9771	5983	1519	798	1471
福 建	Fujian	22684	22512	15769	3086	1421	2236
江 西	Jiangxi	7396	7094	4374	1116	606	998
山 东	Shandong	23630	22789	13761	4192	2072	2764
河 南	Henan	23697	20202	12200	3283	1765	2954
湖 北	Hubei	17402	16638	10317	2911	1339	2071
湖 南	Hunan	11471	10662	6377	1864	889	1532
广 东	Guangdong	22769	22320	14381	3445	1887	2607
广 西	Guangxi	14057	12774	7969	1762	1173	1870
海 南	Hainan	2627	2526	1480	431	200	415
重 庆	Chongqing	5022	4600	2656	858	454	632
四 川	Sichuan	14629	14252	8290	2563	1247	2152
贵 州	Guizhou	8058	7985	5045	1557	513	870
云 南	Yunnan	12443	12121	7262	1838	955	2066
西 藏	Tibet	933	933	621	122	39	151
陕 西	Shaanxi	12723	11740	6646	2270	1112	1712
甘 肃	Gansu	12320	11957	7201	1634	926	2196
青 海	Qinghai	1536	1496	1015	186	63	232
宁 夏	Ningxia	1219	1195	641	194	94	266
新 疆	Xinjiang	8839	8723	5157	1363	688	1515

21-22 各地区普通高等学校和中等专业学校学生数（2003年）

Enrollment of Regular Institutions of Higher Education and Specialized Secondary Schools by Region (2003)

单位：人 (person)

地区	Region	普通高等学校 Regular Institutions of Higher Education			普通中等专业学校 Regular Specialized Secondary Schools		
		毕业生数 Number of Graduates	招生数 New Student Enrollment	在校学生数 Student Enrollment	毕业生数 Number of Graduates	招生数 New Student Enrollment	在校学生数 Student Enrollment
全国	**National Total**	**1877492**	**3821701**	**11085642**	**1484471**	**1838777**	**5023708**
北京	Beijing	82828	141790	454480	29248	35271	116725
天津	Tianjin	40221	86115	245213	23071	23844	73254
河北	Hebei	113442	203826	575542	75276	85235	246956
山西	Shanxi	40779	91283	272967	73444	57295	191902
内蒙古	Inner Mongolia	24919	59450	157602	33516	30102	90415
辽宁	Liaoning	98908	163802	514191	47479	73948	173347
吉林	Jilin	52605	107125	319504	25373	27261	77955
黑龙江	Heilongjiang	69050	121984	392246	45279	36258	111540
上海	Shanghai	71158	120269	378517	33929	43439	136879
江苏	Jiangsu	137048	256595	859674	92456	189064	461328
浙江	Zhejiang	78685	168167	484135	41198	46666	120658
安徽	Anhui	65685	142361	410041	46134	47872	122450
福建	Fujian	47792	106715	257417	105747	136465	358575
江西	Jiangxi	47167	141571	358622	56174	66391	155084
山东	Shandong	117253	273894	761417	89550	122832	336691
河南	Henan	108975	190214	557240	100630	134915	364252
湖北	Hubei	119118	250198	721513	71978	89749	222006
湖南	Hunan	90035	193830	537220	60664	92245	226487
广东	Guangdong	105533	225837	587779	83871	111574	306714
广西	Guangxi	40178	82537	227257	57941	63742	173173
海南	Hainan	5846	17006	43498	9637	13180	36427
重庆	Chongqing	42653	85474	240503	23414	34621	95057
四川	Sichuan	74307	180308	512663	57536	74308	198979
贵州	Guizhou	25362	53318	149444	43248	41592	120635
云南	Yunnan	31337	62176	175255	39355	45394	148407
西藏	Tibet	1745	4279	10409	1938	2093	6519
陕西	Shaanxi	79785	168127	499017	40195	39463	125825
甘肃	Gansu	29582	60069	173391	30383	38215	116439
青海	Qinghai	4771	9075	26124	4596	2691	10184
宁夏	Ningxia	5461	11237	35134	9907	9036	27346
新疆	Xinjiang	25264	43069	147627	31304	24016	71499

21-23 各地区按城乡分普通中学学校及在校学生数（2003年）

Number of Regular Secondary Schools and Student Enrollment by Urban and Rural Areas and by Region (2003)

地区	Region	学校数（所） Number of Regular Secondary Schools (unit)							
		合计		城市		县镇		农村	
		Total	#高中 Senior Secondary Schools	Urban Areas	#高中 Senior Secondary Schools	Counties and Towns	#高中 Senior Secondary Schools	Rural Areas	#高中 Senior Secondary Schools
全国	**National Total**	**79490**	**15779**	**15289**	**6300**	**24662**	**7191**	**39539**	**2288**
北京	Beijing	763	329	347	209	279	103	137	17
天津	Tianjin	664	222	311	134	216	72	137	16
河北	Hebei	5024	810	730	293	1674	428	2620	89
山西	Shanxi	3379	531	577	246	745	222	2057	63
内蒙古	Inner Mongolia	1743	381	428	193	584	169	731	19
辽宁	Liaoning	2341	456	808	285	344	128	1189	43
吉林	Jilin	1698	297	305	104	666	178	727	15
黑龙江	Heilongjiang	2719	481	631	206	552	190	1536	85
上海	Shanghai	858	343	500	209	327	128	31	6
江苏	Jiangsu	3202	845	641	255	650	292	1911	298
浙江	Zhejiang	2695	614	697	270	1638	342	360	2
安徽	Anhui	3820	741	552	245	857	307	2411	189
福建	Fujian	2006	592	331	194	815	332	860	66
江西	Jiangxi	2848	629	370	188	1067	353	1411	88
山东	Shandong	4606	845	1076	380	1965	415	1565	50
河南	Henan	6363	888	909	348	1652	411	3802	129
湖北	Hubei	3305	626	1043	347	639	188	1623	91
湖南	Hunan	4689	765	607	275	1366	358	2716	132
广东	Guangdong	4176	995	1092	389	1440	396	1644	210
广西	Guangxi	2990	519	409	166	1452	329	1129	24
海南	Hainan	542	105	76	32	241	56	225	17
重庆	Chongqing	1564	293	530	158	597	123	437	12
四川	Sichuan	5000	785	470	224	1631	478	2899	83
贵州	Guizhou	2488	420	390	148	832	210	1266	62
云南	Yunnan	2275	421	172	92	778	278	1325	51
西藏	Tibet	105	17	25	10	79	7	1	
陕西	Shaanxi	2714	624	477	269	623	206	1614	149
甘肃	Gansu	2031	453	267	149	394	196	1370	108
青海	Qinghai	504	148	70	42	170	93	264	13
宁夏	Ningxia	446	104	88	37	109	41	249	26
新疆	Xinjiang	1932	500	360	203	280	162	1292	135

21-23 续表 continued

地区	Region	在校学生数（人） Student Enrollment (person) 合计 Total	#高中 Senior Secondary Schools	城市 Urban Areas	#高中 Senior Secondary Schools	县镇 Counties and Towns	#高中 Senior Secondary Schools	农村 Rural Areas	#高中 Senior Secondary Schools
全国	**National Total**	**85832447**	**19648261**	**18530322**	**7090958**	**33594338**	**10453499**	**33707787**	**2103804**
北京	Beijing	704405	250959	346197	151836	283266	92914	74942	6209
天津	Tianjin	615034	182529	272840	102462	209347	58348	132847	21719
河北	Hebei	5437138	1142264	962707	345193	2312746	706745	2161685	90326
山西	Shanxi	2506125	573639	638488	240485	823439	294989	1044198	38165
内蒙古	Inner Mongolia	1543724	420138	542292	207192	656319	201814	345113	11132
辽宁	Liaoning	2410745	602442	963193	326624	498676	230106	948876	45712
吉林	Jilin	1577588	381362	387692	132027	767363	241230	422533	8105
黑龙江	Heilongjiang	2473923	486096	659678	198826	662186	238039	1152059	49231
上海	Shanghai	762356	299095	461144	195145	285556	100798	15656	3152
江苏	Jiangsu	4943557	1240038	857416	301756	1270671	547957	2815470	390325
浙江	Zhejiang	2706635	787249	863277	346043	1684760	439309	158598	1897
安徽	Anhui	4283100	899943	699296	259075	1311915	472320	2271889	168548
福建	Fujian	2471911	575152	459590	174268	1233362	350378	778959	50506
江西	Jiangxi	3010626	724053	428327	198138	1440491	469541	1141808	56374
山东	Shandong	6543372	1690657	1680852	723618	3244512	899861	1618008	67178
河南	Henan	7505132	1464205	1108803	429028	2630258	909020	3766071	126157
湖北	Hubei	4414715	1072914	1285829	532077	1104436	403795	2024450	137042
湖南	Hunan	4887766	1065740	772354	321099	1865046	573563	2250366	171078
广东	Guangdong	5459077	1137234	1399796	410738	2130249	536832	1929032	189664
广西	Guangxi	3034976	585085	438846	171475	1811476	397450	784654	16160
海南	Hainan	507886	88946	91622	28153	299179	54827	117085	5966
重庆	Chongqing	1663728	407905	524504	169355	797624	214390	341600	24160
四川	Sichuan	4810712	1130813	677669	303761	2211050	731226	1921993	95826
贵州	Guizhou	2353007	383052	350050	124431	1004013	231103	998944	27518
云南	Yunnan	2284619	363368	215203	86869	950221	247934	1119195	28565
西藏	Tibet	114136	22076	28061	13372	85402	8704	673	
陕西	Shaanxi	2954061	741329	567899	248261	922357	341865	1463805	151203
甘肃	Gansu	1733035	427011	297373	126523	551562	238892	884100	61596
青海	Qinghai	294400	80310	62187	20089	128208	53868	104005	6353
宁夏	Ningxia	376427	107479	98734	38921	128523	52461	149170	16097
新疆	Xinjiang	1448531	315178	388403	164118	290125	113220	770003	37840

21-24 各地区按城乡分普通中学招生数和毕业生数（2003年）

Number of New Student Enrollment and Graduates of Regular Secondary Schools by Urban and Rural Areas and Region (2003)

单位：人 (person)

地区	Region	招生数 New Student Enrollment							
		合计 Total	#高中 Senior Secondary Schools	城市 Urban Areas	#高中 Senior Secondary Schools	县镇 Counties and Towns	#高中 Senior Secondary Schools	农村 Rural Areas	#高中 Senior Secondary Schools
全国	**National Total**	**29474377**	**7521264**	**6289800**	**2698002**	**11734412**	**4009038**	**11450165**	**814224**
北京	Beijing	218560	94894	108617	55937	88030	35994	21913	2963
天津	Tianjin	198303	69875	86603	38697	68419	22711	43281	8467
河北	Hebei	1879051	449334	332811	136972	816543	273725	729697	38637
山西	Shanxi	802533	217394	202515	90477	280706	111489	319312	15428
内蒙古	Inner Mongolia	519092	165772	182633	81897	223001	79563	113458	4312
辽宁	Liaoning	820180	232730	312558	125733	178772	88629	328850	18368
吉林	Jilin	558905	146132	131724	51026	273226	91793	153955	3313
黑龙江	Heilongjiang	618877	187643	190455	76736	185922	91780	242500	19127
上海	Shanghai	232595	104030	136865	66194	91137	36587	4593	1249
江苏	Jiangsu	1745353	462352	285432	111490	466061	208602	993860	142260
浙江	Zhejiang	909894	302695	300179	135833	560187	166195	49528	667
安徽	Anhui	1514709	344862	246652	98150	472100	183658	795957	63054
福建	Fujian	874825	218414	165031	66496	439202	132990	270592	18928
江西	Jiangxi	1036594	278808	145135	74574	507739	182731	383720	21503
山东	Shandong	1929441	638087	521241	274652	977683	337280	430517	26155
河南	Henan	2531970	537749	379898	159412	897474	329832	1254598	48505
湖北	Hubei	1560675	396137	437518	198287	403149	146255	720008	51595
湖南	Hunan	1714186	422322	275595	125865	675436	228435	763155	68022
广东	Guangdong	1991218	442596	519672	158378	777493	209992	694053	74226
广西	Guangxi	1093165	216817	151941	61449	653924	148696	287300	6672
海南	Hainan	189270	32620	33694	10054	110780	20012	44796	2554
重庆	Chongqing	603658	157825	186294	63389	295018	85497	122346	8939
四川	Sichuan	1746751	458577	242035	117863	823926	299812	680790	40902
贵州	Guizhou	885474	156515	128837	50038	372324	93617	384313	12860
云南	Yunnan	815864	138369	73595	32503	339951	94938	402318	10928
西藏	Tibet	46935	9024	10504	5343	36049	3681	382	
陕西	Shaanxi	1041508	273499	194788	92170	320385	125588	526335	55741
甘肃	Gansu	621290	168181	106670	49920	200393	92873	314227	25388
青海	Qinghai	110325	32785	23039	8218	48019	21811	39267	2756
宁夏	Ningxia	130189	39063	33906	14563	44268	19108	52015	5392
新疆	Xinjiang	532987	126163	143363	65686	107095	45164	282529	15313

21-24 续表 continued

单位: 人 (person)

地区	Region	毕业生数 Number of Graduates 合计 Total	#高中 Senior Secondary Schools	城市 Urban Areas	#高中 Senior Secondary Schools	县镇 Counties and Towns	#高中 Senior Secondary Schools	农村 Rural Areas	#高中 Senior Secondary Schools
全国	**National Total**	**24537060**	**4581235**	**5179807**	**1691793**	**9505536**	**2411586**	**9851717**	**477856**
北京	Beijing	234207	56601	115483	37025	89566	18639	29158	937
天津	Tianjin	184239	44968	87881	25999	60279	14412	36079	4557
河北	Hebei	1630930	264873	269848	80732	656027	164835	705055	19306
山西	Shanxi	589805	138440	147632	60681	213542	69425	228631	8334
内蒙古	Inner Mongolia	402194	102500	139196	51002	168773	49009	94225	2489
辽宁	Liaoning	740994	148501	300997	84931	141823	53422	298174	10148
吉林	Jilin	469686	92934	115887	33008	220585	58055	133214	1871
黑龙江	Heilongjiang	658977	115778	170565	48435	168103	56845	320309	10498
上海	Shanghai	260311	78270	162608	52757	92312	24748	5391	765
江苏	Jiangsu	1321875	291593	256507	75089	308512	123148	756856	93356
浙江	Zhejiang	880868	196142	257326	83985	562886	111492	60656	665
安徽	Anhui	1171890	209603	186557	60902	351222	108306	634111	40395
福建	Fujian	733256	139457	127922	43693	362692	83276	242642	12488
江西	Jiangxi	839577	155520	114163	42876	400363	100817	325051	11827
山东	Shandong	2228167	413708	493234	175982	1102502	222229	632431	15497
河南	Henan	2251557	363787	297726	99886	756812	229910	1197019	33991
湖北	Hubei	1188795	272741	355573	136620	289716	102923	543506	33198
湖南	Hunan	1325552	233929	201220	69725	484157	126834	640175	37370
广东	Guangdong	1557309	274956	367646	99910	614996	129874	574667	45172
广西	Guangxi	888425	140988	122264	40890	527893	96799	238268	3299
海南	Hainan	141421	22299	26313	6993	84264	14070	30844	1236
重庆	Chongqing	475066	74895	160005	34148	215378	37550	99683	3197
四川	Sichuan	1299710	201256	170999	58969	567764	127066	560947	15221
贵州	Guizhou	577392	75141	88565	25684	251647	44872	237180	4585
云南	Yunnan	639359	84456	59860	21550	263861	57065	315638	5841
西藏	Tibet	21290	6022	7154	3679	14071	2343	65	
陕西	Shaanxi	805123	178276	158030	58835	251470	82436	395623	37005
甘肃	Gansu	456044	89040	78978	28050	139433	50315	237633	10675
青海	Qinghai	75421	17626	15590	4329	32497	12104	27334	1193
宁夏	Ningxia	108351	26111	26551	8560	37606	13285	44194	4266
新疆	Xinjiang	379269	70824	97527	36868	74784	25482	206958	8474

21-25 各地区按城乡和主办部门分普通中学教职工数（2003年）

Number of Staff and Full-time Teachers in Regular Secondary Schools by Urban and Rural Areas, by Department and by Region (2003)

单位：人 (person)

地区	Region	教职工数 Number of Teachers and Staff in Regular Secondary Schools						
		合计 Total	按主办部门分 By Departments			按城乡分 By Urban and Rural Areas		
			教育部门和集体办 Schools Run by Educational Departments and Collective Units	社会力量办 Schools Run by Society	其他部门办 Schools Run by Other Departments	城市 Urban Areas	县镇 Counties and Towns	农村 Rural Areas
全国	**National Total**	**5496535**	**4944927**	**291604**	**260004**	**1416121**	**2134433**	**1945981**
北京	Beijing	76484	69899	3169	3416	39385	28589	8510
天津	Tianjin	55107	49788	2542	2777	26794	18250	10063
河北	Hebei	339848	302529	23793	13526	71432	143660	124756
山西	Shanxi	180083	145100	17896	17087	50285	58265	71533
内蒙古	Inner Mongolia	118311	98929	5240	14142	39980	49416	28915
辽宁	Liaoning	179521	169335	4497	5689	75169	37258	67094
吉林	Jilin	122120	104484	4322	13314	32177	57765	32178
黑龙江	Heilongjiang	186384	137934	8448	40002	55332	53252	77800
上海	Shanghai	76853	67031	8465	1357	45611	29592	1650
江苏	Jiangsu	318703	292224	23301	3178	72186	85504	161013
浙江	Zhejiang	187820	166947	19990	883	64938	112222	10660
安徽	Anhui	210197	192040	10560	7597	44727	66912	98558
福建	Fujian	160212	153473	6523	216	35214	79032	45966
江西	Jiangxi	176175	155352	14226	6597	30809	83244	62122
山东	Shandong	468627	429200	26982	12445	137135	221155	110337
河南	Henan	417707	380702	21043	15962	78503	143460	195744
湖北	Hubei	263879	245411	7386	11082	90790	65713	107376
湖南	Hunan	301306	277604	14283	9419	52913	116370	132023
广东	Guangdong	323075	300865	17426	4784	95493	125999	101583
广西	Guangxi	187457	172370	10871	4216	30801	109415	47241
海南	Hainan	31537	24093	2807	4637	6719	17459	7359
重庆	Chongqing	110133	104234	3564	2335	41877	48334	19922
四川	Sichuan	297743	280691	9398	7654	51854	135255	110634
贵州	Guizhou	123132	111622	5905	5605	24115	54208	44809
云南	Yunnan	143290	136539	2881	3870	16351	62084	64855
西藏	Tibet	7334	7079	175	80	2364	4939	31
陕西	Shaanxi	178330	152799	10187	15344	38267	54003	86060
甘肃	Gansu	100004	89521	1633	8850	20901	31925	47178
青海	Qinghai	21257	19821	386	1050	4979	9781	6497
宁夏	Ningxia	25549	23364	418	1767	6856	9107	9586
新疆	Xinjiang	108357	83947	3287	21123	32164	22265	53928

21-25 续表 continued

单位：人 (person)

地区	Region	专任教师数 Number of Full-time Teachers						
		合计 Total	按主办部门分 By Department			按城乡分 By Urban and Rural Areas		
			教育部门和集体办 Schools Run by Educational Departments and Collective Units	社会力量办 Schools Run by Society	其他部门办 Schools Run by Other Departments	城市 Urban Areas	县镇 Counties and Towns	农村 Rural Areas
全国	**National Total**	**4537310**	**4137757**	**201421**	**198132**	**1096706**	**1748178**	**1692426**
北京	Beijing	51448	47100	1924	2424	25551	19977	5920
天津	Tianjin	41422	37814	1429	2179	18549	14002	8871
河北	Hebei	285865	258544	16851	10470	55527	119179	111159
山西	Shanxi	147347	121958	12167	13222	37808	46422	63117
内蒙古	Inner Mongolia	89935	76189	3530	10216	29762	37449	22724
辽宁	Liaoning	144016	136075	3594	4347	59992	28661	55363
吉林	Jilin	92338	79655	2640	10043	23894	43457	24987
黑龙江	Heilongjiang	149629	114337	6289	29003	43645	41523	64461
上海	Shanghai	51455	44768	5723	964	30192	20061	1202
江苏	Jiangsu	259817	240826	16534	2457	56408	68079	135330
浙江	Zhejiang	158305	143287	14353	665	52389	96401	9515
安徽	Anhui	179529	166544	6750	6235	35859	55617	88053
福建	Fujian	135778	131006	4604	168	28739	67385	39654
江西	Jiangxi	155764	140344	10006	5414	25748	73156	56860
山东	Shandong	374811	346647	18937	9227	104520	177167	93124
河南	Henan	358840	331510	14902	12428	61379	121068	176393
湖北	Hubei	223751	210208	4779	8764	72929	56286	94536
湖南	Hunan	259281	241239	10356	7686	42081	97869	119331
广东	Guangdong	271589	256294	11740	3555	75100	107396	89093
广西	Guangxi	144975	134629	7344	3002	23380	84213	37382
海南	Hainan	24903	19892	1671	3340	5080	14091	5732
重庆	Chongqing	89560	85408	2352	1800	32961	39376	17223
四川	Sichuan	247098	235019	6297	5782	40423	110801	95874
贵州	Guizhou	107312	98862	3971	4479	19415	46319	41578
云南	Yunnan	120221	115545	1825	2851	12700	51014	56507
西藏	Tibet	6461	6264	144	53	2009	4422	30
陕西	Shaanxi	148437	129153	7118	12166	29589	45053	73795
甘肃	Gansu	87753	79529	1140	7084	16710	27389	43654
青海	Qinghai	18613	17553	244	816	4057	8402	6154
宁夏	Ningxia	21725	20053	241	1431	5551	7524	8650
新疆	Xinjiang	89332	71505	1966	15861	24759	18419	46154

21-26 各地区职业中学基本情况（2003年）

Basic Statistics on Vocational Secondary Schools by Region (2003)

单位：人 (person)

地 区	Region	学校数（所） Number of Schools	毕业生数 Number of Graduates	招生数 New Student Enrollment	在校学生数 Student Enrollment	教职工数 Number of Staff and Teachers	#专任教师 Full-time Teachers
全 国	**National Total**	**6843**	**1355468**	**2220743**	**5281709**	**399612**	**288723**
北 京	Beijing	99	23266	25947	84273	11244	6634
天 津	Tianjin	103	24065	20231	61415	7559	4637
河 北	Hebei	355	97080	138679	334714	27010	19990
山 西	Shanxi	303	35863	56845	138311	13401	10001
内蒙古	Inner Mongolia	311	43712	61634	176779	16727	12643
辽 宁	Liaoning	298	48605	72508	186817	19743	13073
吉 林	Jilin	147	34863	42608	99522	9477	6231
黑龙江	Heilongjiang	167	25115	31340	88916	10427	7177
上 海	Shanghai	55	21992	21121	70414	5549	3332
江 苏	Jiangsu	258	47587	108184	235876	21527	16509
浙 江	Zhejiang	417	96551	213412	503181	26889	20663
安 徽	Anhui	667	138003	228245	565282	24864	20395
福 建	Fujian	1	108	57	261	29	23
江 西	Jiangxi	220	37806	64184	149402	9658	7102
山 东	Shandong	406	124542	198568	468240	39844	27502
河 南	Henan	462	116753	168518	423172	29117	22068
湖 北	Hubei	187	41468	64522	151725	9950	7466
湖 南	Hunan	464	69488	160504	299145	23702	15814
广 东	Guangdong	279	57893	78218	205800	15863	12267
广 西	Guangxi	221	37856	55262	123030	10411	7043
海 南	Hainan	45	2326	3508	7072	1260	858
重 庆	Chongqing	168	30065	62731	135661	9243	6542
四 川	Sichuan	289	49928	115421	244695	17532	12963
贵 州	Guizhou	189	19467	27964	66310	5131	3953
云 南	Yunnan	181	43023	47267	125190	9771	7167
西 藏	Tibet	2	335	394	2337	13	
陕 西	Shaanxi	304	54929	114473	230506	15172	10357
甘 肃	Gansu	117	12212	14645	38471	3748	2901
青 海	Qinghai	19	1383	1867	5040	536	416
宁 夏	Ningxia	23	3499	6508	14822	1100	899
新 疆	Xinjiang	86	15685	15378	45330	3115	2097

21-27 各地区按城乡分小学学校及学生数（2003年）

Number of Primary Schools and Student Enrollment by Urban and Rural Areas and by Region (2003)

地区	Region	学校数（所）Number of Primary Schools (unit)	城市 Urban Areas	县镇 Counties and Towns	农村 Rural Areas	在校学生数（人）Student Enrollment (person)	城市 Urban Areas	县镇 Counties and Towns	农村 Rural Areas
全国	**National Total**	**425846**	**25473**	**40007**	**360366**	**116897395**	**18076855**	**21929021**	**76891519**
北京	Beijing	1652	482	545	625	546530	258544	179021	108965
天津	Tianjin	1136	332	421	383	585446	217563	206356	161527
河北	Hebei	25700	1098	2409	22193	6065832	776133	1031059	4258640
山西	Shanxi	31126	762	844	29520	3635608	641349	514855	2479404
内蒙古	Inner Mongolia	7763	522	840	6401	1733702	441295	438077	854330
辽宁	Liaoning	11339	1160	572	9607	2891925	880270	372214	1639441
吉林	Jilin	8163	430	776	6957	1833141	348246	503275	981620
黑龙江	Heilongjiang	11400	683	681	10036	2401918	502950	473140	1425828
上海	Shanghai	698	412	241	45	654844	340034	290902	23908
江苏	Jiangsu	7845	1153	768	5924	5793921	904986	869895	4019040
浙江	Zhejiang	7712	1206	5048	1458	3402942	871656	2200088	331198
安徽	Anhui	22328	1038	1370	19920	6612171	715465	794029	5102677
福建	Fujian	12406	749	1896	9761	3119777	472165	928111	1719501
江西	Jiangxi	15862	384	4183	11295	3905386	341621	1265677	2298088
山东	Shandong	18303	1945	1915	14443	6427848	1247259	1137032	4043557
河南	Henan	36379	1277	2080	33022	10586075	942497	1277554	8366024
湖北	Hubei	15746	1926	585	13235	5281177	1150591	548735	3581851
湖南	Hunan	24673	922	2222	21529	4686892	603812	973164	3109916
广东	Guangdong	22792	2820	2215	17757	10253706	2576086	1841902	5835718
广西	Guangxi	16102	815	1271	14016	4918503	435137	782860	3700506
海南	Hainan	3287	160	304	2823	1008860	136246	229977	642637
重庆	Chongqing	10966	2237	1269	7460	2779441	730858	707496	1341087
四川	Sichuan	24573	587	1562	22424	7554308	599469	1482922	5471917
贵州	Guizhou	14504	519	1109	12876	4768740	359881	708936	3699923
云南	Yunnan	20296	261	1163	18872	4418821	202236	572506	3644079
西藏	Tibet	892	27	109	756	322060	25077	59252	237731
陕西	Shaanxi	24922	672	1209	23041	4014754	487511	529964	2997279
甘肃	Gansu	15635	344	1377	13914	3227592	283945	508595	2435052
青海	Qinghai	2998	75	446	2477	506906	81153	125005	300748
宁夏	Ningxia	2816	111	235	2470	669503	105797	129914	433792
新疆	Xinjiang	5832	364	342	5126	2289066	397023	246508	1645535

21-27 续表 continued

地 区	Region	毕业生数（人）Number of Graduates (persons)	城 市 Urban Areas	县 镇 Counties and Towns	农 村 Rural Areas	招生数（人）New Student Enrollment (person)	城 市 Urban Areas	县 镇 Counties and Towns	农 村 Rural Areas
全 国	**National Total**	**22678857**	**3179926**	**4265248**	**15233683**	**18293875**	**2966115**	**3403283**	**11924477**
北 京	Beijing	123580	49816	44143	29621	82631	39906	27394	15331
天 津	Tianjin	132022	47423	42938	41661	84963	31855	30606	22502
河 北	Hebei	1459161	149849	242720	1066592	727434	114986	128255	484193
山 西	Shanxi	597477	97897	86218	413362	734901	118529	103889	512483
内蒙古	Inner Mongolia	388019	83978	94547	209494	294991	75833	73903	145255
辽 宁	Liaoning	595278	179055	71135	345088	432650	133169	55816	243665
吉 林	Jilin	437518	68562	111139	257817	250000	54495	71612	123893
黑龙江	Heilongjiang	438212	103800	72586	261826	405337	86264	78154	240919
上 海	Shanghai	129623	70506	54750	4367	101633	53332	44693	3608
江 苏	Jiangsu	1300348	168788	176737	954823	742117	133736	118304	490077
浙 江	Zhejiang	597818	139198	392270	66350	524509	143467	333026	48016
安 徽	Anhui	1271012	132722	151303	986987	1063988	109816	120568	833604
福 建	Fujian	669693	84968	191195	393530	402276	71391	124552	206333
江 西	Jiangxi	757359	55593	249657	452109	733559	65287	226291	441981
山 东	Shandong	1282382	206585	222230	853567	1078606	233729	197371	647506
河 南	Henan	2041813	179810	240982	1621021	1643456	158472	208488	1276496
湖 北	Hubei	1186986	232227	124185	830574	651856	157477	67009	427370
湖 南	Hunan	1294814	123841	279586	891387	714944	94396	134852	485696
广 东	Guangdong	1586749	363751	300079	922919	1729914	456357	302990	970567
广 西	Guangxi	923669	78588	151612	693469	770795	68369	119333	583093
海 南	Hainan	173992	22392	44555	107045	164629	22757	34975	106897
重 庆	Chongqing	456848	120466	132909	203473	444276	114867	108127	221282
四 川	Sichuan	1324117	94166	284717	945234	1223734	100086	229043	894605
贵 州	Guizhou	805694	58641	126430	620623	827264	65759	114983	646522
云 南	Yunnan	771499	33771	102811	634917	731132	34628	93734	602770
西 藏	Tibet	45695	3786	9709	32200	58913	4279	9884	44750
陕 西	Shaanxi	806239	85517	103676	617046	530089	75719	71470	382900
甘 肃	Gansu	481495	47762	81110	352623	572321	48465	86511	437345
青 海	Qinghai	81467	13628	18524	49315	94559	13886	23701	56972
宁 夏	Ningxia	96835	16566	17507	62762	128779	18834	22630	87315
新 疆	Xinjiang	421443	66274	43288	311881	347619	65969	41119	240531

21-28 各地区按城乡和主办部门分小学教职工数（2003年）

Number of Staff and Full-time Teachers in Primary Schools by Urban and Rural Areas, by Department and by Region (2003)

单位：人 (person)

地区	Region	教职工数 Number of Teachers and Staff in Primary Schools						
			按主办部门分 By Department			按城乡分 By Urban and Rural Areas		
		合计 Total	教育部门和集体办 Schools Run by Educational Departments and Collective Units	社会力量办 Schools Run by Society	其他部门办 Schools Run by Other Departments	城市 Urban Areas	县镇 Counties and Towns	农村 Rural Areas
全国	**National Total**	**6256185**	**5850398**	**162825**	**242962**	**1080931**	**1260445**	**3914809**
北京	Beijing	63174	60453	797	1924	27481	20890	14803
天津	Tianjin	52603	49803	564	2236	22882	17950	11771
河北	Hebei	352846	329301	11650	11895	49638	61677	241531
山西	Shanxi	202648	176338	7445	18865	38440	28721	135487
内蒙古	Inner Mongolia	145166	129023	2999	13144	28141	34518	82507
辽宁	Liaoning	199829	194846	1056	3927	57389	24819	117621
吉林	Jilin	166592	153012	977	12603	26462	42132	97998
黑龙江	Heilongjiang	204820	164596	1594	38630	38230	36617	129973
上海	Shanghai	54157	50381	2591	1185	27772	24342	2043
江苏	Jiangsu	297083	287997	5487	3599	55985	47509	193589
浙江	Zhejiang	175366	166962	7875	529	45817	109202	20347
安徽	Anhui	279648	267394	4331	7923	38108	36398	205142
福建	Fujian	189027	186078	2635	314	26608	54348	108071
江西	Jiangxi	207306	198689	2781	5836	18600	66498	122208
山东	Shandong	410968	393014	9308	8646	83348	76695	250925
河南	Henan	516735	490444	12641	13650	58099	68350	390286
湖北	Hubei	252645	239359	4079	9207	66445	29726	156474
湖南	Hunan	275811	262375	4600	8836	35713	58346	181752
广东	Guangdong	447013	400305	41128	5580	116612	87964	242437
广西	Guangxi	235014	224826	6090	4098	26311	49233	159470
海南	Hainan	54869	42247	4552	8070	7581	13363	33925
重庆	Chongqing	129140	124879	2540	1721	41688	34670	52782
四川	Sichuan	350201	336836	7547	5818	32758	76427	241016
贵州	Guizhou	191695	181266	5788	4641	18963	36328	136404
云南	Yunnan	235740	229386	1521	4833	11565	36003	188172
西藏	Tibet	13767	13526	179	62	1741	3430	8596
陕西	Shaanxi	206447	188932	6368	11147	27963	28725	149759
甘肃	Gansu	131752	123299	714	7739	15722	22939	93091
青海	Qinghai	29692	28287	334	1071	4013	7693	17986
宁夏	Ningxia	35833	33510	279	2044	5643	7241	22949
新疆	Xinjiang	148598	123034	2375	23189	25213	17691	105694

21-28 续表 continued

单位：人 (person)

地区	Region	专任教师数 Number of Full-time Teachers in Primary Schools 合计 Total	按主办部门分 By Department 教育部门和集体办 Schools Run by Educational Departments and Collective Units	社会力量办 Schools Run by Society	其他部门办 Schools Run by Other Departments	按城乡分 By Urban and Rural Areas 城市 Urban Areas	县镇 Counties and Towns	农村 Rural Areas
全 国	**National Total**	**5702750**	**5379242**	**117239**	**206269**	**936396**	**1120663**	**3645691**
北 京	Beijing	49843	47738	540	1565	21642	16088	12113
天 津	Tianjin	43829	41674	236	1919	17905	15275	10649
河 北	Hebei	329165	310763	8150	10252	44017	55685	229463
山 西	Shanxi	188109	166644	5114	16351	33057	25489	129563
内蒙古	Inner Mongolia	127011	114026	2266	10719	24104	28648	74259
辽 宁	Liaoning	170947	166732	955	3260	47763	21409	101775
吉 林	Jilin	141363	130472	685	10206	21852	33117	86394
黑龙江	Heilongjiang	178122	147342	1149	29631	31137	30441	116544
上 海	Shanghai	39408	36345	2091	972	20332	17477	1599
江 苏	Jiangsu	268436	261332	3968	3136	50169	42052	176215
浙 江	Zhejiang	159127	153099	5567	461	40928	99764	18435
安 徽	Anhui	266458	256198	3100	7160	35327	33722	197409
福 建	Fujian	177248	175052	1913	283	24449	49642	103157
江 西	Jiangxi	198513	191015	2126	5372	17241	63894	117378
山 东	Shandong	380066	365610	6720	7736	73052	68294	238720
河 南	Henan	488490	467592	9047	11851	51334	62220	374936
湖 北	Hubei	233902	222755	2962	8185	58881	27422	147599
湖 南	Hunan	260704	249509	3246	7949	32097	54231	174376
广 东	Guangdong	389262	356030	28555	4677	97912	77011	214339
广 西	Guangxi	205142	196832	4831	3479	23263	42617	139262
海 南	Hainan	49367	39436	3047	6884	6199	11917	31251
重 庆	Chongqing	115212	111945	1840	1427	36446	30338	48428
四 川	Sichuan	316029	304853	6116	5060	28450	66470	221109
贵 州	Guizhou	179367	170470	4726	4171	16749	33420	129198
云 南	Yunnan	221589	216541	1012	4036	10366	32522	178701
西 藏	Tibet	13026	12833	137	56	1608	3174	8244
陕 西	Shaanxi	190964	176665	4405	9894	24110	26303	140551
甘 肃	Gansu	126740	119321	504	6915	14310	21772	90658
青 海	Qinghai	28496	27258	269	969	3773	7372	17351
宁 夏	Ningxia	34531	32455	188	1888	5324	6901	22306
新 疆	Xinjiang	132284	110705	1774	19805	22599	15976	93709

21-29 各地区特殊教育情况（2003年）

Basic Statistics on Special Education by Region (2003)

单位：人 (person)

地 区	Region	学校数(所) Number of Schools (unit)	毕业生数 Number of Graduates	招生数 New Student Enrollment	在校学生数 Student Enrollment	教职工数 Number of Staff and Teachers	#专任教师 Full-time Teachers
全 国	**National Total**	**1551**	**44533**	**48840**	**364740**	**40853**	**30349**
北 京	Beijing	25	1007	647	6177	929	667
天 津	Tianjin	22	535	230	3167	711	458
河 北	Hebei	97	1987	1794	13481	2097	1605
山 西	Shanxi	36	422	782	5852	1116	870
内蒙古	Inner Mongolia	31	249	402	3037	813	610
辽 宁	Liaoning	75	790	803	8429	2474	1854
吉 林	Jilin	45	466	477	4748	1775	1237
黑龙江	Heilongjiang	71	536	830	6404	2546	1926
上 海	Shanghai	31	2143	1361	11563	1629	985
江 苏	Jiangsu	108	3988	3857	32222	3346	2456
浙 江	Zhejiang	63	2561	1947	15357	1445	1133
安 徽	Anhui	71	2032	2582	18849	1295	973
福 建	Fujian	77	6677	5270	40921	1505	1251
江 西	Jiangxi	49	1025	2262	14854	509	413
山 东	Shandong	138	2012	2308	17154	5135	3585
河 南	Henan	123	1977	2634	19146	3194	2510
湖 北	Hubei	76	774	1118	7908	1633	1243
湖 南	Hunan	55	2192	2154	13634	1219	923
广 东	Guangdong	67	3396	3462	27073	1655	1311
广 西	Guangxi	47	1579	2918	15874	719	495
海 南	Hainan	4	71	213	1665	100	65
重 庆	Chongqing	41	1891	1513	14483	697	543
四 川	Sichuan	70	2090	2550	15839	1278	994
贵 州	Guizhou	38	1237	2051	13812	675	517
云 南	Yunnan	25	1759	2619	17621	610	442
西 藏	Tibet	2	11	30	162	39	23
陕 西	Shaanxi	28	129	304	2143	662	481
甘 肃	Gansu	14	466	975	7673	394	294
青 海	Qinghai	8	212	240	2383	153	128
宁 夏	Ningxia	6	55	138	1246	149	120
新 疆	Xinjiang	8	264	369	1863	351	237

注：特殊教育指盲、聋、哑和弱智儿童的教育。

a) Special education refers to the education for the blind, deaf, deaf-mute and the mentally retarded.

21-30 各地区幼儿园基本情况（2003年）

Basic Statistics on Kindergartens by Region (2003)

地 区	Region	园 数 (所) Number of Kindergartens (unit)	班 数 (个) Number of Classes (unit)	幼儿数 (人) Student Enrollment (person)	教职工数 (人) Number of Staff and Teachers (person)	#教 师 Teachers
全 国	**National Total**	**116390**	**728511**	**20039061**	**973159**	**612856**
北 京	Beijing	1430	7733	199390	26324	13056
天 津	Tianjin	1778	6703	199551	15309	9737
河 北	Hebei	3765	35957	926076	32822	21688
山 西	Shanxi	5137	29767	680324	29705	19923
内蒙古	Inner Mongolia	1140	12881	290612	15839	9735
辽 宁	Liaoning	7033	29668	675118	42852	24946
吉 林	Jilin	2404	12637	259163	16994	10107
黑龙江	Heilongjiang	2181	15572	345116	20298	11779
上 海	Shanghai	1032	8110	254821	25087	15089
江 苏	Jiangsu	6875	42795	1252515	64317	46239
浙 江	Zhejiang	11560	44651	1179558	83022	54056
安 徽	Anhui	2512	25003	715064	19528	14162
福 建	Fujian	7064	26721	695822	38671	27238
江 西	Jiangxi	4478	22778	633073	26515	17612
山 东	Shandong	17070	54998	1432854	80216	57349
河 南	Henan	2659	47970	1494284	41756	26242
湖 北	Hubei	2258	21422	597841	28905	17815
湖 南	Hunan	2331	25732	657070	24208	12662
广 东	Guangdong	10067	71393	2125196	143381	82186
广 西	Guangxi	2670	31394	843289	23374	13702
海 南	Hainan	662	4790	113367	7685	4308
重 庆	Chongqing	3093	18840	572538	19013	12141
四 川	Sichuan	8109	51272	1536444	49451	31243
贵 州	Guizhou	1319	17532	620089	13994	8751
云 南	Yunnan	1862	24488	706551	23857	15279
西 藏	Tibet	41	204	6901	628	341
陕 西	Shaanxi	2288	8371	231912	21020	12689
甘 肃	Gansu	2276	14834	372225	14568	9614
青 海	Qinghai	220	2908	74075	3243	1825
宁 夏	Ningxia	167	3267	102217	3784	2415
新 疆	Xinjiang	909	8120	246005	16793	8927

21-31 各地区教育经费情况(2002年)

Basic Statistics on Educational Funds by Region (2002)

单位: 万元 (10 000 yuan)

年 份 地 区	Year Region	合 计 Total	国家财政性教育经费 Government Appropriation for Education	# 预算内教育经费 Budgetary	社会团体和公民个人办学经费 Funds of Social Organizations and Citizens for Running Schools	社会捐资和集资办学经费 Donations and Fund-raising for Running Schools	学费和杂费 Tuition and Miscellaneous Fee	其他教育经费 Other Educational Funds
	1991	7315028	6178286	4597308		628210	323476	185057
	1992	8670491	7287506	5387382		696285	439319	247380
	1993	10599374	8677618	6443914	33323	701856	871477	315100
	1994	14887813	11747396	8839795	107795	974487	1469228	588907
	1995	18779501	14115233	10283930	203672	1628414	2012423	819760
	1996	22623394	16717046	12119134	261999	1884190	2610391	1149798
	1997	25317326	18625416	13577262	301746	1706588	3260792	1422783
	1998	29490592	20324526	15655917	480314	1418537	3697474	3569741
	1999	33490416	22871756	18157597	628957	1258694	4636108	4094901
	2000	38490806	25626056	20856792	858537	1139557	5948304	4918352
	2001	46376626	30570100	25823762	1280895	1128852	7456014	5940766
	2002	54800278	34914048	31142383	1725549	1272791	9227792	7660099
北 京	Beijing	3538686	2194373	2017389	34577	103803	386539	819395
天 津	Tianjin	975730	596588	531017	52724	4166	127789	194463
河 北	Hebei	2101072	1373881	1243141	62398	27554	442541	194699
山 西	Shanxi	1176900	774619	665526	39826	48882	203726	109848
内蒙古	Inner Mongolia	854998	641468	575371	7136	4694	130614	71086
辽 宁	Liaoning	1943995	1283470	1135498	40798	6660	374196	238871
吉 林	Jilin	1226407	856766	757043	13881	32373	176366	147021
黑龙江	Heilongjiang	1587805	1096738	902092	33312	4056	266404	187296
上 海	Shanghai	2739674	1740617	1528276	102574	56916	395646	443923
江 苏	Jiangsu	4044278	2336581	2061504	143342	265358	633224	665774
浙 江	Zhejiang	3396099	1973232	1580232	241947	142825	457235	580860
安 徽	Anhui	1640473	1061198	997076	28340	21757	338582	190597
福 建	Fujian	1779257	1149600	1041591	113998	57029	249931	208701
江 西	Jiangxi	1169816	684152	635353	59067	10932	247322	168343
山 东	Shandong	3338764	2094604	1831984	142001	63322	648258	390580
河 南	Henan	2288399	1555518	1437318	51568	30795	413269	237249
湖 北	Hubei	2301981	1292427	1162285	20816	58698	514211	415829
湖 南	Hunan	2104948	1151361	1056543	60760	34565	536794	321468
广 东	Guangdong	5203412	3247693	2910766	252942	118281	1009222	575274
广 西	Guangxi	1346031	924536	824650	20982	11080	233333	156101
海 南	Hainan	297250	195178	161222	11673	6870	49001	34529
重 庆	Chongqing	1066535	645004	593212	19097	35629	161596	205209
四 川	Sichuan	2437437	1519277	1380815	29612	68053	379724	440770
贵 州	Guizhou	867638	660740	601850	11456	6792	122255	66395
云 南	Yunnan	1295046	1071095	987968	15512	17415	105486	85539
西 藏	Tibet	141178	134183	133971		436	4931	1628
陕 西	Shaanxi	1597679	944164	882321	89389	18722	331813	213591
甘 肃	Gansu	836405	606262	538793	8872	9239	132540	79492
青 海	Qinghai	190401	161860	155646	957	328	17769	9487
宁 夏	Ningxia	229623	177182	164007	648	2744	27378	21671
新 疆	Xinjiang	1082359	769681	647925	15345	2820	110100	184413

21-32 各类学校教育经费情况（2002年）

Educational Funds in Various School (2002)

单位：万元 (10 000 yuan)

学校类别	Type of Schools	合计 Total	国家财政性教育经费 Government Appropriation for Education	# 预算内教育经费 Budgetary	社会团体和公民个人办学经费 Funds of Social Organizations and Citizens for Running Schools	社会捐资和集资办学经费 Donations and Fund-Raising for Running Schools	学费和杂费 Tuition and Miscellaneous Fee	其他教育经费 Other Educational Funds
全国总计	**National Total**	**54800278**	**34914048**	**31142383**	**1725549**	**1272791**	**9227792**	**7660099**
#中央	Central Government	6581621	3531595	3042307		206891	872793	1970341
地方	Local Government	48218657	31382452	28100077	1725549	1065900	8354998	5689758
按学校类别分组	**Grouped by Type of Schools**							
高等学校	Institutions of Higher Education	15832129	7875176	7548856	417624	279514	4264517	2995298
普通高等学校	Regular Institutions of Higher Education	14878590	7521463	7243459	331363	278253	3906526	2840985
成人高等学校	Institutions of Higher Education for Adults	953539	353713	305398	86261	1261	357991	154314
中等专业学校	Specialized Secondary Schools	2505374	1356575	1273760	25046	8203	824108	291443
中等技术学校	Technical Schools	1723506	931580	880751	10881	3094	610482	167469
中等师范学校	Teacher Training Schools	375673	198849	185890		2924	128563	45336
成人中专学校	Specialized Secondary Schools for Adults	406195	226145	207119	14165	2185	85063	78638
技工学校	Technical Schools	366761	196714	137485		1159	77189	91700
中学	Secondary Schools	16704638	10623979	9003382	898922	599214	2433371	2149153
普通中学	Regular Secondary Schools	16682290	10613313	8995103	896845	599146	2428480	2144507
高级中学	Senior Secondary Schools	3490128	1651652	1359066	146229	185092	853344	653811
完全中学	Whole Secondary Schools	4595596	2528160	2046847	404974	217738	708894	735829
初级中学	Junior Secondary Schools	8596566	6433501	5589191	345643	196315	866242	754866
#农村	Rural	4270562	3413785	3188333		87628	494221	274928
成人中学	Secondary Schools for Adults	22349	10666	8278	2077	68	4891	4647
职业中学	Vocational Schools	1470024	888019	773303	63429	14042	358984	145551
小学	Primary Schools	14485878	11641507	10473153	320528	327885	1156260	1039698
普通小学	Regular Primary Schools	14480218	11636869	10469011	319902	327885	1156107	1039455
#农村	Rural Areas	8389831	7100911	6709477		175006	743639	370275
成人小学	Primary Schools for Adults	5660	4638	4142	626	1	153	243
特殊教育学校	Special Education Schools	151392	133195	116767		2868	3304	12025
幼儿园	Kindergartens	675844	416389	397253		14908	110061	134486
其它	Others	2608238	1782495	1418424		24998		800744

21-33 科技活动基本情况
Basic Statistics on Scientific and Technological Activities

指标	Item	1999	2000	2001	2002	2003
科技活动人员 （万人）	**Personnel Engaged in S&T Activities (10 000 persons)**	**290.6**	**322.4**	**314.1**	**322.2**	**328.4**
#科学家和工程师	Scientists and Engineers	159.5	204.6	207.2	217.2	225.5
研究与试验发展折合全时人员 （万人年）	**Full-time Equivalent of R&D Personnel (10 000 man-years)**	**82.2**	**92.2**	**95.7**	**103.5**	**109.5**
#科学家和工程师	Scientists and Engineers	53.1	69.5	74.3	81.0	86.2
科技经费筹集额 （亿元）	**Funding for S&T Activities (100 million yuan)**	**1460.6**	**2346.7**	**2589.4**	**2938.0**	**3459.1**
#政府资金	Government Funds	473.0	593.4	656.4	776.2	839.3
企业资金	Self-raised Funds by Enterprises	745.9	1296.4	1458.4	1676.7	2053.5
金融机构贷款	Loans from Finance Institutions	123.0	196.2	190.8	201.9	259.3
科技经费内部支出 （亿元）	**Internal Expenditures on S&T Activities (100 million yuan)**	**1284.9**	**2050.2**	**2312.5**	**2671.5**	**3121.6**
#劳务费	Service Fees	270.2	475.8	549.3	654.6	751.5
固定资产购建费	Purchase or Construction of Fixed Assets	357.4	607.3	692.3	722.6	852.4
研究与试验发展经费支出（亿元）	**Expenditure on R&D (100 million yuan)**	**678.9**	**895.7**	**1042.5**	**1287.6**	**1539.6**
#基础研究	Basic Research	33.9	46.7	52.2	73.8	87.7
应用研究	Applied Research	151.5	151.9	175.9	246.7	311.4
试验发展	Experimental Development	493.5	697.0	814.3	967.2	1140.5
研究与试验发展经费支出相当于国内生产总值比例 （%）	**Proportion of Expenditure on R&D to GDP (%)**	**0.83**	**1.00**	**1.07**	**1.23**	**1.31**
科技成果及获奖数	**Achievements in S&T and National Prizes Won**					
科技成果登记数 （项）	Number of Major Achievements in Science and Technology	31060	32858	28448	26697	30486
国家技术发明奖 （项）	Number of National Invention Prizes Awarded	69	23	14	21	19
国家科学技术进步奖 （项）	Number of National Scientific and Technological Progress Prizes Awarded	476	250	191	218	216
技术市场成交额 （亿元）	**Transaction Value in Technical Market (100 million)**	**523**	**651**	**783**	**884**	**1085**
专利申请受理量 （件）	**Total Patent Applications Examined**	**134239**	**170682**	**203573**	**252631**	**308487**
发明	Inventions	36694	51747	63204	80232	105318
实用新型	Utility Models	57492	68815	79722	93139	109115
外观设计	Designs	40053	50120	60647	79260	94054
专利申请授权量 （件）	**Total Patent Applications Certified**	**100156**	**105345**	**114251**	**132399**	**182226**
发明	Inventions	7637	12683	16296	21473	37154
实用新型	Utility Models	56368	54743	54359	57484	68906
外观设计	Designs	36151	37919	43596	53442	76166

21-34 科学研究与开发机构基本情况
Basic Statistics on Scientific Research and Development Institution

项目	Item	1999	2000	2001	2002	2003
科技活动人员 （万人）	**Personnel Engaged in S&T Activities (10 000 persons)**	**53.5**	**47.2**	**42.7**	**41.5**	**40.6**
#科学家和工程师	Scientists and Engineers	33.6	29.7	27.6	27.1	26.7
研究与试验发展折合全时人员 （万人年）	**Full-time Equivalent of R&D Personnel (10 000 man-years)**	**23.3**	**22.7**	**20.5**	**20.6**	**20.4**
#科学家和工程师	Scientists and Engineers	16.7	15.0	14.8	15.2	15.5
#基础研究	Basic Research	1.9	2.5	2.4	2.3	2.6
应用研究	Applied Research	5.8	7.5	7.6	8.1	7.9
试验发展	Experimental Development	6.0	12.8	10.3	10.2	9.9
科技经费筹集额 （亿元）	**Funding for S&T Activities (100 million yuan)**	**537.6**	**559.4**	**626.0**	**702.7**	**750.6**
#政府拨款	Government Appropriation Funds	338.6	377.4	434.9	498.0	535.0
企业资金	Self-raised Funds by Enterprises	34.3	37.7	25.4	36.3	47.0
金融机构贷款	Loans from Finance Institutions	20.9	10.7	8.6	11.9	11.3
科技经费内部支出 （亿元）	**Internal Expenditures on S&T Activities (100 million yuan)**	**491.7**	**495.7**	**557.9**	**620.2**	**681.3**
#劳务费	Service Fees	115.1	120.4	142.5	159.8	169.1
业务费	Operating Expenses	178.8	245.1	231.9	298.6	313.5
固定资产购建费	Purchase or Construction of Fixed Assets	99.0	99.7	123.9	122.0	138.0
研究与试验发展经费支出（亿元）	**Expenditure on R&D (100 million yuan)**	**260.5**	**258.0**	**288.5**	**351.3**	**399.0**
#基础研究	Basic Research	20.1	25.3	34.6	40.7	46.0
应用研究	Applied Research	88.6	66.7	78.9	121.2	140.3
试验发展	Experimental Development	151.9	166.0	175.0	189.4	212.7

注：数据口径为县以上独立核算研究机构及科技信息与文献机构，不包括转制的研究机构。

a) The coverage of statistics is the research institutions and the science, technology information and literature institutions with independent accounting system at county and higher levels, but excluding the research institutions which system have been reformed.

21-35 大中型工业企业科技活动基本情况

Basic Statistics on Science and Technology Activities of Large-scale and Medium-scale Industrial Enterprises

指　　标	Item	2000	2002	2003
有科技机构的企业　（个）	**Number of Enterprises Having Scientific and Technological Institution (unit)**	**6187**	**5836**	**6424**
有科技机构的企业占全部企业比重　(%)	Percentage of Enterprises Having Scientific and Technological Institutions to Total Number of Enterprises (%)	28.5	25.3	28.8
科技机构数　（个）	**Number of Scientific and Technological Institutions**	**7601**	**7192**	**6841**
科技活动人员　（万人）	**Personnel Engaged in S&T Activities (10 000 persons)**	**138.7**	**136.7**	**141.1**
#科学家和工程师	Scientists and Engineers	76.9	81.3	87.3
研究与试验发展折合全时人员（万人年）	**Full-time Equivalent of R&D Personnel (10 000 man-years)**	**32.9**	**42.4**	**47.8**
科技机构科技活动人员数（万人）	Personnel Engaged in S&T Activities in S&T Institutions (10 000 persons)	44.0	49.8	53.1
#科学家和工程师	Scientists and Engineers	27.5	32.6	35.7
科技经费筹集额　（亿元）	**Funding for S&T Activities (100 million yuan)**	**922.8**	**1213.0**	**1588.6**
#政府资金	Government Funds	43.2	53.7	51.8
企业资金	Self-raised Funds by Enterprises	744.4	1020.3	1339.6
金融机构贷款	Loans from Finance Institutions	97.3	99.9	156.5
科技经费内部支出　（亿元）	**Internal Expenditures on S&T Activities (100 million yuan)**	**823.7**	**1164.1**	**1467.8**
#开发新产品经费支出	Expenditure on New Product Development	388.9	509.2	639.0
科技经费支出占产品销售收入的比重　(%)	Percentage of Expenditures on Science and Technology to Sales Revenue (%)	1.65	1.73	1.52
研究与试验发展经费支出（亿元）	**Expenditure for R&D (100 million yuan)**	**353.4**	**560.2**	**720.8**
科技项目数　（项）	**Number of Scientific and Technological Projects (unit)**	**100099**	**110270**	**121926**
#新产品项目	Projects for New Product Development	55953	59788	68633
技术引进经费支出　（亿元）	**Expenditures for Indraught of Technology (100 million yuan**	**245.4**	**372.5**	**405.4**
消化吸收经费支出　（亿元）	**Expenditures for Absorb and Digest (100 million yuan)**	**18.2**	**25.7**	**27.1**
购买国内技术支出　（亿元）	**Expenditures for Inner Technology (100 million yuan)**	**26.4**	**42.9**	**54.3**

注：2003年大中型工业企业统计范围按《统计上大中小型企业划分办法》进行了调整。

a) Statistical scope of large-scale and medium-scale enterprises has been adjusted by "*grouped means of large-scale, medium-scale and small* enterprises *on statistic*" in 2003.

21-36 高等学校科技活动情况

Basic Statistics on Higher Education for Scientific and Technological Activities

指　　标	Item	1999	2000	2001	2002	2003
科技活动人员　（万人）	**Personnel Engaged in S&T Activities (10 000 persons)**	**34.2**	**35.2**	**36.6**	**38.3**	**41.1**
#科学家和工程师	Scientists and Engineers	32.9	31.5	35.9	37.6	40.4
研究与试验发展机构　（个）	**R&D Institutions (unit)**	**3124**	**3735**	**3481**	**3702**	**3332**
研究与试验发展折合全时人员（万人年）	**Full-time Equivalent of R&D Personnel (10 000 man-years)**	**17.6**	**15.9**	**17.1**	**18.1**	**18.9**
#科学家和工程师	Scientists and Engineers	16.8	14.7	16.8	18.2	18.6
#基础研究	Basic Research	4.7	5.1	5.1	5.6	5.8
应用研究	Applied Research	9.8	8.7	9.2	9.5	10.0
试验发展	Experimental Development	3.1	2.1	2.8	3.1	3.1
科技经费筹集额　（亿元）	**Funding for S&T Activities (100 million yuan)**	**102.9**	**166.8**	**200.0**	**247.7**	**307.8**
#政府拨款	Government Appropriation Funds	49.2	97.5	109.8	137.3	164.8
企业资金	Self-raised Funds by Enterprises	53.2	55.5	72.5	89.6	112.6
金融机构贷款	Loans from Finance Institutions	0.5	1.4	1.0	1.3	1.5
科技经费内部支出　（亿元）	**Internal Expenditures on S&T Activities (100 million yuan)**	**85.1**	**137.1**	**165.9**	**204.2**	**253.9**
#劳务费	Service Fees	8.9	28.5	29.8	38.2	49.1
固定资产购建费	Purchase or Construction of Fixed Assets	17.0	27.4	51.3	38.3	45.1
研究与试验发展经费支出（亿元）	**Expenditure for R&D (100 million yuan)**	**63.5**	**76.7**	**102.4**	**130.5**	**162.3**
#基础研究	Basic Research	11.4	17.8	17.0	27.8	32.9
应用研究	Applied Research	37.7	40.0	59.0	67.1	89.7
试验发展	Experimental Development	14.4	18.9	26.4	35.6	39.7

21-37 高技术行业大中型工业企业科技活动投入情况（2003）

行业	Industry	科技活动人员（人）Personnel Engaged in S&T Activities (person)	研究与试验发展折合全时人员(人年) Full-time Equivalent of R&D Personnel (man.year)
合计	**Total**	**278017**	**127847**
医药制造业	**Medical and Pharmaceutical Products**	**44561**	**17518**
#化学药品原药制造业	Original Chemical Medicine	16925	6529
化学药品制剂制造业	Chemical Medicine Preparation	11748	4884
生物、生化制品制造业	Biology, Biochemistry Products	2533	1147
航空航天器制造业	**Aviation and Aircrafts Manufacturing**	**56554**	**28165**
电子及通信设备制造业	**Electron and Communicate Equipments**	**128068**	**61643**
#通信设备制造业	Communicate Equipments	46932	29053
雷达及配套设备制造业	Radar Equipments	6433	1710
广播电视设备制造业	Broadcast and Television Equipments	942	251
电子器件制造业	Electronic Parts	23381	7486
电子元件制造业	Electronic Organs	27478	10025
家用视听设备制造业	Household Audiovisual	18112	10600
其他电子设备制造	Other Electron Equipment	4790	2518
电子计算机及办公设备制造业		**25886**	**12393**
#电子计算机整机制造业	Electronic Computer	14138	6537
电子计算机外部设备制造业	Electronic Computer Peripheral Equipments	9086	4347
医疗器械及仪器仪表制造业	**Medical Treatment Instrument and Meter**	**22948**	**8128**
#医疗仪器设备及器械制造业	Medical Treatment Equipments and Instruments	2387	840
仪器仪表制造业	Instruments and Meters	20561	7288

21-38 高技术行业大中型工业企业科技活动产出情况（2003）

单位：万元

行业	Industry	工业总产值 Gross Value of Industrial Output	#新产品 New Products
合计	**Total**	**168642214**	**46921587**
医药制造业	**Medical and Pharmaceutical Products**	**18784438**	**3310771**
#化学药品原药制造业	Original Chemical Medicine	5447138	929659
化学药品制剂制造业	Chemical Medicine Preparation	6331487	1375342
生物、生化制品制造业	Biology, Biochemistry Products	1098249	198963
航空航天器制造业	**Aviation and Aircrafts Manufacturing**	**5283027**	**2294171**
电子及通信设备制造业	**Electron and Communicate Equipments**	**86573093**	**28853286**
#通信设备制造业	Communicate Equipments	29918648	11419148
雷达及配套设备制造业	Radar Equipments	590984	212121
广播电视设备制造业	Broadcast and Television Equipments	239267	30919
电子器件制造业	Electronic Parts	15824556	3593196
电子元件制造业	Electronic Organs	16210248	1722723
家用视听设备制造业	Household Audiovisual	21813836	11737748
其他电子设备制造	Other Electron Equipment	1975554	137431
电子计算机及办公设备制造业	**Electronic Computers and Office Equipments**	**53295657**	**11245418**
#电子计算机整机制造业	Electronic Computer	28048669	5793230
电子计算机外部设备制造业	Electronic Computer Peripheral Equipments	19333735	5066979
医疗器械及仪器仪表制造业	**Medical Treatment Instrument and Meter**	**4705999**	**1217941**
#医疗仪器设备及器械制造业	Medical Treatment Equipments and Instruments	912358	121861
仪器仪表制造业	Instruments and Meters	3793641	1096080

Basic Statistics on Scientific and Technological Activities Funds of Large-scale and Medium-scale Industrial Enterprises in High-tech Industry (2003)

#科学家和工程师 Scientists & Engineers	科技活动经费支出(万元) Expenditure on Technological Activities (10 000 yuan)	#R&D经费(万元) R&D Expenditure (10 000 yuan)	#新产品经费(万元) Expenditure for New Products (10 000 yuan)	技术改造经费支出(万元) Expenditure for Technical Renovation (10 000 yuan)
92499	**3990123**	**2224421**	**2075842**	**1550340**
13215	**527349**	**276665**	**228616**	**469164**
4614	175170	79993	61417	206875
3684	153372	87986	65845	119080
921	32613	15238	15946	28836
13220	**424878**	**222590**	**198838**	**342100**
49380	**2151159**	**1385018**	**1187584**	**584797**
26683	1051747	776355	604865	74429
1534	35248	13478	18787	11806
200	8739	5791	6555	3011
5121	328503	210412	140854	248148
6347	238387	126238	125847	162893
7198	394327	225139	268590	72665
2297	94208	27605	22086	11846
10374	**747950**	**257487**	**379391**	**85706**
5625	519828	172070	293477	33888
3523	191263	59556	70162	28045
6310	**138787**	**82661**	**81413**	**68573**
685	23603	10883	13906	14241
5625	115184	71778	67507	54333

Basic Statistics on Scientific and Technological Activities Outputs of Large-scale and Medium-scale Industrial Enterprises in High-tech Industry (2003)

(10 000 yuan)

产品销售收入 Total Revenue from the Sale of Products	#新产品 New Products	#出口 Export	产品销售利润 Profits from the Sale of Products	#新产品 New Products	专利申请(项) Patent Applications (item)	#发明专利数 Invention	拥有发明专利数(项) Patent Owned (item)
168940768	**45150392**	**14168308**	**15446052**	**3521025**	**8270**	**3787**	**3356**
18946084	**3037910**	**382156**	**4024749**	**691592**	**1305**	**757**	**459**
6138364	877349	259586	1135598	225319	143	96	89
6119040	1216432	42685	1185650	237498	347	182	134
1042836	215287	58117	265226	48179	82	54	26
5227228	**2151101**	**89218**	**840494**	**162461**	**282**	**56**	**141**
84736383	**29261861**	**7375847**	**7409876**	**1882689**	**4890**	**2305**	**2100**
30145417	12409300	1589077	2930977	889411	2621	1507	1394
589635	165710	19031	140128	24078	29	3	6
228104	30896	5282	20589	4007	13		8
15398967	3474045	857554	1432774	189327	688	407	313
15749754	1613748	626509	1505721	170142	240	64	176
20641606	11425476	4248648	1120035	587029	1200	301	197
1982900	142687	29747	259652	18696	99	23	6
55414176	**9549549**	**6135727**	**2372402**	**571546**	**1243**	**485**	**271**
30940208	4195102	2051656	1193607	257333	813	389	106
18620663	4994586	3953208	739824	181433	363	94	163
4616897	**1149971**	**185360**	**798531**	**212737**	**550**	**184**	**385**
869452	120543	25673	129585	21751	98	21	49
3747445	1029428	159687	668946	190986	452	163	336

21-39 专利申请受理量

Patent Applications Examined

单位：项 (item)

指　标	Item	1990	1995	2000	2002	2003
申请受理量合计	**Total Applications Examined**	**41469**	**83045**	**170682**	**252631**	**308487**
发　明	**Inventions**	**10137**	**21636**	**51747**	**80232**	**105318**
国　内	Domestic	5832	10018	25346	39806	56769
职　务	Service	2482	2993	12609	22668	34731
大专院校	Universities and Colleges	509	574	1942	4282	7704
科研单位	Research Institutions	805	865	2228	3429	4711
工矿企业	Industrial and Mineral Enterprises	816	1086	8316	14657	21858
机关团体	Government Agencies and Organizations	352	468	123	300	458
非职务	Non-service	3350	7025	12737	17138	22038
国　外	Foreign	4305	11618	26401	40426	48549
职　务	Service	4018	11045	25334	38764	46764
非职务	Non-service	287	573	1067	1662	1785
实用新型	**Utility Models**	**27615**	**43741**	**68815**	**93139**	**109115**
国　内	Domestic	27488	43429	68461	92166	107842
职　务	Service	7424	8727	17792	27612	34044
大专院校	Universities and Colleges	811	771	965	1658	2375
科研单位	Research Institutions	1521	1376	1616	1642	2104
工矿企业	Industrial and Mineral Enterprises	3830	4739	14912	23800	28998
机关团体	Government Agencies and Organizations	1262	1841	299	512	567
非职务	Non-service	20064	34702	50669	64554	73798
国　外	Foreign	127	312	354	973	1273
职　务	Service	55	190	259	640	1076
非职务	Non-service	72	122	95	333	197
外观设计	**Designs**	**3717**	**17668**	**50120**	**79260**	**94054**
国　内	Domestic	3265	15433	46532	73572	86627
职　务	Service	1713	8193	22974	30962	33681
大专院校	Universities and Colleges	13	18	17	41	173
科研单位	Research Institutions	64	104	278	302	183
工矿企业	Industrial and Mineral Enterprises	1310	6031	22634	30505	33261
机关团体	Government Agencies and Organizations	326	2040	45	114	64
非职务	Non-service	1552	7240	23558	42610	52946
国　外	Foreign	452	2235	3588	5688	7427
职　务	Service	418	2013	3432	5458	7192
非职务	Non-service	34	222	156	230	235

21-40 专利申请授权量

Patent Applications Granted

单位：项 (item)

指　标	Item	1990	1995	2000	2002	2003
授权量合计	**Total Applications Certified**	**22588**	**45064**	**105345**	**132399**	**182226**
发　明	**Inventions**	**3838**	**3393**	**12683**	**21473**	**37154**
国　内	Domestic	1149	1530	6177	5868	11404
职　务	Service	908	932	2824	3144	6895
大专院校	Universities and Colleges	326	258	652	697	1730
科研单位	Research Institutions	331	304	910	907	1677
工矿企业	Industrial and Mineral Enterprises	206	205	1016	1461	3382
机关团体	Government Agencies and Organizations	45	165	246	79	106
非职务	Non-service	241	598	3353	2724	4509
国　外	Foreign	2689	1863	6506	15605	25750
职　务	Service	2496	1748	6222	15013	24849
非职务	Non-service	193	115	284	592	901
实用新型	**Utility Models**	**16952**	**30471**	**54743**	**57484**	**68906**
国　内	Domestic	16744	30195	54407	57092	68291
职　务	Service	5100	6766	15519	18369	24008
大专院校	Universities and Colleges	698	623	868	973	1582
科研单位	Research Institutions	1280	1025	1529	1276	1485
工矿企业	Industrial and Mineral Enterprises	2249	2627	12821	15753	20485
机关团体	Government Agencies and Organizations	873	2491	301	367	456
非职务	Non-service	11644	23429	38888	38723	44283
国　外	Foreign	208	276	336	392	615
职　务	Service	132	154	261	252	498
非职务	Non-service	76	122	75	140	117
外观设计	**Designs**	**1798**	**11200**	**37919**	**53442**	**76166**
国　内	Domestic	1411	9523	34652	49143	69893
职　务	Service	751	5344	17789	20020	31465
大专院校	Universities and Colleges	7	10	28	40	104
科研单位	Research Institutions	35	156	248	140	270
工矿企业	Industrial and Mineral Enterprises	598	2554	17482	19802	31002
机关团体	Government Agencies and Organizations	111	2624	31	38	89
非职务	Non-service	660	4179	16863	29123	38428
国　外	Foreign	387	1677	3267	4299	6273
职　务	Service	336	1402	3108	4106	6113
非职务	Non-service	51	275	159	193	160

21-41 各地区专利申请受理和授权量（2003年）

Patent Applications Examined and Granted by Region (2003)

单位：项 (item)

地区	Region	申请受理量 合计 Number of Patent Applications Examined	发明 Inventions	实用新型 Utility Models	外观设计 Designs	授权量合计 Number of Patent Applications Granted	发明 Inventions	实用新型 Utility Models	外观设计 Designs
全国	**National Total**	**251238**	**56769**	**107842**	**86627**	**149588**	**11404**	**68291**	**69893**
北京	Beijing	17003	7833	6665	2505	8248	2261	4244	1743
天津	Tianjin	6812	3328	2713	771	2505	241	1547	717
河北	Hebei	5623	986	3272	1365	3572	275	2197	1100
山西	Shanxi	1743	480	951	312	1175	276	662	237
内蒙古	Inner Mongolia	1393	244	713	436	817	80	423	314
辽宁	Liaoning	13545	2584	7859	3102	5656	644	3905	1107
吉林	Jilin	4267	1172	2268	827	1690	233	1049	408
黑龙江	Heilongjiang	4972	1151	3173	648	2794	229	2097	468
上海	Shanghai	22374	5936	5992	10446	16671	880	3844	11947
江苏	Jiangsu	18393	3279	8228	6886	9840	626	5381	3833
浙江	Zhejiang	21463	2751	7750	10962	14402	429	4947	9026
安徽	Anhui	2676	532	1516	628	1610	139	968	503
福建	Fujian	7236	797	2554	3885	5377	137	1658	3582
江西	Jiangxi	2434	832	1071	531	1238	97	685	456
山东	Shandong	15794	2596	9186	4012	9067	580	5770	2717
河南	Henan	5261	1025	3219	1017	2961	256	1983	722
湖北	Hubei	6635	1627	3406	1602	2871	420	1859	592
湖南	Hunan	6054	1492	3124	1438	3175	346	1888	941
广东	Guangdong	43186	6181	12985	24020	29235	953	7921	20361
广西	Guangxi	2250	452	1212	586	1331	83	790	458
海南	Hainan	445	110	147	188	296	28	97	171
重庆	Chongqing	4589	560	1835	2194	2883	125	1088	1670
四川	Sichuan	7443	1475	2865	3103	4051	342	1722	1987
贵州	Guizhou	1242	385	566	291	723	79	355	289
云南	Yunnan	1966	574	788	604	1213	173	527	513
西藏	Tibet	24	4	12	8	16	4	5	7
陕西	Shaanxi	3421	1191	1737	493	1609	169	1105	335
甘肃	Gansu	961	324	536	101	474	83	307	84
青海	Qinghai	173	70	60	43	90	17	35	38
宁夏	Ningxia	441	101	200	140	338	54	160	124
新疆	Xinjiang	1473	254	938	281	752	75	521	156
香港	Hong Kong	1816	279	441	1096	1565	80	314	1171
澳门	Macao	18	3	8	7	14	1	5	8
台湾	Taiwan	18112	6161	9852	2099	11329	989	8232	2108

21-42 按国别(地区)分专利申请受理量及授权量(2003年)

Patent Applications Examined and Grantedby Country (Region) (2003)

单位：项 (item)

国别（地区）	Country (Region)	申请受理量 合计 Number of Patent Applications Examined	发明 Inventions	实用新型 Utility Models	外观设计 Designs	授权量合计 Number of Patent Applications Grant	发明 Inventions	实用新型 Utility Models	外观设计 Designs
总计	**Total**	**56847**	**48286**	**1240**	**7321**	**32371**	**25627**	**586**	**6158**
日本	Japan	24241	20092	627	3522	12674	9369	205	3100
马来西亚	Malaysia	32	21	4	7	20	6	2	12
新加坡	Singapore	142	83	4	55	66	17	3	46
泰国	Thailand	61	13	9	39	23	5	3	15
韩国	Republic of Korea	5015	4328	139	548	2693	2017	113	563
塞普路斯	Cyprus	14	13	1		4	2	2	
印度	India	118	82	3	33	33	16		17
摩纳哥	Monaco	6	6			5	5		
南非	South Africa	56	52		4	37	32		5
德国	Germany	4522	3993	40	489	2977	2615	14	348
荷兰	Holland	1376	1270	7	99	868	756		112
英国	England	1314	1040	28	246	808	572	19	217
瑞士	Switzerland	1374	1193	10	171	913	762	7	144
丹麦	Denmark	315	251	13	51	217	177	3	37
匈牙利	Hungary	12	12			17	17		
奥地利	Austria	185	173	3	9	124	118	2	4
比利时	Belgium	189	173		16	125	116	1	8
法国	France	1941	1695	2	244	1180	1038		142
挪威	Norway	120	113		7	80	77	1	2
俄罗斯联邦	Russia	57	54	1	2	29	27		2
卢森堡	Luxembourg	42	42			15	15		
列支敦士登	Liechtenstein	79	53	1	25	53	26	1	26
西班牙	Spain	164	104	4	56	90	48	3	39
捷克	Czech	13	11		2	21	14	7	
波兰	Poland	6	6			10	5		5
爱尔兰	Ireland	54	29	7	18	18	14		4
芬兰	Finland	598	510		88	525	433		92
意大利	Italy	765	563	11	191	531	374	12	145
瑞典	Sweden	694	636	1	57	832	791	2	39
以色列	Israel	163	152		11	86	75	1	10
巴西	Brazil	58	46	1	11	34	20		14
美国	United States	12221	10682	310	1229	6835	5733	177	925
加拿大	Canada	407	362	14	31	197	163	3	31
新西兰	New Zealand	43	39		4	20	19		1
澳大利亚	Australia	450	394		56	211	153	5	53

21-43 按国际标准分类的发明、实用新型专利申请量和授权量

Inventions and Utility Models of Patent Applications Examined and Granted by International Classifications

单位：项 (item)

分类	Item	2002 申请量 Applications Examined	2002 授权量 Applications Granted	2003 申请量 Applications Examined	2003 授权量 Applications Granted
合计	**Total**	**181373**	**78957**	**195123**	**106060**
A 部(人类生活需要)	**Section A: Personal Use Items**	**34973**	**16165**	**41507**	**20075**
农、林、牧、渔	Agriculture, Forestry, Animal Husbandry and Fishery	4782	1989	4835	2530
烘烤、食用面团	Baking and Edible Doughs	268	146	276	145
屠宰、加工	Butchering and Meat Processing	40	35	58	24
食品、食物及处理	Foods or Foodstuffs and their Treatment	2503	844	2884	906
烟类及用品	Tobacco, Cigars and Cigarettes	393	170	499	317
服装	Clothing	886	457	1159	528
帽类制品	Headwear	194	88	222	120
鞋类	Footwear	894	472	973	578
男用服饰用品、珠宝	Haberdashery and Jewelry	306	188	295	230
手携及旅行用品	Hand or Traveling Articles	1298	724	1495	841
刷类用品	Brushware	421	186	447	304
家具、家庭日用品或设备	Furniture, Domestic Articles and Appliances	6931	3745	8125	4740
医学、兽医学、卫生学	Medical or Veterinary Science and Hygiene	13196	5418	16583	6838
救生、消防	Life-saving and Fire-fighting	539	285	920	355
体育、游戏、娱乐活动	Sports, Games, and Recreation	2322	1418	2736	1619
B 部(作业、运输)	**Section B: Industrial and Transportation**	**32915**	**17867**	**35126**	**22051**
物理或化学的方法或装置	Physical or Chemical Processes or Apparatus	2795	1664	2796	2396
破碎、研磨、粉碎	Crushing, Pulverizing, or Disintegrating	609	358	521	405
分选、分离	Separation of Solid Materials, Electrostatic Separation	244	125	242	162
离心装置、离心机	Centrifugal Apparatus or Equipment	141	103	113	93
喷射、雾化	Spraying or Atomizing General	895	515	1022	600
机械振动的产生和传递	Generation or Transmission of Mechanical Vibrations	40	16	39	18
固体分离、分选	Separating Solids from Solid Wastes	233	147	286	182
清洁	Janitorial	310	157	308	180
固体废料的处理	Disposal of Solid Waste	218	70	189	109
金属加工、冲裁	Mechanical Metal-working and Stamping	974	524	1053	673
铸造、粉末冶金	Casting and Powder Metallurgy	546	307	730	366
机床、其他金属加工	Machine Tools	1824	1082	1966	1360
磨削、抛光	Grinding and Polishing	379	240	498	268
简单工具	Hand Tools, Portable Power Tools, and Workshop Equipment	899	462	1079	590
手工、切割工具、切断	Hand Cutting Tools, Cutting, and Severing	490	320	595	376
木材加工、保存、钉钉机	Wood Preservation and Nailing or Stapling Machines	509	349	478	319
加工水泥、粘土和石料	Cement, Clay or Stone	496	264	561	332
塑料制品的加工	Plastics	1304	636	1338	828
压力机	Presses	211	159	214	138
纸品制作、纸的加工	Paper Making and Processing Paper	75	64	90	67
叠层产品	Layered Products	489	280	465	332
印刷、打字机、印刷机	Printing, Lining Machines, and Typewriters	1158	632	1363	655
装订、图册、文件夹	Bookbinding, Albums, and Files	560	266	545	269

21-43 续表 1 continued

单位：项 (item)

分 类	Item	2002 申请量 Applications Examined	2002 授权量 Applications Granted	2003 申请量 Applications Examined	2003 授权量 Applications Granted
绘图具、办公附属用品	Writing or Drafting Devices	1608	625	1497	703
装饰艺术	Decorative Arts	570	251	573	267
一般车辆	Vehicles in General	4297	2396	5216	2764
铁 路	Railways	542	238	598	335
无轨陆用车牌	Land Vehicles other than Rail	2675	1509	2823	1731
船舶、船只、有关设备	Ships and Related Equipment	472	180	511	310
飞行器、航空、宇宙航行	Aircraft and Aviation	244	110	219	118
输送、包装、存贮、搬运	Conveying and Packing Inflammatory Materials	5969	3214	6089	4246
卷扬、提升、牵引	Hoisting, Lifting, and Hauling	910	497	843	661
液体的贮运	Opening or Closing Bottles, Jars or Similar Containers	218	104	196	188
鞍具、室内装璜	Saddlery ; Upholstery	11	3	14	8
微观结构技术	Micro-structural Technology			40	2
超微观技术	Nano-Technology			16	
C 部(化学、冶金)	**Section C: Chemistry and Metallurgy**	**18992**	**5804**	**18939**	**8974**
无机化学	Inorganic Chemistry	945	292	924	368
水、废污水、泥浆的处理	Treatment of Water, Waste Water, Sewage or Sludge	2083	752	1733	953
玻璃、石棉和渣棉	Glass; Mineral of Slag Wool	439	135	480	242
水泥、陶瓷等、隔音材料	Cement, Concrete, Artificial Stone; Ceramics, Refractories	831	278	768	273
肥料及制造	Fertilizers and Related Products	339	84	348	108
炸药、火柴	Explosives and Matches	42	13	60	25
有机化学	Organic Chemistry	4164	1148	4075	1993
有机高分子化合物	Organic Macromolecular Compounds	2628	814	2565	1702
染料、涂料、抛光剂等	Dyes, Paints, Polishes, Resins, and Adhesives	1623	459	1857	586
石油、煤气及炼焦工业	Petroleum, Gas or Coke Industries, Inert Gases	1101	511	928	586
动植物油、脂类	Animal or Vegetable Oils, Fats	456	160	397	261
生化、酒、醋、酶、遗传工程	Biochemistry, Beer, Spirits, Wine, Vinegar, Microbiology, Benzymology, Mutation or Genetic Engineering	2308	373	2471	764
糖或淀粉工业	Sugar Industry	27	11	22	19
大小原皮、毛皮、皮革	Skins, Hides, Pelts, Leather	33	5	38	14
黑色冶金	Metallurgy of Iron	400	172	393	221
冶金学、合金或有色合金	Metallurgy, Ferrous or Nonferrous Alloys	617	288	697	367
金属加工涂料、防腐防锈	Coating Metallic Materials	474	105	605	216
电解电泳方法及设备	Electrolytic or Electrophoretic Processes	396	166	427	206
晶体生长	Crystal Growth	86	38	151	70
D 部(纺织、造纸)	**Section D: Textiles and Papers Making**	**7727**	**1645**	**3722**	**1893**
线、纤维、纺纱	Natural or Artificial Threads or Fibers, Spinning	4912	253	699	389
纺纱、整经或络经	Yarns, Mechanical Finishing of Yarns or Rope	98	57	153	60
织 造	Weaving	245	119	305	124
编带、花边、针织、整理	Braiding, Lace-Making, Knitting	354	210	384	209
缝纫、绣花、簇绒	Sewing, Embroidery, Tufting	286	126	309	198
织物等的处理、洗涤	Treatment of Textiles, Laundering	1348	590	1461	624
绳、除电缆外的缆绳	Ropes and Cables, other than Electric	57	13	43	29
造纸、纤维素的生产	Paper making, Production of Cellulose	427	277	368	260
E 部(固定建筑物)	**Section E: Fixed Construction**	**11488**	**6346**	**12313**	**7958**
道路、铁路和桥梁的建筑	Construction of Roads, Railways, or Bridges	1087	466	981	720
水利工程、基础、运土	Hydraulic Engineering, Foundations, Soil-shifting	848	384	958	532
给水、排水	Water Supply, Sewage	1376	888	1605	962

21-43 续表 2 continued

单位：项 (item)

分类	Item	2002		2003	
		申请量 Applications Examined	授权量 Applications Granted	申请量 Applications Examined	授权量 Applications Granted
建筑物	Building	2985	1670	3518	2216
锁、钥匙、门窗、保险箱	Locks, Keys, Windows or Door Fittings; Safes	1868	1062	1873	1172
一般门、窗、百叶窗、梯子	Doors, Windows, Shutters, or Roller Blinds in General; Ladders	1576	1016	1604	1130
钻井、采矿	Well Drilling, Mining	1748	860	1774	1226
F 部(机械工程)	**Section F: Mechanical Engineering**	**21832**	**11936**	**22908**	**14935**
一般机器、发动机、蒸汽机	Machines or Engines in General; Engine Plants in General; Steam Engines	728	463	813	487
内燃机等	Combustion Engines	1420	791	1477	880
液力机械和其他发动机	Machines or Engines for Liquids	490	181	461	184
液体变容机械、泵	Positive-displacement Machines for Liquids; Pumps for Liquid or Elastic Fluids	2089	1119	2399	1541
液压调节器、液压技术	Fluid-pressure Acuators; Hydraulic or Pneumatics in General	184	131	275	146
工程元件或部件	Engineering Elements or Units; General Measures for Producing and Maintaining Effective Functioning of Machines or Installations; Thermal Insulation in General	5434	3052	5809	3908
气体或液体的贮藏或分配	Storage or Distribution of Gases or Liquids	192	150	204	153
照　明	Lighting	1312	796	1479	1084
蒸汽的生产	Steam Generation	137	101	165	123
燃烧设备、燃烧技术	Combustion Apparatus; Combustion Processes	1510	940	1426	1002
采暖、炉灶、通风	Stoves, Ranges, Ventilation	5537	2653	5389	3421
制冷气体的液化和固化	Refrigeration or Cooling, Heat Pump Systems	1173	609	1244	861
干　燥	Drying	215	156	288	178
炉、窑、灶、罐	Furnaces, Kilns, Ovens	340	213	363	234
一般热交换	Heat Exchange in General	708	390	714	513
武　器	Weapons	189	112	209	110
弹药、爆破	Ammunition, Blasting Caps	174	79	193	110
G 部(物理)	**Section G: Physics**	**24102**	**8955**	**29981**	**14301**
测量、测试	Measurements, Testing	6087	2862	7408	4049
光学技术	Optics	2600	806	3729	1482
照相术、电影术、电刻术	Photography, Cinematography, Electrography	1129	493	1909	751
测时技术	Horology	493	144	386	254
控制、调节技术	Controlling, Regulating	624	164	654	375
计算、推算、计数技术	Computing, Calculating, Counting	7408	2315	8876	3620
核算装置	Measurement Devices	414	187	518	264
信号装置	Signaling	645	247	626	405
教育、密码、显示、广告等	Education, Cryptography, Advertising, Seals	2002	760	2375	1061
乐器、声学	Musical Instruments, Acoustics	561	191	651	386
信息的存储	Information Storage	1980	739	2555	1472
仪器的零部件	Instrument Details	91	30	223	96
核物理、核工程	Nuclear physics, Nuclear Engineering	69	17	71	86
H 部(电学)	**Section H: Electricity**	**29344**	**10239**	**30627**	**15873**
基本电器元件	Basic Electric Elements	11646	4607	12529	6658
电力的发电、变电或配电	Generation, Conversion, or Distribution of Electric Power	3751	1414	4011	2000
基本电子电路	Basic Electronic Circuitry	1103	377	1013	809
电信技术	Telecommunications Techniques	10980	3100	10985	5411
其他类不包括的电技术	Electric Techniques Not Otherwise Provided for	1864	741	2089	995

注:此表不包括外观设计分类。

a) Designs patents are excluded in this table.

21-44 国有企事业单位专业技术人员数(年底数)

Number of Scientific and Technical Personnel in State-owned Enterprises and Institutions at the Year-end

单位：人 (person)

年份 地区	Year Region	合计 Total	工程技术人员 Engineering	农业技术人员 Agriculture	科学研究人员 Scientific Research	卫生技术人员 Health Care	教学人员 Teaching
	1990	16483542	4797176	450406	335066	2657588	8243306
	1991	17168413	5024000	463050	341934	2757993	8581436
	1992	17596532	5204950	476853	337146	2827599	8749984
	1993	18124140	5363632	496279	333851	2916255	9014123
	1994	18658689	5535329	519827	321036	2995940	9286557
	1995	19133834	5625850	535731	302879	3035335	9634039
	1996	19920785	5745367	579157	303177	3130788	10162296
	1997	20495006	5719337	611458	302684	3213762	10647765
	1998	20913343	5656735	635929	290537	3254958	11075184
	1999	21430140	5654863	654138	283532	3329706	11507901
	2000	21650807	5551098	670105	274506	3371966	11783132
	2001	21698037	5316327	674644	265554	3390233	12051279
	2002	21860024	5289166	666998	262692	3402326	12238842
	2003	21739699	4992867	683437	275496	3441109	12346790
北京	Beijing	448505	198751	6555	6570	74368	162261
天津	Tianjin	227381	56307	2611	1716	50823	115924
河北	Hebei	981541	147308	25129	3198	132307	673599
山西	Shanxi	619906	124547	18596	3866	90826	382071
内蒙古	Inner Mongolia	439973	68669	22202	2029	72508	274565
辽宁	Liaoning	783087	166335	26215	6297	153782	430458
吉林	Jilin	547570	103418	27903	4456	99159	312634
黑龙江	Heilongjiang	716404	155432	30731	5694	132671	391876
上海	Shanghai	316418	79852	2372	5821	77712	150661
江苏	Jiangsu	1033231	178130	34157	6487	162217	652240
浙江	Zhejiang	657957	110674	18928	5140	130700	392515
安徽	Anhui	709608	98254	19659	2973	92539	496183
福建	Fujian	511062	68822	13859	4132	60623	363626
江西	Jiangxi	576050	79872	18307	2692	98911	376268
山东	Shandong	1506151	282997	48947	9204	250250	914753
河南	Henan	1232272	146998	30345	5434	166048	883447
湖北	Hubei	849806	121557	31939	6964	177229	512117
湖南	Hunan	912746	130482	27886	4512	160695	589171
广东	Guangdong	1090383	135621	12575	4918	202548	734721
广西	Guangxi	654862	109325	22881	2999	105308	414349
海南	Hainan	111452	10707	3389	488	20734	76134
重庆	Chongqing	355110	47596	12606	1930	52757	240221
四川	Sichuan	1001858	127949	43194	5486	155582	669647
贵州	Guizhou	492604	63652	27170	1633	71317	328832
云南	Yunnan	637172	89855	38730	3518	99475	405594
西藏	Tibet	33728	3038	1447	378	7112	21753
陕西	Shaanxi	565724	96386	23668	2648	84113	358909
甘肃	Gansu	382978	64779	19125	2090	53361	243623
青海	Qinghai	92034	12875	5808	569	16915	55867
宁夏	Ningxia	118268	22541	8572	702	19837	66616
新疆	Xinjiang	387778	57599	30813	2399	65715	231252

注：1.1991年起，本表中专业技术人员包括社会科学领域专业技术人员及小学教师，但不包括行政机关专业技术人员。

2.分地区数据中不含中央属国有企事业单位人数。

a) Since 1991, the data include the personnel in the social field and the primary teachers, but exclude the personnel in the administration.

b) The regional data exclude the personnel in the state-owned enterprises and institution under the central government.

21-45 开发区高新技术企业主要经济指标（2003年）

Main Economic Indicators of High-tech Enterprises in Development Areas (2003)

开发区	Development Area	企业数（个）Number of Enterprises (unit)	从业人员（人）Number of Employees (person)	总产值（万元）Gross Output Value (10 000 yuan)	总收入（万元）Total Income (10 000 yuan)	出口总额(万美元) Exports (10 000 US dollars)
全国	**National Total**	**32857**	**3953621**	**172574345**	**209387307**	**5101690**
北京	Beijing	12030	488561	16077549	28864155	329299
天津	Tianjin	1530	125282	4820861	5636396	148573
石家庄	Shijiazhuang	491	56645	1828157	2379593	14162
保定	Baoding	140	31167	1063238	1059828	8031
太原	Taiyuan	532	86639	2362507	2668095	4140
包头	Baotou	266	58803	1611121	1636793	23798
沈阳	Shenyang	1552	57657	2538627	5004202	85301
大连	Dalian	1085	107601	2517310	3399898	66475
鞍山	Anshan	284	62122	1305822	1541878	2206
长春	Changchun	676	113812	6237933	6253800	50703
吉林	Jilin	567	89371	4101602	4200239	5045
哈尔滨	Harbin	247	91567	2781670	3259021	19522
大庆	Daqing	218	43256	1885243	2024477	2431
上海	Shanghai	550	115009	12361533	16109807	663450
南京	Nanjing	213	76014	8082192	8814597	210137
常州	Changzhou	336	57125	1855766	1903135	37446
无锡	Wuxi	460	103413	6467452	8729673	342841
苏州	Suzhou	410	107254	7558655	7509190	473187
杭州	Hangzhou	423	48275	3558274	4782616	61300
合肥	Hefei	198	45433	2070076	2113987	14919
福州	Fuzhou	158	34343	1797267	1833140	80911
厦门	Xiamen	88	27394	3378651	3528015	245540
南昌	Nanchang	172	59018	1075408	1282649	14757
济南	Ji'nan	323	86825	3674994	3836113	19013
青岛	Qingdao	175	65498	5000923	5477145	92519
淄博	Zibo	145	66804	2556035	2775369	32107
潍坊	Weifang	202	49528	2385350	2498182	14205
威海	Weihai	153	40601	1816422	1843364	87081
郑州	Zhengzhou	342	53249	1428473	1878106	18942
洛阳	Luoyang	243	55054	1065255	1376327	8141
武汉	Wuhan	600	115512	3768194	4812906	25357
襄樊	Xiangfan	88	65474	1266825	1615436	2830
长沙	Changsha	732	89188	3521928	4039143	25474
株洲	Zhuzhou	152	50526	1414346	1508129	21404
广州	Guangzhou	918	89211	4230455	5881922	169944
深圳	Shenzhen	273	82716	8957996	8330115	521970
珠海	Zhuhai	266	65194	3865555	3808983	329515
惠州	Huizhou	85	48389	3691331	4539498	259648
中山	Zhongshan	432	97092	3264042	3252510	267015
佛山	Foshan	46	27794	2281357	2112399	91784
南宁	Nanning	273	32589	1073071	1488694	4885
桂林	Guilin	230	51603	1054309	1080108	8172
海南	Hainan	109	16655	1205726	1173138	4436
重庆	Chongqing	539	113025	5115766	5903372	12200
成都	Chengdu	372	108444	2401312	2753955	37157
绵阳	Mianyang	89	45907	2051776	1920663	69618
贵阳	Guiyang	93	46317	1014996	955867	7990
昆明	Kunming	157	31516	982142	1318985	18214
西安	Xi'an	2537	167390	4021402	6264743	33363
宝鸡	Baoji	121	47938	804711	789502	3374
杨凌	Yangling	70	8838	179362	239388	5757
兰州	Lanzhou	366	38711	893083	1022695	2319
乌鲁木齐	Urumqi	100	10272	250298	355373	3086

21-46 各地区技术市场成交额

Transaction Value in Technical Market by Region

单位：万元 (10 000 yuan)

地区	Region	1997	1998	1999	2000	2001	2002	2003
全国	**National Total**	**3513718**	**4358228**	**5234123**	**6507519**	**7827489**	**8841713**	**10846728**
北京	Beijing	543192	815591	921889	1402871	1910065	2211738	2653574
天津	Tianjin	150074	200298	220296	262581	306009	363262	420008
河北	Hebei	115256	139090	153795	94143	46784	60406	67969
山西	Shanxi	10284	9758	3955	5258	14693	39014	32251
内蒙古	Inner Mongolia	28958	31332	29348	60287	62359	58197	108452
辽宁	Liaoning	250372	280977	301546	347817	408698	508326	620200
吉林	Jilin	85793	93167	103498	71390	88543	82921	87292
黑龙江	Heilongjiang	145752	152569	157121	152382	111035	120110	121165
上海	Shanghai	287568	314060	366324	738952	1061603	1202170	1427790
江苏	Jiangsu	284473	330684	416683	449568	529165	594873	765163
浙江	Zhejiang	133232	162275	188496	276275	316652	389438	530353
安徽	Anhui	29585	39545	48544	61012	64145	75423	87960
福建	Fujian	57454	69363	80868	172601	136941	128988	166779
江西	Jiangxi	31058	38332	51444	69299	62724	62891	83323
山东	Shandong	241583	261922	275121	288135	321938	347650	525682
河南	Henan	157766	176492	201661	211621	212589	178506	192690
湖北	Hubei	145733	187596	230161	276000	338597	348603	412538
湖南	Hunan	161392	220189	246605	286833	293887	323422	369306
广东	Guangdong	195993	248122	344528	482104	539722	684532	805730
广西	Guangxi	17293	37021	25344	17741	37753	44406	41808
海南	Hainan	35645	41533	82407		83990	9134	11978
重庆	Chongqing	60628	92951	325345	296594	289484	409433	555083
四川	Sichuan	158004	152000	125931	104150	126311	77524	128686
贵州	Guizhou	1150	14071	762	620	599	13484	17892
云南	Yunnan	54515	127222	172339	187742	255279	179496	228718
西藏	Tibet							
陕西	Shaanxi	71782	57765	82537	92560	84615	151554	168022
甘肃	Gansu	26427	28137	25816	26413	27393	54644	77581
青海	Qinghai	12035	2917	4283		4657	12373	8291
宁夏	Ningxia	2351	2643	4654	6402	8872	8496	10047
新疆	Xinjiang	18370	30606	42822	66168	82387	100699	120395

21-47 各地区测绘部门生产完成情况（2003年）

Statistics on Projects Completed by Surveying and Mapping Departments by Region (2003)

地区	Region	大地测量 Geodesy		测图合计	地图数字化	地图编制 Drawing Map		
		GPS测量（点）Global Positioning System Survey (point)	水准测量（公里）Leveling (kilometer)	（幅）Mapping (unit)	（幅）Digital Map (unit)	地形图（幅）Topographic Map (unit)	专题地图（幅）Special Map (unit)	地图集（册）Atlas (Volume)
全 国	**National Total**	**32363**	**58681**	**228913**	**59137**	**2731**	**2443**	**105**
北 京	Beijing	2582	512	10633	1833		52	1
天 津	Tianjin	841	2572	6883	731	87	2	
河 北	Hebei	157	1320	9865	541		44	4
山 西	Shanxi	1352	3252	5630	1228		58	2
内蒙古	Inner Mongolia	974	839	4910	1246	115	64	1
辽 宁	Liaoning	6670	2484	23851	1827		11	
吉 林	Jilin	193	3112	6045	809		10	1
黑龙江	Heilongjiang	2463	4279	28651	714	803	139	11
上 海	Shanghai			6894			1	
江 苏	Jiangsu	1293	5432	7056	1145	12	28	1
浙 江	Zhejiang	5042	5419	7584	871			
安 徽	Anhui	360	140	5615	2920	27	297	1
福 建	Fujian	273	2600	3843	1687			
江 西	Jiangxi	189	100	3072	1887		23	1
山 东	Shandong	1249	1216	7407	1065	497	57	5
河 南	Henan	575	3213	6429	1922		126	2
湖 北	Hubei	669	1055	3138	2374	126	110	6
湖 南	Hunan	206	1690	8297	3395	263	229	
广 东	Guangdong	1309	3646	5397	6465	22	134	27
广 西	Guangxi	348	189	4871	3082	94	148	
海 南	Hainan	180	1000	1572	713		19	
重 庆	Chongqing	87	50	620	5045	60	12	2
四 川	Sichuan	701	2781	18400	9111	587	196	15
贵 州	Guizhou	380		1025	243		1	1
云 南	Yunnan	46	1109	4529				1
西 藏	Tibet						89	
陕 西	Shaanxi	1219	4144	22878	6809		75	8
甘 肃	Gansu			1993	166		98	1
青 海	Qinghai	2321	1425	1042	146		73	
宁 夏	Ningxia	204	1120	2356	316			1
新 疆	Xinjiang	480	3982	4491	689	38	59	1
国家基础地理信息中心	National Geomatics Center of China							
中国测绘科学研究院	China Academy of Surveying and Mapping Science			3956	157		138	
中国地图出版社	China Atlas Publishing House						150	12

21-48 各地区测绘资料提供情况（2003年）

Statistics on Output of Surveying and Mapping Materials by Region (2003)

地区	Region	地形图合计（张）Topographic Map (unit)	1:10000 (scale)	1:50000 (scale)	大地成果（点）Geodetic Results (point)	航摄成果（片）Aerial Photograph (piece)	挂图（张）Wall Map (unit)	地图集（册）Atlas (volume)
全　国	**National Total**	**693979**	**195642**	**124309**	**147658**	**446685**	**9621**	**5240**
北　京	Beijing	45278	4762	405	16057		483	645
天　津	Tianjin	13665	1980	178	217	68		
河　北	Hebei	9924	6380	2615	2112	90	44	36
山　西	Shanxi	13722	10400	3019	920	3036		
内蒙古	Inner Mongolia	13602	2111	9043	1724			
辽　宁	Liaoning	5086	4306	778	372		2703	1948
吉　林	Jilin	15914	11428	3110	4490	3468	693	17
黑龙江	Heilongjiang	16012	6626	8071	685	105687	262	23
上　海	Shanghai	251936	1786	144	20808	10080		
江　苏	Jiangsu	9464	6746	1961	2093	1058		426
浙　江	Zhejiang	17395	14917	1631	3562	934		
安　徽	Anhui	12322	7644	3914	3886	4771		
福　建	Fujian	9187	6236	1887	2500	1750		
江　西	Jiangxi	10457	8656	1392	47372	8411		
山　东	Shandong	12878	9015	3155		675	126	162
河　南	Henan	3848	1569	1938	705	4588		
湖　北	Hubei	1925	1321	358	555	152		
湖　南	Hunan	16689	12693	3595	622	402		
广　东	Guangdong	14331	12118	1945	3172			
广　西	Guangxi	27254	24394	1307	19911	2842	1646	2
海　南	Hainan	988	642	123	263	5142		
重　庆	Chongqing	17427	783	292	58	3311	7	
四　川	Sichuan	20356	9209	7307	3032	9221	234	452
贵　州	Guizhou	12449	8423	3725	452	34872	392	73
云　南	Yunnan	16918	6076	6552	5850	5597	975	
西　藏	Tibet	14121	143	353	165		597	506
陕　西	Shaanxi	12440	8209	3386	501	73301	46	
甘　肃	Gansu	10765	2138	7175	608	310		
青　海	Qinghai	5695	1096	3332	619		856	950
宁　夏	Ningxia	3924	2549	1089	554		31	
新　疆	Xinjiang	8719	1286	3836	1302	24001	526	
国家基础地理信息中心	National Geomatics Center of China	49288		36693	2491	142918		

21-49 各地区气象台站数和卫星云图接收、使用情况（2003年）

Meteorological Observatories, Stations and The Reception and Use of Satellite Cloud Images by Region (2003)

地区和单位	Region, City and Units	气象台站总数（个） Number of Meteorological Observatories and Station (unit)	#气象台 Meteorological Observatories	#气象站 Meteorological Stations	#大气本底特种观测站 Atmosphere Background Special Observation Station	卫星云图接收站点数（个） Number of Satellite Cloud Images Receiving Station (unit)
全　国	**National Total**	**2632**	**366**	**2481**	**4**	**413**
北　京	Beijing	25	1	22	1	3
天　津	Tianjin	13	2	14		3
河　北	Hebei	147	12	146		14
山　西	Shanxi	117	12	109		7
内蒙古	Inner Mongolia	124	15	124		24
辽　宁	Liaoning	60	14	56		18
吉　林	Jilin	58	9	56		6
黑龙江	Heilongjiang	83	13	86	1	3
上　海	Shanghai	11	1	11		13
江　苏	Jiangsu	81	13	75		49
浙　江	Zhejiang	68	11	63	1	25
安　徽	Anhui	81	18	84		3
福　建	Fujian	77	9	71		24
江　西	Jiangxi	91	12	90		5
山　东	Shandong	119	17	117		23
河　南	Henan	135	18	121		16
湖　北	Hubei	87	14	82		13
湖　南	Hunan	118	15	101		10
广　东	Guangdong	101	21	88		44
广　西	Guangxi	90	15	97		3
海　南	Hainan	22	2	22		2
重　庆	Chongqing	48	4	35		4
四　川	Sichuan	172	22	159		6
贵　州	Guizhou	90	10	85		9
云　南	Yunnan	135	17	130		4
西　藏	Tibet	40	8	40		4
陕　西	Shaanxi	109	11	98		13
甘　肃	Gansu	86	13	84		18
青　海	Qinghai	57	9	56	1	10
宁　夏	Ningxia	24	5	27		3
新　疆	Xinjiang	130	16	106		17
大连市	Dalian	8	3	8		1
宁波市	Ningbo	11	1	8		8
青岛市	Qingdao	8	1	7		4
厦门市	Xiamen	2	1	2		1
国家气象中心	National Mete-Center	1	1			
国家卫星气象中心	National Satellite Meteorological Center	1				3
气象科学研究院	Chinese Academy of Meteorological Science	2		1		

注：气象部门台站总数中已剔除台、站合一的283个站。

a) As many as 283 observatory-station combined units have been excluded from the total number of the observatories and stations in the meteorologica department.

21-50 各地区农业气象业务站点数（2003年）

Agro-Meteorological Observation Stations by Region (2003)

单位：个 (unit)

地区和单位	Region, City and Unit	农业气象观测站点数 Agro-Meteorological Observation Stations	农业气象试验站点 Agro-Meteorological Stations	农业气象情报预报站点 Agro-Meteorological Information Services Stations
全 国	**National Total**	**780**	**66**	**1396**
北 京	Beijing	7		7
天 津	Tianjin	7		1
河 北	Hebei	133		143
山 西	Shanxi	31		33
内蒙古	Inner Mongolia	24	6	57
辽 宁	Liaoning	23	3	52
吉 林	Jilin	22	3	46
黑龙江	Heilongjiang	33	2	37
上 海	Shanghai	1		1
江 苏	Jiangsu	19	3	49
浙 江	Zhejiang	11	1	61
安 徽	Anhui	22	3	22
福 建	Fujian	23	4	28
江 西	Jiangxi	18	1	36
山 东	Shandong	57	1	117
河 南	Henan	30	3	120
湖 北	Hubei	28	2	24
湖 南	Hunan	19	4	36
广 东	Guangdong	25	2	25
广 西	Guangxi	24	5	86
海 南	Hainan	6		7
重庆市	Chongqing	13		36
四 川	Sichuan	45	2	68
贵 州	Guizhou	18	1	86
云 南	Yunnan	21	4	35
西 藏	Tibet	4	1	4
陕 西	Shaanxi	18	1	28
甘 肃	Gansu	22	4	56
青 海	Qinghai	17	2	24
宁 夏	Ningxia	16	3	17
新 疆	Xinjiang	36	4	36
大连市	Dalian	2		6
宁波市	Ningbo	2		7
青岛市	Qingdao	3		5
气象科学研究院	Chinese Academy of Meteorological Science		1	

21-51 各地区地震监测情况(2003年)

Situation of Earthquake Monitoring (2003)

单位: 个 (unit)

地 区	Region	地震台数						强震观测点	骨干测报点	一般测报点
		总 数 Total Number of Earthquake Stations	基准台 Fiducial Stations	基本台 Basic Stations	省级台 Provincial Stations	市、县级台 City and County Stations	企业台 Enterprises Managing Stations	Number of Observation for Spot Strong Earthquake	Number of Main Observation Spots	Number of Normal Observation Spots
全 国	**National Total**	**1098**	**39**	**267**	**230**	**458**	**104**	**307**	**1803**	**5746**
北 京	Beijing	11	1	6	4			1	52	60
天 津	Tianjin	9	1	3	5					
河 北	Hebei	86	1	27	7	34	17	7	248	1084
山 西	Shanxi	94	1	4	9	45	35	10	77	258
内蒙古	Inner Mongolia	61	2	6	13	37	3		40	202
辽 宁	Liaoning	49	2	5	11	26	5	1	100	209
吉 林	Jilin	28	3	3	4	18			25	334
黑龙江	Heilongjiang	86	1	75	5	4	1	142		
上 海	Shanghai	23	1	1	13	8		14	8	9
江 苏	Jiangsu	83	1	7	10	59	6	8	80	138
浙 江	Zhejiang	6	1	3	2				10	24
安 徽	Anhui	29		3	9	12	5		67	168
福 建	Fujian	14	1	3	10			10	60	61
江 西	Jiangxi	10	1	2	1	6			13	8
山 东	Shandong	36	1	5	20	6	4	1	120	973
河 南	Henan	28	1	1	10	11	5	2	109	671
湖 北	Hubei	22	1	4	4	13		3	38	32
湖 南	Hunan	28	1	2	4	18	3		17	44
广 东	Guangdong	45	2	21	1	20	1	6	53	105
广 西	Guangxi	8		1	7				48	210
海 南	Hainan	15	1	2		12		3	12	8
重 庆	Chongqing	1		1				8	5	1
四 川	Sichuan	37	1	16	20				70	171
贵 州	Guizhou	1					1			
云 南	Yunnan	79	2	11	30	36		25	92	54
西 藏	Tibet	8	2	2	4					
陕 西	Shaanxi	40	1	5	8	21	5		100	127
甘 肃	Gansu	89	2	30	10	40	7	24	315	642
青 海	Qinghai	12	1	6		2	3	4	5	2
宁 夏	Ningxia	16	1	3	3	8	1	3	21	96
新 疆	Xinjiang	44	5	9	6	22	2	35	18	55

21-52 国家监督抽查产品质量情况

Results of Sampling Check on Product Quality under State Supervision

年 份 Year	抽查企业 (个) Number of Enterprises Selected	无不合格品企业数(个) Number of Enterprises without Products Unqualified	抽查产品 Products Selected in Sampling		合格产品 (种) Number of Products Qualified (kind)	样品合格率 (%) Rate of Sample Products Qualified (%)
			(类) Number of Types (type))	(种) Number of Kinds (kind)		
1988	2983		181	4031	3072	76.2
1989	3948	2795	180	5437	4092	75.3
1990	2495	1838	131	3457	2657	76.9
1991	2845	2186	138	3902	3122	90.0
1992	6845	4477	231	9007	6312	70.1
1993	8110	5509	281	9915	6980	70.4
1994	4640	3090	164	6036	4216	69.8
1995	5288	3851	185	6713	5061	75.4
1996	6779	5052	217	8318	6420	77.2
1997	5441	4116	187	6590	5162	78.3
1998	5431	4056	176	6770	5269	77.8
1999	7131	5440	207	8345	6562	78.6
2000	8142	6254	235	9705	7655	78.9
2001	8076	5992	207	9906	7513	75.8
2002	7892	6033	222	8850	6942	78.4
2003	10134	7809	249	11152	8738	78.4

21-53 各地区产品质量情况（2003年）

Quality of Products by Region (2003)

单位：% (%)

地 区	Region	产品质量等级品率 Rates of Grade Products			新产品产值率 Rate of New Products	质量损失率 Rate of Loss Due to Bad Quality
		优等品率 Rate of Products with Excellent Quality	一等品率 Rate of Products with First Grade Quality	合格品率 Rate of Products with Qualified Quality		
全 国	**National Total**	**31.49**	**49.39**	**19.12**	**29.77**	**0.46**
北 京	Beijing					
天 津	Tianjin	34.94	53.76	11.31	48.06	0.45
河 北	Hebei	38.40	38.79	22.81	15.39	0.35
山 西	Shanxi	29.52	32.75	37.72	6.98	0.80
内蒙古	Inner Mongolia					
辽 宁	Liaoning					
吉 林	Jilin	35.05	48.48	16.47	14.18	0.15
黑龙江	Heilongjiang	13.59	70.31	16.10	62.29	0.53
上 海	Shanghai	15.30	73.01	11.69	49.95	0.38
江 苏	Jiangsu					
浙 江	Zhejiang	39.13	44.65	16.22	19.63	0.05
安 徽	Anhui	27.21	33.53	39.26	17.65	0.63
福 建	Fujian	50.38	28.93	20.69	6.29	0.56
江 西	Jiangxi	57.74	28.44	13.82	20.16	0.56
山 东	Shandong	37.65	40.95	21.40	34.56	0.67
河 南	Henan	24.65	53.50	21.85	44.76	0.51
湖 北	Hubei	40.02	44.59	15.48	7.60	0.15
湖 南	Hunan	47.58	31.99	20.44	28.96	0.86
广 东	Guangdong	4.58	89.55	5.86	69.79	0.26
广 西	Guangxi					
海 南	Hainan	8.92	70.81	20.27	26.37	0.14
重 庆	Chongqing	23.72	61.89	14.39	43.01	0.53
四 川	Sichuan	53.10	37.12	9.78	31.72	0.41
贵 州	Guizhou	36.72	28.96	34.32	11.49	0.79
云 南	Yunnan	57.63	13.08	29.29	17.82	0.12
西 藏	Tibet					
陕 西	Shaanxi	18.55	40.98	40.47	16.93	1.10
甘 肃	Gansu	66.29	15.26	18.45	13.94	0.08
青 海	Qinghai					
宁 夏	Ningxia					
新 疆	Xinjiang					

注：本资料由73个重点工业城市抽样数据汇总而成。

a) Sampling data in this table are collected from 73 main industrial cities.

21-54 产品、商品质量监督检查情况(2003年)

Results of Sampling Check on The Quality of Products and Commodities under State Supervision (2003)

项目	Item	产品质量 Product Quality			商品质量 Commodity Quality	
		监督检验企业数(个) Number of Enterprises Supervised & Checked (unit)	有不合格产品企业所占比例(%) Proportion of Enterprises with Products Unqualified	批次合格率(%) Rate of Batch-time Qualified (%)	检查商业企业数(个) Number of Commercial Enterprises Checked (unit)	批次合格率(%) Rate of Batch-time Qualified (%)
全国总计	**Total**	**319492**	**17.11**	**86.07**	**244734**	**76.76**
农用产品	**Agricultural Products**	**14559**	**17.23**	**84.44**	**37994**	**77.39**
拖拉机	Tractors	357	12.61	87.32	495	88.41
农用化肥	Chemical Fertilizers	7729	16.43	84.14	22599	71.89
化学农药	Chemical Pesticides	1123	9.35	87.53	7419	90.15
饲料	Forages	4380	20.66	84.56	4387	70.61
农用薄膜	Agricultural Films	635	21.73	76.24	2053	73.41
种子	Seeds	335	13.43	82.60	1041	81.24
加工食品和饮料	**Food and Beverage**	**77813**	**17.69**	**82.59**	**58074**	**82.09**
食用植物油	Edible Vegetable Oil	9542	14.93	85.34	6887	87.46
糕点糖果	Cake	28711	17.83	80.91	12515	78.01
乳制品	Dairy Products	2099	21.68	81.97	3296	77.47
罐头	Canned Food	1081	25.25	77.61	3379	80.01
白酒	White Spirit	31543	16.91	84.25	23089	83.39
啤酒	Beer	1150	7.57	93.96	6100	85.72
冷冻饮料	Frozen Beverage	3687	29.16	74.39	2808	84.45
家用电器	**Household Electric Appliances**	**2503**	**14.38**	**82.80**	**8982**	**80.06**
收录机、音响设备	Radio and Cassette Players, Hi-fi Stereo Component Systems	103	4.85	93.55	667	83.54
电视机、录像机	TV Sets, Videocorders	24	12.50	96.14	789	94.50
洗衣机	Washing Machines	112	9.82	89.19	661	97.92
电风扇	Electric Fans	485	29.90	71.63	1771	62.88
电话机	Telephone Sets	131	6.11	86.00	957	75.81
冰箱、冷藏冷冻箱	Refrigerators, Freezers	10		100.00	321	97.71
电热器具	Electric Heating Appliances	1219	12.14	82.24	1641	67.36
厨房电器具	Elec'ric Cooking Utensils	318	5.66	92.18	1807	88.52
抽油烟机	Smoke Absorbers	101	21.78	78.12	368	75.90
轻工产品	**Light Industry Products**	**19280**	**18.70**	**82.23**	**17477**	**60.58**
纸	Paper	2243	20.95	72.41	1519	64.81
纸制品	Paper Products	5154	20.24	81.91	3022	68.95
玩具	Toys	459	18.95	81.38	1272	72.68

21-54 续表 continued

项 目	Item	产品质量 Product Quality 监督检验企业数(个) Number of Enterprises Supervised & Checked	有不合格产品企业所占比例(%) Proportion of Enterprises with Products Unqualified	批次合格率(%) Rate of Batch-time Qualified (%)	商品质量 Commodity Quality 检查商业企业数(个) Number of Commercial Enterprise Checked	批次合格率(%) Rate of Batch-time Qualified (%)
家具	Furniture	7177	21.11	78.53	3029	66.21
铝制品压力锅	Aluminum Products	306	19.28	92.25	402	66.15
眼镜(架、片)	Spectacles (Glass & Frame)	3147	11.76	90.34	4972	81.84
灯泡灯管	Electric Bulbs & Fluorescence Tubes	537	10.99	89.10	2761	62.03
镇流器	Ballast	45	2.22	94.74	329	52.74
电热、燃气热水器	Water Heaters	212	0.94	97.26	171	84.25
纺织、鞋类产品	**Textile and Shoes**	**10430**	**12.29**	**88.27**	**7882**	**75.88**
布(印染、色织、坯布)	Cloth	991	6.16	93.47	495	79.14
毛织品	Wool Fabrics	214	4.21	94.44	1242	74.96
丝麻织品	Silk & Fabrics	616	7.31	93.10	409	84.09
针织品	Knit Goods	1112	17.27	84.42	2112	75.31
鞋	Shoes	7497	13.01	87.48	3624	75.39
化工产品	**Chemical Products**	**4424**	**12.05**	**89.34**	**3958**	**159.81**
涂料、油漆	Paint	3648	13.57	89.90	3698	83.84
化学试剂	Chemical Reagent	776	4.90	86.80	260	75.97
建材产品	**Building Raw Materials**	**66515**	**10.37**	**92.97**	**15256**	**82.18**
水泥	Cement	9108	6.61	94.25	3414	82.04
水泥预制构件	Cement Prefabricated Components	21554	6.31	92.87	4317	85.46
砖瓦	Bricks & Tiles	32847	12.68	94.93	3498	76.95
油毡油纸	Asphalt Felts & Oilpaper	751	41.41	50.00	1806	87.97
平板玻璃	Plate Glass	40	12.50	84.61	166	75.64
水暖管件	Waterpipe	2215	20.72	83.45	2055	78.39
机械、电器产品	**Mechanical and Electrical Products**	**5700**	**10.75**	**66.98**	**16300**	**62.03**
轴承	Bearings	214	7.01	90.00	981	77.60
阀门、泵	Valves	1440	5.35	92.43	1863	77.65
电线	Electric Wire	2044	15.46	87.61	6912	56.05
低压电器元件	Low-voltage Electric Elements	1134	6.88	94.66	3633	76.40
电动工具	Electric Tools	332	14.76	85.33	2218	76.56
消防器材	Fire-fighting Equipment & Materials	291	23.37	83.08	222	84.04
电动机柴油机	Motors & Diesel Engines	245	4.08	96.63	471	71.23
冶金产品及金属制品	**Metallurgical and Metal Products**	**3213**	**27.42**	**78.92**	**11409**	**78.37**
线材	Wire Rod	2250	30.09	78.62	5877	79.03
型材	Section Steel	963	21.18	79.73	5532	77.74
其他产品	**Others**	**119479**	**20.70**	**84.53**	**71360**	**80.23**

21-55 各地区出入境货物检验检疫情况（2003年）

货值单位：万美元

机构名称	Institute	总计 Total 批次 Number of Batch	#不合格 Disqualification	货值 Value	#不合格 Disqualification	商品检验 Commodity 批次 Number of Batch	#不合格 Disqualification	货值 Value	#不合格 Disqualification
总　计	**National Total**	**11021963**	**69383**	**43584787**	**857650**	**9827977**	**57939**	**39658956**	**388967**
北　京	Beijing	118660	466	644877	2488	102742	385	608328	2412
天　津	Tianjin	276820	766	2067566	25078	239472	208	1857551	572
河　北	Hebei	84594	376	595352	30767	63209	308	483155	17771
山　西	Shanxi	16015	71	91127	155	13834	63	85190	134
内蒙古	Inner Mongolia	126564	1492	230153	279	101926	1461	204772	260
辽　宁	Liaoning	271818	637	1769773	13381	196555	365	1402366	1925
吉　林	Jilin	63677	369	386546	1536	29686	263	272169	1142
黑龙江	Heilongjiang	100699	7051	163733	922	74913	7048	117859	920
上　海	Shanghai	900974	27534	5059733	165395	849553	25539	4861565	139948
江　苏	Jiangsu	798619	2661	4249863	146964	756818	2455	3933917	54957
浙　江	Zhejiang	640797	2383	1990237	12294	594460	2146	1827409	9586
宁　波	Ningbo	262311	774	1503434	40559	246093	545	1419362	8153
安　徽	Anhui	59476	95	208744	813	48359	87	177984	792
福　建	Fujian	435181	1416	1305204	12982	372300	692	1131211	3355
厦　门	Xiamen	187999	1951	733851	11223	169668	1879	687384	7796
江　西	Jiangxi	25686	421	130954	975	21347	387	117001	895
山　东	Shandong	605522	3459	3034348	167496	385688	2518	2192199	59856
河　南	Henan	41646	214	264958	1566	32455	200	213625	1497
湖　北	Hubei	33752	451	241225	1866	27453	405	212813	1554
湖　南	Hunan	56900	418	217829	2041	46435	404	198252	2025
广　东	Guangdong	3887849	7191	9752806	94892	3714039	4410	9275100	35188
深　圳	Guangdong	1249797	2514	5855549	73242	1081187	1766	5570069	18440
珠　海	Guangdong	381607	303	1411108	1409	352744	245	1388052	1023
广　西	Guangxi	78656	733	279475	34499	50539	454	197294	7075
海　南	Hainan	15348	188	111259	2178	11955	100	95306	1867
重　庆	Chongqing	28836	34	143834	56	24385	31	132605	55
四　川	Sichuan	51655	168	317883	388	44391	148	287011	374
贵　州	Guizhou	7834	64	64196	278	7053	48	58871	220
云　南	Yunnan	71198	2345	179844	5109	42345	664	127982	2549
西　藏	Tibet	1781		5969		1098		4661	
陕　西	Shaanxi	20200	106	124334	900	16564	103	108283	900
甘　肃	Gansu	6945	87	77644	588	4236	72	70133	546
青　海	Qinghai	2520	58	23043	214	2392	57	22346	213
宁　夏	Ningxia	4472	39	42247	501	3790	36	40828	495
新　疆	Xinjiang	105555	2548	306089	4617	98293	2447	276307	4473

注：国家出入境货物检验检疫数据是由全国直属的35个检验检疫局直报国家质检总局汇总得到。

General Statistics on Entry-Exit Inspection and Quarantine of Freight by Region

(10 000 US$)

动物及动物产品检疫 Animal and Its Product				植物及植物产品检疫 Plant and Its Product				食 品 Food			
批次 Number of Batch	#不合格 Disqualification	货值 Value	#不合格 Disqualification	批次 Number of Batch	#不合格 Disqualification	货值 Value	#不合格 Disqualification	批次 Number of Batch	#不合格 Disqualification	货值 Value	#不合格 Disqualification
613811	**6413**	**1947663**	**95320**	**1729514**	**23200**	**4198347**	**501794**	**1034267**	**9373**	**3590340**	**449564**
8742	30	31639	59	10002	40	15828	29	14342	52	33168	42
12960	107	81815	1467	84041	437	292719	23053	34648	442	183707	23647
10615	82	52345	455	14745	63	87445	12985	18667	64	94890	12980
2393	1	20783	13	2260	3	8433	2	2126	8	5867	21
3333		15765		95855	716	100808	42	23534	31	22621	20
26808	41	98841	211	83414	336	324852	12363	65624	255	346255	11415
1966	5	4211	15	36242	8	112344	2	33298	106	111545	394
1280		3816		73860	6111	82754	248	25363	3	43680	2
33458	2450	181396	20545	96420	6568	305091	37972	52217	1754	171024	23462
30859	84	139304	754	63431	528	518075	110255	37555	196	291196	91844
32242	148	136589	2158	79318	172	148768	1905	41092	235	141578	2715
4489	89	32990	1381	33798	207	123119	32582	15849	220	82008	32253
1655	19	7301	576	12277	22	30943	21	10229	8	27699	21
18456	381	85874	5038	81713	320	146072	4849	61834	417	158591	5073
6315	6	20895	22	20218	93	51755	3510	14275	70	41505	3426
1989	9	5626	37	4451	31	12028	62	2975	29	12311	77
68295	968	403361	48197	185365	994	619589	111304	214647	871	821189	107026
5103	49	19782	1036	5945	11	34535	86	6876	14	44340	69
3085	75	12431	640	4409	94	17730	160	4572	45	24252	309
3922	3	6737	1	7229	28	13466	115	6418	9	13255	11
145545	624	317228	9445	354870	3723	484794	62139	142730	1859	428094	52598
124078	88	162238	202	261659	836	412210	56280	104972	663	254584	52132
23137	17	13932	17	26620	58	21853	1061	24558	50	21495	371
5182	19	11527	499	32896	251	89040	26929	25170	263	74701	26925
1626	11	6757	49	3207	81	10343	346	3146	84	14786	310
7800	3	13854		2616	2	4883	1	3692	3	6213	1
17210	1	35654	1	5636	12	12836	11	6429	20	25491	14
126		93		679	12	5224	55	389	6	2289	5
5691	812	5355	1561	29998	1325	56456	3242	24420	1489	41450	2222
216		402		644		1268		509		981	
1421		2803		3533	3	15365		3038	3	14502	
123	1	1049	12	2524	15	6614	42	2624	15	7020	42
51	1	572	1	80		80		108	1	532	1
232		2072		693	3	2337	7	638	3	1300	7
3408	289	12631	928	8866	97	28688	134	5703	85	26224	128

a) National data of entry-exit inspection and quarantine of freight are collected from the 35 inspection and quarantine bureaus directly under the national general bureau directly reported.

21-56 中国科协系统科技活动情况（2003年）

项　　目	Item	总计 Total
机构和人员	**Number of Associations or Academic Societies and Personnel**	
机构数　（个）	Number of Associations or Academic Societies (unit)	6988
从业人员　（人）	Number of Employed Persons (person)	48527
学会个人会员　（万人）	Number of Personal Members of Academic Societies (10 000 person)	
学术交流活动	**Academic Exchange**	
境内举办学术交流活动　（次）	Number of Academic Meetings Held in China (time)	23862
参加人数　（万人次）	Number of Participants (10 000 person-time)	323.1
科学技术普及（经常性科普活动）	**S&T Popularization Activities (Frequent Popularization Activities)**	
举办科普讲座　（次）	Number of S&T Popularization Lectures (time)	101903
听讲人数　（万人次）	Number of Participants (10 000 person-time)	2482.9
举办科普展览　（次）	Number of S&T Popularization Exhibitions (time)	29130
参观人数　（万人次）	Number of Participants (10 000 person-time)	6070.1
举办科普宣传　（次）	Number of S&T Popularization Propagation (time)	51094
组织工作人员　（万人次）	Working Staffs (10 000 person-time)	79.8
举办青少年科技竞赛　（次）	Number of S&T Competitions for Adolescent (time)	5735
参加人数　（万人次）	Number of Participants (10 000 person-time)	2950.5
举办青少年科技夏冬令营　（次）	Number of Summer-Winter Camps on S&T Competitions for Adolescent (time)	1804
参加人数　（万人次）	Number of Participants (10 000 person-time)	150.3
科学技术普及（科技周活动）	**S&T Popularization Activities (National S&T Week Activities)**	
举办科普讲座　（次）	Number of S&T Popularization Lectures (time)	15725
听讲人数　（万人次）	Number of Participants (10 000 person-time)	634.0
举办科普展览　（次）	Number of S&T Popularization Exhibitions (time)	12563
参观人数　（万人次）	Number of Participants (10 000 person-time)	2502.2
举办科普宣传　（次）	Number of S&T Popularization Propagation Events (time)	17268
组织工作人员　（万人次）	Working Staffs (10 000 person-time)	68.9
科学技术普及（科技下乡活动）	**S&T Popularization Activities (Popularization Activities Conducted in Rural Section)**	
组织科技下乡次数　（次）	Number of S&T Popularization Programs Conducted in Rural Section (time)	47396
举办科普讲座　（次）	Number of S&T Popularization Lectures (time)	45345
听讲人数　（万人次）	Number of Participants (10 000 person-time)	1262.0
举办科普展览　（次）	Number of S&T Popularization Exhibitions (time)	19903
参观人数　（万人次）	Number of Participants (10 000 person-time)	3474.2
举办科普咨询　（次）	Number of S&T Popularization Consultion (time)	91223
组织工作人员　（万人次）	Working Staffs (10 000 person-time)	57.6
对外交流活动	**International S&T Exchange**	
接待国外及港澳台地区来访科技团组　（个）	Visits from Foreign Countries, Hong Kong, Macao and Taiwan (unit)	2418
接待总人数　（人次）	Total Number of Visitors (person-time)	19096
派往国外及港澳台地区科技团组　（个）	Visits to Foreign Countries, Hong Kong, Macao and Taiwan (unit)	1683
派出总人数　（人次）	Total Number of Visitors (person-time)	12921
社会、科技服务活动	**Public Service on S&T**	
“金桥工程”本年完成数　（项）	Number of Completed "Golden Bridge Program" Projects (item)	9509
完成技术咨询合　（项）	Number of Consultative Contracts Completed (item)	56686
反映科技建议　（项）	Number of S&T Proposals (time)	32455
举办培训班　（个）	Number of Training Courses (unit)	77777
培训人数　（万人次）	Number of Persons Trained in Training Courses (10 000 person-time)	1343.0
科技传媒情况	**S&T Media**	
主办科技期刊　（种）	Number of Scientific & Technological Journals (kind)	2145
发行量　（万册）	Number of Copies Distributed (10 000 copies)	10500.1
主办科技报纸　（种）	Number of Scientific & Technological Newspapers (kind)	102
发行量　（万册）	Number of Copies Distributed (10 000 copies)	25961.2
编著科技图书　（种）	Number of Scientific & Technological books (kind)	1957
发行量　（万册）	Number of Copies Distributed (10 000 copies)	1341.8

注：1.经常性科普活动的数据不含科技周和科技下乡活动数据。
　　2.科协科技周活动数据含所属学会数据。

Basic Statistics on Scientific and Technological Activities of China Associations for Science and Technology (2003)

科协小计					学会小计		
Total Number of Associations	中国科协 China Associations	省级科协 Provincial Associations	地级科协 Prefectural Associations	县级科协 County Associations	Total Number of Learned Societies	全国性学会 National Learned Societies	省学会 Provincial Learned Societies
3207	1	31	396	2779	3781	167	3614
34015	1391	6372	9297	16955	14512	1958	12554
						387	400
13307	38	291	4847	8131	10555	2316	8239
213.7	1.2	8.1	64.7	139.8	109.4	29.1	80.2
86198	132	791	14718	70557	15705	1166	14539
2200.1	7.8	28.4	296.7	1867.2	282.8	31.6	251.2
25962	61	575	5031	20295	3168	197	2971
5500.4	152.0	302.8	1085.5	3960.1	569.7	55.4	514.4
46304	42	766	8344	37152	4790	635	4155
74.0	0.1	0.8	11.5	61.6	5.8	1.4	4.4
5125	2	149	1512	3462	610	46	564
2212.0	0.2	506.2	904.5	801.1	738.5	192.2	546.3
1462		70	499	893	342	57	285
146.4		1.4	126.4	18.6	4.0	0.6	3.4
15725		141	2960	12624			
634.0		200.1	119.6	314.3			
12563		118	2427	10018			
2502.2		160.7	513.3	1828.2			
17268		122	3516	13630			
68.9		0.2	34.0	34.8			
41339	3	588	5744	35004	6057	471	5586
38776	10	269	6655	31842	6569	328	6241
1126.0	0.6	10.4	163.6	951.5	136.0	7.9	128.1
19320	26	442	2807	16045	583	11	572
3396.4	33.7	174.5	747.3	2440.9	77.9	2.6	75.3
87271		2406	10873	73992	3952	270	3682
55.8		0.8	16.6	38.3	1.8	0.1	1.7
221	54	167			2197	669	1528
1755	646	1109			17341	6985	10356
322	138	184			1361	444	917
2698	1245	1453			10223	4065	6158
9509	240	1754	3265	4250			
48776		11998	27781	8997	7910	268	7642
20312	133	377	3864	15938	12143	385	11758
67103	71	1613	11290	54129	10674	1002	9672
1211.0	1.0	8.2	139.3	1062.5	132.0	12.7	119.4
82	14	68			2063	873	1190
2544.2	278.0	2266.2			7955.9	5169.1	2786.8
37	1	36			65	14	51
16249.5	3.2	16246.3			9711.7	3275.6	6436.1
955	21	289	223	422	1002	223	779
882.6	14.3	431.0	178.6	258.7	459.2	118.5	340.7

a) Data of frequent popularization activities excludes data of national S&T week activities, activities of popularization conducted in Rural Section.

b) Associations' data of national S&T week activities includes data of Academic societies.

主要统计指标解释

普通高等学校 指按照国家规定的设置标准和审批程序批准举办的，通过全国普通高等学校统一招生考试，招收高中毕业生为主要培养对象，实施高等教育的全日制大学、独立设置的学院和高等专科学校、高等职业学校和其他机构。

大学、独立设置的学院主要实施本科层次以上教育，高等专科学校、高等职业学校实施专科层次教育，其他机构是承担国家普通招生计划任务不计校数的机构。包括普通高等学校分校和批准筹建的普通高等学校等。

成人高等学校 指按照国家规定的设置标准和审批程序批准举办的，通过全国成人高等学校统一招生考试，招收具有高中毕业或同等学历的在职从业人员为主要培养对象，利用函授、业余、脱产等多种形式对其实施高等学历教育的学校。包括职工高等学校、农民高等学校、管理干部学院、教育学院、独立函授学院、广播电视大学、其他机构等。其他机构是承担国家成人招生计划任务不计校数的机构。

小学学龄儿童入学率 指调查范围内已入小学学习的学龄儿童占校内外学龄儿童总数(包括弱智儿童，不包括盲聋哑儿童)的比重。计算公式为：

$$\text{小学学龄儿童入学率} = \frac{\text{已入学的小学学龄儿童数}}{\text{校内外小学学龄儿童总数}} \times 100\%$$

科技活动 指在自然科学、农业科学、医药科学、工程与技术科学、人文与社会科学领域(简称科学技术领域)中，与科技知识的产生、发展、传播和应用密切相关的有组织的活动。可分为研究与试验发展(R&D)、研究与试验发展成果应用及相关的科技服务三类活动。该定义是联合国教科文组织考虑成员国特别是发展中国家开展科技统计工作的需要，而对科技活动所作的统计界定。

科技活动人员 指直接从事科技活动、以及专门从事科技活动管理和为科技活动提供直接服务，累计的实际工作时间占全年制度工作时间 10%及以上的人员。(1)直接从事科技活动的人员包括：在独立核算的科学研究与技术开发机构、高等学校、各类企业及其他事业单位内设的研究室、实验室、技术开发中心及中试车间(基地)等机构中从事科技活动的研究人员、工程技术人员、技术工人及其它人员；虽不在上述机构工作，但编入科技活动项目(课题)组的人员；科技信息与文献机构中的专业技术人员；从事论文设计的研究生等。(2)专门从事科技活动管理和为科技活动提供直接服务的人员，包括：独立核算的科学研究与技术开发机构、科技信息与文献机构、高等学校、各类企业及其他事业单位主管科技工作的负责人，专门从事科技活动的计划、行政、人事、财务、物资供应、设备维护、图书资料管理等工作的各类人员，但不包括保卫、医疗保健人员、司机、食堂人员、茶炉工、水暖工、清洁工等为科技活动提供间接服务的人员。该指标用来反映投入科技活动人力的规模。

科学家与工程师 指科技活动人员中具有高、中级技术职称(职务)的人员和不具有高、中级技术职称(职务)的大学本科及以上学历人员。该指标用来反映投入科技活动人力的素质。

研究与试验发展(R&D) 指在科学技术领域，为增加知识总量、以及运用这些知识去创造新的应用进行的系统的创造性的活动，包括基础研究、应用研究、试验发展三类活动。国际上通常采用R&D活动的规模和强度指标反映一国的科技实力和核心竞争力。

基础研究 指为了获得关于现象和可观察事实的基本原理的新知识(揭示客观事物的本质、运动规律，获得新发现、新学说)而进行的实验性或理论性研究，它不以任何专门或特定的应用或使用为目的。其成果以科学论文和科学著作为主要形式。用来反映知识的原始创新能力。

应用研究 指为获得新知识而进行的创造性研究，主要针对某一特定的目的或目标。应用研究是为了确定基础研究成果可能的用途，或是为达到预定的目标探索应采取的新方法(原理性)或新途径。其成果形式以科学论文、专著、原理性模型或发明专利为主。用来反映对基础研究成果应用途径的探索。

试验发展 指利用从基础研究、应用研究和实际经验所获得的现有知识，为产生新的产品、材料和装置，建立新的工艺、系统和服务，以及对已产生和建立的上述各项作实质性的改进而进行的系统性工作。其成果形式主要是专利、专有技术、具有新产品基本特征的产品原型或具有新装置基本特征的原始样机等。在社会科学领域，试验发展是指把通过基础研究、应用研究获得的知识转变成可以实施的计划(包括为进行检验和评估实施示范项目)的过程。人文科学领域没有对应的试验发展活动。主要反映将科研成果转化为技术和产品的能力，是科技推动经济社会发展的物化成果。

研究与试验发展人员 指参与研究与试验发展项目研究、管理和辅助工作的人员，包括项目(课题)组人员，企业科技行政管理人员和直接为项目(课题)活动提供服务的辅助人员。反映投入从事拥有自主知识产权的研究开发活动的人力规模。

研究与试验发展人员全时当量 指全时人员数加非全时人员按工作量折算为全时人员数的总和。例如：有两个全时人员和三个非全时人员(工作时间分别为20%、30%和70%)，则全时当量为2+0.2+0.3+0.7=3.2人年。为国际上比较科技人力投入而制定的可比指标。

专业技术人员 指从事专业技术工作和专业技术管理工作的人员，即企事业单位中已经聘任专业技术职务从事专业技术工作和专业技术管理工作的人员，以及未聘任专业技术职务，现在专业技术岗位上工作的人员。包括工程技术人员，农业技术人员，科学研究人员，卫生技术人员，教学人员，经济人员，会计人员，统计人员，翻译人员，图书资料、档案、文博人员，新闻出版人员，律师、公证人员，广播电视播音人员，工艺美术人员，体育人员，艺术人员及企业政治思想工作人员，共十七个专业技术职务类别。用来反映科技人力资源情况。

科技活动经费筹集 指从各种渠道筹集到的计划用于科技活动的经费，包括政府资金、企业资金、事业单位资金、金融机构贷款、国外资金和其他资金等。反映各社会经济主体对促进科技进步所做的努力。

政府资金 指从各级政府部门获得的计划用于科技活动的经费，包括科学事业费、科技三项费、科研基建费、科学基金、教育等部门事业费中计划用于科技活动的经费以及政府部门预算外资金中计划用于科技活动的经费等。

企业资金 指从自有资金中提取或接受其他企业委托的、科研院所和高校等事业单位接受企业委托获得的，计划用于科研和技术开发的经费。不包括来自政府、金融机构及国外的计划用于科技活动的资金。

金融机构贷款 指从各类金融机构获得的用于科技活动的贷款。

科技活动经费内部支出 指报告年内用于科技活动的实际支出，包括劳务费、科研业务费、科研管理费，非基建投资购建的固定资产、科研基建支出以及其他用于科技活动的支出。不包括生产性活动支出、归还贷款支出及转拨外单位支出。反映科技投入实际完成情况。

劳务费 指以货币或实物形式直接或间接支付给从事科技活动人员的劳动报酬及各种费用。包括各种形式的工资、津贴、奖金、福利、离退休人员费用、人民助学金等。反映改善科技人员待遇情况。

固定资产购建费 指报告年内使用非基建投资购建的固定资产和用于科研基建投资的实际支出额，即固定资产实际支出和科研基建投资实际完成额之和。固定资产是指长期使用而不改变原有实物形态的主要物资设备、图书资料、实验材料和标本以及其他设备和家具、房屋、建筑物。反映用于改善科研条件和科研手段方面的投入情况。

新产品 指采用新技术原理、新设计构思研制、生产的全新产品，或在结构、材质、工艺等某一方面比原有产品有明显改进，从而显著提高了产品性能或扩大了使用功能的产品。既包括政府有关部门认定并在有效期内的新产品，也包括企业自行研制开发，未经政府有关部门认定，从投产之日起一年之内的新产品。用来反映科技产出及对经济增长的直接贡献。

专利 是专利权的简称，是对发明人的发明创造经审查合格后，由专利局依据专利法授予发明人和设计人对该项发明创造享有的专有权。包括发明、实用新型和外观设计。反映拥有自主知识产权的科技和设计成果情况。

发明 指对产品、方法或者其改进所提出的新的技术方案。是国际通行的反映拥有自主知识产权技术的核心指标。

实用新型 指对产品的形状、构造或者其结合所提出的适于实用的新的技术方案。反映具有一定技术含量的技术成果情况。

外观设计 指对产品的形状、图案、色彩或者其结合所作出的富有美感并适于工业上应用的新设计。反映拥有自主知识产权的外观设计成果情况。

Explanatory Notes on Main Statistical Indicators

Regular Institutions of Higher Learning refer to educational establishments set up according to the government evaluation and approval procedures, enrolling graduates from senior secondary schools and providing higher education courses and training for senior professionals. They include full-time universities, colleges, high professional schools, high professional vocational schools and others.

Universities and colleges are mainly providing undergraduate courses; those high professional schools and high professional vocational schools are mainly providing professional trainings; and others refer to educational establishments, which are responsible for enrolling students but not covered in the total number of schools, including: branch schools of universities and colleges, and universities and colleges that have been proved and prepared to construct.

Institutions of Higher Learning for Adults refer to educational establishments, set up in line with relevant rules approved by the government, enrolling staff and workers with senior secondary school or equivalent education, and providing higher education courses in many forms of correspondence, spare time, or full time for adults. Professionals thus trained receive a qualification equivalent to graduates studying regular courses at regular universities, colleges and professional colleges. Institutions of higher learning for adults include schools of high education for staff and workers, schools of high education for peasants, colleges for management cadres, pedagogical colleges, independent correspondence colleges, Radio and TV universities and other educational establishments. Other educational establishments are responsible for enrolling adult students but not covered in the number of schools.

Enrollment Rate of Primary School Age Children refers to the proportion of school age children enrolled at schools to the total number of school age children both in and outside schools (including retarded children, but excluding blind, deaf and mute children). The formula is:

Enrollment Rate of Primary School-age Children = (Total Primary School-age Children at Schools)/(Total Primary School age Children Both at and Outside Schools) x 100%

Scientific and Technological Activities (S&T Activities) refer to organized activities which are closely related with the creation, development, dissemination and application of the scientific and technical knowledge in the fields of natural sciences, agricultural science, medical science, engineering and technological science, humanities and social sciences (referred to as scientific and technological fields). S&T activities can be classified in to 3 categories: research and development (R&D) activities, application of R&D results, and related S&T services. This statistical definition is made by UNICHIEF for scientific and technological activities to meet the need of carrying out statistical work in this field for its member countries in particular those developing countries.

Personnel Engaged in S&T Activities refer to personnel directly engaged in S&T activities, in the management of S&T activities, and in providing direct service to S&T activities, who spend over 10% of the total working hours in a year in S&T activities. (1) Personnel directly engaged in S&T activities include researchers, engineers, technicians and other related personnel engaged in S&T activities in independent-accounting R&D institutions, institutions of higher learning, and in research institutes, laboratories, technology development centers and central experiment workshops under enterprises and institutions. Also included are people working in S&T research project teams, professional and technical personnel working in S&T information archiving institutes, and graduate students working on the design of their thesis. (2) Personnel engaged in the management of S&T activities and in providing direct service to S&T activities include senior management people responsible for S&T activities in independent-accounting R&D institutions, S&T information archiving institutes, institutions of higher learning, and in enterprises and institutions where S&T activities are undertaken. Also included are people responsible for the planning, administration, personnel management, financial management, logistics supply, equipment maintenance, information and library management that are related with S&T activities. People providing indirect services are excluded, such as security, medical service, drivers, plumbers, cleaners and those providing catering and related service. This indicator reflects the size of personnel engaged in S&T activities.

Scientists and Engineers refer to persons engaged in S&T activities who have obtained titles of senior and middle level professional positions, and those without such position but have completed university or higher education. This indicator reflects the quality of personnel engaged in S&T activities.

Research and Development (R&D) refers to systematic and creative activities in the field of science and technology aiming at increasing the knowledge and using the knowledge for new application. R&D includes 3 categories of activities: basic research, applied research and experiments and development. The scale and intensity of R&D are widely used internationally to reflect the strength of S&T and the core competitiveness of a country in the world.

Basic Research refers to empirical or theoretical research aiming at obtaining new knowledge on the fundamental principles of phenomena of observable facts to reveal the nature and law of movement of objects and to acquire new discoveries or new theories. Basic research takes no specific or designated application as the aim of the research. Results of basic research are mainly released or disseminated in the form of scientific papers or monographs. This indicator reflects the original innovation capacity of knowledge.

Applied Research refers to creative research aiming at obtaining new knowledge on a specific objective or target. Purpose of the applied research is to identify the possible use of results from basic research, or to explore new (fundamental) methods or new approaches. Results of applied research are expressed in the form of scientific papers, monographs, fundamental models or invention patents. This indicator reflects the exploration of ways to apply the results of basic research.

Experiments and Development refer to systematic activities aiming at using the knowledge from basic and applied researches or from practical experience to develop new products, materials and equipment, to establish new production process, systems and services, or to make substantial improvement on the existing products, process or services. Results of experiment and development activities are embodied in patents, exclusive technology, and monotype of new products or equipment. In social sciences, experiment and development activities refer to the process of converting the knowledge from basic or applied researches into feasible programmes (including conduct of demonstration projects for assessment and evaluation). There are no experiment and development activities in the science of humanities. This indicator reflects the capability of transferring the results of S&T into technique and products, which is the materialized measurement of S&T pushing forward the economic and social development.

R&D Personnel refer to persons engaged in research, management and supporting activities of R&D, including persons in the project teams, persons engaged in the management of S&T activities of enterprises and supporting staff providing direct service to the research projects. This indicator reflects the size of personnel engaged in R&D activities with independent intellectual property.

Full-time Equivalent of R&D Personnel refers to the sum of the full-time persons and the full-time equivalent of part-time persons converted by workload. For instance, if there are 2 full-time persons and 3 part-time workers (20%, 30% and 70% of working hours respectively on R&D activities), the full-time equivalent is 2+0.2+0.3+0.7=3.2 person-years. This is an internationally comparable indicator of input of personnel in S&T activities.

Professional and Technical Personnel refer to persons engaged in professional and technical work or in the management of professional and technical activities, i.e., people with professional or technical positions who are engaged in professional and technical work or in the management of professional and technical activities, and people without professional or technical positions but are working on professional or technical posts. They include professionals and technicians working in 17 categories of technical occupations including engineering, agriculture, scientific researches, medical service, teaching, economic research and application, accounting, statistics, translation, libraries, archives, cultural and museum service, journalism and publication, lawyers, notarization service, radio and television broadcasting, handicraft and fine arts, sports, performing art, and political workers in enterprises. This indicator reflects the condition of human resources in S&T.

Funding for S&T Activities refers to funds obtained from various sources for S&T activities, including government funds, self-raised funds by enterprises, self-raised funds by institutions, loans from financial institutions, foreign funds and other funds. This indicator reflects the efforts made by various social economic entities in promoting the development of S&T.

Government Funds refer to funds obtained from government agencies at all levels to be used for S&T activities, including fund for scientific undertakings, 3 kinds of fund for S&T activities, fund for capital construction for scientific researches, science fund, funds from education expenditures by education departments for S&T activities, and extra-budget fund from government agencies for S&T activities.

Self-raised Funds by Enterprises refers to self-raised funds by enterprises from their own expenditure or from other enterprises and funds received by universities or research institutions from enterprises for scientific research or technical development projects. Excluded in this category are funds from government agencies, financial institutions or from foreign institutions.

Loans from Financial Institutions refer to loans from various financial institutions for S&T activities.

Internal Expenditures on S&T activities refer to the actual expenditures on S&T activities during the reference year, including service fees, expenditure on research activities, expenditure on research management, purchase or construction of fixed assets not included in the investment for capital construction, expenditure on capital construction for scientific researches, and other expenditures on S&T activities. Not included are expenditure on production activities, repayment of loans and transfer expenditure. This indicator reflects the real accomplishment of input in S&T.

Service Fees refer to direct or indirect payment, in cash or in kind, made to personnel engaged in S&T activities as remuneration and other fees. They include, in various forms, salaries, subsidies, bonus, benefits, retirement pension, stipend, etc. This indicator reflects the improvement of treatment toward S&T personnel.

Purchase or Construction of Fixed Assets refers to the fixed assets purchased or constructed using funds other than the investment in capital construction, and the actual expenditure on capital construction for scientific researches. In other words, it is the sum of the actual expenditure on fixed assets and the accomplished investment in capital construction for scientific researches. Fixed assets refer to main materials and equipment, literatures and documents in libraries, materials for experiments, specimen, instruments, furniture, buildings and constructions that can be used for a long time without changing the form and shape of those articles or constructions. This indictor reflects the input in improving the condition of S&T and the means of scientific research.

New Products refer to new products produced with new technology and new design, or products that represent noticeable improvement in terms of structure, material, or production process so as to improve significantly the character or function of the older versions. They include new products certified by relevant government agencies within the period of certification, as well as new products designed and produced by enterprises within a year without certification by government agencies. This indictor reflects the direct contribution of S&T output to economic growth.

Patent is an abbreviation for the patent right and refers to the exclusive right of ownership by the inventors or designers for the creation or inventions, given from the patent offices after due process of assessment and approval in accordance with the Patent Law. Patents are granted for inventions, utility models and designs. This indicator reflects the achievements of S&T and design with independent intellectual property.

Inventions refer to the new technical proposals to the products or methods or their modifications. This is universal core indicator reflecting the technologies with independent intellectual property.

Utility Models refer to the practical and new technical proposals on the shape and structure of the product or the combination of both. This indicator reflects the condition of technological results with certain technical content.

Designs refer to the aesthetics and industrially applicable new designs for the shape, pattern and color of the product, or their combinations. This indicator reflects the appearance design achievements with independent intellectual property.

二十二、文化、体育和卫生

Culture, Sports and Public Health

简要说明

一、本篇资料的主要内容

本篇主要反映文化、体育、卫生、新闻出版、广播电影电视事业的发展情况。

文化部分主要包括艺术表演团体、艺术表演场所、公共图书馆、博物馆、文化馆、档案馆、文化站、广播、电影、电视、新闻出版以及文物等文化事业的机构、人员、经费和业务活动情况。体育部分主要包括群众体育和竞技体育，主要内容有体育系统职工、运动员、教练员和裁判员等情况，体育场地数，竞技体育成绩，体育锻炼达标人数以及与国外体育交往次数和人数等情况。卫生部分主要内容有卫生机构、人员、床位数，医院诊疗人次及入院人数，主要疾病死亡原因及构成，传染病的发病及死亡以及卫生事业费用测算等情况。

二、本篇的资料来源

根据各部门制定的统计报表制度汇总加工整理而成。艺术事业、图书馆事业、群众文化事业的资料主要来自文化部；档案馆资料来自国家档案局；文物资料来自国家文物局；广播、电影、电视资料来自国家广播电影电视总局；新闻出版资料来自国家新闻出版总署；体育部分的资料来自国家体育总局；卫生部分的资料来自卫生部。

三、详细资料分别见《中国文化文物统计年鉴》（文化部计划财务司编）、《中国新闻出版统计资料汇编》（新闻出版署计财司编）、《广播电影电视资料汇编》（广电总局计财司编）和《全国卫生统计年报资料》（卫生部信息中心编）。

Brief Introduction

I. Main Content:

Data in this chapter mainly show the development of culture, sports, public health, news and publication, radio broadcasting, films and televisions.

Data on culture cover mainly the situations on institutions, personnel and business activities of arts (performing groups and venues), libraries, museums, cultural centers, archives, cultural stations, broadcasting, films, televisions, news and publication. Data on sports cover mass sports (sports for all) and athletics sports, including mainly the number of staff and workers in sports departments, number of athletes, coaches and referees, number of stadiums and gymnasiums, achievements in athletic sport events, number of persons who have come up to the National Physical Training Program Standards and the international exchanges of sport delegations. Data on public health include mainly the number of institutions, personnel, hospital beds, number of patients treated and in-patients, major diseases as the causes of death and the proportion to the total deaths, the incidence of, and the deaths caused by infectious diseases, estimation of health cost, etc.

II. Sources of Data

Data are collected and tabulated in accordance with the statistical reporting schemes stipulated by the departments concerned. Data on the causes of arts, libraries, mass culture are provided by the Ministry of Culture. Data on archives are from National Bureau of Archives. Data on broadcasting, film and television are mainly from State Administration of Broadcasting, Film and Television. Data on news and publication are mainly provided by the State Agency of News and Publication. Data on sports are mainly from the State Sports Administration. Data on public health are mainly from the Ministry of Public Health.

III. Detailed information please refer to "China Cultural Relics Yearbook" (Department of Financial Management, Ministry of Culture), "Collection of China News and Publication Statistical Information" (Department of Financial Management, State Agency of News and Publication), "Collection of Broadcasting, Film and Television Statistics" (Department of Financial Management, State Administration of Broadcasting, Film and Television and "Annual Statistical Report on National Health Care" (Information Center, Ministry of Public Health).

22-1 文化、文物事业机构、人员数(2003年)

Number of Institution and Personnel in Culture and Cultural Relics (2003)

机构类别	Category of Institution	机构数（个） Number of Institution (unit)	从业人数（人） Number of Employed Person (person)
文化事业合计	**Culture**	**349055**	**1658793**
艺术事业	Arts	5123	180353
#艺术表演团体	Arts Performance Troupes	2618	137059
话剧、儿童剧、滑稽剧团	Drama, Children, Plays and Comedy Troupes	88	6831
歌剧、舞剧、歌舞剧团	Opera, Ballet and Dance Troupes	104	11576
歌舞团、轻音乐团	Song and Dance Troupe, Light Music Troupe	361	22468
文工团、文宣队、乌兰牧骑	Cultural and Performance Troupes and Ulanmuchi (equestrian art troupes)	361	10186
戏曲剧团	Local Opera Troupes	1483	74283
#京剧	Local Beijing Opera Troupes	104	8689
曲艺、杂技、木偶、皮影团	Recitation and Ballad Troupes, Acrobatics and Circus Troupes, Puppet Show Troupes and Shadow Play Troupes	189	9439
艺术表演场所	Arts Centers	1912	37123
剧场、影剧院	Theaters and Music Halls	1869	36352
书场、曲艺场	Storytelling Places, Recitation and Ballad Places	19	209
杂技、马戏场	Acrobatics, Circus Places	3	166
音乐厅	Concert Halls	13	334
公共图书馆事业	Public Libraries	2709	49646
群众文化事业	Mass Culture	41816	123458
群众艺术馆	Mass Art Centers	382	10627
文化馆	Cultural Centers	2846	41708
文化站	Cultural Stations	38588	71123
#乡文化站	Township Cultural Stations	35138	60516
艺术教育事业	Culture and Education	195	13907
其他文化事业	Other Cultural Units	295903	1230924
艺术创作机构	Art Creation Institutions	404	3017
艺术研究机构	Art Research Institutions	185	3155
艺术展览机构	Art Exhibition Institutions	53	1163
#美术馆	Art Gallery	29	612
文化艺术经纪与代理业	Brokers and Agents for Cultural and Arts Activities	584	5254
其他	Others	294677	1218335
文物事业合计	**Cultural Relics**	**3903**	**66676**
文物保护管理机构	Agency of Historical Relics Preservation	2275	29277
文物科研机构	Scientific and Research Historical Relics Agency	75	3110
其他文物机构	Other Historical Relics Agency	71	3285
博物馆	Museums	1515	34891
综合性博物馆	Comprehensive Museum	846	18674
历史类博物馆	History Museum	450	11200
艺术类博物馆	Arts Museum	56	1898
自然科技类博物馆	Nature Science and Technology Museum	20	532
其他	Other Museum	143	2587
文物商店	Cultural Relics Agencies	113	2508

22-2 文化、文物事业单位数

Number of Institutions for Culture and Cultural Relics

单位: 个 (unit)

地区	Region	艺术表演团体 Art Performance Troupes	艺术表演场所 Art Performance Places	文化馆 Cultural Centers	公共图书馆 Public Libraries	博物馆 Museums
	1978	3150	1095	2748	1218	349
	1979	3482	1255	2892	1651	344
	1980	3533	1444	2912	1732	365
	1985	3317	1673	2965	2344	711
	1989	2850	2011	2955	2512	967
	1990	2805	2011	2955	2527	1013
	1995	2682	1972	2886	2608	1194
	1996	2664	1934	2892	2620	1219
	1997	2663	1947	2901	2628	1282
	1998	2652	1929	2901	2652	1339
	1999	2632	1911	2905	2669	1363
	2000	2630	1912	2907	2677	1392
	2001	2605	1854	2852	2696	1461
	2002	2587	1829	2854	2697	1511
	2003	2618	1912	2846	2709	1515
北　京	Beijing	20	24	19	25	28
天　津	Tianjin	15	32	18	31	17
河　北	Hebei	133	98	165	147	44
山　西	Shanxi	158	48	119	122	86
内蒙古	Inner Mongolia	113	30	103	108	28
辽　宁	Liaoning	74	69	103	128	35
吉　林	Jilin	65	48	62	62	22
黑龙江	Heilongjiang	86	50	125	97	45
上　海	Shanghai	65	180	32	35	23
江　苏	Jiangsu	127	115	113	100	89
浙　江	Zhejiang	77	77	87	83	70
安　徽	Anhui	93	91	99	84	40
福　建	Fujian	94	76	78	82	79
江　西	Jiangxi	78	57	101	104	83
山　东	Shandong	120	104	138	140	73
河　南	Henan	199	159	187	136	75
湖　北	Hubei	98	69	114	103	98
湖　南	Hunan	86	94	125	115	73
广　东	Guangdong	144	70	117	129	144
广　西	Guangxi	117	24	100	96	42
海　南	Hainan	28	19	18	19	17
重　庆	Chongqing	32	25	41	44	16
四　川	Sichuan	89	76	174	132	51
贵　州	Guizhou	26	13	84	90	10
云　南	Yunnan	121	39	128	149	30
西　藏	Tibet	27	37	48	1	2
陕　西	Shaanxi	116	109	110	111	81
甘　肃	Gansu	74	32	84	92	66
青　海	Qinghai	14	1	43	38	16
宁　夏	Ningxia	14	14	21	21	5
新　疆	Xinjiang	88	26	90	84	23

22-3 艺术表演团体演出情况（2003年）

Basic Statistics on Performance of Art Troupes (2003)

种 类	Item	演出场数（万场） Number of Performances (10 000 shows)	#到农村演出 Shows in Rural Areas (10 000)	观众人数（万人次） Number of Spectators (10 000 person-times)
总 计	**Total**	**38.5**	**21.5**	**39163**
#国有剧团	Troupes Sponsored by State-owned Units	25.9	13.2	28086.7
集体经营剧团	Troupes Sponsored by Collective Units	12.2	12.0	10560.6
按剧种分:	**Art Troupes**			
话剧、儿童剧、滑稽剧团	Drama, Children's Play and Comedy Troupes	0.1		1141.4
歌舞剧团	Song and Dance Drama Troupes	0.1		2021.5
歌舞团、轻音乐团	Song and Dance, Light Music	0.3	0.1	4021.5
文工团、宣传队、乌兰牧骑	Cultural and Performance Troupes and Ulanmuchi (equestrian art troupes)	0.3	0.2	2989.3
乐团、合唱团	Philharmonic and Chorus Troupes	0.1		523.5
戏曲剧团	Local Opera Troupes	21.6	15.7	25489.8
#京 剧	Local Beijing Opera Troupes	0.1		1084.5
曲艺、杂技、木偶、皮影团	Recitation and Ballad Troupes, Acrobatics and Circus Troupes, Puppet Show Troupes, and Shadow Play Troupes	0.7	0.2	2976

注：歌舞剧团包括歌剧、舞剧、歌舞剧团(下表同)。

a) Song and dance drama troupes include opera, dance and light music troupes. The same as in the following table.

22-4 艺术表演团体收支情况(2003年)

Income and Expenditures of Art Troupes (2003)

种 类	Item	补贴团数（个） Number of Troupes Receiving Government Subsidies (unit)	总收入（万元） Total Income (10 000 yuan)	#财政补助收入（万元） Government Subsidies (10 000 yuan)	#演出收入 Income from Perform	总支出（万元） Total Expenditures (10 000 yuan)	经费自给率（%） Total Income/Total Expenditures Ratio (%)
总 计	**Total**	**2375**	**400867**	**269640**	**71781**	**397890**	**29.6**
#国有剧团	Troupes Sponsored by State-owned Units	1872	365011	249143	60674	361693	28.5
集体经营剧团	Troupes Sponsored by Collective Units	489	32966	19503	9796	33245	38.1
按剧种分:	**Art Troupes**						
话剧、儿童剧、滑稽剧团	Drama, Children's Play and Comedy Troupes	82	36683	23530	4789	35823	32.8
歌舞剧团	Song and Dance Drama Troupes	95	46706	29089	8427	45135	33.4
歌舞团、轻音乐团	Song and Dance, Light Music	339	73197	50345	15001	72756	31.9
文工团、宣传队、乌兰牧骑	Cultural and Performance Troupes and Ulanmuchi (equestrian art troupes)	332	15536	12947	1148	15205	15.6
乐团、合唱团	Philharmonic and Chorus Troupes	16	22195	11869	5018	21142	35.4
戏曲剧团	Local Opera Troupes	1349	170251	118564	28231	171671	27.4
#京 剧	Local Beijing Opera Troupes	101	33691	25338	3222	33715	21.3
曲艺、杂技、木偶、皮影团	Recitation and Ballad Troupes, Acrobatics and Circus Troupes, Puppet Show Troupes and Shadow Play Troupes	162	36299	23297	9166	36157	34.8

注:本表各项指标仅指文化部系统内的。

a)The data in this table only refer to those under the administration of the cultural departments.

22-5 群众艺术馆、文化馆站业务活动及经费情况(2003年)

Basic Statistics on Activities and Expenditures of Mass Art Centers and Cultural Centers (2003)

项　目	Item	总　计 Total	群众艺术馆 Mass Art Centers	文化馆 Cultural Centers	文化站 Cultural Stations
单位数 (个)	Number of Units (unit)	41816	382	2846	38588
举办展览 (个)	Number of Exhibitions (unit)	93514	1958	14172	77384
组织文艺活动 (次)	Art Performances and Story-Telling Sessions (times)	327306	9466	68578	249262
举办训练班	Training Courses				
班　次 (次)	Number of Classes (times)	154502	10158	39984	104360
结业人次 (万人次)	Number of Persons Completing Courses (10 000 person-times)	519	20	103	396
群众艺术馆、文化馆负责指导单位	Units Responsible for Guiding Mass Art Centers and Cultural Centers				
农村集镇文化中心 (个)	Cultural Centers in County Towns (unit)	21621	2023	19598	
文化俱乐部、室 (个)	Cultural Clubs (unit)	76340	1854	74486	
文化户 (户)	Households Specializing in Cultural Activities (household)	139047	3265	135782	
群众业余演出团(队)(个)	Part-time Art Groups (unit)	37659	1642	36017	
总支出 (万元)	Total Expenditures (10 000 yuan)	265751	45159	109278	111314
#业务费	Professional Expenditures	35887	6024	12365	17498
修缮费	Maintenance Expenses	10398	1618	3817	4963

注:本表各项指标仅指文化部系统内的。

a)The data in this table only refer to those under the administration of the cultural departments.

22-6 公共图书馆业务活动及经费情况(2003年)

Facilities, Services and Expenditures of Public Libraries (2003)

项　目	Item	总　计 Total	#省级公共图书馆 Public Libraries at Provincial Level	#县级公共图书馆 Public Libraries at County Level
总藏量 (万册、件)	Total Collections (10 000 volumes)	43776	13881	15224
书架总长度 (万米)	Total Length of Bookshelves (10 000 m)	1035	292	375
发放借书证数 (万个)	Number of Library Cards Distributed (10 000 units)	943	182	398
图书流通情况	Circulation of Books			
总流通人次 (万人次)	Total Number of Circulation (10 000 person-times)	21440	2557	10960
书刊外借册次(万册次)	Number of Books Borrowed by the Readers (10 000 volume-times)	18775	2010	9793
为读者服务举办各种活动	Service Activities Provided for Readers			
次　数 (次)	Number of Activities (times)	92701	6667	63040
参加人数 (万人次)	Number of Readers Involved (10 000 person-times)	2432	397	945
总支出 (万元)	Total Expenditures (10 000 yuan)	235819	65298	65537
#藏量购置费 (万元)	Purchase Expenses (10 000 yuan)	51097	18832	7256
本年新购藏量 (万册)	Number of Books Purchased During the Year (10 000 volumes)	1406	419	475
公用房屋建筑面积 (万平方米)	Floor Space of Public Buildings Floor Space of Buildings (10 000 sq.m)	589	98	282
#书　库 (万平方米)	Stack Rooms (10 000 sq.m)	156	34	67
阅览室座席 (万个)	Seating Capacity of Reading Rooms (10 000 seats)	46	3	29

22-7 博物馆、文物机构业务活动及经费情况(2003年)

Facilities, Services and Expenditures of Museums and Cultural Relic Agencies (2003)

项目	Item	文物保护管理机构 Protection and Management Agencies	文物科研机构 Scientific and Research Agencies	其他文物机构 Other Agencies	博物馆 Museums
藏品 (件)	Number of Collections (piece)				
传统计量	Tradition Statistics	1789501	755551	55950	10050427
实际数量	Factual Statistics	2193731	763347	56094	12336328
#一级品 (件)	Grade One (piece)				
传统计量	Tradition Statistics	4544	2037	405	29461
实际数量	Factual Statistics	4995	4161	405	44351
业务活动	Operations				
陈列展览 (个)	Number of Displays and Exhibitions (unit)	4153			5809
参观人数 (万人次)	Number of Visitors (10 000 person-times)	3240			6206
经费支出 (万元)	Total Expenditures (10 000 yuan)	88383	27248	9780	226896
#业务费	Professional Expenditures	8126	6432	1490	43345
#考古发掘费	Archaeology and Excavation Expenses	1098	6432	856	4673
修缮费	Maintenance Expenses	13240	1578	919	31086
增加值 (万元)	Value Added (10 000 yuan)	45184	10563	1720	93553

22-8 摄 制 电 影 片 产 量

Film Production

年份 Year	电影故事片厂 (个) Number of Feature Film Studios (unit)	故事片 (部) Feature Films (film)	美术片 (本) Cartoons (reel)	科学教育片 (本) Popular Science Films (reel)	纪录片 (本) Documentary Films (reel)
1952	4	4	2	41	157
1957	11	40	5	84	272
1962	16	34	17	94	133
1965	16	52	21	240	378
1975	15	27	11	214	313
1978	12	46	26	289	202
1979	17	65	25	349	317
1980	17	82	32	337	242
1981	19	105	33	277	276
1982	19	112	33	284	259
1983	19	127	37	343	299
1984	20	144	37	387	337
1985	20	127	45	357	419
1986	20	134	46	383	417
1987	22	146	45	353	347
1988	22	158	38	344	350
1989	22	136	53	334	259
1990	22	134	51	326	296
1991	22	130	46	351	283
1992	22	170	56	354	307
1993	22	154	47	252	300
1994	22	148	32	182	22
1995	30	146	37	40	111
1996	30	110	58	33	39
1997	31	88	28	34	95
1998	31	82	9	30	54
2000	31	91	1	49	10
2001	27	88	1	56	9
2002	31	100	2	60	7
2003	31	140	2	53	6

注：本表电影故事片厂只包括国务院批准的厂。

a) The number of feature film studios in this table only includes those approved by the State Council.

22-9 广播、电视事业发展情况
Basic Statistics on Broadcasting and Television Stations

项 目	Item	2002	2003	2003年比2002年增长% Increase Percentage in 2003 over 2002
广播电视系统职工人数(人)	Number of Staff and Workers (person)	519705	509176	-2.00
广播电台 (座)	Number of Broadcasting Stations (set)	306	277	-9.00
广播发射台及转播台(座)	Number of Broadcast Transmission Stations and Relaying Stations (set)	757	742	-2.00
广播发射机功率 (千瓦)	Broadcast Power of Transmitters (kw)	49396.4	53926.3	9.16
县级广播电视台 (座)	Number of Wire Broadcast Stations in Counties and Cities (set)	1526	1308	-14.28
广播人口覆盖率 (%)	Listener Rating (%)	93.34	93.72	0.38
电视台 (座)	Number of Television Stations (set)	368	317	-13.85
电视发射台及转播台(座)	Television Transmission Stations and Relaying Stations (set)	53668	51659	-3.74
电视发射机功率 (千瓦)	Power of Transmitters (kw)	8247.71	8447.83	2.40
电视人口覆盖率 (%)	Viewer Rating (%)	94.61	94.97	0.36

注：广播电台、电视台未包括县级数。
a) Number of Broadcasting and Television stations excludes that in county level.

22-10 广播、电视节目制作时间
Basic Statistics on Broadcasting and Television

单位：小时 (hour)

项 目	Item	1995	2000	2001	2002	2003
广播节目制作	Production of Broadcasting	2332164	3381466	3494303	3774001	4301505
#新闻	News Programs	353368	449582	483631	531278	628090
专题	Special Subject Programs	565464	821031	861222	942190	1011694
教育	Educational Programs	91240	171057	199239	195932	223467
文艺	Programs of Entertainment	924656	1087252	1096440	1161402	1376816
服务性	Service Programs	397436	554219	517322	565432	627030
电视节目制作	Production of TV Programs	383513	585007	989173	1072704	1185507
#新闻	News Programs	80800	147239	235336	256883	280273
专题	Special Subject Programs	81146	105257	189903	206832	220767
教育	Educational Programs	11630	19255	27526	34842	38639
文艺	Programs of Entertainment	109322	133084	191154	218955	228802
服务性	Service Programs	100615	75104	162061	137575	173677

22-11 广播、电视宣传基本情况（2003年）
Basic Statistics on Broadcasting and Television (2003)

项 目	Item	节目套数（套） Number of Programs (set)	播出时间（小时/日） Broadcasting Hours (hour/ per day)	自办节目时间（小时/日） Self-Produced Programs (hour/per day)	#新闻节目 News Programs	#专题节目 Special Subject Programs	#教育节目 Educational Programs	#文艺节目 Entertainment Programs	#服务性节目 Service Programs
无线广播合计	**All Radio Broadcasting Stations**	**2064**	**26489**	**17986**	**2403**	**3917**	**930**	**6709**	**2316**
中央台和国际台	China Central Broadcasting and China International Broadcasting	9	529	529	200	183	15	116	8
地方台	Local	2053	25960	17457	2203	3734	915	6593	2308
电视播映合计	**All Television Stations**	**2262**	**27499**	**20455**	**1785**	**2422**	**487**	**11618**	**1899**
中央电视台	China Central Television	14	280	280	64	80	9	88	27
地方台	Local Television	2248	27219	20175	1721	2342	478	11530	1872

22-12 各地区新闻出版事业机构和人员数（2003年）

Number of Institutions and Persons Engaged in News and Publishing Undertakings by Region (2003)

地 区	Region	书刊出版社 Publishing Houses		国家定点书刊印刷厂 Printing Houses		书 店 Book Stores	
		机构数（个） Institutions (unit)	从业人员（人） Personnel (person)	机构数（个） Institutions (unit)	从业人员（人） Personnel (person)	机构数（个） Institutions (unit)	从业人员（人） Personnel (person)
全 国	**National Total**	**570**	**50537**	**285**	**113963**	**12867**	**154390**
中 央	Center Institutions	220	21520	35	12982	13	2455
地 方	Local Institutions	350	29017	250	100981	12854	151935
北 京	Beijing	17	857	10	2980	154	4287
天 津	Tianjin	12	1124	6	3425	119	2003
河 北	Hebei	7	822	15	6077	589	8287
山 西	Shanxi	8	638	4	2284	432	4759
内蒙古	Inner Mongolia	7	468	5	1241	279	2797
辽 宁	Liaoning	18	1540	12	4930	242	5968
吉 林	Jilin	14	951	6	2019	183	4059
黑龙江	Heilongjiang	12	671	6	3181	252	4775
上 海	Shanghai	38	3905	16	3805	356	4682
江 苏	Jiangsu	17	1347	13	5387	1030	8390
浙 江	Zhejiang	13	982	8	1392	442	5887
安 徽	Anhui	10	822	7	3072	535	5099
福 建	Fujian	11	498	6	2714	336	4085
江 西	Jiangxi	7	457	10	4921	337	4609
山 东	Shandong	17	1239	17	8440	1024	10290
河 南	Henan	12	791	13	7625	1429	12363
湖 北	Hubei	13	1477	16	5547	585	6696
湖 南	Hunan	12	1148	12	4338	502	6979
广 东	Guangdong	19	1389	15	4840	550	10918
广 西	Guangxi	8	966	6	2609	338	4561
海 南	Hainan	4	565	2	512	52	1263
重 庆	Chongqing	3	520	2	1741	198	3823
四 川	Sichuan	16	1404	11	4114	596	7471
贵 州	Guizhou	4	274	4	2070	448	2206
云 南	Yunnan	8	696	5	1641	514	3971
西 藏	Tibet	2	83	2	417	71	256
陕 西	Shaanxi	17	1746	6	4120	455	4832
甘 肃	Gansu	9	502	6	2884	374	2576
青 海	Qinghai	2	99	3	708	134	1054
宁 夏	Ningxia	3	128	2	404	67	693
新 疆	Xinjiang	10	908	4	1543	231	2296

22-13 图书、杂志和报纸出版情况

Number of Books, Magazines and Newspaper Published in China

年份 地区	Year Region	图书 Books Published				杂志 Magazines Published				报纸 Newspapers Published			
		种数 (种) Number of Publications (kind)	#新出版 New Publications	总印数 (亿册、亿张) Printed Copies (100 million copies)	总印张数 (亿印张) Printed Sheets (100 million sheets)	种数 (种) Number of Publications (kind)	每期平均印数 (万册) Average Printed Copies per Issue (10 000 copies)	总印数 (亿册) Total Printed Copies (100 million copies)	总印张数 (亿印张) Printed Sheets (100 million sheets)	种数 (种) Number of News Publish-ed (kind)	每期平均印数 (万份) Average Printed Copies per Issue (10 000 copies)	总印数 (亿份) Total Printed Copies (100 million copies)	总印张数 (亿印张) Printed Signatures (100 million sheets)
	1978	14987	11888	37.7	135.4	930	6200	7.62	22.74	186	4280	127.8	113.5
	1980	21621	17660	45.9	195.7	2191	10298	11.25	36.72	188	6236	140.4	141.7
	1985	45603	33743	66.7	282.8	4705	23952	25.60	77.29	1445	19107	246.8	202.8
	1989	74973	55475	58.6	243.6	6078	17145	18.40	50.70	1576	15288	207.0	179.5
	1990	80224	55245	56.4	232.1	5751	16156	17.90	48.12	1444	14670	211.3	182.8
	1991	89615	58467	61.4	266.1	6056	18216	20.62	54.44	1524	16393	236.5	205.8
	1992	92148	58169	63.4	280.4	6486	20506	23.60	62.73	1657	18031	257.9	238.8
	1993	96761	66313	59.3	282.3	7011	20780	23.51	64.21	1788	18478	263.8	287.1
	1994	103836	69779	60.1	297.2	7325	19763	22.11	63.86	1953	17736	253.2	310.8
	1995	101381	59159	63.2	316.8	7583	19794	23.37	67.02	2089	17644	263.3	359.6
	1996	112813	63647	71.6	360.5	7916	19300	23.10	68.06	2163	17877	274.3	392.4
	1997	120106	66585	73.1	364.0	7918	20046	24.38	73.30	2149	18259	287.6	459.8
	1998	130613	74719	72.4	373.6	7999	20928	25.37	79.87	2053	18211	300.4	540.0
	1999	141831	83095	73.2	391.4	8187	21845	28.46	96.77	2038	18632	318.4	636.7
	2000	143376	84235	62.7	376.2	8725	21544	29.42	100.04	2007	17914	329.3	799.8
	2001	154526	91416	63.1	406.1	8889	20697	28.90	100.90	2111	18130	351.1	938.9
	2002	170962	100693	68.7	456.4	9029	20406	29.50	106.40	2137	18721	367.8	1067.4
	2003	190391	110812	66.7	462.2	9074	19909	29.50	109.10	2119	19072	383.1	1235.6
北京	Beijing	3416	1562	0.6	5.1	177	342	0.42	2.03	37	510	11.9	50.1
天津	Tianjin	3621	2392	0.7	5.3	245	366	0.46	1.89	27	361	8.2	37.3
河北	Hebei	2265	1343	2.5	13.5	215	380	0.46	1.33	66	559	10.8	27.8
山西	Shanxi	2004	1059	1.1	7.5	198	258	0.42	1.77	67	1771	16.1	19.3
内蒙古	Inner Mongolia	2120	1380	0.8	5.3	160	159	0.21	0.64	68	167	2.9	3.9
辽宁	Liaoning	5167	2751	1.5	10.2	299	1006	1.40	3.39	90	750	13.0	33.1
吉林	Jilin	4025	2152	1.4	9.9	235	483	0.67	2.04	55	562	6.7	12.3
黑龙江	Heilongjiang	2559	1749	0.8	5.2	323	448	0.58	2.16	76	376	7.5	14.7
上海	Shanghai	15613	8721	2.7	23.1	626	1335	1.83	8.51	71	856	17.0	66.1
江苏	Jiangsu	7100	3823	4.6	29.7	462	616	0.99	3.17	94	1192	26.1	76.3
浙江	Zhejiang	5919	2646	3.0	16.4	224	623	0.91	2.44	83	934	24.2	71.5
安徽	Anhui	3003	1673	2.7	14.9	186	478	0.60	1.69	53	388	8.0	22.2
福建	Fujian	2628	1890	1.6	9.2	186	312	0.39	1.45	53	344	8.0	23.5
江西	Jiangxi	1728	1235	1.9	9.5	173	343	0.58	1.37	46	298	5.3	15.6
山东	Shandong	5511	3497	3.2	18.1	285	766	1.35	4.31	106	884	21.5	64.0
河南	Henan	3206	1653	3.2	18.0	258	803	1.18	3.96	81	878	14.9	38.8
湖北	Hubei	5255	2767	2.8	17.1	401	988	1.85	6.56	105	626	16.2	57.0
湖南	Hunan	3715	2371	3.0	16.7	269	1020	1.26	3.19	64	587	11.3	31.5
广东	Guangdong	5439	2990	2.6	17.1	367	1289	2.28	9.31	128	1822	42.5	272.7
广西	Guangxi	3775	1825	2.2	12.8	200	422	0.60	1.96	64	304	6.9	15.5
海南	Hainan	1715	681	0.8	4.7	45	82	0.11	0.52	20	80	1.8	5.3
重庆	Chongqing	1764	795	1.1	6.4	130	287	0.42	2.03	25	252	4.7	25.8
四川	Sichuan	4147	2331	2.6	16.9	293	392	0.52	2.29	89	634	13.9	35.7
贵州	Guizhou	840	499	1.2	5.9	88	85	0.10	0.53	31	131	3.4	9.3
云南	Yunnan	2160	1353	1.5	8.2	134	196	0.27	0.96	50	186	4.2	13.4
西藏	Tibet	327	92	0.1	0.4	34	12	0.01	0.03	19	19	0.3	0.3
陕西	Shaanxi	4230	2485	1.7	10.5	266	383	0.58	2.56	52	289	6.6	31.7
甘肃	Gansu	1047	876	0.4	2.7	130	521	1.08	4.15	55	183	3.8	9.2
青海	Qinghai	294	135	0.1	0.7	41	13	0.01	0.03	19	29	0.5	0.5
宁夏	Ningxia	448	255	0.1	0.9	24	10	0.01	0.04	13	33	0.8	1.5
新疆	Xinjiang	3522	2195	0.7	4.6	195	131	0.14	0.06	99	186	3.7	9.2

22-14 图书出版分类构成情况（2003年）

Composition of Books Published in China (2003)

类　别	Category	种　数 (种) Number of Publication (kind)	印　数 (万册) Printed Copies (10 000 copies)	印　张 (千印张) Printed Sheets (1 000 sheets)
总　计	**Total**	**190391**	**667000**	**46222401**
使用“中国标准书号”合计	Publications with "China International Standard Book Number"	188505	662843	46012398
马列主义、毛泽东思想	Marxism-Leninism, Mao Zedong Thought	496	921	127711
哲　学	Philosophy	2523	2061	250701
社会科学总论	General Social Sciences	2097	1786	209615
政治、法律	Politics and Law	8665	10039	1198205
军　事	Military Affairs	597	474	52414
经　济	Economics	14397	10776	1734366
文化、科学、教育、体育	Culture, Science, Education and Sports	77185	535055	31976461
语言、文字	Languages	8600	13692	1992237
文　学	Literature	11771	14731	1581246
艺　术	Arts	10655	24856	1027502
历史、地理	History and Geography	6046	9899	699482
自然科学总论	General Natural Sciences	921	3590	167377
数理科学、化学	Mathematics and Chemistry	3703	4019	575273
天文学、地球科学	Astronomy and Geology	678	207	26790
生物科学	Biology	800	630	84562
医学、卫生	Medicine and Health Care	8472	7427	900703
农业科学	Agricultural Science	3219	2330	203938
工业技术	Industrial Technology	22508	15818	2710545
交通运输	Transportation	1615	1335	159861
航空、航天	Aeronautics and Aerospace	179	82	9843
环境科学	Environmental Science	747	508	56034
综合性图书	General Books	2631	2607	267532
不使用“中国标准书号”图书	Publications without "China International Standard Book Number"	1886	4157	106054

22-15 各地区少年儿童读物类图书和课本出版情况（2003年）

Number of Books Published for Children and Textbooks by Region (2003)

地 区	Region	种 数(种) Number of Publication (kind)		总 印 数（万册） Printed Copies (10 000 copies)		总 印 张(千印张) Printed Sheets (1 000 sheets)	
		儿童读物 Books for Children	课本 Textbooks	儿童读物 Books for Children	课本 Textbooks	儿童读物 Books for Children	课本 Textbooks
全 国	**National Total**	**7588**	**28789**	**19895**	**325380**	**713282**	**20922860**
中 央	Center Publishing	1038	11740	2498	27315	124765	3036119
地 方	Local Publishing	6550	17049	17397	298065	588517	17886741
北 京	Beijing	193	450	181	399	13326	50044
天 津	Tianjin	253	608	334	2317	19792	167558
河 北	Hebei	181	399	240	18093	10183	977956
山 西	Shanxi	66	38	403	6585	4005	419886
内蒙古	Inner Mongolia	163	559	302	5675	9385	351736
辽 宁	Liaoning	272	974	549	8581	21683	561333
吉 林	Jilin	275	648	638	5826	37182	344037
黑龙江	Heilongjiang	106	304	368	5715	18043	354287
上 海	Shanghai	954	1892	1539	8321	69342	674059
江 苏	Jiangsu	423	1585	1003	23446	37509	1509744
浙 江	Zhejiang	769	853	2069	11141	83364	675798
安 徽	Anhui	273	272	468	18471	10670	1008751
福 建	Fujian	127	284	277	8973	10435	535776
江 西	Jiangxi	332	165	1227	11962	29684	665184
山 东	Shandong	133	598	582	13419	18772	661737
河 南	Henan	170	245	494	21617	12736	1247763
湖 北	Hubei	418	1391	1045	17457	35158	1088559
湖 南	Hunan	80	575	313	19309	7908	1067773
广 东	Guangdong	176	898	510	17691	13047	1144209
广 西	Guangxi	134	268	618	11379	25766	653511
海 南	Hainan	34	12	184	1988	3609	110171
重 庆	Chongqing	98	843	408	7445	6497	458938
四 川	Sichuan	291	892	1057	15382	23392	1015473
贵 州	Guizhou	31	84	397	7496	5691	431162
云 南	Yunnan	63	141	492	8812	13461	473216
西 藏	Tibet	1	216	1	714	43	36932
陕 西	Shaanxi	320	737	1214	10858	32175	642569
甘 肃	Gansu	54	9	101	3450	1615	205487
青 海	Qinghai	2	162	1	755	42	49276
宁 夏	Ningxia	23	7	54	789	1947	52356
新 疆	Xinjiang	135	940	328	3999	12055	251460

22-16 课本出版情况(2003年)
Publication of Textbooks (2003)

项　目	Item	种数（种）Number of Publication (kind)	#新出版 New Publication	总印数（万册）Printed Copies (10 000)	总印张（千印张）Printed Sheets (1 000)	定价总金额（万元）Total Priced Value (10 000 yuan)
总计	**Total**	**28789**	**9106**	**325380**	**20922860**	**1960647**
大专及以上课本	Textbooks for Colleges and Universities	14355	5575	16137	2690255	339872
中专、技校课本	Textbooks for Secondary Technical Schools	2319	509	4716	616772	69043
中学课本	Textbooks for Secondary Schools	3546	1021	138921	11295360	888249
小学课本	Textbooks for Primary Schools	4931	963	161778	5961980	625079
业余教育课本	Textbooks for Spare-time Education	665	286	700	82121	11678
扫盲课本	Textbooks for Eliminating Illiteracy	2	2	40	2700	116
教学用书	Teaching Materials	2971	750	3088	273672	26610

22-17 各地区图书发行流转情况 (2003年)
Basic Statistics on Distribution and Circulation of Books by Region (2003)

单位: 万册、万元 (10 000 copies) (10 000 yuan)

地　区	Region	图书购进 Purchases		图书销售 Sales		图书库存 Stock	
		册数 Copies	金额 Value	册数 Copies	金额 Value	册数 Copies	金额 Value
全　国	**National Total**	**1624146**	**11463286**	**1575423**	**10702012**	**385351**	**4013807**
中　央	Center Distribution Units	146314	2158406	133090	1877457	78111	1439919
地　方	Local Distribution Units	1477832	9304880	1442333	8824555	307240	2573888
北　京	Beijing	19769	248406	16514	220191	9311	126859
天　津	Tianjin	16258	135746	16221	133488	5089	58910
河　北	Hebei	89643	427180	90449	408497	14067	98482
山　西	Shanxi	34998	200380	34037	192021	5753	38339
内蒙古	Inner Mongolia	15353	85036	16097	83218	2689	20995
辽　宁	Liaoning	47790	352569	46805	328200	9360	129932
吉　林	Jilin	25652	175410	24107	153779	14744	80557
黑龙江	Heilongjiang	22483	137395	22276	128394	5361	46893
上　海	Shanghai	44884	569631	46890	536612	22371	290223
江　苏	Jiangsu	133458	935499	129044	894401	22446	166297
浙　江	Zhejiang	71668	511308	65818	454388	20838	190136
安　徽	Anhui	68787	334428	66107	319597	14552	85575
福　建	Fujian	43356	251126	42227	238516	6181	55993
江　西	Jiangxi	47743	271690	47620	267135	6908	51560
山　东	Shandong	104027	645096	100090	602822	21579	168218
河　南	Henan	130928	681448	129509	634831	20119	138334
湖　北	Hubei	52387	363839	50577	344135	11746	109542
湖　南	Hunan	65507	429007	65266	406169	13059	100524
广　东	Guangdong	78619	533588	72268	488904	18910	187664
广　西	Guangxi	49189	267332	51254	279500	6123	58472
海　南	Hainan	9973	67163	10112	67549	2978	12748
重　庆	Chongqing	32755	199263	32864	189679	6125	42307
四　川	Sichuan	89103	549652	88247	538416	13334	111773
贵　州	Guizhou	37341	138086	37517	138314	2055	11171
云　南	Yunnan	40031	204114	37584	193996	9008	55410
西　藏	Tibet	137	1666	189	1468	197	1317
陕　西	Shaanxi	47957	281189	46037	279140	12905	77330
甘　肃	Gansu	26511	129822	26688	129767	2770	20878
青　海	Qinghai	1874	16860	1909	17382	438	4363
宁　夏	Ningxia	5371	24704	4980	22987	1359	7258
新　疆	Xinjiang	24280	136247	23030	131059	4865	25828

22-18 各地区图书纯销售情况(2003年)
Net Sales of Books by Region (2003)

单位：万元 (10 000 yuan)

地区	Region	总计 Total Sales	对居民和社会集团零售 Retail Sales to Households and Institutions				批发 Wholesale		出口 Export
			合计 Total	市 Cities	县 Counties	县以下 Below Counties	供销社 Supply & Marketing Coops	集体和个体 Collectives and Individuals	
全 国	**National Total**	**4616387**	**3438451**	**1711317**	**887202**	**839932**	**254511**	**906795**	**16630**
中 央	Center Distribution Units	403874	112757	110000	2262	495	883	276427	13807
地 方	Local Distribution Units	4212513	3325694	1601317	884940	839437	253628	630368	2823
北 京	Beijing	117116	108016	95415	9568	3033	21	9053	26
天 津	Tianjin	70090	47118	32317	12553	2248	14	22268	690
河 北	Hebei	190457	185107	67381	68190	49536	131	5219	
山 西	Shanxi	103438	89430	33584	22855	32991	1200	12808	
内蒙古	Inner Mongolia	45935	44003	22526	18091	3386	26	1906	
辽 宁	Liaoning	131800	97111	79772	14208	3131	5673	29016	
吉 林	Jilin	56670	54389	35766	15368	3255	14	2267	
黑龙江	Heilongjiang	66719	57481	38261	16651	2569	31	9207	
上 海	Shanghai	222226	129869	113532	15852	485	240	90674	1443
江 苏	Jiangsu	394310	336706	129022	20375	187309	3330	54180	94
浙 江	Zhejiang	214889	179716	119391	36560	23765	4822	30136	215
安 徽	Anhui	180311	125185	49313	38412	37460	1351	53775	
福 建	Fujian	119170	91387	45731	21102	24554	17523	10072	188
江 西	Jiangxi	135063	127100	33906	87552	5642	156	7807	
山 东	Shandong	294238	253961	113462	54802	85697	6210	34067	
河 南	Henan	252049	180726	51061	30680	98985	18510	52807	6
湖 北	Hubei	128166	92141	46764	21498	23879	9832	26193	
湖 南	Hunan	200757	182983	59330	73934	49719	118	17610	46
广 东	Guangdong	332807	157050	138674	14291	4085	157302	18446	9
广 西	Guangxi	98761	66444	35351	14603	16490	3510	28716	91
海 南	Hainan	11883	4207	2845	1362			7676	
重 庆	Chongqing	87489	76674	30491	33614	12569	5573	5242	
四 川	Sichuan	245104	216944	79577	82636	54731	7608	20537	15
贵 州	Guizhou	72422	48616	16169	19062	13385		23806	
云 南	Yunnan	107875	96350	26071	39244	31035	10280	1245	
西 藏	Tibet	1206	1149	1149				57	
陕 西	Shaanxi	167595	122527	41476	52102	28949	150	44918	
甘 肃	Gansu	70012	64193	17815	17059	29319		5819	
青 海	Qinghai	8658	8173	4720	3365	88		485	
宁 夏	Ningxia	12867	12862	6754	5396	712		5	
新 疆	Xinjiang	72430	68076	33691	23955	10430	3	4351	

22-19 各地区录像制品出版情况(2003年)

Publication of Video Products (2003)

地区	Region	录像带 Videotapes		数码激光视盘 VCD		高密度激光视盘 DVD-V	
		种数 (种) Kind	数量 (万盒) Volume (10 000 cassettes)	种数 (种) Kind	数量 (万张) Volume (10 000 disks)	种数 (种) Kind	数量 (万张) Volume (10 000 disks)
全 国	**National Total**	**296**	**16.4**	**12651**	**30483.7**	**1944**	**4851.9**
中 央	Center Publishing House	237	5.1	4001	6748.6	525	811.8
地 方	Local Publishing House	59	11.2	8650	23735.1	1419	4040.2
北 京	Beijing	2	0.1	176	1423.3	50	211.8
天 津	Tianjin			50	52.4	36	61.5
河 北	Hebei	8	1.6	148	476.0	3	27.6
山 西	Shanxi			101	100.0		
内蒙古	Inner Mongolia			57	145.3	5	6.4
辽 宁	Liaoning	1	2.0	876	2967.6	245	1342.5
吉 林	Jilin			218	83.9		
黑龙江	Heilongjiang	5	4.9	185	56.3	7	3.0
上 海	Shanghai	10	0.4	558	502.4	22	67.4
江 苏	Jiangsu			217	237.4	12	33.8
浙 江	Zhejiang			393	233.7	109	7.6
安 徽	Anhui			1081	805.2	2	0.6
福 建	Fujian			734	6514.6	240	651.9
江 西	Jiangxi			284	114.9		
山 东	Shandong			133	1706.2	60	338.9
河 南	Henan			231	78.0	1	0.5
湖 北	Hubei	1	1.5	329	884.2	13	57.4
湖 南	Hunan	30	0.2	312	283.7	14	49.7
广 东	Guangdong	1	…	1324	5961.7	481	1097.8
广 西	Guangxi			101	254.1	11	15.1
海 南	Hainan			57	81.5	7	3.2
重 庆	Chongqing	1	0.5	455	339.7	52	28.0
四 川	Sichuan			85	40.5	13	10.0
贵 州	Guizhou			150	180.2	6	14.5
云 南	Yunnan			198	98.1	3	1.8
西 藏	Tibet			1	2.0	1	0.6
陕 西	Shaanxi			68	63.1	26	8.5
甘 肃	Gansu						
青 海	Qinghai						
宁 夏	Ningxia			97	40.3		
新 疆	Xinjiang			31	9.0		

22-20 各地区录音制品出版情况(2003年)

Publication of Audio Products by Region (2003)

地区	Region	录音带 Audio-tapes		激光唱盘 CDs		高密度激光唱盘 DVD-A	
		种数 (种) Kind	数量 (万盒) Volume (10 000 cassettes)	种数 (种) (Kind)	数量 (万张) Volume (10 000 pieces)	种数 (种) (Kind)	数量 (万张) Volume (10 000 pieces)
全　国	**National Total**	**8502**	**17646.30**	**4810**	**4340.53**	**21**	**17.23**
中　央	Center Publishing House	3281	9149.33	1365	1436.72		
地　方	Local Publishing House	5221	8496.97	3445	2903.81	21	17.23
北　京	Beijing	61	90.55	95	59.70		
天　津	Tianjin	112	210.12	59	61.30		
河　北	Hebei	67	218.43	37	38.80		
山　西	Shanxi	41	59.53	2	2.00		
内蒙古	Inner Mongolia	45	72.50	84	125.20		
辽　宁	Liaoning	80	229.36	42	27.60		
吉　林	Jilin	34	7.10	19	9.90		
黑龙江	Heilongjiang	10	1.28	17	3.65		
上　海	Shanghai	2127	4482.54	755	261.11	6	4.73
江　苏	Jiangsu	181	392.49	132	121.78		
浙　江	Zhejiang	181	40.97	61	20.50		
安　徽	Anhui	199	149.09	65	22.90		
福　建	Fujian	108	278.33	92	303.60	1	4.50
江　西	Jiangxi	149	203.61	104	127.47		
山　东	Shandong	12	3.00	11	7.80		
河　南	Henan	48	17.00	88	11.30		
湖　北	Hubei	299	450.02	75	87.47	1	1.00
湖　南	Hunan	286	193.02	219	76.69		
广　东	Guangdong	727	1103.29	993	1275.39	13	7.00
广　西	Guangxi	67	60.52	168	127.04		
海　南	Hainan	33	22.6	70	37.30		
重　庆	Chongqing	59	20.92	74	38.25		
四　川	Sichuan	81	24.56	87	16.40		
贵　州	Guizhou			23	5.45		
云　南	Yunnan	66	24.00	40	20.00		
西　藏	Tibet			1	2.40		
陕　西	Shaanxi	123	134.92	14	4.46		
甘　肃	Gansu	12	4.12				
青　海	Qinghai						
宁　夏	Ningxia			14	7.30		
新　疆	Xinjiang	13	3.10	4	1.05		

22-21 各地区两级定点书刊印刷企业主要产品产量(2003年)

Production of Designated Book Printing Enterprises by Region (2003)

地区	Region	机构数（个）Number of Enterprise (unit)	书刊排字（万字）Typesetting (10 000 characters)	书刊印刷（万令）Printing of Books (10 000 reams)	胶印印刷（万色令）Off-set Printing (10 000 color-reams)	零件印刷（万千印）Printing of Loose Sheets (10 000 k-prints)	书刊装订（万令）Binding of Books (10 000 reams)
全　国	**National Total**	**1123**	**1603572**	**6425**	**25466**	**938**	**5513**
中　央	Center Book Printing Enterprises	68	295760	687	1039	47	298
地　方	Local Book Printing Enterprises	1055	1307812	5738	24427	890	5215
北　京	Beijing	138	105999	732	1295	94	309
天　津	Tianjin	46	28555	143	677	13	78
河　北	Hebei	70	114945	444	689	20	416
山　西	Shanxi	18	13520	79	260	4	97
内蒙古	Inner Mongolia	18	38006	44	203	8	46
辽　宁	Liaoning	32	52818	170	292	8	201
吉　林	Jilin	24	7355	99	144	6	123
黑龙江	Heilongjiang	20	18809	79	269	11	77
上　海	Shanghai	45	38771	107	1103	50	60
江　苏	Jiangsu	56	78492	396	1123	126	367
浙　江	Zhejiang	33	49297	188	1583	101	227
安　徽	Anhui	39	5321	193	234	30	202
福　建	Fujian	29	41925	131	568	18	139
江　西	Jiangxi	32	10461	127	403	21	134
山　东	Shandong	66	217737	550	1034	78	673
河　南	Henan	61	58976	244	623	48	256
湖　北	Hubei	45	61264	345	658	27	348
湖　南	Hunan	41	42002	369	503	19	225
广　东	Guangdong	62	66203	373	9687	39	379
广　西	Guangxi	28	50222	259	722	53	156
海　南	Hainan	10	3171	21	506	3	13
重　庆	Chongqing	5	5759	39	105		42
四　川	Sichuan	22	20995	117	316	9	155
贵　州	Guizhou	13	21431	57	386	12	85
云　南	Yunnan	24	28114	108	124	20	72
西　藏	Tibet	2	8282	7	11		3
陕　西	Shaanxi	25	18749	143	472	16	143
甘　肃	Gansu	11	26434	102	170	13	94
青　海	Qinghai	9	25239	8	54	22	19
宁　夏	Ningxia	9	3996	11	23	2	7
新　疆	Xinjiang	22	44966	54	189	20	68

22-22 各地区国家定点书刊印刷企业主要财务经济指标(2003年)

Key Financial Indicators of State-designated Book Printing Enterprises by Region (2003)

单位：万元　　(10 000 yuan)

地　区	Region	产品销售收入 Revenue From Sales	产品销售成本 Cost of Sales	产品销售费用 Expenses of Sales	产品销售税金 Taxes From Sales	管理费用 Management Expenses	财务费用 Financial Expenses	利润总额 Total Profit	产成品存货 Stock of Finished Products	工业增加值 Industrial Value-added
全　国	**National Total**	**773949**	**604412**	**13602**	**6360**	**139088**	**21357**	**40616**	**108971**	**335796**
中　央	Center Book Printing Enterprises	80846	63487	1147	699	24247	736	4598	14149	44345
地　方	Local Book Printing Enterprises	693103	540924	12454	5660	114841	20621	36017	94822	291451
北　京	Beijing	24132	18638	563	115	6723	178	834	2579	8512
天　津	Tianjin	49156	38854	782	905	-1893	7199	10958	6780	26521
河　北	Hebei	29404	23953	479	248	6472	908	299	5808	12991
山　西	Shanxi	13207	9868	108	126	3195	419	192	3939	10378
内蒙古	Inner Mongolia	3743	2463	93	27	1377	100	47	982	837
辽　宁	Liaoning	25454	19424	981	269	5959	1400	1288	4358	9692
吉　林	Jilin	9772	7136	112	95	2147	171	611	2361	5576
黑龙江	Heilongjiang	4702	3629	329	59	903	49		2113	2011
上　海	Shanghai	36639	29369	566	218	7099	1115	1315	2153	13438
江　苏	Jiangsu	41346	32004	456	420	7442	1278	1808	3066	24330
浙　江	Zhejiang	27586	15103	312	120	2597	-4	1362	584	5452
安　徽	Anhui	17965	14017	234	166	3066	399	790	522	7647
福　建	Fujian	24002	18788	250	151	3852	565	1213	1158	11619
江　西	Jiangxi	19721	13099	292	134	3545	860	536	3226	5195
山　东	Shandong	62914	49004	1781	676	11301	1116	905	8871	22463
河　南	Henan	25144	19741	519	237	5365	124	1485	5455	15125
湖　北	Hubei	35603	27424	615	260	6851	731	1786	2870	10837
湖　南	Hunan	55315	49545	470	237	4809	552	974	8219	15620
广　东	Guangdong	72543	58396	1102	302	7666	921	4665	9059	27354
广　西	Guangxi	14630	12499	236	129	3487	-499	253	2752	6593
海　南	Hainan	4760	3821	43		1020	516	831	113	2267
重　庆	Chongqing	4186	3023	79	80	2063	177	1670	684	2851
四　川	Sichuan	16577	13605	432	122	3309	476	497	2594	7034
贵　州	Guizhou	6862	5006	16	70	1960	224	212	3419	3854
云　南	Yunnan	11391	7595	170	127	2877	155	630	1398	7015
西　藏	Tibet	3157	2473	26	23	496	-11	113		1374
陕　西	Shaanxi	24658	21147	634	116	3528	930	111	4765	10257
甘　肃	Gansu	15246	11498	572	140	3504	296	136	2849	6538
青　海	Qinghai	2489	2079	29	14	789	56	42	787	2044
宁　夏	Ningxia	2085	1794	8	9	366	9	249	28	1297
新　疆	Xinjiang	8715	5929	167	69	2966	212	205	1331	4730

22-23 我国与外国体育活动交往情况
Visits between Chinese and Foreign Sports Delegations

项　目	Item	1990	1995	2000	2002	2003
来我国的体育团体	Foreign Sports Delegations Visiting China					
次数 (次)	Number of Times (time)	364	1929	1000		
人数 (人次)	Person-Times (person-time)	3171	38700	20320		
我国派出的体育团体	Chinese Sports Delegations Visiting Foreign Countries					
次数 (次)	Number of Times (time)	607	2787	3880	3348	5615
人数 (人次)	Persons-Times (person-time)	5227	18033	22789	11733	7436

注：自1995年起来华、出访次数、人数包括地方各级体委组办数。自2003年起不再统计来我国的体育代表团体人数和次数。

a) Number of times and persons of foreign delegations visiting China and these of Chinese sports delegations visiting foreign countries included the visits organized by the local sports commissions since 1995. Since 2003, the statistics on number of times and person-times offoreign delegations visiting China does not carried out.

22-24 群众体育活动情况
Activities of Mass Sports

项　目	Item	1990	1995	2000	2002	2003
《国家体育锻炼标准》达标人数 (万人)	Number of Persons Who Have Come up to *the State Physical Training Standards* (10 000 persons)	7478	10608	15202	15001	14146
优秀级 (万人)	Excellent (10 000 persons)	1414	1888	2787		
良好级 (万人)	Good (10 000 persons)	2746	3586	5366		
及格级 (万人)	Pass (10 000 persons)	3318	5135	7048		
县以上体委举办运动会次数 (次)	Number of Sports Meets Held by Sports Commissions at and Above County Level (time)	30158	24880	26196	25981	37764
参加运动会的运动员人数 (万人)	Number of Athletes Attending Sports Meets (10 000 persons)	1076	1345	1272	1148	

注：自2003年起达标人数指标统计上不再区分优秀、良好和及格三级。

a) Number of persons who have come up to the State Physical Training Standards since 2003 are not classfied as excellent, good and pass.

22-25 体委系统职工人数(2003年)
Number of Staff and Workers in Sports Commissions (2003)

单位：人 (person)

人员分类	Category of Personnel	合计 Total	#优秀运动队 Excellent Sports Teams	#体育运动学校 Physical Education and Sports Schools	#业余体校 Space-time Sports Schools	#公共体育场馆 Public Stadiums and Gymnasiums	#训练基地 Training Bases
总　计	**Total**	**97062**	**35477**	**17196**	**28976**	**14295**	**1118**
运动员	Athletes	20527	20005	413	40	55	14
专职教练员	Full-time Coaches	23433	3987	4385	14539	472	50
专职文化教师	Full-time Teachers	9951	470	5385	4031	64	1
科技人员	Scientific and Technical Personnel	327	91	114	110	12	
医务人员	Medical Personnel	1300	770	318	159	49	4
管理人员	Administrative Personnel	22474	5578	3734	5683	7024	455
其他	Others	19050	4576	2847	4414	6619	594

注：自2003年起重点业余体校、体育中学和普通业余体校合并为一个指标，称业余体校。

a) Since 2003, key space-time sports schools, physical education middle schools, and popular space-time sports schools are ranked as the space-time sports schools.

22-26 等级运动员、等级裁判员人数（2003年）

Number of Athletes and Referees in Grades by Type of Sports (2003)

单位：人 (person)

运动项目	Item	等级运动员 Number of Athletes in Grades	#国际级运动健将 International Master of Sports	#运动健将 Master of Sports	#一级运动员 First Grade Sportsman	等级裁判员 Number of Referees in Grades	#国际裁判 International Referees	#国家级裁判 National Referees	#一级裁判 First Grade Referees
总计	**Total**		**148**	**1343**				**322**	
#田径	Athletics		6	117				65	
游泳	Swimming		7	26					
跳水	Diving		2	58				6	
水球	Water Polo			15					
举重	Weightlifting		1	51				23	
体操	Gymnastics		4	13				24	
艺术体操	Artistic Gymnastics		4	22				3	
射击	Shooting		14	130					
射箭	Archery			16				5	
国际式摔跤	Wrestling		9	42					
柔道	Judo		5	36					
自行车	Cycling		12	33					
击剑	Fencing		9	40				9	
赛艇	Rowing		3	45				14	
皮划艇	Canoeing		1	29				16	
帆船	Sailing		4	15				12	
冰球	Ice Hockey			35					
速度滑冰	Speed Skating		2	18					
篮球	Basketball		6	48					
排球	Volleyball			28					
足球	Football			26					
乒乓球	Table Tennis		3	37					
羽毛球	Badminton		3	32					
网球	Tennis			9				17	
手球	Handball			17					
棒球	Baseball			13					
垒球	Softball		1	36					
台球	Billiards							1	
技巧	Acrobatic Gymnastics			17					
国际象棋	International Chess			7					
中国象棋	Chinese Chess		1	11				37	
围棋	Weiqi							25	
武术	Wu Shu		3	63					
无线电测向	Radio Goniometry			1					
蹼泳	Web Swimming		9	15				2	
航海模型	Model Ship Sailing		4	4				11	
航空模型	Model Airplane		5	3				1	
花样游泳	Figure Swimming		4	17					
拳击	Boxing			22				3	
短道速滑	Short Skating			20					
花样滑冰	Figure Skating		7	16					
冰球	Ice Hockey			35					
跳伞	Parachute Jump		5	2					
登山	Mountaineering		2	14					
健美	Calisthenics			1				5	
蹦床	Trampoline			26				3	
跆拳道	Taekwondo		5	45				30	
沙滩排球	Beach Volleyball			17				3	
健美操	Aerobics		7	16				4	
马术	Equestrian			4					
体育舞蹈	Physical Dance							3	

注：自2003年起等级运动员指标不再统计三级和少年级运动员；等级裁判员指标不再统计三级裁判员。

a) Since 2003, number of athletes exclude the third grade sportsman and juvenile sportsman, and number of referees exclude the third grade referees.

22-27 运动员创世界纪录情况

World Records Chalked up by Chinese Athletes

单位: 项、人/队、次　　　　(item, person/team, times)

年份 Year	项数 Number of Events	#女子 Female	人、队数 Number of Persons/teams	#女子 Female	次数 Number of Times	#女子 Female
1956	1		1		3	
1957	3	1	3	1	3	1
1963	13	7	14	6	20	13
1965	28	12	66	28	41	20
1970	1		1		1	
1975	6	6	7	7	12	12
1978	3	3	6	6	3	3
1979	13	3	32	5	26	
1980	7		17		15	
1981	8	2	15	3	18	3
1982	11	4	16	8	15	4
1983	13	1	25	1	18	1
1984	12	6	17	10	17	10
1985	5	1	6	1	9	1
1986	7	4	12	4	12	6
1987	22	6	28	6	41	12
1988	33	20	16	13	34	29
1989	36	25	25	14	47	35
1990	14	9	17	10	16	9
1991	31	26	29	24	50	44
1992	42		31/4	27	106	102
1993	57	47	38/7	28/7	124	109
1994	41	39	26/4	24/4	72	69
1995	13	11	14/2	12/2	24	22
1996	22	15	17/1	13/1	30	22
1997	29	24	29/2	24/2	43	38
1998	31	27	30/3	26/3	68	64
1999	24	21	16	13	50	46
2000	22	17	14/2	10/1	30	25
2001	10	10	8/2	8/2	12	12
2002	29	25	17/5	14/4	33	29
2003	13	12	8/1	7	16	15

注: 1990年及以前各年集体项目的队数折合在人数中。

a) The number of teams in the years before 1990 was converted into the number of persons.

22-28 运动员分项创世界纪录情况（2003年）

World Records Chalked up by Chinese Athletes by Event (2003)

单位: 项、人/队、次 (item, person/team, times)

项目	Item	项数 Number of Events	#女子 Female	人数 Number of Persons/teams	#女子 Female	次数 Number of Times	#女子 Female
总计	**Total**	**13**	**12**	**8**	**7**	**16**	**15**
蹼泳	Web Swimming	2	2	2	2	2	2
射击	Shooting	1	1	1	1	1	1
举重	Weightlifting	9	8	5	4	12	11
短道速滑		1	1	1	1	1	1

22-29 运动员获世界冠军情况

World Championships Won by Chinese Athletes

单位: 项、人、个 (item, person, number)

年份 Year	项数 Number of Events	#女子 Female	人数 Number of Persons	#女子 Female	个数 Number of Times	#女子 Female
1959	1		1		1	
1963	4		7		4	
1965	5	2	9	4	5	2
1971	4	2	7	2	4	2
1975	2	1	9	4	2	1
1978	4	2	4	2	4	2
1979	12	6.5	20	11	12	6.5
1980	3		3		3	
1981	25	12.5	53	32	25	12.5
1982	12	2	31	15	13	2
1983	37	15	50	24	39	17
1984	33	10	46	26	37	10
1985	42	20	70	41	46	23
1986	26	14	56	34	26	14
1987	64	39	72	34	69	41.5
1988	54	36.5	59	30	54	36.5
1989	80	49	83	48	82	50
1990	54	33.5	61	30	54	33.5
1991	88	57.5	86	51	93	61.5
1992	86	69.5	68	52	89	72.5
1993	101	66.5	106	70	103	68.5
1994	79	53.5	86	45	79	53.5
1995	98	49.5	187	86	102	51.5
1996	72	55	58	42	75	57
1997	87	46	96	46	92	50.5
1998	75	49	89	59	83	55
1999	91	43	129	72	92	44
2000	92	52	109	60	110	66.5
2001	79	46.5	138	77	90	54.5
2002	99	58	123	81	110	64
2003	17	15.5	94	62.5	86	49

注：男女混合运动项目，女子按半项和半个计算。

a) Mixed doubles table tennis champions count 0.5 for females.

22-30 运动员分项获世界冠军情况（2003年）

World Championships Won by Chinese Athletes by Item (2003)

单位：项、人、个 (item, person, number)

项目	Item	项数 Number of Events	#女子 Female	人数 Number of Persons/teams	#女子 Female	次数 Number of Times	#女子 Female
总计	**Total**	**73**	**41**	**57**	**30**	**73**	**39**
跳水	Diving	4	3	5	4	4	3
举重	Weightlifting	19	12	7	4	19	12
乒乓球	Table Tennis	5	4.5	6	2	5	2.5
射击	Shooting	7	4	6	4	7	4
体操	Gymnastics	5	1	3	1	5	1
跳伞	Parachute	1	1	1	1	1	1
航海模型	Model Ship Sailing	4		3		4	
短道速滑	Short Skating	7	5	3	2	7	5
羽毛球	Badminton	3	2	4	3	3	2
武术	Wu Shu	17	8	17	8	17	8
花样滑冰	Figure Skating	1	0.5	2	1	1	0.5

注：男女混合运动项目，女子按半项和半个计算。

a) The number of events and times of mixed doubles is counted 0.5 for females.

22-31 运动员分项创全国纪录情况（2003年）

National Records Chalked up by Chinese Athletes (2003)

单位：项、人、队、次 (item, person, team, times)

项目	Item	项数 Number of Events	#女子 Female	人数 Number of Persons	#女子 Female	队数 Number of Teams	#女子 Female	次数 Number of Times	#女子 Female
总计	**Total**	**39**	**25**	**22**	**10**	**10**	**6**	**39**	**19**
田径	Athletics	5	3	5	3			5	3
游泳	Swimming	10	10	5	2	2	1	10	4
举重	Weightlifting	4	1	3	1			4	1
射箭	Archery	15	10	6	4	6	4	15	10
射击	Shooting	1				1		1	
自行车	Cycling	1		1				1	
短道速滑	Short Skating	1	1			1	1	1	1
室内田径	Indoor Athletics	2		2				2	

注：人数栏中是个人单项创全国纪录的运动员人数，队数栏中是集体项目创全国纪录的队数，队中人数未计算在人数中。

a) The number of persons refers to the number of persons who have chalked up the national records in single events. The number of teams refers to the number of teams which have chalked up the national records in the collective events. The number of persons in the teams is excluded in the "number of persons".

22-32 卫 生 机 构 数

Number of Health Institutions

单位：个 (unit)

年 份 Year	总 计 Total	医院、卫生院 Hospitals	疗养院 Sanatoriums	门诊部、诊所 Clinics	专科防治院(所、站) Specialized Prevention & Treatment Centers or Stations
1978	169732	64309	389	94395	887
1980	180553	65315	470	102474	1138
1985	200866	59342	640	126604	1566
1989	206724	61613	651	128112	1747
1990	208734	62126	650	129332	1781
1991	209036	62768	642	128665	1818
1992	204787	61006	639	125873	1845
1993	193586	60460	600	115161	1872
1994	191742	67524	587	105984	1905
1995	190057	67460	582	104406	1895
1996	322566	67556	528	237153	1887
1997	315033	67479	506	229474	1893
1998	314097	66614	503	229349	1889
1999	310996	66385	503	226588	1877
2000	324771	65944	471	240934	1839
2001	330348	64840	461	248061	1783
2002	306038	63858	365	219907	1839
2003	291323	62968	305	204468	1749

22-32 续表 continued

单位：个 (unit)

年 份 Year	疾病预防控制中心(防疫站) CDC (Epidemic Prevention Station)	妇幼保健院(所、站) Maternity and Child Care Centers	医学科学研究机构 Research Institutions of Medical Science	其他卫生机构 Other Institutions
1978	2989	2571	219	3973
1980	3105	2745	282	5024
1985	3410	2996	323	5985
1989	3591	3112	328	7570
1990	3618	3148	337	7742
1991	3652	3187	335	7969
1992	3673	3187	339	8225
1993	3609	3115	436	8333
1994	3611	3190	437	8504
1995	3629	3179	427	8479
1996	3635	3172	427	8208
1997	3619	3180	426	8456
1998	3613	3191	423	8515
1999	3627	3180	421	8415
2000	3741	2598	405	8827
2001	3813	3132	397	8124
2002	3580	3067	298	13124
2003	3584	3033	284	14932

注：1.1995年及以前的卫生机构数不含私人诊所。
2.1997年开始原不列入卫生机构的"个体开业人员" 改称"私人办诊所"并列入门诊部（所）中；门诊部（所）包括门诊部、诊所、卫生保健所和医务室；
3.2001年及以前的医院数包括专科疾病防治院；疾病预防控制中心(防疫站)包括预防保健中心；
4.2002年及以后卫生机构数为登记注册数，卫生机构数不包括高中等医学院校、药检机构和非卫生部门办的计划生育指导站。

a) Number of health institutions exclude the private clinics before 1995.
b) "Individual practitioners" that were not included in the number of health institutions were reclassified as "private clinics" and were included in the number of clinics since 1997, Number of clinics include clinics, health care stations, and infirmary.
c) Number of hospitals before 2002 includes specialized prevention and treatment institutions, and CDC (epidemic prevention station) include health prevention and care centers.
d) Number of health institutions since 2002 are the number of registeration and exclude higher and middle medical colleges, drug test institutions and family planning guidance station of non-health dapartment.

22-33 卫生机构的人员数

Number of Employed Personnel in Health Institutions

单位：万人 (10 000 persons)

年 份 Year	总 计 Total	卫生技术人员 Medical and Technical Personnel	#医 生 Doctors	#护师、护士 Senior and Junior Nurses	每千人口医生数(人) Number of Doctors per 1 000 Population
1978	310.6	246.4	103.3	40.7	1.07
1980	353.5	279.8	115.3	46.6	1.17
1985	431.3	341.1	141.3	63.7	1.33
1989	478.7	380.9	171.8	92.2	1.52
1990	490.6	389.8	176.3	97.5	1.54
1991	502.5	398.5	178.0	101.2	1.54
1992	514.0	407.4	180.8	104.0	1.54
1993	521.5	411.7	183.2	105.6	1.55
1994	530.7	419.9	188.2	109.4	1.57
1995	537.3	425.7	191.8	112.6	1.58
1996	541.9	431.2	194.1	116.3	1.59
1997	551.6	439.8	198.5	119.8	1.61
1998	553.6	442.4	200.0	121.9	1.60
1999	557.0	445.9	204.5	124.5	1.67
2000	559.1	449.1	207.6	126.7	1.68
2001	558.4	450.8	210.0	128.7	1.69
2002	523.8	427.0	184.4	124.7	1.47
2003	527.5	430.6	186.8	126.6	1.48

注：2002年及以后医生系执业(助理)医师数，护师(士)系注册护士数，故有所减少。

a) Doctors since 2002 refer to the certified (assistant) doctors, nurses refer to the registration nurses, so the numbers decreased somewhat.

22-34 卫生机构床位数

Number of Beds in Health Institutions

单位：万张 (10 000 units)

年 份 Year	总 计 Total	医院、卫生院 Hospitals	疗养院 Sanatoriums	妇幼保健院(所、站) Maternity and Child Care Centers	其他卫生机构 Other Health Institutions	每千人口医院、卫生院床位数(张) Number of Hospital Beds per 1 000 Population (unit)
1978	204.2	184.7	5.1	1.2	13.2	1.93
1980	218.4	197.1	6.8	1.6	12.9	2.01
1985	248.7	220.5	10.6	3.5	14.1	2.11
1989	286.7	253.7	12.3	4.5	16.2	2.28
1990	292.5	259.2	12.3	4.7	16.3	2.30
1991	299.2	265.6	12.5	4.8	16.3	2.32
1992	304.9	270.9	12.5	5.0	16.5	2.34
1993	309.9	276.7	11.9	4.5	16.8	2.36
1994	313.4	280.2	11.8	4.8	16.6	2.36
1995	314.1	280.6	11.6	5.1	16.8	2.34
1996	310.0	283.4	10.9	5.6	10.1	2.34
1997	313.5	286.9	10.4	6.0	10.2	2.35
1998	314.3	287.8	10.2	6.3	10.0	2.33
1999	315.9	289.0	9.8	6.6	10.5	2.39
2000	317.7	290.8	9.7	7.1	10.1	2.38
2001	320.1	293.5	9.5	7.4	9.7	2.39
2002	313.6	290.7	6.9	8.0	8.0	2.32
2003	316.4	295.5	4.8	8.1	8.0	2.34

22-35 按市县分卫生机构床位数和卫生技术人员

Beds and Medical Technical Personnel in Health Institutions By City and County Areas

年 份 Year	卫生机构床位数(万张) Beds in Health Institutions (10 000 units)		卫生技术人员(万人) Medical Technical Personnel (10 000 persons)		# 医 生 Doctors		# 护师、护士 Senior and Junior Nurses	
	市 City	县 County	市 City	县 County	市 City	县 County	市 City	县 County
1952	12.1	3.9	22.5	46.5	8.1	34.3	4.3	1.8
1957	22.1	7.4	38.2	65.7	13.8	40.8	10.0	2.8
1962	43.7	25.3	57.1	84.3	21.4	47.4	15.5	4.5
1965	45.8	30.8	65.2	88.0	26.9	49.4	17.6	5.9
1970	51.0	59.5	59.6	85.7	24.1	46.1	18.0	11.6
1975	63.7	96.1	95.7	110.0	36.7	51.0	24.0	14.0
1978	71.6	114.0	114.2	132.1	44.2	59.1	25.7	14.9
1980	76.8	121.4	131.3	148.5	52.7	62.6	30.0	16.6
1981	80.3	121.4	143.5	157.6	58.6	65.8	33.4	19.1
1982	83.2	122.1	150.9	163.4	62.8	67.9	35.4	21.0
1983	86.9	124.0	157.4	167.9	66.5	68.7	37.3	22.3
1984	91.9	124.7	164.2	170.2	69.4	68.8	39.3	22.3
1985	96.2	126.7	167.7	173.4	70.9	70.4	39.2	24.5
1986	103.3	126.4	177.4	173.3	74.9	69.5	42.9	25.2
1987	112.7	127.7	188.2	172.6	79.3	68.9	46.1	25.7
1988	125.5	124.8	202.8	169.6	88.6	73.2	53.7	29.2
1989	133.5	123.3	212.1	168.8	95.0	76.8	59.9	32.2
1990	138.7	123.7	218.5	171.3	97.8	78.5	63.4	34.1
1991	144.8	124.0	226.4	172.1	100.3	77.7	66.6	34.6
1992	152.4	122.0	236.3	171.1	104.3	76.5	69.5	34.5
1993	159.6	119.9	243.3	168.5	107.7	75.5	71.5	34.1
1994	170.7	112.4	258.9	161.0	115.0	73.2	76.2	33.2
1995	174.0	109.7	265.9	159.8	118.4	73.4	79.0	33.5
1996	179.1	107.5	272.2	159.0	120.3	73.8	82.3	34.0
1997	184.2	106.1	279.5	160.3	123.5	75.0	85.3	34.6
1998	187.2	104.2	281.9	160.5	124.2	75.7	87.0	34.9
1999	188.7	104.2	283.0	162.9	126.1	78.4	88.6	35.9
2000	191.4	103.4	283.5	165.6	126.8	80.8	89.8	36.9
2001	195.9	101.7	287.2	163.6	129.5	80.5	91.8	36.9
2002								
2003	215.0	101.5	282.8	147.8	121.6	65.2	92.8	33.8

注：2001及以前按市县分的卫生机构床位数为医院、卫生院床位数。

a) Number of beds in health institutions by city and county before 2001 refer to hospital beds.

22-36 医院、卫生院平均每院床位和人员数

Average Number of Beds and Persons Engaged Per Hospital

项 目	Item	2002 床 位(张) Beds (unit)	2002 人 员(人) Personnel (person)	2002 #卫生技术人员 Medical Technical Personnel	2003 床 位(张) Beds (unit)	2003 人 员(人) Personnel (person)	2003 #卫生技术人员 Medical Technical Personnel
医院合计	**Hospitals**	**124.5**	**170.6**	**134.4**	**127.8**	**172.7**	**136.5**
#综合医院	General Hospitals	132.4	185.1	146.6	136.0	187.1	148.5
中医医院	TCM Hospitals	99.0	153.7	124.1	103.3	157.4	127.6
专科医院	Specialized Hospitals	117.2	119.3	86.9	117.6	121.0	88.4
卫生院合计	**Township Hospitals**	**14.9**	**23.8**	**20.4**	**15.2**	**24.0**	**20.6**
城市街道卫生院	Urban Township Hospitals	13.8	28.9	24.6	14.0	30.7	26.2
农村乡(镇)卫生院	Rural Township Hospitals	14.9	23.7	20.3	15.2	23.9	20.5

22-37 各地区卫生机构、床位数(2003年)

Number of Health Institutions, Beds and Employed Personnel by Region (2003)

地 区	Region	卫生机构数（个）Health Institutions (unit)	#医院 Hospital	#卫生院 Health Center	#门诊部、所 Clinics	#疾病预防控制中心(防疫站) CDC	#妇幼保健院(所站) Maternity and Child Care Centers	医疗机构床位数（张）Beds Total (bed)	#医院、卫生院 Hospital and Health Center
全 国	**National Total**	**291323**	**17764**	**45204**	**204468**	**3584**	**3033**	**3144235**	**2955160**
北 京	Beijing	5073	458	187	4204	29	19	74134	70823
天 津	Tianjin	7132	273	212	6183	25	22	40095	38070
河 北	Hebei	9018	770	3227	4313	194	186	157920	149587
山 西	Shanxi	12960	833	1650	9804	150	133	103368	98591
内蒙古	Inner Mongolia	4036	450	1368	1728	146	117	64898	60530
辽 宁	Liaoning	12533	912	1096	8057	129	117	170636	158215
吉 林	Jilin	7695	595	836	4775	75	72	85828	80810
黑龙江	Heilongjiang	8469	831	979	5927	202	150	115594	109073
上 海	Shanghai	7500	219	126	5712	22	23	83360	74731
江 苏	Jiangsu	8870	898	1607	5492	135	110	176101	169247
浙 江	Zhejiang	6261	474	2509	2286	103	88	126363	117644
安 徽	Anhui	15688	615	2147	11872	133	117	118882	112424
福 建	Fujian	8525	338	979	6492	94	91	78309	69991
江 西	Jiangxi	3348	498	1548	763	112	110	82394	77023
山 东	Shandong	4855	1042	1864	1116	175	149	216116	201827
河 南	Henan	13621	1102	2043	9308	180	165	202334	192720
湖 北	Hubei	9498	599	1189	7136	109	92	136002	127999
湖 南	Hunan	14539	717	2628	9839	167	132	143631	133772
广 东	Guangdong	13213	867	1532	9768	131	127	186865	172549
广 西	Guangxi	6610	444	1305	4374	105	103	88081	82206
海 南	Hainan	19470	192	311	18604	31	25	17847	17028
重 庆	Chongqing	3730	363	1318	1864	46	44	62696	59794
四 川	Sichuan	16756	1157	6048	8138	208	198	185423	176616
贵 州	Guizhou	13178	390	1465	10719	99	93	59118	56199
云 南	Yunnan	3006	557	1494	442	151	151	95844	89677
西 藏	Tibet	5166	97	672	4184	81	53	6212	5859
陕 西	Shaanxi	14369	813	1861	10924	128	115	101963	95712
甘 肃	Gansu	8037	382	1478	5684	103	98	60439	56946
青 海	Qinghai	9559	131	406	8824	54	19	15384	15001
宁 夏	Ningxia	8990	122	279	8372	28	25	15740	14815
新 疆	Xinjiang	9618	625	840	7564	239	89	72658	69681

22-38 各地区卫生机构人员数（2003年）

Number of Employed Personnel in Health Institutions by Region (2003)

单位：人 (person)

地　区	Region	人员合计 Total	# 卫生技术人员 Medical Technical Personnel	# 执业(助理)医师 Doctors	# 注册护士 Nurses
全　国	**National Total**	**5274786**	**4306471**	**1867957**	**1265959**
北　京	Beijing	148191	112043	47819	39875
天　津	Tianjin	78286	60795	25808	19633
河　北	Hebei	262278	216962	97141	50992
山　西	Shanxi	169870	143810	66778	39297
内蒙古	Inner Mongolia	120369	101153	49344	25566
辽　宁	Liaoning	269252	210705	92835	71890
吉　林	Jilin	161398	128638	57016	40076
黑龙江	Heilongjiang	192858	149964	63876	44989
上　海	Shanghai	133038	102211	44136	37894
江　苏	Jiangsu	302192	242586	103428	73508
浙　江	Zhejiang	207937	173010	79310	49298
安　徽	Anhui	185916	152665	62112	42306
福　建	Fujian	114893	96902	41252	31545
江　西	Jiangxi	138068	115036	48219	33617
山　东	Shandong	366895	308123	132372	90204
河　南	Henan	348890	278656	106363	72001
湖　北	Hubei	255648	207860	86969	63684
湖　南	Hunan	254697	212126	90507	58235
广　东	Guangdong	336175	273620	108677	88536
广　西	Guangxi	146747	118181	50155	40713
海　南	Hainan	36191	29083	11850	9875
重　庆	Chongqing	92978	77449	36426	20405
四　川	Sichuan	288300	240898	115797	59494
贵　州	Guizhou	91057	77557	36911	21844
云　南	Yunnan	134508	112396	52967	35647
西　藏	Tibet	10058	8287	4299	1756
陕　西	Shaanxi	164398	134732	60294	37183
甘　肃	Gansu	96538	82306	35094	22400
青　海	Qinghai	22987	19822	9099	5940
宁　夏	Ningxia	27589	23126	10666	7274
新　疆	Xinjiang	116584	95769	40437	30282

22-39 卫生机构各类人员数

Employed Persons in Health Care Institutions by Type of Occupation

单位：万人 (10 000 persons)

人员分类	Type of Personnel	1990	1995	2000	2002	2003
总计	**Total**	**490.6**	**537.3**	**559.1**	**523.8**	**527.5**
卫生技术人员	Medical Technical Personnel	389.8	425.7	449.1	427.0	430.6
其他技术人员	Other Technical Personnel	8.6	12.1	15.8	18.0	19.9
管理人员	Managerial Personnel	39.7	45.0	42.7	33.3	31.9
工勤人员	Logistics Workers	52.6	54.5	51.6	45.6	45.2
卫生技术人员	**Medical Technical Personnel**	**389.8**	**425.7**	**449.1**	**427.0**	**430.6**
医生	Doctor & Assistant Doctor	176.3	191.8	207.6	184.4	186.8
其中:医师	of which: Doctor	130.3	145.5	160.3	146.4	148.6
护师、士	Senior Nurse & Nurse	97.5	112.6	126.7	124.7	126.6
药技人员	Pharmacist	40.6	41.9	41.4	35.8	35.7
检验人员	Laboratory Technician	17.0	18.9	20.1	20.9	21.0
其他	Others	58.4	60.5	53.3	61.2	60.6
平均每千人口有卫生技术人员(人)	**Number of Medical Technical Personnel Per 1 000 Population**	**3.4**	**3.5**	**3.6**	**3.4**	**3.4**

22-40 各类医疗机构诊疗人次及入院人数(2003年)

Number of Visits and Inpatients in Medical Institutions (2003)

医疗机构	Medical Institutions	诊疗人次(亿次) Visits (100 million person-times)			入院人数(万人) Inpatients (10 000 persons)		
		合计 Total	非营利 Non- profit	营利 Profit	合计 Total	非营利 Non- profit	营利 Profit
总计	**Total**	**20.96**	**20.33**	**0.56**	**6092**	**5921**	**150**
医院	Hospital	12.13	11.75	0.36	4159	4021	135
#综合医院	General Hospital	9.31	9.04	0.25	3379	3294	82
中医医院	TCM Hospital	1.90	1.87	0.03	462	441	21
专科医院	Specialized Hospital	0.76	0.68	0.07	275	245	30
疗养院	Sanitarium	0.01	0.07		3	3	
社区卫生服务中心	Health Service Center for Community	0.38	0.38		10	10	
卫生院	Health Center	7.10	7.01	0.06	1626	1601	11
#乡镇卫生院	Township Health Center	6.91	6.82	0.06	1608	1583	11
门诊部	Outpatient Department	0.39	0.26	0.13	11	8	3
妇幼保健院(所、站)	MCH Center	0.78	0.76		259	257	
专科疾病防治院(所、站)	Specialized Disease Prevention & Treatment Institute	0.17	0.16		23	21	

22-41 医疗机构病床使用情况(2003年)

Utilization of Beds in Medical Institutions (2003)

医疗机构	Medical Institutions	病床使用率（%） Utilization Rate (%)			出院者平均住院日 Average Stay Days in Hospital		
		合计 Total	非营利 Non- profit	营利 Profit	合计 Total	非营利 Non- profit	营利 Profit
总计	**Total**	**58.7**	**59.0**	**47.7**	**9.0**	**9.0**	**6.4**
医院	Hospital	65.3	65.8	48.7	11.0	11.1	6.9
#综合医院	General Hospital	65.3	65.8	47.5	10.4	10.4	7.0
中医医院	TCM Hospital	59.0	59.4	44.9	10.6	10.9	3.9
专科医院	Specialized Hospital	71.9	73.5	53.3	19.9	21.3	9.1
疗养院	Sanitarium	39.1	39.2	32.2	18.4	18.4	
社区卫生服务中心	Health Service Center for Community	67.1	67.3	31.2	23.8	24.1	4.1
卫生院	Health Center	36.2	36.1	35.5	4.2	4.2	4.7
#乡镇卫生院	Township Health Center	36.2	36.1	35.6	4.2	4.2	4.7
妇幼保健院(所、站)	MCH Center	57.6	57.9	15.8	5.4	5.4	2.2
专科疾病防治院(所、站)	Specialized Disease Prevention & Treatment Institution	55.2	54.8	89.3	16.3	17.9	10.2

22-42 城市前十位疾病死亡原因及构成(2003年)

Death Rate of 10 Major Diseases in Urban Areas (2003)

顺位 No.	疾病死亡原因	Cause of Death	占死亡总人数的% As % of Total Deaths
	十种死因合计	**Total**	**89.09**
1	恶性肿瘤	Malignant Tumour	25.47
2	脑血管病	Cerebrovasular Disease	19.95
3	呼吸系病	Respiratory Disease	14.63
4	心脏病	Heart Trouble	14.43
5	损伤和中毒	Trauma and Toxicosis	6.16
6	消化系病	Digestive Disease	3.66
7	内分泌、营养、代谢及免疫疾病	Internal System, Nutrition, Metabolite and Immunity Disease	2.66
8	泌尿、生殖系病	Urinary Disease	1.34
9	神经病	Neuropathy	0.91
10	围产期病	Disease Originating in the Perinatal Period	0.89
	男性十种死因合计	**Male Total**	**90.14**
1	恶性肿瘤	Malignant Tumour	28.78
2	脑血管病	Cerebrovasular Disease	19.23
3	呼吸系病	Respiratory Disease	15.04
4	心脏病	Heart Trouble	13.22
5	损伤和中毒	Trauma and Toxicosis	6.67
6	消化系病	Digestive Disease	2.75
7	内分泌、营养、代谢及免疫疾病	Internal System, Nutrition, Metabolite and Immunity Disease	2.73
8	泌尿、生殖系病	Urinary Disease	1.28
9	神经病	Neuropathy	0.87
10	围产期病	Disease Originating in the Perinatal Period	0.68
	女性十种死因合计	**Female Total**	**87.87**
1	恶性肿瘤	Malignant Tumour	21.62
2	脑血管病	Cerebrovasular Disease	20.79
3	呼吸系病	Respiratory Disease	16.26
4	心脏病	Heart Trouble	13.71
5	损伤和中毒	Trauma and Toxicosis	5.57
6	内分泌、营养、代谢及免疫疾病	Internal System, Nutrition, Metabolite and Immunity Disease	4.71
7	消化系病	Digestive Disease	2.58
8	泌尿、生殖系病	Urinary Disease	1.41
9	神经病	Neuropathy	0.81
10	围产期病	Disease Originating in the Perinatal Period	0.41

22-43 农村前十位疾病死亡原因及构成(2003年)

Death Rate of 10 Major Diseases in Rural Areas (2003)

顺位 No.	疾病死亡原因	Cause of Death	占死亡总人数的% As % of Total Deaths
	十种死因合计	**Total**	**92.91**
1	恶性肿瘤	Malignant Tumour	25.28
2	脑血管病	Cerebrovascular Disease	23.75
3	呼吸系病	Respiratory Disease	18.72
4	心脏病	Heart Trouble	12.03
5	损伤和中毒	Trauma and Toxicosis	5.69
6	内分泌、营养、代谢及免疫疾病	Internal System, Nutrition, Metabolite and Immunity Disease	3.56
7	消化系病	Digestive Disease	2.78
8	泌尿、生殖系病	Urinary Disease	1.89
9	围产期病	Disease Originating in the Perinatal Period	1.11
10	肺结核	Pulmonary Tuberculosis	1.10
	男性十种死因合计	**Male Total**	**93.35**
1	恶性肿瘤	Malignant Tumour	23.33
2	脑血管病	Cerebrovascular Disease	20.94
3	呼吸系病	Respiratory Disease	18.21
4	心脏病	Heart Trouble	14.87
5	损伤和中毒	Trauma and Toxicosis	8.20
6	消化系病	Digestive Disease	3.41
7	内分泌、营养、代谢及免疫疾病	Internal System, Nutrition, Metabolite and Immunity	1.84
8	泌尿、生殖系病	Disease Urinary Disease	1.60
9	肺结核	Pulmonary Tuberculosis	1.15
10	围产期病	Disease Originating in the Perinatal Period	0.80
	女性十种死因合计	**Female Total**	**90.96**
1	脑血管病	Cerebrovascular Disease	21.35
2	呼吸系病	Respiratory Disease	21.35
3	恶性肿瘤	Malignant Tumour	18.50
4	心脏病	Heart Trouble	18.04
5	损伤和中毒	Trauma and Toxicosis	4.99
6	消化系病	Digestive Disease	3.02
7	内分泌、营养、代谢及免疫疾病	Internal System, Nutrition, Metabolite and Immunity Disease	2.72
8	泌尿、生殖系病	Urinary Disease	1.70
9	围产期病	Disease Originating in the Perinatal Period	0.81
10	精神障碍	Mental Disorders	0.48

注：统计范围包括北京等90个县的资料。

a) Statistics in the table cover full or partial areas of 90 counties, including counties in Beijing.

22-44 法定报告传染病发病及死亡情况（2003年）

Incidence and Death from Infectious Diseases (2003)

病　　名	Item	发病率 (1/10万) Incidence Disease Rate (per 100 000 persons)	死亡率 (1/10万) Death Rate (per 100 000 persons)	病死率 (%) Mortality Rate per 100 Infectious Disease Patients
总计	**Total**	**192.18**	**0.48**	**0.25**
鼠疫	The Plague			7.69
霍乱	Cholera	0.02		0.41
病毒性肝炎	Viral Hepatitis	68.55	0.08	0.12
痢疾	Dysentery	34.52	0.02	0.05
伤寒副伤寒	Typhoid and Paratyphoid Fever	4.17		0.06
艾滋病	AIDS	0.08	0.03	33.10
淋病	Gonorrhea	14.09		
梅毒	Syphilis	4.50		0.05
脊髓灰质炎	Poliomyelitis			
麻疹	Measles	5.55	0.01	0.11
百日咳	Pertussis	0.41		0.05
白喉	Diphtheria			33.33
流脑	Epidemic Encephalitis	0.19	0.01	5.48
猩红热	Scarlet Fever	0.75		0.01
出血热	Hemorrhage Fever	1.68	0.01	0.76
狂犬病	Hydrophobia	0.15	0.15	97.20
钩端螺旋体病	Leptospirosis	0.13		3.33
布氏杆菌病	Brucellosis	0.48		
炭疽	Anthrax	0.04		1.66
斑疹伤寒	Typhus Fever	0.30		0.05
乙脑	Encephalitis B	0.58	0.03	4.66
黑热病	Kala-Azar	0.01		
疟疾	Malaria	3.00		0.14
登革热	Dengue Fever	0.01		
新生儿破伤风	Newborn Baby Tetanus	0.18	0.03	14.51
肺结核	Pulmonary Tuberculosis	52.36	0.08	0.16
传染性非典型肺炎	SARS	0.40	0.03	6.55

注：新生儿破伤风发病率和死亡率单位为1‰。
a) The unit of incidence disease rate and death rate of newborn baby tetanus is 1‰.

22-45 卫 生 总 费 用

Expenditure for Public Health

本表按当年价格计算。
The data in this table are calculated at current prices.

单位：亿元 (100 million yuan)

项目	Item	1997	1998	1999	2000	2001	2002
卫生总费用	**Total Expenditure for Public Health**	**3384.9**	**3776.5**	**4178.6**	**4764.0**	**5150.3**	**5684.6**
政府预算卫生支出	Government Budgetary Expenditure	522.1	587.2	640.9	709.5	800.6	864.5
公共卫生服务经费	Public Health Services	362.3	410.5	449.7	498.5	564.9	
公费医疗经费	Social Medicine	159.8	176.7	191.3	211.0	235.8	
社会卫生支出	Social Expenditure	937.7	1006.0	1064.6	1167.7	1236.4	1503.6
居民个人卫生支出	Resident Individual Expenditure	1925.1	2183.3	2473.1	2886.7	3113.3	3316.5

注：本表卫生费用为测算数。
a) Data in the table are estimated.

主要统计指标解释

文化事业机构 指从事专业文化工作和为专业文化工作服务的独立建制的单位。不包括这些单位另外举办独立核算的其他机构和各部门的业余文化组织。该指标主要反映文化事业机构发展规模水平。

艺术表演团体 指从事戏曲、音乐、舞蹈、杂技等专业艺术表演，有独立帐户的单位，不包括半工半艺、半农半艺和民间职业剧团。该指标主要反映全国专业艺术表演团体发展规模水平。

艺术表演观众人数(人次) 指售票、包场演出或民族地区免费演出的艺术表演观众人次数，不包括彩排审查和内部观摩演出的观看人次数。该指标主要反映全国观看专业艺术表演团体演出的效益规模。

等级运动员人数 指经考核正式批准授予等级运动员称号的人数。运动员等级分为国际级运动健将、运动健将、一级运动员、二级运动员、三级运动员、少年级运动员。该指标主要反映运动员队伍的技术质量水平。

等级裁判员人数 指经考核正式批准授予等级裁判员称号的人数。裁判员等级分为国际裁判、国家级裁判、一级裁判、二级裁判、三级裁判。该指标主要反映裁判员队伍的技术质量水平。

体育场 指有400米跑道(中心含足球场)，有固定道牙，跑道6条以上，并有固定看台的室外田径场地。体育场按看台容纳观众人数分为：甲级25000人以上，乙级15000–25000人，丙级5000–15000人，丁级5000人以下。该指标主要反映大中型体育场数量水平。

体育馆 指有固定看台，可供篮球、排球、羽毛球、乒乓球、体操等项目训练比赛活动用的室内运动场地。体育馆按看台容纳观众人数分为：甲级6000人以上，乙级4000–6000人，丙级2000–4000人，丁级2000人以下。该指标主要反映大中型体育馆数量水平。

卫生机构 包括医疗机构、疾病预防控制中心(防疫站)、采供血机构、卫生监督及监测(检验)机构、医学科研和在职培训机构、健康教育所等。

医疗机构 包括医院、社区卫生服务中心(站)、疗养院、卫生院、门诊部、诊所(卫生所、医务室)、妇幼保健院(所、站)、专科疾病防治院(所、站)、急救中心(站)和临床检验中心。医疗机构分为非赢利性医疗机构和赢利性医疗机构。

医院 包括综合医院、中医医院、中西医结合医院、民族医院、各类专科医院和护理院。

卫生技术人员 指卫生机构中医生、护理人员 、药剂人员、检验人员等卫生技术人员。

医生 指在医疗、预防保健机构工作且取得《执业医师证书》的执业医师和执业助理医师。

卫生服务总费用 反映全国当年用于医疗卫生保健服务所消耗的资金总额，用筹资来源法测算。政府预算卫生支出指各级政府用于卫生事业的财政预算拨款。社会卫生支出指政府预算外的卫生资金投入，主要表现为社会医疗保险。其中包括如企事业单位和乡村集体经济单位举办医疗卫生机构设施建设费，企业职工医疗卫生费，行政事业单位负担的职工公费医疗超支部分等。居民个人卫生支出指城乡居民用自己可支配的经济收入支付的各项医疗卫生费用和医疗保险费用。

Explanatory Notes on Main Statistical Indicators

Cultural Institutions refer to units, which have their own organizational system and independent accounting system and specialize in or serve cultural development. They exclude other establishments run by these cultural institutions and amateur cultural groups established by various departments. This indicator reflects the development of cultural units.

Art Troupe refers to the troupe which is engaged in drama, opera, music, dance, acrobatics or other art performance, opens independent accounts with banks and has self-supporting accounting system; excluding the troupes which are engaged partly in industrial or agricultural activities, partly in art performance and the professional troupes organized by the people. This indicator reflects the development of national professional art troupes.

Number of Audience at Art Performance refers to the number of attendants at commercial shows, completely booked shows or free shows given in minority national areas, and does not include the number of spectators at rehearsals for examination and internal shows for study.

Number of Athletes in Grades refers to the number of athletes who have been given titles through examination. The titles of athletes include international masters of sports, masters of sports, first-grade, second-grade and third-grade sportsmen and young athletes. This indicator reflects skill of the athletes.

Number of Referees in Grades refers to the number of referees who have been given titles after examination. They are classified as international referees, national referees and referees of the first, second and third grades. This indicator reflects the skill of referees.

Stadiums refer to stadiums for track and field events with six lane 400-meter tracks around soccer fields, permanent track marks and permanent bleachers. Stadiums are classified according to seating capacity. They include: Class A stadiums have the capacity of seating 25000 people each. Class B stadiums have the capacity of seating 15000 to 25000 people each. Class C stadiums have the capacity of seating 5000 to 15000 people each, and Class D stadiums have the capacity of seating fewer than 5000 people. This indicator reflects numbers of large and medium-sized stadiums.

Gymnasiums refer to indoor sports grounds with permanent seats in which basketball, volleyball. badminton, table tennis and gymnastics competitions can be held. Gymnasiums are classified according to seating capacity. They include: Class A gymnasiums with seating over 6000 people. Class B gymnasiums with seating 4000 to 6000 people. Class C gymnasiums with seating 2000 to 4000 people, and Class D gymnasiums with eating fewer than 2000 people. This indicator reflects the total number of large and medium-sized gymnasiums

Health Care Institutions include: medical institutions, disease prevention and control centers (epidemic prevention stations), blood gathering and supplying institutions, health supervision and inspection (check up) institutions, medicinal scientific research and on-job training institutions, health education and so on.

Medical Organizations include: hospitals, health service centers (stations) of communities, nursing homes, health centers, clinics, clinics (health stations and infirmaries), maternity and child care agencies (centers and stations), special disease prevention and curing agencies (centers and stations), first aid centers (stations) and clinical inspection centers. Medical organizations are grouped by two types: profit-making and non-profit-making medical organizations.

Hospitals include: polyclinics, traditional Chinese medical hospitals, hospitals integrated with traditional Chinese therapeutics and western therapeutics, ethical hospitals, various specialties hospitals and nursing hospitals.

Medical Technical Personnel refers to doctors, assistant nurses, pharmacists, and laboratory technicians working in medical institutions.

Doctors refer to certified physicians and certified assistant physicians with certifications working in medical and health care and prevention agencies.

Total Cost of Health Services reflects the total expenditures on medical and health care services for the whole country, calculated on basis of sources of funding. Health expenditure from government budget refers to budgetary allocation for health undertakings by governments at all levels. Social health expenditure refers to non-government budgetary capital input, mainly the health insurance. It includes expenditure on health institutions run by enterprises and rural collective entities, expenditure on medical and health care of employees of enterprises, and excessive health expenditure of government employees that could be covered by the government health care system. Health expenditure on individuals refers to expenditure on health service and health insurance paid by residents from their disposable income.

二十三、其他社会活动

Other Social Activities

简要说明

本篇主要包括社会活动参与、公检法司、民政事业、劳动保障、残疾人事业、妇女干部和妇女地位调查等内容。

一、社会活动参与的内容主要包括历届全国人大代表和政协委员情况以及全国工会组织情况。全国人大代表、政协委员数由全国人大和全国政协信息中心提供，依全国人大、政协换届情况每五年更换一次；全国工会组织情况由全国总工会依据统计报表制度整理提供。

二、公检法司的资料主要包括公安机关的刑事案件立案情况和治安案件查处情况，交通、火灾事故情况，检察机关的办案情况，人民法院审理案件和收结案情况，以及律师、公证、调解工作等情况。资料分别由公安部、最高人民法院、最高人民检察院和司法部依据统计报表制度整理提供。

三、民政事业和劳动保障统计资料主要包括社会福利企事业机构、人员、经费情况、优抚和社会救济情况、城镇社区服务和农村社会保障网络情况、婚姻登记情况、离退休人员数量及费用和劳动争议仲裁等情况。资料分别由民政部与劳动和社会保障部依据统计报表制度整理提供。

民政事业统计资料详见《中国民政事业统计年鉴》(民政部财务和机关事务司编)，工会资料详见《中国工会统计年鉴》(全国总工会编)。

四、残疾人资料主要包括残疾人康复、教育、就业、扶贫和残联组织建设等情况。资料由中国残疾人联合会整理提供。

五、妇女干部情况主要包括年龄、学历、政治面貌和妇女干部的流动等情况。资料由全国妇联提供。

妇女社会地位调查主要包括妇女生活时间分配、就业和保健等情况。资料是2000年全国妇联和国家统计局组织的抽样调查资料的部分汇总数据。

Brief Introduction:

Data in this chapter show statistics on participation in social activities, public security, procuratorial, legal and judicial affairs, civil affairs, labor protection, disabled persons, survey on female cadres and female conditions and so on.

I. Data on participation cover mainly information on representatives to the National People's Congress (NPC), members of the Chinese People's Political Consultative Conference (CPPCC) and trade unions. Data on number of NPC and CPPCC representatives are provided by NPC and CPPCC information centers. Data on expiration of office terms of NPC and CPPCC are updated every five years. Data on trade unions are from All-China Federation of Trade Unions based on statistical reporting scheme.

II. Data on public security, procuratorial, legal and judicial affairs cover information such as criminal cases registered and offense cases handled by the public security agencies, traffic or fire accidents, cases handled by procurator's offices, cases accepted and settled by the people's courts, and statistics on lawyers, notarization and mediation. Data are from the Ministry of Public Security, the Supreme People's Procuratorate, the Supreme People's Court and the Ministry of Justice based on statistical reporting scheme.

III. Data on civil affairs and labor protection include: condition of institutions and personnel, budget, social welfare relief, urban welfare facilities, rural network of social security, marriage registration, retirement pensions, arbitration of labor disputes, etc. Data on civil affairs and labor protection are from the Ministry of Civil Affairs and the Ministry of Labor and Social Security based on statistical reporting scheme.

Data on civil affairs refer to "Statistical Yearbook on Civil Affairs of China" (Department of Financial and Departmental Affair, Ministry of Civil Affairs). Data on trade unions refer to "Statistical Yearbook on Chinese Trade Unions" (All-China Federation of Trade Unions).

IV. Data on disabled persons covering information on the rehabilitation, education, employment and poverty alleviation of disabled persons and institutions serving the needs of disabled persons. Data are from the All-China Federation of Disabled Persons,

V. Data on female cadres mainly include the basic information of age, education, membership in political parties and shift of work position. Data are from All-China Federation of Women.

Survey on the Social Status of Chinese Women covers the time allotment, employment and health care of women. Data are from the sample survey conducted jointly by All-China Federation of Women and National Bureau of Statistics in 2000.

23-1 历届全国人民代表大会代表人数

Number of Deputies to All the Previous National People's Congresses

单位：人 (person)

届别	Congress	年份 Year	代表总数 Total Number of Deputies	#女代表 Female Deputies	#少数民族代表 Minority Deputies	占代表总数比重(%) As Percentage to Total Deputies (%) #女代表 Female Deputies	#少数民族代表 Minority Deputies
一届	First Congress	1954	1226	147	178	12.0	14.5
二届	Second Congres	1959	1226	150	179	12.2	14.6
三届	Third Congress	1964	3040	542	372	17.8	12.2
四届	Fourth Congress	1975	2885	653	270	22.6	9.4
五届	Fifth Congress	1978	3497	742	381	21.2	10.9
六届	Sixth Congress	1983	2978	632	403	21.2	13.5
七届	Seventh Congress	1988	2978	634	445	21.3	14.9
八届	Eighth Congress	1993	2978	626	439	21.0	14.8
九届	Ninth Congress	1998	2979	650	428	21.8	14.4
十届	Tenth Congress	2002	2985	604	414	20.2	13.9

23-2 历届全国政治协商会议委员人数

Number of Deputies to All the Previous Chinese People's Political Consultative Conferences

单位：人 (person)

届别	Congress	年份 Year	委员总数 Total Number of Deputies	#中国共产党委员 Deputies from the Communist Party of China	#少数民族委员 Minority Deputies	占委员总数比重(%) As Percentage to Total Deputies (%) #中国共产党委员 Deputies from the Communist Party of China	#少数民族委员 Minority Deputies
一届	First Congress	1954	198		19		9.6
二届	Second Congres	1959	729	40	61	5.5	8.4
三届	Third Congress	1964	1071	60	78	5.6	7.3
四届	Fourth Congress	1975	1199	61	81	5.1	6.8
五届	Fifth Congress	1978	1988	76	143	3.8	7.2
六届	Sixth Congress	1983	2039	76	185	3.7	9.1
七届	Seventh Congress	1988	2083	90	225	4.3	10.8
八届	Eighth Congress	1993	2093	91	241	4.3	11.5
九届	Ninth Congress	1998	2196	92	258	4.2	11.7
十届	Tenth Congress	2002	2238	99	103	4.4	4.6

23-3 妇联干部情况

Cadre of the Women's Federation

单位：人 (person)

项 目	Item	1990	1995	2002	2003
干部总数	**Total Number of Cardres**	**97566**	**82834**	**52529**	**52649**
少数民族干部	Number of Minority Cardre	14638	10834	9008	8999
按行政级别分	By Administration Level				
司局级	Department/Bureau Level	132	321	344	376
县处级	County Level	1013	2739	6027	5809
科以下	Section Chief and Below	96421	79774	46158	46464
按干部年龄分	By Age Group				
35岁以下	35 and Below	56761	24570	21362	25174
36-45岁	36-45	30332	47197	23442	23153
46-55岁	46-55	9512	10349	7332	4039
56岁以上	56 and Over	961	718	393	283
按干部政治面貌分	By Political Status				
共产党员	Chinese Communist Party	59097	54038	40714	41733
共青团员	Communist Youth League	21549	13271	4728	4893
民主党派	Democratic Parties	1136	1281	324	338
群众	Mass	15784	14244	6763	5685
按干部文化程度分	By Education Attainments				
博士生	Ph. Doctor			19	19
研究生	Master		698	709	808
大学本科、大专学历	University / College	17615	30146	36163	38909
高中、中专及以下	Senior Middle School and Below	79951	51990	15638	12913
按行政编制分	By Organization Types				
行政编制	Administration	69158	65336	38541	38616
事业编制	Institution	7217	4944	8930	10473
招聘干部	Recruitment	21191	12554	5058	3560
干部参加学历教育情况	**Cadre Attending the Formal Education**				
博士生	Ph. Doctor			9	6
研究生	Master		149	672	661
大学、大专学历	University / College	6676	4025	10914	6555
干部参加非学历教育情况	**Cadre Attending the Non-formal Education**				
党校培训	Training at Party School			10458	13822
参照公务员管理培训	Training for Civil Servant			13045	13587
岗位培训	Vocational Training	37542	9391	15555	21659
干部流动情况	**Cadre Exchange**				
调入	In	1273	2010	4256	4215
调出	Out	8262	1629	3159	3331
省（区、市）妇联领导进同级	**Cadres at Provincial Level Attending the Same Level**				
党委	CCP Committee	22	13	21	19
人大	People's Congress	24	88	24	25
政协	CPPCC	24	33	23	32

注：妇联干部指在妇联系统工作的专职干部。

a) Cadre of the women's federation refers to the full-time cadres who are working in the system of women's federation.

23-4 工会组织情况

Basic Statistics on Trade Unions

年 份 Year	工会基层组织数 (万个) Number of Grassroots Unions (10 000 units)	全国已建工会组织的基层单位职工与会员人数（万人） Membership and Number of Staff and Workers in Grassroots Unions (10 000 persons)				工会专职工作人员 (万人) Number of Full-time Personnel of Unions(10 000 persons)
		职工人数 Number of Staff and Workers	#女职工 Female	会员人数 Membership	#女会员 Female	
1952	20.7	1393.2		1002.3		5.3
1957	16.5	2158.3		1746.7		
1962	16.5	2667.1		1922.0		8.6
1978						
1979	32.9	6897.2	2171.7	5147.3		17.9
1980	37.6	7448.2	2518.6	6116.5		24.3
1981	41.1	8183.0	2902.0	6843.9	2412.8	29.1
1982	43.3	8586.6	3065.9	7331.6	2629.3	32.2
1983	44.7	8845.7	3191.8	7693.4	2771.4	33.7
1984	46.6	9243.9	3370.3	8029.1	2950.3	41.9
1985	46.5	9643.0	3596.7	8525.8	3149.2	38.1
1986	50.2	9949.6	3664.3	8908.5	3309.2	45.9
1987	53.6	10411.8	3900.4	9336.5	3486.9	47.0
1988	56.4	10747.4	4434.9	9628.9	3647.0	47.4
1989	58.9	10998.6	4178.7	9909.2	3777.7	48.8
1990	60.6	11156.9	4291.0	10135.6	3897.7	55.6
1991	61.4	11351.4	4394.8	10389.1	3991.6	58.0
1992	61.7	11223.9	4377.1	10322.5	3974.0	58.0
1993	62.7	11103.8	4359.9	10176.1	3949.6	55.4
1994	58.3	11269.6	4483.2	10202.5	4018.1	56.0
1995	59.3	11321.4	4515.3	10399.6	4116.5	46.8
1996	58.6	11181.4	4500.0	10211.9	4093.1	60.5
1997	51.0	10111.5	4004.8	9131.0	3579.4	57.7
1998	50.4	9716.5	3882.0	8913.4	3546.7	48.4
1999	50.9	9683.0	3797.9	8689.9	3406.2	49.7
2000	85.9	11472.1	4534.5	10361.5	3917.3	48.2
2001	153.8	12997.0	5087.9	12152.3	4696.6	
2002	171.3	14461.5	5157.6	13397.8	4665.2	47.2
2003	90.6	13301.6	5079.3	12340.5	4601.2	46.5

注：2003年工会基层组织数统计口径有所调整。

a) The statistical standard of number of grassroots unions in 2003 have been adjusted.

23-5 劳动争议处理情况(2003年)

项 目	Item	合计 Total	国有企业 State-owned Enterprises	集体企业 Collective-owned Enterprises
上期未结案数 （件）	**Number of Cases Left Over from Last Period (case)**	**16276**	**4263**	**1483**
案件受理情况	**Cases Accepted**			
当期案件受理数 （件）	Number of Cases (case)	226391	48771	30218
用人单位申诉案件	Number of Cases Appealed by Units	10879	3158	1357
劳动者申诉案件数	Number of Cases Appealed by Laborers	215512	45613	28861
#集体劳动争议数	Number of Collective Labour Disputes	10823	3623	1519
劳动者当事人数 （人）	Number of Persons Involved (person)	801042	309439	97501
#集体争议劳动者当事人数	Number of Persons Involved in Collective Disputes	514573	294794	47796
争议原因 （件）	Cause of the Disputes (case)			
劳动报酬	Labour Remuneration	76774	12637	10168
保险福利	Social Insurance and Welfare	44434	11025	6903
工伤	Work Injury	31747	4936	3586
职业培训	Occupation Training	1211	313	213
变更劳动合同	Change the Labour Contract	5494	1796	684
解除劳动合同	Relieve the Labour Contract	40017	10702	4944
终止劳动合同	End the Labour Contract	12043	3671	1918
下岗	Laid-off	1540	570	438
其他	Others	13131	3121	1364
案件处理情况	**Cases Settled**			
结案数 （件）	**Number of Cases Settled (case)**	**223503**	**49528**	**29376**
按处理方式分	by Manners of Settlement			
仲裁调解	by Mediation	67765	13592	9783
仲裁裁决	by Arbitration Lawsuit	95774	23344	12487
其他方式	Others	59954	12592	7106
按处理结果分	by Result of Settlement			
用人单位胜诉	Won by Units	34272	9375	4370
劳动者胜诉	Lawsuit Won by Laborers	109556	24636	16298
双方部分胜诉	Lawsuit Partly by Both Parties	79475	15517	8708
本期未结案数 （件）	**Number of Cases Dissettled (case)**	**19164**	**3506**	**2325**
案外调解争议数 （件）	**Number of Cases Settled by Other Forms (case)**	**58451**	**11404**	**8231**

The Disposal of Labor Disputes (2003)

港、澳、台及外资企业 Hong Kong, Macao, Taiwan and Foreign Funded Enterprises	股份制联营 Share-holding Joint Ownership Enterprises	有限责任公司 Limited Liability Corporations	私营企业 Private Enterprises	个体工商户 Individual Economy	机关社团事业单位 State Organs and Institutions	其他 Others
2061	**1981**	**3056**	**1895**	**386**	**488**	**663**
23391	23451	47814	31537	9603	5937	5669
1124	884	2438	1257	270	255	136
22264	22567	45376	30280	9333	5682	5536
1121	733	1801	1248	343	221	214
89621	63649	126537	73627	19763	9532	11373
45798	18456	54613	37720	6880	3704	4812
7775	8351	16903	12244	4571	1367	2758
3807	4676	9307	5358	925	1423	1010
3425	2568	7464	6633	2213	390	532
186	221	91	103	30	16	38
480	701	823	513	116	215	166
5090	3561	8310	4231	917	1524	738
1608	1217	1708	1039	281	382	219
49	185	102	44	57	54	41
971	1791	3106	1372	493	566	347
20692	**23557**	**48105**	**31092**	**9312**	**6062**	**5779**
6511	7105	14322	10432	3229	1806	985
9182	10082	20356	11910	3807	2160	2446
4999	6370	13427	8750	2276	2096	2338
3101	4193	6567	3712	880	1239	835
9733	9954	21845	15878	5462	2730	3020
7858	9410	19693	11502	2970	2093	1724
4760	**1875**	**2765**	**2340**	**677**	**363**	**553**
9276	**3897**	**11711**	**8172**	**3848**	**1050**	**862**

23-6 律师、公证、调解工作基本情况

Basic Statistics on Lawyers, Notarization and Mediation

项　目	Item	1999	2000	2001	2002	2003
律师工作	**Lawyers**					
律师事务所　(个)	Number of Law Offices (unit)	9144	9541	10225	10873	11593
律师工作人员　(人)	Number of Lawyers (person)	111433	117260	122585	136684	142534
#专职律师　(人)	Full-time Lawyers (person)	61761	69117	76558	90012	99793
兼职律师　(人)	Part-time Lawyers (person)	17082	15639	13699	12186	6850
聘请担任常年法律顾问的单位　(处)	Number of Units with Permanent Legal Advisors (unit)	238576	247160	254758	265362	271669
民事诉讼代理　(件)	Agent of Civil Cases (case)	592455	640610	667232	767628	781452
经济诉讼代理　(件)	Agent of Economic Cases (case)	426358	438672	402669	381146	405133
刑事辩护　(件)	Defender of Criminal Cases (case)	309767	317108	339549	335267	324454
行政诉讼代理　(件)	Agent of Administrative Action (case)	39006	41785	43800	43703	48115
非诉讼法律事务　(件)	Agent of Non-Litigious Legal Affairs (case)	716287	770087	1162715	827057	876696
涉外及涉港澳台法律事务　(件)	Agent of Foreign-related, Hong Kong, Macao & Taiwan Legal Affairs (case)	18793	30531	10609	26788	20622
解答法律询问　(万件)	Agent of Legal Advisory Services (10 000 cases)	419.20	457.40	403.40	487.41	430.25
代写法律事务文书(万件)	Agent of Legal Documents Written on Behalf of Clients (10 000 cases)	96.64	111.30	113.90	119.70	120.27
公证工作	**Notarization**					
公证处　(个)	Number of Notary Offices (unit)	3189	3189	3186	3157	3175
公证人员　(人)	Notarial Personnel (person)	18654	19211	19303	19460	20015
#公证员　(人)	Notaries (person)	13083	12849	12931	12245	12093
公证员助理　(人)	Assistant Notaries (person)	1584	2103	1995	2556	3018
办理公证文书　(万件)	Number of Notarized Documents (10 000 cases)	1644.6	1249.7	1007.2	1004.5	1010.4
人民调解工作	**Number of People's Mediation**					
专职司法助理员　(人)	Number of Full-time Judicial Assistants (person)	54987	54638	48682	47173	46088
人民调解委员会　(万个)	Number of People's Mediation Committees (10 000 units)	97.41	96.4	92.3	89.1	87.8
调解人员　(万人)	Number of Mediators (10 000 persons)	880.25	844.5	779.3	716.2	669.2
调解民间纠纷　(万件)	Number of Civil Disputes Mediated (10 000 cases)	518.86	503.1	486.1	314.1	449.2

23-7 国内公证文书分类

Domestic Notarial Documents by Type

分 类	Item	2002		2003	
		办证件数(件) Number of Notarial Documents Issued (pieces)	比 重 (%) Percentage	办证件数(件) Number of Notarial Documents Issued (pieces)	比 重 (%) Percentage
经 济 公 证	**Notarized Documents on Economic Affairs**	**3480962**	**100.00**	**3824249**	**100.00**
购 销	Purchases and Sales of Products	92404	2.65	119422	3.12
联 营	Joint Business	6355	0.18	9676	0.25
拍 卖	Auctions	22010	0.63	28374	0.74
贷 款	Loans	1399875	40.16	1851760	48.42
担 保	Guarantees	95476	2.74	94798	2.48
招标、投标	Bidding	55513	1.60	72990	1.91
技术合作	Scientific and Technological Contracts	3406	0.10	1429	0.04
供 用 电	Supply and Use of Electric Power	63754	1.83	14047	0.37
劳务合同	Labor Contracts	112024	3.21	95145	2.49
建筑工程承包	Construction Project Contracts	15128	0.43	19406	0.51
工商服务业承包	Industrial and Commercial Service Contracts	10887	0.31	11830	0.31
农林牧副渔业承包	Farming, Forestry, Animal Husbandry, Sideline Production and Fishery Contracts	164162	4.71	125585	3.28
乡镇企业承包	Township Enterprise Contracts	5342	0.15	9991	0.26
财产租赁	Property Leases	22489	0.65	24546	0.64
企业租赁	Leases of Enterprise	4086	0.12	5391	0.14
资产经营协议	Asset Business Contracts	2757	0.08	4435	0.12
还款协议	Payment Contracts	131405	3.77	110829	2.90
土地使用权出让、转让	Selling or Transfer of Right of Land Utilization	49373	1.42	40792	1.07
其他经济合同	Other Business Contracts	328667	9.43	360705	1.59
法人(代表人)资格	Legal Person (agent) Identification	12839	0.37	13116	0.34
法人委托书	Legal Person Trust Deeds	44700	1.28	86811	2.27
公司章程	Corporation Constitutions	6114	0.18	3779	0.46
执行许可证明	Operating Permits	18010	0.52	19268	0.50
提 存	Consignation	12579	0.36	16794	0.44
抵押登记	Mortgage Registration	87303	2.50	85648	2.24
公司会议记录	Minutes of Corporation Meetings	18842	0.54	9658	0.52
其 他	Others	700472	19.95	587984	15.38
民事法律关系公证	**Notarized Documents on Civil Legal Relations**	**3581641**	**100.00**	**3663716**	**100.00**
收 养	Child Adoption	8924	0.25	6884	0.19
解除收养	Adoption Renouncements	1030	0.03	1273	0.03
继 承 权	Rights of Inheritance	151032	4.22	194478	5.31
遗 嘱	Testaments	65450	1.83	65535	1.79
产 权	Property Rights	31287	0.87	42175	1.13
亲属关系	Kinship Confirmation	50096	1.40	49569	1.35
死 亡	Death Certificates	8865	0.25	14375	3.95
房屋买卖	Purchases and Sales of Houses	332162	9.27	352353	9.62
房屋租赁	House Leases	37286	1.04	23745	0.65
留学协议	Foreign Study Contracts	9634	0.27	9769	0.27
遗赠扶养协议	Donations and Family Fostering	7985	0.22	12976	0.22
委 托 书	Trust Deeds	186369	5.20	373838	10.20
赠 与 书	Presentation Documents	102583	2.86	108398	2.96
声 明 书	Declarations	130992	3.66	176289	4.81
现场监督	Field Supervision	107190	2.99	102125	2.79
签名印鉴属实	Confirmation of Signatures and Seals	41419	1.16	49751	1.36
副本等与原本相符	Confirmation of Copies and Photo-offset Copies to Originals	26191	0.73	37181	1.01
宅基地使用权	Rights to Housing Site	21336	0.60	26906	0.73
证据保全	Evidence Preservation	56804	1.59	73393	2.00
拆迁协议	Housing Demolition Agreements	135886	3.79	287543	7.85
计划生育	Family Planning	547718	15.29	312007	8.52
赡养协议	Agreements on Supporting Parents	30519	0.85	12130	0.33
合伙协议	Partnership Agreements	14832	0.41	26983	0.74
夫妻财产协议	Property Agreements Between Spouses	103412	2.89	163655	4.47
其他民事协议	Other Civil Agreements	530773	14.82	492024	13.43
其 他	Others	841669	23.51	648698	17.71

23-8 涉外公证文书分类（2002年）
Foreign-Related Notarial Documents by Type (2003)

分类	Item	办证件数(件) Number of Notarial Documents Issued (pieces)	比重(%) Percentage	分类	Item	办证件数(件) Number of Notarial Documents Issued (pieces)	比重(%) Percentage
合计	**Total**	**2463540**	**100.00**	委托书	Proxy	24740	1
收养	Child Adoption	14745	0.60	营业证书	Shop Card	11011	0.45
遗嘱	Testaments	2493	0.10	公司章程	Corporation Constitutions	2497	0.1
出生	Births	339100	13.76	其他法律文书	Other Legal Documents	34620	1.41
死亡	Deaths	15278	0.62	职称	Professional Certificates	12371	0.5
生存、居住	Survival and Residence	6683	0.27	法人资格	Legal Person Identification	2625	0.11
学历	Schooling	263055	10.68	商标注册	Trademark Registrations	109	0.00
经历	Personal Histories	46746	1.90	贷款	Loans	7689	0.31
国籍	Nationality	36941	1.50	担保	Guarantees	3346	0.14
婚姻状况	Marital Status	217511	8.83	其他经济合同	Other Business Contracts	31025	1.26
亲属关系	Kinship Confirmation	276811	11.24	副本等与原本相符	Confirmation of Copies and Photo-offset Copies to Originals	299892	12.17
继承权	Rights of Inheritance	2413	0.10				
受、未受刑事处分	Criminal Records	266089	10.80	签名印鉴属实	Confirmation of Copies and Photo-offset Copies to Originals	171969	6.98
声明书	Announcement	39289	1.59	其他	Other	334492	13.58

23-9 调解民间纠纷分类
Number of Civil Disputes Mediated by Type

项目	Item	调解纠纷(件) Civil Disputes (cases)		各类纠纷所占比重(%) Percentage	
		2002	2003	2002	2003
合计	**Total**	**4636157**	**4492157**	**100.0**	**100.0**
婚姻家庭	Family Disputes	1753027	1657030	37.8	36.9
婚姻	Marriages	796279	752010	17.2	16.7
继承	Rights of Inheritance	258058	248858	5.6	5.5
赡抚扶养	Family Fostering	347491	326451	7.5	7.3
其他	Others	351181	329711	7.6	7.3
房屋、宅基地	Housing and Housing Sites	482739	454171	10.4	10.1
债务	Debts	424325	423661	9.2	9.3
生产经营	Business	447529	426279	9.7	9.5
邻里	Neighbor Disputes	694451	690547	15.0	15.4
损害赔偿	Compensation for Damages	353371	335132	7.6	7.5
其他	Others	480733	505337	10.4	11.3

23-10 公安机关立案的刑事案件及构成
Criminal Cases Registered in Public Security Organs and Composition

单位：起 (case)

案件类别	Category of Cases	立案（起） Number of Cases Registered (case)		构成（%） Composition (%)	
		2002	2003	2002	2003
合计	**Total**	**4337036**	**4393893**	**100.00**	**100.00**
杀人	Homicide	26276	24393	0.61	0.56
伤害	Injury	141825	145485	3.27	3.31
抢劫	Robbery	354926	340077	8.18	7.74
强奸	Rape	38209	40088	0.88	0.91
拐卖妇女儿童	Abducting Women or Children	5684	3721	0.13	0.08
盗窃	Larceny	2861727	2940598	65.99	66.92
诈骗	Fraud	191188	193665	4.41	4.41
走私	Smuggling	1149	1178	0.03	0.03
伪造、变造货币,出售、购买、运输、持有、使用假币	Forging Coin, and Selling, Buying, Transporting, Using the False Coin	5238	3151	0.12	0.07
其他	Others	710814	701537	16.39	15.97

注：2003年共破获刑事案件1842699起。

a) The solved criminal cases in 2003 are 1842699 cases.

23-11 公安机关受理、查处治安案件数
Offense Cases Against Public Order Handled by Public Security Organs

单位：起 (case)

案件类别	Category of Cases	2002		2003	
		受理 Number of Cases Accepted to be Treated	查处 Number of Cases Investigated and Treated	受理 Number of Cases Accepted to be Treated	查处 Number of Cases Investigated and Treated
合计	**Total**	**6232350**	**5196998**	**5995594**	**4869591**
扰乱工作、公共秩序	Disturbing Work or Public Order	544363	534504	426962	419237
结伙斗殴、寻衅滋事	Gang Fighting or Picking Quarrels and Making Troubles	147307	126225	131951	113564
侮辱妇女及其他流氓活动	Acting Indecently Towards Women	27468	25335	21391	19593
阻碍国家工作人员执行职务	Obstructing the Government Workers to Perform Their Duty	51917	49599	48209	46123
违反枪支管理规定	Violating Regulations on Management of Firearms	19052	18699	10278	10154
违反爆炸物品管理规定	Violating Regulations on Management of Explosives	71606	70496	61792	60831
殴打他人	Beating Other Body	1135896	881592	1138225	876863
偷窃财物	Robbing Other People of Their Valuables	1001965	470116	1066740	465737
骗取、抢夺、敲榨勒索财物	Defrauding, Snatching or Extorting and Racketeering Valuables	150620	84496	158472	75802
哄抢公私财物	Making Stirs and Then Robbing Public or Private Valuables	6007	4582	5507	4047
故意损坏公私财物	Intentionally Damaging Public or Private Valuables	117672	84051	126688	87463
伪造倒卖票券、证件	Forging and Fraudulently Selling Bills or Certificates	16656	16154	13643	13410
利用迷信扰乱秩序或骗财	Disturbing Public Order or Defrauding People of Their Valuables by Making Use of Their Superstition	11275	10688	8051	7833
卖淫、嫖娼	Prostitution or Going Whoring	224976	221930	172314	171604
赌博	Gambling	446654	438295	447044	439310
违反户口、居民身份证管理	Violating Regulations on Management of Residence or Identity Cards	899068	889793	771341	762695
其他	Others	1359848	1270443	1386986	1295325

23-12 交通事故情况(2003年)

Basic Statistics on Traffic Accidents (2003)

类　别	Type	发生数(起) Number of Traffic Accidents (case)	死亡人数(人) Number of Deaths (person)	受伤人数(人) Number of Injuries (person)	损失折款(万元) Losses Coverted into Cash (10 000 yuan)
总计	**Total**	**667507**	**104372**	**494174**	**336914.6**
#重大事故	Extraordinarily Serious	91758	92594	50116	58312.0
特大事故	Serious	3927	7720	8167	33922.0
机动车	Motor Vehicles	627029	93390	462427	330502.4
#汽车	Automobiles	483197	61869	310963	300164.0
摩托车	Motorcycles	97381	20026	111797	13881.9
拖拉机	Tractors	13859	3294	11882	3823.3
非机动车	Non-motor-driven Vehicles	17393	4018	14918	2535.2
#自行车	Bicycles	14331	3278	12149	2027.5
行人乘车人	Pedestrians and Passengers	18639	6022	14027	2738.3
其他	Others	4446	942	2802	1138.7

注:损失折款指直接损失(下表同)。

a) Losses converted into cash refer to direct losses. The same as in the following table.

23-13 火灾事故情况(2003年)

Basic Statistics on Fires (2003)

项　目	Item	合计 Total	特大 Extraordinarily Serious	重大 Serious	一般 Ordinary
发生(起)	Fires (case)	253932	37	305	253590
死亡(人)	Deaths (person)	2482	94	419	1969
受伤(人)	Injuries (person)	3087	34	167	2886
损失折款(万元)	Losses Converted into Cash (10 000 yuan)	159089	11929	13287	133873
平均每起事故损失(元)	Average Loss per Fire (yuan)	6265	3223946	435636	5279

23-14 各地区交通事故情况（2003年）

Basic Statistics on Traffic Accidents by Region (2003)

地　区	Region	发生数（起）Number of Traffic Accidents (case)	死亡人数（人）Number of Deaths (person)	受伤人数（人）Number of Injuries (person)	损失折款（万元）Losses Coverted into Cash (10000 yuan)
全　国	**National Total**	**667507**	**104372**	**494174**	**336914.6**
北　京	Beijing	10842	1641	9877	4361.4
天　津	Tianjin	10267	1129	5892	5460.5
河　北	Hebei	24333	4789	19260	10642.6
山　西	Shanxi	18556	3623	14145	8783.0
内蒙古	Inner Mongolia	9833	2103	7995	2368.9
辽　宁	Liaoning	18443	3536	12233	8908.6
吉　林	Jilin	11127	2227	8057	5280.1
黑龙江	Heilongjiang	9954	2447	9599	4605.7
上　海	Shanghai	54196	1406	11179	39721.2
江　苏	Jiangsu	40383	6640	21555	24302.0
浙　江	Zhejiang	56975	7149	36086	54268.1
安　徽	Anhui	21791	4155	18572	8561.0
福　建	Fujian	33290	3993	26003	14229.7
江　西	Jiangxi	13998	2818	11542	7783.4
山　东	Shandong	49414	8905	41030	17702.0
河　南	Henan	40477	5756	30925	15529.0
湖　北	Hubei	20047	2729	14251	9671.7
湖　南	Hunan	19414	3664	20562	10547.7
广　东	Guangdong	68903	11151	73170	31387.5
广　西	Guangxi	15221	3607	13915	7066.5
海　南	Hainan	2335	533	2057	1156.4
重　庆	Chongqing	16086	1037	11326	4291.3
四　川	Sichuan	37326	4907	31169	13123.4
贵　州	Guizhou	5005	1976	4260	2815.2
云　南	Yunnan	20676	3138	7083	9783.5
西　藏	Tibet	1317	621	1161	1266.7
陕　西	Shaanxi	12502	2324	9406	3893.3
甘　肃	Gansu	7659	2090	5948	3498.9
青　海	Qinghai	1619	744	1635	737.6
宁　夏	Ningxia	5249	889	4237	1426.1
新　疆	Xinjiang	10269	2645	10044	3741.6

注:损失折款指直接损失。

a) Losses converted into cash refer to direct losses.

23-15 各地区火灾事故情况（2003年）

Basic Statistics on Fires by Region (2003)

地区	Region	发生数（起）Number of Traffic Accidents (case)	死亡人数（人）Number of Deaths (person)	受伤人数（人）Number of Injuries (person)	直接经济损失（万元）Losses Coverted into Cash (10 000 yuan)	人口火灾发生率（1/10万人）Average Number of Fires per 100 Thousand People
全　国	**National Total**	**253932**	**2482**	**3087**	**159088.6**	**20.3**
北　京	Beijing	7548	42	112	2149.6	66.0
天　津	Tianjin	5261	30	23	1843.0	56.8
河　北	Hebei	7746	81	123	4457.7	11.5
山　西	Shanxi	3545	48	74	2425.3	10.9
内蒙古	Inner Mongolia	3523	25	23	1283.2	15.1
辽　宁	Liaoning	22055	113	147	10988.4	53.1
吉　林	Jilin	19200	76	72	3721.4	72.5
黑龙江	Heilongjiang	16681	119	90	9042.2	44.7
上　海	Shanghai	5820	48	88	1887.3	43.6
江　苏	Jiangsu	14011	192	247	8856.0	19.7
浙　江	Zhejiang	27606	236	187	24044.1	60.9
安　徽	Anhui	6683	71	106	4890.9	10.5
福　建	Fujian	8261	95	117	8661.4	24.8
江　西	Jiangxi	8029	72	115	4921.3	18.8
山　东	Shandong	17525	129	97	11224.8	19.3
河　南	Henan	11677	125	137	7330.6	12.1
湖　北	Hubei	5862	47	58	3633.2	9.8
湖　南	Hunan	6221	102	111	6378.5	9.5
广　东	Guangdong	15635	248	334	13752.8	20.4
广　西	Guangxi	2975	100	131	3259.7	6.2
海　南	Hainan	937	12	18	778.8	12.0
重　庆	Chongqing	6973	58	98	3307.3	22.4
四　川	Sichuan	9286	123	150	4656.1	11.0
贵　州	Guizhou	1846	22	18	1160.6	4.9
云　南	Yunnan	3910	107	127	4476.7	9.4
西　藏	Tibet	171	16	19	1393.6	6.7
陕　西	Shaanxi	3947	42	58	2508.2	10.9
甘　肃	Gansu	3058	31	83	2082.8	11.9
青　海	Qinghai	734	13	23	424.0	15.1
宁　夏	Ningxia	2724	9	13	1010.3	47.6
新　疆	Xinjiang	4482	50	88	2538.8	24.1

注:全国总计数据包括发生在铁道、交通、军队的火灾情况。

a) The national data include the fires which happen in railways and other transport process.

23-16 检察机关直接立案侦查案件情况（2003年）

Cases under Direct Investigation by Procurator's Offices(2003)

案件分类	Case Item	受案（件）Cases Accepted (case)	立案件数（件）Number of Cases Registered (case)	立案人数（人）Person of Cases Registered (person)	#要案 Key Case	结案件数（件）Number of Cases Settled (case)	结案人数（人）Person of Cases Settled (person)
合计	**Total**	**71032**	**39562**	**43490**	**2728**	**37042**	**40639**
贪污贿赂案件小计	**Sub-total of Cases on Corruption and Bribery**	**55333**	**31953**	**34922**	**2389**	**29986**	**32707**
贪污	Corruption	29276	14161	16162	632	13172	14979
贿赂	Bribery	16476	10553	10922	1378	9861	10197
挪用公款	Misappropriation of Public Funds	8272	6754	7249	289	6472	6936
集体私分	Collective Illegal Possession of Public Funds	1023	419	515	76	414	512
巨额财产来源不明	Unstated Source of Large Properties	193	32	32	12	18	19
其他	Others	93	34	42	2	49	64
渎职案件小计	**Sub-total of Cases on Abuse and Dereliction of Duty**	**15699**	**7609**	**8568**	**339**	**7056**	**7932**
滥用职权	Abuse of Power	4047	2049	2208	141	1873	2014
玩忽职守	Dereliction of Duty	4029	2545	2743	126	2402	2595
徇私舞弊	Fraudulent Practice	4354	1509	1656	39	1434	1587
其他	Others	3269	1506	1961	33	1347	1736

23-17 检察机关审查批准、决定逮捕犯罪嫌疑人和提起公诉被告人情况（2003年）

Arrests of Criminal Suspects and Defendants Under Public Prosecution Approved by Procurator's Offices (2003)

案件分类	Item	批捕、决定逮捕合计 Total of Arrests		决定起诉合计 Total of Public Prosecutions	
		件 (case)	人 (person)	件 (case)	人 (person)
合计	**Total**	**520481**	**764776**	**560978**	**819217**
公安、安全、监狱机关提请小计	**Sub-total of Requests by Departments of State and Public Security and Prisons**	**505732**	**748756**	**538217**	**793093**
危害国家安全案	Offences Against State Security	180	336	186	456
危害公共安全案	Offences Against Public Security	39641	46506	55245	62543
破坏社会主义市场经济秩序案	Offences Against Socialist Economic Order	12500	19222	12870	21440
侵犯公民人身、民主权利案	Offences Against Citizens' Personal and Democratic Rights	119160	152165	132750	166969
侵犯财产案	Offences Against Properties	262134	407782	265226	414870
妨害社会管理秩序案	Offences Against Social Management of Order	71981	122528	71816	126591
危害国防利益案	Offences Against National Defense	135	216	120	220
军人违反职责案	Offences on Dereliction of Duty by Servicemen	1	1	4	4
检察机关直接立案侦查案件小计	**Sub-total of Cases Handled by Procuratorates**	**14749**	**16020**	**22761**	**26124**
贪污贿赂案	Offences on Corruption and Bribery	13591	14656	19848	22631
渎职案	Offences on Abuse and Dereliction of Duty	1158	1364	2913	3493

23-18 检察机关处理申诉案件情况(2003年)

Appeals Handled by Procurator's Offices (2003)

案件分类	Cases	受案(件) Cases Accepted (case)	立案复查(件) Cases Registered for Reinvestigation (case)	结案(件) Cases Settled (case)	改变原决定 Original Decision Changed
合计	**Total**	**10166**	**5276**	**4465**	**504**
不服检察机关处理决定	Appeals against Decision of Procurator's Offices	4945	3236	2676	381
不服不批捕	Appeals against Rejection of Arrest	803	543	475	34
不服不起诉	Appeals against Rejection of Prosecuting	1796	1361	1143	131
不服撤案	Appeals against Withdrawal of the Case	258	143	129	19
不服原免予起诉	Appeals against Original Exemption of Lawsuit	212	149	116	27
其他	Others	1876	1040	813	170
不服法院刑事判决裁定	Appeals against Judgment of Criminal Case	5221	2040	1789	123
刑罚执行中被害人申诉	Appeals of the Victim at the Punishment	1429	462	415	16
刑罚执行中被告人申诉	Appeals of the Defendant at the Punishment	2247	904	788	89
刑罚执行完毕后被害人申诉	Appeals of the Victim after the Punishment	415	160	141	4
刑罚执行完毕后被告人申诉	Appeals of the Defendant after the Punishment	1130	514	445	14

23-19 人民法院审理一审案件情况

First Trial Cases by Courts

单位: 件 (case)

年份 Year	收案 Cases Accepted	刑事 Criminal	民事 Civil	经济纠纷 Economic Disputes	行政 Administrative	海事海商 Maritime Law and Affairs
1978	447755	146968	300787			
1979	513789	123846	389943			
1980	763535	197856	565679			
1981	906051	232125	673926			
1982	1024160	245219	778941			
1983	1343164	542648	756436	43553	527	
1984	1355460	431357	838307	84813	983	
1985	1319741	246655	846391	225541	916	238
1986	1611282	299720	989409	321220	632	301
1987	1875229	289614	1213219	366110	5940	346
1988	2290624	313306	1455130	513046	8573	569
1989	2913515	392564	1815385	694907	9934	725
1990	2916774	459656	1851897	591462	13006	753
1991	2901685	427840	1880635	566592	25667	951
1992	3051157	422991	1948786	650601	27125	1654
1993	3414845	403267	2089257	892580	27911	1830
1994	3955475	482927	2383764	1051742	35083	1959
1995	4545676	495741	2718533	1275959	52596	2847
1996	5312580	618826	3093995	1515848	79966	3945
1997	5288379	436894	3277572	1478822	90557	4534
1998	5410798	482164	3375069	1450049	98350	5166
1999	5692434	540008	3519244	1529877	97569	5736
2000	5356294	560432	3412259	1290867	85760	6976
2001	5344934	628996	3459025	1149101	100921	6891
2002	5132199	631348	4420123		80728	
2003	5130760	632605	4410236		87919	

注：一审案件指人民法院按照诉讼级别管辖按第一审程序审理的案件。

a) First trial cases refer to cases accepted by people's courts according to the first trial proceedings.

23-20 人民法院审理刑事一审案件收结案情况（2003年）
First Trial Criminal Cases Accepted and Settled by Courts (2003)

单位：件 (case)

项 目	Item	收 案 Cases Accepted	结 案 Cases Settled
合 计	**Total**	**632605**	**634953**
危害公共安全罪	Offences Against Public Security	57369	57505
破坏社会主义市场经济秩序罪	Offences Against Socialist Economic Order	14591	14775
侵犯公民人身权利民主权利罪	Offences Against Citizens' Personal and Democratic Rights	182642	184018
侵犯财产罪	Offences Against Properties	278629	278969
妨害社会管理秩序罪	Offences Against Social Management of Order	76072	76217
危害国防利益罪	Offences Against National Defense	151	155
贪污贿赂罪	Offences on Corruption and Bribery	20765	20933
渎职罪	Offences on Dereliction of Duty	2082	2053
其他	Others	304	328
合计中含自诉案件	Private Prosecution of Total	39464	40250

注：结案中含上年旧存。
a) Cases settled include cases turned over from the previous year.

23-21 人民法院审理刑事案件犯罪情况
Criminal Cases Heard by Courts

单位：人 (person)

年 份 Year	刑事罪犯总数 Number of Offenders	# 青少年罪犯 Young Offenders	不满18岁 Less Than 18 yrs	18岁至25岁 Between 18 and 25 yrs	青少年罪犯占刑事罪犯比重(%) Proportion of Young Offenders to Total (%)
1997	526312	199212	30446	168766	37.9
1998	528301	208076	33612	174464	39.4
1999	602380	221153	40014	181139	36.7
2000	639814	220981	41709	179272	34.5
2001	746328	253465	49883	203582	34.0
2002	701858	217907	50030	167879	31.0
2003	742261	231715	58870	172845	31.2

23-22 人民法院审理婚姻家庭、继承一审案件收结案情况（2003年）
First Trial Civil Cases of Marriages, Family Affairs and Inheritance Accepted and Settled by Courts (2003)

单位：件 (case)

项 目	Item	收 案 Cases Accepted	结 案 Cases Settled	调 解 Mediation	判 决 Judgement	驳 回 Reject	撤 诉 With-drawal	其 他 Other
合 计	**Total**	**1264037**	**1266593**	**552005**	**476010**	**5291**	**222118**	**11169**
婚姻家庭	Marriages and Family Affairs	1244804	1247532	547158	465929	5067	218520	10858
离婚	Divorce	1057864	1060019	492759	369292	4091	185398	8479
解除非法同居关系	Relieving the Relation of Lawless Cohabitation	49509	49729	2967	41783	134	4386	459
赡养纠纷	Support Disputes	38988	39048	12962	14667	134	10762	523
抚养、扶养关系纠纷	Upbringing Disputes	25365	25567	13031	7982	149	4160	245
抚育费纠纷	Upringing Fee Disputes	24636	24686	9282	10594	159	4357	294
其他	Others	48443	48483	16157	21611	400	9457	858
继承	Inheritance	19233	19061	4847	10081	224	3598	311
法定继承	Legal Inheritance	9776	9753	2639	4980	104	1893	137
遗嘱继承	Testament Inheritance	1195	1176	303	631	15	216	11
其他	Others	8262	8132	1905	4470	105	1489	163

注：结案中含上年旧存。
a) Cases settled include cases turned over from the previous year.

23-23 人民法院审理合同纠纷一审案件收结案情况（2003年）

First Trial Cases of Contracts Disputes Accepted and Settled by Courts (2003)

单位：件 (case)

项　目	Item	收　案 Cases Accepted	结　案 Cases Settled	调　解 Mediation	判 决 Judgement	驳 回 Reject	撤 诉 With-drawal	其 他 Other
合计	**Total**	**2266476**	**2269167**	**602251**	**1017418**	**36265**	**554392**	**58841**
借款合同	Loan Contracts	812269	815820	239308	391140	6925	156556	21891
买卖合同	Trade Contracts	523777	525580	146103	233804	8293	124485	12895
电信合同	Telecom Contracts	110864	110813	34851	14152	2994	54355	4461
租赁合同	Lease Contracts	100726	100344	20540	45261	1723	31323	1497
劳动争议	Work Disputes	98112	98159	18957	55831	5025	16207	2139
房地产合同	Real Estate Contracts	93769	92663	13444	55203	2010	20283	1723
供用动力合同	Labor Contracts	71569	71207	15354	23221	845	30936	851
建设工程合同	Construction Contracts	62405	62231	13648	32094	1569	13444	1476
农村承包合同	Rural Contracts	59146	58790	20251	17278	746	19080	1435
承揽合同	Contracts for Work	55753	55407	13878	24296	1249	14642	1342
其他	Others	278086	278153	65917	125138	4886	73081	9131

注：结案中含上年旧存。

a) Cases settled include cases turned over from the previous year.

23-24 人民法院审理权属、侵权纠纷及其他民事一审收结案情况（2003）

First Trial Cases of Disputes of Right, Infringement of Right and Other Civil Affairs Accepted and Settled by Courts (2003)

单位：件 (case)

项　目	Item	收　案 Cases Accepted	结　案 Cases Settled	调　解 Mediation	判　决 Judgement	驳 回 Reject	撤 诉 With-drawal	其 他 Other
合计	**Total**	**879723**	**880408**	**167964**	**383443**	**16442**	**137630**	**174929**
人身损害赔偿	Compensate for Personal Harm	324042	324419	98382	170882	3276	48087	3792
所有权及其相关权利	Ownership and Related Rights	241302	241685	49124	120263	7231	59962	5105
特别程序	Special Proceedings	224587	223020	1835	47860	3127	8734	161464
人身权纠纷	Personal Rights	10713	11242	2070	6043	240	2611	278
特殊侵权纠纷	Disputes of Special Infringement of Right	15297	15287	3255	7874	373	3499	286
不当得利	Unjustified Enrichment	9565	9366	1182	4687	785	2495	217
票据、证券、股票纠纷	Disputes of Bill, Securities and Stocks	8296	8392	1018	3674	280	1609	1811
知识产权案件	Intellectual Rights	5388	5187	601	2066	139	2139	242
海事海商案件	Marttime Affairs	491	414	185	90	18	48	73
其他	Other	40042	41396	10312	20004	973	8446	1661

23-25 人民法院行政一审案件收结案情况(2003年)

First Trial Administrative Cases Accepted and Settled by Courts (2003)

单位: 件 (case)

项 目	Item	收 案 Cases Accepted	结 案 Cases Settled	维 持 Affirmation of Original Judgement	撤 销 Cancel Lation	驳 回 Reject	撤 诉 With-drawal	单独赔偿 Separate Compen-sation	其 他 Other
合计	**Total**	**87919**	**88050**	**16356**	**10337**	**9400**	**27811**	**1023**	**23123**
土地等资源	Land	16750	16804	3054	2467	2006	4348	167	4762
公安	Public Security	10816	10950	3166	1342	1007	3373	179	1883
城建	City Construction	19811	19793	3717	2559	2196	6313	182	4826
交通运输	Traffic and Transport	2570	2610	428	184	177	1261	45	515
工商	Industry and Commerce	2715	2719	580	276	300	974	28	561
环保	Environment Protection	655	619	132	29	19	265	1	173
计划生育	Family Planning	1168	1181	163	80	69	326	11	532
税务	Tax	803	816	126	60	90	225	3	312
卫生	Health	806	801	123	64	62	322	4	226
乡政府	Townships Government	4976	5031	476	467		664	132	3292
劳动和社会保障	Labour and Social Security	4047	4060	1125	628	289	904	18	1096
其他	Other	22802	22666	3266	2181	3185	8836	253	4945

注：结案中含上年旧存。

a) Cases settled include cases turned over from the previous year.

23-26 社会福利事业、企业单位和工作人员数

Number of Social Welfare Institutions and Enterprises and Persons Engaged

项 目	Item	机 构 (个) Number of Institution or Enterprise (unit)		工 作 人 员 (人) Number of Persons Engaged (person)	
		2002	2003	2002	2003
全国总计	**National Total**	**89766**	**87052**	**1895612**	**1882944**
收养性福利事业单位	Adopting Social Welfare Institutions	38200	37294	201097	205352
国家办	Run by Governments	3082	3284	73240	76328
集体	Run by Collective Units	34122	32945	117709	117109
民办	Run by Private Units	996	1065	10148	11915
社会福利企业	Social Welfare Enterprises	35758	33976	1523183	1204860
国有	Run by Governments	1577	1321	100102	80592
集体	Run by Collective Units	28153	26184	1219479	1181285
其他	Run by Private Units	6028	6471	203602	242983
优抚事业单位	Administration Agencies for Martyrs	2826	2927	31788	32470
救助管理单位	Collecting and Repatriation Units	861	914	18036	17799
殡葬事业单位	Funeral and Interment Institutions	2882	2969	55457	59658
募捐单位	Collecting Purse Units	1341	1452	6654	6939
社区服务单位	Community Service Institutions	7898	7520	59397	55866

23-27 收养收容性社会福利事业单位基本情况（2003年）

Basic Statistics on Social Welfare Institution (2003)

项　目	Item	单位数（个） Number of Home (unit)	工作人员（人） Number of Staff and Workers (person)	床　位（张） Number of Bed (bed)	年末收养收容人数（人） Number of Persons Adopted or Housed at the year-end
总　计	**Total**	**38208**	**223151**	**1346774**	**1006339**
收养性福利事业单位	**Adopting Social Welfare Institution**	**37294**	**205352**	**1298097**	**965470**
国家办	Run by Government	3284	76328	282492	211802
集体办	Run by Collective Units	32945	117109	940128	701388
民　办	Run by Private Units	1065	11915	75477	52280
优抚休、疗养院	Convalescent Homes	137	15227	26525	17674
光荣院	Homes for Disabled Veterans	1298	10651	25286	33920
社会福利院	Social Welfare Homes	1508	30401	144656	108940
儿童福利院	Baby Welfare Homes	192	6237	26676	25344
精神病福利院	Psychopathy Welfare Homes	130	11713	28939	24473
城镇老年性福利机构	Urban Elderly Welfare Units	9013	45712	326210	238033
农村老年性福利机构	Rural Elderly Welfare Units	24343	81263	675906	503506
其他收养机构	Other Adopting Units	673	4148	20417	13580
收容性福利事业单位	**Housing Social Welfare Institution**	**914**	**17799**	**48677**	**40869**

23-28 社会福利救济主要费用情况

Basic Statistics on Social Welfare Relief Funds

单位：万元　　(10 000 yuan)

项　目	Item	1999	2000	2001	2002	2003
优抚对象补助金额	**Funds for Family Members of Martyrs and Disabled Veterans**	**914443**	**1076605**	**1080771**	**1121737**	**1271253**
国家支出	Government Funds	511444	607550	694912	746918	879672
集体供给	Collective Funds	402999	469055	385859	374819	391581
城乡各种福利院支出	**Funds for Urban and Rural Welfare Homes of All Types**	**230566**	**286662**	**405275**	**359293**	**384439.5**
国家支出	Government Funds	136863	189599	263791	220842	292913
集体供给	Collective Funds	93703	97063	141484	138451	91527
#光荣院	Homes for the Disabled Veterans	19478	21882	22971	25678	27506
国家支出	Government Funds	18204	20561	21925	24562	26232
集体供给	Collective Funds	1274	1321	1046	1116	1274

23-29 享受补助、救济人员情况

Persons Receiving Subsidies or Relief Funds

单位: 万人 (10 000 persons)

项 目	Item	1999	2000	2001	2002	2003
城乡居民最低生活保障人数	**Number of Persons Receiving Lowest Cost-of-living in Urban Area and Rural Area**	**531.7**	**702.8**	**1475.3**	**2472.5**	**2613.9**
城镇居民最低生活保障人数	Number of Persons Receiving Lowest Cost-of-living in Urban Area	265.9	402.6	1170.7	2064.7	2246.8
农村居民最低生活保障人数	Number of Persons Receiving Lowest Cost-of-living in Rural Area	265.8	300.2	304.6	407.8	367.1
传统救济情况	**Traditional Relief**					
城镇临时救济人次数	Number of Poor Persons Receiving Temporary Almsgiving in Urban Area	157.1	155.6	213.9	321.4	348.3
农村临时救济人数	Number of Poor Persons Receiving Temporary Almsgiving in Rural Area	1659.8	1667.6	1800.5	1677.6	2009.8
农村散居五保户人数	Number of Persons with Livelihood Guaranteed in Five Aspects in Rural Area in Rural Area	303.7	270.6	221.6	162.2	173.9

23-30 社会福利企业基本情况

Basic Statistics on Social Welfare Enterprises

年 份 Year	国有和集体 State-owned and Collective-owned			其 他 Other		
	单 位 (个) Number of Units (unit)	职 工 (人) Number of Staff and Workers (person)	#残疾职工 Disabled Persons	单 位 (个) Number of Units (unit)	职 工 (人) Number of Staff and Workers (person)	#残疾职工 Disabled Persons
1985	2214	219189	83051	12554	448829	151250
1986	2551	236371	89421	17211	637747	225708
1987	2976	250329	96605	24714	875974	337944
1988	3692	282947	106095	36701	1180589	875974
1989	4595	310345	119626	36864	1192179	494182
1990	5208	325461	124630	36517	1245072	512941
1991	6329	352112	136183	37889	1342064	565139
1992	6798	373412	142473	42985	1528266	635700
1993	7232	390619	147211	49649	1672141	695046
1994	7373	382519	151523	52805	1800262	757307
1995	7734	368636	148551	52503	1845838	790671
1996	7364	355864	141831	52033	1811820	794003
1997	8024	351354	141778	47485	1747143	767980
1998	7527	322522	133389	42987	1630654	722656
1999	7819	207271	132330	36809	1594894	657955
2000	31580	1377506	605592	9090	280853	123899
2001	31445	1379008	603447	6535	218626	95203
2002	29730	1319581	591930	6028	203602	90910
2003	27505	1261877	567916	6471	242983	110917

注：国有和集体办的福利企业数据，1999年以前统计范围仅限民政系统，2000年起扩大到全社会范围。

a) The statistical coverage in 2000 have been adjusted. The state-owned and collective-owned social welfare enterprises before 2000 refer to those managed by the system of civil administration, and those in 2000 refer to all state-owned and collective-owned social welfare enterprises.

23-31 各地区城镇社区服务设施和农村社会保障网络基本情况（2003年）

Basic Statistics on Urban Welfare Facilities and Rural Social Security Network (2003)

单位：个 (unit)

地区	Region	城镇社区服务设施数 Number of Urban Welfare Facilities	#社区服务单位个数 Number of Community Service	城镇便民、利民服务网点 Number of Urban Service Points for Civilian
全国	**National Total**	**196452**	**7520**	**668418**
北京	Beijing	1787	143	6230
天津	Tianjin	1913	105	8373
河北	Hebei	9574	190	21109
山西	Shanxi	2983	136	13772
内蒙古	Inner Mongolia	5995	208	41868
辽宁	Liaoning	11679	388	74568
吉林	Jilin	6654	368	25512
黑龙江	Heilongjiang	7735	510	54183
上海	Shanghai	7451	99	12667
江苏	Jiangsu	24974	478	54182
浙江	Zhejiang	26166	217	47181
安徽	Anhui	8488	382	23713
福建	Fujian	3676	238	40230
江西	Jiangxi	2254	308	8982
山东	Shandong	9738	347	42572
河南	Henan	3051	220	17485
湖北	Hubei	7017	239	17129
湖南	Hunan	14112	603	46882
广东	Guangdong	6953	820	8553
广西	Guangxi	1386	101	3367
海南	Hainan	540	6	1210
重庆	Chongqing	1306	71	5175
四川	Sichuan	9674	315	25892
贵州	Guizhou	4873	122	10662
云南	Yunnan	1079	38	1700
西藏	Tibet	42		
陕西	Shaanxi	8197	314	24664
甘肃	Gansu	1888	255	17151
青海	Qinghai	1150		595
宁夏	Ningxia	1813	91	3461
新疆	Xinjiang	2304	208	9350

23-32 各地区离休、退休、退职人员数(2003年底)

Number of Retired and Resigned Persons by Region at the Year-end (2003)

单位: 万人 (10 000 persons)

地 区	Region	合 计 Total	离休人员 Retired Veterans	退休人员 Retired Persons	退职人员 Resigned Persons	企 业 Enterprises	离休人员 Retired Veterans	退休人员 Retired Persons	退职人员 Resigned Persons
全 国	**National Total**	**4523.4**	**140.9**	**4303.1**	**79.4**	**3486.4**	**73.7**	**3345.9**	**66.8**
北 京	Beijing	179.6	5.8	169.0	4.7	146.5	3.2	139.0	4.4
天 津	Tianjin	110.6	2.2	107.1	1.4	94.0	1.2	91.6	1.2
河 北	Hebei	191.1	9.0	178.5	3.6	142.9	4.0	136.0	2.9
山 西	Shanxi	115.2	7.2	106.7	1.4	88.5	3.6	83.9	1.0
内蒙古	Inner Mongolia	78.4	2.8	74.5	1.1	55.1	1.2	53.0	0.9
辽 宁	Liaoning	326.8	11.2	308.8	6.8	280.6	6.8	267.4	6.4
吉 林	Jilin	130.0	5.0	122.7	2.3	104.2	2.6	99.6	1.9
黑龙江	Heilongjiang	228.6	8.7	215.4	4.5	187.1	5.0	178.3	3.7
上 海	Shanghai	254.6	3.4	247.9	3.2	220.0	2.0	215.1	3.0
江 苏	Jiangsu	301.4	7.7	287.0	6.7	240.2	3.6	230.5	6.1
浙 江	Zhejiang	162.4	3.4	154.6	4.4	125.0	1.4	119.9	3.7
安 徽	Anhui	140.5	5.3	132.9	2.3	105.0	2.5	100.6	2.0
福 建	Fujian	85.8	2.0	82.4	1.4	62.6	1.0	60.7	1.0
江 西	Jiangxi	101.9	2.1	98.7	1.1	76.1	1.0	74.1	0.9
山 东	Shandong	211.1	12.2	194.1	4.8	161.8	6.2	152.3	3.3
河 南	Henan	202.7	9.5	190.9	2.3	145.3	4.1	139.2	1.9
湖 北	Hubei	223.9	4.6	215.4	3.8	180.3	2.5	174.4	3.4
湖 南	Hunan	195.3	4.4	188.6	2.2	143.0	2.1	139.0	1.9
广 东	Guangdong	229.3	5.6	222.1	1.6	173.9	2.7	170.1	1.2
广 西	Guangxi	99.5	1.7	96.6	1.2	66.9	0.8	65.3	0.8
海 南	Hainan	32.7	0.5	30.5	1.7	26.4	0.3	24.5	1.6
重 庆	Chongqing	106.6	1.3	103.2	2.0	82.6	0.7	80.1	1.8
四 川	Sichuan	232.5	3.4	225.5	3.7	168.1	1.8	163.3	3.0
贵 州	Guizhou	72.4	1.8	69.9	0.6	47.3	0.8	46.0	0.5
云 南	Yunnan	105.1	3.1	100.9	1.1	72.1	1.3	70.0	0.8
西 藏	Tibet	5.1	0.1	5.1	…	2.5	…	2.5	…
陕 西	Shaanxi	112.5	4.4	105.5	2.6	84.4	2.3	80.3	1.8
甘 肃	Gansu	69.0	2.4	65.4	1.2	50.3	1.4	48.1	0.9
青 海	Qinghai	23.0	0.8	21.8	0.5	15.0	0.4	14.5	0.2
宁 夏	Ningxia	19.2	0.7	18.2	0.4	13.9	0.3	13.4	0.2
新 疆	Xinjiang	149.7	8.4	136.4	4.8	124.7	7.1	113.2	4.4

注:企业数据不包括民政部门支付离休、退休、退职费的人数。

a) The enterprises data excluded retired and resigned staff and workers under civil administration.

23-33 离休、退休、退职费

Pensions for Retired and Resigned Persons

年份 Year	费用总额(亿元) Total Pensions (100 million yuan)	民政部门支付 Paid by Civil Affairs Departments	总后事业单位支付 Paid by Units under the General Logistics Departments of PLA	国有单位 Funds of State-owned Units	#单位支付 Paid by Employer Units	城镇集体单位 Funds of Urban Collective Owned Units	其他单位 Funds of Other Ownership Units	平均每人(元) Per Capita Funds (yuan)
绝对数 Absolute Figure								
1980	50.4	3.3		43.4	40.1	7.0		714
1981	62.3	3.3		53.3	50.0	9.0		706
1982	73.1	3.2		62.1	58.9	11.0		709
1983	87.3	3.2		74.0	70.8	13.3		726
1984	106.1	3.0		84.6	81.6	21.2	0.3	766
1985	145.6	3.7		116.1	112.4	29.1	0.4	935
1986	172.2	3.3		140.6	137.3	31.0	0.6	1001
1987	208.1	4.0		171.9	167.9	35.3	0.8	1103
1988	275.1	6.6		220.5	213.9	53.2	1.4	1346
1989	319.4	7.5		258.9	251.4	59.1	1.4	1478
1990	396.2	7.2		319.7	312.5	74.7	1.8	1760
1991	467.5	7.6		380.7	373.1	84.5	2.3	1975
1992	578.5	9.2		474.3	465.1	100.8	3.4	2300
1993	759.3	12.0		623.2	611.2	123.9	12.2	2824
1994	1043.6	17.5		875.9	858.4	146.2	21.5	3656
1995	1305.6	19.4		1093.1	1073.7	182.4	30.1	4335
1996	1552.2	20.1		1308.2	1288.1	204.0	40.0	4923
1997	1790.8	22.7	1.9	1517.6	1493.0	225.2	48.0	5458
1998	2073.7	26.1	3.6	1726.0	1696.3	229.0	114.8	5972
1999	2420.9	29.6	3.1					6614
2000	2733.3	36.4	3.4					7190
2001	3072.0	44.3	3.4					7784
2002	3659.4	51.0	3.6					8881
2003	4148.9	56.7	3.6					9485
比上年增长(%) Increase over the Preceding Year (%)								
1981	23.6			22.8	24.7	28.6		-1.1
1982	17.3	-3.0		16.5	17.8	22.2		0.4
1983	19.4			19.2	20.2	20.9		2.4
1984	21.5	-6.3		14.3	15.3	59.4		5.5
1985	37.2	23.3		37.2	37.7	37.3	33.3	22.1
1986	18.3	-10.8		21.1	22.2	6.5	50.0	7.1
1987	20.8	21.2		22.3	22.3	13.9	33.3	10.2
1988	32.2	65.0		28.3	27.4	50.7	75.0	22.0
1989	16.1	13.6		17.4	17.5	11.1		9.8
1990	24.0	-4.0		23.5	24.3	26.4	28.6	19.1
1991	18.0	5.6		19.1	19.4	13.1	27.8	12.2
1992	23.7	21.1		24.6	24.7	19.3	47.8	16.5
1993	31.3	30.4		31.4	31.4	22.9	258.8	22.8
1994	37.4	45.8		40.5	40.4	18.0	76.2	29.5
1995	25.1	10.9		24.8	25.1	24.8	40.0	18.6
1996	18.9	3.6		19.7	20.0	11.8	32.9	13.6
1997	15.4	12.9		16.0	15.9	10.4	20.0	10.9
1998	15.8	15.0	89.5	13.7	13.6	1.7	139.2	9.4
1999	16.7	13.4	-13.9					10.8
2000	12.9	23.0	9.7					8.7
2001	12.4	21.7						8.3
2002	19.1	15.1	5.9					14.1
2003	13.4	11.2						6.8

注:1.本表数字不包括离休、退休、退职职工的医疗卫生费。

2.本表1985-1988年的数字不包括根据1985年有关规定发给离休、退休、退职职工的肉类等价格补贴。

a)Figures in this table exclude medical expenditures of retired and resigned workers and staff.

b)Figures of 1985-1988 in this table exclude subsidies on meat, etc. delivered to retired and resigned workers and staff in accordance with relevant regulations issued in 1985.

23-34 离休、退休、退职人员保险福利费用及构成

Historic Figures of Total Social Insurance and Welfare Fund of Retirees

年 份 Year	合 计 Total	离休金 Pensions for Termination	退休金 Retirement Pensions	退职生活费 Resignation Allowances for Living Expenses	医疗卫生费 Medical Care Expenses	其 他 Others
绝对数（亿元） Absolute Figure (100 million yuan)						
1990	465.2	34.6	239.4	5.0	76.2	110.0
1991	554.4	38.6	271.5	5.7	94.5	144.1
1992	685.6	47.1	338.8	6.7	116.3	176.7
1993	901.7	57.1	435.5	8.6	154.3	246.2
1994	1218.9	103.2	766.5	12.4	192.8	144.0
1995	1522.4	121.9	986.3	15.3	236.3	162.6
1996	1797.7	137.7	1199.3	17.1	265.6	178.0
1997	2043.8	162.6	1423.9	23.5	277.6	156.2
1998	2330.9	167.7	1708.5	24.1	286.9	143.7
1999	2708.3	186.1	2035.2	27.2	320.1	139.7
2000	3040.5	201.1	2305.7	30.3	346.9	156.5
2001	3337.2	223.4	2618.7	27.8	312.9	154.4
2002	3870.7	263.7	3143.0	33.4	266.0	164.6
2003	4359.9	269.5	3592.1	37.6	271.3	189.4
比上年增长（%） Increase over Preceding Year (%)						
1991	19.2	11.6	13.4	14.0	24.0	31.0
1992	23.7	22.0	24.8	17.5	23.1	22.6
1993	31.5	21.3	28.5	28.4	32.7	39.3
1994	35.2	80.7	76.0	44.2	25.0	-41.5
1995	24.9	18.1	28.7	23.4	22.6	12.9
1996	18.1	13.0	21.6	11.8	12.4	9.5
1997	13.7	18.1	18.7	37.4	4.5	-12.2
1998	14.0	3.1	20.0	2.6	3.4	-8.0
1999	16.2	11.0	19.1	12.9	11.6	-2.8
2000	12.3	8.1	13.3	11.4	8.4	12.0
2001	9.8	11.1	13.6	-8.3	-9.8	-1.3
2002	16.0	18.0	20.0	20.1	-15.0	6.6
2003	12.6	2.2	14.3	12.6	2.0	15.1
构成（以合计为100） Composition (Total=100)						
1990	100.0	7.4	51.5	1.1	16.4	23.6
1991	100.0	7.0	49.0	1.0	17.0	26.0
1992	100.0	6.9	49.4	1.0	17.0	25.8
1993	100.0	6.3	48.3	1.0	17.1	27.3
1994	100.0	8.5	62.9	1.0	15.8	11.8
1995	100.0	8.0	64.8	1.0	15.5	10.7
1996	100.0	7.7	66.7	1.0	14.8	9.9
1997	100.0	8.0	69.7	1.1	13.6	7.6
1998	100.0	7.2	73.3	1.0	12.3	6.2
1999	100.0	6.9	75.1	1.0	11.8	5.2
2000	100.0	6.6	75.8	1.0	11.4	5.2
2001	100.0	6.7	78.5	0.8	9.4	4.6
2002	100.0	6.8	81.2	0.9	6.9	4.2
2003	100.0	6.2	82.4	0.9	6.2	4.3

注：本表不包括民政部门支付的离休、退休、退职费。

a) Data in the table excluded retired and resigned staff and workers paid by the civil administration organs.

23-35 参加基本养老保险的职工和离休、退休、退职人员数

Employees and Retirees Contributed to Pension Insurance

单位: 万人 (10 000 persons)

年 份 Year	在职职工人数 Formal Employees	企 业(含其他) Enterprises (Included Others)	离休、退休、退职人员数 Number of Retirees	企 业(含其他) Enterprises (Included Others)
1989	4816.9	4816.9	893.4	893.4
1990	5200.7	5200.7	965.3	965.3
1991	5653.7	5653.7	1086.6	1086.6
1992	7774.7	7774.7	1681.5	1681.5
1993	8008.2	8008.2	1839.4	1839.4
1994	8494.1	8494.1	2079.4	2079.4
1995	8737.8	8737.8	2241.2	2241.2
1996	8758.4	8758.4	2358.3	2358.3
1997	8671.0	8671.0	2533.4	2533.4
1998	8475.8	8475.8	2727.3	2727.3
1999	9501.8	8859.1	2983.6	2863.8
2000	10447.5	9469.9	3169.9	3016.5
2001	10801.9	9733.0	3380.6	3171.3
2002	11128.8	9929.4	3607.8	3349.2
2003	11646.5	10324.5	3860.2	3556.9

23-36 失业保险、基本医疗保险基本情况

Historic Figures of Unemployment Insurance，Basic Medical Insurance

年 份 Year	失 业 保 险 Unemployment Insurance			基本医疗保险年末参保人数（万人）Contributors of Basic Medical Insurance at the Year-end (10 000 persons)	
	年末参保职工人数（万人） Contributors at the Year-end (10 000 persons)	全年发放失业保险金人数（万人） Beneficiaries of Unemployment Insurance Funds (10 000 persons)	全年发放失业保险金（万元） Unemployed Relief (10 000 yuan)	职 工 Workers	离休、退休、退职人员 Retirees
绝对数 Absolute Figure					
1994	7968.0	196.5	50755	374.6	25.7
1995	8238.0	261.3	81964	702.6	43.3
1996	8333.1	330.8	138704	791.2	64.5
1997	7961.4	319.0	186780	1588.9	173.1
1998	7927.9	158.1	203907	1508.7	369.0
1999	9852.0	271.4	318722	1509.4	555.9
2000	10408.4	329.7	561984	2862.8	924.2
2001	10354.6	468.5	832563	5470.7	1815.2
2002	10181.6	657.0	1167736	6925.8	2475.4
2003	10372.9	741.6	1314448	7974.9	2926.8
比上年增长 (%) Increase over Preceding Year (%)					
1995		33.0	61.5	87.6	68.0
1996	-12.3	26.6	69.2	12.6	49.0
1997	-4.5	3.6	34.7	63.5	53.9
1998	0.4	-50.4	9.2	-5.1	113.2
1999	24.3	71.7	56.3	0.05	50.7
2000	4.8	21.5	76.3	89.7	66.2
2001	-0.6	42.1	48.1	91.1	96.4
2002	-1.7	40.2	40.2	26.6	36.4
2003	1.9	12.9	12.6	15.1	18.2

23-37 社会保险基金收支及累计结余

Revenue, Expenses and Reserve of Social Insurance Funds

单位:亿元 (100 million yuan)

年份 Year	合计 Total	基本养老保险 Basic Pension Insurance	失业保险 Unemployment Insurance	医疗保险 Medical Insurance	工伤保险 Work Injury Insurance	生育保险 Maternity Insurance
基金收入 Revenue						
1989	153.6	146.7	6.8			
1990	186.8	178.8	8.0			
1991	225.0	215.7	9.3			
1992	377.4	365.8	11.7			
1993	526.1	503.5	17.9	1.4	2.4	0.8
1994	742.0	707.4	25.4	3.2	4.6	1.5
1995	1006.0	950.1	35.3	9.7	8.1	2.9
1996	1252.4	1171.8	45.2	19.0	10.9	5.5
1997	1458.2	1337.9	46.9	52.3	13.6	7.4
1998	1623.1	1459.0	72.6	60.6	21.2	9.8
1999	2211.8	1965.1	125.2	89.9	20.9	10.7
2000	2644.5	2278.1	160.4	170.0	24.8	11.2
2001	3101.9	2489.0	187.3	383.6	28.3	13.7
2002	4048.7	3171.5	215.6	607.8	32.0	21.8
2003	4882.9	3680.0	249.5	890.0	37.6	25.8
基金支出 Expenses						
1989	120.9	118.8	2.0			
1990	151.9	149.3	2.5			
1991	176.1	173.1	3.0			
1992	327.1	321.9	5.1			
1993	482.2	470.6	9.3	1.3	0.4	0.5
1994	680.0	661.1	14.2	2.9	0.9	0.8
1995	877.1	847.6	18.9	7.3	1.8	1.6
1996	1082.4	1031.9	27.3	16.2	3.7	3.3
1997	1339.2	1251.3	36.3	40.5	6.1	4.9
1998	1636.9	1511.6	56.1	53.3	9.0	6.8
1999	2108.1	1924.9	91.6	69.1	15.4	7.1
2000	2385.6	2115.5	123.4	124.5	13.8	8.3
2001	2748.0	2321.3	156.6	244.1	16.5	9.6
2002	3471.5	2842.9	186.6	409.4	19.9	12.8
2003	4016.4	3122.1	199.8	653.9	27.1	13.5
累计结余 Balance at the Year-end						
1989	81.6	68.0	13.6			
1990	117.3	97.9	19.5			
1991	169.7	144.1	25.7			
1992	252.8	220.6	32.1			
1993	303.7	258.6	40.8	0.4	3.1	0.8
1994	365.7	304.8	52.0	0.7	6.8	1.4
1995	516.8	429.8	68.4	3.1	12.7	2.7
1996	696.1	578.6	86.4	6.4	19.7	5.0
1997	831.6	682.8	97.0	16.6	27.7	7.5
1998	791.1	587.8	133.4	20.0	39.5	10.3
1999	1009.8	733.5	159.9	57.6	44.9	13.9
2000	1327.5	947.1	195.9	109.8	57.9	16.8
2001	1622.8	1054.1	226.2	253.0	68.9	20.6
2002	2423.4	1608.0	253.8	450.7	81.1	29.7
2003	3313.9	2206.5	303.6	670.6	91.2	42.0

23-38 分地区基本养老保险情况（2003年）

Conditions of Basic Endowment Insurance (2003)

地区	Region	年末参保职工（万人）Active Contributors at the Year-end (10 000 persons)	#企业（含其他）Enterprise (included others)	年末离休、退休、退职人员人数（万人）Retirees at the Year-end (10 000 persons)	基金收支情况（万元）Revenue and Expenses (10 000 yuan) 基金收入 Revenue	基金支出 Expenses	累计结余 Balance at the Year-end
全国	**National Total**	**11646.5**	**10324.5**	**3860.2**	**36799793**	**31221058**	**22065401**
北京	Beijing	307.0	297.1	141.5	1663306	1475353	378691
天津	Tianjin	185.7	178.4	97.6	852741	817207	221073
河北	Hebei	501.9	410.1	163.6	1487934	1230766	872288
山西	Shanxi	276.3	276.3	88.1	940865	708988	701009
内蒙古	Inner Mongolia	228.3	197.2	72.6	600943	531052	268420
辽宁	Liaoning	754.9	688.6	315.5	2623065	2173763	1557866
吉林	Jilin	311.5	300.3	115.5	923387	811094	258991
黑龙江	Heilongjiang	518.3	468.0	196.0	1547627	1351845	732467
上海	Shanghai	461.1	394.3	254.6	2942041	2895766	743332
江苏	Jiangsu	863.8	775.7	271.4	2615091	2332601	1193700
浙江	Zhejiang	657.0	594.2	144.2	2173528	1493128	2006702
安徽	Anhui	343.1	323.1	113.6	812206	740298	247157
福建	Fujian	284.8	230.8	79.4	731491	663249	464774
江西	Jiangxi	262.5	242.3	93.4	593132	536315	304829
山东	Shandong	916.7	710.9	219.3	2637041	2190979	1754944
河南	Henan	580.0	504.0	171.0	1441656	1203326	971519
湖北	Hubei	554.4	501.1	177.9	1197485	1176227	434851
湖南	Hunan	468.7	317.4	167.5	1363588	1189872	757407
广东	Guangdong	1278.5	1145.7	203.8	3055375	1972110	4567456
广西	Guangxi	198.5	195.0	66.3	502828	462505	333686
海南	Hainan	83.1	62.3	33.6	228031	210100	106219
重庆	Chongqing	187.6	183.3	92.4	575475	536253	155727
四川	Sichuan	418.0	397.2	187.5	1729205	1451783	1111592
贵州	Guizhou	120.0	106.4	48.0	415840	348341	320611
云南	Yunnan	179.6	162.4	77.8	718964	616629	454622
西藏	Tibet	4.4	3.5	2.8	48028	48216	-260
陕西	Shaanxi	265.0	265.0	97.4	742622	685370	207032
甘肃	Gansu	140.8	134.8	51.2	473073	427163	200118
青海	Qinghai	40.5	37.9	15.9	159085	156661	6600
宁夏	Ningxia	46.5	42.9	14.3	165889	114540	157788
新疆	Xinjiang	186.3	178.2	83.0	826213	663502	539624
不分地区	Not Classified by Region	21.6		3.7	12038	6056	34566

注:不分地区合计中，包括中国人民银行、中国农业发展银行数。

a) Data of not classified by region include these of the People's Bank of China and Agricultural Bank of China.

23-39 分地区失业保险基本情况(2003年底)

Basic Conditions of Unemployment Insurance at the Year-end by Region（2003）

单位: 万人 (10 000 persons)

地区	Region	参保人数 Contributors	企业 Enterprises	国有企业 State-owned Enterprises	集体企业 Collective-owned Enterprises	其他企业 Other Enterprises	事业单位 Institutions	领取失业保险金人数 Beneficiaries of Unemployment Insurance
全　国	**National Total**	**10372.9**	**8029.8**	**4884.2**	**1124.6**	**2021.1**	**2175.3**	**414.9**
北　京	Beijing	306.6	231.6	111.2	14.6	105.8	75.0	5.2
天　津	Tianjin	193.5	158.9	102.1	20.6	36.2	34.6	9.4
河　北	Hebei	484.2	364.7	250.1	45.8	68.8	118.5	8.3
山　西	Shanxi	284.1	236.1	210.2	24.1	1.7	47.5	5.7
内蒙古	Inner Mongolia	221.6	157.2	86.2	17.9	53.1	59.8	5.7
辽　宁	Liaoning	622.2	486.3	248.4	124.6	113.3	102.5	67.0
吉　林	Jilin	292.9	245.1	201.7	22.3	21.0	47.5	16.2
黑龙江	Heilongjiang	479.0	429.8	327.7	71.4	30.8	48.6	12.6
上　海	Shanghai	441.1	314.6	112.9	40.3	161.4	66.8	14.0
江　苏	Jiangsu	761.6	606.3	266.4	130.4	209.5	146.1	48.9
浙　江	Zhejiang	396.8	292.5	83.2	43.7	165.7	89.2	17.4
安　徽	Anhui	380.8	290.6	188.8	59.6	42.1	89.5	23.4
福　建	Fujian	266.4	214.2	74.0	24.2	116.0	49.9	10.0
江　西	Jiangxi	215.5	154.6	136.4	11.7	6.4	60.8	5.9
山　东	Shandong	719.1	568.0	389.1	100.3	78.6	149.1	30.1
河　南	Henan	680.0	512.0	343.0	91.5	77.5	163.1	18.7
湖　北	Hubei	390.1	283.5	222.5	30.3	30.7	105.7	18.7
湖　南	Hunan	347.5	228.5	191.5	23.1	13.8	118.6	10.5
广　东	Guangdong	954.1	858.0	262.9	86.8	508.3	72.9	25.9
广　西	Guangxi	219.1	134.3	102.5	13.3	18.6	84.5	8.9
海　南	Hainan	57.7	48.5	42.4	3.2	2.9	8.8	1.8
重　庆	Chongqing	199.5	160.4	119.3	29.1	12.0	36.4	8.1
四　川	Sichuan	400.0	276.6	191.8	22.1	62.8	122.3	12.6
贵　州	Guizhou	128.0	88.6	79.0	5.1	4.5	39.3	1.3
云　南	Yunnan	183.0	125.2	78.2	17.2	29.8	56.8	6.6
西　藏	Tibet	7.1	3.2	3.2			3.9	
陕　西	Shaanxi	323.3	257.1	212.0	31.6	13.5	64.4	8.2
甘　肃	Gansu	162.1	121.3	93.3	12.9	15.1	40.4	3.8
青　海	Qinghai	33.2	22.1	20.2	0.6	1.2	10.8	1.3
宁　夏	Ningxia	36.3	26.6	20.5	1.7	4.4	9.5	1.0
新　疆	Xinjiang	186.5	133.4	113.6	4.5	15.4	52.6	7.4

23-40 分地区基本医疗保险基本情况(2003年)

Basic Medical Insurance by Region (2003)

地 区	Region	年末参保人数（万人）Contributors at the Year-end (10 000 persons)		基金收支情况（万元）Revenue and Expenses（10 000 yuan)		
		职 工 Workers	离休、退休、退职人员 Retirees	基金收入 Revenue	基金支出 Expenses	累计结余 Balance at the Year-end
全 国	**National Total**	**7974.9**	**2926.8**	**8899652**	**6538736**	**6706463**
北 京	Beijing	301.5	134.7	680951	544354	245435
天 津	Tianjin	146.2	108.5	195347	204036	58554
河 北	Hebei	298.4	84.7	266861	178845	224387
山 西	Shanxi	194.2	51.3	102891	48961	89995
内蒙古	Inner Mongolia	186.2	66.1	114895	85804	94648
辽 宁	Liaoning	480.4	217.2	380300	262647	309144
吉 林	Jilin	175.4	55.3	99115	70722	78846
黑龙江	Heilongjiang	313.2	122.1	154843	112356	115326
上 海	Shanghai	459.1	250.6	1215590	1170618	465984
江 苏	Jiangsu	587.4	227.6	733229	555503	519956
浙 江	Zhejiang	370.8	139.5	589217	338695	611633
安 徽	Anhui	238.4	79.8	168696	116234	133246
福 建	Fujian	185.9	61.8	264851	166915	289949
江 西	Jiangxi	142.5	45.7	80489	61669	52079
山 东	Shandong	553.0	138.0	486904	363008	320953
河 南	Henan	441.0	126.9	283377	195924	261344
湖 北	Hubei	306.6	110.1	248495	141552	214573
湖 南	Hunan	307.4	116.1	271930	201598	190474
广 东	Guangdong	730.6	146.4	1009690	573139	1256457
广 西	Guangxi	169.0	66.1	190483	108574	144986
海 南	Hainan	47.7	15.4	40557	33316	25329
重 庆	Chongqing	80.0	41.7	55219	38564	37196
四 川	Sichuan	357.4	173.8	366763	269754	357314
贵 州	Guizhou	95.9	38.2	69346	38323	55444
云 南	Yunnan	200.1	81.4	276196	227008	190686
西 藏	Tibet	4.2	1.8	10866	11160	7373
陕 西	Shaanxi	223.6	77.4	122598	92733	95840
甘 肃	Gansu	113.2	32.8	86925	72231	43956
青 海	Qinghai	38.6	17.8	39193	25120	37616
宁 夏	Ningxia	35.4	12.7	43669	22236	31755
新 疆	Xinjiang	191.4	85.3	250166	207137	145985

23-41 残疾人事业基本情况

Basic Information of People with Disabilities

项目	Item	1999	2000	2001	2002	2003
康复	**Rehabilitation**					
白内障复明手术	Sight-restoring Cataract Surgery					
白内障复明手术(万例)	Sight-restoring Cataract Surgeries (10 000 Cases)	41.7	48.1	49.1	51.3	57.4
人工晶体植入率 (%)	Artificial Intra-ocular Lens Implantation Rate (%)	60.4	71.3	78.3	83.0	88.0
低视力配用助视器 (人)	Vision-aids Provided for Individuals with Low-vision (persons)	22079	21701	26476	28231	30932
聋儿康复	Rehabilitation of Children with Hearing Disability					
年收训聋儿 (人)	Hearing and Speech Training (persons)	17030	16904	17934	18771	18465
聋儿入普幼普小率(%)	Enrollment Rate of Trained Children to Ordinary Kindergartens and Primary Schools (%)		19.4	22.5	23.6	24.5
培训家长 (人)	Parents Trained (persons)	13998	13568	18550	21155	20716
精神病防治康复	Prevention and Treatment of Psychiatric Diseases					
开展精神病防治康复工作市县数 (个)	Counties Carried on the Works of Prevention and Treatment of Psychiatric Diseases (units)	243	243	551	549	582
综合防治康复精神病人数 (万人)	Prevention and Treatment Provided for Patients with Severe Psychiatric Diseases (10 000 persons)	103.3	122.6	133.2	207.3	242.6
监护率 (%)	Guardianship Rate (%)	91.5	93.0	91.3	86.7	90.2
显好率 (%)	Significant Improvement Rate (%)	73.6	71.6	73.6	69.5	71.1
社会参与率 (%)	Social Involvement Rate (%)	64.9	62.7	62.6	58.7	60.6
肇事率 (%)	Violent Events Rate (%)	0.2	0.2	0.2	0.3	0.3
康复训练与服务 (人)	Rehabilitation Training and Service (person)					
肢体残疾康复训练数	Function Training Provided to Persons with Physical Disability	54263	52538	50577	47848	44221
智残儿童康复训练数	Rehabilitation Training Provided to Children with Intellectual Disability	23213	24009	26093	22642	22295
脑瘫儿童康复训练数	Rehabilitation Training Provided to Children with Cerebral Palsy			8607	10003	10539
麻风畸残康复	Rehabilitation of People with Leprosy					
矫治手术 (例)	Orthopaedic Surgeries (case)			1730	5814	3852
发放辅助用具 (件)	Assistant Devices Provided (unit)			5827	30100	35001
康复训练 (人)	Rehabilitation Training (person)			5773	13970	9170
教育	**Education**					
未入学适龄残疾儿童少年 (万人)	School-age Disabled Children without Schooling (10 000 persons)	43.3	39.1	35.6	32.3	30.6
职业教育与培训	Vocational Education and Training					
机构数 (个)	Facilities (unit)	3999	4164	3927	3871	4143
教育与培训人数(万人)	Number of Educated and Trained (10 000 persons)	57.9	65.4	48.1	45.3	49.9
就业	**Employment**					
城镇残疾人就业状况	Employment of Urban Handicappeds					
当年安排就业 (万人)	Persons Employed in the Year (10 000 persons)	26.1	26.6	27.6	30.2	32.7
#按比例就业	Employed by Quota Scheme	5.9	7.2	7.5	7.1	8.4
集中就业	Employed at Welfare Enterprises	6.2	7.1	6.6	8.5	9.8
个体就业	Self-employed	13.9	12.3	13.4	14.6	14.5
未安排就业	Unemployed	116.1	96.2	101.2	103.2	100.4
农村残疾人就业状况	Employment of Rural Handicapped					
就业 (万人)	Employed (10 000 persons)	1568.8	1616.1	1579.5	1717.8	1685.2
未就业 (万人)	Unemployed (10 000 persons)	467.6	358.2	379.8	337.3	370.2
残疾人就业服务机构(个)	Employment Placement Service Facilities for Disabled Jobseekers (unit)	2880	3012	2991	2998	3005
省	Provinces	31	30	30	31	33
地	Prefectures	85	73	71	49	54
市(含县级市)	Cities (inc. Cities at County Level)	610	632	646	652	636
县	County	1497	1550	1497	1505	1517
市辖区	Districts under the Jurisdiction of Cities	653	727	747	761	765
盲人按摩	**Massage by Persons with Visual Disability**					
保健按摩员培训 (人)	Massage Therapists Training (person)	6533	8471	7511	7413	6874
医疗按摩员培训 (人)	Keep-fit Massager Training (person)	1984	2364	3728	3853	4821
扶贫	**Poverty Alleviation**					
扶贫开发解决温饱残疾人 (万人)	Rural Handicappeds Overcomed Poverty by Govern--ment's Poverty Reduction Program(10 000 persons)	251.0	231.6	167.8	151.4	123.3
尚未解决温饱贫困残疾人 (万人)	Rural Handicappeds Remained in Poverty (10 000 persons)	649.5	978.9	1058.4	1022.1	1065.2
#可扶持贫困残疾人	Rural Handicappeds Remained in Poverty Can Be Supported	445.2	682.5	657.7	634.4	673.7
残联组织建设	**Organization Building of Disabled Persons' Federation**					
残疾人工作者数 (万人)	Workers for Handicappeds (10 000 persons)	8.2	8.0	7.3	7.5	7.8

注：根据1987年全国残疾人抽样调查的结果推算，全国各类残疾人的总数共有6000万人。

a) According to the calculation from the handicappeds survey in 1987, total handicappeds in China will be 60 million persons.

23-42 婚姻登记和离婚情况

Number of Marriages and Divorces

年份 Year 地区 Region	结婚登记总对数（万对） Total Number of Registered Marriages (10 000 couples)	内地居民登记结婚 Registered Marriages of Mainland	初婚（万人） First Marriages (10 000 persons)	再婚（万人） Remarriages (10 000 persons)	涉外及港澳台居民登记结婚 Registered Marriages with Foreigner and the Citizen of Hong Kong, Macao, Taiwan	离婚（万对） Divorces (10 000 couples)	离婚率（‰） Divorce Rate (‰)
1985	831.3	829.1	1607.6	50.5	2.2	45.8	0.9
1989	937.2	935.2	1796.0	74.4	2.0	75.3	1.3
1990	951.1	948.7	1819.1	78.2	2.4	80.0	1.4
1991	953.6	951.0	1820.3	81.6	2.6	82.9	1.4
1992	957.5	954.5	1832.1	76.9	3.0	85.0	1.5
1993	915.4	912.2	1747.0	77.3	3.3	90.9	1.5
1994	932.4	929.0	1779.3	78.7	3.4	98.1	1.6
1995	934.1	929.7	1776.1	83.3	4.4	105.5	1.8
1996	938.7	934.0	1781.7	86.2	4.7	113.2	1.9
1997	914.1	909.1	1726.0	92.2	5.1	119.8	1.9
1998	891.7	886.7	1675.4	97.9	5.0	119.0	1.9
1999	885.3	879.9	1659.4	100.5	5.4	120.2	1.9
2000	848.5	842.0	1581.4	102.6	6.5	121.3	1.9
2001	805.0	797.1	1481.7	112.5	7.9	125.0	2.0
2002	786.2	778.8	1440.3	117.1	7.3	117.7	1.8
2003	811.4	803.5	1483.9	123.3	7.8	133.1	2.1
北　京 Beijing	9.4	9.3	15.9	2.7	0.08	3.1	
天　津 Tianjin	6.3	6.3	10.9	1.6	0.03	1.4	
河　北 Hebei	52.4	52.4	95.3	9.5	0.02	5.8	
山　西 Shanxi	14.5	14.5	27.3	1.7	0.01	2.3	
内蒙古 Inner Mongolia	13.1	13.0	24.3	1.8	0.02	3.0	
辽　宁 Liaoning	25.4	25.0	42.7	7.4	0.32	8.3	
吉　林 Jilin	16.2	15.5	27.5	3.6	0.68	4.3	
黑龙江 Heilongjiang	20.5	20.1	34.8	5.4	0.43	7.7	
上　海 Shanghai	10.8	10.5	17.2	3.9	0.24	3.3	
江　苏 Jiangsu	46.1	46.0	85.8	6.2	0.13	6.9	
浙　江 Zhejiang	36.1	35.6	65.8	5.5	0.43	5.6	
安　徽 Anhui	42.3	42.3	81.5	3.2	0.06	4.3	
福　建 Fujian	28.0	25.6	49.4	1.9	2.47	3.9	
江　西 Jiangxi	26.9	26.8	50.8	2.8	0.20	2.9	
山　东 Shandong	79.9	79.9	149.5	10.2	0.09	6.8	
河　南 Henan	57.0	56.9	108.4	5.3	0.12	6.7	
湖　北 Hubei	32.9	32.7	61.0	4.4	0.18	5.3	
湖　南 Hunan	38.4	37.9	69.6	6.3	0.43	5.9	
广　东 Guangdong	57.9	57.0	109.1	4.9	0.86	6.0	
广　西 Guangxi	29.8	29.6	56.6	2.6	0.31	3.3	
海　南 Hainan	3.5	3.4	6.3	0.4	0.11	0.4	
重　庆 Chongqing	18.0	17.9	30.8	4.9	0.17	5.2	
四　川 Sichuan	40.5	40.3	71.5	9.0	0.26	10.7	
贵　州 Guizhou	23.4	23.3	44.7	2.0	0.08	2.8	
云　南 Yunnan	26.5	26.5	49.8	3.1	0.05	3.9	
西　藏 Tibet	0.5	0.5	0.9	0.1	…	0.1	
陕　西 Shaanxi	19.0	19.0	35.6	2.5	0.04	3.4	
甘　肃 Gansu	11.8	11.8	22.2	1.5	0.01	1.9	
青　海 Qinghai	3.3	3.3	6.1	0.5	…	0.7	
宁　夏 Ningxia	3.6	3.6	6.6	0.5	…	0.6	
新　疆 Xinjiang	16.6	16.5	25.6	7.6	0.02	5.9	

23-43 档案馆机构和人员情况

Statistics on Institution and Personnel of Archives Institution

单位：个、人 (unit, person)

年份 Year	国家综合档案馆 National Comprehensive Archives		国家专门档案馆 National Special Archives		部门档案馆 Department Archives		企业档案馆数 Enterprise Archive Institution	文化事业档案馆数 Culture Archive Institution	科技事业单位档案馆数 Science and Technology Archive Institution
	馆数 Number of Institution	专职人员 Full-time Personnel	馆数 Number of Institution	专职人员 Full-time Personnel	馆数 Number of Institution	专职人员 Full-time Personnel			
1991	2957	21657	211	2038	128	2171	229	19	28
1992	2962	22226	206	2082	122	2258	231	19	28
1993	2980	23624	200	2245	122	1448	221	20	31
1994	2983	23568	205	2294	136	2160	209	20	36
1995	3024	24777	216	2484	144	2168	213	27	38
1996	3011	24542	226	2658	134	2072	232	23	44
1997	3021	24904	223	2578	162	2521	228	26	46
1998	3034	24197	232	3200	149	2411	245	27	46
1999	3046	23530	225	3436	142	2123	304	40	59
2000	3070	23701	234	3319	141	1865	307	53	80
2001	3100	23652	243	3448	142	2086	286	47	84
2002	3110	22825	253	3435	148	2109	299	75	93
2003	3121	23086	260	3514	141	1770	300	75	85

23-44 国家综合档案馆馆藏、建筑面积、开放和利用情况

Collection, Floor Space, Opening and Utilization of National Comprehensive Archives

年份 Year	馆藏档案（万卷、万件）Number of Archives (10 000 volume, piece)	照片档案（万张）Photo (10 000 sheet)	开放档案（万卷、万件）Opening Archives (10 000 volume, piece)	利用档案（万卷、万件次）Utilized Archives (10 000 volume, piece)	档案馆建筑面积（万平方米）Floor Space of Archives Institution (10 000 sq.m)
1991	9637.4	371.0	2094.3	937.0	348.1
1992	10003.5	402.4	2018.7	773.8	255.7
1993	10726.8	435.5	2140.7	891.9	275.9
1994	10782.9	449.6	2454.6	674.4	268.3
1995	11318.3	485.5	2790.3	529.3	282.5
1996	11341.4	494.6	2939.2	485.4	297.5
1997	12222.9	553.0	3304.6	501.0	347.6
1998	12276.5	579.7	3556.5	446.5	310.7
1999	12866.8	584.5	3808.2	508.5	328.4
2000	13314.0	631.7	4072.0	494.4	336.2
2001	13756.6	642.8	4129.7	575.4	342.0
2002	14790.7	720.5	4301.1	548.8	351.0
2003	15945.9	797.4	4618.4	602.6	361.4

主要统计指标解释

社会福利事业单位 指集中收养社会孤老、残、幼的机构，包括由民政部门管理的社会福利院、儿童福利院、精神病人福利院和城镇集体举办的福利院及农村集体举办的敬老院以及优抚医院和具有收养能力的社区服务中心等。该指标主要反映我国在社会福利性单位投入的水平。

社会福利事业单位收养人数 包括民政部门管理和城镇、农村集体举办的社会福利事业单位中收养的老人、少年儿童、缺乏生活自理能力的残疾人员和精神病人。该指标主要反映收养性社会福利单位的收养能力。

社会福利企业单位 指以安置城镇有一定劳动能力的盲、聋、哑和肢体残疾人员就业为目的，享受国家减免税待遇的国有或集体企业。包括福利工厂、福利商业和服务业、假肢厂和安置农场等单位。该指标主要反映我国对残疾人照顾的特殊政策。

农村五保户 指农村中既无劳动能力，又无经济来源的老、弱、孤、残的农民，其生活由集体供养，实行保吃、保穿、保住、保医、保葬(孤儿保教)，简称“五保”，享受五保待遇的家庭叫五保户。该指标主要反映农村弱势群体的人员数量。

聋儿入普幼普小率 指本年度内进入普通幼儿园、普通小学的聋儿数与在训聋儿数(不含当年新收训聋儿数)之比。该指标主要反映经过康复训练的聋儿进入普通幼儿园和普通小学的情况。

综合防治康复精神病人数 指在开展精神病防治康复工作地区，采取不同形式，接受综合性防治康复措施、开放式管理的精神病人数。该指标主要反映精神病患者接受治疗康复情况。

监护率 指通过监护小组、家庭病床、工疗站、社会就业以及精神卫生机构，接受社会化、综合性、开放式治疗与康复的精神病人占经调查摸底、登记在册的精神病人数的百分比。该指标主要反映对精神病患者落实治疗康复措施的情况。

社会参与率 指生活能自理，并参加生产劳动和社会生活的精神病人数占监护精神病人数的百分比。该指标主要反映精神病人康复状况和参与社会的情况。

未入学适龄残疾儿童少年 指根据义务教育法规定应接受义务教育，但因各种原因未能入学的适龄视力残疾、听力与言语残疾、智力残疾、肢体残疾、精神残疾、多重残疾儿童少年。适龄残疾儿童少年的年龄段参照各省级人民政府依照义务教育法规定的入学年龄。该指标主要反映因各种原因未能入学的适龄残疾儿童的年度变化,为制定残疾儿童义务教育发展规划及其应采取的方针、政策和措施提供依据,同时为各地开展资助残疾儿童就学工作提供依据。

律师 指依法取得律师执业证书，担任法律顾问，民事(刑事、行政)案件代理人、刑事案件辩护人、办理非诉讼业务，解答法律询问，代写法律事务文书等，为社会提供法律服务的人员。

公证人员 指在公证处工作的人员总称，包括公证处主任、副主任、公证员、公证员助理(助理公证员)和其他从事辅助性工作的人员。

公证文书 指公证处根据当事人申请，依照事实和法律，按照法定程序制作的，具有法律效力的司法证明文书。根据公证书用途和使用地，公证书分为国内公证书、国内经济公证书、涉外民事公证书、涉外经济公证书四类。

调解员 指在人民调解委员会担负调解民间纠纷工作的人员，包括调解委员会的委员和调解小组的调解员。该指标主要反映从事人民调解工作的人员数量。

调解民间纠纷 指调解委员会按照法律规定，根据自愿原则，用说服教育的方法调解民间发生的有关民事权利和义务争执的件数，包括调解成功数和调解未成功数。该指标主要反映人民调解委员会的工作量。

立案 指人民检察院对受理的报案、控告、举报或自首及自行发现的犯罪线索、犯罪嫌疑人进行初步调查后，认为存在职务犯罪事实和应追究刑事责任，并决定作为刑事案件进行侦查的诉讼活动，是追究犯罪的开始。该指标主要反映人民检察院依法将职务犯罪线索作为刑事案件进行侦查的诉讼活动。

大案 指贪污、贿赂案数额在5万元以上，挪用公款案数额在10万元以上，集体私分、巨额财产来源不明、隐瞒境外存款案数额在50万元以上以及按照《人民检察院直接受理的渎职、侵权重、特大案件标准(试行)》认定的案件。该指标主要反映人民检察院立案查办的职务犯罪案件中经济损失大、社会危害严重的案件。

要案 指县、处级以上干部的犯罪案件。该指标主要反映国家工作人员中县、处级以上干部因职务犯罪被人民检察院依法立案侦查的情况。

决定逮捕 指人民检察院对直接受理、自行侦查的案件，认为需要逮捕犯罪嫌疑人时，依据法律做出的逮捕决定。该指标主要反映人民检察院对直接受理的案件行使决定逮捕权的情况。

批准逮捕 指人民检察院对公安机关、国家安全机关、监狱管理机关提出逮捕的犯罪嫌疑人进行审查，根据事实，依法做出逮捕决定。该指标主要反映人民检察院对提请逮捕机关提请逮捕犯罪嫌疑人进行审查后依法做出批准逮捕决定的情况。

决定起诉 指人民检察院对公安机关、国家安全机关、监狱管理机关和检察机关内设机构反贪污贿赂部门等移送起诉的案件进行审查，根据事实，做出提起公诉的案件。该指标主要反映人民检察院对各种刑事案件向人民法院提起公诉的情况。

申诉 指经检察机关信访部门审查处理后，移送到检察机关申诉部门的申诉案件，包括不服检察机关处理决定和不服法院刑事判决和裁定的申诉的案件。

受理劳动争议案件数 指劳动争议仲裁委员会根据国家

有关规定，对劳动争议当事人的申请予以审查，符合受理条件而正式立案、准备处理的劳动争议案件数。

基本养老保险

1.参加保险人数：指报告期末按照国家法律、法规和有关政策规定参加基本养老保险的职工人数。包括不能正常缴费、已中断缴费但未终止保险关系的职工人数。

2.社会统筹基金收入：指根据国家规定，由纳入基本养老保险范围的单位，按照国家规定的缴费基数和缴费比例缴纳的社会统筹基金，以及通过其他方式取得的形成基金来源的收入，包括：单位缴纳的社会统筹基金收入、财政补贴收入、利息收入、其他收入。

3.社会统筹基金支出：指按照国家政策规定的开支范围和开支标准从社会统筹基金中支付给参加基本养老保险的离休、退休、退职人员个人的养老金、丧葬抚恤补助，以及由于保险关系转移、上下级之间调剂资金等原因而发生的支出。包括：基础性养老金、过渡性养老金、离休金、退休金、退职金、补贴、丧葬抚恤补助、其他支出。

4.社会统筹基金结余：指截止报告期末基本养老保险的社会统筹基金结余金额。包括银行存款、财政专户、债券投资和其他。

离休、退休、退职人员 指正式办理了离休、退休、退职手续，并享受相应的离休、退休、退职待遇的人员。

基本医疗保险

1.参加保险人数：指报告期末按国家有关规定参加基本医疗保险的人数。包括参加保险的职工人数和退休人员人数。

2.社会统筹基金收入：指根据国家有关规定，由纳入基本医疗保险范围的缴费单位，按国家规定的缴费基数和缴费比例缴纳的社会统筹基金，以及通过其他方式取得的形成基金来源的款项，包括：单位缴纳的社会统筹基金收入、财政补贴收入、利息收入、其他收入。

3.社会统筹基金支出：指按照国家政策规定的开支范围和开支标准从社会统筹基金中支付给参加基本医疗保险的职工和退休人员的医疗保险待遇支出及其他支出。包括：住院医疗费用支出、门急诊医疗费用支出、其他支出。

4.社会统筹基金结余：指截止报告期末基本医疗保险的社会统筹基金结余金额。包括银行存款、财政专户、债券投资和其他。

失业保险

1.参加保险人数：指报告期末按照国家法律、法规和有关政策规定参加了失业保险的城镇企业事业单位的职工及地方政府规定参加失业保险的其他人员的人数。

2.失业保险金：指为保障失业人员的基本生活而按规定支付的失业保险金金额。

保险福利费用总额 指各单位在工资以外支付给职工和离休、退休、退职人员个人和用于集体的保险福利费用，不包括用于职工的劳动保护费用，由保险福利费用开支的医务人员工资，集体福利机构工作人员和病伤休息期满6个月以上人员的工资。

离休、退休、退职人员保险福利费用包括：

1.离休金：指发给离休干部的工资和按1982年国务院《关于老干部离职休养制度的几项规定的通知》发给符合规定的离休干部相当于一至两个月标准工资的生活补贴及1988年增发的生活补贴。

2.退休金：指按照国家有关规定发给退休职工的退休费和1988年增发的生活补贴。

3.退职生活费：指按照1978年国务院《关于工人退休、退职的暂行办法》发给退职人员的生活费用和1988年增发的生活补贴。

以上离退休、退职人员的离退休金、退职生活费还应包括发给离退休、退职人员的生活补贴和物价补贴。

4.医疗卫生费：指离休、退休、退职人员的医疗费、住院费以及住院伙食补助等费用。

5.其他：指上述费用以外的其他保险福利费用，如丧葬抚恤救济费、交通费补贴、冬季取暖补贴等。

Explanatory Notes on Main Statistical Indicators

Social Welfare Institutions refer to institutions taking care of old people without children, handicapped people and orphans. They include social welfare institutions run by civil affairs departments, children welfare institutions, social welfare institutions for mental patients, collective-owned old peoples homes in rural areas, convalescent homes and community service centers with the capacity of receiving those people. This indicator reflects the input in social welfare institutions.

Number of People Taken in by Social Welfare Institutions refers to the number of old people, children, totally dependent handicapped people and mental patients taken in by social welfare institutions run by civil affairs departments and those run by collective units in urban and rural areas. This indicator reflects the capacity of social welfare institutions.

Social Welfare Enterprises are collective owned enterprises which employ the blind, deaf-mute, and other handicapped people who are able to work in cities and towns and enjoy exemption from state taxes, including welfare plants, welfare commercial services, artificial limb plants and farms, etc. This indicator reflects the preferential policies toward disabled persons.

Rural Households with Livelihood Guaranteed in Five Aspects refer to the households in which there are old people without child, orphans and handicapped people who are unable to work and without financial resources in rural areas. They are taken care of by the collective units and their food, clothing, housing, medical care, funeral expenses (or schooling for orphans) are guaranteed to be provided for. This indicator reflects the total number of disadvantageous groups of rural population.

Proportion of Deaf Children Enrolled in Ordinary Preschool and Primary Education refers to the proportion of deaf children who are enrolled in ordinary kindergartens or primary schools during the year in the total number of deaf children under rehabilitation programs (not including new comers into the rehabilitation programs during the year). This indicator mainly reflects number of rehabilitated deaf children entering ordinary kindergartens or primary schools.

Number of Mental Patients under Integrated Prevention and Rehabilitation Program refers to mental disease patients receiving integrated prevention and rehabilitation treatment of various forms under open environment in areas with mental disease rehabilitation programs. This indicator reflects the condition of metal patients receiving rehabilitation treatment.

Supervision Rate refers to the percentage of patients among the total number of registered mental disease patients, who participate in social integrated and open treatment and rehabilitation programs through various forms such as supervision groups, family treatment, employment or guidance from psychiatric institutions. This indicator reflects the implementation of various measures aimed at rehabilitating those metal patients.

Social Participation Rate refers to proportion of mental disease patients who are able to manage their daily life and participate in economic activities to the total number of mental disease patients under supervision. This indicator reflects the condition of recovery of those metal patients and their participation in social activities.

School-age Disabled Children not in Schools refer to children with disability in sight, listening, speaking, mentality, limbs or multi-disability who are obliged to compulsory education by law but have not been enrolled in schools due to various reasons. The definition of school age for disabled children is decided by the definition of school age as specified by provincial governments in line with the local laws on compulsory education. This indicator reflects the annual change of school-age disable children not entering schools by various reasons. It will provide foundation for the formulation of development plans of compulsory education for those disable children, and for related principles, policies and measures as well. It is also the base for the job of funding those disabled children back to schools across the countries.

Lawyers are certified legal workers according to law, and who are employed by legal counseling firms to act as legal advisers, agents in criminal or civil lawsuits, or defenders in criminal lawsuits, or to handle non-litigious legal affairs, to advise on matters of law or to write legal papers for others, and provide service to the public.

Notary Personnel refers to people working for notary offices including: directors, deputy director, notaries, assistant notaries, and other people providing assistance.

Notary Documents refer to the judicatory notary documents drawn up by the request of the party and are in accordance with facts and laws and following certain legal proceedings. According to usage and locality, the notary documents are divided into following 4 types: domestic notary documents, domestic economic notary documents, foreign-related civil notary documents and foreign-related economic notary documents.

Mediators refer to workers on peoples mediation committees responsible for mediating in civil disputes and cases of slight infraction of the law. They include members of the mediation committees and mediators of mediation groups. This indicator reflects the number of people engaged in meditation.

Mediation of Civil Disputes refers to number of cases made by mediation committees in mediating in civil disputes concerning civil rights and duties through persuasion and education in accordance with the provisions of law on a voluntary basis, so as to solve disputes by helping the parties involved come to an agreement and understanding, including those unsuccessful ones. This indicator reflects the workload of the mediation committees

Acceptance of Case refers to the decision made by the people's procuratorate office on reported cases, prosecution, impeachment, surrender, self-found criminal clues or suspects after initial investigation to confirm the act of crime and to start legal proceedings of the case as criminal case.

Large Cases refer to cases involving a corruption or bribery of over 50,000 yuan, or a misappropriation of over 100,000 yuan. Cases of collectively illegal possession of public funds, unstated sources of large properties, or disguised overseas savings deposits involving 500,000 yuan, or a case that has been defined by the "Standard on Serious and Large Cases of Misconduct and Tortious that Directly Accepted by People's Procurators Office (trial)". This indicator mainly reflects number of accepted cases of job-related criminals that caused serious economic losses or extremely harmful to the society.

Key Cases refer to cases committed by government officials with a ranking of division director or county administrator. This indicator mainly reflects the recorded and spied on cases by the people's procurators offices toward government official with a ranking of division director or county administrator.

Decision on Arrest refers to decision made by people's procurators office, in accordance with laws, to arrest the suspect (s) in the cases that are accepted and to be investigated by procurators office. This indicator mainly reflects the implementation of the decision on arrest by people's procurators office.

Approval for Arrest refers to the decision made by people's procurators office, in accordance with laws and relevant facts, to approve the arrest of the suspect(s) that is proposed by the public security departments, state security departments or authority of prisons. This indicator reflects approved arrests made by people's procurators office that are proposed by related departments.

Decision on Prosecution refers to the decision made by people's procurators office, in accordance with laws and relevant facts, to institute proceedings to the people's court against the suspect(s) of criminal cases handed over by the public security departments, state security departments or authority of prisons, or by the anti-corruption departments within the procurators office. This indicator reflects the condition of the prosecutions made by people's procurators office toward the people's court.

Appeals refer to cases transferred to the appeal departments of procurator's offices after initial review by departments dealing with complaint letters and calls of the public. Included are appeals against decisions made by procurator's offices and appeals against court rules and verdicts.

Number of Labour Dispute Cases Accepted refers to the number of cases of labour dispute submitted that, after being reviewed by the labour dispute arbitration committees in line with the relevant state regulations, are accepted and registered for treatment.

Basic Endowment Insurance

1.Number of people participating in the insurance program: by the end of reference period, number of staff and workers participating in the insurance program in line with national laws, regulations and related policies, including those who can not make regular payment or interrupt payment but not terminate the insurance program.

2.Revenue of social comprehensive funds: according to national provision, payments made by units covered in basic endowment insurance program, and income from other resources, including: income of social comprehensive funds paid by unites, financial subsidies, interest income and others.

3.Expenditure of social comprehensive funds: refer to payment made to those retired and resigned people covered in endowment insurance program in terms of pension or compensation within the expenditure scope and standards according to related national policies, and the expenditure occurred due to shift of the insurance relationship or adjustment funds among agencies, including: basic pension, transitional pension, pension for resigned people, pension for retired people, pension for people quitting jobs, subsidies, funeral subsidies and other expenditure.

4.Balance of social comprehensive funds: refer to the balance of basic endowment insurance of social comprehensive funds at the end of the reference period, including: bank savings, special fiscal account, investment in bonds and others.

Retired or Resigned Personnel refers to people who have formally gone through the formalities for their retirement or quitting work and enjoy the corresponding treatments.

Basic Medical Care Insurance:

1.Number of people participated in the insurance program: refer to number of people participated in the basic medical care insurance program according to related regulation by the end of reference period, including: number of staff and workers and retired persons participated in this insurance program.

2.Revenue of social comprehensive funds: according to national provision, payments made by units covered in basic medical care insurance program, and income from other resources, including: income of social comprehensive funds paid by unites, financial subsidies, interest income and others.

3.Expenditure of social comprehensive funds: refer to payment made to those retired and resigned people covered in basic medical care insurance within the expenditure scope and standards according to related national policies, including: expenditure on fee-for-service in hospital, expenditure on fee-for-service in clinic and other expenditure.

4.Balance of social comprehensive funds: refer to the balance of medical care insurance of social comprehensive funds at the end of the reference period, including: bank savings, special fiscal account, investment in bonds and others.

Unemployment Insurance

1.Number of people participated in unemployment insurance program: number of staff and workers in urban enterprises or institutions and other people according to local government regulations participated in unemployment insurance program in line with national law, regulations and related policies by the end of the reference period.

2.Sum of Unemployment Insurance: refer to total amount of insurance paid to un-employees to guarantee their basic lives according to related regulations.

Insurance and Welfare Funds refers to labour insurance and welfare fund paid by enterprises, organizations and institutions to their staff and workers as well as retired and resigned persons in addition to their wages and salaries£¬ excluding labour protection fees, wages paid to medical workers from insurance and welfare fund and wages paid to staff members working in collective welfare agencies and to people with over 6 months of sick-leave.

Insurance and Welfare Funds for Retired and Resigned Staff and Workers covers:

1.Pensions for retired veteran cadres: They refer to pensions, other subsidies, and additional allowances paid to retired in line with relevant government documents.

2.Pensions for Retirement: They refer to living allowance; other subsidies and additional allowances paid to retired staff and workers in line with the relevant government documents.

3.Resignation Allowances for Living Expenses: They refer to living allowance, and additional allowances subsidies paid to resigned staff and workers in line with relevant government instructions.

It also includes living subsidies and prices subsidies paid to retired and resigned staff and workers.

4.Medical Care Allowance: refer to fee-for-service, cost of medical care and per diem subsidies during hospitalizations of retired and resigned staff and workers.

5.Others: They refer to other expenses, including other types of insurance and welfare fund, fees for funerals, traveling subsidies and heating subsidies during the winter time.

二十四、香港特别行政区主要社会经济指标

Main Social and Economic Indicators of Hong Kong Special Administrative Region

简要说明

一、本章资料反映香港特别行政区主要社会、经济发展情况。内容包括：土地、人口、就业、国民收入、国际收支平衡表、工业、能源、建筑、交通、对外贸易、财政金融、教育、房屋、卫生、社会保障等方面。

二、本章由香港特别行政区政府统计处提供所有数据，国家统计局国际统计信息中心负责整理、编辑。

三、在统计工作方面，按中华人民共和国“香港特别行政区基本法”的有关原则，香港特别行政区保留其单独运作的统计系统，并负责编制和发布反映香港特别行政区情况的统计数据。由于香港和内地在使用统计名词及概念方面会有所不同，读者在比较两地数据时，请参考以下资料：

（1）本章内的“《中国统计年鉴》与香港特别行政区统计刊物中使用的指标对照表”列出两地概念相近但名称不同的词汇。

（2）本章末的“主要统计指标解释”，载有一些重要概念的解释。

四、香港特别行政区是单独的关税地区，香港与内地之间的贸易，亦需办理进出口报关。在贸易统计方面，香港特别行政区对外贸易统计数据亦包括香港特别行政区与内地的贸易。

五、在外汇统计及与之有关的各方面，港币是香港特别行政区的法定货币，因此，除港币以外的货币（包括人民币）均视作外币。

六、更详细的统计资料及有关的技术细节，可参阅香港特别行政区政府统计处出版的《香港统计月刊》、《香港统计年刊》及各专题统计出版物。

七、本章节表中的符号使用说明：“－”表示不适用；“空格” 表示没有数字。

Brief Introduction

I. Data in this chapter show main social and economic developments of the Hong Kong Special Administrative Region, including data on land, population, employment, national income, Balance of Payments account, industry, energy, construction, transportation, external trade, finance and banking, education, housing, health and social security.

II. All data in this chapter are provided by the Census and Statistics Department, the Government of the Hong Kong Special Administrative Region, and further tabulated or edited by the International Statistical Information Centre of the National Bureau of Statistics.

III. According to the Basic Law of the Hong Kong Special Administrative Region of the People's Republic of China, Hong Kong Special Administrative Region maintains its independent statistical system, and compiles and disseminates statistics on the Region. As Hong Kong and the mainland of China use different statistical concepts, definitions and terminologies, users are advised to make reference of the following materials when using and comparing data of the mainland of China and the Hong Kong Special Administrative Region:

1. A Comparison of Common Statistical Terms Used in China Statistical Yearbook and Publications Compiled by the Census and Statistics Department, the Government of the Hong Kong Special Administrative Region, which listed similar statistical concepts using different terms.

2. The Explanatory Note at the end of this chapter which gives explanation on important statistical indicators.

IV. As Hong Kong is a separate custom territory, trade between Hong Kong and the mainland of China needs customs declaration procedures. In terms of trade statistics, data on Hong Kong's imports and exports include Hong Kong's trade with the mainland of China.

V. As HK dollar is the legal tender in the Hong Kong Special Administrative Region, all other currencies (including Renminbi) are regarded as foreign currencies in compiling foreign exchange statistics and related statistics.

VI. For more detailed statistics and technical details, users are advised to read the "Hong Kong Monthly Digest of Statistics", the "Hong Kong Annual Digest of Statistics" and other publications compiled by the Census and Statistics Department, the Government of the Hong Kong Special Administrative Region.

VII. Notations used in this chapter:

"-" indicates not applicable. "(blank)" indicates not available.

24-1 主要统计指标概览

Summary of Key Statistics

项　目	Item	1999	2000	2001	2002	2003
人口及生命事件	**Population and Vital Events**					
年中人口 (万人)	Mid-year Population (10 000 persons)	660.7	666.5	672.5	678.7	680.3
粗出生率 (‰)	Crude Birth Rate (‰)	7.8	8.1	7.2	7.1	6.9
粗死亡率 (‰)	Crude Death Rate (‰)	5.0	5.1	5.0	5.0	5.4^
劳工	**Labour**					
劳动人口 (万人)	Labour Force (10 000 persons)	332.0	337.4	342.7	348.7	350.1
劳动人口参与率 (%)	Labour Force Participation Rate (%)	61.3	61.4	61.4	61.8	61.4
失业率 (%)	Unemployment Rate (%)	6.2	4.9	5.1	7.3	7.9
就业不足率 (%)	Underemployment Rate (%)	2.9	2.8	2.5	3.0	3.5
选定行业的就业人数 (千人)	Number of Employed Persons in Selected Industries (1 000 persons)					
(i)制造业	(i) Manufacturing	353.9	333.7	326.4	290.2	272.4
(ii)建筑业	(ii) Construction	286.8	301.7	291.4	286.5	266.1
(iii)批发、零售、进出口贸易 饮食及酒店业	(iii) Wholesale, Retail and Import/Export Trades, Restaurants and Hotels	935.1	981.7	981.1	983.4	993.2
(iv)运输、仓库及通讯业	(iv) Transport, Storage and Communications	339.4	356.6	353.4	345.8	346.4
(v)金融、保险、地产 及商用服务业	(v) Financing, Insurance, Real Estate and Business Services	437.7	452.7	478.1	474.4	470.2
(vi)社区、社会及个人服务业	(vi) Community, Social and Personal Services	732.9	754.7	798.9	825.1	850.8
实际工资指数 (1992年9月=100)	Real Wage Index (September 1992=100)	109.0	112.8	114.6	117.8	118.6
对外商品贸易	**External Merchandise Trade**					
进口 (亿港元)	Imports (HKD 100 million)	13927.2	16579.6	15681.9	16194.2	18057.7
港产品出口 (亿港元)	Domestic Exports (HKD 100 million)	1706.0	1809.7	1535.2	1309.3	1216.9
转口 (亿港元)	Re-exports (HKD 100 million)	11784.0	13917.2	13274.7	14295.9	16207.5
贸易价格比率指数(2000年=100)①	Terms of Trade Index(2000=100)①	101.0	100.0	100.9	102.1	101.0
对外服务贸易	**External Trade in Services**					
服务出口② (亿港元)	Exports of Services② (HKD 100 million)	2655.4	3018.1	3076.6	3354.1	3473.7@
服务进口 (亿港元)	Imports of Services (HKD 100 million)	1840.5	1915.4	1924.5	1996.8	1960.8@
工业生产	**Industrial Production**					
工业生产指数 (2000年=100)	Index of Industrial Production (2000=100)	100.5	100.0	95.6	86.2	78.3
工业电力消费量 (万亿焦耳)	Industrial Electricity Consumption (terajoules)	17547	17769	16759	16112	14851
工业煤气消费量 (万亿焦耳)	Industrial Gas Consumption (terajoules)	914	982	1011	987	1015
经销贸易业、运输业、服务业	**Distributive Trades, Transport Services and Other Services**					
增加值 (亿港元)	Value Added (HKD 100 million)					
批发贸易业	Wholesale Trade	138	125	136	124	
零售贸易业	Retail Trade	271	288	274	279	
进出口贸易业	Import/Export	1986	2254	2272	2316	
运输及有关服务	Transport and Related Services	803	880	849	895	
仓库、通讯、财务(银行除外) 及商用服务业	Storage, Communications, Financing (Except Banking) and Business Services	863	995	910	896	

24-1 续表 1 continued

项　目	Item	1999	2000	2001	2002	2003
土地、楼宇、建筑	**Land, Building and Construction**					
已登记物业买卖合约涉及的价值（亿港元）	Value of Registered Agreements for Sale and Purchase of Building Units (HKD 100 million)					
住宅	Residential	2119.94	1683.93	1509.16	1542.52	1535.78
非住宅	Non-residential	446.47	541.27	418.92	311.41	358.40
总计	Total	2566.41	2225.20	1928.08	1853.93	1894.18
楼宇售价指数（1999年=100）	Property Price Index (1999=100)					
私人住宅单位	Private Domestic Units	100.0	89.6	78.7	69.9	61.6
私人写字楼（甲级、乙级及丙级）	Private Offices (Grades A, B and C)	100.0	89.9	78.7	68.4	62.5
楼宇租金指数（1999年=100）	Property Rental Index (1999=100)					
私人住宅单位	Private Domestic Units	100.0	98.1	95.4	83.4	73.6
私人写字楼（甲级、乙级及丙级）	Private Offices (Grades A, B and C)	100.0	98.5	101.0	85.4	74.7
建筑工程完成名义总值（亿港元）	Gross Value of Construction Work in Nominal Terms (HKD 100 million)	1264	1221	1140	1060	990
获批准可动工兴建私人居住单位（个）	Private Residential Flats with Consent to Commence Work (number)	44323	31366	27274	18271	30012
房屋	**Housing**					
新落成房屋委员会租住单位③（个）	Housing Authority Rental Flats Newly Completed③ (number)	31806	47552	33629	18290	15148
新落成居者有其屋计划的居住单位③④（个）	Home Ownership Scheme Residential Flats Newly Completed③④ (number)	13778	23542	5080	8272	2848
新落成私人机构参建居屋计划的居住单位③④（个）	Private Sector Participation Scheme Residential Flats Newly Completed③④ (number)	2780	9172	1540	2470	2010
运输、通讯、旅游	**Transport, Communications and Tourism**					
进出香港货运车辆（万辆）	Inward/Outward Movement of Goods Vehicle (10 000 vehicle)	887.48	937.98	912.88	975.51	988.26
进出香港货物	Inward and Outward Movements of Cargo					
总卸下（万吨）	Total Discharged (10 000 tons)	12794	13035	13205	14210	15045
总装上（万吨）	Total Loaded (10 000 tons)	8175	8692	8552	9265	9959
集装箱吞吐量（万标准集装箱单位）	Container Throughput (10 000 TEUs)	1621	1810	1783	1914	2045
领牌车辆（千辆）	Motor Vehicles Licensed (1 000 vehicle)	504.0	516.8	525.4	525.5	524.2
电话服务（万条操作线路）	Telephone Services (10 000 working lines)	384	395	393	384	382
访港旅客⑤（万人次）	Visitor Arrivals⑤ (10 000 person-times)	1132.8	1305.9	1372.5	1656.6	1553.7
酒店入住率（%）	Hotel Room Occupancy Rate (%)	79	83	79	84	70
政府收支、货币、金融（亿港元）	**Public Accounts, Money and Finance (HKD 100 million)**					
政府储备结余③	Government's Reserve Balances③	4443	4303	3725	3114	2753
政府收入总额③	Total Government Revenue③	2330	2251	1756	1775	2073
政府开支及证券投资总额③	Total Government Expenditure and Equity Investments③	2230	2329	2389	2392	2475
货币供应量M3@	Money Supply M3@					
港元⑥	Hong Kong Dollar⑥	19355	20024	20166	20042	21229
外币⑦	Foreign Currency⑦	14990	16904	15775	15576	17352
总计	Total	34345	36928	35941	35619	38580
在港使用的贷款及垫款@	Loans and Advances for Use in Hong Kong@	18198	18615	17901	17429	17085
港汇指数⑧（贸易总值加权）（2000年1月=100）	Effective Exchange Rate Indices for the Hong Kong Dollar⑧ (trade-weighted)(January 2000=100)	100.9	101.7	104.7	104.0	100.7
居民消费价格指数	**Consumer Price Indices**					
（1999年10月至2000年9月=100）	(Oct. 1999-Sep. 2000 =100)					
综合消费价格指数	Composite Consumer Price Index	103.2	99.4	97.8	94.8	92.4
甲类消费价格指数	Consumer Price Index (A)	102.5	99.5	97.8	94.7	92.7
乙类消费价格指数	Consumer Price Index (B)	103.4	99.4	97.7	94.7	92.1
丙类消费价格指数	Consumer Price Index (C)	103.9	99.3	97.8	95.1	92.3

24-1 续表 2 continued

项目	Item	1999	2000	2001	2002	2003
教育	**Education**					
日校小学学生人数 (人)	Student Enrolment in Primary Day School (person)	491851	493979	493075	483218	468792
日校中学学生人数 (人)	Student Enrolment in Secondary Day School (person)	453465	456693	456455	461289	467223
教资会资助院校学生人数(人)	Student Enrolment in UGC-funded Institutions (person)	79917	78295	81664	85602	90355
卫生	**Health**					
登记死亡人数 (人)	Registered Deaths (person)	33387	33993	33305	34316	36421
死于心脏病人数⑨ (人)	Deaths from Heart Diseases⑨ (person)	5220	5537	4730	4969	5236^
死于恶性肿瘤人数⑨ (人)	Deaths from Malignant Neoplasms⑨ (person)	10977	11222	11406	11658	11907^
婴儿死亡率(按每千名登记活产婴儿计算)	Infant Mortality Rate (per 1 000 Registered Live Births)	3.2	2.9	2.7	2.4^	2.3^
社会保障	**Social Security**					
综合社会保障援助③	Comprehensive Social Security Assistance ③					
个案数目⑩ (个)	Number of Cases⑩ (case)	228015	228263	247192	271893	290705
发放款项 (亿港元)	Amount (HKD 100 million)	136.23	135.60+	144.05‡	161.31~	173.06
公共福利金③	Social Security Allowances ③					
个案数目⑩ (个)	Number of Cases⑩ (case)	535452	550585	561208	560215	563908
发放款项 (亿港元)	Amount (HKD 100 million)	48.83	51.30+	52.41‡	52.81~	52.14
交通意外伤亡援助③	Traffic Accident Victims Assistance ③					
获批个案数目 (个)	Number of Cases Authorized for Payment (case)	5797	5998	6733	7102	7190
发放款项 (百万港元)	Amount (HKD million)	133.5	130.0	142.0	151.3	151.1
治安	**Law and Order**					
举报罪案合计 (件)	Overall Reported Crimes (case)	76771	77245	73008	75877	88377
暴力罪案总计 (件)	Total Violent Crimes (case)	15705	14812	13551	14140	14542
犯罪被捕人数总计 (人)	Total Persons Arrested for Crime (person)	40745	40930	38829	39665	42051
本地生产总值	**Gross Domestic Product (GDP)**					
按2000年不变价格计算	At Constant (2000) Market Prices					
年增长率 (%)	Annual Growth Rate (%)	3.4	10.2	0.5	1.9@	3.2@
本地生产总值 (亿港元)	GDP (HKD 100 million)	11695	12883	12943	13187@	13610@
人均本地生产总值 (港元)	Per Capita GDP (HKD)	177019	193299	192465	194304@	200061@
按当年价格计算	At Current Market Prices					
年增长率 (%)	Annual Growth Rate (%)	-2.6	3.4	-1.4	-1.8@	-2.2@
本地生产总值 (亿港元)	GDP (HKD 100 million)	12461	12883	12699	12474@	12198@
人均本地生产总值 (港元)	Per Capita GDP (HKD)	188622	193299	188835	183790@	179308@
本地居民生产总值	**Gross National Product (GNP)**					
按当年价格计算	GNP at Current Market Prices					
本地居民生产总值 (亿港元)	(HKD 100 million)	12809	13101	13111	12641@	12540@
人均本地居民生产总值(港元)	Per Capita GNP at Current Market Prices (HKD)	193886	196565	194958	186250@	184324@
国外净要素收入 (亿港元)	Net External Factor Income Flows (HKD 100 million)	347.77	217.68	411.74	166.98	341.28@
国际收支平衡表	**Balance of Payments Account**					
经常帐(11) (亿港元)	Current Account(11) (HKD 100 million)	798.16	551.93	775.31	982.41@	1257.38@
资本及金融帐(11) (亿港元)	Capital and Financial Account (11) (HKD 100 million)	-833.74	-578.63	-973.59	-1511.79	-1514.50@
净误差及遗漏(12) (亿港元)	Net Errors and Omissions(12) (HKD 100 million)	35.57	26.70	198.29	529.38@	257.12@
整体的国际收支 (亿港元)	Overall Balance of Payments (HKD 100 million)	778.67 (盈余) (in surplus)	783.21 (盈余) (in surplus)	365.30 (盈余) (in surplus)	-185.41@ (赤字) (in surplus)	75.89@ (盈余) (in surplus)
国际投资头寸(13)	**International Investment Position(13)**					
国际投资头寸净值(14) (亿港元)	Net International Investment Position(14) (HKD 100 million)	-	17295.5	20679.6	26773.7	30875.3@
对外金融资产 (亿港元)	External Financial Assets (HKD 100 million)	-	88993.0	83506.2	80327.4	91248.9@
对外金融负债 (亿港元)	External Financial Liabilities (HKD 100 million)	-	71697.5	62826.6	53553.8	60373.6@

注: ①贸易指数已更新,新系列是以 2000 年为基期。2000 年以前的新系列指数是将以往发表的旧系列指数(以 1990 年为基期)按比例换算得来,所用的换算因子是根据新旧系列在 2000 年重叠期间的数值而计算的。

②数字已根据香港旅游发展局在 2003 年 11 月份所发布一套新的到港旅客境内消费开支的数字已作出修订。

③数字是以相应的财政年度为根据。例如 2003 年的数字代表 2003 至 2004 财政年度数字。

④从 2003 年起,居者有其屋计划 / 私人机构参建居屋计划单位已经无限期停止兴建和出售。至于已落成和兴建中的居者有其屋计划私人机构参建居屋计划单位,除了少量剩余及回购单位将会售予现有公屋租户和准公屋租户外,其余则基于不与私人市场直接竞争的原则下改为其它用途。

⑤访港旅客数字包括经澳门访港的非澳门居民。

⑥所列数字已包括外币掉期存款。

⑦所列数字已扣除外币掉期存款。《中华人民共和国香港特别行政区基本法》说明,港元是香港特别行政区的法定货币。外币指港元以外的其他货币,因而人民币亦视作外币。

⑧由 2002 年 1 月 2 日起公布的新系列。详情请参阅刊载于《香港统计月刊》2001 年 12 月号题为「新系列港币汇率指数」的专题文章。

⑨由 2001 年起,疾病及死因分类乃根据《疾病和有关健康问题的国际统计分类》(ICD)第十次修订本。2001 年起的数字未必可与以往年份以(ICD)第九次修订本编制的数字作比较。

⑩于财政年度终结时的数字。

(11)经常帐差额的正数显示盈余而负数则显示赤字。在资本及金融帐方面,正数显示净资金流入而负数则显示净资金流出。由于对外资产的增加是属于借方帐目而减少则属贷方帐目,因此负数的储备资产变动净值显示储备资产的增加,而正数则显示减少。

(12)原则上,贷方和借方各项帐目的净总和应相等于零。但实际上,贷方和借方帐目的资料是通过不同的来源搜集,基于各种原因会有差异。为了令贷方和借方帐目的总和相等,便须加进一个余额项目,以反映平衡表的"净误差及遗漏"。

(13)期末头寸。

(14)国际投资头寸净值是对外金融资产总值与对外金融负债总值之差。

^ 临时数字。

@ 日后会作出修订。

+ 包括 2001 年 4 月 1 日所发放的款项。

‡ 包括 2002 年 4 月 1 日所发放的款项,但不包括 2001 年 4 月 1 日所发放的款项。

~ 不包括 2002 年 4 月 1 日所发放的款项。

Notes: ①The trade index numbers have been updated. The new series has year 2000 as the base year. In the new series, indexes for periods prior to 2000 are obtained by re-scaling the previously published series, which has 1990 as the base year, using a conversion factor derived from the levels of the old and new series in the overlapping period of 2000.

②Figures have been revised to incorporate the new data on destination consumption expenditure of incoming visitors and travelers released by the Hong Kong Tourism Board in November 2003.

③Figures are for the corresponding financial year. For example, figures for 2003 would represent the figures for financial year 2003/04.

④The production and sale of Home Ownership Scheme / Private Sector Participation Scheme flats have ceased indefinitely since 2003, except for a small number of unsold and returned flats which will be sold to sitting tenants of public rental housing and those who are about to be rehoused to public rental housing. For those Home Ownership Scheme/Private Sector Participation Scheme flats that are completed or under construction, these will be disposed of through market-friendly means.

⑤Figures include arrival of non-Macao residents via Macao.

⑥Figures are adjusted to include foreign currency swap deposits.

⑦Figures are adjusted to exclude foreign currency swap deposits. Hong Kong dollar is the legal tender in the Hong Kong Special Administrative Region, as stated in "The Basic Law of the Hong Kong Special Administrative Region of the People's Republic of China". Foreign currency refers to any currency other than the Hong Kong currency. Accordingly Chinese Renminbi is also treated as foreign currency.

⑧New series released since 2 January 2002. For details, please see the feature article entitled "New Series of Effective Exchange Rate Index for the Hong Kong Dollar" in the December 2001 issue of the "Hong Kong Monthly Digest of Statistics".

⑨Classification of diseases and causes of death is based on the International Statistical Classification of Diseases and Related Health Problems (ICD) 10th Revision from 2001 onwards. Figures from 2001 onwards may not be comparable with figures for previous years which were compiled based on the ICD 9th Revision.

⑩Figures are as at end of the financial year..

(11) A positive value for the balance figure in the current account represents a surplus whereas a negative value represents a deficit. For the capital and financial account, a positive value indicates a net capital and financial inflow and a negative value indicates a net outflow. As increases in external assets are debit entries and decreases are credit entries, a negative value for net change in reserve assets represents a net increase and a positive value represents a net decrease.

(12) In principle, the net sum of credit entries and debit entries is zero. In practice, discrepancies between the credit and debit entries may however occur for various reasons as the data are collected from many sources. Equality between the sum of credit entries and debit entries is brought about by the inclusion of a balancing item which reflects net errors and omissions.

(13) Position as at end of period.

(14) Net international investment position is the difference between total external financial assets and total external financial liabilities.

^ Provisional figure.

@ Subject to revision later on.

+ Includes the payments for 1 April 2001.

‡ Includes the payments for 1 April 2002, but excludes the payments for 1 April 2001.

~ Excludes the payments for 1 April 2002.

24-2 按区议会地区划分的香港陆地面积

Land Area of Hong Kong by District Council District

单位: 平方公里 (sq. km)

区议会分区	District Council District+	2000	2001	2002	2003	2004
总计	**Total**	**1098**	**1099**	**1101**	**1102**	**1103**
香港岛	**Hong Kong Island**					
中西区	Central and Western	12	12	12	12	12
湾仔	Wan Chai	10	10	10	10	10
东区	Eastern	19	19	19	19	19
南区	Southern	39	39	39	39	39
小计	Sub-total	80	80	80	80	80
九龙	**Kowloon**					
九龙城	Kowloon City	10	10	10	10	10
观塘	Kwun Tong	11	11	11	11	11
深水埗	Sham Shui Po	9	9	9	9	9
黄大仙	Wong Tai Sin	9	9	9	9	9
油尖旺	Yau Tsim Mong	7	7	7	7	7
小计	Sub-total	47	47	47	47	47
新界	**New Territories**					
离岛	Islands	175	175	176	176	176
北区	North	137	137	137	137	137
西贡	Sai Kung	136	136	136	136	136
沙田	Sha Tin	69	69	69	69	69
大埔	Tai Po	147	148	148	148	148
荃湾	Tsuen Wan	61	61	62	62	62
葵青	Kwai Tsing	22	22	23	23	23
屯门	Tuen Mun	84	84	85	85	85
元朗	Yuen Long	139	139	139	139	139
小计	Sub-total	971	971	974	975	975

注: 1999年至2001年的数字是5月份的数据。2002年及以后的数字则是6月底的数据。
2000年至2003年的数字是根据1999年区议会地区界线计算。而2004年的数字是根据2003年区议会地区界线计算。
2002年及以后的数字是根据地政总署测绘处提供之1:10 000 比例地图数据库的计算。

Notes: Figures from 1999 to 2001 are as at May of the year. Figures for 2002 and onward are as at end-June of the year.
Figures for 2000 to 2003 were computed in accordance with the 1999 District Council boundaries. 2004 figures were computed in accordance with 2003 District Council boundaries.
Figures for 2002 and onward were computed with reference to the 1:10 000 Mapping Database of the Lands Department.
+ Before 2000, 'District Council District' was known as 'District Board District'.

24-3 土地用途分布情况

Land Usage

单位: 平方公里 (sq. km)

类 别	Class	2000	2001	2002	2003
住宅	**Residential**				
私人住宅①	Private Residential①	24	25	25	24
公屋②	Public Residential②	16	17	17	17
乡郊居所③	Rural Settlements③	27	26	26	26
商业	**Commercial**				
商业／商贸和办公室	Commercial/Business and Offices	3	3	3	3
工业	**Industrial**				
工业	Industrial	5	5	5	6
工业村	Industrial Estates	3	3	3	3
货仓和贮物处④	Warehouse and Storage④	11	11	11	12
机构	**Institution**				
政府、机构和社区设施	Government, Institution and Community Facilities	20	20	21	21
运输	**Transportation**				
道路	Roads	35	35	36	37
铁路	Railways	1	1	1	2
机场	Airport	13	13	13	13
休憩用地⑤	**Open Space⑤**	20	20	20	20
空置土地	**Vacant Land**				
空置发展／正在进行建筑工程的土地	Vacant Development Land/Construction in Progress	27	31	33	31
其他都市或已建设土地	**Other Urban or Built-up Land**				
坟场和火葬场	Cemeteries and Crematoriums	5	5	5	6
公用事业设施	Public Utilities	6	6	6	6
其他用途	Other Uses	14	14	14	16
农业用地	**Agricultural Land**				
农地	Agricultural	57	55	54	58
鱼塘／基围	Fish ponds/Gei wais	13	13	13	13
林地／灌丛／草地	**Woodland/ Shrubland/ Grassland**				
林地	Woodland	190	190	190	285
灌丛	Shrubland	241	241	241	230
草地	Grassland	310	308	308	226
湿地	**Wetland**				
红树林和沼泽	Mangrove and Swamp	6	6	6	5
荒地	**Barren Land**				
劣地	Badland	16	16	16	11
石矿场	Quarries	3	3	3	2
石岸	Rocky Shore	5	5	5	2
水体	**Water Area**				
水塘	Reservoirs	24	24	24	24
河道和明渠	Streams and Nullahs	4	4	4	4
总计	**Total**	**1099**	**1100**	**1103**	**1103**

注：由2000年起，规划署采用了新的测量方法，利用遥感技术和新的土地用途分类法作出测量。测量结果就土地用途，特别是未建设乡郊地区的土地用途，提供更详细的分类。因此，本表所载的数字不能与1999年及之前的数字作严格比较。
数字是当年12月的数据。
①由私人发展商发展的住宅用地（乡村屋宇、居屋计划／私人参建计划屋苑和临时房屋区除外）。
②包括居屋计划／私人参建计划屋苑和临时房屋区。
③包括临时构筑物。
④包括露天贮物用地。
⑤包括公园、体育馆和运动场。

Notes: From 2000 onwards, a new survey method by using remote sensing technology and a new classification of land uses have been adopted. The results of the survey provide a set of more detailed land uses, particularly in the rural non-built-up areas. Hence, figures presented above are not strictly comparable with those for years 1999 and before.
Figures are as at December of the year.
①Residential land developed by private developers except village houses, Home Ownership Scheme (HOS)/Private Sector Participation Scheme (PSPS) and temporary housing areas.
②Include HOS/PSPS and temporary housing areas.
③Include temporary structures.
④Include open storage areas.
⑤Include parks, stadiums and playgrounds.

24-4　按不同地区类别及路边情况划分的大气质量(2003年)

Air Quality by Area Type and Roadside Condition (2003)

单位：微克/立方米　(microgram/cu.m.)

地区类别及路边	Area Type and Roadside	全年平均大气污染浓度 Annual Average Air Pollutant Concentrations			
		二氧化硫 Sulphur Dioxide	二氧化氮 Nitrogen Dioxide	总悬浮粒子 Total Suspended Particulates	可吸入悬浮粒子 Respirable Suspended Particulates
市区	Urban	19	63	77	53
新市镇	New Town	16	51	79	56
郊区	Rural	12	13	-	47
路边	Roadside	17	95	116	76

24-5　按种类划分的每日平均产生的固体废物

Daily Average Solid Waste Generation by Type

单位：吨　(ton)

种　类	Type	1999	2000	2001	2002	2003
都市固体废物①	Municipal Solid Waste①					
住宅废物②	Domestic②	7430	7540	7550	7520	7400
商业废物③	Commercial③	1250	1150	1190	1340	1430
工业废物④	Industrial④	590	640	560	560	610
小计	Sub-total	9270	9330	9300	9420	9440
拆建废料①⑤	Construction and Demolition Waste ①⑤	7890	7480	6410	10200	6730
特殊废物⑥	Special Waste ⑥	880	1090	1110	1540	1590
已回收都市固体废物⑦	Recovered Municipal Solid Waste ⑦	4220	4810	5320	5370	6510
总计	**Total**	**22260**	**22710**	**22140**	**26530**	**24270**

注：①都市固体废物包括运往弃置设施的住宅废物、商业废物及工业废物，但不包括拆建废料及已回收都市固体废物。
②住宅废物包括使用后的住宅固体废物，及由公共洁净服务收集的废物。
③商业废物包括所有类型的商业活动产生的固体废物。
④工业废物包括由工业活动产生的固体废物，但不包括化学废物及拆建废料。
⑤拆建废料包括由建筑及拆卸活动所产生的废物，但不包括可运往公众填土区作填海用途的物料。
⑥特殊废物包括弃置于堆填区的动物尸体、屠房废物、报废货物、滤水厂及污水处理后的污泥、污水处理厂的隔滤物、禽畜废物、医疗废物及化学废物。
⑦都市固体废物回收后会在本地或海外循环再造。

Notes:①Municipal solid waste includes domestic waste, commercial waste and industrial waste delivered to disposal facilities but excludes construction and demolition waste and recovered municipal solid waste.
②Domestic waste covers post-consumer residential solid waste and refuse collected in public cleansing activities.
③Commercial waste covers solid waste arising from all forms of commercial activities.
④Industrial waste covers solid waste arising from industrial activities but excludes chemical waste and construction and demolition waste.
⑤Construction and demolition waste covers waste arising from construction and demolition activities but excludes material delivered to public filling areas for land reclamation and formation.
⑥Special waste includes animal carcasses, abattoir waste, condemned goods, waterworks and sewage treatment sludge, sewage works screening, livestock waste, clinical waste and chemical waste delivered to landfills.
⑦Municipal solid waste recovered will be recycled locally or overseas.

24-6 人口主要指标

Main Indicators of Population

项　　目		Item		1999	2000	2001	2002	2003
年中人口	(万人)	Mid-year Population	(10 000 persons)	660.7	666.5	672.5	678.7	680.3
粗出生率	(‰)	Crude Birth Rate	(‰)	7.8	8.1	7.2	7.1	6.9
粗死亡率	(‰)	Crude Death Rate	(‰)	5.0	5.1	5.0	5.0	5.4^
婴儿死亡率	(‰)	Infant Mortality Rate	(‰)	3.1	3.0	2.6	2.3	2.4^
自然增长率	(‰)	Rate of Natural Increase	(‰)	2.7	3.1	2.2	2.1	1.4^
总和生育率①②		Total Fertility Rate①②		965	1024	927	959	941
登记结婚数	(对)	Registered Marriages	(couple)	31287	30879	32825	32070	35439
离婚判令	(对)	Divorce Decrees	(couple)	13408	13247	13425	12943	13829
出生时平均预期寿命	(年)	Expectation of Life at Birth	(years)					
男		Male		77.7	78.0	78.4	78.6	78.6^
女		Female		83.2	83.9	84.6	84.5	84.3^

注：①按每千名15至49岁女性人口计算。

②此数字是以没有包括女性外籍家庭佣工的人口作分母编制。

^ 临时数字。

Notes: ①Per 1000 women aged 15-49.

②These figures have been compiled using a population denominator which has excluded female foreign domestic helpers.

^ Provisional figure.

24-7 劳动人口及失业状况

Labour Force and Unemployment

项　　目		Item		1999	2000	2001	2002	2003
劳动人口数目	(万人)	Labour Force	(10 000 persons)	332.0	337.4	342.7	348.7	350.1
男		Male		195.7	196.4	196.5	196.5	196.2
女		Female		136.2	141.0	146.2	152.2	153.9
就业人数	(万人)	Employed Persons	(10 000 persons)	311.2	320.7	325.2	323.2	322.3
失业人数	(万人)	Unemployed Persons	(10 000 persons)	20.7	16.7	17.5	25.6	27.8
失业率	(%)	Unemployment Rate	(%)	6.2	4.9	5.1	7.3	7.9

24-8 按行业划分的就业人数

Number of Employed Persons by Industry

单位: 万人 (10 000 persons)

行业	Industry	1999	2000	2001	2002	2003
制造业	Manufacturing	35.39	33.37	32.64	29.02	27.24
建筑业	Construction	28.68	30.17	29.14	28.65	26.61
批发、零售、进出口贸易、饮食及酒店业	Wholesale, Retail and Import/Export Trades, Restaurants and Hotels	93.51	98.17	98.11	98.34	99.32
运输、仓库及通讯业	Transport, Storage and Communications	33.94	35.66	35.34	34.58	34.64
金融、保险、地产及商用服务业	Financing, Insurance, Real Estate and Business Services	43.77	45.27	47.81	47.44	47.02
社区、社会及个人服务业	Community, Social and Personal Services	73.29	75.47	79.89	82.51	85.08
其他	Others	2.65	2.62	2.31	2.62	2.41
总计	**Total**	**311.21**	**320.73**	**325.23**	**323.16**	**322.33**

注: 有关就业统计数字，可分别按“综合住户统计调查”及“雇佣及职位空缺按季统计调查”的结果编制。此两套数字用于反映有关就业情况时，各有优点和局限。上表载列了“综合住户统计调查”的估计数字，是由于其包括的就业人口范围较全面。再者，个别人士，包括有多过一份工作的职位持有者，都只计算一次。但“综合住户统计调查”的就业估计数字有一个主要局限，就是被访者有困难准确地提供其本身所属行业的资料，尤以制造业员工为甚。随着香港制造业机构将部分工序移往中国内地，这些机构在香港的传统运作模式已有改变。就一些已将大部分工序移往中国内地的机构而言，他们应归类为进出口贸易业。不过，由于有关机构的员工，尤其是技师及技工级等员工，未必全部都能清楚理解这个统计分类上的改变，有些被访者仍认为他们是属于制造业而非进出口贸易业，因而使“综合住户统计调查”的有关制造业估计就业人数有高估的现象。

Notes: Employment statistics are compiled separately based on the General Household Survey (GHS) and the Quarterly Survey of Employment and Vacancies. Each source has its own merits and limitations in reflecting the employment situation. The GHS estimates are presented here because the omission in terms of coverage of the employed population is negligible. Besides, individual persons, including multiple job holders, are counted only once. However, a major limitation of the GHS estimates is that the respondents might not have reported accurately the industry to which they belong, especially for workers in the manufacturing sector. With the relocation of some production processes to the mainland of China, there is a change in the mode of operation of the traditional manufacturing establishments in Hong Kong. As a result, some of these establishments are more appropriately classified as import/export establishments if the majority of the production activities are carried out in the mainland of China. However, this change in statistical classification may not be readily recognized by all the employed persons, particularly the technicians and craftsmen, of the establishments concerned. Hence, the GHS employment estimate in respect of the manufacturing sector will be overstated to the extent that some respondents mistakenly regard themselves as still being engaged in the manufacturing sector instead of the import/export trades.

24-9 按每月就业收入划分的就业人数

Employed Persons by Monthly Employment Earnings

单位: 万人 (10 000 persons)

每月就业收入(港元)	Monthly Employment Earnings (HK$)	1999	2000	2001	2002	2003
< 3 000	< 3 000	8.64	8.07	9.32	12.58	14.97
3 000 – 3 999	3 000 - 3 999	19.11	20.21	22.74	24.46	25.57
4 000 – 4 999	4 000 - 4 999	9.33	9.50	10.18	11.58	14.45
5 000 – 5 999	5 000 - 5 999	13.44	13.41	14.08	16.92	18.75
6 000 – 6 999	6 000 - 6 999	19.34	19.96	20.52	22.01	22.70
7 000 – 7 999	7 000 - 7 999	20.46	20.21	19.44	20.83	21.38
8 000 – 8 999	8 000 - 8 999	26.68	26.84	25.50	24.61	24.34
9 000 – 9 999	9 000 - 9 999	19.04	18.53	17.83	17.10	17.74
10 000 – 14 999	10 000 - 14 999	74.28	76.56	74.54	66.60	60.67
15 000 – 19 999	15 000 - 19 999	33.79	35.53	36.05	34.31	32.31
20 000 – 29 999	20 000 - 29 999	34.78	36.63	38.07	36.01	34.49
≧ 30 000	≧ 30 000	32.32	35.26	36.98	36.16	34.96
总计	**Total**	**311.21**	**320.73**	**325.23**	**323.16**	**322.33**
每月就业收入中位数(港元)	Median Monthly Employment Earnings (HK$)	10000	10000	10000	10000	10000

注: 数字是指该年四季「综合住户统计调查」所得的数字的平均数。

Notes: Figures are averages of the figures obtained from the General Household Survey for the four quarters of the year.

24-10 本地生产总值
Gross Domestic Product

年 份 Year	本地生产总值(按当年价格计算) Gross Domestic Product (GDP) At Current Market Prices		本地生产总值与上年比较的实际增长(%) GDP Real Growth Rate over the Preceding Year (%)	人均本地生产总值(按当年价格计算) Per Capita GDP At Current Market Prices	
	(亿港元) (HKD 100 million)	(亿美元) (USD 100 million)		(港元) (HKD)	(美元) (USD)
1988	4572	586	8.0	81251	10409
1989	5271	676	2.6	92695	11884
1990	5876	754	3.7	103010	13225
1991	6772	872	5.6	117741	15151
1992	7913	1022	6.6	136423	17623
1993	9128	1180	6.3	154687	19996
1994	10298	1333	5.5	170622	22078
1995	10963	1417	3.9	178078	23019
1996	12109	1566	4.3	188163	24329
1997	13445	1737	5.1	207194	26762
1998	12799	1652	-5.0	195585	25253
1999	12461	1606	3.4	188622	24313
2000	12883	1654	10.2	193299	24811
2001	12699	1628	0.5	188835	24213
2002@	12474	1599	1.9	183790	23566
2003@	12198	1567	3.2	179308	23027

注： @数字在日后得到更多资料时会作出修订。
Notes: @Figures are subject to revision later on as more data become available.

24-11 按当年价格计算生产法本地生产总值
Gross Domestic Product by Economic Activity at Current Prices

单位: 亿港元 (HKD100 million)

经济活动	Economic Activity	1998	1999	2000	2001	2002@
农业及渔业	**Agriculture and Fishing**	**15.30**	**11.71**	**9.20**	**10.03**	**10.02**
工业	**Industry**	**1799.83**	**1722.89**	**1747.76**	**1627.89**	**1496.13**
采矿及采石业	Mining and Quarrying	3.01	3.07	2.41	1.74	1.36
制造业	Manufacturing	726.01	675.40	716.55	635.19	548.48
电力、煤气及水的生产和供应业	Electricity, Gas and Water	360.81	372.11	388.53	401.26	415.40
建筑业	Construction	710.00	672.32	640.26	589.71	530.89
服务业	**Services**	**10238.36**	**10043.35**	**10532.02**	**10515.62**	**10548.64**
批发贸易、零售贸易、进出口贸易、饮食及酒店业	Wholesale, Retail and Import/Export Trades, Restaurants and Hotels	3016.93	2963.18	3246.22	3246.54	3241.31
运输、仓库及通讯业	Transport, Storage and Communications	1114.09	1126.67	1257.24	1242.60	1282.78
金融、保险、地产及商用服务业	Financing, Insurance, Real Estate and Business Services	2963.52	2814.39	2910.62	2740.30	2675.37
社区、社会及个人服务业	Community, Social and Personal Services	2331.69	2460.03	2524.35	2650.81	2676.59
楼宇业权	Ownership of Premises	1706.60	1624.88	1553.03	1591.18	1595.86
减:非直接计算的金融中介服务调整	*Less* : Adjustment for Financial Intermediation Services Indirectly Measured	894.46	945.80	959.45	955.82	923.28
本地生产总值(按要素成本计算)	**GDP at Factor Cost**	**12053.49**	**11777.96**	**12288.97**	**12153.54**	**12054.79**
生产及进口税	**Taxes on Production and Imports**	**603.72**	**534.74**	**579.08**	**539.17**	**433.25**
统计差额①	**Statistical Discrepancy①**	**1.1%**	**1.2%**	**0.1%**	**+**	**-0.1%**
本地生产总值(按当年价格计算)	**GDP at Current Market Prices**	**12798.50**	**12461.34**	**12883.38**	**12698.96**	**12473.81**

注: ①统计差额是以支出法编制的本地生产总值与以生产法编制的本地生产总值的差额。这差额是由于使用不同数据来源及估算方法而引起的。统计差额是以占本地生产总值(按当年价格计算)的百分比形式作表达。
@ 数字在日后得到更多资料时会作出修订。
+ 在 ± 0.05%之内。

Notes:①Statistical discrepancy refers to the difference in values of GDP compiled using the expenditure and production approaches, as a result of the adoption of different data sources and estimation methods. It is expressed as a percentage to GDP at current market prices.
@ Figures are subject to revision later on as more data become available.
+ Within ± 0.05%.

24-12 按2000年不变价格计算生产法本地生产总值

Gross Domestic Product by Economic Activity at Constant (2000) Prices

单位: 亿港元 (HKD 100 million)

经济活动	Economic Activity	2000	2001	2002@	2003@
农业及渔业	**Agriculture and Fishing**	**9.20**	**9.58**	**9.51**	**9.70**
工业	**Industry**	**1747.76**	**1682.75**	**1620.67**	**1545.52**
采矿及采石业	Mining and Quarrying	2.41	2.07	1.84	1.88
制造业	Manufacturing	716.55	655.08	591.07	537.02
电力、煤气及水的生产和供应业	Electricity, Gas and Water	388.53	398.41	410.29	419.81
建筑业	Construction	640.26	627.18	617.47	586.80
服务业	**Services**	**10532.02**	**10704.83**	**11024.07**	**11524.19**
批发贸易、零售贸易、进出口贸易、饮食及酒店业	Wholesale, Retail and Import/Export Trades, Restaurants and Hotels	3246.22	3251.30	3388.23	3726.49
运输、仓库及通讯业	Transport, Storage and Communications	1257.24	1284.17	1363.84	1380.32
金融、保险、地产及商用服务业	Financing, Insurance, Real Estate and Business Services	2910.62	2899.97	2938.62	3083.24
社区、社会及个人服务业	Community, Social and Personal Services	2524.35	2623.94	2606.38	2607.14
楼宇业权	Ownership of Premises	1553.03	1611.68	1651.42	1687.92
减:非直接计算的金融中介服务调整	*Less* : Adjustment for Financial Intermediation Services Indirectly Measured	959.45	966.23	924.41	960.93
生产及进口税	**Taxes on Production and Imports**	**579.08**	**572.82**	**571.09**	**586.66**
统计差额①	**Statistical Discrepancy①**	**0.1%**	**-0.2%**	**-0.3%**	**-0.4%**
本地生产总值（按2000年不变价格计算）	**GDP at Constant (2000) Market Prices**	**12883.38**	**12943.06**	**13187.43**	**13610.36**

注: ①统计差额是以支出法编制的本地生产总值与以生产法编制的本地生产总值的差额。这差额是由于使用不同数据来源及估算方法而引起的。统计差额是以占本地生产总值(按2000年不变价格计算)的百分比形式作表达。

@ 数字在日后得到更多资料时会作出修订。

Notes: ①Statistical discrepancy refers to the difference in values of GDP compiled using the expenditure and production approaches, as a result of the adoption of different data sources and estimation methods. It is expressed as a percentage to GDP at constant (2000) market prices.

@Figures are subject to revision later on as more data become available.

24-13 支出法本地生产总值

Gross Domestic Product by Expenditure Component

单位: 亿港元 (HKD 100 million)

本地生产总值组成部份	GDP Components	1999	2000	2001	2002@	2003@
按当年价格计算	**At Current Market Prices**					
居民消费①	Private Consumption Expenditure ①	7544.50	7601.68	7651.05	7280.92	7048.63
政府消费	Government Consumption Expenditure	1199.84	1201.48	1288.46	1312.79	1300.67
本地固定资本形成总额	Gross Domestic Fixed Capital Formation	3253.28	3473.75	3330.36	2860.20	2691.27
存货变动	Changes in Inventories	-106.12	143.99	-40.60	56.60	94.71
货物出口(离岸价)	Exports of Goods(f.o.b.)	13490.00	15726.89	14809.87	15621.21	17490.89
减:货物进口(离岸价)	Less: Imports of Goods(f.o.b.)	13735.00	16367.11	15492.22	16015.27	17940.59
服务出口①	Exports of Services①	2655.36	3018.13	3076.57	3354.12	3473.71
减:服务进口	Less: Imports of Services	1840.52	1915.43	1924.53	1996.76	1960.80
本地生产总值	**GDP**	**12461.34**	**12883.38**	**12698.96**	**12473.81**	**12198.49**
人均本地生产总值(港元)	**Per Capita GDP (HKD)**	**188622**	**193299**	**188835**	**183790**	**179308**
物量指数(2000年=100)	**Volume Indices (2000=100)**					
居民消费①	Private Consumption Expenditure ①	94.4	100.0	102.0	100.8	100.5
政府消费	Government Consumption Expenditure	98.0	100.0	106.1	108.7	110.7
本地固定资本形成总额	Gross Domestic Fixed Capital Formation	90.1	100.0	102.6	98.0	98.1
存货变动	Changes in Inventories	-84.5	100.0	-34.0	47.8	75.0
货物出口(离岸价)	Exports of Goods(f.o.b.)	85.4	100.0	96.7	105.0	120.0
货物进口(离岸价)	Imports of Goods(f.o.b.)	84.6	100.0	98.1	105.9	119.7
服务出口①	Exports of Services①	88.4	100.0	106.2	118.7	125.4
服务进口	Imports of Services	95.9	100.0	102.0	105.8	101.0
本地生产总值	**GDP**	**90.8**	**100.0**	**100.5**	**102.4**	**105.6**
人均本地生产总值	**Per Capita GDP**	**91.6**	**100.0**	**99.6**	**100.5**	**103.5**

注: ①数字已根据香港旅游发展局在2003年11月份所发布一套新的到港旅客境内消费开支的数字而作出修订。
@数字在日后得到更多资料时会作出修订。

Notes: ①Figures have been revised to incorporate the new data on destination consumption expenditure of incoming visitors and travellers released by the Hong Kong Tourism Board in November 2003.
@Figures are subject to revision later on as more data become available.

24-14 本地居民生产总值

Gross National Product

单位: 亿港元, 另有注明除外 (HKD 100 million, unless otherwise specified)

项 目	Item	1999	2000	2001	2002	2003@
按2000年不变价格计算①	**At Constant (2000) Market Prices①**					
本地生产总值	GDP	11695	12883	12943	13187@	13610
国外净要素收入	Net External Factor Income Flows	331	218	424	181@	383
本地居民生产总值	GNP	12022	13101	13367	13369@	13993
人均本地生产总值 (港元)	Per Capita GDP (HKD)	177019	193299	192465	194304@	200061
人均本地居民生产总值 (港元)	Per Capita GNP (HKD)	181968	196565	198774	196975@	205689
按当年价格计算	**At Current Market Prices**					
本地生产总值	GDP	12461	12883	12699	12474@	12198
国外净要素收入	Net External Factor Income Flows	348	218	412	167	341
本地居民生产总值	GNP	12809	13101	13111	12641@	12540
人均本地生产总值 (港元)	Per Capita GDP (HKD)	188622	193299	188835	183790@	179308
人均本地居民生产总值 (港元)	Per Capita GNP (HKD)	193886	196565	194958	186250@	184324

注: ①由于按不变价格计算的本地生产总值及本地居民生产总值的基年已重订至2000年, 在该基年前的统计期, 按不变价格计算的本地居民生产总值数字和以不变价格计算的本地生产总值及国外净要素收入之和有些微差异。
@数字在日后得到更多资料时会作出修订。

Notes: ①Owing to rebasing of GDP and GNP at constant prices to year 2000, there are slight discrepancies between figures on GNP at constant market prices and the sum of figures on GDP at constant market prices and net external factor income flows for reference periods before the base year of 2000.
@ Figures are subject to revision later on as more data become available.

24-15 国际收支平衡表
Balance of Payments Account

单位：亿港元 (HKD 100 million)

标准组成部分①	Standard Components①	1999	2000	2001	2002@	2003@
经常帐②	**Current Account②**	**798.16**	**551.93**	**775.31**	**982.41**	**1257.38**
货物	Goods	-245.01	-638.32	-649.70	-394.06	-449.70
服务	Services	814.84	1102.70	1152.04	1357.36	1512.91
收益	Income	347.77	217.68	411.74	166.98	341.28
经常转移	Current Transfers	-119.43	-130.13	-138.78	-147.87	-147.11
资本及金融帐②	**Capital and Financial Account②**	**-833.74**	**-578.63**	**-973.59**	**-1511.79**	**-1514.50**
资本转移	Capital Transfers	-138.12	-120.44	-91.55	-156.86	-79.13
直接投资	Direct Investment	405.11	199.76	969.48	-606.85	762.44
有价证券投资	Portfolio Investment	2568.12	1907.82	-3220.45	-3024.84	-2371.43
金融衍生工具	Financial Derivatives	792.25	16.61	396.40	515.63	795.68
其他投资	Other Investment	-3682.43	-1799.17	1337.83	1575.73	-546.18
储备资产(变动净值)③	Reserve Assets (Net Change)③	-778.67	-783.21	-365.30	185.41	-75.89
净误差及遗漏④	**Net Errors and Omissions④**	**35.57**	**26.70**	**198.29**	**529.38**	**257.12**
整体的国际收支	**Overall Balance of Payments**	**778.67**	**783.21**	**365.30**	**-185.41**	**75.89**
		(盈余)	(盈余)	(盈余)	(赤字)	(盈余)
		(in surplus)	(in surplus)	(in surplus)	(in deficit)	(in surplus)

注：①根据国际收支平衡表的核算常规，某标准组成部分的净贷方数字以正数显示，而净借方则以负数显示。

②经常帐差额的正数显示盈余而负数则显示赤字。在资本及金融帐方面，正数显示净资金流入而负数则显示净资金流出。由于对外资产的增加是属于借方帐目而减少则属贷方帐目，因此负数的储备资产变动净值显示储备资产的增加，而正数则显示减少。

③在国际收支平衡架构下储备资产变动净值的估计是指交易数字。因计价方式改变(包括价格变动及汇率变动)及分类重组所导致的影响并不包括在内。

④原则上，贷方和借方各项账目的净总和应相等于零。但实际上，贷方和借方账目的资料是通过不同的来源搜集，基于各种原因会有差异。为了令贷方和借方账目的总和相等，便须加进一个余额项目，以反映平衡表的「净误差及遗漏」。

@数字在日后得到更多资料时会作出修订。

Notes:①In accordance with the Balance of Payments accounting rules, a net credit for a standard component is represented by a positive value, and a net debit a negative value.

②A positive value for the balance figure in the current account represents a surplus whereas a negative value represents a deficit. For the capital and financial account, a positive value indicates a net capital and financial inflow and a negative value indicates a net outflow. As increases in external assets are debit entries and decreases are credit entries, a negative value for net change in reserve assets represents a net increase and a positive value represents a net decrease.

③The estimates on net change in reserve assets under the Balance of Payments framework are transaction figures. Effects from valuation changes (including price changes and exchange rate changes) and reclassifications are excluded.

④In principle, the net sum of credit entries and debit entries is zero. In practice, discrepancies between the credit and debit entries may however occur for various reasons as the data are collected from many sources. Equality between the sum of credit entries and debit entries is brought about by the inclusion of a balancing item which reflects net errors and omissions.

@Figures are subject to revision later on as more data become available.

24-16 国际投资头寸(期末头寸)
International Investment Position (Position as at end of period)

单位：亿港元 (HKD 100 million)

概括组成部分	Broad Components	2000	2001	2002	2003@
香港资产	**Hong Kong Assets**	**88992.95**	**83506.23**	**80327.44**	**91248.94**
在外地的直接投资	Direct Investment Abroad	30278.09	27492.37	24129.32	26091.29
有价证券投资	Portfolio Investment	13943.20	16030.59	19032.41	25755.51
金融衍生工具	Financial Derivatives	1310.63	1366.72	1756.16	1673.77
其它投资	Other Investment	35072.66	29947.34	26681.50	28537.29
储备资产	Reserve Assets	8388.39	8669.22	8728.05	9191.07
香港负债	**Hong Kong Liabilities**	**71697.49**	**62826.62**	**53553.76**	**60373.62**
在香港的直接投资	Direct Investment in Hong Kong	35508.40	32696.53	26222.98	29114.96
有价证券投资	Portfolio Investment	11944.77	9124.93	7294.56	9710.59
金融衍生工具	Financial Derivatives	975.82	940.22	1653.05	1650.46
其它投资	Other Investment	23268.49	20064.94	18383.16	19897.61
国际投资头寸净值①	**Net International Investment Position①**	**17295.47**	**20679.61**	**26773.68**	**30875.32**

注：①国际投资头寸净值是对外金融资产总值与对外金融负债总值之差。
@数字在日后得到更多资料时会作出修订。

Notes: ①Net International Investment Position is the difference between total external financial assets and total external financial liabilities.
@Figures are subject to revision later on as more data become available.

24-17 电力、煤气、水消费量
Electricity, Gas and Water Consumption

用途	Use	1999	2000	2001	2002	2003
电力 (万亿焦耳)	**Electricity (Terajoules)**					
住宅	Domestic	31400	32234	32799	33394	34365
商业	Commercial	76028	80347	84214	87241	88834
工业	Industrial	17547	17769	16759	16112	14851
街灯	Street lighting	312	325	367	365	384
出口往中国内地	Export to the Mainland of China	2279	4253	5692	7830	10827
总计	Total	127566	134928	139830	144942	149261
煤气 (万亿焦耳)	**Gas (Terajoules)**					
住宅	Domestic	13064	13866	14493	14794	15446
商业	Commercial	10709	11209	11060	10860	10542
工业	Industrial	914	982	1011	987	1015
总计	Total	24687	26057	26564	26641	27002
水 (万立方米)	**Water (10 000 Cubic Meters)**	**91100**	**92400**	**94000**	**94900**	**97400**

24-18 工业生产指数
Index of Industrial Production

(2000年=100) (2000=100)

工业组别/组别内选定工业	Industry Group/Selected Component Industry	1999	2000	2001	2002	2003
所有制造行业	**All Manufacturing Industries**	**100.5**	**100.0**	**95.6**	**86.2**	**78.3**
食品、饮品及烟草制品业	Food, Beverages and Tobacco	103.2	100.0	98.4	106.4	94.1
服装制品业(鞋类除外)	Wearing Apparel, Except Footwear	97.1	100.0	99.9	93.3	95.1
纺织制品业(包括针织)	Textiles(Including Knitting)	96.3	100.0	99.7	92.5	82.6
纸品及印刷业	Paper Products and Printing	98.0	100.0	98.8	98.6	98.2
化学产品、橡胶制品、塑胶制品及非金属矿产制品业	Chemical, Rubber, Plastic and Non-metallic Mineral Products	116.8	100.0	92.2	76.3	77.3
塑胶制品业	Plastic Products	112.2	100.0	84.8	75.7	69.6
基本金属及金属制品业	Basic Metals and Fabricated Metal Products	112.6	100.0	84.6	64.5	60.3
金属制品业(机械及设备除外)	Fabricated Metal Products, Except Machinery and Equipment	122.7	100.0	89.8	63.4	48.3
电器及电子制品、机械、专业设备及光学用品制造业	Electrical and Electronic Products, Machinery, Professional Equipment and Optical Goods	99.2	100.0	92.1	71.7	56.4
电器及电子制品制造业	Consumer Electrical and Electronic Products	101.1	100.0	100.0	76.4	65.9
机械、设备、仪器及零件制造业	Machinery, Equipment, Apparatus, Parts and Components	93.5	100.0	91.5	76.1	58.9
其他产品制造行业	Miscellaneous Manufacturing Industries	95.9	100.0	94.9	98.5	91.8

24-19　按楼宇种类划分的新落成私人楼宇

Private Buildings Newly Completed by Type of Building

年　份 Year	住宅楼宇 Residential		商住两用楼宇 Residential/Commercial			商业楼宇 Commercial	
	楼宇数目（栋） Number of Blocks (unit)	实用楼面面积（万平方米） Usable Floor Area (10 000 sq.m.)	楼宇数目（栋） Number of Blocks (unit)	实用楼面面积（万平方米） Usable Floor Area(10 000 sq.m.) 住　宅 Residential	非住宅 Non-residential	楼宇数目（栋） Number of Blocks (unit)	实用楼面面积（万平方米） Usable Floor Area (10 000 sq.m.)
1999	309	57.6	115	67.2	23.5	50	37.1
2000	378	82.2	46	27.2	4.2	26	11.8
2001	184	56.2	56	37.9	8.8	14	8.3
2002	874	94.7	71	36.3	7.8	26	21.0
2003	541	39.6	71	53.1	8.4	18	32.9

24-19　续表　continued

年　份 Year	工业楼宇 Industrial		其他用途楼宇 Others			总　计 Total		
	楼宇数目（栋） Number of Blocks	实用楼面面积（万平方米） Usable Floor Area (10 000 sq.m.)	楼宇数目（栋） Number of Blocks	实用楼面面积（万平方米） Usable Floor Area (10 000 sq.m.) 住　宅 Residential	非住宅 Non-residential	楼宇数目（栋） Number of Blocks	实用楼面面积（万平方米） Usable Floor Area (10 000 sq.m.) 住　宅 Residential	非住宅 Non-residential
1999	26	19.5	146	9.9	48.2	646	134.7	128.3
2000	28	10.4	133	0.7	15.0	611	110.1	41.4
2001	27	7.1	153	2.3	14.8	434	96.3	39.1
2002	18	2.0	119	5.0	24.0	1108	136.0	54.8
2003	6	4.4	141	7.2	13.2	777	99.9	58.8

24-20　按楼宇种类划分的获批准可动工兴建私人楼宇

Private Buildings with Consent to Commence Work by Type of Building

年　份 Year	住宅楼宇 Residential		商住两用楼宇 Residential/Commercial			商业楼宇 Commercial	
	楼宇数目（栋） Number of Blocks	实用楼面面积（万平方米） Usable Floor Area (10 000 sq.m.)	楼宇数目（栋） Number of Blocks	实用楼面面积（万平方米） Usable Floor Area (10 000 sq.m.) 住　宅 Residential	非住宅 Non-residential	楼宇数目（栋） Number of Blocks	实用楼面面积（万平方米） Usable Floor Area (10 000 sq.m.)
1999	244	77.7	98	88.1	9.1	16	19.6
2000	468	69.9	57	40.2	9.9	32	23.9
2001	212	41.0	74	58.4	9.6	12	16.9
2002	604	58.7	36	17.0	5.8	22	30.7
2003	398	58.9	54	34.9	5.4	13	14.6

24-20 续表 continued

年 份 Year	工业楼宇 Industrial		其他用途楼宇 Others			总 计 Total		
	楼宇数目（栋）Number of Blocks	实用楼面面积（万平方米）Usable Floor Area (10 000 sq.m.)	楼宇数目（栋）Number of Blocks	实用楼面面积 （万平方米）Usable Floor Area (10 000 sq.m.)		楼宇数目（栋）Number of Blocks	实用楼面面积 （万平方米）Usable Floor Area (10 000 sq.m.)	
				住 宅 Residential	非住宅 Non-residential		住 宅 Residential	非住宅 Non-residential
1999	18	8.5	113	3.4	12.6	489	169.3	49.8
2000	20	12.9	131	4.3	24.0	708	114.3	70.7
2001	14	4.6	92	0.8	7.5	404	100.3	38.6
2002	17	10.7	125	3.3	10.9	804	79.0	58.2
2003	2	0.1	239	10.0	44.4	706	103.8	64.5

24-21 按类型划分的永久性屋宇单位数量(3月底的数字)

Number of Permanent Quarters by Type (as at End March of the Year)

单位: 万个 (10 000 units)

年 份 Year	总 计 Total	公营租住房屋① Public Rental Housing①	资助出售单位② Subsidized Sale Flats②	私人房屋③ Private Housing③
1999	206.53	70.58	27.03	108.92
2000	213.52	69.11	32.47	111.93
2001	223.66	68.52	38.09	117.06
2002	229.50	68.58	37.17	123.75
2003	236.05	68.53	39.66	127.86

注：永久性屋宇单位的涵盖范围不包括酒店及院舍内的屋宇单位。

①由2000年起，数字不包括在房屋委员会的租者置其屋计划中已出售的单位。

②由2000年起，数字包括在房屋委员会的租者置其屋计划中已出售的单位。在1999年或以前，该单位则包括在公营租住房屋类别内。由2002年起，数字不包括可在公开市场买卖的资助出售单位。

③由2002年起，数字包括可在公开市场买卖的资助出售单位。

Notes:The coverage of the permanent quarters excludes quarters in hotels and institutions.

① Figures from 2000 onwards exclude quarters sold under the Housing Authority Tenants Purchase Scheme.

② Figures from 2000 onwards also cover quarters sold under the Housing Authority Tenants Purchase Scheme which were previously included under public rental housing in 1999 and before. As from 2002, figures exclude subsidized sale flats that can be traded in open market.

③ As from 2002, figures include flats under subsidized sale flats that can be traded in open market.

24-22 按居所租住权划分的家庭住户数目

Domestic Households by Tenure of Accommodation

单位: 万户 (10 000 households)

项 目	Item	1999	2000	2001	2002	2003
总计	**Total**	**199.89**	**203.70**	**207.84**	**213.37**	**217.49**
自置居所住户	Owner-occupier	96.30	104.13	108.43	112.32	115.56
全租户	Sole Tenant	85.34	83.34	83.44	84.72	86.44
合租户	Co-tenant	6.73	6.41	5.45	5.06	4.78
二房东	Main Tenant	0.63	0.48	0.36	0.23	0.23
三房客	Sub-tenant	1.72	1.38	1.20	1.10	0.74
免租	Rent Free	2.63	2.42	3.39	4.54	4.52
居所由雇主提供	Provided by Employer	6.53	5.54	5.56	5.39	5.22

注：数字是指该年四季「综合住户统计调查」所得的数字的平均数。

Note: Figures are averages of the figures obtained from the General Household Survey for the four quarters of the year.

24-23 进出香港货物

Inward and Outward Movements of Cargo

单位: 万吨 (10 000 tons)

项　目	Item	1999	2000	2001	2002	2003
卸下	**Discharged**					
空运	By Air	84.1	95.3	89.4	100.4	103.5
水运	By Water	10630.5	10693.5	11047.2	11972.9	12855.4
海运	By Ocean	8862.1	8800.3	8850.6	9344.4	9936.3
河运	By River	1768.4	1893.2	2196.6	2628.4	2919.1
道路运输①	By Road①	2050.0	2214.2	2040.9	2108.5	2060.6
铁路运输②	By Rail②	29.3	31.8	27.3	28.3	25.3
总计	Total	12794.0	13034.9	13204.8	14210.0	15044.8
装上	**Loaded**					
空运	By Air	113.3	128.8	118.0	147.5	160.7
水运	By Water	6253.3	6770.7	6773.8	7278.2	7905.8
海运	By Ocean	3960.1	4293.4	4217.0	4485.7	4925.5
河运	By River	2293.2	2477.3	2556.8	2792.5	2980.3
道路运输①	By Road①	1791.5	1779.1	1650.9	1828.8	1884.6
铁路运输②	By Rail②	17.3	13.3	9.7	10.2	7.6
总计	Total	8175.4	8691.9	8552.4	9264.7	9958.8

注: ①2001至2003年的数字是根据自2001年4月开始采用的新估计方法编制得来。
②数字不包括家畜。

Notes: ①Figures for 2001-2003 are compiled based on a new estimation method, which has been adopted as from April 2001.
②Figures exclude livestock.

24-24 按主要货物装卸地点划分的集装箱吞吐量

Container Throughput by Main Cargo Handling Location

单位: 万标准集装箱单位 (10 000 TEUs)

项　目	Item	1999	2000	2001	2002	2003
集装箱吞吐量	Container Throughput	1621.1	1809.8	1782.6	1914.4	2044.9
集装箱码头	Container Terminals					
抵港	Inward					
载货集装箱	Laden Container	358.4	386.2	380.2	409.6	433.5
空集装箱	Empty Container	125.1	164.4	157.5	161.0	157.5
离港	Outward					
载货集装箱	Laden Container	507.2	574.7	559.1	583.3	579.9
空集装箱	Empty Container	38.9	34.9	31.7	35.3	36.1
集装箱码头以外	Other than Container Terminals					
海运	Ocean					
抵港	Inward					
载货集装箱	Laden Container	136.0	152.8	153.7	167.2	184.6
空集装箱	Empty Container	18.2	17.1	13.2	10.3	14.2
离港	Outward					
载货集装箱	Laden Container	103.7	112.8	118.5	143.1	180.8
空集装箱	Empty Container	25.9	20.5	15.6	12.0	10.9
河运	River					
抵港	Inward					
载货集装箱	Laden Container	76.5	86.1	98.6	115.3	142.9
空集装箱	Empty Container	88.5	91.2	80.2	85.8	85.9
离港	Outward					
载货集装箱	Laden Container	98.3	112.1	108.8	113.7	131.4
空集装箱	Empty Container	44.4	56.8	65.5	77.9	87.2

注: 标准集装箱单位是以20英尺×8英尺×8英尺的标准集装箱为根据。

Note: TEU refers to Twenty-Foot Equivalent Units (based on a standardized container size of 20 ft. x 8 ft. x 8 ft.).

24-25 通讯及互联网服务
Communications and Internet Services

项　目	Item	1999	2000	2001	2002	2003
邮递服务	**Postal Services**					
信件邮件　(亿件物品)	Letter Mail (100 million articles)	12.7	13.4	13.6	12.7	12.7
包裹　(万件)	Parcels (10 000 pcs)	102.7	97.5	92.3	92.8	94.6
电话服务①（万条操作线路）	**Telephone Services①(10 000 working lines)**					
住宅	Residential	219.0	221.0	216.1	213.4	211.9
商用	Business	164.9	173.6	176.5	170.8	170.1
总计	Total	383.9	394.6	392.6	384.2	382.0
图文传真①（万条操作线路）	**FAX① (10 000 working lines)**	**38.4**	**40.4**	**41.1**	**54.6**	**49.1**
对外电话通讯量　(万分钟)	**External Telephone Traffic Volume (10 000 minutes)**					
拨出②③	Outgoing②③	255011	307489	348729	395090	423260
拨入④	Incoming④	167922	185805	194235	175599	167620
对外专用电报通讯量(万分钟)	**External Telex Traffic Volume (10 000 minutes)**					
发出	Outward	407.3	304.7	195.4	150.1	92.9
收到	Inward	412.9	323.0	247.1	229.1	162.9
转接	Transit	534.8	362.8	303.6	212.2	142.4
本港电报机电讯　(万分钟)	**Internal Telex Traffic (10 000 minutes)**	**983.2**	**728.9**	**530.7**	**294.9**	**206.9**
电报　(万件)	**Public Telegram Traffic (10 000 messages)**					
发出	Outward	2.7	2.1	1.2	0.7	0.5
收到	Inward	1.2	0.8	0.5	0.4	0.2
本港电报　(万件)	**Inland Telegram (10 000 messages)**	**1.5**	**0.1**	**0.3**	0.005	0.007
公共无线电传呼接收器①(户)	**Public Radio Paging Receivers①(numbers)**	**342058**	**327768**	**253215**	**197405**	**177926**
公共流动无线电话用户系统①⑤　(户)	**Public Mobile Radiotelephone Subscriber Units①⑤ (numbers)**	**3650238**	**4173318**	**4256422**	**4207465**	**4407569**
		(3989750)	**(5234370)**	**(5701686)**	**(6218984)**	**(7194335)**
互联网服务	**Internet Services**					
持牌互联网服务供应商数目①	No. of Licensed Internet Service Providers (ISPs)①	**159**	**235**	**259**	**236**	**201**
持牌互联网服务供应商客户数目①⑥	No. of Customers of Licensed Internet Service Providers (ISPs)①⑥					
以拨号接驳的已登记客户户口(不包括互联网储值卡)⑦	Registered Customer Accounts with Dial-up Access (Excluding Internet Pre-paid Calling Cards)⑦	1734254	2283047	2018238	1371705	1084368
作拨号接驳用途的互联网储值卡	Internet Pre-paid Calling Cards for Dial-up Access	117496	38708	18569	14978	20411
以私人租用线路接驳的已登记客户户口⑦	Registered Customer Accounts with Leased Line Access⑦	7495	11527	7066	3439	2739
宽频互联网接驳客户户口⑦⑧⑨	Registered Broadband Internet Access Customer Accounts⑦⑧⑨		392118	623302	989115	1230607
互联网使用量⑥	Internet Traffic Volume⑥					
客户通过公共电话网络接驳⑩　(万分钟)	Customer Access via Public Switched Telephone Networks⑩ (10 000 minutes)	1092312	1498859	1105581	555023	3563943
客户通过宽频网络接驳⑨⑾　(兆兆比特)	Customer Access via Broadband Networks⑨⑾ (terabits)		2909	73607	215296	933728

注：①数字为该年年底数字。 ②数字包括图文传真及数据。③1999年以前的数字只计话音通讯。 ④估计数字。
⑤数字不包括储值智能卡。包括储值智能卡的数字于括号内展示。
⑥数字为根据互联网服务供应商申报的估计数字，并不包括不属于持牌互联网服务供应商客户的使用者。
⑦已登记客户户口指互联网服务供应商的客户户口(包括免费的客户户口)。拥有超过一个客户登入识别码的登记客户户口只算作一个已登记的客户户口。数字不包括只获提供电邮地址的客户户口。
⑧数字自2000年2月开始提供。
⑨宽频互联网接驳指利用导线解调器、异步传输模式(ATM)、非对称数码用户线路(ADSL)、数码用户线路(DSL)或其他技术而下载速度达每秒一兆比特或以上的服务。
⑩不包括通过私人租用线路接驳及使用宽频服务的客户。
⑾数字自2000年11月开始提供。

Notes:①Figures are as at end of the year. ②Figures include facsimile and data. ③Figures prior to 1999 refer to voice traffic only. ④Estimated figures.
⑤Excluding pre-paid SIM cards. Figures including prepaid SIM cards are presented in brackets.
⑥Estimated figures are based on the return from the ISPs and do not include users who are not customers on the licensed ISPs.
⑦Registered customer accounts refer to the customer accounts of ISPs (including those free-of-charge customer accounts). For a registered customer account which has more than one user login ID, it is counted as one registered customer account only. Figures do not include customer accounts which are provided with e-mail addresses only.
⑧Figures were first available in February 2000.
⑨Broadband Internet access refers to services with downloading speed of 1 Mbps or above using cable modem, ATM (asynchronous transfer mode), ADSL (asymmetric digital subscriber line), DSL (digital subscriber line) or other technologies.
⑩ Not including customer access via leased circuits and broadband services.
⑾Figures were first available in November 2000.

24-26 商品进出口贸易总额

Total Imports and Exports of Goods

单位: 亿港元 (HKD 100 million)

贸易种类	Type of Trade	1999	2000	2001	2002	2003
进口	Imports	13927.18	16579.62	15681.94	16194.19	18057.70
港产品出口	Domestic Exports	1706.00	1809.67	1535.20	1309.26	1216.87
转口	Re-exports	11784.00	13917.22	13274.67	14295.90	16207.49
整体出口	Total Exports	13490.00	15726.89	14809.87	15605.17	17424.36
贸易总额	Total Trade	27417.17	32306.52	30491.81	31799.36	35482.06
商品贸易差额	Merchandise Trade Balance	-437.18	-852.73	-872.08	-589.03	-633.34

24-27 主要商品进口供应地和出口去向

Imports and Exports of Goods by Supplier or Destination

单位: 亿港元 (HKD 100 million)

贸易种类/主要国家/地区	Type of Trade/Main Country/Territory	1999	2000	2001	2002	2003
进口(供应地)	**Imports (Supplier)**	**13927.18**	**16579.62**	**15681.94**	**16194.19**	**18057.70**
中国内地	The mainland of China	6075.46	7149.87	6819.80	7170.74	7856.25
日本	Japan	1626.52	1989.76	1765.99	1825.69	2139.95
中国台湾	Taiwan, China	1004.26	1241.72	1079.29	1159.06	1252.03
美国	United States of America	985.72	1128.01	1049.41	914.78	987.30
新加坡	Singapore	600.17	749.98	728.98	757.40	905.70
港产品出口(目的地)	**Domestic Exports (Destination)**	**1706.00**	**1809.67**	**1535.20**	**1309.26**	**1216.87**
美国	United States of America	513.58	544.38	475.89	419.08	391.30
中国内地	The mainland of China	504.14	541.58	495.47	413.74	367.57
英国	United Kingdom	103.92	106.81	85.78	75.88	77.62
德国	Germany	85.43	92.94	58.18	42.73	48.53
中国台湾	Taiwan, China	51.01	61.04	53.46	43.88	36.53

24-28 商品转口的主要来源和去向

Re-Exports of Goods by Origin or Destination

单位:亿港元 (HKD 100 million)

贸易种类/主要国家/地区	Type of Trade/Main Country/Territory	1999	2000	2001	2002	2003
转口(目的地)	**Re-exports (Destination)**	**11784.00**	**13917.22**	**13274.67**	**14295.90**	**16207.49**
中国内地	The mainland of China	3991.88	4888.23	4965.74	5718.70	7057.87
美国	United States of America	2694.44	3110.47	2821.89	2910.43	2850.84
日本	Japan	675.06	820.50	835.51	807.43	911.54
德国	Germany	441.22	505.99	457.74	445.67	513.69
英国	United Kingdom	455.41	523.56	467.64	466.44	496.25
转口(来源地)	**Re-exports (Origin)**	**11784.00**	**13917.22**	**13274.67**	**14295.90**	**16207.49**
中国内地	The mainland of China	7201.26	8495.17	8083.70	8639.67	9671.04
日本	Japan	1212.65	1373.38	1256.49	1357.93	1612.31
中国台湾	Taiwan, China	719.57	879.42	803.21	942.75	1071.44
美国	United States of America	567.37	654.65	651.93	629.00	631.58
韩国	Republic of Korea	388.22	460.57	397.75	472.18	570.00

24-29 涉及外发中国内地加工的贸易

Trade Involving Outward Processing in the Mainland of China

项　目	Item	1999	2000	2001	2002	2003
涉及外发加工贸易的估计货值　(亿港元)	**Estimated Value of Outward Processing Trade (HKD 100 million)**					
输往中国内地的港产出口货物	Domestic Exports to the mainland of China	376.96	393.04	351.72	288.48	249.24
输往中国内地的转口货物	Re-exports to the mainland of China	1978.90	2429.29	2243.81	2488.01	3012.23
输往中国内地的整体出口货物	Total Exports to the mainland of China	2355.86	2822.33	2595.53	2776.50	3261.47
从中国内地进口的货物	Imports from the mainland of China	4875.07	5670.00	5319.60	5310.34	5649.33
原产地为中国内地经香港输往其他地方的转口货物	Re-exports of the mainland of China Origin to Other Places	5701.26	6473.38	5783.29	5947.08	6034.60
涉及外发加工贸易的估计比率 (%)	**Estimated Proportion of Outward Processing Trade (%)**					
输往中国内地的港产出口货物	Domestic Exports to the mainland of China	75.9	72.7	71.0	69.8	68.0
输往中国内地的转口货物	Re-exports to the mainland of China	49.7	49.7	45.2	43.5	42.7
输往中国内地的整体出口货物	Total Exports to the mainland of China	52.6	52.0	47.5	45.3	43.9
从中国内地进口的货物	Imports from the mainland of China	80.5	79.3	78.0	74.0	71.7
原产地为中国内地经香港输往其他地方的转口货物	Re-exports of the mainland of China Origin to Other Places	86.6	85.1	82.2	82.5	79.4

24-30 按主要服务组别划分的服务出口及进口

Exports and Imports of Services by Major Service Group

单位: 亿港元　　(HKD 100 million)

主要服务组别	Major Service Group	1999	2000	2001	2002	2003@
服务出口	**Exports of Services**					
运输	Transportation	892.30	995.13	936.75	1037.51	1056.01
旅游①	Travel①	428.40	460.19	463.62	588.55	555.14
保险服务	Insurance Services	30.65	34.52	35.56	34.21	36.72
金融服务	Financial Services	192.06	208.59	218.23	195.64	201.54
商贸服务及其他与贸易相关的服务	Merchanting and Other Trade-related Services	815.24	976.16	1064.47	1159.96	1286.16
其他服务	Other Services	296.72	343.55	357.94	338.26	338.14
总计①	Total①	2655.36	3018.13	3076.57	3354.12	3473.71
服务进口	**Imports of Services**					
运输	Transportation	392.38	486.28	509.16	485.18	488.12
旅游	Travel	1018.89	974.02	960.57	968.46	891.33
保险服务	Insurance Services	49.75	41.11	40.28	46.18	51.01
金融服务	Financial Services	57.29	55.36	52.42	48.76	54.03
商贸服务及其他与贸易相关的服务	Merchanting and Other Trade-related Services	105.10	111.70	118.02	146.60	168.09
其他服务	Other Services	217.11	246.95	244.08	301.58	308.22
总计	Total	1840.52	1915.43	1924.53	1996.76	1960.80
服务出口净额①	**Net Exports of Services①**	**814.84**	**1102.70**	**1152.04**	**1357.36**	**1512.91**

注: ①旅游服务出口的数字已根据香港旅游发展局在2003年11月份所发布的新一套到港旅客境内消费开支的数字而作出修订。
　　@数字在日后得到更多资料时会作出修订。

Notes: ①Figures for exports of travel services have been revised to incorporate the new data released by the Hong Kong Tourism Board in November 2003 on destination consumption expenditure of incoming visitors and travellers.
　@Figures are subject to revision later on as more data become available.

24-31 按主要目的地和来源地划分的服务出口及进口

Exports and Imports of Services by Main Destination and Source

单位: 亿港元 (HKD 100 million)

目的地/来源地	Destination/Source	1999	2000	2001	2002	2003@
服务出口①	**Exports of Services①**					
中国内地	The mainland of China	636.58	688.44	764.79	952.60	
美国	United States of America	540.53	684.88	702.05	703.57	
日本	Japan	255.77	279.58	269.45	297.56	
中国台湾	Taiwan, China	150.43	204.77	209.38	220.22	
英国	United Kingdom	144.10	189.04	179.66	197.08	
其他	Others	927.94	971.44	951.25	983.09	
所有目的地	All Destinations	2655.36	3018.13	3076.57	3354.12	3473.71
服务进口	**Imports of Services**					
中国内地	The mainland of China	621.88	593.86	596.37	608.76	
美国	United States of America	259.47	301.38	302.41	317.04	
日本	Japan	112.40	131.81	129.63	147.74	
英国	United Kingdom	106.82	121.83	118.00	129.03	
澳大利亚	Australia	97.77	105.68	112.72	116.39	
其他	Others	642.17	660.87	665.41	677.79	
所有来源地	All Sources	1840.52	1915.43	1924.53	1996.76	1960.80

注:①数字已根据香港旅游发展局在2003年11月份所发布一套新的到港旅客境内消费开支的数字而作出修订。

@数字在日后得到更多资料时会作出修订。

Notes: ①Figures have been revised to incorporate the new data on destination consumption expenditure of incoming visitors and travellers released by the Hong Kong Tourism Board in November 2003.

@Figures are subject to revision later on as more data become available.

24-32 按主要投资者国家/地区划分的外来直接投资头寸及流动

Position and Flow of Inward Direct Investment by Major Investor Country/Territory

单位: 亿港元 (HKD 100 million)

主要投资者国家/地区①	Major Investor Country/Territory①	以市值计算的外来直接投资 Inward Direct Investment at Market Value					
		年底头寸 Position at end of year			年间流入 Inflow in year		
		2000	2001	2002	2000	2001	2002
英属维尔京群岛	British Virgin Islands	11314	9436	7794	2384	747	594
中国内地	The mainland of China	11122	9581	5946	1107	385	317
百慕大	Bermuda	3172	3157	2732	369	99	21
荷兰	Netherlands	2248	1999	2049	74	-23	103
美国	United States	1614	1937	1866	188	118	-110
日本	Japan	1132	1166	1414	258	85	153
新加坡	Singapore	982	888	735	600	114	64
英国	United Kingdom	553	454	558	-413	72	86
开曼群岛	Cayman Islands	902	1195	449	111	109	-687
澳大利亚	Australia	323	320	445	-21	23	7
其他	Others	2147	2564	2237	168	126	207
总计	**Total**	**35508**	**32697**	**26223**	**4826**	**1854**	**755**

注: ①国家/地区是指直接来源经济体系。这分类未必反映最初资金流出的国家/地区。

Note: ①Country/territory here refers to the immediate source economy. It does not necessarily reflect the country/territory in which the funds are initially mobilised.

24-33 按主要接受投资国家／地区划分的向外直接投资头寸及流动
Position and Flow of Outward Direct Investment by Major Recipient Country/Territory

单位：亿港元 (HKD 100 million)

主要接受投资国家／地区①	Major Recipient Country/Territory①	以市值计算的向外直接投资 Outward Direct Investment at Market Value					
		年底头寸 Position at end of year			年间流出 Outflow in year		
		2000	2001	2002	2000	2001	2002
英属维尔京群岛	British Virgin Islands	15694	14370	11483	705	254	101
中国内地	The mainland of China	10116	8440	8430	3612	663	1243
百慕大	Bermuda	889	919	768	126	-192	-49
巴拿马	Panama	235	324	390	25	95	22
美国	United States	243	248	322	29	-20	72
马来西亚	Malaysia	202	287	279	30	63	50
开曼群岛	Cayman Islands	711	826	279	-61	-24	-102
新加坡	Singapore	258	245	260	36	42	43
泰国	Thailand	156	206	208	9	22	26
英国	United Kingdom	234	206	205	46	9	36
其他	Others	1540	1421	1506	69	-27	-81
总计	**Total**	**30278**	**27492**	**24129**	**4626**	**885**	**1362**

注：①国家／地区是指首个目的地经济体系。这分类未必反映资金最终被使用的所在国家／地区。

Note: ①Country/territory here refers to the immediate destination economy. It does not necessarily reflect the country/territory in which the funds are ultimately used.

24-34 按母公司注册国家/地区划分的驻港地区总部公司数目
Number of Companies in Hong Kong that are Regional Headquarters by Country/Territory of Incorporation of the Parent Company

项目	Item	1999	2000	2001	2002	2003
驻港地区总部公司数目	**Number of companies in Hong Kong that are regional headquarters**	**840**	**855**	**944**	**948**	**966**
驻港地区总部数目最多的国家/地区	Countries/territories with the largest number of regional headquarters in Hong Kong					
美国	The United States	205	212	221	233	242
日本	Japan	114	127	160	159	168
英国	United Kingdom	82	81	90	80	86
中国内地	The mainland of China	69	69	70	96	84
德国	Germany	55	50	56	52	56
法国	France	36	28	43	35	44
瑞士	Switzerland	32	29	34	36	40
荷兰	Netherlands	32	31	48	39	38
新加坡	Singapore	20	21	25	26	22
澳大利亚	Australia	9	9	15	13	22
加拿大	Canada	19	21	16	23	19
中国台湾	Taiwan,China	28	21	22	21	18
瑞典	Sweden	16	15	16	17	16
韩国	Republic of Korea	14	15	13	17	15
丹麦	Denmark	**	6	10	11	10

注:指有关年度6月首个工作日的数字。
地区总部是指一个办事处有权控制／管理区内(即香港及一个或多个地方)的办事处的运作／业务，而毋须经常请示其香港以外的母公司。
就一家联营的驻港地区总部而言，其母公司注册国家/地区可能会多于一个。
**由于精确度及保密原因，数据不予公布。

Notes: Figures refer to the first working day of June of the year.
A regional headquarters (RHQ) is an office that has control over the operations of offices in the region (i.e. Hong Kong plus one or more other places), and manages the business without frequent referrals to its parent company outside Hong Kong.
In the case of a joint-ventured regional headquarters in Hong Kong, there may be more than one country/territory of incorporation of its parent company/companies.
**Data are not released due to precision and confidentiality considerations.

24-35 按母公司注册国家/地区划分的驻港地区办事处公司数目

Number of Companies in Hong Kong that are Regional Offices by Country/Territory of Incorporation of the Parent Company

项　目	Item	1999	2000	2001	2002	2003
驻港地区办事处公司数目	**Number of companies in Hong Kong that are regional offices**	**1650**	**2146**	**2293**	**2171**	**2241**
驻港地区办事处数目最多的国家/地区	Countries/territories with the largest number of regional offices in Hong Kong					
美国	The United States	278	358	420	437	498
日本	Japan	368	492	533	471	442
英国	United Kingdom	124	155	163	163	196
中国内地	The mainland of China	136	160	172	170	148
德国	Germany	76	93	108	96	122
中国台湾	Taiwan,China	97	113	142	121	111
法国	France	74	88	88	91	101
新加坡	Singapore	39	76	77	79	81
瑞士	Switzerland	50	69	68	61	61
韩国	Republic of Korea	56	71	76	49	60
荷兰	Netherlands	48	65	62	57	55
澳大利亚	Australia	29	42	43	52	45
意大利	Italy	47	43	52	38	41
加拿大	Canada	25	30	34	28	27
奥地利	Austria	19	25	32	26	22

注：指有关年度6月首个工作日的数字。

地区办事处是指一个办事处有权协调/管理区内(即香港及一个或多个地方)的办事处/运作/业务，但须经常请示其地区总部或香港以外的母公司。

就一家联营的驻港地区办事处而言，其母公司注册国家/地区可能会多于一个。

Notes: Figures refer to the first working day of June of the year.

A regional office (RO) is an office that coordinates offices/operations in the region (i.e. Hong Kong plus one or more other places), and manages the business but with frequent referrals to its parent company outside Hong Kong or its regional headquarters .

In the case of a joint-ventured regional office in Hong Kong, there may be more than one country/territory of incorporation of its parent company/companies.

24-36 按居住国家/地区划分的访港旅客人数

Visitor Arrivals by Country/Territory of Residence

单位：万人 (10 000 persons)

居住国家/地区	Country/Territory of residence	1998	2002	2003
中国内地	The mainland of China	267.2	682.5	846.7
中国台湾	Taiwan, China	188.6	242.9	185.2
南亚及东南亚	South & Southeast Asia	127.3	190.5	136.0
北亚	North Asia	129.8	185.2	123.5
美洲	The Americas	110.5	134.7	92.6
欧洲、非洲及中东	Europe, Africa & the Middle East	112.6	126.3	94.6
中国澳门	Macao, China	44.2	53.5	44.4
澳大利亚、新西兰及南太平洋	Australia, New Zealand & South Pacific	35.8	41.0	30.6
总计	**Total**	**1016.0**	**1656.6**	**1533.7**
		(-9.9)	**(+20.7)**	**(-6.2)**

注：括号内数字表示与去年同期比较的变动百分比，并根据未进位的数字计算。

Note: Figures in brackets refer to percentage changes over the same period in preceding year and are calculated based on unrounded figures.

24-37 政府储备结余(一般收入帐目及各基金)

Government's Reserve Balances (General Revenue Account and Funds)

单位: 亿港元 (HKD 100 million)

项　目	Item	1999/2000	2000/2001	2001/2002	2002/2003	2003/2004
期初储备结余	Opening Reserve Balances	4343.02	4442.54	4302.78	3725.03	3154.71*
收入①	Revenue①	2329.95	2250.60	1755.59	1774.89	2073.38
开支①	Expenditure①	2230.43	2328.93	2388.90	2391.77	2474.66
盈余/(赤字)	Surplus/(Deficit)	99.52	(78.33)	(633.31)	(616.88)	(401.28)
在外汇基金的投资亏损储备	Profits-back of Provision for Loss in Investments with the Exchange Fund	-	-61.43	55.56	5.87	-
期末储备结余	Closing Reserve Balances	4442.54	4302.78	3725.03	3114.02	2753.43

注: ①数额不包括“政府一般收入帐目与各基金之间的转拨”。
　　*2003年4月1日的结余包括奖券基金的40.69亿元结余。

Note: ①Figures exclude 'transfers between the General Revenue Account and Funds'.
　　*The balance at 1 April 2003 includes the balance of $4,069 million in the Lotteries Fund.

24-38 政府收入(一般收入帐目及各基金)

Government Revenue (General Revenue Account and Funds)

单位: 亿港元 (HKD 100 million)

项　目	Item	1999/2000	2000/2001	2001/2002	2002/2003	2003/2004
经营收入	**Operating Revenue**					
直接税	Direct Taxes					
入息税及利得税	Earnings and Profits Tax	669.14	738.70	777.49	730.28	804.74
间接税	Indirect Taxes					
博彩及彩票税	Bets and Sweeps Tax	119.38	126.30	115.71	109.21	116.36
酒店房租税	Hotel Accommodation Tax	1.82	2.23	2.03	2.01	1.56
印花税	Stamp Duties	121.16	109.11	86.37	74.58	112.46
飞机乘客离境税	Air Passenger Departure Tax	4.99	5.37	6.66	8.84	7.53
海底隧道使用税	Cross Harbour Tunnel Passage Tax	0.97	-	-	-	-
应课税品税项	Duties	73.77	72.93	69.81	66.20	64.22
一般差饷	General Rates	71.32	144.28	127.27	89.23	111.67
车辆税	Motor Vehicle Taxes	26.13	30.25	26.76	25.10	27.24
专利税及特权税	Royalties and Concessions	15.77	17.67	18.81	17.26	16.76
其他收入	Other Revenue					
罚款、没收及罚金	Fines,Forfeitures and Penalties	10.93	10.61	9.26	8.43	8.46
物业及投资	Properties and Investments	69.86	75.79	86.21	80.15	78.70
贷款、偿款、供款及其他收入	Loans, Reimbursements, Contributions and Other Receipts	56.72	42.10	41.54	44.05	31.33
公用事业	Utilities	33.26	32.97	33.66	20.68	28.77
各项收费	Fees and Charges	108.96	109.73	109.16	96.87	105.49
投资收入	Investment Income					
政府一般收入帐目	General Revenue Account	153.90	68.35	2.25	27.66	59.23
土地基金	Land Fund	213.88	126.81	1.06	132.81	171.59
经营收入总额	Total Operating Revenue	1751.96	1713.20	1514.05	1533.36	1746.11
非经常收入	**Capital Revenue**					
间接税	Indirect Taxes					
遗产税	Estate Duty	12.72	15.03	19.28	14.03	14.55
其他收入	Other Revenue					
其他	Others	13.84	105.25	8.37	5.48	15.40
从房屋委员会收回的款项	Recovery from Housing Authority	6.40	20.67	24.75	22.12	3.27
基金	Funds					
基本工程储备基金(不包括债券收入)	Capital Works Reserve Fund (exclude proceeds of bond issue)	391.11	321.83	106.83	121.90	65.49
资本投资基金	Capital Investment Fund	26.65	29.49	28.16	24.32	24.27
赈灾基金	Disaster Relief Fund	0.04	0.03	0.01	0.02	0.04
贷款基金	Loan Fund	115.15	36.12	53.82	44.64	176.23
公务员退休金储备基金	Civil Service Pension Reserve Fund	10.16	6.02	0.05	6.31	11.46
创新及科技基金	Innovation and Technology Fund	1.92	2.96	0.27	2.71	4.25
奖券基金	Lotteries Fund	-	-	-	-	12.31
非经常收入总额	Total Capital Revenue	577.99	537.40	241.54	241.53	327.27
政府收入总额	**Total Government Revenue**	**2329.95**	**2250.60**	**1755.59**	**1774.89**	**2073.38**

24-39 政府开支(一般收入帐目及各基金)
Government Expenditure (General Revenue Account and Funds)

单位: 亿港元 (HKD 100 million)

项目	Item	1999/2000	2000/2001	2001/2002	2002/2003	2003/2004
经营开支	**Operating Expenditure**					
经常开支	Recurrent Expenditure					
个人薪酬	Personal Emoluments	464.88	504.97	519.09	509.66	492.63
与员工有关联的开支	Personnel Related Expenses	50.35	51.16	48.70	48.30	48.81
退休金	Pensions	82.54	93.81	128.99	121.07	134.82
部门开支	Departmental Expenses	101.84	129.34	143.66	155.63	150.73
其他费用	Other Charges	295.90	303.55	313.28	336.55	346.28
资助金	Subventions					
教育	Education	222.82	238.60	251.37	258.94	257.98
卫生	Health	276.09	282.21	295.46	295.53	291.12
社会福利	Social Welfare	60.65	64.53	69.60	68.18	69.22
大学及理工学院	Universities and Polytechnics	137.11	131.31	132.58	131.89	129.04
职业训练局	Vocational Training Council	21.16	20.39	20.67	20.05	19.26
杂项	Miscellaneous	25.79	25.35	32.52	34.24	33.02
其他非经常开支	Other Non-recurrent	20.08	21.64	31.51	23.06	59.43
经营开支总额	**Total Operating Expenditure**	**1759.21**	**1866.86**	**1987.43**	**2003.10**	**2032.34**
非经常开支	**Capital Expenditure**					
机器、设备及工程资助金	Plant, Equipment and Works Subventions	13.72	8.53	9.84	9.52	7.64
教育	Education	3.85	4.64	3.98	4.13	3.55
卫生	Health	4.11	3.71	3.85	3.99	3.73
职业训练局	Vocational Training Council	0.19	0.67	1.07	0.71	0.37
杂项	Miscellaneous	1.39	1.10	0.70	0.70	2.57
基金	Funds					
基本工程储备基金	Capital Works Reserve Funds	294.90	305.77	303.30	309.19	344.86
资本投资基金(证券投资)	Capital Investment Fund (Equity Investments)	85.10	81.02	3.05	29.40	42.53
贷款基金	Loan Fund	65.80	53.10	72.77	27.89	21.81
赈灾基金	Disaster Relief Fund	0.32	0.43	0.08	0.19	0.16
创新及科技基金	Innovation and Technology Fund	1.84	3.10	2.83	2.95	4.71
奖券基金	Lotteries Fund	-	-	-	-	10.39
非经常开支及证券投资总额	**Total Capital Expenditure and Equity Investments**	**471.22**	**462.07**	**401.47**	**388.67**	**442.32**
政府开支及证券投资总额	**Total Government Expenditure and Equity Investments**	**2230.43**	**2328.93**	**2388.90**	**2391.77**	**2474.66**

24-40 按用途划分的公共开支
Public Expenditure by Function

单位: 亿港元 (HKD 100 million)

项目	Item	1999/2000	2000/2001	2001/2002	2002/2003	2003/2004+
公共及对外事务	Community and External Affairs	91.30	82.62	82.25	80.77	85.26
经济	Economic	122.72	124.86	137.14	137.48	155.61
教育	Education	503.07	514.08	522.32	547.85	577.48
环境及食物	Environment and food	124.96	113.37	112.07	114.43	112.13
卫生	Health	318.94	327.53	342.13	331.99	344.85
房屋	Housing	458.72	426.06	320.55	240.31	278.54
基础建设	Infrastructure	229.33	228.20	248.78	245.90	263.63
保安	Security	258.82	267.43	275.54	270.68	274.56
社会福利	Social Welfare	276.16	281.65	300.59	322.82	339.97
辅助服务	Support	310.82	309.27	352.22	342.97	359.80
总计	**Total**	**2694.84**	**2675.07**	**2693.59**	**2635.20**	**2791.83**

注: 公共开支包括政府开支(即所有记入政府一般收入帐目的开支及由政府的法定基金(不包括资本投资基金)所支付的开支), 以及营运基金及房屋委员会的开支。但政府只享有权益股的机构, 包括法定机构, 例如机场管理局、地铁有限公司和九广铁路公司, 其开支则不包括在内。同样地, 资本投资基金的垫款及股本投资亦不包括在内, 因为这些款项并不代表政府实际所用资源。
+修订预算。

Notes: Public expenditure comprises government expenditure (i.e. all expenditure charged to the General Revenue Account and financed by the Government's statutory funds excluding Capital Investment Fund), and expenditure by the Trading Funds and the Housing Authority. But not included is expenditure by those organisations, including statutory organisations, in which the Government has only an equity position, such as the Airport Authority, the MTR Corporation Ltd and the Kowloon-Canton Railway Corporation. Similarly, advances and equity investments from the Capital Investment Fund are excluded as they do not reflect the actual consumption of resources by the Government.
+Revised estimate.

24-41 外币兑换率及港汇指数

Exchange Rates and the Effective Exchange Rate Indices

(每单位外币兑换港元) (HKD per unit of foreign currency)

项　　目	Item	1999	2000	2001	2002	2003
年内平均数字①	**Average for the year①**					
澳元	Australian Dollar	5.01	4.53	4.04	4.25	5.08
比利时法郎 ②	Belgian Franc②	0.205	0.178	0.173	-	-
加拿大元	Canadian Dollar	5.22	5.25	5.04	4.97	5.58
人民币 (每百港元)	Chinese Renminbi (per HK$100)	106.67	106.17	106.04	105.84	105.86
德国马克 ②	Deutsche Mark②	4.23	3.68	3.57	-	-
荷兰盾 ②	Dutch Guilder②	3.75	3.27	3.17	-	-
法国法郎 ②	French Franc②	1.26	1.10	1.07	-	-
印尼卢比	Indonesian Rupiah	0.0010	0.0009	0.0008	0.0008	0.0009
意大利里拉 ②	Italian Lira②	0.0043	0.0037	0.0036	-	-
日圆	Japanese Yen	0.0685	0.0723	0.0643	0.0625	0.0673
马来西亚林吉特	Malaysian Ringgit	2.04	2.04	2.04	2.04	2.04
新台币	New Taiwan Dollar	0.240	0.248	0.232	0.229	0.227
菲律宾比索	Philippine Peso	0.201	0.18	0.157	0.156	0.146
英镑	Pound Sterling	12.55	11.81	11.24	11.73	12.73
韩圆	Republic of Korea Won	0.0065	0.0069	0.0060	0.0063	0.0065
新加坡元	Singapore Dollar	4.58	4.52	4.36	4.36	4.47
瑞士法郎	Swiss Franc	5.17	4.62	4.63	5.03	5.79
泰铢	Thai Baht	0.205	0.194	0.175	0.182	0.188
美元	US Dollar	7.758	7.791	7.799	7.799	7.787
欧元 ②	Euro②	8.27	7.20	6.99	7.38	8.81
特别提款权	SDR	10.60682	10.27532	9.92836	10.10470	10.90920
港汇指数③ (2000年1月=100)	Effective Exchange Rate Indices for the Hong Kong dollar③ (January 2000=100)					
贸易总值(进口及整体出口)加权	Trade (import and export)-weighted	100.9	101.7	104.7	104.0	100.7
进口货值加权	Import-weighted	101.4	101.5	105.1	104.7	101.6
整体出口货值加权④	Export-weighted④	100.4	101.9	104.3	103.3	99.8
年底数字⑤	**As at end of year⑤**					
澳元	Australian Dollar	5.06	4.35	3.99	4.41	5.83
比利时法郎②	Belgian Franc②	0.194	0.182	0.171	-	-
加拿大元	Canadian Dollar	5.35	5.20	4.90	4.95	6.00
人民币 (每百港元)	Chinese Renminbi (per HK$100)	106.61	106.04	106.04	105.82	106.67

24-41 续表 continued

(每单位外币兑换港元) (HKD per unit of foreign currency)

项　　目	Item	1999	2000	2001	2002	2003
德国马克②	Deutsche Mark②	4.00	3.76	3.53	-	-
荷兰盾②	Dutch Guilder②	3.55	3.33	3.13	-	-
法国法郎②	French Franc②	1.19	1.12	1.05	-	-
印尼卢比	Indonesian Rupiah	0.0011	0.0008	0.0007	0.0009	0.0009
意大利里拉②	Italian Lira②	0.0040	0.0038	0.0036	-	-
日圆	Japanese Yen	0.0761	0.0682	0.0594	0.0657	0.0726
马来西亚林吉特	Malaysian Ringgit	2.04	2.04	2.04	2.04	2.04
新台币	New Taiwan Dollar	0.245	0.238	0.226	0.228	0.227
菲律宾比索	Philippine Peso	0.194	0.168	0.159	0.150	0.143
英镑	Pound Sterling	12.59	11.64	11.31	12.51	13.83
韩圆	Republic of Korea Won	0.0069	0.0062	0.0060	0.0066	0.0065
新加坡元	Singapore Dollar	4.66	4.50	4.21	4.49	4.57
瑞士法郎	Swiss Franc	4.88	4.84	4.67	5.61	6.27
泰铢	Thai Baht	0.207	0.180	0.177	0.181	0.196
美元	US Dollar	7.771	7.796	7.797	7.798	7.763
欧元②	Euro②	7.82	7.34	6.91	8.17	9.77
特别提款权	SDR	10.65370	10.16140	9.79010	10.60154	11.53559
港汇指数③	Effective Exchange Rate Indices					
(2000年1月=100)	for the Hong Kong dollar③					
	(January 2000=100)					
贸易总值(进口及整体出口)加权	Trade (import and export)-weighted	100.1	102.9	105.9	102.0	98.8
进口货值加权	Import-weighted	100.0	103.2	106.7	102.7	99.8
整体出口货值加权④	Export-weighted④	100.2	102.6	105.1	101.2	97.7

注：《中华人民共和国香港特别行政区基本法》说明,港元是香港特别行政区的法定货币。外币指港元以外的其他货币，因而人民币亦视作外币。

①数字是指年内每日电汇或现钞收市中间兑换价的平均值。

②欧元是欧洲的统一货币，于1999年1月1日推出。由2002年1月1日开始，欧元的纸币及硬币已取代各参与国家的货币成为法定货币

③由2002年1月2日起公布的新系列。详情请参阅刊载于《香港统计月刊》2001年12月号题为「新系列港币汇率指数」的专题文章。

④包括转口和港产品出口。

⑤数字是该年最后一个交易日的电汇或现钞收市中间兑换价。

Notes: Hong Kong Dollar is the legal tender in the Hong Kong Special Administrative Region, as stated in "The Basic Law of the Hong Kong Special Administrative Region of the People's Republic of China". Foreign currency refers to any currency other than the Hong Kong currency. Accordingly Chinese Renminbi is also treated as foreign currency.

①Figures are the averages of the daily closing middle-market telegraphic transfer rates or notes rates for the year.

②Figures are the closing middle-market telegraphic transfer rates or notes rates as at the last trading day of the year.

③Euro is a unified European currency launched on 1 January 1999. As from 1 January 2002, Euro notes and coins have replaced notes and coins in national currencies of participating countries of the Euro.

④Including re-exports and domestic exports.

⑤New series released since 2 January 2002. For details, please see the feature article entitled "New Series of Effective Exchange Rate Index for the Hong Kong Dollar" in the December 2001 issue of the "Hong Kong Monthly Digest of Statistics".

24-42 货币供应量
Money Supply

单位：亿港元(年底数字) (HKD 100 million, as at end of year)

项　目	Item	1999	2000	2001	2002	2003
法定纸币及硬币的流通量	Legal Tender Notes and Coins in Circulation					
由商业银行发行	Commercial Bank Issues	1181.95	992.65	1075.45	1184.75	1342.15
由政府发行	Government Issues	60.29	61.70	59.43	61.43	65.50
总计	Total	1242.24	1054.35	1134.88	1246.18	1407.65
由认可机构持有的法定纸币及硬币	Authorized Institutions' Holdings of Legal Tender Notes and Coins	247.05	136.74	118.61	113.84	128.98
由公众持有的法定纸币及硬币	Legal Tender Notes and Coins in Hands of Public	995.19	917.61	1016.27	1132.34	1278.67
货币供应量：就外币掉期存款作出调整	Money Supply: Adjusted for Foreign Currency Swap Deposits					
货币供应量 M1	Money Supply M1					
港元	Hong Kong Dollar	2053.39	2039.66	2299.98	2594.11	3547.52
外币	Foreign Currency	198.18	398.81	282.15	362.39	586.71
总计	Total	2251.56	2438.47	2582.14	2956.50	4134.23
货币供应量 M2	Money Supply M2					
港元①	Hong Kong Dollar①	19234.81	19879.63	19987.74	19840.49	21072.69
外币②	Foreign Currency②	14627.14	16615.29	15512.86	15342.77	17061.73
总计	Total	33861.96	36494.92	35500.60	35183.26	38134.42
货币供应量 M3	Money Supply M3					
港元①	Hong Kong Dollar①	19354.71	20023.58	20166.35	20042.25	21228.61
外币②	Foreign Currency②	14989.95	16903.94	15774.95	15576.27	17351.83
总计	Total	34344.67	36927.53	35941.30	35618.52	38580.44
货币供应量：未就外币掉期存款作出调整	Money Supply: Unadjusted for Foreign Currency Swap Deposits					
货币供应量 M2	Money Supply M2					
港元	Hong Kong Dollar	18951.40	19836.37	19961.38	19821.42	21058.60
外币	Foreign Currency	14910.56	16658.56	15539.23	15361.84	17075.82
总计	Total	33861.96	36494.92	35500.60	35183.26	38134.42
货币供应量 M3	Money Supply M3					
港元	Hong Kong Dollar	19071.30	19980.32	20139.98	20023.18	21214.52
外币	Foreign Currency	15273.37	16947.21	15801.32	15595.34	17365.92
总计	Total	34344.67	36927.53	35941.30	35618.52	38580.44

注：《中华人民共和国香港特别行政区基本法》说明,港元是香港特别行政区的法定货币。外币指港元以外的其他货币,因而人民币亦视作外币。

①所列数字已包括外币掉期存款。

②所列数字已扣除外币掉期存款。

Notes: Hong Kong dollar is the legal tender in the Hong Kong Special Administrative Region, as stated in "The Basic Law of the Hong Kong Special Administrative Region of the People's Republic of China". Foreign currency refers to any currency other than the Hong Kong currency. Accordingly Chinese Renminbi is also treated as foreign currency.

①Figures are adjusted to include foreign currency swap deposits.

②Figures are adjusted to exclude foreign currency swap deposits.

24-43 股票价格指数、证券交易成交额及市场总值

Index of Share Prices, Value of Stock Exchange Turnover and Market Capitalisation

项　目	Item	1999	2000	2001	2002	2003
主板	**Main Board**					
股票价格指数	Index of Share Prices					
恒生指数(1964年7月31日=100)	Hang Seng Index (31.7.1964=100)					
最高	High	16962.1	18301.7	16164.0	11974.6	12594.4
最低	Low	9076.3	13722.7	8934.2	8858.7	8409.0
收市	Closing	16962.1	15095.5	11397.2	9321.3	12575.9
分类指数(1964年7月31日=100)	Sectoral Sub-indices (31.7.1964=100)					
金融	Finance					
最高	High	22388.9	24131.8	24970.6	20852.0	26263.6
最低	Low	12982.6	16891.0	15030.9	17060.7	17316.4
收市	Closing	22388.9	24041.7	19497.7	18231.2	26263.6
公用	Utilities					
最高	High	19799.1	21704.5	22510.2	23666.8	25070.5
最低	Low	10771.8	16160.1	20022.9	20128.6	21611.2
收市	Closing	18999.3	21704.5	20498.9	21970.5	24878.8
地产	Properties					
最高	High	20273.0	20302.1	20096.0	16635.4	15525.5
最低	Low	11806.6	12289.7	10789.8	10264.4	8837.4
收市	Closing	19839.9	18362.4	15554.8	11103.9	14778.7
工商	Commerce and Industry					
最高	High	10753.0	13976.6	9102.6	5765.5	5342.9
最低	Low	4978.9	7906.8	4282.2	3817.6	3485.8
收市	Closing	10753.0	8151.7	5508.8	4044.0	5271.7
恒生综合指数系列①	Hang Seng Composite Index Series①					
(2000年1月3日=2 000)	(3.1.2000=2 000)					
恒生综合指数②	Hang Seng Composite Index②					
最高	High	-	-	1396.8	1444.0	1621.6
最低	Low	-	-	1166.4	1064.5	1031.3
收市	Closing	-	-	1346.2	1130.2	1621.6
恒生香港综合指数②	Hang Seng Hong Kong Composite Index②					
最高	High	-	-	1473.6	1530.3	1688.9
最低	Low	-	-	1214.8	1145.8	1126.9
收市	Closing	-	-	1420.5	1215.8	1688.9
恒生香港大型股指数②	Hang Seng HK LargeCap Index ②					
最高	High	-	-	1498.2	1516.4	1636.5
最低	Low	-	-	1229.0	1145.9	1115.1
收市	Closing	-	-	1442.5	1211.1	1636.5
恒生香港中型股指数②	Hang Seng HK MidCap Index②					
最高	High	-	-	1513.7	1739.8	2049.3
最低	Low	-	-	1261.1	1267.9	1273.8
收市	Closing	-	-	1461.5	1345.9	2024.9
恒生香港小型股指数②	Hang Seng HK SmallCap Index②					
最高	High	-	-	1082.2	1198.7	1573.0
最低	Low	-	-	909.4	842.9	918.2
收市	Closing	-	-	1025.0	956.9	1543.3
恒生中国内地综合指数②	Hang Seng Mainland Composite Index②					
最高	High	-	-	1271.3	1269.0	1503.3
最低	Low	-	-	1003.8	894.0	825.9
收市	Closing	-	-	1198.3	950.6	1503.3
恒生中国企业指数③	Hang Seng China Enterprises Index③					
最高	High	2778.6	2413.3	2562.6	2259.8	5020.2
最低	Low	1268.0	1396.2	1560.6	1754.2	2007.5
收市	Closing	1972.6	1624.1	1757.8	1990.4	5020.2
恒生香港中资企业指数③	Hang Seng China- Affiliated Corp. Index③					
最高	High	2079.0	2577.7	2095.1	1398.9	1455.3
最低	Low	1010.3	1492.7	1098.5	957.2	848.0
收市	Closing	1970.2	1641.2	1340.5	1011.1	1427.7

24-43 续表 1 continued

项　　目	Item	1999	2000	2001	2002	2003
恒生综合行业指数②	Hang Seng Composite Industry Indices②					
资源矿产业	Oil & Resources					
最高	High	-	-	1658.4	2173.8	3974.8
最低	Low	-	-	1476.2	1560.9	1978.4
收市	Closing	-	-	1549.6	1966.1	3974.8
工业制品业	Industrial Goods					
最高	High	-	-	1592.3	1991.0	2732.8
最低	Low	-	-	1177.4	1239.3	1409.4
收市	Closing	-	-	1462.3	1472.2	2732.8
消费品制造业	Consumer Goods					
最高	High	-	-	1274.4	1735.7	2444.7
最低	Low	-	-	1021.9	1232.0	1354.6
收市	Closing	-	-	1238.3	1353.6	2420.0
服务业	Services					
最高	High	-	-	968.7	957.4	900.4
最低	Low	-	-	743.0	631.3	559.6
收市	Closing	-	-	906.1	671.1	900.4
公用事业	Utilities					
最高	High	-	-	2332.4	2596.5	2932.3
最低	Low	-	-	2192.8	2203.1	2398.4
收市	Closing	-	-	2241.5	2418.2	2932.3
金融业	Financials					
最高	High	-	-	1862.0	1869.1	2359.3
最低	Low	-	-	1559.0	1518.2	1546.2
收市	Closing	-	-	1748.4	1628.0	2359.3
地产建筑业	Properties & Construction					
最高	High	-	-	1571.4	1630.5	1590.6
最低	Low	-	-	1192.3	1014.8	896.9
收市	Closing	-	-	1529.2	1100.0	1527.7
资讯科技业	Information Technology					
最高	High	-	-	1132.2	1214.9	1171.6
最低	Low	-	-	837.1	673.8	641.4
收市	Closing	-	-	1113.3	753.4	1124.3
综合企业	Conglomerates					
最高	High	-	-	1441.3	1479.9	1392.7
最低	Low	-	-	1110.4	949.1	919.4
收市	Closing	-	-	1417.4	1027.5	1362.3
恒生流通指数系列④	Hang Seng Freefloat Index Series④					
恒生流通综合指数④	Hang Seng Freefloat Composite Index④					
最高	High	-	-	-	1234.6	1701.2
最低	Low	-	-	-	1074.8	1055.4
收市	Closing	-	-	-	1145.7	1701.2
恒生香港流通指数④	Hang Seng Hong Kong Freefloat Index④					
最高	High	-	-	-	1230.7	1559.4
最低	Low	-	-	-	1071.5	1043.6
收市	Closing	-	-	-	1135.4	1554.3
恒生中国内地流通指数④	Hang Seng Mainland Freefloat Index④					
最高	High	-	-	-	1435.9	2658.7
最低	Low	-	-	-	1252.0	1300.1
收市	Closing	-	-	-	1379.2	2658.7
恒生流通50⑤	Hang Seng Freefloat 50⑤					
最高	High	-	-	-	-	1666.2
最低	Low	-	-	-	-	1053.3
收市	Closing	-	-	-	-	1666.2
恒生流通香港25⑤	Hang Seng Freefloat HK 25⑤					
最高	High	-	-	-	-	1512.2
最低	Low	-	-	-	-	1036.0
收市	Closing	-	-	-	-	1507.9
恒生流通中国内地25⑤	Hang Seng Freefloat Mainland 25⑤					
最高	High	-	-	-	-	3043.3
最低	Low	-	-	-	-	1485.6
收市	Closing	-	-	-	-	3043.3

项 目	Item	1999	2000	2001	2002	2003
标准普尔/香港交易所大型股⑥	S&P/HKEx LargeCap Index⑥					
(2003年2月28日=10 000)	(28.2.2003=10 000)					
最高	High	(7137.1)	(7825.6)	(6503.3)	(5263.1)	13645.2
最低	Low	(3806.9)	(5709.8)	(3866.0)	(3884.1)	9155.3
收市	Closing	(7134.8)	(6107.9)	(4885.6)	(4113.1)	13645.2
成交金额（亿港元)	Turnover (HKD 100 million)	19159.4	30475.7	19500.9	15990.8	25456.8
市价总值⑦(亿港元)	Market Capitalisation⑦(HKD 100 million)	47275.3	47951.5	38853.4	35591.0	54776.7
创业板⑧	**Growth Enterprise Market⑧**					
标准普尔/香港交易所创业板⑨	S&P/HKEx GEM Index⑨					
(2003年2月28日=1 000)	(28.2.2003=1 000)					
最高	High	-	(1021.7)	(324.7)	(217.4)	1252.8
最低	Low	-	(302.5)	(162.4)	(105.5)	901.4
收市	Closing	-	(309.4)	(199.4)	(110.4)	1186.1
成交金额（亿港元)	Turnover (HKD 100 million)	36.0	842.9	394.2	439.8	381.5
市价总值⑦(亿港元)	Market Capitalisation⑦(HKD 100 million)	72.4	672.9	609.6	522.2	701.8

注：所有最高和最低指数是根据期内每日收市指数所编制。

①于2001年10月3日推出。

②2001年的最高及最低指数指由2001年10月至12月期间的数字。

③在「恒生综合指数系列」推出后，指数的成份股已作出修订，而指数亦以2000年1月3日为基日。

④于2002年9月23日推出，2002年的最高及最低指数指由2002年9月23日至12月底期间的数字。

⑤于2003年1月20日推出，2003的最高及最低指数指由2003年1月20日至12月底期间的数字。

⑥于2003年3月3日推出。由2003年4月14日起取代所有普通股指数。括号内数字是指所有普通股指数(1986年4月2日=1 000)。

⑦年底数字。

⑧于1999年11月25日推出。

⑨于2003年3月3日推出。由2003年4月14日起取代创业板指数。括号内数字是指创业板指数(2000年3月17日=1 000)，该指数自2000年3月20日起开始编制。

Notes:All high and low indices are compiled based on the daily closing indices in the period.

①Launched on 3 October 2001.

②High and low indices for 2001 refer to the period from October to December 2001.

③Following the launch of the Hang Seng Composite Index Series, its constituents have been revised and the index has been re-based to 3 January 2000.

④Launched on 23 September 2002, high and low indices for 2002 refer to the period from 23 September to end December 2002.

⑤Launched on 20 January 2003, high and low indices for 2003 refer to the period from 20 January 2003 to end December 2003.

⑥Launched on 3 March 2003 and replaced the All Ordinaries Index with effect from 14 April 2003. Figures in brackets refer to the All Ordinaries Index (2.4.1986=1 000).

⑦Year-end figures.

⑧Launched on 25 November 1999.

⑨Launched on 3 March 2003 and replaced the Growth Enterprise Index with effect from 14 April 2003. Figures in brackets refer to the Growth Enterprise Index (17.3.2000=1 000), which has been compiled since 20 March 2000.

24-44 居民消费价格指数(1999年10月-2000年9月=100)

Consumer Price Indices (Oct. 1999 - Sep. 2000=100)

项　　目	Item	权　数 Weight	1999	2000	2001	2002	2003
综合消费价格指数	**Composite Consumer Price Index**						
总指数	**All Items**	**100.00**	**103.2**	**99.4**	**97.8**	**94.8**	**92.4**
食品	Food	26.67	101.9	99.7	98.9	96.8	95.4
外出用餐	Meals Bought away from Home	[16.39]	100.8	99.9	99.6	98.2	96.7
食品(不包括外出用餐)	Food, Excluding Meals Bought away from Home	[10.28]	103.8	99.4	97.7	94.7	93.1
住房①	Housing①	29.91	107.3	98.5	95.5	90.0	85.7
私人房屋租金	Private Housing Rent	[24.59]	108.8	98.2	95.3	89.2	83.5
公营房屋租金	Public Housing Rent	[2.07]	98.8	99.8	91.6	89.1	97.3
电力、煤气及水	Electricity, Gas and Water	2.98	97.3	100.7	98.7	91.9	93.1
烟酒	Alcoholic Drinks and Tobacco	0.94	101.1	100.1	103.4	105.9	106.0
服装、鞋	Clothing and Footwear	4.13	109.2	97.9	93.4	94.1	91.6
耐用物品	Durable Goods	6.24	103.7	98.7	91.7	85.9	80.4
杂项物品	Miscellaneous Goods	5.70	99.6	100.5	101.8	103.6	106.0
交通	Transport	9.01	99.4	100.3	100.7	100.1	99.6
杂项服务②	Miscellaneous Services②	14.42	100.2	99.9	100.4	98.1	95.0
教育服务	Educational Services	[3.67]	98.8	100.4	102.0	103.5	104.2
电话及其他通讯服务	Telephone and Other Communications Services	[3.27]	103.9	98.6	97.5	86.0	74.6
医疗服务	Medical Services	[1.71]	99.3	100.2	101.1	101.7	103.1
甲类消费价格指数	**Consumer Price Index (A)**						
总指数	**All Items**	**100.00**	**102.5**	**99.5**	**97.8**	**94.7**	**92.7**
食品	Food	31.88	102.0	99.7	98.6	96.4	94.9
外出用餐	Meals Bought away from Home	[17.94]	100.7	99.9	99.4	97.8	96.4
食品(不包括外出用餐)	Food, Excluding Meals Bought away from Home	[13.94]	103.8	99.4	97.6	94.7	93.0
住房①	Housing①	29.13	105.3	98.8	95.2	89.8	87.1
私人房屋租金	Private Housing Rent	[21.76]	107.8	98.4	95.5	89.0	83.7
公营房屋租金	Public Housing Rent	[5.08]	98.8	99.8	91.6	89.1	97.3
电力、煤气及水	Electricity, Gas and Water	3.99	97.0	100.7	98.0	90.0	91.2
烟酒	Alcoholic Drinks and Tobacco	1.50	101.0	100.1	103.7	106.2	106.3
服装、鞋	Clothing and Footwear	3.36	111.5	97.6	93.4	95.9	93.0
耐用物品	Durable Goods	4.96	103.3	98.7	91.9	86.4	80.9
杂项物品	Miscellaneous Goods	5.25	99.4	100.9	103.6	104.7	105.9
交通	Transport	8.23	99.6	100.2	100.7	100.1	99.1
杂项服务②	Miscellaneous Services②	11.70	99.7	99.7	100.3	97.0	93.4
教育服务	Educational Services	[3.35]	98.6	100.3	101.8	103.1	103.7
电话及其他通讯服务	Telephone and Other Communications Services	[3.94]	100.3	98.6	98.3	87.3	76.3
医疗服务	Medical Services	[1.27]	99.2	100.2	101.5	101.5	104.4
乙类消费价格指数	**Consumer Price Index (B)**						
总指数	**All Items**	**100.00**	**103.4**	**99.4**	**97.7**	**94.7**	**92.1**
食品	Food	25.94	101.8	99.7	98.8	96.7	95.1
外出用餐	Meals Bought away from Home	[17.20]	100.8	99.9	99.2	97.4	95.8
食品(不包括外出用餐)	Food, Excluding Meals Bought away from Home	[8.74]	103.8	99.4	97.8	95.3	93.6
住房①	Housing①	29.68	107.3	98.5	95.8	90.1	85.6
私人房屋租金	Private Housing Rent	[25.48]	108.5	98.3	95.5	89.2	83.8
公营房屋租金	Public Housing Rent	[1.03]	98.8	99.8	91.6	89.1	97.3
电力、煤气及水	Electricity, Gas and Water	2.81	97.3	100.7	99.0	92.4	93.7
烟酒	Alcoholic Drinks and Tobacco	0.86	101.3	100.1	103.5	106.0	106.1
服装、鞋	Clothing and Footwear	4.47	111.5	97.9	93.7	95.5	92.9
耐用物品	Durable Goods	6.93	103.9	98.5	91.0	85.1	79.5
杂项物品	Miscellaneous Goods	5.58	99.6	100.5	101.8	103.2	105.4
交通	Transport	9.05	99.6	100.3	100.6	100.1	99.6
杂项服务②	Miscellaneous Services②	14.68	100.3	99.9	100.4	98.1	95.2
教育服务	Educational Services	[3.82]	98.9	100.3	101.7	103.0	103.7
电话及其他通讯服务	Telephone and Other Communications Services	[3.36]	104.8	98.8	97.6	85.6	73.5
医疗服务	Medical Services	[1.74]	99.3	100.2	101.5	102.1	103.5

项　目	Item	权数 Weight	1999	2000	2001	2002	2003
丙类消费价格指数	**Consumer Price Index (C)**						
总指数	**All Items**	**100.00**	**103.9**	**99.3**	**97.8**	**95.1**	**92.3**
食品	Food	21.38	101.7	99.8	99.6	97.9	96.7
外出用餐	Meals Bought away from Home	[13.28]	100.8	99.9	100.7	100.4	99.2
食品(不包括外出用餐)	Food, Excluding Meals Bought away from Home	[8.10]	103.9	99.6	97.8	93.8	92.5
住房①	Housing①	31.22	108.9	98.2	95.5	90.2	84.4
私人房屋租金	Private Housing Rent	[26.67]	109.8	97.9	94.9	89.2	82.9
电力、煤气及水	Electricity, Gas and Water	2.02	97.7	100.6	99.9	94.9	96.3
烟酒	Alcoholic Drinks and Tobacco	0.39	101.3	100.2	101.8	104.1	104.7
服装、鞋	Clothing and Footwear	4.55	104.2	98.2	93.1	90.4	88.2
耐用物品	Durable Goods	6.73	103.7	98.8	92.4	86.7	81.2
杂项物品	Miscellaneous Goods	6.43	100.1	100.1	100.2	103.0	106.8
交通	Transport	9.94	98.7	100.5	100.7	99.8	100.2
杂项服务②	Miscellaneous Services②	17.34	100.3	100.1	100.3	98.9	96.0
教育服务	Educational Services	[3.81]	98.7	100.5	102.6	104.6	105.5
电话及其他通讯服务	Telephone and Other Communications Services	[2.32]	109.9	98.2	95.9	84.4	73.3
医疗服务	Medical Services	[2.19]	99.5	100.2	100.4	101.3	101.5

注：以上的权数是根据1999至2000年间进行的住户开支统计调查结果计算出来。

①除"私人房屋租金"及"公营房屋租金"外，"住房"类别还包括"管理费及其它住房杂费"和"保养住所工具及材料"。而丙类消费价格指数中的"住房"类别并不包括"公营房屋租金"。

②"杂项服务"包括"教育服务"、"电话及其它通讯服务"、"医疗服务"及其它杂项服务。

Notes: The weights are derived from the results of the 1999/2000 Household Expenditure Survey.

①Apart from "Private Housing Rent" and "Public Housing Rent", the "Housing" section also includes "Management Fee and Other Housing Charges" and "Tools and Materials for House Maintenance". For CPI(C), the "Housing" section does not include "Public Housing Rent".

②"Miscellaneous Services" section includes "Educational Services", "Telephone and Other Communications Services", "Medical Services" and other miscellaneous services.

24-45 按四分位开支组别及商品或服务类别划分的住户每月平均开支

Average Monthly Household Expenditure by Commodity/Service Section by Quartile Expenditure Group

商品或服务类别	Commodity/Service Section	四分位开支组别 Quartile Expenditure Group									
		总数 Overall		最低四分位 The Lowest 25%		第二四分位 The Second 25%		第三四分位 The Third 25%		最高四分位 The Highest 25%	
		绝对值 Value	百分比 (percent)	绝对值 Value	百分比 (percent)	绝对值 Value	百分比 (percent)	绝对值 Value	百分比 (percent)	绝对值 Value	百分比 (percent)
食品	Food	5612	25.7	2917	36.3	4650	31.5	5929	27.9	8953	20.8
住房	Housing	7009	32.2	2275	28.3	4539	30.7	6413	30.1	14813	34.4
电力、煤气及水	Electricity, Gas and Water	631	2.9	402	5.0	559	3.8	659	3.1	906	2.1
烟酒	Alcoholic Drinks & Tobacco	226	1.0	150	1.9	211	1.4	213	1.0	331	0.8
服装、鞋	Clothing & Footwear	958	4.4	211	2.6	538	3.6	933	4.4	2150	5.0
耐用物品	Durable Goods	988	4.5	226	2.8	553	3.7	1036	4.9	2136	5.0
杂项物品	Miscellaneous Goods	1053	4.8	397	4.9	715	4.8	1029	4.8	2073	4.8
交通	Transport	2009	9.2	598	7.4	1146	7.8	1869	8.8	4424	10.3
杂项服务	Miscellaneous Services	3310	15.2	851	10.6	1866	12.6	3194	15.0	7329	17.0
总数（港元）	**All Sections (HKD)**	**21797**	**100.0**	**8026**	**100.0**	**14778**	**100.0**	**21275**	**100.0**	**43114**	**100.0**
住户总数（户）	**Number of Households (household)**	**1624000**	**100.0**	**406000**	**25.0**	**406000**	**25.0**	**406000**	**25.0**	**406000**	**25.0**

注：从1999年10月至2000年9月进行的住户开支统计调查获取的结果。

Note: Results are obtained from the Household Expenditure Survey carried out from October 1999 to September 2000.

24-46 按年龄／教育程度／经济活动身分划分的2001年至2003年曾使用个人计算机的10岁及以上人士数目

Persons Aged 10 and Over Having Used Personal Computer by Age/ Educational Attainment/Economic Activity Status, 2001 - 2003

项目	Item	2001			2002			2003		
		人数 Number of persons	百分比 Percent	比率+ Rate+	人数 Number of persons	百分比 Percent	比率+ Rate+	人数 Number of Persons	百分比 Percent	比率+ Rate+
年龄组别	**Age Group**									
10-14	10–14	390200	12.9	90.8	414700	12.7	96.2	422200	12.2	96.3
15-24	15–24	806700	26.7	88.0	823200	25.2	92.3	833300	24.1	94.3
25-34	25–34	810900	26.9	73.6	830800	25.4	76.2	858600	24.8	79.6
35-44	35–44	705600	23.4	52.0	792300	24.2	58.4	856600	24.7	62.9
45-54	45–54	253300	8.4	26.2	317300	9.7	31.2	388500	11.2	36.1
55-64	55–64	44200	1.5	8.8	71300	2.2	13.8	87900	2.5	16.2
65岁及以上	65 and Over	8900	0.3	1.2	20800	0.6	2.8	17200	0.5	2.2
合计	**Overall**	**3020000**	**100.0**	**50.3**	**3270300**	**100.0**	**54.0**	**3464400**	**100.0**	**56.2**
教育程度	**Educational Attainment**									
未受教育／幼儿园／小学	No Schooling/ Kindergarten/Primary	268700	8.9	14.3	308900	9.4	17.0	314100	9.1	17.6
中学／预科	Secondary/Matriculation	1941500	64.3	60.0	2002700	61.2	62.6	2379400	68.7	67.4
专上教育	Tertiary	809800	26.8	91.1	958700	29.3	92.8	770900	22.3	91.6
合计	**Overall**	**3020000**	**100.0**	**50.3**	**3270300**	**100.0**	**54.0**	**3464400**	**100.0**	**56.2**
经济活动身分	**Economic Activity Status**									
从事经济活动	Economically Active	2027900	67.1	57.8	2173500	66.5	61.5	2328500	67.2	64.6
非从事经济活动	Economically Inactive	992100	32.9	39.7	1096800	33.5	43.5	1135900	32.8	44.4
学生	Students	807300	26.7	93.3	860900	26.3	97.5	883200	25.5	97.2
退休人士	Retired Persons	19000	0.6	2.6	35300	1.1	5.3	36700	1.1	4.5
料理家务者	Home-makers	129300	4.3	18.0	186200	5.7	21.1	200700	5.8	26.0
其他	Others	36600	1.2	20.3	14500	0.4	16.5	15300	0.4	22.8
合计	**Overall**	**3020000**	**100.0**	**50.3**	**3270300**	**100.0**	**54.0**	**3464400**	**100.0**	**56.2**

注：数字是来自 2001年4月至6月、2002年5月至7月及2003年5月至8月进行的一项有关信息科技的使用情况和普及程度的住户统计调查，并指在统计前12个月内曾使用个人计算机的10岁及以上人士数目。

+在个别年龄／教育程度／经济活动身分组别中占所有10岁及以上人士的百分比。以所有10至14岁的人士为例，根据2001年的住户统计调查所得，90.8% 在统计前12个月内曾使用个人计算机。

Notes: Figures are based on a Household Survey on Information Technology Usage and Penetration conducted during April to June in 2001, May to July in 2002 and May to August in 2003. They refer to the number of persons aged 10 and over who had used personal computer in the twelve months before enumeration.

\+ As a percentage of all persons aged 10 and over in the respective age/educational attainment/economic activity status groups. For example, among all persons aged 10 – 14, 90.8% had used personal computer in the twelve months before enumeration based on the Household Survey in 2001.

24-47 按年龄／教育程度／经济活动身分划分的2001年至2003年曾使用互联网服务的10岁及以上人士数目

Persons Aged 10 and Over Having Used Internet Service by Age/ Educational Attainment/Economic Activity Status, 2001 - 2003

项目	Item	2001 人数 Number of persons	2001 百分比 Percent	2001 比率+ Rate+	2002 人数 Number of persons	2002 百分比 Percent	2002 比率+ Rate+	2003 人数 Number of Persons	2003 百分比 Percent	2003 比率+ Rate+
年龄组别	**Age Group**									
10－14	10–14	341200	13.1	79.4	387500	13.3	89.9	401700	12.5	91.6
15－24	15–24	743000	28.6	81.1	795100	27.2	89.2	812300	25.3	91.9
25－34	25–34	717100	27.6	65.1	753900	25.8	69.1	810000	25.2	75.1
35－44	35–44	574000	22.1	42.3	659300	22.6	48.6	773400	24.1	56.8
45－54	45–54	189800	7.3	19.6	254300	8.7	25.0	327100	10.2	30.4
55－64	55–64	29800	1.1	6.0	54300	1.9	10.5	74600	2.3	13.8
65岁及以上	65 and Over	6200	0.2	0.8	14400	0.5	1.9	13700	0.4	1.8
合计	**Overall**	**2601300**	**100.0**	**43.3**	**2918800**	**100.0**	**48.2**	**3212800**	**100.0**	**52.2**
教育程度	**Educational Attainment**									
未受教育／幼儿园／小学	No Schooling/ Kindergarten /Primary	207400	8.0	11.1	263100	9.0	14.4	272200	8.5	15.2
中学／预科	Secondary/Matriculation	1621500	62.3	50.1	1736900	59.5	54.3	2192500	68.2	62.1
专上教育	Tertiary	772400	29.7	86.9	918800	31.5	89.0	748100	23.3	88.9
合计	**Overall**	**2601300**	**100.0**	**43.3**	**2918800**	**100.0**	**48.2**	**3212800**	**100.0**	**52.2**
经济活动身分	**Economic Activity Status**									
从事经济活动	Economically Active	1732800	66.6	49.4	1909700	65.4	54.1	2143800	66.7	59.5
非从事经济活动	Economically Inactive	868400	33.4	34.8	1009100	34.6	40.0	1069000	33.3	41.8
学生	Students	733300	28.2	84.7	824200	28.2	93.4	856200	26.7	94.2
退休人士	Retired Persons	13400	0.5	1.8	27500	0.9	4.1	31300	1.0	3.9
料理家务者	Home-makers	91500	3.5	12.7	144900	5.0	16.5	167800	5.2	21.7
其他	Others	30200	1.2	16.8	12400	0.4	14.2	13700	0.4	20.5
合计	**Overall**	**2601300**	**100.0**	**43.3**	**2918800**	**100.0**	**48.2**	**3212800**	**100.0**	**52.2**

注：数字是来自 2001年4月至6月、2002年5月至7月及2003年5月至8月进行的一项有关信息科技的使用情况和普及程度的住户统计调查，并指在统计前12个月内曾使用互联网服务的10岁及以上人士数目。

+在个别年龄／教育程度／经济活动身分组别中占所有10岁及以上人士的百分比。以所有10至14岁的人士为例，根据2001年的住户统计调查所得，79.4% 在统计前12个月内曾使用互联网服务。

Notes: Figures are based on a Household Survey on Information Technology Usage and Penetration conducted during April to June in 2001, May to July in 2002 and May to August in 2003. They refer to the number of persons aged 10 and over who had used Internet service in the twelve months before enumeration.

+ As a percentage of all persons aged 10 and over in the respective age/educational attainment/economic activity status groups. For example, among all persons aged 10 –14, 79.4% had used Internet service in the twelve months before enumeration based on the Household Survey in 2001.

24-48 按行业／就业人数类别划分的2001年至2003年使用个人计算机、连接互联网或有设立网页／网站的机构单位数目

Establishments Using Personal Computers, with Internet Connection or Web Pages/Web Sites by Industry Sector/Employment Size, 2001 - 2003

行业／就业人数	Industry Sector/Employment Size	年份 Year	机构单位数目 Number of Establishments	在机构单位中 Among Establishments		
				使用个人计算机的机构单位的百分比 % using PCs	连接互联网的机构单位的百分比 % with Internet Connection	有设立网页／网站的机构单位的百分比 % with Web Pages/Web Sites
行业类别	**Industry Sector**					
制造业、电力及煤气业	Manufacturing, Electricity and Gas	2001	19999	39.6	27.8	8.0
		2002	20402	40.7	31.2	7.0
		2003	17275	52.7	42.0	13.4
建筑业	Construction	2001	24976	45.8	27.7	3.1
		2002	22959	44.8	36.4	2.4
		2003	25147	55.6	37.9	9.1
批发贸易、零售贸易、进出口贸易、饮食及酒店业	Wholesale, Retail and Import/Export Trades, Restaurants and Hotels	2001	176597	49.5	37.2	11.8
		2002	171508	58.1	45.9	11.9
		2003	165855	54.6	49.4	14.4
运输、仓储及通讯业	Transport, Storage and Communications	2001	36253	29.2	21.0	3.4
		2002	36849	30.6	27.4	7.0
		2003	37220	31.5	26.5	6.6
金融、保险、地产及商用服务业	Financing, Insurance, Real Estate and Business Services	2001	47954	76.1	61.5	17.6
		2002	50784	77.7	66.1	18.6
		2003	48865	76.6	68.9	14.9
社区、社会及个人服务业	Community, Social and Personal Services	2001	29152	43.4	32.2	10.3
		2002	30781	41.4	33.7	15.7
		2003	34829	50.5	40.7	17.4
合计	Overall	2001	334932	49.7	37.2	10.7
		2002	333283	54.5	44.2	11.8
		2003	329191	54.8	47.5	13.5
就业人数类别	**Employment Size**					
大型	Large	2001	5635	93.4	86.0	57.2
		2002	6063	94.6	82.6	61.0
		2003	5836	94.2	85.1	62.4
中型	Medium	2001	32507	79.2	64.2	29.1
		2002	38300	76.6	66.1	31.6
		2003	35125	87.7	78.2	31.7
小型	Small	2001	296790	45.7	33.3	7.8
		2002	288921	50.7	40.5	8.1
		2003	288231	50.0	43.0	10.2
合计	Overall	2001	334932	49.7	37.2	10.7
		2002	333283	54.5	44.2	11.8
		2003	329191	54.8	47.5	13.5

注：数字是来自2001年4月至6月、2002年4月至6月及 2003年5月至8月进行的一项有关信息科技在工商业的使用情况和普及程度的按年统计调查。

Note: Figures are based on the Annual Survey on Information Technology Usage and Penetration in the Business Sector conducted during April to June in 2001, April to June in 2002 and May to August in 2003.

24-49 按行业／就业人数类别划分的2001年至2003年有通过电子途径预订或购买、获取、售卖或递送货物、服务或资料划分的机构单位数目

Establishments Having Ordered or Purchased, Received, Sold or Delivered Goods, Services or Information through Electronic Means by Industry Sector/Employment Size, 2001 - 2003

行业／就业人数	Industry Sector/Employment Size	年份 Year	机构单位数目 Number of Establishments	在机构单位中有通过电子途径进行以下不同层面的商业交易的机构单位数目百分比 Among establishments in column (a),% of establishments having performed the following types of business transactions through electronic means			
				预订或购买 Order or Purchase	获取 Receipt	售卖 Sale	递送 Delivery
行业类别	**Industry Sector**						
制造业、电力及煤气业	Manufacturing, Electricity and Gas	2001	19999	5.3	31.7	0.8	8.1
		2002	20402	6.1	34.3	1.8	7.4
		2003	17275	6.0	45.6	1.6	13.5
建筑业	Construction	2001	24976	3.8	31.9	…	4.0
		2002	22959	2.1	38.5	…	2.4
		2003	25147	9.8	38.4	…	9.1
批发贸易、零售贸易、进出口贸易、饮食及酒店业	Wholesale, Retail and Import/Export Trades, Restaurants and Hotels	2001	176597	5.0	40.1	0.9	13.0
		2002	171508	6.1	46.6	1.2	12.1
		2003	165855	8.7	53.6	1.2	14.4
运输、仓库及通讯业	Transport, Storage and Communications	2001	36253	4.4	24.7	0.6	6.9
		2002	36849	1.8	25.4	0.6	7.0
		2003	37220	4.3	35.1	0.5	6.6
金融、保险、地产及商用服务业	Financing, Insurance, Real Estate and Business Services	2001	47954	13.7	62.8	2.6	21.2
		2002	50784	15.5	67.9	4.3	18.6
		2003	48865	19.1	67.9	1.6	15.6
社区、社会及个人服务业	Community, Social and Personal Services	2001	29152	5.5	33.4	1.2	11.4
		2002	30781	9.2	35.4	0.1	17.5
		2003	34829	7.9	43.4	1.0	17.6
合计	Overall	2001	334932	6.2	40.0	1.1	12.4
		2002	333283	7.1	45.2	1.5	12.1
		2003	329191	9.6	51.0	1.1	13.6
就业人数类别	**Employment Size**						
大型	Large	2001	5635	26.2	85.1	8.5	62.6
		2002	6063	28.6	80.7	6.5	61.3
		2003	5836	27.9	84.7	8.5	62.6
中型	Medium	2001	32507	13.9	65.1	2.4	31.8
		2002	38300	12.0	67.6	1.9	31.8
		2003	35125	15.4	76.2	2.3	32.7
小型	Small	2001	296790	4.9	36.4	0.8	9.3
		2002	288921	6.0	41.4	1.3	8.4
		2003	288231	8.5	47.2	0.8	10.3
合计	Overall	2001	334932	6.2	40.0	1.1	12.4
		2002	333283	7.1	45.2	1.5	12.1
		2003	329191	9.6	51.0	1.1	13.6

注：数字是来自2001年4月至6月、2002年4月至6月及 2003年5月至8月进行的一项有关信息科技在工商业的使用情况和普及程度的按年统计调查。

Note: Figures are based on the Annual Survey on Information Technology Usage and Penetration in the Business Sector conducted during April to June in 2001, April to June in 2002 and May to August in 2003.

24-50 15岁及以上人口教育程度

Educational Attainment of Population Aged 15 and Above

项 目	Item	1999		2000		2001		2002		2003	
		人 数（万人）Number of Persons (10 000 persons)	百分比 (Percent)	人 数（万人）Number of Persons (10 000 persons)	百分比 (Percent)	人 数（万人）Number of Persons (10 000 persons)	百分比 (Percent)	人 数（万人）Number of Persons (10 000 persons)	百分比 (Percent)	人 数（万人）Number of Persons (10 000 persons)	百分比 (Percent)
总计	**Total**										
男	**Male**	**264.50**	**48.85**	**267.08**	**48.57**	**269.39**	**48.28**	**271.09**	**48.04**	**272.56**	**47.77**
女	**Female**	**276.97**	**51.15**	**282.78**	**51.43**	**288.53**	**51.72**	**293.19**	**51.96**	**298.05**	**52.23**
未受教育/幼儿园	No Schooling/Kindergarten										
男	Male	11.31	2.09	9.80	1.78	9.68	1.73	9.34	1.65	9.21	1.61
女	Female	34.28	6.33	31.95	5.81	31.22	5.60	29.90	5.30	30.41	5.33
小学	Primary										
男	Male	59.29	10.95	59.60	10.84	58.05	10.40	56.07	9.94	54.05	9.47
女	Female	61.32	11.33	62.41	11.35	62.63	11.23	62.46	11.07	62.30	10.92
初中	Lower Secondary										
男	Male	51.85	9.58	52.24	9.50	52.93	9.49	52.24	9.26	53.97	9.46
女	Female	37.51	6.93	39.42	7.17	41.08	7.36	42.63	7.56	44.07	7.72
高中	Upper Secondary										
男	Male	79.39	14.66	80.21	14.59	79.60	14.27	80.46	14.26	78.08	13.68
女	Female	87.16	16.10	88.56	16.11	88.76	15.91	88.92	15.76	87.74	15.38
预科	Matriculation										
男	Male	11.77	2.17	11.33	2.06	11.65	2.09	12.57	2.23	13.74	2.41
女	Female	11.91	2.20	12.51	2.28	13.73	2.46	14.09	2.50	16.59	2.91
专上教育	Tertiary										
非学位课程	Non-degree Courses										
男	Male	18.44	3.41	19.18	3.49	19.25	3.45	20.90	3.70	22.05	3.86
女	Female	19.06	3.52	19.92	3.62	19.91	3.57	21.73	3.85	22.18	3.89
学位课程	Degree Courses										
男	Male	32.45	5.99	34.72	6.31	38.23	6.85	39.51	7.00	41.45	7.26
女	Female	25.73	4.75	28.01	5.09	31.21	5.59	33.41	5.93	34.76	6.09

注：数字是指该年四季“综合住户统计调查”所得的数字的平均数。

Note: Figures are averages of the figures obtained from the General Household Survey for the four quarters of the year.

24-51 按教育及培训机构类别划分的学生人数

Student Enrolment by Type of Educational and Training Institution

单位：人 (person)

类别	Type	1999	2000	2001	2002	2003*
幼儿园	Kindergarten	171138	160921	156202	143725	136096
小学	Primary School					
日校	Day School	491851	493979	493075	483218	468792
夜校	Evening School	-	-	-	-	-
中学	Secondary School					
日校	Day School	453465	456693	456455	461289	467223
初中	Lower Secondary	235874	241616	246132	251556	251463
高中	Upper Secondary	159343	155518	150886	150705	157009
中六及中七	Secondary 6 and Secondary 7	58248	59559	59437	59028	58751
夜校	Evening School	11785	10017	8948	4637	3264
特殊教育学校	Special Education School					
日校	Day School	9687	9387	9511	9889	10177
特殊学校	Special School	9499	9181	9354	9648	10082
普通学校内的特殊班	Special Classes in Ordinary School	188	206	157	241	95
职业训练局①②	Vocational Training Council①②	58102	56705	58413	60038	59440
全日制	Full-time					
技工级课程③④	Craft Level Courses③④	3975	4124	3918	4226	4723
技术员级课程⑤	Technician Level Courses⑤	8538	13530	15112	15049	13352
高级技术员／技术员级课程⑥	Higher Technician/Technician Level Course⑥	6298	420	364	373	363
高级技术员级课程⑤	Higher Technician Level Courses⑤	3803	7074	8741	11356	14240
兼读制	Part-time					
技工级课程③	Craft Level Courses③	10941	8835	8073	6030	5079
技术员级课程⑤	Technician Level Courses⑤	14471	12941	10978	10623	10755
高级技术员级课程⑤	Higher Technician Level Courses⑤	10076	9781	11227	12381	10928
认可专上学院	Approved Post-secondary Colleges					
全日制	Full-time	2361	2707	4180	4011	4043
其他学院	Other Colleges					
日间课程	Day Course	3620	4193	2284	1988	1960
夜间课程	Evening Course	953	1065	979	1049	976
教资会资助院校⑦	UGC-funded Institution⑦	79917	78295	81664	85602	90355
全日制	Full-time					
副学位课程⑧	Sub-degree⑧	10887	10284	13830	16668	20034
学士学位课程	Undergraduate	44031	44241	44796	45669	46602
研究院修课课程	Taught Postgraduate	1480	1593	1925	2446	2574
研究院研究课程	Research Postgraduate	3363	3290	3647	3841	4623*
兼读制	Part-time					
副学位课程	Sub-degree	6192	5188	4537	4372	4293
学士学位课程	Undergraduate	3436	3365	3258	3501	3527
研究院修课课程	Taught Postgraduate	9870	9662	9034	8501	8100
研究院研究课程	Research Postgraduate	658	672	637	604	602*
香港演艺学院	The Hong Kong Academy for Performing Arts					
全日制	Full-time	704	712	738	743	749
非学位程度⑨	Non-degree ⑨	433	438	452	446	450
学位程度	Degree	271	274	286	297	299
香港公开大学②⑩	The Open University of Hong Kong ②⑩	38879	46889	49626	47465	40782
全日制	Full-time	-	-	116	113	249
兼读制	Part-time	38879	46889	49510	47352	40533
建造业训练局	Construction Industry Training Authority					
全日制	Full-time	2336	2169	1859	1456	1440
技工级课程③(11)	Craft Level Courses ③(11)	1984	1823	1558	1115	1220
技术员级课程⑤(12)	Technician Level Courses ⑤(12)	352	346	301	341	220
制衣业训练局	Clothing Industry Training Authority	687	525	486	615	853
全日制	Full-time					
技工级课程③	Craft Level Courses ③	55	31	37	47	46
技术员级课程⑤	Technician Level Courses ⑤	398	354	359	441	561
兼读制	Part-time					
技工级课程③	Craft Level Courses ③	234	140	90	127	246

24-51 续表 continued

单位: 人 (person)

类 别	Type	1999	2000	2001	2002	2003^
医院管理局(13)	Hospital Authority (13)					
全日制	Full-time	-	-	-	108	109
毅进计划(14)	Project Yi Jin (14)	-	3267	4293	4170	4529
全日制	Full-time	-	3267	2085	2804	2880
兼读制	Part-time	-	-	2208	1366	1649
提供成人教育/补习/职业课程的院校②	Institutes Offering Adult Education /Tutorial/Vocational Courses②					
日间课程	Day Courses	64293	75241	88251	110916	94552
夜间课程	Evening Courses	77909	100259	94466	99176	106521

注: 数字只包括就读为期一年或以上长期课程的全日制及兼读制的学生人数。「提供成人教育/补习/职业课程的院校」的数字则包括长短期课程。

表内列载有关幼儿园、小学、中学及特殊教育学校的数字是截至该年9月为止。「提供成人教育/补习/职业课程的院校」的数字，是截至该年10月为止。至于有关职业训练及专上教育，学年开始和完结月份则会因应各教育及培训机构而有所不同。

①数字指香港专业教育学院、训练及培训发展中心及专业进修中心的学生人数。另外，职业训练局工商资讯学院于2001年9月开始收生。数字亦包括就读于该学院所开办的自资全日制专上课程的学生人数。

②数字不包括就读毅进计划课程的学生人数。

③技工级课程为中三以上程度课程。

④数字亦包括训练及培训发展中心的操作工级课程。

⑤高级技术员及技术员级课程为中五以上程度课程，而高级技术员级课程为较高程度课程。

⑥高级技术员/技术员级课程为中五以上程度课程，首年须修读共同科目。

⑦2001年前的数字只包括教资会资助课程的学生人数。1996年及以后的数字包括香港教育学院。该学院自1996年7月1日起成为大学教育资助委员会资助院校。

⑧自2001年起，数字亦包括就读自资全日制经评审专上课程的学生人数。

⑨数字包括证书、深造证书、专业证书、文凭、深造文凭及专业文凭课程的学生人数。

⑩香港公开进修学院于1989年6月成立。并于1997年5月30日正名为香港公开大学。数字亦包括李嘉诚专业进修学院（前身为持续及社区教育中心）的学生人数。

(11)数字是指基本工艺课程的学生人数。

(12)数字是指建造业管工/技术员训练课程的学生人数。

(13)数字指护士训练课程，并从2002年起开始提供。

(14)毅进计划于2000年10月推出。

^ 临时数字。

* 自2003年起，数字亦包括在教资会学生人数指标外但受教资会资助的研究院研究课程的学生人数。

Notes: Figures cover both full-time and part-time students attending long programmes lasting for at least one academic year, except for "institutes offering adult education/tutorial/vocational courses" where long and short programmes are included.

Figures for kindergarten, primary, secondary and special education school are as at September of the year. Figures for "institutes offering adult education/tutorial/vocational courses" are as at October of the year. For vocational and post-secondary education, beginning and ending months of academic year vary among educational and training institutions.

①Figures refer to students of the Hong Kong Institute of Vocational Education, Training and Development Centres, and Continuing Professional Development Centre. Students attending full-time self-financing post-secondary programmes run by the Vocational Training Council School of Business and Information Systems are also included since the school started to admit students in September 2001.

②Figures do not include students attending programmes of the Project Yi Jin.

③Craft level courses are post-secondary 3 courses.

④Figures also include operative level courses of Training and Development Centres.

⑤Higher technician and technician level courses are post-secondary 5 courses but higher technician level courses are more advanced courses.

⑥Higher technician/technician level courses are post-secondary 5 courses with common first year curricula.

⑦Figures before 2001 refer to students of UGC-funded programmes only. Figures from 1996 onwards include those for the Hong Kong Institute of Education, which came under the aegis of the University Grants Committee (UGC) with effect from 1 July 1996.

⑧Starting from 2001, figures also include students attending full-time accredited self-financing post-secondary programmes.

⑨Figures include students in certificate, advanced certificate, professional certificate, diploma, advanced diploma and professional diploma courses.

⑩The Open Learning Institute of Hong Kong was established in June 1989. It was retitled The Open University of Hong Kong on 30 May 1997. Figures for Li Ka Shing Institute of Professional and Continuing Education (formerly the Centre for Continuing and Community Education) are also included.

(11)Figures refer to students of basic craft courses.

(12)Figures refer to students of construction supervisor/technician trainee training courses.

(13)Figures refer to nurse training programmes and are available only since 2002.

(14)Project Yi Jin was launched in October 2000.

^ Provisional figure.

* Starting from 2003, figures also include research postgraduate students counted outside the UGC student number target but wholly funded by UGC.

24-52 医疗卫生条件
Conditions of Public Health

项目	Item	1998	1999	2000	2001	2002	2003
注册医护人员① (人)	Number of Registered Medical Personnel①(person)						
医生	Doctors	9527	9818	10130	10412	10731	11016
牙医	Dentists	1724	1779	1826	1855	1907	1848*
药剂师	Pharmacists	1212	1273	1315	1362	1414	1457
护士	Nurses	39250	38960	40388	42032	43383	43782
按每千名人口计算的医生数	Doctors Per Thousand Population	1.4	1.5	1.5	1.5	1.6^	1.6^
医疗机构和病床	Number of Medical Institutions and Hospital Beds						
医疗机构 (个)	Medical Institutions (number)	102	105	102	99	98	97
病床 (张)	Hospital Beds (bed)	32836	34286	35100	34852	35159	35566
按每千名人口计算的病床数	Beds Per Thousand Population	5.0	5.2	5.2	5.2	5.2^	5.2^

注：年底的数字。

①注册医护人员的统计资料取自不同的资料来源。医务委员会提供医生的资料，牙医管理委员会提供牙医的资料，护士管理局提供护士的资料,及药剂业及毒药管理局提供药剂师的资料。医生、牙医及药剂师需要每年重新申请执业证书。医生／牙医的数字包括本地及海外名册的正式注册医生／牙医。护士的数字包括注册护士及登记护士。

^ 临时数字。

* 在2003年，有关当局根据香港法例第156章《牙医注册条例》第15(3)条把154名注册牙医的姓名从名册中除去。计及2003年新增的95名注册牙医后，该年注册牙医的净删减人数为59名。

Notes: Figures are as at end of the year.

①Statistics on the registered medical personnel are maintained by the Medical Council for doctors, Dental Council for dentists, Nursing Council for nurses and Pharmacy and Poisons Board for pharmacists. Annual renewal of practising certificate is required for doctors, dentists and pharmacists. Figures for doctors/dentists refer to the doctors/dentists with full registration on both the local and overseas lists. Figures for nurses refer to both registered nurses and enrolled nurses.

^ Provisional figure.

* In accordance with Section 15(3) of the Dentists Registered Ordinance, Cap. 156 Laws of Hong Kong, 154 names of registered dentists were removed from the register in 2003. Offsetting by 95 new dentists registered in 2003, there was a net decrease of 59 dentists in that year.

24-53 社会保障
Social Security

社会保障计划	Social Security Scheme	1998/1999	1999/2000	2000/2001	2001/2002	2002/2003	2003/2004
综合社会保障援助	Comprehensive Social Security Assistance						
处理中的个案数目①(个)	Number of Active Cases① (case)						
年老	Old Age	124304	133070	135409	139288	143585	147433
失明	Blind	550	283	295	294	313	325
听觉受损	Deaf	210	215	253	278	312	352
肢体残疾	Physically Disabled	4313	2836	3485	3948	4359	4600
精神病患	Mentally Ill	9668	8380	8584	9208	9992	10665
健康欠佳	Temporary Disability/Ill Health	25041	19979	18917	20082	20852	22251
单亲家庭	Single Parent Family	25613	25146	26078	29534	34249	37949
低收入	Low Earnings	7562	8002	8319	9140	10982	14215
失业	Unemployment	31942	26185	23250	31602	43237	48450
其他	Others	3616	3919	3673	3818	4012	4465
总计	Total	232819	228015	228263	247192	271893	290705
发放款项(亿港元)	Amount (HKD 100 million)	130.29	136.23	135.60+	144.05‡	161.31~	173.06
公共福利金	Social Security Allowance						
处理中的个案数目①(个)	Number of Active Cases① (case)						
伤残津贴	Disability Allowance	81741	89617	96851	103167	105282	107110
高龄津贴	Old Age Allowance	445001	445835	453734	458041	454933	456798
总计	Total	526742	535452	550585	561208	560215	563908
发放款项（亿港元）	Amount (HKD 100 million)	47.37	48.83	51.30+	52.41‡	52.81~	52.14
暴力及执法伤亡赔偿	Criminal and Law Enforcement Injuries Compensation						
获批个案数目(个)	Number of Cases Authorized for Payment (case)	557	447	427	399	455	387
交通意外伤亡援助	Traffic Accident Victims Assistance						
获批个案数目(个)	Number of Cases Authorized for Payment (case)	5809	5797	5998	6733	7102	7190
紧急救济	Emergency Relief						
受助灾民人数（人）	Number of Victims Assisted (person)	1097	2643	868	1119	278	93

注：①于财政年度终结时的数字。财政年度是由4月1日至3月31日。处理中的个案包括新申请个案，正在复查中的个案，正领取援助款项的个案和已停止领取援助款项等待复查的个案。

+包括2001年4月1日所发放的款项。

‡包括2002年4月1日所发放的款项，但不包括2001年4月1日所发放的款项。

~不包括2002年4月1日所发放的款项。

Notes: ①Figures are as at end of the financial year. Financial year is from 1 April to 31 March. Active cases refer to cases being handled which include new applications, cases being reviewed, cases being paid and cases suspended for payment pending review.

+Includes the payments for 1 April 2001.

‡Includes the payments for 1 April 2002 but excludes the payments for 1 April 2001.

~Excludes the payments for 1 April 2002.

《中国统计年鉴》与香港特别行政区统计刊物中使用的指标对照表

A Comparison of Common Statistical Terms Used in China Statistical Yearbook and Publications Compiled by the Census and Statistics Department, the Government of the Hong Kong Special Administrative Region

对应表号 Table Number	中国内地统计名词 Statistical Terms Used in China Statistical Yearbook	香港特别行政区统计名词及对应英文 Statistical Terms Used in Publications of the Hong Kong Special Administrative Region
1	实际工资指数	实质工资指数 Real wage index
1, 14	国民总收入	本地居民生产总值 Gross National Product(GNP)
1, 10, 11, 12, 14	国内(地区)生产总值	本地生产总值 Gross Domestic Product(GDP)
1, 10, 12	按当年价格计算	以当时市价计算 At current market prices
1, 11, 12, 14	按不变价格计算	以固定市价计算 At constant market prices
1, 13	支出法国内生产总值	按开支组成部分划分的本地生产总值 GDP by expenditure component
1	增加值	增加价值 Value added
1	批发贸易业	批发业 Wholesale
1	零售贸易业	零售业 Retail
8, 11, 12	建筑业	建造业 Construction
13	居民消费	私人消费开支 Private consumption expenditure
13	政府消费	政府消费开支 Government consumption expenditure
13	国内固定资本形成总额	本地固定资本形成总额 Gross domestic fixed capital formation
13	存货变动(存货增加)	存货增减 Changes in inventories
13	货物出口(离岸价)	货品出口(离岸价) Exports of Goods (f.o.b.)
13	货物进口(离岸价)	货品进口(离岸价) Imports of Goods (f.o.b.)
11, 12	生产法国内生产总值	生产法国内生产总值 GDP by economic activity
11, 12	生产及进口税	生产及入口税 Taxes on production and imports
11, 12	电力、煤气及水的生产和供应业	电力、燃气及水务业 Electricity, gas and water
17	水	食水 Water
17	电力消费量	用电量 Electricity consumption
17	煤气消费量	煤气用量 Gas consumption
28, 35	韩国	大韩民国 Republic of Korea
32, 33	百慕大	百慕达 Bermuda
31, 32, 34, 35	澳大利亚	澳洲 Australia
41	马来西亚林吉特	马来西亚元 Malaysian Ringgit
41	韩圆	南韩圆 Republic of Korea Won
41	菲律宾比索	菲律宾披索 Philippine Peso
44	居民消费价格指数	消费物价指数 Consumer Price Indices
44	外出用餐	外出用膳 Meals bought away from home
44, 45	服装、鞋	衣履 Clothing and footwear
44, 45	电力、煤气及水	电力、燃气及水 Electricity, gas and water
44, 45	住房	住屋 Housing
4	大气	空气 Air
44, 46	计算机	电脑 Computer
46, 47, 50, 51	幼儿园	幼稚园 Kindergarten

主要统计指标解释

粗出生率 是指某一年内的活产婴儿数目与年中人口的比率，一般按每千人口表示。

粗死亡率 是指某一年内的死亡人数与年中人口的比率，一般按每千人口表示。

出生时平均预期寿命 是指某年出生的男、女性，若其一生经历的死亡情况，正如该年的年龄性别死亡率所反映，他／她预期能活的年数。

年中人口 在1996年前是以“广义时点”方法编制，数字包括在统计时点身在香港的永久性居民、非永久性居民和旅客，亦包括暂时离港前往中国内地及澳门的香港永久性居民。自2000年8月起，“居住人口”方法已取代“广义时点”方法用以编制香港的人口数字。追溯至1996年的修订人口数字已经编制。利用“居住人口”方法所编制的人口估计，称“居港人口”。“居港人口”包括“常住居民”和“流动居民”。“常住居民”指两类人士：（一）在统计时点之前的6个月内，在港逗留最少3个月，又或在统计时点之后的6个月内，在港逗留最少3个月的香港永久性居民，不论在统计时点他们是否身在香港；及（二）在统计时点身在香港的香港非永久性居民。至于“流动居民”，是指在统计时点之前的6个月内，在港逗留最少一个月但少于3个月，又或在统计时点之后的6个月内，在港逗留最少1个月但少于3个月的香港永久性居民，不论在统计时点他们是否身在香港。根据新的编制方法，旅客并不包括在香港人口内。

总和生育率 是指某年的每一千名妇女，若他们在生育龄期（即15至49岁）的生育率依循该年的年龄别生育率，一生中活产子女的平均数目。

婴儿死亡率 是以一年内，年龄一岁以下死亡人数与同年出生的每千名活产婴儿的比率。

劳动人口 是指15岁及以上陆上非住院人口，并符合就业人口或失业人口定义的人士。

劳动人口参与率 是指劳动人口占所有15岁及以上陆上非住院人口的比例。

就业人口 包括在统计前7天内有做工赚取薪酬或利润或有一份正式工作的15岁及以上人士。无酬家庭从业员及在统计前7天内正休假的就业人士亦包括在内。

失业人口 包括所有在统计前7天内并无职位，且并无为赚取薪酬或利润而工作及随时可工作，而在统计前30天内有找寻工作的15岁及以上人士。失业人口亦包括那些并无职位，有找寻工作，但由于暂时生病而不能工作的人士；及并无职位，且随时可工作，但由于下列原因而没有找寻工作的人士：（I）已为于稍后时间担当的新工作或开展的业务作出安排；或（II）正期待返回原来的工作岗位；或（III）相信没有工作可做（第III类为“因灰心而不求职的人士”）。

失业率 是指失业人士在劳动人口中所占的比例。

就业不足人口 包括在统计前7天内在非自愿情况下工作少于35小时，而在统计前30天内有找寻更多工作，或即使不是找寻工作，但在统计前7天内可担任更多工作的就业人士。根据此定义，因工作量不足而在统计前7天内放取无薪假期的就业人士，若在该7天期间内工作少于35小时，甚或全段期间都在休假，亦会界定为就业不足人士。

就业不足率 是指就业不足人士在劳动人口中所占的比例。

实际工资指数 是从名义工资指数中，按甲类消费价格指数的变幅，扣除通胀的影响而得出，显示督导级及以下雇员所赚取工资金额购买力的转变。

每月就业收入 是指上月从所有工作所获得的收入。就雇员来说，收入包括工资和薪金、花红、佣金、房屋津贴、逾时工作津贴及勤工津贴，但不包括补薪。就雇主和自营作业人士而言，收入是指从自己拥有的企业提取作个人及家居用途的款额。如果提取作个人及家居用途的款额资料未能提供，则将会搜集有关从业务所得的净收入数据。

本地生产总值 是指一个地区的所有常住生产单位，在一个指定的期间内，未扣除固定资本消耗的生产总值。

人均本地生产总值是指该地区在某统计年的本地生产总值除以该地区在该年的人口总数而得的数字。

本地居民生产总值 是指一个地区的居民从事各项经济活动而赚取的收益，不论该经济活动是否在该地区的经济领域内进行。换言之，编制本地居民生产总值应包括本地居民在经济领域内或领域以外从事各类经济活动的收益，而扣除非本地居民在经济领域内从事经济活动的收益。

计算本地居民生产总值，可用以下方程式：

本地居民生产总值=本地生产总值+本地居民从经济领域外所赚取的要素收益-非本地居民从经济领域内所赚取的要素收益

人均本地居民生产总值是指该地区在某统计年的本地居民生产总值除以该年的人口总数而得的数字。

要素收益组成部分主要分为投资收益及雇员报酬，而投资收益包括了直接投资收益、有价证券投资收益及其它投资收益。

以下指标（“国际收支平衡表”至“储备资产”）适用于国际收支平衡表（表24-15）：

国际收支平衡表 是有系统地载录，在指定期间内，某经济体系与世界各地的各类经济交易的统计表。完整的国际收支平衡表包括以下两个主要核算帐：（甲）经常帐；（乙）资本及金融帐。

经常帐 是主要量度实际资源的流动，包括货物的进出口、服务的进口及出口、从外地应收及应付予外地的收益，以及从外地及往外地的经常转移。

货物 包括所有可移动的货物，其拥有权由本地居民转至非本地居民（出口）及由非本地居民转至本地居民（进口）。

服务 包括由本地居民向非本地居民（出口）和由非本地居民向本地居民（进口）所提供的服务。

收益 是提供生产要素而赚取的所得，包括本地居民从非本地居民（应收收益）或非本地居民从本地居民（应付收益）所赚取的所得。

经常转移 是指一个经济体系，在无同等经济价值回报的情况下，对其它经济体系所提供的实际或金融资源，而且该资源在转移后会被立刻或于短时间内消耗。

资本帐 是用来量度资本转移及非生产／非金融资产的对外交易。

资本转移 是指在无报偿下，固定资产的转移或债务的减免。

金融帐 记录本地居民与非本地居民之间的金融资产及负债交易。它显示某经济体系如何融资以进行其对外交易。金融帐内的交易可归类为直接投资、有价证券投资、金融衍生工具、其它投资及储备资产。

直接投资 是指一个经济体系内的某投资者购买设立在另一经济体系内的企业，兼且对该企业有持久利益和在管理方面具有效的控制权。

有价证券投资 是指对非居民的股本证券及债务证券（例如中长期债券、货币市场工具）所作的投资，而投资者对投资于该企业并无持久的利益或在管理方面具影响力。

金融衍生工具 是一种与某种特定的金融工具、指标或商品有联系的金融工具，使特定的金融风险本身能通过这种工具而进行交易（包括在交易所内及场外）。

其它投资 是指不属于直接投资、有价证券投资、金融衍生工具或储备资产，而对非居民的其它金融申索及负债。

储备资产 是指一个经济体系的金融当局（在香港是指香港金融管理局）可直接用来支付对外收支赤字，且可用于干预外汇市场以影响汇率从而间接调节该赤字的外币资产。

国际投资头寸 是在一特定时点上一个经济体系的对外金融资产及负债存量的资产负债表。对外金融资产涵盖对非居民的申索。另一方面，某经济体系的对外金融负债是指非居民向这经济体系的居民的金融申索。

国际投资头寸净值 是对外金融资产总值与对外金融负债总值之差。国际投资头寸的分类与国际收支平衡表内的金融帐完全一致，资产及负债分为直接投资、有价证券投资、金融衍生工具和其它投资。国际投资头寸的资产项目亦包括储备资产在内。有关投资组成部分的详细解释请参阅国际收支平衡表内金融帐组成部分的解释。

工业生产指数 量度本地制造业生产量的实际变动，即撇除价格调整因素后的本地生产量变动。

楼宇转让契约 是指订明不可分割业权（即楼宇单位）转让的文件。

获批准可动工兴建楼宇 是指获屋宇署签发《同意书》动工兴建的楼宇。这种《同意书》是发给私人发展计划（包括香港房屋协会的计划）及香港房屋委员会的私人机构参建居屋计划，但建于新界区小型屋宇则毋须获取这种《同意书》。

实用楼面面积 指各层楼面面积总和，但不包括楼梯、公共通道空间、升降机（指电梯，下同）等候处、盥洗室、厕所、厨房、及为楼宇提供升降机、空调系统、或类似设施而安装的机械所占用的空间。

居处租住权 是指居所被家庭住户占用的条款和情况。所包括的各项定义如下:

自置居所住户 是指住户拥有其居住的屋宇单位业权。

全租户 是指住户向居于别处的人士租住整个屋宇单位自住，没有分租，单位内也没有其它的住户。

合租户 是指两个或以上的住户，分别向居于别处的人士租用部分单位居住。

二房东 是指住户向居于别处的人士租住整个屋宇单位，并把部分单位分租予其它住户。

三房客 是指住户向居于同一屋宇单位内的人士租用部分单位居住。

免租 是指住户免费在屋宇单位内居住，不论是否获得业主同意，但不包括本身是业主或由雇主提供居所的住户。

居所由雇主提供 是指住户居住在由其成员之一的雇主提供的居所，包括以象征式租金向雇主租住屋宇单位的住户。假如住户使用由雇主提供的房屋津贴租住居所，则租住权不属于“居所由雇主提供”类别。

进出香港的客运火车 是指由九广铁路公司经营来往香港与中国内地的直通火车服务。

进出香港的车辆 是指经落马洲、文锦渡及沙头角出入境管制站往返中国内地的陆路交通。

车辆牌照 给予车辆在道路上行驶的权利，有效期分为4个月及一年两种。领牌车辆总数指年底的数字。

港产品出口货物 是指香港的天然产品或在香港经过制造工序，以致其基本原料的形状、性质、式样或用途受到永久改变的产品。其货值是以离岸价值计算。

转口货物 是指输出曾经自外地输入香港的货物，而这些货物并没有在香港经过任何制造工序，以致永久改变其形状、性质、式样或用途。其货值是以离岸价值计算。

进口货物 是指在香港以外出产或制成的货物，输入香港供本地使用或转口，以及再进口的香港产品。其货值是以到岸价值计算。

输往中国内地作外发加工用途的出口货物 是指那些从香港或经香港出口往中国内地加工的原料或半制成品，经加工后成为制成品，并以合约安排再进口香港。

从中国内地进口与外发中国内地加工有关的货物 是指那些加工后进口香港的货物，其中全部或部分原料或半制成品是以合约安排从香港或经香港出口往中国内地加工。

原产地为中国内地而涉及外发中国内地加工、并经香港输往其它地方的转口货物 是指那些经香港转口的制成品，其中全部或部分原料或半制成品是以合约安排从香港或经香港出口往中国内地加工，而加工后的货物再进口香港。

以下项目（“直接投资”至“直接投资流动”）适用于直接投资（表24-32，24-33）:

直接投资 是指一个经济体系的投资者在另一经济体系的企业所作的投资，而该等投资令该投资者能长期有效地影响有关企业的管理经营决定。在统计上，若投资者持有某一企业10%或以上的股权，便被视为能长期有效地影响有关企业的管理经营决定。直接投资包括股本资本、再投资收益及其它资本。股本资本包括所持有分行的股本，附属及联营公司的股票。再投资收益是指投资者从其附属或联营公司应得但未以股息形式分发的利润。其它资本主要涉及公司之间长期或短期的债务交易，包括母公司与其附属公司、联营公司及分行之间的借贷。

外来直接投资 是指境外居民在香港的企业所作的直接投资。跨国企业在香港经营的分行或附属公司，是外来直接投资的典型例子。

向外直接投资 是指香港居民投资者在境外的企业所作的直接投资。

直接投资头寸 是指某一特定日子香港居民在境外投资的价值或接受外来投资的价值。

直接投资流动 是指某一时段内香港居民于境外的投资或接受境外的投资的投入或撤走。

地区总部 是指一个办事处有权控制／管理区内（即香港及一个或多个地方）的办事处的运作／业务，而毋须经常请示其香港以外的母公司。

地区办事处 是指一个办事处有权协调／管理区内（即香港及一个或多个地方）的办事处／运作／业务，但须经常请示其地区总部或香港以外的母公司。

贷款基金 为香港特别行政区政府贷款计划，例如房屋贷款和学生贷款，提供资金。基金收入主要来自政府一般收入帐目转拨的款项、偿还的贷款及贷款利息。

港汇指数（EERI） 量度港元相对香港主要贸易伙伴货币汇率的加权平均值变动情况。

外币兑换率 指外币兑港元的电汇或现钞收市中间兑换价。

认可机构 包括持牌银行、有限制牌照银行及接受存款公司。

持牌银行 可接受任何金额及期限的存款。在1994年10月1日之前，任何金额的储蓄存款及期限少于15个月的定期存款，除了金额超过港币50万元外，其高利率不得超过香港银行公会所设的利率上限。自1994年10月1日起，《利率规则》开始逐步放宽。随着撤销利率限制的最后阶段在2001年7月3日生效，各类存款利率再无任何限制。

有限制牌照银行 可接受金额不少于港币50万元的任何期限的定期存款，而存款利率并无任何限制。

接受存款公司 可接受金额不少于港币10万元而期限不少于3个月的定期存款，而存款利率并无任何限制。

外币掉期存款 是指顾客在现货市场购买外币，然后存入认可机构，但同时订下远期合约，将该笔外币（本金加利息）在存款到期时售予认可机构。从分析角度来看，这类掉期存款应当作港元定期存款。

货币供应量M1 是指市民持有的法定纸币和硬币加上持牌银行的客户活期存款。

货币供应量M2 是指货币供应量M1所包括的项目，加上持牌银行的客户储蓄及定期存款，再加上持牌银行发行而由非认可机构持有的可转让存款证。

货币供应量M3 是指货币供应量M2所包括的各项，再加上有限制牌照银行及接受存款公司客户的存款，再加上以上两类认可机构发行而由非认可机构持有的可转让存款证。

恒生指数 于1969年11月24日推出，是香港股票市场的主要指标，用以反映股价的一般变动，以及股市的整体表现。

居民消费价格指数 居民消费价格指数在香港特别行政区刊物中称为"消费价格指数"。反映住户一般所购买的消费商品和服务价格水平变动情况。指数的变动反映购买一个固定篮子的消费品和服务的总值的变动。居民消费价格指数的按年变动率是一个重要指标，用以量度通胀对消费者的影响。按年变动率是指当期指数比较早一年同期指数的上升或下降的百分率。

香港特别行政区政府统计处编制不同的居民消费价格指数数列，以反映消费价格变动对不同开支范围的住户的影响。甲类、乙类及丙类消费价格指数分别根据较低、中等及较高开支范围的住户消费模式编制而成。而综合消费价格指数是根据整体住户开支模式而编制，反映消费价格转变对全体住户的影响。

居民消费价格指数的开支权数每五年更新一次，现时采用的权数是根据1999至2000年间进行的住户开支统计调查的结果计算出来的。

教育程度 是指某人在学校或其它教育机构修读达到的最高教育水平，不论他／她有否完成该课程。计算教育程度时，只包括正式课程，即须最少为期一个学年，入学须具指定学历资格（香港公开大学的非学位、副学位、学位及研究生课程除外），以及没有考试或指定评核成绩的程序。

幼儿园 包括所有幼儿园班级。

非学位课程 包括工业学院／科技学院（工业学院及科技学院于1999年已合并为香港专业教育学院）／理工学院（现已改制为大学）的所有高级文凭／增修证书院士课程、理工学院（现已改制为大学）及其它专上学院的院士衔和其它非学位课程。教育学院及工商师范学院的证书／文凭课程及护士训练课程亦包括在内。

学位课程 包括所有在香港及海外专上学院的学士学位课程及研究院课程。

社会保障计划 旨在帮助社会上需要经济或物质援助的人士，应付基本及特别需要。这个毋须供款的社会保障制度，包括综合社会保障援助计划、公共福利金计划、暴力及执法伤亡赔偿计划、交通意外伤亡援助计划和紧急救济。

综合社会保障援助计划 （1993年7月1日前为公共援助计划）是向有需要的个人或家庭提供经济援助，使他们的入息达到一定水平，以应付生活上的基本需要。申请人必须接受经济状况调查。

公共福利金计划 （1993年7月1日前为特别需要津贴计划）包括高龄津贴及伤残津贴。本计划的目的是为65岁或以上或严重残疾的香港居民每月提供现金津贴，以应付因年老或残疾而引致的特别需要。

暴力及执法伤亡赔偿计划 提供现金援助给暴力罪行或执法行动中受害的人士或其遗属。申请人毋需接受经济状况调查。

交通意外伤亡援助计划 为道路交通意外受害人或其遗属迅速提供经济援助。申请人毋需接受经济状况调查，亦不论交通意外是因何人的过失而引致。援助金只按当事人伤亡情况支付，但不包括补偿财物损失。

紧急救济 在香港遇有天灾或其它灾祸时（例如台风、水灾、山泥倾泻、火灾等）为灾民提供膳食（或现金购买膳食）及救济物品。

犯罪被捕人数 的计算方法是按罪犯被捕的次数而定，不论有否遭起诉。若某人在两宗或以上事件中被捕，会于每次事件中分别记录。若某人在一宗事件中因子项罪名被捕，则只选其中可被判最重刑罚的一项罪名作统计之用。

Explanatory Notes on Main Statistical Indicators

Crude birth rate refers to the number of live births occurred during a calendar year to the mid-year population of that year. It is usually expressed in terms of 1000 population.

Crude death rate refers to the number of deaths occurred during a calendar year to the mid-year population of that year. It is usually expressed in terms of 1000 population.

Expectation of life at birth refers to the average number of years of life that a male/female born in a given year can expect to live if he/she were subjected to the prevalent mortality conditions as reflected by the set of age sex specific mortality rates for that year.

Mid-year population before 1996 was compiled using the "extended de facto" approach. It includes Hong Kong Permanent and Non-permanent Residents and visitors who are in Hong Kong at the reference time-point. Hong Kong Permanent Residents temporarily away to the mainland of China and Macao are also included. Since August 2000, the "resident population" approach has been adopted in place of the "extended de facto" approach for compiling Hong Kong population figures. Revised population figures backdated to 1996 have been compiled. The population estimate compiled under the "resident population" approach is referred to as the "Hong Kong Resident Population". The "Hong Kong Resident Population" comprises "Usual Residents" and "Mobile Residents". "Usual Residents" refer to two categories of people : (1) Hong Kong Permanent Residents who have stayed in Hong Kong for at least three months during the six months before or for at least three months during the six months after the reference time-point, regardless of whether they are in Hong Kong or not at the reference time-point; and (2) Hong Kong Non-permanent Residents who are in Hong Kong at the reference time-point. As for "Mobile Residents", they are Hong Kong Permanent Residents who have stayed in Hong Kong for at least one month but less than three months during the six months before or for at least one month but less than three months during the six months after the reference time-point, regardless of whether they are in Hong Kong or not at the reference time-point. Under the new approach, visitors are not included in the Hong Kong Population.

Total fertility rate refers to the average number of children that would be born alive to 1000 women during their lifetime if they were to pass through their childbearing ages 15-49 experiencing the age specific fertility rates prevailing in a given year.

Infant mortality rate refers to the number of deaths aged under one occurred during a calendar year per 1000 live births in the same year.

Labour force refers to the land-based non-institutional population aged 15 and over who satisfy the criteria for inclusion in the employed population or the unemployed population.

Labour force participation rate refers to the proportion of labour force in the land-based non-institutional population aged 15 and over.

Employed population consists of those persons aged 15 and over who have been at work for pay or profit during the seven days before enumeration or have had formal job attachment. Unpaid family workers and employed persons who have been on leave/holiday during the seven days before enumeration are included.

Unemployed population comprises all those persons aged 15 and over who have not had a job, have not performed any work for pay or profit, have been available for work during the seven days before enumeration and have sought work during the thirty days before enumeration. It also includes persons without a job who have sought work but have not been available for work because of temporary sickness; and persons without a job who have been available for work but have not sought work because they (I) have made arrangements to take up a new job or to start business at a subsequent date; or (II) were expecting to return to their original jobs; or (III) believe that work is not available to them (persons in (III) refer to "discouraged workers").

Unemployment rate refers to the proportion of unemployed persons in the labour force.

Underemployed population comprises those employed persons who have involuntarily worked less than thirty-five hours during the seven days before enumeration and have sought additional work during the thirty days before enumeration, or have not sought but have been available for additional work during the seven days before enumeration. Following this definition, employed persons taking no-pay leave due to slack work during the seven days before enumeration are also classified as underemployed if they worked less than thirty-five hours or were on leave even for the whole period during the seven-day period.

Underemployment rate refers to the proportion of underemployed persons in the labour force.

Real wage index indicates changes in the purchasing power of the amount of money earned as wages by employees up to supervisory level and is obtained by deflating the nominal wage index by the Consumer Price Index(A).

Monthly employment earnings refer to earnings from all jobs during the last month. For employees, they include wage and salary, bonus, commission, housing allowance, overtime allowance and attendance allowance. However, back pays are excluded. For employers and self-employed, they refer to amounts drawn from the self-owned enterprise for personal and household use. If information on the amounts drawn for personal and household use is not available, data on net earnings from business would be collected instead.

Gross Domestic Product (GDP) is a measure of the total value of production of all resident producing units of a country or territory in a specified period, before deducting allowance for consumption of fixed capital.

Per capita GDP of a country or territory is obtained by dividing total GDP in a year by the population of that country or territory in the same year.

Gross National Product (GNP) refers to the total income of the residents of a country or region from engaging in various economic activities, irrespective of whether the economic activities are carried out in the economic territory of the country or region or not. In other words, the gross national product should include the income of the residents engaged in various economic activities within or outside the economic territory of the country or region, but exclude the income of non-residents engaged in economic activities in the economic territory of the country or region. The following formula is used in the calculation of the gross national product:

GNP = Gross Domestic Product
+Factor income earned by residents from outside the economic territory of the country or region
-Factor income earned by non-residents from within the economic territory of the country or region.

Per capita GNP of a country or a region refers to the gross national product of the country or region in a year divided by the total population in the same year.

The components of factor income are mainly classified into investment income and compensation of employees. Investment income includes direct investment income, portfolio investment income and other investment income.

The items "Balance of Payments accounts" until "Reserve assets" are applicable to balance of payments account (Table 24-15):

Balance of Payments (BOP) account is a statistical statement that systematically summarizes, for a specific time period, the economic transactions of an economy with the rest of the world. A complete BOP account comprises two broad accounts: (a) Current Account; (b) Capital and Financial Account.

Current account largely measures flow of real resources, including exports and imports of good and services, income receivable and payable abroad, and current transfers from and to abroad.

Goods comprise all movable goods that change ownership from residents to non-residents (exports) and from non-residents to residents (imports).

Services include services rendered by residents to non-residents (exports) and by non-residents to residents (imports).

Income consists of earnings by residents from non-residents (income receivable) and by non-residents from residents (income payable) for the provision of factors of production.

Current transfers are those transactions in which an economy provides to other economies real or financial resources, that are immediately or shortly consumed, without receiving equivalent values in return.

Capital account measures external transactions in capital transfers, and in acquisition or disposal of non-produced, non-financial assets.

Capital transfers are transfers of ownership of a fixed asset or the forgiveness of a liability without receiving any economic value in return.

Financial account records transactions in financial assets and liabilities between residents and non-residents. It shows how an economy's external transactions are financed. Transactions in the financial account are classified into direct investment, portfolio investment, financial derivatives, other investment and reserve assets.

Direct investment refers to external investment in which an investor of an economy acquires a lasting interest and an effective control over the management of an enterprise located in another economy.

Portfolio investment refers to investment in non-resident equity securities and debt securities (e.g. bonds and notes, money market instruments), for which the investors have no lasting interest or influence in the management of the companies they invest.

Financial derivatives are financial instruments that are linked to a specific financial instrument or indicator or commodity, and through which specific financial risks can be traded in financial markets (including on Exchange and over the counter) in their own right.

Other investment refers to other financial claims on and liabilities to non-residents that are not classified as direct investment, portfolio investment, financial derivatives or reserve assets.

Reserve assets consist of foreign currency assets that are readily available to and controlled by the monetary authority of an economy (in the case of Hong Kong, the Hong Kong Monetary Authority) for directly financing payment imbalances and for indirectly regulating the magnitude of such imbalances through intervention in foreign exchange markets to affect the currency exchange rate of that economy.

International Investment Position (IIP) is a balance sheet showing an economy's stock of external financial assets and liabilities at a particular time point. External financial assets consist of claims on non-residents. On the other hand, an economy's external financial liabilities refer to the financial claims of non-residents on residents of the economy.

Net IIP is the difference between total external financial assets and total external financial liabilities. Fully consistent with the balance of payments financial account, IIP is categorized by type of investment. Assets and liabilities are divided into direct investment, portfolio investment, financial derivatives and other investment. The asset side of IIP also includes the reserve assets. For detailed explanation on investment components, please refer to the explanatory notes on the components of the financial account of the Balance of Payments account.

Index of industrial production measures the changes in local manufacturing output in real terms, i.e. changes in the volume of local production after discounting the effect of price changes.

Assignments of building units refer to documents which effect the transfer of ownership of property of undivided shares of a lot, i.e. building units.

Buildings with consents to commence work refer to buildings with consents to commence building works issued by the Buildings Department. Such "consents" are issued to private development projects (including Hong Kong Housing Society's projects) and Hong Kong Housing Authority's development projects under the Private Sector Participation Scheme, except small houses in the New Territories where "consents" are not required.

Usable floor area is defined as the aggregate of the areas of the floor or floors in a storey or a building excluding any staircases, public circulation space, lift landings, lavatories, water-closets, kitchens and any space occupied by machinery for any lift, air-conditioning system or similar service provided for the building.

Tenure of accommodation refers to the terms or conditions under which the accommodation is held by a domestic household. The different terms are defined as follows:

Owner-occupier refers to a household which owns the quarters it occupies.

Sole tenant refers to a household which rents the whole quarters it occupies from someone who lives outside the quarters without sharing it with other household(s) or subletting.

Co-tenant refers to two or more households each of which rents part of the quarters from someone who lives outside the quarters.

Main tenant refers to a household which rents the whole quarters it occupies from someone who lives outside the quarters and sublets part of it to other household(s).

Sub-tenant refers to a household which rents part of the quarters from someone who lives in the same quarters.

Rent free refers to a household which occupies an accommodation free, with or without the owner's permission. This does not include owner-occupiers or households occupying accommodation provided by employers.

Accommodation provided by employer refers to a household which occupies an accommodation provided by the employer of one of the household members. This also includes households occupying quarters leased from employers at a nominal rent. If a household member uses housing allowance given by his/her employer for renting accommodation, the tenure is not regarded as accommodation provided by employer.

Inward and outward movements of passenger trains refer to the through train services operated by the Kowloon-Canton Railway Corporation (KCRC) between Hong Kong and the mainland of China.

Inward and outward movements of motor vehicles refer to traffic through the control points at Lok Ma Chau, Man Kam To and Sha Tau Kok to and from the mainland of China.

Motor vehicle licensing conveys the right for a vehicle to be driven on a road. The valid period is either four months or a year. The total vehicles licensed figure refers to end of the year position.

Domestic exports are the natural produce of Hong Kong or the products of a manufacturing process in Hong Kong which has changed permanently the shape, nature, form or utility of the basic materials used in manufacture. Their values are recorded on f.o.b (free-on-board) basis.

Re-exports are products which have previously been imported into Hong Kong and which are re-exported without having undergone in Hong Kong a manufacturing process which has changed permanently the shape, nature, form or utility of the product. Their values are recorded on f.o.b (free-on-board) basis.

Imports are goods which have been produced or manufactured in places outside the jurisdiction of Hong Kong and brought into Hong Kong for domestic use or for subsequent re-export as well as Hong Kong products re-imported. Their values are recorded on c.i.f. (cost, insurance and freight) basis.

Exports to the mainland of China for outward processing refer to raw materials or semi-manufactures exported from or through Hong Kong to the mainland of China for processing with a contractual arrangement for subsequent re-importation of the processed goods into Hong Kong.

Imports from the mainland of China related to outward processing refer to processed goods imported from the mainland of China of which all or part of the raw materials or semi-manufactures have been under contractual arrangement exported from or through Hong Kong to the mainland of China for processing.

Re-exports of the mainland of China origin to other places involving outward processing in the mainland of China refer to processed goods re-exported through Hong Kong of which all or part of the raw materials or semi-manufactures have been exported from or through Hong Kong to the mainland of China for processing with a contractual arrangement for subsequent re-importation of the processed goods into Hong Kong.

The items "Direct investment" until "Flow of direct investment" are applicable to direct investment (Table 24-32 and 24-33):

Direct investment represents investment which allows investors in one economy, on a long term basis, to influence or have an effective voice in the management of an enterprise in another economy. For statistical purpose, an effective voice is taken as equivalent to a holding of 10% or more of the equity in an enterprise. Direct investment comprises equity capital, reinvested earnings and other capital. Equity capital means equity in branches, stock and shares in subsidiaries and associates. Reinvested earnings consist of investors' share of earnings of their subsidiaries or associates not distributed as dividends. Other capital mainly involves inter-company debt transactions. These include short-term or long-term borrowing and lending of funds between parent companies and their subsidiaries, associates and branches.

Inward direct investment refers to direct investment in a Hong Kong enterprise by a non-Hong Kong resident. Typical examples of inward direct investment are multinational corporations' branches and subsidiaries operating in Hong Kong.

Outward direct investment refers to direct investment by a Hong Kong resident in a non-resident enterprise.

Position of direct investment refers to the value of investment abroad or investment received from abroad of Hong Kong residents at a specified date.

Flow of direct investment refers to the additions/withdrawals of investment abroad or investment received from abroad of Hong Kong residents during a period.

A regional headquarters is an office that has control over the operations of offices in the region (i.e. Hong Kong plus one or more other places), and manages the business without frequent referrals to its parent company outside Hong Kong.

A regional office is an office that coordinates offices/operations in the region (i.e. Hong Kong plus one or more other places), and manages the business but with frequent referrals to its parent company outside Hong Kong or its regional headquarters.

The Loan Fund is used to finance schemes of the HKSAR Government loans, such as housing loans and students loans. The main sources of income are appropriations from the General Revenue Account, loan repayments and interest on loans.

Effective exchange rate index (EERI) measures movements in the weighted average of the exchange rate of Hong Kong Dollar (HKD) against the currencies of major trading partners of Hong Kong.

Exchange rates between Hong Kong Dollar and other currencies refer to the closing middle market telegraphic transfer rates or notes rates.

Authorized institutions include licensed banks, restricted licence banks and deposit-taking companies.

Licensed banks can accept deposits of any size and any term of maturity. Before 1 October 1994, the maximum interest rate payable on savings deposits and time deposits of original maturity of less than 15 months, with the exception of deposits of HK$500,000 or above, were subject to an upper limit set by the Hong Kong Association of Banks. Deregulation of "Interest Rate Rules" has taken place since 1 October 1994. With the final phase of interest rate deregulation came into effect on 3 July 2001, there is no restriction on interest rate payable.

Restricted licence banks can accept time deposits in amounts of not less than HK$500,000 with any term of maturity. There is no restriction on interest rate payable.

Deposit-taking companies can accept time deposits in amounts of not less than HK$100,000 with a term of maturity of at least three months. There is no restriction on interest rate payable.

Foreign currency swap deposits refer to deposits involving customers buying foreign currencies in the spot market and placing them as deposits with authorized institutions, while at the same time entering into a contract to sell such foreign currencies (principal plus interest) forward in line with the maturity of such deposits. For most analytical purpose, they should be regarded as Hong Kong dollar time deposits.

Money Supply M1 refers to the sum of legal tender notes and coins held by the public plus customers' demand deposits placed with licensed banks.

Money Supply M2 refers to the sum of M1 plus customers' savings and time deposits with licensed banks, plus negotiable certificates of deposits issued by licensed banks held by non-authorized institutions.

Money Supply M3 refers to the sum of M2 plus customer deposits with restricted licence banks and deposit-taking companies plus negotiable certificates of deposits issued by restricted licence banks and deposit-taking companies held by non-authorized institutions.

Hang Seng Index launched on 24 November 1969, is the key barometer of the Hong Kong stock market and reflects general price movements and the performance of the market as a whole.

Consumer Price Index (CPI) summarizes changes in the price level of consumer goods and services purchased by households. Its change measures the change over time in the total cost of a given basket of goods and services. Its year-on-year rate of change is an important indicator of inflation affecting consumers. The year-on-year rate of change is the percentage increase or decrease in the current index compared to that in the same period of preceding year.

Different CPIs are compiled by the Census and Statistics Department of the HKSAR to reflect the impact of consumer price changes on households in different expenditure ranges. The CPI(A), CPI(B) and CPI(C) are compiled based on the expenditure patterns of households in the relatively low, medium and relatively high expenditure ranges. A Composite CPI is compiled based on the expenditure patterns of all households taken together to reflect the impact of consumer price changes on the household sector as a whole.

The expenditure weights of the CPIs are updated once every five years. The expenditure weights currently in use are derived from the results of the Household Expenditure Survey conducted in 1999/2000 .

Educational attainment refers to the highest level of education ever attained by a person in school or other educational institution, regardless of whether he/she had completed the course. Only formal courses are counted as educational attainment. A formal course shall be one that lasts for at least one academic year, requires specific academic qualifications for entrance (except sub-degree, associate degree, degree and post-graduate courses offered by the Open University of Hong Kong) and includes examinations or specific academic assessment procedures.

Kindergarten refers to all classes in kindergarten.

Non-degree course refers to all higher diploma/endorsement certificate courses in technical institutes/technical colleges (technical institutes and technical colleges were merged as the Hong Kong Institute of Vocational Education in 1999)/polytechnics (the present universities), associateship and other non-associateship courses in polytechnics (the present universities) and other post-secondary colleges. Certificate/diploma courses in colleges/institute of education and in the Hong Kong Technical Teachers' College and nurse training courses are also included in his category.

Degree course refers to all first degree courses and post-graduate courses in tertiary educational institutions in Hong Kong and overseas.

Social Security Schemes aim to provide for the basic and special needs of the members of our community who are in need of financial or material assistance. The non-contributory social security system comprises: the Comprehensive Social Security Assistance Scheme, the Social Security Allowance Scheme, the Criminal and Law Enforcement Injuries Compensation Scheme, the Traffic Accident Victims Assistance Scheme and Emergency Relief.

The Comprehensive Social Security Assistance (CSSA) Scheme (known as Public Assistance (PA) Scheme before 1 July 1993), which is means-tested, is designed to provide financial assistance to bring the income of needy individuals and families up to a prescribed level to meet their basic needs.

The Social Security Allowance (SSA) Scheme (known as Special Needs Allowance (SNA) Scheme before 1 July 1993) comprises Old Age Allowance (OAA) and Disability Allowance (DA). It provides monthly allowance to Hong Kong residents who are 65 years of age or above or who are severely disabled to meet special needs arising from old age or disability.

The Criminal and Law Enforcement Injuries Compensation (CLEIC) Scheme provides cash assistance for people injured or for dependants of those killed in crimes of violence and law enforcement acts on a non-means-tested basis.

The Traffic Accident Victims Assistance (TAVA) Scheme provides speedy cash assistance for people injured or for dependants of those killed in road traffic accident. It is a non-means-tested scheme which does not take into account the element of fault in causing the accident. Payments cover only personal injury and death but not damage to property.

Emergency relief provides meals or cash-in-lieu of meals and relief articles to victims of natural and other disasters such as typhoon, flood, landslide, fire occurred over the territory.

Persons arrested for crime are counted based on the number of occasions on which the offenders are arrested, whether or not they are prosecuted. If a person is arrested on two or more occasions, each occasion is counted as a 'separate' person. If a person is arrested on one occasion for several offences, the offence with the maximum permissible penalty being the heaviest is chosen for statistical purposes.

二十五、澳门特别行政区主要社会经济指标

Main Social and Economic Indicators of Macao Special Adminstrative Region

简要说明

一、本章资料反映澳门特别行政区主要社会、经济发展情况。内容包括：土地、人口、就业、国民经济核算、工业、能源、建筑、交通通讯、对外贸易、财政金融、物价、教育、卫生、房屋、社会保障等方面。

二、本章涉及的1999年及以前数据均指原名为“澳门地区”的数据。

三、本章由澳门特别行政区政府统计暨普查局提供所有数据，国家统计局国际统计信息中心负责整理、编辑。

四、在统计工作方面，按中华人民共和国“澳门特别行政区基本法”的有关原则，澳门特别行政区保留其单独运作的统计系统，并负责编制和发布反映澳门特别行政区情况的统计数据。由于澳门和内地在使用统计名词及概念方面会有所不同，读者在比较两地数据时，请参考本章末的“主要统计指标解释”。

五、澳门特别行政区是单独的关税地区，澳门与内地之间的贸易，亦需办理进出口报关。在贸易统计方面，澳门特别行政区对外贸易统计数据亦包括澳门特别行政区与内地的贸易。

六、在外汇统计及与之有关的各方面，澳门元是澳门特别行政区的法定货币，因此，除澳门元以外的货币（包括人民币）均视作外币。

七、更详细的统计资料及有关的技术细节，可参阅澳门特别行政区政府统计暨普查局出版的《澳门统计月刊》、《澳门统计年鉴》及各专题统计出版物。

八、本章节表中的符号使用说明：“_”表示绝对数值为零；“空格”表示没有数字或未能提供；“r”表示更正资料；“p”表示临时性数字；“o”表示数据小于本表最小单位半数；“*”或“①”等表示本表下有注解。

Brief Introduction

I. Data in this chapter show main social and economic developments of the Macao Special Administrative Region, including data on land, population, employment, national accounts, industry, energy, construction, transportation, communication, external trade, public finance and banking, prices, education, health, housing and social security.

II. Data of 1999 and previous years in this chapter refer to data of the former Macao region.

III. All data in this chapter are provided by the Statistics and Census Services, the Government of the Macao Special Administrative Region, and further tabulated or edited by the International Statistical Information Centre of the National Bureau of Statistics.

IV. According to the Basic Law of the Macao Special Administrative Region of the People's Republic of China, Macao Special Administrative Region maintains its independent statistical system, and compiles and disseminates statistics on the Region. As Macao and the mainland of China use different statistical concepts, definitions and terminology, users are advised to make reference of the Explanatory Note at the end of this chapter when using and comparing data of the mainland of China and the Macao Special Administrative Region.

V. As Macao is a separate custom territory, trade between Macao and the mainland of China needs customs declaration procedures. In terms of trade statistics, data on Macao's imports and exports include Macao's trade with the mainland of China.

VI. As Pataca (MOP) is the legal tender in the Macao Special Administrative Region, all other currencies (including Renminbi) are regarded as foreign currencies in compiling foreign exchange statistics and related statistics.

VII. For more detailed statistics and technical details, users are advised to read Macao Monthly Bulletin of Statistics, Macao Yearbook of Statistics and other publications compiled by the Statistics and Census Services, the Government of the Macao Special Administrative Region.

VIII. Notations used in this chapter:

"_" Indicates absolute value equals zero; "(blank)" indicates no figure provided or not available; "p" indicates provisional data; " o" indicates less than half of the unit employed; "r" indicates rectified data; "*" or "¢Ù"indicates see footnotes below.

25-1 主要统计指标概况

Principal Statistical Indicators

项　　目	Items	1999	2000	2001	2002	2003
人口及生命事件	**Population and Demographics Characteristics**					
年中人口估计（万人）	Mid-year Estimates of Population (10 000)	42.7	43.1	43.4	43.9	44.5
出生率（‰）	Crude Birth Rate (‰)	9.7	8.9	7.5	7.2	7.2
死亡率（‰）	Crude Death Rate (‰)	3.2	3.1	3.1	3.2	3.3
劳工①	**Labour①**					
劳动人口（万人）	Labour Force (10 000)	20.9	20.9	21.7	21.4	21.6
劳动力参与率（%）	Labour Force Participation Rate (%)	65.5	64.3	64.8	62.3	60.9
失业率（%）	Unemployment Rate (%)	6.3	6.8	6.4	6.3	6.0
就业不足率（%）	Underemployment Rate (%)	1.3	3.0	3.6	3.4	2.7
就业人口（万人）	Employed Population (10 000)	19.6	19.5	20.3	20.1	20.3
制造业	Manufacturing	4.3	3.8	4.4	4.1	3.7
批发及零售业	Wholesale and Retail	3.0	3.0	3.0	3.1	3.3
酒店及饮食业	Hotels and Restaurants	2.1	2.1	2.2	2.3	2.2
公共行政、社会及个人服务业	Public Administration, Community, Social and Personal Services	5.5	5.6	5.6	5.9r	6.0
对外贸易	**External Trade**					
出口（亿澳门元）	Exports (100 million MOP)	176	204	185	189	207
本地产品出口（亿澳门元）	Domestic Exports (100 million MOP)	150	171	151	148	163
再出口（亿澳门元）	Re-exports (100 million MOP)	25	33	33	42	44
进口（亿澳门元）	Imports (100 million MOP)	163	181	192	203	221
贸易条件指数（1996年 ＝ 100）	Terms of Trade Index (1996=100)	103.1	100.7	100.0	99.7	100.9
工业生产	**Industrial Production**					
工业电力消耗量（亿千瓦小时）	Electricity Consumption (100 million kwh)	1.8r	1.6r	1.5r	1.9r	2.0
建筑（私人部门）	**Construction (Private Sector)**					
新建及扩建私人楼宇单位数目（个）	Units Completed and Extended (No.)	5389	3146	2622	381	1566
新建及扩建私人楼宇总面积（万平方米）	Gross Floor Area of Buildings Completed and Extended (10 000 sq.m)	67	37	40	10	24
新动工的私人楼宇单位数目（个）	Units Started (No.)	3619	1167	812	1326	2658
新动工的私人楼宇总面积（万平方米）	Gross Floor Area of Buildings Started (10 000 sq.m)	42	20	16	16	53
楼宇单位买卖数目（个）	Number of Units Sold (No.)	11039	10211	27016	16831r	18556
不动产买卖契约数目（宗）	Deed of Real Estate Transacted (No.)	12230	12484	12992	17513	14400
不动产按揭贷款数目（宗）	Real Estate Mortgage Loans (No.)	7363	7367	8206	9902	9198
运输、通讯、旅游	**Transport, Communications, Tourism**					
进出澳门货运车辆数目（万次）	Lorries Entering and Departing Macao (10 000)	24.2	45.4*	45.8*	47.8*	47.8*
进出澳门的客船班（万次）	Ferry Trips Entering and Departing Macao (10 000)	6.8	7.5	7.4	7.7	7.7
澳门国际机场的商业航班(万次)	Commercial Flights at Macao International Airport (10 000)	2.1	2.4	2.9	3.4	2.9
登记车辆（万辆）	Licensed Vehicles (10 000)	11.4	11.4	11.6	12.4	13.2
电话线（万条）	Telephone Lines (10 000)	30.0	31.8	37.1	45.2	53.9
访澳旅客（万人次）	Visitors (10 000)	744	916	1028	1153	1189
酒店入住率（%）	Hotel Occupancy Rate (%)	54	58	61	67	64
财政收支、货币、金融（亿澳门元）	**Government Accounts, Money and Finance (100 million MOP)**					
财政总收入②	Total Government Revenue②	169	153	156	152r	141
财政总支出②	Total Government Expenditure②	166	150	152	135r	115
货币供应(广义货币供应量M2)	Money Supply (M2)					
澳门元③	MOP③	280	232	261	275	296
港元	HKD	441	445	469	512	594
其他货币	Other Currencies	140	172	185	202	220
总计	Total	861	849	916	990	1111
本地机构及私人贷款及垫款	Loans/Advances to Resident Firms & Individuals	414	382	355	336	331

25-1 续表 Continued

项　　目	Items	1999	2000	2001	2002	2003
居民消费价格指数	**Consumer Price Index**					
（1999年10月至2000年9月=100）	**(October/1999 - September/2000=100)**					
综合消费价格指数	Composite Consumer Price Index	101.1	99.5	97.5	94.9	93.5
甲类消费价格指数	Consumer Price Index (A)	101.0	99.6	98.2	95.9	94.6
乙类消费价格指数	Consumer Price Index (B)	101.0	99.4	97.4	94.6	93.1
房屋（期末值）	**Housing (End of period balance)**					
公共房屋（个）④	Public Housing (No.) ④	9084	9084	9405	9656	7037
教育⑤	**Education ⑤**					
学前教育学生（人）	Pre-primary Education (Students)	16083	14978	13638	12737	
小学生（人）	Primary Education (Students)	47059	45474	43709	41535	
中学生（人）	Secondary Education (Students)	34761	38156	41132	43999	
高等教育学生（人）	Higher Education (Students)	7094	8358	8520	11995	
医疗卫生	**Health**					
死亡登记人数（人）	Registered Deaths (No.)	1374	1338	1327	1415	1474
死于心脏病人数（人）	Deaths of Heart Diseases (No.)	274	326	291	296	329
死于癌症人数（人）	Deaths of Cancers (No.)	366	383	401	439	421
婴儿死亡率	Infant Mortality Rate	4.1	2.9	4.3	3.5	0.6
（按每千名出生登记活产婴儿计算）	(per 1000 registered live births)					
社会保障	**Social Security**					
受益人数目（人）	Beneficiaries (persons)	115698	122327	127703	138514	145677
供款单位数目（个）	Contributors(No.)	7609	8451	8919	9421r	10078
总发放援助次数（万次）	Number of Payments Granted (10 000)	15.8	16.3	17.7	23.6	30.4
总发放金额（万澳门元）	Amount of Payments Granted (10 000 MOP)	14716	20191	22132	34610	53003
治安	**Crime**					
罪案数目（宗）	Number of Crimes	9262	8925	8905	9088	9920
囚犯数目（期末值,人）	Number of Prisoners (as at the end of year)	788	847r	886	928	913
本地生产总值②	**Gross Domestic Product (GDP) ②**					
按1996年不变价格计算	At Constant (1996) Prices					
支出法本地生产总值实际增长率(%)	Expenditure-based GDP Real Growth Rate (%)	-3.0	4.6	2.2	10.0r	15.6
本地生产总值（亿澳门元）	GDP (100 million MOP)	510.2	533.8	545.6	600.3r	694.1
人均本地生产总值（万澳门元）	GDP per Capita (10 000 MOP)	11.9	12.4	12.6	13.7r	15.6
按当年价格计算	At Current Prices					
支出法本地生产总值名义增长率(%)	Expenditure-based GDP Nominal Growth Rate (%)	-5.6	1.5	0.2	8.9r	16.7
本地生产总值（亿澳门元）	GDP (100 million MOP)	490.2	497.4	498.6	542.9r	633.7
人均本地生产总值（万澳门元）	GDP per Capita (10 000 MOP)	11.5	11.6	11.5	12.4r	14.3

注：①‘劳工’资料及报表25-4、25-5及25-6的数据来自就业调查，由于作为就业调查推算基础的人口估计，已根据2001人口普查结果作出修正，因此2001年以前的就业数据亦作出相应修正。

②因2003年自治机构的指定账目未能提供，故2003年的总收入及总支出不能与2002年直接比较。2003年数字在日后得到更多资料时会作出修订。

③《中华人民共和国澳门特别行政区基本法》规定，澳门元是澳门特别行政区的法定货币。

④不包括已出售者。

⑤不包括特殊教育学生。第n年的学生人数是指n/n+1学年年终学生人数。

* 包括关闸及路氹城边检站。

Notes: ①The data referring to 'Labour' and those in Tables 25-4, 25-5 and 25-6 are provided by Employment Survey. Since the population estimates, which serve as the base for statistical inference in the Employment Survey, have been adjusted after Census 2001, the resulting indicators for the previous periods before 2001 were thus revised accordingly.

②Because there are no data available on the revenue and expenditure of autonomous bodies in the specific accounts of 2003, the total revenue and the total expenditure of 2003 are not directly comparable with those of 2002. Figures of 2003 are subject to revisions as more data become available.

③Pataca (MOP) is the legal tender in the Macao Special Administrative Region, as stated in "The Basic Law of the Macao Special Administrative Region of the People's Republic of China".

④Excluding the units that had been sold.

⑤Excluding students in special education. The number of students of year n refer to the students at the end of academic year n/n+1.

*Including the Border gate and the Checkpoint of CoTai.

25-2　按堂区划分的澳门面积

Land Area of Macao by Parish

单位: 平方公里 (sq.km)

分　区	Sub-division	1999	2000	2001	2002	2003
总面积	**Total Land Area**	**23.8**	**25.4**	**25.8**	**26.8**	**27.3**
澳门	**Macao Peninsula**	**7.8**	**8.5**	**8.5**	**8.5**	**8.7**
圣安多尼堂区	Santo Antonio	1.1	1.1	1.1	1.1	1.1
望德堂区	Sao Lazaro	0.6	0.6	0.6	0.6	0.6
风顺堂区	Sao Lourenco	0.9	0.9	0.9	0.9	0.9
大堂区	Se	2.2	2.9	2.9	2.9	3.0
花地玛堂区	N.S. de Fatima	3.0	3.0	3.0	3.0	3.1
氹仔	**Island of Taipa**	**6.2**	**6.2**	**6.2**	**6.2**	**6.3**
路环	**Island of Coloane**	**7.6**	**7.6**	**7.6**	**7.6**	**7.6**
路氹填海区	Reclaimed Land between the Islands of Taipa and Coloane	2.2	3.1	3.5	4.5	4.7

25-3　人口主要指标

Main Demographic Indicator

项　目	Item	1999	2000	2001	2002	2003
年中人口估计　（万人）	Mid-year Estimates of Population (10 000 persons)	42.7	43.1	43.4	43.9	44.5
出生率　（‰）	Crude Birth Rate (‰)	9.7	8.9	7.5	7.2	7.2
死亡率　（‰）	Crude Death Rate (‰)	3.2	3.1	3.1	3.2	3.3
婴儿死亡率　（‰）	Infant Mortality Rate (‰)	4.1	2.9	4.3	3.5	0.6
自然增长率　（‰）	Natural Growth Rate (‰)	6.5	5.8	4.4	4.0r	3.9
总和生育率	Total Fertility Rate	1.0	0.9	0.8	0.8	0.8
登记结婚数　（宗）	No. of Registered Marriages	1367	1222	1222	1209	1309
离婚数目　（宗）	No. of Registered Divorces	283	369	348	385	440
		1994-1997	1995-1998	1996-1999	1997-2000	1998-2001
出生时平均预期寿命(岁)	Life Expectancy at Birth (years)	76.8	77.0	77.9	78.6	78.9
男	Male	75.3	75.5	76.1	76.8	77.2
女	Female	79.9	79.9	80.5	81.3	81.5

25-4　经济活动人口及失业状况

Labour Force and Unemployment

项　目	Item	1999	2000	2001	2002	2003
劳动人口　（万人）	Labour Force (10 000 persons)	20.9	20.9	21.7	21.4	21.6
男	Male	11.3	11.3	11.6	11.3	11.5
女	Female	9.6	9.7	10.1	10.1	10.0
就业人口　（万人）	Employed Population (10 000 persons)	19.6	19.5	20.3	20.1	20.3
失业人口　（万人）	Unemployed Population (10 000 persons)	1.3	1.4	1.4	1.3	1.3
失业率　(%)	Unemployment Rate (%)	6.3	6.8	6.4	6.3	6.0

25-5 按行业划分的就业人口

Employed Population by Industry

单位：万人 (10 000 persons)

行　业	Industry	2001	2002	2003
总数	**Total**	**20.28**	**20.06**	**20.26**
农业、畜牧业、狩猎及林业	Agriculture, Farming of Animals, Hunting and Forestry	o	0.01	0.01
捕渔业	Fishery	0.02	0.02	0.05
采矿业	Mining and Quarrying	o	o	o
制造业	Manufacturing	4.41	4.09	3.71
电力、气体及水的生产与供应业	Electricity, Gas and Water Supply	0.10	0.12	0.13
建筑	Construction	1.69	1.50	1.63
批发及零售业	Wholesale and Retail	3.02	3.08	3.28
酒店及饮食业	Hotels and Restaurants	2.24	2.31	2.21
运输、仓储及通信业	Transport, Storage and Communications	1.45	1.28	1.42
金融、保险业	Financial Intermediation	0.61	0.62	0.62
不动产业务、租赁及向企业提供的服务	Real Estate, Renting and Business Activities	1.07	1.09	1.19
公共行政、社会及个人服务业	Public Administration, Community, Social and personal Services	1.60	1.70	1.78
教育	Education	0.81	0.99	0.96
医疗卫生及社会福利	Health and Social Welfare	0.51	0.42	0.46
团体、社会及个人的其他服务	Other Community, Social and Personal Services	2.21	2.30	2.35
雇用佣人的家庭	Households with Domestic Helpers	0.48	0.48	0.43
国际组织及其他领土以外的机构	International Organizations and Other Extra-territorial Institutions	0.01	0.01	0.01
不详	Unknown	0.03	0.03	0.02

25-6 按行业划分的每月工作收入中位数

Median Monthly Employment Earnings

单位：澳门元 (MOP)

行　业	Industry	2001	2002	2003
总数	**Total**	**4655**	**4672**	**4801**
农业、畜牧业、狩猎及林业	Agriculture, Farming of Animals, Hunting and Forestry	3751	9739	11626
捕渔业	Fishery	3751	4743	4553
采矿业	Mining and Quarrying	5251	8020	25046
制造业	Manufacturing	2760	2766	2840
电力、气体及水的生产与供应业	Electricity, Gas and Water Supply	9950	12827	11526
建筑	Construction	4296	4142	4589
批发及零售业	Wholesale and Retail	4445	4430	4354
酒店及饮食业	Hotels and Restaurants	4001	4050	4075
运输、仓储及通信业	Transport, Storage and Communications	5628	5850	5798
金融、保险业	Financial Intermediation	7704	7941	8652
不动产业务、租赁及向企业提供的服务	Real Estate, Renting and Business Activities	3818	3720	3682
公共行政、社会及个人服务业	Public Administration, Community, Social and Personal Services	13798	13749	14075
教育	Education	8682	8713	9150
医疗卫生及社会福利	Health and Social Welfare	9826	7747	7905
团体、社会及个人的其他服务	Other Community, Social and Personal Services	6183	5974	6481
雇用佣人的家庭	Households with Domestic Helpers	2845	2813	2755
国际组织及其他领土以外的机构	International Organizations and Other Extra-territorial Institutions	12978	7251	4955

25-7　本地生产总值（按当年价格计算）

Gross Domestic Product (At Current Prices)

年份 Year	本地生产总值 GDP		本地生产总值与上年比较的实际增长率 (%)① GDP Real Growth Rate Over the Preceding Year (%)①	人均本地生产总值 GDP per Capita	
	（亿澳门元） (100 million MOP)	（亿美元） (100 million USD)		（澳门元） (MOP)	（美元） (USD)
1990	261.8	32.6	8.0	78144	9740
1991	303.3	37.9	3.7	86242	10775
1992	395.2	49.6	13.3	106555	13365
1993	451.9	56.7	5.2	117695	14772
1994	501.1	63.0	4.3	126303	15867
1995	553.3	69.5	3.3	135190	16970
1996	552.9	69.4	-0.4	133205	16721
1997	558.9	70.1	-0.3	133944	16796
1998	519.0	65.0	-4.6	122901	15403
1999	490.2	61.3	-3.0	114693	14351
2000	497.4	62.0	4.6	115526	14394
2001	498.6	62.1r	2.2	114864	14298
2002r	542.9	67.6	10.0	123862	15418
2003②	633.7	79.0	15.6	142638	17782

注：①实际增长率是按1996年不变价格估算的本地生产总值计算而得。
　　②估算数字在日后得到更多资料时会作出修订。

Notes:①The real growth rates are calculated based on GDP at constant (1996) prices.
　　②The estimates are subject to revisions as more data become available.

25-8　支出法本地生产总值

Gross Domestic Product (Expenditure-based Estimates)

单位：亿澳门元　　(100 million MOP)

本地生产总值组成部份	GDP Components	1999	2000	2001	2002r	2003①
按当年价格计算	**At Current Prices**					
居民消费支出	Private Consumption Expenditure	204.0	203.8	206.5	211.8	219.0
政府最终消费支出	Government Final Consumption Expenditure	67.7	59.0	59.7	61.9	66.0
固定资本形成总额	Gross Fixed Capital Formation	86.7	59.2	51.3	55.8	84.1
存货增加	Changes in Inventories	0.8	0.7	0.3	2.4	2.6
货物出口	Exports of Goods	175.8	203.8	184.7	189.3	207.0
减:货物进口	Less: Imports of Goods	203.3	225.9	234.9	253.1	278.8
服务出口	Exports of Services	216.6	263.3	302.7	356.2	417.7
减:服务进口	Less: Imports of Services	58.1	66.4	71.7	81.2	84.0
本地生产总值	**GDP**	**490.2**	**497.4**	**498.6**	**542.9**	**633.7**
人均本地生产总值（澳门元）	**GDP per Capita (MOP)**	**114693**	**115526**	**114864**	**123862**	**142638**
按1996年不变价格计算	**At Constant (1996) Prices**					
居民消费支出	Private Consumption Expenditure	205.8	207.7	213.8	224.7	235.8
政府最终消费支出	Government Final Consumption Expenditure	64.1	57.8	57.7	59.3	62.9
固定资本形成总额	Gross Fixed Capital Formation	98.1	70.3	63.9	66.0	92.7
存货增加	Changes in Inventories	0.8	0.7	0.3	2.5	2.8
货物出口	Exports of Goods	177.4	202.3	191.8	204.2	223.4
减:货物进口	Less: Imports of Goods	207.9	220.7	239.5	268.4	298.2
服务出口	Exports of Services	227.7	279.5	325.9	391.1	458.9
减:服务进口	Less: Imports of Services	55.8	63.8	68.3	79.1	84.2
本地生产总值	**GDP**	**510.2**	**533.8**	**545.6**	**600.3**	**694.1**
人均本地生产总值（澳门元）	**GDP per Capita (MOP)**	**119373**	**123977**	**125687**	**136950**	**156244**

注：①估算数字在日后得到更多资料时会作出修订。

Notes:①The estimates are subject to revisions as more data become available.

25-9　生产法本地生产总值

Gross Domestic Product(Production-Based Estimates)

单位：亿澳门元　　(100 million MOP)

经济活动	Economic Activities	1998	1999	2000	2001r	2002①
第二产业	**Secondary Sector**	**70.0**	**67.8**	**64.1**	**55.3**	**56.0**
采矿业	Mining and Quarrying	0.1	0.1	o	0.1	0.1
制造业	Manufacturing	40.3	39.1	41.4	34.0	32.2
电力、煤气及水供应业	Electricity, Gas and Water Supply	13.6	13.6	12.2	12.8	12.4
建筑业	Construction	16.0	15.0	10.6	8.4	11.4
第三产业	**Tertiary Sector**	**397.2**	**369.6**	**384.4**	**383.5**	**411.2**
批发零售、维修、酒店、餐厅及酒楼业	Wholesale, Retail, Repair, Hotels and Restaurants	43.0	40.5	45.7	48.6	54.0
运输、仓储及通信业	Transport, Storage and Communications	29.6	29.8	30.9	27.8	30.0
金融保险、不动产、租赁及商业服务	Financial Intermediation, Real Estate, Renting and Business Activities	118.9	107.3	103.3	92.9	94.1
公共行政、社会服务及个人服务（包括博彩业）	Public Administration, Other Community, Social and Personal Services (Including gambling)	205.7	191.9	204.5	214.2	233.1
减调整项：间接计算的金融中介服务	**Less: Adjustment for Financial Intermediation Services Indirectly Measured (FISIM)**	**-27.6**	**-22.7**	**-24.3**	**-23.6**	**-23.4**
以基本价格按生产法估算的本地生产总值	**Production-based GDP at Basic Prices**	**439.6**	**414.6**	**424.2**	**415.2**	**443.8**
加产品税	**Add: Taxes on Products**	**66.0**	**55.4**	**65.8**	**76.7**	**94.5**
以当年价格按生产法估算的本地生产总值	**Production-based GDP at Current Prices**	**505.6**	**470.0**	**490.0**	**491.9**	**538.4**
以当年价格按支出法估算的本地生产总值	**Expenditure-based GDP at Current Prices**	**519.0**	**490.2**	**497.4**	**498.6**	**542.9**
统计差额（%）	Statistical Discrepancy (%)	-2.6	-4.1	-1.5	-1.3	-0.8

注：①估算数字在日后得到更多资料时会作出修订。

Notes:①The estimates are subject to revisions as more data become available.

25-10　生产法本地生产总值结构

Structure of Gross Domestic Product (Production-Based Estimates)

单位：%　　(%)

经济活动	Economic Activities	1998	1999	2000	2001r	2002①
第二产业	**Secondary Sector**	**15.9**	**16.3**	**15.1**	**13.3**	**12.6**
采矿业	Mining and Quarrying	o	o	o	o	o
制造业	Manufacturing	9.2	9.4	9.8	8.2	7.2
电力、煤气及水供应业	Electricity, Gas and Water Supply	3.1	3.3	2.9	3.1	2.8
建筑业	Construction	3.6	3.6	2.5	2.0	2.6
第三产业	**Tertiary Sector**	**90.4**	**89.1**	**90.6**	**92.4**	**92.7**
批发零售、维修、酒店、餐厅及酒楼业	Wholesale, Retail, Repair, Hotels and Restaurants	9.8	9.8	10.8	11.7	12.2
运输、仓库及通信业	Transport, Storage and Communications	6.7	7.2	7.3	6.7	6.8
金融、保险、不动产、租赁及商业服务	Financial Intermediation, Real Estate, Renting and Business Activities	27.0	25.9	24.3	22.4	21.2
公共行政、社会服务及个人服务（包括博彩业）	Public Administration, Other Community, Social and Personal Services (Including gambling)	46.8	46.3	48.2	51.6	52.5
减调整项:间接计算的金融中介服务	**Less: Adjustment for Financial Intermediation Services Indirectly Measured (FISIM)**	**-6.3**	**-5.5**	**-5.7**	**-5.7**	**-5.3**
以基本价格按生产法估算的本地生产总值	**Production-based GDP at Basic Prices**	**100.0**	**100.0**	**100.0**	**100.0**	**100.0**

注：①估算数字在日后得到更多资料时会作出修订。

Notes:①The estimates are subject to revisions as more data become available.

25-11 电力、燃料及水消耗量

Consumption of Electricity, Fuels and Water

项　　目	Item	1999	2000	2001	2002	2003
电力（万千瓦小时）	**Electricity (10 000kwh)**					
住户	Domestic	51292	52270	42068	44329	45278
工业	Industrial	18380r	16167r	15426r	18678r	20289
商业①	Commercial①	85029	90337	104124	109682	111582
燃料	**Fuels**					
重油（万公升）	Fuel Oil (10 000 liters)	30424	31578	31725	32883	30855
轻柴油（万公升）	Gas Oil and Diesel (10 000 liters)	8110	9597	10464	12542	15551
汽油（万公升）	Gasoline (10 000 liters)	4287	4109	4119	4254	4471
液化石油气（吨）	L.P.G. (ton)	24902	24466	24527	26420r	28055
水（万立方米）	**Water (10 000 cu.m)**	**4799**	**4885**	**4837**	**4908**	**5163**

注：①包括公共照明。

Note: ① Including public lighting.

25-12 按用途划分的建成私人房屋单位及建筑面积

Units and Gross Floor Area Completed by End-use

年份 Year	住宅 Residential		商业及写字楼 Commercial and Offices		工业 Industrial		其他用途 Other Uses		总计 Total	
	单位数目（个） No. of Units	建筑面积（万平方米） Gross Floor Area (10 000 m²)	单位数目（个） No. of Units	建筑面积（万平方米） Gross Floor Area (10 000 m²)	单位数目（个） No. of Units	建筑面积（万平方米） Gross Floor Area (10 000 m²)	单位数目（个） No. of Units	建筑面积（万平方米） Gross Floor Area (10 000 m²)	单位数目（个） No. of Units	建筑面积（万平方米） Gross Floor Area (10 000 m²)
1997	6191	57.7	2540	36.3	-	-	365	21.0	9096	115.0
1998	6695	56.0	1562	17.5	4	4.0	60	19.6	8321	96.9
1999	4252	30.8	1085	12.9	2	3.4	50	19.9	5389	66.9
2000	2747	23.0	368	5.5	-	-	31	8.5	3146	37.0
2001	1774	17.4	805	10.8	-	-	43	12.3	2622	40.4
2002	336	3.6	30	0.4	2	0.5	13	5.7	381	10.3
2003	1246	15.4	304	2.5	2	1.4	14	5.0	1566	24.3

25-13 按用途划分的获批准新动工私人房屋单位及建筑面积

Units and Gross Floor Area Started by End-use

年份 Year	住宅 Residential		商业及写字楼 Commercial and Offices		工业 Industrial		其他用途 Other Uses		总计 Total	
	单位数目（个） No. of Units	建筑面积（万平方米） Gross Floor Area (10 000 m²)	单位数目（个） No. of Units	建筑面积（万平方米） Gross Floor Area (10 000 m²)	单位数目（个） No. of Units	建筑面积（万平方米） Gross Floor Area (10 000 m²)	单位数目（个） No. of Units	建筑面积（万平方米） Gross Floor Area (10 000 m²)	单位数目（个） No. of Units	建筑面积（万平方米） Gross Floor Area (10 000 m²)
1997	6299	50.9	1347	12.5	4	4.1	34	17.9	7684	85.3
1998	3308	38.3	482	4.0	2	2.6	33	12.1	3825	57.0
1999	3157	25.0	442	9.7	1	0.4	19	6.7	3619	41.7
2000	1038	9.9	111	2.2	3	0.6	15	7.6	1167	20.3
2001	600	5.3	196	1.2	2	0.3	14	9.0	812	15.8
2002	1196	10.3	116	1.2	-	-	14	4.2	1326	15.7
2003	2430	31.8	211	10.0	-	-	17	11.4	2658	53.3

25-14 零售业销售额

Retail Sales

单位：亿澳门元 (100 million MOP)

项 目	Item	2000	2001	2002	2003
零售业销售总额	**Total Retail Sales**	**45.94**	**48.33**	**52.23**	**62.68**
百货①	Department Stores ①	6.35	6.36	7.20	8.58
超级市场	Supermarkets	5.33	5.64	5.66	7.25
汽车	Motor Vehicles	4.49	5.77	6.48	9.38
钟表金饰	Watches, clocks and jewellery	3.92	4.22	4.94	4.92
成人服装	Adults' clothing	3.48	4.17	4.63	4.16
车辆用燃料	Automotive fuels	2.65	2.47	2.64	3.00
家居用燃料	Fuel for household use	2.45	2.52	2.31	2.83
家庭电器	Household electric appliances	2.38	2.19	2.62	2.71
药房	Pharmacy	1.67	1.73	1.88	1.93
其他	Others	13.22	13.26	13.87	17.92

注:①包括出售粮食、饮品及烟草以外的非专门零售店铺。

Note: ① Including non-specialized retail stores selling merchandise other than food, beverages and tobacco.

25-15 外地进出澳门货物

External Trade by Mode of Transport

单位：万吨 (10 000 tons)

项 目	Mode of Transport	1999	2000	2001	2002	2003
入境①	**Imports ①**					
海路	Sea	156.8	136.5	156.6	153.9	160.7
空路	Air	1.1	1.3	1.7	1.9	1.7
陆路	Land	23.8	43.9	57.3	72.7	110.4
其他②	Others ②	5717.1	5851.1	5453.2	5459.1	5667.2
总数	**Total**	**5898.8**	**6032.9**	**5668.7**	**5687.7r**	**5940.0**
出境①	**Exports ①**					
海路	Sea	47.9	44.1	41.8	26.0	32.2
空路	Air	3.3	3.9	4.0	5.9	6.3
陆路	Land	17.2	16.4	12.6	19.3	16.3
其他②	Others ②	3.6	4.9	4.3	9.6	10.2
总数	**Total**	**72.1**	**69.4**	**62.7**	**60.8**	**65.1**

注：①包括直接转运货物。

②包括邮递及以管道运输方式进出澳门的货物。

Notes:①Including quantities of direct transit.

②Including quantities of external trade in Macao by postal parcels and pipelines.

25-16 集装箱流量

Container Flow

单位：次数 (number)

项 目	Item	1999	2000	2001	2002	2003
入境	Inward	33983	34327	32843	35105	36111
出境	Outward	36106	36934	33527	35706	38932
转口	Trans-shipment	13218	12012	10027	14296	11635

25-17 海路集装箱总吞吐量
Seaborne Container Throughput

单位：标准集装箱单位 (TEU)

项目	Item	1999	2000	2001	2002	2003
入境	Inward	39807	41645	41677	45206	47096
出境	Outward	47836	49639	43783	47485	52819
转口	Trans-shipment	11343	10829	9225	13485	12221

注：标准集装箱单位为 20英尺 x 8英尺 x 8英尺。
Note: TEU - Twenty-foot Equivalent Unit with standard size of 20 feet x 8 feet x 8 feet.

25-18 通信服务
Communications

项目	Item	1999	2000	2001	2002	2003
邮递服务	**Postal Service**					
信件邮件（万件）	Mails (10 000)	1427r	1588	2017r	2090	2107
包裹（万件）	Parcels (10 000)	1.0	0.6	0.5	0.5	0.6
电话服务（万条操作线路）	**Telephone Service (10 000)**					
固定电话线	Fixed Lines	17.8	17.7	17.6	17.6	17.5
移动电话	Mobile Telephone Lines	8.9r	11.8	15.6	17.3	19.9
数码式储值卡	Stored Value GSM Cards	3.0	2.3	3.9	10.3	16.5
对外电话通讯量（万分钟）	**International Calls (10 000 minutes)**					
拨出	Outgoing	13281	15206	15651	15408r	15161
拨入	Incoming	9793	10435	11390	11344r	12524
传呼用户（户）	**Pagers (No.)**	19312	9390	6689	4627	3453
国际互联网	**Internet Service**					
登记用户	Registered Subscribers	17034	27346	34403	41517	48524
总使用时数（万小时）	Total Hours Used (10 000)	338	1082	1812	2707	3812

25-19 主要商品进出口总额
Values of Major Merchandise Trade

单位：亿澳门元 (100 million MOP)

贸易种类	Trade Type	1999	2000	2001	2002	2003
出口	Exports	175.8	203.8	184.7	189.3	207.0
本地产品出口	Domestic Exports	150.4	170.8	151.3	147.7	162.6
再出口	Re-exports	25.4	33.0	33.5	41.5	44.4
进口	Imports	163.0	181.0	191.7	203.2	221.0
进出口总额	Total Trade	338.8	384.8	376.4	392.5	428.0
进出口差额	Trade Balance	12.8	22.8	-7.0	-14.0	-14.0
出口/进口比率 (%)	Exports-to-Imports Ratio(%)	107.9	112.6	96.4	93.1	93.7

25-20 主要商品进口原产地和出口目的地

Values of Imports and Exports by Major Country/Region

单位：亿澳门元 (100 million MOP)

主要国家/地区	Major Country/Region	1999	2000	2001	2002	2003
进口（原产地）	**Imports (Country or Region of Origin)**					
中国内地	Mainland China	58.1	74.3	81.6	84.8	94.9
中国香港	Hong Kong SAR, China	29.5	27.6	26.6	29.6	27.9
欧洲联盟	European Union	21.0	17.4	24.1	23.9	26.4
日本	Japan	10.8	11.4	10.4	13.7	19.9
中国台湾	Taiwan, China	15.5	17.2	12.8	13.6	12.8
美国	United States of America	8.3	8.2	8.0	8.4	8.7
出口（目的地）	**Exports (Country or Region of Destination)**					
美国	United States of America	82.5	98.4	89.1	91.5	103.2
欧洲联盟	European Union	53.0	57.9	49.2	44.0	47.2
中国内地	Mainland China	16.2	20.7	21.5	29.5	28.4
中国香港	Hong Kong SAR, China	12.0	13.3	11.8	11.0	13.6

25-21 财政收入

Government Revenue

单位：万澳门元 (10 000 MOP)

项　目	Items	1999	2000	2001	2002	2003p
经常收入	**Current Revenue**					
直接税	Direct Tax	598736	689544	754742	887623	1134283
间接税	Indirect Tax	49595	53260	84079	92604	98761
费用、罚款及其他金钱制裁	Compulsory Fees, Fines and Penalties	25519	22847	29671	33192	33971
财产收益	Property Income	205873	54545	83898	45458	87209
转移	Transfers	16493	16267	16403	12578	40061
耐用品的出售	Sales of Durable Goods	56	56	67	245	21
劳务及非耐用品的出售	Sales of Services and Non-durable Goods	4581	3470	3374	3997	3938
其他经常收入	Other Current Receipts	6527	4128	1912	23009	2940
资本收入	**Capital Revenue**					
投资资产的出售	Sales of Invested Property	6821	745	99	25	61
转移	Transfers	27893	1914	-	100	-
财务资产	Financial Assets	880	440	440	-	-
财务负债	Financial Liabilities	-	-	-	-	-
其他资本收入	Other Capital Revenue	40000	30642	-	-	-
非从支付中扣减的退回	Reimbursements Not Deducted from Payments	2931	3733	6795	9599	10779
指定帐目	**Specific Accounts**	**708357**	**652261**	**582685**	**414264**	
总数①	**Total①**	**1694260**	**1533850**	**1564165**	**1522692r**	**1412023**

注：①2003年数字在日后得到更多资料时会作出修订。

a) Figures of 2003 are subject to revisions as more data become available.

25-22 财政支出

Government Expenditure

单位：万澳门元

(10 000 MOP)

项　　目	Items	1999	2000	2001	2002	2003p
经常支出	**Current Expenditure**					
人员	Personnel	292701	264848	271964	278525	286983
物品及劳务	Goods and Services	68609	52491	53932	54361	57259
利息	Interest	487	-	-	-	-
经常转移	Current Transfers	423233	425837	496145	439137	525171
其他经常支出	Other Current Expenditure	30234	5232	5456	6834	4808
资本支出	**Capital Payments**					
投资	Investment	112778	87018	99305	135055	236169
资本转移	Capital Transfers	4681	3744	3832	2206	2651
财务活动	Financial Transactions	22538	10998	8761	18314	33217
其他资本支出	Other Capital Expenditure	-	-	-	-	-
指定帐目	**Specific Accounts**	708357	652261	582685	414264	
总数①	**Total①**	1663618	1502427	1522079	1348695r	1146257

注：①2003年数字在日后得到更多资料时会作出修订。

①Figures of 2003 are subject to revisions as more data become available.

25-23 货币供应

Money Supply

单位：亿澳门元（年底数字）

(100 million MOP(as at end of year))

项　　目	Items	1999	2000	2001	2002	2003
狭义货币供应量M1	**Money Supply (M1)**	53.6	49.5	59.2	63.5	87.9
分类一：澳门元	Classification 1: MOP	36.7	31.8	35.2	39.3	48.7
港元	HKD	16.5	17.0	23.3	23.6	35.3
其他货币	Other Currencies	0.4	0.7	0.6	0.6	3.8
分类二：流通货币（澳门元）	Classification 2: Currency in Circulation (MOP)	18.2	17.2	19.0	20.5	23.6
活期存款	Demand Deposits	35.4	32.3	40.2	43.0	64.3
广义货币供应量M2①	**Money Supply (M2) ①**	861.0	849.2	915.5	989.6	1110.9
分类一：澳门元	Classification 1: MOP	279.5	232.2	261.1	275.4	296.4
港元	HKD	441.2	445.1	469.1	512.2	594.4
其他货币	Other Currencies	140.2	171.9	185.4	201.9	220.1
分类二：狭义货币供应量M1②	Classification 2: Money Supply (M1) ②	53.6	49.5	59.2	63.5	87.9
准货币负债③	Quasi-Monetary Liabilities (QML)③	807.3	799.7	856.3	926.1	1023.0
储蓄存款	Savings Deposits	148.8	154.5	193.6	230.7	349.2
通知存款	Notice Deposits	8.8	7.7	8.4	9.3	12.3
定期存款	Time Deposits	649.7	637.5	654.3	686.0	661.5

注：《中华人民共和国澳门特别行政区基本法》规定，澳门元是澳门特别行政区的法定货币。

① M2 = M1 + 准货币负债

② 自2001年1月起，货币供应量M1只包括流通货币及活期存款。储蓄存款则变为准货币负债的组成部份。

③ 准货币负债：包括储蓄存款、通知存款、定期存款及存款证明书。

Notes: Pataca (MOP) is the legal tender in the Macao Special Administrative Region, as stated in "The Basic Law of the Macao Special Administrative Region of the People's Republic of China".

① M2 = M1 + Quasi-Monetary Liabilities (QML)

② Starting from January 2001, the definition of M1 has been revised. Saving Deposits are reclassified as component of the Quasi-Monetary Liabilities (QML); while M1 includes only Currency in Circulation and Demand Deposits.

③ QML: Quasi-Monetary Liabilities, which consist of savings deposits, notice deposits, time deposits and certificate of deposits.

25-24 外币兑换率

Exchange Rates

(一单位外币兑换的澳门元) (MOP to one unit of foreign currency)

项　目	Items	1999	2000	2001	2002	2003
年内平均数字	**Average for the Year**					
澳元	Australian Dollar	5.1574	4.6739	4.1598	4.3703	5.2271
欧元①	Euro ①	8.5277	7.4183	7.1962	7.5984	9.0696
韩圆	South Korean Won	0.0067	0.0071	0.0062	0.0065	0.0067
西班牙比塞塔②	Spanish Peseta②	0.0513	0.0446	0.0433		
美元	US Dollar	7.9918	8.0260	8.0335	8.0334	8.0214
新台币	Taiwan Dollar	0.2477	0.2574	0.2379	0.2328	0.2332
法国法郎②	French Franc②	1.3000	1.1309	1.0971		
英镑	Pound Sterling	12.9284	12.1663	11.5698	12.0766	13.104
港元	Hong Kong Dollar	1.03	1.03	1.03	1.03	1.03
日圆	Japanese Yen	0.0704	0.0745	0.0662	0.0643	0.0692
马来西亚林吉特	Malaysian Ringgit	2.1031	2.1121	2.1141	2.1141	2.1109
新西兰元	New Zealand Dollar	4.2315	3.6684	3.3813	3.7306	4.6671
葡萄牙埃斯库多②	Portuguese Escudo②	0.0425	0.0370	0.0359		
德国马克②	Deutsche Mark②	4.3601	3.7929	3.6794		
人民币	P.R. China Renminbi	0.9654	0.9695	0.9706	0.9706	0.9691
新加坡元	Singapore Dollar	4.7160	4.6553	4.4867	4.4893	4.6034
瑞士法郎	Swiss Franc	5.3278	4.7590	4.7638	5.1812	5.9632
年底数字	**As at End of Year**					
澳元	Australian Dollar	5.2096	4.4888	4.1020	4.5470	5.9869
欧元①	Euro ①	8.0489	7.5665	7.0936	8.4164	10.0413
韩圆	South Korean Won	0.0070	0.0064	0.0061	0.0068	0.0067
西班牙比塞塔②	Spanish Peseta②	0.0484	0.0455	0.0426		
美元	US Dollar	8.0049	8.0337	8.0313	8.0328	7.9969
新台币	Taiwan Dollar	0.2546	0.2426	0.2290	0.2312	0.2351
法国法郎②	French Franc②	1.2271	1.1535	1.0814		
英镑	Pound Sterling	12.9559	11.9951	11.6398	12.8810	14.2269
港元	Hong Kong Dollar	1.03	1.03	1.03	1.03	1.03
日圆	Japanese Yen	0.0782	0.0702	0.0611	0.0678	0.0747
马来西亚林吉特	Malaysian Ringgit	2.1066	2.1141	2.1135	2.1139	2.1044
新西兰元	New Zealand Dollar	4.1682	3.5629	3.3350	4.2333	5.2388
葡萄牙埃斯库多②	Portuguese Escudo②	0.0401	0.0377	0.0354		
德国马克②	Deutsche Mark②	4.1153	3.8688	3.6269		
人民币	P.R. China Renminbi	0.9669	0.9706	0.9704	0.9705	0.9662
新加坡元	Singapore Dollar	4.8054	4.6344	4.3402	4.6331	4.6963
瑞士法郎	Swiss Franc	5.0165	4.9865	4.7942	5.7900	6.4395

注：《中华人民共和国澳门特别行政区基本法》规定，澳门元是澳门特别行政区的法定货币。
外币指澳门元以外的其他货币，因而人民币亦视作外币。
①1999年1月1日之前汇率为欧洲货币单位的兑换率。
②自2002年1月1日开始，欧元区各国均需采用统一的硬币及纸币，而旧有的货币则相继停用。

Notes: Pataca (MOP) is the legal tender in the Macao Special Administrative Region, as stated in "The Basic Law of the Macao Special Administrative Region of the People's Republic of China". Foreign currency refers to any currency other than the Pataca. Accordingly P.R. China Renminbi is also treated as foreign currency.
①Quotations before 1/1/1999 referred to the ECU of the European Union.
②On 1/1/2002, the Euro banknotes and coins were introduced to the Euro zone where member states gradually discontinued the circulations of their original currencies

25-25 居民消费价格指数
（1999年10月至2000年9月=100）
Consumer Price Index
(October/1999 - September/2000=100)

项 目	Items	权数 Weight	1999	2000	2001	2002	2003
综合消费价格指数	**Composite Consumer Price Index**						
总指数	**Global Index**	100.00	101.12	99.49	97.52	94.94	93.46
粮食及饮品	Foodstuff and Beverages	31.35	101.25	99.74	98.30	96.21	95.00
服装和鞋	Clothing and Footwear	5.26	100.84	95.35	90.84	81.56	71.37
租金及住屋开支	Rent and Housing Expenses	29.93	101.31	99.54	97.09	94.05	92.86
烟酒	Tobacco and Alcoholic Beverages	1.23	100.70	99.95	102.59	105.16	105.13
家居用品	Household Goods	3.22	100.80	99.20	94.09	90.59	88.18
医疗	Health	2.42	99.85	100.46	101.30	101.32	100.88
交通及通讯	Transport and Communications	9.81	102.17	100.49	97.35	95.44	94.31
教育及消闲	Education and Leisure	10.89	100.32	99.45	99.02	98.21	98.25
其他商品及服务	Other Goods and Services	5.89	99.30	99.49	98.23	95.42	95.19
甲类消费价格指数	**Consumer Price Index (A)**						
总指数	**Global Index**	100.00	100.99	99.56	98.15	95.90	94.63
粮食及饮品	Foodstuff and Beverages	35.05	101.13	99.58	98.23	95.77	94.39
服装和鞋	Clothing and Footwear	3.34	100.43	95.29	90.44	81.10	71.46
租金及住屋开支	Rent and Housing Expenses	32.88	101.71	99.92	97.89	94.85	93.82
烟酒	Tobacco and Alcoholic Beverages	1.48	100.63	100.00	102.70	105.36	105.29
家居用品	Household Goods	1.47	100.72	98.90	95.32	91.60	88.99
医疗	Health	2.33	100.75	100.94	101.93	102.31	102.13
交通及通讯	Transport and Communications	7.91	101.67	99.53	96.55	94.98	93.70
教育及消闲	Education and Leisure	12.16	99.13	99.63	100.52	101.71	102.13
其他商品及服务	Other Goods and Services	3.38	95.02	98.17	99.42	96.82	95.77
乙类消费价格指数	**Consumer Price Index (B)**						
总指数	**Global Index**	100.00	101.00	99.42	97.36	94.63	93.08
粮食及饮品	Foodstuff and Beverages	31.50	101.37	99.80	98.28	96.25	95.08
服装和鞋	Clothing and Footwear	6.22	100.68	95.53	91.28	82.09	71.29
租金及住屋开支	Rent and Housing Expenses	27.13	101.35	99.60	97.23	94.27	93.24
烟酒	Tobacco and Alcoholic Beverages	1.26	100.91	99.95	102.60	105.22	105.20
家居用品	Household Goods	3.51	101.60	99.68	94.41	90.88	88.36
医疗	Health	2.16	98.84	100.60	101.72	101.84	101.38
交通及通讯	Transport and Communications	10.13	101.63	99.85	96.66	94.57	93.31
教育及消闲	Education and Leisure	11.54	99.61	99.24	98.33	96.43	96.25
其他商品及服务	Other Goods and Services	6.55	99.45	99.46	97.68	94.79	94.98

25-26 按双周开支五等分位及商品与服务分类统计的每户双周平均消费开支

Average Biweekly Household Expenditure by Quintile of Biweekly Expenditure Group and Section of Goods and Services

商品与服务分类	Goods and Services	双周开支五等分位 Quintile of biweekly household expenditure group					
		总数 Total		最低五分位 The Lowest 20%		第二五分位 The Second 20%	
		澳门元 MOP	百分比 (%)	澳门元 MOP	百分比 (%)	澳门元 MOP	百分比 (%)
消费开支	**Total Expenditure**	**5075**	**100.0**	**1454**	**100.0**	**2870**	**100.0**
食物及非酒精饮品	Food and Non-alcoholic Beverages	1396	27.5	495	34.0	899	31.3
烟酒	Tobacco and Alcoholic Beverages	50	1.0	24	1.6	38	1.3
衣着和鞋	Clothing and Footwear	224	4.4	30	2.1	71	2.5
住屋及燃料	Housing and Fuels	1042	20.5	504	34.7	750	26.1
家居设备及日用品	Housing Equipment and Routine Maintenance of the House	142	2.8	17	1.2	33	1.2
医疗	Health	149	2.9	39	2.7	75	2.6
运输	Transport	337	6.6	44	3.0	121	4.2
通讯	Communications	226	4.5	71	4.9	139	4.9
娱乐及文化	Recreation and Culture	324	6.4	45	3.1	160	5.6
教育	Education	483	9.5	70	4.8	311	10.8
杂项商品及服务	Miscellaneous Goods and Services	407	8.0	39	2.7	135	4.7
外地消费	Consumption Expenses Outside Macao	295	5.8	76	5.2	137	4.8
住户数目	**Number of Households**	**134332**	**100.0**	**26867**	**20.0**	**26867**	**20.0**

25-26 续表 continued

商品与服务分类	Goods and Services	双周开支五等分位 Quintile of biweekly household expenditure group					
		第三五分位 The Third 20%		第四五分位 The Fourth 20%		最高五分位 The Highest 20%	
		澳门元 MOP	百分比 (%)	澳门元 MOP	百分比 (%)	澳门元 MOP	百分比 (%)
消费开支	**Total Expenditure**	**4057**	**100.0**	**5674**	**100.0**	**11322**	**100.0**
食物及非酒精饮品	Food and Non-alcoholic Beverages	1263	31.1	1688	29.7	2635	23.3
烟酒	Tobacco and Alcoholic Beverages	48	1.2	61	1.1	78	0.7
衣着和鞋	Clothing and Footwear	130	3.2	231	4.1	660	5.8
住屋及燃料	Housing and Fuels	891	22.0	1156	20.4	1911	16.9
家居设备及日用品	Housing Equipment and Routine Maintenance of the House	55	1.4	128	2.3	475	4.2
医疗	Health	108	2.7	149	2.6	373	3.3
运输	Transport	196	4.8	335	5.9	988	8.7
通讯	Communications	190	4.7	275	4.8	457	4.0
娱乐及文化	Recreation and Culture	260	6.4	348	6.1	808	7.1
教育	Education	473	11.7	559	9.8	1001	8.8
杂项商品及服务	Miscellaneous Goods and Services	247	6.1	439	7.7	1174	10.4
外地消费	Consumption Expenses Outside Macao	195	4.8	305	5.4	761	6.7
住户数目	**Number of Households**	**26866**	**20.0**	**26866**	**20.0**	**26866**	**20.0**

注：从2002年10月至2003年9月进行的住户收支调查获取的结果。
Note: Results are obtained from the Household Budget Survey carried out from October 2002 to September 2003.

25-27 14岁及14岁以上人口教育程度
Education Levels of Population Aged 14 and Over

项　目	Item	1991 人数(万人) (10 000)	1991 百分比 %	1996 人数(万人) (10 000)	1996 百分比 %	2001 人数(万人) (10 000)	2001 百分比 %
总计	**Total**	**28.72**	**100.0**	**31.31**	**100.0**	**34.97**	**100.0**
男	Male	13.74	47.8	14.68	46.9	16.45	47.0
女	Female	14.98	52.2	16.62	53.1	18.52	53.0
从未入学/学前教育	No Education/Pre-primary Education	4.30	15.0	2.63	8.4	2.10	6.0
男	Male	1.51	5.3	0.69	2.2	0.48	1.4
女	Female	2.78	9.7	1.94	6.2	1.62	4.6
小学	Primary Education	12.49	43.5	12.70	40.6	13.64	39.0
男	Male	6.12	21.3	6.08	19.4	6.63	19.0
女	Female	6.38	22.2	6.62	21.1	7.01	20.0
初中	Junior Secondary Education	7.56	26.3	8.93	28.5	9.45	27.0
男	Male	3.75	13.1	4.25	13.6	4.43	12.7
女	Female	3.81	13.3	4.68	14.9	5.02	14.4
高中	Senior Secondary Education	2.88	10.1	4.83	15.4	6.63	19.0
男	Male	1.51	5.3	2.47	7.9	3.32	9.5
女	Female	1.36	4.7	2.36	7.5	3.31	9.5
高等教育	Higher Education						
高等专科	Non-university Degree	0.52	1.8	0.25	0.8	0.75	2.1
男	Male	0.23	0.8	0.09	0.3	0.29	0.8
女	Female	0.28	1.1	0.16	0.5	0.46	1.3
大学	University	0.97	3.4	1.93	6.2	2.39	6.8
男	Male	0.61	2.1	1.09	3.5	1.29	3.7
女	Female	0.36	1.3	0.84	2.7	1.10	3.1
不详	Unknown			0.03	0.1	0.02	0.1
男	Male			0.01		0.01	
女	Female			0.02	0.1		

25-28 按各类型教育机构统计的学生人数①
Students by Type of Educational Institutes①

单位：人　　(No. of Students)

类　别	Type	1998/1999	1999/2000	2000/2001	2001/2002	2002/2003
正规教育	**Regular Education**	105849	104997	106966	106999	110266
学前教育	Pre-Primary Education	17354	16083	14978	13638	12737
小学	Primary Education	48269	47059	45474	43709	41535
中学	Secondary Education	28543	30685	35850	38751	41551
技术及职业中学	Vocational Technical College	3239	4076	2306	2381	2448
高等教育 ②	Higher Education ②	8444	7094	8358	8520	11995
特殊教育	**Special Education**	494	563	560	693	587
学前	Pre-Primary Education	19	19	19	14	26
小学	Primary Education	49	52	63	110	86
中学	Secondary Education	18	20	19	24	30
特殊班	Special Classes in Ordinary School	408	472	459	545	445
成人教育③	**Adult Education③**	47624	46432	65695	82401	86578

注：①学生人数为学年终人数。②只计算政府认可的高等教育机构。③成人教育为注册学生人数。

Notes: ①No. of students as at the end of the school-year.

②Referring only to the higher education institutions recognized by the government.

③In adult education, data refer to student enrollments.

25-29 按住所租住权划分的家庭住户数目
Number of Households by Tenure of Accommodation

单位：户　　(No. of households)

项　目	Item	1993/1994	1998/1999	2002/2003
自置	Owner-occupier	68599	87887	104382
租客	Tenant	20335	21248	17727
二房东	Main tenant	348	233	214
三房客	Sub-tenant	440	269	151
合租者	Co-tenant	4528	6355	3315
由雇主提供	Provided by Employer	4051	2721	1023
免租	Rent-free	8745	9140	7520

25-30 医疗卫生条件

Health

项 目	Items	1999	2000	2001	2002	2003
医护人员（人）	**Medical Personnel in Health Care**					
医生	Doctors	880	895	891	921	1009
牙科技术员	Odontologists	90	86	84	85	83
护士	Nurses	897	943	960	980	1010
诊断及治疗助理员	Diagnostic and Therapeutic Technical Assistants	212	208r	235r	240r	239
卫生服务助理员	Health Service Assistants	360	381	378	388	412
按每千名人口计算的医生数	Number of Doctors per 1000 Residents	2.0r	2.1	2.0	2.1	2.2
医疗机构和病床	**Health Care Establishments and Beds**					
医院（所）	Hospitals (No.)	2	2	2	2	2
病床（张）①	Beds (No.) ①	955	990	980	995	1004
按每千名人口计算的病床数	Number of Beds per 1000 Residents	2.2	2.3	2.2	2.3	2.2

注：①包括普通住院、深切治疗部及新生婴儿的病床。

Notes: ①Including beds for general hospitalization, intensive care and newborns.

25-31 社会保障基金发放次数及金额

Number of Payments and Amounts of Subsidy Granted by Social Security Fund

形 式	Type	2001		2002		2003	
		次数 No. of Payments	金额（万澳门元） Amount (10 000MOP)	次数 No. of Payments	金额（万澳门元） Amount (10 000MOP)	次数 No. of Payments	金额（万澳门元） Amount (10 000MOP)
总计	**Total**	**176647**	**22132**	**236351**	**34610**	**304068**	**53003**
养老金	Old Age Pension	77027	8845	87347	10033	98389	11301
残疾津贴	Disability Pension	7585	866	7594	867	7516	860
社会救济金	Social Security Pension	58652	4373	56749	4240	53836	4024
特别给付	Special Payment	11666	1137	12328	1221	13003	1307
失业津贴	Unemployment Subsidy	7719	1788	11563	2579	12554	2749
疾病津贴	Sickness Subsidy	1127	142	1249	158	1487	181
出生津贴	Birth Subsidy	1947	195	1805	181	1900	190
结婚津贴	Marriage Subsidy	820	82	936	94	917	92
丧葬津贴	Funeral Subsidy	346	45	459	60	500	65
因肺尘埃沉着病的给付	**Payments for Pneumoconiosis**	**7**	**153**	**5**	**52**	**5**	**182**
因工作关系所引起的债权	**Credit Advances to Worker of Financially Troubled Enterprise**	**601**	**1183**	**822**	**1476**	**450**	**809**
援助失业人士	Aid given to the Unemployed	5812	1588	35847r	9995r	69207	20854
援助建造业失业人士	Aid given to the Unemployed Manufacturing and Construction Workers	254	71	-	3	-	-
援助特困行业从业员	Aid given to workers engaged in industires with severe difficulties					5748	277
职业技能培训班和专业知识进修班(4000名额)	Vocational training and professional improvement courses (4000 placements)			19460	3615	38556	10111
根据23/07/97博彩合同修订版第三条款规定给予援助失业人士的款项	Assistance to the Unemployed According to Clause 3 of the Gambling Contract revised on 23/07/97	3084	1733	187	36r	-	-

主要统计指标解释

本地生产总值 反映每年在澳门特区生产的货物和提供各种服务的总量。本年鉴中的本地生产总值用支出法及生产法估算，支出法等于私人消费支出、政府最终消费支出、固定资本形成总额、库存变化和货物及服务出口净值（出口减进口）的总和。而生产法等于各经济行业的增加值总额的总和，这种方法可以评估澳门特区的产业结构。

婴儿死亡率 参考期内年龄在1岁或以下的死亡人数与出生活婴数目的千分比。

自然增长率 参考期内出生人数和死亡人数差额与平均人口之千分比。

出生率 参考期内出生活婴数目与平均人口之千分比。

死亡率 参考期内死亡人数与平均人口之千分比。

正规教育 指有系统的，且主要为儿童及青少年开办的，由学前教育至大学教育之课程。正规教育课程必须符合下列三个条件：

–课程最少为期一学年；

–有规定入学资格；

–有考试或指定程序评核成绩。

学前教育 分为幼儿教育与小学教育预备班。

1)幼儿教育：对象是年龄3–4岁的儿童。在报名当年的12月31日年满3岁的幼儿皆可报读。而晋升方面，则无须进行知识的考核。

2)小学教育预备班：在报名当年的12月31日年满5岁的儿童可报读预备班。为晋升之目的，只设有进度测验。在某些教育机构，小学教育预备班仍被称为学前教育第三年。

小学教育 为期6年，完成小学教育预备班或在报名当年的12月31日年满6岁的儿童可报读小学教育第一年。就读小学的最高年龄为15岁。

中学教育 由两个阶段组成：初中教育及高中教育。大学预科亦被视为中学教育。

1) 初中教育：为期3年，合格完成小学教育者可以入读。就读初中最大年龄为18岁，但在特别情况下，经教育机构决定，可以逾越此年限。

2) 高中教育：为期最少2年，最多3年，合格完成初中教育者可以入读。就读高中最大年龄为21岁，但在特别情况下，经教育机构决定，可以逾越此年限。

技术及职业教育 以培训初级及中级程度的技术及专业人员为目的之课程。

高等教育 由大学、理工学院及相等之学院开办之学位或非学位课程。

特殊教育 指专为有精神、感官、身体、沟通等方面有特殊需要人士所开办的课程。

成人教育 指正规教育系统以外为15岁或以上人士所开办的各种有组织、有系统的学习活动。

劳动人口 在参考期间，可参与生产商品或提供服务之14岁或以上人士的总合。包括就业人口及失业人口。

就业人口 在参考期间，为了金钱或物质的报酬、利润或家庭收入而工作至少1小时的14岁或以上人士的总合。亦包括那些被雇用而没有上班，但与雇主保持正式联系，或拥有1间公司，但因特别原因暂时没有上班的人士。

失业人口 在参考期间，同时符合下列条件的14岁或以上人士的总合。包括：没有工作或与雇主没有正式工作联系；可接受有酬工作或自己做生意；在过去30日曾寻找职业。

就业不足人口 在参考期间，不论其职业身份，非自愿地工作少于35小时，但随时可以接受更多的工作或正在寻找更多工作之就业人口。

劳动力参与率 指劳动人口在14 岁或以上的居住人口中所占的比例。

失业率 指失业人口在劳动人口中所占的比例。

就业不足率 指就业不足人口在劳动人口中所占的比例。

访澳旅客 指任何非以澳门特区为常居地的人士，其连续逗留时间自2000年8月开始由原来少于3个月改为少于12个月，旅客之旅游目的并非在澳门特区参与任何有偿活动。

酒店入住率 入住客房数量与可供应客房数量之百分比。

进口 指将产自外地的货物输入澳门特区，但再进口和转运制度下输入者除外。

出口 指将货物输出澳门特区，但暂时出口和转运制度下输出者除外。

本地产品出口 指将产地为澳门特区的货物输出澳门特区。

再出口 指原进口的货物未经加工输出澳门特区，或虽加工，但不能取得澳门特区产地资格。

转运 指仅为运输之目的，货物在澳门特区经过或转船，且其下目的地应于附同之文件中列明。

原产地 指农产品种植之国家或地区、矿业开采之国家或地区以及工业产品全部或部份生产之国家或地区。若生产产品之部份，负责将产品变成确定形式进入澳门特区前的最后一个生产工序之国家或地区，都可被视为原产地。而再包装、再分类及混合不被视为生产工序。

目的地 目的地是指货物实际最后到达的国家或地区(不论在运输途中有或没有中断)。如有中间国家或地区，只要不在中间国家或地区内进行商业交易，最后到达的国家或地区都可被视为目的地。

贸易条件指数 即出口单位价格指数与进口单位价格指数之比率。

单位 指永久性楼宇之一个或多个间格及其附属建筑物。每一个单位具有独立入口与楼宇内之公用地方相通，具有合法条件进行分层物业登记和作独立转让。

楼宇建筑面积 相等于所有层数之面积总和。楼面面积的计算方法是从外墙起量度，同时亦包括大堂面积、楼梯、升降机所占面积以及所有公用地方面积(两个或以上单位合用)。

居民消费价格指数 反映澳门特区家庭于购买一篮子之指定商品或服务时，在不同时间该等商品或服务之价格变动。

狭义货币供应量M1 为流通货币及活期存款之和。

广义货币供应量M2 指狭义货币供应量M1加上准货币负债。准货币负债指储蓄存款、通知存款、定期存款和存款证明书。

财务活动 由财务资产及财务负债组成。

Explanatory Notes on Main Statistical Indicatiors

Gross Domestic Product (GDP) Reflects the total of goods produced and services provided annually in Macao, China. GDP in this statistical yearbook is estimated by using the expenditure and production approaches. The expenditure-based GDP is measured as the sum of private consumption expenditure, government final consumption expenditure, gross fixed capital formation, changes in inventories, and net exports (exports less imports) of goods and services. The production-based GDP, which is measured as the sum of gross value added of all economic activities, can be used to evaluate the structure of the industrial sectors in Macao, China.

Infant Mortality Rate Deaths of infants under one year old per 1,000 live births within the reference period.

Natural Growth Rate: Surplus (or deficit) of births over deaths per 1,000 residents of the average population within the reference period.

Crude Birth Rate Live births per 1,000 residents of the average population within the reference period.

Crude Mortality Rate Deaths per 1,000 residents of the average population within the reference period.

Regular Education Systematic academic programmes designed in principle, for children and juveniles to access / progress from pre-primary education to university. Three pre-requisites are set up:

-Programme duration of at least one academic year.

-Specific academic qualification for entrance.

-Examination or specific academic assessment procedures included.

Pre-primary Education Composed of 2 stages: infant education and the preparatory level for primary education.

(1)Infant education: Designed for children aged between 3-4 years old. Children aged 3 as at 31st December of the year of enrolment are also eligible. No knowledge assessment tests are required for progression.

(2)Preparatory level for primary education: Designed for children aged 5 as at 31st December of the year of enrolment. Progress examination is a pre-requisite for advancement access. This type of preparatory level is also called the third year of pre-primary education in some educational institutes.

Primary Education Lasts for 6 years. Children having completed the preparatory level or aged 6 as at 31st December of the year of enrolment are eligible to the first year of primary education. The maximum age for primary education is 15.

Secondary Education It is divided into 2 stages: Junior secondary and senior secondary. Pre-university courses are also considered secondary education.

(1)Junior Secondary Education: For a duration of 3 years. Students having successfully completed the primary education are eligible. The maximum age for this level is 18 years old. However, under certain circumstances, the educational institutes can exercise their discretion to accept enrolment beyond the age limit.

(2)Senior Secondary Education: For a duration of 2-3 years. Students having successfully completed the junior secondary level are eligible. The maximum age for this level is 21. However, under certain circumstances, the educational institutes can exercise their discretion to accept enrolment beyond the age limit.

Vocational Technical Secondary Education Programmes aiming at training vocational technical personnels in elementary and intermediate levels.

Higher Education Degree or non-degree programmes offered by universities, polytechnical institutes or equivalent.

Special Education Programmes designed for students with mental, sensory, corporal or communication problems, etc.

Adult Education Practical programmes or courses, outside the regular education, organized for general participation, which are designed for individuals aged 15 and above.

Labour Force Total number of people aged 14 and above who are available to participate in the production of goods and services during the reference period. It comprises employed population and unemployed population.

Employed Population Total number of people aged 14 and above who have worked at least 1 hour during the reference period, for pay, profits or family gains, in cash or in kind. It also includes individuals who have a job and are absent from work but maintain a formal job attachment with the employer, or company owners who are temporarily not working due to specific reasons.

Unemployed Population Total number of people aged 14 and above during the reference period with all of the following conditions:

-Not having a job or any formal job attachment to an employer.

-Available for work with remuneration or running own business.

-Seeking work during the last 30 days.

Underemployed Population Refers to the employed population who, regardless of their status in employment, worked involuntarily for less than 35 hours during the reference period, and have sought or are available to take on additional work.

Labour Force Participation Rate The proportion of labour force in the resident population aged 14 and above in Macao, China.

Unemployment Rate The proportion of unemployed in the labour force.

Underemployment Rate The proportion of underemployed in the labour force.

Visitor Any person travelling to a place (ie Macao, China) other than his/her usual environment and whose main purpose of travel is other than the exercise of an activity remunerated from within the place visited. The maximum length of stay has been amended from 3 consecutive months to 12 consecutive months since August 2000.

Hotel Occupancy Rate The percentage of rooms occupied by guests in the total number of available rooms.

Imports The entry of any commodities into Macao, China, except Re-imports and Transit.

Exports The outgoing from Macao, China, of any commodities, excluding Temporary Exports and Transit.

Domestic Exports The outgoing from Macao, China, of any commodities with the origin of Macao, China.

Re-exports The outgoing from Macao, China of any commodities previously imported, without any transformation or even with transformation, the commodities did not obtain the origin of Macao, China.

Transit Commodities passing through or transhiped in Macao, China for the exclusive purpose of transportation and with their next destination mentioned in the attached documents.

Country of Origin The country or territory where the crops were grown, the minerals were mined and the articles were manufactured wholly or partly. If partly, the origin is considered the country or territory responsible for the last phase of manufacture before the merchandise took its final form. Repacking, sorting or mixing are not considered a manufacture operation.

Country of Destination The final country or territory to which the goods are delivered, whether or not the transport has been interrupted, and without any commercial transaction in the transit country or territory.

Terms of Trade Index GThe ratio of the unit value index of exports to that of imports.

Housing Unit Division(s) or annex of a permanent building. Each housing unit has independent entrance of access to the common area of the building; can be legally registered with the property registry and can be independently transacted.

Gross Floor Area The sum of area of each floor in a building measured to the outer surface of the outer walls including the area of lobbies, stairs, lift landings and communal space (shared by 2 or more housing units).

Consumer Price Index Reflects the price change of a representative "basket" of goods and services consumed by families in Macao, China.

Money Supply (M1) Refers to the sum of currency in circulation and demand deposits.

Money Supply (M2) Refers to the sum of money supply M1 and quasi-monetary liabilities that consist of savings deposits, notice deposits, time deposits and certificates of deposits.

Financial Transactions Comprise financial assets and financial liabilities.

附录一、台湾省主要社会经济指标

APPENDIX I. Main Social and Economic Indicators of Taiwan Province

附录1-1　面积和人口主要指标

Main Indicators of Area and Population

资源来源:台湾省《统计月报》(以下各表同)。

Source: *Monthly Statistics Bulletin,* Taiwan Provice. The same as the following tables.

项　　目	Item	1999	2000	2001	2002	2003
面积　(万平方公里)	Area (10 000 sq.km)	3.6	3.6	3.6	3.6	3.6
年底人口数　(万人)	Year-end Population (10 000 persons)	2209.2	2227.7	2240.6	2252.1	2260.5
男	Male	1131.3	1139.2	1144.2	1148.5	1151.5
女	Female	1078.0	1088.5	1096.4	1103.5	1108.9
出生率　(‰)	Crude Birth Rate (‰)	12.89	13.80	11.65	11.02	10.06
死亡率　(‰)	Crude Death Rate (‰)	5.7	5.7	5.7	5.7	5.8
婴儿死亡率　(‰)	Infant Mortality Rate (‰)	7.23	6.99	6.33		
妇女生育率　(‰)	Fertility Rate (‰)	45	48	41	39	36
人口自然增长率　(‰)	Natural Population Growth Rate (‰)	7.16	8.10	5.94	5.29	4.27
结婚率　(‰)	Marriage Rate (‰)	7.87	8.20	7.63	7.69	7.60
离婚率　(‰)	Divorce Rate (‰)	2.23	2.40	2.53	2.73	2.87
平均期望寿命　(岁)	Life Expectancy at Birth (years)					
男	Male	72.46	72.67	72.80	72.45	73.34
女	Female	78.12	78.44	78.48	78.39	79.33
人口的年龄构成　(%)	Age-specific Distribution (%)					
0-14岁	0-14	21.43	21.11	20.81	20.42	19.83
15-64岁	15-64	70.13	70.26	70.39	70.56	70.94
65岁及以上	65 and Over	8.44	8.62	8.81	9.02	9.24
性别比(女=100)	Sex Ratio (Famel=100)	104.95	104.66	104.36	104.08	103.84
人口密度(人/平方公里)	Population Density (persons/sq.km)	610.5	615.6	619.1	622.3	624.6

附录1-2　劳动力和就业状况

Labor Force and Employment

项　　目	Item	1999	2000	2001	2002	2003
劳动力总人数　(万人)	Labor Force (10 000 persons)	966.8	978.4	983.2	996.9	1007.6
男	Male	581.2	586.7	585.5	589.6	590.4
女	Female	385.6	391.7	397.7	407.4	417.2
就业人数　(万人)	Employment (10 000 persons)	938.5	949.1	938.3	945.4	957.3
男	Male	562.4	567.0	555.3	554.7	557.9
女	Female	376.1	382.1	383.0	390.7	399.4
就业人数部门构成　(%)	Distribution of Employment by Industry (%)	100.0	100.0	100.0	100.0	100.0
农、林、渔、牧业	Agriculture, Forestry, Fishery and Hunting	8.3	7.8	7.5	7.5	7.3
工业	Industry					
采矿业	Mining and Quarrying	0.1	0.1	0.1	0.1	0.1
制造业	Manufacturing	27.7	28.0	27.6	27.1	27.1
电、煤气、水	Electricity, Gas, Water	0.4	0.4	0.4	0.4	0.4
建筑业	Construction	9.0	8.8	8.0	7.7	7.3
服务业	Services					
批发、零售业	Wholesale and Retail Trade	22.7	23.2	23.5	17.9	17.7
运输、仓储和通信业	Transport, Storage, Communications	5.1	5.1	5.2	5.0	5.1
金融、保险业	Financing, Insurance	4.3	4.8	4.7	4.0	3.9
教育服务业	Education	5.1	5.0	5.1	5.2	5.3
住宿及餐饮业	Hotels and Restaurants	5.1	5.3	5.6	6.1	6.1
公共行政业	Public Administration	3.4	3.3	3.5	3.5	3.9
其他	Others	8.8	8.2	8.8	15.5	15.8
失业人数　(万人)	Unemployment (10 000 persons)	28.3	29.3	45.0	51.5	50.3
失业率　(%)	Unemployment Rate (%)	2.9	3.0	4.6	5.2	5.0

附录1-3 本地居民生产总值
Gross National Product

年份 Year	本地居民生产总值 Gross National Product 新台币亿元 NT $100 million	比上年增长% Annual Growth Rate over the Preceding Year %	亿美元① USD 100 million①	人均本地居民生产总值 Per Capita Gross National Product 新台币元 NT $	美元 USD
1992	54598	7.3	2170	264338	10506
1993	60322	6.7	2286	264196	10011
1994	65710	6.8	2483	286191	10812
1995	71291	6.3	2691	336042	12686
1996	77876	5.9	2836	364115	13260
1997	84174	6.3	2933	390103	13592
1998	90066	4.3	2692	413582	12360
1999	93758	5.6	2905	427097	13235
2000	98033	6.4	3139	443087	14188
2001	96980	-1.1	2868	435321	12876
2002	100030	3.1	2893	446636	12916
2003	101814	1.8	2959	452719	13157

注:①按当年价格计算。
Note:①At current market prices.

附录1-4 本地生产总值支出构成
Expenditures on Gross Domestic Product

单位：% (%)

年份 Year	本地生产总值(新台币亿元) Gross Domestic Product (NT$ 100 million)	居民消费 Household Consumption Expenditure	政府消费 Government Consumption Expenditure	固定资本形成总额 Gross Fixed Capital Formation	存货增加 Change in Stocks	货物及服务出口 Exports of Goods and Services	减：货物及服务进口 Minus:Imports of Goods and Services
1992	53376.9	56.0	17.0	23.2	1.7	43.4	41.3
1993	59183.8	56.6	15.6	25.2	1.0	44.1	42.5
1994	64636.0	58.3	14.6	24.6	0.8	43.7	42.0
1995	70179.3	58.8	14.2	25.0	0.4	48.0	46.3
1996	76781.3	59.1	14.3	22.5	0.7	47.4	44.0
1997	83287.8	59.7	14.4	22.8	1.5	48.3	46.2
1998	89389.7	59.7	14.3	23.5	1.4	47.8	46.7
1999	92899.3	60.7	13.2	22.9	0.5	48.3	45.5
2000	96633.9	61.9	12.9	23.5	-0.6	54.4	52.1
2001	95066.2	63.6	13.1	18.7	-1.1	50.9	45.2
2002	97488.1	63.1	12.6	17.7	-0.9	53.8	46.4
2003	98475.6	62.8	12.8	17.5	-0.4	58.1	50.9

附录1-5 本地生产总值及部门构成
Gross Domestic Product by Kind of Economic Activity

单位：% (%)

年份 Year	本地生产总值(新台币亿元) Gross Domestic Product (NT$ 100 million)	农业 Agriculture Forestry, Hunting and Fishery	工业 Industry	制造业 Manufacturing	水、电、煤气业 Electricity Gas & Water	建筑业 Construction
1992	53376.9	3.6	39.9	31.7	2.7	5.0
1993	59183.8	3.6	39.4	20.6	2.7	5.3
1994	64636.0	3.5	37.7	29.0	2.6	5.6
1995	70179.3	3.4	36.4	27.9	2.6	5.4
1996	76781.3	3.2	35.7	27.9	2.5	4.9
1997	83287.8	2.6	35.3	27.8	2.4	4.7
1998	89389.7	2.5	34.6	27.4	2.3	4.4
1999	92899.3	2.6	33.2	26.6	2.2	3.9
2000	96633.9	2.1	32.4	26.4	2.2	3.4
2001	95066.2	2.0	31.1	25.6	2.2	2.9
2002	97488.1	1.9	31.1	25.9	2.2	2.6
2003	98475.6	1.8	30.4	25.5	2.2	2.2

附录1-5 续表 continued

单位：% (%)

年份 Year	服务业 Services	批发、零售及餐饮业 Wholesale and Retail Trade, and Restaurants	运输仓储及通信业 Transport, Storage & Communications	金融保险不动产及工商服务业 Finance, Insurance, Real Estate & Business Services	政府部门服务业 Government Services
1992	56.53	14.98	6.29	18.79	11.02
1993	57.01	15.30	6.40	19.40	10.49
1994	58.77	15.61	6.55	20.96	10.27
1995	60.14	16.35	6.65	21.37	10.35
1996	61.09	16.80	6.78	21.69	10.36
1997	62.13	17.23	6.74	22.83	10.19
1998	62.96	17.77	6.96	22.74	10.02
1999	64.26	18.49	6.73	22.90	10.19
2000	65.53	19.30	6.71	22.76	10.19
2001	66.96	19.29	6.90	20.49	10.64
2002	67.11	19.44		20.87	10.51
2003	67.79	19.85		21.01	10.81

附录1-6 农业生产指数
Index of Agricultural Production

(2001年=100) (2001=100)

年份 Year	总指数 Total	种植业 Crops	林业 Forestry	畜牧业 Livestock	渔业 Fishery
1981	79.1	113.1	704.6	49.3	73.8
1991	100.7	109.6	223.6	92.5	100.2
1993	104.3	112.3	140.9	98.9	102.8
1994	101.1	108.3	106.3	104.5	90.6
1995	104.8	110.5	124.1	109.7	94.4
1996	105.0	110.2	102.2	114.2	90.0
1997	103.6	111.9	115.0	105.7	91.8
1998	97.9	102.7	145.7	97.9	91.9
1999	99.1	109.7	122.4	94.3	90.0
2000	101.2	104.5	120.8	99.7	98.3
2001	100.0	100.0	100.0	100.0	100.0
2002	104.1	105.5	111.6	98.1	108.1

附录1-7 主要农产品产量
Output of Major Crops

单位：万吨 (10 000 tons)

年份 Year	稻米 Rice	小麦(吨) Wheat(ton)	玉米 Maize	花生 Peanuts	香蕉 Banana	茶叶 Tea	甘蔗 Sugarcane	烟叶 Tobacco
1991	181.9	3581	32.1	8.4	19.7	2.1	453.6	2.1
1992	162.8	4326	33.9	7.6	19.6	2.0	585.8	1.6
1993	182.0	4921	34.6	7.6	21.3	2.1	480.3	1.7
1994	167.9	4440	39.7	8.1	18.4	2.4	550.4	1.9
1995	168.7	4429	37.6	9.2	17.3	2.1	486.2	1.3
1996	157.7	193	39.5	8.0	14.1	2.3	419.0	1.1
1997	166.3	85	33.8	8.4	20.5	2.4	390.2	1.0
1998	148.9	66	24.4	6.8	21.6	2.3	355.9	1.0
1999	155.9	88	20.1	6.7	21.3	2.1	325.6	0.9
2000	154.0	127	17.8	7.9	19.8	2.0	289.4	1.2
2001	139.6			5.6	20.5	2.0	218.0	
2002	146.1			7.7	22.7	2.0	197.3	

附录1-8 工业生产指数

Index of Industrial Production

(2001年=100) (2001=100)

年份 Year	总指数 General	矿业 Mining	制造业 Manufacturing	电、煤气、水 Electricity, Gas & Water	建筑业 Construction
1996	86.09	126.55	84.67	77.73	146.79
1997	91.39	126.49	90.79	82.49	123.07
1998	94.49	118.72	93.68	88.79	123.75
1999	101.45	109.20	100.98	91.80	131.93
2000	108.47	99.95	109.12	98.89	112.60
2001	100.00	100.00	100.00	100.00	100.00
2002①	107.92	108.28	109.39	103.31	79.34
2003①	115.58	100.24	117.46	107.20	86.38

注：① 预计数。

Note:①Estimated data.

附录1-9 主要工业产品产量

Output of Major Industrial Products

年份 Year	各种成衣 (万打) Wearing Apparel (10 000 dozens)	人造纤维 (万吨) Yarn of man-made staple (10 000 tons)	木制家具 (新台币亿元) Wood Furniture (NT$100 million)	电风扇 (万台) Electric Fan (10 000 units)	监视器 (万台) Monitor (10 000 units)	缝纫机 (万台) Sewing Machine (10 000 units)	主机板 (万片) Mainboard (10 000 units)	显像管 (万只) Kinescope (10 000 units)
1995	3775.4	258.3	205.6	1993.9	1775.1	321.3	1595.3	1551.8
1996	3329.9	276.6	192.7	2219.7	1866.9	330.5	2343.2	1450.6
1997	3230.0	304.3	188.9	2132.5	2046.1	344.9	3110.3	1537.2
1998	3348.0	319.8	199.3	2034.7	1640.6	329.0	4392.4	1521.7
1999	3175.6	325.5	190.0	2380.0	932.1	277.8	5424.1	2334.4
2000	2760.5	330.8	168.6	2227.9	569.2	294.7	6392.9	2053.8
2001	2188.5	314.9	115.9	2160	675.3	263.0	5528.0	973.9
2002①	1858.1	335.8	95.5	2050	510.5	246.1	4914.5	436.4
2003①	1597.8	333.3			421.5		4671.5	

附录1-9　续表 1 continued

年份 Year	可携式电脑 (万台) Notebook Computer (10 000 units)	手　机 (万部) Mobile Phone (10 000 units)	电子电容器 (亿只) Electron Capacitor (100 million units)	印刷电路板 (万平方英尺) Printing Circuit Board (10000 sq foot)	盐 (万吨) Salt (10 000 tons)	天然气 (亿立方米) Natural Gas (100 million cu.m)	发电量 (亿千瓦小时) Electric Power (100 million K.W.H.)
1995			423.5		22.1	8.9	1178.6
1996	378.6	0.2	450.4	48731	23.3	8.7	1350.0
1997	466.9	2.5	570.9	64202	6.2	8.5	1436.6
1998	702.0	7.9	683.3	79275	0.7	8.7	1554.5
1999	995.3	77.7	824.8	94662	7.7	8.5	1605.7
2000	1306.0	476.1	1144.0	120547	6.9	7.4	1751.7
2001	1413.0	965.4	1217	92541	6.6	8.4	1783.6
2002①	1446.0	2151.4	1500	118005	5.6	8.7	1879.1
2003①	1051.2	3067.7	1991	127722			1971.4

附录1-9　续表 2 continued

年份 Year	汽车外胎 (万条) Tires (10 000 units)	钢　坯 (万吨) Steel (10 000 tons)	水　泥 (万吨) Cement (10 000 tons)	瓷　砖 (万平方米) Tile (10 000 sq.m)	汽车零件 (新台币亿元) Automobile Part (NT$100million)	数控机床 (台) NC Machine Tools (units)	纸　板 (万吨) Paper Board (10 000 tons)	汽车 (万辆) Car (10 000 units)
1995	1218.0		2247.8	13170.4	1203.6	3999		39.0
1996	1332.4	1277.3	2153.7	10969.3	1153.1	4337	321.3	36.7
1997	1446.0	1552.3	2152.2	10666.2	1223.3	4439	325.4	37.6
1998	1573.0	1659.4	1965.2	10172.4	1306.4	5244	297.5	40.3
1999	1702.4	1522.2	1828.3	9234.9	1290.8	4325	307.4	34.5
2000	1755.8	1619.1	1757.2	7153.2	1394.7	5665	323.4	37.1
2001	1679.0	1639.9	1812.8	4726.0	1256.0	3714	259.1	26.9
2002①	1932.6	1742.3	1936.3	3959.8	1527.0	4215	323.5	33.0
2003①	2261.9	1763.8	1847.4	4610.8		5288	340.4	39.2

注：① 预计数。
Note: ①Estimated data.

附录1-10　能 源 生 产 和 消 费
Production and Consumption of Energy

项　目	Item	1998	1999	2000	2001	2002	2003
供给量总计 (亿升标准油)	**Total Supply (100 000 kl oil equivalent)**	**924.6**	**988.8**	**1050.4**	**1085.2**	**1132.3**	**1212.2**
供给量比重(%)	Distribution of Supply (%)	100.0	100.0	100.0	100.0	100.0	100.0
煤炭	Coal	28.9	29.9	31.1	32.3	33.1	32.6
石油	Petroleum	51.4	51.5	50.9	50.4	49.3	50.8
天然气	Natural Gas	7.0	6.7	6.8	7.1	7.6	7.3
水力发电	Hydraulic Power	2.8	2.2	2.1	2.1	1.4	1.4
核能发电	Nuclear Energy Source	9.9	9.7	9.1	8.1	8.7	8.0
消费量总计 (亿升标准油)	**Total Consumption (100 000 kl oil equivalent)**	**807.8**	**851.7**	**906.4**	**948.3**	**1003.1**	**1034.2**
分部门消费比重(%)	Distribution of Consumption (%)	100.0	100.0	100.0	100.0	100.0	100.0
运输	Transportation	17.1	17.0	16.3	15.4	15.3	14.8
工业	Industry	55.3	54.5	55.2	57.1	57.7	51.1
农业	Agriculture	1.5	1.5	1.6	1.6	1.5	1.6
住宅	Residence	11.8	12.6	12.4	12.1	11.8	11.8
商业	Commerce	5.7	5.8	5.8	5.8	5.7	5.8
其他	Other	6.1	5.9	6.1	6.2	6.0	6.7
非能源消费	Non-energy Use	2.5	2.6	2.6	1.8	2.0	2.1
平均每人能源消费量 (千升标准油)	**Per Capita Energy Consumption (kl oil equivalent)**	**3.1**	**3.8**	**4.0**	**4.2**	**4.4**	**4.6**

附录1-11　按用途分的批准动工的建筑面积
Floor Space of Authorized Construction Projects by the Purpose

单位：万平方米　　(10 000 sq.m.)

年份 Year	总计 Total	住宅用 Residential	商业用 Stores & Mercantile	工业用 Industrial	办公用 Office	其他用 Other
1992	3692	1566	898	464	251	153
1993	4754	2177	1264	482	237	203
1994	5816	2858	1536	539	216	236
1995	5526	2646	1534	440	290	268
1996	4571	2063	1086	393	249	345
1997	3846	1459	964	378	290	342
1998	3868	1392	922	461	247	406
1999	4124	1356	894	681	409	360
2000	3502	1037	621	688	304	418
2001	3117	819	438	611	243	585
2002	2439	792	320	331	177	407

附录1-12　铁路和公路客货运量
Railway and Highway Passenger and Freight Traffic

年份 Year	铁路 Railway				公路 Highway			
	客运量 (万人) Passenger Traffic (10 000 persons)	客运周转量 (万人公里) Passenger Kilometers (10 000 p-km)	货运量 (万吨) Freight Traffic (10 000 tons)	货物周转量 (万吨公里) Freight Ton-kilometers (10 000 ton-km)	客运量 (万人) Passenger Traffic (10 000 persons)	客运周转量 (万人公里) Passenger-Kilometers (10 000 p-km)	货运量① (万吨) Freight Traffic① (10 000 tons)	货物周转量① (万吨公里) Freight Ton-kilometers① (10 000 ton-km)
1991	13778	862101	2626	196114	150248	2498117	25430	1181376
1992	14987	935740	2819	213996	142089	2422747	26796	1221989
1993	15803	955227	3058	201778	135556	1941098	30167	1286684
1994	16099	951518	3123	200674	128921	1799516	31340	1309140
1995	16092	949939	3012	189954	120345	1615089	29100	1249150
1996	17100	903200	2741	158486	116716	1542116	28940	1199090
1997	19700	950700	2657	151385	116280	1441704	27700	1216500
1998	23300	1030500	2656	140434	115483	1429848	36000	1742600
1999	31000	1102000	2600	131400	114900	1424673	35000	1847000
2000	46000	1262400	2230	117900	110400	1465716	34400	1818200
2001	47600	1226900	1930	101000	109100	1523654	30000	1773500
2002	50000	1214700	1820	94100	105400	1574680	28900	1773100
2003	47800	1117800	1670	86400	98800	1484700	30400	1816400

注：①仅为民营汽车公司数。

Note: ①Data only refer to private truck companies.

附录1-13 邮政及电信营运量

Telecommunication Services

项目	Item	1999	2000	2001	2002	2003
邮政	**Post**					
函件（亿件）	Letters (100 million pieces)					
收寄	Received	27.1	30.9	28.9	28.8	27.3
投递	Mailing	30.5	34.1	33.1	33.2	32.2
包裹（万件）	Parcels (10 000 pieces)					
收寄	Received	1614.7	1728.7	1063.1	797.3	895.3
投递	Mailing	1653.9	1784.2	1095.2	820.9	918.1
电信	**Telecommunications**					
市内电话用户数（万户）	Number of Local(Urban) Telephone Subscribers (10 000 Subscribers)	1204.4	1264.2	1285.8	1309.9	1335.5
公共电话话机数（万部）	Number of Public Telephones (10 000 Subscribers)	14.5	15.0	13.9	13.5	13.2
移动电话用户数（万户）	Number of Mobile Telephones Subscribers (10 000 Subscribers)	1154.1	1787.4	2163.3	2390.5	2509.0
无线寻呼机用户数（万户）	Number of Subscribers of Pagering Services (10 000 Subscribers)	387.3	281.3	175.6	159.8	141.5
数字式低功率无线电话用户数 （万户）	Digital low-power Wireless Telephones Subscribers (10 000 Subscribers)	6.7	4.4	21.1	52.1	63.4
整体服务数位网络用户数（万户）	Number of Subscribers of Local Area Network (10 000 Subscribers)	2.8	3.8	4.2	3.9	4.8
国际互联网用户数（万户）	Number of Subscribers of Internet Services (10 000 Subscribers)	287.4	465.0	623.2	745.4	782.8
国际电话去话分钟数 （万分钟）	International Call (10 000 minutes)	95826	105838	151442	215391	307674

附录1-14 商品进出口贸易总额

Total Imports and Exports

年份 Year	按新台币计算（亿元） (NT $ 100 million)			按美元计算（亿美元） (USD 100 million)		
	进出口总额 Total	出口额 Exports	进口额 Imports	进出口总额 Total	出口额 Exports	进口额 Imports
1988	31550	17320	14230	1100	610	500
1989	31340	17480	13860	1190	660	520
1990	32750	18030	14720	1220	670	550
1991	37320	20410	16910	1390	760	630
1992	38650	20480	18170	1530	810	720
1993	42740	22390	20350	1620	850	770
1994	47180	24560	22620	1780	930	850
1995	56920	29500	27430	2150	1120	1040
1996	59920	31770	28150	2180	1160	1020
1997	67580	34820	32760	2370	1220	1140
1998	71970	36930	35040	2160	1110	1050
1999	74930	39170	35760	2330	1220	1110
2000	89850	46160	43690	2880	1480	1400
2001	77570	41380	36190	2300	1230	1070
2002	84012	45075	38937	2431	1306	1125
2003	93361	49524	43837	2714	1442	1272

附录1-15　商品进口来源和出口去向

Origin of Imports and Destination of Exports

单位：亿美元　　　　(USD 100 million)

项　目	Item	1999	2000	2001	2002	2003
商品进口来源	**Imports (Major Origin)**					
中国香港	Hong Kong, China	20.9	21.9	18.5	17.4	17.3
日　本	Japan	305.9	385.6	258.5	272.8	326.4
韩　国	Korea, Rep.	71.9	89.9	67.1	77.1	86.9
新加坡	Singapore	33.1	50.1	33.7	35.4	38.6
马来西亚	Malaysia	38.8	53.3	42.1	41.5	47.5
泰　国	Thailand	23.8	27.7	21.8	21.7	23.7
法　国	France	18.9	18.3	21.3	15.5	16.3
德　国	Germany	53.1	55.4	42.5	44.2	49.6
意大利	Italy	13.1	13.9	10.8	10.9	11.3
英　国	United Kingdom	17.2	19.4	14.4	13.6	14.2
加拿大	Canada	11.3	12.8	10.0	9.5	10.8
美　国	United States	196.9	251.3	182.3	180.9	168.2
澳大利亚	Australia	29.6	35.0	30.9	28.3	27.3
印度尼西亚	Indonesia	22.9	30.2	25.2	25.9	29.2
菲律宾	Philippines	21.7	35.9	32.5	36.5	30.8
越　南	Vietnam	3.9	4.7	4.2	4.5	4.5
阿　曼	Oman	3.3	4.0	1.3	5.2	1.1
沙特阿拉伯	Saudi Arabia	13.8	26.9	27.5	24.1	42.8
荷　兰	Netherlands	17.1	20.9	15.2	14.4	13.0
商品出口去向	**Exports (Major Destination)**					
中国香港	Hong Kong, China	260.1	313.4	269.6	308.5	283.5
日　本	Japan	119.0	166.0	127.6	119.8	119.1
韩　国	Korea, Rep.	26.1	89.9	32.8	38.7	45.7
新加坡	Singapore	38.2	50.1	40.5	43.8	49.8
马来西亚	Malaysia	28.5	53.3	30.6	31.3	30.5
泰　国	Thailand	21.0	27.7	21.3	22.9	25.7
法　国	France	15.8	16.4	11.7	11.2	12.5
德　国	Germany	40.8	48.9	44.8	38.4	42.1
意大利	Italy	13.3	14.8	12.6	12.5	14.6
英　国	United Kingdom	38.3	45.1	33.3	29.1	28.8
加拿大	Canada	17.5	18.8	15.6	15.3	14.7
美　国	United States	309.0	348.2	276.5	267.6	259.4
澳大利亚	Australia	18.5	18.3	13.6	15.9	18.8
印度尼西亚	Indonesia	13.0	17.3	14.8	14.6	15.1
菲律宾	Philippines	26.1	30.4	21.5	19.7	23.0
越　南	Vietnam	13.4	16.6	17.3	22.9	26.6
阿　曼	Oman	0.2	0.2	0.2	0.1	0.1
沙特阿拉伯	Saudi Arabia	3.8	3.5	3.5	3.4	3.6
荷　兰	Netherlands	42.1	49.3	42.3	37.7	41.3

附录1-16 出口与进口商品分类
Composition of Exports and Imports

单位：亿美元 (USD 100 million)

年份 Year	出口 Exports: 出口额 Total	农产品 Agricultural Products	农产加工品 Processed Agricultural Products	工业产品 Industrial Products	进口 Imports: 进口额 Total	原材料 Agricultural & Industrial Raw Materials	资本货物 Capital Goods	消费品 Consumer Goods
1992	814.7	5.1	29.8	779.9	720.1	498.7	128.7	92.7
1993	850.9	4.7	30.1	816.1	770.6	541.4	130.1	99.1
1994	930.5	4.6	33.5	892.4	853.5	603.0	136.1	114.4
1995	1116.6	4.8	38.0	1073.8	1035.5	745.6	168.7	121.2
1996	1159.4	4.7	36.2	1118.6	1023.7	706.4	183.6	133.8
1997	1220.8	3.8	21.7	1195.3	1144.3	771.3	217.4	155.6
1998	1105.8	3.2	16.3	1086.3	1046.7	667.7	243.0	135.9
1999	1215.9	3.8	15.7	1196.4	1106.9	709.8	292.4	104.7
2000	1483.2	3.6	17.5	1462.2	1400.1	897.8	392.6	109.8
2001	1228.7	3.0	16.6	1209.1	1072.4	704.8	268.6	98.9
2002	1306.0	3.5	17.0	1285.5	1125.3	761.7	259.2	104.3
2003	1441.8	3.8	17.7	1420.3	1272.5	896.7	260.3	115.5

附录1-17 旅 游 人 数
Visitor Arrivals and International Tourists

单位：万人次 (10 000 person-times)

项 目	Item	1997	1998	1999	2000	2001	2002	2003
总 计	**Total**	**237.2**	**229.9**	**241.1**	**262.4**	**261.7**	**297.8**	**224.8**
华 侨	Overseas Chinese	25.7	26.7	29.6	31.3	32.5	62.4	43.6
外国人	Foreign Tourists	211.6	203.2	211.5	231.1	229.2	235.4	181.2

附录1-18 居民消费价格指数
Consumer Price Indices

(2001年=100) (2001=100)

年份 Year	总指数 General Index	食品类 Food	服装 Clothing	居住 Housing	交 通 Transportation	医药保健 Medicines and Medical Care	教育娱乐 Education and Entertainment	杂 项 Miscellaneous
1995	93.2	94.0	104.9	95.4	95.3	87.5	81.1	95.5
1996	96.1	97.7	107.5	97.4	96.5	89.0	87.0	96.4
1997	97.0	97.0	108.3	98.5	97.6	91.1	90.2	97.3
1998	98.6	101.3	102.8	99.7	96.6	91.9	93.1	98.3
1999	98.8	100.5	101.4	99.8	95.9	95.1	95.1	99.8
2000	100.0	100.9	101.7	100.3	99.0	98.7	97.9	100.4
2001	100.0	100.0	100.0	100.0	100.0	100.0	100.0	100.0
2002	99.8	99.8	100.6	98.9	97.8	101.3	100.1	105.1
2003	99.5	99.7	102.0	97.8	98.4	104.7	98.8	104.7

附录1-19　各级政府财政收入净额

Net Revenue of Treasury

单位：新台币亿元　　(NT $ 100 million)

项　目	Item	1998	1999	2000	2001
总　计	**Total**	**20535**	**20044**	**27849**	**18963**
课税收入	Tax	13396	12997	18525	12003
独占及专卖收入	Revenue from Monopoly	574	553	773	576
营业盈余及事业收入	Revenue from Enterprises and Institutions	3616	3249	4584	3466
其他收入	Other Revenue	2948	3245	3967	2919
财产利息收入	Revenue from Profit of Public Properties	415	254	266	203
规费收入	Fees	689	672	1123	769
罚款及赔偿收入	Revenue from Fines & Indemnities	381	387	597	420
捐赠及赠与收入	Receipts from Donations and Contributions	16	15	27	37
财产收回及售价收入	Return of Properties and Sales of Public Properties	928	1373	1053	872
杂项收入	Miscellaneous Revenues	518	544	901	617

附录1-20　各级政府财政支出净额

Net Expenditures of Treasury

单位：新台币亿元　　(NT $ 100 million)

项　目	Item	1998	1999	2000	2001
总　计	**Total**	**19926**	**20500**	**31409**	**22713**
一般行政支出	General Administration	2573	2791	4680	3287
国防支出	National Defense	3123	2866	3578	2476
教育科学文化支出	Expenditures on Education, Science and Culture	4115	4291	6551	4301
经济发展支出	Economic Development	3350	3511	4749	3988
社会福利支出	Social Welfare	2828	2805	5318	3970
社区发展及环境保护支出	Community Development and Environment Protect	749	903	1061	1091
退休抚恤支出	Retire Pension	1877	1806	2651	1757
债务支出	Obligations	1159	1409	2704	1716
杂项支出	Miscellaneous	153	118	119	127

附录1-21 政 府 公 债
Government Bonds

单位：新台币亿元 (NT $ 100 million)

年份 Year	总计 Total			台湾省级 Taiwan Provincial			省级及"院"辖市级 Sub-provincial and Municipal Gov't		
	发行额 Issues	偿还额 Redemption	余额 Outstanding	发行额 Issues	偿还额 Redemption	余额 Outstanding	发行额 Issues	偿还额 Redemption	余额 Outstanding
1993	2373	665	72223	2100	475	6135	273	189	1087
1994	1480	725	7976	1480	514	7102		211	876
1995	1250	556	8671	1250	300	8051		256	620
1996	2450	1159	9963	2250	940	9361	200	219	601
1997	1740	1354	10348	1600	1208	9754	140	147	594
1998	1460	1369	10439	1200	1260	9694	260	109	745
1999	2828	815	12452	2828	703	11819		112	633
2000	3625	1274	14803	3465	1194	14090	160	80	713
2001	4570	790	18583	4370	734	17736	200	56	857
2002	4362	800	22145	4262	747	21241	100	53	904
2003	4548	808	25885	4548	752	25036		55	849

附录1-22 主 要 金 融 指 标
Principal Financial Indicators

年份 Year	货币供应额 (新台币亿元) Money Supply (NT $100 million)	流动性负债 (新台币亿元) Liquid Liabilities (NT $100 million)	储备货币 (新台币亿元) Reserve Money (NT $100 million)	存 款 (新台币亿元) Deposits (NT $100 million)	放款与投资 (新台币亿元) Loans & Investments (NT $100 million)	再贴现率 (年息%) Rediscount Rate (% annual)	汇率(卖出价) (新台币/美元) Exchange Rates of Selling (NT $/USD)
1991	21584	82874	12653	75728	61897	6.25	25.80
1992	24258	97510	14119	90767	79605	5.63	25.47
1993	27971	113536	15014	104638	95110	5.50	26.72
1994	31393	129901	16688	120405	109556	5.50	26.26
1995	31631	142621	16381	131469	121003	5.50	27.32
1996	34261	156464	16525	142606	130518	5.00	27.54
1997	37153	170188	16413	154213	140847	5.25	32.62
1998	38548	185813	16651	166969	151766	4.75	32.26
1999	45072	206382	16433	180642	156750	4.50	31.44
2000	44921	223182	15834	193087	161757	4.63	33.06
2001	50259	241463	14561	201607	160227	2.13	35.04
2002	54916	257923	15688	206098	159257	1.63	34.81

附录1-23 股 票 交 易
Transactions of Listed Stock

单位：新台币亿元 (NT $ 100 million)

年份 Year	上 市 股 票 Listed Stock				股票成交额 Total Trading Value	股票指数(年平均) (1966年=100) Stock Price Index (year average) (1966=100)
	公司数(家) Number	种类(种) Kind	总面值 Total Par Value	总市值 Total Market Value		
1992	256	286	7360	25460	59170	4271.63
1993	285	325	8910	51450	90570	4214.78
1994	313	354	10710	65020	188120	6252.99
1995	347	383	13250	51080	101520	5543.75
1996	382	425	16270	75240	129080	6003.72
1997	404	470	20660	96960	372410	8410.56
1998	437		26900	83770	296190	7737.68
1999	462		30540	117870	292920	7426.68
2000	531		36300	81910	305270	7847.21
2001	584		40630	102480	183550	4907.43
2002	638		44097	90949	218740	5225.61
2003	669		47051	128691	203332	5161.90

附录1-24 入学率和教育经费

Net Enrollment Rate and Public Expenditures for Education at Current Market Prices

单位：% (%)

年份 Year	粗入学率(6-21岁) Gross Enrollment Rate (age 6-21)			每千人口高等教育学生数	15岁以上人口识字率	公共教育经费 Public Expenditure for Education	
	初等教育 (6-11岁) Primary Education (age 6-11)	中等教育 (12-17岁) Secondary Education (age 12-17)	高等教育 (18-21岁) Higher Education (age 18-21)	Higher Education Student per 1000 Population	Percentage of Literate Aged 15 and Over	总计(新台币亿元) Total (NT $100 million)	占本地居民生产总值% As % of GNP
1991	101.0	95.4	37.9	26.8	92.9	3009.7	6.5
1992	101.3	95.6	42.0	28.9	93.2	3511.4	6.8
1993	101.8	95.3	45.0	30.5	93.4	4011.3	7.0
1994	100.9	95.9	45.3	31.7	93.7	4281.1	6.9
1995	101.4	95.7	46.4	32.7	94.0	4496.9	6.6
1996	101.1	95.8	47.7	34.3	94.3	5008.6	6.8
1997	100.6	97.2	51.1	37.6	94.7	5336.7	6.7
1998	99.8	98.6	56.1	40.7	94.9	5503.1	6.4
1999	99.7	99.6	61.0	44.6	95.3	5815.4	6.4
2000	100.5	99.2	68.4	49.4	95.6	5342.9	5.5
2001	99.7	99.4	77.1	54.1	95.8	5708.0	5.9
2002	100.0	99.3	83.4	56.8	96.0		6.1
2003	99.5	99.0	90.2	58.3	97.0		5.9

附录1-25 科技人员数和科研开发经费

Number of Scientists, Engineers and Technicians and Expenditures for R & D

年份 Year	科技人员数(人) Number of Scientists, Engineers and Technicians Engaged in Research and Experimental Development (Headcount)				科研开发经费 Expenditures for Research and Experimental Development		占科研开发经费比重(%) As % of Expenditures for Research and Development	
	总计 Total	科学家和工程师 Scientists & Engineers	技术员 Technicians	辅助人员 Assistant	总计(新台币亿元) Total (NT $100 million)	占本地生产总值% As % of GDP	政府经费 Government	民间经费 Private
1991	82436	46173	22844	13419	818	1.70	52.1	47.9
1992	77750	48356	22117	7277	948	1.78	52.2	47.8
1993	90918	54905	23720	12293	1036	1.76	49.5	50.5
1994	95088	58156	24067	12865	1147	1.77	48.2	51.8
1995	105822	66478	25635	13709	1250	1.78	45.9	54.1
1996	116853	71611	28987	16255	1380	1.80	42.7	57.3
1997	129165	76588	34021	18556	1563	1.88	40.8	59.2
1998	129305	83209	30535	15561	1765	1.98	38.3	61.7
1999	134845	87454	31465	15926	1905	2.05	37.9	62.1
2000	137622	87394	33713	16515	1976	2.05	37.5	62.5
2001	138409	89118	33007	16283	2050	2.16	37.0	63.0
2002	150200	95421	37448	17331	2244	2.30	38.1	61.9

附录1-26　医院、病床和医务人员情况
Medical Facilities and Health Personnel

年份 Year	医疗机构 (所) Number of Medical Care Facilities	平均每一机构服务人数 (人) Population Served per Medical Care Facility (person)	病床数 (床) Beds (bed)	每万人病床数 (床) Beds per 10 000 Population	从业医务人数 (人) Health Personnel (person)	每万人拥有医务人员 (人) Health Personnel per 10 000 Population
1987	12199	1613	86328	43.88	77246	39.27
1988	12215	1629	88572	44.50	83045	41.72
1989	12267	1639	86693	43.12	85599	42.57
1990	12902	1578	89151	43.80	91153	44.79
1991	13661	1505	92785	45.14	96921	47.15
1992	14468	1434	96084	46.30	102977	49.62
1993	15062	1392	100570	47.90	109538	52.17
1994	15752	1342	103733	48.98	114076	53.87
1995	16109	1326	112379	52.62	118248	55.37
1996	16645	1293	114923	53.39	123829	57.53
1997	17398	1250	121162	55.73	137829	66.72
1998	17731	1237	124564	56.80	144070	65.71
1999	17770	1243	122937	55.65	152385	68.98
2000	18082	1279	126476	56.78	159212	71.47
2001	18265	1271	127676	56.98	165855	74.02
2002	18228	1278	133398	59.23	175444	77.90

附录1-27　家 庭 设 备 普 及 率
Percent of Families Owning Household Appliances

单位：% (%)

年份 Year	彩色电视机 Color TV Sets	有线电视频道设备 Cable TV Sets	空调 Air Conditioners	洗衣机 Washing Machines	电话机 Telephone Sets	汽车 Automobiles	家用电脑 Family Computers
1985	92.31		23.95	77.84	82.12	11.91	2.32
1986	94.42		25.45	79.49	85.25	13.63	2.92
1987	95.78		28.66	81.33	87.20	15.54	3.55
1988	97.34		34.29	83.97	89.11	19.21	3.95
1989	97.80		41.74	86.82	91.51	24.90	5.42
1990	98.26		47.26	88.79	93.08	29.07	6.77
1991	99.16		52.37	89.53	94.75	33.67	9.57
1992	99.30		56.14	90.38	95.13	38.94	11.76
1993	99.25		60.69	91.51	96.00	41.05	13.56
1994	99.36	43.40	64.01	92.31	96.53	45.54	15.29
1995	99.29	54.20	67.08	92.83	96.70	47.95	18.54
1996	99.32	59.60	71.65	93.00	97.49	51.16	22.56
1997	99.47	66.00	73.83	93.99	97.54	53.79	28.39
1998	99.17	68.10	76.20	93.86	97.63	54.52	32.31
1999	99.31	67.90	78.89	94.74	98.00	54.33	38.92
2000	99.45	72.00	79.46	95.36	98.04	55.58	46.49
2001	99.30	72.30	80.50	95.00	97.80	55.60	50.90
2002	99.60	74.80	83.10	96.00	97.90	58.20	56.80

附录二、我国经济、社会统计指标同世界主要国家比较

APPENDIX II. A Comparison of Indicators of Economy and Society Among the People's Republic of China and Other Countries

附录2-1 国土面积和人口

Territory and Population

资料来源：联合国粮农组织数据库。

Sources: FAO Database.

国家	Country	国土面积 (万平方公里) Area (10 000 sq.km)	2002 年中人口数 (万人) Mid-year Population (10 000 persons)	2002 人口增长率(%) Annual Growth Rate(%)	2002 人口密度 (人/平方公里) Population Density (persons/sq.km)
世界	**World**	**13427.9①**	**622497.8**	**1.3**	**46**
亚洲	**Asia**	**3187.0**	**377594.8**	**1.3**	**118**
中国②	China②	960.0	128453	0.6	134
日本	Japan	37.8	12748	0.2	337
印度③	India③	328.7	104955	1.6	319
印度尼西亚	Indonesia	190.5	21713	1.3	114
菲律宾	Philippines	30.0	7858	1.9	262
泰国	Thailand	51.3	6219	1.0	121
马来西亚	Malaysia	33.0	2397	2.0	73
新加坡	Singapore	0.1	418	1.9	6747
巴基斯坦	Pakistan	79.6	14991	2.5	188
缅甸	Myanmar	67.7	4885	1.3	72
孟加拉国	Bangladesh	14.4	14381	2.1	999
土耳其	Turkey	77.5	7032	1.5	91
蒙古	Mongolia	156.7	256	1.2	2
朝鲜	Korea, D.P.Rep.	12.1	2254	0.6	187
韩国	Korea, Rep.	9.9	4743	0.6	478
越南	Vietnam	33.2	8028	1.4	242
非洲	**Africa**	**3030.9**	**83209**	**2.2**	**27**
埃及	Egypt	100.1	7051	2.0	70
尼日利亚	Nigeria	92.4	12091	2.6	131
欧洲	**Europe**	**2297.6**	**72702**	**-0.1**	**32**
德国	Germany	35.7	8241	0.1	231
英国	United Kingdom	24.3	5929	0.3	244
法国	France	55.2	5985	0.5	109
意大利	Italy	30.1	5748	-0.1	191
捷克	Czech Republic	7.9	1025	-0.1	130
波兰	Poland	31.3	3862	-0.1	124
罗马尼亚	Romania	23.8	2239	-0.2	94
保加利亚	Bulgaria	11.1	797	-0.8	72
俄罗斯联邦	Russian Federation	1707.5	14408	-0.5	8
北美洲	**North America**	**2272.5**	**50075**	**1.2**	**22**
美国	United States	962.9	29104	1.0	30
加拿大	Canada	997.1	3127	0.8	3
墨西哥	Mexico	195.8	10197	1.5	52
南美洲	**South America**	**1783.4**	**35733**	**1.4**	**20**
巴西	Brazil	854.7	17626	1.3	21
阿根廷	Argentina	278.0	3798	1.2	14
大洋洲	**Oceania**	**856.4**	**3184**	**1.3**	**4**
澳大利亚	Australia	774.1	1954	1.0	3
新西兰	New Zealand	27.1	385	0.8	14

注：①是指有定居人口的各大洲面积，未包括尚无定居人口的南极洲。如包括南极洲，全世界陆地面积为 14950万平方公里。②中国为年底总人口。③不包括查谟、克什米尔和锡金等地区。

Note: ①Refer to Continents with resident excluding the Antarctica,If included, it would be 149.50 million sq.km. ②China refer to year-end population. ③Excluding Jammu, Kashmir and Sikkim.

附录2-2 按三次产业划分就业构成

Employment by Type of Industry

资料来源：世界银行数据库。

Source: World Bank Database.

单位：% （%）

国 家	Country	第一产业 Primary Industry		第二产业 Secondary Industry		第三产业 Tertiary Industry	
		2000	2001	2000	2001	2000	2001
中 国	China	50.0	50.0	22.5	22.3	27.5	27.7
孟加拉国	Bangladesh	62.1		10.3		23.5	
印度尼西亚	Indonesia	45.3	43.8	17.3	17.0	37.3	37.5
以 色 列	Israel	2.2	19.3	24.0	23.4	73.0	56.0
日 本	Japan	5.1	4.9	31.2	30.5	63.1	63.9
韩 国	Korea,Rep.	10.9	10.3	28.0	27.4	61.0	62.3
马来西亚	Malaysia	18.4		32.2		49.5	
巴基斯坦	Pakistan	48.4		18.0		33.5	
菲 律 宾	Philippines	37.4	37.4	16.0	15.6	46.5	47.0
新 加 坡	Singapore	0.2	0.3	34.2	25.4	65.4	74.2
泰 国	Thailand	48.8	46.6	19.0	19.5	32.2	33.9
土 耳 其	Turkey	34.5	32.6	24.5	24.3	40.9	43.1
埃 及	Egypt	29.6		21.3		49.1	
加 拿 大	Canada	3.3	2.9	22.6	22.7	74.1	74.4
墨 西 哥	Mexico	17.5	17.6	26.9	26.0	55.2	56.0
美 国	United States	2.6	2.4	22.9	22.4	74.5	75.2
阿 根 廷	Argentina	0.7	0.4	22.7	22.9	76.2	76.3
巴 西	Brazil	24.2①	20.6	19.3①	20.0	56.5①	59.2
委内瑞拉	Venezuela	10.6	9.6	22.8	22.1	66.5	68.2
保加利亚	Bulgaria	26.2	26.3	28.3	27.6	45.5	46.0
捷 克	Czech Republic	5.1	4.8	40.0	40.4	54.8	54.8
法 国	France	1.6	1.6	24.5	24.4	73.9	74.1
德 国	Germany	2.7	2.6	33.4	32.5	63.8	64.7
意 大 利	Italy	5.4	5.3	32.4	32.1	62.1	62.5
荷 兰	Netherlands	3.3	2.9	21.3	21.2	72.9	73.4
波 兰	Poland	18.8	19.1	30.9	30.5	50.4	50.4
罗马尼亚	Romania	42.8	42.3	26.2	26.2	31.0	31.5
俄罗斯联邦	Russian Federation	11.5②	11.8①	29.4②	29.4①	59.1②	58.8①
西 班 牙	Spain	6.6	6.4	31.3	31.6	62.0	61.9
乌 克 兰	Ukraine	20.5	19.7	31.4	30.8	42.4	43.9
英 国	United Kingdom	1.5	1.4	25.4	24.9	72.7	73.4
澳大利亚	Australia	4.9	4.9	22.0	20.9	73.1	74.1
新 西 兰	New Zealand	8.7	9.1	23.2	22.8	67.6	67.9

注：①1999年数据。②1998年数据。

Note: ①Data refer to 1999. ②Data refer to 1998.

附录2-3 国内生产总值及其增长率

Gross Domestic Product and Its Growth Rate

资料来源：国际货币基金组织数据库。

Sources: International Monetary Fund Database.

国 家	Country	2003 国内生产总值(亿本币) GDP (national currency 100 million)	国内生产总值增长率(比上年增长%) GDP Growth Rate over the Preceding Year (%)			
			2000	2001	2002	2003
世 界	**World**		**4.7**	**2.4**	**3.0**	**3.9**
中 国	China	117252	8.0	7.5	8.3	9.3
孟加拉国	Bangladesh	31495	5.6	4.8	4.9	5.4
印 度	India	267826	5.4	4.0	4.7	7.4
印度尼西亚	Indonesia	17866909	4.9	3.5	3.7	4.1
伊 朗	Iran	11216936	5.9	5.4	7.2	5.9
以 色 列	Israel	4943	7.5	-0.9	-0.8	1.3
日 本	Japan	4987253	2.8	0.4	-0.3	2.7
哈萨克斯坦	Kazakhstan	43756	9.8	13.5	9.5	9.5
韩 国	Korea,Rep.	7213459	8.5	3.8	7.0	3.1
马来西亚	Malaysia	3920	8.6	0.3	4.1	5.2
蒙 古	Mongolia	13622	1.1	1.0	3.9	5.0
缅 甸	Myanmar	86604	13.7	10.5	5.5	5.1
巴基斯坦	Pakistan	42085	3.4	2.7	4.4	5.5
菲 律 宾	Philippines	42945	4.4	3.0	4.4	4.5
新 加 坡	Singapore	1591	9.7	-1.9	2.2	1.1
斯里兰卡	Sri Lanka	17866	6.0	-1.5	3.9	5.5
泰 国	Thailand	59391	4.8	2.1	5.4	6.7
土 耳 其	Turkey	3586996285	7.4	-7.5	7.9	5.8
越 南	Vietnam	5716290	5.5	5.0	5.8	6.0
埃 及	Egypt	4150	5.1	3.5	3.2	3.1
尼日利亚	Nigeria	72968	5.4	3.0	1.5	10.6
南 非	South Africa	12071	3.5	2.7	3.6	1.9
加 拿 大	Canada	12146	5.3	1.9	3.3	1.7
墨 西 哥	Mexico	67548	6.6	-0.2	0.7	1.3
美 国	United States	109855	3.7	0.5	2.2	3.1
阿 根 廷	Argentina	3762	-0.8	-4.4	-10.9	8.7
巴 西	Brazil	15223	4.4	1.3	1.9	-0.2
委内瑞拉	Venezuela	1365815	3.2	2.8	-8.9	-9.2
白俄罗斯	Belarus	359301	5.8	4.7	5.0	6.8
保加利亚	Bulgaria	347	5.4	4.1	4.8	4.3
捷 克	Czech Republic	24101	3.3	3.1	2.0	2.9
法 国	France	15515	4.2	2.1	1.2	0.2
德 国	Germany	21302	2.9	0.8	0.2	-0.1
意 大 利	Italy	13009	3.0	1.8	0.4	0.3
荷 兰	Netherlands	4534	3.5	1.2	0.2	-0.8
波 兰	Poland	8150	4.0	1.0	1.4	3.7
罗马尼亚	Romania	18907780	2.1	5.7	5.0	4.9
俄罗斯联邦	Russian Federation	133047	10.0	5.1	4.7	7.3
西 班 牙	Spain	7430	4.2	2.8	2.0	2.4
乌 克 兰	Ukraine	2632	5.9	9.2	5.2	9.3
英 国	United Kingdom	11005	3.8	2.1	1.7	2.3
澳大利亚	Australia	7797	3.2	2.5	3.8	3.0
新 西 兰	New Zealand	1489	4.0	2.5	4.3	3.5

附录2-4　农业生产指数(2003年)

Agricultural Production Indices (2003)

资料来源：联合国粮农组织数据库。

Source: FAO Database.

(1999-2001年=100)　　(1999-2001=100)

国　家	Country	农业 Agriculture	种植业 Crops	畜牧业 Livestock	食品 Food	非食品 Non Food
世　界	**World**	**105.1**	**103.9**	**106.5**	**105.3**	**100.6**
发达国家	**Developed Countries**	**99.1**	**96.7**	**101.7**	**99.5**	**88.9**
发展中国家	**Developing Countries**	**108.3**	**107.1**	**110.6**	**108.5**	**104.5**
亚　洲	**Asia**	**108.0**	**106.2**	**111.2**	**108.3**	**104.2**
中　国①	China①	113.6	108.1	120.9		
孟加拉国	Bangladesh	104.1	104.4	102.2	104.0	105.5
印　度	India	103.2	101.1	109.2	103.1	105.5
印度尼西亚	Indonesia	108.5	107.1	118.4	108.3	111.3
伊　朗	Iran	110.2	114.0	102.8	110.7	92.3
以色列	Israel	105.3	97.0	111.2	105.5	95.8
日　本	Japan	96.3	93.6	99.5	96.2	100.5
哈萨克斯坦	Kazakhstan	106.8	112.7	106.5	106.0	126.4
朝　鲜	Korea, D.P.Rep.	107.6	108.9	113.8	107.9	102.8
韩　国	Korea, Rep.	93.8	92.5	101.8	94.1	75.8
马来西亚	Malaysia	113.8	114.3	113.4	115.1	95.0
蒙　古	Mongolia	99.1	121.6	98.2	99.5	92.3
缅　甸	Myanmar	120.6	121.4	119.3	120.9	110.8
巴基斯坦	Pakistan	103.8	98.4	108.7	105.4	91.9
菲律宾	Philippines	111.8	107.7	121.6	112.1	98.6
新加坡	Singapore	75.6	100.0	82.2	75.6	
斯里兰卡	Sri Lanka	102.4	101.5	104.4	102.6	101.6
泰　国	Thailand	106.7	105.6	110.2	106.4	108.7
土耳其	Turkey	99.6	102.5	91.2	99.5	100.5
越　南	Vietnam	117.7	116.0	125.7	118.4	107.5
非　洲	**Africa**	**104.8**	**104.6**	**105.3**	**104.9**	**102.2**
埃　及	Egypt	101.3	100.1	105.5	101.6	94.8
尼日利亚	Nigeria	104.7	104.6	106.4	104.8	97.6
南　非	South Africa	102.0	95.9	109.3	102.5	86.4
北美洲	**North and Central America**	**101.1**	**100.0**	**102.0**	**101.2**	**98.2**
加拿大	Canada	97.5	98.8	98.4	97.5	97.6
墨西哥	Mexico	104.8	105.2	106.0	105.4	78.8
美　国	United States	100.7	98.8	101.9	100.9	96.9
南美洲	**South America**	**111.6**	**115.0**	**110.3**	**112.1**	**103.3**
阿根廷	Argentina	102.7	110.1	97.4	103.2	79.5
巴　西	Brazil	118.1	120.6	117.5	118.6	109.8
委内瑞拉	Venezuela	96.8	97.5	96.6	96.9	91.0
欧　洲	**Europe**	**82.6**	**78.8**	**85.1**	**82.6**	**80.5**
白俄罗斯	Belorussia	109.2	118.1	98.8	109.4	91.4
保加利亚	Bulgaria	100.3	92.2	96.1	98.4	151.0
捷　克	Czech Republic	90.3	76.9	102.6	90.2	99.6
法　国	France	94.4	88.7	100.1	94.3	107.2
德　国	Germany	93.3	87.1	100.8	93.4	59.8
意大利	Italy	91.1	87.6	98.6	91.2	83.8
荷　兰	Netherlands	94.1	94.7	93.6	94.1	95.1
波　兰	Poland	97.2	84.9	101.9	97.3	66.6
罗马尼亚	Romania	105.3	103.5	107.3	105.5	83.1
俄罗斯联邦	Russian Federation	108.7	108.4	109.2	108.7	100.6
西班牙	Spain	107.0	108.6	106.9	107.3	90.2
乌克兰	Ukraine	93.4	88.4	103.1	93.4	98.4
英　国	United Kingdom	97.6	97.9	99.4	97.7	87.5
大洋洲	**Oceania**	**99.0**	**93.8**	**103.6**	**102.5**	**65.4**
澳大利亚	Australia	94.5	92.8	98.1	98.8	59.7
新西兰	New Zealand	111.8	97.0	113.5	113.1	92.4

注：① 2000年为基期的总产值指数。

Note:① Indices of gross agricultural output value, 2000 year=100.

附录2-5 工业生产指数

Industry Production Indices

资料来源：联合国数据库。

Sources: United Nations Database.

(1995年=100) (1995=100)

国家	Country	总指数 General Index			其中：制造业 Of Which: Manufacturing		
		2001	2002	2003	2001	2002	2003
中国①	China①	176.6	194.3	218.8			
孟加拉国	Bangladesh	140.9	147.6	154.3	139.9	146.2	152.8
印度	India	135.4	143.2	165.0②	138.7	147.1	170.0②
印度尼西亚	Indonesia				90.5	84.2	83.8③
以色列	Israel	116.4	114.8	110.2④	116.7	114.8	110.2④
日本	Japan	97.7	97.6	100.6	96.9	96.8	99.8
韩国	Korea, Rep.	156.1	167.6	176.4	156.0	167.5	176.2
马来西亚	Malaysia	142.1	147.8	163.4⑤	149.3	156.0	173.8⑤
蒙古	Mongolia	121.9	122.7	115.2③	81.1	97.8	89.0③
巴基斯坦	Pakistan	122.9	131.5	181.3⑥	124.6	131.7	193.2⑥
新加坡	Singapore	126.6	137	140.8	125.1	135.6	139.5
泰国	Thailand				113.5	123.3	138.4
土耳其	Turkey	107.9	117.8	128.5	106.5	117.9	129.5
南非	South Africa	106.7	111.1	111.5	109.0	114.7	112.1
加拿大	Canada	118.0	124.6	124.8	121.7	133.9	133.5
墨西哥	Mexico	136.4	136.1	135.1	140.3	139.2	136.4
美国	United States	124.9	124.2	124.4	128.0	127.2	127.5
阿根廷	Argentina				90.4	81.4	99.1⑦
巴西	Brazil	111.5	114.1	114.7	107.2	108.8	109.1
捷克	Czech Republic	117.6	123.2	130.4	121.8	128.4	135.8
法国	France	117.6	114.3	113.9	118.8	114.9	114
德国	Germany	117.8	113.5	114.0	120.0	115.5	115.7
匈牙利	Hungary	175.2	180.7	191.5	195.9	201.6	214.8
意大利	Italy	106.8	105.3	104.5	105.8	103.7	102.2
荷兰	Netherlands	112.1	109.5	107.3	114.4	110.8	108.4
波兰	Poland	144.1	146.1	158.9	153.5	156.4	172.8
罗马尼亚	Romania	90.4	94.3	97.5	93.6	99.8	103.7
西班牙	Spain	117.9	118.0	119.9	117.3	117.8	119.5
乌克兰	Ukraine	122.4	131.2	159.3⑧			
英国	United Kingdom	105.4	102.5	102.0	105.2	101.4	101.6
南斯拉夫	Yugoslavia	117.1	116.7	119.6	113.9	119.3	121.4
澳大利亚	Australia	106.7	107.1		105.3	106.7	
新西兰	New Zealand	104.2	106.7	107.1	103.3	105.3	106.7

注：①工业增加值指数。②2004年1月份数字。③2003年第二季度数字。④2003年8月份数字。⑤2003年7月份数字。⑥2003年12月份数字。⑦2003年第三季度数字。⑧2003年9月份数字。

Note: ①Indices of industrial value-added. ②Data refer to Jan.2004.③Data refer to second quarter of 2003.④Data refer to Aug.2003. ⑤Data refer to Jul.2003.⑥Data refer to Dec.2003.⑦Data refer to third quarter of 2003.⑧Data refer to Sep.2003.

附录2-6　我国农业主要产品产量居世界位次

Changes in the Order of Precedence of Output of Major Agricultural Products

资料来源：联合国粮农组织数据库。

Sources: United Nations FAO Database.

项目	Item	1978	1980	1985	1990	1995	2000	2002	2003
谷　物	Cereals	2	1	2	1	1	1	1	1
肉　类①	Meat①	3	3	2	1	1	1	1	1
棉　花	Cotton Lint	3	2	1	1	1	1	1	1
大　豆	Soybeans	3	3	3	3	3	4	4	4
花　生	Groundnuts in Shell	2	2	2	2	1	1	1	1
油菜籽	Rapeseeds	2	2	1	1	1	1	1	1
甘　蔗	Sugar Cane	9	9	4	4	3	3	3	3
茶　叶	Tea	2	2	2	2	2	2	2	2
水　果	Fruit		10	8	4	1	1	1	1

注：①1993年以前为猪、牛、羊肉产量的位次。

Note: ①Data refer to pork, beef and mutton prior to 1993.

附录2-7　我国工业主要产品产量居世界位次

Changes in the Order of Precedence of Output of Major Industrial Products

资料来源：联合国数据库、《工业产品统计年鉴》、粮农组织数据库。

Sources: United Nations Database, "Industrial Commodity Statistics Yearbook", FAO Database.

产品名称	Item	1978	1980	1985	1990	1995	2000	2001	2002
钢	Crude Steel	5	5	4	4	2	1	1	1
煤	Coal	3	3	2	1	1	1	1	1
原　油	Crude Petroleum	8	6	6	5	5	5	5	5
发电量	Electricity	7	6	5	4	2	2	2	2
水　泥	Cement	4	4	1	1	1	1	1	1
化　肥	Fertilizer	3	3	3	3	2	1	1	1
化学纤维	Chemical Fibre	7	5	4	2	2	2		
棉　布	Woven Cotton Fabrics	1	1	1	1	1	2	2	1
糖	Sugar	8	10	6	6	4	4	3	3
电视机	Television	8	5	3	1	1	1	1	1

附录2-8 居民消费价格指数

Consumer Price Indices

资料来源：联合国数据库。

Sources: United Nations Database.

(1990年=100) (1990=100)

国　家	Country	总指数 General Index			其中：食品 Of Which: Food		
		2001	2002	2003	2001	2002	2003
中　国	China	201.8	200.1	202.5			
孟加拉国①	Bangladesh①	142.1	147.0		143.0	147.0	
印　度②	India②	246.2	256.5	267.0	241.9	248.2	257.0
印度尼西亚	Indonesia	387.4	433.5	462.0	462	511.9	516.0
伊　朗	Iran	981.3	1121.9	1307.0	1021.2	1185.7	1398.0
以色列	Israel	248.6	266.0	250.0	223.2	235.0	
日　本	Japan	108.6	107.0	107.0	106.7	105.0	105.0
韩　国	Korea, Rep.	170.9	175.5		176.2	183.4	
马来西亚	Malaysia	143.7	146.3	148.0	162.5	163.6	166.0
蒙　古	Mongolia	193.9	197.6				
缅　甸(仰光)③	Myanmar(Yangon)③	183.8	288.6		252.9	298.6	
巴基斯坦	Pakistan	249	259.0	267.0	250	261.4	267.0
菲律宾	Philippines	240.8	248.3		213.2	217.5	
新加坡	Singapore	119.8	119.7	120.0	117	117.0	118.0
斯里兰卡（科伦坡）	Sri Lanka（Colombo）	287.5	314.9	335.0	297.4	329.1	348.0
泰　国(曼谷)	Thailand（Bangkok）	158.1	161.0	162.0	166.2	170.4	173.0
土耳其①	Turkey①	4586.3	6648.6	9622.0	3886.7	6787.4	7502.0
越　南	Vietnam	417.7	434.0		443.2	465.0	
埃　及	Egypt	229.4	235.7		210.7	219.6	
南　非	South Africa	248.9	287.6	288.0	290.6	357.9	364.0
加拿大	Canada	124.8	127.6	131.0	122.4	125.6	128.0
墨西哥	Mexico	572.9	622.1	629.0	530.5	569.3	580.0
美　国	United States	135.5	137.6	141.0	131.4	133.1	136.0
阿根廷(布宜诺斯艾利斯)	Argentina（Buenos Aires）	397.8	500.7	568.0	362.0	487.0	580.0
巴　西①	Brazil①	254.3	275.8		201.7	221.1	
白俄罗斯④	Belorussia④	17877800	25490200	32718600	21869300	30381100	37310300
保加利亚⑤	Bulgaria⑤	3700.9	3915.9	4008.0	3199.1	3198.6	3186.0
捷　克	Czech Republic	366.5	373.0	371.0	124.7	124.8	124.0
法　国	France	120.5	122.8	125.0	119.4	122.5	125.0
德　国⑥	Germany⑥	125.8	127.4	128.0	111.5	112.3	112.0
匈牙利	Hungary	681.9	740.0		611.6	662.2	
意大利	Italy	144.0	154.0	156.0	135.0	147.8	150.0
荷　兰⑦	Netherlands⑦	127.4	138.7	140.0	115.6	117.6	118.0
波　兰	Poland	124.6	126.9	128.0	116.8	116.4	115.0
罗马尼亚⑥	Romania⑥	55617.4	68152.0	78562.0	46391.4	54879.8	62927.0
俄罗斯联邦	Russian Federation	1135160	1206930		1148100	1208500	
西班牙	Spain	151.6	156.2	107.0	127.8	131.9	109.0
乌克兰	Ukraine	929180	969251		878102	913588	
英　国	United Kingdom	137.5	139.7	144.0	124.0	125.0	127.0
澳大利亚	Australia	124.4	136.9	138.0	129.5	147.7	148.0
新西兰	New Zealand	122.2	125.4	128.0	120.4	123.7	124.0

注：① 1994年=100。②指产业工人。③ 1997年=100。④1992年=100。⑤1995年=100。⑥1991年=100。⑦1996年=100。

Note: ① 1994=100.② Industrial workers.③1997=100.④1992=100.⑤1995=100.⑥1991=100.⑦1996=100.

附录2-9 进出口贸易额

Total Imports and Exports

资料来源：世界贸易组织数据库。

Source: World Trade Organization Database.

单位：亿美元 (USD 100 million)

国家	Country	2002		2003	
		进口 Imports	出口 Exports	进口 Imports	出口 Exports
世界	**World**	**66850.00**	**64240.00**	**77650.00**	**74820.00**
中国	China	2952.03	3255.65	4128.40	4382.00
孟加拉国	Bangladesh	74.78	57.33	96.60	68.20
印度	India	563.15	500.39	697.43	547.40
印度尼西亚	Indonesia	313.28	520.48	323.90	606.50
伊朗	Iran	214.00	229.00	275.80	333.60
以色列	Israel	352.40	294.65	364.30	315.77
日本	Japan	3363.85	4159.85	3829.59	4719.34
哈萨克斯坦	Kazakhstan	65.00	96.00	83.27	129.00
韩国	Korea, Rep.	1521.26	1624.71	1787.84	1943.25
马来西亚	Malaysia	802.19	956.55	810.67	1007.26
蒙古	Mongolia	6.59	5.01	7.87	5.16
缅甸	Myanmar	27.93	27.61	25.15	28.02
巴基斯坦	Pakistan	111.47	98.82	130.34	119.01
菲律宾	Philippines	354.65	356.27	393.01	370.65
新加坡	Singapore	1162.30	1255.86	1278.98	1441.34
斯里兰卡	Sri Lanka	60.55	46.99	64.55	50.60
泰国	Thailand	645.36	686.22	756.79	802.53
埃及	Egypt	123.80	46.50	132.80	57.50
尼日利亚	Nigeria	75.47	151.07	108.90	202.55
南非	South Africa	293.85	297.30	381.41	364.52
加拿大	Canada	2275.89	2525.32	2456.18	2720.54
墨西哥	Mexico	1764.57	1607.87	1789.90	1653.34
美国	United States	12024.99	6935.17	13056.48	7240.06
阿根廷	Argentina	89.88	253.62	138.13	293.49
巴西	Brazil	495.00	603.62	506.65	730.84
委内瑞拉	Venezuela	127.25	268.90	93.06	236.50
保加利亚	Bulgaria	73.07	54.00	107.42	74.39
捷克	Czech Republic	406.46	367.93	513.06	487.23
法国	France	3264.40	3294.97	3883.73	3846.62
德国	Germany	4933.21	6122.36	6016.64	7483.75
意大利	Italy	2410.88	2519.98	2890.17	2902.31
荷兰	Netherlands	2177.00	2433.61	2611.35	2934.37
波兰	Poland	547.67	403.80	668.87	522.85
罗马尼亚	Romania	178.73	136.64	240.03	176.18
俄罗斯联邦	Russian Federation	600.12	1068.58	744.96	1351.62
西班牙	Spain	1536.78	1189.18	2000.88	1518.76
乌克兰	Ukraine	167.00	175.00	230.21	230.80
英国	United Kingdom	3398.13	2759.26	3882.82	3038.90
澳大利亚	Australia	727.36	649.87	886.18	703.58
新西兰	New Zealand	150.09	143.50	185.59	165.05

附录2-10 国际收支（2002年）

Balance of Payments (2002)

资料来源：国际货币基金组织数据库。

Source: International Monetary Fund database.

单位:亿美元 (USD 100 million)

国家	Country	经常帐户 Current Account								资本帐户收支盈余	金融帐户收支盈余	国际收支总盈余
		商品贸易 Merchandise			服务贸易 Services		要素收入 Factor Income		经常帐户收支盈余			
		出口 Exports F.o.b	进口 Imports F.o.b	差额 Trade Balance	贷方 Credit	借方 Debit	贷方 Credit	借方 Debit	Current Account Balance	Capital Account Balance	Fin-ancial Account Balance	Overall Balance
中国	China	3257	-2815	442	397	-465	83	-233	354	…	323	752
美国	United States	6854	-11648	-4794	2887	-2274	2555	-2595	-4809	-13	5317	37
日本	Japan	3956	-3018	938	657	-1079	915	-257	1125	-33	-634	461
德国	Germany	6150	-4928	1222	1060	-1505	1033	-1093	466	-2	-771	-20
英国	United Kingdom	2799	-3500	-702	1304	-1077	1897	-1561	-267	16	89	-6
法国	France	3056	-2966	90	867	-690	808	-679	257	-2	-334	-40
意大利	Italy	2537	-2371	165	603	-635	433	-579	-67	7	112	32
加拿大	Canada	2641	-2272	368	372	-425	202	-377	149	31	-117	-2
澳大利亚	Australia	651	-705	-54	179	-181	82	-199	-174	4	172	1
捷克	Czech Republic	385	-407	-22	71	-64	22	-60	-45	0	112	66
波兰	Poland	467	-540	-72	100	-92	20	-38	-50	0	70	6
匈牙利	Hungary	348	-369	-21	78	-72	12	-28	-26	2	1	-18
罗马尼亚	Romania	139	-165	-26	23	-23	4	-9	-15	1	41	18
印度	India	527	-652	-124	249	-187	23	-62	47	35	81	169
印度尼西亚	Indonesia	592	-357	235	67	-171	13	-84	78	0	-12	50
菲律宾	Philippines	344	-340	4	31	-43	79	-34	42	0	-27	…
泰国	Thailand	668	-570	98	153	-167	34	-47	77	0	-27	55
新加坡	Singapore	1284	-1098	185	297	-273	144	-155	187	-2	-157	13
巴基斯坦	Pakistan	98	-104	-6	24	-22	1	-24	39	0	-8	41
韩国	Korea, Rep.	1626	-1484	142	281	-356	68	-64	61	-11	26	118
埃及	Egypt	71	-129	-58	93	-66	7	-10	6	0	-33	-8
墨西哥	Mexico	1608	-1687	-79	127	-177	41	-155	-141	0	222	74
巴西	Brazil	604	-472	131	96	-146	33	-215	-77	4	-31	-113
阿根廷	Argentina	257	-85	172	30	-46	32	-96	96	0	-234	-153

中国统计出版社最新资料书简目

《中国统计年鉴-2004》
《中国统计摘要-2004》
《国际统计年鉴-2004》
《中国城市统计年鉴-2003》
《中国农村统计年鉴-2004》
《中国劳动统计年鉴-2004》
《中国人口统计年鉴-2004》
《中国工业经济统计年鉴-2001》
《中国市场统计年鉴-2004》
《中国对外经济贸易统计年鉴-2003》
《中国发展报告-2004》
《中国固定资产投资统计年鉴-2004》
《中国基本单位统计年鉴-2001》
《中国建筑业统计年鉴-2003》
《中国民政统计年鉴-2004》
《中国农村乡镇统计概要-2004》
《中国农村住户调查年鉴-2004》
《中国物价及城镇居民家庭收支调查统计年鉴-2004》
《中国高技术产业统计年鉴-2004》

《北京统计年鉴-2004》
《天津统计年鉴-2004》
《河北经济年鉴-2004》
《山西统计年鉴-2004》
《内蒙古统计年鉴-2004》
《辽宁统计年鉴-2004》
《吉林统计年鉴-2004》
《黑龙江统计年鉴-2004》
《上海统计年鉴-2004》
《江苏统计年鉴-2004》
《浙江统计年鉴-2004》
《安徽统计年鉴-2004》
《福建统计年鉴-2004》
《江西统计年鉴-2004》
《山东统计年鉴-2004》
《河南统计年鉴-2004》
《湖北统计年鉴-2004》
《湖南统计年鉴-2004》
《广东统计年鉴-2004》
《广西统计年鉴-2004》
《海南统计年鉴-2004》
《重庆统计年鉴-2004》
《四川统计年鉴-2004》

《贵州统计年鉴-2004》
《云南统计年鉴-2004》
《西藏统计年鉴-2004》
《陕西统计年鉴-2004》
《甘肃年鉴-2004》
《青海统计年鉴-2004》
《宁夏统计年鉴-2004》
《新疆统计年鉴-2004》
《新疆生产建设兵团统计年鉴-2004》

《石家庄统计年鉴-2004》
《唐山统计年鉴-2004》
《邯郸统计年鉴-2004》
《呼和浩特经济统计年鉴-2004》
《鄂尔多斯市统计年鉴-2004》
《包头统计年鉴-2004》
《赤峰统计年鉴-2004》
《沈阳年鉴-2004》
《大连统计年鉴-2004》
《鞍山统计年鉴-2004》
《长春统计年鉴-2004》
《吉林市社会经济统计年鉴-2004》
《四平统计年鉴-2004》
《延吉统计年鉴-2004》
《哈尔滨统计年鉴-2004》
《齐齐哈尔经济统计年鉴-2004》
《牡丹江统计年鉴-2004》
《大庆统计年鉴-2004》
《黑龙江垦区统计年鉴-2004》
《上海浦东新区统计年鉴-2004》
《南京统计年鉴-2004》
《苏州统计年鉴-2004》
《无锡统计年鉴-2004》
《常州统计年鉴-2004》
《徐州统计年鉴-2004》
《南通统计年鉴-2004》
《盐城统计年鉴-2004》
《镇江统计年鉴-2004》
《江阴统计年鉴-2004》
《杭州统计年鉴-2004》
《宁波统计年鉴-2004》
《绍兴统计年鉴-2004》
《台州统计年鉴-2004》
《舟山统计年鉴-2004》

《温州统计年鉴-2004》
《金华统计年鉴-2004》
《嘉兴统计年鉴-2004》
《丽水统计年鉴-2004》
《安庆经济统计年鉴-2004》
《福州年鉴-2004》
《厦门经济特区年鉴-2004》
《福州经济技术开发区年鉴-2004》
《南昌经济社会统计年鉴-2004》
《九江经济统计年鉴-2004》
《济南统计年鉴-2004》
《青岛统计年鉴-2004》
《潍坊统计年鉴-2004》
《淄博统计年鉴-2004》
《郑州统计年鉴-2004》
《洛阳统计年鉴-2004》
《三门峡统计年鉴-2004》
《平顶山统计年鉴-2004》
《南阳经济统计年鉴-2004》
《武汉统计年鉴-2004》
《宜昌统计年鉴-2004》
《十堰统计年鉴-2004》
《荆州统计年鉴-2004》
《长沙统计年鉴-2004》
《广州统计年鉴-2004》
《东莞统计年鉴-2004》
《惠州统计年鉴-2004》
《深圳统计年鉴-2004》
《南宁统计年鉴-2004》
《桂林经济社会统计年鉴-2004》
《柳州经济统计年鉴-2004》
《来宾统计年鉴-2004》
《河池地区经济社会统计年鉴-2004》
《海口统计年鉴-2004》
《成都统计年鉴-2004》
《贵阳统计年鉴-2004》
《昆明统计年鉴-2004》
《西安统计年鉴-2004》
《兰州年鉴-2004》
《西宁统计年鉴-2004》
《银川统计年鉴-2004》
《乌鲁木齐统计年鉴-2004》
《巴音郭楞统计年鉴-2004》
《吐鲁番统计年鉴-2004》

编辑部电话：（010）63321207　63266600—30604　　E-mail: yearbook@stats.gov.cn
欲购以上图书请与中国统计出版社发行部联系。电话：（010）63459084　　同榻行书店电话：68585978
通讯地址：北京市西城区三里河月坛南街75号。邮政编码：100826

New Published Statistical Yearbook by China Statistics Press

China Statistical Yearbook-2004
China Statistical Abstract-2004
China Development Report -2004
China Urban Statistical Yearbook-2003
China Rural Statistical Yearbook-2004
China Labour Statistical Yearbook-2004
China Population Statistical Yearbook-2004
China Industrial Statistical Yearbook-2004
China Market Statistical Yearbook-2004
China Foreign Economic Statistical Yearbook-2001
International Statistical Yearbook-2004
China Development Report -2004
China Fixed Assets Statistical Yearbook-2004
China Basic Statistical Units Yearbook-2001
China Construction Statistical Yearbook-2004
China Civil Affairs's Statistical Yearbook -2004
China Hi-tect Statistical Yearbook -2004

Beijing Statistical Yearbook-2004
Tianjin Statistical Yearbook-2004
Hebei Economic Statistical Yearbook-2004
Shanxi Statistical Yearbook-2004
Inner Mongolia Statistical Yearbook-2004

Liaoning Statistical Yearbook-2004
Jilin Statistical Yearbook-2004
Helongjiang Statistical Yearbook -2004

Shanghai Statistical Yearbook-2004
Jiangsu Statistical Yearbook-2004
Zhejiang Statistical Yearbook-2004
Anhui Statistical Yearbook-2004
Fujian Statistical Yearbook-2004
Jiangxi Statistical Yearbook-2004
Shandong Statistical Yearbook-2004

Henan Statistical Yearbook-2004
Hubei Statistical Yearbook-2004
Hunan Statistical Yearbook-2004
Guangdong Statistical Yearbook-2004
Guangxi Statistical Yearbook-2004
Hainan Statistical Yearbook-2004

Chongqing Statistical Yearbook-2004
Sichuan Statistical Yearbook-2004
Guizhou Statistical Yearbook-2004
Yunnan Statistical Yearbook-2004
Tibet Statistical Yearbook-2004

Shaanxi Statistical Yearbook-2004
Gansu Yearbook-2004
Qinghai Statistical Yearbook-2004
Ningxia Statistical Yearbook-2004
Xinjiang Statistical Yearbook-2004

Xinjiang Production & Construction Group Statistical Yearbook-2004

Anqing Economic Statistical Yearbook-2004
Anshan Statistical Yearbook-2004
Baotou Statistical Yearbook-2004
Bayinguoleng Statistical Yearbook-2004
Changchun Statistical Yearbook-2004
Changsha Statistical Yearbook-2004
Changzhou Statistical Yearbook-2004
Chengdu Statistical Yearbook-2004
Chifeng Statistical Yearbook-2004
Chifeng Statistical Yearbook-2004

Dalian Statistical Yearbook-2004
Daqing Statistical Yearbook-2004
Dongguan Statistical Yearbook-2004
Erdos Statistical Yearbook-2004
Fuzhou Economic & Technical Development District Yearbook -2004
Fuzhou Yearbook-2004
Guangzhou Statistical Yearbook-2004
Guilin Economic Social Statistical Yearbook-2004
Guiyang Statistical Yearbook-2004
Haikou Statistical Yearbook-2004
Handan Statistical Yearbook-2004
Hangzhou Statistical Yearbook-2004
Harbin Statistical Yearbook-2004
Hechi Prefecture Statistical Yearbook-2004
Heilongjiang Assarting District Statistical Yearbook-2004
Hohhot Economic Statistical Yearbook-2004
Huizhou Statistical Yearbook-2004
Jiangyin Statistical Yearbook-2004
Jiaxing Statistical Yearbook-2004
Jilin City Social Economic Statistical Yearbook-2004
Jinan Statistical Yearbook-2004
Jingzhou Statistical Yearbook-2004
Jinhua Statistical Yearbook-2004
Jiujiang Statistical Yearbook-2004
Kunming Statistical Yearbook-2004
Laibing Statistical Yearbook-2004
Lanzhou Yearbook-2004
Lianyungang Statistical Yearbook-2004
Lishui Statistical Yearbook-2004
Liuzhou Economic Statistical Yearbook-2004
Luoyang Statistical Yearbook-2004
Mudanjiang Social Economic Statistical Yearbook-2004
Nanchang Economic and Social Statistical Yearbook-2004
Nanjing Statistical Yearbook-2004
Nanning Statistical Yearbook-2004
Nantong Statistical Yearbook-2004
Nanyang Economic Statistical Yearbook-2004
Ningbo Statistical Yearbook-2004
Pindingshan Statistical Yearbook-2004
Qingdao Statistical Yearbook-2004
Qiqihrer Economic Statistical Yearbook-2004
Sanmenxia Statistical Yearbook-2004
Shaoxing Statistical Yearbook-2004
Shenyang Yearbook-2004
Shenzhen Statistical and Information Yearbook-2004
Shijiazhuang Statistical Yearbook-2004
Shiyan Statistical Yearbook-2004
Siping Statistical Yearbook-2004
Statistical Yearbook of Shanghai Pudong New Area -2004
Suzhou Statistical Yearbook-2004
Taizhou Statistical Yearbook-2004
Tangshan Statistical Yearbook-2004
Tolufan Statistical Yearbook-2004
Urumqi Statistical Yearbook-2004
Weifang Statistical Yearbook-2004
Wenzhou Statistical Yearbook-2004
Wuhan Statistical Yearbook-2004
Wuxi Statistical Yearbook-2004
Xiamen Special Economic Zone Yearbook-2004
Xi'an Statistical Yearbook-2004
Xining Statistical Yearbook-2004
Xuzhou Statistical Yearbook-2004
Yancheng Statistical Yearbook-2004
Yanji Statistical Yearbook-2004
Yinchuan Statistical Yearbook-2004
Zhengjiang Statistical Yearbook-2004
Zhengzhou Statistical Yearbook-2004
Zhoushan Statistical Yearbook-2004
Zibo Statistical Yearbook-2004

Address: No.75 Yuetan Nanjie, Sanlihe, Beijing 100826, P. R. China
China Statistics Press
Editorial Department: Tel: 008610-63321207
E-mail: yearbook@stats.gov.cn
Distribution Department: Tel: 8610-63459084, 68585978